August 13-17, 2016
San Francisco, CA, USA

Association for
Computing Machinery

Advancing Computing as a Science & Profession

San Francisco, CA, USA
KDD 2016

KDD'16

Proceedings of the 22nd ACM SIGKDD International Conference on Knowledge Discovery and Data Mining

Sponsored by:

ACM SIGKDD and ACM SIGMOD

Association for
Computing Machinery

Advancing Computing as a Science & Profession

The Association for Computing Machinery
2 Penn Plaza, Suite 701
New York, New York 10121-0701

ISBN: 978-1-4503-4232-2 (Digital)

ISBN: 978-1-4503-4622-1 (Print)

Additional copies may be ordered prepaid from:

ACM Order Department
PO Box 30777
New York, NY 10087-0777, USA

Phone: 1-800-342-6626 (USA and Canada)
+1-212-626-0500 (Global)
Fax: +1-212-944-1318
E-mail: acmhelp@acm.org
Hours of Operation: 8:30 am – 4:30 pm ET

Printed in the USA

KDD 2016 Chairs' Welcome Message

It is our great pleasure to welcome you to the 2016 ACM Conference on Knowledge Discovery and Data Mining – KDD'16. We hope that the content and the professional network at KDD'16 will help you succeed professionally by enabling you to: identify technology trends early; make new/creative contributions; increase your productivity by using newer/better tools, processes or ways of organizing teams; identify new job opportunities; and hire new team members.

We are living in an exciting time for our profession. On the one hand, we are witnessing the *industrialization of data science*, and the emergence of the *industrial assembly line* processes characterized by the division of labor, integrated processes/pipelines of work, standards, automation, and repeatability. Data science practitioners are organizing themselves in more sophisticated ways, embedding themselves in larger teams in many industry verticals, improving their productivity substantially, and achieving a much larger scale of social impact. On the other hand we are also witnessing astonishing progress from research in algorithms and systems — for example the field of deep neural networks has revolutionized speech recognition, NLP, computer vision, image recognition, etc. By facilitating interaction between practitioners at large companies & startups on the one hand, and the algorithm development researchers including leading academics on the other, KDD'16 fosters technological and entrepreneurial innovation in the area of data science.

This year's conference continues its tradition of being the premier forum for presentation of results in the field of data mining, both in the form of cutting edge research, and in the form of insights from the development and deployment of real world applications. Further, the conference continues with its tradition of a strong tutorial and workshop program on leading edge issues of data mining. The mission of this conference has broadened in recent years even as we placed a significant amount of focus on both the research and applied aspects of data mining. As an example of this broadened focus, this year we have introduced a strong hands-on tutorial program during the conference in which participants will learn how to use practical tools for data mining. KDD'16 also gives researchers and practitioners a unique opportunity to form professional networks, and to share their perspectives with others interested in the various aspects of data mining. For example, we have introduced office hours for budding entrepreneurs from our community to meet leading Venture Capitalists investing in this area. We hope that KDD 2016 conference will serve as a meeting ground for researchers, practitioners, funding agencies, and investors to help create new algorithms and commercial products.

The call for papers attracted a significant number of submissions from countries all over the world. In particular, the research track attracted 784 submissions and the applied data science track attracted 331 submissions. Papers were accepted either as full papers or as posters. The overall acceptance rate either as full papers or posters was less than 20%. For full papers in the research track, the acceptance rate was lower than 10%. This is consistent with the fact that the KDD Conference is a premier conference in data mining and the acceptance rates historically tend to be low. It is noteworthy that the applied data science track received a larger number of submissions compared to previous years. We view this as an encouraging sign that research in data mining is increasingly becoming relevant to industrial applications. All papers were reviewed by at least three program committee members and then discussed by the PC members in a discussion moderated by a meta-reviewer. Borderline papers were thoroughly reviewed by the program chairs before final decisions were made.

In addition, KDD'16 continues to have a strong tutorial and workshop program, as is its tradition since its inception. The program committee reviewed and accepted the following:

Venue or Track	*Reviewed*	*Accepted*	*Acceptance Rate*
Research Track Papers	784	70+72	8.9%+9.2%
Applied Data Science Track Papers	331	40+26	12%+7.9%
Workshops	47	17	36.2%
Tutorials	37	11	29.7%
Applied Data Science Talks	Invited	12	Invited
Hands-on Tutorials	Invited	8	Invited
Regular Keynotes	Invited	4	Invited
Turing Award Winner Talk	Special	1	Special

In the table above the research track papers and applied data science track papers are broken up into the full presentations and poster presentations. We have four excellent keynote presentations from Jennifer Chayes, Joe Hellerstein, Greg Papadopoulous, and Nando de Freitas. In addition, we are honored to have a Turing Award winner, Whitfield Diffie, as one of the keynote speakers. We also encourage attendees to attend the keynote and invited talk presentations.

Putting together *KDD'16* was a team effort. We first thank the authors for providing the content of the program. We are grateful to the program committee and the senior program committee, who worked very hard in reviewing papers and providing feedback for authors. Finally, we thank the numerous sponsors and ACM SIGKDD for their support in hosting the conference.

We hope that you will find this program interesting and thought-provoking and that the conference will provide you with a valuable opportunity to share ideas with other researchers and practitioners from institutions around the world.

Charu Aggarwal
Alex Smola
KDD'16 Research Track Chairs

Rajeev Rastogi
Dou Shen
KDD'16 Applied Data Science Track Chairs

Balaji Krishnapuram
Mohak Shah
KDD'16 General Chairs

Table of Contents

Applied Data Science Track Invited Talks

Applied Data Science Track Posters

Research Track Oral Papers

Research Track Posters

Tutorials

KDD 2016 Conference Organization

General Chairs:	Balaji Krishnapuram *(IBM)* Mohak Shah *(Bosch)*
Research Track Program Chairs:	Alex Smola *(Amazon)* Charu Aggarwal *(IBM)*
Applied Data Science Track Program Chairs:	Dou Shen *(Baidu)* Rajeev Rastogi *(Amazon)*
Associate General Chair	Shipeng Yu (LinkedIn)
Workshop Chairs:	Quoc Le *(Google)* Zhi-Hua Zhou *(Nanjing University)*
Tutorial Chairs:	Hanghang Tong *(Arizona State University)* S V N Vishwanathan *(UCSC)*
KDD Cup Chairs:	Markus Weimer *(Microsoft)* Shou-De Lin *(National Taiwan University)* Vijay Narayanan *(Microsoft)*
Panel Chair:	Andrei Broder *(Google)*
Applied Data Science Invited Talks Chairs:	Evangelos Simoudis *(Synapse Partners)* Usama Fayyad *(Barclays Bank and Oasis500)* Rajesh Parekh *(Facebook)*
Poster Chair:	Jiliang Tang *(Yahoo Labs)*
Best Paper Chairs:	Jiliang Tang *(Yahoo Labs)*
Doctoral Dissertation Award Chair:	Haixun Wang *(Facebook)*
Innovation and Service Award Chair:	Jian Pei *(Simon Fraser University)*
Test-of-Time Award Chair:	Wei Wang *(UCLA)*
Local Arrangements Chairs:	Joaquin Quiñonero Candela *(Facebook)* Olivier Chapelle *(Google)*
Student Travel Award Chairs:	Jure Leskovec *(Stanford University)* Leman Akoglu *(Stony Brook University)*
Media and Publicity Chairs:	Ankur Teredesai *(University of Washington)* Gabor Melli *(Opengov)*
Proceedings Chairs:	Rómer Rosales *(LinkedIn)* Stefanie Jegelka *(MIT)*

Research Track Senior Program Committee (continued):

Jeffrey Yu *(Chinese University of Hong Kong)*
Jennifer Neville *(Purdue)*
Jennifer Dy *(Northeastern University)*
Jian Pei *(Simon Fraser University)*
Jiawei Han *(University of Illinois at Urbana-Champaign)*
Jie Tang *(Tsinghua University)*
Jieping Ye *(University of Michigan at Ann Arbor)*
Jimeng Sun *(Georgia Tech)*
Jing Gao
Johannes Fuernkranz *(TU Darmstadt)*
Johannes Gehrke *(Microsoft Research)*
Jure Leskovec *(Stanford University)*
Karsten Borgwardt *(ETH Zurich)*
Katharina Morik *(TU Dortmund)*
Kristian Kersting *(TU Dortmund)*
Martin Ester *(Simon Fraser University)*
Mohammed Zaki *(RPI)*
Naoki Abe *(IBM T J Watson Research Center)*
Osmar Zaiane *(University of Alberta)*
Paul Bradley *(MethodCare)*
Paul Bennett *(Microsoft Research)*
Peter Flach *(University of Bristol)*
Philip S. Yu *(UI Chicago)*
Qiang Yang *(HKUST)*
Ravi Kumar *(Google)*
Saharon Rosset *(Tel Aviv University)*
Sanjay Chawla
Siegfried Nijssen *(Universiteit Leiden)*
Stefan Wrobel *(Universitaet Bonn)*
Suchi Saria *(Johns Hopkins University)*
Tanya Berger-Wolf *(University of Illinois)*
Thomas Seidl *(LMU Munich)*
Thomas Gaertner *(University of Nottingham)*
Thorsten Joachims *(Cornell University)*
Tie-Yan Liu *(Microsoft Research)*
Tijl De Bie *(Ghen University)*
Vanja Josifovski *(Pinterest)*
Wei Wang *(UC Los Angeles)*
Wray Buntine *(Monash University)*
Xavier Amatriain *(Quora)*
Yan Liu
Yehuda Koren *(Google)*
Yisong Yue *(Caltech)*
Yizhou Sun *(Northeastern University)*
Zhi-Hua Zhou

Applied Data Science Track Senior Program Committee:

Anitha Kannan *(Facebook)*
Balaraman Ravindran *(Indian Institute of Technology Madras)*
Brian D'Alessandro *(Facebook)*
Chao Liu *(Jindi Data Technology Ltd Co.)*
Chiranjib Bhattacharya *(Indian Institute of Science Bangalore)*
Divesh Srivastava *(AT&T Research)*
Gautam Das *(University of Texas Arlington)*
Gautam Shroff *(Tata Consultancy Services Research)*
Graham Williams *(Australian Taxation Office)*
Haixun Wang *(Google)*
Hang Li *(Huawei Technologies)*
Hema Raghavan *(LinkedIn)*
Hui Xiong *(Rutgers University)*
Jan Pedersen *(Microsoft)*
Jeffrey Pan *(Facebook)*
Jun Yan *(Microsoft Research Asia)*
Minos Garofalakis *(University of Chania)*
Ping Luo *(Chinese Academy of Sciences)*
Ralf Herbrich *(Amazon)*
Rayid Ghani *(University of Chicago)*
Roberto Bayardo *(Google)*
S. Muthukrishnan *(Rutgers Univ)*
Sinno Pan *(Nanyang Technological University)*
Tina Eliassi-Rad *(Rutgers Univ)*
Vincent Tseng *(National Chiao Tung University)*
Vipin Kumar *(University of Minnesota)*
Wayne Thompson *(SAS)*
Wei Fan *(Baidu)*
Xiaoming Jin *(Tsinghua University)*
Ying Li *(EV Analysis Corp)*
Yoelle Maarek *(Yahoo! Labs)*
Yu Zheng *(Microsoft Research)*

KDD 2016 Sponsors & Supporters

Sponsor: ACM SIGKDD

KDD

ACM SIGMOD

Supporters: Diamond

DiDi

More than a journey

Supporters: Platinum

Adobe

Microsoft

Supporters: Gold

LinkedIn

BOSCH
Invented for life

Baidu Research

facebook

amazon

IBM Research

Capital One

Supporters: Silver

Supporters: Bronze

Supporters: Lanyard Sponsor

Supporters: KDD CUP Sponsor

Supporters: Student Travel Awards

Supporters: Program Ad Sponsor

Supporters: Media Sponsor

BIG DATA

Mary Ann Liebert, Inc. publishers

Exhibitors:

INDIANA UNIVERSITY

DATA SCIENCE PROGRAM

MORGAN & CLAYPOOL PUBLISHERS

NON SOLUS

ELSEVIER

Springer

MathWorks®

FRONTLINE
solvers
Solver.com • XLMiner.com

spare5

SALFORD
SYSTEMS

Georgia Institute of Technology

TELLIGENT
DATA

Graphons and Machine Learning: Modeling and Estimation of Sparse Massive Networks

Jennifer Chayes
Microsoft Research

ABSTRACT
There are numerous examples of sparse massive networks, in particular the Internet, WWW and online social networks. How do we model and learn these networks? In contrast to conventional learning problems, where we have many independent samples, it is often the case for these networks that we can get only one independent sample. How do we use a single snapshot today to learn a model for the network, and therefore be able to predict a similar, but larger network in the future? In the case of relatively small or moderately sized networks, it's appropriate to model the network parametrically, and attempt to learn these parameters. For massive networks, a non-parametric representation is more appropriate. In this talk, we first review the theory of graphons, developed over the last decade to describe limits of dense graphs, and the more the recent theory describing sparse graphs of unbounded average degree, including power-law graphs. We then show how to use these graphons as non-parametric models for sparse networks. Finally, we show how to get consistent estimators of these non-parametric models, and moreover how to do this in a way that protects the privacy of individuals on the network.

Keywords
Data Mining; Machine Learning; Graphons; Massive Networks; Sparse Networks.

Bio

Jennifer Tour Chayes is Distinguished Scientist and Managing Director of Microsoft Research New England in Cambridge, Massachusetts, which she co-founded in 2008, and Microsoft Research New York City, which she co-founded in 2012. Chayes was Research Area Manager for Mathematics, Theoretical Computer Science and Cryptography at Microsoft Research Redmond until 2008. Chayes joined Microsoft Research in 1997, when she co-founded the Theory Group. Her research areas include phase transitions in discrete mathematics and computer science, structural and dynamical properties of self-engineered networks, and algorithmic game theory. She is the co-author of over 130 scientific papers and the co-inventor of about 30 patents.

Chayes has many ties to the academic community. She was for many years Professor of Mathematics at UCLA. She serves on numerous institute boards, advisory committees and editorial boards, including the Turing Award Selection Committee of the Association for Computing Machinery, the Board of Trustees of the Mathematical Sciences Research Institute and the Institute for Computational and Experimental Research in Mathematics, the Advisory Boards of theCenter for Discrete Mathematics and Computer Science, the Howard Hughes Medical Institute Janelia Farm Research Campus, and Women Entrepreneurs in Science and Technology. Chayes is a past Chair of the Mathematics Section of the American Association for the Advancement of Science, and a past Vice-President of the American Mathematical Society.

Chayes received her B.A. in biology and physics at Wesleyan University, where she graduated first in her class, and her Ph.D. in mathematical physics at Princeton. She did her postdoctoral work in the mathematics and physics departments at Harvard and Cornell. She is the recipient of a National Science Foundation Postdoctoral Fellowship, a Sloan Fellowship, and the UCLA Distinguished Teaching Award. Chayes has recently been the recipient of many leadership awards including the Leadership Award of Women Entrepreneurs in Science and Technology, the Leading Women Award of theGirl Scouts of Eastern Massachusetts, the Women to Watch Award of the Boston Business Journal, and the Women of Leadership Vision Award of the Anita Borg Institute. She has twice been a member of the Institute for Advanced Study in Princeton. Chayes is a Fellow of the American Association for the Advancement of Science, the Fields Institute, the Association for Computing Machinery, the American Mathematical Society, a National Associate of the National Academies, and an Elected Member of the American Academy of Arts and Sciences, and the recipient of the 2015 John von Neumann Lecture Award, the highest honor of the Society for Industrial and Applied Mathematics.

Chayes is well known for her work on phase transitions, in particular for laying the foundation for the study of phase transitions in problems in discrete mathematics and theoretical computer science; this study is now giving rise to some of the fastest known algorithms for fundamental problems in combinatorial optimization. She is also one of the world's experts in the modeling and analysis of random, dynamically growing graphs, which are used to model the Internet, the World Wide Web, social networks, and networks in computational biology. Chayes is one of the inventors of the field of graph limits (graphons), which are now being used extensively in the machine learning of massive networks. Among Chayes' contributions to Microsoft technologies are the development of methods to analyze the structure and behavior of various networks, the design of auction algorithms, and the design and analysis of various business models for the online world.

KDD'16, August 13-17, 2016, San Francisco, CA, USA
ACM 978-1-4503-4232-2/16/08.
http://dx.doi.org/10.1145/2939672.2945357

Learning to Learn and Compositionality with Deep Recurrent Neural Networks

Nando de Freitas
Google DeepMind and University of Oxford

ABSTRACT

Deep neural network representations play an important role in computer vision, speech, computational linguistics, robotics, reinforcement learning and many other data-rich domains. In this talk I will show that learning-to-learn and compositionality are key ingredients for dealing with knowledge transfer so as to solve a wide range of tasks, for dealing with small-data regimes, and for continual learning. I will demonstrate this with several examples from my research team: learning to learn by gradient descent [1], neural programmers and interpreters [3], and learning communication [2].

Keywords

Deep Learning; Recurrent Neural Networks; Compositionality; Transfer Learning; Learning to Learn, Abstraction, Algorithm Induction

Bio

Nando de Freitas is a machine learning professor at Oxford University and a senior staff research scientist at Google DeepMind. He is a fellow of the Canadian Institute For Advanced Research (CIFAR) in the successful Neural Computation and Adaptive Perception program, and an action editor for the Journal of Machine Learning Research. He received his PhD from Trinity College, Cambridge University in 2000 on Bayesian methods for neural networks. From 1999 to 2001, he was a postdoctoral fellow at UC Berkeley in the artificial intelligence group of Stuart Russell. He became a professor at the University of British Columbia from 2001 to 2014. Nando has spun-off a few technology companies, and received several awards, including a few best paper awards, the Charles A. McDowell Award for Excellence in Research, and the Mathematics of Information Technology and Complex Systems Young Researcher Award.

KDD'16, August 13-17, 2016, San Francisco, CA, USA
ACM 978-1-4503-4232-2/16/08.
http://dx.doi.org/10.1145/2939672.2945358

Bibliography

[1] M. Andrychowicz, M. Denil, S. Gomez, M. W. Hoffman, D. Pfau, T. Schaul, and N. de Freitas. Learning to learn by gradient descent by gradient descent. ArXiv preprint 1606.04474, 2016.

[2] J. N. Foerster, Y. M. Assael, N. de Freitas, and S. Whiteson. Learning to communicate with deep multi-agent reinforcement learning. ArXiv preprint 1605.06676, 2016.

[3] S. E. Reed and N. de Freitas. Neural programmer - interpreters. In International Conference on Learning Representations, 2016.

The Evolving Meaning of Information Security

Whitfield Diffie
Stanford University

ABSTRACT

When you are developing security systems, new penetration techniques seem to appear as responses to new security measures but in general the flow is the other way around: security exists and evolves because of the evolution of threats. Beginning with the rise of radio in the 20th Century attacks on communication networks have shown two forms: those that go for the big kill --- such as the breaking of Enigma --- and those that assemble small seemingly innocuous leaks of information into a comprehensive understanding of the target's behavior.

We will analyze the way in which these trends interact with others to create a situation in which what is possible in security and even the meaning of security in communication networks needs reexamination.

Keywords

Information Security; Communication Security; Security Systems

Bio

Whitfield Diffie best known for his 1975 discovery of the concept of public key cryptography, developed jointly with Martin Hellman, which revolutionized not only cryptography but also the cryptographic community and now underlies the security of internet commerce. This work was recognized in 1992 with a Doctorate in Technical Sciences (Honoris Causa) for the creation of a new field of science by the Swiss Federal Institute of Technology in 1992.

During the 1980s, Diffie served as manager of secure systems research at Bell-Northern Research, laboratory of the Canadian telephone system. In 1991, he joined Sun Microsystems as distinguished engineer and remained as Sun fellow and chief security officer until the spring of 2009.

Diffie spent the 1990s working to protect the individual and business right to use cryptography, for which he argues in the book Privacy on the Line, the Politics of Wiretapping and Encryption, written jointly with his Sun colleague Susan Landau. Diffie's role in this policy battle is extensively covered in Steven Levy's book Crypto.

As well as being a winner of the Turing Award, together with Martin Hellman, Diffie has won the ACM Paris Kanellakis Award, the IEEE Hamming Prize, and the Franklin Institute Levy Prize. He is a fellow of the Marconi Society, the International Association for Cryptologic Research, and the Computer History Museum. Diffie is an inductee of the National Inventors Hall of Fame and is particularly proud of receiving the National Computer Systems Security Award, given jointly by NIST and NSA.

Diffie is currently holds the position of consulting scholar at the Center for International Security and Cooperation at Stanford University and is on the advisory boards of a number of startups. His principal interest is the history of cryptography. Along with James Reeds and J.V. Field, he is the editor of Breaking Teleprinter Ciphers at Bletchley Park, an extensively annotated historical edition of the final report of the Newmanry, the group that attacked German systems above the level of Enigma.

KDD '16, August 13-17, 2016, San Francisco, CA, USA
ACM 978-1-4503-4232-2/16/08.
http://dx.doi.org/10.1145/2939672.2949031

People, Computers, and The Hot Mess of Real Data

Joseph M. Hellerstein
University of California, Berkeley / Trifacta

ABSTRACT

In practice, end-to-end data analysis is rarely a cleanly engineered process. Acquiring data can be tricky. Data assessment, wrangling and feature extraction are time-consuming and subjective. Models and algorithms used to derive data products are highly contextualized by time-varying properties of data sources, code and application needs. All of these issues would ideally benefit from an organizational view, but are often driven by individual users.

Viewed holistically, both agile analytics and the establishment of analytic pipelines involve interactions between people, computation and infrastructure. In this talk I'll share some anecdotes from our research, user studies, and field experience with companies (Trifacta, Captricity), as well as an emerging open-source project (Ground).

Keywords

Data Mining; Artificial Intelligence; Real Data; Data Science; User Studies.

KDD '16, August 13-17, 2016, San Francisco, CA, USA
ACM 978-1-4503-4232-2/16/08.
http://dx.doi.org/10.1145/2939672.2945356

Bio

Joseph M. Hellerstein is the Jim Gray Professor of Computer Science at the University of California, Berkeley, whose work focuses on data-centric systems and the way they drive computing. He is an ACM Fellow, an Alfred P. Sloan Research Fellow and the recipient of three ACM-SIGMOD "Test of Time" awards for his research. In 2010, Fortune Magazine included him in their list of 50 smartest people in technology, and MIT's Technology Review magazine included his work on their TR10 list of the 10 technologies "most likely to change our world".

Hellerstein is the co-founder and Chief Strategy Officer of Trifacta, a software vendor providing intelligent interactive solutions to the messy problem of wrangling data. He serves on the technical advisory boards of a number of computing and Internet companies including EMC, SurveyMonkey, Captricity, and Dato, and previously served as the Director of Intel Research, Berkeley.

A VC View of Investing in ML

Greg Papadopoulos
NEA

ABSTRACT

We are seeing a remarkable watershed in the application of data science across markets and industries. A trifecta of advances in algorithms, cheap cycles, and the capture of networked data from everywhere are no doubt the catalysts. The results for many are continuous improvements in efficiencies, and for some are a fundamental re-imagination and disruption of just about every industry. This talk will give examples we are seeing (and funding!) for the latter, and then focus on our views of the ecosystem of value-from-data infrastructure and end-application companies. A big question is whether the enormous collective advances in tools, techniques and education are in-fact converting would-be differentiated products into democratized features used everywhere. We'll follow the value and make our own predictions on future as ML as a business.

Keywords

Data Mining; Machine Learning; Data Science; Investing; Venture.

Bio

Greg joined NEA as Venture Partner in 2010 after more than twenty years of experience in the technology industry and academia. He focuses on early-stage systems, software and semiconductor companies. Prior to NEA, Greg was EVP and CTO of Sun Microsystems, where he guided the company's $2B R&D portfolio. Before Sun, Greg was an Associate Professor of EECS at MIT, where he worked on massively parallel dataflow computing architectures. He also helped found a number of companies, from video conferencing (PictureTel) to computational fluid dynamics (NASDAQ:EXA), and was an engineer with HP and Honeywell.

Greg is an active advisor for the schools of engineering at UCSD, UC Berkeley, and MIT, and is a trustee for the Computer History Museum. Passionate about technology and its possibilities, Greg is a relentless advocate for diversity in engineering and a supporter of open development models that stimulate communication, inclusiveness and innovation. Greg holds an undergraduate degree from UCSD and an S.M. and Ph.D. from MIT. He is also a Senior Fellow of the American Leadership Forum.

KDD '16, August 13-17, 2016, San Francisco, CA, USA
ACM 978-1-4503-4232-2/16/08.
http://dx.doi.org/10.1145/2939672.2945359

Big Data Needs Big Dreamers: Lessons from Successful Big Data Investors

Evangelos Simoudis
Synapse Partners
Palo Alto, CA
esimoudis@corporateinnovation.vc

Mark Gorenberg
Zetta Venture Partners
San Francisco, CA
mark@zettavp.com

Tim Guleri
Sierra Ventures
San Mateo, CA
tguleri@sierraventures.com

Matt Ocko
Data Collective
San Francisco, CA
matt@dcvc.com

Greg Sands
Costanoa Venture Capital
Palo Alto, CA
greg@costanoavc.com

MODERATOR: Evangelos Simoudis

Evangelos Simoudis has been working in Silicon Valley as a technologist, entrepreneur, corporate executive, and VC. Today he advises global corporations on Startup-Driven Innovation and information technology and invests in early stage startups working on big data applications. He is a recognized thought leader on corporate innovation, big data, cloud computing, and digital marketing platforms, a writer and speaker on these topics.

His current directorships include Singtel/Amobee, and Kite Solutions. Prior directorships include Brightroll (acquired by Yahoo!), Bristol Technology (acquired by Hewlett-Packard), Composite Software (acquired by Cisco), Confluent Software (acquired by Oracle Corporation), Exelate (acquired by Nielsen), Extole, Host Analytics, and Princeton Softech (acquired by IBM). Evangelos earned a Ph.D. in computer science from Brandeis University and a BS in electrical engineering from Caltech.

Panelist: Mark Gorenberg

Mark has an enviable track record when it comes to identifying and nurturing enterprise software that delivers exceptional returns. During his 20 years in venture capital, he's generated extraordinary results, particularly in analytics where his portfolio has realized a 149 percent annual rate of return.

Prior to Zetta Venture Partners, Mark served as managing director at Hummer Winblad, the first fund focused on enterprise software. There, his most publicized successes in analytics included Omniture (IPO and acquired by Adobe); AdForce (IPO and acquired by CMGI) and Scopus Technologies (IPO and acquired by Seibel Systems). Today, he sits on the boards of the next generation of leading companies like Domo, Inside Sales, EventBoard and FollowAnalytics.

Mark started his technology career at Sun Microsystems working on its SPARCstation workstations.

Beyond his role as venture capitalist and entrepreneur, Mark is a trusted advisor to some of the country's most influential technology institutions. He serves on the President's Council of Advisors on Science and Technology (PCAST), the Board of Trustees for Massachusetts Institute of Technology and the National Venture Capital Association.

He graduated from MIT and received Masters degrees from the University of Minnesota and Stanford University in Electrical Engineering.

Panelist: Tim Guleri

Tim Guleri is a Managing Director of Sierra Ventures, a California based early stage venture capital fund. Sierra's ten venture funds have committed capital exceeding $1.6 Billion.

Tim's investment focus is Information Technology Software companies. Additionally, Tim has helped execute on Sierra's India strategy and investments. As a venture capitalist, Tim's taken two companies public; Sourcefire in 2007 (Nasdaq: FIRE) which was acquired by Cisco for $2.7B and MakeMyTrip.com (Nasdaq: MMYT). Additional exits have been Greenplum (EMC Corporation), Net6 (Citrix Systems) AirMedia (AOL), Makara (RedHat), Red Aril (Hearst), Runa (Staples), Bina (Roche) and Appcelerator (Axway). Tim currently serves on the BOD of Treasure Data, Alpine Data Labs, Nexenta, Hired, LeadGenius, Phenom People and Shape Security.

Prior to Sierra, Tim learnt the ropes as an entrepreneur. He was founder and CEO of Octane Software from 1996 to 2000. He successfully led Octane's merger with Epiphany (Nasdaq: EPNY), a transaction valued at $3.2 billion in 2000. Before Octane, Tim was Vice President of field operations at Scopus Technology. Scopus went public in 1995 and was acquired by Siebel Systems (Nasdaq: SEBL) in 1997 for $800M. Tim was instrumental in growing the company to $100 million in revenue and to 600 employees from 1992 to 1996.

Tim holds a MS from Virginia Tech, and a BSEE from India.

KDD '16, August 13-17, 2016, San Francisco, CA, USA
ACM 978-1-4503-3664-2/15/08.
http://dx.doi.org/10.1145/2783258.2790456

Panelist: Matt Ocko

Matt Ocko, co-founder and co-Managing Partner of Data Collective (DCVC), has three decades of experience as a technology entrepreneur and VC, in the US and globally. Matt's prior investments include Cotendo (AKAM), Zynga (ZNGA), Facebook (FB), XenSource (CTRX), UltraDNS (NSR), FlashSoft (SDNK), Fortinet (FTNT), Aggregate Knowledge (NSR), Virtuata (CSCO), DataMirror (IBM), Couchbase, Ayasdi, Kenshoo, D-Wave Systems, MetaMarkets, Uber, AngelList, and many others, including multiple additional acquisitions by Google, Facebook, Netapp, and other Fortune 1000 tech companies. Matt founded Da Vinci Systems, a pioneering e-mail software vendor with over 1 million users world-wide prior to its acquisition. He is an inventor on over 40 granted or in-process patents in areas as diverse as enterprise hardware and fraud detection. Matt holds a degree in Physics from Yale University and has been active in helping develop China's venture capital and technology regulatory framework for two decades.

Panelist: Greg Sands

Greg is the Founder and Managing Director at Costanoa Venture Capital, an early stage venture capital firm focused on finding great entrepreneurs using technology to solve real problems and build lasting companies. Prior to founding Costanoa, Greg was a Managing Director at Sutter Hill, where he led early stage investments in Feedburner, QuinStreet, Yokou and Merced Systems. Before Sutter Hill, Greg was the first hire at Netscape Communications after its founding engineering team. Starting as a Product Manager, he wrote the initial business plan, coined the name Netscape, and created the SuiteSpot Business Unit, which he grew from zero to $150m in revenue.

Greg has an MBA from Stanford Graduate School of Business and graduated from Harvard College Magna Cum Laude. He currently serves as President of the Stanford DAPER (Athletics Department) Investment Fund and is a Board Member and Former President of the Western Association of Venture Capitalists.

Designing Policy Recommendations to Reduce Home Abandonment in Mexico*

Klaus Ackermann
Monash University
klaus.ackermann@monash.edu

Eduardo Blancas Reyes
Center for Data Science and Public Policy
University of Chicago
edublancas@uchicago.edu

Sue He
University of Virginia
syh2s@virginia.edu

Thomas Anderson Keller
UC San Diego
andy@keller.org

Paul van der Boor
University of Chicago
pvboor@gmail.com

Romana Khan
Northwestern University
romana.khan@kellogg.northwestern.edu

ABSTRACT

Infonavit[1], the largest provider of mortgages in Mexico, assists working families to obtain low-interest rate housing solutions. An increasingly prevalent problem is home abandonment: when a homeowner decides to leave their property and forego their investment. A major causal factor of this outcome is a mismatch between the homeowner's needs, in terms of access to services and employment, and the location characteristics of the home.

This paper describes our collaboration with Infonavit to reduce home abandonment at two levels: develop policy recommendations for targeted improvements in location characteristics, and develop a decision-support tool to assist the homeowner in the home location decision. Using 20 years of mortgage history data combined with surveys, census, and location information, we develop a model to predict the probability of home abandonment based on both individual and location characteristics. The model is used to develop a tool that provides Infonavit the ability to give advice to Mexican workers when they apply for a loan, evaluate and improve the locations of new housing developments, and provide data-driven recommendations to the federal government to influence local development initiatives and infrastructure investments. The result is improving economic outcomes for the citizens of Mexico by pre-emptively identifying at-risk home mortgages, thereby allowing them to be altered or remedied before they result in abandonment.

*This work was done at the 2015 Eric & Wendy Schmidt Data Science for Social Good Summer Fellowship at the University of Chicago.

[1]Instituto del Fondo Nacional de la Vivienda para los Trabajadores (National Institute of Housing Fund for Workers)

KDD '16, August 13-17, 2016, San Francisco, CA, USA

 ISBN 978-1-4503-4232-2/16/08...$15.00

DOI: http://dx.doi.org/10.1145/2939672.2939702

Figure 1: Abandoned and vandalized house (Zumpango, Mexico)

1. INTRODUCTION

Home abandonment refers to a homeowner's decision to leave their property and forego the financial investment they have already made in the home. This decision imposes negative financial and economic consequences for both individuals and mortgage-financing institutions in Mexico, as well as imposing significant negative externalities on the neighborhood. To date, home abandonment has affected more than 200,000 homes, representing approximately 5% of the homes financed by Infonavit. As the largest provider of mortgages in Mexico, Infonavit serves approximately 70% of the mortgage market in the country. It was created as a public institution for the purpose of assisting lower-income families, who cannot obtain financing from private financing institutions, with home acquisition and other housing solutions.

In Mexico, every employer registered in the National Social Security Institute is required to contribute 5% of each worker's salary to Infonavit, which administers the contributions as a savings account. When employees meet certain

Figure 2: Neighborhoods with high abandonment rate have also high crime rates, which forces the local population to gate entire streets (Zumpango, Mexico)

criteria, they are eligible to apply for a credit, typically to buy a new house.[4]

Most workers who acquire a house through an Infonavit loan come from low-income families. Faced with economic constraints, they tend to buy cheaper houses which are located at a distance from city centers, often in new housing developments in remote suburbs with limited infrastructure and limited access to services and amenities. At the time of purchase, workers may be poorly informed about the day to day realities of their choice. For example, they may fail to properly account for the time and cost involved in commuting to their employment or schooling. It is often the case that families only realize the location does not satisfy their needs after they have moved into their new home, leading to a decision to abandon the house. Previous research indicates that workers abandon their home for several reasons, including long distances to their workplaces and schools, a lack of services, finances, and security concerns.

Infonavit wants to reduce home abandonment, but the current process is reactive and often too late. Loan holders who stop making payments enter a portfolio of low performing loans. Then, payment collectors visit each home and through a lengthy process of extensions and repeated home visits the home is marked as abandoned. This process takes approximately 12-18 months. At this stage the abandoned houses may have already motivated neighbors to leave their house behind as well and neighborhood regeneration programs may be too late to be effective.

1.1 Project objective

This project has the primary objective of reducing home abandonment in Mexico. We address this in two ways:

1. Enable Infonavit to predict the risk of home abandonment for a given individual and home, and use that prediction to provide purchase advice to the individual.
2. Provide policy recommendations to the government using the structure and features of the predictive model.

The first objective is achieved by building a machine learning model that, given an individual applying for a loan and a home location, can predict the risk of abandonment. By evaluating the risk scores over the homes in the individual's choice set, Infonavit can provide advice by identifying which homes would have a lower risk of abandonment in the future. The second objective is to understand the impact of specific location features on home abandonment. Extensive research carried out by Infonavit indicated that distance to employment, and access to facilities such as schools, hospitals and grocery stores were instrumental in the home abandonment decision. What was less well understood was the relative impact of each of these factors, and the maximum distance thresholds that workers were willing to travel. Access to this information will enable Infovanit to improve the location of new housing developments, give data-backed recommendations to the federal government to influence public policy, and provide guidance to improve the home location decisions of Mexican workers.

We believe that these two actions will help prevent the establishment of settlements with high abandonment rates as portrayed in figure 1 and 2. Currently, revitalization eforts in areas with high abandonment rates only begin after the problem has become apparent for years.

2. PROBLEM FORMULATION

Overall, we formulate the abandonment risk prediction problem as a binary classification problem where the outcome variable is whether a person abandons their house. We model this outcome for each year after the loan is granted, either until the end of the observation period or until the home is abandoned.

An alternative is to model the percentage of abandonment for a specific colonia[2]. This would not serve our objectives since the analysis would no longer be focused on the individual decision of a person to abandon their house. Estimation at the colonia level would also require aggregating individual level data to a representative average person, and we would lose the information from individual level variation. Furthermore, as the specific addresses of houses are unknown for a large portion of the data, attempts to geocode these houses were unsuccessful due to the low quality of the address fields[3].

3. DATA SOURCES

To investigate the factors that contribute to home abandonment, we combined data from multiple sources. The primary level of observation is at the individual home owner. This is supplemented with multiple data sources that capture the location characteristics of the house.

3.1 Loans data

The primary data provided by Infonavit includes personal, loan, and house characteristics for every loan granted in the last 20 years. The personal characteristics include demographics such as age and marital status, and financial infor-

[2]Neighborhood

[3]It's important to note that while we are predicting at a home level (to asess which homes are likely to be abandoned in the next year) many of our features are at different levels of aggregation, from the home level up to the municipality level

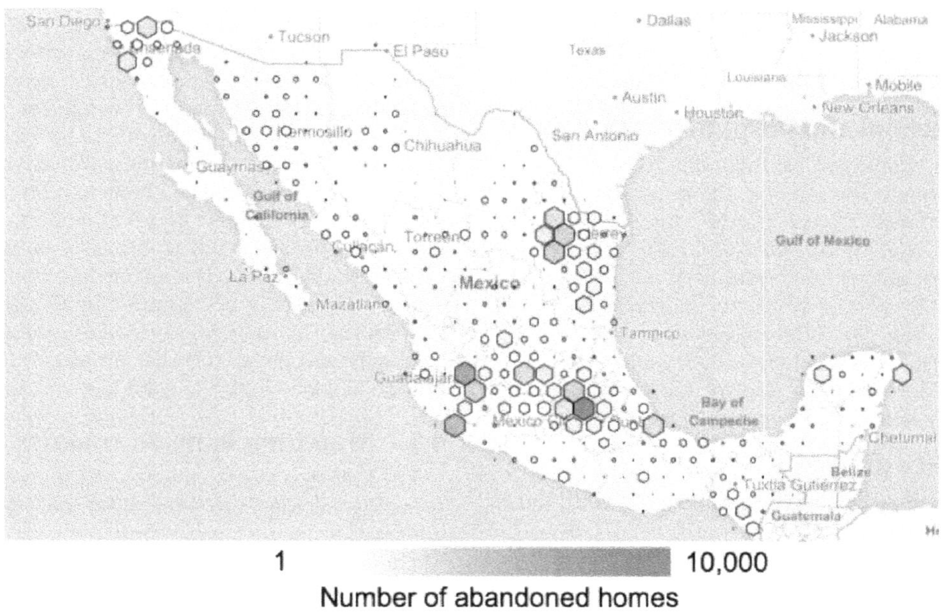

Figure 3: Geographic distribution of home abandonment in Mexico

mation such as wage and the value of accumulated savings. The data also includes a *Risk Index* computed by Infonavit which estimates the risk of employment loss for every credit-holder. The information on the terms of the loan included the interest rate, the value of the loan, and the value of any subsidy received.

We transformed the data so that the unit of observation is at the house level rather than the individual loans, since it is possible for a family to have two loans for a house. We combined their savings and assets so that each observation is representative of one home with its associated characteristics. We excluded joint loans that had mismatched years or prices for the same house. Loans cofinanced with private banks, loans that were granted for the purpose of home improvement, and loans with entries that did not match up with other data sources provided by Infonavit (such as guidelines corresponding to the age of the loan holder) were also excluded. After this cleaning process, we have 4.1 million observations at the house level.

One field in the data that is often missing is the exact location of the house. Unfortunately, geo-coordinates were only available for loans granted in the last 7 years (since 2008), and attempts to geocode the rest of the houses were unsuccessful due to the low quality of the address field. To deal with this practical constraint, we matched loans to colonias[4] using different approaches. A detailed description of this process is described in section 4, Location Matching.

3.2 Approximation of the labeled data

Home abandonment is recorded as a flag in our data but the exact date of abandonment is often unknown. Our loan data (where the abandonment label is located) presents a snapshot of the state of abandonment as of May 2015 and the abandonment flag tells us whether the home is abandoned as of that date.

[4]neighborhoods in Mexico

The abandonment flag can be triggered by different circumstances. The loan repayment occurs through the social security system directly from the employer. Payments cease when a person loses their job, and continue with the uptake of new employment. It is also possible that the person never regains any form of formal employment and joins the informal sector in Mexico. In the first case, a house will be marked as abandoned or vandalized when an inspector visits a colonia. In the second case of no payments, after a grace period an inspector visits the house and tries to locate the owners. Both circumstances are equally devastating for the livelihood of their former owners as well as the remaining occupants in the colonia.

Approximate dates of home abandonment were calculated based on supplemental payment data provided by Infonavit, which recorded payments made for every active loan during the 2010-2014 time period. We assumed that the first interruption in the payments represented the date of home abandonment. There were 4 types of events which were used to identify an interruption in payments:

1. Date of the application for loan extension granted (59%)
2. Date of the first interruption in the payment stream with continued payments after (11%)
3. Date of last payment received (11%)
4. Date the home is marked as abandoned but no single payment entry, date set to 2009 (5%)

For 14% of the data we could not find a pattern and excluded these observations from the study.

3.3 Housing survey data

Infonavit also shared the results of home surveys (ECUVE[5]) conducted by licensed inspectors. This measured housing quality at the municipality[6] level. ECUVE provides an in-

[5]Evaluación cualitativa de la vivienda y su entorno (Quantitative evaluation of housing and its environment)

[6]Municipality is the administrative division of states in Mexico

dex of housing quality based on factors such as construction quality, reliable water and power supply, local access to schools and hospitals, and availability of parks and markets.

3.4 Business, school and hospital location data

Previous research conducted by Infonavit indicated that distance to employment was among the top factors that drive home abandonment. To account for this, we incorporated data from DENUE[7] in our analysis. Every five years, INEGI[8] conducts a census of businesses in Mexico, covering businesses from small grocery stores to multinational corporations. For each business, information such as industry, number of employees, owner, address, and geolocation coordinates is recorded. The data also includes schools and hospitals. The study is updated annually.[9]

3.5 Municipality data

Finally, we included extensive data on the folliwing municipality characteristics:

- Number of Homicides
- Natality
- Mortality
- Natural disaster incidences
- Years of schooling (from the Population Census)
- Households statistics (from the Population Census)
- Literacy rate (from the Population Census)
- Healthcare coverage (from the Population Census)
- Number of vehicles and passenger buses

All the municipality level data comes from INEGI (except for the natural disasters incidence data, which comes from Desinventar [1]). INEGI's datasets are publicly available for download [2].

3.6 Data limitations and project scope

Most of the data available to us is collected annually, except for the Population Census, which occurs every five years. This represented a challenge for feature creation, described in the next section. The loans dataset spans the last 20 years, but house coordinates were only available for loans granted after 2008. Given that location features were critical to our objectives, the scope of the project was limited to loans granted from 2008 to 2015. A timeline of the data is presented in Figure 4.

4. LOCATION MATCHING

One of the biggest challenges for our project was to geolocate granted loans. Since our model depends on spatial-temporal features (e.g. number of schools within 5 Km), we need to obtain coordinates for each loan to be able to compute those features.

Our loans dataset contains more than 4.1 million rows, but location information (coordinates and/or address) is available for only 2 Million (49%) observations. To geolocate address data, a common approach is to obtain geographical coordinates using a geocoding service. In the U.S., for example, the Census Bureau has a geocoding API[7] that given an address returns its coordinates.

Unfortunately, there is no official service for geocoding addresses in Mexico. One of the alternatives is to use Google Maps Geocoding API[6]. The first limitation with Google's service is the rate limit of 2,500 requests per day. Furthermore, the service is not as accurate as in the U.S., mostly because many Infonavit housing developments were built recently and are still not mapped by Google.

With that in mind, we decided to geolocate at the colonia-level only and group together all houses in the same colonia in a point located at the colonia's centroid.

4.1 Matching loans to colonias

The first step to match loans (4.1 million) with their corresponding colonia, is to filter those that have at least address information (some have coordinates).

The next step was to match loans that had geographical coordinates with their corresponding colonia, this was done using PostGIS spatial queries. We matched 740 000 loans using this method. After that we tried locating non-matched loans by finding their closest matching-loan and assigning the same colonia, this process was limited to a distance up to 1km.

The next step to attempt to locate more loans was to use the address field. For each non-matched loan, we compared it to the matched ones and assign the same colonia if the address was the same. We made this comparison using a simple string comparison. Due to time constraints we didn't implement a more robust approach such as entity resolution. In the end we were able to geolocate 2.4 million records (58.5% of total loans).

5. FEATURES

Once we received and cleaned the data (preprocessing such as translation and deflation to account for time variation) and finished the location matching process, we proceeded to build features. Each type of features required a different process, which is described in the following subsections.

5.1 Municipality features

Except for the Population Census, all municipality features are collected yearly. Since some years were missing, the missing values were imputed using linear extrapolation (e.g. to impute a feature for 2010, extrapolate using data from 2008 and 2009). Another approach could be to use interpolation (e.g. to impute a feature for 2010, interpolate using data from 2009 and 2011), this method was rejected since using data from the *future* (in 2010, we don't know the value for 2011 features) would violate our testing and training split paradigm.

Municipalities in Mexico do not have a uniform distribution in terms of area or population. For example, the most populated municipality (Ecatepec) has more than 1.5 million inhabitants, whereas the least populated one (Santa Magdalena Jicotlán) has only 102 inhabitants, in term of land area, the biggest municipality (Ensenada) has an area of roughly 52,000 km^2 and the smallest municipality (San Lorenzo Axocomanitla) has only 4.2 km^2. To account for this, features involving discrete counts were normalized over

[7]Directorio Estadístico Nacional de Unidades Económicas (National Statistical Index of Economic Units)

[8]Instituto Nacional de Estadística y Geografía (National Institute of Statistics and Geography)

[9]Every five years the study is carried out from scratch and every year only a subset of the data (80% of the GDP) is updated. For detailed methodology information refer to [3]

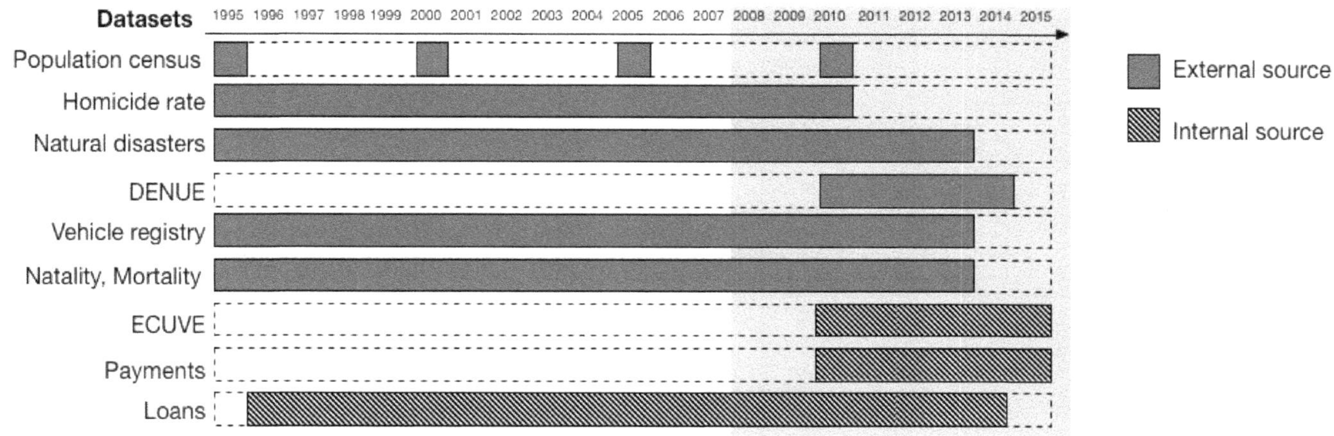

Figure 4: Data timeline summarizing the data sources used and project scoping (2008-2015)

100,000 inhabitants (e.g. number of homicides, births, deaths, households).[10]

5.2 Location features

Location features were critical to our project. They were of strategic value to provide actionable policy recommendations to our partner. Our personal impressions supported this during a site visit to a neighborhood with high abandonment (Zumpango, Mexico). The requirement is to have features that capture the state of the local services and infrastructure in a comparable way across Mexico. We chose to aggregate several types of businesses separately for each colonia, and at various radii (from 0 to 5 km, 5 to 10 km, up to 45 to 50 km). The number of employees for businesses within each concentric circle was also counted. It is an approximation of the actual infrastructure, nevertheless it should be representative across the state.

The accurate distance calculation between approximately 50,000 colonias, spanning some 4 million businesses across Mexico is an extensive endeavor. As we had no road network data to calculate the actual walking or driving time we relied on the air distance corrected by the spheroid distance. Without accounting for the curvature of the earth we might introduce noise in our geometrical aggregation bins, when a business might be counted differently depending on the distance. The challenge that arose was that a single feature calculation for a colonia took between 1 to 5 seconds, depending on the density of businesses. We developed a plsql extension parallelsql[11] for PostgreSQL that allows these distance calculations to be executed in parallel, decreasing the required calculation time by the number of cores available to the database. The input data is partitioned by the primary key in split up in chunks of colonia groups. A load balance implementation submits the chunks to the cores of the database and waits until a sub part is finished and submits the next one until all features are calculated.

5.3 Personal and loan features

Personal and loan features were used for each observation with new aggregate features created to characterize each colonia, taking the colonia average, minimum and maximum for both personal and loan features.

5.4 Merging features

Following the feature engineering step, a master feature table was built to contain all features, with each row having one single loan-year and the following features:

- Credit-holder characteristics
- Loan characteristics
- Average credit-holder characteristics (colonia level)
- Average personal characteristics (colonia level)
- Municipality features
- Location features

6. MODELING

6.1 Model objectives

Our model was created to answer the following question: What is the risk of abandonment for an existing loan in the next year?

We trained a variety of machine learning models on different years and then tested on active loans in the following year (e.g. training from 2008 to 2014 and testing on loans active during 2015). The algorithms tested were Support Vector Machines, Random Forests, AdaBoost, and Logistic Regression.

6.2 Accounting for loan duration

In order to accurately model the effect of loan duration on home abandonment and to be able to easily split our training and testing sets correctly, we duplicated records for each loan from the granting time until the abandonment year (e.g. for a loan granted in 2008 but abandoned in 2010, there will be 3 rows, one for each year), with the most recent row having the abandoned flag as true.

6.3 Generating our training and test sets

To evaluate our models, we had to ensure that we were not violating time-dependent knowledge restrictions between our training and test set. This means using the known economic conditions at the time of *evaluation* rather than at *testing*

[10]INEGI 2010 Population census
[11]https://github.com/k1aus/parallelsql

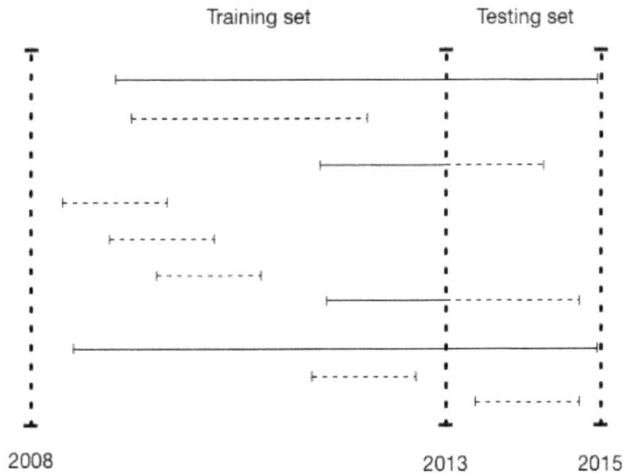

Figure 5: Training (2008-2013)/Testing (2014-2015) splitting example

time. For example, if we wanted to predict home abandonment for 2015, the only information available would be up until 2014, since later information would be using data from the future.

Figure 5 shows a data split using data from 2008 to 2013 for training and 2014 to 2015 for testing. A continuous line means the observation is considered to be inhabited, while a dashed line means the observation is considered abandoned.

To train our models we used scikit-learn[5], a Python library that contains many algorithms for binary classification.

7. RESULTS

Because of the time restrictions on accurate home location data, and our approximation of dates of home abandonment (explained in previous sections), our final models was trained using data from 2008 to 2014 and tested on 2015. This resulted in a 95 to 5 negative to positive class ratio. To tackle this imbalance we oversampled the positive class in our training set to have 50% positive observations, while leaving the test set untouched. Our main evaluation metric was chosen to be AUC given it's interpretation as the probability that a classifier will rank a randomly chosen positive instance higher than a randomly chosen negative one, which could be directly applied to the ranking of risk for multiple loans.

7.1 Model performance

Our best performing model was a Random Forest which achieved an AUC of 0.70 as shown in Figure 6. With a 0.5 threshold, the model captured 55% of abandoned houses. Given the inherent imbalanced nature of the data, this model produced 266,670 false positives in comparison to 4602 true abandoned houses.

While the predictive power of our model is limited, the top predictors (see subsection 7.2) provide substantial deep insights into the data and provide guidance on where resources need to be allocated to address the problem of home abandonment (see section 8.2).

Several factors contribute to the model's limited performance (see subsection 7.3), and suspect that the vast majority of them relate to the fidelity and quality of the data. To address this, we provided Infonavit with a series of data collection recommendations (see section 8.1) to aid in the improvement of the performance of the current model.

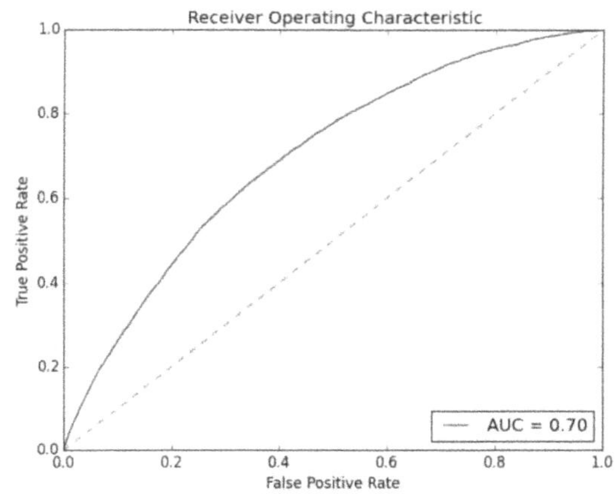

Figure 6: ROC curve for our best model

Risk Index
Years since loan granted
Loan sales price
Daily wage
Loan account value
Colonia minimum sales price
Loan interest rate
Loan holder age

Table 1: Top personal/loan predictors

7.2 Top predictors

Trained models consistently show the same sets of features as important to predict home abandonment. Table 1 shows the top features regarding inherent personal and loan characteristics and Table 2 shows the top features that can potentially be impacted through policy.

7.3 Model limitations due to data quality

Determining accurate coordinates of homes was a major limitation we encountered while attempting to precisely compute location features (such as distance to nearest employment areas). Since we only had exact coordinates for about 740,000 of 4.1 million loans, the most accurate location we could calculate for homes with missing location data was the center of the colonia in which they were located. Using various fuzzy matching methods we retrieved colonia locations for 2.4 million loans, still missing around 1.7

ECUVE index
Number of restaurant employees within 5 km
Number of employees within 5 km
Number of businesses within 5 km
Number of hospitals within 5 km
Loan-holder age * Number of schools within 5 km
Number of churches within 5 km
Municipality Passenger buses over 1000 inhabitants

Table 2: Top predictors that can be improved through policy changes

million. This location approximation introduced a substantial amount of noise into our location features since colonias can stretch multiple kilometers and we had no indication of where a given home was located inside each colonia.

The poor location information created two problems for our analysis. First, we were unable to compute actual distances to nearby businesses in meters, and instead opted to count the number of businesses within distance rings. Second, since we were unable to locate an individual loan within a colonia, we could not compute intra-colonia features which could have helped our model distinguish between homes (especially those with similar loan information) in a given colonia.

Related to the distance features, our model strongly depends on DENUE. This process to update this dataset is carried out every 5 years, so it is possible that the current model does not capture all the economic changes that occur year to year.

Limitations related to data acquisition include our inability to obtain public transportation information (e.g. location of bus stops) and an inability to obtain accurate employment information and location for each loan holder.

Another limitation is the uncertainty of abandonment date within official Infonavit records. Home abandonment is a complex process, so establishing the exact timestamp of when a home was abandoned would is difficult if not impossible without all houses being checked consistently. The only timestamp we had originally from the raw data was the year in which the loan was granted. For our models, the abandonment year needed to be estimated from the loan payment history data.

7.4 Prototype

The predictive model (Figure 7) was deployed as a web application which estimates the risk of abandonment for the next year based only on personal characteristics and a selected colonia for the home. The process to make a prediction is as follows:

1. User selects a colonia
2. User inputs personal characteristics (age, *Risk Index* and daily wage)
3. The web application retrieves the loan characteristics as the average for that colonia
4. Municipality and location features are retrieved from the database
5. The aggregated features are run through the trained model, and the application displays the prediction to the user, along with a map and a summary of the factors driving home abandonment

8. CONCLUSIONS

Our model made a modest but substantive improvement in home abandonment prediction compared to a baseline model of Infonavit's internal *Risk Index* alone. Before our project, the institute had no way to estimate the risk of home abandonment at the loan level. Taking advantage of the insights found, Infonavit will be able to take the following actions:

1. **Advise** Mexican workers when they are applying for a loan, so that home abandonment can be prevented at the loan origination time. Using our model, Infonavit can estimate the risk of home abandonment given personal characteristics and location. With this information, they will be able to suggest alternative locations better suited to the loan applicant and decrease the risk of abandonment. It is important to mention that Infonavit cannot deny loans to formally employed workers by law, so our model results will only be used to provide guidance to potential loan holders and to help them make a better location decision.
2. **Prevent** the spread of home abandonment in certain neighborhoods. By identifying locations which are at risk of abandonment, pre-emptive action can be taken to reduce such risk (e.g. intervention programs).
3. **Improve** planning for new developments. Infonavit does not build houses, but purchases them from development companies. Taking advantage of our work, Infonavit will have enough information to asses the risk associated with a new development in a certain location.
4. **Influence** public policy at the federal level. Solving the problem of home abandonment in Mexico involves many stakeholders such as Infonavit and the federal government. Based on the results of our work, Infonavit will be in a better position to influence public policy and to prioritize changes based on our findings.

8.1 Data collection recommendations

To improve the model's ability to accurately predict abandonment, we recommend Infonavit make certain improvements in the data collection process. Most important is to collect precise geographic coordinates for all houses. Since location related features are important predictors of home abandonment, it is critical to improve the quality of this data.

The second recommendation is to start collecting the loan holder's employment location and school location data. According to previous Infonavit research, commuting time is a top reason for home abandonment, so incorporating this information in the model will provide new insight and may have a significant effect in the model performance.

The interval ECUVE score created at Infonavit is a top predictor of home abandonment but there were many missing values in some component variables (ECUVE measures different variables such as transportation, access to water, parks, markets and aggregates them to provide an overall score). Some were unsuitable for use in our models. Given the promise of the overall ECUVE score as a predictor, it is important to improve the quality of the ECUVE data. One priority could be to increase the sample size to include more municipalities in the country.

Our last recommendation is in regards to the time records. Since the desired output of a model is the risk of abandonment with respect to a change in time (in the current model we predicted abandonment in the next year), it is important to improve the temporal data quality, meaning that Infonavit needs to record important events with more precision such as month of loan granting and if possible, the month of abandonment. At the start of the project the only raw timestamp recorded at Infonavit was the loan granting year. We thus needed to approximate the date of abandonment in order to accurately consider the change in our features over time (e.g. number of jobs within 10 km in 2012 versus 2013).

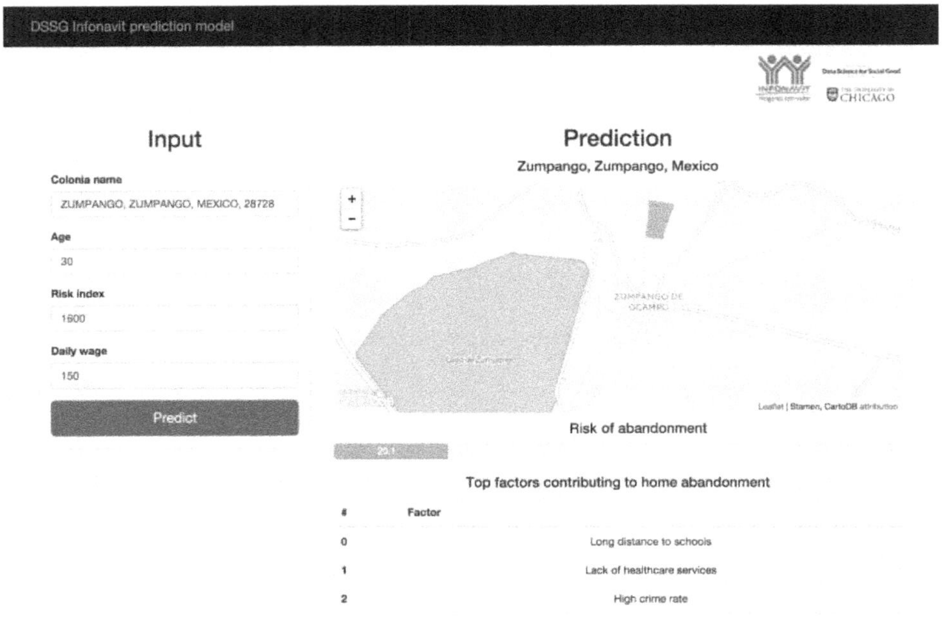

Figure 7: Prototype screenshot

This introduced noise in our model, thus severely affecting the performance.

8.2 Public policy recommendations

Infonavit cannot change public policy as an individual actor, but has a close relationship with the federal government and can advise the them and influence other players to do so. With a considerable spectrum of possible policy changes yet limited resources to deploy them, having a data-backed starting point is crucial to tackling home abandonment.

Our recommendation pinpoints the need for a focus on local rather than regional growth. Our model found that the critical distance for services is within 5 km, so creating large centralized employment and educational centers at distances further than 5km from colonias would not have a significant impact on reducing home abandonment.

Home abandonment is not an intermittent phenomenon across time, instead it spreads inside neighborhoods, so we encourage Infonavit to allocate resources for urban regeneration and intervention programs in neighborhoods that already have higher percentages of abandonment.

9. ACKNOWLEDGMENTS

This project would not have been possible without the financial support provided by the Schmidt Family Foundation, making not only this project possible, but also another eleven in the Data Science For Social Good (DSSG) program.

We would also like to thank DSSG staff for making the program possible and for all the support provided throughout the summer. Their hard work inspired us every day to do our best and to make an impact.

Finally, we are grateful to Infonavit for trusting and actively working with the team to provide valuable insights. We hope our results help the institution better accomplish its social mission and improve the quality of life for many families in Mexico.

10. ADDITIONAL AUTHORS

Rayid Ghani (University of Chicago, email: `rayid@uchicago.edu`) and José Carlos González (Infonavit, email: `josecarlosgonz@gmail.com`).

11. REFERENCES

[1] Desinventar. Inventory system of the effects of disasters. http://www.desinventar.org/en, 2013. [Online; accessed 09-September-2015].

[2] INEGI. Descarga masiva. http://www3.inegi.org.mx/sistemas/descarga/, 2013. [Online; accessed 09-September-2015].

[3] INEGI. Directorio estadístico nactional de unidades económicas. http://www.inegi.org.mx/est/contenidos/proyectos/denue/presentacion.aspx, 2015. [Online; accessed 09-September-2015].

[4] Infonavit. Qué hago para cumplir. http://portal.infonavit.org.mx/wps/wcm/connect/infonavit/patrones/mis_compromisos/que+hago+para+cumplir. [Online; accessed 09-September-2015].

[5] F. Pedregosa, G. Varoquaux, A. Gramfort, V. Michel, B. Thirion, O. Grisel, M. Blondel, P. Prettenhofer, R. Weiss, V. Dubourg, J. Vanderplas, A. Passos, D. Cournapeau, M. Brucher, M. Perrot, and E. Duchesnay. Scikit-learn: Machine learning in Python. *Journal of Machine Learning Research*, 12:2825–2830, 2011.

[6] Google. The Google Maps Geocoding API. https://developers.google.com/maps/documentation/geocoding/intro, 2016. [Online; accessed 15-January-2016].

[7] United States Census Bureau. Geocoder. http://geocoding.geo.census.gov, 2010. [Online; accessed 15-January-2016].

Aircraft Trajectory Prediction *Made Easy* with Predictive Analytics

Samet Ayhan * Hanan Samet
Department of Computer Science
University of Maryland
College Park, MD 20742
{sayhan} {hjs} @cs.umd.edu

ABSTRACT

At the heart of Air Traffic Management (ATM) lies the Decision Support Systems (DST) that rely upon accurate trajectory prediction to determine how the airspace will look like in the future to make better decisions and advisories. Dealing with airspace that is prone to congestion due to environmental factors still remains the challenge especially when a deterministic approach is used in the trajectory prediction process. In this paper, we describe a novel stochastic trajectory prediction approach for ATM that can be used for more efficient and realistic flight planning and to assist airspace flow management, potentially resulting in higher safety, capacity, and efficiency commensurate with fuel savings thereby reducing emissions for a better environment.

Our approach considers airspace as a 3D grid network, where each grid point is a location of a weather observation. We hypothetically build cubes around these grid points, so the entire airspace can be considered as a set of cubes. Each cube is defined by its centroid, the original grid point, and associated weather parameters that remain homogeneous within the cube during a period of time. Then, we align raw trajectories to a set of cube centroids which are basically fixed 3D positions independent of trajectory data. This creates a new form of trajectories which are 4D joint cubes, where each cube is a segment that is associated with not only spatio-temporal attributes but also with weather parameters. Next, we exploit machine learning techniques to train inference models from historical data and apply a stochastic model, a Hidden Markov Model (HMM), to predict trajectories taking environmental uncertainties into account. During the process, we apply time series clustering to generate input observations from an excessive set of weather parameters to feed into the Viterbi algorithm. Our experiments use a real trajectory dataset with pertaining weather observations and demonstrate the effectiveness of our approach to the trajectory prediction process for ATM.

*Senior Engineer at Boeing Research & Technology

KDD '16, August 13-17, 2016, San Francisco, CA, USA

DOI: http://dx.doi.org/10.1145/2939672.2939694

Keywords

Aircraft Trajectory Prediction; Predictive Analytics; Air Traffic Management; Hidden Markov Model; Time Series

1. INTRODUCTION

The goals of Air Traffic Control (ATC) are the safe and efficient management of aircraft. The Air Navigation Service Provider (ANSP) in the USA, the FAA, is concerned with providing optimal airspace capacity and efficiency within the National Airspace System (NAS). These goals require the separation and sequencing of airborne aircraft by controllers who often use DSTs to monitor the progress of each aircraft and resolve conflicts when necessary. Other controllers monitor the future aggregate flows of aircraft traffic and using a DST implement flow management decisions to ensure that the traffic density always remains within safe limits. At the core of these automation tools resides the Trajectory Prediction (TP) tool, that given the aircraft initial state, its flight plan and the wind and temperatures, computes where the aircraft will be in the future in four dimensions. Inaccurate trajectory prediction can have a substantial impact on the performance of the DST and the ATM system, resulting in

- larger separation standards that limit the number of aircraft that can be allowed in controllers' sectors and/or
- increased numbers of conflicts increasing the workload of the controllers and reducing their sector capacity and/or
- inefficient fuel consumption due to continual deviations to avoid other aircraft and/or
- adverse impact on the environment due to more fuel burn leading to more emissions.

As a consequence, the performance of the TP tool which supports the DSTs is critical to the success of the DST functions.

Although prior trajectory prediction research and development activities have been able to address the challenge to some extent, dealing with increasingly congested airspace and new environmental concerns still remains the challenge when deterministic approach is used in trajectory prediction process. Hence due to the nature of uncertainties that contribute to trajectory prediction errors, in our research, we have taken a stochastic approach to address the trajectory prediction issues.

We define airspace as a set of spatio-temporal data cubes where each cube is considered as an atomic unit. Weather parameters such as temperature, wind speed, and wind direction remain homogeneous within the cube during a period of time. Other parameters that describe the cube include its center coordinates (latitude, longitude, altitude) along with a time stamp. These spatio-temporal data cubes form the overall airspace. Then, we adapt raw trajectories to the cubes, by aligning each trajectory vertex to the nearest cube centroid, inspired by the *Realm* method [19]. The process yields 4D joint cubes that can be considered as piecewise trajectory segments. Using adapted trajectories in the form of 4D joint cubes, we train our model with the historical data and choose a state sequence that best explains the current observations, the pertinent weather parameters. This process corresponds to the Problem No.2 described in [33] where it attempts to uncover the hidden part of the model, which is the optimal state sequence, given the observations. Note that in the process, each segment is chosen from one of the many hidden segments and the occurrence of a hidden segment that underlines an observation is dependent on the hidden state of the previous segment. Since our objective is to find the most likely trajectory, we use HMM that is nothing more than a probabilistic function of a Markov process. Due to the nature of interconnected cube centroids forming a trellis, we use the Viterbi algorithm [48] to efficiently generate the optimal trajectory by joining the multiple segments together, where one segment is only dependent on the previous segment.

Now, a critical question arises: *What constitutes the input observations?* or more importantly, *among so many weather observations in the airspace volume of interest during the time period of flight, which ones should be passed to the Viterbi process?* We address this problem by clustering the current weather observations for the cube centroids that were historically traversed. Before the process, we split the current weather observations into buckets and then perform time series clustering [21]. We finally feed the output cluster into the Viterbi algorithm to probabilistically generate the best state sequence.

In summary, the contributions of this paper are as follows:

- We propose a novel way of representing aircraft trajectories, a set of 4D joint cubes generated upon an alignment and fusion process.
- We build a stochastic model, HMM that learns from the combination of historical trajectories and aircraft specifications, and their correlation with the pertinent weather parameters. Then, we perform time series clustering on the trajectory segments that were historically traversed. Finally, we feed the series of cluster centroids as observations into the Viterbi algorithm in order to predict trajectories that can be used as more realistic pre-departure flight plans.
- We conduct experiments based on real host track and aircraft specification data and demonstrate that our system effectively predicts aircraft trajectories.

Although the proposed solution can be adapted for both tactical and strategic trajectory prediction, our experimental study focuses more on a ground-based tactical trajectory prediction system that can be used by both AOC dispatchers to file more realistic flight plans and/or flow managers at the Air Traffic Control System Command Center (ATCSCC) to approve the proposed flight plans based on their conformance to the relatively more realistic predicted trajectories, right before the aircraft departs.

The rest of the paper is organized as follows. Section 2 reviews the related work. Section 3 introduces the preliminary concepts, presents the problem, and overviews the proposed system. Section 4 discusses in the detail the aircraft trajectory prediction system, that we propose. Section 5 presents the results of an experimental evaluation. Section 6 concludes the paper and outlines some future work.

2. RELATED WORK

There has been much work on trajectories in the spatial domain for motor vehicles along roads [40] with an emphasis on their generation (e.g., [41]), queries (e.g., [30, 32, 36, 38, 39]), and matching (e.g., [20, 29, 37]). This is not our subject here. On the other hand, there has been a vast amount of research and abundant literature with regards to predicting aircraft trajectories. Methodologies to attain this goal can be divided into deterministic and probabilistic approaches. Deterministic approaches are made up of nominal and worst-case techniques, and probabilistic techniques include Sequential Monte Carlo (SMC), Hidden Markov Models (HMM) and others.

The nominal technique gives the aircraft position by propagating estimated states into the future along a single trajectory without considering uncertainties of the state estimate and the prediction [13, 22]. Worst-case techniques assume that an aircraft will perform any of a set of maneuvers and the worst case, defined by the application, is considered for aircraft trajectory prediction. Algorithms based on this idea are too conservative since civilian aircraft rarely perform extreme maneuvers [47]. Overall, deterministic techniques [8, 10, 11, 34] suffer from degraded accuracy due to fact that they don't account for uncertainties and address only specific phase(s) of the flight when predicting aircraft trajectories.

Past efforts addressing aircraft trajectory prediction using probabilistic methods are similar to our approach in a way that they aim at modeling uncertainties to describe potential changes in the future trajectory of an aircraft. However, many of them [23, 24, 26, 42, 50, 51] either lack empirical validation or use a simulated set of aircraft trajectories instead of real host track data in their evaluations.

Aside from accounting for uncertainties in the computation, there is considerable research in identifying potential sources of uncertainties in trajectory prediction [12, 27, 45]. In addition to purely deterministic and probabilistic methods, a hybrid method combining the SMC and the worst-case method was also proposed [15]. Although the majority of the research on trajectory prediction is used toward detecting and resolving conflicts with other aircraft, there is also a number of research papers on the same topic from the standpoint of convective weather and Special Use Airspace (SUA) avoidance [25, 28, 43, 44, 46].

Our work is closer in spirit to research [14, 16, 49] that studied the aircraft trajectory prediction problem with machine learning approach, in which they train the model using historical surveillance data and make predictions using various observations. Choi et al [14] present an approach to predict future motion of a moving object based on its past movement. The approach exploits the similarities of short-term movement behaviors by modeling a trajectory as a concatenation of short segments. Although their approach shares some common ground with ours, they have never applied it to aircraft trajectory prediction. Leege et al. [16] specifically propose a machine learning approach to aircraft trajectory prediction. However, unlike our study, they use a stepwise regression approach to systematically determine which input variables to include in the models based on explanatory power. In his PhD. dissertation, Winder et al. [49] present a framework for designing a hazard avoidance alerting system that is based on a Markov decision process model.

The machine learning approach also inspires our study as with our stochastic technique, we leverage the historical Aircraft Situation Display to Industry (ASDI) [3] track data and aircraft specifications to select among the possible intermediate reference points and predict the aircraft trajectory based on meteorological observations. During the process, we assume that the weather observations are realizations of hidden trajectory segments and the transitions between the underlying hidden segments follow a Markov model.

To summarize, our approach is distinguished from the past efforts in at least one of the following four respects: *i)* We use probabilistic approach by taking the uncertainties into account, which yields higher accuracy *ii)* We consider trajectories as a set of 4D joint cubes, which helps us to unify trajectory segments and associate them with pertinent weather parameters, *iii)* We perform time series clustering on the excessive set of current observations to generate time series to feed into the Viterbi algorithm, which is an efficient way to find the optimal state sequence, and *iv)* We use real host track and aircraft specifications data along with weather observations to validate the effectiveness of our approach.

3. PRELIMINARY AND OVERVIEW

In this section we introduce some preliminary concepts, present the problem, and give an overview of the proposed aircraft trajectory prediction system.

3.1 Concepts

The EUROCONTROL/FAA Action Plan 16 (AP16) defines a(n) (aircraft) trajectory as *"the path a moving aircraft follows through the airspace and can be mathematically described by a time-order set of trajectory (state) vectors or the geometry of the flight path"* in the TP Requirements Engineering Methodology paper [1]. The International Civil Aviation Organization (ICAO)'s definition of trajectory is slightly different; *"the description of the movement of an aircraft, both in the air and on the ground, including position, time, and at least via calculation, speed and acceleration"* [4]. Our definition of trajectory, which we call "original trajectory", inspired by Ayhan et al. [9] is slightly different:

Definition 1. An *original trajectory* of an aircraft is a continuous representation of its motion with 4D spatio-temporal parameters *(latitude, longitude, altitude, and time)*, indicating the exact path, traveled by the aircraft.

Due to the fact that there exists no system that continuously records and stores exact positions of an aircraft's original trajectory, only a discrete set of sample data are recorded and stored which presumably represent a close approximation of the original trajectory. We call this a raw trajectory, which we formally define below.

Definition 2. A *raw trajectory* T of an aircraft is a finite sequence of positions with timestamps sampled from the original trajectory. $T = [p_1, p_2, ..., p_n]$, where each point p is defined by its 4D spatio-temporal parameters *(latitude, longitude, altitude, and time)*.

Depending on sampling strategy, which is the way how the position recording is triggered, discrete set of spatio-temporal parameters are captured as the aircraft moves. Among others, the most widely used sampling strategies are time-driven (e.g once every minute), distance-driven (once every mile), and geometry-driven (e.g. once the aircraft deviates from its heading more than 15 degrees). Our study uses ASDI track data which is a form of time-driven raw trajectory, described in detail in Section 4.

Definition 3. A *reference point* r is a fixed spatial location in the 3D space, that is independent of the trajectory data source. A set of evenly distributed reference points form a *reference system* R.

Our study uses the Global Forecast System (GFS) Rapid Refresh (RAP) weather model's 3D grid network [7] as a reference system, described in detail in Section 4. Figure 1.a shows a 2D partial view of the RAP weather model's grid network, which is the reference model overlaid on top of the western Florida area in Google Earth [5].

Definition 4. An *aligned trajectory* $\bar{T}$ is a set of reference points that the raw trajectory points are transformed into. More formally, given a *reference system* R, the aligned trajectory $\bar{T}$ for the *raw trajectory* $T = [p_1, p_2, ..., p_n]$ is $\bar{T} = [r_1, r_2, ..., r_n]$, where $r_i \in R$.

Aligned trajectories must preserve the original trajectories as much as possible. Note that erroneous adjustments are introduced each time original trajectories are turned into raw trajectories and raw trajectories are turned into aligned trajectories. Hence, preserving original trajectories in aligned trajectories is obviously a challenging task. This study uses Euclidean distance as a distance function and searches for the nearest neighboring grid point in the reference system to transform raw trajectory points into reference points. Figure 1.b illustrates 3D partial view of both aligned and raw trajectories with the reference system on top of the western Florida area in Google Earth.

Definition 5. A *spatio-temporal data cube* is an atomic trajectory unit in space, defined by its reference point coordinates *(latitude, longitude, altitude)* where weather parameters (temperature, wind speed, and wind direction) are considered to remain constant within a period of time.

Aligning raw trajectories to reference points is a critical preparation step where all necessary parameters are aggregated per point. However, due to uncertainties, we hypothetically create cubes around reference points, building an entire airspace composed of 3D cubes, where each data cube has homogeneous weather parameters within during a certain period of time. This way, trajectories are defined by a set of cubical segments. In our study, the lateral resolution of each cube is $13km$ and temporal resolution is $1hr$. Figure 1.c is an illustration of a set of spatio-temporal data cubes defining an aligned trajectory transformed from a partial raw trajectory.

Definition 6. An *airspace volume of interest* is a 4D airspace volume in which a number of spatio-temporal data cubes are stacked up horizontally and/or vertically.

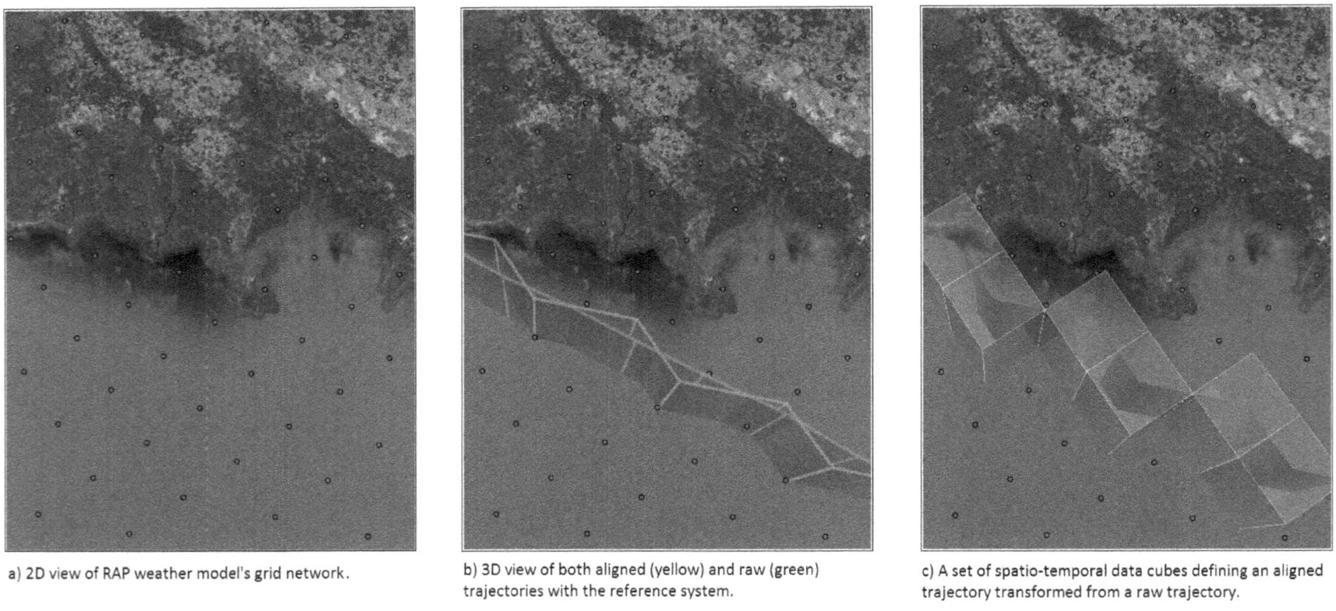

Figure 1: Partial illustration of reference system, raw and aligned trajectories, and spatio-temporal data cubes on top of the western Florida area in Google Earth.

3.2 Problem Statement

Given a set of historical raw trajectories for specific aircraft types along with pertinent historical weather observations, we aim at learning a model that reveals the correlation between weather conditions and aircraft positions and predicts trajectories in the form of a time series. In this problem space, we assume that the weather observations are realizations of hidden aircraft positions i.e. trajectory segments and the transitions between the underlying hidden segments follow a Markov model. This assumption considers a finite set of states, each of which is associated with a probability distribution over all possible trajectory segments. Transitions among the states are managed by a set of probabilities. The states are not visible, but the pertinent observations are. Given a sequence of observations, we want to learn an HMM, a statistical Markov model, and derive a sequence of hidden states that correspond to the sequence of observations.

The Viterbi algorithm [48] is an efficient method to compute this. However, in our problem space, the observation sequence for which we want to predict the state sequence is unknown. In other words, given a set of weather observations for the full set of spatio-temporal cubes covering the airspace volume of interest and approximate time period of flight, we need to identify the ones that we can input into the Viterbi process.

3.3 System Overview

Figure 2 shows the overview of the proposed aircraft trajectory prediction system, which generates the optimal state sequence in three steps:

- In the first step, we perform training data processing by generating the HMM parameters based on a set of historical trajectories and weather parameters.
- In the second step, we perform test data processing by executing time series clustering on weather observations for the entire airspace volume of interest which yields the observation sequence.
- In the final step, we use the output of the first two steps in the Viterbi algorithm to generate the optimal state sequence based on the observation sequence.

In Figure 2, data storage is colored yellow, training data processing is colored red, test data processing is colored blue, and the Viterbi process with the final output is colored green.

4. AIRCRAFT TRAJECTORY PREDICTION

This section presents our approach to aircraft trajectory prediction and elaborates in detail each step of the process.

4.1 Training Data Processing

This step enables us to accurately fuse weather parameters per sample point of a raw trajectory. To attain this goal, we need a weather model with the highest spatio-temporal resolution available and that offers both current and historical weather data. The National Oceanic and Atmospheric Administration (NOAA) GFS RAP product operational at the National Center for Experimental Prediction (NCEP) meets these requirements. Hence, we use GFS RAP weather model's 3D grid network as our reference system.

Training data processing, colored red in Figure 2, is performed as follows: Based on the reference system, grid-based alignment is performed on the historical raw trajectories. The process is based on the simple idea of finding the nearest 3D reference point for each sample point of a raw trajectory and then mapping the original sample point to a nearest 3D reference point, inspired by the *Realm* method [19]. More precisely, each sample point in a raw trajectory is aligned to a nearest 3D reference point. This process generates aligned trajectories for historical trajectory data. Although, this seems to suffer from accuracy, it allows to form a unified set resulting in increased similarity between aligned trajectory

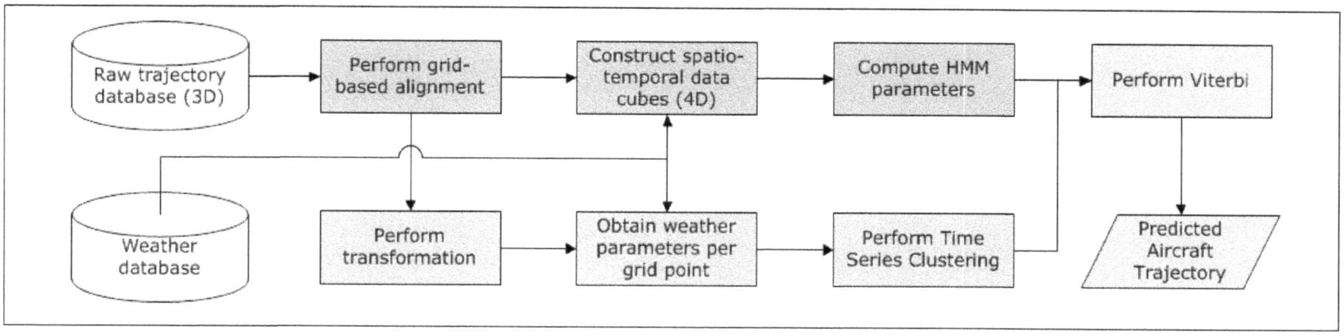

Figure 2: System overview. Data storage is colored yellow, training data processing is colored red, test data processing is colored blue, and the Viterbi process with the final output is colored green

points. Spatio-temporal data cubes are formed in the next step. During this step, weather parameters for the pertinent time window are retrieved from the weather database and re-sampled to generate N buckets with distinct ranges. Then, the weather parameters in distinct buckets are fused with spatial data for each grid point along the aligned trajectory. The process yields training data where each historical raw trajectory becomes a set of 4D joint data cubes.

4.2 Test Data Processing

In order for us to compute the maximum probability of HMM generating the optimal state sequence of $s_1, s_2, ..., s_m$, the observation sequence $o_1, o_2, ..., o_m$ is needed. Although the reference points covering the entire airspace volume of interest are known, we don't know which one of these should be fed into the Viterbi process. To answer this question, we perform time series clustering with Dynamic Time Warping (DTW) on excessive set of observations and generate the input time series.

Test data processing, colored blue in Figure 2, enables us to address this question. In this step, among all reference points between the departure and arrival airports, we consider only the ones that were traversed in the historical trajectories. The first step in the process is to perform transformation on these aligned historical trajectories by replacing the original date per reference point with the current date, presuming the flight is about to depart. In other words, during this step, all aligned historical trajectories are treated as if they are current. In the second step, based on new timestamps, weather parameters are retrieved from the weather database and resampled to generate N buckets with distinct ranges. Next, the weather parameters in distinct buckets are fused with spatial data for each grid point along the aligned trajectory. This step generates hypothetical cubes, in the same way as in the training data processing. The output of this step is an excessive set of spatio-temporal data cubes forming distinct trajectories in the form of a time series.

In the final step of the test data processing, spatial data is omitted and *k-Nearest Neighbors (k-NN)* clustering is performed using DTW on the weather parameters along the time series. The algorithm enforces a *locality* constraint and uses a *LB Keogh* lower bound.

Note that in time series analysis, DTW is an algorithm for measuring similarity between multiple temporal sequences which may vary in time or speed. For simplicity, suppose there are two temporal sequences, Q and C, of length n and m respectively, such that $Q = q_1, q_2, ..., q_i, ..., q_n$ and $C = c_1, c_2, ..., c_i, ..., c_n$. To align two sequences using DTW, n-by-m matrix is constructed where the (i^{th}, j^{th}) element of the matrix contains the distance $d(q_i, c_j)$ between the two points q_i and c_j. Each matrix element (i, j) corresponds to the alignment between the points q_i and c_j. A *warping path* W is a contiguous set of matrix elements that defines a mapping between Q and C. During the process, the warping path is subject to a *locality* constraint. There are exponentially many warping paths that satisfy this constraint. We are only interested in the path that minimizes the warping cost. This path can be found using dynamic programming to evaluate the following recurrence, which defines the cumulative distance $\gamma(i, j)$ as the distance $d(i, j)$ found in the current cell and the minimum of the cumulative distances of the adjacent elements:

$$\gamma(i,j) = d(q_i, c_j) + min\{\gamma(i-1, j-1), \gamma(i-1, j), \gamma(i, j-1)\}$$

By enforcing *locality* constraint through a threshold window, the algorithm ensures that it is unlikely for d_i and t_j to be matched if i and j are too far apart. In this algorithm, the number of clusters is set apriori to 1 and similar time series are clustered together. The process yields an observation sequence in the form of a set of weather parameters which are fed into the Viterbi process, in the next step.

4.3 HMM Processing and Viterbi

We approach the HMM problem by identifying the parameter set computed based on training data as follows:

- States $S = \{S_1, S_2, ..., S_K\}$ are represented by reference points' coordinates *(latitude, longitude, altitude)* that form aligned trajectories.
- Transition probabilities $A = \{a_{ij}\}$, $1 \leq i, j \leq K$, i.e. a_{ij} is the probability of an aircraft discretely transitioning from one state S_i to another S_j along its aligned trajectory, $\bar{T}$.
- Emission probabilities $B = \{b_i(o)\}$, $1 \leq i \leq K$ is the probability of discrete weather parameters having been observed at a specific state, S_i.
- Initial probabilities $\pi = \{\pi_i\}$, $1 \leq i \leq K$ is the probability of an aligned trajectory beginning at a specific state, S_i.

These parameters form an HMM, denoted by $\lambda = \{S, A, B, \pi\}$. The next step in the process is to choose a corresponding state sequence $s = \{s_1, s_2, ..., s_m\}$, that best explains the observation sequence, $O = \{o_1, o_2, ..., o_m\}$. To answer this question, we use the Viterbi algorithm [48], which has a recursive approach that works in parallel for all states in a

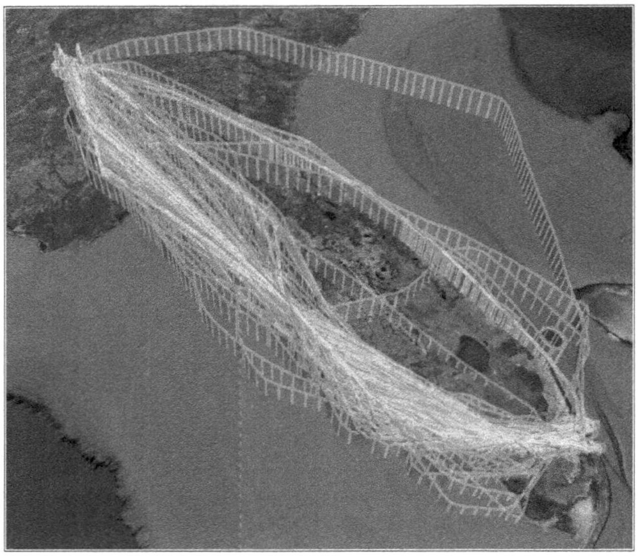

Figure 3: 3D raw trajectories of flight DAL2173 between Atlanta and Miami for the period of May 2010 through December 2011 in Google Earth

strictly time synchronous manner. The key component in the algorithm is the *optimal probability*, denoted as $\delta_m(i)$, which is the maximal probability of HMM generating the observation segment $o_1, o_2, ..., o_m$, along the optimal state sequence $s_1, s_2, ..., s_m$, in which $s_m = i$. Hence, we compute:

$$\delta_m(i) = \max_{s_1,...,s_{m-1}} \pi_{s_1} b_{s_1}(o_1) \prod_{j=2}^{m} (a_{s_{j-1},s_j} b_{s_j}(o_j))$$

The process colored green in Figure 2 yields the predicted aircraft trajectory.

5. EXPERIMENTAL EVALUATION

In this section, we conduct experiments to validate the effectiveness of our aircraft trajectory prediction system. Section 5.1 introduces the experimental dataset. Section 5.2 presents the implementation details and our environment. Section 5.3 discusses the results for our prediction system, and Section 5.4 outlines the discoveries gained by our trajectory prediction system.

5.1 Experimental Dataset

Our empirical evaluation used real host track data along with real weather data: The Delta Airlines' flights DAL2173, departing from Hartsfield-Jackson Atlanta International Airport (ATL) and arriving at Miami International Airport (MIA) for the period of May 2010 through December 2011 were studied. The dataset has a total of 594 trajectories and 56752 points. ATL to MIA is one of the major routes in the NAS due to fact that the departure airport is the busiest airport in the U.S. and the flights are prone to frequent convective weather in the airspace controlled by three Air Route Traffic Control Centers (ARTCC), Atlanta (ZTL), Jacksonville (ZJX), and Miami (ZMA). Figure 3 shows 3D raw trajectories of flight DAL2173 between Atlanta and Miami for the period of May 2010 through December 2011.

Two main data sources to our Aircraft Trajectory Prediction System are the FAA's ASDI and NOAA's RAP data which are colored yellow in Figure 2 and presented next.

5.1.1 ASDI

The source of the raw trajectory data is ASDI, which is a continuous stream of messages delivered over a TCP/IP network socket. Note that a total of over 30 million ASDI messages are processed in any single day. ASDI messages can be flight plan related data, oceanic reports, or host track reports. The host track data is recorded once in every 60 seconds, and provided in near real-time by the FAA. Upon processing, the data is stored in a relational database and made available for use by our trajectory prediction system. Note that surface data is not included in the ASDI feed, although departure and arrival airports remain the same, the positions of the first and last track records may differ over time. The raw trajectory data is generated by joining various ASDI message types including: Track Information and Flight Plan Information. The process generates *source center, date, time, aircraft ID, speed, latitude, longitude, altitude* values from the Track Information and *special aircraft qualifier* from the Flight Plan Information message type.

5.1.2 RAP

The source of the weather data is NOAA National Centers for Environmental Prediction (NCEP) Rapid Refresh (RAP) [7] which is the continental-scale NOAA hourly-updated assimilation/modeling system. RAP covers North America and is comprised primarily of a numerical forecast model and an analysis/assimilation system to initialize that model. It has $13km$ horizontal resolution with 50 vertical levels, ptop=10hPa, sigma vertical coordinate. Although there is an experimental $3km$ hourly updated nest inside of the $13km$ Rapid Refresh, it is not widely available yet. The RAP weather data is stored as a set of *grib2* files [6] each hour and made available for use by our prediction system.

5.2 Implementation

The ASDI host track data is composed of radar recordings at an approximate rate of once every 60 seconds by each Air Route Traffic Control Center (ARTCC) for any aircraft operating under Instrument Flight Rules (IFR) within the confines of an ARTCC's airspace. Our airspace volume of interest is controlled by three separate ARTCCs, due to fact that an aircraft traveling between Atlanta and Miami airports uses Atlanta ARTCC (ZTL), Jacksonville ARTCC (ZJX), and Miami ARTCC (ZMA). The ASDI host track data contains multiple recordings when the aircraft crosses a boundary between multiple ARTCCs. Hence, our initial implementation step filtered these multiple recordings by taking the timestamp and source center (ARTCC) information into account. The filtering process reduced the number of historical recordings from 56752 to 48694. As in rare cases, ARTCCs recorded multiple track data within a relatively short period of time, such as 20 seconds, we also filtered these recordings. The process brought the number of historical recordings down to 44824.

The remaining historical raw trajectory points went through alignment process as elaborated in Section 4.1. During the process, we used GFS RAP weather model's 3D grid network as our reference model, and mapped the raw trajectory points to the nearest reference points. This pro-

Table 1: Buckets for weather parameters

No	Bucket	Value (*kelvin*)
Temperature (*temp*)		
1	$temp \leq 220$	220
2	$220 < temp \leq 240$	240
3	$240 < temp \leq 260$	260
4	$260 < temp \leq 280$	280
5	$280 < temp \leq 300$	300
6	$300 < temp \leq 350$	350

No	Bucket	Value (*knots*)
Wind speed (*ws*)		
1	$ws \leq 30$	30
2	$30 < ws \leq 60$	60
3	$60 < ws \leq 90$	90
4	$90 < ws \leq 120$	120
5	$120 < ws \leq 150$	150

No	Bucket	Value (*degrees*)
Wind direction (*wd*)		
1	$wd \leq 45$	45
2	$45 < wd \leq 90$	90
3	$90 < wd \leq 135$	135
4	$135 < wd \leq 180$	180
5	$180 < wd \leq 225$	225
6	$225 < wd \leq 270$	270
7	$270 < wd \leq 315$	315
8	$315 < wd \leq 360$	360

cess yielded aligned historical trajectories. In the next step, spatio-temporal data cubes were formed and reference points along aligned trajectories were fused with weather parameters. However, due to lack of historical weather data for the flight time window of interest of some aligned trajectories, we were not able to expand their dimensions. Subsequently these aligned historical trajectories were eliminated bringing the total number of reference points down to 37849. Fusing positional data with weather parameters yielded the following attributes per spatio-temporal data cube: *source center, date, time, aircraft id, speed, latitude, longitude, altitude, aircraft type, temperature, wind speed, wind direction.* As the final step of the training data processing, we split the weather parameters into buckets as shown in Table 1.

Next, we computed the following HMM parameters:

- 3698 distinct states, S were generated.
- A sparse transition matrix, A of size 3698 x 3698 = 13675204 was generated.
- An emission matrix, B of size 117 x 3698 = 432666 was generated.
- An initial matrix, π of size 28 x 1 was generated.

Aside from these HMM parameters, we also needed to feed the observation sequence into the Viterbi algorithm.

To evaluate our prediction system, we performed bootstrapping by drawing many trajectory samples with replacement from the historical trajectories. In the meantime, we removed the pertinent track records from the training dataset. The process allowed us to plot 95% confidence interval (CI) for the mean error and standard deviation of our trajectory samples. Note that one of the trajectory samples we draw happened to be May 14, 2011. Hence, we present the process for this particular trajectory sample. The test data processing repeated itself for other trajectory samples.

Test data processing for this particular trajectory sample is as follows: We used aligned trajectories for the same historical data. However, this time we treated each trajectory as if it was flown on May 14, 2011. This required a simple transformation of replacing date value per aligned trajectory point. The next step in the process required that we obtain weather parameters for the positional data. However, in order for us to do that, we needed to identify the time period of the flight. Given the median duration of the flight DAL2173 being 78 minutes, we decided to use two *RAP grib2* weather files, one targeting weather observations recorded at 15:00 UTC and the other targeting weather observations recorded at 16:00 UTC on May 14, 2011. By using these files, we retrieved the pertinent weather parameters per aligned trajectory point. Next, we split the weather parameters into buckets as shown in Table 1. In the final step of test data processing, we performed time series clustering, using DTW. The input to the process was 474 time series of 78 weather observations, where each observation contained *temperature, wind speed, wind direction* parameters. The *k-nearest neighbors (k-NN)* clustering with k=1 used DTW Euclidean distance for similarity measure. To speed up the process, we used *LB Keogh* lower bound. The resulting set of cluster centroids identified by weather parameters defined the observation sequence Y_s.

As the final step of the process, we fed the observation sequence Y_s and HMM parameters, $\lambda = \{S, A, B, \pi\}$ into the Viterbi algorithm. The algorithm worked in parallel for all states in a strictly time synchronous manner and returned the optimal state sequence with the maximum probability.

Our experiments were conducted on a computer with Intel Core i7-3840QM CPU @ 2.80GHz and 16GB memory, running on Linux Ubuntu 14.04.2 64-bit LTS Operating System. All the algorithms were implemented in Python v2.7.

5.3 Results

We evaluated the effectiveness of our prediction system based on bootstrapping by drawing 23 trajectory samples with replacement from the historical trajectories. This way, we compared our prediction with the ground truth, flight DAL2173's aligned trajectory. Next, we computed the mean error and standard deviation per trajectory sample. Then, we ranked order the means to estimate the 2.5 and 97.5 percentile values for 95% CI.

Figure 4 shows actual flown trajectory in red overlaid on top of spatio-temporal data cubes in white predicted by our system for one of the trajectory samples drawn, May 14, 2011 as part of the bootstrapping. Major prediction errors are introduced around top of climb and descent phases.

Our quantitative evaluation is based on trajectory prediction accuracy metrics, including horizontal, along-track, cross-track, and vertical errors, as outlined in [18, 31]. The errors illustrated in Figure 5 are based on the coordinates of the aircraft, denoted as AC, and a trajectory segment containing the points TJ_1 and TJ_2.

Table 2 captures mean error μ and standard deviation σ for horizontal, vertical, along-track, and cross-track errors for the entire set of trajectory samples with 95% CI. The errors were computed based on our prediction versus flight DAL2173's raw trajectory per trajectory sample.

The horizontal error is unsigned whereas the along-track and cross-track errors are signed errors. Note that the mean value for the cross-track error $\mu(e_{cross})$ along the entire tra-

Figure 4: Actual flown trajectory overlaid on top of spatio-temporal data cubes generated for flight DAL2173 on May 14, 2011 by our prediction system

jectory of flight DAL2173 is 6.804nm (=12.601km), when the sign is omitted. Due to fact that spatial resolution of our trajectory prediction system is 13km, which is the horizontal length of each spatio-temporal cube, we can conclude that the mean value $\mu(e_{cross})$ for the cross-track error of 12.601km is within the boundaries of our spatial resolution.

Figure 6 illustrates the pertinent histograms for horizontal, vertical, along-track and cross-track errors for the entire set of trajectory samples with 95% CI. Due to fact that the along-track and cross-track errors are signed errors, they generate a relatively symmetric distribution about the zero, as shown in Figure 6. The area of the histograms provides an indication of overall performance.

To evaluate behavior of trajectory prediction errors over time, we also computed horizontal, along-track, and cross-track errors for the entire set of trajectory samples with 95% CI based on look-ahead time, as shown in Figure 7. Generally, the longer the look-ahead time, the greater the uncertainty, yielding larger errors. However, this is not the case for our system, as shown in Figure 7.

As part of the time-based evaluation, we compared estimated time of arrival initially entered by AOC, predicted time of arrival computed by our system and the actual time of arrival for flight DAL2173.

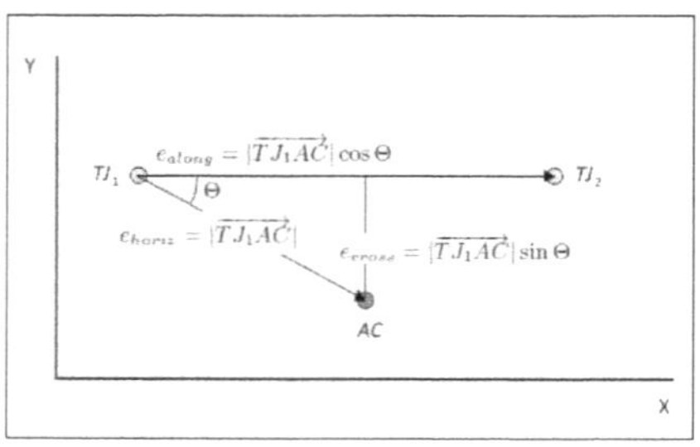

Figure 5: Trajectory prediction accuracy metrics

Table 2: Mean and standard deviation values for horizontal, vertical, along-track, and cross-track errors for flight DAL2173 on trajectory samples

Mean error (μ)			
$\mu(e_{horiz})$	$\mu(e_{along})$	$\mu(e_{cross})$	$\mu(e_{vert})$
12.965nm	1.454nm	-1.859nm	687.497ft
Standard deviation (σ)			
$\sigma(e_{horiz})$	$\sigma(e_{along})$	$\sigma(e_{cross})$	$\sigma(e_{vert})$
12.093nm	13.833nm	10.836nm	4910.691ft

Although our prediction system considers time of last ASDI track record as arrival time, there is an additional 4 minutes in average for the aircraft to actually land. By taking this offset into account, our predicted arrival time virtually matches the actual arrival time. Accurate arrival time prediction is a critical capability in maintaining safe separation and sequencing of aircraft.

5.4 Discoveries

In this section, we present the value our system offers in an operational view of flight planning.

The majority of other ground-based tactical TP tools communicate with the aircraft periodically throughout the flight, obtain and update the following parameters, and predict trajectories: *i*) initial conditions (aircraft's 4D position), *ii*) flight plan, *iii*) aircraft performance model, *iv*) weather observations, and *v*) aircraft intent.

As with proprietary implementations, their prediction accuracy depends on correct initial state values and look-ahead time. Hence, they require frequent parameter updates from the aircraft. Each update requires datalink communication throughout the flight, resulting in high communication costs. To give a notional idea on communication cost, it is safe to assume that a TP tool communicates with an aircraft once every 10 seconds for position and once every 2 minutes for aircraft intent data where each message costs \$0.50, although airlines pay yearly flat rates to data link service providers such as ARINC and SITA that are kept confidential. Based on the assumption, for a single flight of 80-minute duration, the data link communication cost can add up to \$260. Depending on the fleet size and frequency and distance of flights, data link communication cost can easily become millions of dollars per year.

Unlike other TP tools, our system inputs only weather observations and predicts a trajectory, based on an HMM that was learned from the historical trajectories for particular aircraft types. Our prediction system is also ground-based and runs offline requiring no datalink communication with the aircraft. As presented in the analysis of mean error versus look-ahead time, the accuracy of a trajectory predicted by our system is independent of look-ahead time. Our system saves the airlines data communications costs, if deployed.

Initial pre-departure flight plans are filed by the AOC and approved by the FAA, when validated. As presented in the analysis of mean errors and standard deviation values, our system predicts aircraft trajectory within the boundaries of our horizontal spatial resolution of 13km. Hence, when deployed by the airlines, AOC can generate an accurate flight plan and file for approval. In return, the FAA can run our system and validate the filed flight plans, when deployed.

As presented in the analysis of arrival times, our system predicted virtually the same arrival time of flight DAL2173

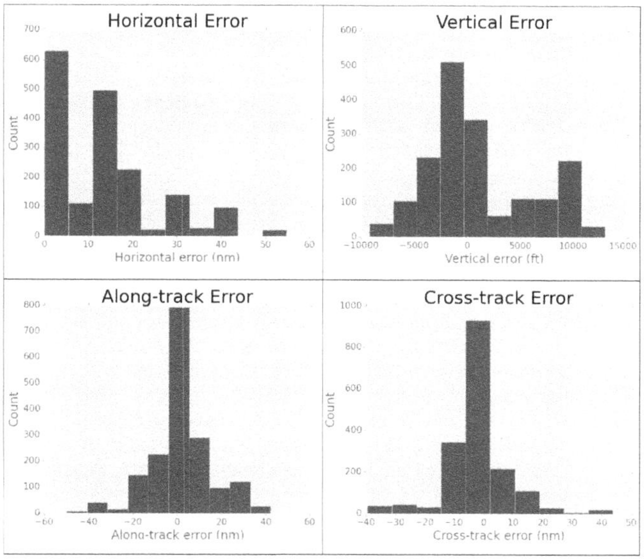

Figure 6: Histograms for horizontal, vertical, along-track, and cross-track errors

as the actual arrival time. The accuracy would help in maintaining separation and sequencing of aircraft in the NAS. Better maintained separation and sequencing means: *i*) higher safety and capacity, *ii*) accurate arrival metering which translates to efficiency and so fuel savings and reduced emissions. An erroneously predicted arrival time would lead the Air Traffic Controller to allot more time or insufficient time and airspace for the flight, and generate the incorrect landing sequence potentially reducing runway acceptance rate and causing other aircraft to be perturbed in their operations resulting in reduced efficiency, waste of resources, and possibly reducing safety. Note that the aircraft type Delta Airlines flown for DAL2173 on May 14, 2011 is Boeing 757-200 and operational cost of this particular aircraft per hour is $8,383.15 [2], or $139.72 each minute of extra flight time due to erroneous arrival prediction plus the cost of the impact on other perturbed dependent flights.

6. CONCLUSIONS

The role and performance of trajectory prediction system is critical to the success of the DST functions which have substantial impact on ATM and airspace flow management. In this paper, we have proposed a novel approach to aircraft trajectory prediction that can be used for more efficient and realistic flight planning by aircraft operators and to assist airspace flow management, potentially achieving higher safety, capacity, and efficiency and commensurate fuel savings and so emission reductions for a better environment.

Our evaluation on a real trajectory dataset verified that our prediction system achieved horizontal accuracy of $12.601km$ which is defined as a mean cross-track error $\mu(e_{cross})$ that is within the boundaries of highest spatial resolution, our trajectory prediction system has to offer. In order for us to achieve higher accuracy, we need weather observations of higher spatial resolution than $13km$, which is the current highest spatial resolution available. We plan to investigate the feasibility of resampling and intelligent interpolation of weather data to generate higher spatial resolution. Another option would be to use the recent High-Resolution Rapid Refresh (HRRR) weather product, which offers $3km$ of spatial resolution for a smaller geographic region, yet still experimental by the NOAA. The introduction of a browsing capability similar to what is available in the spatial domain (e.g., [17, 35]) is also of interest.

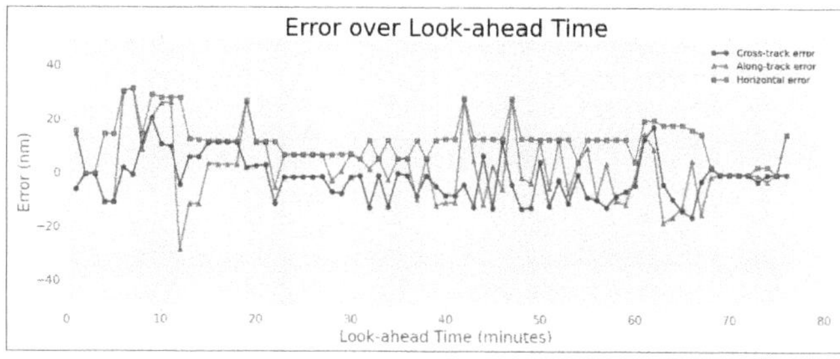

Figure 7: Horizontal, along-track, and cross-track mean errors over look-ahead time

7. ACKNOWLEDGMENTS

The authors would like to thank Milad Gholami and Alexander Wainwright for their assistance with this research. This work was supported in part by the NSF under Grants IIS-12-19023 and IIS-13-20791.

8. REFERENCES

[1] Action plan 16: Common trajectory prediction capability. https://acy.tc.faa.gov/cpat/tjm/TP_Requirements_Engineering_Methodology.pdf.

[2] Aircraft operating expenses. http://www.opshots.net/2015/04/aircraft-operating-series-aircraft-operating-expenses/.

[3] Aircraft situation display to industry. http://www.fly.faa.gov/ASDI/asdi.html.

[4] Definition of an aircraft trajectory by icao. http://ap16.atmrt.org/.

[5] Google earth. https://www.google.com/earth//.

[6] Grib2 documentation. http://www.nco.ncep.noaa.gov/pmb/docs/grib2/grib2_doc.shtml.

[7] Ncep wmo grib2 documentation. http://www.nco.ncep.noaa.gov/pmb/docs/grib2/grib2_doc.shtml.

[8] G. Avanzini. Frenet-based algorithm for trajectory prediction. *Journal of Guidance, Control, and Dynamics*, 27(1):127–135, January 2004.

[9] S. Ayhan and H. Samet. Diclerge: Divide-cluster-merge framework for clustering aircraft trajectories. In *Proceedings of the 8th ACM SIGSPATIAL IWCTS*, Seattle, WA, November 2015.

[10] J. Benavides, J. Kaneshige, S. Sharma, R. Panda, and M. Steglinski. Implementation of trajectory prediction function for trajectory based operations. In *AIAA Atmospheric Flight Mechanics Conference*, Atlanta, GA, 2014.

[11] J. Bronsvoort, G. McDonald, J. Lopez-Leones, and H. Visser. Improved trajectory prediction for air traffic management by simulation of guidance logic and inferred aircraft intent using existing data-link technology. In *AIAA GNC Conference and Exhibit*, Minneapolis, MN, August 2012.

[12] E. Casado, C. Goodchild, and M. Vilaplana. Identification and initial characterization of sources of uncertainty affecting the performance of future trajectory management automation systems. In *Proceedings of the 2nd Int'l Conference on ATACCS*, pages 170–175, Toulouse, France, May 2012.

[13] G. Chatterji. Short-term trajectory prediction methods. In *AIAA GNC Conference and Exhibit*, Portland, OR, August 1999.

[14] P. Y. Choi and M. Hebert. Learning and predicting moving object trajectory: a piecewise trajectory segment approach. Technical report, Carnegie Mellon University School of Computer Science, Pittsburgh, PA, August 2006.

[15] E. Crisostomi, A. Lecchini-visintini, and J. Maciejowski. Combining monte carlo and worst-case methods for trajectory prediction in air traffic control: A case study. *Journal of Guidance, Control and Dynamics*, 43(4), 2008.

[16] A. de Leege, M. van Paassen, and M. Mulder. A machine learning approach to trajectory prediction. In *AIAA GNC Conference and Exhibit*, Boston, MA, August 2013.

[17] C. Esperança and H. Samet. Experience with SAND/Tcl: a scripting tool for spatial databases. *Journal of Visual Languages and Computing*, 13(2):229–255, April 2002.

[18] C. Gong and D. McNally. A methodology for automated trajectory prediction analysis. In *AIAA GNC Conference and Exhibit*, Providence, RI, August 2004.

[19] R. H. Güting and M. Schneider. Realm-based spatial data types: The rose algebra. *The VLDB Journal*, 4(2):243–286, April 1995.

[20] E. Jacox and H. Samet. Metric space similarity joins. *ACM Transactions on Database Systems*, 33(2):7, June 2008.

[21] E. Keogh and C. A. Ratanamahatana. Exact indexing of dynamic time warping. *Knowl. Inf. Syst.*, 7(3):358–386, March 2005.

[22] J. Krozel and D. Andrisani. Intent inference and strategic path prediction. In *AIAA GNC Conference and Exhibit*, San Francisco, CA, August 2005.

[23] Y. Liu and X. R. Li. Intent based trajectory prediction by multiple model prediction and smoothing. In *AIAA GNC Conference and Exhibit*, New Orleans, LA, January 2015.

[24] I. Lymperopoulos, J. Lygeros, and A. Lecchini. Model based aircraft trajectory prediction during takeoff. In *AIAA GNC Conference and Exhibit*, Keystone, CO, August 2006.

[25] S. Mondoloni. A genetic algorithm for determining optimal flight trajectories. In *AIAA GNC Conference and Exhibit*, Boston, MA, August 1998.

[26] S. Mondoloni. A multiple-scale model of wind-prediction uncertainty and application to trajectory prediction. In *6th AIAA Aviation Technology, Integration and Operations Conference*, Wichita, KS, September 2006.

[27] K. T. Mueller, J. A. Sorensen, and G. J. Couluris. Strategic aircraft trajectory prediction uncertainty and statistical sector traffic load modeling. In *AIAA GNC Conference and Exhibit*, Monterey, CA, August 2012.

[28] H. K. Ng, S. Grabbe, and A. Mukherjee. Design and evaluation of a dynamic programming flight routing algorithm using the convective weather avoidance model. In *AIAA GNC Conference and Exhibit*, Chicago, IL, August 2009.

[29] S. Nutanong, E. H. Jacox, and H. Samet. An incremental Hausdorff distance calculation algorithm. *PVLDB*, 4(8):506–517, August 2011.

[30] S. Nutanong and H. Samet. Memory-efficient algorithms for spatial network queries. In *Proceedings of the 29th IEEE Int'l Conference on Data Engineering*, pages 649–660, Brisbane, Australia, April 2013.

[31] M. Paglione and R. Oaks. Implementation and metrics for a trajectory prediction validation methodology. In *AIAA GNC Conference and Exhibit*, Hilton Head, SC, August 2007.

[32] S. Peng, J. Sankaranarayanan, and H. Samet. SPDO: High-throughput road distance computations on spark using distance oracles. In *Proceedings of the 32nd IEEE Int'l Conference on Data Engineering*, pages 1239–1250, Helsinki, Finland, May 2016.

[33] L. R. Rabiner. Readings in speech recognition. chapter A Tutorial on Hidden Markov Models and Selected Applications in Speech Recognition, pages 267–296. Morgan Kaufmann, San Francisco, CA, 1990.

[34] H. Ryan and M. Paglione. State vector based near term trajectory prediction. In *AIAA GNC Conference and Exhibit*, Honolulu, HI, 2008.

[35] H. Samet, H. Alborzi, F. Brabec, C. Esperança, G. R. Hjaltason, F. Morgan, and E. Tanin. Use of the SAND spatial browser for digital government applications. *Communications of the ACM*, 46(1):63–66, January 2003.

[36] J. Sankaranarayanan, H. Alborzi, and H. Samet. Efficient query processing on spatial networks. In *Proceedings of the 13th ACM Int'l Symposium on Advances in Geographic Information Systems*, pages 200–209, Bremen, Germany, November 2005.

[37] J. Sankaranarayanan, H. Alborzi, and H. Samet. Distance join queries on spatial networks. In *Proceedings of the 14th ACM Int'l Symposium on Advances in Geographic Information Systems*, pages 211–218, Arlington, VA, November 2006.

[38] J. Sankaranarayanan and H. Samet. Distance oracles for spatial networks. In *Proceedings of the 25th IEEE Int'l Conference on Data Engineering*, pages 652–663, Shanghai, China, March 2009.

[39] J. Sankaranarayanan and H. Samet. Query processing using distance oracles for spatial networks. *IEEE Transactions on Knowledge and Data Engineering*, 22(8):1158–1175, August 2010.

[40] J. Sankaranarayanan and H. Samet. Roads belong in databases. *IEEE Data Engineering Bulletin*, 33(2):4–11, June 2010.

[41] J. Sankaranarayanan, H. Samet, and H. Alborzi. Path oracles for spatial networks. *PVLDB*, 2(1):1210–1221, August 2009.

[42] C. Schultz, D. Thipphavong, and H. Erzberger. Adaptive trajectory prediction algorithm for climbing flights. In *AIAA GNC Conference and Exhibit*, Minneapolis, MN, August 2012.

[43] T. Stewart, L. Askey, and M. Hokit. A concept for tactical reroute generation, evaluation and coordination. In *12th AIAA ATIO Conference and 14th AIAA/ISSMO Multidisciplinary Analysis and Optimization Conference*, Indianapolis, IN, September 2012.

[44] T. Stewart, J. DeArmon, , and D. Chaloux. Using flight information to improve weather avoidance predictions. In *Aviation Technology, Integration, and Operations Conference*, Los Angeles, CA, August 2013.

[45] S. Swierstra. Common trajectory prediction capability for decision support tools. In *Proceedings of ATM 2003, 5th USA/Europa R&D Seminar*, Budapest, Hungary, June 2003.

[46] C. P. Taylor and C. Wanke. Improved dynamic generation of operationally acceptable reroutes using network optimization. *Journal of Guidance, Control, and Dynamics*, 34(4):961–975, August 2011.

[47] C. Tomlin, G. J. Pappas, and S. Sastry. Conflict resolution for air traffic management: A study in multiagent hybrid systems. *IEEE Transactions on Intelligent Transportation Systems*, 43(4):509–521, April 1998.

[48] A. J. Viterbi. Error bounds for convolutional codes and an asymptotically optimum decoding algorithm. *IEEE Transactions on Information Theory*, 13(2):260–269, April 1967.

[49] L. F. Winder and J. K. Kuchar. *Hazard Avoidance Alerting with Markov Decision Processes.* PhD thesis, Department of Aeronautics and Astronautics, Massachusetts Institute of Technology, Cambridge, MA, August 2004.

[50] J. L. Yepes, I. Hwang, and M. Rotea. An intent-based trajectory prediction algorithm for air traffic control. In *AIAA GNC Conference and Exhibit*, San Francisco, CA, August 2005.

[51] J. L. Yepes, I. Hwang, and M. Rotea. New algorithms for aircraft intnet inference and trajectory prediction. *Journal of Guidance, Control, and Dynamics*, 30(2):370–382, March 2007.

Matrix Computations and Optimization in Apache Spark

Reza Bosagh Zadeh*
Stanford and Matroid
475 Via Ortega
Stanford, CA 94305
rezab@stanford.edu

Xiangrui Meng
Databricks
160 Spear Street, 13th Floor
San Francisco, CA 94105
meng@databricks.com

Alexander Ulanov
HP Labs
1501 Page Mill Rd
Palo Alto, CA 94304
alexander.ulanov@hp.com

Burak Yavuz
Databricks
160 Spear Street, 13th Floor
San Francisco, CA 94105
burak@databricks.com

Li Pu
Twitter
1355 Market Street Suite 900.
San Francisco, CA 94103
li.pu@outlook.com

Shivaram Venkataraman
UC Berkeley
465 Soda Hall
Berkeley, CA 94720
shivaram@eecs.berkeley.edu

Evan Sparks
UC Berkeley
465 Soda Hall
Berkeley, CA 94720
sparks@cs.berkeley.edu

Aaron Staple
Databricks
160 Spear Street, 13th Floor
San Francisco, CA 94105
aaron.staple@gmail.com

Matei Zaharia
MIT and Databricks
160 Spear Street, 13th Floor
San Francisco, CA 94105
matei@mit.edu

ABSTRACT

We describe matrix computations available in the cluster programming framework, Apache Spark. Out of the box, Spark provides abstractions and implementations for distributed matrices and optimization routines using these matrices. When translating single-node algorithms to run on a distributed cluster, we observe that often a simple idea is enough: separating matrix operations from vector operations and shipping the matrix operations to be ran on the cluster, while keeping vector operations local to the driver. In the case of the Singular Value Decomposition, by taking this idea to an extreme, we are able to exploit the computational power of a cluster, while running code written decades ago for a single core. Another example is our Spark port of the popular TFOCS optimization package, originally built for MATLAB, which allows for solving Linear programs as well as a variety of other convex programs. We conclude with a comprehensive set of benchmarks for hardware accelerated matrix computations from the JVM, which is interesting in its own right, as many cluster programming frameworks use the JVM. The contributions described in this paper are already merged into Apache Spark and available on Spark installations by default, and commercially supported by a slew of companies which provide further services.

*Corresponding author.

KDD '16, August 13 - 17, 2016, San Francisco, CA, USA

ISBN 978-1-4503-4232-2/16/08...$15.00
DOI: http://dx.doi.org/10.1145/2939672.2939675

CCS Concepts

•Mathematics of computing → Mathematical software; *Solvers;* **•Computing methodologies → MapReduce algorithms;** *Machine learning algorithms; Concurrent algorithms;*

Keywords

Distributed Linear Algebra, Matrix Computations, Optimization, Machine Learning, MLlib, Spark

1. INTRODUCTION

Modern datasets are rapidly growing in size and many datasets come in the form of matrices. There is a pressing need to handle large matrices spread across many machines with the same familiar linear algebra tools that are available for single-machine analysis. Several 'next generation' data flow engines that generalize MapReduce [5] have been developed for large-scale data processing, and building linear algebra functionality on these engines is a problem of great interest. In particular, Apache Spark [12] has emerged as a widely used open-source engine. Spark is a fault-tolerant and general-purpose cluster computing system providing APIs in Java, Scala, Python, and R, along with an optimized engine that supports general execution graphs.

In this work we present Spark's distributed linear algebra and optimization libraries, the largest concerted cross-institution effort to build a distributed linear algebra and optimization library. The library targets large-scale matrices that benefit from row, column, entry, or block sparsity to store and operate on distributed and local matrices. The library, named LINALG consists of fast and scalable implementations of standard matrix computations for common linear algebra operations including basic operations such as multiplication and more advanced ones such as factorizations. It also provides a variety of underlying primitives such as column and block statistics. Written in Scala and using native (`C++` and fortran based) linear algebra libraries on each node, LINALG includes Java, Scala, and Python APIs, and is released as part of the Spark project under the Apache 2.0 license.

1.1 Apache Spark

We restrict our attention to Spark, because it has several features that are particularly attractive for matrix computations:

1. The Spark storage abstraction called Resilient Distributed Datasets (RDDs) is essentially a distributed fault-tolerant vector on which programmers can perform a subset of operations expected from a regular local vector.

2. RDDs permit user-defined data partitioning, and the execution engine can exploit this to co-partition RDDs and co-schedule tasks to avoid data movement.

3. Spark logs the lineage of operations used to build an RDD, enabling automatic reconstruction of lost partitions upon failures. Since the lineage graph is relatively small even for long-running applications, this approach incurs negligible runtime overhead, unlike checkpointing, and can be left on without concern for performance. Furthermore, Spark supports optional in-memory distributed replication to reduce the amount of recomputation on failure.

4. Spark provides a high-level API in Scala that can be easily extended. This aided in creating a coherent API for both collections and matrix computations.

There exists a history of using clusters of machines for distributed linear algebra, for example [3]. These systems are often not fault-tolerant to hardware failures and assume random access to non-local memory. In contrast, our library is built on Spark, which is a dataflow system without direct access to non-local memory, designed for clusters of *commodity* computers with relatively slow and cheap interconnects, and abundant machines failures. All of the contributions described in this paper are already merged into Apache Spark and available on Spark installations by default, and commercially supported by a slew of companies which provide further services.

1.2 Challenges and Contributions

Given that we have access to RDDs in a JVM environment, four key challenges arise to building a distributed linear algebra library, each of which we address:

1. Data representation: how should one partition the entries of a matrix across machines so that subsequent matrix operations can be implemented as efficiently as possible? This led us to develop three different distributed matrix representations, each of which has benefits depending on the sparsity pattern of the data. We have built

   (a) COORDINATEMATRIX which puts each nonzero into a separate RDD entry.

   (b) BLOCKMATRIX which treats the matrix as dense blocks of non-zeros, each block small enough to fit in memory on a single machine.

   (c) ROWMATRIX which assumes each row is small enough to fit in memory. There is an option to use a sparse or dense representation for each row.

   These matrix types and the design decisions behind them are outlined in Section 2.

2. Matrix Computations must be adapted for running on a cluster, as we cannot readily reuse linear algebra algorithms available for single-machine situations. A key idea that lets us distribute many operations is to separate algorithms into portions that require matrix operations versus vector operations. Since matrices are often quadratically larger than vectors, a reasonable assumption is that vectors fit in memory on a single machine, while matrices do not. Exploiting this idea, we were able to distribute the Singular Value Decomposition via code written decades ago in FORTRAN90, as part of the ARPACK [6] software package. By separating matrix from vector computations, and shipping the matrix computations to the cluster while keeping vector operations local to the driver, we were able to distribute two classes of optimization problems:

   (a) Spectral programs: Singular Value Decomposition (SVD) and PCA

   (b) Convex programs: Gradient Descent, LBFGS, Accelerate Gradient, and other unconstrained optimization methods. We provide a port of the popular TFOCS optimization framework [1], which covers Linear Programs and a variety of other convex objectives

   Separating matrix operations from vector operations helps in the case that vectors fit in memory, but matrices do not. This covers a wide array of applications, since matrices are often quadratically larger. However, there are some cases for which vectors do not fit in memory on a single machine. For such cases, we use an RDD for the vector as well, and use BlockMatrix for data storage.

   We give an outline of the most interesting of these computations in Section 3.

3. Many distributed computing frameworks such as Spark and Hadoop run on the Java Virtual Machine (JVM), which means that achieving hardware-specific acceleration for computation can be difficult. We provide a comprehensive survey of tools that allow matrix computations to be pushed down to hardware via the Basic Linear Algebra Subprograms (BLAS) interface from the JVM. In addition to a comprehensive set of benchmarks, we have made all the code for producing the benchmark public to allow for reproducibility.

   In Section 4 we provide results and pointers to code and benchmarks.

4. Given that there are many cases when distributed matrices and local matrices need to interact (for example multiplying a distributed matrix by a local one), we also briefly describe the local linear algebra library we built to make this possible, although the focus of the paper is distributed linear algebra.

2. DISTRIBUTED MATRIX

Before we can build algorithms to perform distributed matrix computations, we need to lay out the matrix across machines. We do this in several ways, all of which use the sparsity pattern to optimize computation and space usage. A distributed matrix has long-typed row and column indices and double-typed values, stored distributively in one or more RDDs. It is very important to choose the right format to store large and distributed matrices. Converting a distributed matrix to a different format may require a global shuffle, which is quite expensive. Three types of distributed matrices have been implemented so far.

2.1 RowMatrix and IndexedRowMatrix

A RowMatrix is a row-oriented distributed matrix without meaningful row indices, backed by an RDD of its rows, where each row is a local vector. Since each row is represented by a local vector, the number of columns is limited by the integer range but it should be much smaller in practice. We assume that the number of columns is not huge for a RowMatrix so that a single local vector can be reasonably communicated to the driver and can also be stored / operated on using a single machine.

An IndexedRowMatrix is similar to a RowMatrix but with meaningful row indices. It is backed by an RDD of indexed rows, so that each row is represented by its index (long-typed) and a local vector.

2.2 CoordinateMatrix

A CoordinateMatrix is a distributed matrix backed by an RDD of its entries. Each entry is a tuple of (i: Long, j: Long, value: Double), where i is the row index, j is the column index, and value is the entry value.

A CoordinateMatrix should be used only when both dimensions of the matrix are huge and the matrix is very sparse. A CoordinateMatrix can be created from an RDD[MatrixEntry] instance, where MatrixEntry is a wrapper over (Long, Long, Double). A CoordinateMatrix can be converted to an IndexedRowMatrix with sparse rows by calling toIndexedRowMatrix.

2.3 BlockMatrix

A BlockMatrix is a distributed matrix backed by an RDD of MatrixBlocks, where a MatrixBlock is a tuple of ((Int, Int), Matrix), where the (Int, Int) is the index of the block, and Matrix is the sub-matrix at the given index with size rowsPerBlock × colsPerBlock. BlockMatrix supports methods such as add and multiply with another BlockMatrix. BlockMatrix also has a helper function validate which can be used to check whether the BlockMatrix is set up properly.

2.4 Local Vectors and Matrices

Spark supports local vectors and matrices stored on a single machine, as well as distributed matrices backed by one or more RDDs. Local vectors and local matrices are simple data models that serve as public interfaces. The underlying linear algebra operations are provided by Breeze and jblas. A local vector has integer-type and 0-based indices and double-typed values, stored on a single machine. Spark supports two types of local vectors: dense and sparse. A dense vector is backed by a double array representing its entry values, while a sparse vector is backed by two parallel arrays: indices and values. For example, a vector (1.0, 0.0, 3.0) can be represented in dense format as [1.0, 0.0, 3.0] or in sparse format as (3, [0, 2], [1.0, 3.0]), where 3 is the size of the vector.

3. MATRIX COMPUTATIONS

We now move to the most challenging of tasks: rebuilding algorithms from single-core modes of computation to operate on our distributed matrices in parallel. Here we outline some of the more interesting approaches.

3.1 Singular Value Decomposition

The rank k singular value decomposition (SVD) of an $m \times n$ real matrix A is a factorization of the form $A = U \Sigma V^T$, where U is an $m \times k$ unitary matrix, Σ is an $k \times k$ diagonal matrix with non-negative real numbers on the diagonal, and V is an $n \times k$ unitary matrix. The diagonal entries Σ are known as the singular values. The k columns of U and the n columns of V are called the "left-singular vectors" and "right-singular vectors" of A, respectively.

Depending on whether the $m \times n$ input matrix A is tall and skinny ($m \gg n$) or square, we use different algorithms to compute the SVD. In the case that A is roughly square, we use the ARPACK package for computing eigenvalue decompositions, which can then be used to compute a singular value decomposition via the eigenvalue decomposition of $A^T A$. In the case that A is tall and skinny, we compute $A^T A$, which is small, and use it locally. In the following two sections with detail the approaches for each of these two cases. Note that the SVD of a wide and short matrix can be recovered from its transpose, which is tall and skinny, and so we do not consider the wide and short case.

There is a well known connection between the eigen and singular value decompositions of a matrix, that is the two decompositions are the same for positive semidefinite matrices, and $A^T A$ is positive semidefinite with its singular values being squares of the singular values of A. So one can recover the SVD of A from the eigenvalue decomposition of $A^T A$. We exploit this relationship in the following two sections.

3.1.1 *Square SVD with ARPACK*

ARPACK is a collection of Fortran77 subroutines designed to solve eigenvalue problems [6]. Written many decades ago and compiled for specific architectures, it is surprising that it can be effectively distributed on a modern commodity cluster.

The package is designed to compute a few eigenvalues and corresponding eigenvectors of a general $n \times n$ matrix A. In the local setting, it is appropriate for sparse or structured matrices where structured means that a matrix-vector product requires order n rather than the usual order n^2 floating point operations and storage. APRACK is based upon an algorithmic variant of the Arnoldi process called the Implicitly Restarted Arnoldi Method (IRAM). When the matrix A is symmetric it reduces to a variant of the Lanczos process called the Implicitly Restarted Lanczos Method (IRLM). These variants may be viewed as a synthesis of the Arnoldi/Lanczos process with the Implicitly Shifted QR technique. The Arnoldi process only interacts with the matrix via matrix-vector multiplies.

APRACK is designed to compute a few, say k eigenvalues with user specified features such as those of largest real part or largest magnitude. Storage requirements are on the order of nk doubles with no auxiliary storage is required. A set of Schur basis vectors for the desired k-dimensional eigen-space is computed which is numerically orthogonal to working precision. The only interaction that ARPACK needs with a matrix is the result of matrix-vector multiplies.

By separating matrix operations from vector operations, we are able to distribute the computations required by ARPACK. An important feature of ARPACK is its ability to allow for arbitrary matrix formats. This is because it does not operate on the matrix directly, but instead acts on the matrix via prespecified operations, such as matrix-vector multiplies. When a matrix operation is required, ARPACK gives control to the calling program with a request for a matrix-vector multiply. The calling program must then perform the multiply and return the result to ARPACK. By using the distributed-computing utility of Spark, we can distribute the matrix-vector multiplies, and thus exploit the computational resources available in the entire cluster.

Since ARPACK is written in Fortran77, it cannot immediately be used on the Java Virtual Machine. However, through the netlib-java and breeze packages, we use ARPACK on the JVM on the driver node and ship the computations required for matrix-vector multiplies to the cluster. This also means that low-level hardware optimizations can be exploited for any local linear algebraic operations. As with all linear algebraic operations within MLlib, we use hardware acceleration whenever possible. This functionality has been available since Spark 1.1.

We provide experimental results using this idea. A very popular matrix in the recommender systems community is the Netflix Prize Matrix. The matrix has 17,770 rows, 480,189 columns, and 100,480,507 non-zeros. Below we report results on several larger matrices, up to 16x larger.

With the Spark implementation of SVD using ARPACK, calculating wall-clock time with 68 executors and 8GB memory in each, looking for the top 5 singular vectors, we can factorize larger matrices distributed in RAM across a cluster, in a few seconds, with times listed Table 1.

3.1.2 Tall and Skinny SVD

In the case that the input matrix has few enough columns that $A^T A$ can fit in memory on the driver node, we can avoid shipping the eigen-decomposition to the cluster and avoid the associated communication costs.

First we compute Σ and V. We do this by computing $A^T A$, which can be done with one all-to-one communication, details of which are available in [11, 10]. Since $A^T A = V\Sigma^2 V^T$ is of dimension $n \times n$, for small n (for example $n = 10^4$) we can compute the eigen-decomposition of $A^T A$ directly and locally on the driver to retrieve V and Σ.

Once V and Σ are computed, we can recover U. Since in this case n is small enough to fit n^2 doubles in memory, then V and Σ will also fit in memory on the driver. U however will not fit in memory on a single node and will need to be distributed, and we still need to compute it. This can be achieved by computing $U = AV\Sigma^{-1}$ which is derived from $A = U\Sigma V^T$. Σ^{-1} is easy to compute since it is diagonal, and the pseudo-inverse of V is its transpose and also easy to compute. We can distribute the computation of $U = A(V\Sigma^{-1})$ by broadcasting $V\Sigma^{-1}$ to all nodes holding rows of U, and from there it is embarrassingly parallel to compute U.

The method COMPUTESVD on the ROWMATRIX class takes care of which of the tall and skinny or square versions to invoke, so the user does not need to make that decision.

3.2 Spark TFOCS: Templates for First-Order Conic Solvers

To allow users of single-machine optimization algorithms to use commodity clusters, we have developed Spark TFOCS, which is an implementation of the TFOCS convex solver for Apache Spark.

The original Matlab TFOCS library [1] provides building blocks to construct efficient solvers for convex problems. Spark TFOCS implements a useful subset of this functionality, in Scala, and is designed to operate on distributed data using the Spark. Spark TFOCS includes support for:

- Convex optimization using Nesterov's accelerated method (Auslender and Teboulle variant)
- Adaptive step size using backtracking Lipschitz estimation
- Automatic acceleration restart using the gradient test
- Linear operator structure optimizations
- Smoothed Conic Dual (SCD) formulation solver, with continuation support
- Smoothed linear program solver
- Multiple data distribution patterns. (Currently support is only implemented for RDD[VECTOR] row matrices.)

The name "TFOCS" is being used with permission from the original TFOCS developers, who are not involved in the development of this package and hence not responsible for the support. To report issues or download code, please see the project's GitHub page

https://github.com/databricks/spark-tfocs

3.2.1 TFOCS

TFOCS is a state of the art numeric solver; formally, a first order convex solver [1]. This means that it optimizes functions that have a global minimum without additional local minima, and that it operates by evaluating an objective function, and the gradient of that objective function, at a series of probe points. The key optimization algorithm implemented in TFOCS is NesterovÕs accelerated gradient descent method, an extension of the familiar gradient descent algorithm. In traditional gradient descent, optimization is performed by moving "downhill" along a function gradient from one probe point to the next, iteration after iteration. The accelerated gradient descent algorithm tracks a linear combination of prior probe points, rather than only the most recent point, using a clever technique that greatly improves asymptotic performance.

TFOCS fine-tunes the accelerated gradient descent algorithm in several ways to ensure good performance in practice, often with minimal configuration. For example TFOCS supports backtracking line search. Using this technique, the optimizer analyzes the rate of change of an objective function and dynamically adjusts the step size when descending along its gradient. As a result, no explicit step size needs to be provided by the user when running TFOCS.

Matrix size	Number of nonzeros	Time per iteration (s)	Total time (s)
23,000,000 × 38,000	51,000,000	0.2	10
63,000,000 × 49,000	440,000,000	1	50
94,000,000 × 4,000	1,600,000,000	0.5	50

Table 1: Runtimes for ARPACK Singular Value Decomposition

Matlab TFOCS contains an extensive feature set. While the initial version of Spark TFOCS implements only a subset of the many possible features, it contains sufficient functionality to solve several interesting problems.

3.2.2 *Example: LASSO Regression*

A LASSO linear regression problem (otherwise known as L1 regularized least squares regression) can be described and solved easily using TFOCS. Objective functions are provided to TFOCS in three separate parts, which are together referred to as a composite objective function. The complete LASSO objective function can be represented as:

$$\frac{1}{2}||Ax - b||_2^2 + \lambda||x||_1$$

This function is provided to TFOCS in three parts. The first part, the linear component, implements matrix multiplication:

$$Ax$$

The next part, the smooth component, implements quadratic loss:

$$\frac{1}{2}|| \bullet -b||_2^2$$

And the final part, the nonsmooth component, implements L1 regularization:

$$\lambda||x||_1$$

The TFOCS optimizer is specifically implemented to leverage this separation of a composite objective function into component parts. For example, the optimizer may evaluate the (expensive) linear component and cache the result for later use.

Concretely, in Spark TFOCS the above LASSO regression problem can be solved as follows:

TFOCS.optimize(new SmoothQuad(b), new LinopMatrix(A), new ProxL1(lambda), x0)

Here, SmoothQuad is the quadratic loss smooth component, LinopMatrix is the matrix multiplication linear component, and ProxL1 is the $L1$ norm nonsmooth component. The x0 variable is an initial starting point for gradient descent. Spark TFOCS also provides a helper function for solving LASSO problems, which can be called as follows:

SolverL1RLS.run(A, b, lambda)

3.2.3 *Example: Linear Programming*

Solving a linear programming problem requires minimizing a linear objective function subject to a set of linear constraints. TFOCS supports solving smoothed linear programs, which include an approximation term that simplifies finding a solution. Smoothed linear programs can be represented as:

$$\begin{aligned} \text{minimize} \quad & c^T x + \frac{1}{2}||x - x_0||_2^2 \\ \text{subject to} \quad & Ax = b \\ & x \geq 0 \end{aligned}$$

A smoothed linear program can be solved in Spark TFOCS using a helper function as follows:

SolverSLP.run(c, A, b, mu)

A complete linear program example is presented here:

https://github.com/databricks/spark-tfocs

3.3 Convex Optimization

We now focus on Convex optimization via gradient descent for separable objective functions. That is, objective functions that can be written in the form of

$$F(w) = \sum_{i=1}^{n} F_i(w)$$

where w is a d-dimensional vector of parameters to be tuned and each $F_i(w)$ represents the loss of the model for the i'th training point. In the case that d doubles can fit in memory on the driver, the gradient of $F(w)$ can be computed using the computational resources on the cluster, and then collected on the driver, where it will also fit in memory. A simple gradient update can be done locally and then the new guess for w broadcast out to the cluster. This idea is essentially separating the matrix operations from the vector operations, since the vector of optimization variables is much smaller than the data matrix.

Given that the gradient can be computed using the cluster and then collected on the driver, all computations on the driver can proceed oblivious to how the gradient was computed. This means in addition to gradient descent, we can use tradtional single-node implementations of all first-order optimization methods that only use the gradient, such as accelerated gradient methods, LBFGS, and variants thereof. Indeed, we have LBFGS and accelerated gradient methods implemented in this way and available as part of MLlib. For the first time we provide convergence plots for these optimization primitives available in Spark, listed in Figure 1. We have available the following optimization algorithms, with convergence plots in Figure 1:

- gra: gradient descent implementation [7] using full batch
- acc: accelerated descent as in [1], without automatic restart [8]
- acc_r: accelerated descent, with automatic restart [1]
- acc_b: accelerated descent, with backtracking, without automatic restart [1]

- acc_rb: accelerated descent, with backtracking, with automatic restart [1]
- lbfgs: an L-BFGS implementation [13]

In Figure 1 the x axis shows the number of outer loop iterations of the optimization algorithm. Note that for backtracking implementations, the full cost of backtracking is not represented in this outer loop count. For non-backtracking implementations, the number of outer loop iterations is the same as the number of spark map reduce jobs. The y axis is the log of the difference from best determined optimized value. The optimization test runs were:

- linear: A scaled up version of the test data from TFOCS's 'test_LASSO.m' example [1], with 10000 observations on 1024 features. 512 of the features are actually correlated with result. Unregularized linear regression was used. As expected, the Scala/Spark acceleration implementation was observed to be consistent with the TFOCS implementation on this dataset.
- linear l1: The same as 'linear', but with L1 regularization
- logistic: Each feature of each observation is generated by summing a feature gaussian specific to the observation?s binary category with a noise gaussian. 10000 observations on 250 features. Unregularized logistic regression was used.
- logistic l2: Same as 'logistic', but using L2 regularization

For all runs, all optimization methods were given the same initial step size. We now note some observations. First, acceleration consistently converges more quickly than standard gradient descent, given the same initial step size. Second, automatic restarts are indeed helpful for accelerating convergence. Third, Backtracking can significantly boost convergence rates in some cases (measured in terms of outer loop iterations), but the full cost of backtracking was not measured in these runs. Finally, LBFGS generally outperformed accelerated gradient descent in these test runs.

3.4 Other matrix algorithms

There are several matrix computations on distributed matrices that use algorithms previously published, so we only cite them here:

- RowMatrix provides QR decomposition as described in [2]
- RowMatrix provides optimized computation of $A^T A$ via DIMSUM [11]
- BlockMatrix will provide large linear model parallelism [4, 9]

4. HARDWARE ACCELERATION

4.1 CPU and GPU acceleration

To allow full use of hardware-specific linear algebraic operations on a single node, we use the BLAS (Basic Linear Algebra Subroutines) interface with relevant libraries for CPU and GPU acceleration. Native libraries can be used in Scala as follows. First, native libaries must have a C BLAS interface or wrapper. The latter is called through the Java native interface implemented in Netlib-java library and wrapped by the Scala library called Breeze. We consider the following implementations of BLAS like routines:

- f2jblas - Java implementation of Fortran BLAS
- OpenBLAS - open source CPU-optimized C implementation of BLAS
- MKL - proprietary CPU-optimized C and Fortran implementation of BLAS by Intel
- cuBLAS - proprietary GPU-optimized implementation of BLAS like routines by nVidia. nVidia provides a Fortran BLAS wrapper for cuBLAS called NVBLAS. It can be used in Netlib-java through CBLAS interface.

In addition to the mentioned libraries, we also consider the BIDMat matrix library that can use MKL or cuBLAS. Our benchmark includes matrix-matrix multiplication routine called GEMM. This operation comes from BLAS Level 3 and can be hardware optimized as opposed to the operations from the lower BLAS levels. We benchmark GEMM with different matrix sizes both for single and double precision. The system used for benchmark is as follows:

- CPU - 2x Xeon X5650 @ 2.67GHz (32 GB RAM)
- GPU - 3x Tesla M2050 3GB, 575MHz, 448 CUDA cores
- Software - RedHat 6.3, Cuda 7, nVidia driver 346.72, BIDMat 1.0.3

The results for the double precision matrices are depicted on Figure 2. A full spreadsheet of results and code is available at https://github.com/avulanov/scala-blas.

Results show that MKL provides similar performance to OpenBLAS except for tall matrices when the latter is slower. Most of the time GPU is less effective due to overhead of copying matrices to/from GPU. However, when multiplying sufficiently large matrices, i.e. starting from 10000×10000 by 10000×1000, the overhead becomes negligible with respect to the computation complexity. At that point GPU is several times more effective than CPU. Interestingly, adding more GPUs speeds up the computation almost linearly for big matrices.

Because it is unreasonable to expect all machines that Spark is run on to have GPUs, we have made OpenBlas the default method of choice for hardware acceleration in Spark's local matrix computations. Note that these performance numbers are useful anytime the JVM is used for Linear Algebra, including Hadoop, Storm, and popular commodity cluster programming frameworks. As an example of BLAS usage in Spark, Neural Networks available in MLlib use the interface heavily, since the forward and backpropagation steps in neural networks are a series of matrix-vector multiplies.

A full spreadsheet of results and code is available at

https://github.com/avulanov/scala-blas

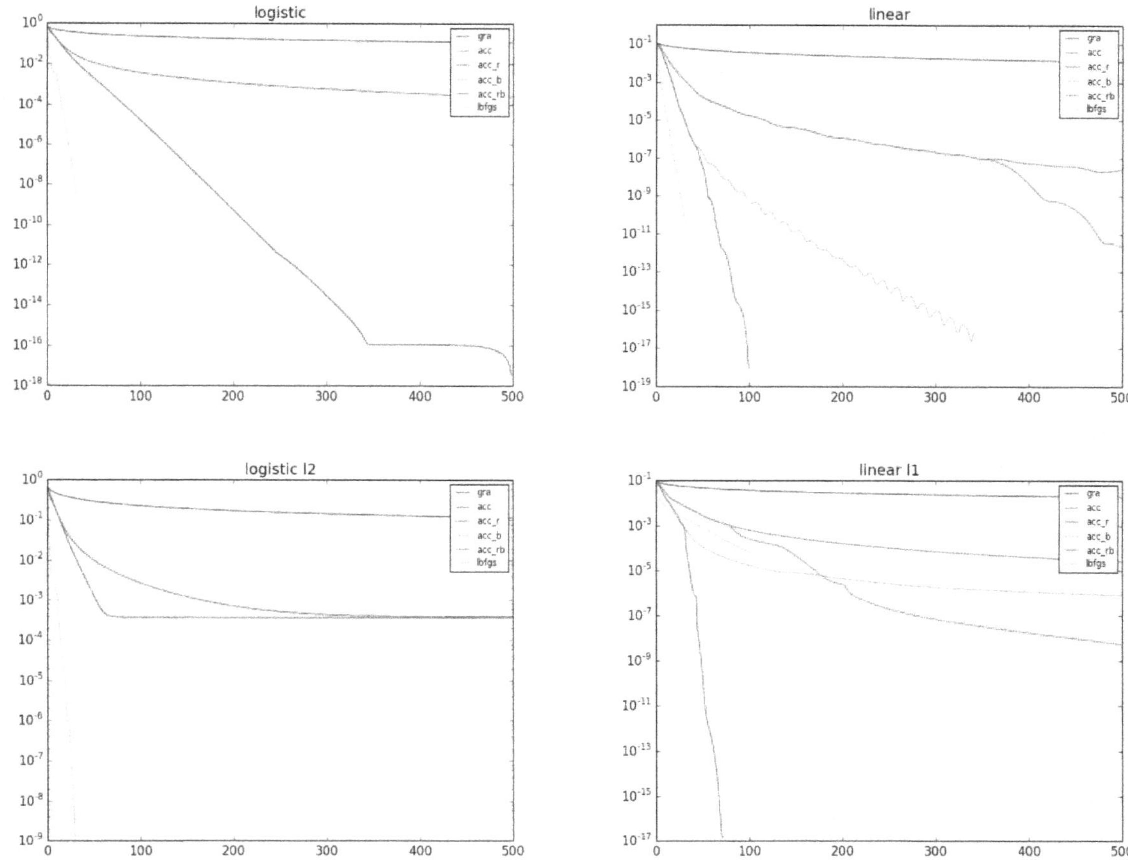

Figure 1: Error per iteration for optimization primitives. From left to right, top to bottom: logistic regression, least squares regression, L2 regularized logistic regression, L1 regularized least squares (LASSO).

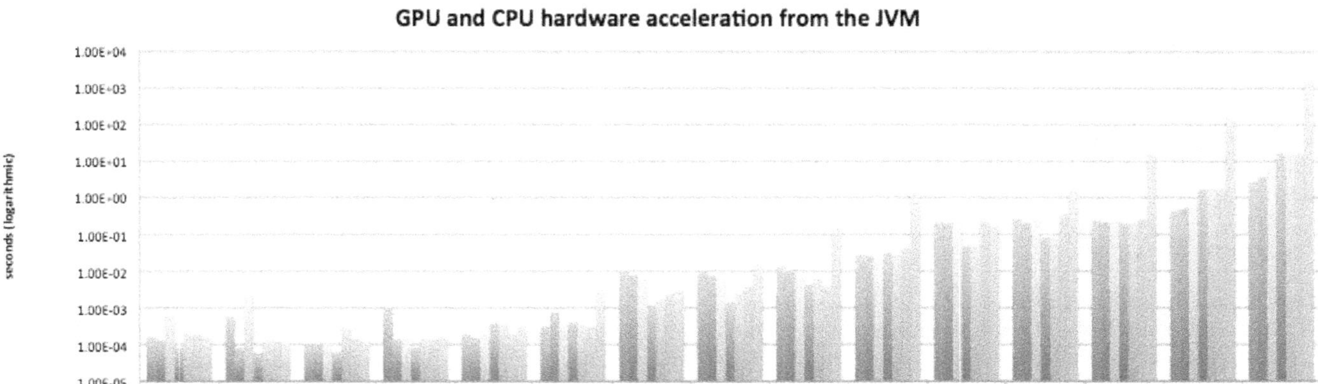

	1x1*1x1	10x10*10x1	10x10*10x10	100x100*100x1	100x100*100x10	100x100*100x100	1000x1000*1000x1	1000x1000*1000x10	1000x1000*1000x100	1000x1000*1000x1000	10000x10000*10000x1	10000x10000*10000x10	10000x10000*10000x100	10000x10000*10000x1000	10000x10000*10000x10000
netlib-nvblas 3 GPU	1.67E-04	5.93E-04	1.07E-04	1.01E-03	1.98E-04	3.27E-04	1.09E-02	1.09E-02	1.38E-02	2.74E-02	2.27E-01	2.62E-01	2.47E-01	4.39E-01	2.75E+00
netlib-nvblas 2 GPU	1.36E-04	8.26E-05	1.02E-04	1.43E-04	1.61E-04	8.02E-04	8.13E-03	8.02E-03	1.12E-02	2.61E-02	2.09E-01	2.12E-01	2.20E-01	5.14E-01	3.73E+00
netlib-nvblas 1 GPU	7.74E-04	2.29E-03	1.03E-04	1.58E-04	1.95E-04	3.48E-04	6.44E-03	6.23E-03	7.95E-03	2.14E-02	2.32E-01	2.51E-01	2.53E-01	7.69E-01	6.73E+00
BIDMat-MKL	8.85E-05	6.11E-05	6.46E-05	8.43E-05	3.98E-04	4.09E-04	1.27E-03	1.42E-03	4.42E-03	3.13E-02	4.79E-02	8.39E-02	2.11E-01	1.72E+00	1.65E+01
netlib-MKL	2.04E-04	1.30E-04	2.88E-04	1.48E-04	3.80E-04	3.66E-04	1.74E-03	2.54E-03	6.07E-03	2.63E-02	4.78E-02	8.09E-02	2.04E-01	1.74E+00	1.64E+01
netlib OpenBLAS	1.90E-04	1.29E-04	1.45E-04	1.45E-04	1.98E-04	3.15E-04	2.56E-03	3.96E-03	3.88E-03	4.01E-02	2.20E-01	3.63E-01	2.60E-01	1.73E+00	1.65E+01
netlib-f2jblas	1.65E-04	1.15E-04	1.26E-04	1.61E-04	3.22E-04	3.28E-03	3.35E-03	1.54E-02	1.49E-01	1.45E+00	1.66E-01	1.61E+00	1.61E+01	1.61E+02	1.61E+03

Figure 2: Benchmarks for hardware acceleration from the JVM. Full results and all numbers are available at https://github.com/avulanov/scala-blas

4.2 Sparse Single-Core Linear Algebra

The BLAS interface is made specifically for *dense* linear algebra. There are not many libraries on the JVM that efficiently handle sparse matrix operations, or even provide the option to store a local matrix in sparse format. MLlib provides SparseMatrix, which provides memory efficient storage in Compressed Column Storage (CCS) format. In this format, a row index and a value is stored for each non-zero element in separate arrays. The columns are formed by storing the first and the last indices of the elements for that column in a separate array.

MLlib has specialized implementations for performing Sparse Matrix × Dense Matrix, and Sparse Matrix × Dense Vector multiplications, where matrices can be optionally transposed. These implementations outperform libraries such as Breeze, and are competitive against libraries like SciPy, where implementations are backed by C. Benchmarks available at https://github.com/apache/spark/pull/2294.

Conclusions

We described the distributed and local matrix computations available in Apache Spark, a widely distributed cluster programming framework. By separating matrix operations from vector operations, we are able to distribute a large number of traditional algorithms meant for single-node usage. This allowed us to solve Spectral and Convex optimization problems, opening to the door to easy distribution of many machine learning algorithms. We conclude by providing a comprehensive set of benchmarks on accessing hardware-level optimizations for matrix computations from the JVM.

Acknowledgments

We thank all Spark contributors, a list of which can be found at:

https://github.com/apache/spark/graphs/contributors

Spark and MLlib are cross-institutional efforts, and we thank the Stanford ICME, Berkeley AMPLab, MIT CSAIL, Databricks, Twitter, HP labs, and many other institutions for their support. We further thank Ion Stoica, Stephen Boyd, Emmanuel Candes, and Steven Diamond for their valuable discussions.

5. REFERENCES

[1] Stephen R Becker, Emmanuel J Candès, and Michael C Grant. Templates for convex cone problems with applications to sparse signal recovery. *Mathematical Programming Computation*, 3(3):165–218, 2011.

[2] Austin R Benson, David F Gleich, and James Demmel. Direct qr factorizations for tall-and-skinny matrices in mapreduce architectures. In *Big Data, 2013 IEEE International Conference on*, pages 264–272. IEEE, 2013.

[3] L Susan Blackford, Jaeyoung Choi, Andy Cleary, Eduardo D'Azevedo, James Demmel, Inderjit Dhillon, Jack Dongarra, Sven Hammarling, Greg Henry, Antoine Petitet, et al. *ScaLAPACK users' guide*, volume 4. siam, 1997.

[4] Weizhu Chen, Zhenghao Wang, and Jingren Zhou. Large-scale l-bfgs using mapreduce. In *Advances in Neural Information Processing Systems*, pages 1332–1340, 2014.

[5] Jeffrey Dean and Sanjay Ghemawat. Mapreduce: simplified data processing on large clusters. *Communications of the ACM*, 51(1):107–113, 2008.

[6] Richard B Lehoucq, Danny C Sorensen, and Chao Yang. *ARPACK users' guide: solution of large-scale eigenvalue problems with implicitly restarted Arnoldi methods*, volume 6. Siam, 1998.

[7] Xiangrui Meng, Joseph Bradley, Burak Yavuz, Evan Sparks, Shivaram Venkataraman, Davies Liu, Jeremy Freeman, DB Tsai, Manish Amde, Sean Owen, Doris Xin, Reynold Xin, Michael J. Franklin, Reza Zadeh, Matei Zaharia, and Ameet Talwalkar. Mllib: Machine learning in apache spark. *arXiv preprint arXiv:1505.06807*, 2015.

[8] Brendan OâĂŹDonoghue and Emmanuel Candes. Adaptive restart for accelerated gradient schemes. *Foundations of computational mathematics*, 15(3):715–732, 2013.

[9] Reza Bosagh Zadeh. Large linear model parallelism via a join and reducebykey. https://issues.apache.org/jira/browse/SPARK-6567, 2015. Accessed: 2015-08-09.

[10] Reza Bosagh Zadeh and Gunnar Carlsson. Dimension independent matrix square using mapreduce. In *Foundations of Computer Science (FOCS 2013) - Poster*, 2013.

[11] Reza Bosagh Zadeh and Ashish Goel. Dimension independent similarity computation. *The Journal of Machine Learning Research*, 14(1):1605–1626, 2013.

[12] Matei Zaharia, Mosharaf Chowdhury, Michael J Franklin, Scott Shenker, and Ion Stoica. Spark: cluster computing with working sets. In *Proceedings of the 2nd USENIX conference on Hot topics in cloud computing*, volume 10, page 10, 2010.

[13] Ciyou Zhu, Richard H Byrd, Peihuang Lu, and Jorge Nocedal. Algorithm 778: L-bfgs-b: Fortran subroutines for large-scale bound-constrained optimization. *ACM Transactions on Mathematical Software (TOMS)*, 23(4):550–560, 1997.

APPENDIX

Appendix A - BLAS references

To find information about the implementations used, here we provide links to implementations used in Figure 2.

1. Netlib, Reference BLAS and CBLAS http://www.netlib.org/blas/
2. Netlib-java https://github.com/fommil/netlib-java
3. Breeze https://github.com/scalanlp/breeze
4. BIDMat https://github.com/BIDData/BIDMat/
5. OpenBLAS https://github.com/xianyi/OpenBLAS
6. CUDA http://www.nvidia.com/object/cuda_home_new.html
7. NVBLAS http://docs.nvidia.com/cuda/nvblas

Predicting Disk Replacement towards Reliable Data Centers

Mirela Botezatu
IBM Research
Zurich Switzerland
bot@zurich.ibm.com

Ioana Giurgiu
IBM Research
Zurich Switzerland
igi@zurich.ibm.com

Jasmina Bogojeska
IBM Research
Zurich Switzerland
jbo@zurich.ibm.com

Dorothea Wiesmann
IBM Research
Zurich Switzerland
dor@zurich.ibm.com

ABSTRACT

Disks are among the most frequently failing components in today's IT environments. Despite a set of defense mechanisms such as RAID, the availability and reliability of the system are still often impacted severely.

In this paper, we present a highly accurate SMART-based analysis pipeline that can correctly predict the necessity of a disk replacement even 10-15 days in advance. Our method has been built and evaluated on more than 30000 disks from two major manufacturers, monitored over 17 months. Our approach employs statistical techniques to automatically detect which SMART parameters correlate with disk replacement and uses them to predict the replacement of a disk with even 98% accuracy.

Keywords

Disk replacement; time series; classification; changepoint

1. INTRODUCTION

Data center downtime costs have increased significantly in the past years from \$5,600/minute in 2010 to \$8,851/minute in 2016 according to a study conducted on 63 data center organizations in the U.S [1]. IT equipment failure is a significant contributor to such downtimes.Disks are among the most frequently failing components in today's IT environments. It appears that field behavior of disks is fairly different than the one described in the datasheet specifications [18]. Factors such as temperature, duty cycles or workloads may significantly affect both the reliability and the performance of hard drives. Reliability issues are by far the most severe and manifest themselves as disk failures leading to replacements.

Disk failures can be either predictable or unpredictable. On the one hand, unpredictable failures, ranging from electronic components becoming defective to sudden crashes due to improper handling, cannot be foreseen by monitoring. On the other hand, predictable failures mainly result from slow processes such as wear-and-tear that typically progress over months or years. The latter ones make it possible for predictive failure analysis.

In this paper, we introduce a novel data mining approach able to automatically predict disk replacements based on historic disk replacement data from an expert-maintained disk environment and hence minimize the effects of component failure as shown in Figure 1.

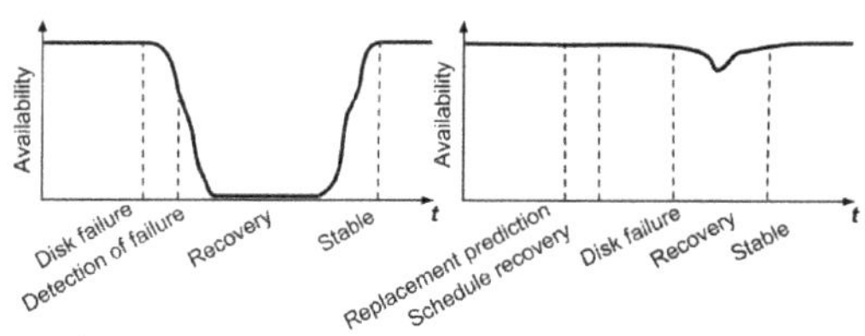

Figure 1: Availability: without proactive replacement (left) vs. with proactive replacement(right)

SMART monitoring (disk sensors' data) can be used to determine when disk failures become more likely. Some manufacturers even use them to deploy drives with embedded predictive models. However, these models are proprietary and often times, simple, threshold-based normalizations, that are designed to avoid false alarms and therefore have a very weak predictive power [18, 17, 12] .

In this paper, we focus on the automatic forecasting of predictable disk replacements using SMART attributes. For this purpose, we use data collected from a large population of disks (>30000) monitored over 17 months. A drive is labeled as failed when it stopped working, it is non-responsive to commands, the RAID system reports that the drive cannot be written or read, or it shows evidence of failing soon [2]. Therefore, the model goes beyond the expert knowledge used in proactive replacements and is able to detect failures that this knowledge can not capture (see Section 3.6).

The goals of our analysis are two-fold: (1) to provide the set of SMART attributes that are informative for disk replacements; (2) to use these attributes to build a statistical model that automatically predicts impending replacements with high accuracy (81-98%). Such a model not only automates the disk replacement decision, but also allows ad-

KDD '16, August 13 - 17, 2016, San Francisco, CA, USA

ISBN 978-1-4503-4232-2/16/08... \$15.00

DOI: http://dx.doi.org/10.1145/2939672.2939699

ministrators to proactively replace disks at risk, days in advance.

To achieve these goals, we employ an approach that comprises four steps. First, we use changepoint detection in time series to identify the SMART attributes indicative of impending replacements. Second, we transform the event sequence into a set of examples [20] by encoding multiple events as individual points such that we achieve a compact, yet informative representation of the time series of each disk. Next, we build a predictive classification model that is able to discriminate between healthy and failure-impending drives, by using these data points as inputs. Finally, we propose a transfer learning approach to enable replacement decision prediction on data from novel disk models.

There are several challenges one may encounter when performing the aforementioned steps. In the following, we list a few of them. Since SMART indicators are manufacturer-specific, their encoding and normalization varies widely across manufacturers. This hinders the possibility to fit one predictive model for all different disk manufacturers. A separate model needs to be trained for each individual disk manufacturer. Further, due to the lack of standards when implementing SMART attributes, one needs to discover the ones that are indicative of failures. Finally, the disk data are highly unbalanced (only about 2% of disks are replaced), which makes the task of fitting high quality models very challenging.

Therefore, we build and evaluate our approach for disks from two individual manufacturers. Following our efforts to choose the right SMART indicators and tuning the predictive model, results show up to 98% accuracy in identifying both disks that are about to be replaced and those that are healthy, when using only a small set of SMART parameters.

The remainder of this paper is organized as follows. In Section 2, we describe the predictive pipeline, whereas in Section 3 we present experimental results. We discuss deployment in Section 4 and finally review the state-of-the-art in Section 5 and conclude in Section 6.

2. PREDICTING DISK REPLACEMENT

Given the longitudinal measurements of the SMART attributes for a large set of disks, from a specific disk model of interest and information on their replacements, we develop a fully automated approach for solving the disk replacement prediction problem. Our method is summarized in Algorithm 1 and consists of four consecutive steps: (1) selection of relevant SMART attributes, (2) compact time-series representation, (3) balancing of the healthy and unhealthy disk classes via informed downsampling, and (4) classification model for disk replacements. In the following, we present the details of each step.

2.1 Selection of relevant SMART attributes

The main goal of this step is to automatically discover the set of SMART attributes that are indicative of impending disk replacements. This will reveal the most informative predictors with respect to the disks at risk to the domain experts. As SMART attribute data are gathered over time, we address this feature selection problem through changepoint detection in time series. More specifically, when a SMART attribute is informative of disk replacement, we expect a significant shift in its values at some time point before the actual replacement, i.e., at the changepoint. Moreover, this shift should be permanent and unrecoverable to be indicative of a disk replacement. In the following we provide a more formal description of the approach for detecting the permanent changepoints for SMART attributes.

Algorithm 1 Disk replacement prediction algorithm

Input: A time series collection of SMART attributes along with the disk replacement information for a given target disk type.

1. Find the subset of SMART attributes indicative of disk replacements by identifying significant changepoints in their corresponding time series;
2. Compute a highly-informative compact representation for the time series corresponding to each relevant attribute from Step 1 via exponential smoothing;
3. Perform informative downsampling via K-means clustering to address the high class imbalance in the disk replacement datasets;
4. Use the training dataset from Step 3 to fit a classification model that predicts disk replacements.

Output: Predictive model for disk replacement using a small set of SMART attributes.

Let $S_i = (s_1, s_2, \cdots, s_p)$ denote the time series for a target SMART attribute comprising p measurements ordered by their timestamps, where s_p is the most recent one when the disk replacement has occurred. If there exists a timestamp $t < p$ when a significant change in the values of the attribute S_i occurs (e.g., the values start increasing), then we consider S_i a potential attribute relevant for the disk replacement. We determine the time point t that indicates a significant change using the approach described in [7]. Briefly, $t = argmax_\tau ML(\tau)$ provided that $ML(t)$ is significantly larger than $\log p(\mathbf{s}_{1:p} \mid \hat{\theta})$, where:

$$ML(\tau) = \log(p(\mathbf{s}_{1:\tau} \mid \hat{\theta_1})) + \log(p(\mathbf{s}_{\tau+1:p} \mid \hat{\theta_2})). \quad (1)$$

Next, we verify whether the change is permanent by checking whether the difference between the time series of the potential SMART attribute and the corresponding time series of the same attribute in the absence of the observed change at time point t is significant. We do this as follows. First, let the time series $\Gamma_t = (s_t, \cdots, s_p)$ denote the subsequent values recorded for the potential SMART indicator S_i starting from the timestamp t to the time of the replacement p. Then, we generate a synthetic time series for the same indicator denoted $\Psi = (\tilde{s}_{t+1}, \cdots, \tilde{s}_p)$ that has no significant change at time point t. More specifically, we compute the posterior distribution of Ψ, $p(\tilde{\mathbf{s}}_{(t+1):p} \mid \mathbf{s}_{1:(t)}, \mathbf{x}_{1:p})$ given the value of the series in the pre-change period $\mathbf{s}_{1:t}$ along with the values of the control time series $\mathbf{x}_{1:p}$ using a Bayesian structural time-series model. The control time series is a sample of the values of the target SMART attribute collected for a healthy disk. Finally, the target SMART attribute is indicative of a disk replacement if the probability distributions of the actual time series measured after the detected change point and the synthetic one generated based on the values of a healthy disk are significantly different. We assess the difference via hypothesis testing. Formally, let Γ_k and

Ψ be samples generated from unknown distributions P and Q, respectively.

The hypothesis to test is the following:

$$\begin{cases} H_0 : P = Q \\ H_1 : P \neq Q \end{cases} \quad (2)$$

Then we check whether we can reject the null hypothesis H_0 that the two probability distributions P and Q are equal with high confidence.

2.2 Compact time series representation

As the previous step results in the set of relevant SMART indicators for the disk replacement problem, the goal of this step is to provide a compact, but highly informative representation the time series of each indicator that can readily be employed in the predictive model.

There are several observations that hint the necessity of a compact representation for the time series data: (i) Each daily observation on its own is not enough - we need to consider a longer time frame - this is because the single day record is not stable due to the recovery mechanisms embedded in the disk. (ii) Also, if we considered as observations for the failed class only the entries from the last day of the life of the disk then the model will not be able to predict replacement in advance as it can only recognize the instances when drive fails not before.

Therefore, we use a window to split the raw data set into segments. We aggregate each of the relevant time series to a single value using exponential smoothing over a specific time window. This way, we assign the highest weights to the most recent observations and exponentially decreasing weights to the remaining observations as they get older. Intuitively we expect that the observations closer to the time point of the disk replacement are more informative compared to the older ones. Formally:

$$S_t = \alpha \cdot Y_t + (1 - \alpha) \cdot S_{t-1} \quad (3)$$

In the equation above, the smoothed value at time t, S_t is computed recursively based on the observation at time t and the smoothed value at time $t-1$. When fixing the width of the window to a value k, S_t becomes the weighted average of a certain number of the past observations up to Y_{t-k}.A smaller value of k causes a weaker smoothing effect which enables higher sensitivity to new changes in the data. The parameter α controls the speed at which the older observations are dampened. A large α is used for assigning lower weights to observations from the more distant past.

For each relevant SMART attribute, the width of the time window used in the smoothing process is chosen as *the median of the distribution of the time stamps of their corresponding significant change* computed as described in Section 2.1.

2.3 Class balancing via informative downsampling

The data to be used in the predictive model is highly imbalanced, as only a small percentage of all disks are replaced over time. Since classification algorithms are typically optimized to maximize the overall accuracy, when trained using imbalanced datasets they exhibit poor predictive performance. To address this issue, we balance the training dataset for our predictive model by using a representative subset of the data for the dense class – in our case the healthy disks. This representative subset is chosen such that it comprises the most informative samples with low or no redundancy. We achieve this by clustering the observations pertaining to the healthy disk set into k clusters using the K-means clustering algorithm [15]. Next, for each cluster, we select the data points closest to the respective cluster centroid as representatives for the healthy disk class. Finally, we generate a balanced training dataset by choosing k close to the number of samples available for the replaced disks.

2.4 Classification for disk replacements

In the final step of our approach we fit a model that utilizes the training dataset generated in the previous step and provides high quality disk replacement predictions for new, unseen data. Formally, let $D = \{(\mathbf{x_i}, y_i)\}_{i=1}^{n}$ denote the training dataset, where $\mathbf{x_i} \in X$ is a multivariate temporal observation aggregating information between time points t_{i-k} and t_i for the set of relevant SMART attributes, and y is a binary response variable ($y \in \{0, 1\}$). We want to learn a function $h\colon X \rightarrow \{0, 1\}$ that minimizes the loss $\ell(h(\mathbf{x}); y)$ that quantifies the prediction quality. Intuitively the goal is to train a model that correctly predicts whether a disk needs replacement ($y = 1$) or not ($y = 0$).

We tackle this problem using the regularized greedy forests (RGF) [14] approach that is a powerful, non-linear classification method. We show that, for this task, it delivers better quality predictions compared to other tree ensemble based methods such as gradient boosted decision trees (GBDT) [21] or random forests [6] and also outperforms other classification methods such as SVM [8], or logistic regression [9].

The RGF algorithm is a variation of GBDT in which the structure search and the optimization are decoupled. More specifically, the main differences are given as follows:

- RGF introduces an explicit regularization term that takes advantage of individual tree structures.

$$\hat{h} = argmin_{h \in H}[\ell(h(\mathbf{x}); y) + R(h)] \quad (4)$$

- RGF employs a *fully-corrective* greedy algorithm which iteratively modifies the weights of all the leaf nodes (decision rules) currently obtained while new rules are added into the forest by greedy search. Here, an explicit regularization is also included to avoid overfitting and very large models.

- RGF utilizes the concept of structured sparsity to perform greedy search directly over the forest nodes based on the forest structure.

The general framework of RGF is given in Algorithm 2 which we describe in the following.

F represents a forest, and each node v of F is associated with the pair (b_v, a_v), where b_v denotes the basis function of node v and a_v the weight assigned to this node. The model of F is given by $h_{F(x)} = \sum_{v \in F} a_v b_v(\mathbf{x})$ with $a_v = 0$ for any internal node v.

In this setting, the regularized loss specified in Eq. 4 is a function of F: $Q(F) = \ell(h_F(\mathbf{x}), y) + R(h_F)$. Further, $S(F)$ represents the set of all structure-changing operations applicable to F (i.e. the split of a node or the addition of a new tree).

Algorithm 2 Regularized Greedy Forest framework

$F \leftarrow \{\}$
while stopping criterion not met **do**
Fix weights and adjust forest structure s:
$\hat{s} \leftarrow argmin_{s \in S(F)} Q(s(F))$ (the optimum s that minimizes $Q(F)$ among all the structures that can be obtained by applying one structure-changing operation to F).
if some criterion is met **then**
Fix the structure and change the weights in F s.t. the loss is minimized in $Q(F)$ (it can be optimized using a standard procedure (such as coordinate descent) if the regularization penalty is standard e.g., *L2-loss*
end if
end while
Optimize leaf weights in F to minimize loss in $Q(F)$
return $h_F(\mathbf{x})$

2.5 Transfer learning

As illustrated in Figure 5 in Section 3.5, the data collected from different disk models are different. We observe the fact that different models of a single disk manufacturer have similar SMART reporting but different distributions of the values reported for the SMART attributes. Therefore, utilizing an existing predictive model created on the training data of a specific disk model will not deliver the optimal predictive performance when directly applied on the data collected from a different disk model from the same manufacturer. In data mining, this problem is referred to as *sample selection bias, covariate shift or dataset shift*. Therefore, we apply a transfer learning approach in order to be able to use a prediction model trained on specific disk model for a new disk model of the same manufacturer.

Note that such an approach is valuable as it transfers the expert knowledge gathered over the years through historic data to a new disk model from a given manufacturer of interest. We tackle the described dataset shift issue we have across disk models of a given manufacturer as follows. We leverage the unlabeled data for the target (new) disk model to conduct a sample selection de-biasing, as described in Algorithm 3. The idea behind the algorithm is to train a classifier that can rank the observations linked to a specific disk model based on their similarity to observations pertaining to the target disk model. Furthermore, this enables to sample the observations from the original disk model (which are already labeled) that are more representative for learning the class labels for the target disk model, i.e. that matches the distribution of the original disk model to the target disk model. Learning a predictive model using a training sample that reflects the distribution of the new disk model results in higher quality predictions.

3. EVALUATION

In the following, we present our experimental setup and the results obtained in each step of our approach.

3.1 Data description and experimental setup

Our analysis is based on the Backblaze dataset[1]. The set contains data collected from 50984 hard disks, monitored over 27 months (April 2013 to June 2015) with daily granularity. The data collected contains the following: (1) timestamp, (2) disk serial number, (3) disk model, (4) disk capacity, (5) failure - '0' if the drive is alive and '1' if the disk has been replaced the following day, and (6) SMART statistics. From the disk models, we extract the manufacturers and we restrict our analysis to Hitachi[2] and Seagate[1] due to the fact that for the other manufacturers there are only few samples in the dataset, or poor population of the SMART parameters. We also exclude all monitoring data between April 2013 and January 2014, as more than 70% of the SMART parameters are not collected. Thus the dataset we consider is gathered over 17 months.

First, we build and evaluate the predictive model described in this paper for Seagate ST4000DM000 (SgtA) and Hitachi HDS722020ALA330 (HitA). Then, we evaluate the transfer learning approach on Seagate ST31500541AS (SgtB) and Hitachi HDS5C3030ALA630 (HitB), respectively. Further details on the data are presented in Table 1.

Algorithm 3 Transfer learning for different models

Input: $D_{DM_1} = \{x_i, y_i\}_i^n$, the labeled data collected from disk model 1, and $D_{DM_2} = \{x'_i, y'_i\}_i^m$ the unlabeled data from disk model 2.

1. Let $D_{DM_1} = \{x_i, y_i\}_i^n$ be the labeled data collected from disk model 1, and $D_{DM_2} = \{x'_i, y'_i\}_i^m$ be the unlabeled data from disk model 2.
2. Let $D_{aug} = \{x_i, \text{“}DM_1\text{”}\}_i^n \cup \{x'_i, \text{“}DM_2\text{”}\}_i^m$
3. Use D_{aug} to learn a function $f : X \to [0,1]$, such that $f(x)$ represents the probability of a disk being of type “DM_1” or “DM_2”.
4. Sample a subset D_{sub} from D_{DM_1} according to f .
5. Use D_{sub} to learn a function $g : X \to [0,1]$ (call the procedure in Algorithm 2) such that $g(x)$ represents the probability of a disk of type DM_2 needing replacement.

Output: Predictive model for disk replacement for disk model 2.

	Original		**Post-aggregation**	
	H	R	H	R
SgtA	247524	543	17769	457
SgtB	30859	375	2188	227
HitA	75618	150	4616	115
HitB	74040	80	4662	73

Table 1: Healthy (H) vs. replaced (R) disks in the raw dataset and after data cleaning and aggregation for Hitachi and Seagate.

3.2 Selection of relevant SMART attributes

First, note that for each SMART indicator there are two values recorded – the raw value, and the normalized value. The raw value often represents counts or a physical unit (e.g., degrees Celsius or milliseconds). The normalized values are a vendor specific mapping of the raw values such that, typically, higher values indicate healthy disks with some exceptions (e.g., the *temperature* attribute for Seagate models). A detailed breakdown of the SMART parameters is found in [4].

[1]https://www.backblaze.com/hard-drive-test-data.html

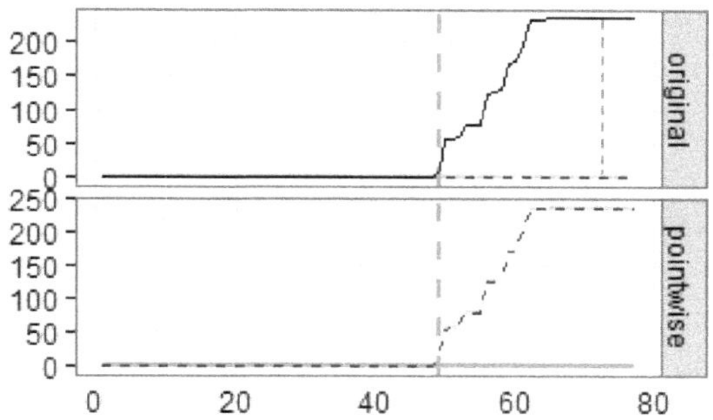

Figure 2: Differences between the forecasted and the observed values for SMART_187_raw.

As presented in Section 2, we find SMART indicators relevant for disk replacements via changepoint analysis.

In Figure 2, we illustrate the evolution of the time series for the parameter SMART_187_raw (reported uncorrectable errors) over 80 days for SgtA disk. Note that after 50 days of usage the disk starts to accumulate uncorrectable errors, up to the point where a replacement is necessary. Since there is a significant difference between the time series observed on days 1 to 50 and the one observed on days 50 to 80, our algorithm detects a changepoint 30 days before the disk has been replaced.

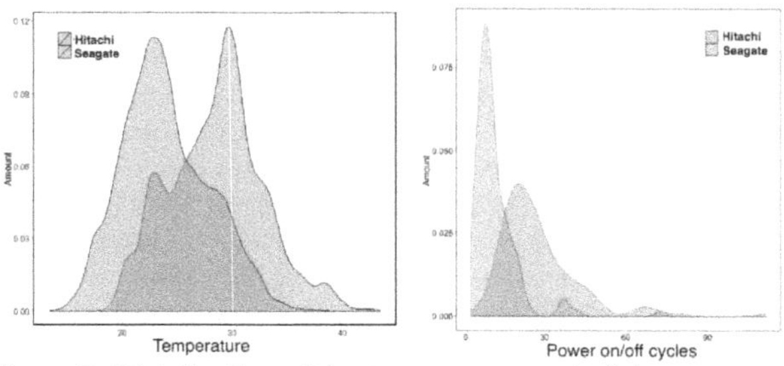

Figure 3: Distribution of the temperature and of the power on off cycles across the replaced disks for Hitachi and Seagate.

We perform the changepoint analysis for both Seagate and Hitachi disks and present the results in Table 2. For each of the considered SMART parameters we report the percentage of drives for which a correlation with disk is observed.

For Seagate, 63% of the replaced drives correlate with an increase in SMART_193_raw (the load cycle count), and between 19 and 26% of them also correlate with SMART_7_raw (seek error count), SMART_1_normalized (read error rate), SMART_240_raw (transfer error rate), SMART_197_raw (nr. of pending sectors), SMART_198_raw (uncorrectable sector count), SMART_187_raw (number of uncorrectable errors), as well as SMART_5_raw (reallocated sector count).

For Hitachi, only some of these SMART parameters are indicative of drive replacements. Among the top correlated indicators for Hitachi (30-47%), we note SMART_196_raw (reallocation event count), SMART_194_normalized (internal temperature), SMART_5_raw and SMART_197_raw.

We also note that it's mostly the raw values of SMART indicators that correlate with impending replacements. This is expected, since, the normalized values are computed based on generous thresholds, where a replacement can also occur *before* the normalized value changes at all.

The changepoint analysis also shows that some SMART indicators correlate stronger with the replacements of the

	SgtA		**HitA**	
	Ratio	Inp.	Ratio	Inp.
SMART_1_norm	23%	✓	28%	✓
SMART_1_raw	2%	✓	15%	✓
SMART_3_norm	–	×	13%	✓
SMART_3_raw	–	×	15%	✓
SMART_5_norm	2%	✓	22%	✓
SMART_5_raw	19%	✓	31%	✓
SMART_7_norm	14%	✓	–	×
SMART_7_raw	26%	✓	–	×
SMART_183_norm	0.5%	×	–	×
SMART_183_raw	0.5%	×	–	×
SMART_184_norm	1%	✓	–	×
SMART_184_raw	1%	✓	–	×
SMART_187_norm	21%	✓	–	×
SMART_187_raw	21%	✓	–	×
SMART_188_norm	0%	×	–	×
SMART_188_raw	10%	✓	–	×
SMART_189_norm	1%	✓	–	×
SMART_189_raw	1%	✓	–	×
SMART_190_norm	2%	✓	–	×
SMART_190_raw	2%	✓	–	×
SMART_193_norm	10%	✓	–	×
SMART_193_raw	63%	✓	–	×
SMART_194_norm	2%	✓	31%	✓
SMART_194_raw	2%	✓	2%	✓
SMART_196_norm	–	×	20%	✓
SMART_196_raw	–	×	26%	✓
SMART_197_norm	5%	✓	4%	✓
SMART_197_raw	27%	✓	22%	✓
SMART_198_norm	6%	✓	–	×
SMART_198_raw	27%	✓	–	×
SMART_199_norm	0%	×	–	×
SMART_199_raw	0.5%	×	–	×
SMART_240_norm	0.5%	×	–	×
SMART_240_raw	21%	✓	–	×
SMART_241_norm	0%	–	–	×
SMART_241_raw	15%	✓	–	×
SMART_242_norm	0%	×	–	×
SMART_242_raw	19%	✓	–	×

Table 2: SMART correlation frequencies for SgtA and HitA. A ✓indicates the predictor is included in the classification task.

Seagate model than with those of the Hitachi model, and vice versa. We discuss these differences in the context of SMART_194 (the disk internal temperature). Relative to temperature, 31% of the Hitachi replaced disks correlate, compared to only 2% for Seagate. We attribute this to the overall higher temperatures that characterize the Hitachi disks, as shown through the comparative plots in Fig. 3. Although the distributions are similar, there is a clear shift towards higher temperature for Hitachi, by 5 to 10 degrees Celsius.

3.3 Compact time series representations

Fig. 4 shows the distribution of the number of days before replacement when the changepoint was observed for six SMART indicators (read error rate, the number of reallocated sectors, the number of pending sectors, the reported uncorrectable errors, the seek error count and the transfer error rate). Note how the median values are different from one predictor to another. We use these median values to select the length of the window of the time series when creating the compact representation.

We notice that on the one hand, for the number of real-

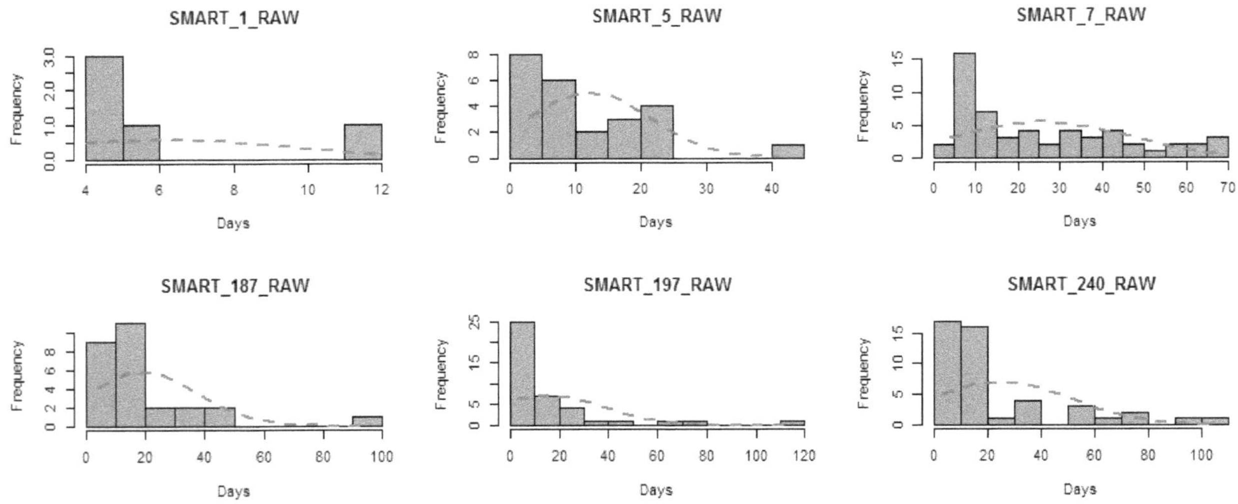

Figure 4: Distribution of the number of days before replacement when the changepoint was observed.

located sectors and of pending sectors (SMART_5_raw and SMART_197_raw), considering the last 12 and 10 days, respectively, before the disk replacement in the predictive model is sufficient. This is because an increase in either of these two parameters indicates that a remapping operation is necessary (i.e., data from the defective sector is transferred to a spare area). As shown in [17], a drive which has had any reallocated or pending sectors at all is significantly more likely to fail in the nearest future. An even stronger indicator for replacement is the read error rate (SMART_1_raw), which represents the rate of hardware read errors while reading data from the disk surface. It indicates a critical problem with the read/write heads (e.g., head resonance or contamination, broken head, etc.) and in most cases an imminent failure. From our dataset, we find that for this predictor, looking back only 4 days in the past is sufficient for the predictive model. Similarly, a drive with uncorrectable errors as indicated by SMART_187_raw (i.e., cannot be recovered using hardware ECC) may need to replaced about 15 days after the event.

On the other hand, for the seek and transfer error rates (SMART_7_raw and SMART_240_raw), the algorithm considers the past 25 days in the aggregation process. Both are indicative of malfunctions of the magnetic heads, but hinder performance primarily and lead to failures only in a second phase. For instance, seek errors hint at the drive overshooting or undershooting the correct track when it moves the heads. This implies it will need to perform another seek to acquire the track before it can read or write data.

3.4 Classification for disk replacements

Since only 2.5 to 3% of the disks for both SgtA and HitA models are replaced, the classifier will be biased towards the healthy drives. Thus, we downsample the healthy class to an amount that is close to the size of the replaced class. We choose to downsample to 1000 for SgtA and to 500 for HitA. These values are chosen based on the error estimate of the Regularized Greedy Forest (RGF) classifier. Consequently, we run K-means with 100 and 50 clusters as inputs and subsequently for each cluster we select the top 10 data points closest to the centroid of each cluster.

The SMART attributes used to build the predictive model correspond to the rows that have non-null entries and values higher than 1% in Table 2. In essence, for the Seagate model we use 26 SMART predictors and for the Hitachi model only 12. This discrepancy in the amount of predictors we feed to the Seagate model versus the Hitachi one will be reflected in the difference in performance of the classifiers.

To evaluate the classifier's performance, we measure precision, recall and F-score as defined below, for both replaced and healthy classes. Precision is used to measure the ability of the classifier to correctly identify disks at risk. Recall measures the classifier's sensitivity, i.e the the ability of the classifier to capture all replaced disks. A higher recall is equivalent to minimizing the number of false negatives (i.e., the number of disks labeled as healthy when they were actually replaced). The F-score is the combined score between precision and recall, or the weighted harmonic mean.

$$P = \frac{tp}{tp + fp} \qquad R = \frac{tp}{tp + fn} \qquad \text{F-score} = \frac{2PR}{P + R}$$

We perform a systematic comparison with different classifiers. In order to assess the goodness of each classifier we run the following experiment. We generate 100 random splits of the dataset into training (80%) and test (20%), and for each such split, we train the model on the training set and evaluate it on the test set and compare the performance of RGF with that of other classifiers such as Random Forests (RF), Gradient Boosted Decision Trees (GBDT), Support Vector Machines (SVM), Logistic Regression (LR) and decision trees (DT).

For a fair comparison, we have performed parameter tuning (grid search on parameter space to maximize accuracy) for all the parametric classifiers. For RGF we have obtained the best performance when using the L2 regularizer. There were two L2 regularization parameters to be tuned: one for weight optimization – which was set to 1 and and the other for tree learning which was set to 0.005. The model size in terms of the number of leaf nodes in the forest was set to 10000 leafs. The results are given in Table 3.

In case of the replaced disks, the model exhibits better prediction quality for Seagate, where we have 4x more data

		RGF		GBDT		RF		SVM		LR		DT	
		SgtA	HitA	SgtA	HitA	SgtA	HitA	SgtA	HitA	SgtA	HitA	SgtA	HitA
Replaced	P	0.98	0.84	0.97	0.82	0.93	0.82	0.93	0.72	0.73	0.72	0.89	0.74
	R	0.98	0.79	0.96	0.78	0.94	0.76	0.95	0.65	0.81	0.59	0.87	0.61
	F	**0.98**	**0.81**	**0.96**	**0.80**	**0.94**	**0.79**	**0.94**	**0.68**	**0.77**	**0.65**	**0.88**	**0.67**
	Sd	**0.01**	**0.02**	0.01	0.04	0.05	0.08	0.02	0.05	0.07	0.1	0.04	0.03
Healthy	P	0.99	0.93	0.98	0.92	0.97	0.92	0.97	0.87	0.89	0.85	0.94	0.86
	R	0.98	0.95	0.98	0.94	0.96	0.93	0.96	0.90	0.85	0.90	0.95	0.91
	F	**0.98**	**0.94**	0.98	0.93	0.97	0.92	0.96	0.88	0.87	0.87	0.94	0.88
	Sd	**0.01**	**0.02**	0.02	0.03	0.04	0.05	0.02	0.04	0.08	0.05	0.02	0.02

Table 3: Precision, Recall, F-score, Deviation of different classifiers - median on 100 runs , each of which using randomly-drawn training and test data points

points and 2x more non-null SMART indicators, with 98% accuracy and 1-2% error over 100 runs. The precision, recall and F-score for Hitachi are lower by 14-19% and the error is higher – 2%, due to a smaller number of drives in the set and 60% less predictors.

For the healthy class, the model achieves similar performance for Seagate as on the replaced class, with 99% precision and 98% recall and F-score. In the case of Hitachi, the model achieves better performance in discriminating the healthy drives as compared to the faulty ones, by 15% on average. We attribute this boost in accuracy to the fact that healthy disks are easier to identify due to the lower variability in the values of the SMART parameters recorded for them.

3.5 Transfer learning

Figure 5 illustrates the covariate shift for various relevant predictors between different disk models from the same manufacturer. This demonstrates that if we want to reuse the data from one model to build a predictive model for another one we need to employ appropriate transfer learning.

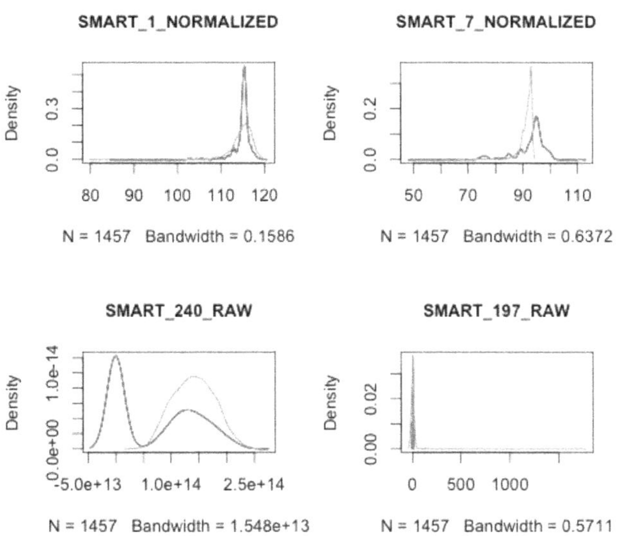

Figure 5: Covariate shift for the two Seagate models

To illustrate the usefulness of our transfer learning approach we compare the models trained and evaluated on SgtA and HitA with the models built with transfer learning and tested on SgtB and HitB, respectively. The results are given in table Table 4.

The gain in predictive performance achieved from using transfer learning when building the new disk models (SgtB and HitB, respectively) compared to directly evaluating the base model (trained on SgtA and HitA, respectively) on the new disk models is shown in Table 4. We obtain 50% increase in the accuracy of the model with transfer learning compared to the accuracy of the base for model SgtA. Also for Hitachi, transfer learning boosts the accuracy of the model by 20%.

		SgtB		HitB	
		Base	Tr. Learn.	Base	Tr. Learn.
Replaced	P	0.65	**0.90**	0.53	**0.76**
	R	0.52	**0.82**	0.84	**0.78**
	F	0.58	**0.86**	0.65	**0.77**
Healthy	P	0.89	0.96	0.92	0.83
	R	0.93	0.98	0.73	0.82
	F	0.91	0.97	0.81	0.83

Table 4: Precision, recall and F-score to illustrate the importance of transfer learning

3.6 Comparison with human designed replacement policies

A drive is labeled as failed when it stopped working, it is non-responsive to commands, the RAID system reports that the drive cannot be written or read, or it shows evidence of failing soon [2]. Currently, datacenter administrators at Backblaze only focus on a very small set of SMART indicators (5, 187, 188, 197, 198) [2]. However, we illustrate that if one were to do proactive replacement using only this small subset of indicators, the number of disks one could correctly identify drops by almost 50%.

In order to mimic a set of such replacement rules we train a decision tree on the aforementioned subset of SMART indicators. We report the results in Table 5.

	DT on the reduced subset		
		SgtA	HitA
Replaced	Precision	0.95	0.66
	Recall	**0.53**	**0.44**
	F-score	0.68	0.51
	Sd	0.06	0.15
Healthy	Precision	0.70	0.84
	Recall	0.98	0.96
	F-score	0.81	0.92
	Sd	0.02	**0.12**

Table 5: Simple decision tree with (insufficient but commonly used) subset of SMART indicators

Note the differences in recall for SgtA and HitA for our model (98% and 81% respectively) compared to a simple rules based model (53% and 44% respectively) – see Table 5 vs. Table 3. Our solution employs powerful learning methods, leverages a larger set of relevant SMART attributes and hence has numerous advantages: captures a higher amount of the failure patterns of disks (high recall), it has low false alarm rate, early detection of disks that need to be replaced, and enables transferring the knowledge acquired by expert data center administrators on specific disk models to new disk models from the same manufacturer.

3.7 Early vs. late replacement detection

While one would prefer to use as much as possible from the lifespan of a disk, being able to detect an impending failure early on allows administrators to plan properly for replacements. Therefore, we evaluate how many of the replaced disks our model correctly captures based on snapshots of the SMART indicators taken 1, 3, 10 and 30 days prior to the actual replacement. We expect this amount to be higher when using the snapshots closer to the failure event, since SMART attributes would become more indicative of the impeding replacement, thus making the model more accurate. Figure 6 shows the results obtained for both Seagate and Hitachi. On the one hand, for SgtA, the model correctly identifies 97% of the faulty disks 3 days prior, 92% of them 10 days in advance and, then, sees a more significant decrease to 73% for up to 30 days in the past. On the other hand, for HitA, the decrease in percentage is less dramatic, as 84% of replaced disks are predicted 3 days before the event and 75% of them 30 days prior. The ratio late vs. early detection is similar for the model built with transfer learning for SgtB and HitB. Compared to the current predictive model implemented in SMART, which mostly warns about a disk failure in the last minute, our model has a major advantage. For both Seagate and Hitachi, an administrator can identify 73 to 75% of the disks to replace a month in advance, which provides her/him with the possibility of planning the replacement in advance, while still using the drives for another 25-30 days.

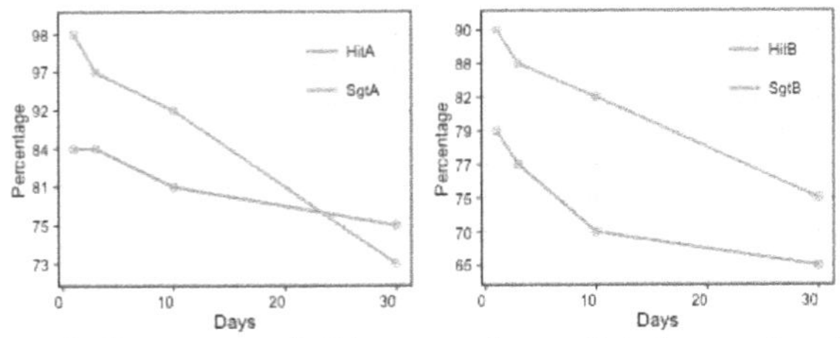

Figure 6: Percentage of disks correctly predicted as replaced on snapshots taken 1,3,10 and 30 days before the actual replacement event.

3.8 SMART indicator rules

Once we have the balanced training dataset comprising the informative SMART attributes in a compact form (this is obtained by running steps 1 through 3 in Algorithm 1) we can use it to fit a decision tree and extract a set of rules that can be used to predict disk replacements. We present rules that are of the form of the underlying learner, more specifically:

$$Rule(\mathbf{x}) = \prod_j \mathcal{I}(\mathbf{x}[i_j] \leq t_j) \prod_k \mathcal{I}(\mathbf{x}[i_k] > t_k) \tag{5}$$

where $\{(i_j, t_j), (i_k, t_k)\}$ represent a set of (smart attribute index, threshold) pairs and $\mathcal{I}(z) = 1$ if z is true and 0 otherwise. The rules provide a detailed insight into the information on the relation among the relevant SMART attributes and the disk replacements available in our training dataset.

Examples of such rules for both SgtA and HitA are provided in Table 6, together with the predicted outcome for the disks adhering to these rules and the prediction confidence. Each rule is composed of one or more single SMART parameter conditions. The fewer conditions, the higher the correlation of the corresponding SMART indicators to the healthy or faulty state of the disks. For instance, in the case of Seagate, the second rule states with 100% confidence that if SMART_197_raw is at least 2, that is the disk has at least two pending sectors, it should be replaced. On the other hand, if its value is below 2, the outcome of the prediction can go both ways, depending on other parameters' values. As an example, consider rules 1 and 3, in which the one indicator that changes the prediction output is the normalized read error rate (SMART_1_normalized). As predicted by our decision tree model, if the number of read errors exceeds 800 thousand, than the disk status is unhealthy.

For Hitachi, the majority contain at most three conditions. As seen in lines 5–8, an indicative combination of attributes is (SMART_197_raw, SMART_3_raw). Line 5 shows that if the number of pending sectors is higher than 1 and the average time spent during a spin up operation exceeds 626 milliseconds, the model predicts an impending faulty state of the disk with 100% confidence. However, if the spin up time is lower, it also considers the number of reallocated sectors in its decision and determines that even with less than 17 such sectors, the disk should be replaced (Line 7). A healthy state is predicted with 97% confidence when the disk has no pending and at most 7200 reallocated sectors, a slow spin up time (i.e., higher than 629 milliseconds) and less than 109 read errors.

Comparing Seagate and Hitachi, we make the following remarks. First, the primarily important SMART indicators are sowewhat different. The pending sector count and the read error rate seem to be model and even manufacturer agnostic, while the command timeout (SMART_188), the average spin up time and the reallocated sectors count are disk model-specific. Second, we note a very large difference in the number of read errors that determine a faulty disk state. For Seagate, this threshold is in hundreds of millions, while for Hitachi they are 6 orders of magnitude lower. We attribute this gap to the fact that this indicator is vendor specific, and therefore a comparison across manufacturers is not feasible.

4. DEPLOYMENT

Our predictive model has been designed to reduce disk failures and allow for more efficient, scheduled maintenance processes in place of the inefficient, reactive repair procedures. Especially for enterprise workloads, where more than 99.9% data availability needs to be guaranteed, current storage systems use incorporated Predictive Failure Analysis (PFA) components to anticipate certain forms of disk failures. Such models are often threshold-based and use only read and write error counts to nominate disks for replacement. As shown in Table 4, thresholds lead to less accurate replacement decisions, therefore integrating our approach enables more precise replacement strategies.

We exemplify how our component could be integrated for rebuilding a RAID 5 array when a disk is signaled as likely to fail, through smart rebuild [3].

An early signal enables the disk to still be available for I/O operations, and thus be kept in the array, rather than

Line	Model	Rule	Outcome	Confidence
1	Seagate	If $SMART\_197\_raw < 2$ and $SMART\_188\_raw > 0$ and $SMART\_1\_normalized \in [0, 117)$	Healthy	100%
2	Seagate	If $SMART\_197\_raw \geq 2$	Replace	100%
3	Seagate	If $SMART\_197\_raw < 2$ and $SMART\_188\_raw > 0$ and $SMART\_1\_normalized > 117$	Replace	80%
4	Seagate	If $SMART\_197\_raw < 2$ and $SMART\_188\_raw = 0$ and $SMART\_187\_normalized < 100$ and $SMART\_240\_raw < 14780$ billion	Replace	97%
5	Hitachi	If $SMART\_197\_raw > 1$ and $SMART\_3\_raw > 626$	Replace	100%
6	Hitachi	If $SMART\_197\_raw > 5$ and $SMART\_3\_raw < 626$ and $SMART\_5\_raw > 17$	Replace	92%
7	Hitachi	If $SMART\_197\_raw > 1$ and $SMART\_3\_raw < 626$ and $SMART\_5\_raw < 17$	Replace	100%
8	Hitachi	If $SMART\_197\_raw < 1$ and $SMART\_5\_raw < 7200$ and $SMART\_3\_raw > 629$ and $SMART\_1\_raw \in [0, 109]$	Healthy	97%

Table 6: Examples of rules extracted from a decision tree model trained on the Seagate and Hitachi datasets obtained with Algorithm 1.

being rejected because of a standard rebuild. A spare disk can be either used from the array or brought in if none is available. The signaled drive and the spare are put in a temporary RAID 1 (full mirroring). This allows the duplication of the faulty drive onto the spare, rather than performing full RAID reconstruction which slows down the entire array's performance. The spare becomes a regular member of the array and the signaled-to-be-faulty disk can be safely removed from the disk, without any risk of data loss. By using such models that can detect failures early in advance and have low ratios of false positives, the array would never have to go through a time consuming $n - 1$ disks stage where it would be exposed to complete RAID failure if an additional drive fails in the meantime. Therefore, the benefits – time saving and increased availability – are substantial.

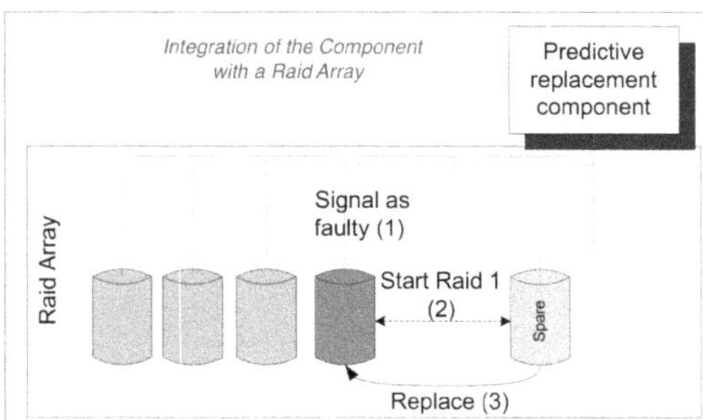

Figure 7: Integration of the predictive replacement component with storage arrays

In Figure 7, we show how our predictive component could be used in interaction with the RAID array and the steps necessary for the automatic rebuild: (i) the predictive component signals a disk with impending failure, (ii) the mirroring process is started on the spare, (iii) the unhealthy disk is replaced by its healthy mirror. In this setting, the process falls back to RAID rebuild only if necessary (e.g., mirroring is not possible).

Our failure model can be deployed in large scale environments (e.g data centers), provided that two conditions are fulfilled. First, the SMART parameters identified as relevant (see Table 2) are continuously measured by the manufacturer. Second in order to learn such model for different manufacturers, even though failed disks represent only a small fraction compared to the healthy ones, in absolute terms, these need to be in the order of hundreds for the model to achieve precision and recall higher than 80%.

5. RELATED WORK

Researchers have performed a couple of large-scale studies on disk failures, the most notable ones pertaining to the authors of [18, 17]. They observed that the field replacement rates of drives are significantly higher than those in the technical datasheets – 2-10 times higher for disks aged less than 5 years and up to 30 times higher for disks between 5 and 8 years. They also demonstrate a significant overestimation of MTTF by the manufacturer. The authors also observed a continuous increase in the replacement rates, starting already in the second year of operation and a high correlation between the first error and a later disk failure. Our analysis also confirms these findings.

This line of research is complemented by works of [5, 11, 13, 16, 19] where the focus is on building a predictive model for the timely discovery of impending disk failures. In [11], the authors employ Bayesian methods to model disk drive failures based on SMART data. First, they solve an anomaly detection problem (i.e., by looking back in the lifespan of the drive and establishing if any of the previous observations is an anomaly). They achieve this by applying a mixture model based on naive Bayes clusters trained using expectation-maximization. Second, they train a naive Bayes classifier which predicts that a drive will fail if any of its snapshots are identified as anomalous or as failures. They evaluate the approach on a smaller dataset, consisting of 1936 drives, out of which only 9 were marked as failed, with a detection rate of up to 55% only.

The authors of [13] explore the capabilities of statistical tests such as the multivariate rank sum test to improve failure warning accuracy and lower false alarms. Their dataset is also fairly small with only 3744 drives (out of which 36 failures), coming from two different models and with each set containing at most 3 months of reliability design test data. The highest accuracies achieved were modest (40%-60%) at 5% AFR. A different model for predicting failures is proposed in [16], comprising of an algorithm based on the multiple-instance learning framework and the naive Bayes classifier. The dataset used was again very small - only data from 369 drives.

There are several key differences between the aforementioned studies and ours. First, the number of disks we consider is significantly larger, with over 23000 drives. Second, our approach focuses on selecting the SMART indicators that correlate with disk replacements and proposes stable representations of the time series data for each disk as input to the predictive model. Last, but not least, some studies are based on monitoring data from drives used in accelerated life tests, whereas we rely only on field data collected when the disks where in actual use. The problem with data collected during testing in uniform controlled environments is that although it can be insightful in understanding the role of certain environmental factors, it has been shown to be not informative enough with respect to actual failure rates observed in the field [10].

Finally, we note that some manufacturers deploy the disks with embedded failure predictive models. However, these models are based on simple methods, such as threshold-based normalizations which according to field observations these models are built such that they avoid false alarms at the expense of a weak predictive power [18, 17, 12].

6. CONCLUSIONS

In this paper, we present a machine learning-based pipeline for predicting disk replacements, built and evaluated on real data from a large disk population from two different manufacturers. We demonstrate the ability of our model built using SMART data to predict disk replacements with high accuracy. A changepoint based feature selection and a compact representation of the time series data for the SMART indicators plugged into a RGF classifier achieves up to 98% accuracy in predicting replacements, 10-15 days in advance. As expected, such models are sensitive to the number of SMART attributes they learn from and the size of the training data. Given that in our original dataset there were considerably less indicators with non-null values for Seagate, we were able to build a model with 24 attributes for Seagate contrary to 12 only for Hitachi. This together with the dataset size explains the 17% difference in accuracy for the two disk models – 98% and 81%, respectively. We also demonstrate how transfer learning can be used to reuse the information available in the labeled dataset for a disk model from a specific manufacturer to build a high quality predictive model for a new disk model from the same manufacturer with no available labeled data.

We believe that such high quality models have many practical benefits. First of all, they can be easily applied to any disk model or manufacturer as long as SMART data is collected. Second, they provide an automatic tool for the disk replacement problem that can be a valuable asset enabling the administrators to identify faulty disks in due time. Last but not least, the predictive models mitigate the reliability issues of storage service providers by allowing administrators to backup the data and plan the actual replacement in advance. Also, note that all these benefits are achievable based only on data that is automatically collected from the disk and no extra effort is necessary.

[1]Seagate is a trademark of Seagate Technology LLC.
[2]Hitachi is a registered trademark of Hitachi, Ltd., and/or its affiliates in the United States and other countries.

7. REFERENCES

[1] Data center downtime costs. http://www.emerson.com/en-us/News/Pages/Net-Power-Study-Data-Center.aspx.

[2] Hard drive smart stats. https://www.backblaze.com/blog/hard-drive-smart-stats/.

[3] IBM system storage DS8000 architecture and implementation. http://www.redbooks.ibm.com/redbooks/pdfs/sg248886.pdf.

[4] S.M.A.R.T. https://en.wikipedia.org/wiki/S.M.A.R.T.

[5] V. Agarwal, C. Bhattacharyya, T. Niranjan, and S. Susarla. Discovering rules from disk events for predicting hard drive failures. ICMLA '09, pages 782–786, Dec 2009.

[6] L. Breiman. Random forests. *Machine Learning*, 45(1):5–32.

[7] K. H. Brodersen, F. Gallusser, J. Koehler, N. Remy, and S. L. Scott. Inferring causal impact using bayesian structural time-series models. *Annals of Applied Statistics*, 9:247–274, 2015.

[8] C. J. C. Burges. A tutorial on support vector machines for pattern recognition. *Data Min. Knowl. Discov.*, 2(2):121–167, June 1998.

[9] D. R. Cox. The regression analysis of binary sequences (with discussion). *J Roy Stat Soc B*, 20:215–242, 1958.

[10] J. Elerath and S. Shah. Server class disk drives: how reliable are they? In *Reliability and Maintainability, 2004 Annual Symposium - RAMS*, pages 151–156.

[11] G. Hamerly and C. Elkan. Bayesian approaches to failure prediction for disk drives. ICML '01, pages 202–209, San Francisco, CA, USA, 2001. Morgan Kaufmann Publishers Inc.

[12] How does S.M.A.R.T. function of hard disks work? www.hdsentinel.com/smart/index.php.

[13] G. F. Hughes, J. F. Murray, K. Kreutz-Delgado, and C. Elkan. Improved disk-drive failure warnings. *IEEE Transactions on Reliability*, 51(3):350–357, 2002.

[14] R. Johnson and T. Zhang. Learning nonlinear functions using regularized greedy forest. *IEEE Transactions on Pattern Analysis and Machine Intelligence*, 36(5):942–954, May 2014.

[15] J. Macqueen. Some methods for classification and analysis of multivariate observations. In *Berkeley Symposium on Mathematical Statistics and Probability*, pages 281–297, 1967.

[16] J. F. Murray, G. F. Hughes, and D. Schuurmans. Machine learning methods for predicting failures in hard drives: A multiple-instance application. *Journal of Machine Learning research*, 6:816, 2005.

[17] E. Pinheiro, W.-D. Weber, and L. A. Barroso. Failure trends in a large disk drive population. FAST 2007, Berkeley, CA, USA, 2007. USENIX Association.

[18] B. Schroeder and G. A. Gibson. Disk failures in the real world: What does an mttf of 1,000,000 hours mean to you? FAST 2007, Berkeley, CA, USA, 2007. USENIX Association.

[19] Y. Tan and X. Gu. On predictability of system anomalies in real world. In *IEEE MASCOTS, 2010*, pages 133–140, Aug 2010.

[20] G. M. Weiss and H. Hirsh. Learning to predict rare events in event sequences. In *KDD 1998*, pages 359–363. AAAI Press, 1998.

[21] J. Ye, J.-H. Chow, J. Chen, and Z. Zheng. Stochastic gradient boosted distributed decision trees. CIKM 2009, pages 2061–2064. ACM, 2009.

Developing a Data-Driven Player Ranking in Soccer Using Predictive Model Weights

Joel Brooks
Massachusetts Institute of Technology
Cambridge, MA
brooksjd@mit.edu

Matthew Kerr
Massachusetts Institute of Technology
Cambridge, MA
mattkerr@alum.mit.edu

John Guttag
Massachusetts Institute of Technology
Cambridge, MA
guttag@mit.edu

ABSTRACT

Quantitative evaluation of the ability of soccer players to contribute to team offensive performance is typically based on goals scored, assists made, and shots taken. In this paper, we describe a novel player ranking system based entirely on the value of passes completed. This value is derived based on the relationship of pass locations in a possession and shot opportunities generated. This relationship is learned by applying a supervised machine learning model to pass locations in event data from the 2012-2013 La Liga season. Interestingly, though this metric is based entirely on passes, the derived player rankings are largely consistent with general perceptions of offensive ability, e.g., Messi and Ronaldo are near the top. Additionally, when used to rank midfielders, it separates the more offensively-minded players from others.

Keywords

machine learning; sports analytics; soccer analytics

1. INTRODUCTION

Although soccer is by far the world's most popular sport [19], published work in soccer analytics has yet to achieve the same level of sophistication as analytics being performed in other professional sports. Crude summary statistics such as goals, shots, and assists are still the most common way to compare player performance analytically. More work is emerging [23] that leverages the rich datasets available to make discoveries about soccer, but there has not been much focus on quantitative metrics for evaluating player performance.

In this paper, we describe a novel way of quantitatively measuring a player's *passing* performance using existing data. We chose to focus on passing because it is one of the more strategic elements of soccer. Currently, players are often considered good passers if they accumulate many assists. Assists identify when a player makes a pass that directly leads to a goal, but this measure alone is quite limited. For example, assists do not capture passes that would have been assists except for an errant shot, or an excellent save by the opposing team's goalkeeper. Opta [17] extends the idea of assists to include all passes that lead to shots (whether or not they lead to a goal) in their "key passes" metric, but both this metric and assists are only applicable to passes immediately preceding a shot. There may be players who are excellent passers that create many opportunities for their team, but rarely make the last pass before a shot or goal.

Instead, we want to be able to quantitatively measure the importance of *any* pass. We accomplish this by first training a classifier that uses information about the locations of a set of passes to identify when that group of passes results in a shot. Since we use a linear classifier, we can directly utilize the model weights to understand the relative importance of pass origins and destinations for generating shot opportunities. These weights allow us to compute an estimated value of any pass for creating shots. We can then rank players by the value of the passes they complete over the course of a season.

In this paper, we use data from the 2012-2013 La Liga season to:

1. Construct a model relating pass origins and destinations during a possession with the probability of a shot. This model accurately identifies whether a possession ends in a shot from the pass locations alone.

2. Show how the resulting weights offer insights into the offensive utility of passes.

3. Utilize this model to rank players by the frequency with which their passes are highly valued by the model.

The rest of the paper is organized as follows. In Section 2, we outline some related work on using machine learning for knowledge discovery in soccer and other sports. In Section 3, we describe our event-based dataset. In Section 4, we present our methodology for building a model for predicting shots at the end of possessions. In Section 5, we demonstrate that this model can be used to rank players in an objective manner by how often they complete passes our model rates as valuable. Finally, in Section 6, we summarize the overall contributions of this paper and discuss possible future work.

2. RELATED WORK

Much of the published research in sports analytics, especially research that utilizes spatiotemporal data, has focused on sports that are easily discretized, such as baseball,

KDD '16 August 13-17, 2016, San Francisco, CA, USA

ACM ISBN 978-1-4503-4232-2/16/08.

DOI: http://dx.doi.org/10.1145/2939672.2939695

American football and tennis [22]. These sports are easily broken up into individual events (e.g. at bats, plays or points) that have immediate outcomes, such as hits, yards gained or a point won. For example, Intille and Bobick used player tracking data to recognize different plays in American football [11]. It is more difficult to perform similar work for sports that are not as easily discretized, such as basketball and soccer, because the continuous nature of play makes the connections to outcomes less obvious. Previous work has used tracking data for basketball to classify offensive plays and the movement patterns of offensive players [12, 18]. Similar work in soccer has proved to be more difficult because there are not as clear distinctions between epochs in play in soccer as there are in basketball.

Soccer analytics has focused on building probabilistic models to simulate game actions and predict the outcomes of matches or goals scored. Reep and Benjamin developed models for the success rates of different length passing sequences [21]. More recently, there has been work on predicting the outcomes of matches by using possession rates of different teams and other historical statistics to develop probabilistic models [7, 8]. Other work has identified a relationship between a goal being scored and the frequency of passes in the 5 minutes preceding that goal [20]. In contrast, our work focuses on predicting shots taken in possessions as opposed to the outcome of games or goals. Additionally, we focus on how these predictions can be useful for ranking players in a quantitative fashion, as opposed to the performance of the predictors themselves.

An increasing amount of spatiotemporal data for soccer is allowing analysts to study the underlying mechanics of the game in a manner that would not be possible with box score statistics alone. Bloomfield *et al.* used player tracking information to investigate the physical demands of soccer and the work rates of different players [3]. Gyarmati *et al.* leveraged ball-event data and passing sequences to cluster the playing styles of different teams [10]. Lucey *et al.* used ball-event data to infer the location of the ball throughout a game. Using this information, they constructed "entropy-maps" to characterize how different teams move the ball during a match [14]. In more recent work, the authors combine match statistics, event data and player tracking data to identify the teams playing in a given game with 70% accuracy [2].

Our feature representation is an extension of previous work we did for using pass locations to identify teams by their passing styles [13]. We also showed that these feature representations are promising for building quantitative player-rankings [4]. However, in this work, we extend these representations to have smarter ways of relating field locations, and a better breakdown of the understanding of offensive performance by different types of positional players.

Other recent work in sports analytics has focused specifically on quantitatively measuring specific player contributions. Macdonald [15] fits a ridge-regression model of a number of statistics of players in a hockey team to their expected goal-scoring rate. This allows a quantitative measure of an individual player's contribution to those expected goals while taking account of the contributions of the other players on the team. Cervone and others [5] fit a model relating actions and movements taken by the ball handler in basketball to the expected number of points scored over the course of a possession. They then demonstrate how this model can rank players based on the average value of every action they take over a course of a season. We similarly utilize predictive models for evaluating player performance, but our metric is focused specifically on the value of the location of a completed pass.

Finally, we draw upon work that trains interpretable discriminative models, and then utilizes those model weights for developing quantitative metrics for stratifying populations. This is commonly done in the medical literature for developing risk scores. Specifically, both the TIMI risk score [1] for risk of adverse cardiac events and the SAPS III score [16] for evaluation of patient status in intensive care units utilize logistic regression models to understand which patient variables have the strongest relationship with adverse outcomes. They then utilize their trained model weights for constructing simple metrics that are both easy to compute manually, and can accurately separate high risk patients from low risk patients. This is analogous to how we use a model trained on predicting shots for identifying important origin and destinations of passes, and then utilize these locations to rank players.

3. THE DATA

3.1 Data Overview

The data we used are hand-labeled annotations of each ball-event that took place during the course of a match (e.g. each pass, tackle, shot, etc). A ball-event is recorded any time a player makes a play on the ball, apart from dribbling. The dataset also includes additional information for each ball-event such as the location, the player involved, and the outcome.

We focused specifically on the *locations* of pass attempt origins and destinations because we hypothesized that pass location is a strong indicator of team strategy and personnel. We use data collected from the 2012-13 La Liga season. La Liga is the premier league in Spain and is comprised of 20 teams. On average, each team in La Liga attempted around 18,000 passes during the entire season, with Barcelona making the most passes by a wide margin at 30,283, and Levante attempting the smallest number of passes at 13,094. We present a complete list of teams ranked by their final standing in La Liga with the number of shots they took in the 2012-13 season in Table 1.

3.2 Pass Location Representation

Each pass event in the dataset has an origin and destination location. To aggregate pass origin or destination locations that are near each other, we discretized the field into 18 zones, as shown in Figure 2. This representation has previously been shown to identify critical zones on the field associated with offensive outcomes such as shots and goals [6]. Additionally, in previous work we showed that by discretizing the field into these 18 zones, we can build representations of pass locations that are highly indicative of team passing styles [4]. However, we did not want to represent each pass location as belonging to a single zone, since we do not believe the hard cutoffs between zones are representative of anything fundamental to the game of soccer.

Instead, we extended our previous representation of each pass location (either a location of a pass origin or a destination) to be a continuous-valued vector of length 18, where each element in the vector represents the closeness of a

Rank	Team	Shots
1	Barcelona	528
2	Real Madrid	710
3	Atletico Madrid	513
4	Real Sociedad	557
5	Valencia	567
6	Malaga	443
7	Betis	456
8	Rayo Vallecano	567
9	Sevilla	553
10	Getafe	473
11	Levante	402
12	Atletico Bilbao	482
13	Espanyol	413
14	Valladolid	393
15	Granada	470
16	Osasuna	514
17	Celta de Vigo	460
18	Mallorca	485
19	Deportiva La Coruna	527
20	Zaragoza	461

Table 1: **Teams in the La Liga 2012-13 season.** Teams are ranked by their final standing in the league at the season end.

given pass location to the corresponding zone. We then compute the vector representation for a pass location l as $\mathbf{r}^l = [r^l_1 \ldots r^l_{18}]$, where each element is

$$r^l_i = \frac{c_i}{max(d(l, z_i), 1)} \tag{1}$$

where $d(l, z_i)$ is the Euclidean distance between the coordinates of l and the center of zone i (z_i), and c_i is an indicator variable that takes the value 1 if zone i is one of the N closest zones (by Euclidean distance to the center of the zone) to l, and 0 otherwise. We utilize the $max(d(l, z_i), 1)$ to prevent passes located very near the center of a zone from leading to extremely large values. Finally, we normalize $\mathbf{r}^l$ by its L1-norm so that the $\sum_{i=1}^{18} r^l_i = 1$.

The resulting vector $\mathbf{r}^l$ has N non-zero values. This vector describes how close a pass location is to the Nth closest zones. For our task, $N = 2$ seemed to provide the best results. Intuitively, this results in a location representation that emphasizes the zone in which the pass occurred, but accounts for cases where a pass location is near the border of two zones. This representation allows aggregation or averaging of multiple passes in a sequence of passes without restricting any one pass in that sequence to have an origin or destination in just a single zone.

4. METHODS

4.1 Feature Extraction

To extract the features that we used to build our predictive models, we first segment each game into a discrete sequence of observations. We segment the game at the level of *possessions*. A possession in soccer is defined as a period of time when a single team retains the ball without an interruption in play or loss of the ball to the opposing team. Possessions contain a sequence of passes between players on

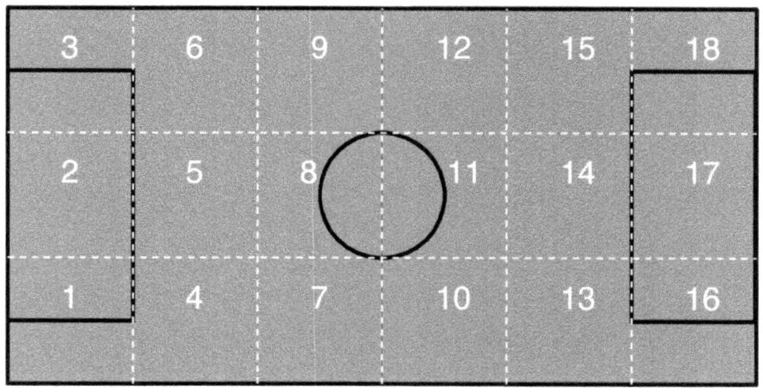

Figure 2: **The playing area split up into 18 zones.** The left side of the field (zones 1-3) is the defensive side of the field, and the right side (zones 16-18) is the offensive area.

the same team. We only considered possessions that had a minimum number of passes in order to remove epochs of play where a team only had the possession of the ball for a short period of time. We set this minimum to be 3 complete passes since we found a minimum of 4 or greater led to a steep drop in overall performance.

We extracted features from each possession to construct the feature vectors for our learning algorithms. We constructed the feature vector for a single pass with origin and destination locations (l_o, l_d) in a possession by:

1. Computing $\mathbf{r}^{l_o}$ and $\mathbf{r}^{l_d}$, the representations of the pass origin and destination, respectively, using the method described in Section 3.2.
2. Constructing the matrix $\mathbf{R}^{l_{od}} = \mathbf{r}^{l_o} \otimes \mathbf{r}^{l_d}$, the outer product of the origin and destination representations. These origin-destination-pair features provide information about which pairs of origins and destinations are more likely to lead to shots (e.g. knowing that the ball was passed into the middle from the corner as opposed to just knowing that the ball reached the middle).
3. Constructing the feature vector as the concatenation of $\mathbf{r}^{l_o}$, $\mathbf{r}^{l_d}$, and a flattened $\mathbf{R}^{l_{od}}$.

The origin and destination representations have one value per zone, so each accounts for 18 features. The flattened origin-destination-pair representation is of length 324. As a result, each pass was converted into a feature vector of length 360. To get a feature vector for a possession, we average the feature vectors across all completed passes in that possession. This feature vector represents a summary of the locations of pass origins and destinations of a possession.

Each feature vector is labeled with $y \in \{1, -1\}$ according to how the possession ended. Possessions that ended in a shot taken by the offensive team were assigned a label of 1, and all others were assigned a label of -1.

4.2 Experimental Design and Testing

Upon converting each possession in a game to a feature vector, we then used these feature vectors to train models to relate passing strategy in a possession to shots taken. We first split the data into a training and holdout set. We split the data by using the first 80% of games chronologically as the training set, and setting aside the final 20% as the holdout set. We did this split to simulate the scenario of applying our models to newly generated data.

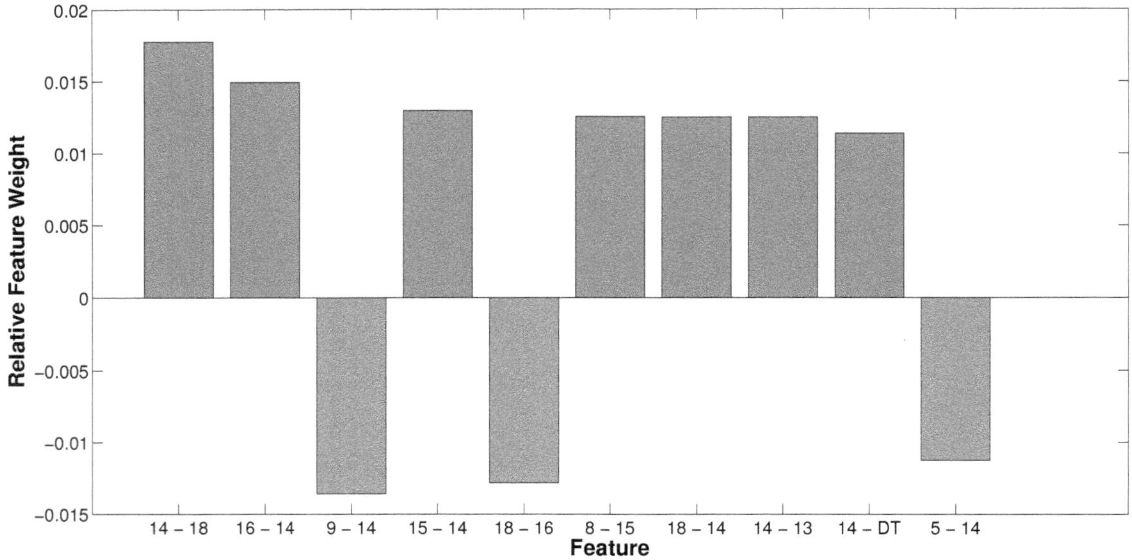

Figure 1: **Top 10 most influential features for predicting when a possession will end in a shot**. All features are normalized by the total sum of absolute weights. Each number corresponds to a zone. "DT" designates a pass destination feature, and features labeled with two zones, "$Zone_1$ - $Zone_2$," designate an origin-destination feature from $Zone_1$ to $Zone_2$.

Using the training set, we trained an L2-regularized Support Vector Machine (SVM) model using the LIBLINEAR package [9]. We used LIBLINEAR's asymmetric cost parameter option in order to account for the extreme class imbalance between positive and negative examples in the training set. We utilized 5-fold cross validation to find the optimal class-specific cost parameters on the training set. The folds were constructed at the *game* level so possessions in a single game were not split across multiple folds. We chose the cost parameters that had the maximum average Area Under the Receiver Operating Characteristic Curve (AUROC) on the five test folds, and used those parameters to train the final model. The final model was then tested on the holdout set.

5. RESULTS

5.1 Classification Results

Our model that predicts whether a possession will end with a shot has an AUROC of 0.79 and an F-score of 0.31. We plot the ROC curve in Figure 3. We used this model to investigate the relationship between our features and shots by looking at the relative importance of each zone. We show the feature weights for the top 10 features in Figure 1. The weights presented in the figure are normalized by the total sum of the absolute value of all the weights to reflect a feature's relative importance. We can see that no single feature dominates and that the top features have a mixture of positive and negative weights. This provides further evidence that our model captures a trade-off between where passes are likely to lead to shot opportunities in the future and is not based solely on simple rules such as "shots happen when there are passes near the opposing team's goal." In fact, zone 17, the area directly in front of the opposing team's goal, does not appear in the top 10 features.

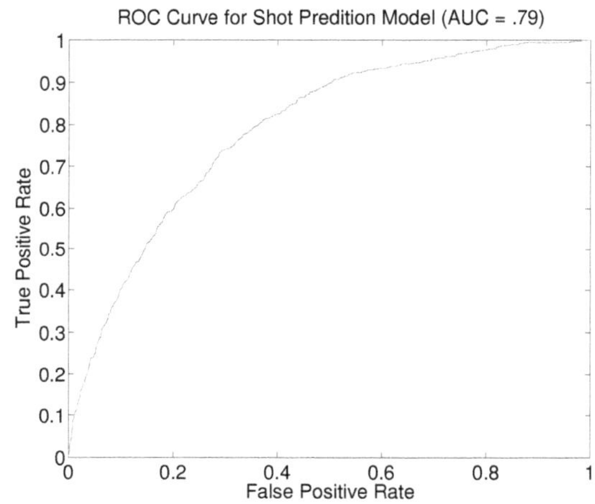

Figure 3: **ROC Curve for the Shot Prediction Model**

Looking at the relative feature importance provides insight into which pass origins and destinations generally lead to shot opportunities. Many of these top features involve zone 14, the "critical zone" centered in the field in front of the penalty box. Possessing the ball in this zone has been strongly identified to be associated with positive offensive outcomes [6]. This is supported by our model, where 6 of the top 10 features are positively associated features that involve zone 14. However, not all of our top features involving zone 14 have positive weights. Passes to zone 14 from either zone 5 or zone 9 both have negative weights. Thus long completed passes to zone 14 are not positively associated with shot opportunities by our model. So while getting the ball into zone 14 can often lead to shot opportunities, it depends a great deal on how you get it there.

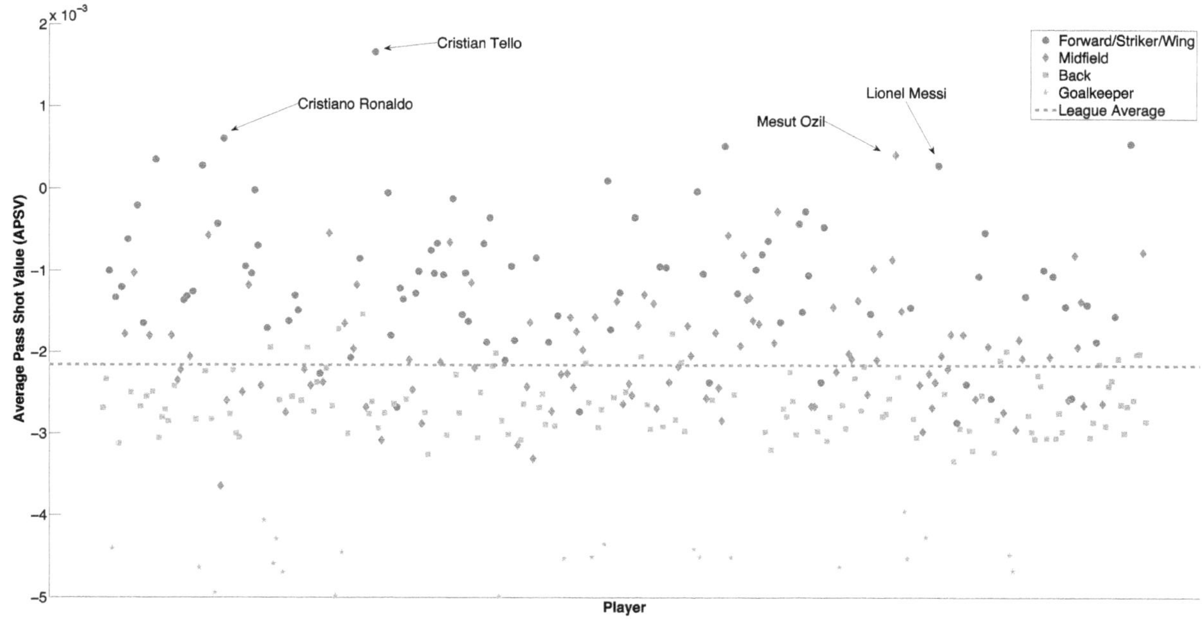

Figure 4: **APSV of passes for all players with more than 200 passes in the 2012-13 La Liga season.** Each item in the plot represents the APSV of a single player. Players have an associated color and shape chosen by their position. The APSV across the entire collection of players is represented by the dashed red line.

Many of the top features also involve the corner areas. The top two features overall are both passes between the corner areas and zone 14. This suggests that many passes that lead to shot opportunities later in the possession involve getting the ball into the corner of the field. However, there is also a strongly negatively associated feature weight with a ball sent from one corner to another (zone 18 to zone 16). This suggests that crosses across the field are harmful for generating shots if they result in the ball being played to the other corner.

5.2 Player Rankings by Shot Prediction Models

In the previous section, we described how we trained a model relating a possession to the outcome of the possession ending in a shot. The resulting model is a vector $\mathbf{w} = [\mathbf{w}^o, \mathbf{w}^d, \mathbf{w}^{od}]$, where $\mathbf{w}^o, \mathbf{w}^d, \mathbf{w}^{od}$ are the vectors of feature weights corresponding to the different zones for pass origins, destinations, and origin-destination pairs, respectively. These weights provide a conceptual map of the field that suggests which pass locations are most likely to lead to a shot opportunity later in the possession. We can use this map to rate a given pass by its association with shot opportunities in our model.

We took every completed pass in the La Liga 2012-13, and using our model computed an estimate of its relative importance for generating a shot. This importance, called Pass Shot Value (PSV), is computed for a pass with an origin in zone i and a destination in zone j as:

$$PSV(i,j) = w_i^o + w_j^d + w_{ij}^{od} \quad (2)$$

Thus, the PSV for a pass is the sum of the feature weights for its corresponding origin, destination and origin-destination pair. For example, a pass from zone 3 to zone 4 would have a PSV of the sum of the model weight for an origin in zone 3, the weight for the destination in zone 4, and the weight of the pair of having an origin of 3 and a destination of 4. We then computed the Average Pass Shot Value (APSV) for all players in La Liga who had over 200 completed passes in the 2012-13 season. We found that 200 passes filtered out everyone besides the top 15-20 players per team by number of completed passes, leaving the main contributors over that season. We again excluded passes that did not occur in a possession of 3 or more completed passes. Note that we only use the closest zone to the origin and destination for computing PSV. This is because we assume the predictive model has accounted for relationships between zones that are near each other.

We plotted the APSV for these players in Figure 4, which shows how our model would rank each player by their average tendency to complete passes that lead to a shot. Unsurprisingly, the APSV metric is biased towards offensive oriented players. In fact, the separation of the different positions by APSV indicates that APSV alone would be a fairly strong predictor of position. The goalkeepers are completely separate from the field position players. As such, APSV is most useful when comparing players within a position.

We ranked the top ten players by position category in Table 2. We also listed the top players by goals and assists in Table 3. Note that APSV is almost always negative. Most possessions do not end in a shot, and thus, most of the model's features are negatively associated with a shot opportunity being generated. Therefore, players make passes with a negative model value the vast majority of the time. In spite of this, some offensive players and one midfielder (Mesut Ozil) have a positive APSV. This suggests that generally their passes were rated by the model to be positively associated with shots at the end of a possession.

Rank	Player
1	Cristian Tello
2	Cristiano Ronaldo
3	Sergio Garcia
4	Karim Benzema
5	Gonzalo Higuain
6	Lionel Messi
7	Jonathan Viera
8	Angel Di Maria
9	Nolito
10	Jorge Molina

(a) **Offense**

Rank	Player
1	Mesut Ozil
2	Diego Buonanotte
3	Kaka
4	Emiliano Armenteros
5	Miguel de las Cuevas
6	Julio Baptista
7	Arda Turan
8	Jose Barkero
9	Cesc Fabregas
10	Ever Banega

(b) **Midfield**

Rank	Player
1	Marcelo Vieira
2	Eliseu
3	Dani Alves
4	Filipe Luis
5	Aly Cissokho
6	Diego Colotto
7	Martin Demichelis
8	Nacho Monreal
9	Sergio Sangez
10	Lolo

(c) **Defense**

Table 2: **Top 10 players in La Liga 2012-13 by APSV**. We separate the positions into three categories: Offense, Midfield, and Defense.

Rank	Player	Goals
1	Lionel Messi	46
2	Cristiano Ronaldo	34
3	Radamel Falcao	28
4	Alvaro Negredo	25
4	Roberto Soldado	24
6	Ruben Castro	18
6	Piti	18
8	Gonzalo Higuain	16
9	Carlos Vela	14
9	Helder Postiga	14
9	Artiz Aduriz	14

(a) **Top Goal Scorers**

Rank	Player	Assists
1	Andres Iniesta	16
2	Mesut Ozil	13
3	Lionel Messi	12
4	Karim Benzema	11
4	Cesc Fabregas	11
6	Cristiano Ronaldo	10
6	Ivan Rakitic	10
8	Ibai Gomez	9
8	Carlos Vela	9
8	Koke	9
8	Alexis Sanchez	9

(b) **Top Players by Assists**

Table 3: **Top 10 players in La Liga 2012-13 by Goals and Assists**

We grouped forwards, strikers, and wingers into an "offense" category. The top players by APSV in the offense category include renowned players such as Ronaldo and Messi. They were the top two scorers in La Liga that season and they both finished the season in the top 10 for assists as well. In fact, we find that a significant ($\rho = 0.27, p < 0.05$) correlation between APSV and goals scored for the season for players in the "offense" category. Notice, however, that neither goals or assists are used in compute APSV, suggesting that these players are not only effective scorers but also effective passers. Others in this category were considered to be strong offensive players and appear in the list of top players by goals and assists as well.

Even within the midfield and defense categories, we see players that are identified to play an "offensive" style. Midfielders in the top 10 by APSV like Ozil and Kaka play most often in the "attacking midfielder" position. Marcelo Viera and Eliseu play as backs, but are known for being capable at playing in the wing position as well. Others like Dani Alves are pure backs but are known for contributing on the offensive end.

6. CONCLUSION

In this paper we presented a novel method of utilizing soccer event data to understand the relationship between pass location and shot opportunities. We showed that the locations of the origins and destinations of passes in a possession relate strongly to whether that possession will end in a shot. Using supervised machine learning techniques, we built a model for predicting whether a possession will end in a shot. The model had an AUROC of 0.79.

We used the features of this model to create a map to understand the relative importance for generating shot opportunities of passing from one location to another. We then used this map to build a data-driven ranking of players by weighing a pass by its relative importance for generating a shot later in the possession. When we ranked all players in La Liga 2012-13 with more than 200 passes with this metric, we see some of the elite attacking players at the top. This ranking also correlates well with standard offensive box score metrics such as goals and assists, even though neither were directly used in its computation. We believe this warrants further investigation into its utility as a player comparison tool. Furthermore, we have outlined a framework for constructing data-driven player metrics. For example, using actions taken by players on defense for predicting *defensive* outcomes may be used to help rank players by defensive ability.

We believe that our results show that appropriate analyses of pass event data in soccer can provide sometimes non-obvious insights. However, soccer is a complicated sport with constantly changing game situations. Incorporating temporal information (e.g. duration of possession, time elapsed between passes) in any analyses would provide more situation-specific insights. Also, utilizing player-tracking data as a source dataset would better allow investigation into the strategic aspects of the game that are not directly involved with the ball. Expanding our features to include sequential information could give a more detailed understanding of how passing strategy relates to outcomes. Lastly, if a team had a large collection of event data from their own games, they could build team-specific models that could provide a better analysis into which strategies are most promising in their system. Further investigation will better reveal how useful this type of analysis can be for gaining a deeper understanding of the world's most popular game.

Finally, we would like to extend this work to other sports, such as basketball. From a technical perspective, this methodology for creating data-driven player metrics could be applied to any sports datasets with events and location information. Just as in soccer, passing performance is primarily measured in basketball by assists. By using the methods from this paper, we could rank players by the value of all passes they complete, and not those just before a shot.

7. REFERENCES

[1] E. M. Antman, M. Cohen, P. J. Bernink, C. H. McCabe, T. Horacek, G. Papuchis, B. Mautner, R. Corbalan, D. Radley, and E. Braunwald. The TIMI risk score for unstable angina/non–st elevation mi: a method for prognostication and therapeutic decision making. *Jama*, 284(7):835–842, 2000.

[2] A. Bialkowski, P. Lucey, P. Carr, Y. Yue, S. Sridharan, and I. Matthews. Identifying team style in soccer using formations learned from spatiotemporal tracking data. In *Data Mining Workshop (ICDMW), 2014 IEEE International Conference on*, pages 9–14. IEEE, 2014.

[3] J. Bloomfield, G. K. Jonsson, R. Polman, K. Houlahan, and P. O'Donoghue. Temporal pattern analysis and its applicability in soccer. In L. Anoilli, S. Duncan Jr., M. Magnusson, and G. Riva, editors, *The Hidden Structure of Interaction: From Neurons to Culture Patterns*. IOS Press, Amsterdam, The Netherlands, 2005.

[4] J. Brooks, M. Kerr, and J. Guttag. Using machine learning to draw inferences from pass location data in soccer. *Statistical Analysis and Data Mining: The ASA Data Science Journal*, forthcoming 2016.

[5] D. Cervone, A. D'Amour, L. Bornn, and K. Goldsberry. Pointwise: Predicting points and valuing decisions in real time with nba optical tracking data. MIT Sloan Sports Analytics Conference, 2014.

[6] A. Coghlan. The secret of zone 14. *New Scientist*, 1999.

[7] C. Collet. The possession game? A comparative analysis of ball retention and team success in European and international football, 2007-2010. *Journal of Sports Sciences*, 31(2):123–136, 2013.

[8] A. C. Constantinou, N. E. Fenton, and M. Neil. pi-football: A Bayesian network model for forecasting Association Football match outcomes. *Knowledge-Based Systems*, 36:322–339, Dec. 2012.

[9] R.-E. Fan, K.-W. Chang, C.-J. Hsieh, X.-R. Wang, and C.-J. Lin. Liblinear: A library for large linear classification. *The Journal of Machine Learning Research*, 9:1871–1874, 2008.

[10] L. Gyarmati, H. Kwak, and P. Rodriguez. Searching for a unique style in soccer. *arXiv:1409.0308 [physics]*, Sept. 2014. arXiv: 1409.0308.

[11] S. S. Intille and A. F. Bobick. A framework for recognizing multi-agent action from visual evidence. In *Proceedings of the Sixteenth National Conference on Artificial Intelligence and the Eleventh Innovative Applications of Artificial Intelligence Conference Innovative Applications of Artificial Intelligence*, AAAI '99/IAAI '99, pages 518–525, Menlo Park, CA, USA, 1999. American Association for Artificial Intelligence.

[12] M. Kates. Player motion analysis: Automatically classifying nba plays. Master's thesis, Massachusetts Institute Of Technology, September 2014.

[13] M. Kerr. Applying machine learning to event data in soccer. Master's thesis, Massachusetts Institute Of Technology, June 2015.

[14] P. Lucey, A. Bialkowski, P. Carr, E. Foote, and I. Matthews. Characterizing multi-agent team behavior from partial team tracings: Evidence from the english premier league. In *AAAI*, 2012.

[15] B. Macdonald. An expected goals model for evaluating nhl teams and players. MIT Sloan Sports Analytics Conference, 2012.

[16] R. P. Moreno, P. G. Metnitz, E. Almeida, B. Jordan, P. Bauer, R. A. Campos, G. Iapichino, D. Edbrooke, M. Capuzzo, J.-R. Le Gall, et al. SAPS 3 - From evaluation of the patient to evaluation of the intensive care unit. part 2: Development of a prognostic model for hospital mortality at icu admission. *Intensive care medicine*, 31(10):1345–1355, 2005.

[17] OptaPro. http://www.optasportspro.com/.

[18] M. Perše, M. Kristan, S. Kovačič, G. Vučkovič, and J. Perš. A trajectory-based analysis of coordinated team activity in a basketball game. *Computer Vision and Image Understanding*, 113(5):612–621, 2009.

[19] B. R. And the silver goes to... *The Economist*, Sept. 2011.

[20] A. Redwood-Brown. Passing patterns before and after goal scoring in FA premier league soccer. *International Journal of Performance Analysis in Sport*, 8(3):172–182, Nov. 2008.

[21] C. Reep and B. Benjamin. Skill and chance in association football. *Journal of the Royal Statistical Society. Series A (General)*, 131(4):581–585, Jan. 1968.

[22] SlamTracker. http://www.wimbledon.com/en_GB/slamtracker/.

[23] Soccer Analytics — Presented by Prozone | MIT Sloan Sports Analytics Conference. http://www.sloansportsconference.com/?p=9740.

The Legislative Influence Detector: Finding Text Reuse in State Legislation

Matthew Burgess
University of Michigan
mattburg@umich.edu

Eugenia Giraudy
UC Berkeley
egiraudy@berkeley.edu

Julian Katz-Samuels
University of Michigan
jkatzsam@umich.edu

Joe Walsh
University of Chicago
jtwalsh@uchicago.edu

Derek Willis
ProPublica
Derek.Willis@propublica.org

Lauren Haynes
University of Chicago
lnhaynes@uchicago.edu

Rayid Ghani
University of Chicago
rayid@uchicago.edu

ABSTRACT

State legislatures introduce at least 45,000 bills each year. However, we lack a clear understanding of who is actually writing those bills. As legislators often lack the time and staff to draft each bill, they frequently copy text written by other states or interest groups.

However, existing approaches to detect text reuse are slow, biased, and incomplete. Journalists or researchers who want to know where a particular bill originated must perform a largely manual search. Watchdog organizations even hire armies of volunteers to monitor legislation for matches. Given the time-consuming nature of the analysis, journalists and researchers tend to limit their analysis to a subset of topics (e.g. abortion or gun control) or a few interest groups.

This paper presents the Legislative Influence Detector (LID). LID uses the Smith-Waterman local alignment algorithm to detect sequences of text that occur in model legislation and state bills. As it is computationally too expensive to run this algorithm on a large corpus of data, we use a search engine built using Elasticsearch to limit the number of comparisons. We show how LID has found 45,405 instances of bill-to-bill text reuse and 14,137 instances of model-legislation-to-bill text reuse. LID reduces the time it takes to manually find text reuse from days to seconds.

Keywords

Social Good; Government Transparency; Text Reuse; Machine Learning

1. INTRODUCTION

State governments have a central yet undervalued role in the United States. Each year, states spend more than $1.5 trillion on programs and services [14] and pass 75 times more bills than Congress [7]. State legislators play a large role by setting budgets, providing oversight, and passing laws. It is a heavy workload given that they lack the time, staff, and expertise compared to their congressional counterparts. According to the National Conference on State Legislatures, only three states have full-time legislatures with large staffs [17].

Rather than writing bills from scratch, legislators increase their productivity by using text written by others. The two most common sources state legislators draw on are legislation from other states and model legislation written by interest groups. Legislation from other states needs adaptation –for example, changing references to existing codes. Of the two, model legislation is especially easy to use: it's "legislative Mad Libs," providing blanks for legislators to fill in (see Figure 1). By lowering the cost of legislating, text reuse can help policies spread.

A BILL TO BAN THE BOX ON EMPLOYMENT APPLICATIONS

The Legislature declares that it is the duty of the state of [Insert State Name] to encourage and contribute to the successful reintegration of people with a criminal history. The ability to procure meaningful employment is essential to reinstating good citizenship. The Legislature also recognizes that reducing barriers to employment for persons with a criminal history is a matter of statewide concern and that increasing employment opportunities will reduce recidivism and improve community stability.

Section 1: Scope

Figure 1: Example model legislation from ALEC

This type of policy diffusion—whether from other states or from lobbyists—can be good. One example might be seat-belt laws, which have been credited with saving thousands of lives. In 1984, New York became the first state to pass a seat-belt law, and over the next 11 years the other 49 states followed. Policy diffusion can also be bad. For example, a relatively small number of powerful people might obtain

KDD '16, August 13-17, 2016, San Francisco, CA, USA

DOI: http://dx.doi.org/10.1145/2939672.2939697

favorable policies at the expense of the majority by writing model legislation for state senators and representatives to turn in to law.

Americans rely on watchdogs to find legislation of questionable origin, but with at least 45,000 bills introduced in state capitols each year (see Figure 2), there is too much legislation for journalists to read, let alone analyze. Even using Google can be slow: to find good matches, the user has to read at least part of the bill to find a short piece of text to search for and then look through the results, many of which will not be legislation. The time-consuming nature of this approach makes it hard for journalists to fully understand where state legislation ideas come from, even for closely watched bills. For example, the media wrote nearly 1,000 stories about the bill Wisconsin Governor Scott Walker signed banning abortions past the 19th week of pregnancy. Some identified the lobby group behind the bill while others noted similar laws had already passed elsewhere, but we have not seen a full legislative accounting in the media, which includes all versions of the bill being introduced in 19 states. This lack of information about who is influencing state laws limits transparency and hinders citizen control, which is the defining feature of democracy.

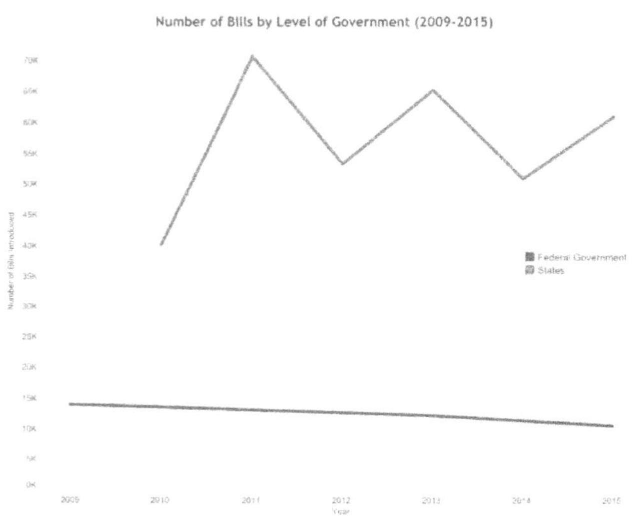

Figure 2: Legislative bills introduced each year

The high cost of analyzing text reuse in state legislative bills also harms social science. Most social scientists limit their inquiries to one or two salient topics (e.g. abortion) or interest groups (e.g. the American Legislative Exchange Council [ALEC]) as one-time studies. At its best, science reproduces findings on new data [4], but reproducibility is difficult when the cost of manual data collection is this high.

This paper presents the Legislative Influence Detector (LID), a tool that helps solve the time-consuming, human-intensive nature of existing approaches by rapidly detecting cases of text reuse in model legislation and state bills. LID uses the Smith-Waterman local alignment algorithm to detect sequences of text that occur in model legislation and state bills. As it is computationally too expensive to run this algorithm on large sets of text, we use a customized search engine built using Elasticsearch to limit the number of documents compared. LID can help journalists, scholars, and concerned citizens shed light on legislative influence by finding legislative text reuse across states and from interest groups.

We ran LID on 550,000 bills collected by the Sunlight Foundation [1] and 2,400 pieces of model legislation collected by our team and found 45,405 instances of bill-to-bill text reuse and 14,137 instances of model-legislation-to-bill text reuse. LID reduces the time it takes to manually find text reuse from minutes, hours, or even days to seconds. We have posted the code[2] and data[3] publicly for download and analysis.

2. SOURCES OF LEGISLATION

Thanks to federalism, states can act as "laboratories of democracy," trying "novel social and economic experiments without risk to the rest of the country" [3]. While this can aid the discovery and adoption of good policies, practical challenges often prevent the dissemination from happening. First, it's rarely clear what good policy is because different people prefer different outcomes [24]. Second, it can be difficult to tell whether a policy is effective. Jurisdictions rarely conduct randomized controlled trials to test policy effectiveness, instead adopting policies from states located nearby [16] or with similar ideology [10] or culture [1], from bills with symbolic value [8], or from bills backed by federal incentives [15]. As the US grew, conducting business and other affairs across state lines grew more difficult, and lawyers began to write model legislation to aid legal standardization across the country [23].

Standardization of law is not the only reason to draft legislation; lobbyists also write model bills to get their preferred policies adopted. Lobbyists have drafted model bills on a range of topics, such as crime, abortion, tax, education, the environment, and health. The goal of lobbying groups is to influence legislators, both at the national and state levels, to introduce and pass bills that resemble their model legislation as completely as possible. To make it easy for legislators and their staffs, lobbying groups provide model legislation that can be easily adapted to each state, as shown in Figure 1.

Whether it comes from state bills or from lobbyists, prewritten legislation makes passing laws easier, especially at the state level. Unlike members of Congress, few state legislators have the expertise, time, and staffs to draft legislation. It is far easier for a legislator to adapt existing legislative text than to write a bill from scratch. Because it is inefficient, if not impossible, to manually find legislative text reuse, legislators can often claim full credit for authoring bills. As lobbyists care more about implementing their preferred policies than getting credit for legislative authorship, and in many cases prefer to remain anonymous, they are often happy to let the legislator claim credit.

Legislative staff also use model legislation and bills from other states. All state legislatures have an office staffed with lawyers through which all legislation must pass before introduction. Senators and representatives can give proposed legislation to the office or ask the office to draft legislation on their behalf. A small staff of lawyers handles these requests,

[1]The Sunlight Foundation is a national, nonpartisan, nonprofit organization that uses the tools of civic tech, open data, policy analysis and journalism to make our government and politics more accountable and transparent to all.
[2]https://github.com/dssg/policy_diffusion
[3]http://dssg.uchicago.edu/lid

and each is tasked with handling a portfolio of legislation that covers several major areas of policy. These legislative staffers do not have the time to draft all original legislation, so they often borrow text from other sources, including lobbyists [2].

A bill's origin provides useful information about its content. For example, a bill written by the banks likely contains bank-friendly policy, and a bill copied from Massachusetts is probably more liberal than a bill copied from Alabama. By arming citizens and journalists with this information, they can exercise more control over their government. This is especially true at the state level, where political knowledge is lesser than at the federal level, and involves less contested issues, such as state-level land zoning.

There is evidence that the importance of model legislation is growing. Through the American Legislative Exchange Council (ALEC) and other professional groups, state-level politicians are organizing and learning from one another, and one of the tools they commonly learn to use is model legislation. In addition, congressional gridlock is encouraging lobbyists to pursue legislation at the state level instead of at the federal level [26].

3. CURRENT APPROACHES

Today, a journalist or member of the public who would like to know where a particular bill originated must perform a largely manual search. The difficult approach would be to read the bill of interest and manually skim and read hundreds of thousands of bills written elsewhere. A smarter approach would use internet search engines, but even those would be slow and tedious. For example, Google limits queries to short text strings, so the user needs to skim the bill to find a text string to search for and then parse through all the results, few of which would be legislation. Some groups use armies of volunteers to monitor legislation for matches, but given this labor-intensive process, they struggle to find all matches in a timely manner. Watchdogs and scholars can further limit the workload by focusing on a single topic (e.g. abortion [19] or crime [13]) or lobbying groups.[4] In addition, manual searches are also unreliable: while one person might flag two bills as a match, another might not. As a consequence, existing analysis tends to be limited and biased.

Political scientists have taken three approaches to automatically detecting legislative text reuse. The first uses a bag of words model. To study whether states are more likely to use model legislation or legislation from other states, Garrett and Jansa [9] use cosine similarity over bags of words to build social networks, finding that model legislation tends to have a larger influence on state legislation than legislation from other states. However, bags of words will often miss the many subtler examples of text reuse that occur in legislation. By the time some bills come to a vote, they can be called "Franken-bills" because they have stitched together legislative text from many sources. In this case, the bills—or even sections of the bills—could have dissimilar bags of words even though parts of the bills match perfectly.

The second approach uses supervised machine learning. Hertel-Fernández and Kashin [11] collected ALEC model legislation, labeled matches from ALEC Exposed—a group dedicated to finding legislative ALEC's legislative fingerprints—and text features to build a match/no match classifier. This approach is more ambitious—it offers the possibility of matching documents with similar intent but dissimilar text—but is also more difficult to use. Their model is ALEC-specific, so it would need to be retrained every time one wants to include new organizations or to compare state-to-state bills. And because it takes a holistic view toward documents, it struggles to find matches in Franken-bills.

The third approach uses a local-alignment algorithm. Local-alignment algorithms were developed to find similar subsequences within longer genetic strings, so they could find short pieces of matching text between two documents, such as those found in legislation stitched together from multiple sources. To study whether congressional bills reuse text from other congressional bills, Wilkerson et al. [27] used the Smith-Waterman algorithm to compare strings of text from congressional bills introduced since the 1990s, finding that the Affordable Care Act borrowed large pieces of text from Republican legislation introduced during the Clinton administration.

The Smith-Waterman algorithm is a good choice for comparing a relatively small number of bills, where matches may be common at the sub-document level. Because the algorithm is $O(n^2)$ costly, it can take a long time to run on a large corpus, such as state legislation. The corpus of federal bills is far smaller and so more amenable to this type of analysis. Including model legislation in the corpus exacerbates the problem. The Smith-Waterman algorithm is impractical for comprehensive analysis at the state level: by our estimates, it would take over 5,000 years for the algorithm to run on the set of bills introduced between 2010 and 2015. A number of researchers have tried this approach and quit when they realized how long it would take.

Our approach aims to overcome the shortcomings of existing approaches. First, we aim to have a generalizable approach that could be used to detect text reuse on all state bills and model legislation without having to limit our analyses to a few topics or to a specific interest group. Second, we aim to have system that will analyze all available state bills and easily update the corpus so it can provide results in near real time. Last, we aim to have our system open and available for all researchers and journalists, so that they no longer need to rely on manual processes.

4. OUR SOLUTION

LID consists of three major components as pictured in Figure 3. Given a query, LID first uses the *search module* to identify documents most likely to contain text reuse. The *alignment module* uses the Smith-Waterman local alignment algorithm to extract parallel passages of text between the query and each of the documents returned from the search module. Alignments are then scored by their probability of being substantive text via the *classification module*. We first describe our process for cleaning and chunking bills into sections and then each of main modules of LID.

All state bills share a similar format, consisting of sections that denote statements of a proposed law. It is often the case that when two documents exhibit text reuse, only certain sections of one bill are copied from the other. Since the format of state legislation is mostly uniform for a given state, our section chunker consists of a regular expression for each state. Most of the regular expressions consist of variations

[4]For example, ALEC Exposed only tries to find matches for American Legislative Exchange Council (ALEC) model legislation.

of the pattern: $\backslash n$ *section*. By splitting the bills by section, LID allows the user to specify a finer granularity at which to identify text reuse since we can run the alignment algorithm on specific sections of a bill.

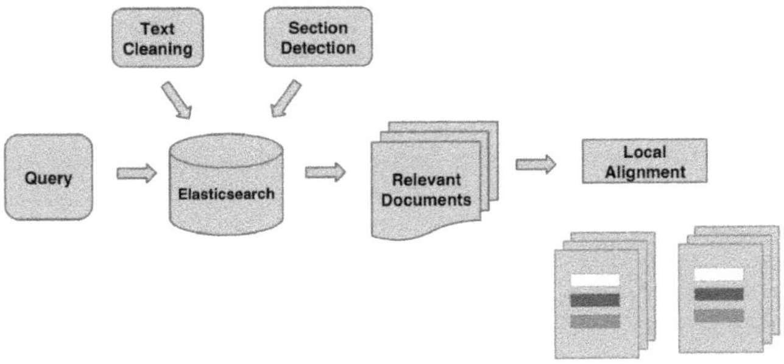

Figure 3: LID system overview.

4.1 Search Module

The local alignment algorithms used to extract the similar bill text is $O(n^2)$ (where n is the length of the longest document), making it computationally too expensive to run on the entire corpus. In order to decrease the computational cost for a given query LID filters the set of documents that we run the local alignment algorithm on. This filter step can be thought of as an information retrieval task where the goal is to identify a subset of bills in the corpus most likely to contain text reuse with the query document.

In the context of this paper, text reuse occurs when two state bills share:

1. Long passages of text, i.e (sections of bills) that can differ in details.

2. Passages which contain text of substantive nature to the topic of the bill.

In addition to text that describe legal directives, state bills also contain boilerplate text that is common to all bills from a particular state or to a particular topic. Examples of legislative boilerplate include: "Read first time 01/29/16. Referred to Committee on Higher Education." and "Safety clause. The general assembly hereby finds, determines, and declares...". The first example is metadata describing where a bill is in legislative process. The second example is a clause included in almost all legislation from Colorado, stating the eligibility of a bill to be petitioned with a referendum.

A common approach for identifying documents that have text reuse is to index the documents using "shingles." Shingles are way of representing a document as a bag of words that comprises of all n-grams of a fixed size. We constructed an inverted index that contains all n-grams of length 3-5. State bills can be long documents, therefore making the computation of similarity between two documents slow. As with previous approaches for detecting text reuse [21] we down-sample the n-grams when computing the similarity between documents. Since our goal is to identify documents that share substantive text, our down-sampling technique is based on ranking the n-grams by their TF-IDF score. Filtering out common terms with high document frequency has been shown to increase efficiency [5] without sacrificing accuracy in document similarity tasks.

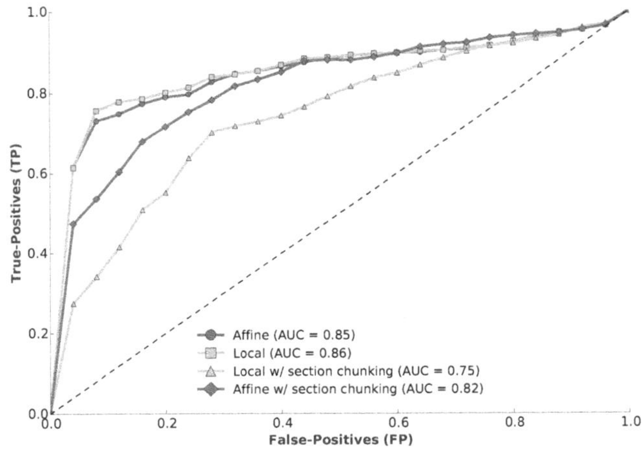

Figure 4: ROC curves for the four variants of the local alignment algorithms.

Our query construction using down-sampling works as follows: for a given query document, we rank the n-grams by their TF-IDF score. We then construct a query of the top 25 n-grams and search our inverted index with this query. We implemented our inverted index using the open-source search engine, Elasticsearch, configured with the standard Lucene scoring function to score the documents for a given query. The resulting list of documents is limited to be at most 300 and to have a Lucene score over 0.01. We chose the values of 300, 0.01, and 25 for the document limit, Lucene threshold and top-k n-grams as we found these values to achieve good results while still being fast.

4.2 Alignment Module

The alignment module uses the Smith-Waterman local alignment algorithm [22] to extract similar passages of text between the query document and each of the documents returned by the search module. The alignment algorithm works by identifying a sub-sequence of words in each document that has the highest alignment score. An alignment score is based on three parameters: word matches, word mismatches (when a word appears in one sub-sequence but not the other), and gaps (when the algorithm inserts a space in one of the sub-sequences). The optimal score is calculated using a dynamic program running in $O(n^2)$, where n is the length of the largest document.

We experimented with many different parameter values, as explained in Section 6. Similar to Smith *et al.* [21], we also implemented a variant of the algorithm with an affine gap penalty that incorporates two gap parameters: An initial *gap* score, and a *extended-gap* score that penalizes all contiguous gaps that follow an initial gap. Using the section chunker, we also implemented a variant of the alignment algorithm where we split the query bill into sections and used the alignment algorithm to extract alignments for each section separately.

4.3 Classification Module

As described previously, state legislation contains a lot of boilerplate text, but the alignment algorithm is indifferent to the substance of the text. An alignment produced by the local alignment algorithm consists of two sequences of text, one that is extracted from the query document and another from the document the query is being aligned to. The classifier module uses a logistic regression classifier to predict the probability that a pair of aligned sequences contains substantive text. The classifier uses features based on the metadata of the alignments such as the mean position of where an two aligned sequences start in a document, and content features such as the Jaccard similarity between the two aligned sequences. We describe each feature used in the classifier below:

We denote a_l and a_r as the left and right sequences respectively and l_{start} and r_{start}

- **alignment length**: Number of words in the alignment
- **jaccard similarity**: Jaccard similarity between the sets of words in a_l and a_r respectively.
- **# matches**: The number of matching words between a_l and a_r.
- **# mismatches**: The number of non-matching words between a_l and a_r.
- **mean distance from top**: average starting position of the sequences, $\frac{l_{\text{start}}+r_{\text{start}}}{2}$
- **n-gram inverted frequency score**: Let N be the total number of n-gram counts in the state legislation corpus and $C(n_i)$ be the number of times the n-gram n_i occurs in the corpus. Let A be the combined set of n-grams that occur in a_l and a_r. We take the average inverted frequency score as a measure of how common the alignment text is.

$$IF(a_l, a_r) = \frac{\sum_{a \in A} \log\left(\frac{N}{C(a)}\right)}{|A|} \tag{1}$$

Our LID implementation uses $n = 4$.

Once the scores are computed, the interface to LID can present a ranking of the alignments to the user, making it easier for the user to find meaningful alignments.

5. DATA SOURCES

We use two main data sources. First, we use the Sunlight Foundation's corpus of state legislation, which includes 550,000 bills and 200,000 resolutions for all 50 states, ranging from 2007 to 2015. While for some states this corpus includes data since 2007, for the majority of states we have data as early as 2010. We do not include in our analysis data from Puerto Rico, where the text is in Spanish, and from DC, whose data includes many idiosyncrasies (e.g. correspondence from city commissions introduced as bills). On average, each state introduced 10,524 bills, with an average length of 1205 words.

Second, we have scraped more than 2400 pieces of model legislation from groups across the political spectrum, including ALEC, the best-known conservative lobbying group; the State Innovation Exchange, the best-known liberal lobbying group; the Council of State Governments; and the Uniform Law Commission.

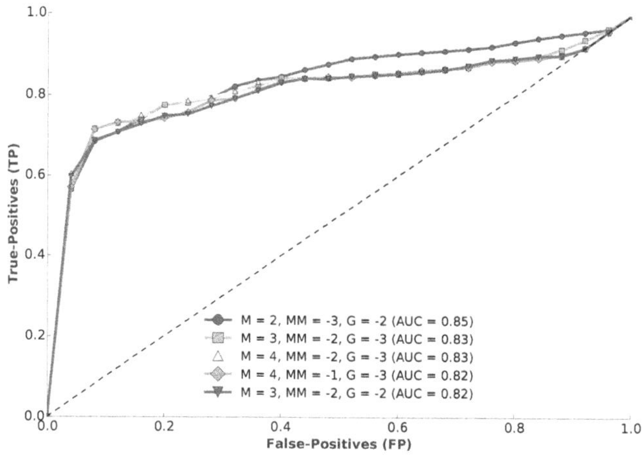

Figure 5: varying the parameters of local alignment algorithm. We denote M for the match score, MM for the missmatch score and G for the gap penalty.

6. RESULTS

6.1 Evaluating Alignment

To evaluate the alignment module we created an evaluation set that includes 165 bills with legislative text reuse. To build this evaluation set we manually read through bills that were highlighted by journalists and experts as cases of text reuse. We then grouped bills into sets with matching text. All pairs of bills within a set are given a positive label, while pairs of documents from different sets are given a negative label. We evaluate the efficacy of the alignment algorithm with ROC analysis using the alignment score as a threshold.

Figures 5 and 4 show the results for the alignment module. Figure 4 provides a comparison of four different kinds of alignment algorithms. On one hand, we vary whether the algorithm has an affine penalty. On the other hand, we vary whether an alignment algorithm finds the alignment with the largest score in a pair of documents or finds alignments by breaking up each document into sections and averaging the score found for each section. The local alignment algorithm performed marginally better than the affine local alignment algorithm. We can also see that sectioning decreased performance as compared to not sectioning. We hypothesize that this is because only certain sections of a document match one another, therefore by averaging the alignment score we may be artificially lowering the score of the few sections that actually match between two documents. Despite these results, we still think that sectioning is an important feature, enabling users to focus the granularity of their intended analysis.

Figure 5 shows how the ROC curve varies for different parameter values for the standard local alignment algorithm. As shown, the algorithms performance does not vary much with respect to the parameter settings. We chose to implement LID with the optimal parameter values: match (3), mismatch(-2), and gap (-3).

6.2 Alignment Classifier Evaluation

To train and evaluate the alignment classifier we labeled a set of alignments produced by LID. Since boilerplate text can come in the form of alignments that have a large score

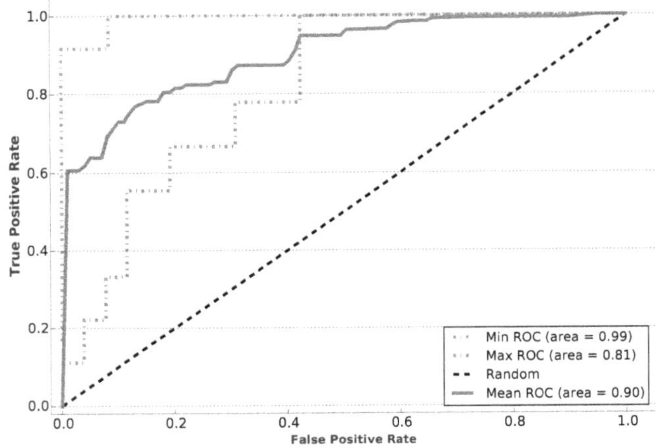

Figure 6: ROC curves for the alignment classifier. The average curve is the mean ROC curve resulting from a 10-fold cross validation.

(e.g. boilerplate sections) or alignments in the form of partial sentences, we wanted to train the classifier on training data that represented both of these scenarios. We obtained these alignments by sampling a set of 400 alignments, 200 with a score above 50 and 200 with a score below 50. We then obtained labels for each training example from 3 human experts (two political science PhD students and one political science post-doc). We only used training examples where all three annotators agreed on the label. Our final training set consisted of 354 examples. The classifier was evaluated using 10-fold cross validation on the training set. Figure 6 shows the mean, min, and max ROC curves resulting from the cross validation. The boilerplate classifier does well on average, and in the worst case still performs substantially better than random guess.

6.3 Interest Group Influence

Using LID we were able to track the influence of interest groups in each of the 50 states. For this, we collected 2400 model bills from websites of different interest groups. These pieces of model legislation can be used as inputs in our system to find state bills that share portions of text.

For the current analysis, we focus on the two largest interest group associations: ALEC (on the conservative side) and ALICE (on the liberal side). Each of these are umbrella associations that represent a large number of interest groups. For instance, ALEC represents the interests of the National Rifle Association (NRA), while ALICE represents several major labor associations. Both ALEC and ALICE have thousands of model bills, on a wide array of topics: labor rights, voting regulations, environmental issues, and economic issues. One of the main goals of both associations is to have a database of model legislation for politicians and activists to enact in state legislatures.

With LID we were able to estimate influence for each interest group. We found 5,557 ALEC bills and 2,307 ALICE bills have been introduced; however, state senators and representatives often introduce slightly different versions of the same bill multiple times. We are not sure how other researchers count these bills, so we conservatively continue the analysis only counting one version per state per year.

Using our stricter definition, LID finds state legislatures have considered 1,816 ALEC-written bills and passed 163 of them (9% success rate). In contrast, the Brookings Institute's manual effort [12] found 132 ALEC bills introduced, 12 of which were enacted (9% success rate). While these differences are large, it is worth noting that Brookings benefited from data precompiled by ALEC Exposed, including copies of ALEC model legislation and a list of ALEC's "most significant" legislation. ALEC Exposed has volunteer researchers in every state to monitor local legislation for ALEC influence.

Hertel-Fernández and Kashin [11] found ALEC introduced 10,370 bills, 1,573 of which were enacted (15%). These larger numbers should come as no surprise: their corpus of state bills is four times larger, their model is trained specifically to find ALEC-written legislation, and they use data labels that include more than word-for-word matches.

Using our stricter definition, LID finds 960 ALICE-written bills that were introduced, 84 of which passed (success rate 9%). We are unaware of another large-scale count of ALICE bills introduced to compare this to, but ALICE's success rate—which is nearly equal to ALEC's—suggests that perhaps this group should receive more attention.

Figures 7 and 8 show how many bills were introduced by state. The darker the color, the more bills introduced. These figures show that states vary in the numbers of bills introduced. For instance, Illinois and Mississippi are both highly influenced by ALEC and ALICE, while Georgia has a great influence from ALEC but a low influence from ALICE.

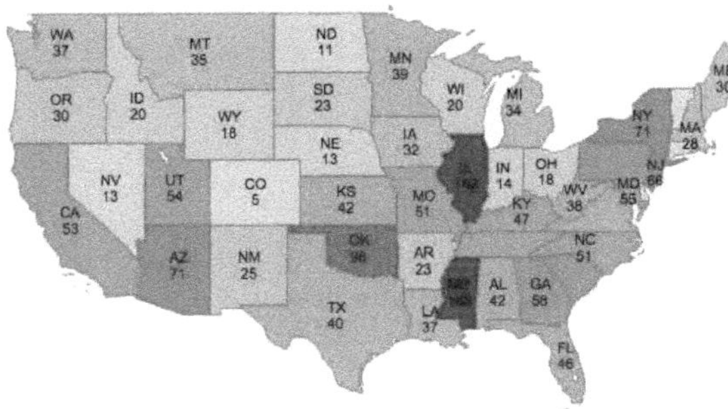

Figure 7: Introduced bills by state from ALEC model legislation

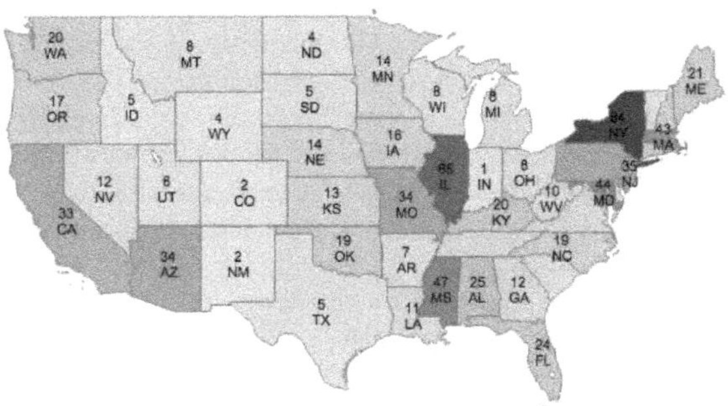

Figure 8: Introduced bills by state from ALICE model legislation

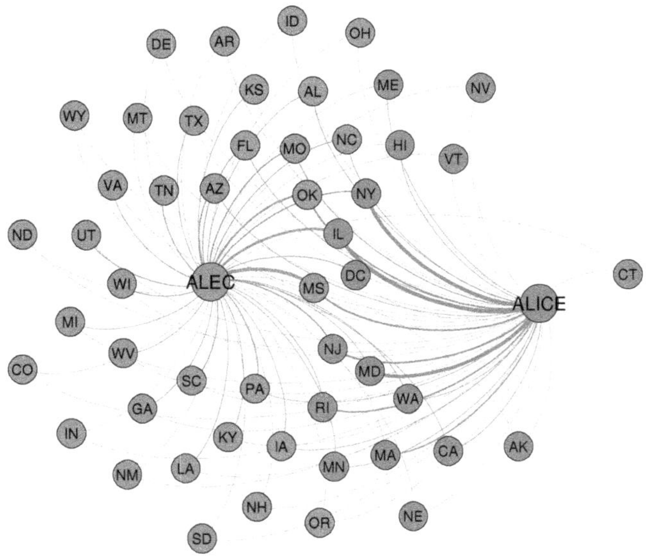

Figure 9: Influence of ALEC and ALICE across States

Figure 9 is another useful way to visualize our analysis. The network shows the influence of both ALEC and ALICE to each state. The thicker the line, the greater the influence. Circle color indicates which group successfully introduced more bills in that state. States more influenced by ALICE are in blue, while the ones more influenced by ALEC are in red. As this figure shows, most conservative states, such as Alabama, Louisiana, and North Dakota, are more influenced by ALEC, while liberal states, as Vermont, Massachusetts, and Connecticut, are more influenced by ALICE. This finding confirms that LID is working accurately.

The analysis here provided can easily be extended to other interest groups. As long as journalist or researchers have model legislation, they can, in a matter of minutes, find all the states' bills that share similar text to the model legislation. One benefit of using the Smith-Waterman algorithm is that it is does not learn from a specific lobbying group. This differs from other existing approaches, resulting in a more useful tool for users to trace the influence of interest groups.

Similarly, researchers can use LID output to go into greater detail on the type of bills that interest groups are pushing across states. LID output allows researchers to analyze the content of those bills that have matches to model legislation. For instance, researchers or journalists can use topic models or cluster analysis to understand what topics (e.g. abortion, taxes, voting rights) are most relevant for each interest group.

6.4 Case Study: Exploring Bills

Last summer, Wisconsin governor Scott Walker signed into law a bill banning non-emergency abortions past the 19th week of pregnancy. Unsurprisingly, Walker's move garnered support from one side, derision from the other, and media attention from both. However, journalists faced a big hurdle when trying to provide context for a story such as this: it is time-consuming to figure out how many states have introduced similar legislation and where it originated.

Abortion is a hotly contested issue, and abortion-related legislation gets far more attention than most. When Walker signed this legislation, journalists wrote nearly 1,000 articles about it, with most only reporting how many other states had similar laws on the books.[5] Few gave a more complete account of the bill's legislative history, such as where similar legislation had been considered and where it originated.

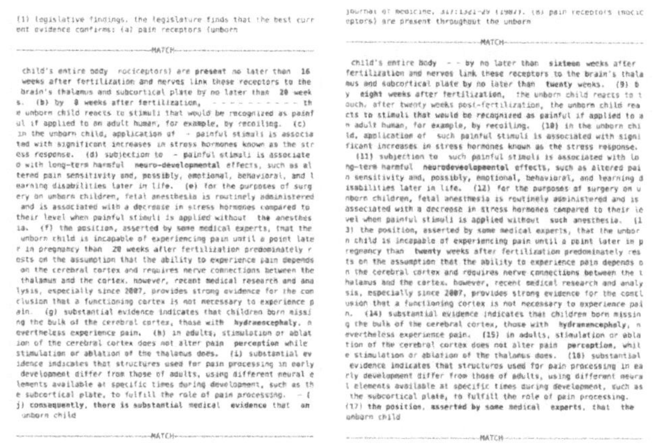

Figure 10: Match between Scott Walker's bill and a highly similar bill from Louisiana. For a detailed view, please visit http://dssg.uchicago.edu/lid/.

Journalists face this challenge every time they want to see if a particular controversial bill has passed in other state. For these cases, LID can be incredibly useful as it can provide a list of bills that share similar text across states in a matter of minutes.

LID allows the user to enter the text of a bill and returns documents that potentially match. The tool highlights similar sections in those documents, allowing the user to quickly evaluate the similarities. With the information about bill number, its state, and its legislative session, users can analyze which bills have passed, which ones have died, and which ones are still under consideration.

Figure 10 is a screen shot of the interactive web application of LID showing the highest-rated match for Walker's bill. The left-hand side displays text from Wisconsin Senate Bill 179 (2015), and the right-hand side displays text from Louisiana Senate Bill 593 (2012). The highlighting shows that these sections match almost perfectly. Where differences exist, they are usually numbers versus spelling (e.g. "16" versus "sixteen") or section identifiers (e.g. "(b)" versus "(9)"). Thanks to LID, we learned that similar bills had passed in Arkansas, Georgia, Idaho, Kansas, Oklahoma, Texas, and West Virginia; that similar bills were under consideration in Illinois, Iowa, Kentucky, Maryland, Oregon, South Carolina, and Virginia; and that similar bills had died in Florida, Michigan, Minnesota, Mississippi, and New Mexico. In summary, different to what all previously mentioned media outlets claimed, 19 states have at least introduced similar bills to Scott Walker's abortion law.

The interactive application of LID can be of particular usefulness for journalists. In a matter of minutes any user can find whether a bill has been introduced in any of the other 49 states in the past 5 years. In addition, the highlighting nature of LID allows user to quickly evaluate simi-

[5]Interestingly, the media gave competing counts: some claimed that 12 [25] states had passed similar measures, others claimed 14 [20], and yet others reported 20 [18].

larities across bills. This tool will be an invaluable resource for journalists covering state politics, who are normally faced with tight budgets to conduct research. As a consequence, LID will (i) increase transparency in state politics by revealing where bills come from and (ii) democratize the process of keeping state lawmakers accountable by enabling any individual to do this work.

7. LIMITATIONS

This tool sheds light on the origins of otherwise untraced state legislation, but it will not find all matches. If the wording changes enough from the first to the second document, LID will not find the match. While this is more likely on very short strings of text, which are perhaps likely to be less important policy ideas, it is a bias to keep in mind.

Many lobbyists intentionally work behind closed doors, and we are unlikely to find their model legislation in the public domain. LID cannot find pieces of model legislation written by clever lobbyists who wish to be invisible, but it can encourage transparency by raising the cost of behind-the-scenes lobbying. Before this tool, a lobbyist might be able to write one piece of model legislation to get a law passed in all 50 states. After this tool, a lobbyist would need to write a separate piece of legislation for each state to avoid detection. By identifying repeating pieces of legislative text across states, this tool can alert journalists to investigate whether there is a common source.

8. IMPLEMENTATION

This section describes how LID can be used by journalists, and what the implications are for coverage of state legislatures and policy. As previously discussed, state legislatures produce more legislation than Congress, yet the number of reporters covering state houses has declined dramatically during the past two decades, according to research by the Pew Research Center [6]. In one state, just two reporters are assigned to cover the state house.

A dwindling press corps demands an approach that maximizes the opportunities for automating portions of the reporting process. The only way for a smaller number of journalists to be able to review and research large amounts of legislation is with the assistance of software and other computational tools. There are several potential uses of LID for journalism, among them detecting similarities within a set of legislation, identifying common phrases or policies across legislatures, and outlier detection, in which the absence of similar legislation can provide insight into the origins and nature of proposed legislation.

The example of model legislation is a primary use of LID, particularly as interest groups seek to make progress in state legislatures (or to block their opponents). A journalist could monitor the spread of model legislation across state lines, enabling her to provide context for how a proposal originated and to explore how it has changed policy outcomes in other states. Ideally, a LID user could rely on model legislation already collected and add new examples to it.

Journalists also could use LID to compare different bills within a topic, whether introduced in the same legislative session or over time. Many legislative proposals are reintroduced repeatedly over time, with the goal of finding the right combination of legislative language and political context to pass the bill. LID could help determine whether proposals are identical or contain differences that might point a journalist toward important additions or deletions compared to earlier versions.

Stories can be found by looking for outliers within a collection of data, or even by the absence of data. If a journalist does not find matching legislative language in a particular state or chamber, that in itself could be a story: is a specific proposal being blocked, or saved for the right moment?

Although the focus of LID is on the legislative text, the tool also could help reveal patterns about legislators who introduce similar bills both within a legislature or across states. LID could be used to determine to what degree the language a lawmaker introduces matches that from other lawmakers of the same party in other legislatures. Combining this information with existing ideological measures and campaign contributions would provide a broader picture of a lawmaker's activity and interests.

In these ways, LID could serve as a general purpose tool for journalists covering topics such as environmental regulation or gun rights, as a resource for reporters seeking to examine a single legislator's interests and devotion to causes, and as a way to identify and trace the activity and success of interest groups seeking to influence public policy.

This tool also has wider applications than state legislation: finding matches among constitutions, referenda, and political speeches, especially during the 2016 campaign. It could be applied to press releases within a state's delegation or among an ideological cohort, or to identify informal coalitions based on the subjects they speak and write about. When political leaders introduce new phrases into a state's policy discussions, LID could be used to track the spread (or lack of it) both inside statehouses and in the wider public sphere.

9. CONCLUSION AND FUTURE WORK

This paper has shown how LID can shed light on a generally neglected topic: who is writing state legislation. In particular, LID can enable researchers, citizens, and journalists to rapidly compare state legislation across states and from model legislation. As a consequence, users will be able to understand who is writing and influencing state policies.

LID solves the shortcomings of existing approaches. First, it creates a generalizable approach that that can be use to detect text reuse on all state bills and model legislation, without limiting the analysis to a subset of topics or interest groups. Second, LID can find sequences of text across documents, which provides more accurate results than a bag of words approach. Third, LID overcomes the computational cost of using the Smith-Waterman local alignment algorithm in a corpus of more than 500,000 state bills. Last, LID is an open system, available for all researchers and journalists, so that they no longer need to rely on manual processes.

Although LID has demonstrated its value, we are planning several improvements that will increase the tool's usefulness:

- We are continuing to develop LID to make it more useful and accessible. First, we are working with journalists and interest groups to produce daily updates. As state legislators introduce bills nearly every day, we would like to run those bills through LID every night and flag text similarities for review. We will set up an alert system to notify users of potential matches.

- Our corpus of model legislation is limited even for the handful of lobbying groups included because it does not include future model legislation. In addition to scraping known lobbying websites for model bills, we are building a tool that automatically queries internet search engines for unique pieces of text in documents that do not match to model legislation in our existing corpus.
- We are improving the quality of the matches. This version of LID only credits exact matches. We would like to credit synonyms and other small differences, which LID currently treats as mismatches. This will help uncover dark-horse lobbying, where people can submit pieces of legislation that they find but are otherwise not available to the public.
- We will make the interactive tool public. At the moment, users can download datasets of potential matches but they can neither perform their own searches nor submit their own documents. We are developing a tool that enables users to provide feedback on the quality of results and then uses that information to weight each user's feedback. For example, this tool gives more weight to a user whose feedback is consistent with other users than a user whose feedback is inconsistent with other users. The tool will also enable LID to weigh user-submitted documents using feedback from other users.

All in all, the main goal of LID is to enable users to better understand who is influencing politics at the state level. We believe that LID can be an essential tool to increase government transparency, enhance accountability, and strengthen democracy.

10. ACKNOWLEDGMENTS

We thank the Eric & Wendy Schmidt Data Science for Social Good Fellowship for generously supporting this work. We also thank Irina Matveeva, James Turk, Paul Tagliamonte, Rachel Shorey, Miles Watkins, and Rob Mitchum for useful discussions. We extend special thanks to those who shared the expertise they gained working on related projects: John Wilkerson, David Smith, Nicholas Stramp, Alexander Hertel-Fernandez, and Konstantin Kashin.

References

[1] A. Abbott and S. DeViney. The welfare state as transnational event: evidence from sequences of policy adoption. *Social Science History*, 16(02):245–274, 1992.

[2] J. Bollman. Michigan legislative process. personal communication, August 12 2015.

[3] L. D. Brandeis. Dissenting opinion. *New State Ice Co. v. Liebmann*, 285, 1932.

[4] C. Drummond. Replicability is not reproducibility: nor is it good science. 2009.

[5] T. Elsayed, J. Lin, and D. W. Oard. Pairwise document similarity in large collections with mapreduce. In *Proceedings of the 46th Annual Meeting of the Association for Computational Linguistics on Human Language Technologies: Short Papers*, HLT-Short '08, pages 265–268, Stroudsburg, PA, USA, 2008. Association for Computational Linguistics.

[6] J. Enda, K. E. Matsa, and J. L. Boyles. *America's Shifting Statehouse Press: Can New Players Compensate for Lost Legacy Reporters?* July 10 2014.

[7] S. I. Exchange. Top ten progressive victories of 2015. https://stateinnovation.org. Accessed January 14, 2016.

[8] R. C. Fording. Laboratories of democracy or symbolic politics. *Race and the politics of welfare reform*, pages 298–319, 2003.

[9] K. N. Garrett and J. M. Jansa. Interest group influence in policy diffusion networks. *State Politics & Policy Quarterly*, page 1532440015592776, 2015.

[10] L. J. Grossback, S. Nicholson-Crotty, and D. A. Peterson. Ideology and learning in policy diffusion. *American Politics Research*, 32(5):521–545, 2004.

[11] A. Hertel-Fernandez and K. Kashin. Capturing business power across the states with text reuse. In *annual conference of the Midwest Political Science Association, Chicago, April*, pages 16–19, 2015.

[12] M. Jackman. Alec's influence over lawmaking in state legislatures. *Brookings*, 2013.

[13] S. L. Kent and J. T. Carmichael. Legislative responses to wrongful conviction: Do partisan principals and advocacy efforts influence state-level criminal justice policy? *Social science research*, 52:147–160, 2015.

[14] C. H. Lee, T. Dyson, M. Park, C. Handy, and M. B. Reynolds. State and local government finances summary: 2013. *Governments Division Briefs*, 2015.

[15] S. F. Liebschutz. The national minimum drinking-age law. *Publius: The Journal of Federalism*, 15(3):39–52, 1985.

[16] C. Z. Mooney. Modeling regional effects on state policy diffusion. *Political Research Quarterly*, 54(1):103–124, 2001.

[17] NCSL. Full- and part-time legislatures, 2014.

[18] F. News. Gop presidential hopeful scott walker signs abortion ban bill, 2015.

[19] D. J. Patton. The effect of united states supreme court intervention on the innovation and diffusion of post-roe abortion policies in the american states-university of kentucky. *National Catholic Bioethics Quarterly*, 2004.

[20] M. J. Sentinel. Scott walker signs 20-week abortion ban, 2015.

[21] D. A. Smith, R. Cordell, E. M. Dillon, N. Stramp, and J. Wilkerson. Detecting and modeling local text reuse. In *Proceedings of the 14th ACM/IEEE-CS Joint Conference on Digital Libraries*, JCDL '14, pages 183–192, Piscataway, NJ, USA, 2014. IEEE Press.

[22] T. Smith and M. Waterman. Identification of common molecular subsequences. *Journal of Molecular Biology*, 147(1):195 – 197, 1981.

[23] R. A. Stein. *Forming a More Perfect Union: A History of the Uniform Law Commission.* Uniform Law Commission, 2013.

[24] D. A. Stone. *Policy paradox: The art of political decision making.* Norton New York, 2002.

[25] N. R. to Life. 12 states have passed measures similar to walker's, 2015.

[26] L. E. Whyte and B. Wieder. Amid federal gridlock, lobbying rises in the states. *The Center for Public Integrity*, February 11 2016.

[27] J. Wilkerson, D. Smith, and N. Stramp. Tracing the flow of policy ideas in legislatures: A text reuse approach. *American Journal of Political Science*, 2015.

Identifying Police Officers at Risk of Adverse Events *

Samuel Carton
University of Michigan
scarton@umich.edu

Jennifer Helsby
University of Chicago
jen@redshiftzero.com

Kenneth Joseph
Carnegie Mellon University
kjoseph@cs.cmu.edu

Ayesha Mahmud
Princeton University
mahmud@princeton.edu

Youngsoo Park
University of Arizona
youngsoo@email.arizona.edu

Joe Walsh
University of Chicago
jtwalsh@uchicago.edu

Crystal Cody
Charlotte-Mecklenburg Police Department
ccody@cmpd.org

CPT Estella Patterson
Charlotte-Mecklenburg Police Department
epatterson@cmpd.org

Lauren Haynes
University of Chicago
lnhaynes@uchicago.edu

Rayid Ghani
University of Chicago
rayid@uchicago.edu

ABSTRACT

Adverse events between police and the public, such as deadly shootings or instances of racial profiling, can cause serious or deadly harm, damage police legitimacy, and result in costly litigation. Evidence suggests these events can be prevented by targeting interventions based on an Early Intervention System (EIS) that flags police officers who are at a high risk for involvement in such adverse events. Today's EIS are not data-driven and typically rely on simple thresholds based entirely on expert intuition. In this paper, we describe our work with the Charlotte-Mecklenburg Police Department (CMPD) to develop a machine learning model to predict which officers are at risk for an adverse event. Our approach significantly outperforms CMPD's existing EIS, increasing true positives by $\sim 12\%$ and decreasing false positives by $\sim 32\%$. Our work also sheds light on features related to officer characteristics, situational factors, and neighborhood factors that are predictive of adverse events. This work provides a starting point for police departments to take a comprehensive, data-driven approach to improve policing and reduce harm to both officers and members of the public.

1. INTRODUCTION

Recent high-profile cases of police officers using deadly force against members of the public have caused a political and public uproar [4, 5]. They have also highlighted and further encouraged tensions between the American police force and citizens. While such violent altercations tend to capture the nation's attention, there is evidence that more mundane interactions between the police and the public can have negative implications as well [13]. *Adverse events* between the police and the public thus come in many different forms, from deadly use of a weapon to a lack of courtesy paid to a victim's family. These events can have negative mental, physical, and emotional consequences on both police officers and citizens. We discuss our precise definition of "adverse event" below as an aspect of our experimental design.

Prior work has shown that a variety of factors are predictive of adverse events [11, 6]. While some of these factors are beyond the control of police officers and their departments, many of them can theoretically be addressed ahead of time. For example, training in appropriate use of force may reduce the odds of an officer deploying an unnecessary level of force in a particular situation.

The incidence of such factors is not randomly distributed among officers or over time [11]. Certain officers, at certain periods of time, can be identified as being more *at risk* of involvement in an adverse event than others. Because police departments have limited resources available for interventions, a system to identify these high-risk officers is vital. Using this kind of *Early Intervention System* (EIS), police departments can provide targeted interventions to prevent adverse events, rather than responsively dealing with them after such an event occurs.

The work described in this paper was initiated as part of the White House's Police Data Initiative[1] launched based on President Obama's Task Force on 21st Century Policing. As part of this effort, we had discussions with several US police departments and it became clear that existing EISs were ineffective in their attempts to identify at risk officers. This paper describes our work with the Charlotte-Mecklenburg Police Department (CMPD) in North Carolina to use machine learning algorithms to improve their existing EIS.

*This work was started at the 2015 Eric & Wendy Schmidt Data Science for Social Good Summer Fellowship at the University of Chicago.

KDD '16, August 13 - 17, 2016, San Francisco, CA, USA

ACM 978-1-4503-4232-2/16/08 $15.00
DOI: http://dx.doi.org/10.1145/2939672.2939698.

[1]https://www.whitehouse.gov/blog/2015/05/18/launching-police-data-initiative

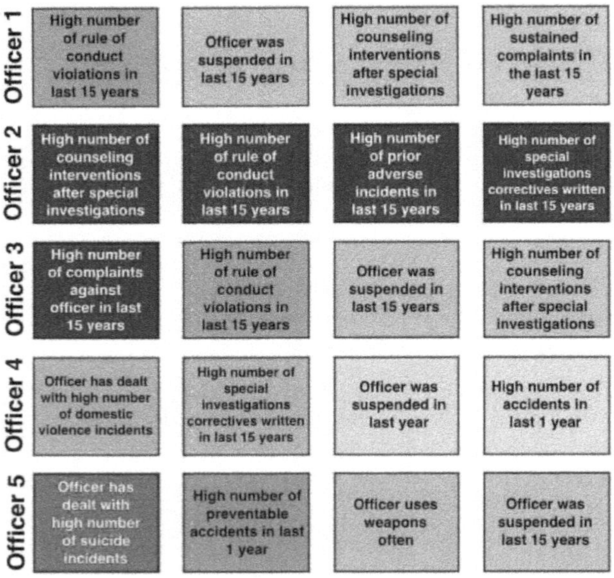

Figure 1: An illustration of five at-risk officers that will go on to have an adverse incident and their risk factors. The darker the red, the stronger the importance of that feature.

CMPD's 1800 officers patrol more than 500 square miles encompassing more than 900,000 people. Over the last ten years, CMPD has become a leader in data-driven policing by investing heavily in a centralized data warehouse and building its own software, including an EIS. Like most EISs, CMPD's system uses behavioral thresholds, chosen through expert intuition, to flag officers. A supervisor then determines whether an intervention is appropriate. Several departments have adopted CMPD's system since it was built more than ten years ago [16]. To improve the current system, we focus on the following prediction task:

> Given the set of all active officers at time t and all data from time periods prior to t, predict which officers will have an adverse interaction in the **next year**.

We show that a random forest model with an extensive set of features significantly outperform the department's existing EIS. Specifically, our model shows a relative increase of $\sim$ 12% in true positive rate and a relative decrease of $\sim$ 32% in false negative rate over the existing EIS in a temporal cross-validation experiment. Unlike the existing system, our approach uses a data-driven approach and can thus be used to explore officer characteristics, neighborhood and environmental factors that are predictive of adverse events.

Figure 1 shows an illustrative chart that shows the individual risk factors that are associated with a high risk of an adverse event for five anonymous officers. Each officer in Figure 1 went on to have an adverse event. These risk factors were met with substantial acceptance by CMPD - an indicator of external validity of our modeling approach.

In addition to factors we discover in our analyses of feature importances from this prediction task, we also provide an exploratory analysis of predictive features at the single event level to better understand situational factors that may play a significant role in scenarios leading to adverse events.

The system described here is the beginning of an effort that has the potential to allow police chiefs across the nation to see which of their officers are in need of training, counseling, or additional assistance to make them better prepared to deal safely and positively with individuals and groups in their communities. Police departments can move from being responsive to negative officer incidents to being proactive and preventing them from happening in the first place.

In summary, the contributions of this paper are the following:

- We apply, to our knowledge, the first use of machine learning toward prediction of adverse incidents from internal police department data.
- We show significant improvement over existing systems at flagging at-risk officers
- We take preliminary steps toward understanding the situational factors that lead to an adverse event.

2. EXISTING EARLY INTERVENTION SYSTEMS

A small minority of officers account for the majority of adverse events, such as citizen complaints or excessive uses of force [11, 6]. EISs, which are designed to detect officers exhibiting alarming behavioral patterns and prompt intervention such as counseling or training before serious problems arise, have been regarded as risk-management tools for countering this issue. The US Commission on Civil Rights [1], the Commission on Accreditation of Law Enforcement Agencies [2], US Department of Justice [3], the International Association of Chiefs of Police, and the Police Foundation have recommended departments use EISs. Most federal consent decrees (legal settlements between the Department of Justice and a police department) to correct problematic policing require an EIS to be in place [19]. A 2007 Law Enforcement Management and Administrative Statistics (LEMAS) survey showed that 65% of surveyed police departments with 250 or more officers had an EIS in place [15].

Current EISs detect officers at risk of adverse events by observing a number of performance indicators and raising a flag when certain selection criteria are met. These criteria are usually thresholds on counts of certain kinds of incidents over a specified time frame, such as two accidents within 180 days or three uses of force within 90 days. Thresholds such as these fail to capture the complex nature of behavioral patterns and the context in which these events play out. For example, CMPD's system uses the same thresholds for officers working the midnight shift in a high-crime area as an officer working in the business district in the morning. More sophisticated systems flag outliers while conditioning on one or two variables, such as the officer's beat[2], but still fail to include many factors. For example, CMPD's indicators include complaints, uses of force, vehicle pursuits & accidents, rule-of-conduct violations, raids and searches of civilians or civilian property, and officer injuries. Important factors, such as prior suspensions from the force, are often not included.

Empirical studies on the effectiveness of these systems have been limited, and their findings give mixed conclusions.

[2]Roughly, an indicator of the area the officer patrols and the time at which they patrol it

Case studies focusing on specific police departments have shown that EISs were effective in decreasing the number of citizen complaints [20, 9], but it is unclear whether this decrease arises from a reduction in problematic behavior or from discouraging officers from proactive policing [23]. A large-scale study of emerging EISs across departments concludes that EIS effectiveness depends on departmental characteristics and details of implementation, such as which indicators are tracked, what thresholds are assigned, and how supervisors handle the system's flags [15].

Beyond their possible ineffectiveness, threshold-based systems pose additional challenges. First, inconsistent use of the system creates an obstacle for threshold-based EISs. Second, threshold-based systems are difficult to customize. At least one vendor hard-codes thresholds into their EIS, making changes difficult and costly—which is good for the vendor but bad for the department. Ideally, the system should improve as the department collects more data, but threshold-based systems require extensive use of heuristics, making such changes unlikely.

Third, threshold systems are easily gamed. Because thresholds are visible and intuitive, officers can modify their behaviors slightly to avoid detection - either not taking an action they should have taken, or by not reporting an action they did take. Finally, output from threshold systems are limited to binary flags instead of risk scores. Risk scores enable the agency to rank officers by risk, to explicitly choose tradeoffs (e.g. precision vs. recall), and to allocate resources in a prioritized manner.

A machine learning system would be able to alleviate many of these issues. With respect to customization, machine learning models can be easily retrained on new data and with new features. Furthermore, given the volume of features and feature interactions that can be used within a machine learning model, parameters are sufficiently complex that the system cannot be easily gamed. Importantly, such models return control to the department, allowing its leaders to choose the right mix of accuracy and interpretability. Finally, machine learning approaches can be used to generate risk scores as opposed to pure binary classification. In addition to being a better fit for the resource constraints faced by today's American police force, risk-score systems can identify which officers are doing well as easily as which are at risk. The department can use this information when assigning officers to partners or when looking for best practices to incorporate into its training programs.

3. POLICE MISCONDUCT

Designing an effective EIS requires knowledge of what factors may be predictive of adverse events. The literature on police behavior and misconduct has focused on three broad sets of potential predictors: officer characteristics, situational factors, and neighborhood factors.

More educated police officers, particularly those with four-year college degrees, tend to have fewer complaints and allegations of misconduct compared to officers with less education [14, 22, 8]. In a study of misconduct in the New York Police Department, White and Kane [22] found that, in addition to education level, prior records of criminal action, prior poor performance and a history of citizen complaints were all significant predictors of misconduct as well.

Situational factors are those specific to particular incidents that (perhaps) result in an adverse event. These factors include demographics and behaviors of the citizen(s) involved in that particular incident as well as features of the incident itself, such as time of day and location. White [21] found that certain categories of incidents, such as robberies and disturbance incidents, were more likely to result in police use of deadly force. However, studies examining the relationship between citizen characteristics (such as race, gender, and age) and police behavior (such as likelihood of arrests and citations, and use of force) have found mixed results [17]. Research on citizen characteristics has, moreover, been limited due to lack of publicly available data.

Finally, neighborhood features have also been studied as a potential predictor of police misconduct. Sobol [17] found that incidents in high-crime neighborhoods have a greater likelihood of ending in interrogation, search and/or arrest. Similarly, Terrill and Reisig [18] found that police officers were more likely to use higher levels of force in disadvantaged and high-crime neighborhoods.

Our models incorporate features at each of these levels of analysis, finding that predictors at each level have a unique and important role in predicting officers at risk of adverse events. We are currently involved in efforts to experimentally distinguish causal factors. In the present work, however, efforts are restricted to understanding only those features correlated with officers at risk of adverse events.

Database	Num. Records	Time Window
Internal Affairs	20K	2002-Now
Dispatch Events	14M	2003-Now
Criminal Complaints	959K	2005-Now
Citations	946K	2006-Now
Traffic Stops	1.6M	2002-Now
Arrests	350K	2005-Now
Field Interviews	180K	2003-Now
Employee Records	20K	2002-Now
Secondary Employment	651K	2009-Now
Training	1.4M	2001-Now
Existing EIS	14K	2005-Now

Table 1: Description of the types of data used, as well as the number of records and the time window over which we have data of that type

4. DATA DESCRIPTION

The data for this work consists of almost all employee information and event records collected by CMPD to manage its day-to-day operations. Certain information, such as employee names, ID numbers, and military veteran status, as well as all narrative fields in the data, were redacted in accordance with North Carolina personnel laws to protect employee privacy and safety. The major types of information present in the dataset, summarized in Table 1, are described in detail in this section. Almost all records are associated with one or more involved officers and include a hashed version of the ID of that officer in addition to any other information.

4.1 Internal Affairs Data

Internal Affairs (IA) records contain the information about adverse events that we use as our outcome variable. Every

IA record pertains to a single officer. When a department employee or member of the public files a complaint or when an officer uses force, engages in a vehicle pursuit, gets into a vehicle accident, commits a rule-of-conduct violation, is injured, or conducts a raid and search, CMPD creates an IA record. Each record contains additional information such as a link to the *dispatch event*[3] during which the incident took place. Finally, each record contains the reviewing supervisor's decision regarding the appropriateness of the officer's actions as well as the recommended intervention if intervention was deemed necessary.

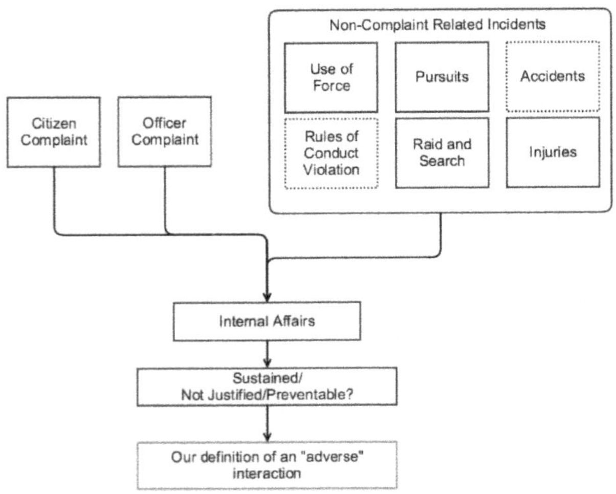

Figure 2: The Internal Affairs process and our definition of an adverse incident.

IA investigations of different event types can carry different outcomes: complaints can be deemed *sustained* or *not sustained*; accidents and injuries can be deemed *preventable* or *not preventable*; and everything else (e.g. use of force) can be deemed *justified* or *not justified*. **We define records with *not justified*, *preventable*, and *sustained* dispositions to define the class of adverse events, with exceptions for a number of internal complaints that we consider less egregious, such as misuse of sick leave.** These data serve as the positive class for our dependent variable. Figure 2 shows the IA process and our definition for an adverse incident, and Table 2 lists the full set of IA outcomes that we label as adverse events.

Notably, we proceed with the assumption that the Internal Affairs (IA) data reasonably represent the true distribution of adverse events and officer fault. For various reasons, this assumption may be flawed. For example, many departments screen complaints before entering them into their IA system, and incidents have been reported in which officers do not faithfully record events. While CMPD encourages good data collection by punishing officers who fail to report adverse incidents, there is no complete guarantee of data accuracy. In addition, almost all IA cases are resolved internally without reference to an external agency. Unfortunately, without similarly comprehensive data from other police departments, it is difficult to estimate what effect these biases might have on the present work. We thus note this point as a condition on which the present analysis should be qualified and plan to investigate this further as we expand our work to other police departments.

[3]defined below

Event	**IA Ruling**
Citizen Complaint*	Sustained
Officer Complaint*	Sustained
Vehicle Accidents	Preventable
Injuries	Preventable
Use of Force	Unjustified
Raid and Search	Unjustified
Pursuit	Unjustified
Discharge of Firearm	Unjustified
Tire Deflation Device	Unjustified

*Minor violations excluded

Table 2: The types of events within the IA database that we define as representative of an *adverse event*

4.2 Other Data

4.2.1 Dispatch Events

CMPD's system creates a dispatch event every time an officer is dispatched to a scene—for example, in response to a 911 call—and every time an officer reports an action to the department. The dispatch system is the backbone of how officer movements are coordinated, and an officer's dispatches provide a rough guide to what the officer did and where the officer did it at all times they are active on the force. Dispatch records include the time and location of all events, as well as the type of event (e.g. robbery) and its priority. Dispatches are often linked in CMPD's system to other types of events, such as arrests or IA cases, that occurred during that dispatch.

4.2.2 Criminal Complaints

The criminal complaints data provided by CMPD contains records of criminal complaints made by citizens. Each record includes a code for the incident, the location of the incident, the type of weapons involved if weapons were involved, and details about victims and responding officers. It also contains flags that include information such as whether the event was associated with gang violence, domestic violence, narcotics activity or hate crimes.

4.2.3 Citations

The citations data provides details of each citation written by officers. Each record contains the date and type of citation, a code corresponding to the division, and additional meta-data such as whether the citation was written on paper or electronically.

4.2.4 Traffic Stops

CMPD officers are required to record information about all traffic stops they conduct. Records include time, location, the reason for and the outcome of the stop, if the traffic stop resulted in the use of force, and the stopped driver's socio-demographic profile.

4.2.5 Arrests

CMPD records every arrest made by its officers, including when and where the arrest took place, what charges were associated, whether a judge deemed the officer to have had probable cause, and the suspect's demographic information.

4.2.6 Field Interviews

A "field interview" is the broad name given by CMPD for any event in which a pedestrian is stopped and/or frisked, or any time an officer enters or attempts to enter the property of an individual. In the latter case, officers may simply be completing a "knock and talk" to request information from a citizen, or be part of a team conducting a "raid and search" of an individual's property. A field interview can also be conducted as result of a traffic stop. Records contain temporal and spatial information as well as information about the demographics about the interviewed person.

4.2.7 Employee Records

The department's employee information includes demographic information on every individual employed by the department, including those that have retired or been fired. The data includes officer education levels, years of service, race, height, weight, and other persistent qualities of officers.

4.2.8 Secondary Employment

CMPD records all events in which officers are hired by external contractors to provide security. These external contractors include, for example, financial institutions, private businesses and professional sports teams. Officers are allowed to sign up for these various opportunities through CMPD and are required to record all events that occur at them, such as disturbances, trespasses or arrests.

4.2.9 Training

CMPD requires officers to receive rigorous training on a variety of topics, from physical fitness to how to interact with members of the public. The department records each officer's training events.

4.2.10 Existing EIS Flags

We were also given the history of EIS flags going back over 10 years to 2005. Each record identifies the relevant officer and supervisor, the threshold triggered (e.g. more than two accidents in a 180 day period or more than three uses of force in an 90 day period) and the selected intervention for each flag, which can include training and counseling.

4.2.11 Neighborhood

In addition to the data provided by CMPD, we also use publicly available data from 2010 and 2012 neighborhood quality-of-life studies[4] to understand the geospatial context of CMPD events. These studies collect data on many neighborhood features including Census/ACS data on neighborhood demographics and data on physical characteristics, crime, and economic vitality.

4.3 Data Limitations

In addition to the potential bias discussed above, the dataset has a few other limitations. First, traffic stops, field interviews, and criminal complaints are entered into the CMPD system by the officers themselves, often in the midst of busy shifts or retroactively after their shifts have ended. Times and locations are often approximate, and these types of events often fail to be properly linked to an associated dispatch call, which limits what other information (such as IA cases) they can be linked to. Other important fields are also missing with relative frequency from the data. We take standard measures to accommodate missing data, and try to mitigate the unreliability of temporal and spatial information by aggregating the data across time and space in our feature generation.

[4] `http://mcmap.org/qol/`

5. METHODS

The goal of the EIS is to predict which officers are likely to have an adverse event in the near future. We formulate it as a binary classification problem where the class of interest is whether a given officer will have an adverse event in a given period of time into the future. In discussions with CMPD and in consideration of the rareness of adverse events, we decided that one year was an appropriate prediction window. Efforts were chiefly geared towards the extraction of these features - in total 432 features were used. For modeling, we tried a variety of model types, including AdaBoost, Random Forests, Logistic Regression, and Support Vector Machines. Random searches over a standard hyperparameter space using 3-fold cross-validation were used to tune each model. Below, we discuss our feature extraction process and how models were evaluated.

5.1 Feature Generation

We generated features based on our expertise as well as on discussions with experts at the Charlotte-Mecklenburg Police Department. Patrol officers, Internal Affairs investigators, members of our officer focus group, and department leadership suggested features that varied across the officer- and neighborhood- levels of analysis. We explore situational factors in Section 7.

At the officer level, we generate behavioral features by aggregating the record of incidents by each officer, establishing a behavioral history. The simplest features are frequencies and fixed-period counts of incidents the officer has been involved in (e.g. arrests, citations, etc.) and incident subtypes (e.g. arrests with only discretionary charges). Broad incident classes we track include arrests, traffic stops, field interviews, IA cases, and external employment.

Notably among incident sub-types, we track incidents we believe are likely to contribute to officer stress, such as events involving suicides, domestic violence, young children, gang violence, or narcotics. In addition, we incorporated features describing the number of credit hours of training officers had in topic areas of relevance: less-than-lethal weapons training, bias training, and physical fitness training.

To these frequencies we add a variety of normalized and higher-order features. To account for high-crime times and locations, we include outlier features, where we compare an officer's event frequencies against the mean frequencies for the officer's assigned division and beat. We generate time-series features from raw event counts (e.g. a sudden increase in the number of arrests in the six-month period prior to the point of analysis) to capture sudden changes in behavior. We also use more static officer features such as demographics, height, weight, and time on the force.

We include the existing EIS thresholds as features in our model. These EIS flags will occur if a threshold number of adverse events occur within a specific timeframe, e.g. 3

Metric	Existing EIS	Improved EIS	Percent Change
True Positives	43	48	+12%
False Positives	624	427	−32%
True Negatives	802	999	+25%
False Negatives	40	35	−8%

Table 3: Comparison of model performance between the existing threshold-based EIS and the improved predictive EIS developed in this work.

uses of force within 90 days, and similarly for other potential warning signs such as complaints and sick leave use.

Finally, we include neighborhood features to capture specific information about the areas where officers patrol. For example, we included the 311 call rate for CMPD patrol areas, which correlates not only with conditions in the neighborhood but also with the residents' willingness to report problems to city government.

5.2 Model Evaluation

We validate our models using temporal cross validation [12], meaning that if, for example, predictions were being made for adverse events in the years 2010-2012, we train our models on data from periods before 2010. With our data ranging from 2009 to 2015, we perform multiple evaluations over the data and aggregate them to come up with the final statistics. For each evaluation, we use precision (percent of officers flagged who actually have an adverse event) and recall (percent of officers with adverse events who are flagged) at various probability (or risk score) thresholds as outcome metrics. We compare various versions of our models and feature sets to each other as well as to a random baseline, to a classifier that exactly replicates the current EIS, and to a logistic regression baseline model using only the officer age, sex, race, years of experience and days since last adverse event as features.

6. RESULTS

In this section we discuss results in terms of performance on the officer-level prediction problem as well as an analysis of highly predictive features.

6.1 Predictive Performance

At the officer level, about $8-9\%$ of officers will have an adverse event of some type in every year. The best binary classification model to predict these events was a Random Forest with 50 estimators. Table 3 shows how our model compares with the EIS baseline in terms of false positives, false negatives, true positives, and true negatives. Our results show that moving beyond the current threshold system and using a broader set of data with more complex models improves accuracy. Our best performing model is able to flag 12% more high-risk officers (true positives) while flagging 32% fewer low-risk officers (false positives), compared to the current system. We show the precision-recall curves for the officer-level prediction problem in Figure 3.

6.2 Feature Analysis

Figure 4 shows the features with the largest feature importances in our best performing random forest model. The most predictive features of the model were those relevant to

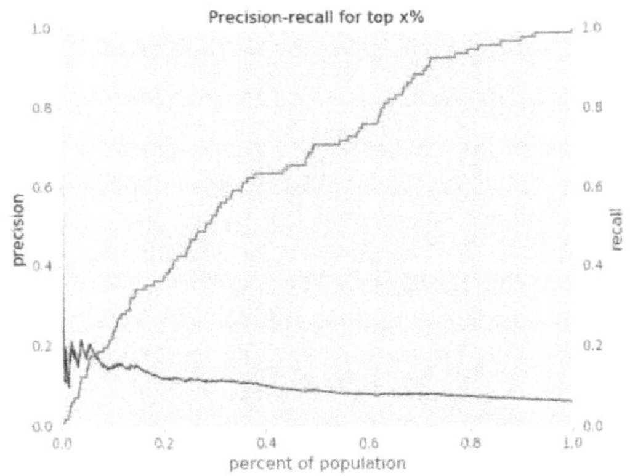

Figure 3: Precision-recall curves for the Random Forest model.

the prior IA history of the officer: officers who are routinely found to have been engaged in an adverse event are likely to engage in another such event in the future. This is fairly typical in behavioral prediction tasks.

Such indicators are complex and overlie a variety of causal factors - for example, officers who are in areas of higher rates of violent crime are more likely to use force because of the area they patrol and perhaps not because of any inherent tendencies. However, two caveats to this notion are in order. First, significant controls at the neighborhood level exist within the model. Such controls have an impact on prediction - for example, vacant land area rates are a significant predictor of officer risk. Second, indicators such as the rates of prior adverse incidents and sustained complaints indicate cases where IA officials previously found officers to be at fault over and above these increased risk rates.

Combined, these observations provide support for the idea that a subset of officers are at particular risk for adverse events, and that an EIS which controls for non-officer level factors may be able to find such officers so that interventions can be applied. Further, these factors are based on *behavioral characteristics of the officer, not demographic information.* While correlations are likely to exist between behavior and demographics, and causal factors may be extremely difficult to untangle, it is preferable to base policy decisions on things officers can remedy (behavior) as opposed to things they cannot easily change.

To maximize the insight gained from the most prominent features, it is ideal to have information on the *directionality* of these features, i.e. whether the changes in one of the features correlate positively or negatively with the corresponding change in the predicted risk score. Such information would clarify how a feature moves the trained model, thereby allowing for a deeper understanding of the underlying phenomenon. Traditional approaches to feature importance in random forest models do not, however, allow us to infer the direction of a feature's effect. In order to address this issue, we perform a Monte Carlo sampling of our model's risk score surface to estimate the conditional distribution of risk scores, or the "risk score curve," on each feature.

We begin with 100,000 Monte Carlo samples generated by drawing from a uniform distribution in the feature space spanning the entire range of feature values in the training data. To analyze the risk score curve of a feature, we di-

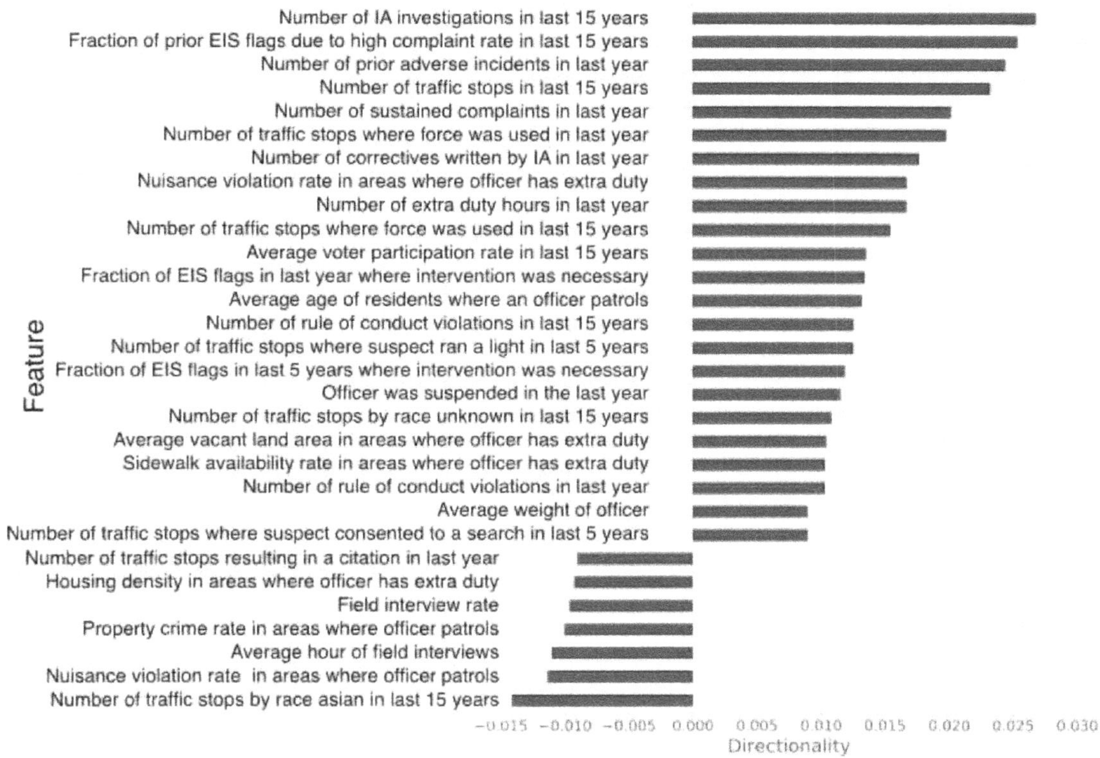

Figure 4: Feature directionalities from the officer-level random forest model

vide the generated samples into 50 bins ranging from the minimum to the maximum value of the feature of interest found in the dataset. Finally, within each bin, the mean and the standard deviation of the risk score distribution are calculated. In Figure 5, we present the risk score curve for the number of uses of force in traffic stops over the last 15 years. It is notable that a sharp transition, or shift, in the risk score distribution occurs around seven traffic stops. This sharp transition aligns with the behavior one would expect from a random forest model, where risk scores are determined via binary selection criteria that act as sharp distributional "switches".

To construct a metric for directionality from the estimated risk score curve, we use the mean risk score difference between the first and last bin. While this metric is arguably less robust for features that undergo multiple transitions of conflicting directions, it is a good first-order proxy for the directionality of the most prominent features. Further, in assessing the resulting data, such multiple transitions were rare in the feature set used for the present work.

After estimating the risk score curve for every feature used, we present in Figure 4 the most prominent directionalities we found in our model. It is worth noting that while there is a strong correspondence between features with high importances and high directionalities, it is not an exact match. This is because the definition of feature importance in random forests depends not only on the strength of the directionality of a feature, but also on the exact configuration of the trees within the forest. We are actively looking at other ways of determining feature importance, such as using additive models [7].

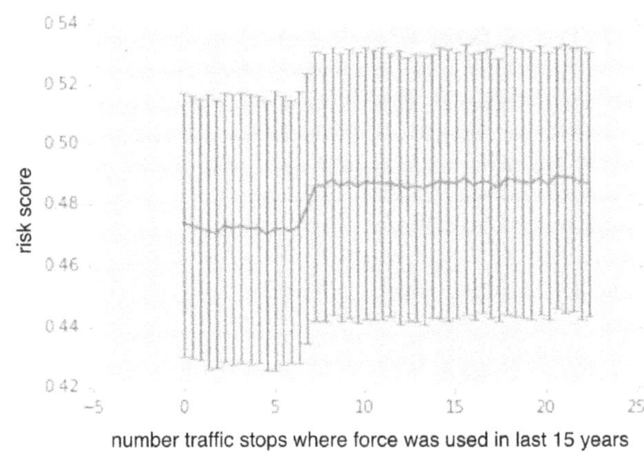

Figure 5: Risk score curve for the number of uses of force in traffic stops over the last 15 years.

7. DISPATCH-LEVEL PREDICTION

As an exploratory exercise to better understand situational, near-term factors that may have an impact on officer risk of adverse events, we attempt to predict which dispatch calls are likely to result in an adverse event. Each dispatch call record in the data contains data that includes time, location, type of call, officers dispatched, and priority (or urgency) of the situation. These environmental factors of a given event could play a significant role in determining whether an event "turns adverse", in addition to the characteristics of officers involved. Furthermore, a history of dispatch calls can be constructed for each officer, from which a general pattern of dispatches leading to an eventual adverse event can be found. For example, overworked officers at the end of a long shift may be more likely to be involved in an adverse event, and this analysis allows us to discern whether such patterns exist.

To make predictions at the dispatch-level, we use most of the features generated for the officer-level experiment. To these we add features of the dispatch event itself, such as its priority level, features of medium and short-term officer stress, such as how many consecutive days the officer had been on duty at the time of the dispatch, and features of the location in which the dispatch takes place. In total, we examine 359 features at the dispatch level.

For this task, there is no existing baseline method analogous to the EIS. Therefore, all comparisons are against a random baseline. Further, and most importantly, adverse events are extremely rare: 1 in 10,000 dispatches end in any type of adverse incident in our dataset. As an exploratory analysis, we subset the data to a ratio where feature analysis can be performed. This means that model performance *should not be expected to hold in realistic settings.*

The positive examples for this prediction task consist of every dispatch from CMPD's database that can be linked to an adverse event. These 929 positive examples are contrasted against 8,361 negative examples (i.e. "non-adverse" events) drawn randomly from the database, for a 10%-90% balanced training set of 9,290 examples. We then split the data temporally, training on all adverse events prior to 2013, and testing on those following 2013.

To understand what types of feature lend utility to this prediction model, we compare performance of different feature subsets. Notable subsets we examine include dispatch features, such as the priority level of the dispatch (1 to 9) or the typecode assigned to it by the dispatcher (e.g. SUSP-SCN for suspect-on-scene), and medium-to-short-term officer stress features, such as how many hours the officer has been on duty at the time of the dispatch.

Figure 6 shows the performance of a tuned random forest on predicting whether dispatch events will result in adverse interactions between the involved officer and a citizen. The full model achieves an F1 of 0.478 with respect to the positive class, significantly better than the 0.18 that would result from random guessing.

Features of the dispatch event itself dominate the model. Used alone, they achieve comparable performance to the full model. Removed from the dataset, they reduce model performance to indistinguishable from random. This suggests that immediate situational factors outweigh longer-term officer- or location-level factors in determining when a dispatch is likely to result in an adverse event.

Figure 7 examines which features are used to the greatest cumulative effect in reducing sample impurity in the random forest model. The clear outlier is travel time, which appears to have a major impact in predicting adverse outcomes. Other significant features include the JST-OCC dispatch typecode, indicating an event that has just occurred, and the career arrest rates, both discretionary and overall, of the officer involved in the dispatch.

Figure 8 further examines feature importance by using the same Monte Carlo sampling method employed in figure 4. Travel time is found to have a positive sign, meaning that longer travel times are associated with a higher risk

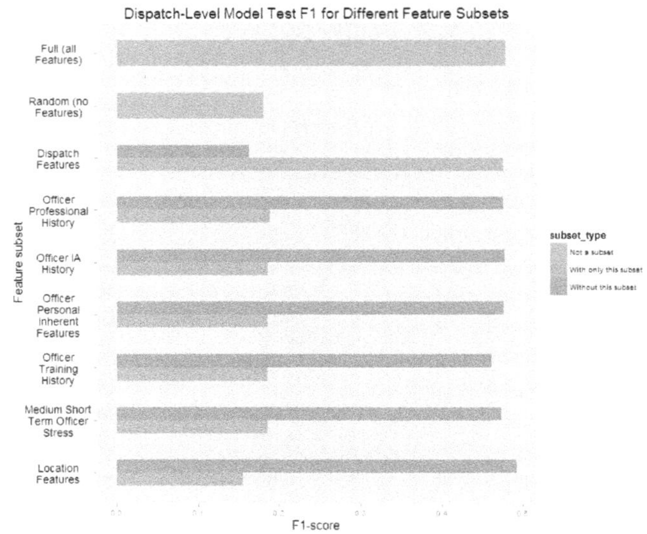

Figure 6: Comparison of model performance (f1-score w/respect to positive class) of feature subsets on dispatch-level adverse-outcome prediction

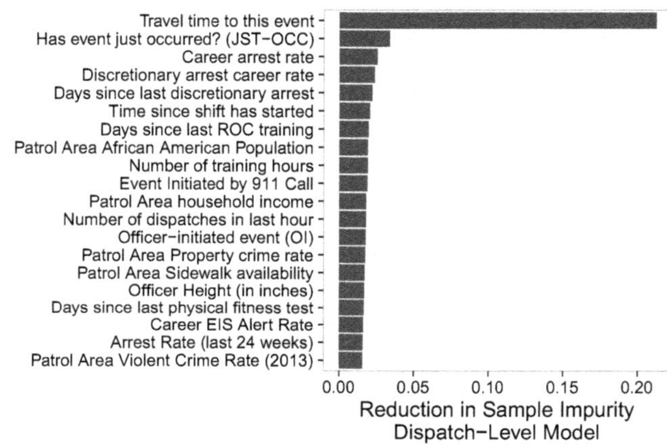

Figure 7: Conventional unsigned feature importances in dispatch-level random forest model

of adverse outcomes in the model. The dominant positive feature by this measure of importance is the REPT-OFC dispatch typecode, indicating that the situation being addressed by the dispatch was reported by the responding police officer. Similar, and also positively contributing, are the OFC-INVL (officer involved) typecode and OI (officer-initiated) dispatch type. Other contributing features include the suspect-on-scene typecode, the number of hours the officer has been on duty, and two features associated with how frequently that officer makes discretionary arrests

Features that contribute negatively to the risk of adverse outcomes include the height and weight of the officer, and the number of days since their last discretionary arrest. Wealthier neighborhoods with a higher age of death are associated with fewer negative outcomes, though interestingly, so are those with a greater number of minor nuisance violations.

Taken together, these results seem to reinforce the conclusion that situational factors are largely, though not ex-

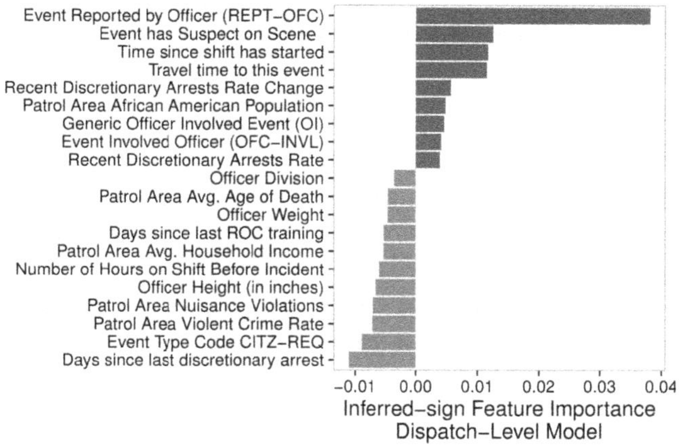

Figure 8: Inferred signed feature importances in dispatch-level random forest model

clusively, predictive of adverse outcomes at the individual dispatch level. "Hot" dispatches initiated by officers themselves (as opposed to citizens by way of 911 calls), seem more likely to end in adverse outcomes. Indicators of heightened officer stress (hours on duty) and aggressive policing style (discretionary arrest rate), seem to also have a positive impact on the risk of adverse outcomes.

8. IMPLEMENTATION AND NEXT STEPS

Next steps include implementation and effect of interventions. There are several ways the risk scores could be used by a police department. However, our primary goal is to develop individually tailored interventions to ensure that each officer receives appropriate training and support. In addition, the risk scores enable the prioritization of resource allocation to the officers that are considered most at-risk.

We are exploring using our model to develop interventions for groups of officers. When risk scores are aggregated over groups defined by unit or division, we find that some divisions and units have a significantly higher risk than others. These divisions and units may benefit from additional group interventions such as group trainings to lower their risk.

In terms of implementation, as always, the utility of the improved EIS will be mediated by social structures within the department. Perhaps most importantly supervisors using the EIS system should also be trained to treat model results similarly. Instructing supervisors on how to understand the meaning of risk scores and how to interpret features will be an important avenue of our implementation approach.

Our dispatch-level models take the first steps toward predictive risk-based dispatch decisions, where an officer who is at higher risk of an adverse incident for that dispatch can potentially be held back and a different officer, at a lower risk score, can be dispatched. For example, in June 2015 a police officer in Texas, Cpl. Eric Casebolt, pulled his weapon on children at a pool party after responding to two suicide calls earlier that shift [10]. Most police departments would like to avoid these situations by dispatching low-risk officers to calls. Risk-based dispatching could enable improved dispatching to match officers and dispatches while minimizing risk of harm to the public and the officer.

Finally, future work will focus on finding the appropriate balance between actionability, transparency, interpretability, and resistance to gaming by officers. A dashboard can help strike a balance between these concerns and communicate model results in easy-to-use and actionable formats, which we are currently developing for use by the CMPD. The proposed system will provide the top feature importances, which will enable officers in the department to understand what factors are typically correlated with adverse incidents without providing a recipe for those that wish to game the system.

9. CONCLUSION

The present work uses a machine learning approach to develop an Early Intervention System for flagging police officers who may be at high risk of involvement in an adverse interaction with a member of the public. Our model significantly outperforms the existing system at the Charlotte-Mecklenburg Police Department (CMPD). Our model also provides risk scores to the department, allowing them to more accurately target training, counseling, and other interventions toward officers who are at highest risk of having an adverse incident. This will allow the department to better allocate resources, reduce the burden on supervisors, and reduce unnecessary administrative work of officers who were not at risk.

Further, our models provide insight into which factors are important in predicting whether an officer is likely to have an adverse event. We find that, largely, intuitive officer-level and neighborhood level features are predictive of adverse events, but also that many features the department had not yet considered are also correlated with future adverse events. This information will hopefully allow this department, and potentially other police departments, to develop more effective early interventions for preventing future adverse events.

To explore the immediate situational factors associated with adverse events, we also engaged in an exploratory analysis at the individual dispatch event level. Results suggest that features of a particular dispatch may be highly predictive of whether or not a dispatch will result in an adverse outcome relative to officer-specific features. Future work will be focused on addressing how to utilize these features more effectively.

At a higher level, our goal is to take this system, developed for CMPD, and extend it to other departments across the US. We already have commitments from Los Angeles Sherriff's Department and Knoxville Police Department to work with us to extend this system. Several other departments across the US are also in discussions with us. We have made our system open source for departments to build upon if they so choose[5]. A tool built across departments is especially important for small departments, which are unlikely to have enough adverse events to build reliable models. We are also implementing the system on CMPD It systems and monitoring the model's performance one year in the future, from July 1, 2015, which is the last day of data we received, to June 30, 2016.

Finally, we are discussing an intervention pilot in partnership with CMPD. Predicting which officers will have adverse events will only be impactful if it is possible to design interventions to prevent those events. Similarly, we realize that while intervention may reduce adverse events between the

[5] `https://github.com/dssg/police-eis`

police and the public, such interventions are only a part of a larger approach to dealing with the complex web of cognitive, interactional, social, and institutional factors affecting the relationship between the police and the public. We are hopeful that work at the intersection of data science, social science and the practice of policing can someday help to advance the work being done in these contexts as well.

10. ACKNOWLEDGMENTS

We thank the Eric & Wendy Schmidt Data Science for Social Good Fellowship for generously supporting this work. We also thank the leadership and officers of the Charlotte-Mecklenburg Police Department for sharing data, expertise, and feedback for this project as well as the White House Office of Science and Technology Policy for their help and support.

References

[1] *Who is Guarding the Guardians?* United States Commission on Civil Rights, Washington, DC, 1981.

[2] *Personnel Early Warning System.* Commission on Accreditation of Law Enforcement Agencies, Fairfax, VA, 2001.

[3] *Principles for Promoting Police Integrity.* United States Department of Justice, Washington, DC, 2001.

[4] Timeline: Recent us police shootings of black suspects. `http://www.abc.net.au/news/2015-04-09/timeline-us-police-shootings-unarmed-black-suspects/6379472`, 2015.

[5] Topic: Police brutality, misconduct and shootings. `http://topics.nytimes.com/top/reference/timestopics/subjects/p/police_brutality_and_misconduct/index.html`, 2016.

[6] R. Arthur. How to predict bad cops in chicago. `http://fivethirtyeight.com/features/how-to-predict-which-chicago-cops-will-commit-misconduct/`, 2015.

[7] R. Caruana, Y. Lou, J. Gehrke, P. Koch, M. Sturm, and N. Elhadad. Intelligible models for healthcare: Predicting pneumonia risk and hospital 30-day readmission. In *Proceedings of the 21th ACM SIGKDD International Conference on Knowledge Discovery and Data Mining*, KDD '15, pages 1721–1730, New York, NY, USA, 2015. ACM.

[8] C. Chapman. Use of force in minority communities is related to police education, age, experience, and ethnicity. *Police Practice and Research*, 13(5):421–436, 2012.

[9] R. C. Davis, N. J. Henderson, J. Mandelstram, C. W. Ortiz, and J. Miller. *Federal Intervention in Local Policing : Pittsburgh's Experience with a Consent Decree.* Office of Community Oriented Policing Services, Washington, D.C, 2003.

[10] M. Fernandez. Texas officer was under stress when he arrived at pool party, lawyer says. *New York Times*, June 10 2015.

[11] H. Goldstein. *Policing a Free Society.* Ballinger Pub. Co, Cambridge, Mass, 1977.

[12] R. J. Hyndman and G. Athanasopoulos. *Forecasting: principles and practice.* OTexts, 2014.

[13] N. Jones. "the regular routine": Proactive policing and adolescent development among young, poor black men. *New directions for child and adolescent development*, 2014(143):33–54, 2014.

[14] J. Manis, C. A. Archbold, and K. D. Hassell. Exploring the impact of police officer education level on allegations of police misconduct. *International Journal of Police Science and Management*, 10(4):509–523, 2008.

[15] J. A. Shjarback. Emerging early intervention systems: An agency-specific pre-post comparison of formal citizen complaints of use of force. *Policing*, 9(4):314–325, mar 2015.

[16] A. Shultz. Early warning systems: What's new? what's working?, 2015.

[17] J. J. Sobol, Y. Wu, and I. Y. Sun. Neighborhood context and police vigor a multilevel analysis. *Crime & Delinquency*, 59(3):344–368, 2013.

[18] W. Terrill and M. D. Reisig. Neighborhood context and police use of force. *Journal of Research in Crime and Delinquency*, 40(3):291–321, 2003.

[19] S. Walker. The new paradigm of police accountability: The u.s. justice department "pattern or practice" suits in context. *Saint Louis University Public Law Review*, 22(3):3–52, 2003.

[20] S. Walker, G. P. Alpert, and D. J. Kenney. *Early warning systems: Responding to the problem police officer.* US Department of Justice, Office of Justice Programs, National Institute of Justice, 2001.

[21] M. D. White. Identifying situational predictors of police shootings using multivariate analysis. *Policing: an international journal of police strategies & management*, 25(4):726–751, 2002.

[22] M. D. White and R. J. Kane. Pathways to career-ending police misconduct an examination of patterns, timing, and organizational responses to officer malfeasance in the nypd. *Criminal Justice and Behavior*, 40(11):1301–1325, 2013.

[23] R. E. Worden, M. Kim, C. J. Harris, M. A. Pratte, S. E. Dorn, and S. S. Hyland. Intervention with problem officers: An outcome evaluation of an EIS intervention. *Criminal Justice and Behavior*, 40(4):409–437, oct 2012.

Data-Driven Metric Development for Online Controlled Experiments: Seven Lessons Learned

Alex Deng *
Microsoft
One Microsoft Way
Redmond, WA 98052
alexdeng@microsoft.com

Xiaolin Shi*†
Yahoo Research
701 1st Ave
Sunnyvale, CA 94089
shixiaolin@gmail.com

ABSTRACT

Online controlled experiments, also called A/B testing, have been established as the mantra for data-driven decision making in many web-facing companies. In recent years, there are emerging research works focusing on building the platform and scaling it up [34], best practices and lessons learned to obtain trustworthy results [19; 20; 23; 26], and experiment design techniques and various issues related to statistical inference and testing [6; 7; 8]. However, despite playing a central role in online controlled experiments, there is little published work on treating metric development itself as a data-driven process. In this paper, we focus on the topic of how to develop meaningful and useful metrics for online services in their online experiments, and show how data-driven techniques and criteria can be applied in metric development process. In particular, we emphasize two fundamental qualities for the goal metrics (or Overall Evaluation Criteria) of any online service: directionality and sensitivity. We share lessons on why these two qualities are critical, how to measure these two qualities of metrics of interest, how to develop metrics with clear directionality and high sensitivity by using approaches based on user behavior models and data-driven calibration, and how to choose the right goal metrics for the entire online services.

Keywords

Controlled experiment; A/B testing; web measurement; online metrics; user experience evaluation

1. INTRODUCTION

As the quote by Lord Kelvin stated, "If you cannot measure it, you cannot improve it", it is also true for online services in industry. For various online services such as search engines, e-commerce sites, and social networking sites, metrics are used to indicate how well the systems are serving real users for their needs. The impact of any feature change of the service can be quantitatively measured by the metrics. Depending on how the scores of metrics are generated, there are two types of metrics for most online services: one type is offline metrics, whose scores are based on labels of offline data sets (usually generated by a small group of judges); and the other type is online metrics, whose scores are usually based on the behavioral data log of millions of users who interact with the system in real time. In industry, the most popular and widely accepted way of monitoring and comparing online metrics is using online controlled experiments (i.e. A/B testing experiments) [5; 22; 34]. Figure 1 shows the relationship between the services and online metrics: based on the data logged by the services, online metrics are able to measure how well the services are doing; and based on the metrics, the online services are able to know the direction of making further improvement.

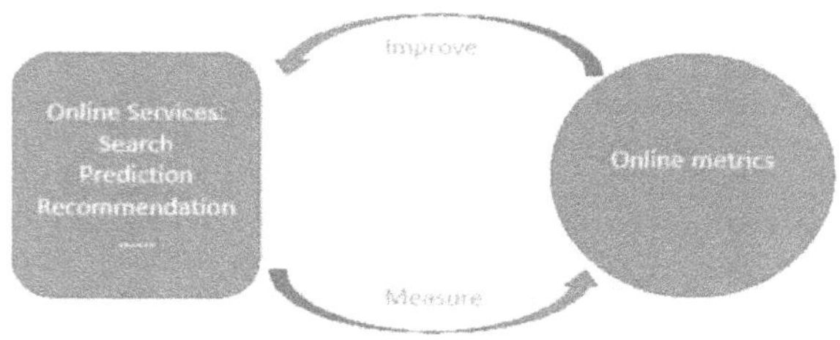

Figure 1: The relationship between online services and online metrics.

Nowadays, many online service companies are using online metrics as the pointers toward the North Star (i.e. the success of the business) to improve their products, including Amazon [21], eBay, Etsy [28], Facebook [3], Google [34], Groupon, Intuit [29], LinkedIn [30], Microsoft [27], Netflix [2], and Yahoo. The *Overall Evaluation Criteria (OEC)* (also known as *goal metrics* or *key metrics*) of an online service are metrics defined to help the system move toward the North Star. The choice of good OEC is not easy. As an online service grows over time, its OEC should also evolve, and the choice of its OEC depends on how far the system is away from the North Star (as shown in Figure 2).

Many previous works have been focusing on the experimentation platform [22; 25; 34], various best practices and lessons learned [20; 24; 26] and various issues related to the statistical inference and testing [3; 7; 8; 13]. Little work has been published on the topic of data driven metric development for online controlled experiments. The work of [31] proposes the metric framework HEART, which first points

*Authors contributed equally to this work.
†Work primarily done when working at Microsoft.

KDD '16, August 13-17, 2016, San Francisco, CA, USA

DOI: http://dx.doi.org/10.1145/2939672.2939700

out that user-centric metrics are more direct in measuring user experience of using the product than metrics focusing on business or technical aspects of the product. Our work further demonstrates how to develop metrics that well align with user experience in a data-driven approach, and how to choose the right metrics for online services. To the best of our knowledge, this paper is the first work on how to develop online metrics systematically in a data-driven way.

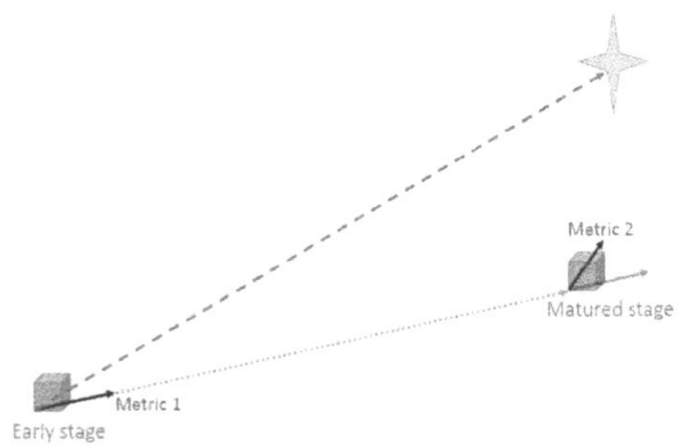

Figure 2: The choice of OEC evolves as the service grows over time toward the North Star. When the service (the cubic) is at an early stage, metric 1 is used as the OEC. Another OEC (metric 2) is used when the service is closer to the North Star.

2. PRELIMINARIES

2.1 Offline metrics vs. online metrics

Before the large-scale online experiments are available, the most popular way to measure the performance of online systems in industry is using offline metrics such as area under curve (AUC), root mean squared error (RMSE), and normalized discounted cumulative gain (NDCG), etc. The evaluation approach of using offline metrics is borrowed from academia, where the sizes of the data sets are much smaller and whose targets are not the real users. However, in industry, when the online services are deployed, the ultimate performance of interest is the success of the business, and the real users are the core of the business. Offline metrics certainly have great values in guiding the services when they are at relatively early stages and not many users are available for experimentation yet. For example, Bing used the offline metric NDCG for a long time at the early stage of the search engine, and NDCG had been playing a critical role in guiding the improvement of the search system for several years. However, at a certain point, it was found that NDCG could not give us the directions with high confidence any more, and very often it did not align with what was shown by online metrics either. In fact, it has been realized that in many scenarios, offline metrics have poor correlations with online metrics. According to [4], it could be due to two reasons. First of all, offline metrics such as AUC and NDCG ignore human factors, and thus cannot capture the qualities of services that are designed for personalization. Another reason is offline metrics are based on incomplete and biased offline data sets, and thus offline metrics cannot always predict the results of online metrics that are based on large-scale real users. It is still an open question in this area on how to correlate offilne metrics with online metrics.

2.2 Types of online metrics

Because of the special role of metrics in online services, most work in this community is done from the business perspective. For example, the AARRR model [1] defines metrics according to their different roles in conversion and monetization in a web service.

However, because of the diversity of online services, the link between user status and monetization is not always as straightforward as the AARRR model describes. Moreover, these standard web metrics may be too generic to be used on online applications with different service purposes. In this paper, we categorize online metrics into the following three types based on how they are defined:

Type 1: Business report driven metrics. This type of metrics are defined based on the long-term goals of the online services, and thus they are usually directly related to the success of the business, such as Revenue per User, Queries or Visits per User. Recently there is growing interest in reporting active user count metrics such as Monthly Active Users (MAU) and Daily Active Users (DAU).

This type of metrics are mainly used as reports to business owners, executives and investors or shareholders as they are directly related to the success of the online services. However, this type of metrics are often not actionable because the short-term movements of these metrics measured in online experiments are often different from the long-term effects. As a result, product teams whose purpose of using online metrics is to chase short-term signals can hardly use these metrics to improve their features efficiently. For example, long-term revenue per user is crucial for the success of a search engine service such as Bing; however, if revenue per user is used as the goal metric, the product teams may find it very hard to tune their ranking algorithms toward the improvement of this goal in short terms (such as a couple of weeks). This is because improved search results may immediately increase the clicks on the search results and decrease the probability of clicking on the ads results, and thus decrease revenue per user in short term. The same reversed direction happens to market share metrics. For a search engine, bad ranking algorithms often result in short-term increases in query volumes [32], since users tend to issue more reformulation queries to satisfy their information needs. Thus, using business report driven metrics to measure the long-term impact usually requires running experiments for long periods of time, which is not desired for agile online experiments whose purpose is to show the impact of new features with limited time and cost.

Type 2: Simple heuristic based metrics. This type of metrics are usually based on the simple facts of the interaction between users and the online services, such as Click-Through Rate (CTR) of a web page, performance delay, count of activities per user.

This type of metrics give us straightforward descriptions on how users interacting with the services. They are mostly actionable and also important for us to monitor the system from different perspectives. For example, the count of activities per user within a certain period of time shows how frequently an average user is active on the service, while performance delay indicates how soon the system responds to users' requests. However, this type of metrics usually lack clear interpretations regarding user experience and are usually ambiguous in the relationship with the North Star. For example, having more spams and misleading captions with the URLs in online service may increase its click through

[1] http://piratemetrics.com/

rate. However, this is actually hurting user experience, and will hurt the revenue and market share of the service eventually. For another example, a longer page load time often is considered bad. However if the delay is caused by a new feature addition that greatly generates user satisfaction, it should be interpreted as a reasonable trade-off.

Business report driven metrics and simple heuristic based metrics represent the first generation of online metrics. They are mostly simple, obvious and align with our common sense. Usually at the early stage of an online service, when it does not have enough users and the improvements are easy to observe, these two types of metrics may be good enough. However, when the service accumulates enough users and the market share is relatively stable, these metrics are either insensitive to small feature improvements (especially for the revenue based metrics), or mis-align with real improvement of user experience (especially for the simple heuristic based metrics). At such stages, a third type of online metrics, user-behavior-driven metrics, are in great need.

Type 3: User-behavior-driven metrics. This type of metrics are based on user behavior models such as satisfaction models and frustration models. Ideally, a well designed user-behavior-driven metric should be able to measure user experience directly, and these experiences are highly correlated with the long-term success of the online service. At the same time, it should be sensitive enough and actionable so that it can be used in agile online experiments with limited time and cost. Metric definitions of this type are often more involved, relying on highly customized rules or algorithms trained from user behavioral models of using the particular online services, and thus more complexity in the design process. For example, we need a user satisfaction model to define whether a search result page satisfies a user. Clicking signals and dwell time signals are used but there are also cases where user can be satisfied by just looking at the page (i.e. good abandonment) [9; 33]. Thus, it is essential to analyze user search behavior instead of simply using clicks as the only heuristic in the metrics of user search satisfaction. More details about the process and rules of designing user-behavior-driven metrics will be described in Section 3.5.

3. SEVEN LESSONS OF ONLINE METRIC DEVELOPMENT

3.1 Lesson 1: Define metrics for metrics

As we have mentioned at the beginning, metrics are used to evaluate the online services quantitatively. However, when we develop online metrics, what are the criteria we can use to evaluate the metrics quantitatively? Especially, how can we make comparison and choose one or a couple of metrics as OEC or the goal metrics for the online service from hundreds or even thousands of metrics we are monitoring? Generally speaking, there are two mandatory qualities we have to take into consideration when choosing the OEC or goal metrics for an online service: directionality and sensitivity. The directionality and sensitivity of a metric are like the direction and magnitude of a vector, as both are critical in pushing the system improving toward the North Star effectively (Figure 2).

Mandatory quality 1 – directionality: a good goal metric (or OEC) should have a clear directional interpretation that aligns with user experience in most common cases. In another word, when the metrics are used in A/B experiments, the goal metric should show consistent direction when the experiments positively impact user experience, and show the opposite direction for the experiments that negatively impact user experience. It is not uncommon to see metrics whose directions are ambiguous in indicating user experience. One example is the metric Distinct Queries per Unique User (DSQ/User) in search. Intuitively, users issue more distinct queries if they are more satisfied with the search results and this is why some search engines gain more market share than others. However, user behavior analysis shows that, in a short term after relevance improved, users tend to issue less queries within a search task while the total number of search tasks remains almost the same [32]. Thus the metric DSQ/User decreases almost immediately after the relevance gets improved. It is important to make sure that the goal metrics should not have such ambiguous directional interpretation and have consistent directions for both short term and long term. A common mistake in picking a goal metric is to beat the control in short term by doing something clearly "wrong" from a business perspective (such as increasing DSQ/User by degrading the relevance of a search engine), as it is quite often that short-term and long-term objectives diverge diametrically [24].

Mandatory quality 2 – sensitivity: a good goal metric (or OEC) needs to be sensitive to most of the improvement of user experience. A sensitive goal metric helps the organization and feature teams being able to make decisions quickly and with limited cost. As we have mentioned before, report or revenue driven metrics usually require long experimentation time and high user traffic to observe the impact of new features. For example, the metric Sessions per User (Sessions/User) is a metric believed to be closely correlated with the market share of a search engine as well as user satisfaction. However, deep-dive analysis shows that instead of improving the total number of sessions, which requires much longer time to change, the search success rate improves more immediately and significantly when search relevance changes [32]. In another word, metrics based on successful sessions are much more sensitive than the metric Sessions/User, and thus we prefer metrics such as Successful Sessions per User or Successful Session Rate as the goal metric for an online service.

In order to measure the two qualities of metrics qualitatively and convince the entire organization to adopt a new metric, a relatively objective and systematical approach for metric evaluation is critical. At Bing, there is an evaluation framework called MetricLab. More details will be discussed in Section 3.3.

In addition to evaluating a new metric by quantitatively reporting its direction and sensitivity based on a validation corpus, it is also very important to have a thorough understanding on the applicability of the metrics. Generally speaking, no metric can be applicable everywhere, even the metrics with the most state-of-the-art models. Thus, it is important to fully evaluate the pros and cons of a new metric, including its *directionality*, *sensitivity* and *applicability*.

3.2 Lesson 2: Understand roles of metrics

In the previous subsections, we have introduced the goal metrics (or OEC) of an online service and the two mandatory qualities of good OEC. We also have pointed out that no metric is applicable in all scenarios and thus in order to have a more objective and complete understanding of the change of user experience with the service, in addition to the goal metrics, it is also very important to have the following two types of metrics: *guardrail metrics* and *debugging metrics*.

Guardrail metrics are metrics that help to guard against situations when the goal metrics may give us wrong signals. They are usually used in two scenarios. The first scenario is to replace the goal metric (or OEC) in cases when the goal metric is not applicable. In this scenario, we should not read too much into the goal metrics, and use the guardrail metrics as substitutes. For example, the entire organization of a search engine service may use the metrics with long dwell time clicks as the goal metrics, as users having more long dwell time clicks in web search usually shows that the search engine is doing a better job. However, this rule is not applicable to the engineering team that works on the instant answers (e.g. weather, stock, dictionary), whose goal is to provide users with the right information without having clicks. Thus, instead of using metrics with long dwell time clicks as the goal metrics, these teams need some guardrail metrics that can better address the user experience in using instant answers. The second scenario of guardrail metrics is to capture the dimensions of user experience that the goal metrics are not able to measure. In this scenario, usually the goal metrics are still the keys to look at, and the guardrail metrics help to make sure that some other important dimensions are not going in the wrong way. For example, metrics such as Revenue per User and performance latency are good candidates for guardrail metrics when the metric of user satisfaction rate is used as the goal metric. These guardrail metrics can make sure that the service is not improving the user experience by sacrificing revenue, nor anything unexpected happening on the server side. Having a clear directional interpretation is very important for a good guardrail metric in both scenarios.

Debugging metrics are usually used to help us understand why some important metrics, especially the goal metrics, move or do not move, and how to interpret their movements. For goal metrics whose models are based on multiple user behavior signals, it is helpful to keep track of how these individual signals contributed to the overall metric movement (and thus, it is desirable for a goal metric to be debuggable or decomposable, which we will discuss more in Section 3.5). Debugging metrics can be as simple as making sure certain assumptions we make are correct. For example, http response size or log size typically should change when new features are added for the treatment. Debugging metrics are especially important for rate metrics. If we use a rate metric such as Query Success Rate for a search engine, it is important to keep track of the change of the plain count of the denominator, which is the total number of queries per user in this case. We will discuss more regard this in Section 3.6. Instead of having an clear directional interpretation, it is more important for a good debugging metric to be sensitive. This is a distinct difference between debugging metrics and guardrail metrics.

In summary, it is always important for us to fully understand the characteristics of each individual metric, including when it is applicable and when it is not, and its direction and sensitivity in different scenarios, so that we are able to assign it to the right role.

3.3 Lesson 3: Evaluate metric qualities

In Lesson 1 we show two mandatory qualities that we need to measure for each metric under development: sensitivity and directionality. If a metric rarely shows movement with statistical significance (i.e. is insensitive), it is not actionable in practice no matter how good the metric is in all other aspects. On the other hand, if a metric frequently gives us statistically significant signals, but we have little confidence on how to relate the movement to the success of the business, then the metric is disqualified to act as a goal metric. The next question is how to measure these two qualities of metrics systematically and convincingly. According to our experience, there are two effective approaches.

3.3.1 Validation Corpus

Motivated by supervised learning, we could have a validation dataset with known labels. In online controlled experiments, this translates to a set of existing experiments for which we know whether the feature is indeed good for the users (in terms of average treatment effect[2]) or not. In reality, we can never be 100% sure about the goodness of the features, so the best we can do is to collect a set of high quality past experiments for which we have high confidence on whether their features are good for the users or not. This set of past experiments is called the *validation corpus*.

Such a validation corpus is extremely valuable as it provides straightforward way for us to systematically test a new metric and see whether the movement of the tested metric agrees with the "labels" in the corpus. In Bing we have developed a tool called MetricLab to routinely measure new and old metrics. There are three cases: (1) the metric shows statistically significant movement with a consistent direction (either positively or negatively correlates with the "labels"), (2) the metric shows statistically significant movement with ambiguous directions and (3) the metric is not statistically significant. Sensitivity can be measured by proportion of cases in (3), or by computing average or medium of t-statistics. If the ratio of average t-statistics between two metrics X and Y are r, then we can say movements of Y *on average* requires r times of traffic than those of X to be detected. More details about developing and using the validation corpus can be found in [10].

3.3.2 Degradation experiment

A problem with the validation corpus described above is that this approach is not applicable when we adventure into a new experimentation scenario. For instance, when we onboard a new partner with a new product, we need to design and implement a set of first generation of metrics to start with. Obviously there exists no validation corpus. People commonly resort to simple business reporting metrics and believe the directions of these metrics are obvious to interpret. However as we mentioned in Section 3.1, even a standard reporting metric as simple as DSQ/User might be misleading[3]. Hence it is important to verify the directions of these metrics before we make any decision based on them. Fortunately there is a way to validate the directions without having the validation corpus. This solution lies in a lesson we learned over years. Most of the time it is hard to come up with a good feature that impacts user experience with statistically detectable improvement in a short period, but it is much easier for us to degrade or even screw up user

[2]Note that there might be heterogeneous treatment effect among users, i.e., some subpopulations of users might like the feature while others dislike. For feature ship decision making, here we only focus on average treatment effect.

[3]Distinct query volume is part of ComScore search share report.

experience deliberately. In another words, it is hard to find positive labels but there are plenty of cases with negative labels. This leads us to the idea of using degradation experiments to validate metric direction and sensitivity[4]. The type of user experience degradation experiments depends on the type of web services. For search engine and online websites, typical degradation experiments include delaying a web page [25], downgrading to a known inferior service [32] to more extreme choices such as deliberately giving user a buggy experience such as crashing a mobile app.

People often feel reluctant to run degradation experiments because deliberately hurting user experience is against the organization goal. We argue that if we control the degradation within an acceptable degree, we only hurt short term user experience without making permanent damage, and the knowledge gained from running such experiment outweighs the short term loss in the long run. In Bing we've experimented delaying return of search result page by 250ms and didn't observe any long term user effect [25]. The long running search relevance degradation experiment [32] showed a short term left over effect on user search behavior but no sign of losing user base. Both experiments successfully helped us validate the directions of many metrics, and also cast lights on the development and adoption of new goal metrics.

3.4 Lesson 4: Decompose metric sensitivity

When there is a good metric candidate that is not sensitive enough to be used as an actionable goal metric, we need to better understand its sensitivity before giving it up. There are two components of metric sensitivity:

1. Statistical Power: Given a true effect moving the metric, how likely are we able to detect the effect?
2. Movement Probability: How often does a change we test really moves the metric (has a treatment effect)?

The separation of the two components above helps us to isolate two sources impacting metric sensitivity. On one hand, statistical power accounts for the probability that we can detect the movement *given that there is a true underlying movement (treatment effect) on a metric.* On the other hand, the movement probability shows *how likely a metric is indeed moved or not.* The two components together help us to compare sensitivity of different metrics. For example, we know Sessions per User is a relatively insensitive metric. Surprisingly, its insensitiveness is not mainly due to its lacking statistical power: its noise level, measured by the coefficient of variations (Standard Deviation divided by Mean), is not among the highest. Instead, the reason we cannot detect its movement is because people's daily search needs are limited and it is hard to change users engagement within a short time. Google [16] reported similar results that even for long running experiments it is hard to move sessions per user. In contrast, metrics like Revenue per User is relatively less sensitive than other revenue focus metrics such as Revenue per Search due to its high variance (highly skewed distribution) and low statistical power. If statistical power is the reason of insensitiveness, we then can focus on *variance reduction.* Increasing traffic size is an obvious option since the variance of a metric decreases at the rate of $\sqrt{N}$ where N is the number of independent samples. Methods such as capping the metric to reduce skewness and other more sophisticated transformation methods may also apply.

[4]We first heard this idea in a discussion with Ron Kohavi and Brian Frasca.

To measure the two components, we first need to lay some foundations. Suppose for both treatment and control groups we observe i.i.d. observations from two distributions with unknown mean τ_T and τ_C respectively. Denote our observations by $Y_i, i = 1, \ldots, N_T$ for treatment group and $X_i, i = 1, \ldots, N_C$ for control group. We want to test the null hypothesis $H_0 : \tau_T - \tau_C = 0$ against the alternative $H_1 : \tau_T \neq \tau_C$.

Without assuming distributions of X and Y, in A/B testing we resort to the central limit theorem and hence use Wald test which can be seen as large sample version of the well-known t-test. The test statistic is

$$Z := \frac{\overline{X} - \overline{Y}}{\sqrt{\sigma_T^2/N_T + \sigma_C^2/N_C}} = \frac{\Delta}{\sqrt{\sigma_T^2/N_T + \sigma_C^2/N_C}},$$

where σ_C and σ_T are variances of X and Y and Δ is the observed metric difference between treatment and control. The variances are unknown but in large sample scenario we can assume they are known by using their estimates which will not change the asymptotic normal approximation. Note that metrics are often in different scales and to evaluate different metrics we need to unify the scale. We first define $N_E = 1/(1/N_T + 1/N_C)$ to be the **effective sample size**. Let σ^2 be the **pooled variance** such that $\sigma^2/N_E = \sigma_T^2/N_T + \sigma_C^2/N_C$. The two definitions above are used to convert a two-sample problem into an equivalent one-sample problem, where we can define **effect size** to be $\delta = \Delta/\sigma$. With these shorthands, Z-statistics can be rewritten as

$$Z = \frac{\delta}{\sqrt{1/N_E}}. \tag{1}$$

Note that the effect size δ is the observed difference Δ scaled by pooled standard deviation σ and thus is scaleless. We also treat σ as a fixed constant. Finally, define

$$\mu := E(\delta) = E(\Delta)/\sigma = (\tau_T - \tau_C)/\sigma \tag{2}$$

is the average treatment effect scaled by σ. When σ is treated as known, inference on $\tau_T - \tau_C$ and μ are equivalent and μ is the scaleless treatment effect.

We adopt a model where we assume there are two states of the truth. When there is no treatment effect $\mu = 0$ and this is the null hypothesis H_0. The alternative hypothesis H_1 is the state where there is non-zero treatment effect μ. Unlike fixing an alternative treatment effect as in most textbook power analysis, we also assume under H_1 μ follows certain distribution g. This is because the true treatment effect in general is unknown.

Recall the Z-statistics is the ratio of δ to $\sqrt{1/N_E}$. We typically declare a metric moved statistically significantly if $|Z| > 1.96$[5]. We see the probability of the event that *a treatment has an effect and we can detect successfully* is

$$P(H_1) \times P(|Z| > 1.96|H_1) \tag{3}$$

where the first term $P(H_1)$ is the probability of a true movement and the second term $P(|Z| > 1.96|H_1)$ is the statistical power. These two terms corresponds to the two components of sensitivity introduced at the beginning.

To calculate the statistical power, one need to know the distribution of δ under alternative H_1. We found it useful

[5]1.96 and the corresponding 0.05 p-value cutoff is arbitrary and we can replace 1.96 by other thresholds in (3)

to assume $\mu \sim N(0, V^2)$ under H_1. The parameter V is unknown and need to be measured and we claim that V is a good quantity to measure the statistical power component of metric sensitivity. The larger the V, the more disperse the treatment effect is under H_1, and hence more easily we can detect the movement. Note that under H_1, $\delta \sim N(0, (1/N_E + V^2))$. Let S be a standard normal random variable,

$$P(|Z| > 1.96|H_1) = P\left(|S| > 1.96 \times \sqrt{\frac{1/N_E}{1/N_E + V^2}}\right) \quad (4)$$

For any given effective sample size N_E, the larger the V, the larger the above probability. We make remark that unlike traditional power analysis concerning sample size needed in an experiment for a given presumed effect size, here we are not interested in the sample size. Instead, we are interested in for any given sample size, how we can compare expected statistical power of different metrics. The result above identified V to be a good metric of metrics for this component.

The component $P(H_1)$ and V together allows us to systematically order and compare sensitivity of metrics. To estimate both quantities for each metric, we can use the same validation corpus mentioned above. However such corpus tend to be small due to the cost of expert labeling. For the sake of decomposing sensitivity, label is not required and we can use a vast unlabeled historical experiments data. The technical detail is in [6]. Note when comparing two metrics, a metric A might have higher $P(H_1)$ but smaller V than metric B. To combine the two sensitivity metrics into one, we fix an effective sample size N_E and use (4) to calculate the expected statistical power for the given sample size and then multiply it with $P(H_1)$ to get (3). The effective sample size is chosen to reflect a typical experiment, e.g. the sample size we typically allocate for an experiment.

Metric	P(True Movement)	$V^2/(1/N_E)$	P(Detect True Movement)
Count Metric A(whole page)	3%	25.1	2.1%
Count Metric A(sub region)	17%	37.2	12.8%
Metric B	31%	2.8	9.8%
Metric B with Utility Weights	45%	3.3	15.6%
Metric C	12%	9.2	5.9%
Metric C with VR	11%	19.7	8.0%
Metric D	13%	29.3	9.4%
Metric D Capped	16%	38.6	12.1%

Table 1: Examples of detailed sensitivity decomposition. Results align with theory and experience.

Table 1 shows results of a few example metrics when we apply the method to Bing historical experiments. We found the results consistent with theory and our experiences and we listed a few here.

1. It is easier to move a metric measuring part of a page than a whole page metric [26]. The sub region version of Metric A is way more sensitive than the whole page version. It has significantly higher $P(H_1)$, which means more experiments can move sub region metric.
2. Carefully designed utility weighting helps improving sensitivity. Metric B is a session level metric and after giving different weights to different sessions according to a custom utility function, we found the revised version significantly improved sensitivity.
3. Variance Reduction (VR) increase sensitivity by reducing variance σ^2 and hence increasing V. The work by Deng et al. [7] proposes a variance reduction framework usng pre-experiment data. In the above table comparing Metric C with and without VR we found V^2 doubled after VR, aligning well with the theory.
4. Capping of highly skewed metrics helps improving sensitivity by reducing variance. Comparing Metric D with and without capping, we also found a significant increase of V^2. See [26] for more details about capping.

We make a remark that there is a naive but relatively biased approach to measure sensitivity using unlabeled historical experiment data. Given a list of historical experiment, just count the proportion of experiments a metric moved statistically significantly. On surface it seems this will give the same measure we tried to calculate in (3). But imagine if a metric never truly moved, i.e. $P(H_1) = 0$, then because of Type-I error, this naive approach will in expectation gives 5%. In other word, the naive approach is biased, with the bias being $P(H_0) \times 5\% \leq 5\%$. Since the bias is bounded, the naive method can still be used to quickly compare sensitivity of different metrics when the more sophisticated measurement (3) is not available. For example, if metric A using the naive approach has a sensitivity score more than 5% higher than another metric B, we can say metric A is more sensitive than metric B, ignoring the estimation error of the two sensitivity measurements, which is often small when the set of unlabeled data is large. The two parameter approach presented here has the advantage that it separates two sources of sensitivity apart. When lack of sensitivity of a metric is due to lack of statistical power, we can then investigate where we can improve the statistical power by ways of reducing variance.

3.5 Lesson 5: Learn from offline data

As we have mentioned in Section 2.2, a more advanced type of metrics – user-behavior-driven metrics – are getting more importance when the systems are at matured stages. User-behavior-driven metrics are based on user behavioral models that can predict or classify user experience of using the system, such as satisfaction, frustration, gain or cost [9; 11; 15; 17]. Thus, a carefully designed user-behavior-driven metric usually has good alignment with user experience and high sensitivity, i.e. the two qualities of good OEC we have described in Section 3.1. However, because users seldom give explicit feedback regarding their experience at the same time of using the online services, we propose the approach of utilizing offline labeled data to associate user behavioral signals (i.e. activity logs collected when they use the services) to their experience in developing this type of metrics.

Generally speaking, there are three major steps in developing user-behavior-driven metrics:

- **Step 1**: Have some hypotheses about the user experience based on preliminary observations. Start with the simplest model.
- **Step 2**: Design user study experiments and collect labeled data sets. Test the model from Step 1 on the collected labeled data sets.
- **Step 3**: Design online metrics based on the model learned from Step 2. Validate the metrics based on the validation corpus and try out the metrics on new A/B testing experiments as much as possible.

Iterate these three steps till satisfying results achieved based on the validation corpus described in Section 3.3. Unlike building user behavioral models for other applications such as prediction or recommendation, during the process of building models for online metrics, there are some principles that we need to follow.

First of all, the hypotheses we start in Step 1 should capture important *collective behavioral patterns* of most users. By "collective behavioral patterns", we mean the behavioral patterns that can be observed from most users. For example, for the majority of users of using a search engine, they spend longer time in reading more relevant documents [11], and issue more reformulation queries when they are not satisfied with the results of previous queries [15]. It is absolutely possible that there are some users whose clicking or reformulation behavior is different from the majority; however, we do not have to worry too much about the behavioral patterns of the minority of the users unless there are some special cases we want to address (such as the feature of instant answer in search). In other words, the behavioral models for online metrics need to capture users' homogeneous behavior instead of their heterogeneous behavior.

Secondly, when we collect labeled offline data and learn models from them in Step 2, we should be extra cautious and keep the following several rules in mind:

Rule 1: If possible, collect the labeled data from multiple different ways. This is because for many inevitable reasons, such as different user populations and data distributions, any user or judge labeled data is biased comparing with the real production data. Thus, the phenomena that can be observed from data sets collected in different ways are more likely to be true for the real production data as well. There are two most common ways to collect labeled data. One is collecting first-hand labels by taking surveys from the users or by doing lab study. The studies in [1; 11; 12] use this approach. The other is using third-party judges to label the logged data by re-presenting the information and behavioral traces to the trained crowd workers, such as the work in [14; 17; 36]. Both approaches have their own pros and cons. For example, using the lab study generates more accurate labels as they are labeled by the users themselves, but this approach can hardly simulate the real scenarios of using the services; on the other hand, employing third-party crowd workers to annotate logged search sessions is inexpensive and can better capture the real usage scenarios, the limitation of this method is being less accurate than real users' own ratings. In the work of [15], multiple labeled data sets collected by both approaches are used to verify the relationship between query reformulation and search success, which makes the conclusion more convincing and reliable, and hence Bing employs this feature in defining the search success model for its OEC.

Rule 2: Avoid making the models as black-boxes. In Section 3.2 we have mentioned that it is important to have debugging metrics for OEC; on the other hand, it is very desirable for OEC to be "debuggable" or "decomposable". By being "debuggable", we mean it is easy and straightforward to define debugging metrics to track and explain the movements of a metric. In order to get a "debuggable" metric, the behavioral model that the metric is based on should be decomposable and intuitive. For example, we learn that both clicking behavior and reformulation behavior are highly correlated with user's search satisfaction [15], a decision tree classifier as Figure 3 is much better than a machine learned classifier when being used as the model for metrics. This is because a decision tree model as Figure 3 is very intuitive and easy to be decomposed into several branches: queries followed by reformulations (unsuccessful queries of branch 1), queries not followed by reformulations and without long-dwell-time clicks (unsuccessful queries of branch 2), and queries not followed by reformulations and with long-dwell-time clicks (successful queries of branch 3). If we use Successful Queries per User as the goal metric, then it is fairly easy to understand the movement of this metric by using Queries per User, Reformulation Queries (i.e. queries followed by reformulations) per User and Queries with Long-dwell-time Clicks per User as the debugging metrics.

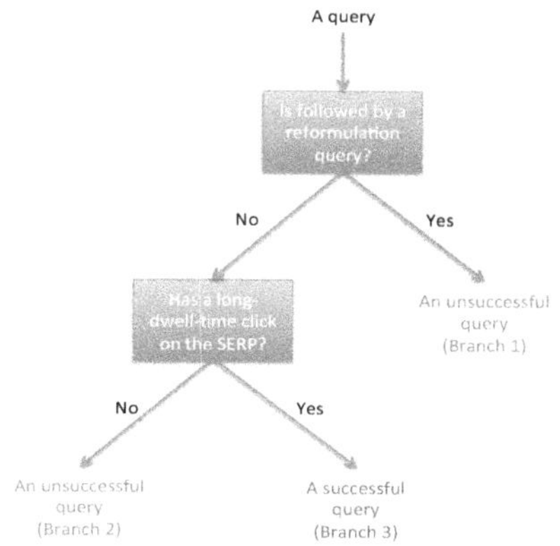

Figure 3: An intuitive and decomposable decision tree model combining two behavioral signals, reformulation and long-dwell-time clicks, to decide if a query is successful or not.

In practice, based on the offline labeled data, we can first have some machine-learned models, and then we simplify and hand-tune the machine-learned models into clear, human-readable models for online metrics. It is acceptable if the human-readable simplified models have reasonably lower accuracies than the machine-learned models when evaluated by the offline labeled data. This is because the goodness of a model for metrics is eventually evaluated by the quality described in Section 3.1 instead of fitting the offline labeled data.

Rule 3: When choose features for the models, make sure that only exogenous features can be used. Exogenous features are features from the user side, such as users' clicking behavior, browsing patterns or dwell time. In contrast, endogenous features are those from the service side, such as the information shown on the webpages. If the endogenous features are used in the models for metrics, then the product teams have the chance of gaming the metrics either intentionally or unintentionally, and thus the metrics lose the required quality of impartiality. For example, it has been shown that displaying good instant answers on the search result pages has high probability in making the users end their search tasks without clicks but with satisfaction [33]. However, if we use an endogenous feature such as "an instant answer of weather being displayed" as a feature in the model shown in Figure 4, then if the feature team has a powerful algorithm in predicting when the user would not have any click, they can manipulate the metric by displaying a weather answer to improve the probably of classifying a query into branch 2 even the query has nothing to do with weather. Although this kind of manipulation is hard in practice, we have seen some "accidental or unintentional" manipulation of our metrics when some endogenous features are employed in the models in reality.

Finally, even with the most state-of-the-art models, it is still halfway to a good metric. Rigorously validating the behavior-driven metrics based on the validation corpus and extensively testing them on new controlled experiments is the must step. Moreover, with the same user behavior model, we can define multiple metrics. For example, with the successful query model shown in Figure 3, we can define metrics such as Successful Queries per User, Successful Query Rate, Successful Sessions per User and Successful Session Rate. When we want to choose the right one for OEC, in addition to the qualities discussed in Section 3.1, there are a few important factors we need to take into consideration. First of all, usually metrics with bounded values are preferred, as metrics without upper bounds are much more sensitive to outliers than those having bounded values [19]. Thus, comparing with the count metrics such as Sessions per User and Queries per User, rate metrics such as Session Success Rate and Query Success Rate have the advantage of being bounded and less likely to be affected by outliers. Second, if we want to use rate metrics for OEC or goal metrics, there are some rules we need to follow, which will be discussed in the next subsection.

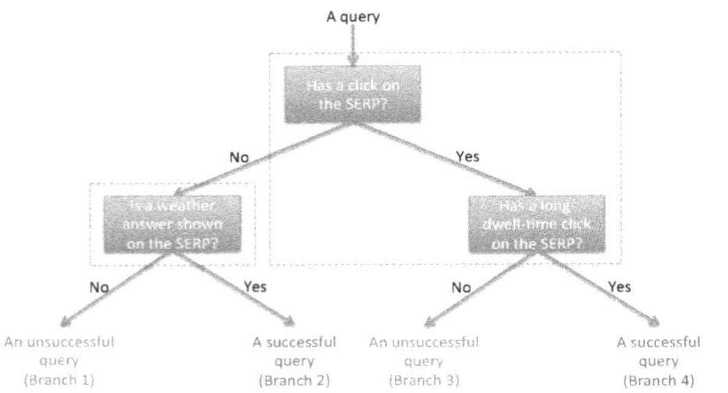

Figure 4: A decision tree model having both exogenous features (within the green dashed box) and an endogenous feature (within the red dashed box). The endogenous feature gives the feature team a chance to manipulate the metric.

3.6 Lesson 6: Choose the right rate metrics

A rate metric is a metric that has two parts in its definition: the numerator and the denominator (and the denominator not be the count of users), such as Click Through Rate, Views per Movie, or Success Query Rate (i.e. the count of success queries divided by the count of total queries). Rate metrics are widely used and in many cases they are good candidates for OEC, as rate metrics have good properties such as with bounded values, less skewed (e.g. the value of rate metric Query Success Rate is bounded between 0 and 1 and its distribution is less skewed than the count metric of Successful Queries per User) and relatively more sensitive. However, when we design and use rate metrics, there are some traps we need to be extremely careful about.

First of all, when a rate metric increases with statistical significance, it could be due to the following reasons: (a) the numerator increases and the denominator remains stable; (b) the denominator decreases and the numerator remains stable; (c) the numerator increases and the denominator decreases; (d) both the numerator and denominator increase, and (e) both the numerator and denominator decrease. Among these five possibilities, except for (a), the goodness of all other cases are ambiguous. Take the rate metric of Query Success Rate as an example, case (a) means that the total number of queries a user issues (i.e. the denominator) remains the same while the number of successful queries a user issues (i.e. the numerator) increases. This is clear and very likely a positive scenario. However, if the denominator (i.e. the total number of queries) is not stable, then it could be due to any reason from (b) to (e). As we have mentioned previously, the move direction of total queries per user is ambiguous, and thus it is hard to decide if any scenario from (b) to (e) is positive, negative or mixed without further analysis. Generally speaking, if the denominator of a rate metric changes between the control and treatment groups, then comparing the rate metric between the control and treatment groups makes as little sense as comparing apples and oranges. Thus, there are two rules we have to follow when dealing with rate metrics:

1. We should always keep the denominator and the numerator as debugging metrics (discussed in Section 3.2) for a rate metric;
2. When we choose a rate metric to be a goal metric, we should choose the one whose denominator is relatively more stable in most cases.

For example, when we want to decide the goal metric between Query Success Rate (QSR) and Session Success Rate (SSR) for Bing, we examined whose denominator is more stable in addition to look at their directions and sensitivities as mentioned in Section 3.1. Based on the observations from hundreds of A/B experiments, we find that the denominator of SSR, i.e. number of sessions per user, is much more stable than the denominator of QSR, i.e. number of queries per user. In fact, 10% of statistically significant QSR movement happened together with statistically significant Distinct Queries per User movement! In other word, interpreting QSR is tricky for 10% of cases. Thus, although QSR is more sensitive than SSR in many cases, SSR is more appropriate for being a goal metric. We use QSR as a debugging metric to help better understand the goal metric.

The second issue is that there are two ways to compute the metrics for rate metrics: Average of Ratios and Ratio of Averages. For instance, Click Through Rate (CTR) can be defined as A) Average CTR per User, and B) #(Clicks of all users)/#(Pageviews of all users). The former is average of ratios where for each individual user we calculate the ratio first and then take average across all users. The latter is equivalent to the ratio of Clicks/User to Pageviews/User, hence is a ratio of averages. Both definitions are used in practice, and sometimes both versions are computed for the same rate metric and therefore it is important to understand the differences. Their main difference is how users are weighted. For average of ratios, users have the same weight on the final metric because each user has a single value of ratio. For ratio of averages, mathematically it is equivalent to weighted average of ratio per user, where weight is proportional to the denominator value for each user, e.g. user with more pageviews will have a higher impact on CTR. Because of the difference in weighting, optimizing ratio of averages puts more emphasize on heavy users while optimizing average of ratios treats each user equally important.

In our experience, these two versions of rate metrics move in the same direction for most experiments. When they don't, we get an interesting signal that the treatment effect is different between heavy users and average users, which begs our further investigation. In general average of ratios tends to be more sensitive than ratio of averages when treatment effects are homogeneous for all users. This is because for ratio of averages, the metric is dominated by those heavy users, and hence the *effective sample size* is the same as the number of heavy users. On the other hand, average of ratios is influenced equally by all the users and its *effective sample size* is the total number of users. The concept of effective sample size is better explained in the literature of weighted samples and importance sampling. As a rule of thumb, when using weights in sample average, effective sample size is smaller than the number of independent samples. The larger the skewness of weight distribution is, the smaller the effective sample size is. Also note that the variance for ratio of averages should be calculated using Delta Method [35] if users are used as the randomization units, while for average of ratio, we just need to use the standard sample variance formula.

3.7 Lesson 7: Use combo metrics as surrogate for OEC

In spite of all the techniques we have stated above, finding a good goal metric that has both clear direction and actionable sensitivity can still be very hard because no metric is applicable in all scenarios. In the absence of a single OEC to use as our guide toward the North Star, one approach is to use a set of success criteria metrics and by looking at these metrics altogether, we can have a better estimation on the experiment result. For this strategy to work, first, we need to have a fairly comprehensive understanding of all the success criteria metrics. For each metric, we need to know the intended direction interpretation and more importantly scenarios where the metric fail to give clear direction and therefore should be either discarded or replaced by another metric in the decision making process. Second, the set of individual metrics should cover all known scenarios. When one metric fail to give clear direction, there must be at least one other metric that can fill the gap. At last, the most ambiguous situation is when two metrics shows different directions, i.e. one shows user experience is improved and the other suggests degradation. In such cases experts' opinions are often required to carefully trade off two things: the signal strength and the signal value.

This procedure described above requires a panel experts to gather together regularly to review the experiment results together and thus is not scalable. For an entire organization to align, a more objective and standardized approach is still preferred. **Combo metrics** are designed to address this issue. It is a derived metric consists of the most important success criteria metrics used in experts' decision rule. Given a set of metrics $X_i, i = 1, \ldots, k$, a combo metric is of the form

$$f(\Delta\%(X_i), \ldots, \Delta\%(X_k))$$

where the $\Delta\%(X_i)$ is the Percent Delta of metric X_i defined as $\frac{X_i^T - X_i^C}{X_i^C} \times 100\%$ (X_i^T and X_i^C here are metric X_i's values for treatment and control). The functional form of f is what we need to design. It is generally recommended to make f differentiable and with continuous first derivative. This is because we need to perform statistical test on the combo metric and continuity makes the test of the combo metric as easy as each component. When f is not differentiable, the metric might not even have an asymptotically normal distribution which significantly complicates the analysis. We show the asymptotic normality of a combo metric when f is differentiable with continuous partial derivatives. Our derivation also gives the formula of the variance. When combo metric is asymptotically normal, Wald's Z-test described in Section 3.4 can be applied.

The key of the derivation is to use the delta method [35]. We can rewrite the combo metric as

$$f(X_1^T, \ldots, X_k^T, X_1^C, \ldots, X_k^C)$$

where X^T and X^C is the component metrics calculated in treatment and control groups respectively. The asymptotic distribution of the vector $X = (X_1^T, \ldots, X_k^T, X_1^C, \ldots, X_k^C)$ is multivariate normal with known covariance matrix from multivariate central limit theorem. Because treatment and control groups are two independent groups of subjects, the covariance matrix of this vector has the structure

$$\begin{pmatrix} \Sigma_T & 0 \\ 0 & \Sigma_C \end{pmatrix}$$

where Σ_T and Σ_C are covariance matrix of $(X_i^T, \ldots, X_k^T)$ and $(X_i^C, \ldots, X_k^C)$ respectively and both can be estimated using sample covariance from the experiment data. From the delta method, the variance of $f(X_i^T, X_i^C, \ldots, X_k^T, X_k^C)$ can be calculated as:

$$\left(\left.\frac{\partial f}{\partial x}\right|_{x=X}\right)^T \times \begin{pmatrix} \Sigma_T & 0 \\ 0 & \Sigma_C \end{pmatrix} \times \left.\frac{\partial f}{\partial x}\right|_{x=X}$$

If the function f does not have a continuous first derivative, then there is no guarantee that the combo metric has a asymptotic normal distribution. An example of such combo metric is any function that involves MAX or MIN, or conditional rules. For those irregular combo metrics, more computationally intensive method such as bootstrap [18] should be used instead.

The simplest type of combo metrics are linear combinations, i.e. combo metrics of the form

$$\sum w_i \Delta\%(X_i)$$

where the weight w_i has a utility based interpretation. If a validation corpus is available to accurately measure direction and sensitivity of a combo metric, then we can try different weights or functional forms and pick the one with the best performance. If such a validation corpus is not available, we can use degradation experiments as described in Section 3.3. For example, if X and Y are two success criteria metrics and from several degradation experiments the ratio of degradation between the two are r, then it means 1% change of Y is comparable to r% change of X. This gives us a good starting point of the weights.

4. SUMMARY

Nowadays, controlled experiments are used heavily by many data-driven Internet companies to understand the impact of the business on real users. In this paper, we present the process of designing online metrics for controlled experiments could also be data-driven by showing methodologies we have adopted and lessons we have learned over years. We define two mandatory qualities that goal metrics (i.e. OEC) have to meet, directionality and sensitivity, and show empirical ways to measure these qualities systematically and effectively. We also show how to design and improve metrics by utilizing user behavior modeling and statistical techniques, and how to choose the right and most appropriate metrics based on different characteristics they have. We hope the insights and lessons we share in this paper could benefit the successful use and deployment of online metrics for controlled experiments in various online services in industry.

Acknowledgment

The authors want to thank Pavel Dmitriev and Xian Wu for their work on MetricLab, Shouyuan Chen for his related internship work in alternative sensitivity and alignment measurement framework not published here, and Patrick Pantel and Yi-Min Wang for discussions and support when one of the authors was working at Microsoft Research. We also thank anonymous reviewers who gave helpful feedback on the presentation and contents of this paper.

References

[1] Mikhail Ageev, Qi Guo, Dmitry Lagun, and Eugene Agichtein. Find it if you can: A game for modeling different types of web search success using interaction data. In *Proceedings of the 34th ACM SIGIR Conference*, pages 345–354, 2011.

[2] Xavier Amatriain and Justin Basilico. Netflix recommendations: beyond the 5 stars. *Netflix Tech Blog*, 6, 2012.

[3] Eytan Bakshy and Dean Eckles. Uncertainty in online experiments with dependent data: an evaluation of bootstrap methods. In *Proceedings of the 19th ACM SIGKDD Conference*, pages 1303–1311, 2013.

[4] Joeran Beel, Marcel Genzmehr, Stefan Langer, Andreas Nürnberger, and Bela Gipp. A comparative analysis of offline and online evaluations and discussion of research paper recommender system evaluation. In *Proceedings of the International Workshop on Reproducibility and Replication in Recommender Systems Evaluation*, RepSys '13, 2013.

[5] Brian Christian. The a/b test: Inside the technology that's changing the rules of business, April 2012. URL http://www.wired.com/business/2012/04/ff_abtesting/.

[6] Alex Deng. Objective bayesian two sample hypothesis testing for online controlled experiments. In *Proceedings of the 24th International Conference on World Wide Web Companion*, pages 923–928, 2015.

[7] Alex Deng, Ya Xu, Ron Kohavi, and Toby Walker. Improving the sensitivity of online controlled experiments by utilizing pre-experiment data. In *Proceedings of the 6th ACM WSDM Conference*, pages 123–132, 2013.

[8] Alex Deng, Tianxi Li, and Yu Guo. Statistical inference in two-stage online controlled experiments with treatment selection and validation. In *Proceedings of the 23rd international conference on World Wide Web*, pages 609–618, 2014.

[9] Abdigani Diriye, Ryen White, Georg Buscher, and Susan Dumais. Leaving so soon?: Understanding and predicting web search abandonment rationales. In *Proceedings of the 21st ACM CIKM*, pages 1025–1034, 2012.

[10] Pavel Dmitriev and Xian Wu. Measuring metrics, 2016. https://archive.org/details/MeasuringMetricsCIKM2016.

[11] Steve Fox, Kuldeep Karnawat, Mark Mydland, Susan Dumais, and Thomas White. Evaluating implicit measures to improve web search. *ACM Trans. Inf. Syst.*, 23(2):147–168, April 2005.

[12] Qi Guo and Eugene Agichtein. Ready to buy or just browsing?: Detecting web searcher goals from interaction data. In *Proceedings of the 33rd ACM SIGIR Conference*, pages 130–137, 2010.

[13] Yu Guo and Alex Deng. Flexible online repeated measures experiment. *arXiv preprint arXiv:1501.00450*, 2015.

[14] Ahmed Hassan, Rosie Jones, and Kristina Lisa Klinkner. Beyond dcg: User behavior as a predictor of a successful search. In *Proceedings of the Third ACM WSDM Conference*, pages 221–230, 2010.

[15] Ahmed Hassan, Xiaolin Shi, Nick Craswell, and Bill Ramsey. Beyond clicks: Query reformulation as a predictor of search satisfaction. In *Proceedings of the 22nd ACM CIKM Conference*, pages 2019–2028, 2013.

[16] Henning Hohnhold, Deirdre O'Brien, and Diane Tang. Focusing on the long-term: It's good for users and business. In *Proceedings of the 21th ACM SIGKDD Conference*, pages 1849–1858, 2015.

[17] Jiepu Jiang, Ahmed Hassan Awadallah, Xiaolin Shi, and Ryen W. White. Understanding and predicting graded search satisfaction. In *Proceedings of the 8th ACM WSDM Conference*, pages 57–66, 2015.

[18] Ariel Kleiner, Ameet Talwalkar, Purnamrita Sarkar, and Michael I Jordan. A scalable bootstrap for massive data. *J. R. Stat. Soc. Ser. B (Statistical Methodol.)*, 2014.

[19] R. Kohavi, R. Longbotham, and T. Walker. Online experiments: Practical lessons. *Computer*, 43(9):82–85, Sept 2010.

[20] Ron Kohavi and Roger Longbotham. Unexpected results in online controlled experiments. *ACM SIGKDD Explorations Newsletter*, 12(2):31–35, 2011.

[21] Ron Kohavi and Matt Round. Front line internet analytics at amazon.com, 2004.

[22] Ron Kohavi, Randal M Henne, and Dan Sommerfield. Practical guide to controlled experiments on the web: listen to your customers not to the hippo. In *Proceedings of the 13th ACM SIGKDD Conference*, pages 959–967, 2007.

[23] Ron Kohavi, Roger Longbotham, Dan Sommerfield, and Randal M. Henne. Controlled experiments on the web: survey and practical guide. *Data Mining Knowledge Discovery*, 18:140–181, 2009.

[24] Ron Kohavi, Alex Deng, Brian Frasca, Roger Longbotham, Toby Walker, and Ya Xu. Trustworthy online controlled experiments: Five puzzling outcomes explained. *Proceedings of the 18th ACM SIGKDD Conference*, 2012.

[25] Ron Kohavi, Alex Deng, Brian Frasca, Toby Walker nd Ya Xu, and Nils Pohlmann. Online controlled experiments at large scale. *Proceedings of the 19th ACM SIGKDD Conference*, 2013.

[26] Ron Kohavi, Alex Deng, Roger Longbotham, and Ya Xu. Seven rules of thumb for web site experimenters. In *Proceedings of the 20th ACM SIGKDD Conference*, KDD '14, pages 1857–1866, 2014.

[27] Ronny Kohavi, Thomas Crook, Roger Longbotham, Brian Frasca, Randy Henne, Juan Lavista Ferres, and Tamir Melamed. Online experimentation at microsoft. In *Proceedings of the Third International Workshop on Data Mining Case Studies, held at the 5th ACM SIGKDD Conference*, pages 11–23, 2009.

[28] Dan McKinley. Design for continuous experimentation: Talk and slides.[online] dec 22, 2012.

[29] Mike Moran. Multivariate testing in action: Quicken loan's regis hadiaris on multivariate testing. *Biznology Blog by Mike Moran*, 2008.

[30] Christian Posse. Key lessons learned building recommender systems for large-scale social networks. In *Proceedings of the 18th ACM SIGKDD Conference*, pages 587–587, 2012.

[31] Kerry Rodden, Hilary Hutchinson, and Xin Fu. Measuring the user experience on a large scale: User-centered metrics for web applications. In *Proceedings of CHI 2010*, 2010.

[32] Yang Song, Xiaolin Shi, and Xin Fu. Evaluating and predicting user engagement change with degraded search relevance. In *Proceedings of the 22nd International Conference on World Wide Web*, WWW '13, pages 1213–1224, 2013.

[33] Yang Song, Xiaolin Shi, Ryen White, and Ahmed Hassan Awadallah. Context-aware web search abandonment prediction. In *Proceedings of the 37th International ACM SIGIR Conference*, pages 93–102, 2014.

[34] Diane Tang, Ashish Agarwal, Deirdre O'Brien, and Mike Meyer. Overlapping experiment infrastructure: More, better, faster experimentation. *Proceedings of the 16th ACM SIGKDD Conference*, 2010.

[35] Aad W Van der Vaart. *Asymptotic statistics*, volume 3. Cambridge university press, 2000. ISBN 0521784506.

[36] Hongning Wang, Yang Song, Ming-Wei Chang, Xiaodong He, Ahmed Hassan, and Ryen W. White. Modeling action-level satisfaction for search task satisfaction prediction. In *Proceedings of the 37th ACM SIGIR Conference*, 2014.

Catch Me If You Can: Detecting Pickpocket Suspects from Large-Scale Transit Records

Bowen Du
State Key Lab of Software Development Environment
Beihang University
Beijing, China
dubowen@buaa.edu.cn

Chuanren Liu
Decision Sciences and MIS
LeBow College of Business
Drexel University
Philadelphia, US
chuanren.liu@drexel.edu

Wenjun Zhou
Business Analytics & Statistics
Haslam College of Business
University of Tennessee
Knoxville, US
wzhou4@utk.edu

Zhenshan Hou
State Key Lab of Software Development Environment
Beihang University
Beijing, China
zhh@buaa.edu.cn

Hui Xiong*
Management Science and Information Systems
Rutgers University
New Jersey, US
hxiong@rutgers.edu

ABSTRACT

Massive data collected by automated fare collection (AFC) systems provide opportunities for studying both personal traveling behaviors and collective mobility patterns in the urban area. Existing studies on the AFC data have primarily focused on identifying passengers' movement patterns. In this paper, however, we creatively leveraged such data for identifying thieves in the public transit systems. Indeed, stopping pickpockets in the public transit systems has been critical for improving passenger satisfaction and public safety. However, it is challenging to tell thieves from regular passengers in practice. To this end, we developed a suspect detection and surveillance system, which can identify pickpocket suspects based on their daily transit records. Specifically, we first extracted a number of features from each passenger's daily activities in the transit systems. Then, we took a two-step approach that exploits the strengths of unsupervised outlier detection and supervised classification models to identify thieves, who exhibit abnormal traveling behaviors. Experimental results demonstrated the effectiveness of our method. We also developed a prototype system with a user-friendly interface for the security personnel.

CCS Concepts

•Information systems → Spatial-temporal systems; Data mining; •Computing methodologies → Anomaly detection;

*Corresponding Author

KDD '16, August 13-17, 2016, San Francisco, CA, USA

DOI: http://dx.doi.org/10.1145/2939672.2939687

Keywords

Automated Fare Collection; Travel Behaviors; Mobility Patterns; Public Safety; Anomaly Detection.

1. INTRODUCTION

Passengers in the public transit systems have been the main target for pickpockets. In many cities, thefts happen frequently in public transit systems, because passengers tend to pay less attention to their belongings when they are in a rush or in a crowded environment. For example, during the first nine months of 2014, 350 pickpockets were caught in the subway system and 490 were caught on buses[1] in Beijing, China. Many other big cities in the world, such as Barcelona, Prague, Rome, and Paris, are also reported to suffer from the pickpocket problem [2], which has led to public safety concerns [23, 7]. Indeed, it is challenging to detect theft activities committed by cunning thieves who know how to escape without being disclosed. Despite the substantial cost in manpower and resources, many thieves are still at large. It is critical to provide a smart surveillance and tracking tool for the security personnel of the transit systems.

With rapid advances in information technology and data processing capacities, transactional records collected by automated fare collection (AFC) systems [20] have become valuable for understanding passengers' mobility patterns and the urban dynamics [6, 3, 20, 29, 18]. However, most of the existing studies focused on identifying regular, collective mobility patterns, such as commute flows and transit networks. Our study is the first to focus on identifying thieves based on AFC data. In fact, it is possible to detect thieves using AFC records because behavioral differences are coined in the mobility footprints, which can help to separate suspects from regular passengers. Examples of such behaviors, which can make suspects notable, include traveling for an extended length of time, making unnecessary transfers, and/or wandering on certain routes while making random stops.

[1] http://www.bjgaj.gov.cn/web/detail_zxftDetail_397242.html

[2] http://abcnews.go.com/Travel/top-10-pickpocket-cities-watch-wallet-avoid-thieves/story?id=11769828

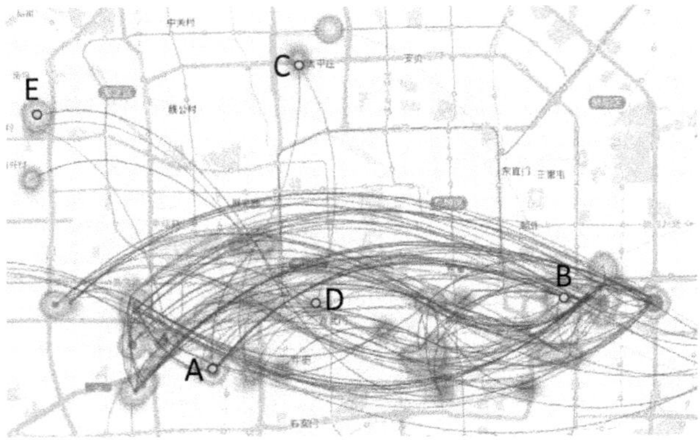

Figure 1: Trajectories of passengers.

However, detecting thieves based on AFC records is not a simple outlier detection problem. Figure 1 shows the difference between a known thief and an outlier. We can see a number of trajectories between hot regions A and B. By careful examination, we can see that most passengers move from one region to another using near-optimal configuration (*e.g.*, shortest time/distance, or a minimal number of transfers). However, a passenger (a known suspect) who took the path $A \rightarrow C \rightarrow D \rightarrow B$ looks suspicious because there is no need to make transfers at C and D in order to reach B. Based on the above observation, passengers who exhibit such abnormal behaviors will be selected for further examination. In contrast, another passenger who travels from E to B is an outlier, since few passengers take the same path. However, this passenger is likely just a regular passenger who originates from a less crowded area.

In summary, to identify thieves from AFC records, we are faced with a number of inherent challenges.

- The first challenge is how to identify useful features to distinguish thieves from regular passengers. These features should not only help us understand the behaviors of pickpockets, but also help us build a suspect detection and tracking system for supporting the security personnel.
- Second, using regular outlier detection methods tends to result in a large number of false positives. In particular, not every trip made by a regular passenger looks normal. Regular commuters may occasionally make trips to visit friends or places of interest, and some of such trips may look suspicious by how much they deviate from regular behaviors.
- Third, a large number of AFC records are being collected from millions of passengers, only a tiny fraction of which are pickpockets. Identifying such a small group of people in such a large-scale dataset is like looking for a needle in the haystack.
- Finally, we also need to effectively transform our knowledge based on model development into a decision support system, so that real-time, personalized deployment recommendations could be made to help to guide security personnel to perform their work more efficiently.

To this end, in this paper, a comprehensive approach is taken to meet the above challenges. Specifically, we first construct a feature representation for profiling passengers. Furthermore, we establish a two-step framework to separate normal movement patterns from irregular behaviors, and eventually, distinguish thieves from regular passengers. Finally, we leverage real-world datasets from multiple sources for model training and validation, and implement a prototype system for end users.

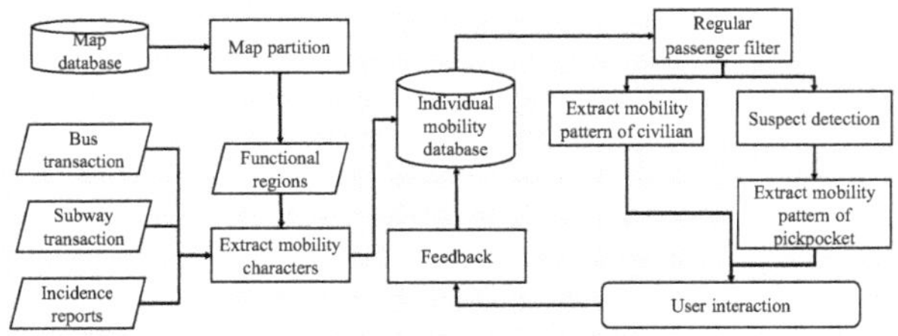

Figure 2: The framework.

Figure 2 shows the overall architecture of our framework. We first partition the city area into regions with functional categories. Then, the mobility characteristics of passengers are extracted from transit records and incident reports. Moreover, we build an individual mobility database to store the profile of each passenger. Next, we implement our framework by regular passenger filtering and suspect detection. The system is efficient and interactive, with both mobile and desktop clients. Finally, the user feedback information, such as newly confirmed thieves, will be entered as ground truth for future model training.

The remaining of this paper is organized as follows. Section 2 provides an overview the AFC datasets, based on which we performed the study. A detailed description of features that we extract to characterize mobility profiles of passengers is presented in Section 3. A two-step framework of the suspect identification system is proposed in Section 4. Experimental results are summarized in Section 5, and an overview of the deployed system is presented in Section 6. Finally, we summarize related work in Section 7, and draw conclusions in Section 8.

2. DATA DESCRIPTION

The data for our study have been collected from multiple sources. These include transit records, geographical information, and theft incident reports. In this section, we provide an overview of the data.

2.1 Transit Records

Our study is based on a large-scale transit records dataset collected from a public transit system that includes buses and subways. Passengers utilizing the transit service are charged by the distance they travel. A rechargeable smart card is issued to each passenger, who has to swipe the card when they board or exit a vehicle. The AFC system then calculates the fare according to the stations of boarding and exiting. As a result, each raw AFC record consists of the smart card ID, the route number, the event (*i.e.*, boarding or exiting), the station, and the time stamp. We transformed the data so that each transit record consists of one boarding and one exiting event of the same ID. There are about 1.7 billion records between April and June in 2014. After removing replicates and extremely infrequent riders, we are left with over 1.6 billion records that involve approximately 6 million passengers (for three months).

In order to describe the data and subsequent feature extraction process clearly, here we clarify two concepts, *transit records* and *trips*, using a concrete example. Figure 3 illustrates an example passenger's activities in a typical day. Part (a) is the actual trajectory on the city's map; Part (b) splits the trajectory into three separate trips; and Part (c) demonstrates the corresponding transit records in our data. In particular, let us say that the passenger holds a smart card with an ID of 4322. He started by taking Route 52 at Station a, which is next to his home, at 7:15 a.m. Having to make a transfer, he exited Route 52 at Station b at 7:40 a.m., and walked across the street to take Route 26 at Station c (7:46 a.m.). Then he got off at Station d, which is next to his workplace, at 8:23 a.m. He completed Trip 1 since the next time he was in the transit system was more than 30 minutes (*i.e.*, our empirical cutoff) later. Similarly, the transit in the afternoon from d to e was considered Trip 2; and the transit from e back home at a, making a transfer at f, was considered Trip 3. As a result, we collected the five transit records that describe three trips.

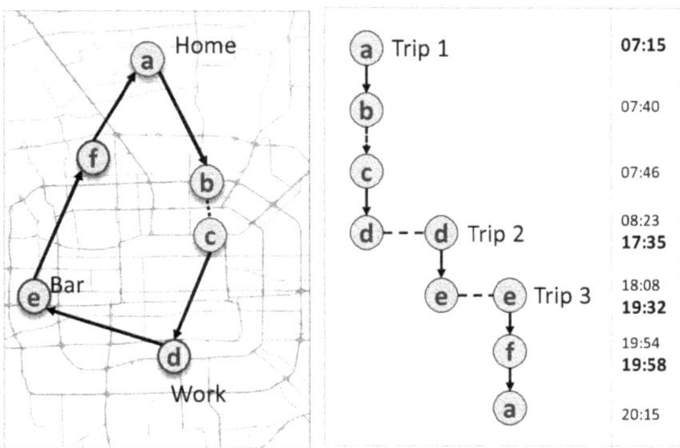

(a) Example Activities (b) Trips

Smart Card ID	Route Number	Boarding Station	Boarding Time	Exiting Station	Exiting Time
4322	Route 52	a	07:15	b	07:40
4322	Route 26	c	07:46	d	08:23
4322	Route 11	d	17:35	e	18:08
4322	Route 11	e	19:32	f	19:54
4322	Route 16	f	19:58	a	20:15

(c) Transit Records

Figure 3: An example of trips and transit records.

Intuitively, a transit record corresponds to one segment of transit between a pair of consecutive boarding and exiting events of the same passenger. Even though this segment of transit may pass a number of stations, the passenger has never left the vehicle during the time. In contrast, a trip consists of one or more such segments, which connect places of interest on the two ends, where the passenger stays for extended periods of time. A trip may include connections or transfers, as long as those breaks are relatively short in time. Formally, we provide the following definitions.

DEFINITION 1 (TRANSIT RECORD). *A transit record tr contains the following information:*

- tr_{route}: *the bus/subway route number;*
- tr_{sboard}, tr_{tboard}: *the boarding station and time; and*
- tr_{sexit}, tr_{texit}: *the exiting station and time.*

As a result, for each transit record, we were able to compute the travel distance tr_{dist}, travel time tr_{time} and number of stops tr_{stops} during the transit.

DEFINITION 2 (TRIP). *A trip Tr is a sequence of transit records $Tr = (tr^1, tr^2, \cdots, tr^n)$, where the passenger's origin location is $Tr_{origin} = tr^1_{vboard}$ and the destination is $Tr_{dest} = tr^n_{sexit}$.*

In practice, we construct one trip record if and only if the time gap between two consecutive transit records is no more than 30 minutes. The trip's time duration is calculated as $Tr_{time} = tr^n_{texit} - tr^1_{tboard}$.

2.2 Geographical Information

To project the transit records to the city map, we made use of two datasets of important geographical information. Namely, the points of interests (POI) data and the public transit network information.

Table 1: Categories of Functional Regions

Category	Examples	Frequency
Home	Apartment buildings	28,731
Work	Government or office buildings	71,364
Education	Schools, training centers	3,527
Food	Restaurants and dining	56,906
Shopping	Shopping malls and outlets	24,310
Entertainment	Museums, theaters, clubs	18,223
Scenic Spot	Parks, sports fields	2,362
Transportation	Airports, transit centers	15,287
Healthcare	Hospitals, pharmacy	8,685
Car services	Car sales, repairs	1,781

With the POI data, we followed Yuan's work [28] to segment the urban area into small regions by major road networks, and then categorize each region into one of ten functions, as listed in Table 1. These regions are then color coded and visualized in Figure 4(a).

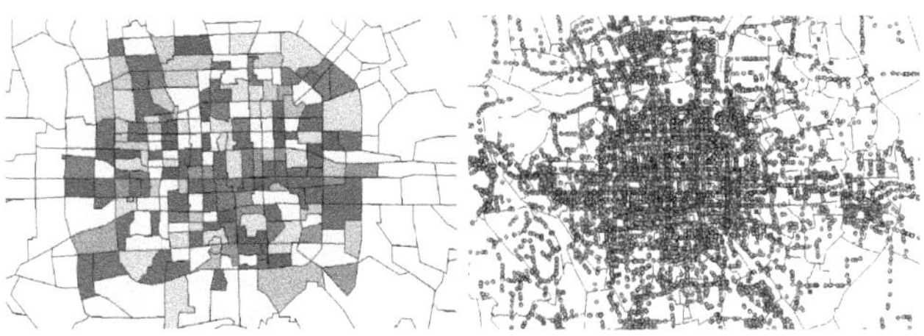

(a) Functional Regions (b) Stations

Figure 4: Geographical information.

The public transit network dataset provides basic information of each route of buses and subways. Each route is a sequence of stations, and the raw data include the route number, the sequence ID in the route, the name of the station, and the geo-location expressed as latitude and longitude. As shown in Figure 4(b), in total, we have 44,524 bus stations (points in gray) covered by 896 bus routes, and 320 subway stations (points in blue) covered by 18 subway routes. To remove the redundancy and better model the human mobility pattern, we merge stations located at the same road intersection.

2.3 Incident Reports

Confirmed pickpocket incidents are publicly announced via Sina Weibo, the primary social network services in China.

It is considered public data since posts are all visible to everyone, just like Twitter in the United States. We included two types of pickpocket reports: official announcements, as announced by the police[3], and personal complaints, as posted by the victims. Figure 5 provides an example of each type of report. We can see that the date, time, and location of the theft events are normally identified in the posts, which has helped us to link such events to other sources of data. We found 10,529 records during our study period.

(a) Police report: "At 7:40 a.m. on July 10th, a thief was caught at Route 349 East Chengzhuanglukou Station."

(b) Victim complaint: "Just now (around 5:20pm), my sister's phone was stolen at the Dashanzi Bridge Bus Station."

Figure 5: Example incident reports on Weibo.

3. MOBILITY CHARACTERISTICS

In this section, we will describe the features we extracted from passengers' AFC records, which are potentially useful for characterizing public transit mobility patters, and thus, will eventually be used for distinguishing pickpocket suspects from regular passengers. As shown in Table 2, our features are grouped into three categories: daily behaviors, social comparisons, and historical behaviors.

3.1 Travel Time and Frequency

The daily travel time is defined as the total duration spent by each passenger in the public transit system, and the daily riding frequency is defined as the number of transit records traveled by each passenger per day.

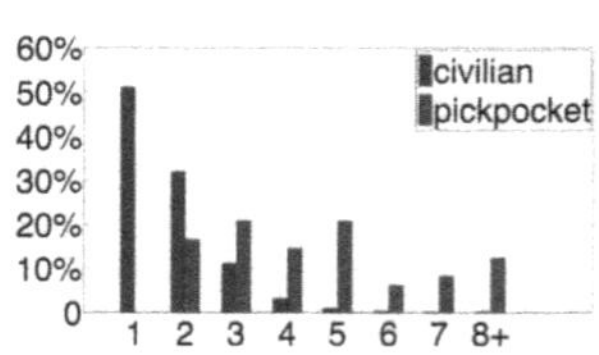

(a) Travel time.

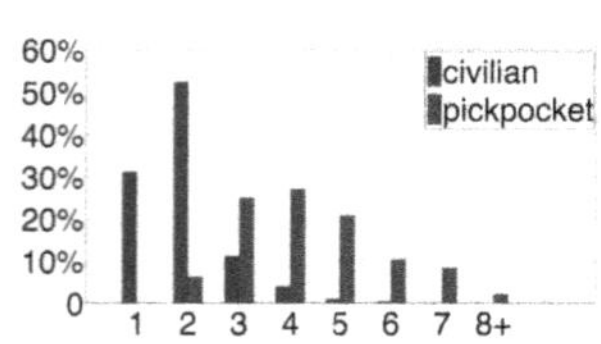

(b) Riding frequency.

Figure 6: Distributions of travel time and the number of transit records.

Indeed, picking pockets is a hard work: a thief has to spend quite long time in the crowded buses, subways, or near the transit stations to find potential victims and better crime moments. Also, in order to have more theft opportunities, a thief (pickpocket) tends to travel between bus/subway stations in random ways without specific destinations. Such abnormal behaviors lead to abnormal daily travel time and riding frequency. Figure 6 plots the distribution of daily travel time and riding frequency, respectively, of passengers traveling around the city with smart cards. We can see that more than 80% passengers finish their travels in 2 hours and within 2 transit records per day. In comparison, the identified thieves often spend more than 3 hours of daily travel time, and their daily riding frequency is also larger.

3.2 Short Rides

A short ride is a transit record tr with less than 3 stops. Regular passengers normally prefer fewer transfers in each trip. Therefore, if a transit has to be made, each transit record will pass several bus/subway stops. In contrast, pickpockets often switch routes within few stops to avoid attracting fellow passengers' attention and being recognized.

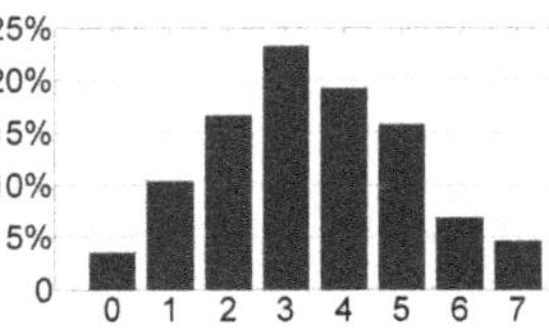

(a)

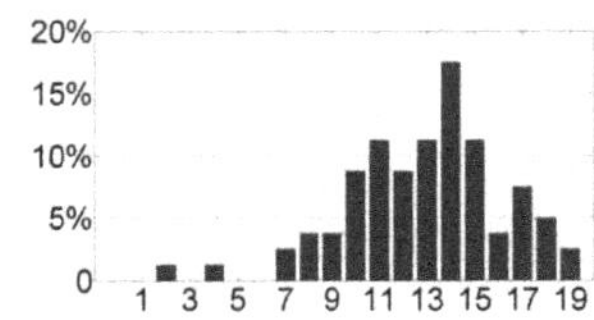

(b)

Figure 7: Distributions of short distance trips.

Figure 7 are the distribution of the daily number of short rides for all passengers with at least 7 and 19 transit records, respectively. The x-axis is the number of short rides and the y-axis is the percentage of passengers. For the passengers with at least 7 transit records in Figure 7(a), the distribution approximates Gaussian with mean around 3. In Figure 7(b), for the passengers with at least 19 transit records, the distribution peak is shifted to the right. It shows that the frequency of short rides increases with increasing number of transit records.

3.3 Functional Transitions

A high-level view of the human mobility patterns can be summarized by transition among regions, where each region covers multiple stations. For example, the morning commuting trips can be abstracted as 'leaving from residence region, then transiting at transfer stations, and arriving at the workplace region at last'. Other examples include 'shopping trips' like `residence` → `shopping facilities` → `residence`, or 'sightseeing trips' like `residence` → `scenic spot` → `scenic spot` → `residence`.

Indeed, such sequential information is very useful for pattern discovery and predictive modeling [14, 12, 30]. To discriminate regular passengers and pickpockets, we observed that there are typical sequential patterns followed by the regular passengers. However, pickpockets tend not to follow the typical patterns, and wander randomly among the functional regions.

As a result, we define features such as the number of boarding stations and the number of boarding regions. Then, we count the transition frequency between any pair of function categories for the daily trip of each passenger.

[3] http://weibo.com/571100476

Table 2: List of extracted features.

Category	Feature Description	Mean	Median
Current Behaviors	Travel time (hours)	1.25	0.976
	Riding frequency	3.93	3
	Number of trips	2.38	2
	Number of short rides	0.81	0
	Number of boarding stations	3.72	3
	Number of regions	3.06	2
	Total number of functional transitions (See Subsection 3.3)	2.26	2
	Number of rides on the most frequent route	2.63	2
	Maximum number of visits of a functional region	2.06	2
	Number of wandering concentration spots (See Subsection 3.4)	2.17	2
Social Comparisons	Time gap of trips (hours) (See Subsection 3.5)	0.49	0.43
	Time gap of region transitions	0.37	0
Historical Behaviors (See Subsection 3.6)	Daily travel time, median	1.14	0.89
	Daily riding frequency, median	3.71	3
	Number of trips, median	2.55	2
	Number of short rides, median	0.83	0
	Number of boarding stations, median	2.89	2
	Number of regions, median	3.16	2
	Functional transitions, median	2.88	2
	Daily travel time(hour), standard deviation	0.36	0.35
	Daily riding frequency, standard deviation	0.79	0.57
	Number of trips, standard deviation	0.89	0.64
	Number of short rides, standard deviation	0.42	0.31
	Number of boarding stations, standard deviation	1.81	1.13
	Number of regions, standard deviation	1.43	0.92
	Functional transitions, standard deviation	1.28	1.17
	Number of days detected as suspect	0.00	0

3.4 Frequently Visited Regions

In practice, the majority of human mobility patterns are regular movements between a small set of locations that the passenger is familiar with. Pickpockets often spend a significant portion of the time within few routes or regions if they intend for opportunities. In particular, once a thief has committed the crime or lost the target, he or she would likely come back to a familiar station for the next target. Thieves know profoundly well about and wander around these areas. Therefore, we can measure such wandering behaviors by counting the maximum number of times a route was taken, or the maximum number of visits made to a region.

Moreover, the wandering behaviors lead to concentration of the passenger's boarding or exiting locations. We use the number of clusters as another feature, which measures the wandering concentration.

3.5 Deviation from the Social Norm

This group of features measures the difference between the individual behaviors and the typical behaviors of the population, so we call them social features. According to our empirical study, two very informative social features are the time gap of trips and the time gap of region transitions. Actually, given the same origin and destination, the trip variation of the majority of the population (i.e., regular passengers) is low. For example, most of the trips will be finished within a specific amount of time given the trip origin and destination, while pickpocket suspects may spend more time in the transit system during the trip.

Thus, for each pair of origin o and destination d, we find the travel time of all trips between this pair. We then convert the time gap significance of a given trip by the quantile of its travel time with respect to the population. Similarly, we also define the time gap significance of region transitions.

3.6 Historical Behaviors

We compute the statistics (e.g., median and standard deviation) of the daily features observed in the last seven days for each passenger, to quantify their historical behaviors. We use the median instead of the mean, because median is more robust in the presence of outliers, especially if the sample size is small. In our case, we only used data from the past seven days, and median can effectively avoid the impact of non-routine passenger behaviors. The standard deviation indicates the degree of variation of the daily behaviors of individual passengers. Regular passengers following routine trajectories normally generate statistics with less variations. Moreover, we also record the number of days (out of the recent seven days) when the passenger was detected as potential pickpocket suspects.

4. SUSPECT IDENTIFICATION

This section presents the key component of our thief footmark detection system. Specifically, in order to distinguish pickpockets from the regular passengers with high accuracy and low false-positives, we develop a two-step framework. The first step adopts anomaly detection techniques to identify thieves as well as some suspects from the passenger population. The second step further distinguishes the pickpockets from the suspects, by mapping the defined features into a high dimensional space and computing the optimal decision surface in support vector machines (SVM).

Suppose there are totally N passengers included in the dataset $\{(x_j, y_j) \mid j = 1, ..., N\}$, where $x_j \in \mathbb{R}^q$ is the extracted features associated with the j-th passenger, and $y_j \in \{0, 1\}$ is the classification label, such that $y_j = 1$ if and only if the passenger is a determined as a pickpocket suspect. Our objective is to develop a predictive model

$$f : x \mapsto y = f(x), \quad (1)$$

which can be used to identify pickpockets from the regular passenger population.

4.1 A Two-Step Framework

In this study, we develop a two-step framework for identifying pickpocket suspects. On one hand, since the dominant majority of the passengers are regular ones, it is non-trivial to use a classification algorithm. Specifically, the percentage of confirmed pickpockets is extremely low in the passenger population. Simple heuristics like over-sampling and under-sampling would only be helpful for handling moderate class imbalance, but not imbalance as extreme as ours. Building robust machine learning models for such unbalanced data is still an active research area in the literature [21, 4, 16, 17]. On the other hand, utilizing anomaly detection algorithms, which are typically unsupervised, not only cannot scale well, but also may lead to significant false-positives, since many regular passengers who occasionally perform irregular activities can be misclassified as suspects.

To address these challenges, we develop a two-step framework by unifying the unsupervised anomaly detection and supervised classification in a novel way. We show that the two steps can effectively utilize the supervised information, overcome the issue of unbalanced data distribution, and reinforce the learning performances. The overall framework can predict the pickpockets with very low false-positives. In the two-step framework, we approximate the predictive function $f(\cdot)$ as $f(x) = g(x)h(x)$, and equivalently:

$$f(x) = \begin{cases} 0 & \text{if } g(x) = 0 \\ h(x) & \text{if } g(x) = 1 \end{cases} \tag{2}$$

This relationship can also be demonstrated in Figure 8.

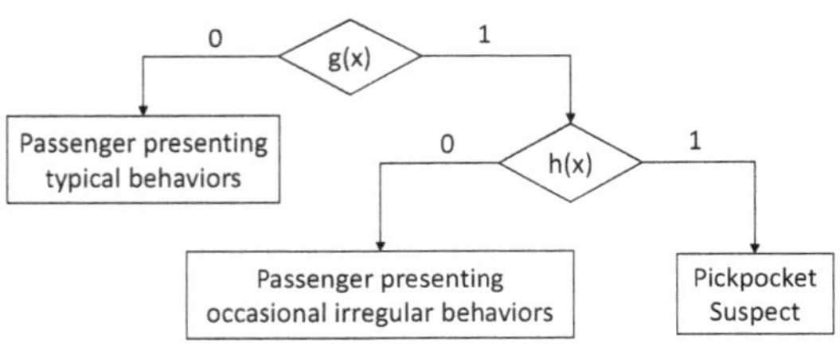

Figure 8: A two-step approach for suspect detection.

In other words, we first use function $g(\cdot)$ (the first step) to filter out regular passengers whose mobility patterns are typical in the majority of the passenger population. If the passenger associated with feature vector x is not filtered out (i.e., $g(x) = 1$), we then use function $h(\cdot)$ (the second step) to detect whether the passenger is a pickpocket suspect. In the following of this section, we develop the two steps (function $g(\cdot)$ and $h(\cdot)$) in our framework.

4.2 Regular Passenger Filtering

The first step in our framework is the regular passenger filtering by anomaly detection algorithm. Its objective is to exclude regular passengers without any suspicious behaviors from later modeling steps. Therefore, we intentionally allow some false-positives in the anomaly detection result.

Many general purpose anomaly detection algorithms can be used to implement the filtering function $g(\cdot)$. In this paper, we use the One-Class SVM (Support Vector Machine) [25] method due to its superior detection accuracy, computing efficiency, and modeling flexibility. One-Class SVM computes non-linear decision boundaries to detect outliers, using appropriate kernel functions and soft margins. The kernel function $\kappa(\cdot,\cdot)$ is defined as

$$\kappa(x_1, x_2) = \langle \phi(x_1), \phi(x_2) \rangle.$$

The function $\phi(\cdot)$ maps the original feature into a high-dimensional kernel space where the optimal decision boundary exists:

$$\widehat{g}(x) = \langle w, \phi(x) \rangle + \rho,$$

and then

$$g(x) = \begin{cases} 1 & \widehat{g}(x) \geq 0 \\ 0 & \widehat{g}(x) < 0 \end{cases} \tag{3}$$

The optimization objective of the One-Class SVM is to:

$$\min_{w,\rho} \frac{1}{2}\|w\|^2 + C\sum_{n=1}^{N} \epsilon_i - \rho$$

subject to $\widehat{g}(x_i) = \langle w, \phi(x_i) \rangle + \rho \leq \epsilon_i$ and $\epsilon_i \geq 0$ for all collected passengers $n = 1, 2, \cdots, N$. The parameter C controls the fraction of anomalies (e.g., x such that $g(x) = 1$) after the filtering.

It can be shown that the optimization process requires $\kappa(\cdot,\cdot)$ instead of an implicit formulation of $\phi(\cdot)$. We use the widely used Gaussian kernel:

$$\kappa(x_1, x_2) = e^{-\|x_1 - x_2\|^2/h}, \tag{4}$$

and learn the best parameter h (bandwidth) by cross-validation.

4.3 Suspect Detection

The second step in our framework is the suspect detection to eventually identify the suspect pickpockets. After the regular passengers filtered by the first step, now we have subjects including the real suspects as well as the false-positives not filtered out by the One-Class SVM. However, by controlling the parameter C of One-Class SVM, the number of the false-positives are limited and comparable with the number of suspects. Now the second step further distinguish these two subsets with supervised information verified by the social media.

Specifically, suppose there are in total M subjects after filtering in the dataset $\{(x_j, y_j) \mid j = 1, \cdots, M\}$, where for the training purpose we have $y_j = 1$ if and only if the passenger associated with feature vector x_j is a verified pickpocket, otherwise $y_j = 0$. Now, to train the suspect detection model, we again use the support vector machine (SVM), where we use the same feature mapping function $\phi(\cdot)$ and kernel function $\kappa(\cdot,\cdot)$ defined in Subsection 4.2. To classify the real suspects and false-positives, the optimal decision hyperplane is: $\widehat{h}(x) = \langle w, \phi(x) \rangle + \rho$ and then $h(x) = \begin{cases} 1 & \widehat{h}(x) \geq 0 \\ 0 & \widehat{h}(x) < 0 \end{cases}$. To compute the optimal w and ρ in $h(\cdot)$, we optimize:

$$\begin{aligned} &\min_{w,\rho,\xi} \frac{1}{2}\|w\|^2 + C\sum_{j=m}^{M} \xi_m \\ &\text{s.t. } \widehat{h}(x) \geq +1 - \xi_i, \forall y_j = 1 \\ &\widehat{h}(x) \leq -1 + \xi_i, \forall y_j = 0 \\ &\xi_j > 0, \forall j \end{aligned} \tag{5}$$

Again, C is trade-off parameter and the computing depends only on the kernel function define in Equation 4.

5. EXPERIMENTAL RESULTS

In this section, we present experimental results with our proposed framework. First, we describe the experimental environments and provide implementation details. Then, in comparison with several baseline methods, we demonstrate the effectiveness of our framework. We will also evaluate the usefulness of feature extracted in Table 2. Finally, we show practical usage of our methods in a real-world system.

5.1 Experiment Settings

Datasets. We conduct our experiments on real-world datasets containing over 1.6 billion transit records, as discussed in Section 2. We split the data into historical training set and evaluation test set. Specifically, training set covers three months (from April to June, 2014) and test set comes from the following two weeks (in July 2014). Also, from the training set, we filter out passengers whose maximum number of daily records is no more than three.

Platform. All experiments were conducted on a Windows Server 2012 64-bit system (4-CPU, each with 2.6GHz with Quad-Core, and 128G main memory). All algorithms and our real-world system were implemented with Java.

Baselines. The method is compared with a variety of competing methods grouped into the following categories:

Classification methods (CM). The classification methods, including logistic regression (LR), decision trees (DT), and support vector machines (SVM), are straightforwardly fitted with the training set and evaluated with the test set. Since the proportion of positive instances are extremely low, the classification problem is unbalanced and it's expected to observe high Type II Error. In experiments, we under-sample the negative instances to balance the data and improve the results. For each method, we repeat the sampling 10 times and report the averaged results.

Anomaly detection (AD). Anomaly detection methods, such as one-class SVM (OCSVM) and local outlier factor (LOF), seem more appropriate for our setting. Among them, LOF is unsupervised, finding outliers by measuring the local deviation of a given data point with respect to its neighbors. OC-SVM can be fitted in a supervised manner, with only the negative instances in the training set, to identify the suspects.

Two-step (TS) methods. As aforementioned, our approach is a TS method, consisting of unsupervised one-class SVM and supervised two-class SVM. For comparison, we also experiment using the LOF as the first step to identify potential suspects, and further use a classification method (*e.g.*, LR or DT) the second step, to filter out the false positives.

For all the methods with parameters, we optimize the parameters with 10-fold cross-validation by further dividing the training set into 80% for model fitting and 20% for parameter validation.

Evaluation metrics. We use *precision, recall, and F-score* computed with test set to evaluate the performances of different methods. The precision is the number of correctly identified positives divided by the number of identified positives instances. The recall is the number of correctly identified positives divided by the number of all positive instances in the test set. Then, the F-score is defined as:

$$\text{F-score} = 2 \times \frac{precision \times recall}{precision + recall}.$$

5.2 Results Summary

Table 3 summarizes the performances of our method and the baselines listed above.

Table 3: A Performance Comparison.

Algorithm	Precision	Recall	F-score	Run Time(s)
		CM Methods		
DT	0.002	0.451	0.004	44.81
LR	0.003	0.476	0.006	36.72
SVM	0.005	0.512	0.009	21.31
		AD Methods		
LOF	0.004	0.560	0.009	300+
OCSVM	0.015	0.583	0.029	39.67
		TS Methods		
LOF+DT	0.011	0.780	0.022	301.18+
LOF+LR	0.016	0.829	0.031	301.16+
OCSVM+DT	0.053	0.878	0.099	41.19
TS-SVM	**0.071**	**0.927**	**0.133**	**41.05**

We have several interesting observations which confirm our research motivation. First, the precisions of all one-step methods are very low, especially for classification methods including DT, LR, and SVM. The AD methods perform somehow better, but still lower than our two-step framework. In contrast, all the two-step combinations significantly improve the precisions, among which, our TS-SVM performs best. This observation shows that the two-step approach can effectively reduce the false-positives. Second, two-step methods also perform better in terms of other metrics. For example, the recall of our TS-SVM is consistently above 90%, by finding the detection/classification boundaries in the non-linear kernel space. Finally, given the excellent recall of TS-SVM, we contend that it's "ground-truth" precision can be higher than the reported 7%. The reason is that not all the suspects have been caught or reported.

5.3 Feature Analysis

To further study the discriminative power of the features, we evaluate the performance of our framework (TS-SVM) with different feature combinations.

As shown in Figure 9, we use Db, Sc, and Hb to represent the *daily behavior*, *social comparison*, and *historical behavior* features, respectively. Most significantly, the precision of the daily behavior features is improved by the social comparison and further the historical behaviors. Such improvements can also be observed for other metrics in the table.

We also empirically compare the modeling performances on weekdays and weekends. As expected, since the human mobilities in weekends are more complicated, the detection accuracy of our method is slightly lower on weekends.

6. DEPLOYMENT AND INSIGHTS

With the automatic feature extraction and two-step suspect detection model described above, we developed a decision support system for the security personnel to easily spot

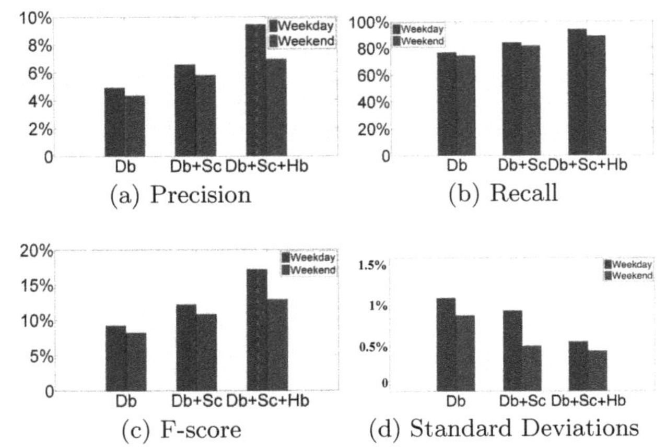

(a) Precision (b) Recall

(c) F-score (d) Standard Deviations

Figure 9: The impact of feature combinations.

pickpocket hotspots, and crack down on the suspects efficiently at the crime scene. In this section, we demonstrate how our system works in practice.

6.1 A Prototype System

The prototype system was implemented using bootstrap[4], Java and SparkQL. Figure 10 is a screenshot of the graphical user interface (GUI), which can be viewed on a computing terminal or a mobile device. The GUI has the following five basic components, which allow users to view suspect analytics at different levels of details.

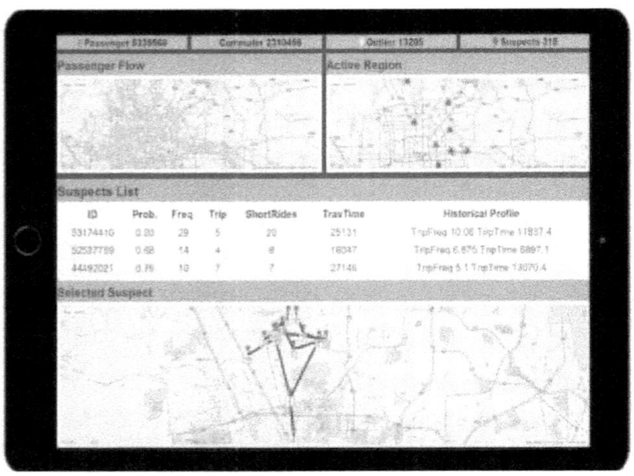

Figure 10: A screenshot of the prototype system.

Statistics. Summary statistics about the transit system status are provided at the top of the screen, which includes the total numbers of passengers, commuters, outliers, and suspects, respectively. The user is allowed to specify the time window for these statistics, in terms of the number of days, in the settings.

Passenger Flows. The density of passenger flows have a high correlation with pickpocket activities. The live state of passenger flow is shown with a heat map, where the density of passenger flow of each station is expressed by blending the color between green and red. (Redder means higher density.) This map helps users find areas with more traffic and thus are more vulnerable to theft.

Active Regions. Active regions of suspects at the city level is visualized in the "active regions" map. These active regions are indicated by the blue flashing circles, which are found by calculating the centroids of a DBSCAN algorithm. The user can inspect a specific area by zooming in.

Suspect List. Passengers identified as suspects will be listed on the "suspect list." Profiles of these suspect, such as smart card ID number, total travel time, riding frequency, the number of trips and the number of short rides, will be displayed by default. Quantile score against the social norm, historical profile information, and system determined likelihood of a suspect, are also available. The user is allowed to choose which features to display and to sort with.

Selected Suspect. When a suspect on the list is selected, his or her trajectory, as represented by linking the boarding and exiting stations, will be displayed in the "selected suspect" panel.

The database which stores identified suspect records is updated every day with newly collected transactions data. The two-step suspect detection model is trained offline, so that detectives can get an instant result when they interact with the system.

6.2 Examples of Passenger Behaviors

As mentioned in the "passenger flow" function above, we visualize the passenger movement patterns on the city map, which will be used for analyzing the behaviors of different types of passengers.

Figure 11 provides examples of representative movement patterns in different passenger groups in Beijing on a typical day from 8:00 a.m. to 11:00 a.m. Recall that each curve in the figure represents the transition between a pair of origin and destination, and the color represents traffic density between regions (red=high, green=low). In addition, the more curves through the same node means the more routes pass through that region.

The overall passenger flow, as shown in Figure 11(a), provides users a bird's view to know which regions have dense traffic at the city level. We can see that the Huilongguan area, Tiantongyuan area, Military Museum, CBD area, and the Dongdan area have the highest density. In order to understand the transit purposes, we classify passengers by the major categories of functional regions they visit. Besides Figure 11(a), which covers primarily regular commuters (*i.e.*, those who visit residence, workplace and transit regions), Figure 11(b) shows that visitors frequently visit Yuanmingyuan, Tiananmen, and Nanluoguxiang, whereas Figure 11(c) shows that shoppers tend to visit regions like Wangfujing and Xidan. Most of the normal travels are one-way or round-trip with clear directions. In contrast, pickpockets behave quite differently. As visualized in Figure 11(d), pickpockets tend to present a wandering pattern without a clear destination. They tend to make frequent, random stops with short travel segments. They also like to visit a variety of functional regions, such as transit hubs (*e.g.*, Xizhimen), shopping regions(*e.g.*, Wangfujing), and scenic spots (*e.g.*,

[4] Bootstrap (https://wrapbootstrap.com) is a web client framework.

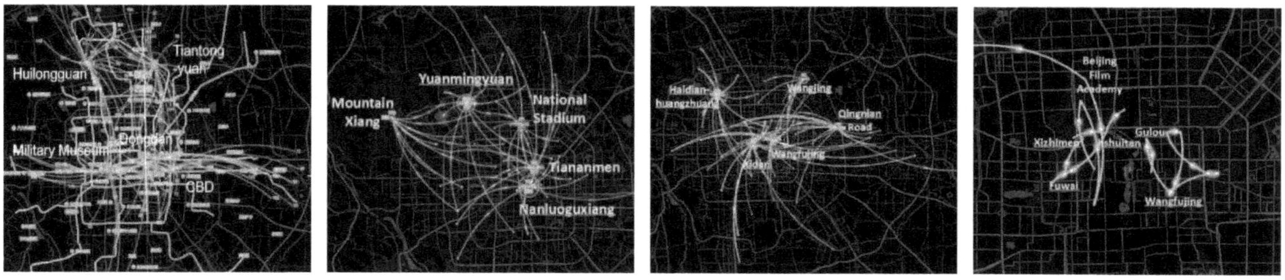

(a) all passengers (b) visitors (c) shoppers (d) thieves

Figure 11: Movement patterns of different type of passengers.

Gulou), whereas most regular passengers only visit one functional region during a short period of time.

7. RELATED WORK

As urban sensing data, such as GPS traces, call details records, and smart card logs, grow ubiquitous, research efforts devoted to analyzing such data has resulted in a number of works in recent years. In this section, we provide a brief review of the related work, categorized into two groups.

7.1 Passengers Activity Patterns

The first group of literature focuses on finding patterns in passenger activity records. Such knowledge can be useful in a variety of applications, and plays a vital role in effectively finding and satisfying passenger needs. Examples include assessing the performance of the transit network, identifying and optimizing problematic or flawed bus routes, improving the accuracy of passenger flow forecast between two regions, and making service adjustments that accommodate variations in ridership on different days. In particular, using AFC data, [3] estimates the crowdedness of various stations in the transportation network. [22] measures the variability of transit behaviors on different days of the week. In addition, different studies have investigated unique characteristics of traveling patterns of the elderly [27], students, and adults [22], which provide interesting insights for understanding behavioral differences of sub-populations.

It has been suggested that human mobility patterns follow a high degree of spatial and temporal regularity, and are thus highly predictable [9, 26]. Existing studies in discovering trip patterns typically aim at discovering movement patterns by finding frequently visited places of regular passengers, who travel with the same sequence of places at the similar time of day. For example, [5] identifies spatiotemporal patterns from GPS traces of taxis for night bus route planning. [19] tries to reflect the common routing preference of the past passengers by finding the most frequent path of a certain time period. [6] discovers and explains movement patterns of a set of moving objects (e.g. traffic management, birds migration, disease spreading).

7.2 Abnormal Traveling Behavior Detection

Existing studies on detecting anomalies in urban sensing data can be divided into two categories: those based on locations, and those on trajectories.

Along the line of location-based anomaly detection, [28] presents a framework that learns the context of different functional regions in a city, which provides the basis of our feature extraction approach. Besides, [15] attempts to discover casual relationships among spatiotemporal outliers. [24] mines representative terms from social media that people posted when location-relevant events happen in the city, such as accidents and protests. [10] discovers black-hole or volcano patterns in human mobility data in a city, which can quickly identify gathering events, such as football matches and concerts. Detection of such anomalies can help sensing abnormal events, and provide input for intelligent decision support, such as smoothing the traffic flow [10].

The main goal of trajectory based anomaly detection is to find a small percentage of individuals, whose movement traces are different from the general population. One example is to identify fraudulent taxi driving behaviors. A large number of studies have investigated trajectory based anomaly detection using data mining techniques, such as graph based [6], clustering based [20, 3, 1], local/context-aware based [2, 13], dimension reduction based [11] and evidence based (*e.g.*, using Dempster-Shafer theory [8]). While the trajectory of pickpockets with features that are implicit, previously unknown, and potentially useful from large datasets, pickpocket suspect detection based on AFC records is a novel problem that has not been considered in the literature, and is quite challenging.

8. CONCLUSION

In this paper, we developed a suspect detection and tracking system by mining large-scale transit records. The system can help identify pickpocket suspects' and enable active surveillance in high-risk areas. Specifically, we first constructed a feature representation for profiling passengers. Then, we established a novel two-step framework to distinguish regular passengers from pickpocket suspects. Finally, we leverage real-world datasets from multiple sources for model training and validation, and implement a prototype system for end users. Experimental results on real-world data showed the effectiveness of our proposed approach.

9. ACKNOWLEDGMENTS

This research was supported in part by National Natural Science Foundation of China (No. 51408018), National Natural Science Foundation of China (No. 71329201), National High Technology Research and Development Program (863, 2013AA01A601).

References

[1] Paul Bouman, Evelien Van der Hurk, Leo Kroon, Ting Li, and Peter Vervest. Detecting activity patterns from smart card data. In *BNAIC*, 2013.

[2] Markus M. Breunig, Hans-Peter Kriegel, Raymond T. Ng, and Jörg Sander. LOF: Identifying density-based local outliers. *SIGMOD Rec.*, 29(2):93–104, May 2000.

[3] Irina Ceapa, Chris Smith, and Licia Capra. Avoiding the crowds: understanding tube station congestion patterns from trip data. In *UrbComp*, pages 134–141, 2012.

[4] Olivier Chapelle, Eren Manavoglu, and Romer Rosales. Simple and scalable response prediction for display advertising. *ACM Trans. Intell. Syst. Technol.*, 5(4):61:1–61:34, 2014.

[5] Chao Chen, Daqing Zhang, Zhi-Hua Zhou, Nan Li, Tülin Atmaca, and Shijian Li. B-planner: Night bus route planning using large-scale taxi gps traces. In *PerCom*, pages 225–233, 2013.

[6] Ticiana L. Coelho da Silva, José A. F. de Macêdo, and Marco A. Casanova. Discovering frequent mobility patterns on moving object data. In *MobiGIS*, pages 60–67, 2014.

[7] Marcus Felson and Ronald V Clarke. Opportunity makes the thief: Practical theory for crime prevention. Report 98, Policing and Reducing Crime Unit: Police Research Series, 1998.

[8] Yong Ge, Hui Xiong, Chuanren Liu, and Zhi-Hua Zhou. A taxi driving fraud detection system. In *ICDM*, pages 181–190, 2011.

[9] Marta C Gonzalez, Cesar A Hidalgo, and Albert-László Barabási. Understanding individual human mobility patterns. *Nature*, 453(7196):779–782, 2008.

[10] Liang Hong, Yu Zheng, Duncan Yung, Jingbo Shang, and Lei Zou. Detecting urban black holes based on human mobility data. In *GIS*, 2015.

[11] Shan Jiang, Joseph Ferreira Jr, and Marta C Gonzalez. Discovering urban spatial-temporal structure from human activity patterns. In *UrbComp*, pages 95–102, 2012.

[12] Chuanren Liu, Fei Wang, Jianying Hu, and Hui Xiong. Temporal phenotyping from longitudinal electronic health records: A graph based framework. In *KDD*, pages 705–714. ACM, 2015.

[13] Chuanren Liu, Hui Xiong, Yong Ge, Wei Geng, and Matt Perkins. A stochastic model for context-aware anomaly detection in indoor location traces. In *ICDM*, pages 449–458, 2012.

[14] Chuanren Liu, Kai Zhang, Hui Xiong, Guofei Jiang, and Qiang Yang. Temporal skeletonization on sequential data: Patterns, categorization, and visualization. *IEEE Transactions on Knowledge and Data Engineering*, 28(1):211–223, Jan 2016.

[15] Wei Liu, Yu Zheng, Sanjay Chawla, Jing Yuan, and Xie Xing. Discovering spatio-temporal causal interactions in traffic data streams. In *KDD*, pages 1010–1018, 2011.

[16] Xianglong Liu, Cheng Deng, Bo Lang, Dacheng Tao, and Xuelong Li. Query-adaptive reciprocal hash tables for nearest neighbor search. *IEEE Transactions on Image Processing*, 25(2):907–919, 2016.

[17] Xianglong Liu, Yadong Mu, Bo Lang, and Shih-Fu Chang. Mixed image-keyword query adaptive hashing over multilabel images. *ACM Transactions on Multimedia Computing, Communications, and Applications*, 10(2):22:1–22:21, 2014.

[18] Yanchi Liu, Chuanren Liu, Jing Yuan, Lian Duan, Yanjie Fu, Hui Xiong, Songhua Xu, and Junjie Wu. Intelligent bus routing with heterogeneous human mobility patterns. *Knowledge and Information Systems*, Forthcoming (Accepted as of Feb 2016).

[19] Wuman Luo, Haoyu Tan, Lei Chen, and Lionel M Ni. Finding time period-based most frequent path in big trajectory data. In *SIGMOD*, pages 713–724, 2013.

[20] Xiaolei Ma, Yao-Jan Wu, Yinhai Wang, Feng Chen, and Jianfeng Liu. Mining smart card data for transit riders travel patterns. *Transportation Research Part C*, 36:1–12, 2013.

[21] H. Brendan McMahan, Gary Holt, D. Sculley, Michael Young, Dietmar Ebner, Julian Grady, Lan Nie, Todd Phillips, Eugene Davydov, Daniel Golovin, Sharat Chikkerur, Dan Liu, Martin Wattenberg, Arnar Mar Hrafnkelsson, Tom Boulos, and Jeremy Kubica. Ad click prediction: A view from the trenches. In *KDD*, pages 1222–1230, 2013.

[22] Catherine Morency, Martin Trépanier, and Bruno Agard. Analysing the variability of transit users behaviour with smart card data. In *ITSC*, pages 44–49, 2006.

[23] Graeme R Newman and Megan M McNally. Identity theft literature review. Report 210459, United States Department of Justice, July 2005.

[24] Bei Pan, Yu Zheng, David Wilkie, and Cyrus Shahabi. Crowd sensing of traffic anomalies based on human mobility and social media. In *GIS*, pages 344–353, 2013.

[25] Bernhard Schölkopf, John C. Platt, John C. Shawe-Taylor, Alex J. Smola, and Robert C. Williamson. Estimating the support of a high-dimensional distribution. *Neural Computation*, 13(7):1443–1471, 2001.

[26] Chaoming Song, Zehui Qu, Nicholas Blumm, and Albert-László Barabási. Limits of predictability in human mobility. *Science*, 327(5968):1018–1021, 2010.

[27] Myung Joon Sung. Analysis of travel patterns of the elderly using transit smart card data. In *TRB*, volume 11-2357, 2011.

[28] Jing Yuan, Yu Zheng, and Xing Xie. Discovering regions of different functions in a city using human mobility and pois. In *KDD*, pages 186–194, 2012.

[29] Kai Zheng, Yu Zheng, Nicholas Jing Yuan, Shuo Shang, and Xiaofang Zhou. Online discovery of gathering patterns over trajectories. *IEEE Transactions on Knowledge and Data Engineering*, 26(8):1974–1988, 2014.

[30] Hengshu Zhu, Chuanren Liu, Yong Ge, Hui Xiong, and Enhong Chen. Popularity modeling for mobile apps: A sequential approach. *Cybernetics, IEEE Transactions on*, 45(7):1303–1314, 2015.

Email Volume Optimization at LinkedIn

Rupesh Gupta, Guanfeng Liang, Hsiao-Ping Tseng,
Ravi Kiran Holur Vijay, Xiaoyu Chen, Rómer Rosales
LinkedIn Corporation
Mountain View, CA, USA
{rugupta, gliang, htseng}@linkedin.com,
rvijay@pinterest.com, {xochen, rrosales}@linkedin.com

ABSTRACT

Online social networking services distribute various types of messages geared towards providing increased value to their members. Common types of messages include news, connection requests, membership notifications, promotions, and event notifications. Such communication, if used judiciously, can provide an enormous value to the members. However sending a message for every instance of news, connection request, or the like can result in an overwhelming number of messages in a member's mailbox. This may result in reduced effectiveness of communication if the messages are not sufficiently relevant to the member's interests, and potentially a poor brand perception. In this paper, we discuss our strategy and experience with regard to the problem of email volume optimization at LinkedIn. In particular, we present a cost-benefit analysis of sending emails, the key factors to administer an effective volume optimization, our algorithm for volume optimization, the architecture of the supporting system, and experimental results from online A/B tests.

Keywords

Machine learning, optimization, email

1. INTRODUCTION

LinkedIn and other online social networking services provide members with an easy way to connect and exchange information. They facilitate exchange of information by giving members the opportunity to send private messages to other members, upload and share rich media with other members, self-organize into interest groups around a subject matter and ask/answer questions, subscribe to channels delivering news on topics of interest, etc. The networking services help members keep up with this information through pull-model based in-app services like feed and in-app notifications, as well as push-model based content distribution services like email and push notifications. Conventionally, members can subscribe to receive email communication regarding news, connection requests, membership and event notifications. At times the social networking service may also use the email communication channel for the purpose of promotions or product marketing. Such email communication is of special interest to a networking service because of its potential in providing valuable information to its members without requiring them to be actively logged in to the mobile or web applications of the networking service. Email communication, if used judiciously, can help provide enormous value to the members and as a consequence increase engagement and value to the networking service. However, sending an email for every instance of news, connection request, or the like can result in a member receiving an overwhelming number of email messages. This can hamper the effectiveness of communication if the email messages are not sufficiently relevant to the member's interests, as the member might start to indiscriminately disregard all messages received from the networking service (including the important ones).

For a social networking service, email communication can help drive mid and long-term value to members. This value can be measured in various ways, including member engagement. Member engagement often relates to members visiting the mobile or web applications of the networking service more often. However since optimizing for member visit frequency is often difficult due to long-term feedback loops, proxies that are readily measurable with little feedback delay are often optimized in practice. Most of the industrial research and development in the area of email optimization has been in the context of driving up click-through rates of email marketing campaigns [1]. These approaches were inadequate for our problem setting.

Email communication from LinkedIn to members comprises of several different types of emails, with each type corresponding to a product vertical as illustrated in Figure 1. Some sample email templates are shown in Figure 2. As highlighted in the email template of Figure 2(b), LinkedIn allows members to control their communication experience of a particular type of email through the *change frequency* or the *unsubscribe* options on any email of that type. Alternatively, members can personalize their communication experience of all types of emails through the communication settings panel under the user account settings tab on the web or mobile application, as shown in Figure 3. In this panel, for each type of email, a member can choose to turn off communication completely, or to receive communication at event-occurrence, daily, weekly or *recommended* cadence. The *recommended* setting is designed to enable the member to receive email communication regarding only the most relevant information in a timely manner. LinkedIn op-

KDD '16, August 13-17, 2016, San Francisco, CA, USA

DOI: http://dx.doi.org/10.1145/2939672.2939692

Figure 1: Types of emails from LinkedIn

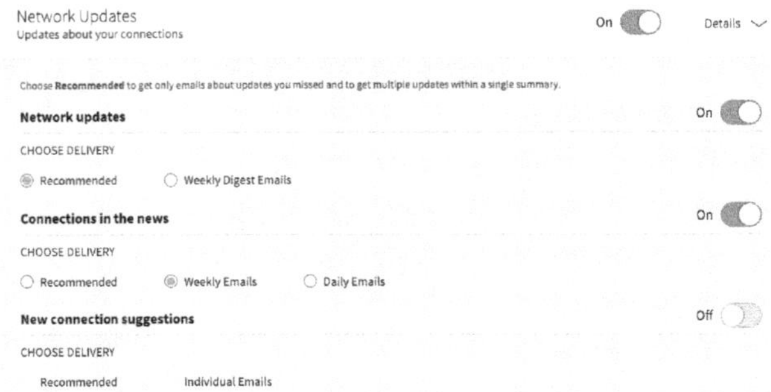

Figure 3: Email communication settings

timizes the communication experience of the member when the member opts-in to this setting.

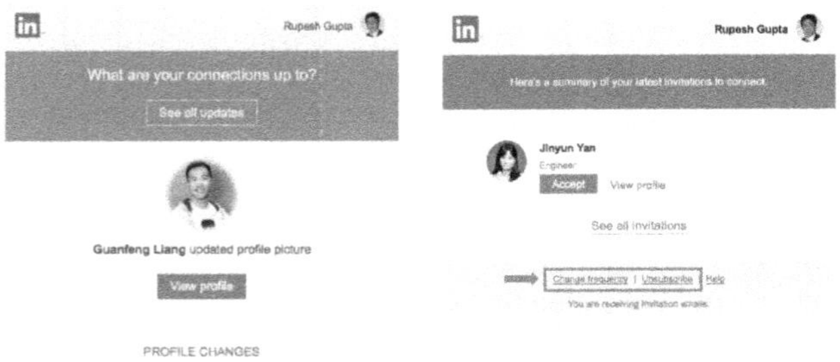

(a) News feed (b) Contacts

Figure 2: Sample email templates

Optimizing the communication experience of a member entails optimization on several fronts, such as, volume optimization, delivery time optimization, frequency control, and channel selection. Each of these problems pose unique challenges which merit careful attention to detail. One of these problems, namely volume optimization, is discussed at length in this paper.

Since email communication can provide a large value to the members, it is worth investing in methods that can maximize this value and at the same time minimize unnecessary email. Naive reduction of email volume can have adverse effects on member value and growth of the service. Hence, intelligent algorithms are required to identify the emails which may be dropped (not sent). The decision to send or drop an email needs be based on the likelihood of the targeted user deriving a high value from the email. We can indirectly infer the value based on the user's reaction to the email. The user may interact positively with the email by either viewing the email or also by clicking a link within the email which will typically bring her to the application. Alternatively, the user may react negatively to the email by either ignoring the email, or by clicking on the *unsubscribe* option within the email, or by reporting the email as spam to her email service provider. Ideally the networking service would like to cut down on email volume in a way such that the positive interactions are maximized and negative interactions are minimized. It is evident that this would require optimizing across multiple different objectives. This paper is about the challenges, approaches, and experiences relating to email volume optimization at LinkedIn. Our contributions are summarized below:

- We present a comprehensive cost-benefit analysis of email communication in Section 3.
- We describe our response prediction modeling process, as well as the mathematical formulation of volume optimization as a multi-objective optimization problem in Section 4.
- We outline the architecture of our system supporting volume optimization in Section 5.
- We report real world experimental results based on online A/B tests in Section 6.

2. RELATED WORK

Whittaker et al. [2] published the first user experience study on email overload in 1996. The study exposed the problem of information management, with the subjects finding it challenging to organize their cluttered inboxes and identifying important emails. Sixteen years later, Grevet et al. [3] conducted a quantitative analysis of users' inboxes on Gmail and concluded that large email volume and poor email organization continue to remain problems. In a unique study published in [4], the authors were able to quantitatively establish the advantages of cutting down emails in a workplace. These included improved work quality and lower stress levels, among others.

In light of the above, several ideas and tools have been conceived to help users manage email overload. Some of the most promising research has been targeted at automated classification of emails into different priority levels or content categories. Early attempts at email prioritization can be found in [5] where the authors train a linear classifier on a small email corpus, using only email features such as text, message length, etc. More recently, Yoo et al. [6] have proposed methods for a more personalized email prioritization where the feature vector is enriched with personal features inferred from the social graph. Lu et al. [7] on the other hand make use of explicit personal features in the form of a user's interaction history with messages.

While email prioritization tries to address email overload from the recipient side, email volume optimization is an attempt to address email overload from the sender side. If the sender had a mechanism to estimate the priority of each email message for its targeted recipient then the sender could decide to drop the messages with low priority, as the recipient is likely to ignore those emails anyway. However the decision to drop messages in the recipient's interest can conflict with the sender's interest. Hence, email volume optimization requires the sender to make a trade-off between multiple different objectives. We have not been able to trace any published literature on email volume optimization *per se*, but there is literature demonstrating effectiveness of multi-objective optimization in various problems pertaining to web applications. Agarwal et al. have employed multi-objective optimization for personalized click shaping in online content recommendation in [8] and for displaying promotional widgets on web applications under business constraints in [9].

3. COST-BENEFIT ANALYSIS

In order to empirically examine the cost and benefit of emails for LinkedIn, we set up a small user bucket as follows. For each member in this bucket, we selected a random number in $[0, 1]$ as the probability with which each email message generated for this member was dropped. We denote this bucket as the *random-drop* bucket. The remaining users received all emails generated for them. We denote this bucket as the *send-all* bucket.

We collected data from this experiment over a period of one week. Over this period, a large number of unique users in the *random-drop* bucket received several different types of emails. Each type of email contained information corresponding to a particular product-vertical and contained at least one link, clicking on which would bring the user to a page under the product-vertical on the mobile or web application. Important user interactions with emails, such as email view, email click, unsubscribing from an email type and reporting an email as spam were tracked. In addition, user sessions were tracked and categorized into two categories, viz., downstream (email triggered) and organic, based on the following attribution model. Any session that a user started within 15 minutes of clicking a link within an email was attributed to that email, and categorized as an email triggered downstream session. Any page view and in-app action performed within a downstream session, such as profile view, job view, search, invitations-to-connect, feed like/comment/share, etc., was also categorized as downstream. All remaining sessions were categorized as organic.

3.1 Benefit of Sending Email

Emails were found to drive a significant percentage of in-app engagement. As tabulated in Table 3.1, we observed 2.6% less page views from members in the *random-drop* bucket compared to the members in the *send-all* bucket. In other words, members who received all email messages generated for them performed 2.6% more page views than the members who randomly received about half of the email messages which were generated for them. Similarly, a substantial loss in page views was observed for pages under various product verticals.

Total	-2.6%
Homepage	-1.4%
Jobs	-4%
Profile	-4.5%
PYMK	-4.5%
Search	-4%

Table 1: Delta in page views for various product-verticals. *random-drop* vs. *send-all*

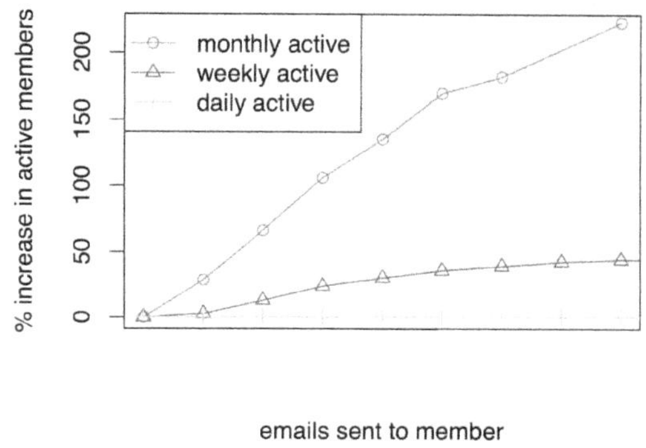

Figure 4: % increase in active members with increase in emails sent to member

Figure 5: % increase in downstream page views by a member with increase in emails sent to member

To understand this better we performed a fine grained analysis of members in the *random-drop* bucket. We divided the members into four segments based on the frequency of their visits to the mobile or web application before the start of the experiment. These four segments were: daily-active (visited everyday), weekly-active (visited once a week), monthly-active (visited once a month) and dormant (remaining). This segmentation is also meaningful from another point of view: about the same number of emails were being generated for members within a given segment. No emails were being generated for a vast majority of members within the dormant segment. As shown in Figure 4, it was found that the number of active members (who visited the application at least once over the course of the experiment) increased with an increase in the number of email messages sent to members. For example, from the plot for monthly-active members, we can say that if x of these members are active when no emails are sent to these members, then more than $2x$ members will be active if a large number of emails are sent to these members. This trend is evident for all member segments except the daily-active segment, in which 100% of the members visit organically without the need for any email triggers. However even within this segment members were found to perform more downstream page views with an increase in the number of emails sent, as shown in Figure 5.

To analyze the impact of downstream page views on in-app actions we computed the contribution of downstream in-app actions towards the overall in-app actions. We found that downstream in-app actions can constitute 10% to 40% of the total in-app actions for certain important actions, such as viewing a job, sending an invitation to connect, etc. These findings are shown in Figure 6. Also shown in the same figure is the percentage of members who performed specific in-app actions only as downstream actions. For example, of all the members who performed action1 on the mobile or web application, about 12% of those performed that action only after clicking a link within an email which brought them to the application. This implies that a significant number of members rely on the receipt of email to carry out certain tasks on LinkedIn.

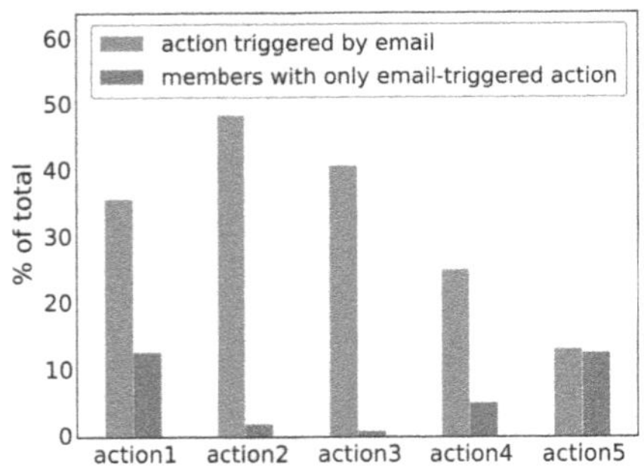

Figure 6: Contribution of downstream in-app actions to overall in-app actions

3.2 Cost of Sending Email

We found that excessive email communication could have several negative consequences. We observed 45% more number of negative responses to emails in the *send-all* bucket compared to the *random-drop* bucket. These negative responses were in the form of clicking the unsubscribe option within an email, or reporting an email as spam to the email service provider. This was not surprising since sending more number of emails is likely to result in more number of responses, positive and negative. However, unlike a positive response to an email, the scope of a negative response to an email does not end at that particular email. If a member clicks the unsubscribe option within an email, we lose the ability to send any emails of that type to that member in the future. If a large number of members report emails from a particular sender as spam to their email service providers, then this can result in an email service provider blocking and filtering all emails from that sender [10]. In general, such deliverability issues are not easy to resolve.

Excessive email communication was also found to result in the members missing important emails. Owing to limited time and attention spans in humans, user attention was found to get divided across important and less important emails. Here is how we discovered this. We picked four types of emails that were designed specifically to serve an important purpose for LinkedIn. We selected members in the *random-drop* bucket who received an equal number (=4) of these important emails but different number of total emails. For this set of members we plotted the average number of clicks on these important emails by a member against the total number of emails received by that member. This plot

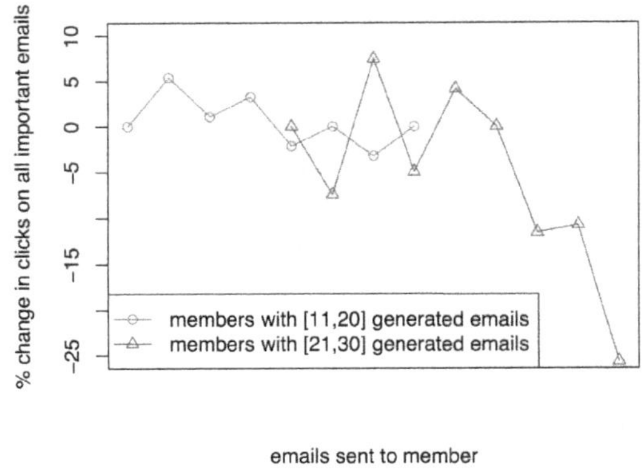

Figure 7: % Δ in clicks on important emails by member with increase in total emails sent to member

is shown in Figure 7 for two groups of members, viz., members for whom a small number of emails were generated, and members for whom a large number of emails were generated. A downward trend is readily visible in both these groups.

Irrelevant email communication (irrelevant to the recipient) can at times also affect the brand perception of a corporation.

4. PROBLEM FORMULATION

As established in the previous section, on the one hand email is an important driver in-app engagement, but on the other hand excessive email can also have severe negative consequences. It goes without saying that the sender needs a way to identify those emails which are important for the sender, and at the same time relevant to the recipient. Then the sender can send only these emails, dropping the rest. In other words, the sender would like to minimize the number of emails sent, in a way so as to maximize the positive outcome and minimize the negative outcome.

In this section, we describe how we formulate email volume optimization at LinkedIn as a Multi-Objective Optimization (MOO) problem in order to obtain optimal trade-off points involving positive and negative outcomes of sending emails. We also describe how the MOO problem is solved and how the solution to the problem is actually used in a production system. But first, we will explain why we think MOO is the right approach.

4.1 Why MOO

For the purpose of simplicity of exposition, let's consider only one kind of positive consequence and only one kind of negative consequence of each email. Let's consider a downstream session as the positive outcome and an unsubscribe or reporting of an email as spam (denoting either one as a complaint) as the negative outcome. Then, on one hand we would like to maximize the number of downstream sessions and on the other hand we would like to minimize the number of emails sent and the number of resulting complaints. For each generated email e, let's assume we can obtain estimates for

$$P_{sess}(\mathbf{x}_e) = \Pr(\text{downstream session from } e \mid e \text{ is sent}) \text{ and}$$
$$P_{comp}(\mathbf{x}_e) = \Pr(\text{complaint from } e \mid e \text{ is sent})$$

by using email features $\mathbf{x}_e$ in the utility prediction models

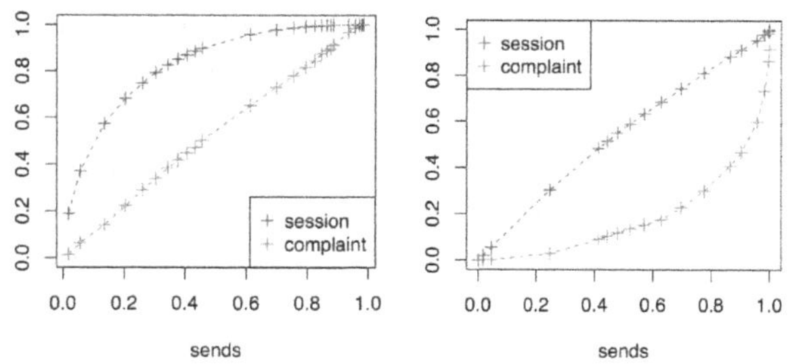

(a) Thresholding on P_{sess} (b) Thresholding on P_{comp}

Figure 8: Trade-off achieved using naive thresholding approach

from Section 4.3. Since each email e is targeted to a particular user, we are assuming that $\mathbf{x}_e$ will also include features of the targeted user.

One simple and intuitive approach for achieving our goal could be to rank-order emails based on P_{sess} and only send the top emails for which P_{sess} is greater than some threshold T_{sess}. Another simple approach could be to only send those emails for which P_{comp} is smaller than a threshold T_{comp}.

In Figure 8 we plot the fraction of sessions and complaints obtained at various threshold values, using these two naive approaches. The points on the curves are computed by simulating the thresholding process with various values of T_{sess} and T_{comp}. Both x and y axes are normalized by the simulation result at the point where no threshold is applied, i.e., the point where no email is dropped.

As we can see from Figure 8(a), thresholding on P_{sess} achieves a very nice trade-off between sessions and sends: we could choose a point on the trade-off curve where the send volume is reduced dramatically with little loss in sessions. For example, we could send only 60% of the emails and still maintain roughly 93% of the maximum achievable sessions. However, this thresholding approach achieves a poor trade-off between complaints and sends: complaints are proportional to sends, which is no better than dropping emails at random. On the other hand thresholding on P_{comp} achieves a good trade-off between complaints and sends but a poor one between sessions and sends, as shown in Figure 8(b).

Clearly, none of these naive thresholding approaches yields a satisfactory trade-off point where the send volume is reduced with a minimal loss in sessions and a significant drop in complaints, simultaneously. Loosely speaking, an ideal solution would achieve a sessions-sends trade-off similar to the blue curve in Figure 8(a), and a complaints-sends trade-off similar to the red curve in Figure 8(b). More formally, we would like a solution to have a mechanism that can output *optimal* combinations of sends, sessions and complaints.

4.2 MOO Formulation

In this section we develop on our running example of finding an optimal trade-off between sends, sessions and complaints and present our MOO methodology for email volume optimization. While the following discussion is based on the example of three utilities it should become clear that the formulation presented here readily generalizes to an arbitrary number of utilities of similar nature.

4.2.1 Primal Formulation

Consider any given window of time starting from now, say, the week starting today. Let's assume we have the entire set of emails which will be generated over this week and denote it as E. Also assume that each email $e \in E$ will be one of T different email types. Let $t = 1, \ldots, T$ be an index over the email types and E_t denote the set of emails of type t. Then $e \in E_t$ would mean that email e is of email type t.

We assign a decision variable $z_e = \Pr(\text{sending } e)$ to each email e. The set $\mathbf{z} = \{z_e : e \in E\}$ is referred to as the serving plan, which is to be optimized. We now formulate this optimization problem as a constrained linear programming problem (LP) as follows.

$$\min_{\mathbf{z}} \quad \sum_{e \in E} z_e \tag{1}$$

$$\text{s.t.} \quad \sum_{e \in E} P_{sess}(\mathbf{x}_e) z_e \geq \alpha_{global} \times \text{maxGlobalSess} \tag{2}$$

$$\sum_{e \in E_t} P_{sess}(\mathbf{x}_e) z_e \geq \alpha_t \times \text{maxLocalSess}_t, \quad \forall t \tag{3}$$

$$\sum_{e \in E} P_{comp}(\mathbf{x}_e) z_e \leq \beta_{global} \times \text{maxGlobalComp} \tag{4}$$

$$\sum_{e \in E_t} P_{comp}(\mathbf{x}_e) z_e \leq \beta_t \times \text{maxLocalComp}_t, \quad \forall t \tag{5}$$

$$0 \leq z_e \leq 1 \quad \forall e \tag{6}$$

In this formulation:

- The objective $\sum_{e \in E} z_e$ in (1) is the expected number of emails sent under serving plan $\mathbf{z}$, across all email types.

- The first constraint (2) specifies the target for the global session count. On the left hand side, $\sum_{e \in E} P_{sess}(\mathbf{x}_e) z_e$ is the expected session count under serving plan $\mathbf{z}$ across all email types. On the right hand side,

  $$\text{maxGlobalSess} = \sum_{e \in E} P_{sess}(\mathbf{x}_e)$$

  is the expected session count if all emails in E are sent and $\alpha_{global} \in [0, 1]$ is the fraction of this maximum achievable session count that we aim to retain.

  It is worth pointing out that in expressing the total session count as a summation over the session probabilities of individual emails we are making an independence assumption between emails. In other words, we are making an assumption that the send/drop decision for an email does not affect the probability of a session from any other email. This may be a strong assumption to make in certain scenarios and our future research is targeted at solutions for such scenarios.

- The second constraint (3) specifies the targets for the local number of sessions originating from each email type t. On the left hand side, $\sum_{e \in E_t} P_{sess}(\mathbf{x}_e) z_e$ is the expected number of sessions originating from type t emails under serving plan $\mathbf{z}$. On the right hand side,

  $$\text{maxLocalSess}_t = \sum_{e \in E_t} P_{sess}(\mathbf{x}_e)$$

is the expected number of sessions originating from type t emails if all those type t emails are sent, and $\alpha_t \in [0,1]$ is the fraction of this maximum achievable number of sessions originating from type t emails that we aim to retain.

- The next two constraints (4) and (5) specify the global and local tolerances for complaints, similar to those for sessions.
- The last constraint (6) enforces that z_e is a probability.

It is worth noting here that:

1. Not all constraints (2)-(5) need to be specified. Only the ones corresponding to actual requirements need to be specified. For example, let us say that we have a strict global sessions target, a strict global complaints tolerance and a strict local sessions target for email type $t = 1$. Then we only need to include the two global constraints and one local constraint corresponding to $t = 1$. In an extreme case if we only care about a global sessions target, then only one constraint (2) needs to be included, and the problem (and its solution) degenerates to the naive approach of thresholding on P_{sess}.
2. Although in the example LP formulation above we consider the send volume as the objective and treat sessions and complaints as constraints, this is not a requirement. Depending on the use case any one of the utilities of interest can become the objective and the rest can be specified as constraints. For our example, it is okay to change the objective to maximizing the total sessions $\sum_{e \in E} P_{sess}(\mathbf{x}_e) z_e$ and have the total send volume as a constraint: $\sum_{e \in E} z_e \leq \omega_{global} \times \text{maxGlobalSend}$, where $\omega_{global} \in (0, 1]$.

4.2.2 *Handling Unseen Emails With Lagrangian Duality*

At first glance, solving the above LP may seem trivial: at the beginning of the upcoming week, gather all emails E which will be generated, solve the LP with any standard LP solver, and use the optimal solution obtained to serve the emails in the week. However, this is unrealistic in practice due to the following challenge: we do not know in advance the set of emails E that will be generated in the upcoming week.

Fortunately, we observe that the distribution of our generated emails does not change significantly week over week. So we use the set of emails generated in the past week as a forecast for E. However, similarity in distribution does not provide us the solution z_e for every email that will actually be generated in the upcoming week. To that end, we make use of the primal-dual technique introduced in [8]. We first add a quadratic regularization term to the objective to make the problem strongly convex. This allows easy conversion from dual solutions to primal solutions.

$$\min_{\mathbf{z}} \quad \sum_{e \in E} \left[z_e + \frac{\gamma}{2}(z_e - q)^2 \right]$$

where $q \in [0, 1]$ is some prior on the send probability, and $\gamma > 0$ is a regularization parameter.

We now solve the dual of the primal problem above for the set of emails generated in the past week. Standard QP solvers are unable to handle a problem of our scale due to the large number of variables in the dual problem corresponding to the probability constraints of (6) (of the order of millions at LinkedIn). We employ an in-house large scale implementation of the Operator Splitting algorithm [11] to solve this QP. Let μ_{global}, μ_t, ν_{global} and ν_t be the solutions to the dual problem corresponding to the global session constraint (2), the local session constraints (3), the global complaint constraint (4) and the local complaint constraints (5) respectively. Then z_e for any newly generated email can be efficiently computed on-the-fly without the dual solutions corresponding to (6) using Algorithm 1 from [8]. That algorithm can be condensed into the following equation for our binary (send or drop) decision case. For an email e of type t:

$$z_e = \Pi_{[0,1]} \left(\frac{\mu_t^* P_{sess}(\mathbf{x}_e) - \nu_t^* P_{comp}(\mathbf{x}_e) - 1}{\gamma} + q \right)$$

where $\mu_t^* = \mu_{global} + \mu_t$, $\nu_t^* = \nu_{global} + \nu_t$, $\Pi_{[0,1]}(\cdot)$ stands for the projection onto $[0, 1]$. If we set $\gamma \to 0^+$ then the send/drop decision is further simplified to the following deterministic rule. For an email e of type t:

$$\text{Send } e \Leftrightarrow \mu_t^* P_{sess}(\mathbf{x}_e) - \nu_t^* P_{comp}(\mathbf{x}_e) - 1 > 0. \tag{7}$$

We use this simplified decision rule in our current implementation. This rule requires us to maintain a set of just a few coefficients $\{\mu_t^*, \nu_t^*\}$ to make a send/drop decision for each individual email. We call these the MOO coefficients.

4.3 Utility Prediction

The solution to the MOO problem above depends on the availability of downstream session prediction $P_{sess}(\mathbf{x}_e)$ and complaint prediction $P_{comp}(\mathbf{x}_e)$ for each generated email. In this section we outline our process for training response prediction models. This includes data collection, large-scale logistic regression model training and model evaluation.

4.3.1 *Training Data Collection*

Collecting unbiased training data for our use case is a non-trivial exercise. A naive approach for collecting training data is to reserve a small fraction of user base to always receive all generated emails, bypassing any volume optimization logic. The responses (downstream session/complaint/no-interaction) thus collected could then form the training dataset. However, this method of data collection can suffer from serving bias due to the following reason. A user's response to an email depends not just on the attributes of that particular email but also on the past experience of the user with similar emails. For example, we have observed that a user's propensity of clicking on an email is correlated with the number of emails received by the user per week over the past few weeks. The click probability is high if the user received few emails in the previous week, but the correlation becomes weaker if the user consistently received few emails each week over the past four weeks. If the serving scheme is unable to produce instances with varying number of emails sent over the past few weeks then we will not be able to capture user behavior in such scenarios. At LinkedIn, at least one email is generated for a vast majority of active members every week which implies that the naive serving scheme will rarely, if ever, create a scenario where an active member received zero emails in the previous week, although it is likely to result in a higher probability of engagement with a candidate email this week.

We developed the following serving scheme to explore the feature space and overcome the aforementioned sparsity problem. For every member, we choose a random number in $[0, 1]$ which is the probability with which a message is dropped for this member, denoted as P_{drop}. We refresh P_{drop} every 4 weeks so as to capture both novelty as well as burn-in effects. As an illustration, suppose that 10 emails are generated for Alfred every week and that the random number generator produces $P_{drop} = 0.8$ for Alfred, then this would mean that Alfred will receive 2 messages per week on average from week 1 to week 4. If the random number generator produces $P_{drop} = 1.0$ for Alfred at the end of week 4, then Alfred will receive 0 messages per week from week 5 to week 8. We do not refresh the random numbers for all members at the same epochs (beginning of week 1, week 5) but rather spread the refresh epochs as described in Algorithm 1. This provides us with the flexibility of choosing any time frame (say one week) for training data collection with adequate coverage of feature space.

Algorithm 1: Choosing P_{drop} for each member

```
if memberId % 4 == weekOfYear % 4 then
    choose a new P_drop for memberId
else
    keep using the previous P_drop for memberId
```

We deploy this model for 1% of our members.

4.3.2 Model and Features

Once we have collected appropriate training data, we train two logistic regression models with ℓ_2 regularization, one for each of the two utilities, viz., downstream session and complaint. Let y denote the response to an email e described by feature vector $\mathbf{x}_e$, then the corresponding Bernoulli random variable $\mathbb{Y}$ is modeled as

$$\mathbb{E}[\mathbb{Y}] = \frac{1}{1 + \exp(-\boldsymbol{\theta}^\top \mathbf{x}_e)}$$

where $\boldsymbol{\theta}$ is the parameter vector which we want to learn. Once $\boldsymbol{\theta}$ has been estimated from the training data, for any new example $\mathbf{x}_e^{\text{new}}$ we simply use the mean of the Bernoulli distribution as the predicted response, i.e.,

$$\begin{aligned} \text{Prediction} &= \Pr(\{\mathbb{Y} = 1\}) \\ &= \mathbb{E}[\mathbb{Y}] = \frac{1}{1 + \exp(-\boldsymbol{\theta}^\top \mathbf{x}_e^{\text{new}})} \end{aligned} \tag{8}$$

We include 4 broad categories of features in the feature vector $\mathbf{x}_e$, viz.,

1. Targeted member's profile features such as member's locale, age, etc.

2. Targeted member's in-app activity features such as member's last visit time, number of sessions over the last week, etc.

3. Targeted member's past experience with emails such as number of emails received in the past week, number of emails clicked, etc.

4. Email message features such as type of message, length, etc.

In addition, we also include interactions between the above features.

We train these logistic regression models on Spark [12] using in-house optimization libraries which implement a distributed version of TRON [13], a trust region Newton method. The distributed optimizer enables model training with a large number of features and training examples on the Spark framework which allows rapid iterations.

4.3.3 Model Validation

We compute 2 metrics to measure the performance of our response prediction models:

1. Area under the receiver operating characteristic curve (AUC): This is to verify whether the model is directionally correct, i.e., larger predictions for positive examples.

2. Observed to expected ratio (O/E ratio): This is to verify the scale of the model. This metric is computed as the number of positive test examples divided by the sum of predicted probabilities for all test examples. An O/E ratio close to 1 is desired. It is important to verify the scale of the model because the sum of the predicted utilities is used to approximate the actual number of sessions and complaints in the constraints of the MOO formulation.

The AUC and O/E ratio metrics for our best utility prediction models are tabulated in Table 2.

Utility	AUC	O/E ratio
Session	0.86	0.99
Complaint	0.81	1.05

Table 2: Validation metrics for prediction models

4.4 Offline Evaluation

As described in Section 4.2.2 we use the set of emails generated in the past week to obtain the MOO coefficients, and then use those for making send/drop decisions for emails which will be generated in the upcoming week. Since there is an element of uncertainty here, we use a simple replay methodology to evaluate the effectiveness of our volume optimization models (response prediction + MOO coefficients) before deploying them to the online serving system.

We collect one week of data from our *send-all* bucket, starting from a point in time after the period over which the training data was collected. The emails e thus collected are annotated with the observed user responses, namely, observed complaints (oc $= 0/1$) and observed downstream sessions (os $= 0/1$). Now Algorithm 2 is used to compute the replay results. Note that we are only maintaining counters for the global utilities in this algorithm, but its extension to include local level utilities should be obvious.

The sends, sessions and complaints ratios thus produced should closely match the expected ratios as per (1)-(6). For example, at the global level the following should hold true:

Algorithm 2: Replay algorithm for global utilities

Data: $d = (x_e, \text{oc}, \text{os})$

complaints = sessions = sends = 0
maxComplaints =maxSessions = maxSends = 0
foreach d **do**
  maxComplaints = maxComplaints + oc
  maxSessions = maxSessions + os
  maxSends = maxSends + 1
  if type(e) == t **then**
    score(e) = $\mu_t^* P_{sess}(\mathbf{x}_e) - \nu_t^* P_{comp}(\mathbf{x}_e) - 1$
  if score(e) > 0 **then**
    complaints = complaints + oc
    sessions = sessions + os
    sends = sends + 1
sendsRatio = sends/maxSends
sessionsRatio = sessions/maxSessions
complaintsRatio = complaints/maxComplaints

$$\left|\text{sendsRatio} - \frac{\sum_e z_e}{\sum_e 1}\right| \to 0$$
$$\text{sessionsRatio} \geq \alpha_{global}$$
$$\text{complaintsRatio} \leq \beta_{global}$$

Although this replayer is a simple and efficient tool for obtaining an estimate of a model's performance in an online A/B test, it is not always accurate due to a shortcoming of this replayer. This replayer need not capture all the dynamics of the population on which the model is going to be deployed. For example, say we are going to deploy our new model to a population which is being served by another model which drops emails with a fixed probability of P_{drop}=0.9. Then the distribution of $P_{sess}(\mathbf{x}_e)$ and $P_{comp}(\mathbf{x}_e)$ for this population is likely to be different from the *send-all* population used in the replayer.

5. SYSTEM ARCHITECTURE

In this section, we outline the important components of our system, as illustrated through a block diagram in Figure 9. The system consists of an online serving system and an offline training system.

Depending on a member's message subscription settings, the message generator will produce a message for the member. For example, if the member subscribes to network updates, then a message is generated once a week which contains important updates pertaining to the member's connections, such as job changes, work anniversaries, profile updates, etc. This message is passed down to the utility prediction engine along with the ID of the target user. The utility prediction engine extracts the message features from the message to create a partial feature vector and appends member features of the targeted user from a tracking data store. This feature vector is used in the utility prediction models to predict the expected utilities as per (8). These predicted utilities are passed to the Volume Optimization (VO) decision engine which makes the final send/drop decision based on the MOO coefficients as per (7). The member's interactions with the received emails, along with member profile and activity data are recorded in the tracking data store.

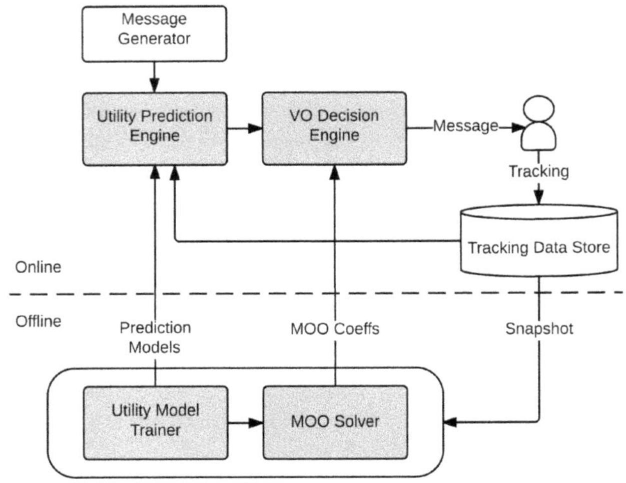

Figure 9: Simplified system architecture

Hourly snapshots of this database are loaded into Hadoop. The snapshot data is used in the utility model trainer for training response prediction models on Spark. These models are fed into the utility prediction engine as well as the MOO solver. The MOO solver employs these models on the training data for predicting expected utilities, which are used in the optimizer to produce optimal MOO coefficients. Note that the beauty of the design lies in the ability to make a send/drop decision for each individual email independently, based on the learned response prediction models and a few MOO coefficients. Further, this simple but effective design is what enables us to scale the online decision making to handle millions of message requests every week.

6. EXPERIMENTS & RESULTS

6.1 Experimental Setup

We set up an online A/B test experiment to evaluate the performance of our volume optimization approach. Members in the treatment bucket received emails based on the output of the volume optimization decision engine. The MOO coefficients used in the decision engine were dual solutions to a MOO problem with constraints listed under the 'Constraint' column of Table 3. The experiment covered several email types which constitute about 70% of the total volume of emails sent by LinkedIn. We collected several metrics of interest from this bucket and compared them against the control *send-all* bucket in which members received all emails generated for them.

6.2 Results And Analysis

Table 3 summarizes the offline replay and A/B test results. The 'Contribution' column shows the contribution of each email type towards the total sends, complaints and downstream sessions in the *send-all* bucket. The 'Constraint' column lists the complaint tolerances and session targets at global and local levels. In this experiment, at the global level we are willing to tolerate no more than 60% of the maximum possible complaints (when all emails are sent) and target at least 98.5% of the maximum achievable sessions. It is quite obvious from Figure 8 that it is impossible to achieve this kind of a trade-off through the naive threshold-

Email Type	Contribution (%)			Constraint (%)		MOO Coeff		Offline Replay (%)			A/B Test (%)		
	send	complaint	session	complaint ($100 \times \beta$)	session ($100 \times \alpha$)	complaint (ν)	session (μ)	send	complaint	session	send	complaint	session
All	100	100	100	60.00	98.50	883.76	360.99	66.46	54.60	95.99	64.51	46.97	98.16
1	3.16	2.14	16.78	80.00	95.00	143	0	96.86	77.42	99.77	95.65	71.67	101.06
2	1.74	0.53	4.84	50.00	85.00	32901.77	0	58.76	45.45	74.88	72.78	30.94	93.92
3	20.05	13.85	24.35	80.00	97.00	0	93.26	68.92	60.07	97.84	73.44	60.56	99.40
Rest	75.05	83.48	54.03	-	-	-	-	65.50	43.37	96.40	61.37	34.97	96.71

Table 3: Comparison of constraints with replay and A/B test results

ing approaches. We have also specified local level constraints for three important email types. There are no local level constraints for the remaining email types. The 'MOO Coeff' column contains the dual solutions (ν_{global}, ν_t, μ_{global}, and μ_t) corresponding to the constraints of the optimization problem. The 'Offline Replay' and 'A/B Test' columns show the sends, complaints and downstream sessions results achieved through our volume optimization model in offline replay and online A/B test respectively. The A/B test results are relative to the *send-all* bucket.

We draw the following observations from the table:

1. The MOO coefficients μ_1 and μ_2 corresponding to the session constraints for email type 1 and 2 respectively are equal to 0. This means that the corresponding local level constraints on session targets were inactive at the point of optimality. This in turn implies that we could achieve more local sessions for these email types than the target. For example, we have specified a session target of 95% under the Constraint column for email type 1 but have achieved 101.06% sessions for this email type in our A/B test. Similarly, we achieve more sessions (93.92%) in the A/B test than our target of 85% for email type 2. The MOO coefficient ν_3 corresponding to the complaint constraint for email type 3 is 0, which implies that we could achieve fewer complaints than our tolerance. We do observe fewer complaints (60.56%) in the A/B test than our tolerance of 80% for this email type.

2. The MOO coefficient ν_2 corresponding to the complaint constraint for email type 2 is orders of magnitude larger than the others. This is because we have specified a very strict constraint on the complaints tolerance (50%) for email type 2. In general, the stricter a constraint the higher are the chances of its corresponding dual solution being larger. This is because a large MOO coefficient will ensure that the corresponding utility prediction plays an important role in the send/drop decision making as per (7). For example, the large ν_2 will ensure that an email e of type 2 is sent only if its predicted complaint probability $P_{comp}(\mathbf{x}_e)$ is very small.

3. All constraints are being satisfied in the A/B test results, except for a minor violation of the global sessions constraint. This violation is not surprising since we solve the MOO problem for emails generated in the previous week and use its solution to make send/drop decisions for emails generated in the following week.

4. The offline replay is making reasonable predictions about the A/B test results but it is not always accurate.

Weekly trends for the global metrics that we directly optimize for, viz., sends, sessions and complaints are shown in Figure 10. The red line in each plot corresponds to the A/B test result while the blue line corresponds to the constraint. Table 3 above was a detailed presentation of results from week 8.

Product	Unique users Δ
Overall	-
Homepage	-
Groups	+0.9%
Profile	+0.1%
Notifications	-1.9%
HelpCenter	-25.5%

Table 4: Change in number of unique users visiting certain product pages due to volume optimization

We also saw an indirect impact of volume optimization on certain metrics that we did not explicitly optimize for. The impact on one such metric, namely, the number of unique users who visited a page is tabulated for some of the product pages in Table 4. A '-' entry in the table indicates that the impact was not statistically significant. We do not observe any statistically significant loss in the total number of unique users visiting the mobile or web applications. This was expected because of our strict constraint on global sessions target. However, we do observe a reshaping of user visits across various products. This is a nice byproduct of volume optimization which eliminates less relevant and poor quality emails. If poor quality emails are dropped, the total email volume received by a member is reduced allowing the member to devote more time and attention to the good quality emails. So although certain products lose out on unique users, the more relevant products gain. This is consistent with our observations in Section 3.2 where we had seen that user attention gets divided between important and less important emails. Here we would like to point out once again that this kind of interaction between emails is ignored in our MOO formulation where we assume that the send/drop decision for an email does not affect the probability of a session or complaint from any other email. Relaxing this independence assumption is the primary target of our future research. On a lighter note, the large drop in unique users visiting the HelpCenter pages is rewarding and also amusing, for reasons which should be obvious to the reader!

7. CONCLUSION

To the best of our knowledge, this is the first work on email volume optimization for a large online social networking service. We have introduced the challenging nature of the problem through a comprehensive cost-benefit analysis of email communication. It has been found that on the one hand emails deliver significant value to the members thereby driving in-app engagement, but on the other hand excessive email volume results in increased negative responses such as

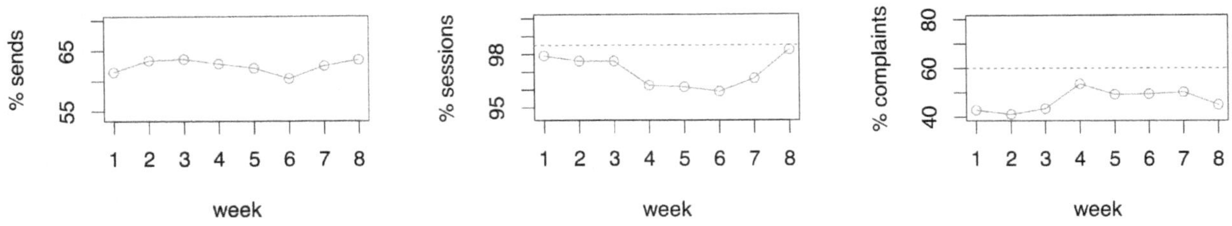

(a) Sends (b) Sessions (c) Compliants

Figure 10: Global email metrics with volume optimization. blue: constraint, red: A/B test result

a member unsubscribing from an email type or reporting an email as spam to her email service provider. Excessive email has also been found to result in the user's attention drifting away from important emails. We have illustrated why naive approaches to volume optimization result in sub-optimal solutions, and presented our formulation of the problem as a multi-objective optimization problem, with the objective of minimizing the number of emails sent in a way so as to maximize the positive outcome and minimize the negative outcome of sending emails. We have discussed the challenges faced in solving the multi-objective optimization problem and our workaround. We have described how we evaluate our volume optimization models offline before deploying them in production. The major components of our volume optimization system, comprising of an online serving system and an offline training system have been outlined. Finally, we have demonstrated the effectiveness of our approach through online A/B test experiments.

8. ACKNOWLEDGMENTS

This work would not have been possible without the invaluable insights from our team at LinkedIn comprising of Ankan Saha, Carl Cummings, Deepak Agarwal, Kinjal Basu, Liang Zhang, Rishi Jobanputra, Shaunak Chatterjee and many others.

9. REFERENCES

[1] Sarah Goliger. 9 Critical Components for Optimized Marketing Emails, 2013. http://blog.hubspot.com/marketing/ 9-components-optimized-marketing-emails-ht.

[2] Steve Whittaker and Candace Sidner. Email overload: Exploring personal information management of email. In *ACM SIGCHI*, 1996.

[3] Catherine Grevet, David Choi, Debra Kumar, and Eric Gilbert. Overload is overloaded: Email in the age of gmail. In *ACM SIGCHI*, 2014.

[4] Gloria Mark, Stephen Voida, and Armand Cardello. "a pace not dictated by electrons": An empirical study of work without email. In *ACM SIGCHI*, 2012.

[5] Eric Horvitz, Andy Jacobs, and David Hovel. Attention-sensitive alerting. In *Proceedings of the Fifteenth Conference on Uncertainty in Artificial Intelligence*, 1999.

[6] Shinjae Yoo, Yiming Yang, Frank Lin, and Il-Chul Moon. Mining social networks for personalized email prioritization. In *ACM SIGKDD*, 2009.

[7] Shinjae Yoo, Yiming Yang, and Jaime Carbonell. Modeling personalized email prioritization: Classification-based and regression-based approaches. In *ACM CIKM*, 2011.

[8] Deepak Agarwal, Bee-Chung Chen, Pradheep Elango, and Xuanhui Wang. Personalized click shaping through lagrangian duality for online recommendation. In *ACM SIGIR*, 2012.

[9] Deepak Agarwal, Shaunak Chatterjee, Yang Yang, and Liang Zhang. Constrained optimization for homepage relevance. In *WWW*, 2015.

[10] SpamCop Blocking List. https://www.spamcop.net/bl.shtml.

[11] Eric Chu, Brendan O'Donoghue, Neal Parikh, and Stephen Boyd. A primal-dual operator splitting method for conic optimization. *Stanford Internal Report*, 2013.

[12] Apache Spark. http://spark.apache.org/.

[13] Chih-Jen Lin and Jorge J. Moré. Newton's method for large bound-constrained optimization problems. *SIAM J. on Optimization*, 9(4), April 1999.

Large-Scale Item Categorization in e-Commerce Using Multiple Recurrent Neural Networks

Jung-Woo Ha*
NAVER LABS
Seongnam, 13561, Korea
jungwoo.ha
@navercorp.com

Hyuna Pyo*
NAVER LABS
Seongnam, 13561, Korea
hyuna.pyo
@navercorp.com

Jeonghee Kim†
NAVER LABS
Seongnam, 13561, Korea
jeonghee.kim
@navercorp.com

ABSTRACT
Precise item categorization is a key issue in e-commerce domains. However, it still remains a challenging problem due to data size, category skewness, and noisy metadata. Here, we demonstrate a successful report on a deep learning-based item categorization method, i.e., deep categorization network (DeepCN), in an e-commerce website. DeepCN is an end-to-end model using multiple recurrent neural networks (RNNs) dedicated to metadata attributes for generating features from text metadata and fully connected layers for classifying item categories from the generated features. The categorization errors are propagated back through the fully connected layers to the RNNs for weight update in the learning process. This deep learning-based approach allows diverse attributes to be integrated into a common representation, thus overcoming sparsity and scalability problems. We evaluate DeepCN on large-scale real-world data including more than 94 million items with approximately 4,100 leaf categories from a Korean e-commerce website. Experiment results show our method improves the categorization accuracy compared to the model using single RNN as well as a standard classification model using unigram-based bag-of-words. Furthermore, we investigate how much the model parameters and the used attributes influence categorization performances.

CCS Concepts
• **Computing methodologies → Neural networks** • **Computing methodologies → Supervised learning by classification** • **Information systems → Online shopping.**

.Keywords
large-scale item categorization; recurrent neural networks; deep learning; e-commerce

1. INTRODUCTION
Recent advances in web and mobile technologies have dramatically increased the e-commerce markets. Many new items are registered in e-commerce websites such as *eBay*, *Amazon*, and *NAVER shopping* every day. Each item is represented by metadata such as its title, category, image, price and so on, and most of them are given manually by human sellers. Dissimilar to attributes including title and price that can only be provided by humans, the item categories can be automatically inferred from the metadata. While automatic item categorization can reduce time and economic costs, the accuracy of the categorization has large influences on customer satisfaction and revenue of e-commerce sites [19, 20]. Therefore, precisely categorizing items emerges as a significant issue in e-commerce domains.

Item categorization is a text classification problem because most metadata of items are represented as textual features. Although many models using support vector machines (SVMs) [14], naïve Bayes classifiers [1], decision trees [6], and latent Dirichlet allocations (LDAs) [3, 18] have been successfully applied to text classification, they are difficult to be applied to item categorization due to scalability, sparsity and skewness. Item categorization is mapping several millions of items to class labels, corresponding to several thousands of leaf categories. Moreover, the distribution of leaf categories is usually severely skewed. Furthermore, many new items continue to be listed in an online commerce site on-the-fly every day. Although a seller inputs metadata on items, the data often includes noisy information. Therefore, precise item categorization still remains a challenging problem in online marketplace domains. Shen et al. proposed a hierarchical item categorization method for large items [19-21]. However, it may be inefficient because it does not use a flat-classifier but conducts two levels of classification. Since the method uses a unigram-based approach for learning from text descriptions, in addition, it is difficult to avoid the sparsity problem and to capture the full meaning of given word sequences [2]. Taxonomy-based methods have also showed competitive performances in category integration [17]. However, they require taxonomy of item categories as prior knowledge. Neural network-based approaches also have been successfully applied to text classification such as sentiment analysis [4, 12]. However, the studies on deep learning-based large-scale item categorization over several tens of million goods are still rare to the best of our belief.

Here we propose a flat categorization model for large-scale items from their metadata using deep learning [13] without prior knowledge, called deep categorization network (DeepCN). The proposed DeepCN uses an end-to-end deep network consisting of multiple recurrent neural networks (RNNs) for feature construction [7, 16] and fully connected layers [22] for item categorization. Each RNN is dedicated to each input metadata attribute composing the item information. For example, the RNNs of DeepCN includes Name-RNN, ShoppingMAll-RNN, and so on.

KDD'16, August 13-17, 2016, San Francisco, CA, USA
© 2016 ACM. ISBN 978-1-4503-4232-2/16/08...$15.00 .
DOI: http://dx.doi.org/10.1145/2939672.2939678
*: Both authors have equally contributed to this work.
†: Corresponding author

Figure 1. Examples of items listed in "NAVER Shopping" website. Red, blue, and green boxes denote the categories, the names, and the shopping malls of items

Dedicating an RNN to each attribute prevents the ambiguity emerging by concatenating the attribute word sequences. Also, the dedication approach keeps the word sequence from being too long. The RNNs generate real-value vectors characterizing the description semantics from given metadata through word embedding. The use of RNNs allows the input node size of the fully connected layers to be fixed regardless of the word sequence length. Also, it enables the model to learn the full meaning of text descriptions while bag of words (BoW) methods using *n*-grams use very restricted sequential information. The features generated by the RNNs move through the multiple fully connected layers and a softmax layer into the output layer correspond to leaf categories. The cost function is defined as the errors of the output layer which are propagated through the fully connected layers to the RNNs to update the weights of the model. This end-to-end structure not only allows the word vectors to characterize the category-sensitive semantics but also renders a pretraining process such as word2vec [15] unnecessary.

We evaluate the proposed DeepCN on large-scale industrial data including more than 94 million items dealt with in a Korean famous online marketplace, "*NAVER Shopping*[1]". The number of leaf categories is approximately 4,100. Experimental results show that our method outperforms a neural categorization model using single RNN as well as the Bayesian networks using bag of words based on unigram. Furthermore, we investigate the effects of each metadata attribute on categorization as well as model parameters for high-level categories.

2. ITEM DATA IN E-COMMERCE

2.1 Item Categorization in Online Marketplaces

Item categorization is defined as a problem to classify the leaf category of items from their metadata. In general, item categories are hierarchical and for convenience we separate them into leaf category and high-level category. In this study, the target classified is the leaf category of an item.

[1] http://shopping.naver.com

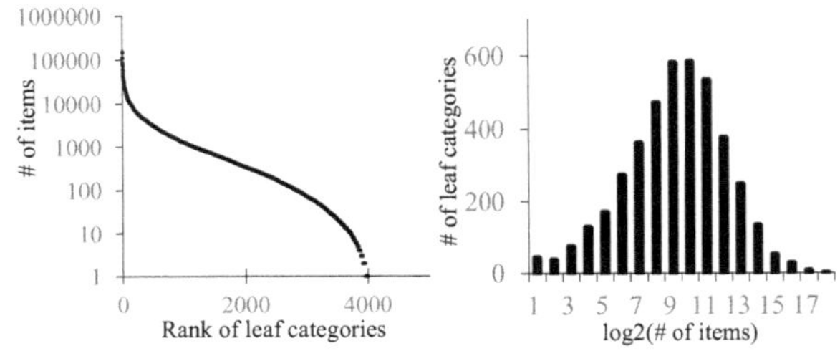

(a) Item-Rank (b) Category-Item

Figure 2. Distributions of the item data used in this study. The data are very large-scale over 94 million items and severely skewed with respect to leaf category.

In most online marketplace sites, sellers register an item by manually feeding metadata as shown in Figure 1. However, these metadata are likely to include lots of intentional or unintentional noisy information. For example, the name of socks is "*Socks, stockings, leggings, ankle socks. Thank you so much. We will do our best*!!" There exist many cases where the leaf category of an item is not related to a high-level category given by a seller and a high-level category registered by a seller is not consistent to the category terms of the online shopping system. Simple unigram-based approaches are not sufficient to precisely categorize items from these metadata.

Categorizing items belongs to text classification because metadata are in general represented by textual description. However, it is more challenging, compared to traditional text classification problems. In e-commerce domains, the data distribution has a long tail, which means that there are many leaf categories including a few items only. The data used in this study also show a long tail distribution according to Figure 2. It is well known that the leaf categories in a long-tail position are difficult to be categorized correctly because it is a severely imbalanced data problem. In addition, many new items continue to be registered every day. Furthermore, the number of leaf categories is over several thousand. Therefore, although a model might initially show good performance, its accuracy could decrease as e-commerce sites add new items with time.

2.2 Online Item Metadata

Item metadata include various attributes such as specification, name, hierarchical category information, image, brand, and so on. However, sellers often register data directly related to sale or search only and omit the rest of them. In this study, therefore, we use six essential attributes including item name, brand name, high-level (HL) category given by sellers, sellers' shopping mall id, maker, and image signature. An image signature is represented by nominal value characterizing the color and the edge patterns of an image. This allows image signatures to be used as a symbolic attribute. Therefore, all the attributes are characterized as textual word sequences or nominal values.

Formally, an item d consists of its leaf category label y and an attribute vector $\mathbf{x}$ represented with a collection of six attributes:

$$d = \{\mathbf{x}, y\} = \{\mathbf{x}^{(1)}, \mathbf{x}^{(2)}, ..., \mathbf{x}^{(6)}, y\}, \quad (1)$$

Table 1. Description of item metadata attributes

Var	Attributes	Values	Example
$\mathbf{x}^{(1)}$	Item name	Word sequence	Stylish wallet
$\mathbf{x}^{(2)}$	Brand name	Word sequence	Louis quatorze
$\mathbf{x}^{(3)}$	High-level category	Word sequence	Miscellaneous goods / Women goods
$\mathbf{x}^{(4)}$	Shopping Mall ID	Nominal	A023012
$\mathbf{x}^{(5)}$	Maker	Word sequence	Louis quatorze
$\mathbf{x}^{(6)}$	Image signature	Nominal	38720307
y	Leaf category	Nominal	3423(Women's wallet)

Shopping mall id is users' unique id, which is automatically generated when a user signs in NAVER Shopping.

$$\mathbf{x} = \{\mathbf{x}^{(1)}, \mathbf{x}^{(2)}, ..., \mathbf{x}^{(6)}\}. \quad (2)$$

Table 1 explains the metadata description in detail. For preprocessing, we eliminate all the symbols that are not characters or numbers from the metadata. In addition, we treat all nominal values as a textual word. Then, the i-th metadata attribute of an item is defined as the sequence of textual words as follows:

$$\mathbf{x}^{(i)} = \{x_1^{(i)} x_2^{(i)} ... x_n^{(i)}\}. \quad (3)$$

3. DEEP LEARNING-BASED ITEM CATEGORIZATION

Deep categorization network (DeepCN) is an end-to-end deep learning model for categorizing large-scale items from their textual and nominal metadata. DeepCN uses multiple RNNs and fully connected layers for learning, thus integrating the processes of metadata attribute-specific feature construction and category classification. The given textual data are transformed into real-valued vectors which precisely distinguish categories by learning.

3.1 Deep Categorization Networks

DeepCN consists of multiple RNNs, fully connected layers, one softmax and an output layer. The RNNs generate real-valued feature vectors from given metadata represented by word sequences. The generated vectors characterize the semantics of a word sequence. Each RNN is dedicated to one attribute composing metadata, and thus DeepCN includes m RNNs when item metadata consist of m attributes. This dedication approach keeps the accuracy from being low by too long word sequence length and the ambiguity emerging by concatenating attribute words. All the output vectors generated from the RNNs are concatenated into one vector, which moves to the fully connected layer. The nodes in the output layer correspond to leaf categories and each output node value is represented the probability of the corresponding leaf category where the given item belongs through fully connected and softmax layers. Figure 3(a) presents the structure of a DeepCN model.

DeepCN is formulated with traditional terms of neural networks. Let ${}^{R}_{m}\mathbf{h}^{(n)}_{t}$ and ${}^{F}\mathbf{h}^{(a)}$ denote the n-th layer at time t of the m-th RNN and the a-th fully connected layer. R and F mean RNN and fully connected, respectively. Like the preceding, ${}^{R}_{m}W^{kn}$ and ${}^{F}W^{kn}$ denote the weight matrix between the k-th and the n-th layers of the m-th RNN and the fully connected layers, respectively. ${}^{R}_{m}\mathbf{h}^{(n)}_{t}$ is defined with a function whose parameters are the hidden layer vector at t-1, ${}^{R}_{m}\mathbf{h}^{(n)}_{t-1}$, and the hidden layer vector of (n-1)-th layer at time t, ${}^{R}_{m}\mathbf{h}^{(n-1)}_{t}$:

$${}^{R}_{m}\mathbf{h}^{(n)}_{t} = {}^{R}_{m}f^{(n)}\left({}^{R}_{m}W^{(n-1)n}\,{}^{R}_{m}\mathbf{h}^{(n-1)}_{t} + {}^{R}_{m}W^{nn}\,{}^{R}_{m}\mathbf{h}^{(n)}_{t-1} + {}^{R}_{m}\mathbf{b}^{(n)}\right), \quad (4)$$

$${}^{R}_{m}\mathbf{h}^{(1)}_{t} = {}^{R}_{m}f^{(1)}\left({}^{R}_{m}W^{x1}\mathbf{x} + {}^{R}_{m}W^{11}\,{}^{R}_{m}\mathbf{h}^{(1)}_{t-1} + {}^{R}_{m}\mathbf{b}^{(1)}\right), \quad (5)$$

where ${}^{R}f^{(n)}$ and ${}^{R}\mathbf{b}^{(n)}$ denote the nonlinear activation function and the bias vector of ${}^{R}\mathbf{h}^{(n)}_{t}$. As defined in (5), the first layer uses the input layer as the (n-1)-th layer and $\mathbf{x}$ denotes the input vector with represented with one hot encoding, which means the index of

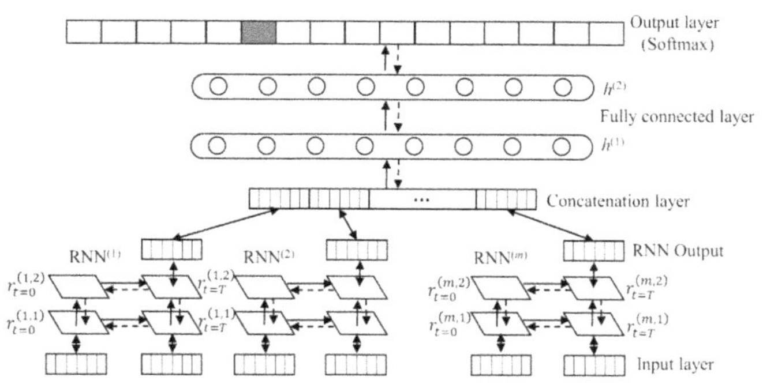

(a) Structure of DeepCN

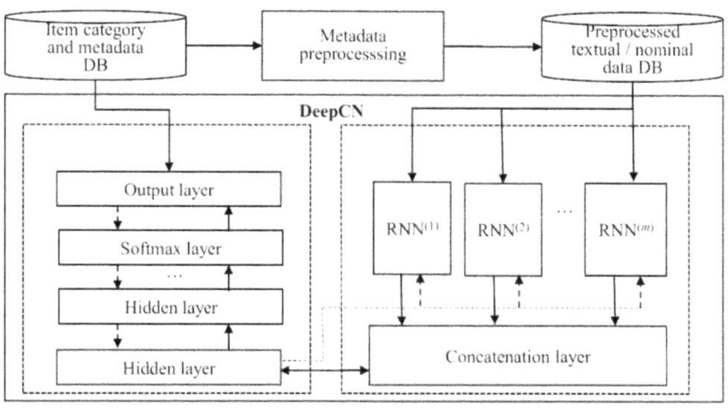

(b) Overall learning flow of DeepCN

Figure 3. Structure (a) and overall learning flow (b) of DeepCN. In (a), the model consists of *m* attribute-specific RNNs with two fully connected layers and a softmax layer for the output layer. Solid and dashed lines denote the flows of data and errors during the learning process, respectively.

the t-th word in a given metadata sequence is only one and the rests are zero. The size of $\mathbf{x}$ is equal to the vocabulary size. The output vectors of all the attribute-RNNs are concatenated into one vector $\mathbf{u}$, which is given to the fully connected layers:

$$\mathbf{u} = {}^{R}_{1}\mathbf{h}^{(n)}_{T_1} \circ \cdots \circ {}^{R}_{m}\mathbf{h}^{(n)}_{T_m}, \tag{6}$$

where T_i denotes the length of the word sequence of the i-th attribute.

The fully connected layer is defined as:

$${}^{F}\mathbf{h}^{(a)} = {}^{F}f^{(a)}\left({}^{F}W^{a(a-1)}\,{}^{F}\mathbf{h}^{(a-1)} + {}^{F}\mathbf{b}^{(a)}\right), \tag{7}$$

$${}^{F}\mathbf{h}^{(1)} = {}^{F}f^{(1)}\left({}^{F}W^{21}\mathbf{u} + {}^{F}\mathbf{b}^{(1)}\right). \tag{8}$$

The hyperbolic tangent function is used for the activation functions of both the RNNs and the fully connected layers in this study since it in general provides better performance in RNN learning than the sigmoid function [10].

For representing the probability for each category, we use the softmax function in the output node of DeepCN:

$$P(y_k \mid {}^{F}\mathbf{h}^{(l)}) = \frac{\exp\left(\mathbf{w}_k\,{}^{F}\mathbf{h}^{(l)}\right)}{\sum_{y\in Y}\exp\left(\mathbf{w}_y\,{}^{F}\mathbf{h}^{(l)}\right)}, \tag{9}$$

where $\mathbf{w}_k$ means the weight vector between the k-th output node and the l-th fully connected layer nodes, and l denotes the number of fully connected layers.

Therefore, given an item metadata represented with textual word sequences, DeepCN calculates the category probability vector of the item, and classifies the category with the maximum probability as the item category.

3.2 DeepCN Learning

The objective function is defined as the categorization errors on the given item metadata dataset, which is minimized by the training process. Figure 3(b) illustrates the learning flow of DeepCN.

Formally, the categorization error is formulated as follows:

$$E = \frac{1}{2}\sum_{n=1}^{N}\left\{y^{(n)} - \hat{y}^{(n)}\right\}^2 \equiv \frac{1}{2}\sum_{n=1}^{N}\left\|\mathbf{y}^{(n)} - \hat{\mathbf{y}}^{(n)}\right\|^2, \tag{10}$$

where $\mathbf{y}^{(n)}$ and $\hat{\mathbf{y}}^{(n)}$ denote the one-hot-encoding vector of the real category of the n-th item and the calculated softmax probability vector, respectively. The errors are propagated from the output layer into the fully connected hidden layers and the weights of the hidden layers are updated as follows:

$$\mathbf{w}_i = \mathbf{w}_i - \eta\frac{\partial E}{\partial \mathbf{w}_i} \text{ and } \frac{\partial E}{\partial \mathbf{w}_i} = \delta_i\mathbf{x}, \tag{11}$$

$$\delta_i = \begin{cases} \left(y_i^{(n)} - \hat{y}_i^{(n)}\right)\left(1 - \tanh^2(net_i)\right), & \text{if } i \in \mathbf{o} \\ \left(\sum_{j\in J}\delta_j w_{ij}\right)\left(1 - \tanh^2(net_i)\right), & \text{if } i \in \mathbf{h} \end{cases}, \tag{12}$$

where $\mathbf{o}$ and $\mathbf{h}$ denote the node set of an output and an inner hidden layer. η is the learning rate and net_i denotes the net value of the i-th node, the weighted sum of the lower layer node values. The backpropagated error gradients are separated into the top hidden node errors of each attribute-RNN. After that, all the weights of the RNNs are updated by backpropagation through time (BPTT) [23]:

$${}^{R}_{m}\mathbf{w}_i^{kk} = {}^{R}_{m}\mathbf{w}_i^{kk} - \eta\sum_{t=1}^{T}\delta_i(t)\,{}^{R}_{m}\mathbf{h}^{(k)}_{t-1}, \tag{13}$$

$$\mathbf{w}_i^{(n-1)n} = \mathbf{w}_i^{(n-1)n} - \eta\sum_{t=1}^{T}\delta_i(t)\,{}^{R}\mathbf{h}_t^{(n-1)}. \tag{14}$$

Therefore, this error propagation allows the word vector representation to capture the information on the category as well as the relationships between words.

Figure 4 shows the algorithm of learning DeepCN. The word sequences of item metadata are given to each attribute-RNN. The

Algorithm 1: Learning of DeepCN

D' / D^{te}: Minibatch trainng dataset / test dataset
M: The number of RNNs (= # of used metadata attributes)
U: The set of concatenated vectors
E: Categorization error
${}^{R}E_m$: Backpropagated error of the m-th RNN
V_m: Word sequence embedding vector set by the m-th RNN
S: The number of separated minibatch datasets
${}^{F}\theta^{i}$ / ${}^{R}\theta^{i}_{m}$: Model parameters of FC layers and the m-th RNN at the i-th iteration
$MAXITER$: The number of maximum iteration for learning

(${}^{R}\theta^{0}_{1}$,..., ${}^{R}\theta^{0}_{M}$, ${}^{F}\theta^{0}$) ← Initialize(M)
for i =1 **to** $MAXITER$
  for j =1 **to** S
    D' ← GetMiniBatch(D, $|D'|$);
    for m=1 **to** M
      V_m ← DeepCN_RNN_Forward(D', ${}^{R}\theta^{i-1}_{m}$);
    endfor
    U ← Concatenate(V_1,...,V_M)
    E ← DeepCN_FC_Softmax_Forward(U, ${}^{F}\theta^{i-1}$);
    (${}^{F}\theta^{i}$, ${}^{R}E$) ← DeepCN_ FC_Softmax_Backward(E, ${}^{F}\theta^{i-1}$);
    for m=1 **to** M
      ${}^{R}E_m$ ← SeparateError(${}^{R}E$, m)
      ${}^{R}\theta^{i}_{m}$ ← DeepCN_RNN_Backward(${}^{R}E_m$, ${}^{R}\theta^{i-1}_{m}$);
    endfor
  endfor
  EvaluateDeepCN(D^{te}, ${}^{R}\theta^{0}_{1}$,..., ${}^{R}\theta^{0}_{M}$, ${}^{F}\theta^{0}$)
endfor

Figure 4. Algorithm of learning DeepCN

Table 2. Composition of item data with respect to high level categories

High-level category	# of leaf categories	Training (8)	Validation (2)	Test (1)	Total	Data size / leaf category
Fashion clothing	103	7,201,594	1,800,399	900,200	9,902,193	**96,138**
Miscellaneous goods	255	12,798,623	3,199,656	1,599,829	17,598,108	**69,012**
Cosmetic / Beauty	156	2,595,834	648,959	324,480	3,569,273	22,880
Digital & home electronic	642	13,341,844	3,335,462	1,667,731	18,345,037	28,575
Furniture / Interior	335	5,159,216	1,289,805	644,903	7,093,924	21,176
Childbirth / Infant care	473	5,162,732	1,290,684	645,342	7,098,758	15,008
Foods	432	1,610,087	402,522	201,261	2,213,870	**5,125**
Sports / Leisure	459	5,255,248	1,313,813	656,907	7,225,968	15,743
Life / Health	1,115	15,104,282	3,776,071	1,888,036	20,768,389	18,626
Trip / Culture	61	748,506	187,127	93,564	1,029,197	16,872
Tax free goods	85	25,196	6,299	3,150	34,645	**408**
Total	4,116	69,003,162	17,250,797	8,625,403	94,879,362	23,051

Bold faces denote high-level categories with a very skewed data size per leaf category. Values in parenthesis of table header mean the ratios of data separated for learning deepCN.

real-valued vectors characterizing the word sequences are generated by the forward mechanism of an RNN. The generated vectors are concatenated into one vector for each item, which is forwarded into the fully connected hidden layers and then is transformed into the probability vector of the leaf categories with the softmax layer. After that, the categorization error is propagated through the fully connected layers into the RNNs and the weights are updated by the BPTT method.

4. EXPERIMENTAL RESULTS

4.1 Data and Parameter Setup

We evaluated the proposed DeepCN on a very large-scale dataset including over 94.8 million items with 4,116 leaf and 11 high-level categories. These items are currently registered in a Korean famous online e-commerce website, "*NAVER Shopping*." The high-level categories of the items are manually given by sellers. The item leaf categories are manually classified by many human experts employed at the website and these were used as the ground truth category for learning and evaluating the models.

The data are randomly separated into training, validation, and test sets, whose ratios are 8/11, 2/11, and 1/11, respectively. Table 2 shows the composition of the data in detail. As shown in Table 2 and Figure 2, we find that the high-level categories are severely imbalanced in both the number of leaf categories and the number of items per leaf category. As preprocessing, we eliminated rare words and sentence symbols including parenthesis, quotation, and period from the metadata. The resulting vocabulary size is 2,836,443.

The fixed model parameters for experiments are learning rate, momentum, and minibatch size, which are 0.001, 0.9 and 100, respectively. These values are selected by many experimental experiences and we focus on main parameters such as the number of hidden layers, hidden node size, and the used metadata attributes in this study. DeepCN was implemented based on CUDA 6.4 using a single GPU, Titan Black with 6GB VRAM.

4.2 Performance Measure and Comparison

We define a new measure, relative accuracy, instead of using conventional accuracy term due to a legal issue in this study. Relative accuracy of a model θ for given data D $\tilde{\psi}(D;\theta)$ is defined as the ratio of an estimated accuracy $\psi(D;\theta)$ to basis accuracy $\bar{\psi}$:

$$\tilde{\psi}(D;\theta) = \frac{\psi(D;\theta)}{\bar{\psi}}. \qquad (15)$$

The basis accuracy is the accuracy of the model using all metadata attributes (DCN-6R) and can be flexibly defined for target categories.

The global mean accuracy can be computed by averaging accuracies for all the leaf categories of DCN-6R on the test dataset. For example, when an estimated accuracy of a model is 0.8 and the global mean accuracy is 0.9, the relative accuracy is 0.889 (0.8/0.9). The relative accuracy is enough to show the improvements by using the proposed DeepCN even if we cannot use the conventional absolute accuracy.

We compare our method to one deep learning-based method and one conventional bag-of-words (BoW) approach. The first is a model using the architecture same as the proposed method except using only single RNN for item metadata (DCN-1R). In this setting, all the word sequences of the item metadata are concatenated into one long sequence, which is given as an input data instance. Comparing DCN-1R, we validate the effects of the approach dedicating an RNN to each metadata attribute. The second is the Bayesian networks using BoW based on uni-gram as the input feature (BN_BoW). In this setting, all the words appearing in the metadata of an item are converted into a TF/IDF vector, which is given as an input. The maximum number of parent nodes of the Bayesian network is set to 2. Comparing BN_BoW, we confirm the effects of word-embedding by deep neural networks as the data representation.

Table 3: Relative accuracies of three methods

High-level category	DCN-6R	DCN-1R	BN_BoW
Fashion clothing	**1.004**	0.984	0.696
Miscellaneous goods	**0.895**	0.866	0.443
Cosmetic / Beauty	**1.011**	0.976	0.823
Digital & home electronic	**1.108**	1.091	0.852
Furniture / Interior	**0.983**	0.952	0.665
Childbirth / Infant care	**0.956**	0.926	0.740
Food	**1.033**	1.005	0.791
Sports / Leisure	**1.016**	0.985	0.713
Life / Health	**0.992**	0.963	0.628
Trip / Culture	**1.197**	1.193	0.930
Tax free goods	**1.027**	1.008	0.101
Total	**1.000***	0.974	0.676

* denotes the basis accuracy for the relative accuracy.

4.3 Categorization Performance

Table 3 presents the relative accuracies of DeepCN compared to the DeepCN using single RNN and the Bayesian networks using BoW. The values are the categorization accuracies of the leaf categories for each high-level category, and are averaged on 10 times of experiments. The basis accuracy for relative accuracy in Table 3 is the conventional mean accuracy, which denotes the ratio of the number of correct categorization to the size of all test data. DCN-6R has six RNNs with two layers and two fully connected hidden layers. DCN-1R use one RNN and the same number of fully connected layers. The word vector size, the hidden node size of the RNNs is 100 and the fully connected layer node size is 600. As shown in Table 3, DCN-6R shows better categorization accuracy as 2.6% and 32.4% on average compared to DCN-1R and BoW-based Bayesian network. This indicates the categorization accuracies are improved by the dedicated RNN approach as well as word-embedding representation using neural networks.

We investigate the improvement of the proposed method in the level of high-level categories. Table 4 shows the decreases of categorization accuracies of two compared methods with respect to high-level categories. Unlike Table 3, the basis accuracy for each high-level category is defined as the mean accuracy of the high-level category. As shown in Table 4, DCN-1R shows even accuracy decreases from 1% to 3.5% for all high-level categories.

Table 4: Accuracy decrements of two methods for each high-level category

High-level category	DCN-1R	BN_BoW
Fashion clothing	0.979	0.693
Miscellaneous goods	0.968	**0.495**
Cosmetic / Beauty	0.966	0.814
Digital & home electronic	0.985	0.769
Furniture / Interior	0.968	0.676
Childbirth / Infant care	0.968	0.774
Food	0.974	0.766
Sports / Leisure	0.969	0.702
Life / Health	0.971	0.633
Trip / Culture	0.996	0.777
Tax free goods	0.982	**0.099**
Average on HL categories	0.975	0.654

Bold face denotes the large decrease of categorization accuracy.

This indicates the dedicated RNN approach is effective for most categories. Unlike the results of DCN-1R, the accuracy decrements of BN_BoW show large disparity. In particular, large decreases appear in *miscellaneous goods* and *tax free items*. In general, *tax free items* are difficult to be discriminated from other categories because they are same to other category items but are dealt with in tax free shop only. In addition, we can imagine that low accuracy of *tax free goods* may be caused by their smaller number of data compared to other categories as shown in Table 2. *Miscellaneous goods* are usually more general than other categories. From Table 4, word-embedding methods by a deep learning approach can resolve these problems which are difficult for conventional BoW-based models.

Figures 5(a) shows the learning curves of DCN-6R and DCN-1R. Two curves show the similar pattern while the learning proceeds and the accuracy differences between two methods are steadily kept. Figures 5(b) and (c) present the distributions of leaf categories with respect to accuracy. In two figures, x-axis values are relative accuracies or accuracy ranges whose basis accuracy is the third quartile of all leaf category accuracies of DCN-6R. We used this 3Q-normalzied relative accuracy in order to investigate the accuracy patterns for the sizes of leaf categories. 1.0 in x-axis

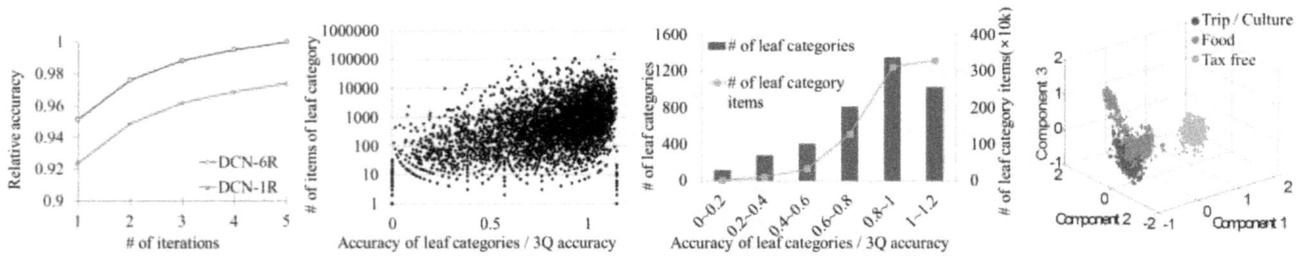

(a) Learning curve (b) Distribution of item number of leaf category for accuracy (c) Distribution of the number of leaf categories and leaf category items for accuracy (d) PCA plot of word-embedding vectors of metadata

Figure 5. Learning curves of DCN-6R and DCN-1R (a), distribution of the numbers of items contained in leaf categories for a normalized categorization accuracy (b), distribution of the numbers of leaf categories (bar) and items contained in leaf categories (line) for a normalized accuracy (c), and three dimensional PCA plot of the concatenated output vectors of the RNNs for three high-level categories (d). The normalized accuracy of a leaf category is the ratio of the accuracy of the leaf category to the third quartile accuracy for all leaf categories of DCN-6R.

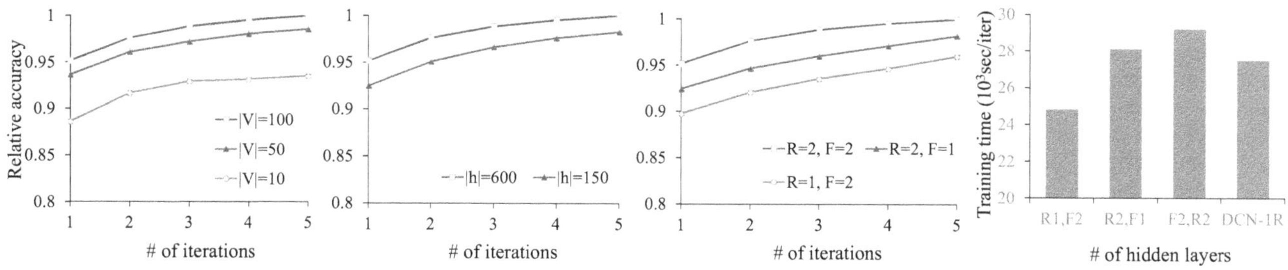

(a) Word vector size (b) Number of hidden nodes (c) Number of hidden layers (d) Training time

Figure 6. Relative accuracies on three model parameters such as word vector size (a), hidden node sizes of the fully connected layers (b), numbers of hidden layers (c), and training time for the number of hidden layers (d). |*V*| and |*h*| are the sizes of the word vector and hidden nodes of the fully connected layers. R*n* and F*n* denote the numbers of hidden layers of the RNNs and the fully connected layers of DeepCN, respectively.

denotes the accuracy equal to the third quartile accuracy. As shown in Figure 5(b), DeepCN in general provides better accuracies for leaf categories containing more items over 10,000 goods. It is known that goods in a long tail are usually difficult to be categorized correctly. Interestingly, we find that DeepCN shows high accuracy for many long tail leaf categories including less than 10 items from figure 5(b) despite low accuracy of many other leaf categories belonging to a long tail. Figure 5(c) shows the distributions of the number of leaf categories and leaf category items for normalized accuracy, respectively. From Figures 5(c), we can confirm that the accuracy variances are not large because the proportion below 0.6 compared to the third quartile accuracy is less than 20% with respect to the number of leaf categories. Considering Figure 5(b) and the distribution of the number of leaf category items in Figure 5(c), we can find that DeepCN provides better accuracy for leaf categories including more items.

Figure 5(d) shows the three-dimensional PCA plot of concatenated word-embedding vectors of item metadata extracted from the learned RNNs for three different high-level categories such as *trip/culture*, *food*, and *tax-free goods*. Similar to many RNN-based language models, item metadata are represented by DeepCN as real-valued vectors whose dimension size is equal to the number of hidden nodes of a top RNN layer. These vectors characterize the semantic and syntactic information of the metadata of an item to discriminate its category more precisely. We can find that the metadata vectors are separately scattered in a three-dimensional space for each high-level category. This indicates that DeepCN generates a category-specific metadata representation, thus enhancing the classification accuracies compared to conventional BoW-based methods.

4.4 Effects of Parameters

We investigate how much model parameters influence categorization accuracy and training time. In this study, we focus on three parameters directly related to model architectures such as word-embedding vector size, the number of hidden layers, and hidden node size of the fully connected layers. The word vector size is equivalent to the hidden node size of the RNNs.

Figure 6 presents the effects of the parameters on the categorization performance, including the word vector size (a), the number of hidden nodes in fully connected layers (b), and the number of hidden layers (c). As shown in Figures 6(a) and (b), larger word vector size and hidden node size provide better categorization accuracy. This is consistent to the results of many deep learning-based language models [14]. In particular, too a small embedding-vector size such as $|V|$=10 makes the accuracy worsen because it is not enough for discriminating categories. Figures 6(c) and (d) shows the effects of the hidden layer numbers on the accuracy and learning time, respectively. As shown in Figures 6(c) and (d), more number of hidden layers provides better accuracy. In particular, comparing the results of R2F1 model and DCN-1R to that of R1F2, we indicate that the number of RNN layers and RNNs has larger influence on accuracy and time cost that the number of fully connected layers.

4.5 Effects of Attributes

Table 5 shows the relative accuracy of using subsets of the metadata attributes. The basis accuracy is same as that of Table 4. The results in Table 5 are from a model using two RNN hidden layers and two fully connected layers (R2F2) with $|V|$=100 and $|\mathbf{h}|$=600. The values in Table 5 are computed by the same way to the results in Table 4. As shown in Table 5, on average, the model using all the metadata attributes shows higher accuracy as 2.3% compared to that of model excluding image signatures. This result

Table 5: Relative accuracy for used metadata attributes

High-level category	Ex Image	Ex Image+ Sm_id
Fashion clothing	0.983	0.901
Miscellaneous goods	**0.958**	**0.870**
Cosmetic / Beauty	0.981	0.908
Digital & home electronic	0.975	0.929
Furniture / Interior	0.965	0.885
Childbirth / Infant care	0.970	0.882
Food	0.980	0.890
Sports / Leisure	0.977	0.888
Life / Health	0.966	0.884
Trip / Culture	0.997	0.974
Tax free goods	0.994	**0.814**
Total	0.977	0.893

Ex denotes excluded attributes. Bold face denotes the large decrease of categorization accuracy.

indicates that image signatures slightly improve the categorization accuracy for all high-level categories. When shopping mall id is excluded in addition to image signature, the mean relative accuracy considerably decreases from 0.977 to 0.893. Interestingly, we find that the accuracy on *tax-free goods* dramatically decreases while those on other high-level categories slightly worsen. This result indicates shopping mall id is a critical attribute for discriminating tax-free goods. Considering the results in Table 4 together, this result indicates that DeepCN effectively uses shopping mall id attribute for categorization unlike BoW-based methods.

5. CONCLUDING REMARKS

Item categorization is a significant but challenging problem in e-commerce domains. We demonstrated a deep learning-based model for categorizing large-scale items reaching 100 million goods from textual metadata in a real-world online shopping website, i.e., a deep categorization network (DeepCN). The proposed DeepCN is an end-to-end model integrating multiple RNNs dedicated to each metadata attribute for feature construction, two fully connected layers, and one softmax layer for item categorization. The categorization errors are propagated back through the fully connected layers to the RNNs to update the weights. This structure enables the model to categorize items using the semantics of the word sequences from the metadata, thus overcoming simple bag of words-based text classification models using an n-gram approach. Also, the proposed method to dedicate each RNN to an attribute composing item metadata not only prohibits the ambiguity emerging by concatenating semantically heterogeneous word sequences describing item attributes and but also keeps the length of word sequences from being too long.

We evaluated DeepCN on large-scale real-world data including 94.9 million items with 4,116 leaf categories from a Korean e-commerce site, *NAVER Shopping*. Experimental results show the proposed DeepCN slightly outperforms the model using single RNN for all metadata attributes and dramatically improves the categorization accuracy compared to conventional BoW-based models using the Bayesian networks. Also, DeepCN can precisely categorize leaf categories in a long tail position, and this means our method can be applied to problems of classifying imbalanced data. Furthermore, we investigated the effects of the key model parameters such as the numbers of hidden layers and hidden nodes. We found that the number of RNN layers is a critical parameter for model performances including categorization accuracy and learning time. In addition, we confirmed the effects of the metadata attributes including image signatures and shopping mall ids on categorization. Furthermore, DeepCN is a general model that can be applied to various text classifications such as sentiment analysis and document classification even if it is applied to large-scale item categorization in this study.

DeepCN has some directions improved despite its encouraging results. Although DeepCN provides relatively good accuracies for more than tens of leaf categories in a long tail, in particular, the performances for more long-tail leaf categories are still not satisfactory. It can be improved by using advanced RNNs such as long short-term memories (LSTMs) [8] and gated recurrent units (GRUs) [5]. The use of the convolutional neural network features [9, 11] for item images would improve the performance instead of image signature. Moreover, the model will be advanced to deal with the problem where new leaf categories continue to increase with time.

6. ACKNOWLEDGMENTS

This work was partly supported by the Creative Industrial Technology Development Program (10053249, Development of Personalized Healthcare System Exploiting User Life-log and Open Government Data for Business Service Model Proof on Whole Life Cycle Care) funded by the Ministry of Trade, Industry & Energy (MOTIE, Korea).

7. REFERENCES

[1] Agrawal, R. and Srikant, R. 2001. On Integrating Catalogs. In *Proceedings of the 10th International Conference on World Wide Web* (*WWW 2001*), 603-612.

[2] Bengio, Y., Ducharme, R., Vincent, P., and Janvin, C. 2003. A Neural Probabilistic Language Model. *The Journal of Machine Learning Research*, 3, 1137-1155.

[3] Blei, D. M., Ng, A. Y. and Jordan, M. I. 2003. Latent Dirichlet Allocation. *The Journal of Machine Learning Research*, 3, 993-1022.

[4] Cao, Z., Li, S., Liu, Y., Li, W., and Ji, H. 2015. A Novel Neural Topic Model and Its Supervised Extension. In *Proccedings of the Twenty-Ninth AAAI Conference on Artificial Intelligence* (*AAAI* 2015), 2210-2216.

[5] Chung, J., Gulcehre, C., Cho, K., & Bengio, Y. 2015. Gated Feedback Recurrent Neural Networks. *arXiv preprint arXiv*:1502.02367.

[6] Dalal, M. K. and Zaveri, M. A. 2011. Automatic Text Classification: a Technical Review. *International Journal of Computer Applications*, 28, 2, 37-40.

[7] Graves, A. 2012. *Supervised Sequence Labelling with Recurrent Neural Networks*, 385. Heidelberg: Springer.

[8] Graves, A. and Schmidhuber, J. 2005. Framewise Phoneme Classification with Bidirectional LSTM and Other Neural Network Architectures. *Neural Networks*, 18, 5, 602-610.

[9] He, K. Zhang, X., Ren, S., and Sun, J. 2016. Deep Residual Learning for Image Recognition. In *Proceedings of IEEE Conference on Computer Vision and Pattern Recognition* (*CVPR 2016*).

[10] Jozefowicz, R., Zaremba, W., and Sutskever, I. 2015. An Empirical Exploration of Recurrent Network Architectures. In *Proceedings of the 32nd International Conference on Machine Learning* (*ICML-15*), 2342-2350.

[11] Krizhevsky, A., Sutskever, I., and Hinton, G. E. 2012. Imagenet Classification with Deep Convolutional Neural Networks. In *Advances in Neural Information Processing Systems*, 1097-1105.

[12] Lai, S., Xu, L., Liu, K., and Zhao, J. 2015. Recurrent convolutional neural networks for text classification. In *Proceedings of Twenty-Ninth AAAI Conference on Artificial Intelligence* (*AAAI 2015*), 2267-2273.

[13] LeCun, Y., Bengio, Y., and Hinton, G. 2015. Deep Learning, *Nature*, 521, 436-444.

[14] Lee, L. H., Wan, C. H., Rajkumar, R., and Isa, D. 2012. An Enhanced Support Vector Machine Classification

Framework by Using Euclidean Distance Function for Text Document Categorization. *Applied Intelligence*, 37, 1, 80-99.

[15] Mikolov, T. Sutskever, I. Chen, K., Corrado, G., and Dean, J. 2013. Distributed Representation of Words and Phrases and Their Compositionality, In *Advances in Neural Information Processing Systems* (*NIPS 2013*), 3111-3119.

[16] Mikolov, T., Kombrink, S., Burget, L., Cernocky, J. H., and Khudanpur, S. 2011. Extensions of Recurrent Neural Network Language Model. In *Proceedings of 2011 IEEE International Conference on Acoustics, Speech and Signal Processing* (*ICASSP* 2011), 5528-5531.

[17] Papadimitriou, P., Tsaparas, P., Fuxman, A., and Getoor, L. 2013. TACI: Taxonomy-Aware Catalog Integration. *Knowledge and Data Engineering, IEEE Transactions on*, 25, 7, 1643-1655.

[18] Paul, M. and Dredze, M. 2012. Factorial LDA: Sparse Multi-Dimensional Text models. In *Advances in Neural Information Processing Systems* (*NIPS 2012*), 2582-2590.

[19] Shen, D., Ruvini, J.-D., Mukherjee, R., and Sundaresan, N. 2012. A Study of Smoothing Algorithms for Item Categorization on e-Commerce sites. *Neurocomputing*, 92, 54-60.

[20] Shen, D., Ruvini, J.-D., Sarwar, B. 2012. Large-scale Item Categorization for e-Commerce. In *Proceedings of International Conference on Information and Knowledge Management* 2012 (*CIKM'*12), 595-604.

[21] Shen, D., Ruvini, J.-D., Somaiya, M. and Sundaresan, N. 2011. Item Categorization in the e-Commerce Domain. In *Proceedings of International Conference on Information and Knowledge Management* 2011 (*CIKM'*11), 1921-1924.

[22] Suykens, J. A., Vandewalle, J. P., and de Moor, B. L. 2012. *Artificial Neural Networks for Modelling and Control of Non-Linear systems*. Springer Science & Business Media.

[23] Werbos, P. J. 1990. Backpropagation through Time: What It Does And How to Do It. In *Proceedings of the IEEE*, 78, 10, 1550-1560.

Online Dual Decomposition for Performance and Delivery-Based Distributed Ad Allocation

Jim C. Huang
Amazon
Seattle, WA, USA
huangjim@amazon.com

Rodolphe Jenatton
Amazon
Berlin, Germany
jenatton@amazon.com

Cédric Archambeau
Amazon
Berlin, Germany
cedrica@amazon.com

ABSTRACT

Online optimization is central to display advertising, where we must sequentially allocate ad impressions to maximize the total welfare among advertisers, while respecting various advertiser-specified long-term constraints (e.g., total amount of the ad's budget that is consumed at the end of the campaign). In this paper, we present the online dual decomposition (ODD) framework for large-scale, online, distributed ad allocation, which combines dual decomposition and online convex optimization. ODD allows us to account for the distributed and the online nature of the ad allocation problem and is extensible to a variety of ad allocation problems arising in real-world display advertising systems. Moreover, ODD does not require assumptions about auction dynamics, stochastic or adversarial feedback, or any other characteristics of the ad marketplace. We further provide guarantees for the online solution as measured by bounds on cumulative regret. The regret analysis accounts for the impact of having to estimate constraints in an online setting before they are observed and for the dependence on the smoothness with which constraints and constraint violations are generated. We provide an extensive set of results from a large-scale production advertising system at Amazon to validate the framework and compare its behavior to various ad allocation algorithms.

Keywords

distributed optimization; display advertising; campaign optimization; ad allocation; budget pacing; long-term constraints; demand-side platform

1. INTRODUCTION

The past few years have seen significant interest and research in ad allocation in online display advertising, where the problem consists of serving ad impressions to users from many competing ads across a large number of websites and mobile apps, subject to a variety of advertiser objectives and constraints. For example, advertisers typically expect that an advertising platform will maximize ad performance (i.e., the ad's effectiveness at driving user behavior), subject to constraints on user targeting and constraints on ad delivery, such that the advertising platform is expected to spend as close to 100% of an ad's budget as possible by the end of the ad's flight time under a cost-per-mille, or CPM, billing model. In the literature on display advertising [3, 6, 17], online ad allocation is typically formulated as an online optimal assignment problem over a bi-partite graph in which nodes correspond to both ads and bid requests (i.e., user visits to a web page). Bid requests are processed sequentially, with edges corresponding to possible assignments of an ad to a bid request with weight equal to the advertiser's welfare for the given ad/bid request pair. In practice, the ad allocation problem is characterized by being 1) online, and 2) distributed (i.e., variable updates must be executed in parallel across large fleets of machines), with 3) potentially multiple long-term constraints that require estimation of quantities at bid request time (e.g., estimating the cost of an ad impression before winning it on external exchanges).

Various algorithms have been proposed for the ad allocation problem in the online display advertising literature [3, 6, 9, 10], but these have largely been derived as either approximation algorithms or heuristics, increasing the difficulty and complexity in extending these methods to a variety of constraints [17]. The distributed aspect of online display advertising has not been explicitly addressed either, especially in the presence of long-term constraints, which leads to further approximations in a production setting. Moreover, algorithms proposed have not accounted for highly variable, dynamic constraint violations (e.g., spend amounts) per ad that are often encountered in practical online ad serving systems. This is one reason why ad allocation solved as an offline problem can often be sub-optimal in practice [6]. Finally, the impact of having to estimate constraints in order to allocate ad impressions (e.g., in real-time bidding, or RTB, exchanges, the clearing price of an ad auction is only revealed to us after we've decided on which ad to show).

To the best of our knowledge, a comprehensive and holistic framework that satisfactorily addresses the above challenges faced in practical web-scale algorithms is still missing. In this paper, we present a general framework for deriving online and distributed ad allocation algorithms for dealing with a variety of online ad allocation problems in display advertising. Our contributions can be summarized as follows:

- We introduce a framework to derive online distributed optimization algorithms applicable to online ad alloca-

KDD '16, August 13 - 17, 2016, San Francisco, CA, USA

ISBN 978-1-4503-4232-2/16/08...$15.00

DOI: http://dx.doi.org/10.1145/2939672.2939691

tion problems with long-term advertiser-specified constraints;

- We account for the impact of having to estimate constraints before they are observed, without explicitly assuming bandit feedback;
- Leveraging the theoretical analysis provided in [12], we show that our approach enjoys bounds on dynamic cumulative regret, which depend on the smoothness with which constraint violations and the constraints themselves occur to the oracle learner over time.These results do not make assumptions about auction dynamics, stochastic or adversarial feedback, or other characteristics of the ad marketplace.
- We validate the framework by reporting results on traffic data collected by a large-scale display advertisement system at Amazon.

We call our framework online dual decomposition (ODD), which allows us to efficiently solve general large-scale optimization problems in a distributed and online fashion.

2. ONLINE DISPLAY ADVERTISING AS AN OPTIMAL ASSIGNMENT PROBLEM

In online advertising, each user visit to a web page triggers a bid request i to be sent in real-time (through possibly complex channels) to a host, or machine, in an ad serving fleet. Each incoming bid request has a set of candidate ads that can be served: the set of candidates that are eligible to be shown for a bid request are determined by several advertiser-specified constraints such as behavioral or demographic targeting (i.e., an ad is to be/not to be shown only to users satisfying targeting criteria), or frequency capping (i.e., an ad is not to be shown more than some number of times to a given unique user over some time period), to name a few. Indexing bid requests by i, we denote by $C_i \subseteq \{1, \cdots, M\}$ the subset of M ads that are eligible to be shown for bid request i as a result of such constraints. Indexing ads by $j = 1, \cdots, M$, the welfare of serving an impression for ad j (i.e., the value of showing the ad once to a user) for bid request i is given by $v_{ij} \geq 0$. The welfare v_{ij} can be set to the expected value of serving one ad impression for ad j for bid request i, but other expressions for welfare may be used as well.

For bid request i, let assignment variable $x_{ij} = 1$ correspond to our decision to allocate ad j an impression, with $x_{ij} = 0$ otherwise. Let w_i be the clearing price associated with allocating an impression for bid request i (e.g., the result of a second-price auction on external ad exchanges). Similarly, let a_{ij} be the some advertising quantity (e.g., budget consumed) incurred a result of allocating an impression for bid request i for ad j, where we generally assume that advertisers are charged per impression (as opposed to, say, a cost-per-click or cost-per-action model). We note at this juncture that a_{ij} and the clearing price w_i can be distinct in practice. In particular, the method by which a_{ij} is computed can vary from ad to ad and from one bid request to the next, depending on contracts that advertisers may hold with the ad serving system.

Given the welfare v_{ij} of serving an impression of ad j for bid request i, we wish to derive an online and distributed algorithm for selecting ads j such that in aggregate, we maximize total welfare across all advertisers subject to long-term constraints specified by the advertisers as a function of all variables x_{ij}. We will also have the constraints that for any bid request i, $\sum_{j \in C_i} x_{ij} \leq 1$, such that we can show at most one ad per bid request (we can also elect to show none). As we assume a distributed and online setting, bid requests are divided across time and among several hosts. Thus, there are two ways to partition bid requests: the first is by time, whereby we can divide the continuous time axis into rounds of T approximately even-sized intervals indexed by $t = 1, \cdots, T$. For a given interval t, let I_t denote the set of bid requests processed across the entire fleet in that interval, such that the sets I_t form a partition of all bid requests. Given the above, let $\mathbf{x}_t, \mathbf{u}_t$ denote assignment and utility[1] vectors whose elements correspond to $x_{ij}, v_{ij} - w_i$ respectively, and define matrices $\mathbf{A}_t$ similarly. For illustration, Figure 1 shows a toy example of an assignment problem with scalar quantities and corresponding matrices and vectors as defined above.

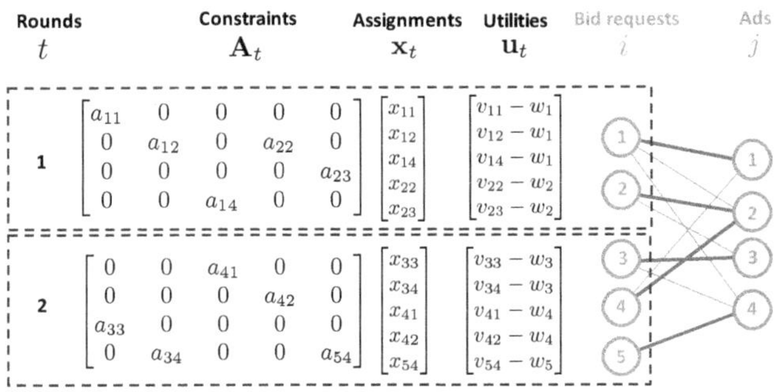

Figure 1: A toy assignment problem consisting of 4 ads and 5 bid requests divided into 2 rounds, with corresponding matrix and vector quantities $\mathbf{A}_t, \mathbf{x}_t, \mathbf{u}_t$. Here, elements a_{ij} correspond to some advertising output of interest (e.g., budget consumed) for bid request i and ad j, with $x_{ij} \in \{0, 1\}$. Dark edges in the bipartite graph on the right correspond to a possible feasible assignment. Figure best seen in color.

As has been commonly done in online display advertising [3, 6, 9], we formulate the canonical problem of allocating ad impressions as an optimal assignment problem, where the goal is to match ads to bid requests such that we maximize the total difference between welfare and clearing price (profit) across all ads and all bid requests for the ad serving platform. The standard optimal assignment problem can be written as a linear program (LP) relaxation of the corresponding combinatorial optimization problem with assignment variables $\mathbf{X} = \{x_{ij}\}$:

$$\underset{\mathbf{X}}{\text{maximize}} \sum_{i, j \in C_i} (v_{ij} - w_i) x_{ij} \text{ with } \begin{cases} \forall\, i, \sum_{j \in C_i} x_{ij} \leq 1 \\ \forall\, i, j \in C_i,\ x_{ij} \geq 0. \end{cases}$$

We now introduce the online aspect of the problem (we postpone discussion of the distributed aspects for later) by partitioning bid requests into sets I_t for $t \in \{1, \cdots, T\}$.

[1]Utility measures the advertiser's preference between bid requests.

Using matrix-vector notation and introducing the quantity $N \equiv \max_t M|I_t|$, we can compactly re-write the optimal assignment problem as $\underset{\mathbf{x}_1 \in \mathcal{X}_1, \cdots, \mathbf{x}_T \in \mathcal{X}_T}{\text{maximize}} \sum_{t=1}^{T} \mathbf{u}_t^\top \mathbf{x}_t$, where we have defined

$$\mathcal{X}_t \equiv \Big\{ \mathbf{x} \in [0,1]^N \Big| \forall\, i \in I_t, \sum_{j \in C_i} x_{ij} \le 1 \text{ and } x_{ij} = 0 \text{ if } j \notin C_i; \\ \forall i \notin I_t, x_{ij} = 0 \Big\},$$

and $\mathbf{x}_t$ is a row in the matrix $\mathbf{X} \in \{0,1\}^{T \times N}$. In the online assignment problem, for round t the external world generates the vector $\mathbf{u}_t$, after which we must make allocation decisions $\mathbf{x}_t$ and obtain reward $\mathbf{u}_t^\top \mathbf{x}_t$. Thus, each element of vector $\mathbf{x}_t \in \mathcal{X}_t$ is an assignment variable x_{ij}, with the elements of vector $\mathbf{u}_t$ similarly ordered to be equal to $v_{ij} - w_i$.

It has been shown [6] that we can solve the optimal assignment problem iteratively for each bid request i by sorting ads $j \in C_i$ by v_{ij}, picking the top-ranking ad and assigning an impression to that ad [6] if $\max_j v_{ij} \ge w_i$. For completeness and due to its central role in what follows, we formalize this result as a Lemma and reproduce the proof (which can also be found in [6]) in the Appendix.

LEMMA 1. *Denote by $\mathbf{x}_t$ to be the set of all x_{ij}'s that are processed in round t. Let $j^\star = \text{argmax}_{j \in C_i} v_{ij}$, and let β_i be a dual variable for enforcing the constraint $\sum_{j \in C_i} x_{ij} \le 1$. Then for each $i \in I_t$, we must have*

$$\beta_i^\star = v_{ij^\star} = \max_{j \in C_i} v_{ij},$$

$$\hat{x}_{ij^\star} = 1, \hat{x}_{ij} = 0\; \forall j \in C_i, j \neq j^\star \text{ if } \beta_i^\star \ge w_i,$$

$$\hat{x}_{ij} = 0\; \forall j \text{ if } \beta_i^\star < w_i,$$

such that $\hat{\mathbf{x}}_t = \text{argmax}_{\mathbf{x}_t \in \mathcal{X}_t} \mathbf{u}_t^\top \mathbf{x}_t$.

Thus, for a given round t, the above online algorithm sequentially allocates impressions such that the optimum $\hat{\mathbf{x}}_t \in \text{argmax}_{\mathbf{x}_t \in \mathcal{X}_t} \mathbf{u}_t^\top \mathbf{x}_t$ is attained. In particular, the quantity $\beta_i^\star$ plays the role of the bid submitted to an auction for a given ad impression opportunity within a larger advertising marketplace. Consistent with the practical reality of ad allocation, if $\beta_i^\star < w_i$, we do not allocate any ad impression (i.e., we lost the auction) and otherwise we get to allocate an ad impression to the winning ad $j^\star \in C_i$. Thus, the calculation of $\hat{\mathbf{x}}_t$ is wholly determined by computing bids $\beta_i^\star$ and finding whether we win an ad impression or not via the clearing price w_i for bid requests $i \in I_t$.

In the sequel, we take advantage of the above result to introduce *concave* functions of $\mathbf{X}$ for modelling long-term constraints and solve the resulting non-linear maximization problems via an online primal-dual method (with guarantees on the resulting solution as compared to the optimal offline solution), whilst preserving the computationally-efficient primal steps with some simple modifications. Under our proposed framework, we will modify each bid as a function of long-term constraints to $\beta_i^\star = \max_j\{v_{ij} - \lambda_{j,t} a_{ij}\}$ such that $\hat{\mathbf{x}}_t = \text{argmax}_{\mathbf{x}_t \in \mathcal{X}_t}\{\mathbf{u}_t^\top \mathbf{x}_t - \boldsymbol{\lambda}^\top \mathbf{A}_t \mathbf{x}_t\}$ for some dual variables $\boldsymbol{\lambda}$ (formally defined in the sequel) that allow us to penalize violations of constraints. Our framework has the property that no knowledge of auction dynamics, assumptions about stochastic or adversarial feedback, or knowledge of other characteristics of the ad marketplace are needed to provide regret guarantees for online ad allocation. Moreover, as we will show, the resulting algorithm can be naturally extended to a distributed setting in which we must allocate ad impressions across a large number of ad serving hosts operating independently, which is key for practical large-scale ad serving systems.

3. OPTIMAL ASSIGNMENT WITH LONG-TERM CONSTRAINTS

As we will show, many online optimization problems of interest in online display advertising will consist of an optimal assignment problem with additional equality and inequality constraints on the primal variables $\mathbf{x}_t$, which introduces non-trivial challenges. We assume that these constraints are 1) measured over T rounds, and 2) are linear in the assignment variables $\mathbf{X}$, such that we can account for such constraints by penalizing some measure of $\frac{1}{T}\sum_{t=1}^{T} \mathbf{A}_t \mathbf{x}_t - \mathbf{b}_t$, where $\mathbf{A}_t \in \mathcal{A} \subseteq \mathbb{R}^{K \times N}, \mathbf{b}_t \in \mathbb{R}^K$. Building on the work from [12], the optimal assignment problem can be modified to:

$$\underset{\mathbf{x}_1 \in \mathcal{X}_1, \cdots, \mathbf{x}_T \in \mathcal{X}_T}{\text{maximize}} \; \frac{1}{T}\sum_{t=1}^{T} \mathbf{u}_t^\top \mathbf{x}_t - \mathcal{E}\left(\frac{1}{T}\sum_{t=1}^{T} \mathbf{A}_t \mathbf{x}_t - \mathbf{b}_t\right) \quad (1)$$

where $\mathcal{E}$ is a convex function measuring the residuals of the constraints. In this paper, we will assume that $\mathcal{E}$ is smooth in the sense that it has Lipschitz continuous gradients over the domain $\mathbb{R}^K$. We note that although the above optimization problem is not linear in all variables in the strict sense of the optimal assignment problem, the corresponding Lagrangian (and primal-dual algorithm that we will derive) remains linear with respect to assignment variables $\mathbf{X}$, which implies that the computationally efficient ranking scheme derived for the optimal assignment problem can be modified to solve for the primal variables in the above problem. Moreover, we note that unlike [2], we are not interested in the (unweighted) average of $\mathbf{x}_t$ vectors insofar as objectives and constraints are concerned, and we are explicitly interested in maximizing functions of $\mathbf{x}_t$ that are time-varying and highly dynamic. Before we continue, we illustrate two common problem classes that arise frequently in online display advertising that can be naturally formulated as optimization problems of the above form.

EXAMPLE 1. *(Max-performance, target delivery ad allocation) In this problem formulation, we wish to maximize ad performance (as measured by welfare v_{ij} for each bid request and eligible ad candidate) subject to the need to consume as close to 100% of each ad's total budget for T rounds. Denoting 1) a_{ij} to be the revenue charged to the advertiser for ad j upon serving an impression for ad j and bid request i and 2) b_j to be ad j's total budget to be delivered over T rounds, we have $K = M$ (one constraint per ad for M ads), $\mathbf{A}_t \in \mathbb{R}^{M \times N}$ is a matrix whose $(j,i)^{th}$ element is a_{ij} and $\mathbf{b}_t \in \mathbb{R}^M$ is a vector whose j^{th} element is b_j, so that $\frac{1}{T}\sum_{t=1}^{T} \mathbf{A}_t \mathbf{x}_t - \mathbf{b}_t$ is the average error between the amount of budget consumed and the target amount of budget to be consumed over T rounds, which we wish to penalize via a suitable choice of $\mathcal{E}$.*

EXAMPLE 2. *(Max-delivery, max cost-per-action ad allocation) Here, we aim to maximize welfare subject to a constraint on the cost-per-action (CPA) for each ad, specified as $c_j > 0$. With $K = M$, let p_{ij} be the probability of user conversion, and let r_{ij} be the amount of revenue charged to* *the advertiser upon serving an ad impression for bid request i and ad j. Given the quantities defined in Example 1, we can formulate the CPA constraint for ad j as*

$$\forall j, \sum_i r_{ij} x_{ij} \le c_j \sum_i p_{ij} x_{ij}.$$

This can be formulated equivalently as $\frac{1}{T}\sum_{t=1}^{T} \mathbf{A}_t \mathbf{x}_t - \mathbf{b}_t$ *where* $\mathbf{A}_t$ *is a matrix whose* $(j,i)^{th}$ *element is* $(r_{ij} - c_j p_{ij})$ *and* $\mathbf{b}_t = \mathbf{0}$ *so that penalizing values of* $\frac{1}{T}\sum_{t=1}^{T} \mathbf{A}_t \mathbf{x}_t - \mathbf{b}_t$ *above* $\mathbf{0}$ *is equivalent to a penalty for violating the CPA constraint for each ad.*

A list of possible instantiations for $\mathcal{E}$ for the above problems can be found in [12]. We highlight that in the general case, we allow $K \neq M$, which allows us to account for multiple constraints per ad, and/or diverse sets of constraints for different ads.

Consider now the Lagrangian, or saddle-point function, for the problem in (1), given by

$$\mathcal{L}(\mathbf{X}, \boldsymbol{\lambda}) = \frac{1}{T}\sum_{t=1}^{T} \mathbf{u}_t^\top \mathbf{x}_t - \boldsymbol{\lambda}^\top \left[\frac{1}{T}\sum_{t=1}^{T} \mathbf{A}_t \mathbf{x}_t - \mathbf{b}_t\right] + \mathcal{E}^\star(\boldsymbol{\lambda}), \quad (2)$$

where $\boldsymbol{\lambda} \in \Lambda$ are dual variables that belong to the domain $\Lambda \subseteq \mathbb{R}^K$ of $\mathcal{E}^*$, where $\mathcal{E}^\star(\boldsymbol{\lambda}) \equiv \sup_{\mathbf{z} \in \mathbb{R}^K} \{\boldsymbol{\lambda}^\top \mathbf{z} - \mathcal{E}(\mathbf{z})\}$ is the Fenchel conjugate [4] of $\mathcal{E}$ for which we assume the domain is compact so that there exists $R_\lambda \equiv \max_{\boldsymbol{\lambda} \in \Lambda} \|\boldsymbol{\lambda}\|_2 < +\infty$. Moreover, we remark that $\mathcal{E}^\star$ is strongly convex by virtue of $\mathcal{E}$ having Lipschitz continuous gradients [14]. We recall that a function $\mathcal{E}^\star$ is strongly convex with modulus $\sigma > 0$ if $\mathcal{E}^\star(\mathbf{u}) \le \mathcal{E}^\star(\mathbf{v}) + \nabla\mathcal{E}^\star(\mathbf{u})^\top(\mathbf{u}-\mathbf{v}) - \frac{\sigma}{2}\|\mathbf{u}-\mathbf{v}\|^2$ for any $\mathbf{u}, \mathbf{v} \in \mathbb{R}^K$. We can rewrite the Lagrangian function described in (2) as $\mathcal{L}(\mathbf{X}, \boldsymbol{\lambda}) = \frac{1}{T}\sum_{t=1}^{T} \mathcal{L}_t(\mathbf{x}_t, \boldsymbol{\lambda})$, where

$$\mathcal{L}_t(\mathbf{x}_t, \boldsymbol{\lambda}) = \begin{cases} \mathbf{u}_t^\top \mathbf{x}_t - \boldsymbol{\lambda}^\top\Big(\mathbf{A}_t \mathbf{x}_t - \mathbf{b}_t\Big) + \mathcal{E}^\star(\boldsymbol{\lambda}) & \text{if } \boldsymbol{\lambda} \in \Lambda \\ -\infty & \text{otherwise.} \end{cases}$$

To maximize $\mathcal{L}_t(\mathbf{x}_t, \boldsymbol{\lambda}_t)$ with respect to $\mathbf{x}_t$, it is straightforward to show that the result of Lemma 1 can be modified to accomplish this by ranking ads for each bid request, but using a modified bid of $v_{ij} - \lambda_{j,t} a_{ij}$. Thus, in the sequel we will appeal to Lemma 1 for a computationally efficient method for solving the problem of computing $\hat{\mathbf{x}}_t \in \mathrm{argmax}_{\mathbf{x}_t \in \mathcal{X}_t} \mathcal{L}_t(\mathbf{x}_t, \boldsymbol{\lambda})$.

In an offline setting where we would have the ability to iteratively update both primal variables $\mathbf{x}_t, t = 1, \cdots, T$ and dual variables $\boldsymbol{\lambda}$, the following canonical[2] primal-dual algorithm would allow us to solve for optimal variables $\mathbf{x}_t^\star$, $\boldsymbol{\lambda}^\star$ by repeating the two steps below until some convergence criterion is met:

- (P-offline) Compute for all $t = 1, \cdots, T$
$$\hat{\mathbf{x}}_t \in \arg\max_{\mathbf{x}_t \in \mathcal{X}_t} \mathcal{L}_t(\mathbf{x}_t, \boldsymbol{\lambda}).$$
- (D-offline) Given $\hat{\mathbf{x}}_t$ for all $t = 1, \cdots, T$, compute $\mathcal{L}_t(\hat{\mathbf{x}}_t, \boldsymbol{\lambda})$ and gradient $\nabla_{\boldsymbol{\lambda}}\mathcal{L}(\hat{\mathbf{X}}, \boldsymbol{\lambda}) = \sum_t \nabla_{\boldsymbol{\lambda}}\mathcal{L}_t(\hat{\mathbf{x}}_t, \boldsymbol{\lambda})$. Update all dual variables $\boldsymbol{\lambda}$ using a projected gradient descent method with step size η. Note that we speak about a project *gradient* scheme (as opposed to a projected *subgradient* method) since the choice of $\mathcal{E}$ we will make in the experiments leads us to consider a function $\mathcal{E}^*$ which is not only strongly convex, but also differentiable on its domain Λ.

[2]There are in fact several primal-dual algorithms that could be used to solve the offline problem; we present a simple method to best illustrate the online method that follows.

The above algorithm is an offline algorithm that iteratively updates primal and dual variables until convergence. However, in practice, ad allocation requires us to make decisions in online, or sequential, fashion, such that the primal and dual steps above must be interleaved over rounds $t = 1, \cdots, T$. We now turn to formulating the ad allocation problem as an online convex optimization problem in which we sequentially update primal and dual variables $\hat{\mathbf{x}}_t$ and $\hat{\boldsymbol{\lambda}}_t$ at each round.

4. OPTIMAL AD ALLOCATION AS ONLINE CONVEX OPTIMIZATION

To move to an online convex optimization formulation, we must also account for the fact that in an online setting, not only must we update primal and dual variables sequentially, but also the constraint matrices $\mathbf{A}_t$ are only observed after we allocate ad impressions for round t (a practical example of this is that we often only find out how much to charge the advertiser once we have won an external RTB auction for a given winning ad). This requires us to estimate such matrices via $\hat{\mathbf{A}}_t$ in order to produce primal variable updates. To this end, we introduce

$$\hat{\mathcal{L}}_t(\mathbf{x}_t, \boldsymbol{\lambda}) = \mathbf{u}_t^\top \mathbf{x}_t - \boldsymbol{\lambda}^\top(\hat{\mathbf{A}}_t \mathbf{x}_t - \mathbf{b}_t) + \mathcal{E}^\star(\boldsymbol{\lambda})$$

as the Lagrangian function for round t using the estimate $\hat{\mathbf{A}}_t$ such that $\hat{\mathcal{L}}_t(\mathbf{x}_t, \boldsymbol{\lambda}) = \mathcal{L}_t(\mathbf{x}_t, \boldsymbol{\lambda}) - \boldsymbol{\lambda}^\top(\hat{\mathbf{A}}_t - \mathbf{A}_t)\mathbf{x}_t$. Then, an online version of the primal-dual method for each round $t = 1, \cdots, T$ can be described as:

- (P-online) Compute $\hat{\mathbf{x}}_t \in \mathrm{argmax}_{\mathbf{x}_t \in \mathcal{X}_t} \hat{\mathcal{L}}_t(\mathbf{x}_t, \hat{\boldsymbol{\lambda}}_t)$.
- (D-online) From $\hat{\mathbf{x}}_t$, compute $\mathcal{L}_t(\hat{\mathbf{x}}_t, \hat{\boldsymbol{\lambda}}_t)$. Given gradients $\nabla\mathcal{L}_t(\hat{\mathbf{x}}_t, \hat{\boldsymbol{\lambda}}_t)$, update dual variables $\hat{\boldsymbol{\lambda}}_{t+1}$ using a projected online gradient descent method as
$$\hat{\boldsymbol{\lambda}}_{t+1} = \Pi_\Lambda\Big[\hat{\boldsymbol{\lambda}}_t - \eta_t \nabla\mathcal{L}_t(\hat{\mathbf{x}}_t, \hat{\boldsymbol{\lambda}}_t)\Big] \text{ with step size } \eta_t.$$
- (A-online) Given $\mathbf{A}_t, \hat{\mathbf{A}}_t$, update $\hat{\mathbf{A}}_{t+1}$ via a projected online subgradient method with step size ν_t.

In the above online optimization problem, we require estimating constraint matrices for each round via $\hat{\mathbf{A}}_t$ *before* we provide primal variable estimates $\hat{\mathbf{x}}_t$. This implies that $\hat{\mathbf{x}}_t$ is obtained from a perturbation of $\mathcal{L}_t(\mathbf{x}_t, \hat{\boldsymbol{\lambda}}_t)$ via $\hat{\mathcal{L}}_t(\mathbf{x}_t, \hat{\boldsymbol{\lambda}}_t)$, with $\mathbf{A}_t$ observed only *after* we have made the ad assignment $\hat{\mathbf{x}}_t$.

Estimating $\mathbf{A}_t$: To estimate constraint matrices $\mathbf{A}_t$ online, we assume that in addition to the dual variables being bounded in ℓ_2 norm with radius R_λ, we also have $\|\mathbf{x}_t\|_2 \le R_x$ for all $t, \mathbf{x}_t \in \mathcal{X}_t$. Similarly, let R_A be such that $\|\mathbf{A}\|_F \le R_A$ for all $\mathbf{A} \in \mathcal{A}$ and $\mathcal{A}$ is convex. We further assume that we perform an online projected subgradient method on matrices $\hat{\mathbf{A}}_t$ to estimate the sequence $\mathbf{A}_1, \ldots, \mathbf{A}_T$ where $\hat{\mathbf{A}}_{t+1} = \Pi_{\mathcal{A}}[\hat{\mathbf{A}}_t - \nu_t \mathbf{G}_t]$, with $\mathbf{G}_t$ a subgradient of $\mathbf{A} \mapsto \|\mathbf{A}_t - \mathbf{A}\|_F$ at $\hat{\mathbf{A}}_t$. With the step size $\nu_t = R_A/\sqrt{t}$, it can be shown [12] that for any sequence $\{\mathbf{A}_t\}_{t=1}^{T}$, the overall cumulative regret bound for the estimation of $\mathbf{x}_t$'s is additively impacted by the term

$$\frac{6R_\lambda R_x}{\sqrt{T}}\left[\sum_{t=1}^{T}\|\mathbf{A}_t-\mathbf{A}_{t+1}\|_F+R_A\right],$$

where $\|\cdot\|_F$ stands for the Frobenius norm. This contribution captures the variations in the constraints $\mathbf{A}_t$ themselves from one round t to the next, plus a function of the largest constraint matrix (as measured by R_A) observed over the course of the algorithm. With the above result and having described our online algorithm, we are now ready to present cumulative regret bounds for the above algorithm as measured by the difference in the primal objectives for the oracle solution and the online solution obtain from the above online algorithm, where both solutions account for advertiser objectives and long-term constraints. That is, we will compare the performance of the online algorithm to that of an oracle algorithm which has complete knowledge of past and future, plus the ability to modify optimization variables in the past, so as to provide primal variables of the form $\mathbf{x}_t^\star \in \operatorname{argmax}_{\mathbf{x}\in\mathcal{X}_t}\mathcal{L}_t(\mathbf{x},\boldsymbol{\lambda}^\star)$ for each round t given the offline dual optimal variables $\boldsymbol{\lambda}^\star$. We expect at the outset that the above algorithm should achieve performance which is a function of the oracle algorithm's performance plus factors that depend on the number of rounds T, as well as variability of constraints as measured by the oracle's ability to satisfy constraints. We present the bound in Theorem 1, and direct the details of the proof (as well as key technical Lemmas) to [12]. We note that the version of the theorem which we state is for instance valid for the choice of $\mathcal{E}$ we make in the experimental section.

THEOREM 1. *Let $\{\mathbf{x}_t^\star\}_{t=1}^T$ be the offline primal optimal assignment variables, and consider the sequence $\{\hat{\mathbf{x}}_t\}_{t=1}^T$ generated by our online algorithm. Let $\mathbf{e}_t^\star=\mathbf{A}_t\mathbf{x}_t^\star-\mathbf{b}_t$ be the corresponding optimal constraint residuals. We denote by*

$$f^\star \equiv f(\mathbf{x}_1^\star,\cdots,\mathbf{x}_T^\star)\equiv\frac{1}{T}\sum_{t=1}^{T}\mathbf{u}_t^\top\mathbf{x}_t^\star-\mathcal{E}\Big(\frac{1}{T}\sum_t\mathbf{A}_t\mathbf{x}_t^\star-\mathbf{b}_t\Big)$$

the optimal primal objective value obtained for the assignments $\{\mathbf{x}_t^\star\}_{t=1}^T$, and define $\hat{f}\equiv f(\hat{\mathbf{x}}_1,\cdots,\hat{\mathbf{x}}_T)$ similarly. Provided that $\max_{t=1,\cdots,T,\mathbf{x}_t\in\mathcal{X}_t,\boldsymbol{\lambda}\in\Lambda}\|\nabla_{\boldsymbol{\lambda}}\mathcal{L}_t(\mathbf{x}_t,\boldsymbol{\lambda})\|_2\le G$ for $G>0$, the projected online gradient descent/subgradients updates for $\hat{\boldsymbol{\lambda}}_t$ and $\hat{\mathbf{A}}_t$ with step sizes $\eta_t=L/t,\nu_t=R_A/\sqrt{t}$ imply

$$f^\star-\hat{f}\le\frac{GL}{T}(1+\log(T))\cdot\max_{t=1,\cdots,T}\left\|\sum_{j=1}^{t}\frac{T-t}{T}\mathbf{e}_j^\star-\sum_{j=t+1}^{T}\frac{t}{T}\mathbf{e}_j^\star\right\|_2$$
$$+\frac{G^2L}{2T}(1+\log(T))+\frac{6R_\lambda R_x}{\sqrt{T}}\left[\sum_{t=1}^{T}\|\mathbf{A}_t-\mathbf{A}_{t+1}\|_F+R_A\right]$$

where $\mathcal{E}$ has Lipschitz gradients with modulus L.

Theorem 1 establishes that the projected online gradient descent updates for dual variables $\hat{\boldsymbol{\lambda}}_t$, along with projected online subgradient updates for constraint matrices $\hat{\mathbf{A}}_t$, yield an overall cumulative regret bound that decomposes into three terms. The first term measures the smoothness, or regularity, of the sequences $\{\mathbf{e}_t^\star\}_{t=1}^T$ (as measured by the oracle's ability to minimize constraint violations) as well as $\{\mathbf{u}_t\}_{t=1}^T$ (which have a direct influence on $\mathbf{x}_t^\star$). We can observe that if the residual vectors are constant $\mathbf{e}_t^\star=\mathbf{e}^\star$ for all t, the first term vanishes.[3] The second term captures the contribution of having to perform online updates, which is is sub-linear in the number of rounds T given previous results in the online convex optimization literature [11, 19]). The third and last term captures the contribution to the regret due to the variation in constraint matrices $\mathbf{A}_t$ as measured by $\sum_{t=1}^T\|\mathbf{A}_t-\mathbf{A}_{t+1}\|_F$.

We note that Theorem 1 does not require any assumptions about the arrival order of bid requests, stationarity, or about the precise mechanisms under which feedback is generated (e.g., specific auction dynamics, marketplace characteristics, etc). Thus, Theorem 1 holds for *any* sequences of $\{\mathbf{A}_t,\mathbf{b}_t\}_{t=1}^T,\{\mathbf{u}_t\}_{t=1}^T$, including those generated by an adversary, with the consequence that if the adversary is sufficiently powerful such that $\{\mathbf{A}_t\mathbf{x}_t^\star-\mathbf{b}_t\}_{t=1}^T,\{\mathbf{u}_t\}_{t=1}^T$ vary wildly (i.e., even the oracle algorithm is unable to obtain a smooth sequence $\{\mathbf{A}_t\mathbf{x}_t^\star-\mathbf{b}_t\}_{t=1}^T$), then the worst-case bound on regret for our proposed online primal-dual method can be large. Conversely, if the oracle algorithm is able to achieve a regular-enough sequence $\{\mathbf{A}_t\mathbf{x}_t^\star-\mathbf{b}_t\}_{t=1}^T$, then our proposed online primal-dual method is able to achieve the same performance plus a factor that is sublinear in the number of rounds.

5. DISTRIBUTED ASPECTS OF ONLINE AD ALLOCATION

Having presented regret bounds for our proposed online algorithm, we now address the distributed aspects of ad allocation, which are a fundamental to the display advertising setting in practice. We note that for the allocation problem, we can write $\mathbf{u}_t^\top\mathbf{x}_t=\sum_{h=1}^H\mathbf{u}_{ht}^\top\mathbf{x}_{ht}$ so that the primal step of computing $\hat{\mathbf{x}}_t\in\operatorname{argmax}_{\mathbf{x}_t\in\mathcal{X}_t}\mathcal{L}_t(\mathbf{x}_t,\hat{\boldsymbol{\lambda}}_t)$ can be decomposed across multiple hosts, each processing disjoint subsets of bid requests for round t by ranking candidate ads for each bid request to be processed on that host. We first present an offline distributed algorithm that leverages this decomposability, which we will quickly incorporate into an online and distributed algorithm.

5.1 Offline dual decomposition

If we temporarily ignore the online aspect of the ad allocation problem, a technique that would allow us to perform distributed optimization is to decompose the ad allocation problem across hosts for a given set of dual variables, collect primal solutions and then update the dual variables. We note that for any round t, we can partition the primal variables $\mathbf{x}_t$ across hosts into disjoint sub-vectors of variables such that $\mathbf{x}_t=[\mathbf{x}_{1t},\cdots,\mathbf{x}_{Ht}]$, where $\mathbf{x}_{ht}$ is the vector of primal variables associated with host $h=1,\cdots,H$. Furthermore, by defining partitions I_h of bid requests across hosts $h=1,\cdots,H$, we can perform similar partitions for $\mathbf{u}_t,\mathbf{A}_t$, $\mathcal{X}_t$ (so that $\mathbf{x}_{ht}\in\mathcal{X}_{ht}$). With these partitions defined, the Lagrangian $\mathcal{L}_t(\mathbf{x},\boldsymbol{\lambda})$ can then be decomposed as

$$\begin{aligned}\mathcal{L}_t(\mathbf{x}_t,\boldsymbol{\lambda})&=\mathbf{u}_t^\top\mathbf{x}_t-\boldsymbol{\lambda}^\top\Big(\mathbf{A}_t\mathbf{x}_t-\mathbf{b}_t\Big)+\mathcal{E}^\star(\boldsymbol{\lambda})\\&=\sum_{h=1}^{H}\mathbf{u}_{ht}^\top\mathbf{x}_{ht}-\boldsymbol{\lambda}^\top\mathbf{A}_{ht}\mathbf{x}_{ht}+\boldsymbol{\lambda}^\top\mathbf{b}_t+\mathcal{E}^\star(\boldsymbol{\lambda})\\&=\sum_{h=1}^{H}F_{ht}(\mathbf{x}_{ht},\boldsymbol{\lambda})+G_t(\boldsymbol{\lambda}),\end{aligned}$$

[3]We refer the reader to [12] for an in-depth discussion.

which is a sum over functions of $\mathbf{x}_{ht}$ with no overlap in primal variable arguments, plus a function of $\boldsymbol{\lambda}$ that is otherwise independent of variables $\mathbf{x}_{ht}$. This implies that we can parallelize the primal step of estimating the allocation $\hat{\mathbf{x}}_t \in \arg\max_{\mathbf{x}_t \in \mathcal{X}_t} \mathcal{L}_t(\mathbf{x}_t, \boldsymbol{\lambda})$ across a number of hosts for a given $\boldsymbol{\lambda}$, collect the solutions $\hat{\mathbf{x}}_{ht}$ and then update $\boldsymbol{\lambda}$. The resulting distributed primal-dual algorithm is then

- (P-offline & distributed) Compute for each round $t = 1, \cdots, T$ and for all hosts $h = 1, \cdots, H$:
$$\hat{\mathbf{x}}_{ht} \in \arg\max_{\mathbf{x}_{ht} \in \mathcal{X}_{ht}} F_{ht}(\mathbf{x}_{ht}, \boldsymbol{\lambda}),$$
- (D-offline) Collect solutions to form $\hat{\mathbf{x}}_t = [\hat{\mathbf{x}}_{1t}, \cdots, \hat{\mathbf{x}}_{Ht}]$ for all $t = 1, \cdots, T$. From $\hat{\mathbf{x}}_t$, compute $\mathcal{L}_t(\hat{\mathbf{x}}_t, \boldsymbol{\lambda})$ and gradient $\nabla \mathcal{L}(\hat{\mathbf{X}}, \boldsymbol{\lambda}) = \sum_t \nabla \mathcal{L}_t(\hat{\mathbf{x}}_t, \boldsymbol{\lambda})$. Given the gradient, update dual variables $\boldsymbol{\lambda}$ using a projected gradient descent method with step size η.

The proposed algorithm consists of iteratively 1) performing a distributed Lagrangian maximization across all hosts to obtain $\max_{\mathbf{x}} \mathcal{L}(\mathbf{x}, \boldsymbol{\lambda})$, followed by 2) a gradient descent method. This technique for solving large-scale convex optimization problems in a distributed setting consists of *dual decomposition* [7, 8, 13], which yields primal and dual-optimal $\mathbf{x}^\star, \boldsymbol{\lambda}^\star$ for a large enough number of iterations. However, in the online advertising setting, we do not have the ability to revise past ad allocations, nor can we realistically anticipate (and hence make allocation decisions for) future bid request opportunities. To address this whilst retaining the ability to decompose the problem across a large number of ad serving hosts, we next present online dual decomposition (ODD), an extension of the dual decomposition technique to the online optimization setting.

5.2 Online dual decomposition (ODD)

Consider now the following distributed and online algorithm for each round $t = 1, \cdots, T$:

- (P-online & distributed) Define
$$\hat{F}_{ht}(\mathbf{x}_{ht}, \boldsymbol{\lambda}) = \mathbf{u}_{ht}^\top \mathbf{x}_{ht} - \boldsymbol{\lambda}^\top \hat{\mathbf{A}}_{ht} \mathbf{x}_{ht}.$$
Compute for all hosts $h = 1, \cdots, H$:
$$\hat{\mathbf{x}}_{ht} = \arg\max_{\mathbf{x}_{ht} \in \mathcal{X}_{ht}} \hat{F}_{ht}(\mathbf{x}_{ht}, \hat{\boldsymbol{\lambda}}_t).$$
- (D-online) Collect solutions to form $\hat{\mathbf{x}}_t = [\hat{\mathbf{x}}_{1t}, \cdots, \hat{\mathbf{x}}_{Ht}]$. From $\hat{\mathbf{x}}_t$ and given $\mathbf{A}_t$, compute $\mathcal{L}_t(\hat{\mathbf{x}}_t, \hat{\boldsymbol{\lambda}}_t)$ and gradient $\nabla \mathcal{L}_t(\hat{\mathbf{x}}_t, \hat{\boldsymbol{\lambda}}_t)$, and update dual variables $\hat{\boldsymbol{\lambda}}_{t+1}$ using a projected gradient descent method with step size η_t.
- (A-online) Given $\mathbf{A}_t, \hat{\mathbf{A}}_t$, update $\hat{\mathbf{A}}_{t+1}$ via a projected online subgradient method with step size ν_t.

The above distributed primal step, combined with the online projected gradient descent for $\hat{\boldsymbol{\lambda}}_t$ and subgradients for $\hat{\mathbf{A}}_t$ together form online dual decomposition (ODD), which extends classical dual decomposition to an online setting in which we must make ad allocations and update dual variables in an online fashion whilst having to use estimates of constraint matrices $\hat{\mathbf{A}}_t$. In ODD, in each round t we 1) solve for allocations $\hat{\mathbf{x}}_{ht}$ that maximize $\hat{F}_{ht}(\mathbf{x}_{ht}, \hat{\boldsymbol{\lambda}}_t)$ (distributed Lagrangian maximization with estimates of constraints $\hat{\mathbf{A}}_t$), followed by 2) updates of the dual variables $\hat{\boldsymbol{\lambda}}_t$ via an online dual gradient descent method on $\mathcal{L}_t(\hat{\mathbf{x}}_t, \hat{\boldsymbol{\lambda}}_t)$ and 3) online updates on $\hat{\mathbf{A}}_{t+1}$. We note that the above algorithm naturally leverages the embarassingly parallel and computationally-efficient ranking algorithm resulting from Lemma 1 for the primal step, and otherwise enjoys the same regret bound as presented in Theorem 1. The only additional assumption we've made for ODD is that there exists a centralized system for aggregating ad allocations, i.e., budget spend per round and per host given by $\sum_{i \in I_t \cap I_h} \mathbf{A}_{ht} \hat{\mathbf{x}}_{ht}$ and constraint matrices $\mathbf{A}_{ht}$ across hosts at the end of each round. From those pieces of information, global constraint violations can be computed for each ad (given centralized knowledge of $\mathbf{b}_t$ for each round) and updates for dual variables can be computed and then propagated back to each host in the ad serving fleet. Such systems are generally used in the online display advertising platforms to track budget spend: we do not discuss details on systems architectures that could be used for this purpose.

6. RESULTS

To validate our proposed online distributed ad allocation algorithm, we conducted three series of experiments with the aim to empirically compare the performance and delivery characteristics of ODD with those of other online algorithms. We focus on the application of max-performance, target delivery ad allocation described in Example 1, for which we consider two key metrics: 1) *performance* as measured by return on ad spend (ROAS), or the ratio of ad-attributed sales to ad spend, and 2) *delivery*, as measured by the fraction of an ad's budget that was successfully consumed relative to the fraction of the ad's flight time that has elapsed. More specifically, the goal in this class of problems is to maximize the ad's performance whilst consuming as close as 100% of the ad's budget by the end of its run time. We chose $\mathcal{E}(\mathbf{z})$ to be the Huber function (see the detailed discussion in [12]) for some non-negative parameters R, L:

$$\mathcal{E}(\mathbf{z}) = \begin{cases} \frac{L}{2}\|\mathbf{z}\|_2^2 & \text{if } \|\mathbf{z}\|_2 \leq \frac{R}{L}, \\ R\|\mathbf{z}\|_2 - \frac{R^2}{2L} & \text{otherwise.} \end{cases}$$

This choice yields the strongly convex dual function $\mathcal{E}^\star(\boldsymbol{\lambda}) = \mathcal{I}_{\mathcal{B}_R}(\boldsymbol{\lambda}) + \frac{1}{2L}\|\boldsymbol{\lambda}\|_2^2$, where $\mathcal{I}_{\mathcal{B}_R}$ is the indicator on the ℓ_2 ball such that $\|\hat{\boldsymbol{\lambda}}_t\|_2 \leq R$ for all rounds.

6.1 Experiment A: Simulation of ad allocation

In this experiment, we simulated ad allocation for a sample of 36 ads configured with a variety of budgets, delivery profiles (i.e., the fraction of budget to be delivered in a given time period) and targeting constraints encountered in our ad serving system, where ad impressions were allocated over a period of 24 hours with over 100MM bid request opportunities. To compare the performance and delivery characteristics of ODD, we examined 1) the proportional control heuristic of [6, 15] and 2) the *pdAvg* approximation algorithm from [10]. The proportional control heuristic consists of modifying the welfare term w_{ij} for each ad by subtracting a term that is proportional to the error in delivery in a given round (the difference between expected budget to be consumed in a round and actual amount delivered). The *pdAvg* approximation algorithm consists of modifying the welfare in similar fashion, but as a function of average welfare gained from allocating impressions for a given ad so far. All algorithmic parameters for the above algorithms were chosen from a discrete set in order to minimize total under- and over-delivery.

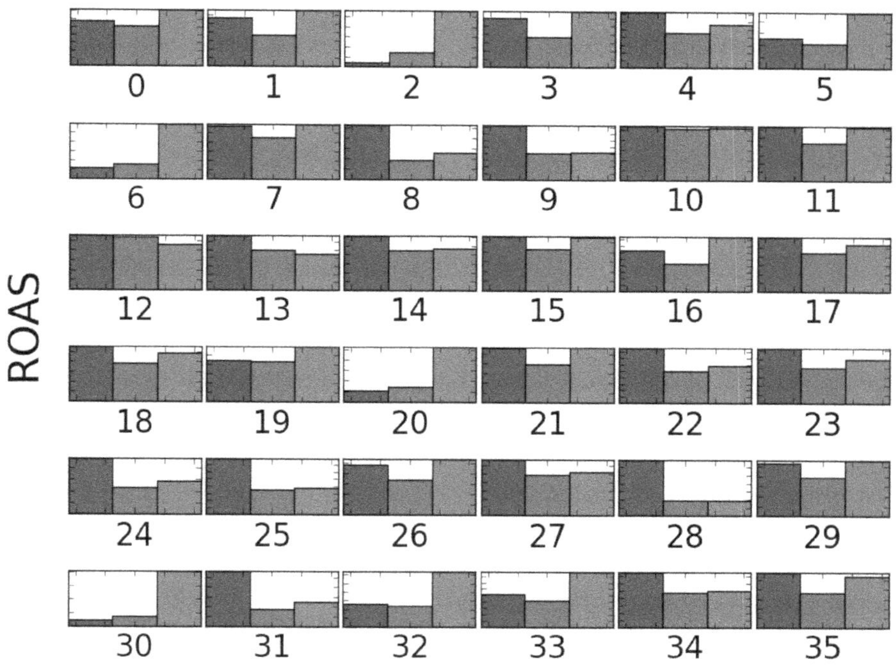

Figure 2: Performance for each of the 36 ads in Experiment A, as measured by return on ad spend (ROAS) obtained by ODD (blue), the proportional control heuristic (green) and the *pdAvg* algorithm of [10] (red). Subplots are numbered by ad to ease comparison between Figures 2 and 3. Figure best seen in color.

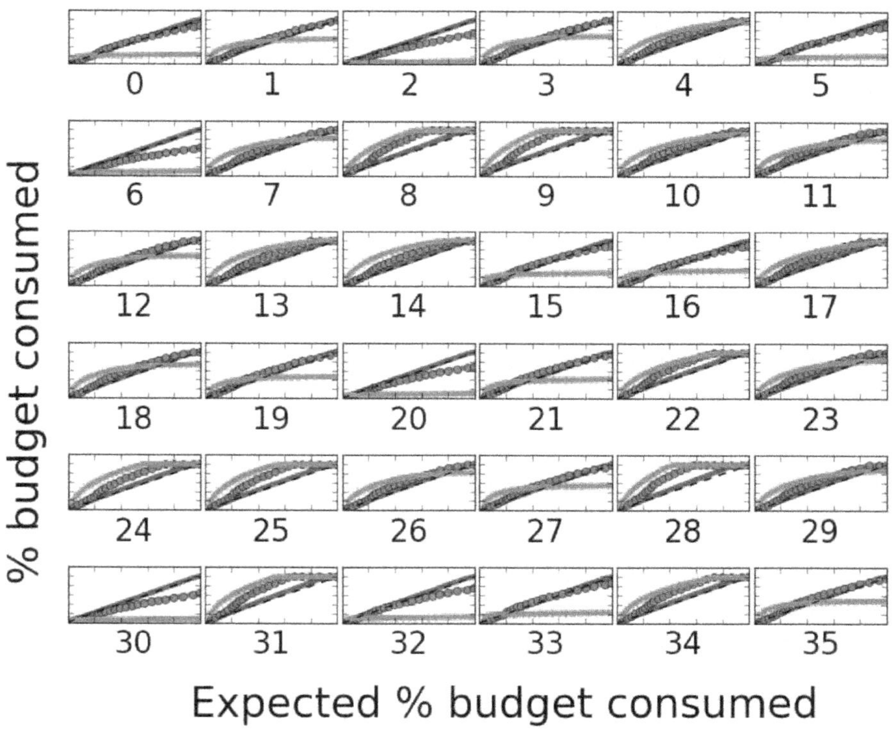

Figure 3: Percent budget delivered as a function of expected percentage of budget consumed over a period of 24 hours for the 36 ads for ODD (blue), the proportional control heuristic (green circles) and the *pdAvg* algorithm of [10] (red) for Experiment A. The black dotted line denotes the delivery profile matching exactly with the expected delivery profile for a given ad. Subplots are numbered by ad to ease comparison between Figures 2 and 3. Figure best seen in color.

Figure 2 shows the performance (ROAS) metrics at the end of the flight time for each of the three algorithms. Figure 3 shows delivery profiles for each one of them as a function of the expected delivery. As can be seen, *pdAvg* is able to achieve improved performance over ODD (for 16/36 ads), but at the cost of under-delivery in such cases (e.g., see ads 2, 5 and 30). This is undesirable from the advertiser's perspective, as under-delivery limits the overall impact of an ad and does not fully utilize the ad's budget to achieve the advertiser's performance goals. Conversely, for cases where *pdAvg* over-delivered (i.e., spent more budget ahead of schedule), such as for ads 25 and 31, the performance obtained was lower than that achieved by ODD. In aggregate, the performance metrics obtained for the ODD and *pdAvg* algorithms were very similar (within 3% of one another), but *pdAvg* demonstrated the highest variability in delivery (consistent with observations in [3]) in the form of over- or under-delivery (standard deviation in percent budget consumed across the 36 ads was 0.16% for ODD, 11.11% for proportional control, 34.2% for *pdAvg*) By comparison, the proportional control heuristic was only able to outperform the ODD technique for 4/36 ads (in all four cases, it under-delivered relative to the expected delivery profile), whilst yielding larger violations of delivery goals across the 36 ads as compared to ODD, but less variability in delivery as compared to *pdAvg*. Overall, ODD yielded a smoother delivery profile for all 36 ads with significantly less over- or under-delivery as compared to the other algorithms, and with performance (reward) equal to that achieved by the best of the algorithms studied.

6.2 Live experiments in a distributed production system at Amazon

The next two experiments were conducted within the distributed ad serving system at Amazon, where we compare the performance and delivery characteristics of ODD relative to a variant of the *pdAvg* algorithm.

6.2.1 Experiment B: Online A/B test at medium-scale

For the second experiment, we ran online tests of the ODD framework in a live production environment at Amazon where we compare our distributed optimization algorithm (treatment) to an ad allocation algorithm derived from *pdAvg* (control). Figure 4 shows results from an online test consisting of 7 pairs of control and treatment ads with a variety of slot positions, slot sizes and use/non-use of targeting, with the ad line items in treatment and control set to be otherwise identical. For this test, the exposure to external and non-stationary ad marketplace dynamics over the duration of the experiment (14 days) can lead to under- and over-delivery (where in practice, advertisers are less sensitive to over-delivery than under-delivery). As can be seen, the use of ODD achieves positive performance lifts, with delivery close to the target of 100% delivery for each ad.

6.2.2 Experiment C: Online A/B test at large-scale

Figures 5 and 6 show the results for the last experiment, where we compare our distributed optimization algorithm (treatment) to an ad allocation algorithm derived from *pdAvg* (control). It is conducted with a larger-scale test (>25X the number of ads from Experiment B) than the previous experiment (leveraging a variety of slot positions, slot sizes and use/non-use of targeting) for a larger set of ads across 8 advertiser pools over a period of 21 days: we see a consistent and significant reduction in both over- and under-delivery for all ads in the treatment set. We also note an overall significant decrease (i.e., 39%) in the number of ads in the treatment group that under-delivered as compared to the control group, and a 22% decrease in the number of ads in the treatment group that over-delivered as compared to the control group, where under- and over-delivery were defined by each advertiser. We also observe an overall 9% decrease in the number of ads that under-perform and a 19% increase in the number of ads that achieve advertiser-specified performance targets (also defined by the advertiser). Last but not least, we observed overall performance lifts in the range of 10% to 193%: these results, taken cumulatively, demonstrate that our algorithm is able to achieve higher advertiser performance whilst being able to better enforce ad delivery constraints as compared to the control treatment.

7. DISCUSSION

In this paper we have presented online dual decompositions as a technique for deriving practical online and distributed ad allocation algorithms for a variety of problems in online display advertising. In addition to having provided several empirical results derived from online advertising data, we have provided a theoretical analysis of the dynamic regret incurred by ODD, which includes a dependence on 1) the ability of an oracle algorithm to smoothly deliver ad impressions and 2) the smoothness with which constraints and constraint violations occur. While our analysis provides a regret bound that otherwise scales sub-linearly with the number of rounds T, there remain several factors that arise in practice that can impact performance and delivery in a production setting outside of the allocation algorithm: examples of these include 1) changes in auction dynamics, 2) changes, misallocations of ad budgets and 3) mis-specification of other campaign-specific parameters, to name a few. The impact of such changes on delivery and performance in practice is not to be discounted (and such impacts captured by our analysis in impacting the ability of an oracle algorithm to achieve smooth delivery) and should be studied as part of future work.

In this paper we have provided regret analysis that does not require making any assumptions about how feedback is generated by the external ad marketplace (e.g., auction dynamics, stochastic versus adversarial pricing). While this provides a robust baseline for performance and delivery characteristics that can be expected from ODD in a practical setting, this does not preclude the use of stable domain knowledge and/or assumptions about the ad marketplace (e.g., forecasting data) that could be useful in practice in improving performance and delivery properties for ODD. We also did not analyze the impact of delays and delayed feedback on the algorithm: we conjecture that adaptive gradient methods [1, 16] for dealing with delays may be appropriate for this setting, which we leave for future work. In terms of dealing with incomplete feedback, we leave as future work an investigation into extensions of ODD into the bandits setting [5]. Last but not least, we did not examine different distributed systems architectures and their impact on both empirical performance and delivery of our framework, which would be fruitful directions for future investigation.

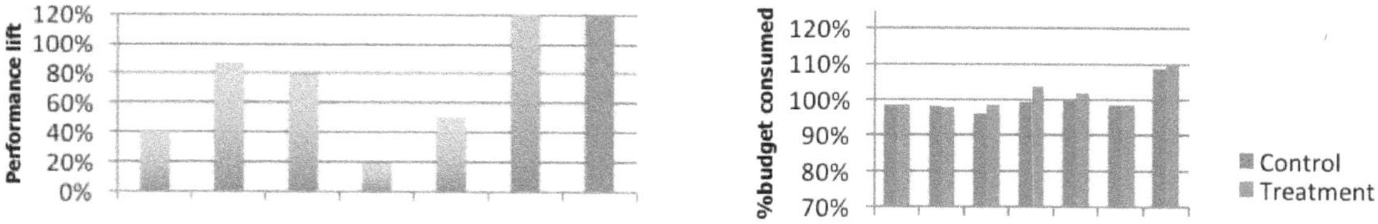

(a) (b)

Figure 4: (a) Performance lift for treatment ads and (b) change in delivery for treatment ads using ODD relative to control ads as a result of ad allocation via ODD in Experiment B. For this test, the exposure to external and non-stationary ad marketplace dynamics over the duration of the experiment (14 days) can lead to under- and over-delivery (in practice, advertisers are less sensitive to over-delivery than under-delivery). Here, the use of ODD achieves positive performance lifts, with delivery close to the target of 100% delivery for each ad. Figure best seen in color.

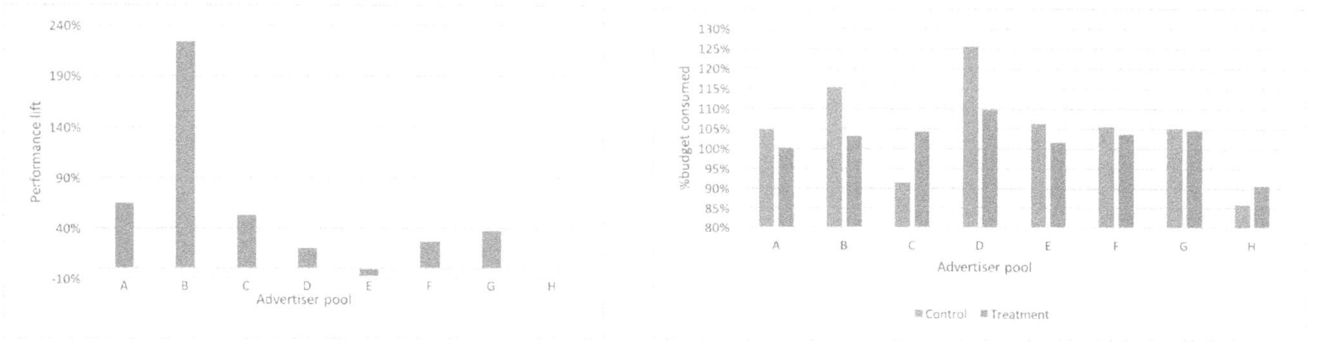

(a) (b)

Figure 5: (a) Performance and (b) delivery characteristics obtained from ODD relative to control ads for Experiment C. For this test, the exposure to external and non-stationary ad marketplace dynamics over the duration of the experiment (21 days) can lead to under- and over-delivery (where in practice, advertisers are less sensitive to over-delivery than under-delivery). Here we see overall performance lifts in the range of 10% to 193% and a consistent and significant reduction in both over- and under-delivery for all ads in the treatment set. Figure best seen in color.

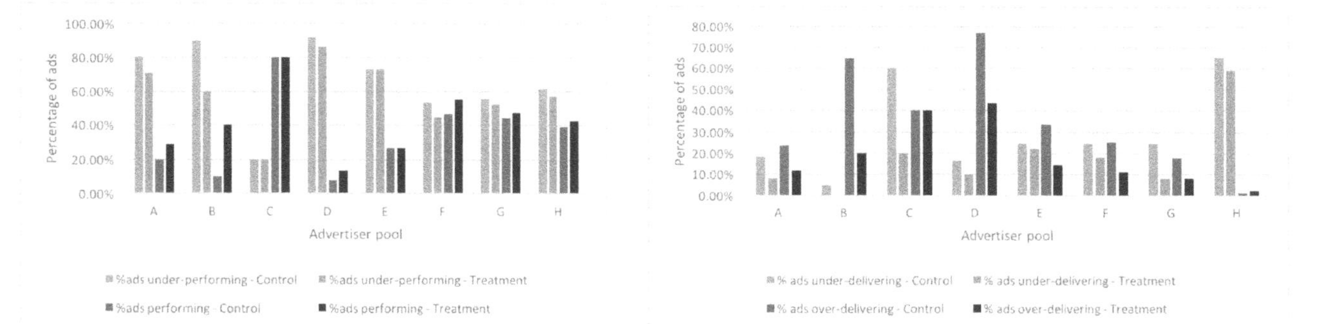

(a) (b)

Figure 6: (a) Lift in performance and (b) change in delivery relative to control ads as a result of ad allocation via ODD for Experiment C. For this test, the exposure to external and non-stationary ad marketplace dynamics over the duration of the experiment (21 days) can lead to under- and over-delivery (in practice, advertisers are less sensitive to over-delivery than under-delivery). Here we see decreases in the fraction of ads that under-perform and/or under-deliver, as well as an increase in the fraction of ads that perform or deliver up to advertiser-specified expectations. Figure best seen in color.

8. REFERENCES

[1] A. Agarwal and J. C. Duchi. Distributed delayed stochastic optimization. In *Advances in Neural Information Processing Systems*, pages 873–881, 2011.

[2] S. Agrawal and N. R. Devanur. Fast algorithms for online stochastic convex programming. In *SODA 2015 (ACM-SIAM Symposium on Discrete Algorithms)*. SIAM-Society for Industrial and Applied Mathematics, January 2015.

[3] A. Bhalgat, J. Feldman, and V. Mirrokni. Online allocation of display ads with smooth delivery. In *Proceedings of the 18th ACM SIGKDD International Conference on Knowledge Discovery and Data Mining (KDD 2012)*, pages 1213–1221, 2012.

[4] S. P. Boyd and L. Vandenberghe. *Convex Optimization*. Cambridge University Press, 2004.

[5] O. Chapelle, E. Manavoglu, and R. Rosales. Simple and scalable response prediction for display advertising. *ACM Trans. Intell. Syst. Technol.*, 5(4):61:1–61:34, Dec. 2014.

[6] Y. Chen, P. Berkhin, B. Anderson, and N. Devanur. Online bidding algorithms for performance-based display ad allocation. In *Proceedings of the 17th ACM SIGKDD International Conference on Knowledge Discovery and Data Mining (KDD)*, pages 1307–1315, 2011.

[7] G. Dantzig and P. Wolfe. Decomposition principle for linear programs. *Operations Research*, 8:101–111, 1960.

[8] H. Everett. Generalized Lagrange multiplier method for solving problems of optimum allocation of resources. *Operations Research*, 11(3):399–417, 1963.

[9] J. Feldman, M. Henzinger, N. Korula, V. Mirrokni, and C. Stein. Online stochastic packing applied to display ad allocation. In *ESA'10 Proceedings of the 18th annual European conference on Algorithms: Part I*, pages 182–194, 2010.

[10] J. Feldman, N. Korula, V. Mirrokni, S. Muthukrishnan, and M. Pal. Online ad assignment with free disposal. In *Proceedings of the 5th conference on Web and Internet Economics (WINE)*, 2009.

[11] E. Hazan, A. Agarwal, and S. Kale. Logarithmic regret algorithms for online convex optimization. *Machine Learning*, 69(2-3):169–192, 2007.

[12] R. Jenatton, J. Huang, C. Archambeau, and D. Csiba. Online optimization and regret guarantees for non-additive long-term constraints. *arXiv:1602.05394*, 2016.

[13] L. Lasdon. *Optimization theory for Large Systems*. MacMillan, 1970.

[14] C. Lemarechal and J.-B. Hiriart-Urruty. *Convex Analysis and Minimization Algorithms II*. Springer-Verlag, 1993.

[15] M. McEachran. Using Proportional Control For Better Pacing. `http://rubiconproject.com/technology-blog/using-proportional-control-for-better-pacing/`, 2012.

[16] B. McMahan and M. Streeter. Delay-tolerant algorithms for asynchronous distributed online learning. In *Advances in Neural Information Processing Systems*, pages 2915–2923, 2014.

[17] A. Mehta. Online matching and ad allocation. *Foundations and Trends in Theoretical Computer Science*, 8(4):265–368, 2012.

[18] A. Schrijver. *Combinatorial Optimization: Polyhedra and Efficiency, Volume A*. Springer, 2003.

[19] M. Zinkevich. Online convex programming and generalized infinitesimal gradient ascent. In *Proceedings of the International Conference on Machine Learning (ICML)*, 2003.

Appendix

PROOF (LEMMA 1). Note that maximizing $\mathbf{u}_t^\top \mathbf{x}_t$ with respect to $\mathbf{x}_t \in \mathcal{X}_t$ is itself an LP, which can be written as:

$$\begin{aligned} \underset{\mathbf{x}_t}{\text{maximize}} \quad & \sum_{i \in I_t, j \in C_i} (v_{ij} - w_i) x_{ij} \\ \text{subject to} \quad & \forall\, i \in I_t,\ \sum_{j \in C_i} x_{ij} \leq 1 \\ & \forall\, i \in I_t, j \in C_i,\ x_{ij} \geq 0. \end{aligned}$$

The dual of the above LP is given by

$$\begin{aligned} \underset{\boldsymbol{\beta}}{\text{minimize}} \quad & \sum_{i \in I_t} \beta_i \\ \text{subject to} \quad & \forall\, i \in I_t, j \in C_i, \beta_i \geq v_{ij}, \\ & \forall\, i \in I_t, \beta_i \geq w_i, \end{aligned}$$

with dual optimum $\boldsymbol{\beta}^\star$. Trivially, for a given i, if $\beta_i^\star \geq w_i$, we must have $\beta_i^\star = \max_{j \in C_i} v_{ij} = v_{ij^\star}$ (otherwise $\beta_i^\star$ would violate the constraint $\beta_i^\star \geq v_{ij}\ \forall\, j \in C_i$, which contradicts dual optimality). Now, since a feasible solution to the above primal LP exists (trivially set all variables $x_{ij} = 0$) and the objective function is bounded, there exists at least one solution $\hat{\mathbf{x}}_t$ that maximizes $\mathbf{u}_t^\top \mathbf{x}_t$. Suppose that for a given i, we have $\beta_i^\star > 0$ and we were to assign $x_{ij'} = 1, x_{ij} = 0\ \forall j \neq j'$ for some $j' \neq j^\star$: call this vector of primal variables $\mathbf{x}_t'$. Then the primal objective here would be $\mathbf{u}_t^\top \mathbf{x}_t' < \mathbf{u}_t^\top \hat{\mathbf{x}}_t$, since $v_{ij^\star} > v_{ij'}$ (assuming no ties), which contradicts. Therefore $x_{ij^\star} = 1, x_{ij} = 0\ \forall\ j \neq j^\star$ maximizes $\mathbf{u}_t^\top \mathbf{x}_t'$. Finally, the $\hat{x}_{ij}$'s are integral 0/1 variables (i.e.: we cannot have fractional x_{ij}'s that maximize $\mathbf{u}_t^\top \mathbf{x}_t$: to see this, we note that the optimal allocation problem is equivalent to matching bid requests $i \in U$ to a single ad $j \in V$ in a bi-partite graph $G = (U, V, E)$ where U is the set of bid requests, V is the set of ads and E is the set of edges connecting nodes in U to nodes in V. In particular, for a given bid request $i \in U$, the set of edges incident on i is C_i. Now, the constraint in the primal LP can be written as $\mathbf{Gx} \leq \mathbf{1}$ with $\mathbf{G}$ being the incidence matrix of G. Since G is (by construction) bi-partite, $\mathbf{G}$ is totally unimodular [18] and so the primal LP only has integral 0/1 solutions. □

Minimizing Legal Exposure of High-Tech Companies through Collaborative Filtering Methods

Bo Jin*
Dalian University of Technology
jinbo@dlut.edu.cn

Chao Che*
Dalian University
chechao@gmail.com

Kuifei Yu
Zhigu Tech
yukf@zhigu.com

Yue Qu
Dalian University of Technology
firestorm@mail.dlut.edu.cn

Li Guo
Dalian University of Technology
guoli@dlpu.edu.cn

Cuili Yao
Dalian University of Technology
yaocuili1984@dlut.edu.cn

ABSTRACT

Patent litigation not only covers legal and technical issues, it is also a key consideration for managers of high-technology (high-tech) companies when making strategic decisions. Patent litigation influences the market value of high-tech companies. However, this raises unique challenges. To this end, in this paper, we develop a novel recommendation framework to solve the problem of litigation risk prediction. We will introduce a specific type of patent-related litigation, that is, Section 337 investigations, which prohibit all acts of unfair competition, or any unfair trade practices, when exporting products to the United States. To build this recommendation framework, we collect and exploit a large amount of published information related to almost all Section 337 investigation cases. This study has two aims: (1) to predict the litigation risk in a specific industry category for high-tech companies and (2) to predict the litigation risk from competitors for high-tech companies. These aims can be achieved by mining historical investigation cases and related patents. Specifically, we propose two methods to meet the needs of both aims: a proximal slope one predictor and a time-aware predictor. Several factors are considered in the proposed methods, including the litigation risk if a company wants to enter a new market and the risk that a potential competitor would file a lawsuit against the new entrant. Comparative experiments using real-world data demonstrate that the proposed methods outperform several baselines with a significant margin.

CCS Concepts

•**Social and professional topics** → **Patents**; •**Applied computing** → **Law**; •**Information systems** → *Data mining; Recommender systems;*

*Corresponding Author

KDD '16, August 13–17, 2016, San Francisco, CA, USA.
© 2016 ACM. ISBN 978-1-4503-4232-2/16/08...$15.00
DOI: http://dx.doi.org/10.1145/2939672.2939708

Keywords

Patent Litigation; Section 337 Investigations; Collaborative Filtering; Proximal Slope One Predictor; Time-aware Predictor

1. INTRODUCTION

When an inventor, business, or other entity owns a patent and that patent is infringed, the patent owner has few alternatives other than to undertake patent litigation. Few entities wish to undertake patent litigation because it is usually lengthy and expensive. For example, Apple and Google spend more money on patent litigation and defensive patent acquisitions than they do on research and development. However, some firms try to *extort* money from others using patent litigation. These firms are known as patent trolls. Such firms collect patents solely for the purpose of litigation to extort money from small companies that cannot afford patent defense. In 2013, the president of the United States, Barack Obama introduced a proposal to crack down on patent trolls. His administration also pledged to protect innovators from frivolous litigation. A country's government rarely talks explicitly about detailed aspects of technology and intellectual property policy. Thus, it is clear that patent litigation is a huge challenge for high-technology (high-tech) companies in the United States.

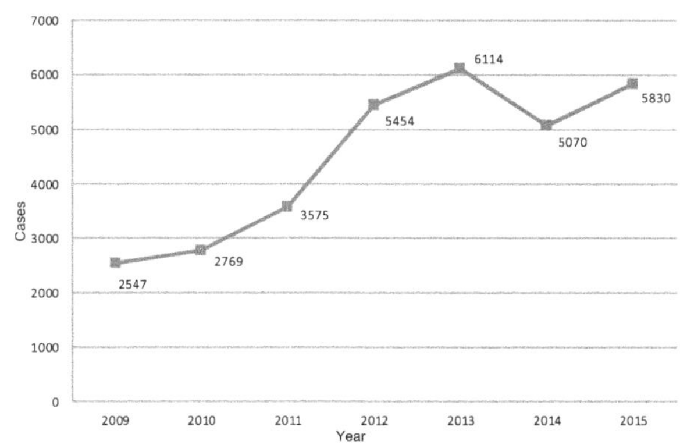

Figure 1: U.S. patent litigation cases filed, 2009–2015.

Patent litigation numbers have increased rapidly in recent years, as shown in Figure 1. This paper focuses on a specific type of litigation: Section 337 investigations. Section 337 investigations refer to investigations conducted according to Section 337 of the Tariff Act of 1930 and its related amendments by the United States International Trade Commission (USITC). Section 337 investigations prohibit all acts of unfair competition, or any unfair trade practices, when exporting products to the United States. If convicted under a Section 337 investigation, the exporter's products may be permanently excluded from the US market, which can result in considerable economic losses. Most Section 337 investigation cases concern patents. As with intellectual property rights, Section 337 investigations are frequently used for blocking purposes. Both parties in a Section 337 investigation are competitors; hence such investigations can be a means of blocking competitors by preventing their market expansion. Therefore, predicting the probability of its involvement in a Section 337 investigation is crucial for the development of a high-tech company.

Section 337 investigations consume precious resources, and the outcome can signify success or failure to a company. Hence, it is critical for high-tech companies to understand their legal exposure in their industry category and from their competitors to be successful in such patent litigations. Despite the increasing number of arguments and lawsuits, there are no reliable unbiased data mining methods on the patterns and trends of patent litigation in the United States[8] This paper aims to enable high-tech companies to develop data-driven intellectual property business strategies to succeed in their challenging environments. For example, the Chinese smartphone giant Xiaomi is being targeted by a U.S.-based patent troll. The troll company (Blue Spike LLS) filed a lawsuit against Xiaomi in a U.S. district court at the end of 2015. Thus, as Forbes reported, Xiaomi may have a major patent problem if it wants to enter the U.S. market. Xiaomi operates as an investment holding company and uses its subsidiaries for the development and transfer of its technologies and intellectual properties.

This paper has two aims: 1) to predict the litigation risk in a specific industry category for high-tech companies, and 2) to predict the litigation risk from competitors for the high-tech companies. To achieve these goals and to identify the risky industry categories and competitors for high-tech companies, we must consider several factors. We must consider the litigation risk if a company wants to enter a new market, and further consider the risk that a potential competitor would file a lawsuit against the new entrant. The risks must be formally estimated. These issues can be answered by mining historical investigation cases and related patents. Specifically, we develop two matrixes: 1) the company–category matrix predicts the litigation risk in a specific industry category for a high-tech company and 2) the complainant–respondent matrix predicts the litigation risk from the competitors for a high-tech company. We propose two methods to meet the needs of both aims: a proximal slope one predictor and a time-aware predictor. The proposed methods can work on different conditions, that is, companies previously engaged in lawsuits and companies never engaged in a lawsuit. Finally, we carry out extensive experiments on a real-world data set collected from the USITC. The experimental results clearly validate the effectiveness of the proposed methods. With the results of this paper, high-tech companies could adjust their strategies for development and explore space for market.

Overview. The paper is organized as follows. Section 2 describes the data used in this paper and introduces the trends of patent litigation in the United States. Section 3 formulates the problem of patent litigation prediction for high-tech companies, and introduces some preliminary matters in prediction. Section 4 and Section 5 describe the proposed methods, the proximal slope one predictor and time-aware predictor, respectively. Section 6 discusses the results of our study. Section 7 outlines some related works. Finally, Section 8 provides a conclusion and some suggestions for future research.

2. DATA DESCRIPTION AND ANALYSIS

2.1 Data Description

This paper uses several data sources. The first comes from USITC Section 337 investigation cases[1]. We analyze Section 337 case data (a sample is shown in Figure 2) for the period of 1982–2014. We find that 857 of the 906 cases in that period concern patent infringements, and 623 of these cases list the related patents. There are 1,654 patents, including design and utility patents. Several patents are used in multiple investigations.

Figure 2: Section 337 investigation: sample HTML document.

We also use patent grants data from USPTO Bulk Downloads[2]. This public dataset is provided by the United States Patent and Trademark Office (USPTO). Each patent publication contains a group of structured and unstructured information. The USPTO updates the patent application publication each week. We first download the patent data package and retrieved the weekly data package files. We then import the patent data (in XML format) to our own local database. Finally, we retrieve the information from this local database using the ID of 1,654 patents as queries.

The final data source used is the industry category for the companies. It is difficult to identify the industry category of a company in relation to its patents. Each of the Section 337 investigation cases of patent infringement is associated

[1] https://www.usitc.gov/

[2] http://www.google.com/googlebooks/uspto-patents.html

with one or more patents, and each U.S. patent has at least one class number. In this study, we determine the industry category by the patents that a company holds. However, US patents have 1,088 classifications in total. Therefore, we reclassify the US patent data according to 56 industry categories with a mapping table.

2.2 Data Analysis

We analyze the Section 337 investigation cases by regions and the companies involved.

Figure 3 shows the top 10 Section 337 investigation regions from 1982–2014. The figure shows that the allegations relating to patent infringements vary across regions over time. In the 1980s and early 1990s, Japan was the most intensively investigated country, accounting for 43.15% of the total number of cases. Mainland China and Chinese Taiwan were also frequently investigated in the period 1982–2004. The Chinese mainland is currently the most frequent respondent in Section 337 investigations. Since 2004, Chinese products and companies have been involved in over 40% of Section 337 investigations, as the export volume of a region to the United States influences the number of patent litigations. When the trade volume of a country or region increases substantially with rapid economic development, the number of Section 337 investigations increases correspondingly. Japan, Chinese Taiwan, and Mainland China are all in the same situation.

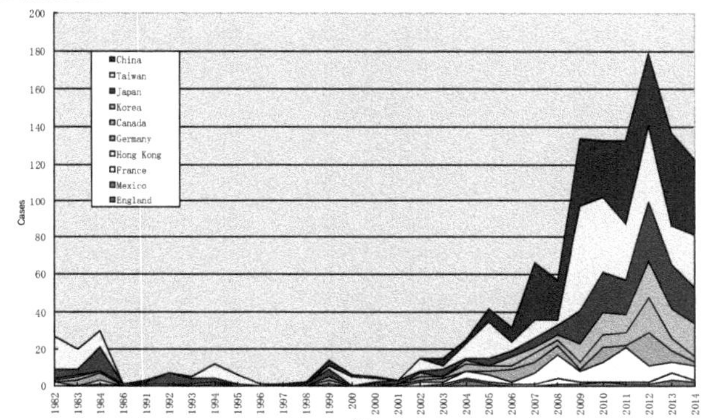

Figure 3: Top 10 respondent regions in Section 337 investigations.

Figure 4 shows the top 10 Section 337 investigation industry categories for 1982–2014. The figure shows that most of the cases are in material equipment domains such as building material processing equipment and assembly and material handling equipment, which are covered by a large number of patents. Electrical communication domains, including image and sound equipment and telecommunication, are also responsible for many Section 337 investigations.

Figure 5 shows the top 10 Section 337 investigation complainants for 1982–2014. We find that most of the complainants are large high-tech companies that hold core technologies and monopolistic advantages in their related domains. Such companies are motivated to retain their dominant position and to exclude competitors from the market.

Figure 6 shows the top 10 Section 337 investigation respondents for 1982–2014. We find that Section 337 investigations are associated with companies that experience explosive growth. The top four respondents are all smartphone companies. The telecommunication sector has undergone

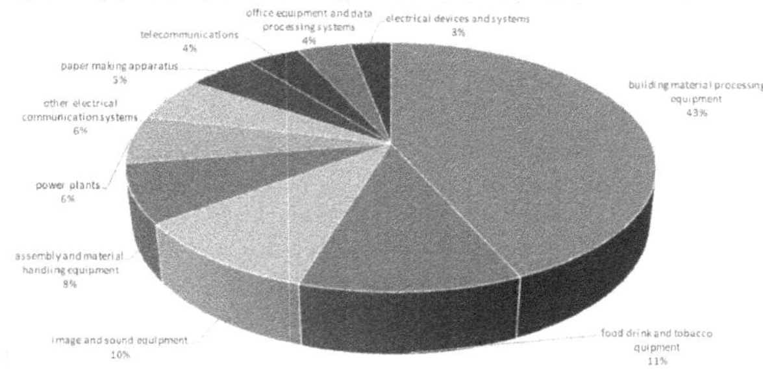

Figure 4: Top 10 industry categories in Section 337 investigations.

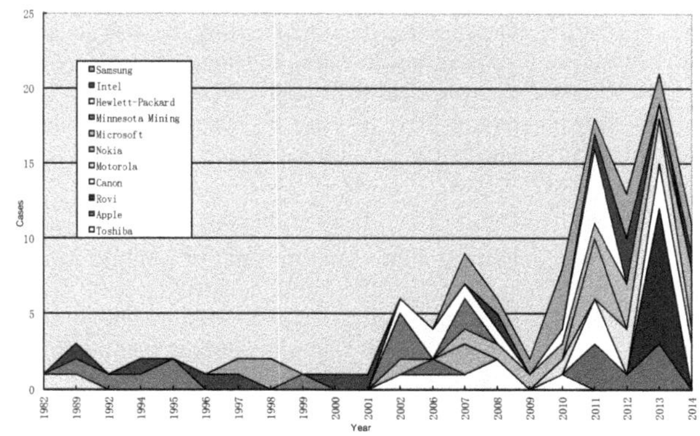

Figure 5: Top 10 complainants in Section 337 investigations.

the most investigations since 2009 because the rapid growth of mobile Internet has resulted in intense competition in the smartphone market. Hence, there has been an increase in lawsuits in this market.

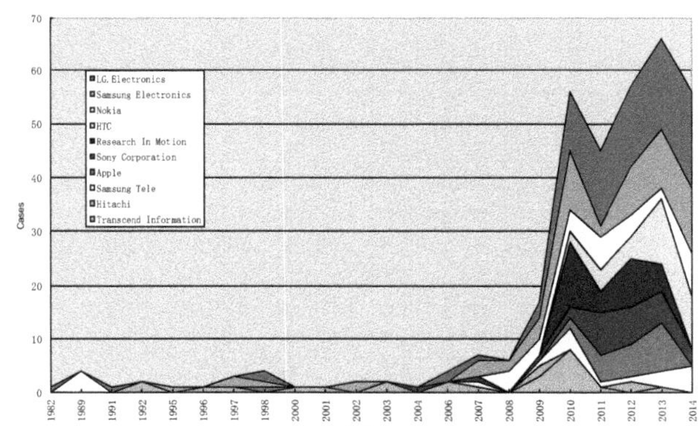

Figure 6: Top 10 respondents in Section 337 investigations.

3. PROBLEM FORMULATION

In this section, we introduce some preliminary matters, and then formally define the problem of minimizing the legal exposure of high-tech companies.

3.1 Preliminary Matters

A relatively small number of companies are involved in Section 337 investigations; however, the number of patents is quite large. To reduce the number of calculations and enhance the precision, we analyze the data by patent category rather than by patent itself. Thus, individual patents are replaced by their corresponding patent classifications. As Section 337 investigations only protect the patents of United States, thus, we use the United States Patent Classification (USPC) system. The USPC system has 1,088 patent classes, making it difficult to identify the patent classification for a company. Thus, we further amalgamate the USPC classifications into industry categories. There are some works on patent classification mapping [13], we employ a common standards to map the USPC classifications into 56 industry categories.

To construct the company–category matrix, we need to first construct the company–classification matrix. The number of times that a company has undergone a Section 337 investigation determines its value in the matrix. After the normalization process, the company–classification value ranges between zero and five. Formula 1 is used to normalize the company-classification value as follows:

$$x_i^* = \frac{x_i - x_{min}}{x_{max} - x_{min}}\beta \tag{1}$$

where x_i indicates the actual number of patents in a patent classification related to Section 337 investigation cases that the company is involved in, x_i^* indicates the normalized value, x_{min} and x_{max} indicate the minimum and maximum number of patents related with Section 337 investigation cases, respectively. β is set to 5 for normalizing the value from 0 to 5.

The company–classification matrix is then transferred into the company–category matrix with a patent classification–industry category mapping table. The proposed methods are used to calculate the prediction values in this matrix.

A sample predicted results of the company–category matrix is shown in Table 1. Let us consider, for example, the 0.326 rating at the intersection between the row of Company ID 51 and column of Category 10. This rating indicates that there is a 0.326 probability that Adidas America Inc. (Company ID 51) may be investigated under the bleaching and dyeing industry category (Category 10).

In the same way we develop the complainant–respondent matrix. The total number of Section 337 investigation cases is not large enough, such that the complainant–respondent matrix is quite sparse. Take cases in 2014 as an example, for company pairs, there are only 564 non-zero values of the 2 million values in the matrix. For the full duration data set used in this paper, there are 3,370 non-zero values for company pairs in the matrix.

3.2 Recommendation Framework

Here, we convert the legal exposure prediction problem to a recommendation problem. We first try to recommend the riskiest industry category and the riskiest competitor for a high-tech company. We then formally define the problem of legal exposure recommendation with time-awareness.

DEFINITION 1. *We have company c, and a set of industry categories $A = a$, each of which contains a set of investigation probabilities p_{ai}. The goal of the legal exposure recommendation is to build an optimal ranked list of industry categories.*

DEFINITION 2. *We have company c, and a set of competitors $B = b$, each of which contains a set of investigation probabilities p_{bi}. The goal of the legal exposure recommendation is to build an optimal ranked list of competitors.*

The above problem statements raise two issues:

- How to mine data relating to the litigation risk of an industry category and how to produce a ranked list $\Lambda^{RiskA} = a|a \in c$ according to their risk scores $RiskA(a)$.
- How to mine data relating to the litigation risk of a competitor and how to produce a ranked list $\Lambda^{RiskB} = b|b \in c$ according to their risk scores $RiskB(b)$.

Although it is desirable to minimize legal exposure for high-tech companies, it is not an easy task to effectively discover and evaluate the litigation risks of both industry category and competitors. Patent litigation is a complex legal action and there are many factors to consider in a recommendation. Thus, it is difficult to answer how to efficiently manage litigation risk for high-tech companies. To this end, in this paper, we propose a novel recommendation framework to solve this problem.

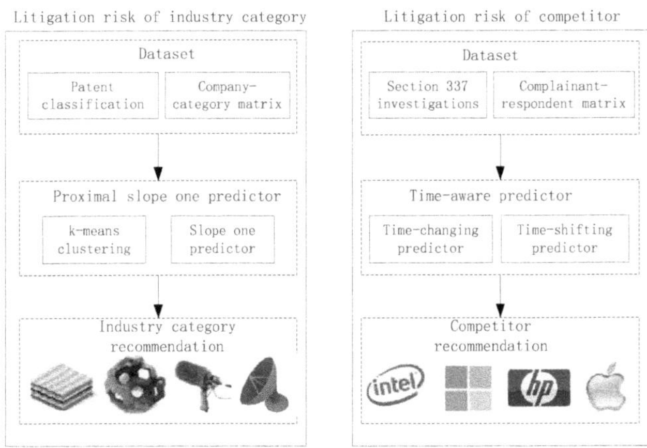

Figure 7: The recommendation framework.

Figure 7 shows the proposed recommendation framework, which consists of the two aims. *Litigation risk of industry category* predicts the legal exposure in a specific industry category for high-tech companies. *Litigation risk of competitor* predicts the litigation risk from competitors for high-tech companies.

4. PROXIMAL SLOPE ONE PREDICTOR

This section proposes a proximal slope one predictor as the recommendation algorithm to predict the litigation risk for high-tech companies in a specific industry category. In Section 337 investigations, the litigation procedures of various companies in an industry category are quite different. Slope One algorithm[9] is suitable to settle this problem. However, Slope One algorithm only improve the problem of item rating deviation without considering the difference between the items. Hence, the quality and performance of the recommender system are unsatisfactory for our problem. Because the investigations of companies other than the target company in different industry categories will affect the prediction accuracy, we therefore improved the Slope One

Table 1: Company–category matrix

Company ID	Category 1		Category 10		Category 23		Category 45		Category 56
1	0	...	0	...	0	...	0	...	0
...	...	...	...	...	...	...	...	...	...
51	...	...	0.326	...	0	...	0	...	...
...	...	...	...	...	...	...	...	...	...
411	0	...	0	...	0	...	0.217	...	0
...	...	...	...	...	...	...	...	...	...
1912	0	...	0	...	0	...	0.109	...	0
...	...	...	...	...	...	...	...	...	...
2338	0	...	0	...	0.109	...	0.217	...	0
...	...	...	...	...	...	...	...	...	...
2805	0	...	0	...	0	...	0	...	0

algorithm using a clustering method. In this paper, the k-means algorithm and the Slope One algorithm are combined to predict the litigation risk. The prediction value of the k-nearest neighbor vectors of the target company should be calculated using a sub-matrix of the company–classification matrix. This not only decreases the amount of calculations, but also relieves the problems caused by data sparseness. Specifically, we first establish patent classification vectors of the companies according to the historical patents related to Section 337 investigation cases. The k-means algorithm is employed to cluster the vectors into K clusterings. Then the k-nearest neighbor companies of the target company are screened and are used to construct the sub-matrix of the company–classification matrix. The prediction value in the sub-matrix is calculated using the Slope One algorithm. Finally, we transfer the company–classification matrix to the company–category matrix. We can predict the litigation risk of the target company based on the company–category matrix.

Suppose the patent classification vector of a company can be denoted as $X = \{x_i, i = 1, 2, \ldots, n\}$, where x_i is a patent classification and n is the total number of U.S. patent classifications. The m vectors X are then clustered into K clusterings as $C = \{c_k, k = 1, 2, \ldots, K\}$, where each c_k denotes a vector group of similar companies. Suppose μ_k is the clustering center of c_k, the distance between each patent classification vector of a company and the clustering center can be calculated as:

$$J(c_k) = \sum_{x_i \in c_k} \|x_i - \mu_{ki}\|^2 \quad (2)$$

where μ_{ki} is the value of the i-th patent classification of μ_k.

For each company, we can obtain k-nearest neighbor patent classification vectors with the result of clusterings, and construct a sub-matrix A_{ij}. The Slope One algorithm is employed to predict the values R_{ij} in the sub-matrix. Basically, a Slope One algorithm is used as follows. Suppose x and y indicate the value of two patent classifications by company u. The two values conform to the linear relation $y = x + b$, where b is the parameter, and we obtain the estimated value $\hat{b}$ of parameter b. After substituting the known value x, we obtain the estimated rating $\hat{y}$ by company u. Formula 3 is used to calculate the value $dev_{j,i}$ between the target item $Item_j$ and item $Item_i$. Formula 4 is then used to obtain the prediction value $P(u)_j$:

$$dev_{j,i} = \sum_{u \in S_{j,i}(x)} \frac{u_j - u_i}{card(S_{j,i}(x))} \quad (3)$$

$$P(u)_j = \frac{\sum_{i \in R_j}(dev_{j,i} + u_i)}{card(R_j)} \quad (4)$$

where $S_{j,i}(x)$ indicates the set of companies who have co-rated items $Item_j$ and $Item_i$ and R_j indicates the set of items that have been rated by user u. The number of elements in a set S is $card(S)$.

As shown in Algorithm 1, in the proposed recommendation algorithm, using the company–classification matrix, $R_{m\times n}$ indicates the historical data of Section 337 investigations. Here m indicates the number of companies, n indicates the number of classifications, and R_{ij} indicates the normalized number of Section 337 investigation cases that company i filed according to the patent classification j.

Algorithm 1 Proximal Slope One Predictor

1: Construct the company–classification matrix A_{ij} with the k-means algorithm;
2: According to the classification i that has been rated by the target company u, select the nearest top k classifications with the classification i, and then produce the set K';
3: Use formula (3) to calculate the value $dev_{j,i}$ with other classifications rating for the target company u in a set K';
4: Use formula (4) to calculate the prediction rating $P(u)_j$, and then obtain the company–classification matrix $R'_{m\times n}$;
5: According to the company–classification matrix $R'_{m\times n}$, transfer into the company–category matrix;
6: Recommend the top r prediction categories for the target company.

5. TIME-AWARE PREDICTORS

This section proposes time-aware predictors as recommendation algorithms to predict the litigation risk for high-tech companies from their competitors. The proposed algorithm is based on a matrix factorization model that has been well studied in recent years. It is a popular model in the area of recommendation because it combines good scalability with predictive accuracy. Additionally, this model is very flexible when modeling various temporal real-life situations. We improve the basic matrix factorization model [7] with a time-shifting baseline predictor. We combine the time-changing baseline predictor and the time-shifting baseline predictor to meet the needs of our problem. There are two different conditions, which are 1) a company pair that has no historical litigations, and 2) a company pair with historical litigations. The first condition is settled with the time-changing baseline predictor, and the second is settled with the time-shifting baseline predictor.

5.1 Static Baseline Predictor

As shown in Figures 5 and 6, the number of Section 337 investigation cases is time-dependent. Before we deal with temporal effects, we would like to establish the foundations of a static baseline predictor. A pure matrix factorization model could serve well in capturing the interaction between the users and items in a recommendation system. However, most of the observed values of litigation cases are due to effects independent of the interaction associated with either complainants or respondents. For example, typical Section 337 investigation data exhibit large complainant and respondent biases. That is, some companies initiate more investigations than other companies, and some companies face more investigations than others. We will encapsulate those effects, which do not involve complainant-respondent interactions, within the baseline predictors [7]. These baseline predictors tend to capture much of the observed values, in particular much of the temporal dynamics within the data. Hence, it is vital to model them accurately, which enables the better identification of the part of the values that truly represents complainant–respondent interactions and should be subject to factorization.

Now we discuss how to construct a static baseline predictor. Suppose each complainant u is associated with vector p_u and each respondent i is associated with vector q_i. The overall average number of investigation cases is denoted by μ. A baseline predictor for an unknown value r_{ui} is denoted by the observed deviations b_u and b_i of complainant u and respondent i, respectively, from the average as follows:

$$b_i = \frac{\sum_{u \in R(i)}(r_{ui} - u)}{\lambda_1 + |R(i)|} \tag{5}$$

$$b_u = \frac{\sum_{u \in R(u)}(r_{ui} - u - b_i)}{\lambda_2 + |R(u)|} \tag{6}$$

where λ_1 and λ_2 are regularization parameters which make the values of b_i and b_u shrink towards zero. Here $\lambda_1 = 10$, $\lambda_2 = 25$.

The static baseline predictor should then be integrated back into a factor model. The value is predicted by the rule:

$$\hat{r}_{ui} = \mu + b_i + b_u + q_i^T p_u \tag{7}$$

To determine the vectors p_u and q_i, we minimize the regularized squared error:

$$\min_{q^*,p^*,b^*} \sum_{(u,i)\in K} (r_{ui} - \mu - b_i - b_u - q_i^T p_u)^2 + \lambda_3(\|q_i\|^2 + \|p_u\|^2 + b_i^2 + b_u^2) \tag{8}$$

where the constant λ_3 controls the extent of regularization, as usually determined by cross validation. In this paper, minimization is performed by typical stochastic gradient descent. The parameters are updated as follows:

$$b_i = b_i + \gamma(e_{ui} - \lambda_3 \cdot b_i) \tag{9}$$

$$b_u = b_u + \gamma(e_{ui} - \lambda_3 \cdot b_u) \tag{10}$$

$$q_i = q_i + \gamma(e_{ui} \cdot p_u - \lambda_4 \cdot p_i) \tag{11}$$

$$p_u = p_u + \gamma(e_{ui} \cdot q_i - \lambda_4 \cdot p_u) \tag{12}$$

where e_{ui} is the prediction error as follows:

$$e_{ui} = r_{ui} - (\mu + b_i + b_u + q_i^T \cdot p_u) \tag{13}$$

5.2 Time-changing Baseline Predictor

In this section, we discuss the following temporal effects which include in the baseline predictors: (1) complainant biases b_u change over time; (2) respondent biases b_i change over time; (3) complainant preferences p_u change over time; and (4) respondent preferences q_i change over time. Hence, in our models we would like to take the parameters as functions of time. For our problem of litigation risk prediction, it's no need to get the finest resolution. Thus, an adequate decision would be to split the biases into time-based bins. We employ a distinct bias for each time period related with a single bin. Such decision should strike a balance for the desire to achieve a finer resolution with enough ratings per bin. Considering the features of Section 337 litigation cases, we select 3 years as the bin size. We define the bias functions $b_i(t)$ of the respondent i, changing by year t, as follows:

$$b_i(t) = b_i + b_{i \cdot Bin(t)} \tag{14}$$

where $b_{i \cdot Bin(t)}$ is the bias of respondent i in those bins that contain year t.

In the same way, we define the bias functions $b_u(t)$ of the complainant u, changing by year t:

$$b_u(t) = b_u + \alpha \cdot dev_u(t) \tag{15}$$

where $dev_u(t)$ is the associated time deviation. If u files a lawsuit in the year t, $dev_u(t)$ is defined as:

$$dev_u(t) = sign(t - t_u) \cdot |t - t_u|^\beta \tag{16}$$

where $|t - t_u|$ measures the time distance between t and t_u. Furthermore, t_u is the average duration of Section 337 investigation cases of complainant u, which can be calculated as:

$$t_u = t_u(\lceil \frac{n_l - 1}{2} \rceil) \tag{17}$$

where n_l denotes the most recent Section 337 investigation case of complainant u.

Moreover, we note that the complainants' preferences change with time, leading to changes in the interactions between complainant and respondent. For example, if one company files a lawsuit against another company several times, the respondent may strike back. Suppose the feature vector of a company has k dimensions, the changing function of preferences is defined as:

$$p_{uk}(t) = p_{uk} + p_{uk \cdot Bin(t)} \tag{18}$$

where p_{uk} captures the stationary portion of the factor and $P_{uk \cdot Bin(t)}$ approximates a possible portion that changes in those bins containing year t.

Thus, the prediction rule is as follows:

$$\hat{r}_{ui} = \mu + b_i(t) + b_u(t) + q_i^T p_u(t) \quad (19)$$

where t indicates the year of the last lawsuit.

To determine the involved parameters $b_{i \cdot Bin(t)}$, α_u and α_{uk}, we should solve:

$$min \sum_{(u,i)\in K} (r_{ui} - \mu - b_i(t) - b_u(t) - q_i^T p_u(t))^2 + \lambda_5(||q_i||^2 + ||p_u||^2 + b_i^2 + b_{i \cdot Bin(t)}^2 + b_u^2 + \alpha_u^2 + p_{uk \cdot Bin(t)}^2) \quad (20)$$

where the constant λ_5 controls the extent of regularization, as usually determined by cross validation. In this paper, minimization is performed by typical stochastic gradient descent. The parameters are updated as follows:

$$b_{i \cdot Bin(t)} = b_{i \cdot Bin(t)} + \gamma(e_{ui} - \lambda_5 \cdot b_{i \cdot Bin(t)}) \quad (21)$$

$$\alpha_u = \alpha_u + \gamma(e_{ui} \cdot dev_u(t) - \lambda_5 \cdot \alpha_u) \quad (22)$$

$$p_{uk \cdot Bin(t)} = p_{uk \cdot Bin(t)} + \gamma(e_{ui} \cdot p_i - \lambda_5 \cdot p_{uk \cdot Bin(t)}) \quad (23)$$

5.3 Time-shifting Baseline Predictor

The time-changing baseline predictor only considers the bias of the complainant and respondent in the current time period. Practical application shows that litigation should be predicted based on the bias in the prior time period. Thus, the time-shift characteristics of bias are studied in this paper: $Shift(t)$ denotes the bias in a period of time, $b_{i \cdot Shift(t)}$ denotes the time-shift bias of the complainant, $b_{u \cdot Shift(t)}$ denotes the time-shift bias of the respondent, and $p_{u \cdot Shift(t)}$ denotes the time-shift bias of the complainant's suppressed feature vector. We then extend the bias functions denoted in the prior section as follows:

$$b_i(t) = b_i + b_{i \cdot Shift(t)} \quad (24)$$

$$b_u(t) = b_u + b_{u \cdot Shift(t)} \quad (25)$$

$$p_u(t) = p_u + p_{u \cdot Shift(t)} \quad (26)$$

Then the prediction rule is as follows:

$$\hat{r}_{ui} = \mu + b_i(t) + b_u(t) + q_i^T p_u(t) \quad (27)$$

We then split the data set into two groups: data of lawsuits before time t and data of lawsuits at time t. For the first data group, we employ a basic matrix algorithm to optimize the parameters b_u, b_i, q_i and p_u. For the second data group, to determine the involved parameters $p_{u \cdot Shift(t)}$, $b_{u \cdot Shift(t)}$, and $b_{i \cdot Shift(t)}$, we need to solve:

$$min \sum_{(u,i)\in K} (r_{ui} - \mu - b_i(t) - b_u(t) - q_i^T p_u(t))^2 + \lambda_6(||p_{u \cdot Shift(t)}||^2 + b_{u \cdot Shift(t)}^2 + b_{i \cdot Shift(t)}^2) \quad (28)$$

where the constant λ_6 controls the extent of regularization, as usually determined by cross validation. In this paper, minimization is performed by stochastic gradient descent. The parameters are updated as follows:

$$b_{i \cdot Shift(t)} = b_{i \cdot Shift(t)} + \gamma(e_{ui} - \lambda_6 \cdot b_{i \cdot Shift(t)}) \quad (29)$$

$$b_{u \cdot Shift(t)} = b_{u \cdot Shift(t)} + \gamma(e_{ui} - \lambda_6 \cdot b_{u \cdot Shift(t)}) \quad (30)$$

$$p_{u \cdot Shift(t)} = p_{u \cdot Shift(t)} + \gamma(e_{ui} \cdot p_i - \lambda_7 \cdot p_{u \cdot Shift(t)}) \quad (31)$$

Furthermore, e_{ui} is the prediction error:

$$e_{ui} = r_{ui} - \hat{r_{ui}} \quad (32)$$

where r_{ui} is the number of lawsuit filed by u against i in year t, $\hat{r}_{ui}$ is the predicted value based on the data before year t. As the exact value and predicted value are obtained from different durations, time-shifting trends are considered in our method.

As shown in Algorithm 2, in the proposed recommendation algorithm, the time-changing predictor trains the bias during a large range of time, and does not distinguish the conditions. Thus, it shows high accuracy for those companies without prior lawsuits. The time-shifting predictor trains the bias in the duration before year t. This indicates the shifting trend from the duration before year t and after year t. It provides high accuracy for those companies with prior lawsuits.

Algorithm 2 Time-aware Predictor

1: Constructs complainant–respondent matrix B_{ij}, and indicates the conditions of a company pair that has no historical litigation and a company pair that has historical litigations;
2: For the conditions of a company pair that has no historical litigation, use Formula 19 to calculate the predicted value $\hat{r}_{ui}$ and update the parameters using Formula 21, 22 and 23;
3: Repeat step (2) until the maximum number of iteration is reached or the changes in the RSME are less than the threshold;
4: Split the data set into D_t' and D_t according to year t, and optimize parameters b_u, b_i, q_i and p_u in data set D_t' before year t;
5: For the conditions of a company pair that has historical litigations, use Formula 27 to calculate the predicted value $\hat{r}_u i$ and update the parameters using Formulas 29, 30 and 31;
6: Repeat step (5) until the maximum number of iteration is reached or the changes in the RSME are less than the threshold;
7: Recommend the top r prediction competitors for the target company using the time-changing predictor and the time-shifting predictor for different conditions.

6. EXPERIMENTAL RESULTS

6.1 Evaluation Metrics

We use root-mean-square error (RMSE) to measure the prediction performance of the proposed algorithms. The smaller the RMSE values, the better the prediction accuracy of the algorithms. The RMSE formula are defined as follows:

$$RMSE = \sqrt{\frac{\sum_{i=1}^{N}(p_i - q_i)^2}{N}} \quad (33)$$

where p_i is the prediction rating of the test set; q_i is the real rating of the test set; and N is the number of ratings of the test set.

6.2 Evaluation of Predictor for Industry Category

In the experiments, we employ k-fold cross-validation. The data is divided into k roughly equal-sized parts ($k = 5$ here). Of the k parts, a single part is retained as the validation data for testing the predictor, and the remaining $k - 1$ parts are used as training data. We use 1691 cases in the test set (out of 8,455 total cases in the data set). We then make recommendations for 2,806 companies, with an average of 2.41 observations per company for the entire training set.

We adopt three state-of-the-art baselines to evaluate the performances of our proximal slope one predictor. The first baseline is a traditional collaborative filtering algorithm, that is, an item-based collaborative filtering algorithm (IBCF). The second baseline is matrix factorization algorithm (MF), which is one of the most popular approaches to collaborative filtering. Moreover, we also use a popular slope one algorithm, that is, a bi-polar slope one algorithm, as the third baseline. All results reported below come from the same test set to facilitate comparison.

6.2.1 *Recommendation Performances*

We set up the evaluation as follows. First, we implemented our proximal slope one predictor and other baselines on the test data set. Specifically, by performing the proximal slope one predictor, we rate the company–category matrix. We then obtain the RMSE value by comparing the results with the original rating. We set the clustering parameters k as 20, and it remained invariant during the experiment.

Figures 8 show the results of each approach. In the figure we can see that our approach consistently outperforms other baselines and the improvement is significant. These results clearly validate the effectiveness of our proximal slope one predictor.

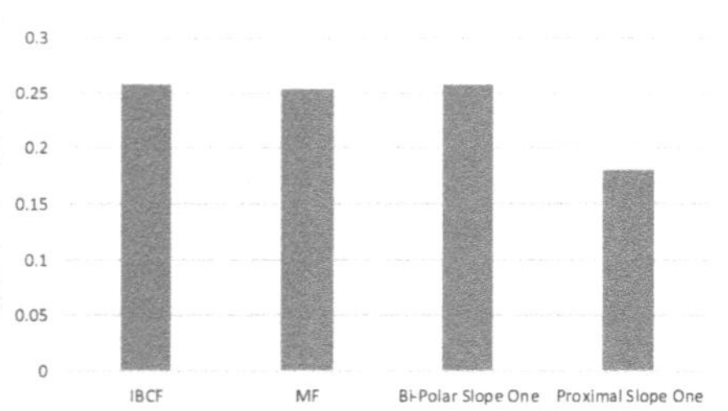

Figure 8: RMSEs of different approaches.

6.2.2 *Case Study*

To further evaluate the performances of the different approaches, we randomly select 10 cases including 8 companies for case study. The results of the case study are shown in Table 2. Two companies (Company ID 200, 587) fall within two categories. The closer the difference between the predicted value and the rating, the better the prediction accuracy of the algorithm. According to the results, the prediction value of Proximal Slope One algorithm is closer to the original rating than that of the other three approaches. The extreme sparseness of the company-category matrix results that the parameters of MF could not be fully trained and optimized. Our approach is superior to matrix factorization algorithm due to no need of parameter training and optimizing. The IBCF and the bi-polar slope one algorithms use all of the data from the training data set as their prediction foundation, without clustering. The IBCF simply analyzes the similarity according to the investigation categories, and does not consider the degree of association between the categories. This means that the result is flawed. The bi-polar slope one algorithm analyzes the rating data that have been divided into two groups, according to the preference of the company regarding category. The disadvantage of this algorithm is that two totally different results will be produced when two ratings are close to the average value, but one is bigger than the average and the other is smaller. In the company–category matrix, there are a lot of data around the average: this leads to large errors when using the bi-polar slope one algorithm. Our approach only considers the data set that belongs to the same category as the target type. This minimizes the influence of unrelated categories, giving the highest prediction accuracy. However, in our approach, because of data sparseness, the nearest neighbor number of some types cannot achieve the number in the experimental setup. Thus, predicted partial results are not sufficiently accurate.

6.3 Evaluation of Predictor for Competitors

In these experiments, we divide the data set into training data and test data according to date. There are two experiments in this section: the first experiment used data from 2000 to 2012 as training data and data from 2013 as test data; the second experiment used data from 2000 to 2013 as training data and data from 2014 as test data. Figure 9 compares the results of the two proposed predictors. We can see that the results for the two years are similar.

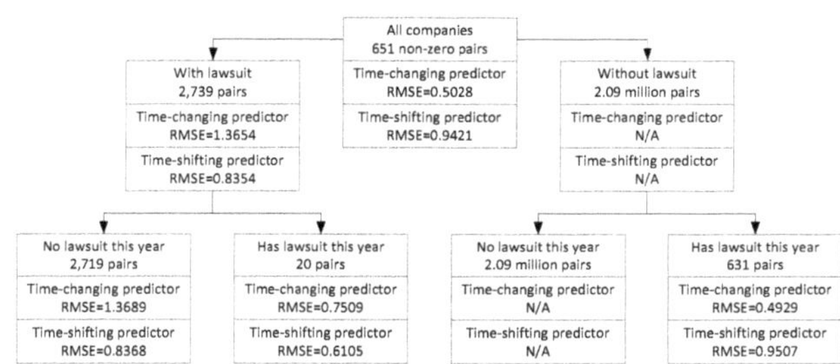

(a) Test data set of 2013

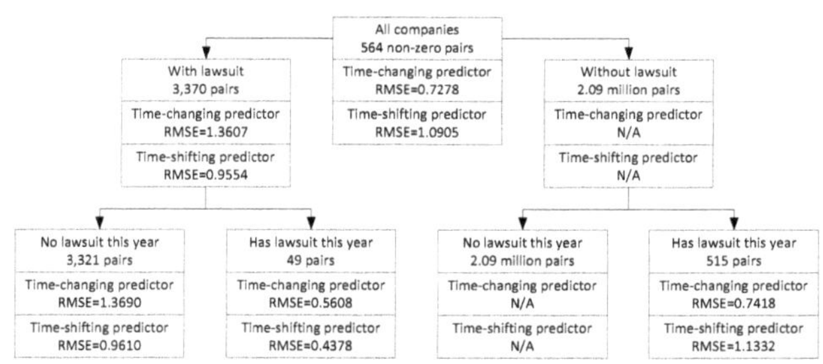

(b) Test data set of 2014

Figure 9: The recommendation performances of different approaches.

Specifically, we set regularization parameters as $\lambda_3 = 0.005$, $\lambda_4 = 0.015$, $\lambda_5 = 0.005$, $\lambda_6 = 0.01$, and $\lambda_7 = 0.03$. The learning rate γ is set to 0.007 for static baseline predictor and time-changing baseline predictor, and 0.01 for time-shifting

Table 2: Prediction results for case study.

Company ID	Class	Category	Rating	IBCF	MF	Bi-polar Slope One	Proximal Slope One
71	258	20	0.109	0.277	0.084	0.249	0.109
200	452	56	0.217	0.168	0.061	0.249	0.217
200	602	53	0.217	0.228	0.085	0.249	0.217
336	11	17	0.109	0.113	0.011	0.249	0.109
587	229	18	0.109	0.129	0.039	0.249	0.109
587	471	17	0.109	0.132	0.027	0.249	0.109
846	448	48	0.109	0.191	0.076	0.203	0.117
1584	564	11	0.326	0.285	0.262	0.217	0.040
1874	526	9	0.217	0.243	0.048	0.249	0.217
2548	624	14	0.109	0.046	0.085	0.109	0.099

baseline predictor. For the setting of the number of iterations, if the number is smaller, the fitting degree of training is not high enough. However, if the number of iterations is larger, there might be overfitting. Thus, based on the results of the test, we set the number of iterations as 40.

As shown in Figure 9, the time-changing predictor performs better than the time-shifting predictor in the conditions of overall company pairs and company pairs with no historical lawsuits. In fact, it's extremely difficult to predict the legal exposure for a company without historical lawsuit data. It's even harder to predict the data in 2014 than in 2013, since there are much more new companies involved in Section 337 investigations in 2014. The rate of new companies (20) out of all companies (651) in 2013 is 0.0307, while the rate of new companies (49) out of all companies (564) in 2014 is 0.0869. On the other hand, the time-shifting predictor performed better in other conditions. This indicates that if a company pair has never been engaged in a lawsuit, and has a lawsuit in the test year, we can predict using the time-changing predictor. If a company pair has been engaged in a lawsuit previously, we can predict using the time-shifting predictor. It should be noted that the proposed approaches do have some limitations. If the company pair has been involved in a lawsuit previously, and has no lawsuit in the test year, it is difficult to predict using either of our approaches.

7. RELATED WORKS

Patent litigation covers both legal and technical issues, and is also a key concern of managers when making strategic decisions. Furthermore, patent litigation influences the market value of a company. Lerner's research[10] shows that patent litigation can decrease the market value of the respondent companies by 2%–3.1%. Such lawsuits are usually used to prevent imitation by other companies. The patentee prevents the infringement use of technology via litigation. The technology barriers constructed by litigation can transform into market entry barriers. Such barriers guarantee that the patentee retains its dominant position in the market. Lanjouw and Schankerman[8] argued there is a relationship between the characteristics of patents and the likelihood that they will become involved in infringement lawsuits. Chien[3] shows that whether a patent is going to be litigated depends on the economic value of the patent, the characteristics of the patent owner, and the owner's propensity to litigate. By studying all of the infringement claims for a sample of recently expired patents, Love[12] found considerable differences in litigation practices between practicing and non-practicing entities. Product-producing companies usually enforce their patents soon after issuance, and complete their enforcement activities well before their patent rights expire.

Existing research on patent recommendation have largely focused on method/approach, system/software, and patent derivatives (e.g., collaborator, maintenance). Most of the patent recommendation methods/approaches have been based on retrieval techniques and ranking methods. Bashir[1] proposed a query-expansion method using pseudo relevance feedback to increase the retrievability of patents. Cao[2] proposed a new user-friendly patent search paradigm and introduced three techniques (error correction, topic-based query suggestion, and query expansion) to improve the usability of patent searches. Oh[16] proposed a CV-PCR framework with a heterogeneous patent citation-bibliographic network that combines both patent citations (reflecting value relation) and bibliographic information (reflecting similarity relation). Based on this network, they proposed value-driven and context-guided features. Magdy[15] reported a comparison between simple and straightforward information retrieval techniques[14] and much more sophisticated techniques[11] in patent searches. Their experiments showed that the advanced search technique is statistically better only when no initial citations are provided.

Jie Tang[17] presented a topic-driven patent analysis and mining system (PatentMiner), which mainly focuses on mining heterogeneous patent networks. They proposed a dynamic probabilistic model to characterize the topical evolution of different objects in a heterogeneous network. The system uses patent summarization and technology trend visualization. Hasan[4]built a patent ranking software (Claim Originality Analysis) that rates a patent based on its value by measuring its age and the impact of the important phrases that appear in the "claims" section of the patent. Bo[5] designed an indicator to understand technology prospecting by studying the evolving distributions of technologies in high tech companies.

The research mentioned above largely focused on patent content. Other relevant studies have also been conducted such as partner recommendation and maintenance decisions. Wu[18] studied the problem of recommending patenting partners in enterprise social networks and proposed a ranking factor graph model to suggest co-invention relationships. Jin[6] proposed a systematic solution to analyze patents to recommend patent maintenance decisions. In their approach, the patents are modeled as a heterogeneous time-evolving information network and new patent features are proposed to build models for a ranked prediction on whether to maintain or abandon a patent.

8. CONCLUSIONS

In this paper, we developed a recommendation framework for patent litigation risk prediction. The proposed framework clearly provides risky industry categories and risky competitors for high-tech companies when entering the US market. The design, analysis, and deployment of our recommendation framework are introduced in this paper. Specifically, we first acquired related information of Section 337 cases from USITC, and integrated it into a data set. We also presented the results of our statistical analysis, at both a regional and company level. Two methods of collaborative filtering, that is, proximal slope one predictor and time-aware predictor, are proposed in this paper. Finally, we evaluated our methods with extensive experiments on the real-world data set. The experimental results clearly validate the effectiveness of our methods.

Potentially, this study has many future research directions. First, it would be interesting to investigate new recommendation models to improve the accuracy of litigation risk prediction. Second, we plan to build a professional recommendation system to predict litigation risk for high-tech companies.

9. ACKNOWLEDGMENTS

The work was supported by the Natural Science Foundation of China (No. 61402068, 61425002) and Fundamental Research Funds for the Central Universities (No. DUT15QY04). It was also partially supported by a research grant from Zhigu Tech.

10. ADDITIONAL AUTHORS

Additional authors: Ruiyun Yu (Northeastern University, email: yury@mail.neu.edu.cn) and Qiang Zhang (Dalian University, email: zhangq26@126.com).

11. REFERENCES

[1] S. Bashir and A. Rauber. Improving retrievability of patents in prior-art search. In *Advances in Information Retrieval*, pages 457–470. Springer, 2010.

[2] Y. Cao, J. Fan, and G. Li. A user-friendly patent search paradigm. *Knowledge and Data Engineering, IEEE Transactions on*, 25(6):1439–1443, 2013.

[3] C. V. Chien. Patent assertion and startup innovation. *New America Foundation, Open Technology Institute White Paper*, 2013.

[4] M. A. Hasan, W. S. Spangler, T. Griffin, and A. Alba. Coa: Finding novel patents through text analysis. In *Proceedings of the 15th ACM SIGKDD international conference on Knowledge discovery and data mining*, pages 1175–1184. ACM, 2009.

[5] B. Jin, Y. Ge, H. Zhu, L. Guo, H. Xiong, and C. Zhang. Technology prospecting for high tech companies through patent mining. In *Data Mining (ICDM), 2014 IEEE International Conference on*, pages 220–229. IEEE, 2014.

[6] X. Jin, S. Spangler, Y. Chen, K. Cai, R. Ma, L. Zhang, X. Wu, and J. Han. Patent maintenance recommendation with patent information network model. In *Data Mining (ICDM), 2011 IEEE 11th International Conference on*, pages 280–289. IEEE, 2011.

[7] Y. Koren. Collaborative filtering with temporal dynamics. In *Proceedings of the 15th ACM SIGKDD International Conference on Knowledge Discovery and Data Mining*, KDD '09, pages 447–456, New York, NY, USA, 2009. ACM.

[8] J. O. Lanjouw and M. Schankerman. Characteristics of patent litigation: a window on competition. *RAND journal of economics*, pages 129–151, 2001.

[9] D. Lemire and A. Maclachlan. Slope one predictors for online rating-based collaborative filtering. In *SDM*, volume 5, pages 1–5. SIAM, 2005.

[10] J. Lerner and A. Seru. The use and misuse of patent data: Issues for corporate finance and beyond. *Booth/Harvard Business School Working Paper*, 2015.

[11] P. Lopez, L. Romary, et al. Experiments with citation mining and key-term extraction for prior art search. In *CLEF 2010-Conference on Multilingual and Multimodal Information Access Evaluation*, 2010.

[12] B. J. Love. An empirical study of patent litigation timing: Could a patent term reduction decimate trolls without harming innovators? *University of Pennsylvania Law Review*, 161:1309, 2013.

[13] T. J. Lybbert and N. J. Zolas. Getting patents and economic data to speak to each other: An ąőalgorithmic links with probabilitiesąŕ approach for joint analyses of patenting and economic activity. *Research Policy*, 43(3):530–542, 2014.

[14] W. Magdy and G. J. Jones. Applying the kiss principle for the clef-ip 2010 prior art candidate patent search task. 2010.

[15] W. Magdy, P. Lopez, and G. J. Jones. Simple vs. sophisticated approaches for patent prior-art search. In *Advances in Information Retrieval*, pages 725–728. Springer, 2011.

[16] S. Oh, Z. Lei, W.-C. Lee, P. Mitra, and J. Yen. Cv-pcr: a context-guided value-driven framework for patent citation recommendation. In *Proceedings of the 22nd ACM international conference on Conference on information & knowledge management*, pages 2291–2296. ACM, 2013.

[17] J. Tang, B. Wang, Y. Yang, P. Hu, Y. Zhao, X. Yan, B. Gao, M. Huang, P. Xu, W. Li, et al. Patentminer: topic-driven patent analysis and mining. In *Proceedings of the 18th ACM SIGKDD international conference on Knowledge discovery and data mining*, pages 1366–1374. ACM, 2012.

[18] S. Wu, J. Sun, and J. Tang. Patent partner recommendation in enterprise social networks. In *Proceedings of the sixth ACM international conference on Web search and data mining*, pages 43–52. ACM, 2013.

Ranking Universities Based on Career Outcomes of Graduates

Navneet Kapur*
GoFundMe
Redwood City, CA, USA
nkapur@gofundme.com

Nikita Lytkin
LinkedIn Corporation
Mountain View, CA, USA
nlytkin@linkedin.com

Bee-Chung Chen
LinkedIn Corporation
Mountain View, CA, USA
bchen@linkedin.com

Deepak Agarwal
LinkedIn Corporation
Mountain View, CA, USA
dagarwal@linkedin.com

Igor Perisic
LinkedIn Corporation
Mountain View, CA, USA
iperisic@linkedin.com

ABSTRACT

Every year, millions of new students enter higher educational programs. Publicly available rankings of academic programs play a key role in prospective students' decisions regarding which universities to apply to and enroll in. While surveys indicate that majority of freshmen enter college to get good jobs after graduation, established methodologies for ranking universities rely on indirect indicators of career outcomes such as reputational assessments of the universities among academic peers, acceptance and graduation rates, learning environment, and availability of research funding. In addition, many of these methodologies rely on arbitrary choices of weighting factors for the different ranking indicators, and suffer from lack of analyses of statistical stability. In this paper, we addresses these challenges holistically by developing a novel methodology for ranking and recommending universities for different professions on the basis of career outcomes of professionals who graduated from those schools. Our methodology incorporates a number of techniques for achieving statistical stability, and represents a step towards personalized educational recommendations based on interests and ambitions of individuals. We have applied this methodology on LinkedIn's Economic Graph data of over 400 million professional from around the world. The resulting university rankings have been made available to the public and demonstrate that there are valuable insights to be gleaned from professional career data on LinkedIn.

Keywords

Educational Recommendations; University Rankings; Company Rankings; Statistics

*Work done while at LinkedIn.

KDD '16, August 13 - 17, 2016, San Francisco, CA, USA

ISBN 978-1-4503-4232-2/16/08...$15.00

DOI: http://dx.doi.org/10.1145/2939672.2939701

1. INTRODUCTION

Millions of high school students (3 million in the US alone in 2015) apply for higher education every year. For each aspiring college student, the application process starts with selecting schools to apply to based on the student's career interests and academic performance. A recent survey [16] conducted by Higher Education Research Institute on hundreds of thousands of entering freshman found that 88% of freshman attend college to get a good job while 81% state the desire to be very well off financially as one of their personal goals. Thus, the ability to recommend schools on the basis of careers and eventually in a personalized manner has potential to provide tremendous value.

On LinkedIn.com, millions of professionals across the world enter rich information about their careers. We propose to leverage this valuable data and convert it into actionable information for LinkedIn's youngest users and drive change through actionable insights at higher education institutions. In this paper, we for the first time present in full detail our novel approach to ranking and recommending universities given a choice of a profession, on the basis of career outcomes of professionals who graduated from those schools.

The notion of ranking universities in itself is not a new concept. Ranking agencies such as US News & World Report, Times Higher Education and QS produce university lists each year - overall and by major. These rankings assess schools on the basis of indicators such as percentages of accepted students who go on to enroll, graduation rates, average SAT scores in addition to somewhat nebulous indicators like reputational assessments by peers at other universities. However, we believe that a more objective way to evaluate a degree program with respect to career outcomes is to measure performance of its graduates in industry. We achieve this by first developing an approach for identifying most desirable companies for different professions. We then present a methodology for ranking universities based on the rates at which their graduates are able to obtain jobs at these desirable companies in a given profession. Such data-driven rankings are a complex data product which requires careful consideration for a number of statistical aspects including representation bias and statistical robustness of results. In following sections, we present our methodology and approaches used for correcting potential representation biases and ensuring statistical robustness of the computed rankings with respect to potential noise in the underlying data.

2. RELATED WORK

Commonly adopted approaches [5, 6, 2, 1] to university rankings typically rely on a mixture of factors such as a university's reputation amongst peer academics (e.g., deans, provosts and faculty), learning environment (e.g., class size), research quality, volume and funding, and student acceptance and graduation rates. While some ranking methodologies focus on a single factor such as quality of research output [19] or reputation among academic peers [4, 3], other methodologies combine multiple factors into a single ranking statistic [5, 6, 2, 1, 12, 18]. In the latter case, the ranking statistic is often based on a weighted combination of scores on each individual factor. For instance, US News 2016 undergraduate rankings [5] place a weight of 22.5% on Undergraduate academic reputation (as judged by surveyed academic peers and high school counselors), and 12.5% on Student selectivity, which includes application acceptance rate as a sub-factor. Another popular ranking of universities produced by Times Higher Education (THE) [2] follows a similar approach to US News.

Both US News and THE methodologies are examples of approaches in which individual factor weights are assigned *arbitrarily* at the ranking agency's discretion - a point of criticism which has also been raised by other researchers [19, 14]. Furthermore, no assessment by the ranking agencies is provided on (a) statistical confidence of the rankings (e.g., due to limited sample sizes, reporting errors, etc.), and (b) the degree of sensitivity of the rankings with respect to changes in the weights assigned to the individual factors[1]. The use of ad-hoc factor weightings coupled with a lack of analyses of statistical stability of the rankings and of their sensitivity to changes in the factor weightings comes at the cost of interpretability of the rankings and makes their reliability (in some sense, trustworthiness) unclear. At the same time, research suggests that university rankings wield significant influence over prospective students' educational choices with the strength of the influence increasing with increasing rank of a university [13]. Researchers have also begun to question the strength of the link between quality of education and the quantitative factors used in common university rankings (see [11] for a methodological critique of the major quality assessments in U.S. higher education).

In order to make university rankings robust to potential noise in the underlying data, in the current work, we integrate statistical stability mechanisms directly into the rankings methodology by making use of confidence intervals and resampling techniques as discussed in subsequent sections. Moreover, instead of attempting to combine multiple different ranking dimensions into one ranking statistic, we focus exclusively on a single ranking criterion based on career outcomes of university graduates, as will be explained in the following sections.

It is worth noting that factors such as academic reputation are prone to manipulation and feedback effects, with the effects getting stronger with increasing influence of the rankings publisher on the general audience. Interestingly and perhaps not surprisingly, broad publicity and the potential for attracting prospective students are cited by ranking and data collection agencies as the key reasons for universities to provide the necessary data[2]. To see the potential for a feedback loop, consider that a better ranking of a university by a prominent ranking agency may lead to increases in the number of applications to that university in subsequent years. This in turn could further increase the university's reputational assessment and acceptance indicators (e.g., lower admission rates). As a result, this university's competitiveness in the rankings could increase over time. In fact, [9] found evidence of strong effects on university acceptance indicators due to ranking by US News. There is also evidence suggesting that the sheer act of publishing a ranking can influence peer assessments of reputability of a university in subsequent surveys [8, 10]. For example, [10] found anchoring effects in peer assessments of university reputation due to the first publication of Times Higher Education Supplement world university rankings. In addition, another study [8] found evidence of significant influence of US News rankings on future peer assessments, *independent of changes in organizational quality and performance.* We therefore refrain from using reputational assessment factors in our ranking methodology.

A major limitation faced by the above ranking methodologies is due to the lack of comprehensive data on career outcomes of university graduates. In contrast, LinkedIn Economic Graph[3] data comprised of over 400 million professional profiles is a unique dataset that provides a view of educational and career paths of individuals across the world at an unprecedented scale and granularity. Not only does this data allow us to rank universities with respect to the overall career outcomes of their graduates, the data also provides the necessary information for ranking universities with respect to career outcomes in specific professions such as Software Developers, Designers, Finance Professionals, etc. This is in stark contrast to rankings focused on academic areas of study. For example, US News engineering rankings, which are based solely on reputational peer assessments [4], may not be as relevant to specific professional outcomes since according to [7] only an estimated 27% of US college graduates end up working in roles related to their undergraduate majors.

There are certainly multiple facets to high quality education, with some researchers proposing multidimensional rankings for higher education [18]. Learning environment, teaching and research excellence, as well as financial returns on investment in education are important factors to consider when evaluating educational opportunities. Compared to university rankings based on the more traditional criteria discussed earlier in this section, the methodology presented in this work brings to light a complementary tool for informing educational decisions on the basis of career outcomes of university graduates. The resulting LinkedIn university rankings based on career outcomes are available to the general public[4]. Next, we present the underlying methodology. Note that we use the terms "profession" and "career" interchangeably.

[1]Unfortunately, the underlying data is not publicly available, which precludes such sensitivity analyses from being conducted by independent researchers.

[2]See a link to a PDF at the bottom of the page at http://www.commondataset.org/

[3]https://www.linkedin.com/company/linkedin-economic-graph

[4]https://www.linkedin.com/edu/

3. METHODOLOGY

3.1 Overview

Our methodology for ranking universities based on career outcomes consists of two main components shown in Figure 1. First, the most desirable companies for a given profession are identified by CompanyRanker based on employee transition dynamics reflected in LinkedIn member data. Universities are then ranked by SchoolRanker based on how successful their graduates are at landing jobs at the most desirable companies in the given profession. There is a number of methodological challenges such as representation bias and robustness to potential noise in the data that are addressed in order to produce statistically sound results. We discuss these in the following subsections where we present CompanyRanker and SchoolRanker in detail.

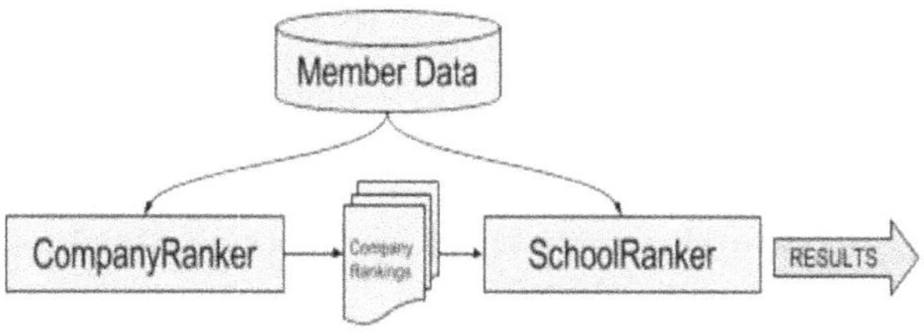

Figure 1: Algorithm architecture overview

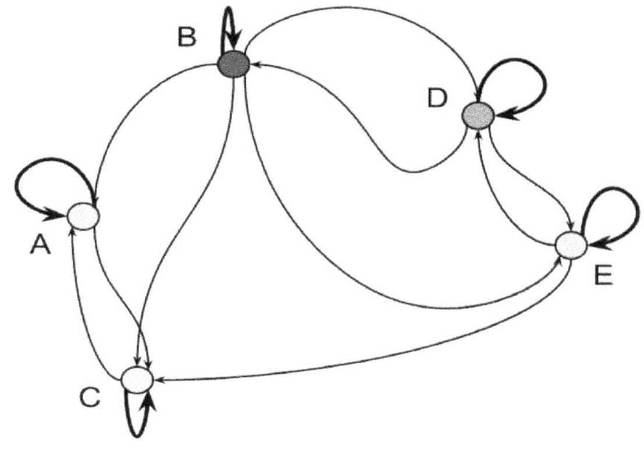

Figure 2: An illustration of a Talent Flow Graph for a given profession. Nodes correspond to companies. Edges are weighted based on numbers of employees transitioning between companies. Variability in edge weights is depicted with different line widths. Weights on self-loops are normalized by the median tenure in the profession. Self-loops typically have higher weights than other edges leaving a node except in cases of significant lay-offs or poor retention.

3.2 CompanyRanker: Determining companies desirable to a career

We define companies desirable for a profession as those which are the best at attracting and retaining talent in that profession. We let the career choices of hundreds of millions of LinkedIn members tell us how desirable it is to work at a company.

To illustrate this, imagine there are two companies, A and B. If more finance professionals are choosing to leave company A to work at company B, the data indicates that getting a finance job at B is more desirable. This is based on the hypothesis that when a professional moves from one company to another, she gives the company she moves to a strong vote of confidence.

Extending the hypothesis further, we posit that attracting employees from other desirable companies makes a company more desirable. Similarly, the ability of a company to retain its employees is a strong indicator of that employer's attractiveness. So, hypothetically, if A and B are both attracting external employees at similar rates, but A has much higher churn than B, A would be deemed to be less desirable than B.

The above model can be conveniently represented using a graph structure. Given a profession and a set of LinkedIn members with their career histories, we define a Talent Flow Graph (TFG) to be a directed graph whose nodes correspond to companies and edges are weighted by the numbers of employment transitions between companies. We restrict the set of eligible employment transitions to those taken by members in the profession of interest. For example, when ranking companies by desirability for software engineers (SWEs), we limit the relevant population of members to those who held a SWE role. The corresponding TFG is then formed on the basis of companies these members have worked at while in SWE roles. Companies with very few professionals contributing to their edges are removed from the graph in order to reduce noise. In order to make company desirability estimates reflective of contemporary labor market conditions, only transitions during the past five years are considered.

We capture employee retention dynamics by introducing one self-loop edge for each company in a TFG. Weights on self-loop edges are normalized for median retention within the profession. This normalization allows us to effectively control for variations in tenure length across different professions. For a given profession P, the self-loop weight for a company A in a TFG is defined as $\sum_{x \in R_P(A)} t_P(x, A)$, where $R_P(A)$ is the set of professionals with tenure at company A longer than median tenure for profession P, and $t_P(x, A)$ equals professional x's tenure at A divided by the median tenure for P.

A schematic illustration of a TFG is shown in Figure 2. Once a TFG is constructed, company desirability scores are determined by applying PageRank [15] on this graph. Note that besides modeling employee transition dynamics more richly, factoring in retention helps mitigate company-size reinforcement caused by the lack of inbound-edge normalization in PageRank.

To see this, consider a hypothetical profession with one big company A, two medium-sized companies B and C, and three small companies D, E and F. Figure 3 shows the corresponding TFG in the form of an employee transition probability matrix and in the absence of self-loops. The transition probability matrix is obtained by representing the TFG by a weighted adjacency matrix with (i, j)-th element encoding the talent flow from company i to company j as discussed above, and with each row normalized to sum to one. For illustrative purposes, the individual probabilities are generated following the observation that bigger companies, besides having more open positions available, have higher brand awareness and generally attract more job applications from aspirants. (Some small companies are acquired by large ones as well.) In row 2 of the transition probability matrix for example, we see that A has higher than three times the rate of attracting talent when compared to small companies (D, E and F) - 0.4 as opposed to 0.13 - and about two times the rate when compared to medium-sized companies (B and C) - 0.4 as opposed to ~0.2.

The computed page rank scores show that company A scores highest with 0.297 while the medium-sized and small companies score 0.165 and 0.124 respectively.

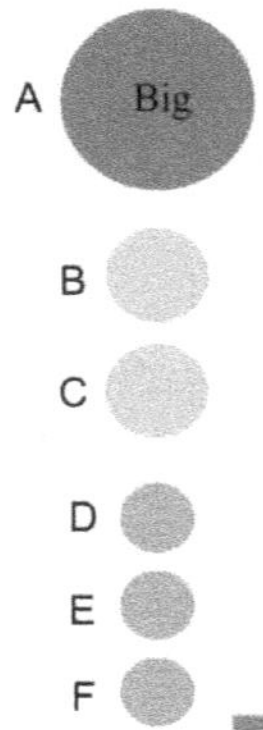

Row-normalized Transition Probability Matrix

	A	B	C	D	E	F
A	0	0.25	0.25	0.167	0.167	0.166
B	0.40	0	0.21	0.13	0.13	0.13
C	0.40	0.21	0	0.13	0.13	0.13
D	0.50	0.15	0.15	0	0.1	0.1
E	0.50	0.15	0.15	0.1	0	0.1
F	0.50	0.15	0.15	0.1	0.1	0
	0.297	0.165	0.165	0.124	0.124	0.124

Figure 3: Transition probability matrix representing a Talent Flow Graph without retention (self-loop edges), for a hypothetical profession. Sizes and colors of the circles encode company sizes from large (A) to medium (B, C), and small (D, E, F). Bottom row shows the corresponding PageRank score for each company from A (left) through F (right).

Now, what if the large company A was experiencing a high employee churn of, say, 20% a year as compared to 5% for the other companies? This would indicate that A may not be such a desirable company to work at and we would like our methodology to reflect this. After representing retention in the form of self-loops, the transition probability matrix and the resulting PageRank scores are shown in Figure 4. With retention factored in, company A now comes in last w.r.t. desirability with a score of 0.13 while the medium-sized companies score the highest with 0.184 due to stronger employee retention. The score for small companies is 0.167.

Note that since we construct different TFGs for different professions, given two companies A and B and professions P_1 and P_2, it is possible for company A to score better than B for desirability for profession P_1 and score worse than B for profession P_2.

In order to account for varying labor market dynamics and professional preferences across countries and educational degree levels (e.g., Bachelors, Masters, etc.), we construct a separate TFG for each (profession, country, degree level) combination. For example, the list of desirable companies for software engineers who studied in the UK will likely differ from the one for those who attended academic programs in the US. Also, the top companies for graduates of Bachelor's programs might differ from those for MBA graduates.

Row-normalized Transition Probability Matrix

	A	B	C	D	E	F
A	**0.8**	0.05	0.05	0.033	0.034	0.033
B	0.02	**0.95**	0.01	0.0067	0.0067	0.0067
C	0.02	0.01	**0.95**	0.0067	0.0067	0.0067
D	0.025	0.0075	0.0075	**0.95**	0.005	0.005
E	0.025	0.0075	0.0075	0.005	**0.95**	0.005
F	0.025	0.0075	0.0075	0.005	0.005	**0.95**
	0.13	0.184	0.184	0.167	0.167	0.167

Figure 4: Transition probability matrix with retention factored in for the hypothetical profession example. Bottom row shows the corresponding PageRank score for each company from A (left) through F (right).

3.3 SchoolRanker: Ranking universities based on career outcomes

The foundational assumption underlying our approach to university rankings is that obtaining employment at some of the most desirable companies for a given profession indicates a favorable career outcome for a university graduate. We therefore derive a university success score based on the proportion of graduates who obtained employment in a given profession at some of the most desirable companies for that profession. However, not all graduates may be interested in pursuing the same profession. Hence, when computing a success score for a university with respect to a profession, we only consider the subpopulation of graduates who went on to obtain a position in that profession. For example, for the profession of software engineering, we consider every graduate who went on to hold a software engineering role at any company post-graduation.

Note that since some university graduates may not be members of LinkedIn professional network, there may be a representation bias in the data. We correct for potential representation bias using the method of post-stratification weighting [17]. In particular, we apply externally reported university graduation data, such as published by the U.S. Department of Education[5], to adjust the sufficient statistics for university success scores by stratifying on gender, graduation year, degree level and university.

Let $\mathcal{X}$ denote the domain of a categorical variable encoding all possible combinations of values of the attributes used for post-stratification weighting. For a given university, let $p(x)$ denote the proportion of graduates who have the particular combination of attributes represented by $x \in \mathcal{X}$, according to data on LinkedIn. Let $q(x)$ denote an externally reported proportion of graduates from the same university and with the same combination of attributes x. Then, the total bias-corrected number of graduates from this university and relevant to the profession is

$$r = \sum_{x \in \mathcal{X}} m(x)w(x),$$

[5]https://nces.ed.gov/ipeds/datacenter/

where $m(x)$ denotes the number of the university's graduates with attributes x on LinkedIn who entered the profession at *any* of the relevant companies, and $w(x) = q(x)/p(x)$ is the corresponding post-stratification weight. Similarly, the bias-corrected number of graduates who obtained employment at any of the top companies is

$$s = \sum_{x \in \mathcal{X}} n(x)w(x), \quad (1)$$

where $n(x) \leq m(x), \forall x \in \mathcal{X}$, denotes the size of the subset of the university's graduates with attributes x on LinkedIn who obtained employment at some of the *top* (i.e., most desirable) companies for the profession.

Finally, we define the *university success score* to be the lower end of the 95% Binomial confidence interval around the bias-corrected ratio

$$\theta = \frac{s}{r} \quad (2)$$

of graduates who obtained employment at top companies out of all graduates who entered the profession from the university. The lower end of the confidence interval is used in order to stabilize the ranking statistic w.r.t. limited sample sizes and ground it in sustained trends in career outcomes of university graduates. Note that given the scale of LinkedIn's professional member base of over 400 million members and because we consider all graduates from the last eight years when ranking universities, sample sizes for most universities ranked are large enough for the lower ends of the confidence intervals to be close to the point estimates in Eqn. 2.

The lists of top (i.e., most desirable) companies are based on the career-wise desirability scores provided by the CompanyRanker. University success score computation by virtue of Eqn. 1, however, requires another parameter to be specified - the number of companies to be considered most desirable out of all companies ranked by CompanyRanker for the profession. We discuss the selection of the number of top companies later in this section. For now, let us assume that this number has been given, and consider the following. The representation bias alluded to earlier may also affect company desirability estimation. Unfortunately, at the present time there is no comprehensive publicly available company data that would allow to correct for possible representation bias during company desirability estimation. Reporting errors in LinkedIn member data may also affect the results. In order to make our methodology robust to potential inaccuracies in member data and company desirability estimates, we (a) only use data from member profiles that have successfully passed stringent spam detection checks, and (b) develop a Monte Carlo resampling technique discussed next.

Given a ranking of companies by desirability and the number K of most desirable companies to be used for computing university success scores, a large number (thousands) of perturbed sets of most desirable companies are generated by repeatedly substituting a randomly chosen subset (e.g., 5-10%) of companies from the original set of K most desirable ones with the same number of companies selected from outside that set (i.e., from those companies which didn't make it into the top K by desirability). Companies from outside the most desirable set are sampled with probabilities proportional to their estimated desirability, so the more desirable companies have a higher chance of being placed into a perturbed set.

For each perturbed set of most desirable companies, university success scores are computed and the universities are ranked based on those scores. Thus, for each university, this procedure results in a distribution over ranks the university attained across perturbed sets of most desirable companies. The 95th percentile rank from this distribution is then taken as the ranking statistic for the university. If two or more universities attain the same 95th percentile rank, the 75th percentile rank is used to resolve the tie. Universities that tie on both 95th and 75th percentile ranks are declared tied and are assigned the same final rank. As a result, universities with larger proportions of graduates obtaining jobs in the more desirable companies for a given profession, rank higher. At the same time, rankings of universities are made robust to potential noise in company desirability estimates. What remains to discuss is the determination of the number K of most desirable companies to use for ranking universities.

Selection of the number of desirable companies: As we vary the number K of the most desirable companies, the resulting university rankings may change. The degree of sensitivity of university rankings to the choice of K is a function of the distributions of university graduates across companies for a given profession. Figure 5 shows an example of the cumulative distributions of graduates from five universities over companies ranked by desirability.

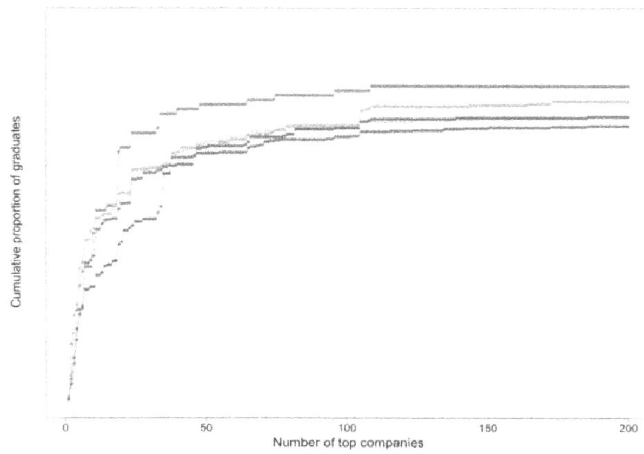

Figure 5: Cumulative distributions of numbers of graduates from five universities across companies ordered by desirability. Large steps in the curves indicate cases where a school feeds strongly into a single company. For example, school plotted in red would rank 4th among presented schools if top 10 companies are chosen and would rank 1st if top 25 companies are chosen.

The jumps in the distributions in Figure 5 indicate that there are cases where a school "feeds" strongly to a single company. Hence, the selection of K is important in determining the final university rankings. We would like to choose a K around which the changes in university ranks due to "single-company effects" are minimized and the rankings are more stable. This is achieved by a grid search over a set of values of K. For each K, we quantify and measure the average pairwise agreement between all pairs of school rankings produced as a result of Monte Carlo resampling of company rankings described above. The agreement between a pair of school rankings is defined as a weighted average of sizes of set intersections between the top N schools in the two rankings and normalized by N, for N=3, 5, 10 and 25. The value of K corresponding to the highest average pairwise agreement is then chosen for defining the set of most desirable companies.

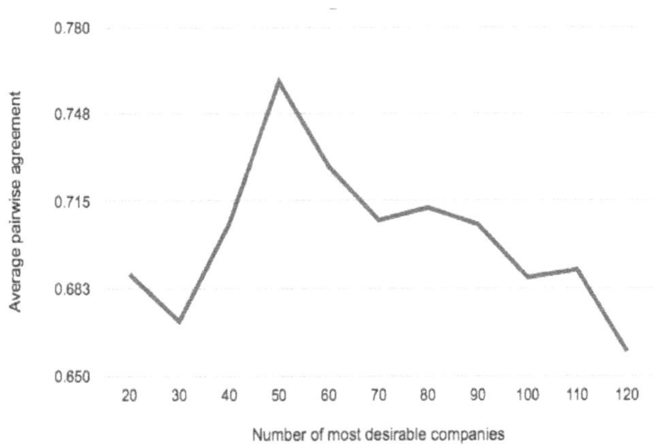

Figure 6: Average pairwise agreement between university rankings across perturbed sets of most desirable companies, as a function of the number of most desirable companies used for determining university success scores.

Figure 6 shows an example of the average pairwise agreement as a function of the number of most desirable companies. In this example, average pairwise agreement is maximized at fifty most desirable companies. In other words, moderate perturbations to the set of most desirable companies affect the resulting university rankings the least at K=50 compared to other values of K. Therefore, in this example, K=50 most desirable companies would subsequently be used for ranking universities.

4. RESULTS AND OBSERVATIONS

Below, we present some of the results obtained by applying our methodology. We discuss company desirability and university rankings for two professions in the US: the Investment Bankers and Software Developers at Startups. For illustrative purposes, Table 1 shows an alphabetically ordered list of the 20 most desirable companies generated by CompanyRanker for Investment Bankers.

It is worth noting that these companies are indeed well-recognized leaders in the investment banking industry. Additionally, we present an alphabetically ordered list of top startups for Software Developers, as of September 2014, in Table 2. Only non-public companies with less than 5,000 employees and less than 10 years in age are considered for this category. Similar to the list of most desirable companies for the Investment Bankers category, the list of top startups is comprised of highly regarded private companies. Note that the above lists of most desirable companies have been identified automatically by our methodology based on the transitions of employees across companies. This further highlights the great potential of LinkedIn's Economic Graph that can be realized through applications of data analytic approaches.

Table 1: Top 20 companies for Investment Bankers (in alphabetical order).

Company
American Express
Bank of America
Citi
Credit Suisse AG
Deutsche Bank
Goldman Sachs
Jefferies
JPMorgan Chase & Co
KPMG
Morgan Stanley
New York Life Insurance Company
Nomura
Piper Jaffray
Raymond James Financial, Inc.
RBC Capital Markets
TIAA-CREF
UBS AG
USAA
Wells Fargo
William Blair

Table 2: Top 20 startups for Software Developers (in alphabetical order)

Company	Type
Airbnb	Hospitality
Braintree	Payments
Clever	Education
CoreOS	Operating Systems
Couchbase	Database Systems
Counsyl	Healthcare
Dropbox	Cloud Storage
Fitbit	Fitness
Flatiron Health	Healthcare
Github	Software Development Tools
Lyft	Transportation and Delivery
Oscar Health	Healthcare
PlanGrid	Industrial Design Software
PlanSource	HR Management Systems
Riot Games	Entertainment
Sovrn Holdings	Online Advertising
Square	Payments
Tapad	Online Advertising
Uber	Transportation and Delivery
Zen Payroll	Payroll Management

University rankings obtained by the SchoolRanker for Investment Bankers and Software Developers at Startups are shown in Tables 3 and 4, resp. As was mentioned in the Methodology section, universities are ranked on the basis of their 95th percentile ranks across perturbed company sets. Ties on the 95th percentile ranks are resolved using the 75th percentile ranks. This can be seen in Table 3, where Columbia University and Duke University both have equal 95th and 75th percentile ranks and are thus considered a tie, both ranking fourth for Investment Bankers. In contrast,

Table 3: **Top ranking undergraduate programs for Investment Bankers**

School	75th Percentile	95th Percentile	Final Rank
Georgetown University	1	2	1
University of Pennsylvania	3	4	2
Yale University	4	7	3
Columbia University in the City of New York	7	9	4
Duke University	7	9	4
Princeton University	9	11	6
New York University	11	11	7
Wellesley College	4	12	8
Cornell University	10	12	9
Dartmouth College	10	13	10

Table 4: **Top ranking undergraduate programs for Software Developers at Startups**

School	75th Percentile	95th Percentile	Final Rank
Stanford University	1	1	1
Massachusetts Institute of Technology	2	2	2
University of California, Berkeley	3	4	3
Carnegie Mellon University	4	5	4
Brown University	6	7	5
Cornell University	6	10	6
The University of Texas at Austin	13	15	7
Rochester Institute of Technology	14	18	8
University of Illinois at Urbana-Champaign	15	18	9
University of Maryland College Park	7	19	10

Table 4 shows Rochester Institute of Technology (RIT) and University of Illinois at Urbana-Champaign (UIUC) achieving the same 95th percentile rank, but different 75th percentile ranks. As a result, RIT's final ranking comes out one step above UIUC's for Software Developers at Startups.

The top universities for Investment Bankers have larger numbers of graduates joining some of the top investment institutions such as Goldman Sachs, JPMorgan Chase & Co and Morgan Stanley. Similarly, for Software Developers at Startups, larger numbers of graduates are helping build some of the top startups such as Airbnb, Dropbox, Uber and others. The complete set of university rankings together with insights about each university and career paths of their graduates can be found via LinkedIn University Rankings, University Finder, and Field of Study Explorer products, which are all part of LinkedIn's suite of educational decision making products[6].

LinkedIn university rankings developed using the methodology presented here based on career outcomes of professionals around the world were first made publicly available in October of 2014 for undergraduate programs with a subsequent expansion into graduate (Masters) programs in March of 2015. The published rankings cover nine professions and three countries - United States, United Kingdom and Canada. The results were viewed by millions of unique users in the first week alone and received broad media coverage including The New York Times, The Wall Street Journal, Inside HigherEd and numerous other publishers.

5. CONCLUSION

We have presented a novel methodology for ranking the world's educational institutions on the basis of career outcomes of their graduates. By leveraging LinkedIn's Economic Graph data on career paths of hundreds of millions of professionals around the world, we are able to rank universities with respect to individual professions - something that the leading ranking agencies such as US News and Times Higher Education are unable to achieve at a comparable scale and granularity. In contrast, these ranking agencies often fall back on reputational assessments instead of directly measuring career outcomes. Our methodology addresses some of the key limitations of the existing approaches such as their heavy reliance on reputational assessments and scarcity of statistical robustness mechanisms, which make the resulting rankings difficult to interpret.

We believe that the methodology we have developed reflects more accurately the impact that universities have on industries and their graduates' careers. Using global career data as a ground-truth for assessing career outcomes makes the resulting university rankings more interpretable and, eventually, more actionable for schools and students alike. Schools can use these rankings as a tool to fine-tune their educational and career development programs while prospective students can choose universities based on professions that excite them. In addition, current students can use the tool in combination with the Alumni Explorer[7] on LinkedIn to connect with alumni and inform the students' career choices and job search.

Even though our methodology improves on the university ranking methodologies used in the industry, the methodology could be enhanced further by incorporating more granular data on job transitions. For example, when considering the flow of employees between companies when ranking companies by desirability, it is sometimes important to know

[6]https://www.linkedin.com/edu/

[7]https://www.linkedin.com/edu/alumni

the circumstances around which the employee leaves an employer. While highly desirable companies have highly competitive hiring processes, in some cases such companies also have stringent employee reevaluation processes. Factoring in information on job application and acceptance rates and reasons for employees' departures would increase the precision of company desirability estimates. Such data would also help further guide selection of subpopulations of graduates interested in a profession when ranking universities. In addition, comprehensive salary data would be a great way to enrich our definition of career outcomes. Finally, additional data from industry experts may help enrich the definition of career outcomes and increase precision of the rankings when coupled with appropriate data analytic methods such as semi-supervised versions of PageRank.

There are multiple facets to high quality education. Learning environment, teaching and research excellence, as well as financial returns on investment in education are important factors to consider when evaluating educational opportunities. The methodology presented in this work brings to light a complementary tool for informing educational decisions on the basis of career outcomes of university graduates.

6. REFERENCES

[1] QS World University Rankings: Methodology. QS, 2015.

[2] World University Rankings 2015-2016 methodology. Times Higher Education, 2015.

[3] Best Undergraduate Business Programs Methodology. U.S. News & World Report, 2016.

[4] Best Undergraduate Engineering Programs Methodology. U.S. News & World Report, 2016.

[5] How U.S. News Calculated the 2016 Best Colleges Rankings. U.S. News & World Report, 2016.

[6] Methodology: 2016 Best Business Schools Rankings. U.S. News & World Report, 2016.

[7] J. R. Abel and R. Deitz. Agglomeration and job matching among college graduates. Staff Report 587, Federal Reserve Bank of New York, December 2012.

[8] M. N. Bastedo and N. A. Bowman. The U.S. News and World Report college rankings: Modeling institutional effects on organizational reputation. *American Journal of Education*, (116):163–184, 2010.

[9] N. A. Bowman and M. N. Bastedo. Getting on the front page: Organizational reputation, status signals, and the impact of u.s. news and world report on student decisions. *Research in Higher Education*, 50(5):415–436, 2009.

[10] N. A. Bowman and M. N. Bastedo. Anchoring effects in world university rankings: exploring biases in reputation scores. *Higher Education*, 61(4):431–444, 2010.

[11] R. Brooks. Measuring university quality. *The Review of Higher Education*, 29(1), Fall 2005.

[12] C. Claassen. Measuring university quality. *Scientometrics*, 104(3):793–807, September 2015.

[13] A. Griffith and K. Rask. The influence of the U.S. News and World Report collegiate rankings on the matriculation decision of high-ability students: 1995-2004. *Economics of Education Review*, (26):244–255, 2007.

[14] S. Lee. Reputation without rigor. https://www.insidehighered.com/news/2009/08/19/rankings September 2009.

[15] L. Page, S. Brin, R. Motwani, and T. Winograd. The pagerank citation ranking: Bringing order to the web. Technical Report 1999-66, Stanford InfoLab, November 1999. Previous number = SIDL-WP-1999-0120.

[16] J. H. Pryor, K. Eagan, L. Palucki Blake, S. Hurtado, J. Berdan, and M. H. Case. The American freshman: National norms fall 2012. Higher Education Research Institute, UCLA, January 2013.

[17] R. Valliant and J. A. Dever. Estimating propensity adjustments for volunteer web surveys. *Sociological Methods & Research*, 40(1):105–137, 2011.

[18] F. A. van Vught and F. Ziegele, editors. *Multidimensional Ranking: The Design and Development of U-Multirank*, volume 37 of *Higher Education Dynamics*. Springer Netherlands, 2012.

[19] L. Waltman, C. Calero-Medina, J. Kosten, E. C. Noyons, R. J. Tijssen, N. J. van Eck, T. N. van Leeuwen, A. F. van Raan, M. S. Visser, and P. Wouters. The leiden ranking 2011/2012: Data collection, indicators, and interpretation. *J. Am. Soc. Inf. Sci. Technol.*, 63(12):2419–2432, Dec. 2012.

Predictors without Borders: Behavioral Modeling of Product Adoption in Three Developing Countries

Muhammad Raza Khan
University of Washington
Seattle, WA 98195
mraza@uw.edu

Joshua E Blumenstock
University of Washington
Seattle, WA 98195
joshblum@uw.edu

ABSTRACT

Billions of people around the world live without access to banks or other formal financial institutions. In the past several years, many mobile operators have launched "Mobile Money" platforms that deliver basic financial services over the mobile phone network. While many believe that these services can improve the lives of the poor, in many countries adoption of Mobile Money still remains anemic. In this paper, we develop a predictive model of Mobile Money adoption that uses billions of mobile phone communications records to understand the behavioral determinants of adoption. We describe a novel approach to feature engineering that uses a Deterministic Finite Automaton to construct thousands of behavioral metrics of phone use from a concise set of recursive rules. These features provide the foundation for a predictive model that is tested on mobile phone operators logs from Ghana, Pakistan, and Zambia, three very different developing-country contexts. The results highlight the key correlates of Mobile Money use in each country, as well as the potential for such methods to predict and drive adoption. More generally, our analysis provides insight into the extent to which homogenized supervised learning methods can generalize across geographic contexts. We find that without careful tuning, a model that performs very well in one country frequently does not generalize to another.

Keywords

Mobile Money; Feature engineering; Gradient boosting; Product adoption; Supervised learning

1. INTRODUCTION

The rapid penetration of mobile phones in developing countries is creating new opportunities to provide basic financial services to billions of individuals who have never before had access to banks or other formal financial institutions (Figure 1). In particular, over the last several years, mobile phone operators across the globe have launched "Mobile Money" platforms, which make it possible for mobile phone subscribers to conduct basic financial transactions from inexpensive feature phones. In several countries, these platforms have been wildly successful: two thirds of all Kenyan adults are active subscribers on the dominant Kenyan Mobile Money system [26]; in Bangladesh and Tanzania the corresponding usage rates are 40% and 50% [6, 9]. Globally, there are 255 live Mobile Money deployments in 89 countries, with an additional 102 planned deployments in the near future. With industry group GSMA estimating that 1 billion individuals currently own a phone but do not have a bank account [27], this presents massive potential to provide useful services to poor customers.

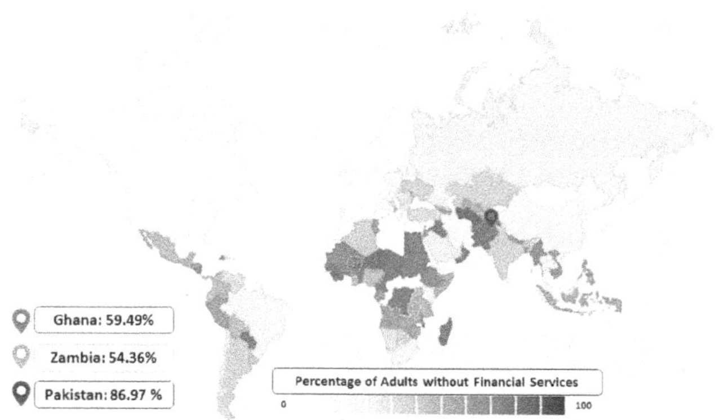

Figure 1: Worldwide access to formal financial services, constructed using data from the Global Financial Inclusion Database [7]. Study locations are identified by pins.

However, outside of the countries mentioned above and a few others, worldwide adoption of Mobile Money has been extremely anemic. The vast majority of deployments have struggled to promote sustained product adoption, and an industry report from 2014 estimates that 66% of registered customers were inactive [27]. An open and important question thus revolves around understanding what drives customers to adopt and use Mobile Money, and whether patterns observed in one country will generalize to another.

In this paper, we use spatio-temporal transactions data on mobile phone activity to model Mobile Money adoption in three developing countries. Our focus is on mining the Call Detail Records (CDR) collected by mobile phone operators, which contain detailed metadata on all events that tran-

KDD '16, August 13 - 17, 2016, San Francisco, CA, USA

ISBN 978-1-4503-4232-2/16/08...$15.00

DOI: http://dx.doi.org/10.1145/2939672.2939710

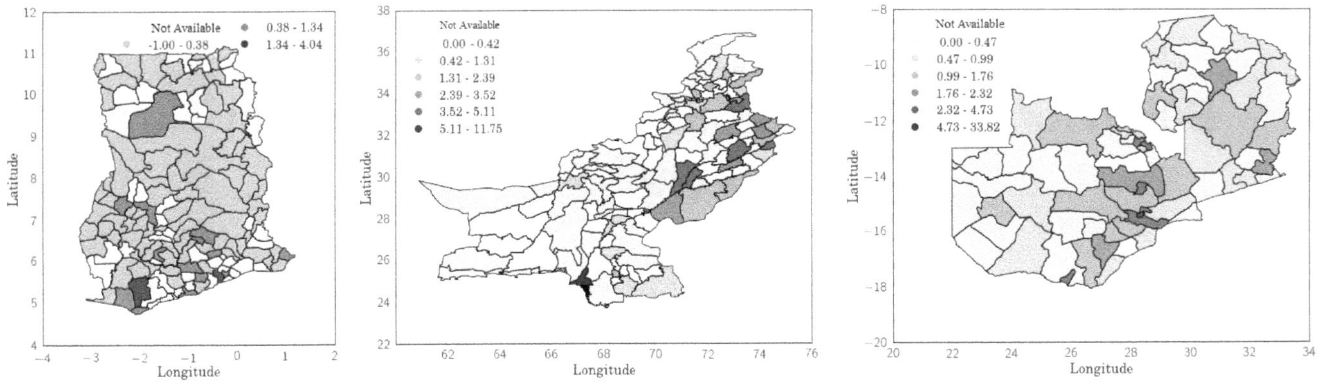

Figure 2: Geographic distribution of registered Mobile Money users in Ghana, Pakistan, and Zambia. Cells are colored according to the fraction of Mobile Money users in each region

spire on the mobile phone network, including phone calls, text messages, and Mobile Money transactions. For thousands of unique individuals in each country, we can thus infer a wealth of information about the structure of their social networks, their daily movements about the country, patterns of communication, and several other behaviors that we discuss in greater detail below. We also know whether each subscribers eventually signs up for Mobile Money, and if so, whether he or she remains an active user on the system. In the three countries we study - Ghana, Pakistan, and Zambia - each Mobile Money platform is owned and operated by a separate, independent mobile phone operator, and the subscriber population in each country has very different social and economic characteristics.

There are three substantive and one methodological contributions of this study. Substantively, we (1) develop a richer understanding of what drives the adoption of Mobile Money, by mining several large databases of transactions data; (2) construct a supervised learner that can predict, to varying degrees of accuracy depending on the prediction task and country context, the likelihood than an individual subscriber will use Mobile Money; and (3) explore the possibility that transfer learning could be used to train models in one country or context and apply them in another. To our knowledge, this is the first study to train and evaluate models of product adoption in three very different contexts. Since Mobile Money adoption is notoriously idiosyncratic, we hope this "cross-cultural" comparison can provide insight into the generalizability of our results, and increase their broader relevance to the policy and business communities working in developing countries.

Methodologically, we develop a novel framework for extracting behavioral metrics from transaction logs, which produces interpretable features that can provide the input data into standard supervised learning algorithms. This framework extends previous efforts described in [2], which used a simplified approach to predict poverty and wealth from mobile phone data. The core of this approach is formalized as a Deterministic Finite Automaton, which provides a structured, recursive grammar that relies on relatively few degrees of freedom to generate a comprehensive and interpretable set of "dense" features from sparse log data. This approach is sufficiently generalizable that we hope it can be further extended to a much broader range of contexts where researchers and data scientists wish to extract interpretable knowledge from transaction log data.

Related Work

Our work builds on several distinct strands in the academic literature. The first is concerned with understanding the determinants of mobile money adoption. This literature has historically been the domain of development researchers, and includes both macroeconomic and ethnographic work. The macro-scale work is concerned with the national and regulatory forces that can promote and hinder the spread of mobile money, such as interoperability regulations, barriers to customer registration, and the need for a robust network of mobile money agents [21, 8, 11]. The ethnographic work has focused primarily on qualitative studies of how mobile money can be integrated into the daily lives of the poor [24, 23, 12].[1]

A second strand of literature seeks to derive general insights from patterns revealed in mobile phone transactions logs. This encompasses a wide array of applications, including predicting the socioeconomic status [2], gender [13], and age [10] of individual mobile phone subscribers. These studies illustrate the rich signal latent in mobile operator data, which reflects social phenomena including the structure of social networks, patterns of mobility and migration, diurnal rhythms of daily activity, and expenditures on communication and airtime.

A third area of prior work, and the one most relevant to our study, contains several papers that use transactions data from mobile operators to study product adoption.[2] For instance, Khan et al. [19] use billing data to predict customer churn in an Afghan telecom, using a brute-force approach to feature generation. Sundsoy et al. [28] construct 350 features from call detail records and compare the performance of basic machine learning algorithms to that of a marketing department in predicting uptake of data plans. Finally, an industry report by CGAP compares the relative influence

[1] A closely related body of work explores the welfare consequences of the spread of Mobile Money [1, 18, 3, 4], though relatively few studies provide rigorous evidence that mobile money has a positive impact on the lives of the poor.

[2] A much broader literature, which we do not review here, studies the role of social networks in the adoption of new technologies [29, 20].

Country	Ghana	Pakistan	Zambia
Panel A: National statistics (Source: World Bank)			
Population	25.90 Million	185.00 Million	15.72 Million
Percent with bank accounts	40.51	13.02	45.64
GDP per capita (PPP adjusted)	$4081.70	$4811.4	$3904.00
Mobile phone subscriptions (per 100 people)	115	73	67
Mobile phone operators	6	6	3
Panel B: Mobile phone use (Source: Call Detail Records)			
Calls per subscriber per day	6.53 (6.99)	7.76 (10.25)	10.26 (102.86)
SMS per subscriber per day	3.10 (100.36)	38.71 (80.83)	10.88 (262.81)
Number of unique contacts	21.66 (24.91)	46.93 (139.67)	17.63 (328.63)
Number of unique Towers	12.98 (16.07)	24.15 (57.30)	7.35 (17.56)

Notes: Standard deviations reported in parenthesis.

Table 1: Summary statistics by country: national indicators and sample CDR metrics

of different types of mobile phone metrics on the adoption of Mobile Money in Africa, using 180 metrics derived from call data [5]. Relative to these studies, our study moves this literature forward by (a) innovating in the method used to generate features, thereby providing a systematic and comprehensive approach to feature engineering; (b) leveraging data from three different contexts to calibrate the external validity and generalizability of our results; and (c) carefully articulating the experimental protocols and algorithms in a way that will enable other researchers to replicate and extend these methods.

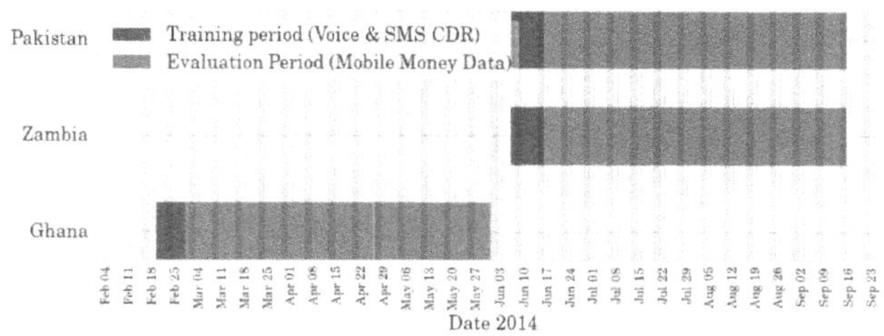

Figure 3: Training and evaluation periods

2. DATA AND CONTEXT

For this study, we worked in collaboration with three mobile phone operators in Ghana, Pakistan, and Zambia. All three countries rank in the bottom third of the Human Development Index, a metric developed by the United Nations to capture a broad range of welfare outcomes such as income, education, inequality, and life expectancy. As can be seen in Figure 1, penetration of financial services is very low in each country. Geographic patterns of Mobile Money adoption also vary greatly within each country, as shown in Figure 2. Additional information on each country is provided in Table 1. Of course, these country-level statistics mask enormous diversity between and within nations in social and demographic characteristics, religious and political attitudes, and general ways of living.

From each mobile phone operator, we obtained the anonymized Call Detail Records (CDR) and Mobile Money Transaction Records (MMTR) of every subscriber on the network. The CDR and MMTR contain basic metadata on every event that occurs on the mobile phone network, including phone calls, text messages, and any form of Mobile Money activity. CDR typically consists of tuples containing `{callerID, recipientID, date, time, duration, callerLocation}`, where the two ID's are anonymized phone numbers, the date and time indicate when the event transpired, the duration of the call is recorded in seconds, and the location field indicates the cellular tower through which the call was routed, which can be used to pinpoint the approximate location of the individual at the time of the call.[3] For the mobile money platforms we study, the MMTR contain similar metadata for basic financial transactions, such as deposits, withdrawals, purchases, balance checks, and so forth.

In total, the original data contains billions of transactions conducted by tens of millions of unique individuals. Each dataset spans several months of activity, which we divide into a "training" period and an "evaluation" period. CDR from a 10-day training period was used to engineer features and fit a predictive model, where the target variables (based on Mobile Money activity) were measured in a subsequent 3-month evaluation period. The timing of these periods is depicted in Figure 3.[4]

Using data from the evaluation period, each subscriber in each sample was labelled as either a "Voice Only" User or a "Registered Mobile Money" user, where Registered Mobile Money users could also be labelled as "Active Mobile Money" users according to the following criteria:

- **Voice Only Users:** If the user did not make any Mobile Money transactions during the evaluation period.
- **Registered Mobile Money User:** If the user made one or more Mobile Money transactions during the evaluation period.
- **Active Mobile Money User:** If the user made at least one Mobile Money transaction in each month of the evaluation period. Note that all Active Mobile Money users are also Registered Mobile Money Users.

[3]In practice, the cell tower is accurate within several hundred meters in urban areas, and tens of kilometers in rural regions. We do not observe the contents of text messages. CDR are only generated when an individual initiates a transaction on the network, so we do not observe, for instance, the individual's location when she is not using her phone.

[4]Our intent was to exactly align the training and evaluation periods across countries, but implementation constraints made this impossible.

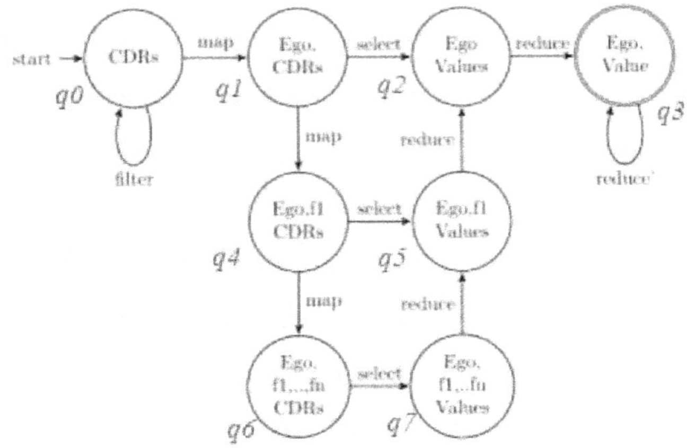

Figure 4: Deterministic Finite Automaton

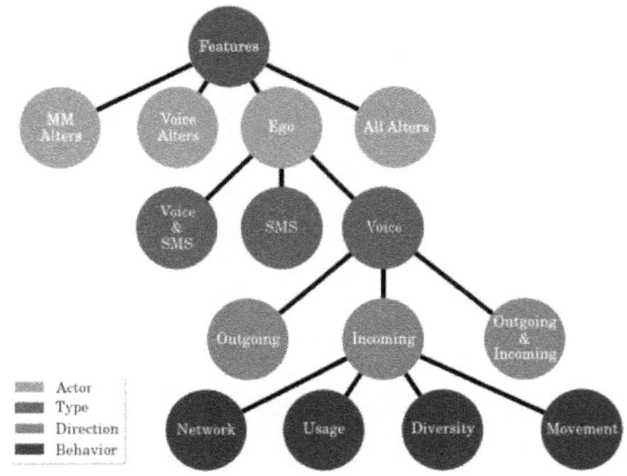

Figure 5: Tree-based feature classification

3. FEATURE ENGINEERING WITH DETERMINISTIC FINITE AUTOMATA

3.1 Approach

As highlighted in the introduction, the CDR contain a wealth of latent information about how people communicate, with whom they interact, the locations they visit, and many other social and behavioral characteristics. Our eventual goal is to leverage this information to better understand why people use Mobile Money, and to develop a predictive model of Mobile Money adoption. However, the raw CDR are not natural inputs to most machine learning algorithms, and interpretable metrics must first be derived from the CDR before inferences can be made.

In the prior literature, the vast majority of studies take a rather ad hoc approach to constructing interpretable metrics ("features") from the phone data. The most common approach is to hand-craft a small number of features that correspond to some intuition of the researcher. For instance, [10] focus on 5 topological properties of the static social network; [17] use two metrics that quantify airtime purchases; and [14] construct 6 measures of physical mobility. Even the more ambitious approaches, such as [28] and [5], which respectively use 350 and 180 CDR-based metrics, employ a large number of idiosyncratic rules to determine which features should be considered by the learning algorithm. These approaches have the advantage of producing metrics that are convenient to interpret, but they may systematically overlook non-intuitive features, mis-attribute relationships (if, for instance, feature A is weakly correlated with the target variable only because an omitted feature B is strongly correlated with both A and the target variable), or fail to maximize the predictive power of a classifier that would perform better with a more comprehensive set of features.

Our approach is different. We develop a method for feature engineering from transactional data that is designed to construct a large and comprehensive set of features from a small number of recursive operations. While the application is to CDR, we believe this method could be used to engineer features from a more diverse class of data including IP logs, social media data, and financial transaction records.

3.2 Deterministic Finite Automaton

We employ a deterministic finite automaton (DFA), a model of computation from automata theory also referred to as a deterministic finite state machine, to formalize the feature generation process [22]. DFA's are typically used in more formal settings to determine whether an expression can be computed, to design circuits, or to operate simple devices. In the abstract, however, DFA's simply define a sequence of legal operations. We appropriate this concept to specify a set of legal operations that can be recursively applied to raw transactional data in order to produce valid features.

Example

As an example, say we are interested in constructing a feature for each individual i that corresponds to, "the variance in the average duration of outgoing calls made by i on different days of the week." We allow for the construction of this feature through the following set of recursive rules:

1. filter *outgoing calls*
2. filter transactions *initiated by i*
3. group by *day of week*
4. focus on *call duration*
5. aggregate by *average* (duration per day of week)
6. aggregate using *variance* (over average daily durations)

By using different filter criteria (or difference group-by and aggregation operations), by adding and removing rules, or by applying the rules in a different order, we produce different features. It is important to note, however, that not all combinations of operations are valid. For instance, it does not make sense to take the variance of a categorical variable (such as `recipientID`), nor does it make sense to group by day of week if a day of week filter has already been applied. The power of the DFA is that it allows us to formalize the set of valid features using a relatively parsimonious specification.

Formalization

The DFA we use to generate features from CDR is shown in Figure 4. In the figure, each circle represents a state, and for convenience we note the data structure expected for each state inside the circle. Valid features are constructed through traversals of the state machine, which start at the start state (q0) and end at the end state (q3) and follow only legal transitions between states (denoted by arrows). For instance, the feature described above would begin with the full CDR in q0, filter outgoing calls and return to q0, map (group by) "ego" i and proceed to q1, map by day of week to q4, select duration and proceed to q5, reduce (aggregate) by average - this produces average call duration for each day of week for each i - and proceed to q2, aggregate by variance and exit at q3.

Formally, the DFA is specified by:

- **Legal states:** `Q = {q0,q1,q2,q3,q4,q5,q6,q7}`
- **Start State:** `q0` $\in$ `Q`
- **End State:** `q3` $\in$ `Q`
- **Alphabet:** $\Sigma =$ {`CDRs, Ego-CDRs, Ego-f-CDRs, Ego-Values, Ego-value`}
- **Transition Functions** ($\delta : Q \times \Sigma \rightarrow Q$): `filter, map, select, reduce`. The set of legal transitions is described in greater detail in Appendix A

In total, there are several thousand valid traversals of the DFA, each of which produces a different feature. Together, the resulting set of features covers almost all of the hand-crafted metrics used in prior work, as well as many, many more.

An additional advantage of the DFA is that it can be efficiently and elegantly implemented. Pseudo-code is provided in Algorithm 1, and the implementation in Spark Python is available from the author's website.[5]

3.3 Feature classification and tree structure

The DFA is a convenient abstraction for generating a very large number of features from a small set of rules. To interpret the set of features produced by the DFA, we label each generated feature with interpretable tags. These tags are determined by the path taken through the automaton, and indicate whether each feature captures information on, for example, incoming vs. outgoing communications, calls vs. text messages, variance vs. volume, and so on. Specifically, we map each feature onto the tree structure shown in Figure 5, which is designed to encapsulate the substantive behavior captured by each feature. Each level of the tree corresponds to a different partition of the feature space:

1. **Actor:** Whether the feature relates to activity of the individual i (the "ego"), or the activity of i's first degree network of connections (the "alters"). We separately look at i's full set of alters, the set who have previously used Mobile Money, and the set that have never used Mobile Money. A simple aggregation operation (such as `mean` or `SD`) is applied to the alter network to produce a feature for i.
2. **Type:** Whether the feature relates to phone calls or text messages (SMS).
3. **Direction:** Whether the feature relates to incoming (e.g., call received) or outgoing (e.g., call placed) activity.
4. **Behavior:** Whether the feature relates to movement (e.g., number of unique cell towers used), network structure (e.g., number of unique contacts in network), phone usage (e.g., number of calls made), or Diversity (e.g., geographic spread of social network). This tag is determined by the data type of the field over which aggregated is performed (e.g., continuous vs. discrete data) and the actual statistical function used in aggregation (`count, unique, min, max, mean, median, SD, variance, radius of gyration`)

Figure 5 is simplified to show only a single expansion along the ego-voice-incoming path. In practice, all nodes on a given level can be expanded analagously to the path shown in Figure 5. For instance, the example feature described in Section 3.2 would be a leaf on the branch of ego-voice-outgoing-usage.

Algorithm 1: Feature Generation Algorithm

Data: cdr,Call Detail Records of all users
Data: opmap,Dictionary of possible operations
cdrtypes ← [Voice, SMS, Voice and SMS]
direction ← [In, Out , In plus Out]
featuresArray ← []
Result: Features

```
Step 1: Perform reduce by grouping only on ego
foreach type, dir1 in cdrtypes,direction do
    filteredCDR ← cdr.filter(type,dir1)
    foreach field in cdr do
        groupeddata ←
          filteredCDR.map([ego]+[combinations(field)])
        foreach op in opmap[field] do
            reduceddata ← groupeddata.reduce(op)
             insert reduceddata in featuresArray
            reducedata2 ←
             reduceddata.map(ego,alters).reduce(op)
             insert reduceddata2 in featuresArray
        end
    end
end
```

4. MODELS AND METHODS

The DFA-based process of feature engineering described above generates thousands of features that quantify patterns of mobile phone use. Armed with these features, our goals are to (a) use these features to understand the determinants of Mobile Money use, (b) build a predictive model that can be used to identify likely adopters, and (c) determine the extent to which models and features from one context can generalize to another.

4.1 Experimental Design

To facilitate our supervised learning experiments, we drew a stratified random sample of 10,000 subscribers from each of the three categories (Voice Only, Registered Mobile Money, Active Mobile Money) from each country. We elected to draw a balanced sample since, as can be seen in Figure 6, the vast majority of subscribers in each country fall into the "Voice Only" category.[6]

[5]http://www.jblumenstock.com

[6]To protect the commercial interests of the operators, we

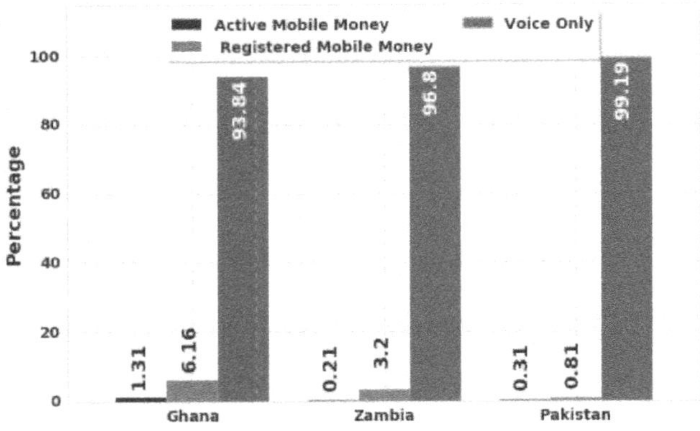

Figure 6: Distribution of user types by country

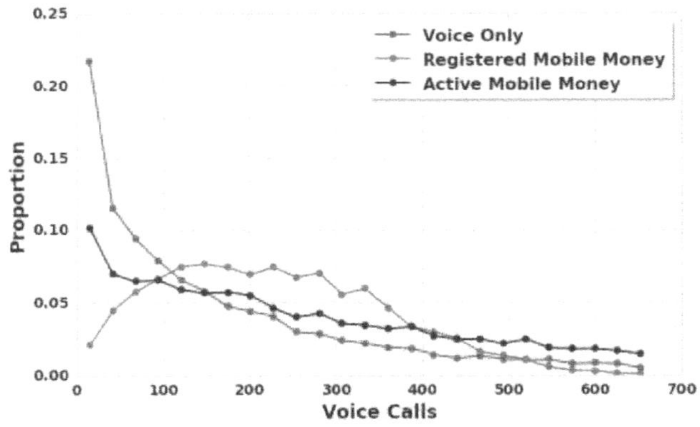

Figure 7: Distribution of calls per subscriber, Ghana

4.2 Classification and Model Selection

We then use a variety of supervised learning algorithms to tackle two classification tasks. First, we seek to differentiate between Voice Only subscribers and Registered Mobile Money Users (one or more Mobile Money transactions); second, we attempt to differentiate between Voice Only and Active Mobile Money users (at least one transaction per month). In all cases, we report the average accuracy across testing sets from 10-fold cross validation.

Since our data has a large number of features relative to observations, we focus on learners that are robust to overfitting, such as regularized and elastic net logistic regression [30], gradient boosting [15], and Extremely Randomized Trees [16]. Performance was comparable across these classifiers, although as expected these methods generally performed better than unregularized alternatives. To streamline the analysis that follows, we report only the results from gradient boosting, which outperformed the other classifiers by a small margin.

4.3 Feature selection and importance

To understand which CDR-based features are related to Mobile Money use, we calculate two metrics:

1. **(Unconditional) AUC**: We run a (cross-validated) bivariate logistic regression of the response variable (one of the above definitions of Mobile Money use) on each feature separately. The provides an indication of the unconditional correlation between each feature and the response variable.
2. **(Conditional) Normalized feature importance**: We calculate the importance of each feature to the final gradient boosting classifier. As we are primarily interested in the *relative* importance, the set of feature importances is standardized to be comparable across countries and classification tasks. Following [15], we denote the relative influence of feature x_j in tree T as

$$\hat{I}_j^2(T) = \sum_{t=1}^{J-1} \hat{i}_t^2 1(v_t = j)$$

where $\hat{i}^2$ is the improvement in (squared) error achieved by splitting feature v_t at node t, summed over all non-terminal nodes $J \in T$. In a collection of gradient-boosted trees, the average feature importance $\bar{I}_j$ is the arithmetic mean of $\hat{I}_j^2(T)$ across all trees, and the *normalized feature importance* is the z-score obtained by subtracting the mean (of all $\bar{I}_j$) and dividing by the standard deviation (of all $\bar{I}_j$) for each $\bar{I}_j$.

show only the fraction of users of each type, rather than the raw numbers, which are in the millions.

5. RESULTS

5.1 Determinants of Mobile Money Adoption

The DFA described in Section 3 produces roughly 3,000 unique features. As one example, Figure 7 shows the distribution of total calls made per subscriber in Ghana, for each of the three subscriber types. There are clear differences between the three user types in this distribution, with Voice Only users making the fewest calls, Registered Mobile Money users concentrated in the range from 100-300 calls (in the 10-day training period), and Active Mobile Money users more evenly distributed across the full range from 100-700 calls.

The distribution of unconditional AUC values for each of the 3,000 features is shown in Figure 8 (left panel), using Ghana as a test case. To construct this figure, we use the feature classification schema from Figure 5 to label each feature with four tags corresponding to the Actor, Type, Direction, and Behavior of the feature. Each violin plot then shows the distribution of AUC values for all features of a given type - such as all "ego" features, or all "movement" features. The left (blue) half of each violin plot indicates the distribution of AUC values for features when discriminating between Voice Only and Registered Mobile Money; the right (red) half shows the distribution when discriminating between Voice Only and Active Mobile Money.

While a large number of features have AUC values near 0.5, indicating they contain little information about the distinction between Voice Only and Mobile Money users, several noteworthy patterns emerge. First, when feature types are defined by the coarse classification tree in Figure 5, no single type dominates; rather, most types of features have a large number of uninformative features and a small number of highly predictive features with AUC≥0.75. At the same time, feature classes do matter. The right panel of Figure 5 shows the distribution of AUC values for the subset of features where Actor="Voice Alters" and Type="All", a subset that are generally more predictive of Mobile Money

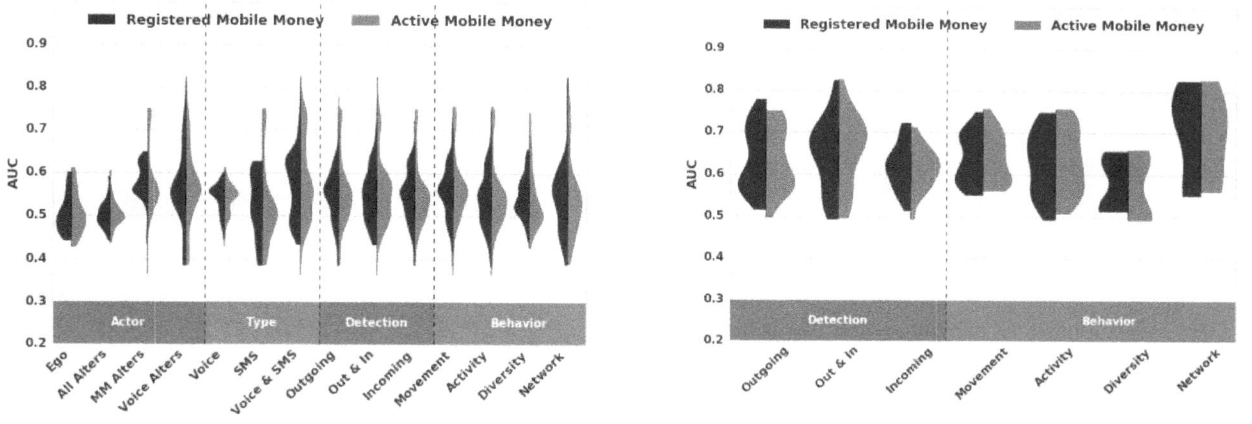

Figure 8: Distribution of AUC values for each feature category. Left figure shows all features in Ghana; Right figure shows the subset of features in Ghana where Actor='Voice Alters' and Type='All'

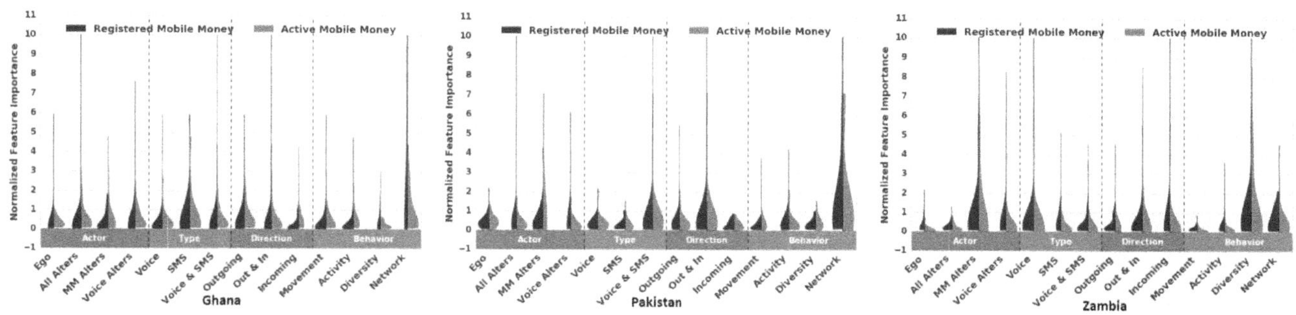

Figure 9: Normalized feature importance

use in Ghana. Here, the range of AUC values is significantly higher than in the full set of features, and some sub-classes such as "Network" have uniformly high predictive power.[7] Finally, the usefulness of each class of features depends on whether the goal is to identify Registered or Active Mobile Money users. For instance, the "MM Alter" features, which capture information about the characteristics of i's network who have previously adopted Mobile Money, are bimodally distributed and on average more useful in predicting Registered users than Active users. However, that same class contains a small number of features that are extremely good predictors of Active Mobile Money use.

A similar approach is taken to construct Figure 9, except here we show the distribution of normalized feature importance values obtained through gradient boosting. The difference between the values in Figure 9 and Figure 8 is that the former are conditional on all features present in the final classification model, which includes several hundred features, whereas the latter are unconditional, i.e., they indicate performance in a univariate model with no other features. As in the uncondititional ranking, each class of features in the conditional ranking contains a mass of features with low predictive power, but closer inspection reveals interpretable patterns.

Perhaps most striking in Figure 9 are the differences between countries in the relative importance of each class of features. For instance, we see that in Ghana and Pakistan the "Network" features are in general more important to the classification model than the other types of Behavior, whereas in Zambia "Diversity" is most important. Zambia is also unique in the higher importance placed on voice calls relative to SMS activity, and in the fact that more signal exists in incoming calls than in outgoing calls. As we discuss below, these cross-country differences imply that models trained in one context may not generalize well to others.

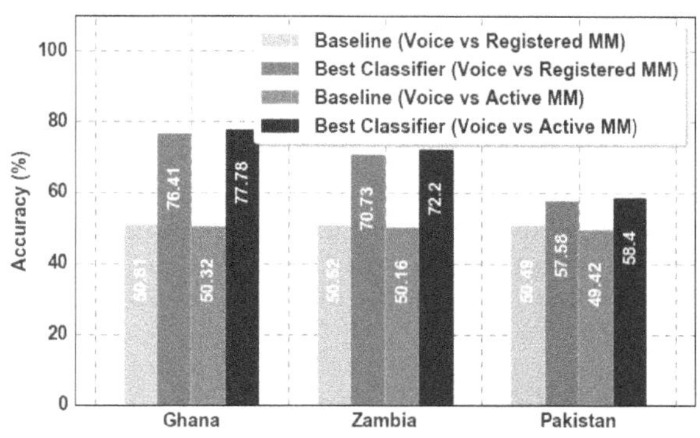

Figure 10: Accuracy in identifying Mobile Money users within each country, using gradient boosting

[7]This particular class, where Actor="Voice Alters," Type="All," and Behavior="Network", corresponds to information about the network structure of i's network; in other words, 2nd degree properties of i's network.

5.2 Predicting Mobile Money Use

As discussed in Section 4.2, we test the ability of several supervised classification models to discriminate between Voice Only and Mobile Money users, using the CDR-based features constructed from the DFA. Cross-validated results from gradient boosting are reported separately for each country in Figure 10. The best-performing models included several hundred features, but in practice there was little difference in performance between models in the range of 50-1000 features. We also include results from a baseline classifier, which uses the same model trained on a single "intuitive" feature – the total number of outgoing calls made by the subscriber, which is the feature shown in Figure 7.

In each country, the DFA-based classifier significantly outperforms the naive baseline, and in all countries, we achieve marginally better success in identifying Active Mobile Money users than Registered Mobile Money users. Across countries, however, there is a great degree of variability in classifier performance, with classification accuracy between 71% and 78% in Ghana and Zambia, but only 58%-59% in Pakistan. We discuss several possible explanations for these results in Section 6.

5.3 "Transfer Learning"

In the proceeding analysis, we have been careful to standardize the methods and analysis performed across all three countries. In each instance, we use the exact same source data, DFA specification, classification algorithm, experimental sample size, and so forth. In some cases, this meant that we knowingly discarded data that might have improved the performance of the classifier in a single country. For example, in some countries we had several months of CDR that could be used for training, additional fields in the CDR metadata, or much larger samples of Mobile Money users available for training and cross-validation. However, our approach reduced everything to the lowest common denominator in order to maintain comparability across contexts.

A key advantage of this approach is that it makes it possible to answer a question that has been elusive in prior studies of the adoption of new technologies in developing countries: *Do the behavioral determinants of adoption identified in one context generalize to another?* Based on the analysis we have performed, our short answer to this question appears to be, "No."

Figure 11 shows the performance of a classifier trained in one country and evaluated in another. Thus, the first set of six bars shows that the classifiers trained in Ghana perform well in Ghana (the first two grey bars), essentially replicating the results in Figure 10. However, that same Ghana model does quite poorly when it is evaluated in Zambia (the next two blue bars) and Pakistan (the final two green bars). While it is almost certain that a more sophisticated approach to transductive transfer learning would perform better [25], the naive application of a model out of context is quite ineffective. We return to these ideas in the discussion that follows.

6. INTERPRETATION AND DISCUSSION

Taken in the broader context of research into the determinants of Mobile Money adoption and use, the preceding results uncover several unexpected patterns. Superficially, it is not surprising that CDR-based metrics can be used to construct classifiers that predict Mobile Money use, though to our knowledge this is the first study to publish performance metrics that can serve as benchmarks in future work in this area. However, in our analysis we were surprised to find that in a given country, the supervised model was only marginally better able to identify Active Mobile Money users (who make at least one transaction per month) than Registered Mobile Money users (who make at least one transaction ever). By contrast, our expectation was that active users, who are quite rare in all three countries, would have distinct patterns of phone use that would make them easier to detect. Since most policymakers agree that true financial inclusion requires active use, this remains an open topic for future work.

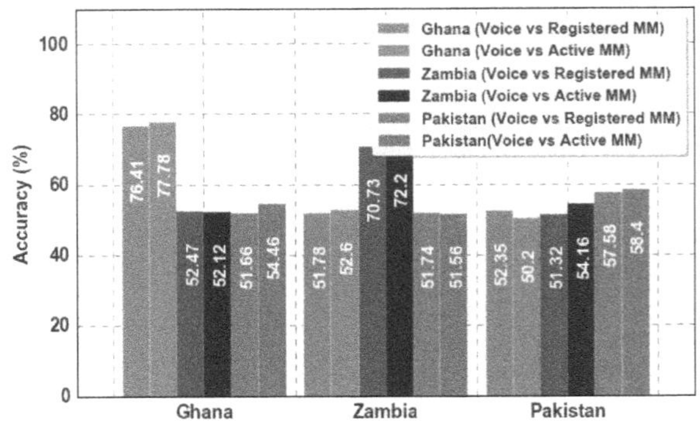

Figure 11: Accuracy when model is trained in one country and evaluated in another

Also interesting are the differences in performance of the same modeling approach applied in different contexts (Figure 10). Most striking here is the relatively poor performance in Pakistan, where the 18% improvement over the baseline is dwarfed by the 55% improvement over the baseline achieved in Ghana.[8] At face value, this finding implies that Mobile Money users in Pakistan are very similar to non-Mobile Money users, or at least that the two groups have similar patterns of mobile phone user. However, looking more carefully at the data, we believe this may also in part be an artifact of the "one size fits all" approach we have taken to standardizing definitions and methods across countries. In particular, there is one type of Mobile Money transaction that is extremely common in Pakistan, which allows a subscriber to add prepaid phone credit to her phone account using Mobile Money. Anecdotally, it is common practice in Pakistan for the retailers of phone credit to perform this Mobile Money transaction on behalf of the subscriber. Thus, a subscriber might appear to be using Mobile Money, though in practice she was not responsible for the transaction. This potential source of bias highlights the brittle nature of the cross-country analysis, which in its current form does not allow for country-specific adaptation.

Perhaps most importantly, our results suggest that across

[8]This result is also unexpected, given the evidence in Figure 9, which indicates that Ghana and Pakistan have very similar profiles in terms of relative feature importance. If anything, this figure might lead one to suspect that Zambia would be an outlier in the analysis, since Zambia's feature profile is distinct from the other two countries.

different countries and cultures in the developing world, no single set of behavioral features is likely to consistently predict Mobile Money adoption and use. This is most clearly evident in Figure 11, which shows that a classifier trained in one country performs very poorly when tested in another country. But the same conclusion may also be drawn from Figure 9, where we see that the same model, when trained in different countries, selects different features and attaches different weights to to those selected features. In results not shown, we further inspect the list of top-ranked features for each country, using both (unconditional) AUC and (conditional) normalized feature importance, and note very few features that appear consistently across countries. However, even though there may not be a "golden" list of features that always predict Mobile Money use, we are optimistic that more generalized insights can be extracted from one context and applied in another. In ongoing work, we are exploring methods for transfer learning that may strike this balance.

More concretely, over the past several months our partner in Ghana has been using the methods we describe to generate "Adoption Scores" that indicate the likelihood that any given mobile subscriber will adopt and use Mobile Money. They recently reported that when using these scores to target promotions, response rates were roughly 30% higher than promotions targeted with traditional methods. Such estimates are notoriously unreliable and subject to many possible sources of bias, but their optimism provides an indication of the potential for this line of research. At the same time, it should be noted that if the end goal is to increase financial inclusion of the poor, further methodological innovation is needed beyond what identifies the "low hanging fruit" subscribers whose behavior indicates that they are likely to adopt of their own volition.

7. CONCLUSION

In this paper, we present a new approach to feature engineering that uses deterministic finite automata to construct a very large number of features from a concise set of rules. In applying this technique to mobile phone data from Ghana, Pakistan, and Zambia, we show that the resultant metrics correlate with, and can be used to predict, both active and passive Mobile Money use in three very different contexts. In so doing, we discover several previously undocumented patterns related to the adoption and use of Mobile Money. Superficially, the analysis makes it possible to highlight specific correlates of Mobile Money use, such as the relative importance of network structure in Ghana and Pakistan, and the relative importance of geographic diversity in Zambia. More fundamentally, the results provide insight into the extent to which standard predictive models can generalize across contexts. Here, it is clear that each population has a unique signature in terms of what metrics are good predictors of adoption, and as a result, models trained in one location do not perform well in another. Retraining the model helps, but does not solve, the underlying issue. Despite the fact that the data structures, experimental design, and Mobile Money products are nearly identical in the three countries, the performance of each country-specific model varies greatly.

8. ACKNOWLEDGMENTS

Financial support for this project was provided by The MasterCard Foundation - IFC Partnership for Financial Inclusion in Sub-Saharan Africa. We are grateful to Sven Harten for providing thoughtful feedback throughout the research process, and to Gabriel Cadamuro and Robert On for help in developing an earlier version of the DFA.

9. REFERENCES

[1] J. Aker, R. Boumnijel, A. McClelland, and N. Tierney. How do electronic transfers compare? Evidence from a mobile money cash transfer experiment in Niger. *CGD Working Paper 268*, Washington, D.C., 2014.

[2] J. Blumenstock, G. Cadamuro, and R. On. Predicting poverty and wealth from mobile phone metadata. *Science*, 350(6264):1073–1076, 2015.

[3] J. E. Blumenstock, M. Callen, T. Ghani, and L. Koepke. Promises and pitfalls of mobile money in afghanistan: evidence from a randomized control trial. In *Proceedings of the Seventh International Conference on Information and Communication Technologies and Development*, page 15. ACM, 2015.

[4] J. E. Blumenstock, N. Eagle, and M. Fafchamps. Airtime transfers and mobile communications: Evidence in the aftermath of natural disasters. *Journal of Development Economics (forthcoming)*, 2016.

[5] CGAP. The Power of Social Networks to Drive Mobile Money Adoption. Technical report, 2013.

[6] G. Chen and S. Rasmussen. bKash Bangladesh: A Fast Start for Mobile Financial Services. Technical report, 2014.

[7] A. Demirguc-Kunt, L. F. Klapper, D. Singer, and P. Van Oudheusden. The global findex database 2014: measuring financial inclusion around the world. *World Bank Policy Research Working Paper*, (7255), 2015.

[8] A. Dermish, C. Kneiding, P. Leishman, and I. Mas. Branchless and mobile banking solutions for the poor: A survey of the literature. *Innovations: Technology, Governance, Globalization*, 6(4):81–98, Oct. 2011.

[9] S. Di Castri and L. Gidvani. Enabling Mobile Money Policies in Tanzania: A "test and learn" approach to enabling market-led digital financial services. Technical report, GSMA, Feb. 2014.

[10] Y. Dong, Y. Yang, J. Tang, Y. Yang, and N. V. Chawla. Inferring user demographics and social strategies in mobile social networks. In *Proceedings of the 20th ACM SIGKDD international conference on Knowledge discovery and data mining*, pages 15–24. ACM, 2014.

[11] K. Donovan. Mobile money for financial inclusion. Information and Communications for Development, pages 61–73. The World Bank, 2012.

[12] A. S. Etim. Mobile banking and mobile money adoption for financial inclusion. *Research in Business and Economics Journal*, 9:1, 2014.

[13] V. Frias-Martinez, E. Frias-Martinez, and N. Oliver. A gender-centric analysis of calling behavior in a developing economy using call detail records. 2010.

[14] V. Frias-Martinez, J. Virseda, and E. Frias-Martinez. Socio-Economic Levels and Human Mobility. *Jourhnal of Information Technology for Development*, pages 1–16, Feb. 2012.

[15] J. H. Friedman. Greedy function approximation: a gradient boosting machine. *Annals of statistics*, pages 1189–1232, 2001.

[16] P. Geurts, D. Ernst, and L. Wehenkel. Extremely randomized trees. *Mach. Learn.*, 63(1):3–42, Apr. 2006.

[17] T. Gutierrez, G. Krings, and V. D. Blondel.

Evaluating socio-economic state of a country analyzing airtime credit and mobile phone datasets. arXiv e-print 1309.4496, Sept. 2013.
[18] W. Jack and T. Suri. Risk sharing and transactions costs: Evidence from Kenya's mobile money revolution. *American Economic Review*, 104(1):183–223, 2014.
[19] M. R. Khan, J. Manoj, A. Singh, and J. Blumenstock. Behavioral modeling for churn prediction: Early indicators and accurate predictors of custom defection and loyalty. In *2015 IEEE International Congress on BigData*, pages 677–680. IEEE, 2015.
[20] J. Leskovec, L. A. Adamic, and B. A. Huberman. The dynamics of viral marketing. *ACM Transactions on the Web (TWEB)*, 1(1):5, 2007.
[21] I. Mas and D. Radcliffe. Scaling mobile money. *Journal of Payments Strategy & Systems*, 5(3):298–315, 2011.
[22] W. S. McCulloch and W. Pitts. A logical calculus of the ideas immanent in nervous activity. *The bulletin of mathematical biophysics*, 5(4):115–133, Dec. 1943.
[23] I. Medhi, A. Ratan, and K. Toyama. Mobile-banking adoption and usage by low-literate, low-income users in the developing world. In *Internationalization, Design and Global Development*, pages 485–494. Springer, 2009.
[24] O. Morawczynski. Exploring the usage and impact of "transformational" mobile financial services: the case of m-PESA in kenya. *Journal of Eastern African Studies*, 3(3):509–525, Oct. 2009.
[25] S. J. Pan, I. Tsang, J. Kwok, and Q. Yang. Domain Adaptation via Transfer Component Analysis. *IEEE Transactions on Neural Networks*, 22(2):199–210, Feb. 2011.
[26] Safaricom. FY14 Presentation, 2014.
[27] C. Scharwatt, A. Katakam, J. Frydrych, A. Murphy, and N. Naghavi. State of the Industry: Mobile Financial Services for the Unbanked. Technical report, GSMA, 2014.
[28] P. Sundsøy, J. Bjelland, A. M. Iqbal, Y.-A. de Montjoye, et al. Big data-driven marketing: How machine learning outperforms marketers' gut-feeling. In *Social Computing, Behavioral-Cultural Modeling and Prediction*, pages 367–374. Springer, 2014.
[29] J. Ugander, L. Backstrom, C. Marlow, and J. Kleinberg. Structural diversity in social contagion. *Proceedings of the National Academy of Sciences*, 109(16):5962–5966, 2012.
[30] H. Zou and T. Hastie. Regularization and variable selection via the Elastic Net. *Journal of the Royal Statistical Society, Series B*, 67:301–320, 2005.

APPENDIX

A. DFA TRANSITION DETAILS

The Deterministic Finite Automaton described in Section A is defined in part by a set of transition functions $\delta : Q \times \Sigma \rightarrow Q$ that define the legal transitions between states Q:

- *Filter*: $Q \times CDR \rightarrow CDR$
  Operations filter the data on the basis of the type of communication (voice, sms) or the direction the activity (incoming, outgoing).
- *Map*: $Q \times CDR \rightarrow (field, CDR)$
  Operations are similar to 'group by' operations, which group the input CDR according to the value of a field in the CDR. All data are initially mapped by ego i, creating N subsets of CDR, one corresponding to each individual. Other common *map* criteria include alter, location, and day-of-week.
- *Select*: $Q \times (field^*, CDR) \rightarrow (field^*, fields)$
  Operations extract a field (or column) from the CDR. Common select criteria are duration, location, and a constant 1 used to count transactions.
- *Reduce*: $Q \times (field^*, fields) \rightarrow (field^*, value)$
  Operations 'aggregate' a set of values into a single value. Valid operations include unique, count, average, standard deviation, radius of gyration, and entropy. Whether a *reduce* operation is legal depends on the data type of the field to which it is being applied. *Reduce'* is a special operation that aggregates values across all of an ego's alters, creating a feature that represents the {average, standard deviation} of the individual's first-degree network.

Repeat Buyer Prediction for E-Commerce

Guimei Liu⋆, Tam T. Nguyen⋆, Gang Zhao#, Wei Zha⋆, Jianbo Yang§
Jianneng Cao⋆, Min Wu⋆, Peilin Zhao⋆, Wei Chen#
⋆Data Analytics Department, Institute for Infocomm Research, Singapore 138632,
{liug,nguyentt,zhaw,caojn,wumin,zhaop}@i2r.a-star.edu.sg
#Development Bank of Singapore, {george.g.zhao, nus.waltchan}@gmail.com
§General Electric, jianbo.yang@ge.com

ABSTRACT

A large number of new buyers are often acquired by merchants during promotions. However, many of the attracted buyers are one-time deal hunters, and the promotions may have little long-lasting impact on sales. It is important for merchants to identify who can be converted to regular loyal buyers and then target them to reduce promotion cost and increase the return on investment (ROI). At International Joint Conferences on Artificial Intelligence (IJCAI) 2015, Alibaba hosted an international competition for repeat buyer prediction based on the sales data of the "Double 11" shopping event in 2014 at Tmall.com. *We won the first place at stage 1 of the competition out of 753 teams.* In this paper, we present our winning solution, which consists of comprehensive feature engineering and model training. We created profiles for users, merchants, brands, categories, items and their interactions via extensive feature engineering. These profiles are not only useful for this particular prediction task, but can also be used for other important tasks in e-commerce, such as customer segmentation, product recommendation, and customer base augmentation for brands. Feature engineering is often the most important factor for the success of a prediction task, but not much work can be found in the literature on feature engineering for prediction tasks in e-commerce. Our work provides some useful hints and insights for data science practitioners in e-commerce.

Keywords

Repeat Buyer Prediction; Feature Engineering; E-commerce

1. INTRODUCTION

Large business-to-consumer (B2C) e-commerce websites, such as Amazon and Alibaba, often run nationwide sales promotions on special days like Black Friday and Double 11 (Singles' Day). Merchants acquire new customers during these events. However, most new customers are one-time deal hunters, and promotions to them usually do not generate *return on investment* (ROI) as expected by merchants. Therefore, merchants need to identify potential loyal ones from these new customers, so as to conduct targeted advertisements (and promotions) towards them to lower the promotion cost. It is difficult for any individual merchant to identify its potential loyal customers as it has little information on its new customers. B2C e-commerce websites instead have the click stream data and purchase history of all the customers at all the merchants on their platforms. Thus, they can learn the preferences and habits of the new customers from their historical data, and then predict how likely a new customer will buy again from a same merchant.

At IJCAI 2015, Alibaba hosted an international competition[1] for repeat buyer prediction based on the sales data of the "Double 11" day of 2014 at Tmall.com—the largest B2C platform in China. Double 11 is the biggest online shopping event in China with sales (in Tmall and Taobao) at US$5.8 billion in 2013, US$9.3 billion in 2014, and over US$14.3 billion in 2015[2]. Data provided to the competition include a number of merchants and their new buyers acquired during the event, and six months of user activity log data before the event. The task is to predict which new customers of a given merchant would buy items from the same merchant again within six months. These new buyers are called *repeat buyers* of the respective merchants.

We won the first place at stage 1 of the competition. Our winning solution consists of comprehensive feature engineering and model training. In particular, we generated various types of features to describe users, merchants, brands, categories, items and their interactions from different aspects. We have trained various classification models, including Factorization Machine [14, 11], Logistic Regression [1, 2], Random Forest [5], GBM [10], and XGBoost [6]. We have also used ensemble techniques to blend multiple classifiers together to further improve the performance.

The repeat buyer prediction problem can be formulated as a typical classification problem, as most of the competition participants did. Model training of this task is not much different from that of other classification tasks. Instead, feature engineering is the main component that distinguishes this task from others. Feature engineering, an integral part of data science, is often the key to the success of a machine learning project. It can be more difficult than learning

KDD '16, August 13-17, 2016, San Francisco, CA, USA
© 2016 ACM. ISBN 978-1-4503-4232-2/16/08... $15.00
DOI: http://dx.doi.org/10.1145/2939672.2939674

[1]http://ijcai-15.org/index.php/repeat-buyers-prediction-competition
[2]https://en.wikipedia.org/wiki/Singles_Day

Table 1: Statistics of training and testing data

data	#users	#merchants	#pairs	#positive pairs	positive%
train	212,062	1,993	260,864	15,952	6.12%
test	212,108	1,993	261,477	16,037	6.13%

because it is domain-specific, while machine learning algorithms are largely general-purpose. Much trial and error can go into feature design, and it is typically where most of the effort in a machine learning project goes [8]. While thousands of classification algorithms have been proposed and studied in the research community, not much work has been reported on feature engineering for prediction tasks in e-commerce. Therefore, in this paper we focus on feature engineering. We will describe how to generate various types of features from user activity log data and study the importance of these features via extensive experiments. The features we generated can be used in all kinds of e-commerce applications, such as customer segmentation, product recommendation, and customer base augmentation for brands. We hope that our work can be valuable for data science practitioners, who need to develop solutions for prediction tasks in e-commerce.

The rest of the paper is organized as follows. Section 2 gives the problem description. Section 3 describes the features we have generated. Model ensemble is briefly described in Section 4. In Section 5, the importance of features is studied and top features are listed. Finally, Section 6 concludes the paper.

2. PROBLEM DESCRIPTION

For the repeat buyer prediction competition, the following data are provided as shown on the top of Figure 1: demographic information of users, six months of user activity log data prior to the "Double 11" promotion, and training and testing ⟨new buyer, merchant⟩ pairs, where the first purchase of the new buyer from the merchant is on the "Double 11" promotion. User demographic data contains the age and gender of users. The age values are divided into seven ranges. The class label of a training ⟨new buyer, merchant⟩ pair is known, and it indicates whether the new buyer bought items from the merchant again within six months after the "Double 11" promotion. The class labels of testing ⟨new buyer, merchant⟩ pairs are hidden. The task is to predict the class labels of the testing pairs. The competition was carried out in two stages. In stage 1, all the data were released to the contestants except for class labels of testing pairs, which were released after stage 1. Stage 2 ran on the cloud platform of Alibaba for bigger data, and the data were not released. Therefore, in this paper, we focus on the data of stage 1.

Table 1 shows the statistics of the training and testing data. The set of merchants in training data and that in testing data are the same except for a single merchant. Users in the training and testing data have no overlap. The second last column is the number of positive ⟨new buyer, merchant⟩ pairs such that the new buyer bought items from the merchant again within six months. The last column is the percentage of such positive pairs. The percentage of positive pairs is around 6%, which indicates that most of the new buyers are indeed one-time deal hunters.

The user activity log data contains the following fields: user_id, merchant_id, item_id, cat_id, brand_id, action_type and time_stamp. Action_type takes four values: 0 for click, 1 for add-to-cart, 2 for purchase and 3 for add-to-favourite. Products sold in different merchants are assigned different item_ids even if the products are exactly the same. Table 2 shows the statistics of the user activity log data. Many merchants in the log data do not have new buyers in the training or testing data. They are included in the log data because some new buyers visited them. The activities of the new buyers at these merchants are valuable information for inferring the preferences and habits of the new buyers.

Table 2: Statistics of log activity data

#rows	#users	#merchants	#items	#categories	#brands
54,925,330	424,170	4,995	1,090,390	1,658	8,444

Table 3: Statistics of action_types

click	add-to-cart	purchase	add-to-favourite
48,550,713 (88.39%)	76,750 (0.14%)	3,292,144 (5.99%)	3,005,723 (5.47%)

Table 3 shows the number of the four types of actions. The majority of actions are clicks. The number of add-to-cart actions is very small, so we merge the add-to-cart actions with click actions.

The user activity log data provided in this competition are very typical in e-commerce prediction tasks. However, the log data are not in a form that is amenable to learning. We need to construct new features from them and then join the new features with the training and testing data. In the next section, we describe how we do this.

3. FEATURE ENGINEERING

The user activity log data contain five entities: users, merchants, brands, categories and items. The characteristics of these entities and their interactions can be predictive of the class labels. For example, users are more likely to buy again from a merchant selling snacks than from a merchant selling electronic products within six months, since snacks are cheaper and are consumed much faster than electronic products. We generated a large number of features to describe the characteristics of the five types of entities and their pairwise interactions. In the rest of this section, we first give an overview of all the generated features, and then describe the features in details.

3.1 Overview of features and profiles

The features we generated range from basic counts to complex features like similarity scores, trends, PCA (Principal Component Analysis) and LDA (Latent Dirichlet allocation) features. All the features of an entity form the profile of the entity. We have five entity profiles and five interaction profiles as shown at the bottom of Figure 1. Table 4 gives a summary of the types of features contained in these profiles. User-merchant interaction is the most important interaction among the five pairwise interaction profiles as the task is to predict whether a user will return to a merchant to buy again. Therefore, user-merchant profile contains more features than the other interaction profiles.

The original training/testing data contain only user_ids and merchant_ids as shown on the top of Figure 1. We expanded the training/testing data by adding age_range and gender of users, item_id, brand_id, and category_id as shown in the middle of Figure 1, where item_id is the id of the item bought by the user from the merchant on the Double 11 day,

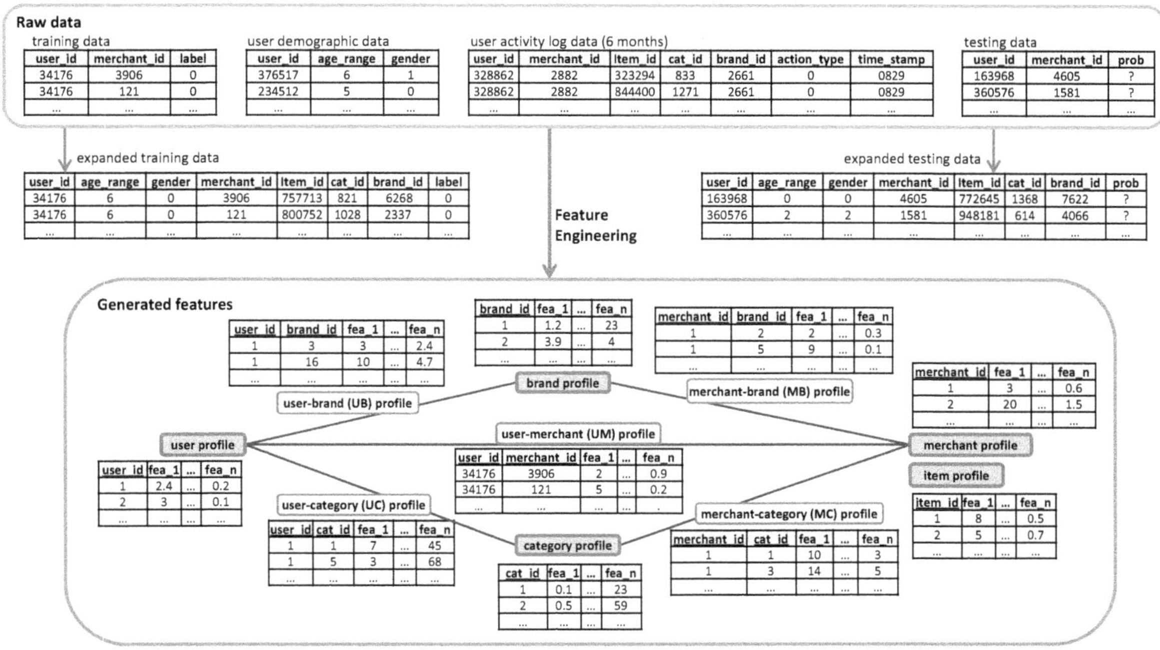

Figure 1: Feature engineering on raw data

Table 4: Summary of features and profiles.

	feature types	user profile	merchant profile	category profile	brand profile	item profile	user-merchant (UM) profile	user-brand (UB) profile	user-category (UC) profile	merchant-brand (MB) profile	merchant-category (MC) profile
count/ratio	overall action count/ratio	✓	✓	✓	✓	✓	✓	✓	✓	✓	✓
	overall day count	✓	✓	✓	✓	✓	✓	✓	✓	✓	✓
	monthly action count/ratio	✓	✓	✓	✓	✓	✓				
	product diversity	✓	✓				✓				
	penetration		✓	✓	✓	✓					
aggregation	monthly aggregation	✓	✓	✓	✓	✓	✓	✓	✓	✓	✓
	merchant aggregation	✓									
	user aggregation		✓								
recent activity	Double 11 features	✓	✓	✓	✓	✓	✓				
	latest one-week	✓	✓	✓	✓	✓	✓				
	latest one-month						✓				
complex features	trend	✓	✓				✓				
	repeat buyer features		✓	✓	✓	✓				✓	✓
	market share									✓	✓
	similarity						✓				
	LDA features	✓	✓								
	PCA features		✓								
age/gender related	age related features		✓	✓	✓	✓					
	gender related features		✓	✓	✓	✓					

and brand_id and category_id are the brand and category of the item. If a user bought multiple items from a merchant on the Double 11 day, then the most frequent one is used. The features are joined with the expanded training/testing data as follows: entity features are joined based on their respective ids; age related features are joined by the respective entity id and age_range; gender related features are joined by the respective entity id and gender; interaction features are joined by the two entity ids involved.

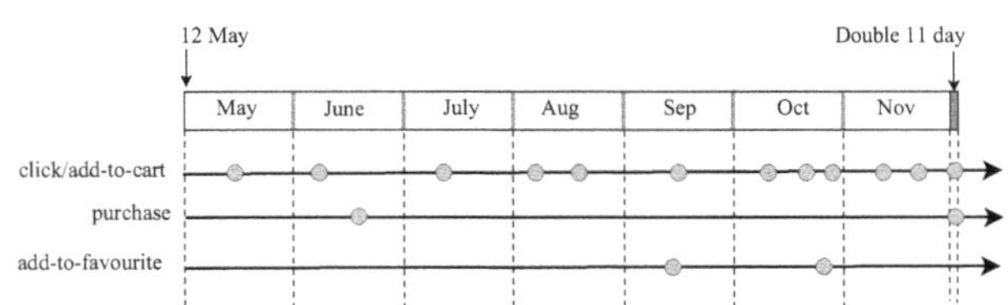

Figure 2: Action history of an example entity

3.2 Count/ratio features

Each entity has three types of actions—click, purchase and add-to-favourites—over the six-month period from 12 May, 2014 to 11 Nov, 2014. Figure 2 shows the action history of an example entity. The three types of actions are represented by green circles.

Action count, action ratio and day count. *Action counts* are number of clicks, purchases, add-to-favourite actions in each month (monthly counts) or over the whole data period (overall count). Count features are the basis for generating more complex features. For the entity shown in Figure 2, the monthly click counts are (1, 1, 1, 2, 1, 3, 3), the monthly purchase counts are (0, 1, 0, 0, 0, 0, 1), and the monthly add-to-favourite counts are (0, 0, 0, 0, 1, 1, 0). The overall counts of click, purchase, and add-to-favorite are 12, 2, and 2, respectively. *Action ratio* is the proportion of a particular action type over all action types, and it can be calculated in each month or over the whole data period. For the entity in Figure 2, the overall click ratio is $12/(12+2+2) = 0.75$, and June click ratio is $1/(1+1+0)=0.5$.

Day counts are the number of days with a particular action type in each month or over the whole data period. Day count features are mainly used to differentiate regular buyers from occasional buyers. For example, a user with 10 purchase actions in one single day is different from another user with the same number of purchase actions that spread over 10 different days. The latter user is considered a more regular buyer than the former.

Action count, action ratio, and day count features can be generated for pairs of entities as well. For example, for each ⟨user, merchant⟩ pair, monthly click counts are the number of times the user clicked some items of the merchant in each month. For a ⟨merchant, brand⟩ pair, overall purchase counts are the number of times products of the brand were purchased from the merchant over the whole data period.

Not all the monthly features are directly used, otherwise there will be too many features. Instead, we use these features to generate more complex features, like monthly aggregation features and trend features as described later.

Product diversity features. For a user, *product diversity* features are the number of unique items, brands and categories that the user clicked, purchased or added to favourites in each month or over the whole data period. For a merchant, product diversity features are defined in a similar way. For a ⟨user, merchant⟩ pair, product diversity features are the number of unique items, brands and categories of the merchant that were clicked, purchased or added to favourites by the user in each month or over the whole data period. The intuition behind product diversity features is that if a user is interested in more items of a merchant, then the user is more likely to buy again from the merchant (see Figures 6(a), 7(d) and 7(i)).

Penetration features. *Penetration* feature of an item is defined as the number of users, who have purchased the item in a given time interval. We have also computed penetration features for merchants, brands and categories. A large customer base usually indicates that the entity has a good reputation, so users are more likely to come back.

3.3 Aggregation features

Monthly aggregation features are mean, standard deviation, max and median of monthly action counts, monthly day counts, monthly product diversity counts and monthly penetration counts.

User aggregation features are calculated for merchants, brands, categories, ⟨merchant, brand⟩ pairs and ⟨merchant, category⟩ pairs. The *user-purchase-day-aggregation features* of a merchant are calculated by first counting the number of days that each individual user bought items from the merchant, and then calculating the mean, standard deviation, max and median over all the users of the merchant. *User-purchase-item-aggregation features* of a merchant are defined in a similar way over the number of unique items that each user purchased from the merchant. For click and add-to-favourite actions, user-action-day-aggregation and user-action-item-aggregation features are calculated in the same way for merchants. For other entities, only the purchase action is considered. User aggregation features are also generated by considering only users of a specific gender or age range.

The intuition behind user aggregation features is — given a merchant, if users visited it or bought items from it more than once on average, then new buyers of the merchant on "Double 11" day are more likely to come back as well (see Figures 5(c), 5(d), 6(e), 6(f), 7(c), 7(e), and 7(f)).

Merchant aggregation features are generated for users. Given a user, his/her *merchant-purchase-day-aggregation* features are calculated by first counting the number of days that the user bought items from each individual merchant, and then calculating the mean, standard deviation, max and median over all the merchants, from which the user had made at least one purchase. *Merchant-purchase-item-aggregation* features are calculated over the number of unique items that the user purchased from each merchant in a similar way. For click and add-to-favourite actions, merchant-action-day-aggregation and merchant-action-item-aggregation features are calculated in the same way.

Merchant aggregation features reflect users' habit. If a user tends to buy from or visit merchants multiple times on average, then he/she is likely to buy from new merchants again (see Figures 5(a), 5(b) and 7(l))

3.4 Recent activity features

Double 11 features are counts of clicks, purchases, add-to-favourites on the Double 11 day. The ratio of the double 11 counts to the overall counts are also calculated. For the entity in Figure 2, its Double 11 click count is 1, its Double 11 click ratio is 1/12=0.083 and its Double 11 buy ratio is 1/2=0.5. If a user has a high Double 11 buy ratio, then the user is more likely to be a one-time deal hunter.

Latest one-week features and **latest one-month features** are counts/ratio of clicks, add-to-favourites, and purchases in the last one week and in the last one month before Double 11, respectively.

3.5 Complex features

Trend features are calculated based on monthly features. Given monthly counts or monthly ratios $y=(y_1, y_2, \cdots, y_7)$ over seven months from May to November, the slope of the trend line is calculated as $\alpha = \frac{n\sum_{i=1}^{n}(x_i y_i)-\sum_{i=1}^{n}(x_i)\sum_{i=1}^{n}(y_i)}{\sum_{i=1}^{n}(x_i^2)-(\sum_{i=1}^{n}(x_i))^2}$, where n=7 and $x_i = i$.

We also calculated the deviation of the latest month from the previous months and normalized it using either mean or standard deviation as follows: $d_1 = \frac{y_7-\mu}{\mu}$ and $d_2 = \frac{y_7-\mu}{\sigma}$, where y_7 is the feature value in November, μ and σ are the mean and standard deviation of the feature values over the previous six months.

Repeat buyer features. *Repeat buyer number* of a merchant is defined as the number of users, who bought on at least two different days from the merchant. For items, brands and categories, *repeat buyer number* is defined as the number of users, who bought the item/brand/category on at least two different days. *Repeat buyer ratio* of a merchant/item/brand/category is defined as the ratio of repeat buyers to all buyers (including non-repeating buyers) of the merchant/item/brand/category.

A *repeat buy day* of a user at a merchant is defined as a day, such that the user bought items from the merchant both before and on the day. *Repeat day number* of a merchant is the sum of the repeat buy day of all its users. *Repeat buy day ratio* is the ratio of the repeat day number of a merchant to the sum of the buy days of all the users of the merchants.

Repeat buyer features are also calculated for pairs of entities. For example, for a ⟨merchant, brand⟩ pair, repeat buyer number is the number of users, who bought items of the brand on at least two different days from the merchant.

A high number or a high proportion of repeat buyers indicates that the entity is widely liked, so the customers are more likely to come back again. Our experiment results confirmed this (see Figures 7(a), 7(g) and 7(j)).

Market share features measure how important a brand/ category is to a merchant, or how important a merchant is to a brand/category. Take a ⟨merchant, brand⟩ pair as an example. Let N_{MB} be the number of purchases of the brand from the merchant, N_M be the total number of purchases from the merchant, and N_B be the number of purchases of the brand from all the merchants. Similarly, we define U_{MB} as the number of users buying the brand from the merchant, U_M the total number of buyers of the merchant, and U_B the number of buyers of the brand from all the merchants. The following four features are then generated:

1) *merchant's market share on the brand* $= N_{MB}/N_B$
2) *merchant's user share on the brand* $= U_{MB}/U_B$
3) *brand's market share within the merchant* $= N_{MB}/N_M$
4) *brand's user share within the merchant* $= U_{MB}/U_M$

The first two features measure how important a merchant is to a brand, and the last two features measure how important a brand is to a merchant. Similarly, we can calculate market share features for ⟨merchant, category⟩ pairs.

User-merchant similarity features measure how similar a user and a merchant are based on brands or categories. They are calculated based on the four market share features defined above and the preferences of users on brands/ categories. The preferences are measured by the times or the number of days the user clicked, purchased, or added to favorites the brand/category. Suppose that a merchant has five brands with respective market shares (0.1, 0.2, 0.05, 0.3, 0.01), and that the number of times of a user buying the five brands are (0, 1, 2, 0, 2). We can compute the inner product of the two vectors, and take it as the similarity score between the user and the merchant, that is, $0.1 \times 0 + 0.2 \times 1 + 0.05 \times 2 + 0.3 \times 0 + 0.01 \times 2 = 0.32$. We can also take the max, instead of sum, over all brands, then the similarity score is $0.2 \times 1 = 0.2$.

Intuitively, the more similar a user and a merchant are, the more likely the user will buy from the merchant again (see Figure 7(h)).

PCA features are generated based on the similarity between merchants. Give a pair of merchants, we use the number of users who bought items from both of them as their similarity score. The total number of merchants is 4,995. Therefore, a matrix of 4,995×4,995 is built. This matrix is highly sparse with most elements equal to 0. Simply adding it into the feature list does not obviously improve the accuracy of classification models, but dramatically increases the model training time. As such, we have applied PCA (principal component analysis) [3, 12] on the similarity matrix. Then for each merchant, the top-10 principal coordinates are used as merchant features.

LDA features. Latent Dirichlet Allocation (LDA) [4] is often used in text mining to retrieve topics from a corpus of documents. It views each document as a mixture of various topics, where each topic is characterized by a distribution over words. The retrieved distribution of the topics can be taken as a feature of the document. We first model users as documents and merchants as words. Given a user, we extract from log activity data all the merchants, from which the user purchased items, and treat these merchants as the words of the user's document. By applying LDA on these created documents, we generate features (i.e., distributions of topics over merchants) for users. Similarly, we model merchants as documents and users as words, and generate features (i.e., distributions of topics over users) for merchants. We set the number of topics to 40 based on the performance of predictive models.

3.6 Age/gender related features

Different user groups may favor different types of products. For example, clothes and cosmetics are more attractive to women while electric products are more appealing to men. As such, we generated features to describe the popularity of merchants, brands, categories, and items within different user groups, where users are grouped based on their gender or age range. These features include overall buy counts, monthly aggregation on monthly buy counts, penetration features and repeat buyer features. Only users of a particular age range or a particular gender are used to calculate these features.

3.7 Feature ranking

We have generated 1364 features in total. It is crucial to identify important ones and remove those that are of little use to reduce the training cost [13, 7]. During the competition, we tested both the wrapper method described in [15, 16] and the feature ranking function provided by XGBoost, and we found that all the methods yield very similar feature rankings. In this paper, we report the results by the feature ranking function of XGBoost. Besides ranking all the features together, we also group features based on their types or the profiles they belong to. We rank the features within each group separately, and output the top features. We have also evaluated the importance of each feature group by leaving it out.

4. MODEL TRAINING

In the competition, we have trained various classification models, including Factorization Machine [14], Logistic Regression [1], Random Forest, GBM [10], and XGBoost [6], where grid search was used to select the optimal parameters. XGBoost performed the best.

To further improve the performance, we used ensemble techniques to blend together the predictions made by the above single classifiers. The blending model is basically a weighted sum as defined below.

$$p(u, m) = \sum_{i=1}^{k} w_i \times p_i(u, m), \tag{1}$$

where $p(u, m)$ is the final probability that a user u will make a repeated purchase from a merchant m, $p_i(u, m)$ is the probability predicted by the i-th single model, w_i is the weight assigned to the i-th single model, and k is the number of single models.

We tested two methods to assign the weight w_i to the i-th single model. For the first method, we manually assign weights to single models, such that single models with higher AUC (the area under the ROC curve) scores receive bigger weights. For the second method, we built a classifier to learn the weights. In particular, we generated a k-dimensional feature vector for each user-merchant pair $(u,\ m)$, where the i-th dimension is the probability $p_i(u, m)$ by the i-th

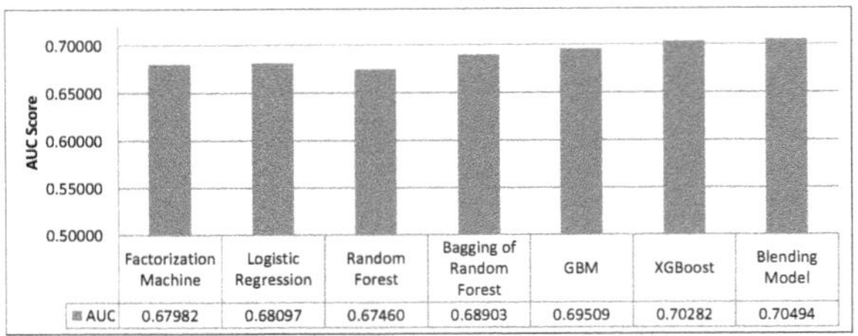

Figure 3: AUC of single models and the blending model

single model. We trained a linear model on these feature vectors to learn the weights.

Our experiments showed that manually assigned weights are often as good as and sometimes even better than the learned weights in this application. Therefore, in the competition, we mainly manually assigned weights to blend the predictions of different models together. We did it in an incremental manner – in each round we kept the best prediction thus far, and blended it with the prediction of a single model. If the resultant AUC score did not improve, we discarded both the blended model and the single model, otherwise, we updated the best prediction using the blended model.

Figure 3 shows the AUC scores of the single models on the testing data. The two linear models, Factorization Machine and Logistic Regression, performed closely. Although their scores are not really high, they contribute to the overall AUC score in the blending model. In ensemble algorithm family, Random Forest has the worst AUC score. However, we found that bagging of Random Forest models can improve the score significantly. XGBoost has the best AUC score of 0.70282. Comparing with the runner up Gradient Boosting Machine, its improvement is more than 0.7%. We have blended around 20 single models with various parameter settings and feature settings, and achieved an AUC score of 0.70494, which is an improvement of 0.21% over the best single model (i.e., XGBoost).

5. A PERFORMANCE STUDY

In this section we evaluate the importance of features in groups. We first conduct the experiments on training data by five-fold cross validation to measure the importance of each group of features (Section 5.1), and to find the top features locally in each group as well as globally in the full feature set (Section 5.2). Extensive experimental results show that some features are less important – removing them has only marginal effect on the performance of the predictive models. Such a finding can help a user to determine the subset of features to be applied in real applications for a good balance between model accuracy and training time. Then, we carry out the experiments on testing data (Section 5.3). We study how the prediction accuracy increases as we incrementally use more features to train models.

5.1 Importance of feature groups

We have generated 1364 features in total. They are organized in groups either by type or by profile as summarized in Table 4 and discussed in Section 3. Features in a same group are generated based on the same hypothesis, and their importance are evaluated together. If one group

Table 5: Feature groups and their AUC scores

	Feature groups	#features	AUC	leave-out AUC
	all features	1364	0.70036	-
entity profiles	user profile	201	0.60442	0.69886
	merchant profile	221	0.6601	0.70096
	brand profile	90	0.65818	0.70071
	category profile	90	0.62087	0.69944
	item profile	70	0.60915	0.70002
interaction profiles	user-merchant profile	107	0.62952	0.69991
	UB and UC profile	26	0.59148	0.70088
	MB and MC profile	58	0.6569	0.69954
count/ratio	monthly action count	161	0.68227	0.70034
	monthly action ratio	163	0.6791	0.70026
	product diversity	61	0.67829	0.70029
	penetration	43	0.66095	0.70001
aggregation features	monthly aggregation	164	0.68729	0.70058
	user aggregation	88	0.66289	0.70031
	merchant aggregation	24	0.58637	0.70039
	all aggregation	276	0.6946	0.69973
recent activity	double 11	79	0.67713	0.69996
	latest one week	24	0.66516	0.69988
	latest one month	10	0.57935	0.70037
complex features	trend	109	0.68234	0.69989
	repeat buyer	72	0.67099	0.70014
	UM similarity score	192	0.64762	0.70043
	PCA	10	0.64546	0.70023
	LDA	80	0.64639	0.69877
age/gender related	age related	30	0.63794	0.70044
	gender related	40	0.65397	0.70017

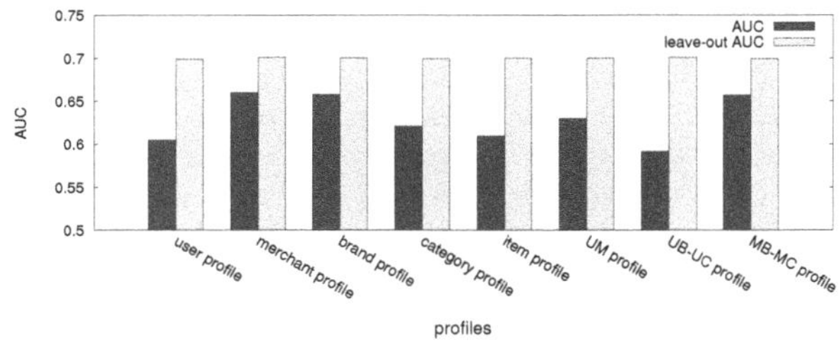

(a) entity and interaction profiles

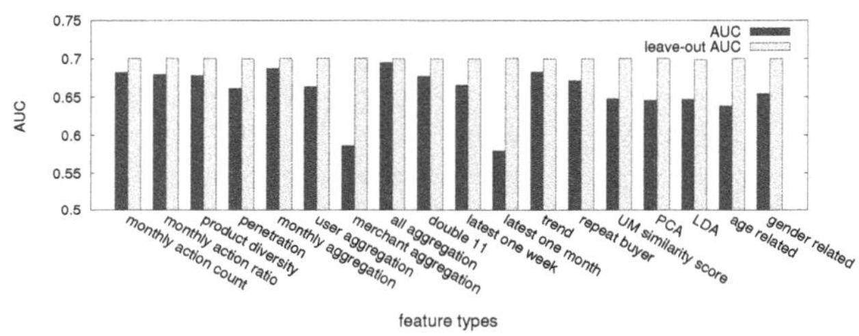

(b) feature types

Figure 4: AUC scores of feature groups

of features turns out to be not important, we can remove the whole group to save the cost of both feature engineering and model training. Table 5 lists the feature groups together with their sizes. The second row shows the AUC score of the full feature set. We study merchant-brand (MB) profile and merchant-category (MC) profile together, since they are of small sizes. Likewise, user-brand (UB) profile and user-category (UC) profile are investigated together.

We use five-fold cross validation to evaluate the importance of each group of features. The predictive model in the experiments is XGBoost with the parameter setting: eta=0.04, nrounds=400, max.depth=7, min_child_weight=200, and subsample=0.8. The five folds are the same for all the experiments, and the reported results are the averages over the five folds. We first train XGBoost by each group of features alone. The "AUC" column in Table 5 and the "AUC" bars in Figure 4 are the averaged AUC scores of XGBoost over the five folds. Clearly, the higher the score, the more important the group of features is. We also evaluate

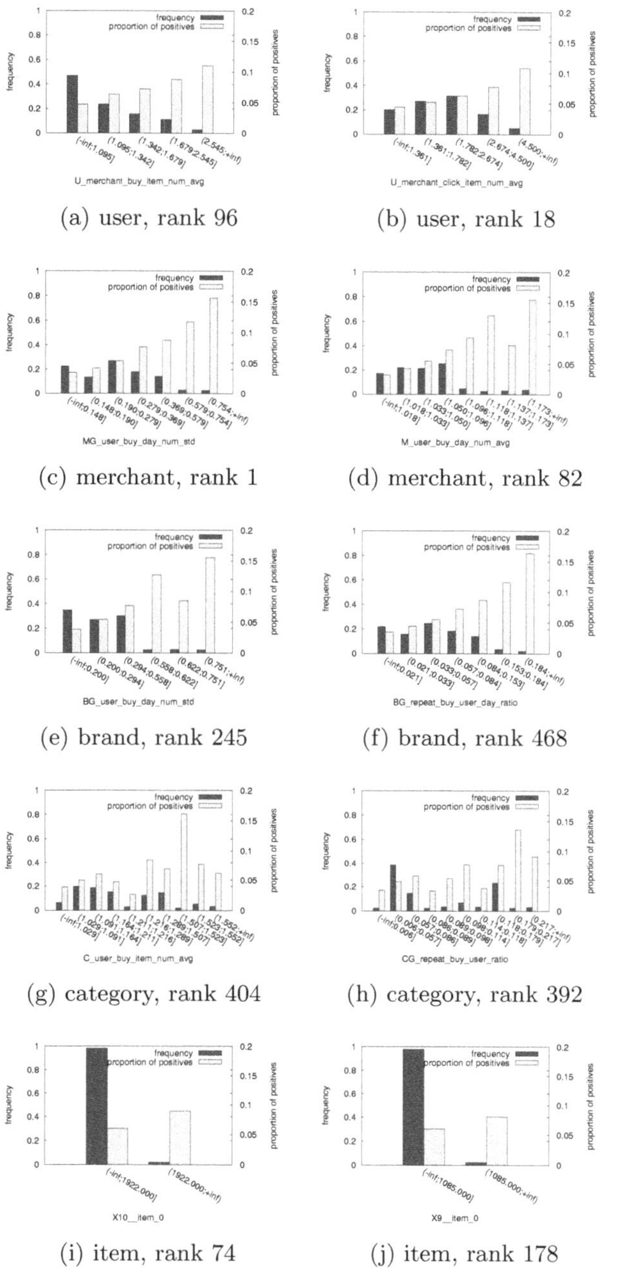

(a) user, rank 96 (b) user, rank 18 (c) merchant, rank 1 (d) merchant, rank 82 (e) brand, rank 245 (f) brand, rank 468 (g) category, rank 404 (h) category, rank 392 (i) item, rank 74 (j) item, rank 178

Figure 5: Top features in entity profiles

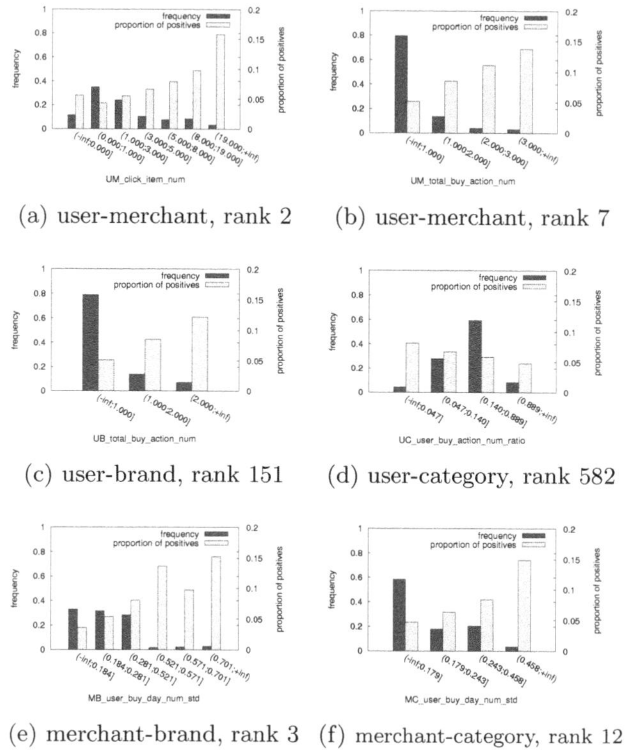

(a) user-merchant, rank 2 (b) user-merchant, rank 7 (c) user-brand, rank 151 (d) user-category, rank 582 (e) merchant-brand, rank 3 (f) merchant-category, rank 12

Figure 6: Top features in interaction profiles

the importance of a group of features by considering the full feature set but excluding the group. In this way, if the AUC score drops more, then the group is more important. The "*leave-out* AUC" column in Table 5 and the "*leave-out* AUC" bars in Figure 4 give the results.

Among the 5 entity profiles in Table 5, merchant profile and brand profile have the highest AUC scores: 0.6601 and 0.65818, respectively. However, if one of them is removed, the leave-out AUC score is even a bit higher than 0.70036—the AUC score of the full feature set. This indicates the redundancy of the two profiles. User profile has the lowest AUC score, but the AUC score drops the most if it is removed. This implies that user profile has important information that does not exist in other profiles. For interaction profiles, MB and MC profiles together have the highest AUC score, and the AUC score drops the most if they are excluded.

Among all the feature types, monthly aggregation has the highest AUC score—0.68729. When all the 276 aggregation features (164 monthly aggregation features, 88 user aggregation features and 24 merchant aggregation features) are used to build XGBoost, the AUC score is 0.6945, which is just 0.82% lower than the AUC score when all the features are used. LDA has the lowest leave-out AUC score (i.e., AUC score drops most if LDA features are excluded), which is still just 0.23% lower than the AUC score of the full feature set. The results above suggest that any feature group can be removed without decreasing the AUC score much.

The "leave-out AUC" column in Table 5 indicates some feature groups may be redundant given all other features, including merchant profile, brand profile, UB and UC profiles, monthly aggregation features, merchant aggregation features, latest-one-month features, user-merchant similarity features and age-related features. The leave-out AUC scores of these feature groups are even slightly higher than that of the full feature set. For example, if we exclude merchant profile from the full feature set, then the leave-out AUC score is 0.70096, which is slightly higher than 0.70036. If we remove all the above seemingly redundant feature groups, the number of remaining features is 691 (50.7% of total features) and the AUC score becomes 0.69936, which is lower than the AUC score of the full feature set.

5.2 Top features

XGBoost calculates a gain score for each feature, which measures how important a feature is to the model. We rank

Table 6: Features with high profile ranking

profile	global rank	type	Feature name	Description
user	96	merchant aggregation	U_merchant_buy_item_num_avg	average number of unique items bought from merchants by the user
	18	merchant aggregation	U_merchant_click_item_num_avg	average number of unique items clicked in merchants by the user
merchant	1	user aggregation & gender related	MG_user_buy_day_num_std	standard deviation of the number of days that users made a purchase from the merchant, only users of a particular gender are considered.
	82	user aggregation	M_user_buy_day_num_avg	average number of days that users made a purchase from the merchant
user-merchant	2	product diversity	UM_click_item_num	number of unique items clicked by the user in the merchant
	7	overall action count	UM_total_buy_action_num	total number of purchases made by the user from the merchant
brand	245	user aggregation & gender related	BG_user_buy_day_num_std	standard deviation of the number of days that users purchased the brand, only users of a particular gender are considered
	468	repeat buyer & gender related	BG_repeat_buy_user_day_ratio	proportion of repeat buy days of the brand, only users of a particular gender are considered.
category	404	user aggregation	C_user_buy_item_num_avg	average number of items in the category that were bought by users
	392	repeat buyer & gender related	CG_repeat_buy_user_ratio	proportion of repeat buyers of the category, only users of a particular gender are considered.
item	74	monthly action count	X10__item_0	times that the item was clicked in October
	178	monthly action count	X9__item_0	times that the item was clicked in September
user-brand	151	overall action count	UB_total_buy_action_num	total times that the user bought the brand
user-category	582	overall action ratio	UC_user_buy_action_num_ratio	ratio of the times that the user purchased the category to the total actions taken by the user on the category
merchant-brand	3	user aggregation	MB_user_buy_day_num_std	standard deviation of the number of days that users bought the brand from the merchant, only users of a particular gender are considered.
merchant-category	12	user aggregation	MC_user_buy_day_num_std	standard deviation of the number of days that users bought the category from the merchant, only users of a particular gender are considered.

Table 7: Features with high global ranking

global rank	profile	type	Feature name	Description
4	merchant-brand	repeat buyer	MB_repeat_buy_day_ratio	proportion of repeat buy days of the brand in the merchant
5	user-merchant	trend	user_seller_store_visit_day_count_MDP	deviation of the number of times the user clicked the merchant in the latest month from the mean of the previous months normalized using mean
6	merchant-brand	user aggregation	MB_user_buy_day_num_avg	average number of days users bought the brand from the merchant
8	user-merchant	product diversity	UM_click_cat_num	number of unique categories clicked by the user in the merchant
9	merchant	user aggregation & gender related	MG_user_buy_day_num_avg	average number of days users bought some item from the merchant, only users of a particular gender are considered
10	merchant-category	user aggregation	MC_user_buy_day_num_avg	average number of days that users bought the category from the merchant.
11	merchant	repeat buyer & age related	MA_repeat_buy_user_day_ratio	proportion of repeat buy days of the merchant, only users of a particular age group are considered.
13	user	monthly aggregation	U_monthly_click_merchant_num_std	standard deviation of the number of merchants clicked by the user every month
14	user-merchant	similarity score	UM_buy_action_num_brand_merchant_user_share_simscore_sum	similarity score between the user and the merchant, and the score is obtained by first calculating the product of the times that the user bought a brand and the brand's user share within the merchant, and then taking sum over all brands in the merchant.
15	user-merchant	product diversity	UM_buy_item_num	number of unique items purchased by the user in the merchant
16	merchant-category	repeat buyer	MC_repeat_buy_day_ratio	proportion of repeat buy days of the category in the merchant
17	category	user aggregation	C_user_buy_day_num_avg	average number of days that users bought the category.
19	user	merchant aggregation	U_merchant_click_day_num_std	standard deviation of the number of days that the user clicked merchants.
20	user	product diversity	U_buy_merchant_ratio	ratio of the number of merchants that the user made a purchase from to the total number of merchants that the user took some actions

features based on their average gain scores over the five folds. Each feature has two rankings: 1) *profile ranking* is the ranking of a feature when only features in the corresponding profile are used to build XGBoost models, and 2) *global ranking* is the ranking of a feature when all of the 1364 features are used to build XGBoost models. Table 6 shows the top one or two features in each profile based on profile ranking. The global rankings of these features are in column "global rank".

All the features we generated are numeric. To visualize their correlations with the class labels, we discretize their values using the method in [9]. To avoid generating too many small bins, we set the minimum number of instances in a bin to 5000. Figure 5 reports the relative frequency of each bin (blue bar with the frequency given by the left y-axis) and the proportion of positive instances therein (green bar with proportion value given by the right y-axis) for top features in entity profiles. Figure 6 reports the top features in interaction profiles. The x-axis in Figures 5 and 6 gives the value ranges of the discretized bins. The proportion of positive instances increases with the feature values in most cases. None of the features is a strong indicator of class labels. The maximal information gain of all features is only 0.00868 after discretization.

Among features in user profile, the average number of items clicked in or purchased from merchants are the top-2 features. For merchant profile, the average and standard deviation of the number of days that users made a purchase in the merchant are the top-2 features in the profile, with the latter being the top feature globally. In profiles of user-merchant, merchant-brand, and merchant-category, top features locally in the profiles also have high global rankings.

Table 7 lists the top-20 features based on global ranking. Those already reported in Table 6 are not repeated in Table 7. Top features are mainly from user aggregation (7 features), repeat buyer (3), and product diversity (3), which account for almost 2/3 of the top-20 features. Figure 7 shows the statistics of the top features, including discretized bins, the frequency, and proportion of positive instances in the bins. Features *U_monthly_click_merchant_num_std* (rank 13) and *U_buy_merchant_ratio* (rank 20) are not shown in the figure, because they have only one bin after discretization. Feature *user_seller_store_visit_day_count_MDP* is set to -999, if a user did not visit the merchant from May to October. This feature is discretized into two bins: (-inf, -999] and (-999, +inf), and the second bin has a higher proportion of positive classes. It indicates that if a user visited a merchant before November, then the user is more likely to buy from the merchant again after Double 11.

Some user aggregation features and repeat buyer features capture like characteristics of entities or interactions from different aspects, and they are highly correlated. For example, feature *MB_repeat_buy_day_ratio* (Figure 7(a)) and feature *MB_user_buy_day_num_avg* (Figure 7(c)) are merchant-brand features, and they show similar patterns. The former

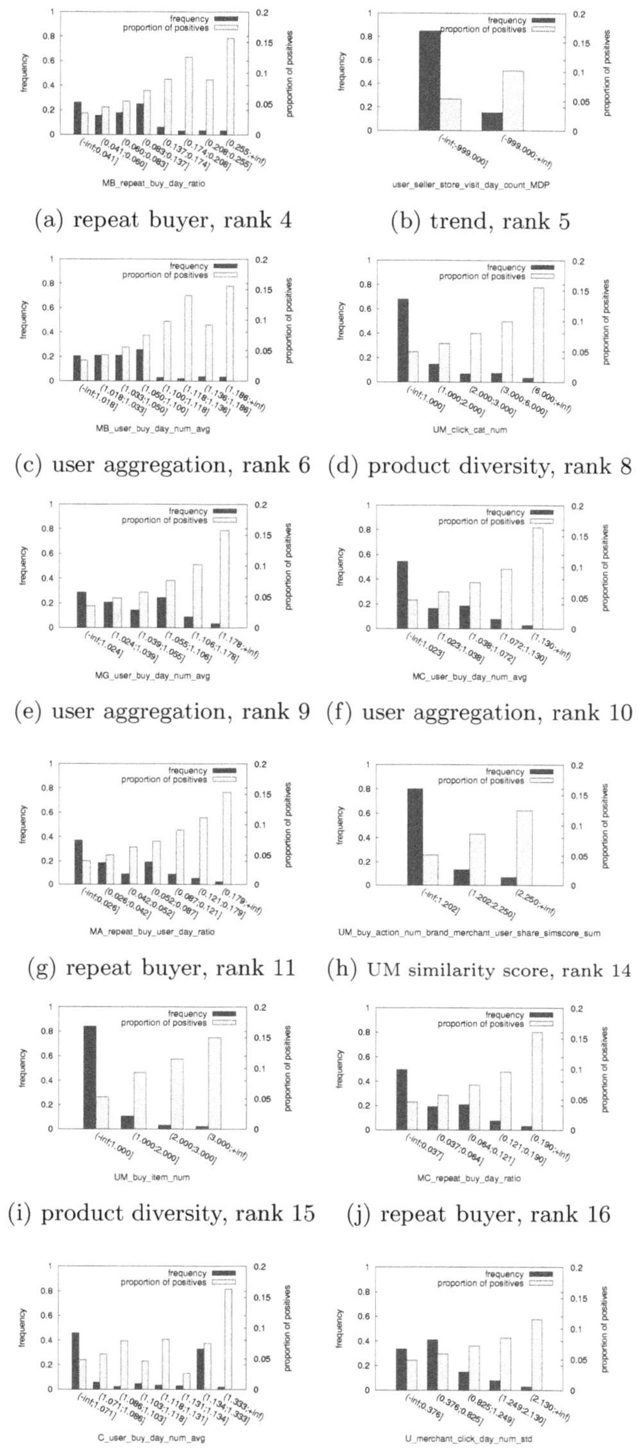

(a) repeat buyer, rank 4 (b) trend, rank 5

(c) user aggregation, rank 6 (d) product diversity, rank 8

(e) user aggregation, rank 9 (f) user aggregation, rank 10

(g) repeat buyer, rank 11 (h) UM similarity score, rank 14

(i) product diversity, rank 15 (j) repeat buyer, rank 16

(k) user aggregation, rank 17 (l) merchant aggregation, rank 19

Figure 7: Features with high global ranking

is the proportion of buyers, who bought the brand from the merchant on at least two different days, among the users who bought the brand from the merchant at least once. The latter is the average number of days that users bought the brand from the merchant. A larger *MB_repeat_buy_day_ratio* value often implies a larger *MB_user_buy_day_num_avg* value

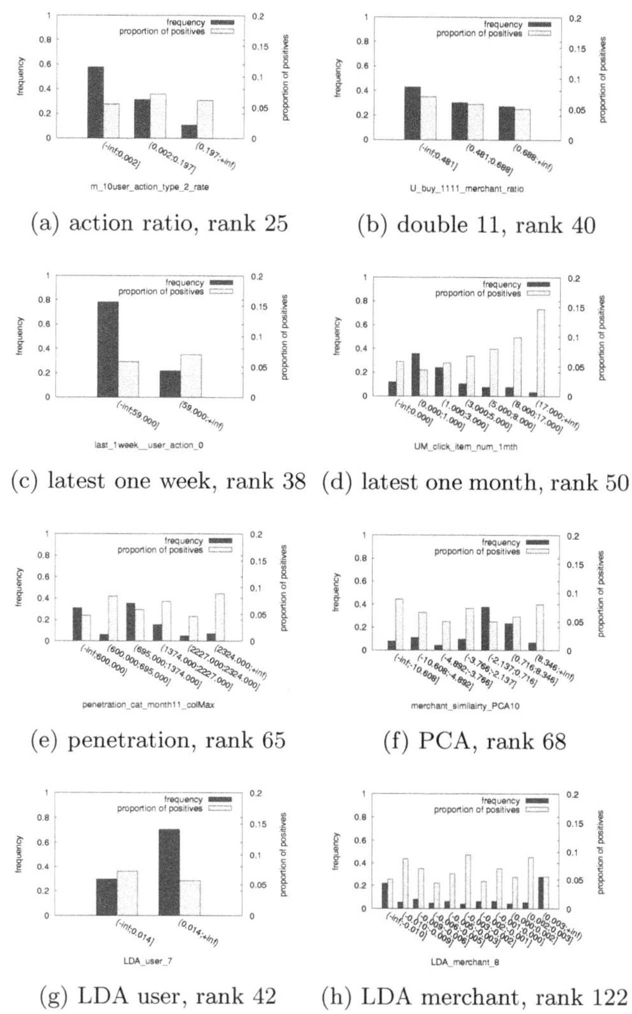

(a) action ratio, rank 25 (b) double 11, rank 40

(c) latest one week, rank 38 (d) latest one month, rank 50

(e) penetration, rank 65 (f) PCA, rank 68

(g) LDA user, rank 42 (h) LDA merchant, rank 122

Figure 8: Top features in other feature type groups

and vice versa. The same correlation is observed for feature *MC_user_buy_day_num_avg* (Figure 7(f)) and feature *MC_repeat_buy_day_ratio* (Figure 7(j)). Both features are merchant-category features.

Several feature types, including monthly action ratio, double 11, latest-one-week, latest-one-month, penetration, PCA and LDA, do not occur in the global top-20 feature list (Table 7). Table 8 reports the top features in these feature groups based on global ranking. Figure 8 shows the statistics of these features.

5.3 Performance on testing data

Section 5.1 and 5.2 evaluate the feature importance on training data by five-fold cross validation. In this subsection, we evaluate the importance of features on the testing data. We set the parameters of XGBoost as follows: eta=0.01, nrounds=2000, max.depth=7, min_child_weight= 200, and subsample=0.8. When all the features are used, the testing AUC score is 0.702508 [3] as shown in the second row of Table 9. The last column of the table is the percentage of AUC

[3] In the competition, we used smaller learning rate and more rounds to achieve the slightly better AUC score of 0.70282.

Table 8: Features with the highest global ranking among features in the remaining feature groups

global rank	profile	type	Feature name	Description
25	user	monthly action ratio	m_10user_action_type_2_rate	ratio of the number of purchases made by the user in October to the total number of actions taken by the user in October
40	user	Double 11	U_buy_1111_merchant_ratio	ratio of the number of merchants that the user made a purchase from on Double 11 to the total number of merchants that the user took some actions on Double 11
38	user	latest one week	last_1week__user_action_0	the number of clicks made by the user in the last week before Double 11
50	user-merchant	latest one month	UM_click_item_num_1mth	the number of unique items clicked by the user in the merchant in the latest one month
65	category	penetration	penetration_cat_month11_colMax	number of users who purchased some item of the category in November
68	merchant	PCA	merchant_similairty_PCA10	the 10-th component of PCA
42	user	LDA user	LDA_user_7	the value of the 7-th topic when users are regarded as documents
122	merchant	LDA merchant	LDA_merchant_8	the value of the 8-th topic when merchants are regarded as documents

Table 9: AUC on testing data

	feature types	profiles	#features	AUC	% of drop
1	all feature types	all profiles	1364	0.702508	-
2	overall action counts/ratio, overall day counts, product diversity, monthly aggregation, user aggregation, merchant aggregation, repeat buyer, double 11, latest one month	user profile, merchant profile, user-merchant profile	354	0.694927	1.08%
3	feature set 2 plus LDA features	same as feature set 2	434	0.696812	0.81%
4	same as feature set 3	feature set 2 plus MB and MC profiles	492	0.699226	0.47%
5	same as feature set 3	feature set 4 plus brand profiles and category profiles	616	0.701392	0.16%
6	feature set 3 plus user-merchant similarity features	all profiles	866	0.701913	0.08%
7	feature set 6 plus monthly action counts, penetration features and PCA features	all profiles	1053	0.702250	0.04%

score drop, when only subsets of features (as specified in the second and third columns of the table) are used.

Feature set 2 contains 354 features from nine feature types and three profiles. Its AUC score is only 1.08% lower than the AUC score when all the 1364 features (i.e., feature set 1) are used. When more feature types and/or profiles are added (top-down in Table 9), the AUC score increases marginally. The results again imply that we can use a smaller number of features to train predictive models without decreasing the AUC score significantly.

6. CONCLUSION

In this paper, we presented our winning solution for the repeat buyer prediction competition hosted at IJCAI 2015 conference. We generated a large number of features to capture the preferences and behaviors of users, characteristics of merchants, brands, categories and items and the interactions among them. Our study shows that none of the features generated is a strong indicator of class labels, so we need hundreds of features to achieve a relatively high AUC score. We hope our winning solution, along with concrete analysis on feature engineering, would serve as a solid stepping stone for practitioners to solving future e-commerce problems. It is a tedious task to generate and manage a large number of features. As our next step, we will explore how to automate the feature generation and selection process for e-commerce prediction tasks.

7. REFERENCES

[1] Fitting generalized linear models. Available on https://stat.ethz.ch/R-manual/R-devel/library/stats/html/glm.html.

[2] Generalized linear models. Available on http://scikit-learn.org/stable/modules/linear_model.html.

[3] H. Abdi and L. J. Williams. Principal component analysis. *Wiley Interdisciplinary Reviews: Computational Statistics*, 2(4):433–459, 2010.

[4] D. M. Blei, A. Y. Ng, and M. I. Jordan. Latent dirichlet allocation. *Journal of Machine Learning Research*, 3(4-5):993–1022, 2003.

[5] L. Breiman. Random forests. *Mach. Learn.*, 45(1):5–32, 2001.

[6] T. Chen and T. He. Xgboost: extreme gradient boosting. Available on https://github.com/dmlc/xgboost.

[7] M. Dash and H. Liu. Feature selection for classification. *Intelligent data analysis*, 1(1):131–156, 1997.

[8] P. Domingos. A few useful things to know about machine learning. *Communications of the ACM*, 55(10):78–87, 2012.

[9] U. M. Fayyad and K. B. Irani. Multi-interval discretization of continuous-valued attributes for classification learning. In *Proc. of the International Joint Conference on Uncertainty in AI*, pages 1022–1027, 1993.

[10] J. H. Friedman. Greedy function approximation: A gradient boosting machine. *Annals of Statistics*, 29:1189–1232, 2000.

[11] Y.-C. Juan, W.-S. Chin, and Y. Zhuang. Field-aware factorization machines. Available on https://github.com/guestwalk/libffm.

[12] S. Lê and F. H. Julie Josse. FactoMineR: an R package for multivariate analysis. *Journal of statistical software*, 25(1):1–18, 2008.

[13] L. C. Molina, L. Belanche, and Àngela Nebot. Feature selection algorithms: A survey and experimental evaluation. In *ICDM*, pages 306–313, 2002.

[14] S. Rendle. Factorization machines with libfm. *ACM Transactions on Intelligent Systems and Technology*, 3(3), 2012.

[15] K.-Q. Shen, C.-J. Ong, X.-P. Li, and E. Wilder-Smith. Feature selection via sensitivity analysis of svm probabilistic outputs. *Machine Learning*, 70(1):1–20, 2008.

[16] J.-B. Yang and C.-J. Ong. An effective feature selection method via mutual information estimation. *IEEE Transactions on Systems, Man and Cybernetics (Part B)*, 42(6):1550 – 1559, 2012.

Audience Expansion for Online Social Network Advertising

Haishan Liu
LinkedIn Corporation
605 W. Maude Avenue
Sunnyvale, CA 94085
haliu@linkedin.com

David Pardoe
LinkedIn Corporation
605 W. Maude Avenue
Sunnyvale, CA 94085
dpardoe@linkedin.com

Kun Liu
LinkedIn Corporation
605 W. Maude Avenue
Sunnyvale, CA 94085
kliu@linkedin.com

Manoj Thakur
LinkedIn Corporation
605 W. Maude Avenue
Sunnyvale, CA 94085
mthakur@linkedin.com

Frank Cao
LinkedIn Corporation
605 W. Maude Avenue
Sunnyvale, CA 94085
fcao@linkedin.com

Chongzhe Li
LinkedIn Corporation
605 W. Maude Avenue
Sunnyvale, CA 94085
ckli@linkedin.com

ABSTRACT

Online social network advertising platforms, such as that provided by LinkedIn, generally allow marketers to specify targeting options so that their ads appear to a desired demographic. Audience Expansion is a technique developed at LinkedIn to simplify targeting and identify new audiences with similar attributes to the original target audience. We developed two methods to achieve Audience Expansion: campaign-agnostic expansion and campaign-aware expansion. In this paper, we describe the details of these methods, present in-depth analysis of their trade-offs, and demonstrate a hybrid strategy that possesses the combined strength of both methods. Through large scale online experiments, we show the effectiveness of the proposed approach, and as a result, the benefits it brings to the whole marketplace including both LinkedIn and advertisers. The achieved benefits can be characterized as: 1) simplified targeting process and increased reach for advertisers, and 2) better utilization of LinkedIn's ads inventory and higher and more efficient market participation.

Keywords

Online advertising; Audience expansion; Lookalike modeling

1. INTRODUCTION

Advertising on social network platforms such as LinkedIn involves interactions between three groups. Users browse and interact with content on the website; in the process they express their intention and preferences. Advertisers seek to show ads to users who are valuable to their marketing campaigns, which usually consist of a set of ads with the goal of promoting products or services. The social network provides "real estate" for placing ads, and matches the ads and the user so that they are relevant to each other.

KDD '16, August 13 - 17, 2016, San Francisco, CA, USA

ISBN 978-1-4503-4232-2/16/08... $15.00

DOI: http://dx.doi.org/10.1145/2939672.2939680

There are two main categories of channels in which ads appear on social network platforms. Sponsored content appears in users' newsfeeds, a sequence of social news items which has become the center of gravity for users' daily traffic. Text or display ads appear in ad slots available on many other parts of the website, such as the top of the page or right column. For both channels, advertisers are able to target specific audiences they want to reach. Unlike the well known sponsored search model for advertising on search engines, where advertisers target a list of keywords that they deem relevant to their campaign, advertisers on social networks are given comprehensive demographic targeting options to precisely define the desired audience. For example, on LinkedIn an advertiser can reach all software engineers having the Machine Learning and Java skills who work in a company located in the US with fewer than 500 employees. However, even with this pinpoint targeting ability, a similar challenge to the coverage problem in search advertising remains, as advertisers usually cannot cover all relevant demographic attributes related to the desired product or service. Indeed, the cardinality of most targeting attributes is well beyond tens of thouands (e.g., titles and skills), and some even rise into multiple millions (e.g., company and group). This makes it costly for advertisers to identify the attributes they wish to target with their campaigns.

To mitigate this problem, we have developed a system, named *Audience Expansion*, to help advertisers on LinkedIn increase the reach of their campaigns. This is achieved by automatically enlarging the original target audience (the exact audience) to include similar, like-minded users. For example, if a campaign targets members with the skill "Online Advertising," the campaign might also be expanded to members who list the skill "Interactive Marketing" on their profiles. This means advertisers can reach the desired target audience with less effort setting up campaigns.

Some advertising platforms have provided similar functionality; however, most commonly the expansion is conversion-oriented. That is, advertisers must provide a list of known users who have prior positive feedback, and this list is then expanded. This requirement limits the usability of the feature to big, savy advertisers who can afford the effort of continuous marketing research and monitoring. Instead, we decided to make LinkedIn's Audience Expansion feature extrememly accessible, as easy as simply checking an option to opt-in at the time advertisers specify the targeting criteria.

Audience Expansion aims to optimize for the joint benefit of advertisers and LinkedIn with minimal impact to the user experience. It benefits advertisers and LinkedIn in the following ways:

- Advertisers – by finding, with only limited advertiser effort, a large audience segment that is likely to engage with advertiser campaigns.
- LinkedIn – by encouraging higher marketplace participation, thus incresing competition and even providing ads for users who were previously untargeted.

In this paper, we propose an efficient system to achieve the above goals. Our main contributions are as follows:

- We present a campaign-agnostic approach to expand user profiles. The expansion is achieved by employing the *Similar-X* recommender system built in-house to generate enriched user profiles with attributes similar to those in a user's original profile. This mechanism is member-oriented, and is thus immediately available for new campaigns with no time required for generating expanded audiences.
- We develop a campaign-aware approach to expand the exact target audience of a campaign to lookalike members. The expansion is based on a nearest neighbor approach where the similarity measure is calculated by *Similar-Profiles*, a custom algorithm in the Similar-X family.
- We present a hybrid system that combines the strength of both the campaign-agnostic and campaign-aware approaches.

This system is now in production for all traffic and has provided significant improvements in key metrics for both advertisers and LinkedIn, such as double-digit percentage increases in impressions served across LinkedIn, and triple-digit percentage increases in value achieved for those advertisers who take advantage of Audience Expansion.

The remainder of this paper is laid out as follows. We describe related work and background in Section 2. Next, Section 3 explains the general architecture of our system and its various components. In Section 4 we describe the modeling aspect of the Similar-X recommender systems and their application in both the campaign-agnostic and campaign-aware expansion approaches. Section 5 details our empirical evaluation over large real-world experiments. Finally, Section 6 concludes the paper and discusses possible future directions.

2. BACKGROUND AND RELATED WORK

Previous work on audience expansion for online advertising has typically fallen into one of two categories: *broad match* in keyword advertising, and *look-alike modeling* in user-targeted advertising. Keyword advertising includes sponsored search advertising, in which ads are placed alongside search results for a relevant query, and contextual display advertising, in which advertisements are placed on a webpage with relevant content. In each case, an advertiser targets its ads by specifying a set of keywords for which it would like to bid. If a keyword occurs in the apropriate context (the search query or the page content), the advertiser then enters an auction to show its ad. The keyword must match exactly, or possibly with minor modification (e.g., different spelling or verb tense). As a result, it can be difficult for an advertiser to enumerate the entire set of keywords for which it would like to bid. In response, many advertising platforms offer broad match, in which each keyword provided by the advertiser is expanded to a larger set of keywords. For example, the keyword "bike repair" might expand to related keywords such as "bicycle repair" and "where to fix my bike".

There are several documented implementations of broad match. Often, these involve doing offline processing and storing the result in a lookup table to be used online. Broder et al. [4] address the issue of broad matches for uncommon "tail" queries that are not present in the table. A system of extracting features from a query is presented; features for common queries are extracted and stored in an inverted index, and at run time the common queries most similar to a given query can be identified using this index. Gupta et al. [9] present a system that performs supervised learning on past ad impressions to learn click probabilities for potential broad matches. The online learning approach described uses a form of max-margin voted perceptron with time decay to rapidly adjust to changes in user and advertiser behavior.

While broad match helps advertisers with the problem of choosing keywords, it does introduce new challenges relating to bid optimization and mechanism design. Even Dar et al. [8] explore the problem of optimal sponsored search bidding in the presence of broad match, where the bid for a single keyword may be applied to many queries of varying value to the advertiser. Amaldoss et al. [1] perform a game-theoretic analysis of broad match for search using a model that incorporates advertisers' bidding cost (i.e., effort expended choosing bids) and identifies the conditions under which advertisers and search engines benefit. Dhangwatnotai [7] studies advertiser welfare under the generalized second price (GSP) auction when broad matches are introduced, while Chen et al. [6] describe a probabilistic mechanism for multi-slot auctions with broad matches that generates larger welfare than the standard GSP.

In user-targeted advertising, advertisers target specific users based on properties such as demographics or interests. These properties may be explicitly specified by the user, or they may be inferred from the user's behavior (this is referred to as *behavioral targeting* [12][15]). As with keyword advertising, enumerating all possible target segments can be difficult for an advertiser. In addition, ideal target segments may contain too few users, while other segments may be too broad. In response, some advertising platforms offer look-alike modeling, which identifies users similar to a given user set. Look-alike modeling can also be used in cases where an advertiser can provide a precise list of users to target, such as in retargeting of website visitors.

Approaches to look-alike modeling include k-means clustering [13] and frequent pattern mining [3]. Mangalampalli et al. [11] show that associative classification (a rule-based form of frequent pattern mining) can be more effective than other common classifiers when training look-alike models for campaigns with few conversions. Bagherjeiran et al. [2] consider the problem of look-alike modeling when both a targeting segment and advertiser conversion data are available. Here expansion is posed as an ensemble learning problem where the goal is to complement the existing segment while minimizing overlap.

Another approach that is related to look-alike modeling is collaborative filtering. A key challenge in applying collaborative filtering to advertising is the extreme sparsity of interaction between users and campaigns. Kanagal et al. [10] address this challenge by using a product taxonomy to identify relationships between campaigns.

Perhaps the most similar method of audience expansion to the one presented in this paper is described in [14]. As at LinkedIn, advertisers can specify a targeting segment as a propositional logic formula based on user properties. This segment is then expanded by finding a new formula describing an expanded set of users. The formula is chosen based on three criteria: 1) similarity, defined as the proportion of the original segment in the expanded segment; 2) novelty, defined as the proportion of the expanded segment not in the original segment; and 3) quality, defined by a performance metric such as CTR or conversion rate.

3. SYSTEM

In this section we give a high-level overview of LinkedIn ads serving and the Audience Expansion system. The next section then provides more details of the proposed methodology from a modeling perspective. Figure 1 shows a diagram of the system overview of Audience Expansion in the ads serving flow.

3.1 Overview

LinkedIn offers multiple ad formats, including *Text Ads* that may appear at the top or side of the page, and *Sponsored Updates* that appear as native content in a user's feed. As ad targeting works the same regardless of format, our Audience Expansion system does not make a distinction between formats. For each format there may be multiple ad slots per page request; for instance, as a user scrolls through their feed they may see several Sponsored Updates.

When an advertiser creates a campaign, they specify the ad format, the ad content (also known as the *creative*), a daily and/or lifetime budget, a bid, and the targeting to use. Bids may either be per thousand impressions (cost per mille or CPM) or per click (CPC). To specify targeting, the advertiser is given choices within a number of categories, such as location, age, company name, and skills. Within each category, the advertiser is presented with a set of standardized choices, and can select options to include and exclude. The included selections in each category are ORed together, and everything is then ANDed together, producing a targeting string that represents a logical formula in conjunctive normal form. For example, a targeting string might be:

(*location* == "USA" OR *location* == "Canada") AND (*location* != "California") AND (*age* == "18-24" OR *age* == "25-34") AND (*seniority* != "unpaid") AND (*seniority* != "training")

Once the targeting has been specified, the estimated size of the audience and a suggested bid are shown to assist the advertiser. They are also given an option to enable Audience Expansion, and may change this setting at any time.

The ads serving flow starts when a member visits a LinkedIn webpage with available ad slots. Together with the page view, an ad request is issued to the backend. The member's profile attributes are fetched, and then matched with the targeting criteria of active ad campaigns to find those that target this member. The matched campaigns then compete in a generalized second price auction, where their predicted CTR and bid jointly determine a rank order, and each campaign's cost is determined by the next-ranked campaign. The winning creatives are sent to the frontend to serve. This workflow is illustrated in the *online processes* (colored in dark grey) in Figure 1.

There are two places where Audience Expansion affects ad targeting in the above workflow. First, when fetching a user's profile attributes, Audience Expansion injects a set of expanded attributes in the return, effectively making the user targetable by more ad campaigns. Second, Audience Expansion explicitly adds a set of campaigns—those not directly targeted at this user, but with an audience that looks alike—to the eligible campaigns of the user. These two different applications correspond to the two frameworks we developed for Audience Expansion. The first kind of expansion is only based upon user attributes, hence we call it *campaign-agnostic*. The second kind of expansion applies *lookalike* modeling on top of campaigns' original target audience, hence we call it *campaign-aware*. Both of these frameworks make use of batch processing carried out in an offline fashion, as illustrated in the *offline processes* (colored in white) in Figure 1. We note that CTR prediction and auction ranking apply as usual to expanded campaigns, and in fact the CTR prediction model uses a feature indicating whether a campaign matches as a result of Audience Expansion. CTR prediction can thus act as a safeguard against showing low-relevance ads due to expansion.

3.2 Campaign-Agnostic Expansion

In the campaign-agnostic framework, profile attribute expansion is achieved by applying LinkedIn's Similar-X algorithm to a set of targetable profile attributes. The "X" refers to any entity of interest, such as company, LinkedIn Group, skill, job title, etc., making Similar-X a collective term for a group of related entity-to-entity recommender systems. For example, from Similar-Skills, we know "Data Mining" is similar to "Big Data" and "Machine Learning." Applying this in profile attribute expansion, now anyone with an explicit "Data Mining" skill will be eligible to see ads targeting "Big Data" and "Machine Learning." The heart of Similar-X is a logistic regression model that takes as input features representing involved entities, and outputs a score aimed at capturing the similarity between the entities learned from historical interaction data, preferably in the ads context.

Campaign-agnostic expansion provides an always-available expansion mechanism that does not require warm-up from the time a campaign is created or expansion is enabled. The downside is the relatively coarse quality of expansion carried out on a per-attribute basis. The campaign-aware expansion described in the next section takes the whole member profile into consideration and is hence more precise. However, the tradeoff is that it takes some time for the offline process to generate the expansion, so the expansion is not available in the short period after a campaign becomes active.

3.3 Campaign-Aware Expansion

In the campaign-aware framework, we view targeting as labeling users; i.e., an advertiser's campaign emits labels for users belonging to the desired audience. We can then pose Audience Expansion as a classification problem to pre-

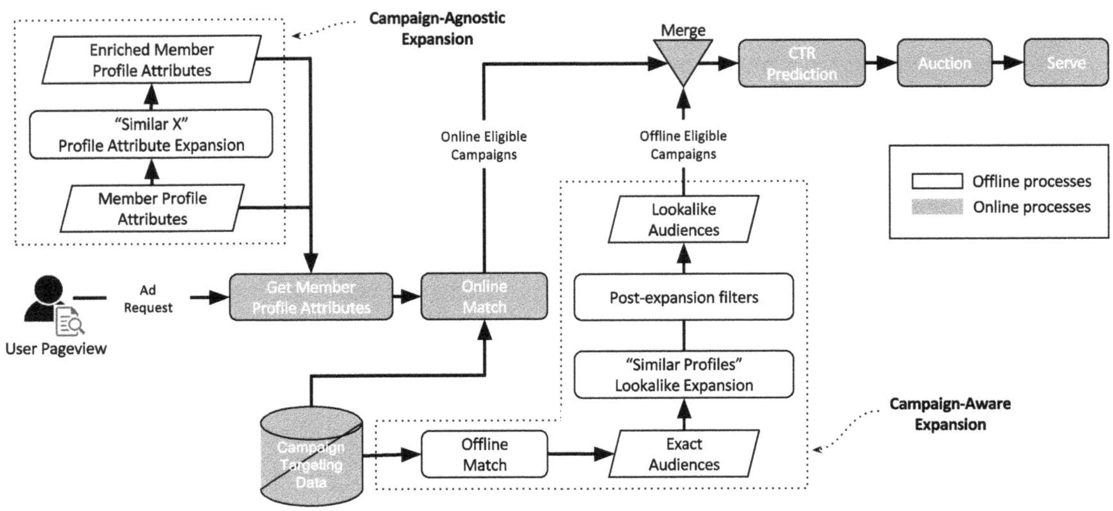

Figure 1: System overview of lookalike expansion in the ads serving workflow.

dict whether or not an untargeted user should be included in the audience for that campaign. The difficulty lies in choosing positive and negative training examples. Labeling targeted users as positive and non-targeted users as negative would simply cause us to learn a model of the original targeting. We could wait until the campaign has run for a while, then collect labels based on users' interactions. However, this takes a prolonged warm-up time for model training, and may require some careful setup to effectively explore-exploit the search space. Therefore we decided to employ a nonparametric method and reduce the problem to nearest neighbor search. This not only simplifies the label gathering process, but also avoids any assumptions that the exact targeted audience is drawn from any distribution or mixture of distributions.

Central to nearest neighbor search is the definition of a similarity measure. We adopt the Similar-Profiles algorithm, a member of the Similar-X family, to model user similarity and retrieve similar users for a given one. Details of the Similar-Profiles algorithm are discussed in Section 4. The workflow of Audience Expansion with Similar-Profiles is depicted in the box labeled "Campaign-Aware Expansion" in Figure 1. The key components of the workflow are:

1. Offline Match: A Hadoop job that calculates exact target audiences for all active campaigns that have enabled expansion by applying their targeting criteria in batch mode; the output is the campaigns' exact audiences.

2. Filter campaigns: Removal of campaigns that are unlikely to benefit from lookalike modeling, such as campaigns that target very broadly or that can easily spend their budget without expansion.

3. Expand audiences to similar profiles: The core step in the expansion, where the exact audiences are expanded to similar users, with the help of the Similar-Profiles algorithm (described in detail below).

4. Filter expansion: Additional filters on top of the expanded audience, such as those to make the new audience comply to campaigns' negative targeting criteria, or to restrict expansion on certain attributes (e.g., location and gender).

The output of the above processes is the lookalike audiences for selected campaigns, grouped by member ID in order to merge easily with the online process, which is pushed to a key-value store accessible by the services in production.

3.4 Hybrid Expansion

As mentioned earlier, campaign-agnostic expansion provides a more readily available mechanism but is relatively less precise. The campaign-aware expansion requires time to process offline but is much finer grained due to the utilization of all profile information. Due to the complementary design of these expansion methods, we can create a hybrid method that includes both the campaign-agnostic and campaign-aware methods, combining the strengths and offsetting the weaknesses of each.

The synergy in the hybrid method is achieved by the fact that both campaign-agnostic and campaign-aware expansion frameworks generate outputs in the same member-oriented fashion. Specifically, the output of campaign-agnostic expansion is an enriched member profile, $U_p = \{A_1^*, A_2^*, \ldots\}$, where A_i^* is an expanded profile attribute. The output of campaign-aware expansion is a list of predicted campaigns, $U_l = \{C_1, C_2, \ldots\}$, where each C_i is a campaign that does not target the member, but should. The enriched profile is used in the online target matching process, the output of which is then directly merged with the list of predicted campaigns. (See Figure 1 for the merge process.) This design provides a straightforward way to conduct A/B tests by selectively making either U_p or U_l available in the ads serving flow. If both U_p and U_l are made available and utilized, this effectively achieves the hybrid method for expansion.

4. MODELING

We now present details of the Similar-X models with their application in both the campaign-agnostic expansion and the campaign-aware expansion. We discuss important factors that need to be considered to bring together the various model components in the practical system.

4.1 Similar-*X* Framework

We model entity similarity through a content-based filtering approach. By treating each entity as a document to be compared against a collection of other entities, we developed a search-based system to find the best-matching entities.

Denote as $\mathcal{X}$ the value space for a given entity type. The problem can be defined as a mapping $\mathcal{X} \rightarrow \mathcal{P}_\kappa(\mathcal{X})$, where $\mathcal{P}_\kappa(\mathcal{X})$ denotes the powerset of $\mathcal{X}$ of cardinality less than κ. Specifically, the Similar-X framework outputs a list of κ target entities $t_1, t_2, \ldots, t_\kappa$ rank-ordered by the similarity scores with regard to the source entity.

4.1.1 *Feature Extraction*

In order to obtain an expressive representation, we model each entity as a structured (multi-fielded) document. We extract four types of fields for each entity, including n-grams / phrases, standardized named data types (e.g., industry), derived data types, and network proximities.

Consider the problem of finding similar companies as an example, where the entities of interest are companies. N-gram/phrase fields are extracted from free text contents of the company meta data, such as description or headline. N-grams are stemmed and a small set of stop words are dropped. Phrases are identified using a dictionary. Standardized named data types are extracted by dedicated classifiers for various predefined types, such as industry type and company size. Derived data types for a company may include additional attributes we infer about the company based on the commonality of its employees or followers. For example, an Internet company may have derived skills such as Network Development or Software Engineering because of the prevalence of those skills among its employees or followers. Network proximities include other related companies determined through various user-company interactions. For example, people who viewed/followed/worked for this company also viewed/followed/worked for other companies.

Table 1 shows an example of the features that may be extracted for LinkedIn as a company.

4.1.2 *The Model*

The fielded document representation of an entity is treated as a query and run against an inverted index of documents generated offline to retrieve similar documents. We employ the vector space model (VSM) to represent fields in documents and queries as weighted vectors in a multi-dimensional space, where each distinct term is a dimension, and we use tf-idf values as the term weights. The VSM similarity between a field f_s in the source entity (query) and a field f_t in the target entity (document) is the Cosine Similarity

$$s(f_s, f_t) = \frac{V(f_s) \cdot V(f_t)}{|V(f_s)||V(f_t)|},$$

where $V(\cdot)$ denotes the VSM representatoin of a field, and will be omitted where there is no confusion.

Note that f_s and f_t can be different fields from the two entities. For example, comparing the past job title from a source member to the current job title of a target member does tell us something useful about the similarity between these two members. In general, it is permissible to compare two fields as long as the terms of the fields (values in the vector space) are of the same type. Specifically, denote as $\mathcal{F}$ the field space of an entity. We can categorize fields based on the type of their term values, which can be either texts (mostly found in n-gram/phrase fields), or IDs (mostly found in standardized, derived, and proximity fields). Denote textual fields as $\mathcal{T}$ and ID fields as $\mathcal{I}$. It follows that $\mathcal{F} = \mathcal{T} \cup \mathcal{I}$. Denote as $G = \{\mathcal{F}_s, \mathcal{F}_t, \mathcal{E}\}$ the bipartite graph between a source and a target entity, in which an edge $(f_s, f_t) \in \mathcal{E}$ if and only if both f_s and f_t are of the same term types, i.e.:

$$\mathcal{E} = \{(f_s, f_t) : (f_s, f_t) \in \mathcal{T} \times \mathcal{T} \vee (f_s, f_t) \in \mathcal{I} \times \mathcal{I}\} .$$

We use $\mathbf{s} = \{s(f_s, f_t) : \forall (f_s, f_t) \in \mathcal{E}\}$ to denote the field based similarities when $s(\cdot)$ is applied to all edges in $\mathcal{E}$.

Given the field similarities, it is natural to characterize the final entity similarity so that it matches the following intuitions: 1) two entities are similar if there are a large number of similar fields; and 2) different fields contribute differently to the final entity similarity. It is then natural to define the entity similarity as a weighted linear combination:

$$S(s, t) = \mathbf{w}^T \mathbf{s} . \tag{1}$$

The coefficients $\mathbf{w}$ can be learned from the historical user-entity interaction log. For example, we take pairs of companies that have been historically co-targeted frequently in ads as positive examples, and companies frequently ignored when recommended to advertisers for inclusion given their existing company targetings as negative examples. We then fit a logistic regression model with elastic net regularization to the training data.

4.1.3 *Personalization*

One potential downside of the naive application of Similar-X attribute expansion is the lack of personalization. For example, if company A is deemed to be similar to company B from Similar-Companies, then A is added to the enriched profile of users who work at B, effectively making everyone from B eligible to see ads targeted at A, which may not be optimal for either users or advertisers. Therefore, we introduce a personalization scheme to rerank each potentially expandabe entity with regard to a given user. We achieve the personalization by employing a learned propensity model to score user-entity pairs. For each user and each entity type $x \in X$, we select the top k_x results from the available Similar-X results.

Taking companies as an example, to build the user-company propensity model we first extract features for users and companies in the same way as described in Section 4.1.1. We gather training examples from historical user-company intractions, for example, a user following a company as a positive example and un-following as negative. A logistic regression model is then trained from these examples.

4.1.4 *Similar-Profiles*

Similar-Profiles is the pinnacle of the Similar-X family of algorithms, with a problem size the square of the number of LinkedIn users (more than 400 million and growing).

Given the large size of the problem, we employ a Locality Sensitive Hashing (LSH) technique, named Arcos [5], to assist in finding members with high cosine similarity. Each member is mapped to one of 2^n clusters, where n is chosen to make our nearest neighbor search manageable. This cluster is built into the member index; this speeds up the subsequent nearest neighbor search because we can restrict our search to members in the same cluster. A member's cluster is specified by n bits, where each bit is determined by the output of a particular hash function. To

Type	Field	Term Values
n-gram/phrase	headline	Internet, professional, Social Network
	description	connection, productive, Talent Solution
standardized	industry	Internet
	type	public company
	company size	5001-10,000 employees
derived	skills	Software Engineering, Management, Marketing
	interests	professional identity, jobs, software development
proximities	view-browsemap	Facebook, Twitter, Pinterest
	occupation-browsemap	Google, Yahoo, Facebook

Table 1: Example features extracted for LinkedIn as a company

obtain each hash function we first choose a random vector $\mathbf{r} \in \mathbb{R}^{|\mathcal{F}|}$ with each component drawn from a Gaussian distribution $\mathcal{N}(0,1)$. The hash function corresponding to the vector $\mathbf{r}$ is defined as $h_{\mathbf{r}}(\mathbf{u}) = sign(\mathbf{r} \cdot \mathbf{u})$, which effectively partitions the space into two half-spaces by a randomly chosen hyperplane. The probability of collision is $Pr_{\mathbf{r}}[h_{\mathbf{r}}(\mathbf{u}) = h_{\mathbf{r}}(\mathbf{v})] = 1 - \theta(\mathbf{u},\mathbf{v})/\pi$, where θ measures the angle between two vectors. It can be shown that $1 - \theta/\pi$ is closely related to the function $\cos(\theta)$. Thus, members with high cosine similarity are likely to be assigned to the same cluster.

4.2 A Note on Implementation

As mentioned earlier, the computation of Similar-X and member-entity propensity is carried out by treating a source entity as a query and performing nearest neighbor search against an index of target documents. The search takes a model configuration that specifies the coefficients ($\mathbf{w}$ in Equation 1) used in the entity similarity function. We implement the feature extraction, indexing, and search process on Hadoop. Indexing is based on Lucene with many features built in house, such as real-time indexing, faceting, etc.

For campaign-agnostic expansion, we use faceted search to achieve personalized Similar-X reranking based on member-entity propensity score, in which case the member profile in the VSM representation acts as a query against the entity index, with the pool of entities to rank being a facet in the search.

For campaign-aware expansion, we first search, for each member in the original targeted audience, for the top k_p similar members using Similar-Profiles. The found members are then considered candidates to be included in the campaign's expanded audience. We set the number of expanded campaigns for each member to be less than a threshold to prevent over-competition on a single member and to control scalability (longer lists incur non-trivial inter-process communication cost). To achieve this we derive a heuristical member-campaign fitness F between a member m and a campaign c, as shown in Equation 2.

$$F(m,c) = \frac{\sum_{m' \in T(c)} S(m,m')}{\sqrt{|T(c)|}}, \tag{2}$$

where $T(c)$ denotes the original targeted audience for the campaign c, and $S(m,m')$ is the Similar-Profiles score (see Equation 1). The intuition for this equation is that the more similar members there are in the targeted audience to an untargeted member, the more fit the untargeted member is to be included in the expanded audience. To make the fitness comparable across campaigns we have to account for the individual campaign characteristics. The numerator in the summation is positively correlated with the size of the targeted audience, hence we normalize away the size in the denominator. We empirically find that adding a square root damping to make the normalization penalize large audiences less works the best in practice.

4.3 Other Considerations

4.3.1 Campaign Selection

Not all campaigns would benefit from Audience Expansion equally. For example, if an advertiser has only a limited budget (e.g., only enough to buy a few clicks in a day), it makes sense to have them prioritize only auctions involving the exact audience, since the value of this audience is explicitly known. As another example, if an advertiser targets a very broad audience (e.g., everyone in the US), then expanding this audience is likely unnecessary, and there may not even be a sensible expansion. Therefore we devise a campaign selection strategy for Audience Expansion in order to identify a subset of the opt-in campaigns that would benefit the most from Audience Expansion. The strategy involves a series of heuristic rules evaluating the suitability of Audience Expansion for a campaign. These rules are checked each time we perform the offline workflow, and for any campaigns that do not satisfy the rules, we do not perform Audience Expansion. In particular, these rules select campaigns that meet the following intuitive requirements:

- They must target a relatively specific audience using fine-grained attributes (e.g., not simply everyone with the same location, gender, or language).
- The size of the audience should not be extremely large, as measured by both the number of matching members and the number of requests matched each day.
- The budget should be enough to afford additional impressions from the expanded audience.

The logic for evaluating the budget is as follows. Each campaign may optionally set a daily budget, and once the budget is spent the campaign no longer participates in the remaining auctions that day. In addition, to prevent campaigns from spending their entire budget early in the day, the ad serving system implements a *pacing* algorithm that randomly removes the campaign from some auctions if it is predicted that the campaign is on pace to exceed its budget. Thus, in a given period a campaign may match M requests, but only participate in $N < M$ auctions due to pacing or having spent its budget. For a campaign that has not yet enabled Audience Expansion, if the ratio of the paced request $r = N/M$ is significantly less than 1 over the past week we can conclude that the campaign has no trouble spending its budget using its original targeting and would not benefit from expansion. For a campaign that has enabled expansion, however, we need to be more careful. We divide M into M_{exact} and $M_{expanded}$, the number of requests matched due to exact and expanded matching, respectively. We then check if $r = N/M_{exact}$ is significantly less than 1 over the past week. The reason we ignore expanded matches is that if a campaign is only able to hit its budget due to expansion, we want to continue to perform expansion, rather than oscillate between turning expansion on and off.

4.3.2 Post-Expansion Filters

After the expanded audience is generated offline, we also apply additional filtering to make sure we do not include any audience that is negatively targeted by the advertiser. We also guarantee certain targeting attributes are not violated in the expanded audience, such as location and gender. The rationale is that attributes such as location and gender are highly specific to a marketing campaign, and if they are specified, we view them as stronger and more exclusive preferences than other targeting attributes (e.g., skill or title).

In addition, as an extra measure to protect advertisers from increased costs due to Audience Expansion, we remove the most expensive members from the expanded audiences. Empirically, the more information we know about a user, the more targetable the user is, resulting in higher competition and cost. Given this intuition, we fit a regression model to predict the bid distribution of a user based on his/her targeting attributes, where the response variable is the log bid, and the explanatory variables are the member's targeting attributes in X:

$$Y = \log Bid = X\beta + \epsilon, \epsilon \sim \mathcal{N}(0, \sigma^2).$$

After we fit the linear regression with coefficient β^*, we estimate the mean log bid μ for member i as $\mu_i = x_i\beta^*$. Given this, we can rank order an expanded audience by μ and remove the top $p\%$ most expensive members.

4.3.3 Online/Offline Sync

Campaign-aware expansion is an offline process that runs multiple times per day and takes a snapshot of our production database (including campaign definitions) as input. If an advertiser updates a campaign's targeting after the snapshot is taken, the expanded audience generated may not be appropriate for that campaign, at least until the next time the expansion process is run. To mitigate the potential descrepancy, we use a mechanism to achieve online/offline synchronization. Specifically, the offline process generates a timestamp along with each output record indicating the time when the input snapshot was taken. Meanwhile, the online serving application maintains a cache of campaign change timestamps. Whenever serving receives an offline-generated member-campaign pair for expansion, it checks the two timestamps, and invalidates the offline result if the offline timestamp predates the online.

5. EXPERIMENTS

5.1 Parameter Setting

Given the many components and algorithms involved in the Audience Expansion system, there are a large number of hyper-parameters to tune. We list a summary of the major parameters in Table 2.

Component	Algorithm	Parameter	Note
campaign-agnostic	personalized Similar-X	$\{k_x : \forall x \in X\}$	top-k_x elements to include from each Similar-X
campaign-aware	Similar-Profiles	k_p	top-k_p elements to include from Similar-Profiles
	campaign selection	t	threshold size of campaign exact audience
		r	ratio of paced requests
	post-expansion filter	p	percentage of most expensive members to remove

Table 2: Summary of parameters in the Audience Expansion system.

For some parameters there is a tradeoff between short term gain and long term platform health. For example, with a larger $\{k_x\}$ we would obtain a larger expansion rate, resulting in increased auction competition, but with potential harm to user experience and advertiser ROI due to the increased possibility of including irrelevant results. Therefore, we conducted many pilot A/B tests on small fractions of members to determine the hyper-parameters, carefully balancing the positive and negative outcomes produced by the system. For example, we arrived at a conservative choice of $\{k_x\}$ for Similar-X algorithms in campaign-agnostic expansion, whereas we chose a larger k_s for Similar-Profiles in campaign-aware expansion. Similarly, we tuned the post-expansion filter threshold p until the increase in campaigns' CPC due to expansion was held to an acceptable level.

5.2 Similar-Profiles in Campaign-Aware Expansion

To evaluate the performance of Similar-Profiles in campaign-aware expansion, we want to compare the quality of expanded audiences with the original targeted audiences. To accurately predict how an advertiser would value individual members in the expanded audience is a challenging task. Instead, we come up with a metric based on connection density to measure how uniform an audience is. The intuition is that the more similar two members are to one another, the more likely they are to connect on LinkedIn. Advertisers are usually interested in members with shared characteristics, therefore the targeted audiences generally have a higher-than-average connection density. If we treat the connection graph for a given audience as an undirected simple graph, then the density is defined as:

$$D = \frac{2|C|}{|M|(|M|-1)},$$

where $|C|$ is the number of connections, and $|M|$ is the number of members in the audience.

In this experiment, we randomly sampled 200 campaigns with campaign-aware expansion enabled. We are interested in two quantities for each campaign: first, the expansion ratio, i.e., the size of the expanded audience over that of the exact audience; second, the density ratio, i.e., the density of the expanded audience over that of the exact audience.

For comparison we also carry out a baseline test by expanding campaigns to a random subset of all members who have actively intracted with ads in a one-month window. We call this method *Active Clickers*-based expansion. We make sure for each campaign that the size of the expanded audience generated by Active Clickers (AC-audience hereafter for simplicity) is roughly the same as that by Similar-Profiles (SP-audience).

To learn the distributions of density ratios for these two methods and how they vary with regard to the expansion ratio, we plot the density ratio against the expansion ratio in Figure 2. From the figure we can see that the SP-audience is on average as dense as the corresponding exact audience (density ratio close to 0 on the log scale). On the other hand, the AC-audience is much more loosely connected. Interestingly, when the expansion ratio is low the SP-audience is even denser than the exact audience.

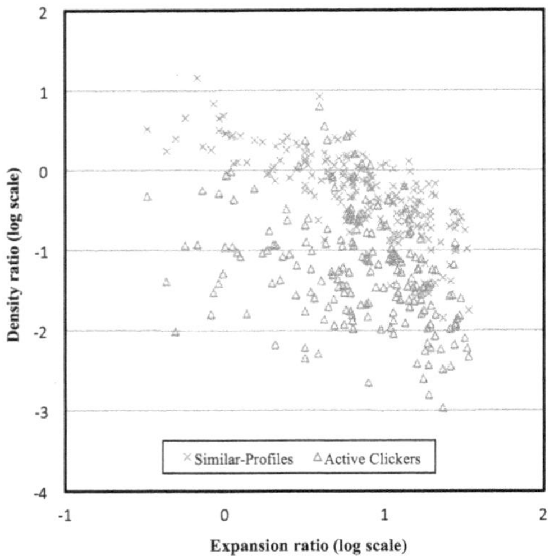

Figure 2: Network density ratio against expansion ratio for Similar-Profiles and Active Clickers.

5.3 Online A/B Test

To test the performance of our Audience Expansion implementations, we ran an experiment for two weeks on live traffic. Traffic was split by user ID across four treatments: control (no expansion, 5% of traffic), campaign-agnostic (5%), campaign-aware (10%), and hybrid (70%). We allocated a large share of traffic to the hybrid treatment because it had performed well in previous smaller tests. The remaining 10% of traffic was allocated to other treatments not described in this paper. We evaluated the results by comparing the following metrics:

- **Impressions:** As previously described, for each request we generate a ranked list of ads to show the user and fill the available ad slots in this order, generating impressions. If too few advertisers target the user, we may not always be able to generate an impression at every opportunity. Thus, we are interested in the number of impressions generated per request, and we hope that expansion would increase this number.
- **Reaches:** We define a reach as a (user, advertiser, date) tuple where the user saw an ad from the advertiser on that date. If the user sees multiple ads from the advertiser on that date, it is unly counted as one reach. By expanding advertisers' targeting, we hope to increase the number of reaches, meaning the average user sees ads from more distinct advertisers and the average advertiser shows ads to more distinct users.
- **Matches:** For each request, we record the number of advertisers whose targeting matches. Clearly, Audience Expansion should increase this number. Having more ads to choose from for a request means that we can hopefully show more relevant ads to the user.
- **Revenue:** Audience Expansion can increase revenue through three means. First, there are impressions where the winning advertiser targeted the user due to audience expansion and where there would othersiwe have been no impression. These new impressions are the ones responsible for increasing the *impressions* metric. Second, there are impressions where the winner targeted the user due to audience expansion and displaced another advertiser by bidding higher. Third, as this is a second-price auction, even if an advertiser targeting the user due to audience expansion does not win the auction, it may place second and increase the cost paid by the winner.
- **Value:** While revenue is naturally important to LinkedIn, a better measure of how well we are meeting the needs of advertisers is their total value (also known as social welfare). We make the assumption, common to second-price auctions, that a bidder's value is equal to its bid. By summing the bid for each impression (counting CPC bids only when the ad is clicked), we obtain the total value. Delivering more value to advertisers is the ultimate goal of audience expansion.
- **CTR (Clickthrough Rate):** Audience Expansion aims to find new users who will be as interested in an advertisement as the originally targeted users. Thus, we hope to see little if any decrease in CTR due to expansion.
- **CPC (Cost per Click):** An advertiser would naturally prefer not to pay more per click when its audience is expanded.
- **Dwell Time:** In addition to clicking at a similar rate, we hope that expanded users will also be similarly interested in the advertiser's landing page. Dwell time is our estimate of the amount of time a user spends on the landing page (capped at 5 minutes), and we hope to see the average dwell time remain steady when audience expansion is applied.

Table 3 shows the relative change in each metric for each expansion method when compared to the control. Due to the proprietary nature of this data, we do not report absolute numbers. Numbers in bold represent statistically significant differences ($p < 0.05$) from the control. (We use a chi-square test of equal proportions for CTR and a Wilcoxon rank sum test for the other metrics. We exclude reaches as it involves counting globally distinct tuples, and thus does not have a clear meaning at the per-request level.)

As expected, all expansion methods increase impressions, reaches, matches, revenue, and value. Campaign-aware expansion produces much larger increases than campaign-agnostic expansion, while combining the two provides some increase beyond campaign-aware expansion alone. It is reassuring that revenue and value show increases of similar magnitude, since this implies that the additional spending by advertisers who enable expansion offers a similar return on investment.

Treatment	Impressions	Reaches	Matches	Revenue	Value	CTR	CPC	Dwell Time
campaign-agnostic	**+1.31%**	+1.35%	**+1.27%**	**+3.08%**	**+3.09%**	**+1.07%**	**+0.67%**	+1.30%
campaign-aware	**+9.76%**	+9.78%	**+11.54%**	**+15.49%**	**+13.98%**	**-1.15%**	**+6.45%**	+0.36%
hybrid	**+10.36%**	+10.40%	**+12.86%**	**+17.47%**	**+15.84%**	-0.44%	**+6.92%**	+0.11%

Table 3: Relative changes in metrics compared to control. Statistically significant differences are in bold.

Treatment	Impressions	Reaches	Revenue	Value	Adj. CTR	Adj. CPC	Adj. Dwell Time
campaign-agnostic	**+7.67%**	+7.77%	**+9.33%**	**+9.72%**	-0.79%	+0.46%	+2.95%
campaign-aware	**+93.85%**	+94.29%	**+105.97%**	**+100.80%**	**-8.56%**	**+6.00%**	-0.39%
hybrid	**+96.97%**	+97.47%	**+111.60%**	**+106.00%**	**-8.08%**	**+6.86%**	-0.44%

Table 4: Relative changes in metrics when only considering impressions won by expansion-enabled campaigns.

CTR and dwell time show only small changes, as hoped, providing evidence that expansion does not hurt the relevance of the advertisements we are showing to users. CPC does increase, but further analysis shows the increase is roughly the same for advertisers who do and do not enable expansion. As a result, we can conclude that the increase is a result of more competitive auctions, and not simply because expansion causes advertisers to target more expensive users.

In addition to looking at global metrics, we can specifically examine how campaigns that enable expansion are affected by computing the same metrics using only the impressions of these campaigns. Table 4 shows the relative changes in metrics (compared to the control) when considering only the impressions of campaigns that did not disable expansion at any time during the two weeks of the experiment. Again, statistically significant changes are shown in bold. Here we use the Mantel-Haenszel adjustment for CTR, CPC, and dwell time metrics, using campaigns as strata. These metrics can differ greatly from one campaign to another, and this adjustment corrects for the different distributions over campaigns in each treatment to give a clearer picture of the change a typical campaign would see. Statistical significance for these metrics is also measured with the appropriate stratified test (Mantel-Haenszel for CTR and stratified Wilcoxon for CPC and dwell time). We omit the matches metric as it is less meaningful when considering a subset of impressions.

From Table 4 we can see that impressions for expansion-enabled campaigns nearly double under the campaign-aware or hybrid treatment, with similarly large increases for reaches, revenue, and value. As before, the change in value roughly keeps up with the change in revenue. Dwell time again shows no statistically significant change. As discussed previously, the increase in CPC for expansion essentially matches the global increase due to increased competition. The relative drop in CTR for the campaign-aware and hybrid treatments is around 8%. Although we would ideally not see any difference in CTR, this drop is not overly large, as users reached through expanded targeting are still clicking on ads at a reasonable rate. Still, improving CTR is the one obvious area for improvement, and we will later present some ideas as part of our future work. It is interesting to note that CTR remains nearly unchanged globally; the explanation is that while a user shown an impression due to expansion may be somewhat less likely to click than the campaign's originally-targeted users, the user is not less likely to click on this impression than on the impression that would otherwise have been shown without expansion.

Overall, our live traffic experiment confirms that our approaches to audience expansion (particularly the campaign-aware and hybrid approaches) are able to greatly increase the reach of campaigns while maintaining reasonable costs and user engagement levels.

Encouraged by the result, we gradually ramped the Audience Expansion system to a full enablement with the hybrid approach being the dominant strategy. The impact of the system to the marketplace has been significant, as can be seen from the change over time in desktop coverage in Figure 3. Coverage is defined as the number of delivered impressions as a percentage of the number of available impressions, which measures how effective the ads inventory is utilized. It is evident that the coverage increases in response to the Audience Expansion ramp-up.

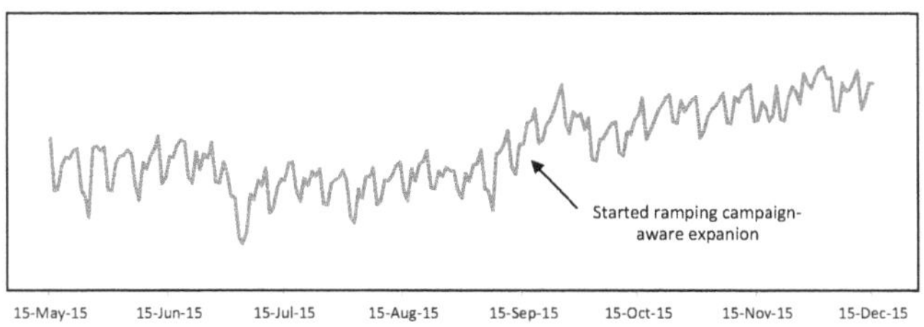

Figure 3: Sponsored Updates coverage on desktop.

5.4 User Similarity and CTR

As described in Section 4.2, campaign-aware expansion computes a similarity score for each user in the expanded audience by summing the Similar-Profile score between that user and all users in the original audience. To determine whether similarity to the original audience is a reasonable predictor of user interest, we can investigate the relationship between this score and clickthrough rates. For each impression shown to a user in a campaign's expanded audience, we look up the similarity score given to that user and then compute the quantile of this score among all of this campaign's impressions. Then, we consider only impressions where the quantile exceeds some threshold and determine the CTR for this subset of expanded impressions. In other words, we can estimate what the CTR of all expanded impressions in our live experiment would have been if, for each campaign, we had only expanded to users with scores above a given quantile for that campaign. Note that this is only possible for impressions where the user was targeted due to campaign-

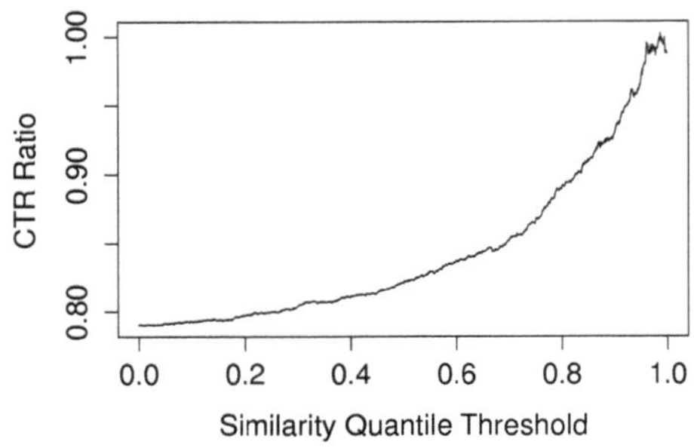

Figure 4: Relative CTR of expanded impressions, thresholded by per-campaign similarity quantile

aware expansion, as campaign-agnostic expansion does not produce a similarity score.

Figure 4 shows the relative CTR (compared to the global CTR of the control treatment) for different quantile thresholds. For a threshold of zero, meaning that all expanded impressions are included, we see a ratio of 0.79. Thus a typical expanded impression would be clicked 79% as often as an impression due to the original targeting. As the threshold increases, the CTR ratio increases, until at thresholds above 0.95 we see a CTR ratio near 1. This means that if we had only expanded each campaign to the most promising 5% of new users, we would likely have seen no significant drop in overall CTR. The clear relationship between similarity score and CTR demonstrates that our similarity scores are indeed useful for identifying promising users for expansion. In addition, if in the future we wish to tune the degree of expansion for individual campaigns, using similarity score thresholds would be a sound approach.

6. CONCLUSION AND FUTURE WORK

We present the Audience Expansion system as a way to optimize ads targeting on social network platforms. We describe two methods for Audience Expansion: campaign-agnostic user attribute expansion, and campaign-aware lookalike expansion. We also demonstrate that due to their complementary nature, we can create a hybrid method to include both approaches, combining the strengths and offsetting the weakness of each. We show the effectiveness of the proposed methods through the large-scale experiment at LinkedIn. Our results indicate significant benefits for both advertisers and LinkedIn achieved by a more accessible and efficient market ecosystem resulted from Audience Expansion.

In future work, we plan to extend the method for campaign-aware expansion to include more behavior-based signals (e.g., ad clicks and social actions). We would like to explore more advanced quality control of the expanded audience. We also want to allow advertisers to optionally include a seed audience, such as known converters, so that we can learn campaign-specific performance-based models.

7. REFERENCES

[1] W. Amaldoss, K. Jerath, and A. Sayedi. Keyword management costs and "broad match" in sponsored search advertising. *Marketing Science*, 2015.

[2] A. Bagherjeiran, A. Hatch, A. Ratnaparkhi, and R. Parekh. Large-scale customized models for advertisers. In *Proceedings of the 2010 IEEE International Conference on Data Mining Workshops*, ICDMW '10, pages 1029–1036. IEEE, 2010.

[3] A. Bindra, S. Pokuri, K. Uppala, and A. Teredesai. Distributed big advertiser data mining. In *Proceedings of the 2012 IEEE International Conference on Data Mining Workshops*, pages 914–914, Dec 2012.

[4] A. Broder, P. Ciccolo, E. Gabrilovich, V. Josifovski, D. Metzler, L. Riedel, and J. Yuan. Online expansion of rare queries for sponsored search. In *Proceedings of the 18th WWW*, pages 511–520. ACM, 2009.

[5] M. S. Charikar. Similarity estimation techniques from rounding algorithms. In *Proceedings of the Thiry-fourth Annual ACM Symposium on Theory of Computing*, STOC '02, pages 380–388. ACM, 2002.

[6] W. Chen, D. He, T.-Y. Liu, T. Qin, Y. Tao, and L. Wang. Generalized second price auction with probabilistic broad match. In *Proceedings of the Fifteenth ACM Conference on Economics and Computation*, EC '14, pages 39–56. ACM, 2014.

[7] P. Dhangwatnotai. Multi-keyword sponsored search. In *Proceedings of the 12th ACM Conference on Electronic Commerce*, EC '11, pages 91–100. ACM, 2011.

[8] E. Even Dar, V. S. Mirrokni, S. Muthukrishnan, Y. Mansour, and U. Nadav. Bid optimization for broad match ad auctions. In *Proceedings of the 18th WWW*, pages 231–240. ACM, 2009.

[9] S. Gupta, M. Bilenko, and M. Richardson. Catching the drift: Learning broad matches from clickthrough data. In *Proceedings of the 15th ACM SIGKDD International Conference on Knowledge Discovery and Data Mining*, KDD '09, pages 1165–1174. ACM, 2009.

[10] B. Kanagal, A. Ahmed, S. Pandey, V. Josifovski, L. Garcia-Pueyo, and J. Yuan. Focused matrix factorization for audience selection in display advertising. In *29th ICDE*, pages 386–397, April 2013.

[11] A. Mangalampalli, A. Ratnaparkhi, A. O. Hatch, A. Bagherjeiran, R. Parekh, and V. Pudi. A feature-pair-based associative classification approach to look-alike modeling for conversion-oriented user-targeting in tail campaigns. In *Proceedings of the 20th WWW*, pages 85–86. ACM, 2011.

[12] S. Pandey, M. Aly, A. Bagherjeiran, A. Hatch, P. Ciccolo, A. Ratnaparkhi, and M. Zinkevich. Learning to target: What works for behavioral targeting. In *Proceedings of the 20th CIKM*, pages 1805–1814, New York, NY, USA, 2011. ACM.

[13] A. Ramesh, A. Teredesai, A. Bindra, S. Pokuri, and K. Uppala. Audience segment expansion using distributed in-database k-means clustering. In *Proceedings of the Seventh International Workshop on Data Mining for Online Advertising*, ADKDD '13, pages 5:1–5:9. ACM, 2013.

[14] J. Shen, S. C. Geyik, and A. Dasdan. Effective audience extension in online advertising. In *Proceedings of the 21th ACM SIGKDD International Conference on Knowledge Discovery and Data Mining*, KDD '15, pages 2099–2108. ACM, 2015.

[15] J. Yan, N. Liu, G. Wang, W. Zhang, Y. Jiang, and Z. Chen. How much can behavioral targeting help online advertising? In *Proceedings of the 18th International Conference on World Wide Web*, WWW '09, pages 261–270. ACM, 2009.

From Online Behaviors to Offline Retailing

Ping Luo[♯], Su Yan[♯♭], Zhiqiang Liu[§], Zhiyong Shen[§], Shengwen Yang[§], Qing He[♯]
[♯]Key Lab of Intelligent Information Processing of Chinese Academy of Sciences
Institute of Computing Technology, CAS, Beijing, China.
[♭]University of Chinese Academy of Sciences, Beijing, China.
[§]Baidu, Inc., Beijing, China.
luop@ict.ac.cn, shenzhiyong@baidu.com

ABSTRACT

To combat the ease of online shopping in pajamas, offline mall owners focus increasingly on driving satisfaction and improving retention by identifying customers' preferences. However, most of these studies are based on customers' offline consuming history only. Benefiting from the internet, we can also get customers' online behaviors, such as the search logs, web browsing logs, online shopping logs, and so on. Might these seemingly irrelevant information from two different modalities (i.e. online and offline) be somehow interrelated? How can we make use of the online behaviors and offline actions jointly to promote recommendation for offline retailing?

In this study, we formulate this task as a cross-modality recommendation problem, and present its solution via a proposed probabilistic graphical model, called *Online-to-Offline Topic Modeling* (O2OTM). Specifically, this method explicitly models the relationships between online and offline topics so that the likelihood of both online and offline behaviors is maximized. Then, the recommendation is made only based on the pairs of online and offline topics, denoted by (t, l), with high values of *lift*, such that the existence of the online topic t greatly increases the response on the corresponding offline topic l compared with the average response for the population without the online topic t. Furthermore, we evaluate this solution in both live and retrospect experiments. The real-world deployment of this model for the anniversary promotion campaign of a famous shopping mall in Beijing shows that our approach increases the occurred customer purchases per promotion message by 29.75% compared with the baseline. Also, our model finds some interesting interpretable relationships between the online search topics and offline brand topics.

Keywords

Brands recommendation, Topic modeling, Recommendation explanation

KDD '16, August 13-17, 2016, San Francisco, CA, USA

DOI: http://dx.doi.org/10.1145/2939672.2939683

1. INTRODUCTION

Recommendation systems (RS) [ ] have been popular for decades, improving the quality of our daily lives by facilitating the item selections from a large set of candidates. Here, we focus on the recommendation systems for *offline retailing*. Although *online shopping* has the tendency of booming development, offline retailing still covers 92% and 90% of the US and China retailing market in 2014 [,], respectively. Thus, small improvements on offline retailing might draw great benefits. Meanwhile, with the penetration of IT systems into this traditional sector, the customers' offline consumption logs can be recorded to better undersatnd customers' interests for driving satisfaction and improving retention. However, previous studies mostly consider the behaviors from offline and online separately [,].

In this paper, we study the online and offline activities from a joint perspective. Here, online behaviors consist of all the activities on Internet, such as web browsing, web searching, online video watching, online music listening, and online shopping etc, while offline behaviors include all the activities in real lives, such as shopping in a mall, traveling, dinning out, watching films etc. Figure 1 shows an example of the data we have from these two modalities. For a small fraction of users, we might know their activities on both online and offline sides. On the online side, we know what they searched in a search engine, what videos they watched, and what items they bought online. On the offline side, we know what brands they consumed in an offline shopping mall. With these data, we might ask could the videos users watch on Youtube interpret the tour sites they select for travelling? Could the news users read on internet be related with the books they borrow in a library? If we connect the online and offline behaviors together, could these two modalities of data fire the chemical reactions for more meaningful recommendation?

This study pioneers towards this direction. As a case study, here we consider the online search logs as the online behaviors, and the offline shopping history as the offline behaviors (note that the proposed model can be applied to any type of online and offline activities). Originally, these two sets of data are owned by Internet companies and local malls, separately. We will show how profitable if Internet companies with online data and local retailers with offline data cooperate for a win-win situation (with the consent from users).

Our basic assumption in this study is that customers' online behaviors could reflect their interests, which in turn influence their offline behaviors. From the real-world data, we

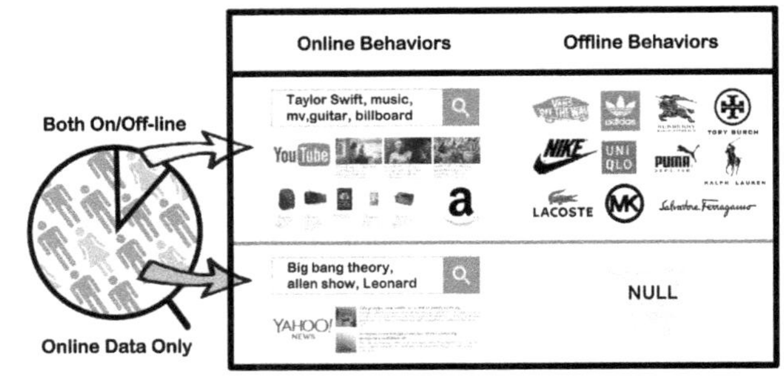

Figure 1: Offline behaviors and online behaviors.

Figure 2: An in-store poster for *EVISU*

Word	Description
火影	*Naruto*, a Japanese anime
海贼王	*One Piece*, Japanese manga series
大学	campus
动漫	animations
lol	*League of Legends*, online battle arena game
ios	iphone operating system
ps4	a video game console from Sony Entertainment

Table 1: The search keywords of EVISU customers

do find some interesting examples which demonstrate that users' search logs are associated with their offline shopping activities (even although people might not search on Internet the exact items they buy offline). Take a clothing brand *EVISU* as an example. Readers can perceive the style of this clothing brand by its in-store advertisement poster, shown in Figure 2. Also, Table 1 shows some key query words issued by the customers of this brand. It clearly demonstrates that people who buy *EVISU* are interested in Japanese animations, computer games, indicating that they are the fashionable new generation. This is consistent with the brand spirit of *EVISU*.

With this assumption, if the relationship between online and offline behaviors can be automatically discovered, it will greatly benefit the mall owners in both offline and online scenarios. A typical offline application is for the sales campaign of a shopping mall. To increase sales revenue, once or twice a year the mall carries out the promotion events by sending coupons to the targeted customers. So, which coupon should be sent to a given user? Setting aside the scale of the discount, it is reasonable to assume that the more a user like a brand the more likely she will use its coupons. Previously, this recommendation for offline coupons is based on users' offline shopping history only. With the support of online behaviors, more accurate recommendation is expected to increase the revenue significantly. This is also validated by the live experiment conducted in a famous shopping center in Beijing (detailed in Section 5).

For the online apllication, with the connection between online and offline behaviors, the local retailers might conduct more effective online advertising to the target customers for a brand. For example, if we know that people who buy *EVISU* often watch Japanese animations, we can directly put the coupons of *EVISU* just before they watch the videos. Also, the representative words of the related topics are the important key words the brand manager should bid for the paid ads shown in the search results.

Motivated by these applications, here we propose the probabilistic graphic model to depict the online and offline behaviors jointly with the goal for offline retailing recommendation. Compared with the previous studies on RS, this task imposes us some new challenges.

- Multiple modalities and modality missing. The online and offline activities actually form the two modalities of user behaviors. Previous studies take use of only one modality (online or offline) for recommendation, but neglect the other part. Additionally, as shown in Figure 1, only a small fraction of users have both the online and offline activities. For the left large amount of users who are potential customers of a mall (living around the mall), they might only leave some online tracks, however, might not consume in the mall before. It means that their offline modality is missing. Thus, we need to transform these online tracks into the intentions and preferences for offline consumption.
- Interpretability. Previous recommendation methods, like matrix factorization [ ], are usually less interpretable. In their methods, since users and items are mapped to the latent vectors, it is hard to explain what each dimension represents. However, for mall owners it will be much more acceptable if the reasons of retail recommendations are provided. Additionally, for the applications of online advertising we need to know the exact key words which are predictive to the consumption of a certain brand. In this study, the online tracks, especially the queries users search, provide us the unique opportunity for the explanation of recommendation. Thus, we need to not only make the recommendations, but also explicitly model the relationships between the online and offline behaviors such that the offline recommendations can be explained by the online search words. Later, we will give more meaningful examples to show the interpretability of our model.
- Predictive vs. unpredictive features. It is also worth emphasizing that not all the online behaviors are predictive to offline activities. For example, most people search the latest news from the search engine. Intuitively, the key words about the news, e.g., the local place names and the people names in breaking news, might not be predictive or causally related to any offline consumptions. Thus, the proposed model needs to automatically distinguish predictive online features from the unpredictive ones so that the recommendation is made only based on the predictive online features.

For past decades, many researches have been conducted for recommendation. The detailed discussion on these related works on recommendation techniques will be presented in Section 7. Here, we argue that although previous studies might address some of the challenges separately there still do not exist a model to tackle them all, especially for the issues of interpretability and predictive features. In this paper, we assume that both online and offline behaviors can be grouped into some semantically related topics. Then, we develop the *lift*-based recommendation method, where the recommendation is made only based on the pairs of online and offline topics, denoted by (t, l), with high values of *lift*, such that the existence of the online topic t greatly increases the response on the corresponding offline topic l compared with the average response of the population without the online topic t. To estimate these lift values, we propose a probabilistic graphic model, called *Online to Offline Topic Model* (O2OTM), to explicitly build the relationships between online and offline topics so that the likelihood to generate all the online and offline behaviors is maximized. We argue that this lift-based recommendation method will be more practically useful for the live recommendation scenarios.

Finally, we evaluate our model by both retrospect and live experiments to show its superiority over several baselines, and also give more examples to show its interpretability. For the live evaluation, we deployed our method into a sales campaign in a famous shopping center in Beijing. We find that for each promotion message our model brings 29.75% more purchases than the random method, and 12.5% revenue more than the method with the offline behaviors only. Therefore, we argue that by combining online and offline behaviors our solution has great potential of business impact for offline retailing.

2. PROBLEM FORMULATION

Here, we recommend brands of offline retailing to customers with the support of their online and offline behaviors. In this section, we describe the data we have and then formulate the problem. All the mathematical symbols are described in Table 2.

In each recommending task, users and items are two indispensable elements. For our problem, users are all the potential customers of a shopping mall while items are the product brands sold in the mall. $\mathcal{B}$ is the set of all the brands, and $\mathcal{U}$ is the set of all the customers. Meanwhile, we might know the search queries issued by these customers in a popular search engine. $\mathcal{V}$ is the vocabulary set of all the search words.

For each customer $u \in \mathcal{U}$, its offline behaviors are represented by $\mathcal{B}_u = \langle b_{u,i} | b_{u,i} \in \mathcal{B} \rangle$, where $b_{u,i}$ is the i-th brand token bought by user u. Meanwhile, the customer's online behaviors are represented by $\mathcal{W}_u = \langle w_{u,j} | w_{u,j} \in \mathcal{V} \rangle$ where $w_{u,j}$ is the j-th word token searched by user u. In other words, both the online and offline behaviors are represented in the bag-of-words manner in this study. Note also that $\mathcal{B}_u$ or $\mathcal{W}_u$ can be an empty set. Based on all these data, we focus on the recommendation of brands. Specifically, we give a ranking of the brands in $\mathcal{B}$ for each user u.

3. ONLINE TO OFFLINE TOPIC MODEL

Before we detail the lift-based recommendation method, we propose the Online to Offline Topic Model (O2OTM), which models the relationships between online and offline topics explicitly based on the data corpus $\{\mathcal{W}_u, \mathcal{B}_u\}_1^U$ from both online and offline sides.

3.1 Modeling online and offline behaviors separately

First, the basic topic modeling method, LDA [ ], can be applied to model the online and offline behaviors separately. LDA is developed to modeling document content based upon

Symbol	Description
$\mathcal{B}$	the set of all the brands
$\mathcal{V}$	the vocabulary set of all the search words
$\mathcal{U}$	the customer set
U	the total number of customers
$\mathcal{B}_u$	the brands bought by customer u
$\mathcal{W}_u$	the words searched by customer u
$\mathcal{P}_u$	the brands which are not consumed by u
θ	distribution over online topics for customers
ϕ	distribution over search words for online topics
π	distribution over offline topics for online topics
φ	distribution over brands for offline topics
π	distribution over offline topics for online topics
$\alpha, \beta, \eta, \lambda$	Dirichlet prior
x, y	online topic variable
z	offline topic variable
w	word variable
b	brand variable
t	index for online topics
l	index for offline topics
v	index for search words
k	index for brands

Table 2: The symbols.

the idea that the probability distribution over words in a document can be expressed as a mixture of topics, where each topic is a probability distribution over words.

In this study, since both online and offline behaviors are represented in a bag-of-words model, we can consider each $\mathcal{W}_u$ or $\mathcal{B}_u$ as a document to form the online corpus $\{\mathcal{W}_u\}_1^U$ and offline corpus $\{\mathcal{B}_u\}_1^U$. Then, LDA can be applied to these two corpora to generate online topics (denoted by x) and offline topics (denoted by z), separately. Here, an online topic $p(w|x)$ is a probability distribution over search words w while an offline topic $p(b|z)$ is a probabilistic distribution over brands b. This method helps to group search words and product brands into semantic topics, and can be used to answer queries about similar online users in terms of search words and similar customers in terms of consumed brands. However, this method does not provide any information about the dependent relationships between the online and offline topics, thus cannot perform modality transformation from online behaviors to offline activities.

3.2 Modeling online and offline behaviors jointly

The proposed O2OTM model draws upon the strengths of probabilistic graphic methods to model the online and offline behaviors jointly by explicitly considering the probabilistic dependency between online and offline topics. As in the O2OTM model, each user u adopts the following probabilistic process to generate its online and offline behaviors, denoted by $(\mathcal{W}_u, \mathcal{B}_u)$. This process can be divided into two parts. First, for each search word $w \in \mathcal{W}_u$, an online topic x is chosen from a distribution over online topics specific to u (denoted by θ_u), and the word is generated from the chose online topic. Second, for each brand $b \in \mathcal{B}_u$, again an online topic y is chose from θ_u. Based on y, an offline topic z is chosen from π_y, which is a distribution over offline topics specific to y; and then the brand is generated from the chose offline topic.

The graphical model corresponding to this process in Figure 3. In this figure, the left part generates the online be-

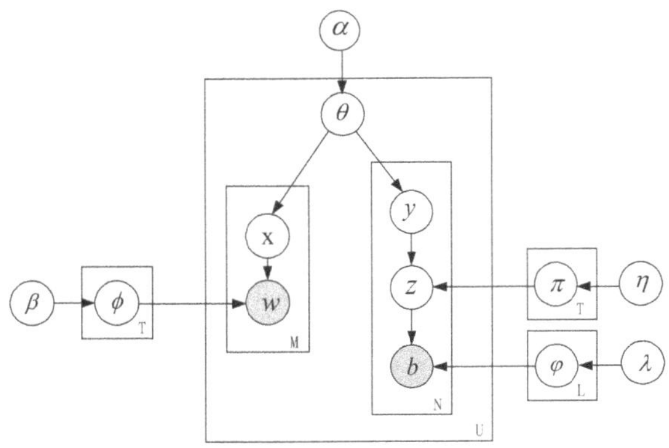

Figure 3: The graphical model of O2OTM

haviors while the right part generates the offline behaviors. In this model, each user u is associated with a distribution over online topics, θ_u (chosen from a symmetric $Dirichlet(\alpha)$ prior). The mixture weights corresponding to u are used to select an online topic x (or y). Then, based on x a search word is generated according to the distribution ϕ_x (drawn from a symmetric $Dirichlet(\beta)$ prior). Meanwhile, based on y an offline topic z is generated according to the distribution π_y (drawn from a symmetric $Dirichlet(\eta)$ prior), and a brand is generated according to the distribution φ_z (drawn from a symmetric $Dirichlet(\lambda)$ prior).

Here, both x and y represent online topics. We use these two different symbols to distinguish the online topics which generates the search words from the ones which generates the offline brands. Additionally, both x and y are generated from the same distribution θ_u. Thus, θ_u is dependent on both online and offline behaviors. It is also worth mentioning that the dependent relationship between online and offline topics is modeled in π. It can be used for online-to-offline modality transformation.

3.3 Gibbs sampling algorithm to O2OTM

In this study we use Gibbs sampling [ ] to estimate the parameters of O2OTM. By applying Gibbs sampling, we construct a Markov chain that converges to the posterior distribution on the latent variables. The transition between successive states of the Markov chain results from repeatedly drawing x, y, z from its distribution conditioned on all other variables, summing out the parameters using standard Dirichlet integrals. Specifically, we have the following three equations to update x, y, z.

First, we have

$$p(x_i = t|\vec{x}_{\neg i}, \vec{y}, \vec{z}, \vec{w}, \vec{b}) = p(x_i = t|\vec{x}_{\neg i}, \vec{y}, w_i = v)$$
$$\propto \frac{O^v_{t,\neg i} + \beta_v}{\sum_{v=1}^{V} O^v_{t,\neg i} + \beta_v} \cdot \frac{O^t_{u,\neg i} + \alpha_t}{\sum_{t=1}^{T} O^t_{u,\neg i} + \alpha_t}, \tag{1}$$

where $x_i = t$ represents the assignment of the i-th word token in the corpus to the t-th online topic, $w_i = v$ represents the observation that the i-th word token is the v-th one in the word lexicon, $\vec{x}_{\neg i}$ represents all assignments of online topics to the words, not including the i-th one. Additionally, $O^v_{t,\neg i}$ denotes the number of times that the v-th word being observed with the t-th online topic, not including the current instance. $O^t_{u,\neg i}$ denotes the number of times that the t-th online topic being observed in user u (who owns the search word w_i), not including the current instance. Here, the online topic x is assigned to each word token in the corpus.

Next, we have

$$p(y_j = t|\vec{y}_{\neg j}, \vec{x}, \vec{z}, \vec{w}, \vec{b}) = p(y_j = t|\vec{y}_{\neg j}, \vec{x}, z_j = l)$$
$$\propto \frac{O^l_{t,\neg j} + \eta_l}{\sum_{l=1}^{L} O^l_{t,\neg j} + \eta_l} \cdot \frac{O^t_{u,\neg j} + \alpha_t}{\sum_{t=1}^{T} O^t_{u,\neg j} + \alpha_t}, \tag{2}$$

where $y_j = t$ represents the assignment of the j-th brand token in the corpus to the t-th online topic, $z_j = l$ represents the observation that the l-th offline topic is assigned to the j-th brand token, $\vec{y}_{\neg j}$ represents all assignments of online topics to the brand tokens, not including the j-th one. Additionally, $O^l_{t,\neg j}$ denotes the number of times that the l-th offline topic being observed with the t-th online topic, not including the current instance. $O^t_{u,\neg j}$ denotes the number of times that the t-th online topic being observed in user u (who buys the brand b_j), not including the current instance. Here, the online topic y is assigned to each brand tokens in the corpus.

Finally, we have

$$p(z_j = l|\vec{z}_{\neg j}, \vec{x}, \vec{y}, \vec{w}, \vec{b}) = p(z_j = l|\vec{z}_{\neg j}, y_j = t, b_j = k)$$
$$\propto \frac{O^k_{l,\neg j} + \lambda_k}{\sum_{k=1}^{B} O^k_{l,\neg j} + \lambda_k} \cdot \frac{O^l_{t,\neg j} + \eta_l}{\sum_{l=1}^{L} O^l_{t,\neg j} + \eta_l} \tag{3}$$

where $z_j = l$ represents the assignment of the j-th brand token to the l-th offline topic, $b_j = k$ represents the observation that the j-th brand token is the k-th brand in the brand lexicon, $y_j = t$ represents the observation that the j-th brand token is assigned to the t-th online topic, $\vec{z}_{\neg j}$ represents all assignments of offline topics to the brand tokens, not including the j-th one. Additionally, $O^k_{l,\neg j}$ denotes the number of times that the l-th offline topic being observed with the k-th brand, not including the current instance. $O^l_{t,\neg j}$ denotes the number of times that the t-th online topic being observed with the l-th offline topic. Here, the offline topic z is assigned to each brand token in the corpus.

After the Markov chain converges, the model parameters can be estimated via

$$\theta_{ut} = \frac{O^t_u + \alpha_t}{\sum_{t=1}^{T} O^t_u + \alpha_t} \tag{4}$$

$$\phi_{tv} = \frac{O^v_t + \beta_v}{\sum_{v=1}^{V} O^v_t + \beta_v} \tag{5}$$

$$\pi_{tl} = \frac{O^l_t + \eta_l}{\sum_{l=1}^{L} O^l_t + \eta_l} \tag{6}$$

$$\varphi_{lk} = \frac{O^k_l + \lambda_k}{\sum_{k=1}^{B} O^k_l + \lambda_k} \tag{7}$$

Here, T, L are the numbers of online and offline topics, respectively. V, B are the sizes of the word vocabulary and brand lexicon.

In this study, we do not estimate the hyperparameters $\alpha, \beta, \eta, \lambda$. Instead, these smoothing parameters are fixed at 0.05, 0.01, 0.01, 0.01, respectively. The algorithm begins by assigning search words to random online topics, and assigning offline brands to random online and offline topics. Each iteration of the algorithm involves applying Equ. (1),(2),(3), to every word token and brand token in the corpus. This sampling process performs at least 2000 rounds until convergence.

3.4 Model Inference

After we learn all the parameters θ, π, φ, we can infer the relationship between a brand and an online topic. Specifically, for an online topic $y = t$ and an offline brand $b = k$, we have

$$\begin{aligned} p(y=t|b=k) &= \sum_{l=1}^{L} p(y=t|z=l)p(z=l|b=k) \\ &\propto \sum_{l=1}^{L} p(y=t)\pi_{tl}\varphi_{lk} \end{aligned} \tag{8}$$

(a) The in-store poster for *Teenie Weenie*

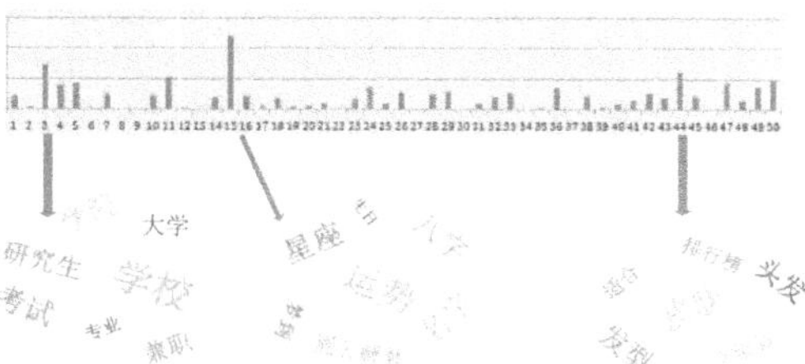

(b) The typical words of the 3 highly-related online topics

Figure 4: The brand *Teenie Weenie* and its related search words. The description of words is listed in Table 3.

Topic #	Word	Description
3	学校	campus
3	学院	school
3	大学	university
3	研究生	graduate students
3	兼职	part-time job
3	专业	majors in school
15	运势	horoscope
15	星座	12 zodiac signs
15	八字	Chinese horoscope according to the birthday
15	名字	name
15	周公解梦	understanding the dreams
44	皮肤	skin
44	头发	hair
44	发型	hair style
44	化妆品	cosmetics
44	排行榜	top charts

Table 3: English translation of words in Figure 4

With this derivation, here we show you an example of the relationship between a brand and online topics. *TEENIE WEENIE* is a Korean brand designed for young girls from 15 to 25 year-old. It is famous for its school-style dress like the poster in Figure 4(a). Figure 4(b) shows the distribution over online topics for this brand, and the representative words for the top 3 topics are also shown with English translation in Table 3. The first topic is mainly about campus life, which indicates that the brand is somehow related to college students. The second topic is about horoscope. Many people especially young women are interested in their horoscopes, which could forecast the love, fortune and career etc. The third topic is about hair style and cosmetics, which shows the brand is related to a group of female people who cares about their appearance. These three topics clearly show that the customers of *TEENIE WEENIE* are a group of young girls, especially college girls, who care about their appearance and long for love and good future. We argue that this kind of relationship could show the characteristics of the consumers of the brand, and help designers to adjust products according to their customers' interests and tastes.

4. CROSS-MODALITY RECOMMENDATION

In this section, we present the methods for cross-modality recommendation.

4.1 Recommendation for Retrospect Evaluation

With all the parameters θ, π, φ, we could make recommendation for customers. The probability of the i-th user buying the k-th brand is calculated as follows:

$$\begin{aligned} & p(b=k|u=i,\theta,\pi,\varphi) \\ &= \sum_{t=1}^{T}\sum_{l=1}^{L} p(b=k|z=l,\varphi)p(z=l|y=t,\pi)p(y=t|u=i,\theta) \\ &= \sum_{t=1}^{T}\sum_{l=1}^{L} \varphi_{lj}\pi_{tl}\theta_{it} \end{aligned} \tag{9}$$

With the estimation of θ_i, this recommendation is made based on both its online and offline behaviors. Since this method can easily generate the ranking of brands for a user, we will evaluate it in the retrospect experiments. This method is deliberately developed only to show the online behaviors might provide extra value for this recommendation task, compared with the method using the offline behaviors only.

4.2 Recommendation for the Live System

The recommendation method in Equ. (9) has the following drawbacks. First, this method uses all the online topics for the offline recommendation although we believe that some online topics are not predictive or causally related to the offline consumption, as mentioned earlier. Additionally, these unpredictive online topics might occupy a large portion of the search content of a user while the topics with the consumption intentions are drowned out. For example, the search content from a primigravid woman might contain little about pregnancy care compared with the large portion about her work and everyday life. Thus, the online topic distribution for this user will have a low value for the topic about pregnancy care, and the brands for babies and pregnant women might not be ranked high based on Equ. (9).

4.2.1 Lift measure

Therefore, we need a measure to automatically identify the pairs of predictive online topic and its corresponding offline one so that the recommendation is made only based on these pairs.

Specifically, we define the following *lift* measure between an online topic t and an offline topic l. Remind that the proposed O2OTM model outputs the relationship between online and offline topics. Namely, the probability of offline topic l given online topic t, denoted by $\pi_{tl} = p(z = l|y = t)$, is assigned so that the likelihood of all the data is maximized. Then, based on π we can also calculate $\pi_{\neg tl} = p(z = l|y = \neg t)$, measuring the probability of offline topic l given all the other online topics t, excluding t. Then, the *lift* is defined as follows

$$lift_{tl} = \frac{p(z = l|y = t)}{p(z = l|y = \neg t)} = \frac{\pi_{tl}}{\pi_{\neg tl}} \tag{10}$$

This lift value is simply the ratio of two values: the target response l with the existence of t divided by the response without t. It actually measures how much enhancement we can get in predicting l conditioned on t compared to the condition without t. The bigger this lift value, the more association between online topic t and offline topic l.

4.2.2 Examples of high-lift pairs

Table 4 shows some examples of high-lift pairs of online and offline topics discovered from our data. These examples are selected so that they can cover different groups of consumers.

- For Group I, the search words are about pet care, and this online topic corresponds with the lift value of 11.5 to the fashioned brands for young girls. Since most of these brands are imported from Japan and Korea, they are more expensive than the regular ones, indicating that these girls are affordable to raise pets.
- For Group II, it is matched to the group of young people (mostly boys) who love Japanese anime series and computer games. What they wear is mostly from some casual brands, such as VANS, ADIDAS ORIGINAL and so on.
- For Group III, it corresponds to the group of pregnant women and young mummies. They search for the knowledge about pregnancy care, newborn baby care and postpartum recovery. Also, they corresponds to two offline topics with high lift values. The first brand group refers to the ones for newborn children, while the second group refers to some brands for young girls, indicating that these new mummies still cannot stop buying something for themselves.
- For Group IV, it refers to the group of housewives with happy lives. On the online side, they search for the materials for keeping fit, popular TV series, netnovels and so on. On the offline side, they buy two groups of brands. One is for their children, and the other is for their husbands with the brands for outdoor sportswear.
- For Group V, we consider the customers of the high-end cosmetic and jewellery brands. We are surprising to find that the lift value reaches 19 when they search for the online materials for gongfu stories, love and urban novels, and literature. Also, the people, who search for the materials about plastic surgery and phone games, like to buy these expensive brands.
- For Group VI, we consider the people who search for stocks, funds, securities, and investment. These are rich people who own some extra money for asset management. The offline topic with the highest lift value to this online topic is about some fancy restaurants in China with different types of cuisines. It indicates that good food is the first priority of these people.

It is worth mentioning that all these pairs of online and offline topics with high values of lift are automatically discovered by the proposed O2OTM model. They are consistent with our basic understandings on online and offline behaviors.

4.2.3 Lift-based recommendation

Then, with a user-specified threshold $\rho > 0$ on lift, we can identify the pairs of online and offline topics whose lift values are not smaller than ρ. Namely, we have

$$\mathcal{R} = \{(t,l)|lift_{tl} \geq \rho\} \tag{11}$$

Then, with these high-lift pairs $\mathcal{R}$ we develop the following recommendation method. Consider the scenario of the recommendation for weekend shopping. The search words in the recent weekdays are collected for inferring their online topics. Once an online topic t appears at least for q times, it is considered to match with $\mathcal{R}$ to check whether t appears in $\mathcal{T} = \{t|(t,l) \in \mathcal{R}\}$. If yes, the top brands in the corresponding offline topics are identified for recommendation. Some postprocessing steps are needed to consider the user's recent shopping history and recommendation logs to avoid repetitive recommendation. In this study, the two thresholds are set as $\rho = 4.5$ and $q = 10$.

In this method, the recommendations are made in a triggering manner. It means that recommendations only happen when the online topics with high lift values appear for enough times and the corresponding recommendations are considered to be reliable enough. It can automatically judge when to recommend, and when not even if many unpredictive search words appear. Since the pairs reflect clear intentions for offline consumption as shown in the examples in Table 4, we believe that the recommendations from this lift-based method will be more attractive to potential customers, while avoiding unnecessary disturbance to users.

5. LIVE EVALUATION

We deployed the proposed lift-based model to a real-world sales campaign in a famous shopping mall in Beijing. In order to celebrate its anniversary, the mall planed to send out lots of coupons from different brands to attract customers. These coupons were sent via short messages 3 days before the anniversary day, and each short message contained 3 coupons of different brands. For the VIP users of this mall, we knew both their offline consumption history and online search queries with their consent. We randomly divided these users into 3 groups, each of which contains around 10,000 users. With this big number of users in each group we assume that the demographic information (e.g. gender, education, spending power, etc.) are the same for these three groups of users.

Then, we evaluated the recommendation performances of three methods, which are responsible for the coupon recommendation for these 3 user groups respectively. These 3 methods include: 1) RAN, representing the random recommendation; 2) LDA, representing the method based on the offline consumption history only. Specifically, the LDA method is applied on $\{\mathcal{B}_u\}_{u=1}^{U}$, and the recommendation for offline retailing can be made by $p(b|u) = \sum_z p(b|z)p(z|u)$; 3) LIFT, representing the lift-based method based on both online and offline data. The 3 methods are deliberately designed to answer the questions on whether the recommendation based on history data is effective compared with the random method, and whether the online behaviors can provide extra value for this recommendation compared with the offline data only.

Methods	IPR	APPC (RMB)	OCPPUP (RMB)
RAN	2.34%	1656.64	38.76
LDA	2.39%	1870.30	44.70
LIFT	**2.59%**	**1942.10**	**50.30**

Table 5: The live evaluation results

In this live evaluation, we recorded the following three 3 measures on the mall consumption for these 3 user groups on the anniversary day:

- IPR, *the instore purchase rate* which means the percentage of people consuming in the mall on the anniversary day.
- APPC, *average purchases per customer.*
- OCPPUP, *occurred customer purchases per unit promotion* which equals to $IPR \times APPC$ and means the purchases each promotion message could bring to the mall.

The results are shown in Table 5. Clearly, the consumptions from the LIFT group are better than the other two groups in terms of all these three measures. Although the increase on IPR is small, the measure of APPC increases greatly. It results in the OCPPUP value of 50.3, meaning that each short message with the coupons recommended by the LIFT method brings 50.3 RMB revenue to the mall in average. For the other two groups of users, the OCPPUP values are 44.7 and 38.76, respectively. Thus, the LIFT group achieves 29.75% increase on OCPPUP compared with the RAN group, and 12.5% increase compared with the LDA group.

Since the demographic statistics are the same for these 3 groups of users, we attribute this purchase increase to better coupon recommendation by LIFT. It indicates that with both the online and offline behaviors O2OTM models the users' preferences more accurately to achieve more attractive recommendations. It clearly shows the great potential business impact if the recommendations based on both online and offline behaviors are introduced to offline retailing.

Furthermore, we check what kind of users the consumption increase comes from. Specifically, for each group of users, we rank them in terms of their purchases. Then, we divide the users, who purchased in this sales campaign, into 10 subgroups by their rankings. Namely, the top 10% users go to the 1st subgroup, the top 10%-20% users go to the 2nd one, and so on. Then, for each subgroup we calculate its APPC value. The results are shown in Figure 5, where the number on each bar represents the purchase percentage of the users in this subgroup compared to the total purchases of all the users.

We have the following observation. First, the users whose spending ranks in the top 10% contribute more that 54.6% of

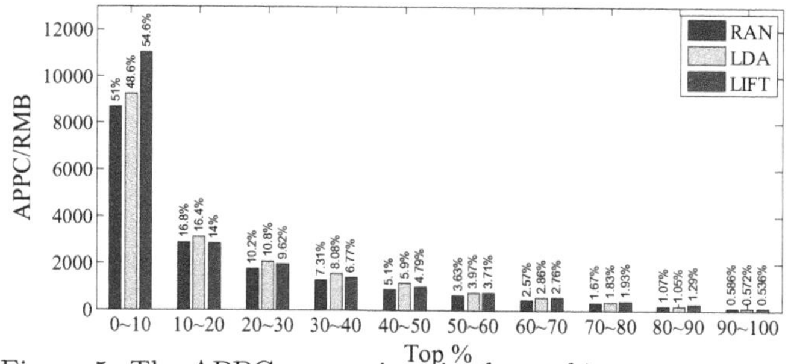

Figure 5: The APPC comparison in the ranking.

the total revenue for the LIFT user group. Second, the APPC increase from LIFT mainly comes from these top ranked high-valued customers. It indicates that these high-valued customers are more sensitive to the performance of coupon recommendation. The better the recommendation serves for high-valued customers, the more purchases it will bring.

6. RETROSPECT EVALUATION

In this section, we compare the performances of the recommendation methods in retrospect evaluation.

Each data set we use consists of online part and offline part. The online part contains users' search queries from a widely used online search engine in China. Each search log has three attributes, namely user id, query and date. Note that a query is parsed into a set of words. The offline part contains consumers' shopping history in a local shopping mall. Each shopping transection consists of consumer id, brand she buys and date.

In this retrospect evaluation, we use two data sets from two different malls in China, denoted by Mall A and Mall B. In total, we get 6539 users from Mall A, with 732 offline brands and 30097 search words. For Mall B, there are 6961 users with 789 offline brands and 103597 search words. For each data set, we use the data from 2013/01/01 to 2014/12/31 for training, and the data from 2015/01/01 to 2015/06/01 for testing.

Many measures [ ] can be used to evaluate the performance of recommendation systems, like mean absolute error (MAE), root mean squared error (RMSE), precision, recall. Since this problem is not for rating prediction, it is not suitable to adopt MAE and RMSE for evaluation. Neither, we cannot use recall since the ground truth for all the brands a user will buy is unknown. We can only calculate the percent of the recommended brands that a user really bought in the testing data. After getting the precision for each customer, we average them and derive the *precision@K* measure for the whole customers.

In this evaluation we focus on recommendation for the products which are not consumed by a user before, since these un-consumed products might reflect users' preferences more precisely. We know that there are some previous studies focusing on repetitive consumption of products [ ], which is mostly decided by the use experiences of the products, the product attributes (e.g. continuous or one-shot usage), and some user psychological issues (e.g. boredom) [ ]. However, the recommendation for repetitive consumptions is beyond the range of this study.

Here, we have the two baseline methods, RAN and LDA, which are the same in the live evaluation. The method of

RAN refers to the random recommendation method, while LDA refers to the one using the offline behaviors only. For the method of RAN, its *precision*@K measure can be analytically estimated as follows,

$$precision@K = \frac{1}{|\mathcal{U}|}\sum_{u\in\mathcal{U}}\frac{|\mathcal{T}_u - \mathcal{B}_u|}{|\mathcal{B} - \mathcal{B}_u|}, \quad (12)$$

where $(\mathcal{B} - \mathcal{B}_u)$ is the set of all the un-consumed brands customer u and $(\mathcal{T}_u - \mathcal{B}_u)$ includes all the un-consumed brands that customer u buys in the testing set. Note that this measure for RAN is independent of K.

In this retrospect evaluation, we compare these two baseline methods with the recommendation method via Equ. (9), denoted as O2OTM. This method can generate the full ranking of all the un-consumed brands. However, the lift-based method might recommend nothing when its online topics do not hit the ones with high lift values. Thus, we do not include it for this retrospect evaluation.

Note also that there exists some strong baseline methods, such as factorization machine [ ], which can embed the features of users and items (e.g. all the search words) for recommendation. However, these methods cannot provide any interpretability for recommendation. Additionally, the goal of this retrospect evaluation is only to show that the online activities can provide extra value for offline retailing. Thus, we do not include these methods for evaluation.

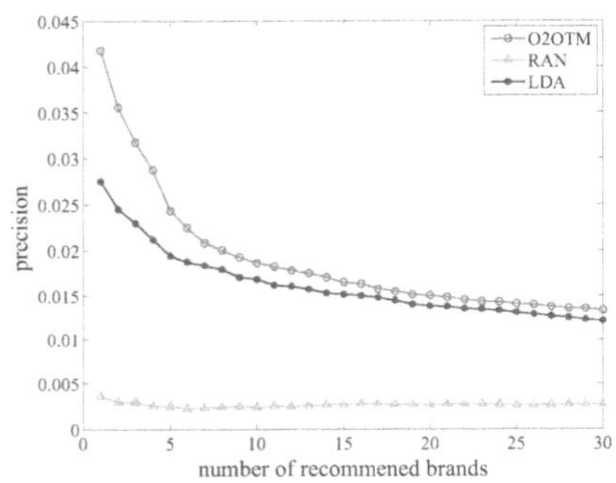

(a) Results on Mall A

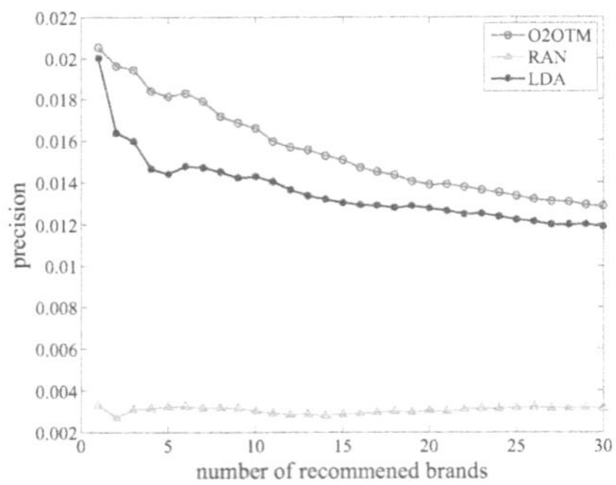

(b) Results on Mall B

Figure 6: precision@K measures for the three methods on two malls

After some initial experiments, we set the number of online topics as $T = 50$, and the number of offline topics as $L = 30$ for this retrospect evaluation. The results of the *precision*@K measure on the two malls are shown in Figure 6. It clearly shows that O2OTM is significantly better than LDA. At Mall A, the improvement from O2OTM is more clear when K is small, while this improvement becomes small after K reaches 15. At Mall B, the performances of O2OTM and LDA are similar when $K = 1$, however, when $K > 1$ the improvement from O2OTM becomes large. Also, the line for the method of RAN is flat, which is consistent with our analytical analysis.

7. RELATED WORKS

Our work is related to three areas, i) recommendation ii) topic modeling methods and iii) multi-modality learning.

Recommendation. Recommendation services have been deployed for many types of items such as books [ ], music [ ], mobile apps [ ] and even point-of-interests [ ]. Collaborative filtering (CF) is the well known recommendation approach with the core idea that users of similar interests may display similar ratings on similar items. Specifically, if a recommendation is made based on similar users (those who have the similar ratings on the same items as the target user has), it is referred to as user-based CF [ ]. On the other hand, if a recommendation is made based on similar items (those that have been rated similarly by the same set of people), it is referred to as item-based CF [ ]. Besides these nearest-neighbor techniques, matrix factorization was developed with the assumption that users and items are associated with latent factors and the observed user-item rating matrix is the multiplication of the two. These latent factors are learned by minimizing a loss function, which is defined as the sum-squared distance between observed and predicted ratings [ ], or by maximizing the likelihood of the regression residual which is assumed to obey the standard Gaussian distribution [ ].

To address the issue of data sparsity, different approaches have been developed to incorporate various features on users and items into recommendation. For example, social network was introduce to constrain the factorization process in such a way that socially connected people tend to have similar user feature vectors [ ]. For the items with rich textual information, the fLDA model was proposed to combine matrix factorization with LDA [ ]. To recommend scientific articles the CTR model was developed with the assumption that the latent factor of items is the sum of its document topic distribution and the latent offset vector [ ]. Yin et al. [ ] developed a model interpreting the silent viewing behaviors to "pseudo vote" to help recommending articles. Also, the general model of factorization machine [ ] was proposed to introduce all kinds of features on both items and users for recommendation with promising performance.

However, all these related works seldom consider the recommendation from the multi-modality perspective, even when the two modalities are only weakly associated. For this cross-modality recommendation task, we explicitly consider the relationships between the two modalities and simultaneously perform topic modeling over the two modalities. The relationships help to not only make cross-modality transformation with clear interpretability, but also identify the associations with high lift values.

Topic modeling. PLSA [ ] and LDA [ ] are popular to find the topics over the co-occurrence matrix. Different variants of topic modeling were proposed to describe the extra features with the data. For example, the author topic model [ ] was developed to consider the author information on the articles. The TOT model [ ] was proposed to describe the topics with its booming time. These previous works provide the basic idea of probabilistic generative process to describe the data we have, but none of them apply it for the cross-modality data.

Multi-modality learning. Multi-modality learning has attracted many attentions recently with the fast accumulation of the data with multiple modalities. Most of these previous works focus on the supervised or semi-supervised learning problems with the features from multiple modalities. Co-training [ ] is the most famous method for this task. Recently, the importance of different modalities was also considered to extract the discriminative features for weak modality with the supervision from strong modality. Note that all these modalities are in the feature space. As to the cross-modality recommendation task in this study, the online modality is used as feature space while the offline modality is considered as labels for prediction.

8. CONCLUSIONS

In this paper, we study the problem of offline retailing recommendation based users' online behaviors. We propose the probabilistic model O2OTM, which performs the topic modeling for both the online and offline activities, and also build the relationships between the online and offline topics. These resultant relationships can directly support cross-modality recommendation, and also provide recommendation explanation. Additionally, the lift measure is developed to identify the pairs of online and offline topics, which have strong or even causally-related associations. The live experiments show that this cross-modality recommendation contains huge business impact. We emphasize that this model for cross-modality recommendation has wide application scenarios. For example, based on the search logs we can perform the recommendations for restaurants, mobile apps, tour sites for traveling, and so on. Also, we will make the proposed model scalable for large-scale data and build the general system for cross-modality recommendation.

Acknowledgements

This work was supported by the National Natural Science Foundation of China (No. 61473274, 91546122, 61573335), National High-tech R&D Program of China (863 Program) (No.2014AA015105), Guangdong provincial science and technology plan projects (No. 2015 B010109005).

9. REFERENCES

[1] http://www.ripenecommerce.com/blog/ecommerce_survey#prettyPhoto.

[2] http://www.pwccn.com/webmedia/doc/635687554653555153_consulting_delivering_o2o_jun2015_chi.pdf.

[3] http://ijcai-15.org/index.php/repeat-buyers-prediction-competition.

[4] D. Agarwal and B.-C. Chen. flda: matrix factorization through latent dirichlet allocation. In *WSDM*, 2010.

[5] D. M. Blei, A. Y. Ng, and M. I. Jordan. Latent dirichlet allocation. *JMLR*, 2003.

[6] A. Blum and T. Mitchell. Combining labeled and unlabeled data with co-training. In *COLT*, 1998.

[7] H.-C. Chen and A. L. Chen. A music recommendation system based on music data grouping and user interests. In *CIKM*. ACM, 2001.

[8] Y. H. Cho and J. K. Kim. Application of web usage mining and product taxonomy to collaborative recommendations in e-commerce. *Expert systems with Applications*, 2004.

[9] G. Heinrich. Parameter estimation for text analysis. Technical report, Fraunhofer IGD, 2009.

[10] J. L. Herlocker, J. A. Konstan, A. Borchers, and J. Riedl. An algorithmic framework for performing collaborative filtering. In *SIGIR*, 1999.

[11] T. Hofmann. Probabilistic latent semantic analysis. In *UAI*, 1999.

[12] Y. Li, J. Hu, C. Zhai, and Y. Chen. Improving one-class collaborative filtering by incorporating rich user information. In *CIKM*, 2010.

[13] H. Ma, H. Yang, M. R. Lyu, and I. King. Sorec: social recommendation using probabilistic matrix factorization. In *CIKM*, 2008.

[14] R. J. Mooney and L. Roy. Content-based book recommending using learning for text categorization. In *Proceedings of the fifth ACM conference on Digital libraries*. ACM, 2000.

[15] S. Rendle. Factorization machines with libFM. *ACM Trans. Intell. Syst. Technol.*, 2012.

[16] P. Resnick, N. Iacovou, M. Suchak, P. Bergstrom, and J. Riedl. Grouplens: An open architecture for collaborative filtering of netnews. In *CSCW*, 1994.

[17] M. Rosen-Zvi, T. Griffiths, M. Steyvers, and P. Smyth. The author-topic model for authors and documents. In *UAI*, 2004.

[18] R. Salakhutdinov and A. Mnih. Probabilistic matrix factorization. In *NIPS*, 2007.

[19] A. D. Sarma, S. Gollapudi, R. Panigrahy, and L. Zhang. Understanding cyclic trends in social choices. In *WSDM*, 2012.

[20] B. Sarwar, G. Karypis, J. Konstan, and J. Riedl. Item-based collaborative filtering recommendation algorithms. In *WWW*, 2001.

[21] G. Shani and A. Gunawardana. Evaluating recommendation systems. In *Recommender systems handbook*. 2011.

[22] N. Srebro and T. Jaakkola. Weighted low-rank approximations. In *ICML*, 2003.

[23] C. Wang and D. Bleig. Collaborative topic modeling for recommending scientific articles. In *KDD*, 2011.

[24] X. Wang and A. McCallum. Topics over time: A non-markov continuous-time model of topical trends. In *KDD*, 2006.

[25] M. Ye, P. Yin, W.-C. Lee, and D. L. Lee. Exploiting geographical influence for collaborative point-of-interest recommendation. In *SIGIR*, 2011.

[26] P. Yin, P. Luo, W.-C. Lee, and M. Wang. App recommendation: a contest between satisfaction and temptation. In *WSDM*, 2013.

[27] P. Yin, P. Luo, W.-C. Lee, and M. Wang. Silence is also evidence: interpreting dwell time for recommendation from psychological perspective. In *KDD*, 2013.

	Online words (English description)	Lift	Offline brands (English description)
I	1. 狗狗 (dogs, puppies) 2. 泰迪 (*Teddy Bear Puppy*, a breed of small dog) 3. 宠物 (pet) 4. 狗粮 (dog food) 5. 绝育 (sterilization for pet) 6. 猫咪 (cats) 7. 宠物医院 (pet hospital) 8. 疫苗 (Pet vaccine) 9. 金毛 (*Golden Retriever*, a breed of large dog with thick yellow hair) 10.拉布拉多 (*Labrador*, a breed of large dog)	11.5	1. TUTUANNA (a Japanese brand famous for lovely girl underwear) 2. PEACH JOHN (girl underwear brand of hot sexy and cute style) 3. INNISFREE (a Korean cosmetics brand) 4. 6IXTY 8IGHT (women fashion brand, famous for women's lingerie, dresses) 5. SNIDEL (a Japanese girl clothing brand) 6. LILY BROWN (a Japanese girl clothing brand) 7. EARTH MUSIC (a Japanese girl clothing brand of simple and natural style) 8. ORBIS (a Japanese cosmetics brand) 9. The Body Shop (natural skin care, make-up brand) 10.Lowrys Farm (a Japanese girl clothing brand)
II	1. 游戏 (games) 2. 漫画 (comic series) 3. 怪物猎人 (*Monster Hunter*, a PSP game) 4. 盗墓笔记 (*The Secret of Grave Robber*, a net-novel) 5. 食尸鬼 (*Tokyo Ghoul*, a Japanese anime) 6. 火影忍者 (*Naruto*, a Japanese anime) 7. 最终幻想 (*Final Fantasy*, a role-playing video game) 8. 暴走 (*Rage Comic*, a comic series) 9. 战争 (wars) 10.上古卷轴 (*The Elder Scrolls*, an action video game)	7.5	1. ADIDAS (a famous brand for sportswear) 2. NIKE (a famous brand for sportswear) 3. VANS (a brand for skate shoes and clothing for the young) 4. CONVERSE (a brand for sportswear and lifestyle footwear) 5. NIKE 360 (a classical sportswear series of NIKE) 6. ADIDAS NEO (a sports and leisure series of ADIDAS) 7. ADIDAS ORIGINAL (a classical sportswear series of ADIDAS) 8. LEVI'S (a famous brand for jeans and jackets) 9. PAUL FRANK (a fashion and lifestyle brand known for its bright color palette and stylish products) 10.MLB (a brand for baseball clothing)
III	1. 新生儿 (newborn baby) 2. 哺乳期 (suckling period) 3. 产后 (postpartum recovery) 4. 奶粉 (milk powder) 5. 母乳 (breast milk) 6. 睡觉 (sleep) 7. 大便 (baby stool) 8. 月子 (confinement in childbirth) 9. 剖腹产 (caesarean birth) 10.满月 (babies' completion of its first month of life)	6.0	1. 乐友 (a brand special for newborn children related products) 2. ORCHESTRA (a children clothing brand) 3. TOYS R US (a kids store for all toys, video games, dolls, etc.) 4. MOTHERCARE (a brand for selected nursery accessories) 5. BABYLAND (a brand for children indoor interactive playground)
		4.6	1. 6IXTY 8IGHT (a women fashion brand, famous for young women's lingerie, dresses) 2. TEENIE WEENIE (a South Korean clothing brand special for the young women) 3. E-LAND (a South Korean clothing brand for the young women) 4. 阿童木 (a women and kids clothing brand) 5. Walker One (a brand for young women's shoes)
IV	1. 郑多燕 (a South Korean diet writer, famous for her fitness exercise) 2. 柔术 (human body flexibility exercise) 3. 天猫 (*TMall*, an online shopping site in China) 4. 奶粉 (milk powder) 5. 奇热 (a website for online TV series) 6. 钟汉良 (a famous TV series actor) 7. 新浪网 (*Sina*, a Chinese online media website) 8. 慢慢 (a shopping guide website) 9. 仙途 (a netnovel) 10. 生肖 (the Chinese zodiac)	7.6	1. 巴拉巴拉 (a brand special for children related products like children's shoes, toys and clothing) 2. OSHKOSH (an American brand for children's clothing) 3. 爱法贝 (a children clothing brand) 4. 法米尼 (a children clothing brand) 5. 斯乃纳 (a brand for pregnant women's clothing and care)
		4.5	1. Columbia (an American outdoor sportswear brand) 2. Jack Wolfskin (a Germany outdoor sportswear brand) 3. 探路者 (a Chinese outdoor sportwear brand) 4. The North Face (an American outdoor sportswear brand, specializing in outerwear and equipment) 5. KAILAS (a brand in the manufacturing of technical climbing gear and apparel)
V	1. 武侠 (Chinese gongfu story series) 2. 文学 (literature) 3. 动漫 (comics and animations) 4. 激情 (emotional love novels) 5. 都市 (urban novels)	19.0	1. Dior (a French fashion brand famous for cosmetics, skin care, makeup and fragrances) 2. Chanel (a French fashion brand for perfume and bags) 3. BIOTHERM (a brand of high-grade skin care products) 4. FANCL (a nature cosmetics brand from Japan)
	1. 幼儿园 (kindergartens) 2. 双眼皮 (double fold eyelid) 3. 保卫萝卜 (*Carrot Fantasy*, a funny phone game) 4. 玻尿酸 (Hyaluronic Acid, used to keep skin elasticity and tension) 5. 整形 (plastic surgery)	5.8	5. DHC (a skincare brand from Japan) 6. Estee Lauder (An American skincare and makeup brand) 7. 周大福 (a Hongkong jewellery brand) 8. 安莉芳 (a Hongkong underwear brand) 9. L'Oreal (a famous French cosmetics, haircare brand) 10.Aupres (a cosmetics brand from Japan)
VI	1. 股票 (stocks) 2. 基金 (funds) 3. 投资 (investment) 4. 股份 (stock shares) 5. 证券 (securities) 6. 阿里巴巴 (*Alibaba*, a Chinese e-commerce company) 7. 金融 (finance) 8. 上市 (IPO) 9. 黄金 (gold) 10. 股价 (stock price)	9.7	1. 唐宫 (a fancy Chinese restaurant brand for Cantonese cuisines) 2. 熔宴 (a Chinese restaurant famous for Hunan cuisines) 3. 便宜坊 (a famous roast duck restaurant in Beijing) 4. 论道茶叶 (a Chinese tea brand) 5. 苗乡楼 (a Chinese restaurant famous for Guizhou cuisines) 6. 鹿港小镇 (a Chinese restaurant famous for Taiwan cuisines) 7. 蕉叶 (a restaurant famous for Thai food) 8. 恒香栈 (a Hongkong tea restaurant) 9. 釜山料理 (a Korean barbecue chain restaurant in China) 10. 至爱 (a Chinese restaurant for mixed cuisines)

Table 4: Example pairs of online and offline topics with the high lift values.

Firebird: Predicting Fire Risk and Prioritizing Fire Inspections in Atlanta

Michael Madaio
Carnegie Mellon University
Pittsburgh, PA, USA
mmadaio@cs.cmu.edu

Shang-Tse Chen
Georgia Tech
Atlanta, GA, USA
schen351@gatech.edu

Oliver L. Haimson
University of California, Irvine
Irvine, CA, USA
ohaimson@uci.edu

Wenwen Zhang
Georgia Tech
Atlanta, GA, USA
wzhang300@gatech.edu

Xiang Cheng
Emory University
Atlanta, GA, USA
xcheng7@emory.edu

Matthew Hinds-Aldrich
Atlanta Fire Rescue Dept.
Atlanta, GA, USA
mhinds-aldrich@atlantaga.gov

Duen Horng Chau
Georgia Tech
Atlanta, GA, USA
polo@gatech.edu

Bistra Dilkina
Georgia Tech
Atlanta, GA, USA
bdilkina@cc.gatech.edu

ABSTRACT

The Atlanta Fire Rescue Department (AFRD), like many municipal fire departments, actively works to reduce fire risk by inspecting commercial properties for potential hazards and fire code violations. However, AFRD's fire inspection practices relied on tradition and intuition, with no existing data-driven process for prioritizing fire inspections or identifying new properties requiring inspection. In collaboration with AFRD, we developed the *Firebird* framework to help municipal fire departments identify and prioritize commercial property fire inspections, using machine learning, geocoding, and information visualization. Firebird computes fire risk scores for over 5,000 buildings in the city, with true positive rates of up to 71% in predicting fires. It has identified 6,096 new potential commercial properties to inspect, based on AFRD's criteria for inspection. Furthermore, through an interactive map, Firebird integrates and visualizes fire incidents, property information and risk scores to help AFRD make informed decisions about fire inspections. Firebird has already begun to make positive impact at both local and national levels. It is improving AFRD's inspection processes and Atlanta residents' safety, and was highlighted by National Fire Protection Association (NFPA) as a best practice for using data to inform fire inspections.

Keywords

Fire risk, predictive modeling, interactive visualization, government innovation, data science

KDD '16, August 13-17, 2016, San Francisco, CA, USA
© 2016 ACM. ISBN 978-1-4503-4232-2/16/08...$15.00
DOI: http://dx.doi.org/10.1145/2939672.2939682

Figure 1: **Firebird Framework Overview.** By combining 8 datasets, Firebird identifies new commercial properties for fire inspections. Its fire risk predictive models (SVM, random forest) and interactive map help AFRD prioritize fire inspections and personnel allocation.

1. INTRODUCTION

In 2014 alone, there were 494,000 structure fires in the United States, causing 2,800 civilian deaths and $9.8 billion in property damage [1]. Municipal fire departments, as the Authority Having Jurisdiction (AHJ), are responsible for enforcing applicable fire codes to reduce the risk of structure fires. The City of Atlanta Fire Rescue Department (AFRD), like many other fire departments, conducts regular commercial property inspections to ensure that they comply with the city's Code of Ordinances [2] for fire prevention and safety. With an annual average of nearly 650 structure fires and 2,573 annual commercial inspections, the AFRD Community Risk Reduction Section wanted to both identify uninspected properties and ensure that the properties being inspected were those at greatest risk of fire. Through a partnership between the City of Atlanta and the Data Science for Social Good (Atlanta) program, our research team developed the *Firebird* framework for identifying and prioritizing property fire inspections, based on fire department criteria and historical fire risk, tackling two important challenges:

Challenge 1: Property Identification. The AFRD Community Risk Reduction Section knew that the 2,573 annually inspected commercial properties were not all of the commercial properties in the city of Atlanta, but they did not have a way to obtain a more complete list of commercial properties that potentially needed inspection. The existing process for AFRD's property inspections involved a legacy system of paper file records and inspections conducted on the basis of pre-existing permits, without a robust process for identification, selection, and prioritization of new properties to inspect. In addition, the variety of data sources AFRD had compiled to inform their inspections were inconsistent, incomplete, and were often at different levels of granularity. Thus, cleaning and merging the datasets to identify which inspectable properties in the city had fallen through the cracks required significant effort. By integrating data from a variety of government and commercial sources, we discovered 19,397 potential new commercial properties to inspect, based on the property usage types that the Atlanta Code of Ordinances specifies require inspection.

Challenge 2: Fire Risk Prediction. Because 19,397 new commercial property inspections is far greater than the current number of annual commercial property inspections, and far more than AFRD's current staff of fire inspectors can reasonably inspect, we developed a method to prioritize those inspections based on their fire risk. First, we created a joined dataset of building- and parcel-level information variables, for 8,223 commercial properties[1]. Then, we built predictive models of fire risk using machine learning approaches, including Support Vector Machine (SVM) [7] and Random Forest [3]. These models achieve true positive rates (TPRs) of up to 71.36% (in predicting fires) at a false positive rate (FPR) of 20%. As our most important goal is to save lives, a higher TPR outweighs the increase in FPR. The resulting fire risk scores were then assigned to over 5,000 commercial properties to help ARFD prioritize inspections.

Contributions & Impact. With Firebird, AFRD can now use data about historical fires to inform their fire inspections and more efficiently utilize their inspection personnel capacity. The challenges that Firebird addresses are not unique to AFRD or the City of Atlanta; many municipal agencies across the country work to integrate a variety of data sources to inform decision-making at all levels of governance. Specifically, many fire safety departments are seeking effective prioritization of property inspections and allocation of inspection resources, given limited inspection personnel and large numbers of inspectable properties. Firebird has already begun to improve AFRD's inspection processes. Its major contributions include:

- **Discovering new properties.** Firebird improves the safety of Atlanta residents and visitors by identifying 19,397 previously unidentified inspectable commercial properties.
- **Predictive fire risk model.** Firebird correctly predicts more than 70% of commercial fires (at 20% FPR), and applies the resulting fire risk scores to over 5,000 properties to help ARFD prioritize inspections.
- **Impact to Atlanta: Firebird at work.** Through an interactive map, Firebird integrates and visualizes fire incidents, property information and inspections, and risk scores to inform the decision-making processes of AFRD fire inspectors, executive staff, and their Community Risk Reduction Section for inspection prioritization and inspection personnel allocation.
- **National impact: reusable end-to-end framework for inspection prioritization.** Firebird provides an explicated model for other municipalities and agencies to use to identify new properties and prioritize commercial property inspections based on fire risk. This project was highlighted by the *National Fire Protection Association* (NFPA) at the *Smart Enforcement Workshop* for fire service professionals across North America as a best practice for using data to inform fire inspections.

[1]We will be referring to *buildings* and *properties* as two distinct concepts throughout this paper. The AFRD conducts property inspections and issues permits to the owners of those "inspectable spaces," which are properties. However, it is the physical structure of buildings that catch fire, and thus, when we built predictive models, we did so with information about the buildings themselves. This is significant because one property may contain multiple buildings, while another building may contain multiple properties.

2. RELATED WORK

Risk prediction models have been widely used in many domains, including health care [15], student performance evaluation [16], and accounting fraud detection [18]. However, urban fire risk prediction has received relatively less attention, despite its obvious importance.

Forest fire prediction. Much of the prior work on data-driven fire risk prediction has targeted woodland and forest fires, such as in Italy [17], Greece [14], and Portugal [9]. They used different methods, such as neural networks [9], fuzzy algebra [14], and decision trees [17] to support the allocation of firefighting, fire prevention, and foliage recuperation resources to the areas of highest fire risk. The features they used, such as soil type and topography, are very different from the ones typically used in urban fire prediction like construction material and property usage type.

Community-level urban fire prediction. Prior work in data-driven urban fire risk prediction tends to work at the region or community level [5, 8], rather than the property- or building-level, which is the unit that the Atlanta fire inspectors are assigned to inspect. For instance, [5] undertook a randomized controlled trial of community fire risk education efforts, targeting high-risk residential communities. However, their method for identifying the high-risk areas was to create a point-distribution map of residential structure fires and draw ellipses to capture the areas of densest concentration of fire incidents. A more methodologically rigorous approach, as seen in [8]'s work on optimizing smoke-alarm inspections, joins data from the American Community Survey and American Housing Survey to predict municipal blocks most likely to have homes without functioning smoke alarms, using a Random Forest. Our work similarly uses publicly available datasets to predict properties most likely to be in need of inspection, but differs in that we offer a fire risk prediction score for individual commercial properties, rather than municipal residential blocks.

Property-level urban fire prediction. There is limited work on predicting fire risk at the property or build-

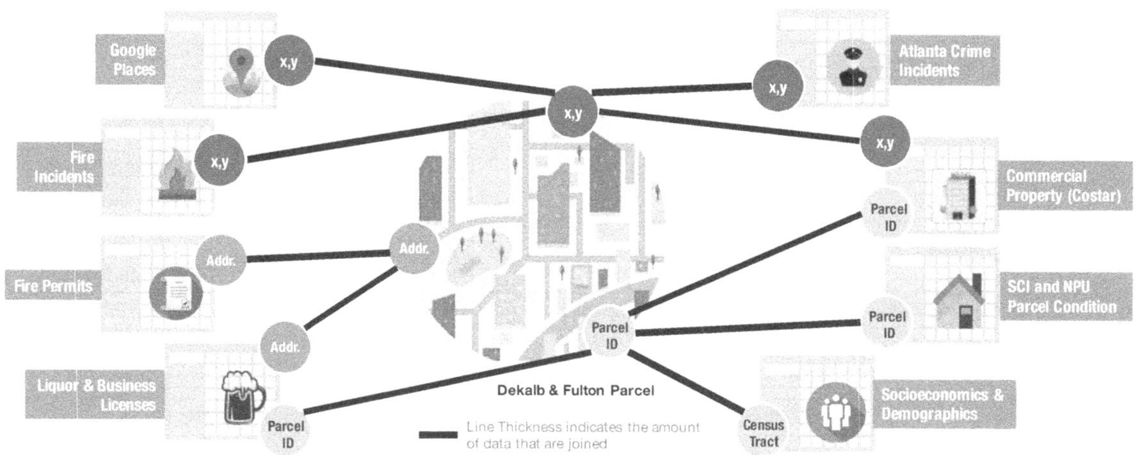

Figure 2: Joining eight datasets using three spatial information types (geocode, address, parcel ID).

ing level. In British Columbia, [12] developed a risk-based model for determining the frequency of commercial property fire inspections, using static and dynamic building-level characteristics. They scored each property by its level of compliance on prior inspections and by a set of risk metric components such as building classification, age, and presence of sprinklers. However, as they acknowledge, the weights and selection of those components were based on their fire code, and not on historical data on features that were highly predictive of fire, such as we utilize in our work.

The nearest precedent for our research with AFRD is the recent work from the New York Mayor's Office of Data Analytics (MODA) with the Fire Department of New York (FDNY) to build a "Risk-Based Inspection System" (RBIS) [6]. They built a data-driven model to identify structures at greatest fire risk, to better prioritize FDNY's inspection process, using a set of structural and behavioral information about those properties. However, due to a lack of detailed information on their technical approach, it is unclear how it may apply to AFRD's scenario.

In both the FDNY RBIS initiative and our work with AFRD, a key challenge emerged: the difficulty of joining disparate datasets about commercial properties, gathered from various city departments without a shared convention for building ID numbers, consistent address formats, or strict internal quality control practices to ensure the datasets are accurate and up-to-date. We differ from [6] and [12] by providing a clear method for identifying new inspectable commercial properties that the fire department is not already aware of. Further, our work goes beyond [6] by presenting a detailed comparison of the performance of several machine learning algorithms for predicting the fire risk of commercial properties, and by incorporating them into an interactive GIS visualization for use by the AFRD fire inspectors and Community Risk Reduction Section, following [10].

3. DATA DESCRIPTION

An essential step before identifying and prioritizing potential properties to inspect is to join the data about commercial properties from multiple sources. This was done to construct as complete a picture as possible for the properties in Atlanta needing inspection, as required by the Atlanta Code of Ordinances. After the data joining, we identified 19,397 new potential commercial properties to inspect, through a process of property discovery that utilized AFRD and City of Atlanta fire code criteria. See Table 1 for a summary of the different lists of total commercial property inspections and commercial buildings we will be referring to throughout this paper.

Name	Count
Current annual inspections	2,573
Long list of potential new inspections[2]	19,397
Short list of potential new inspections	6,096
Current + **short list** inspections	8,669
Current + **short list** inspections with risk score	5,022
Properties for building predictive model	8,223

Table 1: Summary of inspection and building lists

3.1 Data Sources

Firebird uses data from multiple sources, as tabulated in Table 2. AFRD provided us with a dataset of 2,543 historical fire incidents from July 2011 to March 2015, of which 34.3% were commercial fires. This includes information about fire incidents, such as time, location, type, and cause of fire. AFRD also provided a dataset of fire inspections, with 32,488 inspection permit records from 2012 to 2015. The inspection data includes information such as inspected property types, address, and time of inspections. We also obtained structural information about commercial properties from a dataset purchased by AFRD from the CoStar Group, a commercial real estate agency. This dataset includes building-level features such as year built, building material, number of floors and units, building condition and other information. A total of 8,223 commercial properties are documented by the CoStar Group in the City of Atlanta.

While CoStar offers building-level information, parcel data from Atlanta's Office of Buildings provides parcel-level in-

[2]We provided AFRD with two lists of potential properties: one longer list that was the most extensive that we could provide, and another shorter list that was more manageable to display on a map, refined using the most frequently inspected property usage types.

Source	Name	Description
Atlanta Fire Rescue Department	Fire Incidents	Fire incidents from 2011 - 2015
	Fire Permits	All permits filed by AFRD in 2012-2015
City of Atlanta	Parcel	Basic information for each parcel in Atlanta
	Strategic Community Investigation	Information regarding parcel conditions
	Business Licenses	All the business licenses issued in Atlanta
Atlanta Police Department	Crime	2014 crime in Atlanta
	Liquor Licenses	All filed liquor licenses by Police Department
Atlanta Regional Commission	Neighborhood Planning Unit	Boundary data for each Atlanta neighborhood
U.S. Census Bureau	Demographic	Household number, population by race and age
	Socioeconomic	Household median income
CoStar Group, Inc	CoStar Properties	Commercial property information
Google Place APIs	Google Place	Information regarding places from Google Maps

Table 2: Data Sources Summary

formation, such as property value, square footage, address, and other information about each parcel (a unit of land surrounding building(s)). The business license dataset obtained from the City of Atlanta's Office of Revenue provides information about businesses that own commercial properties. The business licenses dataset has 20,020 records with over 20 features including business type, business name, address, owner, etc. For non-business commercial properties (e.g., schools, churches, daycare centers), we obtained such data from Google Places API and State of Georgia Government.

To offer more information about properties for building a predictive risk model, we also obtained socioeconomic and demographic data from the U.S. Census Bureau, liquor license and 2014 crime data from the Atlanta Police Department, and Certificate of Occupancy (CO) data from the Atlanta Office of Buildings. All of these data sources contributed to discovering new inspections and developing our predictive model for commercial fire risk estimation.

3.2 Data Joining

A critical step of this study was to join different datasets together so that data from different sources about the same building or property could be unified to create the most complete picture of a given property. For instance, by joining fire incident and commercial property data together, we can obtain a general idea regarding which commercial properties caught fire in the past five years. Furthermore, by joining commercial property data with data from the commercial real estate reports like the CoStar Group or the SCI Report, we can generate a more comprehensive view regarding specific characteristics of buildings, such as the structure and parcel condition, and even vacancy information.

We joined the datasets together based primarily on spatial location information. There are three types of spatial or location information in our datasets: longitude and latitude, address information, and the parcel identification number, which is a unique ID number created by Fulton and DeKalb county[3] for tax purposes. We then performed a location join based on the above three types of location information. The variety of spatial information types, and our method for joining them is illustrated in Figure 2. One obstacle we encountered was that spatial information had different formatting standards across the datasets. For example, the addresses from the CoStar Group were all in lowercase, with road names abbreviated instead of fully spelled out, while datasets from the multiple departments of the City of Atlanta tend to use a more consistent address format. Therefore, a spatial information cleaning process was conducted before joining the datasets directly. The address location information from different datasets was first validated using Google Geocoding API. The API can auto-correct some misspellings of address information. After validation, addresses were then reformatted using US Postal Service's address validation API. The coordinate information was processed in ESRI ArcGIS software to filter out data points falling outside of the City of Atlanta. The cleaned datasets were then joined together based on the formatted addresses from the USPS API and the coordinate information from ArcGIS.

[3]The City of Atlanta is comprised of two separate counties, Fulton and Dekalb. Although both county governments provided building information, their parcel ID numbering schemes were not consistent. Thus, building information had to joined using addresses and coordinates.

4. IDENTIFYING NEW PROPERTIES NEEDING INSPECTION

To discover new properties, we first needed to understand what types of properties currently required fire inspections according to the Fire Code [2], and we then identified other similar properties. In the current fire inspection permit dataset, we found more than 100 unique occupancy usage types, such as restaurants, motor vehicle repair facilities, textile storage, schools, children's day care centers, etc. To identify other similar commercial properties, we joined the list of currently inspected properties with the Atlanta Business License data by matching both the spatial location (identified through the joining process explained in Section 3.2) and the business name.

We discovered that, in addition to the 2,573 currently inspected properties, there were approximately 19,397 properties of the same occupancy usage types as the city's current inspections. For instance, the Fire Code of Ordinances [2] stipulates that motor vehicle repair facilities require inspection, due to the presence of flammable or combustible materials. However, only 186 of a total of 507 of those facilities in the city were on the list of current annual property inspections, suggesting that many or all of 321 remaining facilities should be inspected. However, because some occupancy types, such as "miscellaneous business service," may have many properties that are not actually required for inspection, we created a shorter, more refined list of 6,096 new potential property inspections (instead of the 19,397 mentioned above), including only the top 100 most frequently inspected property usage types. We discovered these properties from a variety of data sources, including the Atlanta Department of Revenue's Business License dataset, the liquor license dataset from the Atlanta Police Department, the Georgia Department of Education's child care and preschool database, and Google Places API. We used the Google Places API to supplement the other datasets primarily because it provided more up-to-date information about some of our most commonly inspected property types, such as restaurants, bars, nightclubs, schools, churches, gas stations, etc, and because it proved especially useful for discovering properties that required inspection, but were not in the Business License dataset as they did not belong to any "business" category (e.g., churches). Google Places API served as a "bridge" to cross-check properties from different datasets, increasing the accuracy of our property discovery process.

In identifying new properties needing inspection, the most challenging part was to determine how buildings with different names (or IDs, or address formats) in various datasets actually refer to the same building. We had to ensure that properties on our new inspectable property list were unique and not already on the list of currently inspected properties, after the aforementioned datasets were joined together. Different approaches were attempted to ensure the uniqueness and novelty of properties on our potential list. The most reliable and efficient method was found to be joining different datasets in pairs using geocoding and approximate ("fuzzy") string matching to approximately match both the business name and the address. We used Google Maps Geocoding API for geocoding and a Python library [13] to match the strings based on the edit distance. From the joined dataset, a final property list was extracted that contained information from all the available data sources.

5. PREDICTIVE MODEL OF FIRE RISK

However, 19,397 new properties (or even the shorter list of 6,096) is far more than AFRD is able to add to their annual property inspections, and not all of those properties are likely to need inspection at the same priority. We therefore created a predictive model to generate a fire risk score based on the building- and parcel-level characteristics of properties that had fire incidents in the last five years. This model was built using the scikit-learn machine learning package in Python [20]. The model uses 58 independent variables to predict fire as an outcome variable for each property.

5.1 Data Cleaning

After joining various datasets together to obtain building- and parcel-level information, significant data cleaning still needed to occur. The bulk of the data cleaning process involved finding the extent of the missing data and deciding how to deal with that missingness. Our missingness procedures were designed to minimize deletion of properties with missing data, because a significant number of the properties in our model had NA values (not available) for many variables (such as the structure condition of a building, which is only known if the building was inspected by the CoStar Group before). For each property with missing data for a particular feature, we replaced missing values with 0 when appropriate. We also included a binary feature indicating whether each property had missing data for each feature. We used log transformation for variables with a large numerical range, such as the "for sale" price of properties.

5.2 Feature Selection

After merging datasets, we had a total of 252 variables for each property. We manually examined each variable to determine whether it may be relevant to fire prediction, and excluded many obviously non-predictive variables in this initial process (such as the phone number of the property owner, or property ID numbers). We then used forward and backward feature selection processes to determine each variable's contribution to the model, and removed the variables that did not contribute to higher predictive accuracy. Our final model includes only 58 variables. We then expanded categorical variables into binary features. For example, the zip code variable was expanded into 37 binary features, and for each property only one zip code was coded as 1 (all zip codes were designated as 0 if a property's zip code data was missing). After expansion, we had 1127 features in total.

5.3 Evaluation of the Models

We chose to validate our model using a time-partitioned approach. A fire risk model would ideally be tested in practice by predicting which properties would have a fire incident in the following year, and then waiting a year to verify which properties actually did catch fire. Because we wanted to effectively evaluate the accuracy of our model without waiting a year to collect data on new fires, we simulated this approach by using data from fire incidents in July 2011 to March 2014 as training data to predict fires in the last year of our data, April 2014 to March 2015.

We used grid search with 10-fold cross validation on the training dataset to select the best models and parameters. The models we tried included *Logistic Regression* [19], *Gradient Boosting* [11], *Support Vector Machine* (SVM) [7], and *Random Forest* [3]. SVM and Random Forest performed the best, with comparable performances (see Table 3). For SVM, the best configuration is using RBF kernel with $C = 0.5$ and $\gamma = \frac{10}{\#\text{features}}$. For Random Forest, restricting the maximum depth of each tree to be 10 gave the best performance. Increasing the number of trees in general improves the performance, but we only used 200 trees since adding more trees only obtained insignificant improvement.

We then trained SVM and Random Forest on the whole training set using the best parameters and generated predictions on the testing set. Note that training and testing sets include the same set of properties, but different labels correspond to fires in different periods of time. This is a valid approach because we didn't use information that we would only know after the training period, i.e., fires in 2015.

The ROC curves for the training and testing performances are shown in Figure 3. All the results are averaged over 10 trials. The most important metric in this case is the true positive rate (TPR), i.e., how many fires were correctly predicted as positive in our model. The SVM model was able to predict 71.36% of the fires in 2014-2015, at a false positive rate (FPR) of 20%, which was deemed practically useful

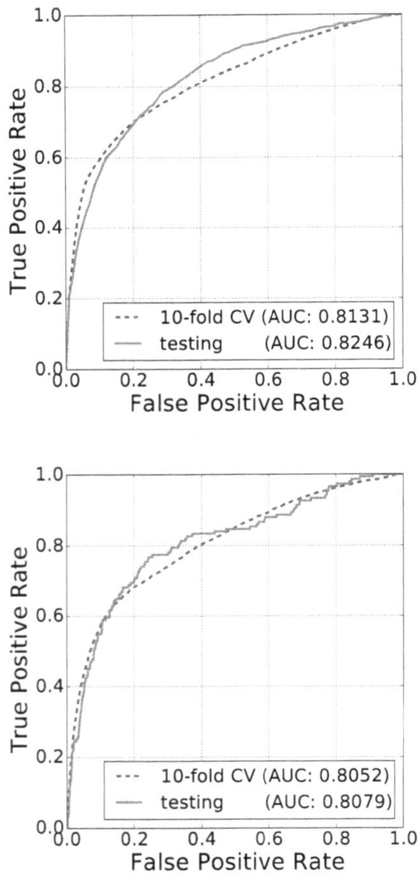

(a) SVM

Figure 3: ROC curves of Random Forest and SVM

for AFRD — potential to save lives (by achieving a higher TPR) significantly outweighs the increase in FPR. At the same time, a high FPR facilitates more inspections of risky buildings, which is also beneficial. In practice, AFRD can adjust the TPR/FPR ratio to match their risk aversity and inspection capacity. The Random Forest model achieved a slightly lower TPR of 69.28% at the same FPR, but had a higher area under the ROC curve (AUC). Considering how few fires occur (only about 6% of the properties in our total dataset had fires), these results are much more predictive than guessing by chance.

False positives (FPs) provide important information to AFRD. As our testing period was the final year in our dataset, it is possible that some of those FP properties may actually catch fire in the near future. These properties share many characteristics with those that did catch fire, and should likely be inspected by AFRD.

5.4 Further Discussion of the Models

In this section, we discuss some insight we obtained while conducting the experiments. First, there is a mismatch between the meaning of labels in the training and testing datasets. The training labels represent fires that happened in a relatively long period of time, whereas the testing labels represent fires in a single year. One way to address this issue would be to expand each properties into multiple examples, one for each year. Each example is then a properties for a particular year, and the corresponding label indicates whether there was a fire in that year. Using this approach, however, did not improve the performance in our experiments. The reason is that most of our variables are static, such as floor size and zip code, and only a few variables are time-dependent, such as the age of the building and the time since last inspection. Therefore, expanding the properties only gives us many similar examples. However, this approach would potentially be helpful after collecting other dynamic information in the future, such as violations of health codes, sanitation ordinances, or other information from relevant city agencies.

Another important issue is whether the performance of predicting fires is consistent in different testing time periods. To test this, we tried different time windows for training, and for each window, we evaluated its prediction performance for the subsequent year. For each time window, we repeated the process described in Section 5.3, including grid search and cross validation, and finally used the best model to predict fires in the following year. The results are shown in Table 3. The performances decrease slightly for shorter training periods. This is due to fewer positive training examples, especially in the period of 2011-2012, which only consists of eight months of data (July 2011 to March 2012). However, this is still significantly better than guessing by chance, which demonstrates that we were not just "lucky" in predicting fires for a particular year.

Finally, it is helpful for us and for AFRD to know which features are the most effective predictors. The Random Forest model presents a natural way to evaluate feature importance: for each decision tree in the Random Forest, the importance of a feature is calculated by the ratio of examples split by it. The final importance is then averaged among all trees. The top ten most predictive features are displayed in Table 4. Collectively, they capture the intuitive insight that buildings of a larger size or those containing more units (thus more people) would have higher probability of catching fire, and those of higher appraised value and higher taxes would have a lower probability of catching fire. The impact of higher appraised property value may be due to more developed fire prevention practices or infrastructure, but this hypothesis has not been empirically validated.

We also tried logistic regression, a linear model, to estimate each feature's importance based on the corresponding weight coefficient in the model. We found that the top features in the logistic regression were very different from the ones in Random Forest. All were binary features indicating either a particular neighborhood or property owner. Some neighborhoods have either very high or low fire rates, and logistic regression tends to assign large positive or negative weights to them, respectively. However, since each of these features is only good at predicting a small number of properties within a certain area but does not predict well on the overall data, they are not chosen in the first few iterations of a decision tree.

5.5 Assignment of Risk Scores

After we built the predictive model, we then applied the fire risk scores of each property to the list of current and potential inspectable properties, so that AFRD could focus on inspecting the properties most at risk of fire. To do this, we first computed the raw output of our predictive model for the

	Testing AUC of the following year	
Training window	Random Forest	SVM
2011-2012	0.7624	0.7614
2011-2013	0.8030	0.7914
2011-2014	0.8246	0.8079

Table 3: Testing AUC of each year

	Top 10 features
1	floor size
2	land area
3	number of units
4	appraised value
5	number of buildings
6	total taxes
7	property type is multi-family
8	lot size
9	number of living units
10	percent leased

Table 4: Top-10 features in Random Forest

list of properties we used to train and test the model. This generated a score between 0 and 1, which we then mapped to the discrete range of 1 to 10 that is easier for our AFRD colleagues to work with. Then, based on visual examination of the clustering of risk scores, we categorized the scores into low risk (1), medium risk (2-5), and high risk (6-10). These risk categorizations were intended to assign a manageable amount of medium risk ($N = 402$) and high risk properties ($N = 69$) for AFRD to prioritize.

We then needed to find out which of the properties with risk scores were in the lists of 2,573 current annually inspected properties and 6,096 potentially inspectable properties. Because of the lack of a consistent property ID across the various datasets used to develop the risk model, the currently inspected and potentially inspectable properties were spatially joined with the properties in the risk model, based on their geo-coordinates or addresses. After joining, we were able to assign risk scores to 5,022 of the 8,669 total commercial properties on the inspection list (both currently inspected [2,573] and potentially inspectable [6,096]).

6. IMPACT ON AFRD AND ATLANTA

6.1 Previous Inspection Process

Our goal in developing the Firebird framework was to help the Atlanta Fire Rescue Department (AFRD) and other municipal fire departments improve their identification and prioritization of commercial property inspections. Before considering the impact our work had on that process, it is important to first describe the previous process of commercial fire inspections in Atlanta. First, fire inspectors at AFRD received a list of properties to inspect every month, which had been inspected during that same month in the previous year. The existing process for adding new commercial properties to the list of required inspections was extremely ad hoc, without a formal notification process from other city departments when new buildings were built or occupied, or new businesses registered. It was largely the responsibility of individual fire inspectors to notice new inspectable properties and initiate an inspection process while driving to another inspection site. Moreover, there was no formal process used by the inspectors to prioritize their monthly inspections based on risk, or even to schedule their daily inspections based on proximity to other inspections. In other words, it is very possible that an inspector could return to the same business complex multiple times throughout the year conducting inspections on adjacent properties, which is not the most effective use of municipal resources. In addition, at present, the City of Atlanta Code of Ordinances does not specify the frequency of inspections based upon risk or other factors. As a result, inspections are effectively binary; regardless of potential fire risk, a property either gets an annual inspection in the same month every year, or it is unlikely to be inspected at all.

6.2 Technology Transfer to AFRD

After developing the Firebird framework, we first provided AFRD's executive staff and Community Risk Reduction Section with a dataset of all commercial properties in Atlanta that fit their criteria for inspection. This included a shorter list of 6,096 new inspectable properties which are of the top 100 currently inspected property usage types (e.g., restaurants, motor vehicle repair facilities, etc), and a longer list of all commercial properties (19,397) that fit any property usage type that had been previously inspected. This dataset included the associated building- and parcel-level information for those properties in the form of a CSV file, with a subset of those properties (5,022) assigned a fire risk score. We then provided AFRD with an interactive map-based visualization tool, as part of the Firebird framework, for the fire inspectors and AFRD executive staff to use to augment their policy and decision-making processes. The map in Figure 4 was made using the open source map-making tools Mapbox and Leaflet to create the base map layer. Then, using the Javascript visualization library D3.js, we displayed differently colored circles on the map to represent fire incidents, currently inspected properties, and potentially inspectable properties in red, green, and blue, respectively, using their longitude and latitude coordinates.

We also built a user interface for the Firebird map developed through discussions with the AFRD Assessment and Planning Section, and refined by incorporating feedback from fire inspectors and AFRD executive staff. The map includes an information panel for displaying property information when hovering over a property on the map, such as its business name, address, occupancy usage type, date since fire incident or inspection, and fire risk score, if available. The map also includes a user interface panel with the ability to filter the fire incidents, the currently inspected, and the potentially inspectable properties according to their property usage type, the date of fire incident or inspection, and their risk score. Finally, we incorporated a set of regional overlays requested by the AFRD executive staff, including the AFRD battalions, and the Atlanta Neighborhood Planning Units (NPU) and Council Districts, which are both political subdivisions of the city. We included dynamically updated counts and percentages for the displayed fire incidents, current inspections, and potential inspections for each regional overlay (Figure 4), so the AFRD executive staff could make decisions at a battalion, NPU, or Council District level.

This map, and the Firebird framework in general, could be used as a powerful tool for supporting data-driven conversations about personnel and resource allocation and in-

Figure 4: **Interactive map of fires and inspections.** The colored circles on the map represent fire incidents, currently inspected properties, and potentially inspectable properties in red, green, and blue, respectively. Inspectors can filter the displayed properties based on property usage type, date of fire or inspection, and fire risk score. *Callout:* activating the Neighborhood Planning Unit overlay allows an inspector to mouse-over a political subdivision of the city to view its aggregate and percentage of the fires, inspections, and potential inspections.

spection decisions, and may even be used to inform decisions regarding community education programs for fire safety and prevention. To ensure AFRD could update the risk model and property visualization as new fire incident and inspection data becomes available, we shared our source code and process with AFRD's Assessment and Planning Section, and made it publicly available on Github.[4]

6.3 Impact on AFRD Processes

After receiving the dataset of properties needing inspection, prioritized according to their fire risk score, AFRD has begun integrating the results of the analytics into their fire inspection process. Increasing the number of annual inspections by 6,096 (237%) overnight was not feasible without significant changes in organizational processes, local ordinances, or increased staffing. As an initial effort, AFRD assigned the 69 high-risk properties to the inspectors covering those respective areas. Of those, 27 had current or out-of-date fire safety permits that required re-inspection, 13 properties required new permits, and 15 properties recently went out of business. The remaining properties were found to not require a fire safety permit. Most significantly, the inspectors assigned to review these properties found a total of 48 violations that needed to be addressed to meet the Fire Code. As AFRD continues working through the list of potentially inspectable properties in descending risk order, the sheer number of additional inspections (increased workload) and potential violations identified and mitigated (positive outcomes) has already had a transformative impact on the daily operations of AFRD's fire inspection process.

In addition to the immediate impact on the daily property inspections, the results of this work have stimulated important conversations within the executive leadership of AFRD and the Assessment and Planning Section about 1) how to more effectively allocate inspection personnel; 2) how to update and utilize the model to provide dynamic risk data in real time (e.g., on a monthly basis when new inspection assignments are given to the inspectors); 3) how to motivate increased data sharing between various government departments such as the Office of Buildings and AFRD; 4) how to give teams of firefighters access to fire safety permit and violation information when they respond to a fire emergency at that commercial property; and 5) how to extend the risk prioritization to residential properties using more behavioral data such as noise or sanitation ordinance violations, and consumer data from companies like Experian or ESRI.

Though there are many more inspectable properties than AFRD currently has the personnel capacity to handle, AFRD has already begun to take steps toward a more efficient use of their existing personnel, by discussing how to assign inspectors to regions with a higher proportion of properties requiring inspection, rather than by the geographical assignment to fire battalions currently in use. In addition, they have begun to discuss altering properties' inspection frequencies to reflect their fire risk levels. By prioritizing future inspections and more efficiently allocating inspection personnel to target the commercial properties most at risk of fire, we hope this work will lead to a reduction in the frequency and severity of fire incidents in Atlanta. We also hope that this framework can be instructive for other municipal fire departments to improve their fire inspection processes.

7. CHALLENGES

As fire departments in many municipalities embark on more data-driven fire risk inspection policies and practices, several challenges we encountered could prove instructive for others. As with many governmental data science initiatives, the practical application of the predictive model has been contingent on local politics, organizational inertia, and existing policies, or what [4] calls the "politics of place.' While AFRD was an active and engaged partner throughout this

[4]https://github.com/DSSG-Firebird

project, securing access to clean and usable data proved a challenge. At the time of this writing, the City of Atlanta's Office of Buildings, Office of Housing, and AFRD do not share a unified database of buildings or a shared building identification numbering convention, and thus, the process of joining various datasets was more technologically difficult than it might otherwise have been. Even the seemingly simple task of discovering which properties in the Office of Building's dataset were also in the AFRD dataset required a rather elaborate process of fuzzy text-matching and address verification. In addition, our ability to leverage regularly updated dynamic data was similarly hindered by the difficulty of data sharing among city departments. For instance, the Office of Building's Business License database may very well be updated regularly, but without a pipeline in place for those updated data to be used by AFRD, businesses may close without AFRD knowing, causing inspectors to waste time attempting to inspect closed businesses. These challenges could be mitigated if each department with a vested interest in municipal commercial properties and structures worked more closely to share their data and information.

Entrenched organizational processes may similarly hinder the adoption of new methods of identifying properties to inspect. While, in theory, the fire inspection process targets properties that are required by city ordinance to have a fire safety permit (e.g., restaurants over a certain capacity, auto repair facilities, etc.), in practice there is no existing organizational procedure at AFRD and in many other cities to systematically add properties to the list of regular inspections, or to determine their frequency of inspection [12]. In this work, while we have created and employed an innovative method of identifying new properties to inspect, until inter-departmental data-sharing becomes widespread, this process would need to be redone on a regular basis as new businesses open, close, or change usage type. Further, though we created an interactive map for visualization of various types of property inspections, such a tool has not previously been part of AFRD fire inspectors' regular workflow, and this novelty presents a barrier for adoption, as seen in [10]. Finally, with the number of inspectable properties increasing by up to 237%, there is no clear incentive for the fire inspectors to work more efficiently to increase their individual number of property inspections per month.

From a policy standpoint, the existing municipal Fire Code in Atlanta [2] requires that inspections occur regularly for a specified set of commercial property types, but it is not clear that those property types require inspection with equal priority or frequency, or that these property types are the most in need of inspection. After using the results of this work for determining individual property fire risk, the AFRD should begin a conversation about how best to revise their municipal fire code to reflect differences in inspection type, priority, and frequency due to the fire risk associated with various property types. Prior work in [12] has similarly suggested revisions of the British Columbian fire code from being a reactive, inflexible document based on tradition and intuition to a data-driven, responsive, and pro-active document that incorporates information about fire risk. Finally, AFRD's policies for property fire inspections are primarily geared towards commercial properties, yet the majority of the fires in Atlanta occur in residential properties. This will require additional rethinking of their residential community fire safety and prevention education programs.

As in many municipalities, fully leveraging the power of analytics to improve fire safety in Atlanta will require a significant rethinking of how to approach and manage city operations such as fire inspections, and how to best facilitate data sharing practices between different city agencies.

8. CONCLUSIONS AND FUTURE WORK

Due to the large number of commercial properties in Atlanta potentially requiring inspection and the limited inspection personnel capacity of the Atlanta Fire Rescue Department (AFRD), as in many other municipalities, there is a need for a data-driven prioritization of commercial property inspections. In this paper, we provide the Firebird framework: a re-usable method for municipal fire departments to identify and prioritize their commercial property fire inspections based on each property's fire risk. Our work first provides a clear process for joining disparate data sources from multiple municipal departments and private sources to identify new inspectable properties based on currently inspected property types. We were able to identify 6,096 new inspectable properties, comprised of the top 100 property types currently inspected by the AFRD, and a total of 19,397 new inspectable properties comprised of all currently inspected property types by AFRD.

We next present a method for predicting fire risk for each commercial property. Our models used 58 building- and parcel-level variables to predict fires in 8,223 properties, 5,022 of which are on the list of properties requiring inspection. Specifically, we trained SVM and Random Forest models using data from 2011-2014 to predict fires in 2015. At a false positive rate of 20%, the SVM and Random Forest models were able to predict 71.36% and 69.28% of the fires in that year, respectively. Furthermore, even the false positives provided valuable insight, since they represent properties with high risk of catching fire, that likely should be inspected by AFRD. We also identified features that are highly related to fires. From the Random Forest model, we learned that features related to building size, number or units, and value were most predictive. On the other hand, the logistic regression model revealed certain neighborhoods and property owners that associate with very high or low fire rates. We then converted these results to a risk score for each property, and were able to apply these scores to 5,022 currently inspected and potentially inspectable properties (1,975 currently annually inspected and 3,047 potentially inspectable), with 454 of those properties having a medium or high risk score (188 currently inspected and 266 potentially inspectable properties). Finally, we incorporated those scores into our joined dataset of property inspections and visualized each of the properties on an interactive map, with their associated property information and risk score, for use by AFRD to augment their inspection decision processes.

Research Directions. Future research should seek to refine, expand, and further validate our prediction model. Due to missing or erroneous entries in the data sources, we could only to incorporate 8,223 properties into our predictive fire risk model, out of the more than 20,000 commercial properties in the city. In addition, because of the lack of integration across city department datasets and a lack of completeness in many of our datasets, we could only provide risk scores for 5,022 of the 8,669 current and potentially inspectable properties in the dataset we provided to AFRD. Researchers working with other municipal fire departments might train their models on a dataset that has fewer building- or parcel-level information variables, but may be applicable to more properties. Other work could improve the accuracy of the model by incorporating additional dynamic sources of data, such as violations of prior fire inspections, data from the Department of Health and Wellness inspections, information from the Certificates of Occupancy, or other, more behavioral sources, such as sanitation or noise violations, as seen in [6], rather than the largely static building- and parcel-level data that we used. In addition, more research needs to be done on the usefulness and usability of an interactive map to display inspection, and how the inspectors or executive staff of a fire department could use it in different ways to inform their day-to-day planning, decisions, and operations. One step that municipal government agencies can take towards implementing this framework is to generate a unique Building Identification Number (BIN), used by all stakeholders, such as the Office of Buildings, Office of Housing or city planning departments, as well as the Fire and Police Departments. This would allow for easier joining of disparate sources of data, without the need for address validation, text matching, and other complex and potentially error-generating processes for joining datasets.

Identification, selection, and prioritization of risky properties for fire inspection can be difficult for cities that do not have an integrated data platform, because some municipal agencies may have relevant property and structure information that is isolated from other local data sources, and which may not have a regular, timely process for updating. Our framework outlined here can be a model for improving the complex process of property inspection, identification, and prioritization. Additionally, our experience joining isolated datasets from different government departments, commercial data, and open data sources could be invaluable for many cities that want to begin utilizing data science for a smarter city, without requiring a significant financial investment. We hope the impact from our work may further promote the beneficial use of open public sector data, both in the city of Atlanta and elsewhere.

9. ACKNOWLEDGMENTS

We thank our partners at the Atlanta Fire Rescue Department for their support and willingness to re-examine their existing processes, especially Chief Baker, Chief Rhodes, and the staff of the Community Risk Reduction Section. We thank the Data Science for Social Good Atlanta program for their support for this research. This work was partially supported by NSF grant IIS-1217559, TWC-1526254, and gifts from Google, Symantec, Yahoo! Labs, eBay.

10. REFERENCES

[1] National Fire Protection Association. Fires in the U.S. http://www.nfpa.org/research/reports-and-statistics/fires-in-the-us. Accessed: 2016-02-09.

[2] City of Atlanta. Code of ordinances: Fire prevention and protection. https://www.municode.com/library/ga/atlanta/codes/code_of_ordinances, 2015.

[3] L. Breiman. Random forests. *Machine learning*, 45(1):5–32, 2001.

[4] J. B. Carr and K. LeRoux. Which local governments cooperate on public safety?: lessons from michigan. *Working Group on Interlocal Services Cooperation*, page 4, 2005.

[5] J. Clare, L. Garis, D. Plecas, and C. Jennings. Reduced frequency and severity of residential fires following delivery of fire prevention education by on-duty fire fighters: Cluster randomized controlled study. *Journal of safety research*, 43(2):123–128, 2012.

[6] E. Copeland. Big data in the big apple. *Capital City Foundation.*, 2015.

[7] C. Cortes and V. Vapnik. Support-vector networks. *Machine learning*, 20(3):273–297, 1995.

[8] M. DaCosta, J. Krinsley, and B. Abelson. Optimizing local smoke alarm inspections with federal data. *Bloomberg Data for Good Exchange*, 2015.

[9] M. P. de Vasconcelos, S. Silva, M. Tome, M. Alvim, and J. C. Pereira. Spatial prediction of fire ignition probabilities: comparing logistic regression and neural networks. *Photogrammetric engineering and remote sensing*, 67(1):73–81, 2001.

[10] L. Dobrică, T. Ionescu, L. Dobrică, and S. Elena. Solutions based on gis technology in components of urban management applications. *U.P.B Scientific Bulletin*, 2010.

[11] J. H. Friedman. Stochastic gradient boosting. *Computational Statistics & Data Analysis*, 38(4):367–378, 2002.

[12] L. Garis and J. Clare. A dynamic risk–based framework for redesigning the scheduling of fire safety inspections. 2014.

[13] J. Gonzalez. Fuzzywuzzy. https://github.com/seatgeek/fuzzywuzzy, 2015.

[14] L. S. Iliadis. A decision support system applying an integrated fuzzy model for long-term forest fire risk estimation. *Environmental Modelling & Software*, 20(5):613–621, 2005.

[15] D. Kansagara, H. Englander, A. Salanitro, D. Kagen, C. Theobald, M. Freeman, and S. Kripalani. Risk prediction models for hospital readmission: a systematic review. *Jama*, 306(15):1688–1698, 2011.

[16] H. Lakkaraju, E. Aguiar, C. Shan, D. Miller, N. Bhanpuri, R. Ghani, and K. L. Addison. A machine learning framework to identify students at risk of adverse academic outcomes. In *KDD*, pages 1909–1918. ACM, 2015.

[17] A. Lapucci, S. Lombardo, M. Petri, and A. Santucci. A KDD based multicriteria decision making model for fire risk evaluation. In *Conference on GIS-cience (AGILE)*, 2005.

[18] M. McGlohon, S. Bay, M. G. Anderle, D. M. Steier, and C. Faloutsos. Snare: a link analytic system for graph labeling and risk detection. In *KDD*, pages 1265–1274. ACM, 2009.

[19] J. A. Nelder and R. J. Baker. Generalized linear models. *Encyclopedia of Statistical Sciences*, 1972.

[20] F. Pedregosa, G. Varoquaux, A. Gramfort, V. Michel, B. Thirion, O. Grisel, M. Blondel, P. Prettenhofer, R. Weiss, V. Dubourg, J. Vanderplas, A. Passos, D. Cournapeau, M. Brucher, M. Perrot, and E. Duchesnay. Scikit-learn: Machine learning in Python. *JMLR*, 12:2825–2830, 2011.

DopeLearning: A Computational Approach to Rap Lyrics Generation*

Eric Malmi
Aalto University and HIIT
Espoo, Finland
eric.malmi@aalto.fi

Pyry Takala
Aalto University
Espoo, Finland
pyry.takala@aalto.fi

Hannu Toivonen
University of Helsinki and HIIT
Helsinki, Finland
hannu.toivonen@cs.helsinki.fi

Tapani Raiko
Aalto University
Espoo, Finland
tapani.raiko@aalto.fi

Aristides Gionis
Aalto University and HIIT
Espoo, Finland
aristides.gionis@aalto.fi

ABSTRACT

Writing rap lyrics requires both creativity to construct a meaningful, interesting story and lyrical skills to produce complex rhyme patterns, which form the cornerstone of good flow. We present a rap lyrics generation method that captures both of these aspects. First, we develop a prediction model to identify the next line of existing lyrics from a set of candidate next lines. This model is based on two machine-learning techniques: the RankSVM algorithm and a deep neural network model with a novel structure. Results show that the prediction model can identify the true next line among 299 randomly selected lines with an accuracy of 17%, i.e., over 50 times more likely than by random. Second, we employ the prediction model to combine lines from existing songs, producing lyrics with rhyme and a meaning. An evaluation of the produced lyrics shows that in terms of quantitative rhyme density, the method outperforms the best human rappers by 21%. The rap lyrics generator has been deployed as an online tool called DeepBeat, and the performance of the tool has been assessed by analyzing its usage logs. This analysis shows that machine-learned rankings correlate with user preferences.

1. INTRODUCTION

Emerging from a hobby of African American youth in the 1970s, rap music has quickly evolved into a mainstream music genre with several artists frequenting Billboard top rankings. Our objective is to study the problem of computational creation of rap lyrics. Our interest in this problem is motivated by two different different perspectives. First, we are interested in analyzing the formal structure of rap lyrics and in developing a model that can lead to generating artistic work. Second, with the number of smart devices increasing that we use on a daily basis, it is expected that the demand will increase for systems that interact with humans in non-mechanical and pleasant ways.

Rap is distinguished from other music genres by the formal structure present in rap lyrics, which makes the lyrics rhyme well and hence provides better flow to the music. Literature professor Adam Bradley compares rap with popular music and traditional poetry, stating that while popular lyrics lack much of the formal structure of literary verse, rap crafts "intricate structures of sound and rhyme, creating some of the most scrupulously formal poetry composed today" [5].

We approach the problem of lyrics creation from an information-retrieval (IR) perspective. We assume that we have access to a large repository of rap-song lyrics. In this paper, we use a dataset containing over half a million lines from lyrics of 104 different rap artists. We then view the lyrics-generation problem as the task of identifying a *relevant next line*. We consider that a rap song has been partially constructed and treat the first m lines of the song as a *query*. The IR task is to identify the most relevant next line from a collection of candidate lines, with respect to the query. Following this approach, new lyrics are constructed line by line, combining lyrics from different artists in order to introduce novelty. A key advantage of this approach is that we can evaluate the performance of the generator by measuring how well it predicts existing songs. While conceptually one could approach the lyrics-generation problem by a word-by-word construction, so as to increase novelty, such an approach would require significantly more complex models and we leave it for future work.

Our work lies in the intersection between the areas of *computational creativity* and *information retrieval*. In our approach, we assume that users have a certain concept in their mind, formulated as a sequence of rap lines, and their information need is to find the missing lines, composing a song. Such an information need does not have a factual answer; nevertheless, users will be able to assess the relevance of the response provided by the system. The relevance of the response depends on factors that include rhyming, vocabulary, unexpectedness, semantic coherence, and humor. Tony Veale [26] illustrates other linguistically creative uses of information retrieval, e.g., for metaphor generation. He argues that phrases extracted from large corpora can be used

*When used as an adjective, *dope* means *cool*, *nice*, or *awesome*.

KDD '16, August 13 - 17, 2016, San Francisco, CA, USA

ISBN 978-1-4503-4232-2/16/08...$15.00

DOI: http://dx.doi.org/10.1145/2939672.2939679

as "readymade" or "found" objects, like *objets trouvés* in arts, that can take on fresh meanings when used in a new context.

From the computational perspective, a major challenge in generating rap lyrics is to produce semantically coherent lines instead of merely generating complex rhymes. As Paul Edwards [9] puts it: "If an artist takes his or her time to craft phrases that rhyme in intricate ways but still gets across the message of the song, that is usually seen as the mark of a highly skilled MC."[1] As a result of record results in computer vision, deep neural networks [1] have become a popular tool for feature learning. To avoid hand-crafting a number of semantic and grammatical features, we introduce a deep neural network model that maps sentences into a high-dimensional vector space. This type of vector-space representations have attracted much attention in recent years and have exhibited great empirical performance in tasks requiring semantic analysis of natural language [19, 20].

While some of the features we extract from the analyzed lyrics are tailored for rap lyrics, a similar approach could be applied to generate lyrics for other music genres. Furthermore, the proposed framework could form the basis for several other text-synthesis problems, such as generation of text or conversation responses. Practical extended applications include automation of tasks, such as customer service, sales, or even news reporting.

Our contributions can be summarized as follows:

(*i*) We propose an information-retrieval approach to rap lyrics generation. A similar approach could be applied to other tasks requiring text synthesis.

(*ii*) We introduce several useful features for predicting the next line of a rap song and hence for generating new lyrics. In particular, we have developed a deep neural network model for capturing the semantic similarity of lines. This feature carries the most predictive power of all the features we have studied.

(*iii*) We present *rhyme density*, a measure for the technical quality of rap lyrics. This measure is validated with a human subject, a native-speaking rap artist.

(*iv*) We have built an online demo of the rap lyrics generator openly available at `deepbeat.org`. The performance of the algorithm has been assessed based on the usage logs of the demo.

The rest of the paper is organized as follows. We start with a brief discussion of relevant work. Next, we discuss the domain of rap lyrics, introduce the dataset that we have used, and describe how rhymes can be analyzed. We proceed by describing the task of NextLine and our approach to solving it, including the used features, the neural language model, and the results of our experiments. We apply the resulting model to the task of lyrics generation, showing also examples of generated lyrics. The final sections discuss further these tasks, our model, and conclusions of the work.

2. RELATED WORK

While the study of human-generated lyrics is of interest to academics in fields such as linguistics and music, artificial rhyme generation is also relevant for various subfields of computer science. Relevant literature can be found under domains of computational creativity, information extraction and natural language processing. Additionally, relevant methods can be found under the domain of machine learning, for instance, in the emerging field of deep learning.

Hirjee and Brown [12, 13] develop a probabilistic method, inspired by local alignment protein homology detection algorithms, for detecting rap rhymes. Their algorithm obtains a high rhyme detection performance, but it requires a training dataset with labeled rhyme pairs. We introduce a simpler, rule-based approach in Section 3.3, which seemed sufficient for our purposes. Hirjee and Brown obtain a phonetic transcription for the lyrics by applying the CMU Pronouncing Dictionary [16], some hand-crafted rules to handle slang words, and text-to-phoneme rules to handle out-of-vocabulary words, whereas we use an open-source speech synthesizer, eSpeak, to produce the transcription. The computational generation of rap lyrics has been previously studied in [29, 28]. These works adopt a machine-translation approach, whereas we view it as an information-retrieval problem. Furthermore, we have deployed our lyrics generator as an openly accessible web tool to assess its performance in the wild.

Automated creation of rap lyrics can also be viewed as a problem within the research field of Computational Creativity, i.e., study of computational systems which exhibit behaviors deemed to be creative [7]. According to Boden [4], creativity is the ability to come up with ideas or artifacts that are new, surprising, and valuable, and there are three different types of creativity. Our work falls into the class of "combinatorial creativity" where creative results are produced as novel combinations of familiar ideas. Combinatorial approaches have been used to create poetry before but were predominantly based on the idea of copying the grammar from existing poetry and then substituting content words with other ones [25].

In the context of web search, it has been shown that document ranking accuracy can be significantly improved by combining multiple features via machine-learning algorithms instead of using a single static ranking, such as PageRank [21]. This *learning-to-rank* approach is very popular nowadays and many methods have been developed for it [17]. In this paper, we use the RankSVM algorithm [14] for combining different relevance features for the next-line prediction problem, which is the basis of our rap-lyrics generator.

Neural networks have been recently applied to various related tasks. For instance, recurrent neural networks (RNNs) have shown promise in predicting text sequences [11, 23]. Other applications include tasks such as information extraction, information retrieval and indexing [8]. Question answering has also been approached by using deep learning to map questions and answers to a latent semantic space, and then either generating a response [27] or selecting one [30]. Our neural network approach has some similarity to response selection as we also learn a mapping to a hidden space. On the other hand, our network architecture uses a feed-forward net—a suitable choice in our context where sentences are often relatively short and equal in length. Also, generation of lyrics is not typically considered as a response-selection task but we interpret it as one.

3. ANATOMY OF RAP LYRICS

In this section, we first describe a typical structure of rap lyrics, as well as different rhyme types that are often used. This information will be the basis for extracting useful fea-

[1]MC, short for master of ceremonies or microphone controller, is essentially a word for a rap artist.

tures for the next-line prediction problem, which we discuss in the next section. Then we introduce a method for automatically detecting rhymes, and we define a measure for rhyme density. We also present experimental results to assess the validity of the rhyme-density measure.

3.1 Rhyming

Various different rhyme types, such as *perfect rhyme*, *alliteration*, and *consonance*, are employed in rap lyrics, but the most common rhyme type nowadays, due to its versatility, is the *assonance* rhyme [2, 9]. In a perfect rhyme, the words share exactly the same end sound, as in "slang – gang," whereas in an assonance rhyme only the vowel sounds are shared. For example, words "crazy" and "baby" have different consonant sounds, but the vowel sounds are the same as can be seen from their phonetic representations "kɹeɪsi" and "beɪbi."

An assonance rhyme does not have to cover only the end of the rhyming words but it can span multiple words as in the example below (rhyming part is highlighted). This type of assonance rhyme is called *multisyllabic rhyme.*

"This is a job — I get paid to **sling some raps**,
What you made last year was less than my **income tax**" [10]

It is stated in [10] that "[Multisyllabic rhymes] are hallmarks of all the dopest flows, and all the best rappers use them,"

3.2 Song structure

A typical rap song follows a pattern of alternating verses and choruses. These in turn consist of lines, which break down to individual words and finally to syllables. A line equals one musical bar, which typically consists of four beats, setting limits to how many syllables can be fit into a single line. Verses, which constitute the main body of a song, are often composed of 16 lines. [9]

Consecutive lines can be joined through rhyme, which is typically placed at the end of the lines but can appear anywhere within the lines. The same end rhyme can be maintained for a couple of lines or even throughout an entire verse. In the verses our algorithm generates, the end rhyme is kept fixed for four consecutive lines unless otherwise specified by the user (see Appendix A for an example).

3.3 Automatic rhyme detection

Our aim is to automatically detect multisyllabic assonance rhymes from lyrics given as text. For this, we first obtain a phonetic transcription of the lyrics by applying the text-to-phonemes functionality of an open source speech synthesizer eSpeak.[2] The synthesizer assumes a typical American–English pronunciation. From the phonetic transcription, we can detect rhymes by finding matching vowel phoneme sequences, ignoring consonant phonemes and spaces.

3.3.1 Rhyme density measure

In order to quantify the technical quality of lyrics from a rhyming perspective, we introduce a measure for the *rhyme density* of the lyrics. A simplified description[3] for the computation of this measure is provided below:

1. Compute the phonetic transcription of the lyrics and remove all but vowel phonemes.
2. Scan the lyrics word by word.
3. For each word, find the longest matching vowel sequence (=multisyllabic assonance rhyme) in the proximity of the word.
4. Compute the rhyme density by averaging the lengths of the longest matching vowel sequences of all words.

The rhyme density of an artist is computed as the average rhyme density of his or her (or its) songs. Intuitively speaking, rhyme density means the average length of the longest rhyme per word.

Table 1: A selection of popular rappers and their rhyme densities, i.e., their average rhyme lengths per word.

Rank	Artist	Rhyme density
1.	Inspectah Deck	1.187
2.	Rakim	1.180
3.	Redrama	1.168
30.	The Notorious B.I.G.	1.059
31.	Lil Wayne	1.056
32.	Nicki Minaj	1.056
33.	2Pac	1.054
39.	Eminem	1.047
40.	Nas	1.043
50.	Jay-Z	1.026
63.	Wu-Tang Clan	1.002
77.	Snoop Dogg	0.967
78.	Dr. Dre	0.966
94.	The Lonely Island	0.870

3.3.2 Data

We compiled a list of 104 popular English-speaking rap artists and scraped all their songs available on a popular lyrics website. In total, we have 583 669 lines from 10 980 songs.

To make the rhyme densities of different artists comparable, we normalize the lyrics by removing all duplicate lines within a single song, as in some cases the lyrics contain the chorus repeated many times, whereas in other cases they might just have "Chorus 4X," depending on the user who has provided the lyrics. Some songs, like intro tracks, often contain more regular speech rather than rapping, and hence, we have removed all songs whose title has one of the following words: "intro," "outro," "skit," or "interlude."

3.3.3 Evaluating human rappers' rhyming skills

We initially computed the rhyme density for 94 rappers, ranked the artists based on this measure, and published the results online [18]. An excerpt of the results is shown in Table 1.

Some of the results are not too surprising; for instance Rakim, who is ranked second, is known for "his pioneering use of internal rhymes and multisyllabic rhymes."[4] On the other hand, a limitation of the results is that some artists, like Eminem, who use a lot of multisyllabic rhymes but construct them often by bending words (pronouncing words un-

[2]http://espeak.sourceforge.net/
[3]For the details, see: https://github.com/ekQ/raplysaattori
[4]The Wikipedia article on Rakim http://en.wikipedia.org/wiki/Rakim (Accessed: 2016-02-11)

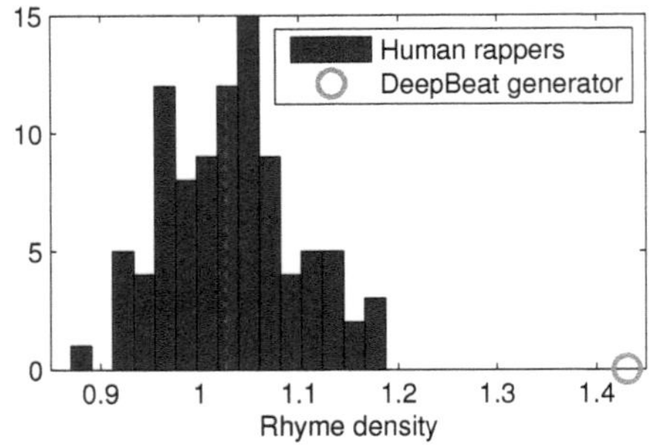

Figure 1: Rhyme density distribution of 105 rappers.

Table 2: List of rap songs ranked by the algorithm and by the artist himself according to how technical he perceives them. Correlation is 0.42.

Rank by artist	Rank by algorithm	Rhyme density
1.	1.	1.542
2.	4.	1.214
3.–4.	9.	0.930
3.–4.	3.	1.492
5.	2.	1.501
6.–7.	10.	0.909
6.–7.	7.	1.047
8.–9.	6.	1.149
8.–9.	5.	1.185
10.	8.	1.009
11.	11.	0.904

usually to make them rhyme), are not as high on the list as one might expect.

In Figure 1, we show the distribution of rhyme densities along with the rhyme density obtained by our lyrics generator algorithm DeepBeat (see Section 5.3 for details).

3.4 Validating the rhyme density measure

After we had published the results shown in Table 1 online, a rap artist called *Ahmen* contacted us, asking us to compute the rhyme density for the lyrics of his debut album. Before revealing the rhyme densities of the 11 individual songs he sent us, we asked the rapper to rank his own lyrics "starting from the most technical according to where you think you have used the most and the longest rhymes." The rankings produced by the artist and by the algorithm are shown in Table 2.

We can compute the correlation between the artist produced and algorithm produced rankings by applying the Kendall tau rank correlation coefficient. Assuming that all ties indicated by the artist are decided unfavorably for the algorithm, the correlation between the two rankings would still be 0.42, and the null hypothesis of the rankings being independent can be rejected ($p < 0.05$). This suggests that the rhyme density measure adequately captures the technical quality of rap lyrics.

4. NEXT LINE PREDICTION

We approach the problem of rap lyrics generation as an information-retrieval task. In short, our approach is as follows: we consider a large repository of rap lyrics, which we treat as training data, and which we use to learn a model between consecutive lines in rap lyrics. Then, given a set of seed lines we can use our model to identify the best next line among a set of candidate next lines taken from the lyrics repository. The method can then be used to construct a song line-by-line, appending relevant lines from different songs.

In order to evaluate this information-retrieval task, we define the problem of *"next-line prediction."*

4.1 Problem definition

As mentioned above, in the core of our algorithm for generating rap lyrics is the task of finding the next line of a given song. This next line prediction problem is defined as follows.

PROBLEM 1. (*NextLine*) *Consider the lyrics of a rap song S, which is a sequence of n lines $(s_1, \ldots, s_n)$. Assume that the first m lines of S, denoted by $B = (s_1, \ldots, s_m)$, are known and are considered as "the query." Consider also that we are given a set of k* candidate next lines $C = \{\ell_1, \ldots, \ell_k\}$, *and the* promise *that $s_{m+1} \in C$. The goal is to identify s_{m+1} in the candidate set C, i.e., pick a line $\ell_i \in C$ such that $\ell_i = s_{m+1}$.*

Our approach to solving the NextLine problem is to compute a relevance score between the query B and each candidate line $\ell \in C$, and return the line that maximizes this relevance score. The performance of the method can be evaluated using standard information retrieval measures, such as mean reciprocal rank. As the relevance score we use a linear model over a set of similarity features between the query song-prefix B and the candidate next lines $\ell \in C$. The weights of the linear model are learned using the RankSVM algorithm, described in Section 4.3.2.

In the next section, we describe a set of features that we use for measuring the similarity between the previous lines B and a candidate next line ℓ.

4.2 Feature extraction

The similarity features we use for the next-line prediction problem can be divided into three groups, capturing (*i*) *rhyming*, (*ii*) *structural similarity*, and (*iii*) *semantic similarity*.

(*i*) We extract three different rhyme features based on the phonetic transcription of the lines, as discussed in Section 3.3.

EndRhyme is the number of matching vowel phonemes at the end of lines ℓ and s_m, i.e., the last line of B. Spaces and consonant phonemes are ignored, so for instance, the following two phrases would have three end rhyme vowels in common.

Line	*Phonetic transcription*
pay for	pe̲ɪ̲ fɔ̲ː̲ɹ
stay warm	ste̲ɪ̲ wɔ̲ː̲ɹm

EndRhyme-1 is the number of matching vowel phonemes at the end of lines ℓ and s_{m-1}, i.e., the line before the last in B. This feature captures alternating rhyme schemes of the form *"abab."*

OtherRhyme is the average number of matching vowel phonemes per word. For each word in ℓ, we find the longest matching vowel sequence in s_m and average the lengths of these sequences. This captures other than end rhymes.

(*ii*) With respect to the structural similarity between lines, we extract one feature measuring the difference of the lengths of the lines.

LineLength. Typically, consecutive lines are roughly the same length since they need to be spoken out within one musical bar of a fixed length. The length similarity of two lines ℓ and s is computed as

$$1 - \frac{|\mathrm{len}(\ell) - \mathrm{len}(s)|}{\max(\mathrm{len}(\ell), \mathrm{len}(s))},$$

where len $(\cdot)$ is the function that returns the number of characters in a line.[5] We compute the length similarity between a candidate line ℓ and the last line s_m of the song prefix B.

(*iii*) Finally, for measuring semantic similarity between lines, we employ four different features.

BOW. First, we tokenize the lines and represent each last line s_m of B as a bag of words S_m. We apply the same procedure and obtain a bag of words L for a candidate line ℓ. We then measure semantic similarity between two lines by computing the Jaccard similarity between the corresponding bags of words

$$\frac{|S_m \cap L|}{|S_m \cup L|}.$$

BOW5. Instead of extracting a bag-of-words representation from only the last line s_m of B, we use the k previous lines.

$$\frac{\left|\left(\bigcup_{j=m-k}^{m} S_j\right) \cap L\right|}{\left|\left(\bigcup_{j=m-k}^{m} S_j\right) \cup L\right|}.$$

In this way we can incorporate a longer context that could be relevant with the next line that we want to identify. We have experimented with various values of k, and we found out that using the $k = 5$ previous lines gives the best results.

LSA. Bag-of-word models are not able to cope with synonymy nor polysemy. To enhance our model with such capabilities of use a simple latent semantic analysis (**LSA**) approach. As a preprocessing step, we remove stop words and words that appear less than three times. Then we use our training data to form a line–term matrix and we compute a rank-100 approximation of this matrix. Each line is represented by a term vector and is projected on the low-rank matrix space. The **LSA** similarity between two lines is computed as the cosine similarity of their projected vectors.

NN5. Our last semantic feature is based on a neural language model. It is described in more detail in the next section.

4.3 Methods

In this section we present two building blocks of our method: the neural language model used to incorporate semantic similarity with the **NN5** feature and the RankSVM method used to combine the various features.

4.3.1 Neural language model

Our knowledge of all possible features can never be comprehensive, and designing a solid extractor for features such as semantic or grammatical similarity would be extremely time-consuming. Thus, attempting to learn additional features appears a promising approach. Since neural networks

[5]We also tested the number of syllables in a line but the results were similar.

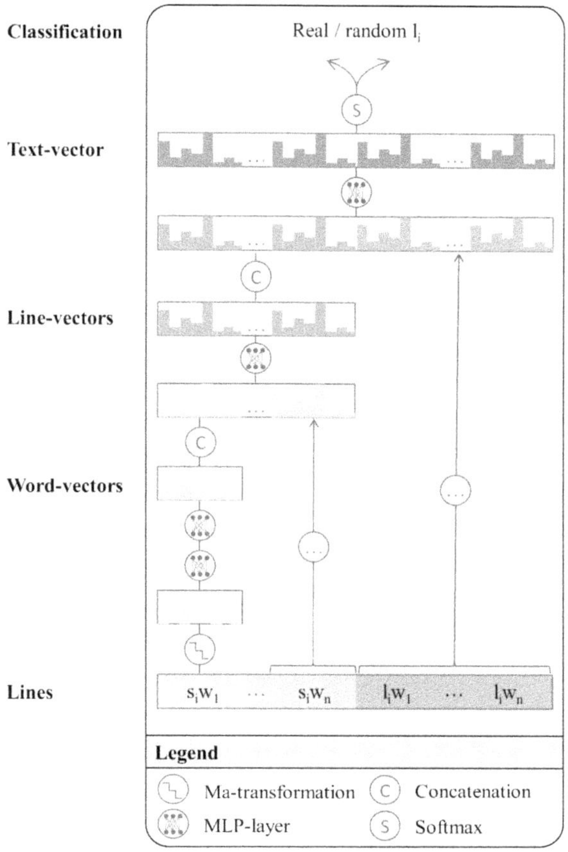

Figure 2: Network architecture

can have a vast number of available parameters and can learn complex nonlinear mappings, we experiment with whether they could be used to automatically extract relevant features. To this end, we design a neural network that learns to use raw text sequences to predict the relevance of a candidate next line given previous lines.

In brief, our neural network starts by finding distributed (vector) representations for words. These are combined to distributed representations of lines, and further combined to vector representations of multiple lines, where the last line may be a real line, or a randomly sampled line. Based on this vector representation of text, our network learns to predict whether it believes that the last line is a suitable next line candidate or not.

Network architecture. At the core of our predictor, we use multi-layered, fully-connected neural networks, trained with backpropagation. While the network structure was originally inspired by the work of Collobert et al. [6], our model differs substantially from theirs. In particular, we have included new input transformations and our input consists of multiple sentences.

The structure of our model is illustrated in Figure 2. We start by preprocessing all text to a format more easily handled by a neural network, removing most non-ascii characters and one-word lines, and stemming and lower-casing all words. Our choice of neural network architecture requires

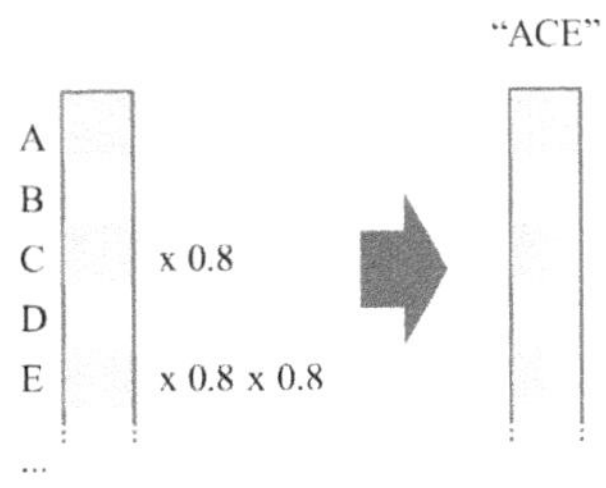

Figure 3: Simplified example of exponential moving-average transformation

fixed line lengths, so we also remove words exceeding 13 words, and pad shorter lines. We build samples in the format: "candidate next line (ℓ_i)"; "previous lines ($s_1, \ldots, s_m$)." For lines with too few previous lines, we add paddings.

The first layers of the network are word-specific: they perform the same transformation for each word in a text, regardless of its position. For each word, we start with an exponential moving average transformation that turns a character sequence into a vector. A simplified example of this is shown in Figure 3 .[6] We use this transformation as it is, compared to one-hot encoding, more robust to different spellings, coping well for instance with slang and spelling errors.

The transformation works as follows: we create a zero-vector, with the length of possible characters. Starting with the first character in a word, we choose its corresponding location in the vector. We increment this value with a value proportional to the character's position in the word, counting from the beginning of the word. We get a word-representation $\mathbf{w} = (w_a\, w_b\, \ldots\, w_z\, \ldots)^T$, where

$$w_a = \sum \frac{(1-\alpha)^{c_a}}{Z},$$

where c is the index of the character at hand, α is a decay hyperparameter, and Z is a normalizer proportional to word length. For further details of this transformation, see [24].

To avoid always giving larger weight to the beginning of a word, we also concatenate to the vector this transformation backwards, and a vector of character counts in the word. Following this transformation, we feed each word vector to a fully-connected neural network.

Our word-specific vectors are next concatenated in the word order to a single line-vector, and fed to a line-level network. Next, the line-vectors are concatenated, so that the candidate next-line is placed first, and preceding lines are then presented in their order of occurrence. This vector is fed to the final layer, and the output is fed to a softmax-function that outputs a binary prediction indicating whether it believes one line follows the next or not. In our ensemble model, we use the activation before the softmax, corresponding to the confidence the network has in a line being the next in the lyrics.

Training. For training the neural network, we retrieve a list of previous lines for each of the lyrics lines. These lyrics are fed to the neural model in small batches, and a corresponding gradient descent update is performed on the weights of the network. To give our network negative examples, we follow an approach similar to [6], and generate fake line examples by choosing for every second example the candidate line uniformly at random from all lyrics.

A set of technical choices is necessary for constructing and training our network. We use two word-specific neural layers (500 neurons each), one line-specific layer (256 neurons, and one final layer (256 neurons). All layers have rectified linear units as the activation function. Our minibatch size is 10, we use the adaptive learning rate Adadelta [31], and we regularize the network with 10% dropout [22]. We train the network for 20 epochs on a GPU machine, taking advantage of the Theano library [3]. Analyzing hyperparameters, we find that we can improve results especially by going from one previous line to a moderately large context (5 previous lines), and by using a larger input window, i.e. giving the network more words from each line.

Manual evaluation. To get some understanding of what our neural network has learnt, we manually analyze 25 random sentences where a random candidate line was falsely classified as being the real next line. For 13 of the lines, we find it difficult to distinguish whether the real or the random line should follow. This often relates to the rapper changing the topic, especially when moving from one verse to another. For the remaining 12 lines, we notice that the neural network has not succeeded in identifying five instances with a rhyme, three instances with repeating words, two instances with consistent sentence styles (lines having always e.g., one sentence per line), one instance with consistent grammar (a sentence continues to next line), and one instance where the pronunciation of words is very similar the previous and the next line. In order to detect the rhymes, the network would need to learn a phonetic representation of the words, but for this problem we have developed other features presented in Section 4.2.

4.3.2 Ranking candidate lines

We take existing rap lyrics as the ground truth for the next line prediction problem. The lyrics are transformed into preferences

$$s_{m+1} \succ_B \ell_i,$$

which are read as "s_{m+1} (the true next line) is preferred over ℓ_i (a randomly sampled line from the set of all available lines) in the context of B (the preceding lines)". When sampling ℓ_i we ensure that $\ell_i \neq s_{m+1}$. Then we extract features $\mathbf{\Phi}(B, \ell)$ listed in Section 4.2 to describe the match between the preceding lines and a candidate next line.

The RankSVM algorithm [14] takes this type of data as input and tries to learn a linear model which gives relevance scores for the candidate lines. These relevance scores should respect the preference relations given as the training data for the algorithm. The relevance scores are given by

$$r(B,\ell) = \mathbf{w}^T \mathbf{\Phi}(B,\ell), \tag{1}$$

where $\mathbf{w}$ is a weight vector of the same length as the number of features.

The advantage of having a simple linear model is that it can be trained very efficiently. We employ the SVM^{rank} software for the learning [15]. Furthermore, we can interpret the weights as importance values for the features. Therefore,

[6]While we achieve our best results using this transformation, a traditional 'one-hot' vector approach yields nearly as good results. A model that learns the transformation, such as a recurrent neural network could also be tested in future work.

Table 3: Next line prediction results for $k = 300$ candidate lines. MRR stands for mean reciprocal rank and Rec@N for recall when retrieving top N lines.

Feature(s)	Mean rank	MRR	Rec@1	Rec@5	Rec@30	Rec@150
Random	150.5	0.021	0.003	0.017	0.010	0.500
LineLength	117.6	0.030	0.002	0.029	0.177	0.657
EndRhyme	103.2	**0.140**	**0.077**	**0.181**	**0.344**	0.480
EndRhyme-1	126.0	0.075	0.037	0.092	0.205	0.347
OtherRhyme	123.3	0.047	0.016	0.055	0.190	0.604
BOW	112.4	0.116	0.074	0.138	0.280	0.516
BOW5	99.1	0.110	0.065	0.129	0.314	0.708
LSA	111.3	0.089	0.051	0.107	0.262	0.662
NN5	**84.7**	0.067	0.020	0.083	0.319	**0.793**
FastFeats	73.5	0.224	0.160	0.272	0.476	0.802
FastFeatsNN5	61.2	**0.244**	**0.172**	**0.306**	0.524	0.853
All features	**60.8**	0.243	0.169	0.304	**0.527**	**0.855**

when the model is later applied to lyrics generation, the user could manually adjust the weights, if he or she, for instance, prefers to have lyrics where the end rhyme plays a larger/smaller role.

4.4 Empirical next line prediction evaluation

Our experimental setup is the following. We split the lyrics by artist randomly into training (50%), validation (25%), and test (25%). The RankSVM model and the neural network model are learned using the training set, while varying a trade-off parameter C among $\{1, 10^1, 10^2, 10^3, 10^4, 10^5\}$ to find the value which maximizes the performance on the validation set. The final performance is evaluated on the unseen test set.

We use a candidate set containing the true next line and 299 randomly chosen lines. The performance is measured using mean rank, mean reciprocal rank (reciprocal value of the harmonic mean of ranks), and recall at N where the value of N is varied. The results are computed based on a random sample of 10 000 queries.

Table 3 shows the test performance for different feature sets. Each feature alone yields a mean rank of < 150 and thus carries some predictive power. The best individual feature with respect to the mean rank is the output of the neural network model. However, if we look at recall at 1 (the probability to rank the true next line first), the best performance, 7.7%, is obtained by EndRhyme which works very well in some cases but is in overall inferior to NN5 since in some cases consecutive lines do not rhyme at all. Combining all features, we achieve a mean rank of 60.8 and can pick the true next line with 16.9% accuracy. The probability to pick the true next line at random is only 0.3%. The features are combined by taking a linear combination of their values according to Equation (1).

To enable the generation of rap lyrics in real time, we also tested employing only the features which are fast to evaluate, i.e., FastFeats = LineLength + EndRhyme + EndRhyme-1 + BOW + BOW5, and FastFeatsNN5 = FastFeats + NN5. With the latter feature set, the performance is almost identical to using the full feature set and even FastFeats works relatively well.

Algorithm 1: Lyrics generation algorithm DeepBeat.

```
Input: Seed line ℓ1, length of the lyrics n.
Output: Lyrics L = (ℓ1, ℓ2, ..., ℓn).
L[1] ← ℓ1 ;                          // Initialize a list of lines.
for i ← 2 to n do
    C ← retrieve_candidates(L[i − 1]) ;     // Sec. 5.2.1
    ĉ ← NaN;
    foreach c ∈ C do
        /* Check relevance and feasibility of the candidate. */
        if rel(c, L) > rel(ĉ, L) & rhyme_ok(c, L) then
            ĉ ← c;
    L[i] ← ĉ;
return L;
```

5. LYRICS GENERATION

5.1 Overview

The lyrics generation is based on the idea of selecting the most relevant line given the previous lines, which is repeated until the whole lyrics have been generated. Our algorithm DeepBeat is summarized in Algorithm 1.

The relevance scores for candidate lines are computed using the RankSVM algorithm described in Section 4. Instead of selecting the candidate with strictly the highest relevance score, we filter some candidates according to `rhyme_ok()` function. It checks that consecutive lines are not from the same song and that they do not end with the same words. Although rhyming the same words can be observed in some contemporary rap lyrics, it has not always been considered a valid technique [9]. While it is straightforward to produce long "rhymes" by repeating the same phrases, it can lead to uninteresting lyrics.

5.2 Online demo

An online demo for the lyrics generation algorithm is available at `deepbeat.org`. This web tool was built in order to (1) make the generator available to the public, (2) provide the users easy ways of customizing the generated lyrics, and (3) collect limited usage logs in order to evaluate and improve the algorithm. The website was launched in November 2015 and as of June 2016 it has been visited by more than 42 000 users.

After the initial launch of the project, we started collaborating with some musicians to record the first songs written by DeepBeat,[7] which showed us the importance of giving the user sufficient customization capabilities instead of merely outputting complete lyrics. With this in mind, we designed the online demo so that users can: (1) define keywords that must appear in the generated lyrics; (2) ask the algorithm to give suggestions for the next line and pick the best suggestion manually; and (3) write some of the lines by themselves. A user can, for example, write the first line by herself and let the algorithm generate the remaining lines. An interesting mode of usage we noticed some users adopting is to write every other line by yourself and generate every other.

[7]The first music video is available at:
https://youtu.be/Js0HYmH31ko
More about the collaboration can be read at:
https://howwegettonext.com/deepbeat-what-happens-when-a-robot-writes-rhymes-for-rappers-77d07c406ff5

When the user generates lyrics line-by-line, asking for suggestions from DeepBeat, we log the selected lines. In Section 5.3.2, we show how to evaluate the algorithm using the log data. Conveniently, we can also use the logs to refine the learned models employing the RankSVM approach as done in [14].

5.2.1 Performance optimization

Candidate set retrieval. Results in Table 3 show that EndRhyme alone is a good predictor. Therefore, we define the set of candidate next lines as the 300 best rhyming lines instead of 300 random lines. This candidate set has to be retrieved quickly without evaluating each of the $n_l = 583\,669$ lines in our database. Conveniently, this can be formulated as the problem of finding k strings with the longest common prefix with respect to a query string, as follows

1. Compute a phonetic transcription for each line.
2. Remove all but vowel phonemes.
3. Reverse phoneme strings.

We solve the longest common prefix problem by first, sorting the phoneme string as a preprocessing step, second, employing binary search[8] to find the line with the longest common prefix (ℓ_{long}), and third, taking the $k-1$ lines with the longest common prefix around ℓ_{long}. The computational complexity of this approach is $\mathcal{O}(\log n_l + k)$. For the online demo, we have set $k = 300$.

Feature selection. By default, `deepbeat.org` employs the FastFeats feature set by which the generation of an 8-line verse takes about 0.3 seconds. The user can additionally enable the NN5 feature in which case the algorithm will retrieve the top-30 lines based on FastFeats and then rerank the top lines based on FastFeatsNN5. We only evaluate 30 lines using NN5 since NN5 is much heavier to compute than the other features (it increases the generation time to about 35 seconds per 8-line verse) and since recall at 30 is only 3.8 percentage points lower for FastFeats compared to FastFeatsNN5. The NN5 feature could be used more heavily by acquiring a server which enables GPU computation or via parallelization (different candidate lines can be evaluated independently).

5.3 Empirical evaluation of generated lyrics

The lyrics generated by DeepBeat are evaluated by the rhyme density measure, introduced in Section 3.3.1, and by measuring the correlation between relevance scores assigned by DeepBeat and human preferences recorded via `deepbeat.org`.

5.3.1 Rhyme density of DeepBeat

We ran a single job to generate a hundred 16-bar verses with random seed lines. A randomly selected example verse from this set is shown in Appendix A. The rhyme density for the hundred verses is 1.431, which is, quite remarkably, 21% higher than the rhyme density of the top ranked human rapper, Inspectah Deck.

One particularly long multisyllabic rhyme created by the algorithm is given below (the rhyming part is highlighted)

"Drink and drown **in my own iniquity**
Never smile style **is wild only grin strictly**"

In this example, the first line is from the song *Rap Game* by *D-12* and the latter from *I Don't Give a F**k* by *AZ*. The rhyme consists of nine consecutive matching vowel phonemes.

5.3.2 Online experiment

In order to evaluate the algorithm, we performed an online experiment using the demo. The idea was to employ an approach which is used for optimizing search engines [14] where the clicked search result r_i is logged and the following pairwise preferences are extracted: $r_i \succ r_j,\ j = 1, \ldots, i-1$ (the lines below the selected line are ignored since we cannot assume that the user has evaluated those). The objective is to learn a ranking model which assigns relevance scores that agree with the extracted preferences.

At `deepbeat.org`, when a user clicks "Suggest Rhyming Line" button, 20 suggested candidate next lines are shown to the user. We wanted to see how often the line selected by the user was assigned a higher score than the lines above the selection. Our hypothesis was that the larger the absolute difference between the algorithm-assigned relevance scores of two lines was, the more likely the user would pick the line preferred by the algorithm.

In the initial data we collected through the website, we noticed that users are more likely to select a line the higher it appears on the list of suggestions. Furthermore, the users tend to prefer the fifth line since it often appears in the same location of the screen as the "Suggest Rhyming Line" button, so if a user is just playing around with the tool without putting much thought to the content of the suggestions, the user is likely to select the fifth suggestion. It is very challenging to get rid of this type of biases entirely when conducting an uncontrolled experiment in the wild but to mitigate the biases, we shuffled the order of the suggested lines and removed the first three selections of each user since we assumed that in the beginning users are more likely to play with the tool without thinking too much. Moreover, we wanted to create more variability among the suggestions, as the top 30 might be almost equally good, so we defined the set of suggested lines as the lines ranked: 1–14., 298–300., and three randomly picked lines from range 15–297.

To avoid degrading the usability of the tool too much, we only applied the aforementioned manipulations when NN5 was not enabled by the user. However, we also stored the text of the selected line and the previous lines to enable the computation of the relevance scores with FastFeatsNN5 as a post-processing step. In total, this experiment resulted in 34 757 pairwise preferences from 1 549 users.[9]

The results of the experiment are shown in Figure 4. They confirm our hypothesis that the higher the difference between the relevance scores of two lines the more likely the users select the line which is evaluated more suitable by the algorithm. Furthermore, including the NN5 feature improves the evaluations, which can be seen by studying the difference of the two data series in the figure. We may conclude that the learned RankSVM model generalizes and is able to successfully learn human preferences from existing rap lyrics, and that the developed deep neural network is an important component of the model.

[8]The candidate set could be found even faster by building a trie data structure of the phoneme strings. However, in our experiments, the binary search approach was fast enough and more memory-efficient.

[9]An anonymized version of the dataset including the scores assigned by DeepBeat is available at: https://github.com/ekQ/dopelearning

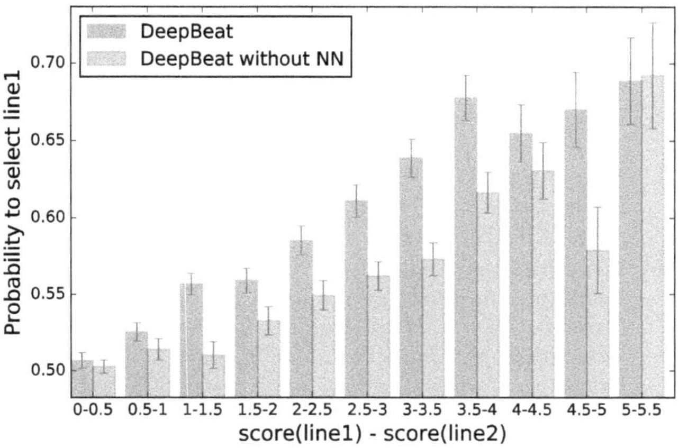

Figure 4: Probability of a `deepbeat.org` user to select a line with a higher score from a pair of lines given the (binned) score difference of the lines. User preferences correlate with the scores assigned by DeepBeat.

6. DISCUSSION

According to Boden [4], creativity is the ability to come up with ideas or artifacts that are (1) new, (2) surprising, and (3) valuable. Here, produced lyrics as a whole are novel by construction as the lines of the lyrics are picked from different original lyrics, even if individual lines are not novel. Lyrics produced with our method are likely to be at least as surprising as the original lyrics.

The (aesthetic) value of rap lyrics is more difficult to estimate objectively. Obvious factors contributing to the value are poetic properties of the lyrics, especially its rhythm and rhyme, quality of the language, and the meaning or message of the lyrics. Rhyme and rhythm can be controlled with relative ease, even outperforming human rappers, as we have demonstrated in our experiments. The quality of individual lines is exactly as good as the dataset used.

The meaning or semantics is the hardest part for computational generation. We have applied standard bag-of-words and LSA methods and additionally introduced a deep neural network model in order to capture the semantics of the lyrics. The importance of these features has been proven by the experimental results for the next line prediction problem and an online experiment. The features together contribute towards the semantic coherence of the produced lyrics even if full control over the meaning is still missing.

The task of predicting the next line can be challenging even for a human, and our model performs relatively well on this task. We have used our models for lyrics prediction, but we see that components that understand semantics could be very relevant also to other text processing tasks, for instance conversation prediction.

This work opens several lines for future work. It would be interesting to study automatic creation of story lines by analyzing existing rap songs and of novel lines by modifying existing lines or creating them from scratch. Even more, it would be exciting to have a fully automatic rap bot which would generate lyrics and rap them synthetically based on some input it receives from the outside world. Alternatively, the findings of this paper could be transferred to other text processing tasks, such as conversation prediction which could carry significant business potential when applied to tasks like customer service automation.

7. CONCLUSIONS

We developed DeepBeat, an algorithm for rap lyrics generation. Lyrics generation was formulated as an information retrieval task where the objective is to find the most relevant next line given the previous lines which are considered as the query. The algorithm extracts three types of features of the lyrics—rhyme, structural, and semantic features—and combines them by employing the RankSVM algorithm. For the semantic features, we developed a deep neural network model, which was the single best predictor for the relevance of a line.

We quantitatively evaluated the algorithm with three measures. First, we evaluated prediction performance by measuring how well the algorithm predicts the next line of an existing rap song. The true next line was identified among 299 randomly selected lines with an accuracy of 17%, i.e., over 50 times more likely than by random, and it was ranked in the top 30 with 53% accuracy. Second, we introduced a rhyme density measure and showed that DeepBeat outperforms the top human rappers by 21% in terms of length and frequency of the rhymes in the produced lyrics. The validity of the rhyme density measure was assessed by conducting a human experiment which showed that the measure correlates with a rapper's own notion of technically skilled lyrics. Third, the rap lyrics generator was deployed as a web tool (`deepbeat.org`) and the analysis of its usage logs showed that machine evaluations of candidate next lines correlate with user preferences.

Acknowledgments

We would like to thank Stephen Fenech for developing the front end for `deepbeat.org` and Jelena Luketina, Miquel Perelló Nieto, and Vikram Kamath for useful comments on the manuscript.

8. REFERENCES

[1] Y. Bengio, I. J. Goodfellow, and A. Courville. Deep learning. Book in preparation for MIT Press, 2015.

[2] D. Berger. Rap genius university: Rhyme types. http://genius.com/posts/24-Rap-genius-university-rhyme-types. Accessed: 2015-05-07.

[3] J. Bergstra, O. Breuleux, F. Bastien, P. Lamblin, R. Pascanu, G. Desjardins, J. Turian, D. Warde-Farley, and Y. Bengio. Theano: a CPU and GPU math expression compiler. *Proceedings of the Python for Scientific Computing Conference (SciPy)*, 2010.

[4] M. A. Boden. *The Creative Mind: Myths and Mechanisms*. Psychology Press, 2004.

[5] A. Bradley. *Book of rhymes: The poetics of hip hop*. Basic Books, 2009.

[6] R. Collobert, J. Weston, L. Bottou, M. Karlen, K. Kavukcuoglu, and P. Kuksa. Natural language processing (almost) from scratch. *Journal of Machine Learning Research*, 12:2493–2537, 2011.

[7] S. Colton and G. A. Wiggins. Computational creativity: The final frontier? In *Proceedings of the*

European Conference on Artificial Intelligence, pages 21–26, 2012.

[8] L. Deng. An overview of deep-structured learning for information processing. In *Proceedings of Asian-Pacific Signal & Information Processing Annual Summit and Conference*, pages 1–14, October 2011.

[9] P. Edwards. *How to rap: the art and science of the hip–hop MC.* Chicago Review Press, 2009.

[10] Flocabulary. How to write rap lyrics and improve your rap skills. https://www.flocabulary.com/multies/. Accessed: 2015-05-07.

[11] A. Graves. Generating sequences with recurrent neural networks. *In Arxiv preprint*, arXiv:1308.0850, 2013.

[12] H. Hirjee and D. G. Brown. Automatic detection of internal and imperfect rhymes in rap lyrics. In *Proceedings of the Tenth International Society for Music Information Retrieval Conference*, pages 711–716, 2009.

[13] H. Hirjee and D. G. Brown. Using automated rhyme detection to characterize rhyming style in rap music. 2010.

[14] T. Joachims. Optimizing search engines using clickthrough data. In *Proceedings of the 8th ACM SIGKDD international conference on Knowledge discovery and data mining*, pages 133–142, 2002.

[15] T. Joachims. Training linear SVMs in linear time. In *Proceedings of the 12th ACM SIGKDD international conference on Knowledge discovery and data mining*, pages 217–226, 2006.

[16] K. Lenzo. The CMU Pronouncing Dictionary. http://www.speech.cs.cmu.edu/cgi-bin/cmudict. Accessed: 2015-05-07.

[17] T.-Y. Liu. Learning to rank for information retrieval. *Foundations and Trends in Information Retrieval*, 3(3):225–331, 2009.

[18] E. Malmi. Algorithm that counts rap rhymes and scouts mad lines. http://mining4meaning.com/2015/02/13/raplyzer/, 2015. Blog post.

[19] T. Mikolov, I. Sutskever, K. Chen, G. S. Corrado, and J. Dean. Distributed representations of words and phrases and their compositionality. In *Advances in Neural Information Processing Systems*, pages 3111–3119, 2013.

[20] J. Pennington, R. Socher, and C. D. Manning. Glove: Global vectors for word representation. *Proceedings of the Empiricial Methods in Natural Language Processing*, 12, 2014.

[21] M. Richardson, A. Prakash, and E. Brill. Beyond pagerank: machine learning for static ranking. In *Proceedings of the 15th international conference on World Wide Web*, pages 707–715. ACM, 2006.

[22] N. Srivastava, G. Hinton, A. Krizhevsky, I. Sutskever, and R. Salakhutdinov. Dropout: A simple way to prevent neural networks from overfitting. *Journal of Machine Learning Research*, 15:1929–1958, 2014.

[23] I. Sutskever, J. Martens, and G. Hinton. Generating text with recurrent neural networks. In *Proceedings of the 28th International Conference on Machine Learning*, pages 1017–1024. ACM, 2011.

[24] P. Takala. Word embeddings for morphologically rich languages. In *Proceedings of European Symposium on Artificial Neural Networks, Computational Intelligence and Machine Learning*, 2016.

[25] J. M. Toivanen, H. Toivonen, A. Valitutti, and O. Gross. Corpus-based generation of content and form in poetry. In *Proceedings of the Third International Conference on Computational Creativity*, pages 175–179, 2012.

[26] T. Veale. Creative language retrieval: A robust hybrid of information retrieval and linguistic creativity. In *Proceedings of the 49th Annual Meeting of the Association for Computational Linguistics: Human Language Technologies–Volume 1*, pages 278–287. Association for Computational Linguistics, 2011.

[27] O. Vinyals and Q. Le. A neural conversational model. In *Proceedings of ICML Deep Learning Workshop*, 2015.

[28] D. Wu and K. Addanki. Learning to rap battle with bilingual recursive neural networks. In *Proceedings of the 24th International Conference on Artificial Intelligence*, pages 2524–2530, 2015.

[29] D. Wu, V. S. K. Addanki, M. S. Saers, and M. Beloucif. Learning to freestyle: Hip hop challenge-response induction via transduction rule segmentation. In *Proceedings of the Empirical Methods in Natural Language Processing Conference*, pages 102–112, 2013.

[30] L. Yu, K. M. Hermann, P. Blunsom, and S. Pulman. Deep Learning for Answer Sentence Selection. In *Proceedings of NIPS Deep Learning Workshop*, 2014.

[31] M. D. Zeiler. Adadelta: an adaptive learning rate method. Technical report, 2012.

APPENDIX

A. SAMPLE VERSES

Table 4 shows an example of a generated verse. It was randomly selected from a set of a hundred verses, excluding the verses with profane language. The other verses are available at: https://github.com/ekQ/dopelearning

Table 4: A randomly selected verse from the set of 100 generated lyrics.

Everybody got one	(2 Chainz - Extremely Blessed)
And all the pretty mommies want some	(Mos Def - Undeniable)
And what i told you all was	(Lil Wayne - Welcome Back)
But you need to stay such do not touch	(Common - Heidi Hoe)
They really do not want you to vote	(KRS One - The Mind)
what do you condone	(Cam'ron - Bubble Music)
Music make you lose control	(Missy Elliot - Lose Control)
What you need is right here ahh oh	(Wiz Khalifa - Right Here)
This is for you and me	(Missy Elliot - Hit Em Wit Da Hee)
I had to dedicate this song to you Mami	(Fat Joe - Bendicion Mami)
Now I see how you can be	(Lil Wayne - How To Hate)
I see u smiling i kno u hattig	(Wiz Khalifa - Damn Thing)
Best I Eva Had x4	(Nicki Minaj - Best I Ever Had)
That I had to pay for	(Ice Cube - X Bitches)
Do I have the right to take yours	(Common - Retrospect For Life)
Trying to stay warm	(Everlast - 2 Pieces Of Drama)

EMBERS at 4 years: Experiences operating an Open Source Indicators Forecasting System

Sathappan Muthiah[1], Patrick Butler[1], Rupinder Paul Khandpur[1], Parang Saraf[1], Nathan Self[1], Alla Rozovskaya[1], Liang Zhao[1], Jose Cadena[2], Chang-Tien Lu[1], Anil Vullikanti[2], Achla Marathe[2], Kristen Summers[‡,**], Graham Katz[‡], Andy Doyle[‡], Jaime Arredondo[¶], Dipak K. Gupta[‖], David Mares[¶], Naren Ramakrishnan[1]
[1] Discovery Analytics Center, Dept. of Comp.Science, Virginia Tech, Arlington, VA 22203
[2] Biocomplexity Institute, Virginia Tech, Blacksburg, VA 24061
[¶] University of California at San Diego, San Diego, CA 92093
[‖] San Diego State University, San Diego, CA 92182
[‡] CACI Inc., Lanham, MD 20706
[**] IBM Watson Group, Chantilly, VA 20151

ABSTRACT

EMBERS is an anticipatory intelligence system forecasting population-level events in multiple countries of Latin America. A deployed system from 2012, EMBERS has been generating alerts 24x7 by ingesting a broad range of data sources including news, blogs, tweets, machine coded events, currency rates, and food prices. In this paper, we describe our experiences operating EMBERS continuously for nearly 4 years, with specific attention to the discoveries it has enabled, correct as well as missed forecasts, lessons learnt from participating in a forecasting tournament, and our perspectives on the limits of forecasting including ethical considerations.

Keywords

civil unrest, event forecasting, open source indicators.

1. INTRODUCTION

Modern communication forms such as social media and microblogs are not only rapidly advancing our understanding of the world but also improving the methods by which we can comprehend, and even forecast, the progression of events. Tracking population-level activities via 'massive passive' data has been shown to quite accurately shed light into large-scale societal movements.

Two years ago, in KDD 2014, we described EMBERS [15], a deployed anticipatory intelligence system [5] that forecasts significant societal events (e.g., civil unrest events such as protests, strikes, and 'occupy' events) using a large set of open source indicators such as news, blogs, tweets, food prices, currency rates, and other public data. The EMBERS system has been running continuously 24x7 for nearly 4 years at this point and our goal in this paper is to present the discoveries it has enabled, both correct as well as missed forecasts, and lessons learned from participating in a forecasting tournament including our perspectives on the limits of forecasting and ethical considerations. In particular, we shed insight into the value proposition to an analyst and how EMBERS forecasts are communicated to its end-users.

The development of EMBERS is supported by the Intelligence Advanced Research Projects Activity (IARPA) Open Source Indicators (OSI) program. EMBERS currently focuses on multiple regions of the world but for the purpose of this paper we focus primarily on the 10 Latin American countries, specifically the countries of Argentina, Brazil, Chile, Colombia, Ecuador, El Salvador, Mexico, Paraguay, Uruguay, and Venezuela. Similarly, EMBERS generates forecasts for multiple event classes—influenza-like-illnesses [3], rare diseases [16], elections [12], domestic political crises [8], and civil unrest—but in this paper we focus primarily on civil unrest as this was the most challenging event class with hundreds of events every month across the countries studied here. EMBERS forecasts are scored against the Gold Standard Report (GSR), a monthly catalog of events as reported in newspapers of record in these 10 countries. The GSR is compiled by MITRE corporation using human analysts.

Our key contributions can be summarized as follows:

1. Unlike retrospective studies of predictability, EMBERS forecasts are communicated in real-time before the event to MITRE/IARPA and scored independently of the authors. (Further, the scoring criteria are set by IARPA.) We present multiple quantitative indicators of EMBERS performance as well as insights into how we made EMBERS forecasts most valuable to analysts. We report two primary ways in which analysts utilize EMBERS and present the use of automated narratives to help make EMBERS forecasts as useful as possible.

KDD '16, August 13-17, 2016, San Francisco, CA, USA
© 2016 ACM. ISBN 978-1-4503-4232-2/16/08...$15.00
DOI: http://dx.doi.org/10.1145/2939672.2939709

2. In an attempt to demystify the state-of-the-art in forecasting and to create an open dialogue in the community, we report both successful forecasts of EMBERS as well as events missed by EMBERS. The events not forecast by EMBERS lead us to considerations of both the limitations of the underlying technology as well as the inherent limits to forecasting large-scale events.
3. While social media is often touted as the key to event forecasting systems such as EMBERS, we present the results of an ablation study to outline the performance degradation that ensues if data sources such as Twitter and Facebook were to be removed from the forecasting pipeline.
4. We consider the separation of civil unrest events into events that happen with a degree of regularity versus rare or significant events, and evaluate the performance of EMBERS in forecasting such surprising events.
5. We describe our current best understanding of the limitations to forecasting civil unrest events using technologies like EMBERS and also consider the ethical considerations of the EMBERS technologies.

2. BACKGROUND

We begin by providing a brief review of forecasting systems, followed by a quick preview of EMBERS, its system architecture, machine learning models, and measures for evaluating its performance. For more details, please see [15].

Forecasting societal events such as civil unrest has a long tradition in the intelligence analysis and political science community. We distinguish between forecasting systems versus event coding systems (systems that provide structured representations of ongoing events reported in newspapers), and focus on the former. Early forecasting systems such as ICEWS [14] provided very broad coverage in countries but were limited by their spatio-temporal resolution (e.g., typically country- and month- level forecasting for specific events of interest [19]). The ICEWS events of interest are domestic political crises, international crises, ethnic/religious violence, insurgencies, and rebellion. A similar project in scope is PITF (Political Instability Task Force) [6] funded by the CIA. To the best of our knowledge, only EMBERS provides the most-specific spatial resolution (city-level) and the most-specific temporal resolution (daily-level) capability in forecasting.

The software architecture of EMBERS (Early Model Based Event Recognition using Surrogates) is designed as a loosely coupled, share-nothing, highly distributed pipeline of processes connected via ZeroMQ. In this manner, the system is both highly scalable and fault tolerant. The EMBERS pipeline can loosely be broken up into four stages: ingestion, enrichment, modeling, and selection. In the first stage, ingestion, data is collected from a variety of sources and streamed into the following stages in real-time. The enrichment stage takes the raw data from the ingestion stage and processes it in various ways including natural language processing, geocoding, and relative time phrase normalization. After enrichment, the modeling stage feeds the enriched data into the various models that make up EMBERS. Unlike other systems which use single monolithic models to make predictions, EMBERS combines the results of several different models to arrive at the most accurate forecasts.

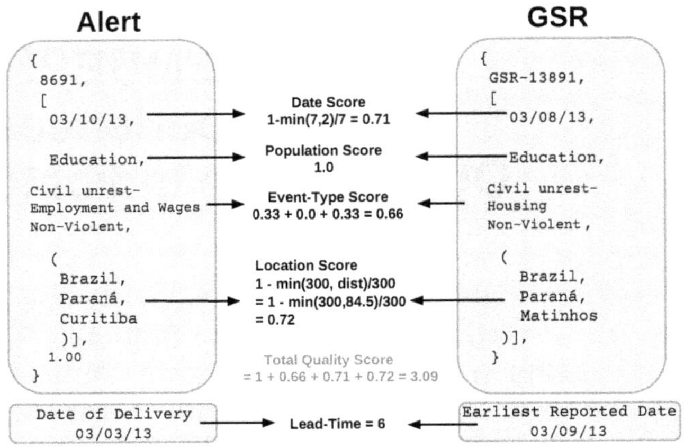

Figure 1: An example depicting how an alert is scored with respect to the ground truth.

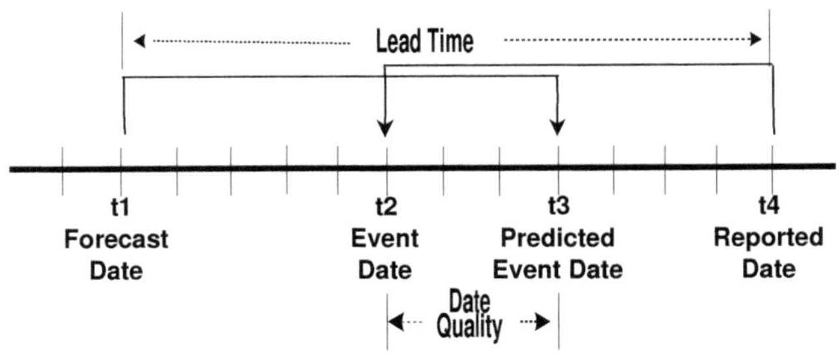

Figure 2: Alert sent at time $t1$ predicting an event at time $t3$ can be matched to a GSR event that happened at time $t2$ and reported at time $t4$ if $t1 < t4$.

In particular, the separate alerts from each model are deduplicated, fused, and selected and finally emitted as a full forecast for a real world event.

The structure of a civil unrest forecast is shown in Figure 1 (left). A forecast constitutes four fields, corresponding to the when, where, who, and why of the protest. These fields are respectively denoted as the date, location, population, and event type. Location is recorded at the city level. Population and event type are fields chosen from a categorical set of possibilities. The figure further shows how an alert with all these fields are scored against a GSR event. In the basic scoring methodology shown in Figure 1 each of the four fields are weighted uniformly and a total quality score out of 4 is obtained. Apart from this each alert also has a lead-time associated with it calculated as shown in Figure 2.

Rather than design one model to integrate all possible data sources, EMBERS adopted a multi-model approach to forecasting. Each model utilized a specific (possibly overlapping) set of data sources and is tuned for high precision, so that the union of these models can be tuned for high recall. A fusion/suppression engine [7] allows a tunable strategy to issue more or fewer alerts depending on whether the analyst's objective is to obtain a higher precision or recall. The underlying models used in EMBERS are: (i) *planned protest model* [13], (ii) *dynamic query expansion* [20], (iii) *volume-based model* [9], (iv) *cascade regression* [2], and (v) a baseline model. The planned protest model, for news and social media (Twitter, Facebook), identifies explicit signs of organization and calls for protest, resolves relative mentions of time (e.g., 'next Saturday') and space (e.g., 'the square') to issue forecasts. The dynamic query expansion (DQE) model uses Twitter as a data source and learns time- and country-specific expansions of a seed set of keywords to identify specific situational circumstances for civil unrest. For instance, in Venezuela (an economy where the government exercises stringent price controls), there were a series of protests in 2014 stemming from the shortage of toilet paper, a novel circumstance that was uncovered by DQE. The volume-based model uses a range of data sources, spanning social, economic and political indicators. It uses classical statistical models (LASSO and hybrid regression models) to forecast civil unrest events using features from social media (Twitter and blogs), news sources, political event databases (ICEWS and GDELT [10]), Tor [4] statistics, food prices, and currency exchange rates. It aims to provide a multi-source perspective into forecasting by leveraging the selective superiorities of different data sources. The cascade regression model aims to model activity related to organization and mobilization in Twitter [2]. Finally, the baseline model uses maximum likelihood estimation over the GSR to issue history-based forecasts.

The EMBERS project is unique not just in its algorithmic underpinnings but also in the use of new measures for evaluation, specifically aimed at determining forecasting performance. As shown in Figure 2, one of the primary measures of EMBERS performance is lead time, the number of days by which a forecast 'beats the news', i.e., the date of reporting of the event. Lead time should not be confused with date quality, i.e., the difference between the predicted date and the actual date of the event. The date quality is one of the components of the quality score, the other components being the location score, event type score, and population score. Figure 1 shows how these other components are scored between an EMBERS forecast and a GSR record.

Given a set of alerts and a set of GSR events for a given month, the lead time is used as a constraint to define legal (alert, event) pairs so that we can construct a bipartite matching to optimize the best quality score. From this bipartite matching, measures of precision and recall can be derived, i.e., by assessing the number of (un)matched events or alerts. Finally, a confidence score is used to assess the quality of probabilities imputed by EMBERS to its forecasts, and measured in terms of the Brier score. For more details, please see [15].

We now turn to a discussion of specific discoveries enabled by EMBERS, into civil unrest in Latin America, and into the complexity of the forecasting enterprise as a whole.

3. PERFORMANCE ANALYSIS

First, we begin with a performance analysis of EMBERS, from both a quantitative point of view with respect to the GSR and with respect to end-user (analyst) goals.

3.1 Quantitative Metrics

Figure 3 depicts both the targets set by the IARPA OSI program as well as the actual measures achieved by the EMBERS system. As shown here, the easiest target to achieve in EMBERS was, surprisingly, the lead time objective. This was feasible due to EMBERS's focus on modeling both planned and spontaneous events. Planned events are sometimes organized with as many as several weeks of

Targets

	Month 12	Month 24	Month 36
Mean Lead-Time	1 day	3 days	7 days
Mean Probability Score	0.60	0.70	0.85
Mean Quality Score	3.0	3.25	3.5
Recall	0.50	0.65	0.80
Precision	0.50	0. 65	0.80

Actual

Metric	Month 12	Month 24	Month 36
Mean Lead-Time	3.89 days	7.54 days	9.76 days
Mean Probability Score	0.72	0.89	0.88
Mean Quality Score	2.57	3.1	3.4
Recall	0.80	0.65	0.79
Precision	0.59	0.94	0.87

Figure 3: IARPA OSI targets and results achieved by EMBERS.

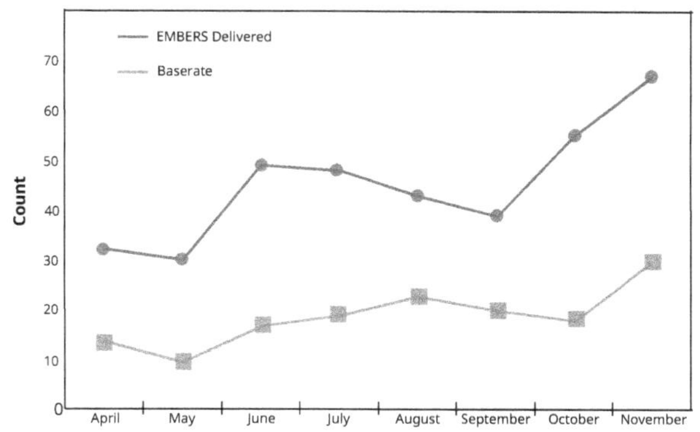

Figure 4: Comparison of number of perfect scores (4.0) obtained by EMBERS vs a baserate model each month in 2013.

lead time and thus identifying indicators of organization was instrumental in achieving lead time objectives. The confidence (mean probability) scores were also achieved by EMBERS and involved careful calibration of probabilities by taking into account estimates of model propensities and data source reliabilities. The measure that was most difficult to achieve was the quality score as it involved a four component additive score and thus tangible improvements in score required more than incremental improvements in forecasting specific components. Finally, recall and precision involve a natural underlying trade-off and the deployment of our fusion/suppression engine provided the ability to balance this trade-off to meet IARPA OSI's objectives. Apart from comparing mean scores another interesting measure is to see how many perfect matches (4.0 quality score) are obtained by EMBERS. Fig. 4 shows the number of alerts issued by EMBERS that matched perfectly to an event in the future on a monthly basis for 2013. It is clear that EMBERS makes almost double the number of fully accurate forecasts as compared to a baserate model.The baserate model generates alerts using the rate of occurrence of events in the past three months.

3.2 Analyst Evaluation

In addition to the quantitative measures above, our experience interacting with analysts demonstrated an interesting dichotomy as to how analysts use EMBERS alerts. Some analysts preferred to use EMBERS in an 'analytic triage' scenario wherein they could tune EMBERS for high recall so that they would apply their traditional measures of filtering

EMBERS forecasts that there will be a violent protest on February, 18th 2014 in Caracas, the capital city of Venezuela. It predicts that the protest will involve people working in the business sector. The protest will be related to discontent about economic policies.
There were 5, 5, and 5 other similar warnings in last 2, 7 and 30 days, respectively.
The forecast date of the warning falls in week 7, which may have historical importance; this week is found to be statistically significant (pval=0.00461919415894, zscore=2.832, avg. count=57.25, mean=21.569 +/- 12.597)
Audit trail of the warning includes an article printed 2014-02-17.
Major players involved in the protest include Venezuelan opposition leader, students, President Nicolas Maduro, and Leopoldo Lopez.
Reasons: Protest against rising inflation and crime; Protestors want a political change; President Nicolas Maduro has accused US consular officials and right-wing.
Protests are characterized by: Venezuelan opposition leader spearheaded days of protest and calling for peaceful demonstration; Maduro accused official on 2014-12-16; Protests have seen several deadly street protests; Three people were killed on 2014-02-12; Demonstrations setting days of clashes; supporters to march to Interior Ministry on 2014-02-18.

Figure 5: An example narrative for an EMBERS alert. Here, color red indicates named entities, green refers to descriptive protest related keywords. Items in blue are historical or real time statistics and those in magenta refer to inferred reasons of the protest.

and analysis to hone in on forecasts of interest. Other analysts instead viewed EMBERS as a data source and preferred to use it in a high precision mode, e.g., wherein they were focused on a specific region of the world (e.g., Venezuela) and/or aimed to investigate a particular social science hypothesis (e.g., whether disruptions in global oil markets led to civil unrest).

To support these diverse classes of users, we implemented two mechanisms in the alert delivery stage. First, we implemented a mechanism wherein in addition to generating alerts, EMBERS also forecasted the expected quality score for each forecast (using machine learning methods trained on past GSR-alert matches). This expected quality score measure provided a way for analysts to use quality directly as a way to tune the system to receive greater or fewer alerts. Second, we implemented an automated narrative generation capability (see Fig. 5) wherein EMBERS auto-generates a summary of the alert in English prose. As shown in Fig. 5, a narrative comprises many parts drawn from different sources of information. One source constitutes the named entities wherein the system uses 'Wikification' to identify definitions and descriptions of named entities on Wikipedia. A second source is historical (or real-time) statistics of warning output and warning performance and situating the alert in this context. The third source pertains to inferred reasons for the protest using knowledge graph identification techniques.

4. EMBERS SUCCESSES AND MISSES

Next, we detail some of the successful as well as not so successful forecasts made by EMBERS over the past few years in Latin America.

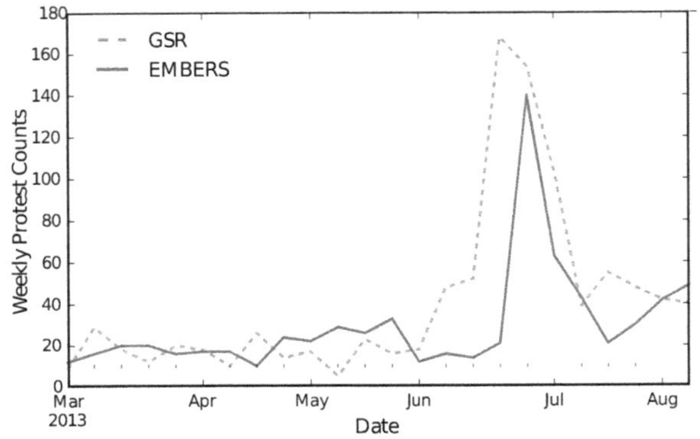

Figure 6: EMBERS performance during the Brazilian Spring (June 2013).

4.1 Successful Forecasts

Brazilian Spring (June 2013)

These protests were the largest and most significant protests in Brazil's recent history and caught worldwide attention. Millions of Brazilians took part in these demonstrations, also known as the Brazilian Spring or the Vinegar Movement (inspired from the use of vinegar soaked cloth by demonstrators to protect themselves from police teargas). These protests were sparked by an increase in public transport fares from *R*\$3 to *R*\$3.20 by the government of President Dilma Rousseff.

As shown in Fig. 6, while missing the initial uptick, EMBERS did forecast the increase in the order-of-magnitude of protest events during the Brazilian Spring and also captured the spatial spread in the events. In addition EMBERS correctly forecast that this event will span the broad Brazilian general population (as opposed to being confined to specific sectors).

Around 68% of EMBERS alerts during this period originated from the planned protest model. This is due to the fact that social networking platforms (Twitter and Facebook) as well as conventional news media played a key role in organization of these uprisings. Although initial protests were primarily due to the bus fare increases, they quickly morphed into more broader dissatisfaction to include wider issues such as government corruption, over-spending, and police brutality. The demonstrators also made calls for political reforms. In response, President Rousseff proposed a plebiscite on widespread political reforms in Brazil (but this was later abandoned). Through its dynamic query expansion model, EMBERS was able to capture such discussions on Twitter (see Fig. 7), and tracked their evolution as events unfolded through June.

The protests intensified in late June (see Fig. 6), which were forecast correctly by EMBERS, and these events also coincided with FIFA 2013 Confederation Cup matches. We believe this was an important factor in helping the protests gain momentum, as the events were covered by international media. A majority of protests occurred in the cities that were hosting FIFA soccer matches. EMBERS issued most of its alerts for these host cities (see Fig. 8), viz. Rio de Janeiro, São Paulo, Belo Horizonte, Salvador, and Porto Alegre, among others. For example, on 27th June during the Confederations Cup semi-final in Fortaleza, around 5000

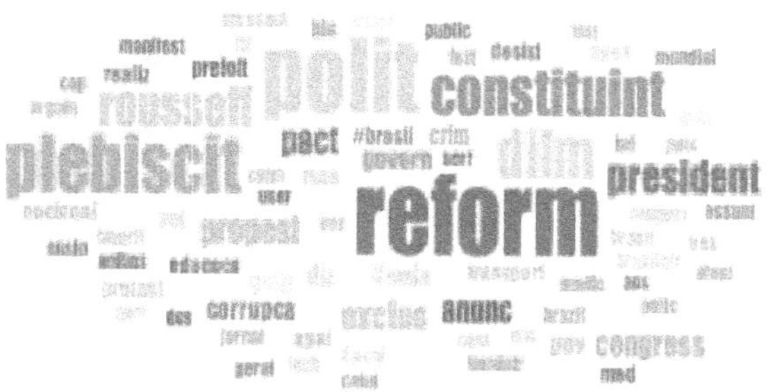

Figure 7: Word cloud representing tweets identified by EMBERS dynamic query expansion model.

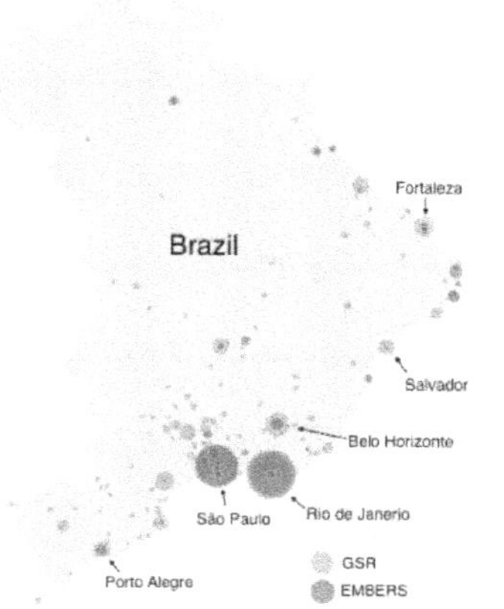

Figure 8: Geographic overlap of protest events (from the GSR) and EMBERS alerts for Brazil during June 2013.

protesters clashed with the police near the Castelao stadium. In this case EMBERS had forecast an alert the day before. Later on the 30th of June, when the last games of the confederation cup took place in Rio de Janeiro and Salvador, they were plagued by mass protests as well; EMBERS predicted these events and submitted multiple alerts for Rio for the 28th and 29th June and one for Salvador for 29th June.

Venezuelan protests (Feb-March 2014)

In early 2014 Venezuela began experiencing a situation of turmoil with a large portion of its population protesting due to insecurity, inflation and shortage of basic goods. This period saw one of the highest levels of civil disobedience in Venezuela with protests beginning in January with the murder of a former Miss Venezuela. However, the protests started gaining more importance and turned violent and more frequent with students joining the movement following an attempted rape of a student on a campus in San Cristobal. EMBERS captured some of these first calls-to-protest at San Cristobal and its nearby surrounding areas and correctly forecast the population (Education) and that the protests would turn violent. A majority of the protesters were demanding that president Nicolas Maduro step down owing to the poor economic policies and widespread corruption. EMBERS succeeded in capturing that the reason behind the protests were mainly against government policies

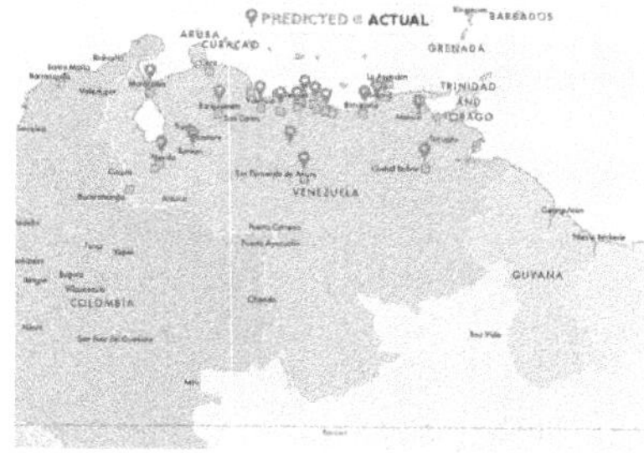

Figure 9: Geographical spread of protests (and forecasts) during the Venezuelan student protests (Feb-Mar 2014).

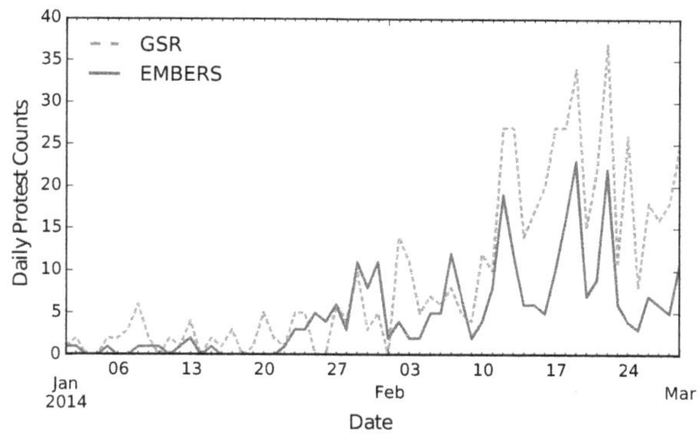

Figure 10: EMBERS performance during the Venezuelan student protests (Feb-Mar 2014).

with corruption being a major theme. The EMBERS models working on Twitter were also clearly able to identify some of the major leaders involved in the protest, such as the key opposition leader Leopoldo Lopez. Though the events mainly began in San Cristobal, they spread widely throughout the country; EMBERS captured this spread very well as shown in Fig. 9. Fig. 10 shows how EMBERS closely forecast the spike in the number of events during this period.

Mexico protests (Oct 2014)

In September 2014, there were some peaceful protests by students from Ayotzinapa in Mexico against discriminatory hiring practices for teachers. During these protests, police opened fire on the students killing around three; 43 students went missing. This poor handling of the protest by the Mexican government caused widespread demonstrations throughout the country over the next few months in support of the families of the 43 missing students. Many of these protests were violent in nature with demonstrators expressing extreme dissatisfaction against the government of president Pena Nieto. EMBERS, as shown in Fig. 16 forecast an uptick in Mexico protests during early October 2014 with a lead time of about three days. It also generated a series of alert spikes coinciding with the first large-scale nationwide protests between October 5th and 8th. Fig. 11 provides a timeline of GSR events and EMBERS alerts for Mexico during this period. This figure provides a detailed comparison of the continuous stream of alerts produced by EMBERS during this period against how the actual events unfolded in the real world.

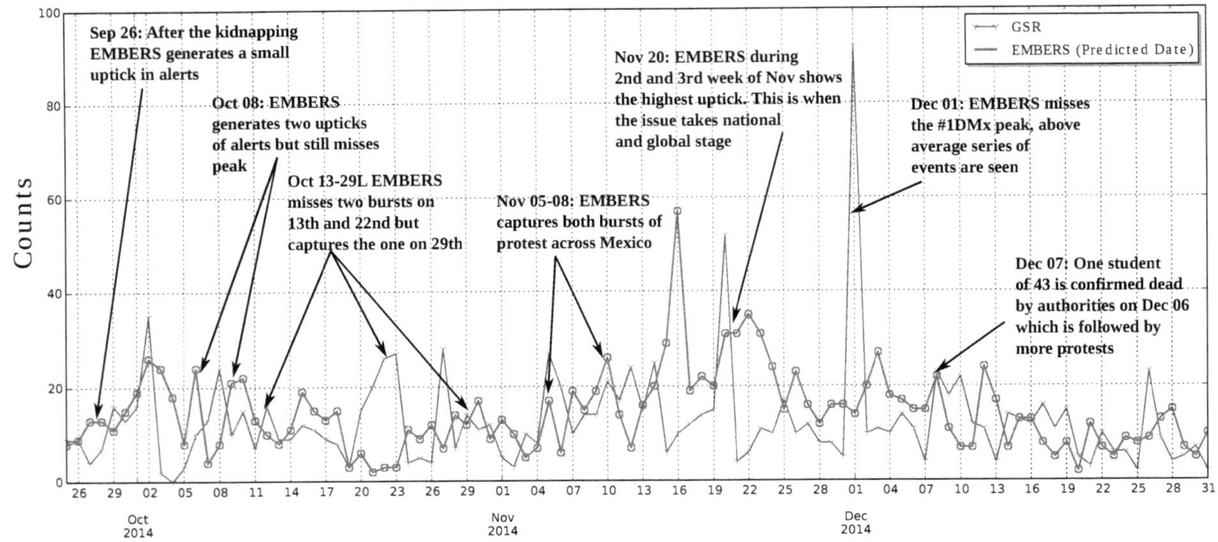

Figure 11: Timeline of Mexico protests, showing the correspondence between counts of GSR events and EMBERS alerts on a daily basis.

Colombia protests (Dec 2014 to March 2015)

Colombia witnessed two different significant protests during this period, one during late December 2014 and the other during February 2015. Towards the end of 2014, the Colombian government was on the process of moving forward with peace negotiations to end 50 years of conflict with the Revolutionary Armed Forces of Colombia (FARC). With the FARC rebels having been associated with various acts of terror, e.g., extortion, armed conflict, kidnapping, ransom, and illegal mining, for a long period, the people of Colombia gathered in huge numbers to protest against possible amnesty for the FARC rebels. EMBERS successfully forecast the uptick in the number of events during the middle of December 2014 as indicated in Fig. 12. This figure also depicts the increase in protest counts during February 2015, although in this case EMBERS over-predicted the counts.

The protests in February 2015 were qualitatively different in nature and were led by truckers unions demanding better freight rates, labor rights, and revolting against high fuel prices. The truckers protests extended for about a month and caused an estimated loss of about $300 million to the Colombian economy. EMBERS forecast the truckers protests accurately at the onset of these events but overestimated the number of protests during February 11-12.

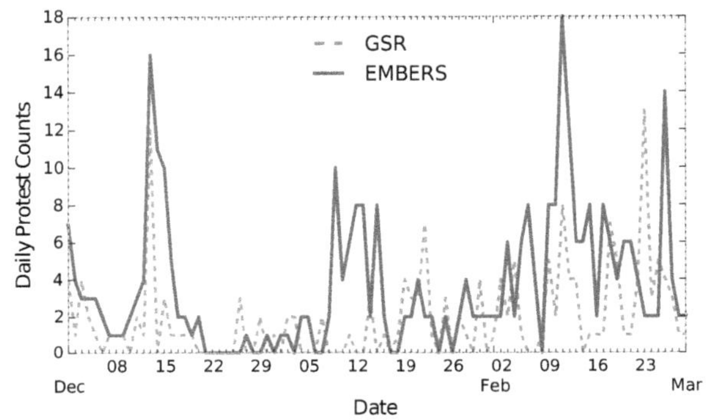

Figure 12: EMBERS performance during the Colombia protests (Dec 2014 to Mar 2015).

Paraguay protests (February 2015)

The February 2015 protests in Paraguay were mainly carried out by peasants against the actions of President Horacio Cartes. The protests were carried out after president Horacio's public revelation that he had opened two private Swiss bank accounts. The protests also had a historical significance. They were also being carried out as a tribute to peasant leaders and activists who were murdered. The peasants also protested against the introduction of a new public-private partnership law. EMBERS forecast the uptick in the number of Paraguay protests during mid February 2015 as shown in Fig. 13.

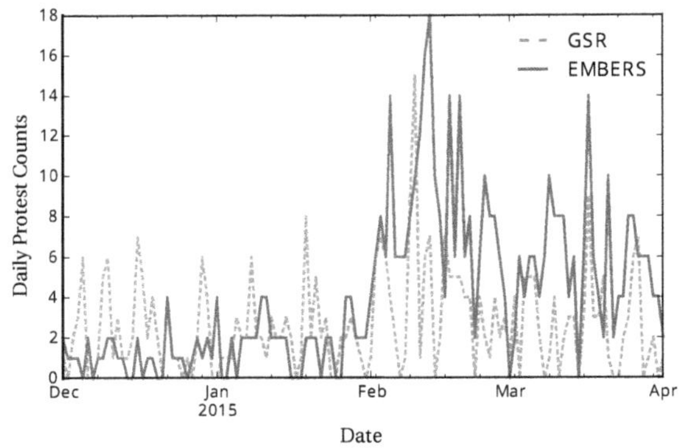

Figure 13: EMBERS performance during the Paraguay protests (Feb. 2015).

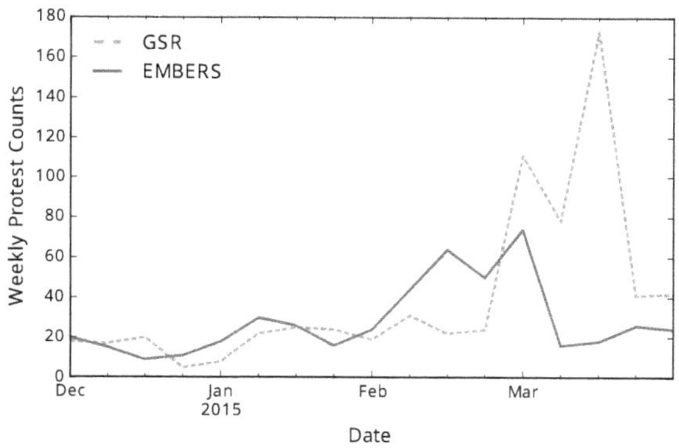

Figure 14: EMBERS performance during the Brazilian protests of March 2015.

4.2 EMBERS Misses

Next, we outline specific large-scale events that EMBERS failed to forecast accurately, along with a discussion of underlying reasons.

4.2.1 Brazilian protests (March 2015)

The beginning of 2015 saw a series of protests in Brazil demanding the removal of president Dilma Roussef amidst much furore against the increasing corruption in the country. The number of protests increased significantly due to the revelations that many politicians belonging to the ruling party accepted bribes from the state-run energy company Petrobas. The protests drew huge participation from the general population, with protesters generally estimated to be around a million. EMBERS, as shown in Figure 14, picked up the onset of events but failed to capture the sudden rise in the number of events.

During this period there was a significant architectural change in the EMBERS processing pipeline. As mentioned in Section 2 the EMBERS system enrichment pipeline consists of the following steps: natural language processing, geocoding, and relative time phrase normalization (temporal tagging). During early 2015 EMBERS had moved to the Heideltime [17] temporal tagger versus the previously used TIMEN [11] temporal tagger. (This choice was made because Heideltime supported more languages and an active development cycle.) Heideltime had no support for Portuguese (the primary language of Brazil) and the EMBERS software development team had extended Heideltime to support Portuguese by translating the underlying resources for Spanish to Portuguese. As it turns out, the simple translation of rules from Spanish to Portuguese was not sufficient and this affected the recall of one of the key models for Brazil, viz. the planned protest model. Since the planned protest model relies almost exclusively on the quality of information (specifically, date) extraction from text, its performance significantly deteriorated. This was subsequently corrected for the future by adding more rules and correcting existing rules (which were translated from Spanish) in Heideltime for Portuguese with the aid of language experts and extensive backtesting. Fig. 15 shows an example detection before and after the changes.

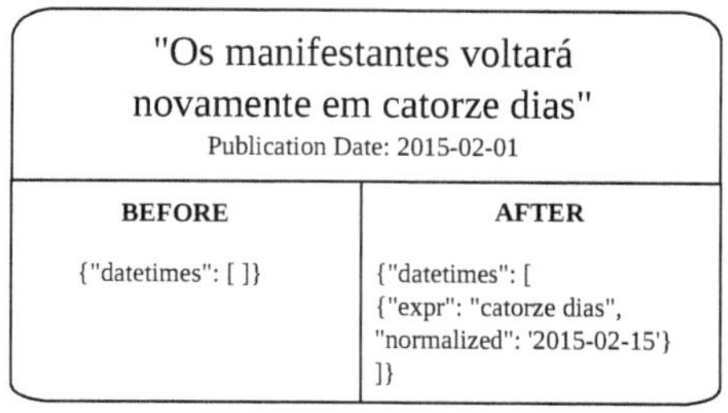

Figure 15: Example depicting the improvement in time phrase recognition after changes to Heideltime.

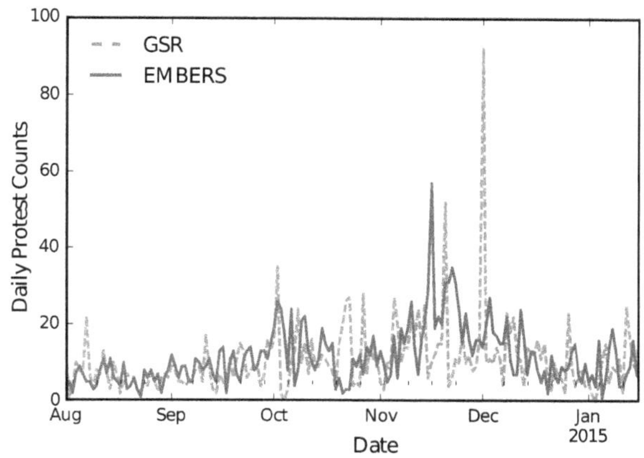

Figure 16: EMBERS performance during Mexico protests (Oct 2014).

4.2.2 Mexico protests (Dec 2014)

The days of December 2014 witnessed a continuation of the series of protests that began in October 2014 as described in Section 4.1. People turned out in huge numbers in different cities of Mexico demanding President Pena Nieto's ouster owing to the manner in which the case of the 43 missing students were handled. The protests were largely peaceful except for a few cases where vehicles were torched and windows and office equipment were broken.

EMBERS missed the huge single day spike on December 1st. Though having predicted a nationwide event for December 1, EMBERS failed to capture the individual cities where the protests would take place out and thus was unable to forecast the number of events accurately. On manual retrospective, it was found that the date, viz. December 1, was picked by the protesters due to its historical significance. This was the day when President Pena Nieto was sworn in (in 2012) amidst much controversy and opposition from many specific constituent groups. The manual analysis also led to the understanding of how special dates were mentioned by the twitterati **#1Dmx**. Dates mentioned using such abbreviations went unrecognized by the EMBERS system and was one of the main reasons for EMBERS not being able to capture the peak on December 1st despite its historical significance.

4.2.3 Brazilian Spring Onset

The EMBERS forecasts during the 2013 Brazilian Spring as shown in Fig. 6 was able to capture the peak but as can be seen the system was unable to capture the initial onset. See Section 7 for a detailed discussion of the limits of forecasting.

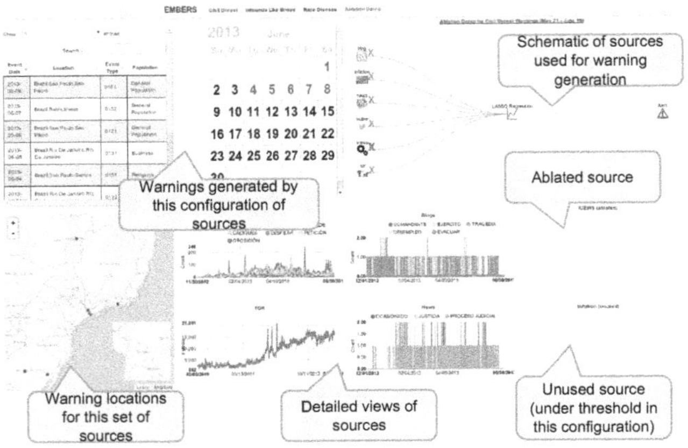

Figure 17: EMBERS ablation visualizer.

Table 1: Comparison of performance measures under ablation testing. Social media sources contribute toward recall but, due to their noisy nature, lower other measures of performance.

Data Source	Quality-Score	Lead-time	Precision	Recall
Removing news and blogs	-16.48%	-55%	+35%	-14%
Removing social media	+8.42%	+30%	+79%	-33%

5. ABLATION TESTING

Different data sources provide different value to the forecasting enterprise. It is important that we understand the value of a data source w.r.t. its forecasting potential. In this section we describe ablation testing in EMBERS where the incremental value addition is evaluated for specific data sources. In particular, we are interested in determining the utility of using social media versus traditional media such as news and blogs. Table 1 shows the percentage improvement or degradation in performance measures when specific sources are removed. It clearly shows that social media sources are mainly necessary in achieving high recall but are not that useful in achieving high lead times, for which traditional media sources are required. This behavior is expected as social media is where daily chatter occurs whereas signs of organization and calls for protest often happen over (or are reported in) traditional meadia. Mainly, Table 1 makes it evident that to build a successful forecasting system we need a good mix of both traditional and social media sources. Fig. 17 shows a snapshot of the EMBERS ablation visualizer. The visualizer provides an analyst with the capability to selectively remove data sources and assess the differences in final alerts.

6. FORECASTING SURPRISING EVENTS

The GSR contains a mix of everyday, mundane, protests as well as surprising events such as the Brazilian Spring. We aimed to ascertain the relative ease of forecasting each class of events with respect to the baserate model described in section 3.1. To define surprising events, we employed a maximum entropy approach. For this purpose, each event is assumed to be describable in terms of three dimensions: country, population, and event type. The GSR can then be conceptualized as a cube. We infer a maximum entropy distribution conditioned on the marginals induced by the cube using iterative proportional fitting [1].

Table 2: Surprising events identified by a maximum entropy analysis over the GSR.

Month	Country	Description
May '13	Colombia	Nationwide protests against administrative policy changes regarding the Youth in Action program and social security pension.
Jun '13	Brazil	Brazilian Spring.
Jul '13	Brazil	Brazilian Spring.
Sep '13	Mexico	Nationwide protests against education and energy reforms.
Oct '13	Mexico	Nationwide protests against education and energy reforms.
Oct '13	Uruguay	Nationwide protests demanding increase in minimum wage.
Feb '14	Venezuela	Venezuelan student protests.
Mar '14	Venezuela	Venezuelan student protests.
May '14	Brazil	Nationwide demonstrations in response to the 2014 FIFA World Cup and other social issues.
Jun '14	Brazil	Nationwide demonstrations in response to the 2014 FIFA World Cup and other social issues.
Aug '14	Argentina	Nationwide protests against drops in wages, employment, and rising inflation.
Sep '14	Ecuador	Nationwide protests to demand changes in labor policies.
Oct '14	Mexico	Nationwide protests after the discovery of mass graves of kidnapped students.

Every month, events from the last three months of the GSR are used to populate the underlying cube of counts and a iterative proportional fitting procedure is used to estimate the expected counts for each cell. The resultant sample counts are then scaled to match the observed number of GSR events in the current month. The cell-wise difference between the inferred maxent distribution and the observed GSR is computed and all cells with significance greater than five standard deviations are classified as containing surprising events. In essence, this approach takes the GSR as input and creates a truncated GSR against which we can evaluate EMBERS (and the baserate model).

In Table 2 we present several inferred events in Latin America from our maximum entropy filter. For all these events, we compare the recall of both EMBERS and baserate model in Figure 18. It is clear that EMBERS is able to forecast these significant upticks consistently and that the baserate model is not able to.

7. UNCERTAINTIES IN FORECASTING

While examining the events of civil unrest closely in the past few years, it was clear to our team that events carry two distinct types of uncertainties: **cause** and **timing**. Fig. 19 summarizes these uncertainties.

Among all the incidents of civil unrest that we encounter, the largest and the most significant ones are planned events. These events are usually organized by political parties, labor and student unions. Since it takes a huge effort to organize protest demonstrations that attract thousands, the organizers must disseminate information regarding the venue and

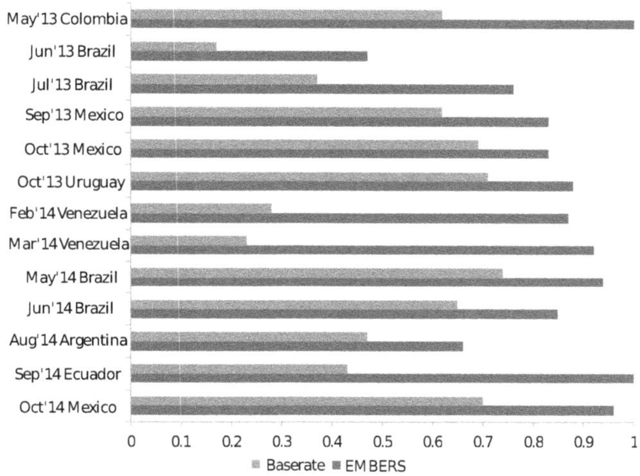

Figure 18: Performance of EMBERS vs a baserate model for surprising events.

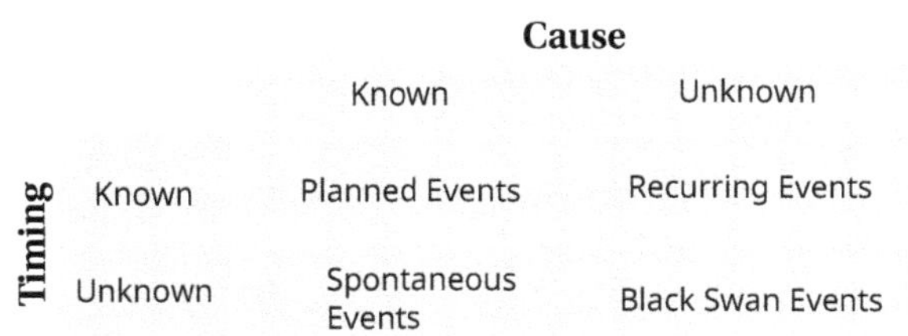

Figure 19: Studying the limitations of event forecasting.

the date and time. These announcements are posted on the organizers' websites and are widely shared on social media. By scouring our sources, it has been possible for EMBERS to accurately forecast the occurrence of these types of protests.

The recurring events take place on a regular basis. For instance, in Chile and Argentina the 'mothers of the disappeared' protest the disappearance of their children by the military dictatorships of the 1970s and 1980s on a certain particular day of the week and in the same plaza. In some countries with large Muslim populations, fighting and protests break out regularly after Friday evening prayer as people stream out of the mosques after listening to fiery sermons. These are typically small events but if they are reported as part of our GSR, EMBERS models will be able to forecast them.

The protests for which the causes are known but not the timing are staged spontaneously. These events are the outcomes of longstanding frustration and anger which fuel widespread protests in response to trigger events. Thus, the viral videos of police brutality or a sudden change in government policy can start a prairie fire of protests. The Brazilian Spring with origins in bus fares and which channeled public anger against corruption and government mismanagement is a classical example. The challenge here is not just to be aware of the underlying tensions that might erupt when an event occurs, but to also distinguish between events that do and do not perform as triggers. Algorithms to better model precursors is an area of further research that will aid further forecasting this class of events.

Finally, *black swan* events [18] are rare and truly unforeseen and can happen as a result of natural disasters, the sudden death of a leader, or even the sudden rise of a small group that can truly destabilize a nation. (Each of these types of events can in turn spark civil unrest.) For instance the rise of the Islamic State in Iraq and Syria (ISIS) has truly confounded policymakers all over the world. While there were other Sunni groups, from al-Qaeda to al-Nusra, that contributed to instability, the rapid ascendance of ISIS, which did not depend on an isolated terrorist attack and burst out with a clear holding of territories as a full-scale insurgency, surprised most observers. It might not be feasible to forecast the beginnings of such events; however, once such movements have been initiated, models should be able to detect and forecast their momentum.

8. ETHICAL ISSUES

EMBERS, as an anticipatory intelligence system, has many powerful legitimate uses but is also susceptible to abuse.

First, it is important to have a discussion of civil unrest and its role in society. In our opinion, under the proper circumstances, civil unrest enhances the ability of citizens to communicate not only their views but also their priorities to those who govern them. Governments constantly need to make choices and find it difficult to know, on specific issues at particular times, how their constituencies value the available options. Elections are retrospective indicators and rarely issue-specific; polling taps into sentiment, but is not a good indicator of priorities or strength of feeling because of the low cost associated with responding. Events, on the other hand, indicate a willingness to bear some costs (organization, mobilization, identification) in support of an issue and thus reveal not only preferences but provide some indication of priorities.

An open sources indicators approach, as we have used here, is a potentially powerful tool for understanding the social construction of meaning and its translation into behavior. EMBERS can contribute to making the transmission of citizen preferences to government less costly to the economy and society as well. There are economic costs to even peaceful disruptions embodied in civil unrest due to lost work hours and the deployment of police to manage traffic and the interactions between protestors and bystanders. Given the vulnerability of large gatherings to provocation by handfuls of violence-oriented protestors (e.g., Black Box anarchists in Brazil) the economic, social and political costs of large-scale public demonstrations are also potentially significant to marchers, bystanders, property owners and the government – democratically elected or not. The right to demonstrate can still be respected but if the government responds to grievances in time, the protestors may cancel the event or fewer people might participate in the event. In today's interconnected society, protests also cause disruptions to supply chain logistics, travel, and other sectors, and anticipating disruptions is key to ensuring safety as well as reliability.

The potential power of civil unrest forecasting systems, like those of most scientific advances, is susceptible to abuse by both democratic and non-democratic governments. The appropriate safeguards require developing transparent and accountable democratic systems, not outlawing science. Non-democratic governments may clearly abuse such forecasting systems. But even here the value of forecasting civil unrest is not simply negative. Many non-democratic regimes transition to democratic ones, often in a violent process but not always (in Latin America, authoritarian regimes negotiated transitions to democracy without a civil war in Mexico, Honduras, Peru, Bolivia, Brazil, Uruguay, Argentina and Chile). The rational choice models of authoritarian decision-making in such crises always explain a dictatorship's collapse rather than accommodation to a transition by pointing to the lack of credible information in a dictatorship regarding citizens' true feelings. EMBERS-like models may thus provide the information that facilitates and encourages some transitions.

9. CONCLUSIONS

We have presented our experiences and lessons learnt from operating EMBERS continuously 24x7 over a period of four years. EMBERS has proven itself to be a reliable predictor of civil unrest events in 10 different countries by ingesting data from multiple languages. EMBERS has been a wonderful testbed for our data science team and even in its misses much has been learnt.

Future work falls primarily in three directions. First, we intend to investigate more formal methods to model precursors to protests, so that better precursor detection can constitute better protest forecasting. Second, we will continue to build a strong systems capability to forecasting societal events, by enlarging the scope of regions and languages covered. Finally, we are investigating techniques to remove or reduce the human element required in generating the GSR. Currently the most human intensive part of the EMBERS project is generating a GSR for training and validation of the models.

Acknowledgments

Supported by the Intelligence Advanced Research Projects Activity (IARPA) via DoI/NBC contract number D12PC000337, the US Government is authorized to reproduce and distribute reprints of this work for Governmental purposes notwithstanding any copyright annotation thereon. Disclaimer: The views and conclusions contained herein are those of the authors and should not be interpreted as necessarily representing the official policies or endorsements, either expressed or implied, of IARPA, DoI/NBC, or the US Government.

10. REFERENCES

[1] Y. M. Bishop, S. E. Fienberg, and P. W. Holland. *Discrete multivariate analysis: theory and practice.* Springer Science & Business Media, 2007.

[2] J. Cadena, G. Korkmaz, C. J. Kuhlman, et al. Forecasting Social Unrest using Activity Cascades. *PLOS One*, 10(6):e0128879, 2015.

[3] P. Chakraborty, P. Khadivi, B. Lewis, A. Mahendiran, et al. Forecasting a Moving Target: Ensemble Models for ILI Case Count Predictions. In *SIAM International Conference on Data Mining, April 24-26, 2014*, pages 262–270, 2014.

[4] R. Dingledine, N. Mathewson, and P. F. Syverson. Tor: The Second-Generation Onion Router. In *USENIX Security Symposium, August 9-13, 2004*, pages 303–320, 2004.

[5] A. Doyle, G. Katz, K. Summers, C. Ackermann, et al. Forecasting Significant Societal Events using The EMBERS Streaming Predictive Analytics System. *Big Data*, 2(4):185–195, dec 2014.

[6] J. A. Goldstone, R. H. Bates, D. L. Epstein, et al. A Global Model for Forecasting Political Instability. *American Journal of Political Science*, 54(1):190–208, 2010.

[7] A. Hoegh, S. Leman, P. Saraf, and N. Ramakrishnan. Bayesian Model Fusion for Forecasting Civil Unrest. *Technometrics*, 57(3):332–340, February 2015.

[8] Y. Keneshloo, J. Cadena, G. Korkmaz, and N. Ramakrishnan. Detecting and Forecasting Domestic Political Crises: A Graph-Based Approach. In *ACM Web Science Conference, WebSci '14, June 23-26, 2014*, pages 192–196, 2014.

[9] G. Korkmaz, J. Cadena, C. J. Kuhlman, A. Marathe, A. Vullikanti, and N. Ramakrishnan. Combining Heterogeneous Data Sources for Civil Unrest Forecasting. In *IEEE/ACM International Conference on Advances in Social Networks Analysis and Mining, ASONAM, August 25 - 28, 2015*, pages 258–265, 2015.

[10] K. Leetaru and P. Schrodt. GDELT: Global Data on Events, Location and Tone, 1979–2012. *ISA Annual Convention*, pages 1979–2012, 2013.

[11] H. Llorens, L. Derczynski, et al. TIMEN: An Open Temporal Expression Normalisation Resource. In *International Conference on Language Resources and Evaluation, LREC, May 23-25, 2012*, pages 3044–3051, 2012.

[12] A. Mahendiran, W. Wang, J. A. S. Lira, et al. Discovering Evolving Political Vocabulary in Social Media. In *International Conference on Behavioral, Economic, and Socio-Cultural Computing, BESC, October 30 - November 1, 2014*, pages 26–32, 2014.

[13] S. Muthiah, B. Huang, J. Arredondo, et al. Planned Protest Modeling in News and Social Media. In *AAAI Conference on Artificial Intelligence, January 25-30, 2015*, pages 3920–3927, 2015.

[14] S. P. O'Brien. Crisis Early Warning and Decision Support: Contemporary Approaches and Thoughts on Future Research. *International Studies Review*, 12(1):87–104, 2010.

[15] N. Ramakrishnan, P. Butler, S. Muthiah, N. Self, et al. 'Beating the news' with EMBERS: Forecasting Civil Unrest using Open Source Indicators. In *International Conference on Knowledge Discovery and Data Mining, KDD, August 24 - 27, 2014*, pages 1799–1808, 2014.

[16] T. Rekatsinas, S. Ghosh, S. R. Mekaru, et al. SourceSeer: Forecasting Rare Disease Outbreaks using Multiple Data Sources. In *SIAM International Conference on Data Mining, April 30 - May 2, 2015*, pages 379–387, 2015.

[17] J. Strötgen and M. Gertz. HeidelTime: High Quality Rule-based Extraction and Normalization of Temporal Expressions. In *International Workshop on Semantic Evaluation*, SemEval '10, pages 321–324, 2010.

[18] N. N. Taleb. *The Black Swan. The Impact of the Highly Improbable.* Random House Inc., 2008.

[19] M. D. Ward, N. W. Metternich, C. Carrington, et al. *Geographical Models of Crises: Evidence from ICEWS*, pages 429–438. CRC Press, Boca Raton, FL, 2012.

[20] L. Zhao, F. Chen, et al. Unsupervised Spatial Event Detection in Targeted Domains with Applications to Civil Unrest Modeling. *PLOS ONE*, 9(10):e110206, 2014.

Anomaly Detection Using Program Control Flow Graph Mining from Execution Logs

Animesh Nandi‡, Atri Mandal‡, Shubham Atreja◇, Gargi B. Dasgupta‡, Subhrajit Bhattacharya‡
‡ IBM Research
◇ IIT Kanpur

ABSTRACT

We focus on the problem of detecting anomalous run-time behavior of distributed applications from their execution logs. Specifically we mine templates and template sequences from logs to form a control flow graph (cfg) spanning distributed components. This cfg represents the baseline healthy system state and is used to flag deviations from the expected behavior of runtime logs. The novelty in our work stems from the new techniques employed to: (1) overcome the instrumentation requirements or application specific assumptions made in prior log mining approaches, (2) improve the accuracy of mined templates and the cfg in the presence of long parameters and high amount of interleaving respectively, and (3) improve by orders of magnitude the scalability of the cfg mining process in terms of volume of log data that can be processed per day.

We evaluate our approach using (a) synthetic log traces and (b) multiple real-world log datasets collected at different layers of application stack. Results demonstrate that our template mining, cfg mining, and anomaly detection algorithms have high accuracy. The distributed implementation of our pipeline is highly scalable and has more than 500 GB/day of log data processing capability even on a 10 low-end VM based (Spark + Hadoop) cluster. We also demonstrate the efficacy of our end-to-end system using a case study with the Openstack VM provisioning system.

1. INTRODUCTION

IT Operational Analytics (ITOA) aims at providing insights into the operational health of IT components deployed in a cloud datacenter. One of the strongest use cases of ITOA is driven by automated problem diagnostics and has recently received a lot of attention as a key differentiator of successful IT service vendors. A very challenging problem in this domain entails troubleshooting a distributed application deployed on the cloud by analyzing large volumes of machine-data collected from the different layers of the application, middleware, and infrastructure.

Not surprisingly, one of the primary sources of data used for mining operational insights is log data, given that execution logs contain rich information about runtime behaviour of a system. For example, warnings and error messages in logs give valuable clues to debugging the cause of the problem. But limiting the analysis to error/warning messages alone has severe limitations since several problems do not manifest as errors/warnings (leading to bad recall). Additionally, many errors/warnings are often benign and get reported even when the system is healthy (leading to bad precision).

We focus on a more robust approach of detecting anomalous runtime behavior by (a) mining/learning a healthy state model, and (b) comparing the runtime behaviour against the healthy-state reference model to locate deviations from expected behaviour. Some prior works [17, 31]) have proposed modeling the healthy state of a distributed system as a *control flow graph (cfg)* that stitches together various log message types or *templates* after mining the execution flows in the distributed system. In this paper, we adopt a similar approach, where we first mine *templates* from raw logs and then mine sequences from the templates in order to create a cfg. But contrary to prior works, we aim to do so without making some of the simplistic assumptions (summarized below and also described in detail in Section 5) made in prior works.

A template is an abstraction of a print statement in source code, which manifests itself in raw logs with different embedded parameter values in different executions. Represented as a set of invariant keywords and parameters (denoted by parameter placeholder $< P >$), a template when accurately identified can be used for summarization of multiple raw log lines that are instances of it. The parameter values change across different instances of same template, while the invariant keywords remain constant. The cfg represents the distributed control flow of a distributed system, where the sequence of templates is stitched together from execution flows. It is a graph where the nodes are templates and the edges represent the transition sequences from one template to another. The cfg graph represents all possible flow paths (within and across components) of a distributed system encountered when the distributed application runs.

The mining of cfg structures from execution logs may seem similar to the network inference problem [1, 10]. This addresses the problem of tracing paths of the underlying network using a generative model of cascades. Given the knowledge of when a particular node is infected (but not by whom), the challenge is to mine the unobserved network topology for each cascade. In comparison, there are two very important differences in the domain of mining cfg structure from execution logs. In the log domain, the nodes of the network are unknown and thus observations about when a particular cascade event occurred on a node cannot be made without mining the nodes themselves. We refer to this sub-problem of mining the nodes as the template mining problem. Secondly, each cascade in the network diffusion is identifiable using a cascade id. The execution logs from the distributed application domain does not guarantee that every transaction or flow through the system will be uniquely identifiable with a transaction id, and this results in interleaving of events across different simultaneously occurring transactions. Thus the cfg mining problem is inherently more complex in the setting of execution logs, since it has to be done without knowing the nodes of the network and without the presence of transaction ids.

To distinguish cfg mining from the process mining literature we note that process mining [6, 11, 18] assumes that the set of nodes is known in advance. It further assumes that recorded events contain a case/transaction id which ties together the set of events occurring

KDD '16, August 13-17, 2016, San Francisco, CA, USA

DOI: http://dx.doi.org/10.1145/2939672.2939712

for each execution of a workflow/process. While this assumption of the presence of a clearly demarcated execution trace per transaction is reasonable for transactional systems like ERP and CRM, for the genre of distributed applications composed of various third-party microservices on the cloud this assumption does not hold.

The goal of this work is to overcome certain limiting assumptions made in the prior works in mining cfg of a distributed application. Firstly, some prior works rely on the availability of source code or binaries [31] to assist in the template mining phase, an assumption that does not hold in today's distributed applications composed of multiple third-party microservices. Amongst approaches that mine cfg from logs only, they make certain assumptions about parameters being small [19] or occurring towards the beginning of a template [9], or make assumptions about the presence of demarcated execution traces through the cfg [11, 18], or rely on explicitly embedding a transaction id parameter thats tracks a transaction flow across the distributed application [2, 13]. The goal of our work is to mine the cfg without making any of these assumptions.

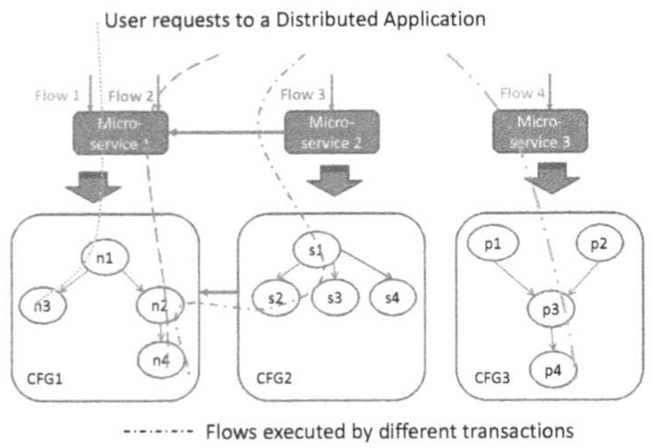

Figure 1: Transaction Flows in a Distributed Application

Figure 1 shows an example of a distributed application whose components are running on the cloud. Based on user requests coming to the application, one or more simultaneous flows are initiated which in turn invokes one or more microservice hosted on the cloud. Each transaction initiates a flow that executes one or more microservice deployed on the cloud infrastructure. The control flow of each microservice is represented as a cfg. The node within a cfg represents a template message that manifests itself in the execution logs of the microservice. The edges represent how the control flow passes between the nodes.

The figure shows four flows Flow 1 - Flow 4. Firstly, different transactions could generate simultaneous flows within the same cfg. For example, Flow 1 comprising (n1, n3) and Flow 2 comprising (n2, n4) traverses through the same cfg 1. The execution logs of microservice 1 will contain interleaved traces from both these flows while executing the same cfg 1. Secondly, transactions could also initiate parallel flows across different cfgs. For example, when Flow 1 and Flow 4 co-occur, cfg 1 and cfg 3 execute in parallel. Lastly, transactions could also initiate flows across microservices. For example, Flow 3 spans across cfg 2 and cfg 1.

To mine flows across cfgs, execution logs of all microservices comprising a distributed application needs to be merged. Our goal in this paper is to mine the cfg structures of the microservices and their cross dependencies from the merged execution logs across all microservices. The two sub-problems we strive to solve here are (a) mining the template messages while assuming no application specific knowledge about the print statements, its invariants or parameters and (b) mining cfg edges connecting the templates in the presence of interleaved logs without assuming the presence of explicit transaction ids demarcating different transactions.

1.1 Challenges in CFG Mining

Figure 2 shows a sample raw log input to our cfg mining methods. The raw logs are interleaved from multiple transaction flows that are executing a ground truth cfg (shown at the bottom of Figure 2). Each raw log statement has some invariant keywords and some variable

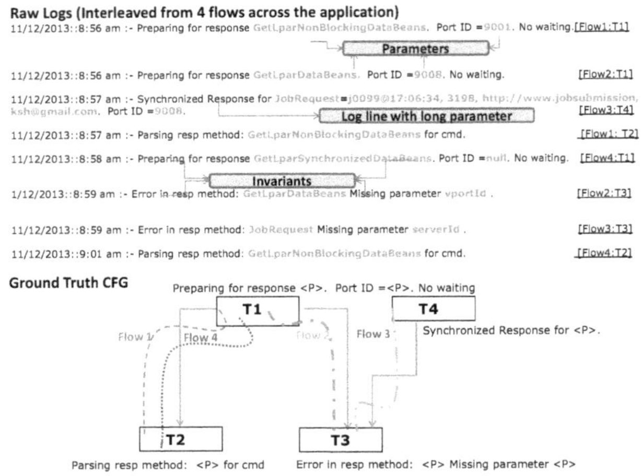

Figure 2: Raw Logs from Interleaved Flows

parameters. Sometimes the parameters can be as long or even longer than the keywords (e.g. Template T4 in [Flow 3: T4]). Each raw log instance is annotated with the tag of transaction-flow id:template id. Note that transaction ids are only present for understanding of the reader and in real logs we do not assume either transaction ids or template ids to be present.

In the absence of application specific knowledge, mining message templates from log lines incurs several challenges. This is because of the fact that parameters are indistinguishable from actual words, and can vary in number, in length, as well as their positions within a print statement. This causes instances of the same template to look very different or different templates with common parameters to look similar (see more examples of two classes of confusion in Section 2.1). For the above reasons, off-the-shelf text clustering techniques on the log lines does not work because of the complexities of semi-structured data with arbitrary behaviour of parameters. Further, running clustering on large volumes (several million lines) of log data does not scale.

In the absence of transaction ids, mining template sequences from interleaved log traces of different components or multi-threaded traces of the same component, also becomes a hard problem. Without clearly distinguishable transaction demarcations, which is a prerequisite for a suite of process mining techniques proposed in literature, the challenge lies in separating the noise from interleaved sequences. For e.g. in Figure 2, in the absence of transaction-flow ids, it is nontrivial to separate the execution path of each flow and build the cfgs. [Flow 3: T4] immediately follows [Flow 2: T1] and gives the false impression of an edge existing between nodes T4 and T1.

1.2 Highlights of our Approach

The key highlights of our end-to-end system called OASIS are –

Template Mining Phase - In the absence of application specific knowledge or assumptions on the usage of parameters, we observe that using text alone is not sufficient to accurately map log lines to a template (see prior works in Section 5.1). We attempt to overcome this challenge by using the multi-modal signal of text and temporal vicinity (i.e. predecessors and successors in the cfg) to further refine the mapping of log lines to templates (see Section 2.1).

CFG Edge Mining Phase - In order to mine the cfg structure from the interleaved logs in the absence of transaction-ids, we propose a novel two-phase approach of mining template sequences that leverages nearest-neighbor-groups (NNS) computed in the first phase to prune away noise due to interleaving, followed by a second phase that mines only immediate predecessors/successors of a template (see Section 2.2).

Anomaly Detection Phase - We describe how the mined cfg structure can be used to identify different classes of anomalies. We describe the architecture and implementation of an end-to-end system that detect anomalies in deployed distributed applications by analyzing their execution logs (see Section 3).

Evaluation of our Approach - We empirically evaluated the effectiveness of our template mining and cfg edge mining algorithms in comparison with alternative design choices, using synthetic log traces and as well as several real-world log datasets. We also demonstrate that our overall cfg mining pipeline has good parallelizability and is able to process more than 500 GB/day of log data even on a 10 low-end VM based (Spark + Hadoop) [24] cluster. Finally, we demonstrate the efficacy of our end-to-end anomaly detection system using a case study with Openstack [21] VM provisioning system.

2. OUR CFG MINING TECHNIQUES

We now describe our offline analytic models of template and sequence mining, both of which together enable us to compute the cfg nodes (templates) and cfg edges (sequences).

2.1 Mining of Templates

The same template would manifest as multiple log lines based on the embedding of the actual values of parameters. There are primarily *two classes of confusion* created by parameters and invariant keywords in a print statement when attempting to mine templates: (i) C1: Log lines resulting from the *same* template can look different textually when the template has multiple or long parameters values, and (ii) C2: Log lines resulting from two *different* templates can look alike textually when they share common long parameters.

Prior works in mining templates from logs (see Section 5.1) largely rely on some form of text-based clustering of similar log lines in order to compute templates. These text-based clustering approaches combat the above two classes of confusion by relying on either application specific knowledge of the types of parameters (such as IP address, requestID etc.), or assume that a template has few parameters and that too comprising of a single word each, or assume that parameters even if long are typically at the end of the print statement. Although these assumptions are indeed true for a subset of datasets, we found these assumptions to *not* hold for many of the datasets we experimented with.

In the absence of application specific knowledge, we make the observation that using text alone is never going to be sufficient to generically map log lines to a template. Building on this intuition, we propose a novel *multi-modal* algorithm for using temporal vicinity of a template (i.e. templates that typically occur in time before it or after it) as an additional signal to textual content of a template, in order to mine high quality templates without making any application specific assumptions. The intuition behind using the joint-signal of text similarity and temporal vicinity similarity is that *ideally* two instances of the same print statement should not only look similar w.r.t. the text-similarity, but they should also have similar temporal vicinities. W.r.t. confusion class C1, observe that although two instances of the same print statement might have a low text similarity, they can still be merged into the same template cluster if their temporal vicinities are very similar. W.r.t confusion class C2, even if two log line instances corresponding to two different print statements might look similar if they share a long common parameter and also have additional overlapping words, their temporal-vicinity will be quite different and thereby will not be eligible for merging. Thereby, using the temporal vicinity similarity information in addition to the text similarity information, we can overcome the fundamental challenges created by the two classes of confusion described above.

Contrary to prior works that mine templates using the textual content of the log lines alone, our multi-modal approach of template mining would require us to mine the temporal vicinity of each log line as well. Given that each log line can be potentially unique because of the unique combination of the multiple embedded parameter values in each print statement, mining temporal vicinity at the granularity a log line would not give us statistically significant information about the observed predecessors and successors of a log line. This leads to a *seemingly* chicken-and-egg situation, wherein mining templates requires us to mine sequences, and mining sequences requires us to mine some notion of template that aggregates multiple instances of the same print statement. We resolve this dilemma by not directly operating on raw logs but transforming the raw logs into an intermediate form of *approximate templates*.

To construct approximate templates, we make a first pass on the raw log lines in order to compute a frequency histogram comprising of every distinct keyword that was observed in the logs. The underlying intuition here is that the invariant template words are much more frequent in the logs than the parameters. A change point detection algorithm that operates on frequency analysis of the unique words in the logs, detects words with frequencies beyond the change point threshold as *dictionary* keywords. We transform the log lines to approximate templates by iterating over the words in the log line in order, and retaining words in the log line that are present in the computed dictionary and replacing the words that are not in the dictionary by a parameter placeholder $< P >$. At the end of this dictionary based log line transformation phase, the output is a list of approximate templates which are several orders of magnitude less than the number of raw log lines. In our experiments, we typically observed more than 1000x compression ratio (i.e. #log-lines : #approximate-templates).

Inspite of this reduction from log lines to approximate templates, we nevertheless observe that in many datasets, a modest fraction of approximate templates still have support values below the minimum threshold (i.e. support) required to mine statistically significant temporal vicinities of these approximate templates (using our algorithm described in the next Section 2.2). To overcome this limitation, we then run a text-based clustering at a very high threshold (here 90%) of edit-distance based similarity to further cluster different approximate templates which correspond to the same ground truth template or print statement. Note that we need to use a very high text-similarity threshold in this phase to ensure that two different print statements are *extremely* unlikely to get mapped to the same *approximate template cluster*.

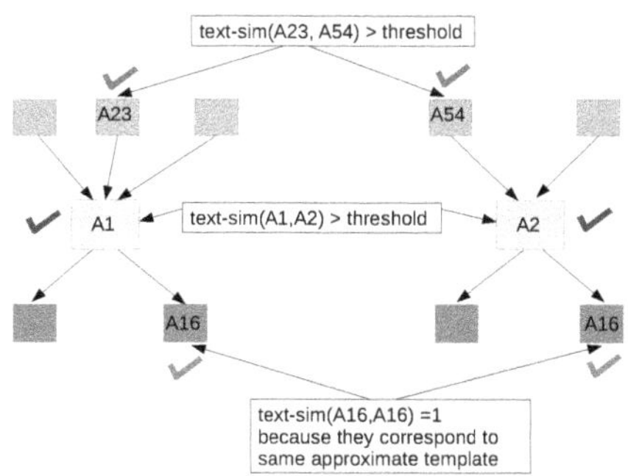

Figure 3: Example multi-modal similarity check

At this point, although the approximate template clusters are quite noise-free (i.e. their constituent members indeed correspond to the same print statement), the issue that needs to be overcomed is that we mine multiple clusters for the same print statement when the number of parameters is large or parameter values are long. Consequently, to refine these text clusters further, we then resort to our multi-modal clustering approach that merges clusters using the multi-modal signal of the textual content of cluster label that is computed using a Longest Common Subsequence (LCS) of the text in the constituent members, coupled with the computed statistically significant predecessor(s) and successor(s) of these clusters.

Figure 3 shows an example *multi-modal similarity check* that is performed for two approximate template clusters A1 and A2. Lets say we mine 3 parents and 2 children of A1, and similarly, 2 parents and 2 children of A2. In contrast to checking the text similarity of the reference cluster labels of A1 and A2 alone (as was done in prior text-alone approaches), we also compute the text similarity between any parent of A1 and A2, and also between any child of A1 and A2. Based on the comparison, if we find that these clusters have a good text similarity match between any of their respective parents (A23 and A54) and also between any of their respective children (here shared approximate template A16), then the two reference approximate clusters A1 and A2 satisfy the multi-modal similarity check.

Note that in comparison to text-only clustering approaches, our multi-modal approach can set relatively lower values of the text similarity threshold in order to combat confusion class C1 described above, and still ensure that we do not succumb to the bad merges that could have been potentially caused by confusion class C2.

Our algorithm however needs to handle a few special scenarios – (a) when both of the clusters being compared do not have a child (this happens for leaves in the cfg), we need to discount the child direction text similarity match, and similarly (b) when both the clusters being compared do not have a parent (this happens for root nodes in a cfg), we need to discount the parent direction check.

Worth admitting here, is that there are some rare scenarios wherein our multi-modal algorithm is unable to merge two instances of the same print statement. This happens when the transaction flows producing the two instances of the same print statement, have different incoming paths and different outgoing paths in the underlying ground truth cfg. In such a scenario, the temporal vicinity of the two instances of the print statement are different in reality and thus the multi-modal check fails. This is the primary reason why our evaluation of our multimodal agorithm in Section 4.4 demonstrates that although multi-modal performs superior to using pure text-based clustering, we still end up with some print statements having multiple unmerged cluster instances (leading to reduced precision).

Additionally, note that our multi-modal algorithm (in contrast to pure text-based clustering) depends on the accuracy of the mined predecessors/successors of the approximate template clusters. We observed that because of this dependence, errors in the mined cfg can negatively affect the accuracy of mined templates in the multi-modal algorithm – leading to occassional merging of two different print statements into a cluster whose's LCS label becomes corrupted (leading to reduced recall) and sometimes also leading to fragmentation of the same print statement into multiple cluster instances (leading to reduced precision).

2.2 Mining of CFG Edges

As described in the previous section, our multi-modal template mining approach requires us to compute the predecessors and successors of the approximate template clusters. Even if we had magically mined the intended ground-truth templates, this sequence mining phase would nevertheless have been needed in order to mine the cfg edges corresponding to the sequences between the mined templates. The challenge of this phase is to be able to robustly mine statistically significant predecessors and successors of the approximate templates when operating on interleaved logs. Interleaved logs result from multi-threaded executions of the same component (*intra-level parallelism*). Further, given our intention of mining control flows across different distributed microservices (e.g. the assignment of map tasks from a Hadoop Jobtracker node to a Datanode), interleaved logs also result from having to intentionally merge logs from different distributed components (*inter-level parallelism*).

As described in Section 5.2, although classical sequence mining approaches are not directly applicable in our problem setting of interleaved logs because of the lack of demarcated transactions, one can adapt these algorithms to work in our setting by chunking the interleaved logstream based on time-windows and creating a transaction id per time-window [20]. The duration of the time-window can be set to maximum (or 99th percentile) edge lag in the application.

Figure 4 describes the inner workings of how such an approach would mine predecessors/successors. As an example, a sub-goal is to mine the children of T2, i.e. mine the existence of the edge T2 → T3 and T2 → T6. Tracking the immediate successor of each template does not work in the interleaved logs setting since the next log line could very well be noise from either intra- or inter- parallelism. What is needed is a lookahead window beyond the immediate next line, and incrementing the counts of all succeeding templates occurring within the lookahead window. Although this lookahead window

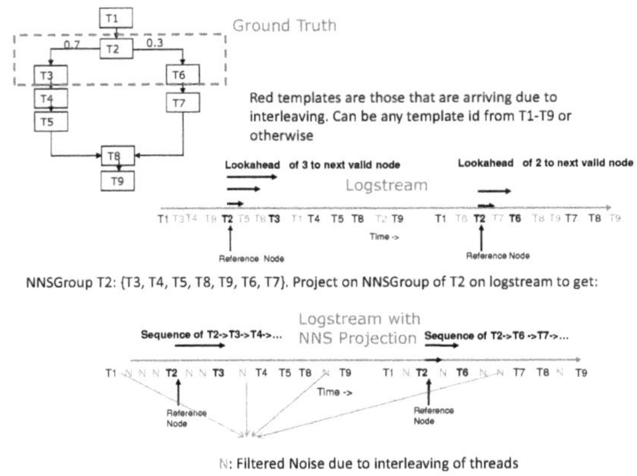

Figure 4: Our two-stage sequence mining algorithm as compared to classical single-stage sequence mining approach

based bookkeeping would enable mining of the edges from the reference node (here T2) to its children (here T2 → T3 and T2 → T6), the limitation and concerning issue with this approach is that the algorithm will also mine edges to the downstream cfg descendants of the reference node (i.e. T4, T5, T7, T8, T9). Consequently, instead of mining the two desired children of T2, the algorithm will end up mining lots of redundant edges from the reference node to the downstream descendants. Although one may envision running a transitive-edge removal algorithm [4] on the bloated cfg mined by this strawman algorithm, note that the transitive-edge removal could end up removing potential *genuine detour paths* from a parent to its downstream grandchild. For many practical datasets, the occurrence of multiple detour paths existing between two nodes is fairly common, and standard transitive edge removal will thereby lead to mining an incorrect cfg.

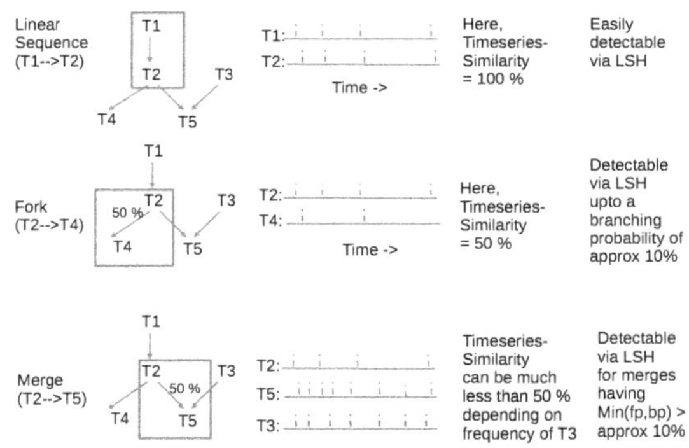

Figure 5: Nearest-Neighbor (NNS) group computation using template time-series

To overcome the limitations of the above strawman approach, we propose a novel two-stage sequence mining approach. In the first-stage, we compute *Nearest-Neighbor-Groups (NNS) groups* of each template, and the second stage leverages this pre-computed NNS group information to mine *only the immediate* successors/predecessors of each template. The intuition behind our two-stage algorithm is that if we find that the immediately succeeding log line of a reference template-id in the input logstream is not a part of the NNS group of that reference template, then it implies that the occurrence of this succeeding log line is essentially noise resulting from the interleaving. Before we describe the details of our approach, we first describe what we mean by NNS groups, followed by how it helps us avoid the limitations of the previous single-stage approach.

The NNS group of a template is a set of other templates that are observed to statistically *temporally co-occur* with the reference template. NNS groups of each reference template can be computed by analyzing the *time-series* of each template which captures the timestamps or chunked time-bins wherein that particular template occurred in the logstream. Given the time-series of each template the algorithm to mine the NNS groups of a template depends on the type of cfg sub-structure we want to mine.

Figure 5 describes the three fundamental *cfg sub-structures* we want to mine, and how the time-series of the nodes in those sub-structures relate to each other, and the algorithm we should use in order to mine these sub-structures. In particular, the cfg comprises of three types of sub-structures – linear sequences, forks, and merges. Depending on the type of sub-structure, the time-series of the nodes in the sub-structure have different extents of similarity. As depicted in the figure, time-series of nodes in the linear sequence have almost a 100% similarity in their respective time-series. For forks, the similarly depends on the branching probability between the parent and the child. For merges however, the time-series similarity can be low inspite of a high branching probability between the parent and child. In general the algorithm to compute the NNS groups depends on the type of sub-structure we want to mine. The scalable Locality-Sensitive-Hashing (LSH) [12] based Minhash [5] algorithm that detects jaccard similarity is a good candidate for detecting the linear sequences, forks, and a constrained setting of merges that are not very skewed (i.e. time-series similarities $>$ approx 10%). To mine arbitrary skew in forks and merges however, one would need to resort to the bayesian approach of mining forward (fp) and backward conditional probabilities (bp) [29].

When mining correlations using either the jaccard similarity or the bayesian conditional probability approach, we ensure that the correlations are not coincidental by incorporating the *null-invariant* check [29]. For this, we measure the ratio of the conditional probability of an event as compared to the independent probability. Essentially, if the ratio of (P(A/B) / P(A)) is above a *non-indepedence threshold*, then it implies that the two events are not independent, since P(A/B) should be approx P(A) if the two events A and B had been independent.

The second-stage of our sequence mining approach leverages the pre-computed information of the NNS group of each template, and only increments the counter of the first template that succeeds the reference template pre-conditioned on the fact that the succeeding template must belong to the NNS group of the reference template (here T2). Further, we can preempt the lookahead, the moment such a template is found, thereby implying that we create a successor edge only to the first NNS group member that follows the reference template. Another way of interpreting this algorithm is that in order to create the successor edges of a reference template, we consider a projection of the input logstream on the NNS group of that reference template, as shown in Figure 4. This projection essentially implies that the noisy candidates due to interleaving do not exist in the projected logstream.

This second-stage of this algorithm can be realized by making a single pass of the input logstream, and tracking for each NNS group, the latest occurring NNS group member ($lastmemberseen$) and the time of this last occurrence ($lasttimeseen$), and creating edges only when the lastmemberseen is the same as the reference template of the NNS group and the ($currenttime$ - $lasttimeseen$) $< lagthreshold$, wherein lagthreshold is an application specific threshold based on expected edge lags. On observing a template, we update the $lastmemberseen$ and $lasttimeseen$ in all the NNS groups this template is part of.

For each template, once the successor/predecessor edges and also the relative normalized values of the counters of the NNS group members is computed, the relative branching probabilities of the CFG edges can be computed. Further, the temporal vicinity of each template can be stitched together to construct the desired CFG.

2.3 Scalability and Parallizability of our CFG Mining Pipeline

Given that the log datasets of typical applications are very voluminous, it is imperative that the algorithms involved in the above different stages of the pipeline be parallelized in order to enable scalable mining of the cfg from large volumes of training data using multiple cores or a cluster of machines (i.e. worker nodes).

(*Stage 1*) The approximate template generation phase can be easily parallelized across multiple worker nodes by splitting the log data into multiple splits. This stage in the first round computes the frequency histogram of the keywords in a MapReduce fashion, followed by broadcasting of the word dictionary computed from the frequency histogram using change point detection, followed by the generation of the approximate templates using the dictionary lookup based transformation of the log lines.

(*Stage 2*) The second stage of high similarity edit-distance based text clustering is done efficiently via Minhashing [5] the tokens of the approximate templates to efficiently identify other potential approximate templates that are very similar. The actual edit-distance is calculated between the Minhash pruned candidates, and members having edit-distance similarity above a threshold are merged to form high-similarity text clusters.

(*Stage 3*) To parallelize the third stage of NNS Group computation, we need to essentially parallelize the computation of the pairwise time-series correlation metric that is based on the bayesian conditional probability coupled with the null-invariant check. To do this, every worker node computes the partial time-series of every template from the timeline fragmented portion of the logs hosted by the worker, followed by $O(N)$ computation of the partial length of each time-series and the $O(N^2)$ computation of the pairwise overlap between the partial time-series of each template. The final pairwise correlation metric (based on entire time-series) can be efficiently computed in a distributed way by leveraging the partial length/overlap statistics computed (in parallel) on the different worker nodes.

(*Stage 4*) The fourth stage of mining the predecessors/successors makes one pass on the logs and this phase can be parallelized by broadcasting the computed nns-matrix (typically sparse) to each worker node, computing the partial edge statistics on respective portions of the timeline based log splits, and then aggregating the partial statistics to compute the relative branching probabilities for each approximate template cluster.

(*Stage 5*) Finally, we have the fifth stage of multimodal template refinement. Since this stage operates only on a small number of high-similarity edit-distance based template clusters and not on the raw logs, we avoid parallelizing this phase. Moreso, this stage cannot be trivially parallelized and thus we intentionally chose to have a centralized implementation only. However, to nevertheless speedup this phase, we employed scalable LSH-based Minhashing [5] on the text tokens of the approximate template cluster labels to efficiently identify potential candidates for the multimodal similarity check.

3. ARCHITECTURE OF OUR END-TO-END ANOMALY DETECTION SYSTEM

In this section, we describe the system architecture and implementation of our end-to-end log analytics system called OASIS (see Figure 6). Logs from various services are ingested using Logstash [16] adapters, routed through Kafka [14], and indexed into ElasticSearch [7]. Data becomes available for search immediately. At the same time, data is also passed onto the (Spark + Hadoop) [24] layer. The two components in OASIS are described below:

3.1 Offline Mining of CFG based Model

At the heart of OASIS lies the offline analytic models comprising of template and cfg mining (shown in blue in Fig.6) using the algorithms we described in Section 2. The offline training models comprise of a set of templates along with the cfg edges having annotations of branching probabilities and expected edge lags.

3.2 Online Anomaly Scoring

The online anomaly scoring module of OASIS uses the offline models of the mined templates and cfg. As shown in Fig.6, this comprises of two modules –

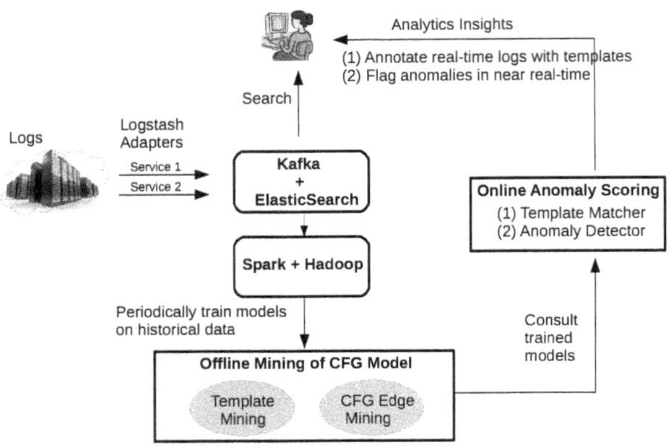

Figure 6: OASIS Architecture

Template Matcher: At runtime, as log lines are ingested, the offline computed dictionary is consulted to detect the invariant keywords in the incoming messages and then mine the approximate template in the same way as in the offline model building phase. Further, using the previously stored mapping of the approximate templates to the final refined templates got via multi-modal template mining, we map in real-time the incoming log line to a previously mined refined templates.

Anomaly Detector: Logs annotated with template ids are passed through an anomaly detection routine. In OASIS, anomalies have two attributes: (1) type of anomaly and (2) score of anomaly. The type of an anomaly signifies the underlying reason of why it is an anomaly. The score of an anomaly signifies its severity. There are two types of anomalies viz. (a) sequence anomaly and (b) distribution anomaly.

A *sequence anomaly* is raised when none of the children of a parent node is seen within an expected time lag interval. These are raised instantaneously when the the expected duration timeout occurs. Hence this type of anomaly messages are more real-time. The advantage of sequence anomalies are that they are very few in number and high precision. Also most sequence anomalies can generate actionable insights i.e. deeper investigation into why a particular control flow was interrupted at a particular node. We also assign a score to the sequence anomaly to denote our confidence that this anomaly was not an artifact of the occurrence of some low branching probability edge that got pruned away as a noisy edge because of its branching probability being below the 10% branching probability threshold. So, we use the aggregate children probability as the anomaly score, with higher scores denoting that we are more confident.

A *distribution anomaly* is raised when the edge probabilities between parent and any of its children changes. This type of anomaly can identify shifts in the observed branching probability distribution at a cfg node. However, its critical that we design the scoring metric in a way, that for inherently fluctuating workloads, we do not raise false positives. To cater to this, we track the observed branching probabibility distributions over the entire course of the healthy run of the system. To do this, for each node, the branch probabilities are calculated periodically on non-overlapping windows over the entire span of the training log, and representative branching distributions materialized in a set called Expected Set. During anomaly detection, we calculate a diff-score of the observed branching distribution with every distribution present in the Expected Set, and use the minimum diff-score as the distribution anomaly score.

4. EVALUATION

4.1 Datasets

We evaluate our system using both real-world and synthetic datasets. For the cfg mining technique, we use two real datasets – (i) *linux*: Linux syslogs, and (ii) *distMW*: a proprietary distributed middleware application. For evaluating our end-to-end anomaly detection system, we do a special case study with a third real-world dataset *openstack* [21]: a popular cloud VM provisioning system which comprises of multiple distributed microservices. Given that our techniques rely on exploiting timing correlations, we ensured that our techniques are not negatively impacted by large machine clock drifts, by running the distributed applications either in standalone mode (i.e. all different microservices running on the same machine) or on machines that are NTP time synchronized (a fairly common scenario).

In addition to the above three real-world log datasets, we evaluate each phase of our pipeline (i.e. template mining, mining of cfg edges, anomaly detection) using synthetic logs generated by a log generator, which we built specifically for this purpose. The synthetic log generator has three modules – the cfg edge generator, the cfg template generator, and the execution simulator.

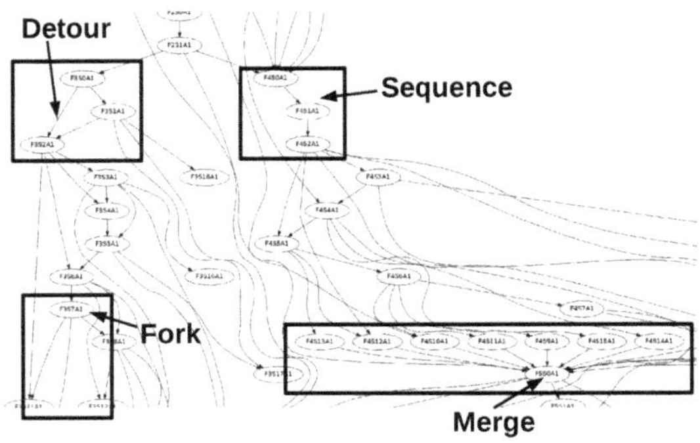

Figure 7: A portion of a synthetically generated cfg

The **CFG Edge Generator** builds the cfg edges for a hypothetical microservice from basic programming constructs. Figure 7 shows a portion of a sample synthetic cfg that is generated. As depicted in it, observe that it models all types of fundamental building blocks like linear sequences, forks, and merges, and also has detour paths. Further, edges are characterized by a lag representing the delay between the two print statements that are executed in succession, and also a branching factor probability.

The **CFG Template Generator** determines the print statement corresponding to every node in the cfg. The invariants are selected from a global dictionary of words and parameters could be fixed or variable length. The number of parameters and their positions and the length of templates are chosen from a Gaussian distribution. Parameter values, determined at runtime are chosen either from a parameter space or inherited from their cfg ancestors.

Once the cfg is generated, the **Execution Simulator** generates paths based on branching probabilities. As the paths are traversed, each path outputs its print statements after simulating time equivalent to the corresponding edge lag. Each path reflects the execution of a thread. Threads arrive into the system according to a Poisson process and are traversed simultaneously, leading to multi threaded behaviour. Multiple cfg executions are also simulated.

4.2 Competitive Approaches

For comparison, we obtained the state-of-the art tools (from authors of prior works, and open source binaries) and ran them against the same datasets.

For template mining, the alternative approaches compared are: (i) *logcluster (lc)*: clustering approach on a set of approximate templates [28], (ii) *loghound (lh)*: frequent item-set mining on the words in each log line [27], (iii) *edit-distance (ed)*: Levenshtein's text similarity metric, (iv) *weighted-edit-distance (wted)*: modified similarity metric with higher weights on words at the beginning of templates [18]. Further, to cover a representative spectrum of possible configurations of competitive approaches, we report high(1%) and low(0.01%) support versions of lc and lh approaches, and high(0.9) and low(0.25) text similarity versions of edit distance algorithm. All

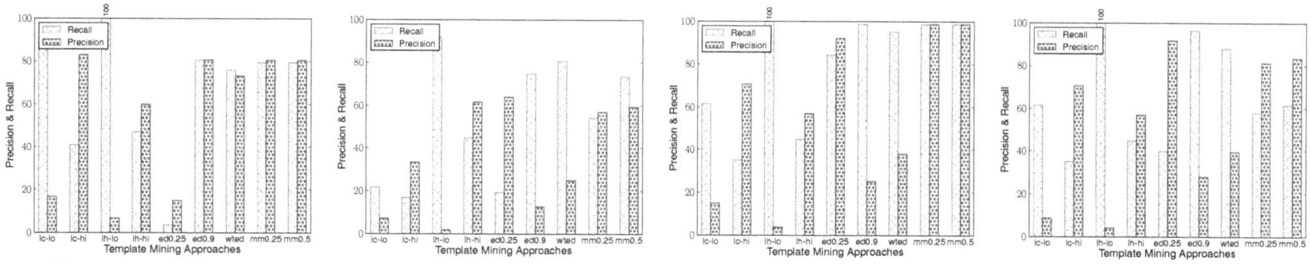

(a) Word:Param=0.9 ($\delta = 0.7$) (b) Word:Param=0.5 ($\delta = 0.7$) (c) $\delta = 0.85$ (Word:Param=0.75) (d) $\delta = 0.5$ (Word:Param=0.75)

Figure 8: Template Mining Precision/Recall as a function of word:parameter ratio and discriminative property in synthetic dataset

these approaches are compared with our multi-modal, which uses temporal vicinity along with text to compute refined templates.

For cfg edge mining, the competitive approaches compared are: (i) *SM-vanilla*: classical sequence mining (SM) algorithm (PrefixSpan [22]), (ii) *SM-tred*: this employs classical sequence mining followed by a step of graph transitive edge reduction in order to remove redundant descendants, (iii) *SM-wtred*: classical sequence mining with the transitive edge reduction step prioritizing which edges to remove based on weights [4] and using Jaccard association-rule mining metric as the weight, (iv) *PM*: classical process mining (PM) using the Fuzzy Miner [11], (v) *PM-noCID*: the MIM process mining tool [8] that attempts mining of process workflows from interleaved logs even in the absence of transaction or case ids, (vi) *WM*: workflow-miner [17]. Note that classical SM and classical PM approaches work on the basis of transaction ids. Since transaction boundaries are not present in interleaved execution logs, our approach for creating transformed inputs for classical SM and PM is to time-slice the logs into chunks based on a configurable time-window [20], and assign the same transaction id for all logs in the same time-window.

4.3 Methodology

We use the standard Precision/Recall metrics for evaluating our template mining, cfg edge mining, and anomaly detection phases. Recall is the fraction of the ground truth templates, edges, or anomalies that were mined. Precision is the fraction of mined templates, edges or anomalies that were present in the ground truth.

For synthetic logs, the comparisons were made with the available ground truth generated by our tool. For ground truth generation on real logs, we took the following approach: (a) subject matter experts were asked to identify the distinct ground truth templates present in the logs, (b) thread ids in real logs were used to separate out the valid ground truth sequences (note that threadids were used only for ground truth sequence generation, but intentionally not leveraged by our sequencing algorithms), (c) For logs where there were no threadids, we asked domain experts for some known sequences and compared our precision in being able to mine them.

4.4 Mining Templates

We now evaluate template mining performance for competitive approaches mentioned in Section 4.2, for different characteristics of the logs: its average word to parameter ratio and the discriminative property of each template that denotes how distinct each template looks from the others. These two metrics captures the confusion added by long parameters or inherited parameters respectively.

Figure 8(a) and Figure 8(b) report how precision/recall vary as average word to parameter ratio changes, keeping discriminative property fixed. In contrast, Figure 8(c) and Figure 8(d) report how precision/recall vary as discriminative property changes, keeping average word to parameter fixed. In these experiments, we intentionally used a single-threaded execution of a single cfg (having 100 templates), so that our proposed multi-modal algorithm has perfect information with respect to temporal vicinities. Note however that the real datasets in contrast have interleaved events from multiple threads and multiple microservices.

In Figure 8(a), we first observe that lh and lc approaches at low support have the best recall but suffer largely in terms of precision because many ground truth templates gets fragmented into multiple mined templates. In contrast, the high support variants have great precision but low recall, implying that they are unable to mine many low frequency patterns. For the edit-distance approaches, they are very much sensitive to the similarity threshold parameter. Edit-distance at 0.25 suffers from poor recall as they create many bad merges of slightly similar looking templates. In contrast, multi-modal even when run at a very low similarity threshold (0.25) effectively filters out noise using the temporal vicinity signal and consistently reports better recall and precision.

In Figure 8(b), where parameters occupy as much as of the log line as invariants, the precision of edit-distance at 0.9 drops severely since different instances of the same print statement look different and result in multiple mined templates. Edit-distance at 0.25 continues to have bad recall since the bad merges causes the cluster labels to become corrupted resulting in several of the ground truth templates not being identifiable in the list of mined templates. The multi-modal is the only approach that does fairly on both recall and precision front (both 60%).

In Figure 8(c), we observe that when templates are highly discriminative ($\delta = 0.85$), even edit-distance at 0.25 works quite well. However, in Figure 8(d) when δ drops ($\delta = 0.5$) and templates start looking similar, the recall begins to degrade. This is because with more confusion, mining actual ground truth templates become harder. However multi-modal even in this setting does fairly well on both recall and precision front.

We now report results on real datasets of distMW and linux in Figure 9(a & b). For distMW, there were 3000 ground truth templates, with word:parameter ratio = 0.5 and $\delta = 0.5$. Consistent with our observation on synthetic logs, multi-modal has relatively better precision and recall, while other approaches suffer either in precision or in recall. This is because the parameters were extremely long and complex. For linux, the computed ground truth templates was 80 while the word:parameter ratio =0.8 and $\delta = 0.6$. Here the edit distance approaches work fairly well w.r.t precision because of relatively shorter parameters. However at $\delta = 0.6$, templates were still fairly similar and the ability of multi-modal to disambiguate using temporal vicinity helped it dominate the results.

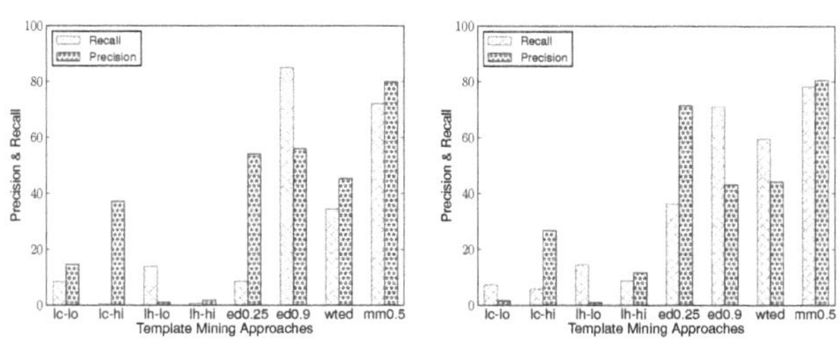

(a) Template Mining: distMW (b) Template Mining:linux

Figure 9: Template Mining on Real Datasets

	Intra-Parallelism Among Threads (varying t)				Inter-Parallelism among CFGs (varying n)		
	(n=1,t=1,s=300)	**(n=1,t=2,s=300)**	**(n=1,t=5,s=300)**	**(n=1,t=10,s=300)**	**(n=2,t=1,s=300)**	**(n=5,t=1,s=300)**	**(n=10,t=1,s=300)**
OASIS	P=100.0,R=97.1	P=100.0,R=96.2	P=99.8, R=91.9	P=98.6,R=88.8	P=100.0,R=97.1	P=100.0,R=92.7	P=100.0,R=82.3
SM-vanilla	P=15.8,R=99.6	P=8.6,R=99.6	P=2.6,R=100.0	P=1.5,R=100.0	P=11.9, R=86.0,	P=6.5,R=87.7	P=3.0,R=88.9
SM-tred	P=66.4,R=47.6	P=56.7,R=43.9	P=43.5,R=36.9	P=32.5, R=31.1	P=76.6, R=51.9	P=49.0,R=37.4	P=45.1, R=37.3
SM-wtred	P=91.8,R=88.6	P=87.5,R=86.9	P=84.2,R=82.7	P=82.9, R=79.8	P=91.1, R=80.6	P=89.3,R=81.4	P=87.1, R=81.3
PM	P=96.8,R=97.7	P=81.3,R=97.1	P=72.5,R=84.6	P=39.0,R=58.6	P=91.0,R=91.8	P=61.9,R=53.0	P=24.0,R=29.3
PM-noCID	P=64.0,R=78.2	P=58.7,R=73.5	P=45.8,R=59.1	P=24.0,R=40.0	P=64.0,R=69.8	P=27.6,R=41.5	P=10.0,R=24.0

Table 1: CFG Edge Mining with various levels of interleaving (n: #cfgs, t: #threads per cfg, s: cfg size)

The overall template mining results show that OASIS's use of multi-modal classification enables it to have better accuracy over other best known alternatives. In our evaluation of multi-modal on the synthetic dataset, we assumed that the ground truth cfg was known. However since multi-modal algorithm depends on the accuracy of the mined cfg in real datasets, the error in the mined cfg can affect the accuracy of mined templates in some cases. We acknowledge that accurately classifying log lines to ground truth templates in the absence of any application-specific knowledge of the usage of parameters, is a hard problem, and call for more further research in this direction.

4.5 Mining CFG Edges

We now evaluate cfg edge mining performance for the different competitive approaches mentioned in Section 4.2, from the perspective of how efficiently they can mine cfg edges from interleaved logs.

We first simulate a distributed application having 10 cfgs executing in parallel, where each cfg has 10 threads executing within it. Keeping the mean cfg size constant at 300 nodes, Figure 10(a) captures the performance of all the competitive approaches in this (10cfg-10thread) setting. Note that the accuracy of PM approaches suffer because they either expect caseIDs to be explicitly present (i.e. PM) or try to implicitly mine them using generative models (i.e. PM-noCID). Classical sequence mining SM-vanilla has high recall but it mines a large number of spurious edges compromising precision. Transitive reduction on the mined edges using SM-tred improves precision to some extent but also removes valid detour paths, thereby lowering recall. But SM-wtred that intelligently decides which edges to remove has a decent precision and recall performance. OASIS significantly out-performs all approaches with a precision $> 90\%$ and recall $> 82\%$. Also note that our branching factor threshold for edges is 10%, which implies that the recall applies to all edges above that. We observed that even setting a branching threshold of 25% results in above 95% recall for OASIS.

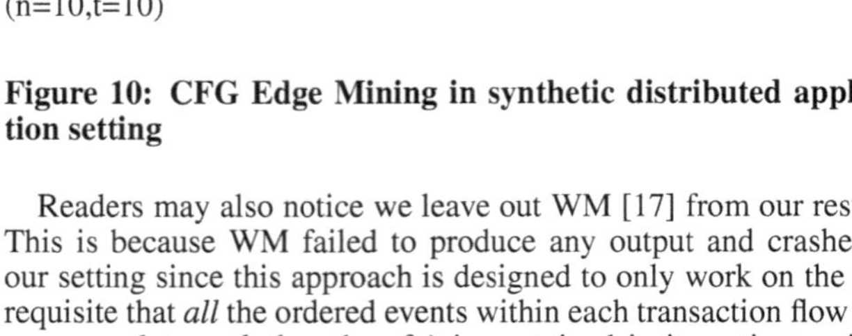

(a) Synthetic Distributed App (n=10,t=10) (b) OASIS (varying cfg size)

Figure 10: CFG Edge Mining in synthetic distributed application setting

Readers may also notice we leave out WM [17] from our results. This is because WM failed to produce any output and crashed in our setting since this approach is designed to only work on the pre-requisite that *all* the ordered events within each transaction flow (i.e. one *complete path* thru the cfg) is contained in its entirety within each trace. In contrast to classical process mining, their work is designed to cope with multiple parallel transactions within each trace, but they require multiple such traces as input to their algorithm. In our setting where we have a single log, our only option of chunking the logstream using our time-windowing approach violates their strict complete-path pre-requisite. We confirmed this limitation of their technique by creating another synthetic dataset that respects complete-path boundaries, and as expected, we observed this approach to run successfully and also give good results.

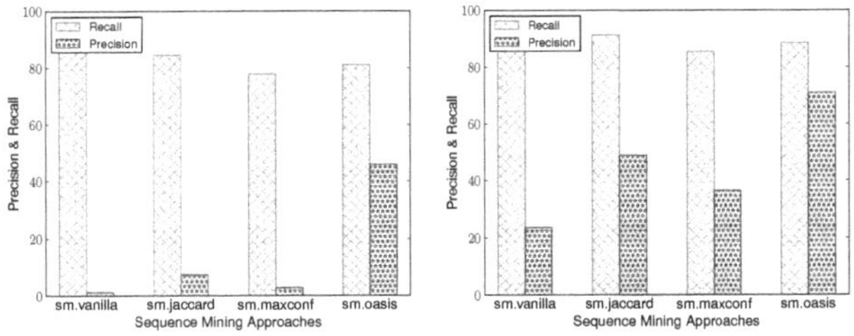

(a) SM: distMW (b) SM: linux

Figure 11: CFG Edge Mining on Real Datasets

Next we delve deeper into trends as a function of amount of intra- and inter- parallelism. Table1 shows the results for (n,t,s) configurations where n: #cfgs, t: #threads per cfg, and s: cfg size. We vary t (intra-level parallelism) and n (inter-level parallelism) at s=300. For a single threaded execution, most approaches do well, with the noted exception being SM-vanilla where precision suffers because of the large number of false edges mined. As t increases, the precision of other algorithms drop considerably, whereas the precision of OASIS remains very high (98.6%). Similar observation is made when n increases viz. the precision of other algorithms drop considerably, whereas OASIS has 100% precision. Overall, amongst the alternative approaches, we observe that SM-wtred is the second best after OASIS in both the intra- and inter- parallelism setting.

We now experiment with differently sized cfgs having 100, 300 and 500 nodes, each of which execute 10 parallel threads. Figure 10(b) shows that interestingly the precision/recall numbers improve with larger cfgs. This is because when the cfg has fewer nodes with a large number of parallel threads executing it, it is harder to distinguish the true neighbor of a log message from noise. For this reason the OASIS precision for 60 nodes drops to 65.8%. But with larger cfgs, OASIS is able to successfully weave out the noise and construct cfgs with very high accuracy.

Having established OASIS's capabilities on simulated logs, we now move to real data. Figure 11(a) and Figure 11(b) show results on distMW and linux respectively. Here we discarded PM because of their very bad performance in synthetic datasets. Overall, we observe that OASIS has the best performance and SM-wtred is second best, as per our observation in synthetic datasets.

The overall cfg edge mining results show that OASIS significantly outperforms best known alternatives. The only threat to validity we acknowledge is when OASIS is unable to disambiguate confusion due to high intra-level parallelism in small sized cfgs.

4.6 Anomalies

In Figure 12 we report the precision and recall on Single-threaded (n=1,t=1,s=300), Intra (n=1,t=10,s=300), Inter (n=10,t=1,s=300) and Realistic (n=10,t=10,s=300) configurations. In these experiments, the anomalies were injected at a small fraction (approx 10%) of random nodes in the cfg.

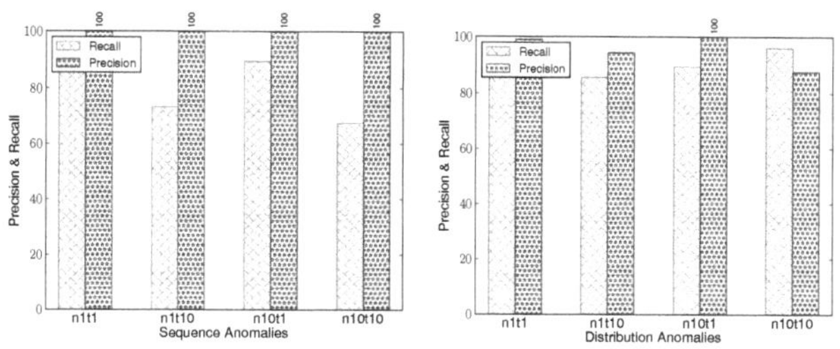

(a) Sequence Anomaly (b) Distribution Anomaly

Figure 12: Anomaly Results

For sequence anomalies (Figure 12(a)), we observe that precision is very high in all settings. In the case of single threaded and inter setting, the recall is approx 90%. The misses happen when the anomalies are generated at parent nodes of popular merge points. This is because, inspite of the injected sequence anomaly at the parent node, a popular merge point is observed to occur via the path of another parent. At this point, the anomaly detection algorithm is unable to differentiate the multiple paths to the merge point and will not raise the anomaly. This occurrence is magnified in the t=10 settings and the lower recall can be explained by multiple threads through the cfg being processed in parallel.

For distribution anomalies (Figure 12(b)), the precision and recall scores are overall quite satisfactory. We observe that the cause of the occasional misses and false alerts are due to the fact that we have not captured the entire spectrum of inherent fluctuations in the workload due to larger time-windows over which the branching probability distributions are being measured. One way to improve performance is to use smaller time-windows. Larger volumes of training data would also improve performance since it would capture all potential benign fluctuations.

4.7 Scalability

Finally we comment on the performance of each of the five stages (see Section 2.3) of our cfg mining technique in terms of their processing time. The pipeline comprises of the Spark [24] implementations of the four stages discussed in Section 2.3 viz. ApproxTemplateMiner, TemplateTextClustering, NNSGroupComputation, CFGEdgeMiner. For the reasons described in Section 2.3, the MultimodalRefinement phase remains a centralized implementation. The pipeline is executed on a 10 VM (Spark + Hadoop) cluster, with 1 dedicated master and 9 workers. Each Spark worker utilizes 1 core and has 4GB memory available to it.

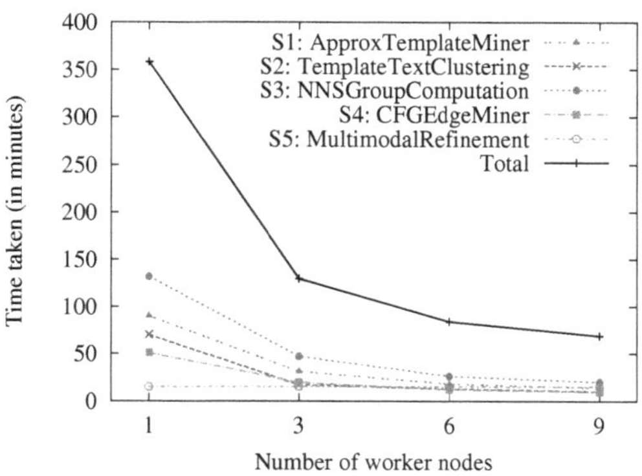

Figure 13: Scalability on (Spark + Hadoop) Setup

Figure 13 shows how the time taken by each stage reduces as the number of Spark workers increase. We use 25 GB subset of *distMW* dataset described in Section 4.1 comprising approx 55 million log lines for this experiment. We get more than 5x speedup when going from single to 9 workers. The total throughput of the entire pipeline is 522 GB/day using our 10 low-end VM setup. Further, we also experimented with the entire 100 GB dataset comprising more than 200 million log lines and got similar throughput (here 508 GB/day).

4.8 Case Study: OpenStack

To evaluate the overall effectiveness of our end-to-end system, we did a case-study with OpenStack [21] VM provisioning system. We drove the input workload by manually creating, suspending, resuming, and terminating multiple VMs randomly via Openstack's Web portal. These meta-level activities were randomly initiated over a period of one week with a total of approximately 50 such activities.

We collected individual logs from all the different microservices of Openstack spanning across nova, glance, keystone, cinder, swift, neutron, and horizon services. We did a timestamp-based merging of these individual logs in order to be able to detect flows across microservices. We used this one-week of logs as training data to mine the healthy-state cfg. We got a cfg with a total of 264 nodes (i.e. templates) and 616 edges.

From this mined cfg, we were specifically interested in the subgraph that corresponded to the popular *create-VM* event since this event requires coordination between most of the microservices. In order to mine the templates that were associated with the create-VM event, we manually created a time-series of this event using the recorded times when we issued this event, and then ran LSH's Minhash [5] with a very high time-series similarity threshold to detect other templates that were tightly correlated with the create-VM event time-series.

A summarized view (depicting module name and important keywords of the main templates only) of the subset of the CFG comprising 44 templates corresponding to create-VM event is shown in Figure 14. The templates belong to different modules of different microservices that participate in the create-VM event, and the cfg structure depicts interactions between them. The actual template pattern for node 8 is shown as example, and it reflects the starting of the nova compute manager instance.

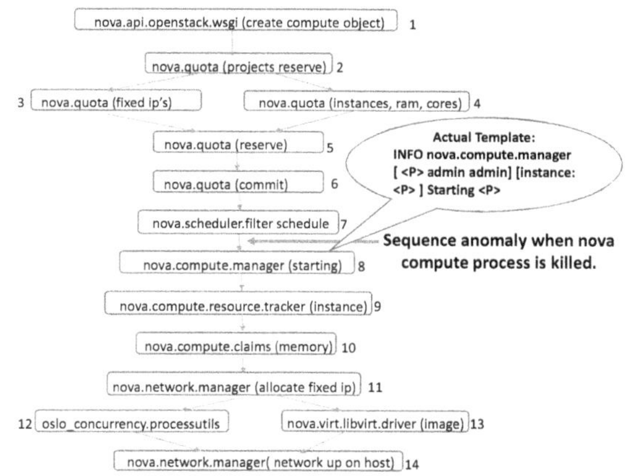

Figure 14: Summarized view of Openstack CFG subgraph related to create-VM event

To verify that our anomaly detection scheme does not throw false alarms when run on another healthy run of the system that is different from the training data, we fired different types of VM events beyond the training period. On running our anomaly detection scheme on these logs, we observed that our system raised only one false-positive sequence anomaly.

We additionally wanted to verify if we can detect anomalies when we manually inject different types of faults in the Openstack cluster. To verify this, we manually disrupted the nova-compute microservice by killing the nova-compute process. Subsequently, we fired a create-VM request. Not surprisingly, the Openstack portal denoted the failure of the create-VM event but was unable to tell us the cause for it. To get insights on the potential cause, we ran our anomaly detector, which reported a sequence anomaly at node-7, since the entire subgraph in Figure 14 from node-8 to node-14 was found missing.

5. RELATED WORK

We organize the related work into the following two main categories –

5.1 Mining of Templates

Contrary to our approach of mining templates from logs using a multi-modal signal of text and temporal-vicinity, all prior approaches use only the textual content of log lines in order to mine templates.

The first subcategory of such works [25, 27] mine templates by leveraging frequent item-set mining approaches wherein the premise is that by mining sets of co-occuring words across a large fraction of logrecords, one can filter out the invariant words in the print statements from the time-varying parameters. Frequent-itemset mining approaches for template mining however suffer from either bad recall or bad precision depending on the support threshold.

The next subcategory of such works [9, 23, 26, 28] employ some mechanism of generating approximate templates using frequency histogram of keywords mined in the first phase, and then further cluster similar approximate templates using some form of text-based similarity metric.

Last but the least, the work of Makanju et al. [19] employs an iterative partitioning technique that recursively partitions the set of log lines, first on number of words in a line, followed by the words in different positions, followed by another partitioning based on association of words in the log lines. But this approach works on impractical assumption that parameters comprise single words only.

5.2 Mining of CFG Edges

Contrary to our two-phase CFG edge mining approach, we describe prior approaches of mining template sequences on interleaved logs and their limitations.

Firstly, classical process mining [6, 11, 18] approaches are not directly applicable to our problem setting since they operate on the prerequisite of clearly demarcated transactions and require an input dataset comprising a set of such transactions.

A second class of approaches [3, 18] exploit temporal dependencies between events to mine control flows under high amount of interleaved traces. Assuming that enough data is available for mining statistically significant dependencies, these approaches use some form of association rule mining [29] to mine correlated events and can then do transitive edge removal. However transitive edge removal will result in removal of genuine detour paths in cfg.

A third class of approaches [17, 30] mine template sequences via stitching together log message templates that share the same parameter. But from our experimentation with real-world log datasets, we observed that parameters unless explicitly embedded (as in [13]), inherently do not flow deep enough. Also, they typically metamorphose, resulting in detection of very short sequences.

Finally, worth mentioning here is that instead of mining sequences, one may mine only the frequency, periodicity, and mutual distribution of different message templates, as proposed in Melody [15]. These models, due to the lack of the underlying cfg structure, are unable to pinpoint the root-cause of the change in the expected distribution of different event types, and end up throwing alerts for every node in the affected subtree of the cfg.

6. CONCLUSION

We have presented an approach of detecting anomalous run-time behaviour in distributed systems from execution logs. We mine a control-flow-graph (cfg) that captures healthy execution flows that span within and across different components of a distributed system, and raise anomaly alerts on observing deviations from this learnt cfg model. We outlined why mining such a cfg from interleaved logs of a distributed application without making any application specific assumptions, is a hard problem. We proposed novel and scalable algorithms to accurately mine the cfg, and based on an extensive evaluation against alternative design choices, depict the superiority of our proposed algorithms.

7. ACKNOWLEDGMENT

We thank our colleagues – Sriram Raghavan, Anindya Neogi, Narendran Sachindran, Pooja Aggarwal and Rahul Chandrakar for valuable discussions at different phases of this project. We thank authors of prior works we compared against, for making their binaries available for experimentation. We also thank the anonymous reviewers for their valuable feedback.

8. REFERENCES

[1] B. Abrahao, F. ChieriChetti, R. Kleinberg, and A. Panconesi. Trace complexity of network inference. In *KDD*, 2013.

[2] Appdynamics. www.appdynamics.com.

[3] I. Beschastnikh, Y. Brun, M. D. Ernst, A. Krishnamurthy, and T. E. Anderson. Mining temporal invariants from partially ordered logs. In *SLAML*, 2011.

[4] D. Bosnacki, W. Lightenberg, M. Odenbrett, A. Wijs, and P. Hilbers. Parallel algorithms for transitive reduction of weighted graphs. In *Math Maced*, 2010.

[5] E. Cohen, M. Datar, S. Fujiwara, A. Gionis, P. Indyk, R. Motwani, J. D. Ullman, and C. Yang. Finding interesting associations without support pruning. In *TKDE*, 2001.

[6] W. V. der Aalst, T. Weijters, and L. Maruster. Workflow mining: Discovering process models from event logs. In *TKDE*, 2004.

[7] Elasticsearch: Search and analyze data in real time. https://www.elastic.co/products/elasticsearch.

[8] D. R. Ferreira and D. Gillblad. Discovering process models from unlabelled event logs. In *BPM*, 2009.

[9] Q. Fu, J.-G. Lou, Y. Wang, and J. Li. Execution anomaly detection in distributed systems through unstructured log analysis. In *ICDM*, 2009.

[10] M. Gomez-Rodriguez, J. Leskovec, and A. Krause. Inferring networks of diffusion and influence. In *KDD*, 2010.

[11] C. W. Gunther and W. M. van der Aalst. Fuzzy mining - adaptive process simplification based on multi-perspective metrics. In *BPM*, 2007.

[12] P. Indyk and R. Motwani. Approximate nearest neighbor - towards removing the curse of dimensionality. In *STOC*, 1998.

[13] X. Ju, L. Soares, K. G. Shin, K. D. Ryu, and D. D. Silva. On fault resilience of openstack. In *SOCC*, 2013.

[14] Kafka: A high-throughput distributed messaging system. http://kafka.apache.org.

[15] T. Li, F. Liang, S. Ma, and W. Peng. An integrated framework on mining log files for computing system management. In *KDD*, 2005.

[16] Logstash: Collect, enrich and transform data. https://www.elastic.co/products/logstash.

[17] J.-G. Lou, Q. Fu, Y. Wang, and J. Li. Mining dependency in distributed systems through unstructured logs analysis. In *SIGOPS Operation Systems Review*, 2010.

[18] J.-G. Lou, Q. Fu, S. Yang, J. Li, and B. Wu. Mining program workflow from interleaved traces. In *KDD*, 2010.

[19] A. Makanju, A. Z. Heywood, and E. E. Milios. Clustering event logs using iterative partitioning. In *KDD*, 2009.

[20] H. Mannila, H. Toivonen, and A. I. Verkamo. Discovery of frequent episodes in event sequences. In *DMKD*, 1997.

[21] Openstack: Open-source software for creating public and private clouds. www.openstack.org.

[22] J. Pei, J. Han, B. Mortazavi, H. Pinto, Q. Chen, U. Dayal, and M.-C. Hsu. Mining sequential patterns efficiently by prefix-projected pattern growth. In *ICDE*, 2001.

[23] T. Reidimeister, M. Jiang, and P. A. Ward. Mining unstructured log files for recurrent fault diagnosis. In *IM*, 2011.

[24] Spark: Lightning-fast cluster computing. http://spark.apache.org.

[25] J. Stearley. Towards informatic analysis of syslogs. In *Cluster*, 2004.

[26] R. Vaarandi. A data clustering algorithm for mining patterns from event logs. In *IPOM*, 2003.

[27] R. Vaarandi. A breadth first algorithm for mining frequent patterns from event logs. In *Intell. Comm.*, 2004.

[28] R. Vaarandi and M. Pihelgas. Logcluster - a data clustering and pattern mining algorithm for event logs. In *CNSM*, 2015.

[29] T. Wu, Y. Chen, and J. Han. Association mining in large datasets: A re-examination of its measures. In *PKDD*, 2009.

[30] W. Xu, L. Huang, A. Fox, D. Patterson, and M. Jordan. Online system problem detection by mining patterns of console logs. In *ICDM*, 2009.

[31] W. Xu, L. Huang, A. Fox, D. Patterson, and M. Jordan. Detecting large scale system problems by mining console logs. In *ICML*, 2010.

Engagement Capacity and Engaging Team Formation for Reach Maximization of Online Social Media Platforms

Alexander Nikolaev*
University at Buffalo
312 Bell Hall
Buffalo, New York 14260
anikolae@buffalo.edu

Shounak Gore
University at Buffalo
113 Davis Hall
Buffalo, New York 14260
shounakg@buffalo.edu

Venu Govindaraju
University at Buffalo
113 Davis Hall
Buffalo, New York 14260
venu@cubs.buffalo.edu

ABSTRACT

The challenges of assessing the "health" of online social media platforms and strategically growing them are recognized by many practitioners and researchers. For those platforms that primarily rely on user-generated content, the *reach* – the degree of participation referring to the percentage and involvement of users – is a key indicator of success. This paper lays a theoretical foundation for measuring *engagement* as a driver of reach that achieves growth via positive externality effects. The paper takes a game theoretic approach to quantifying engagement, viewing a platform's social capital as a cooperatively created value and finding a fair distribution of this value among the contributors. It introduces *engagement capacity*, a measure of the ability of users and user groups to engage peers, and formulates the Engaging Team Formation Problem (EngTFP) to identify the sets of users that "make a platform go". We show how engagement capacity can be useful in characterizing forum user behavior and in the *reach maximization* efforts. We also stress how engagement analysis differs from *influence* measurement. Computational investigations with Twitter and Health Forum data reveal the properties of engagement capacity and the utility of EngTFP.

Keywords

social networks, engagement, reach, team formation problem, influence maximization

1. INTRODUCTION

Measuring social influence online is becoming a sophisticated and granular task. Several new-age companies, e.g., Klout and PeerIndex, are in the business of evaluating the influential power of their clients' online userbases. Social media influence, defined as an individual's ability to affect the thinking or actions of peers, is the driver of success of many of today's online services, apps, ideas, etc.; the identification of influential persons, with the objective of using them to alter political preferences in a community or advertise products to increase sales, is an active research direction.

However, influence measurement is not particularly useful to an online platform manager who does not seek to exploit its userbase, but instead, strives just to maintain/encourage user activity. The purpose of most online activities including sharing pictures or posts, contributing comments or "likes" in response to peers' posts, or exchanging opinions in social forum threads is to share experiences and maintain (friendly) communication between fellow users of the network. This form of communication keeps the users together, and ultimately, defines the influential power of the platform that they use. Take as an example the downfall of MySpace and Orkut with the success of Facebook. As more and more users migrated from Orkut to Facebook, the utilization of Orkut declined, leading to its eventual abandonment. The ability to detect such turns and strategically grow online platforms is of interest to many practitioners, putting the question of assessing the platform's "health" up on the research agenda.

The recently emerging applications of social media analysis shift the focus of investigation from huge populations to well-defined, smaller subpopulations, e.g., interest-based groups, followship bases and health forums, with their own culture and purpose. Such subpopulations are of special interest to the research community, since they may develop their own mechanisms of peer pressure delivery and discourse features, and often, have significant societal value. For example, the forum analyses can aid us in drug safety signal detection efforts (similar to "early warning systems" adopted for disaster prevention [5]), disease symptom profiling, and understanding the concerns and behavior of various patient groups that communicate online [42]. Naturally, for the online health forums that prove to be effective in helping their users, there is a need for the methods and tools to attract more users.

Taking a page from RE-AIM, a widely used systematic program evaluation framework [12], we use the term "reach" to refer to an online platform's ability to attract new users, and define "engagement" as any existing user's degree of involvement in the platform's activities. The interplay between engagement and reach can be understood by leveraging on the research of the structure, stagnation, and growth of consumer markets. Studies of cascade emergence in demand-side economics have found that the customers' willingness to choose (adopt) a product grows with the number of people that have already adopted it; this increase in value, otherwise known as positive network externality, occurs with each sale of a product unit [14]. On an online platform, positive

*Corresponding author.

KDD '16, August 13-17, 2016, San Francisco, CA, USA

DOI: http://dx.doi.org/10.1145/2939672.2939681

network externalities occur in two instances: (1) when a new user joins the network and authors a new post, and (2) when an existing user contributes new user-generated content [37]. Thus, the internal growth of a platform (achieved through added user-generated content) leads to its external growth (the increase in the number of newly registered users): i.e., higher engagement leads to higher reach.

We posit that engagement occurs when a user contributes content in response to someone else's contribution(s). A network of directed relationships reflecting "which post attracts which" captures the sequence and structure of engagement (see Figure 1). An online forum grows through its users: every post (even "weather talk") fosters user "bonding" and creates a positive externality effect, even more so when it is read and responded to. The propagator – the creator of seed content – is said to engage the responder, while the responder is said to engage into the forum's activity.

Addressing the need for theory-supported quantification of engagement, we introduce the term "engagement capacity", interpreted as a user's ability to engage peers and measured as their share in the platform / forum engagement power. We view the value generated by an online social network community as a direct product of communication between its members, attributed to the submitted contributions' content and structure (order), and only in part to the volume (note that irrelevant interactions are promptly removed from pro-health sites, a majority of which are moderated).

In order to assess any individual user's engagement capacity, we employ cooperative game theory. Cooperative game theory is a branch of science that calculates "fair-share" equilibria in settings with agents that form coalitions to achieve a common goal. Its first fundamental advance is due to Shapley [32], who introduced a method for calculating fair contributed values for "players" forming unstructured coalitions, where any contributor can interact or team up with any other contributor with the objective of generating synergistic value. This is a perfect setup for the engagement ability measurement: the un-normalized and normalized (e.g., by the number of contributions or the amount of time spent online) engagement capacity can allow for fair comparison between users as they contribute to the growth of a platform.

It is important to see the potential of studying "engagement" in social networks as opposed to studying "influence" enabled by them. The latter type of analysis requires one to define how the connected agents affect each other's decisions with respect to some query; the former is query-independent. Several recent position papers stress the potential utility of engagement-focused research, citing a series of under-explored questions in this area. The beginnings of this emerging literature, along with other relevant works, are reviewed in Section 2, motivating the investigations in the present paper. Section 3 discusses the details of using cooperative game theory for engagement quantification. Section 4 introduces the concept of targeted engagement capacity and the Engaging Team Formation Problem (EngTFP). Section 5 discusses the insights shed by the engagement capacity calculations with real-world data. Section 6 gives the concluding remarks and discusses future research directions.

2. BACKGROUND AND RELATED WORK

The desire to understand the patterns in the spread of ideas, technologies, and viral product adoption in social networks motivates the modern studies of social influence mechanisms. These studies often use the term "word-of-mouth" [40] and offer diffusion-based models that explain the defining elements of innovation adoption [8], disease spread [22], and other network-driven phenomena in sociology [36] and politics [10]. The developed metrics for quantifying the ability of actors to influence their peers' decision-making, based on the structural properties of the network, in which they are embedded, are known as centrality metrics [7, 28, 23].

The work on "influence maximization" that emerged over the past decade focuses on the problem of selecting a group of the initiators (commonly termed "seeds" or "opinions leaders") to generate the largest influence cascade - by the number of adopters of a product or idea [15]. The ability to identify influential subsets of users of an online resource is particularly valuable for viral marketing [29], personalized recommendation delivery services [33], as well as microblogging [6] and health forum analyses [35].

This paper attacks a new question: "What subset of users is the most important for keeping the whole user base together?" – keeping current users engaged and keeping the platform appealing to potential new users [43].

The more recently published position papers describe the patterns of user activity that can help explain "engagement". These papers emphasize the need for quantifying engagement, and call for systematic approaches to tracking and enhancing it in calculated ways.

Lim et al. distinguish several forms of engagement in analyzing TV-viewership data [19]. They define functional engagement as real-time participation of online media platform users that results in content development; communal engagement is then presented as a consequence of functional engagement: essentially, it is what we refer to as "reach". Li et al. describe engagement as "informedness", i.e., the "ability to inform", distinguishing cognitive, relational and behavioral aspects of engagement [18]. Vydiswaran et al. discuss the reasons why users create new groups and summarize the insights for designers and researchers who desire to build better, larger communities [38]. Online social support provision is a topic of exploration of the recent papers about online health forums [39]; indeed, such forums are known to successfully deal with behavioral aspects of health: they help "e-patients" maintain diets, cope with side effects of medications, quit smoking and remain sober [43].

Several prescriptive research ideas stem from engagement analyses. Stearns et al. call for "smart thread" recommender systems to boost the reach of online health forums [34]. The logic of Bernabe-Moreno et al. [5] suggests that the engagement measurement can inform "early warning" systems signaling changes in the health of an online platform. Another practically useful idea lies in maintaining and/or growing the userbase of a platform by identifying and nurturing the users that are most responsible for its (high) engagement.

The questions of measuring the motivation of a user to contribute to a forum thread first came up in the studies of Question-and-Answer forums [3]. The simple measures, e.g., the number of upvotes on websites like StackOverflow, or the number of "likes" on Facebook and Twitter, reflect forum utilization and signal user interest. Natural language processing (NLP) works with the text of a post to understand its success in attracting responses [4, 39]. In an effort pursuing a similar objective to ours, Lehmann et al. use Twitter data to study "transient crowd-forming" and find most *in-*

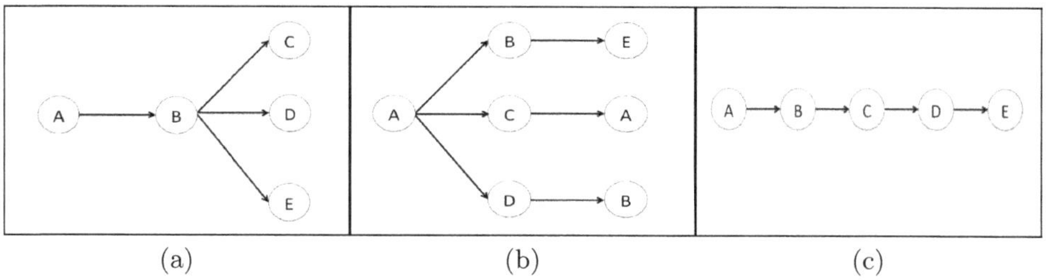

Figure 1: Examples of communication threads of different structure.

fluential/engaging curators of news propagation based solely on text analysis: they find common topics of interest which bind the transient crowd together [16, 17]. The NLP methods, however, do not yet account for the dynamics of users creating posts and interacting with each other; they require much human supervision, and tend to be slow in processing big data. Overall, the above measures and methods serve the purposes different from quantifying how much merit a user deserves for engaging peers in conversation.

The studies of engagement, accounting for the dynamics of interaction, have emerged recently. The terms "engagingness" and "responsiveneness" are used in modeling email message chains [26, 25]. In a study of Twitter, the count of re-tweets is taken as a measure of engagingness [1]. These works, however, are based on direct responses from one user to another, with indirect communication (engaging one user through another) not accounted for. Zhao et al. explore how the structure of online interactions affects the sentiment of the messages posted by a given user [44], considering the situations where the same user appears at least twice in the same thread, e.g., asks a question and then replies to the respondent(s). The work of Yang and Tang on understanding the mechanisms of online influence [43] goes further in exploring the reasons why a user may succeed in attracting responses to their posts. They recognize – as do we – that the contributions of forum thread posts to making the thread engaging must depend on the posts' positions within the thread, with the immediate predecessor deserving more credit for attracting a new (follow-up) post in the thread.

This paper introduces new metrics to quantify engagement by fully exploiting the dynamics of user interactions in online communication-based platforms. The following section describes our methodological approach in detail.

3. MEASURING THE ENGAGEMENT CAPACITY OF A USER

The seminal work on calculating fair shares in cooperatively created value for agents forming unstructured coalitions is due to Shapley [32]. His work was extended by Myerson [21], and later, by other researchers, to problems with constraints on cooperation structure and frequency [27, 24, 41, 9].

The most relevant to our work are the extensions that recognize that in certain situations, the value generated by a coalition may depend on the order in which players interact [24, 30]. We extend and adapt this line of work to render it useful in thread-based communication context, by allowing for multiple interactions between users (as players) in forum threads, accounting for contribution (forum post) order.

Consider a setting where forum users cooperatively generate engagement value: when they contribute posts that attract more posts, they promote the forum growth and increase its reach achieved through positive externality effects. Each post contributed in response to other post(s) is assumed to generate one unit of engagement value for the forum. We define the engagement capacity of a user as their share in the forum's total engagement value, based on all the threads the user has contributed to. The engagement capacity of a user can be positive if and only if the user has been active in at least one thread; the passive readers (lurkers) do not add engagement value to the forum. Moreover, the users who contribute, but are never responded to, have zero engagement capacity; indeed, if a forum consisted of only such members, it would generate no communication at all.

Based on a single thread, the engagement capacity of a user depends on the position(s) of the user's contribution(s) in the thread's flow. As such, a thread starter is (in part) responsible for engaging all the users that have replied to the thread: a user whose post generates further posts gets partial engagement value credit from all such contributions. On the other hand, the posts immediately preceding a newly contributed post get more credit for engaging it than the posts appearing earlier in the thread: otherwise, the new contribution would be expected to have occured earlier or be directly responding to those older posts.

Let us look closely at the examples in Figure 1: assume that three forum threads have been created by the same five users. User A originates each thread. User B replies to A's original messages in all the three threads. In the first thread (Figure 1a), users C, D and E reply to B, instead of directly replying to A. In the second thread (Figure 1b), users C and D also reply to A's question directly. The third thread (Figure 1c) consists of a single "line" thread branch. Based on the directed networks in Figure 1, the averages of some standard centrality metrics are reported in Figure 2 (the detailed explanation of how the engagement capacity metric is computed in the figure and the discussion of how the metrics relate to each other will be given in the subsequent sections). A methodological approach to computing engagement capacity is presented next, followed by a discussion of some computational aspects of the engagement analysis.

3.1 Cooperative Games on k–Coalitions

Nowak and Radzik [24] and Sánchez et al. [30] explain that for a transferable utility (cooperative) game in a directed graph, the worth of a coalition can depend not only on the individual properties of coalition members but also on the order in which they interact in a coalition. Nowak and Radzik [24] define the value Ψ^{NR} that generalizes the Shapley value for transferable utility games. For a game with player set N and value function v, where player subsets $S \subset N$ form ordered coalitions $T \equiv (i_1, ..., i_{|T|})$ from the set of all possible ordered coalitions $\pi(S)$, this value for player i amounts to

$$\Psi_i^{NR}(N, v) = \sum_{S \subset N \setminus \{i\}} \sum_{T \in \pi(S)} \frac{(|N| - |T| - 1)!}{|N|!}(v(T \cup i) - v(T)),$$

which, with $\Omega(N)$ as the set of all possible ordered subsets of N, $H(T)$ as the set of players in coalition T, and $i(T)$ as the position of player i in coalition T, can be concisely re-written as

$$\Psi_i^{NR}(N, v) = \sum_{T \in \Omega(N), i \in H(T), i(T) = |T|} \frac{\Delta_v^*(T)}{|T|!},$$

where $\Delta_v^*(T)_{T \in \Omega(N), T \neq \emptyset}$ are termed the generalized coefficients of v, also known as the coordinates of v in the generalized unanimity basis [13]. Sanchez and Bergantinos [30] define another Shapley value extension, distinguishing coalitions by the players' positions *within* them,

$$\Psi_i^{SB}(N, v) = \sum_{T \in \Omega(N), i \in H(T)} \frac{\Delta_v^*(T)}{|T| \, (|T|!)}.$$

More recently, del Pozo et al. [9] defined a generalization of Ψ^{NR} and Ψ^{SB} as a parametric family of functions $\{\Psi^{\alpha}\}_{\alpha \in [0,1]}$, where the value generated by an ordered coalition is shared proportionally to the positions of its members,

$$\Psi_i^{\alpha}(N, v) = \sum_{T \in \Omega(N), i \in H(T)} \Delta_v^*(T) \frac{\alpha^{|T| - i(T)}}{|T|! \sum_{j=0}^{|T|-1} \alpha^j}.$$

We extend and adapt the line of work on ordered transferable utility games [24, 30, 9] to render it useful in the thread-based communication context, where interactions take place between online platform users (as players) as they contribute posts to forum threads in response to each other, in sequence, and possibly, multiple times to the same thread. To this end, define k-coalition as a connected ordered sequence of player *appearances*. As with the coalitions used to define $\{\Psi^{\alpha}\}_{\alpha \in [0,1]}$, a k-coalition is distinguished not only by its membership, but also, by its ordering. Similarly to $i(T)$, we let $i(T, k)$, $k = 1, 2, ..., K$, denote the position of the k-th appearance of player $i \in H(T)$ in k-coalition $T \in \Omega^K(N)$, with $\Omega^K(N)$ denoting the set of all k-coalitions in which any given player can appear at most K times. The value generated by a k-coalition is shared proportionally to the positions of the appearances of the coalition members,

$$\Psi_i^{K\text{-}\alpha}(N, v) = \sum_{T \in \Omega^K(N), i \in H(T), k = 1, .., K} \Delta_v^*(T) \frac{\alpha^{|T| - i(T,k)}}{|T|! \sum_{j=0}^{|T|-1} \alpha^j}. \quad (1)$$

The family of parametric functions $\{\Psi^{K\text{-}\alpha}\}_{K \in I^+, \alpha \in [0,1]}$ encompasses, as special cases, the conventional Shapley value as well as the functions Ψ^{NR}, Ψ^{SB}, and $\{\Psi^{\alpha}\}_{\alpha \in [0,1]}$.

The concept of engagement capacity is now introduced, in conjunction with the term *engaging subthread* in forum communication. Define subthread as an uninterrupted chain (sequence) of posts of a thread that begins with the first post of the thread; in a directed tree graph, representing a forum thread, every path that begins at the root is a subthread. A subthread is called *engaging* if it is succeeded by at least one post in its respective thread. The number of forum posts contributed in response to or following up on another post (or a sequence of posts) over the whole forum constitutes a total engagement value generated by the forum users; the share of each user in this value is called engagement capacity: it measures each user's ability to engage peers, computed retrospectively, i.e., based on their past activity records.

Given an online forum, let N denote the set of all the users in the forum's userbase. Define (N, v, P) as a game on the set of all the forum's subthreads P. A subthread-restricted game (N, v_U, p) can be interpreted as the game where users $U \subset N$ contribute posts to form $p \in P$; this setup is similar, but not exactly the same, to a game in a communication "situation" described in [9]. Given the forum's historical data, set K to be the largest number of posts contributed by the same user to any subthread; let the *value function* $\Delta_v^*(T)$ return a total number of posts immediately succeeding such *engaging* subthreads $p \in P$ that have the same membership, size and structure as k-coalition $T \in \Omega^K(N)$. The engagement capacity of forum user $i \in N$ is the value that (1) returns for this user as a solution of the game (N, v, P) and is hereafter denoted by η_i, or by $\eta_{i,F}$ to specify that the computation is based on a restricted set of forum threads F.

Note that the coefficient $\alpha \in [0, 1]$ in $\{\Psi^{K\text{-}\alpha}\}_{K \in I^+, \alpha \in [0,1]}$ captures the engagement share tradeoff between thread contributors, as they manage to attract each new post to "their" thread. As such, if a new post is submitted in response to multiple (preceding) consecutive posts, then its immediate predecessor gets more credit for attracting it, with the credit to the earlier predecessors discounted by the factors of α, α^2, α^3, etc., respectively. Note that this property of engagement capacity complies with an observation that the posts, newly attracted to a (long) forum thread, tend to respond to the latest prior contributions in this thread [43].

3.2 Calculating Engagement Capacity

Consider the example in Figure 1a, and denote the thread depicted on it by "(a)". Using (1), the engagement capacity of user A is found to be

$$\eta_{A,(a)} = 1 + 3 * \frac{\alpha}{\alpha + 1},$$

as user A gets the engagement value of 1 by contributing to engaging subthread A with $\Delta_v^*(\{A\}) = 1$, and gets $\frac{3\alpha}{\alpha+1}$ by contributing to engaging subthread AB with $\Delta_v^*(\{AB\}) = 3$; meanwhile, subthreads ABC, ABD and ABE are not engaging. The engagement capacity of user B is

$$\eta_{B,(a)} = 3 * \frac{1}{1 + \alpha}.$$

Note that users C, D and E have zero engagement capacity in this example; also, the total engagement value generated and shared is equal to four, i.e., to the number of posts contributed by all the users in response to their peers. Table 1 gives the engagement capacity values for each thread in Figure 1, with $\alpha = 1$, i.e., giving all the subthread propagators equal credit for engaging a responder. In these examples, the early contributors have higher engagement capacities than the late ones. However, in general, this is not necessarily the case; for example, with $\alpha = 0$, $\eta_{A,(a)} = 1$ and $\eta_{B,(a)} = 3$.

The engagement capacity values can be interpreted directly, or upon normalization. One sensible way is to normalize by the number of contributed posts to identify the

User	(a)	(b)	(c)
A	2.5	4.5	2.083
B	1.5	0.5	1.083
C	0	0.5	0.583
D	0	0.5	0.25
E	0	0	0

Table 1: Engagement capacity values for the threads in Figure 1.

users whose contribution content is engaging irrespective of the volume.

The case where a forum post is immediately followed (in the same thread) by another post of the same user is worth a separate discussion. The treatment of such occurrences is up to the researcher: e.g., one may choose to "merge" such posts and treat them as one. However, in a moderated forum, one may assume that every contribution is distinct, i.e., makes a new point; since every post creates positive externalities, rewarding the user (with a share in the total engagement value) for both posts makes sense. Another issue that becomes apparent in the considered example is that a user may gain a high engagement capacity by engaging themselves (as opposed to others): this issue will be addressed in Section 4, with the introduction of "targeted engagement capacity."

Engagement capacities of users can be, rather conveniently, dynamically computed and updated, as new content is added, without the need to redo the analysis for the whole history of the forum/platform every time it changes. Recall that each new user post submitted in response to another post, or sequence of posts, brings in one unit of engagement value to the communication thread and to the platform as a whole. A newly added post increases the engagement capacity values of all the users contributing to the subthread leading to the new post (but not including it). Consider a k-coalition $T' \in \Omega^K(N)$ with the same membership, size and structure as this subthread. The increase in the engagement capacity of user $i \in H(T')$, resulting from the addition of the new post, is given by

$$\Delta_i = \sum_{k=1,2,\ldots,K} \frac{\alpha^{|T'|-i(T',k)}}{\sum_{j=0}^{|T'|-1} \alpha^j}. \qquad (2)$$

Equation (2) specifies how every new contribution changes the engagement capacity values of the forum users. This equation can be used in real time to efficiently track the contributed engagement dynamics. Note that the expression in (2) can be evaluated in $O(n)$ time: its denominator requires finding the subthread succeeded by a new post, and its numerator requires the information about the positions of user appearances in this subthread.

4. TARGETED ENGAGEMENT CAPACITY AND ENGAGING TEAM FORMATION

Equation (2) of Section 3 specifies how to fairly distribute a unit engagement value, brought to the platform with any new post submitted into an existing thread, between the thread contributors. Naturally, some users may be succesfull in engaging certain peers and not so successful in engaging others. This realization highlights the value of solving a game of engaging one given user j: the peers of j would split the engagement value generated by the j's responses to their posts or post sequences. In this case, only those subthreads that are followed up on by the posts of j would be considered engaging.

More generally, one can address the question of evaluating the ability of a given set of users, $V \in N$, to engage another set of users, $W \in N$, in forum communication. To this end, we introduce the term *targeted engagement capacity*: denoted by $\eta_{V\to W}$, it is defined as the sum of the shares allocated to the members of V in the game of engaging the members of W. In the setting of the game on k-coalitions, described in Section 3.1, one has

$$\eta_{V\to W} = \sum_{i\in V, j\in W} \sum_{i\in H(T), k=1,..,K} \Delta_v^*(T) \frac{\alpha^{|T|-i(T,k)}}{|T|! \sum_{j=0}^{|T|-1} \alpha^j}, \qquad (3)$$

where $\Delta_v^*(T)$ returns a total number of posts by the members of W immediately succeeding such *engaging* subthreads $p \in P$ that have the same membership, size and structure as k-coalition $T \in \Omega^K(N)$. Note that generally, $\eta_i \neq \eta_{i\to N\setminus i}$: the difference between these quantities is $\eta_{i\to i}$ – it indicates how much user i tends to engage in back-and-forth conversations as opposed to occasionally contributing to multiple forum threads. Note also, that targeted engagement capacity can be updated dynamically, as well as the originally defined engagement capacity, by a trivial extension of (2).

Table 2 shows the targeted engagement capacity values, per equation (3), for the users contributing to the threads in Figure 1. The columns of Table 2 are for the the users whose engagement capacity is calculated and the rows are for the targeted users. The sum over each column gives a total engagement capacity of the respective user over all the three thread. Note that $\eta_{A\to A} > 0$: user A self-engaged in the second thread.

User	A	B	C	D	E
A	0.5	0.00	0.5	0.00	0.00
B	3.5	0.00	0.00	0.5	0.00
C	2.00	1.00	0.00	0.00	0.00
D	1.833	0.833	0.333	0.00	0.00
E	1.25	1.25	0.25	0.25	0.00

Table 2: Targeted engagement for the threads in Figure 1

The ability to measure how successful a particular user is in engaging other particular users allows us to attack the following question: "What group (team) of active users is most engaging?" This question is of special interest to any growing online platform, since such teams of users can be rewarded, encouraged, and assisted in further increasing peer engagement and retention. To help this cause, the Engaging Team Formation Problem (EngTFP) is introduced.

The EngTFP objective is to select a subset of users with a maximal targeted engagement capacity towards all the other users: $\max_U \eta_{U\to N\setminus U}$. This problem can be formulated with additional constraints, e.g., those specifying which historical engagement data to take into account and/or the maximum size of the subset to be selected (e.g., $|U| \leq b$).

To set up an instance of EngTFP, first, use (3) to compute all the pairwise targeted engagement capacity values, $\{\eta_{i\to j}\}_{i\in N, j\in N, i\neq j}$. Note that, in general, $\eta_{i\to j} \neq \eta_{j\to i}$ for $i \neq j$. Let X_i, $i \in N$, be binary decision variables such that for any $i \in N$, $X_i = 1$ if i is selected into U, and zero otherwise. Let Y_{ij}, $i \in N$, $j \in N$, $i \neq j$, be auxiliary binary variables that would be set to 1 if and only if $X_i = 1$ and

$X_j = 0$ (at the same time). Then, EngTFP is given,

$$\begin{aligned} \max \quad & \sum_{i \in N} \sum_{j \in N, j \neq i} \eta_{i \to j} Y_{ij} \\ \text{s.t.} \quad & Y_{ij} \le X_i, \quad \forall\, i, j, \\ & Y_{ij} \le 1 - X_j, \quad \forall\, i, j, \\ & X_i, Y_{ij} \in \{0, 1\}, \quad \forall\, i, j. \end{aligned}$$

A non-linear formulation of EngTFP does not use any auxiliary variables and maximizes $\sum_{i \in N, j \in N, j \neq i} \eta_{i \to j} \left(X_i^2 - X_i X_j\right)$; this formulation is quadratic but not convex, and hence, does not allow for a dominant convex decomposition [20], confirming that EngTFP is combinatorially challenging.

EngTFP is a special case of MAX2SAT problem, known to be NP-Hard; for a review of the algorithmic work on MAX2SAT, see [11]. The complexity of EngTFP is due to the fact that, once user i is selected into a team, the team members can no longer be rewarded for engaging i. Indeed, if a platform decides to pay some users for helping grow it, the users to be paid should be good at attracting other users but not each other.

Again, we underline the difference between the EngTFP and the influence maximization problem. Influence maximization strives to enhance a certain effect (e.g., change in political opinion, product adoption, etc.) in a pre-existing and known user network. Meanwhile, EngTFP solutions aim at helping a platform maintain or build its network or non-network userbase. The EngTFP advises a decision-maker on what users should be rewarded, virtually (e.g., via badges, titles, points) or physically (e.g., via gift cards, discount codes, cash), for igniting communication, which the users achieve through content generation, question asking, social support provision, information exchange, etc.

5. COMPUTATIONAL INVESTIGATIONS

This section reports the engagement capacity analyses conducted with the data from two active online communication platforms differing in purpose. We begin with an account of the data collection, and then, present the numerical findings.

5.1 Data Collection

We collected the forum contribution records from an online healthcare platform, one of the biggest active and freely accessible online sites for pro-health social networking. It has about 200 social support forums and about as many "ask an expert" forums. The website has close to 3 Million active and inactive threads and attracts about 8 Million visitors every month. The users in these health forums (HF) interact through discussion boards, contribute personal journal entries exploiting weight and mood tracker features, and post notes on their friends' home pages. The HF data most relevant to the present study are those of the users' interactions on moderated discussion forums.

A web crawler was used to collect the data of the contributed posts, and their sequences, in the "anxiety", "cholesterol control" and "weight-loss & dieting" forums. The anxiety forum has about 33500 threads dating back to the early 2000s. The cholesterol control forum has about 300 threads. The weight-loss & dieting forum has about 7000 threads. Each thread consists of at least one post, however, not all the threads have replies; the unanswered threads do not affect the engagement capacity computation. After cleaning up threads with no replies we end up with a database of about 48800 unique users for the HF data. Note that some of these users have been active on more than one forum.

A data tree is built for each analyzed thread. In each such tree, every user contribution is represented by a node; a directed link is drawn from node A to node B, if B replies to node A. This tree captures the relations between the users who interact in a particular thread discussion. The tree structure also tells us who initiates a particular discussion (e.g., by posting a question), who engages the maximum number of people by furthering a discussion with comments and who interacts frequently in a particular conversation. The engagement capacities computed and presented hereafter are based on both forums (all their threads) together.

Another dataset was created using Twitter, based on about 20,000 tweets, with their re-tweets, related to the 2014 FIFA World Cup. A tweet thread consists of a tweet and all of its re-tweets. A directed link is drawn from node A to node B, if user B re-tweets user A's tweet. Thus, we have a number of communication threads where every root is a particular original tweet and the other nodes are re-tweets. This tree structure, like the HF trees, allows us to identify an initiator, the most engaging user and the person who interacts most frequently in any particular conversation. A total of 31,467 unique Twitter users contributed to these threads.

5.2 Calculations for the Example in Figure 1

Using the dynamic approach to engagement capacity measurement with the collected data, we first assess how the different influence-related measures behave, as compared to the proposed scheme of measuring user engagement.

Figure 2 reports the values of the different metrics for the example in Figure 1, considering that these three threads constitute a whole forum. In Figure 2, the users are arranged over the horizontal axis in the descending order of their engagement capacity values. The other metrics were evaluated in Python [31]. The experiments were run on a Macbook Pro machine with an Intel-i5 2.3GHz processor.

As expected, the engagement capacity values depend on the number of users engaged, the length of the communication branches, and the frequency of communication. The deeper a branch goes, the more value each of the upstream users gains. User A, involved in both engaging a lot of users (Figure 1a) and seeding deeper communication branches (Figure 1c), enjoys the highest engagement capacity. User B also has a high engagement capacity value as it engages a fair number of users directly (Figure 1b) and also gets partial credit whenever the depth of the branch increases (Figure 1c). User E has zero engagement capacity due to failing to engage any peers – this user always stops the communication.

The results in Figure 2 suggest that the calculated engagement capacity values are in line with the intuition. Engagement capacity positively correlates with out-degree: indeed, high engagement capacity signals a high ability of a user to spread information, and thus, highly engaging users are expected to be connected to more peers. Engagement capacity also correlates with betweenness centrality, since the latter indicates how capable users are of transferring information between otherwise disconnected subgroups. The page rank and in-degree behave very differently than engagement capacity since they focus on describing the information flows into a user, not the other way around.

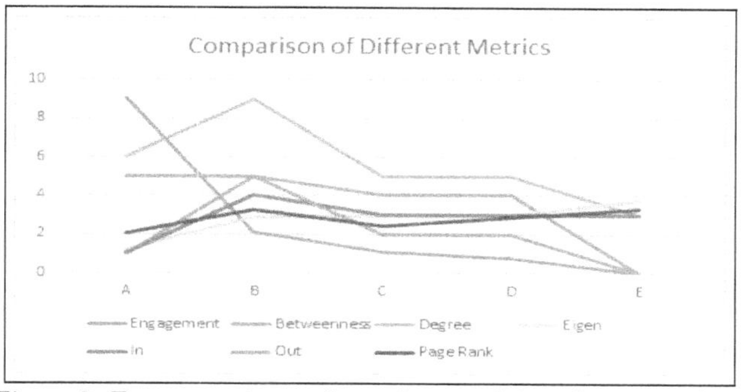

Figure 2: Engagement capacity and network-based metric values for the users of a forum with three threads as depicted in Figure 1 (best viewed in color).

	coeff	std err	t	P
betweenness	3.7676	0.166	22.695	<0.001
degree	3.1465	0.121	26.068	<0.001
eigen	4.2928	0.169	25.352	<0.001
page_rank	10.4100	0.395	26.405	<0.001

Table 3: Linear regression outputs for engagement capacity, with centrality metrics as predictors, based on HF data.

	coeff	std err	t	P
betweenness	0.6716	0.010	68.658	<0.001
degree	0.9212	0.013	71.803	<0.001
eigen	1.0924	0.016	68.685	<0.001
page_rank	1.5579	0.020	78.509	<0.001

Table 4: Linear regression outputs for engagement capacity, with centrality metrics as predictors, based on Twitter data.

5.3 Calculations for the HF and Twitter data

We now turn to the collected HF and Twitter data. In all the subsequent analyses, the (targeted) engagement capacities were computed with $\alpha = 0.99$.

Figure 3(a) shows that the distribution of engagement capacity is Gaussian in the HF and Twitter user bases. Such a good visual fit is surprising, and suggests that this metric may be capturing/revealing something about the personality of each user: indeed, personal characteristics/abilities/talents, e.g., IQ, are typically normally distributed in humans. The engagement capacity values of Twitter users are generally higher than those of the HF users because of the higher overall level of communication (i.e., retweets contributed vs. posts submitted). Figure 3(b) shows that the distribution of the number of contributions per user on each platform is likely a power law: this is common in social media analyses.

Figure 4 depicts the engagement capacity values, normalized by the number of contributions (posts), for the users in the anxiety forum (Figure 4(a)), cholesterol forum (Figure 4(b)), weight loss & dieting forum (Figure 4(c)), and Twitter data (Figure 4(d)). The anxiety forum has the largest number of contributions, however, the average engagement value per contribution in this forum is noticeably lower than in the other forums. The large number of contributions in this forum is attributed to the many discussions it hosts; however, the thread originators tend to leave the threads once they get their concerns resolved (some of them continue socializing but typically with small groups of peers). This is in line with the purpose and function of many social support forums, where users are more comfortable sharing their experiences/thoughts one-on-one, going back and forth in a conversation, so the threads get long. Consequently, the engagement values gained by these users, per contribution, are lower compared to other forums or Twitter, where a single message can engage a larger number of readers/followers. The cholesterol forum exhibits an opposite dynamics: here, the average engagement per contribution is very high, while the number of contributions per user is much smaller. This suggests that the users tend to post content which is found useful by multiple peers, attracting many responses from different sources. One reason for this behavior could be that cholesterol-related issues are much more generic (and hence, one good post can answer the concerns of many), compared to the anxiety-related issues where each case may be unique, i.e., patient-specific, and requires individual attention. The weight loss & dieting forum has a smaller variance for the distribution of engagement values per contribution.

In summary, the discussed figures verify that the user engagement capacity values do not entirely depend on the number of posts; moreover, the correlation between these two quantities is positive on Twitter but negative on HF, signaling that social support provision is difficult to maintain just by increasing the activity. Also, there is a larger variance in the engagement per contribution in the Twitter data, which can be attributed to the shorter and broader communication trees, compared to HF trees. The figures also show that some users manage to be very engaging even though they contribute to relatively few communication trees.

Figures 5(a)-(d) show the average self-engagement against the number of contributions. Users are said to self-engage when they contribute to same threads multiple times, reacting to the peers' responses to their own responses. For example, in Figure 1(b), user C replies to user A, and then, user A replies back to user C. Thus, user A self-engages and increases their own engagement capacity. Figure 5(a) shows that such situations happen frequently in the anxiety forum, thus giving the users higher self-engagement values. The phenomenon of self-engagement is consistent with and reflects the nature/type of social support provision.

Next, the various metrics used for measuring influence are compared against the presented engagement capacity metric, based on the Twitter data: see Figure 6. The Twitter users are first arranged in the increasing order of their engagement capacity values. Then, they are partitioned by the bins of equal width, separated by the percentile points (forming a total of 100 bins). The horizontal axis in Figure 6 contains the percentile values. The highest value in each bin (for each particular metric) was used to plot the graphs in Figure 6. The vertical axis shows the metric values. Figures 6(a)-6(e) present the engagement capacity, page rank, eigenvalue centrality, betweenness centrality and degree centrality values, respectively, for the Twitter users. The results with the HF data are similar, and omitted for brevity. Per Figure 6, none of the other metrics can replace engagement capacity. In order to reveal any relationship between engagement capacity and the other metrics, we perform a simple linear regression and observe a high R^2 value – around 87% for each of the data sets. This shows that engagement capacity captures multiple aspects of what it means for a node to be important in a directed communication tree, as judged by the metrics traditionally used to measure influence. Tables 3 and 4 report the found regression coefficients, standard errors, t-statistic values and p-values for the regression analyses with the HF and Twitter data, respectively.

Now we identify the top 10 engaging users for both HF

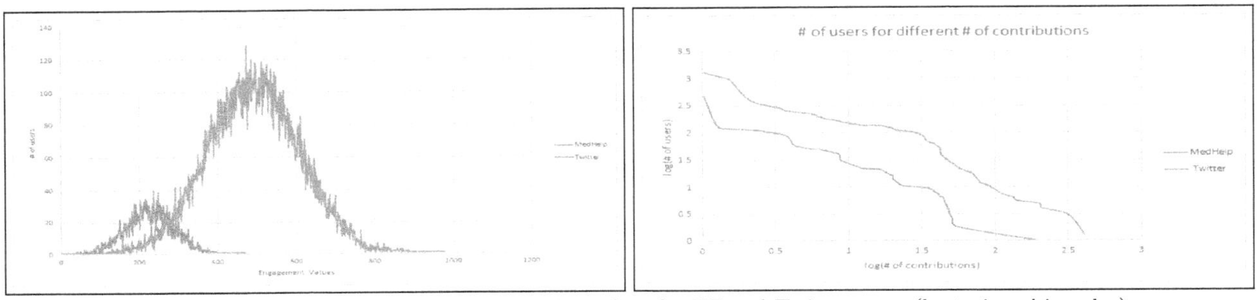

Figure 3: Distribution of engagement capacity values for HF and Twitter users (best viewed in color).

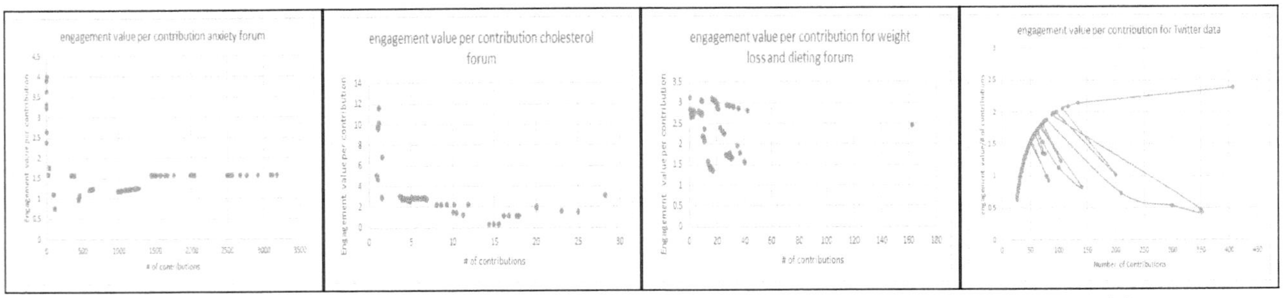

(a) (b) (c) (d)

Figure 4: Engagement capacity per user contribution, for the users ordered by the increasing contribution volume.

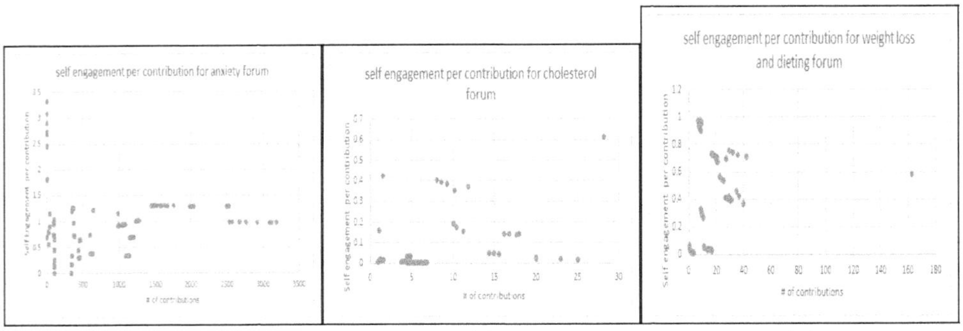

(a) (b) (c)

Figure 5: Self engagement capacity per user contribution, for the users ordered by the increasing contribution volume.

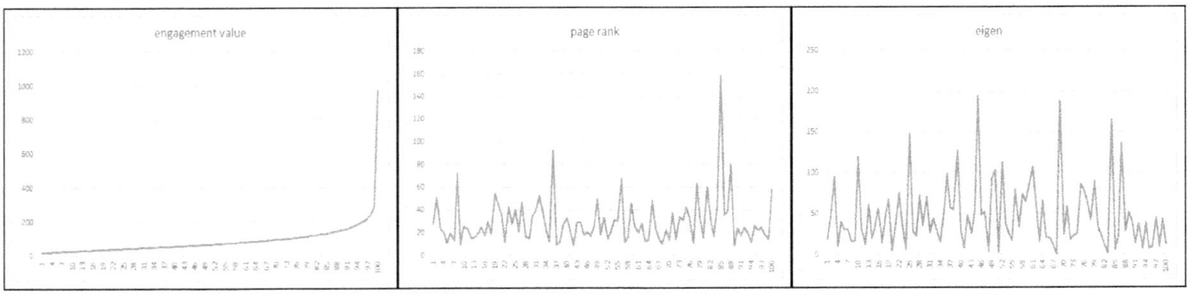

(a) (b) (c)

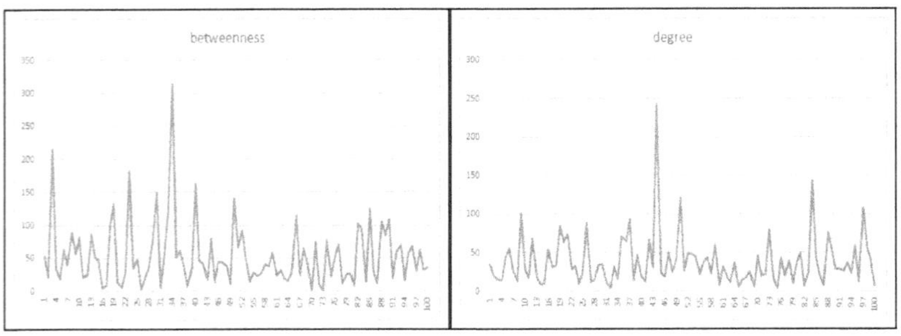

(d) (e)

Figure 6: Comparison of different metrics for the Twitter users arranged according to the increasing engagement capacity.

	A	B	C	D	E	F	G	H
A	3.9	2.3	4.3	4.5	1.2	3.8	1.3	1.3
B	2.9	2.8	3.5	1.9	0.9	1.4	2.5	3.4
C	1.9	3.8	4.6	0	0	1.7	3.4	0
D	2.5	4.4	5	0	2.4	2.6	0.6	2.3
E	1.4	4.4	1.1	1.7	1.5	4.7	2.1	0.2
F	1.2	1	2.2	1	4	5	0.6	0.5
G	0	2.4	3	4.6	4.7	2.2	2.4	0.9
H	2	0	1.5	0.8	2.7	4.5	3.5	1.6

Table 5: Targeted engagement values for top 8 engaging HF users

k	# of users in top 10	Time
2	2	~ 8 hours
3	2	~ 9.5 hours
4	2	~ 10 hours
5	3	~ 11 hours
unconstrained	5	~ 25 hours

Table 6: EngTFP results for the best team of size k.

and Twitter. The HF users can upvote each other's posts; an upvoted post receives a special label. Depending on the number of times their posts are upvoted, a user can be recognized as a top-contributor by a forum. Four of the top 10 engaging users we identify turn out to be such top contributors. This shows that knowledgeable users may earn a high engagement value, albeit without a guarantee. We also find the top 10 tweet creators in the Twitter dataset. Two of these were the accounts associated with news agencies. For an event like the FIFA World Cup, a news agency seems like the right place where other users would go for information. Three of the remaining eight users have a large number of followers and re-tweets. Engagement capacity thus helps reveal the engaging users both in terms of the content they serve as well as the followers they attract.

5.4 Targeted Engagement Capacity Values

Next, we explore what the targeted engagement capacity measure can capture, with the calculations for the top eight engaging users. Using equation (3), we summarize the results for the HF data in Table 5. In this table, users A through H are the top eight most engaging users in each forum, with A being the most engaging, B the second most engaging, etc. The columns in this table are for the users whose engagement is calculated and the rows are for the targeted users. Note that $\eta_{i \to j} \neq \eta_{j \to i}$ for $i \neq j$, i.e., the targeted engagement value from one user i to another user j is not the same as that from user j to user i. Some of the targeted engagement values are zero, signaling no interaction between the user whose engagement capacity was evaluated and the targeted user – in this order. For example, in Table 5, the value for row C and column D is zero. This means there was no communication in the HF forums where D replied to C directly or indirectly. The results with the Twitter data are similar, and omitted for brevity.

5.5 Experiments with EngTFP

Finally, we present the results of solving the EngTFP applied to the HF data. A total of 1,000 random users were selected from the HF dataset, with the objective of finding the most engaging subset of size k among them. The results for several EngTFP instances, solved as integer programs in the SCIP optimization suite [2], are summarized in Table 6. In the instances, the value of k was varied between two and five, and in one instance, k was unrestricted. Comparing the best teams' members against the list of top 10 most engaging HF users, it can be seen the EngTFP does select some highly engaging users but not all. This is because by selecting a pair of users that manage to engage each other, one loses much of targeted engagement. Interestingly, the unconstrained problem optimizes at k as low as 14. Out of the 14 users selected, five are among the top 10 most engaging users, while four others have low engagement values, which indicates that the EngTFP selects some obscure users in order to maximize the reach. The last five users of the 14 have mid-ranged engagement values. Table 6 also shows the time SCIP took to solve each instance. It should be noted that the reported figures included the time to compute the pairwise targeted engagement capacity values for every user pair, before formulating and solving each instance.

6. CONCLUSION

This paper introduces engagement capacity – a metric that serves to measure the ability of online platform users to engage each other in communication on the platform. To this end, we employ co-operative game theory. The presented dynamic method of engagement capacity calculation eliminates the need to re-calculate it from scratch with the addition of new threads and posts to a forum.

The reported experimental results show that engagement capacity can reveal well-interpretable facts about the nature of online communication on different platform types. The observations that one can obtain by calculating the self-engagement and the engagement capacity values, normalized by the number of contributions, are especially insightful. The engagement capacity distribution in a userbase reveals the different dynamics of communication and engagement in two social media, differing in purposes, in HF and Twitter.

We show that targeted engagement capacity can help evaluate the ability of one user to engage another. The targeted engagement studies may facilitate the research of the mechanisms of engagement. Finally, we show how one can use the EngTFP to identify the users who are critical to a platform's success. This work is practically valuable: many online services can rely on it to reward their users in calculated ways.

The paper provides a foundation for future research into *why* engagement occurs. With the engagement capacity metric at hand, various measurable parameters can be explored as its predictors shedding light into user behavior. One might be able to classify engaging users and predict (targeted) engagement capacity by studying its dynamics over time, and by taking into account the activity levels of the users and their followers, their attributes, network positions, behavior, features of posted texts (e.g., sentiment, emotions), etc. For example, studies of engagement predictors (explanatory variables) could distinguish the impact of news media accounts on engagement from that of regular uses; one could determine whether the media texts are any more creative than those of the regular users. The goal of such efforts would be to recognize the *innate abilities* of users to ignite communication, and encourage further activity of such users.

Further experimental work is in order to study how the fluctuations in forum engagement value and user engagement capacity over time correlate with ensuing fluctuations in new user arrival rates, existing user activity levels and turnover. It would also be interesting to see whether these dynamics differ on the Q&A versus social support platforms.

Finally, work can be expanded on more efficient implementations of various versions of constrained EngTFP, coupled with deeper theoretical investigations into its properties. The membership in the most engaging user group, per EngTFP, is likely to vary over time for a given platform. It would be worthwhile to study these dynamics more closely.

7. REFERENCES

[1] P. Achananuparp et al. Who is retweeting the tweeters? modeling, originating, and promoting behaviors in the twitter network. *ACM TMIS*, 3(3):13, 2012.

[2] T. Achterberg. Scip: Solving constraint integer programs. *Mathematical Programming Computation*, 1(1):1–41, 2009.

[3] L. A. Adamic et al. Knowledge sharing and yahoo answers: everyone knows something. In *17th WWW*, pages 665–674. ACM, 2008.

[4] E. Agichtein et al. Modeling information-seeker satisfaction in community question answering. *ACM TKDD*, 3(2):10, 2009.

[5] J. Bernabé-Moreno et al. Caresome: A system to enrich marketing customers acquisition and retention campaigns using social media information. *Knowledge-Based Systems*, 80:163–179, 2015.

[6] F. Bonchi et al. The meme ranking problem: Maximizing microblogging virality. *Journal of Intelligent Information Systems*, page 29, 2013.

[7] S. P. Borgatti. Identifying sets of key players in a social network. *Computational & Mathematical Organization Theory*, 12(1):21–34, 2006.

[8] J. S. Coleman et al. *Medical innovation: A diffusion study.* Bobbs-Merrill Indianapolis, 1966.

[9] M. del Pozo et al. Centrality in directed social networks. a game theoretic approach. *Social Networks*, 33(3):191–200, 2011.

[10] F. DeroıĺLan. Formation of social networks and diffusion of innovations. *Research Policy*, 31(5):835–846, 2002.

[11] M. Fürer et al. *Exact Max 2-Sat: Easier and Faster.* Springer, 2007.

[12] R. E. Glasgow, , et al. Evaluating the public health impact of health promotion interventions: the re-aim framework. *American journal of public health*, 89(9):1322–1327, 1999.

[13] J. C. Harsanyi. A simplified bargaining model for the n-person cooperative game. *International Economic Review*, 4(2):194–220, 1963.

[14] M. L. Katz et al. Network externalities, competition, and compatibility. *The American economic review*, pages 424–440, 1985.

[15] D. Kempe et al. Maximizing the spread of influence through a social network. In *9th ACM SIGKDD*, pages 137–146. ACM, 2003.

[16] J. Lehmann, C. Castillo, M. Lalmas, and E. Zuckerman. Finding news curators in twitter. In *Proceedings of the 22nd international conference on World Wide Web companion*, pages 863–870. International World Wide Web Conferences Steering Committee, 2013.

[17] J. Lehmann, C. Castillo, M. Lalmas, and E. Zuckerman. Transient news crowds in social media. 2013.

[18] T. Li et al. Corporate twitter channels: The impact of engagement and informedness on corporate reputation. *International Journal of Electronic Commerce*, 18(2):97–126, 2013.

[19] J. S. Lim et al. How social media engagement leads to sports channel loyalty: Mediating roles of social presence and channel commitment. *Computers in Human Behavior*, 46:158–167, 2015.

[20] C. C. Moallemi et al. Convergence of min-sum message-passing for convex optimization. *IEEE Transactions on Information Theory*, 56(4):2041–2050, 2010.

[21] R. B. Myerson. Graphs and cooperation in games. *Mathematics of operations research*, 2(3):225–229, 1977.

[22] M. E. Newman. Spread of epidemic disease on networks. *Physical Review E*, 66(1):016128, 2002.

[23] A. Nikolaev et al. On efficient use of entropy centrality for social network analysis and community detection. *Social Networks*, 40:154–162, 2015.

[24] A. S. Nowak et al. The shapley value for n-person games in generalized characteristic function form. *Games and Economic Behavior*, 6(1):150–161, 1994.

[25] B.-W. On et al. Mining interaction behaviors for email reply order prediction. In *ASONAM 2010*, pages 306–310. IEEE, 2010.

[26] B.-W. On et al. *Engagingness and Responsiveness Behavior Models on the Enron Email Network and Its Application to Email Reply Order Prediction.* Springer, 2013.

[27] G. Owen. Values of games with a priori unions. In *Mathematical economics and game theory*, pages 76–88. Springer, 1977.

[28] L. Page et al. The pagerank citation ranking: bringing order to the web. 1999.

[29] M. Samadi et al. A subjective evidence model for influence maximization in social networks. *Omega*, 2015.

[30] E. Sanchez, , et al. On values for generalized characteristic functions. *Operations-Research-Spektrum*, 19(3):229–234, 1997.

[31] D. A. Schult et al. Exploring network structure, dynamics, and function using networkx. In *7th Python in Science Conferences (SciPy 2008)*, volume 2008, pages 11–16, 2008.

[32] L. S. Shapley. A value for n-person games. Technical report, DTIC Document, 1952.

[33] X. Song, , et al. Information flow modeling based on diffusion rate for prediction and ranking. In *16th WWW*, pages 191–200. ACM, 2007.

[34] M. Stearns et al. Towards evaluating and enhancing the reach of online health forums for smoking cessation. *Network Modeling Analysis in Health Informatics and Bioinformatics*, 3(1):1–11, 2014.

[35] X. Tang et al. Identifing influential users in an online healthcare social network. In *ISI 2010*, pages 43–48. IEEE, 2010.

[36] T. W. Valente et al. Network models of the diffusion of innovations. *Nursing Times*, 90(35):52–3, 1994.

[37] T. van Mierlo et al. Mapping power law distributions in digital health social networks: Methods, interpretations, and practical implications. *Journal of medical Internet research*, 17(6), 2015.

[38] V. V. Vydiswaran et al. User-created groups in health forums: What makes them special. In *Proc Conf Weblogs and Social Media (ICWSM) Assoc Adv Artif Intell*, pages 515–24, 2014.

[39] X. Wang et al. Social support and user engagement in online health communities. In *Smart Health*, pages 97–110. Springer, 2014.

[40] W. H. Whyte Jr. The web of word of mouth. *Fortune*, 50(1954):140–143, 1954.

[41] E. Winter. The shapley value. *Handbook of game theory with economic applications*, 3:2025–2054, 2002.

[42] C. C. Yang. Patient centered healthcare informatics.

[43] C. C. Yang et al. Estimating user influence in the medhelp social network. *IEEE Intelligent Systems*, 5(27):44–50, 2012.

[44] K. Zhao et al. Finding influential users of online health communities: a new metric based on sentiment influence. *Journal of the American Medical Informatics Association*, 21(e2):e212–e218, 2014.

Boosted Decision Tree Regression Adjustment for Variance Reduction in Online Controlled Experiments

Alexey Poyarkov
Yandex, Moscow, Russia
alexeypoyarkov@gmail.com

Alexey Drutsa
Yandex, Moscow, Russia
adrutsa@yandex.ru

Andrey Khalyavin
Yandex, Moscow, Russia
halyavin@yandex-team.ru

Gleb Gusev
Yandex, Moscow, Russia
gleb57@yandex-team.ru

Pavel Serdyukov
Yandex, Moscow, Russia
pavser@yandex-team.ru

ABSTRACT

Nowadays, the development of most leading web services is controlled by online experiments that qualify and quantify the steady stream of their updates achieving more than a thousand concurrent experiments per day. Despite the increasing need for running more experiments, these services are limited in their user traffic. This situation leads to the problem of finding a new or improving existing key performance metric with a higher sensitivity and lower variance. We focus on the problem of variance reduction for engagement metrics of user loyalty that are widely used in A/B testing of web services. We develop a general framework that is based on evaluation of the mean difference between the actual and the approximated values of the key performance metric (instead of the mean of this metric). On the one hand, it allows us to incorporate the state-of-the-art techniques widely used in randomized experiments of clinical and social research, but limitedly used in online evaluation. On the other hand, we propose a new class of methods based on advanced machine learning algorithms, including ensembles of decision trees, that, to the best of our knowledge, have not been applied earlier to the problem of variance reduction. We validate the variance reduction approaches on a very large set of real large-scale A/B experiments run at Yandex for different engagement metrics of user loyalty. Our best approach demonstrates 63% average variance reduction (which is equivalent to 63% saved user traffic) and detects the treatment effect in 2 times more A/B experiments.

Keywords: A/B test; variance reduction; prediction

1. INTRODUCTION

Modern Internet companies improve their web services by means of data-driven decisions that are based on *online controlled experiments* also known as *A/B tests* [21]. The scale of use of this state-of-the-art technique, in particular, in search engines is impressive: Bing reported on more than 200 run experiments per day in 2013 (this number grew exponentially over the years [20]), and Google conducted more than 1000 experiments in any day in 2015 [16]. Since the user traffic is limited for a web service, it is vital to effectively use it for maintaining the upward trend of A/B testing.

An A/B test compares two variants of a service at a time, usually its current version (control) and a new one (treatment), by exposing them to two groups of users. The aim of controlled experiments is to detect the causal effect of service updates on its performance relying on an *Overall Evaluation Criterion (OEC)* [23], a user behavior metric (e.g., clicks-per-user, sessions-per-user, etc.) that is assumed to correlate with the quality of the service. The ability of an A/B test to detect the statistically significant difference when the treatment effect exists is referred to as the *sensitivity* [23]. Sensitivity of a particular A/B test could be increased either by a larger sample of participated users, or by a more powerful (more sensitive) OEC. Since user traffic is limited, OEC's sensitivity becomes a crucial aspect that affects the number of experiments with detected treatment effect [23, 21]. That is why a wide set of studies [23, 7, 30, 6, 21, 5, 10, 8, 18, 29, 11] addressed the sensitivity and its improvement.

In this context, the engagement metrics of user loyalty are of greatest interest, since, on the one hand, they are predictive of long-term goals of Internet companies [19, 20, 21] and often considered to be most appropriate for online evaluation (e.g., sessions-per-user [30] is accepted as the "North-star" for online controlled evaluation in major search engine companies like Bing [20, 21]). On the other hand, they are very insensitive to changes of a service [21] what results in utilization of a very large amount of user traffic to achieve a desired level of sensitivity to such small changes (usually, experiments span weeks and cover hundreds of thousands users). Previous work on sensitivity improvement for the loyalty metrics has been limited either to alternative key metrics (periodicity [9, 8] and transformation [11]), evaluation statistics [11], and statistical tests [11], or to a virtual increase of the duration of an experiment by peaking into the future through prediction of the key metric [10].

Since the variance of a key metric reflects its noisiness, a promising way to improve the sensitivity is to decrease the variance [7]. First, the existing studies are limited to only one form of the control variate technique and to only one covariate in the context of large-scale online A/B tests. Second, the empirical validation of the proposed approaches is scant: only a couple of A/B tests is considered and the achieved variance reduction rate is reported only approxi-

KDD '16, August 13–17, 2016, San Francisco, CA, USA.

DOI: http://dx.doi.org/10.1145/2939672.2939688

mately ("up to 40–50%"). Finally, the approaches were not applied to engagement metrics of user loyalty, while, as mentioned above, they are less sensitive than the ones considered in the study, what may have had an effect on the reported variance reduction rate.

Thus, in our study, we address the problem of variance reduction (VR) for user engagement metrics and develop a general framework that allows us to incorporate both the existing state-of-the-art approaches to reduce the variance and some novel ones based on advanced machine learning techniques. We are motivated by the following intuition. The expected value of the key metric for a given user consists of two components: (1) the expected value for this user irrespectively the treatment assignment and (2) the expected bias of the value due to the treatment assignment (i.e., the treatment effect for this user). Since the expectations of the first component does not depend on the treatment assignment, this component does not contribute to the actual average treatment effect, but may increase the variance of its estimation. If we knew the value of the first component, we would subtract it from the key metric and obtain a new metric with decreased variance. However, since we cannot evaluate the first component exactly, we propose to predict it based on the attributes of the user that are independent of the treatment exposure. Therefore, we propose to utilize, as an OEC, instead of the average value of a key metric, its average deviation from its predicted value. We show that the variance of the modified metric is proportional to the mean square error of the predictor. In this way, the problem of VR is reduced to the problem of finding the best predictor for the key metric that is not aware of the treatment exposure.

The framework of our approach covers both the variance reduction technique [7] earlier applied to online evaluation and the ones that are well known in randomized experiments in medicine, social sciences, etc. [14, 28], but, to the best of our knowledge, were never applied in the case of large-scale online A/B tests. At the same time, in our general approach, we apply gradient boosted decision trees (that, as far as we know, were never used to reduce the variance) and achieve a significantly greater variance reduction than the methods of the previous works. In this paper, we conduct our experimental analysis on 161 large-scale A/B experiments run on real users of Yandex (www.yandex.com), one of the most popular global search engines, with duration from one to several weeks and user samples from $5 \cdot 10^5$ to $3 \cdot 10^7$ users. This should make the results of our study more valuable for practical use in modern Internet companies.

To sum up, our study focuses on the problem, which is recognized as fundamental for the *present and emerging Internet companies' needs*: to conduct *more* online controlled experiments per day. Specifically, the major contributions of our work include:

- A new class of variance reduction methods based on advanced machine learning, including ensembles of decision trees, that, to the best of our knowledge, were never used to reduce variance.
- Validation of our variance reduction approach on 161 real online experiments run at Yandex for different engagement metrics of user loyalty, first, demonstrating statistically significant 5.1% improvement of average variance reduction over the best state-of-the-art VR technique (which is equivalent to overall 63% saved user traffic) and, second, detecting the treatment effect in +20% more A/B tests than the best state-of-the-art VR technique.

The rest of the paper is organized as follows. In Sec. 2, the related work on controlled experiments and user engagement is discussed. In Sec. 3, we remind the key points of A/B testing and introduce the general framework of our variance reduction approach. The user engagement metrics and the data (in particular, our 161 A/B experiments) used to validate our approach are described in Sec. 4. In Sec. 5, the details of our prediction task are discussed and our prediction models are evaluated with respect to different settings. In Sec. 6, we validate our approach with respect to variance reduction and sensitivity improvement of key user engagement metrics. In Sec. 7, the study's conclusions and our plans for the future work are presented.

2. RELATED WORK

Online controlled experiment studies. A/B testing methodology achieved a very high popularity in Internet industry over the past few years what is reflected in the recent explosion in the number of published studies on this topic. Early studies [22, 23] were devoted to the theoretical aspects of the methodology. Subsequent work included studies of various aspects of the application of A/B testing in Internet companies: evaluation of changes in various components of web services (e.g., the user interface and ranking algorithms [30, 9, 29]); large-scale experimental infrastructure [31, 20] and optimal scheduling of the experimentation pipeline [17]; different parameters of user interaction with a web service (speed [21], absence [12], abandonment [21], periodicity [9, 8], and engagement [9, 10, 8, 11]); effects of long-term user learning [16]. Many "rules of thumb", pitfalls, and puzzling outcomes of online controlled experimentation were summarized in several studies [4, 19, 21] devoted to the trustworthiness of A/B test results.

A substantial number of studies were devoted to the problem of improving sensitivity of online experiments and saving user traffic in them, what reflects the actual needs of a modern Internet company: to detect the treatment effect in more experiments while expending available resources optimally. Some approaches (to improve sensitivity or to optimize resources) are focused on the alterations of the user groups involved in an A/B experiment (e.g., expanding of user sample [23], elimination of users who were not affected by the service change in the treatment group [30, 5]), as well as changes of the experiment duration (either real increasing [23], or virtual one through the prediction of the future [10]). Some other studies address the problem through a search of more sensitive metrics and their transformations [21, 9, 8] or through the use of more appropriate statistical tests and overall acceptance criteria: statistical tests for two-stage A/B experiments [6], sequential testing for early stopping [18], the optimal distribution decomposition approach [29], and thorough comparison of different evaluation statistics and statistical tests [11]. Finally, this problem is addressed by the variance reduction techniques that are known from Statistics [28] and digital simulation [32]: the stratification and control covariates [7].

Overall, the studies [10] and [7] are the most relevant ones to our work in the context of online controlled experiments. Drutsa et al. in [10] utilized prediction of user engagement to improve sensitivity of an A/B experiment in another way than we do. They used user behaviour observed during the *experiment period* to predict the value of an engagement metric of each individual user in a *future (post-experiment) period*, and, then, they used these values as a *more sensitive key metric.* While, in our study, we use user behaviour observed during the *pre-experiment period* to predict a key engagement metric of each individual user in the *experiment period*, and, then, we improve the sensitivity of the key metric by *subtracting the predicted values* from the actual values of the key metric. Deng et al. in [7] are the first who proposed to utilize pre-experiment data in order to reduce the variance of a key metric. However, their study was limited to the basic forms of control variates techniques that were based only on one feature and were validated via scant empirical analysis (over a pair of A/B tests). This technique is a particular case of our general framework (i.e., the linear model based on one covariate) and, therefore, is considered as a baseline in our study. Besides, we experiment with a very large and diverse set of 161 large-scale A/B tests based on actual interactions of hundreds of thousands of real users.

Randomized experiments in general. Actually, the idea proposed by Deng et al. [7] is not novel in the context of the statistical theory of randomized experiments (randomized control trials, etc.) and their widespread application in clinical researches and other research areas (e.g., the social sciences). Many variance reduction techniques, initially considered in digital simulation [32, 24], were also actively used in the randomized experiments [14, 28]. There are methods that do not change experiment randomization design (e.g., control variates) and methods that change it (blocking, pre-stratification, re-randomization, etc. [1, 27]). Control variates approach is based on a linear model of several covariates (also known as regression adjustment [13]) that approximates the key metric (either by the usual method of ordinary least squares [13, 25], or by a more complex one like Lasso [3]). This technique is a particular case of our general framework (where the learning model built on all available covariates is linear) and, therefore, is also considered as a baseline one in our study (as a straightforward extension of Deng et al.'s approach [7]). In our study, we also consider a technique of matching, which is often used in observational studies [14, 28] to reduce bias in the treatment effect estimation, but could be applied for variance reduction in randomized experiments as well.

Overall, in the context of randomized experiments, on the one hand, our work addresses and provides a verification of the state-of-the-art variance reduction technique on a very large set of large-scale online experiments with at least hundreds of thousands experimental units (in contrast to clinical and social studies). On the other hand, we apply the advanced machine learning method (gradient boosted decision trees[1]) that noticeably improves the state-of-the-art variance reductions, and, thus, it should be of interest from the perspective of randomized experiments in general.

3. FRAMEWORK

3.1 A/B testing background

Assume that we need to compare the performance of a new variant B (*the treatment*) of a web service and the current production variant A (*the control*) w.r.t. a *key metric* X, which quantifies user behavior[2]. Formally, one needs to estimate the *average treatment effect* (*ATE*) defined as

$$\mathrm{ATE}(X) = \mathrm{E}(X \mid B) - \mathrm{E}(X \mid A). \tag{1}$$

In an A/B test (a randomized experiment) [23, 19, 21, 14, 28], users (from a set $\mathcal{U}$ referred to as the *user traffic*), participated in the experiment, are randomly exposed (assigned) to one of the two variants of the service (i.e., $\mathcal{U} = \mathcal{U}_A \sqcup \mathcal{U}_B$). In order to estimate $\mathrm{ATE}(X)$, one estimates each term in Eq. (1) by the average values $\mu_V(X) = \mathrm{avg}_{\mathcal{U}_V} X, V \in \{A, B\}$ (given the observations of metric X for each user group $\mathcal{U}_V, V \in \{A, B\}$), where $\mathrm{avg}_\Omega X = \sum_{\omega \in \Omega} X(\omega)/|\Omega|$ is the *Overall Evaluation Criterion* (*OEC*, also known as the evaluation metric, the online service quality metric, etc. [23]). Their difference $\Delta(X) = \mu_B(X) - \mu_A(X)$ is used as an estimator of $\mathrm{ATE}(X)$ to quantify its sign and magnitude.

The absolute value $|\Delta(X)|$ of the estimator should be controlled by a statistical significance test that provides the probability (called *p-value* and also known [11] as the *achieved significance level*, ASL) to observe this value or larger under *the null hypothesis*, which assumes that the observed difference is caused by random fluctuations, and the variants are not actually different. If the p-value is lower than the threshold $p_{\mathrm{val}} \leq \alpha$ ($\alpha = 0.05$ is commonly used [23, 7, 21, 9, 10]), then the test rejects the null hypothesis, and the difference $\Delta(X)$ is accepted as statistically significant. The pair of an OEC and a statistical test is referred [11] to as an *Overall Acceptance Criterion* (*OAC*). In our study, we utilize the widely applicable *two-sample t-test*[3] (as in [7, 30, 6, 9, 5, 10]). This test is based on the *t-statistic*:

$$\Delta(X)/\sqrt{\sigma_A^2(X) \cdot |\mathcal{U}_A|^{-1} + \sigma_B^2(X) \cdot |\mathcal{U}_B|^{-1}}, \tag{2}$$

where $\sigma_V(X)$ is the standard deviation of the metric X over the users $\mathcal{U}_V, V = A, B$. The larger the absolute value of the t-statistic, the lower the p-value. The additional details of the A/B testing framework could be found in the survey and practical guide on online experiments [23] or in some books on randomized experiments in general like [14, 28]. A practical comparison of different key metrics, evaluation statistics, and statistical tests on a large set of online experiments could be found in [11].

3.2 Variance reduction via subtraction of prediction

In this subsection, we introduce our general framework of the studied variance reduction approach, while, in the next one, we show how it could incorporate different particular cases investigated previously in the literature. To begin, the definition (2) of t-statistic implies that the p-value may be reduced either by an increase of the sample size $|\mathcal{U}|$, or by a reduction of the sample variance $\sigma_{\mathcal{U}}^2(X)$. Hence, a

[1]Similar approaches were applied to reduce bias in the treatment effect estimation in observational studies [26], but, to the best of our knowledge, were not applied to VR problems.

[2]From here on in this paper, we consider "per user metrics" [4, 11], which are calculated for each individual user. This type of metrics (e.g., the number of sessions for a user) is a popular choice for web services [19]. However, there are also frequently used non-per user metrics [4] like presence-time-per-session [11], the annual revenue [21], etc.

[3]The key metric may not follow some assumptions underlying this test, such as the normality of the metric's distribution. However, for large user samples, like those used in our study, the statistical test is correctly applicable [11] for engagement per-user metrics considered in this study.

reduction of the variance by a factor $\varkappa$ allows us to reduce the sample size $|\mathcal{U}|$ by the same factor $\varkappa$ while preserving the sensitivity level achieved before the variance reduction. Hence, *the percent of reduced variance is equal to the percent of saved user traffic, while preserving the same conclusions made in the experiments.*

The motivation. Suppose that we are able to characterize a user u by a set of attributes $\mathbf{F}_u \in \mathbb{R}^n$ that are independent of the treatment assignment $V \in \{A, B\}$. We represent the value of the key metric X as $X = M_1(\mathbf{F}) + M_2(\mathbf{F}, V) + X'$, where $M_1(\mathbf{F}) = \mathrm{E}(X \mid \mathbf{F})$ is the expectation of the key metric X over users with the attributes $\mathbf{F}$, $M_2(\mathbf{F}, V) = \mathrm{E}(X \mid \mathbf{F}, V) - \mathrm{E}(X \mid \mathbf{F})$ is the expectation bias of the metric for users with a given assignment V, and $X' = X - \mathrm{E}(X \mid \mathbf{F}, V)$ is a noise, i.e., the unpredictable part of the key metric. Then the OEC's $\Delta(X)$ consists of three terms: $\mu_B(M_1(\mathbf{F})) - \mu_A(M_1(\mathbf{F}))$, $\mu_B(M_2(\mathbf{F}, B)) - \mu_A(M_2(\mathbf{F}, A))$, and $\mu_B(X') - \mu_A(X')$. The second term is an unbiased estimator of $\mathrm{ATE}(X)$, while the first and the third ones do not affect it, since their expectations are zero. They only make contribution to the variance of the estimate. If we could accurately measure the value of $M_1(\mathbf{F})$ and X' on the basis of the available data about users $(\mathbf{F}_u, V_u)$, we would have subtracted them from our key metric, and, thus, would improve our OEC. In fact, we cannot calculate the third term, but the first term can be *approximated.*

The approach. Let $\widetilde{X}$ be a predictor of the key metric X such that $\widetilde{X}$ does not depend on the treatment exposure. Then *we propose to utilize the difference $\hat{X} = X - \widetilde{X}$ between the actual metric value X and the predicted one $\widetilde{X}$ as a novel key metric in the OEC.* We reveal two properties of the proposed key metric $\hat{X}$, which make it more effective than the original metric X. First, we note that

$$\begin{aligned}\mathrm{ATE}(\hat{X}) &= \mathrm{E}(X - \widetilde{X} \mid B) - \mathrm{E}(X - \widetilde{X} \mid A) \\ &= \mathrm{E}(X \mid B) - \mathrm{E}(X \mid A) - (\mathrm{E}(\widetilde{X} \mid B) - \mathrm{E}(\widetilde{X} \mid A)) \\ &= \mathrm{ATE}(X) - (\mathrm{E}(\widetilde{X}) - \mathrm{E}(\widetilde{X})) = \mathrm{ATE}(X),\end{aligned} \tag{3}$$

where we used the independence of the predictor $\widetilde{X}$ with respect to the treatment. Thus, the difference $\Delta(\hat{X})$ of the novel metric is an unbiased estimator of the treatment effect for the source metric X. Hence, the OEC based on $\hat{X} = X - \widetilde{X}$ could be used instead of the one based on X.

Second, we introduce the following assumptions that may be satisfied by a predictor: (A1) a predictor minimizes the *Root Mean Square Error, RMSE* (i.e., it is optimal) in a class of learning models, which is (A2) closed under addition of a constant and (A3) closed under scalar multiplications.

Then, on the one hand, the variance of the metric $\hat{X}$ is

$$\mathrm{Var}(\hat{X}) = \mathrm{E}\big((X - \widetilde{X})^2\big) - \big(\mathrm{E}(X - \widetilde{X})\big)^2, \tag{4}$$

where the first term is, by definition, the square of the RMSE of the predictor $\widetilde{X}$ and the second term is equal to 0 in the case of an unbiased predictor $\widetilde{X}$ (i.e., if $\mathrm{E}(\widetilde{X}) = \mathrm{E}(X)$, what holds under the assumptions (A1,2)). In this case, the identity (4) transforms to

$$\mathrm{Var}(\hat{X}) = \mathrm{RMSE}^2(X, \widetilde{X}), \tag{5}$$

which states that the variance of the novel metric $\hat{X} = X - \widetilde{X}$ is directly proportional to the loss of the predictor $\widetilde{X}$ (in terms of the MSE). In this way, the better the predictor of the key metric X, the lesser the variance of the modified metric $\hat{X}$, and thus the lesser the volume of the user sample $\mathcal{U}$ required to obtain a certain confidence level.

On the other hand, we know (see, e.g., [10]) that, if the predictor $\widetilde{X}$ is unbiased and satisfies the assumptions (A1,3), then the following identity holds: $\mathrm{Var}(X) = \mathrm{Var}(\widetilde{X}) + \mathrm{Var}(X - \widetilde{X})$, which implies

$$\mathrm{Var}(\hat{X}) = \mathrm{Var}(X) - \mathrm{Var}(\widetilde{X}). \tag{6}$$

Intuitively, the subtracted term $\mathrm{Var}(\widetilde{X})$ corresponds to the variance of the term $M_1(\mathbf{F})$ in the motivation above. The last identity shows that the variance of the difference $\hat{X}$ is lower than the variance of the source metric X in the case when our predictor is not a constant and satisfies (A1,2,3). These conditions are satisfied by a wide range of prediction model classes including linear models and the state-of-the-art ensembles of decision trees [15].

To sum up, (a) Eq. (3) implies that the ATE for the refined metric $\hat{X}$ is equal to the ATE for the source metric X; (b) the direct relationship between the variance of the refined metric $\hat{X}$ and the quality of the unbiased predictor $\widetilde{X}$ is stated in Eq. (5); (c) Eq. (6) guarantees a variance reduction in the case of a non-degenerate predictor $\widetilde{X}$ satisfying the conditions (A1,2,3).

3.3 Details of prediction and special cases

A fundamental approach to obtain a predictor of some target quantity for a set of entities $\mathcal{O}$ is to construct a map M, which depends only on n entity's features $\mathbf{F}(o) = (F_1(o), ..., F_n(o)), o \in \mathcal{O}, n \in \mathbb{N}$. In our case, set $\mathcal{O} = \mathcal{U}$ consists of users, M is referred to as the prediction model, and the target is the key metric X. Thus, $\widetilde{X}(u) = M(\mathbf{F}(u))$. In our approach, it is crucial that the features $\mathbf{F}$ are independent of the treatment assignment. In Sec. 5, we narrowly discuss the targets, features, and models used in our study.

Training set. In order to obtain an optimal map M that has the best prediction quality (i.e., the RMSE in our case) among models from a class $\mathfrak{M}$, a machine learning technique is applied to a training set of examples. According to the usual practice, the prediction process is conducted in the following manner: (a) we train and retrieve an optimal model M based on some examples, whose target is known; (b) we apply this model to the entities whose target is currently unknown. Following this, in our study, we collect some dataset of user behavior observed earlier than the time when our A/B experiments are conducted and use an earlier starting time point when calculating both the feature values and the target to train the model. After that, we use this model to predict the key metric measured in our experiments (e.g., as it is done in [10]). We call such a model a *global predictor.*

However, our VR approach does not require a prediction model prior to a conducted experiment, since the calculation of the OEC (where the predictor $\widetilde{X}$ is used) is performed only after the values of the source metric X are known. At the same time, we know that user behavior significantly depends on a time period, where this behavior is considered [9]. Therefore, the relationship established between features $\mathbf{F}$ and the target X by a model M may differ over different periods. These observations motivate us to train the model on a dataset of examples from the time period, where the obtained predictor will be applied to reduce the variance of the key metric. We expect that this will lead to an improvement of the prediction quality compared to the global predictor. In this way, we obtain a *local predictor*, which is trained individually for each experiment.

Moreover, we can use any subset of the experiment's user traffic (both from the treatment and the control groups) as the training set, since the model outputs $M(\mathbf{F})$ will satisfy the condition of independence of the treatment assignment as far as they depend only on features $\mathbf{F}$ that satisfy this condition themselves (*any map M is independent of users itself and, thus their treatment assignment*). For a large dataset like the one used in our experiments, we did not observe any significant overfitting to the training set and we also did not observe any decrease in the variance reduction rate when using the same dataset of users to train a predictor and to estimate ATE(X). We compare global and local predictors in our experimentation presented in Sec. 5.4 and 6.

Control variates. In a particular case, where we learn a linear predictor $M(F) = \theta F, \theta \in \mathbb{R}$ based on only one feature F, we obtain the approach considered in [7]. The best model is determined as the ordinary least square (OLS) solution with $\theta_0 = \mathrm{Cov}(F, X)/\mathrm{Var}(F)$ estimated either from the considered experiment's data, or from a period before the experiment. This variance reduction technique is known as *control variates*, and, to the best of our knowledge, [7, 5] are the only studies, where this technique is applied to large-scale online experiments (with only one covariate in both cases). However, this technique (also known as linear regression adjustment) is thoroughly studied in the theory of randomized experiments and widely used in offline studies (like clinical or social ones) for more than one covariate as well [13, 14, 25, 28, 3]. Namely, in terms of our general framework, this technique is based on the class of linear models (i.e., $M(\mathbf{F}) = a_0 + \sum_{j=1}^{n} a_j F_j, (a_j)_{j=0}^{k} \in \mathbb{R}^{n+1}$), where the best one is usually determined by the OLS solution [13, 14, 25, 28]. Thus, this state-of-the-art variance reduction technique is a particular case of our approach. To the best of our knowledge, the technique was never previously applied to large-scale online A/B testing studies based on several covariates. We apply it in our empirical study both to one (as in [7]) and to all available features (Sec. 5.4 and 6).

Machine learning. The crucial peculiarity of online experiments is large amounts of user data that need to be processed (usually at least hundreds of thousands experimental units) and complicated dependence of evaluated metrics on covariates, hence we believe that advanced methods of machine learning would work *especially effective* in this case. Therefore, in our paper, we *propose to apply them to the problem of variance reduction.* Namely, we find the optimal prediction model in the class of ensembles of decision trees by means of the state-of-the-art Friedman's gradient boosted decision tree (GBDT) method [15]. To the best of our knowledge, no existing study on variance reduction in randomized experiments (both online and offline) investigated such a machine learned model. The fact that linear regression adjustment [13, 14, 25, 28, 3] uses the same data for learning parameters and for measuring adjusted metric supports our idea to proceed in a similar manner, when we apply GBDTs.

Matching. This approach is based on the idea of finding a similar user (or a set of similar users) from the group $\mathcal{U}_A$ ($\mathcal{U}_B$) for each user from the other group $\mathcal{U}_B$ ($\mathcal{U}_A$ respectively). Matching is usually applied to reduce the bias of a

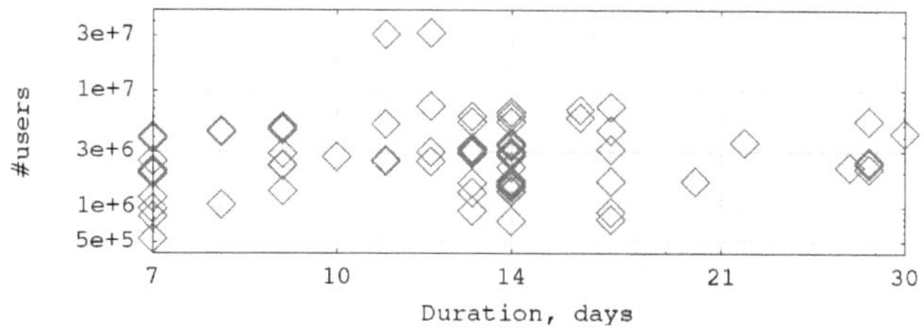

Figure 1: Joint distribution of 161 studied A/B tests w.r.t. their duration and the user traffic.

treatment effect estimation in the context of observational studies, when the randomized assignment is not possible [14, 28], but it also could be used in randomized experiments as a particular case of our general framework. In most matching techniques (e.g., k-nearest neighbours, kNN), the criteria of the similarity is based on a distance in the space of user features $F \in \mathbb{R}^n$. In terms of machine learning, for a user u, the value $X(u_m)$ of the matched user u_m (or a combination of the metric's values for a set of matched users $\{u_m\}$) could be considered simply as a approximated value of the metric for the user u (e.g., estimated by kNN) that could be observed if user u would be assigned to the other group. Hence, first, the machine learning methods used in matching could also be utilized in our approach, and, second, advanced machine learning methods could be applied in matching techniques. In the first case, machine learning methods usually used in matching (like kNN) [14, 28] are very computationally costly considering the sizes of our user samples (from $5 \cdot 10^5$ to $3 \cdot 10^7$, see Sec. 4) and, thus, are infeasible for our large-scale experiments. In the second case, one could apply the state-of-the-art GBDT method [15] to get the following *matching estimator* of the ATE(X)[4]:

$$\Delta_{match}(X) = \frac{|\mathcal{U}_B|}{|\mathcal{U}_A \cup \mathcal{U}_B|}\Delta(\hat{X}_A) + \frac{|\mathcal{U}_A|}{|\mathcal{U}_A \cup \mathcal{U}_B|}\Delta(\hat{X}_B), \quad (7)$$

where $\widetilde{X}_V$ is a predictor of the metric X trained on users $\mathcal{U}_V$, $V = A, B$ (via GBDT, in our study), $\hat{X}_A(u) := X(u) - \widetilde{X}_A(u)$ and $\hat{X}_B(u) := X(u) - \widetilde{X}_B(u)$.

4. STUDIED METRICS AND A/B TESTS

User engagement metrics. In this paper, we concentrate on the study of the loyalty aspect of user engagement [30, 12, 10], since, on the one hand, the metrics measuring this aspect are predictive of long-term goals of Internet companies [19, 20, 21] and are widely used in A/B testing practice [21, 10, 11]. On the other hand, these metrics are difficult to shift by a web service update [21]. Hence, even in the case when such metric X is able to catch the treatment effect during an A/B test, its ATE(X) is expected to be small in comparison with the variance of the metric. Therefore, catching such small effect with a desired statistical significance level will most probably require more resources (more users participating in the experiment over a longer period) than by means of such easily changeable activity-related metrics as, for instance, the number of clicks [21]. This fact was also observed in the recent comparisons [9, 10, 8, 11]: the activity metrics detect the treatment effect in up to 4 times more experiments than the loyalty ones.

[4]Due to space constraints, we omit details and refer a reader to [14, 28], where Eq. (7) is derived for kNN.

Following common practice [19, 12, 30, 10], we define a session as a sequence of user actions whose dwell times are less than 30 minutes. In this paper, we use browser cookie IDs to identify users as done in other studies on user engagement and online A/B testing [31, 12, 30, 9, 16]. We study two key metrics X for a user: the number of her sessions S (as in [30, 9, 10, 11]) and the absence time per session $ATpS$, which is measured as the total absence time (the duration of the whole time period, where the key metric is measured, minus the sum of the durations of all her sessions) divided by the number of sessions S (as in [10, 8, 29]). Due to space constraints, we mainly discuss and analyse the details of our approach for the state-of-the-art sessions-per-user OEC in Sec. 5 and 6. But the final empirical validation of the effectiveness of our approach is also reported for metrics S, $ATpS$, and for some of their modifications (see Sec. 6.3).

Our A/B experiments. In our paper, we consider 161 large-scale A/B experiments conducted on *the users* of Yandex with duration from 7 to 30 days lasted in 2013 and 2014 years. The user samples used in our A/B tests are all uniformly randomly selected, and the control and the treatment groups are approximately of the same size. The total number of users participated in each experiment varies from $5 \cdot 10^5$ to $3 \cdot 10^7$ users. The joint distribution of these 161 A/B tests with respect to their duration and the size of their sample of users is presented in Figure 1. Each experiment evaluates a change in one of the main components of the search engine (including the ranking algorithm, the user interface, the server efficiency, etc). Each of these changes is either an artificial deterioration of a search engine component[5] [20], or its update, which is evaluated before being shipped to production. Each experiment is verified against the absence of a carry-over effect [19] from the past, i.e., we explicitly check that there is no statistically significant difference in the considered OEC between the user groups in the 2-week period before the experiment.

5. PREDICTION

In this section, due to space constraints, only the number of sessions is considered as our *prediction target.*

5.1 Prediction data

The user behavior data are collected both from the period of an experiment (*the experiment period*) and from the 2-week period before the experiment (*the pre-experiment period*). The data from the experiment period are used to obtain the key metric, while both periods are used to obtain features utilized by a predictor of the key metric. Hence, our user engagement prediction problem has the following setting. One has user behavior data observed during two consecutive time periods. Then, one needs to estimate the value of a target engagement metric calculated over the second period for each *individual user* based only on his behavior (observed in both periods) which is not affected by the variant of the web service. Some investigations of the length of the pre-experiment period could be found in the context of the future user experiment prediction in [10] and in the context of variance reduction in [7].

In order to train our prediction models, we either utilize the user behavioral data from the experiments' periods (in this case, we get an individual local predictor for each experiment), or utilize the data collected far before these periods (in this case, we get one global predictor for experiments of the same duration), see Sec. 3.3. For the latter purpose, we additionally collected the behavioral data from 2013, by randomly selecting users and 3-week periods, in which the target is calculated over the last week and the two first weeks are used to calculate features (like for a pre-experiment period in an A/B test). As a result, we obtained a training set with $2.5 \cdot 10^5$ examples, which are then used to train a global predictor for 1-week A/B experiments (see Sec. 5.4 and 6.1).

[5]like the swap of the second and the fourth results in the ranked list returned by the current ranking [9, 29].

Table 1: Comparison of feature sets and models in terms of the average value of nRMSE over 161 A/B tests (relative improvement w.r.t. the first row).

Feature set \ Model	Linear Regression		Decision Trees	
Total	0.8823	(0%)	0.8972	(0%)
Total ∪ TS	0.8594	(−2.59%)	0.8531	(−4.91%)
Total ∪ TS ∪ CT	0.8479	(−3.9%)	0.8213	(−8.46%)
All	0.8418	(−4.59%)	**0.8203**	(−8.57%)

5.2 Features

In our prediction models we utilize the following features to predict the value of the target metric. Note that all of them are measured based on events that are not affected by the service version observed during the experiment.

The total feature. First, we consider the value of the key metric X calculated over the pre-experiment period as our main feature. On the one hand, this feature is reported in [10] as the most predictive one of the value of X in the future period (i.e., the period of an experiment in our case). On the other hand, such feature is known as an effective one in the control variate technique considered to reduce variance in [7]. We denote this feature by **Total**.

The time series. Second, we use the values of the key metric X calculated over each day of the pre-experiment period, obtaining a daily time series of length 14. Then, for each day, except the first day, of the pre-experiment period $t = 2, .., 14$, we calculate the key metric X over the time period that starts on this day t and finishes on the last day of the period. In this way, we obtain the cumulative time series of length 13. Actually, the cumulative time series is a set of features similar to **Total**, but calculated over the shorter pre-experiment periods of length from 1 to 13. The time series are known to be useful to improve the prediction quality of engagement metrics [10]. We refer to these 27 features as **TS**.

The cookie timestamps. Since a user's cookie may be created during an A/B experiment or some days before it, the information presented in the pre-experiment period (the above mentioned features) will not completely describe the actual behavior of the user. For instance, a user could be very active and could use the considered web service each day, but if she clears cookie files in her browser right before the experiment, a new cookie id will be assigned to her, and the number of sessions for this cookie id over 14 days before the experiment's period will be equal to zero, that will represent the user as an inactive one. Hence, in order to distinguish inactive users and users that cleared theirs cookies shortly before the experiment and, thus, assess the confidence in the information contained in the pre-experiment data, we consider, as features important for the prediction

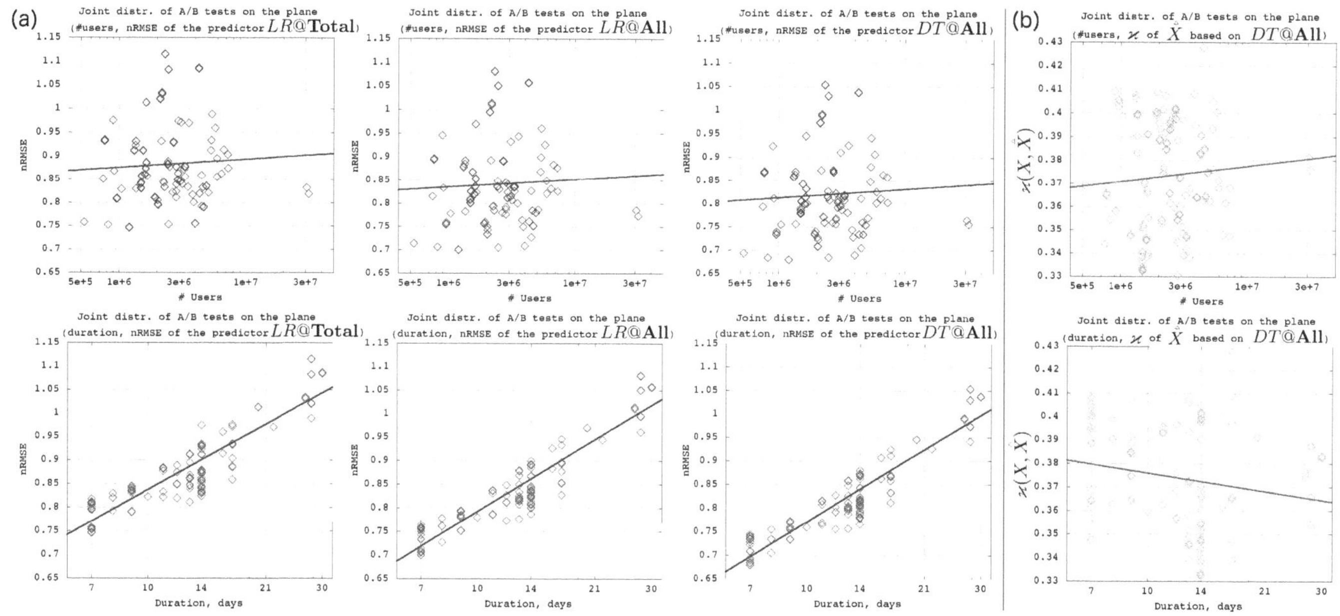

Figure 2: The joint distributions of 161 A/B experiments w.r.t.: (a) (their user traffic; predictor's nRMSE) and (their duration; predictor's nRMSE) for 3 prediction models (LR@Total, LR@All, and DT@All); (b) (their user traffic; the VR rate $\varkappa$) and (their duration; the VR rate $\varkappa$) for the approach based on DT@All.

task, the differences $t_e - t_c$, $t_f - t_e$, and $t_f - t_c$ (denoted by **CT**), where t_c is the creation time of the user cookie; t_f is the time of the first entrance[6] of the user in the experiment[7]; and t_e is the time of the experiment start, which is a constant for all users. Note that the time of the first entrance t_f does not depend on the treatment assignment (although, it is collected during the experiment's period), hence it does not violate the condition of independence of the predictor that is critical for Eq. (3).

The transformation features. The study [10] shows that the prediction quality could be noticeably improved by transformations of the daily time series from **TS**, namely, by the ones that reflect the periodicity (e.g., discrete Fourier amplitudes [9]) and the average amount of information (e.g., different variants of entropy [10]) of user engagement. We utilized 20 most profitable transformations according to the study [10]. We refer to these features as **TrTS**.

We define the set of all features described above by **All** = **Total** ∪ **TS** ∪ **CT** ∪ **TrTS**. Note that features **Total**, **TS**, and **TrTS** are different characteristics of the dynamics of the metric X. We could also use the same characteristics of some other metrics as features to better predict the target value of X. Investigation of this idea in [10] showed that, in the case of $X = S$, these characteristics of other user engagement metrics (considered in [10]) do not noticeably improve the prediction quality, while, in the case of $X = ATpS$, these characteristics of both $ATpS$ and S are useful. Hence, for the absence time per session as the target, we use both $ATpS$ and S to derive the features, while, for the number of sessions as the target, we use only S.

5.3 Models

We utilized two models to predict the values of the targets by minimizing the RMSE as the loss function.

[6]the first activity of the user since the start of the A/B test
[7]This time is more informative than the day of the first entrance (a categorical feature) used as a covariate in [7].

Linear model (LR). The first one is a classical linear regression model, which regards the prediction as an ordinary least square (OLS) problem. When the training set coincides with the data of a considered A/B test (i.e., we deal with a local predictor, see Sec. 3.3), our variance reduction approach in the case of this model becomes the classical linear regression adjustment on a set of covariates that is applied in randomized experiments in clinical studies, social sciences, etc. [14, 28]. Therefore, we consider the linear prediction model built on the feature **Total** (i.e., the total number of sessions during the 14-day pre-experiment period) as our first baseline model (since it coincides with the one applied earlier in online experimentation [7]), and we consider the linear prediction model built on all available features as our second baseline (since it was previously used in randomized experiments [13, 14, 28, 25, 3], but never applied to large-scale *online* A/B tests).

Decision trees' model (DT). The second model is the state-of-the-art Friedman's gradient boosted decision trees [15]. In our experimentation (Sec. 5.4 and 6), we use a proprietary implementation of the machine learning algorithm with 100 iterations and 100 trees, where features were processed by means of the equal frequency binning with 64 bins.

We use the short notation M@**FS** for a model M built on features **FS** (e.g., DT@**All** denotes decision trees built on the features **All** and LR@**Total** denotes the linear regression model based on the feature **Total**).

5.4 Prediction quality

In order to validate the quality of our predictors, we utilize all our 161 A/B experiments. For each experiment, we measure the prediction quality in terms of the normalized RMSE (nRMSE) defined by $\text{nRMSE}(X, \widetilde{X}) := \text{RMSE}(X, \widetilde{X})/\text{E}(X)$ for the actual target X and the predictor $\widetilde{X}$. This allows us, first, to hide the information about the magnitude of the studied metric for confidentiality reasons, and, second, to make the quality measure independent from this magnitude (e.g., when we report the average values), since it significantly depends on the durations of an experiment [9, 10].

Comparison of features and models. In Table 1, we report the average value of the nRMSE for each local prediction model based on different feature sets over all our A/B experiments. All differences between the presented nRMSE are statistically significant with p-value $\leq 10^{-3}$ (measured by paired t-test over the A/B experiments). First, we see that the best predictor is decision trees which is based on the set of all features. Second, our novel timestamps features **CT** noticeably improve the prediction quality w.r.t. **Total** $\cup$ **TS**: by 1.31% for the linear model and by 3.55% for decision trees. The features **CT** carry information about different types of users and, thus, resemble categorical features, so the decision trees may better utilize these features than the linear model. Third, the transformation features **TrTS** improve the prediction quality as well. Note that this improvement is around of 0.11% for decision trees, hence, for this model, one can use the set of features **Total** $\cup$ **TS** $\cup$ **CT** in order to reduce the computational complexity without a critical loss in prediction quality. Summarizing, we conclude that *decision trees built on all features (DT@***All***) significantly outperforms our baselines: LR@***Total** *by 7.2% and LR@***All** *by 2.55%.*

Duration and user traffic. We study the dependence of the prediction quality on the duration of an experiment and on the number of users participated in it. In Figure 2 (a), we report the joint distributions of our 161 A/B experiments w.r.t. the nRMSE and each of these two quantities in the logarithmic scale, due to the space constraints, only for the baseline predictors *LR*@**Total**, *LR*@**All** and for the best one *DT*@**All**. First, we see that the prediction quality only weakly depends on the size of user samples: the slope of the best fit line is very low (from 0.007 to 0.008) and its standard error (SE) is hight (≈ 0.01). It is an expected result, since the prediction quality should not depend on the size of the training and test data, when their sizes (in our case, at least hundreds of thousands users) are large enough w.r.t. the number of features (in our case, no more than a hundred). Second, the prediction quality in terms of the nRMSE clearly linearly depends on the duration of the experiment: the slope of the best fit line is high (from 0.187 to 0.206) and its SE is very low (from 0.006 to 0.007). Thus, we conclude that *the longer an experiment, the worse the quality of prediction*, which is expected since the pre-experiment data of a user becomes more uncertain about her future behavior.

Local vs. global predictor. The results presented above are obtained for local predictors, i.e., the models are trained on all user traffic $\mathcal{U}$[8] for each experiment individually (see Sec. 3.3 for details). In order to understand the advantage of the utilization of a local training w.r.t. to a global one, first, we use the dataset collected from 2013 (described in Sec. 5.1) as the training set for a global predictor. Second, we truncate the duration of all experiments to one week and filter out A/B tests from 2013 year, obtaining a reduced set of 146 experiments of 2014 year. Thus, these experiments occurred later than the training data and have the same duration as the length of the target period of the training examples. On these A/B tests, we compare the nRMSE of the local predictor *DT*@**All** and the global one, which is based on the same learning model and the same feature set, but trained on the above described training set from 2013 year. The average nRMSE of the global predictor is 0.755, while the one of the local predictor is 0.726, which is lower by 3.96%. Thus, we conclude that *a predictor, trained on the data from the experiment's period, definitely outperforms the predictor with the same model and the same set of features, but trained on a dataset collected from a far earlier period.* This has been expected, since user behavior significantly depends on a time period, where this behavior is considered [9] (see Sec. 3.3).

6. A/B EXPERIMENTATION

In the context of variance reduction (VR) and sensitivity improvement, we consider 3 main baseline methods for our approach. The first one is the "zero" baseline, which is our source metric without any modification (e.g., the number of sessions in Sec. 6.1 and 6.2). The other two baseline methods are simplified versions of our approach: one technique coincides with the one applied earlier in online experimentation [7] (it is based on *LR*@**Total**), and the other is its extension based on the practice of randomized experiments in clinical and social studies [14, 28] (it is based on *LR*@**ALL**).

6.1 Variance reduction

We remind, see Sec. 3.2, that the performance of a variance reduction method is measured in terms of the reduction rate $\varkappa(X, \hat{X}) := \mathrm{Var}(\hat{X})/\mathrm{Var}(X)$, where X is the source key metric and $\hat{X}$ is the modified one by the method.

Comparison of features and models. In Table 2, we report the average value of the variance reduction rate $\varkappa$ for each local prediction model[9] based on different feature sets over all our A/B experiments. All differences between the presented VR rates are statistically significant with p-value $\leq 10^{-3}$ (measured as in Sec. 5.4). First, we see that the best VR method is the one which utilizes decision trees based on the set of all features. *It achieves* 62.66% *of saved user traffic on average* (see Eq. (2) and Sec. 3.2). Second, each set of features demonstrates a significant profit in terms of variance reduction: the time series **TS** and our novel timestamps features **CT** noticeably improve the variance reduction rate $\varkappa$ (e.g., for **CT**, by 2.76% and by 7% for *LR* and *DT* models respectively); the transformation features **TrTS** have a lower but positive improvement as well. Third, note that, in all cases except the one with one feature **Total**, decision trees has better performance than the one of the linear regression based on the same set of features. Overall, we conclude that *decision trees built on all features (DT@***All***) significantly outperforms our baselines: LR@***Total** *by 13.9% and LR@***All** *by 5.1% in terms of the variance reduction $\varkappa$ and, hence, in terms of saved user traffic.*

Duration and user traffic. We study the dependence of the variance reduction rate on the duration and the user traffic size of an experiment. In Fig. 2 (b), we plot the joint distributions of our 161 A/B experiments w.r.t. the rate $\varkappa$ and one of these quantities in the logarithmic scale. Due to space constraints, the results are presented only for the best method, which is based on *DT*@**All**, but they are similar for

[8]We considered different user sets as train data (including the control or the treatment user set solely) for local predictors, but the prediction quality was not noticeably different.

[9]Local predictors are better than global ones in terms of nRMSE (see Sec. 5.4) and in terms of $\varkappa$ (e.g., relative difference of $\varkappa$ for *DT*@**All** is 4.71%).

Table 2: Comparison of feature sets and models in terms of the average VR rate $\varkappa$ over 161 A/B test (relative improvement w.r.t. the previous row).

Feature set \ Model	Linear Regression		Decision Trees	
The source metric	1	(0%)	1	(0%)
Total	0.4337	(−56.63%)	0.4481	(−55.19%)
Total ∪ TS	0.4108	(−5.27%)	0.4046	(−9.7%)
Total ∪ TS ∪ CT	0.3995	(−2.76%)	0.3743	(−7.49%)
All	0.3935	(−1.5%)	**0.3734**	(−0.25%)

Table 3: Comparison of feature sets and models in terms of the success sensitivity rate (with $\alpha = 0.05$) over 161 A/B tests.

The source metric:	12 (7.45%)	
Feature set \ Model	Linear Regression	Decision Trees
Total	17 (10.55%)	18 (11.18%)
Total ∪ TS	22 (13.66%)	21 (13.04%)
Total ∪ TS ∪ CT	19 (11.80%)	**24** (**14.91**%)
All	20 (12.42%)	**24** (**14.91**%)

all other methods. First, we see that the variance reduction weakly depends on the size of user samples (the slope of the best fit line ≈ 0.003 with SE ≈ 0.0029). Second, the variance reduction is weakly depends on the duration of the experiment as well (the slope of the best fit line ≈ -0.01 with SE ≈ 0.0043). Thus, we conclude that *the variance reduction rate of our methods weakly depend on the user traffic size and the duration of an experiment.* The last result, together with the dependence of nRMSE on the duration (see Sec. 5.4), implies that this dependence of nRMSE is caused by the dependence of the z-score $z(X) := E(X)/\sqrt{\mathrm{Var}(X)}$ on the duration, since $\mathrm{nRMSE}^2(X, \widetilde{X}) = \varkappa(X, \hat{X})/z^2(X)$ for an unbiased predictor $\widetilde{X}$ (see Eq. (5)). The decrease of our z-score $z(X)$ with the growth of the experiment duration is a reproducing of the well known property of the number-of-sessions metric [19].

Matching. For the matching estimator $\Delta_{match}(X)$ defined by Eq. (7) and described in Sec. 3.3, we obtain the variance reduction rate equal to $\varkappa = 0.3749$. Hence, the relative improvement of the rate $\varkappa$ of the estimator $\Delta(\hat{X})$ based on the predictor *DT*@**All** w.r.t. the one of the matching estimator $\Delta_{match}(X)$ is equal to 0.39%. Thus, we conclude that *our approach based on the classical form of the estimator $\Delta(\hat{X})$ outperforms the matching estimator $\Delta_{match}(X)$ with matching based on the same model (i.e., decision trees) and the same set of features (i.e.,* **All***).*

6.2 Sensitivity improvement

Control of false-positive rates. In A/B testing, correctness of an experimentation is verified by A/A tests (i.e., control experiments) [23, 4]. Each of them compares two identical variants of the service. If a considered OAC (i.e., an OEC with a statistical test, see Sec. 3.1) is valid, then the p-value of this OAC should be uniformly distributed over $[0, 1]$ on A/A tests and the A/A tests should fail in not more than 5% of cases for the p-value threshold $\alpha = 0.05$ [23, 4, 11]. The number of failed A/A tests is referred to as the *false-positive rate* (also known as the type I error). We obtain a thousand of A/A experiments (like in [2, 7, 11]) by randomly splitting users from the control group of one of our A/B experiments. All our source and modified metrics do not fail the predefined false-positive rate threshold.

Success sensitivity rates. Following [9, 10, 8, 29, 11], we compare the sensitivity of our OACs in terms of the *success sensitivity rate*, i.e., the number of A/B tests whose treatment effect is detected by an OAC. In Table 3, we present these rates for our source metric X (i.e., the number of sessions) and for the metrics $\hat{X}$, modified by our approach based on different prediction models and sets of features over all our A/B experiments. We see that *the best variance reduction method, i.e., the one based on DT*@**All**, *has the best sensitivity improvement: the corresponding OAC outperforms the OAC of the source metric by increasing the success sensitivity rate twice and the one of the OAC with LR*@**All** *(baseline VR method) by* 20% (the same improvement is achieved by *DT*@**All** \ **TrTS**).

6.3 Other metrics

In this subsection, we report the results of applying our best variance reduction method (i.e., the one based on *DT*@**All**) to the absence time metric *ATpS*, the other popular engagement metric of user loyalty [12] (see its definition in Sec. 4). We also apply two ways of filtering out users. In the first filter (s-filter), a user with only one session during the experiment period is removed from the user sample $\mathcal{U}$ (as in [11]). The second filter (t-filter) removes any user, who has a browser cookie created later than 24 hours before the experiment start (i.e., the cookie is very "young"). These filters are expected to improve the sensitivity of the source metric, since the removed users are believed to be less affected by the treatment effect.

We report the variance reduction rates $\varkappa$ and the success sensitivity rates in Table 4. The percent of variance reduction is reported relative to the source metric without any user filter. Thus, we are able to understand *the cumulative variance reduction rate* $\varkappa_c$ resulted from applying a user filter and the variance reduction technique together: $\varkappa_c = \varkappa(X, \hat{X}_f) = \varkappa(X, X_f) \cdot \varkappa(X_f, \hat{X}_f)$, where X_f is the source metric X over filtered users. First, the results for the number of sessions S and for the absence time *ATpS* are similar. Second, the best cumulative variance reduction rate is demonstrated by our technique without any filter, while the best $\varkappa$ is demonstrated for the metrics with the t-filter. Note that the increase in variance is expected when we apply the filters, since the removed users have similar or even identical behavior. The user filters really improve the sensitivity of the source metric X, but their combination with the variance reduction technique is not better than the variance reduction technique applied solely. Thus, we conclude that *our technique based on decision trees and all available features noticeably reduces the variance of all engagement metrics of user loyalty (from* 62.66% *to* 58.48% *depending on applied filters) and improves their sensitivity up to twice.*

7. CONCLUSIONS AND FUTURE WORK

In our work, we focused on the problem of variance reduction for engagement metrics of user loyalty that are widely used in A/B testing of web services. We developed a general framework that is based on machine learning techniques, that allowed us, on the one hand, to perform a deep study of existing approaches used in randomized experiments in online and offline studies (like clinical trials), and, on the other hand, to propose a new class of methods based on ensembles of decision trees, that, to the best of our knowledge, have

Table 4: Comparison of source metrics X and their modifications $\hat{X}$ (based on DT@All) in terms of the average VR rate $\varkappa$ (relative improvement w.r.t. non-filtered X) and the success sensitivity rate (with $\alpha = 0.05$) over 161 A/B tests.

Metric $X =$	Variance reduction rate $\varkappa(X, \hat{X})$	Success sensitivity rate for X	for $\hat{X}$
S	0.3734 (**−62.66%**)	12 (7.45%)	**24 (14.91%)**
S (s-filter)	0.4152 (−32.07%)	16 (9.94%)	21 (13.04%)
S (t-filter)	**0.3668** (−33.42%)	15 (9.32%)	21 (13.04%)
$ATpS$	0.3735 (**−62.65%**)	12 (7.45%)	**23 (14.29%)**
$ATpS$ (s-filter)	0.4152 (−32.07%)	16 (9.94%)	22 (13.66%)
$ATpS$ (t-filter)	**0.3668** (−33.42%)	15 (9.32%)	20 (12.42%)

not been applied earlier to problems of variance reduction. We experimented with a very large and diverse set of 161 real large-scale A/B experiments. First, we have shown that our novel variance reduction technique (which is based on decision trees) outperformed state-of-the-art ones. Second, this technique demonstrated 63% average variance reduction (5.1% improvement over the best state-of-the-art technique), which is equivalent to 63% overall (5.1% relative) saved user traffic utilized in online evaluation. Finally, we also applied the method to sensitivity improvement that resulted in the detection of the treatment effect in 2 times more A/B tests than with non-modified user engagement metrics and +20% more A/B tests than the one modified by the state-of-the-art VR technique. Hence, our study produces essential results on effectiveness of different variance reduction techniques applied to user engagement metrics that coincide with the emerging needs of modern Internet companies to run more controlled experiments on a limited number of their users.

Future work. First, we can improve the prediction quality by more complicated models and richer feature sets for further variance reduction and sensitivity improvement. Second, one can further study matching estimators to achieve better sensitivity.

8. REFERENCES

[1] S. Addelman. The generalized randomized block design. *The American Statistician*, 23(4):35–36, 1969.

[2] E. Bakshy and D. Eckles. Uncertainty in online experiments with dependent data: An evaluation of bootstrap methods. In *KDD'2013*, pages 1303–1311, 2013.

[3] A. Bloniarz, H. Liu, C.-H. Zhang, J. Sekhon, and B. Yu. Lasso adjustments of treatment effect estimates in randomized experiments. *arXiv:1507.03652*, 2015.

[4] T. Crook, B. Frasca, R. Kohavi, and R. Longbotham. Seven pitfalls to avoid when running controlled experiments on the web. In *KDD'2009*, pages 1105–1114, 2009.

[5] A. Deng and V. Hu. Diluted treatment effect estimation for trigger analysis in online controlled experiments. In *WSDM'2015*, pages 349–358, 2015.

[6] A. Deng, T. Li, and Y. Guo. Statistical inference in two-stage online controlled experiments with treatment selection and validation. In *WWW'2014*, 2014.

[7] A. Deng, Y. Xu, R. Kohavi, and T. Walker. Improving the sensitivity of online controlled experiments by utilizing pre-experiment data. In *WSDM'2013*, 2013.

[8] A. Drutsa. Sign-aware periodicity metrics of user engagement for online search quality evaluation. In *SIGIR'2015*, pages 779–782, 2015.

[9] A. Drutsa, G. Gusev, and P. Serdyukov. Engagement periodicity in search engine usage: Analysis and its application to search quality evaluation. In *WSDM'2015*, pages 27–36, 2015.

[10] A. Drutsa, G. Gusev, and P. Serdyukov. Future user engagement prediction and its application to improve the sensitivity of online experiments. In *WWW'2015*, pages 256–266, 2015.

[11] A. Drutsa, A. Ufliand, and G. Gusev. Practical aspects of sensitivity in online experimentation with user engagement metrics. In *CIKM'2015*, 2015.

[12] G. Dupret and M. Lalmas. Absence time and user engagement: evaluating ranking functions. In *WSDM'2013*, pages 173–182, 2013.

[13] D. A. Freedman. On regression adjustments to experimental data. *Advances in Applied Mathematics*, 40(2):180–193, 2008.

[14] D. A. Freedman, D. Collier, J. S. Sekhon, and P. B. Stark. *Statistical models and causal inference: a dialogue with the social sciences*. Cambridge University Press, 2010.

[15] J. H. Friedman. Greedy function approximation: a gradient boosting machine. *Annals of Statistics*, 2001.

[16] H. Hohnhold, D. O'Brien, and D. Tang. Focusing on the long-term: It's good for users and business. In *KDD'2015*, pages 1849–1858, 2015.

[17] E. Kharitonov, C. Macdonald, P. Serdyukov, and I. Ounis. Optimised scheduling of online experiments. In *SIGIR'2015*, pages 453–462, 2015.

[18] E. Kharitonov, A. Vorobev, C. Macdonald, P. Serdyukov, and I. Ounis. Sequential testing for early stopping of online experiments. In *SIGIR'2015*, pages 473–482, 2015.

[19] R. Kohavi, A. Deng, B. Frasca, R. Longbotham, T. Walker, and Y. Xu. Trustworthy online controlled experiments: Five puzzling outcomes explained. In *KDD'2012*, 2012.

[20] R. Kohavi, A. Deng, B. Frasca, T. Walker, Y. Xu, and N. Pohlmann. Online controlled experiments at large scale. In *KDD'2013*, pages 1168–1176, 2013.

[21] R. Kohavi, A. Deng, R. Longbotham, and Y. Xu. Seven rules of thumb for web site experimenters. In *KDD'2014*, 2014.

[22] R. Kohavi, R. M. Henne, and D. Sommerfield. Practical guide to controlled experiments on the web: listen to your customers not to the hippo. In *KDD'2007*, pages 959–967, 2007.

[23] R. Kohavi, R. Longbotham, D. Sommerfield, and R. M. Henne. Controlled experiments on the web: survey and practical guide. *DMKD*, 18(1):140–181, 2009.

[24] P. L'Ecuyer. Efficiency improvement and variance reduction. In *Proceedings of the 26th conference on Winter simulation*, pages 122–132. SCSI, 1994.

[25] W. Lin et al. Agnostic notes on regression adjustments to experimental data: Reexamining freedman's critique. *The Annals of Applied Statistics*, 7(1):295–318, 2013.

[26] D. F. McCaffrey, G. Ridgeway, and A. R. Morral. Propensity score estimation with boosted regression for evaluating causal effects in observational studies. *Psychological methods*, 9(4):403, 2004.

[27] K. L. Morgan, D. B. Rubin, et al. Rerandomization to improve covariate balance in experiments. *The Annals of Statistics*, 40(2):1263–1282, 2012.

[28] S. L. Morgan and C. Winship. *Counterfactuals and causal inference*. Cambridge University Press, 2014.

[29] K. Nikolaev, A. Drutsa, E. Gladkikh, A. Ulianov, G. Gusev, and P. Serdyukov. Extreme states distribution decomposition method for search engine online evaluation. In *KDD'2015*, pages 845–854, 2015.

[30] Y. Song, X. Shi, and X. Fu. Evaluating and predicting user engagement change with degraded search relevance. In *WWW'2013*, pages 1213–1224, 2013.

[31] D. Tang, A. Agarwal, D. O'Brien, and M. Meyer. Overlapping experiment infrastructure: More, better, faster experimentation. In *KDD'2010*, pages 17–26, 2010.

[32] J. R. Wilson. Variance reduction techniques for digital simulation. *American Journal of Mathematical and Management Sciences*, 4(3-4):277–312, 1984.

Dynamic and Robust Wildfire Risk Prediction System: An Unsupervised Approach

Mahsa Salehi
IBM Research - Australia
60 City Road, Southbank
Victoria, 3006, Australia
mahsalehi@au1.ibm.com

Laura Irina Rusu
IBM Research - Australia
60 City Road, Southbank
Victoria, 3006, Australia
laurusu@au1.ibm.com

Timothy Lynar
IBM Research - Australia
60 City Road, Southbank
Victoria, 3006, Australia
timlynar@au1.ibm.com

Anna Phan
IBM Research - Australia
60 City Road, Southbank
Victoria, 3006, Australia
anna.phan@au1.ibm.com

ABSTRACT

Ability to predict the risk of damaging events (e.g. wildfires) is crucial in helping emergency services in their decision-making processes, to mitigate and reduce the impact of such events. Today, wildfire rating systems have been in operation extensively in many countries around the world to estimate the danger of wildfires. In this paper we propose a data-driven approach to predict wildfire risk using weather data. We show how we address the inherent challenge arising due to the temporal dynamicity of weather data. Weather observations naturally change in time, with finer-scale variation (e.g. stationary day or night) or large variations (non-stationary day or night), and this determines a temporal variation of the predicted wildfire danger.

We show how our dynamic wildfire danger prediction model addresses the aforementioned challenge using context-based anomaly detection techniques. We call our predictive model a Context-Based Fire Risk (CBFR) model. The advantage of our model is that it maintains multiple historical models for different temporal variations (e.g. day versus night), and uses ensemble learning techniques to predict wildfire risk with high accuracy. In addition, it is completely unsupervised and does not rely on expert knowledge, which makes it flexible and easily applied to any region of interest. Our CBFR model is also scalable and can potentially be parallelised to speed up computation. We have considered multiple wildfire locations in the Blue Mountains, Australia as a case study, and compared the results of our system with the existing well-established Australian wildfire rating system. The experimental results show that our predictive model has a substantially higher accuracy in predicting wildfire risk, which makes it an effective model to supplement the operational Australian wildfire rating system.

KDD '16, August 13 - 17, 2016, San Francisco, CA, USA

ISBN 978-1-4503-4232-2/16/08... $15.00

DOI: http://dx.doi.org/10.1145/2939672.2939685

CCS Concepts

•**Information systems** → **Data streaming;** *Data analytics; Data stream mining;* •**Computing methodologies** → **Anomaly detection;**

Keywords

Wildfires, Bushfires, Risk Prediction, Data Stream Mining, Unsupervised Learning, Context-Based Anomaly Detection

1. INTRODUCTION

Natural disasters are a prevalent reality around the world. Roughly 102 million people worldwide were affected by natural disasters in 2014 alone [8], with a global annual economic loss estimated at over $300B [10]. Researchers link natural disasters with climate change and statistics show that in 2014, 87% of worldwide natural disasters were climate-related [8]. Some countries, including Australia, experience wildfires, locally known as bushfires, as the most damaging disasters. In the Australian state of Victoria, wildfires pose the largest annual risk to the safety of residents [6]. For example, in the recent 'Black Saturday' Victorian wildfire event of February 2009, over 1.1 million acres burnt, 173 people lost their lives and over 400 people were injured [5]. Another notable impactful event was 'Ash Wednesday' in February 1983, with 75 fatalities and over 1 million acres burnt in the states of Victoria and South Australia. The impact of these disasters is multi-dimensional, from social and psychological to economic and environmental.

The reality described above makes a strong case for wildfire research, not only in Australia but also around the world. One of the most pressing problems in this context is the ability to predict the risk of a wildfire event. By knowing the risk, government agencies, communities and individuals can be better informed so they can take the most appropriate measures to mitigate and prepare for of wildfire events, if and when they eventuate (e.g. evacuate people, predeploy firefighting assets etc.).

The McArthur Forest Fire Danger Index (FFDI) [17] is used in Australia by the national Bureau of Meteorology to draw Fire Danger Index maps [2], which in turn are used by state wildfire authorities to determine Fire Danger Ratings (FDR) by taking into account not only the contribution of weather but also other relevant information such as fuel load. The daily FDR are then publicly available and broadcasted to all interested stakeholders.

Along with FFDI, other approaches to predict wildfire danger also exist around the world (summarised later in Section 2, Related Works). However their main drawback, which we address in this paper, is that they generally calculated by feeding the current weather observations into an existing static model, therefore not catering for spatial or temporal variations between observations (e.g. between weather stations due to elevation, or between summer and autumn days). With existing approaches, the danger index on any given day or at any given point in space is calculated using the same models, with static parameters that do not change to reflect the actual context of the danger index calculation. This determines a coarse variation between the danger indices of consecutive days and is not indicative of the temporal development of the wildfire danger, which is actually the case for most wildfire events.

As an exemplar, consider two weeks of weather observations where the current operational mathematical model or other learned/regression models in the literature is used to compute the risk values. Additionally, suppose that in the middle of this period an actual wildfire is happening. Figure 1 depicts an example of risk values computed using the FFDI model for this example time period. In this graph the vertical axis represents the risk values, horizontal axis shows the time in minutes, and the horizontal line in the middle bottom of the graph represents the actual wildfire period. Now suppose there is bad weather conditions one night before the actual wildfire in comparison to other normal nights. The rectangle in this figure shows the described night. Although the night weather information can be used to infer a high risk period in the next few hours, the FFDI model fails to use such information until the actual wildfire is happening. The risk values at night time in this figure (values in the rectangle) are low. Using online learning models which use the whole history of observations cannot be beneficial either, for such models do not differentiate 'night time' from 'day time'. This differentiation is extremely significant, as the decision makers and firefighters need to be able to predict the high risk days beforehand, to enable them to plan strategically in advance.

Since wildfire danger is mainly dependent on the weather and fuel load, and their variability can be observed both spatially and temporally [24, 22], we claim that wildfire risk models should not be static and generic, but dynamic and representative of the spatial and temporal context. That is, we propose a wildfire danger model that considers finer-scale variations in day or night weather observations (stationary observations) or larger variations during day or night (non-stationary observations) and readjusts itself (i.e. its parameters) to the context. In this paper, we consider both the temporal variability and spatial variability of weather observations.

Based on the above, we summarise the novel contributions of this paper as follows:

- We propose a dynamic wildfire risk prediction model to augment the current static operational models;

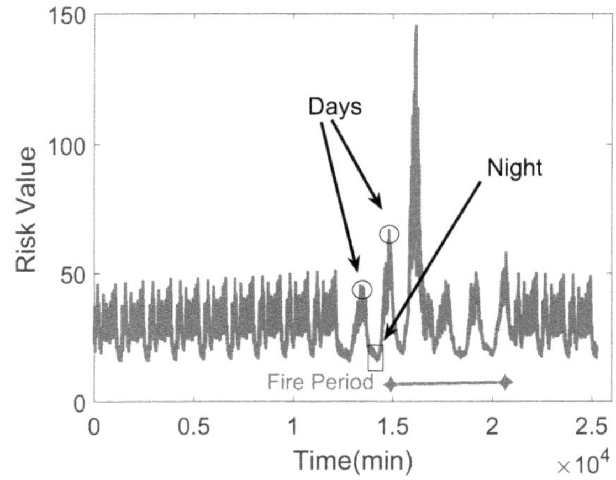

Figure 1: Wildfire risk values over 20 days of weather observations using FFDI

- The solution captures the temporal contextual changes in meteorological observations in determining the applicable risk model;
- The solution is completely unsupervised and it does not rely on expert knowledge or statistics, which makes it flexible and applicable to other areas of interest;
- Since the solution is based on an ensemble learning approach, it is robust and scalable so that it can potentially be parallelised to speed up computation.

This work follows from the project with Fire & Rescue NSW, the largest emergency management agency in Australia and one of the largest in the world, where we looked at the spatiotemporal dynamics of wildfire danger. One challenge we found was the inability of the current wildfire danger models (e.g. FFDI) to incorporate the spatiotemporal context in the modelling, and that issue is addressed in this proposal.

2. RELATED WORKS

There is a vast body of work modelling the risk of wildfires (a.k.a. bushfires) with diverse focus. Some investigate the likelihood of wildfires (that is, probability of ignition or probability of burning), while others study the intensity or effects of wildfires (based on ecological, social or economic values) [18]. This section reviews a few methods currently used for wildfire danger assessment and that are most relevant to the topic of current paper, that is real time assessment of changes in wildfire danger due to weather changes. We then present the McArthur Forest Fire Danger Index (FFDI), which is currently widely used by authorities in Australia and is the starting point for our proposal. Lastly, we highlight why a context based real time assessment of wildfire danger is required to supplement FFDI, and show the real world applicability of the proposed method.

Most of the wildfire danger prediction methods use meteorological observations sourced from weather stations (e.g. temperature, wind speed, wind gust, wind direction relative humidity, precipitations) together with other variables such as topography, vegetation type and vegetation density to predict the wildfire danger/risk for the given conditions based on empirical methods. For example:

- In USA, the National Fire Danger Rating System [11] uses current and historical weather data, fuel type as well as live and dead fuel moisture to come up with a danger rating. The model is 30 years old (1977-1978) and does not capture temporal or spatial dynamics of the meteorological information to fine-tune the model.

- The Canadian Forest Fire Weather Index (FWI) [9] is a numeric rating of wildfire intensity. It uses only four weather variables (temperature, relative humidity, wind speed and 24-hour rainfall) to determine a 'wildfire spread' index and a 'build up' index. These are based on consecutive daily observations of the four above-mentioned variables, and together they give the Fire Weather Index (FWI), used currently as the general index of wildfire danger in the Canadian forests.

In [12], the authors show that there is a correlation between wildfire occurrence and the effect of fuel moisture and thus the rating of wildfire danger. Where wildfire occurrence is given by the frequency of wildfires recorded in a historical period of time, with data often summarised for different time periods, often by daily, weekly, or monthly intervals to help depict variation in wildfire activity through out the season. To counter the issue of spatially limited data (e.g. received from sparse weather stations), a number of studies look at wildfire danger detection using sensor networks. For example, [26] propose a wireless sensor network where sensor nodes are used to collect the data (e.g. temperature, relative humidity) and submit the information to specific cluster nodes. The cluster nodes will then construct neural networks to produce a weather index showing the likelihood for the weather to cause a wildfire. The paper does not describe the actual model hence the spatiotemporal customisation of the model cannot be assessed. In [16], it is claimed that wildfire risk needs to consider both wildfire behaviour probability and effect. The former depends on the spatial and temporal factors controlling wildfire spread, including fuel and weather. Moreover, the authors investigate the burn probability based on historic wildfire data, and highlight the need to move beyond assumptions of spatial and temporal uniformity while modelling that probability. Their approach is in line with [15] that argues that localised spatial properties (topography, fuel, weather) produce local differences in the wildfire behaviour, hence local differences in wildfire risk. This is also in line with our argument towards a customisable model that can cater for local spatial and temporal differences in wildfire danger due to weather.

A scientist from the Commonwealth Scientific and Industrial Research Organisation (CSIRO) developed the McArthur Forest Fire Danger index in the 1960s to measure wildfire danger in Australian forests. The index is currently used by the authorities in Australia to calculate and broadcast wildfire danger ratings during summer. It is based on temperature, humidity, wind speed, dryness and fuel weight as shown in Equations 1 and 2 [21]:

$$FFDI_\gamma = 2e^{-0.45+0.987*ln(DF_\gamma)-0.0345H_\gamma+0.0338T_\gamma+0.0234V_\gamma} \tag{1}$$

$$DF_\gamma = \frac{0.191(I_\gamma + 104)(N_\gamma + 1)^{1.5}}{3.52(N_\gamma + 1)^{1.5} + Pre_\gamma - 1} \tag{2}$$

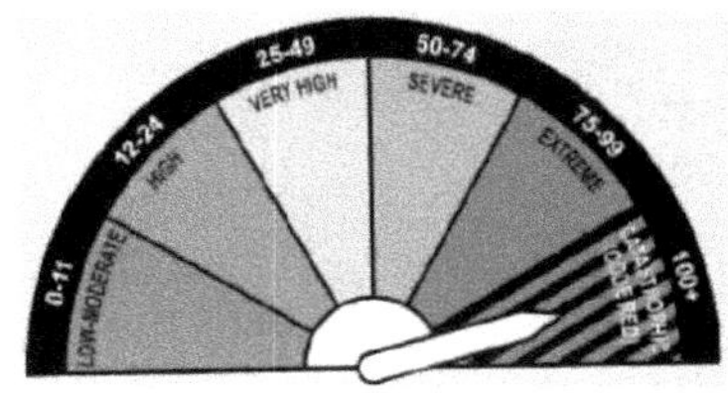

Figure 2: Wildfire Danger Categories in Australia (Figure reproduced from [4])

where H_γ is relative humidity, T_γ is air temperature, V_γ is average wind velocity in the open at the height of 10 m, $FFDI_\gamma$ is forest fire danger index and DF_γ is drought factor which uses precipitation observations Pre_γ, N_γ is time since rain and I_γ is soil's moisture content all at time γ.

The output FFDI values are further interpreted based on a defined categorisation. Figure 2 depicts the six different categories. Using the above equations and these categories, the Australian emergency management agencies find the relevant category and broadcast it daily.

As mentioned in the introduction, the main drawback of operational wildfire rating systems including FFDI is that the danger index is calculated based on the most current weather observations available, using a static model, and not customised to the particular location where the danger index is used. This determines a coarse variation between the danger indices of consecutive days and is not indicative of the temporal development of the wildfire danger conditions, which can be observed prior to wildfire events. To the best of our knowledge there are no current wildfire danger prediction frameworks that consider context-based spatiotemporal variations to fine-tune the models' parameters. Our results, from an Australian case study, show that our proposal does not contradict but rather augment FFDI, giving the decision makers more fine-grained information about the increasing wildfire danger and allowing them to take even better informed decision to protect communities and the environment.

3. OUR PROPOSED CONTEXT-BASED FIRE RISK (CBFR) MODEL

In this section we first formally define the problem, then explain the steps of our context-based fire risk prediction solution (CBFR) in detail.

3.1 Problem Definition

We consider the problem of wildfire risk prediction in dynamically changing environments based on meteorological observations. Specifically, let H be the relative humidity in %, T be the air temperature of the region in °C, V be the average wind velocity in the open at the height of 10 m in $km\ hr^{-1}$ and DF be the drought factor which uses precipitation observations Pre. DF is an indicator of amount of the soil moisture and covering layer of duff moisture in the region of interest R.

Assume that a set of streams of meteorological observations $P^R_{1:\Gamma}$ is collected over time period $[1..\Gamma]$ for a region R. Hence, at time γ a vector $P^R_\gamma = (H_\gamma, T_\gamma, V_\gamma, Pre_\gamma)$ is observed at region R. Our aim is to compute the wildfire risk of observation $CBFR_{P^R_{1..\Gamma}}$ for all of the given observations in a given region R. Note that to make the assumptions

Input: Meteorological data observations $P_{1:\Gamma}$
Context size W
Decaying parameter α
Output: Context-based fire risk $CBFR'_{1:\Gamma}$
$C(1) \longleftarrow Cluster(P_{1:W})$;`// set of clusters C`
$t \longleftarrow 1$;
while $t < \lfloor \frac{\Gamma}{W} \rfloor$ **do**
    `// cluster observations is current context`
    $C(t+1) \longleftarrow Cluster(P_{tW+1:(t+1)W})$;
    `// compute relevancy of historical context models`
    $w_{1:t+1} \longleftarrow Relevancy(C(t+1), C(1:t+1))$;
    foreach $\gamma \in \{tW+1 : (t+1)W\}$ **do**
        `// decay function` $g(x) = 1/x^{\alpha}$
        $$CBFR'_{P_\gamma} = \frac{\sum_{h=1}^{t+1} g(t+1-h) w_h Pr(P_\gamma | C(h))}{\sum_{h=1}^{t+1} g(t+1-h) w_h}$$
    end
    $FFDIfilter(P_{tW+1:(t+1)W})$
    $Smooth(P_{tW+1:(t+1)W})$
    $t \longleftarrow t+1$;
end
return $CBFR'_{1:\Gamma}$;

Algorithm 1: Context-Based Fire Risk (CBFR) Algorithm

more realistic, we consider that the meteorological observations are dynamically changing both temporally and spatially. In other words, first the stream of observations are changing during time, i.e. time changing behaviour can occur in finer-scale variation (e.g., daytime versus nigh-time), or even variations during daytime. Second, the stream of observations can change spatially in different regions.

3.2 Analytical components of our proposed risk model

To develop a predictive risk model, one of the big challenges is lack of label information for building supervised predictive models. In fact, we noticed that in case of wildfire risk, it is really not reasonable to identify which periods of time are risky and which of them are not. One might argue that using wildfire histories can be beneficial. However, we can still have high wildfire risk periods of time where there is no wildfire due to the lack of ignition in the area.

To deal with this challenge an unsupervised algorithm is needed for wildfire risk prediction, where high risk periods are identified without any statistics or expert knowledge. Since wildfire onset is a rare event in comparison to the entire history in time, we believe an anomaly detection algorithm can be a very good candidate solution, where the high risk days can be seen as anomalies and detected in an unsupervised manner. Moreover, to capture the temporal dynamicity of input data streams, our solution would benefit from a stream mining technique. Figure 3 depicts overall schema of the proposed risk model including the analytical components. Algorithm 1 shows the pseudocode of our CBFR model. In the following, we discuss different components of our model in detail.

3.2.1 Data sources

We developed our system based on weather data. Data sources can be any weather company which measures the variables mentioned in problem definition section. In the case study of this paper, weather data was provided by Fire & Rescue NSW from the Bureau of Meteorology (BoM) in Australia [1]. Although we evaluate our model using weather data, our model is not restricted to weather observations and we can incorporate other types of data e.g. vegetation type, fuel load and topographical data into the model to achieve more accurate results.

Reanalysis for high resolution: In addition to the above data sources we conduct a high resolution meteorological reanalysis, running local atmospheric models to resolve smaller phenomena and provide more detailed data than would otherwise be possible from observations. The simulation was conducted with the Weather and Research Forecasting model (WRF-ARW) [14]. The model outputs include temperature, precipitation, pressure, relative humidity and wind speed.

3.2.2 Identify context

As mentioned earlier, the temporal dynamics in input data streams is not considered by current operational wildfire risk systems. To deal with this challenge, we propose exploiting an online anomaly detection algorithm. In addition, we need to deal with the non-stationarity of temporal weather observations in the input data as well. Hence, the proposed online algorithm in this paper should be able to adapt to the non-stationarity behaviour of data.

This can be solved by modelling different contexts in the underlying behaviour of input data stream separately and maintain multiple models over time.

Definition 1. **Context** is a specific period of time in which weather observations remain roughly stationary.

Thus in this step, we identify the defined context based on available resolution of input data. For instance, we may consider day context versus night context in weather observations. If we have finer granularity input data, we can further decompose the temporal context into morning, noon, afternoon, evening and etc. The number of weather observations in a context is denoted by parameter W.

3.2.3 Contextual-Based Anomaly Detection

After identifying the required context and parameter W, we need an anomaly detection algorithm that captures the temporal dynamicity in weather data streams to detect the anomalous patterns (high risk) periods. Our solution is to use an ensemble based anomaly detection algorithm which is proposed for dynamically changing data streams [23]. Figure 3 shows the schematic of this unsupervised learning algorithm in the bottom left of the figure. By dividing data streams into different data chunks based on their contexts, we are able to build anomaly detectors for each context (day and night in Figure 3) separately. Each of these anomaly detectors is a risk predictor. In the current temporal context (last 'night' in the bottom of Figure 3), all relevant historical predictors are considered and a decision on the risk value of current observations are made by participating only the relevant models. We further discuss the subcomponents of this algorithm:

- **Clustering:** A clustering-based anomaly detection technique is used to profile the weather observations for

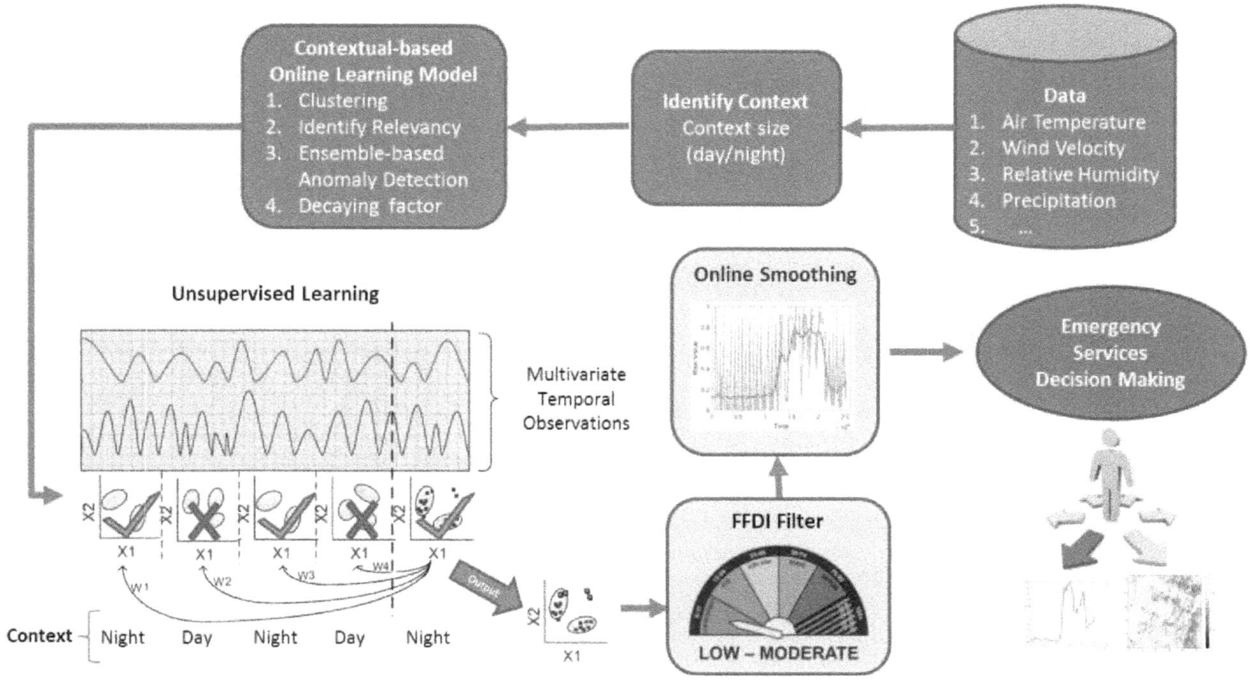

Figure 3: The analytical components of our proposed risk model

each temporal context with size W (called a data chunk). Using a density-based clustering algorithm such as [20] enables on one hand to detect the number of clusters dynamically and on the other hand to speed up the algorithm to near linear. The output of this clustering algorithm is a set of hyper-ellipsoidal boundaries for the current data context. Let $C(t)$ be the tth (current) set of hyper-ellipsoidal boundaries or data clusters. Hence for the tth historical data chunk we only store the clusters centers c^t and covariance matrices Σ^t.

- **Identify relevancy:** To select relevant historical contexts with the current context, at this step we compare the similarity of hyperellipsoidal boundaries of the current model with historical models. The similarity between two hyperellipsoids is computed using a distance measure called focal distance. Interested readers can refer to [19] for more details on this distance measure. The bottom left of Figure 3 depicts this step. In this figure the similarities between the current clustering model and all historical clustering models are computed and weights of similarity are computed (i.e. w_h, $0 < h < t$). Let dis_h be the distance between a past clustering model $C(h)$ and a current clustering model $C(t)$, then $w_h = \begin{cases} \frac{1}{dis_h} & \text{if } dist_h \neq 0 \\ 1 & \text{if } dist_h = 0 \end{cases}$.

- **Ensemble-based anomaly detection:** In this step we incorporate the most relevant historical clustering models and use their weights to compute an anomalous value for all of the weather observations in the current context. Selecting relevant historical models leads to a more effective risk prediction model. Given a set of clusters $C(t)$ and a weather observation P_γ at time γ, an anomalous value of P_γ is computed using the mahalanobis distance of P_γ and all clusters in $C(t)$. The mahalanobis distance of an observation P_γ to i^{th} cluster in $C(t)$ with center c_i^t and covariance Σ_i^t is computed as following:

$$(P_\gamma - c_i^t)^T(\Sigma_i^t)^{-1}(P_\gamma - c_i^t) \tag{3}$$

Using the above formula, if an observation P_γ falls into the .95 percent covered by at least one of the clusters (hyperellipses) in $C(t)$ we do not consider the observation as anomaly, i.e., $Pr(P_\gamma|C(t)) = 0$. Otherwise it is equal to 1.

Finally, an ensemble of relevant (weighted) historical models is used in assigning final anomalous values to the current observations. Given a weather observation P_γ at time γ, the final context-based wildfire risk (or anomalous) value $CBFR_{P_\gamma}$ is computed using all t clustering models $C(h)$ $(0 < h \leq t)$. More specifically:

$$CBFR_{P_\gamma} = \frac{\sum_{h=1}^{t} w_h Pr(P_\gamma|C(h))}{\sum_{h=1}^{t} w_h} \tag{4}$$

- **Identify decaying factor:** We are running our risk model on each weather station and the available memory is limited per station. By modelling the incoming weather data streams, we produce an infinite number of clustering models or profiles over time. This can be problematic both in terms of required memory and time. To deal with this problem, we define a decaying factor [13] which limits the number of clustering models to be stored in memory. We define a *polynomial* decay function $g(x) = 1/x^\alpha$ for a parameter α and $x \geq 0$. Other than relevancy weights which are identified in the above paragraphs, the temporal importance of each clustering model can be calculated as well. At t^{th} step of the clustering model, the importance of historical models h $(0 < h \leq t)$ is computed as $g(t-h)$. Hence the final risk value by integrating the decaying factor is computed using the following:

$$CBFR'_{P_\gamma} = \frac{\sum_{h=1}^{t} g(t-h) w_h Pr(P_\gamma | C(h))}{\sum_{h=1}^{t} g(t-h) w_h} \quad (5)$$

3.2.4 FFDI filter

In order to avoid the false positive rates of our anomaly detection solution in very rare cold days, we suggest using the current operational FFDI system as a filter to our model. This can be simply done by computing the FFDI values for incoming weather observations. If these values fall in one of the top five categories (i.e. high, very high, severe, extreme or catastrophic) according to Figure 2, we keep the wildfire risk values ($CBFR'_{P_\gamma}$) intact. Otherwise, we set the values to zero.

3.2.5 Linear regression smoothing

In this step of the algorithm, while we have the risk values for the current window observations, we smooth the output in order to find a pattern. By smoothing, we can better identify the temporal sequence of risk values. We use 'locally weighted' linear regression smoothing method in this component and a stream of risk values is produced as output.

3.2.6 Scalability of CBFR

The computational complexity of analytical components in CBFR is near linear with respect to the number of weather observations. This matches the real-time requirement of our risk prediction problem. Also CBFR is scalable and we can further speedup the algorithm by parallelising the computation of 'relevancy identification' and 'incorporation of historical data profiles' steps of the algorithm.

4. EVALUATION OF OUR PROPOSED MODEL IN BLUE MOUNTAINS NATIONAL PARK- AUSTRALIA

In this section, we compare our proposed model with the operational McArthur FFDI method described in Section 2.

4.1 Blue Mountains National Park Dataset

The dataset we used in this case study is the meteorological data provided by Fire & Rescue NSW from the Blue Mountains region. The reason why we chose this area for study is that a severe wildfires occurred in this area in 2013 from October 17 until October 21. These days are considered as anomalies and the proportion of anomalies and normal observations in this dataset is 7%. The dataset consists of temperature, relative humidity, wind speed and precipitation measurements from three different BoM weather stations located in this area (Mt Victoria, Richmond Raaf and Penrith Lake). Figure 4 shows the mentioned locations in Blue Mountains of these weather stations. The meteorological measurements are taken every 1 minute and there are 300K observations in total from all stations.

Moreover, we created a higher spatial resolution dataset using our reanalysis model. The model consisted of 3 domains nested at 3:1 grid size ratio, the inner domain had a grid spacing of 5 km and covers an area of 275 km × 275 km centered on the town of Blackheath (-34.80, 138.90) in the Blue Mountains region.

The reanalysis simulated 96 hours from the start of October 13, 2013 UTC to the end of October 17, 2013 UTC. The model was initialised and forced with boundary conditions provided by ERA-Interim reanalysis, this analysis is a global atmospheric reanalysis produced by the European Center for Medium-Range Weather Forecasts (ECMWF), it uses a 30 minutes time step and has a spectral T255 horizontal resolution which is about a 79km and a vertical resolution of 60 layers [14]. The simulation output is provided at frequency of 1 minute.

4.2 Performance measures

In order to compare our model with the operational FFDI, we have used different performance measures: (1) Since our proposed model's output is a fuzzy value between 0 and 1, we used the Area Under ROC curve (AUC) to find the accuracy of our model. The output value of FFDI on the other hand, is a value between 0 to 100+. To compare our model with FFDI, we consider the trend of both FFDI and CBFR values. (2) The second performance measure is accuracy ($\frac{TPos+TNeg}{Pos+Neg}$), where $TPos$ is the number of true positives (the number of episodes that the high risk of wildfire is predicted correctly), $TNeg$ is the number of true negatives (the number of episodes that the low risk of wildfire is predicted correctly), Pos is the number of total episodes where risk of wildfire is high and Neg is the number of total episodes where risk of wildfire is not high. (3) The third performance measure is sensitivity ($\frac{TPos}{Pos}$), which is the ratio of predicting the high risk of wildfire correctly. And finally, (4) Youden Index, which is an optimal point on AUC. This is the farthest point from diagonal line and is computed as following [25]:

$$max(\frac{Sensitivity + Specificity - 1}{\sqrt{2}}) \quad (6)$$

where sensitivity is computed from above, and specificity is $\frac{TNeg}{Neg}$.

4.3 Effectiveness of our CBFR Approach

We apply our proposed CBFR approach on the Blue Mountains dataset. In other words, all of the analytical components and subcomponents of our CBFR model (including, decaying factor, FFDI filter and linear regression smoothing) are applied on the Blue Mountains dataset and the final risk values are calculated for each episode of time in this dataset (every minute). Hence the effectiveness and predictability measures which will be shown in this section, indicate how well the combination of all of these components perform.

According to granularity of the observations (measurements are taken every 1 minute), we decided to set the window size equal to the number of observations which are measured over daytime and nighttime. A total number of 720 observations are measured during each day/night. The reason in selecting such window size is that we want to distinguish between the clustering models of nighttime and daytime. So if the weather is bad in the nighttime context, our model outputs high values which predicts a high wildfire risk in the next day. Whereas in the current FFDI model, the index is computed based on the weather data and independent of the temporal occurrence of historical observations.

While in this case study, we have used nighttime and daytime length as a window size, there might be some important and valuable variations in the daytime as well. Hence, if given higher frequency observations (e.g. every 30 or 10

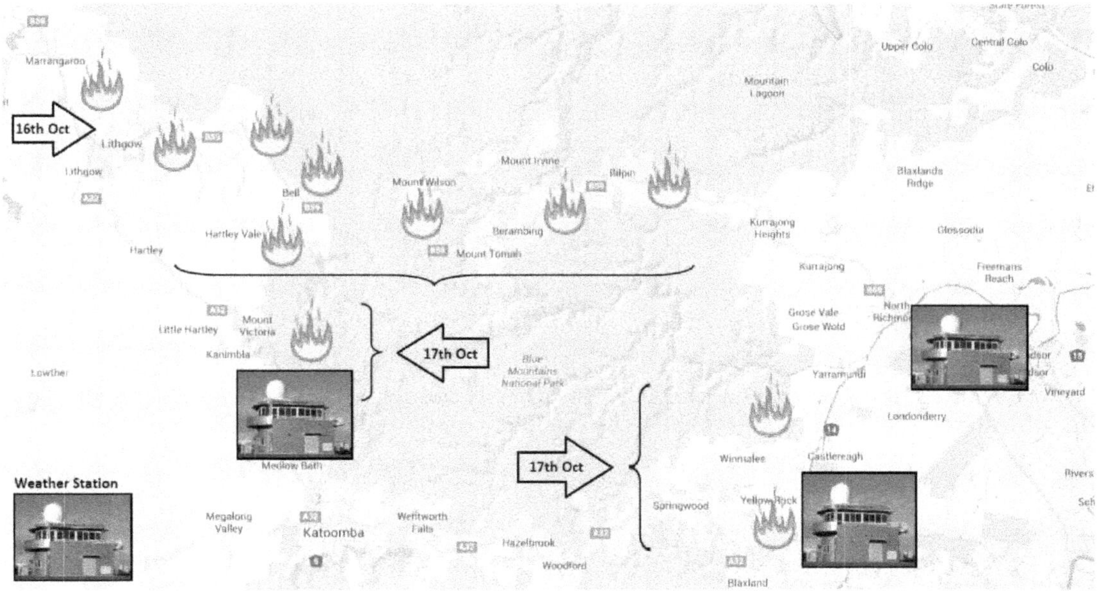

Figure 4: The temporal changes in wildfire onset, Blue mountains region (Figure reproduced from [1, 7])

seconds), multiple models can also be considered for a day that represent different variations in various times. The parameter α in decaying function is set to 2 and we delete the historical data profiles with very low decaying function values to constraint memory and time complexity.

Note that in order to evaluate our model we need to have the ground truth. However, in this specific application, it is very difficult to find the ground truth. One alternative that is used in the literature of disaster management is to label the onset of disasters as high risk episodes. While the episodes of disasters (wildfire in this paper) represent high risk episodes, there might be some other days that have high risk of onset of wildfire, but because no ignition occurs, no wildfire starts. In these situations it is difficult to evaluate whether the proposed model is able to find them as high risk episodes or not. In order to find a more accurate ground truth to evaluate our model with, we decided to further investigate the area of interest.

Figure 4 shows the wildfire onset in different days based on the information provided in the governmental website [3]. On October 16, a wildfire was accidentally sparked in Marrangaroo (top-left of the figure) which continued to travel to the northern regions of Blue Mountains national park. The next day, two major wildfires were reported in the south east (Mount Victoria) and south west (Springwood). These areas are depicted with flames and labeled as '17th Oct' in Figure 4. The sparked wildfires were reported to continue burning until October 21.

Given the wildfire history of the region, we consider two different scenarios for the evaluation purposes:

- **Scenario I**: In this scenario, we follow the evaluation method that is used in literature. This means we use the exact wildfire onset (i.e. October 17 to October 21) to determine which temporal periods of time have high risk.
- **Scenario II**: As mentioned above, a wildfire had already started in the vicinity of the area of interest one day before the wildfire onset (October 16). Hence, in this second scenario we consider October 16 as a high risk day as well. We believe this can be a more realistic assumption.

In both above scenarios, the episodes are labeled based on the presence of wildfire, weather temperature, relative humidity and wind speed. Considering these two scenarios, we want to see how our proposed model is performing in comparison to FFDI model.

For the evaluation purposes, first we applied both our model and FFDI to all observations and compared the output risk of both models. The aim here is to find which model can reflect the high wildfire risk days more accurately. Considering the Scenario I, Figure 5a-c depict the AUC results for three different stations in our area of interest. Each point on the ROC Curve is relevant to sensitivity and 1-specificity of both models considering a certain threshold. The three solid graphs in Figure 5a-c show the results of our model and the three dashed graphs show the results of FFDI method. It is shown that in all three stations, the detection accuracy of wildfire risk by our CBFR model is substantially higher than using the current operational FFDI.

4.3.1 *Predictability*

Considering Scenario II, the aim is to evaluate the predictability of our CBFR model. Figure 6a-c depict the AUC results for three different weather stations in the area of interest. The three solid graphs in Figure 6a-c correspond to the results of our model and the dashed graphs show the results of FFDI method. While the AUC of detecting risk of wildfire by our model is higher than using the current operational FFDI, we noticed that the AUC of our model is either roughly the same as previous scenario for Mt Victoria, or increased by 7% and 8% in Richmond Raaf (Figure 6b) and Penrith Lake (Figure 6c) receptively. Nevertheless, for the FFDI model, the AUC in Mount Victoria increased by 7% but in Richmond Raaf and Penrith Lake, the AUC has

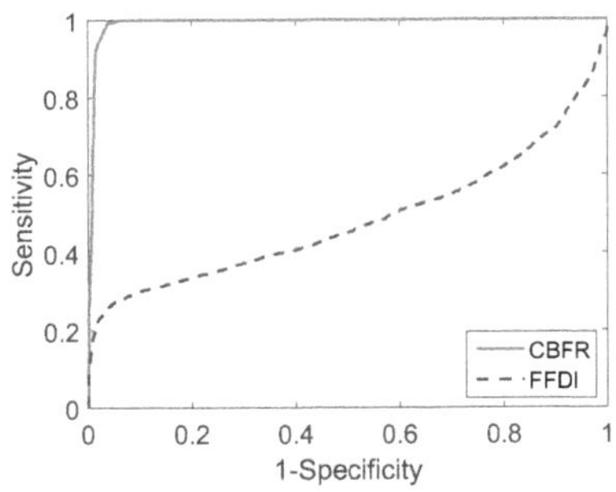

(a) Mount Victoria

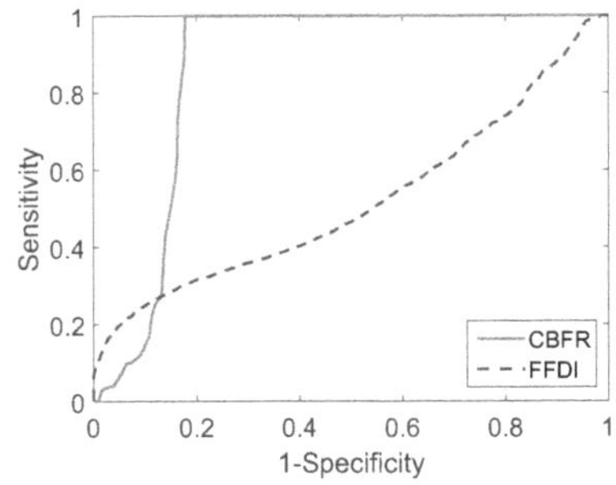

(b) Penrith Lakes

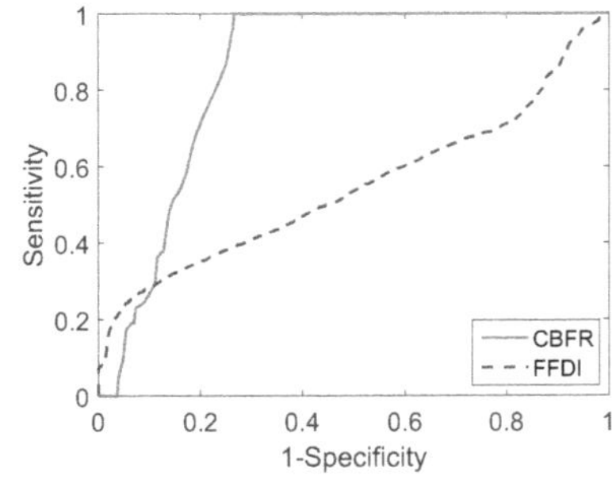

(c) Richmond Raaf

Figure 5: Scenario I Results: Comparing AUC of our CBFR model with FFDI model for all three weather stations. The solid lines represent CBFR while the dashed graphs represent FFDI.

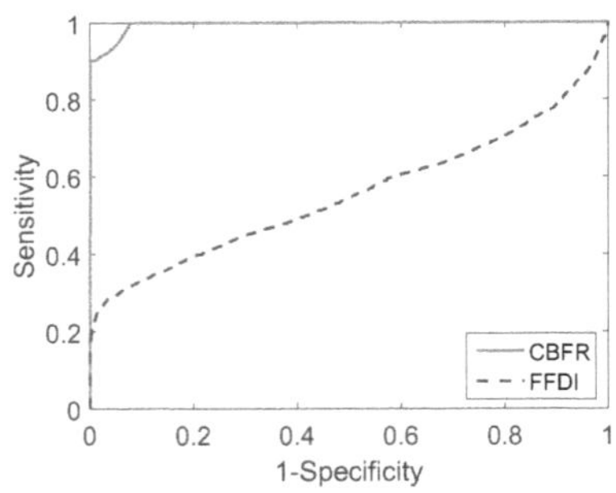

(a) Mount Victoria

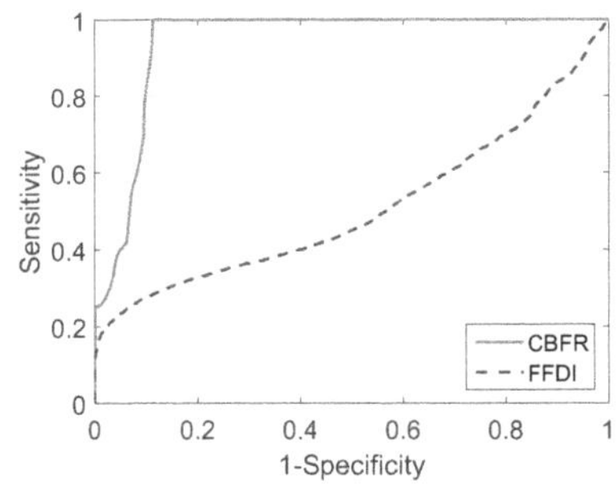

(b) Penrith Lakes

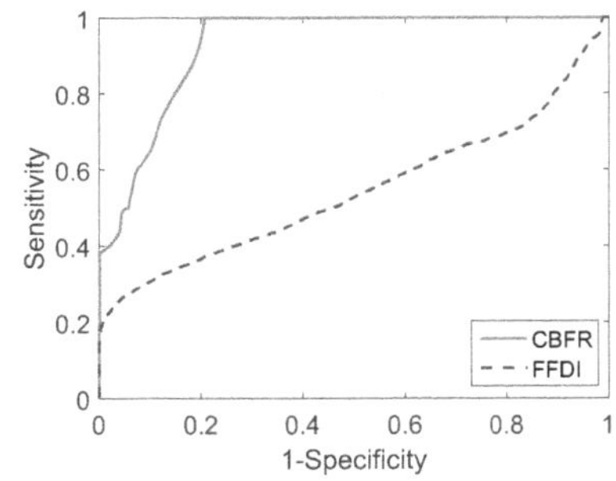

(c) Richmond Raaf

Figure 6: Scenario II Results: Comparing AUC of our CBFR model with FFDI model for all three weather stations. The solid lines represent CBFR while the dashed graphs represent FFDI.

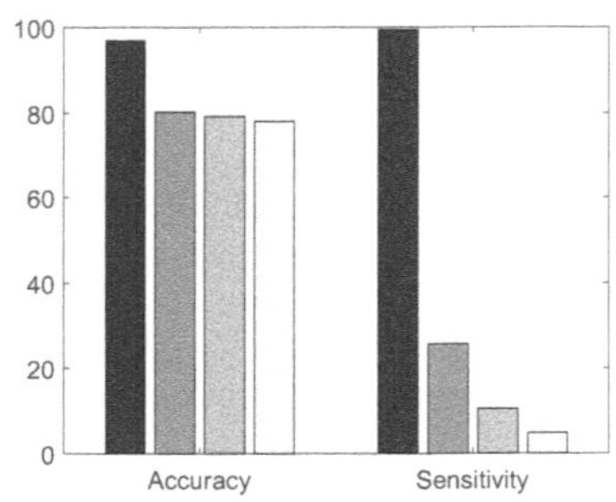

(a) Mount Victoria

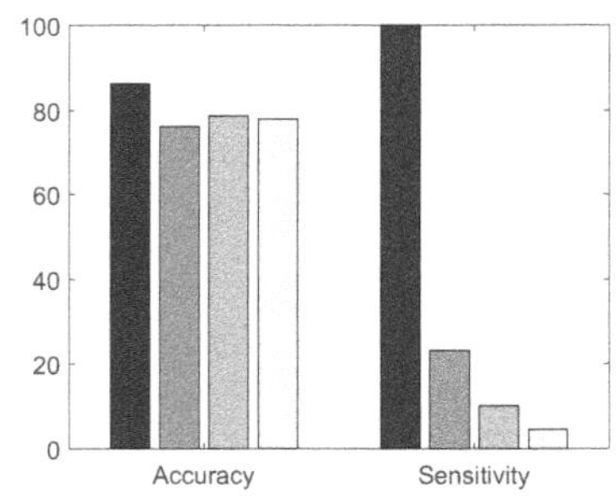

(b) Penrith Lakes

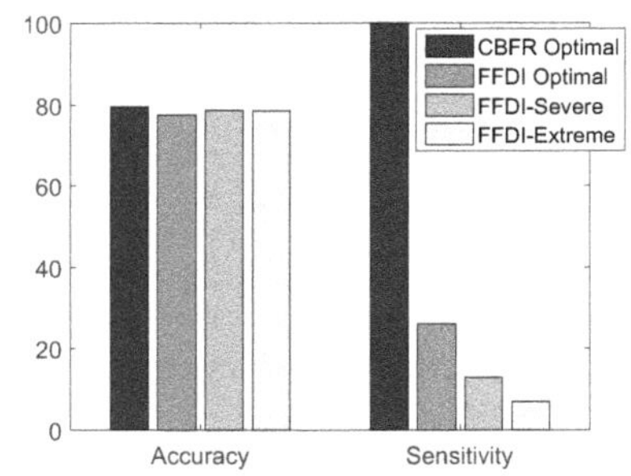

(c) Richmond Raaf

Figure 7: Scenario I Results: Comparing accuracy and sensitivity of CBFR model with FFDI model. Since the fires are rare events, the accuracy is biased towards not-wildfire events and that is why the accuracy comparisons are close even though the CBFR model is more sensitive that the FFDI model.

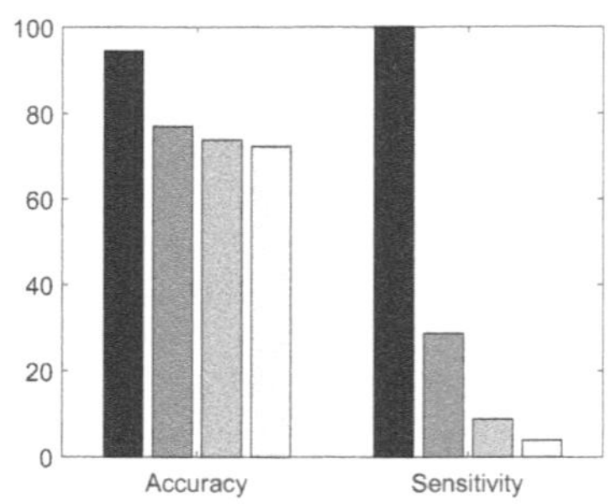

(a) Mount Victoria

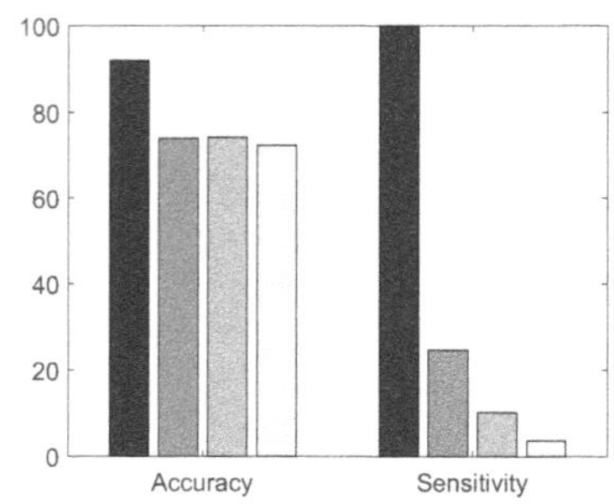

(b) Penrith Lakes

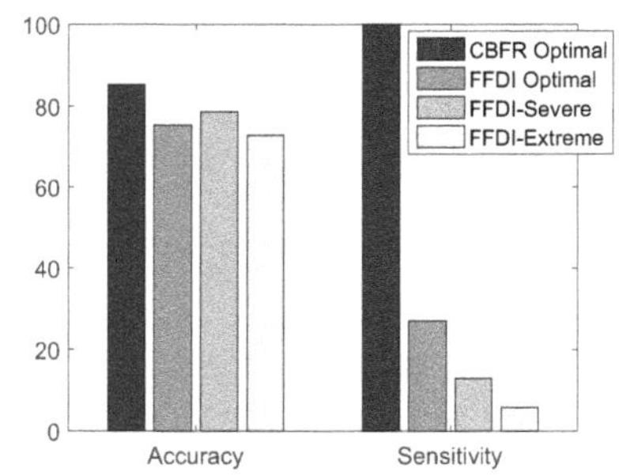

(c) Richmond Raaf

Figure 8: Scenario II Results: Comparing accuracy and sensitivity of CBFR model with FFDI model

even decreased by 2% (Figure 6b) and 1% (Figure 6c) respectively.

Lastly, by comparing the results of both scenarios (Figure 5 and Figure 6) it is clear that the AUC of FFDI drops in Scenario II, which shows that it fails to predict the wildfire risk patterns in advance. The AUC of CBFR on the other hand increases and hence it is more effective in predicting the wildfire risk.

4.4 Considering Risk Threshold

In this section we show how incorporating the FFDI categorisation could help in predicting the wildfire risk. As mentioned earlier, Figure 2 depicts the categorisation and interpretation of different values of the FFDI model. Currently the last two categories, namely *extreme* (FFDI values between 75 and 99) and *catastrophic* (FFDI values above 100) are introduced as very hot, dry and windy conditions for a wildfire in Australia and hence the periods with such characteristics are declared as total fire ban periods. This interpretation however can vary in different states of Australia and sometimes the fourth category i.e., *severe* is also considered as a very bad wildfire condition. Hence, to set a threshold and further evaluate the FFDI's output, we consider both *severe* (above 50) and *extreme* (above 75) as thresholds and further compute the measures introduced in Section 4.2.

In addition we compute the optimal point of ROC curves for both CBFR and FFDI to see how the performance measures change by setting a fixed threshold. Figure 7a-c show the results of setting thresholds for both methods in all three different regions for Scenario I. Similarly, Figure 8a-c depicts the same graphs for scenario II. Our method's optimal point has a very high accuracy and sensitivity in both scenarios and in all regions. FFDI on the other hand, has lower accuracy in all scenarios and regions. Moreover, it has a very low sensitivity, which suggests that it is not able to predict the high risk periods of time. The results comply with the design of the FFDI model. As mentioned in Section 2, this model originally designed for a specific episode in a day without considering spatiotemporal variations.

While all the above results correspond to the dataset provided from Bureau of Meteorology (BoM) in Australia, Figure 9 shows the visualisation of the risk results by CBFR model for the dataset reproduced by high resolution meteorological reanalysis described in Section 3.2.1. As an example, we depict the results at a specific time (12:00:00pm on 16th October 2013), which is related to 12 hours before the actual wildfire in the Blue Mountains. Three arrows in this figure point to the three weather stations depicted in Figure 4. Note that here while building the model, only temporal context is considered.

This visualisation helps in identifying the whole central, northern and western areas on the figure as being at high risk, with a greater level of detail, while FFDI failed to identity all of these areas at risk and only flagged some increased risk in the areas that were already on fire at the time, north of Blue Mountains.

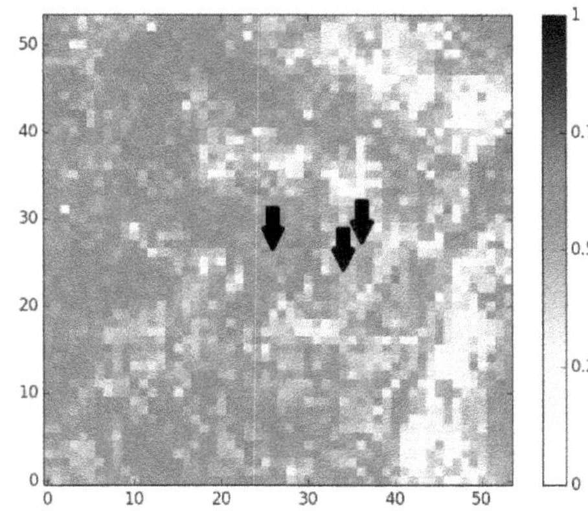

Figure 9: Fire risk values of CBFR model at 12:00:00pm on 16th October 2013- Blue Mountains National Park is located in the center

5. DISCUSSION

In this paper we discussed the problem of wildfire risk prediction using meteorological observations. The first and most significant challenge in this problem is lack of data labels. This is difficult both in terms of designing effective analytical models on one hand, and evaluating the models on the other hand. Even using the past wildfire histories cannot be completely sufficient as there might be some periods of time without a wildfire history but with high wildfire risk. In this paper we propose using an unsupervised learning algorithm (anomaly detection) as a candidate solution to this problem. Our solution does not rely on label information or expert knowledge.

The next challenge is temporal and contextual changes in meteorological observations. The existing operational models or the state-of-the-art methods in wildfire risk literature either focus on the current weather observations and use a mathematical model to estimate the wildfire risk or use the whole historical observations to model risk. However, due to the temporal changes in the context of weather observations, in this paper we proposed to maintain multiple model of historical observations for different contexts. As a result, our context-based fire risk (CBFR) model can predict a high risk day just in advance with 85-90% accuracy and 99% sensitivity in average. Figure 10 shows an example of a situation where our CBFR model estimates high risk values before the actual wildfire period, whereas the operational wildfire danger rating system in Australia postpones it to the actual wildfire day.

One lesson learned from this work was that old models that are used in various contexts and industries can benefit from applying modern analytics techniques (in this case a context-based anomaly detection algorithm) to augment the type of knowledge they can produce and positively impact the final outcome for the benefit of the user (in this case community as a final user of the danger risk prediction techniques). Potential clients of our proposed CBFR model are decision makers in emergency management agencies. Using the CBFR model can significantly help them predict high risk days beforehand and enable them to plan strategically in advance. Wildfire risk values can be also produced in variety of spatial resolutions, which gives decision makers a better understanding of wildfire risk at a high spatial as well as temporal resolution in real-time.

While the proposed CBFR model has a linear time complexity and considers the memory constraints in meteorological stations, we intend to develop the parallelised version of this model using Spark to further speedup the algo-

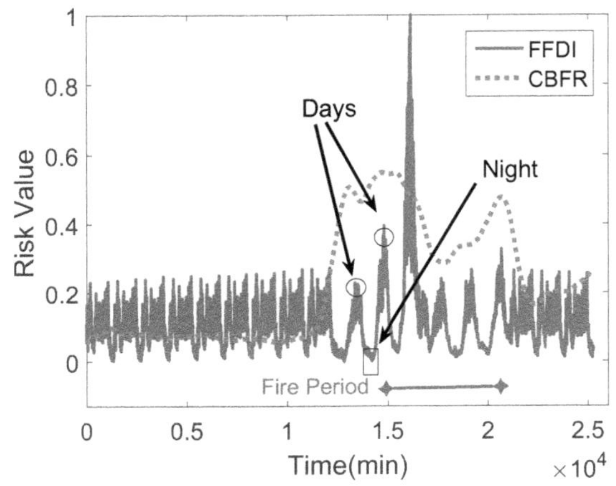

Figure 10: Fire risk values over 20 days of weather observations: FFDI versus CBFR models

rithm. Moreover, spatially specific features (such as vegetation type, fuel load and elevation) can be included as an input to the CBFR algorithm to produce more sophisticated and accurate wildfire risk values in the property levels. We also intend to test our CBFR model on other areas and apply contemporary anomaly detection approaches in comparison to our proposed model.

6. REFERENCES

[1] Australian bureau of meteorology weather stations. http://www.bom.gov.au/climate/cdo/about/sites.shtml.

[2] Australian bureau of meteorology weather stations. http://www.bom.gov.au/vic/forecasts/fire-map.shtml.

[3] Australian emergency management knowledge hub. https://www.emknowledge.gov.au/resource/4781/2013/bushfire-new-south-wales-2013.

[4] Australian fire danger ratings. http://www.esa.act.gov.au/wp-content/uploads/fire-danger-ratings.pdf.

[5] Black saturday bushfires. https://en.wikipedia.org/wiki/black saturday bushfires.

[6] Emergency management victoria strategic action plan. https://www.emv.vic.gov.au/plans/strategic-action-plan/.

[7] Google maps. https://www.google.com.au/maps.

[8] The human cost of natural disasters 2015: a global perspective, http://reliefweb.int/report/world/human-cost-natural-disasters-2015-global-perspective.

[9] Natural resources canada. http://cwfis.cfs.nrcan.gc.ca/background/summary/fwi.

[10] The united nations office for disaster risk reduction, http://www.unisdr.org/archive/42814.

[11] Wildland fire assessment system. fire danger rating. http://www.wfas.net/index.php/fire-danger-rating-fire-potential–danger-32.

[12] P. L. Andrews, D. O. Loftsgaarden, and L. S. Bradshaw. Evaluation of fire danger rating indexes using logistic regression and percentile analysis. *International Journal of Wildland Fire*, 12(2):213–226, 2003.

[13] E. Cohen and M. Strauss. Maintaining time-decaying stream aggregates. In *ACM SIGMOD symposium on Principles of database systems*, pages 223–233, 2003.

[14] D. Dee, S. Uppala, A. Simmons, P. Berrisford, P. Poli, S. Kobayashi, U. Andrae, M. Balmaseda, G. Balsamo, P. Bauer, et al. The era-interim reanalysis: Configuration and performance of the data assimilation system. *Quarterly Journal of the Royal Meteorological Society*, 137(656):553–597, 2011.

[15] C. A. Farris, C. Pezeshki, and L. F. Neuenschwander. A comparison of fire probability maps derived from gis modeling and direct simulation techniques. In *Joint Fire Science Conference and Workshop*, pages 131–138, 1999.

[16] M. A. Finney. The challenge of quantitative risk analysis for wildland fire. *Forest Ecology and Management*, 211(1):97–108, 2005.

[17] A. G. McArthur. Fire behaviour in eucalypt forests. 1967.

[18] C. Miller and A. A. Ager. A review of recent advances in risk analysis for wildfire management. *International journal of wildland fire*, 22(1):1–14, 2013.

[19] M. Moshtaghi, T. C. Havens, J. C. Bezdek, L. Park, C. Leckie, S. Rajasegarar, J. M. Keller, and M. Palaniswami. Clustering ellipses for anomaly detection. *Pattern Recognition*, 44(1):55–69, 2011.

[20] M. Moshtaghi, S. Rajasegarar, C. Leckie, and S. Karunasekera. An efficient hyperellipsoidal clustering algorithm for resource-constrained environments. *Pattern Recognition*, 44(9):2197–2209, 2011.

[21] I. Noble, A. Gill, and G. Bary. Mcarthur's fire-danger meters expressed as equations. *Australian Journal of Ecology*, 5(2):201–203, 1980.

[22] B. Saglam, E. Bilgili, B. Dincdurmaz, A. I. Kadiogulari, and Ö. Küçük. Spatio-temporal analysis of forest fire risk and danger using landsat imagery. *Sensors*, 8(6):3970–3987, 2008.

[23] M. Salehi, C. A. Leckie, M. Moshtaghi, and T. Vaithianathan. A relevance weighted ensemble model for anomaly detection in switching data streams. In *Advances in Knowledge Discovery and Data Mining*, pages 461–473. 2014.

[24] C. Vasilakos, K. Kalabokidis, J. Hatzopoulos, and I. Matsinos. Identifying wildland fire ignition factors through sensitivity analysis of a neural network. *Natural hazards*, 50(1):125–143, 2009.

[25] B. Vidakovic. *Statistics for bioengineering sciences: with MATLAB and WinBUGS support.* Springer Science & Business Media, 2011.

[26] L. Yu, N. Wang, and X. Meng. Real-time forest fire detection with wireless sensor networks. In *International Conference on Wireless Communications, Networking and Mobile Computing*, volume 2, pages 1214–1217, 2005.

Deep Crossing: Web-Scale Modeling without Manually Crafted Combinatorial Features

Ying Shan, T. Ryan Hoens, Jian Jiao, Haijing Wang, Dong Yu*, JC Mao
Bing Ads, Microsoft Research*
Microsoft Corporation
One Microsoft Way, Redmond, WA

ABSTRACT

Manually crafted combinatorial features have been the "secret sauce" behind many successful models. For web-scale applications, however, the variety and volume of features make these manually crafted features expensive to create, maintain, and deploy. This paper proposes the *Deep Crossing* model which is a deep neural network that automatically combines features to produce superior models. The input of Deep Crossing is a set of individual features that can be either dense or sparse. The important crossing features are discovered implicitly by the networks, which are comprised of an embedding and stacking layer, as well as a cascade of *Residual Units*.

Deep Crossing is implemented with a modeling tool called the Computational Network Tool Kit (CNTK), powered by a multi-GPU platform. It was able to build, from scratch, two web-scale models for a major paid search engine, and achieve superior results with only a sub-set of the features used in the production models. This demonstrates the potential of using Deep Crossing as a general modeling paradigm to improve existing products, as well as to speed up the development of new models with a fraction of the investment in feature engineering and acquisition of deep domain knowledge.

Keywords

Neural Networks, Deep Learning, Convolutional Neural Network (CNN), Deep Crossing, Combinatorial Features, DSSM, Residual Net, CNTK, GPU, Multi-GPU Platform

1. INTRODUCTION

Traditional machine learning algorithms are supposed to make the best use of all input features to predict and classify new instances. However simply using raw features rarely provides optimal results. Therefore in both industry and academia, there exists a large body of work on engineering the transformation of raw features. One major type of transformation is to construct functions based on a combination of multiple features, and use their output as the input to a learner. These *combinatorial features*[1] are sometimes called *cross features*, or *multi-way features*.

Combinatorial features are powerful tools, especially in the hands of domain experts. In our own experiences with a major sponsored search engine, they are among the strongest features in many models. In the Kaggle community, top data scientists are the masters of crafting such features, even crossing three to five dimensions[2]. The intuition and the ability to create effective combinatorial features is an essential ingredient in their winning formulas. In the computer vision community, SIFT-like [13] features were the key drivers behind the then state-of-the-art performance of ImageNet competitions. SIFT features are extracted on image patches and are special forms of combinatorial features.

The power of combinatorial features comes with high cost. There is a steep learning curve to climb before an individual can start to create meaningful features. As the number of features grows, managing, maintaining, and deploying them becomes challenging. In web-scale applications, finding additional combinatorial features to improve an existing model is a daunting task due to the large search space, and the slow turnaround in the training and evaluation cycle given billions of samples.

Deep Learning [9, 20, 16] carries the promise of learning from individual features without manual intervention [17, 21]. Speech [8, 4, 18] and image recognition [11] were among the first to demonstrate this potential. Convolution kernels learned from specific tasks through deep Convolutional Neural Networks (CNN) have replaced the hand-crafted SIFT-like features as the state-of-the-art in image recognition. A similar model [3] has been applied to NLP applications to build language processing models from scratch without extensive feature engineering.

Deep Crossing extends the success of deep learning to a more general setting where individual features are of a different nature. More specifically, it takes in individual features such as text, categorical, ID, and numerical features, and searches for the optimal combinations automatically based on the specific task. Furthermore, Deep Crossing is designed to handle web-scale applications and data sizes. This is not only because the authors are primarily interested in such applications, but also because there are not many options for general purpose models operating at this scale. It is

[1]See Sec. 4 for a formal definition and concrete examples.
[2]See github.com/owenzhang/Kaggle-AmazonChallenge2013 for an example of multi-way features in Owen Zhang's winning solution for the Amazon's Employee Access Challenge.

KDD '16, August 13-17, 2016, San Francisco, CA, USA

DOI: http://dx.doi.org/10.1145/2939672.2939704

Feature name	Type	Dimension
Query	Text	49,292
Keyword	Text	49,292
Title	Text	49,292
MatchType	Category	4
CampaignID	ID	10,001
CampaignIDCount	Numerical	5

Table 1: Examples of individual features

worth noting that Deep Crossing does in some way generate combinatorial features during the learning process, although the output of Deep Crossing is a model that does not have explicit representations for these features.

2. RELATED WORK

The idea of learning deep neural network without manually crafted features is not new. In early 80s, Fukushima [6] reported a seven-layer Neocognitron network that recognized digits from raw pixels of images. By utilizing a partially connected structure, Neocognitron achieved shift invariance which is an important property for visual recognition tasks. CNN was invented by LeCun et. al. [12] in the late 90s with a similar architecture, especially the partially connected convolution kernels. Despite the solid foundation of CNN as a recognition engine, classifiers based on SIFT-like [13] features dominated image recognition for nearly a decade. In 2012, Krizhevsky et. al. proposed the AlexNet [11] that beat the SIFT-based baseline error rate by almost 11 absolute percentage points. Recently, a 152-layer Residual Net [7] won both the ImageNet and the MS COCO Competitions in 2015.

The evolution of deep CNN is both inspiring and encouraging. It demonstrated that deep learning is able to improve even in systems in which the best manual features have been finely tuned over a decade. In other words, even the most experienced domain experts could miss the deep interactions among features that were captured by deep CNNs using task-specific filters. Realizing this has profound implications on our work on Deep Crossing.

Deep Semantic Similarity Model (DSSM) [10] learns the semantic similarity between a pair of text strings, each represented by a sparse representation called tri-letter grams. The learning algorithm optimizes an objective function based on cosine distance by embedding the tri-letter grams into two vectors. The learned embedding captures the semantic meaning of words and sentences, and has been applied to sponsored search, question answering, and machine translation with strong results.

Factorization Machines (FM) [15] in their general form models d-way interactions among individual features. In the presence of very sparse inputs, FM shows better results than SVMs but it's unclear how it performs on dense features.

For NLP tasks, [3] built a unified neural network architecture that avoids task-specific feature engineering. Deep Crossing aims at a broader range of input features.

3. SPONSORED SEARCH

Deep Crossing is discussed in the context of *sponsored search* of a major search engine. Readers can refer to [5] for an overview on this subject. In brief, sponsored search is responsible for showing ads alongside organic search results. There are three major agents in the ecosystem: the user, the advertiser, and the search platform. The goal of the platform is to show the user the advertisement that best matches the user's intent, which was expressed mainly through a specific query. Below are the concepts key to the discussion that follows.

Query: A text string a user types into the search box

Keyword: A text string related to a product, specified by an advertiser to match a user query

Title: The title of a sponsored advertisement (referred to as "an ad" hereafter), specified by an advertiser to capture a user's attention

Landing page: A product's web site a user reaches when the corresponding ad is clicked by a user

Match type: An option given to the advertiser on how closely the keyword should be matched by a user query, usually one of four kinds: *exact, phrase, broad* and *contextual*

Campaign: A set of ads that share the same settings such as budget and location targeting, often used to organize products into categories

Impression: An instance of an ad being displayed to a user. An impression is usually logged with other information available at run-time

Click: An indication of whether an impression was clicked by a user. A click is usually logged with other information available at the run-time

Click through rate: Total number of clicks over total number of impressions

Click Prediction: A critical model of the platform that predicts the likelihood a user clicks on a given ad for a given query

Sponsored search is only one kind of web-scale application. However, given the richness of the problem space, the various types of features, and the sheer volume of data, we think our results can be generalized to other applications with similar scale.

4. FEATURE REPRESENTATION

This section defines and compares combinatorial features and individual features, using examples listed in Table 1. The features in the table are available during run-time when an ad is displayed (an impression). They are also available in offline logs for model training, etc.

4.1 Individual Features

Each individual feature X_i is represented as a vector. For text features such as a query, one option is to convert the string into a tri-letter gram with $49,292$ dimensions as in [10]. Categorical input such as `MatchType` is represented by a one-hot vector, where exact match (see Sec. 3) is $[1,0,0,0]$, phrase match is $[0,1,0,0]$, and so on.

There are usually millions of campaigns in a sponsored search system. Simply converting campaign ids into a one-hot vector would significantly increase the size of the model (see Sec. 5.1). One solution is to use a pair of companion features as exemplified in the table, where `CampaignID` is

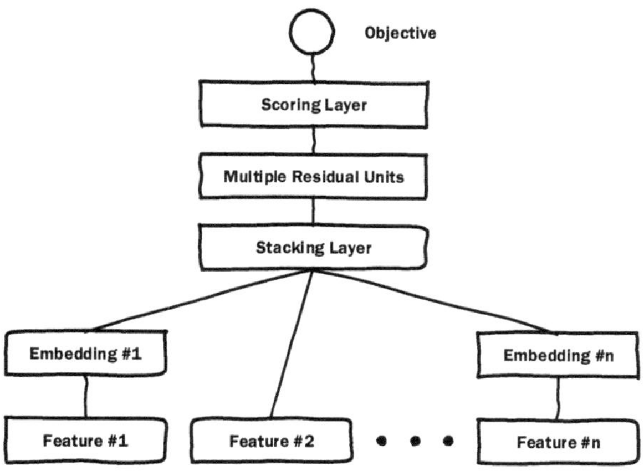

Figure 1: Deep Crossing Model Architecture

a one-hot representation consisting only of the top 10,000 campaigns with the highest number of clicks. The $10,000^{th}$ slot (index starts from 0) is saved for all the remaining campaigns. Other campaigns are covered by `CampaignIDCount`, which is a numerical feature that stores per campaign statistics such as *click through rate*. Such features will be referred as a *counting feature* in the following discussions. All the features introduced so far are sparse features except the counting features.

4.2 Combinatorial Features

Given individual features $X_i \in \mathbb{R}^{n_i}$ and $X_j \in \mathbb{R}^{n_j}$, a *combinatorial feature* $X_{i,j}$ is defined in $\mathbb{R}^{n_i} \times \mathbb{R}^{n_j}$. Combinatorial features also have sparse and dense representations. An example of sparse representation is a `CampaignId`$\times$`MatchType` feature, which is a one-hot vector of $10,001 \times 4 = 40,004$ dimensions. An example of a dense representation counts how many ad clicks for a specific `CampaignId` and `MatchType` combination. The dimension for the dense representation is the same as its sparse counterpart.

Deep Crossing avoids using combinatorial features. It works with both sparse and dense individual features, and supports a broad range of feature types described above. This gives users the freedom to use the features of their choice from their specific application. While collecting features and converting them into the right representations still requires a significant amount of effort, the work stops at the level of individual features. The rest is taken care of by the model.

5. MODEL ARCHITECTURE

Fig. 1 is the model architecture of Deep Crossing, where the input is a set of individual features. The model has four types of layers including the *Embedding*, the *Stacking*, the *Residual Unit*, and the *Scoring Layer*. The objective function is *log loss* for our applications but can be easily customized to soft-max or other functions. Log loss is defined as:

$$logloss = -\frac{1}{N}\sum_{i=1}^{N}(y_i \log(p_i) + (1-y_i)\log(1-p_i)), \quad (1)$$

where i indexes to the training samples, N is the number of samples, y_i is the per sample label, and p_i is the output of the one-node Scoring Layer in Fig. 1, which is a Sigmoid function in this case. The label y_i in the click prediction problem is a user click.

5.1 Embedding and Stacking Layers

Embedding is applied per individual feature to transform the input features. The embedding layer consists of a single layer of a neural network, with the general form:

$$X_j^O = \max(\mathbf{0}, \mathbf{W}_j X_j^I + \mathbf{b}_j), \quad (2)$$

where j indexes the individual feature, $X_j^I \in \mathbb{R}^{n_j}$ is the input feature, $\mathbf{W}_j$ is an $m_j \times n_j$ matrix, $\mathbf{b} \in \mathbb{R}^{n_j}$, and X_j^O is the embedded feature. When $m_j < n_j$, embedding is used to reduce the dimensionality of the input feature. The per element max operator is usually referred to as a *rectified linear unit* (ReLU) in the context of neural networks. The output features are then stacked (concatenated) into one vector as the input to the next layer:

$$X^O = [X_0^O, X_1^O, \cdots, X_K^O], \quad (3)$$

where K is the number of input features. Note that both $\{\mathbf{W}_j\}$ and $\{\mathbf{b}_j\}$ are the parameters of the network, and will be optimized together with the other parameters in the network. This is an important property of embedding in Deep Crossing. Unlike the embedding only approaches such as word2vec [14], it is an integral part of the overall optimization process.

It should be pointed out that the size of the embedding layers has significant impact on the overall size of the model. Even for sparse features, the $m_j \times n_j$ weight matrices are inherently dense. This is why Deep Crossing uses the companion features in Sec. 4 to constrain the dimensionality of high cardinality features. For the click prediction experiments in Sec. 7, the total size of the input features is around 200,000, and the m_j for the high dimensional features such as query and keyword are uniformly set to 256. Features with dimensionality lower than 256 are stacked without embedding. An example is `Feature #2` in Fig. 1.

5.2 Residual Layers

The residual layers are constructed from the *Residual Unit* in Fig. 2. The Residual Unit is the basic building block of the Residual Net [7] that claimed the world record in the ImageNet contest. Deep Crossing uses a slightly modified Residual Unit that doesn't use convolutional kernels. To our knowledge, this is the first time Residual Units have been used to solve problems beyond image recognition.

The unique property of Residual Unit is to add back the original input feature after passing it through two layers of ReLU transformations. Specifically:

$$X^O = \mathcal{F}(X^I, \{\mathbf{W}_0, \mathbf{W}_1\}, \{\mathbf{b}_0, \mathbf{b}_1\}) + X^I, \quad (4)$$

where $\mathbf{W}_{\{0,1\}}$ and $\mathbf{b}_{\{0,1\}}$ are the parameters of the two layers, and $\mathcal{F}$ denotes the function that maps the input X^I of the Residual Unit to the output X^O. Moving X^I to the left side of Eq. 4, $\mathcal{F}(\cdot)$ is essentially fitting the residual of $X^O - X^I$. In [7] the authors believed that fitting residuals has a numerical advantage. While the actual reason why Residual Net could go as deep as 152 layers with high performance is subject to more investigations, Deep Crossing did exhibit a few properties that might benefit from the Residual Units.

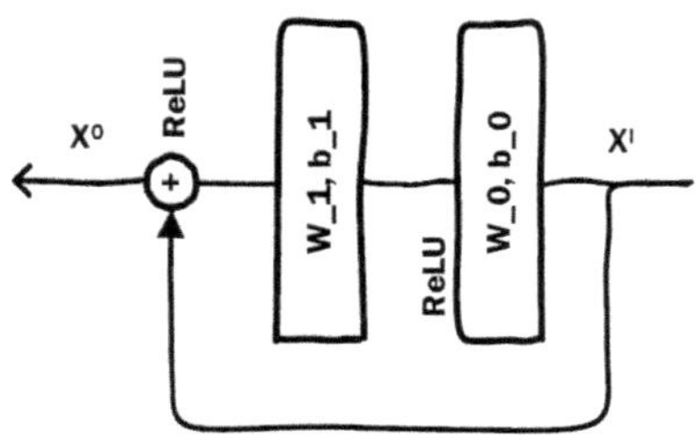

Figure 2: A Residual Unit

Before Deep Crossing, we tried a number of model architectures with deep layers but none of them provided significant gains over a model with two to three layers to justify the added complexity. Deep Crossing is our strongest model that easily beats the performance of its shallower counterparts.

Deep Crossing was applied to a wide variety of tasks. It was also applied to training data with large differences in sample sizes. In all cases, the same model was used without any adjustment in the layers, nodes, and type of nodes. It's likely that the Residual Units are implicitly performing some kind of regularization that leads to such stability.

5.3 Early Crossing vs. Late Crossing

It is worthwhile to compare Deep Crossing with DSSM. Fig. 3 is the architecture of a modified DSSM using log loss as the objective function. The modified DSSM is more closely related to the applications of click prediction. It keeps the basic structure of DSSM on the left side of the green dashed line, but uses log loss to compare the predictions with real-world labels. DSSM allows two text inputs, each represented by its tri-letter gram vector. DSSM has the distinct property of delaying the feature interaction (or crossing) to the late stage of the forward computation. Before reaching the Cosine Distance node, the input features are fully embedded through multiple layers of transformations on two separate routes. In contrast, Deep Crossing adopts at most one layer of single-feature embedding, and starts feature interaction at a much earlier stage of the forward computation.

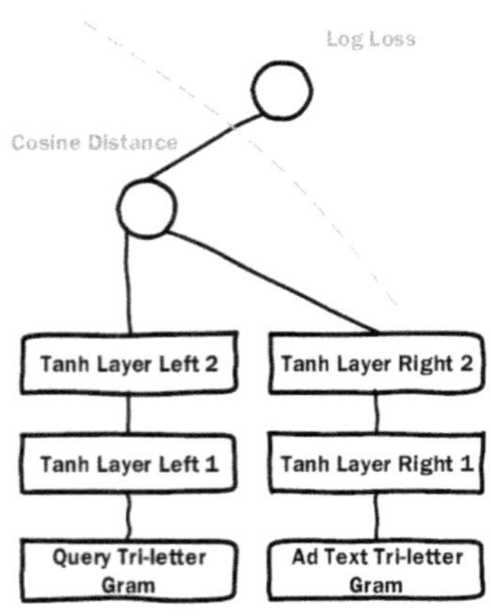

Figure 3: A DSSM Model with Log Loss

DSSM and its convolutional variation (CDSSM [19]) have been proven by many real-world applications to be strong learning machines especially tuned for a pair of text inputs. Still, when comparing Deep Crossing and DSSM in Sec. 7.1 on two text only tasks, the former consistently outperforms the latter. Besides the superior optimization ability of the Residual Units, introducing the feature interaction early on in the forward computation seems to play an important role.

6. IMPLEMENTATION

Deep Crossing is implemented on a multi-GPU platform powered by the Computational Network Toolkit (CNTK)[1][3], which shares the same theoretical foundation of *computational network* with TensorFlow[4].

6.1 Modeling with CNTK

Building the Deep Crossing model is quite straight forward with CNTK. The script below defines a few Macros that will be used later.

```
ONELAYER(Dim_XO, Dim_XI, XI){
    W = Parameter(Dim_XO, Dim_XI)
    b = Parameter(Dim_XO)
    XO = Plus(Times(W, XI), b)
}
ONELAYERSIG(Dim_XO, Dim_XI, XI){
    t = ONELAYER(Dim_XO, Dim_XI, XI)
    XO = Sigmoid(t)
}
ONELAYERRELU(Dim_XO, Dim_XI, XI){
    t = ONELAYER(Dim_XO, Dim_XI, XI)
    XO = ReLU(t)
}
RESIDUALUNIT(Dim_H, Dim_XI, XI){
    l1 = ONELAYERRELU(Dim_H, Dim_XI, XI)
    l2 = ONELAYER(Dim_XI, Dim_H, l1)
    XO = ReLU(Plus(XI, l2))
}
```

The Macro `ONELAYER` creates a weight matrix `W` and a bias vector `b` for one layer of a network. Macros `ONELAYERSIG` and `ONELAYERRELU` apply element-wise Sigmoid and ReLU functions to the output of `ONELAYER` and build a full Sigmoid layer and a ReLU layer, respectively. Comparing side-by-side `ONELAYERRELU` and Equ. 2, `XI`, `XO`, `Dim_XI`, and `Dim_XO` are X_j^I, X_j^O, n_j, and m_j, respectively. The `RESIDUALUNIT` uses a hidden layer of `Dim_H`, but the output has the same dimension as `Dim_XI`. The script in Fig. 4 has the details of the actual Deep Crossing model when applied to the features in Table 1. As can be seen from the script, the full model has five steps. Each step has been described in Sec. 5. Since the MatchType feature `M` has only 4 dimensions, it goes directly to the stacking stage without embedding. This is why the embedding step and the stacking step are regarded as a single, combined step. `Dim_E` and `Dim_CROSS*` are the numbers of nodes in the embedding layer and the hidden layer inside the Residual Unit, respectively. `Dim_L=1` for log loss. Some details such as feature I/O and normalization are not included here for simplicity[5].

[3]http://www.cntk.ai

[4]https://www.tensorflow.org

[5]The full Deep Crossing model will be available at

```
## The Deep Crossing Model
## Step 1: Read in features, omitted
## Step 2A: Embedding
Q = ONELAYERRELU(Dim_E, Dim_Query, Query)
K = ONELAYERRELU(Dim_E, Dim_Keyword, Keyword)
T = ONELAYERRELU(Dim_E, Dim_Title, Title)
C = ONELAYERRELU(Dim_E, Dim_CampaignID, CampaignID)
## Step 2B: Stacking
# M = MatchType, CC = CampaignIDCount
Stack = RowStack(Q, K, T, C, M, CC)
## Step 3: Deep Residual Layers
r1 = RESIDUALUNIT(Dim_CROSS1, Dim_Stack, Stack)
r2 = RESIDUALUNIT(Dim_CROSS2, Dim_Stack, r1)
r3 = RESIDUALUNIT(Dim_CROSS3, Dim_Stack, r2)
r4 = RESIDUALUNIT(Dim_CROSS4, Dim_Stack, r3)
r5 = RESIDUALUNIT(Dim_CROSS5, Dim_Stack, r4)
## Step 4: Final Sigmoid Layer
Predict = ONELAYERSIG(Dim_L, Dim_Stack, r5)
## Step 5: Log Loss Objective
CE = LogLoss(Label, Predict)
CriteriaNodes = (CE)
```

Figure 4: A Deep Crossing Model with five layers of Residual Units, described in the CNTK modeling language

6.2 Multi-GPU Platform

The experiments were carried out on a GPU cluster that is optimized for CNTK for rapid, no-hassle, deep learning model training and evaluation. The cluster, which has high-throughput distributed storage, virtual file systems, and fault tolerance, is managed by specially designed automated cluster management and job/container scheduling software. During experimentation, each GPU machine in the cluster contained four K40 GPU cards. Infiniband is used to connect nearby GPU machines for high-speed data transmission between GPUs across machines.

To speed up the experiments, we have exploited the block-wise model-update filtering (BMUF) distributed training algorithm implemented in CNTK, originally proposed by Chen and Huo [2]. The BMUF algorithm improves over traditional model averaging (MA) and alternating direction method of multipliers (ADMM) while keeping the advantage of the low communication cost of these methods. While MA and ADMM can be easily scaled out, they often under perform single-GPU SGD with regard to the accuracy achievable with the trained model, and require different learning rate schedules than that of single-GPU SGD. The BMUF algorithm, however, does not have these drawbacks. Chen and Huo [2] reported a 28X speedup with 32 GPUs while also achieving better accuracy than the single-GPU SGD on large-scale speech recognition experiments. In our experiments reported in this paper, we reduced training time from *24 days* with a single-GPU, to *20 hours* by exploiting 32 GPUs across 8 machines.

7. EXPERIMENTATION

Deep Crossing was trained and evaluated on impression and click logs of a major search engine. Table 2 lists the data sets used for the experiments in this section. Each

Data Set	Group	Task	Type	Rows	Dims
text_cp1_tn_s	G_1	CP1	train	194	98.5
text_cp1_vd	G_1	CP1	valid	49	98.5
text_cp1_tt	G_1	CP1	test	45	98.5
text_cp1_tn_b	G_1	CP1	train	2,930	98.5
text_cp2_tn	G_2	CP2	train	518	98.5
text_cp2_vd	G_2	CP2	valid	100	98.5
text_cp2_tt	G_2	CP2	test	93	98.5
all_cp1_tn_s	G_3	CP1	train	111	202.7
all_cp1_vd	G_3	CP1	valid	139	202.7
all_cp1_tt	G_3	CP1	test	156	202.7
all_cp1_tn_b	G_3	CP1	train	2,237	202.7

Table 2: Data sets used in this paper, where Rows (in millions) is the number of samples in the data set, while Dims (in thousands) is the total number of feature dimensions

experiment will use a combination of training, validation, and test data sets, referred by the names in the "Data Set" column. Only data sets in the same "Group" are compatible, meaning that there is no overlap in time for different "Types". For example, a model trained with `all_cp1_tn_b` (the last row in the table) can be validated with `all_cp1_vd` and tested with `all_cp1_tt` since they all belong to the `G_3` group.

The "Task" of a data set is either `CP1` or `CP2`. The two tasks represent two different models in the click prediction pipeline. In this case, `CP1` is the more critical model of the two, however the models are complementary in the system.

The Deep Crossing model described in Fig. 4 is used for all the experiments. Model parameters are also fixed to 256, 512, 512, 256, 128, and 64 for `Dim_E`, and `Dim_CROSS[1-5]`, respectively. Readers are encouraged to experiment with these parameters including the number of layers for their specific applications to achieve optimal results.

Note that all experimental results comparing with baselines are statistically significant due to the sheer volume of samples used in the test data. We will not call out individually for simplicity.

7.1 Performance on a Pair of Text Inputs

As briefly mentioned in Sec. 5.3, we are interested in comparing DSSM and Deep Crossing in the setting that DSSM is specialized. To create an apples-to-apples comparison, we trained a DSSM and a Deep Crossing model on data for `CP1` and `CP2`, but limited the Deep Crossing model to the same data as DSSM (i.e., both use a pair of inputs that include query text and keyword or title text, each represented by a tri-letter gram vector).

In the first experiment, click prediction models were trained on task `CP1` on the two data sets listed in Table 3. On both data sets, Deep Crossing outperforms DSSM in terms of rel-

Training Data	DSSM	Deep Crossing
text_cp1_tn_s	100	100.46
text_cp1_tn_b	100	101.02

Table 3: Click prediction results for task CP1 with a pair of text inputs where performance is measured by relative AUC using DSSM as the baseline

https://github.com/Microsoft/CNTK/wiki/Examples. Please check the site for the latest.

Test Data	DSSM	Deep Crossing	Production
text_cp2_tt	98.68	98.99	100

Table 4: Click prediction results for task CP2 with a pair of text inputs where performance is measured by relative AUC using the production model as the baseline

ative AUC as explained in the table. Note that the DSSM model used here is the log loss version detailed in Sec. 5.3.

In the second experiment, both models were trained on task **CP2** on the **text_cp2_tn** dataset, and tested on the **text_cp2_tt** dataset. Table 4 shows the performance results for DSSM, Deep Crossing, and the model currently running inside our production system. The production model is trained on a different data set, but is tested with the same data (**text_cp2_tt**) using the prediction output logged during run-time. It can be seen that Deep Crossing performs better than DSSM but worse than the production model. This is expected since the production model uses many more features – including combinatorial features – and has been refined over many years. Still, by just using individual query and title features, Deep Crossing is only about one percentage point away from the production model.

While we have demonstrated Deep Crossing's ability to learn from simple pairs of text inputs, this is not its main goal. The real power of Deep Crossing is to work with many individual features, as we will see in the subsequent experiments.

7.2 Beyond Text Input

We now consider the performance of Deep Crossing on task **CP1** (training set **all_cp1_tn_s**) with about two dozen features[6] including those listed in Table 1. The experiments in this sub-section don't have external baselines, instead we will only compare Deep Crossing's performance with different combinations of features. Instead of assessing the performance relative to other methods, the goal here is to see Deep Crossing in action, and demonstrate its performance can change significantly as features are added and removed. We will compare the performance of Deep Crossing with production models in the next sub-section, using the same rich set of features.

In the first experiment, we ran Deep Crossing several times with different sets of features turned on and off. Counting features (see Sec. 4 for definition) are always turned off, and will be turned back on in the next experiment. The **All_features** model in Fig. 5 has all the remaining features turned on. As expected, it has the lowest log loss among all the models in this experiment. The **Only_Q_K** model has the highest log loss. This model uses only query text and keyword text, which is similar to the models in the previous sub-section.

Note that the log loss in Fig. 5 is *relative log loss* defined as the actual log loss divided by the lowest log loss of the **All_features** model over all epochs. The gap between **Only_Q_K** and **All_features** in terms of relative log loss is about 0.12. This is roughly a $7-8\%$ improvement in terms of AUC, which is huge given that an improvement of $0.1-0.3\%$ in AUC is usually regarded as significant for click prediction

[6]Unfortunately we were not able to disclose the full feature set but we did our best to make sure the lack of such details has minimal impact on the discussions of the results.

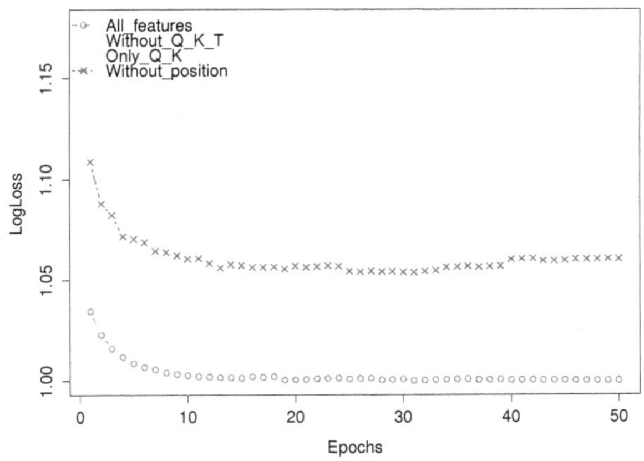

Figure 5: Deep Crossing's performance on task CP1 with different individual feature sets where performance is measured by relative log loss on the validation set over the training epochs (relative log loss is defined in Sec.7.2)

models. **Without_Q_K_T** is a model with query text, keyword text, and title text removed, which means that taking away the majority of text features will increase relative log loss by 0.025. This is a half of the increase with the model **Without_position**, which removes the position feature.

In the second experiment, we study how the counting features interact with the rest of the individual features. As discussed in Sec. 4, counting features play an important role in reducing the dimension of high cardinality features. Our full feature set has five types of counting features. In this experiment we just turned on one of them (referred as *the selected counting feature* hereafter) to demonstrate the effect.

As can be seen from Fig. 6a, the model **Counting_only** with only the selected counting feature is very weak compared with the **All_without_counting** model, which has all of the features except the counting features. Fig. 6b shows the result after adding the selected counting feature, where the new model **All_with_counting** reduced the relative log loss by 0.02. The base point for the relative log loss for both Fig. 6a and Fig. 6b is the lowest log loss of the **All_without_counting** model over all epochs.

7.3 Comparison with Production Models

Up to this point, the question remains whether Deep Crossing can actually beat the production model, which is the ultimate baseline. To answer this question, we trained a Deep Crossing model with 2.2 billion samples, using a subset of the raw features from the production model. As reported in Table 5, the new model has comfortably outperformed the production model in offline AUC on task CP1 (results for task CP2 are not available as of the time of publication). It was trained on the task **CP1** (**all_cp1_tn_b**) data set , and tested on **all_cp1_tt**. The production model was trained on a different (and bigger) data set but was tested with the same data. As in the comparison with the task **CP2** model in Sec. 7.1, the production AUC was based on the prediction output logged during the run-time.

The above result is quite significant since the Deep Cross-

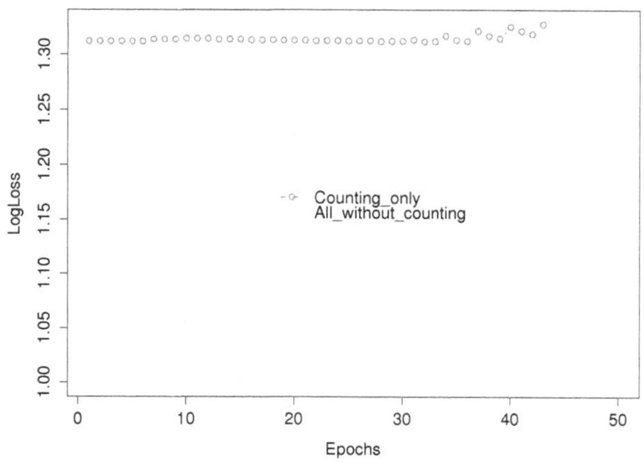

(a) A model (in red) using the selected counting feature only is weak

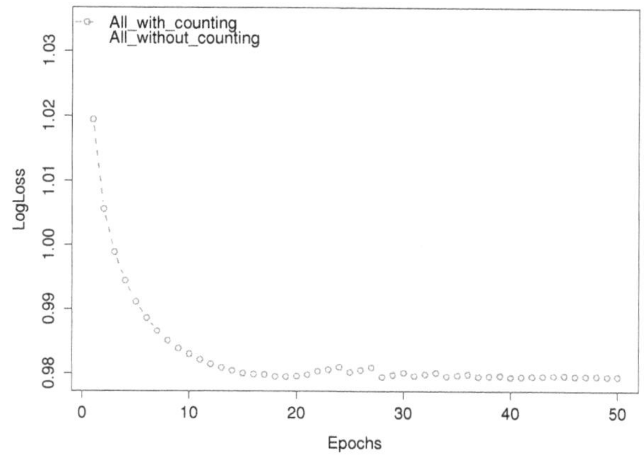

(b) Adding the selected counting feature reduced log loss significantly

Figure 6: The effect of adding the selected counting feature on task CP1 in Deep Crossing where performance is measured by relative log loss on the validation set over training epochs (relative log loss is defined in Sec.7.2)

Test Data	Deep Crossing	Production
all_cp1_tt	101.02	100

Table 5: Click prediction model compared with the production model on task CP1 where performance is measured by relative AUC using production model as the baseline

ing model used only a fraction number of features, and took much less efforts to build and maintain.

8. CONCLUSIONS AND FUTURE WORK

Deep Crossing enables web-scale modeling without extensive feature engineering. It demonstrated that with the recent advance in deep learning algorithms, modeling language, and GPU-based infrastructure, a nearly dummy solution exists for complex modeling tasks at large scale. While such claims require further testing, it does resonate with a key benefit of deep learning envisioned by the pioneers, which is to free people from the tedious work of feature engineering.

Deep Crossing was initially developed in the context of paid search ads, which is a web-application with massive data. When applied to other domains, we expect that most properties will still hold. This is because of the extensive coverage of feature types and the general model representations.

Besides saving effort in building large models, Deep Crossing also helps to decouple the application domains with modeling technologies. To hand craft combinatorial features requires extensive domain knowledge. But if modeling complexity is shifted from feature engineering to modeling technologies, the problem is opened up to the entire world of modeling experts, even those not working in the same domain. As evidence, the BMUF [2] distributed training algorithm developed by a few researchers in speech recognition helped Deep Crossing to fill the last bit of performance gap with a production model for sponsored search. While we don't have an explicit economic study, the compound effect of less efforts in feature engineering and getting more help from others is expected to be significant for a broad range of applications.

Deep Crossing is by design a multi-way fusion engine for heterogeneous features. As we apply it to more application domains, it will be interesting to see how this aspect is fully manifested.

9. ACKNOWLEDGMENTS

The authors would like to thank Chris Basoglu, Yongqiang Wang, Jian Sun, Xiaodong He, Jianfeng Gao, and Qiang Huo for their support and discussions that benefited the development of Deep Crossing.

10. REFERENCES

[1] A. Agarwal, E. Akchurin, C. Basoglu, G. Chen, S. Cyphers, J. Droppo, A. Eversole, B. Guenter, M. Hillebrand, T. R. Hoens, X. Huang, Z. Huang, V. Ivanov, A. Kamenev, P. Kranen, O. Kuchaiev, W. Manousek, A. May, B. Mitra, O. Nano, G. Navarro, A. Orlov, M. Padmilac, H. Parthasarathi, B. Peng, A. Reznichenko, F. Seide, M. L. Seltzer, M. Slaney, A. Stolcke, H. Wang, Y. Wang, K. Yao, D. Yu, Y. Zhang, and G. Zweig. An introduction to computational networks and the computational network toolkit. Technical report, Microsoft Technical Report MSR-TR-2014-112, 2014.

[2] K. Chen and Q. Huo. Scalable training of deep learning machines by incremental block training with intra-block parallel optimization and blockwise model-update filtering. In *Internal Conference on Acoustics, Speech and Signal Processing*, 2016.

[3] R. Collobert, J. Weston, L. Bottou, M. Karlen, K. Kavukcuoglu, and P. Kuksa. Natural language processing (almost) from scratch. *The Journal of Machine Learning Research*, 12:2493–2537, 2011.

[4] G. E. Dahl, D. Yu, L. Deng, and A. Acero. Context-dependent pre-trained deep neural networks

for large-vocabulary speech recognition. *Audio, Speech, and Language Processing, IEEE Transactions on*, 20(1):30–42, 2012.

[5] B. Edelman, M. Ostrovsky, and M. Schwarz. Internet advertising and the generalized second price auction: Selling billions of dollars worth of keywords. Technical report, National Bureau of Economic Research, 2005.

[6] K. Fukushima. Neocognitron: A self-organizing neural network model for a mechanism of pattern recognition unaffected by shift in position. *Biol. Cybernetics*, 36:193–202, 1980.

[7] K. He, X. Zhang, S. Ren, and J. Sun. Deep residual learning for image recognition. *arXiv preprint arXiv:1512.03385*, 2015.

[8] G. Hinton, L. Deng, D. Yu, G. E. Dahl, A.-r. Mohamed, N. Jaitly, A. Senior, V. Vanhoucke, P. Nguyen, T. N. Sainath, et al. Deep neural networks for acoustic modeling in speech recognition: The shared views of four research groups. *Signal Processing Magazine, IEEE*, 29(6):82–97, 2012.

[9] G. E. Hinton, S. Osindero, and Y.-W. Teh. A fast learning algorithm for deep belief nets. *Neural computation*, 18(7):1527–1554, 2006.

[10] P.-S. Huang, X. He, J. Gao, L. Deng, A. Acero, and L. Heck. Learning deep structured semantic models for web search using clickthrough data. In *Proceedings of the 22nd ACM international conference on Conference on information & knowledge management*, pages 2333–2338. ACM, 2013.

[11] A. Krizhevsky, I. Sutskever, and G. E. Hinton. Imagenet classification with deep convolutional neural networks. In *Advances in neural information processing systems*, pages 1097–1105, 2012.

[12] Y. LeCun, L. Bottou, Y. Bengio, and P. Haffner. Gradient-based learning applied to document recognition. *Proceedings of the IEEE*, 86(11):2278–2324, 1998.

[13] D. G. Lowe. Object recognition from local scale-invariant features. In *Computer vision, 1999. The proceedings of the seventh IEEE international conference on*, volume 2, pages 1150–1157. IEEE, 1999.

[14] T. Mikolov, I. Sutskever, K. Chen, G. S. Corrado, and J. Dean. Distributed representations of words and phrases and their compositionality. In *Advances in neural information processing systems*, pages 3111–3119, 2013.

[15] S. Rendle. Factorization machines. In *Data Mining (ICDM), 2010 IEEE 10th International Conference on*, pages 995–1000. IEEE, 2010.

[16] J. Schmidhuber. Deep learning in neural networks: An overview. *Neural Networks*, 61:85–117, 2015.

[17] F. Seide, G. Li, X. Chen, and D. Yu. Feature engineering in context-dependent deep neural networks for conversational speech transcription. In *Automatic Speech Recognition and Understanding (ASRU), 2011 IEEE Workshop on*, pages 24–29. IEEE, 2011.

[18] F. Seide, G. Li, and D. Yu. Conversational speech transcription using context-dependent deep neural networks. In *Interspeech*, pages 437–440, 2011.

[19] Y. Shen, X. He, J. Gao, L. Deng, and G. Mesnil. Learning semantic representations using convolutional neural networks for web search. In *Proceedings of the companion publication of the 23rd international conference on World wide web companion*, pages 373–374. International World Wide Web Conferences Steering Committee, 2014.

[20] D. Yu and L. Deng. Deep learning and its applications to signal and information processing [exploratory dsp]. *Signal Processing Magazine, IEEE*, 28(1):145–154, 2011.

[21] D. Yu, G. Hinton, N. Morgan, J.-T. Chien, and S. Sagayama. Introduction to the special section on deep learning for speech and language processing. *Audio, Speech, and Language Processing, IEEE Transactions on*, 20(1):4–6, 2012.

Question Independent Grading using Machine Learning: The Case of Computer Program Grading

Gursimran Singh, Shashank Srikant, Varun Aggarwal
Aspiring Minds
{gursimran.singh, shashank.srikant, varun}@aspiringminds.com

ABSTRACT

Learning supervised models to grade open-ended responses is an expensive process. A model has to be trained for every prompt/question separately, which in turn requires graded samples. In automatic programming evaluation specifically, the focus of this work, this issue is amplified. The models have to be trained not only for every question but also for every language the question is offered in. Moreover, the availability and time taken by experts to create a labeled set of programs for each question is a major bottleneck in scaling such a system. We address this issue by presenting a method to grade computer programs which requires no manually assigned labeled samples for grading responses to a new, unseen question. We extend our previous work [25] wherein we introduced a grammar of features to learn question specific models. In this work, we propose a method to transform those features into a set of features that maintain their structural relation with the labels across questions. Using these features we learn one supervised model, across questions for a given language, which can then be applied to an ungraded response to an unseen question. We show that our method rivals the performance of both, question specific models and the consensus among human experts while substantially outperforming extant ways of evaluating codes. We demonstrate the system's value by deploying it to grade programs in a high stakes assessment. The learning from this work is transferable to other grading tasks such as math question grading and also provides a new variation to the supervised learning approach.

Keywords

Recruitment; Automatic grading; MOOC; Feature engineering; Supervised learning; One-class learning; Question independent learning

1. INTRODUCTION

The automatic grading of open-ended responses has become the subject of extensive research [9, 27, 10]. Machine learning and other computer science techniques are used to evaluate responses in a variety of domains such as essay writing [11, 24], computer programming [6, 25], spoken English [8, 22, 21] and open response math questions [16]. A number of innovations, in both academia and the industry, are focusing on open-response learning and assessment systems.[4, 2, 5, 1, 3]. MOOCs have a pressing demand for a scalable method of automatic grading of open-ended responses [18] and so does the industry.

Such assessments typically contain questions or prompts regarding a topic (hereafter referred to as *question*) to which test-takers must respond with written answers, for example, essay topics are prompts to test English, whereas programming problems are questions used to test software engineering skills. For each specific question, responses from different test-takers are used to build models that can predict the quality of new, unseen responses. For example, an essay describing a field trip to New York might include terms such as 'Statue of Liberty', 'Niagara', and 'Times Square' which would qualify the response to be rated highly; on the other hand, a *good essay* describing a visit to California might include such terms as 'Silicon Valley', 'Napa valley', or 'Golden Gate Bridge'. For each question, one has to identify such discriminating features and build models using labeled responses, making them specific to the subject matter of the question. The inherent design of such an approach impedes scaling these systems to newer content. Each new question requires a significant number of expert-graded responses to train models. The availability, cost, and time required by the subject matter experts (SMEs) govern the rate at which new questions could be added to the system.

We are interested in the case of automatic programming grading, where the difficulty is two-fold: first, each question needs to have its own predictive model; second, within each question, each specific programming language needs to have separate predictive models. With a programming evaluation platform supporting $5-10$ modern programming languages, scaling to new questions becomes very expensive. Additionally, there are constraints such as the investment of time and resources to train SMEs on the rubrics that they must follow in grading responses; the need to have at least two SMEs evaluating each response to ensure consistency in grading; and the scarcity of qualified SMEs.[1]

In this work, we address the problem of scalability in au-

[1]One cannot make use of a crowdsourcing platform like Amazon Mechanical Turk to source SMEs because evaluating programming assignments are not human-intelligence tasks.

KDD '16, August 13 - 17, 2016, San Francisco, CA, USA

ISBN 978-1-4503-4232-2/16/08...$15.00
DOI: http://dx.doi.org/10.1145/2939672.2939696

tomatic program grading. We present a method to grade computer programs which requires no human-graded samples for grading responses to a new, unseen question. For a given programming language, we transform question specific features to features that maintain their relation with the grade/label across questions. We design such a transformation by exploiting properties specific to the domain of computer programming. We call these transformed features as *expressive structurally invariant features* - their structural relation with the label remains invariant across questions. Using the structurally invariant features we learn a question independent supervised model, which can then be applied to (the automatically transformed features of) an ungraded response to an unseen question. In doing so, we extend our previous work where an expressive grammar of features was proposed and used to train question-specific supervised models. We also suggest how the learning from this work can be transferred to other problems of automatic grading. Specifically, this paper makes the following contributions:

- We present for the first time a machine learning approach to learn question independent models for grading computer programs (or for any domain, to our knowledge) which requires zero human-graded samples for a new question.
- We propose a new machine learning workflow to grade open-response problems, which includes automatic creation of structurally invariant features, normalization, a joint learning across questions with these features, and using them to predict labels for responses to an unseen question.
- Our approach produces a model for which the accuracy rivals the consensus among human experts and we demonstrate its utility in a real world setting to predict grades in high-stakes assessments.

The paper is organized as follows - §2 describes the *question independent* learning approach and related work. In §3, we present the details of our experiments and results. §4 discusses the deployment of our system in a high stakes assessment. §5 concludes the paper and discusses future work.

2. A QUESTION-INDEPENDENT LEARNING APPROACH

We describe in this section how question-independent features are engineered and used in a machine learning framework. We begin by laying out the notation, followed by a summary of the grammar of features proposed in [25]. This provides a context to the discussion in the subsequent sections.

2.1 Notation

For a given programming language, each programming question is referred to as a *question* and a code which attempts this question, as a *response*. The set of questions used in this study is denoted by Q_{all}. Each question $q \in Q_{all}$ has a set of responses $R^{(q)} \in R$ collected on it, where R is the set of responses across all questions. For any given response x, its feature vector is referred to as $\hat{f_x}$.[2] Each feature in feature vector $\hat{f_x}$ belongs to a category in set $\mathbf{C} = \{$B, BC, E, EC, ED, EDC$\}$ (see §2.2 for details). For a *question* $q \in Q_{all}$ having n responses and m unique features, we define the feature matrix $\mathbf{F}^{(q)}_{n\times m}$ as

$$\mathbf{F}^{(q)}_{n\times m} = \begin{bmatrix} \hat{f_1} \\ \vdots \\ \hat{f_n} \end{bmatrix} \quad \text{where } \hat{f_x} \in \mathbb{N}^m \tag{1}$$

where $\hat{f_x}$ is the feature vector of a particular response x to question q.

We define a *good set* for each question (see §2.3 for details) $q \in Q_{all}$ containing k *good responses* as $\mathbf{R}^{(q)}_g$ and the feature matrix of the k *good responses* $\mathbf{G}^{(q)}_{k\times m}$, as

$$\mathbf{G}^{(q)}_{k\times m} = \begin{bmatrix} \hat{g_1} \\ \vdots \\ \hat{g_k} \end{bmatrix} \quad \text{where } \hat{g_y} \in \mathbb{N}^m \tag{2}$$

where $\hat{g_y}$ is the feature vector of a particular *good response* y to question q.

2.2 Feature Grammar

The grammar proposed in [25] generates features that capture the semantic relationships present in a program. The counts and relations of three important properties of a program are extracted - the tokens used in the program, the expressions and the data dependencies.

a) Basic (B) : Examples include counts of all keywords, tokens, operators etc. such as the number of times a '+' operator appears or loop tokens such as '*for*' and '*while*' appear.

b) Expressions (E): Expressions such as $y = x\%2$ are abstracted to a notation such as v:2::op:%::c:'2', which denotes an expression having two variables, one modulus operator and the constant '2'. The number of occurrences of such abstract expressions are counted.

c) Expression Dependency (ED): A data dependency is captured when the variable in one expression is used in another expression. For example, the expression $x < y$, which contains a relational operator (<) and two variables, is dependent on the expression $y{+}{+}$, which contains a post-increment operator (++) and one variable. This is denoted using the notation v:1::op:++← v:2::op:relation. The occurrences of each dependency matching such abstractions is counted. This is repeated for each unique pair of dependencies that appears in a response.

d) Control Context (BC, EC, EDC): Separate counts are maintained for each of the three properties described above according to the control-context (loops and conditional statements) in which they appear. For example, an expression whose abstract notation matches v:2::op:%::c:'2' is counted separately if it appears within an *if* statement as against in a loop like a *for* or a *while* as against in an *if* statement within a *for*.

The grammar of features described above is combinatorial in nature; a $10 - 15$ line program on an average generates 2000 features. A detailed discussion of the features is available in §2.3 of [25].

2.3 Method

The features introduced in [25] predict responses' grades accurately. However, the system requires to build a model

[2]All vectors represented by a cap ($\hat{f_x}$) are row vectors

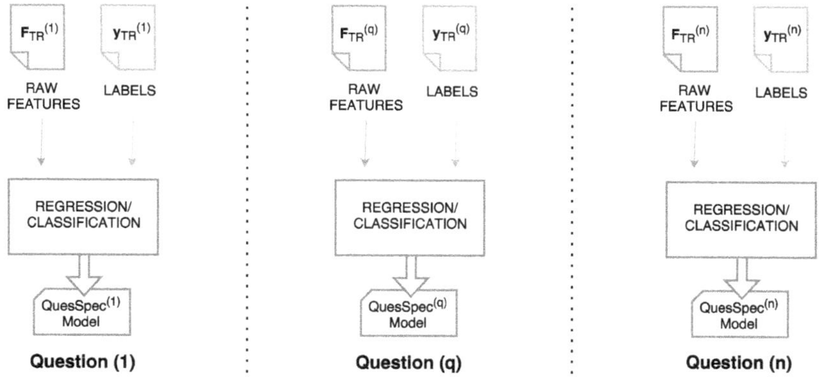

(a) Question dependent model training

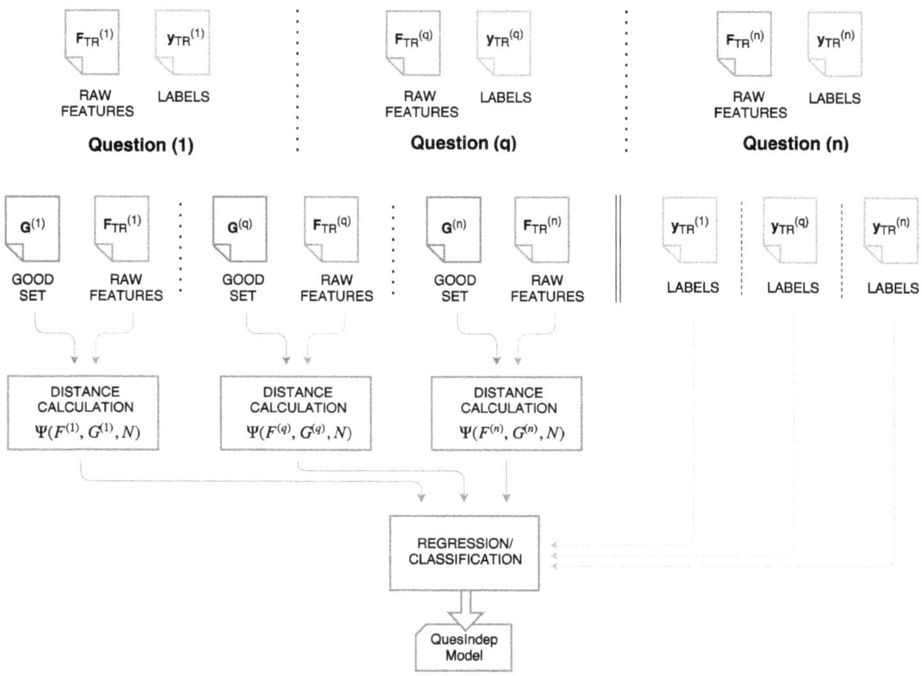

(b) Question independent model training

Figure 1: Question independent model learning

Fig (a) shows how question specific models were learnt in [25]. Each question required a set of grades ($y_{TR}^{(q)}$) corresponding to the feature matrix ($F_{TR}^{(q)}$) to train the models. A model was trained for every question separately. These models predicted grades of unseen responses for their respective questions. Fig (b) shows a modified workflow where only one model is learnt in the training phase. While training, each question's feature matrix first goes through a transformation Ψ before being augmented with the transformed matrices from other questions. This augmented input is used to learn the augmented grades of all responses used in the training phase.

for each question separately using labeled responses (see Fig 1a). Since getting responses labeled is a cost intensive process, we explore the design of a single model that predicts a response's label irrespective of the question it solves. Designing such a model does not fit seamlessly into traditional machine learning approaches since the features which discriminate 'good' responses from 'bad' ones change drastically across questions. For instance, we expect a nested loop in a 'good' response for bubble sort while one loop and other discriminating expressions is expected in a 'good' response to reverse a string. We wish to design features which structurally maintain the same relation with the grades irrespective of the question. One such relationship is an increase in the value of a feature, irrespective of the question, signaling a better grade.[3] We could then learn one model across responses from multiple questions in this invariant feature space and use it to predict grades of responses to unseen questions.

[3]A monotonic relation between a feature and a label is used for a simple illustration; other relations, like a quadratic form, are also acceptable in principle as long as they maintain this form across questions.

Mathematically expressed, we would want to design a transformation Ψ which would transform a *question specific* feature matrix $\mathbf{F}^{(q)}_{n\times m}$, for a given question q, into a structure invariant feature matrix $\mathbf{D}^{(q)}$. Although the transformation Ψ takes in *question specific* parameters, it must be automatic and not require any manually assigned labeled data for a response to an unseen question. The new invariant feature matrix $\mathbf{D}^{(q)}$ can then be augmented across questions and be used as one consolidated input to learn a *question independent* model **QuesInd** (see Fig 1b). The new *question independent* model can then be used to predict the grades of a new question without any human-graded samples.

We describe how we design the transformation Ψ which transforms the question specific features into a set of sufficiently expressive structurally invariant features.

a) Automatic identification of a *good set*: The *good set*, which we define as a subset of the responses that solve a question correctly, is vital in transforming *question specific* features into structurally invariant features (input to Ψ in Fig 1b). Although constructed for every question separately, creating this set does not require manually assigned labeled responses for a question. We posit that a carefully designed test-suite for a question automatically identifies functionally correct responses, which in turn can comprise the *good set*. This is not to say that responses failing a test suite cannot be good - in our approach, it is sufficient to have a subset of such *good responses* (corresponding to labels 4 or 5 of the rubric [25]).[4] We require a sufficient number of such responses so that they capture the variation in possible correct approaches to a question. We exploit the ability to automatically identify such a good set for a question to develop structurally invariant features. We now describe how we develop *structurally invariant* features from such an automatically identified *good set*.

b) Distance from a *good response*: For the sake of simplicity, let us assume the existence of only one possible *good response* to a question. In such a case, an L_1 distance (in the space of m features) between a given response and the *good response* will be a *structurally invariant* feature. A response at a larger distance from the *good response* will have a larger proportion of *different* 'keywords', 'control structures', 'data dependencies' etc. as compared to a response with a lower distance. Thus, responses with higher distances should probably have lower grades as compared to ones with lower distances, irrespective of the question the response and the *good set* belongs to. Such an L_1 distance from an automatically identified *good response* is hypothesized to relate to the grade in a *structurally invariant* way across questions.

We modify the L_1 distance to a one-sided distance ζ, defined as

$$\zeta(\hat{f}_x, \hat{g}_y) = \sum_{i=1}^{m} \beta(g_{yi} - f_{xi})$$
$$\beta(a) = \begin{cases} a & a \geq 0 \\ 0 & otherwise \end{cases} \tag{3}$$

where $\hat{f}_x$ is the feature vector of the response x and $\hat{g}_y$ feature vector of a *good response* y.

We do this guided by the intuition that programming constructs like keywords, control structures etc. not present in the feature vector ($\hat{f}_x$) of response x but present in the feature vector ($\hat{g}_y$) of *good response* y signals a deviation from how response x ought to be written. On the other hand, any excess of such features present in response x might still signal the approach used in *good response* y[5].

This still leaves us with two problems. First, there are usually not one but multiple ways to correctly implement a question. The distance ζ defined above can signal nearness to a specific *good response*. We would want a metric which could signal nearness to one among many such *good responses*. Second, the process of calculating ζ transforms the m dimensional feature space, consisting many interesting and useful features, to just one monolithic distance. We would want to continue having expressive features to learn models which generalize well. We address these problems below.

Algorithm 1 Distance from a *good set*

INPUT:
$\hat{f}_x$: Feature vector of a response x
$G^{(q)}$: *Good set* feature matrix of question q
N: N=1 to normalize distances

OUTPUT:
Distance of a response x from the *good set* of a question q

```
Initialize:
    d̂_x_all ← null    ▷ Dists to all good responses
function goodSetDist(f̂_x, G^(q), N)
    for y ← 1 to k do    ▷ Loop over all good responses
        d_xy ← ζ(f̂_x, ĝ_y)    ▷ See Eq (3)
        if N==1 then
            (d_xy) ← Ω(d_xy, ĝ_y)    ▷ See Eq (4)
        d̂_x_all ← d̂_x_all ∪ (d_xy)
    d_x = meanMin25(_x_all)    ▷ Mean of min 25
return d_x    ▷ Distance from good set
```

c) Distance from a *good set*: A question typically contains multiple *good responses* in its *good set*. A given response has a distance ζ from each of these *good responses*, which we aim to aggregate meaningfully. Such an aggregate could be calculated in many ways, the mean and the minimum of the distances from the *good set*'s responses being two examples. It was shown in [25] that the mean of the 25% minimum distances correlated moderately with the output and outperformed the mean and the minimum. It discussed

[4]There could be cases where a response attempt to trick the system by hard-coding the exact test cases being evaluated. In both, our system and the system proposed in [25], this was handled by keeping a good number of test cases in the test-suite hidden from the respondent, making it hard to guess which specific cases a response would be evaluated on.

[5]We also conducted experiments, not reported for brevity, whose results validate the intuition empirically.

that the mean would dilute the distance metric from matching the closest correct response and the minimum would be too sensitive to outlier responses in the *good set*. We use this mean of the 25% minimum distances across *good responses* as the aggregate measure. Algorithm 1 describes the distance of a response x belonging to a question q from its *good set* $\mathbf{G}^{(q)}$.

d) Expressive distance scores: In our discussions thus far, we obtain a single monolithic distance from Ψ as a feature, for a response, to signal 'goodness'. This distance is aggregated across all features ($\mathbf{F}^{(\mathbf{q})}$) and across the different responses in the *good set*. This is in contrast to the question specific approach, wherein we had the advantage of having several varied features to learn a model. We address this by aggregating the distance across each of the six feature categories one at a time (see §2.2 for a description of the categories). We rewrite the features matrices for the responses and the *good set* as -

$$\mathbf{F}^{(q)} = \left[\mathbf{F}_B^{(q)}\ \mathbf{F}_{BC}^{(q)}\ \mathbf{F}_E^{(q)}\ \mathbf{F}_{EC}^{(q)}\ \mathbf{F}_{ED}^{(q)}\ \mathbf{F}_{EDC}^{(q)}\right]$$
$$\mathbf{G}^{(q)} = \left[\mathbf{G}_B^{(q)}\ \mathbf{G}_{BC}^{(q)}\ \mathbf{G}_E^{(q)}\ \mathbf{G}_{EC}^{(q)}\ \mathbf{G}_{ED}^{(q)}\ \mathbf{G}_{EDC}^{(q)}\right]$$

We then calculate Ψ with each of the six input pairs ($\mathbf{F}_B^{(q)}$, $\mathbf{G}_B^{(q)}$), ($\mathbf{F}_{BC}^{(q)}$, $\mathbf{G}_{BC}^{(q)}$) and so on, resulting in six distance scores for a response. This results in one distance feature corresponding to only *Basic* features like counts and tokens, one corresponding to *Expression* features etc. We hypothesize these categories to have different relations (weights) with the grade despite each of them being structurally invariant across questions. For instance, the *Basic* feature may relate more to gross differences in the responses and thus help signaling large jumps across rubric levels while the distance in the *Expression Dependency* may help quantify fine differences between responses, differentiating at the upper end of the rubric.

e) Transformation, Ψ: The distance score calculated for any response x of question q from the *good set* of q is the transformed feature value which is used to learn question independent models. For a question with n responses, the transformation Ψ converts the feature matrix $\mathbf{F}_{n\times m}^{(q)}$ into a vector of distances $\mathbf{D}_{n\times 1}^{(q)} = \left[d_1 \dots d_n\right]^T$ where each d_i is the distance of response x from the *good set* $\mathbf{G}^{(q)}$.

f) Normalization, Ω: We describe how a distance score is calculated for a response by aggregating its distance from all responses in a *good set* of a question. Although the aggregation ensures that the general relationship between the distances and grades is maintained across questions, the scale of the distances could vary with questions. Specifically, Equation (3) scales up by the number of features which varies across questions. For instance, the set of unique features in responses implementing bubble sort (~11 lines of code, $O(N^2)$) would be much more than to swap two numbers (~4 lines of code, $O(1)$). As a consequence, the magnitude of distance for a 'nearer' response may turn out to be much larger for bubble sort when compared to swapping two numbers. This creates an issue when we augment these differently scaled distances for a joint learning task. A simple way to circumvent this is to normalize the aggregate distance by the total number of features in the *good response* y that it is compared to. We such define a normalization Ω as

$$\Omega(d_{xy}, \hat{g}_y) = \frac{d_{xy}}{\mu_y} \tag{4}$$

where d_{xy} is the distance of response x from *good response* y and $\mu_y = \sum_{i=1}^{m} g_{yi}$ is the sum of features in the *good response* y.

Another normalization strategy could be to normalize by the average distance among responses in the *good set*. One may see this as using distributional properties of an unlabeled sample. We see in the results section §3.3 that some of these normalizations are useful. In summary, by automatically identifying *good responses*, we are able to create six *structurally invariant* features, with a hypothesis that they relate differently and could add incremental value over each other to predict the grade.[6]

2.4 Related Work

Recent work in automated programming grading has focused more on providing feedback than a grade. [23] and [20] propose a program synthesis approach and a static analysis approach respectively to provide feedback for erring programs. These approaches find if small modifications could be made to the program to enable it to pass their respective test cases. They provide a list of such modifications as feedback to students. The systems seemingly perform as expected only on very small and non-complex pieces of code (less than $10-15$ lines implementing simple algorithms) and work only for responses with small deviations from a specified good response. Moreover, they do not focus on evaluation against multiple correct responses. [14] and [15] each propose a system which uses unsupervised learning to cluster together semantically similar codes. An SME provides a grade to any one representative code from each cluster. This grade is then propagated to the rest of the responses in that cluster. These systems have not been designed to automatically grade responses at scale in real time and instead focus on reducing the workload of an SME who is involved in the feedback generation process. This is very different from the business requirements of high-stakes automatic grading of computer programs. In comparison to these systems, ours is the first approach to automatically generate a grade for a program written for a given question without having any manually assigned labeled samples for it. Also, we use supervised learning techniques and derive features from a more expressive feature grammar.

Among machine learning techniques, the literature of domain adaptation [13], which constitutes a sub problem in the field of transfer learning [7, 26], addresses a similar problem as ours. In domain adaptation, a well established model built on data drawn from a *source* distribution is used to learn a model on data drawn from a *target* distribution. The task to be accomplished (e.g. tagging natural language) remains the same across the domains while some distributional properties of the features change. In our problem, unlike in domain adaptation, the learning task changes significantly[7]

[6]In principle, we could treat every original feature separately, convert them into a distance, align them across questions and use them to learn a question independent model. This has issues of high sparsity and learning complications because many features are unique to a question.

[7]Even though the task sounds the same, i.e. to grade pro-

from one question to another. The feature space and the discriminating features drastically change across questions. From the standpoint of domain adaptation, it is hard to say what is the commonality between the source and the target models for different programming questions - there doesn't seem to be any connection between the features or the structure of the models for, say, a bubble sort and a tree traversal. However, if one is able to define structurally invariant features as we do, some learnings from the domain adaptation literature may be useful.

3. EXPERIMENTS

We designed our experiments to address the following questions

- Is the **QuesIndep** model a good predictor of programming performance when compared to human experts? Does it perform well enough to be used in high stakes computer programming assessments?
- How well does the **QuesIndep** perform against **QuesSpec** models and the test case metric? The test case metric provides a baseline while the **QuesSpec** models, with their large feature sets, provide an upper bound on the accuracy of predictions.
- Do normalizing the structurally invariant features help build better models?

To answer these, we analyzed 19 programming questions[8] graded by experts trained on our rubric. The responses to these questions were, on an average, $30 - 35$ lines long and required a variety of data-flow dependencies and control structures to be implemented. We experimented with both, linear and non-linear machine learning techniques. For each question, we learned a specific model and compared its performance on a question-independent model learned on a subset of the questions in the data set. We analyze the performance of the models aggregated over all the questions as well as separately for each question. We now discuss the details of the experiments.

3.1 Data

The experiments were run on a set of programming questions hosted on *Automata*, our automated programming evaluation platform [25]. Respondents, who were college seniors majoring in computer science, took a 90 minute assessment in a proctored environment wherein they attempted two programming questions in a language of their choice. For these questions, the respondents had a choice of C, C++ and Java. A total of 19 questions were used in the study (see Table 1), on which we had an average of 285 responses per question and 5434 responses in all. The topics covered by these questions spanned iterative/ recursive algorithms, trees and graphs and other algorithms like the shortest job first etc.[9]

grams, it actually is different. For instance, the task is to determine whether a response implements bubble sort as against finding whether a number is prime.

[8]Models were built separately on data collected in three languages - C, C++ and Java. Wherever question independent models are mentioned, we refer to the average performance of the models across the three languages.

[9]Due to a paucity of space, we do not list here the details of the question statements.

Table 1: Details of our dataset

Question Name	#Codes	#Good Set	#Features
Qused_tr			
isSameReflection	126	69	2874
waitingTimeSJF	307	31	4513
countCacheMiss	455	93	3682
isTree	420	71	2741
patternPrint	603	211	2945
grayCheck	610	134	1793
transposeMultMatrix	507	183	2728
eliminateVowelString	515	156	2424
Total	**3543**	**948**	
Qunseen_tr			
cellCompete	215	70	2801
insertSortedList	101	22	1154
isSubTree	104	39	1315
minTreePath	189	76	1255
isPath	71	27	4766
lruCountMiss	244	66	4416
generalizedGCD	248	72	3163
distinctElementCount	256	91	1656
rotatePictureMethod	209	83	2085
reverseLinkedList	41	19	1162
balancedParentheses	213	96	1649
Total	**1891**	**661**	

The number of overall responses and the responses in the *good set* for each question is listed. Questions are divided into two sets - Q_{used_tr} and Q_{unseen_tr} based on how they are used in training the models (see §3.2.1)

Three professional software engineers with 3-5 years' experience each, who were also seasoned competitive programmers, shared the task of grading the responses. Each response was graded by two experts. The experts followed the rubric defined in [25] to grade codes on a scale of 1-5. Before beginning the grading exercise, they underwent a one-week workshop wherein they learned how to interpret the rubric and participated in mock grading exercises. The correlation between the grades of any two experts on an average was 0.81 across the questions in the data set.

We note here that grades are required only once for responses to only a subset of these questions. A model built on such responses then predicts grades of responses to any number of unseen questions without manually assigned labeled responses.

3.2 Models

We developed machine learning models on the responses collected on the questions listed in Table 1. We used linear regression, linear regression with L_1 regularization (LASSO), linear regression with L_2 regularization (Ridge regression), decision trees, random forests and SVMs. For LASSO[17] ($\alpha = 1$) we varied λ from 0 to 4. For ridge regression, we varied λ from 0 to 100. For random forests[19], we varied the number of estimators from 15 to 100. For SVMs[19, 12], we tested three kernels - linear, polynomial and RBF. We varied the penalty factor C from 0.125 to 128, and parameters γ from 0.125 to 128 and ϵ from 0.5 to 16. In all these techniques, the model which gave the best cross-validation correlation was selected. For the question specific models, a feature selection step was followed by a 3-fold cross val-

Table 2: Results of LASSO on the test set - Mean values across questions

Metric	Question Set	#Questions	QuesSpec-All	QuesSpec	QuesIndep-N1	QuesIndep-N0	Baseline-TC
Correl	Q_{all}	19	0.84	0.81	0.80	0.76	0.65
Bias	Q_{all}	19	0.14	0.15	0.24	0.28	0.35
MAE	Q_{all}	19	0.41	0.46	0.58	0.66	0.85
Correl	Q_{unseen_tr}	11	0.85	0.81	0.80	0.76	0.65
Bias	Q_{unseen_tr}	11	0.14	0.20	0.27	0.34	0.31
MAE	Q_{unseen_tr}	11	0.43	0.46	0.62	0.70	0.84

idation. The best cross-validation correlation was used for selecting the final model. Similar to what was seen in [25], linear models worked the best among all these techniques, indicating linearity in the inherent structure of this problem space. We report results only for LASSO in this work which outperformed all other techniques. We trained the following models to answer the questions enumerated at the beginning of the section:

- **QuesSpec-All**: We train separate models for each question as described in [25]. The full set of features (with feature selection) were used as inputs. This provides the upper bound on accuracy for our techniques.
- **QuesSpec**: Separate models were trained for every question using the six *expressive distance scores* (see §2.3d) as features. This provides an upper bound on what best we could do with the six categorized features. Our question independent model cannot do better than this (other than in cases where models overtrain). If this model does not perform well, then the technique we introduce in this work cannot be expected to do well either. On the other hand, it is useful to find how the question independent model does in comparison with these.
- **QuesIndep**: Our question independent model was trained across a subset of questions (discussed in §3.2.1) using six of the *expressive distance scores* as features. We train separate models in this category with and without applying the normalization (Ω), discussed in §2.3f. We denote these models by the names **QuesIndep-N1** when normalization is applied and **QuesIndep-N0** when it is not.
- **Baseline-TC**: The baseline for all our experiments is a model trained on just the test-case scores across questions. This mimics a real world scenario where we could have predicted the 'goodness' of a response by its performance on its test-suite. Given that the performance on a test-suite is a metric whose meaning does not change across questions, it too is a *structurally invariant* feature whose values can be used across questions to learn a model.

In all the above models, the percentage of test-cases passed was added as a feature.

3.2.1 Train-Test Split

To learn the **QuesSpecAll** model, we split the responses to each question into a 67−33 train-test set. The selection of the train-test set was nuanced for the **QuestIndep** models. In addition to testing the model on responses belonging to questions already present in the train set, we ensured that there were responses in the test set from unseen questions - those whose responses were not used to train the models at all. The performance on such an unseen set would then demonstrate how well the **QuesIndep** models generalized to questions where we did not have any human-graded samples, the use case expected in a real-world scenario. We also ensured that the responses in the *good set* for each question were not a part of their respective test-sets. We denote those questions whose responses are used to train the question independent models as Q_{used_tr}. Questions whose responses are not used in training the models are denoted as Q_{unseen_tr}. Q_{all} denotes the set of all the questions. In our data-set, we randomly selected 8 questions as part of Q_{used_tr} and the remaining 11 as Q_{unseen_tr}. We trained the **QuesIndep** models on 67% of the responses belonging to Q_{used_tr} (2384 in total) and tested them on the remaining 33% responses of Q_{used_tr} and additionally on all responses of the Q_{unseen_tr} questions (3050 in total).

3.2.2 Evaluation Metric

We use the Pearson correlation coefficient (r) to quantify and measure the similarity between the predicted grades and the experts' grades. While describing the **QuesIndep** model building process (see §2.3), we suggested how the distances calculated from the *good set* could have been on different scales for different questions. For some questions, this could cause the question independent model to scale and/or displace the distribution of grades linearly as compared to their true distribution. As a consequence, the model may still correlate highly with the grade. We hence consider the bias[10] ($\sum \frac{y_{pred} - y}{n}$) and MAE ($\sum \frac{|y_{pred} - y|}{n}$) as evaluation metrics in addition to the correlation coefficient.

3.3 Discussion

We contrast the performance of the **QuesIndep** and **QuesSpec** models on the test set (Table 2). To maintain brevity, we tabulate the mean of the models' performance on each question. We compare the performance of the models on two sets of questions - Q_{all} and Q_{unseen_tr} (see §3.2.1). The baseline results for the Q_{unseen_tr} are calculated by learning a model on the test case scores of only the Q_{used_tr} set and testing on the Q_{unseen_tr} set. The **QuesSpec** results on the Q_{unseen_tr} set correspond to the models learned on each of the Q_{unseen_tr} questions.

We first discuss the aggregate results across questions. We find that the question independent model with normalization (**QuesIndep-N1**) has an r of 0.80 with expert grades on both sets of questions - Q_{all} and Q_{unseen_tr} with a bias of 0.24 and 0.27 on the two sets respectively. This rivals the

[10]The bias in this work does not refer to the bias of learning models. It refers to the observational error.

Table 3: Results of LASSO on the test set - Question-wise results

		QuesIndep-N1			**Baseline-TC**		
	Question Name	Correl	Bias	MAE	Correl	Bias	MAE
	isSameReflection	0.54	0.63	0.73	0.46	0.95	1.10
	waitingTimeSJF	0.80	0.12	0.52	0.65	0.46	0.88
	countCacheMiss	0.82	0.01	0.53	0.52	0.39	1.01
Q_{used_tr}	isTree	0.83	0.23	0.54	0.72	**0.20**	0.74
$(N = 1159)$	patternPrint	0.88	0.14	0.42	0.80	0.32	0.64
	grayCheck	0.84	0.25	0.60	0.72	**0.01**	0.77
	transposeMultMatrix	0.87	0.00	0.37	0.79	0.68	0.81
	eliminateVowelString	0.79	0.15	0.58	0.55	0.16	0.89
	cellCompete	0.73	0.06	0.54	0.60	0.06	0.69
	insertSortedList	0.76	0.33	0.70	0.46	0.55	1.21
	isSubTree	0.75	0.21	0.76	0.60	0.24	1.03
	minTreePath	0.79	0.13	0.61	0.76	0.19	0.68
	isPath	0.86	0.39	0.57	0.73	**0.09**	0.61
Q_{unseen_tr}	lruCountMiss	0.84	0.23	0.51	0.58	0.39	0.87
$(N = 1891)$	generalizedGCD	0.72	0.48	0.90	0.51	0.68	1.20
	distinctElementCount	0.89	0.19	0.43	0.86	**0.12**	0.46
	rotatePictureMethod	0.91	0.28	0.40	0.77	**0.12**	0.74
	reverseLinkedList	0.87	0.23	0.54	0.80	0.62	0.77
	balancedParentheses	0.63	0.49	0.83	0.45	**0.37**	1.00

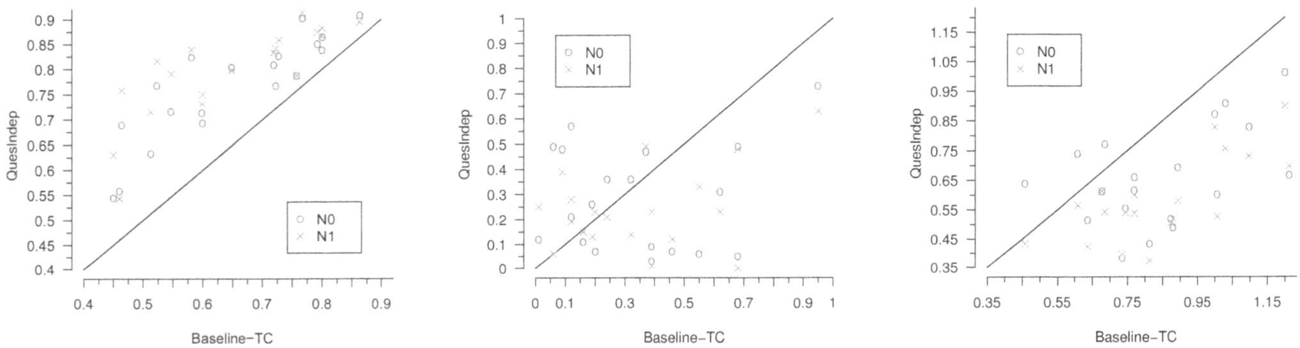

(a) Correlation (b) Bias (c) Mean Absolute Error

Figure 2: Performance of QuesIndep models contrasted against Baseline-TC

agreement of two human experts ($r = 0.81$, $bias = 0.14$) and shows that the model may be used in a real world setting. The Q_{all} and Q_{unseen_tr} sets follow the same trends and we discuss them together. In comparison to the testcase baseline, the question independent model does much better on each of the metrics - r, bias and MAE. When compared to the question specific models (**QuesSpec-All**, **QuesSpec**), the question independent model provides comparable performance in their r. However, it shows a higher bias and MAE. This shows that some scaling issues do creep in while building question independent models and this aspect may further be improved. However, the difference in MAE for question independent and question specific models is not very large and varies between 0.12 and 0.25 points. We find that normalization helps both in terms of r (0.04) and bias $(0.04 - 0.07)$. These observations are as expected.

In summary, we find that the question independent models rival expert grades, largely outperform test case measures, and show higher bias as compared to question specific models. Furthermore, normalizing the structurally invariant features does help build better models.

We now discuss the errors on individual questions. We compare the three error metrics on our best question independent model **QuesIndep-N1** with those on the baseline (Table 3). We find that the r and MAE of the question independent model outperform that of the TC baseline by 0.15 points on an average. This is also distinctly visible in Fig 2a and Fig 2c (X-axis represents the error metric of Baseline-TC and the Y-axis represents the error metric of the models, **QuesIndep-N0** and **QuesIndep-N1**). We see in Fig 2c that the performance on MAE by **QuesIndep-N0** on 3 questions does worse than the baseline. However, the performance on these 3 questions improves on using the model with normalization, reinforcing the utility of normalization in the learning process.

When we compare biases, we see that the question independent model performs better than the test case baseline on 13 of the 19 questions (Fig 2b and Table 3). Out of the 6 questions that underperform: 2 are from the Q_{seen_tr} set and 4 from the Q_{unseen_tr} set (biases marked in boldface). A reason for this under performance could be the normalization technique not being able to get the distances for these questions on the same scale perfectly well. The simple linear scaling demonstrated through our techniques may be replaced by more sophisticated non-linear scaling, warranting a more detailed study.

To conclude, the question independent model consistently outperforms the baseline on correlation, which is expected. As a result of possible normalization issues, the model underperforms in bias in a few cases. However, in no case is the MAE affected and we see it consistently outperform the baseline, demonstrating the utility of the learning technique we introduce in this work.

4. DEPLOYMENT

We deployed the **QuesIndep-N1** model on *Automata*, our online programming evaluation platform. A leading software product company having more than 10,000 employees wanted to use this product for their 2015-2016 hiring cycle of software engineers with 0-2 years' experience. The company wanted to deliver 13 questions developed by them on this platform. Having released the 13 questions in June 2015, we had 68 responses on an average in the *good set* across the questions within 3 weeks. By the first week of July, we had the question independent models live and evaluating responses to the questions. This is in stark contrast to the $4-5$ month process it would typically take to develop question specific models per question. Till December 2015, a total of 3176 candidates had been evaluated on this platform. The company's default shortlisting criterion was to consider candidates passing at least 75% of their test cases, which was followed by an interview where the final hiring decision was made. In this hiring cycle, they shortlisted 468 candidates who had scored 4 or 5 as predicted by the **QuesIndep-N1** model. Had the hiring been done only based on the test-case cut-off, 391 candidates would have made it through. 384 candidates were common to these two sets. Among the 84 candidates $(468-384)$ interviewed by the virtue of **QuesIndep-N1**, the interviewers found the grades of 76 respondents match their evaluation. Hence, 16.5% candidates ($\frac{76}{76+384}$), a sizeable proportion, would not have made it through to the interviews had the criterion been only the test case score. On the other hand, of the 7 candidates who were graded low but had a high testcase score, all were graded 3 by the model, had an average testcase score of 76.3% and seemed to be at the cusp of being graded 3 or 4 on visual inspection by the interviewers. At the end of the process, 136 of the shortlisted 468 candidates were offered a job. 46 of these 136 (33%) were signaled by **QuesIndep-N1**. This case study demonstrates the successful deployment of **QuesIndep-N1** models in a high-stakes assessment, helping save man-hours which would have otherwise gone into designing question specific models. In a separate study done on candidates who have completed 6 months in job, we also found the predictions of **QuesIndep-N1** to correlate significantly ($r = 0.8$) with the manager ratings on job performance.

5. CONCLUSION AND FUTURE WORK

We present in this work a system to grade computer programs using question-independent supervised machine learning models. Building on the grammar of features we introduce in our previous work [25], we engineer *semantically invariant* features which maintain their structural relation with the labels across questions. This is possible because we identify a set of 'good' responses to a question automatically. We show that a single model learned on such features, derived from the responses to a few questions, is able to predict the grades of responses to questions not seen in the model's training. Further, we show that the performance of such a model clearly outperforms extant evaluation techniques, rivals the performance of question-specific models and the consensus of human experts. In doing so, we successfully demonstrate how to grade responses to questions without *any* manually assigned labeled samples. Through a case study, we show how practically efficient the system is when deployed to recruit software engineers, saving significant time and resources in the process.

We see a window for further research in the normalization techniques we lay out and the transformations to create a larger set of structurally invariant features. The relationship of accuracy with the number of train problems, size of data set and the number of good codes for new problems can be studied further. Other learning techniques which model rankings better, like ordinal regression, can also be explored. The automatic identification of functionally correct responses, which we demonstrate in this work, can be extended to other areas as well like open response mathematical questions and electronic circuit solving, where a numeric comparator judges the final answer of a series of equations. It also applies to evaluations whose outcomes are human intelligence tasks (such as evaluating whether a webpage is aesthetically designed); the identification of correct responses then can be crowd-sourced in real time to produce a high quality *good set*. These observations promise interesting opportunities for research in such areas, all of which will help the holy grail of designing fully automated teaching assistants. We look forward to the learning from this work resulting in similar accurate, scalable grading systems being designed in other domains.

6. REFERENCES

[1] Automata. Aspiring Minds http://www.aspiringminds.com/technology/automata.

[2] E-rater. ETS http://www.ets.org/research/topics/as_nlp/writing_quality/.

[3] Intelli metric. Vantage Learning http://www.vantagelearning.com/products/intellimetric/.

[4] Speechrater. ETS https://www.ets.org/research/topics/as_nlp/speech/.

[5] Svar. Aspiring Minds http://www.aspiringminds.com/technology/svar.

[6] V. Aggarwal, S. Srikant, and V. Shashidhar. Principles for using machine learning in the assessment of open response items: Programming assessment as a case study. In *NIPS Workshop on Data Driven Education*, 2013.

[7] J. Baxter. A bayesian/information theoretic model of learning to learn via multiple task sampling. *Machine Learning*, 28(1):7–39, 1997.

[8] J. Bernstein, A. Van Moere, and J. Cheng. Validating automated speaking tests. *Language Testing*, 2010.

[9] M. Birenbaum and K. K. Tatsuoka. Open-ended versus multiple-choice response formatsâĂŤit does make a difference for diagnostic purposes. *Applied Psychological Measurement*, 11(4):385–395, 1987.

[10] H. M. Breland. The direct assessment of writing skill: A measurement review. *ETS Research Report Series*, 1983(2):i–23, 1983.

[11] J. Burstein, L. Braden-Harder, M. Chodorow, S. Hua, B. Kaplan, K. Kukich, C. Lu, J. Nolan, D. Rock, and S. Wolff. Computer analysis of essay content for automated score prediction: A prototype automated scoring system for gmat analytical writing assessment essays. *ETS Research Report Series*, 1998(1):i–67, 1998.

[12] C.-C. Chang and C.-J. Lin. Libsvm: a library for support vector machines. *ACM Transactions on Intelligent Systems and Technology (TIST)*, 2(3):27, 2011.

[13] H. Daume III and D. Marcu. Domain adaptation for statistical classifiers. *Journal of Artificial Intelligence Research*, pages 101–126, 2006.

[14] E. L. Glassman, J. Scott, R. Singh, P. J. Guo, and R. C. Miller. Overcode: Visualizing variation in student solutions to programming problems at scale. *ACM Transactions on Computer-Human Interaction (TOCHI)*, 22(2):7, 2015.

[15] J. Huang, C. Piech, A. Nguyen, and L. Guibas. Syntactic and functional variability of a million code submissions in a machine learning mooc. In *AIED 2013 Workshops Proceedings Volume*, page 25. Citeseer, 2013.

[16] A. S. Lan, D. Vats, A. E. Waters, and R. G. Baraniuk. Mathematical language processing: Automatic grading and feedback for open response mathematical questions. In *Proceedings of the Second (2015) ACM Conference on Learning@ Scale*, pages 167–176. ACM, 2015.

[17] N. Meinshausen and P. Bühlmann. Stability selection. *Journal of the Royal Statistical Society: Series B (Statistical Methodology)*, 72(4):417–473, 2010.

[18] L. Pappano. The year of the mooc. The New York Times (Accessed: 2016-2-2).

[19] F. Pedregosa, G. Varoquaux, A. Gramfort, V. Michel, B. Thirion, O. Grisel, M. Blondel, P. Prettenhofer, R. Weiss, V. Dubourg, et al. Scikit-learn: Machine learning in python. *The Journal of Machine Learning Research*, 12:2825–2830, 2011.

[20] K. Rivers and K. R. Koedinger. Automatic generation of programming feedback: A data-driven approach. In *The First Workshop on AI-supported Education for Computer Science (AIEDCS 2013)*, page 50, 2013.

[21] V. Shashidhar, N. Pandey, and V. Aggarwal. Automatic spontaneous speech grading: A novel feature derivation technique using the crowd. In *Proceedings of the Conference of the Association for Computational Linguistics*. ACL, 2015.

[22] V. Shashidhar, N. Pandey, and V. Aggarwal. Spoken english grading: Machine learning with crowd intelligence. In *Proceedings of the 21th ACM SIGKDD International Conference on Knowledge Discovery and Data Mining*, pages 2089–2097. ACM, 2015.

[23] R. Singh, S. Gulwani, and A. Solar-Lezama. Automated feedback generation for introductory programming assignments. In *ACM SIGPLAN Notices*, volume 48, pages 15–26. ACM, 2013.

[24] V. Southavilay, K. Yacef, P. Reimann, and R. A. Calvo. Analysis of collaborative writing processes using revision maps and probabilistic topic models. In *Proceedings of the Third International Conference on Learning Analytics and Knowledge*, pages 38–47. ACM, 2013.

[25] S. Srikant and V. Aggarwal. A system to grade computer programming skills using machine learning. In *Proceedings of the 20th ACM SIGKDD international conference on Knowledge discovery and data mining*, pages 1887–1896. ACM, 2014.

[26] S. Thrun. Is learning the n-th thing any easier than learning the first? *Advances in neural information processing systems*, pages 640–646, 1996.

[27] C. Vleuten, G. Norman, and E. Graaff. Pitfalls in the pursuit of objectivity: issues of reliability. *Medical education*, 25(2):110–118, 1991.

Contextual Intent Tracking for Personal Assistants

Yu Sun [†1]*, Nicholas Jing Yuan [§2], Yingzi Wang [*‡3], Xing Xie [‡4], Kieran McDonald [§5], Rui Zhang [†6]
[†] Department of Computing and Information Systems, University of Melbourne
{[1] sun.y, [6] rui.zhang}@unimelb.edu.au
[‡] Microsoft Research [§] Microsoft Corporation [*] University of Science and Technology of China
{[2] nicholas.yuan, [4] xing.xie, [5] kieran.mcdonald}@microsoft.com [3] yingzi@mail.ustc.edu.cn

ABSTRACT

A new paradigm of recommendation is emerging in intelligent personal assistants such as Apple's Siri, Google Now, and Microsoft Cortana, which recommends "the right information at the right time" and proactively helps you "get things done". This type of recommendation requires precisely tracking users' contemporaneous intent, i.e., what type of information (e.g., weather, stock prices) users currently intend to know, and what tasks (e.g., playing music, getting taxis) they intend to do. Users' intent is closely related to context, which includes both external environments such as time and location, and users' internal activities that can be sensed by personal assistants. The relationship between context and intent exhibits complicated co-occurring and sequential correlation, and contextual signals are also heterogeneous and sparse, which makes modeling the context-intent relationship a challenging task. To solve the intent tracking problem, we propose the *Kalman filter regularized PARAFAC2* (KP2) nowcasting model, which compactly represents the structure and co-movement of context and intent. The KP2 model utilizes collaborative capabilities among users, and learns for each user a personalized dynamic system that enables efficient nowcasting of users' intent. Extensive experiments using real-world data sets from a commercial personal assistant show that the KP2 model significantly outperforms various methods, and provides inspiring implications for deploying large-scale proactive recommendation systems in personal assistants.

Keywords

Recommendation; nowcasting; multi-task learning

1. INTRODUCTION

Intelligent personal assistants such as Apple's Siri, Google Now, and Microsoft Cortana are widely deployed on mobile devices (Cortana is also on Windows desktops). They offer *proactive experiences* that aim to recommend "the right information at just the right time" [1], and help you "get things done" [2] even "before you ask" [3]. Figure 1 shows examples of such proactive experiences (left to right) from Microsoft Cortana (on desktops), Apple's Siri, and Google Now, respectively. We can see that personal assistants proactively recommend various types of information such as weather, traffic conditions, stock prices, nearby places, and news. They also suggest apps that users probably need to complete certain tasks such as Uber for getting a taxi and Skype for sending a message. Due to limited display sizes (no matter whether on desktops or mobile devices), personal assistants can only effectively present one or two types of information. When they remind users (e.g., of contacting someone), or ask for confirmation to help users proactively complete certain tasks (e.g., playing music), they also only present one reminder or push one notification at the right time. Therefore, to effectively provide such proactive experiences, we need to closely track users' contemporaneous intent, i.e., what users currently *intend to know*, and what they *intend to do*.

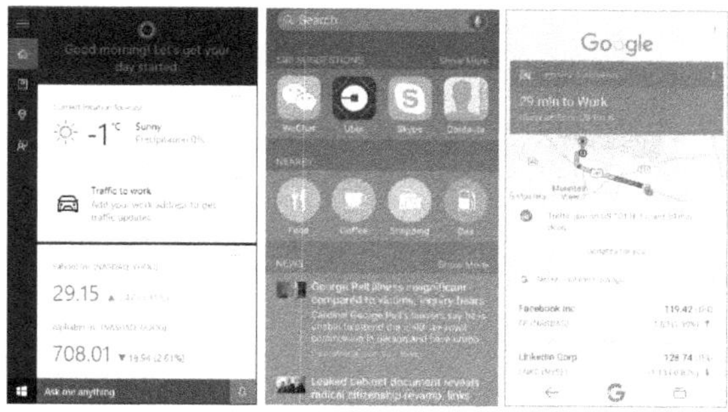

Figure 1: Proactive experiences

Users' contemporaneous intent is closely related to context, which includes not only external environments such as time and location, but users' internal activities that can be effectively sensed by mobile devices such as the apps users use and venues users visit. The relationship between context and intent is complicated, which exhibits complex co-occurring and sequential correlation. For example, users may intend to listen to music while driving or using browsers, or intend to take a taxi when going to or leaving a restaurant. Context itself (e.g., using browsers, driving, and leaving a restaurant) also consists of numerous heterogeneous signals collected from various sources (e.g., the duration of focusing on browsers, distance to home, and time spent at a restaurant), and these signals often contain very sparse records. Therefore, it is challenging to model the context-intent relationship. Moreover, to track users' intent in real-time, we need efficient and robust-to-noise tracking systems, as mobile devices have limited computation capacity and signals collected by mobile devices are prone to be noisy.

*This work was done while the author was an intern at Microsoft Research.

KDD'16, August 13-17, 2016, San Francisco, CA, USA
© 2016 ACM. ISBN 978-1-4503-4232-2/16/08...$15.00
DOI: http://dx.doi.org/10.1145/2939672.2939676

Traditional recommendation models that recommend music tracks [8], movies [6], etc., cannot apply to intent tracking. These models only address one specific type of intent (e.g., to find movies), and for the specific type of intent, they aim at recommending new items, and focus on the content of recommended items. While for intent tracking, the focus is the recurrence of various types of intent, i.e., type of information (e.g., weather, news) users intend to know and tasks (e.g., playing music) they intend to do. Following the line of traditional recommendation, time-aware recommendation models consider the evolving [15] or seasonal variance [24] of user preferences and item attributes. They cannot apply to intent tracking, either. Apart from the above differences, users' intent often changes swiftly in a very short time, rather than varying on a daily or monthly basis. Models [12, 20] that utilize item similarity or item co-occurring and sequential patterns (e.g., next-basket) also cannot apply because they overlook users' context.

We propose solving the intent tracking problem with a nowcasting approach. Nowcasting approaches [5] were originally developed in meteorology and successfully adopted in macroeconomics. Different from forecasting, nowcasting predicts the contemporaneous value of a variable of interest (intent) with more frequently available signals (context). In particular, we propose the KP2 (**K**alman filter regularized **P**ARAFAC**2**) nowcasting model to solve intent tracking. The KP2 model compactly represents the shared structure and co-movement of intent and contextual signals. It utilizes collaborative capabilities among users, and learns, for each user, a personalized dynamic system that effectively models the sequential correlation among contextual signals and intent. The dynamic system is also robust to noise and enables efficient nowcasting of users' real time intent on mobile devices. The contributions are summarized as follows.

- We identify the intent tracking problem for domains of both information intent (i.e., to know) and task-completion intent (i.e., to do), and model intent tracking as a collaborative nowcasting problem.
- We propose a novel KP2 nowcasting model to effectively solve the intent tracking problem. The model compactly represents the structure and sequential correlation of context and intent. Using collaborative capabilities among users, it innovatively learns for each user a personalized dynamic system that enables efficient prediction of users' contemporaneous intent.
- We conduct extensive experiments with real-world data sets from a commercial personal assistant. The results show that KP2 outperforms various methods by a significant margin, and is able to automatically generate intuitive if-do triggers that support large-scale deployment of effective proactive experiences.

The rest of the paper is organized as follows. Section 2 defines the problem. Section 3 analyzes the context and intent. Section 4 discusses the KP2 model. Section 5 presents experiments. Section 6 reviews related work and Section 7 concludes this paper.

2. PRELIMINARIES

2.1 Problem Definition

We study the problem of closely tracking users' contemporaneous intent [10, 21, 22]. The intent can be any tasks users intend to do or any information users intend to know, e.g., to order food, to book a meeting room, to know the headline news or weather conditions. Intent is closely related to context, which includes not only external physical environments, e.g., location and time, but internal states of users indicated by the activities users have recently engaged in, e.g., apps users recently used. Context is also personalized and frequently changed. Using the discrete time model, we denote by ζ a specific type of intent (e.g., listening to music), $\mathbf{x}_t^u$ the context of user u at time step t, and $\mathcal{F}(\zeta, \mathbf{x}_t^u) \in \{0, 1\}$ whether user u has intent ζ at time t given context $\mathbf{x}_t^u$, where $\mathcal{F}(\zeta, \mathbf{x}_t^u) = 1$ means positive and 0 means negative. We formally define the intent tracking problem as follows.

Table 1: Example of a panel

Time step	11 a.m.	12 p.m.	1 p.m.	2 p.m.	Now
Chrome	2345	784	0	435	23
Lync	0	1053	0	0	-
Starbucks	0	1251	766	0	0
Fitness First	0	0	0	143	1334
Dist-to-Home	3.45	5.34	10.3	15.7	-
Day-of-Week	5	5	5	5	5
Taxi intent	1	0	0	1	?

DEFINITION 1 (INTENT TRACKING). *Given a set of M users, a starting time t_0, a tracking granularity Δ, a type of intent ζ, and context $\mathbf{x}_t^u$ of user u, the intent tracking problem is to determine the value of $\mathcal{F}(\zeta, \mathbf{x}_t^u)$ for every time step t of length Δ starting from t_0.*

2.2 Characteristics of Intent Tracking

The intent tracking problem has several challenging characteristics, which requires special attention and careful model design to address simultaneously.

i) **Real-time tracking**. In the current time step, not all contextual signals (e.g., focus time of various apps) are available simultaneously, which requires handling the continuous arrival of contextual signals.

ii) **Complex context-intent correlation**. The relationship between context and intent exhibits complex co-occurring and sequential correlation, e.g., users may intend to check calendar after arriving at offices.

iii) **Efficient and robust computation**. Personal assistants are widely deployed on mobile devices, which have limited computing capabilities, and hence require light-weight computation to response smoothly. Moreover, the data collected by mobile devices are also prone to be noisy.

iv) **Personalized service**. Personal assistants are highly personalized and should be a private friend of users'. We need to pay attention to the contextual signals that are specific to each individual user, e.g., the venues only frequently visited by that user.

v) **Data sparsity**. As with traditional recommendation problems, the contextual data for a single user can be quite sparse and hence have limited predicting power.

3. DATA REPRESENTATION AND ANALYSIS

3.1 Context and Intent as Panel Data

Following existing nowcasting work [5, 9], we model each contextual signal as a random process which produces a time series. The contextual signals we consider include: activities that users engage in such as the apps users use

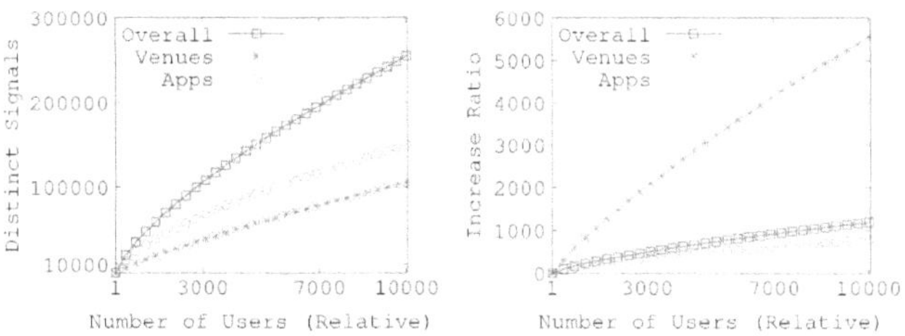

(a) Number of signals (b) Increase rate

Figure 2: Contextual signals v.s. number of users

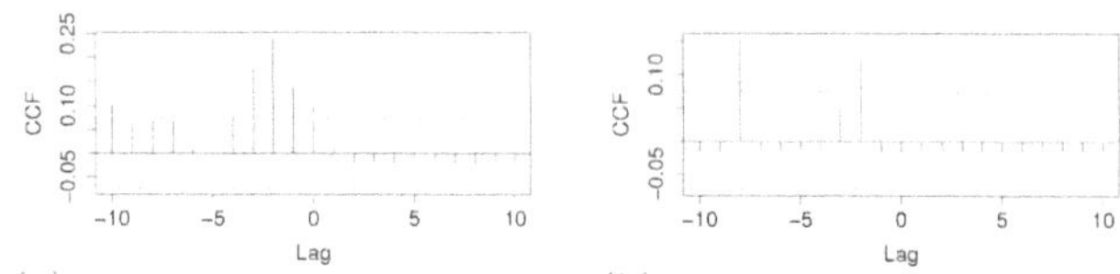

(a) Visit an educational place v.s. Use document editor apps (b) Browse social media apps v.s. Visit a shopping mall

Figure 3: Correlation between contextual signals

and venues users visit, real-time spatial measurements w.r.t. users' home and work locations (e.g., distance to home), temporal dimensions w.r.t. calendars (e.g., day of week), etc. Values in the time series of these contextual signals represent quantities relevant to the intent, e.g., the duration that users focus on an app or visit a venue. We let all the contextual signals for a user u form a *panel*, which is denoted by $\mathbf{X}^u$. Table 1 shows an example of a panel, where there are two app signals Chrome and Lync, two venue signals Starbucks and Fitness First, one spatial signal Dist-to-Home, and one temporal signal Day-of-Week, and the tracking intent is the need for a taxi. Note that to effectively provide personalized services, we use for each user the contextual signals specific to herself, which results in panels of various sizes.

3.2 Context Explosion

Next, to get insight into the data to assist model design, we analyze the size of contextual signals. In particular, we investigate the number of distinct apps used and venues visited by all users. Figures 2(a) and 2(b) plot the number and increase rate of distinct contextual signals against the number of users, respectively (here we use relative number of users to protect the usage statistics of the commercial personal assistant where we obtain the data). From Figure 2(a), we can see that the number of distinct contextual signals, including apps and venues, increases almost linearly with the increase of users. We can also see from Figure 2(b) that venue signals have the highest increase rate. This demonstrates that on average each user visits (resp. uses) a number of venues (resp. apps) different from others. With the fast growth of users, the size of contextual signals will also grow explosively. For example, in a sampled data set of a commercial personal assistant, if we put the contextual signals of all users together, there will be more than $6,000,000$ distinct venues and nearly $700,000$ distinct apps. Therefore, deploying a uniform contextual dimension is not feasible and will cause significant computation problems.

3.3 Sequential Correlation

Correlation between Context and Intent. Next, we investigate the sequential correlation between intent and contextual signals with the cross-correlation coefficient (CCF). CCF, which is also known as sliding inner-product, measures the similarity of two series at different lags, and is widely used to estimate the degree of sequential correlation. Specifically, the CCF between two series $\mathbf{x} = \mathbf{X}^u_{[i]}$ and $\mathbf{y} = \mathbf{X}^u_{[j]}$ from a panel $\mathbf{X}^u$ (here $\mathbf{X}^u_{[k]}$ denotes the kth row of $\mathbf{X}^u$) at lag τ is computed by

$$\mathcal{R}(\tau) = \frac{\sum_t [(\mathbf{x}(t) - \mu_{\mathbf{x}})(\mathbf{y}(t-\tau) - \mu_{\mathbf{y}})]}{\sqrt{\sum_t (\mathbf{x}(t) - \mu_{\mathbf{x}})^2}\sqrt{\sum_t (\mathbf{y}(t-\tau) - \mu_{\mathbf{y}})^2}},$$

where $\mathbf{z}(t)$ indicates the tth element in series $\mathbf{z}$ and $\mu_{\mathbf{z}}$ is the mean of $\mathbf{z}$. Figure 4 shows the CCF at various lags between randomly selected contextual signals and intent. Here each lag is one hour. From Figure 4(a) we can see that while using browsers (context), some users often intend to listen to music (intent) because the two series have a significantly larger CCF at lag zero. We can also see from Figure 4(b) that users often intend to take taxis before and after dining at a restaurant (because at lags around zero the CCFs are significant). Similarly, from Figure 4(c) we know that users often intend to send messages after playing video games. We measure the context "arrive at office" by the distance to office, and we can see from Figure 4(d) that at lag zero the CCF between "arrive at office" and "check calendar" is significantly small. This means that users often intend to check their calendar when their distance to office is small, i.e., arriving at office. From these case studies, we can conclude that users' intent has strong sequential correlation with contextual signals. Note that this does not mean intent is *determined* by only a single signal. Intent in general has a complicated correlation with many signals. Different user groups also have very different patterns.

Correlation between Contextual Signals. We next investigate the correlation between contextual signals. Figure 5 shows the covariance (using heatmap) between contextual signals of a randomly selected panel. We can see that some signals exhibit strong covariance because there are many high heat (bright) points besides the main diagonal (which shows the covariance of a signal with itself, and has the highest heat). This indicates that there is redundancy in contextual signals, and hence we can compactly represent the structure and dynamics of a panel with low-dimensional factors. As with context and intent, we also investigate the sequential correlation between contextual signals. Figure 3 shows the CCF at various lags between randomly selected signals. We can see from Figure 3(a) that users often use document editor apps after they visit an educational place such as a university (as the CCFs from lags -4 to 0 are significant). We can also see from Figure 3(b) that users often visit a shopping mall several hours after using social media apps (e.g., Facebook). From these analyses, we can conclude that contextual signals are also closely correlated.

4. THE KP2 MODEL

The fundamental idea of the KP2 model is to represent the structure and dynamics of panels with low-dimensional latent factors, and utilize the evolution of these latent factors for intent tracking. The structure representation is achieved by techniques inspired by PARAFAC2 tensor decomposition, and the dynamics and sequential correlation in latent factors are enforced by the proposed Kalman filter regularization. To the best of our knowledge, this is the first time Kalman filter is used as a regularizer for tensor decomposition. It needs careful model design to seamlessly join the two components and make them collaborate optimally.

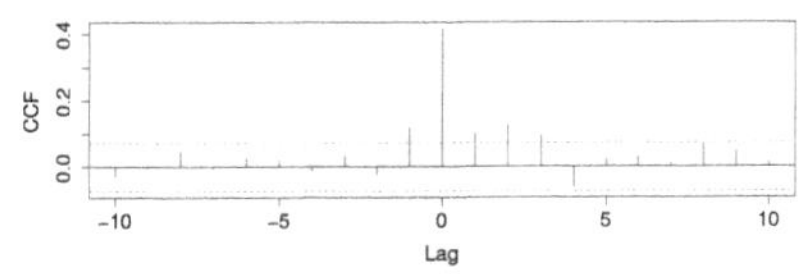

(a) Use browsers v.s. Listen to music

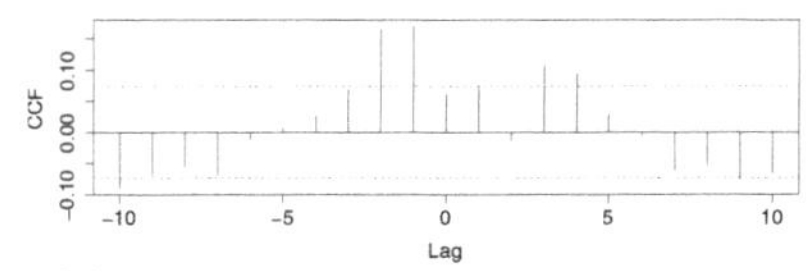

(b) Stay at restaurants v.s. Take taxis

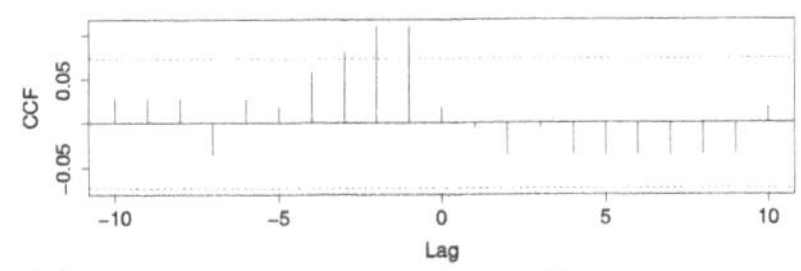

(c) Play video games v.s. Send messages

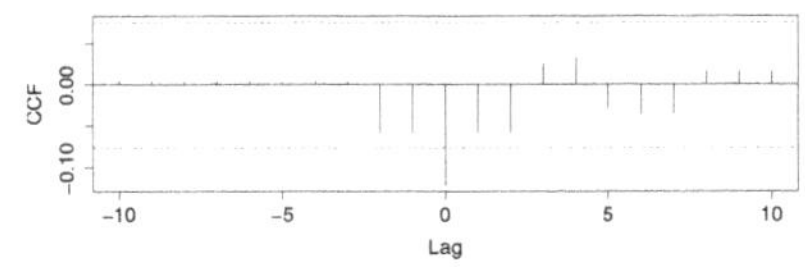

(d) Distance to office v.s. Check calendar

Figure 4: Sequential correlation between contextual signals and intent

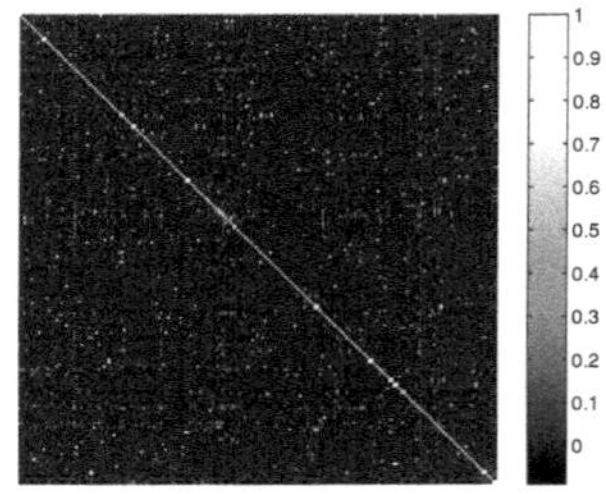

Figure 5: Sample covariance matrix of contextual signals in a randomly selected panel

4.1 Model Formulation

4.1.1 Obtaining Compact Representation

From the above analyses, we have seen that intent and contextual signals exhibit close co-occurring and sequential correlation. To obtain a compact model and hence retain effective prediction power, we assume that the bulk of dynamic interactions among contextual signals and intent can be represented by a few low-dimensional latent factors, i.e.,

$$\mathbf{X}^u \approx \mathbf{\Lambda}^u \mathbf{F}^u ,$$

where $\mathbf{X}^u \in \mathbb{R}^{N^u \times T}$ is the panel of user u with N^u contextual signals, $\mathbf{F}^u \in \mathbb{R}^{R \times T}$ contains the latent factors with $R < N^u$, and $\mathbf{\Lambda}^u \in \mathbb{R}^{N^u \times R}$ is called the factor *loading* matrix. Since the series in a single panel often contain very sparse records, we propose to utilize the collaborative capabilities among users to address the data sparsity problem. Specifically, we propose to represent the common structure of all users' panels with the same set of latent factors, i.e. (note the removal of superscript u from $\mathbf{F}^u$),

$$\mathbf{X}^u \approx \mathbf{\Lambda}^u \mathbf{F} \quad \text{for all} \quad u = 1, 2, \ldots, M .$$

Such latent factors $\mathbf{F}$ are shared by all users. They effectively summarize the dynamic interactions among all panels, and represent the universal co-movement of various series.

We can obtain such latent factors with the PARAFAC2 tensor decomposition [11, 14] by organizing all panels into a tensor and aligning them by the time dimension. Figure 6 illustrates the formed tensor and PARAFAC2 decomposition. In particular, PARAFAC2 decomposition can be formulated as the following optimization problem

$$(\mathbf{F}, \mathbf{\Lambda}^u)_{\{u=1,\ldots,M\}} = \min_{\mathbf{F}, \mathbf{\Lambda}^u} \sum_{u=1}^{M} \|\mathbf{X}^u - \mathbf{\Lambda}^u \mathbf{F}\|_F^2 ,$$

where F stands for the Frobenius norm. An advantage of the above formulation is that it effectively handles the context explosion problem (cf. Section 3.2). The reason is that unlike Tucker or CANDECOMP/PARAFAC (CP) tensor decomposition (cf. [14]), which requires the tensor to be of uniform size in every dimension, this formulation allows the contextual dimension to be of various sizes, and hence avoids deploying a uniform contextual dimension for all users. Another advantage is that, without modifying (e.g., truncating) the panels to form a tensor, it well keeps all the personalized signals of each user, which enables us to provide high-quality personalized services.

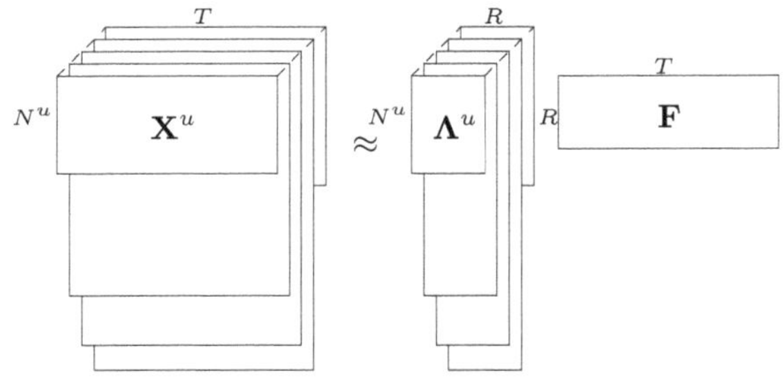

Figure 6: PARAFAC2 decomposition

4.1.2 Regularization with Kalman Filter

Utilizing only the PARAFAC2 decomposition cannot effectively model the sequential correlation within panels. It also cannot support real-time nowcasting because the decomposition is computationally expensive. To enforce sequential correlation, and enable efficient and robust-to-noise intent computation on mobile devices, we propose using Kalman filter to regularize the latent factors, and use the obtained dynamic system for real-time intent nowcasting. Specifically, we consider the linear dynamic system to which Kalman filter applies as follows:

$$\begin{cases} \mathbf{x}_t^u = \mathbf{\Lambda}^u \mathbf{f}_t + \boldsymbol{\xi}_t^u , & t = 1, \ldots, T , \\ \mathbf{f}_t = \mathbf{A}^u \mathbf{f}_{t-1} + \boldsymbol{\omega}_t^u , & t = 2, \ldots, T , \end{cases}$$

where $\mathbf{x}_t^u$ (resp. $\mathbf{f}_t$) is the tth column of matrix $\mathbf{X}^u$ (resp. $\mathbf{F}$), $\mathbf{\Lambda}^u \in \mathbb{R}^{N^u \times R}$ is the loading (observation) matrix, $\mathbf{A}^u \in \mathbb{R}^{R \times R}$ is the transition (system) matrix, and $\boldsymbol{\xi}_t^u$ and $\boldsymbol{\omega}_t^u$ are mutually independent Gaussian random variables with known positive definite covariance matrices $\mathbf{\Psi}^u$ and $\mathbf{Q}^u$, respectively. To further simplify the dynamic system, we assume that the covariance matrix $\mathbf{\Psi}^u$ is diagonal.

Let the vectorization of matrix $\mathbf{U} \in \mathbb{R}^{N \times T}$ be

$$\text{vec}(\mathbf{U}) = \begin{bmatrix} \mathbf{u}_1 \\ \mathbf{u}_2 \\ \vdots \\ \mathbf{u}_T \end{bmatrix}, \text{ and let } \text{diag}(\mathbf{V}, T) = \left.\begin{bmatrix} \mathbf{V} & \mathbf{0} & \cdots & \mathbf{0} \\ \mathbf{0} & \mathbf{V} & \ddots & \vdots \\ \vdots & \ddots & \ddots & \mathbf{0} \\ \mathbf{0} & \cdots & \mathbf{0} & \mathbf{V} \end{bmatrix}\right\} T$$

be the matrix with T input matrices V at the main diagonal. Using Kalman filter as a regularizer, we formulate the following optimization problem for intent tracking:

$$\min_{\mathbf{F}, \mathbf{\Lambda}^u, \mathbf{A}^u} \sum_{u=1}^{M} \|\mathbf{X}^u - \mathbf{\Lambda}^u \mathbf{F}\|_F^2 + \frac{\lambda}{2} \Big(\|\mathbf{H}^u \mathbf{f} - \mathbf{x}^u\|_{\mathbf{\Psi}_u^{-1}}^2 + \|\mathbf{G}^u \mathbf{f} - \mathbf{w}^u\|_{\mathbf{Q}_u^{-1}}^2 \Big) , \quad (1)$$

where $\mathbf{H}^u = \text{diag}(\mathbf{\Lambda}^u, T)$, $\mathbf{f} = \text{vec}(\mathbf{F})$, $\mathbf{x}^u = \text{vec}(\mathbf{X}^u)$,

$$\mathbf{G}^u = \begin{bmatrix} \mathbf{I} & \mathbf{0} & & \\ -\mathbf{A}^u & \mathbf{I} & \ddots & \\ & \ddots & \ddots & \mathbf{0} \\ & & -\mathbf{A}^u & \mathbf{I} \end{bmatrix}, \quad \mathbf{w}^u = \begin{bmatrix} \mathbf{A}^u\mathbf{f}_0 \\ \mathbf{0} \\ \vdots \\ \mathbf{0} \end{bmatrix},$$

$\mathbf{\Psi}_u = \text{diag}(\mathbf{\Psi}^u, T)$, $\mathbf{Q}_u = \text{diag}(\mathbf{Q}^u, T)$, $\mathbf{f}_0$ are initial factors (usually $\mathbf{f}_0 = \mathbf{0}$), and the matrix norm of a vector $\|\mathbf{a}\|^2_{\mathbf{Y}}$ denotes $\mathbf{a}'\mathbf{Y}\mathbf{a}$. Latent factors obtained from the above optimization problem not only compactly represent the panel structure shared by all users, but model the common temporal dynamics and sequential correlation within all panels.

After obtaining the latent factors $\mathbf{F}$ (cf. Section 4.2 for algorithms that solve the optimization problem), transition matrix $\mathbf{A}^u$, loading matrix $\mathbf{\Lambda}^u$, and noise covariance matrices $\mathbf{\Psi}^u$ and $\mathbf{Q}^u$, we can build up a personalized dynamic system for each user, and hence implement efficient real-time intent nowcasting. Specifically, we first estimate a priori latent factors $\tilde{\mathbf{f}}_t$ for the current time step t with system transition $\mathbf{A}^u\mathbf{f}_{t-1}$. When contextual signals $\mathbf{x}^u_t$ are continuously available within t, we compute a posteriori latent factors $\mathbf{f}_t$ with Kalman filter (details on computing a posteriori latent factors with Kalman filter are presented in Appendix A.1), and then use the a posteriori latent factors in the following regression for intent nowcasting.

4.1.3 *Regression for Nowcasting*

With the learned latent factors $\mathbf{F}$, we obtain the relationship between intent and latent factors with regression. In particular, assuming that intent and contextual signals are jointly normal (which is common in the real world), we obtain that the likelihood $\Gamma(\mathcal{F}(\zeta, \mathbf{x}^u_t) = 1)$ of user u has the intent ζ is a linear function of the latent factors $\mathbf{f}_t$ [5], i.e.,

$$\Gamma(\mathcal{F}(\zeta, \mathbf{x}^u_t) = 1) = \alpha^u + \boldsymbol{\beta}^{u\prime}\mathbf{f}_t \,,$$

where α^u and $\boldsymbol{\beta}^u$ are coefficients of the function which can be estimated by regression on historical intent and latent factors. We apply this function to the a posteriori latent factors and obtain the intent likelihood. When the likelihood is above a chosen threshold, we make the prediction that user u has the intent, i.e., $\mathcal{F}(\zeta, \mathbf{x}^u_t) = 1$. The threshold we use is the median of fitted likelihood.

4.2 Optimization Algorithm

We propose solving the optimization problem of Eq. 1 by first estimating noise covariance matrices $\mathbf{\Psi}^u$ and $\mathbf{Q}^u$ with principal component analysis, and then estimating parameters $\mathbf{F}$, $\mathbf{A}^u$, and $\mathbf{\Lambda}^u$ with stochastic gradient descent.

4.2.1 *Estimating Noise Covariance Matrices*

We estimate the observation noise covariance $\mathbf{\Psi}^u$ by residuals of approximating the sample covariance matrix of a panel with its largest R principal components. Specifically, we first standardize signals in a panel so that they have zero sample mean and unitary sample variance, i.e.,

$$x^u_{it} = \frac{1}{\hat{\sigma}^u_i}(\bar{x}^u_{it} - \hat{\mu}^u_i) \,,$$

where $\bar{x}^u_{it}$ means the original data of $\mathbf{X}^u$, $\hat{\mu}^u_i = \frac{1}{T}\sum_{t=1}^T \bar{x}^u_{it}$, and $\hat{\sigma}^u_i = \sqrt{\frac{1}{T}\sum_{t=1}^T (\bar{x}^u_{it} - \hat{\mu}^u_i)^2}$. Let the sample covariance matrix $\mathbf{S}^u$ of panel $\mathbf{X}^u$ be

$$\mathbf{S}^u = \frac{1}{T}\sum_{t=1}^T \mathbf{x}^u_t \mathbf{x}^{u\prime}_t \,.$$

Assuming that noises for different signals are independent, the covariance $\mathbf{\Psi}^u$ is estimated by

$$\mathbf{\Psi}^u \approx \text{Diag}(\mathbf{S}^u - \mathbf{W}^u\mathbf{\Sigma}^u\mathbf{W}^{u\prime}) \,,$$

where $\mathbf{\Sigma}^u \in \mathbb{R}^{R\times R}$ is diagonal and contains the largest R eigenvalues of $\mathbf{S}^u$, $\mathbf{W}^u \in \mathbb{R}^{N^u \times R}$ consists of the corresponding eigenvectors subject to $\mathbf{W}^{u\prime}\mathbf{W}^u = \mathbf{I}$, and "Diag$(\cdot)$" means keeping only the elements on main diagonal.

The transition noise covariance $\mathbf{Q}^u$ is estimated in a similar way, except that we need to first obtain an initial estimate of latent factors $\tilde{\mathbf{F}}^u$ and transition matrix $\tilde{\mathbf{A}}^u$. In particular, we obtain approximated latent factors by projecting the signals to the largest R principle components of $\mathbf{S}^u$ (the space spanned by the largest R eigenvectors), i.e.,

$$\tilde{\mathbf{f}}^u_t = \mathbf{W}^{u\prime}\mathbf{x}^u_t \,,$$

and apply vector auto-regression (VAR) on these approximated latent factors to estimate the transition matrix, i.e.,

$$\tilde{\mathbf{A}}^u = \sum_{t=2}^T \tilde{\mathbf{f}}^u_t \tilde{\mathbf{f}}^{u\prime}_{t-1} \left(\sum_{t=2}^T \tilde{\mathbf{f}}^u_{t-1}\tilde{\mathbf{f}}^{u\prime}_{t-1}\right) .$$

The covariance matrix $\mathbf{Q}^u$ is then estimated by the residuals of VAR

$$\mathbf{Q}^u = \frac{1}{T-1}\sum_{t=2}^T \tilde{\mathbf{f}}^u_t\tilde{\mathbf{f}}^{u\prime}_t - \tilde{\mathbf{A}}^u\left(\frac{1}{T-1}\sum_{t=2}^T \tilde{\mathbf{f}}^u_{t-1}\tilde{\mathbf{f}}^{u\prime}_{t-1}\right)\tilde{\mathbf{A}}^{u\prime} \,.$$

4.2.2 *Gradient Computation*

Next, we estimate parameters $\mathbf{F}$, $\mathbf{A}^u$, and $\mathbf{\Lambda}^u$ with stochastic gradient descent (SGD), where a key task is to obtain the gradient. We mainly use the following theorem [18] to obtain gradients w.r.t. $\mathbf{F}$, $\mathbf{\Lambda}^u$, and $\mathbf{A}^u$ in matrix forms.

THEOREM 1. *For a scalar function g of matrix $\mathbf{Y}$, the following identify holds*

$$\text{d}g = \text{Tr}\left[(\frac{\partial g}{\partial \mathbf{Y}})'\text{d}\mathbf{Y}\right] .$$

PROOF. By the definition of scalar differential, the left hand side equals

$$\text{d}g = \sum_{ij} \frac{\partial g}{\partial \mathbf{Y}_{ij}}\text{d}\mathbf{Y}_{ij} \,.$$

Applying the trace operator, the right hand side equals

$$\text{Tr}\left[(\frac{\partial g}{\partial \mathbf{Y}})'\text{d}\mathbf{Y}\right] = \sum_{ij}(\frac{\partial g}{\partial \mathbf{Y}})_{ij}(\text{d}\mathbf{Y})_{ij} \,.$$

By the definitions of derivative of scalar functions of matrices and matrix differential, we have

$$(\frac{\partial g}{\partial \mathbf{Y}})_{ij} = \frac{\partial g}{\partial \mathbf{Y}_{ij}} \text{ and } (\text{d}\mathbf{Y})_{ij} = \text{d}\mathbf{Y}_{ij} \,,$$

respectively, which completes the proof. □

Applying the above theorem (cf. Appendix A.2 for more details), we obtain the gradients w.r.t. each parameter as

Table 2: Data sets

Name	Data	Time	Intent
Task-completion intent	App-launch log	11/02/2015-11/30/2015	send messages, listen to music, make reservations, get taxis
Information intent	Proactive-card log	08/15/2015-09/10/2015	news, weather, finance, calendar

follows, here J denotes the loss function of Eq. 1.

$$\frac{\partial J}{\partial \mathbf{A}^u} = \lambda \sum_{t=2}^{T} (\mathbf{Q}^u)^{-1}(\mathbf{A}^u \mathbf{f}_{t-1} - \mathbf{f}_t)\mathbf{f}_{t-1}' ,$$

$$\frac{\partial J}{\partial \mathbf{\Lambda}^u} = 2\sum_{t=1}^{T} (\mathbf{\Lambda}^u \mathbf{f}_t - \mathbf{x}_t^u)\mathbf{f}_t' + \lambda \sum_{t=1}^{T} (\mathbf{\Psi}^u)^{-1}(\mathbf{\Lambda}^u \mathbf{f}_t - \mathbf{x}_t^u)\mathbf{f}_t' ,$$

$$\frac{\partial J}{\partial \mathbf{f}_T} = 2\sum_{u=1}^{M} \mathbf{\Lambda}^{u\prime}(\mathbf{\Lambda}^u \mathbf{f}_T - \mathbf{x}_T^u) + \lambda \sum_{u=1}^{M} \mathbf{\Lambda}^{u\prime}(\mathbf{\Psi}^u)^{-1}(\mathbf{\Lambda}^u \mathbf{f}_T - \mathbf{x}_T^u)$$
$$- \lambda \sum_{u=1}^{M} (\mathbf{Q}^u)^{-1}(\mathbf{A}^u \mathbf{f}_{T-1} - \mathbf{f}_T) ,$$

$$\frac{\partial J}{\partial \mathbf{f}_t} = 2\sum_{u=1}^{M} \mathbf{\Lambda}^{u\prime}(\mathbf{\Lambda}^u \mathbf{f}_t - \mathbf{x}_t^u) + \lambda \sum_{u=1}^{M} \mathbf{\Lambda}^{u\prime}(\mathbf{\Psi}^u)^{-1}(\mathbf{\Lambda}^u \mathbf{f}_t - \mathbf{x}_t^u)$$
$$+ \lambda \sum_{u=1}^{M} \mathbf{A}^{u\prime}(\mathbf{Q}^u)^{-1}(\mathbf{A}^u \mathbf{f}_t - \mathbf{f}_{t+1})$$
$$- \lambda \sum_{u=1}^{M} (\mathbf{Q}^u)^{-1}(\mathbf{A}^u \mathbf{f}_{t-1} - \mathbf{f}_t) \quad \text{for } t = 1, \ldots, T-1 .$$

We then apply SGD to estimate these parameters.

5. EXPERIMENTS

5.1 Set-Up

Data Sets. From a commercial personal assistant, we sample two real-world data sets for the two types of intent: task-completion intent and information intent, respectively. The sampled data sets consist of 8,857 anonymous users in total. The data set for task-completion intent contains app-launch log recorded by the personal assistant from November 2nd to November 30th 2015. The app launch log effectively indicates users' task-completion intent because when a user asks the personal assistant to do some job, the personal assistant may open relevant apps to complete the task. In the experiments, we randomly select four types of task-completion intent: sending a message (**Message**), listening to music (**Music**), making a reservation (**Reservation**) and getting a taxi (**Taxi**). The data set for information intent contains proactive-card log of the personal assistant from August 15th to September 10th 2015. The log keeps records of the proactively triggered cards (which present various types of information such as events, sports, food and drinks, and stock prices) that are viewed by users for a certain amount of time or clicked for further information. In the experiments, we randomly pick out four types of cards: news (**News**), weather (**Weather**), stock prices (**Finance**), and calendar (**Calendar**). The details of these data sets are summarized in Table 2.

Contextual Signals. We use contextual signals that can be effectively sensed by mobile devices. In particular, we use the used apps, visited venues, distances to home and work places, time of day, and day of week (a panel example containing such signals is presented in Table 1).

Evaluation Metrics. The metrics we use to evaluate the model include the F-measure and Hit-ratio. The F-measure evaluates the precision and recall of model predicted intent, and hit-ratio measures the model's user coverage. In particular, for a given type of intent ζ, let ϕ be the number of time steps used for testing, $\mathbf{s}^u = (s_1^u, \ldots, s_\phi^u)$ with $s_t^u = F(\zeta, \mathbf{x}_t^u)$ for $t = 1, \ldots, \phi$, i.e., $s_t^u = 1$ means user u has intent ζ at time step t and $s_t^u = 0$ means the opposite. Let $\mathbf{s}_p^u = (s_{p1}^u, \ldots, s_{p\phi}^u)$ be the model's prediction. The precision and recall are computed by

$$\text{Pre} = \frac{\sum_u \mathbf{s}^{u\prime}\mathbf{s}_p^u}{\sum_u \mathbf{1}'\mathbf{s}_p^u} \quad \text{and} \quad \text{Rec} = \frac{\sum_u \mathbf{s}^{u\prime}\mathbf{s}_p^u}{\sum_u \mathbf{1}'\mathbf{s}^u} .$$

respectively, and the F-measure equals

$$\text{F-measure} = 2 \times \frac{\text{Pre} \times \text{Rec}}{\text{Pre} + \text{Rec}} .$$

The Hit-ratio is computed by

$$\text{Hit-ratio} = \frac{|\{u | \mathbf{s}^{u\prime}\mathbf{s}_p^u > 0\}|}{M} ,$$

where the numerator is the cardinality of the set of users having at least one accurate intent prediction and the denominator is the number of all users. The hit-ratio measures the coverage of users who will have at least one pleasant experience with the personal assistant, which is an important factor for real-world product.

Compared Methods. The methods we compare with KP2 include the following

- **LambdaMART (LM).** The LM method is essentially a boosted tree version of LambdaRank. It has strong performance in many real-world applications (e.g., search engines and contextual ranking [21]) and won the 2010 Yahoo! Learning to Rank Challenge.
- **Factorization machine (FM).** FM is a state-of-the-art method for context-aware and sequential recommendations. It performs effectively in personalized item-tag recommendation and sequential next-basket recommendation [20].
- **Kalman filter (K).** K is widely used in time series fore/now-casting. It effectively nowcasts the current gross domestic product (GDP) with the real-time data of various macroeconomic variables [5], and the method is applied in many agencies including Federal Reserve Board and European Central Bank.
- **PARAFAC2+Kalman filter (P2+K).** The P2+K method uses the PARAFAC2 and Kalman filter in a sequential way[1] instead of utilizing the two components in a unified fashion like KP2. P2+K first obtains latent factors with PARAFAC2, and then smooths the transition of latent factors with Kalman filter.

Experiment Setting. For each data set, we use the first three quarters (~three weeks) to train the model, and

[1]We cannot compare with methods utilizing only P2 because the Kalman filter K is essential for prediction.

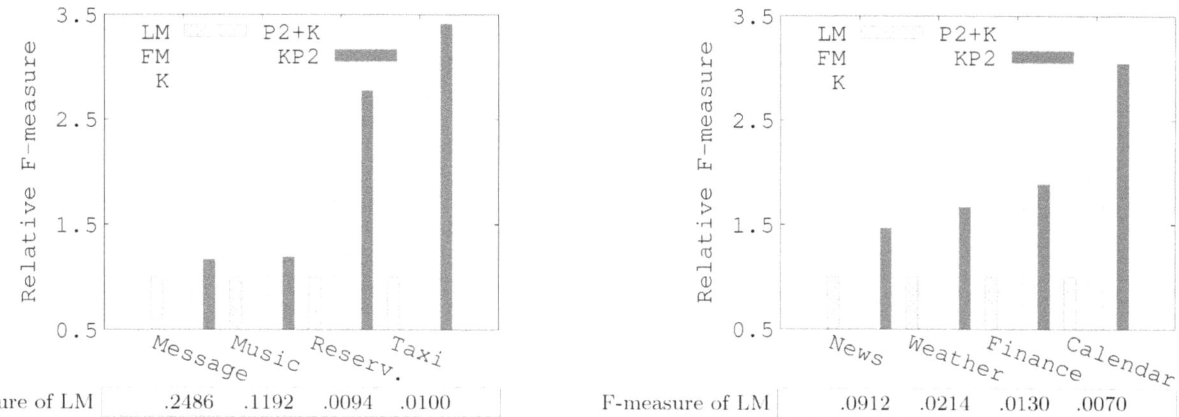

(a) Task-completion intent (b) Information intent

Figure 7: Performance of each method evaluated by F-measure (relative to LM)

the last quarter (~one week) for testing. We use one hour as the tracking granularity. We use mini-batch SGD with a batch size of 30 and an initial learning rate of 10^{-4} with bold driver adaption. We use default parameters for all compared methods, and set $\lambda = 0.5$ and $R = 2$ for KP2 by default. We will study the effect of parameters in Section 5.3.

5.2 Results

5.2.1 *Comparison across Models on F-measure*

In the first set of experiments, we evaluate the performance of KP2 by comparing it with various methods w.r.t. F-measure. Figures 7(a) and 7(b) show the performance of each method (relative to LM) on the four types of task-completion intent and four types of information intent, respectively (the absolute F-measure of LM is shown at the bottom of corresponding intent). From the two figures, we can see that KP2 significantly outperforms all other methods on all types of intent in terms of F-measure.

KP2 v.s. LM. We can see that KP2 largely outperforms LM on every type of intent. Its performance advantage to LM is up to 3.5 times (on Taxi intent) and is greater than 1.5 times on almost all types of information intent. LM is an assemble of decision trees. Although it has best performance in many ranking problems, the poor performance of LM indicates that it fails at building up the complex relationship between context and intent from raw contextual signals. The strong performance of KP2 indicates that it is an effective method to summarize the structure and dynamics of panels with a few latent factors, as it results in a compact model and retains stronger prediction power.

KP2 v.s. FM. We can also see that KP2 performs significantly better than FM on all types of intent, and its performance advantage to FM is up to two times (on Message intent). FM factorizes the panel, takes into account the sequential correlation, and learns an optimal pair-wise ranking model. We can see from Figures 7(a) and 7(b) that except for Message and Music intent, FM has better performance than LM on all other types of intent, which indicates the importance of modeling sequential correlation. The worse performance of FM than KP2, however, indicates that considering only pair-wise correlation is insufficient for intent tracking, which needs to consider longer sequential correlation in the temporal dimension.

KP2 v.s. K. On every type of intent, KP2 also performs considerably better than the K method. Like KP2, the K method also summarizes panels with a few latent factors and considers sequential correlation in the temporal dimension. The drawback of K is that it fails to leverage collaborative capabilities among users because it can only apply to panels of each individual user. By factorizing panels of all users simultaneously with PARAFAC2, KP2 effectively exploits collaborative power among users, captures common temporal recurring patterns, and proficiently handles the data sparsity problem.

KP2 v.s. P2+K. From Figures 7(a) and 7(b), we can also see that KP2 has much better performance than P2+K on all types of intent. Similar to KP2, P2+K is a compact model, considers the sequential correlation and utilizes collaborative capabilities among users. However, using PARAFAC2 and Kalman filter separately, P2+K is unable to control the relative importance of each component, and fails to make them collaborate optimally. On the contrary, KP2 seamlessly joins the two components and is able to fully control their cooperation.

5.2.2 *Comparison across Models on Hit-ratio*

Next, we evaluate KP2 with hit-ratio. The hit-ratio reveals the percentage of users who have (at least one) satisfying proactive experiences with the personal assistant. Such experiences will motivate more interactions and produce a virtuous circle (as more user habits are learned), which is very important for real-world product. Tables 3 and 4 present the hit-ratio of each method on the four types of task-completion intent and four types of information intent, respectively. We can see that KP2 has the highest hit-ratio on all types of intent and significantly outperforms LM and FM. The hit-ratio of KP2 is up to 98.6% (on News intent) and is higher than 50% on almost all types of intent. This indicates that KP2 is able to provide satisfying proactive experiences for a large portion of users and is more suitable than other methods for real-world applications.

We can also see that although the hit-ratios of LM are the lowest among all methods, its hit-ratios on Message, Music, and News intent are higher than other types of intent. This is because these three types of intent correlate with a relatively simpler context, making it relatively less difficult to predict. For example, for the Message intent, some users tend to send messages in regular time windows (e.g., after 9 p.m. or Sunday), which makes the intent closely related to the time of day and day of week. For the Music intent, some users tend to listen to music while driving or using

Table 3: Hit-ratio for task-completion intent

Model	Message	Music	Reservation	Taxi
LM	.6633	.4685	.0104	.0186
FM	.7381	.5925	.1354	.1398
K	.9698	.9331	.4896	.4565
P2+K	.9741	.9547	.4583	.5013
KP2	**.9799**	**.9764**	**.5625**	**.5409**

Table 4: Hit-ratio for information intent

Model	Calendar	Weather	Finance	News
LM	.0056	.0457	.0193	.3748
FM	.0970	.1615	.1273	.6070
K	.4100	.6884	.4790	.9641
P2+K	.4127	.7210	.4874	.9853
KP2	**.4183**	**.7357**	**.5462**	**.9857**

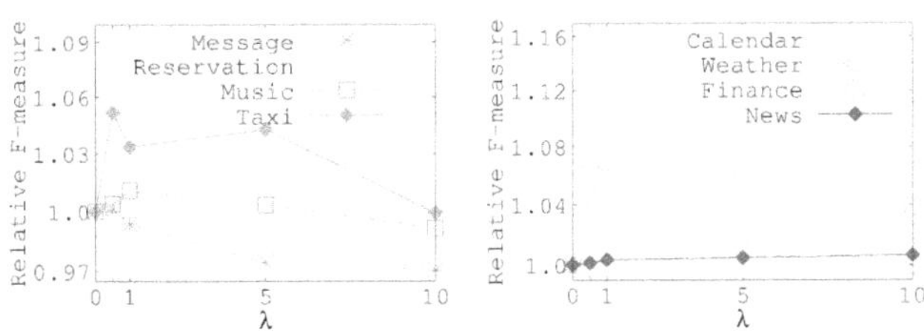

(a) Task-completion intent (b) Information Intent

Figure 8: Relative performance against λ

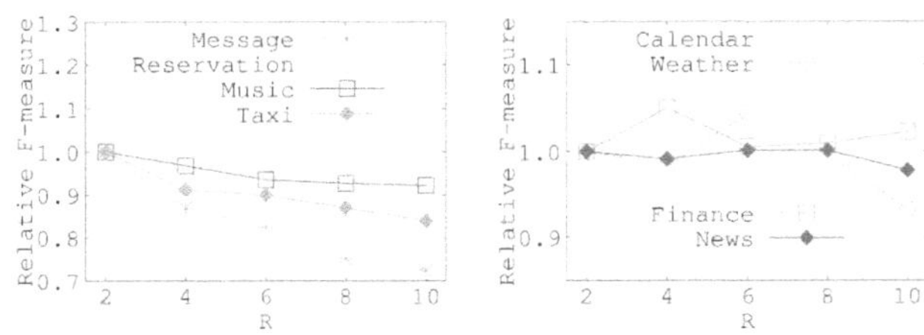

(a) Task-completion intent (b) Information Intent

Figure 9: Relative performance against R

browsers, which relates the intent to the spatial distances and a few widely used apps. Other types of intent such as Reservation and Taxi, however, occur in much more diverse context and are related to much more complex contextual signals. The two tables also show that nowcasting related methods including K, P2+K, and KP2 have a much higher hit-ratio than other methods. This demonstrates that nowcasting methods are more suitable for intent tracking.

From the above experiments, we can see that on all types of intent, KP2 has the strongest performance among all methods in terms of both F-measure and hit-ratio metrics. This demonstrates that KP2 is able to track users intent more accurately and has a very large user coverage for satisfying proactive experiences, which makes KP2 a more appropriate method for real-world applications.

5.3 Effect of Parameters

5.3.1 Effect of λ

Next, we study the performance of KP2 under various settings. We first study the effect of λ by changing λ from 0 to 10. Figures 8(a) and 8(b) plot the F-measure of KP2 (relative to $\lambda = 0$) against λ on task-completion intent and information intent, respectively. The performance measured by hit-ratio is consistent with F-measure, and hence is omitted. Parameter λ controls the degree of Kalman filter regularization, which enforces the sequential correlation of latent factors. From the figures, we can see that with the increase of λ, the performance of KP2 first increases and then decreases on all types of intent (except News). When $\lambda = 0$, there is no enforced sequential correlation for the latent factors, which leads to decreased performance. When λ is greater than 5, the overemphasis on sequential correlation interrupts the utilization of collaborative capabilities and extraction of latent factors. This again demonstrates the significance of modeling sequential correlation and the importance of the ability to fully control the cooperation of PARAFAC2 and Kalman filtering. We can also see that for Taxi, Calendar and Finance intent, the effect of λ is more significant (up to 10%). This shows that these types of intent have a stronger sequential correlation with contextual signals (e.g., such intent often occur when users leave or arrive certain venues). The flexibility of KP2 on modeling such correlation enables us to properly and effectively handle the tracking of such intent.

5.3.2 Effect of R

Next, we study the effect of R by varying R from 2 to 10. Figures 9(a) and 9(b) depict the performance of KP2 with the change of R on task-completion intent and information intent, respectively (relative to $R = 2$). From Figure 9(a), we can see that the performance of KP2 decreases with the increase of R on almost all types of task-completion intent (except Reservation). This is because two-dimensional latent factors are already able to capture the bulk of structure and co-movement of contextual signals related to task-completion intent (which is consistent with the findings in [9]). When R becomes larger, it needs more data to train an effective model because more parameters need to be estimated and the model also tends to overfit to the training data. From Figure 9(b), we can see that the information intent has more complex relationships with R. The performance of KP2 (on average) first increases and then decreases with the increase of R. This indicates that information intent is relevant to a higher dimensional latent space, which has a more complicated structure and the transition of latent factors is more flexible. We can also see that on information intent, the performance variance of KP2 is in most cases within five percent, which means KP2 has the ability to address the different requirements of various information intent.

5.4 If-Do Triggers Generation

Next, we experiment on generating if-do *triggers* from contextual signals. If-do triggers are conditions on which users want certain tasks (resp. information) to be proactively completed (resp. recommended). For instance, in the statement "show me today's headlines every 8:00 a.m. when I am at home", "today's headlines" are the recommended information and "every 8:00 a.m. when I am at home" is the trigger. Automatically generating such triggers (and let users decide which to deploy) will significantly enhance interactions between users and personal assistants. The triggers can also be easily deployed in large-scale applications.

The general methodology of generating triggers is to use decision trees to model the contextual signals in time steps where the intent probability predicted by KP2 is above a certain threshold. The reason we use the predicted probability is because: i) having no record of intent in the log does not imply users do not have such intent, which may

Table 5: If-do triggers for intent

Intent	Triggers
News	Between 6:00 a.m. and 10:00 a.m., Friday, or weekends, distance to office > 10km
Message	Between 5:30 p.m. and 7:30 p.m., weekday, arriving at a food and drink venue
Music	Later than 6:30 p.m., using browsers
Ride	Later than 8:30 p.m., weekday, distance to office > 8km, leaving a supermarket
Reservation	Earlier than 6:30 p.m., Sunday, playing computer games for a long time

be simply because users do not interact with the personal assistant; and ii) the KP2 model effectively generalizes the training instances with common recurring patters and latent characteristics. We follow the paths of decision trees to positive instances to generate the triggers. Table 5 shows one randomly selected trigger for each of the four types of task-completion intent and News intent. We omit certain contextual signals to protect the privacy of anonymous users. We can see that these triggers are quite intuitive for the corresponding intent and can apply to many users with similar habits. This experiment (to some extent) reveals the latent characteristics used by KP2 to predict users intent, and demonstrates the ability of KP2 to automatically generate effective if-do triggers.

6. RELATED WORK

6.1 Context-Aware Recommendation

Traditional recommendation models focus on a specific intent, e.g., to find movies [6], books [19] or music tracks [8], and aim at recommending new items for the intent, which are content-centered. The intent tracking problem, however, focuses on the recurrence of users' intent so as to perform tasks or present information closely related to the intent, which is user-centered. For instance, users may not be interested in watching repeated movies (where content matters), however, they may want to get a taxi every time after shopping (and which taxi does not matter). Following the line of content-centered recommendation, context-aware recommendation [4, 17] further considers users' context, such as time, locations, devices, etc., as users' preferences over new items may be different in different context. Besides the aforementioned difference, the context in context-ware recommendation usually contains only signals about physical environments, and their combinations can be enumerated, e.g., 24 hours × 7 days × location types such as home and office [13, 25]. However, in intent tracking, there are numerous contextual signals even for a single user, and the combinations of context cannot be easily enumerated (as illustrated in Table 5). There are also time-aware models that consider the evolving [15] or seasonal variance [24] of user preferences. These methods cannot apply to intent tracking, because instead of evolving on a weekly or a monthly basis, the intent changes swiftly in very short time.

6.2 Time Series Fore/Now-casting

Similar to KP2, there are methods that use correlated time series to predict the target series. The nowcasting model in [5, 9] utilizes monthly macroeconomic indicators such as industrial production and consumer prices to nowcast the contemporaneous GDP, which is only released quarterly. The model obtains a parsimonious approximation of the available information set by a few common factors and applies Kalman filter for prediction, which is the K method used in our experiments and we have seen that it is outperformed by KP2 because it does not consider collaborative capabilities among users. Similarly, the model in [16] uses the number of tweets containing certain automatically selected tokens to nowcast levels of rainfall; the model in [23] conducts forecast on case counts of influenza-like-illness with dynamic Poisson auto-regression using various indicator data sources such as national case counts and Google Flu Trends; and the model in [7] uses Markov process with additional constraints, e.g., network connections, to model co-evolving of multiple time series of signals from a sensor network. One common difference between these methods and KP2 is that they are well designed for one target variable, but not for use cases that provide personalized services for a large number of users, and hence these methods also do not utilize the collaborative capabilities among users.

6.3 Intent Mining and Ranking

Using search engine query log, the method in [10] identifies sequences of search queries with coherent intent, e.g., a sequence of queries on tasks of planning a wedding, interests of a sports team, or habits of regularly reading a news site. Different from tracking the recurrence of intent, this method is used to obtain coherent search queries, which can be further mined to discover new intent and obtain content relevant to users' long-term interests. Therefore, the method cannot apply to intent tracking. The model in [21] addresses proactive experiences in search engines and personal assistants. It uses users' cross platform behavior patterns to re-rank the proactively triggered information cards, and hence cannot apply to intent tracking, either.

7. CONCLUSIONS

It is important and beneficial for personal assistants to offer high-quality proactive experiences. Closely tracking users' intent helps personal assistants achieve this goal by presenting (resp. completing) the right information (resp. tasks) users intend to know (resp. do) at the right time. Users' intent has complicated correlation with various heterogeneous contextual signals. By modeling the contextual signals and intent as panel data, the proposed KP2 nowcasting model compactly represents the structure and comovement of context and intent by a few latent factors. By applying such representation to all users, the KP2 model effectively utilizes the collaborative capabilities among users. It avoids the context explosion problem with a tensor decomposition technique inspired by PARAFAC2. By regularizing the decomposition with Kalman filter, it enforces sequential correlation into the latent factors, and learns for each user a personalized dynamic system, which is robust to noise and can efficiently nowcast users' intent. Extensive experiments using real-world data sets from a commercial personal assistant have shown that the KP2 model outperforms various methods for both task-completion and information intent, and is able to generate if-do triggers that enable large-scale deployment of effective proactive experiences.

8. REFERENCES

[1] http://www.google.com/landing/now/.
[2] http://dev.windows.com/en-us/cortana.

[3] http://www.apple.com/ios/whats-new/.
[4] G. Adomavicius and A. Tuzhilin. Context-aware recommender systems. In *Recommender systems handbook*, pages 217–253. Springer, 2011.
[5] M. M. Bańbura, D. Giannone, and L. Reichlin. Nowcasting. *The Oxford Handbook of Economic Forecasting*, 2012.
[6] R. M. Bell and Y. Koren. Lessons from the netflix prize challenge. *KDD Explorations*, 9(2):75–79, 2007.
[7] Y. Cai, H. Tong, W. Fan, P. Ji, and Q. He. Facets: Fast comprehensive mining of coevolving high-order time series. In *KDD*, pages 79–88, 2015.
[8] O. Celma. *Music recommendation*. Springer, 2010.
[9] D. Giannone, L. Reichlin, and D. Small. Nowcasting: The real-time informational content of macroeconomic data. *Journal of Monetary Economics*, 55(4):665–676, 2008.
[10] R. Guha, V. Gupta, V. Raghunathan, and R. Srikant. User modeling for a personal assistant. In *WSDM*, pages 275–284, 2015.
[11] R. A. Harshman. Parafac2: Mathematical and technical notes. *UCLA Working Papers in Phonetics*, 22(3044):122215, 1972.
[12] D. Jannach, L. Lerche, and M. Jugovac. Adaptation and evaluation of recommendations for short-term shopping goals. In *RecSys*, pages 211–218, 2015.
[13] A. Karatzoglou, X. Amatriain, L. Baltrunas, and N. Oliver. Multiverse recommendation: N-dimensional tensor factorization for context-aware collaborative filtering. In *RecSys*, pages 79–86, 2010.
[14] T. G. Kolda and B. W. Bader. Tensor decompositions and applications. *SIAM review*, 51(3):455–500, 2009.
[15] Y. Koren. Collaborative filtering with temporal dynamics. In *KDD*, pages 447–456, 2009.
[16] V. Lampos and N. Cristianini. Nowcasting events from the social web with statistical learning. *TIST*, 3(4):72, 2012.
[17] Q. Liu, H. Ma, E. Chen, and H. Xiong. A survey of context-aware mobile recommendations. *International Journal of Information Technology & Decision Making*, 12(01):139–172, 2013.
[18] J. R. Magnus, H. Neudecker, et al. Matrix differential calculus with applications in statistics and econometrics.
[19] R. J. Mooney and L. Roy. Content-based book recommending using learning for text categorization. In *Proceedings of the fifth ACM conference on Digital libraries*, pages 195–204, 2000.
[20] S. Rendle, C. Freudenthaler, and L. Schmidt-Thieme. Factorizing personalized markov chains for next-basket recommendation. In *WWW*, pages 811–820, 2010.
[21] M. Shokouhi and Q. Guo. From queries to cards: Re-ranking proactive card recommendations based on reactive search history. In *SIGIR*, pages 695–704, 2015.
[22] Y. Sun, N. J. Yuan, X. Xie, K. McDonald, and R. Zhang. Collaborative nowcasting for contextual recommendation. In *WWW*, pages 1407–1418, 2016.
[23] Z. Wang, P. Chakraborty, S. R. Mekaru, J. S. Brownstein, J. Ye, and N. Ramakrishnan. Dynamic poisson autoregression for influenza-like-illness case count prediction. In *KDD*, pages 1285–1294, 2015.
[24] Y. Zhang, M. Zhang, Y. Zhang, G. Lai, Y. Liu, H. Zhang, and S. Ma. Daily-aware personalized recommendation based on feature-level time series analysis. In *WWW*, pages 1373–1383, 2015.
[25] H. Zhu, E. Chen, H. Xiong, K. Yu, H. Cao, and J. Tian. Mining mobile user preferences for personalized context-aware recommendation. *TIST*, 5(4):58, 2015.

APPENDIX

A. COMPUTATION DETAILS

A.1 Correcting Factors with Kalman Filter

Let the a priori and a posteriori latent factors and error covariance matrices at time step t be $\tilde{\mathbf{f}}_t$, $\hat{\mathbf{f}}_t$, $\tilde{\mathbf{P}}_t^u$ and $\hat{\mathbf{P}}_t^u$, respectively. In the time update (prediction) step, the a priori factors for the next time step are computed by

$$\tilde{\mathbf{f}}_t = \mathbf{A}^u \hat{\mathbf{f}}_{t-1} + \boldsymbol{\omega}_t^u ,$$

and the a priori error covariance by

$$\tilde{\mathbf{P}}_t^u = \mathbf{A}^u \hat{\mathbf{P}}_{t-1}^u \hat{\mathbf{A}}^{u'} + \mathbf{Q}^u .$$

In the measurement update (correction) step, the Kalman gain $\mathbf{K}_t^u$ equals

$$\mathbf{K}_t^u = \tilde{\mathbf{P}}_t^u \boldsymbol{\Lambda}^{u\prime} (\boldsymbol{\Lambda}^u \tilde{\mathbf{P}}_t^u \boldsymbol{\Lambda}^{u\prime} + \boldsymbol{\Psi}^u)^{-1} .$$

With the Kalman gain, the a priori factors are corrected by available contextual signals (missing signals are assigned a very large variance), and the a posteriori factors equals

$$\hat{\mathbf{f}}_t = \tilde{\mathbf{f}}_t + \mathbf{K}_t^u (\mathbf{x}_t^u - \boldsymbol{\Lambda}^u \tilde{\mathbf{f}}_t) .$$

The a posteriori error covariance for next time step equals

$$\hat{\mathbf{P}}_t^u = (\mathbf{I} - \mathbf{K}_t^u \boldsymbol{\Lambda}^u) \tilde{\mathbf{P}}_t^u .$$

A.2 Details on Computing Gradients

We obtain the differential of the loss function J as follows

$$\begin{aligned}
\mathrm{d}J =& \mathrm{dTr}\Bigg[\sum_{u=1}^{M}\sum_{t=1}^{T}(\boldsymbol{\Lambda}^u\mathbf{f}_t - \mathbf{x}_t^u)'(\boldsymbol{\Lambda}^u\mathbf{f}_t - \mathbf{x}_t^u) \\
&+ \frac{\lambda}{2}\sum_{u=1}^{M}\sum_{t=1}^{T}(\boldsymbol{\Lambda}^u\mathbf{f}_t - \mathbf{x}_t^u)'(\boldsymbol{\Psi}^u)^{-1}(\boldsymbol{\Lambda}^u\mathbf{f}_t - \mathbf{x}_t^u) \\
&+ \frac{\lambda}{2}\sum_{u=1}^{M}\sum_{t=1}^{T}(\mathbf{A}^u\mathbf{f}_{t-1} - \mathbf{f}_t)'(\mathbf{Q}^u)^{-1}(\mathbf{A}^u\mathbf{f}_{t-1} - \mathbf{f}_t)\Bigg] \\
=& \sum_{u=1}^{M}\sum_{t=1}^{T}\mathrm{Tr}\left[\mathrm{d}((\boldsymbol{\Lambda}^u\mathbf{f}_t - \mathbf{x}_t^u)'(\boldsymbol{\Lambda}^u\mathbf{f}_t - \mathbf{x}_t^u))\right] \\
&+ \frac{\lambda}{2}\sum_{u=1}^{M}\sum_{t=1}^{T}\mathrm{Tr}\left[\mathrm{d}((\boldsymbol{\Lambda}^u\mathbf{f}_t - \mathbf{x}_t^u)'(\boldsymbol{\Psi}^u)^{-1}(\boldsymbol{\Lambda}^u\mathbf{f}_t - \mathbf{x}_t^u))\right] \\
&+ \frac{\lambda}{2}\sum_{u=1}^{M}\sum_{t=1}^{T}\mathrm{Tr}\left[\mathrm{d}((\mathbf{A}^u\mathbf{f}_{t-1} - \mathbf{f}_t)'(\mathbf{Q}^u)^{-1}(\mathbf{A}^u\mathbf{f}_{t-1} - \mathbf{f}_t))\right] .
\end{aligned}$$

To obtain the gradient w.r.t. $\mathbf{A}^u$, we have

$$\begin{aligned}
\mathrm{d}J =& \frac{\lambda}{2}\sum_{t=1}^{T}\mathrm{Tr}\left[\mathrm{d}((\mathbf{A}^u\mathbf{f}_{t-1} - \mathbf{f}_t)'(\mathbf{Q}^u)^{-1}(\mathbf{A}^u\mathbf{f}_{t-1} - \mathbf{f}_t))\right] \\
=& \frac{\lambda}{2}\sum_{t=1}^{T}\mathrm{Tr}\left[(\mathrm{d}(\mathbf{A}^u\mathbf{f}_{t-1} - \mathbf{f}_t))'(\mathbf{Q}^u)^{-1}(\mathbf{A}^u\mathbf{f}_{t-1} - \mathbf{f}_t)\right] \\
&+ \frac{\lambda}{2}\sum_{t=1}^{T}\mathrm{Tr}\left[(\mathbf{A}^u\mathbf{f}_{t-1} - \mathbf{f}_t)'(\mathbf{Q}^u)^{-1}\mathrm{d}(\mathbf{A}^u\mathbf{f}_{t-1} - \mathbf{f}_t)\right] \\
=& \lambda\sum_{t=1}^{T}\mathrm{Tr}\left[(\mathbf{A}^u\mathbf{f}_{t-1} - \mathbf{f}_t)'(\mathbf{Q}^u)^{-1}\mathrm{d}(\mathbf{A}^u\mathbf{f}_{t-1} - \mathbf{f}_t)\right] \\
=& \lambda\sum_{t=1}^{T}\mathrm{Tr}\left[\mathbf{f}_{t-1}(\mathbf{A}^u\mathbf{f}_{t-1} - \mathbf{f}_t)'(\mathbf{Q}^u)^{-1}\mathrm{d}\mathbf{A}^u\right] .
\end{aligned}$$

Applying Theorem 1, we obtain

$$\frac{\partial J}{\partial \mathbf{A}^u} = \lambda\sum_{t=2}^{T}(\mathbf{Q}^u)^{-1}(\mathbf{A}^u\mathbf{f}_{t-1} - \mathbf{f}_t)\mathbf{f}_{t-1}' .$$

The gradient w.r.t. other variables is computed similarly.

An Empirical Study on Recommendation with Multiple Types of Feedback

Liang Tang
LinkedIn Corporation
Mountain View, CA, USA
ltang@linkedin.com

Bo Long
Particle Media Inc
Santa Clara, CA, USA
bo.long@particle-inc.com

Bee-Chung Chen
LinkedIn Corporation
Mountain View, CA, USA
bchen@linkedin.com

Deepak Agarwal
LinkedIn Corporation
Mountain View, CA, USA
dagarwal@linkedin.com

ABSTRACT

User feedback like clicks and ratings on recommended items provides important information for recommender systems to predict users' interests in unseen items. Most systems rely on models trained using a single type of feedback, e.g., ratings for movie recommendation and clicks for online news recommendation. However, in addition to the primary feedback, many systems also allow users to provide other types of feedback, e.g., liking or sharing an article, or hiding all articles from a source. These additional feedback potentially provides extra information for the recommendation models. To optimize user experience and business objectives, it is important for a recommender system to use both the primary feedback and additional feedback. This paper presents an empirical study on various training methods for incorporating multiple user feedback types based on LinkedIn recommendation products. We study three important problems that we face at LinkedIn: (1) Whether to send an email based on clicks and complaints, (2) how to rank updates in LinkedIn feeds based on clicks and hides and (3) how jointly optimize for viral actions and clicks in LinkedIn feeds. Extensive offline experiments on historical data show the effectiveness of these methods in different situations. Online A/B testing results further demonstrate the impact of these methods on LinkedIn production systems.

Keywords

Recommender System; Personalized Recommendation; Multi-objective Optimization

1. INTRODUCTION

Recommender systems have been applied to a wide range of applications, such as recommending news articles, movies, books, and research papers. Recommender systems seek to predict the "preference" that a user would give to an item. A typical way for recommender systems to provide recommendations is to build a model based on users' historical feedback (previously clicked, purchased or selected and/or numerical ratings given to those items); then use that model to predict items (or ratings for items) that the users may have an interest in the future.

As modern recommender systems become more complicated and touch more aspects of user experience, there has been a rapid increase in demand for a variety of user feedback to be incorporated into a recommendation model. A few examples are in the follow.

- *News feed*: The news feed of a social network site provides a user with updates from the neighbors of the user in the network. For example, a user's LinkedIn news feed contains articles and images shared, liked or commented on by other users connected to the user. To optimize for user engagement, a recommender system can be built to rank updates based on the predicted click through rate (CTR) for each (user, update) pair. While clicks provide primary feedback for the recommender system, a user can also hide updates from another user indicating strong dissatisfaction, providing additional types of feedback. When the system tries to maximize CTR, it is also important to minimize the hide rate.

- *Email campaign*: Many companies send promotion emails to users to engage with them. A recommender system can be built to decide whether to send a promotion email to a user based on the predicted CTR for each (user, email) pair in order to maximize users' responses to the emails. At the same time, it is important to minimize the chance that a user would unsubscribe all emails from the company or tag the email as a spam, indicating strong dissatisfaction. We call both unsubscriptions and spam tags *complaints*. In this case, clicks provide primary feedback, while complaints provide additional feedback.

- *Online shopping*: Whether a type of feedback is primary or secondary depends on the application. For online shopping, maximizing revenue from purchases is the primary objective. Thus, users' actual purchases provide primary feedback, while clicks on items may provide additional feedback.

Incorporating multiple types of user feedback in a recommendation model has become an important challenge for more and more recommender systems, though the related research is still relatively new in the field of recommendation. An intuitive solution to the problem is simply incorporating different feedback types into labels in training data, e.g., for click and hide feedback, we can label

KDD '16, August 13-17, 2016, San Francisco, CA, USA
© 2016 ACM. ISBN 978-1-4503-4232-2/16/08...$15.00
DOI: http://dx.doi.org/10.1145/2939672.2939690

data instances such that click is 1, non-click is 0, hide is -1. However, this will change the original binary classification model to a multinomial model and a multi-class prediction problem. It is not favorable for the recommendation and ranking purpose, because it generates multiple ranking scores and multiple ranking recommendations for each item. Keeping the same type of models, like binary classification model, and handling an additional feedback inside the model itself is a more preferable and scalable solution for most recommender systems. Furthermore, in a lot of situations, some additional feedback may not be able to put into labels. For example, downstream utilities such as page views are not easily put into binary labels as clicks.

In this paper, we only focus on generalized linear model based recommendation algorithms, which predict the user's interest and rank items based predicted interests. The performance of recommendation heavily depends on the accuracy of prediction. At LinkedIn, this type of algorithms is widely used in many products since content information, such as user profile and job information, are available for models. Collaborative filtering based approaches, such as matrix factorization, are mainly used in feature engineering to generate latent features for the generalized linear models.

The first method we consider is model combination, i.e., training one model for each feedback data then combining all models into a single model. This approach is feasible if the outputs of all models are the ranking scores or recommendation scores for different feedback types. For example, two logistic regression models for click data and hide data can be combined. We can either combine the predicted responses of the models or combine the model coefficients if the two models are in the same feature space and formulations are also the same. Additional weight parameters control the tradeoff of the importance of different types of feedback.

The second method is a sequential training based on Bayesian inference. In the previously mentioned example of the click feedback and hide feedback, we first train a model only using the click data and then use the model as the prior to train the final model using the hide feedback data. The final model fits the hide data but is also regularized by the click model. In general, we sequentially train the model for each feedback type where the prior is utilized to incorporate the previous model.

The third method is joint training, where we put multiple feedback types into a single training problem. The joint training still has one primary feedback to optimize, but we incorporate other secondary feedback as constraints to regularize the optimization problem. This constrained optimization framework can be applied to various recommendation applications. It is capable of incorporating some additional feedback types that are very different from the primary feedback type without changing the original recommendation model; i.e., there is no need to revise the online recommendation system to support multiple models and scorings. Meanwhile, in many applications, a certain correlation exists in different types of user feedback. For example, clicks and hides are often negatively correlated; the likes and clicks are positively correlated.

In this paper, we present an empirical evaluation on the three methods based on LinkedIn recommendation products. We study three important problems that we face at LinkedIn: (1) Whether to send an email based on clicks and complaints, (2) how to rank feed updates in LinkedIn feeds based on clicks and hides and (3) how jointly optimize for the viral actions and clicks in LinkedIn feeds. Extensive offline experiments on historical data show the effectiveness of these methods in different situations. Online A/B testing results further demonstrate the impact to LinkedIn production systems with real traffic. Meanwhile, *model combine* has been adopted by the current LinkedIn feed modeling in both desktop and mobile platforms to promote viral actions and improve the overall liquidity of the users' social network.

The rest of this paper is organized as follows. In Section 2, we formally introduce the problem of recommendation with multiple types of feedback. Detailed description for the three methods that we evaluated is presented in Section 3. Section 4 briefly discusses the implementation of the training algorithm. Extensive empirical evaluation results are reported in Section 5. Section 6 presents a brief summary of prior work relevant to the multi-feedback and multi-criteria recommendation problems, and transfer learning. Finally, Section 7 concludes the paper.

2. PROBLEM FORMULATION

Recommender systems build a model from users' historical impressions and feedback, such as clicks, hides, likes, shares, comments, and purchases etc. In LinkedIn, the recommendation models usually consider multiple user feedback. For instance, LinkedIn feeds models aim to maximize the click per impression (CTR), but also minimize the hide per impression since hide is a strong negative feedback. Meanwhile, like, comment and share are more important than click because they can significantly increase the virality of the contents and the liquidity of the social network. Hence, those actions are important feedback to maximize in recommendation as well. Therefore, our recommendation model has multiple objectives.

We denote our data as $\mathcal{P} = \{(\mathbf{x}_i, y_i^{(1)}, y_i^{(2)}, ..., y_i^{(m)})\}_{i=1}^N$, where where $\mathbf{x}_i$ is the feature vector of the i-th impression, which includes the user features and item features, $y_i^{(1)}$, ... ,$y_i^{(m)}$ are the m different types of feedback received in this impression. All the feedback are represented as binary variables: 1 or 0. For instance, $y_i^{(1)} = 1$ indicates there is a click action and 0 indicates this impression does not receive any click. The recommendation model calculates the ranking score for each impression and selects (or ranks) the items based on the ranking scores. Let $f(\mathbf{x}_i, \beta)$ be the ranking score of a given feature vector $\mathbf{x}_i$, where f is the model function and β is the coefficient vector of the model. For instance, we use the logistic regression to predict the CTR of articles. In this model, the ranking score is the predicted CTR, $f(\mathbf{x}_i, \beta) = 1/(1 + \exp(-\mathbf{x}_i^T \beta))$. Selecting the articles with high predicted CTRs can maximize the received click feedback from the users in future.

The problem that we study in this paper is to build a recommendation model that maximizes (or minimizes) m types of feedback received from users respectively, where the m types of feedback are pre-defined. For instance, for job recommendation at LinkedIn, two typical types of user feedback are click and dismiss. Click is a positive feedback that indicates the user is interested in the recommended job. However, dismiss is a strong negative feedback that indicates the user is upset by seeing this job recommendation. The desired model should be able to maximize the number of received clicks and minimize the number of received dismisses simultaneously. It is worth to mention that we still need a single model to make the recommendation decision for each job posting, which is recommend or not recommend.

3. METHODS

When the number of feedback types $m > 1$, the studied problem is a multi-objective optimization or multi-task learning problem. We explored three potential methods for solving this problem based on LinkedIn products and data. The first simple method is called *model combine*. Basically, this method trains an individual model for each objective. Since there are m feedback types, it has m individual models, $f_1, ..., f_m$. The final model is the combination of

$f_1, ..., f_m$. A simple combination is the weighted linear combination, such that the final model $f(\mathbf{x}_i, \beta) = \sum_{j=1}^{m} w_j \cdot f_j(\mathbf{x}_i, \beta_j)$, where w_j is the weight parameter to control the tradeoff between different objectives and β_j is the model coefficient for the model j, where $j = 1, ..., m$. This method can train the models in parallel and compose the final model in the end.

Besides training the individual models in parallel, we also explored a sequential training method. Let L be the loss function for the training algorithm for each feedback. We sequential solve the model coefficients $\beta_1, ..., \beta_m$ by the following series of optimization problems,

$$\min_{\beta_1} \sum_{i=1}^{N} L(\mathbf{x}_i, y_i^{(1)}; \beta_1),$$
$$\min_{\beta_j} \sum_{i=1}^{N} L(\mathbf{x}_i, y_i^{(j)}; \beta_j) + w_j ||\beta_j - \beta_{j-1}||^2,$$
$$j = 2, ..., m.$$

The final model is the last model with coefficient β_m. The idea of this method is to utilize the previous model as the prior to regularize the next model, so that the training result from the previous model can be transmitted to the next model. The final recommendation model is the last model that should contain the information of all the m models. Thus, we call this method as *prior combine*. Some literatures also mention this method is a warm-start training, in which they consider the old model as the prior or starting point, and use the new training data to train the new model. It is worth to mention that the method has two assumptions. First, the prior model's coefficient is a multivariate normal distribution and second the variance of each dimension is identical and determined by the inverse of w_j. However, the assumption may not exist in many high dimension data. In practice, it is very common that some of the features are sparse and some of the features are dense in real world high dimensional data. Thus, the associate coefficients have very distinct variances.

The third method is the joint training, where all types of feedback are utilized in a single joint optimization problem for the final model. The general form is,

$$\min_{\beta} \sum_{i=1}^{N} L(\mathbf{x}_i, y_i^{(1)}, ..., y_i^{(m)}; \beta),$$

where L is the joint loss function. There are lots of different approaches to compose the joint loss L. For instance, L is a linear combination of a logistic loss and a constraint loss (e.g., the hinge loss). In this instance,

$$L(\mathbf{x}_i, y_i^{(1)}, y_i^{(2)}) = w_1 \cdot \log(1 + \exp(-y_i^{(1)} \cdot f(\mathbf{x}_i, \beta))) + w_2 \cdot \max(0, y_i^{(2)}(c + f(\mathbf{x}_i, \beta))),$$

where w_1, w_2 are the weight parameters, c is a given positive parameter, and $y_i^{(2)}$ is a strong negative feedback from users (e.g., hide and dismiss). The hinge loss, $\max(0, y_i^{(2)}(c + f(\mathbf{x}_i, \beta)))$, forces the ranking score $f(\mathbf{x}_i, \beta) \leq -c$ if $y_i^{(2)} = 1$. Thus, it is a constrained optimization. It aims to minimize the loss from the primary feedback $y_i^{(1)}$ subject to the constraints $f(\mathbf{x}_i, \beta) \leq -c$ if $y_i^{(2)} = 1$. The weight w_2 determines the hardness of the constraints. If w_2 is an arbitrary large number, the constraints are hard constraints. Similarly, if $y_i^{(2)}$ is a strong positive feedback from users (e.g., like or apply a job), an example of L is

$$L(\mathbf{x}_i, y_i^{(1)}, y_i^{(2)}) = w_1 \cdot \log(1 + \exp(-y_i^{(1)} \cdot f(\mathbf{x}_i, \beta))) + w_2 \cdot \max(0, y_i^{(2)}(c - f(\mathbf{x}_i, \beta))),$$

where the hinge loss, $\max(0, y_i^{(2)}(c - f(\mathbf{x}_i, \beta)))$, forces the ranking score $f(\mathbf{x}_i, \beta) \geq c$ if $y_i^{(2)} = 1$. It is common that a recommendation model has one primary type of feedback (e.g., click) with other secondary types of feedback (e.g, hide and dismiss). The secondary types of feedback are either strong positive or strong negative, so we utilize them as constraints to regularize the primary feedback optimization problem. This method is called *constrained regression* in this paper. In many applications, different types of user feedback may have some correlation. For instance, in the LinkedIn feeds, the click and like are positive correlated, while the click and hide are negative correlated. In these situations, the constraints from the secondary types of feedback can help the learning algorithm better regularize the primary feedback learning. At the same time, the primary feedback also helps the learning algorithm find more reliable solutions subject to the constraints. This correlation of feedback is quite useful in some practical scenarios because the strong negative or positive feedback is often very rare in online systems. For instance, the total number of received clicks can be more 100 times larger than the total number of received hides in a same time period. Such rare feedback can hardly build a good recommendation model. But if we add a large amount of correlated feedback data to train jointly, the model performance can be improved. In machine learning, this technique is defined as *Transfer Learning* [8, 32, 10, 2, 3, 4, 27], in which each feedback refers to a domain. In the experimental section, we will discuss several cases where this transfer learning works and several other cases where it does not work based on LinkedIn data. Table 1 shows several loss functions that are widely used in our recommendation models, where y_i is the label of a feedback and $\mathbf{x}_i$ is the corresponding feature vector of the impression. The last loss is a pairwise loss, where $\mathbf{x}_i'$ is the feature vector of another impression.

Table 1: Loss Function

Loss Function	Loss Function Name
$\log(1 + \exp(-y_i f(\mathbf{x}_i, \beta)))$	Logistic Loss
$\lvert y_i - f(\mathbf{x}_i, \beta)\rvert^2$	Square Loss
$1 - I(sign(y_i \cdot f(\mathbf{x}_i, \beta)))$	0-1 Loss
$\max(0, y_i(c + f(\mathbf{x}_i, \beta)))$	Hinge Loss
$\max(0, y_i(c + f(\mathbf{x}_i, \beta)))^2$	Squared Hinge Loss
$\max(0, y_i(f(\mathbf{x}_i, \beta) - f(\mathbf{x}_{i'}, \beta)))$	Pairwise Hinge Loss

The three methods have various advantages and disadvantages in different data sets. *prior combine* takes the trained results from the previous model to regularize the next model's fitting. It has an initiative explanation based on Bayesian inference. *model combine* trains different models separately, where each model only has one objective so its training can easier coverage to its own optimal solution. *constrained regression* is a joint training, which utilizes multiple types of feedback together and is potentially to obtain a better joint optimal solution. It is difficult to theoretically determine which method is the best one in different particular cases. In this paper, we only focus on the empirical evaluation based on LinkedIn data.

4. IMPLEMENTATION

The offline training data is collected from a random bucket of users, where the historical recommended items are randomly selected to the users in order to avoid the sample bias and serving bias. In the algorithm implementation, we only focus on the convex loss function of L. In order to speed up the offline model training, we apply the coordinate gradient descent algorithm [37]. This algorithm minimizes the total loss function along one dimension at a time. On each dimension, it only goes one step along the opposite gradient direction. Recent studies have shown that the efficiency of this coordinate-wise optimization method is superior to many convex optimization algorithms in practice [37, 16]. Another advantage of this algorithm is that, it does not need to employ the backtracking linear search [31] to calculate the appropriate step size. Instead, it fixed the step size to be the inverse of the Lipschitz constant [5] of ∇L. The Lipschitz constant of ∇L provides an upper bound of the step size on each dimension, which is not conservative in coordinate-wise algorithms. We found this trick can significantly improve the efficiency of the algorithms in our model training.

Let d be the dimensionality of the data space, $\beta^{(i)}$ denote the i-th element of the vector β, and l_i be the Lipschitz constant of $\frac{\partial F}{\partial \beta^{(i)}}$, $i = 1, 2, ..., d$. Algorithm 1 presents the pseudocode of the

Algorithm 1 Coordinate Gradient Descent with Lipschitz Constant

Input: $\mathcal{P}$: training data, ϵ: tolerance parameter.

$\beta \leftarrow 0$
$||\nabla L||_{init} \leftarrow ||\nabla L(\beta)||$
while $|||\nabla L(\beta)|| > \epsilon||\nabla L||_{init}$ **do**
  for $i = 1, 2, ..., d$ **do**
    $\beta^{(i)} \leftarrow \beta^{(i)} - \frac{1}{l_i} \cdot \frac{\partial L}{\partial \beta^{(i)}}$
  end for
end while

algorithm, where each dimension's Lipschitz constant l_i is precomputed before entering the algorithm, ϵ is the tolerance parameter for the stopping criteria, which is the same definition for libLinear and libSVM [1]. This algorithm is flexible since it only requires the first order information of the total loss function L and the Lipschitz constant of ∇L. In this paper, for the offline experiments, the training algorithm is implemented in a single machine. For the online A/B testing, we apply the large scale of distributed optimization algorithm ADMM to scale up the production model training [**?**].

5. EXPERIMENTS

We present the empirical evaluation to answer the following important questions for recommendation with multiple types of feedback. First, what kind of feedback is feasible to be incorporated in a practical recommendation model? Second, how to select a suitable method for a particular application? Third, how do the different approaches perform for the real applications?

5.1 Complaints in LinkedIn Emails

Email is one of the most useful channel to improve the user engagement in social network industry. LinkedIn email recommender system aims to rank LinkedIn email candidates, such as news article content, "people you may know" and job postings, and then send top ranked emails to members. The primary feedback is click/non-click from members after they receive the emails. At the same time, the system records other types of feedback, such as complaints. The complaints include the actions of unsubscribing and labeling emails as spams. While the system optimizes CTR to boost member engagement, it is also desirable to minimize the complaints from the users. As described in Section 3, in this problem the number of types of user feedback is $m = 2$, click and complaint. The objective is to maximize the CTR and minimize the complaint rate for each sent email.

We investigate the three potential methods described by Section 3 in the email recommendation experiment. For *prior combine*, we implement two algorithms, "Prior Combine(Click)" and "Prior Combine(Complaint)", where the first one uses the click data to train the prior model and the second one uses the complaint data to train the prior model. For *constrained regression*, we also implement two algorithms, "Constrained(Complaint)" and "Constrained(Click Complaint)", where the first one only uses the complained emails as the constraints and the second one uses both clicked and complaints emails to establish the constraints. We tested the squared hinge loss and logistic loss for the click and complaint feedback, but there is no significant difference for the experimental results. For each algorithm, we vary the weight parameter w_j and regularization weight λ for model training. As a result, for each approach, we obtain 60 - 70 models based on different parameter combinations.

5.1.1 Data

The training and testing data is from the historical logs of a random bucket, i.e., the system randomly sent emails to a group of members and recorded their feedback. Thus, there is no serving bias for the training and testing data. We use around 2.5K features to build the recommendation model for this study. The features mainly consists of the member features, content features and interaction features. The member feature includes the member's profile data, such as the job title, education, company and industry category. The content features describe the content of the emails that we want to notify the member. The interaction feature represents the interests of a particular type of member to a particular category of emails. Table 2 summarizes the details of the data sets. We split the training data and testing data by the member Ids, so that there is no member who both appears in the training and testing data.

Table 2: Email Relevance Modeling Data Summary

Feedback	#Members for Training	# Members for Testing
Click	350K	1.2M
Complaint	460K	1.3M

5.1.2 Performance Metrics

The evaluation metric is AUC (Area Under ROC curve) [**?**]. An intuitive explanation of the AUC is the probability of a positive instance being ranked higher than a negative instance. Since there are two types of feedback, we consider the click AUC and non-complaint AUC at the same time to evaluate the model performance. The non-complaint is the opposite of the complaint. If the user did not complaint an email, the non-complaint feedback is 1, otherwise it is 0. Minimizing the complaint rate is equivalent to maximizing the non-complaint rate. A clicked email should have a higher ranking score than a non-clicked email. A non-complained email also should have a ranking higher core than a complained email. Therefore, click AUC and non-complaint AUC are higher,then the model performance is better. If model A has a both higher click AUC and non-complaint AUC than another model B, then we are sure that model A is better than model B. In multi-objective optimization, we say model A dominates model B [33]. If model A has a higher click AUC but a lower non-complaint AUC than model B, then we do not know A is better or worse than B. In this paper, our goal is to evaluate the potential training methods, not particular models, because two models with different tradeoffs

[1]https://www.csie.ntu.edu.tw/ cjlin/liblinear/

may not be comparable. Since we vary different weights of click and non-complaint feedback, the tradeoff between the click AUC and the non-compliant AUC is also varied. If an algorithm P generates more models that dominate the models generated by algorithm Q, then we can say the algorithm P is better than Q in most cases.

5.1.3 Experimental Results

Figure 1 shows the click AUC and non-complaint AUC of each training method on the test data sets. To protect the user privacy, we show the experiment results in terms of normalized AUC. The normalized click AUC is the click AUC divided by the click model's AUC, where the click model is trained only by the click data. Likewise, the normalized non-complaint AUC is the non-complaint AUC divided by the complaint model's AUC, where the complaint model is trained only by the complaint data.

As shown by Figure 1, we observe that incorporating complaint feedback does not hurt our model's CTR performance too much, but it significantly decreased the complaint rate more than 40% in some area. The *constrained regression* and *model combine* have the best tradeoff between the click AUC and non-complaint AUC. They can improve the non-complaint AUC from 0.4 to 0.7 by sacrificing the click AUC as little as 0.18. For other methods, to achieve the same non-compliant AUC, they have to sacrifice larger click AUC. It is worth to note that the *constrained regression* with only complaint constraints performs worse rapidly when the weight for complaints becomes large. This is because when the complaint weight is larger, the regression algorithm spends more much effort to fit the complaint data points. As a result, the entire data set becomes highly imbalance with more negative feedback. If we put both click and complaint data points into the constraints, constraints set are well balanced as shown by "Constrained(Click Complaint)", then it performs better than "Constrained(Complaint)". The performance of *data combine* approach is almost identical to *constrained regression*. The two algorithms based on *prior combine* perform much worse than the other algorithms. This is because this *prior combine* method only utilizes the coefficient mean of the prior model into the L2 regularizer for the next model training. As we discussed in Section 3, the assumption that the prior model coefficient is a multivariate normal distribution and each dimension has an identical variance may not hold. In the email data, some member and content features are very sparse or very dense so that the corresponding coefficients should have very different variances. Using an inappropriate prior can make the final model worse.

In practice the size of the secondary feedback varies a lot in different applications and time periods, to illustrate the the situation that the secondary feedback data is scarce, we randomly sample only 100 complained emails for training in the experiments. Figure 2 shows another AUC comparison for all the methods. As shown in the figure, *constrained regression* shows a better tradeoff curve of click AUC and non-complaint AUC than other methods. In other words, for the same AUC on non-complaints, *constrained regression* models show a higher AUC on the click feedback. For example, for the models with non-complaint AUC 0.85, the *constrained regression* models achieve around 0.99 on normalized click AUC, while the *model combine* models only achieve around 0.96. Since there are only 100 complained data points, the model for predicting complaint feedback has a high variance, which also hurts the performance of the combined model. A few outliers in the 100 data points can ruin the entire compliant model in *model combine*. On the other hand, *constrained regression* is a joint training that uses the click data and complaint data together. The large number of click data can regularize the joint model to be more robust to these outliers in complaint data. By this way, the correlation between the click feedback and complaint feedback help *constrained regression* achieve better performances than *model combine*.

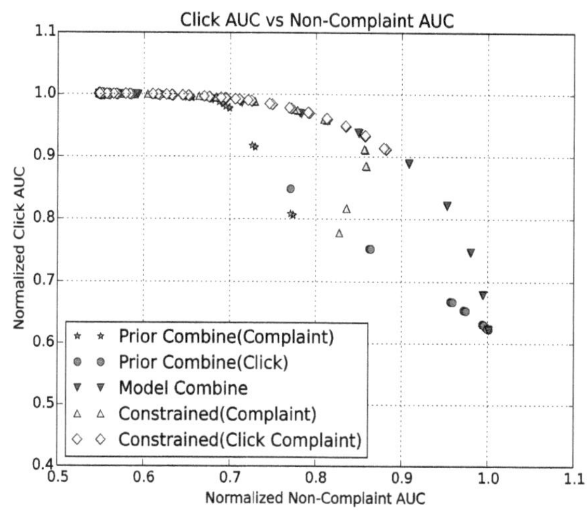

Figure 1: AUC Tradeoff on Email Data

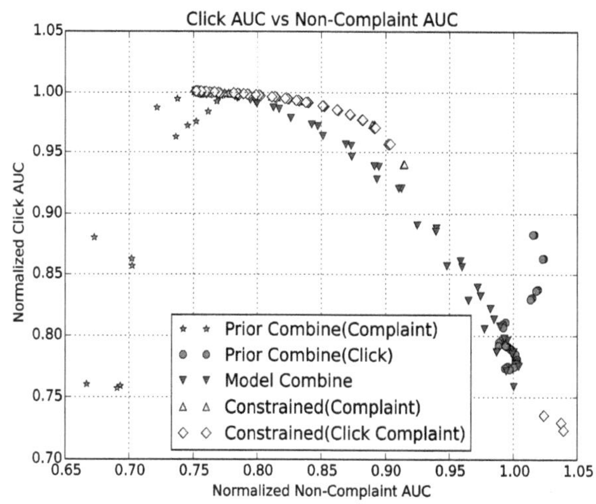

Figure 2: AUC Tradeoff on Email Data (100 Complaints in Train)

5.2 Hides in LinkedIn Feeds

LinkedIn feeds are mainly ranked by relevance models, which aim to maximize the user engagement and other business metrics. The user engagement is represented by the number of user clicks on feed items, which also include like, share, comment and other social actions. We apply the logistic regression model to predict the click probability for each item, and then rank all feed items based on the predicted click probabilities in descending order. Beside like, comment, share and other positive feedback, the users can also provide negative feedback by hiding certain feed items if they do not want to see certain feed updates again. The hide action is a strong negative feedback for user experiences. Therefore, while the ranking system optimizes CTR of feeds, it is also important to eliminate the future user's hide feedback to minimize the negative impact to user experience.

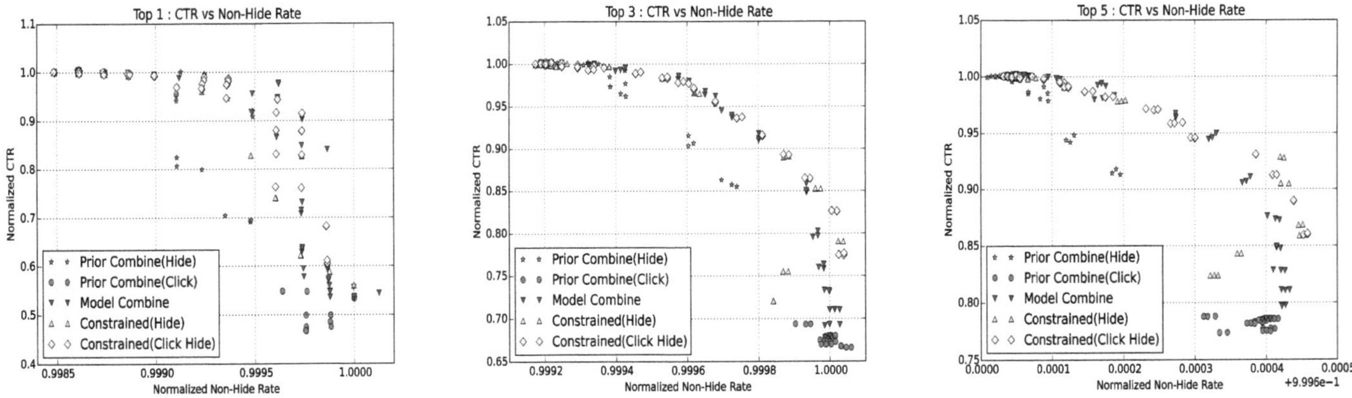

(a) Top 1 Position

(b) Top 3 Positions

(c) Top 5 Positions

Figure 3: CTR and Non-HideRate Tradeoff on Feed Data

We investigate the three methods described by Section 3 in this experiment. Like the LinkedIn email experiment, for *prior combine*, we implement two algorithms, "Prior Combine(Click)" and "Prior Combine(Hide)", where the first one uses the click data to train the prior model and the second one uses the hide data to train the prior model. For *constrained regression*, we also implement two algorithms, "Constrained(Hide)" and "Constrained(Click Hide)", where the first one only uses the hidden impressions as the constraints and the second one uses both clicked and hidden impressions to establish the constraints.

5.2.1 *Offline Experimental Results*

The training data and testing data are summarized in Table 3. Both data sets are sampled from the historical impressions of a random bucket, where we randomly shuffle the ranking list of feeds to a small group of users and collect the feedback in order to avoid the sample bias. The number of features is around 4.5K, which include the member profile features, item's features, and member's past behaviors etc. [?] lists the details of the LinkedIn feeds ranking model in production systems. Since in feed ranking, different

Table 3: Click and Hide Feed Modeling Data Summary

Feedback	#Impression for Training	#Impression for Testing
Click	810K	64.6M
Hide	410K	1.3M

feed positions have different biases to the CTR and hide rate, we select to use *precision at top* K as the evaluation metric instead of AUC, because AUC estimates the classification accuracy of items without considering the feed position. Based on the ranking order of feeds from each model, the CTR and hide rate on top K positions are calculated for each model. If a model A has a higher CTR and a lower hide rate than model B by *precision at top K*, then the model A is better than model B, and A dominates B. For each potential method, we vary different weight parameters and also the regularization weights for model training. As a result, we generate 60 - 70 models for each method based on different parameter combinations.

Figure 3 shows the CTRs and non-hide rates for top 1, 3 and 5 positions by *precision at top* K, $K = 1, 3, 5$ respectively. The non-hide feedback is the opposite of the hide feedback. To protect the user privacy, we only show the normalized CTR and non-hide rate in this paper. The normalized CTR is the CTR divided by the click model's CTR, where the click model is trained only based on the click data. Likewise, the normalized non-hide rate is the non-hide rate divided by the hide model's non-hide rate, where the hide model is trained only based on the hide data. The comparison results are similar as in the experiment for the email recommendations. *prior combine* performs much worse than other methods. *constrained regression* shows slight better tradeoffs than *model combine* on the high non-hide rate areas. It is also interesting to see that, some *constrained regression* models have higher non-hide rates than the hide model that is trained purely based on the hide feedback data. This observation reveals the effect of transfer learning, because the click action and non-hide action have a certain correlation. The large mount of click feedback data helps the joint model to build a better prediction on hide actions.

5.2.2 *Online A/B Testing Results*

To further study the performance of these methods, we conduct online A/B testing experiments in LinkedIn production systems. We launch 4 models of *constrained regression*, where each model is randomly allocated to serve a certain percentage of LinkedIn desktop users. It is worth to note that the members in the training data has no intersection with the members in the online testing. This A/B testing lasts for one week. We set the weight parameter w_2 for the constraints according to α:

$$w_2 = \begin{cases} 0 & \text{if } \alpha = 0 \\ \frac{\alpha N^-_{click}}{N^-_{hide}(1-\alpha)} & \text{if } \alpha > 0, \end{cases} \quad (1)$$

, where N^-_{click} is the number of negative click data points and N^-_{hide} is the number of negative hide data points (or the hided items) in the training data. Meanwhile, $w_1 = 1 - w_2$ is the weight for the logistic loss of the click data. α can be explained as the ratio of the constraint loss to the entire loss from negative data, therefore, it is more intuitive than directly setting up the w_2.

The online testing experiment is deployed on two types of LinkedIn homepage. The first one is the old LinkedIn homepage, which has lower CTRs and hide rates, but the online traffic is large. The other one is the new homepage, which has a smaller online traffic but higher overall user engagements in terms of CTRs and hide rates. Tables 4 and 5 show the online results of the online experiment in the two types of LinkedIn homepage respectively. The control model is the one with $\alpha = 0$, i.e., the control model is trained only with the click data. The CTR and hide rate are calculated in

Table 4: Feed Online A/B Testing Result in Old Homepage

α	CTR Lift	Hide Rate Reduction
0	0	0
0.1	1.1%	1.8%
0.2	0.8%	4.2%
0.5	0.02%	3.6%

Table 5: Feed Relevance Online A/B Testing in New Homepage

α	CTR Lift	Hide Rate Reduction
0	0	0
0.1	2.6%	6.4%
0.2	2.0%	5.0%
0.5	5.2%	12.5%

the page view level, which are the total number of clicks or hides divided by the total number of page views. As shown in the two tables, the CTRs have a small positive lift compared against the control model. It shows that the hide feedback provides additional signals about the member's interest that benefit the click modeling. Meanwhile, the three experimental models decrease the hide rate from 1 to 12 percent. Although the effect of hide rate decreasing is not as large as offline experiments, it is clear enough to demonstrate that this method can successfully incorporate the hide feedback without losing CTR in a real online system.

5.3 Viral Action in LinkedIn Feeds

Like, share and comment are called viral action in LinkedIn feeds, because these actions can generate the new feed updates for the user's neighbors, such as "X shared an article Y", "Y liked an post of Z". Therefore, encouraging viral actions can improve the liquidity of the social network. In LinkedIn feeds, viral actions are more important than the other click actions, such as pure click, connect, follow and play. However, the volume of pure click feedback is much larger than the volume of viral actions in LinkedIn feeds. We cannot only use the viral action feedback to train the ranking model because it would lose plenty of useful signals from the clicks. It is worth to mention that the viral action is a subset of the click action. There are other types of click actions that do not generate new feed updates in the social network.

The objective of the ranking model is to maximize the CTR and viral action rate simultaneously. Compared with the hide action, the viral action is more correlated with the click action since the viral action is a subset of the click action.

Table 6 summarizes the volume of the training data and testing data in the experiment. The features of the feed ranking model are same as in the previous experiment for hide actions. The details of the model can be found in [?].

Table 6: Click and Viral Action Feed Data Summary

Feedback	#Impression for Training	#Impression for Testing
Click	1M	29.5M
Viral Action	1M or 2M	29.5M

In this experiment, the *constrained regression* algorithm considers the click data as the primary feedback and put viral actions as positive constraints. *prior combine* still has two algorithms that consider the click model and viral action model as the prior respectively. We vary the weight parameters to obtain various tradeoff between the CTR and viral action rate for each algorithm.

The performance metric is still the *precision at top K* for clicks and viral actions. Due to the space limitation, we only show the experimental results of $K = 1$.

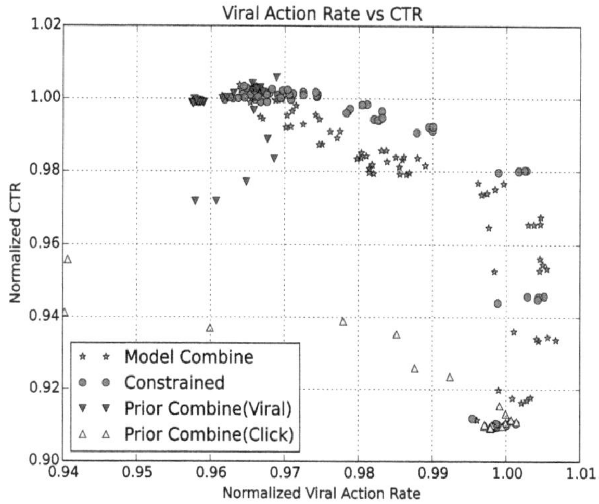

Figure 4: Top 1 Position : CTR and Viral Action Rate (1M Viral Actions in Train)

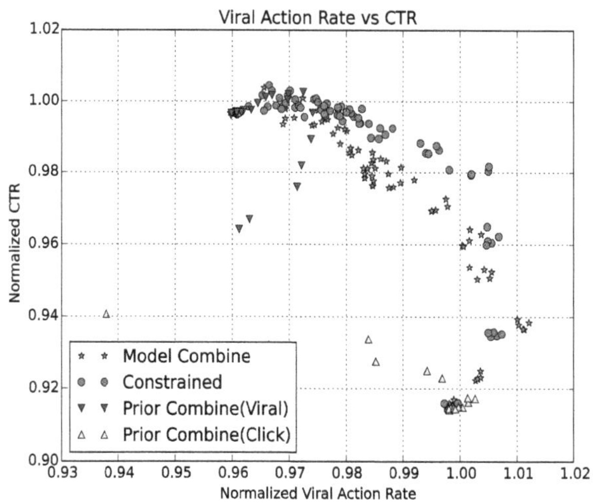

Figure 5: Top 1 Position : CTR and Viral Action Rate (2M Viral Actions in Train)

Figures 4 and 5 show the experimental results for all experimental models, where the number of viral action training data is 1M and 2M respectively in the two figures. To protect the user privacy, we only show the normalized CTR and normalized viral action rate. The normalized CTR is the CTR divided by the click model's CTR, where the click model is trained only based on the click data. Likewise, the normalized viral action rate is the viral action rate divided by the viral model's viral action rate, where the viral model is trained only based on the viral action data. It is clear to see that *constrained regression* achieved a better tradeoff than other algorithms in both figures. For example, to achieve 1.0 normalized viral action rate, *constrained regression* models can maintain 98% of the original CTR, however, *model combine* needs to lose 4% CTR.

Recall that in the previous experiment on hide actions, *constrained regression* and *model combine* have similar performances. However, in this experiment, *constrained regression* performs better than *model combine*. It is probably because the correlation between the click and viral action is larger than the correlation between the click and hide action. Therefore, *constrained regression* obtains a bigger gain from the joint training. Currently, LinkedIn feed production system adopts the *model combine* method to promote viral actions in both desktop and mobile platforms. The major reason is that, *model combine* only needs to train two individual models and vary the weights to obtain various tradeoffs, but *constrained regression* requires to retrain the joint model for each weight parameter and tradeoff. In future, we will conduct the A/B testing experiments to evaluate *constrained regression* for the click/viral action tradeoff in production systems.

In summary, for the three potential methods, *model combine* and *constrained regression* have a clear better performance than *prior combine*. If the multiple types of feedback has a certain correlation and some type of feedback has very small data, *constrained regression* performs better than *model combine*.

6. RELATED WORK

Multi-Criteria Recommendation: Many product recommender systems has different ratings for one product, such as story rating and the visual effect rating for one movie. Users also have different interests and preferences on those aspects. The goal of multi-criteria recommender systems is to maximize interests of all aspects interests at the same time. To achieve this goal, collaborative filtering based algorithms and content based algorithms have different approaches. Collaborative filtering based algorithms construct a rating vector of a user provide for an item. Each user's neighbors are computed based on their rating vectors to items, instead of a single rating variable [24, 1]. The preferences on different rating aspects can be substitute as the weights into the distance function of two rating vectors. Content based algorithms are based on the feature based learning models to predict the user interests. When the user has multiple interests, it can naturally build multiple learning models for predicting those interests [33]. For each user, the algorithms selects the Pareto optimal items to recommend [30]. Those work are similar to the model combine and response combine methods in this paper. They do not explore the benefit of the dependent responses to the user modeling. Besides the accuracy of the user interests, many research studies also consider some item's criteria, such as the item diversity [40, 25] and the novelty [23, 20, 15]. Other criteria including confidence, trust, risk, robustness, and privacy are also mentioned in the survey [35]. Those criteria are the constraints for the recommended items. Our work in this paper focuses on the criteria from the user's explicit feedback or response.

Transfer Learning: Another related field is transfer learning.Transfer learning approaches can be mainly categorized into three classes. A popular class of transfer learning methods is instance-based [6, 11, 28, 7, 19, 13, 36], which assumes that certain parts of the data in the source domain can be reused for the target domain by re-weighting. [21] proposed a heuristic method to remove "misleading" training instances from source domain so as to include "good" instances from labeled source-domain instances and unlabeled target-domain instances. [11] introduced a boosting algorithm, TrAdaBoost, which assumes that the source and target domain data use exactly the same set of features and labels, but the distributions of the data in the two domains are different. TrAdaBoost attempts to iteratively re-weight the source domain data and target domain data to reduce the effect of the "bad" source data while encourage the "good" source data to contribute more for the target domains. [6] proposed a framework to simultaneously re-weight the source domain data and train models on the re-weighted data with a kernel logistic regression classifier.

Another category of approaches can be viewed as model-based approaches [34, 26, 14, 9], which assumes that the source tasks and the target tasks share some parameters or priors of their models. An efficient algorithm MT-IVM [26], which is based on Gaussian Process (GP), was proposed to handle multi-domain learning case. MT-IVM tries to learn parameters of GP over multiple tasks by assigning the same GP prior to the tasks. Similarly, Hierarchical Bayes (HB) is used with GP for multi-task learning [34]. [14] borrowed the idea of [34] and used SVMs for multi-domain learning. The parameters of SVMs for each domain is assumed to be separable into two terms: a common term across tasks and a task specific term. [29] proposed a consensus regularization framework for transfer learning from multiple source domains to a target domain.

The third category of transfer learning approaches are feature based. [8, 32, 10, 2, 3, 4, 27], where a feature representation is learned for the target domain and used to transfer knowledge across domains. A structural correspondence learning (SCL) algorithm [8] is proposed to use unlabeled data from the target domain to extract features so as to reduce the difference between source and target domains. A simple kernel mapping function is introduced in [12], which maps the data from both domains to a high-dimensional feature space. [32] proposed to apply sparse coding, an unsupervised feature construction method, to learning higher level features across domain. On the other hand, heterogeneous transfer learning starts to attract attention very recently. We notice that [39] extends PLSA to a specific application, using social Web data to help image clustering; [38] proposes a manifold alignment based approach for heterogeneous domain adaptation; [18] formulates heterogeneous transfer learning as multi-task and multi-view learning and proposes a graph-based solution; [17] focus on single task learning with multiple outlooks, which is also related to heterogeneous transfer learning.

7. CONCLUSION

Learning multiple user feedback in a recommendation model has become an important challenge for recommender systems. Related research on multiple feedback is relatively new in the empirical study of recommender systems. This paper presents an empirical study on the methods for incorporating multiple types of user feedback into a single recommendation model. We investigate three common training methods, *prior combine*, *model combine* and *constrained regression* in this study. We conduct extensive experiments based on LinkedIn products and real historical data. In the experiments, we show how to use the methods to find the various tradeoff of the click/complaint in LinkedIn email recommendation, click/hide and click/viral action in LinkedIn feeds ranking. Based on our experimental results, *prior combine* does not perform well since its assumption for the prior model and prior distribution often does not hold in many real data. If each user feedback has enough training data, the performance of *model combine* and *constrained regression* are very close. But if some feedback data is rare, another feedback data is large, and the two types of feedback have a certain correlation, then *constrained regression* performs better than *model combine*. In this situation, *constrained regression* is actually doing a transfer learning. The correlated two types of feedback data help the model to better regularize the fitting on each other.

In addition to the offline experiments with historical data, we also conduct the online A/B testing for evaluating the *constrained regression* method for click/hide problem in LinkedIn feeds ranking based on a large amount of real users. The online A/B testing results also confirm the effectiveness of this method. The launched models can reduce 12% of the hide rate without hurting the CTR comparing against the control model.

As for the future work, we consider more advanced joint training methods to incorporate multiple types of feedback into recommendation, such as the constrained matrix factorization in collaborative filtering based on recommendation. Also, we continue to explore more advanced methodologies from transfer learning into the multiple feedback recommendation and utilize the relationship of different types of feedback to provide more accurate personalized recommendation. Meanwhile, we will continue to explore and solve other problems of the multiple types of feedback recommendation. For instance, in LinkedIn job recommendation, the user can apply a job or dismiss the job posting, where apply/not apply is the primary feedback and dismiss/not dismiss is a secondary feedback.

8. REFERENCES

[1] G. Adomavicius and Y. Kwon. New Recommendation Techniques for Multicriteria Rating Systems. *IEEE Expert / IEEE Intelligent Systems*, 22:48–55, 2007.

[2] R. Ando and T. Zhang. A high-performance semi-supervised learning method for text chunking. In *Proceedings of the 43rd Annual Meeting on Association for Computational Linguistics*, pages 1–9. Association for Computational Linguistics Morristown, NJ, USA, 2005.

[3] A. Argyriou, T. Evgeniou, and M. Pontil. Multi-task feature learning. In *Advances in Neural Information Processing Systems: Proceedings of the 2006 Conference*, page 41. MIT Press, 2007.

[4] A. Argyriou, C. Micchelli, M. Pontil, and Y. Ying. A spectral regularization framework for multi-task structure learning. *Advances in Neural Information Processing Systems*, 20, 2008.

[5] A. Beck and M. Teboulle. A fast iterative shrinkage-thresholding algorithm for linear inverse problems. *SIAM Journal on Imaging Sciences*, 2(1):183–202, 2009.

[6] S. Bickel, M. Brückner, and T. Scheffer. Discriminative learning for differing training and test distributions. In *Proceedings of the 24th international conference on Machine learning*, pages 81–88. ACM New York, NY, USA, 2007.

[7] J. Blitzer, K. Crammer, A. Kulesza, F. Pereira, and J. Wortman. Learning bounds for domain adaptation. *Advances in Neural Information Processing Systems*, 20, 2008.

[8] J. Blitzer, R. McDonald, and F. Pereira. Domain adaptation with structural correspondence learning. In *Proceedings of the Empirical Methods in Natural Language Processing (EMNLP)*, 2006.

[9] E. Bonilla, K. Chai, and C. Williams. Multi-task gaussian process prediction. *Advances in Neural Information Processing Systems*, 20:153–160.

[10] W. Dai, G. Xue, Q. Yang, and Y. Yu. Co-clustering based classification for out-of-domain documents. In *Proceedings of the 13th ACM SIGKDD international conference on Knowledge discovery and data mining*, pages 210–219. ACM New York, NY, USA, 2007.

[11] W. Dai, Q. Yang, G. Xue, and Y. Yu. Boosting for transfer learning. In *Proceedings of the 24th international conference on Machine learning*, pages 193–200. ACM New York, NY, USA, 2007.

[12] H. Daume. Frustratingly easy domain adaptation. In *Annual meeting-association for computational linguistics*, volume 45, page 256, 2007.

[13] H. Daume III and D. Marcu. Domain adaptation for statistical classifiers. *Journal of Artificial Intelligence Research*, 26:101–126, 2006.

[14] T. Evgeniou and M. Pontil. Regularized multi-task learning. In *Proceedings of the tenth ACM SIGKDD international conference on Knowledge discovery and data mining*, pages 109–117. ACM New York, NY, USA, 2004.

[15] F. Fouss and M. Saerens. Evaluating performance of recommender systems: An experimental comparison. In *Web Intelligence and Intelligent Agent Technology, 2008. WI-IAT'08. IEEE/WIC/ACM International Conference on*, volume 1, pages 735–738. IEEE, 2008.

[16] J. Friedman, T. Hastie, and R. Tibshirani. Regularization paths for generalized linear models via coordinate descent. *Journal of statistical software*, 33(1):1, 2010.

[17] M. Harel and S. Mannor. Learning from multiple outlooks. In L. Getoor and T. Scheffer, editors, *Proceedings of the 28th International Conference on Machine Learning (ICML-11)*, ICML '11, pages 401–408, New York, NY, USA, June 2011. ACM.

[18] J. He and R. Lawrence. A graph-based framework for multi-task multi-view learning. In L. Getoor and T. Scheffer, editors, *Proceedings of the 28th International Conference on Machine Learning (ICML-11)*, ICML '11, pages 25–32, New York, NY, USA, June 2011. ACM.

[19] J. Huang, A. Smola, A. Gretton, K. Borgwardt, and B. Scholkopf. Correcting sample selection bias by unlabeled data. *Advances in neural information processing systems*, 19:601, 2007.

[20] N. Hurley and M. Zhang. Novelty and diversity in top-n recommendation–analysis and evaluation. *ACM Transactions on Internet Technology (TOIT)*, 10(4):14, 2011.

[21] J. Jiang and C. Zhai. Instance weighting for domain adaptation in NLP. In *Annual meeting-assosciation for computational linguistics*, volume 45, page 264, 2007.

[22] T. Joachims. Optimizing search engines using clickthrough data. In *Proceedings of the Eighth ACM SIGKDD International Conference on Knowledge Discovery and Data Mining, July 23-26, 2002, Edmonton, Alberta, Canada*, pages 133–142, 2002.

[23] N. Kawamae. Serendipitous recommendations via innovators. In *Proceedings of the 33rd international ACM SIGIR conference on Research and development in information retrieval*, pages 218–225. ACM, 2010.

[24] K. Lakiotaki, N. F. Matsatsinis, and A. Tsoukiàs. Multicriteria user modeling in recommender systems. *IEEE Intelligent Systems*, 26(2):64–76, 2011.

[25] N. Lathia, S. Hailes, L. Capra, and X. Amatriain. Temporal diversity in recommender systems. In *Proceedings of the 33rd international ACM SIGIR conference on Research and development in information retrieval*, pages 210–217. ACM, 2010.

[26] N. Lawrence and J. Platt. Learning to learn with the informative vector machine. In *Proceedings of the twenty-first international conference on Machine learning*. ACM New York, NY, USA, 2004.

[27] S. Lee, V. Chatalbashev, D. Vickrey, and D. Koller. Learning a meta-level prior for feature relevance from multiple related tasks. In *Proceedings of the 24th international conference on Machine learning*, pages 489–496. ACM New York, NY, USA, 2007.

[28] X. Liao, Y. Xue, and L. Carin. Logistic regression with an auxiliary data source. In *MACHINE LEARNING-INTERNATIONAL WORKSHOP THEN CONFERENCE-*, volume 22, page 505, 2005.

[29] P. Luo, F. Zhuang, H. Xiong, Y. Xiong, and Q. He. Transfer learning from multiple source domains via consensus regularization. In *CIKM '08: Proceeding of the 17th ACM conference on Information and knowledge management*, pages 103–112, New York, NY, USA, 2008. ACM.

[30] K. Miettinen. *Nonlinear Multiobjective Optimization*. International Series in Operations Research & Management Science. Springer US, 1999.

[31] J. Nocedal and S. Wright. *Numerical Optimization*. Springer series in operations research and financial engineering. Springer, 1999.

[32] R. Raina, A. Battle, H. Lee, B. Packer, and A. Ng. Self-taught learning: Transfer learning from unlabeled data. In *Proceedings of the 24th international conference on Machine learning*, pages 759–766. ACM New York, NY, USA, 2007.

[33] M. T. Ribeiro, A. Lacerda, A. Veloso, and N. Ziviani. Pareto-efficient hybridization for multi-objective recommender systems. In *Proceedings of the Sixth ACM Conference on Recommender Systems*, RecSys '12, pages 19–26, New York, NY, USA, 2012. ACM.

[34] A. Schwaighofer, V. Tresp, and K. Yu. Learning Gaussian process kernels via hierarchical Bayes. *Advances in Neural Information Processing Systems*, 17:1209–1216, 2005.

[35] G. Shani and A. Gunawardana. Evaluating recommendation systems. In *Recommender systems handbook*, pages 257–297. Springer, 2011.

[36] M. Sugiyama, S. Nakajima, H. Kashima, P. von Bunau, and M. Kawanabe. Direct importance estimation with model selection and its application to covariate shift adaptation. *Advances in Neural Information Processing Systems*, 20, 2008.

[37] P. Tseng and S. Yun. A coordinate gradient descent method for nonsmooth separable minimization. *Mathematical Programming*, 117(1-2):387–423, 2009.

[38] C. Wang and S. Mahadevan. Heterogeneous domain adaptation using manifold alignment. In *IJCAI*, pages 1541–1546, 2011.

[39] Q. Yang, Y. Chen, G.-R. Xue, W. Dai, and Y. Yu. Heterogeneous transfer learning for image clustering via the social web. ACL '09, pages 1–9, 2009.

[40] C.-N. Ziegler, S. M. McNee, J. A. Konstan, and G. Lausen. Improving recommendation lists through topic diversification. In *Proceedings of the 14th international conference on World Wide Web*, pages 22–32. ACM, 2005.

An Engagement-Based Customer Lifetime Value System for E-commerce

Ali Vanderveld
Groupon
Chicago, IL
avanderveld@groupon.com

Addhyan Pandey
Groupon
Chicago, IL
adpandey@groupon.com

Angela Han
Groupon
Chicago, IL
angela@groupon.com

Rajesh Parekh*
Facebook
Menlo Park, CA
rgparekh@gmail.com

ABSTRACT

A comprehensive understanding of individual customer value is crucial to any successful customer relationship management strategy. It is also the key to building products for long-term value returns. Modeling customer lifetime value (CLTV) can be fraught with technical difficulties, however, due to both the noisy nature of user-level behavior and the potentially large customer base. Here we describe a new CLTV system that solves these problems. This was built at Groupon, a large global e-commerce company, where confronting the unique challenges of local commerce means quickly iterating on new products and the optimal inventory to appeal to a wide and diverse audience. Given current purchaser frequency we need a faster way to determine the health of individual customers, and given finite resources we need to know where to focus our energy.

Our CLTV system predicts future value on an individual user basis with a random forest model which includes features that account for nearly all aspects of each customer's relationship with our platform. This feature set includes those quantifying engagement via email and our mobile app, which give us the ability to predict changes in value far more quickly than models based solely on purchase behavior. We further model different customer types, such as one-time buyers and power users, separately so as to allow for different feature weights and to enhance the interpretability of our results. Additionally, we developed an economical scoring framework wherein we re-score a user when any trigger events occur and apply a decay function otherwise, to enable frequent scoring of a large customer base with a complex model. This system is deployed, predicting the value of hundreds of millions of users on a daily cadence, and is actively being used across our products and business initiatives.

*This work was done when the author was at Groupon.

KDD '16, August 13 - 17, 2016, San Francisco, CA, USA

ISBN 978-1-4503-4232-2/16/08... $15.00

DOI: http://dx.doi.org/10.1145/2939672.2939693

Keywords

Customer Lifetime Value, E-commerce, Random Forests

1. INTRODUCTION

Groupon[1] is a large global e-commerce company, operating via the web and the popular Groupon Mobile App. Currently serving more than 30 countries and 500 markets, Groupon is the place you start when you want to buy just about anything, anytime, anywhere. We offer physical merchandise through our Goods business, travel deals through our Getaways business, and we are a market leader in Local commerce. As of Q3 of 2015, we have nearly 50 million active customers worldwide, more than one million merchants connected through our suite of online tools, and over 900 million units sold. At Groupon we are trying to develop a robust marketplace, and as such we need to understand at an individual level the supply and service needed to develop a daily habit for our customers. How does featuring the local burger place down the block compare to featuring a big chain when it comes to increasing a user's future spending? Given the number of local choices a customer has, how many Groupon options do we provide to promote a daily habit? What is the added value of providing "white glove" customer service?

Answering such questions requires a comprehensive understanding of user-level value and how it is changing with time. Accordingly, in this paper we tackle the problem of modeling and monitoring customer lifetime value (CLTV) – a prediction of the net dollar value attributed to our future relationship with each individual customer. It is relatively easy to predict aggregate business measures for financial purposes. Accurately modeling the future value of individual users, however, is a far more difficult task, as users spend differing amounts of time on product research and have various engagement levels prior to a final purchase decision. Nonetheless, accurate CLTV predictions can have enormous value for an e-commerce company like Groupon. The historically most common use cases for such a system pertain to marketing and customer relationship management (CRM). With CLTV predictions it is straightforward to find the highest value customers, customers most likely to attrite, and customers most likely to make their first purchase. As

[1]`http://www.groupon.com`

such one can determine the ideal target audiences for promotional offers, personalized customer messaging, exclusive deals, rewards programs, and customer service treatment.

In addition to the huge marketing value, CLTV predictions are generally useful as a powerful performance metric in all areas of the business. For example, in product experimentation we can use CLTV scores to segment users and to build for longer term value returns. We can identify causal versus correlated relationships of certain behaviors with user value by encouraging and incentivising said behaviors and then measuring outcomes. We can also use these predictions in personalization, to tune results to different stages in the customer lifecycle, and for user behavior analysis. How does CLTV change based on offering (e.g. Goods versus Local) or as a result of specific actions? How does the adoption of a new platform change a user's value as a function of time? We can also use CLTV predictions for business unit goal setting; an example of such a goal might be for the CRM team to increase the value of previously one-time buyers by $X\%$ for a given quarter.

Here at Groupon we have developed a new methodology for the modeling and daily tracking of individual customer value. Our system is novel in several ways, including: 1. we engineer features that quantify the level of engagement that each customer has with us on each of our platforms, 2. we build highly accurate two-stage random forest models, 3. we use separate models for different types of purchasers, e.g. one-time buyers versus very active users, and 4. we re-score a user when any trigger events occur and apply a decay function otherwise. Using engagement-based features allows us to detect any changes in value, including attrition, far more quickly than we could otherwise. We have found random forest models to have the best performance over other machine learning frameworks, and modeling different customer types separately allows us to have different feature weights for each while simultaneously overcoming interpretability issues by giving business units a straightforward way to discover and track the most important features for each group. Employing a decay function allows us to efficiently update our scores on a daily cadence despite having a very complex model, leading to a factor of 20 speed up in overall run time. By implementing these model features we are able to achieve Spearman correlations between actual and predicted customer values of 0.53 and 0.77 for quarterly and yearly timeframes, respectively, showing moderate to high correlations at a very high statistical significance ($p < 0.0001$).

In what follows we present our CLTV system, which predicts customer value for three rolling time windows that we will denote as "short," "medium," and "long," that are on the order of a quarter to a year. We use a proxy measure for customer value that we will call "purchase value" that is based on purchasing behavior, focusing on this behavior instead of profit because the latter is subject to margins that can fluctuate and that are not related to user intent. We focus on value over these three time windows as opposed to full lifetime value; given the age of Groupon, a one-year purchase prediction is a significant portion of the overall average customer life as of today. There is not enough training data to make accurate predictions with a longer-term model but the future intent is to add longer time periods as a representative core customer base matures and the data becomes available. Hereafter and we will often refer to these values as the user's "scores." The system described herein is currently deployed in production and successfully running at scale, scoring hundreds of millions of users on a daily cadence and being used by more than half a dozen business and product use cases.

2. RELATED WORK

This work is related to a few different areas in the marketing and machine learning literature, most importantly CLTV, CRM, and random forests.

2.1 Customer Lifetime Value

Gupta *et al.* [9] provide a comprehensive review of different CLTV methodologies, relating them to what they state as the three phases of the relationship between a company and a customer: acquisition, retention, and expansion. They review six basic types of modeling approaches, including the historically popular RFM and related models that deal with the recency, frequency, and value of each customer's purchase history. They present evidence from the literature that machine learned prediction models like the one presented below are superior because they can incorporate a variety of additional variables, and they mention that random forest models had historically performed well in churn prediction competitions. See also [12, 8, 17] for further review on the history behind CLTV prediction. In all of the CLTV literature there is the argument that, rather than focusing on the short-term, CLTV modeling allows us to focus on long-term profitability [19, 2].

There are various methodologies that have been used to model CLTV in a computer science framework, including optimization [7], SVM [6], quantile regression [3], and portfolio analysis [5]. In a 2009 CLTV prediction competition [14], several different frameworks for predicting CLTV on an individual and an aggregate basis were tested against each other. We find that a new approach – two-stage random forest models for each of several user behavior segments, with a comprehensive feature set such as what we have engineered here – performs better than any of the competition entrants. This methodology allows us to incorporate features related to user engagement with our platform, which allow us to quickly detect changes in customer value.

2.2 Customer Relationship Management

The idea that we should invest resources into analyzing customer behavior and maintaining a positive relationship with our customers is nothing new. For example, Kotler and Keller [11] showed that the costs associated with obtaining new customers can be five times larger than the costs associated with maintaining a good relationship with existing customers. A thorough literature review of various subjects related to CRM, including CLTV modeling techniques, can be found in [16]. The need to fully understand our customers so that we can maintain these relationships is one of the strongest motivations for accurate customer lifetime value monitoring. This is the main impetus to build a reliable monitoring system at Groupon.

2.3 Random forests

Random forests is an ensemble learning method that works by producing many random decision trees and then bootstrap aggregating (or "bagging") the results to turn an ensemble of weak learners into a strong one that automatically avoids overfitting. The methodology was developed by Leo Breiman and Adele Cutler [4]. We make use of the functionality in R [13] and the H2O package [1] [2]. H2O is a scalable machine learning framework that supports many of the standard algorithms, including random forests.

3. FEATURE SET

Our model uses over 40 features, which provide a comprehensive view of each user's demographics, general purchasing behavior, engagement, and overall relationship with Groupon. Here we describe each type of feature in turn. A discussion of relative feature importance is in Section 6 below.

3.1 Engagement

The most important features that we include are those that characterize user engagement with our product. These rich features allow us to detect changes in customer value far sooner than we could if we were only relying on purchase history data. In this first version of our model we include engagement scores from email and the mobile app, currently two of our most important sources of traffic. There are various key ways in which users interact with each of these platforms, for example with opens and clicks for email and with deal impressions and searches on the app. We coalesce these behaviors into one composite score for each platform by weighting a quantification of each behavior (e.g. the number of email clicks) by a numerical factor related to the historical conversion coming from that behavior. The final score is then the weighted sum. For example,

$$\text{Email engagement score} = \alpha N_{\text{open}} + \beta N_{\text{click}} ,$$

where N_{open} is the number of email opens, α is the corresponding historical conversion rate (average orders per email open), N_{click} is the number of email clicks, and β is the corresponding historical conversion rate (average orders per email click, given an email open). Note that most emails that are opened are not clicked on, and that a single email can be clicked on multiple times. Thus we consider each behavior (opening and clicking) separately, using the appropriate conversion rates to avoid double counting. We further track email unsubscription and mobile app downloads, and define features related to each.

3.2 User experience

There are many ways in which the Groupon user experience is correlated with future customer value. Firstly, the quantity of available nearby deals can play a large role, especially for newer and re-engaging users. We quantify this local supply by counting the number of deals within a representative radius of the user's home location. We also determine the typical purchase volume in their geographical area, which acts as a proxy for local Groupon brand recognition.

Another key part of the user experience is related to customer service. We track numbers of refunds and customer service tickets, customer service phone and email wait times, and whether the user has given positive or negative responses to post-interaction surveys. We also track average shipping times for our Goods (physical merchandise) business.

[2] `http://www.h2o.ai`

3.3 User behavior

Virtually all CLTV models use purchase history as a key variable, and ours is no exception. We have features relating to purchase value on a variety of historical timescales, along with the number of days since the most recent purchase. We also include Goods versus Local preferences and whether or not those preferences are changing as a function of time. Also redemption behavior can be important, and as such we include as features the typical time between purchase and redemption and the number of unredeemed vouchers that the user is currently holding on to. We further track how much each user is predisposed to using discount codes for their purchases or for purchasing "loss leader" deals.

3.4 Other features

In addition to the aforementioned features we also use basic demographic variables such as gender, age, and location, including city size and the distance between home and city center. We also track the circumstances regarding their original subscription and first purchase, including the cohort years for each.

4. CLTV MODEL

The features in the previous section are used by our series of CLTV models. We train models for each combination of our six user segments and our three time windows – short, medium, and long. Each model is retrained on a quarterly basis due to the relatively young age of our business and the fast pace of business changes. In this section, we describe our user segments, our two-stage random forest model framework, and our empirical seasonality and decay function models. The design of the overall system that calls upon these models is discussed in Section 5 below.

4.1 User segments

Of our 40+ features described above, some will invariably be more important predictors of future purchasing behavior than others. However, which variables are most important will be different for different types of customers. For example, for a user who purchases very frequently we may be able to accurately predict future purchasing behavior largely from previous purchasing behavior. On the contrary, for a user who has not yet purchased we will have to rely entirely on other (non-purchase history) variables. Thus we divide our users into six "purchase cohorts" based on past purchase frequency. Each of these purchase cohorts then is modeled separately from the others to allow for differing feature weights for each.

These cohorts are determined from the past five quarters of data, excluding travel and other outlier price point purchases. The total number of cohorts is six, which was determined based on a balance between model accuracy and re-training time. The time window for cohort determination (five quarters) was determined based on a balance between having enough data to detect a pattern but also allowing for the possibility that users may change their purchasing behavior over their lifetimes.

In this paper, we will focus on a subset of our purchase cohorts, defined and named as follows:

- Unactivated: never purchased
- New users: purchased but insufficient data to determine cohort (requiring at least four quarters)

- One-time buyers: only one purchase ever
- Sporadic buyers: infrequent purchasers (but more than once)
- Power users: very frequent purchasers

The specific thresholds for what constitutes a sporadic buyer versus a power user versus any other cohort will vary for different businesses that have different typical purchase frequencies. We choose thresholds that are optimized for Groupon. Note also that the cohorts developed here are optimized for the purposes of understanding user segments, modeling individual user behavior, and informing product and marketing efforts. These do not reflect the cohort strategy used to assess overall business performance. These separate concerns require very different segmentation strategies.

4.2 Random forest models

For each purchase cohort and time window, we use random forest models in R, using the H2O [1] package. In addition to previous studies finding random forests to be superior for CLTV modeling [9], we further found it to be the most accurate from a series of experiments where we tested various algorithms, including rpart [18] and SVM [15], and various normalizations and parameter tunings. We found that a lower `mtry` (the number of features randomly sampled as candidates at each split) and a higher `ntree` (the number of trees to generate) performed the best for our purposes here. Performance was judged based on a combination of RMSE and Pearson and Spearman correlations between actual and predicted values for our cross-validation data sets.

There are significant benefits and disadvantages of using random forests in this application. The advantages include allowing for missing values, accommodating many nonlinear features (e.g. the number of days since the most recent purchase), and generally better model performance including avoiding overfitting. The main disadvantage relates to interpretability because the result is an average over many decision trees. We overcome this disadvantage by modeling each of our purchase cohorts on its own to extract the most important features. Then we create cohort metrics for our end business partners (marketing, customer service, etc.) so that they can act on these metrics as they change with time. For example, we find that one of the most important features for predicting the future value of our power users is the typical number of days from purchase to redemption. Accordingly we track redemption time and CLTV as we test new redemption-related products, such as redemption reminder emails and expired voucher trade-in programs.

Our model has two stages, each using random forests:

1. Predict purchase propensity, a binary classification for whether or not the user is predicted to purchase, for the time window.
2. Predict the dollar value for users who were predicted to purchase in stage 1.

We use two stages because the data sets tend to be highly imbalanced; for example power users are far more likely to purchase than not, whereas the opposite is true for one-time buyers. Thus for stage 1 we downsample the majority class to get a 50-50 training set. The full combined training sets contain 40,000 samples for each combination of purchase cohort and time window. The classification cutoff has been optimized for each purchase cohort to minimize the bias in the number of purchasers and their overall value. We build separate two-stage models to predict future values for each of the short, medium, and long time windows for each cohort.

4.3 Seasonality and decay models

We employ two additional models which are both built empirically from historical data. Firstly, since our training data is necessarily on at least a quarterly lag, we need to make quarter-to-quarter seasonality adjustments. These adjustment factors are predicted from historical timeseries data for each purchase cohort separately and are re-calculated every quarter.

The second empirical model that we use is related to our scoring procedure. In order to get the most out of a CLTV monitoring system, we require re-scoring on a relatively fast cadence. Ideally we would like daily updates to capture sudden changes in value due to any purchases, engagement, customer service interactions, etc. However, in a large global business such as Groupon we have potentially hundreds of millions of users to score. Doing so with an extensive six-cohort two-stage random forest model would be computationally very expensive. We reduce the computation cost by leveraging our knowledge of customer behavioral patterns.

We note that the value of users who go without any interactions with Groupon, including any engagement, decays in a very predictable manner in line with Figure 1. We measure this decay function as a multiplicative factor, which is a function of the number of days since the last interaction. We calculate this function from historical time-series data and re-calculate it at the start of every quarter. We then use this function as a part of the daily scoring procedure:

1. Find users who had any "trigger events," which we define as any interactions with Groupon related to our feature set (see below).
2. For triggered users, run their updated feature set through the two-stage random forest model to calculate fresh scores.
3. For users without any trigger events, multiply their scores by the appropriate decay functions.

Trigger events include purchases, any interactions with email or the mobile app, and any customer service interactions including calls, emails, and refunds.

With this scoring procedure we reduce our daily scoring time by a factor of 20, a savings of 95%. This time quickly adds up. In this way we are able to update each user's predicted values for each of the short, medium, and long time windows on a daily cadence, with each of these time windows on a rolling basis. For instance, on September 1st, 2015, a quarterly prediction gave the expected purchase value for the current date through the current date plus 90 days, or November 30th. Similarly a one-year prediction gave the expected value until September 1st of 2016.

5. SYSTEM DESIGN

We show a high-level overview of the Groupon CLTV system in Figure 2. The computation and collection of the feature sets is done within Groupon's enterprise data warehouse. We additionally assign purchase cohorts and build

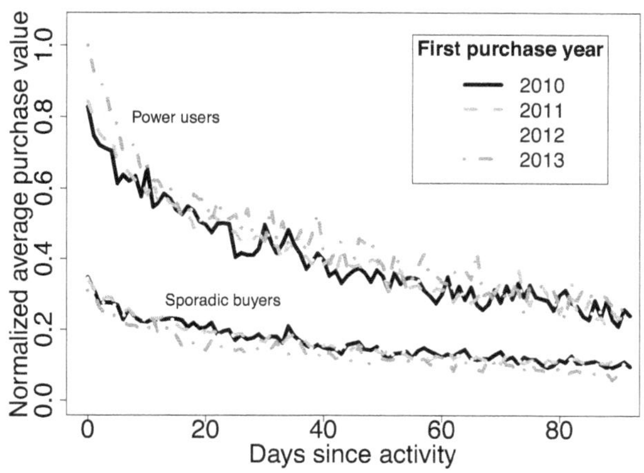

Figure 1: How average quarterly user value decays as a function of the number of days since the last interaction ("trigger event"), shown for various combinations of purchase cohort and first purchase year cohort. All customer values have been normalized by a constant factor such that the average value for 2013 power users is equal to one.

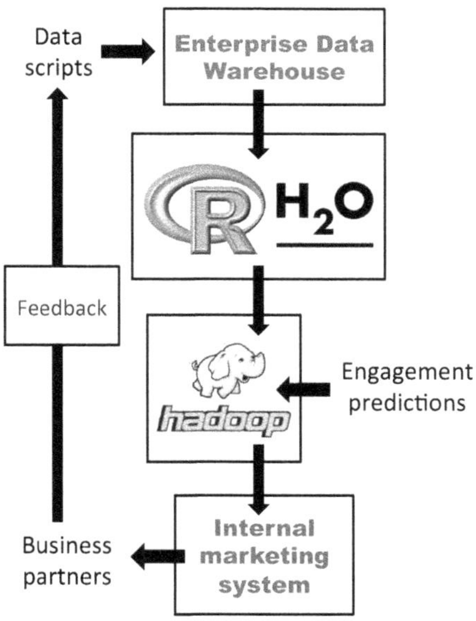

Figure 2: High-level overview of our CLTV system. Timeseries models and features are built within our enterprise data warehouse, then R and H2O [1] are used to build random forest models and calculate user values. Results are stored in our Hadoop cluster, joined with engagement score predictions, and then ported into our internal marketing system for easy access by our business partners.

our timeseries models within this database. Models are built and users are scored using R in conjunction with the H2O package [1] on a server with 44 Gb of RAM and 12 CPU cores. We then store the results in our Hadoop cluster, combine the results with engagement score predictions (from a separate, independent model), and port everything to a Groupon internal marketing system that allows our business partners to segment users for personalized marketing campaigns. Several secondary scores are also calculated, including a predicted percentage value change that compares the past quarter to the future quarter, and an associated binary 0/1 decline alert flag. Feedback from our business partners, typically in the form of feature requests and updates, is fed back into the data model.

We split the CLTV scoring process into a daily process and a quarterly process as described in the subsections below. The quarterly process runs on the first day of each quarter (January 1st, April 1st, July 1st, and October 1st) while the daily process runs on all other days of the year. Both processes have built-in accuracy monitoring and alerts at each stage of each process.

5.1 Quarterly process

On a quarterly basis we complete the following steps:

1. Assign purchase cohorts for each user based on the user's past five quarters of activity.
2. Compute seasonality functions for each purchase cohort from historical data.
3. Compute decay functions for each purchase cohort and time window from historical data.
4. Harvest new training data sets and retrain all models on new data.
5. Calculate all new CLTV scores for everyone with either a purchase in the past six months or any engagement in the past 90 days.
6. Everyone without either a purchase in the past six months or engagement in the past 90 days is predicted to have zero future value for each time window.

The requirements to receive a new score (versus an automatic score of zero value) were determined based on experimentation on the level of inactivity required to be certain of zero value according to our models.

5.2 Daily process

On a daily basis (excluding the first day of the new quarter) we complete the following steps:

1. Update the feature set for all users.
2. Find users with trigger events since the last scoring, which include any interaction with Groupon related to our feature set.
3. Re-score all triggered users for each time window.
4. Apply the decay functions to the scores for all users who were not triggered, for each time window.

As mentioned above, all of these time windows – short, medium, and long – are on a rolling basis and each set of scores is thus updated every night when the CLTV system runs. We are currently building alerts to monitor model drift.

6. SYSTEM PERFORMANCE

The system described herein has been successfully implemented at large scale, scoring hundreds of millions of users on a daily cadence. The system has been stable for several months and takes approximately four hours to run each night. In this section we review 1. the performance of our model using test data, 2. various measures from Q3 of 2015, and 3. the most important features for each stage of our model for our different user segments. In the results below, all metrics are for large random subsets of users and are purely indicative of model performance. Whenever the time window (short, medium, or long) is not specified it is to be assumed that we are defaulting to the short time period; when that is the case then it can further be assumed that the results are similar for the longer time windows.

6.1 Model evaluation

For all of our model experiments we trained with features as of the end of Q1 of 2014, thereby predicting customer values starting from the beginning of Q2 of 2014. We used out-of-time cross-validation data sets that were shifted one quarter later, such that we were predicting values starting from the beginning of Q3 of 2014. We use data from 2014 (as opposed to 2015) in order to have enough data to test the results for our long time window. For each new model experiment we drew new random subsamples of the population to create new random training and cross-validation data sets. Each of our cross-validation and testing data sets contained 10,000 samples from each purchase cohort. We evaluate the performance of Stage 1 based on accuracy, precision, recall, and false positive rate. We evaluate the performance of the overall (stage 1 and 2) model based on Pearson and Spearman correlation coefficients, RMSE, bias in the averages, and a comparison of actual versus predicted distributions.

6.1.1 Stage 1 performance

In the first stage of our model we predict a binary yes/no response for whether each user will make a purchase in the time window of interest. In Figure 3 we show the ROC curves – the true positive rate versus the false positive rate as we vary the cutoff parameter for the binary classification scheme – for each purchase cohort. In this figure the cutoff ranges from 0.2 to 0.8. The shallowness of these curves reflects the inherent difficulty in predicting individual user behavior. The final cutoff parameters are chosen so as to minimize the bias in predicting the total number of purchasers for each cohort.

In Table 1 we show the resulting accuracy, precision, recall, and false positive rate for each purchase cohort for this stage 1 model. The "overall" numbers are for all cohorts combined, with equal numbers of users in each cohort's sample. Note in particular the very high recall and low false positive rate for users who have never purchased, and the very high false positive rate for power users. It is easy to predict when an inactive user will make their first purchase, but it is more difficult to predict when a previously very active user will drop off. This is because we tend to have more advance warning for the former, in the form of increased engagement prior to purchase. In the latter case (when a previously very active user disengages), the shift is typically very sudden. However, we find that a majority of these dropped-off users will return in the following quarter, which means that they will be receptive to CRM efforts once we have enough engagement data to detect the drop-off. Note also that it is very difficult to predict the purchases of sporadic buyers because this is the group with the noisiest purchasing behavior.

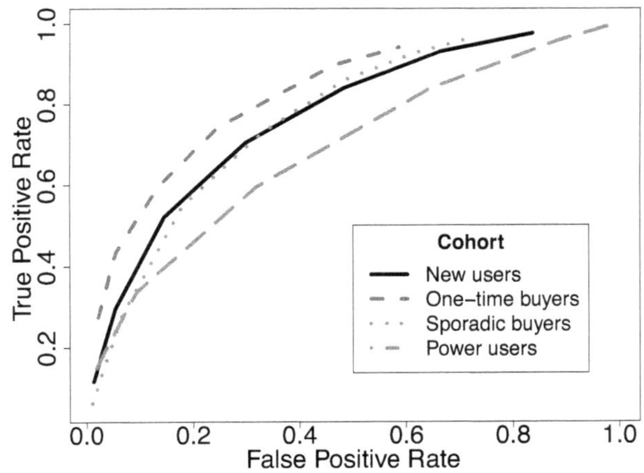

Figure 3: The ROC curves for our stage 1 model for each purchase cohort, showing the true positive rate versus the false positive rate as we vary the classification cutoff parameter from 0.2 to 0.8.

Table 1: The accuracy, precision, recall, and false positive rate (FPR) for each purchase cohort and overall for our stage 1 model. All results are percentages.

Cohort	Accuracy	Precision	Recall	FPR
Unactivated	98	43	100	2
New users	78	50	53	15
One-time buyers	95	37	32	2
Sporadic buyers	81	41	37	10
Power users	77	89	83	64
Overall	93	50	62	4

6.1.2 Overall stage 1 and 2 performance

After we determine a binary classification for which users are predicted to purchase, we then predict the purchase value for the positives and assign a zero value to the negatives to achieve our final results. In Table 2 we show the Pearson and Spearman correlation coefficients between actual and predicted values at the end of this process, for each combination of purchase cohort and time window. All of these show a moderate to high level of correlation [10], all with very high statistical significance ($p < 0.0001$). Typically we find that our accuracy measures tend to improve as the time period is increased. This is because purchase value per user is still a rather noisy measure for the short timeframe for this dataset.

We present the RMSE for each combination of purchase cohort and time window in Table 3. These values are given in units of the average actual purchase value for each combination in question. Once again we see that longer time windows and more active customers are easier to predict, because in these situations we have more data and less noise; the most difficult prediction by far is for the unactivated group over the short time window, whereas the easiest pre-

Table 2: **Pearson (P) and Spearman (S) correlation coefficients for each cohort for each time window.**

Cohort	Short P	Short S	Medium P	Medium S	Long P	Long S
Unactivated	0.38	0.65	0.55	0.95	0.56	0.85
New users	0.33	0.38	0.43	0.46	0.44	0.50
One-time buyers	0.22	0.31	0.36	0.45	0.40	0.51
Sporadic buyers	0.23	0.29	0.31	0.40	0.37	0.46
Power users	0.47	0.40	0.59	0.48	0.61	0.51
Overall	0.45	0.53	0.70	0.72	0.73	0.77

Table 3: RMSE for each cohort for each time window, presented in units of the average actual purchase value for each case.

Cohort	Short	Medium	Long
Unactivated	13.01	7.89	5.46
New users	3.30	2.55	2.44
One-time buyers	7.48	5.15	4.04
Sporadic buyers	4.24	3.07	2.59
Power users	1.20	0.95	0.90
Overall	6.08	1.82	1.67

diction is for the power users over the long time window. For reference, the typical user in our data set purchases 1-2 times over the short time window, with the unactivated users purchasing 0.008 times, the sporadic users purchasing 0.3 times, and the power users purchasing 7 times on average. Our overall results outperform the winner of the 2009 CLTV modeling competition presented in Ref [14].

Because our model was tuned to avoid a systematic bias, we find that the actual and predicted numbers of purchasers are very close, and accordingly that our systematic bias in average purchase value per user is low in each purchase cohort. Overall the bias in average value is less than 1%. This general lack of a systematic bias was verified with testing on a sample to predict Q1 of 2015 (thereby including the confounding factor of the holiday spike).

We further find a good concordance between the actual and predicted distributions of spend per user, as shown in Figure 4. The distribution of actual spend is somewhat more spread out – having both more low- and high-spend users – than the distribution of predicted spend. In particular it is impossible to predict the long tail of very rare high-value purchases. We also find that we are predicting a reduced number of very low-spend users. This is due to our two-stage model, in which these users are typically classified as non-purchasers in stage 1 and thus given an automatic zero value in stage 2. Testing the use of the probability (as opposed to a binary classification) in stage 1 to mitigate this effect is the subject of future work.

6.2 Q3 analysis

This system went live at the start of Q3 of 2015. At the end of the quarter we completed additional validation tests to determine how useful our results were for Q3. Firstly we re-computed the metrics detailed above to successfully confirm that all of our performance metrics were in line with our initial model testing. These computations are automatically checked at the end of every quarter. In particular we find that the correlation coefficients for our entire Q3 customer base are indeed consistent with what we found from

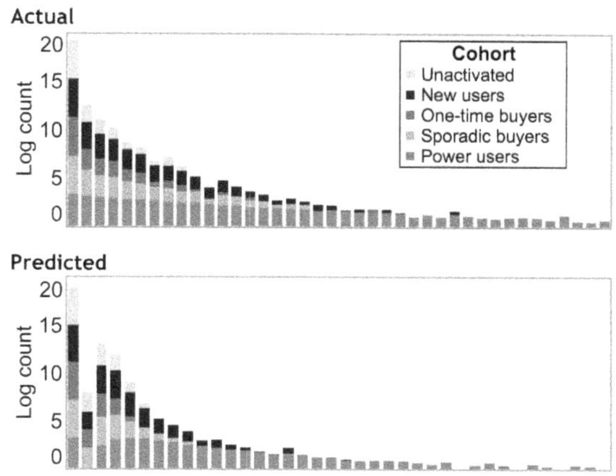

Figure 4: A comparison of the distributions of the actual (top) and the predicted (bottom) purchase value for the short time window, showing logs of counts for clarity. The horizontal and vertical scales are the same for both top and bottom panels and financial information is obfuscated.

our original out-of-time 2014 testing sets. Below we discuss a few additional metrics, all for a random subset of users from Q3 of 2015.

Comparing the top 10% to the bottom, we find that users who were predicted to be in the top 10% ended up spending on average 14 times more than users who were predicted to be in the bottom 90%, and 20 times more than those predicted to be in the bottom 10%. We further find that users who were predicted to decline in their value ended up having on average a 55% decline and users who were predicted to increase in their value ended up having on average a 62% increase.

Furthermore when we predicted that someone would attrite in Q3 of 2015, we ended up being correct 72% of the time. These attriting customers are naturally grouped according to their purchase cohort, which informs our marketing teams as they design CRM campaigns to keep these customers in Q4. We further check the feature set for each user predicted to attrite to find if there are any specific reasons for the disengagement, such as a slow shipping time or an expired voucher. Specific actions include sending promotions for general disengagement and initiating customer service treatment when a disengagement trigger has been identified. Then by tracking CLTV pre- and post-intervention, we determine the efficacy of these different strategies.

We use these predictions to analyze user behavior and to

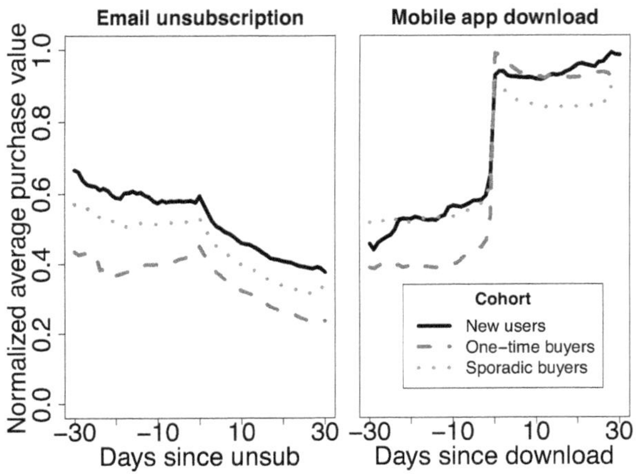

Figure 5: Average purchase value for each purchase cohort for the short time window as a function of the number of days since an unsubscription from emails (left) and a download of the mobile app (right). All customer values have been normalized by a constant factor, and the horizontal and vertical scales are the same for each panel. Power users have been left out because their value is much higher, but their behavior is qualitatively the same.

determine the value changes stemming from various lifecycle events as a function of time. We show two examples in Figure 5. Following an unsubscription from all emails we find a steady decline in predicted value due to a reduction in engagement. On the other hand, a download of our mobile app dramatically increases predicted value, due both to the download itself (a feature in the CLTV model) and due to the increase in app engagement. These behaviors are in line with what we have seen from historical data.

These CLTV predictions are so far being used at Groupon by several of our business units, including our marketing team which uses them for CRM campaigns to find the highest value customers and the customers most likely to attrite. For the sake of illustration we show some examples of the sorts of user segmenting that can be done in Figure 6 with a small sampling of data (how we employ these predictions in practice for user segmenting is outside the scope of this paper). For example, we can use these results to determine which users would benefit most from being sent promotional offers. For Q3 of 2015, users who were characterized as power users who were predicted to purchase in that quarter ended up using \$4.8 million in discounts from promotional offers. That adds up to roughly \$20 million per year in discounts to users who are extremely active and predicted to purchase anyway. Of course, experimentation is required to determine which users would benefit most from promotional offers. These CLTV scores can be used to select a prospective set of users and then the final decision of who gets the promotional offer would be decided based on the responses of user segments in a test campaign.

Also at Groupon we are using these results in product experimentation, both for segmenting users and as a longer-term KPI. For example, products related to redemption are geared towards increasing long-term customer satisfaction and thus cannot be adequately tested using typical shorter-term conversion-based A/B experimentation. For this we use CLTV as a performance metric and track the shifts in redemption-related features in the testing versus control groups over time.

6.3 Feature importance

As discussed above, we build different models for our different "purchase cohorts," with the intuition being that different features will be most important for customers at different stages of their lifecycle. We find that this intuition is indeed correct. For example, the top four most important features for our power users are, in no particular order:

- Purchase value in the past quarter
- Purchase value in the past year
- Lifetime purchase value
- Number of days since most recent purchase

Note that each of these features is related to purchasing behavior. On the other end of the spectrum, we cannot rely on purchase-related features to predict value for our one-time buyers. For these users the most important features include:

- Email engagement score
- Average number of orders per quarter per subscriber in the home city
- Whether or not the user has downloaded the mobile app
- Number of days since the user's last (and only) purchase

7. CONCLUSIONS AND FUTURE WORK

In this paper we have described the challenges faced, the choices made, and the lessons learned in building a customer lifetime value monitoring system for a large global e-commerce company. Our model uses engagement scores for email and our mobile app as features, and this gives us the ability to quickly and accurately detect changes in customer value. We gain additional accuracy by building separate models for differently-behaving sets of customers, such as one-time buyers and power users. We further use a triggering system and an empirical decay function to dramatically speed up the scoring process and make daily re-scoring with such a complex model technologically feasible. This system is currently running in production, scoring hundreds of millions of users on a daily cadence, and the results are being utilized by various business units including our marketing and experimentation teams.

In the future we plan to enhance this system in several ways. These include testing other machine learning algorithms (e.g. zero inflated binomial and gradient boosted decision trees) and adding more features, such as scores for other types of engagement including organic desktop web activity. We also plan to add more information regarding the use of discounts, and other features that other business units request for their specific needs. Our use of scalable technologies means that our system will continue to perform as our business grows. However we will still continue to determine ways to further speed up the system and decrease the use of resources.

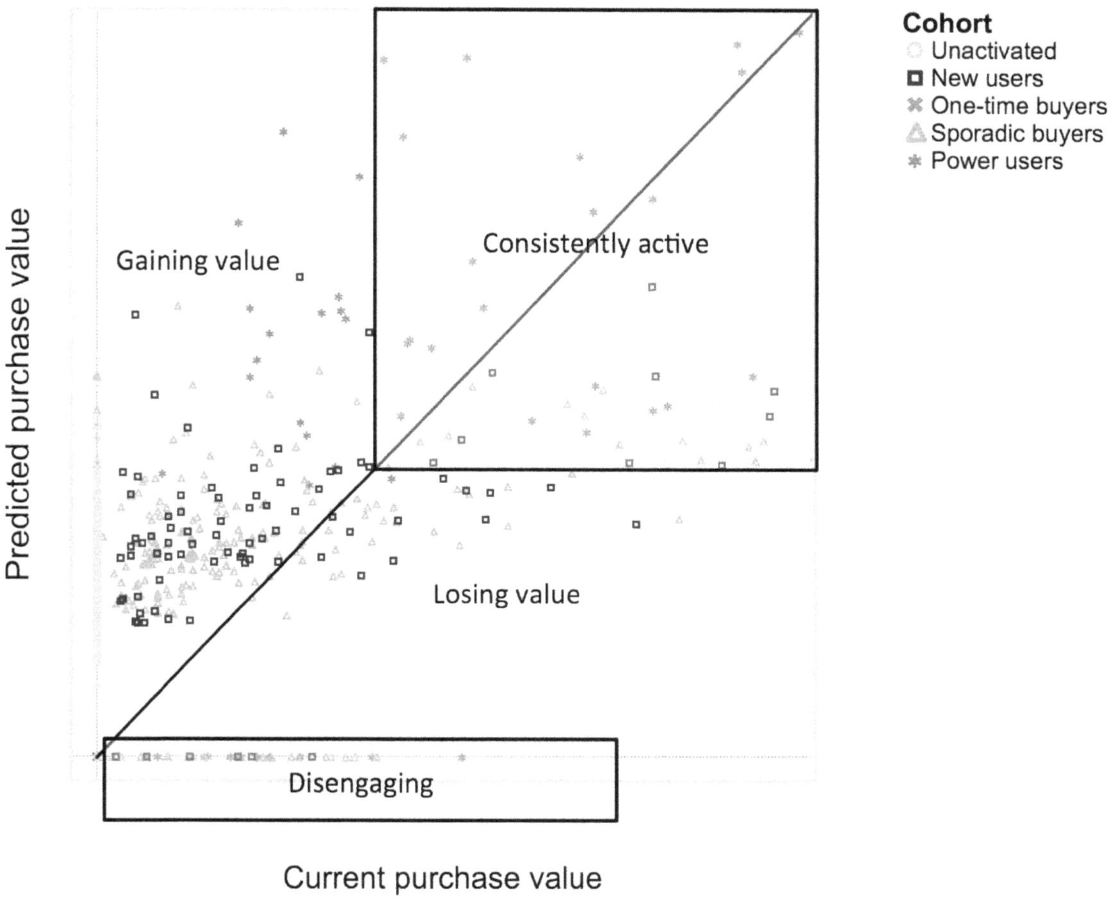

Figure 6: Illustrative scatter plot of predicted future value versus past value for the short time window for a small sample, showing a few different user segments that one could define. The diagonal line denotes a one-to-one correspondence and financial information is obfuscated.

As we continue to gather more data, we will evaluate longer term trends and explore the use of longer time frames for our purchase cohorts. We will also fully quantify the business costs associated with model errors. For example, a false negative for newer users might have larger implications for building a long-tern relationship, whereas it would not be as detrimental to a frequent user. We will further continue to create cohort metrics for our end business users, for instance tracking redemption time for the redemptions team as mentioned above. We plan to similarly track cohort metrics for our other product and marketing partners and continue to iterate to develop the CLTV system and new products in tandem.

8. REFERENCES

[1] S. Aiello, T. Kraljevic, P. Maj, and with contributions from the 0xdata team. h2o: R interface for h2o. 2015. R package version 3.0.0.25.

[2] C. Bailey, P. Baines, H. Wilson, and M. Clark. Segmentation and customer insight in contemporary services marketing practive: why grouping customers is no longer enough. *Journal of Marketing Management*, 25(3/4):227–252, 2009.

[3] D. Benoit and D. V. den Poel. Improving customer retention in financial services using kinship network information. *Expert Systems with Applications*, 39(13):11435–11442, 2012.

[4] L. Breiman. Random forests. *Machine Learning*, 45(1):5–32, 2001.

[5] P. Cermak. Customer profitability analysis and customer life time value models: Portfolio analysis. *Procedia Economics and Finance*, 25:14–25, 2015.

[6] Z.-Y. Chen and Z.-P. Fan. Distributed customer behavior prediction using multiplex data: A collaborative mksvm approach. *Knowledge-Based Systems*, 35:111–119, 2012.

[7] M. Crowder, D. Hand, and W. Krzanowski. On optimal intervention for customer lifetime value. *European Journal of Operational Research*, 183(3):1550–1559, 2007.

[8] F. Dwyer. Customer lifetime valuation for marketing decision making. *Journal of Direct Marketing*, 11(4):6–13, 1997.

[9] S. Gupta, D. Hanssens, B. Hardie, W. Kahn, V. Kumar, N. Lin, N. Ravishanker, and S. Sriram. Modeling customer lifetime value. *Journal of Service Research*, 9(2):139–155, November 2006.

[10] D. Hinkle, W. Wiersma, and S. Jurs. *Applied Statistics for the Behavioral Sciences*. Houghton Mifflin, Boston, 2003.

[11] P. Kotler and K. Keller. *A framework for marketing management*. Pearson Education, England, 2012.

[12] V. Kumar and M. George. Measuring and maximizing customer equity: A critical analysis. *Journal of the Academy of Marketing Science*, 35(2):157–71, 2007.

[13] A. Liaw and M. Wiener. Classification and regression by randomforest. *R News*, 2(3):18–22, 2002.

[14] E. Malthouse. The results from the lifetime value and customer equity modeling competition. *Journal of Interactive Marketing*, 23(3):272–275, 2009.

[15] D. Meyer, E. Dimitriadou, K. Hornik, A. Weingessel, and F. Leisch. *e1071: Misc Functions of the Department of Statistics (e1071), TU Wien*, 2014. R package version 1.6-4.

[16] T. Mirzaei and L. Iyer. Application of predictive analytics in customer relationship management: A literature review and classification. In *Proceedings of the Southern Association for Information Systems Conference*, March 2014.

[17] S. Rosset, E. Neumann, U. Eick, and N. Vatnik. Customer lifetime value models for decision support. *Data Mining and Knowledge Discovery*, 7(3):321–339, July 2003.

[18] T. Therneau, B. Atkinson, and B. Ripley. *rpart: Recursive Partitioning and Regression Trees*, 2014. R package version 4.1-8.

[19] L. Valenzuela, E. Torres, P. Hidalgo, and P. Farias. Salesperson clv orientation's effect on performance. *Journal of Business Research*, 67(4):550–557, 2014.

Identifying Earmarks in Congressional Bills

Ellery Wulczyn*
Stanford University
ellery@cs.stanford.edu

Madian Khabsa*
Microsoft Research
madian.khabsa@microsoft.com

Vrushank Vora
University of Chicago
vvora@uchicago.edu

Matthew Heston
Northwestern University
heston@u.northwestern.edu

Joe Walsh, Christopher Berry, Rayid Ghani
University of Chicago
{jtwalsh,cberry,rayid}@uchicago.edu

ABSTRACT

Earmarks are legislative provisions that direct federal funds to specific projects, circumventing the competitive grant-making process of federal agencies. Identifying and cataloging earmarks is a tedious, time-consuming process carried out by experts from public interest groups. In this paper, we present a machine learning system for automatically extracting earmarks from congressional bills and reports. We first describe a table-parsing algorithm for extracting budget allocations from appropriations tables in congressional bills. We then use machine learning classifiers to identify budget allocations as earmarked objects with an out of sample ROC AUC score of 0.89. Using this system, we construct the first publicly available database of earmarks dating back to 1995. Our machine learning approach adds transparency, accuracy and speed to the congressional appropriations process.

1. INTRODUCTION

An earmark is a legislative provision that directs federal funds to specific projects, circumventing the competitive grant-making process of federal agencies. It has been difficult to study how earmarking has affected the legislative process due to a lack of comprehensive and open data on earmarks. In fact, earmarking is often considered "the best known, most notorious, and most misunderstood aspect of the congressional budgetary process" [14].

In the past, earmark datasets were created manually by experts from governmental agencies, such as the Office of Management and Budget (OMB) and public interest groups such as Taxpayers for Common Sense, Washington Watch, and Citizens Against Government Waste. Congress produces thousands of pages of legal text each year, making the process time-consuming and expensive. As a result, past efforts were limited to short time spans and a limited set of documents. A further issue, is that each of these groups had different definitions, motivations, and processes for identifying and cataloging earmarks.

Given the significant changes in American politics in the last 20 years, e.g. increased polarization, changes to campaign financing, and a recent ban on earmarks [3, 6], datasets with short-term coverage are inadequate for political scientists to draw robust policy conclusions. A consistent, historically complete dataset has the potential to reveal valuable insights on effective governance and answer questions such as: "How instrumental is earmarking to passing controversial legislation?"; "What effect does securing earmarks have on campaign financing and reelection?"; or "Does being a chair of congressional subcommittee affect how funds are appropriated to the legislator's state or district?"

In this paper, we present a machine learning system for automatically extracting earmarks from congressional bills and reports. This approach allows us to cheaply, reliably, and consistently extract earmarks from historical congressional documents. Furthermore, the method is transparent and reproducible, enabling analysts to easily understand, evaluate, and build on our work [7]. Using our system, we construct the first publicly available database of earmarks dating back to 1995.

The dataset is already being used by Harris School of Public Policy researchers of the University of Chicago to do public policy research and analysis. In addition, it is being promoted by both the Center for Data Science and Public Policy, also of the University of Chicago, as well as the Sunlight Foundation to researchers and practitioners interested in government transparency and public policy.

2. SYSTEM OVERVIEW

An overview of the entire system is depicted in Figure 1. The ultimate goal is to be able to take a document, extract all the potential budget allocations that occur in the document, and finally classify which allocations are earmarks. Extracting potential budget allocations involves identifying tables in the document that contain budget allocations and parsing them into rows, where each row is a separate allocation. This process is described in Section 4. Building a classifier for determining which allocations are earmarks requires a labeled set of allocations. We generate a corpus of labeled allocations by matching the extracted allocations to an earmark dataset compiled by the Office of Management and Budget (OMB) in the late 2000s (see Section 5.1). Our method for labeling earmarks involves a combination of hand-labeling and machine learning and is discussed in

*The first two authors contributed equally to this study.

KDD '16, August 13-17, 2016, San Francisco, CA, USA
© 2016 ACM. ISBN 978-1-4503-4232-2/16/08...$15.00
DOI: http://dx.doi.org/10.1145/2939672.2939711

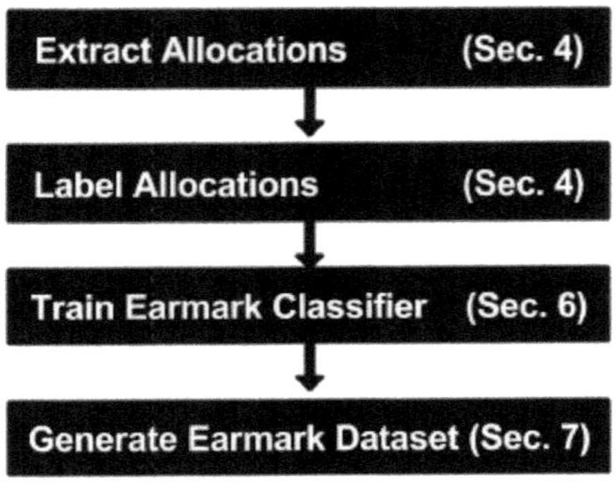

Figure 1: System overview.

Section 5. Given this labeled set of annotations, we train an earmark detection classifier as described in Section 6. Finally, we run our earmark classifier on all congressional bills and reports going back to 1995 and show some preliminary analysis in Section 7.

3. THE BUDGET PROCESS

As many readers may not be familiar with the congressional budgetary process and how earmarking occurs, we provide a brief overview.

At the beginning of each fiscal year, the President submits a proposal for the year's budget to Congress. The budget proposes funding levels for the various government entities and broadly outlines spending limits and revenue expectations for at least the next five years. Next, the House and Senate budget committees review the President's proposal and pass a budget resolution.

Mandatory spending and interest payments account for the majority of federal spending [2]. The House and Senate appropriations committees divide what remains in the budget resolution to their twelve sub-committees. The twelve sub-committees then write the bills that authorize discretionary spending, and each of those bills becomes a law if approved by each chamber and signed by the President. Congress combines those bills into a single omnibus bill and votes on it.

Earmarks can enter at almost any point of the process. Senators and representatives can insert earmarks into the text of appropriations bills, including supplemental appropriations and continuing resolutions [15]. they can place earmarks in the explanatory report attached to the bill. They can also contact bureaucrats directly.

As the budget process has changed over time, so has the placement of earmarks: "During the 19th century, earmarks were often placed in the law. But after the adoption of the Budget and Accounting Act of 1921, most earmarks were included in legislative reports" [8]. Congress officially banned earmarks in 2010, but members have continued to request and receive them [9, 4]. Senators and representatives have increasingly turned to calling and writing federal agencies directly [10].

4. ALLOCATION EXTRACTION

The first step to identifying earmarks is to extract appropriations found in congressional bills and reports. We focus on extracting allocations mentioned within tables, where

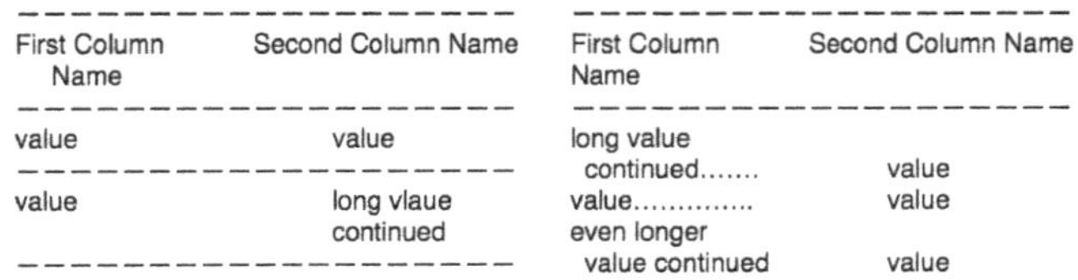

Figure 2: Examples of *dashed* and *dotted* tables.

85% of the earmarks occur (see Sec. 5.4). Future work will identify earmarks in free text to increase the coverage of our dataset.

Several approaches to table parsing have been developed in the field of information retrieval. Pyreddy et al. exploit table layout in text documents and develop a character alignment graph (CAG) that uses heuristic methods to identify tables within documents [13]. They identify sections of tables within documents. Pinto et al. extend the CAG to extract individual cells from tables [11]. Our initial analyses found that many tables shared similar attributes. We thus employ a heuristic based approach described in the following section.

4.1 Table Identification

The Government Printing Office (GPO) provides congressional bills and reports as plain text files where tables appear as blocks of formatted text. Indentation, white space, and dots and dashes are used to format tables. We first segment a document into paragraphs, where paragraphs are separated by two new line characters or more. Then each paragraph is classified as a table or free text. A paragraph is labeled as a table if the percentage of rows satisfying any of the following conditions exceeds a threshold:

- It has numeric characters and three consecutive dots,
- It has numeric characters and at least two consecutive spaces, or
- It has at least three consecutive dashes.

The threshold was set empirically to 0.3. In the experiments section (5.6), we show that this heuristic retrieved more than 98% of the tables in congressional reports and bills.

Furthermore, tables in Congressional bills and reports can be categorized into two main types: *dotted tables* and *dashed tables*. Dashed tables use lines of all dashes to separate rows and whitespaces to separate columns. Dotted tables do not have special lines separating rows: each line is a row or part of a multi-line row, and columns are separated by dots and whitespace. See Figure 2 for examples. We distinguish these two classes of tables because parsing each type requires different rules and heuristics.

4.2 Table Header Detection

Parsing a one-line table header requires splitting on two or more white spaces. In the case where headers span multiple lines, we introduce an algorithm that clusters words in the header based on their vertical overlap. The simple idea is that two words on two consecutive lines that intersect vertically belong to the same header. First, each line is split into cells by two or more consecutive white spaces.

Each cell in every row is represented as a four-dimensional tuple $(text, line, begin, end)$, where $text$ is the clean text of the cell, $line$ is the line number, $begin$ is the offset within the line at which the text begins, and end is the last index within the line at which the cell ends. The tuples are fed into a clustering algorithm 1 to detect headers. The algorithm returns the list of headers of the table.

Algorithm 1: Header Identification Algorithm

```
input : List of cell tuples Cells
output: Table Headers
Sorted = Sort(Cells, key = begin);
Clusters ⟵ List;
C ⟵ List;
Add Sorted[0] to C;
Add C to Clusters;
for i = 1; i < length(Sorted); i++ do
    word ⟵ Sorted[i];
    prev_word ⟵ Sorted[i − 1];
    if word.begin < prev_word.end then
        Add word to Clusters[−1];
    else
        C ⟵ List;
        Add word to C;
        Add C to Clusters;
    end
end
Headers ⟵ List;
for C ∈ Clusters do
    header = Sort(C, key = line);
    Add concat(header) to Headers;
end
return Headers;
```

4.3 Column Detection

Tables are treated as a collection of columns where each column divides rows into multiple cells. The idea behind detecting column dividers is that column boundaries do not contain any text. Instead, they consist of whitespace or other delimiting characters across all the rows. That is, a column divider is a pair of *begin* and *end* positions such that only whitespace is observed within this span for all the lines in the table. Algorithm 2 shows how these tuples are found. In the following section, we discuss how multiline rows are detected and merged.

4.4 Multiline Row Merging

Each line is initially treated as a separate row in the table. Because rows can span multiple lines, we develop heuristics to detect multiline rows and merge the related lines. For dashes tables, identifying multiline rows is trivial because rows are separated by a line of dashes. For dotted tables, things are more involved. The basic concept is that all valid table rows need to have a money allocation in one of their associated lines. This is guaranteed by our table-identification heuristic described earlier. In the case of multiline rows, money allocations can appear either in the first or the last line. Fortunately, the position of the allocation tends to be consistent within a table, which makes it easy to group multiline rows. This heuristic is shown to provide accurate extraction in the experiments section.

Algorithm 2: Column Identification Algorithm

```
input : List of table rows Rows
p ⟵ get_white_space_positions(Rows[0]);
for row ∈ Rows do
    p ⟵ p ∩ get_white_space_positions(row);
end
indices ⟵ Sort(p);
dividers ⟵ list;
if length(indices) = 0 then
    Add (0, length(Rows[0])) to dividers;
else
    i ⟵ 1;
    begin ⟵ indices[0];
    prev ⟵ indices[0];
    while i < length(indices) do
        if indices[i] − prev = 1 then
            prev ⟵ indices[i];
        else
            Add (begin, prev) to dividers;
            begin ⟵ indices[i];
            prev ⟵ indices[i];
        end
        i ⟵ i + 1;
    end
end
return dividers;
```

4.5 Table Parsing Evaluation

To evaluate the the accuracy of our table-identification methodology, we randomly selected 40 documents and tagged all 384 tables in those documents. On this subset, our table-identification heuristic recalled 98.6% of all of true tables, while 89.2% of the predicted tables were true tables. For the table identification task, we value recall higher than precision because an earmark missed in this step will never be recovered and rows that are not allocations can be weeded out later. To evaluate the column-identification and row-merging algorithms, we randomly chose 30 tables from those 40 documents. We correctly identified columns and rows in all 30.

5. ALLOCATION LABELING

The output of the table parsing algorithm, described in Sec. 4, is a collection of tables that are neatly parsed into rows and columns. Each non-header row in an allocation table describes an allocation and is a potential earmark. Eventually, we want to take a supervised learning approach to building a model to classify allocations as earmarks. This approach, however, requires labeling a set of allocations as earmarks or just regular appropriations.

In this section, we describe how we use a corpus of earmarks from the Office of Management and Budget (OMB), described in Sec. 5.1, to generate a labeled set of allocations. In particular, we attempt to match each earmark in the OMB dataset to a corresponding allocation. In order to perform this matching task at scale, we first match a subset by hand (Sec. 5.4) and then train a classifier to predict whether a budget allocation matches an earmark in the OMB dataset (Sec. 5.5 and Sec. 5.6).

5.1 OMB Data

In 2007, the OMB ordered all departments and agencies to identify and catalog earmarks that appeared in appropriations and authorization bills and reports for 2005. Over the course of three months, those departments and agencies sent the OMB congressional funding data. The OMB used this to compile a list of congressional earmarks [12]. This process was repeated in 2008, 2009, and 2010. The OMB posted all the data in CSV format on its website.[1]

For each earmark, the OMB may provide the following:

- The congressional documents it appeared in,
- An excerpt from each of those documents,
- A short description,
- A long description, and
- The recipient of the funds.

See Table 1 for an example OMB record.

Documents	Congress 111, House Bill 3293
Excerpt	...of which $13,455,000 shall be used for the projects, and in the amounts, specified under the heading 'Disease Control, Research, and Training' in the report of the Committee on Appropriations of the House of Representatives to accompany this Act
Short Desc.	Dillard, University, New Orleans, LA for facilities and equipment
Full Desc.	NA
Recipient	NA

Table 1: Sample OMB Record.

5.2 Resolving OMB document references

The first step in matching OMB records to allocations is to map each document cited in the OMB corpus to a congressional document[2]. Unfortunately, there is no unique government document ID, which would make linking trivial. Instead, the OMB references the documents in which an earmark appears in myriad ways, such as specifying a bill number, a report number accompanying a bill, a public law, or a common name for a bill. Table 2 lists typical examples of references. Table 3 describes how references are resolved for OMB data from 2008. The heuristics for the other years are similar.

Earmark ID	Citation Reference
340045	H. Rept. 110-434
235530	P.L. 110-161
235531	Joint Explanatory Statement to accompany H.R. 2764

Table 2: Examples of OMB document references.

[1]http://earmarks.omb.gov/earmarks-public/

[2]We use the Government Printing Office (GPO) as our source of congressional texts.

Citation Reference	Earmark Document
H.Rept. XXX-YYY; S.Rept. XXX-YYY	Mapped to the latest House Report in the XXX Congress that goes to the YYY report; mapping is similar for the Senate
H.R. XXX; S.XXX	Mapped to the latest version of the House or Senate bills of the XXX number in a given Congress and all of the accompanying reports to those bills
P.L. XXX-YYY	Public Laws are bills signed into law by the president of the U.S. We find the latest house version of the law and map it to the bills and all of the relevant documents.
Joint Explanatory Statements	These documents are treated as congressional reports to the bill they are attached to. We map them to those reports accordingly.

Table 3: OMB reference resolution for 2008.

5.3 Matching OMB Records to Allocations

After linking OMB document references to documents in our corpus of congressional texts, we used fields from an OMB record to link OMB records with allocations extracted from the corpus. For example, consider the OMB record in Table 1 and a table extracted from the cited document in Figure 3.

```
------------------------------------------------------------------------
                                                      Committee
                     Project                      recommendation
------------------------------------------------------------------------
Children's Health Fund, New York, NY for health            100,000
 assessments, outreach, and education services for
 children and their families.........................
City of Laredo, TX for a community health assessment.      200,000
County of Marin, San Rafael, CA for research and           200,000
 analysis related to breast cancer incidence and
 mortality in the county and breast cancer screening.
Dillard University, New Orleans, LA for facilities         300,000
Iowa Chronic Care Consortium/Des Moines University,        200,000
 Des Moines, IA for a preventive health initiative...
Iowa State University, Ames, IA for facilities and       1,000,000
 equipment...........................................
Hope Institute for Children and Families,                  100,000
 Springfield, IL for facilities and equipment........
York College of Pennsylvania, York, PA for facilities      300,000
 and equipment.......................................
```

Figure 3: An allocation table.

If an earmark occurs in a table, the OMB does not actually cite the text of the table row the earmark appears in. Instead, they cite part of a bill, which alludes to the fact that an allocation is specified in a report accompanying the bill. This is the case in the example given in Table 1. Even when the excerpt is taken from the report containing the earmark, it will cite the section of the report that alludes to a table which contains the earmark; for example,

> Provided further, That within the amounts appropriated, $3,715,000 shall be used for the projects, and in the amounts, specified in the table titled "Congressionally-designated items" in the report of the Committee on Appropriations of the House of Representatives to accompany this Act. (Page 4 of HR bill 2847)

Thus, the excerpt is of little use in matching the table rows. It would, however, directly provide labels for earmarks that occur in plain text. As a result, we need to use the recipient and description fields for matching. In the example above, there is a perfect string match between the short description and the table cell corresponding to the 11th row of the project column. In general, the short description could be the concatenation of multiple table cells, a single table cell could be the concatenation of the short description and the full description, the description could be a permutation of entities in the table cell text, or the descriptions could contain abbreviations and misspellings of entities in the table cell text.

The matching task is even more complicated when recipients and descriptions are not unique within a document. A recipient can receive multiple earmarks within the same document, and multiple recipients can receive earmarks for the same purpose (e.g. "for equipment and facilities"). Furthermore, the same recipient can receive funding for the same purpose in multiple table rows within the same document. This means there is a one-to-many relationship between an earmark record from the OMB and table rows in a document.

Our matching evaluation works as follows. The matching algorithm is perfect if it matches a row for the earmarked appropriation in the document to its OMB record.

Consider a table row that represents an earmark. It will be incorrectly labeled negative if it does not get matched to a record from OMB either because the record is missing or because the matching was done incorrectly. It will correctly receive a positive label if it matches with a record from the OMB. Note that even if it was matched with the wrong OMB record, it would still be correctly labeled. So if we do matching for the purpose of labeling only, then for the algorithm to perfectly label the table rows, it must only match every table row that represents an earmark to some earmark.

Let's now consider a row that does not represent an earmark. It will correctly receive a negative label if it does not get matched with a record from OMB. It will be incorrectly labeled positive if it matches with a record from OMB, either because the matching was done incorrectly or because the OMB contained a record that is not really an earmark.

For the purposes of this paper, we treat the database from OMB as definitional. We do not exert our own judgment in adding or removing earmarks from their records. We attempt to get the best labels we can by building the best matching algorithm that we can.

As mentioned above, multiple table rows can map to the same OMB record and mapping two OMB records to the same table row does not necessarily imply a labeling error. Because there are no clear constraints on the mapping from OMB records to table rows, we treat the matching problem as a simple classification problem.

5.4 Learning to Match: Training Data

As mentioned above, our goal is to build a classifier that, given an OMB record and a table row, predicts whether they match. We generated a training set to train this matching classifier in a semi-manual fashion. We first take an OMB record r and extract the set of documents D_r in which r occurs. Then for each document $d_r \in D_r$, we compute a similarity score $SIM(t_{d_r}, r)$ between every table row t_{d_r} and r. The similarity score is the maximum of the Jaccard similarities between the bigrams in t_r and the bigrams in r's short description $r.sd$, full description $r.fd$ and recipient $r.rec$. For convenience lets define $F_r = \{r.sd, r.fd, r.rec\}$

$$JS(t_1, t_2) = \frac{|bigrams(t1) \cap bigrams(t2)|}{|bigrams(t1) \cup bigrams(t2)|} \tag{1}$$

$$SIM(t_{d_r}, r) = \max_{f_r \in F_r} JS(t_{d_r}, f_r) \tag{2}$$

Within each document, pairs of the OMB record and the table rows are ranked according to the similarity score SIM. We then looked at the top 20 pairs and hand label them as being a match or not. All other pairs are automatically labeled as not matching. Table 4 gives an example of descriptions from an OMB record and the five most similar table rows. Cells within the table are separated by the | symbol and are removed before computing similarities.

Short Desc	Trimble Local School District, Glouster, OH for an after-school program
Full Desc	NA
1	Trimble Local School District, Glouster, OH for an after-school program
2	Elementary and Secondary Education (includes FIE) | Trimble Local School District, Glouster, OH for an after-school program | Space
3	YMCA of Warren, Warren, OH for an after-school program
4	City of Newark, CA for an after-school program
5	Memphis City Schools, Memphis, TN for an after-school program

Table 4: Descriptions from an OMB record along with the top 5 most similar rows defined by SIM.

In this example, the earmark occurs in two tables within the same document, and the two corresponding rows are ranked highest. The other rows are also earmarks for after-school programs, but they are for different districts or organizations. We applied this labeling procedure to 516 randomly selected OMB records and found at least one matching table row 438 times, thereby giving 85% as an estimated lower bound of earmarks in tables. Because the OMB may cite multiple documents for every record, there were 840 cases in which we tried to match a record to a table row within a specific document, and we found at least one matching row 534 times. There are at least seven possible reasons an OMB record is not matched with a table row within a document that the OMB cites. For each error, assume the previous errors where not made:

1. The document is actually a bill that cites a report which contains the earmark.
2. The document is a public law or resolution; we do not include these documents in our analysis.
3. The citation was parsed incorrectly; we are looking in the wrong document.
4. The earmark does not appear in a table but in plain text.

5. The table was not parsed correctly, so the matching row is not available.
6. The matching row did not appear in the top 20.
7. The matching row was hand-labeled as not matching.

Although one might like to find every occurrence of every earmark, we are most concerned with finding every earmark at least once. The only issue is that if we fail to identify an earmark in a correctly parsed table, we would have an incorrectly labeled table row. This can only happen if errors 1-5 are not made and either error 6 or error 7 seven is made. If our matching algorithm is as good as the gold-standard human labels and the statistics above generalize, then we can estimate the upper bound of incorrectly labeled rows. We extracted 530k table rows and the OMB gives 122k occurrences of earmarks. In the worst case, where errors 1-5 are never made, we would have 8.4% of data mislabeled.

5.5 Learning to Match: Features

In this section, we describe the feature sets we designed for the matching task. Features are computed over pairs of table rows and OMB record pairs. For ease of notation, fix the OMB record r as well as the document d_r it appears in. Let T be the set of table rows t in d_r. Let F be defined as above as the set containing the short description, full description, and recipient texts from r. Let C_t be the set of table cells in table row t.

Jaccard Similarity Features:
Jaccard similarity between the table row and each field of the OMB record:

$$JS(t, f) \text{ for } f \in F \tag{3}$$

Maximum similarity between the table row and each field of the OMB record:

$$\max_{f_r \in F_r} JS(t, f_r) \tag{4}$$

Maximum Jaccard similarity between a field of an OMB record and each cell in the table row for each field of the OMB record:

$$\max_{c_t \in C_t} JS(c_t, f_r) \text{ for} f_r \in F_r \tag{5}$$

Maximum Jaccard similarity between all pairs of cells in the table row and fields of the OMB record:

$$\max_{(c,f) \in C x F} JS(c, f) \tag{6}$$

Relative Performance Features:
For any of the similarity features above, one can compare similarity scores for pairs of table rows and a particular OMB record within a document. A simple way to do this is to take the difference in similarity feature scores between a particular pair and the highest scoring pair. Alternatively, one can find the rank of a pair in the list of all pairs of table rows and a specific OMB record, where the order is determined by a similarity feature score. Here is an example of a difference feature:

$$SIM(t, r) - \max_{t' \in T} SIM(t', r) \tag{7}$$

Because the classification task is really a matching task, a particular OMB record will usually have only one matching table row per document. Providing information about how similar a table row is to an OMB record compared to others provides a way of normalizing similarity scores within the context of a particular OMB record and document.

5.6 Learning to Match: Experiments

As mentioned, the hand-labeling procedure was applied to 516 OMB records. It resulted in 769 matching pairs of OMB records and table rows and 647,157 non-matching pairs. There can be more matching pairs than OMB records because in some reports the same earmark can occur in two tables, resulting in two matches for a single record.

Out of the matching pairs, the lowest SIM score observed was 0.077. To reduce the number of negative examples, we only include pairs with SIM scores greater than 0.05. This reduced the number of negative instances to 32,715. One can think of this threshold as a high-recall, low-precision filter. Correspondingly, when we use the model to match all remaining pairs beyond the ones that were hand labeled, we compute SIM and label the pair negative if the value is less than 0.05. If the score is greater than 0.05, we use the model to label the pair. We present the result of our SVM classifier in Table 5. Varying the weight parameter on the sum of the slack variables in the SVM objective function in the range [0.001, 100] did not change performance.

	Mean Value (se)
AUC	0.9966 (0.08)
Precision: non-matching pairs	0.9203, (4.19)
Precision: matching pairs	0.9955, (0.26)
Recall: non-matching pairs	0.9373, (1.52)
Recall: matching pairs	0.9961, (0.12)
F-Score: non-matching pairs	0.9961, (0.12)
F-Score: matching pairs	0.9280, (2.02)

Table 5: Average Precision, Recall and F1 scores computed via 5 fold cross-validation.

To evaluate the quality of our features, we train a model using all the features described above as well as training a model on just the Jaccard similarity features, just the ranking features, and just the difference features. Figure 4 shows an ROC curve for each set of features. The ranking features are the best individual feature set, but including the difference features and the Jaccard similarity features gives a small but significant increase in the ROC AUC. The results show our algorithm can perform the matching task almost as well as an expert human annotator.

We applied the matching algorithm to all OMB records. For every OMB record r and for every document d referenced by r, we computed the features described above over pairs of table rows in d and r and record whether the matching algorithm predicts a match for each pair. Table 6 shows the number of OMB records, the number of OMB records that have at least one matching table row, and the percentage of OMB records that have at least one matching table row by year. The results for 2005 are dramatically worse, which we traced back to errors in linking documents in our corpus to documents that the OMB cites for earmarks in 2005.

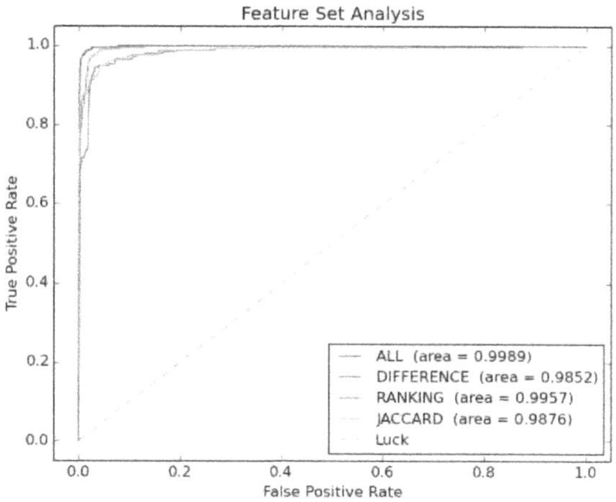

Figure 4: ROC curves for each feature set.

Enacted Year	OMB Records	Distinct	% Matched
2010	9785	9280	94.8 %
2009	11577	9181	79.8 %
2008	11503	10919	94.9 %
2005	14977	7624	50.1%

Table 6: Annual matching performance on OMB data.

6. EARMARK CLASSIFICATION

Given the labels on table rows induced by matching, we build a classifier that takes as input features computed over the table row and predicts earmark characteristics.

6.1 Earmark Classification Features

We compute four broad categories of features for the earmark classification task, which include geographic features, sponsor features, unigrams, and simple string heuristics.

Geo Features: presence of a city, presence of a county, and presence of a state

Sponsor Features: presence of a senator's last name and presence of a representative's last name

Unigrams: indicator variables for all unigrams in the training data except states, cities, counties, and last names of members of Congress.

Simple Heuristic Features:

- number of tokens
- number and percentage of tokens that are numbers
- number of percentage of tokens that are words
- number and percentage of characters that are of dots
- percentage of characters capitalized

6.2 Earmark Classification Experiments

To measure the generalization performance of our earmark classifier over time, we would like to train on documents from one year and test on documents from another. This is complicated by the fact that an earmark can occur in a document from the year it was enacted or the previous year. For example, when looking at the documents that the OMB references for earmarks enacted in 2009, we find that 3786 references are from documents dating from 2008 and 8500 references are dating from 2009. When grouping documents by year, we cannot use documents from 2010 since they could contain earmarks enacted in 2011, for which there is no OMB data. Our labeling policy is that an allocation is labeled as an earmark if and only if it matches an OMB record. Hence, we will mislabel all earmarks enacted in 2011, leading to poor training data and a poor classifier. We can however, use documents from 2008 and 2009.

Table 7 shows the results of training an SVM on the features described above. We are most interested in measuring how a model trained on one year performs on prior years, since most of the OMB data we need to fill in is from before 2008. We report cross-validated metrics for a model tuned and trained on 2009 documents. We also report the metrics for the 2009 model applied to documents from 2008. As a reference point for the generalization performance, we also include cross-validated metrics for a model tuned and trained on 2008 documents.

	CV 2009	**CV 2008**	**Train: 2009 Test: 2008**
Precision	0.74 (0.017)	0.85 (0.014)	0.72
Recall	0.71 (0.042)	0.87 (0.017)	0.48
F-Score	0.72 (0.016)	0.86 (0.007)	0.58
ROC	0.93 (0.001)	0.97 (0.002)	0.91

Table 7: Metrics for documents grouped by document year.

The data suggest that if a document contains OMB earmarks, they were all enacted in the same year. Hence, we can assign an enacted year to those documents referenced by OMB earmarks. This allows us to group documents by the inferred enacted year and assign negative examples to the enacted year of the document they are in. This approach leaves out documents that are not referenced by any OMB records. Hence we may lose negative examples from omitted documents. The advantage is that we can increase our dataset by using documents enacted in 2008, 2009 and 2010. Table 8 shows results analogous to table 7.

	CV 10/09	**CV 2008**	**Train:10/09 Test: 2008**
Precision	0.92(0.012)	0.90 (0.005)	0.87
Recall	0.93 (0.042)	0.93 (0.014)	0.84
F-Score	0.92 (0.016)	0.92 (0.005)	0.85
ROC	0.96 (0.004)	0.94 (0.004)	0.89

Table 8: Metrics for document grouped by enacted year.

Although there appears to be little difference in results between the two grouping approaches as measured by the area under the ROC curve, grouping by enacted year gives a much better F1. In both cases, cross-validation overestimates the generalization error, suggesting that locations, entities, and sponsors indicative of earmarks vary from year to year.

To evaluate the quality of our features, we train a model using all the features described above as well as training a

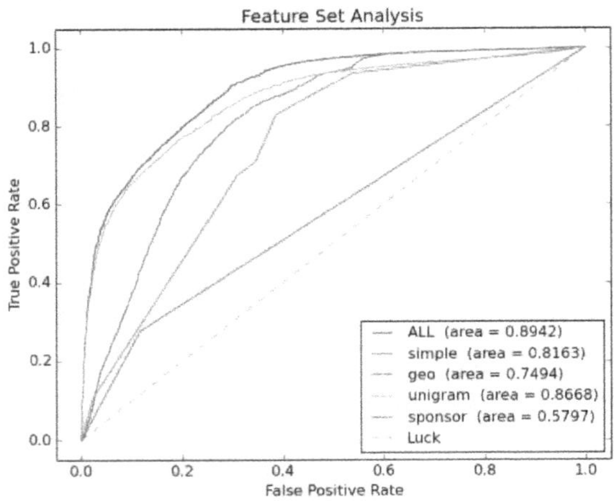

Figure 5: ROC curves for each feature set, trained on documents enacted in 2010 and 2009 and tested on documents enacted in 2008.

model on each set individually. Figure 5 shows an ROC curve for each feature set for a model trained on data enacted in 2009 and 2010 and tested on data enacted in 2008. Unigrams are the most powerful feature set, followed by the set of simple string heuristics.

7. A NEW EARMARKS DATASET

After retraining our model on all years, we applied our system, to documents going back to 1995. For each extracted allocation, we include:

Earmark Confidence Score: The score is the signed distance of the candidate earmark from the SVM margin. Positive scores reflect allocations predicted to be earmarks. The magnitude of the score corresponds to confidence in the prediction.

Allocation Location: We used OpenCalais, an off-the-shelf named-entity recognizer (NER), to geotag allocations. We obtained state-level locations for at least 85% of the earmarks and district-level associations for nearly 45% of the earmarks. Future work will include more sophisticated geotagging based on the location of entities mentioned in the text.

Allocation Topic: The original OMB data includes the spending committee associated with each earmark, such as Agriculture, Commerce, Education, Energy and Water, etc. We trained a spending committee classifier on the OMB data using a Softmax Regression. Before training, we collapsed spending committees related to Homeland Security, Military and Veterans Affairs, and Defense into a single category: Defense and Military Affairs. The average of the out-of-sample precision and recall scores for each class was approximately 85%. Using this classifier, we assigned spending committee labels to each allocation.

Figure 6 compares our generated dataset (DSSG) with the existing databases of earmarks from Citizens Against Government Waste (CAGW) and the Congressional Research Service (CRS). On average, our dataset includes approximately 3,000 more earmarks than CAGW and approximately 2,100 fewer earmarks than CRS. Our dataset also contains five times more earmarks in 2007 than CAGW. CAGW identified only 2,658 earmarks that year because of a "joint resolution that excluded pork from every appropriations bill except Defense and Homeland Security."[5] Our system, however, identified budget items from the appropriation bills in 2007 that very closely resembled earmarked projects from other years.

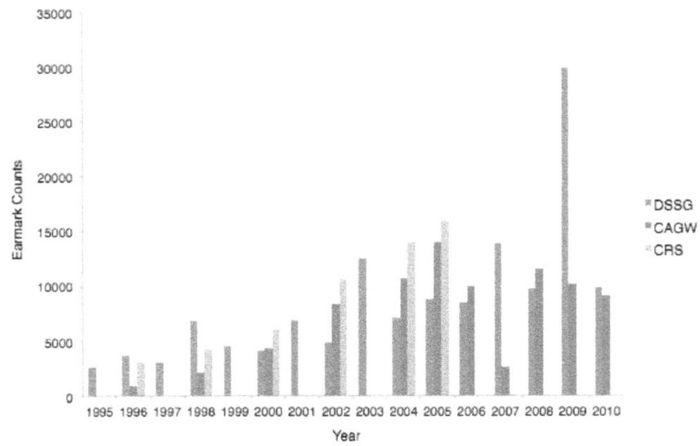

Figure 6: Comparison of our earmarks database (DSSG) with CAGW and CRS databases. Missing bars imply that the database doesn't contain earmark counts for that particular year or those years couldn't be retrieved easily.

The 2009 results look like an outlier, but we randomly examined 100 of those identified earmarks, and 95% of them were correct. We interviewed a K Street lobbyist, and he confirmed that these results are consistent with his impression of earmark behavior over the last decade. He said the big spike in 2009 earmarks is what led Republicans to ban earmarks in the House the following year [1]. Rather than finding too many earmarks in 2009, it may be that we found too few in other years.

From the 1990s through 2005, there is an upward trend in the number of earmarks in all three datasets. Then the use of earmarks appears to have declined except in 2009. The up-and-down trends in earmarks suggests a shift in the nature and processes of earmarking projects over time.

Using our dataset, we can conduct more longitudinal analyses of congressional processes. One outstanding question that has huge implications for political scientists and public policy is whether chairing an appropriations committee impacts the number earmarks granted to the chair's state. Figure 7 shows the results of a difference-in-differences analysis for the nine times a chair of a House or Senate Appropriations committee changed hands between 1995 and 2010. Before a state gained the chair, it could be expected to have the same number of earmarks as other states that lacked the chair. But after a state gained the chair, it could expect about 15 more earmarks than the states that did not gain the chair—a 6% bump over the baseline. This relationship holds when leaving the 111th congress (which covered 2009 and 2010) out of the analysis.

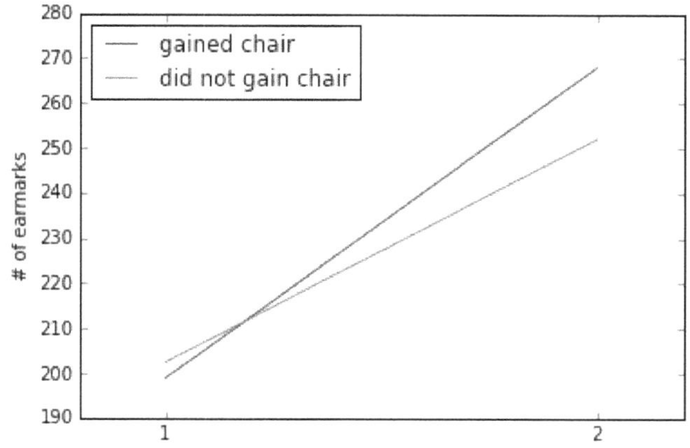

Figure 7: The number of expected earmarks before and after a state gained a chair of Appropriations (blue) and the number of expected earmarks before and after another state gained a chair of Appropriations.

8. FUTURE WORK

Our focus in this work has been on extracting earmarks from tables. We built the allocation table parser based on documents from 2005 and 2008-2010. If Congress used different formats in other years, the parser may fail to extract all allocations, leading to incomplete data. We plan to make a more in-depth survey of table formats used in congressional texts and generalize our table parser if necessary. Another avenue of future research involves identifying earmarks in free text. We believe the direct citations of free-text earmarks provided by the OMB make this task tractable. Finally, we hope to augment our earmarks dataset with more fields. In the current release, we provide the state and district the earmark went to if it is explicitly mentioned in the extracted allocation. We would like to provide more detailed geo-coding by locating the entities mentioned in the allocation. We also plan to include the dollar amount of the earmark, which involves determining the units the allocation is in.

9. CONCLUSION

It has been difficult to study how earmarking affects the legislative process due to the lack of comprehensive and open data on earmarks. This is mainly due to the immense amount of effort required by humans to sift through the thousands of pages of legal text produced by Congress each year. For the fiscal years 2005 and 2008–2010 the Office of Management and Budget (OMB) published a comprehensive dataset of earmarks through a massive inter-agency effort. We developed an automated system that learned how the OMB classifies budget allocations as earmarks. As a result, we were able to extend the scope of the OMB effort to additional fiscal years.

More generally, we have presented an example of how data mining and machine learning can be used to glean structured data from congressional documents. This structured data can be used to make transparent and quantitatively evaluate the functioning of legislative processes. Much of the difficulty in our work arose from the lack common table formats, document identifiers and document structure. These problems would be solved by Congress adopting machine-readable formats.

Our system is available at the Data Science for Social Good (DSSG) GitHub repository, and our dataset is available at the DSSG website: http://dssg.uchicago.edu/earmarks/. The dataset is already being used by Harris School of Public Policy researchers to do public policy research and analysis. In addition, it is being promoted by both the Center for Data Science and Public Policy as well as the Sunlight Foundation to researchers and practitioners interested in government transparency and public policy.

10. ACKNOWLEDGMENTS

We thank the Eric & Wendy Schmidt Data Science for Social Good Fellowship for generously supporting this work. We also thank Irina Matveeva and Rob Mitchum for useful discussions.

11. REFERENCES

[1] Anonymous Republican Lobbyist. Interview. Washington, D.C., October 30 2014.

[2] D. A. Austin and M. R. Levit. Mandatory spending since 1962. *Congressional Research Service*, March 23 2012.

[3] A. Bonica. Mapping the ideological marketplace. *American Journal of Political Science*, 58(2):367–386, 2014.

[4] S. Condon. Ron paul, don young, and joseph cao ignore gop earmark ban, risk reprimand. *CBS News*, April 2 2010.

[5] T. Finnigan. All about pork: The abuse of earmarks and the needed reforms. *Policy Briefing Series*, 2007.

[6] C. Hare and K. T. Poole. The polarization of contemporary american politics. *Polity*, 46(3):411–429, 2014.

[7] G. King. Replication, replication. *PS: Political Science & Politics*, 28(03):444–452, 1995.

[8] R. T. Meyers. *Strategic Budgeting*. Ann Arbor: University of Michigan, 1996.

[9] B. Montopoli. House republicans adopt earmarks ban in new congress. *CBS News*, November 18 2010.

[10] R. Nixon. Lawmakers finance pet projects without earmarks. *New York Times*, December 27 2010.

[11] D. Pinto, A. McCallum, X. Wei, and W. B. Croft. Table extraction using conditional random fields. In *Proceedings of the 26th annual international ACM SIGIR conference on Research and development in informaion retrieval*, pages 235–242. ACM, 2003.

[12] R. Portman. Memorandum for the heads of departments and agencies. *Office of Management and Budget*, January 25 2007.

[13] P. Pyreddy and W. B. Croft. Tintin: A system for retrieval in text tables. In *Proceedings of the second ACM international conference on Digital libraries*, pages 193–200. ACM, 1997.

[14] B. Sinclair. *Unorthodox Lawmaking: New Legislative Processes in the US Congress*. CQ Press, 2011.

[15] S. Streeter. Earmarks and limitations in appropriations bills. *Congressional Research Service*, December 7 2004.

Evaluating Mobile Apps with A/B and Quasi A/B Tests

Ya Xu
LinkedIn Corporation
2029 Stierlin Court
Mountain View, CA, 94043
yaxu@linkedin.com

Nanyu Chen
LinkedIn Corporation
2029 Stierlin Court
Mountain View, CA, 94043
nchen@linkedin.com

ABSTRACT
We have seen an explosive growth of mobile usage, particularly on mobile apps. It is more important than ever to be able to properly evaluate mobile app release. A/B testing is a standard framework to evaluate new ideas. We have seen much of its applications in the online world across the industry [9,10,12]. Running A/B tests on mobile apps turns out to be quite different, and much of it is attributed to the fact that we cannot ship code easily to mobile apps other than going through a lengthy build, review and release process. Mobile infrastructure and user behavior differences also contribute to how A/B tests are conducted differently on mobile apps, which will be discussed in details in this paper. In addition to measuring features individually in the new app version through *randomized* A/B tests, we have a unique opportunity to evaluate the mobile app as a whole using the *quasi-experimental* framework [21]. Not all features can be A/B tested due to infrastructure changes and wholistic product redesign. We propose and establish quasi-experimental techniques for measuring impact from mobile app release, with results shared from a recent major app launch at LinkedIn.

Keywords
A/B testing, mobile, quasi-experiments, causal inference

1. INTRODUCTION
It is clear that mobile is taking over the Internet. In the U.S., two out of three digital media minutes is now happening on mobile. Without question, mobile app usage has been the single most important driver by far, contributing to nearly 90% of the massive mobile growth in the past two years [5]. At LinkedIn, more than 50% our traffic is now coming from mobile, similar to other social networking companies such as Facebook and Pinterest [3].

Many companies, including LinkedIn, have shifted to a "mobile first" mindset, focusing their product strategies around mobile. As a consequence, optimizing for the best user experience in mobile has been more important than ever. However, mobile optimization is a space that is a lot less mature than web optimization. Because of how users consume information on mobile differently, many lessons learnt by optimizing on the web no longer apply. So even companies most experienced with web optimization have to start from the bottom and relearn in the mobile space.

It is not just about coming up with "what" works in mobile, but more importantly, we need to have methodology and system in place to "measure" whether an idea works. A/B testing, also known as controlled experiment, is a standard, widely used framework to evaluate new ideas and to make data driven decisions. We have seen much of its applications in the online world discussed in recent publications, including several past KDD papers from Google, Microsoft and LinkedIn [9,10,12]. However, none of these papers have a focus on mobile, or mobile apps.

At LinkedIn, we have seen a drastic increase of mobile experiments. The growth is more than just proportional to the amount of development work relative to desktop. We have learnt that because the real estate on mobile is limited, small changes tend to have big impact. In addition, A/B testing on mobile is used even more extensively than it is on desktop, and much of it is attributed to a key difference between desktop and mobile development process. Because we cannot ship code to the mobile app other than building and releasing a new app version, feature releases in general involve not just the app developers, but also the app stores (e.g. Google Play or Apple App Store), and the end users. The app store usually requires a review of the build submitted, and a new app version is not effective until the end users update the app. The consequence is that it may take two weeks or more for any change to reach the majority of users, and even longer for a coverage of greater than 90%. A/B testing is hence heavily leveraged to mitigate risk, as it allows us to evaluate the new feature and gradually release it accordingly, without having to release a new version.

The fact that we cannot ship code easily to mobile apps, together with mobile infrastructure and user behavior differences, strongly influences how A/B tests are conducted on mobile apps. We will discuss them in depth in Section 4, following the three steps in the A/B testing process: design, deployment and offline analysis.

In addition to measuring features individually in the new app version through *randomized* A/B tests, we also have a unique opportunity to evaluate the mobile app as a whole using the *quasi-experimental* framework [21]. Not all features can be A/B tested due to infrastructure changes and limitations. For example, LinkedIn recently rewrote the entire flagship app (Project Voyager [3]). Even though some new features were tested and evaluated independently in the old app, many features were launched for the very first time with the new app release. How all the features work together was a key question, but unfortunately we were not able to conduct a randomized experiment on the new app as a whole. However, because not all users adopt the new version at the same time, there is a period of time where we have both versions of the app serving real users. Obviously, simply comparing the adopters with the non-adopters will suffer from self-selection bias. However, we can still reasonably establish causal relationship by carefully removing such bias using quasi-experimental techniques (also called observational causal inference methods in some disciplines).

To set the notation and context for both A/B and quasi A/B testing, we review the Rubin Causal Model [23], a widely used framework to estimate causal effect. Let Y_i be the outcome

KDD '16, August 13-17, 2016, San Francisco, CA, USA
 ISBN 978-1-4503-4232-2/16/08 $15.00
DOI: http://dx.doi.org/10.1145/2939672.2939703

variable for user i, e.g. pageviews, clicks. Let $Z_i \in \{0, 1\}$ be the treatment variable, where $Z_i = 1$ if a user is in treatment (adopted the new app), and $Z_i = 0$ otherwise. Note that in the case of mobile adoption, Z_i is *observed* rather than randomly generated. We also observe $\boldsymbol{X_i}$, a vector of pre-exposure covariates, such as industry or connection counts. In summary, we observe $(Y_i, Z_i, \boldsymbol{X_i})\ for\ i = 1, \dots, n$. Under the Rubin Causal framework, each user has two potential outcomes

$$Y_i = \begin{cases} Y_{i1} & if\ \ Z_i = 1 \\ Y_{i0} & if\ \ Z_i = 0 \end{cases}$$

We are interested in knowing the Average Treatment Effect (ATE), the difference of the average outcomes between applying treatment to the *entire* user population and applying control to the *entire* user population. By definition,

$$\Delta_{ATE} = \frac{1}{n}\sum_{1}^{n} Y_{i1} - \frac{1}{n}\sum_{1}^{n} Y_{i0}$$

Of course, Δ_{ATE} is never known because only one of Y_{i1} and Y_{i0} can be observed (The fundamental problem of causal inference [22]). Instead, it is usually estimated by

$$\widehat{\Delta}_{ATE} = \frac{1}{n_1}\sum_{\{i, Z_i=1\}} Y_{i1} - \frac{1}{n_0}\sum_{\{i, Z_i=0\}} Y_{i0} = \bar{Y}^1 - \bar{Y}^0$$

Two important assumptions are required for $\widehat{\Delta}_{ATE}$ to be an unbiased estimator of Δ_{ATE}. (1) Stable Unit Treatment Value Assumption *(SUTVA),* which states that the behavior of each user in the experiment depends only on his own treatment and not on the treatments of others. (2) Ignorable Treatment Assignment Assumption (also known as *unconfoundedness*) [21], which states that treatment assignment is independent of the two potential outcomes, i.e.

$$(Y_{i0}, Y_{i1}) \perp Z_i$$

Both assumptions are naturally satisfied in most controlled experiments. However, the unconfoundedness assumption is often violated when there exists variables that correlate with both (Y_{i0}, Y_{i1}) and Z_i. As an example, we have observed that LinkedIn members with premium accounts are more likely to adopt a new version faster. Since premium members are in general more engaged on the site, we are likely to conclude a significantly positive impact even if the true Δ_{ATE} is 0 or negative. In fact, the unconfoundedness assumption can be extended to

$$(Y_{i0}, Y_{i1}) \perp Z_i \mid \boldsymbol{X_i}$$

where $\boldsymbol{X_i}$ are the confounding covariates. As a result, if we can identify all such covariates, we can still postulate a model for $E(Y_i|Z_i, X_i)$ and estimate ATE based on

$$\Delta'_{ATE} = \frac{1}{n}\sum_{i=1}^{n}(E(Y_i \mid Z_i = 1, X_i) - E(Y_i \mid Z_i = 0, X_i))$$

This is a fundamental concept of quasi-experimental framework. We will discuss more formally on this in Section 5.

Here is a summary of our contributions in this paper:

- As far as we know, we are the first to study extensively how to evaluate mobile app through both A/B testing and quasi A/B testing. Moreover, we are the first to propose and establish a quasi A/B testing framework to evaluate mobile app release.
- We identify the key differences of conducting A/B tests on mobile vs. on desktop.
- We compare and propose quasi-experimental techniques that have shown to be very successful in removing adoption bias, and are used in major mobile app release at LinkedIn.
- We share insights on how users adopt new app versions, including insights on how to measure novelty effect.

The paper is organized as follows. Section 2 starts with a review of the existing literature in all the three areas of A/B testing, mobile A/B testing and quasi A/B testing. Section 3 describes the process for mobile app releases and its implications on how we evaluate a new release. Section 4 focuses on A/B testing in mobile app and how it is different from testing on the web. Section 5 proposes a quasi A/B testing framework to evaluate app release, with results shared from evaluating Voyager [3]. Section 6 concludes with future work.

2. LITERATURE REVIEW

In this section we review the theoretical foundations and applications of A/B testing and quasi A/B testing as well as existing tools and products for mobile testing.

The theory of controlled experiment dates back to Sir Ronald A. Fisher's experiments at the Rothamsted Agricultural Experimental Station in England in the 1920s [6]. Since then, many textbooks and papers from different fields have provided theoretical foundations [7,8] for running controlled experiments, including the most widely adopted Rubin Causal Model [22,23]. While the theory may be straightforward, the deployment and mining of experiments in practice and at scale can be complex and challenging [15]. In particular, several past KDD papers have discussed at length the experimentation systems used at Microsoft Bing, Google, Facebook and LinkedIn [9,10,11,12], including best practices and pitfalls [13,14].

On the other hand, there are many situations where running a controlled experiment is infeasible and one has to study causal impact based on observed data. [21] discusses the assumptions of applying the Rubin Causal Model to real evaluations. [24, 25] show that the Ignorable Treatment Assignment Assumption is associated with the assumptions of OLS regression. Many models have been developed to address the challenges of observational studies, such as propensity score models [21], Heckman's sample selection model [19] and Doubly Robust Estimation [18]. As far as we know, quasi-experiment techniques have been more widely utilized in econometrics and clinical studies [20,26], and there are few studies of natural experiment in the Internet world. A recent work in this area [17] described a framework for estimating causal effect through identifying mediators and its application to advertising.

While we focus on in-house A/B testing solutions for mobile app development, there are companies specializing in mobile A/B testing, such as Apptimize [27], Optimizely [28] and Mixpanel [29]. These companies provide third party platforms and tools that help mobile developers test in mobile. Other than these commercial products, there seems to be very little literature focusing on mobile A/B testing that we are able to find.

3. MOBILE APP RELEASE PROCESS AND ITS IMPLICATIONS

In most online web development, agile software development process is highly promoted. Being able to iterate fast and improve continuously is crucial for both risk minimization and feature development. Most importantly, it is key to ensure the best user experience because any unexpected issues can be fixed or mitigated as soon as possible. Such fast iterations are feasible for an online website because all changes are controlled on the server side. When a user visits a site, the server pushes the data to the browser to render. New feature releases can happen constantly and continuously without interruption on the end users. In an A/B test, whether the user sees A or B is fully managed by the server and is entirely independent of the end users behavior. Take Linkedin.com as an example. Whether to show a red or yellow button, whether to show a newly revamped homepage or not - these are all changes that can happen instantaneously after server side deployment.

However, feature release process and experimentation in a mobile app are quite different. Instead of the app developers having full control over the deployment and release cycle, the app release process involves all three parties, the app owner (in our case, LinkedIn), the app store (e.g. Google Play or Apple App Store), and the end users. After all the code is ready, the app owner needs to submit a build to the app store for review. Assuming the build passes review (which in the case of iOS takes about a week), releasing it to everyone does not mean that everyone who visits the app will have the new version. Getting the new version is a software upgrade, same as updates we get on our desktops where we can delay or ignore while continuing to use the old version. Some end users take weeks to adopt.

It is worth pointing out that Google and Apple have very different review policies. While it takes about a week to go through Apple's review process, Google Play store's review is almost instantaneous [1]. In addition, Google allows staged roll out of a new version [2], while Apple app store only supports full roll out. Such differences have important implication on app development and evaluation, as we will cover in Sections 4 and 5.

For most web facing companies who truly believe in agile development, it is painful to have to wait for 2+ weeks for a change to take effect, especially when our end users are dealing with a buggy app. What's worse, depending on how fast users adopt new versions, it may take even longer to reach more than 90% users. We have more details on the adoption process in Section 5.1. Moreover, even if new app versions can be built and released every other week, it is annoying from the users' perspective to have to constantly update the app.

This is not to say that we cannot A/B test on mobile. As a matter of fact, there are by and large three kinds of experiments that we can conduct on mobile app.

1. **Server-side changes**: There are many features on mobile that are backend driven. Relevance features are good examples in this category. Experiments on such changes are conducted the same way as experiments on the web [9,10]. Because the code changes happen on the server side only, it only takes server side deployment for the changes to take effect, which can happen independent of the app release.
2. **Client-side changes**: There are many features that need to be controlled from the app itself, including, for example, the look and feel of a button and the number of feed items to fetch from the backend at a time. Any code changes on these features need to be coupled with an app release, and hence are subject to the potential delay. Because of this, there are quite some differences when conducting A/B tests on the app itself. We have devoted Section 4 to go into depth on this topic.
3. **Big changes that cannot be A/B tested**: There are cases where many changes have to be bundled together and it is impossible to put them all behind an A/B test due to infrastructure changes and limitations. For example, LinkedIn recently rewrote the entire flagship app (Project Voyager [3]) and we were not able to experiment the new app as a whole. In the web world, if we cannot split the traffic to two different versions of the site, we are out of luck - once we flip the switch to the new site, we lose the ability to measure the performance of the old site side-by-side. The only comparison that is possible between the new & old sites is a before & after comparison, which is known to suffer from confounding effects such as seasonality. However, for mobile app releases, because not all users adopt the new version at the same time, there is a period of time where we have both versions of the app serving real users. This gives us an opportunity to conduct a quasi-experiment. Details are discussed in Section 5.

4. MOBILE A/B TESTING

As we have mentioned in Section 3, whenever possible, features on mobile apps are tested through controlled experiments. Since server-side changes are usually experimented the same way on app and web, and we have already shared in details how web A/B tests are conducted at LinkedIn in KDD'15 [12], we focus our discussion in this section on the kind of experiments that are more specific to mobile - experiments on the client-side features. Recall that these are features that are controlled from the app, and any code changes on these features require a new app release.

The architecture for a web-based A/B testing system usually has the three essential components, also corresponding to the three steps in an A/B testing process: (1) design (2) deployment (3) offline analysis [9,12]. The same three components are needed for a mobile A/B test. Therefore, we follow a similar structure for our discussion in this section. We focus on highlighting the key differences between app and web testing, while leaving the similarities for readers to follow up in other papers [10, 11].

4.1 Design

Experimental design is arguably the most important step in the testing workflow to get good and meaningful results. As Sir R. A. Fisher put it [13] "To consult the statistician after an experiment is finished is often merely to ask him to conduct a post mortem examination. He can perhaps say what the experiment died of." To be more concrete, design is usually the phase when we determine what we want to experiment on, the goal, the targeted population, the traffic split among variants, and the duration of the experiment.

As described in Section 3, because of the constraint with the mobile app release process (new code cannot be shipped to end users easily), A/B testing on any client-side changes needs to be "planned ahead". In other words, all experiments, including all the variants for each of these experiments, need to be coded and shipped with the current app build. Any new variants, including bug fixes on any existing variant, have to wait for the next app release. This has the following two implications: (1) A/B testing has become more extensive. Whenever possible, new features are always rolled out under A/B tests. One essential function of A/B tests is risk minimization. It allows us to roll out a new feature to a small, randomized user group to evaluate. More importantly, in a mobile world, if a feature doesn't perform as we intended, we can instantly revert back to an equivalent of the older app version by shutting down the traffic to the test, without having to go through a client release cycle (which can take weeks for slowly adopting users). The benefit of preventing our end users from being stuck with a faulty app for weeks really helps promote a truly "test everything" culture among our developers. (2) Parameterization is used extensively to allow flexibility in creating new variants without a client release. This is because even though new code cannot be pushed to the client easily, new configurations can be passed in payload, which effectively creates a new variant as long as the client understands how to parse the configurations. For instance, we want to experiment on the number of feed items to fetch from the backend at a time. We can put our best guesses in the code and experiment only with what we have planned in place, or we can parameterize the number and have the freedom to experiment on any numbers after the release.

Real time targeting is more prevalent in mobile experiments, as the three most widely used targeting attributes (platform, operating systems and app version) are only available at runtime. Many features are unique to a particular platform and OS. Moreover, the same feature usually performs very differently between tablet and phone, and between iPhone and Android. Therefore, when designing a mobile experiment, we usually need to consider targeting a specific platform and OS combination. In addition, many experiments only exist in certain app versions. Obviously, newly added experiments do not apply to older app versions. At the same time, some experiments may only exist in older versions. It is important to target the correct version when rolling out an experiment.

4.2 Deployment

After design is complete, deploying an experiment in web setting usually just involves two components, the application layer that implements the alternative variant behavior according to experiment assignment, and the service layer that is a distributed cache and experiment definition provider [12]. In the mobile setting, the application layer is logically broken into two parts:

1. Server side: It communicates with the service layer, passes experiment assignment information to the mobile client, and logs the experiment event.
2. Mobile client side: It periodically fetches the experiment assignment information from the server and executes it accordingly.

As we mentioned earlier, the experiment implementation on the mobile client side needs to be shipped with the new app version. Once that is done, we can activate the experiment to enable a small percentage of traffic on treatment. Similar to web applications, the activation information propagates from the service layer to the application server every 5 minutes. However, this does not mean the experiment is fully deployed. As a matter of fact, the deployment is usually delayed on the mobile client by at least one user session. This is because new assignment information is usually only fetched at the beginning of each session. In addition, these new assignment usually does not take effect till the next session. This is because we do not want to change a user's experience after they have started the session already. For heavy users who visit multiple sessions a day, such delay is small, but for light users visiting once a week, the experiment does not actually take place till a week later. Such delay and how it depends on user's visitation frequency imply that not only does the signal appear to be weaker at the beginning of the experiment, it is also more biased towards reactions from heavy users.

Moreover, to reduce the number of communications with the server, assignment information is fetched for all active experiments at once and then cached on the mobile client. This is the case regardless of whether an experiment is actually triggered or not. For example, there is an experiment that only affects users who visit the "Me" tab. However, the assignment for that experiment will still be fetched even if a user doesn't visit "Me" during that session. Because experiment information is tracked on the server side, such "over fetching" means we are marking more users as affected by the experiment than there actually are, effectively diluting the signal when we want to evaluate the "real" impact. One potential fix to this problem is to only track experiment event after an experiment assignment is actually used, not when it is fetched.

4.3 Offline Analysis

By and large, the analysis of mobile app A/B tests is done similarly as web experiments. As mentioned in Section 4.1, experiments can be ramped differently for different platforms and operating systems. Even experiments that are ramped uniformly across the population, the performance in these segments can be drastically different. In many experiments we have conducted, it is not unusual to see a positive lift on one platform and a negative impact on the other. It is therefore important to always drill down to examine the per-segment impact in addition to the overall site-wide impact.

Besides the dilution and the delay effect discussed in Section 4.2, one thing to watch out for is the potential interactions between different user interfaces. Many of our members access LinkedIn through desktop, mobile app and mobile web. While it is unusual to drive traffic between desktop and mobile in a session or a day (we don't expect to change user's mobile usage drastically in a short period of time), it is, however, common to shift traffic between mobile app and mobile web. For example, many mobile users visit LinkedIn via clicking on their emails. The email link can either take the user directly to the app (assuming he or she has the app installed), or to the mobile web. When analyzing an experiment, it is important to know whether an experiment may cause or suffer from such an interaction, in which case, we cannot evaluate app performance in isolation, but need to look at user behavior holistically on both mobile app and mobile web. In addition, because user experience on the app tends to be better, directing traffic from the app to the web tends to bring down the total engagement, which may be a confounding effect not intended by the experiment itself.

5. MOBILE QUASI A/B TESTING

We have so far highlighted the special challenges when conducting randomized experiments on mobile app compared with web testing. Most of the differences result from the fact that mobile app release cycle involves not just the app owner, but also app stores and end users. On the other hand, the exact same differences also create an opportunity to evaluate changes that we are not able to A/B test on. These tend to be big changes that involve fundamental infrastructure improvements and holistic product redesign. One such example is LinkedIn's recent release of the new flagship app (Project Voyager [3]).

To be more concrete, the opportunity to evaluate such big releases exists because of the following: First, users take time to adopt the new app. The adoption period creates a natural experiment. Second, Google supports staged roll out of an app. Even though neither enables a fully randomized experiment, we can leverage both to measure the performance of a new app version through a quasi-experimental study. As we will lay out in this section, such quasi-experiment, coupled with thorough validation, is able to estimate the impact from a new app release with little bias, as demonstrated by results from our recent Voyager launch.

This section is organized as follows. We start in Section 5.1 with a deep dive into how mobile app adoption works, who the adopters are and how the adopter group evolves over time. This is crucial in helping us come up with quasi-experimental techniques to adjust for adoption bias. Section 5.2 reviews the basic quasi-experiment methods in the context of evaluating app release. This is not meant to be a comprehensive literature review, but to establish the notation and building blocks for the next section. In the final Section 5.3, we go into depth discussing and comparing the techniques we use to evaluate the Voyager release. Separate methods are needed for iOS and Android, as the Android release was a 20% staged roll out during the evaluation period.

5.1 Mobile App Adoption

Every new app version takes a while to propagate through the user population, as it requires upgrade from the end users. Both Android and iOS give users a lot of flexibility in managing how they want to upgrade. By and large, there are three options: (1) automatically update (2) automatically update only if there is Wi-Fi access (3) manually update. Obviously the choice affects the probability to adopt. The default setting of both operating systems is option (2), with the difference that Android notifies users after the update completes, but iOS updates quietly in background.

The choice of the update options and the ease of access to Wi-Fi are the two most important variables that impact the likelihood of adoption over time. To add to the complexity, we have no visibility into whether a user has updated to the new version until he or she visits the app. One can think of modeling such mechanisms and relationships with a Latent Factor Model (with missing data) to reveal and understand these underlying variables [30]. Since our focus is to evaluate the app performance by adjusting for the intrinsic adoption bias, we instead look to understand who these adopters are and what the key differences are between the adopters and non-adopters.

5.1.1 Adoption Over Time

Because our member populations are intrinsically different across OS, we observe very different adoption curves between Android and iPhone (Figure 1, Left). Adoption is much faster on iPhone, especially during the first couple of days. As we can see in Figure 1, the adoption rate that takes Android a week to reach takes only about three days on iPhone. In general, adoption tends to slow down after a week on both OS. There are some people who stays on the older version for weeks or months before they adopt, and they tend to be the same group of users for each release, likely those who select manual update option on their device. Note that even though the plot only uses data from the recent major release with significant PR pushes, almost exact same plots are observed from other minor historical releases, indicating little social effects on adoption of newer app versions.

From the adoption mechanism described above, it is not surprising to see that adopters tend to consistently adopt through multiple historical app releases. As shown in Figure 1 (Right), a previous adopter is in general 2 – 3 times more likely to adopt again than a previous non-adopter. Note that the risk ratio tends to be smaller in the earlier days. This indicates that historical adoption pattern is less predictive of future adoption shortly after launch. This can be explained by the fact that whether a user adopts or not is largely driven by his or her choice of auto-update options and access to Wi-Fi. Conditional on the same user, we can treat the Wi-Fi availability as a random process independent of users' visit to LinkedIn. Therefore, whether a user adopts *shortly after release* has a large random component and is hard to predict based on historical adoptions.

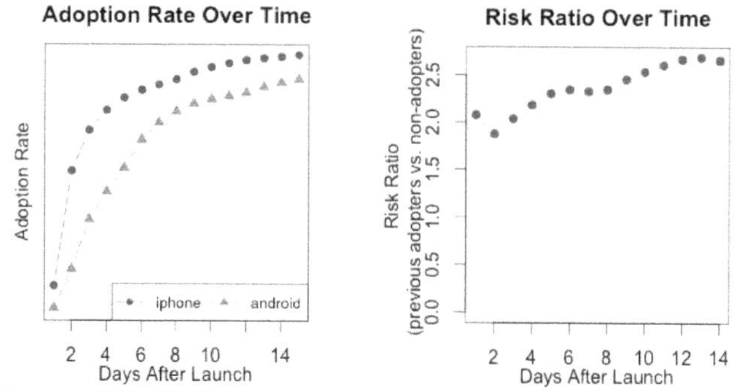

Figure 1. Left: adoption rate over time. Right: the probability of adopting in current release is higher for previous adopters than for previous non-adopters.

5.1.2 Adopters vs. Non-adopters

Among the adopters, there is a big difference between those who adopt on day one and those who adopt on day 14. We group the adopters into cohort 1 through 14 depending on the day they adopt. As show in the heatmap (Figure 2), it is clear that users who adopt earlier are more engaged than the users who adopt later. Also note that even though the diagonal has higher values, it is not an indication that users are more engaged on adoption day. It is an artifact that we don't know users' adoption status until they visit the app, and hence by definition users are active on their adoption day.

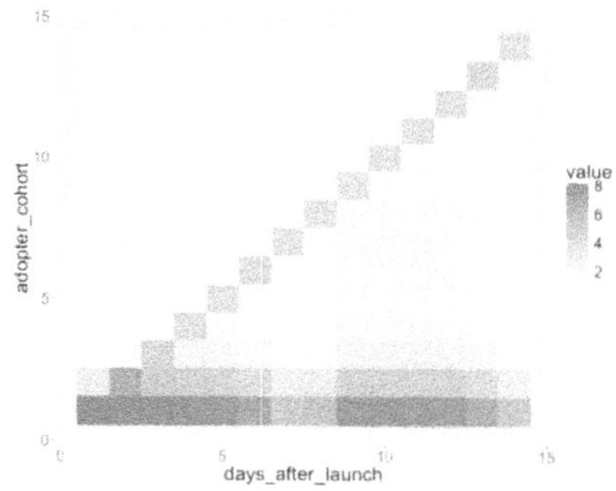

Figure 2. Engagement by adopter cohort. Earlier adopters are more engaged.

Now let's turn to adopter and non-adopter differences. Note that both adopters and non-adopters are active during the analysis period, and their adoption labels can change over time as more people adopt. Figure 3 (Left) plots the difference as percentage delta of a key engagement metric between adopters and non-adopters. The data used is from a minor historical release that is not supposed to create any actual impact on metrics. Interestingly enough, when the analysis period is a single day, the difference starts at over 50%, then drastically decreases to below 10% after a week. However, if we look at cumulative differences cross day, the percentage delta stays at above 30% throughout the entire week! Similar trend is observed for almost all metrics we looked at. It turns out adopters tend to be active on more days. So if we accumulate their activities over time, the adoption bias is bigger. This can be explained by the simple equation below, where the cumulative metric can be decomposed as users' engagement on an active day with a multiplier of total active days. Indeed, by day seven, an average adopter is active on 62% more days, explaining the majority of the difference in the cumulative engagement.

$$\frac{Engagement}{UU} = \frac{Engagement}{ActiveDays} * \frac{ActiveDays}{UU}$$

There are two implications. First, without modeling for adoption bias, we can effectively mitigate it by comparing adopters and non-adopters in a smaller time window. However it assumes the number of visit days is not impacted by the treatment, which should be tested separately. Second, as shown in Figure 3 (Right), if we control for the days users are active, the difference between adopters and non-adopters become much smaller (from over 50% to less than 20% for day one), indicating historical active days is a strong covariate for adjusting adoption bias.

It is worth noting that some users take more than two weeks to adopt, but they are as active as the adopters. These are likely users with auto-update off. It seems that users' choice of auto-update option is fairly independent of their engagement with LinkedIn.

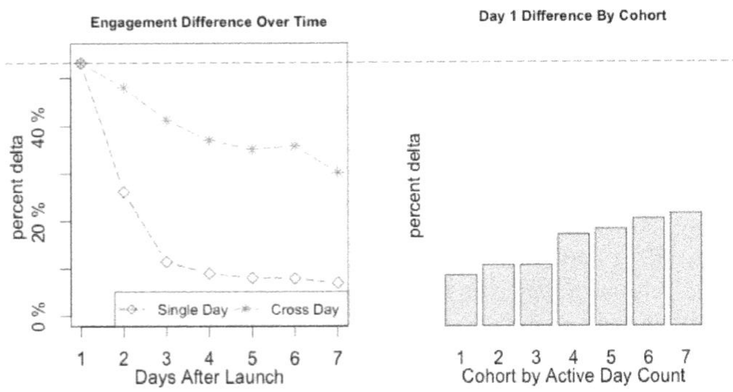

Figure 3. Left: Engagement differences between adopters and non-adopters (A/A). Single-day difference decreases drastically over time. Right: The within cohort differences between adopters and non-adopters are much smaller.

5.2 Common Quasi-Experiment Techniques

As we have already seen in Section 5.1, there are big differences between adopters and non-adopters. Simply comparing those who are on the new app with those on the old app will give a misleading estimate of treatment effect. In this section, we evaluate common statistical techniques to reduce adoption bias; in particular, methods based on OLS regression and propensity score models.

5.2.1 OLS Based Methods

Assume our metric of interest follows a linear model:

$$\boldsymbol{Y} = \beta_0 + Z\beta_1 + \boldsymbol{X}\boldsymbol{\beta_2} + \epsilon \quad (1)$$

where $\boldsymbol{Y} = (Y_1, \dots Y_n)^T$ is the outcome vector for users $i = 1, \dots, n$, $\boldsymbol{Z} = (Z_1, \dots Z_n)^T$ is the dichotomous variable of treatment, and $\boldsymbol{X} = (\boldsymbol{X_1}, \dots \boldsymbol{X_n})^T$ is a matrix representing all the covariates that correlates with both $\boldsymbol{Z}$ and $\boldsymbol{Y}$ (e.g. historical engagement metrics). Under this model, the coefficient β_1 is the ATE under the Rubin Causal framework. If the covariates $\boldsymbol{X}$ are omitted, the OLS estimator of β_1 can be biased, and

$$bias = (\boldsymbol{D}^T\boldsymbol{D})^{-1}\boldsymbol{D}^T\boldsymbol{X}\boldsymbol{\beta_2} \quad (2)$$

where $\boldsymbol{D} = (\boldsymbol{1}, \boldsymbol{Z})$. Note that the bias is zero only if **X** is independent of **D** (so $\boldsymbol{D}^T\boldsymbol{X} = \boldsymbol{0}$, which is true for randomized experiments) or that **X** does not predict **Y** (so $\boldsymbol{\beta_2} = \boldsymbol{0}$).

Practically such bias gets smaller if major covariates that confound the treatment assignment ($\boldsymbol{Z}$) and outcome variable ($\boldsymbol{Y}$) are included in the regression model. However, it is not possible to prove that all non-ignorable covariates are included. In our applications, we are able to evaluate the models based on a validation framework to be discussed in Section 5.3.

There are some potential improvements on the OLS model:

1. It is unlikely that the relationship between the response variable and the covariates is linear. We can consider applying Box-Cox transformation [31] before fitting the model.
2. We can generalize the treatment model (1) to an endogenous switching model by allowing for interactions between the treatment variable and the covariates. The model can then be rewritten as

$$\boldsymbol{Y_1} = \boldsymbol{X_1}\boldsymbol{\beta_1} + \boldsymbol{\epsilon_1} \; if \; Z = 1 \quad (3)$$

$$\boldsymbol{Y_0} = \boldsymbol{X_0}\boldsymbol{\beta_0} + \boldsymbol{\epsilon_0} \; if \; Z = 0 \quad (4)$$

where two equations are fitted separately using data from adopters and non-adopters respectively.

Interestingly, looking at Equation (3) alone, the problem becomes a classical missing value problem where non-adopters are clearly missing at "non-random". Therefore, we can also apply many techniques that address missing value problems to estimate Equation (3) and (4) separately. The method we considered in Section 5.3 is the one proposed by Heckman [19], which models the selection process based on probit regression and assumes that the error term in the probit model and the linear regression are bivariate normally distributed.

5.2.2 Propensity Score Based Methods

Another family of approaches that have been developed to correct for selection bias is through the propensity score, i.e. the probability of receiving treatment. The propensity score is usually estimated through a logistic regression, defined as

$$P(Z = 1|X = x) = \frac{e^{x\beta}}{1 + e^{x\beta}}$$

The score can be used for

1. **Matching or subclassification.** The intuition is that samples with similar propensity scores can be considered as counterfactuals. By reducing to a one-dimensional score, one can incorporate potentially many covariates that have predictive power on treatment selection and still obtain reasonable matched sample sizes.
2. **Weighting.** With the Rubin-causal counterfactual framework, one can show that given the true probability of being treated we have $E(\frac{Y_i}{P(Z_i=1)}) = E(Y_{i1})$ [16]. Hence we can use $\frac{1}{P(Z_i = 1|X)}$ as weight for adopters (and $\frac{1}{1-P(Z_i = 1|X)}$ as weight for non-adopters). However, such inverse weighing mechanism assumes that the propensity score is the true probability of being treated. A more recent class of estimators combines the OLS method and propensity score inverse weighing models. Such Doubly Robust Estimators are consistent as long as at least one of the linear model or the propensity score model is correctly specified [18].

5.3 Evaluating Voyager Release

As we have mentioned earlier, LinkedIn has recently redesigned and rebuilt our flagship app from scratch [3]. The new app, code name "Voyager", should be considerably more intuitive and useful. One key challenge we faced was how to evaluate whether users indeed are benefiting from using the new app. If we were able to A/B test the app, it would have been an easy question to answer. However, with the drastic changes on both backend and frontend infrastructure, it is impossible to test all the changes in a randomized, controlled setting. The closest to A/B test we can get is to leverage Google Play store's staged roll out functionality. But even with the staged roll out, we still have to face adoption bias, and therefore cannot analyze the results as a simple A/B comparison.

As we mentioned earlier, the biggest challenge of any quasi-experimental method is how to validate that the causal relationship is indeed true and not due to some omitted variables in the model. Fortunately, we are able to have a validation framework based on historical data. Historically, we release new app versions to app stores periodically. These regular releases usually ship no more than minor bug fixes, which create a unique opportunity to (1) understand the adoption behavior (section 5.1) and consequently utilize it to build better quasi experiment models; (2) evaluate the validity of a model. These historical releases essentially serve as A/A tests, as it is reasonable to assume that such incremental releases only cause minor impact and the true average treatment effect (ATE) is close to 0. In addition, we have also observed that those validation results hold consistently across multiple historical versions.

Unless specified, all results discussed from here on are cumulative up till a specific day. Even though single-day results tend to suffer less from adoption bias (as seen in Section 5.1), it makes the assumption that the new app does not make users visit more (or less) days. With a release as big as Voyager, it is not a plausible assumption.

Because of the differences in how we roll out the app in iOS and in Android, we have to use different quasi A/B methodologies to evaluate iOS and Android separately, which we share in sections below.

5.3.1 iOS

Unlike in Android, there is no opportunity to release an app version to a randomized percent of users in iOS. This makes the adoption process fully observational. Evaluating Voyager in iOS becomes a "classical" quasi-experiment problem and existing techniques discussed in Section 5.2 should apply directly with only minor improvements. In this section, we compute the bias of each method during the week after release (in terms of percentage delta) for a key engagement metric. To make the comparison fair, the same set of covariates are used across methods. All results are based on a minor historical iOS release (an A/A release).

Before we get to the comparison results, there are a couple of key learning from building the quasi-experiment models.

First of all, many non-adopters become adopters after a couple of days. As we have observed in Section 5.1, whether a user adopts *shortly after release* is somewhat random due to Wi-Fi availability. Such random perturbation creates samples that are very similar in terms of covariates, but with opposite adoption status. These samples confuse the propensity model and make it harder to predict, as we can see in Figure 4 (Left). The baseline AUC is only at 0.65 in the first day compared with 0.82 on day seven. This observation leads us to remove from the non-adopter group those users who in fact are very likely to adopt based on historical adoptions. By removing these "random" non-adopters in the early days, we are able to get an AUC score of close to 0.8 even on day one (green curve). Any improvement for the early days is substantially more valuable in the production environment, as it really helps identify problems early and iterate fast.

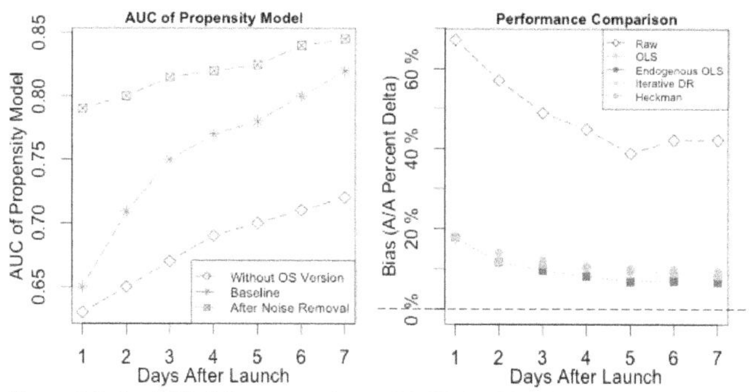

Figure 4. Left: AUC of the propensity model; Right: Bias of various quasi methods evaluated for the iOS release.

Second, it is crucial to include the right features. We have explained the rationale on the choice of some features based on users' adoption behavior in Section 5.1. As directly illustrated in Figure 4 (left), removing one covariate (e.g. OS Version) can decrease the AUC substantially.

As shown in Figure 4 (Right), the raw comparisons are extremely biased, especially in the first days after launch. The amount of adoption bias reduces from about 65% to 40% after a week. The various methods have similar performance over time, with the endogenous OLS model having a slightly smaller bias. Overall, these methods are able to largely reduce adoption bias to about 18% on day one to about 7% on day seven.

5.3.2 Android

Play store makes it easy for app developers to do a staged roll out [2]. We can choose to make the new version available to only a percentage of users. This applies to both existing app users and new users downloading from the Play store. It is a great way to minimize risk and collect feedback from real users. It may not be intuitive at first, but even though these users are randomly selected, we are not able to measure the staged roll out as a regular A/B test. The reason is because from our own tracking, we can only tell whether a user visits with a new app or an old app, but not their actual randomized experiment assignment. As demonstrated in Figure 5, among those visiting with an old app, we cannot differentiate those who are in the control bucket (entire B group) from those who are non-adopters in the "eligible" bucket (A_2 group). If we naively compare members on the new app with members on the old app, we would be comparing A_1 with the rest, and hence suffer from the same adoption bias (or self-selection bias) as a full roll out.

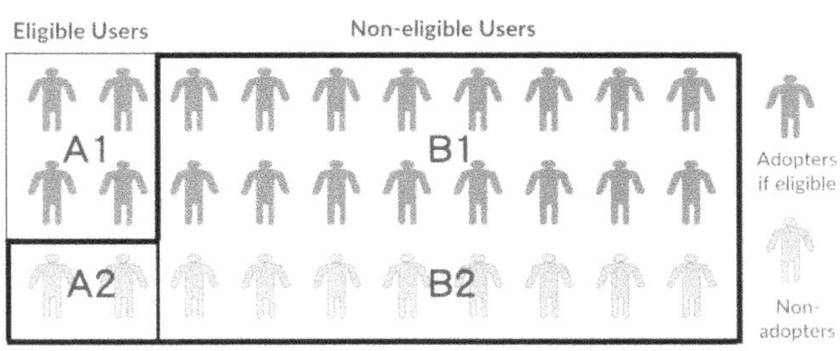

Figure 5. Illustrate how adoption bias exists even in Google staged roll out.

The problem, however, is a little different. In a full roll out, other than the minor random perturbation to the label during the first couple of days (due to Wi-Fi access), the adopters are intrinsically different from non-adopters. Most quasi-experiment techniques described in Section 5.2 try to remove such intrinsic difference by modeling directly on adoption status. For example, propensity score models build a logistic regression using adoption status as response. When the actual adoption status is determined by a combination of randomization and user intrinsic behavior, such models work poorly. This is because the signal that comes with the status is weak. The B_1 users who were non-adopters can become adopters with simply a reshuffle, which obviously cannot be modeled by any user variables.

At the same time, there is a bright side to the unique situation. In a 20% roll out, for every adopter we expect there to be four non-adopters who are similar to him. If we have a methodology that can identify those "would-be" adopters, we are all set. To successfully reduce adoption bias, such method needs to have an extremely low false positive rate, even if that leads to more false negatives. We illustrate the idea in the following.

Assume we have a selection criteria S to pick out potential adopters. Apply such criteria to the two groups of users observed (A_1 vs. $A_2 + B_1 + B_2$). With high false positives and zero false negatives, we have $S(A_1) = A_1$, and

$$S(A_2 + B_1 + B_2) = S(A_2) + B_1 + S(B_2) > B_1$$

Since A_1 and B_1 are the two comparable user groups, such selection criteria create bias. The higher the false positive rate is, the worse the bias gets. On the other hand, if we have only false negatives and no false positives, we get $S(A_1) \subset A_1$, and

$$S(A_2 + B_1 + B_2) = S(B_1) \subset B_1$$

Since A_1 and B_1 are comparable, $S(A_1)$ and $S(B_1)$ are comparable as well. As long as the false negative rate is not too high and $S(A_1)$ is still a representative subset of A_1 (i.e. out-of-sample bias is small), the comparison between $S(A_1)$ and $S(B_1)$ is meaningful. In Section 5.3.2.1 and 5.3.2.2 below, we propose two methods that are guided by such intuition.

5.3.2.1 Geometric Distribution Model

The idea is to separate the "would-be" adopters (B_1) from the rest of the non-adopters by directly modeling their adoption probabilities. By selecting only users with high propensity to adopt in both adopter and non-adopter groups, we hope to achieve high precision in identifying comparable users. Note that different from the usual propensity score modeling, we only use historical data to model the adoption probabilities. The actual adoption status itself is only used in the final step as treatment assignment label.

As we discussed in Section 5.1, the adoption probability increases as time goes by. We therefore need to model p_{it}, the probability for member i to adopt on day t. As described in section 5.1, we do not know whether a member has adopted the new app version until he or she visits our app. To simplify the problem, we assume that every member i has a chance of p_i to show up as an adopter each day they visit, and that the probability of adopting on day t follows a geometric distribution

$$p_{it} = (1 - p_i)^{a_{it}-1} p_i$$

where a_{it} is the number of active days a user has had by day t.

Based on data from historical adoptions, we can compute the maximum likelihood estimator (MLE) for p_i to be

$$\hat{p}_i = \underset{p_i}{\operatorname{argmax}} \prod_{j=1}^{s} (1 - p_i)^{k_{ij}-1} p_i^{I_{ij}} = \frac{\sum_j I_{ij}}{\sum_j I_{ij} + \sum_j k_{ij}}$$

where k_{ij} is the number of active days user i had before adopting historical app version j, with $j = 1, 2 \dots s$, and I_{ij} be the indicator function of whether user i adopted version j. Note that in our application, we capped k_{ij} at 14 days, so if user i did not adopt by day 14 for version j, we have $k_{ij} = 14$ and $I_{ij} = 0$.

Finally, on each day t after Voyager release, we compute the probability that user i adopts *by* day t to be $1 - (1 - \hat{p}_i)^{a_{it}}$, which is the cumulative probability based on the actual number of active days we observe. To get the treatment effect, we only select users with $1 - (1 - \hat{p}_i)^{a_{it}} >$ threshold. The threshold is chosen based on A/A cross-validation results.

The results (Figure 6, Left) show that such method is able to correct for almost all the selection bias towards the end of the adoption week. However, regardless of how high a threshold we pick, the precision in the first few days is poor. This echoes our analysis in Section 5.1 where we observed that adoption in the first days is hard to predict.

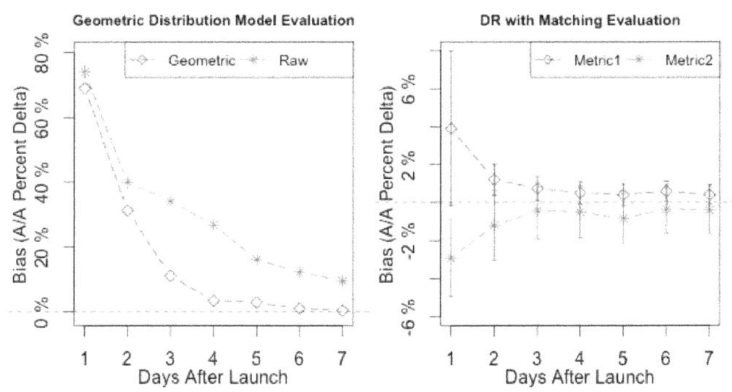

Figure 6. Left: Bias of the geometric distribution model. Right: Bias of the doubly robust with matching model. Both are for Android 20% roll out.

5.3.2.2 Doubly Robust with Matching

As we mentioned early, propensity score models do not work well in the randomized setting. However, because there is supposed to be more users in the non-adopter group who are similar to the adopters, matching directly on covariates themselves is supposed to be an easier task than it is in the full roll out case (as in iOS). There are various methods that perform matching based on covariates, and they all trace back to two that are the most fundamental:

1. **Exact matching**: This is the technique that matches each adopted user to all possible non-adopters with exactly the same values on all the covariates.
2. **Nearest neighbor matching**: This method selects the non-adopters who are closest to each individual in the adopter group in terms of a distance measure specified. The selection process can be done in a couple of ways: (1) a "local" greedy approach that chooses the closest match one at a time, in which case it matters which adopter gets processed first; (2) a "global" optimal approach that finds the matched users with the smallest average absolute distance across all the matched pairs [2].

Neither the local nor the global nearest neighbor approaches can be easily computed in a parallelizable fashion, which makes scaling it to millions of users a hard problem of its own. In addition, on a smaller test data set we tried, the nearest neighbor technique tends to under perform, and highly affected by the distance measure chosen, particularly because we have many categorical covariates. Exact matching, on the other hand, does not work well when there are many covariates (or when some covariates can take many values, such as continuous variables), as it becomes impossible to find sufficient exact matches. Continuous or ordinal variables have an additional challenge in exact matching because of the lack of distance measures. A difference of 1 pageview is treated the same as a difference of 1000 pageviews, which is clearly suboptimal.

Because of these challenges, we have decided to go with a "Doubly Robust" approach [18], where we fit an exact matching model first and then fits a linear regression model on the matched user sets. The exact matching takes in only about 10 important covariates with the continuous variables carefully bucketized to ensure sufficient matched samples. The regression model has a lot more covariates, including several continuous variables, which can compensate for the somewhat coarse matching and offers more granularity into the covariates. Because of its good performance in validation from first day after release, this is the approach we used in production.

Here are the steps we took for the Doubly Robust estimation:

1. Only variables that cannot be impacted by the treatment itself are included as covariates, including variables collected before the new app version release or stable member attributes such as country or language.
2. For all the variables, ensure common support in both adopter and non-adopter groups by pruning the observations where the empirical densities do not overlap. This is to avoid extrapolation.
3. Select a small set of variables (about 10) to be used for exact matching. We first select representative variables to cover a wide range of member attributes and engagement characteristics. Further reduction is then done by dropping one variable at a time and is cross-validated based on A/A test results (described earlier). The goal is to produce as many matched samples as possible without increasing bias.
4. Covariates used in exact matching are bucketized to reduce their cardinalities. We have noticed that using quantiles to bucketize does not work well for a lot of covariates because of their skewed distributions. For example, the difference between the 10th and the 20th percentiles of several variables has no practical significance. Artificially treating them as two entirely different buckets creates inefficiency when matching the samples.
5. Feed the matched samples into a weighted linear regression model, using the weights produced from the exact matching. We use the endogenous switching model described in Equation (3) and (4), building one model for adopters and one for non-adopters. The models are then used to predict on the entire matched user samples. For example, the model trained on adopters is used to produce $\hat{y}_i^{(1)}$, the estimated response under the new version (treatment), for both adopters and non-adopters. The final doubly robust estimator of the treatment effect is a weighted average difference between a world where everyone has adopted and a world where no one has adopted:

$$DRE = \frac{1}{(\sum_{i=1}^{n} w_i)} \left(\sum_{i=1}^{m} w_i \left(y_i - \hat{y}_i^{(0)}\right) + \sum_{i=m+1}^{n} w_i \left(\hat{y}_i^{(1)} - y_i\right) \right)$$

where w_i is the weight from matching and y_i is the observed value. WLOG we assume users $i = 1, \dots, m$ are adopters.

We have noticed that it is important to have sufficient number of samples that are matched. During the first day post launch, as the number of adopters is still relatively small (especially in 20% roll out), the set of variables we include in the matching step is much smaller. As a result, we matched about 60% of adopters on day one, while that number reduces to 20% after day one. On the other hand, the matched non-adopters went from about 5% to 10%. The median number of non-adopters matched per adopter is 3.

The validation results look very positive. As shown in Figure 6 (Right), for the two key metrics we tracked, we had only about 3 – 4 % bias on the first day, compared with an over 70% bias in the raw comparison shown in the left plot. The bias reduces to less than 1% after day three.

5.3.3 Novelty Effect

For big releases that involve drastically different user experience, we usually expect strong novelty effect, as users tend to explore the new experience more at the beginning. One obvious question when it comes to evaluating the performance of a new app version is: is there novelty effect and if so, how long does it take for it to go away? In a randomized A/B test, a simple and practical approach is to check whether the daily treatment effect, measured as the percentage delta between treatment and control, dies down as days go by. With adoption bias, novelty effect is confounded by the fact that people who adopt earlier are simply different from people who adopt later. The quasi-A/B framework in Section 5.3.2.2 provides us with a way to separate out the inconsistent adoption bias and the novelty effect.

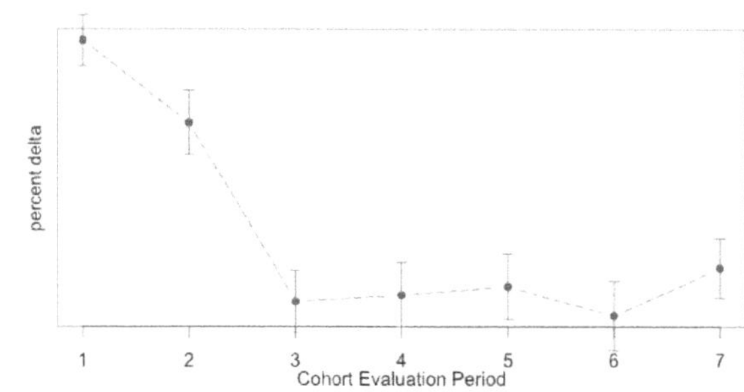

Figure 7. Novelty effect goes away after the first couple of days.

We start with identifying two cohorts of users: the adopter cohort and the non-adopter cohort. Obviously, if we construct the cohorts on day one, we will have some of the non-adopters converted to be adopters during the period of evaluation. Because this is a retrospective study, we can overcome this problem by removing users who ended up adopting during this period from the non-adopter cohort (we can safely assume there is no conversion the other way around, going from adopter to non-adopter). As a second step, we match the cohorts using the same exact matching method as outlined in Section 5.3.2.2. This gives us two matched cohorts with weights. Finally, we remove further bias by applying a weighted linear regression on the matched cohorts as in the doubly robust approach. It is important to note that even though the matched cohorts are constructed once, the evaluation is done on the same cohorts daily, regardless whether a cohort user is active in that particular day. As shown in Figure 7, the treatment effect (measured as percent delta) is much larger in the first couple of days and then settles down to a smaller, consistent value, providing compelling evidence that the novelty effect lasted for just a couple of days.

6. SUMMARY AND FUTURE WORK

In this paper we discussed many differences when experimenting on mobile compared with on desktop. We also proposed and established a quasi A/B testing framework to evaluate mobile app release. Many insights around how users adopt a new app version were shared and discussed.

One very interesting problem that we didn't cover is to understand the latent factors underlying users' adoption behavior (Section 5.1), which should help further improve the quasi models. Moreover, notice how the quasi models have a lot less bias for Android (Figure 6) than they have for iOS (Figure 4). It is because Android was a randomized 20% roll out. If Apple App Store also supports a staged roll out feature, it will greatly benefit not only the app developers, but also app users, as they will get apps that are better evaluated and optimized.

7. ACKNOWLEDGEMENT

The authors wish to thank Bryan Ng, Aarthi Jayaram, Yael Garten and Kiran Prasad for insightful discussions, Romer Rosales and Eytan Bakshy for feedback. We would also like to thank all members of the experimentation team, especially Weitao Duan who was involved in the quasi A/B effort. Finally this work wouldn't have been possible without the guidance and support of Igor Perisic.

8. REFERENCES

[1] Sarah Perez [Online] http://techcrunch.com/2015/03/17/app-submissions-on-google-play-now-reviewed-by-staff-will-include-age-based-ratings/

[2] Google Play [Online] https://support.google.com/googleplay/android-developer/answer/6346149?hl=en&ref_topic=3450989

[3] Jordan Novet "LinkedIn shows off Project Voyager, its new flagship mobile app" [Online] http://venturebeat.com/2015/10/14/linkedin-shows-off-project-voyager-its-new-flagship-mobile-app/

[4] Fisher, Ronald A. Presidential Address. *Sankhya: The Indian Journal of Statistics.* 1938, Vol. 4, 1.

[5] The 2015 U.S. Mobile App Report [Online] https://www.comscore.com/Insights/Presentations-and-Whitepapers/2015/The-2015-US-Mobile-App-Report

[6] Yates, Frank, Sir Ronald Fisher and the Design of Experiments. *Biometrics,* 20(2):307–321, 1964.

[7] Box, George EP, J. Stuart Hunter, and William Gordon Hunter. *Statistics for experimenters: design, innovation, and discovery.* Vol. 2. New York: Wiley-Interscience, 2005.

[8] Gerber, A. S., and Green, D. P. Field Experiments: Design, Analysis, and Interpretation. WW Norton, 2012

[9] Tang, Diane, et al. Overlapping Experiment Infrastructure: More, Better, Faster Experimentation. *Proceedings of the 16th Conference on Knowledge Discovery and Data Mining.* ACM, 2010.

[10] Kohavi, Ron, et al. Online Controlled Experiments at Large Scale. KDD 2013: Proceedings of the 19th ACM SIGKDD international conference on Knowledge discovery and data mining. 2013. http://bit.ly/ExPScale.

[11] Bakshy, Eytan, Eckles, Dean and Bernstein, Michael S. Designing and Deploying Online Field Experiments. *Proceedings of the 23rd international conference on World Wide Web,* pages 283-292, ACM, 2014

[12] Xu, Ya, et al. "From Infrastructure to Culture: A/B Testing Challenges in Large Scale Social Networks." *Proceedings of the 21th ACM SIGKDD International Conference on Knowledge Discovery and Data Mining.* ACM, 2015.

[13] Kohavi, Ron, et al. Trustworthy online controlled experiments: Five puzzling outcomes explained. *Proceedings of the 18th Conference on Knowledge Discovery and Data Mining.* 2012, www.exp-platform.com/Pages/PuzzingOutcomesExplained.aspx.

[14] Kohavi, Ron, et al. Seven Rules of Thumb for Web Site Experimenters. KDD 2014: Proceedings of the 20th ACM SIGKDD international conference on Knowledge discovery and data mining. 2014.

[15] Kohavi, Ron. et al. Controlled experiments on the web: survey and practical guide. *Data Mining and Knowledge Discovery.* February 2009, Vol. 18, 1, pp. 140-181. http://www.exp-platform.com/Pages/hippo_long.aspx.

[16] Imbens, Guido M., and Jeffrey M. Wooldridge. *Recent developments in the econometrics of program evaluation.* No. w14251. National Bureau of Economic Research, 2008.

[17] Hill, Daniel N., et al. "Measuring Causal Impact of Online Actions via Natural Experiments: Application to Display Advertising." *Proceedings of the 21th ACM SIGKDD International Conference on Knowledge Discovery and Data Mining.* ACM, 2015.

[18] Funk, Michele Jonsson, et al. "Doubly robust estimation of causal effects."*American journal of epidemiology* 173.7 (2011): 761-767.

[19] Heckman, James J. "Sample selection bias as a specification error (with an application to the estimation of labor supply functions)." (1977).

[20] Heckman, James J., and Richard Robb. "Alternative methods for evaluating the impact of interventions: An overview." *Journal of econometrics* 30.1 (1985): 239-267.

[21] Rosenbaum, Paul R., and Donald B. Rubin. "The central role of the propensity score in observational studies for causal effects." *Biometrika* 70.1 (1983): 41-55.

[22] Holland, Paul W. "Statistics and causal inference." *Journal of the American statistical Association* 81.396 (1986): 945-960.

[23] Rubin, Donald B. "Estimating causal effects of treatments in randomized and nonrandomized studies." *Journal of educational Psychology* 66.5 (1974): 688.

[24] Kennedy, Peter. *A guide to econometrics.* MIT press, 2003.

[25] Greene, William H. *Econometric analysis.* Pearson Education India, 2003.

[26] Harris, Anthony D., et al. "The use and interpretation of quasi-experimental studies in medical informatics." *Journal of the American Medical Informatics Association* 13.1 (2006): 16-23.

[27] Apptimize [Online] http://apptimize.com/

[28] Optimizely [Online] http://optimizely.com/

[29] Mixpanel [Online] https://mixpanel.com/

[30] Agarwal, Deepak, and Bee-Chung Chen. "Regression-based latent factor models." *Proceedings of the 15th ACM SIGKDD international conference on Knowledge discovery and data mining.* ACM, 2009

[31] Box, George EP, and David R. Cox. "An analysis of transformations." *Journal of the Royal Statistical Society. Series B (Methodological)* (1964): 211-252

Ranking Relevance in Yahoo Search

Dawei Yin†, Yuening Hu†, Jiliang Tang†, Tim Daly Jr., Mianwei Zhou, Hua Ouyang, Jianhui Chen, Changsung Kang, Hongbo Deng, Chikashi Nobata, Jean-Marc Langlois, Yi Chang†
Relevance Science, Yahoo! Inc.
†{daweiy,ynhu,jlt,yichang}@yahoo-inc.com

ABSTRACT

Search engines play a crucial role in our daily lives. Relevance is the core problem of a commercial search engine. It has attracted thousands of researchers from both academia and industry and has been studied for decades. Relevance in a modern search engine has gone far beyond text matching, and now involves tremendous challenges. The semantic gap between queries and URLs is the main barrier for improving base relevance. Clicks help provide hints to improve relevance, but unfortunately for most tail queries, the click information is too sparse, noisy, or missing entirely. For comprehensive relevance, the recency and location sensitivity of results is also critical.

In this paper, we give an overview of the solutions for relevance in the Yahoo search engine. We introduce three key techniques for base relevance – ranking functions, semantic matching features and query rewriting. We also describe solutions for recency sensitive relevance and location sensitive relevance. This work builds upon 20 years of existing efforts on Yahoo search, summarizes the most recent advances and provides a series of practical relevance solutions. The reported performance is based on Yahoo's commercial search engine, where tens of billions of URLs are indexed and served by the ranking system.

Keywords

learning to rank; query rewriting; semantic matching; deep learning

1. INTRODUCTION

The continuing growth of the web consistently expands the information pool available to us and we must increasingly rely on search engines to find useful web documents. Indeed, search engines play an ever more crucial role in information consumption in our daily lives. Meanwhile, search engines are one of the most successful businesses in industry, where the sponsored search model is a predominant form of online advertising.

Ranking relevance has been the most critical problem since the birth of web search. As web content was explosively generated, modern search engines have been required to efficiently and effectively retrieve the relevant URLs from a prohibitively large corpus. This raises tremendous challenges for both industrial and academic researchers. Early works on search relevance concentrated on text matching between queries and web documents such as BM25 [28], probabilistic retrieval model [22], and vector space model [22]. Subsequently, user behavior demonstrated great potential for relevance improvement in the industrial setting, and user behavior modeling has been extensively explored for improving search relevance, e.g., click modeling [9, 20, 19, 31, 26].

The advancing state of the art for search engines presents new relevance challenges, which drives us to think beyond direct text matching and click modeling. First, the semantic gap between queries and web documents is a major barrier for improving base relevance [24]. Query language is usually different from document language. For instance, for the query "how much tesla", relevant documents may contain the term "price" rather than "how much", so direct text matching methods do not work well. Second, search queries follow a long tail distribution and the majority of queries are tail queries that have very low frequency or are completely new to the search engine. As a result, user behavioral information (e.g., clicks) is often not available so click modeling is not applicable to these queries. Third, users tend to treat search engines as general Q&A systems where they can locate useful information directly; thus an increasing number of queries are in the style of natural language, which presents obstacles to many aspects of search technology such as query understanding and semantic matching.

In addition to base relevance, comprehensive relevance includes both temporal and spatial dimensions. First, many queries are best served with up-to-date information, requiring search engines to take freshness into account. For example, for the the query "safest cars", users prefer information about the latest tests for recent car models. It would be a poor user experience if a search engine returned a page stating "the safest car is the 1998 toyota celica". Second, with the increasing use of mobile search, more queries are location sensitive, such as "walmart" and "restaurant", requiring search engines to consider location information in relevance.

This paper focuses on sharing our experiences in tackling these relevance issues and introduces a series of practical techniques that have been successfully implemented and deployed to power the Yahoo search engine. We first revisit the state of the art ranking functions on both offline static evaluation data and the Yahoo search engine. We reveal the key factor leading to the performance difference of ranking functions in these two scenarios, which motivates us to design an effective ranking function for a real web-scale search engine. Second, to bridge the semantic gap between queries and web documents, we take full advantage of users' behavior data in various ways, and develop three types of semantic matching features to transfer click information from head queries to tail queries. Finally, we present a rewriting system that remarkably boosts rel-

KDD '16, August 13-17, 2016, San Francisco, CA, USA

DOI: http://dx.doi.org/10.1145/2939672.2939677

evance performance, especially for tail queries. The three components together significantly enhance the Yahoo search engine. In addition, we provide solutions for recency sensitive relevance and location sensitive relevance. The key contributions include,

- Designing a novel learning to rank algorithm for core ranking and a framework of contextual reranking algorithms.
- Developing semantic matching features including click similarity, deep semantic matching, and translated text matching.
- Building an innovative framework to understand user queries with query rewriting and its ranking strategy.
- Proposing solutions to recency sensitive ranking and location sensitive ranking.

2. BACKGROUND

2.1 Overview of Architecture

The Yahoo search engine can retrieve the most relevant documents from a corpus of billions within a fraction of a second. It achieves this by (1) parallelizing the work for one query across many servers; and (2) repeatedly taking the best candidate documents from a cheaper ranking function and reranking them using a better one. The corpus is segmented into equal-sized shards which are served by index servers. Documents are assigned to a shard based upon the MD5 of their URL. Each query is processed by one complete set of shards, each of which returns its best candidate documents. These are then merged and reranked to produce the final result set.

Within a shard, the first step is to find all documents that match the query. This is called *recall*. Typically, document sets for each query term are intersected to obtain documents containing all terms. These documents are then sorted by the *first round*, a lightweight function that scores each document. Here *uniquing* is then applied, enforcing simple diversity constraints such as a limit on the number of documents from a single host or domain. In addition, query-dependent features are extracted from the top candidates, which are then ranked using a much more expensive *second round* function, also named *Core Ranking Function* [33].

To build a core ranking function, the model performance strongly depends on the distribution and the number of labeled samples in the training set. Obtaining labeled samples is very expensive and time-consuming, and active learning plays an important role in selecting informative and representative samples with limited budget as suggested by previous works [21].

2.2 Ranking Features

There are several major groups of features in traditional search engines, which, when taken together, comprise thousands of features [6]. The ranking functions are built on top of these features. **Web graph**: This type of feature tries to determine the quality or the popularity of a document based on its connectivity in the web graph. A famous example is PageRank [25]. Other features include distance or propagation of a score from known good or bad documents [12, 18]. **Document statistics**: These features compute some basic statistics of the document such as the number of words in various fields. **Document classifier**: Various classifiers are applied to the document, such as spam, adult, language, main topic, quality, type of page (e.g., navigational destination vs informational). **Query Features**: which help in characterizing the query type: number of terms, frequency of the query and of its terms, click-through rate of the query. **Text match**: Basic text matching features are computed from different sections of the document (title, body, abstract, keywords) as well as from the anchor text and the URL. These features are then aggregated to form new composite features. The match score can be as simple as a count or can be more complex such as BM25 [28]. There are also proximity features which try to quantify how far in the document are the query terms (the closer the better) [23]. **Topical matching**: This type of feature tries to go beyond similarity at the word level and compute similarity at the topic level. In the context of contextual advertising, details can be found in [2]. **Click**: These features try to incorporate user feedback, most importantly the clicked results [1]. They are derived either from the search or the toolbar logs. For a given query and document, different click probabilities can be computed: probability of click, first click, last click, long dwell time click or only click. **Time** For time-sensitive queries, the freshness of a page is important. There are several features which measure the age of a document as well as the one of its inlinks and outlinks. More information on such features can be found in [7].

2.3 Evaluation of Search Relevance

There are several ways to evaluate search results, including human labeling (e.g., professional editor's judgment) and user behavioral metrics (e.g., click-through rate, query reformulation rate, dwell time). Usually, user behavioral metrics are complicated, since they may be affected by other factors, such as presentation (e.g., fonts, bold, size, abstract summary etc.) and result diversity. In this paper, we focus on base relevance, which is the most important aspect of search results. Good, relevant URLs are a necessary foundation for impacting behavioral metrics.

To assess base relevance, we leverage professional editors' judgment. Editors manually judge each query-URL pair, assigning one of five grades: Perfect, Excellent, Good, Fair or Bad. We then use Discounted Cumulative Gain (DCG) as the metric to evaluate the search relevance performance. DCG has been widely used to assess relevance in the context of search engines [15]. For a ranked list of N documents, we use the following variation of DCG,

$$\mathrm{DCG}_N = \sum_{i=1}^{N} \frac{G_i}{\log_2(i+1)}$$

where G_i represents the weight assigned to the label of the document at position i. Higher degrees of relevance correspond to higher values of the weight. We use the symbol DCG to indicate the average of this value over a set of test queries in our experiments. DCG will be reported only when absolute relevance judgments are available. In the following sections, we will report DCG1, DCG3, DCG5 with N in $\{1,3,5\}$, respectively. For significance, we employ the Wilcoxon T-test to report p-value.

We sample 2,000 queries from a one year query log as our test queries and evaluate their search results in the Yahoo search engine by capturing the results (query-URL pairs) real time and asking editors to judge them. According to the popularity of the query, the evaluation query set is split into three parts: top, torso and tail. Top queries have very high impressions and, in terms of relevance, they are relatively easy, since lots of click information provides hints for ranking. For torso queries, the click information is very limited and sparse because torso queries occur only a few times in a year. Tail queries generally recur less than once a year, so click information is not available. Tail and torso queries are relatively hard queries for search relevance [8]. Lots of efforts on tail and torso queries have been made [32, 34, 14]. In this paper, we mainly focus on performance of torso and tail queries and introduce the practical solutions in Yahoo's web search engine, where we have taken implementation and efficiency into consideration.

3. MACHINE LEARNED RANKING

In a realistic scenario such as a commercial search engine, given a query, there is a seeming infinity of irrelevant documents which may dominate the relevant results. However, it is infeasible to use only negatives to train the model, and negative results in training data usually cannot cover all aspects of irrelevancy. As a result, at run time, the percentage of bad results is often higher than we expect. The percentage of bad results is also very important – when users see embarrassing results at top positions, they may abandon the current search engine and switch to its competitors.

Search can be treated as a binary problem. In our experiments, we observe that gradient boosting trees (GBDT) with logistic loss usually are able to reduce the bad URLs at top positions. It finds the decision boundary between relevant and irrelevant URLs for a given query. However, this binary classification cannot rank URLs perfectly. We here introduce a unified method for web search which is based on logistic loss and incorporates the Perfect, Excellent and Good information into the model though scaling the gradient for GBDT. Online evaluation of the Yahoo search engine shows that this framework decreases the percent of bad URLs by 40% and increases relevance by 5% in terms of DCG5, compared to the leading ranking algorithms [33, 4].

3.1 Core Ranking

We adopt GBDT (Gradient Boosting Decision Tree) [10] into the framework. Based on the gradient boosting framework, we first introduce logistic loss at the core ranking where we aim to reduce bad/fair URLs in top results. We first flat the labels "Perfect", "Excellent" and "Good" to "Positive" (+1) and "Fair", "Bad" to "Negative" (-1). The log likelihood (loss) is

$$L(y, F) = \log(1 + \exp(-yF)), \quad y \in \{1, -1\} \tag{1}$$

Then the pseudo-response of stage m is

$$-g_m(\mathbf{x}_i) = -\left[\frac{\partial L(y_i, F(\mathbf{x}_i))}{\partial F(\mathbf{x}_i)}\right]_{F(\mathbf{x})=F_{m-1}(\mathbf{x})} \tag{2}$$

$$= y_i/(1 + \exp(y_i F_{m-1}(\mathbf{x}_i))) \tag{3}$$

Logistic loss targets on binary classification, which can decrease the number of bad URLs for top retrieved results. Logistic loss is not limited to classification, and it can provide reasonable ranking, comparing to other classification loss such as hinge loss since it always places the force on positive/negative towards positive/negative infinite. For the samples far from the decision boundary (e.g., 'Perfect" samples are usually far apart from decision boundary), it is highly likely that the predicted values have larger absolute values (very positive/negative). However, only simple binary classification is insufficient for ranking. To bring the orders of "Perfect", "Excellent" and "Good" back to the model, we introduce gradient scale for GBDT. According to the gradient of logistic loss, given a Perfect/Excellent/Good sample, we know that the gradient is always positive, while for Fair/Bad URLs, the gradient of logistic loss is always negative. To distinguish Perfect/Excellent/Good, we scale the gradient, (which is also known as the pseudo-response of stage i), in different levels (e.g., 3 for Perfect, 2 for Excellent, and 1 for Good). As a result, Perfect data samples get relatively higher forces to positive infinite than Excellent ones, which are higher than the Good ones. The pseudo-response of stage m will become

$$\text{pseudo\_response}(x) = -g_m(\mathbf{x}_i) \times \text{scale}(label)$$

where $\text{scale}(label)$ can be empirically set $\text{scale}(Perfect) = 3$, $\text{scale}(Excellent) = 2$ and $\text{scale}(Good/Fair/Bad) = 1$ to distinguish Perfect/Excellent/Good. This loss function takes advantage of both gradient boosting and logistic loss. It not only is a binary classification but also has ability to distinguish the different positive samples. For Fair and Bad samples, since their gradients are always negative, we needn't make any modification/scale for each pseudo-response. This method is actually equivalent to adding different weights on loss for different labels, but it is different from adding sample weights, which actually affect the tree growth of each stage m but do not change pseudo-response.

query	methods	DCG1	DCG3	DCG5
all	LogisticRank	4.31	7.74	9.78
	GBRank	4.26 (-1.19%)	7.52 (-2.81%)*	9.51 (-2.81%)*
	LambdaMart	4.24 (-1.60%)	7.36 (-4.84%)*	9.21 (-5.83%)*
top	LogisticRank	5.69	9.67	12.08
	GBRank	5.56 (-2.22%)	9.25 (-4.29%)*	11.51 (-4.67%)*
	LambdaMart	5.59 (-1.72%)	9.08 (-6.04%)*	11.02 (-8.75%)*
torso	LogisticRank	3.88	7.23	9.26
	GBRank	3.88 (-1.77%)	7.065 (-2.30%)*	9.08 (-2.03%)*
	LambdaMart	3.81 (-1.88%)	6.97 (-3.64%)†	8.92 (-3.64%)*
tail	LogisticRank	2.91	5.65	7.16
	GBRank	2.99 (3.06%)	5.65 (0.01%)	7.19 (0.37%)
	LambdaMart	2.88 (-0.71%)	5.42 (-4.15%)†	6.91 (-2.78%)†

Table 1: Performance comparison of models using different learning algorithms. * denotes p-value<=0.01; † denotes p-value<=0.05.

We name our learning algorithm *LogisticRank* and compare with the leading ranking algorithms: *GBRank* [33] and *LambdaMart* [4] in the Yahoo search engine. All three methods share the same training data, which is collected through active learning and editor labels and includes about 2 million query-URL pairs. The parameters are carefully tuned on a validation query set. The results are shown in Table 1. Interestingly, the overall performance of LogisticRank is the best and significantly better than GBRank and LambdaMart. Especially, on top queries, we obtain the largest improvement through LogisticRank. GBRank, which mixes pairwise loss and pointwise loss, performs consistently better than LambdaMart, which is a listwise loss function and only learns relative orders. In tail queries, GBRank is able to generate similar performance (no significance) as LogisticRank. On the other aspect, the percentage of bad/embarrassing results is reduced by 40% through LogisticRank. We observe that the improvement of LogisticRank is mainly from bad results removal.

We tried to further understand the above results by performing experiments on an offline dataset—the learning to rank challenge data set (LTR) [6]. The results of LambdaMart and GBRank are consistent with [6], where LambdaMart is around 2% better than GBRank in terms of DCG5. However, we find that both LambdaMart and GBRank are better than LogisticRank on this task: LambdaMart is 2.6% better than LogisticRank while GBRank is 0.6% better than LogisticRank in terms of DCG5. The main difference between LTR data and a real search engine is the data distribution. In static LTR data, there are 27% "Bad" query-URL pairs, compared to >99% "Bad" query-URL pairs in the real search engine, since for a given query, there are usually only tens of relevant URLs among tens of billions of indexed URLs. The performance on the static LTR data set is not matched by real search engine performance due to this big difference in data distribution. Unfortunately, it is prohibitively expensive to generate a static data set with editorial labels which has the same distribution as the real search engine.

In the remaining sections of this paper, we use LogisticRank with the existing features described in Section 2 as our base model, which is referred to as 'base'.

query	methods	DCG1	DCG3	DCG5
all	base	4.31	7.74	9.78
	base+reranking	4.34 (0.79%)	7.78 (0.52%)	9.91 (1.30%)*
top	base	5.69	9.67	12.08
	base+reranking	5.72 (0.60%)	9.75 (0.88%)	12.24 (1.33%)†
torso	base	3.88	7.23	9.26
	base+reranking	3.88 (-0.18%)	7.27 (0.49%)	9.38 (1.23%)
tail	base	2.91	5.65	7.16
	base+reranking	3.00 (3.40%)	5.63 (-0.34%)	7.26 (1.38%)

Table 2: Performance of systems with and without contextual reranking. * denotes p-value<=0.01; † denotes p-value<=0.05.

3.2 Contextual Reranking

The core ranking only considers query-URL pair features, while ignoring contextual information from other candidate results for the same query. There are practical reasons – the result set at this point is very large, and it is distributed over hundreds of machines, hence calculating even a very simple feature like the average popularity of all candidate documents would be prohibitively slow.

The reranking phase is applied after the results from the core-ranking phase have been sorted, aggregated on one machine, and trimmed down to the best tens of results, e.g., 30. That allows us to extract features capturing contextual information about the entire result set, which turn out to be the most important features in the model.

Based on the top tens of results (e.g., 30) of a given query, we extract following contextual features for specific existing features – (1) *Rank*: sorting URLs by the feature value in ascending order to get the ranks of specific URLs. (2) *Mean*: calculating the mean of the feature values of top 30 URLs. (3) *Variance*: calculating the variance of the feature values of top 30 URLs. (4) *Normalized feature*: normalizing the feature by using mean and standard deviation. (5) *Topic model feature*: aggregating the topical distributions of 30 URLs to create a query topic model vector, and calculating similarity with each individual result.

Beside contextual features, another advantage of reranking is that the training data for this phase is less prone to sample selection bias, since it is possible to label a complete set of candidate documents for a given query. By contrast, for the core ranking phase, this is infeasible since the candidate set could consist of hundreds of thousands of documents. In practice, we found that it is more robust to use the ranks of the results as a feature instead of directly using the core-ranking function's scores. Though the core-ranking phase score is more informative than the rank, its value can drift as the index refreshes, degrading third phase performance. Since the reranking function is running on top 30 results, its main purpose is to further distinguish relevant results ("Perfect", "Excellent", "Good") rather than to identify and remove bad results. The impact is shown in Table 2. We see that the overall performance is significantly and consistently improved by reranking.

3.3 Implementation and deployment

The core ranking function is run on the index serving nodes. This allows it to run in parallel on billions of documents, and to have local access to posting lists and document properties for quick feature generation. By contrast, the third phase ranking function must be run on a single *blending node*, after merging and sorting the top results from each index serving node, in order to calculate the contextual features. To support this, we have added the ability to *export* features from the index serving nodes. When processing the query, we augment it with the list of primitive features that are used to calculate contextual features. Each index serving node includes the requested features of its top-k documents in its response. This approach is feasible because the reranking phase also has access to the rank and ranking score of each document in core-ranking phase, so it typically requires only between 30 and 50 primitive features, keeping communication overhead to a minimum.

4. SEMANTIC MATCHING FEATURES

The features described in Section 2 have some failings. For tail queries, the user behavior features do not work well due to sparsity and noise. The documents relevant to tail queries are often lacking anchor text. Text matching features suffer from the vocabulary gap between queries and documents [24]. To overcome these issues, we introduce three novel features: click similarity, translated text matching and deep semantic matching, which are calculated from click logs in different ways and complement each other.

4.1 Click Similarity

From the click log, we can extract a bipartite click graph to connect queries and documents by gross judgments from users. A vector propagation framework is developed on this graph to learn vector representations for both queries and documents in a shared space. Based on these vectors, relevance scores can be calculated. Traditional content-based models such as VSM [30] represent queries and documents in a vector space by merging their vocabularies. One weakness of such models is the mismatch between query vocabulary and document vocabulary [24]. To bridge this gap, the proposed model represents both queries and documents using terms in query vocabulary.

Edges in the bipartite click graph link queries and their correspondingly clicked documents. They are weighted by the number of clicks since more clicks could imply more confidence in potential relevance. We extract terms from co-clicked queries to represent documents. Terms that are from more co-clicked queries are likely to be more representative of documents. In such a space, the more queries two documents share, the "closer" they are. Similarly, queries that share many co-clicked documents are likely to share similar intent that should also be reflected by the query vectors. Thus we in turn propagate terms in document vectors to their co-clicked queries so that related queries can share high similarity in this vector space as desired.

With aforementioned assumptions, a vector propagation algorithm is proposed in this section. We first construct the bipartite click graph $\mathcal{G}$ with nodes $\mathcal{V} = \mathcal{D} \cup \mathcal{Q}$, where $\mathcal{D}$ and $\mathcal{Q}$ are the sets of documents and queries, respectively. For a document $d \in \mathcal{D}$ and a query $q \in \mathcal{Q}$, an edge is formed between them if there are co-clicks between them. The weight of the edge is indicated by the number of co-clicks. We use $\mathcal{E}$ to denote the set of edges and C to represent the adjacency matrix of $\mathcal{G}$. An example of the bipartite click graph is shown in Figure 1. QV^n is a $|\mathcal{Q}|\times\, V$ matrix where the i-th row QV_i^n is the query vector of q_i at iteration n and V is the vocabulary size. Likewise, DV is a $|\mathcal{D}|\times\, V$ matrix where each row is a document vector.

We initialize the representation of each query by its terms with weights proportional to their frequencies in the query. Each vector is normalized to 1. The initial matrix for the queries is QV^0. In the n-th iteration, we compute document vectors DV^n by aggregating their co-clicked queries. Formally, DV_j^n of d_j is calculated as:

$$DV_j^n = \frac{1}{\|\sum_{i=1}^{|\mathcal{Q}|} C_{ij} \cdot QV_i^n\|_2} \sum_{i=1}^{|\mathcal{Q}|} C_{i,j} \cdot QV_i^n \qquad (4)$$

where DV_j^n is normalized by ℓ_2 norm. Then the query vectors in

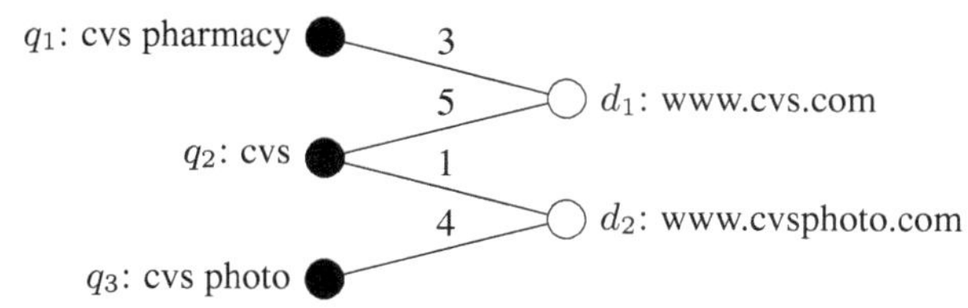

Figure 1: An example of click-through bipartite graph.

QV^{n+1} are updated with their co-clicked document vectors:

$$QV_i^{n+1} = \frac{1}{\|\sum_j^{|\mathcal{D}|} C_{i,j} \cdot DV_j^n\|_2} \sum_{j=1}^{|\mathcal{D}|} C_{i,j} \cdot DV_j^n \quad (5)$$

During the propagation process, queries are enriched with new and relevant terms. The propagation also re-learns the weights to indicate term importance that helps distinguish the informative terms, and is especially helpful for short queries. Document vectors are enriched with terms in queries and adjusted in a similar manner. In this way, query and document vectors mutually enhance each other towards a better representation that reveals more reliable query-document relevance. More details about the proposed framework can be found in [16].

In practice, we use a sparse representation by only considering terms with non-zero weights. The set of non-zero terms could be still quite large. If we use their weights to rank the terms in a vector, we can observe – the first few terms have large weights and the rest are very small. We find that we can keep the top K terms with the highest weight for both query and document vectors in each iteration without losing much accuracy. This optimization is vital for very large click logs. In addition, we have noted that this simple trimming speeds up the convergence of the vectors. Both query and document vectors stay stable after a few iterations.

Evaluation Given the learned query and document vectors in the same space, we can simply compute the inner product as a click similarity feature between queries and documents, which is referred as **CS** and evaluated in a real search engine. As shown in Table 3, through **CS** feature, the overall performance obtains 2.87% relative DCG5 gain, comparing with the base model (LogisticRank with the existing features described in Sec 2). For all query bands (top, torso and tail), CS significantly and consistently improves the performance, especially on the torso and tail queries where 4.18% and 5.14% DCG5 gain respectively. This improvement shows that this vector propagation algorithm successfully reduces the vocabulary gap between queries and documents, and also introduces related terms to learn better representations for both queries and documents. We also study the importance of features and the proposed **CS** feature is ranked as the *top one* feature among thousands.

Implementation and deployment We have created a pipeline that refreshes the query and document vectors monthly to include the latest click log data. This pipeline automatically constructs the click graph from the click log and generates the query and document vectors, which are further quantized to bytes to save space. The quantized document vectors are stored in the forward index on the index serving nodes, and the quantized query vectors are maintained in a table on a blending node. At run time, the similarity between the query and the document is computed as a ranking feature, which is used in the ranking models.

4.2 Translated Text Matching

The click similarity feature, although very effective, cannot be directly calculated for queries and documents that have never been observed in the click log. Statistical machine translation—translating queries to documents or reverse—provides an intuitive method to reduce the vocabulary gap, and it can be applied to all queries and documents. We harness the power of machine translation by introducing a set of new features, named "Translated Text Matching" (TTM).

query	methods	DCG1	DCG3	DCG5
all	base	4.31	7.74	9.78
	base+CS	4.39 (1.97%)†	7.91 (2.18%)*	10.06 (2.87%)*
	base+TTM	4.36 (1.31%)†	7.84 (1.36%)*	9.96 (1.79%)*
	base+DSM	4.37 (1.46%)†	7.87 (1.77%)*	9.95 (1.69%)*
top	base	5.69	9.67	12.08
	base+CS	5.66 (-0.40%)	9.75 (0.84%)†	12.20 (0.98%)†
	base+TTM	5.68 (-0.01%)	9.86 (1.99%)*	12.34 (2.14%)*
	base+DSM	5.70 (0.31%)	9.86 (2.01%)*	12.31 (1.94%)*
torso	base	3.88	7.23	9.26
	base+CS	4.02 (3.54%)†	7.47 (3.33%)*	9.65 (4.18%)*
	base+TTM	3.98 (2.34%)†	7.35 (1.57%)†	9.41 (1.55%)*
	base+DSM	3.94 (1.33%)†	7.36 (1.84%)†	9.37 (1.18%)†
tail	base	2.91	5.65	7.16
	base+CS	3.07 (5.75%)	5.84 (3.40%)†	7.53 (5.14%)*
	base+TTM	3.00 (3.10%)	5.61 (-0.73%)	7.26 (1.40%)
	base+DSM	3.05 (5.15%)†	5.71 (1.01%)*	7.31 (2.15%)*

Table 3: Performance of models with and without new features. * denotes p-value<=0.01; † denotes p-value<=0.05.

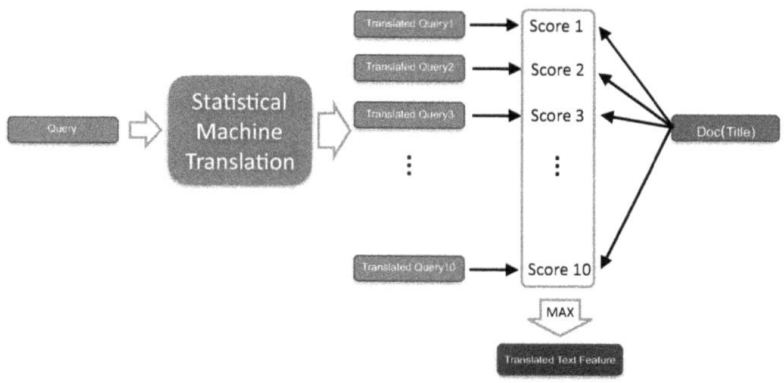

Figure 2: Translated Text Matching (TTM) feature.

The TTM features are constructed as shown in Figure 2. We first create a translation model, using clicked (query, document title) pairs as the bitext. [1] We use this model to translate each query q into k alternate queries $\{q_w^1, \ldots, q_w^k\}$, which are in document title space. Given a document d, we then compute a cosine similarity s_i between the i-th alternate query q_w^i and the document title as the similarity between q_w^i and d. The final similarity score $S(q, d)$ between the original query q and the document d is computed as: $S(q, d) = F(\{s_1, s_2, \ldots, s_k\})$ where F denotes a function to aggregate scores in $\{s_1, s_2, \ldots, s_k\}$ e.g., max, average, median, etc.

In our experiments, we consider various strategies to construct the translation features and we choose $k = 10$ written candidates. Due to space limits, we omit the details and only report the successful features: EXT_Q_TLM_1 is the maximum cosine similarity scores $\{\text{t\_qlm}_i\}_{i=1}^{10}$ between the rewritten queries and document titles, where the rewritten queries are obtained using a translation model and a language model based on document titles; AGG_Q_TLM is obtained by computing the cosine similarity between the rewritten queries (of the original query) using a title language model and the set of the 10 rewritten titles (of the document) using a query language model.

[1]The details of translation model are presented in Section 5.

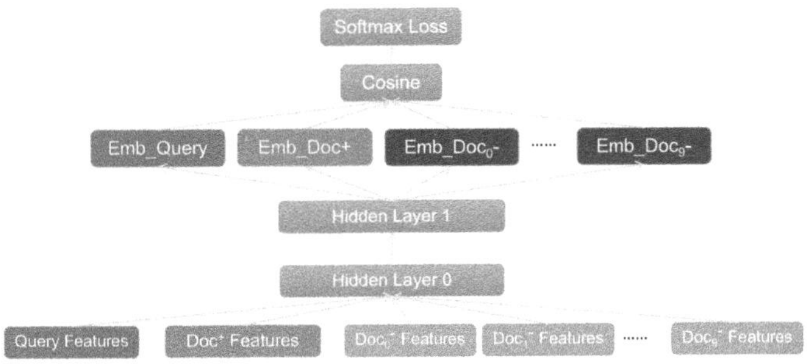

Figure 3: Network structure of the proposed model.

Evaluation We combine the proposed features EXT_Q_TLM$_1$ and AGG_Q_TLM with existing features described in Section 2 to train a ranking function and evaluate the test data by DCG scores. The results are reported in Table 3, which show that the proposed TTM features significantly and consistently improve the relevance performance, compared with the baseline (LogisticRank with the existing features described in Sec 2). We also evaluate the feature importance, and the proposed two features EXT_Q_TLM$_1$ and AGG_Q_TLM are ranked 7th and 10th respectively. These results show that the proposed translation features contain valuable discriminative information for the core relevance modeling task.

Implementation and deployment The implementation of the TTM features is based on a caching strategy which is described in more depth in Section 5. For cache misses, we use a pruned version of the translation model to keep latency low.

4.3 Deep Semantic Matching

Top queries are relatively easier in machine learning based ranking, since many text or click-through features can be used. It may face challenges for torso and tail queries since they occurred only few times in users' historic log. The aforementioned CS and TTM features to some extent mitigate the problem: the CS feature smooths the click information and removes the noise of clicks, while the TTM features are the soft version of query rewriting and record the equivalence of n-grams. However, both methods stay on the word level. To further improve the ranking results, we need to deeply understand the semantic information and users' intentions behind them. Deep learning techniques can help extract semantic and contextual information from top queries, and then we can generalize such information for torso and tail queries.

The rareness of torso and tail queries are mainly caused by misspelling, synonyms, abbreviations, long or descriptive queries. Generally speaking, tail queries tend to be substantially longer than top ones. For example, tail queries on average have four to five words. Longer queries are harder to be matched with the title or content of a web page. However, it might contain more semantic information, compared against shorter queries with one or two words.

We adopted a feed-forward neural network following the work of DSSM [13] as our ranking model. The structure of our network is illustrated in Figure 3. The queries Q and their candidate documents $D_{\pm}$ are fed as inputs, and the embedded vectors V_Q and $V_{D_{\pm}}$ are used to calculate the likelihood function of a clicked document D_+, given by the following softmax:

$$L(D_+|Q) = \frac{exp(-cos(V_Q, V_{D_+}))}{\sum_{D_{\pm}} exp(-cos(V_Q, V_{D_{\pm}}))} \quad (6)$$

For the training purpose, we collected one year of users' query logs of Yahoo's desktop search (US market), from May 1st 2014 to May 1st 2015. We removed spamming queries using simple rules, e.g., whether the number of displayed results per page is larger than 100. A query session is generated by aggregating logs which have the same key of "browser_cookie+time_stamp+view_id". We then aggregated all query sessions based on the query text. We discarded all abandoned sessions, where users did not click on any of the displayed documents. After aggregation, we obtained more than 20 billion unique query-document pairs.

To generate a list of positive and negative documents for training, we use a 10-slot window and slide it down from the top ranked document. The document in the first slot of this window is a positive D_+, and the following ones are regarded as negative D_-. As a result, we generate a large training set of 3 billion query-10-documents samples. The input feature representation is crucial in this model. For documents, we include both document titles and domain names as inputs. As discussed in section 4.2, title is the most informative and representative content about the document, but in a deep understanding model, domain provides another important signal for specific queries, e.g., wiki, weather, imdb, etc. To reduce the vocabulary size, we use 3-letter shingling of words as proposed in DSSM [13], and normalized bag-of-words vectors of dimension $30,000$ are used as input features. The neural network is then trained on a GPU cluster. After training the deep neural network, at runtime, the top level neurons will generate the embeddings of queries and URLs. Then the deep semantic matching (DSM) value is calculated by the inner product of the embeddings of queries and URLs.

Evaluation We evaluate the proposed **DSM** in our ranking framework on the Yahoo search engine. As shown in Table 3, **DSM** obtains 1.69% relative DCG5 gain. It shows significant DCG improvement on all three query bands (top, torso and tail). We also study the importance of features and the proposed **DSM** ranked as the eighth feature among thousands of features.

Implementation and deployment Deploying the deep neural network model is an engineering challenge. Latent vector embeddings of document titles and domain names are pre-computed via forward propagation and stored on index servers. In order to reduce memory footprint, we have to utilize vector quantization to further compress the features represented as vectors of single precision floats. At runtime, we only need to obtain the embedded vector V_Q for the query on the fly. The dot product between V_Q and the embedded document vector V_D is used as the deep learning feature, which is then fed to the GBDT model to calculate the final relevance scores.

5. QUERY REWRITING

Online users play two roles in commercial search engines. Users are information creators that generate web documents and they are also information consumers that retrieve documents for their information needs. Hence web documents and queries often use different language styles and vocabularies; consequently search engines could be unable to retrieve documents matching queries even when queries can perfectly describe users' information needs. For example, a user forms a query " how much tesla", but web documents in search engines use the expression "price tesla". In previous sections, semantic matching features try to solve this issue in a soft way that is mainly focused on improving precision. However, in a commercial web-scale search engine, to boost efficiency, before feeding the query-URL pairs into the ranking function, some steps, e.g., filtering, preselection, are performed. For instance, typically only URLs which contain all query terms are allowed to pass the preselection phase. This results in a recall problem. Query rewriting (QRW) is the task of altering a given query so that it will get better results and, more importantly, to help solve the recall problem. Query rewriting has been proven to be effective in improving search performance [27, 11]. In this section, we will describe the techniques and deployment of QRW in the Yahoo search engine.

5.1 Methodology

We treat query rewriting as a machine translation (MT) problem which translates from a source language of user queries S into a target language of web documents T. In other words, we use QRW to bridge the language gap between queries and documents for search engines. The proposed framework consists of two phases – (1) the learning phase that learns phrase-level translations from queries to documents; and (2) the decoding phase that generates candidates for a given query. Next we detail each phase.

The Learning Phase: The immediate challenge for the learning phase is to obtain a large parallel training data with queries and the corresponding rewritten queries that improve relevance. It is difficult, if not impossible, to use human labeling for the training data because (a) a good translation model requires a prohibitively large bitext; and (b) editors are not very effective at choosing which query will improve relevance. To tackle this challenge, we make use of click graphs. A click graph is a bipartite weighted graph where queries and documents are nodes, edges indicate the co-click between queries and documents and weights are co-click numbers. Typically titles of documents are very informative and representative while queries are usually very short. Titles are more similar to queries than body texts, which suggests that we consider titles of documents as rewritten queries. These observations motivate us to extract query-title pairs from click graphs. Since it is highly possible for us to collect a click graph with millions of queries and titles, we can prepare a very large-scale parallel training data for the learning phase. With query-title pairs, we follow the common steps for a typical phrase-based machine translation framework to learn phrase-level translations – word alignment, phrase extraction and phrase scoring. Note that titles are usually longer than queries; hence we need to adjust the null-word alignment probability to relative large values (say 0.9) to filter out noisy alignments.

The Decoding Phase: Given a query q, there could be many ways to segment it into phrases, and each phrase could then have many translations, leading to hundreds of candidates. The decoding phase should generate the most confident candidate q_w. Typically each candidate q_c is scored via a linear combination of m feature functions and the decoding is formally defined as:

$$q_w = \arg\max_{q_c} \sum\nolimits_{i=1}^{m} \lambda_i h_i(q_c, q)$$

where $h_i(q_c, q)$ is the i-th feature function and λ_i controls the contribution of $h_i(q_c, q)$. λ_i can be either manually tuned or learned through a defined loss function. We here adopt widely used feature functions in traditional statistical machine translation systems including translation scores provided by the learning phase, language model of original queries, word penalty, phrase penalty and distortion. We also develop feature functions specific to the QRW problem that aim to improve search relevance performance. For each pair (q_c, q), we can build three groups of feature functions:

Query feature functions: h_1-number of words in q, h_2-number of stop words in q, h_3-language model score of the query q, h_4-query frequency of q, h_5-average length of words in q;

Rewrite query feature functions: h_6-number of words in q_c, h_7-number of stop words in q_c, h_8-language model score of the query rewrite q_c, h_9-query frequencies of the query rewrite q_c, h_{10}-average length of words in q_c and

Pair feature functions: h_{11}-Jaccard similarity of URLs shared by q and q_c in the query-URL graph, h_{12}-difference between the frequencies of the original query q and the rewrite candidate q_c, h_{13}-word-level cosine similarity between q and q_c, h_{14}-difference between the number of words between q and q_c, h_{15}-number of common words in q and q_c, h_{16}-difference of language model scores between q and q_c, h_{17}-difference between the number of stop words between q and q_c, h_{18}-difference between the average length of words in q and q_c.

From our empirical study, we found that h_{11}, h_{12}, h_{13} are the top three most influential feature functions.

5.2 Ranking Strategy

As mentioned earlier, it is difficult to prepare training data for QRW by human labeling. It is also challenging to assess the performance of QRW by comparing original queries and rewritten queries directly via editors. For example, it is hard for editors to reach an agreement about the quality of "how much tesla" vs. "price tesla" as queries. Intuitively a good QRW should lead to an improvement in search performance. Given the original query and rewritten query, we have two options for ranking strategies. Intuitively, we can replace the original query with the rewritten query. However, our empirical finding is that direct replacement is risky, since sometimes some poor rewrites will hurt relevance significantly. Hence we evaluate the quality of QRW in a blending mode, which is able to overcome most poor rewrites: (1) Suppose that q and q_w are the original and rewritten queries, respectively. We use q and q_w to retrieve top-N documents from a search engine separately. Assume that $\mathcal{O} = \{D_i, S_i\}_{i=1}^{N}$ is the set of documents and their corresponding scores (which is from the ranking function described in Section 3) for q and $\mathcal{R} = \{D_j^w, S_j^w\}_{j=1}^{N}$ for q_w; (2) We join $\mathcal{O}$ and $\mathcal{R}$ – if a document D appears in both, i.e., (D, S_i) and (D, S_j^w), $\max(S_i, S_j^w)$ is the ranking score of D after joining; and (3) We rank documents in the union according to their ranking scores in a descending order and choose the Top-N documents as final results for the original query q.

The DCG improvement over the set of queries is demonstrated in Table 4. Note that QRW is the blending mode while QRW-RE is using the rewritten queries to replace original queries for ranking. Both QRW and QRW-RE are able to significantly improve relevance especially for tail queries, and over 5% DCG5 gain is obtained through QRW. Since rewritten queries may change the intent of original queries, the performance of QRW-RE is worse than QRW.

Implementation and deployment The main issue that needs to be handled before deploying statistical machine translation-based QRW is the latency impact of running the decoder. To minimize latency, we cache the best translation candidate for each query after decoding it. Since the rewrites generated by a given model are constant, the cache entries only expire when a new model is deployed. In addition, we preload the cache with rewrites of the most frequent 100 million queries. For cache misses, there is still some latency impact, however, we are able to keep it within our limit by pruning the phrase table before deployment, limiting beam width in the decoder, and simply abandoning the rewrite in the few cases where it is too slow.

6. COMPREHENSIVE EXPERIMENTS

We here report on the performance of all of the proposed techniques when used together. Performance numbers are shown in Table 5. "GBRank" is the GBRank loss function with the baseline features, essentially a snapshot of Yahoo Search in 2010 [6]; "base" is the LogisticRank with the baseline features; "base+feat" is the LogisticRank with both baseline features and the three types of se-

Query	DCG1		DCG3		DCG5	
	QRW	QRW-RE	QRW	QRW-RE	QRW	QRW-RE
Top	+0.82%	-0.51%	+2.22%	+0.77%	+1.58%	+0.07%
Torso	+2.82%	+2.55%	+2.79%	+1.42%	+2.12%	+0.88%
Tail	+10.42%	+9.15%	+7.03%	+4.58%	+5.56%	+3.13%

Table 4: The relative DCG performance improvement for QRW.

query	methods	DCG1	DCG3	DCG5
all	base	4.31	7.74	9.78
	GBRank	4.26 (-1.19%)	7.52 (-2.81%)*	9.51 (-2.81%)*
	base+feat	4.41 (2.34%)†	7.95 (2.74%)*	10.06 (2.89%)*
	base+all	4.44 (%)*	8.05 (4.09%)*	10.20 (4.25%)*
top	base	5.69	9.67	12.08
	GBRank	5.56 (-2.22%)	9.25 (-4.29%)*	11.51 (-4.67%)*
	base+feat	5.72 (0.65%)	9.82 (1.58%)†	12.22 (1.16%)
	base+all	5.73 (0.83%)	9.89 (2.32%)*	12.27 (1.62%)
torso	base	3.88	7.23	9.26
	GBRank	3.88 (-1.77%)	7.065 (-2.30%)*	9.08 (-2.03%)*
	base+feat	3.96 (1.98%)	7.47 (3.33%)*	9.59 (3.53%)*
	base+all	4.02 (3.42%)	7.58 (4.87%)*	9.75 (5.21%)*
tail	base	2.91	5.65	7.16
	GBRank	2.99 (3.06%)	5.65 (0.01%)	7.19 (0.37%)
	base+feat	3.14 (8.14%)†	5.91 (4.59%)*	7.60 (6.09%)*
	base+all	3.18 (9.48%)*	6.06 (7.20%)*	7.81 (9.09%)*

Table 5: Performance comparison of models with and without the proposed components. "feat" includes CS, TTM and DSM; "all" includes feat, query rewriting and logistic rank. * denotes p-value<=0.01; † denotes p-value<=0.05.

mantic matching features (CS, TTM and DSM); and "base+all" combines all techniques, including proposed ranking functions, semantic matching features and query rewriting. All relative performance numbers are calculated with respect to "base".

The combination of all new features "base+feat" significantly and consistently outperforms the baseline "base" on all the three DCG scores and all three query groups. The semantic matching features together also perform better than each individual semantic matching feature. This confirms that the three semantic matching features are complementary to each other. When we combine QRW models described in Section 5 with the new features in "base+all", the results are further improved. Comparing with "GBRank", the proposed framework improves the performance by 7% in terms of DCG5. For tail queries, it achieves 9% improvement in DCG5. As Table 6 shows, with the help of the proposed ranking function, new semantic features and the query writing, our search engine significantly improves the ranking result for query "how much tesla".

So far, we have discussed only base relevance issues, the most fundamental aspect of a commercial search engine. In the following sections, we discuss the solutions for recency sensitive ranking and location sensitive ranking in Yahoo Search.

7. RECENCY-SENSITIVE RANKING

In this section, we discuss how to improve ranking quality for recency-sensitive queries, which covers a large portion of users' daily search activities. For such queries, users need the search results to be not only relevant, but also fresh. For example, for the query "safest cars", users prefer information about latest tests for recent car models; for "superbowl", it is likely that users search for the last or next superbowl. If a search engine were to return a page that said "the next superbowl will be in 1989" or "the safest car is the 1988 toyota celica", it could lead to poor user experience.

In order to jointly optimize the relevance and freshness of ranking results for recency-sensitive queries, we define a metric called *recency-demoted relevance* to integrate both relevance and recency scores. Specifically, for each document, we characterize its recency with a five-level label:"very fresh (VF)", "fresh (F)", "slightly outdated (SO)", "stale (S)" and "non-time-sensitive (NT)", and adjust its relevance as follows,

	VF	F	SO	S	NT
Perfect	Perfect	Perfect	Excellent	Good	Perfect
Excellent	Perfect	Excellent	Good	Fair	Excellent
Good	Good	Good	Fair	Bad	Good
Fair	Fair	Fair	Bad	Bad	Fair
Bad	Bad	Bad	Bad	Bad	Bad

As the table shows, we keep or promote a document's relevance score when it is a very fresh, fresh, or non-time-sensitive document, and demote its score when its slightly outdated or stale. Our goal is to optimize the DCG metric defined based on the relevance score after adjustment, i.e., *recency-demoted DCG*.

To build such a new ranker with distinct goal, the challenge lies in the cost of collecting training data. It is not possible to have as many recency labels as relevance labels, because the recency labels quickly go stale. We must somehow leverage both a large relevance dataset without recency labels and a small recency dataset for building the recency ranker.

We create the recency-sensitive ranker upon the base relevance ranker by learning an additive freshness component to adjust document score based on its freshness. The freshness component is trained based on the recency dataset. We use a time-sensitive classifier to decide whether the component should be added, which prevents changing the score of non-recency queries and non-time-sensitive documents. The new recency ranker $f(x)$ for query-URL feature vector x is formally defined as,

$$f(x) = \begin{cases} f_{\text{rel}}(x) + r_{\text{fresh}}(x) & \text{if } c_{\text{ts}}(x) > 0 \\ f_{\text{rel}}(x) & \text{elsewise.} \end{cases}$$

where $f_{\text{rel}}(x)$ represents the base ranker trained from general relevance labels, $r_{\text{fresh}}(x)$ denotes the freshness component and c_{ts} denotes the time-sensitivity classifier . $r_{\text{fresh}}(x)$ is added only when c_{ts} shows that x is time-sensitive query-URL pair.

Based on the equation, the problem boils down to training time-sensitivity classifier $c_{\text{ts}}(x)$ and freshness component $r_{\text{fresh}}(x)$. To train $c_{\text{ts}}(x)$, we use the recency dataset and transform the freshness labels into binary labels, i.e., "non-time-sensitive (NT)" to negative and other labels to positive and train a binary classifier. To build $r_{\text{fresh}}(x)$, we use $f_{\text{rel}}(x)$ as the base ranker, and add more trees to optimize the goal of *recency-demoted relevance* – the newly added trees become $c_{\text{ts}}(x)$.

We compare the performance of recency ranker $f(x)$ with base ranker $f_{\text{rel}}(x)$ on 500 recency-sensitive queries, which are also sampled and selected from the whole year query log. We compute three different metrics: 1) DCG to measure the result relevance; 2) DCR, which uses the same formula with DCG but replaces the relevance label with a freshness label, to measure result freshness; 3) RD-DCG (Recency-demoted DCG) to measure overall quality considering both relevance and freshness.

The result in Table 7 shows consistent improvement by the recency ranker on relevance and freshness metrics for recency-sensitive queries, verifying the effectiveness of our proposed method. Table 8 compares the recency ranking example of a newsy query "holly bobo", which shows that our algorithm helps boost fresher results to the top. The deployment of recency ranking is relatively easy, since it shares the same framework with the core ranking function. Note that this recency ranker is only triggered when the query is

ranking		GBRank	base+all
1	Title	TSLA News: How Much Does a Tesla P85D Cost? | InvestorPlace	Tesla Cars: 2016 Tesla Prices, Reviews, Specs
	URL	http://investorplace.com/2014/1...	http://www.autoguide.com/new-cars/tesla/
2	Title	Here's How Much Tesla Is Worth - NASDAQ.com	New 2015 Tesla Prices w/ MSRP & Invoice
	URL	http://www.nasdaq.com/article/...	https://www.truecar.com/prices-new/tesla/
3	Title	How much Mercedes is in a Tesla? | Forums | Tesla Motors	2013 Model S Price Increase | Tesla Motors
	URL	http://www.teslamotors.com/foru...	https://www.teslamotors.com/blog/2013-mo...

Table 6: Compare the ranking results of query "how much tesla".

methods	DCG5	DCR5	RDDCG5
Base Ranker	9.175	11.549	7.875
Recency Ranker	9.334 (+1.74%)	12.355 (+6.98%)	8.264 (4.94%)

Table 7: Performance comparison: recency ranker v.s. base ranker.

classified as a recency-sensitive query by a run time recency classifier.

8. LOCATION-SENSITIVE RANKING

Web search results typically are identical for all users. However, for some queries, *contextualized* search results are more useful for users. In this section, we will discuss location sensitive ranking. For example, given the query "restaurants", users want to find the pages of restaurants which are near to their current locations. We refer to such queries that are closely related with locations as *location-sensitive queries*. Queries with specific location names (e.g., "restaurants Boston") are referred to as *explicit local queries*, and queries without locations but with location-sensitive intention (e.g., "restaurants") are referred to as *implicit local queries*.

To improve the ranking for location-sensitive queries, a straightforward way is to treat the distance $d(\text{QUERY}, \text{URL})$ between the query and the URL as an extra feature in the learning-to-rank framework [3, 5]. However, typically the text-matching features [29] and the click-based features [17] dominate learning-to-rank models, thus this distance feature is likely to be buried due to the its coverage. To overcome this problem, we propose a novel location boosting ranking model to improve the ranking for location-sensitive queries.

To compute the distance between queries and web pages, we first need to extract the locations from both sides. We parse the location from the explicit local queries and use users' locations as the query locations for implicit local queries. The locations of web pages are extracted based on the query-URL click graph from search logs. Given a URL, we parse the locations from the queries that this URL is connected to, and use these locations to describe the URL. We keep all the locations as a location vector weighted by the clicks. In addition, we also parse the locations from URLs directly.

Once we have the locations for both queries and URLs, we can easily compute the distance $d(\text{QUERY}, \text{URL})$, which is further normalized to the range of $[0, 1]$, denoted as $\hat{d}(\text{QUERY}, \text{URL})$. Note that when $d(\text{QUERY}, \text{URL}) = 0$, $\hat{d}(\text{QUERY}, \text{URL}) = 1$. The query-URL relevance is measured by the existing *base ranking function* denoted as $f_b(\mathbf{x})$, where $\mathbf{x} \in \mathbb{R}^n$ is the input feature vector. We assume $f_b(\mathbf{x})$ is already available (trained by learning-to-rank methods [3, 5]). We then introduce the logistic function to combine the two conditions and define the ranking function $f(\mathbf{x})$ for location-sensitive queries as follows:

$$f(\mathbf{x}) = f_b(\mathbf{x}) + w \frac{1}{1 + e^{\alpha f_b(\mathbf{x}) + \beta}} \hat{d}(\text{QUERY}, \text{URL}) \quad (7)$$

The idea is similar to recency ranking. Here, the logistic function controls the distance boosting based on the base relevance score $f_b(\mathbf{x})$ – if the URL is close to user and the content well matches the query, the boosting term (second term in Equation 7) is more positive, thus the total ranking score $f(\mathbf{x})$ for this URL is larger and the ranking for this URL is boosted; however, if the URL is very close to the user but is not relevant to the query, or if the URL matches the query well but it is too far from the user, the boosting term is close to 0, thus the ranking score is only decided by the base ranking function and the ranking for this URL is not boosted.

The parameters w, α and β are trained using pair-wise data by minimizing:

$$\sum_{(p_i, p_j) \in P} \max(0, 1 - f(\mathbf{x}_i) + f(\mathbf{x}_j))^2 \quad (8)$$

where $P = \{(p_i, p_j) \mid p_i \succ p_j\}$ is a set of preference URL pairs to the same query, obtained by human experts; $p_i \succ p_j$ denotes that p_i is more preferred than p_j. We solve the above optimization problem by a standard gradient descent approach.

Evaluation We compare the search relevance of our new ranking function $f(\mathbf{x})$ and the base ranking function $f_b(\mathbf{x})$ on 500 location-sensitive queries, which are sampled from query logs. The URLs are judged by human experts. The new ranking function improves DCG5 compared to the base ranking function by **+6.92%**. We also conduct online experiments to observe how users interact with the new ranking function. We perform "bucket tests" in a certain period to compare the base ranking function and the new ranking function in the Yahoo search engine. We use click-through rate (CTR) as our user experience metric to compare the two functions. Higher CTR implies a better user experience. The bucket test result shows that our new ranking function improves CTR by **+4.78%** compared to the base ranking function. This result is consistent with the offline experimental results (DCG) and shows that the new ranking function outperforms the base ranking function due to the effective location features. Table 9 compares the search results for a query "cvs" from a user in "Sunnyvale, CA". While the baseline ranks URLs with no specific location context on top (Note that cvs is a chain business that has many locations), the proposed distance boosting function ranks local results relatively higher.

Implementation and deployment To implement this location boosting model at run time, we extract the URL locations offline and store them in the forward index. The model parameters w, α and β are learned offline and stored in a dictionary. At run time, the implementation is similar to the core ranking function introduced in Sec 3. The distance between queries and URLs and the location boosting scores are computed in parallel on distributed index serving nodes. Then the boosting scores are added to the base ranking function to get the final ranking score. For URLs that are not labeled with a location, the distance is set to be zero, $\hat{d}(\text{QUERY}, \text{URL}) = 0$, thus only the base ranking function is used for ranking. Note that this location boosting module is only triggered when the query is classified as a location-sensitive query by a run time classifier.

9. CONCLUSION

In this paper, we introduce the comprehensive relevance solutions of Yahoo search. The proposed solutions are effective, prac-

ranking		baseline	recency ranking
1	Title	Murder of Holly Bobo - Wikipedia, the free encyclopedia	Murder of Holly Bobo - Wikipedia, the free encyclopedia
	URL	https://en.wikipedia.org/wiki/Murder_of_...	https://en.wikipedia.org/wiki/Murder_of_...
2	Title	Holly Bobo News, Photos and Videos - ABC News	Status hearing in Holly Bobo case... (published on 11/18/2015)
	URL	http://abcnews.go.com/topics/news/holly-...	http://wkrn.com/2015/11/18/status-hearing-...
3	Title	Man granted immunity in Holly ... (published on 02/24/2015)	Defense attorney in Holly Bobo cas... (published on 02/03/2016)
	URL	http://www.cnn.com/2015/02/24/us/holly-...	http://www.jacksonsun.com/story/news/crim...

Table 8: Compare the ranking results of query "holly bobo" with and without recency ranking.

ranking		baseline	with location boosting
1	Title	CVS pharmacy - Online Pharmacy - Shop for Wellness and Beauty	CVS pharmacy - Online Pharmacy - Shop for Wellness and Beauty
	URL	http://www.cvs.com	http://www.cvs.com
2	Title	CVS Pharmacy - Wikipedia, the free encyclopedia	CVS | Facebook
	URL	http://en.wikipedia.org/wiki/CVS_Pharmacy	https://www.facebook.com/CVS
3	Title	CVS/pharmacy (CVS_Extra) | Twitter	CVS/Pharmacy - Sunnyvale, CA | Yelp
	URL	https://twitter.com/cvs_extra	http://www.yelp.com/biz/cvs-pharmacy-sunnyvale-3

Table 9: Compare the ranking results of query "cvs" with and without location boosting.

tical, and have been deployed and tested at scale in Yahoo's commercial search engine.

The proposed solutions are not limited to web search relevance, but also can be leveraged for vertical search engines, e.g., shopping, news, local, etc. We hope this work is able to provide useful insights to the whole research community for both industry and academia.

10. REFERENCES

[1] E. Agichtein, E. Brill, and S. Dumais. Improving web search ranking by incorporating user behavior information. In *SIGIR '06*.

[2] A. Broder, M. Fontoura, V. Josifovski, and L. Riedel. A semantic approach to contextual advertising. In *SIGIR '07*.

[3] C. Burges, T. Shaked, E. Renshaw, A. Lazier, M. Deeds, N. Hamilton, and G. Hullender. Learning to rank using gradient descent. In *ICML '05*.

[4] C. J. C. Burges. From RankNet to LambdaRank to LambdaMART: An overview. Technical report, Microsoft Research, 2010.

[5] Z. Cao, T. Qin, T.-Y. Liu, M.-F. Tsai, and H. Li. Learning to rank: from pairwise approach to listwise approach. In *ICML '07*.

[6] O. Chapelle and Y. Chang. Yahoo! learning to rank challenge overview. In *JMLR: Workshop and Conference Proceedings*, pages 1–24, 2011.

[7] A. Dong, Y. Chang, Z. Zheng, G. Mishne, J. Bai, R. Zhang, K. Buchner, C. Liao, and F. Diaz. Towards recency ranking in web search. In *WSDM '10*.

[8] D. Downey, S. Dumais, and E. Horvitz. Heads and tails: Studies of web search with common and rare queries. In *SIGIR '07*.

[9] G. E. Dupret and B. Piwowarski. A user browsing model to predict search engine click data from past observations. In *SIGIR '08*.

[10] J. Friedman. Greedy function approximation: a gradient boosting machine. *Annals of Statistics*, 2001.

[11] J. Gao, X. He, S. Xie, and A. Ali. Learning lexicon models from search logs for query expansion. In *EMNLP-CoNLL '12*.

[12] Z. Gyöngyi, H. Garcia-Molina, and J. Pedersen. Combating web spam with trustrank. In *VLDB '04*.

[13] P.-S. Huang, X. He, J. Gao, L. Deng, A. Acero, and L. Heck. Learning deep structured semantic models for web search using clickthrough data. In *CIKM '13*.

[14] S. Huo, M. Zhang, Y. Liu, and S. Ma. Improving tail query performance by fusion model. In *CIKM '14*.

[15] K. Järvelin and J. Kekäläinen. Cumulated gain-based evaluation of ir techniques. *ACM Transactions on Information Systems*, 20(4):422–446, Oct. 2002.

[16] S. Jiang, Y. Hu, C. Kang, T. Daly Jr., D. Yin, Y. Chang and C. Zhai. Learning Query and Document Relevance from a Web-scale Click Graph. In *SIGIR '16*.

[17] T. Joachims. Optimizing search engines using clickthrough data. In *KDD '02*.

[18] A. Joshi, R. Kumar, B. Reed, and A. Tomkins. Anchor-based proximity measures. In *WWW '07*.

[19] C. Liu, F. Guo, and C. Faloutsos. Bbm: bayesian browsing model from petabyte-scale data. In *KDD '09*.

[20] C. Liu, F. Guo, and C. Faloutsos. Bayesian browsing model: Exact inference of document relevancfe from petabyte-scale data. *ACM TKDD*, 4(4):19:1–19:26, Oct. 2010.

[21] B. Long, O. Chapelle, Y. Zhang, Y. Chang, Z. Zheng, and B. Tseng. Active learning for ranking through expected loss optimization. In *SIGIR '10*.

[22] C. D. Manning, P. Raghavan, and H. Schütze. *Introduction to Information Retrieval*. Cambridge University Press, New York, NY, USA, 2008.

[23] D. Metzler and W. B. Croft. A markov random field model for term dependencies. In *SIGIR '05*.

[24] C. Müller and I. Gurevych. A study on the semantic relatedness of query and document terms in information retrieval. In *EMNLP '09*.

[25] L. Page, S. Brin, R. Motwani, and T. Winograd. The pagerank citation ranking: Bringing order to the web. Technical Report 1999-66, Stanford InfoLab, November 1999. Previous number = SIDL-WP-1999-0120.

[26] M. Richardson, E. Dominowska, and R. Ragno. Predicting clicks: estimating the click-through rate for new ads. In *WWW '07*.

[27] S. Riezler and Y. Liu. Query rewriting using monolingual statistical machine translation. *Computational Linguistics*, 2010.

[28] S. Robertson and H. Zaragoza. The probabilistic relevance framework: Bm25 and beyond. *Found. Trends Inf. Retr.*, 3(4):333–389, Apr. 2009.

[29] S. E. Robertson, S. Walker, S. Jones, M. Hancock-Beaulieu, and M. Gatford. Okapi at trec-3. *Trec*, 1994.

[30] G. Salton, A. Wong, and C.-S. Yang. A vector space model for automatic indexing. *Communications of the ACM*, 18(11):613–620, Nov. 1975.

[31] R. Srikant, S. Basu, N. Wang, and D. Pregibon. User browsing models: relevance versus examination. In *KDD '10*.

[32] I. Szpektor, A. Gionis, and Y. Maarek. Improving recommendation for long-tail queries via templates. In *WWW '11*.

[33] Z. Zheng, K. Chen, G. Sun, and H. Zha. A regression framework for learning ranking functions using relative relevance judgments. In *SIGIR '07*.

[34] K. Zhou, X. Li, and H. Zha. Collaborative ranking: Improving the relevance for tail queries. In *CIKM '12*.

Identifying Decision Makers from Professional Social Networks

Shipeng Yu
LinkedIn, Inc.
siyu@linkedin.com

Evangelia Christakopoulou
University of Minnesota
evangel@cs.umn.edu

Abhishek Gupta
LinkedIn, Inc.
agupta@linkedin.com

ABSTRACT

Sales professionals help organizations win clients for products and services. Generating new clients starts with identifying the right decision makers at the target organization. For the past decade, online professional networks have collected tremendous amount of data on people's identity, their network and behavior data of buyers and sellers building relationships with each other for a variety of use-cases. Sales professionals are increasingly relying on these networks to research, identify and reach out to potential prospects, but it is often hard to find the right people effectively and efficiently. In this paper we present LDMS, the LinkedIn Decision Maker Score, to quantify the ability of making a sales decision for each of the 400M+ LinkedIn members. It is the key data-driven technology underlying Sales Navigator, a proprietary LinkedIn product that is designed for sales professionals. We will specifically discuss the modeling challenges of LDMS, and present two graph-based approaches to tackle this problem by leveraging the professional network data at LinkedIn. Both approaches are able to leverage both the graph information and the contextual information on the vertices, deal with small amount of labels on the graph, and handle heterogeneous graphs among different types of vertices. We will show some offline evaluations of LDMS on historical data, and also discuss its online usage in multiple applications in live production systems as well as future use cases within the LinkedIn ecosystem.

Keywords

Decision Makers, Social Network Mining, Graph Mining

1. INTRODUCTION

As a crucial part of any for-profit organizations, sales professionals help to win customers for products and services. For B2B selling,[1] their job typically starts from identifying the right decision makers at the client organizations. This process is often called *prospecting* or *lead generation*. The ability to do this well is arguably the most important skill set that any successful sales professional need to have [6, 10, 12].

As we have entered into the social era, sales professionals started to pay more attention to developing relationships with potential clients as part of the sales process. This is often referred to as *social selling*, and includes components such as social prospecting, personal branding, employee advocacy, and social relationship management.[2] Among these components, *social prospecting* involves monitoring and searching social networks for signs of customer interest, immediate buying intent, or qualified prospect status based on industry, role, geography, etc. It's the entry point of identifying potential clients in the modern sales process.

Nowadays, social prospecting often takes place via social networks such as LinkedIn, Twitter and Facebook. Sales professionals are increasingly checking on member's profile, social connections, and blogs/updates on these social networks. However, they often find it hard to identify prospects they are interested in, despite the large amount of data available in various sources. They need intelligent data tools to help them find the target clients effectively and efficiently.

In this paper we present LDMS, the LinkedIn Decision Maker Score, to capture the fundamental notion of *decision makers* in the sales context by leveraging the professional members data on LinkedIn. The goal of LDMS is to consolidate all member's profile data with social graphs data and calculate a score for each of the 400M+ LinkedIn members, quantifying his or her ability of make or influence a sales decision. We will specifically discuss the modeling challenges of developing LDMS, and present two approaches to tackle the problem, a graph summarization approach and a bipartite graph learning approach. Both approaches are able to leverage both the graph information and the contextual information on the vertices, deal with small amount of labels on the graph, and handle heterogeneous graphs among different types of vertices. These methods are discussed in the LDMS context, but they can be applied to many other ranking or influence extraction problems on social networks or graphs in general. We will show performance of both approaches on LinkedIn data, and also discuss how LDMS is currently used in LinkedIn production systems.

The rest of the paper is organized as follows. In Section 2 we cover the related work on graph-based learning methods for influential node discovery, and in Section 3 we present

[1] Business to Business Selling, https://en.wikipedia.org/wiki/Business-to-business

[2] https://en.wikipedia.org/wiki/Social_selling

KDD '16, August 13-17, 2016, San Francisco, CA, USA

DOI: http://dx.doi.org/10.1145/2939672.2939707

the overview of the problem and the general setup. Then in Section 4 we present two learning approaches to tackle this challenging problem, and in Section 5 we show some experimental results on some offline data. Finally we discuss applications of LDMS within the LinkedIn ecosystem in Section 6, and conclude the paper in Section 7.

2. RELATED WORK

There has been a rich literature on identifying important or influential nodes in a network, both in an unsupervised setting and a semi-supervised setting. We briefly describe some of the work in this section, and also discuss the importance of decision maker identification for sales use cases.

2.1 Unsupervised graph-based ranking

The identification of decision makers can be viewed as finding the most important nodes in a graph. If treated as an unlabeled problem, the most popular graph-based algorithms are PageRank [2] and HITS [11], both in the context of web page ranking. PageRank is an iterative algorithm behind Google search engine, in which the rank of a web page is the probability that a random surfer would visit that page starting from a random page. HITS, on the other hand, tries to answer the question of how authoritative a given web page is. The model assumes that there exist authority pages and pages that link to many related authorities, referred to as hubs, interconnected by a mutually reinforcing relationship.

Several algorithms have been proposed to enhance PageRank and HITS. Haveliwala et al. [8] presented different approaches to personalize PageRank. TrustRank [7] was proposed for spam detection using a seed of expert-verified trusted pages. BrowseRank [14] also incorporates the time component by taking into account how much time users spend on a web site. It uses continuous time Markov process instead of the discrete time Markov process that PageRank uses. An application of PageRank-based algorithm for identifying trendsetters was presented by Trumper et al. [18]. They identify the trendsetters in information networks by using temporal attributes of nodes and edges, and rank users based on their ability to promote new ideas which will be adopted by many other users later.

2.2 Context-aware graph algorithms

Instead of only considering the link structure of the network, several papers also investigated how to incorporate contextual attributes of the nodes into learning and ranking. Topic-sensitive PageRank [9] pre-computes a set of biased PageRank vectors using a set of representative topics. It then uses these to generate query-specific importance scores at query time. Richardson et al. [17] proposed an intelligent surfer which is a query-dependent, content-sensitive version of PageRank. The surfer probabilistically hops from page to page, depending on the content of the page and the query terms the user is searching. TwitterRank [19] ranks users by taking into account the topical similarity between users based on their tweets besides the graph information. The random surfer performs a topic-specific walk and then the overall influence is measured by aggregating the topic-specific TwitterRank over all the topics. Pal et al. [16] identified authorities in Twitter by performing probabilistic clustering over the feature space and then rank the users inside the cluster, under the assumption that features follow a Gaussian distribution.

2.3 Bipartite graph mining

Several work explored the bipartite graphical structure to identify important nodes. The majority of them have been developed in the context of co-authorship and citation networks. Zhou et al. [23] proposed an approach to combine two random walks, one as intra-class walk between same-type entities (authors or documents) and the other as inter-class walk across the two sides of the bipartite graph. The random surfer has a certain probability of taking intra- or inter-class steps at any vertex. Meng et al. [15] developed a rule-based method which iteratively ranks authors and publications following a mutual-reinforcement strategy until convergence. There has also been work on influence mining on a heterogeneous graph by Liu et al. [13], using both the link information and the textual content. They proposed a generative graphical model to find the topic-level direct influence and subsequently the indirect influence between nodes.

2.4 Semi-supervised label propagation

Another work stream on graphs is to start from a small set of labeled vertices, and leverage the graphical structure to propagate the labels to other unlabeled vertices. The main assumption is that similar vertices are more likely to have the same label. Following these principles, approaches for undirected graphs have been developed [24, 20], as well as a HITS-inspired algorithm for directed graphs [21] and a method motivated by PageRank to identify the unknown labels in a directed graph [22].

2.5 Application to sales use case

Many books and articles have discussed the specific skills a sales professional should have. A crucial one among them is to identify real decision makers and to present their products or services to them [4, 6, 10, 12]. However there has not been many work in the data mining community that aims to help sales professionals tackle this problem (see a recent paper in [5]).

For the decision maker identification problem in our context, we cannot simply run a PageRank or HITS type algorithm to identify the important nodes. Such algorithms typically find influential or popular people on our network (such as celebrities), not necessarily the people who can make sales decisions. We require some labels to guide the algorithms, hence need to combine the labels with the graph structure. Also we will need to deal with heterogeneous graphs within our professional network. With this in mind, the approaches we propose in this paper are able to leverage both the graph information and the contextual information, deal with small amount of labels on the graph, and handle heterogeneous graphs among different types of vertices. We believe they will have positive impact in many sales use cases and other application areas beyond the context we discuss in this paper.

3. PROBLEM SETTING

In this section we give a high-level overview of the social network environment in our context, and discuss mechanisms to obtain ground truth and features for developing LDMS. Although the context is within LinkedIn ecosystem, many of the attributes and insights apply to other social network settings.

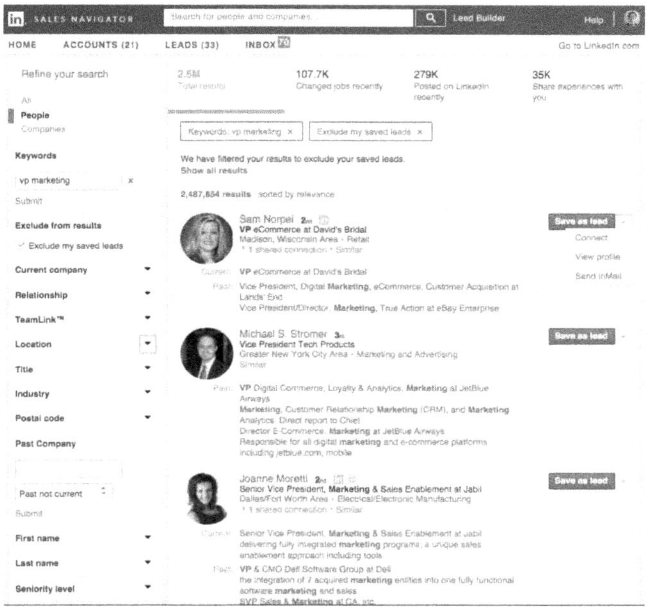

(a) Sales-focused search page

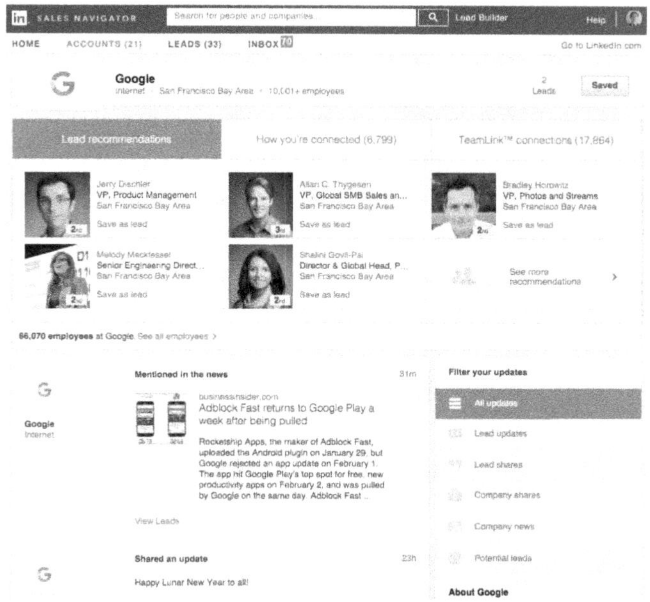

(b) Company page with lead recommendation

Figure 1: Screen shots of LinkedIn Sales Navigator, both leveraging LDMS in live production system. (a) shows the refined search page for sales use case, with sales-focused re-ranking of results and other advanced features (spotlight highlights, advanced filters, "save as lead" option for future follow-up). (b) shows the refined company page, with recommended leads on top that are tailored to the specific sales professional user.

3.1 Social network environment

LinkedIn is the largest professional social network in the world with more than 400M members to date. Most sales professionals have already started using LinkedIn to research, identify, and reach out to potential clients. With a premium subscription, they can view members' profiles, follow them, get introduced to connect to them, send private messages (called *inMails*) to them, etc.

LinkedIn also has a proprietary product called Sales Navigator, which is designed specifically for sales professionals. It combines LinkedIn's network data, relevant news sources, and the accounts, leads, and preferences set by the sales professionals to produce customized recommendations and insights. See Figure 1 for two screen shots of Sales Navigator on sales-focused search and lead recommendation on company page. Both of them are currently leveraging LDMS in live production systems. We will discuss these specific applications in more detail in Section 6.

3.2 Goal

In this work, we focus on identifying decision makers in the professional social networks within the LinkedIn ecosystem. The decision makers in our context are people who can make or influence a sales decision. Note that we are not interested in influence within the social graph, but rather within the sales context. That's why we are leveraging social data from both the LinkedIn.com and LinkedIn Sales Navigator. Both platforms share certain data elements (e.g., member profiles, connections), but Sales Navigator has its own characteristics (see Figure 1(a)):

- Most users are sales professionals
- On top of LinkedIn.com actions (e.g., view profile, send connection request, send inMails), users can save potential prospects as *leads* for future follow-up
- Users have sales-focused member and company search functionalities

Our goal is to learn a scoring function to assign a LinkedIn Decision Maker Score to each of the 400M+ LinkedIn members. We intentionally make the score *global*, in that every member has *one* score regardless of what his or her industry, company, or function is. In other words, we do not aim to develop a specialized score for members within each industry, each company, or each function. This has broader usage for our context, and can be used within a special setting if needed. One can, for instance, use the score to refine search ranking such that higher-scored members are shown at the top. We can also sort members by this score for a given company to measure decision-making power within the company. Both use cases will be discussed further in Section 6.

3.3 Ground truth

One challenge in the LDMS offline training is the unavailability of the actual ground truth. In other words, we do not have definitive answer on who is and who is not a decision maker. We also do not have access to our customer's CRM (i.e., customer relationship management) data to know exactly who made or influenced a buying decision. Therefore, we seek to use a surrogate ground truth from LinkedIn data. In this section we describe the definition details and the rationale behind it.

3.3.1 The key signal

When a sales professional is interested in a particular individual on LinkedIn, here are the major signals we can collect depending on how he or she expresses interest:

- *Profile View*: view the individual's profile to find out more about the individual,
- *Save as Lead*: within Sales Navigator, save this individual as a lead for future follow-up,
- *Connection Request*: reach out to the individual with a connection request,
- *inMail*: send a direct, private message to the individual.

Going from *Profile View* to *inMail*, the sales professional is getting more serious about this individual. He or she also needs to do more work with the interaction - from simply viewing a LinkedIn profile to carefully drafting a message. Since the *inMail* signal is the most effective way of reaching out through the LinkedIn and Sales Navigator platform, in the LDMS training pipeline we chose the *number of inMails from distinct sales professionals within a specified time frame*, denoted as $N_{in}(x, T)$ for member x in time frame T, to be the signal for ground truth definition. The higher this number, the more likely the recipient is truly a prospect. Note that we only count inMails from one sales professional once for each recipient.

3.3.2 *Discount factors*

Inbound inMails alone is not sufficient to identify key decision makers for sales use-case as this leads to a lot of false positives. For example, on LinkedIn platform, recruiters also receive high number of inbound inmails. Not surprisingly, they also send out a lot of inMails to prospective candidates. On the contrary, decision makers tend to receive disproportionately more inbound inMails when compared to the amount of inMails that they send out themselves. Additionally, since our motivation is to compute Decision Maker Score across organizations so in our ground truth we discount for organization's popularity amongst sales professionals. Therefore we considered the following discount factors:

- *High-outgoing-inMail discount*:

$$D_1(x, T) = \frac{N_{in}(x, T)}{N_{in}(x, T) + N_{out}(x, T) + 1},$$

to penalize members who send many inMails out (regardless to whom). Here $N_{out}(x, T)$ denotes the number of inMails sent out by member x in time frame T.

- *Peer-comparison discount*:

$$D_2(x, T) = \frac{N_{in}(x, T)}{\max_{y \sim x} N_{in}(y, T) + 1},$$

to discount members who have some of their peers getting more sales inMails than themselves. Here $y \sim x$ denotes the co-worker relationship (within the same company). The rationale is that the absolute number of sales inMails only makes complete sense within the context of the same company. In other words, if there are peers from the same company getting more sales inMails, the *decision-makerness* of the current member is lower compared to the situation where no one within the same company gets more sales inMails.

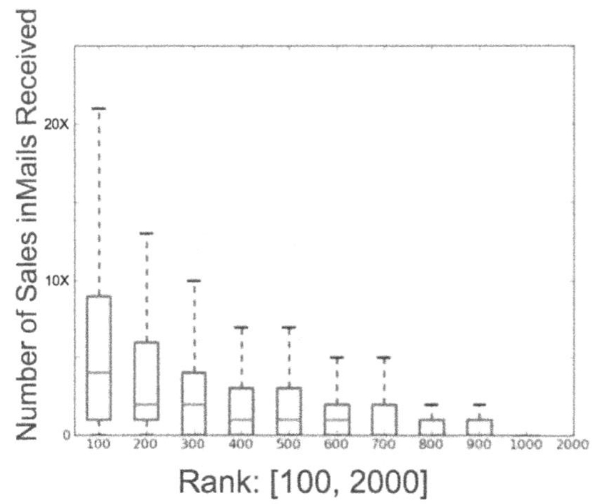

(a) sales inMail signal

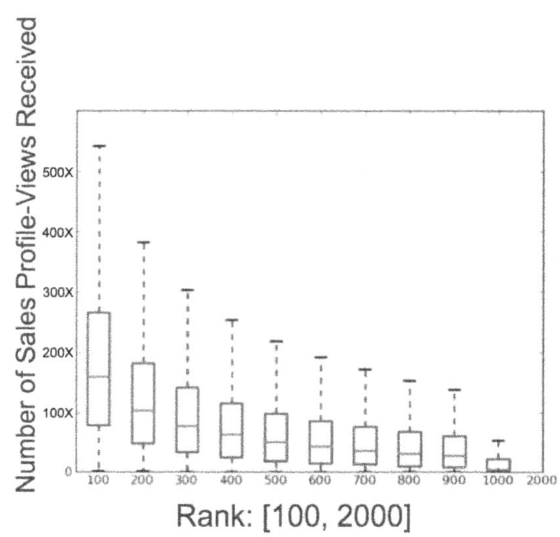

(b) sales Profile View signal

Figure 2: Sparsity of different graph signals. At the per-company level, we show the number of (a) inMail signals and (b) Profile View signals the top-ranked people (from 100th to 2000th) received from sales professionals within the calendar year of 2015. The box plots averaged all companies with more than 5000 employees based on LinkedIn data. On the y-axis we highlight the scale difference of the two box plots instead of the actual number. It can be seen that Profile View signals are ~50 folds larger than inMail signals.

Furthermore, across various time-window we see large changes in the absolute number of inMails that individuals get. Therefore to add robustness to our ground-truth, we consider percentiles within the company for these two discount factors instead of the actual discount values. The final ground truth definition for member x in time frame T is:

$$\mathcal{GT}(x, T) = N_{in}(x, T) * Perc(D_1(x, T)) * Perc(D_2(x, T)),$$

where $Perc$ denotes the percentile which takes value between 0 (0%) and 1 (100%).

3.3.3 Sparsity

One may wonder why not simply use this ground truth definition as the LDMS score (hence no need for supervised learning!). The reason is *data sparsity.* Very few LinkedIn members have ever received an inMail from a sales professional. Figure 2 also shows, at a per-company level, how many inMails and Profile Views top-ranked people received within a 12-month period. It can be seen that other signals, Profile Views in this case, do not suffer as much from sparsity problem. Therefore, to robustly rank a broader set of member base, we need to identify other non-sparse signals that correlate with the ground truth.

3.4 Features

In the LDMS offline training pipeline we considered various information about the member and the social graphs from LinkedIn.com and Sales Navigator. The following are the high-level categories:

- *Member Profile*: title, position, seniority, and related working experience of the member
- *Connection Graph*: an undirected member graph in which each edge is a first-degree connection between two members
- *Invitation Graph*: a directed member graph in which each edge is a connection invite action
- *Profile View Graph*: a directed member graph in which each edge is a profile view action
- *Lead Save Graph*: a directed bipartite graph between members and sales professionals in which each edge is a lead save action in Sales Navigator
- *inMail Graph*: a directed member graph in which each edge means an inMail was sent

All graph edges have a time stamp associated with it, and for some graphs there might be multiple edges between two nodes (e.g. *Profile View Graph*). There are other social graphs within the LinkedIn ecosystem, such as the Follower Graph, Endorsement Graph, etc. We currently do not use them but the framework is easy to extend to these additional graphs. Also note that we make an explicit distinction among various graphs on LinkedIn instead of blending all the actions into one graph. In Section 5.3 we will explore why this is helpful. We also want to emphasize that these heterogeneous graphs cover different types of graphs we normally see in social networks and include undirected, uni-directional and bipartitie graphs.

4. LEARNING APPROACH

Given the aforementioned ground truth and feature groups, in this section we introduce two algorithms for LDMS training, mainly based on how we encode the graph information into the learning process. The graph summarization approach summarizes each graph into specific features, and then adapts state-of-the-art supervised learning algorithms. The bipartite graph learning approach leverages the graphical structure explicitly and presents a novel graph propagation algorithm. Though we focus our algorithmic descriptions within the LinkedIn context, the approaches are general and should be applicable to other applications.

4.1 Learning with Graph Summarization

In this approach we cast the problem to a classification problem, i.e., we are training a classifier to categorize each member to be a decision maker (+1) or not (-1). The key here is how to leverage various social graphs for classifier training on top of the member-profile-based features. In the following we discuss the details for three different types of graphs. Since all the graphs evolve with time, we fix a specific time frame for each graph.

For undirected graphs (e.g., *Connection Graph*), we extract the following information from the graph for each member:

- *All-Degree*: Degree of the member in the graph,
- *Sales-Degree*: Degree of the member considering only neighbors who are sales professionals,
- *Ratio-Sales-All*: The ratio of *Sales-Degree* and *All-Degree*.

For non-bipartite, directed graphs (e.g., *Profile View Graph*, *Invitation Graph*, *inMail Graph*), we compute the following information from the graph for each member:

- *All-In*: Indegree from all members,
- *All-Out*: Outdegree to all members,
- *Sales-In*: Indegree from sales professionals,
- *Ratio-Sales-In*: The ratio of *Sales-In* and *All-In*,
- *Ratio-In-Out*: The ratio of *All-In* and *All-Out*.

For the bipartite directed graph (e.g., *Lead Saves*) between members and sales professionals, we only compute the *Sales-In* feature.

One key insight from this graph summarization approach is that the ratio features are more relevant to distinguish good and not-so-good decision makers, as good decision makers tend to have more in-bound interest (which can be profile views, lead saves, inMails, etc.) and less out-bound signals.

For supervised learning, we created binary labels based on the ground truth values, and combined all the graph-based features with the member-profile-based features. We can use any classification algorithm for training – for comparison in this paper we used elastic net classifier [25], which is a combination of L2 and L1 regularization. From our experience it was shown to be more flexible and can strike the right balance between goodness-of-fit and sparsity. One may also adapt Learning-To-Rank methods to learn the overall ranking of the members based on LDMS ground truth.

4.2 Bipartite Graph Learning

One issue the graph summarization approach does not take into account is the *quality* or *competency* of sales professionals. In the graph features computed from each of the graphs, we effectively weigh each sales professional equally. This may not be ideal as the signal, say a Profile View, from a novice sales professional should carry much less weight compared to that from an experienced and active sales professional. In this subsection we formulate this as a bipartite graph learning problem which explicitly takes into account the LDMS for a member and the competency assessment for a sales professional, which we call the *LinkedIn Sales*

Competency Score (LSCS). The motivation is that when we compute the LDMS score for a member, the incoming signals from the sales professionals should be weighted by their respective LSCS score. Likewise we can also take into account members' LDMS score when updating the LSCS score for a sales professional.

Formally, let $\mathcal{X} = \{x_i\}$ and $\mathcal{Z} = \{z_j\}$ be two disjoint sets of nodes in the network. With a slight abuse of notation we use x_i and z_j to denote both the nodes in the network as well as the contextual feature vectors they represent. We assume there are K bipartite graphs between nodes $\mathcal{X}$ and $\mathcal{Z}$. For the k-th graph $G_k = (V_k, E_k)$, we have vertices $V_k = \mathcal{X} \cup \mathcal{Z}$, and edges $E_k = \{e_{k(ij)} : x_i \in \mathcal{X}, z_j \in \mathcal{Z}\}$. We allow the edges to be undirected ($e_{k(ij)}$), uni-directional ($e_{k(i\to j)}$), or bi-directional ($e_{k(i\leftrightarrow j)}$). In the following we use the uni-directional edges to describe the approach but it can take all three types of edges.

For the bipartite graph construction we assume $\mathcal{X} \cap \mathcal{Z} = \emptyset$. In our context $\mathcal{X}$ can be the members, and $\mathcal{Z}$ the sales professionals. Since sales professionals are also members, in our context they have a representation on both sides.

Let p_i be the p-score for x_i, and q_j be the q-score for z_j. These, in our context, can be LDMS for members and LSCS for sales professionals. We define the following models for p_i and q_j:

$$p_i = f\left(w_{pc}x_i + \sum_{k=1}^{K} w_{pk} \sum_{j:e_{k(j\to i)}\in E_k} q_j \cdot t(j,i)\right), \quad (1)$$

$$q_j = g\left(w_{qc}z_j + \sum_{k=1}^{K} w_{qk} \sum_{i:e_{k(i\to j)}\in E_k} p_i \cdot t(i,j)\right). \quad (2)$$

Here $f(\cdot)$ and $g(\cdot)$ denote non-linear transformation functions from the continuous space to $[0,1]$. We assume they are both sigmoid functions in this paper. w_{pc} and w_{qc} are the weight vectors for all constant (individual) features of x_i and z_j that are not based on the bipartite graphs. In our context these features include profile-based features such as title, position and seniority. Note that they are multi-dimensional and can be of different length for x and z. w_{pk} and w_{qk} are the weights for graph G_k and they measure how graph G_k contributes to the overall model regardless of index i or j. $t(j,i)$ is a pre-defined transformation function for pairs (z_j, x_i). In the simplest case it can be the count of signals z_j sent to x_i in the given time frame.

This model can be seen as a generalization of many existing supervised learning and graph-based methods. With $q_j \equiv 1$, the model goes back to standard supervised learning with summarization features from the bipartite graphs, as we discussed in Section 4.1. If $K = 1$ and we have no constant features, i.e., $x_i \equiv z_j \equiv 0$, the model is an extension of the label propagation approach [24], where any label (of p_i) is first propagated to the other side of the bipartite graph (to q_j's), and then propagated back (to update all p_i's). If we remove the ground truth labels and make this an unsupervised learning problem, the model is an extension of the well-known HITS algorithm [11] to bipartite graphs, in which p_i and q_j can be thought of as the authority and hub scores, respectively.

For learning, we are given ground truth labels for the p-score, and need to estimate $\mathcal{W} = \{w_{pc}, \{w_{pk}\}, w_{qc}, \{w_{qk}\}\}$ (with parameter regularizations). Instead of directly optimizing the problem which is non-convex, in this paper we present an iterative approach and introduce an intertwined elastic net solver to solve the problem. The iterative algorithm is shown in Algorithm 1. As a starting point we initialize the q-score by fixing $w_{qc} \equiv w_{qk} \equiv 1$. Then we solve an optimization problem for w_{pc} and w_{pk} by fixing q_j scores. This can be done exactly the same way as what we discussed in Section 4.1. After that we propagate p_i and q_j scores throughout the entire network by iterating equations (2) and (1), with fixed model parameters $\mathcal{W}$. Note that the unlabeled x_i's within $\mathcal{X}$ will also get propagated p_i scores. We iterate until we reach a stable state of p_i and q_j scores across the entire network. Then we repeat the process of optimizing p_i and q_j separately for the respective parameters, and propagating the labels through the network with the learned parameters. In Step 6 where we optimize the q_j scores, since we do not have ground truth labels for q_j's, we take a heuristic approach and label the top 20% percentile as +1 and bottom 20% percentile as −1. From our experiments we see the results and convergence rate are not sensitive to the specific percentile choice. The algorithm typically converges within 20 iterations from our experience.

Algorithm 1 The Bipartite Graph Learning algorithm

1: Initialization: $w_{pc} = w_{qc} = 1, w_{pk} = w_{qk} = 1, \forall k$.
2: Compute q_j using (2), $\forall j$.
3: (**Optimization**) Solve elastic net problem in (1) for w_{pc} and w_{pk}, $\forall k$.
4: (**Propagation**) Iterate (2) and (1) till convergence with fixed $\mathcal{W}$, obtaining p_i and q_j, $\forall i, j$.
5: **repeat**
6: (**Optimization**) Solve (2) for w_{qc} and w_{qk}, $\forall k$.
7: (**Optimization**) Solve (1) for w_{pc} and w_{pk}, $\forall k$.
8: (**Propagation**) Iterate (2) and (1) till convergence with fixed $\mathcal{W}$, obtaining p_i and q_j, $\forall i, j$.
9: **until** convergence

5. METHODOLOGY AND RESULTS

For the results we show in this paper, we collected all LinkedIn network data over the calendar year of 2015. The ground truth was defined based on Section 3.3 with this time frame, and all the feature groups defined in Section 3.4 were captured for this time frame. There were around 400M members in the pipeline, and the total number of signals (e.g., profile views) for most of the graphs is in the hundreds of millions. For learning and parameter estimation, we leveraged our internal Hadoop infrastructure at LinkedIn for distributed learning.

5.1 Offline Training Methodology

For offline evaluation we randomly split the LinkedIn member base into training (70%) and testing (30%). Based on the ground truth definition in Section 3.3, we assign a (+1/0/-1) label to each member based on two pre-selected thresholds T_+ and T_-:

$$\mathcal{L}(x,T) = \begin{cases} +1, & \text{if } \mathcal{GT}(x,T) \geq T_+, \\ -1, & \text{if } \mathcal{GT}(x,T) < T_-, \\ 0, & \text{otherwise.} \end{cases}$$

For the graph summarization approach, we ignored the members who have label 0 to remove noisy data. For bipartite

Table 1: NDCG results for graph summarization (Summarization) and bipartite graph learning (Bipartite)

NDCG@K	10	20	50	100	500	1,000	5,000	10,000	50,000	100,000	500,000	1,000,000
Summarization	**1**	0.963	0.9084	0.8593	0.9039	0.8684	0.8682	0.7987	0.8339	0.8701	0.9336	0.9344
Bipartite	**1**	**0.9664**	**0.9665**	**0.9063**	**0.9183**	**0.878**	**0.871**	**0.8043**	**0.8412**	**0.8778**	**0.9367**	**0.9373**

Table 2: Kendall's τ results for graph summarization (Summarization) and bipartite graph learning (Bipartite)

Kendall's τ@K	10	20	50	100	500	1,000	5,000	10,000
Summarization	**0.5394**	**0.5769**	**0.5185**	**0.6365**	**0.5681**	0.4829	0.4717	0.4956
Bipartite	0.4045	0.4476	0.5135	0.6253	0.5605	**0.4855**	**0.4746**	**0.5043**

graph learning approach, we only used members with labels $(+1/-1)$ in each round of elastic net training for LDMS (Step 7 in Algorithm 1), but let the labels propagate to the other members throughout the iterations (in all propagation steps).

5.1.1 Metrics

For offline evaluation we need to compare the ranked list of decision makers from the algorithm with that from the ground truth definition. We are more interested in the relative ranking of members rather than the absolute predictive scores. Therefore we chose NDCG (normalized discounted cumulative gain) and Kendall's τ with our own adaptions.

NDCG is widely used in the Learning-To-Rank literature [1, 3] to measure ranking performance. For a ranked list and position k, $NDCG@k$ is the ratio of $DCG@k$ to the ideal $DCG@k$, where the latter is obtained had the list been sorted by the ground truth label. $DCG@k$ is formally given by:

$$DCG@k = \sum_{r=1}^{k} \frac{2^{rel(r)} - 1}{log_2(r+1)}, \quad (3)$$

which captures the importance of finding the correct ordering among the top ranked decision makers. Since the ranked list is very long in our case, we chose various k position from 10 all the way to $1,000,000$. Note that we have only one very long ranked list to evaluate, unlike the typical search scenario that multiple search sessions contribute to the NDCG metric. The gain function $rel(r)$ is defined by binning the ground truth label into different buckets.

Kendall's τ is a standard way of measuring correlation, which has also been extensively used in the literature of identifying the most influential people [15, 16, 19] in order to compare the ranking lists of different algorithms. Formally, it is defined as:

$$\tau(k) = \frac{(\#\text{concordant pairs}) - (\#\text{discordant pairs})}{\frac{1}{2}k(k-1)}$$

at position k, where $\#pairs$ represents the number of pairs. A pair of members are *concordant* if they are ranked the same way in the predictive algorithm and the ground truth, and are *discordant* if they are not. Note that unlike NDCG which is between 0 and 1, $\tau(k)$ is between -1 (i.e., perfect disagreement) and 1 (i.e., perfect agreement). One key difference of Kendall's τ from NDCG is that in Kendall's τ each member pair has the same weight as opposed to a discounted weighting scheme in NDCG. In our experiments we compute $\tau(k)$ for k between 10 and 10,000 to measure the metrics at different scales.

5.2 Overall Results

The performance of the two approaches described in Sections 4.1 and 4.2 is shown in Table 1 and Table 2. First of all, both approaches performed very well for the LDMS ranking problem. Between these two methods, we can see that the bipartite graph learning approach outperformed the graph summarization approach in terms of NDCG for all list sizes. For Kendall's τ, the results show that the graph summarization approach had better Kendall's τ than the bipartite graph learning method for small list sizes $(10-500)$, but was inferior to bipartite graph learning method for large list sizes $(1,000-10,000)$. As we are more interested in how the model would perform with a reasonably large amount of member base for the decision maker ranking, the bipartite graph learning approach is superior overall. Also keep in mind that even a small improvement in these two metrics will typically lead to significant improvement in downstream applications. We will cover one such case in Section 6.

One reason why the improvement tended to be small is that the inMail graph features are more important from both approaches due to the fact that the ground truth definition also leveraged the inMail information. The additional improvements over the graph summarization approach from the bipartite graph learning approach is significant in that it shows a bootstrap from the basic graph summaries with the help of the LSCS score for the sales professionals will lead to a better ranking result overall. We also get the side-benefit of having a ranking among the sales professionals, which by itself has many downstream applications. The details of this are beyond the scope of this paper.

5.3 Leveraging Different Social Graphs

In Tables 1 and 2, we used all the social graphs we have introduced in Section 3.4. In this subsection we evaluate how much each social graph contributes to the overall performance on top of the inMail graph. In Figure 3, we compare NDCG and Kendall's τ results for the following graph configurations:

- using only the inMail graph
- using the inMail and Profile View graph
- using all social graphs

We can see that in the majority of the cases the addition of more graphs helps improve the performance when K is reasonably large. This agrees with our intuition that considering more social graphs leads to a better ranking of LDMS among decision makers, and also stronger signal for the strength of the relationship between a decision maker and a sales professional. The additional social graphs not only

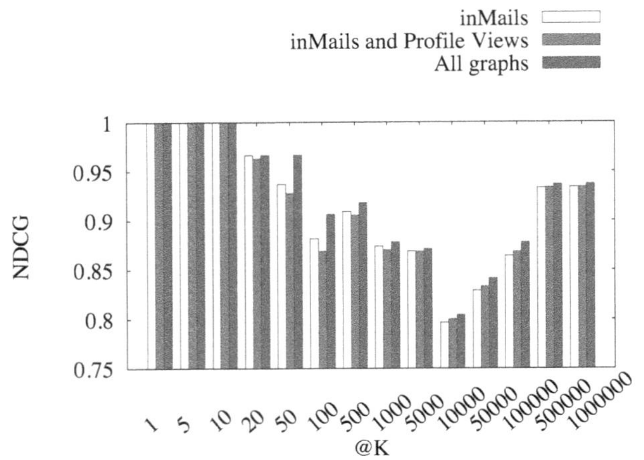

(a) NDCG

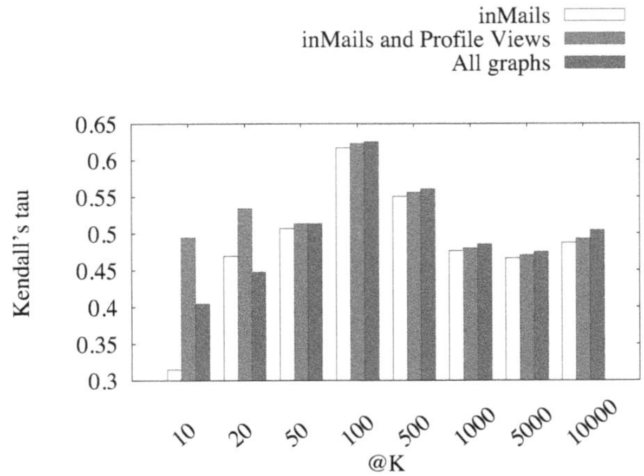

(b) Kendall's τ

Figure 3: NDCG and Kendall τ results for bipartite graph learning approach using different graphs

resolved the sparsity problem we mentioned in Section 3.3.3, but also improved the overall performance.

5.4 Score Distributions

Last but certainly not the least, we plot the histograms of the LDMS score for members and LSCS scores for sales professionals in Figures 4 for the bipartite graph learning approach. The LDMS score for the graph summarization approach follow a similar pattern. We want to highlight that the two scores behave in a totally different way. LDMS scores follow a power law distribution, where the majority of people have scores close to 0. This agrees with our intuition that decision makers are a small percentages of the member base. On the other hand, LSCS scores follow a normal distribution, with the majority of sales professionals around 0.5. This indicates that the majority of sales professionals perform neutrally, with some distinguished and some not very experienced. This is also intuitive and can be supported by various reports [4, 6].

6. APPLICATIONS

One key component of social prospecting is to identify people with influence in the sales process. This is one of the core components of the LinkedIn Sales Navigator product. We discuss some of the applications of LDMS in this section, all of which are currently running live on the Sales Navigator product. On the offline side, the aforementioned offline training algorithms are computed weekly on our internal Hadoop infrastructure. Once it is completed, both versions of the LDMS scores are pushed to a key-value store for online consumption.

6.1 Sales Navigator Search

Search is one of the key building blocks of Sales Navigator. We have integrated the LDMS score into Sales Navigator Search to allow the users to find decision makers faster, which differentiates Sales Navigator search to the LinkedIn.com search (see Figure 1(a)). We first investigated the integration performance offline using the NDCG metric, for which we wanted to test whether the LDMS-enabled search ranking is better than the baseline model (which was already fine-tuned with years of effort). Note this is the NDCG metric on search rankings, not on LDMS ranking as we presented in Section 5. The baseline NDCG performance was 67.3%, LDMS score from the graph summarization approach yielded 68.6%, and the LDMS from the bipartite graph learning approach yielded 69.8%. This seemingly small improvement on offline NDCG turns out to have a significant impact on online search metrics. Compared to the baseline search metrics, the A/B test for the graph summarization approach has shown 4.5% improvement on lead saves from search, which is the key metric for Sales Navigator search. The A/B test for the bipartite graph learning over the graph summarization approach has shown an additional 10.6% improvement on lead saves from search. These metric improvements are the key drivers of improving the Sales Navigator ecosystem.

6.2 Lead Recommendation

Lead recommendation module in Sales Navigator recommends potential leads to the user based on the decision making power those individuals have and the user's past activities on LinkedIn and Sales Navigator, such as profile views, lead saves, and the specified sales preferences. See Figure 1(b) for lead recommendation module on the company page. In the simplest implementation, it is extracted from the top decision makers for the specific company and then filtered by the users activities and their sales preferences. This is a new module that was recently launched, and was made available because of the LDMS score. This is also one of the differentiating factors of the Sales Navigator company page compared to LinkedIn.com. So far we are seeing that this module has the largest user engagement on the company page.

6.3 Decision Maker Insights

Another LDMS application is on the Sales Navigator Insights module, which is a feed system that aims to keep the users informed about latest updates on leads and companies they care about. This includs job changes, article shares, mentions in the news, company updates, etc. LDMS is leveraged to boost rankings of those updates from key decision makers.

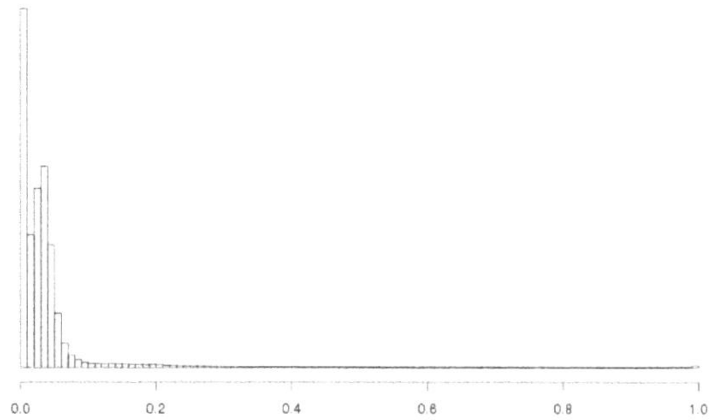

(a) LDMS scores

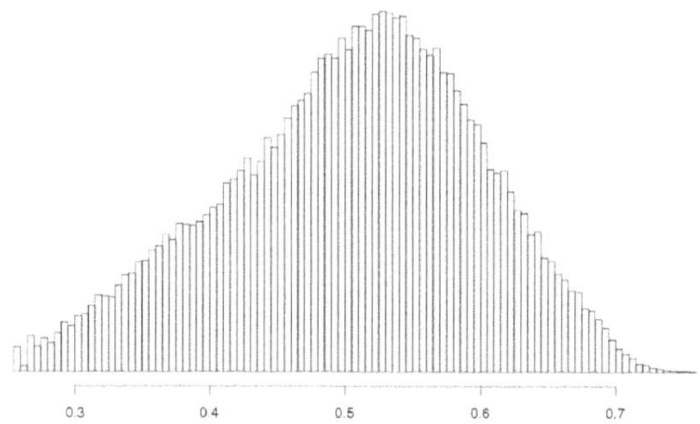

(b) LSCS scores

Figure 4: Histogram of the (a) LDMS scores for members and (b) LSCS scores for sales professionals

7. CONCLUSION

In this paper we presented LDMS, the LinkedIn Decision Maker Score, to capture the ability to make or influence a buying decision for each of the 400M+ LinkedIn member. We proposed two learning approaches to tackle this problem, which are able to leverage both the graph information and the contextual information on the vertices, deal with small amount of labels on the graph, and handle heterogeneous graphs among different types of vertices. Although the approaches were presented in the LinkedIn context, they are general methods and can be applied to other social network settings.

Within LinkedIn Sales Navigator, this score is used in refining search ranking, improving lead recommendations and providing additional insights about decision maker activity on LinkedIn. More broadly for LinkedIn, we are building upon this work to do more holistic optimization to improve overall LinkedIn experience for key decision makers across all enterprise products.

8. REFERENCES

[1] S. Boyd, C. Cortes, M. Mohri, and A. Radovanovic. Accuracy at the top. In *Advances in neural information processing systems*, pages 953–961, 2012.

[2] S. Brin and L. Page. The anatomy of a large-scale hypertextual web search engine. In *Proceedings of the Seventh World Wide Web Conference*, 1998.

[3] O. Chapelle and Y. Chang. Yahoo! learning to rank challenge overview. In *Yahoo! Learning to Rank Challenge*, pages 1–24, 2011.

[4] T. Connor. *91 Mistakes Smart Salespeople Make.* Sourcebooks, Inc., 2006.

[5] B. A. Duncan and C. P. Elkan. Probabilistic modeling of a sales funnel to prioritize leads. In *Proceedings of the 21th ACM SIGKDD International Conference on Knowledge Discovery and Data Mining*, pages 1751–1758. ACM, 2015.

[6] J. J. Fox. *Secrets of Great Rainmakers: The Keys to Success and Wealth.* Hachette Books, 2006.

[7] Z. Gyöngyi, H. Garcia-Molina, and J. Pedersen. Combating web spam with trustrank. In *Proceedings of the Thirtieth international conference on Very large data bases-Volume 30*, pages 576–587. VLDB Endowment, 2004.

[8] T. Haveliwala, S. Kamvar, and G. Jeh. An analytical comparison of approaches to personalizing pagerank. 2003.

[9] T. H. Haveliwala. Topic-sensitive pagerank. In *Proceedings of the 11th international conference on World Wide Web*, pages 517–526. ACM, 2002.

[10] A. B. Karl Schmidt, Brent Adamson. Making the consensus sale. https://hbr.org/2015/03/making-the-consensus-sale, 2015. [Online].

[11] J. M. Kleinberg. Authoritative sources in a hyperlinked environment. *Journal of the ACM (JACM)*, 46(5):604–632, 1999.

[12] D. Kurlan. Top 4 reasons salespeople struggle to reach decision makers. https://www.salesforce.com/blog/2014/03/sales-decision-makers-gp.html, 2014. [Online].

[13] L. Liu, J. Tang, J. Han, M. Jiang, and S. Yang. Mining topic-level influence in heterogeneous networks. In *Proceedings of the 19th ACM international conference on Information and knowledge management*, pages 199–208. ACM, 2010.

[14] Y. Liu, B. Gao, T.-Y. Liu, Y. Zhang, Z. Ma, S. He, and H. Li. Browserank: letting web users vote for page importance. In *Proceedings of the 31st annual international ACM SIGIR conference on Research and development in information retrieval*, pages 451–458. ACM, 2008.

[15] Q. Meng and P. J. Kennedy. Discovering influential authors in heterogeneous academic networks by a co-ranking method. In *Proceedings of the 22nd ACM international conference on Conference on information & knowledge management*, pages 1029–1036. ACM, 2013.

[16] A. Pal and S. Counts. Identifying topical authorities in microblogs. In *Proceedings of the fourth ACM international conference on Web search and data mining*, pages 45–54. ACM, 2011.

[17] M. Richardson and P. Domingos. The intelligent surfer: Probabilistic combination of link and content information in pagerank. In *NIPS*, 2001.

[18] D. Saez-Trumper, G. Comarela, V. Almeida, R. Baeza-Yates, and F. Benevenuto. Finding trendsetters in information networks. In *Proceedings of the 18th ACM SIGKDD international conference on Knowledge discovery and data mining*, pages 1014–1022. ACM, 2012.

[19] J. Weng, E.-P. Lim, J. Jiang, and Q. He. Twitterrank: finding topic-sensitive influential twitterers. In *Proceedings of the third ACM international conference on Web search and data mining*, pages 261–270. ACM, 2010.

[20] D. Zhou, O. Bousquet, T. N. Lal, J. Weston, and B. Schölkopf. Learning with local and global consistency. *Advances in neural information processing systems*, 16(16):321–328, 2004.

[21] D. Zhou, T. Hofmann, and B. Schölkopf. Semi-supervised learning on directed graphs. In *Advances in neural information processing systems*, pages 1633–1640, 2004.

[22] D. Zhou, J. Huang, and B. Schölkopf. Learning from labeled and unlabeled data on a directed graph. In *Proceedings of the 22nd international conference on Machine learning*, pages 1036–1043. ACM, 2005.

[23] D. Zhou, S. Orshanskiy, H. Zha, C. L. Giles, et al. Co-ranking authors and documents in a heterogeneous network. In *Data Mining, 2007. ICDM 2007. Seventh IEEE International Conference on*, pages 739–744. IEEE, 2007.

[24] X. Zhu, Z. Ghahramani, and J. Lafferty. Semi-supervised learning using gaussian fields and harmonic functions. In *Proceedings of the Twentieth International Conference on Machine Learning (IC ML-2003)*, 2003.

[25] H. Zou and T. Hastie. Regularization and variable selection via the elastic net. *Journal of the Royal Statistical Society: Series B (Statistical Methodology)*, 67(2):301–320, 2005.

Batch Model for Batched Timestamps Data Analysis with Application to the SSA Disability Program

Qingqi Yue[1]
qingqi.yue@nih.gov

Ao Yuan[1]
ao.yuan@nih.gov

Xuan Che[1]
xuan.che@nih.gov

Minh Huynh[1,2]
mhuynh@impaqint.com

Chunxiao Zhou[1]
chunxiao.zhou@nih.gov

[1]Epidemiology and Biostatistics Section, Rehabilitation Medicine Department
Clinical Center, National Institutes of Health, Bethesda MD 20892, USA.
[2] Impac International LLC, Washington, DC 20005, USA.

ABSTRACT

The Office of Disability Adjudication and Review (ODAR) is responsible for holding hearings, issuing decisions, and reviewing appeals as part of the Social Security Administration's disability determining process. In order to control and process cases, the ODAR has established a Case Processing and Management System (CPMS) to record management information since December 2003. The CPMS provides a detailed case status history for each case. Due to the large number of appeal requests and limited resources, the number of pending claims at ODAR was over one million cases by March 31, 2015. Our National Institutes of Health (NIH) team collaborated with SSA and developed a Case Status Change Model (CSCM) project to meet the ODAR's urgent need of reducing backlogs and improve hearings and appeals process. One of the key issues in our CSCM project is to estimate the expected service time and its variation for each case status code. The challenge is that the systems recorded job departure times may not be the true job finished times. As the CPMS timestamps data of case status codes showed apparent batch patterns, we proposed a batch model and applied the constrained least squares method to estimate the mean service times and the variances. We also proposed a batch search algorithm to determine the optimal batch partition, as no batch partition was given in the real data. Simulation studies were conducted to evaluate the performance of the proposed methods. Finally, we applied the method to analyze a real CPMS data from ODAR/SSA.

Keywords

batch model; batch information matrix; batched timestamps data; constrained least squares estimation; disability determining process; Case Processing and Management System; service time.

KDD '16, August 13 - 17, 2016, San Francisco, CA, USA

ACM ISBN 978-1-4503-4232-2/16/08...$15.00

DOI: http://dx.doi.org/10.1145/2939672.2939706

1. INTRODUCTION

The United States Social Security Administration (SSA) administers two of the largest federal programs that provide assistance to people with disabilities: the Social Security disability insurance (SSDI) program and the supplemental security income (SSI) program. SSA's disability determination services (DDS) process is complex and involves five levels. The first level is to make the initial disability determination by state DDS staff after a claimant meets all non-medical eligibility criteria at a SSA field office. There are four levels of appeals, namely reconsideration, hearing, appeals council, and federal court, from one level to the next. A claimant may request a next level appeal if she or he disagrees with the decision of the current level. The Office of Disability Adjudication and Review (ODAR) is responsible for hearing and appeals council. Due to the large number of appeal requests and limited resources, SSA is facing many challenges now. As the Office of Inspector General (OIG) report [20] pointed out, one of the biggest challenges is "While SSA continues focusing on the quality and consistency of hearing decisions, it is facing worsening average processing times and increasing pending hearings". In order to control and process cases, the ODAR has established a Case Processing and Management System (CPMS) to record management information since December 2003. The CPMS provides a detailed case status history for each hearing case, from establishing a case to final decision or dismissal.

Our NIH team collaborated with SSA and developed a Case Status Change Model (CSCM) project to meet the ODAR's urgent need of reducing backlogs and improving hearings process. One of the key issues in our CSCM project is to estimate the expected service time and its variation for each case status code. The major information we extracted from CPMS are case status code (job type) , staff ID, staff type, arrival timestamps, and departure timestamps of each status for each case. This is a problem of statistical parameter estimation in queueing model [2], [8], [15], [19], [25]. The work flow recorded by CPMS can be considered as a complex queueing network with multi-stage, multi-task, multi-type, and multi-server [14].

This is a challenging problem, as the complex hearing process system may not follow the typical assumptions used in classical queueing models, such as Poisson arrival processes, exponential service time, and first-come-first-served (FCFS) policy. This is because staff members in the CPMS may freely choose their own service policy; may work on multiple jobs "simultaneously"; they may also switch among multiple unfinished jobs, instead of starting a new job after finished the previous one. However, the CPMS does not record how and when each staff member switches her/ his jobs. We only observe the arrival and the departure timestamps of each job (case status in our system). Note that the arrival time does not necessarily mean the time the staff member starts working on the corresponding job. Since there might be other jobs on the staff member's desk, she/he may continue to work on the unfinished job after the new job arrives. Similarly, the staff member may also hold a finished job for a while and submit it later together with other finished jobs so the departure times may not be the true job finished times.

In this paper, we propose a batch model to make this ill-posed problem tractable. For all the jobs assigned to the same staff, we sort all the departure timestamps of the jobs and cluster the consecutive ones into groups. Then the jobs whose departure timestamps fall into the same group form a batch. For each batch, we build an equality between the batch time interval, i.e., the time between the latest departure timestamps of the previous batch and of the current batch, and the total service time for all jobs within this batch. Then we can estimate the means and the variances of the service time for each case status code once we have enough equalities. However, due to the complexity of the real data, direct estimation using the least square estimate (LSE) often result in large bias and variance. Our method is based the constrained LSE ([7], [22], [23],[26], [27],), with some special features incorporated, the resulting estimates are accurate and robust as demonstrated by our simulation studies.

The major assumption we use in our batch model is that the staff member approximately spends the whole batch time interval to finish the corresponding batch jobs. The batch service policy can be considered as a batched FCFS in the sense that after the jobs in a batch are processed and recorded, the jobs in the next batch will immediately be processed. We assume that the staff member prefers to finish one batch of jobs before moving to the next batch and have the flexibility to apply arbitrary service policy within a batch. We expect that our assumption may be violated by timestamps recording noise and imperfect batch partition where some jobs may not be completely processed within one batch. We do not require that the batch assumption should be strictly satisfied. Instead, we assume that the time the staff spend on the current batch in past batch time intervals and the time the staff spend on future submitted jobs within the current batch interval follow the same distribution. Then these left-hand and right-hand time truncation error effects may cancel out each other statistically. Our batch model idea has been motivated by mainly two facts. One is the timestamps batch pattern, which is due to some batch processing in the system ([1], [5]); the other is the staff service policy pattern although we cannot observe the ground truth service policy. The departure timestamps for each staff member present apparent clustered pattern. In addition, there are several reasons batches may occur: supervisor may allocate more than one job to a staff member at a time; the staff member may also choose to save finished jobs to be reported jointly to meet periodical job quotas.

To the best of our knowledge, this is the first study on estimating service time of batched timestamps data with unknown service policy, which allow switching among unfinished jobs. Our problem is related to the transactional queue inferences, which deals with the instances when only the service times are observed but not the waiting times [8], [15]. However, transactional queues assume FCFS, and it puts distributional assumptions to the arrival and service times. All of these are unknown in our model. For more details, interested readers in this area may consult the comprehensive list composed by Nazarathy and Pollet [19]. This problem is also similar to the blind source separations [6], notably to the applications on independent component analysis (ICA) [6], principal component analysis [6], and non-negative matrix factorizations (NMF) [16], [17]. The objective for blind source separations is to recover unobserved random processes based on partial observation. For instance, when unobserved sources are linearly combined to form observable outputs, ICA can distinguish both the sources and the combination matrix based on the outputs. In order to obtain the estimates, it is required that the outputs to be repeatedly recorded by the same combination mechanics over variable sources. The similarity between blind source separations and our problem is that we also observe a partial output (service time + waiting time) and attempt to estimate the unobservable sources (service time). The difference is that our batch model does not have repeated measurements based on the same combination of sources. The combination of different status codes within a batch is always varying. If we model our problem as separating service times and waiting times from the arrival/departure time interval, we only have one setup for all paired arrival and departure timestamps. Extra assumptions are still needed to make this problem tractable.

The rest of the paper is organized as follows. In Section 2 we describe our method for estimating the means and variances of the service times for all the job types; In Section 3 we present results from our simulation studies; Application of the method to a real data is demonstrated in Section 4; In the final Section 5, we summarize the results and discuss some of the possible further researches.

2. THE METHODS

As mentioned in the introduction, the data from a batch processing system may not provide all within batch information such as the true job starting/finished time for each job. In the following subsections we will use the inherited batch pattern due to the batch process to extract the batch level information to overcome the challenge.

2.1 The Batch Information Matrix

As some of the terms in this paper are generally used in both social service (eg. US Social Security Administration and Immigration services) and academic research (eg. Queueing Theory and Computer System) environments, we first clarify these terms by a series of definitions so that they can be consistently understood without confusion for the general readers.

Definition 1: A case processing and management system (CPMS) is a (generally computer and human) system which allows its components to control and process cases and to produce management information, including the arrival times, departure times and possible types of jobs (statuses of the cases) in the system. For a CPMS system, the *processing time* for a status (job) is the time difference between the departure time and the arrival time of the job; the *service time* for a job is the time actually spent to serve and finish the job; the *waiting time* for a job is the time difference of the processing time and the service time for the job; the *system idle time* (after all jobs are finished) is the time the system is waiting for the next job to arrive; the *system service time on a time interval* I is the sum of the total service times for all the jobs on I; the *system resting time on a time interval* I is the total time on I when the system is not available; and the *system idle time on a time interval* I is the sum of all the system idle times (after those jobs that finished in I). If the CPMS system allows batch processing where the jobs are grouped in processing through some way, the data from such a system will be called *batched timestamps data*

The system idle time is the time when the system is available to process jobs but there is no job to process; while the system resting time is the time when the system is not available to process jobs no matter if there are jobs to process or not. For example, a law firm processes its cases and records the processing information in a computer system. If this law firm finished all its cases on May 1, 2015 and did not receive new cases until May 7, 2015, then the time period between May 1, 2015 and May 7, 2015 will be the system idle time for this law firm. If this law firm does not work on weekends, then the weekends will be the system resting time. Noticing that the system idle time and the system resting time may have overlap periods as in the above law firm example, where the seven days' idle time period at least has one day overlap with the weekends' days, the system resting time, we need to take care of the overlap time when we calculate the system's non-service time.

Remark 1. By Definition 1, we have the following relationships:

The processing time for a case = the waiting time for the case + the service time for the case.

The total time on a time interval I (which is the interval length of I) = the system service time on I+ the system resting time on I+ the system idle time on I - the overlap time of the system resting on I and the system idle time on I.

Now we introduce some terms related to batched timestamps data, in particular the timestamps batch patterns inherited from the batch processing which partitions the jobs into batches so that each batch of jobs may be processed or recorded by a special pattern. For example, in an education system where each teacher grades students' homeworks and records the scores in the system, if the homeworks are collected and graded weekly, then the homeworks for each week can be viewed as a batch of homeworks which will be likely graded and recorded based on the teacher's own schedule before the next class. If we check for the timestamps for the students' homework scores in this education system, we would find that the timestamps might have some patterns due to the weekly batch (of homeworks) processing in the system. In the following, we will focus on the timestamps pattern due to the job batches in a batch processing system. For simplicity, we only consider the batched timestamps data with three columns: arrival time, departure time and job type, and we only use the departure time to analyze the batch pattern.

Definition 2. Let $X := \{(a_l, d_l, g_l) | l = 1, 2, ..., L\}$ be a batched timestamps dataset from a batch processing CPMS system with the departure timestamps column $D = \{d_l | l = 1, 2, ..., L\}$, let $J := \{J_i, i = 1, 2, ..., n\}$ be the job batches in the CPMS system which is a partition of all the jobs whose timestamps records form the dataset X. A *batch partition* B for the departure timestamps D is a partition of $D := \cup_{i=1}^{n} B_i$, where B_i is the departure timestamps in the job batch $J_i, i = 1, ..., n$; the $B_i's$ are also called the batches of the batch partition B; the largest timestamps t_i in B_i, $t_i = max\{B_i\}$, is called the *departure time of* B_i; the number of timestamps in the batch B_i is called the *size of batch* B_i $(i = 1, ..., n)$; and n the *number of the batches* of B.

The jobs whose departure timestamps are in each B_i are usually processed together in one batch in the CPMS system. For example, if a CPMS system consists of human servers (e.g. reviewers) with computer recording and scheduling program and it allows weekly job submissions by servers, then the weekly finished jobs can be viewed as the weekly job batches and their submission timestamps will have a weekly batch partition, which will be most likely clustered around the ends of the weeks.

Definition 3: For a given batched timestamps dataset, a batch partition $B := \{B_i, i = 1, 2, ..., n\}$ for the departure timestamps *is in order* if $max\{B_{i-1}\} < min\{B_i\}$, for $i = 2, ..., n$.

Remark 2. By Definitions 2 and 3, that a batch partition $B := \{B_i, i = 1, 2, ..., n\}$ for the departure timestamps is in order is exactly what we mean to say that the corresponding job batches $J := \{J_i, i = 1, 2, ..., n\}$ are batched FCFS as we mentioned in the introduction. In the following, we always assume the batched FCFS policy and the batched timestamps data is always sorted by the departure timestamps.

Often a batch contains some departure time(s) of jobs partially finished in the previous batch, and there maybe some jobs unfinished with their departure time(s) moved to the next batch. For many batches, the amount of departure times "inherited" from the previous batch and those moved to the next batch are not equal, while in some other batches, these the "inherited" and moved out departure times are of the same amount, and so their effects are canceled out. This leads to the following two definitions.

Definition 4: For a given batched timestamps dataset, a batch partition $B := \{B_i, i = 1, 2, ..., n\}$ for the departure timestamps is called *balanced* if the unfinished jobs in each batch B_i, $i = 1, 2, ..., n$, are the same in terms of the consumed service time.

Definition 5: For a given batched timestamps dataset, a batch partition $B := \{B_i, i = 1, 2, ..., n\}$ for the departure timestamps is called *complete* if there is no unfinished jobs in each batch B_i, $i = 1, 2, ..., n$.

For a batched timestamps dataset, we find that a particular batch partition will be associated with such a dataset, which is inherited from the batch processing in the corresponding CPMS system. As the timestamps within each batch in the batch partition may not be the true job finished timestamps and tend to clustered at the ends of the batches, batch level information may be more reliable for batched timestamps data. Since a batched timestamps dataset often associates a batch partition which can be viewed as a grouping variable to extract the batch level information as in the following two definitions.

Definition 6: Let $X := \{(a_l, d_l, g_l)|l = 1, 2, ..., L\}$ be a batched timestamps dataset with sample size L, where a_l, d_l, and g_l are the arrival time, departure time and the type of the l-th job. Let $B := \{B_i, i = 1, 2, ..., n\}$ be a batch partition for the departure timestamps $T := \{d_l|l = 1, 2, ..., L\}$, and m be the number of types in the type column $\{g_l|l = 1, 2, ..., L\}$ of X and $G_1, \ldots, G_m$ be the m job types. Then the batch counting matrix, $C := (c_{ij})_{n\times m}$ is defined by $c_{ij} =$ the number of elements in $\{(a_l, d_l, g_l)|d_l \in B_i, g_l = G_j, l = 1, 2, ..., L\}$ i.e. c_{ij} is the number of all the j-th type G_j jobs whose departure times are in the i-th batch B_i for $i = 1, 2, ..., n$ and $j = 1, 2, ..., m$.

Definition 7: Let $B := \{B_i, i = 1, 2, ..., n\}$ be a batch partition for the departure timestamps $\{d_l|l = 1, 2, ..., L\}$, $t_i = \max\{t|t \in B_i\}$, for $i = 1, 2, ..., n$ are the batch departure times, the interval $(t_{i-1}, t_i]$ is called the interval of B_i for $i = 1, 2, ..., n$; the batch service time $b := (b_1, ..., b_n)$ is defined to be the system service times on each of the batch intervals $(t_{i-1}, t_i]$ of B, where $t_0 = \min\{t|t \in B_1\}$.

By Definition 7 and Remark 1, the batch service time $b := (b_1, ..., b_n)$ can be expressed as $b_i = t_i - t_{i-1}-$ the system idle time on $(t_{i-1}, t_i]-$ the system resting time on $(t_{i-1}, t_i]$, for $i = 1, 2, ..., n$, where t_0 is the initial time to start the service for the first case in the dataset, or $t_0 = \min\{t|t \in B_1\}$ if the service initial true starting time is not given.

Proposition 1: Let $X := \{(a_l, d_l, g_l)|l = 1, 2, ..., L\}$ be a batched timestamps dataset from a CPMS system. If the CPMS system has the policy that when the system is in idle state (i.e. there is no case to process), it will follow the FCFS policy to serve the first coming case, then the system idle time after the case $(a_{l-1}, d_{l-1}, g_{l-1})$ can be calculated by

$$v_{l,l-1} = \max\{0, \min\{a_i|i > l-1\} - d_{l-1}\}.$$

Definition 8: Let $X := \{(a_l, d_l, g_l)|l = 1, 2, ..., L\}$ be a batched timestamps dataset with a batch partition $B := \{B_i, i = 1, 2, ..., n\}$, $C := (c_{ij})_{n\times m}$ be the batch counting matrix corresponding to B, and $b := (b_1, b_2, ..., b_n)'$ be the batch service time vector. We call the combined $n \times (m+1)$ matrix $[C, b]$ the *batch information matrix* of X corresponding to the batch partition B.

Proposition 2: Let $X := \{(a_l, d_l, g_l)|l = 1, 2, ..., L\}$ be a batched timestamps dataset from a CPMS system which has no system resting time on any time intervals between $\min\{a_l|l = 1, 2, ..., L\}$ and $max\{d_l|l = 1, 2, ..., L\}$. Let $B := \{B_i, i = 1, 2, ..., n\}$ be a batch partition with initial service arrival time. If the CPMS system has the policy that is FCFS when it is in idle state, then the batch information matrix $[C, b]$ of X with the batch partition B can be obtained, where C is the batch counting matrix and the batch service time vector $b := (b_1, b_2, ..., b_n)'$ is calculated by $b_i = t_i - t_{i-1} - \sum_{d_l \in B_i} v_{l,l-1}$ with $t_i = \max\{t|t \in B_i\}$ as in Definition 6 , 7 and Proposition 1.

In the following, we will use the batch information matrix for further analysis.

2.2 The Batch Model

We will continue to use the aforementioned notations. Let $[C, b]$ be the batch information matrix for a given batched timestamps dataset with a given batch partition B. Let S_{ijk} be the random variables representing the k-th service time in the i-th batch for the j-th job type, $(k = 1, 2, ..., c_{ij})$, then one can model the batch service times, viewed as random variables, to be the sum of the individual job service times within the batches, i.e.

$$b_i = \sum_{j=1}^{m}\sum_{k=1}^{c_{ij}} S_{ijk} + \epsilon_i, \quad (i = 1, 2, ..., n) \tag{1}$$

where ϵ_i is the total error including the net time spent for all the partially finished jobs in the i-th batch B_i.

If the batch $B := \{B_i, i = 1, 2, ..., n\}$ is complete, then there will be no unfinished job and the error terms ϵ_i's can be dropped. If $B := \{B_i, i = 1, 2, ..., n\}$ is balanced then the net time on all the unfinished jobs can be canceled out and the error terms ϵ_i's also can be dropped. In general, we may assume that the ϵ_i's are zero-mean independent random noises. To further simplify model (1), we assume that the service time random variables S_{ijk}'s are independent and stationary across (i, k) for the 1st and 2nd moments, i.e.

$$E[S_{ijk}] = \mu_j, \qquad Var[S_{ijk}] = \sigma_j^2$$

For all (i, k)'s, $i = 1, 2, ..., n; j = 1, 2, ..., m; k = 1, 2, ..., c_{ij}$.

In the next subsection, we will use batch model (1) to construct two linear models whose parameters are the means and variances of the service times for each job type.

2.3 The Mean and Variance Estimations by the Least Square Estimator (LSE)

With the above batch model assumptions, we take the expectations and variances respectively on both sides of equation (1) to obtain the following two linear system of equations:

$$E[b_i] = \sum_{j=1}^{m} c_{ij}\mu_j, \qquad (i = 1, 2, ..., n), \tag{2}$$

$$Var[b_i] = \sum_{j=1}^{m} c_{ij}\sigma_j^2 + Var[\epsilon_i], \qquad (i = 1, 2, ..., n), \tag{3}$$

In matrix forms, (2) and (3) can be rewritten as

$$C\mu = E[b], \text{ and } C\sigma^2 = Var[b] - Var[\epsilon], \tag{4}$$

where $C := (c_{ij})_{n\times m}$ is the batch counting matrix, $\mu = (\mu_1, ..., \mu_m)'$ is the vector of the mean service times for the m job types, $\sigma^2 = (\sigma_1^2, ..., \sigma_m^2)'$ is the vector of the corresponding variances, $E[b] = (E[b_1], ..., E[b_n])'$, and $Var[b] =$

$(Var[b_1], ..., Var[b_n])'$, $Var[\epsilon] = (Var[\epsilon_1], ..., Var[\epsilon_n])'$, are the vectors of the means and the variances for the service times of the n batches. From the systems of equations (4), we can use the Least Square method to obtain the solutions as follows:

$$\mu = (C'C)^{-1}C'E[b], \text{ and } \sigma^2 = (C'C)^{-1}C'(Var[b] - Var[\epsilon]). \quad (5)$$

The mean and variance of the batch service time $E[b]$ and $Var[b]$ as well as the variance of the batch error $Var[\epsilon]$ are unknown. We use the batch service time $b = (b_1, ..., b_n)'$ as an approximation to $E[b]$ in (4) so that μ can be estimated by

$$\hat{\mu} = (C'C)^{-1}C'b \quad (6)$$

Similarly we can obtain an estimation for σ^2 as follows. From (4), $E[b]$ can be estimated by

$$\widehat{E[b]} = C\hat{\mu} = C(C'C)^{-1}C'b.$$

Now we use

$$[b - \widehat{E[b]}]^2 = [b - C(C'C)^{-1}C'b]^2 = [(I_n - C(C'C)^{-1}C')b]^2$$

as an approximation to $Var[b] - Var[\epsilon]$ in (5) so that σ^2 can be estimated by

$$\hat{\sigma}^2 = (C'C)^{-1}C'[(I_n - C(C'C)^{-1}C')b]^2 \quad (7)$$

where I_n is the $n \times n$ identity matrix.

With the above assumptions and notations, we obtain the estimated mean service times $\hat{\mu}$ (for the job types) and the estimated variances $\hat{\sigma}^2$ from (6) and (7), which depend on the given batch partition B. The following proposition shows that for a special batch partition, the estimation formulas will be reduced into the sample mean and variance formulas.

Proposition 3: If the given batch partition has the Batch Counting Matrix C of an n by 1 matrix of 1's, then the mean and variance estimation formulas (6) and (7) become

$$\bar{m} = 1/n \sum_{i=1}^{n} b_i, \quad \text{and} \quad \hat{s}^2 = 1/n \sum_{i=1}^{n} (b_i - \bar{m})^2.$$

Now we consider the quality of the batch based mean and variance estimators (6) and (7). Since our estimators are based on a two-step procedure: the batch service time modeling (1) and the linear regression batch service time model $b = C\mu + \eta$, the quality of estimator (6) depends on modeling (1) assumptions, the Batch Counting Matrix C and the variance of the zero-mean error η. Under certain regularity conditions, estimator (6) can be proved to be consistent.

As all samples are finite, the standard errors of the estimators $\hat{\mu}$ and $\hat{\sigma}^2$ for a given sample may provide actual information about the quality of the estimators. From the theory of generalized LSE, the estimated standard errors of the estimators $\hat{\mu}$ and $\hat{\sigma}^2$ are approximated as below.

Proposition 4: *The standard errors of $\hat{\mu}$ and $\hat{\sigma}^2$ are approximated by*

$$se(\hat{\mu}) \approx \sqrt{diag\{C'C)^{-1}C'D(\hat{\mu})C(C'C)^{-1}\}},$$

$$se(\hat{\sigma}^2) \approx \sqrt{diag\{(C'C)^{-1}C'D(\hat{\sigma}^2)C(C'C)^{-1}\}}$$

where $D(\hat{\mu}) = Diag\{[(I_n - C(C'C)^{-1}C')b]^2\}$, and $D(\hat{\sigma}^2) = diag\{[(I_n - C(C'C)^{-1}C')[(I_n - C(C'C)^{-1}C')b]^2]^2\}$ with the $diag(M)$ being the vector of diagonal elements of the matrix M, $DiagV$ being the diagonal matrix obtained form the vector V, and for a non-negative vector $a = (a_1, ..., a_m)$, $\sqrt{a} = (\sqrt{a_1}, ..., \sqrt{a_m})$.

Corollary 1: *If the diagonal matrices $D(\hat{\mu})$ and $D(\hat{\sigma}^2)$ in the above Proposition are replaced by the scaler matrices $k_1 I_n$ and $k_2 I_n$ respectively, where*

$$k_1 = ||[(I_n - C(C'C)^{-1}C')b]^2||^2/(n-m),$$

and $k_2 = ||[(I_n - C(C'C)^{-1}C')[(I_n - C(C'C)^{-1}C')b]^2]^2||^2 /(n-m)$ with $||V||^2$ being the L^2 norm, then the above approximations are reduced to

$$\bar{se}(\hat{\mu}) \approx \sqrt{(diag(k_1(C'C)^{-1})}, \quad \bar{se}(\hat{\sigma}^2) \approx \sqrt{diag(k_2(C'C)^{-1})}$$

which are the estimation formulas for the corresponding Ordinary Least Square Estimators (OLEs).

2.4 The Mean and Variance Estimations by the LSE with Constraints

In section 2.3, we formulated the mean and variance as the coefficient parameters in linear models and use the LSE to estimate them as in (6) and (7). In real data, there are some natural constraints the parameters have to follow. Since our estimated parameters are the mean service times, so their variances should satisfy the constraint of non-negativity. As the mean service time is part of the processing time, it is an upper bound for the parameters. Another natural constraint is based on the global service time decomposition that the total service time (for all the jobs in the dataset) is the sum of the sub-total service time for each of the job types. If the Batch Information Matrix $[C, b]$ is given, then the total service time in the dataset, and that of the jobs for all the job types can be easily obtained by the sums of the columns of $[C, b]$, from which the total service time for each type of job can be calculated if the mean service time for each job is given. With those constraints, the mean estimation formula (6) can be improved by the following constrained LSE:

$$\begin{cases} b = C\mu + \eta \\ 0 \le \mu_j \le \pi_j, \quad j = 1, 2, ..., m \\ \sum_{j=1}^{m} C_j \mu_j = \sum_{i=1}^{n} b_i \end{cases} \quad (9)$$

where $\eta = b - E[b]$, $C_j = \sum_{i=1}^{n} c_{ij}$ is the sum of the j-th column of the batch counting matrix; π_j is the mean processing time for the type j jobs, $j = 1, 2..., m$, which can be easily calculated as the processing time (defined as departure time − arrival time) are observable for each data record. Let $\tilde{\mu}$ be the least squares estimate of μ under model (5) with constraints (9), and $\tilde{\sigma}^2$ be its estimated variance, which can be solved by the R package limSolve [23].

2.5 A Batch Searching Algorithm for 1-dimensional batched timestamps data

In previous subsections, we obtained the mean (service time) and variance estimation formulas for batched timestamps data with a given batch partition. However, in real timestamps data from a CPMS system the batch partition is not given and needs to be found. Even though we know that the timestamps data are batch submitted, due to various reasons (flexible scheduling, individual variabilities, job complexities, etc.) the batch patterns can be complicated and difficult to detect. From our Definition 1, a batch partition is just a special clustering on 1-dimensional data, and in theory any clustering algorithm can be applied for a batch searching. Also, the change detection analysis can be used to find the boundaries of the batches as the change-points. However, as our batch based estimators use the LSE in the second step modeling, and the consistency of the LSE requires that the number of batches should be able to go to infinity in order for the estimators to approach the true parameter values. Therefore, the number of batches should be large in general, as in weekly or daily batch patterns, and the sizes of the batches can be as small as 1, which are not the features that the existing clustering or change detection methods ([3], [4], [9], [10], [11], [12], [13], [18], [21], [24]) are designed for. In the following, we propose a simple batch searching algorithm for 1-dimensional data. From Remark 2, we know that the pattern for a batch partition that is in order should consists of a series of ordered between-batch "jumps" that separate the batches so that the between-batch "jumps" are significantly larger than all those of the within batch "jumps". The key point is to find the most significant minimum between-batch "jumps" so that we have maximum number of significant batches. The main idea is to use the data's natural order to define a kind of "z-value" for each "jump" between two successive numbers in the sorted data. Using those "z-values", we can select the minimum "jump" that is the most significant or by any given significant level, which determine a unique batch partition so that the between batch "jumps" are greater or equal to the minimum "jump". To define the " z-value", we sort all the jumps in decreasing order and compare each jump with all the other smaller jumps, which can be viewed as all the within batch jumps. The first level "z-value" for each jump can be defined as the normalized z-value by the within batch jumps. As we try to find as many as possible number of batches, it is important to determine the last significant z-value like a waterfall for a mountain stream. We use two way to find this "waterfall location" by using the differences of successive first level z-values to define the final "z-value" for each original jump. This final "z-value" will be used to select the minimum between batch jump.

Let $X := \{x_i | i = 1, 2, ..., L\}$ be a numeric vector of length L and $\alpha (< 1)$ be a given significance level, or a range of K is given instead of α. The batch searching algorithm is as follows:

Step 1: Sort X in increasing order $X := \{x_{(i)} | i = 1, 2, ..., L\}$.
Step 2: Form the "jumps" as a new numeric vector of length $L-1$, $Y := \{y_i = x_{(i+1)} - x_{(i)} | i = 1, 2, ..., L-1\}$, where $y_i \geq 0$, $i = 1, 2, ..., L-1$.
Step 3: Choose the unique numbers in Y and sort the resulting vector in decreasing order to get $U := \{u_k | k = 1, 2, ..., K\}$, where $u_k > u_{k+1}$, for $k = 1, 2, ..., K-1$, and $u_K \geq 0$.
Step 4: Define $V := \{v_k | k = 1, 2, ..., K-1\}$ by

$$v_k = \frac{u_k - mean(U_k)}{\sqrt{Var(U_k)}},$$

where $U_k = \{y_i | y_i < u_k, i = 1, 2, ..., L-1\} \cup \{u_k exp(-n_k u_k)\}$, n_k is the length of $\{y_i | y_i < u_k, i = 1, 2, ..., L-1\}$, which is viewed as a vector, and the mean(·) and Var(·) are the sample mean and variance estimators.

Step 5: Define $\bar{V} := \{\bar{v}_k | k = 1, 2, ..., K-2\}$ by $\bar{v}_1 = v_1 - v_2$, $\bar{v}_{K-2} = v_{K-1} - v_{K-2}$, $\bar{v}_k = (2v_k - v_{k+1} - v_{k-1})/2$, for $k = 2, ..., K-3$,
Step 5': Define $\bar{V} := \{\bar{v}_k | k = 1, 2, ..., K-2\}$ by $\bar{v}_k = v_k - v_{k+1}$, for $k = 1, 2, ..., K-2$.
Step 6: Normalize the $\bar{V} := \{\bar{v}_k | k = 1, 2, ..., K-2\}$ to get the "z-values", $Z := \{z_k | k = 1, 2, ..., K-2\}$, where

$$z_k = \frac{\bar{v}_k - mean(\bar{V})}{\sqrt{Var(\bar{V})}}.$$

Step 7: Let $k_\alpha = \max\{k | z_k > Z_\alpha\}$, where Z_α is the one-sided cut-off z-value of the standard normal corresponding to the significant level α with default value of 0.05, or $k_\alpha = \arg\max\{z_k | k \in R_k\}$ if a range of k, R_k, is given instead of a significant level α, and let $Y_\alpha = \{y_{i_r} = x_{(i_r+1)} - x_{(i_r)} | y_{i_r} \geq u_{k_\alpha}, r = 1, 2, ..., N_\alpha\}$, then the batch partition with the given significant level α can be defined by

$$B_\alpha = \{\min(X) \leq x_{(i_1)} < x_{(i_2)} < \cdots < x_{(i_{N_\alpha})} < x_{(L)} = \max(X)\},$$

and the corresponding $N_\alpha + 1$ batches are given by

$$B_1 = \{x_{(i)} | i \leq i_1\}, \ B_r = \{x_{(i)} | i_{r-1} < i \leq i_r\}, \ r = 2, ..., N_\alpha,$$

$$B_{N_\alpha+1} = \{x_{(i)} | i_{N_\alpha} < i \leq L\}.$$

Remark 3: The above algorithm provides an alternative Step (5') to Step (5) while the rest of Steps being the same to search the most significant batch partition, which we will call kBatch1 and kBatch2 in the simulation section below.

In this section, we established the theoretical basis and practical procedures for the analysis of the batched timestamps data from a CPMS system. Using our batch searching algorithm, we can find a batch partition B if it is not provided. With reasonable conditions (Proposition 2), we can calculate the corresponding Batch Information Matrix $[C, b]$. Using our batch model (1) (see Section 2.1), we formulate the mean service time $\hat{\mu}$ as the coefficient parameter in the linear regression model $b = C\mu + \eta$. Similar formulas are also provided for the service time variance $\hat{\sigma}^2$. With some assumptions, the LSE (6) or the constrained LSE (9) will be a consistent estimator $\hat{\mu}$ for μ. The quality of the estimator $\hat{\mu}$ depends on the degree of how well the assumptions are met.

3. SIMULATION STUDY

The simulations consist of the following four parts of evaluations: 1) the performance of the LSE estimators $\hat{\mu}$ and $\hat{\sigma}^2$ in (6) and (7); 2) the performance using the constrained LSE estimators $\tilde{\mu}$ and $\tilde{\sigma}^2$ in (9) when the true batch partitions are given; 3) the performance of our batch searching algorithms by comparing with other existing clustering methods; and 4) the performance of the estimators $\hat{\mu}$ and $\hat{\sigma}^2$ when the batch partitions are not given and are determined by our batch searching algorithms.

3.1 The Performance of $\hat{\mu}$ and $\hat{\sigma}^2$ with Given True Batch Partitions

In the simulations, we used the ideal service policy, FCFS, to generate the batched timestamps data with different parameters using two service time distributions, Exponential

Table 1. The means of the 100 mean and variance estimations for the Poisson distribution with number of batches $n = 250$.

Typ	Frq	$\hat{\mu}$	μ_1	μ_0	$\hat{\sigma}^2$	σ_1^2	σ_0^2
1	980	5.33	5.96	6.00	26.01	35.53	36.00
2	910	7.28	8.00	8.00	49.71	64.19	64.00
3	170	9.20	10.03	10.00	76.98	99.53	100.00
4	50	10.59	11.01	11.00	83.57	118.59	121.00

Table 2. The estimation (mean and variance) standard errors with the same 100 simulated datasets as in Table 1.

Typ	Frq	$se(\mu_1)$	$\bar{se}(\hat{\mu})$	$se(\hat{\mu})$	$se(\sigma_1^2)$	$\bar{se}(\hat{\sigma}^2)$	$se(\hat{\sigma}^2)$
1	980	0.51	0.50	0.47	13.30	15.38	12.57
2	910	0.48	0.54	0.52	16.26	16.64	14.21
3	170	1.57	1.55	1.53	45.10	47.46	43.89
4	50	2.63	2.97	2.86	73.34	90.86	80.94

(for Poisson process) and Normal, with the Uniform distribution for arrival times.

We ran 100 replications to report the average estimation results $(\hat{\mu}, \hat{\sigma}^2)$ for the estimations of the mean and the variance respectively. The parameters in the simulated data for the replications are as follows: the samples size is 2110 with four job types with frequencies 980, 910, 170, 50, the true means are 6, 8, 10, 11 respectively for the four job type in both the Poisson and Normal data, and the variances of 4, 9, 16, 9 for the Normal. The number of batches in the data are 250. The parameters are chosen based on a yearly workload with daily batches. The 250 batches are determined by equal length intervals so that each batch consists of all the jobs whose departure timestamps fall into each of the equal interval. As the within batch timestamps can only provide information for the job types and batch departure time, we only use the batch information by Eq. (6) and Eq. (7) to estimate the means and variances for the four job types. We use all the true simulated timestamps to get the sample mean and variance (μ_1 and σ_1^2) as the "Ground truth" for comparisons. The true mean and variance parameters (μ_0 and σ_0^2) as well as the frequency parameters (Frq) for each type (Typ) in the simulation are also listed in Table 1.

The mean and variance estimations have the following estimated standard errors as listed in Table 2, where $se(\mu_1)$ and $se(\sigma_1^2)$, which serve as the "Ground truth" for error estimation comparison, are the standard deviations of the 100 mean and variance estimations used in Table 1, $\bar{se}(\hat{\mu})$ and $\bar{se}(\hat{\sigma}^2)$ are the means of the estimated standard errors from Corollary 1, $se(\hat{\mu})$ and $se(\hat{\sigma}^2)$ are the means of the 100 estimated standard errors by Proposition 4.

Similar results for Normal distribution are listed in Tables 3 and 4.

Table 3. The means of the 100 mean and variance estimations for the Normal distribution with number of batches $n = 250$.

Typ	Frq	$\hat{\mu}$	μ_1	μ_0	$\hat{\sigma}^2$	σ_1^2	σ_0^2
1	980	5.92	5.99	6.00	3.87	4.00	4.00
2	910	7.87	8.01	8.00	8.79	9.01	9.00
3	170	9.83	9.97	10.00	14.30	15.77	16.00
4	50	11.01	11.03	11.00	9.23	8.92	9.00

Table 4. The estimation (mean and variance) errors with the same 100 simulated datasets as in Table 3.

Typ	Frq	$se(\mu_1)$	$\bar{se}(\hat{\mu})$	$se(\hat{\mu})$	$se(\sigma_1^2)$	$\bar{se}(\hat{\sigma}^2)$	$se(\hat{\sigma}^2)$
1	980	0.18	0.19	0.18	1.99	2.05	1.90
2	910	0.19	0.20	0.21	2.13	2.21	2.25
3	170	0.66	0.58	0.59	6.59	6.22	6.44
4	50	0.97	1.09	1.06	10.13	11.75	11.27

Table 5. For Poisson distribution.

Typ	Frq	$\hat{\mu}$	$\tilde{\mu}$	μ_1	$\hat{\sigma}^2$	$\tilde{\sigma}^2$	σ_1^2
1	980	5.33	5.90	5.96	26.08	35.10	35.53
2	910	7.28	8.03	8.00	49.86	63.83	64.19
3	170	9.20	10.11	10.03	76.60	95.11	99.53
4	50	10.59	11.60	11.01	79.33	99.10	118.59

Note. The frequencies in the tables are close to a real dataset while the true mean and variance parameters are hypothetical. As the number of batches ($n = 250$ as in the above Tables) is the actual sample size in the LSE (6) based on the linear model $b = C\mu + \eta$, the accuracy of the estimations will depend on the number of batches.

3.2 The Improvements of the Constrained LSE (Eq. 9)

The constrained LSE (Eq. 9) is more appropriate due to the meanings of the linear coefficient parameters in our batch model. With the same mean and variance parameters as in Tables 1-4, we calculated the mean and variance estimations by using the constrained LSE ($\tilde{\mu}$ and $\tilde{\sigma}^2$) as well as $\hat{\mu}$, $\hat{\sigma}^2$, μ_1 and σ_1^2 as in Tables 1 and 3 for each one of the 100 simulated datasets. Tables 5 and 6 list their mean values for Poisson and Normal distributions respectively.

From these Tables, we see that the simulations show improvements of the (unconstrained) LSE over the Constrained LSE (Tables 5-6, column 3 and 4 respectively), in particular for the Poisson distribution (Table 5). Especially, the Constrained LSE method overcomes the weakness of the LSE method in variance estimation for the Poisson distributed data as we noticed from the last subsection. Thus, we improved the method so that the estimations will not be affected too much due to the known data distributions.

3.3 The Performance of the Batch Searching Algorithm

With each of the given mean number of centers, we simulated 100 batched datasets whose true number of batches are generated by a Poisson sampling with the given mean number of centers as the parameter. The first part of the simulation is to see if our new methods (kBatch1 and kBatch2) can find the true number of batches. Table 7 lists the results based on the 100 datasets in each of the five mean centers(MC) for five different methods [3], [9], [10], [11], [12],

Table 6. For Normal distribution.

Typ	Frq	$\hat{\mu}$	$\tilde{\mu}$	μ_1	$\hat{\sigma}^2$	$\tilde{\sigma}^2$	σ_1^2
1	980	5.92	6.01	5.99	3.90	4.09	4.00
2	910	7.87	7.99	8.01	8.83	9.18	9.01
3	170	9.83	9.97	9.97	14.35	14.87	15.77
4	50	11.01	11.17	11.03	7.41	7.74	8.92

Table 7. The square roots of MSE for the batch number determinations

MC	apclust	pamk	Mclust	kBatch1	kBatch2
5	0	0.1	3.33	0	0
20	9.17	11.53	1.11	0	0
50	39.03	48.38	1.36	0	0
100	88.68	99.13	13.90	0	0
200	186.46	197.57	58.17	0.1	0.1

Table 8. Computational times (in seconds) for the above simulations for each methods

MC	apclust	pamk	Mclust	kBatch1	kBatch2
5	295.04	192.19	14.78	3.62	3.90
20	325.23	128.21	143.85	3.6	4.00
50	368.09	188.31	831.62	4.15	4.00
100	399.56	271.51	6487.86	4.38	4.43
200	527.41	426.01	21071.60	5.24	5.38

[13], where the square root of Mean Square Error (MSE) is reported, which can be viewed as the (number of center) estimation standard error.

The speed for a searching algorithm is also an important issue. During the above simulations, we recorded the times for each methods and each mean centers on our machine, as in the following Table 8.

The second part of the simulation is to see the accuracy of the batch (cluster) classification when the true number of batches is given. With the same simulated datasets as above, we compare the classification errors of our methods with two commonly used methods, the Mclust and kmeans. Table 9 lists the mean classification error rates for the four methods.

Based on the simulated results in this subsection, we see that our batch searching methods (kBatch1 and kBatch2) perform better than the commonly used existing methods. Table1 shows that our methods are more accurate in finding the true numbers of clusters (batches); Table 2 shows that our methods are quicker to find the numbers of centers; and Table 3 shows that when the true number of clusters are given, our methods have smaller classification errors.

4. REAL DATA APPLICATION

As the methodology is motivated from the data from the SSAs CPMS system, we apply the method to one dataset from the system. The dataset consists of all the jobs from one reviewer within a specified period. It has three columns: arrival time (or receiving time), departure time (or submission time) and types of the jobs. Each job type represents a sub-job, which we call the status of a case, for the job of processing the whole case. Figure 1 below plots about 100 samples in the data, where each horizontal segment represents

Table 9. Mean classification error rates for 4 methods

MC	Mclust	kmeans	kBatch1	kBatch2
5	0	0.37	0	0
20	0.09	0.37	0	0
50	0.14	0.37	0	0
100	0.16	0.36	0	0
200	0.17	0.35	0	0

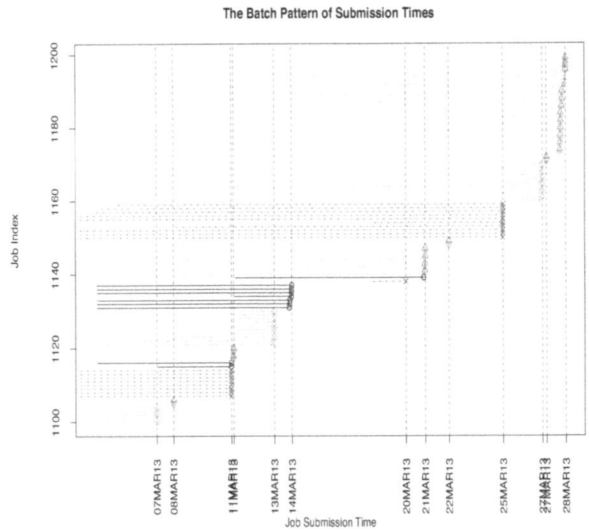

Figure 1: The plot for job arrival and departure times

the arrival and departure times and its color and line style represent the job type (or status). The submission times (departure times) in the data show an approximately daily batch pattern. The vertical dotted blue lines are drawn at the ends of the batches, which are determined by our batch searching algorithm (see section 2.4) and labeled by the submission dates.

From the Figure, we see that the jobs within each of the batches were submitted at almost the same time, and the submitted time for each individual job in each batch might not be the true finished time of the job. Therefore, the sample mean and variance calculations cannot be directly applied to the data.

For illustration, a monthly batch (combining the batches whose departure times are in the same month) is constructed and the estimated and observed batch times are plotted in the following Figure 2.

In the Figure, the estimated batch times, the blue triangles, are calculated as $\hat{b}_i = \sum_{j=1}^{m} c_{i,j}\hat{\mu}_j$, where $C = \left(c_{i,j}\right)_{14,6}$ is the Batch Counting Matrix (data not shown here), $\hat{\mu} = (\hat{\mu}_1, \hat{\mu}_2, ..., \hat{\mu}_6)'$ is the vector of the estimated mean service times for the 6 job types. The estimated batch times would reflect the equivalent working time for the jobs in the batches if the true mean working time were the estimated mean, and the observed batch times, the red circles, are the calendar times of the batches. So the interpretation of the Figure is that if a blue triangle (the estimated batch time) is above the corresponding red circle (the observed batch time), the reviewer worked more than his/her own yearly average on that batch (month). For example, in Figure 2, it seems that this reviewer worked more on most of the months except on the two Novembers (29Nov12, 21NOV13), further information is needed to fully understand the monthly variations for the reviewer.

Based on the simulation in the last section, our Batch method can be used to estimate the means and variances

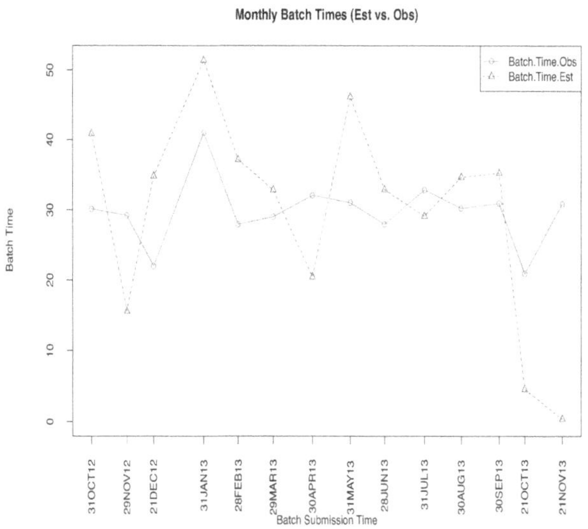

Figure 2: Monthly batch times (Estimated vs. Observed)

(of the service time in the process system) for all the major job types in the batched timestamps data. The following results are based on our Batch method applied on this real dataset. In brackets are the estimated standard errors.

In the table, the column names (Type1, Type2, Type3, Type4, Type5, Type6) are the job types (the true status codes are not used), where Type6 is the combined other job types in the dataset with small frequencies. The time unit in the table is Calendar day. For example, in average this reviewer can finish "Type3" about 8 ($\approx 1/0.12352$) "Type3" jobs per Calendar day while the same reviewer could finish about 80 "Type2" jobs per Calendar day if s/he would have worked on a single job type. For this reviewer, the flexible working schedule (Type5 = 0.32 day) seems more efficient than the regular schedule (Type4 = 0.38 day), where Type4 and Type5 are the same type of job with different working schedules. From the standard errors of the mean estimations, one can see the estimations for Type1,Type4 and Type5 are more accurate than those for Type2, Type3, and Type6, which may reflect the nature of the job types. The estimations for the variances and their standard errors have similar pattern but with less accuracy than that for the mean estimation as we observed in the simulations of the method. Since we used the non-negative constraints in our parameter estimation, the estimation of 0 for the variance of Type2 is likely due to the small mean estimation of Type2, the non-negative constraints and some possible outlier batches where the reviewer might take leaves. As we do not have further information about the reviewers working time over all the periods covered in the data, we can not give any further explanations. The batch information matrix, including the number of jobs for each type, the batch time and the batch departure time, is not shown here and can be obtained by request. Using the estimated mean service times as in Table 5 and the numbers of jobs for each job types, we can estimate batch time for each batch.

Table 10. The mean and variance estimation based on our Batch model method

Est.	Type1	Type2	Type3	Type4	Type5	Type6
mean	0.12	0.01	0.12	0.38	0.32	0.17
se_m	(0.02)	(0.19)	(0.19)	(0.03)	(0.04)	(0.11)
var	0.10	0.00	0.21	0.25	0.13	1.01
se_v	(0.04)	(0.38)	(0.39)	(0.07)	(0.08)	(0.34)
Freq	585	493	422	367	330	232

5. DISCUSSION

We introduced a batch model for batched timestamps data analysis using the batch information matrix to overcome the challenge due to the unreliable information within each batch. In particular, when the batched timestamps data comes from a case processing system with three columns (arrival time, departure time, and job type), our method can be used to estimate the means and variances of the service time for each of the major job types. When each data record is a true observation (the arrival time and departure time are the true arrival and departure time of the job), one can use the single timestamps batch partition and our method becomes the sample mean and variance formula. Our simulations shown the method gives reasonable estimations under various typical situations. As the batch partition is not given in real data, we developed a batch searching algorithm, which fully take the advantage of the 1-dimensional batched timestamps data to make the algorithm more accurate and computationally more efficient than some existing clustering algorithms. The results from the real data application will be further verified. As our batch method just uses the LSE for linear model with the batch information matrix extracted from batched timestamps data, there are certainly a lot of different ways to further improve the method. We suggest two directions for further developments. The first is to find ways to improve the quality of the batch information matrix. The more accurate the time spent on the jobs within a batch represents the time of the batch, the higher the quality is. The second is to find more effective ways for the analysis of the batch information matrix extracted from some batched timestamps data. While we choose the generalized LSE method due to the fact that in the batch information matrix, the numbers of the jobs for the types are linearly related to the total times of the batches, there are certainly many other ways, parametric or non-parametric, to explore for the improvements of the method. After the method is fully developed, it can be applied to analyze the large scale batched timestamps data like the one we currently have as well as to other Federal Agency's data.

6. ACKNOWLEDGMENTS

This research was supported by Social Security Administration and National Institutes of Health (SSA-NIH) Interagency Agreements and by the NIH intramural research program. The authors and co-authors have no financial or other conflicts of interest to disclose that may bias the reporting of the results presented in this study.

7. REFERENCES

[1] Ahmadi, J.H., Ahmadi, R.H., Dasu, S., Tang, C.S. (1992). Batching and scheduling jobs on batch and discrete processors, *Operations Research*, **39**, 750-763.

[2] Armero, C., & Conesa, D. (2004). Statistical performance of a multiclass bulk production queueing system, *European Journal of Operational Research*, **158**(3), 649-661.

[3] Bodenhofer, U., Kothmeier, A. and Hochreiter, S. (2011). APCluster: an R package for affinity propagation clustering. *Bioinformatics*, **27**, 2463-2464. doi:10.1093/bioinformatics/btr406.

[4] Chen, J. and Gupta, A. K. (2000) Parametric statistical change point analysis, Birkhauser

[5] Cheng, T.C.E. and Wang, G. (1998). Batching and scheduling to minimize the makespan in the two-machine flowshop, *IIE Transactions*, **30**, 447-453.

[6] Comon, P., & Jutten, C. (2010). *Handbook of Blind Source Separation: Independent component analysis and applications*, Academic press.

[7] Coons, S.A. (1978). Constrained least-squares, *Computers & Graphics*, **3** (1), 43-47.

[8] Daley, D. J., & Servi, L. D. (1992). Exploiting Markov chains to infer queue length from transactional data, *Journal of applied probability*, 713-732.

[9] Fraley, C. and Raftery, A.E. (2002). Model-based clustering, discriminant analysis and density estimation, *Journal of the American Statistical Association*, **97**, 611-631.

[10] Fraley, C., Raftery, A.E., Murphy, T.B., and Scrucca, L. (2012). *mclust Version 4 for R: Normal Mixture Modeling for Model-Based Clustering, Classification, and Density Estimation.* Technical Report No. 597, Department of Statistics, University of Washington

[11] Frey, B.J. and Dueck, D. (2007). Clustering by passing messages between data points. *Science*, **315**, 972-977. doi:10.1126/science.1136800.

[12] Hennig, C. (2004) Asymmetric linear dimension reduction for classification. *Journal of Computational and Graphical Statistics*, **13**, 930-945 .

[13] Hennig, C. (2005) A method for visual cluster validation. In: Weihs, C. and Gaul, W. (eds.): *Classification - The Ubiquitous Challenge.* Springer, Heidelberg, 153-160.

[14] Kleinrock, L. (1976). *Queueing Systems Volume 1-2: Theory and Computer Applications*, John Wiley & Sons New York.

[15] Larson, R. C. (1990). The queue inference engine: deducing queue statistics from transactional data. *Management Science*, **36**(5), 586-601.

[16] Lee, D. D., & Seung, H. S. (1999) Learning the parts of objects by non-negative matrix factorization. *Nature*, **401**(6755), 788-791.

[17] Lee, D. D., & Seung, H. S. (2001) Algorithms for non-negative matrix factorization. *Advances in neural information processing systems*, **13**, 556-562.

[18] Liu, H., Liu, T., Wu, J., Tao, D., & Fu, Y. (2015). Spectral ensemble clustering. *In Proceedings of the 21th ACM SIGKDD International Conference on Knowledge Discovery and Data Mining*, 715-724. ACM.

[19] Nazarathy, Y., & Pollet, P. K. (2011). Parameter and State Estimation in Queues and Related Stochastic Models: A Bibliography. *http : //www.maths.uq.edu.au/ pkp/papers/Qest/ QEstAnnBib.pdf*

[20] (2015). OIG report: Fiscal Year 2015 Inspector General Statement on the Social Security Administration's Major Management and Performance Challenges. *https : //oig.ssa.gov/sites/default/files/audit/full/pdf/ A − 02 − 16 − 50118_0.pdf*

[21] Qahtan, A. A., Alharbi, B., Wang, S., & Zhang, X. (2015). A pca-based change detection framework for multidimensional data streams: Change detection in multidimensional data streams. *In Proceedings of the 21th ACM SIGKDD International Conference on Knowledge Discovery and Data Mining*, 935-944. ACM.

[22] Rao, C. R., Toutenburg, H., & Shalabh, H. (2008). *Linear Models and Generalizations: Least Squares and Alternatives.*

[23] Soetaert K., Van den Meersche, K., van Oevelen, D. (2009). limSolve: Solving Linear Inverse Models. R-package version 1.5.1

[24] Song, X., Wu, M., Jermaine, C., & Ranka, S. (2007). Statistical change detection for multi-dimensional data. *In Proceedings of the 13th ACM SIGKDD international conference on Knowledge discovery and data mining*, 667-676. ACM.

[25] Sutton, C., & Jordan, M. I. (2011). Bayesian inference for queueing networks and modeling of internet services. *The Annals of Applied Statistics*, **5**(1), 254-282.

[26] Van De Geer, S. (2005). Least squares estimation, *Encyclopedia of Statistics in Behavioral Science*, John Wiley & Sons, Ltd, Chichester.

[27] Wakefield, J. (2013). *Bayesian and frequentist regression methods*, Springer Science & Business Media.

Collaborative Knowledge Base Embedding for Recommender Systems

Fuzheng Zhang[†], Nicholas Jing Yuan[†], Defu Lian[‡], Xing Xie[†], Wei-Ying Ma[†]
[†]Microsoft Research
[‡]Big Data Research Center, University of Electronic Science and Technology of China
{fuzzhang,nicholas.yuan,xingx,wyma}@microsoft.com,
dove.ustc@gmail.com

ABSTRACT

Among different recommendation techniques, collaborative filtering usually suffer from limited performance due to the sparsity of user-item interactions. To address the issues, auxiliary information is usually used to boost the performance. Due to the rapid collection of information on the web, the knowledge base provides heterogeneous information including both structured and unstructured data with different semantics, which can be consumed by various applications. In this paper, we investigate how to leverage the heterogeneous information in a knowledge base to improve the quality of recommender systems. First, by exploiting the knowledge base, we design three components to extract items' semantic representations from structural content, textual content and visual content, respectively. To be specific, we adopt a heterogeneous network embedding method, termed as TransR, to extract items' structural representations by considering the heterogeneity of both nodes and relationships. We apply stacked denoising auto-encoders and stacked convolutional auto-encoders, which are two types of deep learning based embedding techniques, to extract items' textual representations and visual representations, respectively. Finally, we propose our final integrated framework, which is termed as **C**ollaborative **K**nowledge Base **E**mbedding (**CKE**), to jointly learn the latent representations in collaborative filtering as well as items' semantic representations from the knowledge base. To evaluate the performance of each embedding component as well as the whole system, we conduct extensive experiments with two real-world datasets from different scenarios. The results reveal that our approaches outperform several widely adopted state-of-the-art recommendation methods.

Keywords

Recommender Systems, Knowledge Base Embedding, Collaborative Joint Learning

1. INTRODUCTION

Due to the explosive growth of information, recommender systems have been playing an increasingly important role in online services. Among different recommendation strategies, collaborative filtering (CF) based methods, which make use of historical interactions or preferences, have made significant success [23]. However, CF methods usually suffer from limited performance when user-item interactions are very sparse, which is very common for scenarios such as online shopping where the item set is extremely large. In addition, CF methods can not recommend new items since these items have never received any feedbacks from users in the past. To tackle these problems, hybrid recommender systems, which combine collaborative filtering and auxiliary information such as item content, can usually achieve better recommendation results and have gained increasing popularity in recent years [2].

Over the past years, more and more semantic data are published following the Linked Data principles[1], by connecting various information from different topic domains such as people, books, musics, movies and geographical locations in a unified global data space. These heterogeneous data, interlinked with each other, forms a huge information resource repository called knowledge base. Several typical knowledge bases have been constructed, including academic projects such as YAGO[2], NELL[3], DBpedia[4], and DeepDive[5], as well as commercial projects, such as Microsoft's Satori[6] and Google's Knowledge Graph[7]. Using the heterogeneous connected information from the knowledge base can help to develop insights on problems which are difficult to uncover with data from a single domain [6]. To date, information retrieval [9], community detection [25], sentiment analysis [4] - to name a few - are the noteworthy applications that successfully leverage the knowledge base.

Actually, since a knowledge base provides rich information including both structured and unstructured data with different semantics, the usage of the knowledge base within the context of hybrid recommender systems are attracting increasing attention. For example, Yu et al. [30] uses a heterogeneous information network to represent users, items, item attributes, and the interlinked relationships in a knowledge base. They extract meta-path based latent features from the network structure and apply Bayesian ranking optimization based collaborative filtering to solve the entity recommendation problem. Grad-Gyenge et al. [11] extended collaborative filtering by adopting a spreading activation based technique to incorporate a knowledge base's network features for recommender systems' rating prediction task. However, previous studies have not

KDD '16, August 13-17, 2016, San Francisco, CA, USA

DOI: http://dx.doi.org/10.1145/2939672.2939673

[1] http://linkeddata.org/
[2] https://www.mpi-inf.mpg.de/departments/databases-and-information-systems/research/yago-naga/yago/
[3] http://rtw.ml.cmu.edu/rtw/
[4] http://wiki.dbpedia.org/
[5] http://i.stanford.edu/hazy/deepdive/
[6] http://searchengineland.com/library/bing/bing-satori
[7] http://www.google.com/insidesearch/features/search/knowledge.html

fully exploited the potential of the knowledge base since they suffer from the following limitations: 1) only utilize the single network structure information of the knowledge base while ignore other important signals such as items' textual and visual information. 2) rely on heavy and tedious feature engineering process to extract features from the knowledge base.

To address the above issues, in this paper, we propose a novel recommendation framework to integrate collaborative filtering with items' different semantic representations from the knowledge base. For a knowledge base, except for the network structure information, we also consider items' textual content and visual content (e.g., movie's poster). To avoid heavy and tedious manual feature extractions, we design three embedding components to automatically extract items' semantic representations from the knowledge base's structural content, textual content and visual content, respectively. To be specific, we first apply a network embedding approach to extract items' structural representations by considering the heterogeneity of both nodes and relationships. Next, we adopt stacked denoising auto-encoders and stacked convolutional auto-encoders, which are two types of deep learning based embedding techniques, to extract items' textual representations and visual representations, respectively. Finally, to integrate collaborative filtering with items' semantic representations from the knowledge base smoothly, we propose our final framework, which is termed as Collaborative Knowledge Base Embedding (**CKE**), to learn different representations in a unified model jointly.

Our empirical studies consist of multiple parts. First, we conduct several experiments to evaluate the performance of three knowledge base embedding components, respectively. Next, we evaluate the effectiveness of our integrated framework by comparing with several competitive baselines.

The key contributions of this paper are summarized as the following:

- To the best of our knowledge, this is the first work leveraging structural content, textual content and visual content from the knowledge base for recommender systems.
- We apply embedding methods including heterogeneous network embedding and deep learning embedding to automatically extract semantic representations from the knowledge base. The learned representations may also be used for tasks other than recommendation.
- By performing knowledge base embedding and collaborative filtering jointly, **CKE** can simultaneously extract feature representations from the knowledge base and capture the implicit relationship between users and items.
- Based on two real-word datasets, we have conducted extensive experiments to evaluate the effectiveness of our framework. The results reveal that our approaches significantly outperform baseline methods.

The rest of this paper is organized as follows. Section 2 introduces the preliminary concepts and present our recommendation problem. Section 3 gives an overview of our framework. Section 4 delves into the usage of embedding components to extract representations from the knowledge base. In Section 5, we discuss how to effectively integrate collaborative filtering with knowledge base embedding into a unified model. The empirical results are discussed in Section 6, followed by a brief review of related work in Section 7 and a conclusion of this paper in Section 8.

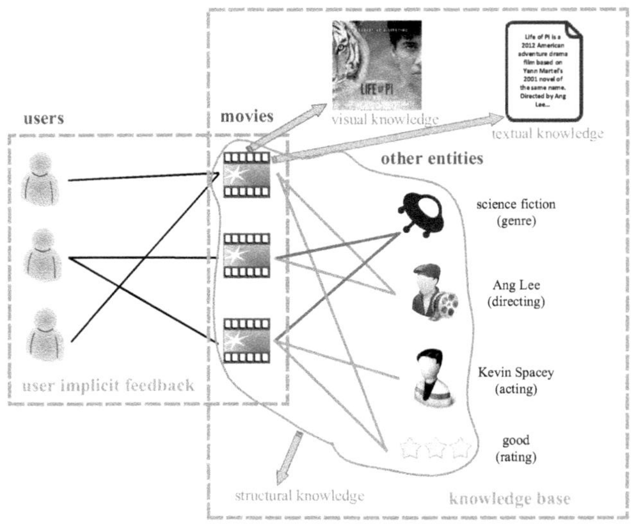

Figure 1: Illustration of a snippet of user implicit feedback data and knowledge base data.

2. PRELIMINARY

In this section, we will first clarify some terminologies used in this paper, and then explicitly present our problem.

2.1 User Implicit Feedback

The recommendation task considered in this paper are targeted for implicit feedback. Assume there are m users and n items, we define the user implicit feedback matrix $\mathbf{R} \in \mathbb{R}^{m \times n}$ as

$$R_{ij} = \begin{cases} 1, & \text{if (user } i, \text{item } j) \text{ interactions have been observed;} \\ 0, & \text{otherwise.} \end{cases} \tag{1}$$

where the value 1 in matrix $\mathbf{R}$ represents the interactions between users and items, e.g., users watched a movie or users searched a book in the search engine. Note that the value 1 in the implicit feedback data does not mean that users actually like the items. Actually a user searched a book because he is interested in the book but he might probably dislike the book after browsing the related information on the Internet. Similarly, the value 0 in $\mathbf{R}$ does not mean that the users dislike the items, but can be regarded as a mixture of negative feedbacks (users are not interested in such items) and potential interactions (users are not aware of such items).

2.2 Knowledge Base

Actually, we are interested in leveraging the knowledge base for enhancing the quality of recommender systems, therefore items in recommender systems are mapped to entities in the knowledge base (e.g., a movie item can usually be mapped to an entity describing this movie), and these entities are termed as **item entities** in this article.

We consider the information stored in the knowledge base can be divided into three parts: structural knowledge, textual knowledge and visual knowledge. The detailed definition of each part is given as follows:

Definition 1: ***Structural knowledge***. This knowledge can be regarded as a heterogeneous network with multiple types of entities and multiple types of links to express the structure of the knowledge base. For movie recommendation, entities usually include movie items and corresponding attributes (e.g., the genre "science fiction" and the actor "Kevin Space"), and links describe the relationship between these entities (e.g., "acting" behavior and "rating" behav-

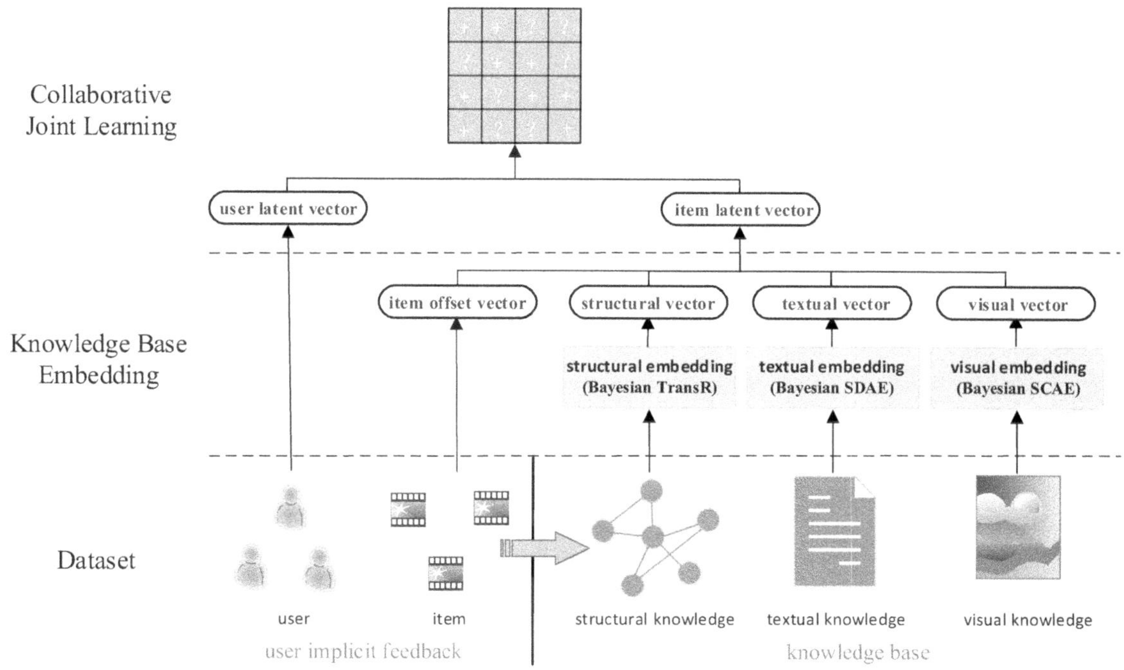

Figure 2: The flowchart of the proposed Collaborative Knowledge Base Embedding (CKE) framework for recommender systems

ior). The network structure implies some similarity between item entities, which is most probably useful for recommendation.

Definition 2: ***Textual Knowledge***. For an item entity such as book or movie in the knowledge base, we use the textual summary to represent the textual knowledge, which usually gives the main topics of this book or this movie.

Definition 3: ***Visual Knowledge***. For an item entity, except for previous textual description, there are usually some images in the knowledge base, we use a book's front cover image or a movie's poster image to represent its visual knowledge.

User implicit feedback interactions and structural knowledge serve as the structural features of an item, while textual knowledge and visual knowledge serve as the content features. A snippet of the knowledge base with three kinds of knowledge as well as user implicit feedback are presented in Figure 1.

2.3 Problem Formulation

We define our recommendation problem in this paper as follows: Given a knowledge base with structural knowledge, textual knowledge and visual knowledge, as well as user implicit feedback, we aim to recommend each user with a ranked list of items he will be interested.

3. OVERVIEW

In this article, by fully exploiting the structural knowledge, textual knowledge and visual knowledge in the knowledge base, we propose a Collaborative Knowledge Base Embedding model (**CKE**) for supporting our recommendation task. Our model mainly consists of two steps: 1) knowledge base embedding and 2) collaborative joint learning.

In the knowledge base embedding step, we extract an item entity's three embedding vectors from structural knowledge, textual knowledge and visual knowledge, respectively. These embedding vectors indicate an item entity's latent representation in each domain. For structural embedding component, we apply a network embedding procedure (Bayesian TransR) to find the latent representation from the heterogeneous network in the structural knowledge. For textual embedding component, we apply an unsupervised deep learning model called Bayesian stacked denoising auto-encoder (Bayesian SDAE) [29] to find the latent representation from the textual knowledge. Similarly, we apply another unsupervised deep learning model called Bayesian stacked convolutional autoencoder (Bayesian SCAE) to find the latent representation from the visual knowledge.

In the collaborative joint learning step, an item's latent vector is finally represented as the integration of three embedding vectors from the knowledge base as well as a latent offset vector. The final item latent vector represents an item's knowledge from structural content, textual content, visual content as well as historical user-item interactions. Then we use collaborative filtering by optimizing the pair-wise ranking between items to learn both user latent vectors and item latent vectors. Final recommendation is generated from these user latent vectors and item latent vectors.

The flowchart of our framework is presented in Figure 2. Knowledge base embedding and collaborative joint learning will be detailed in Section 4 and Section 5, respectively.

4. KNOWLEDGE BASE EMBEDDING

In this section, by leveraging network embedding and deep learning embedding, we present the details of how we extract an item entity's representations from structural knowledge, textual knowledge and visual knowledge, respectively.

4.1 Structural Embedding

The heterogeneous network encodes structured information of entities and their rich relations. To capture this structured knowledge, a promising approach is to embed this heterogeneous network into a continuous vector space while preserving certain information of the network. In this subsection, we first briefly review a state-of-the-art network embedding method called TransR [15], and then give a Bayesian formulation of TransR for our task.

First, to represent the structural knowledge, we use an undirected

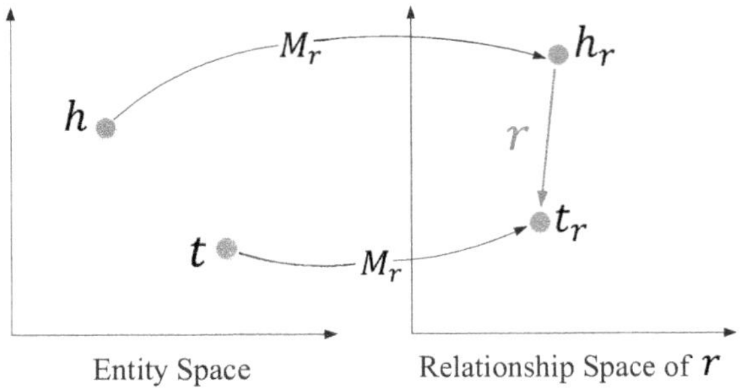

Figure 3: Illustration of TransR for structural embedding

graph $G = (\mathcal{V}, \mathcal{E})$, where $\mathcal{V} = \{v_1, \ldots, v_{|V|}\}$ is a set of vertices referring to different entities and $\mathcal{E}$ is a set of edges referring to different types of relation between these entities.

TransR [15] is a state-of-the-art embedding approach for heterogeneous network. Being different from other methods which assume embedding of entities and relations within the same space $\mathbb{R}^k$, TransR represents entities and relations in distinct semantic space bridged by relation-specific matrices. In TransR, for each triple (v_h, r, v_t) in the network (v_h and v_t are two linked entities, r is the type of edge between them), entities are embedded into vectors $\mathbf{v}_h, \mathbf{v}_t \in \mathbb{R}^k$ and relation is embedded into $\mathbf{r} \in \mathbb{R}^d$. For each relation r, we set a projection matrix $\mathbf{M}_r \in \mathbb{R}^{k\times d}$, which projects entities from entity space to relation space. As shown in Figure 3, the projected vectors of entities are defined as

$$\mathbf{v}_h^r = \mathbf{v}_h \mathbf{M}_r, \qquad \mathbf{v}_t^r = \mathbf{v}_t \mathbf{M}_r. \tag{2}$$

The score function of this triple is correspondingly defined as

$$f_r(v_h, v_t) = ||\mathbf{v}_h^r + \mathbf{r} - \mathbf{v}_t^r||_2^2. \tag{3}$$

Similar to [22], we use a sigmoid function to calculate the pairwise triple ranking probability instead of margin-based objective function adopted in original TransR. Then we extend TransR to a Bayesian version and propose the generative process as follows:

1. For each entity v, draw $\mathbf{v} \sim \mathcal{N}(\mathbf{0}, \lambda_v^{-1}\mathbf{I})$.
2. For each relation r, draw $\mathbf{r} \sim \mathcal{N}(\mathbf{0}, \lambda_r^{-1}\mathbf{I})$ and $\mathbf{M}_r \sim \mathcal{N}(\mathbf{0}, \lambda_M^{-1}\mathbf{I})$, respectively.
3. For each quadruple $(v_h, r, v_t, v_{t'}) \in \mathcal{S}$, draw from the probability $\sigma(f_r(v_h, v_t) - f_r(v_h, v_{t'}))$, where $\mathcal{S}$ is the set of quadruples satisfying that (v_h, r, v_t) is a correct triple and $(v_h, r, v_{t'})$ is an incorrect triple. $\sigma(x) := \frac{1}{1+e^{-x}}$ is the logistic sigmoid function.

It is routine to corrupt correct triple (v_h, r, v_t) by replacing one entity with another entity of the same type, and construct incorrect triple $(v_h, r, v_{t'})$. Note that step 3 implies the fact that when score function of a correct triple is larger than that of an incorrect triple, the quadruple is more likely to be sampled.

For each item entity j, we use embedding vector $\mathbf{v}_j$ from Bayesian TransR to denote its structural representation.

4.2 Textual Embedding

In this subsection, we investigate how to apply an unsupervised deep learning model called stacked denoising auto-encoders (SDAE) to get item entities' textual representations from the textual knowledge.

SDAE [27] is a feedback neural network for learning the representation of the corrupted input data by learning to predict the clean itself in the output. Before presenting the model detail, we give the notations used in SDAE. Assume the number of network layers is L_t, we use matrix $\mathbf{X}_l$ to represent the output of layer l in SDAE. Note that we use the last layer output $\mathbf{X}_{L_t}$ to represent the original clean textual knowledge of all item entities, where the j-th row is the bag-of-words vector $\mathbf{X}_{L_t,j*}$ for item entity j. Similarly, we use matrix $\mathbf{X}_0$ to represent the noise-corrupted matrix (randomly masking some entries of $\mathbf{X}_{L_t}$ by making them zero). $\mathbf{W}_l$ and $\mathbf{b}_l$ are weight parameter and bias parameter, respectively, for layer l.

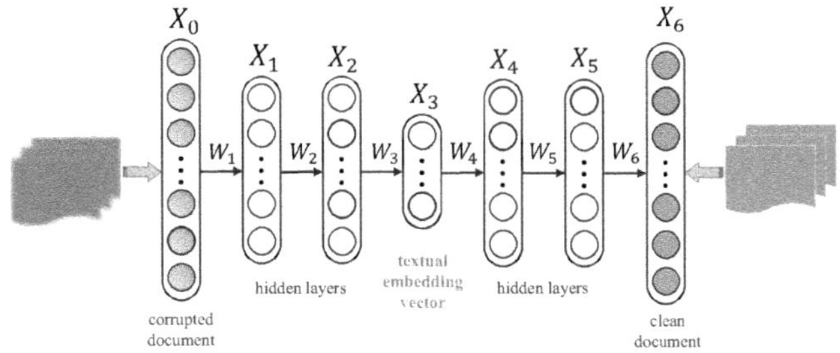

Figure 4: Illustration of a 6-layer SDAE for textual embedding

Figure 4 gives the illustration of a 6-layer SDAE for our textual embedding component. As shown in this figure, the first $\frac{L_t}{2}$ layers of the network (from $\mathbf{X}_0$ to $\mathbf{X}_3$) usually acts as encoder part, which maps the corrupted input $\mathbf{X}_0$ to a latent compact representation $\mathbf{X}_3$, and the last $\frac{L_t}{2}$ layers (from $\mathbf{X}_3$ to $\mathbf{X}_6$) usually acts as the decoder part, which recovers the clean input $\mathbf{X}_6$ from the latent representation $\mathbf{X}_3$.

Similar to [29], given that both the clean input $\mathbf{X}_{L_t}$ and the corrupted input $\mathbf{X}_0$ are observed, we present the generative process of each layer l in Bayesian SDAE as follows:

1. For weight parameter $\mathbf{W}_l$, draw $\mathbf{W}_l \sim \mathcal{N}(\mathbf{0}, \lambda_W^{-1}\mathbf{I})$.
2. For bias parameter, draw $\mathbf{b}_l \sim \mathcal{N}(\mathbf{0}, \lambda_b^{-1}\mathbf{I})$.
3. For the output of the layer, draw $\mathbf{X}_l \sim \mathcal{N}(\sigma(\mathbf{X}_{l-1}\mathbf{W}_l + \mathbf{b}_l), \lambda_X^{-1}\mathbf{I})$

The embedding vector in the middle layer, i.e., $\mathbf{X}_{3,j*}$ in Figure 4, is used as the textual representation for item entity j.

4.3 Visual Embedding

In this subsection, similar to previous textual embedding part, we apply another unsupervised deep learning model, termed as stacked convolutional auto-encoders (SCAE), to extract item entities' semantic representations from the visual knowledge.

For visual objects, convolutional layers based deep learning architectures often beat the common fully connected architectures due to the fact that they can preserve the image's neighborhood relations and spatial locality in the latent higher-level feature representation [7]. Furthermore, convolutional layers restrict the number of free parameters by sharing weights so that they scale well to high-dimensional image content. Given above, by following the work in [16], we adopt the stacked convolutional auto-encoders (SCAE) by using convolutional hidden layers to replace fully-connected layers in previous SDAE.

Assume that there are L_v layers in SCAE, similar to the notation in SDAE, we use a 4-dimensional tensor $\mathbf{Z}_{L_v}$ to denote the collection of clean images, where the j-th row is a 3-dimensional tensor $\mathbf{Z}_{L_v,j*}$ of raw pixel representation in RGB color space for item entity j. Similarly, we use $\mathbf{Z}_0$ to denote the corrupted images (randomly masking some entries of $\mathbf{Z}_{L_v}$ by adding Gaussian noise). Next, for each layer l, we use $\mathbf{Z}_l$ to represent the output, $\mathbf{Q}_l$ to represent the weight parameter, and $\mathbf{c}_l$ to represent the bias parameter.

In SCAE, we set layer $\frac{L_v}{2}$ and layer $\frac{L_v}{2} + 1$ as fully connected layers, while other layers as convolutional layers. Figure 5 gives

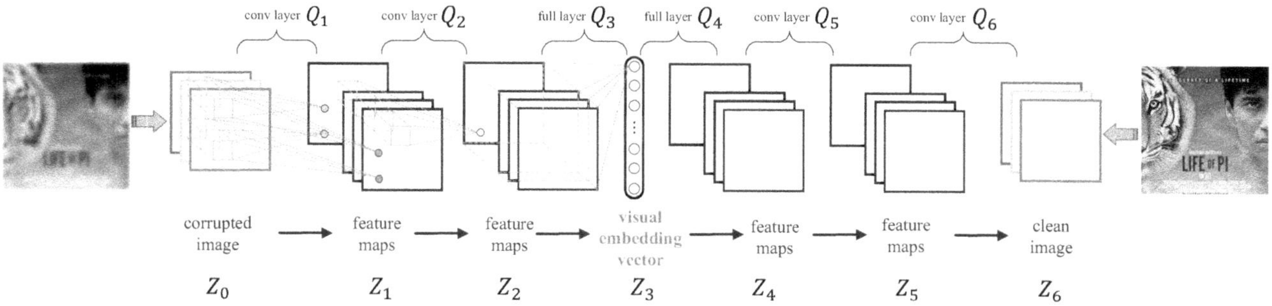

Figure 5: Illustration of a 6-layer SCAE for visual embedding

the illustration of a 6-layer SCAE, which also consists of encoder part and decoder part. As shown in the figure, encoder part consists of two convolutional layers (from $\mathbf{Z}_0$ to $\mathbf{Z}_2$) and a fully connected layers ($\mathbf{Z}_2$ to $\mathbf{Z}_3$). Similarly, decoder part consists of a fully connected layer ($\mathbf{Z}_3$ to $\mathbf{Z}_4$) and two following deconvolutional layers (from $\mathbf{Z}_4$ to $\mathbf{Z}_6$). Note that the output of the middle hidden layer $\mathbf{Z}_3$ is a matrix, which denotes the collection of all item entities' visual embedding vectors, while the output of other hidden layers are usually termed as feature maps [7], which are 4-dimensional tensors generated from convolutional layers. The mapping for a convolutional layer is given as

$$\mathbf{Z}_l = \sigma(\mathbf{Q} * \mathbf{Z}_{l-1} + \mathbf{c}_l) \quad (4)$$

where $*$ denotes the convolutional operator, which can preserve the local connectivity of previous output. More details about convolutional operator can be referred to [20].

Similar to textual embedding component, given both clean image input $\mathbf{Z}_{L_v}$ and corrupted input $\mathbf{Z}_0$, we present the generative process of each layer l in Bayesian SCAE as follows:

1. For weight parameter, draw $\mathbf{Q}_l \sim \mathcal{N}(\mathbf{0}, \lambda_Q^{-1}\mathbf{I})$.
2. For bias parameter, draw $\mathbf{c}_l \sim \mathcal{N}(\mathbf{0}, \lambda_c^{-1}\mathbf{I})$.
3. For the output of the layer,
   (a) If layer l is a fully connected layer: draw $\mathbf{Z}_l \sim \mathcal{N}(\sigma(\mathbf{Z}_{l-1}\mathbf{Q}_l + \mathbf{c}_l), \lambda_Z^{-1}\mathbf{I})$,
   (b) Else: draw $\mathbf{Z}_l \sim \mathcal{N}(\sigma(\mathbf{Z}_{l-1} * \mathbf{Q}_l + \mathbf{c}_l), \lambda_Z^{-1}\mathbf{I})$.

The embedding vector in the middle layer, i.e., $\mathbf{Z}_{3,j*}$ in Figure 5, is used as the visual representation for item entity j.

5. COLLABORATIVE JOINT LEARNING

In this section, in order to integrate collaborative filtering with items' embedding representations from the knowledge base, we propose the collaborative joint learning procedure in our **CKE** framework.

Given user implicit feedback $\mathbf{R}$, motivated by [22], we consider the pair-wise ranking between items for the learning approach. To be more specific, when $R_{ij} = 1$ and $R_{ij'} = 0$, we say that user i prefers item j over j', and then use $p(j > j'; i|\theta)$ to denote the pair-wise preference probability, where θ represents the model parameters. In collaborative filtering, we use a latent vector $\mathbf{u}_i$ as the representation for user i, and a latent vector $\boldsymbol{\eta}_j$ as the representation for item j. To simultaneously capture an item's latent representation in collaborative filtering and representations in the knowledge base, the item latent vector can be re-expressed as

$$\mathbf{e}_j = \boldsymbol{\eta}_j + \mathbf{v}_j + \mathbf{X}_{\frac{L_t}{2},j*} + \mathbf{Z}_{\frac{L_v}{2},j*} \quad (5)$$

Then the pair-wise preference probability can be given as

$$p(j > j'; i|\theta) = \sigma(\mathbf{u}_i^T\mathbf{e}_j - \mathbf{u}_i^T\mathbf{e}_{j'}) \quad (6)$$

Using Bayesian TransR, Bayesian SDAE, and Bayesian SCAE in knowledge base embedding step as components, the generative process of our framework **CKE** by using collaborative join learning is given as follows:

1. Considering the structural knowledge,
   (a) For each entity v, draw $\mathbf{v} \sim \mathcal{N}(\mathbf{0}, \lambda_v^{-1}\mathbf{I})$.
   (b) For each relation r, draw $\mathbf{r} \sim \mathcal{N}(\mathbf{0}, \lambda_r^{-1}\mathbf{I})$ and $\mathbf{M}_r \sim \mathcal{N}(\mathbf{0}, \lambda_M^{-1}\mathbf{I})$, respectively.
   (c) For each quadruple $(v_h, r, v_t, v_{t'}) \in \mathcal{S}$, draw from the probability $\sigma(f_r(v_h, v_t) - f_r(v_h, v_{t'}))$.
2. Considering the textual knowledge, for each layer l in SDAE,
   (a) For weight parameter $\mathbf{W}_l$, draw $\mathbf{W}_l \sim \mathcal{N}(\mathbf{0}, \lambda_W^{-1}\mathbf{I})$.
   (b) For bias parameter, draw $\mathbf{b}_l \sim \mathcal{N}(\mathbf{0}, \lambda_b^{-1}\mathbf{I})$.
   (c) For the output of the layer, draw $\mathbf{X}_l \sim \mathcal{N}(\sigma(\mathbf{X}_{l-1}\mathbf{W}_l + \mathbf{b}_l), \lambda_X^{-1}\mathbf{I})$
3. Considering the visual knowledge, for each layer l in SCAE,
   (a) For weight parameter, draw $\mathbf{Q}_l \sim \mathcal{N}(\mathbf{0}, \lambda_Q^{-1}\mathbf{I})$.
   (b) For bias parameter, draw $\mathbf{c}_l \sim \mathcal{N}(\mathbf{0}, \lambda_c^{-1}\mathbf{I})$.
   (c) For the output of the layer,
      i. If layer l is a fully connected layer: draw $\mathbf{Z}_l \sim \mathcal{N}(\sigma(\mathbf{Z}_{l-1}\mathbf{Q}_l + \mathbf{c}_l), \lambda_Z^{-1}\mathbf{I})$,
      ii. Else: draw $\mathbf{Z}_l \sim \mathcal{N}(\sigma(\mathbf{Z}_{l-1} * \mathbf{Q}_l + \mathbf{c}_l), \lambda_Z^{-1}\mathbf{I})$.
4. For each item j, draw a latent item offset vector $\boldsymbol{\eta}_j \sim \mathcal{N}(\mathbf{0}, \lambda_I^{-1}\mathbf{I})$, and then set the item latent vector as: $\mathbf{e}_j = \boldsymbol{\eta}_j + \mathbf{v}_j + \mathbf{X}_{\frac{L_t}{2},j*} + \mathbf{Z}_{\frac{L_v}{2},j*}$.
5. For each user i, draw a user latent vector as $\mathbf{u}_i \sim \mathcal{N}(\mathbf{0}, \lambda_U^{-1}\mathbf{I})$.
6. For each triple $(i, j, j') \in \mathcal{D}$, draw from the probability $\sigma(\mathbf{u}_i^T\mathbf{e}_j - \mathbf{u}_i^T\mathbf{e}_{j'})$.

Here, $\mathcal{D}$ is a collection of triples, where each triple (i, j, j') satisfies that $R_{ij} = 1$ and $R_{ij'} = 0$ (j' is randomly sampled from user i's uninterested items). Note that $\mathbf{v}_j$, $\mathbf{X}_{\frac{L_t}{2},j*}$ and $\mathbf{Z}_{\frac{L_v}{2},j*}$ serve as the bridges between implicit feedback preference and structural knowledge, textual knowledge as well as visual knowledge, respectively.

Learning the parameters. Computing the full posterior of the parameters is intractable. Like [28], maximizing the posterior probability of $\mathbf{u}$, $\mathbf{e}$, $\mathbf{r}$, $\mathbf{M}$, $\mathbf{W}$, $\mathbf{b}$, $\mathbf{Q}$ and $\mathbf{c}$ is equivalent to maximizing the log-likelihood as follows:

$$\begin{aligned}
\mathcal{L} = & \sum_{(i,j,j')\in\mathcal{D}} \ln\sigma(\mathbf{u}_i^T\mathbf{e}_j - \mathbf{u}_i^T\mathbf{e}_{j'}) - \frac{\lambda_X}{2}\sum_l ||\sigma(\mathbf{X}_{l-1}\mathbf{W}_l + \mathbf{b}_l) - \mathbf{X}_l||_2^2 \\
+ & \sum_{(v_h,r,v_t,v_{t'})\in\mathcal{S}} \ln\sigma(||\mathbf{v}_h\mathbf{M}_r + \mathbf{r} - \mathbf{v}_t\mathbf{M}_r||_2^2 - ||\mathbf{v}_h\mathbf{M}_r + \mathbf{r} - \mathbf{v}_{t'}\mathbf{M}_r||_2^2) \\
- & \frac{\lambda_Z}{2} \sum_{l\notin\{\frac{L_v}{2},\frac{L_v}{2}+1\}} ||\sigma(\mathbf{Z}_{l-1} * \mathbf{Q}_l + \mathbf{c}_l) - \mathbf{Z}_l||_2^2 - \frac{\lambda_U}{2}\sum_i ||\mathbf{u}_i||_2^2 \\
- & \frac{\lambda_Z}{2} \sum_{l\in\{\frac{L_v}{2},\frac{L_v}{2}+1\}} ||\sigma(\mathbf{Z}_{l-1}\mathbf{Q}_l + \mathbf{c}_l) - \mathbf{Z}_l||_2^2 - \frac{\lambda_v}{2}\sum_v ||\mathbf{v}||_2^2 \\
- & \frac{1}{2}\sum_l(\lambda_W||\mathbf{W}_l||_2^2 + \lambda_b||\mathbf{b}_l||_2^2) - \frac{1}{2}\sum_l(\lambda_Q||\mathbf{Q}_l||_2^2 + \lambda_c||\mathbf{c}_l||_2^2) \\
- & \frac{\lambda_I}{2}\sum_j ||\mathbf{e}_j - \mathbf{v}_j - \mathbf{X}_{\frac{L_t}{2},j*} - \mathbf{Z}_{\frac{L_v}{2},j*}||_2^2 \\
- & \frac{\lambda_r}{2}\sum_r ||\mathbf{r}||_2^2 - \frac{\lambda_M}{2}\sum_r ||\mathbf{M}_r||_2^2
\end{aligned} \tag{7}$$

To maximize the objective in Eq. (7), we employ a stochastic gradient descent (SGD) algorithm similar to [22]. In each iteration, for a randomly sampled triple $(i, j, j') \in \mathcal{D}$, we find the subset $\mathcal{S}_{j,j'} \in \mathcal{S}$ satisfying that each quadruple in $\mathcal{S}_{j,j'}$ contains item j or item j'. Then we perform a SGD update for each parameter using the gradient of the corresponding objective function [10].

Prediction The final item recommendation for a user i is given according to the following ranking criterion:

$$i : j_1 > j_2 > \ldots > j_n \rightarrow \mathbf{u}_i^T\mathbf{e}_{j_1} > \mathbf{u}_i^T\mathbf{e}_{j_2} > \ldots > \mathbf{u}_i^T\mathbf{e}_{j_n} \tag{8}$$

6. EXPERIMENTS

In this section, we evaluate our proposed framework on two real-world datasets for both movie and book recommendation scenarios. The experimental results demonstrate evidence of significant improvement over many competitive baselines.

6.1 Datasets Description

To demonstrate the effectiveness of the proposed collaborative knowledge base embedding for recommendation framework, we use two datasets from different domains (movie and book) for empirical studies. The first dataset, MovieLens-1M[8], consists of $1M$ ratings with 6,040 users and 3,706 movies. Similar to [31], in order to be consistent with the implicit feedback setting, we extract only positive ratings (rating 5) for training and testing. After removing users with less than 3 positive ratings, we have 5,883 users, 3,230 movies, and 226,101 ratings in the final dataset. The second dataset, termed as IntentBooks, is collected from Microsoft's Bing search engine and Microsoft's Satori knowledge base [1]. In this dataset, users' interests for books are extracted from click/query actions, e.g., if a user has conducted queries with "Harry Potter" or clicked documents containing that name, this user might be interested for the related book entity. To reduce the name conflict issue (e.g., instead of the book, "Harry Potter" might actually mean the related movie), we extracted user's book interests by combining unsupervised similarity computation with supervised classification by following [13]. Moreover, to validate the effectiveness of book interest extraction, we randomly selected 200 extracted book interest instances and manually labeled each one as true or false. The result shows that the precision is 91.5%, which we believe is accurate enough for subsequent experiments. We sample the user implicit feedback data from Bing's search log from Sep. 2014 to Jun. 2015. After removing users with less than 5 book interests, we finally have 92,564 users, 18,475 books, and 897,871 user-book interests.

[8]http://grouplens.org/datasets/movielens/1m/

Table 1: Detailed statistics of the two datasets

	MovieLens-1M	IntentBooks
#user	5,883	92,564
#item	3,230	18,475
#interactions	226,101	897,871
#sk nodes	84,011	26,337
#sk edges	169,368	57,408
#sk edge types	10	6
#tk items	2,752	17,331
#vk items	2,958	16,719

We also use Satori knowledge base to extract structural knowledge, textual knowledge and visual knowledge for these two datasets. First, we applied a two staged method described in [24] (including both title match and attributes match) to map each movie from MovieLens-1M dataset to an entity in the knowledge base (note that a book in the IntentBooks dataset is already an entity in the knowledge base, therefore matching step is ignored). We explicitly observed 200 paired results, where 92% of the pairs are correctly matched (the match precision is good enough for later process). In addition, we find that only 134 movies can not be mapped to any movie entities from the knowledge base. Next, to build the structural knowledge, we extract a subgraph from the knowledge base which contains item entities, entities which are 1-step away from item entities, and the corresponding relationships. For movie entities, the 1-step entities include genre, director, writer, actors, language, country, production date, rating, nominated awards, and received awards; for book entities, the 1-step entities include genre, author, publish date, belonged series, language, and rating. Then for text knowledge, we follow the word hashing procedure as that in [12] to preprocess the text information extracted from the plots of the movies and the descriptions of the books. Finally, for visual knowledge, we use the poster image of a movie entity and the front cover image of a book entity, where the finally used visual input are images that are reshaped to the $3 \times 64 \times 64$ tensor format in the RGB space. Some detailed statistics of the two datasets are summarized in Table 1. For example, "#sk nodes" indicates the total number of nodes in the extracted structural knowledge, "#tk items" indicates the number of items having textual knowledge, and "#vk items" indicates the number of items having visual knowledge.

6.2 Evaluation Schema

As discussed in [19], precision is not a suitable performance measure for implicit feedback recommendation. Therefore, in our experiments, we use MAP@K (mean average precision) [26] and Recall@K to evaluate the performance of the top K recommendation. For each dataset, similar to [14], we randomly select 70% items associated with each user to constitute the training set and use all the remaining as the test set. For each evaluation scenario, we repeat the evaluation five times with different randomly selected training sets and the average performance is reported in the following parts. For each dataset, we also use a validation set from the training set to find the optimal hyperparameters for our methods as well as baselines introduced in later parts. In the following reported results, hyperparameter settings of our methods are given in Table 2 since best performance is achieved. In Table 2, dim denotes the latent dimension, ϵ denotes the noise masking level, σ denotes the

Table 2: Hyperparameter settings of our framework for the two datasets. cf, sk, tk and vk indicate the parameters in the component of collaborative filtering, structural knowledge embedding, textual knowledge embedding and visual knowledge embedding, respectively.

	MovieLens-1M	IntentBooks
cf	dim=150,λ_U=λ_I=0.0025	dim=100,λ_U=λ_I=0.005
sk	λ_v=λ_r=0.001,λ_M=0.01	λ_v=λ_r=0.001,λ_M=0.1
tk	λ_W=λ_b=0.01, λ_X=0.0001, ϵ=0.2, L_t=4, N_l=300	λ_W=λ_b=0.01, λ_X=0.001, ϵ=0.1, L_t=6, N_l=200
vk	λ_Q=λ_c=0.01, λ_Z=0.0001, σ=3, $L_v = 6$, N_f=20, S_f=(5,5)	λ_Q=λ_c=0.01, λ_Z=0.001, σ=2, $L_v = 8$, N_f=20, S_f=(5,5)

standard deviation for image's Gaussian filter noise, L_t and L_v denote the number of layers, N_l denotes the number of hidden units when layer l is not a middle layer or an output layer in textual embedding's SDAE step, N_f and S_f denote the number and the size of filter maps in each convolutional layer of visual embedding's SCAE step, respectively. Note that for the purpose of keeping the collaborative filtering part the same in different factorization methods, the latent dimension of compared baselines in the following subsections are set the same as that in Table 2, other hyperparameters of baselines are determined by grid search.

In the following subsections, we will evaluate the proposed framework according to four aspects. First, we evaluate the recommendation performance with regard to structural knowledge usage, textual knowledge usage, and visual knowledge usage, respectively. Then, we compare the joint model **CKE** with state-of-the-art baselines to demonstrate the effectiveness of our system.

6.3 Study of Structural Knowledge Usage

In this subsection, to study the performance of our structural knowledge usage, we only incorporate structural knowledge embedding component into collaborative filtering in the joint learning process. We compare our method, termed as "CKE(S)", against the following baselines:

- **BPRMF**: We use Bayesian Personalized Ranking based Matrix Factorization [22], which is based on users' pair-wise preference, as the single collaborative filtering method. Compared with our method CKE(S), this baseline completely ignores the usage of structural knowledge.
- **BPRMF+TransE**: This method combines BPRMF and a network embedding method called TransE [3] for joint learning. This baseline actually uses the same settings as our method CKE(S), except that it uses TransE, which ignores the heterogeneity of entities and relations, instead of TransR to embed structural knowledge.
- **PRP**: PageRank with Priors [17] integrates user-item relation and structural knowledge into a unified homogeneous graph and then perform pagerank for each user with a personalized initial probability distribution.
- **PER**: Personalized Entity Recommendation [30] treats the structural knowledge as a heterogeneous information network and extract meta-path based latent features to represent the connectivity between users and items along different types of relation paths. In this paper, we use all the item-attribute-item formatted meta-path features (e.g., "movie-genre-movie").
- **LIBFM(S)**: LIBFM [21] is a state-of-the-art feature based factorization model. In this paper, LIBFM(S) implies that we use an item's attributes in the structural knowledge as raw features to feed into LIBFM.

The results of different methods are given in Figure 6(a), Figure 7(a), Figure 8(a), and Figure 9(a). The results precipitate several observations for both two datasets, which we summarize as: 1) BPRMF performs the worst among all approaches. Since BPRMF is the only one which totally ignores structural knowledge, the results imply that the additional usage of structural knowledge can significantly improve the recommendation performance. 2) PRP performs worse than other approaches leveraging structural knowledge. This is because among these, PRP is the only one which does not leverage factorization, which can capture the latent low-rank approximation of user-item interactions under the sparseness of the datasets. 3) BPRMF+TransE outperforms LIBFM(S) and PER, which demonstrates that instead of directly using structural knowledge in a feature-engineering way, network embedding can capture the semantic representation in a more reasonable way and thus improve the recommendation quality. 4) Our method CKE(S) beats BPRMF+TransE, which implies that by using TransR, there is still room for improvement when considering the heterogeneity of network embedding.

6.4 Study of Textual Knowledge Usage

In this subsection, we investigate the performance of our textual knowledge usage. Specifically, we use the textual knowledge embedding component and collaborative filtering in the joint learning process. We compare our method, which is termed as "CKE(T)", against BPRMF as well as the following baselines:

- **LIBFM(T)**: This method is the same as LIBFM(S) introduced in Section 6.3, except that bag of words in the textual knowledge are now used as raw features to feed into LIBFM.
- **CMF(T)**: Collective Matrix Factorization [21] combines different kinds of data sources by simultaneously factorizing multiple matrix. In this paper, CMF(T) implies that the two matrices we use are user-item matrix and item-word matrix.
- **CTR**: Collaborative Topic Regression [28], which is state-of-the-art method leveraging textual information for recommendation, integrates collaborative filtering and topic modeling simultaneously.

As shown in Figure 6(b), Figure 7(b), Figure 8(b), and Figure 9(b), the comparison of the results presents the following observations: 1) CKE(S) outperforms CKE(T) and LIBFM(S) outperforms LIBFM(T), which implies that compared to structural knowledge, textual knowledge has weaker improvement on recommendation performance. 2) LIBFM(T), CTR and CKE(T) usually give better performance than CMF, which reveals that the direct factorization of item-word matrix can not make the full use of textual information. 3) CTR is a strong baseline and sometimes even achieve the best performance in the IntentBooks dataset. However, our method CKE(T) can beat CTR most of the time, which demonstrates that compared to topic modeling, deep learning embedding are really good at extracting text's semantic representation by delving into deep structure.

6.5 Study of Visual Knowledge Usage

In this subsection, we focus on studying the performance of our visual knowledge usage. As before, we use the visual knowledge embedding component and collaborative filtering in the joint learning. We compare our method, which is named as "CKE(V)" against BPRMF as well as the following baselines:

- **LIBFM(V)**: This method is the same as LIBFM(S) in Section 6.3, except that flattened raw pixel representation in RGB color space are used as raw features.

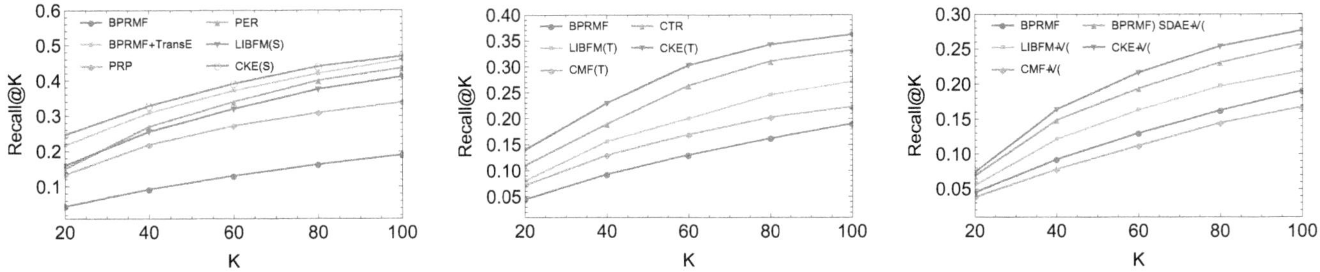

(a) Usage of Structural Knowledge (b) Usage of Textual Knowledge (c) Usage of Visual Knowledge

Figure 6: Recall@K results comparison between our methods using each component in knowledge base embedding and related baselines for dataset MovieLens-1M.

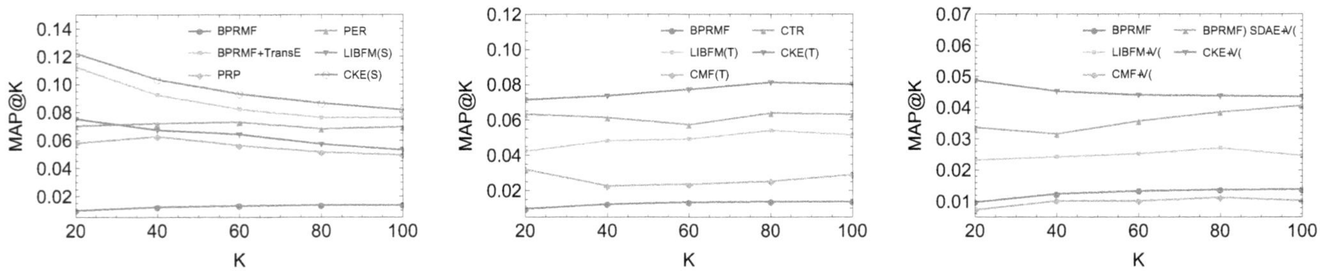

(a) Usage of Structural Knowledge (b) Usage of Textual Knowledge (c) Usage of Visual Knowledge

Figure 7: MAP@K results comparison between our methods using each component in knowledge base embedding and related baselines for dataset MovieLens-1M.

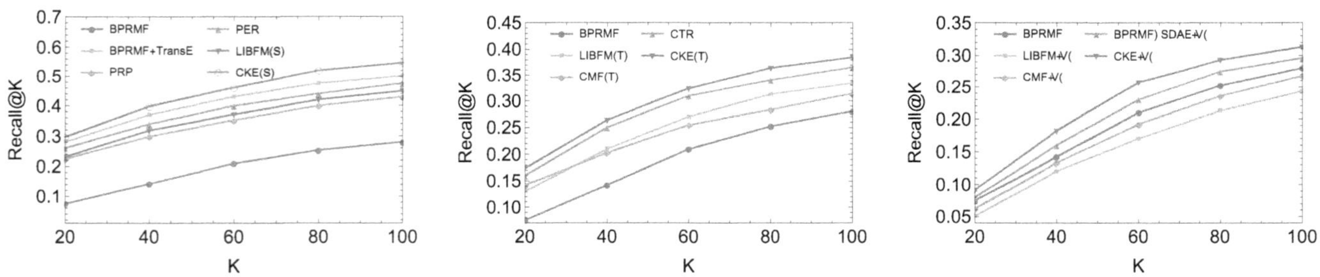

(a) Usage of Structural Knowledge (b) Usage of Textual Knowledge (c) Usage of Visual Knowledge

Figure 8: Recall@K results comparison between our methods using each component in knowledge base embedding and related baselines for dataset IntentBooks.

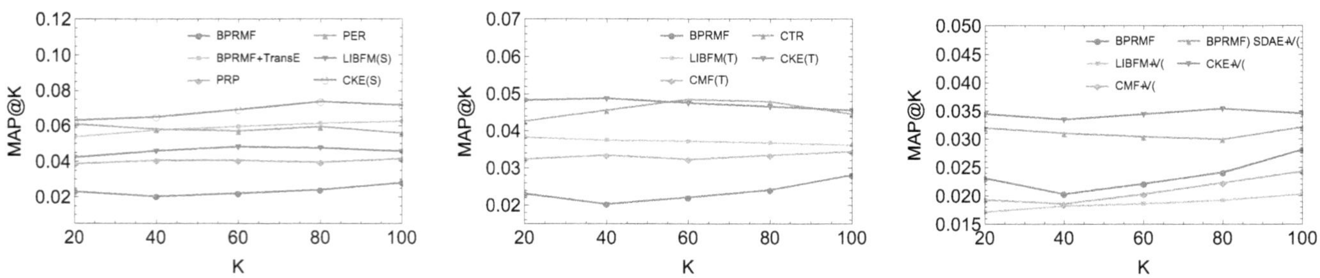

(a) Usage of Structural Knowledge (b) Usage of Textual Knowledge (c) Usage of Visual Knowledge

Figure 9: MAP@K results comparison between our methods using each component in knowledge base embedding and related baselines for dataset IntentBooks.

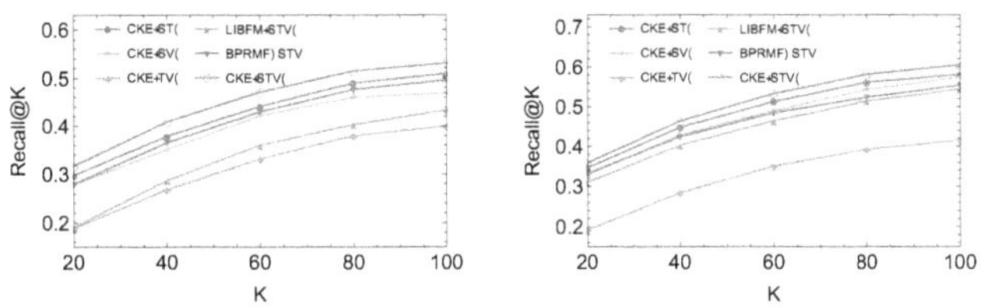

(a) MovieLens-1M (b) IntentBooks

Figure 10: Recall@K results comparison between our framework and related baselines for both datasets.

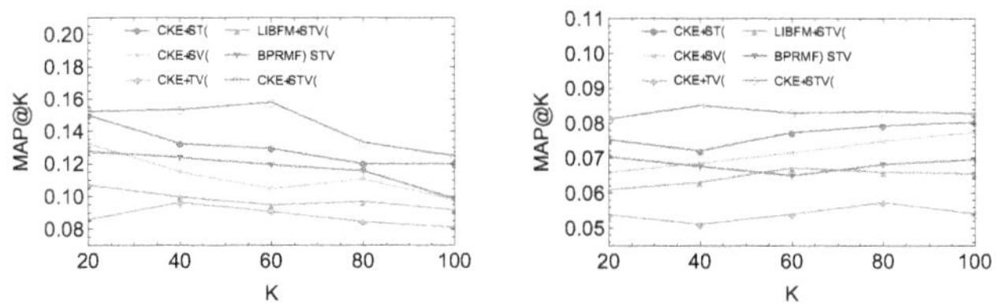

(a) MovieLens-1M (b) IntentBooks

Figure 11: MAP@K results comparison between our framework and related baselines for both datasets.

- **CMF(V)**: This method uses the same setting as CMF(T) described in Section 6.4, except that we use user-item matrix and item-pixel matrix for simultaneous factorization.
- **BPRMF+SDAE(V)**: This method uses the same settings as our method CKE(V), except that it uses stacked denoising auto-encoder to embed visual knowledge. This is for evaluating whether the convolutional layers are effective for visual knowledge embedding.

The results of different approaches are shown in Figure 6(c), Figure 7(c), Figure 8(c), and Figure 9(c), which provide us the following observations: 1) Compared to structural knowledge and textual knowledge, the performance improvement with the usage of visual knowledge is limited but still significant. 2) CKE(V) and BPRMF+SDAE(V) outperform other approaches, which demonstrates the superiority of deep network for visual knowledge embedding. 3) The performance gap between CKE(V) and BPRMF+SDAE(V) is still significant, which reveals that convolutional layers are more suitable for extracting visual representation.

6.6 Study of The Whole Framework

Finally, we evaluate the performance of our whole framework. We compare our ultimate model using three components in knowledge base embedding, denoted as "CKE(STV)" against the following baselines:

- **CKE(ST), CKE(SV), CKE(TV)**: CKE(ST) uses the same setting as CKE(STV), except that it only incorporates structural knowledge and textual knowledge, this is for evaluating whether the additional usage of visual knowledge is effective. The definition is similar to CKE(SV) and CKE(TV).
- **LIBFM(STV)**: This method uses the same setting as LIBFM(S) mentioned in Section 6.4, except that structural knowledge, textual knowledge and visual knowledge are all used as features.
- **BPRMF+STV**: This method uses the same setting as CKE(STV), except that it learns collaborative filtering and three knowledge base embedding components separately. This is for evaluating whether joint learning is effective.

The results are shown in Figure 10 and Figure 11, which give the following observations: 1) CKE(STV) outperforms CKE(ST), CKE(SV) and CKE(TV). This implies that the additional usage of each kind of knowledge can improve the recommendation performance, which demonstrate the insight of our framework combining different kinds of knowledge together for enhancing recommendation. 2) CKE(STV) outperforms LIBFM(STV), which demonstrates that compared to direct usage of the knowledge base in a feature-engineering way, the embedding components can capture the knowledge base's semantic representations more effectively and thus improve the recommendation performance. 3) CKE(STV) still archives better performance than BPRMF+STV, which suggests that the joint learning of collaborative filtering and knowledge base embedding can target the recommendation optimization task in a more direct way and thus improve the recommendation quality.

7. RELATED WORK

7.1 Knowledge Base for Recommendation

The usage of the knowledge base within the context of recommender systems are attracting increasing attention in recent years. For example, Cheekula et al. [5] explores the hierarchical category knowledge derived from the pruned DBpedia knowledge base and applies the spreading activation algorithm to identify personalized entities as recommendation. Passant [18] computes the semantic distance in the graphical structure of a knowledge base and used this distance measure to build music recommendation systems. Compared to previous works which investigated this problem mainly by leveraging the structure of a knowledge base, we present a framework to integrate the heterogeneous knowledge from structure, text as well as visual content for recommendation.

7.2 Structural Knowledge Embedding

Previous works of structural knowledge embedding mainly aim to embed entities and relations into a continuous vector space and model the semantics of structure in that space. For example, TransE [3] represents a relation by a translation vector so that the pair of embedded entities in a triple can be connected with low error. However, TransE has flaws in dealing with many-to-many relations for the heterogeneity of structural information in a knowledge base. To solve the issue of TransE, TransR [15] steps to propose that entities and relations are completely different objects and models entities and relations in distinct spaces and performs translation in relation space by using a translation matrix. In this paper, we integrate TransR with our recommendation task to fully leverage the structural knowledge in the knowledge base.

7.3 Deep Learning for Recommendation

With the success of deep learning in recent years, there is a marked switch from hand-crafted features to those that are learned from raw data in recommendation research. For example, Elkahky et al. [8] proposes a multi-view deep learning model to learn user features and item features from different domains, and uses the enriched feature representation to improve the recommendation quality across all the domains. Wang [29] significantly improve the recommendation performance by jointly performing deep representation learning for the textual content information and collaborative filtering for the ratings matrix. Our framework distinguishes itself from the above-mentioned works in the following aspects: 1) We specifically apply stacked convolutional auto-encoder to extract the semantic representation of visual content, which has not been exploited in previous works. 2) We design a joint model by integrating collaborative filtering and the heterogeneity of structural, textual and visual knowledge to boost the recommendation quality.

8. CONCLUSION

This paper proposes a hybrid recommender system termed as **CKE**, which integrates collaborative filtering and knowledge base for recommendation. Following this framework, we first design three components, which leverage heterogeneous network embedding and deep learning embedding approaches, to automatically extract semantic representations from structural knowledge, textual knowledge and visual knowledge in the knowledge base, respectively. Next, we combine collaborative filtering and knowledge base embedding components into a unified framework and learn different representations jointly. The extensive experiments we have conducted validated the effectiveness of our **CKE** framework. Besides, this research sheds new light on the usage of heterogeneous information in the knowledge base, which can be consumed in more application scenarios.

9. REFERENCES

[1] ahmet uyar, f. m. a. Evaluating search features of google knowledge graph and bing satori. *Online Information Review* (2015).

[2] Bobadilla, J., Ortega, F., Hernando, A., and Gutiérrez, A. Recommender systems survey. *Knowledge-Based Systems 46* (2013), 109–132.

[3] Bordes, A., Usunier, N., Garcia-Duran, A., Weston, J., and Yakhnenko, O. Translating embeddings for modeling multi-relational data. In *Advances in Neural Information Processing Systems* (2013), 2787–2795.

[4] Cambria, E., Schuller, B., Liu, B., Wang, H., and Havasi, C. Knowledge-based approaches to concept-level sentiment analysis. *IEEE Intelligent Systems*, 2 (2013), 12–14.

[5] Cheekula, S. K., Kapanipathi, P., Doran, D., Jain, P., and Sheth, A. Entity recommendations using hierarchical knowledge bases.

[6] Chui, M., Manyika, J., and Kuiken, S. What executives should know about open data. *McKinsey Quarterly, January 2014* (2014).

[7] Ciresan, D. C., Meier, U., Masci, J., Maria Gambardella, L., and Schmidhuber, J. Flexible, high performance convolutional neural networks for image classification. In *IJCAI Proceedings-International Joint Conference on Artificial Intelligence*, vol. 22 (2011), 1237.

[8] Elkahky, A. M., Song, Y., and He, X. A multi-view deep learning approach for cross domain user modeling in recommendation systems. In *Proceedings of the 24th International Conference on World Wide Web*, International World Wide Web Conferences Steering Committee (2015), 278–288.

[9] Freitas, A., Oliveira, J. G., OâĂŹRiain, S., Curry, E., and Da Silva, J. C. P. Querying linked data using semantic relatedness: a vocabulary independent approach. In *Natural Language Processing and Information Systems*. Springer, 2011, 40–51.

[10] Gantner, Z., Rendle, S., Freudenthaler, C., and Schmidt-Thieme, L. Mymedialite: A free recommender system library. In *Proceedings of the fifth ACM conference on Recommender systems*, ACM (2011), 305–308.

[11] Grad-Gyenge, L., Filzmoser, P., and Werthner, H. Recommendations on a knowledge graph.

[12] Huang, P.-S., He, X., Gao, J., Deng, L., Acero, A., and Heck, L. Learning deep structured semantic models for web search using clickthrough data. In *Proceedings of the 22nd ACM international conference on Conference on information & knowledge management*, ACM (2013), 2333–2338.

[13] Ji, H., and Grishman, R. Knowledge base population: Successful approaches and challenges. In *Proceedings of the 49th Annual Meeting of the Association for Computational Linguistics: Human Language Technologies-Volume 1*, Association for Computational Linguistics (2011), 1148–1158.

[14] Lian, D., Zhao, C., Xie, X., Sun, G., Chen, E., and Rui, Y. Geomf: joint geographical modeling and matrix factorization for point-of-interest recommendation. In *Proceedings of the 20th ACM SIGKDD international conference on Knowledge discovery and data mining*, ACM (2014), 831–840.

[15] Lin, Y., Liu, Z., Sun, M., Liu, Y., and Zhu, X. Learning entity and relation embeddings for knowledge graph completion. In *Proceedings of AAAI* (2015).

[16] Masci, J., Meier, U., Cireşan, D., and Schmidhuber, J. Stacked convolutional auto-encoders for hierarchical feature extraction. In *Artificial Neural Networks and Machine Learning–ICANN 2011*. Springer, 2011, 52–59.

[17] Nguyen, P., Tomeo, P., Di Noia, T., and Di Sciascio, E. An evaluation of simrank and personalized pagerank to build a recommender system for the web of data. In *Proceedings of the 24th International Conference on World Wide Web Companion*, International World Wide Web Conferences Steering Committee (2015), 1477–1482.

[18] Passant, A. dbrecâĂŤmusic recommendations using dbpedia. In *The Semantic Web–ISWC 2010*. Springer, 2010, 209–224.

[19] Purushotham, S., Liu, Y., and Kuo, C.-C. J. Collaborative topic regression with social matrix factorization for recommendation systems. *arXiv preprint arXiv:1206.4684* (2012).

[20] Ren, J. S., and Xu, L. On vectorization of deep convolutional neural networks for vision tasks. In *Twenty-Ninth AAAI Conference on Artificial Intelligence* (2015).

[21] Rendle, S. Factorization machines with libfm. *ACM Transactions on Intelligent Systems and Technology (TIST) 3*, 3 (2012), 57.

[22] Rendle, S., Freudenthaler, C., Gantner, Z., and Schmidt-Thieme, L. Bpr: Bayesian personalized ranking from implicit feedback. In *Proceedings of the Twenty-Fifth Conference on Uncertainty in Artificial Intelligence*, AUAI Press (2009), 452–461.

[23] Schafer, J. B., Frankowski, D., Herlocker, J., and Sen, S. Collaborative filtering recommender systems. In *The adaptive web*. Springer, 2007, 291–324.

[24] Scheffler, T., Schirru, R., and Lehmann, P. Matching points of interest from different social networking sites. In *KI 2012: Advances in Artificial Intelligence*. Springer, 2012, 245–248.

[25] Tiddi, I., d'Aquin, M., and Motta, E. Using linked data traversal to label academic communities. In *Proceedings of the 24th International Conference on World Wide Web Companion*, International World Wide Web Conferences Steering Committee (2015), 1029–1034.

[26] Van den Oord, A., Dieleman, S., and Schrauwen, B. Deep content-based music recommendation. In *Advances in Neural Information Processing Systems* (2013), 2643–2651.

[27] Vincent, P., Larochelle, H., Lajoie, I., Bengio, Y., and Manzagol, P.-A. Stacked denoising autoencoders: Learning useful representations in a deep network with a local denoising criterion. *The Journal of Machine Learning Research 11* (2010), 3371–3408.

[28] Wang, C., and Blei, D. M. Collaborative topic modeling for recommending scientific articles. In *Proceedings of the 17th ACM SIGKDD international conference on Knowledge discovery and data mining*, ACM (2011), 448–456.

[29] Wang, H., Wang, N., and Yeung, D.-Y. Collaborative deep learning for recommender systems. In *Proceedings of the 21th ACM SIGKDD International Conference on Knowledge Discovery and Data Mining*, KDD '15, ACM (New York, NY, USA, 2015), 1235–1244.

[30] Yu, X., Ren, X., Sun, Y., Gu, Q., Sturt, B., Khandelwal, U., Norick, B., and Han, J. Personalized entity recommendation: A heterogeneous information network approach. In *Proceedings of the 7th ACM international conference on Web search and data mining*, ACM (2014), 283–292.

[31] Zhou, K., and Zha, H. Learning binary codes for collaborative filtering. In *Proceedings of the 18th ACM SIGKDD international conference on Knowledge discovery and data mining*, ACM (2012), 498–506.

GLMix: Generalized Linear Mixed Models For Large-Scale Response Prediction

Xianxing Zhang, Yitong Zhou, Yiming Ma, Bee-Chung Chen, Liang Zhang, Deepak Agarwal
LinkedIn
Mountain View, CA, USA
{xazhang, yizhou, yma, bchen, lizhang, dagarwal}@linkedin.com

ABSTRACT

Generalized linear model (GLM) is a widely used class of models for statistical inference and response prediction problems. For instance, in order to recommend relevant content to a user or optimize for revenue, many web companies use logistic regression models to predict the probability of the user's clicking on an item (e.g., ad, news article, job). In scenarios where the data is abundant, having a more fine-grained model at the user or item level would potentially lead to more accurate prediction, as the user's personal preferences on items and the item's specific attraction for users can be better captured. One common approach is to introduce ID-level regression coefficients in addition to the global regression coefficients in a GLM setting, and such models are called generalized linear mixed models (GLMix) in the statistical literature. However, for big data sets with a large number of ID-level coefficients, fitting a GLMix model can be computationally challenging. In this paper, we report how we successfully overcame the scalability bottleneck by applying parallelized block coordinate descent under the Bulk Synchronous Parallel (BSP) paradigm. We deployed the model in the LinkedIn job recommender system, and generated 20% to 40% more job applications for job seekers on LinkedIn.

1. INTRODUCTION

Accurate prediction of users' responses to items is one of the core functions of many recommendation applications. Examples include recommending movies, news articles, songs, jobs, advertisements, and so forth. Given a set of features, a common approach is to apply generalized linear models (GLM). For example, when the response is numeric (e.g., rating of a user to a movie), a linear regression on the features is commonly used to predict the response. For the binary response scenario (e.g. whether to click or not when a user sees a job recommendation), logistic regression is often used. Sometimes the response is a count (e.g., number of times a user listens to a song), and Poisson regression becomes a natural choice. All of the above models are special cases of GLM.

The features available in recommender systems often include user features (*e.g.,* age, gender, industry, job function) and item features (*e.g.,* title and skills for jobs, title and named entities for news articles). An approach that is widely adopted in industry to model interactions between users and items is to form the outer (cross) product of user and item features, followed by feature selection to reduce the dimensionality and mitigate the problem of overfitting. In reality, we often observe a lot of heterogeneity in the amount of data per user or item that cannot be sufficiently modeled by user/item features alone, which provides an opportunity to improve model accuracy by adding more granularity to the model. Specifically, for a user who has interacted with many items in the past, we should have sufficient data to fit regression coefficients that are specific to that user to capture his/her personal interests. Similarly, for an item that has received many users' responses, it is beneficial to model its popularity and interactions with user features through regression coefficients that are specific to the item.

One common approach to capture such behavior of each individual user and item is to use ID-level features, i.e., the outer product of user IDs and item features, and the outer product of item IDs and user features. Models with ID-level features are usually referred to as generalized linear mixed models (GLMix) in Statistics [15]. Although conceptually simple, it can generate a very large number of regression coefficients to be learned. For example, for a data set of 10 million users, and each user with 1,000 non-zero coefficients on item features, the total number of regression coefficients can easily go beyond 10^{10}. Therefore, fitting GLMix models for big data is computationally challenging. Dimension reduction methods such as feature hashing [1] or principal component analysis can reduce the number of features. However, they also reduce our ability to interpret the model or explain the predictions in the original feature space (*e.g.,* at the user's ID level), making it difficult to debug or investigate system issues or user complaints.

1.1 Our contributions

In this paper we develop a parallel block-wise coordinate descent (PBCD) algorithm under the Bulk Synchronous Parallel (BSP) paradigm [21] for GLMix model, with a novel model score movement scheme that allows both the coefficients and the data to stay in local nodes. We show that our algorithm successfully scales model fitting of GLMix for very large data sets. We empirically demonstrate that this conceptually simple class of models achieves high accuracy

KDD '16 Aug 13–17, 2016, San Francisco, CA, USA

DOI: http://dx.doi.org/10.1145/2939672.2939684

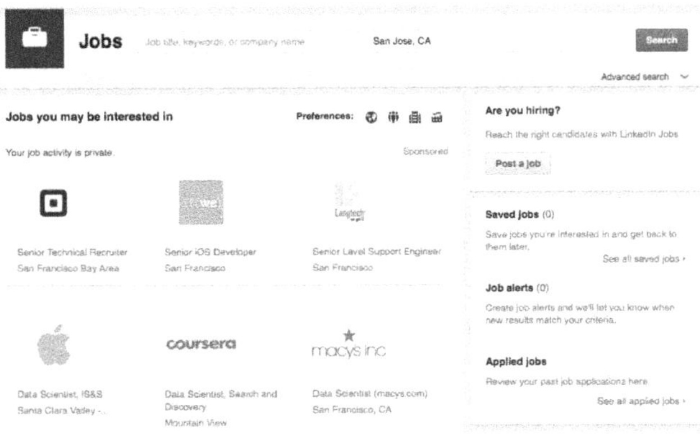

Figure 1: A snapshot of the LinkedIn jobs homepage.

on two public data sets and the LinkedIn job recommendation data set. We also report our successful deployment of GLMix in LinkedIn's job recommendation production system, which improved the total number of job applications from active job seekers by 20% to 40%. To our knowledge, this is the first paper that discusses the practical lessons learned to scale GLMix in real web recommender system applications.

We also extend GLMix by adding a matrix factorization component in order to further leverage recent advancements in scaling up matrix factorization in the distributed environment [24], and see some slight improvement on LinkedIn job recommendation data. Since the parallelization of matrix factorization is well studied, in this paper we mainly focus on the scalability and parallelization of fitting GLMix.

We provide an implementation of the GLMix model with Apache Spark[1], and the code base is open sourced as part of the Photon-ML library[2].

1.2 Organization

The paper is organized as follows. We start by introducing the LinkedIn job recommendation problem as our motivating example and describing the formulation of the GLMix model in such a context in Section 2. The fitting algorithm using PBCD and the implementation details are described in Section 3. We show our offline and online experiments for LinkedIn job recommendation in Section 4, and show results for the other two public data sets in Section 5. We review the literature background of GLMix and related work in Section 6. We conclude the paper in Section 7.

2. OUR MODEL

In this section, we describe the generalized linear mixed model (GLMix) in detail. We start with our motivating example in Section 2.1, the LinkedIn job recommendation problem, to provide the context for GLMix. We introduce the model in Section 2.2 and later describe a general formulation in Section 2.3. Section 2.4 describes extensions of GLMix such as adding a matrix factorization component.

2.1 Job Recommendation at LinkedIn

As the world's largest professional social network, LinkedIn provides a unique value proposition for its over 400M members to connect with all kinds of professional opportunities for their career growth. One of the most important products is the Jobs Homepage, which serves as a central place for members with job seeking intention to come and find good jobs to apply for. Figure 1 is a snapshot of the LinkedIn Jobs Homepage. One of the main modules on the page is "Jobs you may be interested in", where relevant job thumbnails are recommended to members based on their public profile data and past activity on the site. If a member is interested in a recommended job, she can click on it to go to the job detail page, where the original job post is shown with information such as the job title, description, responsibilities, required skills and qualifications. The job detail page also has an "apply" button which allows the member to apply for the job with one click, either on LinkedIn or on the website of the company posting the job. One of the key success metrics for LinkedIn jobs business is the total number of *job application clicks* (i.e the number of clicks on the "apply" button), which is the focus for the job recommendation problem in this paper. Another second-order metric is called "job detail views", which represents the total number of clicks generated from the "Jobs you may be interested in" module to the job details pages. We consider job application clicks to be the key metric to optimize for, instead of job detail views, because the job posters mostly care about how many applications they receive, instead of how many people view their job postings.

2.2 GLMix Model

Now we consider the GLMix model for the job recommendation problem. To measure whether job j is a good match for a member m and to select the best jobs according to this measure, the key is to predict the probability that member m would apply for job j given an impression on the "Jobs you may be interested in" module. Let y_{mjt} denote the binary response of whether member m would apply for job j in context t, where the context usually includes the time and location where the job is shown. We use $\boldsymbol{q}_m$ to denote the feature vector of member m, which includes the features extracted from the member's public profile, e.g., the member's title, job function, education history, industry, etc. We use $\boldsymbol{s}_j$ to denote the feature vector of job j, which includes features extracted from the job post, e.g. the job title, desired skills and experiences, etc. Let $\boldsymbol{x}_{mjt}$ represent the overall feature vector for the (m, j, t) triple, which can include $\boldsymbol{q}_m$ and $\boldsymbol{s}_j$ for feature-level main effects, the outer product between $\boldsymbol{q}_m$ and $\boldsymbol{s}_j$ for interactions among member and job features, and features of the context. We assume that $\boldsymbol{x}_{mjt}$ does not contain member IDs or item IDs as features, because IDs will be treated differently from regular features.

The GLMix model for predicting the probability of member m applying for job j using logistic regression is:

$$g(E[y_{mjt}]) = \boldsymbol{x}'_{mjt}\boldsymbol{b} + \boldsymbol{s}'_j\boldsymbol{\alpha}_m + \boldsymbol{q}'_m\boldsymbol{\beta}_j, \tag{1}$$

where $g(E[y_{mjt}]) = \log \frac{E[y_{mjt}]}{1-E[y_{mjt}]}$ is the link function, $\boldsymbol{b}$ is the global coefficient vector (also called *fixed effect* coefficients in the statistical literature); and $\boldsymbol{\alpha}_m$ and $\boldsymbol{\beta}_j$ are the coefficient vectors specific to member m and job j, respectively. $\boldsymbol{\alpha}_m$ and $\boldsymbol{\beta}_j$ are called *random effects* coefficients, which capture member m's personal preference on different item features and item j's attraction for different member features.

[1]https://spark.apache.org
[2]https://github.com/linkedin/photon-ml

Priors: To mitigate the risk of overfitting due to the large number of parameters and sparsity of the data, we put the following Gaussian priors on both fixed effects and random effects:

$$\boldsymbol{b} \sim N(0, \tfrac{1}{\lambda_b}I), \quad \boldsymbol{\alpha}_m \sim N(0, \tfrac{1}{\lambda_\alpha}I), \quad \boldsymbol{\beta}_j \sim N(0, \tfrac{1}{\lambda_\beta}I), \quad (2)$$

where I is the identity matrix, $\frac{1}{\lambda_b}$ is the prior variance of $\boldsymbol{b}$, and $\frac{1}{\lambda_\alpha}$ and $\frac{1}{\lambda_\beta}$ are the prior variances of $\boldsymbol{\alpha}_m$ and $\boldsymbol{\beta}_j$.

Model behavior: Like many other recommender system applications, we observe a lot of heterogeneity in the amount of data per member or job. There are new members to the site (hence almost no data) as well as members who have strong job search intentions and applied for many jobs in the past. Similarly, for jobs there are both popular and unpopular ones. For a member m with many responses to different items in the past, we are able to accurately estimate her personal coefficient vector $\boldsymbol{\alpha}_m$ and provide personalized predictions. On the other hand, if member m does not have much past response data, the posterior mean of $\boldsymbol{\alpha}_m$ will be close to zero, and the model for member m will fall back to the global fixed effect component $\boldsymbol{x}'_{mjt}\boldsymbol{b}$. The same behavior applies to the per-job coefficient vector $\boldsymbol{\beta}_j$.

2.3 General Formulation

We now consider a more generic formulation of GLMix where more than two sets of random effects can be present in the model. This is useful for scenarios such as multi-context modeling, where we can have random effects to model the interactions between the context id and user/item features. The general formulation of GLMix is provided in the following equation:

$$\begin{aligned} g(E[y_n]) &= \boldsymbol{x}'_n\boldsymbol{b} + \sum_{r\in\mathcal{R}} \boldsymbol{z}'_{rn}\boldsymbol{\gamma}_{r,i(r,n)}, \\ \boldsymbol{b} &\sim p(\boldsymbol{b}), \quad \boldsymbol{\gamma}_{rl} \sim p(\boldsymbol{\gamma}_{rl}), \quad \forall r \in \mathcal{R}, 1 \le l \le N_r \end{aligned} \quad (3)$$

Comparing equation (3) with (1), the following new notations are introduced: Let $\mathcal{R}$ denote the collection of random effect types being modeled. Also let $i(r,n)$ denote an indexing function that retrieves the index of random effect type r in the n-th training sample; for example, if random effect type r corresponds to the per-job random effect, $i(r,n)$ then returns the job ID associated with sample n. Given the definition of the indices, we use $\boldsymbol{\gamma}_{r,i(r,n)}$ to denote random effect coefficient vector and $\boldsymbol{z}_{rn}$ as the corresponding feature vector, for random effect type r in the n-th sample. For the specific case of job recommendations, there are two types of random effects: $\mathcal{R} = \{\text{member}, \text{job}\}$, and n is a per-sample index that represents the triple (m,j,t). For the member-level random effect (i.e., r=member), $\boldsymbol{z}_{rn}$ represents $\boldsymbol{s}_j$ and $\boldsymbol{\gamma}_{r,i(r,n)}$ represents $\boldsymbol{\alpha}_m$. For the job-level random effect (i.e., r=job), $\boldsymbol{z}_{rn}$ represents $\boldsymbol{q}_m$ and $\boldsymbol{\gamma}_{r,i(r,n)}$ represents $\boldsymbol{\beta}_j$.

We generalize the Gaussian priors of fixed effects $\boldsymbol{b}$ and random effects to $p(\cdot)$, and also use N_r to denote the total number of instances for random effect type r, e.g., when r represents member, N_r represents the total number of members in the data set.

2.4 Extensions

We note that GLMix can be extended by incorporating other popular modeling approaches in recommender systems, such as matrix factorization [11]. For example, for the job recommendation application, a simple extension to the model in Equation (1) with an additional matrix factorization component is:

$$g(E[y_{mjt}]) = \boldsymbol{x}'_{mjt}\boldsymbol{b} + \boldsymbol{s}'_j\boldsymbol{\alpha}_m + \boldsymbol{q}'_m\boldsymbol{\beta}_j + \boldsymbol{u}'_m\boldsymbol{v}_j, \quad (4)$$

where $\boldsymbol{u}'_m$ and $\boldsymbol{v}_j$ are k-dimensional member and job factors, respectively.

3. ALGORITHM

In this section we describe our scalable algorithm for the GLMix model using parallel block-wise coordinate descent (PBCD). We start with the algorithm itself in Section 3.1, and in Section 3.2 we discuss the implementation details under the Bulk Synchronous Parallel (BSP) [21] paradigm and lessons learned, such as how to take the network I/O communication complexity into account and how to reduce the size of the random effect coefficients.

Throughout the section, we use the notation of the general formulation described in Section 2.3. Given the set of sample responses $\boldsymbol{y}(\Omega) = \{y_n\}_{n\in\Omega}$, where Ω is the set of sample indices, the main parameters to learn are the fixed effect coefficients $\boldsymbol{b}$ and random effect coefficients $\boldsymbol{\Gamma} = \{\Gamma_r\}_{r\in\mathcal{R}}$, where $\Gamma_r = \{\boldsymbol{\gamma}_{rl}\}_{l=1}^{N_r}$. The hyper-parameters for the priors of $\boldsymbol{b}$ and $\boldsymbol{\Gamma}$, such as λ_b, λ_α and λ_β for the job recommendation case, can be tuned through cross-validation.

For the general formulation of the GLMix model specified in Equation (3), the posterior mode of $\boldsymbol{b}$ and $\boldsymbol{\Gamma}$ can be found through the following optimization problem:

$$\max_{\boldsymbol{b}, \{\Gamma_r\}_{r\in\mathcal{R}}} \sum_{n\in\Omega} \log p(y_n|s_n) + \log p(\boldsymbol{b}) + \sum_{r\in\mathcal{R}}\sum_{l=1}^{N_r} \log p(\boldsymbol{\gamma}_{rl}), \quad (5)$$

where s_n is defined as

$$s_n = \boldsymbol{x}'_n\boldsymbol{b} + \sum_{r\in\mathcal{R}} \boldsymbol{z}'_{rn}\boldsymbol{\gamma}_{r,i(r,n)}, \quad (6)$$

and $p(y_n|s_n)$ is the underlying likelihood function of the link function $g[E[y_n]]$ for response y_n given $\boldsymbol{b}$ and $\boldsymbol{\Gamma}$.

3.1 Parallel Block-wise Coordinate Descent

Traditionally, the fitting algorithms for random effect models require $\boldsymbol{\Gamma}$ to be integrated out either analytically or numerically (literature review can be found in Section 6), which becomes infeasible when facing industry-scale large data sets. Similarly, both deterministic and MCMC sampling based algorithms that operate on $\boldsymbol{\Gamma}$ as a whole become cumbersome.

In Algorithm 1, we propose a parallel block-wise coordinate descent based iterative conditional mode algorithm, where the posterior mode of the random effect coefficients Γ_r for each random effect r is treated as a block-wise coordinate to be optimized in the space of unknown parameters. Given the scores $\boldsymbol{s}$ defined in equation (6), the optimization problems for updating the fixed effects $\boldsymbol{b}$ and the random effects $\boldsymbol{\Gamma}$ are provided in Equation (7) and (8), respectively:

$$\boldsymbol{b} = \arg\max_{\boldsymbol{b}} \left\{ \log p(\boldsymbol{b}) + \sum_{n\in\Omega} \log p(y_n|s_n - \boldsymbol{x}'_n\boldsymbol{b}^{old} + \boldsymbol{x}'_n\boldsymbol{b}) \right\} \quad (7)$$

Algorithm 1: Parallel block-wise coordinate descent (PBCD) for GLMix

while *not converged* **do**
  Update fixed effect $\boldsymbol{b}$ as in (7)
  foreach $n \in \Omega$ *in parallel* **do**
    Update s_n as in (9)
  foreach $r \in \mathcal{R}$ **do**
    foreach $l \in \{1, \dots, N_r\}$ *in parallel* **do**
      Update random effect $\boldsymbol{\gamma}_{rl}$ as in (8)
    foreach $n \in \Omega$ *in parallel* **do**
      Update s_n as in (10)

$$\boldsymbol{\gamma}_{rl} = \arg\max_{\boldsymbol{\gamma}_{rl}} \Big\{ \log p(\boldsymbol{\gamma}_{rl}) + \sum_{n|i(r,n)=l} \log p(y_n | s_n - \boldsymbol{z}'_{rn}\boldsymbol{\gamma}^{old}_{rl} + \boldsymbol{z}'_{rn}\boldsymbol{\gamma}_{rl}) \Big\} \quad (8)$$

As in most coordinate descent algorithms, we perform incremental updates for $\boldsymbol{s} = \{s_n\}_{n\in\Omega}$ for computational efficiency. More specifically, when the fixed effects $\boldsymbol{b}$ get updated, Equation (9) is applied for updating $\boldsymbol{s}$; and when the random effects $\boldsymbol{\Gamma}$ get updated, Equation (10) is used.

$$s^{new}_n = s^{old}_n - \boldsymbol{x}'_n\boldsymbol{b}^{old} + \boldsymbol{x}'_n\boldsymbol{b}^{new} \quad (9)$$

$$s^{new}_n = s^{old}_n - \boldsymbol{z}'_{rn}\boldsymbol{\gamma}^{old}_{r,i(r,n)} + \boldsymbol{z}'_{rn}\boldsymbol{\gamma}^{new}_{r,i(r,n)} \quad (10)$$

Note that Equation (7) and (8) are both standard optimization problems for generalized linear model, for which many numerical optimizers are available for large data sets, such as L-BFGS, SGD, or TRON, and they can be easily parallelized for scalability [9, 14].

3.2 Implementation Details

In this section, we discuss some details on how to implement the parallel block-wise coordinate descent algorithm (PBCD) for GLMix described in Algorithm 1 under the BSP paradigm. Other alternatives for implementing PBCD such as using parameter server are discussed in Section 6.

We first introduce some additional notation, and then discuss the implementation details for updating the fixed effects and the random effects, respectively. An overview of the k-th iteration of the block coordinate descent algorithm for GLMix is given in Figure 2.

3.2.1 Some Notations

At iteration k of Algorithm 1, let $\boldsymbol{s}^k$ denote the current value of $\boldsymbol{s} = \{s_n\}_{n\in\Omega}$. Let P denote the dimension of the fixed effect feature space, i.e., $\boldsymbol{x}_n \in \mathbb{R}^P$, and P_r denote the dimension of the feature space for random effect r, i.e., $\boldsymbol{z}_{rn} \in \mathbb{R}^{P_r}$. And we use C to denote the overall dimension of the feature space, that is:

$$C = P + \sum_{r\in\mathcal{R}} P_r N_r, \quad (11)$$

where N_r denotes the number of random effects of type r (e.g., number of users). For the set of sample responses $\boldsymbol{y}(\Omega) = \{y_n\}_{n\in\Omega}$, we use $|\Omega|$ to denote the size of Ω, i.e. the total number of training samples. We also let $|\mathcal{R}|$ be the number of types of random effects, and M be the number of computing nodes in the cluster. These numbers will be used to compute and discuss the network I/O cost of our proposed approach, which is usually one of the major bottlenecks for an algorithm to scale up in a distributed computing environment [27, 16]

3.2.2 Updating Fixed Effects

We consider the details of updating the fixed effect $\boldsymbol{b}$ at iteration k, following Equation (7). We start with preparing the training data with both the feature set $\boldsymbol{x}_n$ and the latest score s^k_n, and partition them into M nodes. This is identified as Superstep 1 in Figure 2. Given the training data, numerous types of distributed algorithms can be applied to learn $\boldsymbol{b}$, such as [16, 6]. Here we adopt the all-reduce [1] type of implementation for generalized linear models as in MLlib [12]. First, the gradient of $\boldsymbol{b}$ for each sample n is computed and aggregated from each node to the master node. The master node computes the total gradient and updates $\boldsymbol{b}$ using optimizers such as L-BFGS. This corresponds to Superstep 2 in Figure 2. The new coefficients $\boldsymbol{b}^{new}$ are then broadcast back to each node together with $\boldsymbol{b}^{old}$ to update the score $\boldsymbol{s}$ as in Equation (9), in order to prepare for the next effect's update. This phase corresponds to Superstep 3 in Figure 2. Since the main network communication here is the transmission of $\boldsymbol{b}$ from the master node to the worker nodes, the overall network communication cost for one iteration of updating the fixed effects is $\mathcal{O}(MP)$. One trick we found empirically useful is that it sometimes improves convergence to update $\boldsymbol{b}$ multiple times before we update the random effects, for each iteration in Algorithm 1.

In summary, updating the fixed effects consists of three supersteps: (1) Preparing the training data with scores $\boldsymbol{s}$. (2) Updating the coefficients $\boldsymbol{b}$. (3) Updating the scores $\boldsymbol{s}$.

3.2.3 Updating Random Effects

The main challenge in designing a scalable algorithm for GLMix on data sets with a huge number of random effects is that the dimension of the random effect coefficient space can potentially be as large as $N_r P_r$. Therefore, if we naively apply the same approach as the one used in updating fixed effects, the network communication cost for updating the random effects for r becomes MN_rP_r. Given some data of moderate size for example, if $N_r = 10^6$, $P_r = 10^5$ and a cluster with $M = 100$, the network I/O cost amounts to 10^{13}! As a result, the key to making the algorithm scalable is to avoid communicating or broadcasting the random effect coefficient across the computing nodes in the cluster.

Before the random effect updating phase and as a preprocessing step, for each random effect r and ID l, we group the feature vectors $\boldsymbol{z}_{rn}$ to form a feature matrix $\boldsymbol{Z}_{rl}$, which consists of all the $\boldsymbol{z}_{rn}$ that satisfy $i(r,n) = l$. At iteration k and for random effect r, we shuffle the current values of $\boldsymbol{s} = \{s^k_n\}_{n\in\Omega}$ using the same strategy, *i.e.* for ID l we group s^k_n to form a vector $\boldsymbol{S}^k_l$, which consists of all the s^k_n that satisfies $i(r,n) = l$. With the right partitioning strategies, $\boldsymbol{S}^k_l$ can be made to collocate with the corresponding feature matrix $\boldsymbol{Z}_{rl}$, to prepare the training data for updating the random effects r, using Equation (8). This step corresponds to Superstep 4 in Figure 2. With the training data ready for each ID l, any optimizer (*e.g.*, L-BFGS) can be applied again to solve the optimization problem locally, such that the random effects $\boldsymbol{\gamma}_{rl}$ can be learned in parallel without

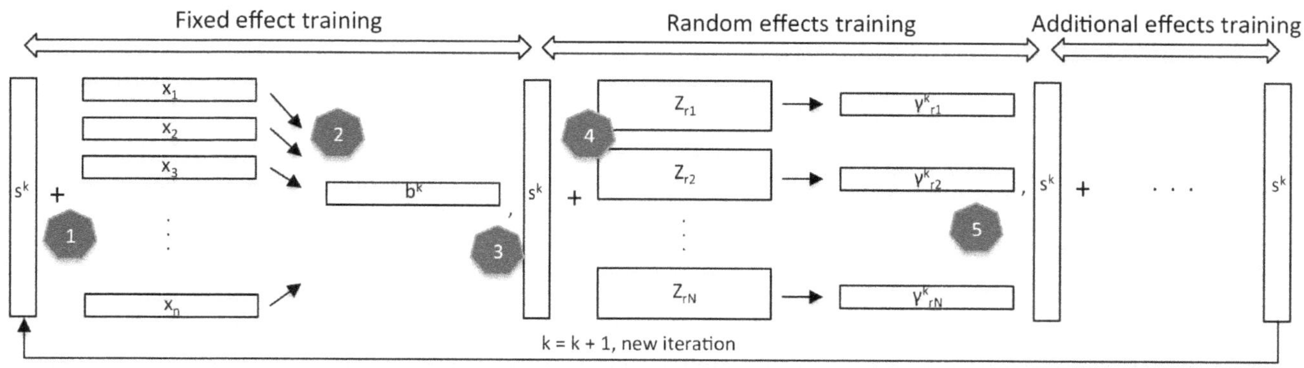

Figure 2: Overview of the kth iteration of the PBCD in BSP paradigm, with five supersteps highlighted in the blue boxes.

any additional network communication cost. Note that because both the coefficients and data collocate in the same node, the scores can be updated locally within the same step, and this phase corresponds to Superstep 5 in Figure 2. Also note that during the whole process, the random effect coefficients γ_{rl} live with the data and would never get communicated through the network; only $\boldsymbol{s}$ would get shuffled around the nodes through network I/O. As a result, the overall network communication cost for one iteration of updating one random effects is $\mathcal{O}(|\Omega|)$, and $\mathcal{O}(|\mathcal{R}||\Omega|)$ for $|\mathcal{R}|$ random effects.

Since the optimization problem in Equation (8) can be solved locally, we have an opportunity to apply some tricks that can further reduce the memory complexity C as defined in Equation (11). Note that although the overall feature space size is P_r for random effect r, sometimes the underlying dimension of the feature matrix $\boldsymbol{Z}_{rl}$ could be smaller than P_r, due to the lack of support for certain features. For example, a member who is a software engineer is unlikely to be served jobs with the required skill "medicine". Hence there will not be any data for the feature "job skill=medicine" for this member's random effects, and in such a scenario, $\boldsymbol{Z}_{rl}$ would end up with an empty column. As a result, for each random effect r and ID l, we can condense $\boldsymbol{Z}_{rl}$ by removing all the empty columns and reindexing the features to form a more compact feature matrix, which would also reduce the size of random effect coefficients γ_{rl} and potentially improve the overall efficiency of solving the local optimization problem in Equation (8). An example is shown in Figure 3, where we compare the random effect coefficient size before and after applying such a condensed data storage strategy on a data set consisting of four months' worth of LinkedIn's job recommendations. More details on the data set can be found in Section 4.

In summary, the updating of random effects consists of two supersteps: (1) Prepare the training data with scores $\boldsymbol{s}$. (2) Update the random effect coefficients and also the scores.

3.2.4 Summary

The overall I/O communication cost for our implementation for GLMix is $\mathcal{O}(MP + |\mathcal{R}||\Omega|)$. Since $|\mathcal{R}|$ is a small constant (usually less than 5), the communication cost is mainly bounded by the number of training instances $|\Omega|$.

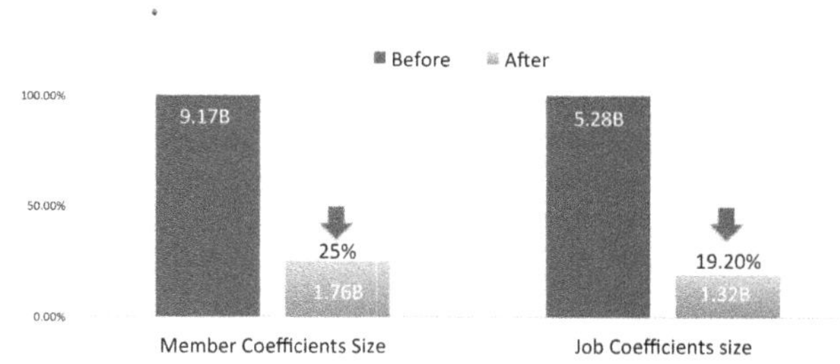

Figure 3: The member and job coefficient size before and after the reindexing and compression with the LinkedIn Job Recommendation data set.

This is a significant improvement compared to the naive implementation with a cost of $\mathcal{O}(MC)$, where C is defined in (11), which could approach $\mathcal{O}(MP_r|\Omega|)$ if we have a large number of random effects N_r that is of the same order as the number of the training instances $|\Omega|$ (*e.g.*, power law distribution). On the other hand, note that even with a large scale data set with *trillions* of training samples, the size of $\boldsymbol{s}$ is bounded to be a couple of terabytes. Given the recent advances in shuffling techniques [26], shuffling terabytes of data is no longer a significant challenge. At the same time, since the total number of random effects N_r no longer depends on the number of nodes in the cluster M, our algorithm has the chance to scale linearly with the number of executors.

4. EXPERIMENTS OF LINKEDIN JOB RECOMMENDATION

In this section, we describe our experiments for the LinkedIn job recommendation problem. Section 4.1 starts with the offline experimental results to compare several variations of GLMix models with a couple of baselines for prediction accuracy, and also experiments on scalability of GLMix in Section 4.1. In Section 4.2 we share implementation details of how we launched GLMix in LinkedIn's production system. We discuss the online A/B test results in Section 4.3.

4.1 Offline Experiments

4.1.1 Setup

All the methods used in the offline experiments are implemented using Apache Spark. In particular, the baseline methods such as ridge regression, ℓ_2-regularized logistic regression, matrix factorization with alternating least squares are from Spark's open source machine learning library MLlib. The experiments were conducted on a cluster consisting of 135 nodes managed by Apache YARN [3]. Each node has 24 Intel Xeon(R) CPU E5-2640 processors with 6 cores at 2.50GHz each, and every node has 250GB memory. In the following experiments, Spark is running on top of YARN as a client, and the memory for each Spark executor is configured to 10GB, where each executor corresponds to a container (e.g., a core of the node) in YARN.

4.1.2 Our Data

Our offline experiments are conducted using a sample of the four months' worth of data (07/2015 - 11/2015) of member's interactions on the "Jobs You May Be Interested In" module on the LinkedIn jobs homepage. The data include 500M samples with 5M members and 3M jobs. We split the data by time into training (90%), validation (5%) and test (5%).

Impressions that resulted in application clicks provide the positive responses, and impressions that did not result in application clicks provide the negative responses. Note that the detail job views are not considered in this experiment, since that is not the metric to optimize for. There are about $2K$ member features for $\boldsymbol{q}_m$, mostly extracted from public member profiles, e.g. industry, job function, education history, skills, and so forth. There are also around $2K$ job features for $\boldsymbol{s}_j$, e.g. the job title, key words in the description, required skills and qualifications etc. We consider two types of interactions among the member and job features: a) The cosine-similarity of the member and job features in the same domain, e.g. keywords in the summary of the member/job profile, or the skills of the member / job requirement. There are around 100 such cosine-similarity features, and we denote the feature vector as $\boldsymbol{f}_c$. b) The simple outer-product of the member and job features. After applying standard feature selection techniques we obtained 20K outer-product features (denoted as $\boldsymbol{f}_o$).

4.1.3 Experiments of Performance

We consider the following models in our offline experiments (where g denotes the link function $g(E[y_{mjt}])$):

- LR-Cosine: The baseline logistic regression model that only includes the cosine-similarity features $g = \boldsymbol{f}_c'\boldsymbol{b}$.
- LR-Full: The logistic regression model that includes all global features, $\boldsymbol{x}_{mjt} = \{\boldsymbol{q}_m, \boldsymbol{s}_j, \boldsymbol{f}_c, \boldsymbol{f}_o\}$, $g = \boldsymbol{x}_{mjt}'\boldsymbol{b}$.
- MF: A baseline matrix factorization model, $g = \boldsymbol{x}_{mjt}'\boldsymbol{b} + \boldsymbol{u}_m'\boldsymbol{v}_j$.
- GLMix-Member: The GLMix model which includes only the member-level random effects: $g = \boldsymbol{x}_{mjt}'\boldsymbol{b} + \boldsymbol{s}_j'\boldsymbol{\alpha}_m$.
- GLMix-Job: The GLMix model which includes only the job-level random effects: $g = \boldsymbol{x}_{mjt}'\boldsymbol{b} + \boldsymbol{q}_m'\boldsymbol{\beta}_j$.
- GLMix-Full: The full GLMix model as described in Equation (1).

[3]https://hadoop.apache.org

- GLMix-Full+MF: An extension of GLMix which adds an additional matrix factorization component, as in Equation (4).

For each model listed above, we tried multiple values of hyper-parameters for the priors (i.e. λ_b, λ_α and λ_β), picked the ones with the best AUC performance on the validation data, and then report their AUC on the test data in Table 1. It is not surprising that adding the member and job random effects to the model dramatically improves the AUC performance (0.723 for LR-Full vs 0.799 for GLMix-Full). There are also two other interesting observations: a) GLMix-Full significantly outperforms MF, which indicates that for this data, using features to interact with member/job IDs is more effective than the interactions among member IDs and job IDs. We believe this is due to the sparse structure of the data and also because the features are very useful. b) Adding matrix factorization to GLMix-Full provides very little improvement in terms of AUC (0.799 to 0.801). This indicates that GLMix already captures most signals of the data, and adding matrix factorization for additional signals in the residual is not effective.

4.1.4 Experiments of Scalability

In this section, we study a) how GLMix scales up with the increase of both data size and the number of Spark executors used, and b) how GLMix speeds up with the increase of number of Spark executors, while fixing the data size. In this experiment, the size of data is controlled by the number of days used to collect the data, e.g., 60 days of the data is about half of the size of 120 days of the data. The experiment results can be found in Figure 4. In general, we find that our proposed algorithm has good scalability properties, and achieves roughly linear speed-up on the Spark cluster, provided that the amount of data processed per executor does not become so small that system overheads start to dominate.

In Figure 4, we also provide the details on the change of the data complexity C, as defined in Equation (11), as the data size increases. We note that the scalability of our implementation is quite robust to the increasing complexity of the data set. If we had used the naive implementation where the network I/O complexity is proportional to the data complexity, it would have been much worse.

4.2 GLMix in Production System

LinkedIn operates one of the largest job recommendation systems in the world, which serves relevant jobs to members who visit the Job Homepage every day. For each member visit, it is required that we rank millions of jobs using relevance models and serve the top ranked ones in less than a second. Apart from model training challenges, to productionize a GLMix model with a huge number of features and random effects, the scoring and ranking become another critical challenge to overcome.

Our approach to mitigate such a challenge is to have a two-stage ranking strategy. In the first stage of the ranking, we convert it to a search-like problem by leveraging the open-source library Apache Lucene [4]. In this stage, an inverted job index is built, where keys are the job features and values are the corresponding job IDs. We run the baseline model LR-Cosine in this stage, which works efficiently with

[4]https://lucene.apache.org/

Model	LR-Cosine	LR-Full	MF	GLMix-Member	GLMix-Job	GLMix-Full	GLMix-Full+MF
AUC	0.664	0.723	0.772	0.780	0.758	0.799	**0.801**

Table 1: Offline model performance for LinkedIn Job Recommendation data.

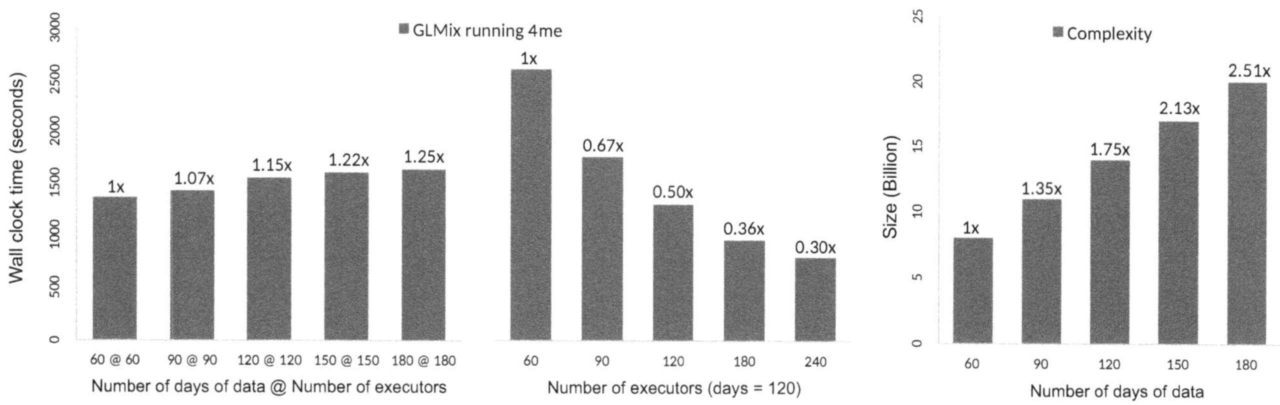

Figure 4: Left and Mid panel: Scale up and speed up results on the Spark cluster. The scale-up experiment is shown on the left panel, where we increase the number of days of data and the amount of Spark executors used at the same time, and the speed-up experiment is shown on the mid panel, where we fix the number of days of data and increase the number of Spark executors used. Right panel: Data complexity as a function of number of days of data.

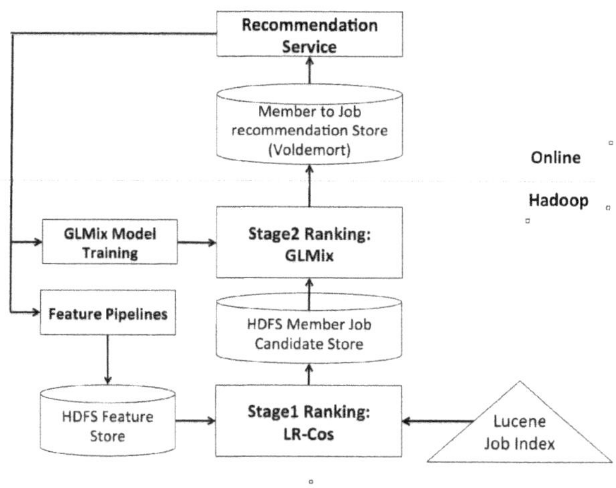

Figure 5: High-level architecture of GLMix in job recommendation production system

Lucene (since all the features are cosine-similarity based), and select the top K results (e.g. K=1000) for the second stage ranking. In the second stage, we re-score the top K results using the full GLMix model and show the top-ranked jobs to the member.

Although such a two-stage strategy can be implemented online, at this time we choose an offline approach as in Figure 5, for more flexibility in experimentation and because of the fact that jobs are usually more evergreen than news articles. Through Hadoop Map-Reduce, we pre-generate the top job recommendations for all members, and push them to an online distributed key-value store using Voldemort [5], where the keys are member IDs and the values are the recommended job IDs. When a member visits the Jobs Homepage, we simply retrieve the recommended jobs from the store, do some post-processing (e.g. freshness control), and show them to the members. This offline-based approach to serve online recommendations has proven to be very valuable in facilitating our experimentation and exploration of new features. Through A/B tests, whatever member or job features that become available on our Hadoop system, we can quickly test them before fully implementing the features in the online retrieval systems, which usually takes much more time.

Note that the two-stage scoring approach is very important even if we move the computation offline: Although it is possible to use Hadoop Map-Reduce to score millions of jobs for each of the 400M LinkedIn members using GLMix, the amount of Hadoop resources it consumes is too high to be cost-efficient.

We also note that it is required to retrain the GLMix model frequently (e.g. every hour or every day). Our offline experiments show that the AUC of GLMix-Full drops from 0.799 to 0.765 if we do not update the model for 20 days.

4.3 Online Experimental Results

We deployed the GLMix-Full model to the LinkedIn job recommendation system as described in Section 4.2 and ran an A/B test to compare with the existing baseline model in the production system, which uses the LR-Cosine model. Each model served a randomly-selected 2% of members, and we report the online experimental results for a week's data in November 2015.

In Figure 6 we show the lift of the job application clicks and job detail views comparing the GLMix model against the baseline LR-Cosine model, for each day of the week. We observe that every day there is a 20%-40% lift of the job application clicks, and interestingly also a consistent 10%-20% lift of job detail views. This shows that a more relevant job recommendation model, which is optimized for job applications, can also dramatically increase the number of times

[5]http://www.project-voldemort.com/voldemort/

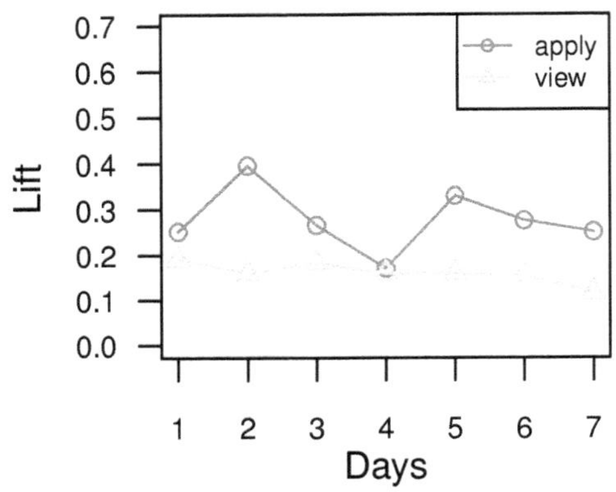

Figure 6: The lift of job application clicks and job detail views comparing GLMix-Full and the baseline model LR-Cosine, for each day of the week.

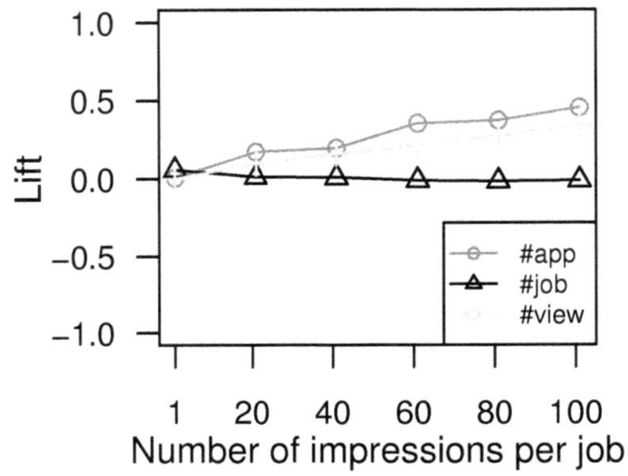

Figure 7: The #app and #view curves are the lift of job application clicks and job detail views comparing GLMix-Full against the baseline model LR-Cosine, for different segments of jobs with different numbers of impressions. The curve of #job shows the lift of the number of jobs per segment comparing GLMix-Full and LR-Cosine.

people click on the job thumbnails to view a given job posting in detail. To further understand the experimental results and investigate the effectiveness of the job random effects in the GLMix model, we segment our online A/B test data by the number of impressions per job, ranging from 1 to 100, and show the lift of job application clicks and detail views comparing GLMix with LR-Cosine in Figure 7. It is interesting to observe that as a job gets more impressions (which is when the per-job random effects become more effective), GLMix generates more lifts compared to the baseline. In the meantime, note that the distribution of the number of impressions per job changes very little, indicating that the GLMix model does not simply serve more popular jobs to members to obtain such a lift in application clicks (in that case the total number of jobs that receive one impression would have dramatically shrunk), instead it tries to serve more relevant jobs to members while keeping the distribution of impressions per job unchanged.

Similarly, we study the effectiveness of the member random effects by segmenting the data into 8 buckets based on the number of visits per member in Figure 8. We observe similar rising patterns for the lift of job application clicks as the number of visits per member increases. There is some slight up patterns of the job detail view curve too but not very significant. The distribution of total number of visits per member remains unchanged since this is a randomized A/B test experiment.

5. EXPERIMENTS ON PUBLIC DATA SETS

In this section, we report the performance of GLMix on two public data sets to demonstrate its modeling capability.

KDD Cup 2012 Track 2: We obtain this data set from https://www.kddcup2012.org/c/kddcup2012-track2. Recall that N_r and P_r denote the random effect size and feature dimension of random effect of type $r \in \mathcal{R}$ respectively, and complexity $= N_r * P_r$, which represents the size of the design matrix resulting from the outer product between the random effect IDs and the features. Basic statistics of the data set is summarized in Table 2.

All the features used through the experiments are raw features from the data set. No feature engineering has been conducted for two reasons: (*i*) to compare GLMix against models with less granularity but trained on well-engineered features as reported in [22] and [18]; and (*ii*) to make it more clear whether the lift results from the well-engineered features, or from GLMix itself. Nevertheless, we believe the best performance could come from the combination of well-engineered features and fine-grained modeling. We leave such study as future work. The features provided in the data set include the position of the ad, the user's age and gender, the tokens of the query, the ad keyword, and the title. The details of the features can be found on the website above.

The accuracy results of different models, measured by AUC are shown in Table 3. The GLMix model with all random effects (G-All) significantly outperforms LR and other variants of GLMix with fewer random effects (*e.g.*, G-Query, which only contains the per-query random effect coefficients). This shows that adding random effects can usually improve model accuracy. We also compare GLMix to other existing methods. In particular, G-All outperforms both RankMF [22] and FM [18] based on their published results. When comparing to the best models in the KDD Cup competition, G-All is ranked between top 5 to top 10.

One thing to note is that all of the models that outperform G-All are ensemble methods, and G-All is the best among the single models.

Type	N_r	$N_r P_r$
user	22,023,547	286,306,111
advertiser	14,847	14,450,644,488
ad	641,707	624,575,989,928
query	24,122,076	4.5192951e+12
title	3,735,796	115,809,676
description	2,934,101	90,957,131
keyword	1,188,089	36,830,759

Table 2: Summary of KDD Cup 2012 Track 2 Data

Yahoo! Music: We obtain this data set from Yahoo! Web-

Model	LR	G-Advertiser	G-Ad	G-Query	G-All	RankMF	FM	Top 5	Top 10	Top 50
Public AUC	0.7497	0.7696	0.7716	0.7698	**0.7982**	0.7968	0.7901	0.7987	0.7925	0.7563
Private AUC	0.7503	0.7645	0.7703	0.7729	**0.7940**	-	0.7932	**0.8017**	0.7938	0.7565

Table 3: Model performance on KDD Cup 2012 Track 2. LR stands for logistic regression, G-name stands for GLMix model with random effect of type name included, G-All stands for GLMix model with all random effects included. RankMF is the best single model reported in [22], FM is the factorization machine reported in [18], Top K means the top k model performance reported on the public/private leaderboard.

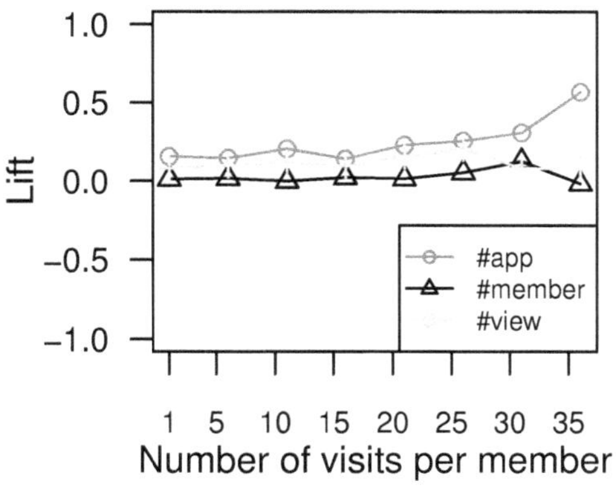

Figure 8: The #app and #view curves are the lift of job application clicks and job detail views comparing GLMix-Full and the baseline model LR-Cosine, for different segments of members with different number of visits. The curve of #member shows the lift of the number of members per segment comparing GLMix-Full and LR-Cosine.

scope (http://webscope.sandbox.yahoo.com): R2 - Yahoo! Music User Ratings of Songs with Artist, Album, and Genre Meta Information, v.1.0. Basic statistics of the data set can be found in Table 4. Features used in this experiment are listed as follows:

- Song attributes: Artist ID, album ID, and genre ID. The total number of such features used is 30,065.
- User latent features and song latent features: Since there is no user feature provided by the data set, we use matrix factorization with rank 30 to generate latent factors for users and songs, and treat them as features.

The root mean squared errors (RMSEs) of these models are reported in Table 5, where the linear model without random effects (RR) does not perform well and MF performs better than GLMix with either only user random effects or only song random effects. However, when both random effects are included, GLMix-Full outperforms MF.

Type	N_r	$N_r P_r$
User	1,623,179	48,833,340,215
Song	136,736	4,113,702,560

Table 4: Summary of Yahoo! Music Data

6. RELATED WORK

Generalized linear mixed models (GLMix) have been thoroughly studied in Statistics [15] and widely applied in many applications. For recommender systems, the full GLMix model that is described in this paper was originally introduced in [3]. There are also many other works with similar or related ideas. For example, [2] used item-level random effects to model the per-ad-campaign interactions with user features,[25] considered recommender system problems such as the Netflix challenge from the perspective of multi-task learning, and described a hierarchical per-item random effect model restricted to the Gaussian case. Our model differs from previous approaches mostly in that our method scales GLMix to industry-scale data sets with an efficient parallel block-wise coordinate descent algorithm.

Traditionally the model fitting approaches for GLMix have relied on Gibbs sampling [3, 10] or trying to integrate the log likelihood over the random effect and obtaining the marginal maximum likelihood estimates of the hyper-parameters [4, 8]. However, for non-Gaussian scenarios, the integral is often not closed form; thus approximations such as adaptive Gauss-Hermite quadrature need to be applied. Note that such approximations only work for scalar random effects, not the multi-dimensional cases where we need to model per-user/item interactions with features. Scaling to large data sets is a problem that none of the above approaches have addressed.

Block coordinate descent algorithms (BCD) have been a natural choice for generalized linear models with certain structures. For example, [17] used BCD for group lasso in logistic regression, and [5] applied BCD for multi-class classification. [19] tried to leverage repeated patterns in the design matrix to create blocks to boost the efficiency of the learning algorithms. [20] used BCD for a mixed effects model that contains only the scalar random effects for Gaussian responses. Therefore, we consider BCD as a natural choice for the GLMix model (more general than the ones with only scalar random effects) in this paper as well.

The parallelization of the BCD algorithms is also a popular area in machine learning research, aiming to speed up parameter learning for loss functions that are separable or partially separable [7]. The ideas are generally to update blocks of parameter estimates in parallel, and the blocks are formed either by natural structure or random sets of parameters. In this paper, since the user/item-level random effects have a natural block structure, the parallelization becomes trivial.

The use of a parameter server [23, 13] is an active research area, which can be used to fit models with a large number of features. In this work we choose to focus on the BSP paradigm and work with Apache Spark because it fits naturally into LinkedIn's distributed computing ecosystem. However, investigating GLMix with parameter server is a promising future direction for research.

7. CONCLUSION

Generalized linear models (GLMs) have been successfully applied to a wide range of applications such as response

Model	MF (rank = 30)	RR	GLMix-User	GLMix-Song	GLMix-Full
RMSE	1.07	1.2734	1.0716	1.0911	**1.0510**

Table 5: Model performance on Yahoo! Music data, MF is trained with Spark MLlib's ALS, RR is a linear model without random effects, GLMix-User and GLMix-Song only models user and song as random effect, respectively, while GLMix-Full models both user and song as random effects.

prediction. However, when the data is abundant at the user/item level, more fine-grained modeling strategies are desired since capturing signals from the user/item's idiosyncrasies in addition to the global pattern could lead to a potentially considerable performance gain. Although it is tempting to apply GLMix on large scale data set, it is also challenging because scalability becomes a problem as the number of parameters of GLMix grows with the size of the data.

In this paper we propose to use GLMix to extend GLM in a way such that the user/item-level idiosyncrasies are captured by the random effects, as a complement to the fixed effect which is responsible for modeling the global pattern. To address the scalability challenge when applying GLMix to the large-scale data, we propose a parallel block-wise coordinate descent algorithm under the bulk synchronous parallel paradigm, and implemented it using Apache Spark. Through extensive experiments we demonstrated the effectiveness, efficiency and scalability of the proposed approach. We also shared our experience of deploying GLMix in the LinkedIn job recommendation system, and showed significant lifts of job applications over the production baseline.

8. REFERENCES

[1] A. Agarwal, O. Chapelle, M. Dudík, and J. Langford. A reliable effective terascale linear learning system. *J. Mach. Learn. Res.*, 2014.

[2] D. Agarwal, B. Long, J. Traupman, D. Xin, and L. Zhang. Laser: A scalable response prediction platform for online advertising. In *WSDM*, 2014.

[3] A. Ansari, S. Essegaier, and R. Kohli. Internet recommendation systems. *Journal of Marketing research*, 2000.

[4] D. Bates, M. Mächler, B. Bolker, and S. Walker. Fitting linear mixed-effects models using lme4. *arXiv preprint arXiv:1406.5823*, 2014.

[5] M. Blondel, K. Seki, and K. Uehara. Block coordinate descent algorithms for large-scale sparse multiclass classification. *Machine learning*, 2013.

[6] S. Boyd, N. Parikh, E. Chu, B. Peleato, and J. Eckstein. Distributed optimization and statistical learning via the alternating direction method of multipliers. *Found. Trends Mach. Learn.*, 2011.

[7] J. K. Bradley, A. Kyrola, D. Bickson, and C. Guestrin. Parallel coordinate descent for l1-regularized loss minimization. *arXiv preprint arXiv:1105.5379*, 2011.

[8] N. E. Breslow and D. G. Clayton. Approximate inference in generalized linear mixed models. *Journal of the American Statistical association*, 1993.

[9] R. Fan, K. Chang, C. Hsieh, X. Wang, and C. Lin. LIBLINEAR: A library for large linear classification. *Journal of Machine Learning Research*, 2008.

[10] P. D. Hoff. Bilinear mixed-effects models for dyadic data. *Journal of the American Statistical association*, 2005.

[11] Y. Koren, R. Bell, and C. Volinsky. Matrix factorization techniques for recommender systems. *Computer*, 2009.

[12] T. Kraska, A. Talwalkar, J. C. Duchi, R. Griffith, M. J. Franklin, and M. I. Jordan. Mlbase: A distributed machine-learning system. In *CIDR*.

[13] M. Li, D. G. Andersen, J. W. Park, A. J. Smola, A. Ahmed, V. Josifovski, J. Long, E. J. Shekita, and B.-Y. Su. Scaling distributed machine learning with the parameter server. In *OSDI*, 2014.

[14] J. Liu, J. Chen, and J. Ye. Large-scale sparse logistic regression. In *KDD*, 2009.

[15] C. E. McCulloch and J. M. Neuhaus. *Generalized linear mixed models.* 2003.

[16] R. Mcdonald, M. Mohri, N. Silberman, D. Walker, and G. S. Mann. Efficient large-scale distributed training of conditional maximum entropy models. In *NIPS*. 2009.

[17] L. Meier, S. Van De Geer, and P. Bühlmann. The group lasso for logistic regression. *Journal of the Royal Statistical Society: Series B*, 2008.

[18] S. Rendle. Social network and click-through prediction with factorization machines. In *KDD Cup 2012 Workshop*.

[19] S. Rendle. Scaling factorization machines to relational data. In *PVLDB*, 2013.

[20] J. Schelldorfer, P. Bühlmann, G. DE, and S. VAN. Estimation for high-dimensional linear mixed-effects models using l1-penalization. *Scandinavian Journal of Statistics*, 2011.

[21] L. G. Valiant. A bridging model for parallel computation. *Commun. ACM*, 1990.

[22] K.-W. Wu, C.-S. Ferng, and et al. A two-stage ensemble of diverse models for advertisement ranking in kdd cup 2012. In *KDD Cup 2012 Workshop*.

[23] E. P. Xing, Q. Ho, W. Dai, J. K. Kim, J. Wei, S. Lee, X. Zheng, P. Xie, A. Kumar, and Y. Yu. Petuum: A new platform for distributed machine learning on big data. In *KDD*, 2015.

[24] H.-F. Yu, C.-J. Hsieh, S. Si, and I. Dhillon. Scalable coordinate descent approaches to parallel matrix factorization for recommender systems. In *ICDM*, 2012.

[25] K. Yu, J. Lafferty, S. Zhu, and Y. Gong. Large-scale collaborative prediction using a nonparametric random effects model. In *ICML*, 2009.

[26] M. Zaharia, M. Chowdhury, M. J. Franklin, S. Shenker, and I. Stoica. Spark: Cluster computing with working sets. *HotCloud*, 2010.

[27] Y. Zhang, M. J. Wainwright, and J. C. Duchi. Communication-efficient algorithms for statistical optimization. In *NIPS*. 2012.

A Non-parametric Approach to Detect Epileptogenic Lesions Using Restricted Boltzmann Machines

Yijun Zhao
CS Department
Tufts University
yzhao@cs.tufts.edu

Bilal Ahmed
CS Department
Tufts University
bahmed01@cs.tufts.edu

Thomas Thesen
Comprehensive Epilepsy Center
New York University
thomas.thesen@med.nyu.edu

Karen E. Blackmon
Comprehensive Epilepsy Center
New York University
karen.blackmon@nyumc.org

Jennifer G. Dy
ECE Department
Northeastern University
jdy@ece.neu.edu

Carla E. Brodley
College of Computer and Information Science
Northeastern University
c.brodley@neu.edu

ABSTRACT

Visual detection of lesional areas on a cortical surface is critical in rendering a successful surgical operation for Treatment Resistant Epilepsy (TRE) patients. Unfortunately, 45% of Focal Cortical Dysplasia (FCD, the most common kind of TRE) patients have no visual abnormalities in their brains' 3D-MRI images. We collaborate with doctors from NYU Langone's Comprehensive Epilepsy Center and apply machine learning methodologies to identify the resective zones for these *MRI-negative* FCD patients. Our task is particularly challenging because MRI images can only provide a limited number of features. Furthermore, data from different patients often exhibit inter-patient variabilities due to age, gender, left/right handedness, etc. In this paper, we introduce a new approach which combines the restricted Boltzmann machines and a Bayesian non-parametric mixture model to address these issues. We demonstrate the efficacy of our model by applying it to a retrospective dataset of MRI-negative FCD patients who are seizure free after surgery.

Keywords

mixture models, Bayesian non-parametric, Restricted Boltzmann Machine, predictive medicine, semi-supervised learning and application

1. INTRODUCTION

Epilepsy is a common neurological disorder, affecting approximately 1% of the population [14]. It is characterized by profound abnormal neural activity during seizures and interictal (between seizures) periods. Uncontrolled epilepsy can have harmful effects on the brain and has increased risk of injuries and sudden death [3]. About one third of epilepsy patients remain resistant to medical treatment [21]. Our research addresses the identification of lesions in the MRI's of patients with focal cortical dysplasia (FCD), which is recognized as the most common source of pediatric epilepsy [3, 35] and the third most common source in adults having medically intractable seizures [20, 22]. Early detection and subsequent surgical removal of the FCD lesion area is the most effective and is often the last hope for these patients.

The most widely used technology in identifying the epileptic lesions is MRI coupled with intracranial EEG (iEEG). For *MRI-positive* patients, (i.e., patients with visible abnormal areas in the MRI), the placement of electrodes on the cortex is informed by the pinpointed problematic regions detected by visual inspection of the MRI. However, for *MRI-negative* patients there is no visible lesion to guide precise electrode implantation [17]. The final target for surgical resection is based on both of these findings if available coupled with other clinical data. Consequently, the post-surgical success (i.e., seizure-freedom after surgery) ratio of MRI-positive to MRI-negative patients is 66% to 29%. Unfortunately, 45% of FCD patients are MRI-negative [37]. For this reason the surgical resection procedure remains highly underutilized as most practitioners are unwilling to operate in the absence of a visually detected lesion [34].

The machine learning task is to detect the lesional region(s) in MRI-negative patients. Specifically, our model identifies the abnormal areas in a patient's brain which in turn serve as a focus of attention mechanism for the neuroradiologists in placing the iEEG sensors on the patient's cortex. The work presented in this paper adopts a new Bayesian non-parametric approach as compared to our previous logistic regression (LR) based model [1]. Our LR model has been in use at NYU's Comprehensive Epilepsy Center since 2013. The new approach, as we present in Section 6, achieves improved performance compared to the LR model.

Our training data comes from the 3D-MRI images of MRI-negative FCD patients who underwent resective brain surgery at NYU and were seizure free after surgery. Furthermore, the resected tissue was histopathologically verified to contain FCD. We also have access to the MRI's of healthy controls who underwent the same MRI protocol. One challenge in applying machine learning to this dataset is the paucity

KDD '16, August 13-17, 2016, San Francisco, CA, USA

DOI: http://dx.doi.org/10.1145/2939672.2939705

of features available from the MRI that are predictive of lesional tissue (see Section 2.1 for a complete list of the available features). To address this issue, we employ the Restricted Boltzmann Machines (RBMs) [32, 40] to learn a new set of nonlinear features. An RBM is an undirected graphical model [18] which can be interpreted as a stochastic neural network. Through training, an RBM learns a closed-form distribution of the input data. The units in the bottom layer of the network correspond to the observable attributes and the top layer consists of hidden units that can be viewed as nonlinear feature detectors [16]. Thus, an RBM is often employed to extract more meaningful features from input data [29].

Another challenge while learning with this dataset is the impact of inter-patient variability, i.e., each human brain has its own characteristics depending on the severity of the disease, age, gender, left/right handedness, lifestyle and genetics many of which are not uniformly available in our data. Thus, learning from data collected from all patients does not lead to satisfactory performance. To address this issue, we partition the data into subgroups with the goal that each subgroup will contain instances with similar brain characteristics. Because we do not have sufficient domain knowledge to estimate the number of subgroups, we employ a Bayesian non-parametric Dirichlet process mixture model (DPM, [33]) to infer the number of clusters automatically from the data.

Our proposed approach leads to an infinite mixture of RBMs. Because a typical mixture (finite or infinite) of RBMs is computationally intractable [23], we propose a two-stage method. We first apply an RBM to the entire dataset and cluster the patients based on the hidden layer of this model using a DPM. The second stage applies a weighted version of RBM to each non-empty cluster using the weights obtained from the DPM model. We discuss the rationale behind this two-stage method in Section 5.1.

We evaluate our model on MRI-negative patients from NYU who were seizure free after resective surgery. Our evaluation includes a successful detection indicator (Y or N) within the resected region and the performance (true negative rate, TNR) outside the resection zone. We need to measure the performance of the two regions separately because we not only want to locate the lesion but also don't want to misclassify non-lesional benign tissue. Note that, instead of using the true positive rate (TPR), we use an indication to measure whether there is any lesion detected inside the resection zone. This is because in the absence of any visual information to locate the lesion precisely, very generous margins are employed during the surgery to ensure that the patient is seizure free afterwards. As a result, the TPR is not a meaningful evaluation metric because the resection zone is much larger than the actual lesion and contains benign areas. Instead, we are interested in assessing whether there is any detection that can potentially guide the placement of iEEG sensors with the ultimate goal of reducing the size of the resection zone, which will lead to a much safer yet effective surgery. In our experiments, our model has accuracies of greater than 99.4% in the benign region and a successful detection in the *resection region* in 7 out of 12 (i.e., 58%) patients (see details in Section 6). This is in contrast to neuroradiologists' visual MRI inspections that have a detection rate of 0 out 12.

In this paper, we first describe our method of constructing training data from 3D-MRI images of human brains using surface morphometry [10, 12]. We then present a brief introduction to RBM and DPM models in Sections 3 and 4 respectively. In Section 5, we outline our model which integrates the RBM and DPM algorithms. We present and discuss our results in Section 6 and conclude in Section 7.

2. SURFACE BASED MORPHOMETRY

Surface based morphometry (SBM) provides the means to characterize and analyze the human brain by explicitly modeling the cortex using a suitable geometric model [10]. The cortical surface represents the outer layer of the brain modeled as a folded two-dimensional surface. It is extracted by delineating the boundary between the gray and white matter using T1-weighted MRI images [10]. The reconstructed surface is represented as a triangulated surface [10], and at each vertex on the surface different morphological features such as cortical thickness, curvature, sulcal depth, etc., can be calculated to characterize the cortex. Similarly, different morphological transforms can be applied to register the cortical surface to a standard surface also known as a group-atlas. Registration is achieved by aligning specific sulcal and gyral landmarks across the *reconstructed* cortical surfaces allowing for a precise comparison of individual cortical structures across subjects [11]. SBM has been used successfully for analyzing and detecting neurological abnormalities in various neurological disorders such as schizophrenia [28], autism [25], and epilepsy [35, 17].

2.1 Feature Extraction

In this work we use five features to represent each vertex on the reconstructed surface:

1. *Cortical thickness* represents the thickness of the cortex which is defined as the distance between the gray/white matter boundary and the outermost surface of the gray matter (pial surface). It is calculated at each vertex using an average of two measurements [11]: (a) the shortest distance from the white matter surface to the pial surface; and (b) the shortest distance from the pial surface at each point to the white matter surface.

2. *Gray/white-matter contrast (GWC)* represents the degree of blurring at the gray/white-matter boundary. GWC is estimated by calculating the non-normalized T1 image intensity contrast at 0.5mm above and below the gray/white boundary with trilinear interpolation of the images. The range of GWC values lies in $[-1, 0]$, with values near zero indicating a higher degree of blurring of the gray/white boundary.

3. *Sulcal depth* characterizes the folded structure of the cortex. It is estimated by calculating the dot product of the movement vectors with the surface normal [12], and results in the calculation of the depth/height of each point above the average surface. The values of sulcal depth lie in the range $[-2, 2]$ with lower values indicating a location in the sulcus whereas higher values indicate a location on the gyral crown.

4. *Curvature* is measured as $\frac{1}{r}$, where r is the radius of an inscribed circle and mean curvature represents the average of two principal curvatures with a unit of 1/mm

[27]. Mean curvature quantifies the sharpness of cortical folding at the gyral crown or within the sulcus, and can be used to assess the folding of small secondary and tertiary folds in the cortical surface.

5. *Jacobian distortion* measures the magnitude of the nonlinear transform needed to wrap each vertex on the subject's brain to a target vetex on the average surface, as part of the registration process. This nonlinear transform is needed to align the gyral and sulcal landmarks between the source and the target brain. Jacobian distortion is a measure of global brain deformation, and has been used to characterize the cortex for analyzing a number of neurological disorders [13].

2.2 Automated FCD Lesion Detection

The machine learning task is to develop a classifier that can distinguish between normal and abnormal cortical tissue using the patient's MRI data. SBM has been used in conjunction with machine learning and statistical techniques to identify lesions in FCD patients. Besson et al. [4] use texture, GWC and a number of morphological features including cortical thickness to represent each vertex on the reconstructed cortical surface. They then train a neural network to classify each vertex as being normal or lesional. Similarly, Thesen et al. [35] use a univariate z-score based thresholding approach on registered SBM data to classify each vertex as being lesional or normal. Recently, Hong et al. [17] developed a two-stage Fisher linear discriminant analysis (LDA) [5] classifier to detect FCD lesions in MRI-negative patients. Initially they train a vertex-level classifier that classifies each vertex on the reconstructed cortical surface as being lesional or non-lesional for both controls and patients. These detections are further refined using another LDA classifier that is trained to distinguish between actual FCD lesions (detections made inside the manually refined resection zones of patients) and false lesional detections made on controls.

One of the major confounding factors inhibiting the development of an effective classifier for detecting FCD lesions is *inter-patient variability*. The morphology of the human brain such as its thickness, curvature and the overall structure in general are affected by different factors such as age, gender, handedness, etc. [30]. This causes a co-variate shift in data as the data from different patients is pooled to learn a common classifier. Similarly, the distribution of pathological features that define an FCD lesion differs across FCD subtypes. For example in addition to causing other morphological abnormalities, FCD type I lesions appear on MRI as abnormally thin regions of cortex, while FCD type II is characterized by abnormally thick regions. This heterogeneity of feature distributions that define the target concept (FCD lesion) for the learner must be taken into account to develop an effective supervised lesion detection scheme.

To counter the effects of differences in feature distributions across FCD subtypes, Hong et al. deal only with FCD type-II [17], while Ahmed et al. [1], stratify the training data into thick and thin lesions based on manual inspection of data, while other schemes bypass this training bias by posing lesion detection as an outlier/anomaly detection problem [35, 2]. However, none of the lesion detection schemes cited previously explicitly address the co-variate shift arising from inter-patient variability. To overcome this co-variate shift in the underlying data distributions, we train an ensemble of classifiers on a training set consisting of an equal number of patients from each of the three FCD subtypes, and control data taken from fifty neurotypical controls. In order to discover subgroups in data, that align with meaningful combinations of patient and FCD subtype characteristics we use a Dirichlet process based mixture of RBMs.

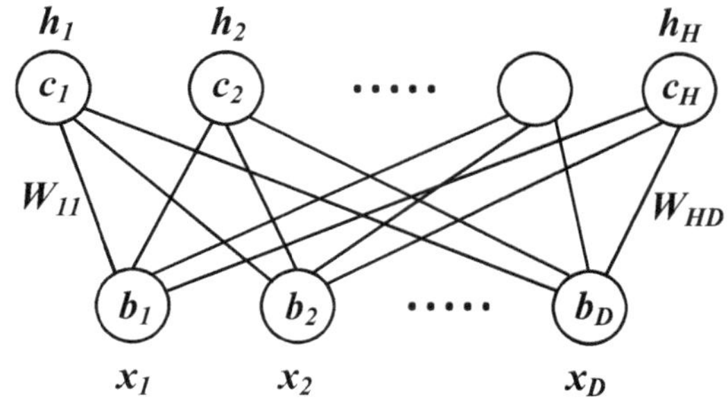

Figure 1: An RBM with D visible units and H hidden units

3. RESTRICTED BOLTZMANN MACHINES

Before describing our method in detail, we first review RBMs and DP mixture models.

3.1 Definition

A restricted Boltzmann machine (RBM, [32, 40]), illustrated in Figure 1, is an undirected graphic model that consists of two layers: a visible layer $\mathbf{x} = \{x_1, x_2, \ldots, x_D\}$, which represents the attributes of the input data, and a hidden layer $\mathbf{h} = \{h_1, h_2, \ldots, h_H\}$. Units across different layers are fully connected. However, connections within the same layer are restricted. The goal of an RBM is to model the distribution of the observations $\mathbf{x}$ with the help of hidden units $\mathbf{h}$.

We define the energy of an RBM as:

$$E(\mathbf{x}, \mathbf{h}) = -\mathbf{h}^\mathbf{T}\mathbf{W}\mathbf{x} - \mathbf{c}^\mathbf{T}\mathbf{x} - \mathbf{b}^\mathbf{T}\mathbf{h} \tag{1}$$

where $\mathbf{W} \in R^{H \times D}$ represents the weights connecting hidden and visible units and $\mathbf{b} \in R^D$, and $\mathbf{c} \in R^H$ are the offsets of the visible and hidden layers respectively. (1) directly leads to the following formulation for the probability density of $\mathbf{x}$:

$$p(\mathbf{x}) = e^{-F(\mathbf{x})}/\mathcal{Z} \tag{2}$$

where

$$F(\mathbf{x}) = \mathbf{c}^T\mathbf{x} + \sum_{j=1}^{H} \ln\left(1 + e^{(b_j + \mathbf{W}_j\mathbf{x})}\right) \tag{3}$$

$F(\mathbf{x})$ is often referred to as the free energy. H is the total number of hidden units and $\mathcal{Z} = \sum_{\mathbf{x}} e^{-F(\mathbf{x})}$ is the partition function. It can be shown that the conditional probability of h_i's given $\mathbf{x}$ is independent, i.e.,

$$p(\mathbf{h}|\mathbf{x}) = \prod_j p(h_j|\mathbf{x}) \tag{4}$$

and furthermore,

$$p(h_j = 1|\mathbf{x}) = \frac{1}{1 + exp(-(b_j + \mathbf{W}_j\mathbf{x}))} = \sigma(b_j + \mathbf{W}_j\mathbf{x}) \tag{5}$$

where $\sigma(\cdot)$ is the sigmoid function. Similarly, we have

$$p(\mathbf{x}|\mathbf{h}) = \prod_k p(x_k|\mathbf{h}) \quad (6)$$

$$p(x_k = 1|\mathbf{h}) = \frac{1}{1 + exp(-(c_k + \mathbf{h}^T\mathbf{W}_k))} = \sigma(c_k + \mathbf{h}^T\mathbf{W}_k) \quad (7)$$

Equations (4) - (7) allow us to make approximations to the inference algorithm described next.

3.2 Inference

Given the training data, the learning objective of an RBM is to adjust parameters $\{\mathbf{W}, \mathbf{b}, \mathbf{c}\}$ such that the free energy defined in (3) is minimized, which is equivalent to maximizing $p(\mathbf{x})$. A standard approach is to use stochastic gradient descent to minimize the average negative log-likelihood $\frac{1}{T}\sum_{t=1}^{T} - \ln p(\mathbf{x}^t)$. Thus, we calculate the partial derivatives with respect to each parameter and set them to zero to obtain a set of update rules. A learning algorithm iteratively updates the parameters until convergence. Specifically,

$$\begin{aligned} -\frac{\partial \ln p(\mathbf{x})}{\partial \theta} &= \frac{\partial F(\mathbf{x})}{\partial \theta} + \frac{1}{\mathcal{Z}}\frac{\partial \mathcal{Z}}{\partial \theta} \\ &= \frac{\partial F(\mathbf{x})}{\partial \theta} + \frac{1}{\mathcal{Z}}\sum_{\mathbf{x}} e^{-F(\mathbf{x})}\frac{\partial(-F(\mathbf{x}))}{\partial \theta} \\ &= \frac{\partial F(\mathbf{x})}{\partial \theta} - \sum_{\mathbf{x}} p(\mathbf{x})\frac{\partial F(\mathbf{x})}{\partial \theta} \end{aligned} \quad (8)$$

where $\theta \in \{\mathbf{c}, \mathbf{b}, \mathbf{W}\}$. The computational difficulty in (8) is the second term which is an expectation over an exponential number of configurations of the input $\mathbf{x}$ under $p(\mathbf{x})$. Hinton introduced the Contrastive Divergence (CD) learning algorithm [15] which makes this computation tractable by estimating the expectation using a sample, $\tilde{\mathbf{x}}$ from the model. This sample is obtained using k-steps of Gibbs sampling. Thus, (8) can be simplified to:

$$-\frac{\partial \ln p(\mathbf{x})}{\partial \theta} = \frac{\partial F(\mathbf{x})}{\partial \theta} - \frac{\partial F(\tilde{\mathbf{x}})}{\partial \theta} \quad (9)$$

For RBMs, because the hidden and visible units are conditionally independent (Equation (4), (6)), we can perform block Gibbs sampling, i.e., we sample all hidden (visible) units simultaneously given the values of the visible (hidden) units. In particular, starting with a given visible observation $\mathbf{x}^{(n)}$, we have:

$$\mathbf{h}^{(n+1)} \sim \sigma(\mathbf{W}'\mathbf{x}^{(n)} + \mathbf{c})$$

$$\mathbf{x}^{(n+1)} \sim \sigma(\mathbf{W}\mathbf{h}^{(n+1)} + \mathbf{b})$$

Consequently, the Contrastive Divergence learning algorithm with k steps of Gibbs sampling (CD-k) can be summarized as follows:

1. For each training example $\mathbf{x}^{(t)}$

   (a) Starting at $\mathbf{x}^{(t)}$, generate a sample $\tilde{\mathbf{x}}$ using k steps of Gibbs sampling.

   (b) Update parameters

$$\mathbf{W} \Longleftarrow \mathbf{W} + \alpha\left(h(\mathbf{x}^{(t)})\mathbf{x}^{(t)^T} - h(\tilde{\mathbf{x}})\tilde{\mathbf{x}}^T)\right)$$

$$\mathbf{b} \Longleftarrow \mathbf{b} + \alpha\left(h(\mathbf{x}^{(t)}) - h(\tilde{\mathbf{x}}))\right)$$

$$\mathbf{c} \Longleftarrow \mathbf{c} + \alpha\left(\mathbf{x}^{(t)} - \tilde{\mathbf{x}})\right)$$

   where $h(\mathbf{x}) = \sigma(\mathbf{b} + \mathbf{W}\mathbf{x})$ and α is the learning rate.

2. Go to Step 1 until the stopping criterion is met.

We set $k = 1$ in our model because it has been shown empirically that even when k is not large (e.g., $k = 1$), the CD-k algorithms often gives good results [9].

4. DIRICHLET PROCESS (DP) MIXTURE MODEL

Dirichlet process is a family of Bayesian nonparametric models in which the model representations grow as more data are observed [39, 38, 26]. In particular, DP used as a prior in a generative mixture model allows the number of mixing components to adapt to the individual dataset automatically. DP can be interpreted as an extension to the traditional generative model with an arbitrary (infinite) number of mixing components.

Formally, a Dirichlet process is an infinite dimensional discrete distribution with two parameters α and H denoted as:

$$G \sim DP(\alpha, H)$$

where H is the base distribution and scalar α is the strength parameter. H serves as the mean of G and α controls the convergence of G towards H. A Dirichlet process can be constructed using the stick-breaking process [31] as follows:

$$\theta_k^* \sim H \qquad v_k \sim Beta(1, \alpha)$$

$$\pi_k^* = v_k \prod_{j=1}^{k-1}(1 - v_j) \qquad G = \sum_{k=1}^{\infty} \pi_k^* \delta(\theta_k^*) \quad (10)$$

where $k = 1, 2, \ldots.$ and δ is the Dirac delta function.

A DP mixture model uses $G(\alpha, H)$ as the prior under the Bayesian framework. The entire dataset is modeled as a mixture of components and each component is parameterized by a random draw (θ) from G. Each data observation belongs to one of the components and is modeled as a function of the parameter of its component, i.e., $f_i(\theta_i)$. Specifically,

$$G|\alpha, H \sim DP(\alpha, H) \qquad \theta_i|G \sim G$$

$$x_i|\theta_i \sim f_i(\theta_i)$$

Consider drawing N samples of θ_i ($i = 1, 2, \ldots, N$) from G. Because G is a discrete distribution, the probability at any given point in the probability space can be non-zero. This implies that the values of the θ_i's will repeat with a positive probability. Hence, these θ_i's exhibit clustering behavior (Polya Urn Scheme)[33]. Given the first N samples of θ_i from G, we assume they have produced a set of k distinct values:

$$\Theta^* = \{\theta_1^*, \theta_2^*, \ldots, \theta_k^*\} \text{ where } k < N.$$

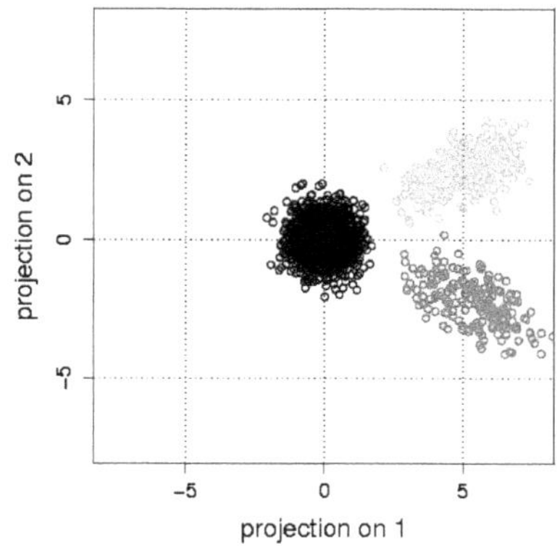

Figure 2: Projection of Clusters

It can be shown that the next new sample θ_{N+1} can be either a new value drawn from base distribution H with probability $\propto \alpha$ or can be taken from one of the existing members from Θ^* with probability $\propto c_i$, where c_i is the number of times θ_i^* has been repeated. Specifically,

$$\theta_{N+1}|\theta_1, \theta_2, \dots, \theta_N \sim \frac{\alpha}{\alpha+N}H + \sum_{i=1}^{n} \frac{c_i}{\alpha+N}\delta_{\theta_i} \tag{11}$$

where δ_{θ_i} denotes the distribution concentrated at a single point θ_i.

Equation (11) illustrates two important properties of a DP. First, the concentration parameter α controls the number of distinct values of θ_i's, i.e., the number of mixing components. Second, DP exhibits a "rich get richer" property: the more frequently a θ_i^* has been adopted (i.e., the larger the c_i), the more likely it will be chosen again as the next θ_i value.

There are various techniques such as Markov chain Monte Carlo (MCMC) sampling[24] and variational inference[7] to conduct inference for a non-parametric model under the Bayesian framework. The variational approach can be more advantageous due to its scalability and guaranteed convergence. In this paper, we adopt the mean-field variational approach outlined in [7].

5. RBM-DPM MODEL

In this section, we describe how to combine the RBM and DPM algorithms for our classification task, including a modified weighted RBM training algorithm.

5.1 Integrating RBM and DPM

The inference of a typical mixture (finite or infinite) of RBMs is intractable due to the difficulty of estimating the partition function $\mathcal{Z}$ in density function $p(\mathbf{x})$ defined in Equation (2). We propose to take a two-stage approach. We first employ a DPM model to partition the data into k clusters. We then apply a modified version of RBM training algorithm to each non-empty cluster using the weights obtained from the DPM model.

For stage one, we note that it is the top layer hidden units (i.e., the non-linear features extracted by the RBM) that serve as the input to our classifier. Thus, directly clustering in the input $\mathbf{x}$ may not be effective for a task for which the inputs are the $\mathbf{h}$'s. For example, in image processing, we can interpret the $\mathbf{h}$'s as a projection of $\mathbf{x}$'s on some other dimension. In Figure 2, the three clusters in the original input space are no longer valid when projected to either of the two dimensions. Input data, therefore, should be partitioned according to the characteristics of the projections (i.e., the top layer hidden units) rather than the original observations.

We propose applying an infinite mixture model to cluster the data at the top layer of the neural network, i.e., the $\mathbf{h}$'s in an RBM, and then learn k classifiers for those partitions produced by the clustering algorithm. To predict the label for a new instance, we will feed the instance to each classifier and take a majority vote from their predictions. Our RBM-DPM model can be outlined as follows:

RBM-DPM Classification Model

INPUT: Instances $\mathbf{x} = \{\mathbf{x}_1, \mathbf{x}_2, \dots, \mathbf{x}_n\}$
Labels $\mathbf{L} = \{\mathbf{l}_1, \mathbf{l}_2, \dots, \mathbf{l}_n\}$

1. Train an RBM R_0 $(\mathbf{W_0}, \mathbf{b_0}, \mathbf{c_0})$ using the entire input dataset $\mathbf{x} = \{\mathbf{x}_1, \mathbf{x}_2, \dots, \mathbf{x}_n\}$.
2. Compute the set of hidden units values, $\mathbf{h} = \{\mathbf{h}_1, \mathbf{h}_2, \dots, \mathbf{h}_n\}$, where $\mathbf{h}_i = \mathbf{W}\mathbf{x}_i + \mathbf{b}$ and $\mathbf{W}, \mathbf{b}$ are learned parameters from R_0.
3. Train a DPM mixture model (see Section 5.2) on $\mathbf{h} = \{\mathbf{h}_1, \mathbf{h}_2, \dots, \mathbf{h}_n\}$, producing k non-empty clusters.
4. Train k weighted RBMs (see Section 5.3) $R_1, R_2, \dots R_k$ for each non-empty cluster from Step 3.
5. Transform each R_i $(i = 1, 2, \dots, k)$ into a classifier by augmenting an output layer of units. Adjust parameters $(\mathbf{W}_i, \mathbf{b}_i, \mathbf{c}_i)$ using labels $\mathbf{L}$ and the backpropagation algorithm.

OUTPUT: Classifiers $R_1, R_2, \dots, R_k$ on input domain $\mathbf{x}$.

5.2 Mixture of Hidden Units

In this section, we give the formulation of the DP mixture model of the hidden units $\mathbf{h} = \{\mathbf{h}_1, \mathbf{h}_2, \dots, \mathbf{h}_n\}$. It corresponds to Step 3 of the RBM-DPM model. We assume instances in the kth cluster follow a multivariate Gaussian distribution $\mathcal{N}(\mu_k, \Sigma_k)$. Our model employs the latent variables $\mathbf{z} = \{z_1, z_2, \dots\}$ (z_i's are the rows of the indicator matrix $\mathbf{z}$ mentioned previously), $\mathbf{v} = \{v_1, v_2, \dots, \}$ (v_i's are the stick-breaking proportions [31] in a DP) and $\Theta = \{\mu_1, \mu_2, \dots, \Sigma_1, \Sigma_2, \dots\}$. Hyper-parameters are α, μ_0 and Σ_0.

The joint distribution $p(\mathbf{h}, \mathbf{z}, \mathbf{v}, \Theta|\mathbf{x})$ can be factored as follows:

$$p(\mathbf{h}, \mathbf{z}, \mathbf{v}, \Theta|\mathbf{x}) = p(\mathbf{h}|\mathbf{z}, \boldsymbol{\Theta}, \mathbf{x})p(\Theta)p(\mathbf{z}|\mathbf{v})p(\mathbf{v}|\alpha) \tag{12}$$

where

$$p(\mathbf{v}|\alpha) = \prod_{k=1}^{\infty} \text{Beta}(v_k|1,\alpha)$$
$$p(\mathbf{z}|\mathbf{v}) = \prod_{n=1}^{N}\prod_{k=1}^{\infty}\left(v_k \prod_{j=1}^{k-1}(1-v_j)\right)^{z_{n,k}}$$
$$p(\Theta) = \prod_{k=1}^{\infty} \mathcal{N}(\Theta_k|\mu_0,\Sigma_0)$$
$$p(\mathbf{h}|\mathbf{z},\Theta,\mathbf{x}) = \prod_{n=1}^{N}\prod_{k=1}^{\infty}\mathcal{N}(\mathbf{h}_n|\mu_k,\Sigma_k)^{z_{n,k}}$$

This is a standard DPM of Gaussian distributions, for which we use the variational inference method [6, 7] to estimate the parameters. The inference algorithm iteratively computes the values of latent variables until convergence. In particular, the mixture model produces a soft mixture of $\mathbf{h}$'s as follows:

$$\begin{bmatrix} z_{1,1}\cdot\mathbf{h}_1 & z_{1,2}\cdot\mathbf{h}_1 & \dots & z_{1,k}\cdot\mathbf{h}_1 & \dots \\ z_{2,1}\cdot\mathbf{h}_2 & z_{2,2}\cdot\mathbf{h}_2 & \dots & z_{2,k}\cdot\mathbf{h}_2 & \dots \\ \vdots & \vdots & \ddots & \vdots & \\ z_{n,1}\cdot\mathbf{h}_n & z_{n,2}\cdot\mathbf{h}_n & \dots & z_{n,k}\cdot\mathbf{h}_n & \dots \end{bmatrix}$$

where each column is a cluster and $\sum_j z_{i,j} = 1$ for $i = 1, 2, \dots, n$.

We next proceed to the second stage, i.e., Step 4 of the RBM-DPM model, and train a weighted RBM (described below) for each non-empty cluster. The weights for cluster k are defined by the $z_{i,k}$'s ($i = 1, 2, \dots, n$).

5.3 Weighted RBM

The mixing proportions for the ith cluster are:

$$\begin{bmatrix} z_{1,i} \\ z_{2,i} \\ \vdots \\ z_{n,i} \end{bmatrix}$$

Because the $\mathbf{h}_i$'s are obtained from the corresponding $\mathbf{x}_i$'s, we modify the energy function using weighted $\mathbf{x}_i$'s:

$$F(\mathbf{x}) = \mathbf{c}^T D\mathbf{x} + \sum_{j=1}^{H} \ln\left(1 + e^{(b_j + \mathbf{W}_j D\mathbf{x})}\right)$$

$$\text{where} \quad D = \begin{bmatrix} z_{1,i} & & & \\ & z_{2,i} & & \\ & & \ddots & \\ & & & z_{n,i} \end{bmatrix}$$

Consequently, we can modify the CD-k learning algorithm as follows:

Table 1: Epilepsy Type and Data Instances Contributed from Each Patient

Patient	Type	Positive Instances	Negative Instances
NY143	2	629	629 * 50
NY148	1	6,569	6,569 * 50
NY149	2	7,035	7,035 * 50
NY159	1	5,111	5,111 * 50
NY186	3	5,869	5,869 * 50
NY294	3	14,107	14,107 * 50
NY226	1	6,485	6,485 * 50
NY255	2	14,394	14,394 * 50
NY259	1	6,792	6,792 * 50
NY315	2	3,434	3,434 * 50
NY338	3	9,046	9,064 * 50
NY343	3	10,463	10,463 * 50
NY351	1	3,522	3,522 * 50
NY371	2	6,915	6,915 * 50
NY394	2	14,197	14,197 * 50
NY46	1	18,972	18,972 * 50
NY67	3	14,932	14,932 * 50
NY72	3	15,448	15,448 * 50
Total		163,920	8,196,000

Weighted CD-k Learning Algorithm

1. For each training example $\mathbf{x}^{(t)}$
   (a) Starting at $\mathbf{x}^{(t)}$, generate a sample $\tilde{\mathbf{x}}$ using k steps of Gibbs sampling.
   (b) Update parameters
   $$\mathbf{W} \Longleftarrow \mathbf{W} + \alpha D\left(h(\mathbf{x}^{(t)})\mathbf{x}^{(t)^T} - h(\tilde{\mathbf{x}})\tilde{\mathbf{x}}^T)\right)$$
   $$\mathbf{b} \Longleftarrow \mathbf{b} + \alpha D\left(h(\mathbf{x}^{(t)}) - h(\tilde{\mathbf{x}}))\right)$$
   $$\mathbf{c} \Longleftarrow \mathbf{c} + \alpha D\left(\mathbf{x}^{(t)} - \tilde{\mathbf{x}})\right)$$
   where $h(\mathbf{x}) = \sigma(\mathbf{b} + \mathbf{W}\mathbf{x})$, α is the learning rate and D is the weight matrix.
2. Go to Step 1 until stopping criterion is met.

6. EXPERIMENTAL RESULTS

In this section we describe in detail the construction of our dataset, the machine learning techniques used to address domain-specific issues related to our task, and the performance evaluation of our proposed RBM-DPM model.

6.1 Patient and Data Description

As described in Section 1, we had access to the MRI data of MRI-negative patients from NYU's Comprehensive

Table 2: **RBM-DPM Model Compared to LR and RBM Models with Different Ensemble Thresholds**

Patient	Threshold = 90						Threshold = 95					
	LR		RBM		RBM+DPM		LR		RBM		RBM+DPM	
	-		# Classifiers*: 18		# Classifiers: 25		-		# Classifiers: 12		# Classifiers: 17	
	Detected	TNR	Detected	TNR	Detected	TNR	Detected	TNR	Detected	TNR	Detected	TNR
NY226	Y	96.3	Y	99.0	Y	99.6	Y	98.7	N	98.3	Y	99.9
NY255	Y	96.8	Y	97.5	Y	99.6	Y	98.6	Y	99.3	Y	99.9
NY259	N	96.3	Y	98.3	Y	99.7	N	99.4	N	97.6	Y	99.9
NY315	N	97.7	Y	97.9	N	99.6	N	98.5	N	99.0	N	99.9
NY338	Y	98.5	Y	97.6	Y	99.4	N	99.8	Y	99.3	Y	99.8
NY343	Y	97.1	Y	97.6	Y	99.6	Y	99.1	Y	98.4	Y	99.9
NY351	N	97.9	N	97.2	N	99.7	N	98.3	N	98.3	N	99.9
NY371	Y	97.5	Y	97.2	N	99.6	Y	99.5	Y	98.1	N	99.9
NY394	N	98.1	N	97.5	N	99.7	N	99.6	N	98.1	N	99.9
NY46	Y	97.4	Y	98.7	Y	99.7	Y	99.2	Y	97.9	Y	99.9
NY67	Y	97.3	Y	98.6	Y	99.6	Y	99.3	Y	99.3	Y	99.8
NY72	N	98.1	N	99.8	N	99.8	N	99.7	N	98.4	N	99.9
Mean	58%	97.4	75%	98.1	58%	99.6	50%	99.1	50%	98.6	58%	99.9

*number of retained classifiers after the selective ensemble described in Section 6.3.

Epilepsy Center who underwent resective surgery and were completely seizure free after surgery. Furthermore, their resected cortical tissue was histopathologically verified to contain FCD. These patients are further categorized into three subtypes (type I, II and III) [8]. Six representative patients were selected from each subtype group resulting in a total of eighteen patients available to our research. This might seem like a small collection of patients, however it should be noted that only a few MRI-negative patients proceed to surgical resection and out of these few only a third achieve complete post-surgical seizure freedom. *Indeed, the six type II patients in our collection represent the entire population of FCD type-II MRI-negative patients treated at NYU during the past three years.*

In terms of the actual data instances, each patient contributes a different number of positive instances to our dataset, depending on the size of his/her resection area. All the vertices within the resected region are labeled as positive (lesional, label = 1). The negative (non-lesional, label = 0) instances for our dataset are extracted from the MRI scans of fifty neurotypical healthy controls who underwent the same MRI protocol. In particular, for each patient, we extract data from each healthy image from the same location as the patient's resection region. As a result, if a patient contributes n lesional samples to our dataset, we will have fifty corresponding sets of non-lesional samples with n instances in each set (i.e., a total of $50 * n$ instances). Table 1 presents the subgroup type, total number of positive and negative instances associated with each patient. We have a total of 163,920 and 8,196,000 positive and negative instances respectively. Note that the negative instances in our dataset are taken from the healthy controls instead of from non-lesional areas outside the patient resection zones. This approach encourages our model to learn a more accurate representation of normal human brains, which is essential to our task of abnormality detection.

6.2 Constructing Training Set

The majority of the FCD patients in our dataset have temporal lobe resections, which is the most prevalent localization of FCD in adults [19]. Training on all patients would therefore be biased toward a specific cortical region limiting its generalization to differentiate between lesional and non-lesional vertices in other cortical regions. Training on all patients (and performing evaluation via leave-one-patient out cross validation) would result in low accuracy in regions other than the temporal lobe. Furthermore, it is desirable to have a balanced training set of patients from the three different FCD subtypes to give a good distribution over different FCD lesion types. Under these two constraints, we selected two patients from each FCD subtype (i.e., six patients in total) as our training patients such that their resected regions optimize coverage of the cortex beyond the temporal lobe [1].

6.3 Selective Ensemble of Classifiers

There is a fifty to one ratio between negative and positive instances in our data. In order to overcome this class imbalance, we apply bagging with under-sampling [36]. Each bag includes all positive instances from our training patients (i.e., all minority instances). At the same time, we randomly pick one control for each patient and include all the corresponding negative instances from the selected control.

[1]In experiments, not reported in this paper due to space, we later verified our assumptions that training on a distribution skewed toward lesions in the temporal lobe did indeed lead to lower performance than a more balanced dataset. We omit these results due to space limitations.

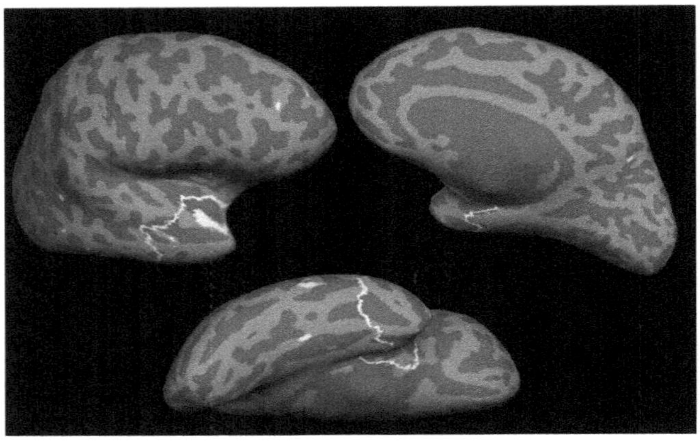

(a) Threshold=90

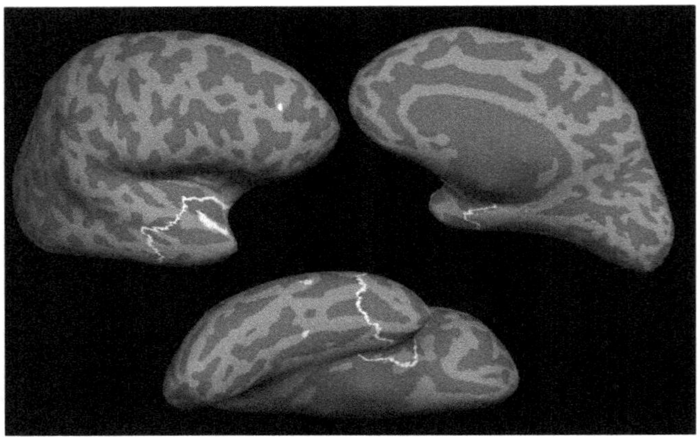

(b) Threshold=95

Figure 3: Detection Results for NY255 using the proposed scheme, at two different thresholds of bag selection, plotted on the inflated cortical surface. The detected clusters are depicted as the solid yellow regions, while the white outlined region represents the actual resected region.

We repeat this process fifty times and create fifty balanced training sets. We learn a classifier for each training set resulting in fifty independent classifiers. A standard ensemble method in machine learning will perform a majority vote among all fifty classifiers when making a prediction. In our case, however, we are biased towards the learners that boast high TNRs on the training data. This is because, although we are aiming at a high lesion detection rate, our detection is only meaningful if we don't sacrifice the performance on non-lesional areas. To address this preference issue specific to our task, we establish an *Ensemble Threshold* and discard classifiers whose TNRs fall below this threshold *on the training data*. The goal is to weed out classifiers that fail to capture the characteristics of healthy cortical tissue.

6.4 Evaluation Method

We have twelve test patients (excluding the six training patients) and we present our model's performance on each test patient's entire brain i.e., vertices from both inside and outside the resected region.We measure the performance on the lesional and non-lesional instances separately to ensure that we are not only detecting the lesions, but also are not misclassifying normal cortical vertices. As discussed in Section 1, we use an indication flag to signal a successful detection within the resection zone and a TNR to measure our performance on non-lesional instances. Note that the benign instances of the patients are not part of our dataset constructed in Section 6.1. Thus, a good performance on these instances (i.e., a high TNR) demonstrates the efficacy of our model in recognizing new healthy brain structures.

We compare the performance of our RBM-DPM model to two baseline models. The first is our recently reported logistic regression (LR) based approach [1] which deals exclusively with MRI-negative patients. This model has been in use at NYU's Comprehensive Epilepsy Center since 2013 and entails a number of pre-processing steps which include manual reduction of the resected region, stratifying the data based on sulcal depth, and a post-processing step that manually discards all detected clusters that fall below a surface area of $50mm^2$. The performance of this model reported in Table 2 which includes all the pre-processing and post-processing steps, and thus represents this method's best performance.

For the second baseline model, we choose to train an RBM over the entire dataset without applying the DPM clustering algorithm to the data. The purpose of the comparison is to verify our conjecture that DPM is able to capture the interpersonal variations arising from different morphologies among the patients.

6.5 Discussion

Table 2 presents the main results of our model on the twelve test patients. We experimented with two thresholds (90 and 95, indicated by the first row) for retaining the classifiers (see details in Section 6.3). Lower thresholds are not interesting because they lead to lower TNR. For each threshold value, we compare the performance of our model to the two baseline models. The third row shows the number of classifiers retained in each case. Under columns "Detected", a value 'Y' indicates a successful detection. The corresponding entry in the last row shows the successful detection rate out of the twelve patients in each model.

We have developed our approach keeping in mind its final use as a focus of attention mechanism for neuroradiologists. The detections made using our model would be used to inform effective electrode placement in iEEG, and constitute a source of secondary evidence for determining the resection target with an ultimate goal of reducing the resection region which leads to a safer and effective surgery. Thus, there are two performance metrics that need to be analyzed: i) performance on the non-lesional regions (i.e., TNR) and ii) detection rate on the lesional regions.

- A high true negative rate is essential in defining success in our task as it alludes to the number of false detections that a neuroradiologist needs to inspect. Indeed, a model with a TNR rate below 99% is impractical because there will be too many false positive regions. One way to increase the TNR rate is to raise the *Ensemble Threshold* to a more stringent value (e.g., from 90 to 95). As we observe in Table 2, the TNR rates improve across all models as we move the threshold from 90 to 95.

- The RBM-DPM approach dominates both RBM and LR models by delivering the highest TNR rates (99.6% and 99.9%) in both threshold settings. Although the RBM model has a higher detection rate at threshold 90, its corresponding TNR rate (98.1%) is too low to be effective for the neuroradiologists. The LR model achieves satisfactory TNR performance at threshold 95, which is the setting that is currently used by NYU's Comprehensive Epilepsy Center.

- Detection rate is defined as the number of patients for whom an abnormal region is detected within their resected region. Although the detection rates presented in Table 2 seem low (50% to 75%), it is worth noting that the detections are made from MRI images of MRI-negative patients, which means the doctors have no identification of any abnormality in these MRI images.

- We observe from Table 2, that RBM-DPM model delivers a more stable performance compared to the other two models at the two threshold settings. In particular, RBM-DPM maintained a detection rate of 58% (7/12 patients) when the threshold changed from 90 to a more stringent value 95. On the other hand, both RBM and LR models sufferred a drop in their detection rates in the process. For the RBM model, the detection rate changed from 75% to 50% and for the LR model, the change was from 58% to 50%. This stable performance coupled with its near perfect TNR accuracies makes RBM-DPM a desirable tool in the pre-surgical evaluation process.

- Even though resective surgery is a viable option for FCD patients, it remains underutilized as most practitioners are unwilling to perform surgery in the absence of a visually detected lesion. This limits the number of available patients whose data can be used to build automated lesion detection models. Our model has the potential to increase the number of patients who are referred to surgery by locating the lesion during the pre-surgical evaluation process. Although the current sample may seem small, the results are significant since a board of experienced neuroradiologists failed to locate the lesion for all these patients, and our approach is able to detect the lesion in 58% of the patients with a near perfect TNR.

Figures 3(a) and 3(b) plot the detection results of RBM-DPM model on a test patient for the two different threshold values using an inflated model of their cortical surface. The yellow areas are detected lesional regions from the model and the white outlined region indicates the actual resected area. Thus, yellow clusters within the resected zone are correct detections, while those outside the zone are false positives. As explained in Section 1, the resection zones are determined in a "generous" manner for MRI-negative patients to maximize the chances of a seizure free outcome. Indeed, we observe in Figures 3(a) and 3(b) that the detected lesional regions are considerably smaller than the size of the actual resection. Thus, the results of our model can be used to guide electrode placement during a patient's iEEG evaluation and obtain a potentially refined resection target, which leads to reduced chances of removing healthy cortical tissue.

7. CONCLUSION

In this paper, we proposed a non-parametric approach to detect MRI-elusive epilepsy lesions using restricted Boltzmann machines (RBMs). In particular, we transform 3D-MRI images of human brains into a standard 2D surface using the Surface-Based Morphometry methodology and extract five features that characterize human cortical surfaces. Our model addresses both issues of limited available features and inter-patient variabilities in the input data. For the former, we used an RBM as a pre-training step. For the latter, we applied a Dirichlet process based clustering algorithm and estimated its parameters via variational inference. To accomplish our classification task, we collect multiple classifiers by training an augmented RBM for each non-empty component from the clustering algorithm and take a majority vote among all classifiers while making a prediction. We evaluated our model on brain images of twelve MRI-negative patients Our model correctly detected abnormal regions within the resected areas in 58% of the patients, with 99.9% accuracy of correctly classifying the non-lesional vertices. Based on these findings, we are evaluating a replacement of our current LR model with our new approach in the clinical treatment for epilepsy patients at NYU's Comprehensive Epilepsy Center.

8. ACKNOWLEDGMENTS

This work is partially supported by NSF IIS-1546428. We would like to thank Hugh Wang at the neurocognitive laboratory, New York University for his help with mapping the resection masks.

9. ADDITIONAL AUTHORS

Additional authors: Ruben Kuzniekcy (New York University, email: `ruben.kuzniecky@nyumc.edu`) and Orrin Devinsky (New York University, email: `od4@med.nyu.edu`).

10. REFERENCES

[1] B. Ahmed, C. E. Brodley, K. E. Blackmon, R. Kuzniecky, G. Barash, C. Carlson, B. T. Quinn, W. Doyle, J. French, O. Devinsky, and T. Thesen. Cortical feature analysis and machine learning improves detection of mri-negative focal cortical dysplasia. *Epilepsy & Behavior*, 48:21 – 28, 2015.

[2] B. Ahmed, T. Thesen, K. Blackmon, Y. Zhao, O. Devinsky, R. Kuzniecky, and C. Brodley. Hierarchical conditional random fields for outlier detection: An application to detecting epileptogenic cortical malformations. In *Proceedings of the 31st International Conference on Machine Learning (ICML-14)*, pages 1080–1088, 2014.

[3] A. Bernasconi, N. Bernasconi, B. Bernhardt, and D. Schrader. Advances in mri for 'cryptogenic' epilepsies. *Nat Rev Neurol.*, 7(2):99–108, 2011.

[4] P. Besson, N. Bernasconi, O. Colliot, et al. Surface-based texture and morphological analysis detects subtle cortical dysplasia. In *MICCAI*, pages 645–652, 2008.

[5] C. M. Bishop. *Pattern Recognition and Machine Learning (Information Science and Statistics)*. Springer-Verlag New York, Inc., 2006.

[6] D. M. Blei and M. I. Jordan. Variational methods for the dirichlet process. *Proceedings of the twenty-first*

international conference on Machine learning, page 12, 2004.
[7] D. M. Blei and M. I. Jordan. Variational inference for dirichlet process mixtures. *Bayesian analysis*, 1.1:121–143, 2006.
[8] I. Blumcke, M. Thom, E. Aronica, et al. The clinicopathologic spectrum of focal cortical dysplasias: A consensus classification proposed by an ad hoc task force of the ILAE diagnostic methods commission. *Epilepsia*, 52(1):158–174, 2011.
[9] M. A. Carreira-Perpinan and G. Hinton. On contrastive divergence learning. *AISTATS*, 10:33–40, 2005.
[10] A. Dale, B. Fischl, and M. Sereno. Cortical surface-based analysis: I. segmentation and surface reconstruction. *NeuroImage*, 9(2):179–194, 1999.
[11] B. Fischl and A. Dale. Measuring the thickness of the human cerebral cortex from magnetic resonance images. *PNAS*, 97(20):11050–11055, 2000.
[12] B. Fischl, M. Sereno, and A. Dale. Cortical surface-based analysis: II: Inflation, flattening, and a surface-based coordinate system. *NeuroImage*, 9(2):195–207, 1999.
[13] C. D. Good, J. Ashburner, and R. Frackowiak. Computational neuroanatomy: new perspectives for neuroradiology. *Revue Neurologique*, 157:685–700, 2001.
[14] W. A. Hauser and D. C. Hesdorffer. *Epilepsy: frequency, causes and consequences*. Epilepsy Foundation of America, 1990.
[15] G. E. Hinton. Training products of experts by minimizing contrastive divergence. *Neural computation*, 14.8:1771–1800, 2002.
[16] G. E. Hinton. Boltzmann machine. *Scholarpedia*, 2(5):1668, 2007.
[17] S. J. Hong, H. Kim, D. Schrader, N. Bernasconi, B. C. Bernhardt, and A. Bernasconi. Automated detection of cortical dysplasia type II in MRI-negative epilepsy. *Neurology*, 83(1):48–55, 2014.
[18] D. Killer and N. Friedman. Probabilistic graphical models: Principles and techniques. *MIT Press*, 2009.
[19] P. Krsek, B. Maton, B. Korman, E. Pacheco-Jacome, P. Jayakar, C. Dunoyer, et al. Different features of histopathological subtypes of pediatric focal cortical dysplasia. *Annals of Neurology*, 63(6):758–769, 2008.
[20] R. I. Kuzniecky and A. Barkovich. Malformations of cortical development and epilepsy. *Brain and Development*, 23(1):2 – 11, 2001.
[21] P. Kwan and M. J. Brodie. Early identification of refractory epilepsy. *New England Journal Of Medicine*, 342(5):314–319, 2000.
[22] J. T. Lerner et al. Assessment and surgical outcomes for mild type I and severe type II cortical dysplasia: a critical review and the UCLA experience. *Epilepsia*, 50(6):1310–1335, 2009.
[23] V. Nair and G. E. Hinton. Implicit mixtures of restricted boltzmann machines. *dvances in neural information processing systems*, pages 1145–1152, 2009.
[24] R. M. Neal. Markov chain sampling methods for dirichlet process mixture models. *Journal of computational and graphical statistics*, 9.2:249–265, 2000.
[25] C. Nordahl, D. Dierker, I. Mostafavi, et al. Cortical folding abnormalities in autism revealed by surface-based morphometry. *J Neurosci.*, 27(43):11725–11735, 2007.
[26] J. Paisley, C. Wang, D. Blei, and M. I. Jordan. A nested hdp for hierarchical topic models. *arXiv preprint arXiv:1301.3570*, 2013.
[27] R. P. R, B. Fischl, V. C. V, N. Makris, and P. E. Grant. A methodology for analyzing curvature in the developing brain from preterm to adult. *International Journal of Imaging Systems and Technology*, 18(1):42–68, 2008.
[28] L. Rimol, R. NesvÃĕg, D. Hagler Jr., et al. Cortical volume, surface area, and thickness in schizophrenia and bipolar disorder. *Biological Psychiatry*, 71(6):552–560, 2012.
[29] D. Rumelhart, G. Hinton, and R. Williams. Learning internal representations by error propagation. *Parallel Distributed Processing: Explorations in the Microstructure of Cognition*, 1:318–362, 1986.
[30] D. H. Salat, R. L. Buckner, A. Snyder, et al. Thinning of the cerebral cortex in aging. *Cerebral Cortex*, 14(7):721–730, 2004.
[31] J. Sethuraman. A constructive definition of dirichlet priors. *FLORIDA STATE UNIV TALLAHASSEE DEPT OF STATISTICS*, No. FSU-TR-M-843, 1991.
[32] P. Smolensky. Information processing in dynamical systems: Foundations of harmony theory. *Parallel Distributed Computing: Explorations in the Microstructure of Cognition*, 1, 1986.
[33] Y. W. Teh. Dirichlet process. *Encyclopedia of machine learning. Springer US*, pages 280–287, 2010.
[34] J. F. Tellez-Zenteno, R. Dhar, and S. Wiebe. Long-term seizure outcomes following epilepsy surgery: a systematic review and meta-analysis. *Brain*, 128(5):1188–1198, 2005.
[35] T. Thesen, B. Quinn, C. Carlson, et al. Detection of epileptogenic cortical malformations with surface-based MRI morphometry. *PLoS ONE*, 6(2):e16430, 2011.
[36] B. C. Wallace, K. Small, C. E. Brodley, and T. A. Trikalinos. Class imbalance, redux. *In Data Mining (ICDM), 2011 IEEE 11th International Conference on*, pages 754–763, 2011.
[37] Z. I. Wang, A. V. Alexopoulos, S. E. Jones, Z. Jaisani, I. M. Najm, and R. A. Prayson. The pathology of magnetic-resonance-imaging-negative epilepsy. *Mod Pathol*, 26(8):1051–1058, 2013.
[38] E. P. Xing, M. I. Jordan, and R. Sharan. Bayesian haplotype inference via the dirichlet process. *Journal of Computational Biology*, 14.3:267–284, 2007.
[39] Y. Xue, X. Liao, L. Carin, and B. Krishnapuram. Multi-task learning for classification with dirichlet process priors. *The Journal of Machine Learning Research*, 8:35–63, 2007.
[40] F. Y. and D. Haussler. Unsupervised learning of distributions on binary vectors using 2-layer networks. *NIPS*, pages 912–919, 1992.

Recruitment Market Trend Analysis with Sequential Latent Variable Models

Chen Zhu[1], Hengshu Zhu[1,2], Hui Xiong[3]*, Pengliang Ding[1], Fang Xie[1]
[1]Baidu Inc., [2]Baidu Research-Big Data Lab, [3]Rutgers University,
{zhuchen02, zhuhengshu, dingpengliang, xiefang}@baidu.com, hxiong@rutgers.edu

ABSTRACT

Recruitment market analysis provides valuable understanding of industry-specific economic growth and plays an important role for both employers and job seekers. With the rapid development of online recruitment services, massive recruitment data have been accumulated and enable a new paradigm for recruitment market analysis. However, traditional methods for recruitment market analysis largely rely on the knowledge of domain experts and classic statistical models, which are usually too general to model large-scale dynamic recruitment data, and have difficulties to capture the fine-grained market trends. To this end, in this paper, we propose a new research paradigm for recruitment market analysis by leveraging unsupervised learning techniques for automatically discovering recruitment market trends based on large-scale recruitment data. Specifically, we develop a novel sequential latent variable model, named MTLVM, which is designed for capturing the sequential dependencies of corporate recruitment states and is able to automatically learn the latent recruitment topics within a Bayesian generative framework. In particular, to capture the variability of recruitment topics over time, we design hierarchical dirichlet processes for MTLVM. These processes allow to dynamically generate the evolving recruitment topics. Finally, we implement a prototype system to empirically evaluate our approach based on real-world recruitment data in China. Indeed, by visualizing the results from MTLVM, we can successfully reveal many interesting findings, such as *the popularity of LBS related jobs reached the peak in the 2nd half of 2014, and decreased in 2015.*

Keywords

Trend Analysis, Recruitment Market, Latent Variable Model

1. INTRODUCTION

The scarcity of skilled talents has stimulated the global recruitment industry in the past few years. An article from Forbes reported that, US corporations spend nearly $ 72 billion each year on a variety of recruiting services, and the worldwide number is likely three times bigger [4]. Along this line, a growing challenge is to provide an effective trend analysis of recruitment market, such as forecasting recruitment demand and predicting market status. Both employers and job seekers can benefit from the study of recruitment market trends. Moreover, at the macro level, this analysis can also provide valuable understanding of industry-specific economic growth for business analysts.

With the rapid development of online recruitment services, such as Linkedin [7], Dice [3], and Lagou [6], massive recruitment posting data have been accumulated. For example, as of the end of 2015, there are more than 1.3 million job positions from 100K+ companies across more than 20 Internet-related industries, such as mobile Internet, online-to-offline (O2O), and cloud computing, available at Lagou [6]-a Chinese tech hiring service website. These huge data enable a new paradigm for studying recruitment market trends in a holistic and fine-grained manner.

Recruitment market analysis is a classic topic in human capital economics, where recruitment market is either treated as a factor of macro economic phenomenons or the analysis is focused on advising people to make the best job decisions in a general economic framework [26, 27, 29]. However, previous studies rely largely on the knowledge of domain experts and classic statistical models, and thus usually too general to capture the high variability of recruitment market (e.g., the evolution of recruitment topics). Also, these studies have limited efforts on understanding the fine-grained market trends, such as forecasting the recruitment situation for a specific company in the next few months. Therefore, it is very appealing to design a new research paradigm for recruitment market analysis through large-scale analysis on massive recruitment data. Along this line, there are some major challenges. First, how to model the intrinsically sequential dependency of recruitment states (e.g., Hiring Freeze) forming the market trend? Second, how to model the semantic relationship between the market trend and job postings from different companies? Finally, how to model the variability of recruitment postings for a long time period?

To tackle these challenges, we propose an unsupervised learning approach for recruitment market trend analysis, which can automatically discern the underlying trend of recruitment market. First, we develop a novel sequential market trend latent variable model (MTLVM), which is designed for capturing the temporal dependencies of recruitment states of companies and is able to automatically learn

*Corresponding Author.

KDD '16, August 13-17, 2016, San Francisco, CA, USA
© 2016 ACM. ISBN 978-1-4503-4232-2/16/08...$15.00
DOI: http://dx.doi.org/10.1145/2939672.2939689

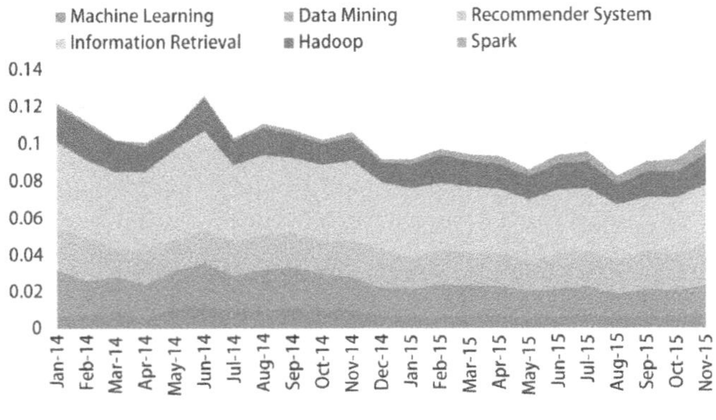

Figure 1: The trend of the number of job postings related to different skill requirements over two years, which indicates the demands of recruitment market.

the latent recruitment topics and demands from recruitment data within a Bayesian generative framework. To be more specific, we assume that the current recruitment state of a specific company is influenced by its state in previous epoch, and it will impel the company to review appropriate recruitment demands (e.g., R&D recruitment). Then, different recruitment demands will generate different recruitment topics (e.g., experienced algorithm engineer), which will finally generate the recruitment postings. In particular, to capture the variability of recruitment topics over time, we design a hierarchical dirichlet processes for MTLVM, which can dynamically generate recruitment topics. Finally, we implement an intelligent prototype system to empirically evaluate our approach based on a real-world recruitment data set collected from China for the time period from 2014 to 2015. Indeed, by visualizing the results from MTLVM, we can successfully observe many interesting discoveries, such as *the popularity of LBS related jobs reaches the peak in the 2nd half of 2014, and decreases in 2015.* Generally, the contributions of this paper can be summarized as follows.

- To the best of our knowledge, this paper is the first attempt to leverage unsupervised learning approach for automatically modeling the trend of recruit market. This work provides a new research paradigm for recruitment market analysis.
- We propose a sequential latent variable model, named MTLVM, for learning the latent recruitment states, demands, and topics simultaneously. Particularly, MTLVM can dynamically generate recruitment topics by integrating hierarchical dirichlet processes.
- We develop a prototype system for empirically evaluate our approach. Indeed, by visualizing the results obtained from MTLVM, we can successfully observe many interesting and useful findings.

2. OVERVIEW

In this section, we first introduce some preliminaries of recruitment market modeling, and then formally present the overview of our model MTLVM.

2.1 Preliminaries

Recent years have witnessed the rapid development of online recruitment services, which have already become the most important venue of talent seeking, especially for high-tech companies. Therefore, the job posting data from these services can help researchers better understand the trend of recruitment market from the perspectives of not only an individual company but also the whole industry.

(a) Jan, 2014-Jun, 2014 (b) Jul, 2014-Dec, 2014 (c) Jan, 2015-Jun, 2015 (d) Jul, 2015-Nov, 2015

Figure 2: The word cloud representation of job postings related to "Mobile Software Engineer" with respect to different epochs in our data set, where the size of each keyword is proportional to its frequency.

Intuitively, different job postings can indicate different ***recruitment demands*** of companies, such as R&D related positions, which usually change over different epochs. For example, Figure 1 demonstrates the trend of the number of job postings related to different skill requirements during January 2014 to November 2015 based on our real-world data set. We can observe that skill "Information Retrieval" becomes less popular, compared with other skills, such as "Data Mining", and "Machine Learning". Meanwhile, "Spark", an emerging technique for big data processing, has attracted more and more attention during these years. Indeed, such evolution of recruitment demands is inherently determined by the change of latent ***recruitment states*** of companies at different epochs, which have strong sequential dependency. For example, Alibaba, one of the largest E-Commerce companies in China, hugely enlarged the recruitment in 2014, which is followed by the recruitment state "Hiring Freeze" in 2015. As a result, its recruitment demands related to E-Commerce largely shrank in 2015. To capture the change of recruitment states, and model the semantic relationship between recruitment demand and state, our model MTLVM follows the Beysian latent variable model with first-order Markov assumption, where current state is only determined by the state at previous epoch.

Indeed, by further analyzing the descriptions of job postings, we observe that the detail of similar recruitment demands (e.g., Recruiting Mobile Software Engineer) will be influenced by the corresponding recruitment states. Thus the corresponding demands usually have high variability, and generate different ***recruitment topics***. For example, Figure 2 shows the word cloud representation [1] of job postings related to "Mobile Software Engineer" with respect to

[1]All the words are originally in Chinese, and are automatically translated by a commercial translation tool [1].

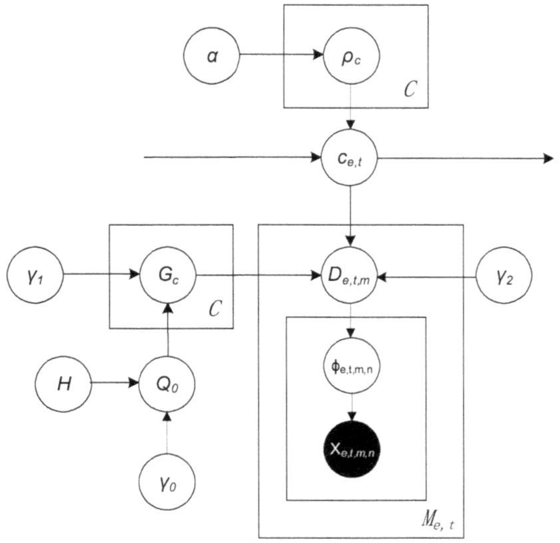

Figure 3: The graphical representation of MTLVM.

different epochs. We can observe that, "Mobile Game Development" is a hot topic in the second half of 2014, while "Android based Web Technology" becomes popular in the first half 2015. To model the semantic relationships among recruitment states, recruitment demands, and recruitment topics, our model, MTLVM, follows the idea of Hierarchical Dirichlet Processes, an infinity version of topic modeling, to model the job postings. Therefore the topic number can be automatically determined.

2.2 Overview of MTLVM

Formally, we regard the m-th job posting of company e at epoch t as a bag of words $\chi_{e,t,m} = \{\chi_{e,t,m,n}\}_n$, where $\chi_{e,t,m,n}$ is the basic observation in job postings (e.g., keywords in job description), and $|\chi_{e,t,m}| = N_{e,t,m}$. For modeling the trend of recruitment market, we first divide all job postings into different data units $\{\chi_{e,t}\}_{e,t}$ with respect to companies and timestamps, which contain job postings of company e at epoch t.

As introduced above, we assume that the current recruitment state of a specific company is influenced by its state in previous epoch, and it will impel the company to review appropriate recruitment demands. Then, different recruitment demands will generate different recruitment topics, which will finally generate the recruitment postings. Therefore, we define a parameter $c_{e,t}$ to represent the recruitment state of company e at epoch t, where the number of unique recruitment states is C. Specifically, at the first epoch, the corresponding $c_{e,1}$ for all companies is sampled from a uniform distribution. For the following epochs, if company e releases some job postings at previous epoch $t-1$, namely that $\chi_{e,t-1}$ exists, its current recruitment state $c_{e,t}$ is sampled from a multinomial distribution determined by previous state $c_{e,t-1}$. Otherwise, $c_{e,t}$ is drawn from the overall recruitment state at epoch $t-1$, i.e., $P(c_{e,t}) = \sum_{c=1}^{C} P(c_{e,t}|c_{t-1}=c)P(c_{t-1}=c)$, where $P(c_{t-1}=c)$ is the average $P(c_{e',t-1})$ of company e' who has market state c at epoch $t-1$. In addition, we name the chains consisting of neighbouring $\chi_{e,t-1}$ that belong to the same company as a data chain. Therefore, if a company only occasionally releases jobs, it may have more than one data chain according to our formulation.

Furthermore, we define the generative process of job posting $\chi_{e,t,m} \in \chi_{e,t}$ of company e at epoch t as follows. First, a recruitment demand $D_{e,t,m}$ is generated from the latent factor G_c which is sampled from a Dirichlet Process and determined by the current recruitment state $c_{e,t}$. Then, we sample a recruitment topic $\phi_{e,t,m,n}$ from the demand $D_{e,t,m}$ for each observation $\chi_{e,t,m,n}$. Finally, each observation $\chi_{e,t,m,n}$ is generated from a multinomial distribution determined by corresponding topic $\phi_{e,t,m,n}$. Specifically, Figure 3 shows the graphical representation of MTLVM.

3. MODELING THE TREND OF RECRUITMENT MARKET

In this section, we will introduce the technical details of our model MTLVM. And we illustrate the important mathematical notations in Table 1.

3.1 Model Inference

According to the introduction in Section 2, we can summarize the parameterizations of MTLVM as follows,

$$\begin{aligned}
\rho_c|\alpha &\sim \text{Diri}(\alpha),\\
c_{e,t}|\{\rho_c\}_{c=1}^{C}, c_{e,t-1} &\sim \text{Multi}(\rho_{c_{e,t-1}}),\\
Q_0|H,\gamma_0 &\sim \text{DP}(\gamma_0, H),\\
G_c|Q_0,\gamma_1 &\sim \text{DP}(\gamma_1, Q_0),\\
D_{e,t,m}|\{G_c\}_{c=1}^{C}, \gamma_2, c_{e,t} &\sim \text{DP}(\gamma_2, G_{c_{e,t}}),\\
\phi_{e,t,m,n}|G_{e,t,m} &\sim D_{e,t,m},\\
\chi_{e,t,m,n}|\phi_{e,t,m,n} &\sim \text{Multi}(\phi_{e,t,m,n}).
\end{aligned}$$

Following the above parameterizations, we can get the joint probability distribution of χ and c as

$$P(\chi, c|\Lambda) = \prod_{e,t} \Big(P(c_{e,t}|c_{e,t-1}, \Lambda) P(\chi_{e,t}|\Lambda, c_{e,t}) \Big), \quad (1)$$

where Λ is a set of hyper-parameters, including α, H, γ_0, γ_1, γ_2, and c_0. Specifically, c_0 is a default initial recruitment state and ρ_{c_0} is fixed to $(1/C, ..., 1/C)$. Indeed, the above equation can be divided into two parts, i.e., $P(c_{e,t}|c_{e,t-1}, \Lambda)$ that follows a multinomial distribution $\text{Multi}(\rho_{c_{e,t-1}})$, and $P(\chi_{e,t}|\Lambda, c_{e,t})$ that follows Dirichlet Processes, respectively. Specifically, $P(\chi_{e,t}|\Lambda, c_{e,t})$ can be computed by

$$P(\chi_{e,t}|\Lambda, c_{e,t}) = \prod_{m=1}^{M_{e,t}} \Big(P(D_{e,t,m}|\Lambda, G_{c_{e,t}}) \times$$

$$\prod_{n=1}^{N_{e,t,m}} P(\phi_{e,t,m,n}|\Lambda, D_{e,t,m}) P(\chi_{e,t,m,n}|\phi_{e,t,m,n}) \Big). \quad (2)$$

Therefore, the objective of learning MTLVM is to find a set of optimal parameters in $P(c_{e,t}|c_{e,t-1}, \Lambda)$, $P(D_{e,t,m}|\Lambda, G_{c_{e,t}})$, $P(\phi_{e,t,m,n}|\Lambda, D_{e,t,m})$, and $P(\chi_{e,t,m,n}|\phi_{e,t,m,n})$, which can maximize the probability of Equation 1. In this paper, we propose a two-step framework to learn our model by a Gibbs Sampling method.

In the first step, we introduce how to optimize the transition matrix ρ, which is constituted of $P(c_{e,t}|c_{e,t-1}, \Lambda)$, given $P(\chi_{e,t}|\Lambda, c_{e,t})$. Depending on equation 1, we could get the conditional distribution of $c_{e,t}$

Table 1: Mathematical Notations.

Symbol	Description
$\chi_{e,t,m,n}$	The n-th tokens at m-th job posting of company e at epoch t.
$\chi_{e,t,m}$	The m-th job posting of company e at epoch t.
$\chi_{e,t}$	The observation unit containing job postings of company e at epoch t.
χ	The entire data set of job postings.
$c_{e,t}$	The recruitment state of company e at epoch t.
α	The hyperparameter of the Dirichlet prior on ρ_c.
ρ	The transition matrix of recruitment state c.
G_c	The probability measure representing the recruitment strategy of state c.
$D_{e,t,m}$	The probability measure representing the recruitment demand of $\chi_{e,t,m}$.
$\phi_{e,t,m,n}$	The recruitment topic of the n-th tokens at m-th job posting of company e at epoch t.
Q_0	The base measure for Dirichlet Process generating G_c.
γ_0	The concentration parameter for Dirichlet Process generating Q_0.
γ_1	The concentration parameter for Dirichlet Process generating G_c.
γ_2	The concentration parameter for Dirichlet Process generating $D_{e,t,m}$.
H	The base measure for Dirichlet Process generating Q_0.
Λ	A set of hyperparameters, including α, H, γ_0, γ_1, γ_2, and c_0.
c_0	The default initial recruitment state.
$N_{e,t,m}$	The number of tokens at m-th job posting of company e at epoch t.
$M_{e,t}$	The number of job postings of company e at epoch t.
C	The number of unique recruitment states.

$$P(c_{e,t}=c|c^{-e,t},\chi,\Lambda)=\frac{P(c_{e,t}=c,\chi_{e,t}|\chi^{-e,t},\Lambda)}{P(\chi_{e,t}|c^{-e,t},\chi^{-e,t},\Lambda)} \propto P(\chi_{e,t}|c_{e,t}=c,\Lambda)P(c_{e,t}=c|c^{-e,t},\Lambda). \quad (3)$$

Since $P(\chi_{e,t}|c_{e,t}=c,\Lambda)$ is given, the only challenge is to calculate $P(c_{e,t}=c|c^{-e,t},\Lambda)$. Here we follow the inference in [16] and give it directly.

$$P(c_{e,t}=c|c^{-e,t},\chi,\Lambda)=P(\chi_{e,t}|c_{e,t}=c,\Lambda)\cdot \frac{q^{-e,t}_{(c_{e,t-1},c)}+\alpha}{q^{-e,t}_{(c_{e,t-1})}+C\alpha}\frac{q^{-e,t}_{(c,c_{e,t+1})}+I(c_{t-1}=c=c_{t+1})+\alpha}{q^{-e,t}_{(c)}+I(c_{t-1}=c)+C\alpha}, \quad (4)$$

where $q^{-e,t}_{(c)}$ means the number of recruitment states c appearing except $c_{e,t}$, and $q^{-e,t}_{(c_{e,t-1},c)}$ means the number of pair $c_{e,t-1},c$ appearing except $c_{e,t}$.

In the second step, we introduce how to compute the parameters related to Dirichlet Process in Equation 2. Indeed, this task can be regarded as an analog of the Chinese Restaurant Process (CRP) [8], and the metaphor can be explained as follows. We have C cuisine styles (i.e., recruitment state) and a franchise (i.e., company) with $M_{e,t}$ restaurants (i.e., job postings). Everyday, the franchise will change its cuisine style according to the cuisine styles on last day. In Particular, the menus of different restaurants may be different, even if they share the same cuisine style. At each table of each restaurant, the dish (i.e., topic) is determined by the first customer (i.e., the basic observation in job postings) sitting there, and it is shared among all customers who sit at that table. When a new customer enters the restaurant, she can sit at an occupied table or a new table. If she chooses a new table, she can order a new dish from the menu. According to the above metaphor of CRP, we can easily obtained a Gibbs sampling scheme for posterior sampling given χ [28]. The detailed definition and inference can be found in Appendix.

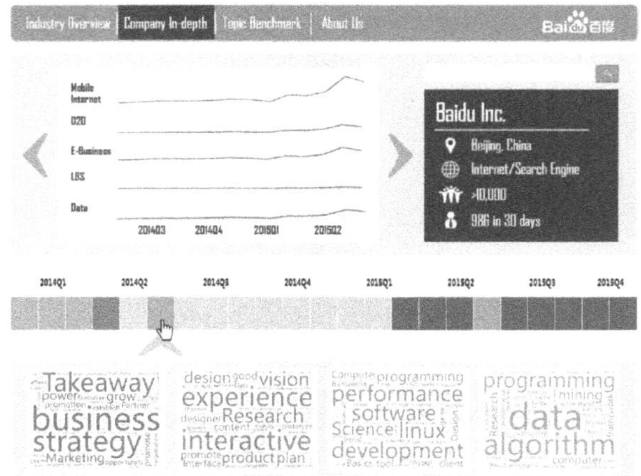

Figure 4: A screenshot of our system for recruitment market analysis.

3.2 The Application of MTLVM

After learning stage, MTLVM can be used for predicting the future trend of recruitment market, e.g., recruitment states, demands, topics, and basic observations. Specifically, given a company e, we can estimate its current recruitment state $c_{e,t}$ by

$$c_{e,t}=\arg\max_{c} P(c|\chi_{e,t},c_{e,t-1},\rho,\Lambda), \quad (5)$$

where ρ is the transition matrix, and

$$P(c_{e,t}|\chi_{e,t},c_{e,t-1},\rho,\Lambda)\propto P(c_{e,t},\chi_{e,t}|c_{e,t-1},\rho,\Lambda) = P(\chi_{e,t}|c_{e,t},\Lambda)P(c_{e,t}|c_{e,t-1},\rho). \quad (6)$$

Therefore, the probability of recruitment state at the next epoch $c_{e,t+1}$ can be obtained by $P(c_{e,t+1})=\text{Multi}(\rho_{c_{e,t}})$. Furthermore, the recruitment topics can be obtained in the same way introduced in Section 3.1. Thus, the probability of a basic observation $\chi_{e,t+1,k}$ (e.g., keywords in job description) from company e appearing at epoch $t+1$ can be computed by

$$P(\chi_{e,t+1,k}|\Lambda)=\sum_{c_{e,t+1}=1}^{C} P(\chi_{e,t+1,k}|c_{e,t+1},\Lambda)P(c_{e,t+1}), \quad (7)$$

where $P(\chi_{e,t+1,k}|c_{e,t+1})$ can be obtained by Equation 2.

4. EXPERIMENTS

In this section, we will study the performance of our model MTLVM on a huge data set collected from a major online recruitment website in China.

Furthermore, we have developed a web-based prototype system to empirically evaluate our model. This system can visualize the results of our model, provide in-depth analysis of recruitment market analysis, and help people understand the high variability of recruitment market. Figure 4 shows a screenshot of this prototype system. In this system, we show the trend analysis of the entire recruitment market and the detail evolution of recruitment state of companies. All of following visualization results in this section can be obtained by this prototype system.

Table 2: The statistics of our real-world data set.

	Raw Data	Filtered Data
# job postings	934,761	257,166
# unique companies	68,302	997
# data units	191,549	13,209
# data chains	116,392	2,557

4.1 Data Set and Experimental Setup

The data set used in our experiments is collected from a major online recruitment website in China and contains 934,761 job postings from 68,302 companies released from January 2014 to November 2015. Specially, Figure 5(a) to 5(d) demonstrate some statistics of our data set. As mentioned above, "data unit" in Figure 5(c) means a job posting set $\chi_{e,t}$ released by company e at epoch t and "data chain" means chains consisting of neighbouring $\chi_{e,t-1}$ that belong to the same company. From these statistics we can observe that most of companies only randomly release very few job postings, and therefore cannot represent the trend of recruitment market. To avoid such bias, we only conserve companies which have released more than 100 job postings. Table 2 shows the detailed statistics of our raw data set and the filtered data set. By the above pre-process, we filtered about 72% original data; and the number of companies declined by 98.6%. However, the average number of job postings per company increases from 13.7 to 258, and the average length of chain also increases from 1.65 to 5.16, which make it more reasonable for training MTLVM.

In particular, in each job posting, the keywords in job description (e.g., job responsibility, skill requirements) are treated as basic observations, and all stop words are removed to guarantee the modeling performance. Note that, our model is trained with original Chinese words, and all experimental results were translated into English by a commercial translation tool [1] for facilitating demonstration.

In the following subsections, we will comprehensively study the performance of MTLVM in term of trend analysis (e.g., learning recruitment states and recruitment topics). Specially, following [28], we set a symmetric Dirichlet distribution with parameters of 0.5 for the prior H over topic distributions. For simplicity, γ_0, γ_1, and γ_2 are set to 1 directly, and another hyperparameter α is also be set to 1 empirically.

4.2 Evaluation of Recruitment Topics

How to quantitatively evaluate the performance of latent variable models is always an open problem. Although perplexity and held-out likelihood are common measures for evaluating prediction results, they cannot demonstrate how coherent and meaningful the latent factors (e.g., recruitment states and topics) are.

Therefore, in this paper, we follow the measures introduced in [31], which is inspired by [30, 13], for evaluating MTLVM. Specifically, we picked up top 10 keywords for each learned recruitment topic and asked 4 senior experts of human resource to evaluate its value. These experts are first

Table 3: Average VM/CM comparison.

	K	VM	CM
MTLVM (C=5)	105	0.464	5.044
MTLVM (C=10)	100	0.682	**6.783**
MTLVM (C=20)	118	**0.688**	6.279
LDA	100	0.637	6.722

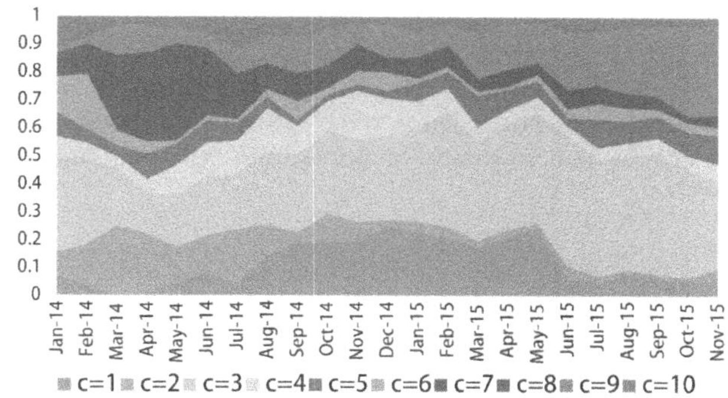

Figure 6: The trend of popularity of recruitment states discovered by our model over time.

required to judge whether this topic is *valuable*. If a topic is *valuable*, they need continue to judge how many words are *relevant* in the top 10 keyword list. Based on these manually labeled results, the metrics Validity Measure (VM) and Coherence Measure (CM) are defined as

$$VM = \frac{\#\text{ of } valid \text{ topics}}{\#\text{ of topics}}, CM = \frac{\#\text{ of } relevant \text{ words}}{\#\text{ of words in } valid \text{ topics}}.$$

Besides, to evaluate how the number of recruitment states affects the performance, we train MTLVM with different settings of state number, i.e., $C = 5, 10, 20$ respectively. Furthermore, we select widely used topic model Latent Dirichlet Allocation (LDA) [12] as baseline. After convergence, the numbers of topic in all our models, i.e., K, are automatically determined as about 100. Therefore, we set K as 100 for LDA.

Table 3 shows the average results of VM and CM. We can observe that in terms of VM, both of MTLVM (C=20) and MTLVM (C=10) outperform LDA a lot, and MTLVM (C=20) has the best performance. In terms of CM, the performance of MTLVM (C=10) is the best, while that of MTLVM (C=20) is worse than LDA. It may be because that too many states will make the model relatively sparse, and thus will make relevant words scattered in different topics. In particular, the performance of MTLVM (C=5) is the worst, which may be because that few states cannot accurately describe the market trend well. Overall, since MTLVM (C=10) has the most balanced results, we set state number $C = 10$ in all of following experiments.

4.3 Evaluation of Recruitment States

Here, we will empirically evaluate the learned recruitment states from several aspects.

Figure 6 shows the trend of popularity of recruitment states discovered by MTLVM over time. It is obvious that these states change over time dramatically. Specifically, state #3 keeps a relative high popularity over the long period, while popularity of #6 is always low. Meanwhile, the popularity of state #9 is rising dramatically since February

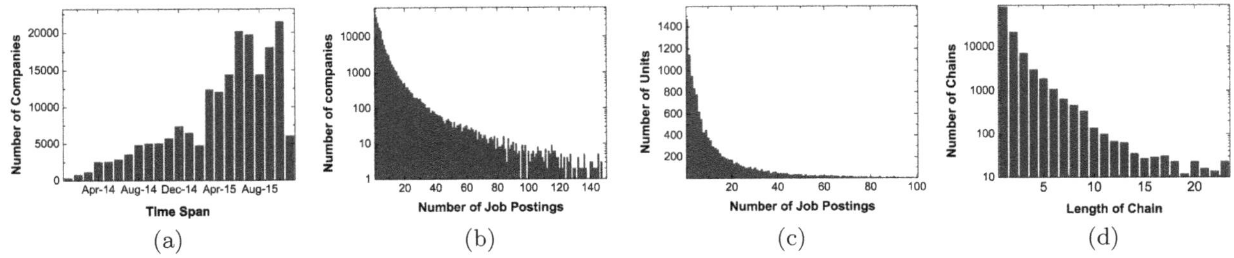

Figure 5: The distribution of (a) the number of companies that release job posting in different epochs, (b) the number of companies with respect to the number of their job postings, (c) the number of data units with respect to the number of contained job postings, and (d) the number of data chains with respect to their length.

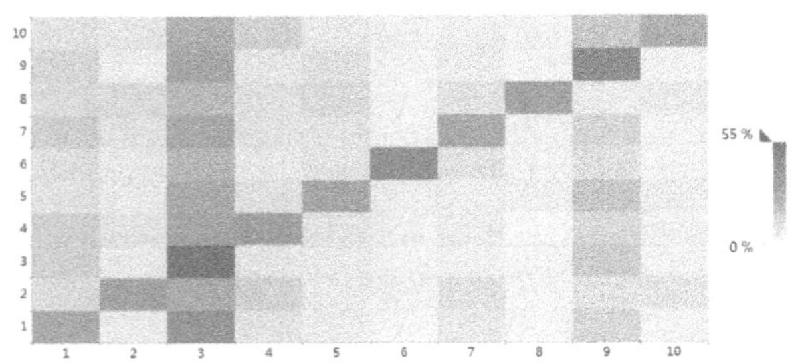

Figure 7: The transition matrix of recruitment states, where the i, j element means the transition probability from i-th state to j-th state, and deeper color means higher probability.

2015. Several other states, such as state #2, #7, and #10, represent totally opposite trends. Furthermore, Figure 7 shows the transition matrix of recruitment states, where the element of i-th row and j-th column represents the transition probability from state i to state j. We can observe that, all states have the highest transition probabilities to themselves, which is due to the momentum of recruitment market. Also, the color of 3-th, and 9-th columns is relatively deeper, which indicates the importance of states #3, and #9. All of above results show that our model MTLVM has the ability to capture the high variability of recruitment market by discovering these latent recruitment states.

4.3.1 Recruitment State Inspection

Here, we will test whether the recruitment states discovered by our model are comprehensible. To solve this problem, we select 4 representative recruitment states according to above analysis and show their top 4 topics in figure 8 by word cloud representations, where the larger words have higher generative probabilities. Meanwhile, Table 4 shows the corresponding generative probabilities of these topics.

We can find that the topic about "programming" always has very high probability in every state. In particular, the top #1 topics in state #1, state #3, and state #9 are the same. That means the demands for R&D related positions are always exuberant, since the high-probability words, "linux" and "mysql", directly indicate the fundamental skill requirements of R&D. Actually, the salary of software engineer has kept rising for a long time, which can support this discovery of our model. These states also show that the work about games and front-end are also very popular, which is consistent with our real-world observations. Next, we further inspect states illustrated in figure 8.

Table 4: The probabilities of top recruitment topics of selected recruitment states (e.g., #1, #3, #4, #9). The corresponding word cloud representations of these topics are shown in figure 8.

	state #3	state #4	state #5	state #9
top #1	0.22493	0.22172	0.18185	0.19441
top #2	0.12399	0.17637	0.10126	0.12350
top #3	0.10064	0.11360	0.07735	0.10018
top #4	0.08932	0.08725	0.07242	0.08021

- **State #3.** It is obvious that the top #1 topic is about R&D. The top #3 topic, containing "data", "analysis", "research", and "algorithm", indicates the demand of recruiting senior researchers or algorithmic engineers. The top #4 topic may be about propaganda (e.g., public relationship), because it contains several paperwork and advertising related words, such as "compose", "edit", "WeChat" and "blog"(e.g., social network based advertising). Besides, what makes this state different is the top #2 topic, which contains "human", "resource", "office", and "assist". All of them are about administrative management obviously. Actually, in our model, this topic only exists in this state. Since research development, propagandism, and administrative management are essential to any companies, we can conclude that this state covers the fundamental talent demands for most by high-tech companies. And figure 6 also indicates state #3 is the most popular.

- **State #4.** This state is closely related to state #5. We can find that the top #2, #3, and #4 topics are relative normal. And the top #1 topic, which contains "data", "programming", and "algorithm", is apparently about R&D, too. However, what makes this topic different is word "lbs". Location-based Service (LBS), such as map navigation or map localization, is the cornerstone of O2O, which is a kind of business model that uses online and mobile to drive offline local sales and become more and more popular since 2014. In figure 6, we notice that the popularity of this topic increased in 2014 and declined in 2015. This may be because the industry doorsill of this field is related high, so only a few large companies have capability to get into this field. Actually, only the largest IT companies in China, such as Baidu, Tencent, and sogou, provide such service now.

(a) state #3 (b) state #4 (c) state #5 (d) state #9

Figure 8: The word cloud representations of top 4 topics of selected recruitment states (e.g., #3, #4, #5, #9), where the size of each keyword is proportional to its generative provability. The generative probabilities of these recruitment topics are shown in table 4.

- **State #5.** This is a very Chinese-style recruitment state. In top #4 topic, we find word "O2O" as well as "merchant" and "business". Actually, with the proposal of "Internet Plus" [5], thousands of start-up companies, focusing on O2O, sprung up across the country. Meanwhile, the others topics in this state are related normal in terms of technology. The top #1 and #3 topics are just about some popular programming language, web-framework, and database. It may indicate that "O2O" is just a business concept rather than a technology concept.

- **State #9.** As shown in figure 6, this state exploded since February 2015. In the word cloud representations of its topics, the top #4 is related meaningful. These high frequency words ("Baidu", "data", "mining", "large", "distributed") indicate this is a big data related topic (e.g., large-scale machine learning and data mining). Its trend directly reveals that high-tech companies, such as Baidu, have paid more attention to big data related fields.

4.3.2 Visualization of Trend over Companies

Here, we evaluate our model by checking the trend of several representative companies from a few important fields, such as Baidu is a famous high-tech company and Alibaba is the largest E-Commerce company in China. We visualize the evolution of the recruitment states of these companies in figure 9.

From figure 9, we can first observe that state #3 is a very common state among most of companies. It is consistent with the analysis from topics of this state. Besides, we find that state #4, which is relevant to LBS, appears relatively frequently among Baidu, Sogou, and Tencent in 2014. Actually, all of these companies provide map service in China, especially Baidu. Baidu Map is the most popular navigation tool in China and many O2O companies use LBS API provided by Baidu to improve their services. So Baidu has remarkable strengths in LBS and has paid much attention to it indeed. Furthermore, Tencent, as one of the largest IT companies in China, its business is very scattered and covers many fields, such as game, social network, media, and entertainment. This kind of business strategy is directly reflected in Figure 9, where the recruitment state of Tencent changes frequently. Meanwhile, Baidu, Alibaba and Sogou (another search engine) prefer state #9, which is relevant to big data (e.g., large-scale machine learning and data mining), in 2015. Considering that their core business (search engine and E-commerce) has several data-related practical applications (advertising and recommender system), the preference is also reasonable. In addition, we happened to find an interesting company, Zuora, whose state is almost state #9. Actually, Zuora is an enterprise software company that aim to automate billing, commerce, and finance operations with a subscription business model. Such business model is naturally related to big data processing and thus has need for senior data-related talents.

Furthermore, we can observe that state #5, which is related to O2O, appears in company Tuniu, Qunar, and Feiniu frequently. Indeed, all of these companies aim to connect offline merchants and online customers, which is high consistent with O2O. Both of Tuniu and Qunar aim to provide one-stop travel booking service, such as hotel, ticket, car rental, and so on. And Feiniu is a B2C E-commerce wesite which is invested by a large retail corporation. The goal of its establishment is to fuse traditional offline service channel with online sale channel.

4.4 Evaluation of of Model Application

Here, we will evaluate the proposed model by predicting basic observations in future.

As introduced in Section 3, we make prediction by calculating the probability of basic observations with equation 7. So in this experiment, we will compare the likelihood of overall observations in test set to prove the performance of our model. The test set is built up by the following approach. We extract the recruitment postings in November 2015, the companies of which had also released some jobs in October 2015. It means all of companies in test set have recruitment states in the previous time span. In the end, the test set contains 350 companies and 4002 recruitment postings. Besides, all of recruitment postings between January 2014 and October 2015 are treated as train data.

We select two model as baselines. One is dynamic Topic Model (DTM) [11]. DTM is a classic topic model for analyzing evolution of topics. It assumes topics evolve smoothly with respect to time and thus chains topics in adjacent epochs by state space models. Its performance was proved by predicting the next year of Science given all the articles from the previous years in [11]. It is obvious that DTM cannot be used for prediction directly, but due to its assumption, the topics extracted by it can model future data better than static topic models in some cases. In this experiment, we follow this method to prove the assumption of DTM is not very solid in our problem and indicate the necessity of our model. The code of DTM was got from [2]. The number of topics is set to 100 and all of other parameters are set to default values.

In addition, we developed a simple sequence approach, called Byesian multivariate Hidden Markov Model (B-mHMM), as the other baseline. Compared with MTLVM, this baseline associates states with words directly. The joint probability distribution of B-mHMM is as follows

$$P(\chi, c|\rho, \iota) = \prod_{e,t} \Big(P(c_{e,t}|c_{e,t-1}, \rho) \prod_{m,n} P(\chi_{e,t,m,n}|c_{e,t}, \iota) \Big), \quad (8)$$

where the first term is the same to equation 1. And as shown in second term, we assume that given the recruitment state, all of observations $\chi_{e,t,m,n}$ are conditionally independent in B-mHMM and $P(\chi_{e,t,m,n}|c_{e,t}, \iota) = Multi(\iota_{c_{e,t}})$. By this baseline, we aim to prove the latent hierarchical structure of our model are meaningful for modeling recruitment markets. Because of the similarity of B-mHMM and MTLVM, The details and inference of B-mHMM follow those of MTLVM and are omitted here.

Table 5 shows the log likelihood of prediction with respect to different models. The larger number means better performance. Both of B-mHMM and MTLVM outperform DTM largely. It indicates it is reasonable to employ latent recruitment states to model the trend of recruitment markets. And the performance of MTLVM is also better than that of B-mHMM. All of these clearly validate the effectiveness of the proposed model.

Table 5: The prediction performance of MTLVM and baseline methods in terms of log likelihood.

	log likelihood
MTLVM	**-2095737.793**
B-mHMM	-2133504.721
DTM	-2599529.728

5. RELATED WORK

Generally, the related works of this paper can be grouped into two categories, namely recruitment market analysis, and sequential latent variable model.

5.1 Recruitment Market Analysis

Traditionally, recruitment market analysis can be regarded as a classic topic in human capital economics, which attracts generations of researchers to contribute ever since Adam Smith. From the Macro perspective, labor is always a crucial element in studying gross economy growth, money market, exchange market and the equilibrium [26], ever since Solow proposed his growth model. Therefore, economists usually study topics about, for example, the demographic structure and participation rate of labor, the relation between inflation and unemployment rate, and how labor contributes in gross productivity or expenditures, etc [27]. In another Micro perspective, which is more relevant to our paper, all studies are set off from a basic market cleaning framework [29], where all employees choose their best balance between leisure and work, while all employers hire with budget constrain, and consequently the wage is derived as the marginal labor cost. Later researches improve our understandings by releasing constraints [19] (e.g., acknowledging the market with segmentations/barriers and as non-cleaning), or by detailed investigations (e.g., forming better utility functions of employees, and studying the actions of employees with game theory). Recently, several researchers in computer science try to employ data mining technology to solve these problems, such as offer categorization [24], job skill analysis [22].

However, previous research in economics efforts relies largely on the knowledge of domain experts or classic statistical models, and thus are usually too general to capture the high variability of recruitment market, and neglect the fine-grained market trend. On the other hand, the recent research in computer science still focuses on those traditional human resource problems. Therefore, in this paper we propose a new research paradigm for recruitment market analysis by leveraging unsupervised learning approach.

5.2 Sequential Latent Variable Model

Indeed, our novel sequential latent variable model MTLVM can be regarded as a combination of both Hidden Markov Model (HMM) and Hierarchical Dirichlet Processes (HDP) within a Bayesian generative framework, which can intrinsically capture the sequential dependency and variability of latent variable (e.g., recruitment states and topics).

Specially, HMM based sequential latent variable models have been successfully applied to problems in a variety of fields, such as signal processing and speech recognition [25, 21], biometrics [15], genetics [14, 23], economics [18], and mobile Internet mining [20, 9, 33]. For much of their history, HMMs have been implemented by using recursive algorithms developed for parameter estimation [10], which are viewed as "black boxes" by many statisticians. In recent years, some researchers proposed to use Bayesian methods to simulate HMM parameters from the posterior distribution, which can

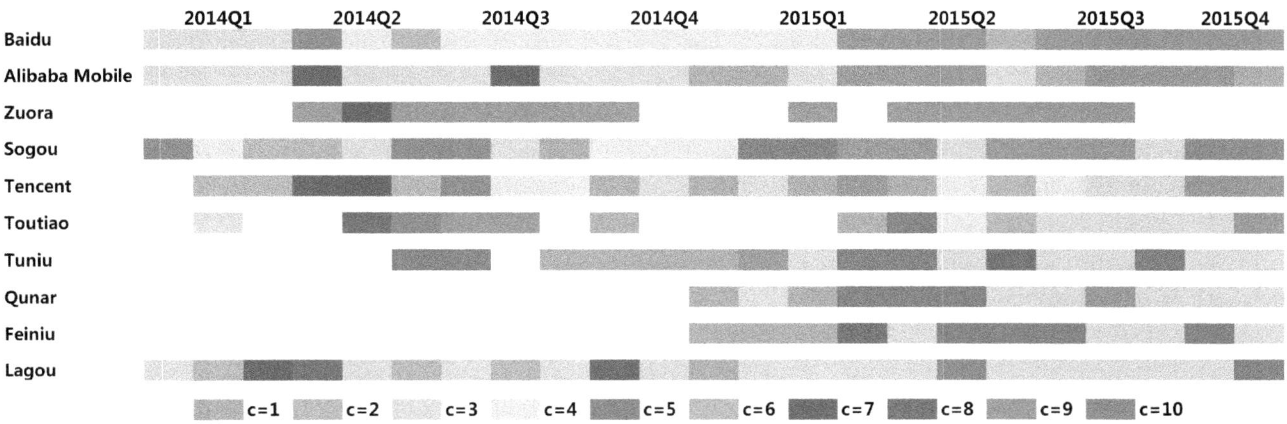

Figure 9: Visualization of the change of recruitment states over several companies, with different colors representing different states.

provide more scalable and stable process of parameter estimation for HMM [16, 17]. Compared with the traditional maximum-likelihood estimation (MLE) based HMM learning solution, the Bayesian methods can directly maximize the probability of the hidden variables given the observed data by integrating over all possible parameter values rather than searching for an optimal set of parameter values. To this end, the model proposed in this paper also follows a Bayesian generative framework.

Latent Dirichlet Allocation (LDA) [12] based latent variable models, have become one of the most powerful tools for mining textual data. However, most topic models [11, 31, 32] need a predefined parameter to indicate the number of topics, and thus fail to capture the variability of topics. To this end, the Hierarchical Dirichlet Processes (HDP) [28] is proposed as an infinity version of topic model, which can automatically learn the number of topics. Therefore, in this paper we propose to ingrate HDP into our MTLVM for capturing the variability of latent recruitment topics.

6. CONCLUSION

In this paper, we provided a large-scale data driven analysis of recruitment market trends. Specifically, we developed a novel sequential latent variable model, named MTLVM, which is designed for capturing the temporal dependencies of corporate recruitment states and is able to automatically learn the latent recruitment topics within a Bayesian generative framework. Moreover, to capture the variability of recruitment topics over time, we designed hierarchical dirichlet processes for MTLVM. These processes allow to dynamically generate recruitment topics. Finally, we implemented a prototype system to empirically evaluate our approach based on large-scale real-world recruitment data. The results showed that our approach could effectively discover recruitment market trends and provide guidances for both job recruiters and job seekers.

7. APPENDIX

Here, we will describe an analog of Chinese Restaurant Process (CRP) for $P(\chi_{e,t}|\Lambda, c_{e,t})$ and corresponding inference in detail. Specifically, we first define $\{\psi_{e,t,m,z}\}_z$ as variables sampled from $G_{c_{e,t}}$ for each job posting and $|\psi_{e,t,m}| = Z_{e,t,m}$. Each $\phi_{e,t,m,n}$ is linked with a $\psi_{e,t,m,z}$ and $z_{e,t,m,n}$ is the index of $\psi_{e,t,m,z}$ for $\phi_{e,t,m,n}$. In other words, we have $\phi_{e,t,m,n} = \psi_{e,t,m,z_{e,t,m,n}}$. Besides, let $i_{e,t,m,z}$ denote the number of $\{\phi_{e,t,m,n}\}_n$ linked with $\psi_{e,t,m,z}$. According to CRP, we can integrate out the $D_{e,t,m}$ and get the conditional distribution of $\phi_{e,t,m,n}$ as follows.

$$\phi_{e,t,m,n}|\phi_{e,t,m,1},...,\phi_{e,t,m,n-1},\{G_c\}_c,c_{e,t},\gamma_2 \sim \sum_{z=1}^{Z_{e,t,m}} \frac{i_{e,t,m,z}}{n-1+\gamma_2}\delta_{\psi_{e,t,m,z}} + \frac{\gamma_2}{n-1+\gamma_2}G_{c_{e,t}}, \tag{9}$$

where δ_ψ is a probability measure concentrated at ψ.

If a new ψ is sampled, it indicates the second term on the right-hand side of equation 9 is chosen. Then we need to add $Z_{e,t,m}$ by 1, sample a new ψ by equation 10, and allocate $\phi_{e,t,m,n}$ to it. If the sampled value is an existed ϕ, we just need allocate $\phi_{e,t,m,n}$ to it.

Second, we define $\{\eta_{c,s}\}_s$ as variables sampled from G_0 for each recruitment state and $|\eta_c| = S_c$. Each $\psi_{e,t,m,z}$ is linked with a $\eta_{c,s}$ and $s_{e,t,m,z}$ is the index of $\eta_{c,s}$ for $\psi_{e,t,m,z}$. In other words, $\psi_{e,t,m,z} = \eta_{c,s_{e,t,m,z}}$. Besides, let $j_{c,s}$ denote the number of $\{\psi_{e,t,m,z}\}_{e,t,m}$, which is linked with $\eta_{c,s}$ and $c_{e,t} = c$. Similarly, we can integrate out G_c and get the conditional distribution of $\psi_{e,t,m,z}$ as follows.

$$\psi_{e,t,m,z}|\psi_{1,1,1,1},...,\psi_{e,t,m,z-1},Q_0,\gamma_1 \sim \sum_{s=1}^{s_c} \frac{j_{c,s}}{\sum_{s=1}^{s_c} j_{c,s}+\gamma_1}\delta_{\eta_{c,s}} + \frac{j_{c,s}}{\sum_{s=1}^{s_c} j_{c,s}+\gamma_1}Q_0. \tag{10}$$

The sampling process is similar to ϕ.

Third, we let $\{\theta_k\}_k$ denote the variables sampled from H and $|\theta|$ is K. Each $\eta_{c,s}$ is linked with a θ_k and $k_{c,s}$ is the index of θ_k for $\eta_{c,s}$, i.e., $\eta_{c,s} = \theta_{k_{c,s}}$. And we also let o_k denote the number of $\{\eta_{c,s}\}_{c,s}$. Now we can write the conditional distribution of $\eta_{c,s}$ directly as

$$\eta_{c,s}|\eta_{1,1},...,\eta_{c,s-1},H,\gamma_0 \sim \sum_{k=1}^{K} \frac{o_k}{\sum_{k=1}^{K} o_k+\gamma_0}\delta_{\theta_k} + \frac{o_k}{\sum_{k=1}^{K} o_k+\gamma_0}H. \tag{11}$$

Next, we will describe a Gibbs sampling method yielded from above. Specifically, we follow the inference method in [28] and sample z, s, k and θ, rather than dealing with ϕ, ψ and η directly.

Sampling z, s, and k. Relying on equation 9, we can easily compute the conditional distribution of $z_{e,t,m,n}$ by

$$P(z_{e,t,m,n} = z|z^{-e,t,m,n}, s, k, \theta, \chi) \propto \begin{cases} \gamma_2 P(\chi_{e,t,m,n}|\theta_{k_{e,s_{e,t,m,z}}}) & \text{new}, \\ i_{e,t,m,z}^{-e,t,m,n} P(\chi_{e,t,m,n}|\theta_{k_{e,s_{e,t,m,z}}}) & \text{used}, \end{cases} \tag{12}$$

where $i_{e,t,m,z}^{-e,t,m,n}$ is $i_{e,t,m,z}$ except the variable $\phi_{e,t,m,n}$. The likelihood of $z_{e,t,m,n} = z$ is simply $P(\chi_{e,t,m,n}|\theta_{k_{e,s_{e,t,m,z}}})$ given all of other variables. And the prior probability that $z_{e,t,m,n}$ samples an existed $\psi_{e,t,m,z}$ is proportional to $i_{e,t,m,z}^{-e,t,m,n}$ is $i_{e,t,m,z}$. Its prior probability for a new ψ is proportional to γ_2. The process of sampling s and k is similar to that of sampling z.

Sampling θ. Given z, s, and k, $\{\theta_k\}_k$ are mutually independent. So the conditional distribution for each θ_k is only related with all of χ that linked with it. It follows

$$P(\theta_k|z, t, k, \theta^{-k}, \chi) \propto h(\theta_k) \cdot$$
$$\prod_{c,s:k_{c,s}=k} \prod_{e,t:c_{e,t}=c} \prod_{m,z:s_{e,t,m,z}=s} \prod_{n:z_{e,t,m,n}=z} P(\chi_{e,t,m,n}|\theta_k), \quad (13)$$

where $h(\theta_k)$ is the density of measure H at parameter θ_k.

8. REFERENCES

[1] Baidu translation. http://fanyi.baidu.com/.

[2] Code of dynamic topic model. https://code.google.com/archive/p/princeton-statistical-learning/downloads.

[3] Dice. http://www.dice.com/.

[4] Forbes article. http://suo.im/gxxz0.

[5] Internet plus. https://en.wikipedia.org/wiki/Internet_Plus.

[6] Lagou. http://www.lagou.com/.

[7] Linkedin. http://www.linkedin.com/.

[8] D. J. Aldous. *Exchangeability and related topics.* Springer, 1985.

[9] T. Bao, H. Cao, E. Chen, J. Tian, and H. Xiong. An unsupervised approach to modeling personalized contexts of mobile users. *Knowledge and Information Systems*, 31(2):345–370, 2012.

[10] L. E. Baum, T. Petrie, G. Soules, and N. Weiss. A maximization technique occurring in the statistical analysis of probabilistic functions of markov chains. *The annals of mathematical statistics*, 41(1):164–171, 1970.

[11] D. M. Blei and J. D. Lafferty. Dynamic topic models. In *Proceedings of the 23rd international conference on Machine learning*, pages 113–120. ACM, 2006.

[12] D. M. Blei, A. Y. Ng, and M. I. Jordan. Latent dirichlet allocation. *the Journal of machine Learning research*, 3:993–1022, 2003.

[13] J. Chang, S. Gerrish, C. Wang, J. L. Boyd-Graber, and D. M. Blei. Reading tea leaves: How humans interpret topic models. In *Advances in neural information processing systems*, pages 288–296, 2009.

[14] G. A. Churchill. Stochastic models for heterogeneous dna sequences. *Bulletin of mathematical biology*, 51(1):79–94, 1989.

[15] D. R. Fredkin and J. A. Rice. Bayesian restoration of single-channel patch clamp recordings. *Biometrics*, pages 427–448, 1992.

[16] S. Goldwater and T. Griffiths. A fully bayesian approach to unsupervised part-of-speech tagging. In *Annual meeting-association for computational linguistics*, volume 45, page 744. Citeseer, 2007.

[17] S. Guha, L. Yi, and D. Neuberg. Bayesian hidden markov modeling of array cgh data. *Journal of the American Statistical Association*, 103:485–497, 2008.

[18] J. D. Hamilton. A new approach to the economic analysis of nonstationary time series and the business cycle. *Econometrica: Journal of the Econometric Society*, pages 357–384, 1989.

[19] T. Hayashi and T. Sakai. Nash implementation of competitive equilibria in the job-matching market. *International Journal of Game Theory*, 38(4):453–467, 2009.

[20] B. Huai, E. Chen, H. Zhu, H. Xiong, T. Bao, Q. Liu, and J. Tian. Toward personalized context recognition for mobile users: a semisupervised bayesian hmm approach. *ACM Transactions on Knowledge Discovery from Data (TKDD)*, 9(2):10, 2014.

[21] B.-H. Juang and L. R. Rabiner. Hidden markov models for speech recognition. *Technometrics*, 33(3):251–272, 1991.

[22] C. Litecky, A. J. Igou, and A. Aken. Skills in the management oriented is and enterprise system job markets. In *Proceedings of the 50th annual conference on Computers and People Research*, pages 35–44. ACM, 2012.

[23] J. S. Liu, A. F. Neuwald, and C. E. Lawrence. Markovian structures in biological sequence alignments. *Journal of the American Statistical Association*, 94(445):1–15, 1999.

[24] E. Malherbe, M. Cataldi, and A. Ballatore. Bringing order to the job market: Efficient job offer categorization in e-recruitment. In *Proceedings of the 38th International ACM SIGIR Conference on Research and Development in Information Retrieval*, pages 1101–1104. ACM, 2015.

[25] L. R. Rabiner. A tutorial on hidden markov models and selected applications in speech recognition. *Proceedings of the IEEE*, 77(2):257–286, 1989.

[26] D. Romer and C. Chow. *Advanced Macroeconomic Theory.* Mcgraw-hill, 1996.

[27] C. Shapiro and J. E. Stiglitz. Equilibrium unemployment as a worker discipline device. *The American Economic Review*, 74(3):433–444, 1984.

[28] Y. W. Teh, M. I. Jordan, M. J. Beal, and D. M. Blei. Hierarchical dirichlet processes. *Journal of the american statistical association*, 101(476), 2006.

[29] H. R. Varian and J. Repcheck. *Intermediate microeconomics: a modern approach*, volume 6. WW Norton & Company New York, NY, 2010.

[30] P. Xie and E. P. Xing. Integrating document clustering and topic modeling. *arXiv preprint arXiv:1309.6874*, 2013.

[31] H. Zhang, G. Kim, and E. P. Xing. Dynamic topic modeling for monitoring market competition from online text and image data. In *Proceedings of the 21th ACM SIGKDD International Conference on Knowledge Discovery and Data Mining*, pages 1425–1434. ACM, 2015.

[32] C. Zhu, H. Zhu, Y. Ge, E. Chen, Q. Liu, T. Xu, and H. Xiong. Tracking the evolution of social emotions with topic models. *Knowledge and Information Systems*, pages 1–28, 2015.

[33] H. Zhu, C. Liu, Y. Ge, H. Xiong, and E. Chen. Popularity modeling for mobile apps: A sequential approach. *Cybernetics, IEEE Transactions on*, 45(7):1303–1314, 2015.

Days on Market: Measuring Liquidity in Real Estate Markets

Hengshu Zhu[1], Hui Xiong[2], Fangshuang Tang[3], Qi Liu[3], Yong Ge[4], Enhong Chen[3], Yanjie Fu[5]

[1]Baidu Research-Big Data Lab, [2]Rutgers University, [3]University of Science and Technology of China, [4]University of Arizona, [5]Missouri University of Science and Technology

[1]zhuhengshu@baidu.com, [2]hxiong@rutgers.edu, [3]{fstang,qiliuql,cheneh}@ustc.edu.cn, [4]ygestrive@gmail.com, [5]yanjiefoo@gmail.com

ABSTRACT

Days on Market (DOM) refers to the number of days a property is on the active market, which is an important measurement of market liquidity in real estate industry. Indeed, at the micro level, DOM is not only a special concern of house sellers, but also a useful indicator for potential buyers to evaluate the popularity of a house. At the macro level, DOM is an important indicator of real estate market status. However, it is very challenging to measure DOM, since there are a variety of factors which can impact on the DOM of a property. To this end, in this paper, we aim to measure real estate liquidity by examining multiple factors in a holistic manner. A special goal is to predict the DOM of a given property listing. Specifically, we first extract key features from multiple types of heterogeneous real estate-related data, such as house profiles and geo-social information of residential communities. Then, based on these features, we develop a multi-task learning based regression approach for predicting the DOM of real estates. This approach can effectively learn district-aware models for different property listings by considering multiple factors. Finally, we conduct extensive experiments on real-world real estate data collected in Beijing and develop a prototype system for practical use. The experimental results clearly validate the effectiveness of the proposed approach for measuring liquidity in real estate markets.

Keywords

Days on Market, Real Estate, Multi-Task Learning

1. INTRODUCTION

Real estate is an important investment option in many countries and has traditionally outperformed the stock market [1]. However, real estate has limited liquidity compared to other investments [28]. Days on Market (DOM) is an important measurement for market liquidity in real estate industry, as it refers to the number of days a property is on the active market. At the micro level, DOM is a special concern of property sellers because real estate is highly cash flow dependent [1]. Also, it is a useful indicator for potential buyers to evaluate the popularity of the estate [25, 28]. Moreover, at the macro level, DOM is an important indicator of the liquidity of the real estate market and shows the level of risk associated with real estate investments.

In the literature, there are a number of studies about DOM related topics [27, 18, 25, 28, 16]. However, most of existing works focus on developing interpretable models for discerning the relationship between DOM and marketing features, such as listing/selling prices. Less efforts have been made for developing predictive methods for measuring DOM, which is very critical for many parties in real estate industry. To this end, in this paper, we aim to measure real estate liquidity by examining multiple underlying factors in a holistic manner. Along this line, an important objective is to model and predict the DOM of a given property listing. The right prediction of DOM could provide valuable insights for both sellers and buyers of real estates and enable the information transparency between sellers and buyers. For example, a seller would know how long it will probably take to sell the house at a certain price using our system. Therefore, the seller could adjust the price to influence the expected DOM. If it turns out that well-decorated houses are more popular (with short DOM) on the market, the seller could also decorate the house to make it more popular. In addition, the developed system can help identify the deceptive manipulations [28] on DOM, and thus could lead to the healthy development of the real estate industry.

However, it is very challenging to predict the DOM of a property because DOM is potentially affected by many factors, such as price, location, and the year of completion in a complicated and involved way. To this end, we first collect and investigate a variety of real estate-related data including transaction records, estate profiles and geo-social information of residential communities. By carefully studying our real-world data, we find that some of these factors are only weakly correlated with DOM. For instance, although some attributes from property profiles (e.g., unit price) can be regarded as intuitively discriminant information for DOM prediction, it turns out that they have limited prediction power for DOM because most property listings within the same urban district have very similar profile attributes. Therefore, we extract various contextual features for establishing the key factors that affect the sale of real estates. These feature include the heterogeneous house profile and the geo-

KDD '16, August 13-17, 2016, San Francisco, CA, USA

DOI: http://dx.doi.org/10.1145/2939672.2939686

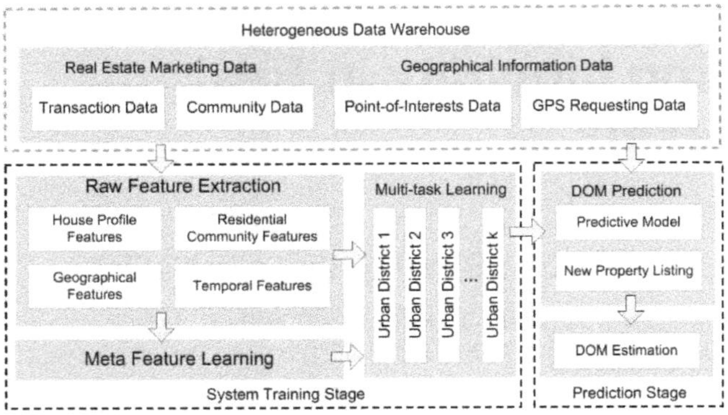

Figure 1: An overview of the framework.

social information of residential communities, such as the number of available facilities (e.g., school and hospital) in the neighborhood, population density, news, and the average monthly DOM of housing sales in the same community. Then, to make full use of all relevant features, we develop a multi-task learning based regression approach for DOM prediction, which can effectively learn district-aware prediction models capturing the geographical correlations of real estates. Figure 1 demonstrates the work flow overview of our approach. Finally, we evaluate our approach by conducting extensive experiments with a large amount of real-world estate related data in Beijing, which include 10K+ residential communities, 145K+ transaction records, 740K+ real estate news, 500K+ points of interests (POIs), and 59M+ GPS requests. Experimental results have demonstrated the effectiveness of the proposed method. In addition, we develop a prototype system for practical use, which clearly shows the value of the proposed decision support system.

Overview. The remainder of this paper is organized as follows. In Section 2, we introduce the details of large-scale real estate data sets. Section 3 presents how to extract contextual features for DOM prediction. In Section 4, we introduce the technical details of our DOM prediction model by exploiting multi-task learning. In Section 5, we report the experimental results of DOM prediction. Section 6 provides a brief review of related works. Finally, in Section 7, we conclude the paper.

2. DATA DESCRIPTION

In this section, we introduce a variety of real-estate related data sets that we have used in developing our multi-task learning based regression method and the DOM decision support system. In summary, Table 2 shows the statistics of our real-world data sets.

2.1 Real Estate Marketing Data

In this study, we use two sets of marketing data collected from a major commercial real estate agency in China.

The first one is a long-term real estate transaction data set, which contains 145,932 transaction records from October 2011 to November 2013 in Beijing. Figure 2 (a) shows the distribution of the number of transactions with respect to different length of DOM. We can observe that most of house listings only have very short DOM, which clearly indicates the prosperity of real estate markets in China. Indeed, this distribution is quite different from that of another data set from Realtor [3] in US, shown in Figure 2 (b). Therefore, we believe, this study can provide valuable insights into Chinese real estate markets.

Table 2: A Summary of Data Statistics.

Data Type	Amount
Raw Transactions	145,932
Community Profiles	10,425
Real Estate News	740,434
Point-of-Interests	510,747
GPS Requesting	59,638,947

Each transaction record in our data set also contains the profile of the listed house, including the residential community the house belongs to [1], DOM, price, location, room number, area, list date, whether it is free of sales tax, orientation, the realtor who facilitated this transaction, etc. Specifically, the top part of Table 1 shows some basic statistics of the above attributes in our data set. Figure 3 shows the distributions of DOM, unit price and transaction number with respect to list time in our data set. From these figures, we can have some very interesting findings. First, the average unit price has grown steadily in Beijing. Second, there is a burst of transaction volume in March 2013, which is due to the "*five policies and measures to regulate real estate market*" by Chinese government [4]. Furthermore, Figure 4 shows the heat map of the geographical distributions of DOM, unit price and transaction numbers in our data set. We can observe that the DOM distribution is relatively even, and the locations with high unit prices usually have a low number of transaction records, which is most prominent when comparing the upper left part of Figure 4 (b), (c).

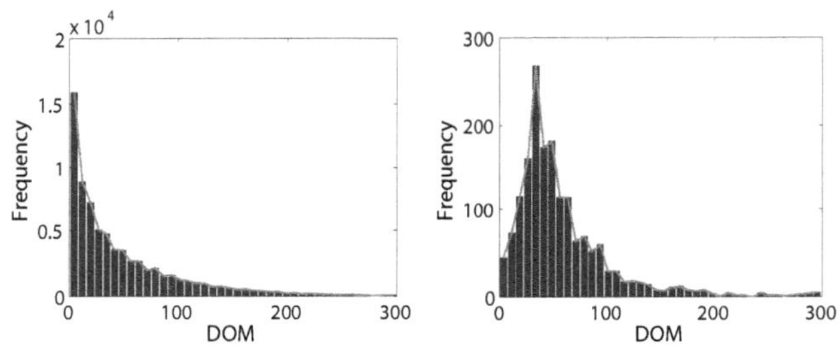

(a) Our Data Set (b) Realtor Data Set

Figure 2: The DOM distribution.

Another market data set includes the profile information of 10,425 residential communities in Beijing, including building number, greening rate, plot ratio, completion year, etc. Particularly, since the real estate market is usually influenced by public opinions, we also collected a large number of real estate news from a variety of portal websites. By using a commercial API of named entity recognition [2], we finally obtained 740,434 news that can be linked to the communities in our data set. Detailed data descriptions are shown at the middle part of Table 1. Moreover, the data set also contains the neighboring facility information of each community, including Transport (e.g., bus stations), School, Hospital, Entertainment (e.g., cinemas), Shopping, Scenery and Unpleasant Facilities (e.g., factories). Some statistics are shown at the bottom part of Table 1, and Figure 3 (d) shows the heat map of the geographical distribution of residential communities.

[1]In the cities of China, a house usually belongs to a specific residential community.

Table 1: **The statistics of some basic attributes of our real estate marketing data sets.**

Data Type	Attributes	Min	Max	Mean	Median	Description
Transaction Profile	Room Number		8			Number of rooms in the house
	Price (0^4 RMB)	0	4,380	4	96	Total price of the house
	Unit Price (RMB)	,4	380,000	8, 88	6,3 6	Price of the house per square meter
	Area (m^2)	5	996	8	74	Area of the house
	DOM		737	53	30	Days on Market of the house
Community Profile	Building Num		363		7	Number of buildings in the community
	Greening Rate	0.00	0.89	0.3	0.3	Greening rate of the community
	Plot Ratio	0.	8 .0	.4	.	Plot ratio of the community
	News Num	0	,396	7	3	Number of news published about the community
	Completion Year	963	0 5	00	003	Completion year of the community
Neighboring Facilities	Transport	0	3	4	3	Number of transport stations nearby
	School	0	6	5		Number of schools nearby
	Hospital	0	53	5	3	Number of hospitals nearby
	Entertainment	0	7	9	5	Number of entertainment facilities nearby
	Shopping	0	45			Number of shopping malls nearby
	Scenery	0	0			Number of sightseeing spots nearby
	Unpleasant	0	0	5	4	Number of unpleasant facilities nearby

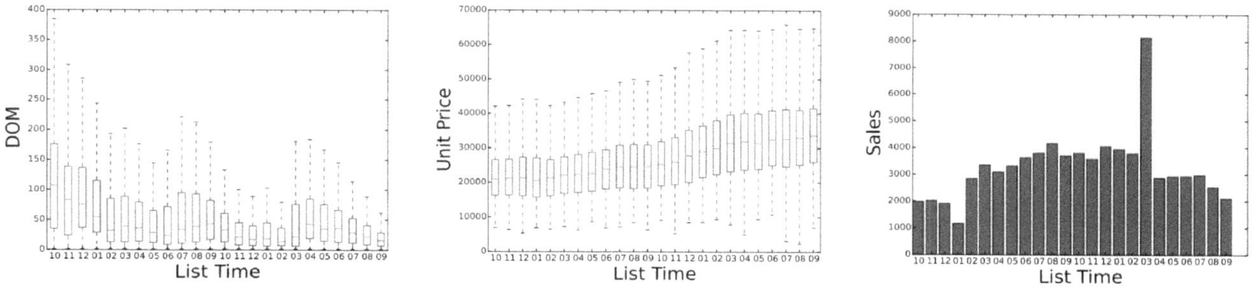

(a) DOM (b) Unit Price (c) Transaction Number

Figure 3: The distributions of DOM, unit price and transaction number w.r.t list time (grouped by month), ranging from Oct. 2011 to Sept. 2013. For brevity, we only show the "month" in x-axis.

2.2 Geographical Information Data

Other than the transaction data, we also collected two sets of large-scale geographical information from a major commercial online map service provider in China. These data sets contain two kinds of geographical information, namely Points Of Interest (POIs) and GPS requests of mobile users.

Specifically, there are totally 510,747 POIs of Beijing in our data set, which can help us further analyze the functionality and convenience of real estates. For example, more POIs generally indicate more convenient living environment, thus the density of POIs is an important factor in influencing people's buying decisions. Figure 4 (e) shows the heat map of the geographical distributions of residential community and POI in our data set.

In another data set, we have the fine-grained daily GPS requesting records of mobile users in Beijing. To be specific, in our experiments, we filtered in total 59,638,947 GPS requests of mobile users from 18:00PM to 23:59PM of some workdays in Beijing. The heat map of the geographical distribution of GPS request is shown in Figure 4 (f). Since most people would stay at home during this time period, we believe that this distribution could roughly reflect the population distribution of Beijing. These results can help us evaluate the occupancy rate and popularity of each residential community.

3. FEATURE EXTRACTION

In this section, we introduce the feature extraction from our data for DOM prediction. Specifically, we group all features into five categories, namely *house profile features*, *residential community features*, *geographical features*, *temporal features*, and *meta features*. While some are simple transformations of house/community attributes, others are implicit features that require the mining of raw data.

3.1 House Profile Features

We obtain 11 house profile features such as area, price, and decoration, which describe the basic characteristics of the house. The details of these features are illustrated in Table 3. Particularly, the feature "Free of Tax" is a dummy variable indicating the seller has to pay sales tax or not. In China, if a residential house is resold by a seller within 5 years since the seller bought it, the seller has to pay sales tax. Otherwise, the seller will be free of sale tax. It is a policy of Chinese government to discourage transactions of residential houses for investment purposes. All of house profile features in Table 3 are directly available from the raw data, except the feature "Historical DOM of Same Realtor", which is used to represent the experience of realtors on DOM. The assumption here is that there exist hard-working or highly skilled realtors who are more likely able to sell a house in a short time, while a less-motivated or inexperienced realtor may spend a long time to find a buyer for the same house. For each transaction, this feature is calculated by averaging the DOM of houses sold by the same realtor.

What should be noted here is that, in the prediction model, we implement classic standardization for all numerical features. And we convert each categorical feature into N binary-valued features using one-hot encoding (i.e., dummy feature), where N is the number of possible values that feature

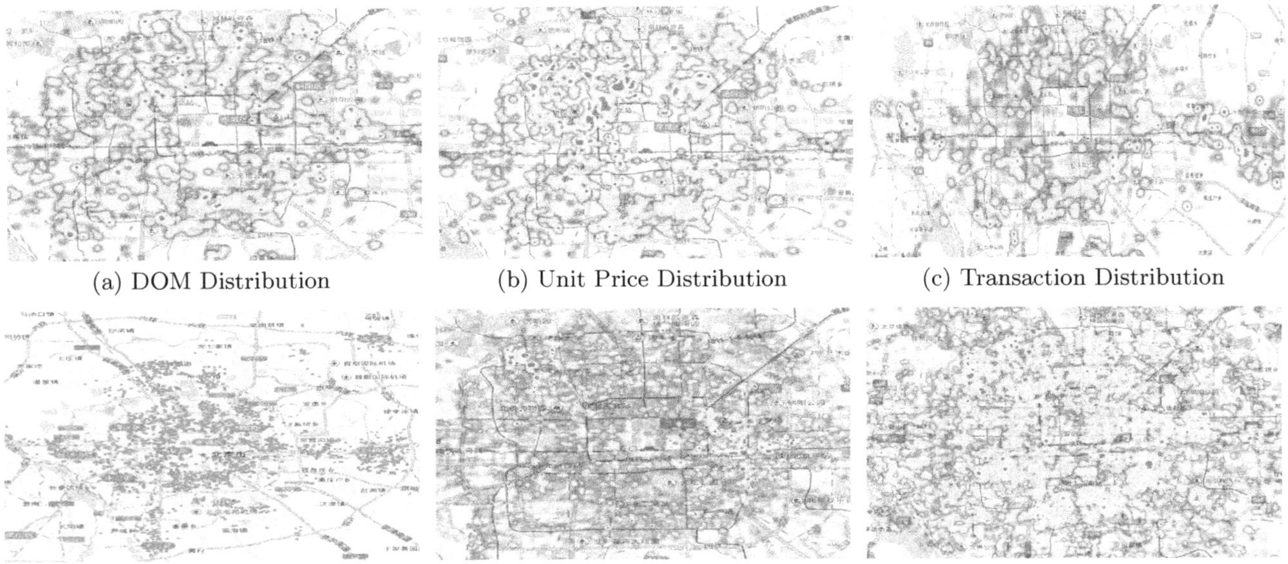

(a) DOM Distribution (b) Unit Price Distribution (c) Transaction Distribution

(d) Community Distribution (e) POI Distribution (f) GPS Request Distribution

Figure 4: The geographical distributions of DOM, unit price, transaction number, residential community, POIs and GPS requests.

could be. Unless specified otherwise, we employ the same recipe to transform other features in this section.

3.2 Residential Community Features

When buying a property, people usually consider not only the house profile, but also the profile of residential community where the house is located. The features we select to describe the profile of residential communities are illustrated in Table 3. To reflect the unique characteristics of each residential community, for each transaction record, we calculate a feature "Historical DOM of Same Community" to indicate the average DOM of historical house transactions in the same community. Since houses in the same community are usually similar in functionality, it is possible that their DOMs are also similar. In such case, this feature could serve as a useful predictor.

Particularly, "District" is an important characteristic of residential communities. Indeed, each city in China is always segmented into different urban districts for administration, which usually have unique urban functionalities, such as business and education. Therefore, we ague that houses in different districts will have different DOM distributions. For example, in our data, there are transaction records from 10 districts out of the 16 districts in Beijing (e.g., as shown in Figure 5 (a)), and the corresponding DOM distribution with respect to different districts is shown in Figure 5 (b). Besides extracting features from district information for DOM prediction, we also use district information as a criterion to split tasks when performing multi-task learning.

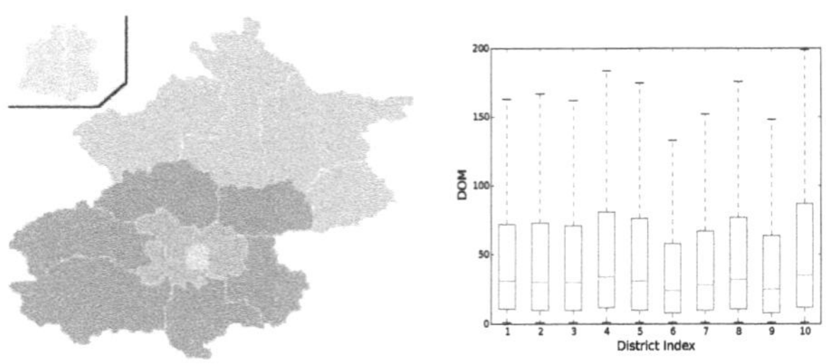

(a) (b)

Figure 5: The DOM distribution with respect to different urban districts.

3.3 Geographical Features

Here we extract several geographical features to capture the spatial characteristics of real estate market. The details are shown in Table 3 and explained as follows.

Surrounding Facilities. The surrounding facilities are important when people consider buying a house, since most of our living services are not directly from the house or the residential community, but from the surrounding facilities. In our data sets, we have seven kinds of facilities, including Transport, School, Hospital, Entertainment, Shopping, Scenery and Unpleasant Facilities. Therefore, for each house, we count the number of each kind of facilities near the house, and use them as geographical features.

Population Density. Indeed, the surrounding population density of house is also useful for DOM prediction, because a residential community that has more people indicates that it is more popular and thus may have smaller DOM. By using the large-scale data set of GPS requests, we can effectively estimate the population density of different areas. Specifically, we first use the widely-adopted grid based method to partition the city area of Beijing into fine-grained grids. Then, we consider the number of requests within each grid as an estimate of population density. For each listed house, we use the density of the grid where it is located as the corresponding geographical feature.

POI Density. As mentioned in Section 2.2, the POI density is an important criterion when people decide to buy the house or not. Therefore, here we extract this geographical feature in a similar way to the population density.

3.4 Temporal Features

To fully explore the temporal characteristics of real estate

Table 3: The description of features.

Feature Type	Feature	Description
House Profile	Room Number	Number of rooms in this house
	Total Price	Total price of the house (0^4 RMB)
	Area	Number of square meters of the house
	Unit Price	Price of the house per square meter (RMB)
	Free of Tax	Dummy variable indicating the house is free of sales tax
	Floor Number	Number of floors of the building where the house is located
	Floor Type	Type of the floor of the house: high, medium, low, or in the basement
	Orientation	Orientation of the house: south, north, east, west, etc.
	Decoration	Type of decoration: well-decorated, simply-decorated, not decorated
	Building Type	Building type: slab-type building, tower building, mixed-type building, etc.
	Historical DOM of Same Realtor	Average DOM of houses employing the same realtor
Residential Community Profile	District	The district of the house: Haidian, Chaoyang, Xicheng, etc
	Completion Year	Completion year of the community
	Greening Rate	Greening rate of the community
	Plot Ratio	Plot ratio of the community
	News Number	Current number of news published about the community
	Historical DOM of Same Community	Average DOM of sold houses in the same community
Geographical Feature	Within School District	Dummy variable indicating whether the house is near school
	Transport	Number of transport stations nearby
	School	Number of schools nearby
	Hospital	Number of hospitals nearby
	Entertainment	Number of entertainment facilities nearby
	Shopping	Number of shopping malls nearby
	Scenery	Number of sightseeing spots nearby
	Unpleasant	Number of unpleasant facilities nearby
	Population Density	Estimated population density within nearest km× km grid
	POI Density	POI density within nearest km× km grid
Temporal Feature	List Date	The date of corresponding property (only day and month information is used)
	DOM of Recently Sold Houses	The DOM of the most recent sold house
	Average DOM of Recently Sold Houses	In recent N days, the average DOM of sold houses
	Percentage of Recently Sold Houses	In recent N days, the percent of listed houses that are sold
	DRPAP	Unit price minus the average unit price of sold houses in recent N days
Meta Feature	RF Feature	Results of random trees trained on original data

market, we also extract the following temporal features for DOM prediction. The details of these features are shown in Table 3 and explained as follows.

DOM of Recently Sold Houses. Two houses that are temporally near to each other may have similar DOM values, since they share similar market conditions. To capture such correlation, for each listed house, we retrieve the most recent N (e.g., 5 in our experiments) sold houses in the same community before its list date, and use the DOM's of those N houses as N numeric features. Note that, if we cannot find such N houses in the same community, we directly use the average DOM of recently sold houses as the default value.

Average DOM of Recently Sold Houses. The intuition behind this feature is similar to that of "DOM of Recent Sold", but differs in that it uses fixed time spans. Specifically, for each listed house, we calculate the average DOM of the houses sold in the same community within the past N days. If no house is sold within that period, the average DOM of all sold houses in the same community is used as the default value. Indeed, this feature can be regarded as complementary to the previous feature. In our experiments, we choose N to be 3, 10, 20, 30, 50 to get 5 different features.

Percentage of Recently Sold Houses. To reflect the temperature of real estate market, we also propose to calculate the percentage of recent sold houses. Specifically, for each listed house, we calculate how much percent of the houses listed within past N days has been sold. If there is no houses listed within this period, this feature is set to a default value (i.e., 0.5 in our experiments). In our experiments, we choose N to be 10, 30, 50 to get 3 different features.

Difference of the Recent Price and the Average Price (DRPAP). Although the price of a house has been widely recognized as a critical variable in influencing DOM [8], it often changes over time. Therefore, we believe that the relative price difference is a better predictor of DOM than the absolute price value. Specifically, for each listed house, we calculate the difference between unit price of current transaction record and the average unit price of the houses sold within past N days. If there is no house listed within this period, this feature is set to a default value (i.e., 0 in our experiments). In experiments, we set N to be 10.

When extracting temporal features, we should be very careful not to use future information, especially when we use default average to fill missing features, since this may cause test data to be used in the training process.

3.5 Meta Features

To improve the accuracy of DOM prediction, we also design some meta features by borrowing the idea of ensemble learning, i.e., training a model on the training data, using the model to predict the DOM of all the instances, and using the prediction value of each instance as a feature. Indeed, such meta features can be regarded as the effective substitutes of manual-selected feature combinations, and thus can help to avoid the "Curse of Dimensionality" problem in feature engineering. In this study, we choose the random forest model for generating meta features due to two reasons: 1) random forest model explores random feature combinations, which can generate diverse structures and avoid homogeneity; 2) the superior performance of random forest model on both classification and regression tasks has been well proved by previous research [24]. Specifically, we first choose the model parameters (e.g. number of trees, max depth of trees) using validation set that can produce best results. Then, after fitting the random forest model on our training data, we use the trained decision trees in the forest to predict DOM for each listed house, and append the prediction results as meta features to other features.

4. MULTI-TASK LEARNING FOR DOM PREDICTION

In this section, we introduce our DOM prediction model, which is built upon multi-task learning.

4.1 Motivation

An intuitive idea for DOM prediction is directly training a regression model with historical transaction records. However, as a kind of geographical asset, real estate usually has unique dependency on locations. For example, as discussed in Section 3, a city in China is always partitioned into different urban districts for administration, which usually have unique urban functionalities and result in different DOM distributions. Therefore, a more reasonable solution is to learn different prediction models for different districts. Figure 6 visualizes the coefficient vectors of linear regression models learned from transaction records of different districts. We can observe that, the coefficient vectors do have different characteristics from each other, which clearly indicates the location dependency of real estates. Although learning a unique model for each district seems to be an effective way for DOM prediction, such solution fails to capture the commonality of different districts and hence has inferior generalization ability. In fact, according to the ***Tobler's First Law of Geography*** [26], "*everything is related to everything else, but near things are more related than distant things*". Therefore, in this study we propose to leverage multi-task learning for addressing this challenge, which can be seen as a trade-off between the previously mentioned two "extreme" solutions. In our approach, we can learn different district-aware models for DOM prediction, and control the distance-aware similarities of different models by using different regularization parameters.

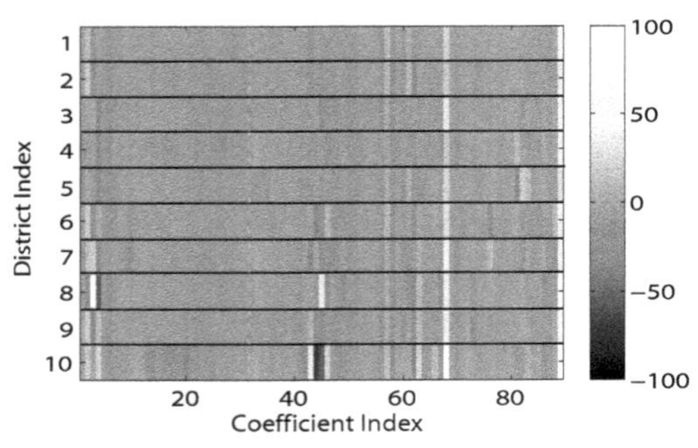

Figure 6: The heat map visualization of coefficient vectors of district-specific linear regression models.

4.2 A DOM Prediction Model

Given a set of N historical transaction records, i.e., $\mathcal{H} \equiv \{(\mathbf{x}_i, y_i)|i = 1, 2, 3, \ldots, N\}$, where $\mathbf{x}_i \in \mathbb{R}^d$ and y_i represent the extracted feature vector and the DOM of the i-th record, respectively. In our approach, we first divide $\mathcal{H}$ into M disjoint subsets by districts: $\mathcal{H} = \mathcal{H}^1 \cup \mathcal{H}^2 \cdots \cup \mathcal{H}^M$, where $\mathcal{H}^t$ $(1 \leq t \leq M)$ denotes the data set of historical transaction records within the t-th urban district. Then, the problem of DOM prediction can be modeled by minimizing the squared error and regularization term of all the tasks, that is,

$$\min_W f = \sum_{t=1}^{M} ||Y^t - X^t W_{t,:}^T||_2^2 + R(W), \tag{1}$$

where t is the index of task; $Y^t = [y_1^t, \cdot, y_{n_t}^t]^T$; $X^t = [\mathbf{x}_1^t, \cdot, \mathbf{x}_{n_t}^t]^T$; $R(x)$ is the regularization term; W is a coefficient matrix and $W_{t,:}$ is the coefficient vector of regression model for the t-th task. The first term represents the squared error and the second term is used to impose the similarity regularization.

Different choices of regularization terms may reflect different types of task relationships. In this study, we formulate our model by graph regularizer combined with L1 regularizer, as shown in Equation 2.

$$\begin{aligned} \min_W f = &\sum_{t=1}^{M} ||Y^t - X^t W_{t,:}^T||_2^2 + \rho||W||_1 + \\ &\frac{\lambda}{2} \sum_{t_1=1}^{M} \sum_{t_2=1}^{M} S_{t_1 t_2} ||W_{t_1,:} - W_{t_2,:}||_2^2, \lambda > 0, \rho > 0, \end{aligned} \tag{2}$$

where S is an $M \times M$ matrix to capture the similarities between different tasks; ρ and λ are hyper-parameters. Specifically, in our model the L1 regularizer controlled by ρ is used to induce a sparse model and avoid over-fitting, and the graph regularizer controlled by λ is used to capture the geographical correlations among tasks, since the tasks are partitioned with respect to urban district. Furthermore, we can find that the graph regularizer is very suitable for representing our idea of trade-off. Specifically, if we omit the L1 regularizer and choose $\lambda = 0$, the formulation is equivalent to training unique prediction model for each district; while if we omit the L1 regularizer and choose $\lambda = +\infty$, the formulation is equal to training a single model on all historical transaction records.

The graph regularizer in Equation 2 can be represented by $\lambda \cdot tr(W^T L W)$, where L is the Laplacian matrix, i.e., $L_{ij} = \delta_{ij} \sum_{k=1}^{M} S_{ik} - S_{ij}$, $\delta_{ij} = 1$ if $i = j$ and 0 otherwise. Indeed, the task similarity matrix S can be computed or learned in various ways. In this paper we develop a novel similarity matrix based on the *Tobler's First Law of Geography*. Specifically, we first compute the distance matrix D for all districts, where $D_{i,j}$ is the distance between district i and district j that can be calculated by the average mutual distance of residential communities located in the two districts. If we denote the set of residential communities located in district i and j by C_i and C_j, we have

$$D_{i,j} = \frac{1}{|C_i| \cdot |C_j|} \sum_{c_i \in C_i} \sum_{c_j \in C_j} dist(c_i, c_j), \tag{3}$$

where $c_i \in C_i$ means c_i is a residential community in C_i, and $dist(c_i, c_j)$ is the geographical distance between c_i and c_j. Then, we can compute the similarity matrix S by

$$S = 1 - D/(D_{max} + \delta), \tag{4}$$

where D_{max} is the maximum value in D, and δ is a small positive constant for smoothing.

Note that the first term of f in Equation 2 is a continuous differentiable convex function, and the regularization term is also convex, thus we can use the canonical accelerated gradient method to obtain the global minimum of f. Specifically, let $f = g + h$, where $g = \sum_{t=1}^{M} ||Y^t - X^t W_{t,:}^T||_2^2 + \lambda \cdot tr(W^T LW)$, $h = \rho||W||_1$, we have

$$\begin{aligned}\nabla g(W)_{ij} &= \frac{\partial g}{\partial W_{ij}} = \frac{\partial ||Y^i - X^i W_{i,:}^T||_2^2}{\partial W_{ij}} + \lambda(LW + L^T W)_{ij} \\ &= \frac{\partial \sum_{k=1}^{K_i} (Y_k^i - X_{k,:}^i W_{i,:}^T)^2}{\partial W_{ij}} + \lambda(LW + L^T W)_{ij} \\ &= \sum_{k=1}^{K} 2(Y_k^i - X_{k,:}^i W_{i,:}^T)(-X_{kj}^i) + \lambda(LW + L^T W)_{ij}.\end{aligned}$$

The detailed algorithm for learning our prediction model is described in Algorithm 1.

Algorithm 1 Accelerated Gradient Method

Input: $S, X, Y, tol, maxIter$
Output: W

$W, W_{old} \Leftarrow \mathbf{0}, t \Leftarrow 1.0$
$\beta \in (0, 1)$
for $k = 1$ *to* $maxIter$ **do**
  $W_{in} \Leftarrow W + \frac{k-2}{k+1}(W - W_{old})$
  $W_{new} \Leftarrow prox_t(W_{in} - t\nabla g(W_{in}))$
  while $g(W_{new}) > g(W_{in}) + \nabla g(W_{in})^T (W_{new} - W_{in}) + \frac{1}{2t}||W_{new} - W_{in}||_F^2$ **do**
    $t = \beta t$
    $W_{new} \Leftarrow prox_t(W_{in} - t\nabla g(W_{in}))$
  end while
  $W_{old} \Leftarrow W$
  $W \Leftarrow W_{new}$
  if $\frac{|f(W_{old}) - f(W)|}{|f(W_{old})| + \epsilon} < tol$ **then**
    Break
  end if
end for
return W

Note that in Algorithm 1, $prox_t(V) = \arg\min_Z \frac{1}{2t}||V - Z||_2^2 + \rho||Z||_1$ has a closed-form solution, which could be used to design an efficient implementation. The solution is shown as follows.

$$Z_{ij} = \begin{cases} V_{ij} - \rho t, & \text{if } V_{ij} > \rho t; \\ V_{ij} + \rho t, & \text{if } V_{ij} < -\rho t; \\ 0, & \text{otherwise.} \end{cases}$$

5. EXPERIMENTAL RESULTS

In this section, we present experimental results to demonstrate the performances of our DOM prediction approach.

5.1 The Experimental Setup

In our experiments, we removed noisy transaction records of which the DOM or other basic profile information (e.g., price) of property is missing. Meanwhile, we also removed some sparse transaction records if the total number of transaction records in the same residential community is less than a threshold (e.g., 10 in our experiments). To avoid the government-driven (i.e., policy) transactions (i.e., as illustrated in Figure 3 (c)), which may introduce strong bias during model training, we further filtered some transaction records with very short DOM (e.g., 1 day) in March 2013. After the above data pre-processing, this data set has totally 70,149 transaction records remained.

Table 4: Data partitioning.

Data Set	Train	Validation	Test
D#1	9,347 (13.3%)	6,407 (9.1%)	54,395 (77.5%)
D#2	23,192 (33.1%)	7,867 (11.2%)	39,090 (55.7%)
D#3	46,431 (66.2%)	11,915 (17.0%)	11,803 (16.8%)

Due to the temporal property of our transaction data set, we propose to use a pair of dates for splitting the data set into training data, validation data, and test data. Specifically, in our experiment, we choose 3 different pairs of dates for data splitting, i.e., (Apr. 1st, 2012, June 1st, 2012), (Aug. 1st, 2012, Oct. 1st, 2012), and (Feb. 1st, 2013, Apr. 1st, 2013), and thus obtain three evaluation data sets D#1, D#2, and D#3. The statistics of each data set (number of instances and corresponding percentage) are illustrated in Table 4. And all the experiments were conducted on a 2.5GHZ×4-Core CPU, 4G main memory PC with Python 2.7 and Matlab 2012 under Windows 7 64bit system.

In the experiments, our approach is called **Multi-task Linear Regression for DOM prediction (MLR-DOM)**, where all the hyper-parameters are learned by using validation data set.

5.1.1 Evaluation Baselines

To verify the effectiveness of our approach, we also chose several state-of-the-art regression methods as baselines.

- **Linear Regression (LR)**: training a linear regression model for DOM prediction.
- **Ridge**: training a ridge regression model (i.e., LR with L2-norm regularizer) for DOM prediction.
- **Lasso**: training a Lasso regression model (i.e., LR with L1-norm regularizer) for DOM prediction.
- **Location-specific Linear Regression (LsLR)**: training different linear regression models for transaction records in different district.
- **Decision Tree (DT)**: training a CART tree for DOM prediction.
- **Random Forest (RF)**: training a random forest regressor for DOM prediction.
- **Support Vector Regression (SVR)**: training a Support Vector Regression model for DOM prediction.

Note that, all the hyper-parameters of baselines are selected by using validation data set.

5.1.2 Evaluation Metrics

To evaluate the prediction performance of different methods, here we select two widely used metrics from general regression analysis, i.e., the root mean squared error (rMSE) and mean absolute error (MAE), and another widely used metric from multi-task learning, i.e., normalized mean squared error (nMSE) [12] for evaluation.

5.2 Overall Results

Here we present the overall performance comparison between our approach and different baselines. Specifically, Table 5 shows the results of different approaches with respect to different evaluation metrics. From this table, we can have several insightful observations.

Table 5: The performance of different methods.

Data Set	Method	rMSE	nMSE	MAE
D#1	LR	111.2758	4.2616	94.1635
	Ridge	58.4916	1.1775	42.0547
	Lasso	58.6558	1.1841	42.1507
	LsLR	147.2266	7.4599	119.4437
	DT	74.4944	1.9099	56.7929
	RF	76.5393	2.0162	63.0411
	SVR	54.9765	1.0402	43.5489
	MLR-DOM	**54.7480**	**1.0316**	**36.4876**
D#2	LR	66.5383	1.9559	52.1974
	Ridge	48.8114	1.0526	37.6255
	Lasso	49.3662	1.0766	37.8580
	LsLR	115.6633	5.9100	93.3486
	DT	55.5625	1.3639	45.9868
	RF	72.3710	2.3139	61.2322
	SVR	49.4277	1.0793	40.4608
	MLR-DOM	**46.3684**	**0.9498**	**32.7723**
D#3	LR	49.7731	1.5896	38.2208
	Ridge	50.1686	1.6150	39.0059
	Lasso	50.0549	1.6076	38.8514
	LsLR	60.3555	2.3372	41.3725
	DT	39.2197	0.9870	31.8181
	RF	38.7276	0.9624	31.7265
	SVR	39.4896	1.0006	31.6821
	MLR-DOM	**38.5147**	**0.9517**	**30.7996**

First, our approach MLR-DOM consistently outperforms other baselines on all data sets in terms of all evaluation metrics, which clearly validates the effectiveness of our multi-task learning based regression model. Second, the district-aware model LsLR cannot achieve good prediction performance, which is even worse than the basic LR model. It may be because of the imbalanced distribution of training data on different districts. Therefore, using similarity matrix for controlling parameter learning is very important for training district-aware models (i.e., just as our approach MLR-DOM). Third, Ridge and Lasso are two competitive methods on D1 and D2, while DT and RF are two competitive methods on D3. Therefore, although some state-of-the-art methods can perform good on some data sets, their performances are actually not stable or robust.

Furthermore, we have also conducted a series of paired T-test of 0.95 confidence level for the experimental results. The results have shown that the improvements of our approaches to other baselines are all statistically significant.

5.3 Feature Contribution Analysis

To evaluate the effect of different feature integrations, we conducted our multi-task learning approach with three different sets of features, as described below.

- **Raw**: Using raw attributes of house and residential community as features.
- **Raw+ST**: Besides features in **Raw**, geographical and temporal features are also included.
- **Raw+ST+M**: Besides features in **Raw+ST**, meta features are also included.

The experimental results are shown in Table 6, where we can have several observation as follows. First, **Raw+ST+M** almost always has the best performance, which indicates the effectiveness of our feature extraction. Second, on D#1 and D#2, adding geographical and temporal features to raw features will not improve the performance much, while adding meta features seems to have produced a noticeable

Table 6: Evaluation of feature combinations.

Data Set	Feature	rMSE	nMSE	MAE
D#1	Raw	55.6912	1.0674	36.5032
	Raw+ST	55.6013	1.0668	36.5616
	Raw+ST+M	**54.7480**	**1.0316**	**36.4876**
D#2	Raw	47.4254	0.9936	34.7932
	Raw+ST	47.4334	0.9881	34.7838
	Raw+ST+M	**46.3684**	**0.9498**	**32.7723**
D#3	Raw	39.2821	0.9900	**30.7882**
	Raw+ST	38.5222	0.9521	30.8136
	Raw+ST+M	**38.5147**	**0.9517**	30.7996

improvement. Third, on D#3 the situation is totally reversed, adding geographical temporal features can improve the prediction performance, while meta features have little effect. Therefore, we can argue that the features are internally correlated, and our model can have the best performance only when combining all kinds of contextual features.

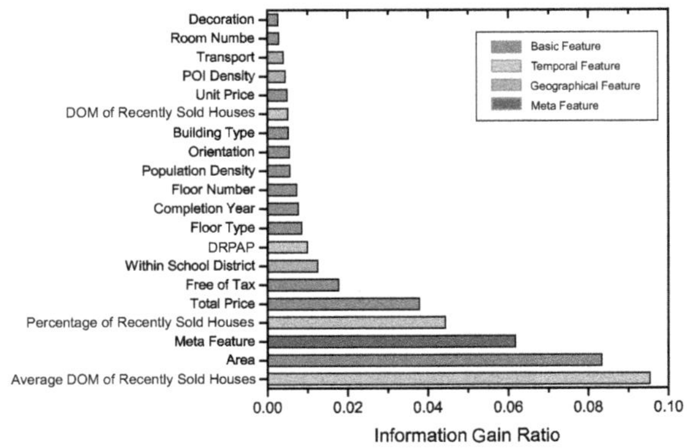

Figure 7: The top 20 features ranked by their information gain ratio.

We further examine the contributions of each individual feature. Specifically, we leverage the widely-used information gain ratio (IGR) as metric to determine which of the features are the most important. Figure 7 demonstrates the top 20 features ranked by their IGR (i.e., higher IGR indicates greater importance). In particular, for each feature that can be parameterized with different time span to generate different features (e.g., "Recent Sold DOM Average"), we only show the value of the most important one. From these results, we can find that the top 5 features that are most correlated with DOM are "Average DOM of Recent Sold", "Area", "Meta Feature", " Percentage of Recent Sold", and "Total Price" in which there are two temporal features, two raw attributes of houses, and the meta feature extracted using random forest. Interestingly, we find that the intuitive feature "Unit Price" has limited contribution to DOM prediction, which is because that most property listings within the same urban district have very similar unit price.

5.4 Evaluation of Different Regularizers

Here, we evaluate the effectiveness of different regularizers in our multi-task learning approach. To be specific, we compare our approach MLR-DOM with $L_{2,1}$ and L_1 regularizers, which are frequently used in multi-task learning. The results are shown in Table 7. We could observe that MLR-DOM has the best prediction performance in terms of MAE on all data sets, and MLR-DOM is always better than

Table 7: The Performance of different regularizers.

Data Set	Method	rMSE	nMSE	MAE
D#1	L_1	60.7496	1.2701	49.2641
	$L_{2,1}$	**54.7373**	**1.0312**	38.8330
	MLR-DOM	54.7480	1.0316	**36.4876**
D#2	L_1	52.2400	1.2056	35.9265
	$L_{2,1}$	48.9935	1.0604	39.3837
	MLR-DOM	**46.3684**	**0.9498**	**32.7723**
D#3	L_1	41.3422	1.0966	31.3027
	$L_{2,1}$	39.3669	0.9943	31.7593
	MLR-DOM	**38.5147**	**0.9517**	**30.7996**

$L_{2,1}$ on each evaluation metric. Furthermore, with regard to rMSE and nMSE metrics, MLR-DOM always outperforms L_1 on all data sets, while MLR-DOM outperforms $L_{2,1}$ and have comparable performance with L_1 on D#2. Based on the above analysis, choosing graph regularizer and L_1 regularizer is reasonable for our multi-task learning approach.

5.5 The Prototype System

We have implemented a prototype system for DOM prediction using bootstrap (front-end framework for web development), angularJS (JavaScript MVW framework), and Django (a web framework in Python) along with MySQL. Specifically, when the user searches a community on the map, the system will show its position and detailed information, such as completion year and plot ratio. It also allows users to input profile information of their house, such as area, price, and then predict the DOM of the house given that information. If the user has not provided complete information, default average values will be used. We regularly update the database with new transaction data and train a new model upon each data refresh. The prediction model is trained offline so that users can get an instant result after submitting house profile information. Furthermore, the system also allows the visualization of real-estate data, such as visualizing the distribution of house prices in Beijing. Some screenshots of our demo system is shown in Figure 8.

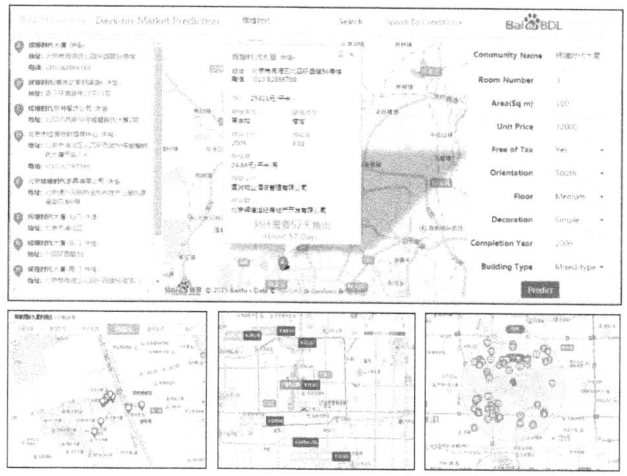

Figure 8: The screenshots of our prototype system for DOM prediction.

6. RELATED WORK

In general, the related work can be grouped into two categories. The first category includes the studies of real estate DOM analysis and the second category includes the studies of multi-task learning.

6.1 Real Estate DOM Analysis

Analyzing the liquidity and popularity of markets is always important for different business sectors [32, 30, 27, 18, 6, 11]. In this paper, we focus on DOM of real estate, which measures the liquidity of real estate markets and shows the level of risk associated with real estate investments. There are a number of studies focused on analyzing the relationship between DOM and prices (both listed prices and sale prices). While there are studies to show positive relationships between sale prices and DOM [27, 18], some other studies claimed that the relationship between two variables is not significant [6]. In this paper, our focus is not on the relationship between these two variables. Instead, we focus on providing a solution to accurately predict DOM with extensive contextual information, such as house profile information and geo-social information.

Specifically, there are three types of methods for the DOM analysis. The first method is Ordinary Least Squares (OLS), which has the ability to test and make corrections for self-selection issues and is equally flexible in dealing with endogeneity issues, which are two major issues with the DOM analysis. However, non-normal error terms can lead to biased OLS coefficient estimates. Second, hazard models, often assuming a Weibull distribution of property marketing time, offer highly flexible functional specifications. However, there are the aforementioned self-selection and endogeneity problems with these models. Finally, instrumental variables models, usually in the form of 2SLS, allow for the joint estimation of simultaneously determined property price and property selling time. Nonetheless, there are criticisms related to the non-normality of the error term and the difficulty in calculating required inverse Mills ratios (IMR) to control for self-selection issues between variables of interest and property marketing time.

In this paper, our work is based on OLS and aims to improve its performance using machine learning techniques, such as feature engineering and multi-task learning. For OLS, there are two variants. For the first type of OLS, feature values (independent variables) and target variables appear in the model without non-linear transformation [28]. This is different from second type of OLS, where sale price, DOM, and some other variables will take logarithm before regression [22]. However, the second type of OLS usually performs very poor on MSE or MAE metrics, since the regression target is the logarithm of DOM rather than DOM. Therefore, we choose the first type of OLS as our baseline in this paper.

6.2 Multi-task Learning

Multi-task learning is a well-known machine learning methods to improve classification and regression performances by utilizing cross-task information. It first appears in the context of neural networks [10, 9]. Later, regularization-based multi-task learning starts to appear and forms an important research area [15, 14, 5].

Usually, regularization-based multi-task learning methods share the same framework, but differ in the choice of regularization terms used to represent assumptions of different types of task relationships. There are works which assume that all tasks are related and share a low-dimensional representation across a set of multiple related tasks. These works often select or learn a common set of shared features among the tasks [14, 5, 21]. Also, Obozinski and Argyriou *et al.* proposed joint feature learning for multi-task methods [5, 23]. Argyriou *et al.* generalized the well-known Lasso from single task case to multiple task case. [14]. In addition, some researchers believe that the assumption that all tasks are related is too strong and may not hold in real world. Therefore, they proposed other task relationship structures, such as clustered structures [17], tree structures [20], and graph structures [19, 13].

Finally, multi-task learning methods have been used in various fields, such as education, disease control, and computer vision. For instance, Argyriou has exploited multi-task learning for predicting students' exam scores. Bickel *et al.* has employed multi-task learning for HIV therapy screening [7] and Zhou *et al.* have proposed a multi-task formulation for predicting disease progression [31]. At last, Wang *et al.* have explored boosted multitask learning for web image and video search [29].

7. CONCLUSION

In this paper, we developed a comprehensive approach for measuring the liquidity of real estate markets. This approach provides a critical capacity for predicting the DOM of a given property listing, and thus enhances the information transparency between sellers and buyers. Specifically, we first investigated various contextual features for identifying the key factors that can affect the sale of real estates. Then, we developed a multi-task learning based regression approach for DOM prediction, which can effectively learn district-aware models for different property listings by integrating extracted contextual features. Finally, we presented experimental results to demonstrate the performance of our method with a large amount of real-world real estate data, and designed a prototype system showing the practical use of the liquidity analysis for real estate markets.

Acknowledgments

This work was partially supported by grants from National Science Foundation for Distinguished Young Scholars of China (Grant No. 61325010), the Natural Science Foundation of China (NSFC, Grant No.s 71329201, 61403358, 61572032, 71571093), and the Youth Innovation Promotion Association of CAS.

8. REFERENCES

[1] http://en.wikipedia.org/wiki/real_estate_investing.
[2] https://nlp.baidu.com.
[3] https://www.realtor.com.
[4] http://wiki.china.org.cn/wiki/index.php/five_policies_a-nd_measures_to_regulate_real_estate_market.
[5] A. Argyriou, T. Evgeniou, and M. Pontil. Convex multi-task feature learning. In *Machine Learning*, 73(3):243–272, 2008.
[6] J. D. Benefield and W. G. Hardin III. Does time-on-market measurement matter? In *The Journal of Real Estate Finance and Economics*, pages 1–22, 2013.
[7] S. Bickel, J. Bogojeska, T. Lengauer, and T. Scheffer. Multi-task learning for hiv therapy screening. In ICML'2008, pages 56–63. ACM, 2008.
[8] K. Björklund, J. Alex Dadzie, and M. Wilhelmsson. Offer price, transaction price and time-on-market. In *Property Management*, 24(4):415–426, 2006.
[9] R. Caruana. Multitask learning. In *Machine learning*, 28(1):41–75, 1997.
[10] R. Caruna. Multitask learning: A knowledge-based source of inductive bias. In *ICML'1993*, pages 41–48, 1993.
[11] B. Chang, H. Zhu, Y. Ge, E. Chen, H. Xiong, and C. Tan. Predicting the popularity of online serials with autoregressive models. In *CIKM'2014*, pages 1339–1348. ACM, 2014.
[12] J. Chen, J. Zhou, and J. Ye. Integrating low-rank and group-sparse structures for robust multi-task learning. In *KDD'2011*, pages 42–50. ACM, 2011.
[13] X. Chen, Q. Lin, S. Kim, J. G. Carbonell, E. P. Xing, et al. Smoothing proximal gradient method for general structured sparse regression. In *The Annals of Applied Statistics*, 6(2):719–752, 2012.
[14] A. Evgeniou and M. Pontil. Multi-task feature learning. In *NIPS'2007*, 19:41, 2007.
[15] T. Evgeniou and M. Pontil. Regularized multi–task learning. In *KDD'2004*, pages 109–117. ACM, 2004.
[16] Y. Fu, G. Liu, S. Papadimitriou, H. Xiong, Y. Ge, H. Zhu, and C. Zhu. Real estate ranking via mixed land-use latent models. In *KDD'2015*, ACM, pages 299–308, 2015.
[17] L. Jacob, J.-p. Vert, and F. R. Bach. Clustered multi-task learning: A convex formulation. In *NIPS'2009*, pages 745–752, 2009.
[18] R. Kalra, K. C. Chan, and P. Lai. Time on market and sales price of residential housing: A note. In *Journal of Economics and Finance*, 21(2):63–66, 1997.
[19] S. Kim and E. P. Xing. Statistical estimation of correlated genome associations to a quantitative trait network. In *PLoS genetics*, 5(8):e1000587, 2009.
[20] S. Kim and E. P. Xing. Tree-guided group lasso for multi-task regression with structured sparsity. In *ICML'2010*, pages 543–550, 2010.
[21] J. Liu, S. Ji, and J. Ye. Multi-task feature learning via efficient l 2, 1-norm minimization. In *UAI'2009*, pages 339–348. AUAI Press, 2009.
[22] H. J. Munneke and A. Yavas. Incentives and performance in real estate brokerage. In *The Journal of Real Estate Finance and Economics*, 22(1):5–21, 2001.
[23] G. Obozinski, B. Taskar, and M. I. Jordan. Joint covariate selection and joint subspace selection for multiple classification problems. In *Statistics and Computing*, 20(2):231–252, 2010.
[24] M. R. Segal. Machine learning benchmarks and random forest regression. In *Center for Bioinformatics & Molecular Biostatistics*, 2004.
[25] C. R. Taylor. Time-on-the-market as a sign of quality. In *The Review of Economic Studies*, 66(3):555–578, 1999.
[26] W. R. Tobler. A computer movie simulating urban growth in the detroit region. In *Economic geography*, pages 234–240, 1970.
[27] R. R. Trippi. Estimating the relationship between price and time to sale for investment property. In *Management Science*, 23(8):838–842, 1977.
[28] C. Tucker, J. Zhang, and T. Zhu. Days on market and home sales. In *The RAND Journal of Economics*, 44(2):337–360, 2013.
[29] X. Wang, C. Zhang, and Z. Zhang. Boosted multi-task learning for face verification with applications to web image and video search. In *CVPR'2009*, pages 142–149. IEEE, 2009.
[30] L. Wu, Q. Liu, E. Chen, X. Xie, and C. Tan. Product adoption rate prediction: A multi-factor view. In *SDM'2015*, pages 154–162, 2015.
[31] J. Zhou, L. Yuan, J. Liu, and J. Ye. A multi-task learning formulation for predicting disease progression. In *KDD'2011*, pages 814–822. ACM, 2011.
[32] H. Zhu, C. Liu, Y. Ge, H. Xiong, and E. Chen. Popularity modeling for mobile apps: A sequential approach. *IEEE Trans. Cybernetics*, 45(7):1303–1314, 2015.

Can You Teach the Elephant to Dance?
AKA: Culture Eats Data Science for Breakfast

Jonathan Becher
SAP
Palo Alto, CA
jonathan.becher@sap.com

ABSTRACT

In the past 20 years, the practical examples of KDD/data mining have become so ubiquitous that it's almost impossible to imagine a new venture that isn't based on data science. Uber, Facebook, 23andMe, Tesla – they aren't just technology companies; they are data companies. And yet the reality is that these companies are still anomalies. Large, successful companies usually still treat KDD as either an afterthought or as an experiment. It's not core to how they run the business.

As practitioners we compound this problem by concentrating our efforts on valuable business problems; but ones which are usually on the periphery of the business. We do this because changing the heart of how a company operates requires more than just process or technology changes. It requires cultural changes. And these cultural changes usually trigger corporate antibodies adverse to anything new.

This talk will review some practical realities of instituting data-driven decisions in a very large multi-national company.

Keywords

Enterprise Software; Analytics; Mobile Technology.

KDD'16, August 13-17, 2016, San Francisco, CA, USA
ACM 978-1-4503-3664-2/15/08.
http://dx.doi.org/10.1145/2783258.2790456

Bio

Jonathan Becher serves as Chief Digital Officer and head of the SAP Digital business unit, which allows individuals to discover, buy, use, and renew SAP and third-party offerings with minimal human interaction. Jonathan reports to Bill McDermott, CEO of SAP.

Jonathan joined SAP from its acquisition of Pilot Software, where he was chief executive officer. Beforehand, he was CEO of Accrue Software, a publically-traded Web site analytics company, and CEO and co-founder of NeoVista Software, a pioneer in predictive analytics and data mining.

Jonathan authors the popular blog, Managing By Walking Around, is a contributor to LinkedIn Today, and a published author on multiple subjects. Jonathan is a board member for the Churchill Club, Silicon Valley's premier business forum, and an advisor for numerous early-stage technology companies.

Jonathan holds a master's degree in computer science from Duke University, and a bachelor's degree in computer engineering from the University of Virginia.

How Machine Learning has Finally Solved Wanamaker's Dilemma

Oliver Downs
Amplero
Seattle, WA
olly@amplero.com

ABSTRACT

We are all familiar with John Wanamaker's famous quote: "Half the money I spend on advertising is wasted; the trouble is I don't know which half." What's ironic is that Wanamaker's dilemma is as much the marketer's dilemma today as it was in the 1900's. In an increasingly sophisticated marketing environment, where new marketing tools have enabled more precise targeting and marketing measurement than ever before, the challenge of solving Wanamaker's dilemma has still loomed – that is, until now. In this talk, I will show you how at Amplero we have solved what's not humanly possible to solve, making available to marketers an AI-powered marketing technology that makes use of dynamic machine learning at massive scale to enable smarter, more effective marketing. In particular, I will focus on the revolution of multi-armed bandit experimentation coupled with machine learning, highlighting what it means for today's marketer, and specifically the marketer's ability to directly impact business KPIs and customer lifetime value. As part of my presentation I will share experiences and examples from our work with BtoC enterprises with 10M's of customers.

Keywords

Marketing Optimization; Multi-armed Bandit Experimentation; Wanamaker's Dilemma.

KDD '16, August 13-17, 2016, San Francisco, CA, USA
ACM 978-1-4503-4232-2/16/08.
http://dx.doi.org/10.1145/2939672.2945363

Bio

As Amplero's Chief Scientist and CTO, Dr. Olly Downs leads the data science, technology and product teams responsible for building the company's AI-based marketing technology platform. Olly is a machine learning scientist and serial technology entrepreneur, credited with bringing advanced analytics and machine learning methods to bear as the creative spark behind numerous early-stage technology companies. Olly specializes in applying abstract analytical ideas from mathematical, physical and statistical science to problems in the real world and commercializing them into significant businesses. He has recently served as Chief Scientist at Atigeo, Chief Scientist at Mindset Media (sold to Meebo, February 2011) and Director of Research at Pelago (sold to GroupOn, April 2011). As Principal Scientist at INRIX, the first technology spin-out from Microsoft Research, Olly delivered a world-first in the provision of real-time traffic information using a nationwide network of GPS-enabled probe vehicles. To date Olly's work has resulted in more than 25 granted patents. Based in Seattle, Olly holds Ph.D. and MA degrees in Applied & Computational Mathematics from Princeton University, and BA, MA and MSci degrees in Experimental & Theoretical Physics from the University of Cambridge, UK.

Learning Sparse Models at Scale

Ralf Herbrich
Amazon
Germany
herbrich@amaon.com

ABSTRACT

Recently, learning deep models from dense data has received a lot of attention in tasks such as object recognition and signal processing. However, when dealing with non-sensory data about real-world entities, data is often sparse; for example people interaction with products in e-Commerce, people interacting with each other in social networks or word sequences in natural language. In this talk, I will share lessons learned over the past 10 years when learning predictive models based on sparse data: 1) how to scale the inference algorithms to distributed data setting, 2) how to automate the learning process by reducing the amount of hyper-parameters to zero, 3) how to deal with Zipf distributions when learning resource-constrained models, and 4) how to combine dense and sparse-learning algorithms. The talk will be drawing from many real-world experiences I gathered over the past decade in applications of the techniques in gaming, search, advertising and recommendations of systems developed at Microsoft, Facebook and Amazon.

Keywords

Scalable machine learning; Sparse models; Optimizing Hyper-Parameters; Zipf Distribution; Advertising; Recommendations.

Bio

Ralf is Director of Machine Learning at Amazon and Managing Director of the Amazon Development Center Germany. He works on problems of demand forecasting, scalable machine learning, computer vision and linking structured content. In 2011, he worked at Facebook leading the Unified Ranking and Allocation team. From 2000 - 2011, he worked at Microsoft Research and was co-leading the Applied Games and Online Services and Advertising group which engaged in research at the intersection of machine learning and computer games and in the areas of online services, search and online advertising combining insights from machine learning, information retrieval, game theory, artificial intelligence and social network analysis. Ralf was Research Fellow of the Darwin College Cambridge from 2000 - 2003. He has a diploma degree in Computer Science (1997) and a Ph.D. in Statistics (2000). Ralf's research interests include Bayesian inference and decision making, computer games, kernel methods and statistical learning theory. He is one of the inventors of the Drivatars system in the Forza Motorsport series as well as the TrueSkill ranking and matchmaking system in Xbox 360 Live. He also co-invented the adPredictor click-prediction technology launched in 2009 in Bing's online advertising system.

KDD '16, August 13-17, 2016, San Francisco, CA, USA
ACM 978-1-4503-4232-2/16/08.
http://dx.doi.org/10.1145/2939672.2945362

Profiling Users from Online Social Behaviors with Applications for Tencent Social Ads

Ching Law
Shenzhen, China
chinglaw@tencent.com

ABSTRACT

QQ and Wechat are the two largest instant messaging & social networks in China. Tencent Social Ads is the advertising platform for both Wechat and QQ, serving over 10B page views per day for several hundred million users.

We strive to understand as much as possible on our users' characteristics, so as to serve the best personalized ads for them. The rich user behaviors on Tencent's diverse products lay a foundation in our user profiles on many dimensions, including demographics, interests, intents, transactions, physical locations, and devices, etc.

In this talk, we will share our experience in large scale user data mining based on online social activities. We will discuss the challenges we face and the solutions we have devised so far.

- Some demographics data are obtained from user input, and thus would have gaps in both accuracy and coverage. We discuss the techniques in calibrating and verifying these data.
- We infer user interests from their social behaviors. For example, most QQ groups are not labelled properly, but by applying a large-scale topic model on the QQ memberships, we can effectively classify most QQ groups into an interest taxonomy. We also infer user interests from user's physical location check-ins and uploaded photos.
- User data can be collected from many diverse sources, including behaviors in various Tencent products, click and conversion in ad platform, and even seed customers collected by advertisers. We'll discuss the systems to merge these diverse data to provide a coherent view for our advertisers.
- High quality user labels are usually sparse. We implemented an algorithm for advertisers to reach more potential customers through user similarity computation based on user features as well as social graph inferences. We'll describe the system's contributions to ads quality.
- Top advertisers demand rich audience targeting solutions in combination of their own customer data, Tencent data, and possibly 3rd-party data. We'll discuss the data exchange platform that can facilitate collaborative applications with 3rd-party DSPs and DMPs.

Keywords

Advertising Technology; Audience Targeting; Social Networks;

Bio

Ching Law is General Manager of Social & Performance Ads Department at Tencent, overseeing engineering, marketing, operations, and products. Ching is instrumental in the development of GDT, the data and technology platform for Tencent Social Ads.

Ching has over ten years of experience in digital marketing and online advertising systems. Before joining Tencent in 2012, Ching worked at Google for eight years, where he led multiple audience & contextual targeting projects in AdSense, Google dictionary and Cantonese input system.

Ching received his Ph.D. in Computer Science from Massachusetts Institute of Technology.

KDD '16, August 13-17, 2016, San Francisco, CA, USA
ACM 978-1-4503-4232-2/16/08.
http://dx.doi.org/10.1145/2939672.2945368

The Wisdom of Crowds: Best Practices for Data Prep & Machine Learning derived from Millions of Data Science Workflows

Ingo Mierswa
RapidMiner
Boston, MA
imierswa@rapidminer.com

ABSTRACT
With hundreds of thousands of users, RapidMiner is the most frequently used visual workflow platform for machine learning. It covers the full spectrum of analytics from data preparation to machine learning and model validation. In this presentation, I will take you on a tour of machine learning which spans the last 15 years of research and industry applications and share key insights with you about how data scientists perform their daily analysis tasks. These patterns are extracted from mining millions of analytical workflows that have been created with RapidMiner over the past years. This talk will address important questions around the data mining process such as: What are the most frequently used solutions for typical data quality problems? How often are analysts using decision trees or neural networks? And does this behavior change over time or depend on the users experience level?

Keywords
Visual Workflow; Machine Learning Tools; Analytics; Data Visualization; Wisdom of the Crowds.

KDD '16, August 13-17, 2016, San Francisco, CA, USA
ACM 978-1-4503-4232-2/16/08.
http://dx.doi.org/10.1145/2939672.2945365

Bio
Dr. Ingo Mierswa is the founder and CTO of RapidMiner and as such responsible for the strategic innovation of the open source machine learning platform. Ingo is an industry-veteran data scientist since starting to develop RapidMiner at the Artificial Intelligence Division of the TU Dortmund University in Germany. Ingo, the scientist, has authored numerous award-winning publications about predictive analytics and big data. Ingo, the entrepreneur, has been leading the company with growth rates of up to 300 percent per year over the first seven years. In 2012, he spearheaded the go-international strategy with the opening of offices in the U.S. as well as the UK and Hungary. After two rounds of fundraising, the acquisition of Radoop, and supporting the positioning of RapidMiner with leading analyst firms like Gartner and Forrester, Ingo takes a lot of pride in bringing the world's best team to RapidMiner.

Bayesian Optimization and Embedded Learning Systems

Jeff Schneider
Pittsburgh, PA
jschneider@uberatc.com

ABSTRACT

An important property of embedded learning systems is the ever-changing environment they create for all algorithms operating in the system. Optimizing the performance of those algorithms becomes a perpetual on-line activity rather than a one-off task. I will review some of these challenges in autonomous vehicles. I will discuss Bayesian optimization methods and their application in robotics and scientific applications, focusing on scaling up the dimensionality and managing multi-fidelity evaluations. I will finish with lessons learned and thoughts on future directions as these methods move into embedded systems.

Keywords

Bayesian Systems; Autonomous Vehicles; Robotics

KDD '16, August 13-17, 2016, San Francisco, CA, USA
ACM 978-1-4503-4232-2/16/08.
http://dx.doi.org/10.1145/2939672.2945367

Bio

Dr. Jeff Schneider is the engineering lead for machine learning at Uber's Advanced Technologies Center. He is currently on leave from Carnegie Mellon University where he is a research professor in the school of computer science. He has 20 years experience developing, publishing, and applying machine learning algorithms in government, science, and industry.. He has over 100 publications and regularly gives talks and tutorials on the subject.

Previously, Jeff was the co-founder and CEO of Schenley Park Research, a company dedicated to bringing machine learning to industry. Later, he developed a machine learning based CNS drug discovery system and commercialized it during two years as Psychogenics' Chief Informatics Officer. Through his research, commercial, and consulting efforts, he has worked with dozens of companies and government agencies around the world.

Accelerating the Race to Autonomous Cars

Danny Shapiro
NVIDIA
Santa Clara, CA
dshapiro@nvidia.com

ABSTRACT

Every automaker is working on driver assistance systems and self-driving cars. Conventional computer vision used for ADAS is reaching its threshold because it is impossible to write code for every possible scenario as a vehicle navigates. In order to develop a truly autonomous car, deep learning and artificial intelligence are required. With deep learning, the vehicle can be trained to have super human levels of perception, driving safer than anyone on the road. An end-to-end artificial intelligence platform based on supercomputers in the cloud and in the vehicle enables cars to get smarter and smarter. Coupled with an extensive software development kit with vision and AI libraries and software modules, automakers, tier 1s, and startups can build scalable systems from ADAS to full autonomy.

KDD '16, August 13-17, 2016, San Francisco, CA, USA
ACM 978-1-4503-4232-2/16/08.
http://dx.doi.org/10.1145/2939672.2945360

Keywords

Self-driving cars; Deep Learning; Artificial Intelligence; Scalability

Bio

Danny Shapiro is Senior Director of NVIDIA's Automotive Business Unit, focusing on solutions that enable faster and better design of automobiles, as well as in-vehicle solutions for self-driving cars, infotainment systems, and digital instrument clusters. Danny holds a BSE in Electrical Engineering and Computer Science from Princeton University and an MBA from the Hass School of Business at UC Berkeley. Danny serves on the Advisory Boards for the LA Auto Show, the Connected Car Council and the NVIDIA foundation that focuses on computational solutions for cancer research.

Large-Scale Machine Learning at Verizon: Theory and Applications

Ashok Srivastava
Verizon
Palo Alto, CA
ashok.n.srivastava@gmail.com

ABSTRACT
This talk will cover recent innovations in large-scale machine learning and their applications on massive, real-world data sets at Verizon. These applications power new revenue generating products and services for the company and are hosted on a massive computing and storage platform known as Orion. We will discuss the architecture of Orion and the underlying algorithmic framework. We will also cover some of the real-world aspects of building a new organization dedicated to creating new product lines based on data science.

Keywords
Large-scale machine learning; Orion; Revenue Generation

Bio
Ashok N. Srivastava, Ph.D. is the Chief Data Scientist at Verizon. He leads a new research and development center in Palo Alto focusing on building revenue generating products and services powered by big data and analytics. He is a Consulting Professor at Stanford in the Electrical Engineering Department and is the Editor-in-Chief of the AIAA Journal of Aerospace Information Systems. Ashok is a Fellow of the IEEE, the American Association for the Advancement of Science (AAAS), and the American Institute of Aeronautics and Astronautics (AIAA).

Formerly he was the Principal Scientist for Data Sciences at NASA Ames Research Center and led the System-Wide Safety and Assurance Technologies project at NASA which has a 5 year budget of nearly $150M.

Ashok has significant experience in the internet, adtech, e-commerce, banking, finance, and securities areas. He has lead major engagements as a private consultant and as Senior Director at Blue Martini Software and Senior Consultant at IBM. He is a thought leader in the area of big data analytics, social media, optimization, machine learning, and data mining and has given presentations worldwide on these subjects. He served as a Venture Advisor focusing on big-data analytics at Trident Capital, and was on the advisory board of several startups. He is the author of over 100 research articles, 4 books, and over 30 patents.

KDD '16, August 13-17, 2016, San Francisco, CA, USA
ACM 978-1-4503-4232-2/16/08.
http://dx.doi.org/10.1145/2939672.2945361

Computational Social Science: Exciting Progress and Future Challenges

Duncan Watts
Microsoft
New York City, NY
duncan@microsoft.com

ABSTRACT

The past 15 years have witnessed a remarkable increase in both the scale and scope of social and behavioral data available to researchers, leading some to herald the emergence of a new field: "computational social science." Against these exciting developments stands a stubborn fact: that in spite of many thousands of published papers, there has been surprisingly little progress on the "big" questions that motivated the field in the first place—questions concerning systemic risk in financial systems, problem solving in complex organizations, and the dynamics of epidemics or social movements, among others. In this talk I highlight some examples of research that would not have been possible just a handful of years ago and that illustrate the promise of CSS. At the same time, they illustrate its limitations. I then conclude with some thoughts on how CSS can bridge the gap between its current state and its potential.

Keywords

Social data; Computational Social Science;

KDD '16, August 13-17, 2016, San Francisco, CA, USA
ACM 978-1-4503-4232-2/16/08.
http://dx.doi.org/10.1145/2939672.2945366

Bio

Duncan Watts is a principal researcher at Microsoft Research and an AD White Professor at Large at Cornell University. Prior to joining MSR in 2012, he was from 2000-2007 a professor of Sociology at Columbia University, and then a principal research scientist at Yahoo! Research, where he directed the Human Social Dynamics group.

Watts' research on social networks and collective dynamics has appeared in a wide range of journals, from Nature, Science, and Physical Review Letters to the American Journal of Sociology and Harvard Business Review, and has been recognized by the 2009 German Physical Society Young Scientist Award for Socio and Econophysics, the 2013 Lagrange-CRT Foundation Prize for Complexity Science, and the 2014 Everett Rogers Prize.

Watts is the author of three books: Six Degrees: The Science of a Connected Age (W.W. Norton, 2003); Small Worlds: The Dynamics of Networks between Order and Randomness (Princeton University Press, 1999); and most recently Everything is Obvious: Once You Know The Answer (Crown Business, 2011). He holds a B.Sc. in Physics from the Australian Defence Force Academy, from which he also received his officer's commission in the Royal Australian Navy, and a Ph.D. in Theoretical and Applied Mechanics from Cornell University.

MAP: Frequency-Based Maximization of Airline Profits based on an Ensemble Forecasting Approach

Bo An
School of Computer Science and Engineering
Nanyang Technological University
boan@ntu.edu.sg

Haipeng Chen
Interdisciplinary Graduate School
Nanyang Technological University
chen0939@ntu.edu.sg

Noseong Park, V.S. Subrahmanian
UMIACS & Department of Computer Science
University of Maryland
{npark,vs}@cs.umd.edu

ABSTRACT

Though there are numerous traditional models to predict market share and demand along airline routes, the prediction of existing models is not precise enough and, to the best of our knowledge, there is no use of data-mining based forecasting techniques to improve airline profitability. We propose the MAP (Maximizing Airline Profits) architecture designed to help airlines and make two key contributions in *airline market share and route demand prediction* and *prediction-based airline profit optimization*. Compared with past methods to forecast market share and demand along airline routes, we introduce a novel Ensemble Forecasting (MAP-EF) approach considering two new classes of features: (i) features derived from clusters of similar routes, and (ii) features based on equilibrium pricing. We show that MAP-EF achieves much better Pearson Correlation Coefficients (over 0.95 vs. 0.82 for market share, 0.98 vs. 0.77 for demand) and R^2-values compared with three state-of-the-art works for forecasting market share and demand, while showing much lower variance. Using the results of MAP-EF, we develop MAP-Bilevel Branch and Bound (MAP-BBB) and MAP-Greedy (MAP-G) algorithms to optimally allocate flight frequencies over multiple routes, to maximize an airline's profit. Experimental results show that airlines can increase profits by a significant margin. All experiments were conducted with data aggregated from four sources: US Bureau of Transportation Statistics (BTS), US Bureau of Economic Analysis (BEA), the National Transportation Safety Board (NTSB), and the US Census Bureau (CB).

Keywords

Ensemble Prediction; Regression; Airline Demand and Market Share Prediction; Airline Profit Maximization;

1. INTRODUCTION

Since the deregulation of US airlines in 1978, there has been intense competition amongst airlines for market share and, eventually, profitability. While there is considerable work on predicting market share and demand along airline routes, the prediction of existing models is not precise enough and, to the best of our knowledge, there is no use of data-mining based forecasting techniques to improve airline profitability. In this paper, we formally define the MAP problem by allowing airlines to decide the flight frequencies on their flying routes in order to maximize their profits, subject to cost constraints. For instance, if there is a set $\mathcal{R}$ of routes in the world, and the airline can fly up to n routes where $n \leq |\mathcal{R}|$, then our MAP problem would capture both route selection (which routes to fly) and frequency[1].

The first key contribution of this paper is a precise route-specific prediction of both total demand of an origin-destination market and an airline's market share. Existing related works only use simple regression methods and focus on a limited number of variables. Our studies of three major route market share [16, 24, 26] and demand prediction [6, 8, 9] methods show that the Pearson Correlation Coefficients between the predicted values and the actual values are a max of 0.82 (for one market share method) and 0.77 (for one demand model). Other existing models predict much lower numbers. Although one of these regression methods [16] outputs satisfactory prediction results in our experiments, there is still a gap between the prediction and the real value. The relatively "small" prediction gap can lead to a huge revenue loss if airlines make decisions based on the prediction. Worse still, due to the inflexibility of existing models, the prediction gap can be large for some routes. We propose a new ensemble-based prediction method for forecasting total demand and market share, which uses an extensive number of features and several state-of-the-art clustering and regression algorithms that have never been adopted for MAP. The new ensemble method builds upon existing models, but also collects several new features, together with novel clustering and game theoretic methods. We are the first to propose a prediction method, for a broad set of routes (around 700 - past works stopped at 200), which considers the predictions of both total demand (demand generation) of a route and market share (demand allocation) of each airline operating in that route (13 airlines in total).

The second key contribution is two novel algorithms for solving MAP, which becomes computationally intractable with brute-force search when the number of routes is large. This is because: 1) the solution space is exponential w.r.t. the number of routes, 2) the profit-frequency function, which is generated by our proposed prediction method, is neither convex nor concave (and thus not linear). We show in Section 2 that MAP belongs to the hardest subclass of *Knapsack Problems* (KPs) and *Resource Allocation Problems* (RAPs), and despite a vast amount of existing works [11, 12, 20, 21] for both KPs and RAPs, all previous algorithms fail to solve it

[1]Because the airline industry is very complex, it is difficult to model all other sources of profit that might be available (e.g., in-flight sales, baggage fees, etc.) to the airline, especially as such data is not freely available.

KDD '16, August 13-17, 2016, San Francisco, CA, USA

© 2016 ACM. ISBN 978-1-4503-4232-2/16/08... $15.00

DOI: http://dx.doi.org/10.1145/2939672.2939726

efficiently. Based on predictions made by MAP-EF, we come up with two optimization algorithms to solve the raised profit maximization problem. We present an exact algorithm to solve MAP based on a novel Bilevel-Branch and Bound approach (MAP-BBB) that computes the true optimal solution, as well as a Greedy algorithm (MAP-G) that more quickly computes suboptimal solutions.

Third, we conduct extensive experimental evaluations to compare MAP's prediction results with those of past works. We show that past prediction models are significantly "beaten" by MAP, which increases these predictive accuracies to over 0.95, while significantly reducing the variance in our prediction error compared with past works. We also compare both the optimality and scalability of our proposed profit maximization algorithms with several benchmarks. The result shows that our predictions are far superior to past efforts. Moreover, by using MAP, an airline can averagely increase its profit by at least 55% under mild conditions.[2]

The rest of this paper is organized as follows. Section 2 introduces related works. Section 3 discusses the data set used in our study. Section 4 shows our proposed prediction framework based on our ensemble method. Section 5 presents our proposed algorithms for the profit maximization problem. Section 6 conducts extensive experimental evaluations. *For notational convenience, Table 1 summarizes all the notations used in this paper.*

2. RELATED WORK

Existing airline market share and demand prediction models try to write down math formulas for market share/demand and then use regression to find values of the parameters in these formulas that minimize the sum of the squared errors between the predicted values and the true values. *We therefore call these **math models** to indicate that the structural form of these models is written down* a priori *without reference to any data and that the parameter values that minimize error are then computed using available data.*

Airline market share prediction. Most works on airline market share prediction use a multinomial logit (MNL) regression model [16, 24, 26]. For a set $\mathcal{A}$ of airlines in a given route, an airline A_i's market share m_i is modeled as:

$$m_i = \frac{e^{V_i}}{\sum_{A_j \in \mathcal{A}} e^{V_j}}. \tag{1}$$

Here $V_i = \sum_k \eta_k X_{ik}$ is the customer's utility for choosing airline A_i's service, X_{ik} is the value of the kth variable for airline A_i and η_k is its corresponding weight to be learnt from data. Various variables have been studied. In Market1 [16], the authors consider a route's price, frequency, and the number of stops. Based on the prediction, they analyze competition among airlines. Market2 [24] considers an airline's frequency, delay, and safety. Market3 [26] studies the effect of aircraft size and seat availability on market share and considers other variables such as price and frequency.

Total demand prediction. For total demand of a route, a multiplicative [6, 8, 9] regression model is the most frequently adopted. Formally, a route's total demand is represented as:

$$d = \prod_k Y_k^{\lambda_k}, \tag{2}$$

where Y_k is a value of the kth variable and λ_k is a parameter to be learnt from data which measures the importance of Y_k. Demand1 [6] considers wealth related variables such as price, income and CPI (consumer price index). Demand2 [9] studies the influence of demographic variables such as price, income and population, as well as hub status (i.e., large, medium, small or non-hub) on passenger demand. Demand3 [8] focuses on variables such as price, income, population and origin-destination distance.

In this paper, we show that our prediction models build on all of these methods, but use an ensemble approach to achieve not only much higher predictive accuracy, but also much greater robustness.

KPs and RAPs. Airline profit maximization through optimal frequency allocation over multiple routes, given a certain budget constraint, belongs to the family of KPs and RAPs, which have been extensively studied ever since the work of Dantzig [13] in 1957. While all variants of KPs are known to be *NP-hard*, MAP, which has bounded integer variables, and a non-concave (arbitrary) objective function, is notoriously hard [11].

There are some Polynomial Time Approximate Schemes (PTAS) and even Fully-PTAS to solve bounded knapsack problems (BKPs), using greedy algorithms [17], dynamic programming [21] and branch and bound [19]. The first two methods assume linear objective functions, while the last approach uses linear relaxation. Several algorithms have been proposed to solve KPs/RAPs with non-linear objective functions, especially for a concave and non-decreasing

[2]Like all past models, our analysis of airline profits is only based on publicly available data, so the true number might be smaller. Nevertheless, even a 10% improvement in the real-world would be substantial.

Table 1: Summary of Notations

$\mathcal{A}$	a set of airlines
A_i	i^{th} airline of $\mathcal{A}$
$\mathcal{R}$	a set of routes
R_i	i^{th} route of $\mathcal{R}$
Symbols related to predict market share of route R	
X_{ik}	the value of the kth variable, e.g., price, of airline A_i
η_k	the weight of X_{ik}
V_i	airline A_i's customer utility in R
m_i	market share of airline A_i in R
Symbols related to predict demand of route R	
Y_k	the value of the kth variable, e.g., population
λ_k	the exponent of Y_k
d	total demand (the number of passengers) of route R
Symbols related to calculate Nash Equilibrium of route R	
p_i	average ticket price of A_i for route R
c_i^{psg}	unit passenger related cost of A_i in route R
$N(A_i)$	utility (profit) of A_i in route R
Symbols related to Profit Maximization of airline A	
C_i	per flight cost of route R_i for a given airline A
f_i	flight frequency of route R_i for a given airline A
$r_i(f_i)$	revenue when A operates f_i flights on route R_i
$N_i(f_i)$	profit (revenue minus total cost) when A operates f_i flights on route R_i
$\langle f_i \rangle$	frequency strategy for all routes in $\mathcal{R}$ of airline A
$\langle f_i^* \rangle$	optimal frequency strategy of airline A
$N(\langle f_i \rangle)$	profit of frequency strategy $\langle f_i \rangle$
b	budget limit of the Profit Maximization problem
K	the number of routes to optimize profit of airline
Symbols related to MAP-BBB in Algorithm 2	
n_p	parent node
c	child node
c_l, c_r	left and right children of a parent node
N^*	optimal profit sought by the algorithm
$MaxLB$	bounding threshold
UB_c, LB_c	lower bound and upper bound profit of node c
C_c	lower bound cost of node c
Symbols related to MAP-G in Algorithm 3	
g	a group of route
q	the number of routes in a group g
$\mathcal{G}$	a set of route groups, $\mathcal{R}$ is divided into $\lvert\mathcal{G}\rvert$ groups
δ	budget allocation unit
$\langle f_g^* \rangle$	optimal frequency strategy of group g

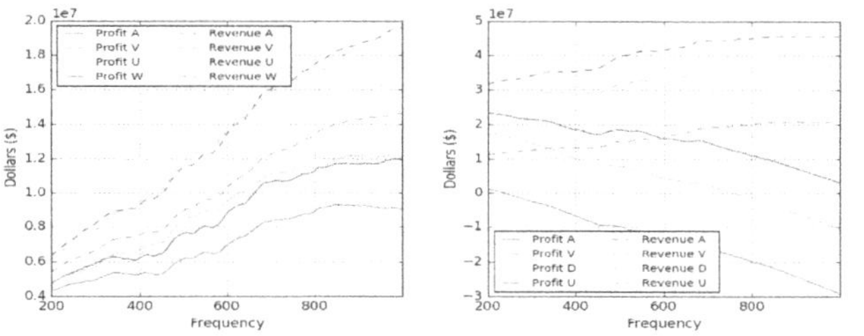

Figure 1: Quarterly revenue (dashed lines) and profit (solid lines) in 10 million dollars generated by MAP-EF. Revenue is defined as average ticket price multiplied by the number of passengers. Cost is per flight cost multiplied by frequency. Note that the profit-frequency curve (revenue minus cost) is very irregular even though the revenue-frequency curve is monotonically increasing. The shapes of the curves are quite different.

objective function [11]. The common idea is to decompose the original objective function into a set of approximated piecewise linear functions. Unfortunately, none of these works for our problem. This is because the profit-frequency function in our problem is neither concave nor convex (thus not linear), varies from one route to another, and cannot be described by a simple math formula but by a series of clustering, regression, and other types of functions[3]. As shown in Figure 1 where the x-axis is the frequency and the y-axis is the profit (or revenue), the two graphs are for two routes (SFO-LAX route on the left and JFK-LAX route on the right) and 4 major US airlines. We see that the shapes of the curve on the left (SFO-LAX) is quite different from another on the right (JFK-LAX). In fact, across the 700 routes we studied, there was huge variation in the actual profit/revenue curves. Thus, any method specially devised for a certain form of objective functions (e.g., linear, concave or convex) cannot be applied.

Optimal decision making based on data-mining. Data-mining based optimization has been implemented by many existing KDD papers, including optimal bidding [28, 29], smart pacing [27] and optimal recommendation systems [18]. In the first step of these works, a predicted objective function is learned using regression analysis techniques. Based on the prediction results, an optimization problem is solved, either analytically [18, 28] or via optimization algorithms [27, 29]. While our MAP framework follows this general scheme, it differs in many ways, including the fact that the predicted objective function is in a very complicated linear algebra form.

3. THE MAP DATASET

We have created an integrated "MAP" data set by aggregating information from 4 publicly available data sources, viz. the Bureau of Transportation Statistics (BTS) [3], the Bureau of Economic Analysis (BEA) [2], the National Transportation Safety Board (NTSB) [4], and the U.S. Census Bureau (Census) [5]. BTS provides almost all aspects of airline market information such as ticket price[4], frequency, number of stops, delay records, aircraft size and available seats. The BEA and the Census release regional income, economic state, and population information while the NTSB provides all safety and accident related information. The BTS provides a quarterly dataset. A detailed description of the variables we consider is presented in Table 2. We plan to publicly release our tools

[3]We will revisit this point after Definition 5.2.

[4]BTS releases a 10% sample of route and airline specific ticket sales logs, from which average ticket price is obtained.

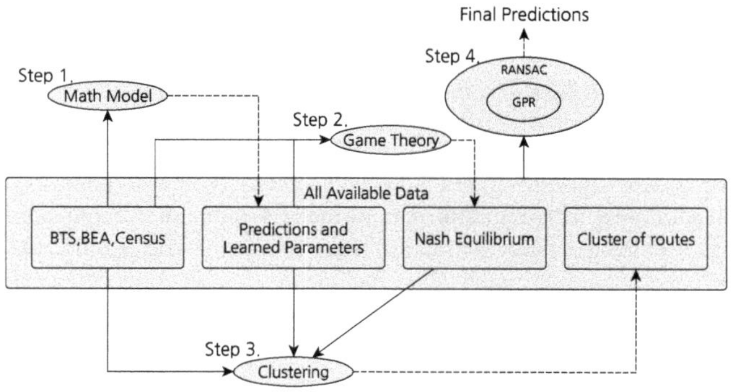

Figure 2: Structure of the MAP-EF prediction model. Rectangles mean data and elipses algorithms. Each algorithm is marked with a processing sequence number. Solid lines mean inputs and dashed lines outputs.

and data set in 2016. Our training data includes 10 years (40 quarters) of data on 13 airlines and 700 routes. Our validation data includes one quarter (all 700 routes and 13 airlines' market share and profits are predicted, leading to a total 9100 predictions in total). This is consistent with most corporate forecasts where forecasts are made for the next quarter[5].

Table 2: Variables used to make predictions by related works

Market Share	
ticket price	average price of tickets sold by airline
frequency	number of flights operated by airline
delay time	average delay time of all flights operated by airline
delay ratio	ratio of delayed flights to total number of flights by airline
cancel ratio	ratio of canceled flights to total number of flights by airline
stop	average number of stops of all flights by airline
safety	number of casualties caused by past accidents of airline
craftsize	average number of seats for a flight of airline
total seat	total number of seats provided by airline during a quarter
Total Demand	
avg. price	average of all airlines' ticket prices
population	geometric mean of origin and destinations' population
income	geometric mean of origin and destinations' income
CPI	geometric mean of origin and destinations' CPI
distance	distance between origin and destination

4. ENSEMBLE PREDICTION MODEL

In this section, we design an ensemble-based predictor MAP-EF that produces highly accurate route-specific predictions.

Overall architecture. Figure 2 shows the architecture of our ensemble model which runs through 4 major steps.

Step 1 - Past Models with Regularization. In the first step, we use the MAP-dataset, in conjunction with existing market share models (Market1 [16], Market2 [24], Market3 [26]) and demand models (Demand1 [6], Demand2 [9], Demand3 [8]) in order to generate the predictions made by models developed previously in the literature. These predictions are used as additional features. In addition, we augment past models with regularization [10].[6] Because this step

[5]These predictions exceed that of related work, e.g., [26], which predicted for 10 airlines with a 10 year history for 200 routes.

[6]In past works for market share prediction, the authors minimize sum-squared-error (SSE), i.e. they try to find parameter values for the math models that minimize $\Sigma_{A_i}(m_i - \hat{m_i})^2$ where m_i (resp. $\hat{m_i}$) is the true (resp. predicted) market share. In addition to this, regularization minimizes $\sum_{A_i}(m_i - \hat{m_i})^2 + ||W||$, where W is a

is straightforwardly built on top of past works, we do not go into it in further detail.

Step 2 - Nash Equilibrium. Ticket pricing clearly influences both market share and demand. At the same time, the competitive pricing behavior among airlines would have further influence. Thus, we include equilibrium pricing calculated based on past models as an additional feature in MAP-EF. At the end of this step, each route has one feature table for market share prediction and another for demand prediction. Each table[7] includes a set of features collected from the MAP-dataset and from Steps 1 and 2.

Step 3 - Clustering of Similar Routes. We cluster all routes into groups of similar routes with the features of the quarter we predict. For each group of routes, we concatenate all the individual route tables constructed in Step 2 for all routes in that group. The merged tables are then used for training within MAP-EF. We describe this step in further detail.

Step 4 - Iterative Gaussian Process Regression (GPR) and Random Sample Consensus (RANSAC). At the end of Step 3, we have a comprehensive *MAP Feature Table*. We use a combination of the well-known methods of GPR [22] and RANSAC [15]. To make market share/demand predictions for a route R, this step trains only on data about the group that contains route R, removes outliers using RANSAC, and then uses GPR to make the final prediction.

Nash equilibrium price feature. In a competitive airline market, the pricing behaviors of airlines are strategic. To capture the competitive nature of the market, we include equilibrium price as an additional feature[8]. The rationale behind this is that when an airline's quoted price is higher/lower than its equilibrium price, the customer might lose/gain utility, which has influence on the customer's choice and thus further affects an airline's market share. Therefore, we use the gap between equilibrium price and real price as an additional feature. The utility (net income) $N(A_i)$ of an airline A_i w.r.t. a specific route is $N(A_i) = (p_i - c_i^{psg}) \cdot d \cdot m_i$, where p_i is the ticket price and c_i^{psg} is the passenger-related per ticket cost obtained from the BTS dataset. d and m_i are a route's total demand and airline A_i's market share as described in Section 2. Recall that Nash equilibrium is an equilibrium situation in a multi-player non-cooperative game, where each player is assumed to know the equilibrium strategies of the other players, and no player has anything to gain by changing only its own strategy. Following this definition, we formulate the computation of Nash equilibrium strategy of each airline $A_i \in \mathcal{A}$ w.r.t. a given route:

$$\max_{p_i} \quad N(A_i), \tag{3}$$

$$\text{subject to} \quad p_i^{min} \leq p_i \leq p_i^{max}, \tag{4}$$

$$d \cdot m_i \leq Q_i. \tag{5}$$

Eq.(4) specifies the feasible section of price, and Eq.(5) indicates that the total number of passengers cannot exceed its capacity Q_i.

vector that consists of parameters η_k (or λ_k for demand prediction) and $||W||$ is the norm of W. $||W||$ can be defined using either the L^1 or L^2 norm. Thus, we have three options: SSE, SSE+L^1 regularization, and SSE+L^2 regularization. In order to decide the best model among these, we use grid search and cross-validation. For cross-validation, we predict a quarter of the training data after training with the remaining quarters regardless of temporal sequence, which creates n-fold cross validation, where n is the number of quarters in the training data.

[7]Please refer to the Appendix [1] for detailed examples of the merged table.

[8]Note that when computing the equilibrium price, the market share and total demand is the math formula obtained in Step 1, and the competition is only within a route.

Algorithm 1: ITER

1 Randomly assign values to $\mathbf{p}_{t-1}$ within $[p_i^{min}, p_i^{max}]$
2 **repeat**
3   **for** $A_i \in \mathcal{A}$ **do**
4     $counter \leftarrow 0$
5     $p_{i,t} \leftarrow$ Solution of Eqs.(3)-(5)
6   **if** $|p_{i,t} - p_{i,t-1}| \leq \varepsilon$ **then** $counter++$
7   $\mathbf{p}_{t-1} \leftarrow \mathbf{p}_t$
8 **until** $counter = n$
9 **return** $\mathbf{p}_t$

To compute equilibrium price on a route, we propose ITER (Iterative meThod for nash EquilibRium computation) in Algorithm 1, where $\mathbf{p}_{t-1}$ and $\mathbf{p}_t$ denote the optimal price vectors of two subsequent "virtual" periods. The algorithm starts with an initialization of $\mathbf{p}_{t-1}$ within $[p_i^{min}, p_i^{max}]$, where p_i^{min} and p_i^{max} are the minimum and maximum possible prices quoted by airline A_i. After this, iteration proceeds. In each repeat loop (Lines 2-9), the algorithm updates optimal prices of all the airlines. Within each repeat loop, there is a for loop (Lines 3-7). In the for loop, each airline alternately updates its optimal price $p_{i,t}$ based on the previous price vector $\mathbf{p}_{-i,t-1}$ of the other airlines in the last virtual period. It iterates until for each airline $A_i \in \mathcal{A}$, the price is not updating in two subsequent virtual periods (i.e., the difference between the two prices is no larger than a small threshold $|p_{i,t} - p_{i,t-1}| \leq \varepsilon$), which means a Nash equilibrium is obtained.

THEOREM 4.1. *If ITER returns a solution, then that solution is the Nash equilibrium price.*

Proof sketch. In each repeat loop, ITER finds the best response of all players (airlines) given the strategies of the last virtual period. When the best response strategies of all players in the current virtual period are equal to the best response strategies of the last virtual period, a Nash equilibrium is found according to the definition of Nash equilibrium. □

Clustering similar routes. Some routes are more similar than others, e.g., LAX-JFK may show more similar market attributes to SFO-JFK than LAX-SFO because the first two are long-haul routes from west to east and the last one is a short-haul local route, and estimating market share/demand would probably benefit from examining all of similar routes. In order to cluster routes, we use all features gathered in the MAP-dataset, Steps 1 and 2. As we do not know the "ground truth" definition of whether a cluster is correct or not, we evaluate cluster quality via *silhouette score*[9] [23]. The silhouette score tends to keep increasing (with some glitches) as the number of clusters increases. The elbow method [25] chooses the optimal number of clusters when silhouette scores stabilize. We tested several clustering methods including K-Means^{++}[7] and connectivity-based and density-based clustering algorithms such as DBSCAN [14]. Of these, we achieved the best result with K-Means^{++}.

RANSAC/GPR regression. Training with similar routes does not always contribute positively to predictive accuracy. In several cases,

[9]The silhouette score is to calculate the consistency of clusters. As more similar routes are contained by a cluster, its silhouette score is higher. If $\mathbf{G}$ is a set of clusters, dis is some distance (dissimilarity) measure, and e is some data item, the silhouette score $SS(e) = \frac{b(e)-a(e)}{\max\{a(e),b(e)\}}$ where $a(e)$ is the average distance between e and the data items of the cluster it belongs to, and $b(e)$ is the minimum average distance between e and the data items of clusters it does not belong to.

it incurs additional error. We tested many linear regression algorithms such as Ridge, Lasso, and Lars [10]. None of them could produce stable performance across multiple routes. We then tested a specially devised structure that consists of RANSAC and GPR. RANSAC removes outliers from training data and GPR makes the final prediction only with inliers. GPR is known to be robust because it is much less parametric than the others. Intuitively, GPR says that if features of two airlines are similar, their market shares should also be similar. It assumes that priors follow a Gaussian distribution. After that, GPR also calculates posteriors using the famous bayes rule, $\mathbb{P}(posterior) \propto \mathbb{P}(likelihood)\mathbb{P}(prior)$ that can be analytically calculated using a covariance matrix fitted to the training data. To predict, GPR, using the learned covariance matrix, calculates similarities between a test case and all training cases, and makes a prediction. The entire process can be described by a very complicated linear algebra form. RANSAC Regression is known to be robust w.r.t. noise. In the first step, RANSAC performs regression with a small random subset of training data. In the second step, all training data that does not fit the model constructed during the first step is classified as outliers and others as inliers. These two processes are iterated over time to refine the set of inliers called the *consensus set*. Thus, MAP-EF uses RANSAC with GPR as a base estimator. We show prediction results of other regression techniques in the Appendix [1].

Time Overheads. In comparison with past models, MAP-EF should spend additional time for clustering and more advanced regression methods, which takes cubic time of training data size.

5. AIRLINE PROFIT MAXIMIZATION VIA FREQUENCY ALLOCATION

In this section, we suggest how to maximize an airline's profit by optimally allocating quarterly frequencies to routes.

DEFINITION 5.1 (FREQUENCY STRATEGY). *A frequency strategy of an airline A for a given set $\mathcal{R} = \{R_1, \ldots, R_n\}$ of routes is a vector $\langle f_i \rangle$ of non-negative integers.*

Intuitively, the i'th element f_i of the frequency strategy denotes the number of times the airline should fly route R_i in a quarter. For a given airline A, a set $\mathcal{R} = \{R_1, \ldots, R_n\}$, per flight cost C_i for each route R_i, and total operation budget b, the profit maximization problem finds the frequency allocation $\langle f_i \rangle$ of A assuming its competitors' behaviors are fixed. We also conduct experiments to test the robustness of this approach when competitors change their strategies simultaneously.

DEFINITION 5.2. *The* ***Frequency-based Profit Maximization Problem*** *can be encoded as the optimization problem:*

$$\max_{\langle f_i \rangle} \quad \sum_{R_i \in \mathcal{R}} N_i(f_i) \tag{6}$$

$$\text{subject to} \quad 0 \le f_i \le f_i^{max}, f_i \in \mathbb{N}, \forall R_i \in \mathcal{R} \tag{7}$$

$$\sum_{R_i \in \mathcal{R}} C_i f_i \le b. \tag{8}$$

$N_i(f_i)$ is the profit of route R_i given frequency f_i, which is ticket revenue $r_i(f_i)$ minus total operation cost $C_i f_i$ and can be calculated by the market share and total demand predicted by MAP-EF. The ticket revenue is defined as price per ticket multiplied by airline A's total passenger demand on route R_i. $\sum_{R_i \in \mathcal{R}} N_i(f_i)$ is the sum of profits for all routes. Because routes (such as the SFO-LAX and JFK-LAX routes shown in Figure 1) can differ dramatically in profitability, and as these numbers are basically estimated by our market share and demand prediction algorithms, it follows that the individual terms $N_i(f_i)$ in our objective function can vary dramatically in form from one route to another. This is what makes using a single form of objective function difficult. Constraint (7) specifies the bound of frequency for each route as f_i^{max} and that the frequencies are non-negative integers. The frequency bound $f_i^{max} = \min(\lfloor \frac{b}{C_i} \rfloor, f^{BTS})$, where f^{BTS} is the maximum frequency discovered in the BTS dataset, so that we prevent f_i from exceeding the feasible frequency bound. Constraint (8) indicates the budget constraint. As discussed in Section 2, this optimization problem belongs to the hardest class of KPs and RAPs, mainly due to two reasons: i) the solution space is exponentially large as $\Pi_i f_i^{max}$, and ii) the objective function is neither convex nor concave (thus not linear).

Before presenting the complexity analysis and the algorithms to solve MAP, we introduce two important assumptions. First, we assume that varying the frequency of a route does not affect other routes' total demand and market share — *Independence of Routes*. This assumption is valid for most cases where the passenger's traveling pattern on one route is independent of the other routes. Second, we assume revenue (resp. cost) is a monotonically increasing non-linear (resp. linear) function of frequency — *Monotonicity of Revenue and Cost*. As shown in Figure 1, this assumption is intuitive. Increasing frequency leads to larger market share (thus higher revenue) and higher operation cost. Therefore, the monotonicity of revenue and cost does not imply the monotonicity of profit. This prevents us from applying many well-developed algorithms for KPs and RAPs. We show the computational hardness of the MAP problem with the following theorem.

THEOREM 5.3. *The decision version of MAP (D-MAP) which answers the question* "Is there a frequency strategy whose profit exceeds a threshold P without violating budget b?" *is NP-complete.*

Proof sketch. We first show that there is a polynomial reduction from the Knapsack problem to D-MAP. In the Knapsack problem, there are n items (each has p_i profit and w_i cost), budget limit W, a threshold V, and the objective is to find a set of items whose profit is no smaller than V without violating budget W. This a special instance of D-MAP where $b = W, P = V, C_i = w_i$ and the profit-frequency function of route R_i is linear with the slope of p_i; and the reduction from the Knapsack problem to profit maximization can be done in polynomial time.

Next, we show its correctness, i.e., Y is a *yes* instance of the Knapsack problem $\Longleftrightarrow$ X reduced from Y is a *yes* instance for D-MAP.

"if" direction. Assume that there exists a solution s for a Knapsack problem instance. We can create a frequency strategy $\langle f_i \rangle$, where f_i is the number of ith item in the solution s. s can achieve a profit of at least V without violating budget W, and so is $\langle f_i \rangle$ because $b = W, P = V, C_i = w_i$ and the same linear profit function.

"only if" direction. Assume that a frequency strategy $\langle f_i \rangle$ can achieve a profit of at least P without violating budget b. We can create a Knapsack solution s to select f_i items for i^{th} item. s is a valid solution of the Knapsack problem because $b = W, P = V$, $C_i = w_i$ and the same linear profit function.

Finally, D-MAP is in $\mathcal{NP}$ because the verification process to check whether a frequency strategy's profit exceeds a threshold requires $|\mathcal{R}|$ oracle queries. Note that each oracle query takes a constant time for a given route and airline. Thus, the verification process takes polynomial time. □

Due to the computational complexity, it is intractable to find an optimal solution of the MAP problem by performing brute-force search. As a result, we propose two new approaches: i) MAP-BBB is a bi-level branch and bound method, and ii) MAP-G is a greedy algorithm operating over groups of routes. Section 6 shows that these two algorithms have complementary performance in terms of runtime (scalability) and optimality.

5.1 Bilevel Branch and Bound (MAP-BBB)

Branch and bound (BB) is a popular search algorithm for combinatorial optimization to efficiently enumerate the entire solution space and find the optimal solution. The solution space of BB can be represented by a rooted tree and each child of a parent node considers a subset of solution space of its parent node. BB consists of a series of repeated branching and bounding processes. In the branching process, the feasible solution space is divided into a number of smaller subsets, while in the bounding process, an upper and a lower bound of the objective (airline profit in this problem) is derived for each subset of solution space. The largest lower bound is updated and, when the upper bound of a certain subset is smaller than the current largest lower bound, that subset is pruned since it does not contain the optimal solution. As we can see, the key of BB lies in finding a tight upper and lower bound for the bounding process, especially for upper bound. While most of the BB algorithms for Knapsack problems find upper bounds through linear relaxation [19], the complicated form of our prediction model prevents us from implementing such upper bounds. As a result, we propose a novel *Bilevel branch and bound* (MAP-BBB) algorithm, which uses another sub-BB search to find an upper bound for the main BB process.

Algorithm 2 shows the MAP-BBB algorithm that builds on classical branch and bound methods. The search for an optimal solution explores a tree whose nodes are labeled with n intervals, one for each of the routes $R_1, \ldots, R_n$ under consideration. Intuitively, if a node is labeled with the interval $[\ell, u]$ for a particular route R_i, it means that we are currently restricting the frequency in the interval $[\ell, u]$ for that route. MAP-BBB also maintains a priority queue Q of all the nodes where the head has the largest *upper bound* profit. The root node has the full range of $[0, f_i^{max}]$ for each route $R_i \in \mathcal{R}$. As we descend the tree, these intervals get smaller. In Figure 3, for example, the parent node n_p is divided into two children nodes c_l and c_r, where the frequency range of the last route of n_p is divided into two halves.

For the bounding process of child node $c \in \{c_l, c_r\}$, upper and lower bound profits of the optimal strategy that can be defined with the frequency range of c are calculated (to be further described below). If its lower bound LB_c is larger than the temporary maximum lower bound, denoted as $MaxLB$ in Algorithm 2, and its lower bound cost C_c of the optimal strategy does not violate the budget b, then we update $MaxLB$ (line 11). If its upper bound UB_c is no larger than $MaxLB$ or its lower bound cost C_c violates budget b, we prune this node (line 12). Once we find a node that consists of only non-divisible ranges, i.e., min and max of ranges are all the same, and its cost is within budget b, it is a candidate of the optimal frequency strategy. The optimal strategy is selected among them (line 13). N^* and $\langle f_i^* \rangle$ stand for the obtained optimal profit and optimal frequency strategy, respectively.

Lower bound profit and lower bound cost. Calculating a lower bound of profit LB_c and cost C_c of node c is a key to the MAP-BBB algorithm. We choose the min frequency value for each route's range and calculate its lower bound profit and cost with MAP-EF. This is valid because the optimal profit and the associated cost of node c are always no smaller than that.

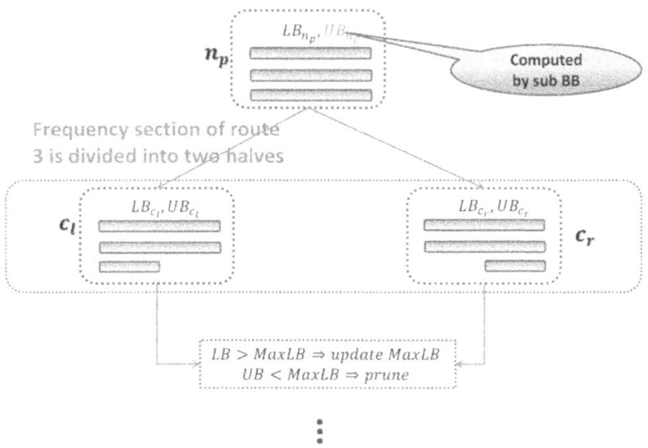

Figure 3: An example branch and bound process for MAP-BBB with three routes. Each blue bar of node represents a frequency range. Lower BB is used to calculate an upper bound profit of a node. c_l and c_r are two children of the parent node n_p.

Algorithm 2: MAP-Bilevel Branch and Bound (MAP-BBB)

1 $N^* \leftarrow 0, \langle f_i^* \rangle \leftarrow \mathbf{0}$
2 Create $root$
3 $MaxLB \leftarrow LB_{root}$
4 PriorityQueue $Q \leftarrow \emptyset$
5 $Q.enque(root)$
6 **while** $|Q| > 0$ **do**
7 $\quad n_p \leftarrow Q.poll()$
8 $\quad$ **if** n_p *is divisible* **then**
9 $\quad\quad$ Create c_l, c_r
10 $\quad\quad$ **for** $c \in \{c_l, c_r\}$ **do**
11 $\quad\quad\quad$ **if** $LB_c > MaxLB$ *and* $C_c \leq b$ **then** $MaxLB \leftarrow LB_c$
12 $\quad\quad\quad$ **if** $UB_c \geq MaxLB$ *and* $C_c \leq b$ **then** $Q.enque(c)$
13 $\quad$ **else if** $N^* < N(n_p)$ *and* $C_{n_p} \leq b$ **then**
14 $\quad\quad$ $N^* \leftarrow N(n_p)$
15 $\quad\quad$ $\langle f_i^* \rangle \leftarrow$ frequency strategy of n_p
16 **return** $\langle f_i^* \rangle, N^*$

Upper bound. As we cannot employ linear relaxation, upper bound calculation is more challenging. For this, we use another branch and bound process, which is why the proposed algorithm is called a *bilevel branch and bound*. For each range of R_i in node c, we perform the following sub branch and bound process to find its optimal frequency within the range **without a budget constraint**. This is good because the optimal profit without budget limit is definitely no smaller than the optimal profit with budget constraint and it is much faster than the upper bound with budget check across multiple routes. We omit its pseudo code because it is more or less the same as Algorithm 2 except that the sub branch and bound does not check budget violation. In order to distinguish two branch and bounds, we use different terms *sub* and *main*. The sub root node is initialized with the specified range of R_i. During the sub branching process, we equally divide a sub node interval into two halves and create two sub children nodes. In the sub bounding process of a sub node, the heuristic for computing a lower bound of the sub branch and bound is defined as $r_i(f_{random}) - C_i f_{random}$, where f_{random} is a random frequency in the frequency range. This holds since any feasible frequency generates a lower bound of the optimal profit. The heuristic for computing an upper bound of the sub branch and bound is $r_i(f_{max}) - C_i f_{min}$, where f_{max} and f_{min} are the maximum and minimum frequency of the sub node, which utilizes the monotonicity of revenue and cost. The sum of maximum profits calculated for each route with the sub branch-and-bound without budget constraint is always no smaller than that with a budget, thus sub branch-and-bound provides an upper bound profit of the main node. With the lower and upper bounds derived above, MAP-BBB eliminates only non-optimal frequency strategies of routes, which proves correctness and optimality of MAP-BBB. We show the best-case complexity analysis of MAP-BBB:

THEOREM 5.4. *The best-case runtime complexity of MAP-BBB is $O((\log(\max\{f_i^{max}\}))^2 \times n)$, where n is the number of routes.*

Proof sketch. The best-case complexity of the bi-level branch and bound algorithm happens when in each branch and bound process, one of the children nodes is pruned. For each route R_i, its maximum frequency is f_i^{max} and it takes $\log(f_i^{max})$ branches until the frequency in this route is nondivisible; for all routes, it takes $\max\{f_i^{max}\} \times n$ time. While for each branch it needs at least $O(\log(\max\{f_i^{max}\}))$ time to solve one sub branch and bound. Thus, the total complexity is $O((\log(\max\{f_i^{max}\}))^2 \times n)$. □

The worst-case complexity happens when there is no pruning in each branch and bound process. however, the experimental results in Section 6 show that this never happens and the average runtime of MAP-BBB is promising.

5.2 Greedy Algorithm (MAP-G)

As MAP is NP-hard, it is clear that the exact algorithm MAP-BBB may not be scalable. In this section, we propose a greedy algorithm to solve MAP more efficiently while sacrificing optimality. A naive greedy algorithm is to increase the frequency of the route with the largest marginal profit/cost ratio (PCR) which is known to work very well for conventional knapsack problems. However, unlike conventional knapsack problems where PCR is fixed (i.e., linear objective function), the PCR in our problem fluctuates as can be seen from the example in Figure 4. According to our experiments, this naive greedy approach on average achieves only 0.66 of the optimal profit.

To address the fluctuating PCRs, we suggest an improved "Group-Greedy" algorithm (MAP-G). The basic idea of MAP-G is that, instead of greedily raising the frequency of a single route with the largest PCR, MAP-G first divides routes into groups, and then compares the PCRs of different groups and raises frequencies of the group of routes with the largest PCR. As shown in Algorithm 3, it randomly divides n routes into $\lfloor \frac{n}{q} \rfloor$ groups (line 2), each consisting of q routes[10]. Initially, each group is assigned small budget δ (line 3) and we independently solve MAP within each group, using exact algorithms such as MAP-BBB as a sub-routine (line 6). We merge all groups' most recent frequency strategy to create a complete frequency strategy of all routes (line 8), and its profit is compared with the temporary maximum profit (line 10). The budget of the group that creates the largest marginal profit density is increased by δ (line 9). This process iterates until the sum of groups' budgets equals to the total budget b. This method is robust w.r.t. the fluctuating PCR because we calculate the optimal strategy for each group in each iteration. On the other hand, calculating optimal frequency strategy for a group of routes is much faster than that of all routes because the solution space is much smaller. We set $\delta = b \times \frac{1}{h}$, where $h > 1$ is an integer. The quality of the solution increases as q increases — if $q = n$ and $h = 1$, it finds the optimal solution. The benefit of a small q is the short runtime, while sacrificing optimality. By adjusting q, MAP-G can trade-off between runtime and optimality.

[10]The actual number of routes in a group may slightly vary due to the floor operation.

Algorithm 3: MAP-G

1 $N^* \leftarrow 0, \langle f_i^* \rangle \leftarrow \mathbf{0}$
2 $\mathcal{G} \leftarrow$ divide $\mathcal{R}$ into $\lfloor \frac{n}{k} \rfloor$ groups
3 $b_g \leftarrow \delta, \forall g \in \mathcal{G}$;
4 **while** $\sum_{g \in G} b_g \leq b$ **do**
5   **for** $g \in \mathcal{G}$ **do**
6     $\langle f_g^* \rangle \leftarrow$ solve MAP of g with budget b_g
7   $g^* \leftarrow$ the best PCR group
8   $\langle f_i \rangle \leftarrow merge(\{\langle f_g^* \rangle | g \in \mathcal{G}\})$
9   $b_{g^*} \leftarrow b_{g^*} + \delta$;
10   **if** $N^* < N(\langle f_i \rangle)$ **then** $\langle f_i^* \rangle \leftarrow \langle f_i \rangle$
11 **return** $\langle f_i^* \rangle, N^*$

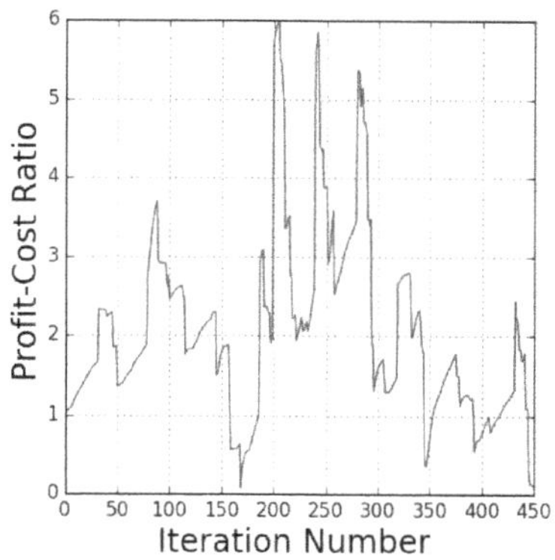

Figure 4: Best Profit-Cost Ratio among all routes in each iteration of the naive greedy Knapsack algorithm.

6. EXPERIMENTAL RESULTS

In this section, we first compare MAP-EF with several benchmark methods for both route demand and airline market share prediction. We then show the improvement of the optimal profit obtained based on MAP-EF prediction compared with that based on traditional methods. Last, we compare both scalability and optimality of our proposed algorithms with several benchmarks.

6.1 Market Share & Total Demand Prediction

6.1.1 Experimental Environment

For route-specific predictions, we selected the 700 largest routes in terms of the number of passengers. We predicted market share and total demand for the first quarter of 2015, the most recent period for which all data are available, after training with 10 years data. We tested 3 pre-existing prediction models for both market share and total demand as described in Section 2, and our proposed method MAP-EF.

For each route, we evaluated with the following three criteria: i) Correlation Coefficient (CC), ii) R^2, and iii) Mean Absolute Error (MAE) divided by the maximum market share value of a route or divided by true total demand value. These two metrics are much stricter than pure MAE values. A good predictor will perform well under all three metrics.

6.1.2 Experiment Results

Market Share. Table 3 (resp. Table 4) summarizes mean values (resp. variances) of the three metrics for all routes (All) and for routes with 4 or more operating airlines ($|\mathcal{A}| \geq 4$) — as the number of airlines increases, predictions become more challenging. Among existing models, Market1 shows the best performance. Its CC of 0.82 is quite reasonable with low variance around 0.18, but its poor R^2 of -0.84 indicates some issues. Two metrics revealing contradictory results indicates that the rise/decline of the predicted values may have high error. Thus, Market1 can tell us which airline has larger market share than another, but its absolute market share value is not reliable. Profit optimization based on the best competitor, Market1, does not make sense because even a small error in predicting market share may lead to a high loss in profit. As shown in Table 3, MAP-EF shows very stable performance in terms of both mean and variance for all metrics, especially when $|\mathcal{A}| \geq 4$.

Table 3: Mean values of CC, R^2 and MAE/Max for market share predictions. ↑ indicates that larger values are preferred and vice versa. The best method is highlighted in yellow.

	All			$\|\mathcal{A}\| \geq 4$		
	CC(↑)	R^2(↑)	MAE /Max(↓)	CC(↑)	R^2(↑)	MAE /Max(↓)
Market1	0.82	-0.84	0.133	0.82	0.18	0.157
Market2	0.48	-3.51	0.188	0.62	-1.92	0.212
Market3	0.34	-6.96	0.27	0.44	-3.99	0.32
MAP-EF	0.96	0.88	0.052	0.95	0.89	0.046

Table 4: Variance of CC, R^2 and MAE/Max of Market Share Predictions.

	All			$\|\mathcal{A}\| \geq 4$		
	CC(↓)	R^2(↓)	MAE /Max(↓)	CC(↓)	R^2(↓)	MAE /Max(↓)
Market1	0.18	132.2	0.06	0.09	4.29	0.08
Market2	0.54	109.7	0.08	0.31	26.77	0.09
Market3	0.55	964.9	0.10	0.35	38.66	0.10
MAP-EF	0.03	0.12	0.01	0.01	0.05	0.01

Total Demand. Whereas route-specific market share prediction is a list (one value for each airline), total demand prediction of a route is a scalar value. Thus, we create two lists, one of true demand and one of predicted demand, and perform CC and R^2 analysis. MAE divided by true demand can be measured for each route and its mean and variance are also summarized in Table 5. Again, MAP-EF shows better performance than all other methods.

All these results indicate that profit maximization should be based on the prediction results of MAP-EF, while "optimal" strategies obtained with other models are more likely to be far from real optimal strategies. Nevertheless, we note that MAP-EF builds upon other pre-existing prediction models' findings and hence we build on top of these prior scientists' work.

6.2 Profit Maximization

6.2.1 Experimental Environment

We performed experiments on a cluster of 64 machines running Linux with 2.4GHz Xeon CPU and 24GB RAMs. We selected six major airlines and calculated the optimal frequency allocation strategy for their top K biggest markets (a market means an origin-destination pair, i.e., a route). We retrieved real budget information of routes from the BTS dataset such that budget for a set of routes is the sum of their real budgets. For the scalability test, we chose the number of markets $K = \{2, 3, 4, 5, 6, 7, 8, 9, 10, 20, 30\}$. We compare the proposed MAP-BBB and MAP-G with two benchmark algorithms, namely N-Greedy (naive greedy algorithm) and DP (dynamic programming). DP is a well-known approach for KPs and RAPS and we refer to Appendix [1] for a detailed description of DP. MAP-BBB is the proposed bilevel branch-and-bound algorithm. We used MAP-BBB as subroutine for MAP-G to solve the profit maximization subproblem in each group.

Table 5: CC, R^2 and MAE divided by true demand of Total Demand Predictions. Note that the variance of CC and R^2 cannot be defined because it predicts a scalar value for each route.

	CC(↑)	R^2(↑)	MAE/True (Mean,↓)	MAE/True (Variance,↓)
Demand1	0.77	0.31	0.29	0.06
Demand2	0.49	-1.4	0.57	0.1
Demand3	0.56	-0.8	0.49	0.08
MAP-EF	0.98	0.96	0.07	0.004

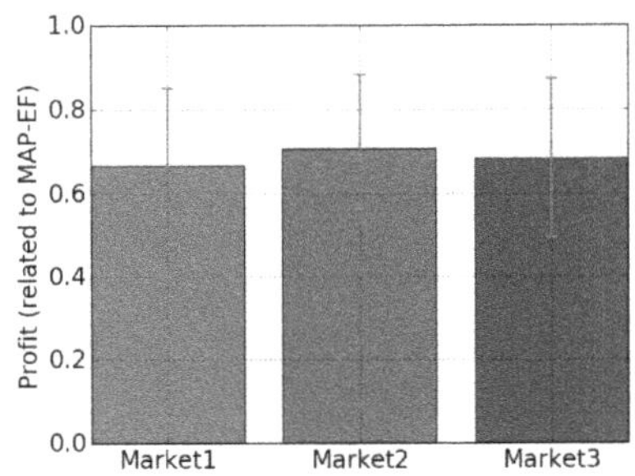

Figure 5: Profit maximization with different prediction methods (relative to MAP-EF) and 90% confidence interval is shown.

6.2.2 Maximum Profit of Different Predictors

Ground truth is not available for the true maximal profit an airline could possibly make as their actual quarterly profit may not reflect the total profit that they could have maade. In theory, MAP-BBB is guaranteed to produce the maximal profit *under the assumptions made in our model.* As we see below, MAP-BBB works when the number of markets is relatively small. In order to explore the profits obtained using predictions made by pre-existing market share predictors [16, 24, 26], we compare them with the profits obtained using the MAP-EF predictor. We also obtain the optimal frequency allocation strategies using MAP-BBB for $K \leq 6$ based on different prediction methods, and then calculate the corresponding profit of these strategies using MAP-EF (for larger K, MAP-BBB, as an exact algorithm, takes an inordinate amount of time). As shown in Figure 5, the optimal profit obtained by all existing methods has a gap of around 30% compared with MAP-EF, which is a huge amount considering the scale of profit (typically on the order of millions of dollars per route per quarter).

6.2.3 Comparing Different Optimization Algorithms

In this subsection, we first compare several algorithms which are targeted at small K (number of markets) values, such as DP, MAP-BBB, and N-Greedy. Using these algorithms as subroutines, we then tested the performance of MAP-G with large K values. Average optimized profits of airlines and runtime are summarized in Figures 6 and 7. "Real" stands for the average profit of airlines calculated with real frequency strategies in the BTS dataset. Interestingly, "Real" shows worse results than even the simple N-Greedy.

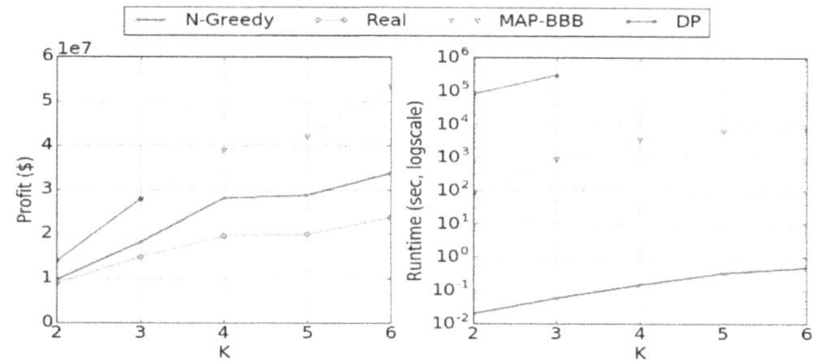

(a) (b)

Figure 6: (a) Optimized profits and (b) Runtime for $K \leq 6$. K is the number of routes.

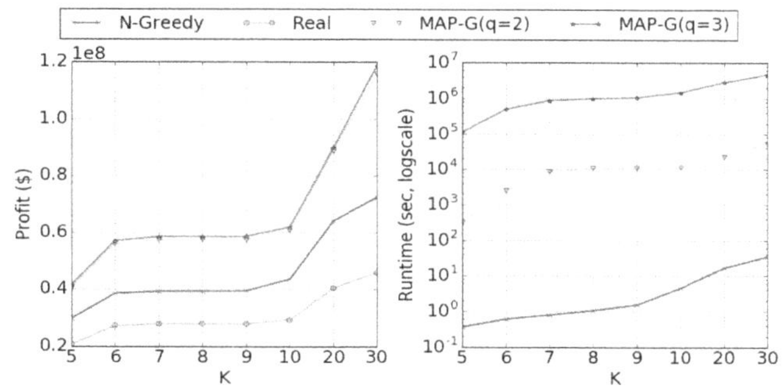

(a) (b)

Figure 7: (a) Optimized profits and (b) Runtime for $K \geq 5$, with the number of routes in a group as $h = 100$.

We see that past market share models can only capture about 75% of the profit generated by MAP-EF. This is a substantial loss in absolute dollars.

Profit and Runtime Analysis for $K \leq 6$. As we can see from Figure 6 (a), since both DP and MAP-BBB are exact algorithms, their maximum profit values are the same and are the largest. However, DP's runtime, shown in Figure 6 (b), grows exponentially and we could not finish it on time for $K \geq 4$. N-Greedy cannot achieve a reasonable profit. When $K = 2$, it has around 70% of the optimal profit calculated with exact algorithms; as K increases, however, it decreases to only 60%. Before $K = 5$, MAP-BBB can find the optimal profit in a few seconds while DP takes around 10,000 seconds in average. This is due to its pseudo polynomial runtime, which behaves more like exponential runtime than polynomial time. This indicates that MAP-BBB scales really well. The MAP-BBB is more suitable as the subsolver of MAP-G.

Profit and Runtime Analysis for $K \geq 5$. Table 6 shows the optimality of MAP-G when $K = 4$, 5 or 6. The exact maximum profit when $K \geq 7$ cannot be computed as the exact algorithms either run out of memory or take inordinately long. But in cases when $K \leq 6$, MAP-G achieves 99% of the maximum profit suggesting that it does very well. As expected, MAP-G is robust w.r.t. the problem of fluctuating profit and independent processing of each route from which N-Greedy suffers. Figure 7 (a) shows that MAP-G is consistently better than N-Greedy and N-Greedy obtains only about 70% of MAP-G's profit, suggesting that MAP-G is far superior. We confirm that $q = 3$ (i.e. groups of similar routes are limited to have 3 routes in them) leads to an increase in profit than when $q = 2$ for MAP-G — in Figure 7 (a), MAP-G with $q = 3$ is consistently better than $q = 2$ — which corresponds to our conjecture that optimality will be improved as the size of groups increases.

The profit increase from "Real" to the optimized one is quite impressive. Airlines can increase their profits by at least 55% by adopting MAP based on our model with available data. But please note that we assume the behaviors of other airlines are fixed, which is not the case in reality. In the following, we will test the robustness of MAP, i.e., when the frequency and pricing strategies of other airlines also vary (and not known in advance), how much profit can be achieved by the airline to be optimized.

Table 6: Profit maximization of MAP-G(BBB) with $q = 3$ (relative to the optimal profit) when $K = 4$, 5 or 6. K is the total number of routes, q is the number of routes allowed in a group.

	$K=4$	$K=5$	$K=6$
Profit	0.99	0.97	0.99

Robustness Analysis. In the above experiments, we assume that the frequency allocation and pricing strategies of all other airlines are fixed and known in advance. We now test the robustness of our approach, i.e., we test the airline profits obtained by our approach when the frequency and pricing strategies of other airlines vary. To do this, we randomly varied price (resp. frequency) by a rate in $\{[-20\%, -10\%), [-10\%, 0), 0, [0, 10\%), [10\%, 20\%]\}$. We first compute the optimal strategy by assuming that the other airlines' behaviors are fixed (because they are unknown). We then evaluate this obtained optimal strategy with the prediction model of the changed price and frequency strategies of other airlines. We computed the ratio of the sub-optimal profit (not knowing other airlines' price/frequency changes) to the optimal profit (knowing the changed price/frequency strategies of other airlines) — in order to calculate the exact optimal profit on time we tested K up to 6. For each frequency and price change rate combination, we generated 30 scenarios with all different random seeds and profits are averaged on them. As is shown in Figure 8, this profit ratio is always larger than 0.8, which indicates robustness of our MAP approach even with a 40% fluctuation of both price and frequency. Moreover, it is shown that for a fixed frequency change rate, the profit ratio is almost the same for all price change rates, which means that frequency change is more effective in airlines' competition. Last, the largest ratio happens in the case that competitors increase frequencies, which means MAP is more effective at competitive markets.

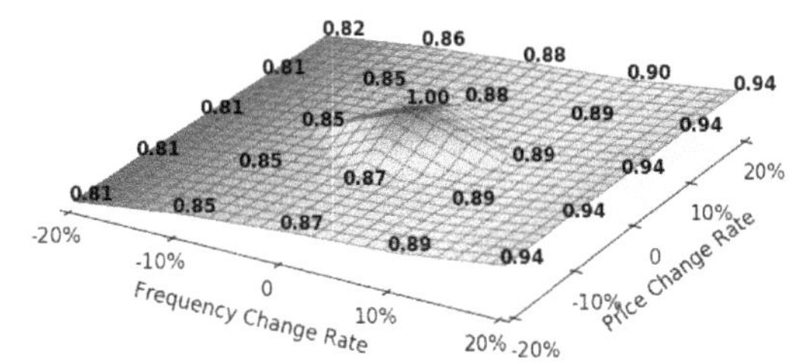

Figure 8: Profits by varying price and frequency of other competitors

7. CONCLUSION AND FUTURE WORK

In this paper, we propose the MAP framework for optimal frequency allocation over multiple routes. We make three key contributions. i) We design a novel ensemble predictor based on past regression-based work, clustering techniques and game theoretic analysis, which have never been utilized for this purpose; ii) based on the prediction, we design several algorithms to solve the profit maximization problem; iii) we conduct extensive experiments. We show that the prediction performance of MAP-EF is much better than past methods. We also compare runtime and optimality of our proposed optimization algorithms with benchmarks. We also show that MAP increases profitability per route by at least 55%. Even if there are factors we did not consider on the basis of open source data and these numbers are reduced substantially if private airline data was to be used, the increased profitability would still be substantial.

We consider two potential directions for future work. First, our current optimization considers only frequency allocation. In the future, we may also consider joint-optimization over frequency and pricing. However, the monotonicity property of revenue and cost is not guaranteed with ticket pricing[11] and it is already one of the hardest KPs and RAPs with only frequency being considered. Second, this paper assumes the behaviors of all other competing airlines are fixed. When other airlines are also strategic, game theory would be a natural methodology to solve the problem, where instead of a single-airline-centric optimization, a Nash equilibrium will be defined.

Acknowledgements

This research is supported by the National Research Foundation Singapore under its Interactive Digital Media (IDM) Strategic Research Programme.

8. REFERENCES

[1] Appendix. http://all-is-well-everyday.weebly.com or http://www.cs.umd.edu/~npark/kdd2016.pdf.

[2] Bureau of Economic Analysis. http://www.bea.gov/regional/downloadzip.cfm.

[3] Bureau of Transportation Statistics. http://www.rita.dot.gov/bts/data_and_statistics/by_mode/airline_and_airports/index.html.

[4] National Transportation Safety Board. http://www.ntsb.gov/_layouts/ntsb.aviation/index.aspx.

[5] U.S. Census Bureau. https://www.census.gov/population/metro/data/.

[6] G. Alperovich and Y. Machnes. The role of wealth in the demand for international air travel. *Journal of Transport Economics and Policy*, 28(2):163–173, 1994.

[7] D. Arthur and S. Vassilvitskii. K-Means++: The advantages of careful seeding. In *Proceedings of the 18th Annual ACM-SIAM Symposium on Discrete Algorithms (SODA)*, pages 1027–1035, 2007.

[8] D. Bhadra and J. Kee. Structure and dynamics of the core us air travel markets: A basic empirical analysis of domestic passenger demand. *Journal of Air Transport Management*, 14(1):27–39, 2008.

[9] D. Bhadra and M. Wells. Air travel by state its determinants and contributions in the United States. *Public Works Management & Policy*, 10(2):119–137, 2005.

[10] C. M. Bishop. *Pattern Recognition and Machine Learning (Information Science and Statistics)*. Springer-Verlag New York, Inc., 2006.

[11] K. M. Bretthauer and B. Shetty. The nonlinear knapsack problem – algorithms and applications. *European Journal of Operational Research*, 138(3):459–472, 2002.

[12] A. Caprara, H. Kellerer, U. Pferschy, and D. Pisinger. Approximation algorithms for knapsack problems with cardinality constraints. *European Journal of Operational Research*, 123(2):333–345, 2000.

[11]By decreasing ticket price, market share will increase but revenue may or may not increase due to the change of price.

[13] G. B. Dantzig. Discrete-variable extremum problems. *Operations research*, 5(2):266–288, 1957.

[14] M. Ester, H.-P. Kriegel, J. Sander, and X. Xu. A density-based algorithm for discovering clusters in large spatial databases with noise. In *Proceedings of the ACM International Conference on Knowledge Discovery and Data Mining (SIGKDD)*, pages 226–231, 1996.

[15] M. A. Fischler and R. C. Bolles. Random sample consensus: A paradigm for model fitting with applications to image analysis and automated cartography. *Communications of the ACM*, 24(6):381–395, June 1981.

[16] M. Hansen. Airline competition in a hub-dominated environment: An application of noncooperative game theory. *Transportation Research Part B: Methodological*, 24(1):27–43, 1990.

[17] H. Keller, U. Pferschy, and D. Pisinger. *Knapsack problems*. Springer-Verlag Berlin, 2004.

[18] W. Lu, S. Ioannidis, S. Bhagat, and L. V. Lakshmanan. Optimal recommendations under attraction, aversion, and social influence. In *Proceedings of the ACM International Conference on Knowledge Discovery and Data Mining (SIGKDD)*, pages 811–820, 2014.

[19] S. Martello and P. Toth. Branch-and-bound algorithms for the solution of the general unidimensional knapsack problem. *Advances in Operations Research*, 13(9):295–301, 1977.

[20] U. Pferschy. Dynamic programming revisited: Improving knapsack algorithms. *Computing*, 63(4):419–430, 1999.

[21] D. Pisinger. A minimal algorithm for the bounded knapsack problem. *INFORMS Journal on Computing*, 12(1):75–82, 2000.

[22] C. Rasmussen and C. Williams. *Gaussian Processes for Machine Learning*. Adaptive Computation and Machine Learning. MIT Press, 2006.

[23] P. J. Rousseeuw. Silhouettes: A graphical aid to the interpretation and validation of cluster analysis. *Journal of Computational and Applied Mathematics*, 20:53–65, 1987.

[24] Y. Suzuki. The relationship between on-time performance and airline market share: A new approach. *Transportation Research Part E: Logistics and Transportation Review*, 36(2):139–154, 2000.

[25] R. L. Thorndike. Who belongs in the family. *Psychometrika*, 18(4):267–276, 1953.

[26] W. Wei and M. Hansen. Impact of aircraft size and seat availability on airlines demand and market share in duopoly markets. *Transportation Research Part E: Logistics and Transportation Review*, 41(4):315–327, 2005.

[27] J. Xu, K.-c. Lee, W. Li, H. Qi, and Q. Lu. Smart pacing for effective online ad campaign optimization. In *Proceedings of the ACM International Conference on Knowledge Discovery and Data Mining (SIGKDD)*, pages 2217–2226, 2015.

[28] W. Zhang, S. Yuan, and J. Wang. Optimal real-time bidding for display advertising. In *Proceedings of the ACM International Conference on Knowledge Discovery and Data Mining (SIGKDD)*, pages 1077–1086, 2014.

[29] Y. Zhu, H. Yang, and J. He. Co-clustering based dual prediction for cargo pricing optimization. In *Proceedings of the ACM International Conference on Knowledge Discovery and Data Mining (SIGKDD)*, pages 1583–1592, 2015.

Gemello: Creating a Detailed Energy Breakdown from just the Monthly Electricity Bill

Nipun Batra
IIIT Delhi
nipunb@iiitd.ac.in

Amarjeet Singh
IIIT Delhi
amarjeet@iiitd.ac.in

Kamin Whitehouse
University of Virginia
whitehouse@virginia.edu

ABSTRACT

The first step to saving energy in the home is often to create an *energy breakdown*: the amount of energy used by each individual appliance in the home. Unfortunately, current techniques that produce an energy breakdown are not *scalable*: they require hardware to be installed in each and every home. In this paper, we propose a more scalable solution called *Gemello* that estimates the energy breakdown for one home by matching it with similar homes for which the breakdown is already known. This matching requires only the monthly energy bill and household characteristics such as square footage of the home and the size of the household. We evaluate this approach using 57 homes and results indicate that the accuracy of Gemello is comparable to or better than existing techniques that use sensing infrastructure in each home. The information required by Gemello is often publicly available and, as such, it can be immediately applied to many homes around the world.

CCS Concepts

•Hardware → Energy metering; •Information systems → *Nearest-neighbor search;*

Keywords

Energy metering; Energy disaggregation; NILM; Feedback

1. INTRODUCTION

Buildings account for more than 30% of total energy usage around the world, of which up to 93% is due to residential buildings [41, 18, 42]. Some of this energy can be saved by producing an *energy breakdown*: the amount of energy used by each individual appliance in the home, akin to the itemised bills we get from grocery stores. With such a breakdown, utility companies can focus conservation programs on homes that have an especially inefficient appliance, such as a fridge, water heater, or air conditioner. Energy feedback can also help induce energy-saving behaviour in the occupants themselves [15, 4, 30, 43, 24].

KDD '16, August 13 - 17, 2016, San Francisco, CA, USA

ISBN 978-1-4503-4232-2/16/08...$15.00

DOI: http://dx.doi.org/10.1145/2939672.2939735

Unfortunately, current techniques that produce an energy breakdown are not *scalable*: they require hardware to be installed in each home and/or intensive manual training of the system. One approach, called non-intrusive load monitoring (NILM), tries to infer the energy breakdown based on the aggregate power trace from a single smart meter installed in the home. This approach is perhaps the most practical because smart meters are already being rolled out in millions of homes worldwide. However, current techniques require high resolution data (1 minute sampling frequency or higher) [39, 11, 4] while most smart meters today only support 15-minute or hourly sample rates to support time-of-use energy pricing. Even if smart meters had a higher sampling rate, most of the world does not yet have smart meters and many places do not even have plans to deploy them. Alternatives to NILM are more accurate but require specialized sensors to be installed inside the home [20], on each individual appliance [32, 26, 16], or on each circuit in the breaker box [37]. All of these solutions are limited by the need for instrumentation to be deployed in every home.

In this paper, we propose a more scalable solution called *Gemello* that produces an energy breakdown in homes without requiring new hardware to be installed in each home. Instead, Gemello estimates the energy breakdown for a home by matching it with similar homes that do have a hardware-based disaggregation solution. This matching requires only the monthly energy bill and household characteristics such as square footage of the home and the size of the household. From an energy perspective, homes in the same geographic region are often very similar because they have similar construction methods, use the same heating fuels, and contain similar fridges, washing machines, and other appliances. Gemello exploits this fact to provide an energy breakdown for many homes in a region by instrumenting only a fraction of them.

Of course, no two homes are exactly identical and finding a perfect twin is unlikely. Therefore, Gemello uses a different set of matching homes to estimate the energy usage of each individual appliance. The key to success is the ability to define 'similarity' on a per-appliance basis. For example, homes with similar seasonal trends in their monthly energy bill are expected to have similar heating/cooling energy (referred as heating, ventilation, and air conditioning [HVAC] from now on); homes with similar square footage are expected to have similar lighting loads; and homes with a similar number of occupants are expected to have similar washing machine energy usage because that is driven by the amount of clothes worn each day. The energy usage of each appliance is predicted by a different set of features, and so Gemello finds a different set of homes to predict the energy usage of each appliance.

We evaluate this approach using 57 homes from the publicly available Dataport data set [38], in which the ground truth energy breakdown is measured by metering each appliance of the home individually for one year or more. Results show that the accuracy of Gemello is comparable to or better than established NILM techniques called FHMM and LBM, both of which require on-site, high-frequency power metering in each home [33, 45]. Gemello can achieve 76% and 69% accuracy on HVAC and fridge, compared to 61% and 39% for FHMM and 56% and 72% for LBM. Furthermore, it achieves up to 57% accuracy on washing machine, dryer, dishwasher, and lighting loads, which is higher than previously reported results. Many existing techniques are not able to disaggregate these loads at all. Our analysis shows that these results are robust with as few as 7 instrumented homes: the accuracy for HVAC loads is ≈69%, still 8% better than state-of-the-art approaches. The accuracy of Gemello becomes higher in homes with smart meters that provide power readings at 15-minute resolution.

The Gemello technique has potential for immediate impact because all of the information it requires is already available. Essentially all homes already have a standard power meter that provides total monthly energy usage for billing purposes, and in many regions this information can be downloaded online[1]. Household characteristics such as the size of the home and the number of people in the household are often publicly available and are already being used by companies to match homes for other types of eco-feedback[2]. Finally, many companies are already collecting submetering information from thousands of homes around the world[3]. By combining these three sources of information, Gemello could be used to provide an energy breakdown for homes around the world without the need to install new instrumentation in each location.

2. RELATED WORK

Various techniques for measuring appliance level energy consumption have been studied in the past. The simplest technique is to install appliance level sensors that monitor and report appliance energy consumption [26, 16, 23]. Many commercial vendors are also selling appliance level sensors such as Kill-A-Watt[4] and Hobo plug load data logger[5]. Instead of directly monitoring the appliance of interest, a few recent systems have looked into *indirect* sensing techniques. Kim et al. [32] develop a system called Viridiscope that leverages the correlation amongst sensor streams, like using a vibration sensor on a fridge to tell if the compressor is running or not, and then using a model to determine fridge's power. Similarly, Clark et al. [13] develop a system called Deltaflow that employs energy harvesting sensors and performs computation on the activation of these sensors to determine appliance power draw. Jain et al. [25] install temperature sensors inside a home to estimate air conditioner energy usage. Gupta et al. [20], Chen et al. [12] and Gulati et al. [19] use the electromagnetic interference typically generated by electronic appliances to determine appliance usages. Previous work has also looked into using sensors deployed at household circuits (lesser in number than individual appliances) to infer per-appliance energy usage [37]. All these solutions are limited by the need for instrumentation to be deployed in every home. Previous research has shown that there are various challenges beyond cost of the system that prevent such systems from being scaled [23].

NILM is often considered the most practical approach towards generating energy breakdown. However, like other approaches mentioned above, it also requires instrumentation in each home. While the effort of deploying a smart meter may be less in comparison to other related approaches, most of the world still does not have smart meter infrastructure.

Since its inception in the early 1980s by George Hart [21], the field of NILM has seen various approaches based on different machine learning techniques leveraging different features of the power trace. However, many of these approaches require submetered data to learn a model of each appliance and these models have not been shown to generalize well across homes. Even if the models did generalise, NILM approaches require high frequency power metering with resolutions of 1-minute or higher. Very high frequency approaches (>10 kHz) [11] use features such as voltage-current trajectories to detect events in aggregate power time series. However, current smart meters do not collect data at such high rates because they are designed and deployed for the purposes of time-of-use pricing and there are currently no efforts to deploy devices suitable for energy disaggregation on a large scale. Therefore, these techniques, while promising, face real practical barriers before being used at scale.

Additionally, existing approaches for energy disaggregation [33, 39, 21, 45, 35] require a model of each appliance. The main differences between these techniques are how they are created and how they are used to infer the hidden states of the appliances based on the aggregate power readings. For example, some systems model appliances as finite state machines (FSMs). However, such approaches generally show poor accuracy on complex appliances such as washing machine and other electronics, as a FSM is a poor model for such appliances. Some systems assume the model is manually generated, learned from training data [21, 33], and in rare cases learned automatically [5]. In all cases, however, the accuracy of these models depends on how well the model approximates the true appliances in the home and it has not yet been demonstrated that these model-based approaches generalize well across homes. Only recently, researchers have started looking into *automatically* learning arbitrarily complex appliances using deep neural networks [29]. However, as claimed by the authors themselves, the work is just scratching the surface. These challenges are likely to impact the generalisability and applicability of existing approaches towards solving the energy breakdown problem.

3. APPROACH

The goal of Gemello is to predict the energy consumption of household appliances given easy to collect information such as a single aggregate energy reading per month and static household characteristics. The key intuition be-

[1]http://www.greenbuttondata.org/
[2]https://opower.com/
[3]http://powerhousedynamics.com/
[4]http://www.p3international.com/products/p4400.html
[5]http://www.onsetcomp.com/products/data-loggers/ux120-018

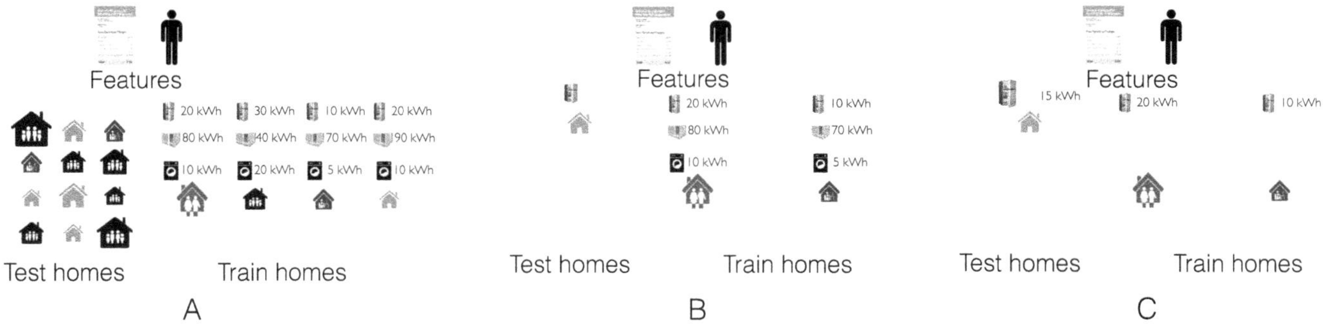

Figure 1: Overview of Gemello. A) We assume a small set of submetered homes (train homes) for which we have access to appliance level energy consumption. Both submetered homes and test homes (for which we need to predict per-appliance energy consumption) have access to monthly energy and static household features; B) We match a given test home to k closest train homes on monthly energy and static household features; C) We predict the appliance energy consumption of the test home as a function of the energy consumption of that appliance across the k closest train homes chosen in the previous step.

hind Gemello is that if per appliance energy consumption is available for a home then any other home that is 'similar' in nature will also have the same energy consumption for that appliance. This intuition leads to the following specific requirements for Gemello to work:

1. Small set of submetered homes (SH) for which per appliance energy consumption is directly measured.
2. Easy to collect information for all the homes in the universal set U - This includes monthly energy consumption (j^{th} home represented by a vector $[EM_{j_1}, \ldots, EM_{j_{12}}]$) which is anyway collected for billing purposes and static household information such as size and number of occupants (represented by a vector $[S_{j_1}, S_{j_2}, \ldots]$).

For each target home i ($i \subset U$), we first derive the feature set (as discussed later) using vectors $[EM_{i_1}, \ldots, EM_{i_{12}}]$ and $[S_{i_1}, S_{i_2}, \ldots]$. Let these feature set be represented by $[I_{i_1}, I_{i_2}, \ldots]$. We next derive the K nearest neighbours for the ith home from amongst the submetered homes in SH by comparing the feature set $[I_{i_1}, I_{i_2}, \ldots]$ with the feature sets derived for the remaining homes SH. Let this set of 'similar' homes be $[N_1, \ldots, N_K]$. Monthly energy consumption for kth appliance (L_k) for ith home is then calculated as:

$$L_{k_i} = \frac{L_{k_1} + L_{k_2} + \cdots + L_{k_K}}{K}$$

where $L_{k_1}, \ldots, L_{k_K}$ represent the monthly energy consumption for the same kth appliance from K identified 'neighbours' which are already sub-metered (and hence this information is directly measured). Figure 1 outlines the proposed Gemello algorithm.

We define 'similarity' differently for each electrical load. For example, homes having 'similar' monthly energy consumption are likely to have similar heating/cooling energy as the monthly energy consumption in many countries is often dominated by heating/cooling loads. Homes having 'similar' area are likely to have 'similar' lighting fixtures and thus may consume similar lighting energy. Homes having a 'similar' number of occupants may have 'similar' dish washer and washing machine energy usage, as clothes and dishes loads is likely to be proportional to the number of occupants. By defining 'similarity' differently for each load, we leverage the fact that no two homes are exactly identical in all respects, but that every home is likely to have a set of similar homes that can be leveraged for predicting energy consumption at the load level.

For an electrical utility that has no smart metering infrastructure or homes in their customer base that already have appliance level monitors already installed, it can chose these set of homes in a way that all the remaining (large number of) homes are 'similar' to one or more of these neighbourhood homes. Standard clustering techniques can be used on the feature set derived from already available information, as is used in Gemello for estimating K neighbours, to create cluster of homes from their customer base and then a small set of homes can be selected from each cluster for installing sub-metering infrastructure.

We develop further understanding of operation of Gemello by answering the questions below.

Q1. What features are derived from the monthly consumption and the static household information?
Monthly energy consumption, $[EM_{i_1}, \ldots, EM_{i_12}]$, is used to derive features such as seasonal trend, variance, range (difference between maximum and minimum) , ratio of minimum to maximum monthly energy consumption, skew, kurtosis and the 25th and 75th percentile. Static household features, $[S_{i_1}, S_{i_2}, \ldots]$ include area, number of occupants and number of rooms. In total, we have 17 features from monthly data and 3 corresponding to static household properties. These are summarised in Table 1.

Q2. When higher resolution information, such as 15-minute AMI data is available, can it be leveraged in Gemello ?
Since 15-minute AMI data is very rich compared to monthly energy consumption, we divide the features derived from AMI data into the following three broad classes:

1. Seasonal and Trend - To derive these features, we first decompose the 15-minute AMI data time series using Seasonal Decomposition of Time Series by Loess (STL) [14] into seasonal and a trend 15-minute time-series. We chose the period of 1 week for STL de-

Feature category	Feature sub category	Features (f)	#f
Monthly energy	Raw monthly energy	12 month household energy aggregate	12
	Derived monthly energy	Variance over 12 month aggregate energy, Min. energy/Max. energy across 12 months, Max. energy-Min. energy across 12 months, (Max. energy - Min. energy)/Max. energy, Skew, Kurtosis, 25th, and 75th percentile of 12 months energy	9
Static household characteristics		Household area, # occupants, # rooms	3
15 min AMI data	Time series decomposition	Max. of seasonal and trend component, Energy of seasonal component across months of HVAC usage, Top-7 Fourier transform coefficients of seasonal component	14
	Weather correlation	Correlation between hourly aggregate energy and external temperature	1
	Usage patterns	Autocorrelation (lag 1 day), Fraction of energy used across 24 hours, Fraction of energy used across 7 days	32
	Step changes	Proportion of step changes in 3 bins (<500 Watts, >500 and <1000 Watts; >1000 Watts), Cluster centers of above 3 bins	6

Table 1: The features above are used to define similarity between homes. Gemello primarily uses features of the monthly energy bill and static household characteristics. However, it can also use features of 15-minute AMI power data if the home has a smart meter installed.

composition as homes show weekly patterns. Features derived in this class include max., energy and first 7 coefficients obtained from the Fourier transform of the seasonal component. These 7 coefficients correspond to periods of 1 through 7 days. This class will be broadly useful to estimate HVAC energy consumption since homes similar in the seasonal and the trend component are likely to be similar in HVAC energy consumption.

2. Temporal Patterns - Features derived in this class include fraction of energy usage across the 7 days of the week, energy usage across the 24 hours of the day and energy usage during the night time. Such features can be used to derive energy consumption of appliances showing temporal usage patterns. For example, certain working class populations may do their groceries, clothes and dishes on weekends and thus would have higher fridge, washing machine and dryer energy consumption on weekends. Further, fridge being a background load, running even in the night time when most other loads would be off, its energy can be easily derived by exploiting similarity in night hours energy usage.

3. Step changes - A step change is likely to be caused by an appliance changing its state. For example, washing machine turning ON could cause a step change of 500 Watts. We compute the fraction of step changes whose magnitude are less than 500 Watts, between 500 and 1000 Watts and greater than 1000 Watts. Step changes greater than 1000 Watts are caused by high power appliances such as HVAC, while step changes less than 500 Watts are caused by low power appliances such as fridge. On similar lines, we find find the cluster centres of the step changes in these three bins. The cluster centres will likely indicate the power of the most frequently cycling appliance (typically fridge).

4. Weather correlation - In addition to 15-minute AMI data, we also use 15-minute weather information as a feature. Homes having similar HVAC energy are likely to have similar response to weather and thus similar correlation between aggregate and temperature.

In total we derive 53 features from 15-minute AMI data. These are summarised in Table 1. Since these features are on different scales, we normalise them in the range 0 to 1 using standard scaling procedures[6].

Q3. From amongst all the features that we derive, how do we decide which features to use for estimating energy consumption of a particular appliance? Using the entire set of features may cause our model to overfit and give poor generalisation. Thus, we select the top-N features from the given feature set using standard feature selection algorithms.

Q4. Once we have selected the feature set, how do we select the neighbouring homes from where the average sub-metered information is available? Given a set of selected features, 'similarity' between homes can be found using distance functions. Standard distance functions such as Euclidean, Manhattan, etc. can be used. For each test home, we find its 'neigh bourhood' by finding its K nearest neighbours from the set of submetered homes, akin the well-known K nearest neighbours algorithm.

[6]https://github.com/robjhyndman/anomalous-acm

HVAC	Lights	Fridge	Dryer	Dish washer	Washing machine
31	12	21	32	26	16

Table 2: Number of homes in the dataset with ground truth values for each appliance

Q5. Once the neighbouring homes are selected, how do we estimate the monthly energy consumption for a particular appliance in the selected home?
Having found K nearest neighbours for the test home, we predict the energy consumption of an appliance in the selected home as the average of energy consumption of that appliance across the K submetered homes. While we use the regular average, we can also use weighted average, which assigns higher weights to closer neighbours while making the prediction. We leave using weighted average for future work.

4. EVALUATION

4.1 Data set

We use the publicly available Dataport data set [38] for evaluating our approach. Dataport data set contains aggregate and appliance level power information for more than 600 homes in Texas, USA for up to 3 years. Submetered and household aggregate power data was collected at 1-minute resolution. 57 homes contain data for 1 year (2013) across 6 appliances of interest (fridge, HVAC, lights, dryer, washing machine and dish washer) and house metadata such as the number of occupants, area of the home and number of rooms. While the data set contains submetered data from a large number of appliances, only the chosen 6 appliances had data across significant number of homes[7]. Not all of these 57 homes monitored all these 6 appliances. Table 2 shows the number of homes for each of these 6 appliance types.

While many NILM data sets have been released in the past, none of the other data set satisfied the requirements of containing both aggregate and submetered power data for a large number of homes for at least one year. While the HES data set [46] contains data from a large number of homes for a large time, it does not contain aggregate power data. Given the high variability present in submetering across homes, we can't assume the aggregate to be the sum of submetered loads. The ECO data set [10] contains data from 6 homes for 8 months. But, there is no single load which is submetered across all these 6 homes. AMPds [36], iAWE [7], Blued [2] contain data only from a single home. REDD [34] contains data for a very short duration from 6 homes. While UK-DALE [28] contains data from 6 homes, only one of them has year long data.

We compare the attributes of our sample (57 homes) to the population (homes in the Texas and USA region). Figure 2a shows the distribution of annual energy usage across the 57 homes with a mean of 9923 kWh, the mean of Texas region is 13896 kWh [17]. Figure 2b shows the distribution of square footage area of households in our sample, with a mean of 2021 sq. ft. The mean for Texas region as reported in two different reports is 2393[8] and 1757 sq. ft [17]. The

[7]http://bit.ly/1QZKwG2
[8]http://1.usa.gov/1LRS08D

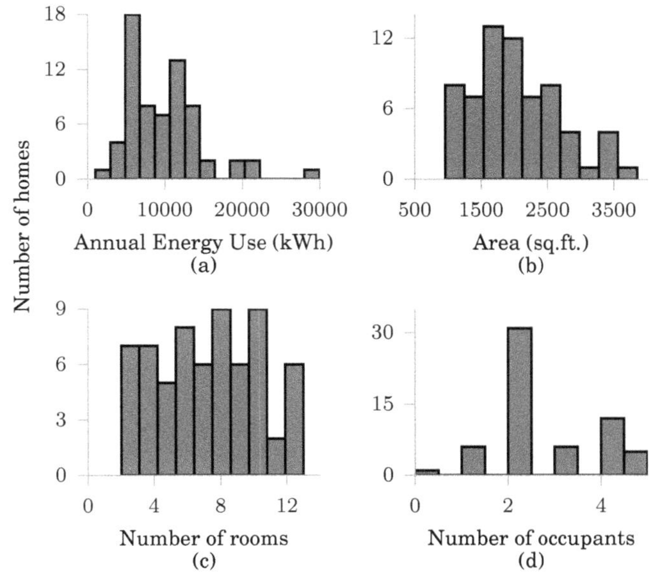

Figure 2: Our dataset has a wide diversity of homes, including very small homes/households as well as very large ones.

distribution of number of rooms in our sample is shown in Figure 2c having a mean of 7.3 rooms. While the statistics for average number of rooms per home in Texas are not available, a survey reports an average of ≈3 bedrooms per homes in the US[9]. Figure 2d shows the distribution of number of occupants per home with a mean of 2.6, the mean for Texas is 2.7.[10]

4.2 Baseline approaches

We compare the accuracy of our approach against the following two approaches:

4.2.1 *Factorial Hidden Markov Model (FHMM)*

FHMM is a well known NILM technique [33, 39] and commonly used as a benchmark by energy disaggregation researchers [8, 45, 34, 9, 35]. In this approach, each appliance is modelled as a hidden Markov model (HMM) containing 'n' states, where a state indicates mode of operation of the appliance. Many appliances can be modelled as 2 state appliances (ON or OFF). The HMM for each appliance is described by 3 parameters: 1) Initial probability (π)- containing the probability of each state at the initial time; 2) Transition matrix (A)- containing the probability of transition between states (e.g. ON to OFF); and 3) Emission matrix (B)- containing the power draw distribution of different states of the appliance. Energy disaggregation is done by performing a joint optimisation over the individual HMMs.

4.2.2 *Latent Bayesian Melding (LBM)*

In recent state-of-the-art work, Zhong et al. [45, 44] propose a method of melding models such as FHMM with prior information from population. Such prior information introduces constraints such as the expected number of cycles per

[9]http://1.usa.gov/1oaaa1K
[10]http://1.usa.gov/1oyImh3

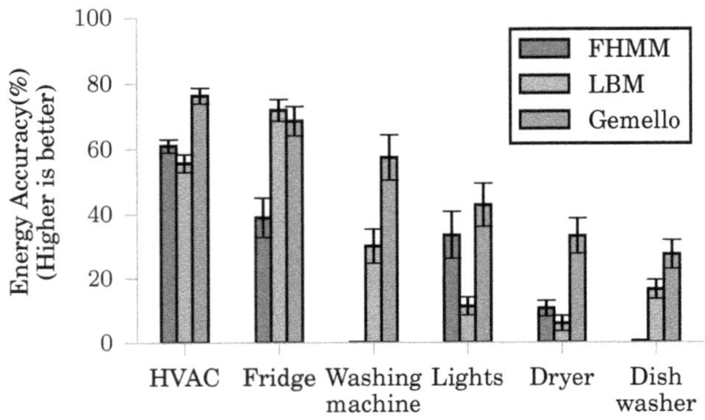

Figure 3: Gemello achieves Energy Accuracy that is comparable to or better than the baseline approaches across all appliances

day of an appliance, expected duration of usage per day and expected energy usage of an appliance per day. Their analysis shows upto 50% accuracy improvement over other approaches.

4.3 Evaluation metric

We define our metric based on prior work [33, 8]. Let the predicted and ground truth appliance energy for an appliance a in home h for month m be $Pred(h, a, m)$ and $GT(h, a, m)$ respectively. The absolute percentage error (PE) for the h, a, m triplet is given by:

$$\mathrm{PE(h,a,m)} = \frac{|\mathrm{Pred(h,a,m)} - \mathrm{GT(h,a,m)}|}{\mathrm{GT(h,a,m)}} \times 100\%$$

The percentage accuracy (PA) for h, a, m triplet is given by:

$$\mathrm{PA(h,a,m)} = \begin{cases} 100 - \mathrm{PE(h,a,m)}, & \text{if } \mathrm{PE(h,a,m)} \leq 100 \\ 0, & \text{otherwise} \end{cases}$$

The percentage accuracy ($PA(h, a)$) for an appliance a in home h is given by the mean of $PA(h, a, m)$ across all months.

$$PA(h,a) = \overline{PA(h,a,m)}$$

We now define our main metric Energy accuracy (%) for an appliance a to be the mean of $PA(h, a)$ across all homes.

$$\text{Energy accuracy}(a) = \overline{PA(h,a)}$$

In our results, we also calculate the standard error to show the variation in energy accuracy across homes. Higher 'Energy accuracy' indicates better disaggregation performance.

4.4 Experimental setup

Our experimental setup tries to replicate the following real world scenario- we have a small subset of submetered homes and a large number of homes without smart meters. However, our data set has the limitation that only a small number of homes (Table 2) containing aggregate and appliance energy for long duration (1 year) and household characteristics is available. Thus, we use the *leave-one-out* cross validation technique to evaluate our approach, where we assume the set of submetered homes to be all the homes except the test home. Since we also want to tune the parameters of our model, we do a nested cross-validation [22], where the inner loop of cross validation is used for model tuning. We tune our model on two parameters- the number of neighbours (K) and the top-N features. We vary K from 1 to 6 and N from 1 to max(number of features, 10). The top-N features are learnt using the ExtraTreeRegressor[11] using the default parameters provided in the Scikit-learn [40] implementation.

We perform this nested cross validation for each of the three feature sets- *monthly*, *static* and *monthly+static* features. We chose to perform nested cross validation on these three sets separately to ensure that we don't overfit when given *monthly+static* features. Of these three feature sets, the feature giving highest training cross-validation accuracy is chosen for reporting the accuracy on the test households [22].

We use data from 2013 for our evaluation. For all homes, we had aggregate and appliance monthly energy consumption for the 12 months. For the HVAC, the evaluation was done only on the months (May-October) in which it is typically used in Texas.

To compare our performance with FHMM, we train an FHMM on 15-minute appliance level data from all homes across the dataset using nilmtk [8, 27]. Each appliance is modelled as a 3 state HMM, as is commonly done in the literature [45, 8]. The FHMM is composed of an HMM for each home contains the 6 appliances of interest. It must be noted that the result of FHMM disaggregation is a 15-minute power signal for each appliance. We calculate the per month energy from this power signal.

To compare our performance with LBM, we use the implementation provided by the paper authors. The FHMM is trained on 15-minute appliance level data from the dataset. Population statistics such as appliance number of cycles, duration of usage are computed on the entire dataset. The LBM paper authors confirmed that the parameters and hyper-parameters we learnt were reasonable. Like FHMM, LBM outputs a 15-minute power timeseries, from which we calculate the monthly energy consumption per appliance.

We have made our code public and provided easy to reproduce IPython notebooks on Github[12].

4.5 Results

Our main result in Figure 3 shows that Gemello gives comparable or better disaggregation performance across all loads in comparison to the 2 baseline approaches. Gemello can achieve 76% and 69% accuracy on HVAC and fridge, compared to 61% and 39% for FHMM and 56% and 72% for latent bayesian melding based approach. Furthermore, it achieves up to 57% accuracy on washing machine, dryer, dishwasher, and lighting loads, which is higher than previously reported results. Many existing techniques are not able to disaggregate these loads at all.

We discussed the results of the benchmark algorithms with several energy disaggregation researchers. We found that there are several reasons why the performance of FHMM and LBM is poor in comparison to our approach. First, FHMM is known to work poorly when the 'unexplained' energy is high. Unexplained energy is the proportion of energy consumed by loads other than that in the model. While one may argue for the incorporation of additional loads, previous research has shown that FHMM performance degrades

[11] http://bit.ly/20Qd50F

[12] https://github.com/nipunbatra/Gemello

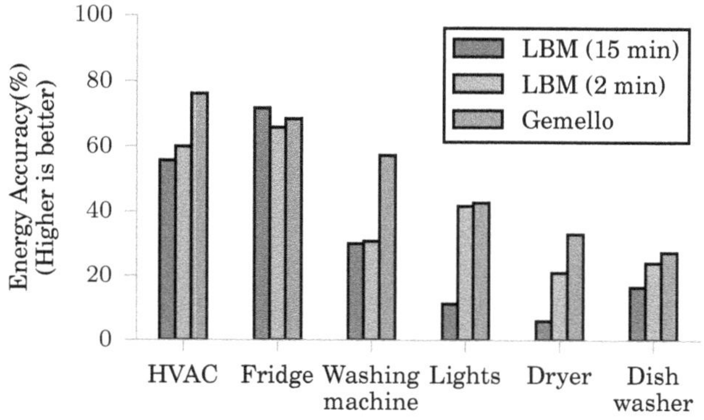

Figure 4: Gemello achieves higher accuracy with monthly sampling frequency than the state-of-the-art LBM algorithm achieves with 15-minute or even 2-minute sampling frequency.

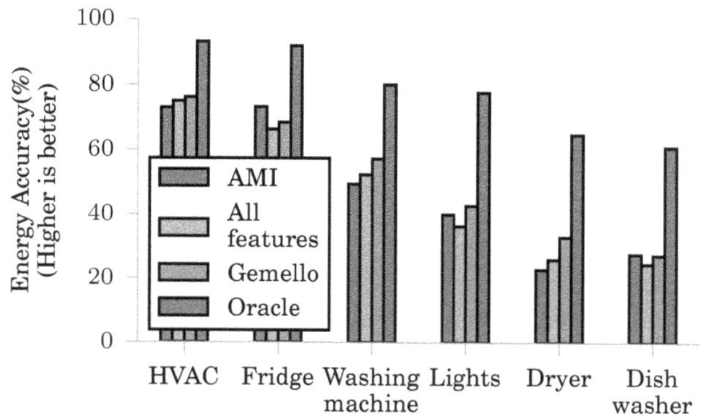

Figure 5: The performance of Gemello can be improved by up to 5% for some appliances if 15-minute AMI data is available. The Oracle illustrates the upper bound on accuracy that can be achieved with this data set if the neighbour selection algorithm were perfect.

as number of appliances increases [31, 8]. It is also generally not feasible to create FHMMs with a large set of appliances as FHMMs have time complexity exponential in the number of appliances. Second, at 15-minute resolution, many appliance lose their distinctive electrical features. For example, a compressor cycle of a fridge may last than 15 minutes and may get confused with noise when data is sampled at 15-minutes interval. Third, FHMMs and in general signature based NILM approaches are prone to poor accuracy when appliances of similar signature are present. In our data set, the dish washer and the dryer had similar electrical signature. Fourth, FHMM is expected to do well for appliances such as fridge and HVAC which have dense usage. But, sparsely used appliances such as dryer and washing machine show poor accuracy. Fifth, appliances such as washing machine, dish washer also exhibit complex electrical signatures, such as spin cycle, dry cycle, rinse cycle [5], which make an HMM based model unsuitable. Most of these limitations are common across all energy disaggregation approaches.

We next evaluated the performance of our approach in comparison to LBM in the case higher resolution data was available to LBM. The LBM authors report high accuracy with 2-minute data. In Figure 4, we see that with an increase in resolution from 15 to 2 minutes, the accuracy of LBM improves. However, our approach still performs comparable or better across all appliances.

4.6 Analysis

4.6.1 Sensitivity analysis on feature space

Having established that Gemello gives better or comparable accuracy than state-of-the-art algorithms, we now analyse the performance of Gemello if additional data such as 15-minute AMI is also available. Figure 5 shows the performance of Gemello across different feature sets. 'All' set of features contains features from AMI data in addition to static household and monthly features. For fridge, the AMI features increase accuracy by 5%. On analysing the optimal set of features selected during nested cross validation when fed AMI features, we found that in 20/21 homes, proportion of step changes that are less than 500 Watts was among the optimal features. As we had hypothesised earlier, fridge is a duty cycled appliance often consuming less than 500 Watts. Thus, homes similar in proportion of step changes less than 500 Watts are similar in fridge consumption. We also found the fraction of energy consumed in afternoon hours to be an important feature as it occurs in 19/21 homes. Homes typically show low electrical activity during afternoon hours, which is often dominated by the always-on appliance fridge. Thus, fraction of energy in afternoon hours is useful for finding homes with similar fridge energy.

We now discuss the optimum set of features learnt by our approach. Table 3 shows the top features learnt over monthly and static features. For the HVAC, washing machine, lights and dryer the features match our intuition, as discussed earlier in Section 3. For dish washer, the top features include the aggregate monthly energy consumption in winter months (December and January). The mean correlation between dish washer energy usage across the months and aggregate energy in December and January is 0.49 and 0.43 respectively. We currently do not have an explanation for this correlation. Further, we find that the top features for fridge shown in the table do not have a high correlation with fridge energy consumption. However, these features do a good job in clustering homes, which ensures that homes similar in the feature are similar in fridge energy.

To find the best possible performance of Gemello on our dataset, we define the 'Oracle'. The 'Oracle' finds the 'optimal' subset of 'neighbourhood' homes from all possible sub sets of homes for each home for each load. The appliance energy data from these 'optimal' homes is then averaged to predict the appliance energy consumption for the test home. Here, 'optimality' is defined as giving the best energy breakdown accuracy. The substantially high accuracy of the 'Oracle' only highlights the potential of Gemello . That is to say, if we were to find *better* features for defining similarity between homes, our accuracies would tend towards the accuracy of the 'Oracle'.

4.6.2 Sensitivity analysis on number of submetered homes

We now discuss the impact of number of submetered homes

Appliance	Top features (prop. of homes present)
HVAC	Aggregate energy in summer months (.94), 75th percentile of 12 month aggregate (.94)
Fridge	Area (1), Kurtosis of 12 month aggregate (.9), Range of 12 month aggregate (.86)
Washing machine	Area (1), Num. rooms (.94)
Lights	Area (1)
Dryer	Num. occupants (1), Area (1)
Dish washer	Monthly aggregate in December (.92), January (.77)

Table 3: Gemello automatically figures out which features are most effective at predicting energy usage for each appliance.

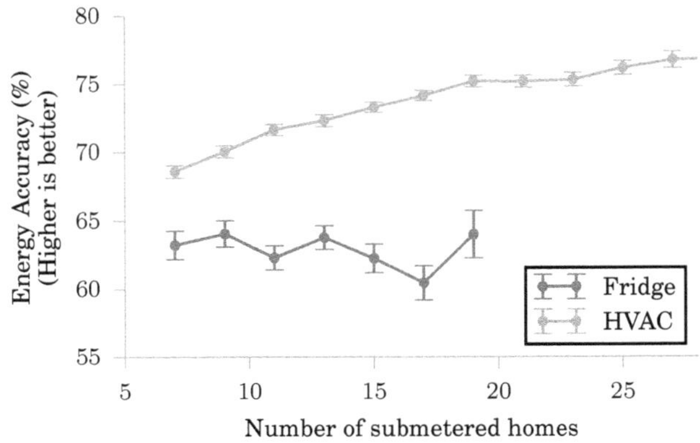

Figure 6: Gemello achieves high accuracy even with only a small fraction of submetered homes, making it a cost-effective and scalable solution. (There are fewer homes in the dataset with fridge data, thus fridge curve ends earlier.)

($\#SH$) on the accuracy of Gemello. A low number of homes is highly desirable as it will make the approach more cost-effective and thus scalable. To find the accuracy if only $\#SH$ homes were submetered, we do a cross-validation to tune our model (inner loop of the nested cross-validation described earlier). Then, on the remaining $Total - \#SH$ homes, we predict using the tuned model. We repeat this procedure 100 times ensuring that we pick different subsets of $\#SH$ homes randomly. Figure 6 shows the accuracy of HVAC and fridge with number of submetered homes ($\#SH$). We chose the starting $\#SH$ as 7, as we have defined 6 as the maximum number of neighbours. We find that even with only 7 submetered homes, Gemello achieves $\approx$ 69% and $\approx$ 65% accuracy on HVAC and fridge respectively. The HVAC accuracy is still 8% better than the state-of-the-art. For the fridge, the accuracy is only 4% off from the accuracy when 21 homes were available. While we don't show the impact of number of submetered homes on accuracy for other appliances in interest of space, time and aesthetics, the conclusion holds that even with low number of submetered homes, our approach gives good performance.

5. LIMITATIONS AND FUTURE WORK

Our work has four major limitations, described below:

1. Since our approach only uses single reading per month, it can only estimate the monthly energy consumed by individual appliances, and cannot estimate the finer grained power signal. Estimating the fine grained signal has been shown to enable various applications such as activity recognition [1], anomaly detection [9, 3] and predicting household occupancy [6]. However, in homes that do have AMI metering infrastructure, the results of Gemello could potentially improve. This is a direction of future work. We believe that incorporating some of our features in the LBM approach could yield good results.

2. This approach is less likely to work for very uncommon appliances. It is likely limited to appliances which are commonly present across a large number of homes. This concern is common to current NILM algorithms as well, which are typically suited for more common appliances. The generality of this approach will grow linearly with the number of homes on which submetering infrastructure is deployed.

3. If people respond to energy breakdown and change their energy consumption, our feature vector consisting of historical energy usage is likely to be less effective. We believe that such changes can be captured by running changepoint detection algorithms over longer duration historical energy data.

4. 'Outlier' homes (such as homes consuming very high energy), which are likely candidates for energy feedback may have wrong predictions owing to the fact that 'neighbouring' homes are not representative of their energy consumption. We plan to address this concern in future work by first segregating these 'outlier' homes based on a model of home's energy consumption as a factor of various static and dynamic characteristics such as: area, number of occupants, etc.

6. CONCLUSIONS

A detailed energy breakdown is the first step towards saving energy in a home. We started with the goal of creating an energy breakdown solution that - works with whatever data is easily accessible, is able to scale across large number of homes and requires minimal capital expenditure involved. In order to achieve these objectives, we completely flipped the way we look at the problem. Rather than the existing bottom-up approach of using modelling to identify electrical signatures, we used the top-down approach of using modelling to identify home level characteristics that correlate well with appliance level energy consumption. We show that such home level characteristics can be easily calculated with static household information and monthly electricity data both of which are readily available. Results show that our proposed approach that satisfies the objectives we started off with, gives comparable or better energy breakdown accuracy than the state-of-the-art NILM techniques which rely on high resolution power consumption data from smart meters. Further, we found that our approach is robust with a small number of instrumented homes. We believe that Gemello has potential for immediate impact because all the information it requires is already available.

7. ACKNOWLEDGEMENTS

We would like to sincerely thank Fred Jiang, Nic Lane, Taiwoo Park, Polly Huang and Wen Hu who provided feedback on an early version of this work at Sensys 2015 PhD forum. Arunchandar Vasan, Venkatesh Sarangan and Mario Berges provided useful suggestions. Jack Kelly, Oliver Parson, Mingjun Zhong, Manoj Gulati, Milan Jain provided detailed pre-submission reviews for our paper, in addition to deep technical discussions. Mingjun Zhong very kindly helped us use his LBM algorithm through Skype discussions and 100+ emails. Grant Fisher provided information about the dataset.

This work was funded in part by NSF awards 1305362, 1038271, and 0845761. The first author is supported by TCS Research and Development PhD fellowship. We also thank Department of Electronics and Information Technology (Government of India) for funding the project (Grant Number DeitY/R&D/ITEA/4(2)/2012 and Grant Number ITRA/15(57)/Mobile/HumanSense/01). We would also like to thank Google for providing support for the conference.

8. REFERENCES

[1] J. Alcalá, O. Parson, and A. Rogers. Detecting anomalies in activities of daily living of elderly residents via energy disaggregation and cox processes. In *Proceedings of the 2nd ACM International Conference on Embedded Systems for Energy-Efficient Built Environments*, pages 225–234. ACM, 2015.

[2] K. Anderson, A. Ocneanu, D. Benitez, D. Carlson, A. Rowe, and M. Bergés. BLUED: A fully labeled public dataset for Event-Based Non-Intrusive load monitoring research. In *Proceedings of 2nd KDD Workshop on Data Mining Applications in Sustainability*, pages 12–16, Beijing, China, 2012.

[3] P. Arjunan, H. D. Khadilkar, T. Ganu, Z. M. Charbiwala, A. Singh, and P. Singh. Multi-user energy consumption monitoring and anomaly detection with partial context information. In *Proceedings of the 2nd ACM International Conference on Embedded Systems for Energy-Efficient Built Environments*, pages 35–44. ACM, 2015.

[4] K. C. Armel, A. Gupta, G. Shrimali, and A. Albert. Is disaggregation the holy grail of energy efficiency? The case of electricity. *Energy Policy*, 52:213–234, 2013.

[5] S. Barker, S. Kalra, D. Irwin, and P. Shenoy. Empirical characterization and modeling of electrical loads in smart homes. In *IEEE International Green Computing Conference*, pages 1–10, Arlington, VA, USA, 2013.

[6] N. Batra, R. Baijal, A. Singh, and K. Whitehouse. How good is good enough? re-evaluating the bar for energy disaggregation. *arXiv preprint arXiv:1510.08713*, 2015.

[7] N. Batra, M. Gulati, A. Singh, and M. B. Srivastava. It's Different: Insights into home energy consumption in India. In *Proceedings of the Fifth ACM Workshop on Embedded Sensing Systems for Energy-Efficiency in Buildings*, 2013.

[8] N. Batra, J. Kelly, O. Parson, H. Dutta, W. Knottenbelt, A. Rogers, A. Singh, and M. Srivastava. NILMTK: An Open Source Toolkit for Non-intrusive Load Monitoring. In *Fifth International Conference on Future Energy Systems (ACM e-Energy)*, Cambridge, UK, 2014.

[9] N. Batra, A. Singh, and K. Whitehouse. If you measure it, can you improve it? exploring the value of energy disaggregation. In *Proceedings of the second ACM International Conference on Embedded Systems For Energy-Efficient Built Environments*. ACM, 2015.

[10] C. Beckel, W. Kleiminger, R. Cicchetti, T. Staake, and S. Santini. The eco data set and the performance of non-intrusive load monitoring algorithms. In *Proceedings of the First ACM International Conference on Embedded Systems For Energy-Efficient Buildings*. ACM, 2014.

[11] M. E. Berges, E. Goldman, H. S. Matthews, and L. Soibelman. Enhancing electricity audits in residential buildings with nonintrusive load monitoring. *Journal of industrial ecology*, 14(5):844–858, 2010.

[12] K.-Y. Chen, S. Gupta, E. C. Larson, and S. Patel. Dose: Detecting user-driven operating states of electronic devices from a single sensing point. In *Pervasive Computing and Communications (PerCom), 2015 IEEE International Conference on*, pages 46–54. IEEE, 2015.

[13] M. Clark, B. Campbell, and P. Dutta. Deltaflow: submetering by synthesizing uncalibrated pulse sensor streams. In *Proceedings of the 5th international conference on Future energy systems*, pages 301–311. ACM, 2014.

[14] R. B. Cleveland, W. S. Cleveland, J. E. McRae, and I. Terpenning. Stl: A seasonal-trend decomposition procedure based on loess. *Journal of Official Statistics*, 6(1):3–73, 1990.

[15] S. Darby. The effectiveness of feedback on energy consumption. *A Review for DEFRA of the Literature on Metering, Billing and direct Displays*, 2006.

[16] S. DeBruin, B. Ghena, Y.-S. Kuo, and P. Dutta. Powerblade: A low-profile, true-power, plug-through energy meter. In *Proceedings of the 13th ACM Conference on Embedded Networked Sensor Systems*, pages 17–29. ACM, 2015.

[17] EIA. Household energy use in texas, 2014.

[18] M. Evans, B. Shui, and S. Somasundaram. *Country report on building energy codes in india*. Pacific Northwest National Laboratory, 2009.

[19] M. Gulati, S. Sundar Ram, A. Majumdar, and A. Singh. Detecting it and lighting loads using common mode conducted emi signals.

[20] S. Gupta, M. S. Reynolds, and S. N. Patel. Electrisense: single-point sensing using emi for electrical event detection and classification in the home. In *Proceedings of the 12th ACM international conference on Ubiquitous computing*, pages 139–148. ACM, 2010.

[21] G. W. Hart. Nonintrusive appliance load monitoring. *Proceedings of the IEEE*, 80(12):1870–1891, 1992.

[22] T. Hastie, R. Tibshirani, J. Friedman, and J. Franklin. The elements of statistical learning: data mining, inference and prediction. *The Mathematical Intelligencer*, 27(2):83–85, 2005.

[23] T. W. Hnat, V. Srinivasan, J. Lu, T. I. Sookoor, R. Dawson, J. Stankovic, and K. Whitehouse. The hitchhiker's guide to successful residential sensing deployments. In *Proceedings of the 9th ACM Conference on Embedded Networked Sensor Systems*, pages 232–245. ACM, 2011.

[24] M. Iyer, W. Kempton, and C. Payne. Comparison groups on bills: Automated, personalized energy information. *Energy and Buildings*, 38(8):988–996, 2006.

[25] M. Jain, A. Singh, and V. Chandan. Non-intrusive estimation and prediction of residential ac energy consumption. In *2016 IEEE International Conference on Pervasive Computing and Communications (PerCom)*, pages 1–9. IEEE, 2016.

[26] X. Jiang, S. Dawson-Haggerty, P. Dutta, and D. Culler. Design and implementation of a high-fidelity ac metering network. In *Information Processing in Sensor Networks, 2009. IPSN 2009. International Conference on*, pages 253–264. IEEE, 2009.

[27] J. Kelly, N. Batra, O. Parson, H. Dutta, W. Knottenbelt, A. Rogers, A. Singh, and M. Srivastava. Nilmtk v0. 2: a non-intrusive load monitoring toolkit for large scale data sets: demo abstract. In *Proceedings of the 1st ACM Conference on Embedded Systems for Energy-Efficient Buildings*, pages 182–183. ACM, 2014.

[28] J. Kelly and W. Knottenbelt. UK-DALE: A dataset recording UK Domestic Appliance-Level Electricity demand and whole-house demand. *ArXiv e-prints*, 2014.

[29] J. Kelly and W. Knottenbelt. Neural nilm: Deep neural networks applied to energy disaggregation. *arXiv preprint arXiv:1507.06594*, 2015.

[30] J. Kelly and W. Knottenbelt. Does disaggregated electricity feedback reduce domestic electricity consumption? a systematic review of the literature. In *3rd International NILM Workshop*, 2016.

[31] H. Kim, M. Marwah, M. F. Arlitt, G. Lyon, and J. Han. Unsupervised disaggregation of low frequency power measurements. SIAM.

[32] Y. Kim, T. Schmid, Z. M. Charbiwala, and M. B. Srivastava. Viridiscope: design and implementation of a fine grained power monitoring system for homes. In *Proceedings of the 11th international conference on Ubiquitous computing*, pages 245–254. ACM, 2009.

[33] J. Z. Kolter and T. Jaakkola. Approximate Inference in Additive Factorial HMMs with Application to Energy Disaggregation. In *Proceedings of the International Conference on Artificial Intelligence and Statistics*, pages 1472–1482, La Palma, Canary Islands, 2012.

[34] J. Z. Kolter and M. J. Johnson. REDD: A public data set for energy disaggregation research. In *Proceedings of 1st KDD Workshop on Data Mining Applications in Sustainability*, San Diego, CA, USA, 2011.

[35] S. Makonin, F. Popowich, I. V. Bajic, B. Gill, and L. Bartram. Exploiting hmm sparsity to perform online real-time nonintrusive load monitoring.

[36] S. Makonin, F. Popowich, L. Bartram, B. Gill, and I. V. Bajic. AMPds: A Public Dataset for Load Disaggregation and Eco-Feedback Research. In *IEEE Electrical Power and Energy Conference*, Halifax, NS, Canada, 2013.

[37] A. Marchiori, D. Hakkarinen, Q. Han, and L. Earle. Circuit-level load monitoring for household energy management. *Pervasive Computing, IEEE*, 10(1):40–48, 2011.

[38] O. Parson, G. Fisher, A. Hersey, N. Batra, J. Kelly, A. Singh, W. Knottenbelt, and A. Rogers. Dataport and nilmtk: a building data set designed for non-intrusive load monitoring. 2015.

[39] O. Parson, S. Ghosh, M. Weal, and A. Rogers. Non-intrusive load monitoring using prior models of general appliance types. In *Proceedings of the 26th AAAI Conference on Artificial Intelligence*, pages 356–362, Toronto, ON, Canada, 2012.

[40] F. Pedregosa, G. Varoquaux, A. Gramfort, V. Michel, B. Thirion, O. Grisel, M. Blondel, P. Prettenhofer, R. Weiss, V. Dubourg, J. Vanderplas, A. Passos, D. Cournapeau, M. Brucher, M. Perrot, and E. Duchesnay. Scikit-learn: Machine learning in Python. *Journal of Machine Learning Research*, 12:2825–2830, 2011.

[41] L. Pérez-Lombard, J. Ortiz, and C. Pout. A review on buildings energy consumption information. *Energy and buildings*, 40(3):394–398, 2008.

[42] B. Shui, M. Evans, H. Lin, W. Jiang, B. Liu, B. Song, and S. Somasundaram. *Country Report on Building Energy Codes in China*. Citeseer, 2009.

[43] H. Wilhite and R. Ling. Measured energy savings from a more informative energy bill. *Energy and buildings*, 22(2):145–155, 1995.

[44] M. Zhong, N. Goddard, and C. Sutton. Signal aggregate constraints in additive factorial hmms, with application to energy disaggregation. In *Advances in Neural Information Processing Systems*, pages 3590–3598, 2014.

[45] M. Zhong, N. Goddard, and C. Sutton. Latent bayesian melding for integrating individual and population models. In C. Cortes, N. Lawrence, D. Lee, M. Sugiyama, and R. Garnett, editors, *Advances in Neural Information Processing Systems 28*, pages 3617–3625. Curran Associates, Inc., 2015.

[46] J.-P. Zimmermann, M. Evans, J. Griggs, N. King, L. Harding, P. Roberts, and C. Evans. Household Electricity Survey. A study of domestic electrical product usage. Technical Report R66141, DEFRA, May 2012.

CaSMoS: A Framework for Learning Candidate Selection Models over Structured Queries and Documents

Fedor Borisyuk Krishnaram Kenthapadi David Stein Bo Zhao
LinkedIn Corporation
Mountain View, CA, USA
{fborisyuk, kkenthapadi, dstein, bozhao}@linkedin.com

ABSTRACT

User experience at social media and web platforms such as LinkedIn is heavily dependent on the performance and scalability of its products. Applications such as personalized search and recommendations require real-time scoring of millions of structured candidate documents associated with each query, with strict latency constraints. In such applications, the query incorporates the context of the user (in addition to search keywords if present), and hence can become very large, comprising of thousands of Boolean clauses over hundreds of document attributes. Consequently, candidate selection techniques need to be applied since it is infeasible to retrieve and score all matching documents from the underlying inverted index. We propose *CaSMoS*, a machine learned candidate selection framework that makes use of Weighted AND (WAND) query. Our framework is designed to prune irrelevant documents and retrieve documents that are likely to be part of the top-k results for the query. We apply a constrained feature selection algorithm to learn positive weights for feature combinations that are used as part of the weighted candidate selection query. We have implemented and deployed this system to be executed in real time using LinkedIn's Galene search platform. We perform extensive evaluation with different training data approaches and parameter settings, and investigate the scalability of the proposed candidate selection model. Our deployment of this system as part of LinkedIn's job recommendation engine has resulted in significant reduction in latency (up to 25%) without sacrificing the quality of the retrieved results, thereby paving the way for more sophisticated scoring models.

Keywords

Candidate selection; Learning query models; Personalized search and recommendation systems

1. INTRODUCTION

Real-time large-scale personalized search and recommendation systems play a key role at Internet companies like LinkedIn. At scale, these systems pose unique challenges, particularly where personalized search results or recommendations must be computed from extremely large populations of candidate items, and where both the items and user context data are highly dynamic. At LinkedIn, we have multiple such large-scale applications, and have developed methods for addressing these challenges using information retrieval and machine learning.

To meet business requirements, some personalized search and recommendation systems must meet tight constraints that they compute results in real time, offer a high degree of data freshness, and respond with low latency. An example of such an application at LinkedIn is the job recommendations product, which computes personalized sets of recommended job postings for users on the site based on the structured, context data present in the publicly available fields of their user profiles. We can train machine-learned scoring functions that predict whether an item (*e.g.*, a job posting) is a good match for a given user, but in large-scale use cases it is not feasible to compute the scores for all possible items in real-time to serve a page load. Instead, we use a two-stage retrieval process where we first invoke a computationally inexpensive model to select a small candidate set of relevant items from the set of all documents that match the query, and then perform a more computationally expensive second pass scoring and ranking on the obtained candidate set.

Search engines are known to be good at retrieving a small set of relevant documents matching a given query out of a huge document set, so for real-time large-scale recommenders it is a natural choice to model the recommendable items as structured documents and define a function to construct queries for selecting candidates. But making effective use of a search engine to produce viable candidate sets (having good precision and recall, and a small candidate set size) is non-trivial. One could naively construct large disjunction queries using all the publicly available keywords in a user's profile, for example, but such an approach would likely match too many items and fail to reject many of the irrelevant ones.

In some cases, ad-hoc heuristics and business rules can allow us to reduce somewhat the size of the candidate set; for example, for a job recommendations system, we could construct a query that selects the jobs in the same geographic region as the user, or the jobs that are in the same industry as the user. But these approaches would not work well in all industries or geographic locations: in some cases, the queries could still match too many jobs, while in some others, more relevant jobs that did not match the ad-hoc criteria could be rejected.

In this paper, we propose *CaSMoS*, a machine learning framework for constructing effective models for candidate selection in personalized search and recommendation systems. We present techniques for learning candidate selection models expressed using Weighted AND (WAND) Boolean predicates [9]. In our approach, we use a constrained feature selection algorithm to learn positive weights for feature combinations that are used as part of the weighted

KDD'16, August 13–17, 2016, San Francisco, CA, USA.
© 2016 ACM. ISBN 978-1-4503-4232-2/16/08. . . $15.00
DOI: http://dx.doi.org/10.1145/2939672.2939718

candidate selection query. We have implemented this system to be executed in real time using LinkedIn's Galene search engine, and deployed in production. We perform extensive evaluation with different training data approaches and parameter settings, and investigate the scalability of the proposed candidate selection model. Our online experiments demonstrate the efficacy of our framework in achieving significant drop in latency (up to 25%) without sacrificing the quality of the retrieved results, thereby paving the way for more sophisticated scoring models. We finally present the lessons learned from the deployment of our system as part of LinkedIn's job recommendation engine that serves millions of job recommendations to millions of users.

2. RELATED WORK

Query optimization has been well studied in relational databases for structured queries [10]. Information retrieval (IR) systems are different from traditional databases in that, inverted indexes are typically used to support keyword queries, and only top-k results need to be returned. One well known work for query optimization and candidate generation in IR systems is [9], in which the authors proposed the formulation of queries in the format of Weighted AND (WAND) predicates and described an efficient algorithm to execute such queries. There has been a lot of follow-up work: using SVM to learn WAND queries towards generation of candidates for document classification was proposed in [4]; the approach in [9] was compared with other algorithms for candidate generation in learning-to-rank systems and determined to be the most efficient among the compared algorithms in [6]; more aggressive pruning stategies on a per-query-basis were proposed in [16]. In this work, we propose methods to learn WAND queries for candidate generation for personalized search and recommendation systems, where both query and document data are semi-structured. The semi-structured data in our scenario is different from traditional web search engines in the sense that there are multiple fields of text in both queries and documents, and it is more important to learn which fields of queries and documents should match instead of which keywords should match. This is the main difference between our work and previous candidate selection methods in web search. Also, in this paper we focus on how to generate the query instead of query execution, since conceptually the underlying search engine can be treated as an independent component, where previous work on optimizing WAND query execution can be applied.

Other types of queries have also been investigated for candidate generation. An approach for constructing query modifications in the web search domain using corpus-based SVM models was introduced in [12]. Boolean models for obtaining the set of minimal terms using an approximate Markov blanket feature selection technique and a decision tree to build the corresponding Boolean query were proposed in [5]. Genetic algorithms were investigated in [3, 13] to find query alterations for faster execution in IR systems.

Candidate generation is also related to blocking methods in the setting of record linkage and entity matching. A dynamic blocking algorithm to choose the blocking keys based on the data characteristics at run time, together with a MapReduce implementation, was proposed in [14]. The construction of blocking functions based on sets of blocking predicates was proposed in [8]. In that paper, the authors formulate the problem of learning an optimal blocking function as the task of finding a combination of blocking predicates. However, for blocking in entity matching systems, high recall is very important, since the goal is to try to match all records in one database with another. In personalized search and recommendation systems, the objective is very different, since we focus more on retrieving top-k relevant results instead of all relevant results.

Table 1: Structured representation of a hypothetical user profile

User field	Value of field
Title	Software Engineer
Company	LinkedIn Corporation
Industry	Internet
Location	San Francisco Bay Area, CA, USA
Skills	C++, Java, Linux, Machine Learning
Position summary	recommendation systems, professional content

Finally, the notion of contextual information has been investigated in varied disciplines such as psychology [7, 11] and computer science (see [2] and the references therein, for example). While these investigations pertain to defining and modeling different types of user context, we focus on the orthogonal problem of constructing effective candidate selection models in personalized search and recommendation systems, wherein the queries incorporate user context.

3. PROBLEM SETTING

Personalized search and recommendation systems form the backbone of several user-facing products at Internet companies such as LinkedIn. The underlying search / recommendation tasks can be modeled as information retrieval problems, wherein the query consists of the user context / interests expressed through user profile and (user provided) search keywords, if present, and the document corpus consists of millions of items of a particular type depending on the application (*e.g.*, the set of job postings in the case of personalized job search/recommendations). Due to the product and business requirements, we typically need to compute the results in real time, under strict latency constraints. While it is evident that the results need to be generated on the fly for search systems, one may wonder whether the results can be precomputed in the case of recommendation systems. However, in several recommendation scenarios, both the user context and the set of items are highly dynamic, necessitating the need for real time computation. On the one hand, relevant results need to be available as soon as a new user creates a profile, or a user changes the profile. On the other hand, the set of valid items may change frequently over time (*e.g.*, due to the arrival of new job postings or the expiration of job postings), and hence the freshness of results is crucial (*e.g.*, users would like to see recommendations of relevant jobs as soon as they are posted). Hereafter, we present in terms of recommendation systems, although our motivation and modeling are applicable for personalized search systems as well.

We next motivate the need for candidate selection as part of a two-stage retrieval process, especially considering the long, complex structured queries and the infeasibility of scoring millions of matching structured documents. Consider, for example, the task of recommending jobs to a hypothetical user who is currently employed as a Software Engineer at LinkedIn in San Francisco Bay Area, with expertise in C++, Java, Linux, and Machine Learning, and works on building recommendation systems for displaying professional content. The structured representation of this user's profile is shown in Table 1. Suppose that the items (jobs) are scored based on the following similarity features: (user_title, job_title), (user_skills, job_skills), (user_position_summary, job_skills). Even assuming such a simplistic scoring model and a relatively minimal user profile context, the number of jobs that need to be scored be-

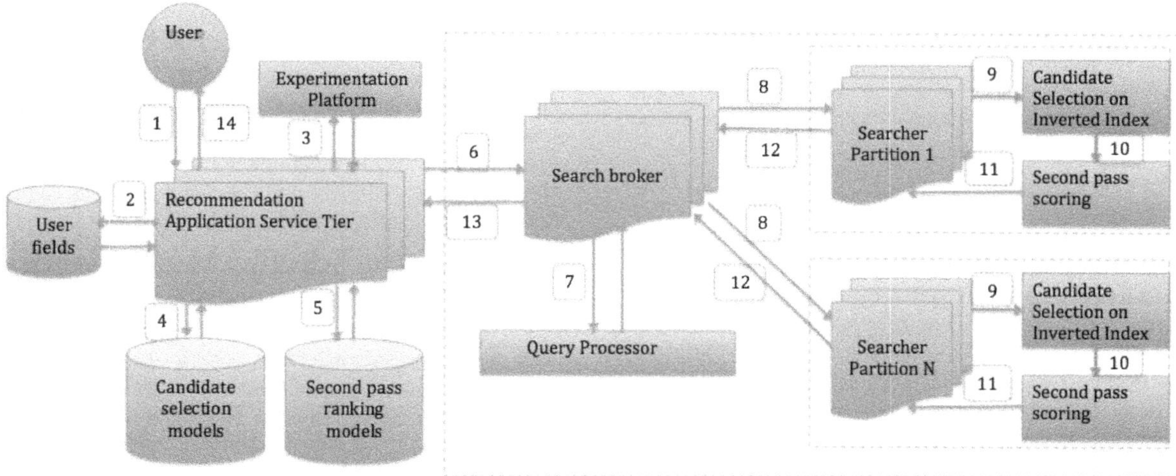

Figure 1: Online query processing and recommendation system.

comes very large, since any job whose structured representation includes one of {job_title: "Software Engineer", job_skills: "C++", . . ., job_skills: "Machine Learning", job_skills: "recommendation systems", job_skills: "professional content"} is a plausible recommendation. This problem is further compounded by the fact that the query may need to be expanded for robust match (*e.g.*, we can include titles similar to the user title, or locations similar to the user location). In practice, a rich user profile may consist of several structured attributes, and there could be hundreds of (user, item) features. Consequently, millions of items may need to be scored for a single user, which is not possible given the latency constraints, thereby highlighting the need for a two-stage retrieval process. Since our goal is to present a small set of most relevant results to the user, we would like to prune a large subset of the matching items that are not likely to be scored high, using a first stage, computationally inexpensive candidate selection model. Our problem can be stated as follows:

Given a long, complex structured query, select a small set of matching documents that are likely candidates for the top-k results for the query, while pruning matching documents that are not likely to be part of the top-k results.

4. RECOMMENDATION SYSTEM DESIGN AND ARCHITECTURE

We describe the overall design and architecture of the recommendation system deployed at LinkedIn, focusing on how candidate selection is performed. We first give an overview of LinkedIn's Galene search platform, followed by the description of the online recommendation system.

4.1 Galene Search Platform

In our deployment, we use LinkedIn's Galene search platform [15]. Galene uses Lucene-based inverted indexes at its core, and provides several functionalities desirable for our applications. The Galene platform supports periodic rebuilding of the entire index data offline in Hadoop, and offers a distributed service architecture with index partitioning and shard replication. The offline-built static base index when deployed in the online service is complemented by an online live-index tier, which consumes from a live Kafka [1] stream of document update events. The static base index and live index tiers together provide a single dynamic view of the search index to upstream callers of the service. Galene provides a rich query language that supports Weighted AND (WAND) queries [9]. Galene also offers a flexible API that allows for individual applications to define query expansion and query rewriting operations, as well as arbitrary scoring functions for ranking the matched documents. These APIs allow for easy integration of machine-learned scoring and candidate selection modules into Galene deployments, including those powering the methodologies discussed in this paper.

4.2 Online Query Processing and Recommendation System

Our online recommendation system uses a multi-tiered service oriented architecture (see Figure 1), and consists of a recommendation application service tier and a distributed search service tier. In this section, we provide an overview of the process by which these services respond to live requests for real-time recommendations. The description is annotated with references to the step numbers found in Figure 1.

4.2.1 *Recommendation Application Service Tier*

The recommendation application service mid-tier accepts requests from the front-end systems that are responsible for the user-facing LinkedIn web applications (step 1). Recommendation requests include the identifier of the entity for which recommendations are to be computed (in the example of job recommendations, this is the ID of the user visiting the site).

The recommendation service then retrieves the structured user fields data from a key-value store (step 2). It then obtains the experimental treatment for the user from an external A/B testing platform service (step 3). The experimental treatment identifies which machine-learned models should be used to compute the recommendations for the user. The recommendation service uses this information to retrieve the first-pass candidate selection model (step 4) and to retrieve the second-pass ranking model (step 5) from respective key-value stores. The models and the user data are then wrapped into a request object that is issued to the search broker service (step 6).

User field data is represented in a term-vector format, and consists largely of natural-language text-based fields including weighted uni-grams and bi-grams. Also included are non-text categorical derived fields (*e.g.*, which industries or geographic locations in our fixed taxonomy is a particular user associated with; the canonical version of user's current position title string, wherein the canonical version is obtained with respect to a large taxonomy of canonical titles; the set of skills for a user) along with corresponding weights.

4.2.2 *Search Service Tier*

The distributed search service tier consists of the following key components.

Search Broker: Search requests issued by the Recommendation Application Service are handled by the search broker service. The search broker applies the candidate selection model to the structured user fields data submitted with the request to synthesize a candidate selection query in the Galene query language (step 7). While the candidate selection model may be expressed in terms of (user, item) feature definitions, the constructed Galene query must be expressed in terms of item fields and values, possibly as a weighted Boolean predicate. For instance, for the task of recommending jobs to the hypothetical user in §3, the constructed Galene query could be a weighted Boolean predicate over literals such as job_title: "Software Engineer", job_skills: "C++", ..., job_skills: "Machine Learning", job_skills: "recommendation systems", and job_skills: "professional content".

The request object is then decorated with the synthesized candidate selection query and is issued by the broker to the distributed set of search nodes, each of which contains one partition of the distributed index (step 8). Upon receiving the responses from the search nodes, the broker service merges the hits from the partitions and returns a list of the top-k items to the recommendation application service.

Searcher Node: A cluster of searcher node machines forms a partitioned and replicated distributed search index service. Each node runs as a stand-alone service, capable of answering queries against its own partition of the search index.

Upon receipt of the search request from the broker, the search node executes the Galene search query against its partition of the inverted index (step 9). In the typical example, the query is a Weighted AND query. As the matching documents are found via the information retrieval process, they are scored according to the second-pass ranking model provided with the request (step 10).

During second-pass ranking, interaction features are computed on-the-fly according to the second-pass ranking model, based on:

- the structured user fields contained in the request (*e.g.*, based on the user's profile data)
- the item (document) fields obtained via Galene's forward-index data

Documents whose scores exceed a defined threshold are inserted into a max-heap (step 11). When all the matching documents have been processed, the top-k documents in the max-heap are returned to the search broker (step 12).

The top documents returned by the searcher node (step 12) are subsequently merged with the results from other searcher nodes by the broker (step 13), and are passed back to the recommendation application service for post-processing. Post-processing may include applying filters and rules required for business reasons (for example, remove recommendations for ineligible jobs). Finally, the recommendation application service returns the finished list of recommended items to the front-end service for rendering on the site (step 14).

5. CaSMoS: CANDIDATE SELECTION MODEL LEARNING FRAMEWORK

We next present an overview of our candidate selection model, and describe the offline framework for learning this model based on user-item interaction log data. This offline framework is implemented in a distributed computing environment using Hadoop infrastructure, and makes use of LinkedIn's machine learning platform, based on Spark.

5.1 Candidate Selection Model Overview

We first present the intuition underlying our candidate selection model. As discussed in §3, for each user, millions of items could match with respect to each (user, item) feature used in the scoring model. However, the most relevant items are very likely to match on multiple (user, item) features. Thus, requiring an item to match on multiple features drastically prunes the number of items to be scored, while retaining the most relevant items. Further, it may be desirable to give different weights to different combinations of features: In an application scenario such as job recommendations, a match on the combination {(user_title, job_title), (user_skills, job_skills)} is more important than a match on the combination {(user_industry, job_industry), (user_seniority, job_seniority)}. Hence, we choose to represent the candidate selection model based on the Weighted AND (WAND) query operator [9].

Let F denote the set of (user, item) feature definitions. For $1 \leq i \leq k$, let C_i be a Boolean variable denoting whether an item matches on a combination $F_i \subseteq F$ of (user, item) features. Equivalently, C_i can be viewed as a conjunction over Boolean version of the corresponding features in F_i. Each clause C_i is associated with a positive weight w_i. An item is selected if the sum of weights associated with clauses that are true exceeds a threshold, θ. Thus, we specify the candidate selection model in terms of WAND Boolean predicate: For a given item, $WAND(C_1, w_1, \ldots, C_k, w_k, \theta)$ is true if and only if

$$\sum_{1 \leq i \leq k} w_i \cdot x_i \geq \theta,$$

where c_i is an indicator variable for C_i ($c_i = 1$ if C_i is true, and 0 otherwise).

We give an illustration using a toy candidate selection model and the hypothetical user profile in Table 1. Suppose that the model is specified with a threshold of 0.5, and in terms of just four (clause, weight) pairs:

1. ((user_title, job_title) $\wedge$ (user_skills, job_skills), 0.55)
2. ((user_title, job_title) $\wedge$ (user_position_summary, job_skills), 0.35)
3. ((user_industry, job_industry) $\wedge$ (user_position_summary, job_skills), 0.25)
4. ((user_industry, job_industry) $\wedge$ (user_seniority, job_seniority), 0.05)

Here, a job posting (item) satisfies a clause if the underlying features will all be non-zero. For instance, a job posting would satisfy the first clause if its title matches the user's title and there is at least one skill in common between the job and the user. We can observe that, for a job posting to be selected, it must either satisfy the first clause or satisfy both the second and the third clauses. For the user in Table 1, a job posting for "Software Engineer" (title) with "Java" as one of the skills will satisfy the first clause, and hence will be selected. Similarly, a job posting for "Software Engineer" at a company in the Internet industry that lists "recommender systems" as

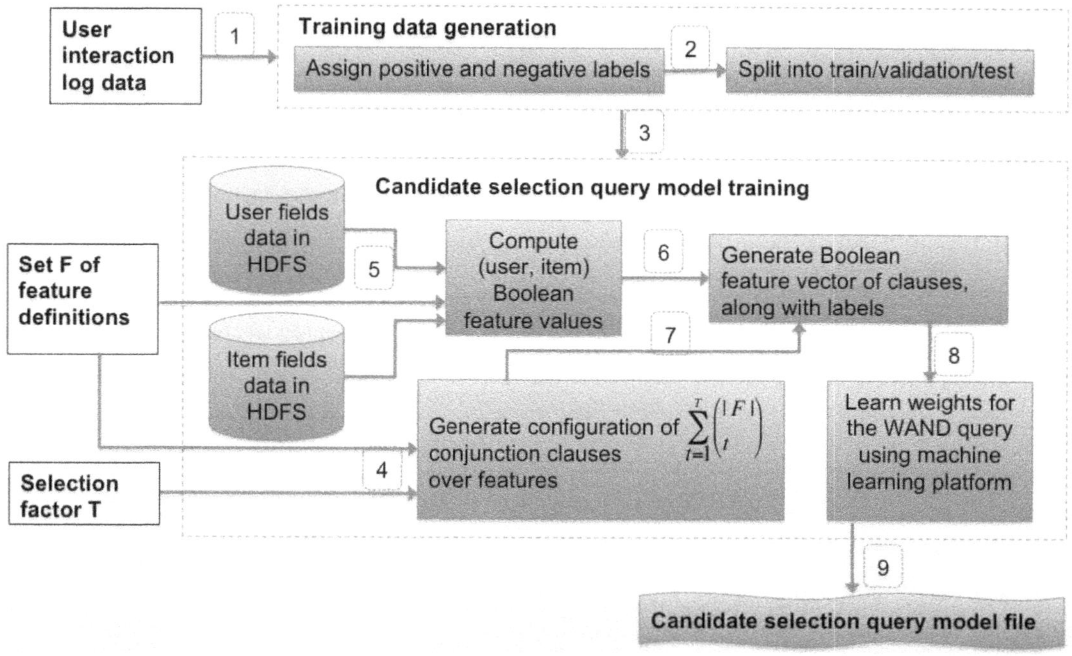

Figure 2: Offline framework for learning candidate selection query model.

one of the skills will satisfy both the second and the third clauses, and hence will be selected. However, a job posting for "Product Manager" at a company in the Internet industry will not be selected even if it lists any of the user's skills. Note that in this example, the fourth clause does not have any effect on whether a job posting will be selected, given the choice of the above threshold.

We next highlight the benefit of the above representation for the candidate selection model.

We are able to make use of WAND query operator, that is supported by LinkedIn's Galene search platform. Galene applies various optimization techniques as part of WAND query execution. For example, since the weights associated with the clauses are positive in WAND query, the retrieval system can select a document as soon as the sum of the weights for the satisfied clauses so far evaluated surpasses the threshold. In this case, there is no need to evaluate the remaining query clauses. This optimization would not be possible in case negative clause weights are allowed since the retrieval system would then need to evaluate all the clauses.

5.2 Candidate Selection Model Training using User-Item Interaction Log Data

We next describe our offline system for learning the candidate selection model. Given a long, complex structured query, the goal of candidate selection can be viewed as achieving a separation between items that could be potentially in the top-k results and the items that are very unlikely to be in the top-k results. Hence, we adopt a supervised machine learning approach to train the candidate selection model. We present the components underlying our system in Algorithm 1, and the overall architecture in Figure 2. We elaborate on the key components below.

Generation of training data: This component assigns positive and negative labels to (user, item) pairs, based on user-item interaction log data, and splits this data into train/validation/test sets. The log data contains events of user interactions with the recommendation application. The events could correspond to an item impression (indicating that the item was recommended to the user) as well as different types of interaction such as clicking (indicating the user clicked on the item snippet to view more details), saving (indicating that the user saved the item for later reference), and other application specific interactions (*e.g.*, applying for a job). We can infer positive and negative labels for (user, item) pairs in several ways, possibly depending on the specific application. For example, for a given user, items that were clicked by the user could be treated as positive examples and the items that were never shown to the user could be treated as negative examples. Our experimentation choices are described in §6.4.

Algorithm 1 Algorithm for Learning Candidate Selection Model

Input: Set F of (user, item) feature definitions; User-item interaction log data; Selection factor, T.
Output: Candidate selection query model, specified as WAND query predicate.

1: Generate training data (labeled (user, item) pairs) from user-item interaction log data.
2: Create the configuration set of possible conjunction clauses, by taking combinations of up to T (user, item) feature definitions.
3: Compute Boolean feature values for the (user, item) pairs present in the training data.
4: Generate Boolean feature vector of conjunction clauses, along with labels.
5: Learn weights for the WAND query.

Configuration of potential clauses for WAND Query: Given the set F of (user, item) feature definitions and the selection factor, T, we create the configuration set of possible clauses for WAND query by taking combinations of up to T feature definitions ($\sum_{1\leq t\leq T}\binom{|F|}{t}$ clauses in total).

Consider the job recommendation example discussed in §3, and assume that there are just three feature definitions: (user_title, job_title), (user_skills, job_skills), (user_position_summary, job_skills). If the selection factor equals 2, the set of potential clauses would be: {(user_title, job_title), (user_skills, job_skills), (user_position_summary, job_skills), (user_title, job_title) ∧ (user_skills, job_skills), (user_title, job_title) ∧ (user_position_summary, job_skills), (user_skills, job_skills) ∧ (user_position_summary, job_skills)}. At first, the last three clauses containing two features each may seem redundant since any item that matches these clauses would have been matched by at least one of the first three singleton clauses. However, since a conjunction of two Boolean features is more selective (and usually more discriminative at identifying relevant items) than either feature, the conjunction could be assigned a significantly larger weight compared to the singleton clauses, and thus could determine whether an item gets selected or not. In our implementation, we set the selection factor, $T = 2$.

Computation of Boolean feature values: Given the set of feature definitions, we next generate the Boolean version of the corresponding features for the (user, item) pairs present in the training data. In the job recommendation example above, the feature (user_skills, job_skills) would evaluate to *true* if and only if there is at least one skill in common between the user and the job. To enable this computation, the system that generates the structured field data for the users writes a copy of this data to HDFS, in addition to populating/updating the user fields store (used by the online query processing recommendation system). Similarly, the system that generates the item fields data writes a copy of the data to HDFS, in addition to updating the corresponding search index online. User fields may include publicly available parts of a user's LinkedIn profile such as the current job title of the user, seniority, function, industry, skills, and key terms extracted from descriptive fields such as the position summary of the user, current job description, and past job descriptions. In the case of job recommendation application, the item (job posting) fields may include the job title, seniority, function, industry, skills, and key terms extracted from the job description.

Generation of Boolean feature vector of conjunction clauses: This component generates the dataset needed for the machine learning algorithm, based on the following inputs: the training data, the Boolean feature values, and the configuration set of conjunction clauses. Each row corresponds to a (user, item) pair. The columns correspond to the conjunction clauses of (user, item) features, with the last column indicating the label. A conjunction clause is set to 1 *(true)* if and only if the user and the item match on all the features present in the clause.

Learning WAND query model: We use LinkedIn's machine learning platform to learn the weights and determine the optimal threshold for the candidate selection model expressed as a Boolean WAND query. Since the weights associated with the clauses need to be positive in the WAND query, we cannot directly use off-the-shelf machine learning techniques. Instead, we formulate our learning task in terms of logistic regression with positive coefficient constraints.

To satisfy this requirement, we experimented with two different algorithmic implementations of our learning task. The first algorithm can be thought of as performing constrained feature selection, treating the logistic regression training procedure as a blackbox. The second algorithm modifies the internals of the training procedure towards achieving positive coefficient weights.

Algorithm 2 Constrained Feature Selection Algorithm

Input: Dataset comprising Boolean feature vector of conjunction clauses, along with labels.
Output: Candidate selection query model, specified as WAND query predicate.

Train the logistic regression model with all features (Boolean conjunction clauses).
repeat
    Remove features whose coefficients are below a small (positive) threshold.
    Retrain the model without the removed features.
until Desired number of conjunction clauses are left.

Algorithm 3 Non-negative Coefficient Constrained Boundary Algorithm

Input: Dataset comprising Boolean feature vector of conjunction clauses, along with labels.
Output: Candidate selection query model, specified as WAND query predicate.

repeat
    Perform a step of the gradient descent algorithm, and update the coefficients of the features (Boolean conjunction clauses).
    Assign negative coefficients to zero.
until The training procedure converges, or the number of iterations reaches a limit.

We describe the two algorithms formally below.

Constrained Feature Selection Algorithm: Algorithm 2 first trains the logistic regression model with all features (Boolean conjunction clauses), and then iteratively prunes features with coefficient weights below a small positive threshold. Thus, both features with negative coefficient weights and very small weights are removed. This process is terminated upon reaching the desired number of conjunction clauses. In our implementation, we tune the desired number of clauses based on the observed latency over a set of queries.

Non-negative Coefficient Constrained Boundary Algorithm: Algorithm 3 performs modification to the gradient descent algorithm so that the negative coefficients are set to zero after each gradient descent step. This process is repeated until either the training procedure converges, or the number of iterations reaches a limit.

We experimentally observed that Algorithm 3 performed similarly as Algorithm 2 in terms of quality metrics. Hence, considering the added complexity associated with modifying the internals of the training procedure, we decided to use Algorithm 2 in our deployed production system. We used precision-recall (PR) curve to select the threshold parameter, θ for the learned WAND query. PR curve can be constructed by measuring precision and recall with respect to different choices of the threshold. We experiment with four different choices of threshold, corresponding to recall values of 0.85, 0.90, 0.95, and 0.99 respectively, and discuss the effect of varying threshold on the performance of candidate selection in §6.

6. EXPERIMENTS

We next present an extensive evaluation of our candidate selection model learning framework. We evaluate both efficiency (query processing time / latency) and effectiveness (quality) of the proposed candidate selection method, in offline as well as online settings. We also investigate the effect of varying training data and features used on the quality of the resulting candidate selection model, as well as the effect of varying index size and traffic loads on the query processing time.

6.1 Experimental Setup

As described earlier, we implemented our techniques to be executed in real time using LinkedIn's Galene search engine, and deployed in production as part of LinkedIn's job recommendation system. Our offline learning framework is implemented in a distributed computing environment using Hadoop, and uses LinkedIn's machine learning platform, based on Spark.

We performed our experiments over two weeks of job recommendations log data, collected during July 2015. This data is part of the user-interaction log data, which contains events of user interactions with various LinkedIn applications. The following types of user-job interaction events were used to train the candidate selection models:

- job impression (whether a job was shown to a particular LinkedIn user),
- job click (whether the user clicked on the job and viewed the details of the job), and
- job application (whether the user applied for the job).

The training data was generated from this log data, and was divided into three subsets: training set, validation set, and test set. We trained the models using the training set, selected the best model based on the validation set, and computed the metrics on the test set. Our baseline model does not use candidate selection, and instead scores all job documents that match structured attribute keywords from the user profile. This model is implemented by constructing a Boolean disjunction query from the structured fields in the user profile to the relevant structured fields in the job documents.

Our online experiments were performed using LinkedIn's A/B testing platform [17]. LinkedIn users were partitioned randomly into different buckets, and different random buckets of users were presented with job recommendation results obtained using different models, over a period of several weeks. The users in the control group were shown results obtained without using candidate selection (our baseline model), while the treatment buckets corresponded to different candidate selection models. Through these online experiments, we compared different models (including the one with no candidate selection) with respect to both efficiency and effectiveness, as explained below.

6.2 Metrics

We used the following metrics for measuring the efficiency as well as effectiveness of our system. We report these metrics relative to the baseline model (for business confidentiality reasons).

Efficiency metrics: We used LinkedIn's internal online performance monitoring tools to measure the query processing time (latency) metric, which represents the time lag between a request to the our system and the response back. We use 90th percentile latency as the efficiency metric (the time taken to process a query is less than this latency 90% of the time). Lower latency corresponds to faster page load times for the users, and hence is desirable from both business objective and user experience/engagement perspectives.

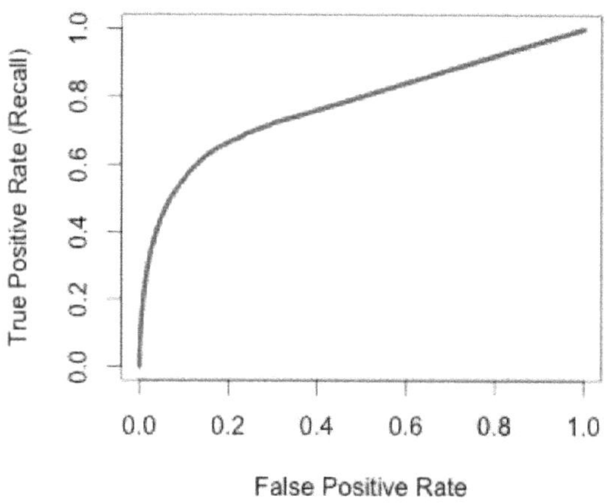

Figure 3: Receiver operating characteristic (ROC) curve for the candidate selection model.

Effectiveness metrics: We used both offline and online measures to quantify the effectiveness (quality) of the candidate selection models.

For offline evaluation, we computed the area under receiver operating characteristic curve (ROC AUC) and the area under precision-recall curve (PR AUC), both of which represent the quality of the candidate selection model (viewed as a binary classifier). The ROC curve is obtained by plotting the true positive rate (recall) against the false positive rate at various choices of the threshold, θ. The PR curve is obtained by plotting the precision against the true positive rate (recall) for various threshold choices.

For online evaluation, we computed the job application rate, which is defined as the ratio of the number of job applications (number of jobs applied to by users) to the number of job impressions (number of jobs presented to users). Higher job application rate corresponds to more relevant jobs being shown to users, and hence is desirable from both business objective and user experience/engagement perspectives.

6.3 Effectiveness and Efficiency of Learned Candidate Selection

We first present the results from offline analysis of the candidate selection model, viewing it as a binary classifier (type 2 training data approach is used for assigning positive and negative labels – see §6.4). Figure 3 shows the receiver operating characteristic (ROC) curve for the candidate selection model at various choices of the threshold. We can observe that a recall of 0.85 can be achieved with a false positive rate close to 0.65. Note that false positive rate is not a significant concern since the false positives can be eliminated as part of the scoring and ranking performed by the second pass ranking model. Further, note that our goal is to retrieve the top-k relevant results for each query, rather than to ensure high recall. For the online experiments, we selected four candidate selection models (varying just in the threshold) corresponding to recall values of 0.85, 0.90, 0.95, and 0.99 respectively, along with the baseline model with no candidate selection.

We measured the efficiency of the candidate selection models with respect to online production traffic. To ensure fair comparison, we allocated the same fraction of users (randomly partitioned)

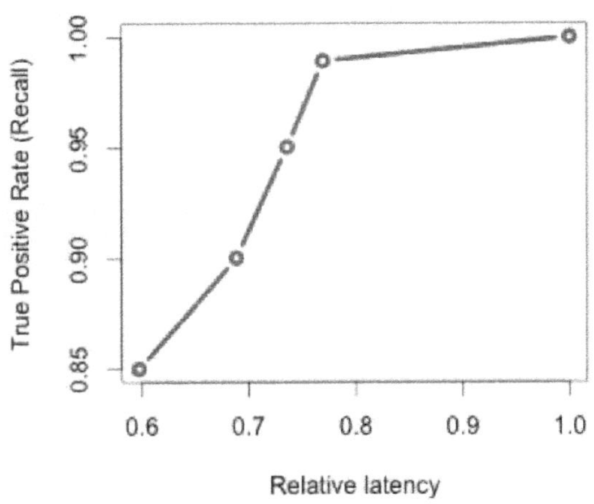

Figure 4: Effectiveness (recall) vs efficiency (relative 90th percentile latency).

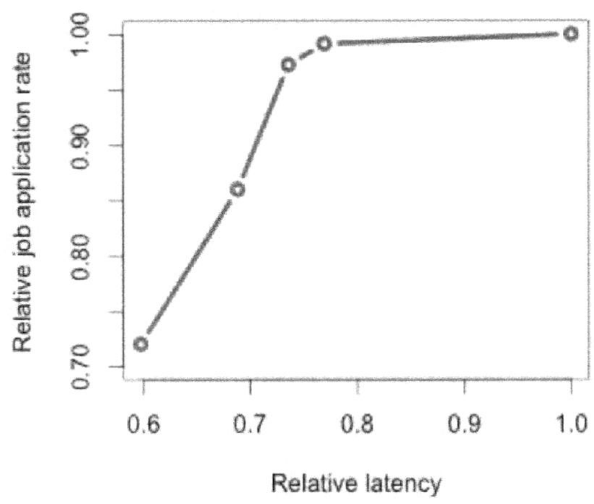

Figure 5: Effectiveness (relative job application rate) vs efficiency (relative 90th percentile latency).

to each of the five models above, so that each model is subject to the same amount of live traffic load. Figure 4 shows the plot of recall vs. 90th percentile latency for the four candidate selection models, relative to those of the baseline model. The top right data point (with relative recall and latency both equal to 1) represents the baseline model. As we increase the threshold parameter of the model, fewer documents are selected, thereby resulting in improved query processing time (latency) but reduced recall. However, we observe that the introduction of the candidate selection model with (a threshold corresponding to) recall value of 0.99 reduces latency by more than 20%. Choosing the models with recall values of 0.95 and 0.90 reduce latency by more than 25% and 30% respectively. These results demonstrate the potential to significantly reduce latency without sacrificing quality.

We next present the trade-off between effectiveness and efficiency for the candidate selection models, focusing on the metrics that directly impact user experience and business objectives. Figure 5 shows the plot of the job application rate vs. 90th percentile latency for the four candidate selection models, relative to those of the baseline model (the top right data point in the plot). We observe that the best balance can be achieved by choosing the candidate selection model that achieves more than 25% latency reduction with less than 3% drop in the job application rate. Comparing Figures 4 and 5, we observe that a small reduction in (offline) recall does not translate to as much drop in the (online) job application rate. On the other hand, a more aggressive candidate selection model (with slightly larger reduction in recall) has a disproportionately worse job application rate when deployed online.

6.4 Effect of Varying Training Data and Choice of Features

We experimented with two methods for generating training data from the user-job interaction logs.

- Type 1. Jobs with clicks + random negatives
  - Positive labels are assigned to (user u, job j) pairs where user u clicked on job j.
  - Negative labels are assigned to (user u, job j) pairs where j is a randomly sampled job that was never shown to u.
- Type 2. Job impressions + random negatives
  - Positive labels are assigned to (user u, job j) pairs where job j is part of the top recommendation results (referred as "impressions") shown to user u using the baseline model.
  - Negative labels are assigned to (user u, job j) pairs where j is a randomly sampled job that was never shown to u.

The intuition underlying type 1 training data is that we want to directly optimize for retrieving jobs that users are more likely to click. Type 2 training data is based on the premise that it is sufficient to optimize for retrieving jobs that would be returned and ranked at the top by the baseline model. The underlying assumption is that this task should be easier than predicting jobs that will get clicked, which would instead be taken care of by the more complicated second pass scoring and ranking model.

Table 2 presents the effectiveness (in terms of ROC AUC and PR AUC) of the models trained with Type 1 and Type 2 training data respectively. We observed better performance using Type 2 training data compared to Type 1 training data (ROC AUC of 0.775 vs. 0.742). Type 2 training data approach also resulted in better online A/B testing performance. Hence, we chose this approach for reporting other experimental results, and also in the deployed production system.

We also measured the impact of using only features with positive coefficient weights in the candidate selection model. From the last two rows in Table 2, we notice that the offline effectiveness (ROC AUC) with this restriction is 0.775, compared to 0.812 when using all features. However, this restriction is needed for the optimization techniques performed by Galene as part of WAND query execution (see §5.1).

Table 2: Dependence of candidate selection model performance on the training data and choice of features.

Method	ROC AUC	PR AUC
Type 1: Clicks + random negatives + only features with positive coefficients	0.742	0.927
Type 2: Impressions + random negatives + only features with positive coefficients	0.775	0.933
Type 2: Impressions + random negatives + all features with positive and negative coefficients	0.812	0.943

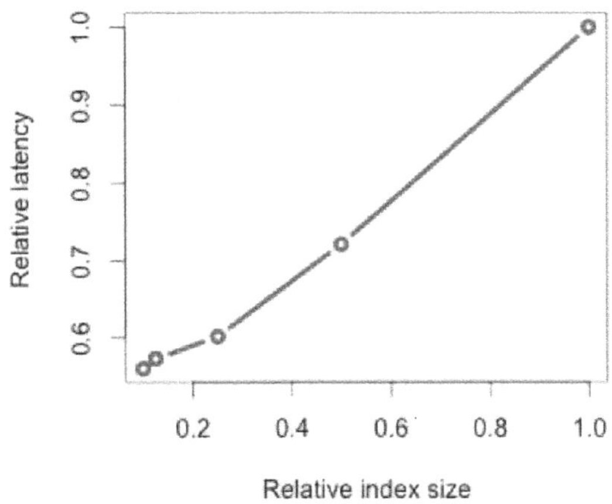

Figure 6: Efficiency (relative 90th percentile latency) vs relative index size.

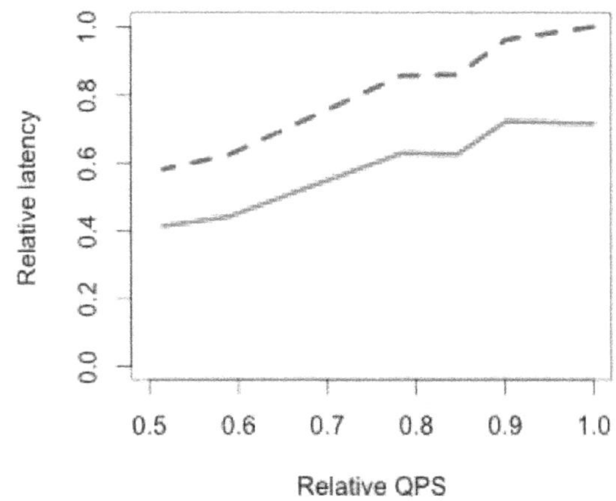

Figure 7: Efficiency (relative 90th percentile latency) vs. relative QPS. Dashed blue line represents baseline, red line represents learned candidate selection model.

6.5 Effect of Varying Index Sizes and Traffic Loads

We also investigated the scalability of our framework by varying index sizes and traffic loads and measuring the impact on the efficiency (latency) in the online system. For these experiments, we used the candidate selection model with (offline) recall value of 0.90.

Figure 6 shows the plot of relative latency vs. relative index size. We observed roughly linear increase in latency as the index size was increased (keeping other parameters such as the number of machines and the traffic load fixed). Since the inverted index is distributed across multiple machines in our architecture, the problem of growing index size can be mitigated by increasing the number of searcher nodes.

Figure 7 presents the effect of increasing traffic load (QPS) on latency. For both the baseline model (dashed blue line) and the candidate selection model (red line), we observed about 65% to 70% increase in latency when QPS was doubled. In particular, the extent of latency reduction for the candidate selection model compared to the baseline remained about the same, demonstrating that the efficiency gain of our proposed framework is robust under different traffic loads.

7. DEPLOYMENT LESSONS

We have deployed our candidate selection strategies as part of the job recommendation system at LinkedIn. Deployment procedure was incremental, where we rolled out the model in several steps to a progressively larger proportion of LinkedIn users. As the amount of traffic to our online system varies depending on the day of the week (for example, relatively large traffic on Mondays compared to the weekends), we carefully monitored the load on the production system upon any deployment changes and gradually increased the traffic allocation on a weekly basis. We noticed that the freshness of the data was very critical to the relevance quality of our system, and hence scheduled major index updates to occur at least daily.

Our experience also highlights the crucial need to leave a certain percent of traffic (*e.g.*, 5%) served by the baseline model, which has highest recall. This traffic allocation is needed to generate unbiased training data for retraining and refreshing the candidate selection model in the future. Otherwise, false negative results from the current model will never be shown to users and hence cannot serve as positive examples during future model training.

During deployment, we also measured the quality of retrieved results in different user segments. A large fraction of the requests for job recommendations comes from active job seekers on LinkedIn. Typically such users tend to have richer and more complete profiles. As a result, the constructed Galene query associated with an active user typically is longer, and consists of Boolean clauses over a significantly large number of literals (item field/value pairs). As discussed in §6, our candidate selection query model favorably helped to serve job recommendations to active users with reduced latency, without sacrificing the quality of the results. At the same time, there are also users on LinkedIn with relatively less rich and complete profiles, for whom we need to serve job recommendations. During initial stages of deployment, we noticed that lesser number of job documents were retrieved for users with lower profile completion when the learned candidate selection model was used, thereby potentially resulting in lower quality of recommendations. Towards better understanding and quantification of this issue, we compared the number of users that are served job recommendation

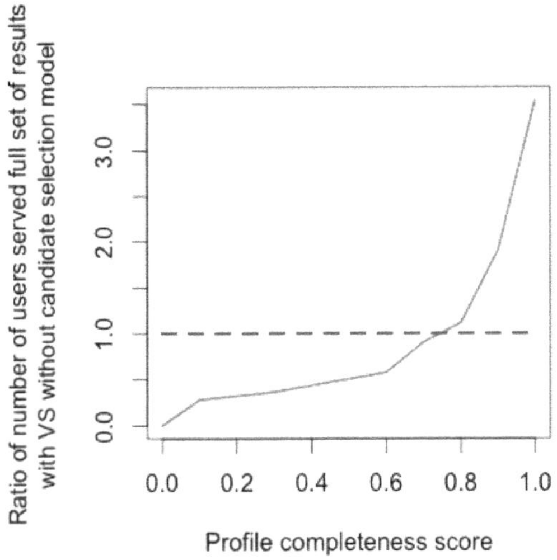

Figure 8: Dependency of ratio of number of users served on profile completeness score.

results with and without learned candidate selection models as a function of a score indicating the extent of richness/completion of a user's profile ('profile completeness score'). More precisely, for each score value, we computed the ratio of (1) the fraction of users within a narrow range of this score that are being served job recommendations using candidate selection model to (2) the fraction of users within a narrow range of this score that are being served job recommendations without candidate selection model. In Figure 8, the X-axis denotes the 'profile completeness score' and the Y-axis denotes the above ratio. We observe that for users with relatively low profile completeness score, the candidate selection based model resulted in a reduced chance of getting a full set of job recommendations (represented as the region where the red line is below the dashed blue line). An explanation is that our initial model was trained with data mostly from active users with relatively high profile completeness score.

Our solution to address this problem was to target users differently depending on their profile completeness score, by using different candidate selection models and/or lowering threshold for the candidate selection model, and in particular, to train a less strict candidate selection model for users with low profile completeness scores.

8. CONCLUSION

Motivated by the requirements of real-time personalized search and recommendation systems at LinkedIn, we studied the problem of building candidate selection models over structured queries and documents. We proposed *CaSMoS*, a machine learned candidate selection framework that makes use of Weighted AND (WAND) query. We developed and deployed our framework as part of the production system that powers LinkedIn's job recommendation engine, resulting in significant reduction in latency (up to 25%) without sacrificing the quality of the retrieved results. We showed the efficacy of the proposed framework through extensive experiments on real datasets using offline metrics as well as online A/B testing evaluation. We also presented the design decisions and tradeoffs faced while building and evaluating our framework, and highlighted the lessons learned through the production deployment of our system.

9. ACKNOWLEDGMENTS

The authors would like to thank Parul Jain, Kaushik Rangadurai, and Lance Wall for their help in the implementation and deployment of our system as part of LinkedIn's job recommendation engine, and David Hardtke and Liang Zhang for insightful feedback.

10. REFERENCES

[1] Apache Kafka. http://kafka.apache.org/.

[2] G. Adomavicius and A. Tuzhilin. Context-aware recommender systems. In *Recommender systems handbook*. Springer, 2015.

[3] E. Al Mashagba, F. Al Mashagba, and M. O. Nassar. Query optimization using genetic algorithms in the vector space model. *International Journal of Computer Science Issues (IJCSI)*, 8(5), 2011.

[4] A. Anagnostopoulos, A. Z. Broder, and K. Punera. Effective and efficient classification on a search-engine model. In *CIKM*, 2006.

[5] Y. Aphinyanaphongs and C. Aliferis. Learning Boolean queries for article quality filtering. In *MEDINFO*, 2004.

[6] N. Asadi and J. Lin. Effectiveness/efficiency tradeoffs for candidate generation in multi-stage retrieval architectures. In *SIGIR*, 2013.

[7] M. Bazire and P. Brézillon. Understanding context before using it. In *CONTEXT*, 2005.

[8] M. Bilenko, B. Kamath, and R. J. Mooney. Adaptive blocking: Learning to scale up record linkage. In *ICDM*, 2006.

[9] A. Z. Broder, D. Carmel, M. Herscovici, A. Soffer, and J. Zien. Efficient query evaluation using a two-level retrieval process. In *CIKM*, 2003.

[10] S. Chaudhuri. An overview of query optimization in relational systems. In *PODS*, 1998.

[11] P. Dourish. What we talk about when we talk about context. *Personal and ubiquitous computing*, 8(1), 2004.

[12] G. W. Flake, E. J. Glover, S. Lawrence, and C. L. Giles. Extracting query modifications from nonlinear SVMs. In *WWW*, 2002.

[13] J.-T. Horng and C.-C. Yeh. Applying genetic algorithms to query optimization in document retrieval. *Information processing & management*, 36(5), 2000.

[14] N. McNeill, H. Kardes, and A. Borthwick. Dynamic record blocking: Efficient linking of massive databases in MapReduce. In *QDB*, 2012.

[15] S. Sriram and A. Makhani. LinkedIn's Galene Search engine, 2014. https: //engineering.linkedin.com/search/did-you-mean-galene.

[16] N. Tonellotto, C. Macdonald, and I. Ounis. Efficient and effective retrieval using selective pruning. In *WSDM*, 2013.

[17] Y. Xu, N. Chen, A. Fernandez, O. Sinno, and A. Bhasin. From infrastructure to culture: A/B testing challenges in large scale social networks. In *KDD*, 2015.

Domain Adaptation in the Absence of Source Domain Data

Boris Chidlovskii, Stéphane Clinchant and Gabriela Csurka
Xerox Research Centre Europe
6 chemin Maupertuis, Meylan, France

ABSTRACT

The overwhelming majority of existing domain adaptation methods makes an assumption of freely available source domain data. An equal access to both source and target data makes it possible to measure the discrepancy between their distributions and to build representations common to both target and source domains. In reality, such a simplifying assumption rarely holds, since source data are routinely a subject of legal and contractual constraints between data owners and data customers. When source domain data can not be accessed, decision making procedures are often available for adaptation nevertheless. These procedures are often presented in the form of classification, identification, ranking etc. rules trained on source data and made ready for a direct deployment and later reuse. In other cases, the owner of a source data is allowed to share a few representative examples such as class means.

In this paper we address the domain adaptation problem in real world applications, where the reuse of source domain data is limited to classification rules or a few representative examples. We extend the recent techniques of *feature corruption* and their *marginalization*, both in supervised and unsupervised settings. We test and compare them on private and publicly available source datasets and show that significant performance gains can be achieved despite the absence of source data and shortage of labeled target data.

Keywords

Domain adaptation; classification; machine learning; marginalization; emerging applications

1. INTRODUCTION

While huge volumes of unlabeled data are generated and made available in many domains, the cost of acquiring data labels remains high. Domain Adaptation (DA) problems arise each time when we need to leverage labeled data in one or more related *source* domains, to learn a classifier for unseen data in a *target* domain. The domains are assumed to be related, but not identical in which case it becomes a standard machine learning problem. Such a situation occurs in multiple real world applications. Examples include named entity recognition across different text corpora, object recognition in images acquired in different conditions (like background scene, object location and pose, view angle changes), and many others (see [25, 34, 39] for a survey on transfer learning and domain adaptation methods).

Domain adaptation is particularly critical for service companies operating customer business processes in customer care, human resource and finance. All machine learning components deployed in a given service solution should be customized to a new customer. This entails re-annotating data or calibrating the models in order to achieve a contractual performance. For example, in vehicle classification, when an image classification algorithm is re-deployed in a new location, better performance is obtained by annotating samples collected on the field. In the brand sentiment management, when a sentiment classifier is re-deployed for a new customer, it is critical to tune the classifier to the manner how users talk about their experience with a particular product, etc.

Numerous approaches have been proposed in the last years to address the text and visual domain adaptation to cite just a few [3, 6, 18, 19, 20, 22, 23, 24, 30, 32, 36]. The majority of existing methods makes an assumption of freely available source domain data. An equal access to both source and target data allows to measure the discrepancy between their distributions and 1) either build representations common to both target and sources, or 2) directly reuse some source instances for a better target classification [43].

In reality, such a simplifying assumption rarely holds. Source data are often a subject of legal, technical and contractual constraints between data owners and data customers. Beyond privacy and disclosure obligations, customers are often reluctant to share their data. When operating customer care, collected data may include information on recent technical problems which is a highly sensitive topic that companies are not willing to share.

It is more common that just *decision making procedures* but not source domain data are available for adaptation. These procedures are often presented in the form of classification, identification, ranking etc. rules trained on source data and made ready for a direct deployment and later reuse. In other cases, the owner of a source data is not allowed to share the entire dataset, but some representative source examples such as class means.

In this paper we address the domain adaptation problem in real world applications, where the reuse of source data is limited to classification rules or a few representative examples. We adopt the recent techniques of *feature corruption* and their *marginalization*, both in the supervised (the Marginalized Corrupted Features [31]) and unsupervised (stacked Marginalized Denoising Autoencoder [7]) frameworks. We propose several extensions to MCF ad sMDA methods in order to address the adaptation needs with no access to source domain data. We cope with three most typical cases of what is available for adaptation: 1) classifiers as a black box, 2)

KDD '16, August 13–17, 2016, San Francisco, CA, USA

DOI: http://dx.doi.org/10.1145/2939672.2939716

classifiers with known models and parameters, and 3) class representatives.

The remainder of the paper is organized as follows. In Section 2 we present several industrial applications on customer data with a critical need for domain adaptation. In Section 3 we revise the prior art and Section 4 presents how to extend MCF ad sMDA methods to address these adaptation needs, in both supervised and unsupervised settings. Publicly available datasets of Office and Amazon, as well on Xerox's Smart Document Management data are described in Section 5.1. In Section 5, we describe the experimental setting and report the evaluation results of adapting the source classifiers and representatives on the selected datasets. Section 6 discusses the open questions and concludes the paper.

2. TARGET APPLICATIONS

In this section, we present three real world applications with a strong domain adaptation need and no access to source domain instances.

2.1 Vehicle Passenger Detection System

Upon a strong demand for *vehicle occupancy count* (VOC) automation in the US tolling and European border crossing, Xerox has developed *Vehicle Passenger Detection System* (VPDS)[1]

Figure 1: VPDS annotation/classification interface at French-Swiss border.

The VPDS is a two-camera system that takes one photograph through the front windscreen of the car, and another one on the side of the car, looking into the back seat. Using the two photos, the system calculates whether the car contains just the driver, the driver plus one passenger, or the driver plus two or more passengers. The project started with one week of "training" the system on the field. Compliance with data protection law is ensured by applying non-reversible blurring techniques to the photographs to prevent facial and number plate recognition; and by retaining the photographs for no more than five days. The results proved the system to be 95% accurate in counting occupants.

The technical solution consists of the car detection, car location in the image, and the VOC classifiers. When the front and side cameras take a photo, the object detectors first localize the information zones in these images. In particular, the visor breeze to the front image and the rear window to the side image. The front and side classifiers then estimate probability of passenger presence in the car. The last module aggregates these probabilities into a final estimate of the vehicle occupancy rate.

[1]http://www.xerox.com/downloads/usa/en/bpo/casestudies/bpo_casestudy_jougne.pdf

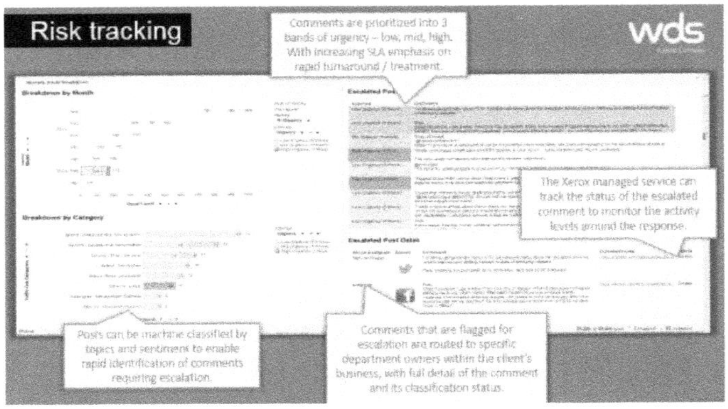

Figure 2: EMPATH Text Analytics GUI.

All classifiers are learned during the training period, when the image annotation tool (see Figure 1) is used to screen the images and to associate each car image with one of the labels, 1, 2 or "3 or more". The training of the algorithm includes annotating the image pairs and estimating optimum parameters to classify the new images.

When a new VPDS installation is requested, the "training" period and annotation cost is expected to be reduced by emerging domain adaptation techniques. As all images are destroyed after five days, the VOC classifiers are the only components to be reused from one VPDS installation to another.

2.2 EMPATH

EMPATH is a product developed by Xerox for customer analytics[2] It aims to understand customers' experiences, needs, and opinions in order to improve operations, products and services offered to customers. EMPATH starts by gathering data from a range of text sources (social media, news feeds, emails, chat and surveys). Collected data is then analyzed by an operator with the help of a text analytics engine. The operator tags one to two hundred posts, which are then used for training statistical models. This analysis helps operators better answer customer requests, to report upcoming issues and to provide valuable insights on product development.

In the text analytics engine, topic models, categories and sentiment classifiers are treated as domain and customer dependent. For some domains (such as *IT* and *mobile phone*), major concerns are similar and domain adaptation has been shown to reduce the annotation burden.

The main text analytics GUI is presented in Figure 2. Using the interface, the operator extracts topics from the text, creates categories to detect coming issues and monitors customer satisfaction with the sentiment predictions. As customers disallow to share their data, operators face the problem of wasting their time and resource by starting the analytics processes from scratch. As certain components, topics, categories and sentiments are common to many brand customers, the adaptation of classifiers across domain and customers represents a strong opportunity for the EMPATH product.

2.3 Print and Document Usage Analytics

As a part of Print and Document Management Services, Xerox offers to their customers facilities to automate and simplify the management of paper and electronic documents. The dematerialization services and process automation offered by Xerox help

[2]http://www.wds.co/product/contact-center/social-media/

streamline client's business processes to drive growth, and to reduce costs.

As documents vary a lot by their origin, layout and content, there exists a strong need to evolve a workflow for the same client, as well as to redeploy the workflow for new clients, under all legal obligations.

In Section 5, document collections from three customers and evaluation results of domain adaptation are presented in more details.

3. STATE OF THE ART

Domain adaptation for text data has been studied for more than a decade, with applications in statistical machine translation, opinion mining, part of speech tagging and document ranking [15, 32, 44]. Most effective techniques include feature replication [14, 15], pivot features [4, 32] and finding topic models shared by source and target collections [9, 10]. Domain adaptation has equally received a lot of attention in computer vision [3, 6, 17, 18, 19, 20, 22, 23, 24, 30, 32, 36, 38] where *domain shift* is a consequence of changing conditions, such as background, location and pose, etc. and, more generally, a strong bias between datasets.

A considerable effort to systematize different domain adaptation and transfer learning techniques has been undertaken in [25, 34, 39]. These studies distinguish three main categories of domain adaptation methods. The first category aims at correcting sampling bias and this family of models gives more weight in the classification loss to instances more similar to the target collection [43]. The second category is in the line with multi-task learning where a common predictor is learned for all domains, which makes it robust to domain shift [6]. The third family seeks to find common representation between source and target examples so that the classification task is eased [33]. In a nutshell, models of this family aim at inferring *domain invariant features*. Finally, an important research direction deals with the theory of domain adaptation; it studies conditions and assumptions for which the adaptation can be effective and generalization bounds can be provided [2].

More recently, deep learning has been proposed as a generic solution to domain adaptation and transfer learning problems [11, 22, 29]. One successful method which aims to find common features between source and target collection relies on *denoising autoencoders*. In deep learning, a denoising autoencoder is a one-layer neural network trained to reconstruct input data from partial random corruption [40]. The denoisers can be stacked into multi-layered architectures where the weights are fine-tuned with back-propagation. Alternatively, outputs of intermediate layers can be used as input features to other learning algorithms. This learned feature representation has been applied to domain adaptation [22], where stacked denoising autoencoders (SDA) achieved top performance in sentiment analysis tasks. The main drawback of SDAs is the long training time and Chen et al. [7] proposed a variation of SDA where the random corruption is *marginalized out*. This crucial step yields a unique optimal solution which is computed in closed form and eliminates therefore the back-propagation. In addition, features learned with such an approach lead to classification accuracy comparable with SDAs, with a remarkable reduction of the training time [7, 42].

Several deep learning approaches have demonstrated their ability to learn robust features and that good transfer performance could be obtained by just fine tuning the neural network on the target task [11]. While such solutions perform relatively well on some tasks, the refinement may require a significant amount of new labeled data. Recent works by Ganin et al. [20, 21] have proposed better strategies than fine tuning: adding a domain prediction task while learning the deep neural network leads to better domain-invariant feature representation. Their approach obtained a significant performance gain which shows that transfer learning is not completely solved by fine tuning and that transfer tasks should be addressed by appropriate deep learning representations.

Nevertheless, the majority of domain adaptation methods makes an assumption of largely available source collections. Such assumption rarely holds in reality. The source instances may become unavailable for technical reasons, or are disallowed to store for legal and contractual reasons. When objects are to be removed from a database, it also makes privacy preserving machine learning methods inapplicable [1, 5].

The case of available source classifiers have been considered by Duan et al. in [17], where their contribution is limited to regularizing the supervised target classifier. On the other hand, this case has been studied by domain adaptation theory [28]. Particularly, a theoretical analysis was conducted by considering the algorithmic stability of source classifiers. It was shown that the relatedness of source and target domains accelerates the convergence of the Leave-One-Out (LOO) error to the generalization error, thus enabling the use of the LOO error to stop the adaptation learning. In case of unrelated domains, it also suggests how to prevent negative transfer, so that in the limit it does not hurt the performance in the target domain.

4. DOMAIN ADAPTATION WITH CLASSIFIERS

We define a domain $\mathcal{D}$ as composed of a feature space $\mathcal{X} \subset R^D$ and a label space $\mathcal{Y}$. Any given task in domain $\mathcal{D}$ (classification, regression, ranking, etc.) is defined by a function $h : \mathcal{X} \to \mathcal{Y}$.

In the domain adaptation setting, we assume working with n_S+1 domains, including n_S source domains $\mathcal{D}^s, s = 1, \ldots, n_S$ and a target domain $\mathcal{D}^t$. In conventional setting the source data $X^s = [X_1, \ldots, X_{n_S}]$, with the corresponding labels $Y^s = [Y_1, \ldots Y_{n_S}]$ are available. In the absence of source data, we assume to have at our disposal either 1) a set $\mathcal{F}$ of classifiers f_k, $k = 1, \ldots, K$, each being trained on source data where at least one classifier is available for source domain $\mathcal{D}^s$, or 2) a set of representatives for each $\mathcal{D}^s$, $s = 1, \ldots, n_S$.

A close analysis of target applications (see Section 2) reveals three important cases to consider; they reflect different situations and complexity levels, as follows:

1. Models and parameters θ_k of source classifiers $f_k \in \mathcal{F}$ are known; for example we might know they are linear and have access to their parameter vectors $\theta_k = \mathbf{w}_k$;
2. Models of classifiers $f_k \in \mathcal{F}$ are unknown; they are used as a black box and, for a target instance $\mathbf{x}_i^t$, predict a class c probabilities $P(y_i^t = c|\mathbf{x}_i^t; \mathcal{F})$;
3. In the target domain, we may have access to both labeled and unlabeled instances, denoted X_l^t and X_u^t accordingly.

The domain adaptation problem then consists of leveraging the source labeled and target unlabeled data to derive a hypothesis performing well on the target domain. To achieve this goal, most DA methods compute covariance or correlation between features from source and target domains. With no or limited access to source data, we argue that the above principle can be extended to *the correlation between target features and the source class decisions*. We thus tune the *adaptation trick* by considering predicted class probabilities as augmented features for target data. Domain adaptation algorithms can then be used to find relations between features which were related in the source with features which seem also related in the target collection. In other words, we use the source classifiers *as a pivot* to transfer knowledge from source to target.

In the following section, we propose solutions to address the three cases mentioned above:

1. When source classifiers are known and they are linear, we extend the Marginalized Corrupted Features (MCF) method [31] to jointly marginalize the corrupted features and predictions;
2. When source classifiers are used as a black box, we can either a) marginalize their predictions with labeled data or b) denoise these predictions with unlabeled target data and Marginalized Denoising Autoencoders;
3. When class means are available as source representatives, we can use them as a Domain Specific Class Means classifier, and denoise their predictions jointly with unlabeled target data.

In the following we will discuss the unsupervised setting where no target instance is labeled, $\mathbf{X}_l^t = \emptyset$, and the supervised setting where a few target examples (for each class) are labeled. To address these problems, we adapt on one hand the Marginalized Corrupted Features that allows to address the problem when target labels are available and, on the other hand, the stacked Marginalized Denoising Autoencoder (sMDA) [7] framework to address the case when no labeled target instances are available.

4.1 Supervised Adaptation with MCF

First, we assume that a set of target instances were manually labeled and we consider the Marginalized Corrupted Features framework to address our specific domain adaptation cases.

To marginalize the corrupted features in the MCF, a corrupting distribution is first defined to transform observations $\mathbf{x}$ into corrupted versions $\tilde{\mathbf{x}}$. The corrupting distribution is assumed to factorize over all feature dimensions and, each individual distribution is assumed to be a member of the natural exponential family, $p(\tilde{\mathbf{x}}|\mathbf{x}) = \prod_{d=1}^{D} P(\tilde{x}_d|x_d;\theta_d)$, where $\mathbf{x} = (x_1,\ldots,x_D)$ and $\theta_d, d = 1,\ldots,D$ is a parameter of the corrupting distribution on dimension d.

The corrupting distribution can be unbiased ($\mathbb{E}[\tilde{\mathbf{x}}]_{p(\tilde{\mathbf{x}}|\mathbf{x})} = \mathbf{x}$) or biased. Known examples of distribution P are the blankout [40], Gaussian, Laplace and Poisson noise [31]. For example, in the unbiased blankout noise, $p(\tilde{x} = 0) = q$ and $p(\tilde{x} = \frac{x}{1-q}) = 1 - q$, with expectation $\mathbb{E}[\tilde{x}] = x$ and variance $Var[\tilde{x}] = \frac{q}{1-q}x^2$.

For the generalization of a classifier using corrupting distribution P, the direct approach is to corrupt each element of the target training set $\mathcal{D}^t = \{(\mathbf{x}_n, y_n)\}, n = 1,\ldots,N$. The extended data set $\tilde{\mathcal{D}}^t$ can be used for training the model by minimizing

$$\mathcal{L}(\tilde{\mathcal{D}}^t;\Theta) = \sum_{n=1}^{N}\frac{1}{M}\sum_{m=1}^{M} L(\tilde{\mathbf{x}}_{nm}, y_n;\Theta), \quad (1)$$

where $\tilde{\mathbf{x}}_{nm} \sim p(\tilde{\mathbf{x}}_{nm}|\mathbf{x}_n)$ is the m-th corrupted observation of $\mathbf{x}_n$ and Θ is the set of model parameters. As explicit corruption comes at a high computational cost, the *marginalization trick* is to consider the limiting case $M \to \infty$, where the weak law of large numbers is applied to rewrite $\frac{1}{M}\sum_{m=1}^{M} L(\tilde{\mathbf{x}}_{nm}, y_n;\Theta)$ as its expectation $\mathbb{E}[L(\tilde{\mathbf{x}}_{nm}, y_n;\Theta)]$. It has been shown that dropout marginalization plays the role of regularization [41]. Classifiers can be trained efficiently with quadratic, exponential, logistic [31] and hinge loss [8], they generalize better and are more robust to missing feature values at test time. In this paper we focus on the quadratic loss which allows a closed form solution[3].

Driven by our target applications in Section 2, we consider the multi-class case where label space $\mathcal{Y}$ includes C classes. We denote by $\mathbf{y}_n$ the vector of size C, where the component c corresponding to the class label of $\mathbf{x}_n$ is set to 1, and all others set to 0.

The expected value of the quadratic loss under corrupting distribution $p(\tilde{\mathbf{x}}|\mathbf{x})$ is given by [4]

$$\begin{aligned}\mathcal{L}(\mathcal{D};\mathbf{\Omega}) &= \mathbb{E}[\textstyle\sum_n \|\mathbf{\Omega}^\top\tilde{\mathbf{x}}_n - \mathbf{y}_n\|^2] \\ &= tr(\textstyle\sum_n (\mathbf{\Omega}^\top\mathbb{E}[\tilde{\mathbf{x}}_n\tilde{\mathbf{x}}_n^\top]\mathbf{\Omega} - \mathbf{\Omega}^\top\mathbb{E}[\tilde{\mathbf{x}}_n]\mathbf{y}_n^\top \\ &\quad -\mathbf{y}_n\mathbb{E}[\tilde{\mathbf{x}}_n^\top]\mathbf{\Omega} + \mathbb{E}[\mathbf{y}_n\mathbf{y}_n^\top])),\end{aligned} \quad (2)$$

where $\mathbf{\Omega}$ is a $D\times C$ parameter matrix with column c seen as a linear classifier corresponding to the class c, and $tr(\cdot)$ is the matrix trace. The optimal solution for $\mathbf{\Omega}^*$ can be given in a closed form [31]

$$\mathbf{\Omega}^* = \left(\sum_{n=1}^{N}\mathbb{E}[\tilde{\mathbf{x}}_n\tilde{\mathbf{x}}_n^\top]\right)^{-1}\left(\sum_{n=1}^{N}\mathbb{E}[\tilde{\mathbf{x}}_n]\mathbf{y}_n^\top\right). \quad (3)$$

As the corruption distribution factorizes over all dimensions, $\mathbf{\Omega}^*$ depends only on the expectations $\mathbb{E}[\tilde{x}_{nd}]$ and variances $Var[\tilde{x}_{nd}]$ over individual dimensions d. Hence, for the unbiased distribution P we can write $\mathbf{\Omega}^* = \mathbf{Q}^{-1}\mathbf{P}$, where

$$\mathbf{P} = \sum_{n=1}^{N}\mathbf{x}_n\mathbf{y}_n^\top, \quad \mathbf{Q} = \textstyle\sum_{n=1}^{N}\left(\mathbf{x}_n\mathbf{x}_n^\top + diag\left(Var[\mathbf{x}_n]\right)\right), \quad (4)$$

and $diag(Var[\mathbf{x}_n])$ denotes the $D\times D$ diagonal matrix constructed with the variances $Var[\mathbf{x}_n]$.

4.2 Integrating source classifiers in MCF

In the case of available source classifiers, the explicit corruption (1) takes into account their predictions on corrupted instances, as $L(\tilde{\mathbf{x}}_{nm}, y_n, \mathcal{F};\mathbf{\Omega})$.

In the limiting case $M \to \infty$, we obtain the loss expectation

$$\mathcal{L}(\mathcal{D}^t, \mathcal{F};\mathbf{\Omega}) = \sum_{n=1}^{N}\mathbb{E}[L(\tilde{\mathbf{x}}_n, y_n, \mathcal{F};\mathbf{\Omega})], \quad (5)$$

where the corrupting distribution $p(\tilde{\mathbf{x}}_n|\mathbf{x}_n)$ factorizes over d dimensions.

Minimizing the expected loss value under the corruption model leads to learning with *marginalized corrupted features and source predictors*. The tractability of (5) depends on the choice of the loss function L and the corrupting distribution.

Let us denote the vector of all the predictions for a given corrupted target instance $\tilde{\mathbf{x}}_n$ by $\mathbf{f}(\tilde{\mathbf{x}}_n)$ and let $\mathbf{\Gamma}$ be the corresponding parameter matrix to be learned. The quadratic loss can then be written as

$$\begin{aligned}\mathcal{L}(\mathcal{D};\mathbf{\Omega},\mathbf{\Gamma}) &= \textstyle\sum_n \mathbb{E}\left[\left(\mathbf{\Omega}^\top\tilde{\mathbf{x}}_n + \mathbf{\Gamma}^\top\mathbf{f}(\tilde{\mathbf{x}}_n) - \mathbf{y}_n^\top\right)^2\right] \\ &= \textstyle\sum_n \mathbb{E}\left[\left(\begin{bmatrix}\mathbf{\Omega}\\ \mathbf{\Gamma}\end{bmatrix}^\top\begin{bmatrix}\tilde{\mathbf{x}}_n\\ \mathbf{f}(\tilde{\mathbf{x}}_n)\end{bmatrix} - \mathbf{y}_n^\top\right)^2\right],\end{aligned}$$

where source predictions $\mathbf{f}(\tilde{\mathbf{x}}_n)$ can be seen as augmented corrupted features under the same distribution $p(\tilde{\mathbf{x}}_n|\mathbf{x}_n)$.

[3]Other losses have been tested as well; the minimization with the exponential loss requires a gradient descent technique, the logistic and hinge losses are approximated by the upper bounds; they will be included in the extended version.

[4]For the notation simplicity, we omit subscript $p(\tilde{\mathbf{x}}|\mathbf{x})$ in $\mathbb{E}[\cdot]_{p(\tilde{\mathbf{x}}|\mathbf{x})}$.

The corresponding closed form solution can be written as:

$$\left[\begin{array}{c}\boldsymbol{\Omega}^* \\ \boldsymbol{\Gamma}^*\end{array}\right]^\top = \mathbf{Q}_\mathcal{F}^{-1}\mathbf{P}_\mathcal{F}, \tag{6}$$

$$\begin{aligned}\mathbf{Q}_\mathcal{F} &= \sum_n \mathbb{E}\left[\left[\begin{array}{c}\tilde{\mathbf{x}}_n \\ \mathbf{f}(\tilde{\mathbf{x}}_n)\end{array}\right]\left[\begin{array}{c}\tilde{\mathbf{x}}_n \\ \mathbf{f}(\tilde{\mathbf{x}}_n)\end{array}\right]^\top\right], \\ \mathbf{P}_\mathcal{F} &= \sum_n \mathbb{E}\left[\begin{array}{c}\tilde{\mathbf{x}}_n \\ \mathbf{f}(\tilde{\mathbf{x}}_n)\end{array}\right]\mathbf{y}_n^\top.\end{aligned}$$

Linear source classifiers. If source classifiers are known to be linear functions (Case 1 in Section 4), we can marginalize them out jointly with the corrupted features. If we know that $\mathbf{f}(\mathbf{x}) = \mathbf{A}^\top\mathbf{x}$, then we can estimate their expectation on a corrupted instance $\mathbf{x}$, $\mathbb{E}(f(\tilde{\mathbf{x}})) = \mathbb{E}(\mathbf{A}^\top\tilde{\mathbf{x}}) = \mathbf{A}^\top\mathbb{E}(\tilde{\mathbf{x}}) = f(\mathbb{E}(\tilde{\mathbf{x}}))$ and variance

$$\mathbb{E}[\mathbf{f}(\tilde{\mathbf{x}}_n)\mathbf{f}(\tilde{\mathbf{x}}_n)^\top] = \mathbb{E}[\mathbf{A}\tilde{\mathbf{x}}_n\tilde{\mathbf{x}}_n^\top\mathbf{A}^\top] = \mathbf{A}\,\mathbb{E}[\tilde{\mathbf{x}}_n\tilde{\mathbf{x}}_n^\top]\mathbf{A}^\top.$$

Hence, we can derive that

$$\begin{aligned}\mathbf{Q}_\mathcal{F} &= \sum_n \left[\begin{array}{cc}\mathbb{E}[\tilde{\mathbf{x}}_n\tilde{\mathbf{x}}_n^\top] & \mathbb{E}[\tilde{\mathbf{x}}_n\tilde{\mathbf{x}}_n^\top]\mathbf{A}^\top \\ \mathbf{A}\,\mathbb{E}[\tilde{\mathbf{x}}_n\tilde{\mathbf{x}}_n^\top] & \mathbf{A}\,\mathbb{E}[\tilde{\mathbf{x}}_n\tilde{\mathbf{x}}_n^\top]\mathbf{A}^\top\end{array}\right] \\ &= \sum_n \left[\begin{array}{c}\mathbf{I}_D \\ \mathbf{A}\end{array}\right]\mathbb{E}\left[\tilde{\mathbf{x}}_n\tilde{\mathbf{x}}_n^\top\right]\left[\begin{array}{c}\mathbf{I}_D \\ \mathbf{A}\end{array}\right]^\top = \mathbf{B}\mathbf{Q}\mathbf{B}^T \end{aligned} \tag{7}$$

and $\mathbf{P}_\mathcal{F} = \mathbf{B}\mathbf{P}$, where $\mathbf{B}$ denotes $[\begin{array}{c}\mathbf{I}_D \\ \mathbf{A}\end{array}]$.

Algorithm 1 Marginalized corrupted features and source predictions (MCFA).

Require: Labeled target dataset $X_l^t \in \mathbb{R}^{N_l \times D}$ with labels $\mathbf{Y}^t$
Require: Unlabeled target dataset $X_u^t \in \mathbb{R}^{N_u \times D}$
Require: Source classifiers $f_k \in \mathbb{R}^D \to [0..1]^C$
Generate class predictions $\mathbf{f}(\mathbf{x}_n^t)$ for labeled $\mathbf{x}_n^t \in X_l^t$
if f_k are known linear functions **then**
  Estimate $[\ \boldsymbol{\Omega}^*; \boldsymbol{\Gamma}^*\ ]$ by using (7)
else
  Compose an augmented dataset with $\mathbf{u}_\mathbf{n}^\mathbf{t} = [\mathbf{x}_n^t; \mathbf{f}(\mathbf{x}_n^t)]$
  Estimate $[\ \boldsymbol{\Omega}^*; \boldsymbol{\Gamma}^*\ ]$ by using (4) with $\mathbf{u}_\mathbf{n}^\mathbf{t}$.
end if
Generate class predictions $\mathbf{f}(\mathbf{x}_n^t)$ for unlabeled $\mathbf{x}_n^t \in X_u^t$
Estimate class labels as $\mathbf{y}^t = [\boldsymbol{\Omega}^*; \boldsymbol{\Gamma}^*]^\top[\mathbf{x}^t; \mathbf{f}(\mathbf{x}^t)]$
Label each $\mathbf{x}^t$ with $c^* = \text{argmax}_c\{y_c^t|\mathbf{y}^t\}$
return Labels for X_u^t

Classifiers as a black box. If the classifier parameters are unknown or they are complex nonlinear functions, it is hard to directly estimate their expectation and variance. Used as black boxes, they can generate class prediction for target instances.

In such a case, we approximate (6) by considering any $f_k(\mathbf{x}_n)$ as an additional feature for $\mathbf{x}_n$. We generate an augmented representation of the target instance as $\mathbf{u}_n = [\mathbf{x}_n, f_1(\mathbf{x}_n), \ldots, f_K(\mathbf{x}_n)]$. Instead of corrupting features $\tilde{\mathbf{x}}_n$ and marginalizing over known classifiers f_k, we assume that the corruption distribution P factorizes over augmented representation $\mathbf{u}_n$ as $p(\tilde{\mathbf{u}}|\mathbf{u}) = \prod_{d=1}^{D+K} P(\tilde{u}_d|u_d;\theta_d)$. In this case, (4) can be directly applied, where $\tilde{\mathbf{x}}_n$ is replaced by $\tilde{\mathbf{u}}_n$. Algorithm 1 summarizes all steps of joint marginalization of corrupted features and source predictions (MCFA). Figure 3 schematically shows the diagrams of training MCFA with known linear and black box classifiers.

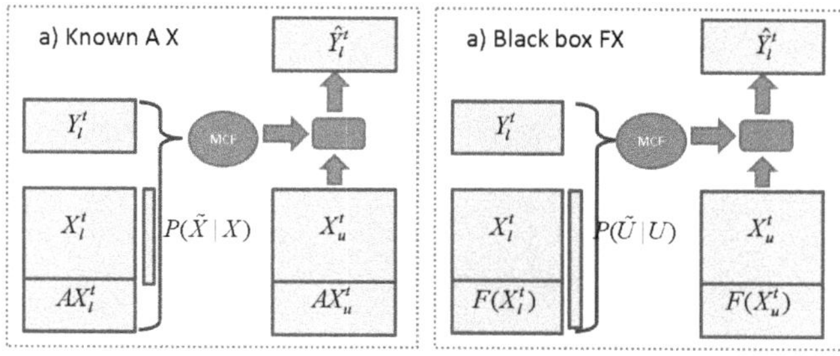

Figure 3: MCFA diagrams. Training with a) known linear classifiers and b) black box classifiers.

4.3 Unsupervised Adaptation

The main drawback of supervised setting presented in the previous section is that it requires target labels and does not exploit the unlabeled target instances X_u^t, which is generally much larger set than X_l^t. In this section we address the unsupervised domain adaptation case by marginalizing corrupted features in the denoising autoencoder framework.

The *stacked Marginalized Denoising Autoencoder* (sMDA) is a version of the multi-layer neural network trained to reconstruct input data from partial random corruption [40] proposed by Chen *et al.* [7] where the random corruption is marginalized out yielding the optimal reconstruction weights in the closed form.

The basic building block of the method is a one-layer linear denoising autoencoder where a set of sample inputs $\mathbf{x}_n$ are corrupted M times by random feature dropout with the probability p and reconstructed with a linear mapping $\mathbf{W} : R^D \to R^D$ by minimizing the squared reconstruction loss[5] :

$$\mathcal{L}(\mathbf{W}) = \sum_{n=1}^{N}\sum_{m=1}^{M} ||\mathbf{x}_n - \mathbf{W}\tilde{\mathbf{x}}_{nm}||^2. \tag{8}$$

By applying the marginalization trick described for MCF, the mapping $\mathbf{W}$ can be expressed in closed form as $\mathbf{W} = \mathbb{E}[\mathbf{P}]\,\mathbb{E}[\mathbf{Q}]^{-1}$, where

$$\mathbb{E}[\mathbf{Q}]_{ij} = \left[\begin{array}{ll}\mathbf{S}_{ij}q_iq_j, & \text{if} \quad i \neq j, \\ \mathbf{S}_{ij}q_i, & \text{if} \quad i = j,\end{array}\right. \quad \text{and} \quad \mathbb{E}[\mathbf{P}]_{ij} = \mathbf{S}_{ij}q_j, \tag{9}$$

where $q = [1-p, \ldots, 1-p, 1] \in R^{D+1}$, p is the dropout probability, D is the feature dimension and $\mathbf{S} = \mathbf{X}\mathbf{X}^T$ is the covariance matrix of the uncorrupted data $\mathbf{X}$.

Stacking together several MDA layers can create a *deep* architecture where we feed the representations of the $(l-1)^{th}$ denoising layer as the input to the lth layer and learn the transformation $\mathbf{W}^l$ to reconstruct the previous output from its corrupted equivalent. In order to extend the mapping beyond a linear transformation, between layers we apply on each output either a hyperbolic tangent function $\mathbf{h}_l = \texttt{tanh}(\mathbf{W}^l\mathbf{h}_{l-1})$ or rectified linear units (RELU) $\mathbf{h}_l = max(\mathbf{W}^t\mathbf{h}_{l-1}, 0)$. We will denote the final output $\mathbf{h}_l$ corresponding to the input $\mathbf{x}_n$ by $\hat{\mathbf{x}}_n$.

The main advantage of sMDA is that it does not require class labels; hence we can take advantage of the unlabeled target data and apply it for unsupervised domain adaptation. Indeed, [7] applied sMDA to the union of target and source datasets in order to learn domain invariant features.

In our case, X^S is unavailable, we have either access to source classifiers $\mathcal{F}$ or a set of representative source examples. We are

[5]A constant is added to the input, $\mathbf{x}_n = [\mathbf{x}_n; 1]$, and an appropriate bias incorporated within $\mathbf{W}$ which is is never corrupted.

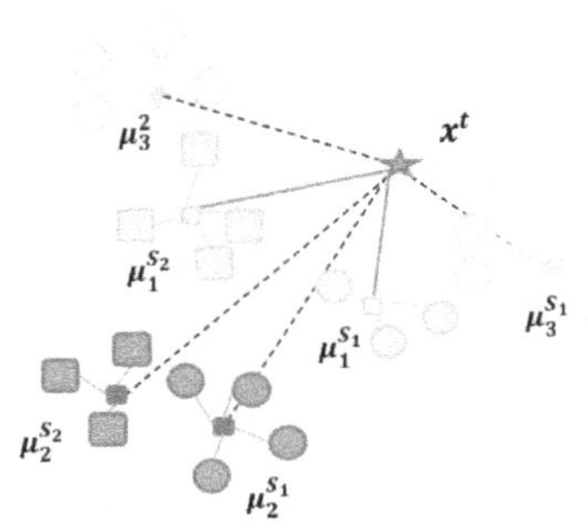

Figure 4: The DSCM class mean classifier.

interested in one particular case, when the representative examples are the class means for each domain X_s. Below we propose two different extensions of sMDA to these two cases.

4.4 Adaptation with Class Means

Class Means. If class means are available, they can be used both as classifiers and as data points. Used as classifiers, the class means can directly predict labels with a weighted softmax distance [13]. Used as representatives of source data, the class means can be concatenated with the target data and fed to sMDA for a joint denoising. The denoised class means can then classify the target test instances [12]. These two ways of using the class means are described in what follows.

The DSCM [13] classifier (see Figure 4) generates the class means per domain as

$$\boldsymbol{\mu}_c^d = \frac{1}{N_d^c} \sum_{\boldsymbol{x}_i \in \mathcal{D}_d \cap \mathcal{C}_c} \boldsymbol{x}_i, \tag{10}$$

where N_d^c is the number of instances from class $\mathcal{C}_c$ in the domain $\mathcal{D}_d$. Then it can predict the class label for an unlabeled target instance using a weighted softmax distance to these domain-specific class means:

$$p(c|\boldsymbol{x}_i) = \frac{\sum_d w_d e^{(-\|\boldsymbol{x}_i - \boldsymbol{\mu}_c^d\|)}}{\sum_{c'} \sum_d w_d e^{(-\|\boldsymbol{x}_i - \boldsymbol{\mu}_{c'}^d\|)}},$$

where w_d is the domain weight. In unsupervised domain adaptation, the DSCM make predictions with source class means μ_c^s. If some target instances are labeled, the classifier can additionally use the target class means μ_c^t.

The Adapted Class Means [12] classifier (ACM) is an extension of DSCM to unsupervised and semi-supervised settings. First, a sMDA is used to denoise the source class means. Instead of full source data $\mathbf{X}^S$, the source class means $[\mu_1^s, \ldots, \mu_C^s]$ concatenated with the unlabeled target data $\mathbf{X}_u^t$ are fed into the sMDA. The transformation matrix $\mathbf{W}$ obtained by (9) (or the set of stacked transformation matrices $\mathbf{W}^l$) is then used to jointly denoise the source class means $\hat{\mu}_c^s$ and the target examples $\hat{\mathbf{x}}_n^t$. The denoised class means $\hat{\mu}_c^s$ are then used by the classifier to predict labels for denoised target data.

Algorithm 2 reports all steps for the case of a single source; the generalization to multiple sources is straightforward.

4.5 Transductive domain adaptation

In the previous section we addressed the case of source representatives, available in the form of class means. Now we address the case of source classifiers available as a black box. They can be solely used for predicting labels, including for target domain instances. Such an unsupervised domain adaptation is of high interest for us, and we propose a Transductive Domain Adaptation (TDA) method which also relies on sMDA but uses it in the way different from the ACM.

Algorithm 2 Adapting Domain Specific Class Means (ACM).

Require: A large set of unlabeled target dataset $\mathbf{X}_u^t$ and optionally a small set of labeled $\mathbf{X}_l^t$
Require: A set of source class means $\mu_1^s, \ldots \mu_C^s$
Compute $\mathbf{W}$ using (9) with $\mathbf{X} = [\mu_1^s, \ldots \mu_C^s, \mathbf{x}_1^t, \ldots, \mathbf{x}_N^t]$ and noise level p
(Optionally) repeat l times, while alternating with $\mathbf{h}_l = \texttt{tanh}(\mathbf{W}^l \mathbf{h}_{l-1})$
Decompose $\mathbf{h}_l$ into reconstructed class means $\hat{\mu}_c^s$ and reconstructed targets $\hat{\mathbf{x}}_n^t$. (Optionally concatenate $\hat{\mathbf{x}}_n^t$ with the original features $\mathbf{x}_n^t$, and $\hat{\mu}_c^s$ with μ_c^s)
if Labeled target examples **then**
  $p(c|\mathbf{x}_n^t) = \frac{e^{(-\|\hat{\mathbf{x}}_n^t - \hat{\mu}_c^s\|)} + e^{(-\|\hat{\mathbf{x}}_n^t - \hat{\mu}_c^t\|)}}{\sum_{c'} \left(e^{(-\|\hat{\mathbf{x}}_n^t - \hat{\mu}_{c'}^s\|)} + e^{(-\|\hat{\mathbf{x}}_n^t - \hat{\mu}_{c'}^t\|)}\right)}$
else
  $p(c|\mathbf{x}_n^t) = \frac{e^{(-\|\hat{\mathbf{x}}_n^t - \hat{\mu}_c^s\|)}}{\sum_{c'} e^{(-\|\hat{\mathbf{x}}_n^t - \hat{\mu}_{c'}^s\|)}}$
end if
Label $\mathbf{x}_n^t$ with $c^* = \mathrm{argmax}_c\, p(c|\mathbf{x}_n^t)$
return Labels for X_u^t.

Like in Section 4.1, we consider class predictions $f_k(\mathbf{x}_n)$ as relevant but corrupted by the domain shift. Hence, we can exploit the correlation between the target data $\mathbf{x}_n$ and source predictions $\mathbf{f}(\mathbf{x}_n^t)$ to reconstruct (or denoise) both the target data and the source classifiers predictions of these target data. We apply the sMDA to the augmented dataset $U^t = [\mathbf{u}_1, \ldots \mathbf{u}_N]$ and compute $\mathbf{W}$; or stack several layers interleaved with nonlinear functions. We denote by $\hat{\mathbf{u}}_n$ the final output corresponding to the input $\mathbf{u}_n$.

In this case, we can directly use the reconstructed class predictions $\hat{\mathbf{f}}(\mathbf{x}_n^t)$ to make the classification decisions. If the set $\mathcal{F}$ includes a single source classifier f_1 with one prediction per class, the class with the maximum reconstructed value, $c^* = \mathrm{argmax}_c\, \mathbf{u}_n^{D+c}$ is assigned as label to $\mathbf{x}_n^t$. In the case of multiple classifiers f_k in $\mathcal{F}$, the maximum of the averaged predictions should be considered. Algorithm 3 summarizes all the steps of this transductive version of domain adaptation.

Algorithm 3 Transductive domain adaptation with mSDA (TDA).

Require: Target dataset $\mathbf{X}_t \in \mathbb{R}^{N \times D}$ without labels
Require: Source classifiers $f_k \in \mathbb{R}^D \to [0..1]^C$
Generate class predictions $\mathbf{f}(\mathbf{x}_n^t)$ for all $\mathbf{x}_n^t \in \mathbf{X}^t$
Compose an augmented dataset $\mathbf{U}$ with $\mathbf{u}_n^t = [\mathbf{x}_n^t; \mathbf{f}(\mathbf{x}_n^t)]$
Use sMDA to estimate $\mathbf{W} = min_{\mathbf{W}} ||\mathbf{U} - \mathbf{W}\tilde{\mathbf{U}}||^2$
Get denoised class predictions for $\mathbf{x}^t$ as $\mathbf{y}^t = \sum \mathbf{W}_{:,D+1:D+C} \mathbf{f}(\mathbf{x})$
Label $\mathbf{x}^t$ with $c^* = \mathrm{argmax}_c \{y_c^t | \mathbf{y}^t\}$.
return Labels for X_u^t

5. EXPERIMENTAL RESULTS

In this section we present a series of experiments to cope with domain adaptation tasks, along several important dimensions:

1. The amount of supervision in target domain; we consider *unsupervised, supervised and semi-supervised* settings.

2. Information available from the sources: *source linear classi-*

fier, source classifier as a black box, and source representatives in the form of *class means*.

3. When the classifier is a black box, we test different classification models, including common ones like SVM and Logistic Regression, and specific ones like MCF and DSCM.

We recall briefly all algorithms proposed in the previous sections:

MCFA (Section 4.2) is primarily *supervised domain adaptation* algorithm described in Algorithm 1. It includes two versions, **mcfal** when the source classifiers $f_k(\mathbf{x})$ are linear, and **mcfab** when $f_k(\mathbf{x})$ are used as a black box to predict class labels for a target example.

ACM (Section 4.4) assumes that *class means* are available from the source data. In the unsupervised setting, it uses the sMDA reconstructions of the class means to predict the class. In the semi-supervised setting, the target class means (μ_c^t) are learned from labeled target data; then, together with the source class means (μ_c^s), they are used to predict the class labels for target data (see Algorithm 2).

TDA (Section 4.5) is the transductive algorithm to denoise source class predictions with target data in unsupervised setting (see Algorithm 3).

The experiments are organized by the supervision type (unsupervised, supervised and semi-supervised); they aim to test performance of all algorithms on different datasets. Below we describe two image and one text datasets used in the experiments.

5.1 Datasets and Experimental Framework

XS3. This collection is a part of the Xerox's Smart Document Management data; it contains printed/scanned documents from three Xerox customers denoted by C_1, C_2 and C_3. The three datasets contain different types of documents such as invoices, contracts, IDs, filled forms, etc. All the documents have been grouped into 21 different classes, all well represented in each dataset (see examples in the Figure 5). Amongst these classes, some refer to generic concepts such as printed emails, computer programs, drawings, handwritten letters; some others (*contracts* and *filled forms*) form a more fine-grained class hierarchy, according to the customers' requirements. We manually aligned between the fine-grain classes have been manually aligned by their visual similarities as the correspondences is often not obvious.

The number of documents per class and per customer varies from 24 to 859; around 2.5K documents are available for each customer. As image representations we use deep convolutional activation features [16]. These features are obtained using publicly available Caffe CNN models[6] [27] trained on the 1000 classes of ImageNet [35] and fine-tuned for document images on the RVL-CDIP document image dataset[7] [26]. In our experiments we use the fully connected layer (caffe_fc6) of dimensionality 4096.

Due to the confidentiality clauses on X3S collection, we also run experiments on two publicly available benchmark datasets:

OFF31. One of the most popular datasets for comparing visual domain adaptation methods is the Office31 collection [36]. It consists of four domains: Amazon (A), Caltech (C), dslr (D) and Webcam (W) with images of 31 products (classes). Each domain is considered in its turn as a *target*, with the other domains considered as *sources*. For the target set we select 3 instances per class to

[6]https://github.com/BVLC/caffe/

[7]http://scs.ryerson.ca/~aharley/rvl-cdip/

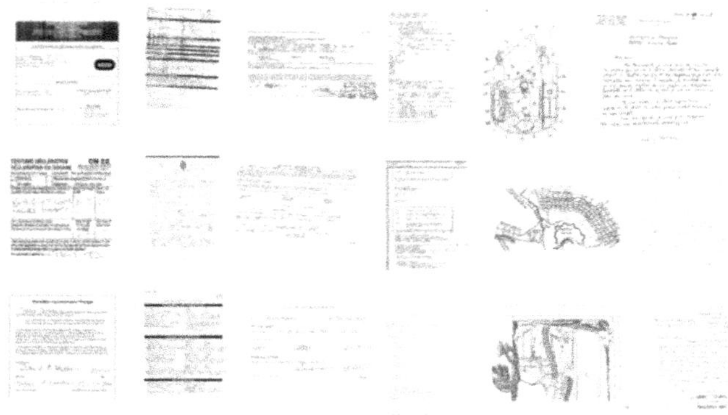

Figure 5: Examples from the XC3 datasets. Each line corresponds to one customer and each column refers to one document class (documents are intentionally blurred for privacy reasons).

form the training set, all other instances form the test set. We use the caffe_fc6 deep convolutional activation features [16] we obtain with the publicly available VGGNET (16 layer) CNN model [37] with no fine-tuning.

AMT. The Amazon text dataset consists of products reviews in four domains: Books (b), Dvd (d), Kitchen (k) and Electronics (e). While a book review can be quite different from a kitchen item review, there are nevertheless some common features to assess whether the users were satisfied with their purchase. A part of this collection was preprocessed by Blitzer et al. [3] and used subsequently in several domain adaptation studies. The task is to predict whether a customer review is positive or negative, where a review with more than 3 stars is considered as positive and (strictly) less than 3 as negative. Documents are represented by a bag of unigrams and bigrams. In our experiments, we only considered the top 10,000 most-frequent features for each domain. In all experiments, we use the whole source and target collections whereas other studies use a predefined split of 2000 documents per domain.

Finally, we list four classification models tested as source classifiers:

DSCM classifier [13] uses a softmax distance to the class specific means to classify a test example.

MCF [31] is a multi-class linear classifier with dropout noise probability fixed to 0.5 for image datasets (OFF31 and XC3) and 0.9 for text dataset (Amazon). Need for a stronger dropout level on text data is explained by its sparsity [12].

LR refers to a l_2 regularized Logistic Regression, cross-validated with the regularization parameter C, where $C \in [0.0001, 0.001, 0.1, 1, 10, 50, 100]$.

SVM is used with the RBF kernel, two main hyperparameters C and γ are fit by a random search, $C \sim Exp(scale = 100)$ and $\gamma \sim Exp(scale = .1)$. For both SVM and LR, the Scikit learn implementation is used [8].

5.2 Unsupervised Setting

In this setting, the baseline consists in classifying target data without any domain adaptation. We compare the performance of the unsupervised ACM with available class means to the TDA with the black box classifier.

[8]http://scikit-learn.org/stable/index.html

Table 1: Unsupervised adaptation in XS3 and OFF31 datasets with DSCM and TDA methods. Underline indicates improvement over the baseline and bold indicates the best performance per task.

f_s	dscm				mcf	
f_t	**smda***	$f_s(X^t)$	**acm**	**tda**	$f_s(X^t)$	**tda**
$S \rightarrow T$						
$C_2 \rightarrow C_1$	*37.18*	30.75	**41.11**	33.36	33.65	34.75
$C_3 \rightarrow C_1$	*37.58*	39.24	41.18	37.14	46.18	**47.8**
$C_1 \rightarrow C_2$	*53.92*	47.59	53.32	51.91	52.5	**54.1**
$C_3 \rightarrow C_2$	*62.16*	57.92	**66.07**	61.29	58.88	60.15
$C_1 \rightarrow C_3$	*36.11*	31.31	**47.34**	36.53	38.02	39.4
$C_2 \rightarrow C_3$	*38.64*	30.09	**41.74**	36.03	35.07	36.83
$D \rightarrow A$	*60.18*	56.91	**60.62**	59.71	56.4	57.83
$W \rightarrow A$	*60.07*	55.74	**61.88**	60.74	55.07	56.65
$A \rightarrow D$	*69.88*	71.36	67.65	70.12	72.84	**73.83**
$W \rightarrow D$	*95.56*	97.04	95.31	95.56	**99.75**	99.51
$A \rightarrow W$	*65.95*	64.1	67.24	68.8	67.95	**69.52**
$D \rightarrow W$	*93.16*	93.59	92.88	93.02	**96.87**	96.3

Table 1 reports results for 6 domain adaptation tasks in XS3 and 6 tasks in OFF31 dataset. Each line indicates an adaptation task $S \rightarrow T$, from source S to target T. Column 1, sMDA*, refers to the *dream case* of fully available source data; it shows classification accuracy of sMDA on full source and target data. Columns 3 to 5 correspond to cases where the source classifier f_s is a DSCM classifier. Column 3 reports the *baseline* accuracy when the source classifier is applied on the target test without adaptation, $f_s(X^t)$. Columns 4 (ACM) and 5 (TDA) show the results of applying the respective domain adaptation. Both methods in general outperform the baseline and achieve the accuracy values comparable with the dream case with full access to source data, and in general ACM outperforms TDA, showing that it is more interesting to adapt the class means (if available) than the softmax scores we obtain with. Finally, columns 6 and 7 show the classification accuracy when the source classifier is the MCF classifier and the source class means are unavailable. The TDA method outperforms the baseline MCF in most cases except the adaptation between D and W, that can be explained by the fact we have almost no domain shift between these two domains.

Table 2 shows the performance of the TDA model on the 12 adaptation tasks of the AMT dataset. We include accuracy values for MCF and LR source classifiers, but exclude results for DSCM and ACM as the class means classifier performs poorly on text data. On average, the LR classifier performs better. Compared to the baseline $f_s(X^t)$ and the dream case sMDA*, TDA always improves over the baseline and is often close to the dream case.

To sum up, domain adaptation with TDA is successful when the classification predictions are obtained with DSCM, MCF or LR. When we have access to the class means, adapting them with ACM seems to be a better strategy for image datasets. For the text dataset, TDA combined with LR predictions performs the best. In all cases, the performance of TDA and ACM is close to the dream case.

5.3 Supervised Setting

We assume now that some of the target instances are labeled, but no unlabeled target instances are given at the training time. For each adaptation task, there are *two baselines*. The first one consists in training the classifier on the labeled target instances; the second

Table 2: Unsupervised adaptation in AMT dataset with TDA method and MCF/LR source classifiers. Underline indicates improvement over the baseline and bold indicates the best performance per task.

f_s	mcf			lr		
f_t	**smda***	$f_s(X^t)$	**tda**	**smda***	$f_s(X^t)$	**tda**
$S \rightarrow T$						
$d \rightarrow b$	*80.81*	80.08	81.66	*84.59*	81.36	**82.61**
$e \rightarrow b$	*73.39*	71.22	73.25	*78.07*	73.87	**75.93**
$k \rightarrow b$	*74.93*	71.17	74.27	*78.75*	73.50	**75.02**
$b \rightarrow d$	*81.96*	80.31	82.07	*85.07*	82.54	**83.56**
$e \rightarrow d$	*75.91*	74.20	76.18	*79.99*	76.46	**77.67**
$k \rightarrow d$	*77.47*	76.03	78.39	*80.76*	77.58	**79.16**
$b \rightarrow e$	*77.47*	74.53	76.75	*80.32*	76.44	**78.54**
$d \rightarrow e$	*79.02*	76.03	78.62	*83.70*	78.65	**80.75**
$k \rightarrow e$	*87.16*	86.28	87.39	*89.05*	87.55	**88.38**
$b \rightarrow k$	*80.45*	76.86	79.31	*84.00*	79.46	**81.44**
$d \rightarrow k$	*81.44*	77.64	80.47	*86.08*	80.83	**83.15**
$e \rightarrow k$	*88.59*	87.72	88.87	*90.76*	89.97	**91.10**

one relies on the logistic regression model[9] trained on the concatenation of the raw target features and the source predictions. Both baselines are shown in italic in the tables. We run experiments with different source classifiers (MCF, SVM, DSCM) and evaluate the two proposed MCF extensions: MCFAl and MCFAb.

Table 3 presents evaluation results on XS3 and OFF31 datasets. Each column in the table shows the accuracy of the target classification using linear classifiers (Column 1) and the black box classifiers (Columns 2 to 4). For all tasks, the first supervised baseline is denoted as $T \rightarrow T$ (for ex., $C_1 \rightarrow C_1$), it refers to learning from labeled target data only. The second baseline is reported in the last column, it uses LR as the target classifier (f_t) that is trained on the target features concatenated with the source classifier predictions obtained with DSCM (f_s).

We can observe that both MCF extensions outperform the baseline LR trained on the concatenated features. Given the small amount of labeled data, the MCF is more appropriate to handle the noise and variability in data, which makes it better suited for domain adaptation and transfer tasks. We can see that MCFAb with SVM or DSCM predictions provide even better results and outperform both baselines; this witnesses a successful adaptation independently of which classifier is used in the black-box (f_s).

We have also conducted experiments on the AMT dataset where 10 target labels per class were used to compare several source classifiers. We do not include results here but report the main findings. MCF shows a better classification performance than LR when using the target features only (similarly to the image datasets). However, when the target data get combined with the source predictions, the LR baseline obtains better results than MCFAb. Adding the source classifier's predictions to the original target features brings an improvement over the supervised $T \rightarrow T$ baseline, for both LR and MCFA. However, due to a small amount of target labels, the $T \rightarrow T$ baseline is worse than the $S \rightarrow T$ one, and none approach is able to outperform the results obtained with the source classifier's predictions (f_s).

On the other hand, as shown in Table 2, combining the source predictions with the unlabeled target data outperforms significantly the results obtained with source predictions f_s. It points out that using the source predictions and the unsupervised denoising with TDA is a *much better* option than using any supervised method

[9]Experiments with SVM give very similar results.

Table 3: **Supervised adaptation in XS3 and OFF31 datasets with MCFA, using 3 labels per class. Underline indicates improvement over both baselines and bold indicates the best performance per task.**

f_s / f_t	mcf / mcfal	mcf / mcfab	svm / mcfab	dscm / mcfab	dscm / lr
XS3 Tasks					
$C_1 \to C_1$	*95.19*	*95.19*	*95.15*	*95.15*	*90.07*
$C_1, C_2 \to C_1$	95.41	94.75	**95.3**	95	*91.18*
$C_1, C_3 \to C_1$	95.44	95.3	95.41	**95.78**	*91.18*
$C_2 \to C_2$	*86.38*	*86.38*	*86.38*	*86.38*	*81.7*
$C_2, C_1 \to C_2$	86.48	86.98	87.75	**88.21**	*83.3*
$C_2, C_3 \to C_2$	86.61	88.8	87.93	**89.25**	*85.8*
$C_3 \to C_3$	*85.78*	*85.78*	*85.78*	*85.78*	*85.6*
$C_3, C_1 \to C_3$	86.01	86.09	**86.16**	**86.16**	*85.6*
$C_3, C_2 \to C_3$	86.05	85.97	**86.2**	86.09	*85.7*
OFF31 Tasks					
$A \to A$	*69.38*	*69.38*	*69.38*	*69.38*	*62.7*
$A, D \to A$	70.29	69.63	70.59	**70.96**	*66*
$A, W \to A$	70.44	**70.66**	70.07	70	*66.1*
$D \to D$	*89.63*	*89.63*	*89.63*	*89.63*	*87.9*
$D, A \to D$	89.14	**91.36**	90.12	90.37	*87.9*
$D, W \to D$	88.89	95.56	**96.05**	94.81	*89.6*
$W \to W$	*84.05*	*84.05*	*84.05*	*84.05*	*88.3*
$W, A \to W$	85.33	85.04	86.61	84.47	*87.3*
$W, D \to W$	84.76	91.03	90.46	**90.74**	*88.7*

Table 4: Semi-Supervised adaptation in XS3 and OFF31 datasets.

f_s	dscm			dscm	svm
X in smda	$[X^s, x^t]$	-	$[\mu^s, X^t]$	X^t $f_s(X^t)$	X^t $f_s(X^t)$
f_t	dscm*	dscm	acm	mcfab	mcfab
XS3 Task					
$C_1 \to C_1$	*96.51*	*94.16*	*96.51*	*96.51*	*96.51*
$C_1, C_2 \to C_1$	*95.52*	91.92	**96.47**	95.66	96.36
$C_1, C_3 \to C_1$	*96.36*	90.63	**96.66**	96.14	96.44
$C_2 \to C_2$	*92.26*	*86.93*	*92.26*	*92.26*	*92.26*
$C_2, C_1 \to C_2$	*92.99*	88.57	**93.58**	84.06	88.43
$C_2, C_3 \to C_2$	*94.08*	88.39	**94.54**	85.29	88.66
$C_3 \to C_3$	*88.31*	*86.78*	*88.31*	*88.31*	*88.31*
$C_3, C_1 \to C_3$	*87.39*	83.14	**86.62**	86.16	85.47
$C_3, C_2 \to C_3$	*86.81*	84.44	**88.46**	86.09	85.74
OFF31 Task					
$A \to A$	*69.49*	*70.33*	*69.49*	*69.49*	*69.49*
$A, D \to A$	*71.84*	**72.32**	71.95	70.96	70.55
$A, W \to A$	*71.91*	71.99	**72.21**	70.0	70.63
$D \to D$	*89.88*	*89.38*	*89.88*	*89.88*	*89.88*
$D, A \to D$	*89.14*	89.63	**90.37**	**90.37**	89.38
$D, W \to D$	*95.06*	**95.06**	94.57	94.81	92.59
$W \to W$	*84.33*	*83.76*	*84.33*	*84.33*	*84.33*
$W, A \to W$	*84.33*	85.04	85.61	84.47	**87.04**
$W, D \to W$	*91.03*	**92.02**	91.45	90.74	88.89

including the baselines. This clearly demonstrates the importance of having access to the unlabeled target data. It shows that the unsupervised domain adaptation can be highly beneficial for the accuracy gain and can considerably reduce the annotation cost.

5.4 Semi-supervised Setting

Lastly, we consider here a transductive semi-supervised setting. We assume that a large set of unlabeled target set $\mathbf{X}_u^t$ is available at the training time. The supervised baseline which uses only target labeled data and our algorithm MCFAb are used as baselines. They are compared to the semi-supervised version of ACM, which assumes available source class means. Despite this requirement, it is still interesting to compare these approaches to understand which classifiers can be more amenable to transfer.

Table 4 shows the evaluation results for 12 domain adaptation tasks in XS3 and OFF31 datasets. For each adaptation task, the supervised baseline is denoted $T \to T$; it trains a classifier on target labeled data only. Column 2 in the table reports the results of DSCM classifier in the supervised setting. Column 3 indicates the performance of sMDA with a DSCM classifier with *full access to source data*. The sMDA results help us measure the performance or adaptation methods under the limited or no access to the source data. Column 4 indicates the performance of the ACM model and Column 5 reports the supervised baseline MCFAB. The table reveals two important findings. First, the semi-supervised ACM brings additional gains comparing to the baselines. But the most important finding is that methods *without access* to source data (ACM, MFCAb) achieve performances close to the methods *with access* to source data (sMDA+DSCM, Column 2). This indicates that the classifier contains enough information for adaptation and upholds the result in unsupervised adaptation.

6. CONCLUSION

In this paper we address the problem of domain adaptation in real world applications, where the reuse of source data is limited, due to legal and contractual obligations, to classification rules or a few representative examples. We adapt the recent techniques of *feature corruption* and their *marginalization* developed for the supervised (MCF) and unsupervised (sMDA) settings. We propose several extensions to MCF and sMDA methods in order to address cases when the source classifiers are available either as a black box or with known parameters, or a few class representatives are from a source domain. We conduct a series of experiments on two public and one in-house datasets in supervised and unsupervised settings. We present the evaluation results and show that significant performance gains can be achieved despite the absence of source data and shortage of labeled target data. This result is an highly encouraging for a range of applications with machine learning components, whose adaptation to new domains and customers is expected to be low and without sacrificing the stated performance.

7. REFERENCES

[1] R. Agrawal and R. Srikant. Privacy-preserving data mining. In *Proc. of SIGMOD/PODS, (ACM)*, pages 439–450, 2000.

[2] S. Ben-David, J. Blitzer, K. Crammer, and F. Pereira. Analysis of representations for domain adaptation. In *Proc. of NIPS, (Curran Associates)*, pages 137–144, 2007.

[3] J. Blitzer, S. Kakade, and D. P. Foster. Domain adaptation with coupled subspaces. In *Proc. of AISTATS*, pages 173–181, 2011.

[4] J. Blitzer, R. McDonald, and F. Pereira. Domain adaptation with structural correspondence learning. In *Proc of EMNLP*, pages 120–128, 2006.

[5] K. Chaudhuri and C. Monteleoni. Privacy-preserving logistic regression. In *Proc. of NIPS, (Curran Associates)*, pages 289–296, 2008.

[6] M. Chen, K. Q. Weinberger, and J. Blitzer. Co-training for domain adaptation. In *Proc. of NIPS, (Curran Associates)*, pages 2456–2464, 2011.

[7] M. Chen, Z. Xu, K. Q. Weinberger, and F. Sha. Marginalized denoising autoencoders for domain adaptation. In *Proc. of ICML*, pages 767–774, 2012.
[8] N. Chen, J. Zhu, J. Chen, and B. Zhang. Dropout training for support vector machines. In *Proc. of AAAI*, pages 1752–1759, 2014.
[9] Z. Chen and B. Liu. Topic modeling using topics from many domains, lifelong learning and big data. In *Proc. of ICML*, pages 703–711, 2014.
[10] Z. Chen, A. Mukherjee, B. Liu, M. Hsu, M. Castellanos, and R. Ghosh. Leveraging multi-domain prior knowledge in topic models. In *Proc. of IJCAI, (AAAI)*, pages 2071–2077, 2013.
[11] S. Chopra, S. Balakrishnan, and R. Gopalan. DLID: Deep learning for domain adaptation by interpolating between domains. In *ICML Workshop on Challenges in Representation Learning (WREPL)*, 2013.
[12] G. Csurka, B. Chidlovskii, and S. Clinchant. Adapted domain specific class means. In *TASK-CV, ICCV workshop*, 2015.
[13] G. Csurka, B. Chidlovskii, and F. perronnin. Domain adaptation with a domain specific class means classifier. In *TASK-CV, ECCV workshop*, 2014.
[14] H. Daumé. Frustratingly easy domain adaptation. *CoRR*, arXiv:0907.1815, 2009.
[15] H. Daume III and D. Marcu. Domain adaptation for statistical classifiers. *Journal of Artificial Intelligence Research*, 26(1):101–126, 2006.
[16] J. Donahue, Y. Jia, O. Vinyals, J. Hoffman, N. Zhang, E. Tzeng, and T. Darrell. Decaf: A deep convolutional activation feature for generic visual recognition. *CoRR*, arXiv:1310.1531, 2013.
[17] L. Duan, I. W. Tsang, D. Xu, and T.-S. Chua. Domain adaptation from multiple sources via auxiliary classifiers. In *Proc. of ICML*, pages 289–296, 2009.
[18] L. Duan, D. Xu, and S.-F. Chang. Exploiting web images for event recognition in consumer videos: A multiple source domain adaptation approach. In *Proc. of CVPR, (IEEE)*, pages 1338–1345, 2012.
[19] B. Fernando, A. Habrard, M. Sebban, and T. Tuytelaars. Unsupervised visual domain adaptation using subspace alignment. In *Proc. of ICCV, (IEEE)*, pages 2960–2967, 2013.
[20] Y. Ganin and V. Lempitsky. Unsupervised domain adaptation by backpropagation. In *Proc. of ICML*, pages 1180–1189, 2015.
[21] Y. Ganin, E. Ustinova, H. Ajakan, P. Germain, H. Larochelle, F. Laviolette, M. Marchand, and V. S. Lempitsky. Domain-adversarial training of neural networks. *CoRR*, arXiv:1505.07818, 2015.
[22] X. Glorot, A. Bordes, and Y. Bengio. Domain adaptation for large-scale sentiment classification: A deep learning approach. In *Proc. of ICML*, pages 513–520, 2011.
[23] B. Gong, Y. Shi, F. Sha, and K. Grauman. Geodesic flow kernel for unsupervised domain adaptation. In *Proc. of CVPR, (IEEE)*, pages 2066–2073, 2012.
[24] R. Gopalan, R. Li, and R. Chellappa. Domain adaptation for object recognition: An unsupervised approach. In *Proc. of ICCV, (IEEE)*, pages 999–1006, 2011.
[25] R. Gopalan, R. Li, V. M. Patel, and R. Chellappa. Domain adaptation for visual recognition. *Foundations and Trends in Computer Graphics and Vision*, 8(4), 2015.
[26] A. W. Harley, A. Ufkes, and K. G. Derpanis. Evaluation of deep convolutional nets for document image classification and retrieval. In *Proc. of ICDAR*, pages 991–995, 2015.
[27] A. Krizhevsky, I. Sutskever, and G. Hinton. ImageNet classification with deep Convolutional Neural Networks. In *Proc. of NIPS, (Curran Associates)*, 2012.
[28] I. Kuzborskij and F. Orabona. Stability and hypothesis transfer learning. In *Proc. of ICML*, pages 942–950, 2013.
[29] M. Long, Y. Cao, J. Wang, and M. I. Jordan. Learning transferable features with deep adaptation networks. In *Proc. of ICML*, 2015.
[30] M. Long, J. Wang, G. Ding, J. Sun, and P. S. Yu. Transfer joint matching for unsupervised domain adaptation. In *Proc. of CVPR, (IEEE)*, 2014.
[31] L. v. d. Maaten, M. Chen, S. Tyree, and K. Weinberger. Learning with marginalized corrupted features. In *Proc. of ICML*, 2013.
[32] S. J. Pan, X. Ni, J.-T. Sun, Q. Yang, and Z. Chen. Cross-domain sentiment classification via spectral feature alignment. In *Proc. of WWW*, 2010.
[33] S. J. Pan, J. T. Tsang, Ivor W.and Kwok, and Q. Yang. Domain adaptation via transfer component analysis. *Transactions on Neural Networks*, 22(2):199 – 210, 2011.
[34] S. J. Pan and Q. Yang. A survey on transfer learning. *Transactions on Knowledge and Data Engineering*, 22(10):1345–1359, 2010.
[35] O. Russakovsky, J. Deng, H. Su, J. Krause, S. Satheesh, S. Ma, Z. Huang, A. Karpathy, A. Khosla, M. Bernstein, A. C. Berg, and L. Fei-Fei. Imagenet large scale visual recognition challenge. *International Journal of Computer Vision*, 115(3):211–252, 2015.
[36] K. Saenko, B. Kulis, M. Fritz, and T. Darrell. Adapting visual category models to new domains. In *Proc. of ECCV, (Springer)*, pages 213–226, 2010.
[37] K. Simonyan and A. Zisserman. Very deep convolutional networks for large-scale image recognition. *CoRR*, arXiv:1409.1556, 2014.
[38] B. Sun, J. Feng, and K. Saenko. Return of frustratingly easy domain adaptation. *CoRR*, arXiv:1511.05547, 2015.
[39] S. S. Sun, H. Shi, and Y. Wu. A survey of multi-source domain adaptation. *Information Fusion*, 24:84–92, 2015.
[40] P. Vincent, H. Larochelle, Y. Bengio, and P.-A. Manzagol. Extracting and composing robust features with denoising autoencoders. In *Proc. of ICML*, 2008.
[41] S. Wager, S. I. Wang, and P. Liang. Dropout training as adaptive regularization. In *Proc. of NIPS, (Curran Associates)*, pages 351–359, 2013.
[42] Z. Xu, M. Chen, K. Q. Weinberger, and F. Sha. From sBoW to dCoT marginalized encoders for text representation. In *Proc. of CIKM, (ACM)*, 2012.
[43] Z. Xu and S. Sun. Multi-source transfer learning with multi-view adaboost. In *Proc. of NIPS, (Curran Associates)*, pages 332–339, 2012.
[44] M. Zhou and K. C. Chang. Unifying learning to rank and domain adaptation: Enabling cross-task document scoring. In *Proc. of SIGKDD (ACM)*, pages 781–790, 2014.

Kam1n0: MapReduce-based Assembly Clone Search for Reverse Engineering

Steven H. H. Ding* Benjamin C. M. Fung* Philippe Charland†

*School of Information Studies, McGill University, Montreal, QC, Canada
†Mission Critical Cyber Security Section, Defence R&D Canada - Valcartier, Quebec, QC, Canada
steven.h.ding@mail.mcgill.ca ben.fung@mcgill.ca philippe.charland@drdc-rddc.gc.ca

ABSTRACT

Assembly code analysis is one of the critical processes for detecting and proving software plagiarism and software patent infringements when the source code is unavailable. It is also a common practice to discover exploits and vulnerabilities in existing software. However, it is a manually intensive and time-consuming process even for experienced reverse engineers. An effective and efficient assembly code clone search engine can greatly reduce the effort of this process, since it can identify the cloned parts that have been previously analyzed. The assembly code clone search problem belongs to the field of software engineering. However, it strongly depends on practical nearest neighbor search techniques in data mining and databases. By closely collaborating with reverse engineers and *Defence Research and Development Canada (DRDC)*, we study the concerns and challenges that make existing assembly code clone approaches not practically applicable from the perspective of data mining. We propose a new variant of LSH scheme and incorporate it with graph matching to address these challenges. We implement an integrated assembly clone search engine called *Kam1n0*. It is the first clone search engine that can efficiently identify the given query assembly function's *subgraph clones* from a large assembly code repository. Kam1n0 is built upon the Apache Spark computation framework and Cassandra-like key-value distributed storage. A deployed demo system is publicly available.[1] Extensive experimental results suggest that Kam1n0 is accurate, efficient, and scalable for handling large volume of assembly code.

Keywords

Assembly clone search; Information retrieval; Mining software repositories

[1]Kam1n0 online demo (no installation required). Both the user name and password are "sigkdd2016". Use Chrome for best experience. http://dmas.lab.mcgill.ca/projects/kam1n0.htm

KDD '16 August 13–17, 2016, San Francisco, CA, USA

ISBN 978-1-4503-4232-2/16/08...$15.00

http://dx.doi.org/10.1145/2939672.2939719

1. INTRODUCTION

Code reuse is a common but uncontrolled issue in software engineering [15]. Mockus [25] found that more than 50% of files were reused in more than one open source project. Sojer's survey [29] indicates that more than 50% of the developers modify the components before reusing them. This massively uncontrolled reuse of source code does not only introduce legal issues such as GNU General Public License (GPL) violation [36, 17]. It also implies security concerns, as the source code and the vulnerabilities are uncontrollably shared between projects [4].

Identifying all these infringements and vulnerabilities requires intensive effort from reverse engineers. However, the learning curve to master reverse engineering is much steeper than for programming [4]. Reverse engineering is a time consuming process which involves inspecting the execution flow of the program in assembly code and determining the functionalities of the components. Given the fact that code reuse is prevalent in software development, there is a pressing need to develop an efficient and effective assembly clone search engine for reverse engineers. Previous clone search approaches only focus on the search accuracy. However, designing a practically useful clone search engine is a nontrivial task which involves multiple factors to be considered. By closely collaborating with reverse engineers and *Defence Research and Development Canada (DRDC)*, we outline the deployment challenges and requirements as follows:

Interpretability and usability: An assembly function can be represented as a control flow graph consisting of connected basic blocks. Given an assembly function as query, all of the previous assembly code clone search approaches [7, 6, 18, 26] only provide the top-listed candidate assembly functions. They are useful when there exists a function in the repository that shares a high degree of similarity with the query. However, due to the unpredictable effects of different compilers, compiler optimization, and obfuscation techniques, given an unknown function, it is less probable to have a very similar function in the repository. Returning a list of clones with a low degree of similarity values is not useful. As per our discussions with DRDC, a practical search engine should be able to decompose the given query assembly function to different known subgraph clones which can help reverse engineers better understand the function's composition. We define a *subgraph clone* as one of its subgraphs that can be found in the other function. Refer to the example in Figure 1. The previous clone search approaches cannot address this challenge.

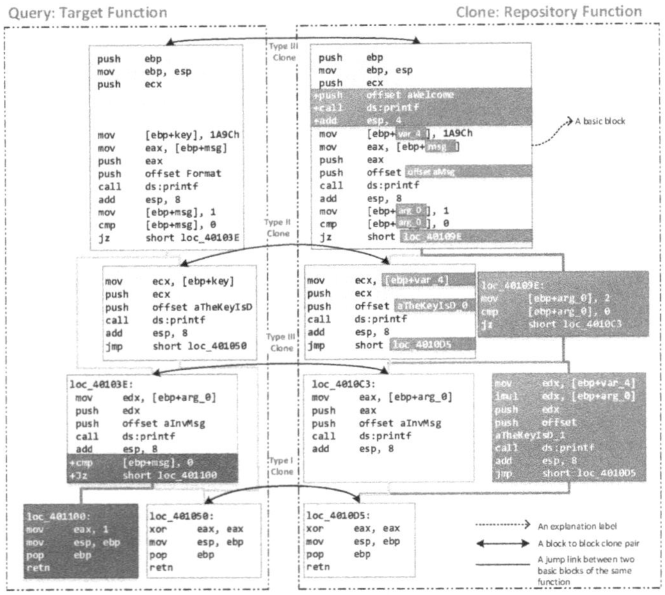

Figure 1: An example of the clone search problem. Basic blocks with a white background form a *subgraph clone* between two functions. Three types of code clones are considered in this paper. Type I: literally identical; Type II: syntactically equivalent; and Type III: minor modifications.

Efficiency and Scalability: An efficient engine can help reverse engineers retrieve clone search results on-the-fly when they are conducting an analysis. Instant feedback tells the reverse engineer the composition of a given function that is under investigation. Scalability is a critical factor as the number of assembly functions in the repository needs to scale up to millions. The degradation of search performance against the repository size has to be considered. Previous approaches in [6, 7], which trade efficiency and scalability for better accuracy, have a high latency for queries and are thus not practically applicable.

Incremental updates: The clone search engine should support incremental updates to the repository, without re-indexing existing assembly functions. [7] requires median statistics to index each vector and [26] requires data-dependent settings for its index, so they do not satisfy this requirement.

Clone search quality: Practically, clones among assembly functions are one-to-many mappings, i.e., a function has multiple cloned functions with different degrees of similarity. However, all previous approaches [6, 7, 18, 26] assume that clones are one-to-one mappings in the experiment. This is due to the difficulty of acquiring such a one-to-many labeled dataset. Moreover, they use different evaluation metrics. Therefore, it is difficult to have a direct comparison among them with respect to the search quality. We need to develop a one-to-many labeled dataset and an unified evaluation framework to quantify the clone search quality.

To address the above requirements and challenges, we propose a new variant of LSH scheme and incorporate it with a graph matching technique. We also develop and deploy a new assembly clone search engine called *Kam1n0*. Our major contributions can be summarized as follows:

- **Solved a challenging problem for the reverse engineering community:** Kam1n0 is the first assembly code clone search engine that supports subgraph clone search. Refer to the example in Figure 1. It promotes the interpretability and usability by providing subgraph clones as results, which helps reverse engineers analyzing new and unknown assembly functions. Kam1n0 won the second prize at the 2015 Hex-Rays plugin Contest[2] and its code is publicly accessible on GitHub.[3]

- **Efficient inexact assembly code search:** The assembly code vector space is highly skewed. Small blocks tend to be similar to each other and large blocks tend to be sparsely distributed in the space. Original hyperplane hashing with banding technique equally partitions the space and does not handle the unevenly distributed data well. We propose a new *adaptive locality sensitive hashing* (*ALSH*) scheme to approximate the cosine similarity. To our best knowledge, ALSH is the first incremental locality sensitive hashing scheme that solves this issue specifically for cosine space with theoretical guarantee. It retrieves fewer points for dense areas and more points for sparse ones in the cosine space. It is therefore efficient in searching nearest neighbors.

- **Scalable sub-linear subgraph search:** We propose a *MapReduce* subgraph search algorithm based on the *Apache Spark* computational framework without an additional index. Different to the existing subgraph isomorphism search problem in data mining, we need to retrieve subgraphs that are both isomorphic to the query and the repository functions as graphs. Thus, existing algorithms are not directly applicable. Algorithmically, our approach is bounded by polynomial complexity. However, our experiment suggests that it is sub-linear in practice.

- **Accurate and robust function clone search:** Kam1n0 is the first approach that integrates both the inexact assembly code and subgraph search. Previous solutions do not consider both of them together. Our extensive experiments suggest that it boosts the clone search quality and yields stable results across different datasets and metrics.

- **Develop a labeled dataset and benchmark state-of-the-art assembly code clone solutions.** We carefully construct a new *labeled* one-to-many assembly code clone dataset that is available to the research community by linking the source code and assembly function level clones. We benchmark and report the performance of twelve existing state-of-the-art solutions with Kam1n0 on the dataset using several metrics. We also setup a mini-cluster to evaluate the scalability of Kam1n0.

The remainder of this paper is organized as follows. Section 2 situates our study within the literature of three different research problems. Section 3 formally defines the studied problem. Section 4 provides an overview of our solution and system design. Section 5 presents the preprocessing steps and the chosen vector space. Section 6 introduces our proposed locality sensitive hashing scheme. Section 7 presents our graph search algorithm. Section 8 presents our benchmark experiments. Section 9 provides the conclusion.

[2]https://hex-rays.com/contests/2015/#kam1n0
[3]https://github.com/McGill-DMaS/Kam1n0-Plugin-IDA-Pro

2. RELATED WORK

Locality sensitive hashing. *Locality sensitive hashing (LSH)* has been studied for decades to solve the ϵ-approximated Nearest Neighbor (ϵNN) problem, since exact nearest neighbor is not scalable to high dimensional data. One of the prevalent problems of LSH is the *uneven data distribution issue*, as LSH equally partitions the data space. To mitigate this issue, several approaches have been proposed including the *LSH-Forest* [2], *LSB-Forest* [32], *C2LSH* [10] and *SK-LSH* [22]. It has been shown that the cosine vector space is robust to different compiler settings [18] in assembly code clone search. However, LSH-Forest, C2LSH and SK-LSH are designed for the p-stable distribution, which does not fit the cosine space. LSB-Forest dynamically and unequally partition the data space. As pointed out by [33], it requires the hash family to possess the $(\epsilon, f(\epsilon))$ property. However, to our best knowledge, such a family in cosine space is still unknown. There are other learning-based approaches [11], which do not meet our incremental requirement. Wang et al. [35] provide a more comprehensive survey on LSH. To satisfy our requirements, we propose the ALSH scheme specifically for the cosine space. Different to the LSH-Forest, ALSH takes more than one bit when going down the tree structure and does not require the $(\epsilon, f(\epsilon))$ property for the LSH family to have theoretical guarantee. Unlike LSB forest [2], we dynamically construct the buckets to adapt to different data distributions.

Subgraph isomorphism. Ullmann [34] proposed the first practical subgraph isomorphism algorithm for small graphs. Several approaches were proposed afterwards for large scale graph data, such as *TurboISO* [13] and *STwig* [31]. It has been shown that they can solve the subgraph isomorphism problem in a reasonable time. However, they do not completely meet our problem settings. The subgraph isomorphism problem needs to retrieve subgraphs that are isomorphic to the graphs in the repository and identical to the query. However, we need to retrieve subgraphs that are isomorphic to the graphs in the repository and isomorphic to the graph of the query, which significantly increases the complexity. More details will be discussed in Section 7. Such a difference requires us to propose a specialized search algorithm. Lee et al. [21] provide a comprehensive survey and performance benchmark on subgraph isomorphism.

Assembly code clone search. The studies on the assembly code clone search problem are recent. Only a few approaches exist [6, 7, 18, 26]. They all rely on the inexact text search techniques of data mining. *BinClone* [7] models assembly code into an Euclidean space based on frequency values of selected features. It is inefficient and not scalable due to the exponential 2-combination of features which approximates the 2-norm distance. *LSH-S* in [26] models assembly code into a cosine space based on token frequency and approximate the distance by hyperplane hashing and banding scheme. It equally partitions the space and suffers from the uneven data distribution problem. *Graphlet* [18] models assembly code into a cosine space based on extracted signatures from assembly code. However, it cannot detect any subgraph clones that is smaller than the graphlet size. *Tracelet* [6] models assembly code according to string editing distance. It compares function one by one, which is not scalable. Kam1n0 is fundamentally different to the previous approaches. It is an integration of inexact assembly code search and the subgraph search. It enables clone subgraph search of any size.

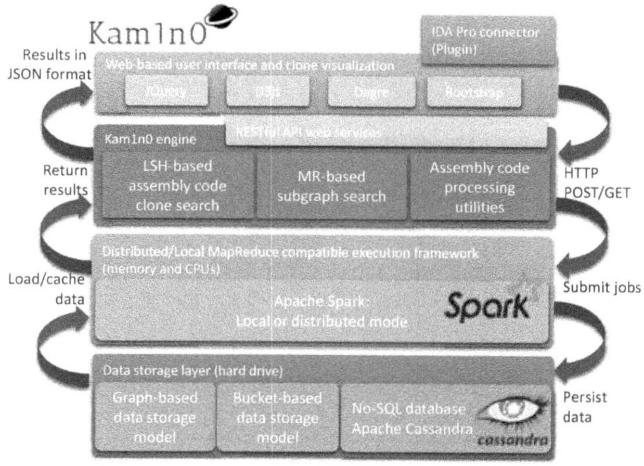

Figure 2: The overall solution stack of the Kam1n0 engine.

3. PROBLEM STATEMENT

Reverse engineering starts from a binary file. After being unpacked and disassembled, it becomes a list of assembly functions. In this paper, *function* represents an assembly function; *block* represents a basic block; *source function* represents the actual function written in source code, such as C++; *repository function* stands for the assembly function that is indexed inside the repository; *target function* denotes the assembly function that is given as a query; and correspondingly, *repository blocks* and *target blocks* refer to their respective basic blocks. Each function f is represented as a control flow graph denoted by (B, E), where B indicates its basic blocks and E, indicates the edges that connect the blocks. Let $B(\mathrm{RP})$ be the complete set of basic blocks in the repository and $F(\mathrm{RP})$ be the complete set of functions in the repository. Given an assembly function, our goal is to search all its subgraph clones inside the repository RP. We formally define the search problem as follows:

Definition 1. (Assembly function subgraph clone search) Given a target function f_t and its control flow graph (B_t, E_t), the search problem is to retrieve all the repository functions $f_s \in \mathrm{RP}$, which share at least one subgraph clone with f_t. The shared list of subgraph clones between f_s and f_t is denoted by $sg_s[1 : a]$, where $sg_s[a]$ represents one of them. A subgraph clone is a set of basic block clone pairs $sg_s[a] = \{\langle b_t, b_s \rangle, \dots\}$ between f_s and f_t, where $b_t \in B_t$, $b_s \in B_s$, and $\langle b_t, b_s \rangle$ is a type I, type II, or type III clone (see Figure 1). Formally, given f_t, the problem is to retrieve all $\{f_s | f_s \in \mathrm{RP} \text{ and } |sg_s| > 0\}$. □

4. OVERALL ARCHITECTURE

The Kam1n0 engine is designed for general key-value storage and the *Apache Spark*[4] computational framework. Its solution stack, as shown in Figure 2, consists of three layers. The data storage layer is concerned with how the data is stored and indexed. The distributed/local execution layer manages and executes the jobs submitted by the Kam1n0

[4]Apache Spark, available at: http://spark.apache.org/

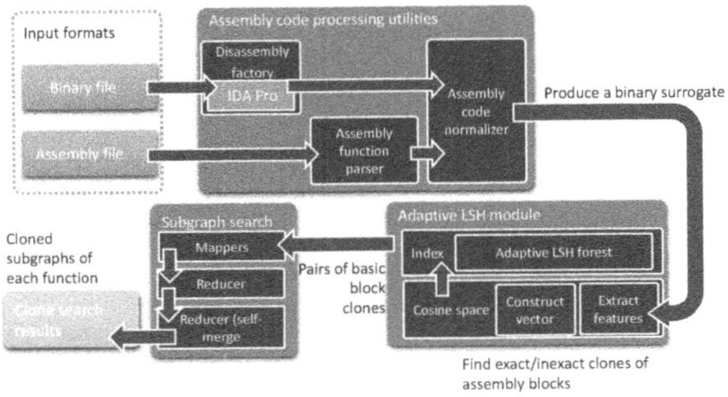

Figure 3: Assembly clone search data flow.

engine. The Kam1n0 engine splits a search query into multiple jobs and coordinates their execution flow. It also provides the RESTful APIs. We have implemented a web-based user interface and an *Hex-Rays IDA Pro* plugin[5] as clients. IDA Pro is a popular interactive disassembler that is used by reverse engineers.

Figure 3 depicts the data flow of the clone search process. It consists of the following steps. *Preprocessing*: After parsing the input (either a binary file or assembly functions) into control flow graphs, this step normalizes assembly code into a general form, which will be elaborated in Section 5. *Find basic blocks clone pairs:* Given a list of assembly basic blocks from the previous step, it finds all the clone pairs of blocks using ALSH. *Search the subgraph clones:* Given the list of clone block pairs, the MapReduce module merges and constructs the subgraph clones. Note that this clone search process does not require any source code.

5. PREPROCESSING AND VECTOR SPACE

We choose the cosine vector space to characterize the semantic similarity of assembly code. It has been shown that the cosine vector space is robust to different compiler settings [18]. It can mitigate the linear transformation of assembly code. For example, to optimize the program for speed, the compiler may unroll and flatten a loop structure in assembly code by repeating the code inside the loop multiple times. In this case, the cosine similarity between the unrolled and original loop is still high, due to the fact that the cosine distance only considers the included angle between two vectors. The features selected in Kam1n0 include mnemonics, combinations of mnemonics and operands, as well as mnemonics n-gram, which are typically used in assembly code analysis [7, 26]. The equivalent assembly code fragments can be represented in different forms. To mitigate this issue, we normalize the operands in assembly code during the preprocessing. We extend the normalization tree used in BinClone [7] with more types. There are three normalization levels: *root*, *type*, and *specific*. Each of them corresponds to a different generalization level of assembly code. More details can be found in our technical report.[6]

6. LOCALITY SENSITIVE HASHING

In this section, we introduce an *Adaptive Locality Sensitive Hashing (ALSH)* scheme for searching the block-level semantic clones. As discussed in Section 2, exact nearest neighbor search is not scalable. Thus, we started from the reduction of the ϵ-approximated k-NN problem:

Definition 2. (*ϵ-approximated NN search problem*) Given a dataset $D \subset \mathbb{R}^d$ ($\mathbb{R}$ denotes real numbers) and a query point q, let r denote the distance between the query point q and its nearest neighbor o^*. This problem is to find an approximated data point within the distance $\epsilon \times r$ where $\epsilon > 1$ □

The ϵ-approximated k-NN search problem can be reduced to the ϵNN problem by finding the k data points where each is an ϵ-approximated point of the exact k-NN of q [10]. The locality sensitive hashing approaches do not solve the ϵNN problem directly. ϵNN is further reduced into another problem: (ϵ, r)-approximated ball cover problem [1, 14].

Definition 3. (*(ϵ, r)-approximated ball cover problem*) Given a dataset $D \subset \mathbb{R}^d$ and a query point q, let $B(q, r)$ denote a ball with center q and radius r. The query q returns the results as follows:

- if there exists a point $o^* \in B(q, R)$, then return a data point from $B(q, \epsilon R)$
- if $B(q, \epsilon R)$ does not contain any data object in D, then return nothing. □

One can solve the (ϵ, r) ball cover problem by using the Locality Sensitive Hashing (LSH) families. A locality sensitive hashing family consists of hashing functions that can preserve the distance between points.

Definition 4. (*Locality Sensitive Hashing Family*) Given a distance r under a specific metric space, an approximation ratio ϵ, and two probabilities $p_1 > p_2$, a hash function family $\mathcal{H} \rightarrow \{h : \mathbb{R}^d \rightarrow U\}$ is $(r, \epsilon r, p1, p2)$-sensitive such that:

- if $o \in B(q, r)$, then $Pr_{\mathcal{H}}[h(q) = h(o)] \geqslant p_1$
- if $o \notin B(q, \epsilon r)$, then $Pr_{\mathcal{H}}[h(q) = h(o)] \leqslant p_2$ □

LSH families are available for many metric spaces such as cosine similarity [3], hamming distance [14], Jaccard coefficient, and p-stable distributions [5]. Based on our chosen cosine vector space, we adopt the random hyperplane hash [3] family, where $sign(\cdot)$ output the sign of the input.

$$h(\vec{o}) = sign(\vec{o} \cdot \vec{a}) \tag{1}$$

By substituting the random vector $\vec{a}$ we can obtain different hash functions in the family. The collision probability of two data points $\vec{o_1}$ and $\vec{o_2}$ on Equation 1 can be formulated as:

$$P[h(\vec{o_1}) = h(\vec{o_2})] = 1 - \frac{\theta_{\vec{o_1}, \vec{o_2}}}{\pi} \tag{2}$$

$\theta_{\vec{o_1}, \vec{o_2}}$ is the included angle between $\vec{o_1}$ and $\vec{o_2}$. The probability that two vectors have the same projected direction on a random hyperplane is high when their included angle is small.

THEOREM 1. *The random hyperplane hash function is a $(r, \epsilon r, 1 - r/\pi, 1 - \epsilon r/\pi)$ sensitive hashing family.* □

PROOF. According to Definition 4 and Equation 2: $p_1 = 1 - r/\pi$ and $p_2 = 1 - \epsilon r/\pi$ □

To use the locality sensitive hashing families to solve the ball cover problem, it needs a hashing scheme to meet the quality requirement. The *E2LSH* approach was originally proposed by [14] and extended by[5]. It concatenates k different hash functions $[h_1, \dots, h_k]$ from a given LSH family $\mathcal{H}$ into a function $g(o) = (h_1(o), \dots, h_k(o))$, and adopts l such functions. The parameters k and l are chosen to ensure the following two properties are satisfied:

Property 1. (P_1): if there exists $p^* \in B(q, r)$, then $g_j(p^*) = g_j(q)$ from some $j = 1 \dots l$. □

Property 2. (P_2): the total number of points $\notin B(q, \epsilon r)$ that collides with q is less than $2l$. □

[5]IDA Pro, available at: http://www.hex-rays.com/

[6]Kam1n0 technical report, available at: http://dmas.lab.mcgill.ca/fung/pub/DFC16kdd.pdf

It is proven that if the above two properties hold with constant probability, the algorithm can correctly solve the (ϵ, r)-approximated ball cover problem [14]. For E2LSH, by picking $k = log_{p_2}(1/n)$ and $l = n^\rho$ where $\rho = \frac{ln 1/p_1}{ln 1/p_2}$, both Properties 1 and 2 hold with constant probability.

However, the ball cover problem is a strong reduction to the NN problem since it adopts the same radius r for all points. Real-life data cannot always be evenly distributed. Therefore, it is difficult to pick an appropriate r. We denote this as the *uneven data distribution issue*. In [12], a magic r_m is adopted heuristically. But as pointed out by [32], such a magic radius may not exist. A weaker reduction was proposed in [14], where the NN problem is reduced to multiple (r, ϵ)-NN ball cover problems with varying $r = \{1, \epsilon^2, \epsilon^3, \dots\}$. The intuition is that points in different density areas can find a suitable r. However, such a reduction requires a large space consumption and longer response time. Other indexing structures have been proposed to solve this issue. Per our discussion in Section 2, existing techniques do not meet our requirement. Thus, we customize the LSH-forest approach and propose the ALSH structure.

6.1 Adaptive LSH Structure

We found that the limitation of the expanding sequence of r in previous section is too strong. It is unnecessary to *exactly* follow the sequence $r = \{1, \epsilon^2, \epsilon^3, \dots\}$, as long as r is increasing in a similar manner to $r_{t+1} = r_t \times \epsilon$. Thus, we customize the ϵ-approximated NN problem as follows:

Definition 5. ($f(r)$-approximated NN search problem) Given a dataset $D \subset \mathbb{R}^d$ and a query point q, let r denote the distance between the query point q and its nearest neighbor o^*. The problem is to find an approximated data point within the distance $f(r)$, where $f(r)/r > 1$ □

Instead of using a fix approximation ratio, we approximate the search by using a function on r. We issue a different sequence of expanding r. The expanding sequence of r is formulated as $r_0, r_1, \dots, r_t, r_{t+1}, \dots, r_m$, where $r_t < r_{t+1}$. Similar to the E2LSH approach, we concatenate multiple hash functions from the random hyperplane hash family $\mathcal{H}$ into one. However, we concatenate different number of hash functions for different values of r. This number is denoted by k_t for r_t, and the sequence of k is denoted by $k_0, k_1, \dots, k_t, k_{t+1}, \dots, k_m$, where $k_t > k_{t+1}$. Recall that the concatenated function is denoted by g. Consequently, there will be a different function g at position t, which is denoted by g_t. Yet, function g_t and function $g_{(t+1)}$ can share k_{t+1} hash functions. With p_m to be specified later, we set the r value at position t as follows:

$$r_t = \pi \times (1 - p_m^{(1/k_t)}) \tag{3}$$

This allows us to have the effect of increasing the r value by decreasing the k value. We calculate the value of k at position t as follows:

$$k_t = c \times k_{t+1}, \text{where } \ c > 1 \tag{4}$$

By getting t_{t+1} from Equation 3, substituting k_t using Equation 4, and substituting p_m using Equation 3, we have:

$$r_{t+1} = \pi \times \left(1 - (1 - \frac{r_t}{\pi})^c\right) = f_c(r_t) \quad f_c(r_t)/r_t > 1 \tag{5}$$

By setting c equals to 2, we can get an approximately similar curve of r sequence to the original sequence $r_{t+1} = r_t \times \epsilon$

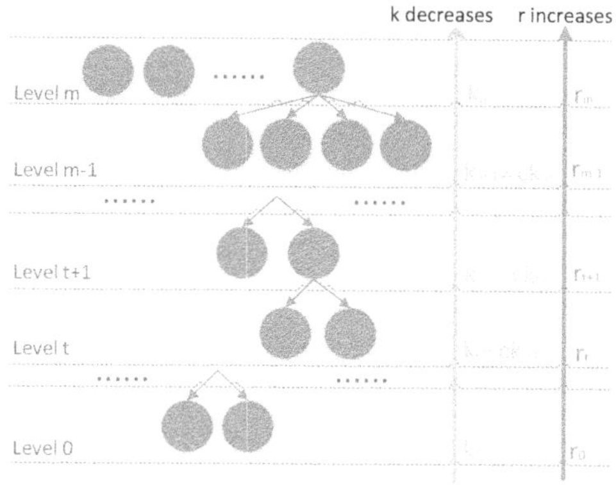

Figure 4: The index structure for the Adaptive Locality Sensitive Hashing (ALSH). There are $m+1$ levels on this tree. Moving from level t to level $t+1$ is equivalent of increasing the search radius from r_t to r_{t+1}.

where ϵ equals to 2. Following the aforementioned logic, we construct an Adaptive Locality Sensitive Hashing (ALSH) index in the form of prefix trees.

As shown in Figure 4, the index structure is a prefix tree of the signature values calculated by $\mathcal{G} = \{g_m, g_{m-1}, \dots, g_0\}$. Level t corresponds to the position t in the r expanding sequence. By introducing different values of k_t, each level represents a different radius r_t. Each level denotes a different g_t function and the g_t function is a concatenation of k_t hash functions. Moving up from a node at level t to its parent at level $t+1$ indicates that it requires a shorter matched prefix. The nodes which have the same parent at level t share the same prefix that is generated by g_t.

To locate the leaf for a given data point $q \in \mathbb{R}^d$, ALSH dynamically constructs the hash functions by trying $g_t \in \mathcal{G}$ in sequence. The signature of g_t can be generated by padding additional hash values to g_{t+1} since $k_t = c \times k_{t+1}$. Following [14, 32], with l to be specified later, we adopt l such prefix trees as the ALSH's index. Given a query point q, we first locate the corresponding leaves in all prefix trees. With l to be specified later, we collect the first $2l$ points from all the leaf buckets. To index a point, we locate its corresponding leaf in each tree and insert it to the leaf bucket. Suppose a leaf is on level t_{t+1}. If the number of points in that leaf is more than $2l$, we split all the data points of that leaf into the next level t by using g_t. All the trees are dynamically constructed based on the incoming points to be indexed in sequence. Therefore, they can be incrementally maintained. Unlike the learning-based LSH [11], Kamln0 does not require the whole repository to estimate the hash functions to build the index.

It can be easily proved that g_t is a $(r_t, r_{t+1}, p_m, p_m^c)$-sensitive hash family and g_t can correctly solve the $(r_{t+1}/r_t, r_t)$-approximated ball cover problem by setting $p_m^c = 1/n$ and $l = n^{1/c}$. The proof follows [14]. Details and implementation on key-value data store can be found in our technical report.[6] Another parameter r_m controls the starting k_m value at the root value. It indicates the maximum distance that two points can be considered as valid neighbors. For sparse points far away from each other, they are not considered as neighbors unless their distance is within r_m.

For a single ALSH tree, the depth in the worst case is k_0, and all the leaves are at level 0. In this case, the tree is equivalent to the E2LSH with $k = k_0$. Therefore, the

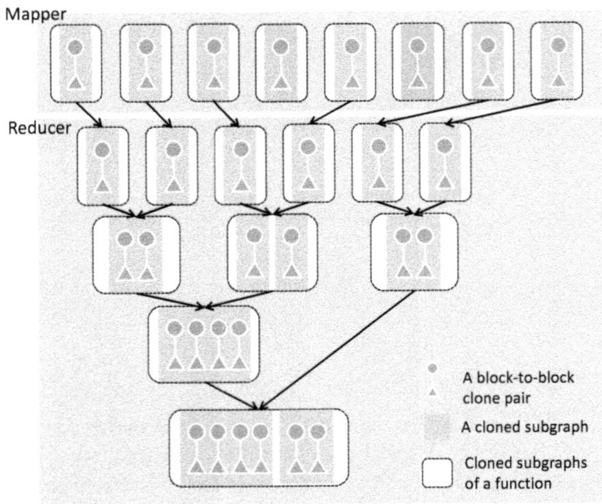

Figure 5: The MapReduce-based subgraph clone construction process.

space consumption for $l = n^{1/c}$ ALSH trees are bounded by $O(dn + n^{1+1/c})$, where $O(dn)$ is the data points in a dataset and $O(n^{1+1/c})$ is the space of indexes for the trees. The query time for a single ALSH prefix tree is bounded by its height. Given the maximum k value k_0 and the minimum k value k_m, its depth in the worst case is $log_c(k_0/k_m) + 1$. Thus, the query time for $l = n^{1/c}$ prefix trees is bounded by $O(log_c(k_0/k_m) \times n^{1/c})$. The ALSH index needs to build $n^{1/c}$ prefix trees for the full theoretical quality to be guaranteed. Based on our observation, setting l to 1 and 2 is already sufficient for providing good quality assembly code clones.

7. SUBGRAPH CLONE SEARCH

Even subgraph isomorphism is NP-hard in theory [21, 28], many algorithms have been proposed to solve it in a reasonable time. Formally, the subgraph isomorphism algorithm solved by most of these systems [13, 21, 31] is defined as:

Definition 6. (*Subgraph Isomorphism Search*) A graph is denoted by a triplet (V, E, L) where V represents the set of vertices, E represents the set of edges, and L represents the labels for each vertex. Given a query graph $q = (V, E, L)$ and a data graph $g = (V', E', L')$ a subgraph isomorphism (also known as *embedding*) is an injective function $M : V \rightarrow V'$ such that the following conditions hold: (1) $\forall u \in V, L(u) \in L'(M(u))$, (2) $\forall(u_i, u_j) \in E, (M(u_i), M(u_j)) \in E'$, and (3) $L(u_i, u_j) = L'(M(u_i), M(u_j))$. The search problem is to find all distinct embeddings of q in g. □

The difference between this problem and ours in Definition 1 is two-fold. First, our problem is to retrieve *all the subgraph clones* of the target function f_t's control flow graph from the repository. In contrast, this problem only needs to retrieve the exact matches of query graph q within g. Refer to Conditions 1, 2, and 3 in Definition 6, or the termination condition of the procedure on Line 1 of subroutine *SubgraphSearch* in [21]. Our problem is more challenging and can be reduced to the problem in Definition 6 by issuing all the subgraphs of f_t as queries, which introduces a higher algorithmic complexity. Second, there is no such L data label attribute in our problem, but two types of edges: the control flow graph which links the basic blocks and the semantic relationship between basic blocks which is evaluated at the querying phase. Existing algorithms for subgraph isomorphism are not directly applicable. Assembly code control graphs are sparser than other graph data as there are less number of links between vertices and typically, basic blocks are only linked to each other within the same function. Given such properties, we can efficiently construct the subgraph clones respectively for each repository function f_s if it has more than one clone blocks in the previous step.

Algorithm 1 Mapper

Input A basic block clone pair $\langle b_t, b_s \rangle$
Output A pair consisting of $\langle f_s, sg_s \rangle$

```
f_s ← getFunctionId(b_s)
sg_s ← [ ]                    ▷ create an empty list of subgraph clones
cloneGraph ← {⟨b_t, b_s⟩}     ▷ create a subgraph clone with one clone pair
sg_s[0] ← cloneGraph          ▷ list of subgraph clones but at this moment, it has only one.
return ⟨f_s, sg_s⟩ with f_s as key index
```

7.1 MapReduce Subgraph Search

We adopt two functions in the Apache Spark MapReduce execution framework, namely the *map* function and the *reduce-by-key* function. In our case, the map function transforms the clone pairs generated by ALSH (refer to the data flow in Figure 3) and the reduce-by-key function constructs subgraph clone respectively for different repository function f_s. Figure 5 shows the overview of our subgraph clone search approach.

The signature for the map function (Algorithm 1) is $\langle b_t, b_s \rangle \rightarrow \langle f_s, sg_s[1 : a] \rangle$. Each execution of the map function takes a clone pair $\langle b_t, b_s \rangle$ produced by ALSH and transforms it to $\langle f_s, sg_s[1 : a] \rangle$, which is a pair of repository function id f_s and its list of subgraph clones sg_s in Definition 1. The map functions are independent to each other.

The outputs of the map functions correspond to the first row in Figure 5. A red circle represents a target basic block b_s and a green triangle represents a source basic block b_t. The link between them indicates that they are a block-to-block clone pair $\langle b_t, b_s \rangle$, which is produced in the previous step. A white rectangle represents a list of subgraph clones and the colored rectangle inside it represents a subgraph clone. Algorithm 1 maps each clone pair into a list of subgraph clones which contains only one subgraph clone. Each subgraph clone is initialized with only one clone pair.

After the map transformation functions, the reduce-by-key function reduces the produced lists of subgraph clones. The reducer merges a pair of lists sg_s^1 and sg_s^2 into a single one, by considering their subgraph clones' connectivity. The reduce process is executed for the links from the second row to the last row in Figure 5. Only the lists of subgraph clones with the same f_s will be merged. As indicated by the links between the first and second row in Figure 5, only rectangles with the same orange background can be reduced together. Rectangles with other background colors are reduced with their own group.

Algorithm 2 shows the reduce function in details. Given two lists of subgraph clones under the same repository function f_s, the reduce function compares their subgraph clones (Lines 1 and 2) and checks if two graphs can be connected (Lines 4 to 13) by referring to the the control flow graph edges E_s and E_t . If the two subgraph clones can be connected by one clone pair, then they can be merged into a single one (Lines 6 and 7). If a subgraph clone from sg_s^2 cannot be merged into any subgraph clones in sg_s^2, it will be appended to the list sg_s^1 (Lines 20 and 21). At the end of the

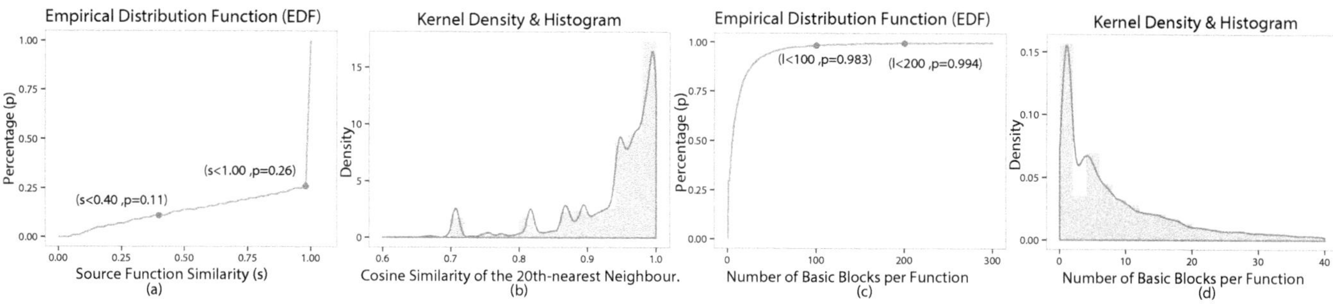

Figure 6: (a) the EDF function on repository function clone pair similarity, (b) the kernel density & histogram of the cosine similarity of each basic block's 20th-nearest neighbor, (c) the EDF on per assembly function block count $|B_s|$, and (d) the kernel density & histogram on assembly function block count $|B_s| < 40$.

Algorithm 2 Reducer

```
Input subgraph lists of same f_s: sg_s^1[1 : a_1] and sg_s^2[1 : a_2]
Output a single subgraph list sg_s^1[1 : a]
 1: for a_1 → |sg_s^1| do
 2:     for a_2 → |sg_s^2| do
 3:         canMerge ← false
 4:         for each ⟨b_t^{a1}, b_s^{a1}⟩ ∈ sg_s^1[a_1] do
 5:             for each ⟨b_t^{a2}, b_s^{a2}⟩ ∈ sg_s^2[a_2] do
 6:                 if E_t(b_t^{a1}, b_t^{a2}) exists then
 7:                     if E_s(b_s^{a1}, b_s^{a2}) exists then
 8:                         canMerge ← true
 9:                         goto Line 14.
10:                     end if
11:                 end if
12:             end for
13:         end for
14:         if canMerge is true then
15:             sg_s^1[a_1] ← sg_s^1[a_1] ∪ sg_s^2[a_2]
16:             sg_s^2 ← sg_s^2 − sg_s^2[a_2]
17:         end if
18:     end for
19: end for
20: if sg_s^2 is not ∅ then     ▷ for graphs in sg_s^2 that cannot be
                                  merged, append them to the list
21:     sg_s^1 ← sg_s^1 ∪ sg_s^2
22: end if
23: return sg_s^1
```

graph search algorithm, we solve the problem in Definition 1. In order to obtain a ranked list of repository functions for f_s, we calculate the similarity value by checking how much its subgraphs sg_s cover the graph of the query f_t: $sim_s = (|\text{uniqueEdges}(sg_s)| + |\text{uniqueNodes}(sg_s)|)/(|B_t| + |E_t|)$.

Compared to other join-based or graph-exploration-based search approach, our MapReduce-based search procedure avoids recursive search and is bounded by polynomial complexity. Let m_s be the number of clone pairs for a target function f_t. There are at most $O(m_s^2)$ connectivity checks between the clone pairs (no merge can be found) and the map function requires $O(m_s)$ executions. m_s corresponds to the number of rectangles in the second row of Figure 5. Refer from the second row to the last one. The reduce function are bounded by $O(m_s^2)$ comparisons. m_s is bounded by $O(|B_t| \times |B_s|)$, which implies that each basic block of f_t is a clone with all the basic blocks of f_s. However, this extreme case rarely happens. Given the nature of assembly functions and search scenarios, m_s is sufficiently bounded by $O(max(|B_t|, |B_s|))$. According to the descriptive statistics of our experiment, 99% of them have less than 200 basic blocks.

8. EXPERIMENTS

This section presents comprehensive experimental results for the task of assembly code clone search. First, we explain how to construct a labeled dataset that can be used for benchmarking in future research. Then, we evaluate the effect of assembly code normalization. Although normalization has been extensively used in previous works, its effects have not been thoroughly studied yet. Next, we present the benchmark results which compares Kam1n0 with state-of-the-art clone search approaches in terms of clone search quality. Finally, we demonstrate the scalability and capacity of the Kam1n0 engine by presenting the experimental results from a mini-cluster.

Library Name	Branch Count	Function Count	Block Count	Clone Pair Count
bzip2	5	590	15,181	1,329
curl	16	9,468	176,174	49,317
expat	3	2,025	35,801	14,054
jsoncpp	14	11,779	43,734	204,701
libpng	9	4,605	82,257	18,946
libtiff	13	7,276	124,974	51,925
openssl	9	13,732	200,415	29,767
sqlite	12	9,437	202,777	23,674
tinyxml	7	3,286	30,401	22,798
zlib	8	1,741	30,585	6,854
total	96	63,939	942,299	423,365

Table 1: The assembly code clone dataset summary.

8.1 Labeled Dataset Generation

One of the challenging problems for assembly code clone search is the lack of labeled (ground truth) dataset, since the most effective labeled dataset requires intensive manual identification of assembly code clones [7]. To facilitate future studies on assembly clone search, we have developed a tool to systematically generate the assembly function clones based on source code clones. The tool performs four steps: *Step 1:* Parse all the source code functions from different branches or versions of a project and identify all the function-to-function clones using CCFINDERX [16], which estimates source code similarity based on the sequence of normalized tokens. *Step 2:* Compile the given branches or versions of a project with an additional debug flag to enable the compiler output debug symbols. *Step 3:* Link the source code functions to the assembly code functions using the compiler output debug symbols, where such information is available. *Step 4:* For each pair of source code clone, generate a pair of assembly function clone and transfer the similarity to the new pair.

The intuition is that the source code function-level clones indicate the functional clones between their corresponding assembly code. In [7, 25], the source code and assembly code are manually linked with an injected identifier in the form of variable declarations. However, after the automation of such process, we find that the link rate is very low due to the impact of compiler optimizations. The generated

M	Approach	Bzip2	Curl	Expat	Jsoncpp	Libpng	Libtiff	Openssl	Sqlite	Tinyxml	Zlib	Avg.
AUROC	BinClone	.985	Ø	Ø	Ø	Ø	Ø	Ø	Ø	Ø	***.894**	.188
	Composite	.857	.766	.693	.725	.814	.772	.688	.726	.688	.729	.746
	Constant	.769	.759	.723	.665	.829	.764	.689	.776	.683	.768	.743
	Graphlet	.775	.688	.673	.563	.714	.653	.682	.746	.676	.685	.685
	Graphlet-C	.743	.761	.705	.604	.764	.729	.731	.748	.677	.668	.713
	Graphlet-E	.523	.526	.505	.516	.519	.521	.512	.513	.524	.514	.517
	MixGram	.900	.840	.728	.726	.830	.808	.809	.765	.707	.732	.785
	MixGraph	.769	.733	.706	.587	.755	.692	.713	.765	.674	.708	.710
	N-gram	.950	.860	.727	.713	.843	.809	.819	.789	.714	.766	.799
	N-perm	.886	.847	.731	.729	.834	.813	.811	.769	.709	.736	.787
	Tracelet	.830	Ø	Ø	Ø	Ø	Ø	Ø	Ø	Ø	.799	.163
	LSH-S	.965	.901	.794	.854	.894	.922	.882	.845	.768	.758	.858
	Kam1n0	***.992**	***.989**	***.843**	***.890**	***.944**	***.967**	***.891**	***.895**	***.864**	.830	***.911**
AUPR	BinClone	.294	Ø	Ø	Ø	Ø	Ø	Ø	Ø	Ø	.091	.038
	Composite	.645	.495	.375	.353	***.541**	.482	.288	.405	.261	.409	.425
	Constant	.247	.280	.301	.158	.311	.349	.072	.157	.142	.240	.226
	Graphlet	.162	.133	.138	.051	.115	.103	.041	.108	.150	.106	.111
	Graphlet-C	.455	.482	.296	.176	.413	.369	.366	.437	.245	.338	.358
	Graphlet-E	.022	.024	.013	.020	.012	.015	.004	.010	.020	.026	.017
	MixGram	.727	.598	.363	.337	.513	.512	***.464**	.471	.286	.383	.465
	MixGraph	.247	.242	.228	.098	.196	.184	.078	.180	.163	.175	.179
	N-gram	.638	.491	.297	.275	.408	.428	.301	.417	.264	.314	.383
	N-perm	.613	.589	.360	.344	.523	***.515**	.438	.465	.288	.370	.450
	Tracelet	.057	Ø	Ø	Ø	Ø	Ø	Ø	Ø	Ø	.027	.008
	LSH-S	.227	.014	.095	.049	.035	.038	.012	.018	.079	.041	.061
	Kam1n0	***.780**	***.633**	***.473**	***.504**	.477	.387	.411	***.610**	***.413**	***.465**	***.515**
MAP@10	BinClone	.495	Ø	Ø	Ø	Ø	Ø	Ø	Ø	Ø	.398	.089
	Composite	.505	.525	.489	.190	.493	.536	.238	.382	.303	.472	.413
	Constant	.354	.459	.539	.132	.473	.502	.199	.379	.229	.495	.376
	Graphlet	.274	.309	.408	.030	.264	.276	.154	.303	.233	.302	.255
	Graphlet-C	.339	.499	.586	.084	.412	.449	.284	.416	.272	.361	.370
	Graphlet-E	.021	.053	.010	.011	.024	.040	.012	.019	.039	.028	.026
	MixGram	.559	.641	.625	.191	.511	.589	.392	.445	.321	.474	.475
	MixGraph	.334	.407	.572	.064	.345	.351	.211	.387	.244	.371	.329
	N-gram	.620	.636	.615	.176	.512	.567	.398	.481	.310	.506	.482
	N-perm	.532	.653	.628	.191	.516	.597	.394	.452	.317	.483	.476
	Tracelet	.228	Ø	Ø	Ø	Ø	Ø	Ø	Ø	Ø	.265	.049
	LSH-S	.322	.069	.198	.032	.145	.078	.086	.111	.130	.101	.127
	Kam1n0	***.672**	***.680**	***.690**	***.196**	***.548**	***.587**	***.434**	***.605**	***.375**	***.573**	***.536**

Table 2: Benchmark results of different assembly code clone search approaches. We employed three evaluation metrics: the *Area Under the Receiver Operating Characteristic Curve* (*AUROC*), the *Area Under the Precision-Recall Curve* (*AUPR*), and the *Mean Average Precision at Position 10* (*MAP@10*). Ø denotes that the method is not scalable and we cannot obtain a result for this dataset within 24 hours.

assembly code clone is in fact the combined result of source code patches and compiler optimizations. The source code evolves from version to version, and different versions may have different default compiler settings. Thus, the labeled dataset simulates the real-world assembly clone evolvement. This tool is applicable only if the source code is available.

Refer to Table 1 for some popular open source libraries with different versions. We applied the aforementioned tool on them to generate the labeled dataset for the experiments. There are 63,939 assembly functions which successfully link to the source code functions. The labeled dataset is a list of one-to-multiple assembly function clones with the transferred similarity from their source code clones.

See Figure 6c and Figure 6d. The assembly function basic block count follows a long-tail distribution. Most of them have between 0 and 5 assembly basic blocks, and 99% of them is bounded by 200. We find that this is the typical distribution of assembly function block count. This distribution facilitates our graph search because the worst case is bounded by $O(|B_t| \times |B_s|)$ and $P[|B_s| < 200] > 0.99$. Figure 6b shows the cosine similarity distribution of each basic block's 20th-nearest neighbor. It reflects variations of density in the vector space and calls for an adaptive LSH.

74% of the source code clones given by CCFINDERX are exact clones (see Figure 6a). However, by applying a strong hash on their assembly code, we find that only 30% of them are exact clones (Type I clones). Thus, the total percentage of inexact clones is $70\% \times 74\% + 26\% = 77.8\%$. CCFINDERX classifies tokens in source code into different types before clone detection. If two source code fragments are identified as clones with a low similarity, there is a higher chance that the underlying assembly code is indeed not a clone due to the normalization of the source code. To mitigate this issue, we heuristically set a 0.4 threshold for clones to be included in our dataset. Thus, we have 66.8% of inexact clones.

8.2 Normalization Level

	None	Root	Specific
Root	$< 2e^{-16}$	-	-
Specific	$< 2e^{-16}$	1	-
Type	$< 2e^{-16}$	1	1

Table 3: Paired t-test on the normalization level.

Assembly code normalization is used in [7, 27]. However, its effects were not formally studied. In this section, we present the results of the statistical test on the effects of the normalization level. Details on normalization can be found in our technical report.[6] We start by using a strong hash clone search with different normalization levels on each of the generated datasets. Then, we collect the corresponding precision value to the given normalization level as samples and test the relationship between precision and the chosen normalization level. Normalization can increase the recall, but we want to evaluate the trade-off between the precision and different normalization levels. According to the ANOVA

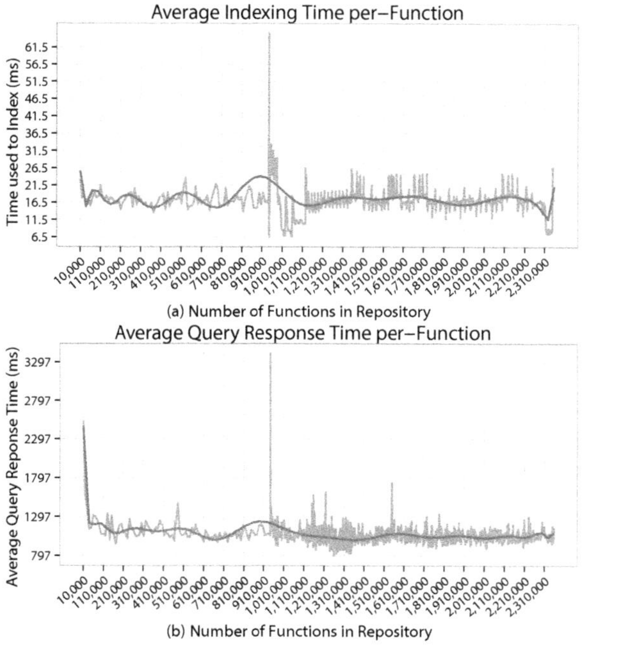

Figure 7: Scalability study. (a): Average Indexing Time vs. Number of Functions in the Repository. (b): Average Query Response Time vs. Number of Functions in the Repository. The red line represents the plotted time and the blue line represents the smoothed polynomial approximation.

test ($p < 2e^{-16}$), the difference of applying normalization or not is statistically significant. Consider Table 3. However, the difference of applying different levels, namely *Root*, *Type*, or *Specific*, is not statistically significant.

8.3 Clone Search Approach Benchmark

In this section, we benchmark twelve assembly code clone search approaches: BinClone [8, 19], Graphlets [17, 18], LSH-S [29], and Tracelet [6]. [18] includes several approaches: mnemonic n-grams (denoted as n-gram), mnemonic n-perms (denoted as n-perm), Graphlets (denoted as Graphlet), Extended Graphlets (denoted as Graphlet-E), Colored Graphlets (denoted as Graphlet-C), Mixed Graphlets (denoted as Mix-Graph), Mixed n-grams/perms (denoted as MixGram), Constants, and the Composite of n-grams/perms and Graphlets (denoted as Composite). The idea of using Graphlet originated from [20]. We re-implemented all these approaches under a unified evaluation framework and all parameters were configured according to the papers. We did not include the re-write engine in [6] because it is not scalable.

Several metrics are used in previous research to evaluate the clone search quality, but there is no common agreement on what should be used. Precision, recall and F1 are used in BinClone [7], while [36] maintains that a F2 measure is more appropriate. However, these two values will change as the search similarity threshold value changes. To evaluate the trade-off between recall and precision, we use three typical information retrieval metrics, namely *Area Under the Receiver Operating Characteristic Curve (AUROC)*, *Area Under the Precision-Recall Curve (AUPR)*, and *Mean Average Precision at Position 10 (MAP@10)*. These three metrics flavor different information retrieval scenarios. Therefore, we employ all of them. AUROC and AUPR can test a classifier by issuing different threshold values consecutively [9, 24, 30], while MAP@10 can evaluate the quality of the top-ranked list simulating the real user experience [23].

Table 2 presents the benchmark results. The highest score of each evaluation metric is highlighted for each dataset. Also, the micro-average of all the results for each approach is given in the *Avg* column. Kam1n0 out-performs the other approaches in almost every case for all evaluation metrics. Kam1n0 also achieves the best averaged AUROC, AUPRC, and MAP@10 scores. The overall performance also suggests that it is the most stable one. Each approach is given a 24-hour time frame to finish the clone search and it is only allowed to use a single thread. Some results for BinClone and Tracelet are empty, which indicate that they are not scalable enough to obtain the search result within the given time frame. Also, we notice that BinClone consumes more memory than the others for building the index, due to its combination of features which enlarges the feature space. We notice that the experimental results are limited within the context of CCFinder. In the future, we will investigate other source code clone detection techniques to generate the ground truth data.

8.4 Scalability Study

In this section, we evaluate Kam1n0's scalability on a large repository of assembly functions. We set up a mini-cluster on *Google Cloud* with four computational nodes. Each of them is a *n1-highmem-4* machine with 2 virtual cores and 13 GB of RAM. We only use regular persistent disks rather than solid state drives. Each machine is given 500 GB of disk storage. All the machines run on *CentOS*. Three machines run the *Spark Computation Framework* and the *Apache Cassandra Database* and the other runs our Kam1n0 engine. To conduct the experiment, we prepare a large collection of binary files. All these files are either open source libraries or applications, such as *Chromium*. In total, there are more than 2,310,000 assembly functions and 27,666,692 basic blocks. Altogether, there are more than 8 GB of assembly code. We gradually index this collection of binaries in random order, and query the zlib binary file of version 2.7.0 on Kam1n0 at every 10,000 assembly function indexing interval. As zlib is a widely used library, it is expected that it has a large number of clones in the repository. We collect the average indexing time for each function to be indexed, as well as the average time it takes to respond to a function query. Figure 7 depicts the average indexing and query response time for each function. The two diagrams suggest that Kam1n0 has a good scalability with respect to the repository size. Even as the number of functions in the repository increases from 10,000 to 2,310,000, the impact on the response time is negligible. There is a spike up at 910,000 due to the regular compaction routine in Cassandra, which increases I/O contention in the database.

9. CONCLUSION AND LESSON LEARNED

Through the collaboration with Defence Research and Development Canada (DRDC), we learned that scalability, which was not considered in previous studies, is a critical issue for deploying a successful assembly clone search engine. To address this, we present the first assembly search engine that combines LSH and subgraph search. Existing off-the-shelf LSH nearest neighbor algorithms and subgraph isomorphism search techniques do not fit our problem setting. Therefore, we propose new variants of LSH scheme and incorporate it with graph search to address the challenges. Experimental results suggest that our proposed MapReduce-based system, Kam1n0, is accurate, efficient, and scalable. Currently Kam1n0 can only identify clones for x86/amd64 processor. In the future, we will extend it to the other processors and investigate approaches that can find clones between different processors. Kam1n0 provides a practical solution of assembly clone search for both DRDC and the reverse engineering community. The contribution is partially reflected by the award received at the 2015 Hex-Rays Plug-In Contest.

10. ACKNOWLEDGMENT

The authors would like to thank the reviewers for the thorough reviews and valuable comments. This research is supported by Defence Research and Development Canada (contract no. W7701-155902/001/QCL) and Canada Research Chairs Program (950-230623).

11. REFERENCES

[1] A. Andoni and P. Indyk. Near-optimal hashing algorithms for approximate nearest neighbor in high dimensions. *Commun. ACM*, 51(1), 2008.

[2] M. Bawa, T. Condie, and P. Ganesan. LSH forest: self-tuning indexes for similarity search. In *Proc. of WWW'05*, 2005.

[3] M. Charikar. Similarity estimation techniques from rounding algorithms. In *Proceedings on 34th Annual ACM STOC'02*, 2002.

[4] P. Charland, B. C. M. Fung, and M. R. Farhadi. Clone search for malicious code correlation. In *Proc. of the NATO RTO Symposium on Information Assurance and Cyber Defense (IST-111)*, 2012.

[5] M. Datar, N. Immorlica, P. Indyk, and V. S. Mirrokni. Locality-sensitive hashing scheme based on p-stable distributions. In *Proc. of ACM SoCG'04*, 2004.

[6] Y. David and E. Yahav. Tracelet-based code search in executables. In *Proc. of SIGPLAN'14*, 2014.

[7] M. R. Farhadi, B. C. M. Fung, P. Charland, and M. Debbabi. Binclone: Detecting code clones in malware. In *Proc. of the 8th International Conference on Software Security and Reliability*, 2014.

[8] M. R. Farhadi, B. C. M. Fung, Y. B. Fung, P. Charland, S. Preda, and M. Debbabi. Scalable code clone search for malware analysis. *Digital Investigation*, 2015.

[9] T. Fawcett. An introduction to roc analysis. *Pattern recognition letters*, 27(8), 2006.

[10] J. Gan, J. Feng, Q. Fang, and W. Ng. Locality-sensitive hashing scheme based on dynamic collision counting. In *Proc. of SIGMOD'12*, 2012.

[11] J. Gao, H. V. Jagadish, W. Lu, and B. C. Ooi. Dsh: Data sensitive hashing for high-dimensional k-nnsearch. In *Proc. of SIGMOD'14*. ACM, 2014.

[12] A. Gionis, P. Indyk, and R. Motwani. Similarity search in high dimensions via hashing. In *Proc. of the VLDB*, 1999.

[13] W. Han, J. Lee, and J. Lee. Turbo$_{\text{iso}}$: towards ultrafast and robust subgraph isomorphism search in large graph databases. In *Proc. of SIGMOD'13*, 2013.

[14] S. Har-Peled, P. Indyk, and R. Motwani. Approximate nearest neighbor: Towards removing the curse of dimensionality. *Theory of Computing*, 8(1), 2012.

[15] E. Juergens et al. Why and how to control cloning in software artifacts. *Technische Universität München*, 2011.

[16] T. Kamiya, S. Kusumoto, and K. Inoue. Ccfinder: a multilinguistic token-based code clone detection system for large scale source code. *IEEE TSE*, 28(7), 2002.

[17] W. M. Khoo. Decompilation as search. *University of Cambridge, Computer Laboratory, Technical Report*, 2013.

[18] W. M. Khoo, A. Mycroft, and R. J. Anderson. Rendezvous: a search engine for binary code. In *Proc. of MSR'13*, 2013.

[19] V. Komsiyski. Binary differencing for media files. 2013.

[20] C. Kruegel, E. Kirda, D. Mutz, W. Robertson, and G. Vigna. Polymorphic worm detection using structural information of executables. In *Proc. of RAID'06*. Springer, 2006.

[21] J. Lee, W. Han, R. Kasperovics, and J. Lee. An in-depth comparison of subgraph isomorphism algorithms in graph databases. *PVLDB*, 6(2), 2012.

[22] Y. Liu, J. Cui, Z. Huang, H. Li, and H. T. Shen. SK-LSH: an efficient index structure for approximate nearest neighbor search. *PVLDB*, 7(9), 2014.

[23] C. D. Manning, P. Raghavan, H. Schütze, et al. *Introduction to information retrieval*, volume 1. Cambridge University Press, 2008.

[24] C. D. Manning and H. Schütze. *Foundations of statistical natural language processing*. MIT press, 1999.

[25] A. Mockus. Large-scale code reuse in open source software. In *Proc. of FLOSS'07*. IEEE, 2007.

[26] A. Saebjornsen. *Detecting Fine-Grained Similarity in Binaries*. PhD thesis, UC Davis, 2014.

[27] A. Sæbjørnsen, J. Willcock, T. Panas, D. J. Quinlan, and Z. Su. Detecting code clones in binary executables. In *Proc. of the 18th International Symposium on Software Testing and Analysis*, 2009.

[28] R. Shamir and D. Tsur. Faster subtree isomorphism. In *Proc. of IEEE ISTCS'97*, 1997.

[29] M. Sojer and J. Henkel. Code reuse in open source software development: Quantitative evidence, drivers, and impediments. *JAIS*, 11(12), 2010.

[30] S. Sonnenburg, G. Rätsch, C. Schäfer, and B. Schölkopf. Large scale multiple kernel learning. *JMLR*, 7, 2006.

[31] Z. Sun, H. Wang, H. Wang, B. Shao, and J. Li. Efficient subgraph matching on billion node graphs. *The VLDB Endowment*, 5(9), 2012.

[32] Y. Tao, K. Yi, C. Sheng, and P. Kalnis. Quality and efficiency in high dimensional nearest neighbor search. In *Proc. of SIGMOD'09*, 2009.

[33] Y. Tao, K. Yi, C. Sheng, and P. Kalnis. Efficient and accurate nearest neighbor and closest pair search in high-dimensional space. *ACM TODS*, 35(3), 2010.

[34] J. R. Ullmann. An algorithm for subgraph isomorphism. *ACM JACM*, 23(1), 1976.

[35] J. Wang, H. T. Shen, J. Song, and J. Ji. Hashing for similarity search: A survey. *arXiv:1408.2927*, 2014.

[36] H. Welte. Current developments in GPL compliance, 2012.

Joint Optimization of Multiple Performance Metrics in Online Video Advertising

Sahin Cem Geyik *, Sergey Faleev *, Jianqiang Shen, Sean O'Donnell, Santanu Kolay
Turn Inc.
901 Marshall Street, Redwood City, CA, USA
{sgeyik, sfaleev, jshen, sodonnell, skolay}@turn.com

ABSTRACT

The field of online advertising, in essence, deals with the problem of presenting ads to online users in the most appropriate contexts to achieve a multitude of advertiser goals. A vast amount of work in online advertising has been focused on optimizing banner display advertising campaigns where the main goal lies in direct response metrics, often as clicks or conversions. In this paper, we explore the newly popularized space of online video advertising, where brand recognition is the key focus. We propose a framework based on a feedback mechanism where we optimize multiple video specific performance indicators while making sure the delivery constraints (budget and user reach) of advertisers are satisfied. While our main focus is on improving metrics such as engagement (amount of view time), and viewability (whether a campaign is within eyesight of a user), we also discuss the possibilities of expanding to other metrics. We demonstrate the benefit of our framework via empirical results in multiple real-world advertising campaigns. To the best of our knowledge, this is the first paper that deals with the unique challenges arising from the nature of online video advertising.

CCS Concepts

•Information systems → Computational advertising; *Expert systems;*

Keywords

Online Advertising; Video Advertising; Performance Optimization

1. INTRODUCTION

Online advertising aims to match advertisers with the most beneficial online users through the most appropriate contexts (websites, mobile applications etc.) in order to maximize their campaign specific goals. These campaign specific goals are often one of two kinds: brand recognition metrics, i.e. any metric which serves to indicate whether or not an audience's opinion of an advertiser's product has improved, or whether or not the size of the audience that knows about an advertiser (or a specific product) has increased; and direct response metrics, which can be directly measured in terms of monetary value, such as a click or a conversion (product purchase, subscription to a newsletter, etc.) [11].

The online advertising ecosystem is generally accepted to be comprised of components which collectively enable advertisers to reach their aforementioned goals: *Demand-side Platforms* (DSPs) strive to find opportunities on behalf of advertisers to show an ad (impression) to a user beneficial to a specific advertiser; *Supply-side Platforms* (SSPs) are publishers (websites or mobile application providers) or intermediary platforms (which publishers connect to) that supply advertising opportunities for multiple competing DSPs (often in a second-price auction) to capture and show an advertisement on; *Data Management Platforms* (DMPs) deal with processing first-party and third-party data for advertisers in order to enable business and analytical inferences for more effective advertising.

By the help of the above three components, the online advertising domain has experienced tremendous growth in the past few years, both in terms of the quality of ads and the amount of Internet traffic allocated to online advertising [19]. In terms of the media type used for advertising, banner display ads have been the main industry standard for the past two decades [4], which are graphic ads designed to achieve user attention, and whose components can also be calibrated for further optimization [9]. In accordance with this trend, a vast amount of literature has been focused towards optimizing direct response metrics which are clicks [6] or conversions [11], since it is not trivial to estimate brand recognition metrics for banner ads. This is especially true for evaluating whether the users' opinions of an advertiser improved or not, which is even more complex.

In this paper, our efforts are mainly focused on optimizing video advertising campaigns where the ads shown to users are in the form of videos, which can have a variety of durations. The key difference for this type of advertising (compared to display ads) is that brand recognition metrics are used much more commonly compared to direct response metrics. Our focus is on two metrics whose detail is given in the next section: (*i*) *Engagement*, which depends on the

* The authors contributed to this work equally.

KDD '16, August 13-17, 2016, San Francisco, CA, USA

DOI: http://dx.doi.org/10.1145/2939672.2939724

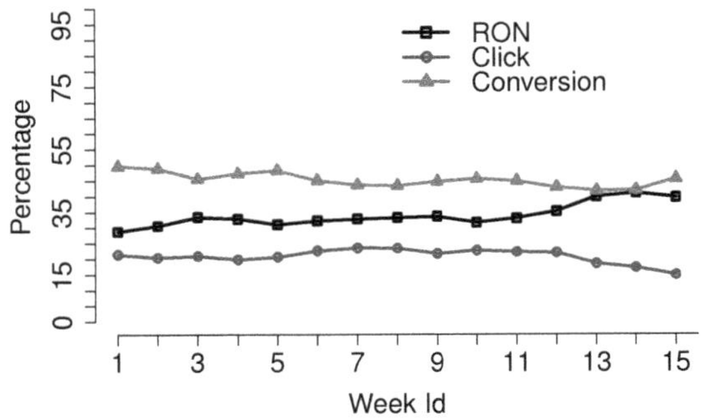

Figure 1: Spend distribution over metric priorities for banner display advertising.

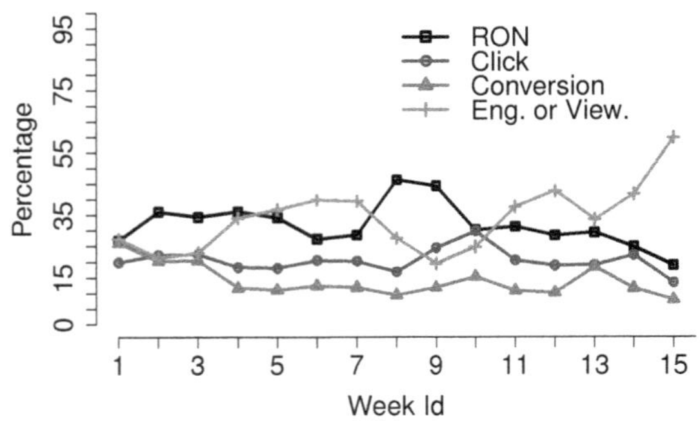

Figure 2: Spend distribution over metric priorities for video advertising.

length of time a video ad is watched, and *(ii) Viewability*, which depends on the location of the video ad inside a webpage or an application. We also propose a feedback-based mechanism that both optimizes the aforementioned two metrics, and satisfies the advertisers' delivery constraints. To the best of our knowledge this is the first work that deals with the specific challenges of online video advertising.

The main contributions of this work include:

- A detailed examination of challenges that arise from online video advertising,
- A multi-criteria optimization framework specific to video advertising which aims to also satisfy advertisers' delivery constraints, and,
- Real-world experiments and results that demonstrate the advantages of our approach.

2. BACKGROUND AND CHALLENGES OF VIDEO ADVERTISING

As aforementioned, we explore the details of video advertising in this work, which is inherently different compared to banner display advertising. First of all, the advertisers that follow the path of display advertising* often utilize click or conversion optimization campaigns. While the advertisers also wish to receive brand recognition through run-of-network campaigns (RON) where no optimization is implied with fixed bid values, aiming to explore new audiences via relaxed user targeting constraints, they have no way to measure whether the users were indeed interested in their product, except for the direct response metrics. Please see Figure 1 for the distribution of campaign spending for display advertising on Turn's platform for a 15-week period within 2015 over different metric prioritizations which supports our claim. In online video advertising however, the advertisers are mainly concerned with brand recognition. This makes it necessary to use metrics which are more closely tied to evaluating the brand recognition performance of a campaign. In this paper we are mainly focusing on three such metrics (the first one specific to video advertising):

- **Engagement** metric measures the percentage of the total duration of a video ad that has been actively watched by the user. There can be multiple types of engagement events (e.g. 25%, 50%, 75%). In the context of our current work, we take engagement to be a binary event where 1 represents that the user watched the whole (100%) of the video ad, and 0 otherwise. Please note that, intuitively, engagement metric measures users' opinion of an advertiser, since it indicates the steady interest (as measured by the amount of time ad was watched) of the user towards the ad.
- **Viewability** indicates the goodness of the ad's location, hence its *viewability* by the online user. Formally, the *view* event of an ad impression is 1 if the video ad is within eye-sight of the user during some time interval (industry standard is 2 seconds with at least 50% of ad area is within eye-sight). This metric suggests size of the audience knowing about an advertiser or product, since the knowledge of a user on an advertiser has not formed if the user has not *viewed* the ad.
- **User Reach** indicates how many users have watched the ads. Formally, since it is common for advertisers to put a frequency cap on the number of impressions delivered to one single user, *User Reach* can be calculated as the number of delivered impressions.

Figure 2 shows the distribution of spending for the video campaigns within Turn that signals importance on different metrics for the same 15-week period as in Figure 1. It can be seen that there is a clear upwards trend of advertisers utilizing viewability and engagement optimization tactics. Furthermore, we can also observe that the amount of budget spent for conversion campaigns holds a much smaller portion of the total video spend compared to display campaigns.

Lack of interest in direct response metric for video advertising has both advantages and disadvantages. A significant advantage comes from the fact that several problems arising for campaigns that value conversions are no longer of concern. First of all, one of the greatest problems related to conversion prediction/tracking is delayed feedback [2], since it takes a significant amount of time for a user to act (in terms of *conversion*, i.e. product purchase etc.) after seeing an ad, or clicking it. Secondly, tracking conversions requires a methodical way to attribute the conversion to the campaigns that show the ad to the user [17, 5], which is not trivial. This means that when we have a campaign that prioritizes conversions as its performance metric, there will be times when it will not even be able to register those conversions (because they have been attributed to another campaign) for accurate performance estimation.

* Within this paper, from time to time, we will use the term *display advertising*, for short, instead of *banner display advertising*.

The main disadvantage of having campaigns that prioritize brand recognition (not direct response) metrics is the ambiguity in assigning a monetary value to the evaluated metrics. While it is trickier for an advertiser to give a monetary value for a click, it is often trivial to see how much monetary value an advertiser should assign to a conversion. For example, the amount of money spent by the user when s/he purchases a product, or the profit made by the advertiser for that conversion, can yield a very intuitive monetary value which can be assigned to a certain conversion. This way, we can look at return-on-investment (ROI) for a specific campaign, which is the ratio of monetary value received (via clicks or conversions) by the campaign to the total amount of money spent for impressions by the campaign. Therefore, in some cases, we do not even have to have a great reach (number of unique users which are shown an impression) or delivery (the amount of money spent for advertising via impressions), as long as we can get a sufficient number of direct responses. This however is not the case for brand recognition metrics. There is no trivial way to assign monetary value to an engagement or view event by a user. Hence, the problem we need to solve for online video advertising includes both optimization of brand recognition metrics, as well as satisfying user reach and delivery criteria set by the advertiser. Please note that satisfying the delivery constraints of an advertiser campaign by itself is a difficult problem which is severely affected by the characteristics of the audience that the advertiser wants to reach [7, 18]. This difficulty gets further aggravated in video advertising campaigns where we aim to improve brand recognition metrics as well.

As mentioned in the previous section, coming up with a system that optimizes brand recognition metrics as well as delivery is our focus. After the literature survey in the next section, we will first delve into the formal definition of the problem we are trying to solve. We then will present our proposed methodology which aims to perform a constant trade-off between the delivery of a campaign and engagement as well as view events received by that campaign.

3. PREVIOUS WORK

Based on the domain-specific goals and metrics of success for online video advertising, we have introduced the challenges that are significantly different from those of the current mainstream approach, which is display advertising. As expected, display advertising has also been much more extensively studied in literature. To the best of our knowledge, our current work is the first to address the specific challenges arising in online video advertising. However, considering that our work also employs a joint optimization over various metrics, we will detail prior research done and approaches taken to jointly optimize performance and/or delivery metrics in online advertising. Please note that there are very few works detailing optimization efforts in online *video* advertising, and these in general exist in the substantially different context of online video advertising infrastructure. One such work deals with jointly optimizing the allocation of video rates and inserted advertisement duration in a wireless broadcast network to maximize profit [8].

Online Video Advertising: There have been a variety of proposed systems to implement effective forms of online video advertising, focused on insertion scheduling, video context similarity, and user relevancy issues. Inserting advertisements into a video stream is an especially complicated problem, as video advertisements are likely to degrade user experience if done clumsily, reducing the effectiveness of a campaign and potentially driving away users. Intuitively, advertisements are less disruptive when they are contextually relevant, with one proposed system [12] using advertiser-provided images (relevant to their own brand/message) to be compared against sampled video frames to determine the best candidate advertisements to show in a given video.

Another previous effort [14] focused on detecting sets of non-intrusive advertisement insertion points within a video, in addition to using contextual and visual-aural relevance to select the best advertisements to place. The authors demonstrated that this approach improved user viewing experience. A similar work [20] chose to introduce the ability to bookmark or delay interaction with an advertisement, in order to avoid video viewing interruption partially or entirely. Finally, in [22], the authors focus on *user's attention relevancy*, where assuming a video ad triggered by a user can be considered relevant to a user's attention, they propose a framework that generates semantic concepts from video broadcasts, which are subsequently used to rank video advertisements by relevancy concepts to find the most relevant video advertisements to ones triggered by a user previously. This paper presented findings which suggested that such an approach was regarded as less intrusive and more satisfying.

Compared to previous work in online advertising, our current effort differs in multiple ways. First of all, the listed literature is mostly involved with systems for scheduling and presenting video content, and have access to the actual video content to parse and analyze ahead of time; this is not applicable to a system like ours, which participates in the online advertising auction process in real-time under strict constraints. Additionally, most previous work is evaluated based on user studies and subjective measures, without much of a feedback loop or evaluation metric to evolve their systems' algorithms or models over time. As a DSP, we are essentially solving a different set of problems in online video advertising, which are necessarily complicated by the evaluation metrics that we are striving to satisfy.

Joint Optimization in Online Advertising: In our current proposal, we are not claiming to introduce new methods of joint optimization, but rather, demonstrating a novel application for joint optimization of desired metrics in online video advertising and its empirical effectiveness. To the best of our knowledge, our proposed use of joint optimization over multiple brand recognition metrics for online video advertising is a novel effort, whereas joint optimization techniques have seen historical use in more traditional areas of online advertising. Perhaps the closest such use to our approach is a framework for the joint optimization of guaranteed delivery (often a brand advertiser's goal) and pay-per-click (a performance-centric goal) auctions in sponsored search, with the objective of increasing search engine revenue [16]. This effort demonstrated the effectiveness of joint optimization compared to many baseline strategies. Additional efforts in sponsored search included jointly optimizing budget allocation and bid price setting, while presenting that it outperformed both bid price optimization and campaign budget optimization done separately [24].

A multi-objective programming approach [1] to optimizing click-through rate and downstream engagement metrics (e.g. a third-party reported time spent on a page), with constraints on how much click volume can be lost, is analogous to our approach, except for direct-response metrics and advertisers. Finally, previous research at the intersection of joint optimization applications and online video advertising seems to exist in a complete different facet of the online advertising industry (in this case, the actual provisioners of video traffic, i.e. the wireless video broadcast network itself) [8], and is not applicable to our challenges.

4. RESEARCH PROBLEMS

Optimization Goals of Video Advertising. Real-time Bidding enables advertisers to target their ads to specific users and cherry-pick only the impressions they deem most valuable to them. The core of our system is a bidding algorithm that computes an appropriate bid for an ad to be submitted to a webpage or mobile app that is being presented to an online user. There is a plethora of efforts in the literature addressing the problem of *bid estimation*. For traditional display advertising, bid optimization can be modeled as a linear programming problem where the objective is to maximize the expected revenue and the constraint is the budget of an advertiser [3]. The bid or the cost per impression is then modeled as:

$$\text{bid} = P(\text{outcome} \mid \text{user, page, ad}) \times \text{Goal}, \quad (1)$$

where the outcome is usually a click or conversion (i.e. direct responses, which we mentioned previously to be the main focus of display advertising) and the *Goal* is defined by the advertiser and indicates the monetary value of such an outcome. *User* and *page* dimensions are provided by the incoming bid request. The majority of research is focused on estimating the probability of a click or conversion. Researchers typically employ logistic regression and its variants or frequency-based features to estimate this probability [11, 15, 6, 13].

Applying the above approach directly to video advertising is not feasible. First of all, as we explained in sections 1 and 2, video advertising campaigns mainly deal with brand-recognition metrics as a priority, which are harder to assign a monetary value. Furthermore, instead of having one single goal, video advertisers typically have multiple performance metrics that can be challenging to be optimized simultaneously. Such metrics can be calculated in multiple ways, depending on the advertiser's preferences. Popular ones include *engagement rate* (ER), *viewability rate* (VR), *user reach* (UR), *cost per click* (CPC), *cost per action* (CPA), and *return-on-investment* (ROI). Assuming we get T bid requests $X = \{\mathbf{x}_1, \mathbf{x}_2, .., \mathbf{x}_T\}$, we can calculate the performance of a bid model $f_\mathcal{A}$ for advertiser $\mathcal{A}$ as follows:

$$\text{ER}(f_\mathcal{A}, X) = \frac{\sum_{\mathbf{x} \in win(f_\mathcal{A}, X)} complete(\mathcal{A}, \mathbf{x})}{|win(f_\mathcal{A}, X)|} ,$$

$$\text{VR}(f_\mathcal{A}, X) = \frac{\sum_{\mathbf{x} \in win(f_\mathcal{A}, X)} viewable(\mathcal{A}, \mathbf{x})}{|win(f_\mathcal{A}, X)|} ,$$

$$\text{UR}(f_\mathcal{A}, X) = |win(f_\mathcal{A}, X)| ,$$

$$\text{CPC}(f_\mathcal{A}, X) = \frac{\sum_{\mathbf{x} \in win(f_\mathcal{A}, X)} cost(f_\mathcal{A}, \mathbf{x})}{\sum_{\mathbf{x} \in win(f_\mathcal{A}, X)} click(\mathcal{A}, \mathbf{x})} ,$$

$$\text{CPA}(f_\mathcal{A}, X) = \frac{\sum_{\mathbf{x} \in win(f_\mathcal{A}, X)} cost(f_\mathcal{A}, \mathbf{x})}{\sum_{\mathbf{x} \in win(f_\mathcal{A}, X)} conv(\mathcal{A}, \mathbf{x})} ,$$

$$\text{ROI}(f_\mathcal{A}, X) = \frac{\sum_{\mathbf{x} \in win(f_\mathcal{A}, X)} value(\mathcal{A}, \mathbf{x})}{\sum_{\mathbf{x} \in win(f_\mathcal{A}, X)} cost(f_\mathcal{A}, \mathbf{x})} . \quad (2)$$

Above,

- $win(f_\mathcal{A}, X)$ denotes the set of bid requests that are won by model $f_\mathcal{A}$ and have been shown some impressions of $\mathcal{A}$, and $|win(f_\mathcal{A}, X)|$ is the number of impressions shown to users by advertiser $\mathcal{A}$,
- $complete(\mathcal{A}, \mathbf{x})$ indicates whether the impression of $\mathcal{A}$ on $\mathbf{x}$ was watched by the user for its whole duration, and $viewable(\mathcal{A}, \mathbf{x})$ indicates whether the impression of $\mathcal{A}$ on $\mathbf{x}$ is within eye-sight of the user reported by the third-party,
- $click(\mathcal{A}, \mathbf{x})$ is a binary indicator on whether the impression on $\mathbf{x}$ leads to a click for $\mathcal{A}$, and $conv(\mathcal{A}, \mathbf{x})$ indicates whether the impression on $\mathbf{x}$ leads to a conversion for $\mathcal{A}$,
- $cost(f_\mathcal{A}, \mathbf{x})$ is the amount of money spent by model $f_\mathcal{A}$ to win bid request $\mathbf{x}$, and $value(\mathcal{A}, \mathbf{x})$ is the amount of value (by the clicks and conversions performed) provided by winning bid request $\mathbf{x}$ to advertiser $\mathcal{A}$.

Optimizing Multiple Goals. Given advertiser $\mathcal{A}$ with budget B and optimization goals $\langle \phi_1, \phi_2, .., \phi_L \rangle$ where each element is one of the metrics defined in Equation 2, our ultimate objective can be formulated as in the following:

DEFINITION 1. The video bidding optimization algorithm *tries to search for a model f that calculates and submits bids for requests $X = \{\mathbf{x}_1, \mathbf{x}_2, .., \mathbf{x}_T\}$ for advertiser $\mathcal{A}$, so that*

$$\max_{f:\mathbf{x}\to\mathbb{R}} \langle \phi_1(f, X), \phi_2(f, X), .., \phi_L(f, X) \rangle$$
$$s.t. \quad f(\mathbf{x}_t) \geq 0 \quad , \forall\, 1 \leq t \leq T ,$$
$$\sum_{\mathbf{x} \in win(f, X)} cost(f, \mathbf{x}) \leq B , \quad (3)$$

In other words, given the constraints on budget and inventory, we seek an optimal bidding strategy to maximize multiple returns for our customers.

DEFINITION 2. *A bid model f is* sound *if it satisfies both budget and inventory constraints; a sound model $f^1 : \mathbf{x} \to \mathbb{R}$* dominates *another sound model $f^2 : \mathbf{x} \to \mathbb{R}$ iff*

$$\phi_l(f^1, X) \geq \phi_l(f^2, X) \quad , \forall\, 1 \leq l \leq L ;$$

A sound model f^* is utopian *iff f^* dominates any other sound model f.*

In most cases, given the optimization goals $\langle \phi_1, \phi_2, ..., \phi_L \rangle$, it is infeasible to find a *utopian* bidding model for the advertiser. For example, assume advertiser $\mathcal{A}$ wants to optimize both the click rate and the engagement rate. It is clear that they can be contradictory to each other: to maximize clicks, we want to make the ads as eye-catching as possible; however, once the ads get attention, it is inevitable that some users will skip the video play. On the other hand, the video ads could finish without skipping (100% engagement event) if they are invisible but in such cases the click rate will be hurt.

Since *utopian* bidding models rarely exist for video advertising, searching for appropriate models is not as straightforward as for the conventional optimization problems of display advertising. In some cases, the advertiser is neutral about the priority of optimization goals and does not require an absolute ranking order. We can then search for the optimal bidding model by formulating a single-objective optimization problem such that the optimal solution to the single-objective optimization problem cannot be dominated by any sound model of the multi-objective optimization problem. This can be achieved by proper scalarization of the objectives:

$$\max_{f:\mathbf{x}\to\mathbb{R}} \; w_1 \cdot \phi_1(f,X) + w_2 \cdot \phi_2(f,X) + \ldots + w_L \cdot \phi_L(f,X)$$
$$s.t. \; f(\mathbf{x}_t) \geq 0 \quad , \forall\, 1 \leq t \leq T \; ,$$
$$\sum_{\mathbf{x}\in win(f,X)} cost(f,\mathbf{x}) \leq B \; , \tag{4}$$

Here, w_l is the advertiser's preferences for different optimization goals. By choosing different parameters for the scalarization, we can produce bidding models with emphases on different goals. However, in many cases the above scalarization approach is not applicable due to two reasons: first, many advertisers have sufficient preference and the optimization goals can be ranked in the order of importance; second, the choice of weight w_l has a significant impact on the generated bidding model and it is not straightforward for advertisers to choose weighting parameters that make the most sense to them.

In this paper, we focus on the case where an advertiser's optimization goals can be ranked in order of importance. Let's assume, without loss of generality, that the performance goals are in an order of importance so that ϕ_1 is the most important and ϕ_L is the least important to the advertiser. Then searching for the optimal bidding models becomes solving a sequence of L single-objective optimization problems of the form

$$\max_{f:\mathbf{x}\to\mathbb{R}} \; \phi_l(f,X)$$
$$s.t. \phi_j(f,X) \geq y_j^* \quad , \forall\, 1 \leq j \leq l-1 \; ,$$
$$f(\mathbf{x}_t) \geq 0 \quad , \forall\, 1 \leq t \leq T \; ,$$
$$\sum_{\mathbf{x}\in win(f,X)} cost(f,\mathbf{x}) \leq B \; , \tag{5}$$

where y_j^* is the optimal performance value of the above problem with $l = j$. In other words, in each iteration we estimate the optimal performance value and use it as the constraint in the next iteration. Let us give an example to make this optimization scheme clearer - suppose we solve the optimization problem for the first objective, and we find f_1 which gives the optimal $\phi_1(f_1, X) = y_1^*$. Then, in the next iteration, we will find the best f_2 to optimize $\phi_2(f_2, X) = y_2^*$, such that f_2 also satisfies $\phi_1(f_2, X) \geq \phi_1(f_1, X) = y_1^*$. We obtain the final bidding model after the Lth problem is solved. Please note that this optimization scheme only makes sense if the function f_l we find in each iteration is not unique, otherwise we will not update the solution for the rest of the iterations (no other f will be feasible for any other iterations). Practically, the nonuniqueness of bidding models f_l could be realized as a quasi-random (with respect to optimization goals ϕ_{l+1}, ϕ_{l+2}, etc) choice of the bidding opportunities in which the ad actually participates when the budget could be satisfied by bidding on a fraction of the available to a bidding opportunity.

In this paper, we will discuss how to approximately solve the above problem and calculate the bidding model for video advertising when an advertiser's optimization goals are strictly ranked in order of importance.

Special Case of Dual Goals. In general, the most important goal of display advertising is to acquire as many clicks/actions as possible. It is different for online video advertising: like traditional TV advertising, its major purpose is branding – utilizing video impressions to create a differentiated name and image of products in order to establish a presence in the consumer's mind, hence attracting and retaining customers. To achieve this, advertisers usually want to maximize user reach (UR) and deliver as many impressions as possible. Besides maximizing user reach, video advertisers also tend to want a secondary performance goal, which can further indicate brand-recognition, such as engagement rate (ER) and viewability rate (VR). Although less common, as aforementioned, some advertisers do value direct response metrics in video advertising, such as cost per click (CPC) and cost per action (CPA). Thus, the most common case for optimizing video advertising has dual goals: one is UR and another is ER/VR/CPC/CPA.

As an emerging media, the winning price of video advertising impressions is usually high and predictable [23]. Given that an advertiser's budget is limited, maximizing impressions is then equivalent to spending all of the available budget. From this it follows that the optimization problem of dual goals given in (5) can be formulated as:

$$\max_{f:\mathbf{x}\to\mathbb{R}} \; \phi(f,X)$$
$$s.t. \; f(\mathbf{x}_t) \geq 0 \quad , \forall\, 1 \leq t \leq T \; ,$$
$$\sum_{\mathbf{x}\in win(f,X)} cost(f,\mathbf{x}) = B \; , \tag{6}$$

Here, ϕ is the secondary (after UR) metric of importance, which are VR, ER, CPC, or CPA. The bidding model needs to spend the entire budget to ensure maximum audience reach. However, solving the above problem directly is challenging: first of all, the expected value for a bid request $(\mathbf{x}_t)$ is hard to forecast, especially for a newly created ad; second, the huge size of bid request patterns, as well as the real-time nature (as we do not have a global view of the bid requests, and these come in a sequence) of online advertising, make direct search prohibitively expensive. It is necessary to adopt an efficient approximate solution, which we will introduce in the next section. Our methodology relies on a feedback mechanism that constantly changes the manner with which we optimize the secondary goal, based on the current status of the UR satisfaction (since this is our first priority).

5. METHODOLOGY

In order to improve both user reach and other performance metrics (e.g. viewability rate, engagement rate, CPC, or CPA), we adopt an approximation of the sequential goal optimization. Within this approach, advertisers are allowed to set different priorities for different metric goals. The goal with the highest priority is always assigned to the user reach, hence our algorithm first tries to satisfy the user reach goal (in terms of budget to be delivered). Once we estimate that the primary goal can be satisfied, the algorithm tries to improve the second priority goal (e.g. viewability rate), and this process keeps iterating until we find a balance point where the goals are optimized. In each step, the algorithm tries to adjust the bidding model while keeping the higher priority goal satisfied. Such adjustments end when the metric with lower priority cannot be improved without trading-off the metric with higher priority.

5.1 Framework of Dual Optimization

As discussed above, we first focus on the case of dual goals and later describe case with more then two goals. Our approach to solving the dual optimization problem can be considered as a special case of *reinforcement learning* [21]: the bidding model makes a bid based on the system dynamics, hoping to achieve optimal rewards; based on the received feedback, we might need to constantly adjust the bidding model. It is a continuous evolutionary process in the Markovian environment. Like other reinforcement learning problems, we rely on accurate modeling of the environment to improve the secondary goal of a campaign while optimizing the primary goal. Having such models allows the system to generate virtual experience and predict the consequences of actions before they are taken. Our models of the world consist of two components:

- **Estimation of Impression Need β,** which is a numerical value between 0 and 1, where the larger value indicates more desire for impressions. We take the historical bid traffic and win rate as input to calculate the delivery expectation in real-time for the campaign. Such signals enable the platform to understand how well the acquisition of impressions goes,
- **Estimation of Goal Metric ϕ,** which maps each perceived <BidRequest, Bid> pair to a single number, a *reward*, indicating the intrinsic desirability of the bid. We apply machine learning algorithms on historical bidding data in order to train hierarchical prediction models [11].

Impression Need β for a campaign indicates its user reach satisfaction, and our system then cherry-picks bid requests according to their expected performance for ϕ. Here, we give an illustrative example before the formal explanation of our algorithm. Suppose that the advertiser sets the primary campaign goal to be user reach (UR), and the secondary goal to be viewability rate (VR). As we noted above, the user reach goal will be satisfied if Impression Need $\beta < 1$ (ideally, $\beta \ll 1$). The viewability rate goal is satisfied by introducing a dynamic filtering threshold for the viewability rate, θ_v. For each bid request, the website and user information is extracted from the bid request parameters, and expected viewability rate ϕ_v is estimated for the qualified campaign utilizing the <ad, website, user> combination. The campaign will not submit a bid for the request if $\phi_v < \theta_v$.

The framework for calculating the dynamic filtering threshold θ is given in Algorithm 1, which performs the secondary goal optimization, while satisfying the primary goal of user reach. For every campaign, θ is calculated periodically in real-time together with β. We start with a conservative θ at the beginning of the campaign to give it a boost in spending. After a new β is calculated for a given campaign, the θ increases accordingly if β is in the *comfortable delivery* mode region, and decreases if β is in the *risky delivery* mode region, and does not change otherwise. These regions (the function *classify* in Algorithm 1) are calculated based on the hypothesis checking for upper and lower limits for each region. If the user reach or delivery situation is constantly good (β is in the comfortable delivery region), then the secondary goal is improved in a methodical manner by consistently increasing the threshold.

Algorithm 1: Optimization of Dual Goals

Input: θ: Current threshold for the secondary goal
Output: θ': New threshold for the secondary goal

$\beta \leftarrow$ calculate Impression Need ;
status = classify(β) ;
$\Delta \leftarrow$ calculate the moving step based on β ;
if *status is* Comfortable Delivery **then**
  $\theta' = \theta + \Delta$;
else if *status is* Risky Delivery **then**
  $\theta' = \theta - \Delta$;
else
  $\theta' = \theta$;
$\theta' = \min(1, \max(\theta', 0))$;
return θ'

5.2 Estimating Impression Need

We need a proxy variable in real-time to evaluate how well we are satisfying the user reach goals, which is our first priority, of a campaign. Before explaining the design of Impression Need, we would like to first explain the life cycle for a bid request, which ends in an advertisement shown (which is the 'impression' event) to the user. When a Real-Time Bid exchange (RTB exchange, which is a part of the SSP component of the online advertising ecosystem) sends a bid request to the DSP, several campaigns are usually qualified (through passing targeting criteria set by the advertisers) for bidding. These campaigns participate in an internal auction performed by the DSP, where they are evaluated based on multiple criteria set by the advertisers, and the advertisement belonging to the campaign with the highest score (for CPA or CPC campaigns this score is proportional to the value returned by Equation 1) is sent (together with the bid price in the bid response) back from the DSP. The bid responses sent to the RTB exchange by several DSPs participate in the RTB Exchange's auction (which is usually *second price*), where the ad with the highest bid wins the auction and is served to the online user.

Usually advertisers want their campaign budgets to be delivered fully with more or less steady pacing within a day (similar amounts of user reach achieved for different periods of the day) [10]. In such a case, in order to ensure steady pacing of the budget, the campaign only participates in β fraction of internal DSP auctions for which it qualifies (according to the targeting criteria set by the advertiser). This dynamic parameter β $[0 \leq \beta \leq 1]$ directly reflects an advertiser's need for impressions. We heuristically adjust β at time period $t+1$ based on "ideal" pacing of the remaining daily budget, the amount of user reach (hence budget spent) in the previous time interval, and traffic:

$$\beta_{t+1} \propto \beta_t \frac{B_{t+1}}{S_t} \frac{BidRequest(t)}{BidRequest(t+1)} \frac{WinRate(t)}{WinRate(t+1)} \tag{7}$$

where B_{t+1} is the budget to be spent at $t+1$, S_t is the spending at t, $BidRequest$ is the number of bid requests (we calculate $BidRequest(t+1)$, i.e. number of bid requests that is predicted to be achieved in time $t+1$, using historical data) and $WinRate$ is the average probability of winning a bid. Impression Need, β, can be applied to ensure smooth budget pacing within a day while finishing the daily budget by the end of the day (this would indeed qualify as satisfying the user reach, UR, as explained in § 4). The case when $\beta \ll 1$ indicates a good delivery situation (i.e. the campaign participates in only a very small fraction of qualified internal DSP auctions, because it is comfortably satisfying its UR constraint), and the case when $\beta \approx 1$ (the campaign participates in all qualified internal auctions) indicates a poor delivery situation, when the campaign has the risk of not satisfying budget constraints in (5) and (6).

5.3 Improving Brand Recognition

Please note that the framework given in Algorithm 1 improves the secondary goal if and only if we have a comfortable delivery pattern for the campaign. When the campaign struggles to attain its delivery or user reach goals, we need a methodical way to increase the bids for the campaign, since higher bid amounts increase a campaign's chances of winning the RTB exchange's auctions.

LEMMA 1. *When the budget is not fully spent, higher bid prices will obtain more impressions.*

PROOF. Real-time bidding follows a second price auction mechanism, therefore increasing the bid prices would not affect our cost on those impressions that had been acquired before. On the other hand, given higher bid prices, some bids that we lost before could have been won. □

This in a way causes the campaign to pay higher than its expected value for each impression; however, it also helps the campaign to satisfy its primary goal, which is user reach. There is clearly a trade-off between the primary and secondary goals of a campaign. In this case, our proposed approach calculates the bid (b) (for the bid request that this campaign qualifies for) as a function of three parameters, ϕ_v, θ_v, and the maximum average bid price specified by the advertiser, b_m:

$$b = f(b_m, \phi_v, \theta_v), \tag{8}$$

where b_m is provided for a campaign when the advertiser does not want to pay more than b_m per served impression on average.

For proprietary reasons and company policy, we are not able to give the exact details of the function f, however, in general, $f(b_m, \phi_v, \theta_v)$ monotonically increases with increasing ϕ_v or b_m. We would like to emphasize here that this function $f(b_m, \phi_v, \theta_v)$ is used for brand-recognition metrics (e.g. viewability and engagements) when there is no trivial way to assign a monetary value for the events seen.

We utilize the threshold θ_v as the parameter that describes current delivery situation, instead of *Impression Need*, β, in f. This is due to the statistical nature of Impression Need which is caused by the internet traffic. We have observed that β could fluctuate in a broad range within a day, while the threshold θ_v incrementally changes with time and therefore has a more smooth behavior that reflects the delivery trends at a larger time scale.

An illustrative example of f is shown in Figure 3. In a comfortable delivery situation ($\theta_v > 0$), the bidding function $f(b_m, \phi_v, \theta_v)$ decreases in the region of small and intermediate ϕ_v, therefore shifting the average in-view rate to higher values for won impressions. This has a similar effect of cherry-picking bid requests with predicted high viewability. In risky delivery situations ($\theta_v \approx 0$), the function $f(b_m, \phi_v, \theta_v)$ increases in the region of small and intermediate ϕ_v, and eventually, at $\theta_v = 0$ reaches maximum value of b_m for $\phi_v = 0$. Please note that $f(b_m, \phi_v, \theta_v \approx 0)$ still increases for increasing ϕ_v, hence improving the secondary goal of the campaign. Such behavior reflects the fact that the advertiser's primary goal is user reach or delivery, and if delivery is bad, the bidding function should be as high as possible (restricted only by maximum average bid price), even for bid-requests with a small probability of success. Note that for $\phi_v > 0$, the bidding function could be larger than b_m only if the average price per impression for the given campaign over several days is less than b_m, hence we have some relaxation in bidding.

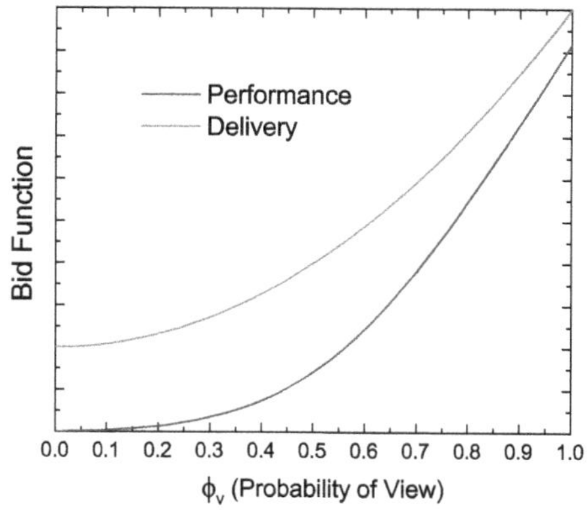

Figure 3: Illustration of bidding functions of dynamic model in performance and delivery limits.

In the above example, the secondary goal is completely ignored (bid is simply $b = b_m$) if the campaign has extremely tight targeting and therefore the delivery goal is hard to satisfy ($\beta = 1$ and therefore $\theta_v \approx 0$) and also if the average price per impression in last several days is close to the limit of b_m. On the other hand, if delivery is good ($\beta \ll 1$), the secondary goal is fully considered and θ_v approaches the maximum possible value (constrained by delivery staying in a neutral region), hence cherry-picking good bid requests to improve the secondary goal.

5.4 Improving Direct Response

Note that the bid function f described in the previous subsection is for brand recognition metrics (i.e. viewability and engagement). This approach significantly differs from the bid function for conventional CPC or CPA optimization goal types. For these goal types, the advertiser sets the maximum average bid price, b_m, as well as the dollar goal value, *Goal*, which indicates the monetary value each click or action is worth. In such a case, due to the second price nature of RTB exchange auctions, the optimal strategy is to bid as given in Equation 1. We can still use the methodology given in § 5.1 to receive more clicks and conversions per ad shown to online users by a campaign. However, modification of the shape of the bidding function of Equation 1 is suboptimal since it may either reduce the return on investment (ROI) below 100% in the case of bidding higher than optimal, or lead to possible underdelivery (user reach goal is not satisfied) in the case of bidding lower than optimal.

In the case of the viewability or engagement goal types, there is no monetary goal value assigned to a view or an engagement event, and therefore there is no consistent ROI definition. This means that we can utilize different shapes of the bidding function due to what the advertiser may prefer to optimize towards - higher delivery or higher performance. The extreme case of the delivery optimization bidding function is the constant bidding function, $b = b_m$, whereas the extreme case of the performance optimization bidding function is a function that is very small in the region of small and intermediate ϕ_v, and increases only in the region of large probabilities of success, $\phi_v \approx 1$.

As we detailed in § 5.3, based on the current delivery situation (described by the dynamic filtering threshold θ_v), our bidding function dynamically changes in a range - from a constant bidding strategy, i.e. $b = b_m$, in the case of bad delivery, to the secondary goal optimizing bidding strategy in the case of good delivery. As we will demonstrate in the experiments section, this dynamic bidding approach turns out to give a better combination of delivery and performance compared to static bidding functions that are set towards the optimization of either delivery or performance.

5.5 Beyond Dual Goals

Currently we implemented the above goal optimization algorithm with only first and second priority goals. The expansion to larger than two goals makes sense only if the targeting criteria set by the advertiser for a campaign is loose enough compared to its budget (user reach or delivery goal), therefore enough inventory is available for the campaign to enable optimization of more than two goals. While this is an open problem, we will sketch here an idea which may indeed help with optimizing towards multiple goals while the user reach constraint is achieved.

In the case of more than two optimization goals, we believe that the bidding function should be chosen based on the second priority goal. If the second priority goal is viewability or engagement, then the bidding function from Equation 8 is used. If the secondary goal is a direct response metric such as CPC or CPA, then the bidding function of Equation 1 is used with dynamic thresholding for *click-through rate*, θ_c, or *conversion rate*, θ_a. After the second priority goal is improved, i.e. if we have high values of θ_2, we can utilize Impression Need β to optimize towards the next priority goals by utilizing θ_i where $i > 2$. (Here θ_i is the dynamic threshold for goal i.) At any time period when Impression Need enters a risky delivery region, the thresholds for the lower priority goals should be reduced first until the comfortable delivery region is reached, obeying the goal priorities set by the advertiser.

Practically, the system should estimate some maximum threshold set, $\hat{\theta}_i < 1$, such that achieving $\theta_i \approx \hat{\theta}_i$ will be considered as satisfaction of the goal i. This allows the system to progress to the next optimization goal. Indeed, for dual-goal optimization with set $\hat{\theta_2}$, then $\theta_2 = \hat{\theta_2}$ and $\beta << 1$ could be the final equilibrium state for well-spending campaigns, while without $\hat{\theta_2}$, θ_2 will increase until reaching the limit of $\theta_2 \approx 1$ while β being still in comfortable delivery zone (but not $\beta << 1$ anymore).

6. EXPERIMENTAL RESULTS

In this section, we will present some preliminary results on real-world campaigns that employ the filtering and bidding methodologies listed in § 5. In Figure 4, we demonstrate the delivery and viewability rate for three models: (*i*) dynamic model, (*ii*) static performance model, and (*iii*) static delivery model. Among these, the *dynamic model* is the sequential goal optimization scheme described in § 5, where the primary goal is delivery and secondary goal is the viewability rate. The bidding function of this model is dynamically adjusted based on the current delivery situation (which is approximated by the proxy variable θ_v, viewability rate filtering threshold). The two static models given in the figure are the viewability optimization models that are similar to the dynamic model in all aspects (i.e. they have the same mechanism for the cherry-picking of bid requests with threshold θ_v as the dynamic model) except that the bidding function is static, hence it does not depend on θ_v (bids do not change with the current delivery situation, i.e. how well we are on track to satisfy the delivery or user reach constraint). The static performance model has a bidding function which is optimized for higher performance (we only bid high when the predicted viewability rate is significantly high), while the static delivery model has a bidding function which is optimized for higher delivery (aims for delivery by bidding higher even for bid requests with low estimated viewability). The bidding function of the static performance model can be given as $f_p(b_m, \phi_v) = f(b_m, \phi_v, \theta_v = 1)$ (from § 5). The bidding function of the static delivery model, $f_d(b_m, \phi_v)$, has larger values than $f_p(b_m, \phi_v)$ in the region of small and intermediate ϕ_v (while still $f_d(b_m, \phi_v = 0) = f_p(b_m, \phi_v = 0) = 0$), but these functions have similar values in the region of large ϕ_v.

The dynamic and the two static models were run for the same campaign and the same daily budget during an 11-day period within 2015 (we replicated all the properties of these campaigns, such as targeting, while only tweaking the bidding strategy). We applied a tight targeting constraint on all the campaigns for the first five days to study the performance of all the listed models in a potentially risky delivery situation. In the last six days, a loose targeting tactic has been applied to the campaigns to see the outcome of the models in a comfortable delivery setting. It can be observed from Figure 4(a) that in the first five days, the delivery of the dynamic model is better than both of the static models*. In the tight targeting situation, the dynamic model fully delivers its daily budget while the static delivery model delivers about 80% of its daily budget, and the static performance model delivers less than 30%. While it seems counter-intuitive to see the dynamic model deliver better than the static *delivery* model, this behavior is expected due to the utilized bidding functions. The dynamic model bids higher (especially in the region of small ϕ_v) than *both* of the static models in a bad delivery situation. Figure 4(b) shows viewability rate for the three models, where we can observe that the dynamic bidding model performs nearly as good as the static performance model. In summary, it is apparent that the dynamic model spends better than both the static models (and, in particular, much better

* Please note that due to the company's privacy policy, we have applied a normalizing factor to all the results presented in this section. The *Delivery* axis in the graphs represents the monetary amount spent on bid requests by each of the campaigns, which is limited by their daily budget.

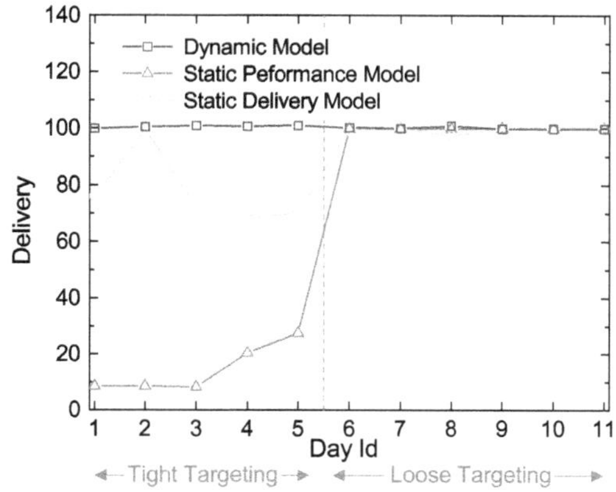

(a) Delivery of Models

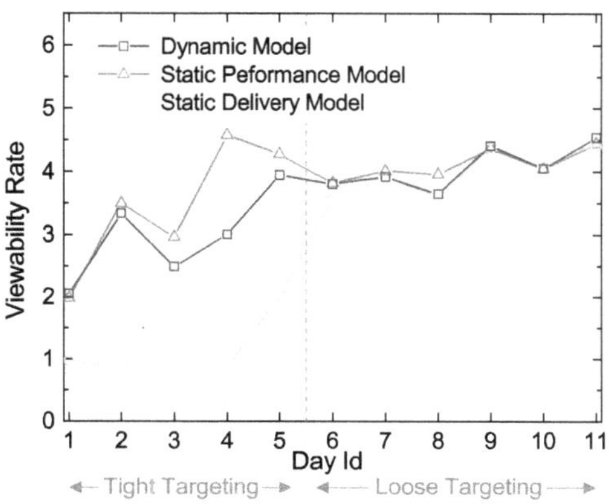

(b) Viewability Rate of Models

Figure 4: Delivery and viewability rate of the dynamic and static models applied to the same campaign with the same daily budget for 11 days. For the first 5 days, tight targeting has been applied on the campaign, and for the last 6 days, loose targeting has been applied.

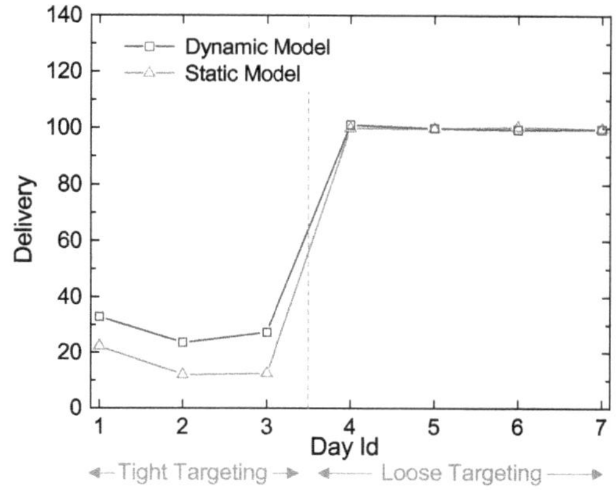

(a) Delivery of Models

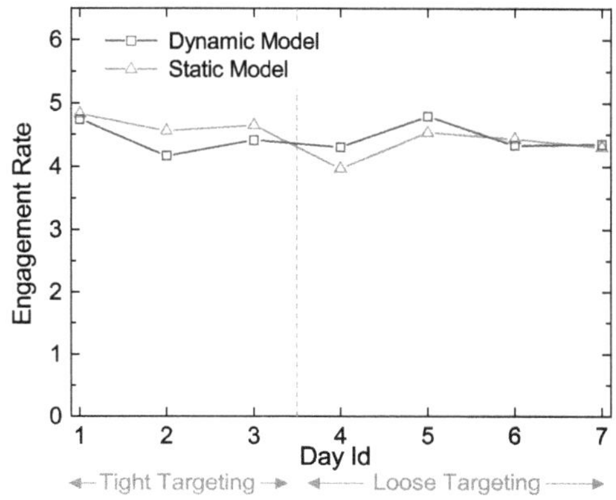

(b) Engagement Rate of Models

Figure 5: Delivery and engagement rate of the dynamic and the static models applied to the same campaign with the same daily budget for 7 days. For the first 3 days, tight targeting has been applied on the campaign, and for the last 4 days, loose targeting has been applied.

than the static performance model) and provides a viewability rate very close to the static performance model in the tight targeting case.

If we examine the results from the last six days when the loose targeting criteria were applied to the campaigns, we can see from Figure 4(a) that all three campaigns performed in a very similar manner. This is a consequence of the fact that, in a comfortable delivery situation, the filtering threshold θ_v is high and all three models only bid on bid-requests with large ϕ_v. Since the bidding functions of all three models behave similarly in the region of large ϕ_v, the delivery and viewability rates of all three models are similar.

We present the delivery as well as the engagement rates of the dynamic model and the baseline static engagement model (which does not adjust its bid values, but rather only applies filtering through θ_e, i.e. engagement rate filtering threshold) in Figure 5 for a 7-day period within 2015. Again, we replicated the same campaign with the same daily budget, where only the bidding functions differ. The primary goal of the dynamic model is delivery, and the secondary goal is the engagement rate. The bidding function of the dynamic model is similar to the bidding function of the static model for intermediate and large values of ϕ_e (predicted engagement rate for a bid request). In the region of small ϕ_e, the bidding functions differ. In particular, similar to the viewability case, the bidding function of the dynamic model is equal to b_m in the limit of $\theta_e = 0$ and $\phi_e = 0$, while the bidding function of the static model (which is independent of θ_e) is equal to 0 in the limit of $\phi_e = 0$.

For the engagement model evaluation campaigns, we applied three days of tight targeting, and four days of loose targeting, to see the effects of both comfortable and risky delivery situations. Since the targeting criteria applied to the identical campaigns were extremely tight during the first three days, both models could not satisfy their daily budget, yet the dynamic model still delivered twice as much advertising budget due to bidding higher on bid-requests with small ϕ_e. During the last four days, when looser targeting criteria had been applied to the campaigns, both models spent their daily budget and showed similar engagement rates. We can observe from Figure 5(b) that engagement rates stayed pretty much the same during the whole seven days, including the tight targeting period. This shows that the engagement rate for the user set reached by the campaigns was quite homogeneous, and further demonstrates that even by increasing the bid values and delivering higher amounts of budget, the dynamic model indeed did not hurt performance in terms of engagement rate.

7. CONCLUSIONS AND FUTURE WORK

In this paper, we focused on the recently popularized domain of online video advertising. We listed the challenges and peculiarities related to video advertising which are inherently different compared to the more traditional banner display advertising approach. We also proposed a multi-objective optimization scheme for online video campaigns, which has a compelling theoretical foundation in its problem definition but is also quite challenging to implement considering the real-time nature of online advertising. We presented a methodology to approximately perform this joint optimization, and demonstrated via real-world experiments that the proposed framework improves delivery and brand recognition metrics, such as viewability and engagement rates for video campaigns. To the best of our knowledge, this is the first work to examine the difficulties that arise due to the nature of online video advertising and present ways to improve advertiser metrics specific to online video campaigns.

As mentioned in the introduction of our methodology, the first future work we would like to propose is extending the number of prioritized goals as opposed to the dual-objective optimization we focused on in this paper. We have presented an initial idea on this work, but nevertheless, this is an interesting direction to follow. Furthermore, we did not perform a deep-dive into the problem of predicting viewability or engagement rates of bid requests for video campaigns. It is our belief that the effective methods to be applied for this purpose could prove to be radically different compared to the previous efforts in literature on click and conversion estimation, and would be an exciting subject to pursue.

Acknowledgments

We thank many talented scientists and engineers at Turn for their help and feedback in this work.

8. REFERENCES

[1] D. Agarwal, B.-C. Chen, P. Elango, and X. Wang. Click shaping to optimize multiple objectives. In *Proc. ACM KDD*, pages 132–140, 2011.

[2] O. Chapelle. Modeling delayed feedback in display advertising. In *Proc. KDD*, pages 1097–1105, 2014.

[3] Y. Chen, P. Berkhin, B. Anderson, and N. R. Devanur. Real-time bidding algorithms for performance-based display ad allocation. In *Proc. ACM KDD*, pages 1307–1315, 2011.

[4] D. S. Evans. The online advertising industry: Economics, evolution, and privacy. *The Journal of Economic Perspectives*, 23:37–60, 2009.

[5] S. C. Geyik, A. Saxena, and A. Dasdan. Multi-touch attribution based budget allocation in online advertising. In *Proc. ACM ADKDD*, pages 1–9, 2014.

[6] X. He et al. Practical lessons from predicting clicks on ads at facebook. In *Proc. ADKDD*, pages 1–9, 2014.

[7] A. Jalali, S. Kolay, P. Foldes, and A. Dasdan. Scalable audience reach estimation in real-time online advertising. In *Proc. ICDMW*, pages 629–637, 2013.

[8] W. Ji, Y. Chen, M. Chen, B.-W. Chen, Y. Chen, and S.-Y. Kung. Profit maximization through online advertising scheduling for a wireless video broadcast network. *IEEE TMC*, 2015.

[9] G. G. Karuga, A. M. Khraban, S. K. Nair, and D. O. Rice. Adpalette: An algorithm for customizing online advertisements on the fly. *Decision Support Systems*, 32:85–106, 2001.

[10] K.-C. Lee, A. Jalali, and A. Dasdan. Real time bid optimization with smooth budget delivery in online advertising. In *Proc. ACM ADKDD*, pages 1–9, 2013.

[11] K.-C. Lee, B. Orten, A. Dasdan, and W. Li. Estimating conversion rate in display advertising from past performance data. In *Proc. ACM KDD*, pages 768–776, 2012.

[12] W.-S. Liao, K.-T. Chen, and W. H. Hsu. Adimage: Video advertising by image matching and ad scheduling optimization. In *Proc. ACM SIGIR*, pages 767–768, 2008.

[13] H. B. McMahan et al. Ad click prediction: a view from the trenches. In *Proc. ACM KDD*, pages 1222–1230, 2013.

[14] T. Mei, X.-S. Hua, L. Yang, and S. Li. Videosense: Towards effective online video advertising. In *Proc. ACM MM*, pages 1075–1084, 2007.

[15] C. Perlich, B. Dalessandro, R. Hook, O. Stitelman, T. Raeder, and F. Provost. Bid optimizing and inventory scoring in targeted online advertising. In *Proc. ACM KDD*, pages 804–812, 2012.

[16] K. Salomatin, T.-Y. Liu, and Y. Yang. A unified optimization framework for auction and guaranteed delivery in online advertising. In *Proc. ACM CIKM*, pages 2005–2009, 2012.

[17] X. Shao and L. Li. Data-driven multi-touch attribution models. In *Proc. ACM KDD*, pages 258–264, 2011.

[18] J. Shen, S. C. Geyik, and A. Dasdan. Effective audience extension in online advertising. In *Proc. ACM KDD*, pages 2099–2108, 2015.

[19] J. Shen, B. Orten, S. C. Geyik, D. Liu, S. Shariat, F. Bian, and A. Dasdan. From 0.5 million to 2.5 million: Efficiently scaling up real-time bidding. In *Proc. IEEE ICDM*, 2015.

[20] S. H. Srinivasan, N. Sawant, and S. Wadhwa. vadeo: Video advertising system. In *Proc. ACM MM*, pages 455–456, 2007.

[21] R. S. Sutton and A. G. Barto. *Reinforcement learning: An introduction.* MIT press, 1998.

[22] J. Wang, Y. Fang, and H. Lu. Online video advertising based on user's attention relavancy computing. In *Proc. IEEE ICME*, pages 1161–1164, 2008.

[23] W. C.-H. Wu, M.-Y. Yeh, and M.-S. Chen. Predicting winning price in real time bidding with censored data. In *Proc. of ACM KDD*, pages 1305–1314, 2015.

[24] W. Zhang, Y. Zhang, B. Gao, Y. Yu, X. Yuan, and T.-Y. Liu. Joint optimization of bid and budget allocation in sponsored search. In *Proc. ACM KDD*, pages 1177–1185, 2012.

Convolutional Neural Networks for Steady Flow Approximation

Xiaoxiao Guo
University of Michigan
guoxiao@umich.edu

Wei Li
Autodesk Research
Wei.Li@autodesk.com

Francesco Iorio
Autodesk Research
Francesco.Iorio@autodesk.com

ABSTRACT

In aerodynamics related design, analysis and optimization problems, flow fields are simulated using computational fluid dynamics (CFD) solvers. However, CFD simulation is usually a computationally expensive, memory demanding and time consuming iterative process. These drawbacks of CFD limit opportunities for design space exploration and forbid interactive design. We propose a general and flexible approximation model for real-time prediction of non-uniform steady laminar flow in a 2D or 3D domain based on convolutional neural networks (CNNs). We explored alternatives for the geometry representation and the network architecture of CNNs. We show that convolutional neural networks can estimate the velocity field two orders of magnitude faster than a GPU-accelerated CFD solver and four orders of magnitude faster than a CPU-based CFD solver at a cost of a low error rate. This approach can provide immediate feedback for real-time design iterations at the early stage of design. Compared with existing approximation models in the aerodynamics domain, CNNs enable an efficient estimation for the entire velocity field. Furthermore, designers and engineers can directly apply the CNN approximation model in their design space exploration algorithms without training extra lower-dimensional surrogate models.

Keywords

Convolutional Neural Networks; Surrogate Models; Computational Fluid Dynamics; Machine Learning

1. INTRODUCTION

Computational fluid dynamics (CFD) analysis performs the calculations required to simulate the physical interaction of liquids and gases with surfaces defined by prescribed boundary conditions. This analysis process typically involves the solution of partial differential equations, such as the Navier-Stokes equations of fluid flow. The focus of our work is the analysis of non-uniform steady laminar flow (Figure 1).

KDD '16, August 13-17, 2016, San Francisco, CA, USA

DOI: http://dx.doi.org/10.1145/2939672.2939738

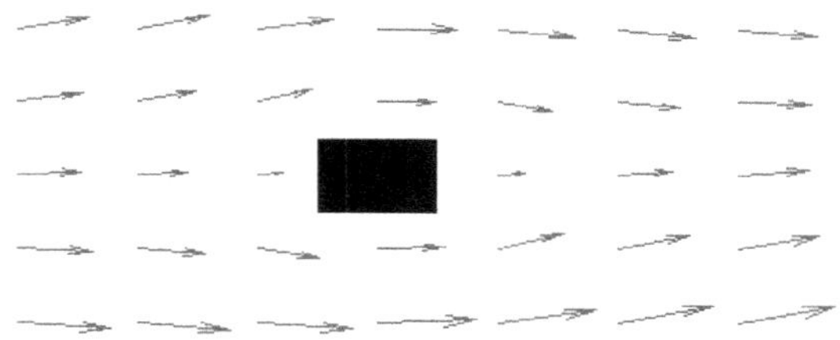

Figure 1: Non-uniform steady laminar flow for 2D geometry. The black box shows the object and the arrows show the velocity field in the laminar flow.

Laminar flow occurs when a fluid flows in parallel layers, with no disruption between the layers [2]. There are no cross-currents perpendicular to the direction of flow, nor eddies or swirls of fluids. Non-uniform steady flow occurs when the flow exhibits differences from point to point, but these differences do not vary over time. The non-uniform steady laminar flow is most often found at the front of a streamlined body and it is an important factor in flight and automobile design. [1]

While traditional CFD methods produce high-accuracy results, they are computationally expensive and the time required to obtain results is often measured in hours, or even days for complex prototypes. In many domains, CFD analysis becomes one of the most intensive and time consuming processes; therefore it is typically used only for final design validation.

During the early design stages, designers often need to quickly iterate over multiple design alternatives to make preliminary decisions and they usually do not require high-fidelity simulations. Significant efforts have been made to make conceptual design software environments interactive, so that designers can get immediate or real-time feedback for continuous design iterations. One of the alternatives to high accuracy CFD simulation is the use of fast approximation models, or surrogates.

In the design optimization practice, multiple design alternatives are explored, evaluated and optimized at the same time [1]. Guiding this process with fluid dynamics-based performance is difficult due to the slow feedback from conventional CFD solvers. The idea of speed-accuracy tradeoffs

[1]The geometry and velocity field representations and the approximation method would be much different if we attempted to model time-dependent unsteady flow and turbulent flow.

[6] also leads to practical design space exploration and design optimization in the aerodynamics domain by using fast surrogate models.

Data-driven surrogate models become more and more practical and important because many design, analysis and optimization processes generate high volume CFD physical or simulation data. Over the past years, deep learning approaches (see [5, 26] for survey) have shown great successes in learning representations from data, where features are learned end-to-end in a compositional hierarchy. This is in contrast to the traditional approach which requires the hand-crafting of features by domain experts. For data that have strong spatial and/or temporal dependencies, Convolutional Neural Networks (CNNs) [20] have been shown to learn invariant high-level features that are informative for supervised tasks.

In particular, we propose a general CNN-based approximation model for predicting the velocity field in 2D or 3D non-uniform steady laminar flow. We show that CNN based surrogate models can estimate the velocity field two orders of magnitude faster than a GPU-accelerated CFD solver or four orders of magnitude faster than a CPU-based CFD solver at a cost of a low error rate. Another benefit of using a CNN-based surrogate model is that we can collect training data from either physical or simulation results. The knowledge of fluid dynamics behavior can then be extracted from data sets generated by different CFD solvers, using different solution methods. Traditional high accuracy simulation is still an important step to validate the final design, but fast CFD approximation models have wide applications in the conceptual design and the design optimization process.

2. RELATED WORK

2.1 CFD Analysis

Computational methods have emerged as powerful techniques for exploring physical and chemical phenomena and for solving real engineering problems. In traditional CFD methods, Navier-Stokes equations solve mass, momentum and energy conservation equations on discrete nodes (the finite difference method, FDM) [11], elements (the finite element method, FEM) [29], or volumes (the finite volume method, FVM) [24]. In other words, the nonlinear partial differential equations are converted into a set of non-linear algebraic equations, which are solved iteratively. Traditional CFD simulation suffers from long response time, predominantly because of the complexity of the underlying physics and the historical focus on accuracy.

The Lattice Boltzmann Method (LBM) [22] was introduced to overcome the drawbacks of the lattice gas cellular automata. In LBM, the fluid is replaced by fractious particles. These particles stream along given directions (lattice links) and collide at the lattice sites. LBM can be considered as an explicit physical-based approximation method. The collision and streaming processes are local [23]. LBM emerged as an alternative powerful method for solving fluid dynamics problems, due to its ability to operate with complex geometry shapes and to its trivially parallel implementation nature [31, 21]. Since distinct particle motion can be decomposed over many processor cores or other hardware units, efficient implementations on parallel computers are relatively easy. LBM can also handle complex boundary conditions. However, LBM still requires numerous iterations and its convergence speed depends on the geometry boundaries. In this paper, we use LBM to generate all the training data for the CNNs, and we compare the speed of our CNN based surrogate models with both traditional CPU LBM solvers and GPU-accelerated LBM solvers.

Compared with physical-based simulation and approximation methods, our approach falls into the category of data-driven surrogate models (or supervised learning in machine learning). The knowledge of fluid dynamics behavior can be extracted from large data sets of simulation data by learning the relationship between an input feature vector extracted from geometry and the ground truth data output from a full CFD simulation. Then, without the computationally expensive iterations that a CFD solver requires to allow the flow to converge to its steady state, we can directly predict the steady flow behavior in a fraction of the time. The number of iterations and runtime in a CFD solver is usually dependent on the complexity of geometries and boundary conditions, but they are irrelevant to those factors in the prediction process. Note that only the prediction runtime of surrogate models has a significant impact on the design processes. The training time of the surrogate models is irrelevant.

2.2 Surrogate Modeling in CFD-based Design Optimization

The role of design optimization has been rapidly increasing and evolving in aerodynamics related fields, such as aerospace and architecture design [1]. CFD solvers have been widely used in design optimization (finding the best design parameters that satisfy project requirements) and design space exploration (finding multiple designs that satisfy the requirements). However, the direct application of a CFD solver in design optimization is usually computationally expensive, memory demanding and time consuming. The basic idea of using surrogates (approximation models) is to replace a high-accuracy, expensive analysis process with a less expensive approximation. CFD surrogate models can be constructed from physical experiments [30]. However, high-fidelity numerical simulation proves to be reliable, flexible, and relatively cheap compared with physical experiments (see [1] and references therein).

Various surrogate models have been explored for design processes, such as polynomial regression [12, 3], multiple adaptive regression splines (MARS) [10], Kriging [12, 16], radial basis function network [19], and artificial neural networks [7, 4]. The existing approaches only predict a restricted subset of the whole CFD velocity field. For example, predict the pressure on a set of points on an object surface [32]. Most existing approaches also depend on domain-specific geometry representations and can only be applied to low-order nonlinear problems or small scale applications [10, 18]. The models are usually constructed by modeling the response of a simulator on a limited number of intelligently chosen data points. Instead of modeling each individual low-dimensional design problem, we model the general non-uniform steady laminar CFD analysis solution, so that our model can be reused in multiple different, lower-dimensional optimization processes, and predict the whole velocity field.

2.3 Convolutional Neural Networks

Convolutional neural networks have been proven successful in learning geometry representations [27, 13]. CNNs also enable per-pixel predictions in images. For example, FlowNet [8] predicts the optical flow field from a pair of images. Eigen, Puhrsch and Fergus [9] estimate depth from a single image. Recently, CNNs are applied on voxel to voxel prediction problems, such as video coloring [28].

Our approach applies CNNs to model large-scale nonlinear general CFD analysis for a restricted class of flow conditions. Our method obtains a surrogate model of the general high-dimensional CFD analysis of arbitrary geometry immersed in a flow for a class of flow conditions, and not a model based on predetermined low-dimensional inputs. For this reason, our model subsumes a multitude of lower-dimensional models, as it only requires training once and can be interrogated by mapping lower-dimensional problems into its high-dimensional input space. The main contribution of our CNN based CFD prediction is to achieve up to two to four orders of magnitude speedup compared to traditional Lattice Boltzmann Method (LBM) for CFD analysis at a cost of low error rates.

3. CONVOLUTIONAL NEURAL NETWORK SURROGATE MODELS FOR CFD

We propose a computational fluid dynamics surrogate model based on deep convolutional neural networks (CNNs). CNNs have been proven successful in geometry representation learning and per-pixel prediction in images. The other motivation of adopting CNNs is its memory efficiency. Memory requirement is a bottleneck to build whole velocity field surrogate models for large geometry shapes. The sparse connectivity and weight-sharing property of CNNs reduce the GPU memory cost greatly.

Our surrogate models have three key components. First, we adopt signed distance functions as a flexible and general geometric representation for convolutional neural networks. Second, we use multiple convolutional encoding layers to extract abstract and high-level geometric representations. Finally, there are multiple convolutional decoding layers that map the abstract geometric representations into the computational fluid dynamics velocity field.

In the rest of this section, we describe the key components in turn.

3.1 Geometry Representation

Geometry can be represented in multiple ways, such as boundaries and geometric parameters. However, those representations are not effective for neural networks since the vectors' semantic meaning varies. In this paper, we use a Signed Distance Function (SDF) sampled on a Cartesian grid as the geometry representation. SDF provides a universal representation for different geometry shapes and works efficiently with neural networks.

Given a discrete representation of a 2D geometry on a Cartesian grid, in order to compute the signed distance function, we first create the *zero level set*, which is a set of points (i,j) that give the geometry boundary (surface) in a domain $\Omega \subset R^2$:

$$Z = \{(i,j) \in R^2 : f(i,j) = 0\} \tag{1}$$

where f is the level set function s.t. $f(i,j) = 0$ if and only if (i,j) is on the geometry boundary, $f(i,j) < 0$ if and only if (i,j) is inside the geometry and $f(i,j) > 0$ if and only if (i,j) is outside the geometry.

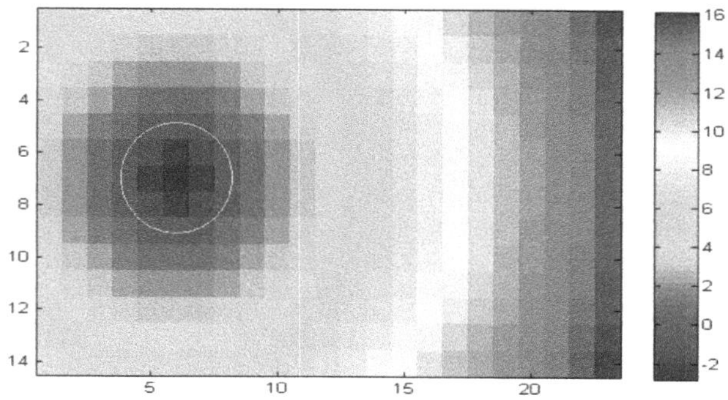

Figure 2: A discrete SDF representation of a circle shape (zero level set) in a 23x14 Cartesian grid. The circle is shown in white. The magnitude of the SDF values on the Cartesian grid equals the minimal distance to the circle.

A signed distance function $D(i,j)$ associated to a level set function $f(i,j)$ is defined by

$$D(i,j) = \min_{(i',j') \in Z} |(i,j) - (i',j')| \operatorname{sign}(f(i,j)) \tag{2}$$

$D(i,j)$ is an oriented distance function and it measures the distance of a given point (i,j) from the nearest boundary of a closed geometrical shape Z, with the sign determined by whether *(i,j)* is inside or outside the shape. Also, every point outside of the boundary has a value equal to its distance from the interface (see Figure 2 for a 2D SDF example).

Similarly, given a discrete representation of a 3D geometry on a Cartesian grid, the signed distance function is

$$D(i,j,k) = \min_{(i',j',k') \in Z} |(i,j,k) - (i',j',k')| \operatorname{sign}(f(i,j,k)) \tag{3}$$

A demonstration of 3D SDF is shown in Figure 3, where SDF equals to zero on the cube surface. In this paper, we use the Gudonov Method [14, 25] to compute the signed distance functions.

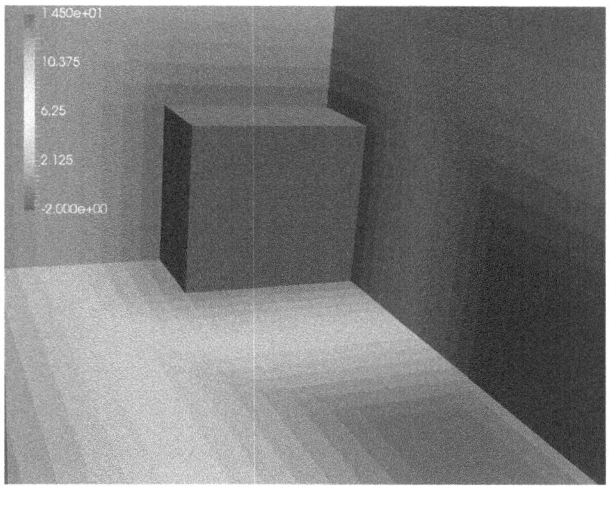

Figure 3: Signed distance function for a cube in 3D domain

The values of SDF on the sampled Cartesian grid not only provide local geometry details, but also contain additional information of the global geometry structure. To validate the efforts of computing SDF values in our experiments, we compare the geometry representiveness of SDF and a simple binary representation, where a grid value is 1 if and only if it is within or on the boundary of geometry shapes. Such binary representations are easier to compute, but the values do not provide any global structure information. We empirically show that SDF is more effective in representing the geometry shapes for convolutional neural networks.

3.2 CFD Simulation

In this paper, we intend to leverage deep neural networks as real-time surrogate models to substitute traditional time-consuming Lattice Boltzmann Method (LBM) CFD simulation [22]. LBM represents velocity fields as regular Cartesian grids, or lattices, where each lattice cell represents the velocity field at that location. The LBM procedure updates the lattice iteratively, and usually the amount of required iterations for the flow field to stabilize from a cold start is large.

In LBM, geometry is represented by assigning an identifier to each lattice cell. This specific identifier defines whether a cell lies on the boundary or in the fluid domain. Figure 4 illustrates this using an example of a 2D cylinder in a channel. In general, the LBM lattice cell resolution does not necessarily equal to the SDF resolution. In this work, we use the same geometry resolution in the LBM simulation and in the SDF representation. Thus, for a geometry with $H \times W \times D$ SDF representation, its CFD velocity field is also $H \times W \times D$. A 2D velocity field consists of two components x and y to represent the velocity components in x-direction and y-direction respectively. The velocity field for 3D geometry has one additional z-component to represent the velocity component in the z-direction.

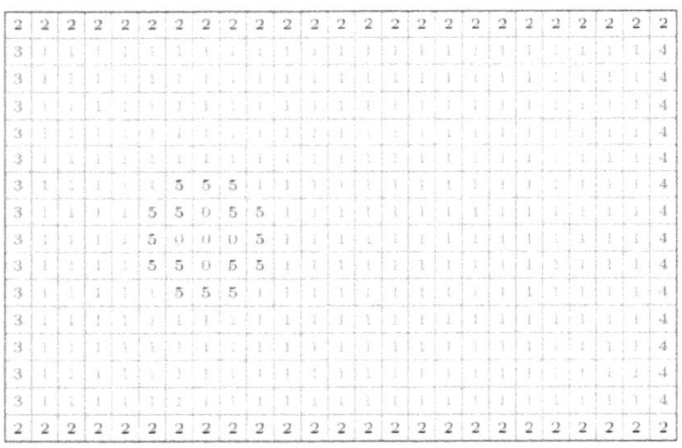

Figure 4: 2D channel flow definition for LBM (1=fluid, 2=no-slip boundary, 3=velocity boundary, 4=constant pressure boundary, 5=object boundary, 0=internal)

3.3 Convolution Encoding

The encoding part takes the SDF, s, as an input, and stacked convolution layers extract geometry features directly from the SDF representation. For 2D geometry, s is a matrix that $s_{ij} = D(i,j)$ and the 2D convolution operations are used for encoding. For 3D geometry, s is a 3D tensor that $s_{ijk} = D(i,j,k)$, and the encoding uses 3D convolution. The

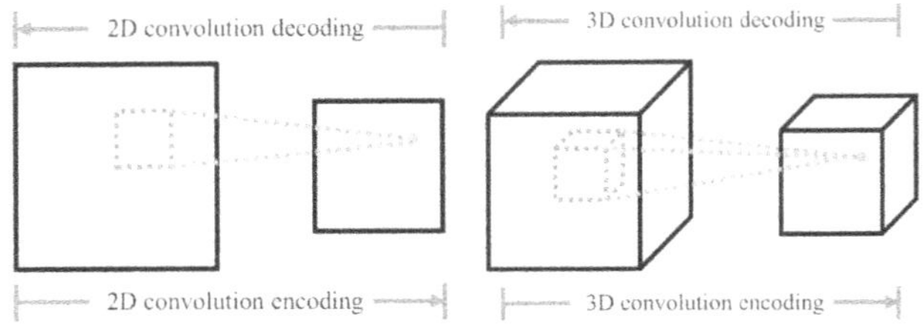

Figure 5: Convolution encoding and decoding.

encoded feature vector $h^{enc}(s)$ can be formulated as:

$$h^{enc}(s) = \text{ConvNN}(s) \quad (4)$$

where ConvNN(.) denotes the mapping from the SDF to a geometry representation vector using multiple convolution layers and a fully connected layer at the end, each of which is followed by a rectifier non-linearity (ReLU).

3.4 Convolutional Decoding

We use the 'inverse' operation of convolution, called deconvolution, to construct multiple stacked decoding layers. Deconvolution layers multiply each input value by a filter elementwise, and sum over the resulting output windows. In other words, a deconvolution layer is a convolution layer with the forward and backward passes reversed. 2D deconvolution maps 1×1 spatial region of the input to $w \times h$ convolution kernels. 3D deconvolution maps $1 \times 1 \times 1$ spatial region of the input to $w \times h \times d$ convolution kernels, as shown in Figure 5.

In our method, deconvolution operations are used to decode high-level features encoded and transformed by the encoding layers. The decoding procedure can be represented as:

$$\hat{t}^x(s) = \text{DeconvNN}(h^{enc}(s)) \quad (5)$$

where $\hat{t}^x(s)$ denotes the x-component prediction of the CFD velocity field. DeconvNN(.) is a mapping from the extracted geometry representation vector to CFD velocity field component using multiple deconvolution layers, each of which is followed by a rectifier non-linearity (ReLU). We decode the y-component (and z-component for 3D geometry) of the CFD velocity field in the same way.

3.5 Network Architecture and End-To-End Training

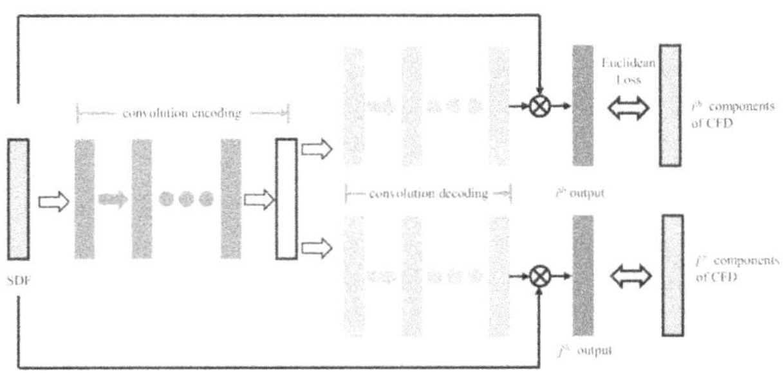

Figure 6: CNN based CFD surrogate model architecture

We use a shared-encoding and separated-decoding architecture for our CFD surrogate model in Figure 6. The shared-encoding saves computations compared to separated-encoding alternatives. Unlike encoding layers, decoding layers are interfered by different velocity field components when a shared-decoding structure is used. In our shared-encoding and separated-decoding architecture, multiple convolutional layers are used to extract an abstract geometry representation, and the abstract geometry representation is used by multiple decoding parts to generate the various components of the CFD velocity field. There are two decoding parts for 2D geometry shapes and three for 3D geometry shapes. An alternative encoding structure is to use separated encoding layers for each decoding part. In the experiment section, we show that the prediction accuracy of the separated encoding structure is similar to the shared encoding structure.

Further, we condition our CFD prediction based on the SDF to reduce errors. By definition, the velocity inside and on the boundary of geometry shapes is zero. Thus, the velocity field values change dramatically on the boundary of geometry shapes. SDF itself fully represents the boundary information and our neural networks could condition the prediction by masking out the pixel or voxel inside or on the boundary of the geometry. Such conditioned prediction eases the training and improve the prediction accuracy. The final prediction of our model is $\hat{t^x} \otimes \mathbb{1}\{s > 0\}$, where $\mathbb{1}\{s > 0\}$ is a binary mask and has the same size as s. Its element is 1 if and only if the corresponding signed distance function value is greater than 0. $\otimes$ denotes element-wise product.

We train our model to minimize the mean squared error:

$$\mathbf{L}(\theta) = \frac{1}{N}\sum_{n=1}^{N} |\hat{t^x}(s_n) \otimes \mathbb{1}\{s_n > 0\} - t^x(s_n)|^2 + |\hat{t^y}(s_n) \otimes \mathbb{1}\{s_n > 0\} - t^y(s_n)|^2 \quad (6)$$

A similar loss function is defined for 3D geometry shapes:

$$\mathbf{L}(\theta) = \frac{1}{N}\sum_{n=1}^{N} |\hat{t^x}(s_n) \otimes \mathbb{1}\{s_n > 0\} - t^x(s_n)|^2 + |\hat{t^y}(s_n) \otimes \mathbb{1}\{s_n > 0\} - t^y(s_n)|^2 + |\hat{t^z}(s_n) \otimes \mathbb{1}\{s_n > 0\} - t^z(s_n)|^2 \quad (7)$$

4. EXPERIMENT SETUP

In the experiments, we evaluate our proposed method in both 2D and 3D geometry domains. In the 2D domain, we train the convolutional neural networks using a collection of 2D geometric primitives and evaluate the prediction over a validation dataset of 2D primitives and a test dataset of 2D car shapes (see Figure 7 for examples). We then train a separate network using a collection of 3D geometry shapes inside a channel (see Figure 8 for examples) and evaluate the prediction over a validation dataset of 3D geometry shapes.

We first empirically compare the representiveness of SDF with the simple binary representations and show that SDF outperforms binary representations in CFD prediction. Second, our CNN based surrogate model outperforms a patch-based linear regression baseline in predicting CFD for both 2D and 3D geometry shapes. Finally, we compare the time cost of our proposed method with traditional LBM solvers to highlight the speedup of our proposed method.

We begin by describing the details of the datasets, LBM data generation, convolutional neural network architectures, and training parameters.

4.1 Data and Preprocessing

Figure 7: 2D car dataset visualization.

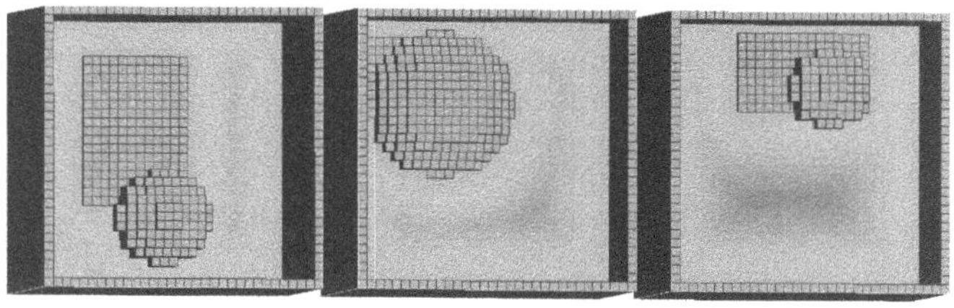

Figure 8: 3D channel dataset: two 3D primitives (a rectangular box and a sphere) in a 32-by-32-by-32 channel and the visualization of their SDF on the Y-Z plane

2D data set. The 2D training and validation datasets consist of 5 types of simple parametric geometric 2D primitives: triangles, quadrilaterals, pentagons, hexagons and dodecagons. Each set of primitives contains samples that are different in size, shape, orientation and location. The training dataset contains 100,000 samples (20,000 random samples for each kind of primitives), and the validation dataset contains 10,000 samples (2,000 random samples for each kind of primitives). The 2D primitives are projected into a 256-by-128 Cartesian grid and the LBM simulation computes a 256-by-128 velocity field as labels. We construct two kinds of 2D primitive datasets for different boundary conditions. In **Type I**, the primitives are always connected to the lower boundary. In **Type II**, the primitives are always above the lower boundary, and the gap ranges from 15 to 25 pixels.

2D car test data set. This data set is dedicated to test the generalization ability of our trained models. It contains various kinds of car prototypes, such as jeeps, vans and sport cars. The car samples are not visible in the training. Similar to 2D primitives, the car samples are projected into a 256-by-128 Cartesian grid and the LBM simulation computes a 256-by-128 velocity field. We also create two boundary conditions for the car samples.

3D data set. In order to understand whether interactions of flow with sets of multiple boundaries can be learned effectively, the 3D dataset contains 0.4 million sphere and rectangular prism pairs. Each sphere-prism pair is positioned in a 32×32×32 channel. Both the location and the parameters of each 3D object are randomly generated. Then a LBM simulation is performed on the 3D channel, where the fluid enters the channel along the *x axile*.

SDF preprocessing. We performed pixel/voxel-wise mean removal for SDF and scaled the resulting representation by 0.01 as inputs to the CNNs.

4.2 CFD Solver Configuration

Laminar flow occurs at low Reynolds numbers[2], where viscous forces are dominant, and is characterized by a fluid flowing in parallel layers, with no disruption between the layers. In all the experiments, we used a Reynolds number of 20. For our 2D experiments, we used OpenLB [15], a C++ Lattice Boltzmann library, to generate CFD velocity field. Because of the lack of GPU support in OpenLB, we ran each simulation on a single core on a Intel Xeon E5-2640V2 processor. For our 3D experiments, we used a proprietary GPU-accelerated LBM solver.

4.3 Network Architectures and Training

The architectures and hyper-parameters of our CNN surrogate models for 2D and 3D CFD are shown in Figure 9. In the CNN architectures, the encoding part is **shared** by decoding parts for different CFD dimensions. Alternative architectures could use a **separated** encoding part for each decoding part where each separated encoding part has the same architecture and hyper-parameters as the shared encoding part. We compare these two encoding paradigms in our experiments.

We implemented the CNNs using Caffe [17]. The parameters of the networks were initialized using Xavier method in Caffe. We used RMSProp with a batch size of 64 to optimize the parameters of the convolutional neural networks. The RMS decay parameter was set to 0.05. We set the initial learning rate to be 10^{-4} and multiplied the learning rate by 0.8 for every 2500 iterations.

5. EXPERIMENT RESULTS

We use the average relative error [1] in the CFD literature to evaluate our prediction. We first compute the difference between the predicted velocity field and the LBM generated velocity field. For a pixel/voxel, the relative error is defined as the ratio of the magnitude of the difference to the LBM generated velocity field. For 2D geometry shapes, the relative error at pixel (i, j) in n-th test case is represented as:

$$\text{err}^n(i,j) = \frac{\sqrt{(t_{ij}^{\hat{x}}(s_n) - t_{ij}^{x}(s_n))^2 + (t_{ij}^{\hat{y}}(s_n) - t_{ij}^{y}(s_n))^2}}{\sqrt{t_{ij}^{x}(s_n)^2 + t_{ij}^{y}(s_n)^2}} \tag{8}$$

The average relative error of n-th data case is the mean value of all the pixels outside the geometry shape:

$$\text{err}^n = \frac{\sum_i \sum_j \text{err}^n(i,j)\mathbb{1}_{ij}(s_n > 0)}{\sum_i \sum_j \mathbb{1}_{ij}(s_n > 0)} \tag{9}$$

where $\mathbb{1}_{ij}(s_n > 0)$ is 1 if and only if (i, j) is outside of the geometry boundary of s_n. err^n can be extended to 3D geometry shapes straightforwardly by considering the z-component.

[2]In CFD modeling, the Reynolds number is defined as a non-dimensional ratio of the inertial forces to viscous forces and quantifies their relevance for the prescribed flow condition [2].

The average relative error over the test data set is the mean of all the test cases:

$$\text{err} = \frac{1}{N}\sum_{n=1}^{N} \text{err}^{\text{n}} \tag{10}$$

5.1 Signed Distance Function vs. Binary Representation

One contribution of this paper is proposing using SDF as geometric representations for the CNN models. We evaluate the effectiveness of SDF geometric representations by comparing with the binary representations in the same CNN architectures. In the experiments, the binary representations use a 256 × 128 binary matrix to represent the geometry. Its element is 1 if and only if the corresponding position is on the geometry boundary or inside the geometry.

The results of prediction on 2D primitives are summarized in the Table 1.

DataSet	Encoding Type	SDF	Binary
2D Type I	shared	1.98%	54.60%
	separated	1.76%	55.25%
2D Type II	shared	2.86%	74.52%
	separated	3.08%	80.71%

Table 1: 2D CFD prediction results of SDF and binary representations.

The results show that the errors of using SDF are significantly smaller than the errors of using binary representations. Given that the deep neural networks are the same, the results imply that the SDF representations are more effective than the binary representations. Each value in the SDF representations carries a certain level global information while the values in binary representations only carry restricted local information. Due to such difference, binary representations may require more complex architectures to capture whole geometric information properly. We also compare the SDF representations to the first order gradients of the SDF representations, the prediction accuracy improvement is not significant, so we focus our contributions on using SDF because of its computation simplicity. The results also show that the prediction accuracy of shared encoding is similar to that of separated encoding.

5.2 Patch-wise Linear Regression Baseline

A patch-wise linear regression model is applied as a baseline to evaluate our proposed models. For 2D geometry shapes, the 256 × 128 SDF inputs are divided into 32 × 32 patches without overlap. The patch-wise linear regression model takes 32 × 32 patches as inputs and predicts 32 × 32 patches to construct the CFD velocity field for each component. The predicted 32 × 32 patches are concatenated without overlap to form the x-component or y-component of the CFD velocity field. For 3D geometry shapes, the 32 × 32 × 32 SDF inputs are divided into 8 × 8 × 8 patches without overlap, and the predicted 8 × 8 × 8 patches are then concatenated to form the velocity field.

The prediction results of CNNs and baseline are summarized in Table 2. The results show that our proposed CNN models outperform the patch-wise linear regression models. The CNN's prediction errors are significantly smaller than

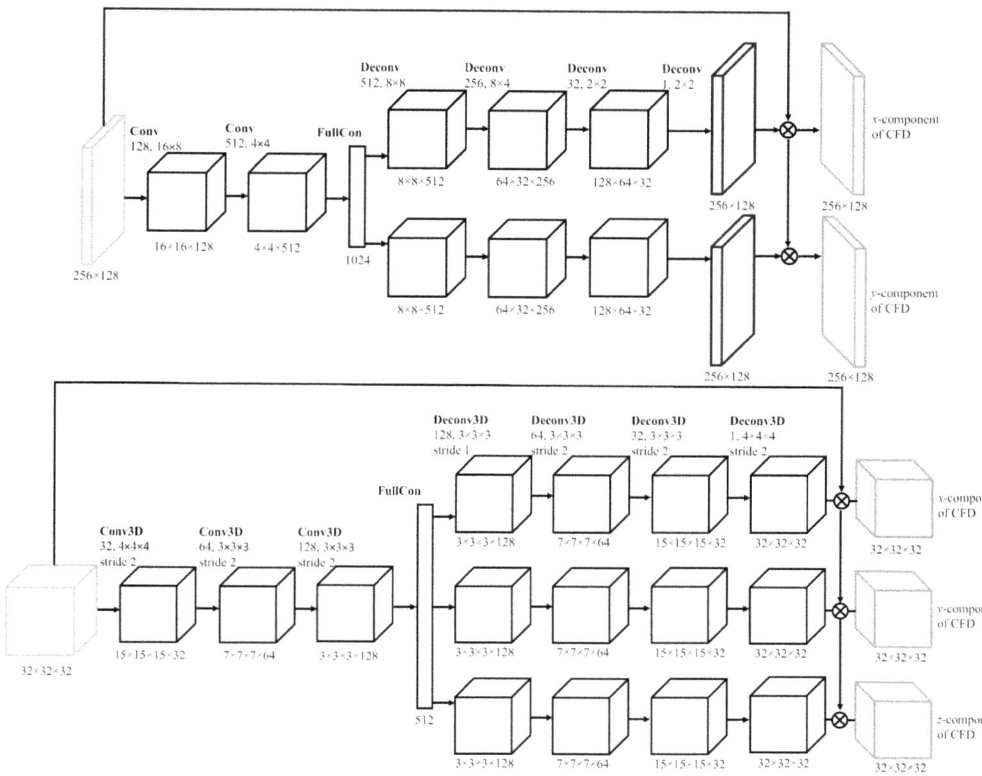

Figure 9: (Top) Network architecture for 2D geometry, (Bottom) Network architecture for 3D geometry. Black cubes/rectangles represent the feature maps. The dimensionalities of feature maps are indicated below. Brown cubes are for SDF and CFD components. Conv, Conv3D, Deconv and Deconv3D represent 2D/3D convolutions and 2D/3D deconvolutions respectively. The number of filters and the kernel size are shown below the operations. The strides for 2D convolutional and deconvolutional layers are the same as kernel sizes. All layers are followed by a rectifier non-linearity except output layers. Arrows indicate the forward operation directions.

the ones reported by the patch-wise linear regression. The prediction accuracy advantage comes from the fact that our CNN models learn a high-level representation of the entire geometry, while the patch-wise linear regression model only takes a local region of SDF as input, thus the input information may not be sufficient to provide accurate prediction for the CFD components. The loss of global geometry information degrades the prediction accuracy much more for 3D case because there are two geometry shapes and the global structure information is even more critical for CFD prediction. Even though a non-patch-wise linear regression model could also take the entire SDF as input, the number of parameters would be too large to handle and thus it is not applicable in practice.

We visualize the CNN's output in Figure 10 and Figure 11 for understanding of the errors from our model. Figure 10 visualizes the CNN prediction on 2D geometry. We visualize the LBM ground truth, the CNN prediction and prediction errors in columns. The shared encoding model's predictions are used in generating the CNN's results. The geometry shapes are visualized in dark blue. The results show that the errors are centered on the geometry boundaries, and the errors are much less than the CFD ground truth. Following the same column order, in our 3D visualization (Figure 11), we show three slices of the velocity fields on the X-Y, X-Z and Y-Z planes.

Data Set	Separated	Shared	PatchLR
2D Type I	1.76%	1.98%	22.86%
Car Type I	11.09%	9.04%	29.03%
2D Type II	3.08%	2.86%	27.66%
Car Type II	15.34%	16.53%	35.96%
3D	-	2.69%	334.19%*

Table 2: CFD prediction results of CNNs and patch-wise linear regression baseline. (*Based on Equation 10, if the error is larger than the true value, then error is larger than 1.)

5.3 Performance Analysis

The main motivation for our surrogate models is that CNN prediction of non-uniform steady laminar flow is considerably faster than traditional LBM solvers. Furthermore CNNs utilize GPU to evaluate the CFD results and the computation overhead per instance could therefore be reduced by allowing multiple predictions to be executed in parallel.

LBM are well suited to massively parallel architectures, as each cell in the lattice can be updated independently at every time step. A widely accepted performance metric for LBM based solvers is Million Lattice Updates per Second (MLUPS). For example, if a 2D LBM solver achieves a per-

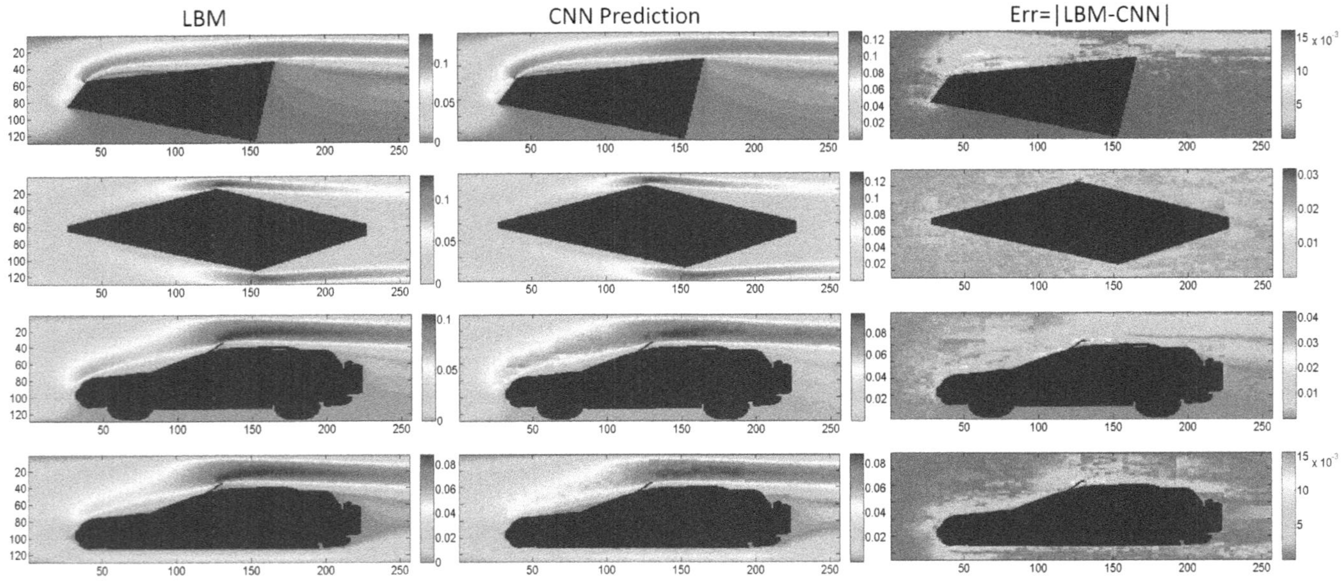

Figure 10: 2D prediction result visualization. The first column shows the magnitude of the LBM ground truth. The second column shows the magnitude of the CNN prediction. The third column shows the magnitude of the difference between the CNN prediction and LBM results.

formance of up to 20 MLUPS, it is the equivalent of performing 1000 time steps per second at a resolution of 200 × 100 lattice points. Modern LBM solvers that are algorithmically optimized for GPU hardware can achieve 820 MLUPS [31, 21]. Using MLUPS as the performance metric, we can estimate the run time of each individual LBM experiment we performed if they had been running at the speed of the state-of-the-art GPU optimized LBM solvers, which is approximately 2 seconds. The average time cost per instance results for LBM solvers are summarized in Table 3.

Methods	LBM CPU	LBM GPU
Time cost	82.64s	2.02s
MLUPS	20.11	820

Table 3: Time of LBM solver on CPU and GPU.

The time results of our CNNs are in Table 4. The time cost measures the average time to generate the CFD given the geometry shape's SDF input. Since CNN based surrogate models could amortize computational overhead per instance by predicting multiple instance in parallel. We measure the average time cost for different batch sizes. Moreover, we compare the time cost of the shared encoding and separated encoding[3]. First, the results show that the average time cost decreases significantly as the batch size becomes larger. Second, the separated encoding takes more time than the shared encoding on different batch sizes. The prediction accuracy of shared and separated encoding architectures is close, but the shared encoding outperforms the separated encoding in terms of time cost.

We use the shared encoding CNNs to compute the speedup,

[3]The time cost of separated encoding measures the total time of sequential prediction of different CFD components.

CNN batch size	1	10	100
shared encoding	0.0145s	0.0077s	0.0069s
separated encoding	0.0182s	0.0085s	0.0072s

Table 4: Time of CNN models on GPU.

compared to LBM on CPU and GPU. The speedup results are summarized in Table 5.

Batch Size	Speedup (CPU)	Speedup (GPU)
1	5699	139
10	10732	262
100	11977	292

Table 5: Speedup results of our CNN surrogate models compared to LBM for different batch sizes.

The speedup results show that (1) GPU accelerated CNN model achieves up to 12K speedup compared to traditional LBM solvers running on a single CPU core, (2) the CNN model achieves up to 292 speedup compared to GPU-accelerated LBM solver, and (3) the speedup increases as batch size increases because the overtime in using GPU is amortized.

6. FUTURE WORK AND CONCLUSION

Even though for many domains, such as architectural design, low Reynolds number flows [2] are usually sufficient, we intend to explore higher Reynolds number flows in the future, to extend the approach to other areas of design optimization.

It would also be worthwhile investigating whether we could use the results from our approximation models as an initial setup to warm start high-accuracy CFD simulations. Since the predictions are fairly close representations of the final, fully converged results, the number of iterations required to converge to steady state could be greatly reduced, and therefore high-accuracy traditional CFD methods could be made to converge much more quickly.

In this paper, we apply deep Convolutional Neural Networks to Computation Fluid Dynamics modeling. Our main motivation is to provide lightweight (fast and less-accurate) interior and exterior flow performance feedback to improve interactivity of early design stages, design exploration and optimization. Using this approach, designers can easily generate immense amounts of design alternatives without facing the time-consuming task of evaluation and selection. Our results show that our CNN based CFD predictions achieve 2-4 orders of magnitude speedup compared to traditional CFD methods to model steady state laminar flow at a cost of low error rates.

7. REFERENCES

[1] M. Ahmed and N. Qin. *Surrogate-Based Aerodynamic Design Optimization: Use of Surrogates in Aerodynamic Design Optimization.* Aerospace Sciences and Aviation Technology, ASAT-13, 2009.

[2] J. Anderson. *Computational Fluid Dynamics.* 1995.

[3] V. Balabanov, A. Giunta, O. Golovidov, B. Grossman, H. Mason, T. Watson, and T. Haftkalf. Reasonable design space approach to response surface approximation. *Journal of Aircraft*, 1999.

[4] M. Batill, A. Stelmack, and S. Sellar. Framework for multidisciplinary design based on response-surface approximations. *Journal of Aircraft*, 1999.

[5] Y. Bengio. *Learning deep architectures for AI, Foundations and trends in Machine Learning.* 2009.

[6] L. Chittka, P. Skorupski, and E. Raine. Speed-accuracy tradeoffs in animal decision making. *Trends in Ecology and Evolution*, 2009.

[7] D. Daberkow and D. N. *New Approaches to Conceptual and Preliminary Aircraft Design: A Comparative Assessment of a Neural Network Formulation and a Response Surface Methodology.* World Aviation Conference, 1998.

[8] A. Dosovitskiy, P. Fischer, E. Ilg, P. Hausser, C. Hazrba, V. Golkov, P. v.d. Smagt, D. Cremers, and T. Brox. Flownet: Learning optical flow with convolutional networks. In *IEEE International Conference on Computer Vision (ICCV)*, 2015.

[9] D. Eigen, C. Puhrsch, and R. Fergus. Depth map prediction from a single image using a multi-scale deep network. In *Advances in neural information processing systems*, 2014.

[10] H. Fang, M. Rais-Rohani, Z. Liu, and M. Horstemeyer. A comparative study of metamodeling methods for multiobjective crashworthiness optimization. *Computers & Structures*, 2005.

[11] G. Forsythe and W. Wasow. *Finite-Difference Methods for Partial Differential Equations.* 1960.

[12] A. Giunta. *Aircraft Multidisciplinary Design Optimization Using Design of Experiments Theory and Response Surface Modeling Methods.* 1997.

[13] S. Gupta, R. Girshick, P. Arbeláez, and J. Malik. Learning rich features from RGB-D images for object detection and segmentation. In *Computer Vision–ECCV*. 2014.

[14] D. Hartmann, M. Meinke, and W. Schröder. Differential equation based constrained reinitialization for level set methods. *Journal of Computational Physics*, 2008.

[15] V. Heuveline and J. Latt. *The OpenLB project: an open source and object oriented implementation of lattice Boltzmann methods.* International Journal of Modern Physics, 2007.

[16] S. Jeong, M. Murayama, and K. Yamamoto. Efficient optimization design method using kriging model. *Journal of Aircraft*, 2005.

[17] Y. Jia, E. Shelhamer, J. Donahue, S. Karayev, J. Long, R. Girshick, and T. Darrell. Caffe: Convolutional architecture for fast feature embedding. In *Proceedings of the ACM International Conference on Multimedia*. 2014.

[18] A. Keane and P. Nair. *Computational approaches for aerospace design.* 2005.

[19] S. J. Leary, A. Bhaskar, and A. J. Keane. Global approximation and optimization using adjoint computational fluid dynamics codes. *AIAA journal*, 2004.

[20] Y. LeCun, L. Bottou, Y. Bengio, and P. Haffner. Gradient-based learning applied to document recognition. *Proceedings of the IEEE*, 1998.

[21] M. Mawson, G. Leaver, and A. Revell. Real-time flow computations using an image based depth sensor and GPU acceleration. 2013.

[22] G. R. McNamara and G. Zanetti. Use of the boltzmann equation to simulate lattice-gas automata. *Physical Review Letters*, 1988.

[23] A. Mohamad. *Lattice Boltzmann Method.* 2011.

[24] S. Patankar. *Numerical heat transfer and fluid flow.* CRC Press, 1980.

[25] G. Russo and P. Smereka. A remark on computing distance functions. *Journal of Computational Physics*, 2000.

[26] J. Schmidhuber. Deep learning in neural networks: An overview. *Neural Networks*, 2015.

[27] R. Socher, B. Huval, B. Bath, C. D. Manning, and A. Y. Ng. Convolutional-recursive deep learning for 3d object classification. In *Advances in Neural Information Processing Systems*, 2012.

[28] D. Tran, L. Bourdev, R. Fergus, L. Torresani, and M. Paluri. Deep end2end voxel2voxel prediction. *arXiv preprint arXiv:1511.06681*, 2015.

[29] J. Turner, W. Clough, C. Martin, and J. Topp. Stiffness and deflection analysis of complex structures. *Journal of the Aeronautical Sciences*, 1956.

[30] N. Umetani, Y. Koyama, R. Schmidt, and T. Igarashi. Pteromys: interactive design and optimization of free-formed free-flight model airplanes. *ACM Trans. Graph.*, 2014.

[31] K. Valderhaug. *The Lattice Boltzmann Simulation on Multi-GPU Systems.* 2011.

[32] S. Wilkinson, G. Bradbury, and H. S. *Reduced-Order Urban Wind Interference, Simulation: Transactions of the Society for Modeling and Simulation International.* 2015.

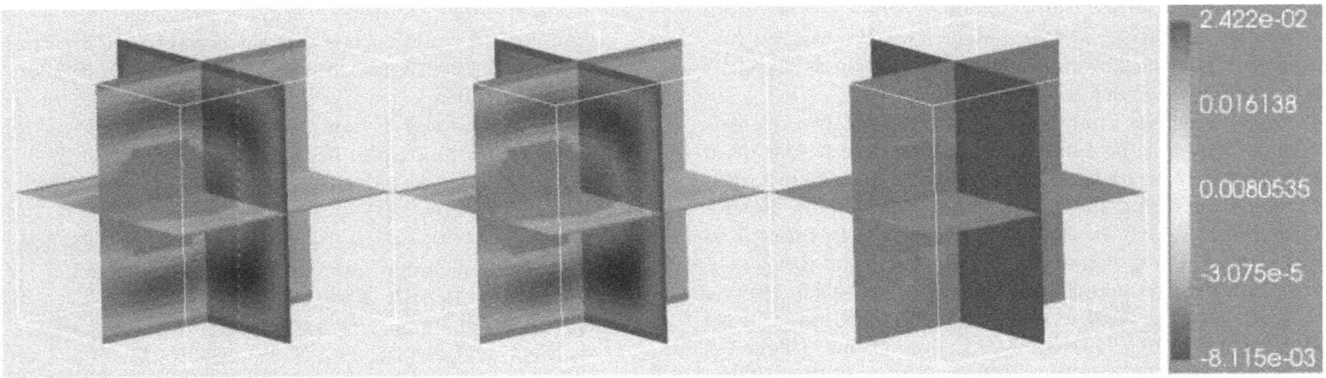

Magnitude of Velocity: ***CFD(LBM) Simulation*** *(left),* ***CNN Prediction*** *(middle),* ***Error*** *(right)*

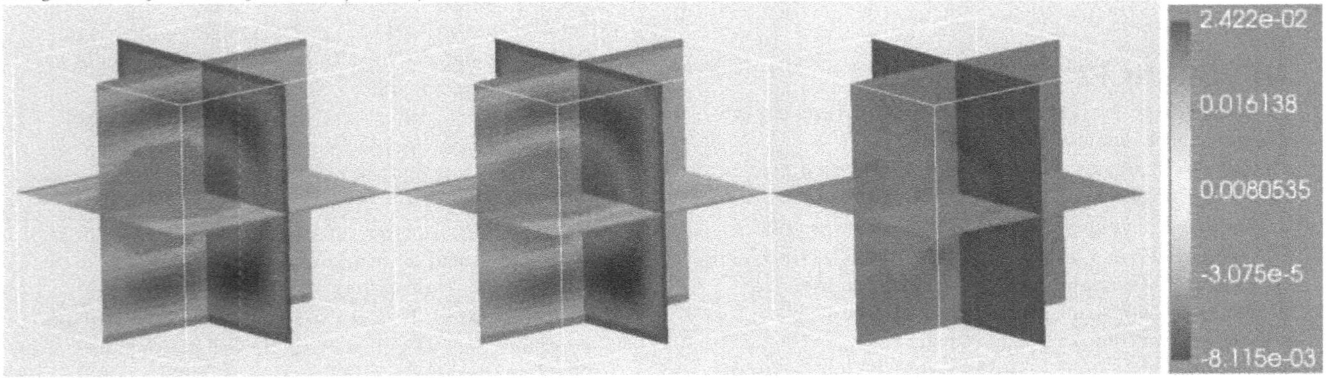

Velocity X component: ***CFD(LBM) Simulation*** *(left),* ***CNN Prediction*** *(middle),* ***Error*** *(right)*

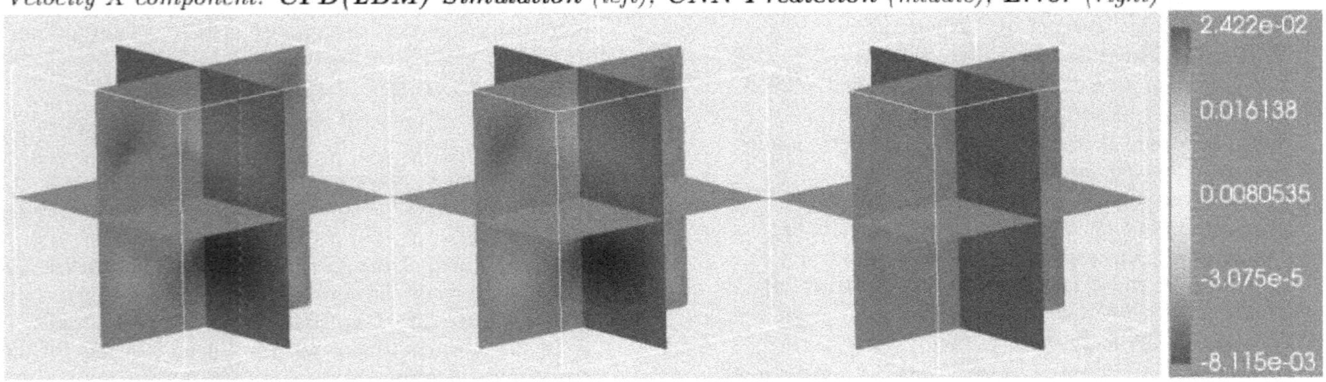

Velocity Y component: ***CFD(LBM) Simulation*** *(left),* ***CNN Prediction*** *(middle),* ***Error*** *(right)*

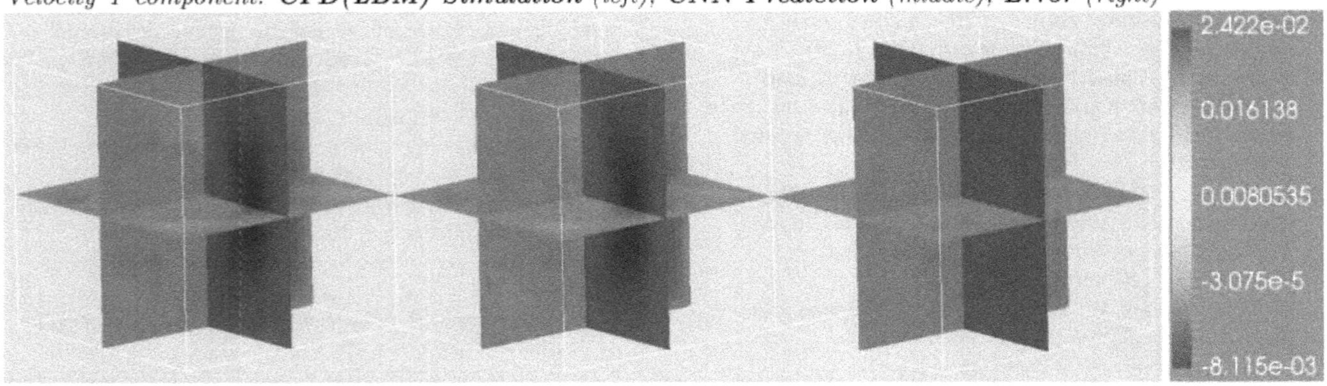

Velocity Z component: ***CFD(LBM) Simulation*** *(left),* ***CNN Prediction*** *(middle),* ***Error*** *(right)*

Figure 11: 3D prediction visualization. The first column shows the magnitude of the LBM ground truth. The second column shows the magnitude of the CNN prediction. The third column shows the magnitude of the difference between the CNN prediction and LBM results.

Computational Drug Repositioning Using Continuous Self-Controlled Case Series

Zhaobin Kuang[1], James Thomson[2], Michael Caldwell[3], Peggy Peissig[4], Ron Stewart[5], David Page[6]
University of Wisconsin[1,6], Morgridge Institute[2,5], Marshfield Clinic[3,4]
zkuang@wisc.edu[1], page@biostat.wisc.edu[6], JThomson@morgridge.org[2], RStewart@morgridgeinstitute.org[5], caldwell.michael@marshfieldclinic.org[3], Peissig.Peggy@mcrf.mfldclin.edu[4]

ABSTRACT

Computational Drug Repositioning (CDR) is the task of discovering potential new indications for existing drugs by mining large-scale heterogeneous drug-related data sources. Leveraging the patient-level temporal ordering information between numeric physiological measurements and various drug prescriptions provided in Electronic Health Records (EHRs), we propose a Continuous Self-controlled Case Series (CSCCS) model for CDR. As an initial evaluation, we look for drugs that can control Fasting Blood Glucose (FBG) level in our experiments. Applying CSCCS to the Marshfield Clinic EHR, well-known drugs that are indicated for controlling blood glucose level are rediscovered. Furthermore, some drugs with recent literature support for the potential effect of blood glucose level control are also identified.

CCS Concepts

•Mathematics of computing → Regression analysis; **•Applied computing → Health care information systems; Health informatics;**

Keywords

Longitudinal Data; Self-Controlled Case Series; Computational Drug Repositioning

1. INTRODUCTION

Drug repositioning is the task of identifying new potential indications for existing drugs. This task has been steadily rising to prominence because the traditional process of *de novo* drug discovery can be slow, expensive, and risky [1]. Moreover, with the advent of the big data era, abundant data sources that collect rich drug-related information are emerging. Mining large-scale heterogeneous drug-related data sources, Computational Drug Repositioning (CDR) has become an active research area that has the potential to deliver more effective drug repositioning. There have been several comprehensive reviews in the literature on CDR [2, 3]. Many methods leverage genotypic and transcriptomic information [4, 5], as well as drug molecular structure and drug combination information [6, 7]. A prior study that used Electronic Health Records (EHRs) to validate a potential indication of *one* existing drug has also been reported [8].

We are interested in mining EHRs in order to identify a potential indication from *multiple* existing drugs simultaneously. As an initial attempt, we examine the *numeric* values of Fasting Blood Glucose (FBG) level recorded in patients' EHRs *before* and *after* some drugs are prescribed to those patients, in the hope of identifying previously unknown potential uses of drugs to control blood glucose level.

For this purpose, we extend the Self-Controlled Case Series (SCCS) [9] model that has been widely used in the Adverse Drug Reactions (ADRs) discovery community to handle *continuous* numeric response, hence the name of our model, Continuous Self-Controlled Case Series (CSCCS).

The cornerstone of a self-controlled method is an understanding of how drug prescription history will potentially influence the FBG level every time such a measurement is taken. For example, an antibiotic drug taken ten years ago might have less, if any, influence on the FBG level than an anti-diabetic drug taken a day before that FBG level is measured. To determine how long a drug can potentially influence a patient, we furthermore propose a data-driven approach that leverages change point detection [10], resulting in estimations of different time spans of influence for different drugs.

Our contributions are three-fold:

- To the best of our knowledge, this is the first translation of SCCS methodology from ADR discovery to CDR. Our work is a pilot study evaluating the use of temporal ordering information between numeric physical measurements and drug prescriptions available in EHRs for the knowledge discovery process of CDR.
- Based on the insightful observations of [11], we derive our CSCCS model from a fixed effect model and hence extend the original SCCS model to address continuous numeric response variables.
- We introduce to the CDR and ADR discovery community a data-driven approach for adaptively determining the time spans of influence of different drugs to the patients.

KDD '16 August 13-17, 2016, San Francisco, CA, USA

ACM ISBN 978-1-4503-4232-2/16/08.
DOI: http://dx.doi.org/10.1145/2939672.2939715

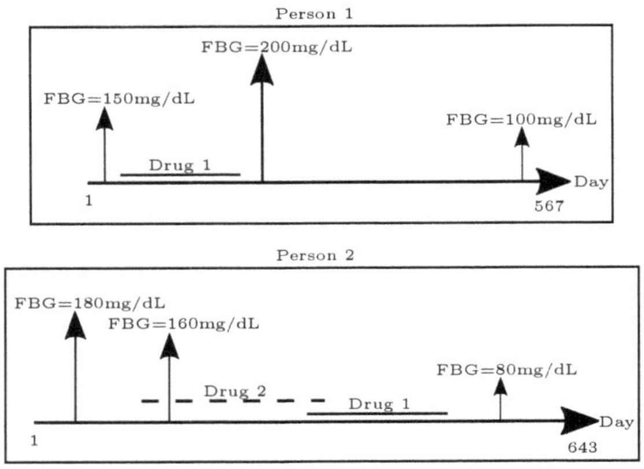

Figure 1: An example of EHRs

2. CONTINUOUS SELF-CONTROLLED CASE SERIES (CSCCS) MODEL

2.1 Notation

Figure 1 visualizes an example of health records for two patients. To confine the time span of a drug that has potential influence on that patient, we use the concept of *drug era*, which is recorded with its start date, end date and the name (or id) of the drug. We consider a patient to be under consistent influence of a drug during a drug era of that drug. However, drug era information is not readily available in most EHRs. Instead, drug prescription information with the name of a drug and the start date of the prescription is usually provided in observational data. How to construct drug eras from prescription records is a challenging and significant task for both CDR and ADR discovery [12, 13]. We provide a data-driven approach to this task in Section 4.

Measurements of FBG level might also be taken from time to time and are recorded with the date taken, as well as their numeric measurement values. We assume that at most one FBG measurement is taken for a particular patient on a particular day.

Let there be N patients with FBG measurements and M different drugs in the EHR. We construct a cohort using all the FBG measurement records as well as all the drug era records from all the N patients. Furthermore, we use a continuous random variable y_{ij}, where $i \in \{1, 2, \cdots, N\}$, $j \in \{1, 2, \cdots, J_i\}$, to denote the value of the jth FBG measurement taken among a total number of J_i measurements during the observation period of the ith person. Similarly, we use a binary variable x_{ijm}, $i \in \{1, 2, \cdots, N\}, j \in \{1, 2, \cdots, J_i\}$, $m \in \{1, 2, \cdots, M\}$ to denote the exposure status of the mth drug of the ith person at the date when the jth FBG measurement is taken, with 1 representing exposure and 0 otherwise.

2.2 The Linear Fixed Effect Model

We treat the y_{ij}'s as the response variables and first consider the following linear regression model:

$$y_{ij}|\boldsymbol{x}_{ij} = \alpha_i + \boldsymbol{\beta}^\top \boldsymbol{x}_{ij} + \epsilon_{ij}, \quad \epsilon_{ij} \overset{iid}{\sim} N\left(0, \sigma^2\right), \tag{1}$$

where

$$\boldsymbol{\beta} = \begin{bmatrix}\beta_1 & \beta_2 & \cdots & \beta_M\end{bmatrix}^\top, \quad \boldsymbol{x}_{ij} = \begin{bmatrix}x_{ij1} & x_{ij2} & \cdots & x_{ijM}\end{bmatrix}^\top,$$

α_i, which is called the *nuisance parameter*, represents the individual effect of the ith person on the value of y_{ij}, invariant to day j, drug m, and other patients, and ϵ_{ij}'s are independent and identically distributed Gaussian noises with zero mean and fixed but unknown variance σ^2.

The parameter of interest in this problem is $\boldsymbol{\beta}$, which represents the effect of each of the M drugs on the response $\boldsymbol{y}$ when a patient is under the joint exposure statuses specified by $\boldsymbol{x}_{ij}$. More specifically, suppose the mth component of $\boldsymbol{\beta}$, β_m, is evaluated to a negative number, that is to say, exposure to the mth drug will cause the FBG level to decrease. If this drug is not known to be prescribed for lowering FBG, such a decrease is an indicator that this drug might have the potential to be repositioned to help diabetic patients control their blood glucose level, given further investigation.

In this setting, fitting a linear regression model is equivalent to solving the following least squares problem:

$$\arg\min_{\boldsymbol{\alpha},\boldsymbol{\beta}} \frac{1}{2}\left\|\boldsymbol{y} - \begin{bmatrix}\boldsymbol{Z} & \boldsymbol{X}\end{bmatrix}\begin{bmatrix}\boldsymbol{\alpha}\\ \boldsymbol{\beta}\end{bmatrix}\right\|_2^2, \tag{2}$$

where

$$\boldsymbol{\alpha} = \begin{bmatrix}\alpha_1 & \alpha_2 & \cdots & \alpha_N\end{bmatrix}^\top, \quad \boldsymbol{Z} = \operatorname{diag}\left(\boldsymbol{1}_1, \cdots, \boldsymbol{1}_N\right),$$
$$\boldsymbol{y} = \begin{bmatrix}y_{11} & \cdots & y_{1J_1} & \cdots & y_{N1} & \cdots & y_{NJ_N}\end{bmatrix}^\top,$$
$$\boldsymbol{X} = \begin{bmatrix}\boldsymbol{x}_{11} & \cdots & \boldsymbol{x}_{1J_1} & \cdots & \boldsymbol{x}_{N1} & \cdots & \boldsymbol{x}_{NJ_N}\end{bmatrix}^\top,$$

where $\boldsymbol{Z}$ is a block diagonal matrix with $\boldsymbol{1}_i$ being a $J_i \times 1$ vector where all the components are 1. The least squares problem in (2) is a linear *fixed effect model* with $\boldsymbol{\alpha}$ being a nonrandom quantity whose i^{th} component α_i, can be interpreted as the *average* FBG measurement level of the ith patient taken over time without exposing to any drugs.

2.3 Deriving the CSCCS Model from the Linear Fixed Effect Model

Like the SCCS model, the motivation behind the CSCCS model is to use only $\boldsymbol{\beta}$ as a parsimonious parameterization to predict the response vector $\boldsymbol{y}$. Inspired by the work in [11], where the equivalence between the Poisson fixed effect model and the SCCS model is established, we are able to derive the CSCCS model from the linear fixed effect model in (2) in a similar fashion. Let

$$\ell\left(\boldsymbol{\alpha}, \boldsymbol{\beta}\right) = \frac{1}{2}\left\|\boldsymbol{y} - \begin{bmatrix}\boldsymbol{Z} & \boldsymbol{X}\end{bmatrix}\begin{bmatrix}\boldsymbol{\alpha}\\ \boldsymbol{\beta}\end{bmatrix}\right\|_2^2.$$

We consider,

$$\frac{\partial \ell\left(\boldsymbol{\alpha}, \boldsymbol{\beta}\right)}{\partial \boldsymbol{\alpha}} = \boldsymbol{0} \Rightarrow \boldsymbol{\alpha} = \left(\boldsymbol{Z}^\top \boldsymbol{Z}\right)^{-1} \boldsymbol{Z}^\top \left(\boldsymbol{y} - \boldsymbol{X}\boldsymbol{\beta}\right) = \bar{\boldsymbol{y}} - \bar{\boldsymbol{X}}\boldsymbol{\beta}, \tag{3}$$

where $\bar{\boldsymbol{y}}$ is an $N \times 1$ vector with the ith component, $\bar{y}_i = \frac{1}{J_i}\sum_{j=1}^{J_i} y_{ij}$, and $\bar{\boldsymbol{X}}$ is an $N \times M$ matrix with the ith row, $\bar{\boldsymbol{X}}_{i\cdot} = \frac{1}{J_i}\sum_{j=1}^{J_i} \boldsymbol{x}_{ij}^\top$. Substitute (3) into (2) results in the CSCCS model:

$$\arg\min_{\boldsymbol{\beta}} \frac{1}{2}\left\|\boldsymbol{y} - \boldsymbol{Z}\bar{\boldsymbol{y}} - \left(\boldsymbol{X} - \boldsymbol{Z}\bar{\boldsymbol{X}}\right)\boldsymbol{\beta}\right\|_2^2. \tag{4}$$

The model in (4) is in the desired form of parsimonious parameterization in that the optimization problem is defined only in the space of $\boldsymbol{\beta}$, and the nuisance parameter $\boldsymbol{\alpha}$ is eliminated.

The CSCCS model is a linear model and hence CSCCS is able to predict *continuous* response $\boldsymbol{y}$. The model is *self-controlled* in that each FBG measurement and their corresponding drug exposure statuses are adjusted by their mean within each individual. The model also utilizes *case series* in that only cases (patients that have at least one FBG measurement) are admitted in the cohort.

CSCCS is derived from its linear fixed effect model counterpart. This derivation shares the same spirit with the equivalence between the original SCCS and the Poisson fixed effect model; in this sense, CSCCS extends SCCS to address numeric response in the new setting.

Although both models in (2) and (4) can be considered as linear models, from the perspective of implementation efficiency, the explicit form of CSCCS in (4) is of vital importance for the task of CDR using large-scale EHRs. This is because the parameter of interest in our task is $\boldsymbol{\beta}$ and the nuisance parameters do not provide direct information in evaluating the impact of a drug in changing FBG level. In the setting of large-scale EHRs, where tens of thousands of patient records might be admitted into the cohort as cases, the dimension of the nuisance parameter can potentially be very high. In this scenario, without the access to a special purpose solver for the fixed effect model, solving a model in the form of (2) using only a general purpose linear model solver can be time consuming or even infeasible. On the contrary, using the explicit form of CSCCS in (4), a general purpose linear model solver only needs to find solutions in the space of $\boldsymbol{\beta}$, a parameter whose dimension is only as large as the number of drugs available in the cohort, which is a much smaller number than the dimension of nuisance parameters.

3. CHALLENGES IN EHR DATA

Several challenges arise when we apply CSCCS to EHR data. In this section, we present the further refinements we perform on the CSCCS model presented in (4) in order to address these challenges.

3.1 High Dimensionality

EHR data is a type of high-dimensional longitudinal data. While tens of thousands of patient records might be admitted into the cohort, effects of thousands of drugs on the FBG level need to be evaluated simultaneously, introducing a high-dimensional problem. This motivates us to incorporate sparsity into our model using the penalty [14],

$$\arg\min_{\boldsymbol{\beta}} \frac{1}{2}\|\boldsymbol{y} - \boldsymbol{Z}\bar{\boldsymbol{y}} - \left(\boldsymbol{X} - \boldsymbol{Z}\bar{\boldsymbol{X}}\right)\boldsymbol{\beta}\|_2^2 + \lambda\|\boldsymbol{\beta}\|_1, \quad (5)$$

where $\lambda > 0$ is a tuning parameter determining the level of sparsity.

The incorporation of this penalty essentially assumes that only a small portion of drugs are related to the change of FBG level, and the rest of them do not have significant effect on changing FBG level when patients are exposed to those drugs. With the L_1 penalization, most components of $\boldsymbol{\beta}$ will be evaluated to zero or a number that is close to zero. The result is, instead of evaluating the effect of *each* of the M drugs on FBG level, L_1 penalized CSCCS only selects a subset of drugs that, in some sense, are most correlated to the change of FBG level, and estimates their relative strength and direction of change among the drugs chosen.

3.2 Irregular Time Dependency

The linear fixed effect model assumes that all responses are independent of each other. The meaning of independence is two-fold. On one hand, responses from different patients are independent of each other. To explain differences across patients (e.g. some patients tend to have higher FBG levels than others in general), $\boldsymbol{\alpha}$ is used with each component representing the time-invariant effect of each patient on the response. On the other hand, responses observed at different time are independent of each other. To explain differences across time (e.g. FBG levels observed in early age *might be* lower than those in old age), a time-dependent variable that has the same value across all patients can be introduced. That is to say:

$$y_{ij}|\boldsymbol{x}_{ij} = \alpha_i + t_j + \boldsymbol{\beta}^\top \boldsymbol{x}_{ij} + \epsilon_{ij}, \quad (6)$$

where t_j is the time-dependent nuisance parameter whose value depends only on the time when the jth measurement is taken. If observations are recorded regularly across time, (6) defines a *two-way fixed effect model*, as opposed to the *one-way fixed effect model* defined in (2) [15].

In practice, a one-way model might be preferred over a two-way model if we assume that the heterogeneity across different individuals is much more significant than that across time. However, in the task of CDR from EHRs, this assumption might be too restrictive. To begin with, EHRs usually contain observational data of patients that are recorded over decades. Therefore, it is probable that the baseline FBG levels of patients change significantly over the years. This is especially true when some persistent FBG level altering events, such as the diagnosis of diabetes, occur to some patients. Furthermore, the length of observation periods varies dramatically among patients. Therefore, we do not have a fully observed and consistent dataset to model the set of time-dependent nuisance parameters. Last but not least, the incorporation of time-dependent nuisance parameters is proposed in a setting where data are collected regularly. With the irregular nature of EHR data, modeling time-dependent nuisance parameters directly with a classic two-way fixed effect model is impractical.

To address the aforementioned challenges without much loss in efficiency, we consider a reasonable assumption: given y_{ij} and $y_{ij'}$, where $j \neq j'$, but the dates of the two measurements taken are very close to each other, we assume the two corresponding time-dependent nuisance parameters are equal to each other, i.e. $t_j = t_{j'}$. More specifically,

$$\begin{aligned} y_{ij}|\boldsymbol{x}_{ij} &= \alpha_i + t_j + \boldsymbol{\beta}^\top \boldsymbol{x}_{ij} + \epsilon_{ij}, \\ y_{ij'}|\boldsymbol{x}_{ij'} &= \alpha_i + t_{j'} + \boldsymbol{\beta}^\top \boldsymbol{x}_{ij'} + \epsilon_{ij'}, \\ |d_{ij} - d_{ij'}| &\leq \tau \Rightarrow t_j = t_{j'}, \end{aligned}$$

where d_{ij} and $d_{ij'}$ represent that the jth and j'^{th} measurements of the ith patient are taken at the d_{ij}^{th} day and $d_{ij'}^{th}$ day of the observation period, and τ is a predetermined threshold. Then,

$$\mathbb{E}\left[y_{ij} - y_{ij'}|\boldsymbol{x}_{ij}, \boldsymbol{x}_{ij'}\right] = \boldsymbol{\beta}^\top\left(\boldsymbol{x}_{ij} - \boldsymbol{x}_{ij'}\right) \equiv \boldsymbol{\beta}^\top \boldsymbol{\delta}_{ij}, \quad (7)$$

where the nuisance parameters are eliminated. Therefore, the quantity in (7) depends only on $\boldsymbol{\beta}$ and the data.

Based on this formulation, we can reconstruct the CSCCS model to address irregular time dependency as follow: firstly, given τ, construct a cohort where only patients with at least a pair of FBG measurements taken within τ days are admitted; only adjacent pairs are used. Secondly, solve the following lasso problem:

$$\arg\min_{\boldsymbol{\beta}} \frac{1}{2}\|\boldsymbol{D}\boldsymbol{y} - \boldsymbol{D}\boldsymbol{X}\boldsymbol{\beta}\|_2^2 + \lambda\|\boldsymbol{\beta}\|_1, \quad (8)$$

where $\boldsymbol{D}$, when multiplied with $\boldsymbol{y}$ or $\boldsymbol{X}$, generates the difference between the measurement of an earlier record and the corresponding measurement of its adjacent later-measured record of the same patient, with the constraint that the two records are collected within a time span of τ days.

Note that the model in (8) is not equivalent to the model in (5). However, the model in (8) can still be considered as a variant of CSCCS in that its parameterization is still restricted to $\boldsymbol{\beta}$, with the goal of predicting a continuous response, using data subtraction within the *same* patient as a self-controlled mechanism, and only admitting cases into the cohort. We call the the model in (8) as CSCCS for Adjacent response, or CSCCSA.

3.3 Confounding

Another challenge an algorithm must tackle is the confounding issue arises due to the complex nature of clinical observational data. In the setting of EHRs, one important confounding issue is called *confounding by co-medication.* Consider drug A and drug B, where only drug A can lower FBG level and drug B has no significant effect on changing blood sugar. However, drug B is usually prescribed with drug A. In this case, drug B can be a confounder if we only evaluate the marginal correlation between each drug and FBG level. Another confounding issue in this setting is *confounding by comorbidity.* Consider the FBG-lowering drug A given to a diabetic patient. Following the prescription of drug A, some other conditions could occur to this patient since diabetes can lead to various comorbidities [16]. To treat a newly introduced condition, drug B is prescribed to the patient. In this case, if we again consider only the marginal correlation between drug B and FBG level, one might draw the conclusion that drug B could lower FBG level since after the prescription of drug A, the FBG level has decreased.

In the two aforementioned confounding issues, drug B is called an *innocent bystander.* Like multiple SCCS [9], multiple CSCCS can effectively handle the innocent bystander confounding problem (a.k.a. Simpson's Paradox). This is because the confounder seems to spuriously correlated to the FBG level when we consider their marginal correlation. However, using a multiple linear model like CSCCS, the joint exposure statuses of both drug A and drug B can be considered simultaneously. Therefore, CSCCS might be able to identify that the decrease of FBG level occurs only when conditioning on the exposure of drug A and hence rule out drug B in the model.

In terms of addressing various confounding issues, CSCCS inherits most of the strengths and weaknesses from SCCS, due to the close relationship between the two models. While CSCCS might address reasonably well the innocent bystander confounding problem, it might not be well suited to handle confounding issues such as time-varying confounding [17]. In Section 5, we empirically evaluate the performance of CSCCS in the CDR task and illustrate how its performance is related to its capabilities of addressing various confounding issues.

4. BUILDING DRUG ERAS FROM DRUG PRESCRIPTION RECORDS

A prerequisite of CSCCS is the availability of drug era information of each drug prescribed to each patient. However, drug era information is usually not provided in most EHRs. Instead, drug prescription records of each patient are kept, usually with the name (or id) of the drug and the date of prescription. Constructing drug eras from drug prescription records is an important but challenging task for both CDR using CSCCS and ADR discovery.

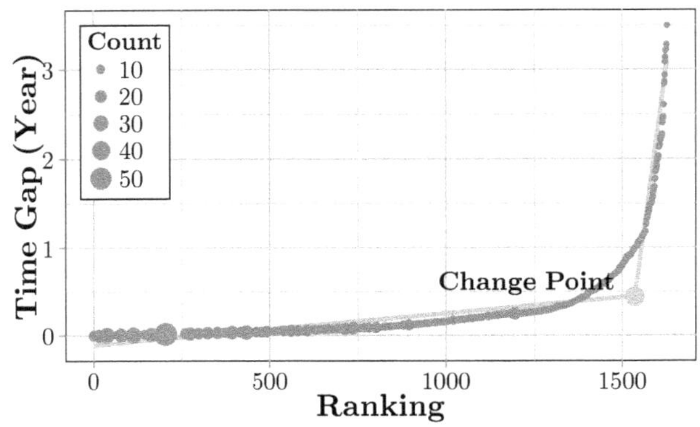

Figure 2: Time gap of Humalog in ascending order: the size of dots represents the number of time gaps that share the same value

4.1 Drug Era in Common Data Model

A heuristic proposed in the Common Data Model (CDM) [18] by Observational Medical Outcome Partnership (OMOP) is to first consider the prescription dates of each prescription record as the start date of the drug era. It then assumes that each drug era lasts n days and hence computes the end date of the drug era accordingly. Within the same patient, we assume there is only one drug prescription record of the same drug in a given date. In this way, drug eras of the same drug within each patient constructed as before start from different dates. For an adjacent pair of drug eras of the same drug within the same patient, we call the drug era that starts earlier a *former era,* and the other a *latter era.* CDM defines a parameter called *persistence window.* If the start date of the latter era, subtracted by the end date of the former era, is no larger than the persistence window, CDM merges the two drug eras into one, using the start date of the former era as the start date of the new era and the end date of the latter era as the end date of the new era. CDM tries to merge as many drug eras of the same drug within the same patient as possible in this fashion, until every resultant drug era of the same drug within the same patient is separated by more than persistence window amount of time. In CDM, both n and the persistence window are usually set to thirty days.

The intuition behind this heuristic is to build a longer drug era if the prescription date of an adjacent pair of records of the same drug are close enough to each other. A natural question to ask is *how large* the time gap between the two adjacent prescription records can be for us to still consider them close enough?

4.2 Constructing Drug Eras via Change Point Analysis

Instead of specifying a predetermined threshold on time gap as it is in CDM, we answer this question via a data-driven approach: for each drug, we compute the time gaps between all adjacent pairs of prescription records. We then sort these time gaps in ascending order. A visualization of

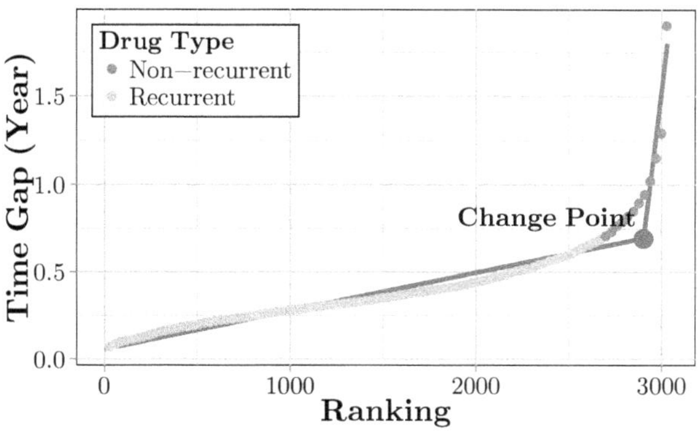

Figure 3: Change points of all drugs in the EHRs in ascending order

the values of the time gaps of Humalog against their relative rankings is given in Figure 2. From Figure 2, we notice that the distribution of time gaps can be approximated by a piecewise linear model with a change point close to the end of the sample with large time gap values. The smaller time gaps can be fitted well by the flat linear segment of the model while the larger time gaps can be fitted well by the steep linear segment. This phenomenon leads to a reasonable assumption that the smaller time gaps are sampling from a different underlying distribution than that of the larger time gaps. The smaller time gaps sampling from the same distribution correspond to the adjacent pairs of prescription records that we can consider close enough to each other to construct a lasting drug era. A threshold we can use to distinguish the two types of time gaps is the change point of the piecewise linear model.

For each drug with at least fifty prescription records in the EHRs, we perform change point detection analysis in the aforementioned fashion using `R` package `segmented`. We plot the change points of all the drugs against their relative rankings after sorting them in ascending order in Figure 3. Interestingly, there is also a change point in Figure 3. A possible explanation of the existence of a change point in Figure 3 is that in EHR data, drug prescriptions of some particular drugs are recurrent in order to battle chronic disease. For example, a diabetic patient needs long-term prescriptions of some FBG lowering drugs. On the other hand, the prescriptions of some other drugs are non-recurrent, such as antibiotics. We consider the change point in Figure 3 as a threshold to distinguish recurrent drugs from non-recurrent drugs in the EHR because a reasonable expectation is that if a drug is recurrent, the gap between an adjacent pair of prescription records of that drug from the same patient will tend not to be too large and hopefully under the change point specified in Figure 3.

We extend the heuristic provided in CDM as follow: We first denote the mean of all change point values of the recurrent drugs in the EHR as γ. For all the recurrent drugs, we set their corresponding n's and the value of their persistence windows to $\frac{\gamma}{2}$. We then set $n = 0.04$year (approximately two weeks) for all non-recurrent drugs and 0 as the value of their persistence windows.

5. EXPERIMENTS

As far as we know, our CSCCS model is the first of its kind to explicitly use temporal ordering information in EHRs for CDR. How do we evaluate the performance of a method that utilizes this type of information? As a preliminary endeavor, we try to answer this question by addressing two major challenges for our experiments.

5.1 Lack of a Baseline Method

The first challenge we need to handle is the lack of a baseline method that also utilizes temporal ordering information in an EHR for CDR. Inspired by the idea of disproportionality analysis from the pharmacovigilance literature [19], we propose the *Pairwise Mean* (PM) method as a baseline method. PM assigns a real-valued score to each of the M drugs in the EHR to represent how likely the drug decreases FBG level, and a smaller score implies a stronger decreasing tendency. The score of the mth drug, s_m, is computed as follow: first, for the ith patient who has FBG measurements within two years before *and* after the *first* prescription of the mth drug, we compute the mean of those FBG measurements before and after the first prescription, denoted as b_{mi} and a_{mi}, respectively; second, compute s_m as:

$$s_m = \frac{1}{N_m} \sum_{i=1}^{N_m} (a_{mi} - b_{mi}),$$

where N_m is the number of patients that have FBG measurements two years before and after the first prescription of the mth drug.

5.2 Incomplete Ground Truth

Unlike the task of ADR discovery from the EHR, where numerous research efforts have been invested on developing a set of ground truth [20] drug-adverse-reaction pairs so that algorithms can be run and evaluated, we do not have access to such a ground truth set for the task of CDR from EHRs. We use Marshfield Clinic EHR as our data source and there are about two thousand drugs for evaluation. To evaluate the performance of our algorithm without knowing the glucose altering effect of every drug, we focus on the top forty most promising drugs generated by PM, CSCCS, and CSCCSA, as shown in Table 2, Table 3, and Table 4, respectively.

In these three tables, rows that are shaded in green represent the drugs commonly prescribed for lowering glucose while rows that are shaded in red represent the drugs commonly prescribed for increasing glucose. The two types of drugs in the three tables are all manually labeled. Drugs in the unshaded rows might potentially be irrelevant, or might constitute new discoveries. These drugs are discussed in further detail in Section 5.7. A summary of the number of each of the three types of drugs discovered by the three algorithms are given in Table 1.

In CSCCSA, we set τ defined in Section 3.2 to four years. In Table 2, the counts and scores are N_m's and s_m's defined in Section 5.1, while in Table 3 and Table 4, the counts are the L_1 norm of the columns in $\boldsymbol{X}$ corresponding to different drugs, and the scores are the regression coefficients of different drugs. We only consider drugs with counts greater than or equal to eight. For CSCCS and CSCCSA, we first construct drug eras using the method described in Section 4, where we determine that $\gamma = 0.34$ years. We then use a lasso penalty for variable selection to generate a long list of about two hundred drugs, and we present the top forty among those selected drugs as the short list. The number eight and forty could be tuned to optimize accuracy but

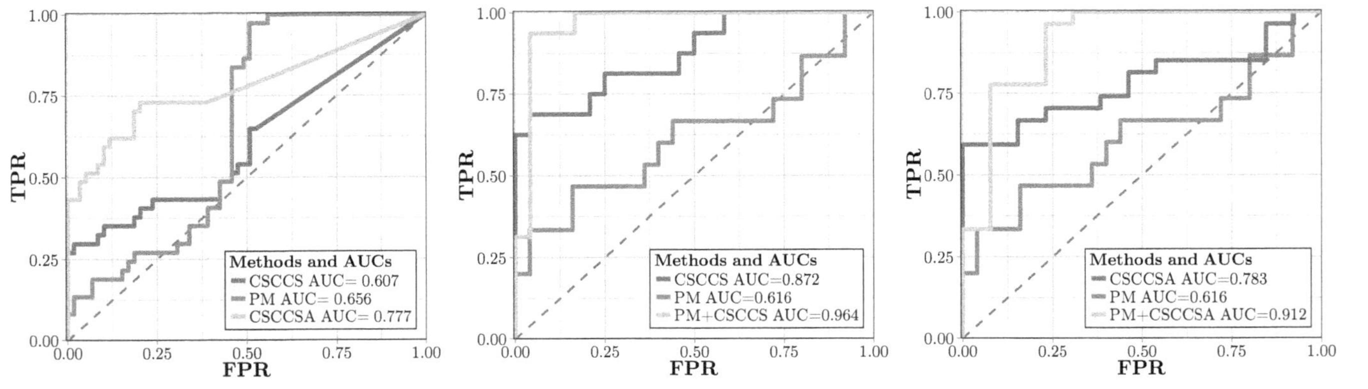

(a) PM, CSCCS, and CSCCSA (b) CSCCS (c) CSCCSA

Figure 4: ROC curves

were fixed here beforehand for practical reasons. Drugs with fewer than eight prescriptions might not have sufficient evidence to support a new use. Evaluating more than forty results per method was too large a burden for human literature review.

Table 1: A summary of three types of drugs discovered by the three algorithms

	PM	CSCCS	CSCCSA
decrease	15	16	27
increase	1	1	0
potential	24	23	13

5.3 Dataset

EHRs of 64515 patients from Marshfield Clinic are used in the CSCCS and CSCCSA experiments, providing 219306 FBG measurement records and 2980 drug candidates.

5.4 Receiver Operating Characteristic

As shown in Tables 2–4, all three methods capture a reasonable number of drugs that are prescribed for lowering glucose among their top forty candidates. We therefore consider identifying drugs prescribed for glucose-lowering as a binary classification task and use Receiver Operating Characteristics (ROC) curves as well as Area Under ROC (AUROC) to evaluate the performance of each algorithm.

We first construct the ROC curves of the three methods using the union list of drugs from Tables 2–4. The three ROC curves are presented in Figure 4(a). Since we perform variable selection in CSCCS and CSCCSA, some drugs might be assigned scores of zero and hence are considered irrelevant to the prediction of FBG level. In these cases, we put these drugs at the bottom of the union list and consider them to be identified as positive examples by the algorithms only at the very end. This results in the straight line segment of the ROC curves of CSCCS and CSCCSA at the liberal region. Figure 4(a) shows that CSCCSA has the highest AUC, outperforming CSCCS and PM by a significant margin, while PM and CSCCS have similar AUCs. However, in the more conservative region where there is drug support for all three methods, CSCCS outperforms PM while CSCCSA maintains the best performance. This phenomenon suggests that the modeling assumptions of CSCCS and CSCCSA are able to provide insights into making reasonable prediction of FBG level.

Figure 4(b) uses the forty drugs in Tables 2 and 3 to generate the ROC curves, in red for PM and in blue for CSCCS. As a comparison, we also plot the ROC curve of the following ensemble strategy: we first use the top forty drugs in Table 3 as a result of variable selection via CSCCS, then we compute the PM scores over the selected drugs. By comparing the AUCs of the three curves, we notice that the ensemble method outperforms CSCCS and PM, while CSCCS outperforms PM. Since the scores used to construct the CSCCS ROC curve are regression coefficients of drug exposure statuses under a lasso penalty, the lack of an oracle property for the lasso [21] might potentially trade off the inherent order among drugs for a sparse model. However, such a trade-off is arguably beneficial, based on the significant improvement of AUC of CSCCS compared with the AUC of PM.

Figure 4(c) is generated similarly as Figure 4(b). The ensemble of CSCCSA with PM outperforms the two individual algorithms. Although the AUC of CSCCSA is less than that of CSCCS, it is worthy to notice that all but one true positive drugs in Table 3 are discovered in Table 4 at the top fifteen positions. Other than that, CSCCSA is also able to discover twelve more true positives that CSCCS does not capture among its top forty discoveries.

5.5 Precision at K

The task of CDR from EHRs is somewhat analogous to web search. Specifically, the algorithm should select only a few drugs that have interesting unexpected effects on the response: returning too many results makes it infeasible for human experts to evaluate the potential effect of the selected drugs. This is similar to users performing web search on a search engine, where typically only the quality of the results on the first page, or the first K results, matters. Based on this observation, an algorithm with a high precision-at-K value is desirable. Figure 5 shows the precision of each of the three algorithms at different positions (K) in the task of identifying drugs prescribed for lowering glucose. CSCCSA achieves the highest performance at all positions. CSCCS outperforms PM significantly at smaller K's, but the performances of the two algorithms are similar at larger K's. This is consistent with results in Table 1, showing that CSCCSA is able to identify more prescribed drugs for lowering glucose than the other two methods. Moreover, these drugs are at the very top of Table 4. Therefore, precision-at-K provides evidence for CSCCSA's utility for CDR from EHRs.

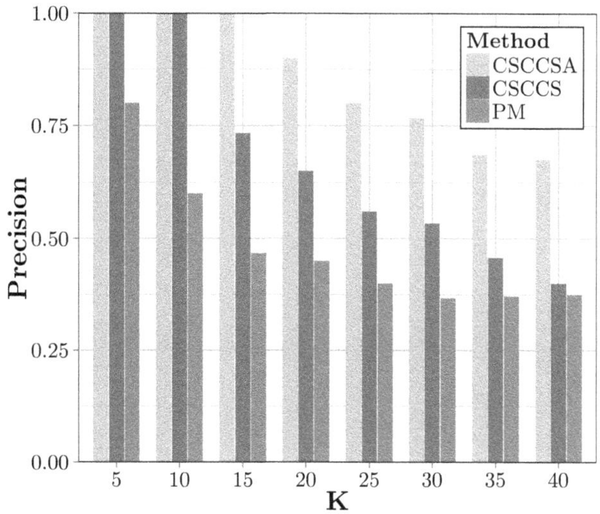

Figure 5: Precision at K of PM, CSCCS, and CSCCSA

5.6 Drugs with Known Glucose Increasing/ Decreasing Effects

From Tables 2–4, we notice that CSCCSA discovers the most number of drugs prescribed for lowering glucose among the three methods under consideration. This reaffirms our belief that CSCCSA is a promising method for CDR from EHR. Furthermore, we also notice that drugs prescribed for increasing glucose are reported in all but the table of CSCCSA.

In Table 2, sucrose is observed as a false positive using PM. Based on its count, this might be a spurious correlation in the data. This is even more probable when we consider the fact that the effect of sucrose on blood glucose level is short-term, and sucrose is not a drug that consistently enter patients' EHR for a long period of time. However, PM considers the glucose measurement records of the patients within two years before and after the first prescription of sucrose, during which many stronger confounding factors could have occurred to alter the glucose level.

In Table 3, glucagon is identified. Glucagon is given to diabetic patients that take glucose-lowering drugs to avoid hypoglycemia. However, glucagon alone is not frequently administered. Therefore, in the data, we observe the co-occurrence of glucagon with various glucose-lowering drugs. While glucagon alone increase blood glucose, combining with glucose-lowering drugs usually results in the decrease of blood sugar. On the other hand, we did not have enough data where glucagon is prescribed alone to observe the responses. Therefore, the algorithm will consider glucagon to have glucose-lowering effects since most of the time the occurrence of glucagon is accompanied by blood sugar decreasing medications. The algorithm might even consider it as a strong glucose-lowering drug because the actual glucose-lowering drugs are coded in various names in the EHR, hence dispersing the effect, while glucagon is coded only by a few different names.

5.7 Confounding and Potential Drugs

We now turn to the discussion of the drugs discovered by the three algorithms in Table 2–4 that are not prescribed for glucose increasing/decreasing. We will make use of a list providing drugs that can influence blood glucose level available in [22] to aid our evaluation process.

5.7.1 *The Blessing and the Curse of Marginal Correlations*

According to [22], in Table 2, Actigall can cause blood glucose level to increase while amphotericin B can cause blood glucose level to decrease. An interesting drug that is also brought to our attention is buderprion SR. Buderprion SR is an antidepressant prescribed for the treatment of depressive disorder. For diabetic patients with depression, buderprion SR can help to alleviate their depressive symptom, making them in a better mood. This in turn has a positive effect on better controlling blood glucose level for longer period of time [23]. PM is able to discover the blood glucose lowering effect of buderprion SR, even with a mere support of nine patients. The fact that PM considers the marginal correlation of each drug-indication pair independently makes it more likely to discover interesting drug-indication pairs with a weaker support. However, spurious correlations, especially those caused by the innocent bystander problem, are also more likely to be reported this way.

Comparing the results from Table 2 with those from Table 3 and Table 4 could justify our argument. In Table 2, Habitrol is a nicotine patch, and Monistat, Voriconazole, amphotericin B, and Hibiclens are all used to treat fungal infection. Interestingly, fungal infection is a comorbidity of diabetes [24, 25], and smokers are also more inclined to be diabetic [26]. On the other hand, we cannot find any drugs that are related to fungal infection or quitting smoke in Table 3 and Table 4. This comparison suggests that the aforementioned drugs in Table 2 generated by marginal association methods like PM might be innocent bystanders while a multiple regression approach such as CSCCS and CSCCSA might significantly help to alleviate this type of confounding issue.

5.7.2 *Potential drugs found by CSCCS and CSCCSA*

In Table 3, a study [27] indicates that enalapril helps to decrease the occurrence rate of diabetes in patients with chronic heart failure. Tricor might also have the potential to lower blood sugar level, based on the findings in [28] and [29]. Vitamin B12 is another interesting drug for consideration. In a rat model used by [30], deficiency in vitamin B12 is linked to hyperglycemia. However, blood glucose level can be decreased by providing vitamin B12. A recent study suggests that diabetic patients under metformin might experience vitamin B12 deficiency [31]. In a study on depressive patients, Zoloft, which is an antidepressant, is linked to the increase of insulin level after its prescription [32]. Zestril, which is the brand name of lisinopril, is found to inhibit high blood sugar level in rats [29]. Captopril is also reported to improve daily glucose profile among non-insulin-dependent patients [33]. However, hydralazine HCl is linked to glucose-increasing in a rat model, according to the findings in [34]. Nifedipine, verapamil HCl, and morphine sulfate can decrease blood sugar while captopril interacting with hydrochlorothiazide could cause high blood sugar, according to the list in [22]. The potential glucose-lowering drugs discovered indicate that CSCCS is a reasonable method for the task of CDR.

In Table 4, Pravachol is a member of a popular class of drugs called statins which are prescribed to lower cholesterol

Table 2: Top forty drugs: PM-Glucose

INDX	CODE	DRUG NAME	SCORE	COUNT
1	5226	LANTUS	-41.672	34
2	6646	NOVOFINE 31	-38.709	33
3	5789	METFORMIN HYDROCHLORIDE	-38.623	10
4	5806	METHENAM/MBLU/BA/SAL/ATROP/HYO	-36.710	10
5	4811	INSULIN NPH	-34.573	23
6	6652	NOVOLOG	-29.895	54
7	4336	HABITROL	-29.871	16
8	6044	MONISTAT	-29.721	14
9	9080	SURFAK	-29.655	14
10	9155	SYRNG W-NDL DISP INSUL 0.333ML	-29.439	30
11	4500	HUMULIN	-29.186	36
12	9008	SUGAR SUBSTITUTE	-28.971	10
13	10176	VORICONAZOLE	-28.538	10
14	1305	BUDEPRION SR	-27.444	9
15	8450	ROXICODONE	-27.428	12
16	9534	TRANDATE	-25.978	8
17	4802	INSULIN	-24.507	697
18	3849	FLURBIPROFEN SODIUM	-24.403	11
19	8316	REZULIN	-24.287	135
20	5257	LENALIDOMIDE	-22.875	8
21	4485	HUMALOG	-22.852	67
22	1389	CAL	-22.817	61
23	144	ACTIGALL	-22.237	36
24	8998	SUCROSE	-22.125	18
25	3843	FLUPHENAZINE HCL	-22.094	8
26	3682	FERROUS FUMARATE	-21.225	10
27	9104	SYMLINPEN 120	-20.333	12
28	1868	CHLORAMBUCIL	-20.268	14
29	4171	GLUCOTROL XL	-19.719	828
30	504	AMPHOTERICIN B	-19.672	24
31	3778	FLEXOR	-19.287	14
32	8241	REGULAR INSULIN	-19.205	39
33	824	AVANDIA	-19.140	487
34	5783	METAPROTERENOL	-18.920	10
35	4434	HIBICLENS	-18.863	10
36	5815	METH/ME BLUE/BA/PHENY/ATP/HYOS	-18.727	11
37	5010	JANUVIA	-18.716	11
38	4813	INSULIN NPL/INSULIN LISPRO	-18.515	126
39	4595	HYDROMORPHONE	-18.470	17
40	7626	POLYMYXIN B SULFATE MICRONIZED	-18.456	11

Table 3: Top forty drugs: CSCCS-Glucose

INDX	CODE	DRUG NAME	SCORE	COUNT
1	7470	PIOGLITAZONE HCL	-13.502	3075
2	8437	ROSIGLITAZONE MALEATE	-13.465	1019
3	6656	NPH HUMAN INSULIN ISOPHANE	-10.963	2874
4	4497	HUM INSULIN NPH/REG INSULIN HM	-10.869	1829
5	160	ACTOS	-7.665	1125
6	824	AVANDIA	-7.543	1239
7	4837	INSULN ASP PRT/INSULIN ASPART	-7.067	258
8	4806	INSULIN GLARGINE HUM.REC.ANLOG	-5.571	4213
9	9152	SYRING W-NDL DISP INSUL 0.5ML	-5.301	4186
10	8316	REZULIN	-3.611	444
11	3227	ENALAPRIL	-3.218	1103
12	6382	NEEDLES INSULIN DISPOSABLE	-3.148	2827
13	4970	ISOSORBIDE DINITRATE	-3.122	1220
14	9623	TRICOR	-3.119	821
15	3686	FERROUS SULFATE	-2.898	4820
16	1760	CELEXA	-2.887	1473
17	4802	INSULIN	-2.806	1526
18	4118	GLUCAGON HUMAN RECOMBINANT	-2.722	1639
19	5786	METFORMIN	-2.625	3838
20	7731	PRAVACHOL	-2.458	1700
21	2512	DARBEPOETIN ALFA IN ALBUMN SOL	-2.359	426
22	6210	MYCOPHENOLATE MOFETIL	-2.253	724
23	2830	DILTIAZEM	-2.216	1021
24	5636	MAVIK	-2.150	2242
25	4132	GLUCOPHAGE	-2.133	6736
26	4525	HYDRALAZINE HCL	-2.095	792
27	4106	GLIMEPIRIDE	-2.034	3384
28	7129	PAXIL	-2.033	2021
29	2426	CYANOCOBALAMIN (VITAMIN B-12)	-1.992	4080
30	4833	INSULIN ZINC HUMAN REC	-1.945	116
31	10392	ZOLOFT	-1.926	2417
32	6069	MORPHINE SULFATE	-1.889	899
33	10333	ZESTRIL	-1.787	2032
34	1216	BLOOD SUGAR DIAGNOSTIC	-1.665	19832
35	10199	WARFARIN SODIUM	-1.632	9223
36	3937	FOSINOPRIL SODIUM	-1.540	2660
37	6499	NIFEDIPINE	-1.524	1472
38	1003	BENAZEPRIL HCL	-1.462	1586
39	9994	VERAPAMIL HCL	-1.433	1856
40	1573	CAPTOPRIL	-1.418	1989

Table 4: Top forty drugs: CSCCSA-Glucose

INDX	CODE	DRUG NAME	SCORE	COUNT
1	4485	HUMALOG	-11.786	124
2	7470	PIOGLITAZONE HCL	-10.220	3075
3	8437	ROSIGLITAZONE MALEATE	-9.731	1019
4	4837	INSULN ASP PRT/INSULIN ASPART	-9.658	258
5	6382	NEEDLES INSULIN DISPOSABLE	-9.464	2827
6	4171	GLUCOTROL XL	-8.117	2853
7	4106	GLIMEPIRIDE	-7.940	3384
8	160	ACTOS	-7.721	1125
9	824	AVANDIA	-6.802	1239
10	9152	SYRING W-NDL DISP INSUL 0.5ML	-6.623	4186
11	4132	GLUCOPHAGE	-6.322	6736
12	4184	GLYBURIDE	-6.021	8879
13	4170	GLUCOTROL	-5.721	1259
14	4208	GLYNASE	-5.670	591
15	416	AMARYL	-5.599	2240
16	4107	GLIPIZIDE	-5.563	9993
17	844	AXID	-4.682	189
18	2830	DILTIAZEM	-4.297	1021
19	4806	INSULIN GLARGINE HUM.REC.ANLOG	-4.175	4213
20	5787	METFORMIN HCL	-4.147	19584
21	2824	DILAUDID	-4.076	39
22	5786	METFORMIN	-3.890	3838
23	7731	PRAVACHOL	-3.532	1700
24	1760	CELEXA	-3.517	1473
25	4497	HUM INSULIN NPH/REG INSULIN HM	-3.501	1829
26	9889	URSODIOL	-3.132	376
27	4813	INSULIN NPL/INSULIN LISPRO	-2.972	623
28	4133	GLUCOPHAGE XR	-2.845	765
29	6445	NEURONTIN	-2.615	1418
30	6656	NPH HUMAN INSULIN ISOPHANE	-2.500	2874
31	9379	THIAMINE HCL	-2.383	341
32	1636	CARDURA	-2.198	1079
33	1218	BLOOD SUGAR DIAGNOSTIC DRUM	-2.073	2593
34	8025	PROZAC	-2.037	1525
35	8316	REZULIN	-1.895	444
36	9136	SYRINGE & NEEDLE INSULIN 1 ML	-1.885	3542
37	4802	INSULIN	-1.812	1526
38	7674	POTASSIUM CHLORIDE	-1.779	9842
39	4804	INSULIN ASPART	-1.752	2476
40	1200	BLOOD-GLUCOSE METER	-1.719	5289

Table 5: Top forty drugs: CSCCSA-LDL

INDX	CODE	DRUG NAME	SCORE	COUNT
1	8444	ROSUVASTATIN CALCIUM	-17.052	27122
2	5368	LIPITOR	-16.908	118468
3	2395	CRESTOR	-16.234	3535
4	8720	SIMVASTATIN	-15.790	206064
5	3584	EZETIMIBE/SIMVASTATIN	-14.721	19396
6	790	ATORVASTATIN CALCIUM	-13.982	151106
7	941	BAYCOL	-12.924	1236
8	10383	ZOCOR	-11.451	26514
9	10186	VYTORIN	-9.877	9047
10	5487	LOVASTATIN	-9.238	45286
11	3583	EZETIMIBE	-8.093	32595
12	7731	PRAVACHOL	-6.729	16525
13	10336	ZETIA	-6.678	6623
14	7733	PRAVASTATIN SODIUM	-6.638	33708
15	5261	LESCOL XL	-6.358	873
16	9183	TAMOXIFEN CITRATE	-4.777	3095
17	5893	MEVACOR	-4.172	4205
18	2175	COLACE	-4.016	4349
19	9182	TAMOXIFEN	-3.764	2048
20	5260	LESCOL	-3.716	6251
21	475	AMLODIPINE/ATORVASTATIN	-2.779	1272
22	494	AMOXICILLIN/POTASSIUM CLAV	-2.495	4186
23	2110	CLOPIDOGREL BISULFATE	-2.271	50059
24	4616	HYDROXYCHLOROQUINE SULFATE	-2.240	5888
25	5281	LEVAQUIN	-2.194	1464
26	3471	ESTROGEN CON/M-PROGEST ACET	-1.929	5896
27	7496	PLAVIX	-1.471	14220
28	8225	RED YEAST RICE	-1.345	5468
29	3746	FLAGYL	-1.169	278
30	6540	NITROGLYCERIN	-1.103	94747
31	2959	DOCUSATE SODIUM	-1.084	32872
32	3475	ESTROGENS CONJUGATED	-1.033	22480
33	3686	FERROUS SULFATE	-0.990	32496
34	7768	PREMARIN	-0.969	5513
35	865	AZITHROMYCIN	-0.959	9861
36	2811	DIGOXIN	-0.908	31353
37	4132	GLUCOPHAGE	-0.779	14764
38	493	AMOXICILLIN	-0.715	11214
39	1985	CIPROFLOXACIN	-0.651	989
40	9946	VARENICLINE TARTRATE	-0.636	10794

level. Although the Food and Drug Administration (FDA) has added blood-glucose-increase warnings to all the drugs in the statin class [35], Pravachol itself has been considered to have blood-glucose lowering effects [36, 37]. The fact that CSCCSA can single out this particular drug from other statin class drug members indicates the potential of the algorithm to distinguish among similar drugs that have subtle differences. Celexa has a mild but non-significant effect on FBG level reduction in a study with seventeen depressive patients [38]. Several cases of hypoglycemia linked to the use of Neurontin have also been reported [39]. Thiamine is reported to reduce the adverse effect of hyperglycemia by inhibiting certain biological pathways [40] and deficiency of thiamine is observed in diabetic patients [41]. Cardura is found to reduce insulin resilience in a study on hypertensive patients with diabetes [42]. According to [22], Prozac can cause both high or lower blood sugar while diltiazem is linked to low blood glucose level.

5.8 Experiments on Low-density Lipoprotein

To demonstrate the potential of our methodology, we also apply our method to predict the numeric value of low-density lipoprotein (LDL). We first construct drug eras from drug prescription records with the approach proposed in Section 4, where γ is computed as 0.36 years. We then run CSCCSA and generate a long list of about two hundred drugs. We report the top forty drugs from the list in Table 5. No confirmed false positives are discovered in the table while all the confirmed true positives are reported at the very top of the list. Some entries of hormone are discovered, which are linked to the decrease of LDL in drug/laboratory tests [43]. Interestingly, many entries of antibiotics are discovered, and all of them are classified as non-recurrent drugs by the algorithm in Section 4. This is consistent with the clinical practice that antibiotics are usually not prescribed for long-term use. Some antibiotics have also been considered to manage cholesterol level, with literature support dating back to the 1950's [44, 45, 46]. The experimental results on LDL suggest that our algorithm is not fine-tuned to boost the performance on discovering drugs that control FBG level. Instead, it is readily applicable to other important numeric clinical measurements that might lead to interesting discoveries in drug repositioning.

6. DISCUSSION

We have introduced the CSCCS model for the task of CDR using EHRs. To our best knowledge, the proposed model is the first of its kind to extensively leverage temporal ordering information from EHR to predict indications for multiple drugs at the same time. The CSCCS model extends the SCCS model that is popular in the ADR community to address a continuous response. As an initial effort, we evaluate our methodology on the task of discovering potential blood-sugar-lowering indications for a variety of drugs in a real world EHR. We develop a set of experimental evaluation methods specific to this problem in order to estimate the performance of our method. Our experimental results suggest that CSCCS can not only discover existing indications but is also able to identify potentially new use of drugs. We hence believe that CSCCS is a promising model to aid the knowledge discovery process in CDR.

Future applications and extensions of the CSCCS model are exciting. To begin with, CSCCS can be applied to a broad variety of numeric responses such as blood pressure level, cholesterol level, or body weight, to name a few. Therefore, potentially new indications of drugs to control the aforementioned important physical measurements can be examined in the same paradigm. Furthermore, many other sources of patient information, such as demographic information, diagnosis codes, other type of lab measurements, as well as interactions among all these information sources can be taken into consideration to facilitate the prediction of the physical measurement level. Last but not least, although the proposed CSCCS model in its simplest form is a linear model, the history of SCCS model development [47] could help guide on future development of CSCCS model. More complicated models can be derived from its simpler counterparts for better predictive performance in more specific and refined applications.

Acknowledgments

The authors would like to gratefully acknowledge the anonymous reviewers for their reviewing efforts and invaluable suggestions. This research is funded by the NIH BD2K Initiative grant U54 AI117924, and the NIGMS grant 2RO1 GM097618. The authors would also like to acknowledge the supports from these two grants.

References

[1] Ted T Ashburn and Karl B Thor. Drug repositioning: identifying and developing new uses for existing drugs. *Nature Reviews Drug Discovery*, 2004.

[2] MR Hurle, L Yang, Q Xie, DK Rajpal, P Sanseau, and P Agarwal. Computational drug repositioning: from data to therapeutics. *Clinical Pharmacology & Therapeutics*, 2013.

[3] Jiao Li, Si Zheng, Bin Chen, Atul J. Butte, S. Joshua Swamidass, and Zhiyong Lu. A survey of current trends in computational drug repositioning. *Briefings in Bioinformatics*, 2015.

[4] Justin Lamb. The connectivity map: a new tool for biomedical research. *Nature Reviews Cancer*, 2007.

[5] Michael Kuhn, Monica Campillos, Ivica Letunic, Lars Juhl Jensen, and Peer Bork. A side effect resource to capture phenotypic effects of drugs. *Molecular Systems Biology*, 2010.

[6] Yanbin Liu, Bin Hu, Chengxin Fu, and Xin Chen. Dcdb: drug combination database. *Bioinformatics*, 2010.

[7] Craig Knox, Vivian Law, Timothy Jewison, Philip Liu, Son Ly, Alex Frolkis, Allison Pon, Kelly Banco, Christine Mak, Vanessa Neveu, et al. Drugbank 3.0: a comprehensive resource for omics research on drugs. *Nucleic Acids Research*, 2011.

[8] Hua Xu, Melinda C Aldrich, Qingxia Chen, Hongfang Liu, Neeraja B Peterson, Qi Dai, Mia Levy, Anushi Shah, Xue Han, Xiaoyang Ruan, Min Jiang, Ying Li, Jamii St Julien, Jeremy Warner, Carol Friedman, Dan M Roden, and Joshua C Denny. Validating drug repurposing signals using electronic health records: a case study of metformin associated with reduced cancer mortality. *Journal of the American Medical Informatics Association*, 2014.

[9] Shawn E Simpson, David Madigan, Ivan Zorych, Martijn J Schuemie, Patrick B Ryan, and Marc A Suchard. Multiple self controlled case series for large scale longitudinal observational databases. *Biometrics*, 2013.

[10] Vito MR Muggeo. Estimating regression models with unknown break points. *Statistics in Medicine*, 2003.

[11] Stanley Xu, Chan Zeng, Sophia Newcomer, Jennifer Nelson, and Jason Glanz. Use of fixed effects models to analyze self-controlled case series data in vaccine safety studies. *Journal of Biometrics & Biostatistics*, 2012.

[12] Prakash M Nadkarni. Drug safety surveillance using de-identified EMR and claims data: issues and challenges. *Journal of the American Medical Informatics Association*, 2010.

[13] PB Ryan. Establishing a drug era persistence window for active surveillance. *White Papers*, 2010.

[14] Robert Tibshirani. Regression shrinkage and selection via the lasso. *Journal of the Royal Statistical Society. Series B (Methodological)*, 1996.

[15] Edward W Frees. *Longitudinal and panel data: analysis and applications in the social sciences.* Cambridge University Press, 2004.

[16] AACE. Management of common comorbidities of diabetes. http://outpatient.aace.com/type-2-diabetes/management-of-common-comorbidities-of-diabetes. (Visited on 02/06/2016).

[17] RM Daniel, SN Cousens, De BL Stavola, MG Kenward, and JAC Sterne. Methods for dealing with time dependent confounding. *Statistics in Medicine*, 2013.

[18] Stephanie J Reisinger, Patrick B Ryan, Donald J O'Hara, Gregory E Powell, Jeffery L Painter, Edward N Pattishall, and Jonathan A Morris. Development and evaluation of a common data model enabling active drug safety surveillance using disparate healthcare databases. *Journal of the American Medical Informatics Association*, 2010.

[19] Jean-Louis Montastruc, Agnès Sommet, Haleh Bagheri, and Maryse Lapeyre-Mestre. Benefits and strengths of the disproportionality analysis for identification of adverse drug reactions in a pharmacovigilance database. *British Journal of Clinical Pharmacology*, 2011.

[20] OMOP. Ground truth for monitoring health outcomes of interest. http://omop.org/sites/default/files/ground%20truth.pdf, 2015. (Visited on 09/28/2015).

[21] Martin J Wainwright. Sharp thresholds for high-dimensional and noisy recovery of sparsity using l1-constrained quadratic programming. *IEEE Transactions on Information Theory*, 2009.

[22] DiabetesInControl. Drugs that can affect blood glucose levels. http://www.diabetesincontrol.com/wp-content/uploads/2010/07/www.diabetesincontrol.com_images_tools_druglistaffectingbloodglucose.pdf, 2015. (Visited on 09/28/2015).

[23] Patrick J Lustman, Monique M Williams, Gregory S Sayuk, Billy D Nix, and Ray E Clouse. Factors influencing glycemic control in type 2 diabetes during acute-and maintenance-phase treatment of major depressive disorder with bupropion. *Diabetes Care*, 2007.

[24] Jose A Vazquez and Jack D Sobel. Fungal infections in diabetes. *Infectious Disease Clinics of North America*, 1995.

[25] ADA. Skin complications. http://www.diabetes.org/living-with-diabetes/complications/skin-complications.html?referrer=https://www.google.com/. (Visited on 01/19/2016).

[26] CDC. Smoking and diabetes. http://www.cdc.gov/tobacco/campaign/tips/diseases/diabetes.html. (Visited on 01/19/2016).

[27] Emmanuelle Vermes, Anique Ducharme, Martial G Bourassa, Myriam Lessard, Michel White, and Jean-Claude Tardif. Enalapril reduces the incidence of diabetes in patients with chronic heart failure insight from the studies of left ventricular dysfunction (solvd). *Circulation*, 2003.

[28] Taner Damci, Serkan Tatliagac, Zeynep Osar, and Hasan Ilkova. Fenofibrate treatment is associated with better glycemic control and lower serum leptin and insulin levels in type 2 diabetic patients with hypertriglyceridemia. *European Journal of Internal Medicine*, 2003.

[29] Pitchai Balakumar, Rajavel Varatharajan, Ying Nyo, Raja Renushia, Devarajan Raaginey, Ann Oh, Shaikh Akhtar, Mani Rupeshkumar, Karupiah Sundram, and Sokkalingam A Dhanaraj. Fenofibrate and dipyridamole treatments in low-doses either alone or in combination blunted the development of nephropathy in diabetic rats. *Pharmacological Research*, 2014.

[30] Bacon F Chow and Howard H Stone. The relationship of vitamin b12 to carbohydrate metabolism and diabetes mellitus. *The American Journal of Clinical Nutrition*, 1957.

[31] Rose Zhao-Wei Ting, Cheuk Chun Szeto, Michael Ho-Ming Chan, Kwok Kuen Ma, and Kai Ming Chow. Risk factors of vitamin b12 deficiency in patients receiving metformin. *Archives of Internal Medicine*, 2006.

[32] Murat Kesim, Ahmet Tiryaki, Mine Kadioglu, Efnan Muci, Nuri Ihsan Kalyoncu, and Ersin Yaris. The effects of sertraline on blood lipids, glucose, insulin and hba1c levels: A prospective clinical trial on depressive patients. *Journal of Research in Medical Sciences: the Official Journal of Isfahan University of Medical Sciences*, 2011.

[33] Junichi Kodama, Shigehiro Katayama, Kiyoshi Tanaka, Akira Itabashi, Shyoji Kawazu, and Jun Ishii. Effect of captopril on glucose concentration: possible role of augmented postprandial forearm blood flow. *Diabetes Care*, 1990.

[34] Tetsuo Satoh, Shuichi Hara, Midori Takashima, and Haruo Kitagawa. Hyperglycemic effect of hydralazine in rats. *Journal of Pharmacobio-Dynamics*, 1980.

[35] FDA. Consumer updates: FDA expands advice on statin risks. http://www.fda.gov/ForConsumers/ConsumerUpdates/ucm293330.htm, 2014. (Visited on 09/28/2015).

[36] Dilys J Freeman, John Norrie, Naveed Sattar, R Dermot G Neely, Stuart M Cobbe, Ian Ford, Christopher Isles, A Ross Lorimer, Peter W Macfarlane, James H McKillop, et al. Pravastatin and the development of diabetes mellitus evidence for a protective treatment effect in the west of scotland coronary prevention study. *Circulation*, 2001.

[37] Aleesa A Carter, Tara Gomes, Ximena Camacho, David N Juurlink, Baiju R Shah, and Muhammad M Mamdani. Risk of incident diabetes among patients treated with statins: population based study. *BMJ*, 2013.

[38] Jay D Amsterdam, Justine Shults, Nancy Rutherford, and Stanley Schwartz. Safety and efficacy of s-citalopram in patients with co-morbid major depression and diabetes mellitus. *Neuropsychobiology*, 2006.

[39] Joep HG Scholl, Rike van Eekeren, and Eugène P van Puijenbroek. Six cases of (severe) hypoglycaemia associated with gabapentin use in both diabetic and non-diabetic patients. *British Journal of Clinical Pharmacology*, 2015.

[40] Khanh vinh quoc Luong and Lan Thi Hoang Nguyen. The impact of thiamine treatment in the diabetes mellitus. *Journal of Clinical Medicine Research*, 2012.

[41] GLJ Page, David Laight, and MH Cummings. Thiamine deficiency in diabetes mellitus and the impact of thiamine replacement on glucose metabolism and vascular disease. *International Journal of Clinical Practice*, 2011.

[42] T Inukai, Y Inukai, R Matsutomo, K Okumura, K Takanashi, K Takebayashi, K Tayama, Y Aso, and Y Takemura. Clinical usefulness of doxazosin in patients with type 2 diabetes complicated by hypertension: effects on glucose and lipid metabolism. *The Journal of International Medical Research*, 2004.

[43] FDA. Premarin (conjugated estrogens tablets, usp). http://www.accessdata.fda.gov/drugsatfda_docs/label/2006/004782s147lbl.pdf. (Visited on 02/08/2016).

[44] Paul Samuel. Treatment of hypercholesterolemia with neomycin-a time for reappraisal. *New England Journal of Medicine*, 1979.

[45] YA Kesäniemi and Scott M Grundy. Turnover of low density lipoproteins during inhibition of cholesterol absorption by neomycin. *Arteriosclerosis, Thrombosis, and Vascular Biology*, 1984.

[46] David JA Jenkins, Cyril WC Kendall, Maryam Hamidi, Edward Vidgen, Dorothea Faulkner, Tina Parker, Nalini Irani, Thomas MS Wolever, Ignatius Fong, Peter Kopplin, et al. Effect of antibiotics as cholesterol-lowering agents. *Metabolism*, 2005.

[47] David Madigan, Shawn Simpson, Wei Hua, Antonio Paredes, Bruce Fireman, and Malcolm Maclure. The self-controlled case series: Recent developments. *Submitted*, 2015. URL http://www.stat.columbia.edu/~madigan/PAPERS/DrugSafety.pdf.

How to Get Them a Dream Job?

Entity-Aware Features for Personalized Job Search Ranking

Jia Li
University of Illinois at Chicago
1200 W Harrison St
Chicago, IL, USA
jli213@uic.edu

Dhruv Arya
LinkedIn
2029 Stierlin Ct
Mountain View, CA, USA
darya@linkedin.com

Viet Ha-Thuc
LinkedIn
2029 Stierlin Ct
Mountain View, CA, USA
vhathuc@linkedin.com

Shakti Sinha
LinkedIn
2029 Stierlin Ct
Mountain View, CA, USA
ssinha@linkedin.com

ABSTRACT

This paper proposes an approach to applying standardized entity data to improve job search quality and to make search results more personalized. Specifically, we explore three types of entity-aware features and incorporate them into the job search ranking function. The first is query-job matching features which extract and standardize entities mentioned in queries and documents, then semantically match them based on these entities. The second type, searcher-job expertise homophily, aims to capture the fact that job searchers tend to be interested in the jobs requiring similar expertise as theirs. To measure the similarity, we use standardized skills in job descriptions and searchers' profiles as well as skills that we infer searchers might have but not explicitly list in their profiles. Third, we propose a concept of entity-faceted historical click-through-rates (CTRs) to capture job document quality. Faceting jobs by their standardized companies, titles, locations, etc., and computing historical CTRs at the facet level instead of individual job level alleviate sparseness issue in historical action data. This is particularly important in job search where job lifetime is typically short. Both offline and online experiments confirm the effectiveness of the features. In offline experiment, using the entity-aware features gives improvements of +20%, +12.1% and +8.3% on Precision@1, MRR and NDCG@25, respectively. Online A/B test shows that a new model with these features is +11.3% and +5.3% better than the baseline in terms of click-through-rate and apply rate.

Categories and Subject Descriptors

H.3.3 [**Information Search and Retrieval**]: [Search process]

KDD '16, August 13 - 17, 2016, San Francisco, CA, USA

ISBN 978-1-4503-4232-2/16/08...$15.00

DOI: http://dx.doi.org/10.1145/2939672.2939721

Keywords

Information Retrieval; Learning-to-Ranking; Personalization

1. INTRODUCTION

Traditional information retrieval systems, and particularly Web search engines, have focused on keyword-matching. In this search paradigm, users typically input their information needs as a set of keywords and the search engines match the keywords with documents and use some additional signals, such as document popularity (e.g., document historical click through rate, PageRank etc.) to find relevant documents. This paradigm makes it very simple and easy for users to use. Moreover, it allows the efficient retrieval of documents at the Web scale. However, while this paradigm has been effective for the majority of the queries on generic Web search engines, it does not work that well for LinkedIn job search. In our use case, user information needs are typically rather complicated. For example, when a user issues query "software engineer Cambridge Microsoft", he or she does not mean to find a job that its description contains these keywords. Instead, he or she looks for a job with *title* software engineer at *company* Microsoft in Cambridge *city*. Thus, it is important to understand the structure of the information need. Moreover, even if we can structure the query as above, it is still unclear which city does "Cambridge" refers to. Even assuming we know that "Cambridge" refers to the city in Massachusetts (USA), there could still be plenty of Microsoft software engineer jobs in the city. In this case, which specific ones match best with the user's interests and expertise? Thus, it is crucial to go beyond keyword-matching when scoring documents to provide personally relevant results on LinkedIn job search.

Semantic search, on the other hand, represents information needs and documents in a structured way and semantically matches the information needs with the documents. A challenge with semantic search is that it is typically difficult for an end-user to describe his or her information need in a semantic representation. Moreover, semantic search is often restricted by concepts and relations predefined in a knowledge base. Thus, it does not scale well to open and dynamic document sets like the Web.

This work aims to bridge the two search paradigms to make LinkedIn job search experience more relevant and personalized yet still simple to use while keeping it efficient at the Web scale. From a user perspective, he or she is still able to describe their information needs in a free-text form. Given user queries, we extract and standardize the entities, such as, *job title*, *company*, *skills* and *location*. On the document side, we leverage standardized entities mentioned in job descriptions and include them in the search index. Based on the standardization information, we construct entity-aware features matching queries and documents as well as entity-faceted historical CTR features capturing global document qualities (query-independent). Moreover, as mentioned in the motivating example above, even when a query is perfectly understood, the query is not enough to represent user information need. To overcome this issue, we leverage standardized skills in members' profiles and job descriptions to capture searcher-job expertise homophily. For instance, if the searcher is a machine learning expert, he or she will be more likely to apply for software engineer jobs focusing on machine learning domain rather than on software system infrastructure. Thus, the ranking function should rank the former higher than the latter. Finally, to combine these features, we apply learning to rank technique to automatically learn a personalized search ranking function.

We conduct offline and online experiments on LinkedIn job search. Our experiments confirm the benefit of using standardized entities in the ranking function to make job search results more relevant and personalized. Specifically, in offline experiment on randomized data, a new model with the proposed features improves over the baseline without the features +20%, +12.1% and +8.3% in terms of Precision@1, MRR and NDCG@25, respectively. Online A/B test shows that the features can improve click-through-rate and apply rate, the two most important metrics of the product, +11.3% and +5.3%, respectively. At the time of this writing, the new ranking model has served all of LinkedIn job search traffic.

The main contributions of this paper are the following:

1. Proposing a new approach to incorporating entity data into personalized ranking functions for job search. Specifically, we propose three classes of entity-aware features including:
    - Query-job matching: Extract and standardize entities mentioned in queries and documents, such as, job titles, skills, companies and locations. Then, construct features matching queries and documents based on these entities.
    - Searcher-job expertise homophily: Analyzing log data, we discover that job searchers tend to be interested in the jobs requiring similar expertise as theirs. Thus, we propose features capturing searcher-document expertise homophily based on the standardized skills in job descriptions and users' profiles as well as the skills that members might have but not explicitly list. These features make results more personalized to the searchers.
    - Job historical CTRs: We introduce a concept of entity-faceted historical CTRs to capture job document popularity. Job documents are faceted on job attributes like company, title or location. Then, historical CTRs are computed as the facet level to overcome data sparseness issue.
2. Presenting practical challenges when deploying the entity-aware features in LinkedIn job search engine such as ambiguity, missing values, sparseness, parameter tuning, scalability, online efficiency, biases in log data and how to combine the new features with existing ones in an optimal way as well as solutions for these challenges.
3. Experimenting and demonstrating significant benefit of using standardized entity data for personalized search ranking in an industrial setting serving hundreds of millions of users.

The rest of the paper will be organized as follows. Section 2 reviews related work. Section 3 presents query-document matching features based on standardized entities in queries and documents. Section 4 discusses searcher-document features capturing expertise homophily. Section 5 details how we construct entity-faceted historical click-through-rate features. In Section 6, we present a learning-to-rank approach to combine the proposed features and the existing ones. Offline and online experimental results are discussed in Section 7. Finally, concluding remarks are in Section 8.

2. RELATED WORK

2.1 Semantic search

Semantic search has been an active research area recently. Generally speaking, semantic search uses semantics to make search systems more effective. More specifically, semantic search approaches extract semantic meanings and structures from search queries and documents and exploits them in search process [6]. The main approach to semantic search typically represents queries and documents in a structured way and applies semantic query languages like SPARQL [19] to retrieve results.

SHOE system [12] is one of the early work in this direction. It annotates Web pages with semantic information. On query side, users specify their information needs based on nodes and relations in an ontology. Swoogle [8] and Corese [4] are Semantic Web search engines. These engines store documents in Resource Description Framework (RDF) format and provide structured query languages to retrieve the documents. Similarly, Zhong et al. [28] represent queries and documents by conceptual graphs then propose an ontology-based matching algorithm estimating the similarity between a query and a document.

A common problem of these approaches is that it is challenging for end users to specify their information needs in such structured ways [24]. Also, these approaches are often restricted by concepts and relations predefined in ontologies. Thus, they do not scale to open and dynamic document sets like the Web [7]. Moreover the algorithm matching queries and documents in the structured representation are typically computationally expensive. Thus, it is challenging for industrial search engines to apply them in real time at the Web scale.

2.2 Enhancing traditional IR with semantics

Another research direction related to our work is using semantic technology to enhance traditional keyword-based information retrieval. Guha et al. [9] propose an approach to improve keyword-based search by using data retrieved from the Semantic Web. Specifically, given a text query, the terms in the query are then mapped to nodes in the Semantic Web. They also propose heuristics to resolve ambiguity when mapping. Then, the nodes are used to augment the query. SemSearch [24] also allows users to specify their information needs by free text. Then, it maps the terms into classes, properties or instances in a knowledge base. A novel aspect of the work is that for a query containing multiple terms, the whole semantic meanings of all of the terms are taken into account. Fernandez et al . [7] introduce a new architecture to scale semantic search by supporting both pure semantic search on ontologies and enhancing traditional keyword search with semantics. In particular, their approach deals with knowledge incompleteness by switching from the former to the later search paradigm when there is no match in the ontologies. Buscaldi et al. [2] use semantic relationship such as synonymy in WordNet to compute similarity of a document and a query and then to rank the results. More recently, Dalton et al. [5] propose an approach called entity feature query expansion that expands user queries by structured data in knowledge bases. Given a query, the approach first annotates it with both explicit and latent entities and link them to two knowledge bases including Wikipedia and Freebase. Then, the corresponding structured data is used to do query expansion. The expanded queries are used to match with documents in retrieval phase. They show effectiveness of the approach on TREC text collections.

Compared to the previous work, our work is different to them in the following aspects. First, unlike the most of the previous approaches focusing on semantically matching documents and queries, our work goes beyond that. In particular, our work exploits standardized entities to match a searcher and documents to make results personalized as well as to model document popularities (query-independent) on various facets. As shown in evaluation section, these feature categories give even higher impacts than document-query matching. Second, even though our document-query matching approach is similar to the ones in the literature, our approach is customized for job search domain. To the best of our knowledge, there is no prior work focusing on using semantic knowledge in job search. Third, our approach uses entity data at a feature level in personalized ranking function (as opposed to query expansion level in some previous work). At the feature level, by applying learning to rank, our approach can softly combine semantic features and traditional features in an optimal way learnt from training data instead of making a hard switch between semantic search and keyword search as in some previous work, such as [7]. Finally, besides typical offline experiments, we experiment on live traffic on an industrial search engine. The online metrics are derived from searcher actions, thus they allow demonstrating effectiveness of the approach in a personalized setting.

2.3 Personalized Search

An important aspect of our work is personalization, which is also an active research area in the literature. The key idea behind personalized search is that different users might have different backgrounds and interests. As a result, they might look for different results even when issuing the same queries [1]. Thus, the one-size-fit-all model is not effective. There are multiple ways to achieve personalization in search. One direction is to ask users to describe their interests. For instance, Google personalized web search allows users to explicitly select some of the predefined topics to specify their interests. Another direction is to implicitly model user's interests. Sugiyama et al. [22] and Sontag et al. [21] propose approaches to model user's long-term interests. Some other work like [20, 25] focuses on immediate history to represent user's short-term interests. When data is too sparse to model user's interests individually, personalization could be achieved by grouping users in cohorts [27]. When a user issues a query, the corresponding cohorts can be used to customize results for the user.

A novel aspect of our work in terms of personalization is that we propose a new concept of expertise homophily to personalize job search results. Expertise homophily is measured by similarity between user's expertise and expertise requirement of each job. Moreover, to represent user's expertise, we do not only use standardized skills explicitly in a user profile but also infer skills that the user might have. The inference step is done by collaborative filtering technique exploiting skill co-occurrence patterns in the whole member base.

3. ENTITY-AWARE DOCUMENT-QUERY MATCHING

As mentioned before, when a user issues a query like "software engineer Microsoft", the user implicitly links the keywords to different typed entities, such as, title and company and expects the results matching with the information need in terms of the structure he or she has in mind. To satisfy this, we propose an approach that indexes documents in a structured way. At searching time, the user query is segmented and linked to one of the typed entities used in the document index. Then, we construct various features matching typed entities mentioned in the query with the corresponding ones in the documents. In the next subsections, we describe how documents are structured and indexed, how to segment a query and link the segments to entities and how to construct features semantically matching the query and documents.

3.1 Job Document Indexing

To help job seekers search and discover jobs, we build a search index on some of the key attributes of the job. Jobs on LinkedIn are structured to present the following key attributes: *job title*, *company*, *location*, *industry* and *skills*. An example is shown in Figure 1. When a job is posted on LinkedIn, it goes through a standardizer which looks at above mentioned fields to extract out standardized entities. The extracted entities are based on curated dictionaries built over time from our member profiles. The standardizer has been engineered through multiple iterations to understand what parts of the job posting are critical for different entities. The standardized job is then indexed and is searchable both on the entities as well as the free text as entered by the job poster. Since there is huge research literature on mapping textual mentions to entities, this paper does not emphasize this step. Instead, through out the paper, we focus on how to use these entities in job search ranking.

3.2 Query Processing

When a searcher enters a query, e.g. "software engineer Microsoft Cambridge", we first apply a query tagger to segment the query and tag the segments into entity types that

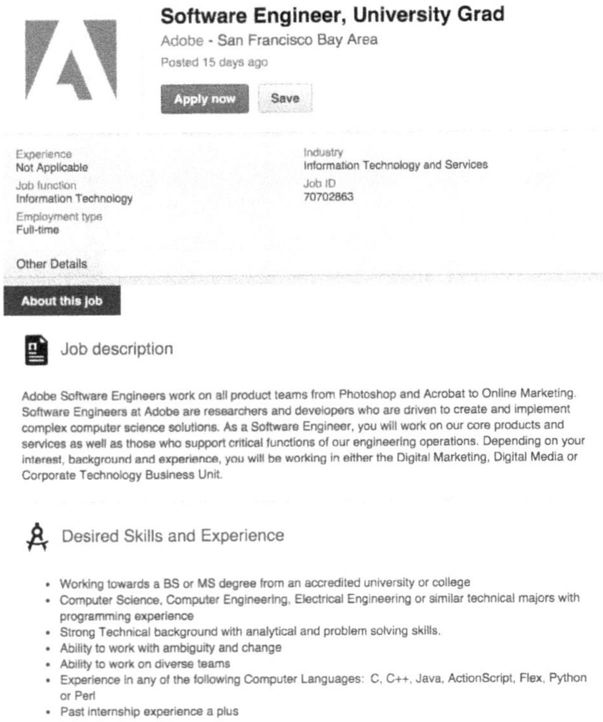

Figure 1: A job posting on LinkedIn. Entities in the job such as title, skills, company and location are extracted, standardized and indexed.

are important to the job search domain, such as, *job title*, *skill*, *company* and *location*, etc. For instance, the query above is segmented into "software engineer", "Microsoft" and "Cambridge" segments. These segments are then tagged into types of *job title*, *company* and *location*, respectively. Our query segmentation approach is similar to [23]. We refer interested readers to the reference for more details.

Given entity types of query segments, the next step is to map the segments into specific entities. The segments are matched against the dictionary of the corresponding types. In ambiguous cases, e.g., "security" (ambiguous title) or "Cambridge" (ambiguous location), the standardized entities in the searcher's profile are then used to resolve the ambiguity in a personalized way. For example, if the standardized location in the searcher's profile is Massachusetts (USA), "Cambridge" in his or her query is more likely to refer to the city in the US rather than the one in the UK. Similarly, if the searcher has title of computer security or related skills, such as, computer security or fraud detection, the term "security" in his or her query is more likely to refer to "computer security" title rather than "physical security".

3.3 Query-Document Matching Features

Given typed entities mentioned in user queries and in documents, we construct entity-aware features to capture the semantic similarity between the queries and the documents. In particular, we match entities in the queries and the ones with the same *types* in the documents. For instance, for the query "software engineer Microsoft Cambridge", after extracting standardized entities from the query as described above, we match title entity ("software engineer") with the title entity in each job document. Similarly, we match company entity and location entity with the corresponding ones in the job description. We consider two types of entity-matching: hard matching and soft matching. The former checks if the two entities (in the query and in the document) have the same identifier. This matching is able to capture synonymy relationship amongst different textual forms of the same entities, e.g., "software engineer" and "software developer".

We also consider the semantic similarity (soft matching) between two different but related standardized entities, such as, between title "software engineer" and title "software architect" or between skill "information retrieval" and skill "Web search". To measure such similarity, we use an approach leveraging the uniqueness of LinkedIn data collection including entity co-occurrence and career trajectory of more than 400 million members on LinkedIn. Intuitively, if two skills tend to co-occur in similar groups of members, they are likely to be related. Likewise, if there are a significant number of employees transferring between two companies, they are also likely to be similar.

4. SEARCHER-DOCUMENT EXPERTISE HOMOPHILY

As briefly presented before, for a query like "software engineer Microsoft" the searcher is not equally interested in every software engineer job at the company. Instead, if the searcher happens to be a machine learning expert, he or she is much more likely to be interested in software engineer jobs related to this field rather than software engineer jobs focusing on other domains. Thus, in many cases, user queries are not enough to represent user information need and interest. To complement the query, we exploit an idea of expertise homophily that captures the similarity between searcher's expertise and job expertise requirements to make job search results more personally relevant.

Homophily has been extensively studied in the context of social networks analysis [17, 14]. The main idea is that in a social network, a node tends to be connected or interact with other nodes that are similar to it. In the context of job search, we hypothesize that a job searcher tends to be interested in the jobs requiring similar expertise as his or hers. In this section, we first present how we represent expertise of searchers and expertise requirement of jobs via standardized skills. Then, we conduct an analysis to verify the hypothesis. Finally, we propose features capturing searcher-document expertise homophily.

LinkedIn allows members to add *skills* to their profiles. Typical example of skills for a software engineer would be - "Algorithm", "Data Mining", "Python", etc. On LinkedIn, there are about 35 thousand standardized skills. Members can also *endorse* skills of other members in their network. Thus, skills are an integral part of members' profiles to help them showcase their professional expertise (see Figure 2). On document side, as described in Section 3, each job description also associates with a set of standardized skills. Thus, in this paper, we use skills to represent searcher's expertise and job expertise requirement.

We conduct an analysis to verify the hypothesis that a job searcher tends to be interested in the jobs similar to his or her expertise using search logs. To avoid confounding factors, e.g., a feature in the original ranking function produc-

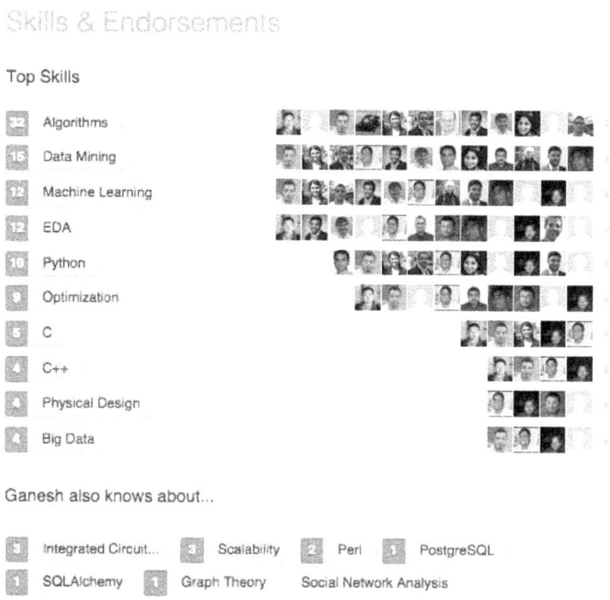

Figure 2: Example of Skill Section with Endorsements.

	Difference between overlapping bucket and non-overlapping bucket
CTR	+ 55%
Apply Rate	+ >100%

Table 1: CTRs and Apply Rates of job results with overlapping skills and job results without overlapping skills.

ing the logs that is correlated with searcher-result skill homophily and also impacts searcher's actions on results (since it impacts result rankings and searchers are biased towards top results), we use randomized data as described in details in Section 6.2. The data contains about 200 thousand searches from tens of thousands unique searchers. The results of the searches are divided into two buckets. The first bucket contains job results that their required skills overlap with the searcher's skills. The second bucket includes job results that do not require any skills the searcher has. The overlapping bucket ends up with about 16% and the non-overlapping bucket has 84% of the total number of results. For each bucket, we compute *CTR* and *apply rate*, which are defined as ratios of the number of job results that the searcher clicks (views) or applies, respectively, to the total number of results shown (the number of result impressions). As shown in Table 1, CTR and apply rate of the jobs with overlapping skills are 55% and more than 100%, respectively, higher than the jobs without overlapping skills. Thus, this analysis confirms the importance of skill homophily between searcher and results.

A key challenge of generating the expertise homophily feature is that searchers may not explicitly list all the skills they have on profiles. On the other hand, some of their skills might not be relevant to their core expertise. For instance, a machine learning researcher could have "nonprofit fundraising" skill [11]. To overcome these challenges, we estimate expertise scores of a member on the explicit skills and the ones he might have. Figure 3 describes the offline process to estimate the expertise scores. In the first step, we use a supervised learning algorithm combining various signals on LinkedIn such as skill-endorsement graph page rank, skill-profile textual similarity, member's seniority, etc. to estimate the expertise score, i.e., $p(expert|member, skill)$. After this step, the expertise matrix (E_0) is very sparse since we can be certain only for a small percentage of the pairs. In the second step, we factorize the matrix into member and skill matrices in K-dimensional latent space. Then, we compute the dot-product of the matrices to fill in the "unknown" cells. The intuition is that if a member have "machine learning" and "information retrieval" skills, based on skill co-occurrence patterns from all of our member base, we could infer that the member is likely to also know "learning-to-rank".

Since the dot-product results in a large number of non-zero scores of each member on the 35K skills, the scores are then thresholded. If a member's score on a skill is less than a threshold, the member is assumed not to know the skill and the score is zeroed out. Thus, outlier skills are removed. At the same time, the final expertise matrix (E_1) is still relatively denser than E_0 since it includes scores of inferred skills. We refer interested readers to our recent work [10] for more details.

Since matrix factorization is computationally complex, to guarantee efficiency, we apply a two-phase approach. An offline process periodically runs on distributed computing platforms like Hadoop to infer member skills. The online phase then simply consumes the latest version of the data at ranking time. Given a set of skills that a searcher has and a set of skills that a job requires, we compute Jaccard similarity between the the two sets. One future direction is to use weighted Jaccard similarity in which the weights are determined by searcher's expertise scores on the skills.

5. ENTITY-FACETED HISTORICAL CLICK-THROUGH-RATE

In this section, we propose entity-faceted document-popularity features based on user past behaviors. These features aim to indicate the quality of documents and are independent of query and searcher. The idea of using user's historical actions on documents in Web search ranking functions has been shown effective in the literature [3]. However, a key challenge when deploying these features is the sparseness of data. The challenge is even more serious for job search since the lifetime of a job document is much shorter. To overcome this, instead of computing a single historical CTR separately for every job in the corpus, we estimate historical CTRs of a job on different entity-facets, such as, title, company or location. Please also note that in this paper we use historical CTR as an example, the idea is also applicable to other user-action based popularity features where data sparseness is an issue.

5.1 Feature Definition

Given a job corpus, we compute multiple historical CTRs on different facets of the jobs. These facets are defined based on standardized entities mentioned in the jobs, such as, ti-

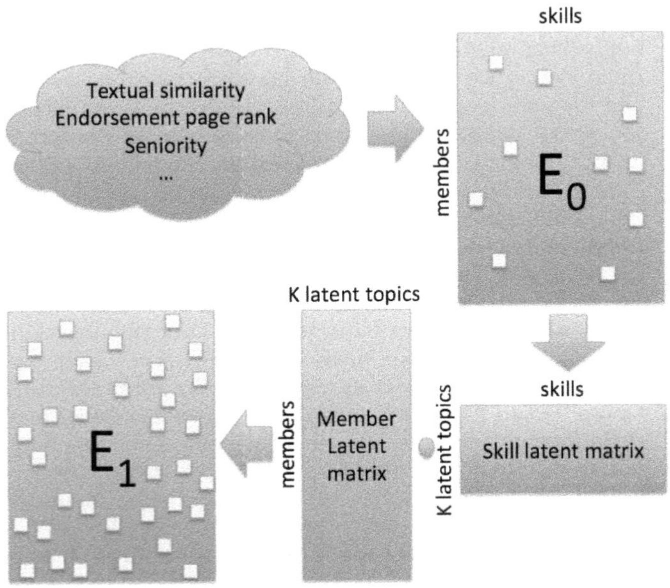

Figure 3: Member-skill matrix factorization to infer skills that members might have but do not explicit list on profiles.

tle, company or location. Specifically, we estimate historical CTR of jobs with a certain title like "data scientist", historical CTR of jobs at a company or historical CTR of jobs at some location. Then, given a specific job, for instance, a data scientist job at company LinkedIn in the city of Mountain View (California - USA), we use applicable entity-faceted historical CTRs including CTR_{title}*(data scientist)*, $CTR_{company}$*(LinkedIn)* and $CTR_{location}$*(Mountain View (California - USA))* as features to indicate the popularity of the jobs on the corresponding aspects.

It is worth noting that when computing historical CTRs, the jobs are grouped at entity level (e.g., company Ids), not at text level (e.g., company names in job postings). Thus jobs listing different names of the same company such as "International Business Machines", "IBM Corporation", "IBM corp." or "IBM" are grouped together in the same bucket. Similarly, jobs with different title variations of the same title entity like "software engineer", "software developer", "software development engineer" or "SDE" are also grouped together. Grouping the jobs at entity level does not only make the facet more meaningful, but also further reduces the issue of data sparseness. One future direction is to consider related entities, such as subsidiary companies (e.g., "Google", "Youtube" and "Alphabet") or neighboring cities (like "Mountain View" and "Sunnyvale" - both are in Silicon Valley) when estimating historical CTRs.

The entity-faceted historical CTRs are computed based on the number of times the jobs belonging to the entity got clicked and the number of times these jobs were shown on search results (See Equation 1). Smoothing factor N and default value λ are parameters. For entity that the jobs belonging to it have zero or a small number of impressions compared to N, historical CTR corresponding to it will have value equal or closed to the default value λ. Once again, for efficiency purpose, we build an offline process running on a distributed system to estimate the entity-faceted historical CTRs at a large scale. At ranking time, the online process takes the latest data to compute features in realtime.

$$CTR = \frac{(\#clicks + \lambda * N)}{(\#impressions + N)} \quad (1)$$

5.2 Parameter Tuning

The default value λ controls an interesting trade off for the cases where the number of impressions are low, e.g., jobs from a new company. If we use a too small default value, the new jobs that were not previously shown have little chance to be shown. Thus, we could not *explore* these results. However, many of these jobs could be good results and could get clicked if they are shown to the users. On the other hand, if we assign λ to a too high value, historical CTRs become too smooth and we do not *exploit* much of the insight from user historical actions.

$$\lambda = \underset{\lambda}{\operatorname{argmax}} \quad Correlation(CTR, label) \quad (2)$$

We tune the values of λ on validation set. Each instance in the data set, which corresponds to a search result, contains a feature vector and a graded relevance label. The label indicates how relevant the result is to the query and the searcher. The details on how the data set is generated will be described in Section 6.2. For each entity-faceted historical CTR (e.g., company-faceted historical CTR), we select the value for λ that maximizes the correlation between the CTR and the labels (See Equation 2).

To illustrate the effect of parameter tuning, Figures 4 and 5 show company-faceted historical CTRs with λ equaling to zero and the optimal value. In each figure, the upper plot shows the relationship between the CTR feature and labels and the lower plot reveals company distribution over CTR values. On Figure 4, when the default value is zero, there are a significant number of companies having the historical CTR of zero because they have zero or few impressions in the period before we collect the training data. However, the average label of these results is not low (the first data point in Figure 4(a)), i.e., many of them are actually good results. Thus, as shown in the figure, the CTR does not strongly predict result relevance. When we assign λ to the optimal value (Figure 5), however, the company-faceted historical CTR becomes strongly correlated with the label. Quantitatively, between the two values for λ, the later improves Pearson correlation coefficient between the feature and the label by 55%.

6. MODEL TRAINING

This section describes how the proposed features are integrated into the job search ranking function. Specifically, we apply learning-to-rank approach to learn a new ranking function combining the entity-aware features with the existing ones. We first give a high level description on the existing features. Then, we present an approach for extracting personalized training data from search log and the learning-to-rank algorithm used to learn a new ranking function from the training data.

6.1 Existing Features

The existing features are generally divided into the following categories.

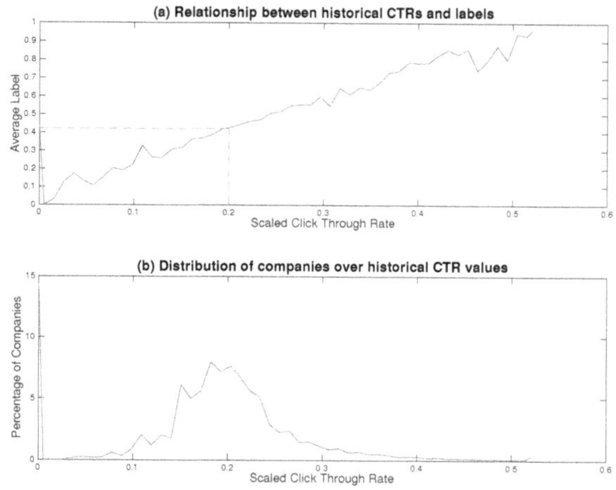

Figure 4: Company-Faceted Historical CTR with $\lambda = 0$. With this setting, the historical CTR does not predict result relevance well.

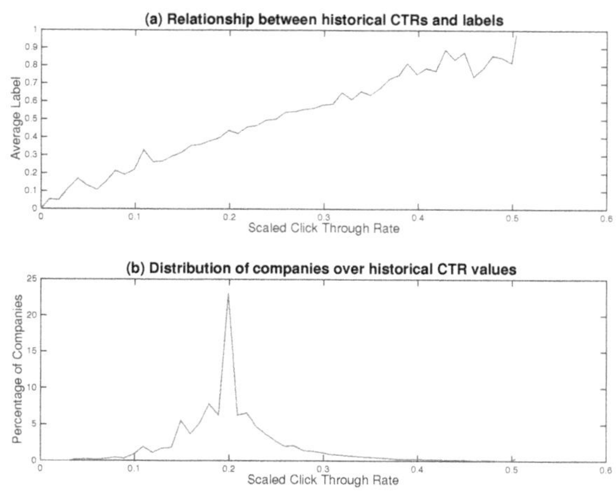

Figure 5: Company-Faceted Historical CTR with the optimal value for λ. With this setting, the historical CTR is strongly correlated with labels.

Textual features The most traditional type of features in information retrieval is textual features. These features match the keywords in queries with different sections of job descriptions, such as, title, company, etc. The key difference between these features and entity-aware matching features in Section 3 is that the former does not take into account standardized entity information when matching queries and documents.

Geographic features (personalized features) Job search on LinkedIn is highly personalized. For instance, a query like "software developer" from a job seeker will produce very different results if the searcher is in New York City, USA as opposed to (say) Montreal, Canada. Location plays an important role in personalizing the results. We create multiple features capturing this.

Social features (personalized features) Another important aspect of personalization is to capture how the results socially relate to the searcher. We leverage a variety of the signals on LinkedIn, such as, how the searcher socially connects with the company posting the job, e.g., if he or she follows the company or he or she has friends working at the company, etc. to generate the features in this category. We refer the readers to [10] for a more detailed description of the existing features.

6.2 Training Data and Learning Algorithm

A traditional way to obtain training data is to use human experts to label the results. However, as we are dealing with a large amount training data for personalized search, it is expensive to use human experts. At the same time, it is very hard for people other than the searcher to know the true relevance judgment of the results. For example, for the same query "software engineer", a new college graduate in the US and an experienced candidate in Canada could be interested in very different results. Thus, similar to [13], we use log data as implicit feedback from searchers to generate training data.

One problem with the log data is position bias as the users tend to interact (e.g., click) on top results. Thus, labels inferred from the user actions are biased towards the ranking function generating the data. In order to counter the position bias, we randomize the ranking of search results and show them to a small percentage of traffic. Then, we collect user actions on the results. For instance, as shown in Figure 6, a user issues query "software engineer", and six results are shown. There are different actions the user can take on the results and the corresponding ones will have different graded relevance labels based on the importance of the actions. In the example shown, the searcher clicks on the second result and decides to apply to the job at the fourth position. Since applying to a job is a stronger signal of relevance than clicking on a job, we assign a higher label to applied results (label=3, i.e., considered as perfect results) and a lower label to clicked results (label=1, i.e., good results). For the first and third results, the searcher scans through them but chooses not to take any action. Thus, we consider that these results are irrelevant (label=0, i.e., bad results). For the results ranked below the last interacted one (below result 4 in the Figure), we cannot be certain about the relevance judgement of them since the searcher may not have looked at them. Therefore, we discard these results.

It is worth noting that when collecting the data, we count every query issued as a unique search. For instance, if the

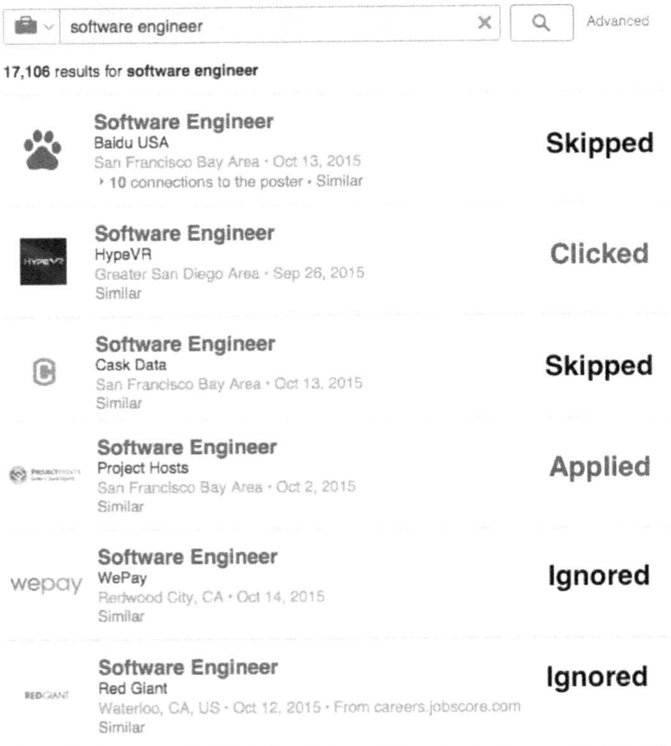

Figure 6: Example of how the labels are generated from user actions. Applied results are considered as perfect, clicked results are good and skipped results are bad. The results under the last interacted ones are ignored since the searcher may not have looked at them.

query "software engineer" is issued five times, they are considered as five distinct searches. The reason for this is that even though the query being searched for is identical across the five searches, they might have different search contexts when considering other dimensions such as searcher, location or time, etc. Moreover, this keeps the query distribution in the labeled data the same as in our live search traffic. We run the randomization bucket as mentioned above for two full weeks. The reason we keep the period in order of weeks is to iron out strong weekly patterns. For example, if the labeled data is collected only during weekdays, it will be biased towards weekday search patterns and will not represent weekend search traffic. After two weeks, the randomization bucket ends up with about two hundred thousand searches with at least one searcher's action. The labeled data is then divided into training, validation and test sets.

Given the training dataset, we apply Coordinate Ascent [18], a listwise learning-to-rank algorithm, to search for an optimal model. For efficiency purpose, we use linear models in our work. Coordinate Ascent algorithm has also been shown to be effective for learning linear ranking functions in some other search domains [18]. One key benefit of listwise learning-to-rank approach over pointwise and pairwise ones is that the listwise approach can optimize ranking-based metrics directly [15, 16]. The objective function we optimize in the learning process is normalized discounted accumulative gain (NDCG@K) defined on the graded relevance labels as described above. Parameter K is set to *25*, which is the number of results shown in the first result page of LinkedIn job search.

7. EVALUATION

In this section, we evaluate the proposed features in both offline testing and online A/B testing.

7.1 Offline Experiment

7.1.1 Models to Compare

Baseline: The baseline model uses all of the existing features described in Section 6.1 and does not contain any entity-aware features.

Entity-Aware Document-Query Matching (DQM): This model uses the existing features and entity-aware document-query matching features discussed in Section 3.

Document-Searcher Expertise Homophily (DSH): This model uses the existing features and searcher-document expertise homophily features described in Section 4.

Entity-Faceted Historical CTR (ECTR): This model uses the existing features and entity-facted histotical CTRs described in Section 5. In this paper, we experiment with company and title facets.

All of Entity-Aware Features (ALL): This model uses the existing features and all of the entity-aware features.

All of the models are trained on the same training set and are tuned extensively on the validation set to get the optimal parameter setting for each of them.

7.1.2 Offline Results

The Figure 7 shows performance lifts of the proposed models over the baseline on the test set in terms of Precision at 1 (P@1), Mean Reciprocal Rank (MRR), NDCG@15 and NDCG@25. As shown in the figure, all of the models with entity-aware features (DQM, DSH and ECTR) are consistently better than the baseline across all of the metrics. This confirms the benefit of using entity-aware features in job search. For instance, on NDCG@25, entity-aware document-query matching features, document-searcher expertise homophily features and entity-faceted historical CTR features can improve the baseline by 1.2%, 5.4% and 4.8% respectively.

Interestingly, amongst the three feature categories, document-query matching features yield the least improvement and document-searcher matching features achieve the highest improvement. This emphasizes the importance of using standardized entities to personalize search results. Finally, when combining all of the features together, not so surprisingly ALL model has the best performance. Compared to the baseline, ALL model is 20%, 12.1%, 8.3% and 7.9% better in terms of P@1, MRR, NDCG@15 and NDCG@25.

7.2 Online Experiment

In our online experiment, we take the model with the best offline performance, which is the one using all of the entity-aware features and compare it with the model currently in production. The model in production uses the features in Section 6.1 and some simple entity-aware document-query matching features. The later could be viewed as a simplified version of the features described in Section 3. The model

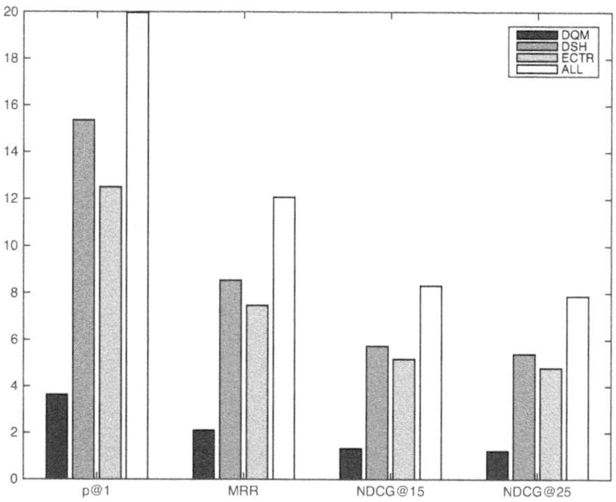

Figure 7: Percentage improvements over the baseline model on offline experiment. All of the improvements are statistically significant.

is also linear and trained by the same approach. Thus, the difference between the new model and the current one essentially demonstrates the effectiveness of the proposed features.

We take a random portion of LinkedIn job search live traffic and randomly split the searchers in the experiment traffic into control and treatment buckets. To guarantee consistent experience, each of the searchers is either control or treatment bucket (not both) throughout the whole experiment period. The control bucket is served by the current ranking model and the treatment bucket is served by the new model. We run the A/B test on LinkedIn experiment platform [26] for a reasonably long period of time (4 weeks) and ignore results in the first week to eliminate the novelty effect. During the three-week period, each bucket ends up with more than one million unique searchers and tens of millions of searches.

We evaluate the buckets by two metrics: click-through-rate and apply rate as defined in Section 4. These are the most important metrics from our business perspective. It is worth emphasizing that these are ranking-based metrics, not set-based metrics. In *online* experiments, even if two ranking functions produce exactly the same set of results on first result page (top 25 results), the one that ranks relevant results at higher positions on the page will be likely to achieve higher numbers of job views and applications. Thus, these metrics discount document relevance by positions, just like the NDCG metric that we use as the objective function in the offline training. In fact, we find that the NDCG metric in offline experiments is directionally inline with these metrics in online experiments, i.e., if a model A is better than a model B in terms of the NDCG metric in offline experiments, model A is likely to perform better than model B on click-through-rate and apply rate in online experiments.

Table 2 shows online A/B test results. Because of business sensitivity, we only report the relative improvements. On click-through-rate and apply rate, the new model with the proposed entity-aware features is 11.3% and 5.3% better than the current ranking model in production. Both of the improvements are statistically significant (details of the statistical testing is described in [26]) This re-confirms the advantage of entity-aware features in personalized job search ranking.

Metric	Improvement of Treatment over Control
Click-Through-Rate	11.3%
Apply Rate	5.3%

Table 2: Online A/B test results on click-through-rate and apply rate metrics. Both of the improvements are statistically significant.

8. CONCLUSION

In this paper, we propose an approach to applying standardized entity data to improve job search quality and to personalize search results. To match queries and job documents, we structure the queries and the documents in a schema specific to job search domain including critical entity types in the domain such as job title, skill, company and location, etc. Then, we construct various features semantically matching the queries and the job documents based on the structured schema. To close the gap between a query and the searcher's information need and also to personalize search results, we propose a concept of expertise homphily capturing the similarity between the searcher's expertise and the requirement of the job. We use standardized skills to represent searcher's expertise and job expertise requirement and measure the similarity based on these skills. Finally, to model document popularity, we introduce an idea of entity-faceted historical CTRs. These capture quality of each job on different aspects such as job title, company and location, etc. Grouping job documents based on the entities does not only make the groups meaningful but also alleviates the data sparseness issue when estimating historical CTRs.

Throughout the paper, we also detail how we resolve practical challenges when deploying standardized entities in job search ranking, including: ambiguity, missing values (such as members' skills), scalability and online efficiency (especially for sophisticated signals such as skill expertise scores), sparseness of historical searchers' actions (particularly in job search domain where job lifetime is typically short), parameter tuning for feature engineering, confounding factors and biases in log data and how to optimally combine the new features with the current ones in the existing ranking function.

We conduct offline experiment on randomized data and online A/B test to understand the effectiveness of the entity-aware features. In offline experiment, a new model with the features improves over the baseline +20%, +12.1% and +8.3% in terms of Precision@1, MRR and NDCG@25, respectively. Online A/B test shows that the features can improve click-through-rate and apply rate, the two most important metrics of the product, +11.3% and +5.3%, respectively. The results confirm the benefits of the proposed features in job search. As of this writing, the new model serves all live traffic on LinkedIn job search.

ACKNOWLEDGMENT: We would like to thank Deepak Agarwal for his valuable feedback during the course of this work.

9. REFERENCES

[1] D. Arya, V. Ha-Thuc, and S. Sinha. Personalized federated search at linkedin. In *Proceedings of the 24th ACM International on Conference on Information and Knowledge Management (CIKM)*, pages 1699–1702, 2015.

[2] D. Buscaldi and P. Rosso. Using geowordnet for geographical information retrieval. In *Evaluating Systems for Multilingual and Multimodal Information Access*, pages 863–866, 2008.

[3] O. Chapelle and Y. Chang. Yahoo! learning to rank challenge overview. In *Proceedings of the Yahoo Learning to Rank Challenge, held at ICML*, pages 1–24, 2011.

[4] O. Corby, R. Dieng-Kuntz, and C. Faron-Zucker. Querying the semantic web with corese search engine. In *Proceedings of the 16th European Conference on Artificial Intelligence*, pages 705–709, 2005.

[5] J. Dalton, L. Dietz, and J. Allan. Entity query feature expansion using knowledge base links. In *The 37th ACM SIGIR Conference on Research and Development in Information Retrieval*, pages 365–374, 2014.

[6] B. Fazzinga and T. Lukasiewicz. Semantic search on the web. *Semantic Web*, 1(1-2):89–96, 2010.

[7] M. Fernandez, V. Lopez, M. Sabou, V. Uren, D. Vallet, E. Motta, and P. Castells. Semantic search meets the web. In *2008 IEEE International Conference on Semantic Computing (ICSC)*, pages 253–260, 2008.

[8] T. W. Finin, L. Ding, R. Pan, A. Joshi, P. Kolari, A. Java, and Y. Peng. Swoogle: Searching for knowledge on the semantic web. In *Proceedings of the Twentieth National Conference on Artificial Intelligence*, pages 1682–1683, 2005.

[9] R. Guha, R. McCool, and E. Miller. Semantic search. In *Proceedings of the 12th ACM International Conference on World Wide Web (WWW)*, pages 700–709, 2003.

[10] V. Ha-Thuc, G. Venkataraman, M. Rodriguez, S. Sinha, S. Sundaram, and L. Guo. Personalized expertise search at linkedin. In *Proceedings of the 4th IEEE International Conference Big Data*, 2015.

[11] V. Ha-Thuc, Y. Xu, S. P. Kanduri, X. Wu, V. Dialani, Y. Yan, A. Gupta, and S. Sinha. Search by ideal candidates: Next generation of talent search at linkedin. In *Proceedings of the 25th International Conference on World Wide Web (WWW)*, pages 195–198, 2016.

[12] J. Heflin, J. A. Hendler, and S. Luke. SHOE: A blueprint for the semantic web. In *Spinning the Semantic Web: Bringing the World Wide Web to Its Full Potential*, pages 29–63, 2003.

[13] T. Joachims. Optimizing search engines using clickthrough data. In *Proceedings of the eighth ACM SIGKDD International Conference on Knowledge Discovery and Data Mining*, pages 133–142, 2002.

[14] P. F. Lazarsfeld and R. K. Merton. Friendship as a social process: A substantive and methodological analysis. *Freedom and control in modern society*, 18:18–66, 1954.

[15] H. Li. A short introduction to learning to rank. *IEICE Transactions*, 94-D(10):1854–1862, 2011.

[16] T. Liu, T. Joachims, H. Li, and C. Zhai. Introduction to special issue on learning to rank for information retrieval. *Information Retrieval*, 13(3):197–200, 2010.

[17] M. McPherson, L. Smith-Lovin, and J. M. Cook. Birds of a feather: Homophily in social networks. *Annual Review of Sociology*, 27(1):415–444, 2001.

[18] D. Metzler and W. B. Croft. Linear feature-based models for information retrieval. *Information Retrieval*, 10(3):257–274, 2007.

[19] E. Prud'Hommeaux, A. Seaborne, et al. Sparql query language for rdf. *W3C recommendation*, 15, 2008.

[20] X. Shen, B. Tan, and C. Zhai. Implicit user modeling for personalized search. In *Proceedings of the ACM International Conference on Information and Knowledge Management (CIKM)*, pages 824–831, 2005.

[21] D. Sontag, K. Collins-Thompson, P. N. Bennett, R. W. White, S. Dumais, and B. Billerbeck. Probabilistic models for personalizing web search. In *Proceedings of the fifth ACM International Conference on Web Search and Data Mining (WSDM)*, pages 433–442, 2012.

[22] K. Sugiyama, K. Hatano, and M. Yoshikawa. Adaptive web search based on user profile constructed without any effort from users. In *Proceedings of the 13th ACM International Conference on World Wide Web (WWW)*, pages 675–684, 2004.

[23] B. Tan and F. Peng. Unsupervised query segmentation using generative language models and wikipedia. In *Proceedings of the 17th ACM International Conference on World Wide Web (WWW)*, pages 347–356, 2008.

[24] V. S. Uren, Y. Lei, and E. Motta. Semsearch: Refining semantic search. In *The Semantic Web: Research and Applications, 5th European Semantic Web Conference*, pages 874–878, 2008.

[25] R. W. White, P. N. Bennett, and S. T. Dumais. Predicting short-term interests using activity-based search context. In *Proceedings of the 19th ACM International Conference on Information and Knowledge Management (CIKM)*, pages 1009–1018, 2010.

[26] Y. Xu, N. Chen, A. Fernandez, O. Sinno, and A. Bhasin. From infrastructure to culture: A/B testing challenges in large scale social networks. In *Proceedings of the 21th ACM SIGKDD International Conference on Knowledge Discovery and Data Mining*, pages 2227–2236, 2015.

[27] J. Yan, W. Chu, and R. W. White. Cohort modeling for enhanced personalized search. In *Proceedings of the 37th ACM SIGIR Conference on Research and Development in Information Retrieval*, pages 505–514, 2014.

[28] J. Zhong, H. Zhu, J. Li, and Y. Yu. Conceptual graph matching for semantic search. In *Conceptual Structures: Integration and Interfaces, 10th International Conference on Conceptual Structures*, pages 92–196, 2002.

Scalable Fast Rank-1 Dictionary Learning for fMRI Big Data Analysis

Xiang Li[1*], Milad Makkie[1*], Binbin Lin[2], Mojtaba Sedigh Fazli[1], Ian Davidson[3]
Jieping Ye[2#], Tianming Liu[1#], Shannon Quinn[1#]

[1]Department of Computer Science, University of Georgia, Athens, GA
[2]Department of Computational Medicine and Bioinformatics, University of Michigan, Ann Arbor, MI
[3]Department of Computer Science, University of California, Davis, CA
[*]Equal contributions; [#]Joint corresponding authors.

ABSTRACT
It has been shown from various functional neuroimaging studies that sparsity-regularized dictionary learning could achieve superior performance in decomposing comprehensive and neuroscientifically meaningful functional networks from massive fMRI signals. However, the computational cost for solving the dictionary learning problem has been known to be very demanding, especially when dealing with large-scale data sets. Thus in this work, we propose a novel distributed rank-1 dictionary learning (D-r1DL) model and apply it for fMRI big data analysis. The model estimates one rank-1 basis vector with sparsity constraint on its loading coefficient from the input data at each learning step through alternating least squares updates. By iteratively learning the rank-1 basis and deflating the input data at each step, the model is then capable of decomposing the whole set of functional networks. We implement and parallelize the rank-1 dictionary learning algorithm using Spark engine and deployed the resilient distributed dataset (RDDs) abstracts for the data distribution and operations. Experimental results from applying the model on the Human Connectome Project (HCP) data show that the proposed D-r1DL model is efficient and scalable towards fMRI big data analytics, thus enabling data-driven neuroscientific discovery from massive fMRI big data in the future.

Categories and Subject Descriptors
• **Information systems~Data mining** • Computing methodologies~Machine learning

General Terms
Algorithms, Performances

Keywords
fMRI; Sparse coding; Distributed computation; Algorithm parallelization

KDD '16, August 13-17, 2016, San Francisco, CA, USA
 ISBN 978-1-4503-4232-2/16/08...$15.00
DOI: http://dx.doi.org/10.1145/2939672.2939730

1. INTRODUCTION
In recent years, the field of neuroimaging studies based on functional magnetic resonance imaging (fMRI) has featured unprecedented large-scale data availability thanks to the efforts from a series of data collection works including Human Connectome Project [26], 1000 Functional Connectomes [19] and OpenfMRI Project [20]. The rapidly growing data characterized different aspects of brain cognitive processes as well as various disorders, thus providing a great opportunity for decoding and identification of potential functional biomarkers for brain diseases. Consequently, there is an urgent call for more efficient and scalable data analytics and knowledge discovery methods, especially for dealing with fMRI big data. Functional network analysis has become an important and popular approach for discovering the underlying organization structures and meaningful dynamic patterns from the vast and noisy functional brain signals. Focusing on understanding the functional aggregation/co-activation among brain regions through quantitative and data-driven approaches, researchers have employed various types of matrix decomposition methods for the functional network analysis studies, including Independent Component Analysis (ICA) [24], Principal Component Analysis (PCA) [23] and Dictionary Learning [11]. Dictionary learning in particular has been shown to be a powerful tool in image compressed sensing [21], classification [14] and de-noising [8], and has shown superior performance in decomposing the meaningful and comprehensive functional networks from various types of fMRI signals [15]. However, the computational cost for solving the sparse coding problem for dictionary learning has been known to be very demanding [12], especially when dealing with large-scale data sets. Furthermore, most of current dictionary learning methods for fMRI data analysis are only implemented for local application without any parallelization scheme. Facing with the rapidly growing fMRI data and the needs for population-level analysis with terabytes or even petabytes of data size [23], the computation power limit of a single machine will eventually become the bottleneck for efficient and effective knowledge discovery from the fMRI big data.

Following the previous success in using dictionary learning for functional network decomposition [15], in this work we devolved a novel distributed rank-1 dictionary learning (D-r1DL) model, leveraging the power of distributed computing for handling large-scale fMRI big data. Compared to the gradient-based dictionary learning algorithms such as the online dictionary learning [18] (based on stochastic gradient descent) and the K-SVD [4] (based on gradient descent), the proposed rank-1 dictionary learning algorithm has a few critical advantages: 1) The learning process is a fix-point algorithm by alternating least squares updates, thus avoiding the tuning of the learning rate/step size while also avoiding the slow convergence near the solution; 2) The memory cost of the proposed algorithm is very low because it needs not to maintain the potentially large gradient matrix in the memory. The intermediate results will be discarded after each rank-1 basis is learned and stored, which further reduce the memory cost. More importantly, the rank-1 dictionary learning algorithm is very light-weighted regarding to the operational complexities: besides the input data, most of the routines in the algorithm will only take one vector as input and one vector as output. This feature helps the r1DL algorithm to be easily parallelized to its distributed version.

For the algorithm parallelization, in this work we used the Spark engine [3] to implement the D-r1DL algorithm. Spark is a high-performance distributed compute engine for large-scale data processing. It is similar to MapReduce, but has several distinct advantages that make it ideal for the deployment of large-scale analytics frameworks. First, its basic abstraction for distributed data, the resilient distributed dataset (RDD) [27], combines robust fault-tolerance with highly efficient data layout strategies. RDDs track their computation lineage as a directed acyclic graph; therefore, if a segment is lost, it can be easily recomputed from the lineage. These lineages can be optimized on-the-fly to minimize the overhead of the prescribed computations. Second, all operations in Spark are performed in-memory, thus significantly improving throughput of data pipelines. This is a departure from Hadoop MapReduce, in which data are serialized to disk in between map and reduce steps. Third, the Spark compute engine is much more generalizable than MapReduce, and can efficiently support highly diverse workloads. While Spark supports the map and reduce primitives from Hadoop MapReduce, it also supports graph processing [10] and streaming [28] APIs on the same compute engine, in addition to numerous functional primitives beyond *map* and *reduce*. This structural flexibility is crucial to the efficient implementation of a wide variety of distributed algorithms.

An illustration for the operational and algorithmic pipeline consisting of three layers of model specification is shown in Fig. 1. The first and foremost deliverable of this work is to provide an integrated solution for the large-scale fMRI big data analysis. Therefore, we initially deployed the proposed D-r1DL model on our in-house server (termed "in-house solution") with an integrated neuroinformatics system [17]. The neuroinformatics system provides a web-based user interface for fMRI data uploading, hosting and result post-processing [17], as illustrated in Fig. 1(a). Alternatively, we also tested deploying the D-r1DL model on the cloud computing service provided by Amazon Web Services Elastic Compute Cloud (AWS-EC2) [1], which has been widely applied for biomedical imaging researches due to its resource flexibility and ease of use. For the "AWS-EC2 solution", the data preprocessing was performed before running the D-r1DL model on it. Subroutines of the r1DL algorithm and its logic flow are illustrated in Fig. 1(b). The parallelization subroutines and its relationship with the r1DL algorithm are illustrated in Fig. 1(c).

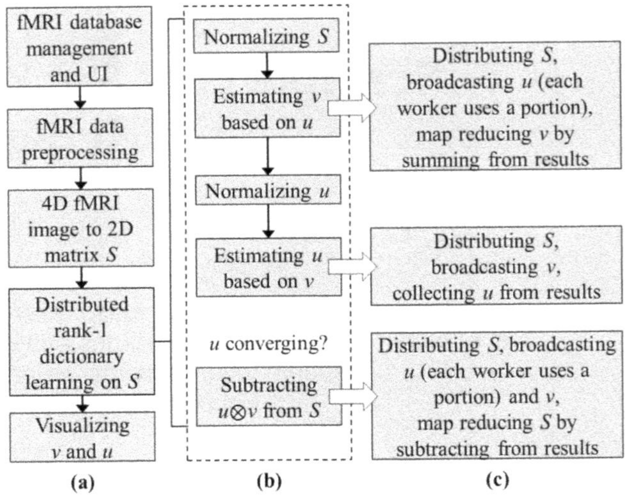

Figure 1. (a): Operations on the neuroinformatics system for preparing the application of D-r1DL and post-analysis. (b): Algorithm pipeline of the rank-1 dictionary learning. (c): Parallelization subroutines of the D-r1DL model derived from the corresponding subroutines of the r1DL using Spark. The distribution of input data *S* is based on RDDs.

2. BACKGROUND AND RELATED WORK

Functional network analysis based on matrix decomposition methods has the basic premise: the observed functional signals are the result of the linear combination from the signals of many latent source (i.e. functional networks), plus noises and/or artifacts signals [5]. The methods then aim to identify the latent source signals as well as the loading matrix based on various learning priors including spatial/temporal independence [5; 24] (for ICA), or the sparsity in the loading coefficients [11; 15] (for dictionary learning). The decomposition results consist of two parts: the signals of the latent sources (i.e. temporal pattern of the functional networks) that are regarded as basis activation patterns, and the loading matrix characterizing how each source contributes to the formation of each observed signal across voxels/ brain regions (i.e. spatial pattern of the functional networks). The spatial and temporal pattern of a sample network decomposed result is shown in Fig. 2.

Several sets of consistent and meaningful functional networks have been identified in the previous literature: including the 10 well-established resting-state networks (RSNs) [24] obtained using ICA, the task-related patterns obtained using PCA [25], and the HAFNI (holistic atlases of functional networks and interactions) atlases [15] featuring 32 group-wise consistent patterns during both task and resting-state using dictionary learning [2]. Visualization of one functional network from the matrix decomposition results using the proposed r1DL method is shown below, to illustrate the temporal (the time series curve) and spatial (on cortical volumetric space) patterns of the brain functional networks.

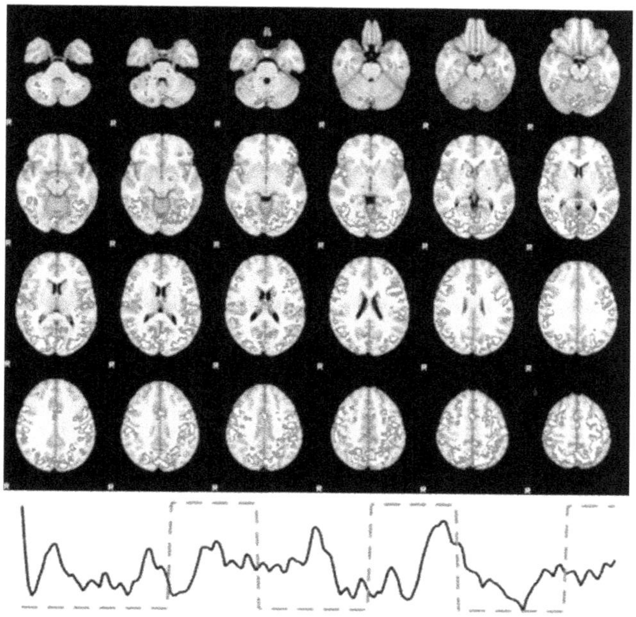

Figure 2. Top: spatial pattern visualized on cortical volumetric space of one decomposed network. Bottom: visualization of its temporal pattern.

While dictionary learning in general is an active area of research, there has been significantly less effort in scaling the algorithm. One of the few methods proposed was [22], in which the authors designed a sparse coding framework on Hadoop MapReduce. The method was parallelized by splitting the core operations in two main phases: the sparse coding phase, in which the loading weights were learned in parallel; and the dictionary learning phase, in which the dictionary atoms were updated. By taking advantage of hard sparsity constraints, the authors avoided materializing the entire data matrix in memory at once, instead operating on blocks of the matrix in parallel and constructing the loading matrix row by row. In this work we undertook the similar dataflow optimization techniques: the sparse coding and dictionary atoms are assumed to fit easily in memory for fast and efficient computation. However, using the Spark framework instead of Hadoop MapReduce provides us intrinsic speedups. Where Hadoop MapReduce excels in batch processing, Spark is optimized for iterative computation: intermediate results are cached in-memory on the workers and re-used in subsequent iterations, and the updates are efficiently broadcasted to the workers. Most importantly, the RDDs abstraction pipelines the requested operations and lazily executes them after determining the optimal computational path using the least amount of resources. We leverage these advantages to provide a substantial performance gain in our D-r1DL dictionary learning implementation.

3. RANK-1 DICTIONARY LEARNING FOR FMRI DATA ANALYSIS

The rank-1 dictionary learning algorithm aims to iteratively estimate multiple rank-1 basis vector u ($T\times 1$ vector with unit length) and its loading coefficient vector v ($P\times 1$ vector) to decompose the input signal matrix S of dimension $T\times P$, by minimizing the following energy function $L(u, v)$:

$$L(u,v) = \|S - uv^T\|_F, \text{s.t.} \|u\| = 1, \|v\|_0 \leq r. \quad (1)$$

Eq. 1 indicates that the product of u and v is supposed to well-fit the input S while the total number of non-zero elements in v should be smaller than or equal to the given sparsity constraint parameter r. The minimization problem in Eq. 1 can be solved by alternatively updating u (randomly initialized before the first iteration) and v until convergence:

$$v = \underset{v}{\operatorname{argmin}} \|S - uv^T\|_F, s.t. \|v\|_0 \leq r,$$

$$u = \underset{u}{\operatorname{argmin}} \|S - uv^T\|_F = \frac{Sv}{\|Sv\|}, \quad (2)$$

$$\text{Converging at step } j \text{ if: } \left\|u^{j+1} - u^j\right\| < \varepsilon, \varepsilon = 0.01.$$

Eq. 2 involves multiplication between input matrix S and vector u, followed by setting all elements in the resulting vector smaller than its r-th largest value to zero, essentially performing the vector partition operation. One rank-1 basis $[u, v]$ can be estimated in each step; afterwards the input matrix S will be deflated to its residual R:

$$R^n = R^{n-1} - v^T R^{n-1}, R^0 = S, 1 < n \leq K, \quad (3)$$

where K is the total number of expected basis (i.e. dictionary atoms) to be discovered from the input data. It could be seen that the formulation of the proposed rank-1 dictionary learning algorithm is similar to the sparse PCA problem [6]. However, the goal of PCA and sparse PCA is to derive a low-dimensional basis (i.e. learning a smaller set of high representative basis); in contrast, the goal in dictionary learning is to learn an over-complete dictionary set [12]. Regarding the algorithm convergence, it is easy to show that the value of the energy function as in Eq. 1 decreases at each iteration (until convergence), thus the objective is guaranteed to converge. The convergence of the learning in Eq. 2 was also empirically tested in this work. The deflation operation in Eq. 3 is based on Hotelling's deflation method for estimating the eigenvectors, where each step of deflation leads to the corresponding eigenvalue replaced by zero. The validity of using Hotelling's deflation for sparse PCA was provided in [6], while better deflation methods were also discussed in [16]. Fig. 3 shows a running example illustrating the data preparation and networks decomposed by r1DL.

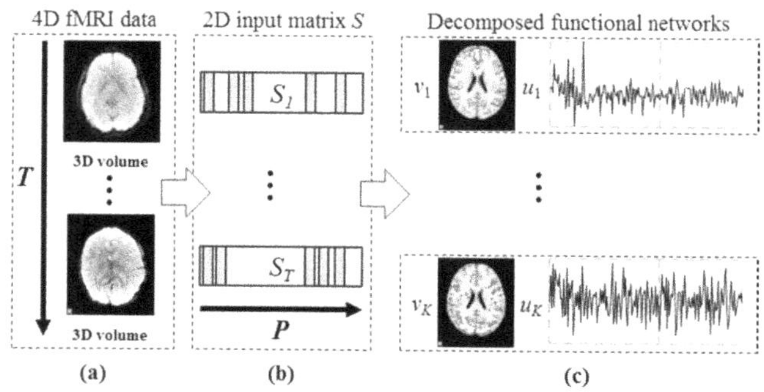

Figure 3. Illustration of the r1DL model applied on fMRI data as a running example. (a) 4D fMRI data represented as a series of 3D volume images. (b) Converting 4D data into 2D input matrix *S*. (c) Spatial ($v_1...v_K$) and temporal ($u_1...u_K$) patterns of the decomposed functional networks from *S* using r1DL dictionary learning.

4. ALGORITHM PARALLLIZTAION AND DEPLOYMENT ON SPARK

In this work, the rank-1 dictionary learning algorithm introduced above was implemented and parallelized on the Spark engine. Specifically, the vector-matrix multiplication and the matrix-vector multiplication steps in Eq. 2 were implemented by their corresponding distributed primitives in Spark. Reading and partitioning the input data S is supported by the RDD abstraction; therefore, the distribution of S to each node as a series of key-value pairs is inherently straight forward: data formation of the current work is based on row-vectors. In other words, each column in S contains the T number of observations for one specific feature, to the total of P features. While S was maintained as an RDD, the vectors u and v were broadcast to all nodes. Thus during the vector-matrix multiplication, each node will use its portion of the updated u vector, and then estimate the v vector based on the multiplication of portions of S and u. The resulting v vectors from all the nodes will be then map-reduced by the summation operation. The matrix-vector multiplication is relatively easier, where each node will use all the updated v vector then estimate its corresponding portion of the u vector. The resulting u vector is just the collection of the results from each node. In addition, the matrix deflation operation in Eq. 3 was also parallelized by broadcasting both the u and v vectors learned from Eq. 2, and then estimating the outer produce between portion of u vector and the whole v vector at each node. The S matrix is then subtracted by the results of each node through mapping over each row and deflating it in parallel. This implementation of the r1DL algorithm after parallelization is termed as the "Distributed rank-1 dictionary learning" (D-r1DL) model.

4.1 Complexity of the distributed primitives

The computational complexity of the original (un-parallelized) rank-1 dictionary learning algorithm is quite obvious: all the major subroutines including matrix-vector multiplication, vector-matrix multiplications and deflation have complexity of $T*P$, essentially traversing through input matrix S. However, the distributed primitives added for the parallelization in D-r1DL will potentially cause large extra computations and/or data transfers across nodes. The problem will be magnified when such transfer occurs over a network (e.g. worker nodes are distributed across Internet). Thus we analyzed the extra complexity induced by the parallelization of the three subroutines, assuming that there are M number of nodes. It should be noted that the estimations are upper bounds for the complexity; the empirical performance will be largely dependent on how Spark optimizes the transformation lineage for the RDD, and how the RDD is distributed across the cluster.

- For the vector-matrix multiplication for estimating v, the total complexity is $(T*M + P*M+T\log(T) + P)$: $T*M$ caused by the broadcasting, $P*M+T\log(T)$ caused by the map reduce and network shuffle, and P caused by the updating of v.
- For the matrix-vector multiplication, the total complexity is $(P*M + T)$: $P*M$ caused by the broadcasting, and T caused by the updating of u.
- For the matrix deflation, the total complexity is $(P*M+T*M)$: both u and v will be broadcasted to all M nodes.

4.2 Deployment and configuration

The D-r1DL model was deployed on two different sets of server clusters, leading to two solutions for the data analysis. The first set is based on the in-house server, called the "in-house solution". Spark version 1.5.2 pre-built for Hadoop 1.X and python version 2.7.11 with all the required dependencies were installed on the in-house server. We setup one standalone spark cluster on the server with a master node consisting of 16 cores and 16GB RAM. The in-house solution also featured an integrated neuroinformatics system named HELPNI (HAFNI-enabled largescale platform for neuroimaging informatics) as introduced in [17]. Authorized users of the system can upload, manage, and perform the preparations of the fMRI data for the model analysis. For running the D-r1DL model, the preparation steps include fMRI signal preprocessing (gradient distortion correction, motion correction, bias field reduction, and high pass filtering) [9], converting the 4D fMRI images to 2D data matrix, as well as the generation of shell scripts according to user specifications. When the computations by D-r1DL are finished, the reports of the results (consisting of the statistics and visualizations of the decomposed functional networks) will be automatically generated by the HELPNI neuroinformatics system [17] and uploaded to the server, accessible via web interface for viewing and sharing. The in-house solution is mainly used for testing the single-server (on the local threads), standalone mode performance of the D-r1DL algorithm.

The second set was based on the computational resources provided by AWS-EC2 service. For the AWS-EC2 implementations, we used the provided EC2 deployment scripts with the Spark distribution. These created a Spark cluster on EC2 with one master node and 16 workers. Each worker consisted of 2 cores and 7.5GB memory. EC2 clusters are highly scalable, as the number of workers recruited could be adjusted within the cluster. The preprocessed and converted fMRI data was stored at the cloud through Amazon S3 and accessible by the EC2 cluster. The nodes featured Hadoop distributed file system (HDFS), which ensured data consistency and improved I/O speed. Hadoop version 1.0, Spark version 1.5.2, and Python version 2.7.11 with the Anaconda scientific programming stack (e.g. NumPy, SciPy) were installed on EC2 cluster. An illustrative diagram showing the organization and execution architecture of the two solutions are shown below.

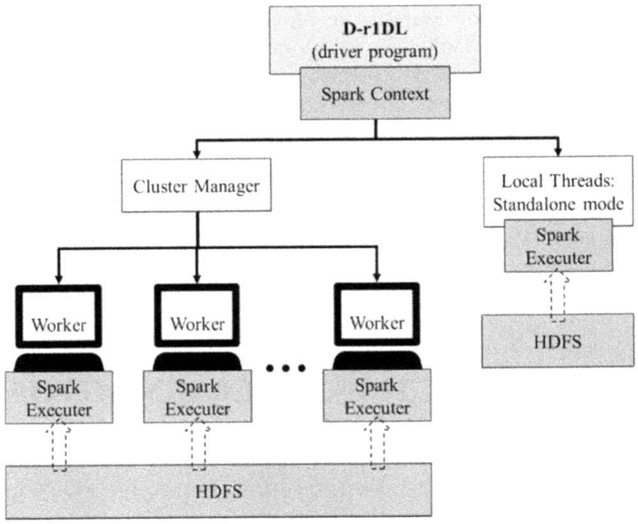

Figure 4. Illustrative diagram showing the organization and execution architectures for the standalone local mode and the multi-worker cluster mode.

5. EXPERIMENTAL APPLICATION ON BRAIN FUNCTIONAL IMAGING DATA

5.1 Validation of the D-r1DL model

To validate the effectiveness of the proposed D-r1DL model in terms of its capability of decomposing fMRI data into meaningful functional networks, we applied the framework on the fMRI data acquired during multiple tasks from the Human Connectome Project (HCP) Q1 release dataset [26]. The HCP dataset is advantageous in its high temporal and spatial resolution (TR=0.72s, varied temporal length from 176 to 1200 volumes; 2mm isotropic voxels, to the total of over 200,000 voxels), which enables more detailed characterization of the brain's functional behavior. Additionally, the HCP dataset includes acquisitions of fMRI data during 7 tasks and resting-state from 68 subjects, to the total of over 500 individual data, which matches the aim of the proposed framework for population-level fMRI big data analysis.

The learned collection of functional networks represented by rank-1 dictionary basis was then compared with the HAFNI atlases [15]. The HAFNI atlas was obtained by applying online dictionary learning method [18] on all the individual fMRI data in the same HCP Q1 dataset. Subsequently, 32 group-wise consistent networks were identified through manual inspection over more than 200,000 decomposed networks [15]. Thus our aim in this validation was to identify the presence (or absence) of those atlas networks from the results of D-r1DL. The main rationale of performing comparison with network templates and atlas network for the model validation in this work was due to the lack of ground truth in fMRI data. At this stage, the capability and accuracy of the proposed model could only be validated by comparing with the previously-reported and well-established results from the same dataset.

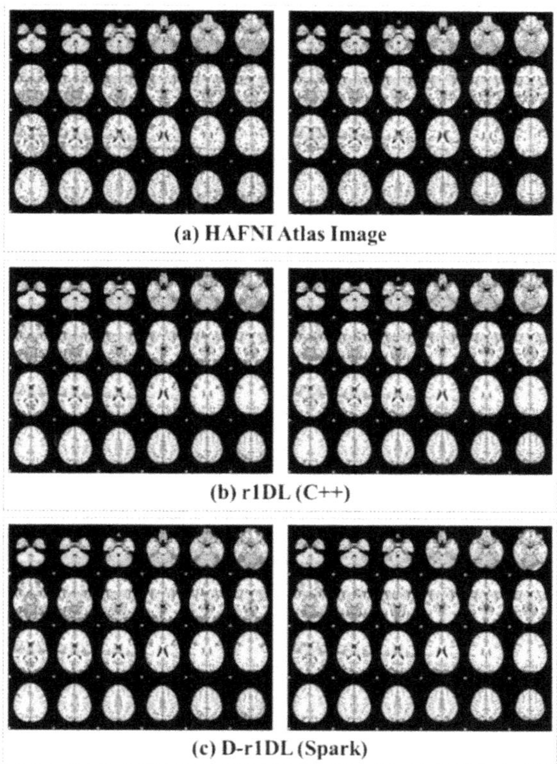

Figure 5. Spatial maps obtained from applying the dictionary learning method on the same fMRI dataset implemented by SPAMS, r1DL in C++, and D-r1DL in Spark.

In addition, the D-r1DL model was compared with the rank-1 dictionary learning algorithm implemented in C++ without any parallelization, in order to investigate whether the parallelization would affect the model performance. Both of the implementations were deployed on the same in-house server and applied on the HCP Q1 individual resting-state fMRI data as well as two task fMRI datasets ("Emotion" and "Working Memory") using the same parameter setting (r=0.07, K=80). An illustration for the spatial maps of two sample networks decomposed by r1DL implemented in C++ and D-r1DL, as well as the corresponding individual-level atlas network in HAFNI, is shown in the three panels in Fig. 5 (a)-(c), respectively.

The obtained functional networks from D-r1DL were then matched to the individual-level atlas networks on the same subjects of the same tasks (or resting-state) by maximizing the spatial similarity between them:

$$R(P_1, P_2) = |P_1 \cap P_2|/|P_2|, \quad (4)$$

where P_1 and P_2 are the spatial map vectors of the two networks. In this work P_1 is the network decomposed by D-r1DL and P_2 is the atlas network. Operator $|\bullet|$ counts the total number of voxels with non-zero values in the given spatial pattern. R ranges from 0 (no voxels overlapping) to 1 (exactly the same maps). The spatial similarity results show that all of the atlas networks defined in HAFNI could be found from the results of D-r1DL. Specifically, the 3 atlas networks from Emotion dataset were identified from D-r1DL results with average spatial similarity of 0.82. The 6 atlas networks from WM dataset were identified with average spatial similarity of 0.79. The 10 resting-state networks, originally reported in [7] and later included in the HAFNI atlas were identified from the results of applying D-r1DL on resting state fMRI data with average spatial similarity of 0.70. The spatial similarity results also show that the networks decomposed by r1DL implemented in C++ and D-r1DL implemented in Spark are almost identical, with average spatial similarity of 0.99.

5.2 Experiment on algorithm convergence

As discussed in section 3 for the algorithm description, we have performed extensive experiments for testing the convergence of alternating least squares with l-0 constraint problem in Eq. 2. By running the r1DL algorithm on each individual fMRI dataset in the HCP Q1 release across 7 tasks with dictionary size parameter K=400 (i.e. decomposing 400 functional networks from each fMRI data), we found that the learning of u and v converged for all the 190,400 networks decomposed. The average number of alternative updates needed for learning one network for different datasets of 5 randomly selected sample subjects is listed in Table 1 below. It can be seen that regardless of the input data size, the majority of the learning would be finished within only a few iterations.

Table 1. Average number of iterations needed for convergence across 7 tasks of 5 subjects

	sbj1	sbj2	sbj3	sbj4	sbj5
Emotion	6.1	6.1	6.2	6.1	6.2
Gambling	6.3	6.3	6.5	6.3	6.2
Language	6.4	6.3	6.4	6.3	6.3
Motor	6.4	6.2	6.3	6.5	6.3
Relational	6.2	6.2	6.2	6.2	6.2
Social	6.3	6.3	6.2	6.3	6.3
WM	6.4	6.3	6.4	6.4	6.4

5.3 Performance boost by r1DL comparing with other dictionary learning algorithms

One of a major premise of the proposed r1DL algorithm is that because of its smaller memory cost and robust learning mechanism (no need to set learning rate), the algorithm should have similar or faster running speed, compared with other dictionary learning methods, even without the parallelization. Based on the performance statistics from running r1DL over the whole HCP task fMRI (tfMRI) dataset as introduced above, we compare the r1DL with the other two dictionary learning algorithms: online dictionary learning implemented in SPAMS package [18] and the stochastic coordinate coding (SCC) algorithm introduced in [13], by applying these two methods on the same HCP Q1 dataset using the same in-house server. The performance comparison is shown in Fig. 6 (averaged across all 68 subjects). From the comparison, it can be seen that r1DL has exhibited improved computational speed over the other two methods in all the 7 tfMRI datasets. It should be noted that we used the r1DL implemented in C++ for the testing in this experiment, and in the same way the other two methods were implemented to ensure consistency in the comparison.

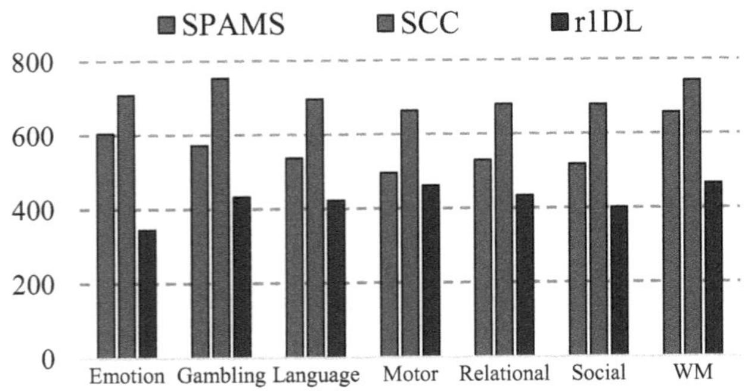

Figure 6. Average time cost (measured in seconds) for functional network decomposition from individual tfMRI data during 7 tasks across 68 subjects, using the three dictionary learning methods.

5.4 Performance and scalability analysis for D-r1DL using the in-house solution

As introduced in 5.1, in this work we applied the D-r1DL model on the three types of datasets for functional network decompositions: tfMRI data of Emotion task with dimension of 176*2M, tfMRI data of Working Memory (WM) task with dimension of 405*2M, and resting state fMRI (rsfMRI) data with dimension of 1200*2M. The testing input files sizes of the three types of dataset were 300MB, 700MB and 2GB, respectively. Using the in-house solution as specified in 4.2, we firstly analyzed the performance of the D-r1DL model using different numbers of cores on a single machine. The performance statistics measured in time cost are shown in Fig. 7.

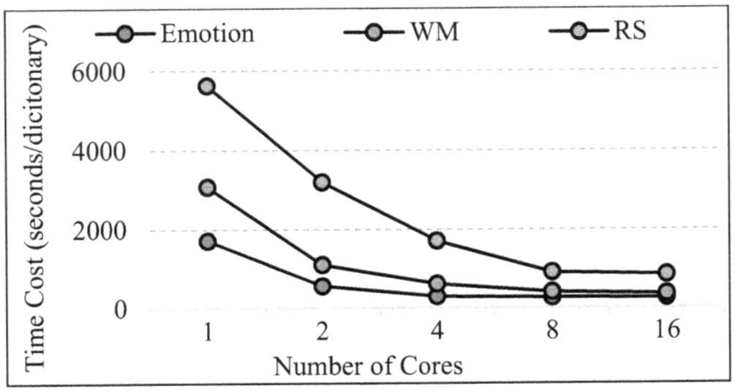

Figure 7. Time cost for decomposing one functional network from three different fMRI datasets by recruiting varying number of cores, using the in-house solution.

For all the three datasets, there exists clear logarithmic relationship (R^2=0.84, 0.89 and 0.92) between the number of cores recruited and the total time cost for the decomposition. The speed boosts by recruiting more cores for the computation comparing with the baseline (1-core) configuration for the three datasets using the in-house solution are listed in Table 2, showing the ratio between the time cost using 1 core and the time cost using multiple cores.

Table 2. Ratios of time cost decreases by recruiting more cores comparing with the single-core configuration

	Emotion	WM	RS
2 cores	3.1	2.8	1.8
4 cores	6.0	5.1	3.3
8 cores	6.6	7.7	6.3
16 cores	6.8	8.6	6.7

As the configuration for using only one core for D-r1DL is equivalent to the non-parallel algorithm, the performance statists indicate that the parallelization based on Spark could greatly improve the performance of the rank-1 dictionary learning algorithm. Specifically, the better performance gain on larger dataset indicates that the parallelization of the rank-1 dictionary learning could potentially overcome the computational bottleneck for analyzing big neuroimaging data, potentially enabling high-throughput analysis on a locally-deployed high-performance computation cluster in the future.

Another analysis of the performance of D-r1DL on the in-house server was aiming at investigating the relationship between dictionary size K (i.e. number of functional networks to be decomposed) and the time/memory cost. The rationale is that, as discussed in 3.1, the rank-1 dictionary learning algorithm has advantages in the iterative estimation of the basis vectors [u, v]. Thus the program does not need to maintain the learning results in the memory. As shown in Fig. 8, the average time cost for estimating one dictionary only marginally increased when using larger dictionary sizes K. Further, the total memory cost of running the D-r1DL was independent with K. This feature is especially useful when the spatial dimension of the input data is large, either because of the higher spatial resolution or because of the aggregated dataset from multiple subjects in a population. As in such cases, the size of all decomposed networks, which equals to $P*K$, could be very large.

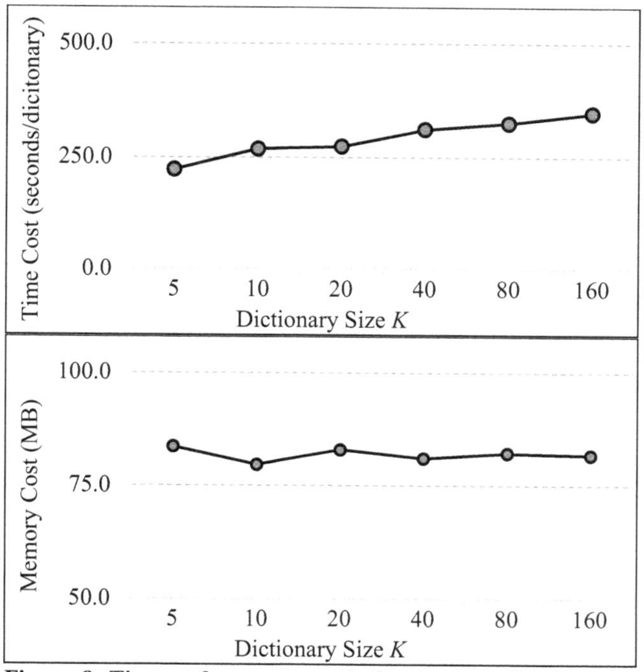

Figure 8. Time and memory costs for decomposing Emotion tfMRI datasets with varying dictionary size *K*, recruiting 16 cores, using the in-house solution.

5.5 Performance of D-r1DL in multi-worker mode using AWS-EC2 solution

In addition to the experiments of the single-machine multi-core configurations conducted using the in-house solution, we have also applied the D-r1DL on the same datasets using the cloud computing service provided by AWS-EC2 as introduced in 4.2. We aimed to investigate the performance of D-r1DL when applied over multiple machines through a network interface. Specifically, as the Spark Python architecture and the resilient distributed dataset abstracts have been designed for supporting large-scale, high efficient analytic framework, we are interested to test its capability of utilizing the distributed computational resources provided by AWS-EC2. In this work, we tested the performance in terms of time and memory cost of the D-r1DL model using 1, 2, 4, 8 and 16 workers on three datasets, while each worker has two cores for the computation. It should be noted that for normal usage, 16 is the maximum number of workers allowed for one instance for the EC2 configuration. The D-r1DL would be running in stand-alone mode under single-worker configuration, similar to the configuration used in the in-house solution. As discussed in 4.1, the communications through network interfaces caused by the parallelization of computation (e.g. the broadcasting of u and v) will potentially increase the time cost mainly due to latencies. Thus the single-worker configuration serves as the baseline for testing whether recruiting more workers will be beneficial from the performance perspective. The performance results of the time and memory cost are summarized in Fig. 9, with the baseline results from single-worker configuration highlighted.

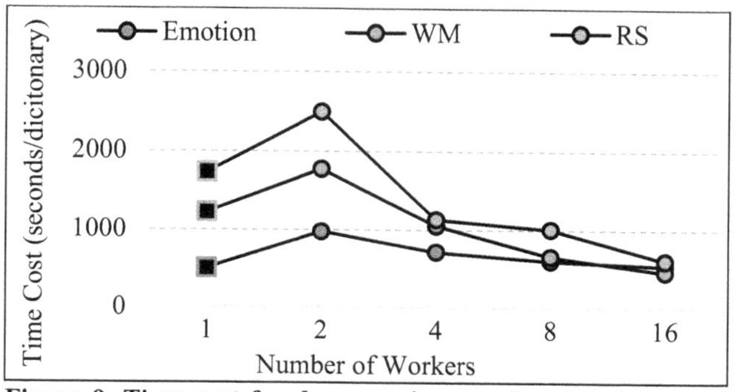

Figure 9. Time cost for decomposing one functional network from three different fMRI datasets by recruiting varying numbers of workers, using the AWS-EC2 solution. The results from single-worker (standalone mode) configuration are highlighted as blocked markers.

First of all, from the results it can be seen that the AWS-EC2 solution recorded faster computation speed (10%~80% faster) comparing with the in-house solution, especially on larger dataset, when both of them use two cores. Considering the fact that the hardware configuration of AWS-EC2 features larger memory capacity better optimized for computation purposes, such difference in performance is within our expectation.

On the other hand, it is interesting to observe that for AWS-EC2 solution, there exists the break-even point at which the multiple-worker mode outperformed the stand-alone mode, but only for the two larger datasets. The ratio between the time cost using standalone mode and the time cost using multiple workers are for the three datasets summarized in Table 3. It can be observed that, for the 700MB WM and the 2GB RS dataset, using 4 or more workers could lead to faster speed comparing with the standalone mode using 1 worker. While for the smaller 300MB Emotion data, the standalone mode is the fastest among all experiments. Thus it can be concluded that the multi-worker configuration will be more suitable for analyzing larger datasets, while standalone mode or the simpler in-house server solution might be preferred for datasets with typically smaller sizes.

Table 3. Ratios of time cost changes by recruiting various number of workers comparing with standalone mode

	Emotion	WM	RS
2 workers	3.1	2.8	1.8
4 workers	6.0	5.1	3.3
8 workers	6.6	7.7	6.3
16 workers	6.8	8.6	6.7

The memory cost on each worker as summarized in Fig. 10 indicates that the multi-worker mode under AWS-EC2 solution scales good with the increasing input file size, as it maintains reasonable small (~100MB) memory cost for all configurations including the single-worker standalone mode. That is the major advantage of using Spark Python model and its resilient distributed dataset for the parallelization: one or multiple workers need not to load the whole dataset at once, but only its corresponding portion of the data according to the data partitioning strategy implemented in the RDDs abstract.

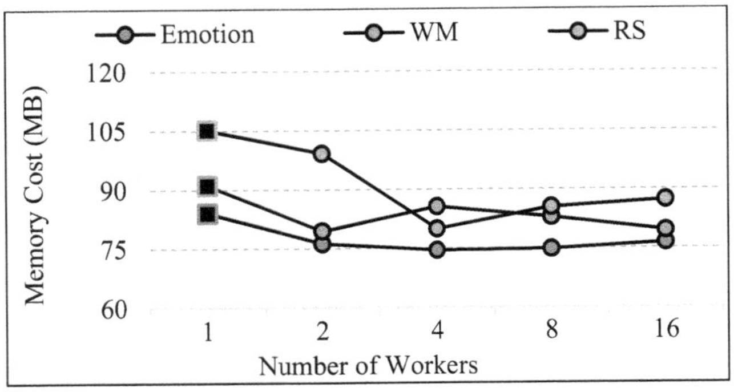

Figure 10. Memory cost for decomposing three different fMRI datasets by recruiting varying number of workers, using the AWS-EC2 solution. The results from single-worker (standalone mode) configuration are highlighted as blocked markers.

6. CONCLUSIONS

In this paper, we proposed a novel and effective distributed dictionary learning model based on iterative rank-1 basis estimation. The model was implemented and parallelized in Spark, and then deployed using the in-house solution as well as the AWS-EC2 solution. The aim of this work is to meet the challenges posed by fMRI big data for more efficient and scalable data analytics methods. The testing results from running both solutions on the HCP Q1 dataset show that functional network decomposition using rank-1 dictionary learning could benefit from parallelization for both single-worker multi-core configuration and the multi-worker cluster configuration, with significant performance improvement especially on larger datasets. In the current work, we have only analyzed individual-level fMRI data, with the largest data size of 2GB. As it has been shown from the performance statistics that the Spark engine supported by RDDs abstract could effectively perform the data partition and reduce the memory cost for large-scale input data, we will test the model performance on larger, population-level datasets (e.g., the HCP full dataset) with the size of dozens or hundreds of terabytes in the near future. The ultimate goal of the proposed D-r1DL model with the HELPNI neuroinformatics system is to provide an integrated solution for functional neuroimaging big data management and analysis, enabling high-throughput neuroscientific knowledge discovery. In addition, the similar parallelization scheme used in this work for D-r1DL could be implemented on other algorithms as well. Thus the experience of this work also offers a practical perspective for improving the efficiency and scalability of general machine learning and data mining algorithm developments.

7. REFERENCES

[1] https://aws.amazon.com/ec2/

[2] http://hafni.cs.uga.edu

[3] https://spark.apache.org

[4] Aharon, M., Elad, M., and Bruckstein, A., 2006. K-SVD: An Algorithm for Designing Overcomplete Dictionaries for Sparse Representation. *Signal Processing, IEEE Transactions on 54*, 11, 4311-4322. DOI= http://dx.doi.org/10.1109/TSP.2006.881199.

[5] Biswal, B.B. and Ulmer, J.L., 1999. Blind Source Separation of Multiple Signal Sources of fMRI Data Sets Using Independent Component Analysis. *Journal of Computer Assisted Tomography 23*, 2, 265-271.

[6] D'aspremont, A., Ghaoui, L.E., Jordan, M.I., and Lanckreit, G.R., 2004. A Direct Formulation for Sparse PCA Using Semidefinite Programming. In *Advances in Neural Information Processing Systems.*

[7] Damoiseaux, J.S., Rombouts, S.A.R.B., Barkhof, F., Scheltens, P., Stam, C.J., Smith, S.M., and Beckmann, C.F., 2006. Consistent resting-state networks across healthy subjects. *Proceedings of the National Academy of Sciences of the United States of America 103*, 37, 02/20/received), 13848-13853. DOI= http://dx.doi.org/10.1073/pnas.0601417103.

[8] Elad, M. and Aharon, M., 2006. Image Denoising Via Sparse and Redundant Representations Over Learned Dictionaries. *Image Processing, IEEE Transactions on 15*, 12, 3736-3745. DOI= http://dx.doi.org/10.1109/TIP.2006.881969.

[9] Glasser, M.F., Sotiropoulos, S.N., Wilson, J.A., Coalson, T.S., Fischl, B., Anderson, J.L., Xu, J., Jbabdi, S., Webster, M., Polimeni, J.R., Van Essen, D.C., and Jenkinson, M., 2013. The minimal preprocessing pipelines for the Human Connectome Project. *NeuroImage 80,* 105-124. DOI= http://dx.doi.org/http://dx.doi.org/10.1016/j.neuroimage.2013.04.127.

[10] Gonzalez, J.E., Xin, R.S., Dave A., Crankshaw, D., Franklin, M.J., and Stoica, I., 2014. GraphX: graph processing in a distributed dataflow framework. In *Proceedings of the Proceedings of the 11th USENIX conference on Operating Systems Design and Implementation*, USENIX Association, 2685096, 599-613.

[11] Kangjoo, L., Sungho, T., and Jong Chul, Y., 2011. A Data-Driven Sparse GLM for fMRI Analysis Using Sparse Dictionary Learning With MDL Criterion. *Medical Imaging, IEEE Transactions on 30*, 5, 1076-1089. DOI= http://dx.doi.org/10.1109/TMI.2010.2097275.

[12] Lee, H., Battle, A., Raina, R., and NG, A.Y., 2006. Efficient sparse coding algorithms. In *Advances in Neural Information Processing Systems.*

[13] Lin, B., Li, Q., Sun, Q., Lai, M.-J., Davidson, I., Fan, W., and Ye, J., 2014. Stochastic Coordinate Coding and Its Application for Drosophila Gene Expression Pattern Annotation. *arXiv:1407.8147.*

[14] Liu, B.-D., Wang, Y.-X., Zhang, Y.-J., and Shen, B., 2013. Learning dictionary on manifolds for image classification. *Pattern Recognition 46*, 7, 1879-1890. DOI= http://dx.doi.org/10.1016/j.patcog.2012.11.018.

[15] Lv, J., Jiang, X., Li, X., Zhu, D., Zhang, S., Zhao, S., Chen, H., Zhang, T., Hu, X., Han, J., Ye, J., Guo, L., and Liu, T., 2015. Holistic atlases of functional networks and interactions reveal reciprocal organizational architecture of cortical function. *Biomedical Engineering, IEEE Transactions on 62*, 4, 1120-1131. DOI= http://dx.doi.org/10.1109/TBME.2014.2369495.

[16] Mackey, L.W., 2008. Deflation Methods for Sparse PCA. In *Advances in Neural Information Processing Systems.*

[17] Makkie, M., Zhao, S., Jiang , X., Lv , J., Zhao, Y., Ge, B., Li, X., Han, J., and Liu, T., 2015. HAFNI-enabled largescale

platform for neuroimaging informatics (HELPNI). Brain Informatics 2, 4, 225-238. DOI= http://dx.doi.org/10.1007/s40708-015-0024-0.

[18] Mairal, J., Bach, F., Ponce, J., and Sapiro, G., 2010. Online Learning for Matrix Factorization and Sparse Coding. *J. Mach. Learn. Res. 11*, 19-60.

[19] Mennes, M., Biswal, B.B., Castellanos, F.X., and Milham, M.P., 2013. Making data sharing work: The FCP/INDI experience. *NeuroImage 82*, 683-691. DOI= http://dx.doi.org/ 10.1016/j.neuroimage.2012.10.064.

[20] Poldrack, R.A., Barch, D.M., Mitchell, J.P., Wager, T.D., Wagner, A.D., Devlin, J.T., Cumba, C., Koyejo, O., and Milham, M.P., 2013. Toward open sharing of task-based fMRI data: the OpenfMRI project. *Frontiers in Neuroinformatics 7*, 12. DOI= http://dx.doi.org/10.3389/fninf.2013.00012.

[21] Ravishankar, S. and Bresler, Y., 2011. MR Image Reconstruction From Highly Undersampled k-Space Data by Dictionary Learning. *Medical Imaging, IEEE Transactions on 30*, 5, 1028-1041. DOI= http://dx.doi.org/10.1109/TMI.2010.2090538.

[22] Sindhwani, V. and Ghoting, A., 2012. Large-scale distributed non-negative sparse coding and sparse dictionary learning. In *Proceedings of the Proceedings of the 18th ACM SIGKDD international conference on Knowledge discovery and data mining* 2339610, 489-497. DOI= http://dx.doi.org/10.1145/2339530.2339610.

[23] Smith, S.M., Hyvarinen, A., Varoquaux, G., Miller, K.L., and Beckmann, C.F., 2014. Group-PCA for very large fMRI datasets. *NeuroImage 101*, 0, 738-749. DOI= http://dx.doi.org/ 10.1016/j.neuroimage.2014.07.051.

[24] Smith, S.M., Miller, K.L., Moeller, S., XU, J., Auerbach, E.J., Woolrich, M.W., Beckmann, C.F., Jenkinson, M., Andersson, J., Glasser, M.F., Van Essen, D.C., Feinberg, D.A., Yacoub, E.S., and Ugurbil, K., 2012. Temporally-independent functional modes of spontaneous brain activity. *Proceedings of the National Academy of Sciences 109*, 8, 3131-3136. DOI= http://dx.doi.org/10.1073/pnas.1121329109.

[25] Thirion, B. and Faugeras, O., 2003. Dynamical components analysis of fMRI data through kernel PCA. *NeuroImage 20*, 1, 34-49. DOI= http://dx.doi.org/ 10.1016/S1053-8119(03)00316-1.

[26] Van Essen, D.C., Smith, S.M., Barch, D.M., Behrens, T.E.J., Yacoub, E., and Ugurbil, K., 2013. The WU-Minn Human Connectome Project: An overview. *NeuroImage 80*, 0, 62-79. DOI= http://dx.doi.org/ 10.1016/j.neuroimage.2013.05.041.

[27] Zharia, M., Chowdhury, M., Das, T., Dave, A., MA, J., Mccauley, M., Franklin, M.J., Shenker, S., and Stoica, I., 2012. Resilient distributed datasets: a fault-tolerant abstraction for in-memory cluster computing. In *Proceedings of the Proceedings of the 9th USENIX conference on Networked Systems Design and Implementation*, 2228301, 2-2.

[28] Zaharia, M., Das, T., Li, H., Hunter, T., Shenker, S., and Stoica, I., 2013. Discretized streams: fault-tolerant streaming computation at scale. In *Proceedings of the Proceedings of the Twenty-Fourth ACM Symposium on Operating Systems Principles*, 2522737, 423-438. DOI= http://dx.doi.org/10.1145/2517349.2522737.

CompanyDepot: Employer Name Normalization in the Online Recruitment Industry

Qiaoling Liu, Faizan Javed, and Matt Mcnair
CareerBuilder LLC
5550-A Peachtree Parkway Suite 200, Norcross, GA 30092
{qiaoling.liu, faizan.javed, matt.mcnair}@careerbuilder.com

ABSTRACT

Entity linking links entity mentions in text to the corresponding entities in a knowledge base (KB) and has many applications in both open domain and specific domains. For example, in the recruitment domain, linking employer names in job postings or resumes to entities in an employer KB is very important to many business applications. In this paper, we focus on this employer name normalization task, which has several unique challenges: handling employer names from both job postings and resumes, leveraging the corresponding location context, and handling name variations, irrelevant input data, and noises in the KB. We present a system called CompanyDepot which contains a machine learning based approach CompanyDepot-ML and a heuristic approach CompanyDepot-H to address these challenges in three steps: (1) searching for candidate entities based on a customized search engine for the KB; (2) ranking the candidate entities using learning-to-rank methods or heuristics; and (3) validating the top-ranked entity via binary classification or heuristics. While CompanyDepot-ML shows better extendability and flexibility, CompanyDepot-H serves as a strong baseline and useful way to collect training data for CompanyDepot-ML. The proposed system achieves 2.5%-21.4% higher coverage at the same precision level compared to an existing system used at CareerBuilder over multiple real-world datasets. Applying the system to a similar task of academic institution name normalization further shows the generalization ability of the method.

Keywords

employer name normalization; entity linking; named entity disambiguation; learning to rank

1. INTRODUCTION

Entity linking links entity mentions in text to the corresponding entities in a knowledge base (KB) and has many applications such as information extraction and content analysis [22], in both open domain and specific domains. For example, in the recruitment domain, linking the company name on a user's professional profile position to a company entity is very important to many business applications [24].

The mission of CareerBuilder[1], a company providing human capital solutions globally, is to empower employment. Its online career site contains over 45 million candidate resumes and 1.6 million jobs. One of its products is Supply & Demand which performs big data analytics on the supply and demand of jobs. For example, on one hand it computes the demand (i.e., the number of open positions) for specific jobs and the top employers with such demand; on the other hand, it also computes the supply (i.e., the number of candidates) for specific jobs and the top places such supply come from. Such analytics are achievable by parsing and analyzing a large number of job postings and candidate resumes related to specific jobs. To enable accurate computation, besides a KB of employers [15] we need a system that can do employer name normalization, i.e., linking the employer names in the job postings and the resumes to the employer entities in the KB. In this paper, we focus on this employer name normalization task, which is illustrated in Figure 1.

Some key challenges of the task are summarized below based on the applications at CareerBuilder. An effective employer name normalization system should be able to:

1. Handle employer names from both job postings and resumes, which are in semi-structured format and could come from different sources. Therefore, the employer name fields could contain varying degrees of noises.

2. Leverage the location context. Jobs are often associated with locations, and so are the employer names in job postings and resumes. The location information associated with an employer name could be useful for normalization, but it could be empty or inaccurate.

3. Handle name variations. An employer entity can have legacy names, nicknames, acronyms (e.g., "Beaver College" vs. "Arcadia University", "Gatech" vs. "Georgia Institute of Technology", "IBM" vs. "International Business Machines"). An employer name could also be wrongly typed (e.g., "macy's" vs. "macys", "wells fargo" vs. "wellsfargo").

4. Handle irrelevant or unlinkable input data. There are two cases: (a) the input does not mean any employer, e.g., "Not specified", "self-employed"; (b) the input means an employer, but it does not refer to any known entity in the KB.

[1]http://www.careerbuilder.com/

KDD '16, August 13-17, 2016, San Francisco, CA, USA
 ISBN 978-1-4503-4232-2/16/08... $15.00
DOI: http://dx.doi.org/10.1145/2939672.2939727

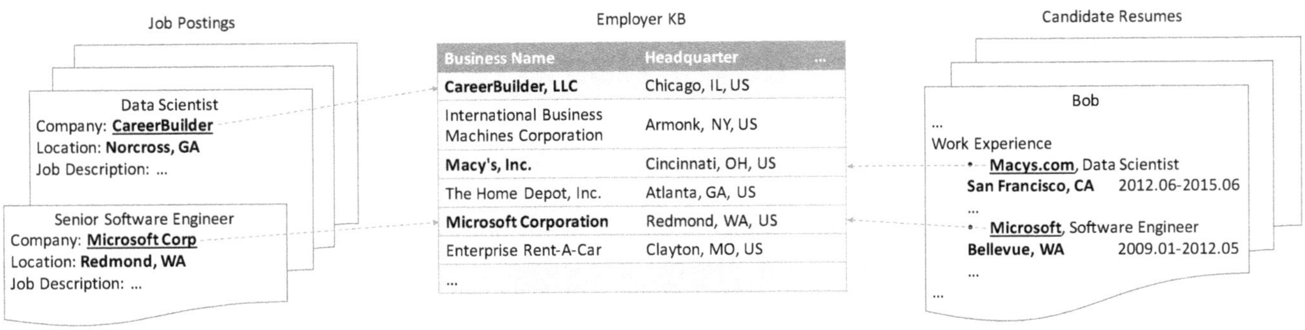

Figure 1: Illustration of employer name normalization in jobs and resumes

5. Handle noises in the KB. The employer KB used in this paper is derived from a database which may contain duplicate records referring to the same employer. For example, it contains different records named "Enterprise Rent A Car", "Enterprise Rentacar", and "Enterprise Rent-A-Car Company" respectively.

Some of these challenges (3 and 4) also exist in the typical entity linking task [8, 22]. Yet, other challenges (1, 2, and 5) are rather unique in the recruitment domain. This paper describes a system called CompanyDepot which aims to address all these challenges. The system takes an employer name and its associated location from job postings or resumes as input and normalizes it into entities in an employer KB. We develop two approaches, one based on machine learning techniques and the other based on heuristics, which address the proposed task in three steps: entity retrieval, reranking, and validation. The retrieval step searches for candidate entities based on a customized search engine for the KB, the reranking step ranks the candidate entities based on learning-to-rank methods or heuristics, and the validation step validates the top-ranked entity based on binary classification or heuristics. We experiment with the proposed system over multiple real-world datasets and compare its performance with an existing employer name normalization system used at CareerBuilder. Our system achieves 2.5%-21.4% higher coverage at the same precision level. We also apply it to a similar task of academic institution name normalization and compare its performance with a state-of-the-art method. The experimental results show the effectiveness, robustness, and generalization ability of our system. Its fast query response time allows the system to be applied to online employer name normalization.

The major contributions of this paper are as follows:

- Proposing a novel employer name normalization task.
- Presenting a system called CompanyDepot with a machine learning based approach and a heuristic approach.
- Comparing its performance on multiple real-world datasets with the existing systems used at CareerBuilder.

The rest of the paper is organized as follows. Section 2 discusses the related work. Next, we provide the problem definition in Section 3 and some preliminaries in Section 4. Then Section 5 describes the system and Section 6 details the experiments. Finally, we conclude the paper in Section 7.

2. RELATED WORK

2.1 Entity Linking with a Knowledge Base

Entity linking [22], also called named entity disambiguation (NED) or named entity normalization (NEN), which links entity mentions in text to the corresponding entities in a KB, has attracted much research effort since the availability of large KBs such as Wikipedia[2] and Freebase [2]. It is a key step to understand and annotate the raw and noisy data in many applications.

A comprehensive survey of the issues and methods about entity linking is provided in [22]. As it summarized, a typical entity linking system has three modules: candidate entity generation, candidate entity ranking, and unlinkable mention prediction. To generate candidate entities, many methods have been proposed, e.g., building a table of mappings from surface forms to the possible entities [26, 28], extracted expanded forms for entity mentions from the local document [25, 27, 28], and finding relevant entity pages via search engines (such as Google API [8] and Wikipedia search engine [26]). To rank the candidate entities, many systems used supervised ranking methods and the most popular two are binary classification [24, 26, 27] and learning to rank [8, 21, 25, 27, 28]. To predict unlinkable mentions, many methods used binary classification to decide whether to output the top-ranked entity or NIL (Not-In-Lexicon) as the final result [21, 25, 27, 28], while some methods integrated NIL prediction into the learning-to-rank process [8].

The employer name normalization task proposed in this paper can be viewed as a general entity linking problem, yet it differs from the traditional entity linking task [22] in three aspects: (1) different data sources: entity linking takes an entity mention recognized in text as input while our task takes an employer name parsed from a semi-structured job posting or resume as input; (2) different contexts: in entity linking the document where an entity mention appears serves as the context, while in our task the location associated with an employer name extracted from the job posting or the resume is used as the context; (3) different KBs: entity linking often focuses on a global KB and multiple types of entities while our task is concerned with a domain-specific KB and a single type of entities.

Because of these differences, the employer name normalization task has unique challenges such as handling the location context and noises in the KB. Our system adapts the three-module framework used in the entity linking systems.

[2]https://www.wikipedia.org/

First, we build our own search engine customized for the KB, which enables us to efficiently retrieve relevant entities by tuning the suitable search algorithms. Then we use learning-to-rank methods to rank the candidate entities and a binary classifier to validate the top-ranked entity. Compared to the entity linking systems, our system has a novel candidate entity generation process. We also design novel features (such as query complexity and location matching) for learning based entity ranking and validation. Moreover, we develop a heuristic approach which serves as a practical and strong baseline for the machine learning based approach.

2.2 Domain-Specific Name Normalization

Our work is also related to a set of domain-specific name normalization applications. For example, within the same recruitment domain, Yan et al. described how to normalize the company name on a LinkedIn member's profile position using social graphs based on binary classification [24]. Although their application is within the same domain as ours, a few differences exist: (1) LinkedIn only considers input from member profiles while we need to normalize company names in both job postings and resumes; (2) LinkedIn has the whole profile as the context which makes the important social features derived from member-to-member links available, while we only have the location corresponding to an employer name as the context; (3) LinkedIn has a Typeahead Assist which allows users to select the correct company entity from a suggested list, thus automatically reducing input noises and creating training data, which is unfortunately not available in our application and many other applications.

The problem of academic institution name normalization discussed by Jacob et al. [11] is very similar to ours. Instead of an employer KB used in our work, they used a KB of academic institutions. Their method, named sCooL, consists of two steps: retrieval and reranking. The retrieval step is also based on building a search engine for the KB. However, sCooL treated each mapping from a surface form to an entity as a document, while our system treats each entity as a document, which leads to very different indexing structures and search processes. The reranking step of sCooL is based purely on heuristics, while we develop a machine learning based approach besides the heuristic approach.

NEMO [13] addressed a related task of extracting and normalizing organization names from PubMed articles. The method first uses multi-layered rule matching to extract entity mentions and then leverages unsupervised clustering to identify entity mentions referring to the same entity.

Besides organization name normalization, there are also many other domain-specific name normalization applications, e.g., product item name normalization [3], gene name normalization [23], disease name normalization [16], and person name normalization [18]. The main differences of these applications with ours lie in different data sources, contexts, and KBs, which often bring some different challenges.

2.3 Deduplicating Domain-Specific Knowledge Bases

The task of employer name normalization depends on an employer KB, and a key step in building such domain-specific KBs is de-duplication [15]. Kardes et al. proposed graph-based blocking and clustering strategies for organization entity resolution [14]. McNeill et al. proposed a dynamic blocking method to efficiently deduplicate around 5 billion people records [19]. The book by Christen summarizes more methods for general duplicate detection [6].

This paper focuses on the task of employer name normalization, for which we performed simple deduplication of the records in an employer database based on their business names. More complex deduplication will be the future work.

3. PROBLEM DEFINITION

Our task is to link the employer names in job postings or resumes to entities in an employer KB, as illustrated in Figure 1. We next describe the problem more formally. The entities in the employer KB are denoted by $E = \{e_1, e_2, ..., e_k\}$. The employer names and the associated location contexts extracted from job postings and resumes[3] are denoted by $Q = \{q_1, q_2, ..., q_c\}$, where $q_i = (n_i, l_i)$ is a pair of employer name and the associated location. In the rest of the paper, we call n_i the query name and l_i the query location. We represent a query location as a triple: $l_i = (City_i, State_i, Country_i)$, where the city, state, country information could be empty. The problem of employer name normalization can then be summarized as inferring a mapping function $f(q_i) \Rightarrow e_j$, where $q_i \in Q$ and $e_j \in E \cup \{NIL\}$. Note that NIL (Not-In-Lexicon) means the input query does not refer to any known entity in the KB.

As discussed in Section 2, our task can be viewed as a general entity linking problem, but is different from the traditional entity linking task for documents [22] and other domain-specific name normalization tasks [24] in terms of different data sources, contexts, and KBs.

4. PRELIMINARIES

4.1 Employer Knowledge Base

The employer KB we used in this paper is based on a third-party employer database, which contains about 21 million employer records. Each record represents an employer with a set of attributes like business name, location, industry code, and company size. Branches of a company are represented as different records, often with the same business name. The database has a good coverage of employers in US, however, it is noisy and may contain duplicate records for the same employer entity. For example, it contains different records named "Enterprise Rent A Car", "Enterprise Rentacar", and "Enterprise Rent-A-Car Company" respectively.

To make an employer KB for the employer name normalization system, we performed simple deduplication of the above employer database. We merged all the records with the same business name into a single entity (by assuming that two records with the same business name refer to the same employer entity) and kept a list of all the original locations. We also computed the number of the original records merged into an entity as the entity popularity. This resulted in a set of around 18 million employer entities that serves as our final employer KB. Note that the noises still exist in the KB, which needs to be considered in the employer name normalization system.

Note that in this KB we treat the business name of an entity as its normalized form and there are no surface forms

[3]The extraction of the employer names and the associated locations is done by in-house job parsers and resume parsers at CareerBuilder, which is out of the scope of this paper.

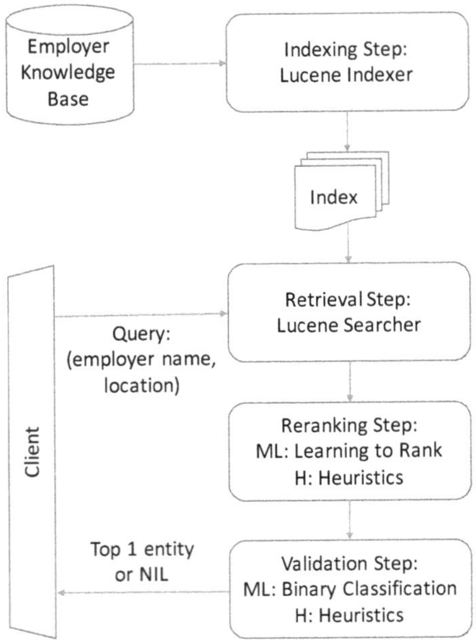

Figure 2: Architecture of the CompanyDepot system.

associated with it. Yet, the proposed system can also make use of the available surface forms in other KBs [11, 15].

4.2 Lucene Search Engine

Our system uses Apache Lucene[4] to index and retrieve the employer entities respectively. Lucene is a high-performance text search engine library. A document in Lucene is a set of fields. Each field has a name and a textual value, with semantics about how it is parsed (e.g., tokenized vs. untokenized, stopwords kept vs. removed). Lucene scoring first works on fields and then combines the results to return documents, allowing giving different weights to different fields.

Lucene supports a wide variety of query implementations, which can be combined to provide complex querying capabilities. For example, it supports the following searches:

- Keyword search which finds documents containing any of the query terms.
- Fuzzy search which finds documents containing terms similar in spelling to a query term.
- Phrase search which finds documents containing all the query terms occurring in the same order as in the query (the number of other terms permitted between terms in the query phrase can be controlled).
- Aggregated search which finds documents satisfying any of the individual searches.

All the above searches are used in our system to retrieve relevant employer entities for a given query.

5. THE COMPANYDEPOT SYSTEM

The architecture of our system is shown in Figure 2. Before taking any queries, the system needs to index the employer KB using a Lucene indexer. Once the index is ready,

[4]https://lucene.apache.org/

Field	Value
id	15
normalized_form	International Business Machines Corporation
surface_forms[5]	International Business Machines Corporation; IBM; International Business Machines; ...
calibrated_name	internationalbusinessmachines
json	{"id": "15", "normalized_form": "International Business Machines Corporation", "surface_forms": [...], ...}

Table 1: An example document created for an employer entity.

the system can take normalization requests. Each request consists of an employer name and its location context (part of or whole location information could be empty). The system then uses a Lucene searcher to retrieve a list of N employer entities. We then send these N candidate entities to the reranking step, which first generates a feature vector for each entity and then uses either a machine learning based ranking model or some feature-based heuristics to rank them. Finally, the top-ranked entity is sent to the validation step to decide whether it is a correct result for the query using either a binary classifier or some heuristics. If it says yes, we output this entity to the user; otherwise, we output NIL. We will next describe each step in more detail.

5.1 Indexing Step

The purpose of this step is to index all the entities in the employer KB so that they can be efficiently retrieved in the next step. For each entity, we created a document which contains five fields: id, normalized form, surface forms, calibrated name, and json. An example document is shown in Figure 1. The id field is used to locate an entity. The fields of normalized form and surface forms are used to match the query name in the retrieval step. Distinguishing these two fields allows us to give higher weights to matches in the normalized field. The calibrated name field is used to enable better fuzzy match, derived by compact calibration of the normalized form (details in Section 5.1.1). The json field is a stored field, which is used to get all the detailed information about an entity, e.g., locations and popularity, for computing features used for the machine learning techniques.

Then all these documents are sent to the Lucene indexer to build an index, which is then used by the Lucene searcher in the retrieval step.

5.1.1 Calibration of Employer Names

Proper parsing and pre-processing of text is an important step in building effective search engines [7]. Inspired by this, we propose to calibrate entity names and query names to make them more comparable. The calibration of an employer name works as follows:

1. Convert the name to lowercase, and replace "'s" with "s" (e.g., "Macy's" -> "macys").
2. Convert all the non-alphanumeric characters to space.

[5]We always include the normalized form of an entity as one of its surface forms.

Employer name	After calibration	After compact calibration
International Business Machines Corporation	international business machines	internationalbusinessmachines
Sherman & Howard L.L.C.	sherman howard	shermanhoward
Oxnard Police Dept	oxnard police department	oxnardpolicedepartment
Macy's, Inc.	macys	macys

Table 2: Examples of calibration and compact calibration of employer names.

3. Remove stop-phrases (e.g., "pvt ltd" and "l l c") and stop-words (e.g., "inc", "corporation", "incorporated", and "the").
4. Expand commonly used abbreviations, e.g., "ctr" -> "center", "svc" -> "services", "dept" -> "department".
5. (Optionally) remove all spaces in the name.

Table 2 shows some calibration examples. Considering that a query name is often short while the official name of an entity could be tedious, comparing two calibrated forms often enables more accurate match detection than comparing the two original names.

5.2 Retrieval Step

The purpose of this step is to efficiently generate a pool of N candidate entities so that the correct result is included. To generate this pool, we first use Lucene's powerful querying capabilities to retrieve a large set of entities that are possibly relevant to the query name, and then apply several filters to this entity set and keep only the most likely correct results in the pool.

Specifically, we first search for the query name against all the entity documents via an aggregated search in Lucene which combines (1) keyword searches in the normalized form and surface forms fields; (2) fuzzy searches in the surface forms and calibrated name fields; and (3) phrase searches in the surface forms field. After obtaining top N_0 (e.g., N_0=1000) entities from the Lucene searcher, we then generate the pool of candidate entities as follows:

- From the N_0 results, add to the pool the top N_1 (e.g., N_1=10) entities that have the highest Lucene score.
- From the N_0 results, use Levenshtein Distance to compute the top N_2 (e.g., N_2=2) results whose surface forms have the minimum distance with the query name, and add them to the pool.
- From the N_0 results, use Levenshtein Distance to compute the top N_3 (e.g., N_3=2) results whose compactly calibrated surface forms have the minimum distance with the compactly calibrated query name, and add them to the pool.
- From the N_0 results, add to the pool the N_4 entities obtained by querying a legacy mapping table (details in Section 6.3) which contains mappings from surface forms to the possible linked entities.

The resulted pool contains $N = N_1 + N_2 + N_3 + N_4$ candidate entities, which will be reranked in the next step. Note that the query location is not used in this step because we believe it is more helpful in ranking rather than generating candidate entities.

5.3 Reranking Step: Learning to Rank

The purpose of this step is to effectively rerank the N candidate entities obtained in the previous step so that the correct result is ranked top.

We use supervised learning-to-rank methods to automatically build the ranking model based on training data [17]. A key to the success of such methods is the features used, so next we describe the features used in our system.

5.3.1 *Feature Generation*

For each (query, candidate entity) pair, we generate a vector of features, which can be grouped into three categories:

- **Query features** indicate the complexity of finding a correct result for this query, which include the length of the query name, whether it indicates irrelevant input, and whether the query location is specified.
- **Query-entity features** indicate the likelihood that the entity is a correct result for the query, which include the score of the Lucene searcher, string comparison of the query name and the normalized form (or the surface forms) of the entity, matching between the query location and the location list of the entity, whether there is a mapping from the query name to the entity in the legacy mapping table.
- **Entity features** indicate the prior knowledge about the entity being a correct result for some query, which include the entity popularity, the number of locations of the entity, whether the normalized form of the entity contains a legal word such as "inc" or "llc".

A full list of the features is shown in Table 3. In Section 6, we will do feature ablation tests to see how each feature group contributes to the learning performance.

5.3.2 *Learning Algorithm*

Based on the above features, our system uses a listwise learning-to-rank method, coordinate ascent [20], to rerank the candidate employer entities. Coordinate ascent can directly optimize any user specified ranking measure, by updating one parameter at a time while holding other parameters fixed. It has been shown to provide superior performance compared to some other learning-to-rank models [4]. Specifically, we use the coordinate ascent implementation provided in the RankLib[6] library for our experiments.

Before training and testing, we normalize each feature by its mean and standard deviation. Since only the top-ranked entity matters in our task, we choose P@1 to optimize on the training data. To increase the chances of finding a global solution, we use 10 random restarts. For other parameters, the default values provided in RankLib are used.

[6]http://sourceforge.net/p/lemur/wiki/RankLib/

Query features (8 total)
• length of query name in characters. • length of query name in words. • whether query name contains specific phrases or words (e.g., "self employed", "freelancer"). • whether query location (city, state, country) is specified.

Query-entity features (32 total)
• score by Lucene searcher. • whether query name equals entity normalized form by ignoring case. • whether query name equals entity normalized form by considering only alphanumeric characters. • whether query name equals any entity surface form by ignoring case. • whether (compactly) calibrated query name is prefix (suffix) of (compactly) calibrated entity normalized form, or vice versa. • number (percentage) of common words between calibrated query name and calibrated entity normalized name. • Levenshtein (and Jaro-Winkler) distance between (compactly) (calibrated) query name and (compactly) (calibrated) entity normalized form (surface forms). • Jaccard similarity between the two 4-gram sets of (compactly) (calibrated) query name and (compactly) (calibrated) entity normalized form (surface forms). • whether query location (city, state, country) matches entity location (city, state, country). • whether a mapping from query name to entity exists in the legacy mapping table.

Entity features (5 total)
• how many surface forms this entity has. • entity popularity. • length of entity normalized form in characters. • whether entity normalized form contains a legal word like "inc" or "llc". • how many locations this entity has.

Table 3: Features used for learning to rank.

The output of the reranking step is a ranked list of the N candidate entities. Yet, only the top-ranked candidate entity will be sent to the next validation step.

5.4 Validation Step: Binary Classification

The purpose of this step is to validate the top-ranked result so that either a correct result or NIL is sent to the user.

We use a binary classifier to do the validation. The features used for this classification include the features derived in Section 5.3.1 as well as the score output of the learning-to-rank method. We used LibSVM [5] as our binary classifier. In the future, we could add more features indicating NIL such as how similar the top N candidate entities are.

5.5 Heuristic Method

The supervised learning methods above cannot be applied without training data. For the employer name normalization task discussed in this paper, there is no off-the-shelf ground-truth data available. Therefore, we also develop a heuristic method within the system framework, which does not require training data.

The heuristic method shares the same indexing and retrieval steps as the machine learning based approach while having a different process in the reranking and validation steps. In the reranking step, the heuristic method ranks the candidate entities based on the following three feature values (which are also listed in Table 3):

- s_1: Jaccard similarity between the 4-gram sets of the compactly calibrated query name and the compactly calibrated entity normalized form.
- s_2: Entity popularity.
- s_3: Jaccard similarity between the 4-gram sets of the calibrated query name and the calibrated entity normalized form.

In the validation step, the heuristic method simply outputs the top-ranked entity and outputs s_1 as its score.

As will be shown in Section 6, this heuristic method is used to collect manual labels as our training data for the machine learning based approach and serves as a strong baseline compared to other methods.

5.6 Discussion

The Lucene search engine is also used in sCooL [11] to retrieve the candidate entities for academic institution name normalization. However, the index structure in our system is different from the one used in sCooL. While sCooL treats each mapping from a surface form to a normalized form as a document, our system treats each entity as a document. This leads to several benefits. First, fewer documents need to be indexed, which often results in more efficient retrieval. Second, the documents returned by the Lucene searcher directly correspond to a set of entities, which does not need an extra step to compute a list of entities from the returned mappings. In addition, more information of an entity (e.g., the normalized form together with all the surface forms) can be used for computing the matching between the entity and the query in the retrieval process.

Ranking candidate entities based on learning to rank and validating the top-ranked entity based on binary classification have been shown to be effective choices in previous research [21, 25, 27, 28]. We derived similar features (such as name string comparison and entity popularity) that have been shown to be effective, as well as novel features (such as query complexity and location matching) designed for the employer name normalization task. For learning to rank, we choose the coordinate ascent algorithm [20] which can directly optimize the P@1 metric we care most in our task, instead of the more popularly used ranking SVM algorithm [12] in previous work [21, 25, 27, 28]. Our preliminary experiments suggest that coordinate ascent gives better performance than ranking SVM for our task.

6. EXPERIMENTS

In this section, we conduct experiments to answer the following questions: (1) How do the proposed methods compare to the existing employer name normalization systems used at CareerBuilder? (2) How do the proposed methods compare to the state-of-the-art methods on similar tasks? (3) What are the effects of different feature groups on the performance of the machine learning based approach?

6.1 Test Suite

6.1.1 Job and Resume Datasets

To evaluate the performance of the proposed employer name normalization system CompanyDepot, we sampled two resume datasets and two job datasets from real applications at CareerBuilder. The two resume datasets (RDB, EDGE)

Dataset	#Queries	%Country	%US	%State
RDB	1098	58.5%	96.4%	50.9%
EDGE	1093	97.3%	45.3%	20.8%
JOB1	1100	100%	100%	99.7%
JOB2	500	100%	98.4%	100%

Table 4: Statistics about the job and resume datasets (%Country means the percentage of queries with country specified, %US means the percentage of queries with country=US when country is specified, %State means the percentage of queries with state specified).

are sampled from two resume databases respectively. The two job datasets are sampled from a database of job postings based on a legacy normalization system: JOB1 (JOB2) was sampled from cases for which the legacy system returned some (no) result at some time. The datasets were sampled using weighted random sampling techniques [9] so that queries that are more frequent are more likely to be chosen. We believe this sampling strategy would enable more realistic evaluation, better reflecting the overall impact on user experience. The statistics of the datasets are shown in Table 4. We can see that different datasets have different characteristics in terms of the percentage of queries with location specified and the percentage of international queries.

After the query sets were ready, we generated results using three systems: CompanyDepot-H, Legacy, and WService, which will be described in Section 6.3 in more detail. Each system generated a single result or NIL for each query. Each result has information such as business name, location, company size, and industry.

We then asked a group of raters at CareerBuilder to judge the correctness of the results. We showed each (query, result) pair in a random order to the rater, and asked the rater to choose from the following scoring options:

- 3 = Result name correct, location is headquarter.
- 2 = Result name correct, location is not headquarter.
- 1 = Result name acceptable although not perfect.
- 0 = Result name wrong.
- -1 = Query ambiguous (hard to understand the need).

Based on the above scoring options, we consider a result as a correct result if it gets score>=1.

6.1.2 Academic Institution Datasets

To understand the generalization ability of CompanyDepot, we apply it to a similar task of academic institution name normalization [11]. We used the same five datasets that are used in the previous work:

- 4icu-uk: a list of 145 popular universities and colleges in UK from the website of 4ICU [1].
- guardian: a list of 135 universities in UK from the website of TheGuardian [10].
- g1-6: randomly sampled 780 academic institution names that occurred 1-6 times in a resume database for UK.
- g7-39: randomly sampled 736 academic institution names that occurred 7-39 times in a resume database for UK.
- g40-max: randomly sampled 653 academic institution names that occurred 40 or more times in a resume database for UK.

.

6.2 Metrics

To evaluate the performance of different employer name normalization systems, we used the same precision and coverage metrics as used in [11, 24]. For a set of queries, suppose a normalization system returns I_c correct results, I_w wrong results, and I_n null results (i.e., NIL), then the following metrics are computed:

- Precision is the percentage of correct results out of all non-null results generated by the system.

$$Precision = I_c/(I_c + I_w)$$

- Coverage[7] is the percentage of queries that the system returns a non-null result.

$$Coverage = (I_c + I_w)/(I_c + I_w + I_n)$$

Besides the above two metrics, we also add the following two metrics that serve as a combination of precision and coverage to show the overall performance of the system:

$$SuccessRate = Precision * Coverage$$

$$F1 = 2 * Precision * Coverage/(Precision + Coverage)$$

The success rate of a system indicates how likely the system succeeds to generate a correct result, which is important for many applications at CareerBuilder.

6.3 Systems in Comparison

The following systems are compared in the experiments:

- **CompanyDepot-ML**: the machine learning based approach within CompanyDepot that is described in Section 5. For each dataset, we run a model trained on another dataset to generate its results, which are then evaluated as the performance on this dataset. Detailed assignment is shown in Table 5.
- **CompanyDepot-H**: the heuristic method within CompanyDepot that is described in Section 5.5.
- **Legacy**: a system used at CareerBuilder for employer name normalization. It is based on a mapping table which contains a large number of mappings from surface forms to their linked entities, generated via some black-box algorithms with manual corrections.
- **WService**: a third-party web service that supports employer name normalization, with two special characteristics: (1) It requires an employer name and a specified country to return any result; (2) It uses its

[7]Note that coverage here is not the same as recall, because the computation of recall requires that all the true answers of a query (which are very hard to obtain) are known, while the computation of coverage only checks whether a non-null result is returned by the system.

Train	Test
EDGE	RDB
RDB	EDGE
RDB	JOB1
RDB	JOB2

Table 5: Training and test datasets for CompanyDepot-ML.

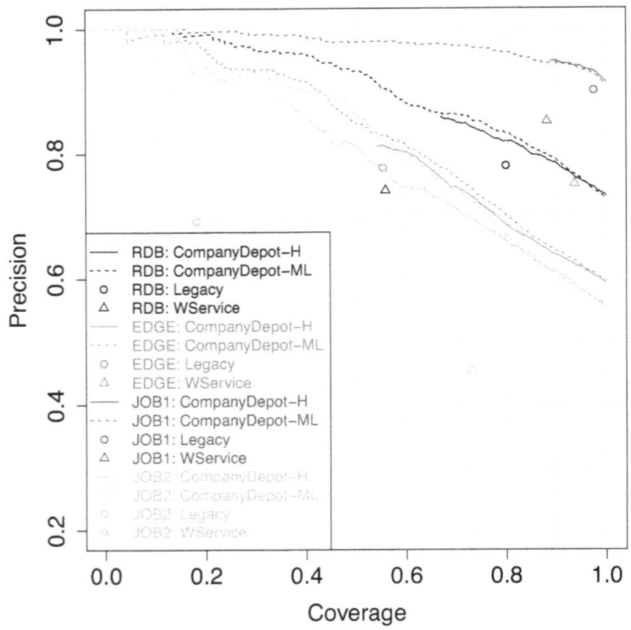

Figure 3: Performance comparison on the job and resume datasets.

own KB, which is a superset of the KB used by other systems, with a much better coverage of international employers.

- **sCooL** [11]: a system used at CareerBuilder for academic institution name normalization.

6.4 Results

6.4.1 Results on Job and Resume Datasets

We compared the results of four methods, CompanyDepot-ML, CompanyDepot-H, Legacy, and WService, on the job and resume datasets. For the two CompanyDepot methods (CompanyDepot-H and CompanyDepot-ML), the output contains a confidence score along with the result. By varying the threshold on the confidence score, we can plot a precision-coverage curve. For Legacy and WService, however, the confidence score is not available, so we can only derive a single precision and coverage value.

Figure 3 shows the precision-coverage values of the four methods. We can see that CompanyDepot-ML has the best performance over three datasets (RDB, JOB1, and JOB2), while WService performs best on the EDGE dataset. Moreover, CompanyDepot-ML achieves 2.5%, 14.2%, and 21.4% higher coverage at the same precision level compared to Legacy over JOB1, RDB, and EDGE respectively.

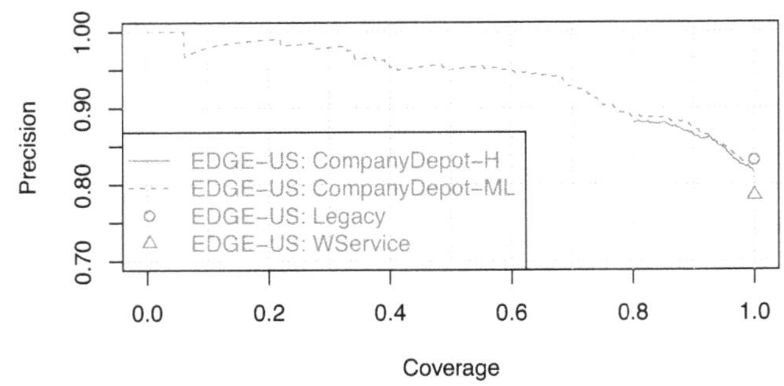

Figure 4: Performance comparison on the EDGE-US dataset (which contains all the US queries in the EDGE dataset).

As shown in Table 4, the EDGE dataset contains a larger percentage of international queries (smaller percentage of US queries, 45.3%) compared to the other datasets. Recall that compared to the KB used by WService, the KB used by CompanyDepot-ML, CompanyDepot-H, and Legacy has a rather poor coverage on international employers. This could be the main reason why these three systems have worse performance than WService on the EDGE dataset. To verify this conjecture, we derived a subset of EDGE called EDGE-US which contains only its US queries. On this subset, we observed that these three systems have better performance than WService, as shown in Figure 4.

The RDB dataset contains a larger percentage of queries with empty country information (smaller percentage of queries with country, 58.5%). Recall that WService requires a country parameter to return any result. This is why WService has a low coverage (55.9%) compared to other systems.

The JOB1 dataset contains the cleanest queries, all about US employers that proactively published job postings. Therefore, all the four systems show the best performance on this dataset compared to on other datasets.

In contrast, the JOB2 dataset contains a set of very hard queries. We can see that both Legacy and WService have very bad performance. Legacy has a low coverage (18%) because the dataset was sampled from the cases that Legacy failed to normalize at some time (which may have been corrected). WService has a low precision (46%), mostly because it puts too much weight on location match as we found many wrong results returned by WService have the same location as the query location (note that all the queries in this dataset have the state specified).

By comparing the two CompanyDepot methods closely, we can see that CompanyDepot-ML performs better on three datasets: RDB, EDGE, and JOB2. While CompanyDepot-H cannot achieve a precision of 90% on these three datasets, CompanyDepot-ML can achieve a 90% precision at a 40% or higher coverage. The main reason is that CompanyDepot-H mostly depends on a single feature while CompanyDepot-ML is able to use all the available features for entity ranking and validation. As shown in Section 5.5, the final score of CompanyDepot-H is the Jaccard similarity between the 4-gram sets of the compactly calibrated versions of the query name and the entity normalized form. However, even with perfect similarity (i.e., score=1), a result can be wrong. In contrast, CompanyDepot-ML can learn these situations based on many other features, e.g., the popularity of the en-

Dataset	Method	Cov	Pre	SR	F1
4icu-uk	sCooL	95.2	92.8	88.3	94.0
	CompanyDepot-H	100	96.6	**96.6**	**98.3**
guardian	sCooL	93.3	92.8	86.6	93.0
	CompanyDepot-H	100	91.8	**91.8**	**95.7**
s40-max	sCooL	99.1	91.7	90.9	95.3
	CompanyDepot-H	100	96.1	**96.1**	**98.0**
s7-39	sCooL	99.3	96.2	95.5	97.7
	CompanyDepot-H	100	97.5	**97.5**	**98.7**
s1-6	sCooL	97.7	94.0	91.8	95.8
	CompanyDepot-H	100	93.5	**93.5**	**96.6**

Table 6: Performance comparison on the academic institution datasets (Cov means coverage; Pre means precision; SR means success rate).

tity or whether a mapping from the query name to the entity exists in the mapping table. This shows that the machine learning based approach is quite promising. It is also easier to extend and improve, because more features can be easily added and automatically integrated, while the optimization of the heuristic approach depends on pure manual effort.

6.4.2 *Results on Academic Institution Datasets*

We compared the results of two systems, CompanyDepot-H and sCooL, on the academic institution datasets. The two systems used the same KB derived in [11] for normalization and the same classifier to detect K-12 schools. A new set of stop-words (e.g., "college", "university", "school") is used in CompanyDepot-H for calibration of academic institution names.

Table 6 shows the performance of these two systems. We can see that CompanyDepot-H achieves better success rate and F1 score over all the five datasets. Specifically, it achieves comparable or higher precisions at better coverages. Note that CompanyDepot-ML was not deployed here as our error analysis revealed that the main room to improve is the quality of the underlying KB.

6.4.3 *Effects of Feature Groups*

We would like to understand how each of the following feature groups contributes to the learning performance: (1) query features; (2) query-entity features; and (3) entity features. Figure 5 shows the performance of CompanyDepot-ML over the EDGE dataset based on different feature groups. We can see that the best performance is achieved using all feature groups, which shows that all the feature groups are contributing to the learning process. Considering a single feature group, query-entity features is the most effective one. Without this feature group, the performance is very bad. Next, we compare the effects of the query feature group and the entity feature group. We see that removing the group of entity features (green curve) from all feature groups leads to a higher decrease in performance than removing the group of query features (red curve). This indicates that the entity feature group is more effective than the query feature group for our task, especially considering the noisy KB which contains entities with varying degrees of quality.

6.5 Discussion

The job and resume datasets used in this paper were originally built for the purpose of creating benchmark datasets for comparing the performance of CompanyDepot-H, Legacy, and WService. For each query, we received up to three re-

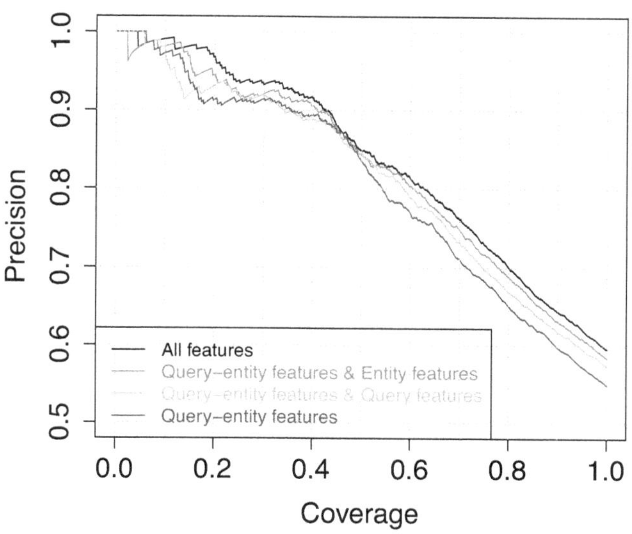

Figure 5: Effects of feature groups on performance of CompanyDepot-ML over the EDGE dataset.

sults in total, and collected manual judgments about them. With such limited labeled data, the correctness of many results returned by CompanyDepot-ML are unknown, which however were counted as wrong results in our evaluation. Although this setting brings limitations on the training and test data for CompanyDepot-ML, the experimental results still show that the machine learning based approach is quite promising. The performance numbers we computed for it are actually the lower bounds of the performance given better training and test data. While the machine learning based approach has advantages such as extendability and flexibility, the heuristic approach has its own advantage of being a strong baseline and eliciting ground-truth data for CompanyDepot-ML. Both the two methods have query response time within a second, showing the feasibility of applying the system to online employer name normalization.

7. CONCLUSION AND FUTURE WORK

In this paper, we proposed a novel employer name normalization task which takes an employer name and its associated location from job postings or resumes as input and normalizes it into entities in an employer KB. We then presented a system called CompanyDepot which contains a machine learning based approach CompanyDepot-ML and a heuristic approach CompanyDepot-H to address the task in three steps: entity retrieval, reranking, and validation. We compared its performance with existing employer name normalization systems used at CareerBuilder, applied it to a similar task of academic institution name normalization, and compared its performance with a state-of-the-art method. The experimental results over multiple real-world datasets showed the effectiveness, robustness, and generalization ability of our system.

In our future work, we plan to use more contextual information (e.g., employer address and website) if available. We also intend to develop more features to handle entity quality and query segmentation. Another branch of potential work is to improve the quality and coverage of the employer KB.

8. ACKNOWLEDGMENTS

We would like to thank Kyle Diemer for his help with building the benchmark datasets. We would also like to thank Yun Zhu for his helpful discussions about the project.

9. REFERENCES

[1] 4ICU. Top universities in the united kingdom. http://www.4icu.org/gb/. accessed 2014-01.

[2] K. Bollacker, C. Evans, P. Paritosh, T. Sturge, and J. Taylor. Freebase: A collaboratively created graph database for structuring human knowledge. In *Proceedings of the 2008 ACM SIGMOD International Conference on Management of Data*, SIGMOD '08, pages 1247–1250, New York, NY, USA, 2008. ACM.

[3] A. Borkovsky. Item name normalization, Apr. 29 2003. US Patent 6,556,991.

[4] R. Busa-Fekete, G. Szarvas, T. Éltető, and B. Kégl. An apple-to-apple comparison of learning-to-rank algorithms in terms of normalized discounted cumulative gain. In *B. Proceedings of ECAI-12 Workshop, Preference Learning: Problems and Applications in AI*, 2012.

[5] C.-C. Chang and C.-J. Lin. LIBSVM: A library for support vector machines. *ACM Transactions on Intelligent Systems and Technology*, 2:27:1–27:27, 2011. Software available at http://www.csie.ntu.edu.tw/~cjlin/libsvm.

[6] P. Christen. *Data Matching: Concepts and Techniques for Record Linkage, Entity Resolution, and Duplicate Detection*. Springer Publishing Company, Incorporated, 2012.

[7] B. Croft, D. Metzler, and T. Strohman. *Search Engines: Information Retrieval in Practice*. Addison-Wesley Publishing Company, USA, 2009.

[8] M. Dredze, P. McNamee, D. Rao, A. Gerber, and T. Finin. Entity disambiguation for knowledge base population. In *Proceedings of the 23rd International Conference on Computational Linguistics*, COLING '10, pages 277–285, 2010.

[9] P. S. Efraimidis and P. G. Spirakis. Weighted random sampling with a reservoir. *Inf. Process. Lett.*, 97(5):181–185, Mar. 2006.

[10] Guardian. Universities. http://www.theguardian.com/education/list/educationinstitution. accessed 2014-01.

[11] F. Jacob, F. Javed, M. Zhao, and M. Mcnair. sCooL: A system for academic institution name normalization. In *Collaboration Technologies and Systems (CTS), 2014 International Conference on*, pages 86–93, 2014.

[12] T. Joachims. Optimizing search engines using clickthrough data. In *Proceedings of the Eighth ACM SIGKDD International Conference on Knowledge Discovery and Data Mining*, KDD '02, pages 133–142, New York, NY, USA, 2002. ACM.

[13] S. Jonnalagadda and P. Topham. NEMO: Extraction and normalization of organization names from PubMed affiliation strings. *Journal of Biomedical Discovery and Collaboration*, 5:50, 2010.

[14] H. Kardes, D. Konidena, S. Agrawal, M. Huff, and A. Sun. Graph-based approaches for organization entity resolution in MapReduce. In *Proceedings of TextGraphs-8 Graph-based Methods for Natural Language Processing Workshop at EMNLP*, 2013.

[15] M. Kejriwal, Q. Liu, F. Jacob, and F. Javed. A pipeline for extracting and deduplicating domain-specific knowledge bases. In *Proceedings of 2015 IEEE International Conference on Big Data*, 2015.

[16] R. Leaman, R. I. Dogan, and Z. Lu. Dnorm: disease name normalization with pairwise learning to rank. *Bioinformatics*, 29(22):2909–2917, 2013.

[17] T.-Y. Liu. Learning to rank for information retrieval. *Found. Trends Inf. Retr.*, 3(3):225–331, Mar. 2009.

[18] W. Magdy, K. Darwish, O. Emam, and H. Hassan. Arabic cross-document person name normalization. In *Proceedings of the 2007 Workshop on Computational Approaches to Semitic Languages: Common Issues and Resources*, Semitic '07, pages 25–32, 2007.

[19] W. P. McNeill, H. Kardes, and A. Borthwick. Dynamic record blocking: Efficient linking of massive databases in mapreduce. In *Proceedings of 10th International Workshop on Quality in Databases (QDB) at VLDB*, 2012.

[20] D. Metzler and W. Bruce Croft. Linear feature-based models for information retrieval. *Inf. Retr.*, 10(3):257–274, June 2007.

[21] L. Ratinov, D. Roth, D. Downey, and M. Anderson. Local and global algorithms for disambiguation to wikipedia. In *Proceedings of the 49th Annual Meeting of the Association for Computational Linguistics: Human Language Technologies - Volume 1*, HLT '11, pages 1375–1384, 2011.

[22] W. Shen, J. Wang, and J. Han. Entity linking with a knowledge base: Issues, techniques, and solutions. *IEEE Trans. Knowl. Data Eng.*, 27(2):443–460, 2015.

[23] J. Wermter, K. Tomanek, and U. Hahn. High-performance gene name normalization with GENO. *Bioinformatics*, 25(6):815–821, 2009.

[24] B. Yan, L. Bajaj, and A. Bhasin. Entity resolution using social graphs for business applications. In *International Conference on Advances in Social Networks Analysis and Mining, ASONAM 2011*, pages 220–227, 2011.

[25] W. Zhang, Y. C. Sim, J. Su, and C. L. Tan. Entity linking with effective acronym expansion, instance selection and topic modeling. In *Proceedings of the Twenty-Second International Joint Conference on Artificial Intelligence - Volume Volume Three*, IJCAI'11, pages 1909–1914. AAAI Press, 2011.

[26] W. Zhang, J. Su, C. L. Tan, and W. T. Wang. Entity linking leveraging: Automatically generated annotation. In *Proceedings of the 23rd International Conference on Computational Linguistics*, COLING '10, pages 1290–1298, 2010.

[27] W. Zhang, C. L. Tan, Y. C. Sim, and J. Su. NUS-I2R: learning a combined system for entity linking. In *Proceedings of the Third Text Analysis Conference, TAC 2010*, 2010.

[28] Z. Zheng, F. Li, M. Huang, and X. Zhu. Learning to link entities with knowledge base. In *Human Language Technologies: The 2010 Annual Conference of the North American Chapter of the Association for Computational Linguistics*, HLT '10, pages 483–491, 2010.

Understanding Behaviors that Lead to Purchasing: A Case Study of Pinterest

Caroline Lo*
Stanford University
clo@cs.stanford.edu

Dan Frankowski
Pinterest
dan@pinterest.com

Jure Leskovec
Pinterest & Stanford University
jure@cs.stanford.edu

ABSTRACT

Online e-commerce applications are becoming a primary vehicle for people to find, compare, and ultimately purchase products. One of the fundamental questions that arises in e-commerce is to characterize, understand, and model user long-term purchasing intent, which is important as it allows for personalized and context relevant e-commerce services.

In this paper we study user activity and purchasing behavior with the goal of building models of time-varying user purchasing intent. We analyze the purchasing behavior of nearly three million Pinterest users to determine short-term and long-term signals in user behavior that indicate higher purchase intent. We find that users with long-term purchasing intent tend to save and clickthrough on more content. However, as users approach the time of purchase their activity becomes more topically focused and actions shift from saves to searches. We further find that purchase signals in online behavior can exist weeks before a purchase is made and can also be traced across different purchase categories. Finally, we synthesize these insights in predictive models of user purchasing intent. Taken together, our work identifies a set of general principles and signals that can be used to model user purchasing intent across many content discovery applications.

1. INTRODUCTION

E-commerce has drastically changed traditional buyer-seller relationships, as well as the shopping process for many consumers [4]; today, consumers are able to browse and compare endless product catalogs, create wishlists, and enjoy powerful features such as search, personalization, and the benefits of social networks [5, 12, 21, 26]. As the complexity of online shopping behaviors has increased, it has become increasingly important to understand and characterize consumer online purchasing behavior. In particular, it is essential to understand how user activity might build up over time into purchase intent, and ultimately, a purchase. Here, purchase intent is defined as a predictive measure, at a given time, of subsequent purchasing behavior [23].

*Research partly done while at Pinterest.

KDD '16, August 13 - 17, 2016, San Francisco, CA, USA

ISBN 978-1-4503-4232-2/16/08...$15.00

DOI: http://dx.doi.org/10.1145/2939672.2939729

Understanding online purchase intent and its buildup over time is important because individuals spend large amounts of time and resources on online shopping—in the U.S. alone, e-commerce sales have reached over 350 billion USD per year and are expected to grow at around 15% annually [8]. Modeling and recognizing purchase intent is vital for providing better services, more usable e-commerce platforms, and improved personalization in content and search result rankings, as well as advertising.

However, there are several challenges in studying the purchase intent of online users. Generally, most prior work has examined short-term user activity and considered predicting whether a given user session will result in a purchase [18, 22, 29, 30, 32]. But the purchase intent of a consumer may slowly build up over time, and may not instantaneously lead to a purchase. Furthermore, traditional studies often examine user behavior on a single e-commerce platform, while users may use several different services and move across e-commerce platforms when deciding which product to purchase and where. Thus, what is missing from the picture is a cross-platform analysis of how user purchase intent varies over time. To this end, it is important to contrast the population of purchasing users with the population of non-purchasing users, and then also identify how purchasers' online behavior changes over time from the norm as a result of impending purchases.

Present work: Understanding cross-platform purchasing behavior. Here we perform a large-scale cross-platform longitudinal study of user purchase intent and how it builds and varies over time. We adopt the definition of purchase intent as a predictive measure of subsequent purchasing behavior [23] and estimate it by tracking anonymized user activity on a content discovery application. We identify four general classes of actions that users on content discovery applications engage in: closing-up on a piece of content, clicking through a link to an external website, searching for content, and saving content for later retrieval. We then analyze how engagement in these actions predicts users' future purchasing activity on a number of e-commerce platforms.

In particular, we study how the usage of Pinterest [17], a content discovery application, relates with future user shopping behavior. On Pinterest, users engage with visual bookmarks, called pins, which can be saved into collections of pins, called boards. In order for users to discover pins to save to boards, users can search, closeup, and clickthrough on pins. We analyze the detailed activity traces of over two million Pinterest users over a one month time period and partner with external e-commerce sites in order to identify how Pinterest usage activity related to the future purchasing activity of those users.

We discover general cross-platform signals which characterize how purchase intent builds over time. While we created the dataset such that the number of active days in our observation period of purchasers and non-purchasers is the same, we surprisingly found that the total number of raw actions is slightly smaller for purchasers. In fact, we find that a trivial hypothesis that purchasers are simply more engaged users is not true, and our analyses reveal a much richer picture about the behavioral differences between the two populations. In particular, we find that purchasers engage in more high-effort actions. For example, purchasers tend to clickthrough on on-site content to visit external websites about 25% more, and engage in about 5% more saving behavior. On the other hand, purchasers tend to engage in about 5% fewer search and content closeup actions.

Users on Pinterest engage with a broad and diverse set of content, such as food and drinks, fashion, travel, gadgets, arts and crafts, as well as decorations and interior design. From analyzing the content users engage with, we find that users with purchase intent tend to disproportionately focus on content related to their purchase. In particular, we find a strong correlation between content engagement and purchasing behavior for content related to weddings, kids, travel, holidays, events, and health & fitness.

Importantly, in general we find that signals for purchase intent tend to slowly build up over time, and sharply increases about 3 to 5 days before a purchase. For example, we observe that about three days before the purchase, users with purchase intent start being more active. At that time we also observe that the number of searches and clickthrough actions to external websites sharply increases at the expense of browsing and content saving. Likewise, the focus on purchase content is frequently amplified about three days before the purchase, and on the day of purchase, users are on average nearly twice as likely to engage in commercial content (i.e., pins that are related to buyable products) of the same type as the category of the product they eventually buy.

To understand the dynamics of purchase intent over time and how it builds up, we formulate a prediction task aiming to detect whether a given user is going to make a purchase online k days or hours in the future. We find that purchasers can be identified with medium accuracy as early as 28-days before their purchase date. Again, we find that about three days before the purchase, users with purchase intent are easier to identify, with the last day being the easiest. By increasing the temporal resolution to hours, we find that behavioral characteristics of purchasers get very specific about three hours before the purchase and that such users can be relatively reliably identified. We further examine whether not just the purchase intent but also the category of purchase can be reliably modeled. Here we find that purchasers in weddings, home and decor, holidays, events, and cosmetics are easiest to identify.

Taken together, our study provides one of the first windows into how usage patterns on content discovery applications relates to user long-term purchasing behavior on external e-commerce platforms, and how user purchase intent builds up. In general, our work has many practical applications in that the identification of users with purchase intent can be used to improve personalization, search, and content ranking efforts. Applications can also focus on promoting commercial content (e.g., buyable pins, or pins from which a direct purchase can be made on Pinterest) towards the users who would be interested, i.e., users with identified purchase intent.

2. RELATED WORK

Research on the purchasing behavior of online shoppers has a long tradition and dates back to the early days of e-commerce on the Web [4, 24]. Studies have investigated how motivations, privacy/security considerations, as well as demographic factors, such as gender and age, determine online shopping behavior [5, 9, 10, 14, 16, 19, 26, 27, 28, 31, 33]. Our work here adds to this line of work by performing a longitudinal analysis of how long-term as well as short-term usage patterns of a content discovery application differ between populations of purchasers and non-purchasers.

Another line of related work focuses on using machine learning methods to predict purchasing behavior. Prior work has considered predicting the purchase propensity of a given user for a given product in a given time window [18, 22] as well as predicting whether or not a purchase will be made during the next visit to the website [32]. In terms of features used for making such predictions, prior research has investigated user demographics and interests [34], user purchase patterns [18], product characteristics [5], as well as detailed navigational click-stream and web search data [22, 29, 30, 32]. Purchasing intent has been especially well studied in the context of search engines in order to identify user search goals [1, 6, 11, 20, 25]. There are many similarities as well as differences with our work here. While the above studies often focus on short-term user behavior on a website and try to predict a user's purchasing intent on that same website, our work here is different. We observe a user's actions and activity on one application, and then aim to correlate behavior on that application with the user's purchasing behavior on different, external websites. Also, our goal here is broader as we aim to understand how the use of content discovery applications relates to shopping behavior. In particular, we are not interested in just predicting whether a given usage session will result in a purchase, but rather aim to characterize how the overall behavior and usage of a content discovery application differs for online purchasers and how purchase intent builds up over time.

More recently, social media has opened a new avenue for research on the behaviors of online purchasers and several interesting problems have been studied. Works have focused on modeling correlations between users' social media profiles and their e-commerce behaviors [35] as well as understanding the linguistic relationships between users' purchasing intent and their social media posts [3, 7, 13, 15]. Another interesting aspect is the role of social networks in online shopping in terms of user-to-user communication [12] as well as the diffusion of product adoption in social networks [2, 21]. Our work adds to this line of work by performing a large-scale longitudinal study of the dynamics of user purchase intent across a number of e-commerce sites. In contrast to previous work, our user activity data is resolved down to single actions and we not only observe user posting behavior but also clicking, searching, and browsing. Taken together, our work identifies a set of general principles and signals that can be used for modeling user purchasing intent across many social media and content discovery applications.

3. DATASET DESCRIPTION

Our analysis focuses on the behavior of users on Pinterest, a content discovery application founded in 2010. While the concept of boards and pins is unique to Pinterest, many of the actions surrounding these concepts are analogous to actions that can be taken by different content discovery applications, making our subsequent findings generalizable.

3.1 Mechanics of a Content Discovery Application

We characterize four broad classes of actions that users in many content discovery applications take. Example content discovery applications include YouTube and Instagram, and even traditional social networking applications such as Facebook and Twitter have features that allow them to be considered as content discovery applications. Here we use Pinterest as a concrete instance in our analysis.

On Pinterest, specifically, users can browse, zoom-in on, and save/bookmark images—referred to as pins. These pins can be collected into boards, which are then shared with other users of the service. The four classes of actions are as follows:

- **Search**: Nearly every content discovery application possesses search functionality that allows users to *discover* previously unseen content. For example, users can search YouTube for videos, and Twitter for tweets and other users. On Pinterest, users may enter search queries (e.g., "christmas ornaments"), and pins that are related to the search query are subsequently displayed.
- **Closeup**: Applications allow users to engage *on-site* with specific content to reveal more information; we call this action a closeup. For example, on Facebook, Twitter, and Instagram, users can closeup on a post to receive detailed information. On Pinterest, users may choose to closeup on a pin so that a higher resolution image with text information is displayed.
- **Clickthrough**: Content discovery applications also allow users to engage *off-site* with content; we call such actions clickthroughs. For example, on Facebook and Twitter, this translates to clicking on a link to an external news article, and on Pinterest, users can click on links to external sites such as recipe blogs or e-commerce sites.
- **Save**: Many content discovery applications allow users to bookmark or save content for later retrieval and viewing. For example, YouTube allows users to organize and save videos into playlists, and Twitter allows users to create curated lists of other Twitter users. On Pinterest, users save pins by collecting them in boards.

3.2 Pinterest Dataset Preparation

Our dataset focuses on the anonymized activity and purchase data of Pinterest users in the United States in May of 2015. Users who make online purchases on one of Pinterest's external partner companies (*e.g.*, wedding invitation and footwear retailers) are referred to as *purchasers*. These purchasers buy items that span across a broad spectrum of categories, ranging from fashion to sports.

Statistic	Value
Number of purchasers	1.3M
Number of non-purchasers	1.3M
Number of users (total)	2.6M
Number of actions (total)	0.5B
Time duration	28 days
Month when purchases were made	May 2015

Table 1: Dataset statistics.

Purchasers and non-purchasers. Our sample dataset includes 1.3M unique users who purchased one or more items from partner companies in the month of May 2015. Each of these users was active on Pinterest at some point in the 28 days prior to a purchase (Table 1).

We find that the number of purchases made per user follows a heavy-tailed distribution with exponent 1.5 (Figure 1(a)). Less than 40% of users make more than one purchase in our observation period, and for these users we only consider a single randomly sampled purchase. We refer to the day on which this purchase takes place as the *purchase date*.

In subsequent analyses we compare the population of purchasers with the population of non-purchasers. For the purpose of this analysis we define *non-purchasers* to be users who do not purchase anything from one of Pinterest's partner companies in the month of May 2015. (Note, however, that these users may have made purchases outside our observation window or while logged out of Pinterest.)

In general, we find that purchasers log on to Pinterest more frequently than non-purchasers. In order to conduct a more nuanced analysis that observes beyond such zero-order effects, we carefully match each purchaser with a non-purchaser by controlling for three potentially confounding factors: (1) registration month, to minimize sign-up cohort effects; (2) the number of days active 28 days prior to a purchase, so that similar long-term activity levels are maintained, and (3) gender, to minimize unrelated population-based effects, which we also minimize by considering only U.S.-based users. The benefit of matching is that we now have a paired and aligned population, which means that we can compare the dynamics of activity between each purchaser and her matched non-purchaser over time.

Time span. We refer to the 24 hour period of time prior to a purchase as day 0. Our analysis of user behavior spans the 28 day time period prior to purchase. In our analysis, N days prior to day 0 is referred to as day $-N$; thus, our analysis spans from day -27 to day 0.

3.3 User Activity Characteristics

To better understand user activity on Pinterest and how it varies in aggregate between purchasers and non-purchasers, we conduct an initial analysis of overall user activity.

We first examine overall activity levels by computing the number of days purchasers and non-purchasers are active within our 28-day dataset. A CCDF plot is shown in Figure 1(b). Cumulative density is practically identical between purchasers and non-purchasers, validating our matching process (as number of days active was used as a criteria for matching). More importantly, we observe that users in our dataset are, on the whole, regularly active. In fact, 50% of users are active at least 7 out of 28 days (i.e., approximately

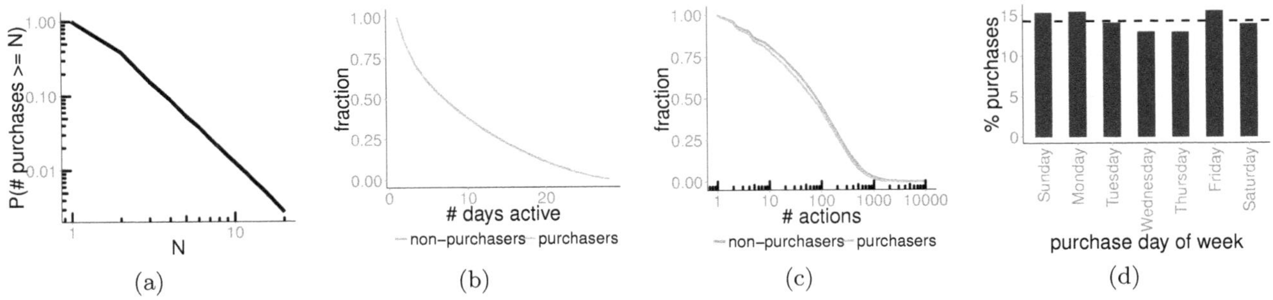

Figure 1: (a) CCDF of number of purchases made by purchasers in May 2015, capped at 20 purchases. (b) CCDF of number of days purchasers and non-purchasers are active in our analysis. Note that lines are identical. (c) CCDF of number of actions taken by purchasers and non-purchasers, capped at 10^4 actions. (d) Percentage of purchases made on any given day of the week.

every four days), and 25% are active 14 out of 28 days, i.e., approximately every other day.

Interestingly, we also notice that non-purchasers take slightly more actions than purchasers in aggregate (Figure 1(c)). Here, we define an action to be one of the four identified actions described in Sec. 3.1: search, closeup, clickthrough, or save. We also find that the amount of saved content, expressed as the number of saved boards and pins, is virtually identical between purchasers and non-purchasers (plots not shown for brevity). These observations are particularly interesting as they invalidate a trivial hypothesis that purchasers tend to be more engaged users. Moreover, these observations motivate our work because they suggest that on the surface purchasers seem to be no different from non-purchasers. In what follows, we develop a methodology that allows us to reveal a richer and more fine-grained picture about behavioral differences between the two populations.

4. DYNAMICS OF PURCHASE INTENT

Motivated by our observations, we now aim to develop a deeper understanding of how user purchase intent evolves over time, *i.e.*, how it builds up and ultimately results in an online purchase. Specifically, we examine user activity levels, types of actions taken, and content users interact with.

4.1 User Activity Level

In Section 3.3 we saw that in aggregate, purchasers are no more active than non-purchasers. However, we would expect that behavioral differences in activity emerge as the time of purchase approaches.

In order to see if such differences exist, we first note that seasonal cycles impact user online activity. To prevent such global changes from impacting our analysis, we compute the relative activity level of purchasers when compared to non-purchasers. We call this metric the *activity ratio* (AR) for each day d:

$$AR(d) = \frac{\text{\% purchasers active on day } d}{\text{\% non-purchasers active on day } d}. \quad (1)$$

Users are considered active on a certain day if they took at least one action on Pinterest on that day.

Figure 2(a) shows the activity ratio in the 28 days before purchase. Recall that we match purchasers with non-purchasers based on the number of days active in the 28 days before a purchase is made. If the intent to purchase did not impact user activity, we should see comparable levels of activity between purchasers and non-purchasers throughout the entire time duration analyzed, i.e., the activity ratio should remain at approximately 1 throughout the entire time span. However, we instead observe interesting phenomena. First, we note that purchaser activity follows a weekly cycle, peaking on the purchase date's day of week, meaning that purchasers are more likely to be on Pinterest on the day of week in which a purchase takes place. Figure 1(d) shows that while there is some variation, overall, purchases take place at every day of the week. In contrast, non-purchaser activity peaks only on weekend days, explaining the cyclic nature of the figure.

Second, we observe a slow but significant buildup of user activity. In fact, we notice a sharp increase in activity levels

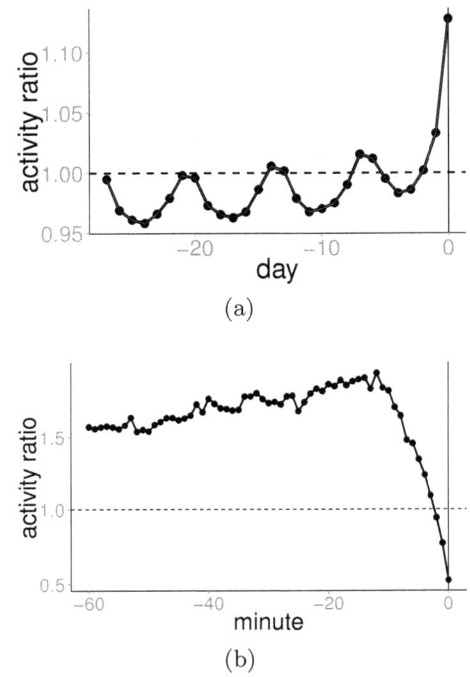

Figure 2: (a) Activity ratio of purchasers over time by day. Dashed line indicates comparable activity levels between purchasers and non-purchasers. (b) Activity ratio computed by minute.

in the three days right before a purchase—in particular, on the day of purchase, the activity ratio is 1.2, meaning that on that day, purchasers are 20% more likely to be active on Pinterest. The phenomenon of signals for purchase intent increasing sharply 3-5 days before a purchase is one that we observe multiple times throughout our analysis.

The fact that purchasers are more active on Pinterest closer to the purchase date remains true even when we closely zoom in to the period of time right before a purchase. To confirm this, we examine the ratio of users active on the site minutes before a purchase is made (Figure 2(b)). Here we compute activity ratio, where we compare the number of purchasers and non-purchasers active on a given *minute* as opposed to a day. We observe that purchasers are increasingly likely (nearly 2 times as likely) to visit Pinterest as the purchase time approaches, with a sharp but natural dropoff to account for time spent on the e-commerce site when actually making the purchase.

From our analysis of purchaser activity levels over time, we can conclude that in aggregate, purchasing intent can be reflected via a user's activity on a content discovery application. In short, as purchase intent increases and manifests itself as a purchase, purchasers are more likely to be active on a relevant content discovery application. This observation, however, raises the question: How exactly might a purchaser's specific behavior on the application change as a result of increasing purchase intent?

4.2 Types of User Actions

On many online applications, users can take different actions, which represent varying levels of effort. We would expect that the distribution over actions that purchasers take changes as the purchase time approaches.

We consider the four types of actions that users can take on social applications, as discussed in Section 3.1: search, closeup, clickthrough, and save. Note that on Pinterest, all these actions are taken by users intentionally, as opposed to passive actions such as viewing a pin that is recommended on a user's home page. Among these four types of actions, searching and clickthroughing are typically used to browse and examine content. Both clickthroughing and saving are considered actions that suggest higher levels of engagement in specific content.

To determine the extent to which each user prioritizes each type of action, we compute an *action score* (AS) for each user u, day d, and action type a, defined as follows:

$$AS(u,d,a) = \frac{\#\text{ actions } u \text{ took on day } d \text{ of type } a}{\#\text{ actions } u \text{ took overall on day } d}. \quad (2)$$

For each action type a, we can then compare the action scores of purchasers and non-purchasers for each day d by computing an *action score ratio* (ASR):

$$ASR(d,a) = \frac{avg_{u \in \text{purchasers}} AS(u,d,a)}{avg_{u \in \text{non-purchasers}} AS(u,d,a)}. \quad (3)$$

Long-term behavior. Figure 3 plots the action score ratio for each action type over time (with day 0 being the day of purchase). As with our earlier analyses, if purchasers used Pinterest in the same manner as non-purchasers, one would expect the ASR to remain at approximately 1 at all times, for all action types. However, again we see that this is not the case; throughout the entire time period, purchasers have a higher save and clickthrough ASR, and a lower closeup and search ASR. As saves and clickthroughs are actions that suggest higher engagement with specific content, we conclude that purchasers are as a whole more focused on specific content, rather than casually interacting with many different types of content. We next take note of the substantially higher overall clickthrough ASR (1.25 average), when compared with the save ASR (1.06 average), which suggests that examining content is a stronger potential signal of long-term purchase intent than saving content.

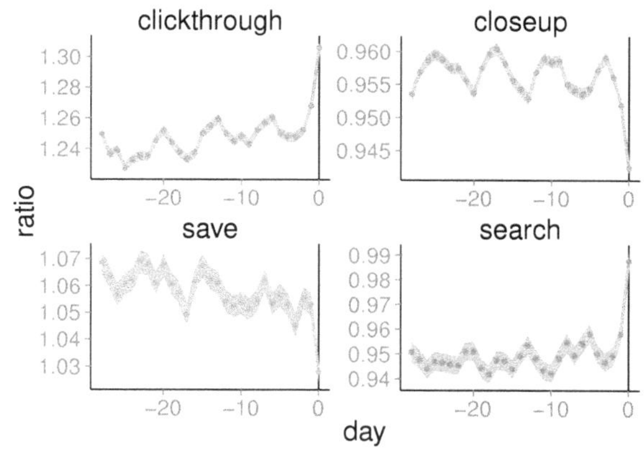

Figure 3: Action score ratios for each day. Shaded area represents standard error.

Lastly, we observe that the actions that purchasers take relative to non-purchasers change over time. Clickthrough ASR, for example, increases noticeably from 1.26 to 1.30 in the three days right before purchase and peaks on the purchase date itself. In contrast, in the 28 days prior to purchase date, the clickthrough action scores of non-purhasers remain relatively constant (plot not shown). We observe similar behavior for searches, while the amount of save and closeup actions drops in the last three days before the purchase. Over 28 days, search action ratios increase and save action ratios decrease very slightly for all users, but the corresponding increase and decrease among searches and saves for purchasers in the three days before purchase is much more prominent, which results in the trends observed in Figure 3.

We find it especially intriguing that many of the temporal changes in ASR occur surrounding the purchase date. In fact, the spikes in ASR on the date of purchase suggest that purchaser behavior does change right before a purchase.

Short-term behavior. To further examine temporal trends in behavior, we next focus on just the 24 hours before the purchase. Figure 4 plots the ASR per hour for this time frame. Here we immediately observe that the spikes in clickthrough and search ASR seen on day 0 (Figure 3) spike even more sharply as the purchaser approaches the hour of purchase (Figure 4). For example, the likelihood that purchasers will engage in clickthrough actions increases from 30% at the start of the day to 50% at the time of purchase. We furthermore observe an interesting unimodal pattern for closeups, where the ASR peaks within 8 to 15 hours before purchase.

Most interesting is the fact that for several hours before a purchase, purchasers are *more* likely to conduct search actions. In the majority of our analysis we found that differences between purchaser and non-purchaser behavior are

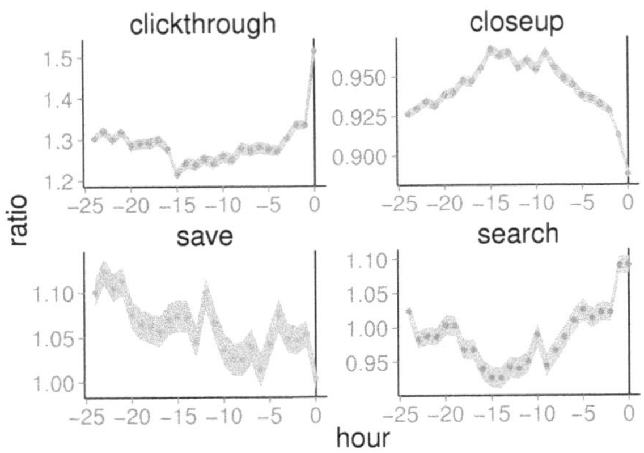

Figure 4: Action score ratios for the hours before a purchase. Shaded area represents standard error.

amplified towards the date of purchase, but in this case, recall from Figure 3 that purchasers are actually *less* likely to search for content in the long-term. This shows that searching is most likely to provide direct utility for purchasers in the short term.

From our analysis of different action types taken by users on Pinterest, we conclude that there exist two overarching characteristics in the behavior of purchasers. First is an increased investment in specific content over a lengthy period of time. Second is a sharp increase in searching for and browsing through content on the purchase date relative to the purchasers' behavior on other days. Put together, we can conclude that purchasers seek out content over time in a more frequent and more focused manner than their non-purchaser counterparts.

4.3 Content Users Interact With

Our above conclusions motivate our next question: What types of content do purchasers seek out over time, and how might this reflect upon their purchase intent? We aim to examine whether purchasers are more likely to focus on content relating to their future purchases.

On Pinterest, specifically, all content falls under one of 32 predetermined high-level categories, ranging from "Women's fashion" to "Travel" to "Weddings". Using these high-level categories, we can characterize the topicality of pins users engage with. Similarly, by examining the category of pins that are owned by Pinterest's partner companies, we also assign a category to each partner company by finding the most common category of the pins owned by the partner company. We find that all partner companies fall within 10 high-level categories.

For each purchaser, we then compare her level of interaction in her purchase category with the average non-purchaser's level of interaction in that category. Specifically, let

$$I(u,d,c) = \frac{\text{\# actions } u \text{ takes in category } c \text{ on day } d}{\text{\# actions taken in total on day } d}. \quad (4)$$

$I(u,d,c)$ (*category interaction score*) is the fraction of actions taken by a user u on day d that fall under some category c. Here, we define an action to be a closeup, save, or clickthrough, all of which are actions that involve interacting with a single pin. We define an action to be taken in a certain category c if the pin interacted with belongs to that

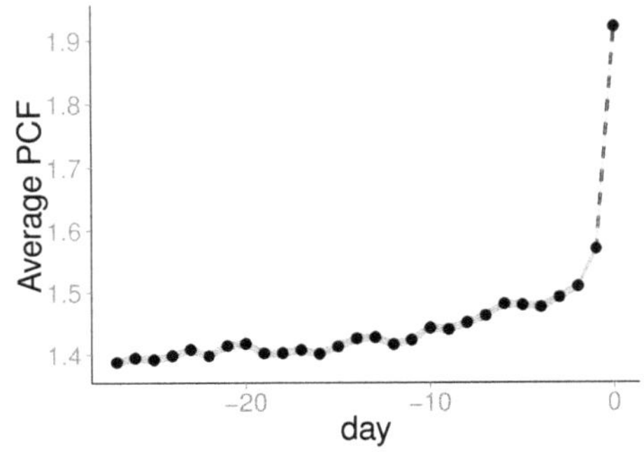

Figure 5: Average purchase category focus (PCF) score for purchasers active on Pinterest, by day. Shaded area represents standard error.

category. We can define for each purchaser p, category c, and day d the *purchase category focus* (PCF) score:

$$PCF(p,d,c) = \frac{I(p,d,c)}{avg_{u \in non-purchasers} I(u,d,c)}. \quad (5)$$

The PCF score directly evaluates the relative amount of interaction a purchaser devotes to her purchase category as compared to a baseline user. If purchasers were not more focused on their purchase category than the average user, one would expect the average PCF over time to be 1.

Figure 5 plots the average PCF for the 28 days prior to purchase. We make several observations. First, the average PCF remains noticeably above the baseline of 1 for the entire time duration. In other words, purchasers are already predisposed to interacting with content in their purchase category, well before a purchase is made. We also observe a steady rise in the PCF throughout the entire 4 week period, in which the PCF increases from 1.4 to 1.5. Most interestingly, we observe a sharp increase in the last three days before the purchase. Overall, PCF provides a reliable signal for growing user purchase intent, both as a long-term signal as well as a useful short-term signal.

Per-category PCF. Thus far we only examined the interaction of all purchasers with their purchase category, in aggregate. Thus, a natural follow-up question is: How does the purchase category focus (PCF) differ between categories? In particular, we are interested in understanding how much more engaged are purchasers in specific categories.

To answer this question, we compute the average PCF for purchasers, split by purchase category (Figure 6). We observe that for the vast majority of categories, the average PCF remains above 1, which means that purchasers are generally more focused on their purchase category.

We next observe that overall PCF levels vary widely between different categories. Purchasers in specialized categories, such as "Holidays & Events" and "Weddings" have a higher overall PCF, whereas broader categories with more general appeal, such as "Food & Drink" and "Women's Fashion" have lower overall PCF scores. The PCF score can therefore be considered comparatively as a measure of how much general appeal (to purchasers and non-purchasers alike) a category may have; higher PCF scores overall mean that those who interact with that category may be that much more inclined to make a purchase.

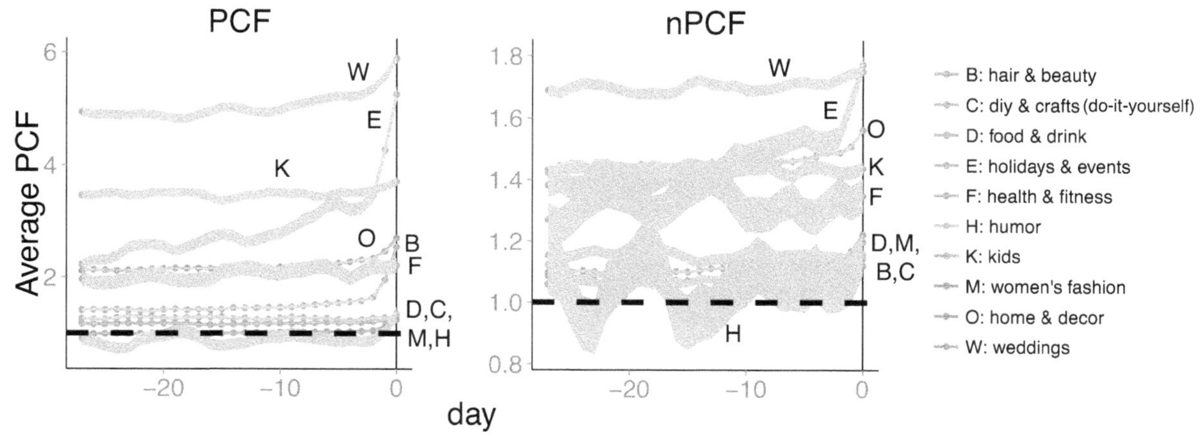

Figure 6: Left: Average purchase category focus (PCF) scores for purchasers in each purchase category. Right: Average normalized purchase category focus (nPCF) scores for purchasers in each purchase category. Shaded area represents standard error.

Furthermore, we also observe that while many categories experience a spike in PCF right before the purchase date, this behavior differs across category. "Holidays & Events" and "Hair & Beauty", for example, experience a more dramatic spike, whereas "DIY Crafts" barely experiences a spike at all. One explanation is that there may exist a correlation between the size of a spike in PCF on the purchase date and the tendency for users to make an impulse or sudden purchase in that category. For example, one may decide, after browsing for a short while on Pinterest, to purchase a Christmas card or a hair curler on a whim, but because DIY projects can span a lengthy period of time and may require pre-planning, it is less likely that a brief online browsing session will be sufficient to determine what to purchase.

While PCF is a good measure to gauge a purchaser's focus on her purchase category in comparison with the global population, an important question remains unanswered: What happens when we compare how interested a purchaser is in her purchase category with users on Pinterest who we already know are interested in that category? To compare these two types of users, we introduce the *interest-normalized purchase category focus* (nPCF) score:

$$nPCF(p,d,c) = \frac{I(p,d,c)}{avg_{u \in interested\_np} I(u,d,c)}, \qquad (6)$$

where *interested_np* is the set of non-purchasers who interacted with category c on Pinterest on day d. In essence, $nPCF$ allows us to determine whether interested purchasers might be even more interested in their purchase category than interested non-purchasers.

Figure 6 plots the nPCF over time. Here, an nPCF score of 1 would indicate that interested purchasers are approximately as focused on their purchase category as non-purchasers interested in that purchase category are. Surprisingly, we see that across the board, even within only the population of users who are already interested in their purchase category, purchasers are even more focused on their purchase category than average. They are in fact extra dedicated to their purchase category, which further highlights the potential effectiveness of targeted advertising efforts.

In summary, our analysis here shows that 1) users with purchase intent focus on content related to their purchase, and increasingly so as the purchase date approaches, and that 2) the extent to which purchase intent is expressed varies by category.

5. MODELING PURCHASE INTENT

Our analysis thus far points to noticeable differences in the online behavior of purchasers, which grow slowly over weeks and are amplified in the days right before a purchase. To better understand the dynamics of how purchase intent grows over time, we build on the insights and signals developed in Section 4 to formulate the following general prediction task: Can we identify purchasers based on their behavior k days before purchase?

Here, we are interested in seeing how predictive performance might change over time, or by category, to reflect purchase intent. If purchasers are easy to identify (predictive performance is high) then their behavior is very different from users with no purchasing intent. Similarly, if purchasers are hard to identify (low predictive performance), then their purchasing intent is also low since the activity patterns closely match those of non-purchasers.

Features used for learning. Based on our insights from Sections 3 and 4 we identify five general classes of features that can be extracted in any content discovery application, including Pinterest. Note that here, none of the computed features rely on prior knowledge of whether a user is a purchaser, and can be computed on an individual basis.

- **Demographics (4 features)**: Demographic information used most frequently in computational advertising. It forms a useful baseline because it contains static, infrequently changing information. We include gender and geographic region as well as long-term user profile information, namely the number of boards and pins created by a user to date (Sec. 3).
- **Activity (2 features)**: In Sec. 4.1 we observed that activity levels of purchasers change as the purchase date approaches. We formalize this as two features: the number of days active in the previous 7 days and the number of actions taken in a day.

- **Action-type (2 features)**: We also observed that a user's mix of actions changes are the purchase date approaches (Sec. 4.2). We capture this via each user's action ratio across each of the four action types, as well as platform usage information (*e.g.*, mobile, desktop).
- **Content (2 features)**: Sec. 4.3 showed that purchase intent is revealed through the type of content users interact with. We capture this signal by computing category interaction scores as seen in Eq. (4). We do not include PCF scores, as they indicate knowledge of a purchase category. We instead include category interaction scores, normalized by a user's activity level, from a set of approximately 500 LDA-trained topics, which Pinterest uses internally as sub-categories.
- **Temporal (3 features)**: Throughout Sec. 4 we observed consistent temporal dynamics where purchase intent can build slowly over time. Thus, we include temporal features based on Action-type and Content features, which compare each user's feature values at a given time with earlier feature values. Specifically, we compare feature values with the values 3 days prior. We also compare feature values between the last two quarters of a day. Finally, we compare the current day's feature values with the feature values from the entire week prior.

5.1 Modeling Purchasing Intent Over Time

We first aim to understand how well we can identify purchasers as their day of purchase approaches. Our goal is to use changes in classification performance by day to understand changes in user purchasing intent.

We proceed as follows. We train multiple classifiers, one for each day before a purchase. For each day k, we sample 250K purchasers and 250K non-purchasers who were active on Pinterest on that day and our goal is to determine whether a given user is a purchaser (that is, whether the user will engage in e-commerce activity k days in the future). Note that user populations may differ between classifiers, because different subsets of users are active on different days. For each of the 28 days in our analysis we train a separate logistic regression classifier and report the 10-fold cross validated AUC ROC score. A random baseline has a score of 0.50 under this setup.

Figure 7 plots the results over time. We immediately observe that throughout the entire analysis duration, the ROC AUC remains above the random baseline, ranging from approximately 0.62 to 0.66. These results confirm that there exist long-term differences in the online behavior of purchasers, and that these differences provide a non-random signal in identifying them weeks before the purchase. We also note a sharp increase in classification performance in the 3 days preceding the purchase, which parallels the way signals of purchase intent (e.g., activity of purchasers) also pick up in the last three days, as shown in Section 4. As with Figure 4.1, we also observe weekly patterns in our results. Overall, our results suggest that purchase intent slowly builds up over time and significantly increases in the last three days right before purchase.

Next, we focus on user purchase intent dynamics in the 12 hours right before purchase. Our aim is to better understand the extent to which purchaser behavior deviates right before a purchase is made. Here we predict whether a user active in a given hour prior to purchase is a purchaser.

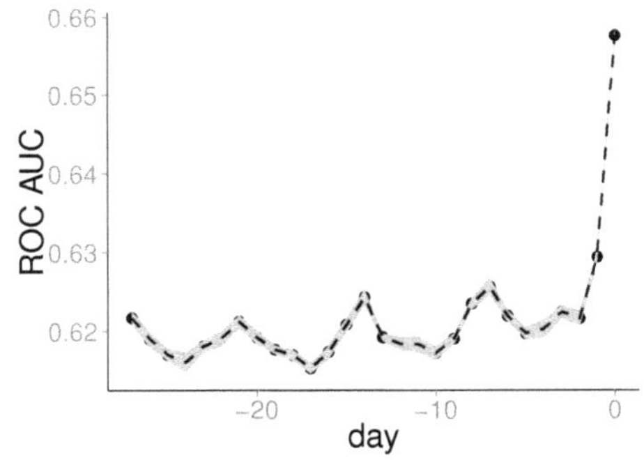

Figure 7: The ROC AUC for predicting whether a given user is a purchaser. Shaded area represents standard error.

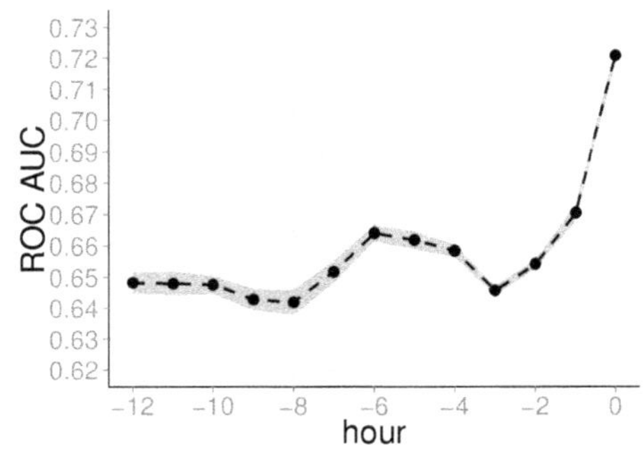

Figure 8: The ROC AUC for predicting whether a given user active on a certain hour is a purchaser.

Figure 8 displays the results. We observe that performance increases significantly as the purchase time approaches. In fact, the ROC AUC for the hour right before the time of purchase is 0.72 (up from 0.65). This result demonstrates that strong short-term differences in online behavior of purchasers exist shortly before a purchase is made.

Overall, we conclude that purchase intent builds slowly over time and starts getting stronger approximately 3 days before the time of purchase. Interestingly, we also observe that last few hours before a purchase, shoppers become easier to identify.

5.2 Importance of Different Signals

To better understand the role that different behavioral signals play in the buildup of purchase intent, we examine separate models trained on different groups of features. We focus on two prediction tasks: identifying purchasers active on day 0, and identifying purchasers active on hour 0.

Results are shown in Table 2. First, we observe that demographics is a very bad predictor of user purchase intent. Content and overall activity have similar predictive performance. The types of actions that users take are the best individual predictors of purchasing behavior (0.63 AUC ROC for day 0 and 0.70 for hour 0). We see that features which represent *how* the user is using the application (Activity, Demographics, and Action-type) are collectively more predictive of user purchasing intent than features that represent *what* the user is looking at (Content). However, we also note that *how* and *what* features seem to be somewhat orthogo-

Features	Day 0	Hour 0
Random Baseline	0.500	0.500
Demographics (d)	0.513 ± 0.0007	0.513 ± 0.0024
Activity (a)	0.591 ± 0.0008	0.625 ± 0.0015
Action-type (A)	0.633 ± 0.0008	0.698 ± 0.0020
Content (C)	0.577 ± 0.0008	0.617 ± 0.0020
Temporal (T)	0.544 ± 0.0007	0.581 ± 0.0019
d + a + A (*how*)	0.642 ± 0.0009	0.702 ± 0.0017
d + a + A + C + T	**0.657**$\pm$0.0007	**0.721**$\pm$0.0026

Table 2: Performance results (ROC AUC) for predicting whether a user is a purchaser based on user behavior at the purchase time.

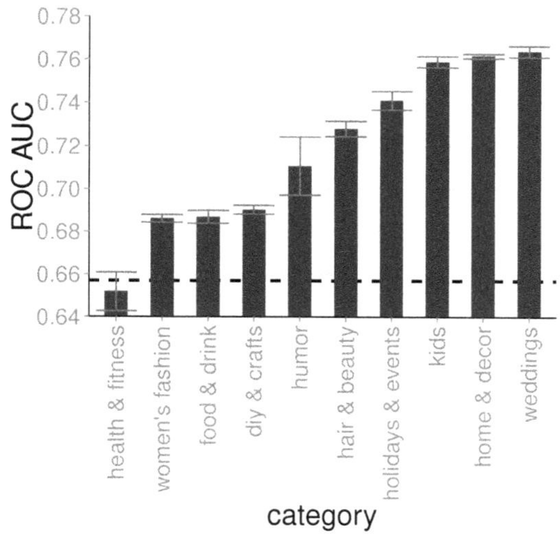

Figure 9: The ROC AUC for predicting whether a given user is a purchaser in a specific category. Error bars represent standard error. Dashed line represents baseline ROC AUC for predicting whether a given user is a purchaser in any category.

nal, as their combination gives best results (0.66 for Day 0, and 0.72 for Hour 0).

5.3 Modeling Per-Category Purchase Intent

Lastly, we consider modeling the intent of users to purchase products in a given product category. Here we formulate a task to predict whether a user will purchase an item in a specific category (e.g., Women's Fashion) given her activity data on Pinterest.

As before, we only focus on users who are active on the purchase date for each category. We sample an equivalent number of non-purchasers and purchasers in each given category and build one binary classifier per category. Our goal here is to predict whether a user is a purchaser in a given product category.

Figure 9 gives the results. We note that in almost all cases, the ROC AUC is noticeably higher for our category-based classifiers than in our original day-based classifier described in Section 5.1. We interpret differences in ROC values between categories as an indication that purchase intent is easier to identify in some categories than in others. Several large and important categories (e.g., Weddings, Home & Decor) have respectable ROC AUCs, suggesting that in most cases, category-based classification provides higher utility than general purchaser classification. Finally, we observe that although PCF scores were specifically excluded as a feature in all discussed prediction tasks, generally speaking, higher average PCF scores lead to higher ROC AUC scores in our category-based classification. In fact, the Spearman rank correlation coefficient between the PCF scores and the AUC ROC scores is 0.75, indicating a strong positive correlation. This demonstrates that the content viewed by users can be used to provide insights into their purchase decisions.

Taken together, our results show that purchase intent can be modeled both over time, as well as within a specific category. Our results are also an encouraging proof-of-concept that a user's online activity in a content discovery application can be used as signals in determining the user's inclination to purchase online.

6. DISCUSSION & CONCLUSION

In this paper we conducted a data-driven cross-platform analysis of the behavioral and usage patterns of purchasers with the goal of modeling time-varying user purchasing intent. We analyzed the purchasing behavior of over two million Pinterest users to determine short-term and long-term signals in user behavior that suggest strong purchase intent.

We found that users with long-term purchasing intent tend to save and clickthrough more on content. However, as users approach the time of purchase their activity gets more topically focused and actions shift from saves to searches. We also showed that purchase intent can be traced across different purchase categories. Overall, we found that purchase signals in online behavior can exist weeks before a purchase is made and are amplified in the last three days before purchase. Finally, we synthesized these insights into a predictive model of user purchasing intent.

Our study opens the door for many important applications. It provides a promising starting point in terms of identifying potential purchasers and better understanding their long-term behavior. Predictions based on our models show a clear path for identifying users with purchase intent. On Pinterest, this can be used to surface buyable pins only to users whose experience would be improved by their presence, *i.e.*, users with potential purchase intent. Buyable pins are pins that allow a user to purchase products directly from Pinterest's interface. In general, the identification of users with purchase intent can also be used to improve personalization and search result ranking to provide increased value to users, *e.g.*, users with identified purchase intent in the wedding category can be shown other useful wedding-related content. Finally, our models allow us to better understand how purchasing intent forms around certain topics, as well as brands. Surfacing such analytic results can be very useful to commercial partners as well as to Pinterest itself.

There are also many fruitful avenues for future work. In particular, there is a large opportunity to study how user behavioral data can be used to recognize purchasers in content discovery applications. We believe that an in-depth textual analysis of the content that purchasers on such applications interact with can further increase our understanding of user purchasing intent. And last, further work is needed on how to recognize purchasers based on their online behavior; in particular, we are curious whether long-term behavioral differences exist between impulse shoppers, and shoppers who carefully make well-researched purchase decisions.

Taken together, our work identifies a set of general principles and signals that can be used for modeling user purchasing intent across many social media and content discovery applications. We hope that the present work will serve as a useful basis for future studies on the intersection of online user behavior and purchasing patterns.

Acknowledgements

We thank Edmarc Hedrick, Tara Syed, Andrea Burbank, Julie Park, Tim Althoff, Rok Sosic, and David Lo for their help and useful discussions.

7. REFERENCES

[1] E. Agichtein, E. Brill, S. Dumais, and R. Ragno. Learning user interaction models for predicting web search result preferences. In *Proc. of the 29th ACM SIGIR conf. on Research and Development in Information Retrieval*, 2006.

[2] S. Aral and D. Walker. Creating social contagion through viral product design: A randomized trial of peer influence in networks. *Management Science*, 57(9), 2011.

[3] N. Banerjee, D. Chakraborty, A. Joshi, S. Mittal, A. Rai, and B. Ravindran. Towards analyzing micro-blogs for detection and classification of real-time intentions. In *Int'l Conf. on Web and Social Media*, 2012.

[4] S. Bellman, G. L. Lohse, and E. J. Johnson. Predictors of online buying behavior. *Communications of the ACM*, 42(12), 1999.

[5] M. Brown, N. Pope, and K. Voges. Buying or browsing? an exploration of shopping orientations and online purchase intention. *European Journal of Marketing*, 37(11/12), 2003.

[6] H. K. Dai, L. Zhao, Z. Nie, J.-R. Wen, L. Wang, and Y. Li. Detecting online commercial intention. In *Proc. of the 15th Conf. on World Wide Web*, 2006.

[7] X. Ding, T. Liu, J. Duan, and J.-Y. Nie. Mining user consumption intention from social media using domain adaptive convolutional neural network. In *Proc. 29th AAAI Conf. on Artificial Intelligence*, 2015.

[8] eMarketer. US retail commerce sales highest for computers, consumer electronics, April 2014.

[9] A. Farahat and M. C. Bailey. How effective is targeted advertising? In *Proc. of the 21st Conf. on World Wide Web*, 2012.

[10] J. F. George. Influences on the intent to make internet purchases. *Internet Research*, 12(2), 2002.

[11] Q. Guo and E. Agichtein. Ready to buy or just browsing?: detecting web searcher goals from interaction data. In *Proc. of the 33rd ACM SIGIR conf. on Research and development in Information Retrieval*, 2010.

[12] S. Guo, M. Wang, and J. Leskovec. The role of social networks in online shopping: information passing, price of trust, and consumer choice. In *Proc. of the 12th ACM Conf. on Electronic commerce*, 2011.

[13] V. Gupta, D. Varshney, H. Jhamtani, D. Kedia, and S. Karwa. Identifying purchase intent from social posts. In *Int'l Conf. on Web and Social Media*, 2014.

[14] B. Hernández, J. Jiménez, and M. José Martín. Age, gender and income: do they really moderate online shopping behaviour? *Online Information Review*, 35(1), 2011.

[15] B. Hollerit, M. Kröll, and M. Strohmaier. Towards linking buyers and sellers: detecting commercial intent on twitter. In *Proc. of the 22nd Conf. on World Wide Web*, 2013.

[16] M.-H. Hsu, C.-H. Yen, C.-M. Chiu, and C.-M. Chang. A longitudinal investigation of continued online shopping behavior: An extension of the theory of planned behavior. *Int'l Journal of Human-Computer Studies*, 64(9), 2006.

[17] E. Hwang. 100 million of the most interesting people we know, September 2015. https://blog.pinterest.com/en/100-million-most-interesting-people-we-know.

[18] E. Kim, W. Kim, and Y. Lee. Combination of multiple classifiers for the customer's purchase behavior prediction. *Decision Support Systems*, 34(2), 2003.

[19] M. L. Korzaan. Going with the flow: Predicting online purchase intentions. *The Journal of Computer Information Systems*, 43(4), 2003.

[20] U. Lee, Z. Liu, and J. Cho. Automatic identification of user goals in web search. In *Proc. of the 14th Conf. on World Wide Web*, 2005.

[21] J. Leskovec, L. A. Adamic, and B. A. Huberman. The dynamics of viral marketing. *ACM Transactions on the Web*, 1(1), 2007.

[22] R. Lukose, J. Li, J. Zhou, and S. R. Penmetsa. Learning user purchase intent from user-centric data. In *Advances in Knowledge Discovery and Data Mining*. 2008.

[23] V. G. Morwitz and D. Schmittlein. Using segmentation to improve sales forecasts based on purchase intent: Which" intenders" actually buy? *Journal of Marketing Research*, 1992.

[24] A. O'cass and T. Fenech. Web retailing adoption: exploring the nature of internet users web retailing behaviour. *Journal of Retailing and Consumer Services*, 10(2), 2003.

[25] D. E. Rose and D. Levinson. Understanding user goals in web search. In *Proc. of the 13th Conf. on World Wide Web*, 2004.

[26] R. Roy Dholakia. Going shopping: key determinants of shopping behaviors and motivations. *Int'l Journal of Retail & Distribution Management*, 27(4), 1999.

[27] W. D. Salisbury, R. A. Pearson, A. W. Pearson, and D. W. Miller. Perceived security and world wide web purchase intention. *Industrial Management & Data Systems*, 101(4), 2001.

[28] S. Senecal, P. J. Kalczynski, and J. Nantel. Consumers' decision-making process and their online shopping behavior: a clickstream analysis. *Journal of Business Research*, 58(11), 2005.

[29] C. Sismeiro and R. E. Bucklin. Modeling purchase behavior at an e-commerce web site: A task-completion approach. *Journal of Marketing Research*, 41(3), 2004.

[30] E. Suh, S. Lim, H. Hwang, and S. Kim. A prediction model for the purchase probability of anonymous customers to support real time web marketing: a case study. *Expert Systems with Applications*, 27(2), 2004.

[31] W. R. Swinyard and S. M. Smith. Activities, interests, and opinions of online shoppers and non-shoppers. *Int'l Business & Economics Research Journal (IBER)*, 3(4), 2011.

[32] D. Van den Poel and W. Buckinx. Predicting online-purchasing behaviour. *European Journal of Operational Research*, 166(2), 2005.

[33] C. Van Slyke, C. L. Comunale, and F. Belanger. Gender differences in perceptions of web-based shopping. *Communications of the ACM*, 45(8), 2002.

[34] E. Young Kim and Y.-K. Kim. Predicting online purchase intentions for clothing products. *European Journal of Marketing*, 38(7), 2004.

[35] Y. Zhang and M. Pennacchiotti. Predicting purchase behaviors from social media. In *Proc. of the 22nd Conf. on World Wide Web*, 2013.

Images Don't Lie: Transferring Deep Visual Semantic Features to Large-Scale Multimodal Learning to Rank

Corey Lynch
Etsy
55 Washington Street
Brooklyn, New York
clynch@etsy.com

Kamelia Aryafar
Etsy
55 Washington Street
Brooklyn, New York
karyafar@etsy.com

Josh Attenberg
Etsy
55 Washington Street
Brooklyn, New York
jattenberg@etsy.com

ABSTRACT

Search is at the heart of modern e-commerce. As a result, the task of ranking search results automatically (learning to rank) is a multibillion dollar machine learning problem. Traditional models optimize over a few hand-constructed features based on the item's text. In this paper, we introduce a multimodal learning to rank model that combines these traditional features with visual semantic features transferred from a deep convolutional neural network. In a large scale experiment using data from the online marketplace Etsy [1], we verify that moving to a multimodal representation significantly improves ranking quality. We show how image features can capture fine-grained style information not available in a text-only representation. In addition, we show concrete examples of how image information can successfully disentangle pairs of highly different items that are ranked similarly by a text-only model.

Keywords

Learning to rank; Computer vision; Deep learning;

1. INTRODUCTION

Etsy [1] is a global marketplace where people buy and sell unique goods: handmade items, vintage goods, and craft supplies. Users come to Etsy to search for and buy listings other users offer for sale. A *listing* on Etsy consists of an image of the item for sale along with some text describing it. With 35 million listings for sale [2], correctly ranking search results for a user's query is Etsy's most important problem. Currently Etsy treats the ranking problem as an example of supervised learning: learn a query-listing relevance function from data with listing feature representations derived from listings' titles and tags. However, with over 90 million listing images, we wonder: *is there useful untapped information hiding in Etsy's images that isn't well captured by the descriptive text?* If so, how can we integrate this new data modality into Etsy's existing ranking models in a principled way? In this paper we attempt to explore these two major questions on a real world dataset containing over 1.4 million Etsy listings with images. Specifically, we describe a multimodal learning to rank method which integrates both visual and text information. We show experimentally that this new multimodal model significantly improves the quality of search results.

[1] www.etsy.com

[2] The statistics reported in this paper are accurate at the time of submission of this paper.

KDD '16, August 13-17, 2016, San Francisco, CA, USA
© 2016 ACM. ISBN 978-1-4503-4232-2/16/08...$15.00
DOI: http://dx.doi.org/10.1145/2939672.2939728

Figure 1: **Irrelevant search results for the query "wedding dress":** Even though it's apparent in the images that these are not wedding dresses, each listing's descriptive title contains the phrase "wedding dress", allowing it to show in search results for the query.

We motivate this paper with a real example of a problem in search ranking. Figure 1 shows listings that appear in the results for the query "wedding dress". Even though it is clear from looking at the images that they aren't wedding dresses, each listing's title contains the term "wedding dress", causing it to appear in the results. This kind of term noise in listing descriptions is pervasive. Sellers write their own descriptions and are motivated to include high traffic query terms to boost the visibility of their listings in search. It is obvious that there is *complementary information* in the listing images that is either unavailable in the text or is even in contrast to the text. Our hypothesis is that if we can mine this complementary high-level visual information, we can incorporate it into our models to improve search ranking as suggested by multimodal embeddings literature [, , , , , , ,].

With the goal of learning high-level content directly from the image, deep convolutional neural networks (CNN) [,] are an obvious model choice. CNNs are a powerful class of models in-

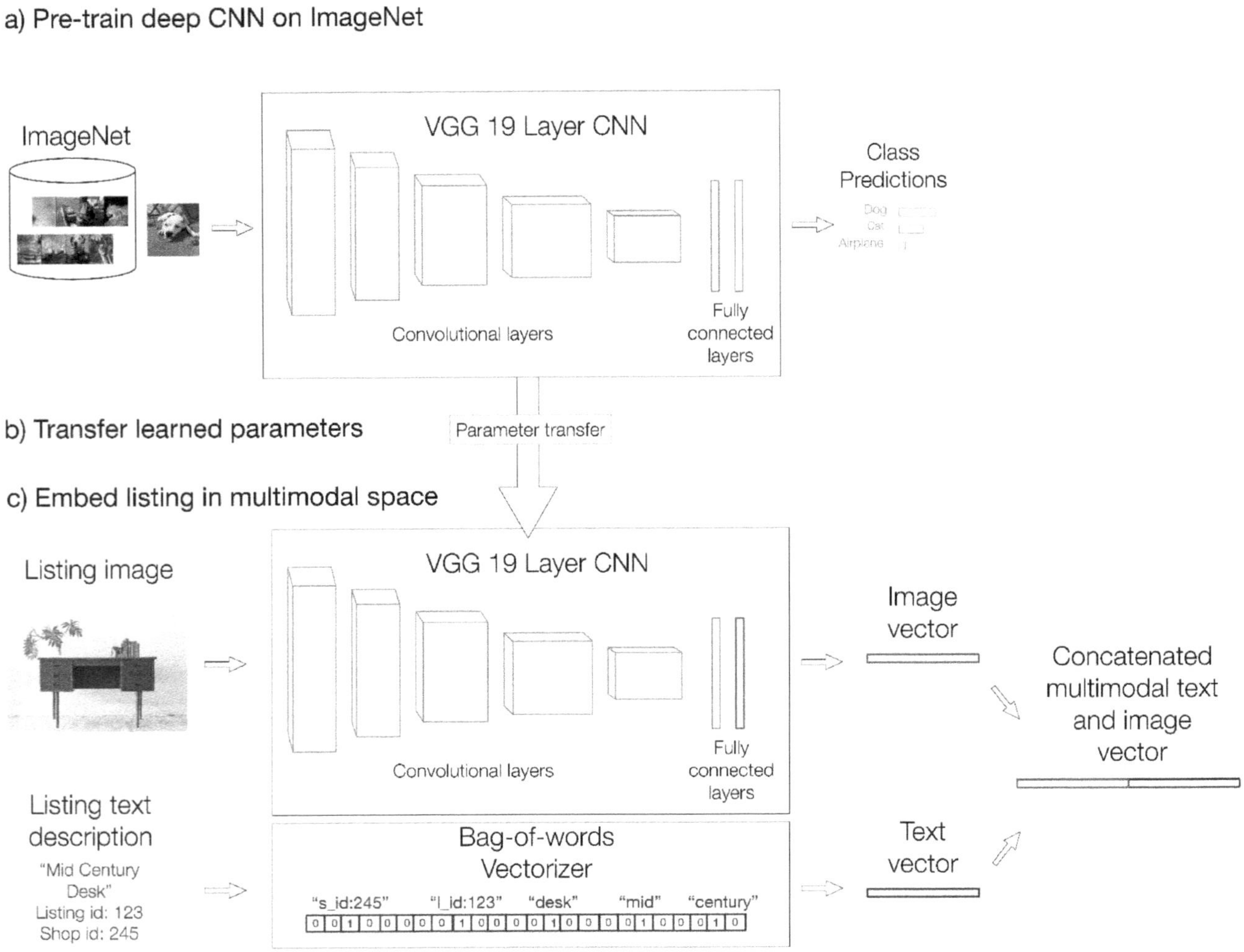

Figure 2: **Transferring parameters of a CNN to the task of multimodal embedding:** In a) we utilize a pre-trained 19 layer VGG-style network that is trained on a large scale object recognition task (ImageNet challenge). In b) we remove the last layer (containing scores for the different object classes) and transfer the parameters of the modified network to our task. In c) we use the modified network as a fixed feature extractor of high-level image content information, taking the last fully connected layer as an image embedding. We simultaneously embed the listing's text in a bag of words space, then concatenate the two embeddings to form a single multimodal descriptor of a listing.

spired by the human visual cortex that rivals human-level performance on difficult perceptual inference tasks such as object recognition [ ]. [ ] shows that image feature representations learned on large scale object recognition tasks are powerful and highly interpretable. The lower layers of the network learn low-level features like color blobs, lines, corners; middle layers combine lower layers into textures; higher layers combine middle layers into higher-level image content like objects. High-level visual information is made increasingly explicit along the model's processing hierarchy [ ]. This high-level description formed in the deep layers of the network is what we are interested in mining as a rival source of information to the listing's text description.

One consideration to make is that large modern CNNs require large amounts of training data [,]. Even though Etsy's production search system generates millions of training examples per day in aggregate, the amount of examples available to an individual query model can be in the low hundreds, particularly for queries in the long tail. This makes training one deep CNN per query from scratch prone to overfitting. Transfer learning is a popular method for dealing with this problem, with many examples in computer vision [, ,]. We take the pre-trained 19-layer VGG net [,] as a fixed extractor of general high-level image features. We chose this model due to it's impressive performance on a difficult 1000-way object classification task. Our assumption is that the activations of it's neurons immediately prior to the classification task contain general high-level information that may be useful to our ranking task. Figure 2 gives a high-level overview of our multimodal feature extraction process.

Learning to rank search results has received considerable attention over the past decade [, , ,], and it is at the core of modern information retrieval. A typical setting of learning to rank for search is to: (i) embed documents in some feature space, (ii) learn a ranking function for each query that operates in this feature space over documents. Early approaches optimized over a few

Algorithm 1 Multimodal Embedding of Listings

procedure EMBEDMULTIMODAL($\mathbf{d}_i$)
  $\mathbf{d}_{T_i} \leftarrow \mathbf{BoW}(text)$
  $\mathbf{d}_{I_i} \leftarrow \mathbf{VGG}(image)$
  $\mathbf{d}_{MM_i} \leftarrow [\mathbf{d}_{T_i}, \mathbf{d}_{T_i}]$
  return $\mathbf{d}_{MM_i}$

hand-constructed features, e.g. item title, URL, PageRank [ ]. More recent approaches optimize over much larger sets of orthogonal features based on query and item text [ ]. Our research follows this orthogonal approach and explores the value of a large set of image features. Our baseline listing representation consists of features for a listing's terms, a listing's id, and a listing's shop id. The presence of the latter two features captures historical popularity information at the listing and shop level respectively for the query.

To our knowledge, this is the first investigation of the value of transferring deep visual semantic features to the problem of learning to rank for search. The results of a large-scale learning to rank experiment on Etsy data confirms that moving from a text-only representation to a multimodal representation significantly improves search ranking. We visualize how the multimodal representation provides complementary style information to the ranking models. We also show concrete examples of how pairs of highly different listings ranked similarly by a text model get disentangled with the addition of image information. We feel this, along with significant quantitative improvements in offline ranking metrics demonstrates the value of the image modality.

This paper is organized as follows: In Section 2 we describe our multimodal ranking framework. Section 2.1 gives a detailed explanation of how we obtain multimodal embeddings for each listing. Section 2.2 gives a brief introduction to learning to rank and describes how these embeddings are incorporated into a pairwise learning to rank model. Section 3 describes a large scale experiment where we compare multimodal models to text models. Finally in Section 4, we discuss how moving to a multimodal representation affects ranking with qualitative examples and visualizations.

2. METHODOLOGY

Here we describe how we extend our existing learning to rank models with image information. We first explain how we embed listings for the learning to rank task in both single modality and multimodal settings. Then we explain how listings embedded in both modalities are incorporated into a learning to rank framework.

2.1 Multimodal Listing Embedding

Each Etsy listing contains text information such as a descriptive title and tags, as well as an image of the item for sale. To measure the value of including image information, we embed listings in a multimodal space (consisting of high-level text and image information), then compare the multimodal representation to the baseline single modality model. Let $\mathbf{d}_i$ denote each listing document. We then use $\mathbf{d}_{T_i} \in \mathbb{R}^{|T|}$ and $\mathbf{d}_{I_i} \in \mathbb{R}^{|I|}$ to denote the text and image representation of $\mathbf{d}_i$ respectively. $|T|$ denotes the dimensionality of the traditional feature space which is a sparse representation of term occurrences in each $\mathbf{d}_i$. $|I|$ denotes the dimensionality of the image feature space which in contrast to text is a dense feature space. The goal of multimodal embedding is then to represent a listing through text and image modalities in a single vector, i.e. the $\mathbf{d}_{MM_i} \in \mathbb{R}^{|M|}$ where $|M|$ is the dimensionality of the final embedding.

Given a listing document $\mathbf{d}_i$ consisting of the title and tag words, a numerical listing id, a numerical shop id, and a listing image,

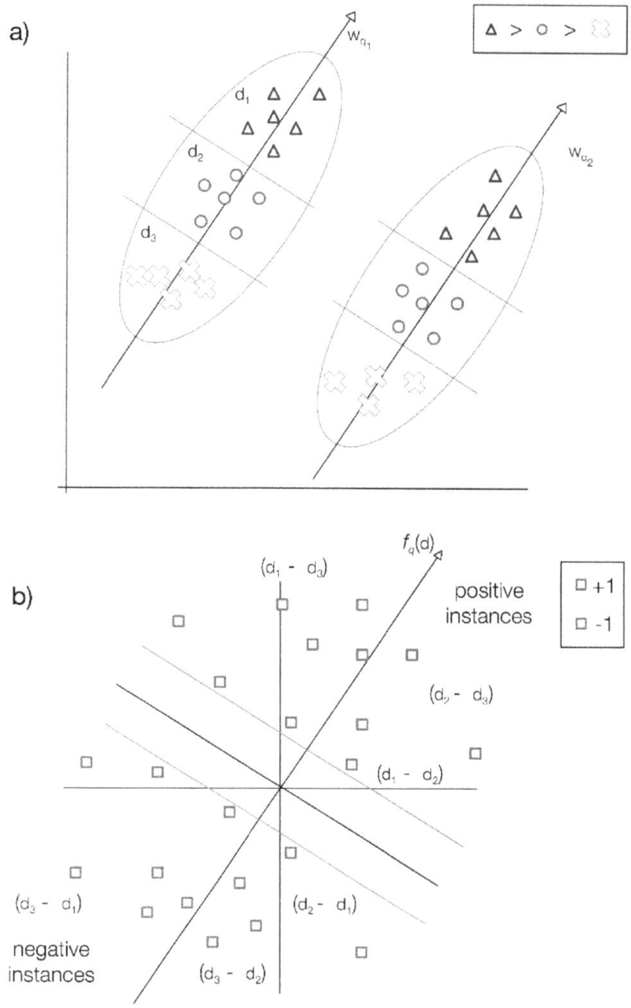

Figure 3: **Transformation to Pairwise Classification [ ]:** a) Shows a synthetic example of the ranking problem. There are two groups of documents (associated with different queries) embedded in some feature space. Documents within each group have different relevance grades: $relevance(\mathbf{d}_1) > relevance(\mathbf{d}_2) > relevance(\mathbf{d}_3)$. The weight vector w corresponds to a linear ranking function $f(\mathbf{d}) = \langle w, \mathbf{d} \rangle$ which can score and rank documents. Ranking documents with this function is equivalent to projecting the documents onto the vector and sorting documents according to the projections. A good ranking function is one where documents in $\mathbf{d}_1$ are ranked higher than documents in $\mathbf{d}_3$, and so on. Documents belonging to different query groups are incomparable. b) shows how the ranking problem in (a) can be transformed into a pairwise classification task: separate well-ordered and non-well ordered pairs. In this task, well-ordered pairs are represented as the vector difference between more relevant and less relevant document vectors, e.g., $\mathbf{d}_1 - \mathbf{d}_2$, $\mathbf{d}_1 - \mathbf{d}_3$, and $\mathbf{d}_2 - \mathbf{d}_3$. Non-well ordered-pairs are represented as the vector difference between less relevant and more relevant document vectors, e.g., $\mathbf{d}_3 - \mathbf{d}_1$, $\mathbf{d}_2 - \mathbf{d}_1$, and $\mathbf{d}_3 - \mathbf{d}_2$. We label well-ordered instances $+1$, non-well-ordered -1, and train a linear SVM, $f_q(\mathbf{d})$, which separates the new feature vectors. The weight vector w of the SVM classifier corresponds to the ranking function w in (a).

Algorithm 2 Generate Pairwise Classification Instances

procedure GETPAIRWISEINSTANCES($\{\langle \mathbf{d}_i^+, \mathbf{d}_i^- \rangle\}$)
  $L \leftarrow \{\}$
  for $i = 1 \ldots |P|$ **do** ▷ $|P|$ labeled tuples
    $\mathbf{d}_{MM_i}^+ \leftarrow$ **EmbedMultimodal**($\mathbf{d}_i^+$)
    $\mathbf{d}_{MM_i}^- \leftarrow$ **EmbedMultimodal**($\mathbf{d}_i^-$)
    Draw r uniformly at random from $[0, 1)$
    if $r > 0.5$ **then**
      $x_i \leftarrow \mathbf{d}_{MM_i}^+ - \mathbf{d}_{MM_i}^-$
      $y_i \leftarrow +1$
    else
      $x_i \leftarrow \mathbf{d}_{MM_i}^- - \mathbf{d}_{MM_i}^+$
      $y_i \leftarrow -1$
  $L = L.append(\langle x_i, y_i \rangle)$
  return L ▷ The list of classification instances.

we obtain a multimodal feature vector $\mathbf{d}_{MM_i}$ by embedding traditional terms in a text vector space, embedding the image in an image vector space, then concatenating the two vectors. Algorithm 1 describes this multimodal embedding. The text-based features are based on the set of title and tag unigram and bigrams, the listing id, and the shop id for each $\mathbf{d}_i$. These baseline features are then represented in a bag-of-words (BoW) [ ] space as $\mathbf{d}_{T_i} \in \mathbb{R}^{|T|}$. $|T| = |D| + |L| + |S|$, where $|D|$ is the size of the dictionary, $|L|$ is the cardinality of the set of listings, and $|S|$ is the cardinality of the set of shops. Each element in $\mathbf{d}_{T_i}$ is 1 if $\mathbf{d}_i$ contains the term, and is 0 otherwise.

Each $\mathbf{d}_i$ is also represented in the image space as $\mathbf{d}_{I_i} \in \mathbb{R}^{|I|}$. To obtain $\mathbf{d}_{I_i}$, we adopt a transfer learning approach. Oquab *et al.* [ ] shows that the internal layers of a convolutional neural network pre-trained on ImageNet can act as a generic extractor of a mid-level image representation and then re-used on other tasks. In our model, we utilize the VGG-19 network [ ] and remove the last fully-connected layer. For every listing $\mathbf{d}_i$, we scale it's image uniformly so that its shortest spatial dimension is 256 pixels, then take the center 224×224 crop. We then pass the cropped image through the modified VGG network to get a 4096 dimensional feature vector [3]. This vector contains the activations fed to the original object classifier. We ℓ_2 normalize the activations, then use the normalized vector as the final 4096 dimensional image representation $\mathbf{d}_{I_i}$. The multimodal representation of the document $\mathbf{d}_i$ can now be obtained simply as $\mathbf{d}_{MM_i} \in \mathbb{R}^{|M|} = [\mathbf{d}_{T_i}, \mathbf{d}_{I_i}]$ where $|M| = |T| + |I|$ is the dimensionality of the final multimodal representation. Figure 2 illustrates this process in details.

2.2 Learning To Rank

E-commerce search is a task that can be described as follows: (i) Query: a user comes to the site and enters a query, q, e.g. "desk". (ii) Retrieval: the search engine finds all listing documents that contain terms from the query in their title or tag descriptions, such as "mid century desk", "red desk lamp", etc. (iii) Ranking: the search engine uses a ranking function to score each listing document, where a higher score expresses that a listing document is more relevant to the query. The search engine sorts listings by that score, and presents the results to the user. The goal of learning to rank [ ] is to automatically learn (iii), the ranking function, from historical search log data.

In this paper, we restrict our attention to the *pairwise preference* approach to learning a ranking function [ ]. That is, given a set of labeled tuples P, where each tuple contains a query q, a relevant document $\mathbf{d}^+$ and an irrelevant document $\mathbf{d}^-$, we want to learn a function $f_q(\mathbf{d})$ such that $f_q(\mathbf{d}^+) > f_q(\mathbf{d}^-)$. In our case, relevance is binary and determined by the user: a user is said to judge a search result relevant if she purchases the listing, adds it to her cart, or clicks on the listing and dwells on it for longer than 30 seconds.

As shown by Herbrich *et al.* [ ], the ranking problem can be transformed into a two-class classification: learn a linear classifier that separates well-ordered pairs from non-well-ordered pairs. This is illustrated in Figure 3. To achieve this, we can transform any implicit relevance judgement pair $(\mathbf{d}^+, \mathbf{d}^-)$ into either a well-ordered or non-well ordered instance. Specifically, suppose for each preference pair $(q, \mathbf{d}^+, \mathbf{d}^-)$ we flip a coin. If heads the preference pair $(q, \mathbf{d}^+, \mathbf{d}^-) \mapsto (\mathbf{d}^+ - \mathbf{d}^-, +1)$ (a well-ordered pair), else $(q, \mathbf{d}^+, \mathbf{d}^-) \mapsto (\mathbf{d}^- - \mathbf{d}^+, -1)$ (a poorly ordered pair).

This results in an evenly balanced pairwise classification dataset for each query q. Algorithm 2 explains the process of generating classification instances for input pairwise preference tuples. The new classification task can now be solved by minimizing the regularized hinge classification loss:

$$\min_w \sum_{i=1}^{m} max([1 - y_i \langle w, x_i \rangle], 0) + \lambda_1 \|w\|^1 + \lambda_2 \|w\|^2$$

via stochastic gradient descent. A well trained pairwise classifier minimizes the number of pairs which are ranked out of order, i.e. the ranking loss. To rank a new set of listing documents for a query, we embed them in the feature space, then use output of the trained classifier to obtain ranking scores for each. This method, also known as RankingSVM, is used extensively in the ranking literature [, ,].

Following [ ], we can obtain large quantities of *implicit* pairwise preference instances cheaply by mining Etsy's search logs [4].

The process for doing so is as follows: A user comes to the site, enters a query, and is presented with a page of results. If she interacts with listing $\mathbf{d}_i$ and ignores the adjacent listing $\mathbf{d}_j$, a reasonable assumption is that she prefers $\mathbf{d}_i$ over $\mathbf{d}_j$ in the context of query q. We call this an implicit relevance judgement, mapping $(q, \mathbf{d}_i, \mathbf{d}_j) \mapsto (q, \mathbf{d}^+, \mathbf{d}^-)$, forming the necessary input for Algorithm 2. Figure 4 illustrates how we move from search logs to multimodal pairwise classification instances.

3. RESULTS AND DISCUSSION

This section describes a large scale experiment to determine how a multimodal listing representation impacts ranking quality. In Section 3.1, we describe our ranking quality evaluation metric. In Section 3.2 we describe our dataset. Finally we present our findings in Section 3.3.

[3] We make our scalable VGG-19 feature extractor available at: https://github.com/coreylynch/vgg-19-feature-extractor

[4] We obtain labeled pairs for each query using the FairPairs method. A well known and significant problem in collecting training data from search is presentation bias [ ]: users click on higher presented results irrespective of query relevance. Ignoring this bias and training on naively collected data can lead to models that just learn the existing global ranking function. The FairPairs method modifies search results in a non-invasive manner that allows us to collect pairs of (preferred listing, ignored listing) that are unaffected by this presentation bias.

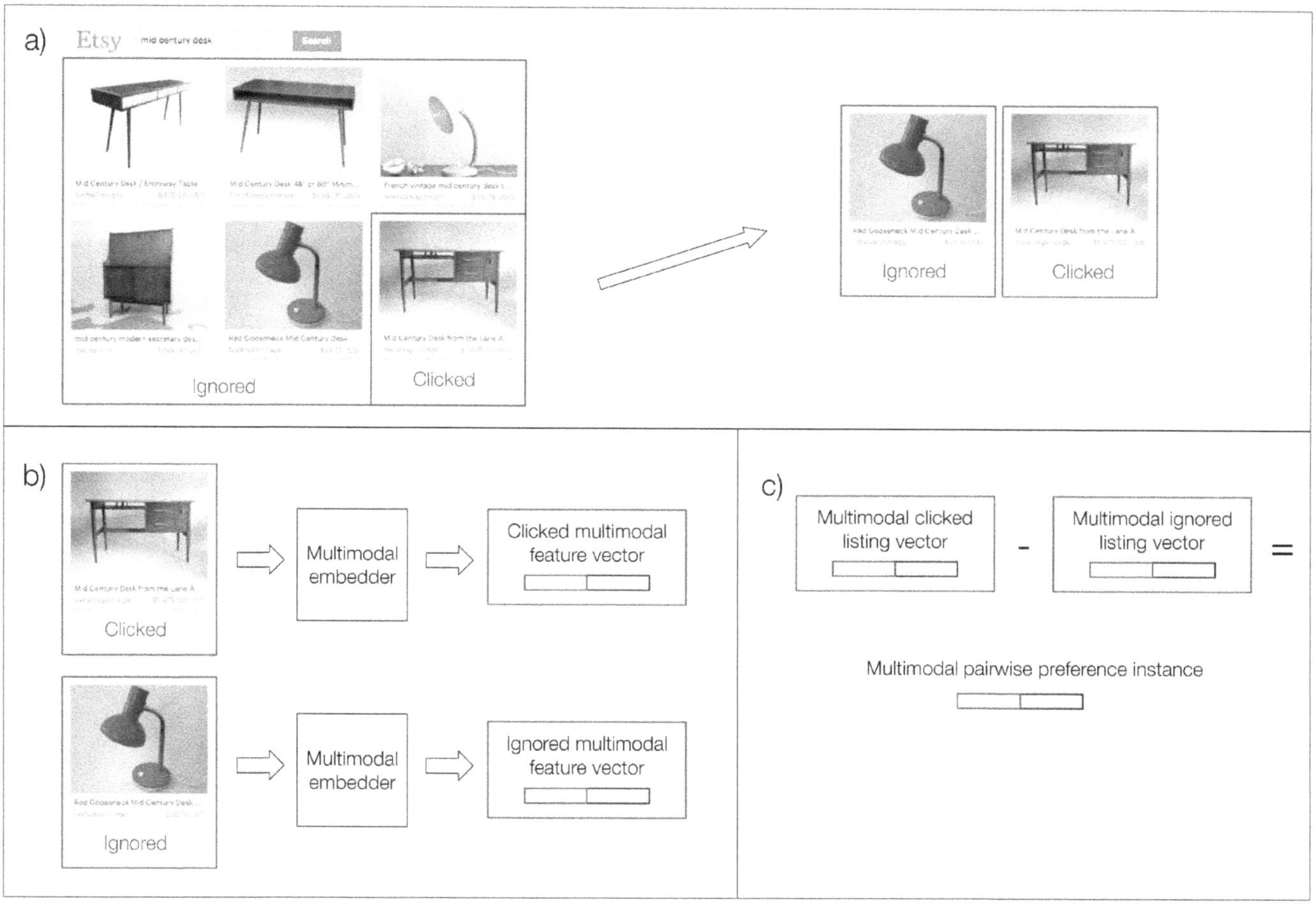

Figure 4: **From search logs to multimodal pairwise classification instances:** a) A user comes to the site, enters the search query **mid century desk**, is presented with some results, clicks one and ignores the others. We take the listing she clicked and an adjacent listing she ignored as an instance of implicit pairwise preference in the context of the query **mid century desk** forming a training triplet $(q, \mathbf{d}^+, \mathbf{d}^-)$ from (**mid century desk**, clicked listing, ignored listing). b) We embed both listings in the pair in multimodal space. c) Map labeled embedded pair to a single pairwise classification instance. We flip a coin. If heads, create a well-ordered pairwise instance (clicked vector - ignored vector) and label it $+1$; if tails, create a non-well-ordered pairwise instance (ignored vector - clicked vector) and label it -1.

3.1 Evaluation metrics

To evaluate the quality of one modality ranking model over another, we measure the model's average *Normalized Discounted Cumulative Gain* (NDCG) [ ] on holdout search sessions. NDCG is the standard measure of a model's ranking quality in information retrieval. It lies in the $[0, 1]$ range, where a higher NDCG denotes a better holdout ranking quality. Here we give a brief background on NDCG and why it is a good choice for quantifying ranking quality.

The cumulative gain (CG) of a ranking model's ordering is the sum of relevance scores over the ranked listings. The CG at a particular rank position p is defined as:

$$\mathrm{CG_p} = \sum_{i=1}^{p} rel_i,$$

where rel_i is the *implicit* relevance of the result at position i.

CG on its own isn't a particularly good measure of the quality of a model's ordering: moving a relevant document above an irrelevant document does not change the summed value.

This motivates discounted cumulative gain (DCG) [ ] as a ranking measure. DCG is the sum of each listing's relevance score *discounted by the position it was shown*. DCG is therefore higher when more relevant listings are ranked higher in results, and lower when they are ranked lower. The DCG is defined as:

$$\mathrm{DCG_p} = \sum_{i=1}^{p} \frac{2^{rel_i} - 1}{\log_2(i+1)}.$$

Finally, we arrive at Normalized Discounted Cumulative Gain (NDCG) by dividing a model's DCG by the ideal DCG (IDCG) for the session:

$$\mathrm{nDCG_p} = \frac{DCG_p}{IDCG_p}$$

This gives us a number between 0 and 1 for the model's ranking of a holdout search result set, where a higher NDCG approaches the ideal DCG, denoting a better ranking quality.

Our holdout data (both validation and test) are in the form of a list of labeled sessions for each query q. A labeled session is a page of search results presented to a user for the query q, where the user

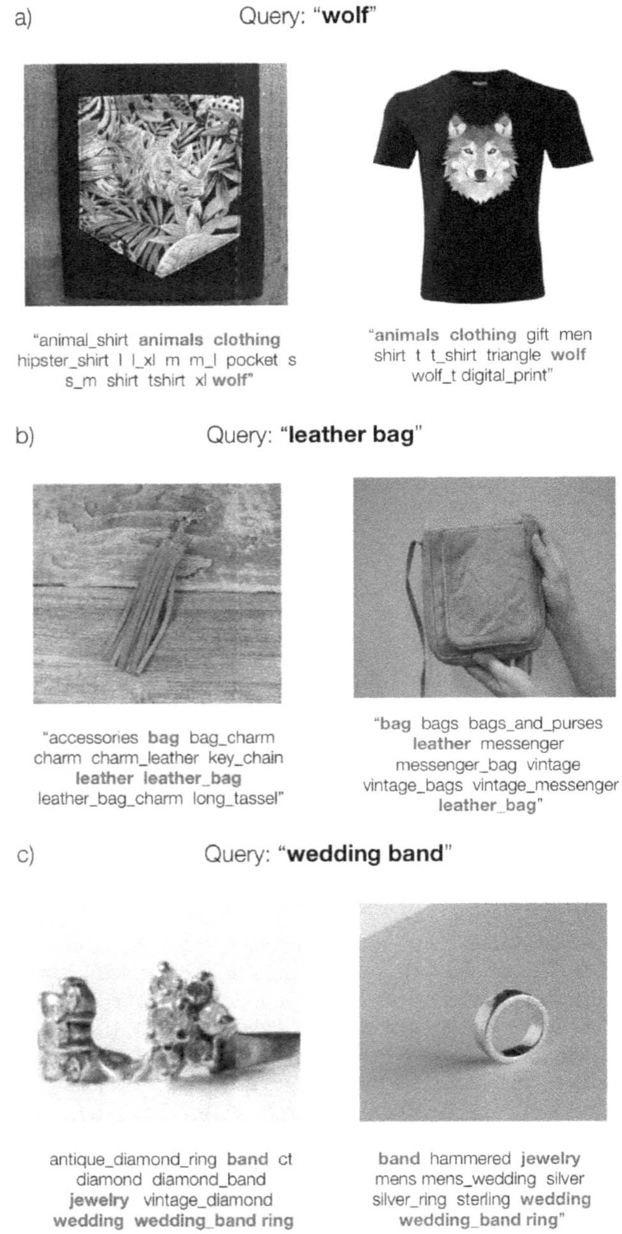

Figure 5: **Image information can help disentangle different listings considered similar by a text model:** Here are three pairs of highly different listings that were ranked similarly by a text model, and far apart by a multimodal model. Title terms that both listings have in common are bolded, showing how text-only models can be confused. In every case, the multimodal model ranks the right listing higher. All three queries benefit from substantial gains in ranking quality (NDCG) by moving to a multimodal representation. In a) for example, we see two listings returned for the query "wolf": the left listing's image shows a picture of a rhino, while the right listing's image shows a t-shirt with a wolf on it. A text-only model ranked these listings only 2 positions apart, likely due to the overlapping words in their titles. A multimodal model, on the other hand, ranked the right listing 394 positions higher than the left. The query "wolf" saw a 3.07% increase in NDCG by moving to a multimodal representation.

has provided implicit relevance judgements.[5] We evaluate a trained query model f_q by computing its average NDCG over all labeled holdout sessions for the query q. To achieve this, we first compute each session's NDCG as follows: i) embed all the session's listing documents in the model space, ii) score and rank embedded listings with the model, and iii) compute the labeled session NDCG. Then we average over session NDCG to get average query NDCG. Finally, to compare the ranking ability of models based in one modality vs. another, we report the average modality NDCG across query NDCGs.

3.2 Dataset

For our experiment, we select a random 2 week period in our search logs to obtain training, validation, and test data. We mine query preference pairs from the first week as *training data*. We mine labeled holdout sessions from the following week, splitting it evenly into *validation* and *test* sessions. This results in 8.82 million training preference pairs, 1.9 million validation sessions, and 1.9 million test sessions. Across training and test there are roughly 1.4 million unique listing images.

We tune model learning rates, λ_1 and λ_2 regularization strengths on our validation data. We also allow queries to select the best modality based on validation NDCG from the set of multiple modalities : *text-only*, *image-only*, and *multimodal* prior to test. Of the 1394 total queries we built models for, 51.4% saw an increase in validation NDCG by utilizing the multimodal representation over the baseline representation. We present results in Section 3.3.

3.3 Results

Here we present and discuss the results of incorporating image information into our ranking models. Table 1 summarizes the results of our experiment for queries that moved from a text-only representation to a multimodal one. For each modality, we present the average lift in NDCG over our baseline text-only models. We find that consistent with our expectations, switching from a text-only ranking modality to one that uses image information as well (MM) yields a statistically significant **1.7% gain in average ranking quality**. We find it interesting that a purely image-based representation, while strictly worse than both other modalities, only underperforms the baseline representation by 2.2%.

Table 1: Lift in Average NDCG, relative to baseline (%), on sample dataset is compared across various modalities. * indicates the change over baseline method is statistically significant according to Wilcoxon signed rank test at the significance level of 0.0001.

Modality	Text	Image	MM
Relative lift in NDCG	+0.0%	−2.2%*	**+1.7%***

We can explore how incorporating image information changes the ranking by looking at a continuum visualization of how the two modality models rank listings for a query: The top row shows the top 90th percentile of ranked listings, the bottom row shows the 50th percentile of ranked listings, and every row in between is a continuum. Figure 6 illustrates a continuum visualization for the query bar "bar necklace". We observe that by moving from a text-only to a multimodal representation, the top ranked listings in each

[5]We collect implicit relevance judgments in the test period the same as in training: documents are labeled 0.0 if ignored and 1.0 if the user purchased the listing, added the listing to their cart, or clicked on the listing and dwelled for more than 30 seconds.

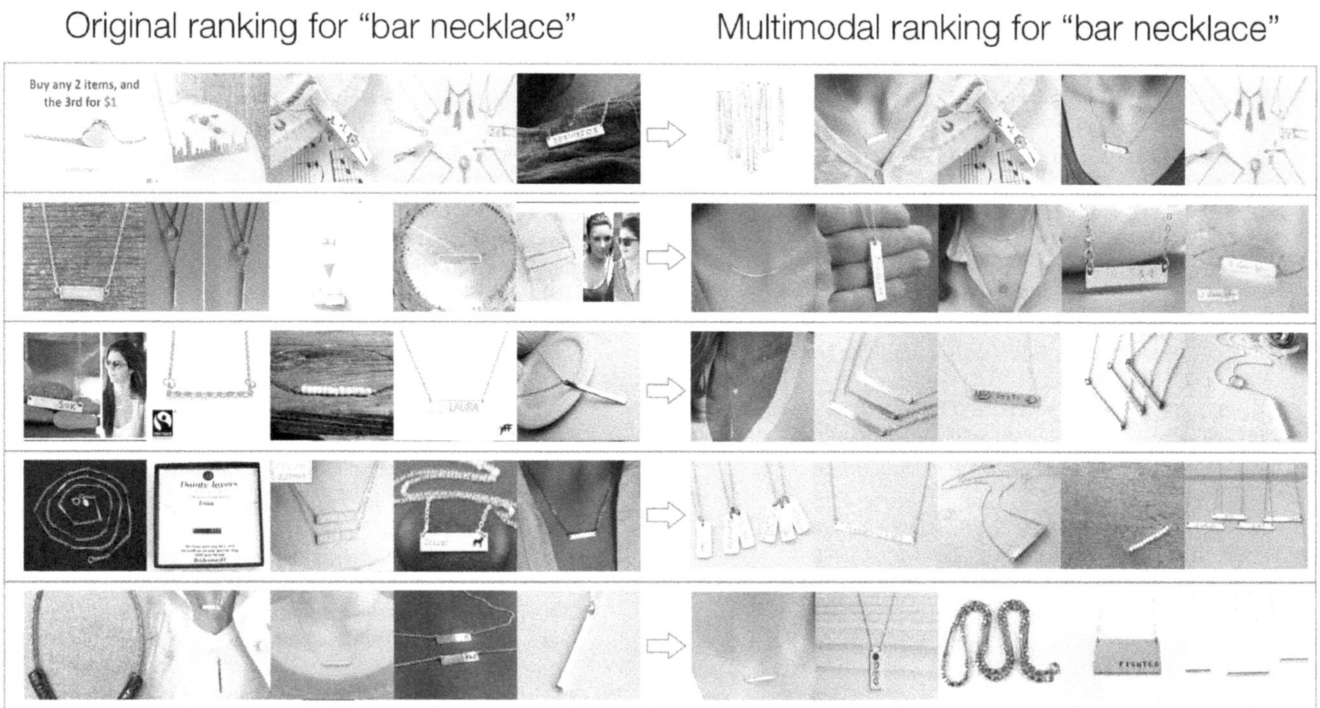

Figure 6: **Visualizing ranking changes by incorporating image information:** Here we visualize how moving from a text-only representation to a multimodal one impacted the ranking for the query "bar necklace". Each row shows the top ranked listings for the query by percentile, from 90th percentile on the top to 50th percentile on the bottom. We observe that the images in each row show more visual consistency under a multimodal ranking than a text-only ranking. That, along with the fact that the query saw a 6.62% increase in ranking quality (NDCG) by moving to a multimodal representation, suggests that the multimodal representation captures relevant visual style information not available in the text.

band show greater visual consistency. This suggests that there is *relevant style information* captured in the image representation that is not available, or not well described in the text representation. Incorporating this complementary side information leads to a $\mathbf{6.62\%}$ **increase** in offline NDCG.

We can also see concrete examples of the image representation providing valuable complementary information to the ranking function. Figure 5 shows three examples of listings that were ranked similarly under a text model and very differently under a multimodal model. For example, Figure 5 (a) shows two listings that match the query "wolf". It is apparent by looking at the two listing images that only the right listing is relevant to the query: the left shows a picture of a rhino; the right is a t-shirt with a wolf on it. The text-only model ranked these two listings only two positions apart. In contrast, the multimodal model ranked the relevant right-hand listing 394 positions higher. We can see by looking at the bolded terms in common how the text model could be confused: as points embedded in text space, these listings are essentially on top of each other. It is clear that the images contain enough information to differentiate them: one contains a wolf, one contains a rhino. By embedding listings in a space that preserves this difference, the multimodal model can effectively disentangle these two listings and provide a more accurate ranking. The query "wolf" saw an overall $\mathbf{3.07\%}$ **increase** in NDCG by moving to a multimodal representation. Similarly for Figure 5 (b), a text model for the query "leather bag" ranked the two listings 1 position apart, while the multimodal model ranked the right listing 660 positions higher. "leather bag" saw a $\mathbf{2.56\%}$ **increase** in NDCG by moving to a multimodal representation. For Figure 5 (c) a text model for the query "wedding band" ranked the left and right listing 4 positions apart, while the multimodal model ranked the right listing 427 positions higher. "wedding band" saw a $\mathbf{1.55\%}$ **increase** in NDCG by moving to a multimodal representation.

4. CONCLUSION

Learning to rank search results is one of Etsy and other e-commerce sites' most fundamental problems. In this paper we describe how deep visual semantic features can be transferred successfully to multimodal learning to rank framework. We verify in a large-scale experiment that there is indeed significant complementary information present in images that can be used to improve search ranking quality. We visualize concrete examples of this marginal value: (i) the ability of the image modality to capture style information not well described in text. (ii) The ability of the image modality to disentangle highly different listings considered similar under a text-only modality.

Acknowledgments

The authors would like to thank Arjun Raj Rajanna, Christopher Kanan and Robert Hall for fruitful discussions during the course of this paper. We would also like to thank Ryan Frantz and Will Gallego for their insight and help in building the infrastructure required for running our experiments.

5. REFERENCES

[1] AYTAR, Y., AND ZISSERMAN, A. Tabula rasa: Model transfer for object category detection. In *Computer Vision (ICCV), 2011 IEEE International Conference on* (2011), IEEE, pp. 2252–2259.

[2] BAI, B., WESTON, J., GRANGIER, D., COLLOBERT, R., SADAMASA, K., QI, Y., CHAPELLE, O., AND WEINBERGER, K. Learning to rank with (a lot of) word features. *Information retrieval 13*, 3 (2010), 291–314.

[3] BURGES, C., SHAKED, T., RENSHAW, E., LAZIER, A., DEEDS, M., HAMILTON, N., AND HULLENDER, G. Learning to rank using gradient descent. In *Proceedings of the 22nd international conference on Machine learning* (2005), ACM, pp. 89–96.

[4] CHATFIELD, K., SIMONYAN, K., VEDALDI, A., AND ZISSERMAN, A. Return of the devil in the details: Delving deep into convolutional nets. *arXiv preprint arXiv:1405.3531* (2014).

[5] FROME, A., CORRADO, G. S., SHLENS, J., BENGIO, S., DEAN, J., MIKOLOV, T., ET AL. Devise: A deep visual-semantic embedding model. In *Advances in Neural Information Processing Systems* (2013), pp. 2121–2129.

[6] GATYS, L. A., ECKER, A. S., AND BETHGE, M. Texture synthesis and the controlled generation of natural stimuli using convolutional neural networks. *arXiv preprint arXiv:1505.07376* (2015).

[7] GONG, Y., WANG, L., HODOSH, M., HOCKENMAIER, J., AND LAZEBNIK, S. Improving image-sentence embeddings using large weakly annotated photo collections. In *Computer Vision–ECCV 2014*. Springer, 2014, pp. 529–545.

[8] GUILLAUMIN, M., VERBEEK, J., AND SCHMID, C. Multimodal semi-supervised learning for image classification. In *CVPR 2010-23rd IEEE Conference on Computer Vision & Pattern Recognition* (2010), IEEE Computer Society, pp. 902–909.

[9] HANG, L. A short introduction to learning to rank. *IEICE TRANSACTIONS on Information and Systems 94*, 10 (2011), 1854–1862.

[10] HERBRICH, R., GRAEPEL, T., AND OBERMAYER, K. Large margin rank boundaries for ordinal regression. *Advances in neural information processing systems* (1999), 115–132.

[11] JÄRVELIN, K., AND KEKÄLÄINEN, J. Cumulated gain-based evaluation of ir techniques. *ACM Transactions on Information Systems (TOIS) 20*, 4 (2002), 422–446.

[12] JOACHIMS, T. Optimizing search engines using clickthrough data. In *Proceedings of the eighth ACM SIGKDD international conference on Knowledge discovery and data mining* (2002), ACM, pp. 133–142.

[13] KANNAN, A., TALUKDAR, P. P., RASIWASIA, N., AND KE, Q. Improving product classification using images. In *Data Mining (ICDM), 2011 IEEE 11th International Conference on* (2011), IEEE, pp. 310–319.

[14] KARPATHY, A., JOULIN, A., AND LI, F. F. F. Deep fragment embeddings for bidirectional image sentence mapping. In *Advances in neural information processing systems* (2014), pp. 1889–1897.

[15] KIROS, R., SALAKHUTDINOV, R., AND ZEMEL, R. Multimodal neural language models. In *Proceedings of the 31st International Conference on Machine Learning (ICML-14)* (2014), pp. 595–603.

[16] KRIZHEVSKY, A., SUTSKEVER, I., AND HINTON, G. E. Imagenet classification with deep convolutional neural networks. In *Advances in neural information processing systems* (2012), pp. 1097–1105.

[17] MIKOLOV, T., SUTSKEVER, I., CHEN, K., CORRADO, G. S., AND DEAN, J. Distributed representations of words and phrases and their compositionality. In *Advances in neural information processing systems* (2013), pp. 3111–3119.

[18] OQUAB, M., BOTTOU, L., LAPTEV, I., AND SIVIC, J. Learning and transferring mid-level image representations using convolutional neural networks. In *Computer Vision and Pattern Recognition (CVPR), 2014 IEEE Conference on* (2014), IEEE, pp. 1717–1724.

[19] PAN, S. J., AND YANG, Q. A survey on transfer learning. *Knowledge and Data Engineering, IEEE Transactions on 22*, 10 (2010), 1345–1359.

[20] PEREIRA, J. C., AND VASCONCELOS, N. On the regularization of image semantics by modal expansion. In *Computer Vision and Pattern Recognition (CVPR), 2012 IEEE Conference on* (2012), IEEE, pp. 3093–3099.

[21] RADLINSKI, F., AND JOACHIMS, T. Minimally invasive randomization for collecting unbiased preferences from clickthrough logs. In *Proceedings of the National Conference on Artificial Intelligence* (2006), vol. 21, Menlo Park, CA; Cambridge, MA; London; AAAI Press; MIT Press; 1999, p. 1406.

[22] RAZAVIAN, A., AZIZPOUR, H., SULLIVAN, J., AND CARLSSON, S. Cnn features off-the-shelf: an astounding baseline for recognition. In *Proceedings of the IEEE Conference on Computer Vision and Pattern Recognition Workshops* (2014), pp. 806–813.

[23] SIMONYAN, K., AND ZISSERMAN, A. Very deep convolutional networks for large-scale image recognition. *arXiv preprint arXiv:1409.1556* (2014).

[24] SRIVASTAVA, N., HINTON, G., KRIZHEVSKY, A., SUTSKEVER, I., AND SALAKHUTDINOV, R. Dropout: A simple way to prevent neural networks from overfitting. *The Journal of Machine Learning Research 15*, 1 (2014), 1929–1958.

[25] TOMMASI, T., ORABONA, F., AND CAPUTO, B. Learning categories from few examples with multi model knowledge transfer. *Pattern Analysis and Machine Intelligence, IEEE Transactions on 36*, 5 (2014), 928–941.

[26] WANG, G., HOIEM, D., AND FORSYTH, D. Building text features for object image classification. In *Computer Vision and Pattern Recognition, 2009. CVPR 2009. IEEE Conference on* (2009), IEEE, pp. 1367–1374.

[27] WEINBERGER, K., DASGUPTA, A., LANGFORD, J., SMOLA, A., AND ATTENBERG, J. Feature hashing for large scale multitask learning. In *Proceedings of the 26th Annual International Conference on Machine Learning* (2009), ACM, pp. 1113–1120.

[28] WESTON, J., BENGIO, S., AND USUNIER, N. Large scale image annotation: learning to rank with joint word-image embeddings. *Machine learning 81*, 1 (2010), 21–35.

[29] ZEILER, M. D., AND FERGUS, R. Visualizing and understanding convolutional networks. In *Computer Vision–ECCV 2014*. Springer, 2014, pp. 818–833.

Text Mining in Clinical Domain: Dealing with Noise

Hoang Nguyen
Data61 - CSIRO
13 Garden Street
Eveleigh, NSW 2015, Australia
hoang.nguyen@data61.csiro.au

Jon Patrick
University of Sydney
1 Cleveland Street
Sydney, NSW 2006, Australia
jonpat@it.usyd.edu.au

ABSTRACT

Text mining in clinical domain is usually more difficult than general domains (e.g. newswire reports and scientific literature) because of the high level of noise in both the corpus and training data for machine learning (ML). A large number of unknown word, non-word and poor grammatical sentences made up the noise in the clinical corpus. Unknown words are usually complex medical vocabularies, misspellings, acronyms and abbreviations where unknown non-words are generally the clinical patterns including scores and measures. This noise produces obstacles in the initial lexical processing step as well as subsequent semantic analysis. Furthermore, the labelled data used to build ML models is very costly to obtain because it requires intensive clinical knowledge from the annotators. And even created by experts, the training examples usually contain errors and inconsistencies due to the variations in human annotators' attentiveness. Clinical domain also suffers from the nature of the imbalanced data distribution problem. These kinds of noise are very popular and potentially affect the overall information extraction performance but they were not carefully investigated in most presented health informatics systems.

This paper introduces a general clinical data mining architecture which is potential of addressing all of these challenges using: automatic proof-reading process, trainable finite state pattern recogniser, iterative model development and active learning. The reportability classifier based on this architecture achieved 98.25% sensitivity and 96.14% specificity on an Australian cancer registry's held-out test set and up to 92% of training data provided for supervised ML was saved by active learning.

Keywords

Clinical, active learning, text classification, named-entity recognition, natural languages processing

KDD '16, August 13-17, 2016, San Francisco, CA, USA
© 2016 ACM. ISBN 978-1-4503-4232-2/16/08...$15.00
DOI: http://dx.doi.org/10.1145/2939672.2939720

1. INTRODUCTION

Processing clinical texts is quite challenging. Firstly, clinical records comprise idiosyncratic spellings, abbreviations, acronyms, poor grammatical structure, and up to 30 percent of non-word tokens. Besides resolving misspellings, knowing the correct expansions of abbreviations and acronyms is critical to understanding the document for both automatic natural language processing as well as human comprehension and interpretation [27]. Secondly, an important part of narrative reports that needs to be captured is clinical scores and measures as doctors infer a patient's status by analyzing these complex patterns. For example, BP 140/65 (84) is an example of Blood Pressure; HR 72 is pattern of Heart Rate. These lexical obstacles in the clinical corpus should be addressed at an early step of processing to avoid inherited chain of errors.

Our research focuses on supervised ML approaches because designing rules and patterns is time consuming and complicated process for human experts to complete. The basic advantage of ML is that the concept characteristics and classification rules can be automatically learnt through training examples. Therefore, the high quality of a semantically classified and annotated corpus is mandatory to contribute to the success of supervised learning algorithms. However, the training examples are usually not free and obtaining these labels is a time consuming and high labour cost process. Narrative reports usually take longer time to annotate as they require expertise knowledge in the field. Even if tagging is provided by human experts, there is a high level of inconsistency in the labelled data because some instances are implicitly difficult for annotators and also they become distracted or fatigued over time, introducing variability in the quality of their annotations [29]. Besides the noise caused during the annotation process, the train set of clinical ML also suffers from the problem of imbalanced data distribution: one class (usually negative class) may have many more instances that dominate all other classes (e.g. non-cancer cases vs cancer cases in radiology reports). This can cause a bias in the training process and may require a special active learning method for the sample data to improve the overall ML performance.

To the best of our knowledge, none of the published health information system is capable of addressing all of the above challenges. In the present paper, we propose the novel data mining system that employed natural language processing techniques, supervised ML and active learning approaches to overcome the difficulties when working with clinical text.

Our system focuses on clinical text classification and named-entity recognition and includes three main components:

- The specialised pre-processing system to deal with noise in the corpus.
- The iterative model development process to reduce both the noise and cost of manual annotations.
- Active learning infrastructure to optimise the training production of supervised learning. The main purpose of the optimisation process is to achieve the best performance with a smaller number but higher quality training examples, hence minimising labelling costs. The problem of imbalanced data distribution is also improved by applying special active learning strategies (Section 3.3).

The rest of the paper is structured as follows. Section 2 gives an overview of the previous clinical and radiological information extraction systems. Our system architecture is presented in Section 3. The proposed system demonstrated the high performance in classifying real-world and large scale radiology reports provided by Australian Cancer Registries. Experiments and results related to the Cancer Council's project are reported in Section 4. We conclude in Section 5 with directions for future work.

2. RELATED WORK

A variety of methods and systems have been implemented in the clinical domain to extract information from free text. The popular learning tasks include document classification, named-entity recognition (NER) and classification of relationship between the entities (medical concepts).

Friedman et al. (1994) [9] developed the medical language extraction and encoding (MedLEE) system, which used a domain-specific vocabulary and semantic grammar to process radiology reports. It was initially used to participate in an automated decision-support system, and to allow natural language queries. MedLEE was then adapted to automatically identify the concepts in clinical documents, map the concepts to semantic categories and semantic structures [10]. The final semantic representation of each concept contained information on status, location and certainty of each concept instance. Haug et al. (1995) [12] introduced symbolic text processor (SymText), a natural language understanding system for chest x-ray reports. SymText processes each sentence in a document independently with syntactic and probabilistic semantic analysis. Bayesian networks are used in SymText to determine the probability that a disease is present in the patient.

An early combined classifier approach in biomedical NER proposed a two-state model in which boundary recognition and term classification are separated into two phases [17]. In each classification phase, different feature sets were selected independently, which is more efficient for each task. A comparative study between two classical ML methods, Conditional Random Fields (CRFs) and Support Vector Machines (SVMs) for clinical NER shows that the CRFs outperformed SVMs in clinical NER [19].

When extracting information from narrative text documents, the context or assertion of the concepts extracted play a critical role. The NegEx algorithm of [3] implements dictionaries of pre-UMLS and post-UMLS phrases that are indicative of negation to identify positive and negative assertions. NegEx uses a rule-based method and heuristics to limit the scope of indicative phrases. The i2b2 challenge's assertion classification is an extension of a previous system designed by [35], in the new specification an uncertainty assertion is divided into values of hypothetical, conditional and possible. A combination of ML and rule-based approaches is utilised in the system of [35]. One of these approaches extends the rule-based NegEx algorithm to capture alter-association in addition to positive, negative and uncertain assertions; the other employs an SVM to present a ML solution to assertion classification.

For the relationship classification task, there are many definitions of relationships between concepts in which each system classifies different relationship types. In general, relevant features are extracted from the text and are usually selected on the basis of the experimental results and intuition, or by statistical techniques [11]. First, by experience and intuition, we designed feature sets that were expected to have a strong correlation with the target classification. Forward selection was applied by sequentially adding each feature set to the model and evaluating its performance. The feature set is retained if a better result is achieved otherwise it is discarded before the next cycle is repeated.

ML systems have demonstrated high accuracy in information extraction and classification from radiology reports. It has also been used for automatic structuring of important medical information from radiology reports [15, 30]. Thomas et al. used Boolean logic built from 512 consecutive ankle radiography reports to create a text search algorithm and then applied to a different set of 750 radiology reports with a sensitivity of 87.8% and specificity of 91.3% [31]. The LEXIMER automated engine classified 1059 unstructured reports of radiography examinations based on the presence of important findings and suggestions for further actions with 94.9% and 97.7% sensitivity and specificity respectively [6]. In other research specialised on lung cancer reports, McCowan el at. used SVM learning techniques to investigate the classification of cancer stages [21, 20]. This system achieved an accuracy of 74% for tumour (T) staging and 87% for node (N) staging on the complete 179-case trial data set. In recent work published by Cheng et al., they first accessed whether the text contains sufficient information for a classification process then the tumour status and progression was determined by utilizing the SVMs models that reached 80.6% sensitivity and 91.6% specificity [4]. However, the sizes of the corpora used in previous research were relatively small compared to the number of reports processed by a registry each year.

3. SYSTEM ARCHITECTURE

Figure 1 presents the system architecture which comprises of three phases: pre-processing, iterative model development and active learning. The electronic medical records (EMRs) are retrieved from the database then passed into the pre-processing phase for proof-reading, lexical verification and medical concepts identification. At the end of this step, the records are cleaned and annotated with the medical concepts hence they are ready to be used to develop training data for ML models. At each development cycle, the model's performance is evaluated using n-fold cross-validation method then more data will be added to the train set with the support of active learning algorithms to query the most infor-

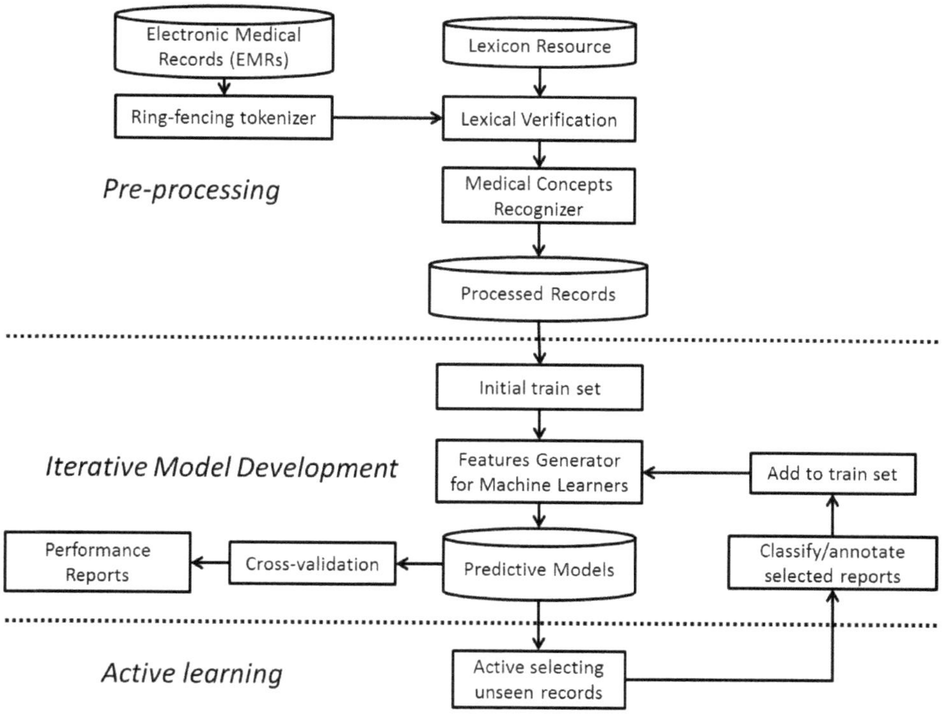

Figure 1: System architecture.

mative instances. This process is repeated until the desired performance is met.

3.1 Proof-reading (pre-processing system)

Proof-reading is a process whereby a clinical text is validated to identify unknown tokens/words and their valid forms. There are two principal tasks to be achieved, these are normalisation and standardisation. The normalisation process changes the texts in a way so that a human reader would consider it as normal, such as correcting spelling, expanding abbreviations and acronyms. The standardisation process converts the text into certain formats that an expert community has defined as standard; a good example is converting scores and measures into a standard layout.

3.1.1 Standardisation

The ring-fencing tokeniser is capable of capturing popular basic and complex patterns in clinical text. It is a cascaded Finite State Recognizer (FSR) which uses training examples to recognize token patterns constituting a score or measurement that requires standardisation [26]. There are a large number of different scores and measurements in clinical notes. Some other types of measurements and scores in the training patterns are illustrated in Table 1.

When using regular expressions (REs) to describe patterns as more rules are developed to capture missed items, the rules became so complicated that it makes them difficult to update as any change has the risk of losing previously recognized patterns or introducing new false positives. Another problem is that the rule updating task requires an exhaustive knowledge of REs and a considerable amount of time modifying the rules. Consequently, the automated learning process to capture patterns using REs is particularly difficult. On the other hand, a trainable FSR can be built directly from training examples of data with high accuracy and efficient computational time.

Type	Pattern
BP	BP 140/65(84)
ABG	ABG's: 0355 7.41/41/103/26/2
Lipids	Lipids 10% at 20mls/hr
Measurement	7mg/hr
SaO2	O2 sats 91%

Table 1: Examples of clinical measures and scores can be recognized by FSR.

To capture composite patterns in clinical text, the cascaded FSR is generated by several levels of generalisation. The basic patterns is recognised first by simple FSR and then passed to complex FSR to capture the final complicated patterns. The example of applying a cascaded FSR to capture complex patterns in the text is showed in Figure 2.

3.1.2 Normalisation

After standardisation, each token is passed through the lexical verification process and then inserted into the Lexicon Management System (LMS) which supports automated and manual resolution of unknown tokens. The LMS is a system developed to store the accumulated lexical knowledge and contains categorizations of spelling errors, abbreviations, acronyms and a variety of non-word tokens. It also has a web interface that supports rapid manual correction of unknown words with a high accuracy clinical spelling suggestor plus the addition of grammatical information and the categorization of such words into gazetteers [25]. The method of the clinical spelling suggestor is based on combining heuristic-based suggestion generation and ranking algo-

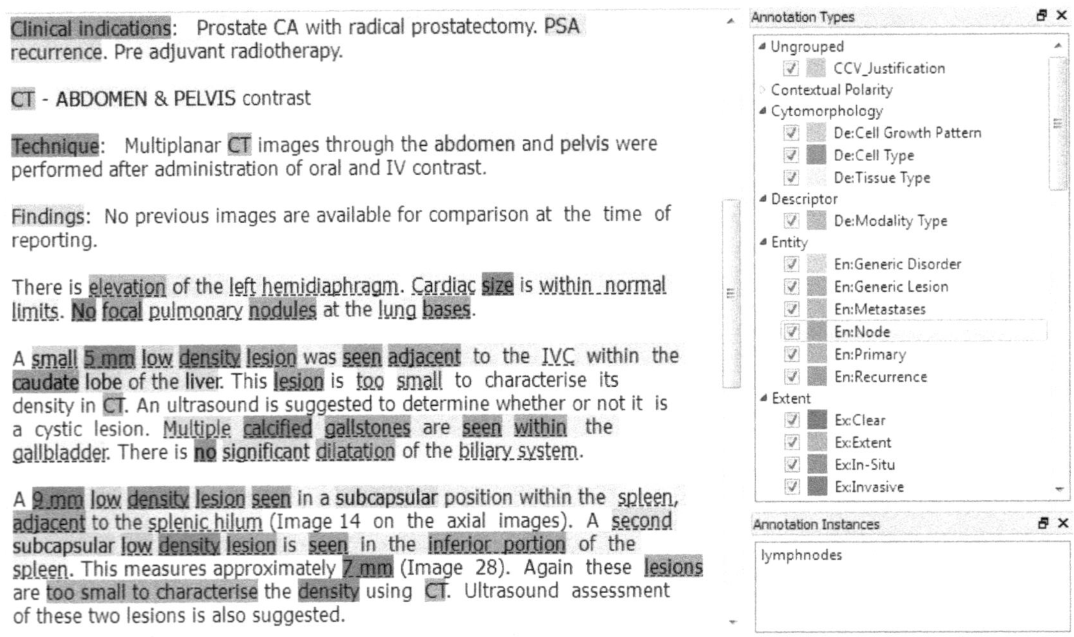

Figure 3: Example of annotated clinical report with in-house design of annotation schema for cancer radiology reports classification case study.

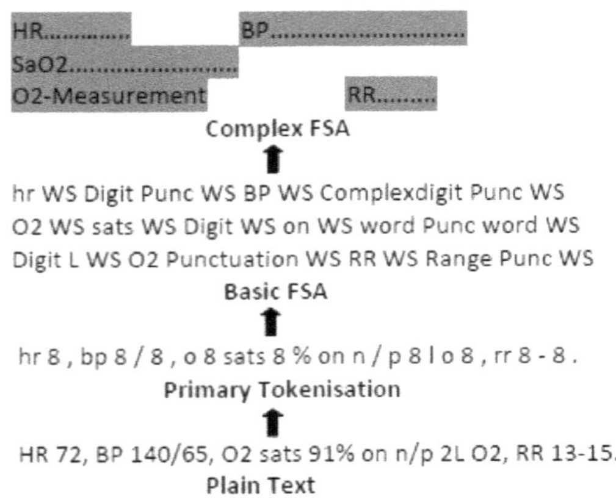

Figure 2: Example of cascaded FSR.

rithms based on word frequencies and trigram probabilities. The lexical verification process contains an additional step to resolve misplaced whitespace (e.g. 'looka fter' should be 'look after') and punctuation (e.g. 'natio;n' should be 'nation' or 'nation.The' should be 'nation. The').

3.1.3 Clinical Concepts Recognition

In EMRs, the same clinical concepts are usually expressed in different ways causing the models interpreted them as different features. Hence, there is a need for normalization of the medical concept using universal terminologies such as $UMLS^{®}$, $SNOMED-CT^{®}$ or their subsets. Besides general medical terminologies, the in-house design tag set was utilised in many studies because it is better controlled and more relevant to the predictive tasks, or to identify specific clinical entities in the text. Figure 3 illustrates the example annotation schema which was specially designed for classification of cancer radiology reports.

A detailed and well-designed tagging system can contribute significantly to the classification and extraction results. For example, the sentence 'There is no convincing metastatic bone lesion' in the conclusion will be tagged as:

$$\text{There is } \underbrace{\text{no}}_{\text{LPN}}\ \underbrace{\text{convincing}}_{\text{Modality}}\ \underbrace{\text{metastatic}}_{\text{Metastases}}\ \underbrace{\text{bone}}_{\text{Site}}\ \underbrace{\text{lesion}}_{\text{Lesion}}.$$

The occurrence of popular cancer terms (e.g. metastatic, lesion) in a sentence in the conclusion section is not enough to conclude that the cancer is reportable. The complete investigation has to consider whether the cancer term is negated or modalised on the basis of linguistic tags such as Lexical Polarity Negative (LPN) and Modality in the classification process.

3.2 Iterative Model Development

In the annotation process, free-text reports are annotated for examples of the information to be extracted and then algorithms are developed that use the examples to compute a more general model of the desired content. The small initial data set is selected to train the first model. The model is evaluated and the algorithm is revised in a feedback process to produce a more accurate result. This is continued over a series of experiments until an optimal model is identified.

In our model of iterative development, the annotators use a Visual Annotator (VA) tool as shown in Figure 3 which contains computational models of the tag set so as to support the manual annotation and classification processing. Hence, they no longer need to annotate each report de novo but employ knowledge from previously annotated instances and knowledge from all annotators as learnt by the computational model. This not only reduces the workload and annotation time per report but also reduces the error rate and inconsistencies of human annotation which were generated by different levels of expertise.

After each cross-validation cycle, the new model is delivered to the VA to perform manual correction of the current gold-standard with the support of an annotation validation tool. This model is further supported by active learning algorithms to query the most informative instances to enrich the train set. The active learning selection process can query instances as a group in batch-mode which are suitable for parallel processing environment.

SVMs combined with CRFs are the main ML methods proposed for text classification and named-entity recognition for clinical textual data [14, 16]. For a large-scale classification problem with millions of instances and features such as in the radiology reports classification task, a linear kernel is usually a promising learning technique. Experiments were therefore performed with optimized linear kernel as the base classifier rather than SVMs with non-linear kernels [8]. The recommended sets for feature selection experiments include but not limited to:

- Bag of words (BOW): the feature value of the binary term weight is 0 or 1 corresponding to the existence of that feature in the text. The frequency term weight with normalised vector can also be applied.

- Proof reading: corrections and expansions, when used as features, will support the model in learning correct forms of misspelt words ('medicla' and 'medcial' refer to the same word 'medical') and variations of abbreviations ('amnt' and 'amt' are both 'amount'), and multiple acronyms of the same term ('ABG', 'ABGs' are both 'arterial blood gases').

- Ring-fencing: the basic patterns (date, time, number, etc) and standard patterns (blood pressure, heart rate, cancer stage, etc) are used as features to indicate whether a token belongs to any kind of scores or measures.

- Lemma, part of speech, chunk from the GENIA tagger: The GENIA tagger analyses English sentences and outputs the base forms, part-of-speech tags, chunk tags. The tagger is specifically tuned for biomedical text and is a useful pre-processing tool to extract information from biomedical documents [33].

- Medical terminology and gazetteer: checks whether a term belongs to a specialized clinical concept (UMLS, SNOMED-CT) or gazetteer (e.g. cancer terminology).

- Bag of tags (BOT): this feature indicates the clinical entities tagged by the computational annotation model. Entity is the generalisation of the frequent key words used to report a medical concept.

- Context feature: adds features to indicate whether a word belongs to a specific context (e.g. clinical indication, conclusion).

- Negation and modality feature: the occurrence of negation and modality tags help to identify whether a phrase is modalised or negated.

3.3 Active Learning

Active learning (AL) is a subfield of ML where the learner is allowed to query the most informative instances to retrain the model instead of making a random selection. Based on this approach, with the same number of sample selections, the performance of active learners dominates random learners in most cases [29]. This approach requires significantly fewer sample reports while maintaining comparable performance to traditional supervised learning with all training data or even bettering it.

In the present work, the main focus is on pool-based sampling which was introduced by Lewis and Catlett [18]. In this scenario, the learner has access to a pool of unlabelled instances and can request the labels for some number of them. Among many AL algorithms have been introduced in the literature, the four algorithms investigated and suggested for clinical text classification in this paper are Simple, Self-Confident (Self-Conf), Kernel Farthest-First (KFF), and Balanced Exploration and Exploitation (Balance-EE). These algorithms appear to be among the best performers based on empirical studies. Furthermore, they are reasonably well motivated and achieved high performance on real-world data sets [1, 24].

3.3.1 Simple AL

The Simple algorithm is based on the kernel machines and was independently proposed by three different research groups [28, 32, 2]. The name Simple (simple margin) used uncertainty estimation as its selection strategy [32]. In SVMs kernel space, the highest uncertain instance, which is defined as the most informative instance, is the one that lies closest to the decision hyperplane. For each unlabelled instance x, the shortest distance between the feature vector $\Phi(x)$ and the hyperplane w_i in the feature space is easily computed by $|w_i \cdot \Phi(x)|$. Hence, the querying function of Simple uses the current classifier to choose an unlabeled instance which is closest to the decision boundary.

3.3.2 Self Confident

The Self-Conf algorithm chooses the next example to be labeled so that, when it is added to the training data, the future generalization error probability is minimized [1]. Since true future error rates are unknown, the learner attempts to estimate them using a 'self-confidence' heuristic, which uses its current classifier for probability measurements. The future error rate is estimated by a log-loss function, which uses the entropy of the posterior class distribution on a sample of the unlabeled instances. Each instance from the unseen pool is examined by adding it to the training set with a sample of its possible labels and estimating the resulting future error rate as described in equation 1; the instance with the smallest expected log is then chosen.

Let $P(y|x)$ be an unknown conditional distribution over inputs x, and output $y \in \{y_1, y_2, ..., y_n\}$. At each query, a trained probabilistic (soft) classifier given by $\hat{P}(y|x)$ is already built from current training data. For each instance x from the unseen pool U, the algorithm trains a new classifier P' over $L'(x, y) = L \bigcup \{(x, y)\}$ and the expected log-loss is defined as:

$$E(\hat{P'}_{L'}(x, y)) = \frac{1}{|U|} \sum_{y' \in Y, x' \in U} \hat{P'}(y'|x') \log \hat{P'}(y'|x') \quad (1)$$

The original SELF-CONF employed Naive Bayes probability estimates. In the experiments described in this chapter, [1] implemented SELF-CONF using soft (confidence rated) SVMs. Probabilistic estimates are obtained in a standard way using the logistic regression transform. However, in each selection round, the expected log-loss is re-calculated for all instances in the unseen pool based on their possible labels and then the model is re-trained.

3.3.3 Kernel Farthest-First

The KFF algorithm uses a simple AL heuristic based on the 'farthest-first' traversal sequence in kernel space [13]. In this algorithm, the most informative instance is the farthest instance in the unseen pool from the current training set, where the distance from a point to a set is defined as the Euclidean distance to the closest point in the set. The assumption behind the KFF heuristic is that the farthest instance is considered to be the most dissimilar to the current training data and needs to be learned first.

Given a set L of labelled examples, KFF chooses the next farthest example x from L in the feature space induced by the SVM's kernel K to be labelled:

$$argmax_{x \in U}(min_{y \in L}||\Phi_K(x) - \Phi_K(y)||), \quad (2)$$

where

$$||\Phi_K(x) - \Phi_K(y)|| = \sqrt{K(x,x) + K(y,y) - 2K(x,y)} \quad (3)$$

is the Euclidean distance from $\Phi_K(x)$ to $\Phi_K(y)$, which are the projections of x and y in the feature space induced by the kernel K.

The advantage of KFF over Simple and Self-Conf algorithms is that it does not use the model to evaluate the unseen pool during the querying process. Hence, there is no need to retrain the model after each AL trial, and it can be applied to any learning algorithms.

3.3.4 Balanced Exploration and Exploitation

The Simple active learner is good at 'exploitation' by selecting the examples near the boundary, but it does not carry out 'exploration' by searching for large regions in the instance space that it might incorrectly predict. The Balance-EE method, which is based on a combination of Simple and KFF, to address the problem of balancing between exploitation of labeling instances that are near the current decision boundary (Simple) and exploration by searching for instances that are far from the already labeled points (KFF) [24]. At each trial, Balance-EE randomly decides whether exploration (Simple) or exploitation (KFF) will be used. If the choice is exploration (Simple), the algorithm evaluates the efficiency of the exploration to adjust its probability of exploring again.

Let h and h' be the hypothesis before and after the new example from Simple is added. The change induced from h to h' $d(h,h') \in [-1,+1]$ is evaluated. If $d(h,h')$ is positive, the exploration was efficient and p will be kept high and vice versa.

Let $S = x_1, x_2, ..., x_n = L \cup U$ be the set of labelled and unlabelled instances. For each of the hypotheses $h(\cdot), h'(\cdot)$, vectors of the predictions of h and h' on S are defined as $H = (h(x_1), h(x_2), ..., h(x_n))$ and $H' = (h'(x_1), h'(x_2), ..., h'(x_n))$. Then $d(h,h')$ is defined as:

$$d(h,h') = 3 - 4\frac{\langle H, H'\rangle}{||H||||H'||}, \quad (4)$$

The probability p for exploration will be updated as:

$$p' = \max(\min(p\lambda \exp(d(h,h')), 1-\epsilon), \epsilon), \quad (5)$$

where ϵ defines the upper and lower-bounds for the value of p, and λ is a learning rate for updating p.

3.3.5 Imbalanced Data Problem and AL

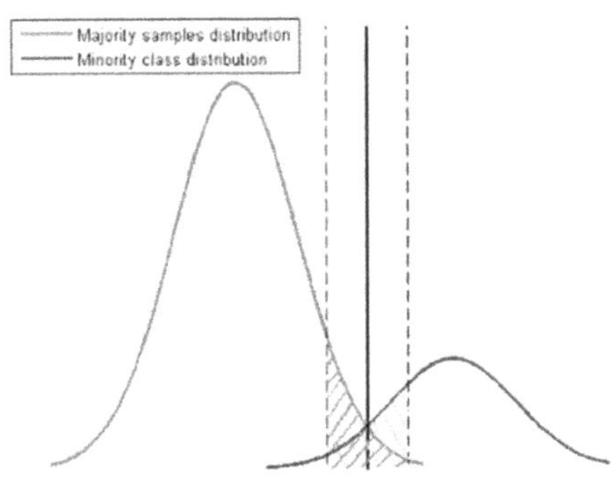

Figure 4: Data within the margin is less imbalanced than the entire data.

Ertekin et al. demonstrated that Simple method has the capability of overcoming the imbalanced data problem by providing the learner with much better balanced classes. Figure 4 presents an example of the imbalanced data distribution (image source [7]). Uncertainty AL tends to select the instances that are close to the decision boundary (within the margin), this selection strategy more likely ends up with a better balanced class distribution than that of the entire data set. This problem can also be improved by not querying the redundant samples from the dominated class or querying the positive and negative examples repeatedly from the labelled pool.

4. EXPERIMENTS AND RESULTS

Patrick and Nguyen (2011) conducted the evaluation for the role of pre-processing phase in improving the ML performance [25]. System performance was evaluated before and after an automatic proof reading process by comparing the computed SNOMED-CT codes to the coding created originally by the clinical staff. The automatic coding of the texts increased the coded content by 15% after the automatic correction process and the number of unique codes increased by approximately 5%.

The early design of our system without the integration of AL was initially ranked among the top three teams in the i2b2 2010 international challenge on clinical information extraction [25, 34]. Our follow-up challenge experiments with AL methods recorded the equivalent performance to the winning team with 15% less training data used [22, 5].

In this section, we focus on the evaluation of the general system which was fully developed for a project with Victorian Cancer Council in Australia[1]. This project has the

[1]http://www.cancervic.org.au/research/registry-statistics/capture-stage-recurrence

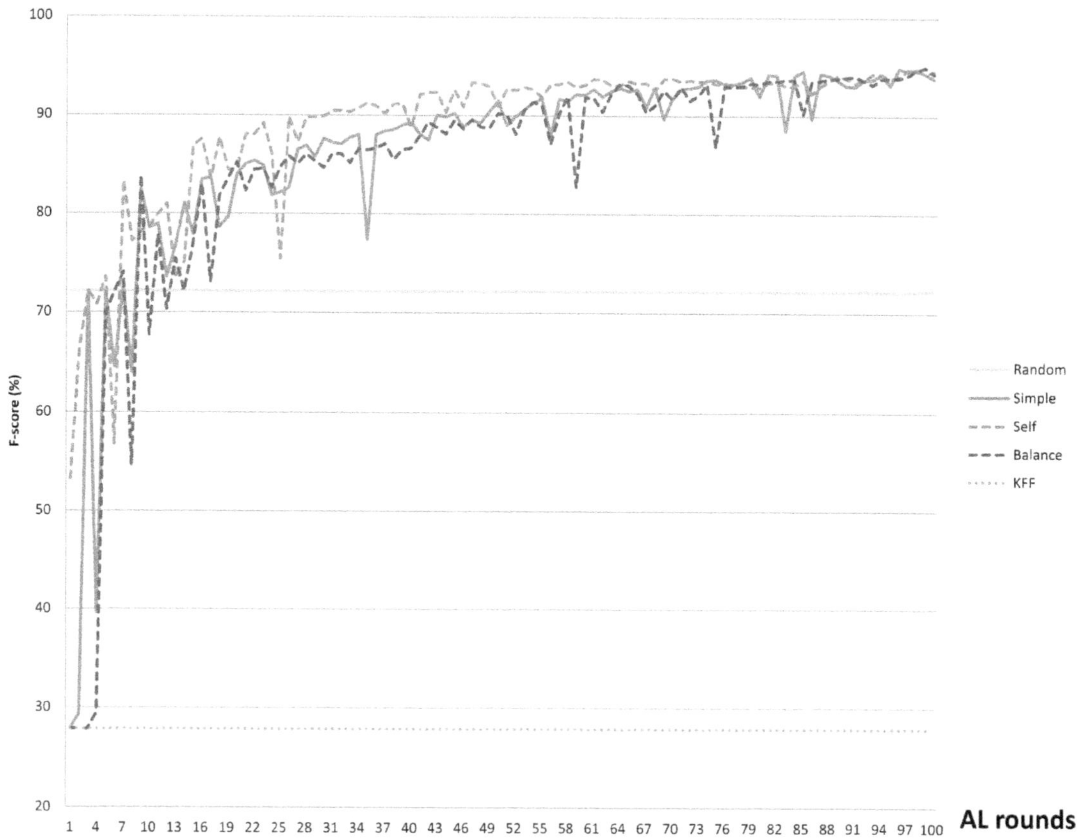

Figure 5: Evaluation of active and random sampling on test data.

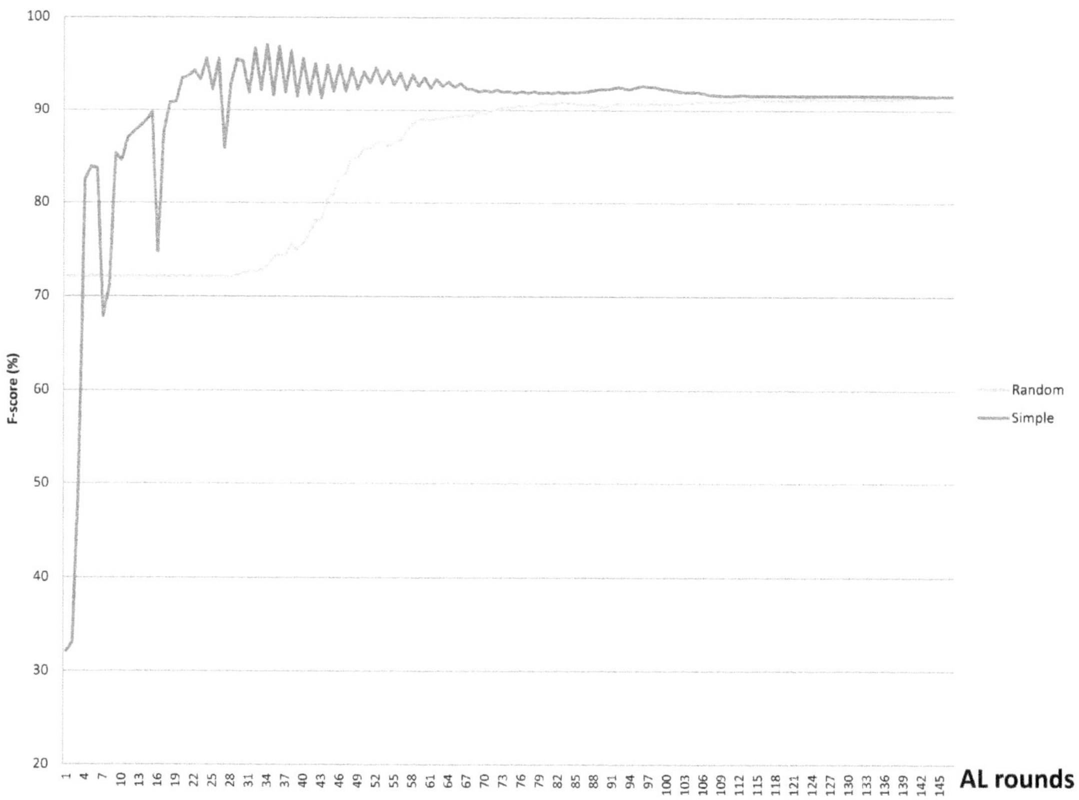

Figure 6: Full learning curves for Simple active learning and random learning with a batch size of 100.

Tag	TPs	FPs	FNs	P	R	F
De	230615	17980	16682	0.928	0.933	0.930
En	71340	6214	7640	0.920	0.903	0.912
Ra	1417	114	182	0.926	0.886	0.905
Li	141257	8464	8948	0.944	0.940	0.942
St	20370	204	391	0.990	0.981	0.986
All	464999	32976	33843	**0.934**	**0.932**	**0.933**

Table 2: Fivefold cross-validation tagging performance.

special requirement of separating the cancer and non-cancer reports by using a deliberate bias to ensure virtually all cancer reports are recognised. It has the consequence of producing as high an accuracy for sensitivity as possible with the challenge of maintaining reasonable specificity for the classifier. Ideally, the cancer registry does not want to miss any cancer cases, however they have accepted a sensitivity greater than 98% and specificity greater than 96%.

4.1 Data Description

The cancer cases covered in this study included all reports provided in a year's data collection by the imaging services in Australia. The pilot sites were Lake Imaging, Ballarat, Peter MacCallum Cancer Centre, Melbourne, and Westmead Hospital, Sydney in conjunction with the Cancer Institute of NSW. The process of creating the classifiers relied on using a manually trained corpus drawn from each site. Initially, a sample of 16 472 reports was drawn from Lake Imaging and assigned to cancer (4784 reports) or non-cancer (11 688 reports) classes by the cancer registry and then incrementally delivered to our system.

4.2 Named-Entity Recognition

To support the classification process, the training reports were tagged to identify structure and cancer-related information based on an in house design annotation schema. More than 3000 cancer reports were annotated with approximately 500 000 tag instances. The overall F-score for fivefold cross-validation of the Named-Entity Recognizer (NER) is 93%. The CRF++ tool was used in our NER experiments[2].

Our designed tag sets for cancer information extraction are well controlled and do not contain superfluous information, which can mislead the classification process. Table 2 presents the 5-fold cross validation performance of the computational tagger. In this table, the tags are divided into five subsets:

- Descriptor (De): morphology, topography, cytomorphology and modality type tags.
- Entity (En): objects of interest within a report. They are usually the subject of the report, which is cancer in this case.
- Linguistic (Li): includes lexical polarity, normality and modifier tags. Linguistic tags are not directly related to cancer content, but they are crucial for the confirmation of reportability.
- Radiologist's coding (Ra): includes cancer stage, TNM (tumor-nodal-metastases) values which are recorded directly in the text.
- Structure (St): includes heading tags. The structure tags are not directly related to the cancer content but support the use of context as features in the classification process. These headings are also used to structure the report body when populating the output in an XML format.

[2]http://crfpp.googlecode.com/svn/trunk/doc/index.html

4.3 Classification and Active Learning

Figure 5 shows the accuracy of the four AL algorithms and random sampling in classifying the radiology reports. The AL experiment was executed in batch mode with 10 reports/round for 100 rounds. Random sampling gave a consistent performance of 72.13% throughout the learning process; this accuracy is equal to the rate of non-reportable instances in the test set (1188/1647). Except for the last few cycles which can only capture one or two positive instances, the random classifier predicted every instance in the test set as non-reportable. This is because of imbalanced data distribution problem, e.g. the number of non-reportables in the training set is 2.6 times greater than the number of reportables, so they exceeded the reportable instances in the early cycles of random selection. The worst performance can be seen with the KFF algorithm, with 27.87% over time; this accuracy is equal to the rate of reportables in the test set (459/1647). Different from the random sampling, the KFF algorithm mostly selected the positive class (766 positives out of 1002 selected examples). Hence, the KFF classifier categorized all instances in the test set as reportable.

The three other AL algorithms show comparable results, with over 94.5% accuracy at the peak points. Balance-EE is a combination of Simple and KFF with a choice of algorithm in each trial. In this experiment, KFF was selected by Balance-EE for the first six trials for 60 examples, and then Simple was applied for the subsequent instances. As a result, except for several 'drop points', Balance-EE had a similar learning curve to Simple because most examples were selected using the 'exploitation' (Simple) strategy. The Self-Conf algorithm showed consistently higher accuracy than Simple and Balance-EE for the initial AL queries, and it quickly reached the top performance with only 60% queries used.

From these analyses, the Simple algorithm was chosen as the AL strategy for generating the priority list for manual reportability classification of radiology reports. As seen in Figure 5, the Simple method had comparable results to Self-Conf and Balanced-EE, but its implementation was simpler and more efficient. For 100 trials, Balanced-EE was slightly slower than Simple, while Self-Conf was five times slower than Simple.

The full learning curves for Simple active sampling and random sampling with a batch size of 100 reports per round for 145 rounds are presented in Figure 6. The batch size was increased from 10 to 100 to speed up the process in order to generate an overview of the comprehensive learning curves. However, the performance of the active learner with the same training size was reduced as compared to batch of 10 results because the model was updated 10 times less frequently. Figure 6 shows that the performance of the random sampler increased only when it had 3000 reports. At that point, the Simple active learner had already reached its top performance, which was over 23% higher than the random learner. There was not much difference in the performances of the two methods since 10 000 reports had been selected.

A known problem with many AL algorithms, especially in the early steps of learning, is that they are prone to generate a biased training set rather than representative of the true underlying data distribution. As can be seen in Figure 6, there are a few points where the performance of the active learner dropped dramatically - for example, the performance fell below 80% when 1600 samples were used. This is due to limitations in the initial model that will perform AL. Many algorithms just randomly select a few instances to train the first model, which is usually not a good starting point for the real data distribution [22].

4.4 Held-out Test Set Result

The evaluation of the reportability classifier presented here was executed independently at the Cancer Registry. They used sensitivity and specificity as evaluation metrics, while precision, recall, and F1-score were calculated in our experiments. For the binary classification problem, 'sensitivity' is equal to 'recall' of the positive class (reportable), and 'specificity' is the 'recall' of the negative class (non-reportable). The Registry maintains the held-out test set to evaluate the system independently until the required sensitivity and specificity are achieved. None of the held-out test set was used for any part of the system development - for example, they were not used to build the gazetteers or the ML models. This held-out test set comprised 400 reportables and 2100 non-reportables, which is a similar distribution to the released data.

The approved version of the classifier achieved the sensitivity of 98.25% and specificity of 96.14% (Table 3). The final version is implemented based on two ML algorithms, they are CRFs and SVMs. In addition, the special cancer gazetteers collected by the linguists who have experience at interpreting the reports are used to support the ML models. The addition of gazetteer features slightly increased the sensitivity of the model (1.5%) while decreased the specificity level (2.2%). The significant improvement of nearly 5.3% in the targeted sensitivity score was experienced when the classifier was supported with the tagging features (BOT) generated by the computational annotation models. Furthermore, the specificity was still maintained at over 96% which was fulfilled the requirement of the project.

Sensitivity	Specificity	BOW	Gaz	BOT
91.46%	98.76%	Yes		
92.96%	96.53%	Yes	Yes	
98.25%	**96.14%**	**Yes**	**Yes**	**Yes**

Table 3: Reportability classifier's performance on evaluation (held-out) set for Lake Imaging

5. CONCLUSIONS

This paper presents a general system for text mining in clinical domain with a focus on dealing with multiple frequent kinds of noise. This system is then become part of an industrial-strength processing pipeline built to extract content from radiology reports for use in the Victorian Cancer Registry. The most important practical application of the reportability classifier is that it can dramatically reduce human effort in identifying relevant reports from the large imaging pool for further investigation of cancer. The classifier is built on a large real-world dataset and can achieve high performance in filtering relevant reports.

In future work, we will investigate the specialised parser to deal with the problem of poor grammatical sentences in the clinical corpus. In the patient notes, very few sentences could be successfully explored by full constituent parse tree due to the frequent ungrammatical notes written by the doctors. However, the partial trees are usually utilised when the complete parse could not be generated. Exploring the subtrees between two target concepts can help to better classify the relationship between them.

In the present system, the models stopped learning when it reached the pre-defined performance. However, it is more ideal if the model only finishes the querying process when the best performance is archived. We plan to improve the current system by introducing the stopping criteria during the AL process. Several stopping criteria have been introduced and are based on measures of stability or self-confidence within the learner [36, 23].

6. ACKNOWLEDGEMENTS

This work was supported by the Victorian Cancer Registry, Cancer Australia (2012-2013) and Data61 - CSIRO (2015). The authors would like to thank Helen Farrugia and Georgina Marr of the Cancer Council of Victoria, who provided the funding for this project and the registry expertise, and Dr Alex Pitman of Lake Imaging for contributing his radiological expertise.

7. REFERENCES

[1] Y. Baram, R. El-Yaniv, and K. Luz. Online choice of active learning algorithms. *Journal of Machine Learning Research*, 5:255–291, 2004.

[2] C. Campbell, N. Cristianini, A. Smola, et al. Query learning with large margin classifiers. In *Machine Learning-International Workshop then Conference*, pages 111–118, 2000.

[3] W. Chapman, W. Bridewell, P. Hanbury, G. Cooper, and B. Buchanan. A simple algorithm for identifying negated findings and diseases in discharge summaries. *Journal of Biomedical Informatics*, 34(5):301–310, 2001.

[4] L. Cheng, J. Zheng, G. Savova, and B. Erickson. Discerning tumor status from unstructured mri reports-completeness of information in existing reports and utility of automated natural language processing. *Journal of Digital Imaging*, 23:119–132, 2010.

[5] B. de Bruijn, C. Cherry, S. Kiritchenko, J. Martin, and X. Zhu. Machine-learned solutions for three stages of clinical information extraction: the state of the art at i2b2 2010. *Journal of the American Medical Informatics Association*, 18(5):557–562, 2011.

[6] K. Dreyer, M. Kalra, M. Maher, A. Hurier, B. a. Asfaw, T. Schultz, E. Halpern, and J. Thrall. Application of recently developed computer algorithm for automatic classification of unstructured radiology reports: validation study. *Radiology*, 234(2):323–9, Mar. 2005.

[7] S. Ertekin, J. Huang, L. Bottou, and L. Giles. Learning on the border: active learning in imbalanced data classification. In *Proceedings of the sixteenth*

ACM conference on Conference on information and knowledge management, pages 127–136. ACM, 2007.

[8] R. Fan, K. Chang, C. Hsieh, X. Wang, and C. Lin. Liblinear: A library for large linear classification. *J. Mach. Learn. Res.*, 9:1871–1874, June 2008.

[9] C. Friedman, P. Alderson, J. Austin, J. Cimino, and S. Johnson. A general natural-language text processor for clinical radiology. *Journal of the American Medical Informatics Association*, 1(2):161–174, 1994.

[10] C. Friedman, L. Shagina, Y. Lussier, and G. Hripcsak. Automated encoding of clinical documents based on natural language processing. *Journal of the American Medical Informatics Association*, 11(5):392–402, 2004.

[11] B. Haddow. Using automated feature optimisation to create an adaptable relation extraction system. In *Proceedings of the Workshop on Current Trends in Biomedical Natural Language Processing*, BioNLP '08, pages 19–27, Stroudsburg, PA, USA, 2008. Association for Computational Linguistics.

[12] P. Haug, S. Koehler, L. Lau, P. Wang, R. Rocha, and S. Huff. Experience with a mixed semantic/syntactic parser. page 284, 1995.

[13] D. Hochbaum and D. Shmoys. A best possible heuristic for the k-center problem. *Mathematics of operations research*, 10(2):180–184, 1985.

[14] T. Joachims. Text categorization with support vector machines: Learning with many relevant features. *Machine learning: ECML-98*, pages 137–142, 1998.

[15] D. Johnson, R. Taira, A. Cardenas, and D. Aberle. Extracting information from free text radiology reports. *International Journal on Digital Libraries*, 1(3):297–308, Dec. 1997.

[16] J. Lafferty, A. McCallum, and F. Pereira. Conditional random fields: Probabilistic models for segmenting and labeling sequence data. 2001.

[17] K. Lee, Y. Hwang, and H. Rim. Two-phase biomedical ne recognition based on svms. In *Proceedings of the ACL 2003 workshop on Natural language processing in biomedicine - Volume 13*, BioMed '03, pages 33–40, Stroudsburg, PA, USA, 2003. Association for Computational Linguistics.

[18] D. Lewis and J. Catlett. Heterogeneous uncertainty sampling for supervised learning. In *Proceedings of the eleventh international conference on machine learning*, pages 148–156, 1994.

[19] D. Li, K. Kipper-Schuler, and G. Savova. Conditional random fields and support vector machines for disorder named entity recognition in clinical texts. In *Proceedings of the Workshop on Current Trends in Biomedical Natural Language Processing*, BioNLP '08, pages 94–95, Stroudsburg, PA, USA, 2008. Association for Computational Linguistics.

[20] I. McCowan and D. Moore. Collection of Cancer Stage Data by Classifying Free-text Medical Reports. *Journal of American Medical Informatics Association*, pages 736–745, 2007.

[21] I. McCowan, D. Moore, and M. Fry. Classification of cancer stage from free-text histology reports. *Conference proceedings : Annual International Conference of the IEEE Engineering in Medicine and Biology Society*, 1:5153–6, Jan. 2006.

[22] D. Nguyen and J. Patrick. Reverse active learning for optimising information extraction training production. In *AI 2012: Advances in Artificial Intelligence*, pages 445–456. Springer, 2012.

[23] F. Olsson and K. Tomanek. An intrinsic stopping criterion for committee-based active learning. In *Proceedings of the Thirteenth Conference on Computational Natural Language Learning*, CoNLL '09, pages 138–146, Stroudsburg, PA, USA, 2009. Association for Computational Linguistics.

[24] T. Osugi, D. Kun, and S. Scott. Balancing exploration and exploitation: A new algorithm for active machine learning. In *Proceedings of the Fifth IEEE International Conference on Data Mining*, pages 330–337, 2005.

[25] J. Patrick and D. Nguyen. Automated proof reading of clinical notes. In *25th Pacific Asia Conference on Language, Information and Computation (PACLIC 25)*, pages 303–312. aclweb, 2011.

[26] J. Patrick and M. Sabbagh. An active learning process for extraction and standardisation of medical measurements by a trainable fsa. In A. Gelbukh, editor, *Computational Linguistics and Intelligent Text Processing*, volume 6609 of *Lecture Notes in Computer Science*, pages 151–162. Springer Berlin / Heidelberg, 2011.

[27] J. Patrick, M. Sabbagh, S. Jain, and H. Zheng. Spelling correction in clinical notes with emphasis on first suggestion accuracy. *2nd Workshop on Building and Evaluating Re-sources for Biomedical Text Mining*, pages 2–8, 2010.

[28] G. Schohn and D. Cohn. Less is more: Active learning with support vector machines. In *Machine Learning-International Workshop then Conference*, pages 839–846. Citeseer, 2000.

[29] B. Settles. Active learning literature survey. Computer Sciences Technical Report 1648, University of Wisconsin–Madison, 2009.

[30] R. Taira. Automatic Structuring of Radiology Free-Text Reports. *Radiographics*, 98105:237–245, 2001.

[31] B. Thomas, H. Ouellette, E. Halpern, and D. Rosenthal. Automated computer-assisted categorization of radiology reports. *American Journal of Roentgenology*, 184(2):687–690, 2005.

[32] S. Tong and D. Koller. Support vector machine active learning with applications to text classification. *Journal of Machine Learning Research*, 2:45–66, 2002.

[33] Y. Tsuruoka, Y. Tateishi, J. Kim, T. Ohta, J. McNaught, S. Ananiadou, and J. Tsujii. Developing a robust part-of-speech tagger for biomedical text. *Advances in informatics*, pages 382–392, 2005.

[34] O. Uzuner, B. South, S. Shen, and S. DuVall. 2010 i2b2/va challenge on concepts, assertions, and relations in clinical text. *Journal of the American Medical Informatics Association*, 18(5):552–556, 2011.

[35] O. Uzuner, X. Zhang, and T. Sibanda. Machine learning and rule-based approaches to assertion classification. *Journal of the American Medical Informatics Association*, 16(1):109–115, 2009.

[36] A. Vlachos. A stopping criterion for active learning. *Computer Speech & Language*, 22(3):295–312, 2008.

Detecting Devastating Diseases in Search Logs

John Paparrizos*
Columbia University
jopa@cs.columbia.edu

Ryen W. White
Microsoft Research
ryenw@microsoft.com

Eric Horvitz
Microsoft Research
horvitz@microsoft.com

ABSTRACT

Web search queries can offer a unique population-scale window onto streams of evidence that are useful for detecting the emergence of health conditions. We explore the promise of harnessing behavioral signals in search logs to provide advance warning about the presence of devastating diseases such as pancreatic cancer. Pancreatic cancer is often diagnosed too late to be treated effectively as the cancer has usually metastasized by the time of diagnosis. Symptoms of the early stages of the illness are often subtle and nonspecific. We identify searchers who issue credible, first-person diagnostic queries for pancreatic cancer and we learn models from prior search histories that predict which searchers will later input such queries. We show that we can infer the likelihood of seeing the rise of diagnostic queries months before they appear and characterize the tradeoff between predictivity and false positive rate. The findings highlight the potential of harnessing search logs for the early detection of pancreatic cancer and more generally for harnessing search systems to reduce health risks for individuals.

Keywords

Health screening; Search logs; Behavioral data; Digital disease detection; Pancreatic cancer; Temporal analysis

1. INTRODUCTION

Web search is a primary resource for people concerned about the significance of health-related symptoms [16]. Researchers have studied symptom and illness-related searches in pursuit of insights about how people search about health concerns, including patterns of querying and review of information in pursuit of diagnoses [54], healthcare utilization signals [55], traces of therapeutic decision making for challenging illnesses [40], and identification of new adverse effects of medications [56, 57]. Prior studies have examined how population-level signals in social media can be used to detect the emergence of diseases [10, 19].

*Work conducted during a Microsoft Research internship. John Paparrizos is an Alexander S. Onassis Foundation Scholar.

KDD '16, August 13-17, 2016, San Francisco, CA, USA

DOI: http://dx.doi.org/10.1145/2939672.2939722

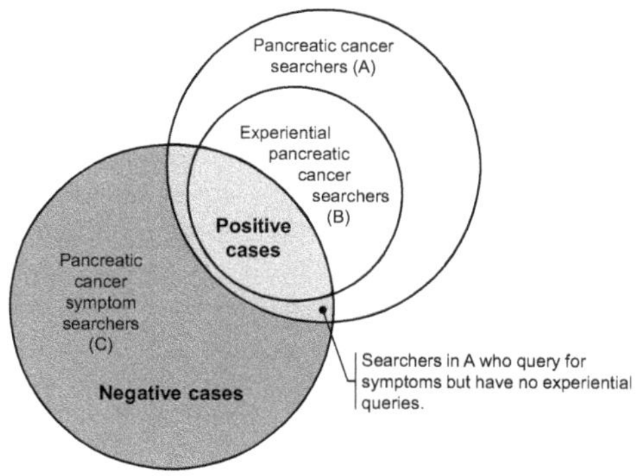

Figure 1: Venn diagram depicting sets of users employed in analyses: pancreatic cancer searchers (A), pancreatic cancer searchers exhibiting experiential diagnostic queries (B), and those who search for the symptoms of pancreatic cancer (C). $|A \cup C|$ (i.e., number of users in original, pre-filtered dataset) is 9.2 million. Positives and negatives are sourced from $B \cap C$ and $C \setminus A$, respectively. Relative set sizes are not to scale.

We explore the prospect of harnessing anonymized long-term sequences of health-related search queries to yield information that could provide valuable signals for detection of illness in advance of traditional diagnosis. Leveraging online behavioral data to provide earlier detection of a disease or of the raised risk of illness on a large scale can make significant contributions to healthcare. Better outcomes can be achieved by earlier confirmation of illnesses and risks via gaining access to more timely diagnoses, treatments, and other proactive interventions. As an example, such capabilities might help to identify those at significant risk of suffering the onset of advance of chronic disease processes such as diabetes or heart disease or the rise of acute processes such as atrial fibrillation or more severe cardiac arrhythmias. Interventional programs ranging from changes in diet or exercise to taking (or avoiding) certain medications can yield significant health benefits.

The diagnosis for certain medical conditions can be particularly devastating if the chances of survival are typically low at the time of diagnosis. Survival rates may be improved significantly via earlier detection and treatment. With many cancers, screening methods can be effective for early detection and therapy [41], but they involve explicit testing prompted by policies around risk factors such as family history [33] or medical history [14, 32]. Ideally, health screening systems would be able to observe people passively as they engage in their normal activities and alert them (per their preferences on vigilance) to potential health risks without requiring the investment of time and effort in special screening activities. Individual-level postings on social media have been mined for this purpose [10, 46], but may not have representative coverage of symptoms associated with social stigma [11].

We present a study of the feasibility of doing early detection of devastating diseases based on large-scale logs of health-related Web search activity. We consider the content of queries over time, and the prospect that temporal relationships and patterns among queries over multiple sessions over several months provide subtle fingerprints of lurking illness. We focus on the early detection of the presence of pancreatic cancer, a devastating diagnosis given the typical progression of the disease to an inoperable situation by the time it is found. Our work showcases the potential value of innovative approaches for speeding up the time to diagnosis of this deadly disease.

Pancreatic cancer is the fourth leading cause of cancer death in men and women in the United States and the sixth leading cause in Europe [36]. The illness is widely known as being difficult to detect and is frequently diagnosed too late to be treated effectively [22, 30]. A recent study found that the progression of pancreatic cancer from stage I to stage IV happens in just over one year [59]. Approximately 75% of pancreatic cancer patients die within a year of diagnosis, and only about 4% survive for five years post diagnosis. Exploration of the possibility that a patient has pancreatic cancer involves a careful and costly consideration of history, labwork, and imaging studies (in contrast to the passive screening methods described in this paper) [45]. Screening is largely performed to detect the disease at an early phase (pre-invasive or early invasive) when it is still curable by surgical intervention and chemotherapy. Earlier diagnosis of pancreatic cancer improves the feasibility of discovering the illness at an earlier stage [7]. For patients diagnosed early who undergo curative surgery (e.g., a Whipple procedure), five-year survival rate is higher, but it remains less than 25% [58].

We take as a proxy for ground truth of a diagnosis of pancreatic cancer the detection of *experiential diagnostic* queries issued by searchers. Experiential queries show strong evidence of being linked to the actual presence of symptomatology or conditions versus less directly involved, more distant *exploratory* queries seeking information about symptoms or diseases [40]. Experiential diagnostic queries for pancreatic cancer are identified via consideration of the structure of queries and of patterns of information gathering over multiple users in search logs. Experiential queries often include first-person assertions such as [*i was just diagnosed with pancreatic cancer*], which when associated with prior queries about symptoms identifies the positive cases.

We construct models to predict the future rise of experiential queries from longitudinal search data. Figure 1 shows the different subsets of users in our analysis, including people who search for pancreatic cancer (A), the subset of these searchers who issue experiential diagnostic queries (B), and those who search for a set of symptoms linked to pancreatic cancer (C). Those who *only* search for one or more related symptoms with no evidence of pancreatic cancer searching constitute the negative cases. We find that our methods can detect cases where people show evidence of being diagnosed with pancreatic cancer many months in advance of their experiential diagnostic queries.

We make the following contributions with this research:

- Introduce early detection of diseases as a promising new application of search log mining and machine learning that scales to millions of searchers.
- Present a case study on the early detection of pancreatic cancer from longitudinal individual search activity.
- Forecast with significant lead times that users will later input experiential queries for pancreatic cancer.
- Explore the influence of different factors, such as the lead time or the presence of specific symptoms in the search activity, on the predictive performance of our learned models, including true positive rates when false positive rates are strictly controlled. Controlling false positives is especially important to reduce unnecessary costs and concerns given potential future applications such as providing early warnings and suggestions to searchers about undertaking more formal screenings.

We now describe related research in this important area.

2. RELATED WORK

Related research in a number of areas is relevant to our work. These include (i) health searching; (ii) large-scale analysis of search behavior; and (iii) methods for the early detection of disease, with a focus on pancreatic cancer.

The Web is an important source of health-related information for many people. To better understand how people pursue health information, studies have examined online health search using a variety of methods, including interviews [42], surveys [49], and analyses of large-scale search log data [2, 5]. According to a 2013 survey, 59% of American adults had used the Web to find health information in the year preceding the survey, 35% of those adults engaged in self-diagnosis, and over half of these self-diagnosing searchers then discussed the matter with a clinician following the search [16]. Despite the potential benefits, concerns have been raised about the quality of online health information [8]. In a large-scale survey of the use of search for self-diagnosis, White and Horvitz [53] found that almost 40% of participants experienced increased anxiety from searching health information online. Studies have characterized problems with symptom search, including the influence of poor accounting for base rates of diseases and people's bias to focus on results covering serious illnesses versus more likely benign explanations. Such biases can lead to inappropriate anxiety [28, 53] and highlight the criticality of studying how patients use the Web, including the nature and dynamics of queries, and content delivered in response.

There has been a large amount of research on the analysis of search behavior from search engine logs. Log analysis provides insights to understand how people engage in information seeking in online settings [51], while also having applications for tasks such as result ranking [1, 24], query suggestion [25], prediction of future search actions and interests [13, 27], and detection of real-world events and activities [44]. Given access to population-scale data on how people search for health information, this can be applied for important tasks such as the detection of influenza [19], the detection of adverse drug reactions [56], population-scale studies of nutrition [50], epidemiology [19], and studies of chronic medical conditions such as pregnancy [15]. Related to this research, but focused on activity post-diagnosis, are studies of cancer-related searching [3, 6, 21], some of which have revealed strong similarities between temporal patterns in search logs and those in practice [38, 40]. Studies have leveraged online behavioral signals for early disease detection at the population level [19], and individually [11, 46].

Screening high-risk individuals for pancreatic cancer is the only practical approach to detect precancerous or cancerous changes in the pancreas at the phase in which surgical intervention will have a high chance of cure [26]. Risk level can be determined by factors such as race [9], family history [33], and a history of pancreatitis [32]. Imaging studies via methods such as endoscopic ultrasound, computer tomography scans, and magnetic resonance imaging [35, 37] have been useful to diagnose pancreatic cancer once the tumor is large enough to cause unusual, salient symptoms that induce people to seek medical attention (e.g., yellow eyes, changes in stool), but at this point the disease is more likely to be at an advanced and unresectable stage (i.e., locally advanced or metastatic, when it cannot be removed by surgery) [29]. Common, seemingly innocuous symptoms such as back pain, abdominal pain, itchy skin, unexplained weight loss and nausea (and combinations and temporal patterns of these and other symptoms) may also be observed in the query stream. Such symptom searches can provide patterns of symptoms that might one day be employed in new kinds of health surveillance systems. Such systems could be used to alert people who would otherwise not feel moved to see a healthcare professional.

Active, explicit screening for early signs of pancreatic cancer is not cost effective unless there is a reasonable probability of detecting invasive or pre-invasive disease (at least 16% according to one study [45]). A log-based methodology provides scale that is not achievable with more traditional epidemiological studies, which tend to be on the order of tens or hundreds of participants, e.g., [23, 43].

3. DATASET CREATION

We now describe the data used, starting with a description of the logs (Section 3.1). We then discuss the creation of an ontology with symptoms commonly experienced by people with pancreatic cancer (Section 3.2) and provide details on extracting pancreatic cancer and symptom searchers (Section 3.3). We review the augmentation, tagging, and filtering steps for our dataset (Section 3.4). Finally, we summarize the creation of query timelines for the positive cases (i.e., experiential diagnostic searchers who also search for pancreatic cancer symptoms) and the negative cases (i.e., those who only search for the symptoms) (Section 3.5). Since reliable labels cannot be determined for the non-experiential pancreatic cancer searchers, we exclude them to create a cleaner dataset for training and testing. We show later (see Section 5.6) that predictive performance is largely unchanged if these searchers are included as negative examples during the application of the model in a realistic scenario.

3.1 Anonymized Web Search Engine Logs

Search engines track various characteristics during their interaction with users so as to better capture information needs, improve their responses, and personalize the content. Every such interaction corresponds to a log entry that includes a unique, anonymized user identifier based on a Web browser cookie. This enables the extraction of the search history comprising queries and clicks from an identifier for up to 18 months. Note that the identifier may comprise the search activity of multiple users on shared machines and does not consolidate activity from a user across multiple machines. We use the logs of a randomly-selected subset of Bing search engine users in the English-speaking United States locale from October 2013 to May 2015 inclusive.

3.2 Symptoms and Risk Factors

Warning signs and symptoms for pancreatic cancer usually include generic, subtle signs and symptoms, such as abdominal and back pain, loss of appetite, and unexplained weight loss. We performed an extensive review of possible signs, symptoms, and risk factors associated with pancreatic cancer and developed an ontology with 21 categories of symptoms. This manually-curated ontology consists of two levels. The first level includes the names of the symptoms and the second level includes multiple names, synonyms, and expressions with which the corresponding symptom in the first level may appear in our data. We performed multiple iterations of refinements of this ontology to remove noise and to minimize erroneous query matches. Table 1 presents the 21 symptom categories with some representative examples of associated query expressions. Also shown are 12 risk factors and associated synonyms, derived from the literature (e.g., [31]), describing attributes, characteristics, or exposures that may increase the likelihood of pancreatic cancer. The symptoms and the risk factors are featurized in predictive models, and they are also used in policies to determine when predictive models should be applied (see Section 5.5).

3.3 Extraction of Searchers

In order to identify positive and negative cases for the generation of our learned model, we built a dataset comprising two groups of users (Figure 1). The *pancreatic cancer searchers* group, denoted as A in the figure, includes all searchers with at least one query explicitly on pancreatic cancer (i.e., a query matches this expression [('pancreas' *OR* 'pancreatic') *AND* 'cancer']). The *symptom searchers* group, denoted as C, includes all users with at least one query related to symptoms linked to pancreatic cancer, as captured by the symptoms and synonyms described in Section 3.2.

Having unique identifiers for each user in the union of A and C (i.e., $A \cup C$) permits the extraction of the full query histories of 9.2 million searchers. We first sought to remove searchers who are likely healthcare professionals (HCPs). To do this, we employed a proprietary Bing classifier that identifies health-related queries to remove users from the study for whom 20% or more of queries are health related. This threshold was based on a prior analysis of identifying health professionals in search logs [52].

3.4 Dataset Augmentation

Age and gender are important factors associated with developing pancreatic cancer [31, 36]. As such, we augmented the dataset with demographic information from proprietary search engine classifiers that estimate age (discretized as $<$ 18, 18–24, 25–34, 35–50, or 50–85) and the gender for each user. The classifiers are trained on data where ground truth of demographic details are provided explicitly by users. The predictions are based on signals derived from searchers' long-term search activity, including their search queries and Web domains of their clicked results. Since pancreatic cancer incidence rates vary by geographic location, we also annotated searchers with the U.S. state from which they searched most (based on reverse Internet provider (IP) lookup data).

Table 1: Ontology with symptoms, risk factors, and examples of associated synonyms for pancreatic cancer.

Type	Name	Example synonyms
Symptom	back pain	pain in lower back, lowback pain
	blood clot	blood clots, thrombosis
	dark or tarry stool	dark poop, tarry feces
	dark urine	orange pee, brown urine
	enlarged gall bladder	swollen gallbladder, inflamed gallbladder
	floating stool	floating stool, floaters
	greasy stool	greasy poop, oily feces
	high blood sugar	frequent urination, sudden diabetes
	itchy skin	skin itching, hands itchy
	yellow skin or eyes	jaundice, yellow eyes
	light stool	pale stool, white crap
	loss of appetite	poor appetite, decreased appetite, not hungry
	nausea or vomiting	throwing up, nauseous
	smelly stool	stinky feces, smelly poop
	sudden weight loss	unexplained weight loss, weight loss sudden
	taste changes	changes in taste, dysgeusia
	loose stool	loose feces, loose stool, diarrhea
	constipation	constipated, backed up
	indigestion	acid reflux, heartburn
	abdominal swelling or pressure	swollen stomach, pressure abdomen
	abdominal pain	belly pain, stomach ache
Risk factor	alcoholism	heavy drinking, alcoholics anonymous, alcoholic
	hepatitis	hep b, hep c
	pancreatitis	–
	ulcers	ulcer
	obesity	obese, very fat, extremely fat
	smoking	smoker, cigarette, cigar
	chills or fever	chills, fever
	multiple endocrine neoplasia	men1
	hereditary nonpolyposis colorectal cancer	lynch syndrome, hnpcc
	von hippel-lindau syndrome	hippel-lindau syndrome
	hereditary intestinal polyposis syndrome	peutz-jeghers syndrome
	familial atypical multiple mole melanoma syndrome	fammm, b-k mole syndrome

Beyond the demographic information, we are also interested in the subject matter of the queries and results that were visited over searchers' timelines. We augmented each query and corresponding clicked websites with their estimated Open Directory Project (ODP, dmoz.org) category. We used a text-based classifier, similar to [4], that uses logistic regression to predict the ODP categories. When optimized for the score in each category, this classifier has a micro-averaged F1 score of 0.60. For queries, the ODP category is that of the top-ranked search result. The remaining users after the augmentation and filtering steps total 7.4 million, from which 479,787 are pancreatic cancer searchers.

3.5 Positive and Negative Cases

We create *query timelines* for experiential pancreatic cancer searchers and experiential symptom searchers which we then featurize for the early detection task. Figure 2 summarizes the strategies for identifying positives and negatives. To avoid including users with very short histories, we filter out all users with less than five search sessions[1] spanning five different days. This reduced the population to 6.4 million users, with a mean total duration (time from first to last query for a user) of 210.32 days, standard deviation (SD) of 182.93 days, and interquartile range of 120 days.

Positive Cases: To identify experiential pancreatic cancer users, we created a set of first-person diagnostic queries for pancreatic cancer (denoted Exp_0). Some examples of such diagnostic queries are [*just diagnosed with pancreatic cancer*], [*why did i get cancer in pancreas*], and [*i was told i have pancreatic cancer what to expect*].

From the set of 479,787 pancreatic cancer searchers, 3,203 match the pattern of diagnostic queries. In order to consider them as experiential users, we require them to have searched at least for one symptom *prior to* the diagnosis query. This

[1] *Session* is a query sequence with $\leq$ 30 minutes between queries [51].

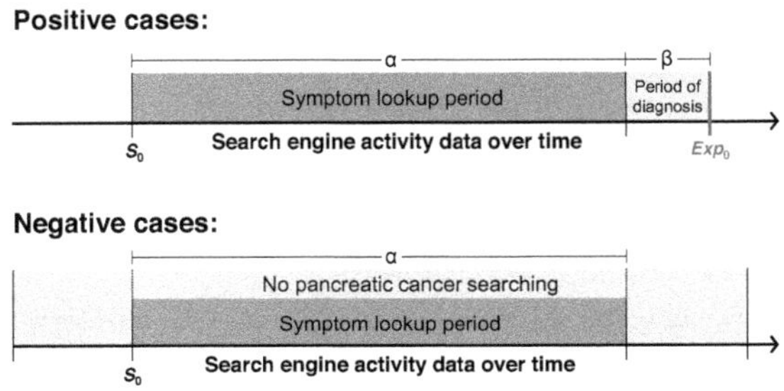

Figure 2: Schematic illustration of the query timelines used in the selection of positive and negative cases. S_0 refers to the first symptom query and Exp_0 is the first experiential diagnostic query. α is the duration of the symptom lookup period, which was approximately equal in the aggregate for the positives and negatives. β is the duration of the period of diagnosis, set to one week in this study.

step generates a set of 1,072 query timelines of experiential searchers that contain periods of *symptom lookup* followed by the diagnostic query. The symptom lookup period starts when the first symptom is detected as matching terms represented in the symptom ontology. For positive cases, the symptom lookup period completes at least one week before diagnosis (i.e., we consider the week before the diagnostic query as the period of diagnosis in real life and do not count queries in that time since they may be polluted with ground truth signals). For reliability, especially given the need to compute *Temporal* features (Section 4.2), the minimum time period for which our features are computed is four weeks.

Negative Cases: To generate the negative set, we sample from the users who searched for pancreatic cancer symptoms but did not search for pancreatic cancer anywhere in their timeline (i.e., $C \setminus A$), either before or after the symptom lookup period. Performing this additional check on data

Table 2: Summary statistics, namely, mean (M), standard deviation (SD), and number of cases (N), of durations and numbers of queries in positive and negative datasets.

Class	Duration (days)		Total # queries		N
	M	SD	M	SD	
Positives	109.34	49.66	380.66	150.83	1,072
Negatives	108.04	48.35	378.09	151.01	3,025,046

from outside the lookup period is required to increase the likelihood that the negative cases are indeed negative. Users who searched for pancreatic cancer and its symptoms, but did not issue an experiential query (the gray subset in Figure 1 representing $(A \cap C) \setminus B$), were excluded since a label could not be reliably determined. In Section 5.6 we describe an additional experiment where pancreatic cancer searchers were included during model testing.

We were concerned that rudimentary behavioral differences that may reflect artifacts in the data could invalidate the learning task. For example, if our experiential users were just more active generally, then a feature that computed the total number of queries would have strong predictive value, yet would be uninteresting scientifically. We sought to address this by downsampling the negative cases to attain a similar distribution of symptom lookup periods in terms of the temporal duration and query volume as observed for the positive cases.[2] We did this by selecting users with a symptom lookup period duration within three standard deviations of the mean of the positive cases. This reduces the number of negative cases to 3,025,046. Table 2 presents the summary statistics on the symptom lookup periods in terms of the number of days and the number of queries in the two datasets. The table shows that the distributions for positive and negative cases (in terms of number of days and number of queries) are similar. The distributions are statistically indistinguishable using two-sample Kolmogorov-Smirnov tests for temporal duration ($D = 0.005; p = 0.7017$) and number of queries ($D = 0.003; p = 0.7681$), even though the latter was not a filtering criterion. We note that query timelines are not aligned: the absolute point in time where people issue the experiential diagnostic query, and the accompanying symptom lookup period can differ between searchers.

4. EARLY DETECTION

We now present the problem, summarize features extracted from query timelines, and review the prediction model.

4.1 Problem Description

We address the problem of early detection of experiential searchers for pancreatic cancer via anonymized Web search engine logs. We cast this as a binary classification task, where the model is trained on features extracted from search log query timelines of experiential pancreatic cancer searchers and symptom-only searchers. We focus on maintaining very low false-positive rates (i.e., 1 misprediction in 100k correctly identified cases) while keeping high the imbalance ratio of positive and negative cases (i.e., one thousand positives vs. millions of negative cases); these properties are important for potential future large-scale real-world applications such as an alerting mechanism in search engines.

[2]We could also have addressed this by making all features relative percentages. Sampling gave us more flexibility in feature construction. As an additional check, we included features such as the number of queries in the symptom lookup period; those were found to carry little evidential weight in the learned model.

4.2 Features

We now describe the features extracted from query timelines. We group our features into five different categories: (i) demographic information about the user; (ii) characteristics about user sessions, query classes, and URL classes; (iii) characteristics about symptoms; (iv) features that capture the temporal dynamics, and (v) risk factors.

Demographics: Cancer statistics from the U.S. National Cancer Institute[3] show that pancreatic cancer is more common with increasing age, is slightly more common in men than in women, and varies by geographic location. As such, we develop features related to the demographics of the users. In particular, we use the estimated age bucket and gender (see Section 3.4) along with the classifier's probabilities as confidence values. The dominant location (U.S. state) of a searcher is also included as a feature.

Search Characteristics: People express their information needs and preferences through queries and click behavior (i.e., the website visits). We extract various features to capture these search and retrieval activities. As we discussed previously, the queries, as well as the visited websites, were tagged with their ODP category in an attempt to identify domains of interest (see Section 3.4). A first set of features *SearchHistory* contains several generic statistics, such as counts, ratios, and percentages, which are characteristics of the global behavior of the user. For example, we compute the number of queries, sessions, and clicks, as well as ratios of clicks per query for each user. Then, we compute a large number of features with respect to the ODP categories of queries *QueryTopic*, clicked search results *URLTopic*, and the combination *QueryURLTopic*. These include compute counts and percentage of queries and sessions in each ODP category, the average time until queries appear in the same category, as well as the time of the day that queries appear in each category. Similar features are also computed for each category of the visited websites (e.g., counts, ratios, and percentages of visited websites that belong to each category). We additionally compute features to characterize the user sessions, including features that capture the click behavior of users associated with queries. For example, we compute counts and percentages of all the combinations of query categories that led to visits in website categories.

Symptoms: Features described above attempt to capture generic characteristics from user sessions. However, for the problem of interest, we seek to also leverage features from queries containing terms captured in the symptom ontology for pancreatic cancer (Section 3.2). The symptom features are divided into two classes: (i) *SymptomGeneric* and (ii) *SymptomSpecific*. Generic symptom features contain counts and percentages for the queries and sessions matching symptoms in our ontology, the average time between symptom queries, as well as the average number of symptom queries that are issued daily. Specific symptom features are generated per symptom category. For example, for each symptom, we compute counts and percentages of appearance, the time between distinct symptoms, and the time of day such symptom queries are issued. As with the user session features, we combine symptoms to capture the click behavior and, hence, we compute counts and percentages of each symptom query leading to a visit on a website belonging to particular ODP categories. Finally, we define features that capture the *se-*

[3]http://seer.cancer.gov/statfacts/html/pancreas.html

Table 3: Performance at four-week intervals for users where features can be computed from Exp_0 – 1 week to Exp_0 – 21 weeks. Values averaged across the ten folds of cross-validation. The significance of differences in AUROC and TPR using paired t-tests for each week versus Exp_0 – 1 indicated * $p < 0.01$, ** $p < 0.001$, and *** $p < 0.0001$. Weeks denote lead time before Exp_0 (β in Figure 2).

Weeks before Exp_0	TPR (as %) at FPRs ranging from 0.00001–0.1					AUROC
	0.00001	0.0001	0.001	0.01	0.1	
1 week	7.122	10.386	20.772	36.202	71.810	0.9112
5 weeks	7.122	10.979	20.178	34.421	70.620	0.9047
9 weeks	7.122	10.683	18.991*	33.234*	70.023	0.8854*
13 weeks	7.122	9.792	17.804*	32.937*	67.359*	0.8700*
17 weeks	6.825	9.199*	17.209*	32.640**	64.688**	0.8539**
21 weeks	6.528*	9.199*	16.319**	32.345**	61.424***	0.8315**

quence in which symptoms appear in query timelines.

Temporal: All previous features produce aggregated statistics over the full time window under consideration. Following [34], we include a set of features to capture the temporal variation of these statistics over misaligned query timelines with noise and missing values. For every feature, we generate a time series with points that represent aggregated values for intervals of the time window. For example, each feature can be computed per month, per week, or per day, depending on the level of granularity we seek to capture. Since the occurrence of specific features can be sparse, we set the time window to four weeks for temporal features. For features that are not percentages or ratios, we also compute the cumulative time series. For each time series, we use the first coefficient of the linear least-square estimates to devise features that capture the trend (i.e., increasing, decreasing, and unchanged) and the rate of change (i.e., slope).

Risk Factors: This class contains features related to the presence of terms representing risk factors in the symptom lookup period. For each risk factor, we note its presence or absence, and also the number of queries containing that risk factor and the fraction of all queries from that user that these risk factor queries represents. Total number of distinct risk factors in the symptom lookup period is also a feature.

4.3 Prediction Model

The prediction model uses the features outlined in the previous section, computed for each searcher, to make predictions about the future occurrence of experiential diagnostic searches in each searcher's query timeline. We use gradient boosted trees [17], which employ an ensemble of decision trees to construct a better learned model. Advantages include the ability to capture non-linear relationships, model interpretability (e.g., a ranked list of important features is generated), facility for rapid training and testing, and robustness against noisy labels and missing values. We experimented with different learning algorithms, but gradient boosted trees yielded superior accuracy.

5. EXPERIMENTAL RESULTS

We now present the findings of our experiments. We report the overall performance in Section 5.1 and the performance as we increase the lead time before the first experiential diagnostic query (Section 5.2). We then inspect the model to understand the contributions that each feature makes towards early detection (Section 5.3) and the performance of different feature *classes* (Section 5.4). We examine the effect on model performance of conditioning on symptoms and risk factors (Section 5.5) and consider a realistic deployment scenario (Section 5.6). We use the area under the receiver operating characteristic curve (AUROC) and recall (TPR, true positive rate) at fixed, extremely low false positive rates (FPRs) as our primary evaluation metrics. We applied 10-fold cross validation, stratified by user to evaluate the generalizability of the model when applied to new users. Significance level is $p < 0.05$ unless stated.

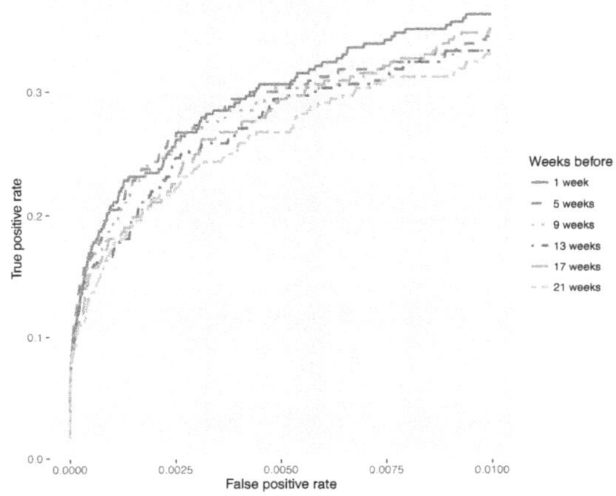

Figure 3: Average partial ROC curves in the FPR range 0–0.01, for models learned using data up to 21 weeks before the first experiential diagnostic query (error bars excluded for clarity). Variance in FPR and TPR is minor.

5.1 Overall

The overall performance of the classifier in making predictions based on data up to the beginning of the period of diagnosis (i.e., Exp_0 – 1 week) in AUROC is 0.9003. Given that low error rates would be vital in practice to avoid unnecessary patient alarm, we focus on the true positive rate (fraction of all positives that are recalled by the model) at low false positive rates (FPR). Focusing on FPR in the range 0.00001–0.01, the model is able to recall 5–30% of the positive cases, depending on the specific FPR. We see this performance as promising given the limited information (primarily search-related activity) available to the model.

5.2 Performance by Week

A key part of early detection is being able to predict the emergence of the disease well in advance. To understand how prediction performance changed as we move further back in time before the first experiential diagnostic query we selected the set of 337 positive searchers and 945,394 negative searchers who were still observed in the logs many weeks prior to the experiential diagnostic query. We report results from one week before the experiential diagnostic query, all the way up to 21 weeks before the diagnostic query. To count as being present at Exp_0 – 21 weeks, a searcher needs to have symptom queries extending back at least four weeks before that point (i.e., to Exp_0 – 25 weeks, or approximately six months before the first experiential diagnostic query).

We trained a model for these users in the same way as we did for Section 5.1. The ratio between positive and negative searchers remains similar to that for all users (i.e., approximately 1:3000). Table 3 reports the TPR at different false positive rates for this same set of users at different four-week increments, as well as the AUROC. The general trend is that the performance drops fairly consistently as we increase the lead time, but even 20 or so weeks before the first experiential diagnostic query the predictive perfor-

Table 4: Top 10 features by evidential weight relative to the top feature. "Positive" or "Negative" direction means that a feature correlates positively or negatively, respectively, with the rise of experiential queries.

Feature	Weight	Direction	Class
NumOfDistinctSymptoms	1.0000	Positive	SymptomGeneral
NumOfQueriesInHealthCategory	0.8253	Positive	QueryTopic
NumOfDistinctSymptomsVariants	0.6899	Positive	SymptomGeneral
AgeClassProbability_5085	0.6889	Positive	Demographic
HasBackPain	0.6622	Negative	SymptomSpecific
HasIndigestion	0.6432	Negative	SymptomSpecific
HasIndigestionThenAbdominalPain	0.6349	Positive	Temporal
SlopeNumOfDistinctSymptoms	0.6154	Positive	Temporal
HasBackPainThenYellowSkinOrEyes	0.6004	Positive	Temporal
AgeClassProbability_LT18	0.5869	Negative	Demographic

mance is still quite strong (AUROC=0.8315, TPR=6.528% at FPR=0.00001). Assuming that pancreatic cancer progresses steadily from stage I to stage IV in just over one year (as has been previously reported [59]), accurate predictions 20 weeks in advance of the diagnostic period could lead to a sizable increase in the five-year survival rate (e.g., moving the point of diagnosis from Stage III to Stage II could increase the survival rate from 3% to 5–7% [47]).

Focusing on the FPR region from 0 to 0.01 (i.e., false positives occur less than 1 in 100 times) and visualizing that part of the ROC curve (Figure 3) we observe some clear differences in the performance of the models in this important region. The average normalized partial AUROC ranges from 0.292 ($Expo - 1$ week) to 0.231 ($Expo - 21$ weeks). All differences in AUROC for $Expo - 5$ or more weeks versus $Expo - 1$ week are significant ($p < 0.01$ using paired t-tests).

5.3 Feature Contributions

In addition to understanding the overall performance, we are also interested in understanding the features that are most important in the learned model for predicting the future issuance of experiential queries. Table 4 shows the top 10 features with the highest weight, along with their weight relative to the top-ranked feature (*NumOfDistinctSymptoms*) and the feature class. The direction is based on the correlation between the feature value and the labels in the training data, using Pearson biserial correlation or the phi coefficient, depending on whether or not the feature data is binary. Table 4 shows that there is a broad range of features. The number of distinct pancreatic cancer symptoms was the most important feature. Temporal features representing changes over time and sequence ordering of symptom pairs are also important. Age is important, and it is positively correlated if the searcher is older and is negatively correlated if they are younger. Individual symptom features related to back pain and indigestion are important but have a negative influence on predicting future experiential queries, likely because (i) there are many explanations for why these symptoms appear in a query timeline, and (ii) they are positive for many negative cases (16.7% of negatives search for back pain, 7.4% search for indigestion).

5.4 Feature Classes

Beyond the individual features, we can also consider the accuracy of the models based on feature classes. This can be particularly important when some classes of features are easy to obtain in practice, e.g., the demographic features may be available for all searchers without the need to perform temporal modeling of query patterns. Table 5 presents the AUROC for models trained on each of the feature classes. The findings show that the *Temporal* class is particularly important, signifying the key role of temporal dynamics for this prediction task. The model is still accurate solely with access

Table 5: Performance of individual feature classes (as AUROC and TPR at a FPR of 0.00001) averaged across the 10 experimental folds. The performance differences against the *Overall* performance are statistically significant using paired t-tests at * $p < 0.01$, ** $p < 0.001$, and *** $p < 0.0001$.

Feature Class	AUROC	TPR (as a %) at FPR=0.00001
Demographic	0.6565***	0.280%***
RiskFactor	0.6988***	0.653%**
SearchHistory	0.7202***	1.399%**
QueryURLTopic	0.7597**	2.052%**
SymptomGeneral	0.7672**	2.146%**
URLTopic	0.7753**	2.332%*
SymptomSpecific	0.8176*	2.800%*
QueryTopic	0.8137*	2.892%*
Temporal	0.8391*	2.985%*
Overall	0.9003	4.851%

to demographics and basic features about general searching. However, performance improves considerably if we consider the specifics of the symptoms searched (*SymptomSpecific*) or the topics of the queries and results clicked (*QueryTopic*).

5.5 Symptoms and Risk Factors

We also considered the impact of the presence of symptoms and risk factors on the performance of the model.

- *Symptoms*: We filtered the positive and negative cases to those where a symptom was present in query timelines.
- *Risk factors*: These are risk factors corresponding to the presence of factors such as pancreatitis, smoking, and obesity, as well as cancer syndromes such as hereditary intestinal polyposis syndrome or familial atypical multiple mole melanoma syndrome (i.e., genetic disorders that predispose individuals to develop pancreatic cancer), all of which have been shown to lead to increased likelihood of developing pancreatic cancer [18, 20, 32, 48].

Recall that our cross-validation was stratified by user. During cross validation, we learned a model on the users in the training folds and then for testing we limited to users with evidence of the specific symptoms or risk factors in their search history prior to the experiential diagnostic query. In each case the number of positives and negatives is less than the full set.[4] Table 6 presents statistics on the performance for each model where the number of positive examples was at least 10 (to help ensure that AUROC calculations were meaningful). The table also presents TPRs at different false positive rates, as well as the percentage of positive or negative cases that have the symptom or risk factor searches. Finally, the last three columns shows the estimated number of true positives (capture) and false positives (cost) that would be observed, assuming a FPR of 0.00001, and the associated capture-cost ratio. Ideal targets for rates of capture versus cost in a deployed service can be derived via a decision analysis that considers the net expected value of the early detection and the expected costs of unnecessary anxiety. Such an optimization would leverage a careful characterization of the value of early intervention and details of designs of methods for engaging people.

Table 6 shows that focusing on users who search for risk factors such as smoking, hepatitis, and obesity leads to better overall performance. There were fewer than ten users searching for each of the cancer syndromes (e.g., hereditary nonpolyposis colorectal cancer) and, hence, they were excluded from Table 6. Focusing on the percentage of posi-

[4] An alternative would be to train a separate model for symptom or risk factor. An issue with doing that is there are insufficient positive examples about each dataset with which to train a robust model.

Table 6: Performance of the models conditioned on a variety of symptom (S) and risk factors (RF). Values below the dashed line have a higher AUROC than *Overall*. Capture represents the number of TP cases in the cohort of positives ∪ negatives at FPR=0.00001. Cost is computed as the target FPR (.00001) multiplied by the size of the negative set in each subgroup. Since this exact FPR may not be attainable in each subgroup, cost may not be an integer. A capture-cost ratio of > 1.0 means that more people would benefit from an alert than would be mistakenly alerted. Statistically significant differences with *Overall* model (DeLong's test [12]) are marked ** $p < 0.001$ and *** $p < 0.0001$ (where α following a Bonferroni correction is 0.002).

Symptom or Risk Factor	TPR at FPRs ranging from 0.00001–0.1					AUROC	# pos (%)	# neg (%)	FPR = 0.00001		
	0.00001	0.0001	0.001	0.01	0.1				Capture	Cost	Capture/Cost
Dark or tarry stool (S)	7.692	7.692	23.077	38.462	46.154	0.7173***	13 (1.2%)	58,597 (1.9%)	1	0.5860	1.7066
Abdominal swelling (S)	4.167	8.333	16.667	20.833	45.833	0.7735***	24 (2.2%)	45083 (1.5%)	1	0.4508	2.2183
Ulcers (RF)	0.000	0.000	0.000	7.895	50.000	0.7894***	38 (3.5%)	16,081 (0.5%)	0	0.1608	0.0000
Dark urine (S)	0.000	5.556	16.667	27.778	50.000	0.8129**	18 (1.7%)	51,236 (1.7%)	0	0.5124	0.0000
Pancreatitis (RF)	6.061	9.091	12.121	24.242	54.546	0.8220**	33 (3.1%)	34,184 (1.1%)	2	0.3418	5.8514
Abdominal pain (S)	5.385	10.000	16.923	32.308	60.000	0.8343**	130 (12.1%)	311,266 (10.3%)	7	3.1127	2.2489
Enlarged gallbladder (S)	0.885	2.655	9.735	25.664	53.982	0.8358**	113 (10.5%)	98,454 (3.3%)	1	0.9845	1.0157
Constipation (S)	3.529	7.059	9.412	22.353	57.647	0.8469**	85 (7.9%)	317,300 (10.5%)	3	3.1730	0.9455
Smoking (RF)	3.846	3.846	7.692	15.385	53.846	0.8585	26 (2.4%)	27,817 (0.9%)	1	0.2782	3.5945
Blood clot (S)	4.494	10.112	14.607	31.461	61.798	0.8589	89 (8.3%)	351,385 (11.6%)	4	3.5139	1.1383
High blood sugar (S)	6.135	8.896	16.564	31.595	60.429	0.8611	326 (30.4%)	429,543 (14.2%)	20	4.2954	4.6561
Nausea or vomiting (S)	3.200	8.800	17.600	30.400	63.200	0.8706	125 (11.7%)	639,502 (21.1%)	4	6.3950	0.6255
Chills or fever (RF)	3.636	7.273	20.909	30.909	65.455	0.8727	110 (10.3%)	357,536 (11.8%)	4	3.5754	1.1188
Loose stool (S)	4.615	7.692	18.462	35.385	72.308	0.8756	65 (6%)	74,720 (2.5%)	3	0.7472	4.0150
Indigestion (S)	7.547	12.264	20.755	38.679	68.868	0.8932	106 (9.9%)	504,462 (16.7%)	8	5.0446	1.5859
Itchy skin (S)	18.750	25.000	25.000	25.000	75.000	0.8982	16 (1.5%)	79,448 (2.6%)	3	0.7945	3.7760
Back pain (S)	7.801	14.184	19.858	34.752	69.504	0.9047	141 (13.2%)	223,586 (7.4%)	11	2.2359	4.9197
Yellow skin or eyes (S)	2.174	5.439	19.565	38.044	73.913	0.9217	92 (8.6%)	85,805 (2.8%)	2	0.8581	2.3307
Hepatitis (RF)	7.692	10.256	20.513	38.462	71.795	0.9275	39 (3.6%)	25,158 (0.8%)	3	0.2516	11.9237
Alcoholism (RF)	12.500	16.667	27.083	41.667	89.583	0.9494**	48 (4.5%)	32,333 (1.1%)	6	0.3233	18.5586
Obesity (RF)	20.690	20.690	37.931	62.069	82.7590	0.9572**	29 (2.7%)	22,153 (0.7%)	6	0.2215	27.0880
Overall	4.851	8.302	17.258	36.474	72.015	0.9003	1,072 (100%)	3,025,046 (100%)	52	30.2505	1.7190

tives and negatives that contain each of the symptoms or risk factors, we observe that there are some that are much more likely to occur in positives (e.g., pancreatitis and smoking are 5.9 and 3.6 times as likely, respectively). Focusing on the utility, we find that if we set the FPR to 0.00001, overall we would find 52 positives in the union of positives and negatives at the expense of 30 negatives, who would be altered mistakenly. There are some symptoms and risk factors for which the capture-cost is more favorable. For example, in the case of alcoholism or obesity, we would find 20–30 times as many TPs as FPs. There are others symptoms such as nausea or vomiting, or chills or fever, where the costs in mistakenly alerting users equal or outweigh the benefits. Presence of symptoms or risk factors could help decide whether to apply early detection models for a searcher.

5.6 Applying Learned Model in Practice

Up to now, our model considers experiential diagnostic users as positives and symptom-only users as negatives. This is a clean dataset for algorithm training and testing but it ignores the symptom searchers who issue non-experiential pancreatic cancer searches (gray region in Figure 1). These users may have been diagnosed or may simply be exploring. Regardless, they should be considered in practice.

We perform an additional experiment on a separate set of symptom searchers that included non-experiential pancreatic cancer searchers as negatives. We trained a model on all data described thus far and applied it to identify (i) experiential and (ii) experiential+treatment users in a new held out dataset in advance of their first experiential diagnostic query. We generated the test set from logs of a separate randomly selected subset of Bing users, over an 18-month period from August 2014 to January 2016 inclusive. There was no overlap in users with the set used for training. We identified positive cases as earlier and expanded the definition of negatives to include pancreatic cancer searchers. This resulted in 2.9 million negatives, including 48,221 non-experiential pancreatic cancer searchers, and 945 experiential searchers with preceding symptom searches. To help target the identification of cases where experiential queries are issued, we created a subset of the positives who issued treatment-related queries following Exp_0 (e.g., whipple procedure, 5-fu); in total, 494 users (52%) met this requirement.

Table 7: Average AUROC and average TPR (as %) at FPR=0.00001 for identifying experiential users and experiential+treatment users from held out dataset. Differences in AUROC and TPR between Exp_0 – 1 week and other weeks noted (*** $p < 0.001$, ** $p < 0.001$, and * $p < 0.01$).

Weeks before Exp_0	Experiential		Experiential+Treatment	
	AUROC	TPR (%)	AUROC	TPR (%)
1 week	0.9012	8.677	0.9225	12.145
5 weeks	0.8892	8.571	0.9089*	11.943
9 weeks	0.8754**	8.278*	0.8902**	11.343*
13 weeks	0.8611**	8.018**	0.8795**	10.738**
17 weeks	0.8456***	7.666**	0.8683***	10.400***
21 weeks	0.8330***	7.438***	0.8508***	9.645***

The symptom lookup durations for positives and negatives were similar to Section 3.5. We randomly split the test data into ten equally-sized subsets for significance testing. Table 7 reports the predictive performance at different lead times.

Table 7 shows that the performance of the model remains strong on this held-out set and is comparable to that reported in the earlier sections. The performance decreases with increased lead time as noted previously (see Table 3). Interestingly, the performance in identifying the subset of experiential diagnostic users who subsequently searched for treatments is higher than for the experiential-only set. This is promising confirmatory evidence as these users are assumed to have experienced a cancer diagnosis, per definitions of experiential queries [40].[5]

6. DISCUSSION AND CONCLUSIONS

We studied the potential feasibility of learning from search engine logs to predict future issuance of experiential queries about pancreatic cancer at a low error rate. The success of these methods has implications for online methods that would provide passive screening of searchers to provide early warning about potential signs of pancreatic cancer and other devastating diseases. We discovered that conditionalization on different symptoms and risk factors can enhance predictive power. We found capture-cost tradeoffs associated with

[5]For completeness, we also trained a model on all data from earlier in the paper, including the non-experiential pancreatic cancer searchers as negative cases, and tested it on this held-out set. The performance is around 5% lower than reported in Table 7, for both AUROC and TPR, across all weeks. Including the non-experiential pancreatic cancer searchers may add noise to model training.

different symptoms and risk factors in terms of the total number of truly positive cases identified versus the number of searchers who would be mistakenly alerted. We characterized model performance as we increase lead time and we found that we can attain a TPR in region of 5–30%, while controlling the FPR to 0.00001–0.01 months before a diagnostic query is observed. Looking forward, we seek to understand the costs and clinical significance of these methods, including how they might offer early warning of devastating disease onset to enhance outcomes (e.g., quality of life).

Despite the promising findings, we note several important limitations. First, we lack explicit ground truth about diagnoses per the anonymity of our logs. We rely on models of self-reporting in queries. We have found that streams of queries following the experiential queries can provide confirmatory evidence of pancreatic cancer diagnoses. Indeed, in the weeks immediately following the experiential diagnostic query, over 40% of searchers queried for treatment options, with many using sophisticated terminology (e.g., Whipple procedure, pancreaticoduodenectomy, neoadjuvant therapy) and over 20% of searchers searched for pancreatic cancer medications (e.g., gemcitabine, 5-fu). In contrast, only 0.5% and 0.02% of searchers in our negative set searched for treatments and medications, respectively, at any point in their query timeline. We need to work with diagnosed patients to understand (i) the relationship between experiential searching and diagnosis; and (ii) the model performance with the use of traditional data as ground truth about diagnoses (e.g., medical records). We also need to understand the role of factors such as race [9], family history [33], medical histories [32], diabetes [14], and other factors (e.g., smoking [18]). Some of these can be crudely estimated from geographic and census data (race), whereas others (family and medical histories) are best sought from searchers directly. To reflect anticipated performance in a natural setting, we focused on our imbalanced dataset. We re-ran the analysis with a balanced set, with highly similar results. Finally, we note that this is a retrospective analysis for model training/testing and we need to consider its representativeness for real-time screening, e.g., identifying negative cases in the retrospective study relies on symptom lookup durations. Potential additional analyses include explorations of predicting on fixed dates versus at the end of the observation period.

We are interested in several research directions. We believe it would be valuable to collect ground truth data, e.g., via targeted surveys, where responses and electronic health records could be linked (given consent) to long-term search activity. There is opportunity to develop more sophisticated time-series models and with applying our methods to other diseases. We leave to future reflection and efforts the design of methods for fielding the methods. We seek to engage with the medical community on directions for deploying the technology. In a recent sister publication, we shared these findings with practicing oncologists [39]. For real-world deployment, we need to consider whether online services would wish to provide individuals with early warnings about undiagnosed diseases given false positive rates, anxiety and associated costs of ruling out illness, privacy implications, and liability concerns. Beyond alerting searchers, a system could provide summaries of symptom searches as talking points for dialog with a medical professional, or contact a physician on the individual's behalf. One could imagine services enabling users to opt-in to such screening programs with appropriate education and caveats about false-positive rates and their associated costs. In another approach, models could be trained from anonymized data yet fielded in a private manner, e.g., as an application on a searcher's smartphone. Future work should consider the value of the search-centric analyses in the context of more traditional screening methods such as direct (active) cancer screening. Larger designs would consider how the search-based methods could be integrated with traditional screening to develop a more cost-effective screening program. Such work would require a careful consideration of the accuracies and costs of pre-screening and screening and the expected benefits of increased rates of survival associated with different policies.

7. REFERENCES

[1] E. Agichtein, E. Brill, and S. Dumais. Improving web search ranking by incorporating user behavior information. *SIGIR*, 19–26, 2006.

[2] S. L. Ayers and J. J. Kronenfeld. Chronic illness and health-seeking information on the internet. *Health*, 11(3): 327–347, 2007.

[3] J. L. Bader and M. F. Theofanos. Searching for cancer information on the internet: Analyzing natural language search queries. *JMIR*, 5(4), 2003.

[4] P. Bennett, K. Svore, and S. Dumais. Classification -enhanced ranking. *WWW*, 111–120, 2010.

[5] E. V. Bernstam, J. R. Herskovic, and W. R. Hersh. Query log analysis in biomedicine. *Handbook of Research on Web Log Analysis*, 359–377, 2009.

[6] K. Castleton et al. A survey of internet utilization among patients with cancer. *Supportive Care in Cancer*, 19(8): 1183–1190, 2011.

[7] S. T. Chari et al. Early detection of sporadic pancreatic cancer: Summative review. *Pancreas*, 44(5): 693, 2015.

[8] R. J. Cline and K. M. Haynes. Consumer health information seeking on the internet: The state of the art. *Health Education Research*, 16(6): 671–692, 2001.

[9] S. S. Coughlin et al. Predictors of pancreatic cancer mortality among a large cohort of united states adults. *Cancer Causes & Control*, 11(10): 915–923, 2000.

[10] M. De Choudhury, S. Counts, and E. Horvitz. Predicting postpartum changes in emotion and behavior via social media. *SIGCHI*, 3267–3276, 2013.

[11] M. De Choudhury, M. R. Morris, and R. W. White. Seeking and sharing health information online: Comparing search engines and social media. *SIGCHI*, 1365–1376, 2014.

[12] E. R. DeLong, D. M. DeLong, and D. L. Clarke-Pearson. Comparing the areas under two or more correlated receiver operating characteristic curves: A nonparametric approach. *Biometrics*, 837–845, 1988.

[13] D. Downey, S. T. Dumais, and E. Horvitz. Models of searching and browsing: Languages, studies, and application. *IJCAI*, 2740–2747, 2007.

[14] J. Everhart and D. Wright. Diabetes mellitus as a risk factor for pancreatic cancer: A meta-analysis. *JAMA*, 273(20): 1605–1609, 1995.

[15] A. Fourney, R. W. White, and E. Horvitz. Exploring time-dependent concerns about pregnancy and childbirth from search logs. *SIGCHI*, 737–746, 2015.

[16] S. Fox and M. Duggan. Health online 2013, 2013.
[17] J. H. Friedman. Greedy function approximation: A gradient boosting machine. *Annals of Statistics*, 1189–1232, 2001.
[18] C. S. Fuchs et al. A prospective study of cigarette smoking and the risk of pancreatic cancer. *Archives of Int. Med.*, 156(19): 2255–2260, 1996.
[19] J. Ginsberg et al. Detecting influenza epidemics using search engine query data. *Nature*, 457(7232): 1012–1014, 2009.
[20] A. M. Goldstein et al. Increased risk of pancreatic cancer in melanoma-prone kindreds with p16 ink4 mutations. *NEJM*, 333(15): 970–975, 1995.
[21] P. R. Helft. Patients with cancer, internet information, and the clinical encounter: a taxonomy of patient users. *American Society of Clinical Oncology Educational Book*, pages e89–92, 2011.
[22] R. H. Hruban et al. Progression model for pancreatic cancer. *Clin. Cancer Res.*, 6(8): 2969–2972, 2000.
[23] R. Huxley et al. Type-II diabetes and pancreatic cancer: a meta-analysis of 36 studies. *British J. of Cancer*, 92(11): 2076–2083, 2005.
[24] T. Joachims. Optimizing search engines using clickthrough data. *SIGKDD*, 133–142, 2002.
[25] R. Jones et al. Generating query substitutions. *WWW*, 387–396, 2006.
[26] J. Klapman and M. P. Malafa. Early detection of pancreatic cancer: Why, who, and how to screen. *Cancer Control*, 15(4): 280–287, 2008.
[27] T. Lau and E. Horvitz. Patterns of search: Analyzing and modeling web query refinement. *UMAP*, 1999.
[28] C. Lauckner and G. Hsieh. The presentation of health-related search results and its impact on negative emotional outcomes. *SIGCHI*, 333–342, 2013.
[29] P. Legmann et al. Pancreatic tumors: comparison of dual-phase helical CT and endoscopic sonography. *American J. Roentgenology*, 170(5): 1315–1322, 1998.
[30] D. Li et al. Pancreatic cancer. *The Lancet*, 363(9414): 1049–1057, 2004.
[31] A. B. Lowenfels and P. Maisonneuve. Epidemiology and risk factors for pancreatic cancer. *Best Practice & Research Clinical Gastro.*, 20(2):197–209, 2006.
[32] A. B. Lowenfels et al. Pancreatitis and the risk of pancreatic cancer. *NEJM*, 328(20): 1433–1437, 1993.
[33] H. T. Lynch et al. Familial pancreatic cancer: A review. *Seminars in Oncology*, 23: 251–275, 1996.
[34] K. McKeown et al. Predicting the impact of scientific concepts using full-text features. *JASIST*, 2016.
[35] H. R. Mertz et al. EUS, PET, and CT scanning for evaluation of pancreatic adenocarcinoma. *Gastrointestinal Endoscopy*, 52(3): 367–371, 2000.
[36] D. Michaud. Epidemiology of pancreatic cancer. *Minerva Chirurgica*, 59(2): 99–111, 2004.
[37] M. Müller et al. Pancreatic tumors: Evaluation with endoscopic US, CT, and MR imaging. *Radiology*, 190(3):745–751, 1994.
[38] Y. Ofran et al. Patterns of information-seeking for cancer on the internet: An analysis of real world data. *PLoS One*, 2012.
[39] J. Paparrizos, R. W. White, and E. Horvitz. Screening for pancreatic adenocarcinoma using signals from web search logs: Feasibility study and results. *JOP*, 2016.
[40] M. J. Paul, R. W. White, and E. Horvitz. Search and breast cancer: On disruptive shifts of attention over life histories of an illness. *TWEB*, 10(2): 13, 2016.
[41] M. S. Pepe et al. Phases of biomarker development for early detection of cancer. *J. Nat. Cancer Inst.*, 93(14): 1054–1061, 2001.
[42] G. Peterson, P. Aslani, and K. A. Williams. How do consumers search for and appraise information on medicines on the internet? A qualitative study using focus groups. *JMIR*, 5(4), 2003.
[43] A. G. Renehan et al. Body-mass index and incidence of cancer: A systematic review and meta-analysis of prospective observational studies. *The Lancet*, 371(9612): 569–578, 2008.
[44] M. Richardson. Learning about the world from long-term query logs. *TWEB*, 2(4): 21, 2009.
[45] S. J. Rulyak et al. Cost-effectiveness of pancreatic cancer screening in familial pancreatic cancer kindreds. *Gastrointestinal Endoscopy*, 57(1): 23–29, 2003.
[46] A. Sadilek, H. Kautz, and V. Silenzio. Modeling spread of disease from social interactions. *ICWSM*, 2012.
[47] American Cancer Society. Staging pancreatic cancer. http://www.cancer.org/cancer/pancreaticcancer/detailedguide/pancreatic-cancer-pdf, 2014.
[48] G. Talamin et al. Alcohol and smoking as risk factors in chronic pancreatitis and pancreatic cancer. *Digestive Diseases and Sci.*, 44(7): 1303–1311, 1999.
[49] M. I. Trotter and D. W. Morgan. Patients' use of the internet for health related matters: A study of internet usage in 2000 & 2006. *Health Inf.*, 14(3):175–181, 2008.
[50] R. West, R. W. White, and E. Horvitz. From cookies to cooks: Insights on dietary patterns via analysis of web usage logs. *WWW*, 1399–1410, 2013.
[51] R. White and S. Drucker. Investigating behavioral variability in web search. *WWW*, 21–30, 2007.
[52] R. W. White et al. Toward enhanced pharmacovigilance using patient-generated data on the internet. *Nature CPT*, 96(2): 239–246, 2014.
[53] R. W. White and E. Horvitz. Cyberchondria: Studies of the escalation of medical concerns in web search. *TOIS*, 27(4): 23, 2009.
[54] R. W. White and E. Horvitz. Studies of the onset and persistence of medical concerns in search logs. *SIGIR*, 265–274, 2012.
[55] R. W. White and E. Horvitz. From health search to healthcare: Explorations of intention and utilization via query logs and user surveys. *JAMIA*, 21(1): 49–55, 2014.
[56] R. W. White et al. Web-scale pharmacovigilance: Listening to signals from the crowd. *JAMIA*, 20(3): 404–408, 2013.
[57] R. W. White et al. Early identification of adverse drug reactions from search log data. *JBI*, 59: 42–48, 2016.
[58] C. J. Yeo et al. Pancreaticoduodenectomy for pancreatic adenocarcinoma: Postoperative adjuvant chemoradiation improves survival. *Annals of Surgery*, 225(5): 621, 1997.
[59] J. Yu et al. Time to progression of pancreatic ductal adenocarcinoma from low-to-high tumour stages. *Gut*, 2015.

When Recommendation Goes Wrong - Anomalous Link Discovery in Recommendation Networks

Bryan Perozzi*
Stony Brook University
bperozzi@cs.stonybrook.edu

Michael Schueppert
Google New York
mschueppert@google.com

Jack Saalweachter
Google New York
saalweachter@google.com

Mayur Thakur*
maythakur@gmail.com

ABSTRACT

We present a secondary ranking system to find and remove erroneous suggestions from a geospatial recommendation system. We discover such anomalous links by "double checking" the recommendation system's output to ensure that it is both structurally cohesive, and semantically consistent.

Our approach is designed for the Google Related Places Graph, a geographic recommendation system which provides results for hundreds of millions of queries a day. We model the quality of a recommendation between two geographic entities as a function of their structure in the Related Places Graph, and their semantic relationship in the Google Knowledge Graph.

To evaluate our approach, we perform a large scale *human evaluation* of such an anomalous link detection system. For the long tail of unpopular entities, our models can predict the recommendations users will consider poor with up to 42% higher mean precision (29 raw points) than the live system.

Results from our study reveal that structural and semantic features capture different facets of relatedness to human judges. We characterize our performance with a qualitative analysis detailing the categories of real-world anomalies our system is able to detect, and provide a discussion of additional applications of our method.

Categories and Subject Descriptors

D.2.8 [**Database Management**]: Database applications—*Data mining*

Keywords

anomaly detection; knowledge graph; link prediction; recommendation systems

*Work performed while at Google, Inc.

KDD '16 August 13-17, 2016, San Francisco, CA, USA

ACM ISBN 978-1-4503-4232-2/16/08.

DOI: http://dx.doi.org/10.1145/2939672.2939734

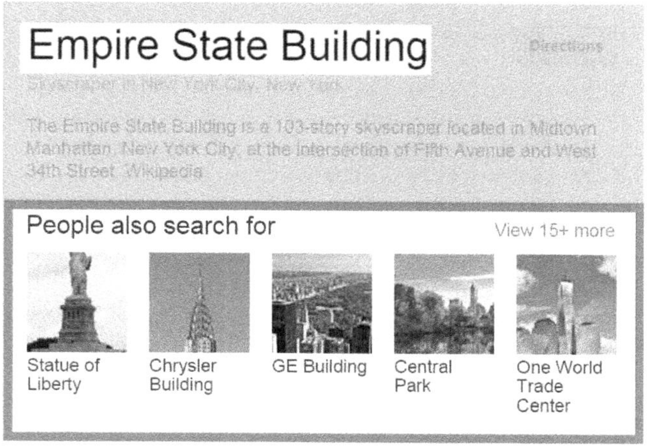

Figure 1: The *People Also Search For* feature, showing five good recommendations from the Related Places Graph for the `Empire State Building`. Prominent use of recommendations raises the risk of bad suggestions negatively affecting a user's product experience.

1. INTRODUCTION

Recommendation systems have become an integral part of modern information retrieval systems. They are used to suggest almost anything to users, including places, products, publications, and on social networks - even friends.

Despite their prevalence, recommendation systems are still capable of making recommendations that users might find irrelevant or unhelpful. These bad recommendations can occur from noise in the real world processes that generate the data that they are trained on, or can be the result of a subtle dependency that the recommendation system doesn't properly model. As the size of a dataset grows, so does its long tail of less popular items, which worsens both problems. Not only do spurious correlations occur more often, but the effects of improperly modeled dependencies become more apparent. These sources of error directly affects the utility of these recommendation systems for information retrieval and content recommendation tasks.

In the literature this problem is usually addressed by changing the original model to include additional features and dependencies. Unfortunately, the cost of properly engineering and validating such an enhanced model for web-scale

t	Query	Entity
1	taj mahal	`taj mahal` (*landmark*)
		`trump taj mahal` (*casino*)
		`taj mahal` (*restaurant*)
2	atlantic city casinos	`borgota` (*casino*)
		`trump taj mahal` (*casino*)
		`trump plaza` (*casino*)
3	trump plaza	`trump plaza` (*casino*)
		`trump taj mahal` (*casino*)
		`borgata` (*casino*)

(a) Hypothetical session queries

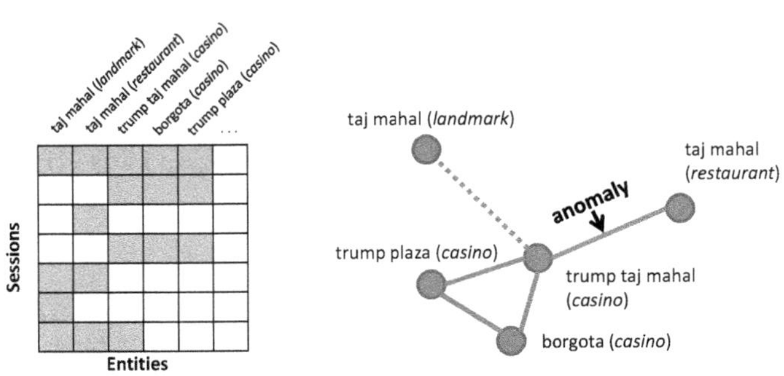

(b) Session-Entity Matrix (c) Related Places Graph

Figure 2: Overview: The Related Places Graph is formed by observing entity co-occurrence in web sessions (2a), constructing a Session-Entity matrix (2b), and estimating an entity similarity score (2c). This graph can be filtered by distance (dashed lines), but more subtle anomalies (red) may remain.

recommendation is frequently not justified by speculative performance gains.[1] However, simply ignoring the problem is often equally undesirable as incorrect recommendations have been shown to lower a user's opinion of the system [6].

In this work, we present a secondary ranking system for the detection of such erroneous recommendations in the Google Related Places Graph, a large geographic recommendation system which provides recommendations for hundreds of millions of queries a day. Our approach detects anomalous entity recommendations by fusing semantic information from the Google Knowledge Graph with network features from the Related Places Graph. While we focus on a specific problem instance, the approach we present is general, and can be used with any similarly constructed recommendation network and knowledge graph (e.g. Freebase [5]).

To evaluate our approach, we perform what is (to our knowledge) the first comprehensive human evaluation of such an anomalous link detection system, and show that we are able to achieve relative increases of 9% to 42% in mean precision (7 to 29 raw points, respectfully) in an anomaly detection task against a very challenging baseline - the live system itself. We also perform a qualitative evaluation which illustrates the categories of anomalies our system is able to detect.

Specifically, our contributions are the following:

- **Unified Approach**: We fuse *semantic information* from a knowledge graph, with *structural features* from the recommendation network to detect bad recommendations with much higher precision (9% to 42% relative improvement in mean precision) over the base recommendation system.
- **Human Evaluation**: To capture the nuanced semantics assigned with geographic similarity, we evaluate our approach using trained human raters. Results from our study reveal that structural and semantic features capture different facets of relatedness to human judges.
- **Qualitative Analysis**: We provide a comprehensive qualitative analysis of the capabilities and limitations of our system, along with example applications for our system's output. We believe this will motivate further research in this area.

[1] For example, the winning algorithm for the Netflix Challenge was never launched into production [3].

2. RELATED PLACES GRAPH

Our dataset for this paper is the Google Related Places Graph, a very large geographic recommendation system with hundreds of millions of entities and tens of billions of similarity relations. It is used to provide pairwise geographic entity similarity results for hundreds of millions of search queries a day. In this section, we briefly describe its construction and challenges associated with web-scale geographic recommendation.

2.1 Overview

The Google Related Places Graph $G = (V, E)$ is a similarity network composed of V entities which are geolocated businesses or organizations, and E edges which encode a similarity score between them (i.e. edge $E_{ij} = s(i, j)$, the similarity between entities v_i, and v_j). It is an instance of an item-based collaborative filtering system [24], which intuitively captures how related two places are for the purposes of web search. Exact details of the similarity function are proprietary, but a number of memory and model based approaches to similar problems have been discussed in the literature [28]. The top k highest weighted outgoing edges of an entity can be used to return ranked lists of similar places for geographic recommendation. A typical result of such use is shown in Figure 1.

An outline of the Related Places Graph is shown in Figure 2. The process starts by collecting entities associated with user search sessions (2a). This is used to populate a Sessions-Entity matrix M from the set of sessions S and establishments V (2b). Finally a similarity function $s : V \times V \to \mathbb{R}$ is used to construct the recommendation network (2c).

2.2 Challenges

Unfortunately, the relations captured by the Related Places Graph are not perfect. In particular, there are a number of adverse effects which make it difficult to correctly model establishment similarity, including:

- **Distance is relative**: The distance which an individual considers two things to be related varies greatly with location and intent. A pizza restaurant two blocks away may be too far in New York City, but perfectly reasonable in rural Montana. This variance poses challenges for simple thresholding methods.
- **Frequency Imbalance**: Some entities (such as the `Empire State Building`) are much more popular than

many of their surrounding establishments. This imbalance can result in low quality similarity links for less popular establishments.

- **Geographic Sparsity**: Geographic regions with smaller populations have correspondingly lower query volume. Statistical estimates for establishments in these regions are therefore more prone to noise.
- **Conglomerate Entities**: An entity may have multiple semantic senses associated with it. For example, a grocery store might have an automated teller machine (ATM), a pharmacy, or a coffee shop in addition to food products. Composite relationships like this can greatly broaden the scope of entities considered to be related.
- **Ambiguous Queries**: Similarly, the ambiguity of natural language used for search itself poses issues. Consider the `Taj Mahal`, which is both the name of a famous mausoleum and a common name for restaurants which serve Indian cuisine. This polysemy creates superficial similarity.

Dealing with such challenges is a non-trivial task, and geographic recommendation systems are is the subject of active research [15, 33]. The most straightforward strategy is to discard all relationships with low similarity ($E_{ij} < \epsilon_S$) or high distance ($\text{dist}(i,j) > \epsilon_D$). While this thresholding strategy can mitigate some forms of errors (e.g. from frequency imbalance), it adversely effects recall (especially for establishments with low volume). Additionally, it does nothing to address other, more semantic, sources of error. These remaining errors can have an extremely negative influence on how users perceive some queries, typically when multiple semantic meanings or polysemous queries link two seemingly dissimilar places. Examples of anomalous relationships detected by our system are shown in Section 7.2.

2.3 Definition of 'Relatedness'

We note that there are many possible definitions of what might be considered a 'related place'. For the purposes of this work, we consider a place to be 'related' when it is:

- **Relevant**: A relevant recommendation captures a user's internal sense of the similarity between two places.
- **Useful**: A useful recommendation is one which is helpful if shown to users in addition to place they are searching for.

These attributes are subjective, and can vary with the type of entity. For example, whether a business is 'useful' will vary based on location (2 blocks may be too far in NYC, while ten miles may be reasonable in rural Kentucky), or its type (two amusement parks may be far away and still be related). The concept of 'relevance' is also deeply integrated with the nature of the search task which a user is performing at the time of query. For example, when searching for a hotel to stay in, a user might wish to see alternative hotels in the area. However, a user who has already chosen a hotel (and may be already staying there) might prefer to see nearby restaurants or tourist attractions.

In order to capture this relation in all of its nuance, the evaluation of our system utilizes human raters. More details are discussed in Section 5.

3. ANOMALOUS LINK DISCOVERY

Given a graph $G = (V, E)$, the Anomalous Link Discovery (ALD) problem is to find a set of anomalous edges $E_a \subset E$ which represent a deviation from the dominant patterns in G [21]. ALD is related to the link prediction problem [13], which models the evolution of the network by predicting unseen edges.

3.1 Class Imbalance

Link prediction can be viewed as classifying the set of possible edges of G to those that existent and should nonexistent. Many real world graphs are sparse, and so the existent edges (positive label) are a small fraction ($m \approx O(n)$) out of all possible edges ($O(n^2)$) This asymptotically skewed class distribution is a core challenge of link prediction, increasing the variance of link models, and making complete model evaluation computationally expensive.

Unlike link prediction, ALD focuses on the m edges which actually exist - a distinction which becomes increasingly important in sparse real world graphs. We note that this does not eliminate class skew entirely, as most graphs of interest will have more good edges than noisy ones. As such, ALD models must also account for variance arising from both the structure and higher-order semantic properties of a network.

3.2 ALD Modeling

Just as with link prediction, early approaches to ALD consisted of using individual connectedness metrics to provide a ranking of edges by their anomaly value (i.e. edges with $\text{score}(i,j) < \epsilon$ are returned as the anomalies). Modern link prediction uses supervised learning [14], which provides much more flexibility for link modeling. We apply a similar supervised approach in our ALD model, extracting multiple topological properties as features, and seamlessly combining them with additional semantic information.

Specifically, we seek to model $P(E_{ij})$, the probability of an edge found between v_i and v_j in G. We assume that edges are a function of topological properties from G, and the intrinsic semantic attributes of the nodes in our network as represented in the Google Knowledge Graph (denoted X_{KG}), and therefore concern ourselves with $P(E_{ij}|G, X_{KG})$. We assume that the input to our process is a similarity graph where edges are weighted with $E_{ij} = s(i,j)$ and that G has already been appropriately thresholded to only contain high similarity edges (i.e. $E_{ij} > \epsilon$).

4. FEATURES

In this section we discuss the features used for link modeling in our anomalous link detection system for recommendation networks. Our choice of features is based on the assumption that recommendation networks should contain strong homophily - that is they should exhibit both structural transitivity, and semantic consistency. We model structural transitivity through features derived from the network itself and model semantic consistency through features captured by the Google Knowledge Graph. For each feature we briefly discuss its motivation and outline the its construction function $f(v_i, v_j) \mapsto \mathbb{R}$.

4.1 Structural Transitivity

Our first assumption is that a recommendation network should exhibit homophily through transitivity. That is, if entity A is related to entity B and C, then items B and C should have a much higher chance of being related. We quantify this relationship by introducing topological features from the recommendation network representing the structural connectedness of two entities. These network features are very valuable, and can implicitly capture information which has not been explicitly annotated.

4.1.1 Neighborhood

The simplest measures of structural transitivity can be derived from the neighborhoods of two vertices. Features of this variety have been widely used in link prediction[13]. We denote the neighbors of a node v by $\mathcal{N}(v)$, (i.e. $\mathcal{N}(v) = \{i; (i,v) \in E \ \vee (v,i) \in E\}$).

- **Common Neighbors**: $f(x,y) = |\mathcal{N}(x) \cap \mathcal{N}(y)|$
  The simplest link prediction feature is the size of the intersection between two neighborhoods.
- **Jaccard Index**: $f(x,y) = \frac{|\mathcal{N}(x) \cap \mathcal{N}(y)|}{|\mathcal{N}(x) \cup \mathcal{N}(y)|}$
  To avoid bias towards neighborhoods with high size, this measure normalizes the size of the intersection by the total size of the combined neighborhood.
- **Preferential Attachment**: $f(x,y) = |\mathcal{N}(x)| * |\mathcal{N}(y)|$
  In this measure, the size of each neighborhood determines the creation of a link.

4.1.2 Graph Distance

More advanced measures of structural equivalence consider information beyond the node neighborhoods.

- **Personalized PageRank**: $f(x,y) = PPR_x(y)$
  The Personalized PageRank vector[10] PPR_x captures information about probability that node y will be reached in a random walk started at node x.

We note that many additional features have been proposed for link modeling, but limit our discussion to the techniques listed here.

4.2 Semantic Consistency

Our second assumption is that good recommendations are those which are semantically consistent with the entity of interest. This semantic consistency varies with both the type of entity being considered and the location of the entity. For example, consider two medical practitioners: one who specializes in cardiology, and the other in pediatrics. Although they are both doctors, they might be bad recommendations for one another in an area with many doctors. However, they might well be reasonable recommendations if they were the only two doctors in town. Fine grained semantic consistency can be quite nuanced in other domains as well, such as food service. To capture these relationships, we annotated entities in our recommendation network with information from the Google Knowledge Graph.

4.2.1 Knowledge Graph

The Google Knowledge Graph is a comprehensive knowledge store that contains semantic information about entities in the real world [26]. Storing information on people, places, and things, it aids in query disambiguation and summarization.

In this work, we are concerned with the subset of the knowledge graph which refers to places. For our purposes, a place is a location entity which people may wish to visit such as a business, monument, or school. Each place in the

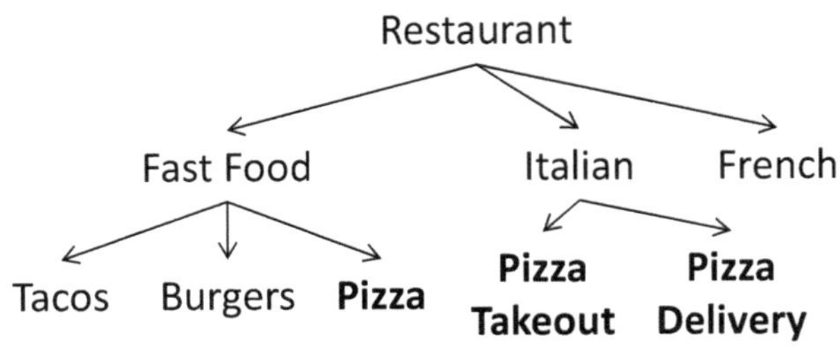

(a) Idealized Knowledge Graph Category Hierarchy

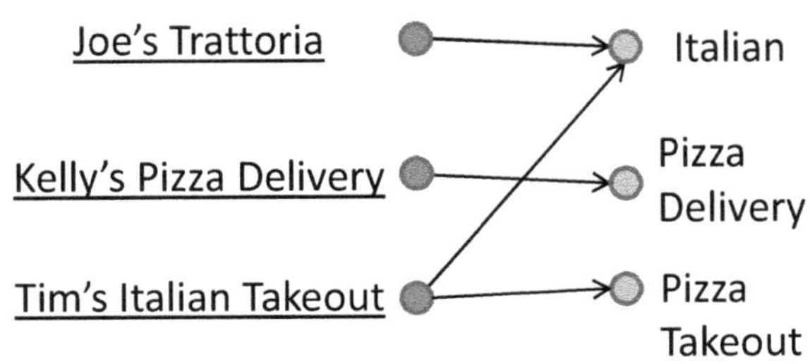

(b) Example: Three businesses which all offer pizza (left), connected to their corresponding semantic labels (right).

Figure 3: An idealized hierarchy of entity categories in the Knowledge Graph (a), showing how even a seemingly straightforward concept like *pizza restaurant* can be encoded in a number of different ways. In (b), an example of 3 hypothetical businesses which all offer pizza, but due to noise in the labeling process, have different sets of semantic categories.

knowledge graph has an associated set of semantic categories associated with it. These categories are related to each other through a hierarchy ranging from the specific (e.g. pizza-delivery, French restaurant) to general (store). Figure 3 illustrates an example of an idealized hierarchy (3a) and the semantic labels for several similar hypothetical businesses (3b). Notice how related entities do not necessarily share the same semantic categories.

The size and scope of the Knowledge Graph afford a variety of ways to create features for classification tasks. We briefly discuss some of them below:

- **Distance**: $f(x,y) = dist(x,y)$
  The distance between two locations is an important part of geographic recommendation. By itself weak (not all close businesses are related), it can be powerful when combined with other features.
- **Common Categories**: $f(x,y) = |\text{Cat}(x) \cap \text{Cat}(y)|$
  The categories which two entities have in common is also very relevant to recommendations. Similar to the common neighbors, this metric can also be normalized using Jaccard similarity $\left(f(x,y) = \frac{|\text{Cat}(x) \cap \text{Cat}(y)|}{|\text{Cat}(x) \cup \text{Cat}(y)|}\right)$ or related measures.
- **Categorical Hierarchy**
  In some cases, there may be no exact overlap between two entities' categories, although they are related (Figure 3b). To capture broader senses of relation, we can expand the set of categories each entity has by traversing upwards through the categorical hierarchy (Figure

3a), searching for common ancestors. The overlap between these expanded sets can be normalized based on their size, or based on the distance up the hierarchy the terms are added at.

We note that the inclusion of categorical features from the Knowledge Graph has the potential to greatly increase a model's complexity. Our approach relies on using a small number of training examples, and so we have discussed aggregating categorical information. However, as available training data grows, model complexity can be easily increased by treating each particular category (or pairwise combination of categories) as separate features.

5. EXPERIMENTAL DESIGN

Our approach to Anomalous Link Discovery uses user input to train discriminative link models. This user input is collected during the course of routine product quality evaluations. The anomalies detected by these models are then evaluated by human raters to determine model performance. In this section, we briefly discuss the process used to construct datasets and link models, the design of the experiments, and our human evaluations.

5.1 Training Dataset Construction

We use human evaluations of the similarity between two place entities as our training data. This data was collected in the course of routine product quality evaluations.

For each pair of entities, at least three different human raters were asked to judge the recommendation (on a scale of {*Not*, *Somewhat*, *Very*}) based on its *relevance* (their internal view of how analogous the two places were), and its *usefulness* (how helpful it would be to a user searching for a the original place). The distinction between relevance and usefulness is elaborated on in Section 2.3.

To convert their ratings to binary labels, a value of {1,2,3} was assigned to each judgment of {*Not*, *Somewhat*, *Very*}. An edge was labeled as relevant (or useful) when its respective average score for that category was above 2. As we assume that a good geographic recommendation is both relevant and useful, we labeled an edge as related only when judged as having both properties.

Using this process, we distilled over 28,800 human ratings into 9,600 labeled examples pairs for training. Of these 7,637 pairs were labeled as related and 1,963 labeled as not-related (a positive class label imbalance of 5:1).

5.2 Classification

Having discussed our method for generating training data, we turn to our choice of classifier for link modeling.

5.2.1 Models Considered

We compared the performance of Logistic Regression (regularized with the L_2 loss), and Random Forest Classifiers to model the probability of a recommendation link being related. We used stratified 5-fold cross validation for model selection, where Random Forests significantly out performed Logistic Regression (shown in Table 1). For the remainder of our paper, we present results using models trained with Random Forests, which we abbreviate RFC.

The baseline models we consider in decreasing order of difficulty:

- **RFC$_{\textbf{Related}}$**: This model uses the raw similarity score (edge weight) of the existing relatedness estimate from the Related Places Graph. This estimate is computed from a very large sample of web traffic, and is a very competitive baseline.
- **RFC$_{\textbf{Common}}$**: A model which considers only the common neighbors between entities.
- **RFC$_{\textbf{Distance}}$**: A model which considers only the distance between two entities.
- **Random**: This model simply returns the links under consideration in an random order, which illustrates the difficulty of the task.

The method under consideration are:

- **RFC$_{\textbf{Network}}$**: This model considers a number of network features designed to capture structural transitivity (Section 4.1).
- **RFC$_{\textbf{Knowledge}}$**: This model considers a number of features derived from the Knowledge Graph, in order to capture semantic similarity (Section 4.2).
- **RFC$_{\textbf{All}}$**: This model is trained on both semantic and structural features.

Classifier	Feature Set	ROC AUC
Logistic Regression	Structural	0.621
Random Forest	Structural	**0.656**
Logistic Regression	Semantic	0.696
Random Forest	Semantic	**0.723**
Logistic Regression	All	0.713
Random Forest	All	**0.778**

Table 1: Average model performance with different feature sets in stratified 5-fold cross validation.

5.3 Human Evaluation

The decision as to whether two geographic entities are related is nuanced, varying with their location, the entities, and ultimately the individual. In order to satisfactorily capture this relation, we evaluate our model's performance using human evaluation.

The human raters we use in our experiments are paid evaluators used for product quality assessment. These raters have been professionally trained using a rigorous process and guidelines. They all reside in the region where our study takes place (United States), and have a full proficiency in English. These vetted raters allow us to avoid some of the quality issues which may be present in other large scale human evaluations (e.g. Mechanical Turk [12]).

We generate test datasets for our evaluation by sampling entities from a subgraph of the Related Places Graph containing only entities located in the United States. This subgraph is large enough to be interesting (millions of nodes and billions of edges), but it eliminates some cultural variance which might complicate evaluation. Our test datasets are generated in one of two ways:

- **Uniform**: Our first test dataset is created by uniform random sampling of entities without replacement. It consists of 12,593 nodes and their top 5 best recommendations (highest weighted edges).
- **Traffic Weighted** - Our second test dataset is created by random sampling of entities in proportional to their average web traffic volume (without replace-

ment). It consists of 1,187 nodes and their top 5 best recommendations (highest weighted edges).

To evaluate the performance of a model, we score the entire test datasets, and send each of the 200 most anomalous edges (highest $P(E_{ij} = 0|G, X_{KG})$) out to three human raters. An individual rater was allowed to answer a maximum of 20 out of the 600 judgments per model, ensuring that at least 30 unique raters contributed to each assessment. The raters were instructed to perform research (e.g. visit an entity homepage, read reviews, etc.) about the two entities and then to deliver a judgment. The raters results are converted to labels (as discussed in Section 5.1), which we use to calculate the area under the precision curve.[2]

6. EXPERIMENTS

After evaluating our models through cross validation, we conducted two large scale human evaluations of feature quality from links present in the Google Related Places Graph. As described in Section 5.2, one evaluation consists of location entities which were sampled uniformly at random and the other of entities sampled in proportion to their web traffic volume.

6.1 Uniform Sampling

The results of our uniform sampling evaluation are presented in Figure 2. Here, we briefly discuss some observations in terms of *relevance* and *usefulness*.

Of all the features considered, we find that the those from the Knowledge Graph perform best for detection of links which are not relevant, initially outperforming the strong $\text{RFC}_{\text{Related}}$ baseline by 14 precision points (k=25), and narrowing to 5 at k=200. Structural features were much less competitive on this task, failing to outperform the baseline at all. A final observation is that the distance model is not able to determine relevance (as judged by humans) significantly better than random.

In contrast, we find that structural features are much better predictors of recommendations which are not useful. We attribute the strong performance of structural features for k<=50 to those features (e.g. a low number of common neighbors) which can provide strong evidence for non-relation. As k grows larger, the network structure's signal is less valuable, and performance degrades.

Both models perform well on detecting recommendations which are not related, with $\text{RFC}_{\text{Network}}$ initially beating the baseline by 42% at k=25, but again degrading as more results are returned. The joint model (RFC_{All}) performs generally well on this task, leveraging the strengths of both the structural and semantic features to beat the baseline by 37% at k=25, to 9% at k=200. However, we note that in some cases the model performs worse than its constituent parts. This occurs when the structural features provide poor discriminating power, and is a result of the highly heterogeneous phenomenon we are modeling. The performance of the joint model will improve as our system collects more human judgments.

We remark that the use of uniform sampling emphasizes entities which lie in the *long tail* of popularity. These relatively unpopularity entities have similarity estimates based on weaker statistical evidence, and are more likely to have data quality issues. Lower popularity then, impacts both structural and semantic feature quality. Our results show that even under such constraints, it is indeed possible to identify anomalous recommendations with a high degree of precision.

[2]As our task is anomaly detection, we consider the positive class label to be 0 when calculating the mean precision.

6.2 Traffic Weighted Sampling

In order to better understand the user impact of our system, we designed an evaluation where the entities were sampled in proportion to their percentage of total search volume. This experiment reflects the real world situation in which our product is used. Instead of dealing with unpopular entities, this experiment allows us to understand how our approach works when the entities have both good similarity estimates and detailed Knowledge Graph entries. This allow the study of nuanced anomalies (and not those that are simply a result of noise). The results of this evaluation are presented in Table 3.

With respect to detecting relations categorized as not relevant, we find that models using features from the Knowledge Graph ($\text{RFC}_{\text{Knowledge}}$, RFC_{All}) again perform much better than $\text{RFC}_{\text{Network}}$. We also see that the relative performance of the baseline is much stronger on this task, and that only the combination of topological and semantic features (RFC_{All}) is able to exceed it (by up to 12% at k=200)

For not useful recommendations, we again see that network features are very strong indicators of whether users consider a recommendation to be useful. When entities have good similarity estimates, the network features much more closely model user behavior. Conversely, the relatively poor performance of the Knowledge Graph features on this task can be explained by the more robust semantic similarities captured between entities. For example, when given an airport, we may recommend nearby hotels. Such a recommendation is quite useful, but may be flagged as an anomaly because it is between two very distinct semantic categories (and there was a lack of training data indicating that these types of entities are appropriate to recommend for each other). We discuss this further in Section 7.

Finally we see that the performance of structural features again carries over to detecting entities which are not related, beating the baseline by 19% at $k = 25$ and still by 5% at $k = 200$. We see that RFC_{All} initially suffers from its reliance on semantic features, but recovers and is superior to both methods by k=200. The worst performing model is $\text{RFC}_{\text{Knowledge}}$, as it can not take advantage of the enhanced similarity estimates available for popular entities.

7. DISCUSSION

Here we discuss the conclusions we have derived from our experiments, provide a qualitative analysis of the types of anomalies we detect, and discuss applications of our work.

7.1 Results

As seen in Section 6, our experiments show that our proposed approach is able to detect erroneous recommendations on a very large recommendation system with much higher precision than any of the baselines we consider. In addition to the raw performance benefits, we have draw several higher-level conclusions from our human evaluation, which we highlight here:

Structural and semantic features are not equal. Our results on the long tail of entities (Uniform Random Sampling) show

	Model	Mean Precision @k				% vs $RFC_{Related}$			
		k=25	k=50	k=100	k=200	k=25	k=50	k=100	k=200
Not Relevant	Random	0.147	0.146	0.200	0.235	-75.7	-76.3	-69.4	-63.9
	$RFC_{Distance}$	0.154	0.165	0.179	0.191	-74.5	-73.2	-72.6	-70.7
	RFC_{Common}	0.297	0.294	0.265	0.250	-50.8	-52.4	-59.4	-61.6
	$RFC_{Related}$	0.604	0.618	0.654	0.653	-	-	-	-
	$RFC_{Network}$	0.603	0.516	0.461	0.437	-0.18	-16.6	-29.5	-33.1
	$RFC_{Knowledge}$	**0.748**	**0.715**	**0.695**	**0.703**	**23.7**	**15.6**	**6.26**	**7.67**
	RFC_{All}	0.766	0.714	0.679	0.654	26.7	15.5	3.89	0.21
Not Useful	Random	0.468	0.417	0.433	0.444	-29.6	-38.1	-39.0	-37.6
	$RFC_{Distance}$	0.285	0.351	0.399	0.443	-57.2	-47.9	-43.8	-37.7
	RFC_{Common}	0.456	0.498	0.478	0.446	-31.5	-26.2	-32.6	-37.2
	$RFC_{Related}$	0.666	0.675	0.710	0.711	-	-	-	-
	$RFC_{Network}$	**0.858**	**0.807**	0.731	0.683	**28.8**	**19.5**	2.89	-3.90
	$RFC_{Knowledge}$	0.779	0.771	**0.762**	**0.785**	17.1	14.2	**7.36**	**10.4**
	RFC_{All}	0.893	0.820	0.773	0.745	34.2	21.46	8.87	4.85
Not Related	Random	0.468	0.423	0.443	0.452	-29.6	-37.3	-37.7	-36.8
	$RFC_{Distance}$	0.285	0.358	0.409	0.451	-57.2	-46.9	-42.5	-36.9
	RFC_{Common}	0.456	0.502	0.489	0.462	-31.5	-25.6	-31.3	-35.4
	$RFC_{Related}$	0.666	0.675	0.712	0.715	-	-	-	-
	$RFC_{Network}$	**0.951**	**0.867**	**0.767**	0.708	**42.8**	**28.4**	**7.85**	-0.95
	$RFC_{Knowledge}$	0.779	0.771	0.762	**0.785**	17.1	14.2	7.14	**9.74**
	RFC_{All}	0.912	0.856	0.812	0.779	37.0	26.9	14.1	8.98

Table 2: Anomaly detection results for our Uniform Random Sampling experiment. Bold indicates whether structure or semantics ($RFC_{Network}$ or $RFC_{Knowledge}$) performed best on the task. For the long tail of unpopular entities, our proposed models can predict the recommendations users will consider not related up to 42% better than our strongest baseline.

	Model	Mean Precision @k				Relative % to $RFC_{Related}$			
		k=25	k=50	k=100	k=200	k=25	k=50	k=100	k=200
Not Relevant	Random	0.145	0.152	0.171	0.179	-75.9	-74.9	-71.9	-70.8
	$RFC_{Distance}$	0.195	0.207	0.207	0.210	-67.5	-66.0	-66.1	-65.7
	RFC_{Common}	0.399	0.354	0.329	0.311	-33.5	-41.7	-46.1	-49.2
	$RFC_{Related}$	0.601	0.608	0.612	0.613	-	-	-	-
	$RFC_{Network}$	0.454	0.411	0.394	0.374	-24.4	-32.3	-35.5	-39.0
	$RFC_{Knowledge}$	0.580	0.593	0.592	**0.620**	-3.55	-2.54	-3.18	**1.13**
	RFC_{All}	0.560	0.618	0.653	0.692	-6.88	1.68	6.86	12.8
Not Useful	Random	0.273	0.260	0.258	0.260	-60.8	-62.6	-62.8	-62.4
	$RFC_{Distance}$	0.543	0.517	0.509	0.510	-22.2	-25.6	-26.6	-26.4
	RFC_{Common}	0.675	0.637	0.574	0.527	-3.27	-8.29	-17.1	-23.9
	$RFC_{Related}$	0.698	0.695	0.693	0.693	-	-	-	-
	$RFC_{Network}$	**0.864**	**0.819**	**0.767**	**0.722**	**23.8**	**17.9**	**10.7**	**4.25**
	$RFC_{Knowledge}$	0.649	0.672	0.677	0.697	-6.98	-3.26	-2.31	0.66
	RFC_{All}	0.682	0.725	0.751	0.769	-2.30	4.39	8.31	11.0
Not Related	Random	0.359	0.299	0.301	0.325	-50.5	-57.8	-57.0	-53.3
	$RFC_{Distance}$	0.543	0.523	0.519	0.518	-25.2	-26.1	-25.9	-25.5
	RFC_{Common}	0.675	0.637	0.579	0.536	-6.96	-10.1	-17.3	-23.0
	$RFC_{Related}$	0.725	0.709	0.700	0.696	-	-	-	-
	$RFC_{Network}$	**0.864**	**0.819**	**0.769**	**0.730**	**19.0**	**15.6**	**9.81**	**4.93**
	$RFC_{Knowledge}$	0.649	0.689	0.699	0.716	-10.53	-2.84	-0.14	2.89
	RFC_{All}	0.682	0.725	0.751	0.774	-6.03	2.36	7.24	11.2

Table 3: Anomaly detection results for our Traffic Weighted Sampling experiment. Bold indicates whether structure or semantics ($RFC_{Network}$ or $RFC_{Knowledge}$) performed best on the task. For popular entities, the combination of structural and semantic features is necessary to discover relations which are not relevant, while structural features provide a strong signal for entity pairs which are not useful.

that semantic features from the Knowledge Graph are good at identifying recommendations which are judged as not relevant, while structural features from the recommendation network are good at determining relationships which judged to be are not useful.

Network features help, regardless of location popularity. As locations receive more web traffic, we are able to build a recommendation network that more accurately models the underlying relationships. This decreases the noise of features directly derived from the network, allowing them to perform well even as the number of anomalies decreases (as in our traffic weighted experiment).

Distance alone is not enough. Many geographic recommendation systems simply include distance-based constraints or regularization to model geospatial dependencies. Our results show that these models can be improved by using structural features of the network, and semantic features of locations.

7.2 Qualitative Analysis

We have performed a qualitative analysis of the types of anomalies our approach is able to capture, which we briefly

Entity Location (*Category*)	Anomalous Recommendation(s) in Top-5 (*Category*)	Reason
`IBM` New York, NY (*Software Company*)	`Victoria's Secret` (*Intimate Apparel Store*)	Nearby
`Boys and Girls Club` Orlando, FL (*Youth Organization*)	`3 Strip Clubs` (*Adult Entertainment*)	Auto-Completion & Polysemy
`Mom's Bar` Los Angeles, CA (*Bar*)	`Los Angeles County Bar Association` (*Professional Association*)	Ambiguous Phrases
`Tony's Small Engine Services` Ashland, KY (*Auto Repair Shop*)	`Academy Animal Hospital` (*Veterinarian*)	Data Sparsity
`IKEA` Canton, MI (*Home Furnishings Store*)	`Comfort Suites` (*Hotel*) `Hampton Inn` (*Hotel*) `La Quinta Inn` (*Hotel*) `Fairfield Inn` (*Hotel*) `Extend Stay America` (*Hotel*)	Unmodeled Phenomenon

`Florida Department of Agriculture`
Tampa, FL
(*State Government Agency*)
	`Tampa Private Investigators`
	(*Private Detectives*)
	`Equip 2 Conceal Firearms`
	(*Gun shop*)
	`Shoot Straight`
	(*Gun shop*)
	`Florida Firearms Academy`
	(*Shooting Range*)
		Conglomerate (issues firearm permits)

Table 4: Representative examples of real anomalies detected by our system, and our categorization of their cause.

discuss here. Table 4 shows a summary of representative examples of actual anomalies we have detected using our approach. Specifically, the variety of anomalies which we were able to discover included those due to:

Unmodeled Phenomena: Unmodeled interactions between entities can lead to very interesting anomalies, such as the recommendation between IKEA and hotels. We discuss how this class of anomalies can be used for targeted ontology improvements in Section 7.3.2.

Ambiguous Phrases: We are able to detect anomalies created both polysemous words and phrases (e.g. `Mom's Bar` / `Bar Association`).

Conglomerate entities Multi-sense entities can result in surprising recommendations. For example, normally one would not expect recommendations between a government entity and firearm clubs. However, as the `Florida Department of Agriculture` also issues gun permits, several such recommendation links appear. We note that such recommendations for conglomerate entities may in fact be useful to users. In such cases, (as with unmodeled phenomena) the anomalies we find can be used to improve the quality of data stored in the Knowledge Graph itself.

Data-sparsity: In some rural locations, there is not enough data for confident estimates of similarity (e.g. `Tony's Small Engine Services` / `Academy Animal Hospital`). When this happens, features from the Knowledge Graph allow detection of entities which are not related.

Mobile users & Search Completion: Finally, two sources of anomalies seemed tied to mobile users and search completion technologies. First are *auto-completion errors*. This category of errors seemed due to substring similarity between entity names. Examples include people's names to locations (e.g. `Tuscano` / `Tuscany`), and between very unrelated entity types (e.g. `Boy's and Girls Club` / `Girls Club`). Second, are *nearby entities*. This category of anomalies contained dissimilar businesses entities which are very close to each other. We suspect this behavior is due to individuals searching for information about that location (e.g. in order to plan a shopping trip).

Our qualitative analysis shows that our approach is able to address the challenges we outlined earlier in Section 2.2, and that we are able to discover anomalous links across a variety of categories, causes, and geographic locations.

7.3 Applications and Future Work

Although our work has thus far focused on a specific problem instance, we believe that the approach we present is general, and has applications to any recommendation network which has structured information available. In this section we highlight additional applications of our method which go beyond the simple removal of low-quality recommendations.

7.3.1 Entity Outlier Score

In our qualitative analysis, we have seen that anomalous links (specifically due to unmodeled phenomena, multi-sense entities, and data sparsity) tend to come in 'clumps' for an entity. A natural extension of our approach, then, is to consider the detection of anomalous entities in addition to anomalous links. We note that an outlier score for an entity may be constructed as a function of it's link probabilities, for example:

$$score(i) = \frac{\sum_{j \in \mathcal{N}(i)} Pr(E_{ij} = 0 | G, X_{KG})}{|\mathcal{N}(i)|} \tag{1}$$

Maintaining an accurate web-scale knowledge base is a very challenging endeavor, and this score could be useful for highlighting entities which have incorrect information about them (perhaps from recent changes). Entities flagged as anomalous by this measure could then be prioritized to be investigated by the relevant data quality team.

7.3.2 Targeted Ontology Improvements

When an anomalous entity is not the result of incorrect information, it can indicate that our underlying semantic

Entity	Location	Anomalous Recommendation(s) in Top-5 (*Category*)
`IKEA`	Brooklyn, NY	`IKEA Dock` (*Transportation*) `Wall Street-Pier 11` (*Transportation*) `New York Water Taxi` (*Transportation*) `St. George Terminal` (*Transportation*) `Hoboken Terminal` (*Transportation*)
`IKEA`	Centennial, CO	`Embassy Suites Denver - Tech Center` (*Hotel*) `Comfort Suites Denver Tech Center` (*Hotel*)
`IKEA`	Charlotte, NC	`Hilton Charlotte University Place` (*Hotel*) `Comfort Suites University Area` (*Hotel*)
`IKEA`	West Chester, OH	`Kings Island` (*Amusement Park*) `Newport Aquarium` (*Aquarium*)

Table 5: Additional examples of the `IKEA` store anomaly, found during our qualitative evaluation. Our investigation reveals that in many areas, users treat `IKEA` more like a *Tourist Attraction* or *Travel Destination* than a normal furniture store.

model is not expressive enough. These data-driven improvements can result in groups of entities acquiring new semantic categories, or even changes to the hierarchical relationships between categories.

As a case study, we return to the furniture store `IKEA`. Table 5 illustrates some highlights from our investigation into the `IKEA` store anomaly found during our qualitative analysis. Interestingly, we see two things. First, in areas of high density (such as Brooklyn, NY), users focus on transportation methods to/from the store. This is understandable, as many residents of New York City do not have cars capable of transporting large furniture. Second, in areas adjacent to large rural regions, `IKEA` is treated as a travel destination. Top recommendations include *Hotels* and tourist attractions like *Amusement Parks* or *Aquariums*. These anomalies suggest that `IKEA` should be modeled differently than a traditional furniture store, perhaps with additional semantic senses (such as a *Tourist Attraction* or *Travel Destination*).

We believe that the investigative analysis of anomalies exposed by our approach will allow us to not only improve the quality of our recommendation system, but also extend the expressiveness of the Knowledge Graph itself. Such improvements can allow a better understanding of user intent and improve user experience across a variety of products.

8. RELATED WORK

The problem of detecting anomalous links touches on the domains of Link Prediction, and Recommender Systems, which we briefly discuss here.

Link Prediction models the strength of relations, usually in order to find high probability links which are missing from a network. Early work on link prediction was unsupervised, using topological features [13]. More recently, the problem has been addressed as in a supervised fashion [2, 14]. Supervision allows the blending of topological features with semantic ones, and a number of methods doing such have been proposed. Semantic features used in the literature include textual features (e.g. paper titles or keywords[2], sometimes with TF-IDF weighting [30]), location features, [7, 18], or social interactions [32]. Other recent work examines using community information [27] or transferability of models across networks [29]. More information is available from several surveys [9, 16, 22].

Although there has been considerable work on link prediction, the vast majority of the literature deals with the discovery of non-existent links and not the detection and removal of anomalous ones. The anomalous link discovery problem was introduced by Rattigan and Jensen [21], who noted that topological measures of similarity performed well for anomalous co-authorship detection. Relatively little work followed. In [11] Huang and Zeng examined anomalous links in an email network, and Ding et al. [8] examined clustering and betweenness centrality for detecting links that represented network intrusion. Our work helps address this gap in the literature by analyzing the performance of an anomalous link discovery system in a very large industrial setting. Furthermore, our comprehensive human evaluation is the first such human evaluation (to our knowledge) of any anomalous link detection approach.

More recent work in graph anomaly detection has focused on discovering anomalous communities [19, 20]. A comprehensive survey is available from Akoglu et al. [1].

Recommender Systems model user/item interactions to suggest additional content to users. Similar to link prediction, the focus is on finding highly confident recommendations (i.e. those which future users will have the highest likelihood of interacting with). Item based filtering was introduced in [24]. Since then, entity recommendation has been proposed for use in search in a variety of different settings [4, 34, 35]. Removal of anomalous recommendations is typically performed implicitly during model improvement, usually through the inclusion of additional features to the model , and several recent works target geographic recommendation [15, 33].

We view our work as complementary to that of the existing recommender system development process for two reasons. First, by explicitly modeling the detection of anomalous links, our approach provides an insightful view of what is being effectively captured by a recommendation system. This analysis is quite useful for understanding the limits of an existing system, and where likely areas of the best improvements are (e.g. Qualitative Analysis in Section 7.2). Second, it is sometimes impossible to replace an entire recommender system used in production as substantial model changes require validation (which can be both expensive and time consuming). Our lightweight modeling of anomalous link discovery approach allows for high precision *focused changes* changes to existing models, which can allow for easier validation.

Finally, we note that the disambiguation of user intent from keyword search is a mainstay of research in information retrieval [17, 23, 25, 31]. We believe that our work helps further the discussion on this important problem.

9. CONCLUSIONS

In this work, we have proposed and evaluated a unified approach for anomalous link discovery in recommendation systems. Given a recommendation system, we treat its output as a network and extract graph features which quantify the structural transitivity present in the recommendations. We fuse this information with features constructed from an appropriate knowledge graph, which capture the semantic consistency of the entities.

Experiments on the Google Related Places Graph using human raters show the effectiveness of our approach on a very large geographic recommendation system. Interestingly, our experiments also show that structural features from the recommendation network capture a sense of a recommendation's *usefulness* to users, while semantic features better capture a sense of the *relevance* of a recommendation.

In addition to strong quantitative results, our qualitative analysis illustrates how the anomalies exposed by our system provide a valuable lens to study a recommendation system's behavior. Investigating such anomalies can enhance understanding of user intent and has the potential to improve user experience across all information retrieval systems leveraging the same knowledge graph.

Acknowledgments

We thank the anonymous reviewers for their comments.

References

[1] L. Akoglu, H. Tong, and D. Koutra. Graph based anomaly detection and description: a survey. *Data Mining and Knowledge Discovery*, 29(3), 2015.

[2] M. Al Hasan, V. Chaoji, S. Salem, and M. Zaki. Link prediction using supervised learning. In *SDM'06: Workshop on Link Analysis, Counter-terrorism and Security*, 2006.

[3] X. Amatriain and J. Basilico. Netflix recommendations: Beyond the 5 stars (part 1). http://techblog.netflix.com/2012/04/netflix-recommendations-beyond-5-stars.html, May 2012.

[4] R. Blanco, B. B. Cambazoglu, P. Mika, and N. Torzec. Entity recommendations in web search. In *The Semantic Web–ISWC 2013*, pages 33–48. Springer, 2013.

[5] K. Bollacker, C. Evans, P. Paritosh, T. Sturge, and J. Taylor. Freebase: a collaboratively created graph database for structuring human knowledge. SIGMOD'08, pages 1247–1250, 2008.

[6] D. Cosley, S. K. Lam, I. Albert, J. A. Konstan, and J. Riedl. Is seeing believing?: How recommender system interfaces affect users' opinions. CHI '03, pages 585–592, 2003.

[7] D. J. Crandall, L. Backstrom, D. Cosley, S. Suri, D. Huttenlocher, and J. Kleinberg. Inferring social ties from geographic coincidences. *Proceedings of the National Academy of Sciences*, 107(52):22436–22441, 2010.

[8] Q. Ding, N. Katenka, P. Barford, E. Kolaczyk, and M. Crovella. Intrusion as (anti)social communication: Characterization and detection. KDD '12, pages 886–894, 2012.

[9] M. Hasan and M. Zaki. A survey of link prediction in social networks. In C. C. Aggarwal, editor, *Social Network Data Analytics*, pages 243–275. Springer US, 2011.

[10] T. Haveliwala, S. Kamvar, and G. Jeh. An analytical comparison of approaches to personalizing pagerank. 2003.

[11] Z. Huang and D. Zeng. A link prediction approach to anomalous email detection. volume 2 of *SMC '06*, pages 1131–1136, Oct 2006.

[12] P. G. Ipeirotis, F. Provost, and J. Wang. Quality management on amazon mechanical turk. HCOMP '10, pages 64–67, 2010.

[13] D. Liben-Nowell and J. Kleinberg. The link-prediction problem for social networks. *Journal of the American society for information science and technology*, 58(7):1019–1031, 2007.

[14] R. N. Lichtenwalter, J. T. Lussier, and N. V. Chawla. New perspectives and methods in link prediction. KDD '10, pages 243–252, 2010.

[15] B. Liu, Y. Fu, Z. Yao, and H. Xiong. Learning geographical preferences for point-of-interest recommendation. KDD '13, pages 1043–1051, 2013.

[16] L. Lü and T. Zhou. Link prediction in complex networks: A survey. *Physica A: Statistical Mechanics and its Applications*, 390(6):1150–1170, 2011.

[17] M. Mitra, A. Singhal, and C. Buckley. Improving automatic query expansion. SIGIR '98, 1998.

[18] J. O'Madadhain, J. Hutchins, and P. Smyth. Prediction and ranking algorithms for event-based network data. *SIGKDD Explor. Newsl.*, 7(2):23–30, Dec. 2005.

[19] B. Perozzi and L. Akoglu. Scalable anomaly ranking of attributed neighborhoods. SIAM SDM, 2016.

[20] B. Perozzi, L. Akoglu, P. Iglesias Sánchez, and E. Müller. Focused clustering and outlier detection in large attributed graphs. KDD, 2014.

[21] M. J. Rattigan and D. Jensen. The case for anomalous link discovery. *SIGKDD Explor. Newsl.*, 7(2):41–47, Dec. 2005.

[22] R. A. Rossi, L. K. McDowell, D. W. Aha, and J. Neville. Transforming graph data for statistical relational learning. *J. Artif. Int. Res.*, 45(1):363–441, Sept. 2012.

[23] M. Sahami and T. D. Heilman. A web-based kernel function for measuring the similarity of short text snippets. WWW '06, 2006.

[24] B. Sarwar, G. Karypis, J. Konstan, and J. Riedl. Item-based collaborative filtering recommendation algorithms. WWW '01, pages 285–295, 2001.

[25] M. Shokouhi, M. Sloan, P. N. Bennett, K. Collins-Thompson, and S. Sarkizova. Query suggestion and data fusion in contextual disambiguation. In *Proceedings of the 24th International Conference on World Wide Web*, WWW '15, 2015.

[26] A. Singhal. Introducing the knowledge graph: things, not strings. http://googleblog.blogspot.com/2012/05/introducing-knowledge-graph-things-not.html, May 2012.

[27] S. Soundarajan and J. Hopcroft. Using community information to improve the precision of link prediction methods. WWW '12 Companion, pages 607–608, 2012.

[28] X. Su and T. M. Khoshgoftaar. A survey of collaborative filtering techniques. *Adv. in Artif. Intell.*, 2009:4:2–4:2, Jan. 2009.

[29] J. Tang, T. Lou, and J. Kleinberg. Inferring social ties across heterogenous networks. WSDM, 2012.

[30] C. Wang, V. Satuluri, and S. Parthasarathy. Local probabilistic models for link prediction. ICDM '07, pages 322–331, Washington, DC, USA, 2007. IEEE Computer Society.

[31] X. Wang and C. Zhai. Mining term association patterns from search logs for effective query reformulation. CIKM '08, 2008.

[32] R. Xiang, J. Neville, and M. Rogati. Modeling relationship strength in online social networks. WWW '10, pages 981–990, 2010.

[33] M. Ye, P. Yin, W.-C. Lee, and D.-L. Lee. Exploiting geographical influence for collaborative point-of-interest recommendation. SIGIR '11, pages 325–334, 2011.

[34] X. Yu, H. Ma, B.-J. P. Hsu, and J. Han. On building entity recommender systems using user click log and freebase knowledge. WSDM '14, pages 263–272, 2014.

[35] X. Yu, X. Ren, Y. Sun, Q. Gu, B. Sturt, U. Khandelwal, B. Norick, and J. Han. Personalized entity recommendation: A heterogeneous information network approach. WSDM '14, pages 283–292, 2014.

Deploying Analytics with the Portable Format for Analytics (PFA)

Jim Pivarski
Open Data Group Inc.
400 Lathrop Ave Suite 90
River Forest IL USA

Collin Bennett
Open Data Group Inc.
400 Lathrop Ave Suite 90
River Forest IL USA

Robert L. Grossman*
Open Data Group Inc.
400 Lathrop Ave Suite 90
River Forest IL USA

ABSTRACT

We introduce a new language for deploying analytic models into products, services and operational systems called the Portable Format for Analytics (PFA). PFA is an example of what is sometimes called a model interchange format, a language for describing analytic models that is independent of specific tools, applications or systems. Model interchange formats allow one application (the model producer) to export models and another application (the model consumer or scoring engine) to import models. The core idea behind PFA is to support the safe execution of statistical functions, mathematical functions, and machine learning algorithms and their compositions within a safe execution environment. With this approach, the common analytic models used in data science can be implemented, as well as the data transformations and data aggregations required for pre- and post-processing data. PFA compliant scoring engines can be extended by adding new user defined functions described in PFA. We describe the design of PFA. A Data Mining Group (DMG) Working Group is developing the PFA standard. The current version is 0.8.1 and contains many of the commonly used statistical and machine learning models, including regression, clustering, support vector machines, neural networks, etc. We also describe two implementations of Hadrian, one in Scala and one in Python. We discuss four case studies that use PFA and Hadrian to specify analytic models, including two that are deployed in operations at client sites.

Keywords

model producers, scoring engines, Portable Format for Analytics, PFA, PMML, deploying analytics

*RLG is also a faculty member at the University of Chicago.

KDD '16, August 13-17, 2016, San Francisco, CA, USA
ACM 978-1-4503-4232-2/16/08.
http://dx.doi.org/10.1145/2939672.2939731

1. INTRODUCTION

The KDD research community has traditionally been focused on developing new algorithms and developing systems for managing and analyzing data. This is the one of the cores of data science. Technology is also required for deploying algorithms and statistical models in analytic products, analytic services, and operational systems. Sometimes the term *analytic operations* is used for this component of the KDD process.

A problem that has haunted the KDD community for the last twenty years is how to efficiently deploy the analytic models developed by data scientists into products and services that must live in operational environments, which usually have stringent service level requirements. Because of these requirements, most organizations do not allow code to be integrated into operations without careful and extensive testing. See Figure 1.

In this paper, we introduce a new language called the Portable Format for Analytics (PFA), describe some of the ways that PFA differs from the Predictive Model Markup Language (PMML), the current dominant standard for describing analytic models [1], and discuss some of the lessons that we have learned working with PFA over the past two years in various deployed analytic applications.

Contributions of this Paper This paper makes four main contributions to the KDD community. The first contribution is that we introduce a language (PFA) for describing statistical and data mining models that overcomes some of the important limitations of PMML. The second contribution is that we have developed and deployed *two* implementations of PFA-compliant scoring engines (one in Scala and one in Python), which are available to KDD community for personal and research use. The third contribution is that we have described two deployments into production sites of the Scala scoring engine and discussed some of the lessons learned from these deployments. The fourth contribution is calling attention to PFA and to the Data Mining Group (DMG) PFA Working Group so that others in the KDD research community can contribute to the further development of the PFA standard.

2. ARCHITECTURES FOR DEPLOYING ANALYTICS

An analytic architecture was developed over fifteen years ago that separated systems, applications and tools that produced analytic models from those that consumed analytic models [2, 3]. Model producers are part of the development

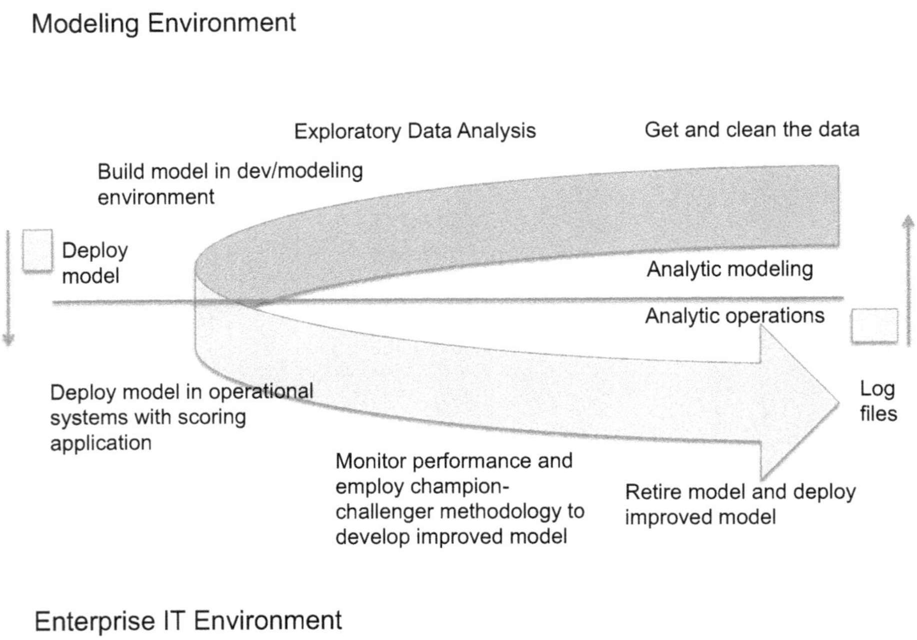

Figure 1: Analytic model producers and analytic model consumers (scoring engines).

or data modeling environment, while model consumers are part of the operational environment. See Figure 1.

Model producers export models in a language for analytic models (sometimes called a model interchange format), while model consumers import analytic models. With this approach, multiple systems, applications and tools can be used by data scientists for exporting models, and a single scoring engine can consume all of them in an operational environment.

Over time, the term *scoring engine* began to be used as a synonym for model consumer. As shown in Figure 3, the scoring engine is usually embedded in deployment environment that includes the inputs and outputs of the scoring engine. For example, scoring engines may be integrated with web applications and services, with databases, with enterprise service buses, with distributed data processing systems, with real time distributed messaging systems, etc.

It is important to note that with this architecture, the analytic models that are described in the model interchange format are designed to be written and read by programs, not by humans. In other words, models in the model interchange format are designed to be machine readable, not human readable.

3. LANGUAGES FOR DEPLOYING ANALYTICS

The model interchange format that has gained the most adoption is the Predictive Model Markup Language (PMML) [3], which is an XML-based markup language for describing statistical and data mining models. The PMML standard [1, 4] supports the models most commonly used by data scientists, including regression, clustering, support vector machines, neural networks, etc.

PMML represented a significant step forward in terms of providing a mechanism for different systems, applications and tools to exchange analytic models. On the other hand, over time limitations of PMML became apparent. Perhaps, the most common was that PMML was not extensible and did not support all the code required to deploy analytic models, since it has relatively limited functionality for the pre- and post-processing required by most deployed applications, and many deployed applications did not use a single PMML model, but rather workflows built from multiple PMML models.

PMML is a *specification* for a model interchange format. Once the PMML Working Group approves a specification for a new PMML model, PMML-compliant scoring engines are updated by their vendors or developers to add support for that model. Although the PMML Working Group works hard on the standard, overtime the specification grew more and more complicated, raising the work required to develop a PMML compliant scoring engine.

The goals for PFA were to define a language for analytic models with the following properties:

1. The language should be extensible so that users and system developers can define their models and pre- and post-processing code.

2. The language should allow models to be composed so that chains of models and hierarchical models can be supported and allow multiple models to be combined into workflows.

3. The language should be easy to integrate into today's distributed and event-based data processing platforms, such as Hadoop [5], Spark and Storm [6].

4. The language should be "safe" to deploy in IT operational environments.

As mentioned, PMML struggled with the first three requirements. The approach taken with PFA was to define a language in which JSON-based functions could be safely composed and the functions were rich enough to define the common analytic models, as well as the common pre- and post- processing used by data scientists. The language and standard support user defined functions, which supports Requirements 1 and 2. Since the language is JSON-based and uses Avro for data serialization, it integrates easily into today's distributed and event based data processing platforms (Requirement 3).

Although PFA is essentially a programming language, it is limited in ways that make it safer to use than conventional programming languages (Requirement 4). A scoring engine implemented in C, Python, or Java could access the underlying file system, operating system, or network, but a scoring engine implemented in PFA can only transform the data that it is given. Therefore, the security issues involved in running arbitrary code are not raised by PFA.

As we will see below, PFA supports functions for data transformations, data aggregations, data filtering, as well as the basic mathematical and statistical functions. Since these core functions ("data mining or analytic primitives") can be composed, the models in the PMML standard can be easily defined [7]. Specifically, the current version of PFA contains all of the analytic models in the current version of PMML [7]. In addition, compositions of the analytic primitives can be used so that any pre-processing or post-processing code can be expressed in PFA.

PFA is a model interchange format based upon *analytic primitives*. A developer or vendor can add support for a new mathematical or statistical function, model, data transformation or data aggregation at any time simply by expressing it in the PFA language. The more common models can be adapted as a standard by the PFA Working Group. This approach makes adding new functionality to PFA-compliant scoring engines relatively easy and reduces to work required to develop PFA-compliant scoring engines.

To summarize, the main benefit provided by scoring engines is that models can be quickly added to operational environments. With a PMML-compliant scoring engine, any model that is specified in the standard can be quickly added to operational environments. With PFA-compliant scoring engines, any model that can be described in the PFA language can be quickly added to operational environments.

4. OVERVIEW OF PFA

The Portable Format for Analytics (PFA) is a domain-specific language that describes scoring engines. A scoring engine is a high-throughput data processor, usually generated by a statistical analysis. For instance, an analysis might describe a dataset using decision trees; its scoring engine is an algorithm that walks down each tree, classifying data. Another analysis might use k-means to summarize a dataset as a code book of cluster centers; its scoring engine would associate new data to their closest clusters. PFA provides a uniform way to implement and transport these scoring engines.

PFA is portable because it is a simple language whose syntax is a strict subset of JSON. JSON is a widely-used serialization format consisting of only four primitives (string, number, boolean, and null) and two container types (array and string-based map). PFA data transformations and models are all implemented as a syntax tree of nested JSON objects. Any program or library that can manipulate JSON can manipulate PFA. Thus, one only needs to add JSON output to existing data analysis software for it to generate PFA-based scoring engines.

The smallest possible PFA document is:
`{"input": "null", "output": "null", "action": null}`, which inputs nothing, outputs nothing, and does nothing. But, this presents the three necessary parts of a PFA Engine: an input, output, and action. Input and output define the data into and out of the PFA engine. This can be a type, like `double` or a schema defining a structure. The action routine is called once for every input datum. The action can be any PFA primitive or user-defined function. For example, here is a trivial model

```
input: double
output: double
action:
  - {m.round: {"*": [{m.sin:
      {+: [input, 1]}}, 2]}}
```

This PFA engine takes a double as input, adds 1 to that, multiples the sine of that addition by 2 and returns the closest whole number as a double.

Simple engines, like the mathematical function above, transform one input into one output. In practice, you sometimes need to filter data (one input to zero or one outputs) or aggregate data (an entire dataset to one output). To handle these cases, PFA has three methods: `map`, `emit`, and `fold`, which are described later in this section.

Also, PFA has a centralized concept of state that can be shared among multiple instances of a scoring engine. These scoring engines can be stopped, resumed, rolled back to a previous state, or analyzed offline in ways that would be impossible for arbitrary code written in a conventional language. A PFA-based scoring engine is essentially a lightweight, human-readable virtual machine capable only of transforming data.

Persistent storage in PFA is handled by cells and pools. Cells are global variables that cannot be created or destroyed at run-time, only reassigned. Pools are collections of key-value pairs that can be created and destroyed at run-time. This is similar to environments in R. For a pool, the granularity of concurrent access is at the level of a single pool item.

Cells and pools are both specified as JSON objects with the same fields, but initialization is only required for cells.

Extensibility. With PMML, when a function not in the specification is needed, people write a custom extension in their PMML-application and submit to the PMML Working Group the new desired functionality as a Request for Comments. This is a reasonable balancing of a developer's immediate needs and the community's goal of moving from one stable release of the specification to the next. The draw back is that in the interim, the model is not valid PMML and cannot be used in another PMML application.

To achieve PFA's first goal of extensibility and to remove this obstacle to vendor portability, PFA is made of up analytic primitives. Its functions are designed as "building blocks" and as with a general programming language, user-defined functions can be written in PFA, that are themselves valid PFA, and used across any PFA application.

For example, in the PFA time module, there is no function that returns the UTC offset when given a timestamp and timezone. This functionality was requested by a client and will be submitted to the PFA Working Group for consideration, but in the mean time, we wrote the user-defined function in Figure 2 that can run inside any PFA application.

Post-processing. Extensibility can also be considered in terms of pre- and post-processing. PFA has `before` and `end` that allows for hooks to be written that are outside of the scoring process. Sometimes, there is a need to post-process the scored event or its score.

Within a PFA scoring engine, post-processing can be performed by including logic in the PFA action. As a simple example, consider the post-processing logic of only wanting:

1. To alert when at least three scores over some threshold have been seen in a 1 minute time window; and
2. Not alert for a given entity more than once in a 24-hour period.

This can be accomplished by defining a record and pool as follows:

```
types:
 record(Counter,
        event_counter: int,
        alert_counter: int,
        first_timestamp: double,
        last_alert_time: double);

pools:
 window(type: Counter,
        shared: true) = {};
```

and including calls to a check and update in the action, rather than just emitting a score:

```
action:
  window[id] to fcn(old: Counter -> Counter) {
    if u.checConditionMet(old) {
      // send alert and update counter
    } else {
      //update counter
      new(Counter,
          event_counter: 1,
          alert_counter: old["alert_counter"] + 1,
          first_timestamp: ts,
          last_alert_time: old["last_alert_time"]);
    }
```

Composing PFA functions. As mentioned above, an important goal of PFA is supporting the composition of any PFA functions. This means that, unlike PMML where compositions are restricted to certain scopes and between certain components, PFA primitives, functions, and user-defined functions can be composed where ever it makes sense. For example, if you have a decision tree defined by:

```
types:
  record(TreeNode,
         field: enum([x,y, z]),
         operator: string,
         value: double,
         pass: union(TreeNode,string),
         fail: union(TreeNode,string))
```

You can add a regression at each leaf node by defining the regression and embedding it in the leaves:

```
types:
   record(Regression,
          const: double,
          coeff: array(double));

   record(TreeNode,
         field: enum([x,y, z]),
         operator: string,
         value: double,
         pass: union(TreeNode,Regression),
         fail: union(TreeNode,Regression))
```

The models are composed, so the action becomes a 2-step process. Instead of returning a label from the tree walk, the leaf is now a regression that needs to be scored:

```
action:
  var leaf = model.tree.simpleWalk(input, tree,
               fcn(d: Datum, t: TreeNode -> boolean)
                 model.tree.simpleTest(d,t));
  leaf
```

becomes:

```
action:
  var leaf = model.tree.simpleWalk(input, tree,
               fcn(d: Datum, t: TreeNode -> boolean)
                 model.tree.simpleTest(d,t));

  var vector = new(array(double), input.x,
               input.y, input.z);
  model.reg.linear(vector, leaf)
```

For completeness, in the decision tree PFA, the regression needs to be defined at each TreeNode:

```
  {TreeNode:
     {field: y,
      operator: "<",
      value: 2.2,
      pass: {string: "pass-pass"},
      fail: {string: "pass-fail"}}},
```

becomes, for example,

```
  {TreeNode:
     {field: y,
      operator: "<",
      value: 2.2,
      pass: {Regression:
         {const: 0.0,
          coeff: [0.1,0.2, 0.3]}}}}
      fail: {Regression:
         {const: -1.0,
          coeff: [0.1,-0.2, 0.0]}}}}
```

PFA outputs. PFA views data as a possibly infinite stream of inputs, and produces a corresponding stream of outputs. The author of a PFA document may define a `begin` method, which is evaluated before seeing any data. This author must define an `action` method, which is evaluated on every input, and may define an `end` method, which is evaluated after all the data, if any such time exists. PFA is a stream processor, like the UNIX command `awk`.

Most scoring engines produce one output for every input, like the `map` or `lapply` functor found in array processing languages. Some scoring engines, however, filter the data,

```
fcns:
  getUTCOffset = fcn(x: double, zone: string -> double) {
    // get minuteOfDay in the time zone
    var hourOfDay_zone = time.hourOfDay(x, zone);
    var minuteOfHour_zone = time.minuteOfHour(x, zone);
    var minuteOfDay_zone = hourOfDay_zone * 60 + minuteOfHour_zone;

    // get minuteOfDay in UTC
    var hourOfDay_UTC = time.hourOfDay(x, "");
    var minuteOfHour_UTC = time.minuteOfHour(x, "");
    var minuteOfDay_UTC = hourOfDay_UTC * 60 + minuteOfHour_UTC;

    // difference modulo the number of minutes in a day
    var minuteDiff = (minuteOfDay_zone - minuteOfDay_UTC) % (24 * 60);

    // difference in hours
    var hourDiff = minuteDiff / 60.0;

    // cycled to a number in the range (-12, 12]
    if (hourDiff > 12.0)
      hourDiff - 24.0
    else
      hourDiff
  }
```

Figure 2: A user defined PFA function to supplement the PFA time module.

producing zero or one outputs for each input, while others expand tables, potentially producing more than one output per input (such as Hadoop mappers). Still other scoring engines reduce a data stream to a single value or structure, such as `reduce` functors or `GROUP BY` in SQL. These cases cover all three types of functions in SQL (transformers, table generating functions, and aggregations).

PFA provides for the three cases with a top-level field called `method`, which may be `"map"`, `"emit"`, or `"fold"`. In `"map"` mode, the `action` is an expression that evaluates to the output. In `"emit"` mode, the `action` may call an `emit` function zero or more times to produce outputs. In `"fold"` mode, the `action` returns a partial aggregation for each input and also updates a `tally` that can be used in later steps of the aggregation. To reduce a dataset, one could ignore all outputs except the last. The `"fold"` mode also requires a `merge` method that combines partial aggregations from independent processors, allowing the aggregation to be scaled out, and a `zero` value for starting the aggregation.

5. PFA LANGUAGE DETAILS

A PFA-based scoring engine is a JSON object with fields for general information like model name, version, and metadata, and a single execution path of expressions to be applied to the input data. These expressions consist of constants, such as numbers, data field references, which are JSON strings, and function calls, which are JSON objects with the following structure: `{"functionName": [arguments]}`. Basic features of the langage are special forms with multiple keys: `{"if": predicate, "then": consequent}`.

PFA is a statically typed language with immutable data structures and restricted function objects. This strictness makes it possible to analyze a scoring engine before it is executed. For instance, a semantically valid PFA scoring engine can never pass a string where a number is expected, can never introduce long-range dependencies between data structures, and can modify shared state without the possibility of deadlock.

5.1 Static typing

The PFA type system is inherited from Avro, a serialization format that imposes structure on JSON by requiring explicitly typed number formats (integer, long, single-precision, and double-precision floating point numbers), a distinction between Unicode strings and raw byte arrays, homogeneous arrays and maps, heterogeneous records, enumeration types, and tagged unions of any of the above. An Avro type is specified as a JSON object, with schemae like `{"type": "array", "items": "int"}` to specify an array of integers, for instance.

Avro schemae are included within PFA as type declarations. Input data, function parameters, and global state require explicit types, declared with Avro schemae, and PFA infers the types of all other expressions and checks them against the declared output types.

PFA can downcast types to allow, for instance, a variable declared as a union of null and integer to be passed to a function that expects an integer, but it always splits the program flow into cases— one path is followed if the variable is null and another is followed if it is an integer. Therefore, PFA can use null to signify missing data without ever encountering a null pointer exception at runtime.

Static typing also provides a performance boost: PFA can be compiled into bytecode that does not need to check types at runtime. Only the structure of the input data must be checked; the rest is guaranteed.

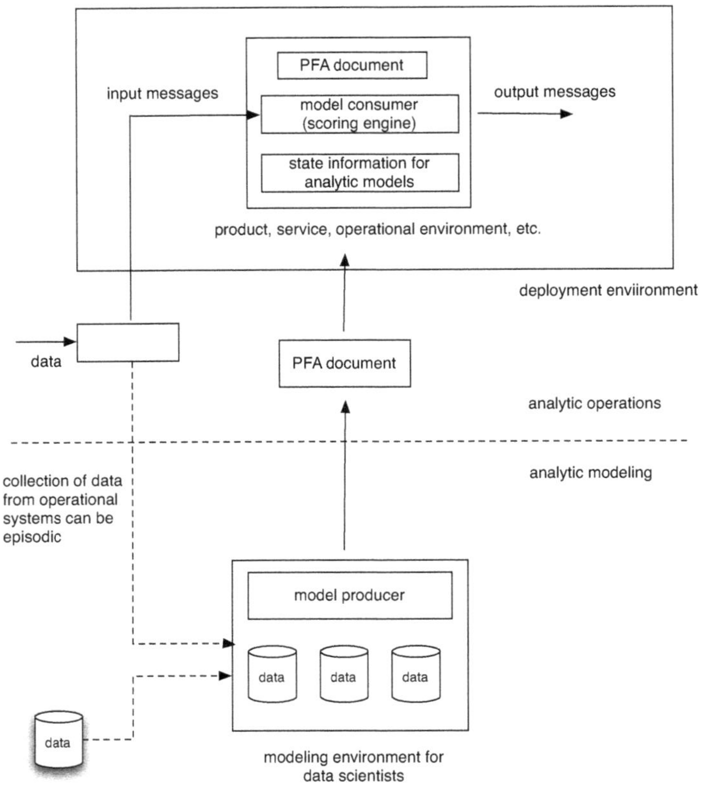

Figure 3: Analytic model producers and analytic model consumers (scoring engines) exchanging a PFA model.

5.2 Immutable data

Immutable data structures can be replaced but not modified in-place. For instance, items in an immutable array cannot be changed, but the whole array can be replaced with one that has different elements. Immutable data structures have several conceptual advantages: there is no distinction between references and values, so two data structures cannot be linked in such a way that modifications of one implicity change the other, and data can be passed from one scoring engine to another without needing to defensively copy it.

Immutability is particularly useful for sharing data among many scoring engines running in parallel. PFA defines copy-on-write semantics for modifications of shared engine state that allows non-blocking, consistent reads of the shared data while one of the scoring engines is processing a transaction to replace it. Since there is no distinction between references and values, PFA implementations can re-use parts of a data structure among different versions of that structure to avoid deep copying and increase both memory and computational performance.

5.3 Function objects

The ability to define functions and pass them as objects is an incredibly useful aspect of many high-level languages. They allow for generic functional programming, such as transforming one structure into another structure by applying a function to each element (map) or summarizing a structure by iteratively applying an aggregation function (reduce). They also allow the programmer to specify the beginning and ending of a transaction on shared data by wrapping it in a function, perhaps closing over local variables.

However, if functions are freely passed as objects, then it can become impossible to statically determine which functions can be executed in a given context. This is particularly problematic when functions are used as transactions on shared data, since this can lead to deadlock— two scoring engines might end up waiting for each other when attempting to process mutually dependent transactions. Therefore, PFA does not allow unrestricted function objects, but only enough functionality to achieve the benefits of functional programming and shared data transactions without the disadvantages.

Functions can be expressed as inline arguments to functors such as map and reduce, and they can be named as globally accessible user-defined functions that are referenced in arguments to functors. Shared data can be modified by passing it a function that transforms the old value into a new value, but these transactions are not allowed to modify any other shared data.

Since function references can only appear in argument lists, a PFA validator can exhaustively determine which functions can ever be called from a function, thereby ensuring that a transaction can never call anything that, through a chain of other function calls, attempts another transaction. These functions are allowed to read any thread-local variables (as closures) and read any shared global data because PFA's concurrency semantics allow reading without blocking.

With these restrictions, functions do not need to be implemented as objects in compiled PFA, which allows for another performance boost: all user-defined functions could be implemented as inlined bytecode.

6. PFA FOR MODEL DEVELOPMENT

Unlike a conventional program, a scoring engine typically implements a simple or well-known algorithm with a large store of parameter data. For example, a random forest may include megabytes or gigabytes of tree parameters, but the scoring procedure simply walks down each tree and reports the average or most common result. A PFA document wraps up the algorithm and the parameter data into one JSON object, which eliminates the bookkeeping involved in coordinating programs with their parameters.

Usually, scoring engines are produced by other programs—for instance, a library package in R derives a random forest and creates a function that can be used in R to score new data. The only problem is that this scoring engine cannot be used outside of the R environment. However, by iterating over the R function's internal parameters, we can convert it to JSON and insert that JSON into a PFA document.

Even though the algorithmic part of a PFA document tends to be a short list of library function calls, it can be difficult to write an algorithm purely out of function calls. Programmers want to write `x + y` rather than `{"+": ["x", "y"]}`. For this reason, there are several converters from conventional programming languages such as Python and Javascript into PFA, but the most fully featured is PrettyPFA, which provides a C-like syntax for all PFA features. In PrettyPFA, the random forest algorithm is

```
input:
  record(Datum, inputPlaceholder: double)

output: Score

types:
  enum([scorePlaceholder], Score);

  record(TreeNode,
         field: enum([inputPlaceholder]),
         operator: string,
         value: double,
         pass: union(Score, TreeNode),
         fail: union(Score, TreeNode))

cells:
  // declare an empty forest, to be filled in by R
  forest(type: array(TreeNode), shared: true) = []

action:
  // apply a tree-scoring function to each tree
  var scores = a.map(forest, u.score(x: input));

  // output the majority vote
  a.mode(scores)

fcns:
  // tree-scoring composes simpleWalk and simpleTest
  score = fcn(x: Datum, tree: TreeNode -> Score)
    model.tree.simpleWalk(x, tree,
      fcn(d: Datum, t: TreeNode -> boolean)
        model.tree.simpleTest(d, t))
```

The `input` and `output` sections declare data fields and the `TreeNode` type declares the structure of a tree. This scoring engine has one globally shared quantity (a `cell`), the array of trees that comprise the random forest. Its action on input data consists of three function calls:

- `a.map` maps a user-defined tree-scoring function (`u.score`) to each tree in the forest, producing an array of each tree's scores;
- `a.mode` computes the mode of this distribution (a majority vote).

The `u.score` function calls two library functions, `simpleWalk` and `simpleTest` (fully qualified), which together describe the global process of walking over the tree and the local process of deciding how to step from node to node. Different choices of library functions or even user-defined functions can be used to augment this process.

Once written, the PrettyPFA is transformed into a JSON object that is more easily manipulated by a script. The above example translates into the PFA in Figure 6. In this form, the forest produced by R can be inserted into the tree by reassigning

```
pfa["cells"]["forest"]["init"] = myForest
```

and changing the `inputPlaceholder` and `scorePlaceholder` field names. We have developed many tools for manipulating JSON, including regular expression patterns that can map

```
{some: ([...]), thing: (# < 12)}
```

(a JSON object with keys `"some"` and `"thing"`, the first pointing to an array and the second to a number under 12) into

```
{another: (1), thing: (2)}
```

(a new JSON object with keys `"another"`, `"thing"` and the same values). These patterns transform PFA structures anywhere in a PFA document, and are thus insensitive to modifications upstream.

7. PFA IMPLEMENTATIONS

We have implemented PFA in two environments: Python and Scala (for the Java Virtual Machine). These two libraries implement version 0.8.1 of the PFA specification [7]. The two implementations agree as determined by the PFA conformance tests that are available from the PFA Working Group website [7].

The Python implementation, called Titus, is more often used for model development, so it includes producers such as regression, k-means clustering, and CART trees, converters such as PMML trees to PFA, Python to PFA, and PrettyPFA, and tools for manipulating structure, such as JSON regular expressions and a command-line driven tool called the PFA Inspector.

The Scala implementation, called Hadrian, is more often used for model deployment, so it compiles PFA documents into Java bytecode on-the-fly (without requiring disk access) and is embedded in many systems. To date, Hadrian has been embedded as a command-line tool that transforms data from standard input to standard output (Hadrian-Standalone), a scoring engine container that builds a directed acyclic {"input": {"fields": [{"type": "double", "name": "inputPlaceholder"}], "type": "record", "name": "Datum"}, "output": {"symbols": ["scorePlaceholder"], "type": "enum", "name": "Score"}, "cells": {"forest": {"type": {"items": "TreeNode", "type": "array"}, "init": [], "shared": true, "rollback": false}}, "action": [{"let": {"scores": {"a.map": [{"cell": "forest"}, {"fcn": "u.score", "fill": {"x": "input"}}]}}}, {"a.mode": ["scores"]}], "fcns": {"score": {"params": [{"x": "Datum"}, {"tree": {"fields": [{"type": {"symbols": ["inputPlaceholder"], "type": "enum", "name": "Enum_1"}, "name": "field"}, {"type": "string", "name": "operator"}, {"type": "double", "name": "value"}, {"type": ["Score", "TreeNode"], "name": "pass"}, {"type": ["Score", "TreeNode"], "name": "fail"}], "type": "record", "name": "TreeNode"}}], "ret": "Score", "do": [{"model.tree.simpleWalk": ["x", "tree", {"params": [{"d": "Datum"}, {"t": "TreeNode"}], "ret": "boolean", "do": [{"model.tree.simpleTest": ["d", "t"]}]}]}]}}}

Figure 4: The PFA for the random forest example.

topology of interacting scoring engines (Hadrian-Actors), a servlet that can be used in Google App Engine or a generic servlet container like Tomcat (Hadrian-GAE), and a map-reduce processor that can score or train models in Hadoop (Hadrian-MR). Any big-data tool that runs on the Java Virtual Machine can be wired into Hadrian.

There is also a version for R, called Aurelius, that is a toolkit for generating PFA in the R programming language. It focuses on porting models to PFA from their R equivalents. However, to validate or execute a execute scoring engines, Aurelius sends them to Titus through rPython (a 3rd party library).

The choice of JSON model serialization allows for easy integration into other big-data toolsets. For instance, the MongoDB database system stores data as JSON-like objects and permits deep inspection of those objects. Titus and Hadrian both have a snapshot feature that serializes the state of a running scoring engine as a new PFA document that could resume processing from the frozen state— MongoDB could be used to store an ensemble of scoring engine states and inspect their contents.

Similarly, the use of Avro as a type system smooths the way to integration with big-data tools. Avro is a popular serialization format in the Hadoop ecosystem, so data transfer to and from these tools is easiest with Avro and possible for any format that can be mapped to Avro. For instance, a CSV file or the tuples passed through a Storm topology could be viewed as a series of flat, heterogeneous Avro records, and the data structures manipulated by Hive SQL are a perfect conceptual match to Avro's nested data types, even though their byte-serializations differ. With a small transformation before and after the scoring engine call, Hadrian could be inserted into a Storm topology or used to write Hive user-defined functions.

Hadrian has been used in high-throughput environments in which hundreds of thousands of records are processed per second. In particular, Hadrian-Actors has been deployed on a 32 CPU machine to perform cluster-based classification and anomaly detection using 4 scoring engines (4 PFA files), distributed as 32 instances, listening to 8 high-speed data pipelines. Map-reduce jobs involving Hadrian-Hadoop and Titus have been used to build models on a MapR cluster, passing data as Avro and JSON.

8. CASE STUDIES

8.1 Case Study 1: Tracking Topical Interest in Proteins Using Wikipedia

In the first case study, we describe a PFA topic tracking model. This model tracked hourly page view statistics (December 2007 through August 2015) for all Wikipedia pages in the category "Human Proteins." There were 11,273 such

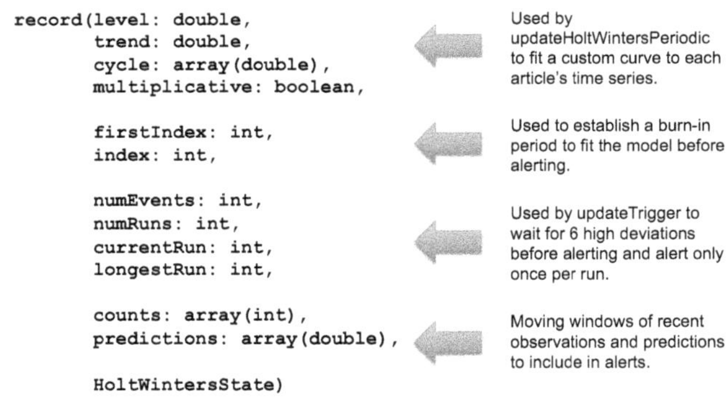

Figure 5: The PFA record structure for the protein topic tracking.

Wikipedia pages and we built a separate segmented PFA model for each page. The purpose of this study was to identify changes in interest that might be related to scientific discoveries. Part of the project was to detect changes representing an increase of interest by scientists vs an increase in interest from more general non-technical audiences, such as occurs when the general press picks up a story.

Interest varies wildly from one page (one protein) to another. Some protein's pages were clearly only of interest to practicing biologists, while others, such as insulin, are well-known to the public. It was for this reason that we used a separate model for each page, which we trained and scored independently.

PFA segments models by placing them in arrays (for models we wish to iterate over, such as decision trees in a random forest), key-value maps (for models that we want to look up quickly, such as the example above), and "pools." Pools act like key-value maps, but have a concurrency granularity at the level of individual key-value pairs, not the whole map. This allows for high-speed training and scoring of submodels by a collection of cooperative scoring engines. For this project, we put the page view models for each Wikipedia page into a pool, and let PFA ensure that contributions from different scoring engines would not conflict.

For the submodels, we noticed that page view trends have a strong day-night effect, since the majority of viewers are on one or two continents. For some pages, there is also a week-long trend, since some pages would only be viewed during the work week.

The record structure used by the models is shown in Figure 7.

We used PFA's Holt-Winters model, also known as a triply exponential moving average, to track the periodicity and slow trends. Interesting events are defined to be cases where this model is suddenly a poor predictor of page view behav-

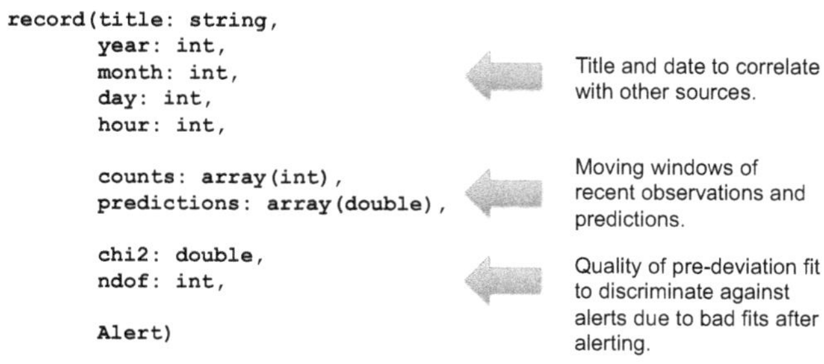

Figure 6: The PFA record structure for alerts for the protein topic tracking.

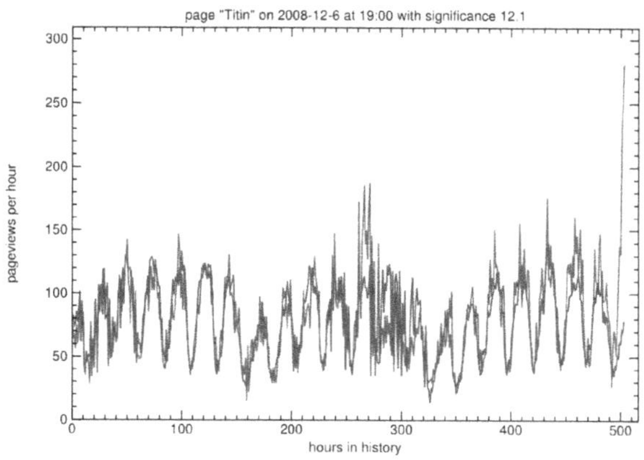

Figure 7: A visualization of the output of the PFA for the segment associated with the titin protein. The blue is the predicted number of page views of the model, the red is the actual observed number of page views. When the observed number of page views differs signifcantly from the predicted view, the model emits an alert.

iors, such as a burst of interest or interest at odd times of day.

Dozens of outliers were discovered, some dramatic and some subtle, and about half could be correlated with relevant news events. The others are potentially interesting cases of rumor or word-of-mouth news in the scientific community.

8.2 Case Study 2: Gaussian Process Model

One of the many models included in the PFA specification is the Gaussian Process [8]. Its inclusion was originally motivated by a request to the PFA Working Group by NIST, but it is a generally useful model— or model component— and therefore should be available as a global library function.

A Gaussian Process essentially smooths a (scalar or vector) function from a given set of sampled points. If these sampled points are taken to be truth from a training phase, the Gaussian Process is a supervised learning technique. However, it could just as easily be a pre- or post-processing step, approximating input data with a curve or reducing noise in scored outputs from another model.

Gaussian Processes also provide a good example of the separation of concerns between the mathematical abstraction presented to the data analyst and vendor-specific optimizations on the backend. The way that it is usually presented, there is no clear separation between training a Gaussian Process model and using it for predictions. Given a training dataset, the Gaussian Process produces a non-parametric fit without an agreed-upon specification for how that PFA must ask for the original training data, not a fit in some vendor-specific coordinates. The PFA `gaussianProcess` function [7, model.reg.gaussianProcess] accepts training data as an array of points and yields predictions.

However, an implementation that re-fits the training data every time a prediction is requested would be very slow. Therefore, Hadrian internally performs the fit once and attaches its non-parametric fit result to the training data array. When the same training data are provided, the implementation first checks for a cached fit result. This fit result never gets out of date because the training data array is immutable.

A similar optimization is provided for k-nearest neighbor models, which are also described by raw training data but are more efficiently searched if the training data are re-cast as a tree. These optimizations are toggled through the top-level PFA field `options`.

The Gaussian Process Model provides a good example of leveraging PFA's ability to compose functions to define new models. In the following code fragment, the math function `m.kernel.rbf` was developed for the Support Vector Machine model, but can be reused to define the Gaussian Process Model as follows:

```
model.reg.gaussianProcess:
    - input
    - {cell: table}
    - null
    - {fcn: m.kernel.rbf, fill: {gamma: 2.0}}
```

Any kernel function could be used here, including user defined PFA functions. Also, the Gaussian Process Model can be used in other PFA functions or in PFA pre- or post-processing code.

8.3 Case Study 3: Supporting Diverse Development Environments

In this case study, we describe a deployed instance of PFA using the Hadrian scoring engine at a client site. The description is high level in order to protect the confidentiality of the client and the project.

The client offered scoring as a service to its customers. A team of data scientists developed models for customers using a variety of different applications and libraries, including R, Scikit-learn and Python. Hadrian was integrated once into the scoring as a service application. PFA exporters were used to export PFA models from the various tools and applications used by the data science team.

Recall that Hadrian is a PFA application written in Scala. For this reason, any J2EE stack to import it as a JAR dependency. For this project, we exposed the scoring function through the Hadrian container's API. Operationally, PFA model files are uploaded to a servlet container, compiled by Hadrian into scoring engines, and exposed to the Java code running in the scoring as a service application. The score function takes an event as a map, validates it against the schema, scores it, and returns the result. Multiple models can be run, and the Java container can provide any pre- or post-processing that is not part of the model. With this approach, a single web-application can be used to score all of the models used by the client in production, independent of what tool or application was used to develop the model and what pre- or post-processing is required.

The exporters used for this project have two parts: the first is written in the native language of the model (R, Python, etc) and goes into the trained models, pulls out the values required in the PFA version, and writes them as JSON while the second takes a PFA template, the input and output schema, and the extract model values as JSON and generates a valid PFA model. This second part is generally written in Python.

After the model is exported, the native and PFA versions are compared on a validation data set and when the model is approved, it is saved with the date and performance metrics so that it can be compared with future candidate models, as part of Champion-Challenger methodology.

8.4 Case Study 4: Scoring over an Enterprise Service Bus

In this case study, we describe a second deployed instance of PFA using the Hadrian scoring engine at a client site. As with the previous case study, the description is high level in order to protect the confidentiality of the client and the project.

In this deployment, MapReduce is used to process large amounts of network data that have been stored in a Hadoop cluster. An application called Hadrian-MR is used to process the data using MapReduce and to produce PFA blocks. These blocks may need to be assembled into a PFA model, depending on the type of MapReduce job run and the statistics calculated. In this way, data scientists can build models over data in the Hadoop cluster and export models in PFA.

The operational systems use a real time distributed messaging platform (an enterprise service bus) that processes billions of messages per day. An application called Hadrian-Actors interfaces to the message platform, listens for messages on the relevant topics, and scores the messages using Hadrian. The output messages are then returned to the messaging platform. In this way, PFA models developed by the data scientists can be easily deployed simply by importing them into the Hadrian-Actor application. The main benefit of this architecture is the ease and speed in which new models can be introduced into the operational environment, even when the models require user defined PFA functions.

9. STATUS OF PFA AND HADRIAN

As of February, 2016, the DMG PFA Working Group has approved version 0.8.1 of the standard. The current standard can be found on the DMG website (www.dmg.org).

To ensure compatibility of PFA implementations, a suite of full-coverage tests were generated for each library function. Since many PFA functions are polymorphic, they are each tested for a broad, representative set of compatible signatures. Each of these signatures are tested for a broad, representative set of values (including infinity, `NaN`, and every possible runtime error). These tests were generated algorithmically, using an XML description of the PFA standard. In all, the tests comprise over 6000 scoring engines, evaluated for more than 1 million sets of values. The JSON file describing these tests is currently 238 MB in size. New PFA implementations can check their compatibility and coverage by evaluating these tests.

Hadrian is available from Github:

`github.com/opendatagroup/hadrian,`

with an open source license. The current version of Hadrian is 0.8.4.

10. SUMMARY AND CONCLUSION

We have described the design of a new extensible language for describing mathematical, statistical and machine learning models called the Portable Format for Analytics (PFA). PFA supports the compositions of models, data transformations, data filtering, data aggregations, and user defined functions, allowing very general user defined models to be described in PFA, as well as the pre- and post-processing required by most deployed models. This represents a significant advance over current standards for describing analytic models. The Data Mining Group is developing the PFA standard and the current version is 0.8.1 and contains over 400 functions. We have also discussed two implementations of PFA conformant scoring engines, one in Scala and one in Python. Finally, we have described four case studies of PFA models that have been deployed using Hadrian.

11. REFERENCES

[1] Data Mining Group, "Predictive Model Markup Language (PMML)," www.dmg.org.

[2] R. Grossman, S. Bailey, A. Ramu, B. Malhi, P. Hallstrom, I. Pulleyn, and X. Qin, "The management and mining of multiple predictive models using the predictive modeling markup language," *Information and Software Technology*, vol. 41, no. 9, pp. 589–595, 1999.

[3] R. L. Grossman, M. Hornick, and G. Mayer, "Data mining standards initiatives," *Communications of the ACM*, vol. 45, no. 8, pp. 59–61, 2002.

[4] A. Guazzelli, W.-C. Lin, and T. Jena, *PMML in action: unleashing the power of open standards for data mining and predictive analytics.* CreateSpace, 2012.

[5] T. White, *Hadoop: The Definitive Guide, 4th Edition.* O'Reilly Media, Inc., 2015.

[6] S. T. Allen, M. Jankowski, and P. Pathirana, *Storm Applied: Strategies for real-time event processing.* Manning Publications Co., 2015.

[7] Data Mining Group, "Portable Format for Analytics (PFA)," www.dmg.org.

[8] C. E. Rasmussen, "Gaussian processes for machine learning," 2006.

Singapore in Motion: Insights on Public Transport Service Level Through Farecard and Mobile Data Analytics

Hasan Poonawala
IBM Research
9 Changi Business Park
Singapore
hasanp@sg.ibm.com

Vinay Kolar
Cisco Systems Inc.
170 West Tasman Dr.
San Jose, CA
vinkolar@cisco.com

Sebastien Blandin
IBM Research
9 Changi Business Park
Singapore
sblandin@sg.ibm.com

Laura Wynter
IBM Research
9, Changi Business Park
Singapore
lwynter@sg.ibm.com

Sambit Sahu
IBM Research
1101 Kitchawan Road
Yorktown Heights, NY
sambits@us.ibm.com

Abstract

Given the changing dynamics of mobility patterns and rapid growth of cities, transport agencies seek to respond more rapidly to needs of the public with the goal of offering an effective and competitive public transport system. A more data-centric approach for transport planning is part of the evolution of this process. In particular, the vast penetration of mobile phones provides an opportunity to monitor and derive insights on transport usage. Real time and historical analyses of such data can give a detailed understanding of mobility patterns of people and also suggest improvements to current transit systems. On its own, however, mobile geolocation data has a number of limitations. We thus propose a joint telco-and-farecard-based learning approach to understanding urban mobility. The approach enhances telecommunications data by leveraging it jointly with other sources of real-time data. The approach is illustrated on the first- and last-mile problem as well as route choice estimation within a densely-connected train network.

Keywords

big data; mobility ; public transport route choice; map-matching

1. INTRODUCTION

1.1 Background

Traditional transportation planning processes can be costly and resource intensive since they are typically based on survey data. However, given the changing dynamics of mobility patterns, it is important for cities to maintain a comprehensive and high-frequency knowledge of mobility patterns. A data-driven approach to the monitoring, analysis, and planning of transport operations is paramount for smart cities.

The deep penetration of mobile phones provides an opportunity for transport agencies to monitor and derive valuable insights from commuters, and across their entire trips. With the proper analytics, anonymized mobile geolocation data has the potential for providing a detailed understanding of mobility patterns, with visibility on the trip segments traditionally un-observed, such as the first and last miles part of the trip. This understanding could then trigger a data-driven feedback for public transit improvements.

On its own, however, mobile geolocation data has a number of limitations. For example, the spatial resolution of the mobile geolocation data, for records without GPS information, may lead to high uncertainty in derived movement patterns. Secondly, the uncertainty in the penetration of mobile devices means that quantitative assessments of densities or volumes cannot be known precisely. Lastly, the heterogeneity of those two sources of errors over space (and time, for the latter) adds further difficulty to the results obtained from mobile geolocation data.

We thus propose a farecard-based learning approach to understand urban mobility from telecommunications data. Fusion with farecard data allows for harnessing the power of the mobile geolocation data while compensating for its limitations. In particular farecard data provides highly accurate quantitative knowledge on station to station travel-times and volumes, which can help anchor end-to-end trajectory information provided by mobile geolocation data.

We are also interested in designing Big Data models for two main types of analyses, namely the so-called first and last mile of public transport users, and the route choice of public transport users in the public transport network. Both require trajectory analytics and data fusion, which are described in this article.

First and last mile analysis is of importance to transport authorities to aid in defining services to and from train stations, including feeder bus routes and on-demand minibus service. The route choice of train passengers in a train network such as Singapore's is not directly available from the farecard data and so must be deduced from other sources. It is valuable to transport authorities in understanding route

KDD '16, August 13-17, 2016, San Francisco, CA, USA

DOI: http://dx.doi.org/10.1145/2939672.2939723

crowding within the network, and adjusting accordingly route information systems. Additionally, the understanding of explanatory factors for route choice (travel-time, fare, etc.) is fundamental for planning.

1.2 Related work

With the increase of mobile data, the concept of crowd and *community sensing* [20] has seen a growing popularity in the recent decades. With the availability of GPS chips and additional sensors indirectly providing location contexts on most smartphones, spatio-temporal analytics which used to rely on inaccurate low-sample cellphone data has seen renewed interest for this new *analytic superfood* [17]. Mobile geolocation data has been used for instance for real-time traffic monitoring [36], adaptive routing [6, 30] and path inference [15] in the context of GPS-based participatory sensing, combined with other sources for city planning [28], and even as a potential replacement for the fixed sensing infrastructure, in particular on expressways [25].

A considerable amount of literature has been focused on extracting spatio-temporal activity patterns from large cellular network datasets [1], in combination with social media [11], and in some cases leveraging models from statistical physics [10]. Remarkable structure and consistency has been exhibited within mobile datasets [4, 31], supporting the design of long-term mobility forecast models able to achieve unexpectedly high accuracy [29]. It has been shown that based on mobile data, it is possible to identify tourists from residents, identify hotspots within a city, and detect preferred activity sequences, see for instance [3, 8, 34].

In the recent years, a growing literature has been concerned with augmenting geospatial and mobility insights with semantics information [18], in particular using social media during events [27] and for prediction of level of service on public transport networks [26].

In Singapore, the large penetration of mobile phones and the relatively high population density have been conducive to a number of studies analyzing public mobility patterns [21], deriving insights on the network resilience [14] based on network connectivity indicators and crowding. In [13] a system was developed to derive passenger traffic and route recommendations for the train network, using train network specific cell tower information. These studies serve as a building block for nation-wide simulation engines [24, 32], which can in turn support enhanced response to incidents [12, 16, 33].

In parallel, Big Data and cloud computing platforms have emerged leveraging fast and efficient frameworks able to run spatio-temporal and statistical models at scale [19] on terabytes of data.

We focus on the study of travel patterns which usie the public transit network. This requires the development of novel analytics for travel mode detection in the context of spatially uncertain mobile geolocation data. We further derive new actionable insights by fusion of mobile geolocation data with farecard data, and show that such insights can support the deployment of new data-driven practices for real-time monitoring and transit planning.

1.3 Contributions

In this work, we generate insights on the Singapore public transport mobility patterns through a fusion approach which includes mobile geolocation data as well as farecard data from the public transport network. The contributions of this work include:

- the development of trajectory analytics for mobile geolocation data calibrated automatically from farecard data, allowing for both high accuracy and high spatial coverage,
- application of the calibrated travel pattern model to the analysis of the first and last mile problem, with categorization of train stations according to their accessibility properties,
- the development and calibration of data-driven route choice models and the resulting analyses of public transport route choices, in particular explanatory features, by using the calibrated travel pattern model.

The remainder of the paper is organized as follows. Section 2 describes the data characteristics, Section 3 presents our Big Data platform, and Section 4 introduces the core analytics developed for the particular use cases of interest, as well as our calibration procedure. Section 5 presents the insights obtained on the problem of the *first and last mile*, and Section 6 addresses the problem of understanding the explanatory factors of public transport route choices. Finally, Section 7 provides concluding remarks.

2. DATASET

In this section, we describe our two main sources of movement data: the anonymized StarHub mobile geolocation data and the anonymized Singapore Land Transport Authority (LTA) farecard data, as well as the key characteristics of the public transport network.

2.1 Public transport network characteristics

The public rail network used in this study is composed of five *Mass Rapid Transit* (MRT) lines: the North-South, East-West, North-East, Circle and Downtown lines. There are 123 stations on the five lines, of which 15 are interchange stations connecting two or more lines. The network boasts a ridership of over 2 million passengers per day.

2.2 Farecard data

All train fares on the Singapore public transport network are paid using cashless smart cards which require a passenger to tap in to enter the network and tap out to exit the network, thus providing the origin, destination, time, and travel-time, of every journey within the train network. The anonymized farecard data thus has a unique entry for each origin-destination journey made by a commuter including the following data fields for each journey (1) anonymized card ID, (2) origin MRT station, (3) destination MRT station, (4) entry timestamp, (5) exit timestamp.

2.3 Mobile geolocation data

The StarHub mobile geolocation data format includes a unique anonymized entry for each geo-localized record generated from a StarHub anonymized customer mobile phone, including the following fields; (1) record time, (2), anonymized user ID, (3) latitude, (4) longitude, (5) accuracy, (7) network event type, where the various network events are further described in the following section.

3. BIG DATA PLATFORM

In this section, we describe the Big Data platform supporting the analytics components. We use IBM *City in Motion* (CiM) system. The system is built on a Hadoop-based platform with a custom spatio-temporal engine.

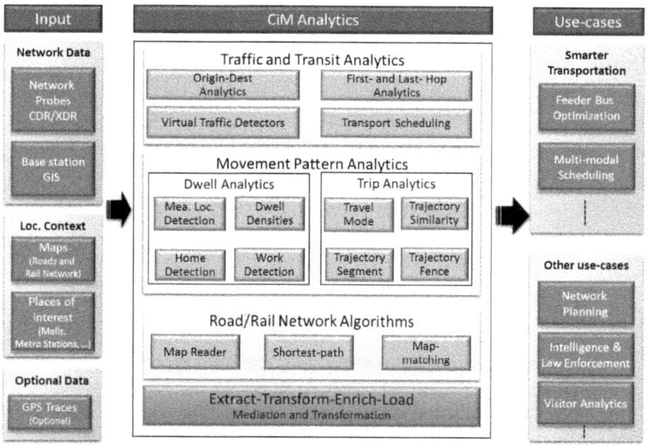

Figure 1: **IBM City in Motion:** Conceptual Architecture.

The conceptual architecture of CiM is shown in Figure 1. The CiM acts on mobile geolocation data to provide meaningful insights about movement patterns in a city. Core algorithms are generically constructed such that CiM can be used as a fundamental system for spatio-temporal analytics in various domains such as Smarter Transportation Planning, Cellular Network Planning, Visitor Analytics for different points-of-interest, and Law Enforcement. We now briefly explain the main components of the system.

3.1 Data and Ingestion

CiM ingests generically available mobile geolocation data including network events, and other forms of openly available data such as maps.

Generic mobile geolocation inputs.

Network event data consists of anonymized subscriber-level events that are recorded by the network. Network events are usually generated under the following conditions: (1) place or receive a call or SMS, (2) periodic log of mobile data usage, (3) location update (typically, when anonymized user moves from one region of the city to another), or (4) network event such as network congestion, call drop, etc.

In addition to the network events, CiM ingests location context and map data. The map data provides CiM with details about the road and the rail network, and is used by the analytics engine to reason about the mode of transport of the anonymized user. Point-of-interest data provides information about important locations to be analyzed, such as malls and train stations.

Extract, Transform, Enrich, Load.

One of the most challenging tasks in ingesting network events is handling the scale, which may range from hundreds of millions to over a billion records per day. CiM ingests network events using Apache Flume and Kafka thus allowing CiM to reach this scale.

Network event data is enriched and converted to a standard format called the *Denormalized Network Event* (DNE). Here, only selective fields required for analysis (anonymized user identifier, time-of-the-event, and event type) are used and the rest of the record is excluded. In this study, we ingest close to 3 billion records for around 2.6 million anonymized users.

The multi-dimensional DNE data is indexed and stored in Hive tables [7]. Indexing the data is not a trivial task. Each analytic component may query the data using different dimensions; certain analytics require all events of an anonymized user for a given time-frame, others may require all events within a certain space-time window. Thus there is no single optimal way to index and cluster the data. We partition the DNE first by time (at date granularity), and then cluster by the user id. This enables the core algorithms – the dwell and trip analytics – to compute meaningful locations and trips of an anonymized user in a given time period.

3.2 Road/Rail Network Algorithms

Several analytics require basic spatio-temporal algorithms on graphs, such as the road and rail network, to determine the location context of the user. Examples of such analytics in CiM include detection of mode of transportation used and computation of the shortest path on the rail network. The main graph-based spatio-temporal functionalities in CiM are: (1) ingestion of the road and rail network; (2) fast shortest-path algorithms on the graph between two points using constrained graph search; (3) *Hidden Markov Model* (HMM) based map-matching algorithm to identify the most likely trajectory on a road or rail network given mobile geolocation data [23]. On the Hadoop platform, the road and rail network are stored in Hive tables. The algorithms for shortest-path and map-matching are exposed as Hive User Defined Functions (UDFs).

3.3 Visualization

For visualization purposes, we aggregate trajectories by origin zone-destination zone (OD) pairs, where zones are 250m x 250m squares. The start and the end point of the trip computed by the *trajectory cut* algorithm, described in the following section, are mapped to their respective zones. We aggregate the number of trajectories at 1 hour interval periods for each day and the estimated aggregate origin destination flow is used by the application-specific modules. We also provide the mean and median measures for the trip distance and duration, along with the number of trips for an OD pair. Figure 2 corresponds to the OD visualization described, for various times of day.

4. MOVEMENT PATTERN ANALYTICS

CiM consists of two types of fundamental spatio-temporal analytics: (1) Dwell analytics determine the meaningful locations where people spend time, and (2) Trip Analytics determine how people move. Properties of mobile geolocation data render these analytics non-trivial.

First, mobile geolocation data is very sparse (around 40 events per person per day) compared to GPS location traces, typically sampled around 1 Hz. In addition, geolocation uncertainty in cellular data typically ranges in the hundreds of meters, whereas GPS data uncertainty is less than 10 meters. Hence, our cellular spatio-temporal analytics compo-

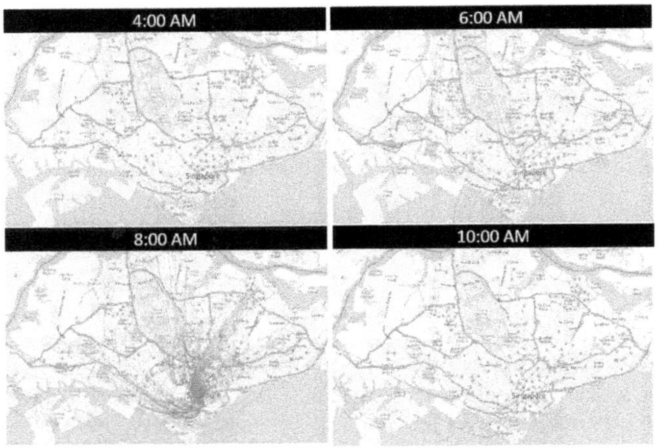

(a) Morning traffic flow

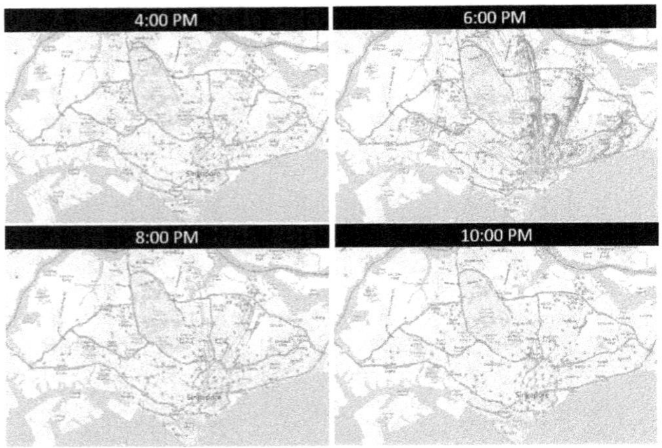

(b) Evening traffic flow

Figure 2: **Origin Destination weekday traffic**: represented by a green arrow from the origin with red head at the destination. The morning traffic toward the Central Business District and evening traffic from the Central Business District on the South can be observed at peak times.

nents are tailored to spatially uncertain and under-sampled geolocation data.

4.1 Dwell analytics

Dwell analytics estimate user home and work location based on the duration of stay at different times of the day. Dwell analytics also estimate additional anonymized user-specific *meaningful locations*, where an anonymized user spends significant time during weekdays and weekends. Home, work and meaningful locations can be aggregated and visualized as a heatmap of where people live, work or spend time. Important places of an anonymized user are stored into HDFS as Hive tables. They are also stored in Elastic-Search, which is an indexed storage for fast retrieval [5]. Home, work and meaningful locations are indexed by the anonymized user identifier and the spatial zone coordinate. In addition, meaningful locations are also indexed by type of day (weekday/weekend) and 90th percentile of the time range of visits to the given location.

4.2 Trip analytics

The Trip Analytics component estimates anonymized user trajectories from raw DNE data. We describe some of the core trajectory algorithms below, focusing on the scalability and Big Data aspects.

Trajectory segmentation.

We utilize stay-point detection algorithms [37] to detect the start and end of a meaningful trip of a user. All the trips of a user are stored into the Hive table. This table serves as a foundation for all trajectory-related algorithms in CiM, such as origin-destination analysis.

Trajectory fencing.

A common requirement consists of assessing whether a trajectory intersects a point of interest. For example, to determine if a user has possibly traveled in a train, it may be useful to compute if the user trip intersects a train station polygon. We have developed *trajectory fence* algorithms to determine if a trajectory cuts a polygon. The polygon of interest is divided into disjoint triangles and a trajectory into a set of lines between hops. The algorithm checks if any line of a trajectory cuts at least one triangle using a fast line cutting polygon algorithm [22].

Trajectory similarity.

It is often required to estimate the distance between two trajectories, for instance a user trip and a train route. We have developed trajectory similarity algorithms based on *least common substring* (LCSS) [35].

4.3 Travel mode detection

In order to provide public transit specific travel patterns insights from mobile geolocation data, it is necessary to identify the subset of the total daily trips including a public transit network segment. To this end, we propose a four-phase approach to process the time-series of sparse mobile geolocation data network events and leveraging the farecard and potentially other sources of real-time data.

In this work, we focus on identifying trajectories where a significant sub-trajectory aligns with a train network segment. Applying a map-matching algorithm on all the trips being prohibitively expensive from a computational standpoint, we propose instead a fast two-step heuristic to efficiently filter out trajectories that are unlikely to correspond to a trip on the train network. A map-matching algorithm is then applied to these filtered trajectories. Lastly, we join the estimated train network trips with patterns estimated from the farecard data, and iterate until a target accuracy has been achieved.

Step 1: determine start and end train stations.

We recognize that a sampled trajectory trace can be a trajectory on a train only if it cuts through at least two train stations. We use the *trajectory fence* algorithm described above to check if the trip cuts train station polygons. For the filtered trajectories, we determine the start and the end train stations in this step. Next steps are executed only for trajectories filtered in this stage.

Step 2: filter based on intermediate points.

We use a heuristic that all points of a trip between the start and end train stations should be *close* to the rail network. We store all line segments of the rail network within a spatial index, such as r-Tree [9]. For each trajectory filtered in step 1, we determine if any point between the start and end train stations is farther than a threshold (1km in this study) from the rail network segments. It that is the case, we conclude that the trip does not correspond to a train trip since at least one point between the candidate start and end train stations is far from the rail network. Step 3 is only applied to the trajectory successfully filtered by both step 1 and step 2.

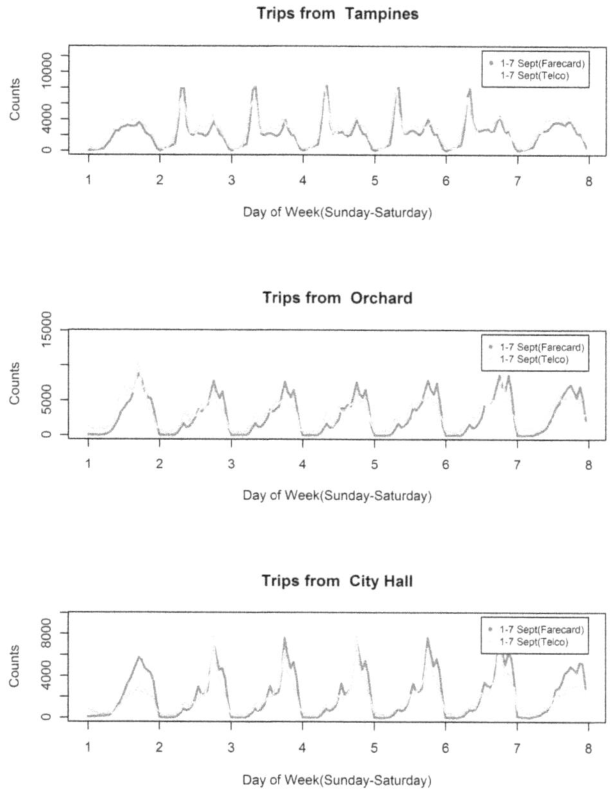

Figure 3: **Farecard-based learning:** for a popular residential station (Tampines), a popular commercial/shopping zone (Orchard) and a busy commercial station in the Central Business District (City Hall).

Step 3: map-matching and similarity test.

We then *snap* the candidate trajectory on the rail-network using the map-matching algorithm described in Section 3.2. The HMM-based map-matching algorithm uses an adequate observation noise model with a 1km variance. This relatively large observation noise also causes scenarios where trips corresponding to nearby roads may be falsely categorized as train trips by the map-matching module. Hence, we utilize a heuristic wherein we compare the sampled sub-trajectory between the start and the end train station with the map-matched sub-trajectory using a *trajectory similarity* algorithm. If the similarity is sufficiently high, we accept the trajectory as a train trip.

Step 4: farecard-based learning.

The output from step 3 is then appropriately scaled based on estimated device penetration rate, and is compared against similar observed quantities from farecard data. CiM iterates if the error metric is too high. This process is illustrated in Figure 3, representing a week of farecard tap-in data and the corresponding tap-in as per step 3. Travel mode detection parameters are updated via local search based on the observed discrepancy until convergence.

For each trip including a train network leg, we eventually obtain from the travel mode detection component both a sub-trajectory corresponding to the train segment, and an entire end-to-end trajectory of the anonymized user trip as per the DNE data. Both trajectories are stored in Hive tables clustered by start and end train stations.

4.4 Evaluation

The general statistics of the dataset and movement patterns are presented in Table 1 and Table 2.

Number of records	3089 M
Number of subscribers	1.7 M
Number of records per user	1800

Table 1: **General Statistics for 15 days of data.**

Number of Trips	33 M
Number of Trips after MRT Filter	27 M
Number of MRT Trips after Map-matching	21.1 M
Number of MRT Trips after Calibration	14 M
Number of MRT Trips after scaling by penetration factor	46.6 M
Number of MRT Trips as per Farecard Data	40 M

Table 2: **Movement Patterns (15 days)**

The evaluation of the performance of the trajectory analytics can be measured quantitatively on a network level by computation of standard rank correlation, such as Spearman rank correlation coefficient or Kendall rank correlation coefficient, presented in Table 3. Specifically, we compare the ranked correlation coefficient for the origin-destination flows, estimated on one hand from the farecard data, and on the other hand from the mobile geolocation data.

Spearman rank correlation coefficient	Kendall rank correlation coefficient
0.60	0.44

Table 3: **Top ODs matching:** between farecard-based top ODs and mobile geolocation-based top ODs.

For completeness, we also present in Table 4 typical values for the qualitative similarity between origin-destination flow rankings from mobile geolocation and farecard data.
In the following section, we present applications of the cal-

Top ODs	Matching between cellular and farecard
100	40
500	225
1000	526
2000	1185

Table 4: **Top ODs matching:** qualitative metric.

ibrated mobile geolocation-based public transit travel patterns model.

5. FIRST AND LAST MILE

5.1 Motivation

Using the results of the trajectory analytics, we analyze the spatial distribution of the initial (first mile) and final (last mile) segment of user trajectories before and after completing a probable train journey. The first and last mile are key quantities for public transit planners, since (1) a significant part of the trip travel-time can be associated with the first and last mile travel-time, and hence improvements to first or last-mile segments can have a large impact to public transport quality of service, and (2) there is currently very little data about these trip segments. In this section, we present our results for the spatial distribution of first and last mile segments as well as for the average first and last mile travel distances.

5.2 Residential vs shopping stations

The distribution of first mile locations of passengers boarding at Tampines MRT, a highly residential area, as estimated from trajectory analytics applied to geolocation data, is presented as a heatmap in Figure 4. Using the same visualization format, we present in Figure 5 the estimated distribution of first mile locations of passengers boarding at Bugis MRT, a popular commercial and shopping area. One can observe that the origin for the shopping area are qualitatively much closer to the train station. This is confirmed by the actual distances to the station for the first mile segments, presented in Table 5. Such insights can be derived in quasi real-time via fusion of mobile geolocation data with farecard, and thus supports frequent analyses, relevant for a fast-paced nation such as Singapore.

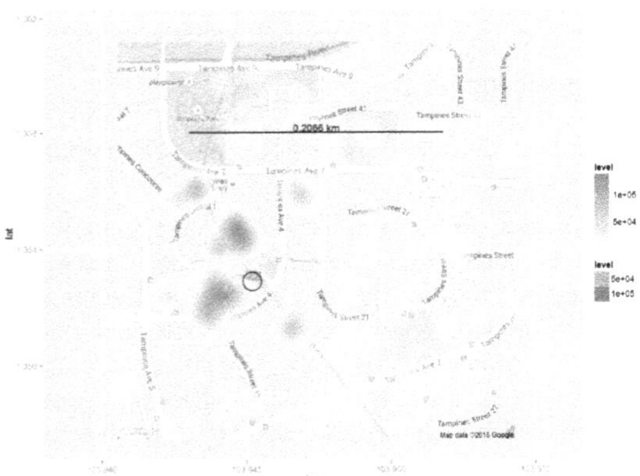

Figure 4: **First mile origin points at residential station:** Tampines MRT (represented as a circle on the map).

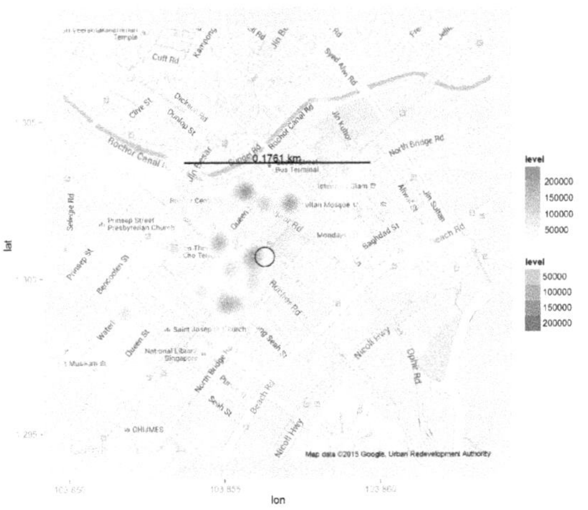

Figure 5: **First mile origin points at a shopping area station:** Bugis MRT (represented as a circle on the map).

Distance (kms)	Percentage Trips Tampines MRT	Percentage Trips Bugis MRT
0-1	39	75
1-2	51	24
2-3	7	1

Table 5: **First mile length:** for residential (Tampines) and shopping (Bugis) stations.

5.3 Analysis of first and last mile

The insights presented in the previous section for two stations can be reproduced for the entire train network. In Figure 6, we present a histogram of the percentage of commuters at each train station for which the trip origin is located within 1 km of the station. The left side of the histogram corresponds to stations with relatively low accessibility (percentage of commuters starting their trip within 1 km of the station is low), whereas the right hand side of the histogram corresponds to stations with relatively high accessibility (percentage of commuters starting their trip within 1 km of the station is higher). Figure 7 presents the analogous histogram for the last mile of the trip. The breakdown of the first mile histogram over a larger set of 42 train stations is provided in Table 6. In Figure 8, we illustrate the impact

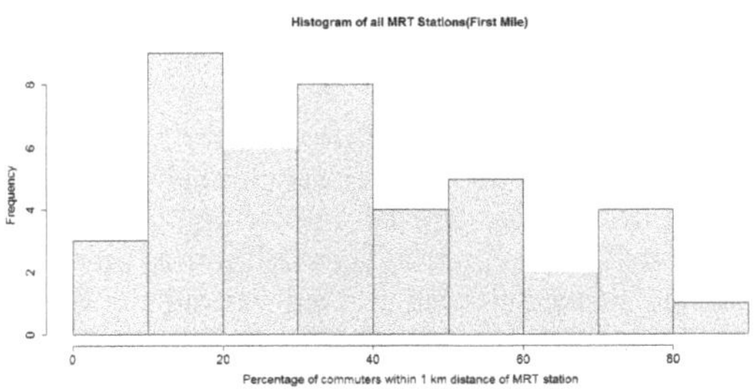

Figure 6: **Distribution of first mile shorter than 1 km:** across 42 MRT stations.

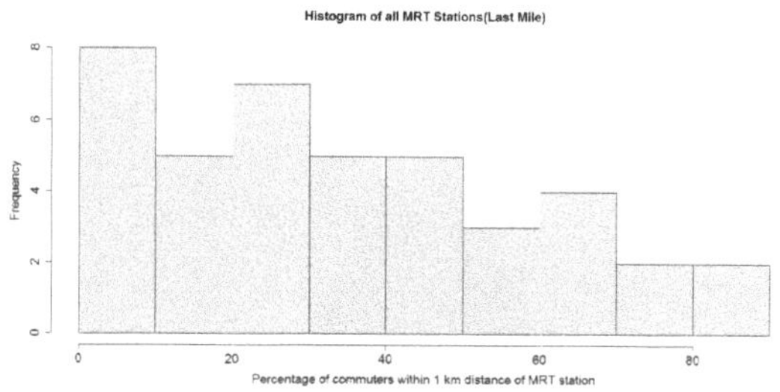

Figure 7: **Distribution of last mile shorter than 1 km:** across 42 MRT stations.

Station	Percent trips within 1 km	Station	Percent trips within 1 km
Admiralty	84	Ang Mo Kio	33
Redhill	78	Orchard	30
Bugis	74	Bishan	30
Bukit Gombak	71	Bukit Batok	27
Lavender	71	City Hall	24
Yio Chu Kang	66	Pasir Ris	23
Commonwealth	63	Buona Vista	23
Tanjong Pagar	59	Jurong East	23
Aljuned	56	Yishun	21
Novena	55	Marina Bay	19
Dhoby Ghaut	53	Clementi	18
Somerset	50	Tampines	17
Braddell	42	Lakeside	15
Boon Lay	40	Toa Payoh	13
Eunos	40	Bedok	12
Queenstown	40	Paya Lebar	11
Kembangan	39	Newton	11
Kallang	38	Chinese Garden	7

Table 6: **Percentage of First Mile trips** within 1 km of MRT station.

of advantageous vs disadvantageous first (and last) mile on the population of Singapore commuters. An origin station is "advantageous" if the true origin is within 1 km for the top quartile, and disadvantageous if the station is in the bottom quartile. We obtain the affected population of commuters from the farecard data. Note that perhaps surprisingly, the two subsets are nearly the same size, at about 24% of the total commuter trip population.

Figure 9 shows interestingly that the impact to Singapore commuters in terms of both origin and destination being advantageous is again nearly the same, since those commuters whose O and D are both disadvantageous correspond to about 7% of all commuters for both groups.

Such insights are of use in new transit initiatives such as Beeline [2] which aims to dynamically adapt direct bus routes for high demand and high travel time origin-destination pairs. Similarly, first and last mile results can also help identify suitable locations to target pilot green and light modes deployment like bike-share and car-share facilities.

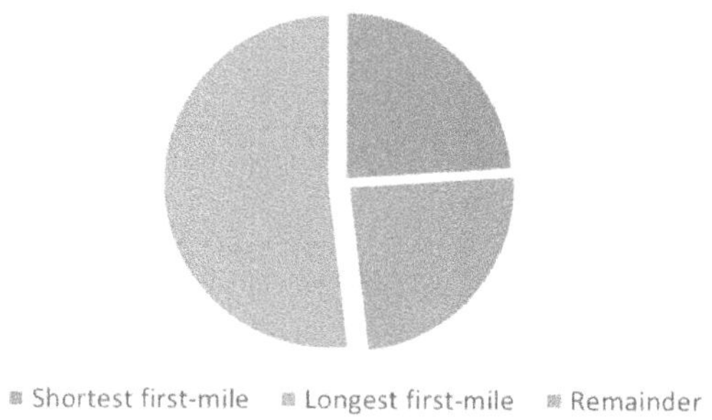

Figure 8: **Roughly equal proportion of commuters have advantageous vs disadvantageous origin stations**, in terms of first mile.

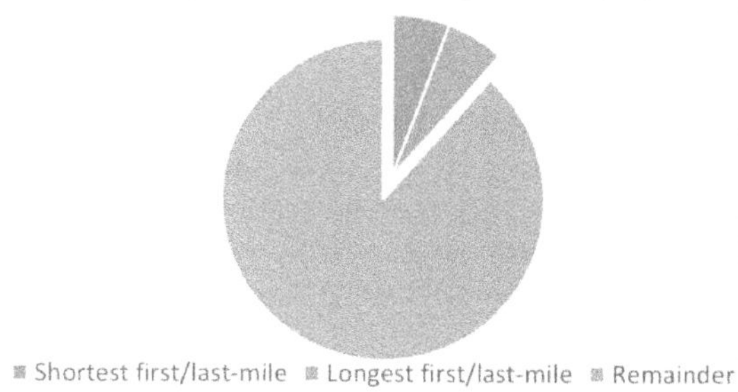

Figure 9: **Roughly equal proportion of commuters have both advantageous vs both disadvantageous Origin and Destination**, in terms of first and last mile.

6. REVEALING ROUTE CHOICE FACTORS

6.1 Motivation

Commuters often decide between several possible train routes from their origin to destination. The route choice may be motivated by a number of factors: distance, travel-time, comfort, crowdedness, cost. Estimating the sensitivity of commuters to specific factors is a valuable aspect of public transit planning, which can inform fare policy, service augmentation decisions, and network extensions plans. Additionally, a proper understanding of route choice is useful in the real-time management of incidents and events on the public transit network.

However, route choices and explanatory factors are not directly observable from farecard data which provides origin and destination, but does not identify the route taken. We leverage our trajectory analytics on mobile geolocation data, described in Section 4, to provide complete estimates of public transit trajectories, as a means to model the route choice process.

For a given origin-destination pair, the probability of a route within the public network being selected by commmuters is an output of the trajectory analytics component. Figure 10 shows the distribution of likely number of used routes across all OD pairs in the network, where a route was assumed likely to be used in practice if the route choice probability was at least 5%. In this section, we present a discrete choice model for revealing the important explanatory features (and their relative importance) governing commuter decision of route choice in the train network.

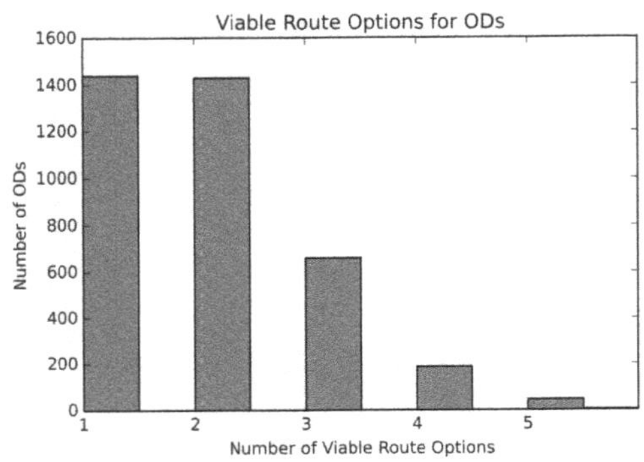

Figure 10: **Probability of route options set size** across all origin-destination pairs, as estimated from mobile geolocation data.

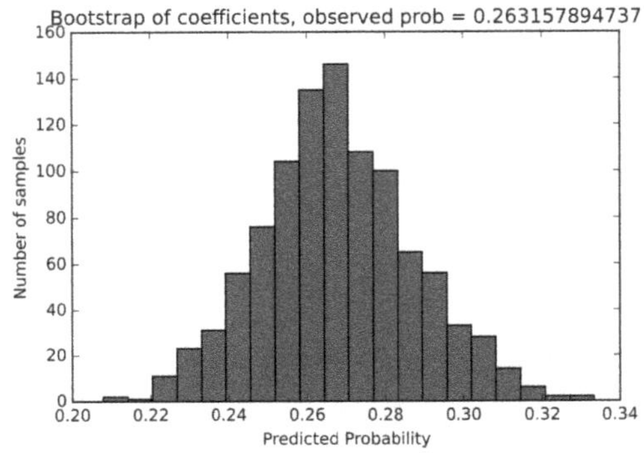

Figure 11: **Bootstrap simulation:** for a given route.

6.2 Discrete choice model

Let the graph $G = (V, E)$ represent the train network, where $V = [v_1, \cdots, v_n]$ are the stations and edges $E = (v_i, v_j)$ exist between connected stations s_i, s_j. Edge attributes include line id, distance, and other available features such as crowd level.

For each station pair, we compute a set P_{v_i,v_j} of at most $p_{\max}$ candidate paths which inherit the features of its edges. We set an upper bound for the maximum path length in order to avoid unreasonably long paths. For each station pair v_i, v_j, the discrete choice set consists of the path set P_{v_i,v_j}. The utility $U_{i,j,k}$ of using path k is a function of the path features and the origin-destination pair. The probability of choosing path k reads $p_{ijk} = Pr(U_{ijk} > U_{ijl,l \neq k}) = e^{U_{ijk}} / \sum_{l=1 \dots p_{\max}} e^{U_{ijl}}$.

We use the following network features: (1) path length, (2) number of interchanges, (3) mean frequency of the trains, and (4) number of crowded interchanges, the latter two features being estimated from farecard data. Specifically, an interchange is labelled crowded for a candidate path if the number of commuters for the intended station-line combination exceeds a threshold at that time of the day.

For consistency, for each OD pair, we normalize the features in the interval $[0, 1]$. The model parameters are the weights associated with each feature in the utility function. The model is calibrated using the number of passengers for a given origin-destination pair from the farecard data, while the candidate paths and the proportion of commuters using a candidate path are provided by the trajectory analytics described in Section 4.

Given the expected distinct route choices at different times, we calibrate two distinct models for (1) morning peak on a non-holiday week day, (2) off-peak on a non-holiday week day. The morning peak model uses 13000 data points, and we obtain $R^2 = 0.56$. The off-peak model uses 28000 data points, and we obtain $R^2 = 0.55$.

We generate confidence intervals via bootstrapping of the model coefficients using a normal distribution with mean equal to the coefficient value and standard deviation equal to the standard error of the coefficient estimation. We bootstrap 1000 model executions and output a distribution of probabilities for every route and origin-destination pair. Figure 11 shows an example bootstrap simulation for a given route with choice probability 0.26.

6.3 Example: route choice set

We illustrate one set of results from the route choice model on high occupancy routes from Ang Mo Kio, a popular residential station to Tanjong Pagar, a popular office location in the Central Business District of Singapore. Figure 12 depicts the route 1, with an estimated 52% of the commuters; Figure 13 shows route 2 with an estimated 24% of the commuters having one extra line change. Figure 14 shows route 3, with an estimated 15 % of the commuters and two extra line changes.

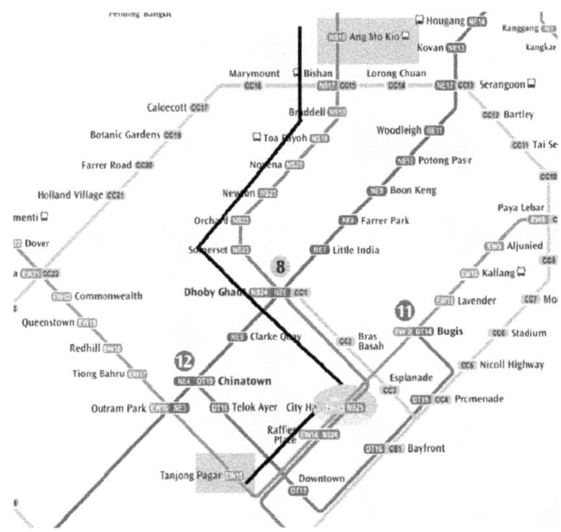

Figure 12: **Route 1:** with 52 percent Ang Mo Kio to Tanjong Pagar.

6.4 Explanatory features

The model feature coefficients and standard errors are listed in Table 7. The results illustrate that path distance remains the most important explanatory factor of the route choice, both during the morning peak and off-peak. One can also observe the relative increase of the sensitivity to crowd level during peak times, indicating the preference for low crowd level. The route choice model can be further improved by considering specific commuter types, regular commuters who know the network and would evaluate more advanced features (such as interchange distance, queues at train doors,

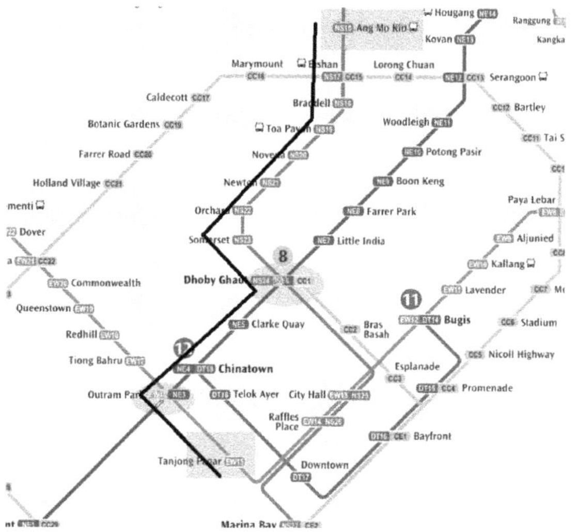

Figure 13: **Route 2:** with 24 percent Ang Mo Kio to Tanjong Pagar.

Feature	Peak coefficient	Off-peak coefficient
Intercept	2.91	3.00
# Interchanges	-1.22	-2.08
Distance	-3.08	-3.07
Train frequency	-0.64	-0.61
Crowd level	-0.59	-0.26

Table 7: **Feature importance:** for both the peak and off-peak models.

etc.) and non-regular commuters such as tourists with additional activity-specific considerations (hotspots on route, station attractivity, etc.)

7. CONCLUSIONS

We use mobile geolocation data and public transit data for generating complete insights on public transit travel patterns. We applied trajectory analytics on mobile geolocation data and showed that the limitations of mobile geolocation data can be addressed by leveraging the complementary strengths of public transit data via appropriate calibration and learning. We have shown that combining these data sources helps provide an accurate and complete picture of public transit trips, including first and last mile. The value of these insights was illustrated on two typical transport applications. Our conclusions on the estimation of first and last mile travel patterns show that the output of our system can be used for the design of on-demand public transit feeders and main public transit lines. We have also shown that parameters that are critical for optimal public transit planning, such as explanatory covariates for route choice, can be estimated from the adequate combination of mobile geolocation and public transit data via advanced learning analytics.

8. ACKNOWLEDGMENTS

We are grateful to the Singapore *Land Transport Authority* for sharing the anonymized farecard data and to *StarHub* for providing the anonymized mobile geolocation data used in this work. We acknowledge the support of the Singapore *Economic Development Board*.

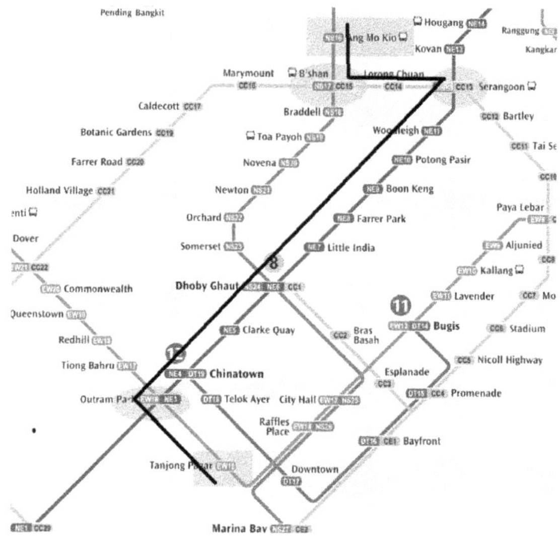

Figure 14: **Route 3:** with 15 percent Ang Mo Kio to Tanjong Pagar.

9. REFERENCES

[1] R. Becker, R. Cáceres, K. Hanson, S. Isaacman, J. M. Loh, M. Martonosi, J. Rowland, S. Urbanek, A. Varshavsky, and C. Volinsky. Human mobility characterization from cellular network data. *Communications of the ACM*, 56(1):74–82, 2013.

[2] Beeline. Beeline. https://www.beeline.sg/.

[3] F. Calabrese, M. Colonna, P. Lovisolo, D. Parata, and C. Ratti. Real-time urban monitoring using cell phones: A case study in rome. *Intelligent Transportation Systems, IEEE Transactions on*, 12(1):141–151, 2011.

[4] N. Eagle and A. S. Pentland. Eigenbehaviors: Identifying structure in routine. *Behavioral Ecology and Sociobiology*, 63(7):1057–1066, 2009.

[5] Elastic. Elastic search. https://www.elastic.co/products/elasticsearch.

[6] A. Flajolet, S. Blandin, and P. Jaillet. Robust Adaptive Routing Under Uncertainty. *submitted to Operations Research*, 2016.

[7] A. Foundation. Apache hive. https://hive.apache.org.

[8] F. Girardin, F. Calabrese, F. D. Fiore, C. Ratti, and J. Blat. Digital footprinting: Uncovering tourists with user-generated content. *Pervasive Computing, IEEE*, 7(4):36–43, 2008.

[9] A. Guttman. R-trees: A dynamic index structure for spatial searching. *SIGMOD Rec.*, 14(2):47–57, June 1984.

[10] S. Hasan, C. M. Schneider, S. V. Ukkusuri, and M. C. González. Spatiotemporal patterns of urban human mobility. *Journal of Statistical Physics*, 151(1-2):304–318, 2013.

[11] S. Hasan, X. Zhan, and S. V. Ukkusuri. Understanding urban human activity and mobility

patterns using large-scale location-based data from online social media. In *Proceedings of the 2nd ACM SIGKDD international workshop on urban computing*, page 6. ACM, 2013.

[12] Y. He, S. Blandin, L. Wynter, and B. Trager. Analysis and real-time prediction of local incident impact on transportation networks. In *Data Mining Workshop (ICDMW), 2014 IEEE International Conference on*, pages 158–166. IEEE, 2014.

[13] T. Holleczek, S. Yin, Y. Jin, S. Antonatos, H. L. Goh, S. Low, A. Shi-Nash, et al. Traffic measurement and route recommendation system for mass rapid transit (mrt). In *Proceedings of the 21th ACM SIGKDD International Conference on Knowledge Discovery and Data Mining*, pages 1859–1868. ACM, 2015.

[14] T. Holleczek, L. Yu, J. K. Lee, O. Senn, C. Ratti, and P. Jaillet. Detecting weak public transport connections from cellphone and public transport data. In *Proceedings of the 2014 International Conference on Big Data Science and Computing*, page 9. ACM, 2014.

[15] T. Hunter, P. Abbeel, and A. Bayen. The path inference filter: model-based low-latency map matching of probe vehicle data. *Intelligent Transportation Systems, IEEE Transactions on*, 15(2):507–529, 2014.

[16] J. G. Jin, K. M. Teo, and L. Sun. Disruption response planning for an urban mass rapid transit network. In *transportation research board 92nd annual meeting, Washington DC*, 2013.

[17] J. Jonas. Analytic superfood. http://jeffjonas.typepad.com/jeff_jonas/2009/08/your-movements-speak-for-themselves-spacetime\\-travel-data-is-analytic-superfood.html.

[18] F. Kling and A. Pozdnoukhov. When a city tells a story: urban topic analysis. In *Proceedings of the 20th International Conference on Advances in Geographic Information Systems*, pages 482–485. ACM, 2012.

[19] V. Kolar, S. Ranu, A. P. Subramainan, Y. Shrinivasan, A. Telang, R. Kokku, and S. Raghavan. People in motion: Spatio-temporal analytics on call detail records. In *Communication Systems and Networks (COMSNETS), 2014 Sixth International Conference on*, pages 1–4. IEEE, 2014.

[20] A. Krause, E. Horvitz, A. Kansal, and F. Zhao. Toward community sensing. In *Proceedings of the 7th international conference on Information processing in sensor networks*, pages 481–492. IEEE Computer Society, 2008.

[21] R. K.-W. Lee, T. S. Kam, et al. Time-series data mining in transportation: A case study on singapore public train commuter travel patterns. *International Journal of Engineering and Technology*, 6(5):431, 2014.

[22] T. Möller and B. Trumbore. Fast, minimum storage ray/triangle intersection. In *ACM SIGGRAPH 2005 Courses*, SIGGRAPH '05, New York, NY, USA, 2005. ACM.

[23] P. Newson and J. Krumm. Hidden markov map matching through noise and sparseness. In *Proceedings of the 17th ACM SIGSPATIAL International Conference on Advances in Geographic Information Systems*, GIS '09, pages 336–343, New York, NY, USA, 2009. ACM.

[24] N. B. Othman, E. F. Legara, V. Selvam, and C. Monterola. Simulating congestion dynamics of train rapid transit using smart card data. *Procedia Computer Science*, 29:1610–1620, 2014.

[25] A. D. Patire, M. Wright, B. Prodhomme, and A. M. Bayen. How much gps data do we need? *Transportation Research Part C: Emerging Technologies*, 2015.

[26] F. C. Pereira, F. Rodrigues, and M. Ben-Akiva. Using data from the web to predict public transport arrivals under special events scenarios. *Journal of Intelligent Transportation Systems*, 19(3):273–288, 2015.

[27] A. Pozdnoukhov and C. Kaiser. Space-time dynamics of topics in streaming text. In *Proceedings of the 3rd ACM SIGSPATIAL international workshop on location-based social networks*, pages 1–8. ACM, 2011.

[28] J. Reades, F. Calabrese, A. Sevtsuk, and C. Ratti. Cellular census: Explorations in urban data collection. *Pervasive Computing, IEEE*, 6(3):30–38, 2007.

[29] A. Sadilek and J. Krumm. Far out: Predicting long-term human mobility. In *AAAI*, 2012.

[30] S. Samaranayake, S. Blandin, and A. Bayen. A tractable class of algorithms for reliable routing in stochastic networks. *International Symposium on Transportation and Trafic Theory (ISTTT), Procedia Social and Behavioral Sciences*, 17:341–363, 2011, doi:10.1016/j.sbspro.2011.04.521.

[31] C. Song, Z. Qu, N. Blumm, and A.-L. Barabási. Limits of predictability in human mobility. *Science*, 327(5968):1018–1021, 2010.

[32] L. Sun, D.-H. Lee, A. Erath, and X. Huang. Using smart card data to extract passenger's spatio-temporal density and train's trajectory of mrt system. In *Proceedings of the ACM SIGKDD international workshop on urban computing*, pages 142–148. ACM, 2012.

[33] X. Tang, S. Blandin, and L. Wynter. A fast decomposition approach for transportation network optimization. In *World Congress*, volume 19, pages 5109–5114, 2014.

[34] A. Vaccari, L. Liu, A. Biderman, C. Ratti, F. Pereira, J. Oliveirinha, and A. Gerber. A holistic framework for the study of urban traces and the profiling of urban processes and dynamics. In *Intelligent Transportation Systems, 2009. ITSC'09. 12th International IEEE Conference on*, pages 1–6. IEEE, 2009.

[35] M. Vlachos, G. Kollios, and D. Gunopulos. Discovering similar multidimensional trajectories. In *Data Engineering, 2002. Proceedings. 18th International Conference on*, pages 673–684, 2002.

[36] D. B. Work, O.-P. Tossavainen, S. Blandin, A. M. Bayen, T. Iwuchukwu, and K. Tracton. An ensemble kalman filtering approach to highway traffic estimation using gps enabled mobile devices. In *Decision and Control, 2008. CDC 2008. 47th IEEE Conference on*, pages 5062–5068. IEEE, 2008.

[37] Y. Zheng. Trajectory data mining: An overview. *ACM Transaction on Intelligent Systems and Technology*, September 2015.

EMBERS AutoGSR: Automated Coding of Civil Unrest Events

Parang Saraf
Discovery Analytics Center
Department of Computer Science
Virginia Tech
parang@cs.vt.edu

Naren Ramakrishnan
Discovery Analytics Center
Department of Computer Science
Virginia Tech
naren@cs.vt.edu

ABSTRACT

We describe the EMBERS AutoGSR system that conducts automated coding of civil unrest events from news articles published in multiple languages. The nuts and bolts of the AutoGSR system constitute an ecosystem of filtering, ranking, and recommendation models to determine if an article reports a civil unrest event and, if so, proceed to identify and encode specific characteristics of the civil unrest event such as the when, where, who, and why of the protest. AutoGSR is a deployed system for the past 6 months continually processing data 24x7 in languages such as Spanish, Portuguese, English and encoding civil unrest events in 10 countries of Latin America: Argentina, Brazil, Chile, Colombia, Ecuador, El Salvador, Mexico, Paraguay, Uruguay, and Venezuela. We demonstrate the superiority of AutoGSR over both manual approaches and other state-of-the-art encoding systems for civil unrest.

Keywords

event extraction, event encoding, text mining

1. INTRODUCTION

The computational modeling and interpretation of societal events has been a holy grail in social science research. Beginning in the 1980s, there have been significant efforts in computational analysis of societal events supported by government programs such as DARPA's ICEWS (Integrated Conflict Early Warning System) and CIA's PITF (Political Instability Task Force). Projects of similar (and more ambitious) scope continues to this day, and offer greater specificity, both spatially and temporally into modeling global events.

We are part of the EMBERS consortium [13] that aims to forecast civil unrest phenomena (protests, strikes, and 'occupy' events) in multiple countries of Latin America, specifically Argentina, Brazil, Chile, Colombia, Ecuador, El Salvador, Mexico, Paraguay, Uruguay, and Venezuela. In our earlier KDD 2014 paper [13] we demonstrated how we can use open source indicators such as news, blogs, Twitter, food prices, and economic data, to forecast civil unrest events. EMBERS forecasts have been evaluated by a third party (MITRE) wherein human analysts prepared a ground truth dataset (called the GSR, or 'Gold Standard report') of reported protests in newspapers of record. The GSR is compared against EMBERS forecasts using metrics introduced in [13].

KDD '16, August 13-17, 2016, San Francisco, CA, USA

DOI: http://dx.doi.org/10.1145/2939672.2939737

As the EMBERS project matures, we realized that we must pay attention to not just forecasting events but also to coding ongoing events, i.e., the process of constructing the GSR on a regular basis. For instance, see Fig. 2. Such coded data serves two uses in EMBERS: to help evaluate EMBERS forecasts, and to support the regular re-training and tuning of the machine learning models. Accordingly, we launched a parallel effort, referred to as the EMEBRS AutoGSR, that conducts automated coding of civil unrest events from news articles published in multiple languages. Like EMBERS, the AutoGSR is also a deployed system continually processing data 24x7 in languages such as Spanish, Portuguese, English. Our key contributions can be summarized as follows:

1. To the best of our knowledge, the AutoGSR is the only/first system to be able to automatically encode civil unrest events across 10 countries in languages local to these countries. This gives a significant advantage over systems that are manual or systems that are automatic but restricted to English.
2. The nuts and bolts of the AutoGSR system constitute an ecosystem of filtering, ranking, and recommendation models to determine if an article reports a civil unrest event and, if so, proceed to identify and encode specific characteristics of a civil unrest event such as the when, where, who, and why of the protest. We present an exhaustive evaluation of the performance of AutoGSR using metrics in the large (e.g., does the system track ongoing happenings in countries of interest?) as well as metrics in the small (e.g., does the system identify specific events of interest?).
3. AutoGSR is meant to be used in both a fully automated and an analyst assisted mode. Through detailed analysis of hours logged in both the manual process and in the AutoGSR system, we quantify the performance gains of our approach.

2. RELATED WORK

The challenges associated with a system like AutoGSR can be broadly classified in two categories: event encoders and event databases. While the event encoders are not freely available, the event databases constructed around them are more available.

Table 1: Sample erroneous encodings by ICEWS and GDELT.

Source	ID	Representative Paragraph	Reason for Error
GDELT	299144197	Pope Francis is hoping to demonstrate the power of prayer next week when Israeli President Shimon Peres and Palestinian President Mahmoud Abbas join the pontiff at the Vatican for an exercise in peace building.	Presence of the word 'demonstrate' results in a false positive.
GDELT	256666928 and 256814375	U.N. Secretary-General Ban Ki-moon on Tuesday expressed alarm at the violence in Turkey as confrontations between Turkish security forces and protesters continued after three weeks of demonstrations against Prime Minister Tayyip Erdogan.	No Duplicate Detection. Two events extracted from two articles covering the same story but published on different days.
ICEWS	23909784	Since its inception, the Islamic State group has demonstrated the firmness of its structure and the strength of its organizational composition.	Presence of word 'demonstrate' results in a false positive.
ICEWS	19873295	Capriles has called off a march by his supporters in Caracas, saying that his rivals were plotting to "infiltrate" the rally to trigger violence.	The protest was called off.

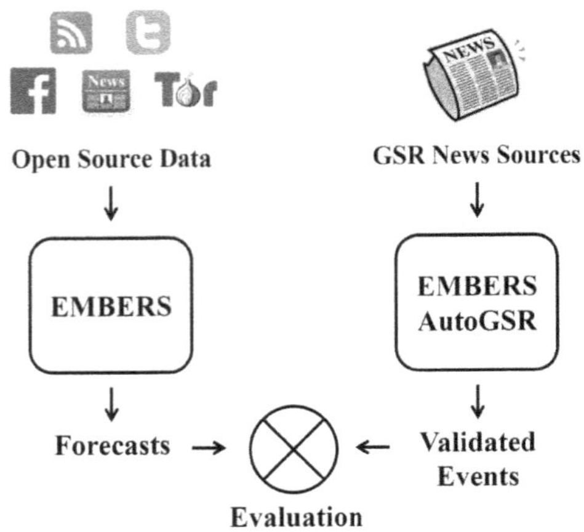

Figure 1: The EMBERS system forecasts civil unrest events from open source indicators while the EMBERS AutoGSR system encodes civil unrest events as they are reported in newspapers. Output from the AutoGSR system is used to both evaluate EMBERS forecasts and to retrain EMBERS models on a periodic basis.

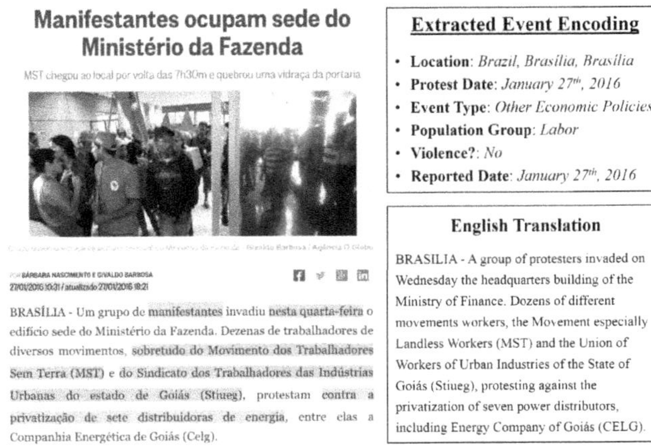

Figure 2: A sample event extracted from a news article.

Table 2: Comparison of automated event encoders.

System	Protest Encoding	Language Agnostic	Tunability	Duplicate Detection
ICEWS	✓			✓
GDELT	✓			
AutoGSR	✓	✓	✓	✓

2.1 Event Encoders

Hogenboom et. al.[3] provides an overview of different extraction methodologies used by the current state-of-the-art systems. The methodologies used here include statistical as well as linguistic and lexicographical approaches for event extraction. TABARI (Textual Analysis by Augmented Replacement Instructions) [15] and BBN's SERIF (Statistical Entity and Relation Information Finder) [1, 14] are two state-of-the-art event encoders. These encoders not only extract events but also encode them via a mapping to an event taxonomy. Such mappings add structure to the extracted event thereby making it feasible to perform systematic studies. CAMEO [16] is one such widely used event taxonomy and is used by both TABARI and SERIF.

TABARI is one of the earlier open source event extraction systems that uses sparse parsing to recognize patterns in text. These patterns are hand coded and identify three types of information: actors, verbs, and actions. For a given text, only a few initial sentences are used for event extraction, to support high throughput applications. Several improved versions of TABARI have been proposed. JABARI is one such system, which is a Java implementation of TABARI and uses a few advanced NLP techniques in addition to pattern matching. More recently, PETRARCH has emerged as the successor of TABARI. Instead of conducting a pattern based extraction, PETRARCH uses the full parsed Penn TreeBank as input to perform a parser-based encoding.

BBN's SERIF is another state-of-the-art event encoder that uses a series of NLP components to capture representations of type *'who did what to whom'* in article text. The encoder works at both the sentence and document level and is able to identify and resolve entities between sentences. Once the entities are resolved, the encoder detects and characterizes the relationship between entities. Finally the encoder maps these relationships to the CAMEO taxonomy using an externally provided list of actor dictionaries and event patterns.

2.2 Event Databases

The origins of automated event databases can be attributed primarily to political scientists and intelligence agencies who over the years have envisioned systems that can perform large scale encoding of events by mining million of news articles. ICEWS (Integrated Crisis Early Warning System) [11] and GDELT (Global Database of Events, Language and Tone)[6] are two such systems that analyze hundreds of news sources from all over the world in order to generate a database of events.

ICEWS, which began in 2007, is a DARPA funded project that focuses primarily on monitoring, accessing and forecasting events of interests for military commanders. Internally, ICEWS employs TABARI and SERIF to encode news articles. ICEWS focuses primarily on generating high quality, reliable events and uses several mechanisms to filter the raw stream of reported stories into a unique stream of events. Events are encoded in accordance to the CAMEO taxonomy.

GDELT, on the other hand focuses on capturing an extensive set of events both in terms of categories and geographical spread. By design, the goal of GDELT is to collect a large number of events without worrying about false positives. Internally, it uses an enhanced version of TABARI and maps events to the CAMEO taxonomy.

Although both these systems are considered state-of-the-art, in our experiments we have found that they perform poorly in comparison to manually generated ground truth data. See Table 1 for examples of erroneous encodings in ICEWS and GDELT. This is primarily because of the fully automated event generation process that yields false positives. Hence, there is a need for a semi-automated system that can generate validated event encodings with minimal human effort. Table 2 contrasts ICEWS and GDELT against our AutoGSR system.

3. SYSTEM ARCHITECTURE

EMBERS AutoGSR is a web based system that generates validated civil unrest events extracted from news articles. The system architecture is shown in Fig. 3.

3.1 Data Sources

News articles are collected every day from three data sources: 1) Site specific Google Search 2) RSS feeds subscribed to individual news websites, and 3) News databases. Articles are filtered if they contain a protest related keyword. With the help of subject matter experts, we created a list of protest keywords for each language.

3.2 Data Processing

This stage of EMBERS AutoGSR is responsible for running and managing the sophisticated *models ecosystem*, along with performing standard tasks like data cleaning and enrichment.

3.2.1 Fetch and Clean

The *fetch and clean* component fetches the article from the original web source and performs a boilerplate removal in order to extract the full article text. On this extracted full text, keyword based search is performed once again to make sure that at least one protest related keyword is present in the text. This component also fetches SEO meta tags, if present for each article. (These meta tags are added by news websites in order to improve their search ranking and includes several key information about the article such as publish date, keywords, summary, and description.)

3.2.2 Data Enrichment

This component enriches news articles by performing various kinds of linguistic processing. The enrichment comprises named entity extraction, lemmatization, location identification, geo-reference resolution, and translation of article text

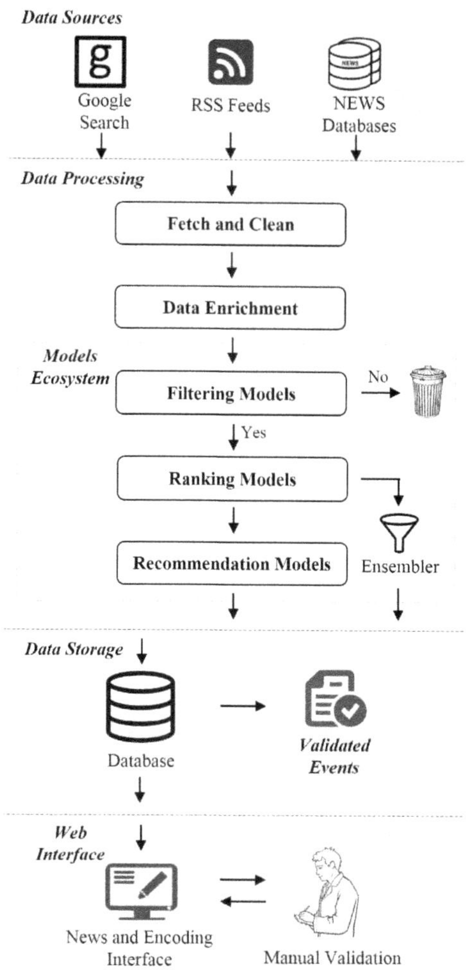

Figure 3: EMBERS AutoGSR System Architecture.

to English. This enriched information is used by models in the *models ecosystem*.

Words or noun phrases identified as a location by the named entity resolver are passed through a geo reference resolver to resolve ambiguity, if any. Many a times, locations are referred by their alternate name(s), for example: *LA* for *City of Los Angeles* or *America/US/USA* for *The United States of America*. Alternatively, several times, famous landmarks like *Times Square, White House, etc* are used to denote a location. The geo-reference resolver goes through a world gazetteer[1] to resolve these phrases and maps them to the official name.

Please note that articles are translated into english only to enhance the readability of an end user. The translated text is not used by any of the models. The models are designed to work with native language.

3.2.3 Models Ecosystem

This component, explained in much detail in a subsequent section, applies several machine learning models on news articles. A first set of models classify an incoming article into protest or non protest. If the article is classified as a protest article, then it passes through a second set of models that recommend event encoding(s) for the article.

[1]GeoNames: http://www.geonames.org/

Filtering Models. These models are based on hand coded rules that perform a hard classification into protest or non protest. The models are applied in a series, where if the article fails one of the models, the article is classified as a non protest article. When an article successfully passes all the filtering models, it is processed through the subsequent ranking and recommendation models.

Ranking Models. These models work independently of each other and assign a probability score for classifying the article as a protest article. The individual probability scores generated by each model are fed to an ensembler which generates a representative ensembled probability score for the article. The accuracy of individual models in the past is also used as an input by the ensembler.

Recommendation Models. The recommendation models assume that the article is a protest article and based on this assumption extracts & recommends both full event encoding(s) and individual encoding components. Elaborating on what was mentioned earlier, a full event encoding comprises of the following components: 1) protest location, 2) protest date, 3) participating population group, 4) reason for protest, 5) violent or peaceful protest, and 6) protest reported date. These models work in tandem to generate the full event encoding. If there are multiple models generating recommendations for a particular encoding component then an ensembler is used to determine a representative value.

3.3 Database

The output of the *data processing* component containing clean, enriched news articles along with the individual and ensembled values generated by the *model ecosystem* is stored in a database. This database acts as the primary data source for the AutoGSR Web Interface which displays news articles along with the associated data. For each article, the database also stores validated encoding results generated by the manual validation process.

3.4 Web Interface

The web interface shown in Fig. 4 displays enriched news articles; output from the *models ecosystem*; and controls to validate recommended encodings. More specifically the interface displays the following (the numerical labeling of the components in the image corresponds with the list numbers below):

1. Allows the user to specify the filtering criteria for displaying news articles. The sytem also allows a user to specify filtering criteria for displaying news articles. An important criterion is the cutoff probability with values between 0 and 1 and is used to classify an article as protest or non-protest. If the representative ensembled probability of an article, generated by the ranking models ensembler, is greater than this cutoff probability, then the article is classified as a protest article; otherwise it gets labeled as a non protest article. Using this control, the user can also tune the precision and recall of the system.
2. The articles satisfying the filtering criteria are clustered in real time to generate news clusters. Each news cluster brings together related stories. For each cluster, a representative label is also generated. The real time clustering is performed using the Lingo3G clustering suite[2]. A summary text is also generated for each article in the cluster, using the *description* meta tag.
3. For each article, the detailed view shows the full article text, article image and translated english text along with recommended event encoding and the output of the models ecosystem as described next.
4. Event encodings are recommended in following three ways – a) *Ensembled Recommendations*: These full encoding recommendations are generated by putting together the recommendations for individual encoding components as generated by the recommendation models from the ecosystem. In the case of automated event extraction, these recommended encodings are considered as the extracted encoding for the article. b) *Clustering Based Recommendations*: Full encoding recommendations are generated using related articles with validated encodings in the dynamically generated news clusters. These recommendations assume that similar/related articles will result in almost similar encodings. c) *Individual Recommendations*: The individual components in the encoding validation form show component specific recommendations.
5. All sentences used by the system to generate recommendations are highlighted for the user's reference. There is an option to toggle the reading view, where only the highlighted sentences of the article are shown. The 'Highlighted Text' view assumes that, in the ideal scenario, the highlighted sentences will provide complete information about the article. Hovering the mouse over the article shows the kind of information that the system extracted from a particular sentence. If the user doesn't agree with the highlighted sentence or the kind of information identified by it, then he can click on that particular sentence and modify the information type through the popover. This active feedback helps the system to learn.

3.5 Encoding Validation

For each article classified as a protest article, recommended encodings are validated manually by subject matter experts. During the validation process, the experts can either accept the recommended encoding or modify it. The validation process is performed using the validation controls of the interface. Encodings for each article are validated by at least two analysts. If the analysts agree on the encoding then that encoding is considered as the final encoding. However, in case of a conflict, the final encoding is decided by a quality control analyst.

3.6 Event Generation

Based on the validated records, a final set of events is generated by performing duplicate detection. As there can be multiple articles reporting the same protest, duplicate detection is performed. During duplicate detection, unique event encoding tuples comprising ≪protest location, protest date, protest reason, participating population group, violence/peaceful≫ are identified and resolved.

4. MODELS ECOSYSTEM

In civil unrest encoding, the ratio of positive to negative articles is highly skewed towards negative articles. Based on

[2]Lingo3G: https://carrotsearch.com/

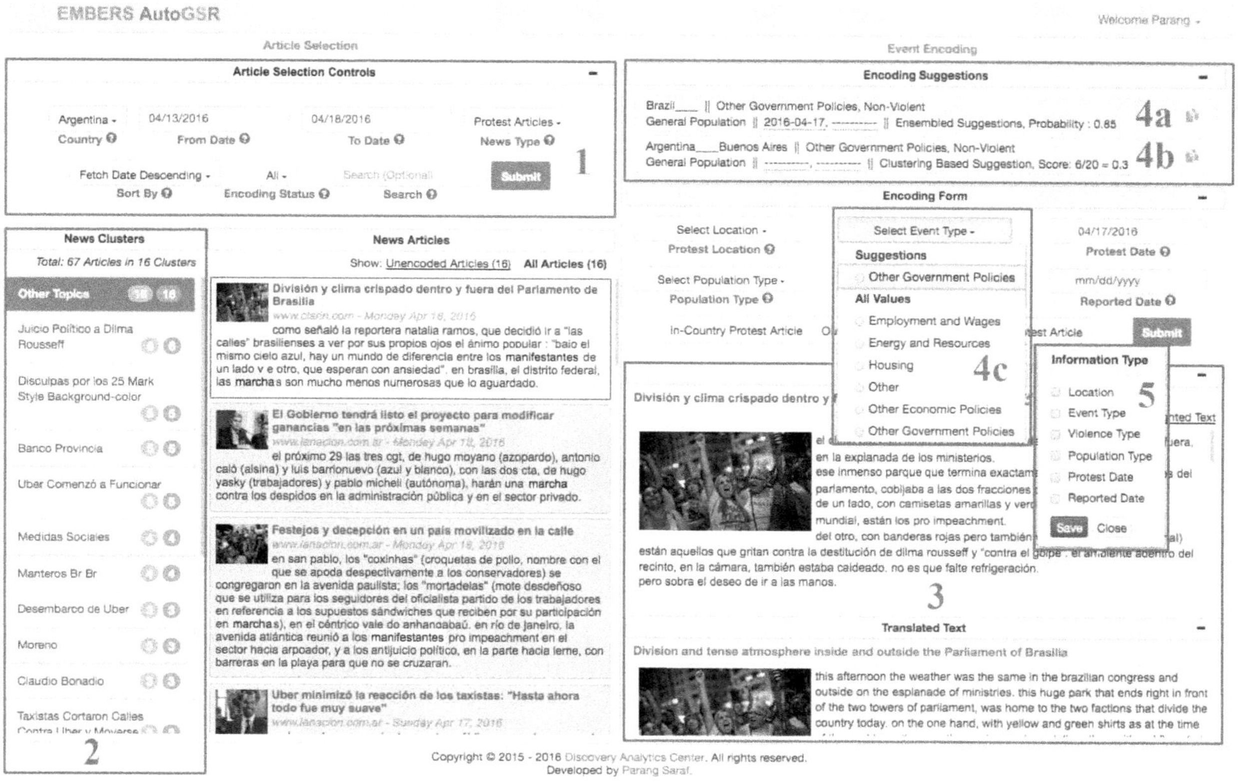

Figure 4: EMBERS AutoGSR Web Interface. 1) Filtering Controls 2) Real time Clustering of News Articles 3) Full Text, Translated Text 4) Full and Partial Encoding Recommendations 5) Model Outputs.

our experience, given a set of articles containing at least one protest keyword, this ratio is somewhere around 1:8. Due to this skewness, an analyst has to typically skim through a huge number of negative articles just to identify a few protest articles. What makes this problem even more challenging is the inherent inability to characterize negative articles. While we know what constitutes a protest article, there is no simple way to describe a non protest article. Given these challenges, the aim of the models ecosystem is two fold: 1) reduce the number of negative articles while minimizing the loss of positive articles, and 2) generate event encoding recommendations for positive articles.

Both of these are non-trivial problems and therefore the solution requires an ensemble of models, each with its own selective superiorities, focus area, and performance. The models as shown in Table 3 and categorized into three compartments: 1) Filtering Models, 2) Ranking Models, and 3) Recommendation Models.

4.1 Filtering Models

These are rules based models that perform hard classification of news articles into protest and non protest. If the article fails even one of these models, then the article is classified as a non protest article.

4.1.1 Sub Domain Based Filtering

Many of the sub domains, for example entertainment, technology, sports, etc. are tagged as non relevant. If an article is published in any of these sub domains then the article is not considered relevant and gets classified as non protest. In this context, a sub domain worth mentioning is *sports*. Sports articles use a lot of protest keywords like *attack*, *surrounded*, etc. to describe competition between two teams/players.

4.1.2 URL Based Filtering

There are several URL structures that list multiple articles on a single page. For example, URLs listing top stories of the day[3], or URLs listing stories by topic[4], or URLs corresponding to search terms[5], etc. All such URLs are considered irrelevant for the this task, and any article with URL matching one of these types is discarded.

4.1.3 Negative Keywords Based Filtering

For many of the protest keywords, there exist words, called Negative Keywords which when used in the vicinity of a protest word can completely alter the meaning. A few such negative keywords are described in Table 4. If any such negative keyword is present in the vicinity of the protest keyword in the same sentence, then such matches are not considered as a positive keyword match and are ignored. After ignoring all such false matches, if the article still contains any other protest keyword, only then the article is allowed to pass. Otherwise, the article is reported as a non protest article.

4.2 Ranking Models

Each of these models assign a probability score of classi-

[3]http://www.clarin.com/politica/
[4]http://www.clarin.com/tema/manifestaciones.html
[5]http://www.clarin.com/buscador?q=protesta

Table 3: EMBERS AutoGSR: Models Ecosystem

Filtering Models	Ranking Models	Recommendations Models
These are rules based models that classify incoming news articles into protest and non protest with a 0 or 1 certainty	These models use standard machine learning algorithms on different components of an incoming article for classification.	These models assume that the incoming article is a protest article and tries to recommend complete or partial encoding(s) for the article
1. Sub Domain Based Filtering 2. URL Based Filtering 3. Negative Keywords Based Filtering	1. Labeled Unlabeled Text Classifier 2. Entity Based Classifier 3. Distributed Representation Classifier 4. MetaTags Based Classifier	Protest Identification Models: 1. Geo Location Recommender 2. Temporal Recommender Protest Characterization Models: 3. Entity Based Naïve Bayes Recommender 4. MetaTags Based Recommender Usability Models: 5. Clustering Based Recommender
Approach: Articles are passed through these models sequentially. If any of these models classifies the article as non protest then the article is labeled as a non protest article in the interface	***Approach***: Each of these models assign individual probabilities to an incoming article. An article's final probability is calculated using 'model ensemble' approach. In the interface user can specify a cutoff probability score. Articles that have probability greater than the cutoff will appear as protest articles.	***Approach***: These recommendations appear in the interface for each article. The recommendations are generated for both full encodings and individual encoding components.

Table 4: Example Negative Keywords

Protest Keyword	Negative Keyword Phrase	Altered Meaning
marcha	ponar en marcha	to start; to set in motion
protesta	tomar protesta	to swear in (public official)
protesta	rendir protesta	to swear in (public official)

fying the article as a protest article. The models focus on different indicators for classifying the article.

4.2.1 *Labeled Unlabeled Text Classifier*

This model implements a LU Classifier as proposed by [9, 10] to work with a set of labeled and unlabeled articles. The model is adapted to work in a binary class setting and implements an Expectation Maximization procedure with a Naïve Bayes Classifier.

4.2.2 *Entity Based Classifier*

This model is designed to work with named entities and protest keywords and can be considered as a special case of the NB classifier built earlier. Using extracted entities and protest keywords as evidences, this model employs a multinomial naïve Bayes method with Laplace smoothing to determine the posterior probability of classifying an article as a protest article. The entities include name, location and organization along with the protest keywords found in the article.

4.2.3 *Distributed Representation Classifier*

This model takes a step away from the bag of words models and aims to capture the ordering of words while generating distributed vector representations for the articles. The model builds upon recent advancements in learning vector representations of words using neural networks [7, 8]. Mikolov et al. show that such vector representations not only capture syntactic and semantic information but is also aware of '*distance*' in the N dimensional representation space. The model was adapted further by [5] to generate distributed representations of documents and was shown to be *distance aware* similar to word vectors.

These models have been designed primarily to work with large datasets and have been shown in [7] to perform better with larger corpora, as they allow the layer weights to stabilize. Therefore, we train this model on an unlabeled corpus of $\sim$250k Spanish and $\sim$100k Portuguese news articles. To increase relevance, we made sure that these articles contain at least one protest keyword. To this set, we added $\sim$20k labeled articles. Each of the labeled articles contains two labels: 1) Unique label identifying the article; and 2) Class label identifying the article as protest or non protest. This way, we not only identify vector representations for each document but also vector representations for labels '*protest*' and '*non protest*'.

Once the distributed vector representations for '*protest*' and '*non protest*' labels have been identified, we classify an incoming article as follows: 1) Generate a distributed vector representation of the article using the trained model; 2) Calculate the *cosine distance* of the article vector from *protest* and *non protest* labels; 3) Classify the article based on closeness and assign a posterior probability.

4.2.4 *MetaTags based Classifier*

In the literature, much of effort in classification of web pages or news articles has focused only on full *article text*. Almost little to no work exists in the domain of using HTML meta tags as input. HTML meta tags provide a wide variety of structured information about a web page, which is primarily used by search engine crawlers. In our scenario, tags of much importance are the ones that are used to generate rich text snippets. Rich text snippet is a short summary description of a web page that is shown when the page appears in search engine results and/or social media websites. Generally, this short description is manually provided by the author of the news article to succinctly describe the article. Google uses meta tags *description* and *title*, along with several other latent parameters to generate snippets. Facebook has created the Open Graph Protocol that describes guidelines for meta tags. These guidelines allow content creators to control the display of their content on social networking websites.

Similarly, Twitter which supports the open graph protocol, also has its own guidelines for content sharing.

Table 5: Metatags used by AutoGSR.

Targeted For	Tag Name
Search Engines	title, description
Facebook	og:title, og:description
Twitter	twitter:title, twitter:description

Table 5 lists the various standard meta tags that we extract information from. In this model, we work on the text extracted from only these tags. We train a vanilla SVM classifier [2] with a linear kernel that has been shown to work exceptionally well with text classification tasks [4].

4.2.5 *Ensembler*

The goal of the ensembler is to take output probabilities from the individual ranking models and fuse them together to generate a final representative probability of the article. The representative probability score should provide a better classification accuracy than any of the models individually. We generate the representative probability score by performing a weighted average of the individual outputs, where weights correspond to the accuracy of each model:

$$P(l_p) = \frac{\sum_{i=i}^{|M|} c_i o_i}{\sum_{i=i}^{|M|} c_i}$$

where, $P(l_p)$ is the probability of classifying the article as protest article, c_i is the accuracy and o_i is the output of model i. The accuracy of a model is derived empirically based on manual validation.

4.3 Recommendation Models

The goal of the recommendation models is to generate partial or complete encoding suggestions for a given article. Broadly speaking these models can be grouped in three categories: 1) Protest Identification, 2) Protest Characterization, and 3) Usability. The *Protest Identification* models aim to identify when and where a protest happened: Geo Location Recommender along with Temporal Recommender identify city and date of protest. Once a protest has been identified, the *Protest Characterization* models work on characterizing a protest event by identifying the reason behind protest and the participating population group. Entity Based Naïve Bayes Recommender and MetaTags based recommender are two such models. The output from these models is passed through an *ensembler*, that combines these individual suggestions into a complete encoding. The interface shows both complete as well as individual encoding suggestions. Lastly, the *usability models* aim to improve the ease of using the interface, by generating clustering based full encoding recommendations.

4.3.1 *Geo-location Recommender*

This is a *protest identification* model, and aims to identify protest location(s) from a news article. The model begins by geo resolving the 'location' named entities found in the article. Geo resolving involves mapping location named entities to cities. These location entities can correspond to local points of interest, alternative name for the city or the official city name. The points of interest pose an interesting challenge as they tend to match to multiple cities. For example: *Main St.* can be found in almost every US city. The goal of the geo resolution is to map these location entities to a minimum number of cities with an assumption that generally a given news article refers only to a focused set of locations. We use the GeoNames database and perform the resolution in a top down fashion. First, all the cities are identified and then the ambiguous points of interest are mapped to these cities. The cities are assigned a confidence rankings based on the total number of mapping location entities. The case where the same city name is present in multiple states is resolved by selecting the most probable city based on past validated encodings.

Frequently, articles report a statewide or a nationwide protest. Such cases are identified by searching for various language specific forms of the keywords: statewide and nationwide, in the article. If such words are found, then we add the top level state/country to our list of location recommendations.

4.3.2 *Temporal Recommender*

This is another *protest identification* model that focuses on identifying protest date(s) from a news article. Article publish date is used as a date of reference and is identified either by the publish date meta tag or is inferred by the article fetch date. The reference date allows the model to resolve words like *yesterday* or *last Tuesday*. The temporal keywords are searched in following places: title, description meta tag and the sentences containing protest keyword(s). Temporal keywords found in title and description carry more confidence score as compared to the ones found in article text. Also, multiple mentions of the same date, increases the confidence score of that date.

4.3.3 *Entity Based Recommender*

This is a *protest characterization* model that identifies the salient features of a protest such as the reason of protest, participating population group and whether the protest was violent or peaceful. In context of AutoGSR, the reason behind a protest can be defined in only following six categories: 1) Employment and Wages, 2) Housing, 3) Energy and Resources, 4) Other Economic Policies, 5) Other Government Policies, and 6) Other. Similarly, the participating population group can be one among the following eleven: Agriculture, Business, Education, Ethnic, General Population, Labor, Legal, Media, Medical, Refugees and Religious. This model employs a multi class Naïve Bayes model trained on named entities extracted from article text and past protest encodings to generate probability score for event Type and population group categories.

4.3.4 *MetaTags Based Recommender*

This model is also a *protest characterization* model, and works very similar to the Entity Based Recommender in principle, but uses only the entities extracted from the title and the description MetaTag to determine event type and population group categories.

4.3.5 *Ensembler*

The task of the ensembler is to take the probabilistic outputs of the *protest identification and characterizations* models and generate complete encoding recommendations. The complete encoding recommendation includes location, date, event type and population group and is generated by finding the most probable individual recommendations in each category. Top two such complete recommendations are shown in the interface.

4.3.6 *Clustering Based Recommender*

This is a *usability model* that aims to increase the ease of using the system in two ways: first, by clustering similar news articles together and second by generating full tuple encoding recommendations based on validated encodings of other articles in the article cluster. Article clusters are generated in real time using the Lingo3G document clustering engine[12]. These clusters allow an analyst to work on related news articles together. Encoding recommendations are generated for un-validated documents using the validated encodings of other documents in the cluster. These recommendations are generated assuming that articles in the clusters are related and hence will have similar encoding. Please note that these recommendations are in addition to the recommendations generated by the ensembler.

5. EVALUATION RESULTS

As stated earlier, the goal of the EMBERS AutoGSR is to develop reliable ground truth civil unrest events while minimizing the manual effort required to do so. With this goal in mind, we evaluate our system alongside four aspects:

1. What is the reduction in number of articles realized after each step of the models ecosystem? (Section 5.1)
2. How does AutoGSR compare w.r.t. manually generated ground truth data? (Section 5.2)
3. What is the reduction in manual effort afforded by AutoGSR? (Section 5.3)
4. How does AutoGSR compare with state-of-the-art systems like ICEWS and GDELT? (Section 5.4)

The evaluation is performed using a manually generated list of civil unrest events for the same period, countries and news sources. These events are hand coded by a team of 15-18 political scientists and subject matter experts working for an independent agency (MITRE). As stated earlier, we refer to the MITRE organized set of ground truth events as GSR, to distinguish them from our AutoGSR system. We focus here primarily on 3 recent months: October, November and December, 2015 for the 10 Latin American countries mentioned earlier, viz. Argentina, Brazil, Chile, Colombia, Ecuador, El Salvador, Mexico, Paraguay, Uruguay, and Venezuela. The news articles are primarily reported in two languages: Spanish and Portuguese, with some English sources as well.

5.1 Reduction in number of articles

Here we present the overall reduction in number of articles for both protest and non protest articles after each stage of the AutoGSR pipeline for both Spanish (ES) and Portuguese (PT), fig. 5. For Spanish, the reduction in non protest articles after filtering models is 60% and after ranking models is 64%, thereby leading to a net reduction of 86%. Similarly, for Portuguese, the reduction in non protest articles after filtering models is 34% and after ranking models is 60%, thereby leading to a net reduction of 74%.

5.2 Quality and Coverage Evaluation

In order to determine quality, we need to identify how similar GSR and AutoGSR encoding extractions are for a given civil unrest event. As mentioned before, an event encoding consists of the following four entities – protest location (city level), protest date, reason of protest along with violence identification (event type) and protesting population group.

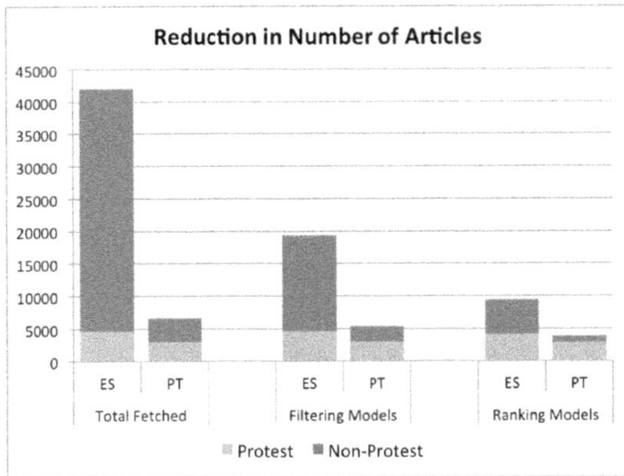

Figure 5: Reduction in number of protest and non-protest articles after each step.

We define Quality Score (QS) on a 4 point scale where each point correspond to how similar each of the encoding entity is as explained below:

$$QualityScore(QS) = DS + LS + ES + PS$$

where DS, LS, ES and PS denote the date score, location score, event type score and population score respectively. Each of these scores are defined next:

$$DS = 1 - min(|GSR_{eventdate} - AutoGSR_{eventdate}|, 7)/7$$

In other words, if the date of the event identified by the GSR is same as AutoGSR then DS is 1. Otherwise if they are further apart by 7 days, then DS is 0.

Location score (LS) is defined as:

$$LS = 0.33 + 0.66(1 - min(dist, 300)/300)$$

where dist denotes the distance (in km) between the city identified by GSR and AutoGSR city. Both GSR and AutoGSR use standardized city names from a World Gazetteer that also provides latitude and longitude values, required for the distance computation. Cities outside 300 km get a score of 0.33; same cities get 1 and cities within 300km get scores in the range [0.33, 1].

Event type score (ES) is defined in terms of triples (e_1, e_2, e_3) where e_1 is the event granularity, e_2 is the protest reason, and e_3 is the violence status. Each of these scores have a value of 0 if they don't match and 1 if they match.

$$ES = \frac{1}{3}e_1 + \frac{1}{3}e_2 + \frac{1}{3}e_3$$

Population score (PS) is simply a binary (0/1) score denoting whether we identified the correct population group or not. Finally, note that QS is designed to take values in the range [0, 4].

Note that the above mentioned Quality Score is generated only between a pair of event encodings for gsr and autogsr. For a given month, there can be thousands of such pairs and hence we need to find the most optimal mapping pairs. We resolve this issue by first constructing a bipartite graph between GSR and AutoGSR events where edge weights correspond to Quality Score between each pair. Then we construct a maximum weighted bipartite matching and consider this the most optimal mapping between GSR and AutoGSR events.

Table 6 shows the Average Quality Score, Precision and Recall for each of the ten countries for three months: Oct

Table 6: Quality and Coverage Evaluation for AutoGSR vs Manual GSR*.

Country	Quality Score			Precision			Recall		
	Oct	Nov	Dec	Oct	Nov	Dec	Oct	Nov	Dec
Argentina	-	3.24	3.21	-	0.85	0.94	-	0.53	0.49
Brazil	-	3.53	3.58	-	0.27	0.21	-	1.00	0.99
Chile	3.24	3.19	3.35	0.53	0.90	0.87	0.84	0.81	1.00
Colombia	3.17	3.24	2.71	0.95	0.97	0.94	0.81	0.63	0.92
Ecuador	3.09	3.20	3.20	0.60	1.00	0.86	1.00	0.84	1.00
El Salvador	3.33	3.09	3.10	1.00	0.89	0.80	0.91	1.00	1.00
Mexico	3.13	3.36	3.16	0.92	0.73	0.93	0.95	0.83	0.86
Paraguay	3.60	3.42	3.39	0.74	0.82	0.78	1.00	1.00	1.00
Uruguay	3.17	3.07	3.12	0.53	0.77	1.00	1.00	0.85	0.73
Venezuela	-	3.48	3.39	-	1.00	0.86	-	0.59	0.93

*In October no manual GSR was generated for Argentina, Brazil and Venezuela. Hence, we are unable to evaluate AutoGSR's performance

Table 7: Daily Time Series Correlation Comparison of ICEWS, GDELT and AutoGSR with Manual GSR.

Country	ICEWS vs. GSR	GDELT vs. GSR	AutoGSR vs. GSR
Argentina	0.13	0.26	**0.49**
Brazil	0.35	0.29	**0.70**
Chile	0.21	0.28	**0.51**
Colombia	0.33	0.23	**0.48**
Ecuador	0.50	0.19	**0.73**
El Salvador	nan	0.06	**0.57**
Mexico	-0.09	**0.35**	0.26
Paraguay	-0.12	0.10	**0.86**
Uruguay	-0.11	0.00	**0.41**
Venezuela	0.08	-0.08	**0.68**

2015, Nov 2015, and Dec 2015. Here recall corresponds to the number of events identified by the GSR that were also identified by AutoGSR; and precision corresponds to the number of events identified by AutoGSR that were also found in the GSR. As the results in Table 6 demonstrate, the AutoGSR system has a near perfect precision and recall, thereby indicating that the system identified almost all civil unrest events reported by the GSR while maintaining a really low false positive rate. Further, for these identified events, the quality of the extracted encodings is very close to the true GSR encodings.

Brazil is the only country which appears to have a high false positive rate which can be attributed to an incorrectly added news source. *Globo* is a big media conglomerate in Brazil that owns newspapers, news channels, and online real time news portals. While MITRE focuses only on the electronic version of the print newspaper (*oglobo.globo.com*), the AutoGSR system was fetching articles from **.globo.com*. These also included articles from the real time news portal *g1.globo.com* which reports events in real time without much verification. Hence, we identified several more protests because the evolving news stories were considered as different events. This is also corroborated by the fact that many of the g1.globo.com links are dead or have a short life span as links pointing to intermittent stories are removed once all the details about an event are known. Interestingly, Brazil has the highest Quality Score with a perfect recall pointing to the fact that all the events reported by GSR were still correctly identified by AutoGSR, and with very high quality. These extraneous sub domains were removed from the system in mid January 2016.

5.3 Reduction in Manual Effort

We evaluate both objectively and subjectively the reduction in manual effort. The objective evaluation is performed by comparing total resource hours required to generate GSR and AutoGSR, while subjective evaluation is done by surveying MITRE's analysts.

Tables 8 and 9 list the number of hours used by analysts to generate GSR and AutoGSR events. Table 10 shows minimum and maximum number of *resource hours* required per week by GSR and AutoGSR teams. The table also lists reduction figures. AutoGSR achieves an average reduction of 71-72% in manual effort.

In order to develop intuition behind this reduction in manual efforts, we surveyed the analysts from the MITRE team.

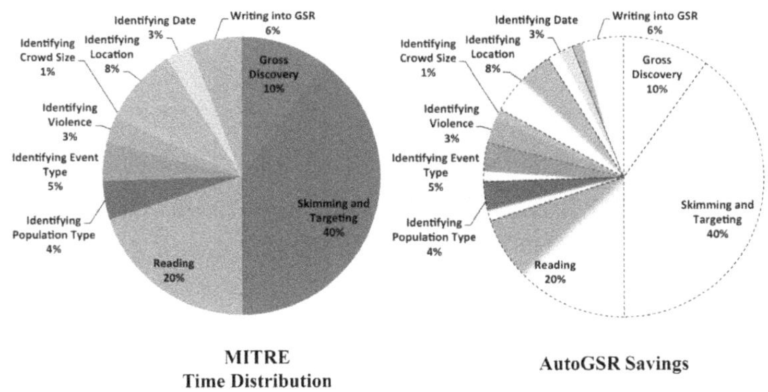

Figure 6: Time Distribution of MITRE's Analysts across various tasks of the GSR generation pipeline.

We requested them for an estimate of time that they spend in performing various sub tasks of the GSR generation process. Fig. 6 shows a rough sketch of the time distribution as reported by them. The figure also shows individual reductions provided for each of these sub tasks by AutoGSR. For each pie, the missing color corresponds to the provided savings: 1) *Gross Discovery*: 100% reduction as articles are fetched and loaded automatically into the system, 2) *Skimming and Targeting*: 100% reduction as articles with cumulative probability score greater than equal to 0.5 are automatically classified as protest articles, 3) *Writing into GSR*: almost 100% reduction as recording an extracted encoding is just a matter of few clicks, and 4) *Reading and Encoding Extraction*: based on the left over reduction percentage ($\sim$15%), it appears that the automatically generated encoding recommendations are providing almost 33% reduction for this task.

5.4 Comparison with ICEWS and GDELT

Finally, we evaluate AutoGSR's performance against the current state of the art systems: ICEWS and GDELT. For each of these systems, for the given countries and time period, we compare the daily events counts. Table 7 shows the Pearson correlation values between daily time series for each of the ten countries for ICEWS-GSR, GDELT-GSR and AutoGSR-GSR combinations. While AutoGSR shows high correlation with the GSR time series, the same is not true for ICEWS and GDELT thereby presenting a strong case in the favor of a system such as AutoGSR to generate reliable ground truth data. Figure 7a compares the daily counts

Table 8: Resource Distribution for GSR

Resource Type	#Resources	#Hours per Week
Analysts	10-15	20
Q. C. Analyst	2	24
Manager	1	10

Table 9: Resource Distribution for AutoGSR

Resource Type	#Resources	#Hours per Week
Analysts	4	15-20
Q. C. Analyst	1	15-20

Table 10: Total Resource Hours required per Week

	Min.	Max.
GSR	258 hrs	358 hrs
AutoGSR	75 hrs	100 hrs
Reduction	71%	72%

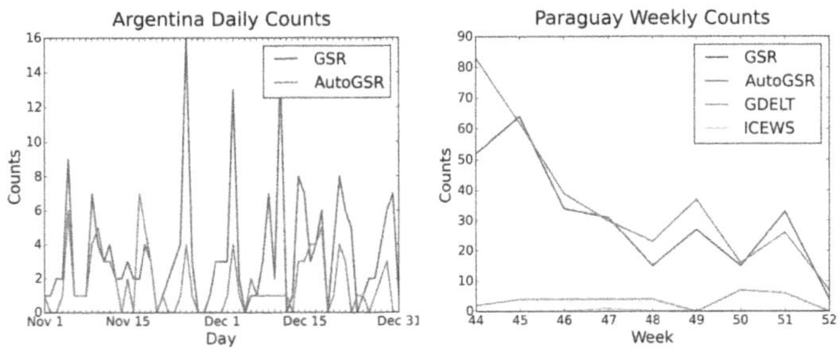

(a) Argentina Daily Counts Comparison

(b) Weekly Time Series Comparison for Paraguay

Figure 7: Daily and Weekly Time Series Comparison

between GSR and AutoGSR and Figure 7b compares the weekly time series for all the four systems.

6. DISCUSSION

We have presented AutoGSR, an automated event coding system for civil unrest events that is now in full continuous production use. In addition to developing and deploying the system, we have undertaken an entire life cycle analysis of how such a system would fit in an analyst's pipeline, with a view to quantify benefits over a purely manual approach. The results from our deployment indicate that the performance measures obtained by AutoGSR are compelling to support their continued use in an event modeling setting. Future work is now focused on expanding the scope of AutoGSR to new regions of the world, and to new classes of events, beyond civil unrest.

Acknowledgments

Supported by the Intelligence Advanced Research Projects Activity (IARPA) via DoI/NBC contract number D12PC000337, the US Government is authorized to reproduce and distribute reprints of this work for Governmental purposes notwithstanding any copyright annotation thereon. Disclaimer: The views and conclusions contained herein are those of the authors and should not be interpreted as necessarily representing the official policies or endorsements, either expressed or implied, of IARPA, DoI/NBC, or the US Government.

7. REFERENCES

[1] E. Boschee, P. Natarajan, and R. Weischedel. Automatic extraction of events from open source text for predictive forecasting. In *Handbook of Computational Approaches to Counterterrorism*, pages 51–67. Springer, 2013.

[2] C. Cortes and V. Vapnik. Support-vector networks. *Mach. Learn.*, 20(3):273–297, Sept. 1995.

[3] F. Hogenboom, F. Frasincar, U. Kaymak, and F. De Jong. An overview of event extraction from text. In *DeRiVE Workshop at ISWC 2011*, volume 779, pages 48–57. Citeseer, 2011.

[4] T. Joachims. Text categorization with suport vector machines: Learning with many relevant features. In *ECML '98*, ECML '98, pages 137–142, London, UK, UK, 1998. Springer-Verlag.

[5] Q. V. Le and T. Mikolov. Distributed representations of sentences and documents. *arXiv preprint arXiv:1405.4053*, 2014.

[6] K. Leetaru and P. A. Schrodt. Gdelt: Global data on events, location, and tone, 1979–2012. In *ISA Annual Convention*, volume 2. Citeseer, 2013.

[7] T. Mikolov, K. Chen, G. Corrado, and J. Dean. Efficient estimation of word representations in vector space. *arXiv preprint arXiv:1301.3781*, 2013.

[8] T. Mikolov, I. Sutskever, K. Chen, G. S. Corrado, and J. Dean. Distributed representations of words and phrases and their compositionality. In *Advances in neural information processing systems*, pages 3111–3119, 2013.

[9] K. Nigam, A. McCallum, S. Thrun, and T. Mitchell. Learning to classify text from labeled and unlabeled documents. In *AAAI '98*, AAAI '98/IAAI '98, pages 792–799, Menlo Park, CA, USA, 1998. American Association for Artificial Intelligence.

[10] K. Nigam, A. K. McCallum, S. Thrun, and T. Mitchell. Text classification from labeled and unlabeled documents using em. *Mach. Learn.*, 39(2-3):103–134, May 2000.

[11] S. P. O'brien. Crisis early warning and decision support: Contemporary approaches and thoughts on future research. *International Studies Review*, 12(1):87–104, 2010.

[12] S. Osinski and D. Weiss. A concept-driven algorithm for clustering search results. *IEEE Intelligent Systems*, 20(3):48–54, May 2005.

[13] N. Ramakrishnan and P. Butler et. al. 'beating the news' with embers: Forecasting civil unrest using open source indicators. In *KDD '14*, KDD '14, pages 1799–1808, New York, NY, USA, 2014. ACM.

[14] L. Ramshaw, E. Boschee, M. Freedman, J. MacBride, R. Weischedel, and A. Zamanian. Serif language processing effective trainable language understanding. *Handbook of Natural Language Processing and Machine Translation: DARPA Global Autonomous Language Exploitation*, pages 636–644, 2011.

[15] P. A. Schrodt. Tabari: Textual analysis by augmented replacement instructions. *Dept. of Political Science, University of Kansas, Blake Hall, Version 0.7. 3B3*, pages 1–137, 2009.

[16] P. A. Schrodt. Cameo: Conflict and mediation event observations event and actor codebook. *Pennsylvania State University*, 2012.

Compute Job Memory Recommender System Using Machine Learning

Taraneh Taghavi
Qualcomm Technologies Inc.
San Diego, CA, USA
ttaghavi@qti.qualcomm.com

Maria Lupetini
Qualcomm Technologies Inc.
San Diego, CA, USA
marial@qti.qualcomm.com

Yaron Kretchmer
Qualcomm Technologies Inc.
Santa Clara, CA, USA
yaronk@qti.qualcomm.com

ABSTRACT

This paper presents a machine learning approach to predict the amount of compute memory needed by jobs which are submitted to Load Sharing Facility (LSF®) with a high level of accuracy. LSF® is the compute resource manager and job scheduler for Qualcomm chip design process. It schedules the jobs based on available resources: CPU, memory, storage, and software licenses. Memory is one of the key resources and its proper utilization leads to a substantial improvement in saving machine resources which in turn results in a significant reduction in overall job pending time. In addition, efficient memory utilization helps to reduce the operations cost by decreasing the number of servers needed for the end-to-end design process.

In this paper, we explored a suite of statistical and machine learning techniques to develop a Compute Memory Recommender System for the Qualcomm chip design process with over 90% accuracy in predicting the amount of memory a job needs. Moreover, it demonstrates the potential to significantly reduce job pending time.

Keywords

Memory Utilization; Compute Memory Recommender System; Statistical and Machine Learning Techniques; Grid Computing

1. INTRODUCTION

In a large scale semiconductor firm like Qualcomm, compute and license environment provides the infrastructure and resources to enable the full cycle of the chip design process. These resources include hardware infrastructure (CPU, storage, memory), software licenses, and etc. The amount of compute resources needed by an end-to-end chip design process is substantially dependent on the design complexity through the entire design cycle and specifically prior to the final stage of it where the design is shipped for manufacturing, also known as "Tapeout".

A key challenge in any large scale semiconductor company is to effectively utilize the compute resources and optimally allocate them to parallel chip design processes. Effective utilization of compute resources yields a significant impact on setting the cost of the end-user devices which helps improving company's position in today's competitive market.

KDD '16, August 13–17, 2016, San Francisco, CA, USA.
 ISBN 978-1-4503-4232-2/16/08…$15.00.
DOI: http://dx.doi.org/10.1145/2939672.2939717

Machine memory, as one of the key compute resources of any job execution, needs to be utilized effectively to improve the efficiency of the design process and prevents any major slowdown or halt in the design flow. Over-requesting memory by a job causes other jobs to go into a pending state since they are using shared pools of resources. On the other hand, under-requesting memory by a job may lead to forceful exit of the job due to lack of required memory to successfully finish the job. Hence an effective and asymmetric memory allocation methodology needs to be adopted to ensure that all the jobs are receiving their needed memory requirement for proper execution.

In this paper, we explored several different models from classic statistical methods to more modern machine learning techniques to develop a memory recommender system based on the historical job execution data on a grid computing platform. Our model is capable of handling large volume of data for training and prediction and can be easily ported to a cloud computing architecture platform.

2. BUSINESS OPERATIONS OVERVIEW

2.1 Chip Design Process

Integrated circuit design, or IC design, is a subset of electronics engineering, which consists of logic and circuit design techniques required to develop and build an IC [1]. The initial chip design process begins with system-level design and architecture planning. This step is where a chip functionality and design is decided. Upon agreement of a system design, the engineers implement the functional models in a hardware description language like Verilog, System Verilog, or VHDL. The next step in the IC design process, physical design phase, is to map the design into actual geometric representations of all electronics devices, such as capacitors, resistors, logic gates, and transistors that will go on the chip. Since errors are expensive, time consuming and hard to spot, extensive testing needs to be done to make sure the mapping to transistors was done correctly and the manufacturing rules were followed faithfully. At the final stage of the design cycle for ICs, Tapeout, the artwork for the silicon photomask of the circuit is sent to be manufactured. After the chip is manufactured and returned back to the design company, massive testing is done to make sure all parts are working according to the specifications. Figure 1 shows the high level chip design process.

One of the main differences between chip and software design is the high cost of fixing design errors. Errors that are not corrected by the time silicon masks are manufactured usually require re-spins of some or all of the masks associated with significant capital expense and opportunity costs, frequently exceeding $10 million. As a result, much of the discipline of chip design is involved with early and frequent verification of the chip as it goes through the design process. The complexity of modern chip design, as well as market pressure to produce designs rapidly, has led to the extensive use of Electronic Design Automation (EDA) software for design, verification andp simulation of different steps

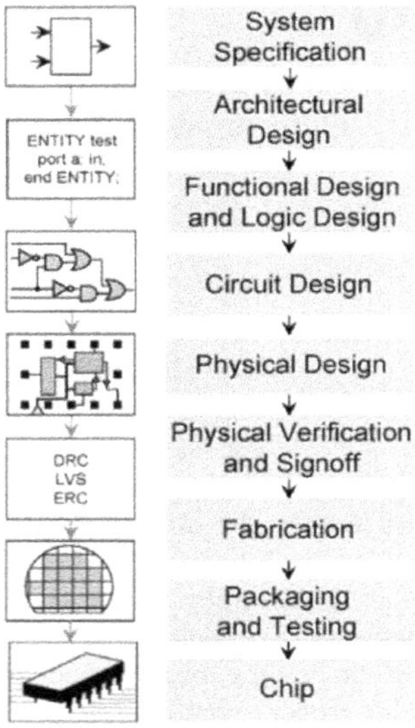

Figure 1. Major Chip Design Steps [1]

of the process. This entails utilizing massive amount of compute resources such as hardware, operating software, and EDA software licenses for simulation, design, and testing stages needed for a full cycle of a chip design. To have a successful and cost efficient design process, available compute resources such as CPU, memory, storage and automation tools and licenses have to be optimally utilized.

2.2 Load Sharing Facility (LSF®[1]) Scheduler in a Grid Environment

IBM Load Sharing Facility (LSF®) is a workload management platform and job scheduler for distributed high performance computing environments. It can be used to execute batch jobs on networked UNIX and Windows systems on many different architectures. It provides a comprehensive set of policy-driven scheduling features that enable users to take full advantage of the available compute infrastructure resources needed for successful job execution [2][10].

In a large scale design process with massive amounts of compute resources, there is a need for a scalable, fault-tolerant, and cost efficient computing power, such as that provided by a grid environment. Grid environments consist of a collection of clustered computers which form a heterogeneous grid computing foundation for a full cycle of design process. The grid environment can be thought of as a distributed system with non-interactive workloads and the ability to perform different tasks and applications [2][12].

The ability to handle scheduling of massive number of jobs on a heterogeneous network of resources make LSF® a viable choice as a workload manager to be utilized by chip design process in many semiconductor companies including Qualcomm Incorporation.

[1] LSF® is a trademark of Platform Computing Corporation and is licensed exclusively to IBM.

2.3 Compute Resource Management

Compute infrastructure and resources used in the chip design process make up a big portion of the total cost of the chip. An inefficient allocation of resources can cause a significant increase in job pending time which leads to inevitable delays in Tapeouts. Furthermore, it can reduce the productivity of the engineers while they wait a longer time for job completion. For these reasons, sustainable solutions for optimal utilization of compute resources are of utmost importance in a competitive market.

Using manual or trial and error methods to allocate compute resources needed for jobs are not regarded to be effective. In addition, due to the volume and complexity of the submitted jobs in a chip design cycle, it is very difficult, inefficient, and at times impossible for users to accurately predict the needed compute resources for successful job executions based on their experience. Hence, a need for machine learning intelligence emerges to effectively predict the resources needed in the chip design process.

3. BUSINESS CHALLENGE

In a grid environment, workload scheduling is done at global and local levels to increase efficiency and scalability. Job submission scripts are responsible for requesting computing resources at the local level and LSF® scheduler is responsible for communicating with all job submission scripts to manage the workload at the grid level. Hence, smart resource requesting mechanisms by job submission scripts enable efficient resource allocation by the LSF® scheduler.

Every job submissions script is configured for a specific type of job and includes the job parameters and paths, files and formats, selected EDA software products, and required compute resources. Job submission scripts are generally developed and maintained within design teams and are specific to each team's requirements. Compute resource requirements for each job is then specified by the team lead or the engineer based on their knowledge of past jobs and priority of the submitted job.

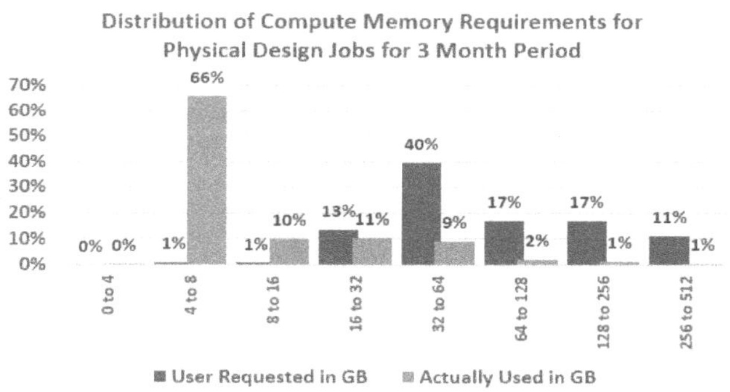

Figure 2. User Requested vs Actually Used Memory (GB)

In general, engineers tend to over-request the amount of compute resources including memory in order to make sure their jobs execute successfully. This phenomena can result in a substantial over-request of memory requirements once they get accumulated over all the jobs submitted in a grid environment. Figure 2 shows that 87% of a specific type of EDA jobs (physical design) for a three month period actually consumed 1MB to 32GB memory, while the users requested 1MB to 32GB of memory for only 17% of the jobs.

Figure 3 illustrates the same point from another perspective, memory by run time. It shows 36% of jobs actually need more

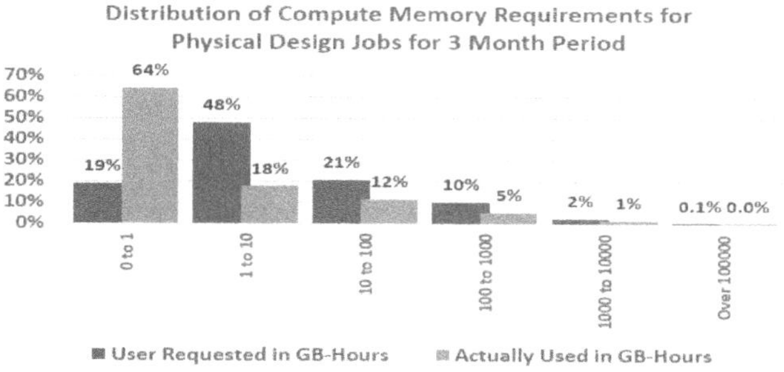

Figure 3. User Requested vs Actually Used Memory x Run Time (GB x Hour)

than 1 GB-Hour memory, in comparison to 81% of jobs requested more than 1 GB-Hour memory. These statistics exhibits great amount of memory over request. The main consequence of this over-request is that jobs have to wait for longer times in a pending state for memory resources to become available which results in longer design cycles. It also impacts engineer's efficiency as they have to wait longer for their jobs to complete which contributes to higher labor cost. Moreover, to accommodate for the peak request of memory resources, servers with larger memory blocks have to be purchased which leads to significant increase in operations cost, potentially resulting in higher price point for end-user devices, or lower profit margins.

These statistics demonstrates the huge potential for improvement in the memory allocation efficiency within Qualcomm's grid environment. An initiative was launched to explore this potential with the goal of closing the gap between the amount of memory requested by a job and the actual memory a job utilizes after it completes. A set of historical data on job submission was collected and an entire suite of techniques from statistical and machine learning paradigms were explored to build an efficient and accurate memory recommender system which includes dynamic user and management level dashboards, memory violation alerting system, and memory recommender engine. In the next two sections we explain the content of the data and the development of our recommender system.

4. DATA ANALYSIS, VISUALIZATION AND FEATURE SELECTION

At the start of the project, our approach was to build a predictive model that would consider the phase and week of the chip design life cycle, the intensity of the chip design analysis and testing at that point in time, plus the EDA software being used at that phase.

As shown in Figure 1, major chips follow this design flow. However, each chip is unique in the pace of its project plan and amount of required software licenses and compute resources. Within the available real-time data, the knowledge of how much of each resource is needed for the individual chip design was not readily available.

To better understand the basic patterns in the data we used descriptive statistics, machine learning, and visualization methods to mine the raw data. Some of our early findings were:

- Some design centers consume more memory than others for similar jobs
- Some contracting firm's temporary workers wasted more memory than others firms
- There are different patterns of memory requested by employees versus non-employees
- Work experience reflected by engineer title correlates with different memory use patterns
- The task influenced the amount of needed memory
- Individual user patterns are distinct
- The number of processors influence memory needs for a job
- The memory used in prior jobs is a good guess for subsequent jobs

The last four points from above became crucial features (variables) for our modeling efforts. These early findings confirmed our understanding of the behavior of a chip designer and test engineer. An engineer typically executes one design task or testing task for several hours up to several days. Their work will require the executions of computer jobs using only a few EDA tools out of many available.

We were able to exploit fields in the job submission scripts captured in the database that indicated the chip project under development, the phase of effort, (i.e., physical design vs physical implementation), the EDA software used, and the specific task (i.e., timing analysis vs floor-planning) for every engineer.

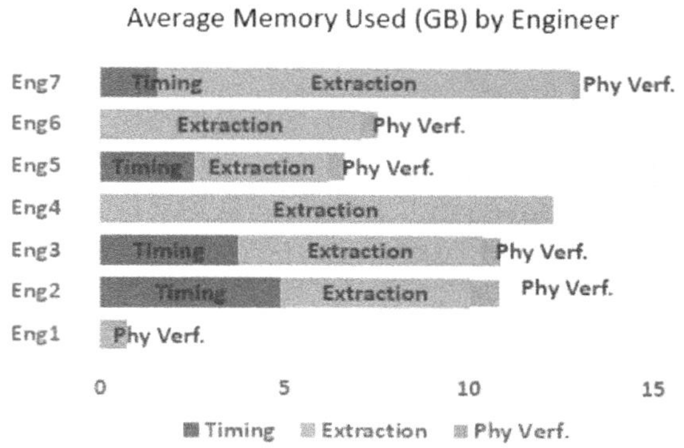

Figure 4. Sample of Memory Use by Physical Design Engineers for Project A during One Month.

Capturing this behavior was an essential factor in developing our compute memory prediction model. Figure 4 demonstrates the unique behavior for seven engineers during the same month for the same project. Some physical design engineers carried out all three tasks: chip timing, parasitic extraction and physical verification, some only one or two of these tasks. In addition, one can see, the average number of memory in gigabytes (GB) varied by task and engineer.

We also considered the number of compute processors requested for each job, the user's location, employment status (employee vs contractor), and engineer's department as possible predictors. In the end, the engineer's department, title, and employment status did not become part of the predictive model. The number of compute processors needed for the job did become an important variable in the model.

Finally, a key behavior captured in the model was the memory needed by past similar jobs. Memory used by past computer jobs, project, phase, task, and number of needed processors submitted by an engineer became the main variables in our predictive model.

5. BUSINESS REQUIREMENTS

One of the main business requirements was to build a predictive model which substantially minimizes compute memory waste over current method driven by engineering teams based on their project needs. In addition, the model should be robust enough to predict the amount of memory a job needs with high accuracy consistently over varying chip projects and time frames. The model and its subsequent implementation should be easy to understand, deploy and maintain and must be able to handle the data volume of more than 1.4 billion computer jobs executed by Qualcomm every year.

Another important business requirement was to limit under-prediction below a certain threshold. If a job is not assigned enough memory for its completion, the LSF® scheduler can be configured to gracefully grant more memory blocks to that job if the machine has enough available memory resources at run time. But if the machine is running out of memory resources, the job is terminated if it does not have enough memory reserved for its execution a priori. Job interruption carries an extremely exorbitant cost due to the high potential of delaying chip design.

6. STATISTICAL AND MACHINE LEARNING METHODS EXPLORED

In order to fulfill our business challenge with the given requirements, we explored an entire suite of models from classical statistics to more modern machine learning paradigms. Below we discuss the pros and cons of some of the best performing models we explored for this problem. In the next sections, we will explain the model selection process considering the tradeoffs between parsimony versus accuracy of different models. Here is the list of all models we explored:

1. *Neural Network (NN):* We used a multi-layer perceptron with one hidden layer. Neural network is generally very effective on a wide range of problems and can detect non-linear patterns very well even for very noisy or dirty data [15]. Although NN is a quite powerful tool to explore the patterns in the data, it has several disadvantages. The main disadvantage is that the generated model is not easily representable and is generally treated as a black box. Furthermore, due to the iterative nature of model training, the training run time is generally large specifically for big size data sets [3]. For these reasons, NN is not the best solution for our problem unless it shows a clear performance improvement compared to other models.
2. *Autoregressive Integrated Moving Average (ARIMA):* ARIMA is a time series analysis technique which can be tuned by using autoregressive, differencing and moving average parameters [4]. We built ARIMA models separately for every different task after we sorted our data by user, number of processors, and project in decreasing order of job submission time. After investigating stationarity and seasonality in our data, we determined that autoregressive models show the best performance among all ARIMA models, hence we included AR(3) and AR(11) in our model comparison. The main advantages of AR models are that they are simple and can easily be maintained. However, the main disadvantage is that they assume the same fundamental patterns exist over time which makes it somewhat not suitable for our purpose due to the change in requirements for different projects at different points of time.
3. *Kalman Filter (KF):* This time series analysis technique uses a series of measurements observed over time, containing statistical noise and other inaccuracies, and produces estimates of unknown variables that tend to be more precise than those based on a single measurement alone [5][13]. We used "astsa" package in R for our analysis of Kalman Filter. Like ARIMA, we build separate KF models by task. Even though KF models proved to be effective, model complexity is their major drawback.
4. *Multivariate Adaptive Regression Spline (MARS®)*[2]*:* This technique is a multivariate piecewise linear regression with adaptive knot selection process [6][14]. MARS® model is a very powerful tool to estimate non-linear patterns with piece wise splines and provides a somewhat light-weight model that can easily be deployed in real-time applications.
5. *Linear Regression (LR):* Least squares linear regression model is a simple and easy to deploy and maintain model which makes it a viable option for our problem. However, it is not capable of finding non-linear patterns in the data if they exist. Similar to the ARIMA model, we applied a linear regression model with an option of look backs of 3 and 11 lags. In addition, we build individual linear regression models for a combination of user, project, task and number of processors at each phase.
6. *Classification and Regression Trees (CART®)*[3]: Decision tree models are recursively partition the data space and fit a simple prediction model within each partition [16]. The main advantage of a CART® decision tree is its interpretability which makes it a suitable option for our problem, but the down side is that the tree size can get large quickly even with pruning.
7. *Chi-square Automatic Interaction Detector (CHAID):* CHAID performs multi-way split and uses Bonferroni adjustment to control tree size to overcome the disadvantage of the CART® model [7]. Unlike linear regression models, decision trees are capable of detecting non-linear patterns in the data, but generate more complex models.

7. EXPERIMENTAL RESULTS

To perform our experiments, we used the R statistical software and its packages and SPM Salford Predictive Modeler®[4]. We compared all the models we explored to the existing solution, which is to allocate memory based on user's request, specified in submission script. The results in this paper are based on the training data set of size over 0.5 million records which are collected for July 1 to Sep 30, 2015 time frame. The trained models were then used to predict the amount of memory needed on the testing set collected for Oct 1, 2015 for one major compute grid on all tasks for one specific phase, Physical Design. Table 1 captures the statistical metrics to compare different models using the test set. Training time for each model is also reported in the last column of this table.

As described in business requirements section, our major challenge was to make sure we limit under-prediction below a selected threshold due to severe consequence of under-allocation of memory slots to a job. Since currently about 5% of the jobs are submitted with memory request less than what actually is needed by those jobs, it is reasonable to set the threshold for under-prediction to be 5%. For this purpose, we build a 95% statistical upper prediction interval for our linear regression models using (1), where n is the data set size, X is the design matrix, S is the model standard deviation, and $t(0.05, n-2)$ is the upper 95% quantile from t-distribution with $n-2$ degrees of freedom [8].

---

[2] MARS® is a trademark of Jeril, Inc. and is licensed exclusively to Salford Systems.

[3] CART® is a trademark of California Statistical Software, Inc. and is licensed exclusively to Salford Systems.

[4] SPM Salford Predictive Modeler® is a registered trademark of Salford Systems.

Table 1. Statistical Metrics for Model Comparison

Model	R-SQ	RMSE (GB)	AIC	% Under Predicted Jobs	Training Time (min)
Requested by User	12%	84.3	NA	5%	NA
NN	88%	34.7	9330	58%	33
AR(3)	92%	32.6	9148	18%	8.5
AR(11)	93%	32.4	9152	16%	9.5
KF	94%	32.0	9118	49%	15
MARS®	92%	32.5	9158	54%	3
LR(3)+UPI$_{95}$	93%	32.6	9149	5%	1.1
LR(11)+UPI$_{95}$	93%	32.5	9156	5%	1.2
CART®	87%	35.2	9366	26%	5.5
CHAID	90%	33.8	9260	17%	6

$$UPI_{95} = t(0.05, n-2)\sqrt{S^2(1 + [1\ x](X^tX)'[1\ x]^t)} \quad (1)$$

We added the calculated prediction interval to our predicted values generated by the linear regression model to statistically guarantee that 95% of the jobs will be allocated memory more than what they actually need using our recommendations. Percentage of jobs with under-predicted amount of memory for each model is also reported for comparison.

In addition to minimizing the number of jobs which over-request memory, the recommender system must also minimize the amount of memory over-requested by long-running jobs. Once a job with a large run time acquires the memory amount it asks for, it will hold on to this amount until the job finishes. There are scenarios where a model results in smaller number of jobs with memory over-request compared to another model, but the jobs in the first model which over-requested memory might run for a longer time. To make sure we account for this situation we used a second set of metrics to compare different models as shown in Table 2.

These measures evaluate the ability of each memory recommender model to reduce wasted memory (GB) times the hours of the jobs' run time. We evaluated our models' behavior over different data sets over time. Average amount of over-prediction (GB) and over-prediction by run time (GB x Hour) are shown in Table 2. Average amount of under-prediction (GB) and under-prediction by run time (GB x Hr) is also recorded in this table so we can compare the behavior of different models in terms of under-prediction, specifically due to its potential sever consequences as described in section 5.

7.1 Model Selection Trade-offs

As Table 1 illustrates KF model shows the best R-SQ and the lowest RMSE. On the other hand, AR, MARS® and LR+UPI$_{95}$ model performances are also close to that of KF in these regards. The disqualifying factor for using KF and MARS® models is their high percentage of under-predicted jobs which violates our business constraints. AR models show significantly better result on their percentage of under-predicted jobs, but they are still above the threshold of currently used method which is requested by user. NN, CART® and CHAID model performances are not up to par with other models.

Table 2 shows the average under and over prediction per user for both memory (GB) and memory by run time (GB x Hr) which are consistent with the model performance results of Table 1. All models significantly improve the amount of over prediction over the current model. The KF model results in the least amount of over-prediction trading off larger amounts of under-prediction compared to AR and LR models. LR(11)+UPI$_{95}$ shows the lowest values on average under-prediction both for memory (GB) and memory by run time (GB x Hr), but it shows an slight increase in AIC/BIC values compared to LR(3)+UPI$_{95}$ model as shown in Table 1.

Considering all the trade-offs of model performance, parsimony, fulfillment of business constraints, and maintainability, overall we determined the LR(3)+UPI$_{95}$ model to be the most suitable solution for our memory recommender engine. Figure 5 shows the distribution of requested versus actual and predicted versus actual memory using LR(3)+ UPI$_{95}$ model for "Physical Design" phase on one compute grid which represents about 13% of all jobs submitted using EDA software in Qualcomm. As it can be seen in this figure, the predicted versus actual plot shows a significant performance improvement over the requested versus actual plot. The correlation of determination (R-squared) of the requested to actual memory was a dismal 12%, whereas the R-squared of the predicted to actual memory was an impressive 93%.

Table 2. Operational Metrics for Model Comparison

Model	Average Over Prediction (GB)	Average Over Prediction (GB x Hr)	Average Under Prediction (GB)	Average Under Prediction (GB x Hr)
Requested by User	365.6	1948.3	13.1	108.0
NN	138.7	1071.4	45.5	399.6
AR(3)	65.7	759.7	16.9	194.4
AR(11)	62.0	681.8	14.3	183.6
KF	47.4	642.8	42.9	324.0
MARS®	64.2	818.2	36.4	291.6
LR(3)+UPI$_{95}$	66.8	769.5	14.3	109.1
LR(11)+UPI$_{95}$	65.7	701.3	13.6	108.5
CART®	135.0	1032.4	41.6	388.8
CHAID	127.7	993.5	40.3	378.0

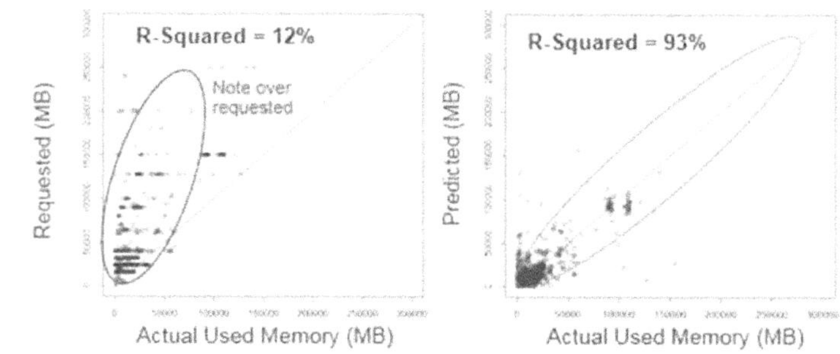

Figure 5. Plots of Requested by User and Predicted using LR(3)+UPI$_{95}$ Model versus Actual Memory Used

Besides memory requirements, another constraint which a job scheduler like LSF® needs to consider is the amount of CPU resources on a machine at the time of scheduling a job. Since CPU resources are associated with blocks of memory of size 4 or 16 GB, a useful metric to compare performance of a model is the histogram of the mismatch between predicted and actual memory built by discretizing the range of memory into bins similar to a confusion matrix. Figure 6 demonstrates the improvement in histogram of mismatch of memory bins between what a job requests versus what it actually uses when we use LR(3)+UPI_{95} prediction model. The figure clearly points out the substantial improvement in terms of matching the predicted and actually used memory bins of size 16GB.

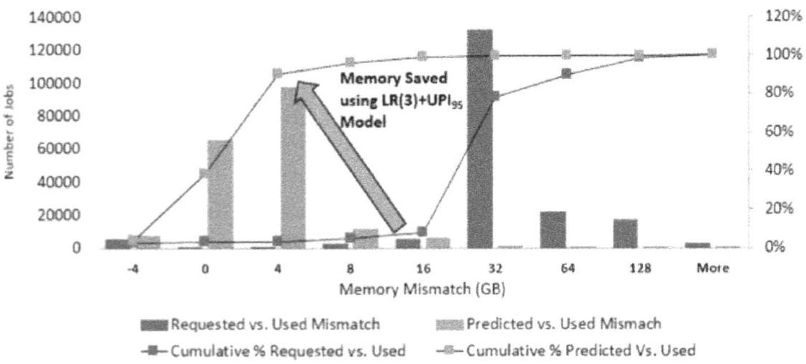

Figure 6. Improvement in Distribution of Memory Mismatch between Actual versus Predicted using LR(3)+UPI_{95}

Furthermore, to investigate the average performance of our model over time, we executed a comprehensive experiment which simulates the use of our model on a rolling window of 50 days. For the first day of the experiment, we built a model based on the data of last three months and applied the model to predict the amount of memory needed for all the jobs ran on that day for "Physical Design" task. Then we advanced our training set forward by one day, meaning we included the data of the actual memory used in that day in the training set. We re-modeled using this incremental change in our training set and applied the model to predict the amount of memory needed for the jobs ran on the second day and so on. Figure 7 illustrates the result of this comprehensive experiment. It compares the percentage of correct bins on the diagonal of confusion matrix of our model (shown in blue) versus the same value when the memory is requested by the user (shown in red). It can be seen that the percentage of entries on the diagonal of the confusion matrix improved from 15% to 91% on average by using our predictive model.

In the next section we describe the alerting system we developed based on the above predictive model using Splunk®[5] software.

[5] Splunk® is a trademark of Splunk Inc.

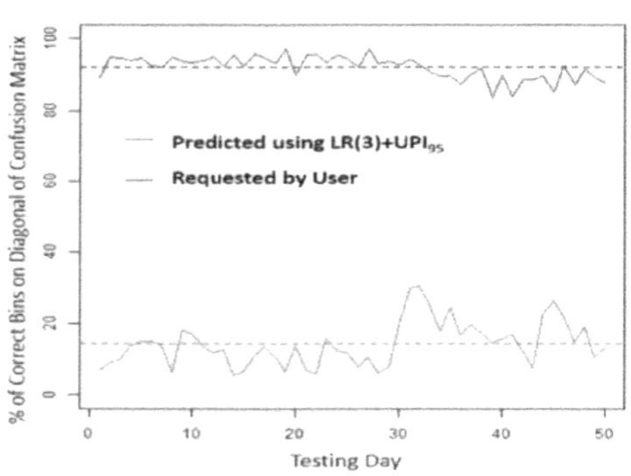

Figure 7. Comprehensive Experiment to Assess Overall Performance of our Prediction Model (LR(3)+UPI_{95})

8. SPLUNK® ALERTING SYSTEM

Splunk® is a software developed by the Splunk Corporation for searching, monitoring, and analyzing machine-generated big data, via a web-style interface. Splunk® captures indexes and correlates real-time data in a searchable repository from which it can generate graphs, reports, alerts, dashboards and visualizations [9][11].

We developed our alerting system through the Splunk® alerting application in two parts: model training and alert triggering. Model training is setup as a cron job using Splunk® scheduler which triggers every day at a specific time. This time is different for every grid depending on geographical location of that grid. We will be able to capture engineers' daily behavior of job submission to different projects and design phases. Once the model training completes, the linear regression model coefficients and upper prediction interval values for every combination of user, project, phase, task, and number of processors is populated into a Splunk® index for that day. The alerting application then gets triggered which queries this index to predict the amount of needed memory for every submitted job by every user and returns back the top 10% violators, users with highest mismatch between their requested and actually used memory. Those users receive an automated email with a report of the jobs they submitted and the amount of memory they requested and used along with our recommendation. They also receive a Splunk® dashboard which visualizes their memory usage and our recommendations over the jobs they submitted on that day.

9. SPLUNK® MANAGEMENT DASHBOARDS

Besides user dashboards, a suite of management dashboards were developed which aggregates and summarizes the memory usage at different hierarchical levels. Figures 8 and 9 illustrate an example of such dashboards. The amount of used, requested and recommended memory in terabytes (TB), and memory by run time (TB x Hour), aggregated by project are shown in these tables. Figures 10 and 11 show the same statistics aggregated at user level shown for top 10 violators. To preserve confidentiality, we substituted project and user names with generic names. It can greatly improve the memory allocation efficiency. Daily dashboards of these sorts are helping management team with tracking problematic areas from memory allocation efficiency standpoint leading to substantially optimizing operational cost.

10. DEPLOYMENT OF COMPUTE MEMORY RECOMMENDER SYSTEM

In order to integrate our recommender system as part of the chip design process with minimal disruption to this process, we decided to develop and deploy this system in three phases. Full development of this system was done using Python SciPy library in conjunction with the Splunk® alerting and dashboarding application.

Here are the deployment phases of our recommender system:

Phase 1. We developed a comprehensive monitoring system to detect the behavior of individual engineers in terms of their memory requests. For this purpose, we set up an informational alerting mechanism to alert the top 10% worst violators. Alerts were sent through the Splunk® alerting application as explained in previous section. The alerts are originally targeted for engineers who submit jobs in "Physical Design" phase on two major grids, but are intended to be expanded to other grids and to other functional areas in third phase. Besides the alerting system, we provided visualization dashboards for both engineers and management teams through the Splunk® dashboarding application.

Phase 2. In this phase we develop a memory recommender engine using Python Sci-Py libray and deploy this engine as part of the EDA flow for "Physical Design" tasks to substitute the user-specified requests for memory with the automated recommendations generated by this engine. We provide users with the capability of overwriting our recommendations with their own memory requests if they choose to do such. However, they will be alerted if they have over-requested memory greatly.

Phase 3. In the last phase we will expand deployment of our memory recommender system (including the automation engine and monitoring and alerting system) to other design phases besides "Physical Design".

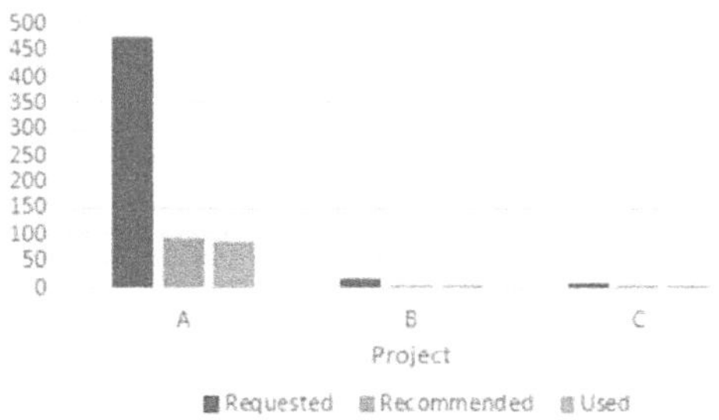

Figure 8. Requested vs. Recommended vs. Used Memory (TB) by Project

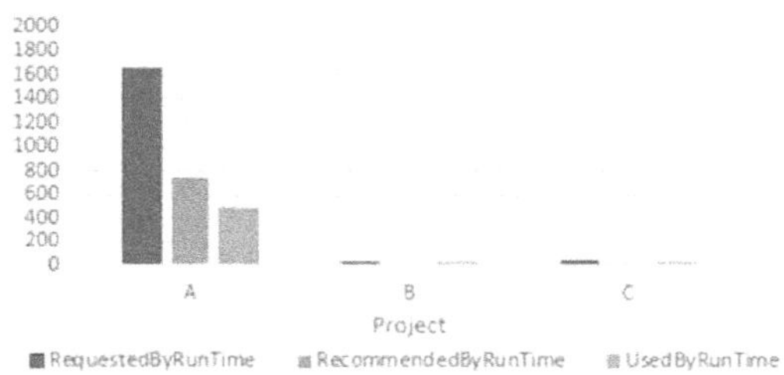

Figure 9. Requested vs. Recommended vs. Used Memory x Run Time (TB x Hour) by Project

11. IMPROVEMENT OF JOB PENDING TIME

Submitted jobs compete with each other to acquire their requested compute resources such as processors and memory. They are dispatched for execution by LSF® scheduler which evaluates the jobs' priority and resource needs. When jobs are highly over-requesting memory, they have to wait longer to acquire their requested amount of memory to be executed. The situation gets even worse when a job with a long run time over-requests memory. Since run time of jobs are not known a priori, the scheduler cannot plan ahead for these types of jobs. Once these jobs get launched, they cause other jobs to wait in a pending state for a longer time before the scheduler is able to dispatch them for execution. To evaluate the effect of using our prediction model on reducing job pending time, i.e., the time computer jobs wait to be dispatched for execution, we need to simulate LSF® behavior. IBM has developed a simulator for LSF® for their internal use, but do not provide it to external customers. For this reason, we developed an in-house basic version of the LSF® scheduler and compared our model performance on job pending time reduction with status quo situation on a suite of real jobs.

11.1.1 Basic LSF® Scheduler Simulator

We imitated similar scheduling behavior of the real LSF® scheduler with less number of resources in our basic simulator. This simulator composed of two servers parameterized to be of different sizes (128GB and 256 GB) and three queues with different priorities: high, medium and low. The job scheduling method is FIFO in each queue with highest probability of scheduling a job from high priority queue versus medium priority queue and so on. We filled up the queues in our simulator using real jobs submitted for the "Physical Design" phase on our major grid. Table 3 compares the effect of using our memory recommender engine on job pending time versus what is currently

Figure 10. Requested vs. Recommended vs. Used Memory (TB) for Top 10 Violators

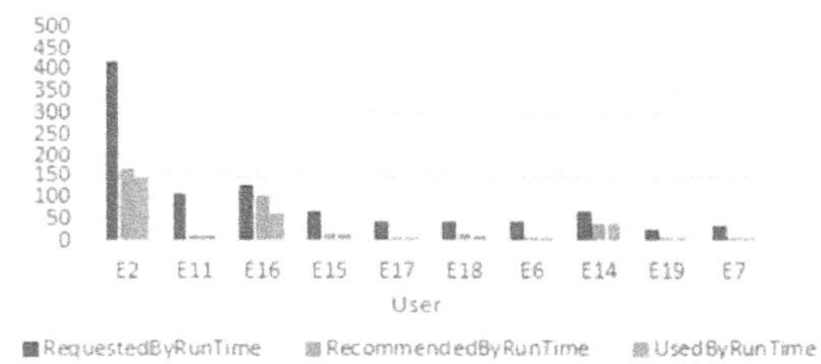

Figure 11. Requested vs. Recommended vs. Used Memory x Run Time (TB x Hour) for Top 10 Violators

requested by user using our basic LSF simulator. Note that these simulations are done using a mock-up version of the LSF® scheduler on much limited number of servers and considers memory as the only compute resource needed for job submission. The experiment clearly demonstrates the high potential for improvement in job pending time, however the actual improvement percentages should be looked at with caution and shall not be considered as standard.

Table 3. Average Pending Time Reduction for Physical Design Jobs on Grid 1

Server Size	Requested by User	LR(3)+UPI_{95}	Improvement (%)
128 GB	43 min	28 min	34%
256 GB	47 min	27 min	27%

12. BENEFITS OF IMPROVING MEMORY UTILIZATION

There are multiple benefits to Qualcomm if compute memory is optimally resourced. The first benefit is the reduced annual cost of compute hosts with high quantities of installed memory. Whenever possible, it is desirable to purchase cheaper computers with 16GB memory and four processors, rather than computers with high level of memory resources. It is estimated that the annual savings could be in the millions of dollars. This predictive model could also be leveraged to minimize compute costs for jobs that could be run in a cloud environment.

As demonstrated by simulations discussed in the preceding section, pending time can potentially be reduced 27% to 34% for a subset of the jobs. Thus, another benefit of improved memory allocation utilization is the potential for the reduced wait time of jobs. Reducing pending time will greatly improve the throughput of compute jobs, thus enabling more chip design and test jobs to be executed resulting in a better quality for the chip. This reduces the wait time for an engineer to get results back and improves the engineer's productivity. Finally, this new system can contribute by helping to bring the chip to market faster, which is an essential advantage in today's competitive markets. Qualcomm places a high value on all these contributions.

13. LESSONS LEARNED

This Compute Memory Recommender project showed that the computer memory needs could be predicted with an acceptable level of accuracy and be leveraged to improve throughput efficiency. This is in addition to the benefits achieved by reduction in computer resource cost. We confirmed that cleverly constructed simple predictive models, like linear regression, could provide the solid business value, and is easier to deploy than more sophisticated machine learning and statistical models like neural nets, Kalman filters, and ARIMA. The main advantage of using a linear regression model is that it is simple, parsimonious, a good predictor, easy to understand, and easy to implement.

Another lesson learned, (or rather re-enforced) is to take novel approaches to defining the problem, rather than tackling a challenge with an expected "chip-design life cycle" approach. We found we could use a recommender model approach that recognized the unique tasks and cadences of each engineer's work, along with their immediate past tasks to predict their next computer job's needs. Thinking more like a "social media" modeler lead us to construct many simple individual models. An alternate "life cycle" approach which was not feasible with our available data would have been to create a model that predicted a standard memory need for a chip project in the Nth week of the design cycle for a given task. With the high level of accuracy and flexibility which our recommender model provides, a "life cycle" model is not necessary.

14. SUMMARY

The implementation plan for our Compute Memory Recommender system is to deploy it across all chip design phases in 2016. At the time of writing this paper, we demonstrated the ability to create predictive models with R-squared of over 90% for the "Physical Design" phase. The tasks done in "Physical Design" phase are some of the most compute intensive jobs in semiconductor development. We believe we will see similar good results with other design phases.

In the course of the analysis and model development, we found we needed to take a "recommender" model approach that predicts the needs of compute memory for jobs which run the next day for an engineer doing a specific task for a given project. We tested many statistical models and machine learning techniques which produced similar results. In order to provide a simple, understandable model that could be readily implemented and updated, we chose a linear regression model with lagged variables capturing prior usage by the individual engineer. An upper 95% statistical prediction interval was added to our model recommendation to ensure jobs do not under-request memory more than 5% of the time based on the business requirements.

The implementation of the recommender model used the Splunk® data repository and software. Predictive models were written in Python code, and deployed in conjunction with the Splunk® application. This system is run daily to train and build unique prediction models for each user by project, EDA software, number of processors, and compute grid. The Splunk® alerting system contacts the engineers with the greatest mismatch of requested and actual compute memory usage on a daily basis.

Our long term goal is to incorporate our compute memory recommendations from the model into job submission scripts for all design phases. This would make the job resource requests at runtime efficient. Having these capabilities will not only save Qualcomm on the cost of computer hardware, but improve job turn-around time thus saving engineering time. Potentially, the greatest contribution of improving the utilization of all these resources, is expediting the semiconductor's time to market.

15. REFERENCES

[1] Lavagno, L., Martin, G., Scheffer, L., 2006. Electronic Design Automation for Integrated Circuits Handbook, Taylor & Francis.

[2] Goering, Richard, March 8, 1999. Load Sharing Brings Kudos, EE Times Online.

[3] Haykin, S., 2007. Neural Networks, a Comprehensive Foundation, Second edition, Prentice Hall of India.

[4] Shumway, R., Stpffer, D., 2011. Time Series Analysis and Its Applications, Third edition, Springer.

[5] Simon, D., 2006. Optimal State Estimation: Kalman, H Infinity, and Nonlinear Approaches. Wiley-Interscience.

[6] Hastie T., Tibshirani R., and Friedman J.H., 2009. The Elements of Statistical Learning, 2nd edition. Springer.

[7] Kass, G. V., 1980. An Exploratory Technique for Investigating Large Quantities of Categorical Data, Applied Statistics, Vol. 29, No. 2, pp. 119–127.

[8] Sheather S., 2009. A Modern Approach to Regression with R, Springer.

[9] Carasso, D. 2012. Exploring Splunk: Search Processing Language (SPL) Primer and Cookbook. New York, NY: CITO Research.

[10] Zhou, S., Zheng, X., Wang, J., and Delisle, P. 1994. Utopia: A Load Sharing Facility for Large, Heterogeneous Distributed Computer Systems. Software-Practice and Experience, Vol 23, No. 2, pp. 1305-1336.

[11] Zadrozny, P., Kodali, R., 2013. Big Data Analytics using Splunk. Apress.

[12] Foster, I., Zhao, Y., Raicu, I., Lu S., 2008. Cloud Computing and Grid Computing 360-Degree Compared, Grid Computing Environments Workshop, GCE'08, pp. 1-10, doi: 10.1109/GCE.2008.4738445.

[13] Grewal, M.S., Andrews A.P., 2014. Kalman Filtering Theory and Practice Using MATLAB, 4th Edition. John Wiley and Sons.

[14] Friedman, J. H. 1991. Multivariate Adaptive Regression Splines. The Annals of Statistics Vol 19, No 1. doi:10.1214/aos/1176347963.

[15] Widrow B., Rumelhard D.E., and Lehr M.A., Neural Networks: Applications in Industry, Business and Science, 1994, Communications of the ACM, Vol. 37, pp. 93-105. doi: 10.1145/175247.175257.

[16] Loh W.Y., 2011. Classification and regression trees. WIREs Data Mining and Knowledge Discovery, Vol 1, pp 14–23

Scalable Time-Decaying Adaptive Prediction Algorithm

Yinyan Tan[1], Zhe Fan[1], Guilin Li[1], Fangshan Wang[1], Zhengbing Li[1], Shikai Liu[1], Qiuling Pan[1]
Eric P. Xing[2], Qirong Ho[2]
[1]Research and Standard Department, Huawei Software Technologies CO. LTD
[2]School of Computer Science, Carnegie Mellon University
tanyinyan, fanzhe, liguilin, wangfangshan, zhengbing.li, liushikai, panqiuling@huawei.com
epxing, qho@cs.cmu.edu

ABSTRACT

Online learning is used in a wide range of real applications, *e.g.*, predicting ad click-through rates (CTR) and personalized recommendations. Based on the analysis of users' behaviors in Video-On-Demand (VoD) recommender systems, we discover that the most recent users' actions can better reflect users' current intentions and preferences. Under this observation, we thereby propose a novel time-decaying online learning algorithm derived from the state-of-the-art FTRL-proximal algorithm, called Time-Decaying Adaptive Prediction (TDAP) algorithm.

To scale Big Data, we further parallelize our algorithm following the data parallel scheme under both BSP and SSP consistency model. We experimentally evaluate our TDAP algorithm on real IPTV VoD datasets using two state-of-the-art distributed computing platforms, *i.e.*, Spark and Petuum. TDAP achieves good accuracy: it improves at least *5.6%* in terms of prediction accuracy, compared to FTRL-proximal algorithm; and TDAP scales well: it runs 4 times faster when the number of machines increases from 2 to 10. In our real running business cases, TDAP significantly increases the degree of user activity, which brings more revenue than existing ones for our customers.

1. INTRODUCTION

Online learning techniques [3, 9, 19, 24, 26, 30, 32] are powerful tools for a wide range of emerging applications, from online advertising [25] and personalized recommendation [2, 28], to unusual events detection [35] and suspicious URLs identification [23]. For example, in an online IPTV Video-On-Demand (VoD) recommender system for one of our customers, a giant Telcom company from Mainland China, the accuracy of prediction (*e.g.*, AUC) can be significantly improved at least 4% using online learning techniques compared to traditional batch (offline) learning techniques [12, 18, 37].

KDD '16, August 13–17, 2016, San Francisco, CA, USA

ISBN 978-1-4503-4232-2/16/08...$15.00
DOI: http://dx.doi.org/10.1145/2939672.2939714

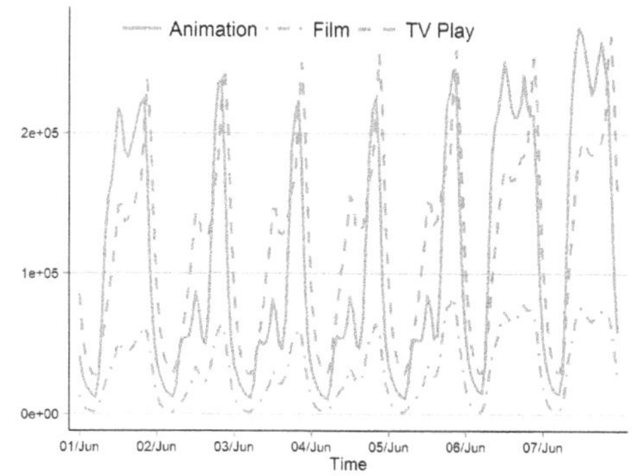

Figure 1: The fast changing users' watching counts on different types of videos (Film, TV play and Animation) from 2015-06-01 to 2015-06-07 on an online IPTV VoD service.

To date, people and devices (from smart phones, to VR Boxes, to coffee machines and cars) generate large volume of data every day, which are with *fast-varying* (or *fast-changing*) nature (*a.k.a.* concept drifting [11]). However, existing online learning techniques may *not* be a good fit for such fast-changing data, which are usually in form of examples with features and labels in practice. Let's first illustrate one of such data taken from a real-world application,

Example 1: Figure 1 shows features about users' watching counts on three different types of videos (Film, TV play and Animation) during the time period from 2015-06-01 to 2015-06-07 on an online IPTV VoD recommender system in a Telcom company from Mainland China.

From Figure 1, we observe that the watching counts on different types of videos vary a lot under different time period. In particular, in weekdays (from 2015-06-02 to 2015-06-05), the watching counts of TV play at working hours (08:00-18:00) on average are larger than those of the other two types of videos (*i.e.*, Animation and Film); Animation views are the most from 18:00 to 20:00; and the number of TV play increases again after 20:00. Besides, Animation views from 08:00 to 18:00 on weekends (from 2015-06-06 to 2015-06-07) and Children's day (2015-06-01) are larger than those of the other two, which typically differ from the case in weekdays (as above).

In short, from the above observation, we note that the varying of users' watching counts on different types of videos between day and night, or between weekdays and holidays, typically implies that the users' watching preferences are changing rapidly along the time series, which in fact brings a big challenge to the design of the online learning algorithm for the recommender system. □

The above example raises one crucial concern to the existing online learning algorithm design: *how to fit and scale those big and fast-changing online data efficiently and practically?* To answer the question, a *scalable time-decaying online learning algorithm* is in need. However, two challenges need to be addressed.

The first challenge is that the time-decaying algorithm requires to *fit the fast-changing online data*. Unfortunately, up to date, previous works [19,24,25,30,32] have *not* addressed it well. On one hand, previous time-decaying algorithms either weight data (or examples) by time-decaying functions (*e.g.*, [16,17]) or just discard outdated examples (*e.g.*, [3]), which require full memory or keep only recent examples, respectively. On the other hand, existing online learning algorithms (*e.g.*, mirror descent (MD) algorithm like TGD [19] and FOBOS [30], and follow-the-regularized-leader (FTRL) algorithm like RDA [32] and FTRL-proximal [24,25]), which do *not* take the changes of the data into account, may *not* respond the changes correctly. And worse still, the target model generated from the existing online learning algorithms may no longer be suitable for current data distribution, since older history of models are equally weighted as the recent ones in the learning procedure, which may decrease its (*i.e.*, the target model's) effectiveness.

For the second challenge, the time-decaying algorithm needs to *scale the big fast-changing online data*. To the best of our knowledge, previous works [34,36,37] only study the parallelism of MD-like algorithms. And the parallelism of FTRL-like algorithms are mentioned in [25] only, *no* detailed solution is provided.

Contributions. This paper addresses scalable online learning problem with fast-changing data. The contributions are characterized as below.

(1) We define a problem called *time-decaying online convex optimization* TOCO problem (Section 2), where the target model approaches to the most recent models while older history of the models are deemphasized, following a user-defined time-decaying function.

(2) We propose a *time-decaying adaptive prediction* TDAP algorithm to solve TOCO problem (Section 3), which incorporates with both the state-of-the-art FTRL-proximal algorithm and an *exponential time-decaying* mechanism over model update. *Recursive closed forms* of the model update functions are proposed for computational efficiency and memory saving.

(3) To scale big data, we first parallelize the TDAP algorithm following the *data parallel* scheme [14] under *bulk synchronous parallel* (BSP) [6] consistency model (Section 4), in which recursive update methods considering time-decaying factors are proposed, and detailed implementations are provided. To avoid the unnecessary costs due to the synchronization policy ("blocking" of stragglers) of BSP, we further parallelize the algorithm under *stale synchronous parallel* (SSP) model, with accuracy guarantees from [13].

(4) Under real-world datasets, we experimentally evaluate our algorithm on top of two well-known platforms (Section 5): (a) general big data analytic platform Spark [27] under BSP model; and (b) specific machine learning platform Petuum [33] under SSP model. It is worth highlighting that TDAP achieves good accuracy: it improves *5.6%* prediction accuracy, compared to FTRL-proximal algorithm, on both platforms; and TDAP *scales* well: it runs 4x speedup when the number of machines increases from 2 to 10. We further observe that TDAP on Petuum runs faster than that on Spark, and the former enjoys better scalability with more machines.

In our production IPTV VoD service, when we switched from FTRL-proximal to TDAP, we observed *5% more users engaging* on our service, and *10% longer engagement time* per user, approximately. We also observed that TDAP on Petuum can process approximately *one order of magnitude* more users than Spark, with the same cluster setup. While both TDAP on Petuum and Spark are viable, we found that deployment was easier and more efficient using Petuum.

Organization. This paper is organized as below: In Section 2, we review some related work and formulate our TOCO problem; We propose our TDAP algorithm to solve the problem in Section 3; Section 4 then parallelize the TDAP algorithm under both BSP and SSP consistency model; We experimentally verify our algorithm in Section 5 and conclude this paper in Section 6.

2. ONLINE LEARNING ALGORITHM

In this section, we first introduce the related work. We then give some details of the FTRL-proximal algorithm since our algorithm are derived from the FTRL-proximal algorithm due to its superior performance. We end this section by formulating our problem.

2.1 Related Work

We characterize related work as follows.

Algorithms with time-decaying property. Numbers of time-decaying algorithms are proposed to address the concept drifting [11] problem. On one hand, for gradual concept drifting, *full* memory based approaches (*e.g.*, [16] and [17]) use exponential or linear time-decaying functions to weight data (or examples), *i.e.*, the older the example, the smaller the impact. For abrupt ones, on the other hand, *partial* memory based methods (*e.g.*, [3]) are proposed by discarding examples outside a pre-defined window, only recent examples in the window are taken into account.

In contrast, we differ from the above as: (a) unlike full memory based methods, we do *not* require to store all examples, which saves memory; (b) We consider all examples in model training, such that information in previous examples are not discarded; and (c) Our algorithms are able to tackle *both* gradual and abrupt concept drifting problems, with tuning the time-decaying factor (to be seen in Section 3).

Online convex learning algorithms. Various online learning algorithms are proposed to solve the online convex optimization problem. We characterize it as the following two types: (a) Mirror descent (MD) algorithms like truncated gradient descent [19] and FOBOS [30]; and (b) Follow-the-regularized-leader (FTRL) algorithms like RDA [32] and FTRL-proximal [26]. Moreover, [24] proves the equivalence between the mirror descent algorithms and the FTRL algorithms, and in particular, FTRL-proximal outperforms the others in terms of accuracy and sparsity [25], and are widely used in industry, *e.g.*, recommender system [2,28] and Advertisement system [25].

However, our algorithms differ from the previous ones in the followings: (a) The effects of the older history of the models on target model are *scaled down* with an exponential time-decaying function, while existing methods do *not*; and (b) The time-decaying factors are embedded into the recursive closed form of model update functions, similar to the FTRL-proximal algorithm in [25].

Parallelism of online learning algorithm. In the literature, there are various existing works on parallelized machine learning algorithm [10, 12, 18]. Meanwhile, lots of machine learning platforms are proposed [1, 8, 22]. Among others, relate to online learning context, techniques for parallelizing mirror descent (MD) algorithms, in particular, stochastic gradient descent (SGD) algorithm have been intensively studied. [36] proves that parallelized SGD converges well with decayed updates. [37] presents the first parallelized SGD including a detailed analysis and experimental evidence. [34] proposes a user-friendly programming interface for parallelizing SGD. [25] also mentions the parallelism of the FTRL-like algorithms, but *no* detailed solution is given.

However, in contrast to previous works, we (a) propose *recursive* model parameters update functions embedded with exponential time-decaying factors in distributed (multi-machines) setting; (b) provide practical implementations of our algorithm (FTRL-like algorithm) for parallelism on both BSP [6] and SSP [13] consistency model in online learning scenario; and (c) compare the performance on two well-known platforms: (i) general big data analytic platform (*i.e.*, Spark [27]) for BSP model; and (ii) specific machine learning platform (*i.e.*, Petuum [33]) for SSP model. We conclude some interesting results in the experiments and hope that all practitioners get enlightened from it.

2.2 FTRL-Proximal Algorithm

In this subsection, we give the details of the FTRL-proximal algorithm. We start with the optimization problem that the algorithm is proposed for. We first establish some notations to be used in the following. We denote a vector $\mathbf{g}^{(t)} \in \mathbb{R}^d$, where t indicates the t-th training examples. The i-th entry in vector $\mathbf{g}^{(t)}$ is defined as $g_i^{(t)}$, and $\mathbf{g}^{(1:t)} = \sum_{s=1}^{t} \mathbf{g}^{(s)}$. We use data and examples interchangeably if the context is clear.

Optimization problem. Given a time step $T \geq 1$, a sequence of training examples with features $\mathbf{x}^{(t)} \in \mathbb{R}^d$ and labels $\mathbf{y}^{(t)}$, $t \in [1, T]$, the optimization problem that FTRL-proximal algorithm solved takes the form of

$$\mathbf{w}^{(T)} = \arg\min_{\mathbf{w}} \Big\{ \sum_{t=1}^{T} L(\mathbf{w}, \mathbf{x}^{(t)}, \mathbf{y}^{(t)}) + R(\mathbf{w}) \Big\}, \quad (1)$$

in particular,

- $\mathbf{w}^{(T)} \in \mathbb{R}^d$ is the target model parameters to be computed;
- $L(,,)$ is a convex loss function of the prediction function, *e.g.*, least square loss in linear regression, or logistic loss in logistic regression; and
- $R(\mathbf{w})$ is a convex regularization term, *e.g.*, L_1-norm, L_2-norm or a linear combination of both.

Model update function. To solve the optimization problem in Equation 1, at each iteration $t \in [1, T]$, the FTRL-proximal algorithm updates the model parameters iteratively, *i.e.*, $\mathbf{w}^{(t+1)}$ takes the form of

$$\arg\min_{\mathbf{w}} \Big\{ \mathbf{g}^{(1:t)} \cdot \mathbf{w} + \lambda_1 \|\mathbf{w}\|_1 + \lambda_2 \|\mathbf{w}\|_2^2 + \frac{1}{2} \sum_{s=1}^{t} \sigma^{(s)} \|\mathbf{w} - \mathbf{w}^{(s)}\|_2^2 \Big\}, \quad (2)$$

where

- $\mathbf{g}^{(t)} \in \mathbb{R}^d$ is a vector of gradients of loss function $L(\mathbf{w}, \mathbf{x}^{(t)}, \mathbf{y}^{(t)})$ in Equation 1;
- $(\lambda_1 \|\mathbf{w}\|_1 + \lambda_2 \|\mathbf{w}\|_2^2)$ is the regularization term corresponding to $R(\mathbf{w})$ in Equation 1; and
- $\frac{1}{2} \sum_{s=1}^{t} \sigma^{(s)} \|\mathbf{w} - \mathbf{w}^{(s)}\|_2^2$ is a *smoothing term*, importantly, such smoothing term does not change the optimum of the original problem in Equation 1, it aims to speed up convergence and improve accuracy.

  Moreover, the vector $\sigma^{(t)}$ is defined in terms of the learning-rate schedule, *i.e.*, $\sigma^{(t)} = \frac{1}{\eta^{(t)}} - \frac{1}{\eta^{(t-1)}}$, such that $\sigma^{(1:t)} = \frac{1}{\eta^{(t)}}$. And $\eta_i^{(t)}$ is a *per-coordinate learning rate* proposed in [25] as,

$$\eta_i^{(t)} = \frac{\alpha}{\sqrt{\sum_{s=1}^{t} (g_i^{(s)})^2}}, \quad (3)$$

  where α is set as twice the maximum allowed magnitude for $\mathbf{w}_i$ to give the best possible regret bound [25].

As reported in [25], the update function in Equation 2 can be transformed into a recursive closed form, *i.e.*, the value $\mathbf{w}^{(t)}$ can be recursively computed from $\mathbf{w}^{(t-1)}$. An efficient implementation with pseudocode is then provided based on the recursive form. And better still, FTRL-proximal algorithm outperforms the other classical online learning algorithms (*e.g.*, FOBOS and RDA) in terms of accuracy and sparsity, Therefore, in this paper, we derive our techniques from the FTRL-proximal algorithm. We consider a possible intuitive modification to FTRL-proximal, that lets it adapt faster to changes in data distribution.

2.3 Problem Definition

As motivated in Sec. 1, we want to tackle the data with fast-changing nature for online learning scenario, which indicates that the target model approaches to the most recent model while older history of the model can be deemphasized. Thus, we state the time-decaying online convex optimization TOCO problem as below.

Definition 1: Given a time step $T \geq 1$, a sequence of training examples with features $\mathbf{x}^{(t)}$ and labels $\mathbf{y}^{(t)}$, $t \in [1, T]$, the time-decaying online convex optimization, denoted as TOCO, is stated as

$$\mathbf{w}^{(T)} = \arg\min_{\mathbf{w}} \Big\{ \sum_{t=1}^{T} L(\mathbf{w}, \mathbf{x}^{(t)}, \mathbf{y}^{(t)}) + R(\mathbf{w}) + \sum_{t=1}^{T} F^{(T)}(t) S(\mathbf{w}, \mathbf{w}^{(t)}) \Big\}. \quad (4)$$

□

The objective function in Equation 4 is similar to that of Equation 1, except that we introduce an additional term as $\sum_{t=1}^{T} F^{(T)}(t) S(\mathbf{w}, \mathbf{w}^{(t)})$ to model the time decay of our target model. More specifically, (a) $F^{(T)}(t)$ is a *monotonic increasing time-decay function* (to be defined shortly) with independent variable t, and (b) $S(\mathbf{w}, \mathbf{w}^{(t)})$ is a smoothing term, *i.e.*, $\frac{1}{2}\|\mathbf{w} - \mathbf{w}^{(t)}\|_2^2$.

The intuition here is that with the help of time-decaying function, the target model $\mathbf{w}^{(T)}$ *cannot* differ too much compared to those recent model, while the effects from older history of the model can be decreased. Such corresponds to the objective of our problem.

3. TIME-DECAYING ADAPTIVE PREDICTION ALGORITHM

In order to solve TOCO problem, in this section, we present the details of the proposed time-decaying adaptive prediction (TDAP) algorithm. We first introduce the time-decaying function. We then give a formal definition of the model update function with recursive closed form. Details of the algorithm are finally presented.

Time-Decaying function. We note that there are numbers of time-decaying function in the literature, such as polynomial decay and exponential decay [7]. In this paper, we use *exponential* decay function as $F^{(T)}(t)$ in Definition 1. The reasons are two folds: (a) it is widely used in both industry [20, 31] and academia [5, 29]; and (b) the recursive closed form of the model update function (to be seen shortly) can be derived under the exponential term [1].

In particular, the exponential time-decaying function takes the form of

$$F^{(T)}(t) = \exp(-\frac{|T+1-t|}{(2\tau)^2}), \tag{5}$$

where $T \geq 1$ is current time step, and t is time step of the history model, $t \in [1, T]$. Note that $F^{(T)}(t)$ is a monotonic increasing function with independent variable t, *i.e.*, the larger the t, the larger the returned value.

Model update function. Based on the exponential decay function in Equation 5, we define the iterative model update function in each iteration t to solve TOCO, where $\mathbf{w}^{(t+1)}$ takes the form of

$$\arg\min_{\mathbf{w}} \left\{ \mathbf{g}^{(1:t)} \cdot \mathbf{w} + \lambda_1 \|\mathbf{w}\|_1 + \lambda_2 \|\mathbf{w}\|_2^2 + \frac{1}{2} \sum_{s=1}^{t} \delta^{(s,t)} \|\mathbf{w} - \mathbf{w}^{(s)}\|_2^2 \right\}. \tag{6}$$

Note that $\delta^{(s,t)} = \sigma^{(s)} \cdot F^{(t)}(s)$, which can be extended on per-coordinate base as

$$\begin{aligned} \delta_i^{(s,t)} &= \sigma_i^{(s)} \exp(-\tfrac{|t+1-s|}{(2\tau)^2}) \\ &= \tfrac{1}{\alpha}\left(\sqrt{\textstyle\sum_{j=1}^{s}(g_i^{(j)})^2} - \sqrt{\textstyle\sum_{j=1}^{s-1}(g_i^{(j)})^2}\right) \exp(-\tfrac{|t+1-s|}{(2\tau)^2}) \end{aligned} \tag{7}$$

We let $\gamma = \frac{1}{(2\tau)^2}$, then $\delta^{(s,t)} = \sigma^{(s)} \exp(-\gamma(t+1-s))$. Here, $\gamma > 0$ is a decay rate, and the bigger the γ, the faster decaying of the history model. It is easy to see that in case of $\lim_{\tau \to +\infty} \gamma = 0$, Equation 6 is equivalent to that of FTRL-proximal algorithm in Equation 2.

It is worth highlighting that the update function for TDAP algorithm differs from that of the FTRL-proximal algorithm as we introduce the time-decaying factor to the smoothing term, *i.e.*, the quadratic term $\frac{1}{2}\sum_{s=1}^{t} \delta^{(s,t)} \|\mathbf{w} - \mathbf{w}^{(s)}\|_2^2$.

Closed form. Similar to FTRL-proximal algorithm, we next derive a recursive closed form of the update function in Equation 6 following the flow in [25].

[1] In this work, we take the first step to study the TOCO problem with exponential decay, other time-decaying functions (*e.g.*, polynomial decay) are refered to the future work.

Algorithm Per-Coordinate TDAP algorithm with L_1 and L_2 Regularization for Logistic Regression
Input: Parameters α, λ_1, λ_2 and γ

($\forall i \in \{1, \cdots, d\}$), initialize $u_i^{(0)} = v_i^{(0)} = \delta_i^{(0)} = h_i^{(0)} = 0$
for each $t = 1$ to T, **do**

  /* features receiving */
  receive feature vector $\mathbf{x}^{(t)}$ and let $I = \{i | x_i^{(t)} \neq 0\}$

  /* model parameters update */
  for each $i \in I$, **do**
    update $w_i^{(t)}$ with closed form /* Equation 9 */

  /* prediction */
  predict $p^{(t)} = \frac{1}{1+\exp(-\mathbf{x}^{(t)} \cdot \mathbf{w}^{(t)})}$ /* logistic regression */

  /* labels observation */
  observe label $y^{(t)} \in \{0, 1\}$

  /* recursive form update for future model update */
  for each $i \in I$, **do**
    $g_i^{(t)} = (p^{(t)} - y^{(t)}) x_i^{(t)}$ /* gradient of loss w.r.t. $\mathbf{w}$ */
    $\sigma_i^{(t)} = \frac{1}{\alpha}(\sqrt{u_i^{(t-1)} + (g_i{}^{(t)})^2} - \sqrt{u_i^{(t-1)}})$ /* $\frac{1}{\eta_i^{(t)}} - \frac{1}{\eta_i^{(t-1)}}$ *
    $u_i^{(t)} = u_i^{(t-1)} + (g_i^{(t)})^2$ /* sum of gradient */
    $\delta_i^{(t)} = \exp(-\gamma)(\delta_i^{(t-1)} + \sigma_i^{(t)})$ /* Equation 10 */
    $v_i^{(t)} = v_i^{(t-1)} + g_i^{(t)}$ /* sum of gradient square */
    $h_i^{(t)} = \exp(-\gamma)(h_i^{(t-1)} + \sigma_i^{(t)} w_i^{(t)})$ /* Equation 11 */
    $z_i^{(t)} = v_i^{(t)} - h_i^{(t)}$ /* Equation 12 */

Figure 2: TDAP Algorithm

We rewrite the Equation 6 *w.r.t.* the arg min over $\mathbf{w}$ as

$$\left\{ (\mathbf{g}^{(1:t)} - \sum_{s=1}^{t} \delta^{(s,t)} \mathbf{w}^{(s)}) \cdot \mathbf{w} + \lambda_1 \|\mathbf{w}\|_1 + \frac{1}{2}(\lambda_2 + \sum_{s=1}^{t} \delta^{(s,t)}) \cdot \mathbf{w}^2 + (const \right. \tag{8}$$

By storing $\mathbf{z}^{(t)} = \mathbf{g}^{(1:t)} - \sum_{s=1}^{t} \delta^{(s,t)} \mathbf{w}^{(s)}$, one can solve $\mathbf{w}^{(t+1)}$ in a recursive closed form on a per-coordinate base as follows,

$$\begin{cases} 0 & \text{if } |z_i^{(t)}| \leq \lambda_1 \\ -(\lambda_2 + \sum_{s=1}^{t} \delta_i^{(s,t)})^{-1}(z_i^{(t)} - \lambda_1 sign(z_i^{(t)})) & \text{if } |z_i^{(t)}| > \lambda_1 \end{cases} \tag{9}$$

From Equation 9, in iteration t, we are required to store $\sum_{s=1}^{t} \delta_i^{(s,t)}$ and $z_i^{(t)}$ in memory *only*. However, how can we update both values in t-th iteration with *only* the values of $(t-1)$-th iteration? Next, we focus on the *recursive form* for updating both $\sum_{s=1}^{t} \delta_i^{(s,t)}$ and $z_i^{(t)}$.

Recursive form of $\sum_{s=1}^{t} \delta_i^{(s,t)}$. $\sum_{s=1}^{t} \delta_i^{(s,t)}$ can be computed in a recursive form:

$$\begin{aligned} \textstyle\sum_{s=1}^{t} \delta_i^{(s,t)} &= \textstyle\sum_{s=1}^{t} \left(\sigma_i^{(s)} \cdot exp\big(-\gamma(t+1-s)\big)\right) \\ &= \exp(-\gamma) \cdot (\textstyle\sum_{s=1}^{t-1} \delta_i^{(s,t-1)} + \sigma_i^{(t)}) \end{aligned} \tag{10}$$

Recursive form of $z_i^{(t)}$. Since $z_i^{(t)} = g_i^{(1:t)} - \sum_{s=1}^{t} \delta_i^{(s,t)} w_i^{(s)}$, we let $h_i^{(t)} = \sum_{s=1}^{t} \delta_i^{(s,t)} w_i^{(s)}$, $h_i^{(t)}$ can then be computed in a recursive form

$$\begin{aligned} h_i^{(t)} &= \textstyle\sum_{s=1}^{t} \delta_i^{(s,t)} w_i^{(s)} \\ &= \textstyle\sum_{s=1}^{t} \sigma_i^{(s)} exp\big(-\gamma(t+1-s)\big) w_i^{(s)} \\ &= \exp(-\gamma)\big(\textstyle\sum_{s=1}^{t-1} (\delta_i^{(s,t-1)} w_i^{(s)}) + \sigma_i^{(t)} w_i^{(t)}\big) \\ &= \exp(-\gamma)(h_i^{(t-1)} + \sigma_i^{(t)} w_i^{(t)}) \end{aligned} \tag{11}$$

Thus, the recursive form of $z_i^{(t)}$ becomes

$$\begin{aligned} z_i^{(t)} &= g_i^{(1:t)} - \sum_{s=1}^{t} \delta_i^{(s,t)} w_i^{(s)} \\ &= g_i^{(1:t-1)} + g_i^{(t)} - \exp(-\gamma)(h_i^{(t-1)} + \sigma_i^{(t)} w_i^{(t)}) \end{aligned} \quad (12)$$

Detailed algorithm. Putting all together, in iteration t, from Equation 10 and 12, we note that our algorithm is required to keep track of $u_i^{(t)}$, $v_i^{(t)}$, $\delta_i^{(t)}$ and $h_i^{(t)}$ on per-coordinate base *only*. We show the pseudocode of TDAP algorithm using the example of logistic regression in Figure 2. The algorithm first initializes the parameters in Line 1. Then, upon receiving the features (Lines 2-3) for each iteration, TDAP updates the model parameters and does the prediction (Lines 4-6). It then updates the parameters for further usage by observing the labels (Lines 7-15).

Advantages. It is worth remarking that (a) the effects of older history models on target model are scaled down with the help of time-decaying function, which leads to adapt fast changes (gradual or abrupt) of data; (b) all examples are used for model training while there is *no* need to record them, which significantly saves the memory; and (c) it is efficient to update the models due to the recursive closed form, as shown in Section 5.

4. PARALLELISM OF TDAP ALGORITHM

In this section, we show the parallelism of TDAP algorithm. We first introduce the data model and the system model. We then present the parallel TDAP under data parallel scheme with *bulk synchronized parallel* (BSP) consistency model, as TDAP_{BSP}. We end this section by showing how we can extend the TDAP_{BSP} to *stale synchronized parallel* (SSP) model, as TDAP_{SSP}.

4.1 Data Model and System Model

Data model. We follow the *data parallel* [14] model in online learning scenario. In particular, the data (examples with features and labels) take the form of stream, which is divided into a sequence of mini-batch $D^{(t)}$ in each iteration $t \in [1, T]$, $|D^{(t)}| \geq 1$. The mini-batch $D^{(t)}$ is then partitioned and assigned to computational workers indexed by p for further computations (to be seen shortly).

System model. The system model follows the state-of-the-art parameter server paradigm *e.g.,* [8,13,22], which are widely used to tackle the large scale iterative machine learning problem [15,18,37]. It comprises of the following three major components:

Driver. The driver is to initiate the algorithm and control the parameters updates via *parameter consistency controller* for each iteration $t \in [1, T]$ under the bulk synchronized parallel (BSP) or stale synchronized parallel (SSP).

Parameter servers. The parameter servers (PS) provide a global access to model parameters via a *parameter synchronization interface* like that of table-based or key-value stores. Note that in practice, the PS can also be the driver.

Workers. Let P be all workers. For each iteration t, each worker $p \in P$ receives the model parameters from PS via the parameter synchronization interface (*i.e.,* pull()), and updates the model locally *in parallel* using the received examples $D_p^{(t)}$ partitioned by mini-batch $D^{(t)}$, *i.e.,* $D_p^{(t)} \subset D^{(t)}$.

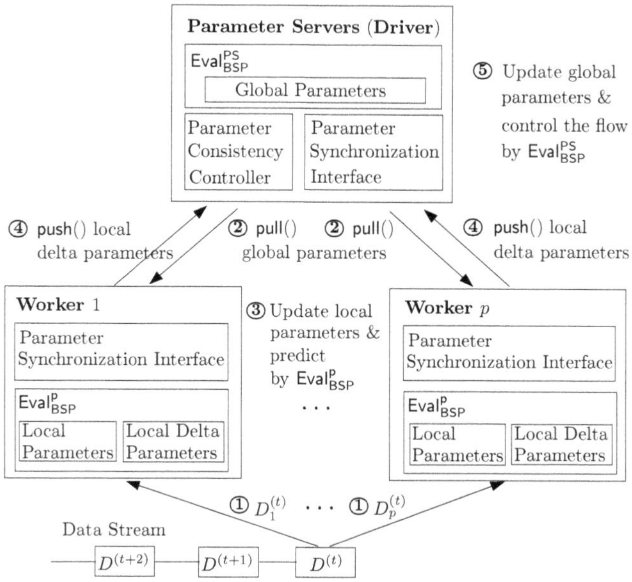

Figure 3: Data model, system model and working flow of TDAP_{BSP} algorithm.

Note that each example in $D^{(t)}$ is allocated to one worker *only*. After the update is done, the worker p then synchronizes the newly updated model parameters to the PS via the synchronization interface push(). The driver (or PS) then generates future decisions.

Example 2: Figure 3 depicts an example of the data model and system model. Three parties of the system, *i.e.,* driver, PS and workers are shown. For simplicity, here, the PS also represents the driver. The examples coming to the system take the form of a stream of mini-batch $D^{(t)}$ in each iteration t. Collections of examples $D_p^{(t)} \in D^{(t)}$ are then sent to the worker p for later computations. □

4.2 Parallel TDAP Algorithm Under BSP

Data structure. We first introduce three types of data structures that facilitate TDAP_{BSP}.

Global parameters on PS. The global parameters are stored in PS, which keep track of the global model states. In particular, in iteration t, the global parameters to be saved are $(u_i^{(t)}, v_i^{(t)}, h_i^{(t)\prime}, \delta_i^{(t)\prime})$ on per-coordinate base, where

- $u_i^{(t)} = u_i^{(t-1)} + \sum_{p \in P} \sum_{d \in D_p^{(t)}} (g_{p,d,i}^{(t)})^2$;
- $v_i^{(t)} = v_i^{(t-1)} + \sum_{p \in P} \sum_{d \in D_p^{(t)}} g_{p,d,i}^{(t)}$;
- $h_i^{(t)\prime} = h_i^{(t-1)\prime} + \sum_{p \in P} \sum_{d \in D_p^{(t)}} \sigma_{p,d,i}^{(t)} w_{p,i}^{(t)}$; and
- $\delta_i^{(t)\prime} = \delta_i^{(t-1)\prime} + \sum_{p \in P} \sum_{d \in D_p^{(t)}} \sigma_{p,d,i}^{(t)}$.

Note that $g_{p,d,i}^{(t)}$ (*resp.* $\sigma_{p,d,i}^{(t)}$ and $w_{p,i}^{(t)}$) are gradient (*resp.* learning-rate schedule and model parameter) with i-th coordinate in t-th iteration computed under example $d \in D_p^{(t)}$ at worker p. And $h_i^{(t)\prime}$ and $\delta_i^{(t)\prime}$ do *not* introduce the time-decaying factor, which are different to $h_i^{(t)}$ and $\delta_i^{(t)}$.

Local parameters at workers. Each worker p stores its local parameters, which can be derived from global parameters on PS. Specifically, in iteration t, the local

Algorithm $\mathsf{Eval}^{\mathsf{P}}_{\mathsf{BSP}}$
Input: A collection of examples $D_p^{(t)}$

/* receiving global parameters from PS */
1. $\mathsf{pull}(u_i^{(t)}, v_i^{(t)}, h_i^{(t)'}, \delta_i^{(t)'})$ on per-coordinate base

/* local parameters update */
2. **for each** coordinate i, **do**
3. $\quad u_{p,i}^{(t)} = u_i^{(t)}$
4. $\quad v_{p,i}^{(t)} = v_i^{(t)}$
5. $\quad h_{p,i}^{(t)} = \exp(-\gamma)(h_{p,i}^{(t-1)} + (h_i^{(t)'} - h_i^{(t-1)'}))$
6. $\quad \delta_{p,i}^{(t)} = \exp(-\gamma)(\delta_{p,i}^{(t-1)} + (\delta_i^{(t)'} - \delta_i^{(t-1)'}))$
7. $\quad$ store $h_i^{(t)'}$ and $\delta_i^{(t)'}$ locally for next iteration

/* computing model parameters */
8. **for each** coordinate i, **do**
9. $\quad$ compute $w_{p,i}^{(t)}$ with closed form /* Equation 9 */

10. **for each** $d \in D_p^{(t)}$, where $d = (\mathbf{x}, y)$, **do**
/* prediction using model parameters */
11. $\quad$ predict $p_{p,d}^{(t)} = \frac{1}{1+\exp(-\mathbf{x}\cdot\mathbf{w}_p^{(t)})}$
/* local delta parameters computation */
12. $\quad$ **for each** coordinate i, **do**
13. $\quad\quad$ compute $g_{p,d,i}^{(t)}$ and $\sigma_{p,d,i}^{(t)}$
14. $\quad\quad \Delta u_{p,i}^{(t)} = \Delta u_{p,i}^{(t)} + (g_{p,d,i}^{(t)})^2$
15. $\quad\quad \Delta v_{p,i}^{(t)} = \Delta v_{p,i}^{(t)} + g_{p,d,i}^{(t)}$
16. $\quad\quad \Delta h_{p,i}^{(t)'} = \Delta h_{p,i}^{(t)'} + \sigma_{p,d,i}^{(t)} w_{p,i}^{(t)}$
17. $\quad\quad \Delta \delta_{p,i}^{(t)'} = \Delta \delta_{p,i}^{(t)'} + \sigma_{p,d,i}^{(t)}$

/* sending local delta parameters to PS */
18. $\mathsf{push}(\Delta u_{p,i}^{(t)}, \Delta v_{p,i}^{(t)}, \Delta h_{p,i}^{(t)'}, \Delta \delta_{p,i}^{(t)'})$ to PS

Figure 4: $\mathsf{Eval}^{\mathsf{P}}_{\mathsf{BSP}}$ at Worker p in iteration t

parameters to be saved at worker p take the form of $(u_{p,i}^{(t)}, v_{p,i}^{(t)}, h_{p,i}^{(t)}, h_i^{(t-1)'}, \delta_{p,i}^{(t)}, \delta_i^{(t-1)'})$ on per-coordinate base, where

- $u_{p,i}^{(t)} = u_i^{(t)}$;
- $v_{p,i}^{(t)} = v_i^{(t)}$;
- $h_{p,i}^{(t)} = \exp(-\gamma)(h_{p,i}^{(t-1)} + \sum_{p' \in P} \sum_{d \in D_{p'}^{(t)}} \sigma_{p',d,i}^{(t)} w_{p',i}^{(t)})$; and
- $\delta_{p,i}^{(t)} = \exp(-\gamma)(\delta_{p,i}^{(t-1)} + \sum_{p' \in P} \sum_{d \in D_{p'}^{(t)}} \sigma_{p',d,i}^{(t)})$.

It is worth highlighting that $h_i^{(t-1)'}$ is recorded in order to compute $\sum_{d \in D_{p'}^{(t)}} \sigma_{p',d,i}^{(t)} w_{p',i}^{(t)}$ (to be seen shortly). Similar for $\delta_i^{(t-1)'}$.

Local delta parameters. Intuitively, for each worker p, it computes the local delta parameters which is to incrementally update the global parameters on PS. More specifically, the local delta parameters for work p in iteration t are $(\Delta u_{p,i}^{(t)}, \Delta v_{p,i}^{(t)}, \Delta h_{p,i}^{(t)'}, \Delta \delta_{p,i}^{(t)'})$ on per-coordinate base, where

- $\Delta u_{p,i}^{(t)} = \sum_{d \in D_p^{(t)}} (g_{p,d,i}^{(t)})^2$;
- $\Delta v_{p,i}^{(t)} = \sum_{d \in D_p^{(t)}} g_{p,d,i}^{(t)}$;
- $\Delta h_{p,i}^{(t)'} = \sum_{d \in D_p^{(t)}} \sigma_{p,d,i}^{(t)} w_{p,i}^{(t)}$; and
- $\Delta \delta_{p,i}^{(t)'} = \sum_{d \in D_p^{(t)}} \sigma_{p,d,i}^{(t)}$.

Algorithm $\mathsf{Eval}^{\mathsf{PS}}_{\mathsf{BSP}}$
Input: Local delta parameters from all workers

/* global parameters update */
1. **for each** worker p, **do**
2. $\quad$ **for each** coordinate i, **do**
3. $\quad\quad u_i^{(t)} = u_i^{(t)} + \Delta u_{p,i}^{(t)}$
4. $\quad\quad v_i^{(t)} = v_i^{(t)} + \Delta v_{p,i}^{(t)}$
5. $\quad\quad h_i^{(t)'} = h_i^{(t)'} + \Delta h_{p,i}^{(t)'}$
6. $\quad\quad \delta_i^{(t)'} = \delta_i^{(t)'} + \Delta \delta_{p,i}^{(t)'}$

Figure 5: $\mathsf{Eval}^{\mathsf{PS}}_{\mathsf{BSP}}$ at PS in iteration t

$\mathsf{TDAP}_{\mathsf{BSP}}$ algorithm. We show the details of $\mathsf{TDAP}_{\mathsf{BSP}}$ using the logistic regression, which is controlled by a driver function $\mathsf{Driver}_{\mathsf{BSP}}$. $\mathsf{Driver}_{\mathsf{BSP}}$ initiates the $\mathsf{TDAP}_{\mathsf{BSP}}$, and triggers $\mathsf{Eval}^{\mathsf{P}}_{\mathsf{BSP}}$ (Figure 4) and $\mathsf{Eval}^{\mathsf{PS}}_{\mathsf{BSP}}$ (Figure 5) functions in each iteration between workers and PS. All parameters are updated *iteratively* under BSP model, *no need* to compute from scratch.

In particular, all global parameters and local (delta) parameters are initiated as zero. Then given a collection of examples in iteration t, each worker p computes the local (delta) parameters by $\mathsf{Eval}^{\mathsf{P}}_{\mathsf{BSP}}$, *in parallel*, based on the global parameters computed in previous iteration. The global parameters are then updated by $\mathsf{Eval}^{\mathsf{PS}}_{\mathsf{BSP}}$ at PS using the newly computed local delta parameters. $\mathsf{Driver}_{\mathsf{BSP}}$ *terminates* the whole procedure manually, or until there is no data coming.

$\underline{\mathsf{Eval}^{\mathsf{P}}_{\mathsf{BSP}}}$. Given a collection of examples $D_p^{(t)} \subset D^{(t)}$ in t-th iteration at worker p, $\mathsf{Eval}^{\mathsf{P}}_{\mathsf{BSP}}$ first receives all global parameters from PS by $\mathsf{pull}()$ function (Line 1). It then updates the local parameters and computes local delta parameters iteratively, based on the parameters in $(t-1)$-th iteration (Lines 2-7). The model parameters $\mathbf{w}^{(t)}$ are then constructed using the newly updated local parameters, and the prediction are conducted (Lines 8-11). $\mathsf{Eval}^{\mathsf{P}}_{\mathsf{BSP}}$ finally computes the local delta parameters (Lines 12-17) and sends them to PS by $\mathsf{push}()$ function for incrementally updating the global parameters (Line 18).

$\underline{\mathsf{Eval}^{\mathsf{PS}}_{\mathsf{BSP}}}$. Upon receiving all local delta parameters from each worker p in iteration t, $\mathsf{Eval}^{\mathsf{PS}}_{\mathsf{BSP}}$ increments global parameters by summing up all those received local delta parameters. The updated global parameters are used for next iteration (Lines 1-6).

Example 3: Figure 3 illustrates the working flow of $\mathsf{TDAP}_{\mathsf{BSP}}$ algorithm in t-th iteration given a mini-batch $D^{(t)}$. All local and global parameters are recored in PS and workers, respectively, which are initialized as zero.

Upon receiving a collection of examples $D_p^{(t)} \subset D^{(t)}$, the worker p invokes $\mathsf{Eval}^{\mathsf{P}}_{\mathsf{BSP}}$. It pulls the global parameters from PS, and updates the local (delta) parameters accordingly. The prediction are conducted based on the newly computed model parameters. After the computations, $\mathsf{Eval}^{\mathsf{P}}_{\mathsf{BSP}}$ pushes the local delta parameters to the PS.

Based on the local delta parameters received from all workers (required by BSP consistency model), the PS then invokes $\mathsf{Eval}^{\mathsf{PS}}_{\mathsf{BSP}}$ to augment the global parameters accordingly. Afterwards, the PS (*a.k.a.* the Driver) then invokes next iteration of the computation, or abort. □

4.3 Parallel TDAP Algorithm Under SSP

The performance of $\mathsf{TDAP_{BSP}}$ may be significantly hampered by the *stragglers* in each iteration that may hold up the process, such costs are inherent to the synchronization policy of BSP. To reduce the costs, one possible solution is to use *asynchronous parallel strategy*, however, *no* performance guarantee is provided [33] in terms of correctness.

In this subsection, we introduce TDAP under SSP consistency model [33], denoted as $\mathsf{TDAP_{SSP}}$, whose accuracy can be theoretically preserved by [13]. Since $\mathsf{TDAP_{SSP}}$ is an extension from $\mathsf{TDAP_{BSP}}$, for presentation simplicity, we avoid repeating the same details, but highlight the major differences between two.

Data structure. We first present the difference on data structure. The local delta parameters for $\mathsf{TDAP_{SSP}}$ are the same to those of $\mathsf{TDAP_{BSP}}$, while local and global parameters involve more components, as described below.

Global parameters on PS. Besides the global parameters used in $\mathsf{TDAP_{BSP}}$, $\mathsf{TDAP_{SSP}}$ introduces two more types of global parameters on PS: (a) The time step t_p for each worker p, which encodes the *latest* time step that worker p synchronizes (via push interface) its local delta parameters to the PS; and (b) The minimum time step t_{PS} for all workers p, *i.e.*, $t_{PS} = \min\{t_p | \forall p \in P\}$.

Local parameters at workers. At worker p, except for those parameters in $\mathsf{TDAP_{BSP}}$, $\mathsf{TDAP_{SSP}}$ requires to record (a) the *latest* time step t_p that the local parameters been updated; and (b) the *latest* time step $t_{(p,PS)}$ that worker p synchronizes global parameters (via pull interface) from PS.

$\mathsf{TDAP_{SSP}}$ algorithm. Based on the newly introduced parameters, we are ready to show the algorithm. Similar to $\mathsf{TDAP_{BSP}}$, $\mathsf{TDAP_{SSP}}$ is also controlled by a driver $\mathsf{Driver_{SSP}}$, which is for initialization and triggering $\mathsf{Eval^{p}_{SSP}}$ and $\mathsf{Eval^{PS}_{SSP}}$ functions under the SSP consistency model. In particular, compared to BSP, workers may compute advance ahead of each other up to s iterations apart, where s is called *staleness threshold* (in short stale), under SSP. Workers that go too far away (s iterations faster than the slowest one) are forced to wait, until slower workers catch up. Note that SSP is equivalent to BSP when $s = 0$.

$\mathsf{Eval^{p}_{SSP}}$. Given a collection of examples $D_p^{(t)}$, $\mathsf{Eval^{p}_{SSP}}$ first checks whether the local parameters are delayed or stale, by evaluating the value of $(t_p - t_{p,PS})$. (a) If $(t_p - t_{p,PS}) > s$ (*i.e.*, local parameters at worker p are delayed at least s iterations), $\mathsf{Eval^{p}_{SSP}}$ yields to synchronize global parameters from PS via pull interface (like Line 1 in Figure 4) and conducts the procedures that are the same to Lines 2-17. The time step $t_{p,PS}$ is then updated as t_{PS}, *i.e.*, $t_{p,PS} = t_{PS}$, where t_{PS} is within those returned global parameters; (b) Otherwise, *no need* to update the local parameters, $\mathsf{Eval^{p}_{SSP}}$ just computes the local delta parameters, the same to Lines 12-17 in Figure 4.

Note that the time step t_p for worker p is incremented by 1 after the above procedure, and all local delta parameters are then sent to PS via push interface, as Line 18 in Figure 4.

$\mathsf{Eval^{PS}_{SSP}}$. Compared to $\mathsf{Eval^{PS}_{BSP}}$, $\mathsf{Eval^{PS}_{SSP}}$ is invoked *once* receiving (a) the local delta parameters, or (b) a pull request for global parameters, from a worker p.

- (a) Upon receiving the local delta parameters from the worker p, $\mathsf{Eval^{PS}_{SSP}}$ conducts the update functions as Lines 2-6 in Figure 5. The time step t_p for worker p is added by 1, and t_{PS} is updated accordingly;
- (b) Otherwise, *i.e.*, receiving a pull request for global parameters from the worker p, $\mathsf{Eval^{PS}_{SSP}}$ is required to evaluate the value of $(t_p - t_{PS})$. (a) If $(t_p - t_{PS}) \leq s$, $\mathsf{Eval^{PS}_{SSP}}$ returns the global parameters directly; (b) Otherwise, which implies that worker p runs too far away, $\mathsf{Eval^{p}_{SSP}}$ has to wait until the slower workers catch up. Once $(t_p - t_{PS}) = s$, $\mathsf{Eval^{PS}_{SSP}}$ proceeds the request again and returns the global parameters.

5. EXPERIMENTAL STUDY

In this section, we experimentally study the performance between FTRL-Proximal and TDAP using real-world datasets. In short, we evaluate (a) the *accuracy* of TDAP; (b) the *scalability* of TDAP; and (c) the *efficiency* between $\mathsf{TDAP_{Spark}}$ and $\mathsf{TDAP_{Petuum}}$. The results exhibit the algorithm with good accuracy, scalability and efficiency.

5.1 Experimental Setup

Datasets. We benchmarked 8 real-world datasets in total, which can be classified into the following categories. Some detailed statistics of the datasets are illustrated in Table 1.

Public non-time series datasets. We used 6 datasets without time series, namely Books, DVD, Electronics, Kitchen, RCV1 and News. Among them, Books, Dvd, Electronics and Kitchen are first used in [4], representing Amazon product reviews of four different product types. RCV1 and News are scaled versions of rcv1.binary [21] and news20.binary [15] datasets for binomial classification, respectively.

Public time series dataset. We used a public dataset with time series on suspicious URLs detection, called URLs which is available from [23]. It is an anonymized 120-day subsets with around 2.4 million URLs detection records. Each day contains about 6,580 positives and 13,223 negatives examples on average.

IPTV VoD time series dataset. We collected a dataset with 7-day IPTV VoD (Video On Demand) program (*e.g.*, movies and TV plays) views, named as IPTV, from a giant Telecom company in Mainland China. It involves 72,350,479 view records from 4,446,247 users.

To generate the examples, we construct a feature label pair $(\mathbf{x}^{(t)}, \mathbf{y}^{(t)})$ for each VoD program view record at time t. In particular, $\mathbf{x}^{(t)}$ is a sparse feature vector, with size of 1,321,393 (as shown in Table 1), encoding the characteristics of both program and user, *e.g.*, program information, user properties, user behaviors and time stamp of user's view. The label $\mathbf{y}^{(t)}$ is 1 if the program was viewed by the user at least 20 minutes or half of the total length of the program; and 0 otherwise.

Algorithm settings. We implemented the following algorithms: (a) Algorithms on Spark 1.5.1 under BSP model: (i) $\mathsf{FTRLProx_{Spark}}$, the FTRL-Proximal algorithm [25], where α, λ_1 and λ_2 are all set as 0.1 [2]; and (ii) $\mathsf{TDAP_{Spark}}$ of Sec. 3, where the settings for α, λ_1, λ_2 are taken from $\mathsf{FTRLProx_{Spark}}$. The parameter γ is carefully chosen for different datasets (to been seen shortly); and (b) Algorithms on

[2]We have varied α, λ_1 and λ_2 from 0.0001 to 1 on all the above datasets, and 0.1 brings the best accuracy on average.

Table 1: Statistics of the datasets

Dataset	# of features	# of positive examples	# of negative examples
Books	332,439	2,264	2,201
DVD	282,899	1,807	1,779
Electronics	235,796	2,857	2,824
Kitchen	205,664	2,954	2,991
RCV1	47,236	355,460	321,939
News	1,355,192	9,999	9,997
URLs	3,231,961	786,182	1,593,948
IPTV	1,321,393	32,869,901	39,480,578

Petuum 1.1 under SSP model [3] (i) $\mathsf{FTRLProx}_{\mathsf{Petuum}}$; and (ii) $\mathsf{TDAP}_{\mathsf{Petuum}}$, the *stale* is set to 2 (as recommended in [33]), other parameter settings are the same to those on Spark (BSP).

Evaluation framework. We conducted the evaluation of the algorithms using three different frameworks in terms of different datasets, where the accuracy metrics used include AUC (Area Under the ROC Curve) and AER [23] (Accumulative Error Rate). Details are as below.

Framework for public non-time series datasets. The framework is designed for public non-time series datasets, where the size of mini-batch is set as one, *i.e.,* once coming one example, the framework conducts prediction and trains the model. The metric, AUC, is calculated after all examples have been traversed.

Framework for URLs dataset. We follow the evaluation framework for URLs as [23], where each mini-batch consists of one example, similar to the above framework. However, the AUC for *both* FTRL-Proximal algorithm and TDAP are very close, which approach to 0.999 (0.999214 for TDAP and 0.999057 for FTRL-Proximal), we thereby use AER instead. The AER is then aggregated and reported in terms of days.

Framework for IPTV dataset. This framework, on the other hand, performs prediction and updates the model on IPTV over each mini-batch formed by time slot with 15 minutes, which follows our business requirements. And still, the AUC is then aggregated and compared in terms of days.

Distributed settings. To evaluate the accuracy of the algorithms, we deployed all algorithms on a mini cluster with $p = 3$ machines, each of which has 24 cores, 96GB memory and 18TB disk. To further study the scalability, we deployed a cluster with $p = 10$ machines, where each is with 8 cores, 64GB memory and 500GB disk. Each experiment is repeated 10 times and the average is reported.

5.2 Experimental Results

Parameter Choosing for TDAP. We first study the accuracy of TDAP by varying the parameter γ, in order to choose good γ for each dataset. We fix the parameters α, λ_1 and λ_2 as mentioned above, for fair comparison.

Figure 6 shows the AUC on Kitchen dataset using $\mathsf{TDAP}_{\mathsf{Spark}}$. The x-axis is γ and y-axis represents the AUC. In particular, by varying γ from 0.1 to 0.000001, the AUC of TDAP becomes stable (approaching 94%) once $\gamma > 0.0005$, and similar for $\mathsf{TDAP}_{\mathsf{Petuum}}$. Hence, we determine $\gamma = 0.0005$ for Kitchen. Note that we conducted the same sets of experiments to determine the value of γ for other datasets (not shown), which are used in later evaluations.

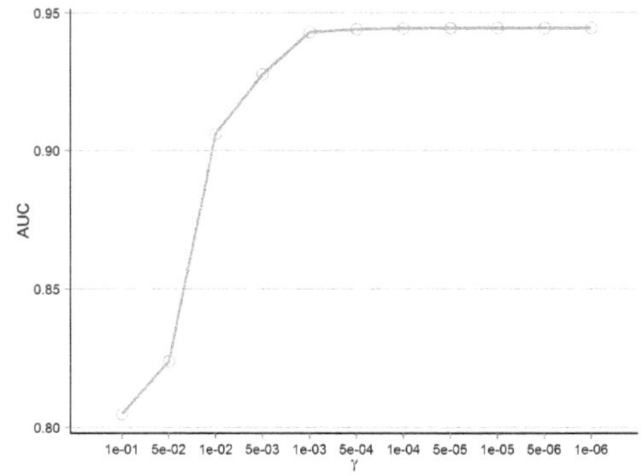

Figure 6: The AUC of TDAP by varying parameter γ on Kitchen dataset using $\mathsf{TDAP}_{\mathsf{Spark}}$; Similar for $\mathsf{TDAP}_{\mathsf{Petuum}}$.

Accuracy Comparison Between FTRL-Proximal and TDAP. After determining γ of TDAP for each dataset, we are ready to compare its accuracy to FTRL-Proximal. As the comparison between $\mathsf{FTRLProx}_{\mathsf{Petuum}}$ and $\mathsf{TDAP}_{\mathsf{Petuum}}$ shows similar results, for space constraints, we only report the results on $\mathsf{FTRLProx}_{\mathsf{Spark}}$ and $\mathsf{TDAP}_{\mathsf{Spark}}$.

Accuracy on public non-time series datasets. Table 2 reports the AUC comparison between $\mathsf{FTRLProx}_{\mathsf{Spark}}$ and $\mathsf{TDAP}_{\mathsf{Spark}}$ on public non-time series datasets. We note that $\mathsf{TDAP}_{\mathsf{Spark}}$ performs nearly the same as $\mathsf{FTRLProx}_{\mathsf{Spark}}$ on Books, Dvd, Electronics, Kitchen and RCV1. However, for News, $\mathsf{TDAP}_{\mathsf{Spark}}$ improves the accuracy by at most 12%. The hypothesis held by FTRL-Proximal is that the effects of all historical models are equivalent. Although this might be suitable for most non-time series datasets, we still believe that, according to "no free lunch" theorem, treating historical models differently can lead to better performance in some datasets, *e.g.,* News in our experiments.

Table 2: The AUC of $\mathsf{TDAP}_{\mathsf{Spark}}$ and $\mathsf{FTRLProx}_{\mathsf{Spark}}$ on all public non-time series datasets. The best value for each dataset is in bold.

Dataset	$\mathsf{FTRLProx}_{\mathsf{Spark}}$	$\mathsf{TDAP}_{\mathsf{Spark}}$
Books	**0.8944**	0.8914 ($\gamma = 0.0005$)
Dvd	**0.8838**	0.8792 ($\gamma = 0.0005$)
Electronics	**0.9278**	0.9249 ($\gamma = 0.0005$)
Kitchen	**0.9448**	0.9440 ($\gamma = 0.0005$)
RCV1	0.9904	**0.9936** ($\gamma = 0.05$)
News	0.8885	**0.9952** ($\gamma = 0.1$)

Accuracy on URLs dataset. Figure 7 shows the AER, *i.e.,* the percentage of misclassified examples for all URLs encountered up to date, for $\mathsf{TDAP}_{\mathsf{Spark}}$ and $\mathsf{FTRLProx}_{\mathsf{Spark}}$ on URLs. The x-axis is the number of days and y-axis is the AER. From the figure, we find out that the AER of $\mathsf{TDAP}_{\mathsf{Spark}}$ approaches 1.4%, which outperforms $\mathsf{FTRLProx}_{\mathsf{Spark}}$ (AER with 1.6%) by 12.5% on average. It is worth remarking that the AUC for both algorithms are very close, both approach 0.999, and the value of $\mathsf{TDAP}_{\mathsf{Spark}}$ increases 0.016% compared to that of $\mathsf{FTRLProx}_{\mathsf{Spark}}$. Hence, we only report the AER in this part.

Accuracy on IPTV dataset. Figure 8 shows the AUC on

[3] We use Petuum for the implementation of SSP as it is not known how to realize it under Spark.

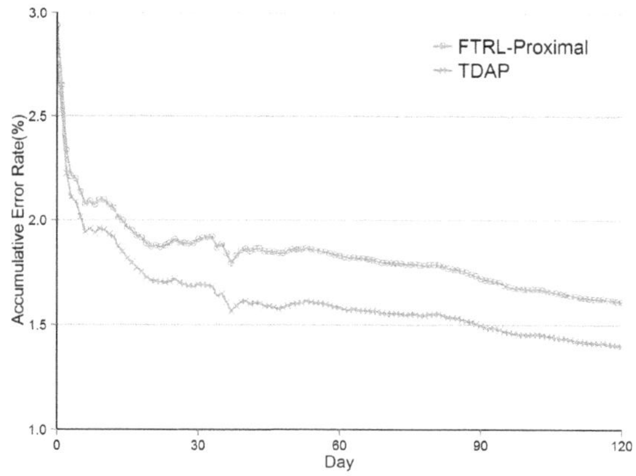

Figure 7: The AER of $\mathsf{TDAP}_{\mathsf{Spark}}$ (with $\gamma = 0.00001$) and $\mathsf{FTRLProx}_{\mathsf{Spark}}$ on URLs dataset.

IPTV time series dataset. Not surprisingly, the results show that $\mathsf{TDAP}_{\mathsf{Spark}}$ outperforms $\mathsf{FTRLProx}_{\mathsf{Spark}}$ by around 5.6% on average. Such indicates that our strategy to deemphasize the effects of historical models in model training can definitely improve the accuracy, when the data are changing fast as motivated in Figure 1.

In our running production service, when we switched from FTRL-Proximal to TDAP, TDAP significantly increased the degree of user activity, *i.e.,* there were approximately 5% more users engaged and each user took 10% more time than ever, due to the accuracy improvement compared to the former one. Such accordingly brought more revenue than the existing one (using FTRL-Proximal) for our customers.

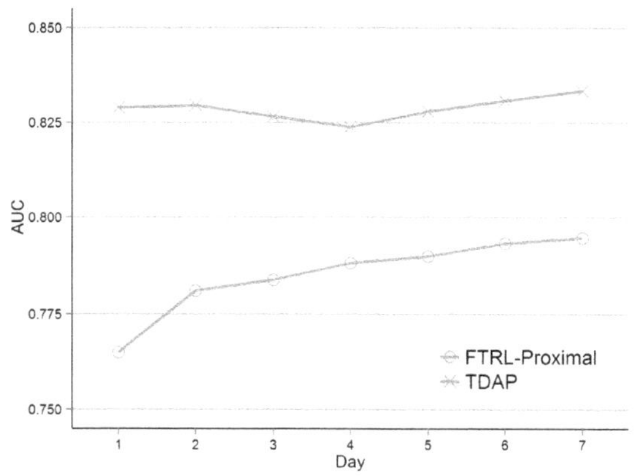

Figure 8: The AUC of $\mathsf{TDAP}_{\mathsf{Spark}}$ ($\gamma = 0.0005$) and $\mathsf{FTRLProx}_{\mathsf{Spark}}$ on IPTV dataset.

Scalability of TDAP. As TDAP shows good accuracy, we next verify its scalability. We conducted the experiments on IPTV dataset by varying $p \in [2, 10]$ using $\mathsf{TDAP}_{\mathsf{Spark}}$ and $\mathsf{TDAP}_{\mathsf{Petuum}}$, the results are shown in Figure 9.

As expected, $\mathsf{TDAP}_{\mathsf{Petuum}}$ shows an excellent scalability, which achieves 4x speedup when p increases from 2 to 10. However, $\mathsf{TDAP}_{\mathsf{Spark}}$ can only achieve 3x speedup, no matter how we increase the machines, *i.e.,*$\mathsf{TDAP}_{\mathsf{Petuum}}$ enjoys better scalability with more machines than $\mathsf{TDAP}_{\mathsf{Spark}}$. The major reasons are two folds: (a) SSP avoids the "blocking" of stragglers in each BSP round, by setting the staleness (as revealed in [13]); (b) Petuum uses fine-grained caching strategies and distributed shared memory to further reduce the costs of network communication [33], whereas Spark's RDD system performs caching at a coarser granularity [27] and thus requires more communication.

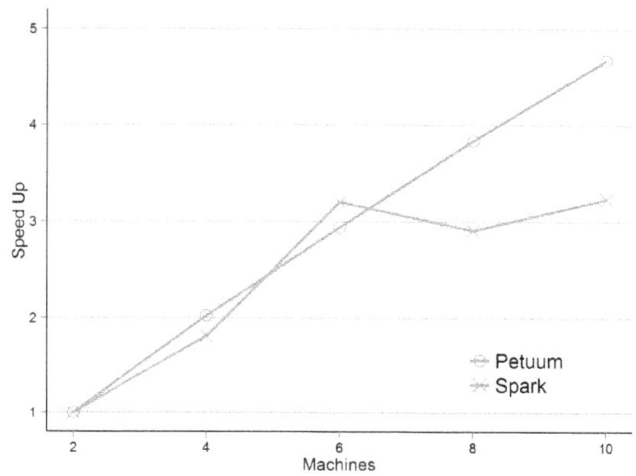

Figure 9: Speed-Up of $\mathsf{TDAP}_{\mathsf{Spark}}$ and $\mathsf{TDAP}_{\mathsf{Petuum}}$. The higher the slope of curve, the better the scalability. Both of them show good scalability, but $\mathsf{TDAP}_{\mathsf{Petuum}}$ is better.

Efficiency Comparison between $\mathsf{TDAP}_{\mathsf{Spark}}$ and $\mathsf{TDAP}_{\mathsf{Petuum}}$. We next focus on the efficiency comparison between $\mathsf{TDAP}_{\mathsf{Spark}}$ and $\mathsf{TDAP}_{\mathsf{Petuum}}$. Figure 10 shows the training time of both algorithms under the same setting (using $p = 3$ machines). We highlight that the training time of $\mathsf{TDAP}_{\mathsf{Petuum}}$ is *at least* 1/20 of that of $\mathsf{TDAP}_{\mathsf{Spark}}$, which is also exhibited in [33] due to the same reasons explained above.

Still in our production service, we observed that Petuum can process approximately *one order of magnitude* more users than Spark, with the same cluster setup, *i.e.,* the throughput of Petuum was at least 10 times larger than that of Spark. Hence, TDAP on Spark was possible, but the deployment was easier and more efficient using Petuum.

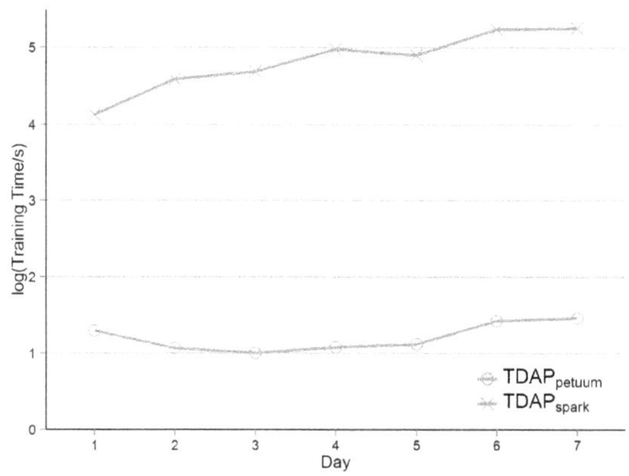

Figure 10: Training time (s) of $\mathsf{TDAP}_{\mathsf{Spark}}$ and $\mathsf{TDAP}_{\mathsf{Petuum}}$.

Summary. We find the followings: (a) TDAP gives better accuracy than FTRL-Proximal: TDAP improves 5.6% prediction accuracy on average over our datasets; (b) TDAP has good scalability: $\mathsf{TDAP}_{\mathsf{Petuum}}$ (resp. $\mathsf{TDAP}_{\mathsf{Spark}}$) is 4 (resp. 3) times faster when p increases from 2 to 10; and (c) $\mathsf{TDAP}_{\mathsf{Petuum}}$ outperforms $\mathsf{TDAP}_{\mathsf{Spark}}$ in terms of efficiency: $\mathsf{TDAP}_{\mathsf{Petuum}}$ runs at least 20 times faster than $\mathsf{TDAP}_{\mathsf{Spark}}$.

6. CONCLUSIONS AND DISCUSSION

Conclusions. In this paper, we have defined time-decaying online convex optimization TOCO problem, where the target model approaches to the most recent models while older history of the models are deemphasized, to tackle the fast-changing data. We have proposed a time-decaying adaptive prediction TDAP algorithm to solve TOCO problem, where recursive closed forms of the model update functions have been designed. To scale big data, we have parallelized the TDAP algorithm under both BSP and SSP consistency model. Using real-world datasets, we have experimentally verified that TDAP achieves good accuracy, scalability and efficiency, on both models. We further observe that TDAP on Spark is possible, but it is easier and more efficient for deployment on Petuum in practice.

Discussion. We note that the proof of *regret bounds* for TDAP, as well as TDAP_{BSP} and TDAP_{SSP}, are *not* the focus of this paper. We refer these to the future work.

7. REFERENCES

[1] A. Agarwal, O. Chapelle, M. Dudík, and J. Langford. A reliable effective terascale linear learning system. *JMLR*, 15(1):1111–1133, 2014.

[2] D. Agarwal, B.-C. Chen, and P. Elango. Fast online learning through offline initialization for time-sensitive recommendation. In *SIGKDD*, pages 703–712, 2010.

[3] B. Babcock, S. Babu, M. Datar, R. Motwani, and J. Widom. Models and issues in data stream systems. In *PODS*, 2002.

[4] D. M. Blitzer J and P. F. Biographies, bollywood, boom-boxes and blenders: Domain adaptation for sentiment classification. *ACL*, 7:440–447, 2007.

[5] H.-I. Choi and W. J. Williams. Improved time-frequency representation of multicomponent signals using exponential kernels. *TSP*, 37(6):862–871, 1989.

[6] T. H. Cormen and M. T. Goodrich. A bridging model for parallel computation, communication, and i/o. *CSUR*, 28:208, 1996.

[7] S. V. S. D. Cormode, G. and B. Xu. Forward decay: A practical time decay model for streaming systems. In *ICDE*, pages 138–149, 2009.

[8] W. Dai, A. Kumar, J. Wei, Q. Ho, G. Gibson, and E. P. Xing. High-performance distributed ml at scale through parameter server consistency models. In *AAAI*, 2015.

[9] C. B. Do, Q. V. Le, and C.-S. Foo. Proximal regularization for online and batch learning. In *ICML*, pages 257–264, 2009.

[10] J. C. Duchi, A. Agarwal, and M. J. Wainwright. Dual averaging for distributed optimization: convergence analysis and network scaling. *Automatic control, IEEE Transactions on*, 57(3):592–606, 2012.

[11] J. Gama, I. Žliobaitė, A. Bifet, M. Pechenizkiy, and A. Bouchachia. A survey on concept drift adaptation. *ACM Computing Surveys*, 46, 2014.

[12] R. Gemulla, E. Nijkamp, P. J. Haas, and Y. Sismanis. Large-scale matrix factorization with distributed stochastic gradient descent. In *SIGKDD*, pages 69–77, 2011.

[13] Q. Ho, J. Cipar, H. Cui, S. Lee, J. K. Kim, P. B. Gibbons, G. A. Gibson, G. Ganger, and E. P. Xing. More effective distributed ml via a stale synchronous parallel parameter server. In *NIPS*, pages 1223–1231, 2013.

[14] M. Isard, M. Budiu, Y. Yu, A. Birrell, and D. Fetterly. Dryad: distributed data-parallel programs from sequential building blocks. In *SIGOPS Review*, volume 41, pages 59–72, 2007.

[15] S. S. Keerthi and D. D. A modified finite newton method for fast solution of large scale linear svms. In *JMLR*, volume 6, pages 341–361, 2005.

[16] R. Klinkenberg. Learning drifting concepts: Example selection vs. example weighting. *Intelligent Data Analysis*, 8:281–300, 2004.

[17] I. Koychev. Gradual forgetting for adaptation to concept drift. ECAI Workshop, 2000.

[18] A. Kyrola, D. Bickson, C. Guestrin, and J. K. Bradley. Parallel coordinate descent for l1-regularized loss minimization. In *ICML*, pages 321–328, 2011.

[19] J. Langford, L. Li, and T. Zhang. Sparse online learning via truncated gradient. In *NIPS*, pages 905–912, 2009.

[20] K. B. Lee, J. Siegel, S. Webb, S. Leveque-Fort, M. Cole, R. Jones, K. Dowling, M. Lever, and P. French. Application of the stretched exponential function to fluorescence lifetime imaging. *Biophysical Journal*, 81(3):1265–1274, 2001.

[21] R. T. G. e. a. Lewis D D, Yang Y. Rcv1: A new benchmark collection for text categorization research. In *JMLR*, volume 5, pages 361–397, 2004.

[22] M. Li, D. G. Andersen, J. W. Park, A. J. Smola, A. Ahmed, V. Josifovski, J. Long, E. J. Shekita, and B.-Y. Su. Scaling distributed machine learning with the parameter server. In *OSDI*, pages 583–598, 2014.

[23] J. Ma, L. K. Saul, S. Savage, and G. M. Voelker. Identifying suspicious urls: an application of large-scale online learning. In *ICML*, pages 681–688, 2009.

[24] H. B. McMahan. Follow-the-regularized-leader and mirror descent: Equivalence theorems and l1 regularization. In *AISTATS*, pages 525–533, 2011.

[25] H. B. McMahan, G. Holt, D. Sculley, M. Young, D. Ebner, J. Grady, L. Nie, T. Phillips, E. Davydov, D. Golovin, et al. Ad click prediction: a view from the trenches. In *SIGKDD*, pages 1222–1230, 2013.

[26] H. B. McMahan and M. Streeter. Adaptive bound optimization for online convex optimization. *COLT*, 2010.

[27] X. Meng, J. Bradley, B. Yavuz, E. Sparks, S. Venkataraman, D. Liu, J. Freeman, D. Tsai, M. Amde, S. Owen, et al. Mllib: Machine learning in apache spark. *arXiv preprint arXiv:1505.06807*, 2015.

[28] T. Moon, L. Li, W. Chu, C. Liao, Z. Zheng, and Y. Chang. Online learning for recency search ranking using real-time user feedback. In *CIKM*, pages 1501–1504, 2010.

[29] S. Provencher. A fourier method for the analysis of exponential decay curves. *Biophysical journal*, 16(1):27, 1976.

[30] Y. Singer and J. C. Duchi. Efficient learning using forward-backward splitting. In *NIPS*, pages 495–503, 2009.

[31] W. Windig and B. Antalek. Direct exponential curve resolution algorithm (decra): a novel application of the generalized rank annihilation method for a single spectral mixture data set with exponentially decaying contribution profiles. *Chemometrics and Intelligent Laboratory Systems*, 37(2):241–254, 1997.

[32] L. Xiao. Dual averaging method for regularized stochastic learning and online optimization. In *NIPS*, pages 2116–2124, 2009.

[33] E. P. Xing, Q. Ho, W. Dai, J. K. Kim, J. Wei, S. Lee, X. Zheng, P. Xie, A. Kumar, and Y. Yu. Petuum: A new platform for distributed machine learning on big data. *SIGKDD*, 2015.

[34] Y. Zhang and M. I. Jordan. Splash: User-friendly programming interface for parallelizing stochastic algorithms. *arXiv preprint arXiv:1506.07552*, 2015.

[35] B. Zhao, L. Fei-Fei, and E. P. Xing. Online detection of unusual events in videos via dynamic sparse coding. In *CVPR*, pages 3313–3320, 2011.

[36] M. Zinkevich, J. Langford, and A. J. Smola. Slow learners are fast. In *NIPS*, pages 2331–2339, 2009.

[37] M. Zinkevich, M. Weimer, L. Li, and A. J. Smola. Parallelized stochastic gradient descent. In *NIPS*, 2010.

Analyzing Volleyball Match Data from the 2014 World Championships Using Machine Learning Techniques

Jan Van Haaren
KU Leuven — Department of Computer Science
Celestijnenlaan 200A, 3001 Leuven, Belgium
jan.vanhaaren@cs.kuleuven.be

Horesh Ben Shitrit
PlayfulVision
Ch. de la Raye 13, 1024 Ecublens, Switzerland
horeshb@playfulvision.com

Jesse Davis
KU Leuven — Department of Computer Science
Celestijnenlaan 200A, 3001 Leuven, Belgium
jesse.davis@cs.kuleuven.be

Pascal Fua
EPFL — Computer Vision Laboratory
Station 14, 1015 Lausanne, Switzerland
pascal.fua@epfl.ch

ABSTRACT

This paper proposes a relational-learning based approach for discovering strategies in volleyball matches based on optical tracking data. In contrast to most existing methods, our approach permits discovering patterns that account for both **spatial** (that is, partial configurations of the players on the court) and **temporal** (that is, the order of events and positions) aspects of the game. We analyze both the men's and women's final match from the 2014 FIVB Volleyball World Championships, and are able to identify several interesting and relevant strategies from the matches.

Keywords

Sports analytics, Spatial data, Strategy detection

1. INTRODUCTION

Optical tracking enables analyses that go beyond descriptive statistics based on event data by providing sufficient context about the game state such that it is possible to gain insights into tactics and strategies. However, automatically detecting and understanding tactics in dynamic sports such as volleyball is a challenging problem as tactics comprise complex interactions among multiple players that evolve across both time and space. Hence, strategy detection must consider and evaluate a huge number of possible spatio-temporal movement patterns. Existing approaches, which largely look at basketball and soccer, tackle this problem by restricting the analysis in some way such as only considering a specific strategy [9], a short time window [4], or a small subset of players [5, 3].

This paper addresses automatically discovering attacking strategies in volleyball matches based on camera-tracking data of the players and the ball as a pattern mining task [1]. Specifically, we consider the following two tasks:

Task 1: Identify a team's attacking patterns in volleyball matches that occur frequently in *won* rallies and infrequently in *lost* rallies.

Task 2: Identify attacking patterns in a volleyball match that are used by one team but not the opposing team.

In contrast to most existing approaches, we attempt to identify patterns that account for both **spatial** and **temporal** aspects of the game. That is, we want to model (partial) configurations of players' positions on the court as well as how play evolves over time. To illustrate this, consider the following simple pattern automatically discovered by our approach:

```
IF player #13 performs the dig  AND NEXT
   player #1 performs the set
      in the front center zone AND NEXT
   player #8 performs the spike
      in position 81 of the court
THEN the attack is likely to be successful.
```

This pattern is temporal as the dig occurs first, the set second, and the spike third. The pattern is spatial as it states the location on the court where the set and spike occur (see Figure 1 for a description of the locations).

In order to automatically identify patterns like the one just shown, we use a relational-learning based approach. As much as possible, we attempt to employ a data-driven approach that can automatically determine which players and characteristics of the game state are relevant to the strategy and should be included in the pattern. We analyze data from both the men's and women's final match from the 2014 FIVB Volleyball World Championships. Our top-ranked discovered patterns represent strategies that are both interesting and relevant from a volleyball perspective.

2. BACKGROUND ON VOLLEYBALL

Volleyball [10, 2] is a ball sport that is played by two teams of six players each. A volleyball court is 18 meters (59 feet) long and 9 meters (29.5 feet) wide. Each team occupies one half of the court, which is 9 meters by 9 meters. The halves are separated by a net whose top is 2.43 meters above the floor in men's competitions and 2.24 meters in women's competitions. The overall goal is to score points by grounding the ball on the opponent's court.

KDD '16, August 13 - 17, 2016, San Francisco, CA, USA

ISBN 978-1-4503-4232-2/16/08...$15.00

DOI: http://dx.doi.org/10.1145/2939672.2939725

Figure 1: The division of the pitch in higher-level zones (left) and lower-level positions (right). The direction of play is from bottom to top, where the thick orange line at the top represents the net.

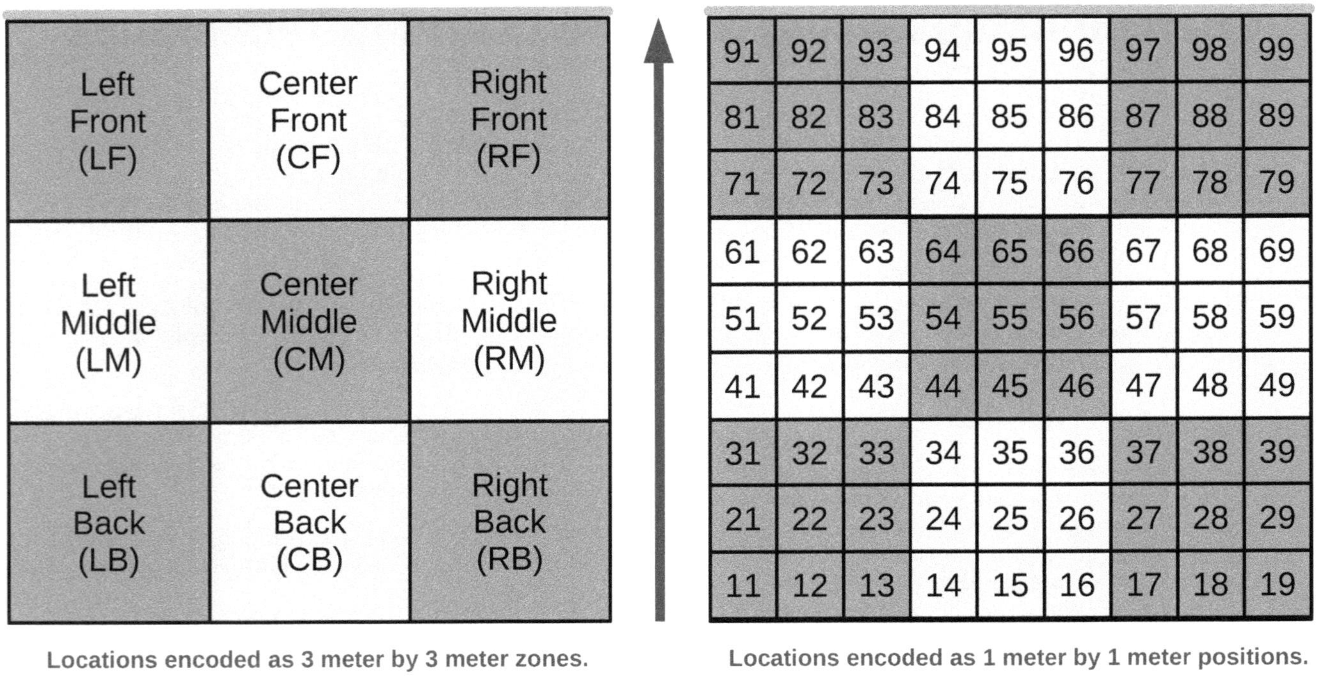

Volleyball matches are won by the first team to win three sets. A set is won by the first team to score 25 points and lead by two points. However, the fifth set is typically played to only 15 points. Each set consists of rallies and one team is awarded a point at the end of each rally. A rally starts by serving the ball from behind the back-line over the net into the opponent's court. The opponent may touch the ball up to three times to prevent it from hitting the court and to get the ball back over the net. A rally ends either when one of the teams makes a kill by grounding the ball on the opponent's court or when a team makes a foul.

The players follow a rotation scheme, where they must rotate one time in clockwise direction after their team wins the serve. Nevertheless, players do have different roles in the team and are free to move within their half of the court after the serve. Typically, the best offensive players will move towards the net, while the best defensive players will move to the back of the court. Although the rotation scheme imposes some restrictions, this tactical freedom allows teams to adopt a wide variety of match strategies. Therefore, volleyball players need to master the following six basic skills:

Serve The serve is the skill of moving the ball from behind the back-line into the opponent's court. While many different types of serves are used, the most popular type is the jump serve, where the server first tosses the ball high in the air and then jumps to hit it.

Dig The dig is the defensive skill of preventing the ball from hitting the court when the ball is nearly touching the floor after a serve or attack from the opponent. The dig is a reflex-based skill which often requires a player to dive towards the ball.

Pass The pass is very similar to the dig. However, in addition to preventing the ball from hitting the court, this defensive skill also involves moving the ball towards a team mate that is well-placed to set up an attack.

Set The set is the offensive skill of pushing the ball into the air such that a team mate can hit it into the opponent's court. The *setter*, who is the player performing the set, coordinates the offensive play of the team by deciding who will eventually attack the ball.

Spike The spike is the offensive skill of hitting the ball such that the opponent cannot prevent it from touching their court. The *spiker*, who is the player performing the spike, first makes a few steps and then jumps to swing at the ball.

Block The block is the skill of stopping or altering an opponent's attack by players standing at the net. An *offensive* block aims at keeping the ball into the opponent's court, while a *defensive* block aims at getting the ball under control by slowing it down.

Typically, the dig or pass is the first contact that the team makes with the ball, the set the second contact, and the spike the third contact. In this paper, we will focus on these three skills.

3. DATA

The data were collected at the FIVB Volleyball World Championships finals that were held in Poland[1] and Italy[2] in 2014. PlayfulVision [7] recorded several men's and women's

[1] http://poland2014.fivb.org/en
[2] http://italy2014.fivb.org/en

matches, including the final matches of both tournaments. They first captured each match using 8 video cameras placed at different angles at 30 frames per second and then used their ball and player tracking code to automatically determine the locations of the players and the ball in each frame. Furthermore, a human manually annotated each frame with the skills performed by the players (i.e., serve, dig, set, spike, and block) for both finals. The data set does not distinguish between digs and passes.

In this paper, we focus on the final matches of the world championships for which both the tracking information and the annotations are available. Table 1 shows the number of sets, rallies, and attacks in both matches as well as relevant statistics for each team such as the number of won rallies and how often they performed each of the skills.

We divide each rally into a series of attacks, where each attack consists of a sequence of consecutive skills performed by the same team. In this work, we only consider attacks that involve each of a dig, a set, and a spike. Based on this preprocessing, we construct positive and negative examples for four settings on each task. In task 1, the positive examples are a team's attacks that result in a point, while the negatives are all the team's other attacks. In task 2, the positives are the attacks from one team (e.g., Brazil), while the negatives are the attacks from the opponent (e.g., Poland). Table 2 lists the number of positive and negative examples for each setup.

To represent an attack, we take a snapshot of the pitch configuration at the time that a skill is performed. Each snapshot is described by the performed skill (dig, set or spike) as well as information about the location of each player and the ball. Each snapshot describes the locations on two levels of granularities: high-level zones (see Figure 1 left) and lower-level positions (see Figure 1 right).

4. RELATIONAL-LEARNING APPROACH TO STRATEGY DISCOVERY

Pattern mining typically focuses on finding patterns that occur frequently (that is, many times) in the data. Our problem has several other important characteristics that we must account for and which distinguish it from standard pattern mining. First, each of our tasks requires differentiating between two classes of examples, either successful and unsuccessful attacks or attacks done by two different teams. Second, we want to be able to simultaneously reason about multiple different levels of granularity in the data. For example, we may want to represent the court with both high-level zones and lower-level positions as illustrated in Figure 1. Furthermore, we would like to be able to discover patterns that involve specific players in a specific position as well as patterns that involve any player in a specific position. Third, this problem is inherently relational and it is crucial to find patterns that account for relationships such as changes over time. For example, we may want to know how the configuration of players changes between a dig and a set. Finally, we have specific knowledge about the game of volleyball and we would like to be able to incorporate it into the pattern mining process.

Based on the above requirements, we pursue an approach based on inductive logic programming (ILP) [6]. ILP is a relational learning approach that permits modeling multiple granularities, capturing relationships, and incorporating background knowledge. ILP represents data using a subset of first-order logic, which is a commonly used representation language for relational data. Interestingly, this subset is equivalent to relational algebra, which forms the basis for relational databases and the SQL query language. Thus, another way to view ILP's approach to rule construction is that it learns the WHERE clause of an SQL query for a given set of tables in a relational database (the FROM part of the query), and a target attribute (the SELECT part of the query).

The goal of ILP is to learn a model that distinguishes positive examples from negative examples. The model is a set of IF-THEN rules. The IF portion of a rule is a set of conditions and the THEN portion has an outcome. If all the conditions in the IF portion are met, then the outcome can be expected (usually with a certain probability). An advantage of rules of this form is that they are easy for domain experts to interpret. However, we do have to make a number of modifications to the standard ILP setup to adapt it to our needs. ILP is traditionally used for learning classifiers, and hence it has a preference for smaller models. That is, models with as few rules as possible with each rule being as short as possible. In contrast, for knowledge discovery we want to find all interesting rules. Furthermore, all other things being equal, we would prefer a detailed pattern that gave as much information about the strategy (e.g., assigns positions and actions to as many players as possible). Thus, unlike model learning, we tend to prefer more specific or detailed patterns to more general ones. To address these problems, we use a two-step process involving pattern generation and pattern post processing.

Pattern Generation

We use the well-known and publicly available Aleph ILP system [8] to generate rules. Depending on the task, we define a set of positive and negative examples as described in the Data section. Aleph constructs one rule at a time, with the goal of discovering a set of conditions such that the condition applies to as many positive and as few negative examples as possible. In other words, it tries to maximize the precision of the rule or the conditional probability that the outcome is true given that the condition is true.

Instead of learning one rule at a time, we define a set of criteria and attempt to identify rules that satisfy the criteria. We consider patterns of up to size 15. Each pattern must apply to at least five examples (i.e., a frequency threshold). Each pattern must have a precision of at least 25%. Given the size of the search space (e.g., there are on the order of 10^{22} patterns of size 15 alone), an exhaustive approach is infeasible so we employ a beam search. We collect all rules found by the beam search that meet these conditions.

When constructing a pattern, the learning algorithm can make use of both levels of granularity for the location and it automatically decides, based on the data, which to use. In fact, a single pattern can simultaneously make use of both granularities. The patterns can refer to specific players (e.g., player 1 is in the front center zone) or generic ones (e.g., a player is in the front center zone). Referring to generic players allows us to find patterns that generalize across different lineups for a team as teams may substitute during the match.

		Men's final		Women's final	
		Brazil	Poland	China	USA
Sets	Total sets	4	4	4	4
	Won sets	1	3	1	3
	Lost sets	3	1	3	1
Rallies	Total rallies	185	185	188	188
	Won rallies	92	93	94	94
	Lost rallies	93	92	94	94
Attacks	Total attacks	246	248	300	306
Skills	Total serves	86	89	95	93
	Total digs	124	120	167	173
	Total sets	105	106	145	154
	Total spikes	112	112	148	156
	Total blocks	39	42	51	52

Table 1: Statistics for the men's and women's final at the 2014 World Championships.

		Men's final		Women's final	
		Brazil	Poland	China	USA
Task 1	Positive examples	51	49	55	61
	Negative examples	18	17	25	36
Task 2	Positive examples	96	95	132	144
	Negative examples	95	96	144	132

Table 2: The number of positive and negative examples for each task.

Pattern Post Processing

Even with our constraints, a huge number of patterns were generated. For task 1, there were 53,212 patterns generated for Brazil, 79,907 for Poland, 51,593 for China, and 77,509 for the USA. For task 2, there were 190,956 patterns generated for Brazil, 197,467 for Poland, 269,753 for China, and 327,731 for the USA. We post processed the patterns and only retained those that included all three skills (dig, set, and spike) we were interested in. This resulted in 1,527 patterns for Brazil, 1,301 for Poland, 242 for China, and 2,037 for the USA in task 1. For task 2, there were 65,484 patterns generated for Brazil, 41,763 for Poland, 73,011 for China, and 84,639 for the USA.

Then, we ranked the patterns by the number of specific players and locations the patterns contained. This enforces a preference for longer, more specific patterns. We broke ties by considering pattern coverage (number of positives the pattern applies to), pattern precision, and pattern length.

5. RESULTS AND DISCUSSION

We present the top-ranked pattern for each of the eight setups we consider. Most of these patterns capture the same offensive strategy, which involves attacking over one side of the court. The patterns do have some small variations, such as about whether the attack is on the left or right side. This attacking pattern is a well-known volleyball strategy. Next, we discuss the top-ranked pattern in each setup in more detail.

Task 1: Which offensive strategy is most successful for each team?

Figures 2 through 5 visualize the offensive patterns that occur in successful attacks but not unsuccessful ones. In all figures, numbers represent specific players, the capital letter X represents the location of the ball, and other capital letters (A, B, and C) represent generic players. That is, they denote the presence of a player in that location, but do not specify which player is there, and hence account for the fact that teams can substitute players. The net is shown in orange at the top of the image.

Figure 2 shows the top-ranked pattern for the Poland men's team. The setter, who is the player with jersey number 5, is already close to the net at the time of the dig. He sets the ball to the front left zone, where another player B spikes it. The pattern covers five successful attacks and no unsuccessful ones. Looking at the location of the spike, the Polish team had 36 successful (including the five covered by this pattern) and 16 unsuccessful spikes in the front left zone.

Figure 3 shows the top-ranked pattern for the Brazil men's team. This pattern is very similar to the one for the Polish team, but with two important exceptions. First, the spike occurs on the right side of the court. Second, the spike occurs in a very specific location, at the back right corner of the front right zone. The pattern covers five successful attacks and no unsuccessful ones. Here, the specific location is important to the pattern as, in the entire front right zone, Brazil had 22 successful attacks (including the five covered by this pattern) and 13 unsuccessful attacks. In terms of the specific position where player 4 was located, Brazil attempted 11 spikes of which nine were successful. Thus the team was much more successful in this location than in the zone in general. The Polish team was less successful from this specific location, attempting 15 spikes of which 10 were successful. Also, in contrast to the women's final, the USA and China only attempted four spikes in aggregate in this specific location and none of them were successful.

Figure 4 shows the top-ranked pattern for the USA women's team. This again illustrates an attack from the side of the court at the front. Given that player B spikes the ball and the ball is located in the front left zone, that is the location where the spike was performed. Notice that a player denoted A moves from the left middle to the left front between the dig and the set. Thus, the setter could have set to either side for the spike. The pattern covers five successful attacks and no unsuccessful ones. The USA attempted 56 spikes in the front right zone of which 37 were successful (including the five covered by this pattern) and 19 were unsuccessful.

Figure 5 shows the top-ranked pattern for the China women's team. This pattern is less specific than the previous three, but it still shows the same general scheme of attacking from the side of the court on the front. Given that the ball is in the front rightmost corner next to the net at the time of the spike, we can infer that this is where player 8 is located. The pattern covers five successful attacks and no unsuccessful ones. Over all spikes in this specific position, China had eight successful spikes (including the five covered by this pattern) and two unsuccessful ones.

Task 2: Which common offensive strategy distinguishes a team from its opponent?

Figures 6 through 9 show the offensive patterns that distinguish between two teams playing against each other. The patterns are illustrated in the same manner as for Task 1.

Figure 6 shows the top-ranked pattern employed by the Poland men's team that is not used by the Brazilian team in their match. Figure 7 shows the top-ranked pattern for the Brazil men's team that is not used by the Polish team. These patterns are quite similar, with a set in the middle and a spike by player 10 on the outside in the front. The difference is that the Polish number 10 attacks on the right and the Brazilian number 10 on the left. One possible explanation is that these players have different dominant hands. Typically in volleyball the spiker wants his dominant hand closest to where the ball is coming from (that is, right-handed players want to spike from the front left, and left-handed players want to spike from the front right). We could not verify this hypothesis.

Figure 8 shows the top-ranked pattern for the USA women's team that is not used by the Chinese team. Figure 9 shows the top-ranked pattern for the China women's team that is not used by the USA team. These patterns are slightly less informative as they do not indicate the location of the spike. All the patterns tell is that the ball is set in the front center zone.

How do men's and women's volleyball compare to each other?

Another natural question to ask is how do the men's and women's game compare to each other. The statistics in Table 1 show that there are some commonalities between them. Namely, the number of rallies is roughly the same in both finals. However, the women's match features many more attacks than the men's final. Furthermore, the number of digs, set, spikes, and blocks is much higher in the women's final than in the men's final. This is most likely due to the faster pace of men's volleyball, which makes it harder to gain control of the ball after an attack from the opponent.

6. CONCLUSION

We proposed a relational-learning based approach to identifying different strategies based on optical tracking data from volleyball matches. In contrast to most existing work, our approach is able to discover spatio-temporal patterns on multiple different levels of granularity that characterize successful attacking play in volleyball. Specifically, it discovered several strategies that make sense from a volleyball perspective. Ultimately, knowledge about what types of patterns work well can be used to alter match tactics and training sessions.

Acknowledgments

We thank the International Volleyball Federation (FIVB) for supporting the Volleyball Tracking System-project (VTS) and allowing PlayfulVision to use their video footage and data for academic research. Jan Van Haaren is supported by the Agency for Innovation by Science and Technology (IWT). Jesse Davis is partially supported by the KU Leuven Research Fund (C22/15/015), and FWO-Vlaanderen (G.0356.12, SBO-150033).

7. REFERENCES

[1] C. Aggarwal and J. Han, editors. *Frequent Pattern Mining*. Springer, 2014.

[2] FIVB. Official Volleyball Rules, 2015. [Online; accessed 12-February-2016].

[3] K. Knauf and U. Brefeld. Spatio-Temporal Convolution Kernels for Clustering Trajectories. In *Proceedings of the KDD Workshop on Large-Scale Sports Analytics*, 2014.

[4] P. Lucey, A. Bialkowski, P. Carr, Y. Yue, and I. Matthews. "How to Get an Open Shot:" Analyzing Team Movement in Basketball Using Tracking Data. In *Proceedings of the MIT Sloan Sports Analytics Conference 2014*, 2014.

[5] P. Lucey, D. Oliver, P. Carr, J. Roth, and I. Matthews. Assessing Strategy Using Spatio-Temporal Data. In *Proceedings of the ACM SIGKDD Conference on Knowledge Discovery and Data Mining*, 2013.

[6] S. Muggleton and L. De Raedt. Inductive Logic Programming: Theory and Methods. *The Journal of Logic Programming*, 19:629–679, 1994.

[7] PlayfulVision. Volleyball Tracking System (VTS), 2016. [Online; accessed 10-February-2016].

[8] A. Srinivasan. The Aleph Manual. *Machine Learning at the Computing Laboratory, Oxford University*, 2001.

[9] J. Wiens, G. Balakrishnan, J. Brooks, and J. Guttag. To Crash or Not to Crash: A Quantitative Look at the Relationship Between Offensive Rebounding and Transition Defense in the NBA. In *Proceedings of the MIT Sloan Sports Analytics Conference 2013*, 2013.

[10] Wikipedia. Volleyball — Wikipedia, The Free Encyclopedia, 2015. [Online; accessed 7-December-2015].

Figure 2: Frequent successful offensive pattern by Poland in the men's final. The setter, who is the player with jersey number 5, is already close to the net at the time of the dig. He sets the ball to the front left zone, where another player B spikes it. Here, player B could denote any other Polish player.

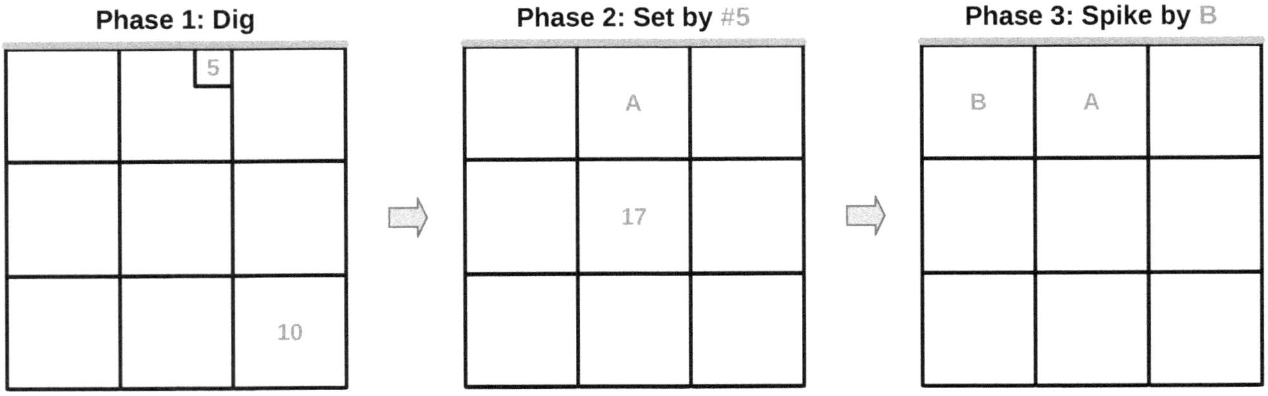

Figure 3: Frequent successful offensive pattern by Brazil in the men's final. The setter, who is the player with jersey number 1, is already close to the net at the time of the dig. He sets the ball from the front center zone to the back right corner of the front right zone, where the player with jersey number 4 spikes it. X denotes the location of the ball.

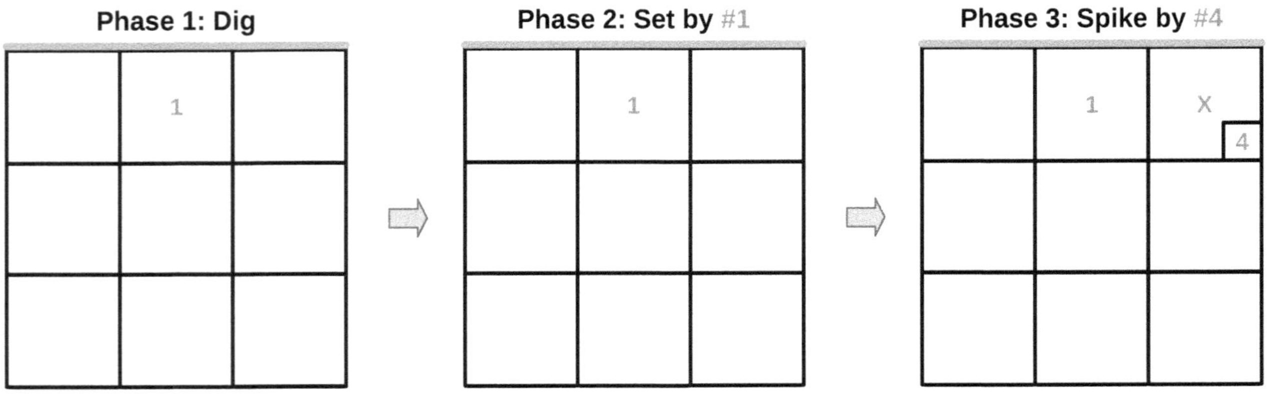

Figure 4: Frequent successful offensive pattern by the USA in the women's final. Player 1, who is the setter, is in the front center at the time of the dig. Player 1 sets the ball to the front left where player B spikes it. A player denoted A moves from the left center to the left front between the dig and the set. It appears that the setter could set to either side for a spike. X denotes the location of the ball.

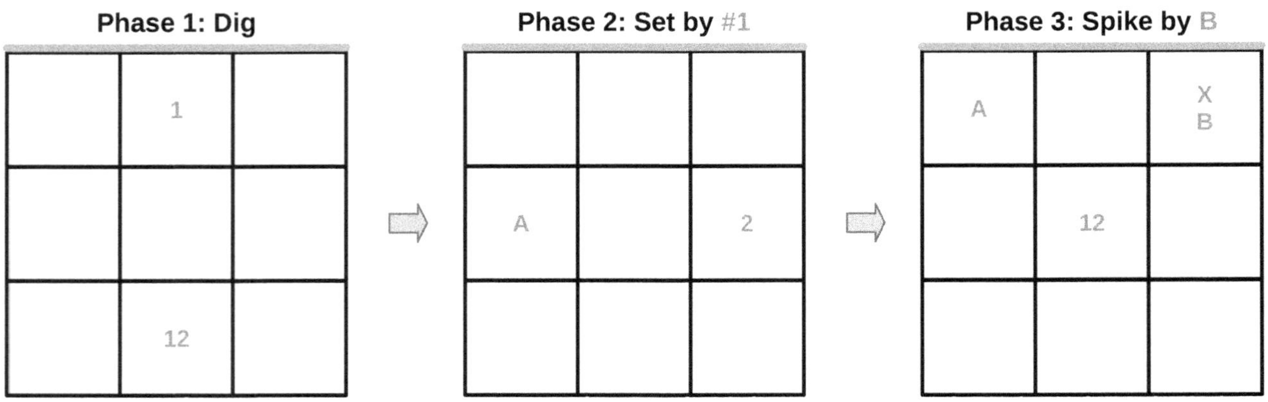

Figure 5: Frequent successful offensive pattern by China in the women's final. In this pattern, player 5 sets the ball and it is spiked by player 8 in the front right corner of the court. X denotes the location of the ball.

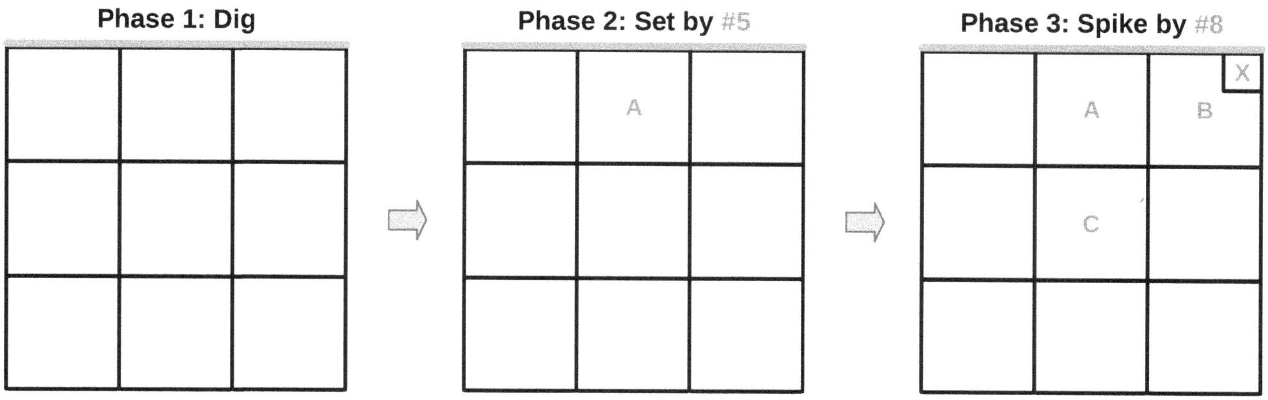

Figure 6: Frequent offensive pattern by Poland that Brazil does not frequently employ in the men's final. Player with jersey number 5 sets the ball from the front center to the front right where it is spiked by player number 10. X denotes the location of the ball.

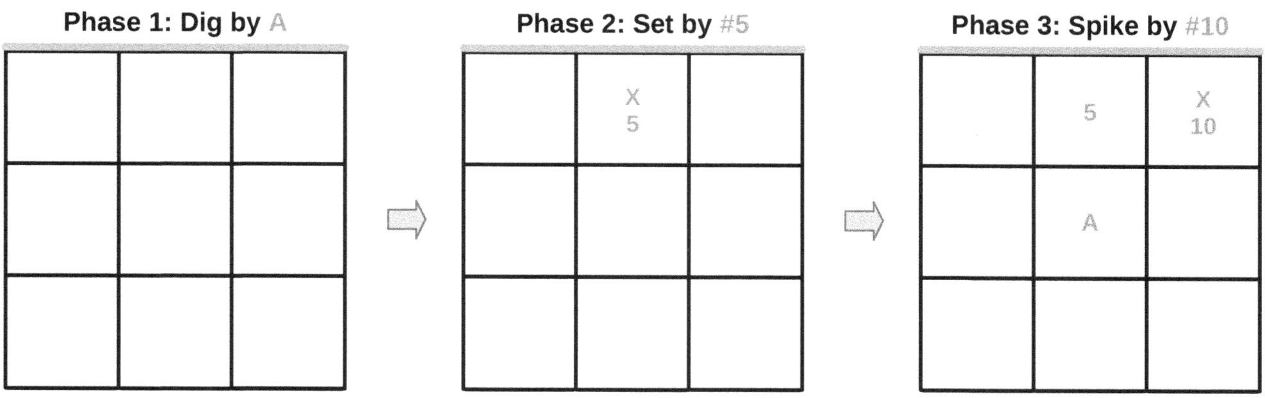

Figure 7: Frequent offensive pattern by Brazil that Poland does not frequently use in the men's final. The player with jersey number 1 is located in the front center at the time of the dig. He sets the ball from the front center to the front left. Player 10 moved from the middle left zone at the time of the dig to the front left zone, where he spiked the ball.

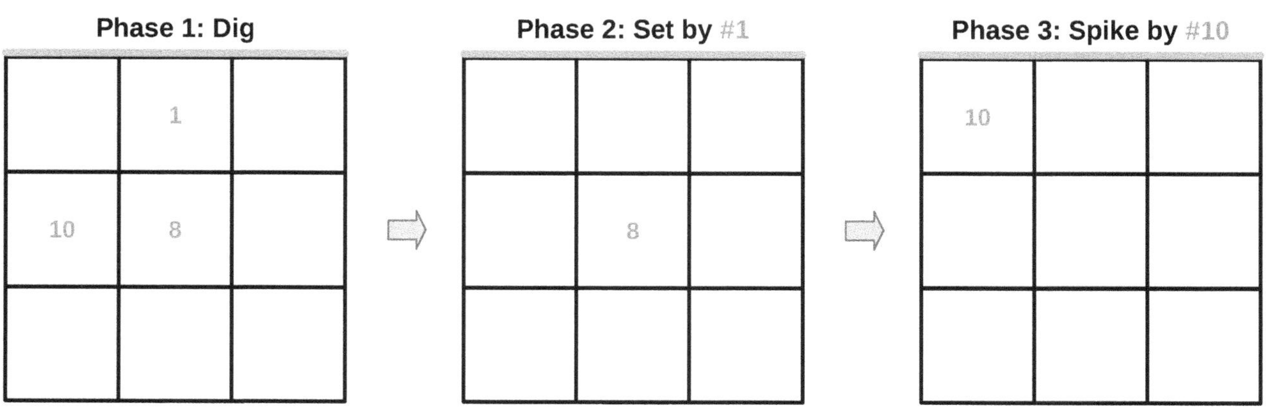

Figure 8: Frequent offensive pattern by the USA not used by China in the women's final. The ball is set by the player with jersey number 1 in the front center zone. Afterwards, another player spikes the ball. X denotes the location of the ball.

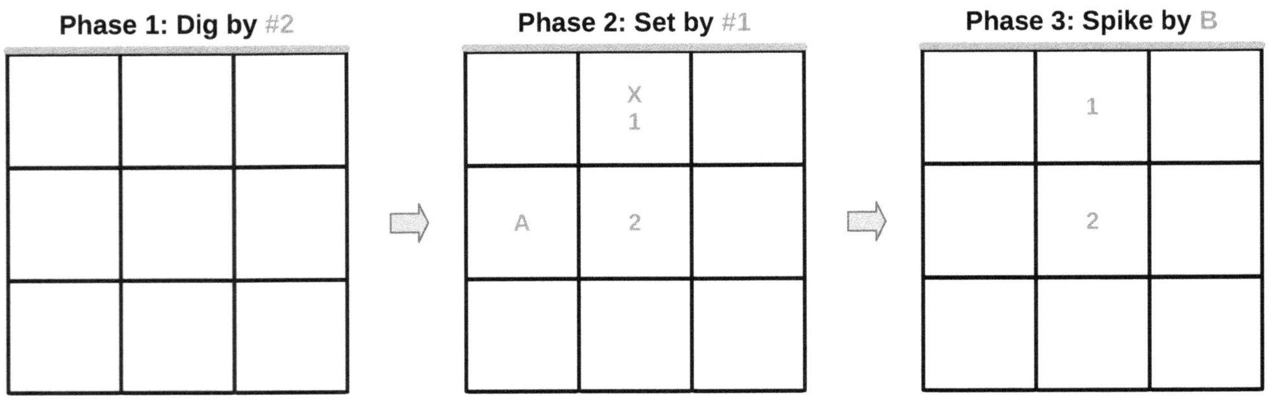

Figure 9: Frequent offensive pattern by China not used by the USA in the women's final. The ball is set by player 5 in the front center zone. Afterwards, player 1 spikes the ball. X denotes the location of the ball.

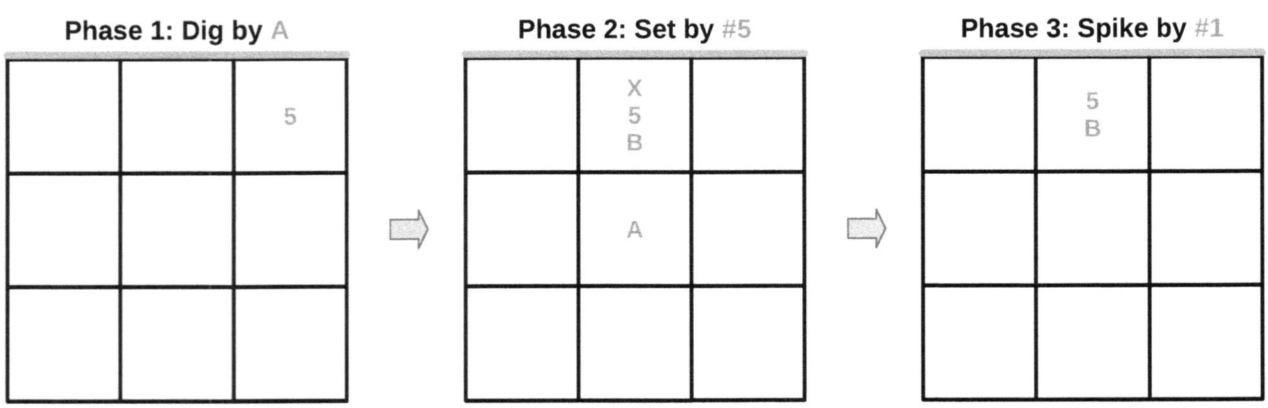

Crime Rate Inference with Big Data

Hongjian Wang†, Daniel Kifer‡, Corina Graif§, Zhenhui Li†
†College of Information Sciences and Technology
‡Department of Computer Science & Engineering
§Department of Sociology and Criminology
Pennsylvania State University, University Park, PA, USA
{hxw186, jessieli}@ist.psu.edu, dkifer@cse.psu.edu, corina.graif@psu.edu

ABSTRACT

Crime is one of the most important social problems in the country, affecting public safety, children development, and adult socioeconomic status. Understanding what factors cause higher crime is critical for policy makers in their efforts to reduce crime and increase citizens' life quality. We tackle a fundamental problem in our paper: crime rate inference at the neighborhood level. Traditional approaches have used demographics and geographical influences to estimate crime rates in a region. With the fast development of positioning technology and prevalence of mobile devices, a large amount of modern urban data have been collected and such big data can provide new perspectives for understanding crime. In this paper, we used large-scale Point-Of-Interest data and taxi flow data in the city of Chicago, IL in the USA. We observed significantly improved performance in crime rate inference compared to using traditional features. Such an improvement is consistent over multiple years. We also show that these new features are significant in the feature importance analysis.

1. INTRODUCTION

Understanding how to control crime is important because exposures to violence and crime have been unusually high in the U.S. for several decades and, while declining, they remain high [6, 16]. Over half a million children and youth aged 10-24 years were treated in 2012 in emergency departments for nonfatal physical assault injuries related to gun shots, cuts and stabbings, among others [17]. Understanding the neighborhood context of crime is particularly important because victimization and other forms of crime exposures have many severe consequences. Beyond the high medical bills and violent death, consequences include behavioral and mental health problems, aggression, substance abuse, post-traumatic stress disorder, and suicide, lower academic achievement, and engaging in further violence [22].

In this paper, we study the problem of crime rate inference of communities. We select Chicago as the target of study for the following reason. Chicago has more homicides and non-negligent manslaughter rates (15.2) per 100,000 residents than New York (4.0) and Los Angeles (6.5) according to the FBI crime statistics for 2013 and has experienced no decline in the past decade compared to the other two large cities, which have been on a slow declining slope [39].

KDD'16 August 13-17, 2016, San Francisco, CA, USA
 ISBN 978-1-4503-4232-2/16/08. . . $15.00
DOI: http://dx.doi.org/10.1145/2939672.2939736

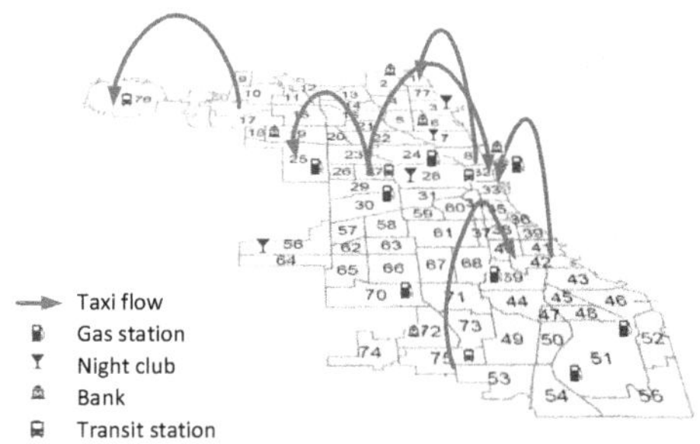

Figure 1: An illustration of various types of features we used in Chicago. The POI distribution across community areas reflects profiles of the region functionality. The taxi flow connects non-adjacent regions and act as "hyperlinks" on the space.

Traditionally, researchers have used demographic information (e.g., population poverty level, socioeconomic disadvantage, racial composition of population) to estimate the crime rate in a community [24]. However, such demographic information only contains partial information about the neighborhoods and does not dynamically reflect the changes in the community (e.g., official counts are collected by the U.S. Census Bureau every 10 years). Using only demographic information will result in a relative error of at least 30% for crime rate estimation in Chicago (refer to experiment section in the paper). Existing studies also use the geographical influence [4] to estimate the crime rate, i.e., the crime in the nearby communities can be propagated to the focal community. But this geographical influence is of little help in improving the crime inference on top of demographic feature, with at most 0.4% relative improvement in our experiments. This is probably because the nearby communities also share similar demographics, which limits the additional benefit of geographical influence.

Recently, big data reflecting city dynamics have become widely available [45], e.g., traffic flow, human mobility, social media, and crowd-generated Points-Of-Interest (POI). As shown in Figure 1, such newer types of big data could provide us new insights to understand some traditional socioeconomic urban problems, such as the crime rate inference problem we focus on in this paper. In particular, we propose to study two newer types of urban data: POI and taxi flow.

POI data. POI data provide venue information such as GPS coordinates, category, popularity, and reviews. These POIs mostly belong to categories such as food, shop, transit, education, etc. Recent studies have shown that using such categorical information of POIs are useful to profile neighborhood functions [44]. Such neighborhood functions could further help us predict crime rate (e.g., communities with less education or entertainment facilities may have a higher rate of crime). Our experiments show that incorporating POI features significantly improve the crime rate inference. Adding POI features in addition to demographics features reduces the relative error by at least 5% in our experiments. This demonstrates that POI data provide additional information about the communities that is not covered by the demographics.

Taxi flow data. A huge amount of taxi flow data reflect how people commute in the city. In previous studies, when using geographical influence [4], people assume that a community is affected by the spatially nearby communities. However, communities are not only affected by spatially-close communities. Even if two communities are distant in geographical space, they could have a strong correlation if many people frequently travel between these two communities [23]. We hypothesize that taxi flows may be considered as "hyperlinks" in the city that connect the locations and we use such data to estimate crime rates. Taxis may be preferred to public transportation by offenders traveling to a crime location as they offer more privacy and more flexible pick-up and drop-off points. Even if taxis do not constitute the main transportation mode in committing crime, taxi flows may be a proxy for broader patterns of population routine activity and mobility, commuting flows, and other forms of social and economic exchanges between two communities over space. Such exchanges may increase the number of potential targets and opportunities for crime [13, 9] or contribute to inter-community diffusion of information about successful local strategies to control or prevent crime (e.g., successful features of neighborhood watch programs). Our experiments show very promising results – adding taxi flow data on top of all other features can further decrease the error by 5%.

We conduct extensive experiments including a systematic comparison between linear regression and negative binomial models, tests of different combinations of features, detailed discussions of how to construct features, analysis of the relative importance of features, and theoretical interpretations of the results from a social scientist (a co-author in the paper). The experiments are conducted on the crime data over multiple years. We demonstrate that using the big urban data shows significant improvements.

In summary, the contribution of this paper are: 1) We study an old but very important crime inference problem by utilizing new urban data: POIs and taxi flows. 2) We find that utilizing these new types of big urban data significantly improves the crime rate inference. 3) We conduct systematic experiments to compare different results and feature combinations. The significantly better performance could serve as a new baseline for future crime inference problems.

The rest of this paper is organized as follows. We first review the related work in Section 2. The crime inference problem is formulated in Section 3. We discuss the inference model in Section 4 and feature extraction procedure in Section 5. The Section 6 presents the quantitative evaluation results on real data. Finally, we conclude the paper in Section 7.

2. RELATED WORK

In the criminology literature researchers have studied the relationship between crime and various features. Examples are historical crime records [28, 40], education [15], ethnicity [8], income level [32], unemployment [18], and spatial proximity [4]. In data mining, newer types of data are used in the study. For example, there are studies using twitter to predict crime [41, 20], and studies using cellphone data [38, 7] to evaluate crime and social theories at scale. Overall, the existing work on crime prediction can be categorized into three paradigms.

Time-centric paradigm. This line of work focuses on the temporal dimension of crime incidents. For example, in a study [28], the authors propose to use a self-exciting point process to model the crime and gain insights into the temporal trends in the rate of burglary. In another study [33], the authors investigate the temporal constraints on crime, and propose an offender travel and opportunity model. This paper validates the claim that a proportion of offending is driven by the availability of opportunities presented in the routine lives of offenders.

Place-centric paradigm. Most existing work adopt a place-centric paradigm, where the research question is to predict the location of crime incidents. The predicted crime location is usually referred by the term *hotspot*, which has various geographical size. There are plenty of studies on exploration of the crime hotspots. For example, in a study [37] the authors use criminal offense records to identify spatio-temporal patterns at multiple scales. They employ various quantitative tools from mathematics and physics and identify significant correlation in both space and time in the crime behavioral data. Short *et al.* [36] use a simple model to study the dynamics of crime hotspots and identify stable hotspots, where criminals are modeled as random walkers. Bogomolov *et al.* [7] use human behavioral data derived from mobile network and demographic sources, together with open crime data to predict crime hotspots. They compare various classifiers and find random forests have the best prediction performance. The paper [41] uses automatic semantic analysis to understand natural language Twitter posts from which the crime incidents are reported. Some other work [12, 14] employ kernel density estimation (KDE) to identify and analyze crime hotspots. Those studies form another form of crime prediction, which relies on the retrospective crime data to identify areas of high concentrations of crime. In [30], the authors extend the crime cluster analysis with a temporal dimension. They employ the space-time variants of KDE to simultaneously visualize geographical extent and duration of crime clusters.

Population-centric paradigm. In the last paradigm, research focuses on the criminal profiling at individual and community levels. At the individual level, [40] aim to automatically identify crimes committed by the same individual from a historical crime database. The proposed system, called *Series Finder*, is designed to find and classify modus operandi (M.O.) of criminals. At the community level, Buczak *et al.* [10] use fuzzy association rule mining to find crime patterns. The rules they found are consistent across all regions. The paper constructs association rules from population demographics in communities. In another paper [38], the authors use computational methods to validate various social theories at a large scale. They used mobile phone data in London, from which they mine the people dynamics as features to correlate with crime.

Our problem is different from the first two categories of work, mainly because our innovation lies in using newer type of data to enhance the commonly used traditional counterparts. More specifically, we use POI to enhance the demographics information and use taxi flow as hyperlinks to enhance the geographical proximity correlation. Although our problem does not consider the temporal dimension of crime in depth, it could be a promising supplement to better profile crime. Our problem does not predict the location of any particular crime incident. Therefore the methods proposed in place-centric methods are not applicable in our problem. However, the features we proposed may be incorporated in those crime prediction models.

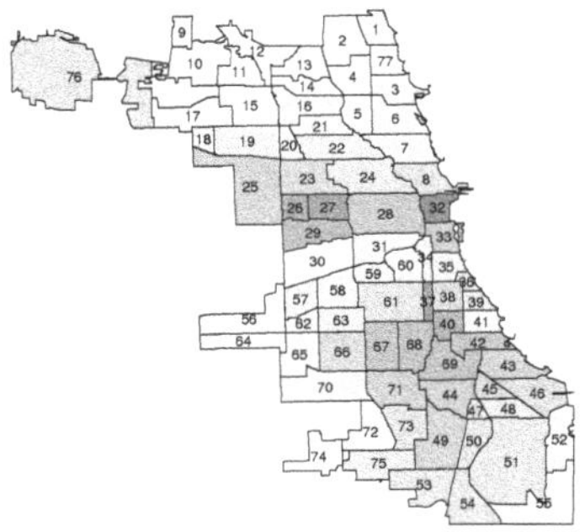

Figure 2: Crime rate of Chicago by community areas. The community area #32 is Chicago downtown, which has the highest crime rate.

Our problem falls into the third paradigm because we try to profile the crime rate for Chicago community areas. In our problem, the community areas are well-defined and stable geographical regions. The newly proposed POI features and taxi links providenew perspectives in profiling the crime rate across community areas.

3. OVERVIEW

The crime data collected in Chicago has detailed information about the time and location (i.e., latitude and longitude) of crime and the types of crime. In our problem, the term crime count refers to number of crime incidents in a region (i.e., community area) in a year. The *community area* is used as our geographical unit of study, since it is well-defined, historically recognized and stable over time [42]. In total, there are 77 community areas in Chicago. Crime rate is the crime count normalized by the population in a region. We use vector $\vec{y} = [y_1, y_2, \dots, y_n]$ to denote the crime rates in regions. The crime rate inference problem is to estimate the crime rate in one region using the crime rate of other regions in the same year by considering the features of regions and correlations between regions.

The crime data of Chicago are obtained from the City of Chicago data portal [3]. Chicago is the city with most complete crime data that are made public online. The crime dataset contains the incident date, location (strict name and GPS coordinates), and primary type from year 2001 to 2015. In total there are 5,856,414 recorded crime incidents over 15 years, which is an average 390,417 crimes incidents per year. We visualize the crime normalized by population in Figure 2, from which we can see that the downtown area has the highest crime rate.

In this paper we study the crime rate inference problem. More specifically, we estimate the crime rate of some regions given the information of all the other regions. Without loss of generality, we assume there is one community area t with crime rate y_t missing, and we use the crime rate of all the other regions $\{y_i\}\backslash y_t$ to infer this missing value. Our problem is mathematically formalized as follows

$$\hat{y}_t = f(\{y_i\}\backslash y_t, X), \tag{1}$$

where X refers to observed extra information of all those community areas.

We consider two types of features X for inference:

- Nodal feature. Nodal features describe the characteristics of the focal region. Such features include demographic information and Point-of-Interest (POI) distribution. Demographics are frequently used in literature, but POI is a newer type of big data, which we find significantly improve the crime inference accuracy.
- Edge feature: (1) Geographical influence. Geographical influence considers the crime rate of the nearby locations. This feature has been extensively used in literature as well. To estimate the focal region, the crime rate of nearby regions are weighted according to spatial distances. (2) Hyperlink by taxi flow. Locations are connected through the frequent trips made by humans, which can be considered as the hyperlinks in space. This type of feature has never been studied in literature. We propose to use taxi trips to construct the social flow. Our hypothesis is that two regions that are more strongly connected through social flow will influence each other's crime rate.

In the following sections, we first discuss the inference models based on these three types of features in Section 4 and then discuss how to construct these features using the real-world data in Section 5.

4. INFERENCE MODEL

4.1 Linear Regression

The most straightforward prediction model is the linear regression. This model assumes the error terms follow a Gaussian distribution $\epsilon \sim \mathcal{N}(0, \sigma^2)$.

Equation 2 gives the linear regression formulation of our problem.

$$\vec{y} = \vec{\alpha}^T \vec{x} + \beta^f W^f \vec{y} + \beta^g W^g \vec{y} + \vec{\epsilon}, \tag{2}$$

where $\vec{x}$ represents the nodal features, including demographics and POI distribution, W^f is the flow matrix of taxi flow, and W^g is the spatial matrix representing the geographical adjacency. On the right-hand side, ϵ is the only stochastic variable, and all other terms are fixed observation values. Therefore, we incorporate all the fixed observations into one term X, and we get the standard regression problem

$$E(y) = Xw + \epsilon.$$

4.2 Negative Binomial Regression

In our problem, we aim to infer the crime rate, which is guaranteed to be a non-negative integer. However, linear regression does not ensure this property. *Poisson regression* is another form of regression, more appropriate for count data than linear regression [19][27]. With shortened notation X, the Poisson regression model has the exponential function as link function

$$E(y) = e^{Xw}. \tag{3}$$

This comes from the assumption that y follows Poisson distribution with mean λ. Additionally, the mean λ is determined by observed independent variables X, with the link function $\lambda = e^{Xw}$. Adding all together, the joint probability of y is

$$P(y|w) = \frac{e^{-e^{Xw}} (e^{Xw})^y}{y!}. \tag{4}$$

However, Poisson regression enforces the mean and variance of dependent variable y to be equal. This restriction leads to the "over-dispersion" issue for some real problems, that is the presence of larger variability in data set than the statistical model expected. To address this, we use the Poisson-Gamma mixture model, which is also known as *negative binomial regression*. Negative binomial regression has been used in similar work [31].

Given that the crime rate y follows Poisson distribution with mean λ, in order to allow for larger variance, λ itself is a random variable having a Gamma distribution with shape $k = r$ and scale $\theta = \frac{1-p}{p}$. The probability function of y becomes

$$\begin{aligned} P(y|r,p) &= \int_0^\infty P_{Poisson}(y|\lambda) \cdot P_{Gamma}(\lambda|r,p) d\lambda \\ &= \frac{\Gamma(r+y)}{y!\Gamma(r)} p^k (1-p)^y \end{aligned} \quad (5)$$

This is exactly the probability density function of negative binomial distribution.

In negative binomial regression, the link function is

$$E(y) = e^{Xw+\epsilon}. \quad (6)$$

The error term e^ϵ is the mixture prior, and we assume it follows Gamma distribution with shape parameter $k = \frac{1}{\theta}$, so that it has mean $E(e^\epsilon) = k\theta = 1$ and variance $Var(e^\epsilon) = k\theta^2 = \theta$. This setting ensures the $E(y) = e^{Xw} \cdot e^\epsilon = e^{Xw}$.

5. FEATURE EXTRACTION

In this section, we will discuss the details of features used in our method. The two types of new features we use are extracted from Point-Of-Interest data and taxi flow data. Below we describe the datasets used to construct features and the characteristics of these features.

5.1 Nodal Feature: Demographics

Socioeconomic and demographic features of neighborhoods have been widely used to predict crime [7, 25, 43, 34]. Previous studies have shown that crime rate correlates with certain demographics. For example, [26, 24] suggests that population diversity leads to less crime in certain neighborhoods. In our study, we include demographic information from the US Census Bureau's Decennial Census [2]. Using 2010 census information would overlap with the time in which crime is measured. Instead, we use year 2000 demographic data because we are interested in predictors that precede temporally the period in which crime rates are evaluated. The demographics include the following features:

total population, population density, poverty, disadvantage index, residential stability, ethnic diversity, race distribution.

The poverty index measures the proportion of community area residents with income below the poverty level. The disadvantage index is a composite scale based on prior work [35], a function of poverty, unemployment rate, proportions of families with public assistance income, and proportion of female headed households. The residential stability measures home ownership and proportion of residents who lived in the neighborhood for more than one year. Racial and ethnic diversity is an index of heterogeneity [24] based on six population groups, including: Hispanics, non-Hispanic Blacks, Whites, Asians, Pacific Islanders and others.

Figure 3 visualizes the crime rate and demographics features in Chicago by community areas. Comparing with Figure 2, it is clear that the crime rate and poverty index and disadvantage index are consistent, the ethnic diversity shows an inverse correlation, and the total population has little correlation with crime.

Table 1 shows the Pearson correlation coefficient between various demographics features and the crime rate at community area level. The corresponding p-value is also calculated and shown in the table to indicate the significance of the correlation coefficient. There are in total 77 community areas in Chicago. Table 1 shows such correlation with several most correlated features. We can see that the poverty index and disadvantage index positively and strongly correlate with crime, while the ethnic diversity negatively correlates with crime. Other features such as total population, population density, and residential stability have weaker correlations. One counter-intuitive observation is that the total population has a weak and negative correlation with crime. The reason is that we use crime rate in each community area, which is already normalized by the population, and therefore the total population and population density have less impact.

Table 1: Pearson correlation between demographic features and crime rate (* indicates significant correlations with p-value less than 5%).

Feature	Correlation	p-value
Total Population	-0.1269	0.2716
Population Density	-0.1972	0.0855
Poverty Index	**0.5573***	1.403e-07
Disadvantage Index	**0.5959***	1.082e-08
Residential Stability	-0.0453	0.6965
Ethnic Diversity	**-0.5545***	1.678e-07
Percentage of Black	**0.6696***	2.779e-11
Percentage of Hispanic	**-0.3820***	0.0006

5.2 Nodal Feature: Point-of-Interest (POI)

While demographics are traditional census data, POI is a type of modern data that provide fine-grained information about locations. We collect POI from FourSquare [1]. POI data from FourSquare provide the venue information including venue name, category, number of check-ins, and number of unique visitors. We mainly use the major category information because categories can characterize the neighborhood functions. There are 10 major categories defined by FourSquare:

food, residence, travel, arts & entertainment, outdoors & recreation, college & education, nightlife, professional, shops, and event.

In total, we have crawled 112,000 POIs from FourSquare for Chicago. Most of these POIs are in the downtown area of Chicago. For the purpose of visualization, we normalize the POIs count per category by the total POI count in a neighborhood and plot two selected categories, i.e. nightlife and professional, in Figure 4. The darker colored neighborhoods in Figure 4 are the ones with a higher proportion of residence POIs.

Table 2: Pearson correlation between POI category and crime rate (* indicates significant correlations with p-value less than 5%).

POI category	Correlation	p-value
Food	-0.1543	0.1803
Residence	-0.0610	0.5984
Travel	-0.0017	0.9883
Arts & Entertainment	-0.0049	0.9661
Outdoors & Recreation	0.0668	0.5637
College & Education	-0.0078	0.9473
Nightlife	-0.1553	0.1775
Professional	**0.3221***	0.0043
Shops	-0.1676	0.1450
Event	0.2196	0.0549

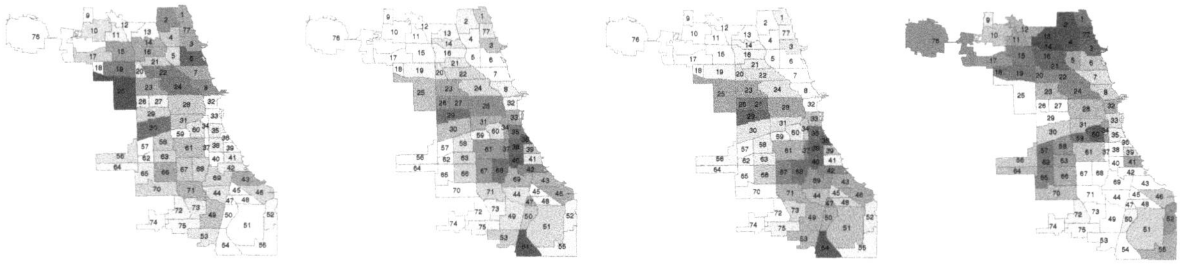

(a) Total population (b) Poverty index (c) Disadvantage index (d) Ethnic diversity

Figure 3: (a)-(d) Demographics in Chicago by community areas. Darker colors indicate higher values. Each demographic feature is normalized into $[0, 1]$.

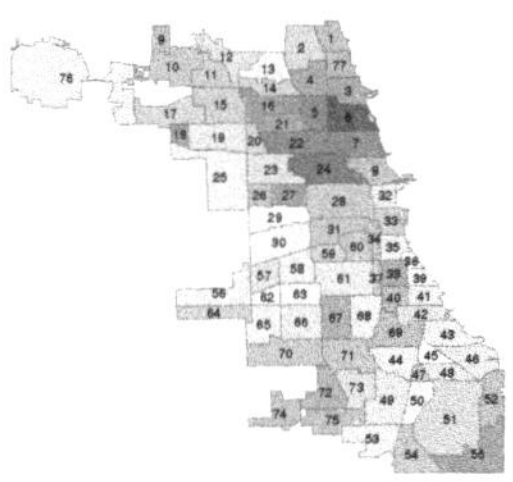

(a) Nightlife (b) Professional

Figure 4: POI ratio per neighborhood. The saturation of color is proportional to the ratio value. The "professional" category distribution is more consistent with the crime distribution, and therefore it is the most correlated with crime. Meanwhile, the "nightlife" category is negatively correlated with Chicago crime. The POI ratios are independently normalized for different POI categories.

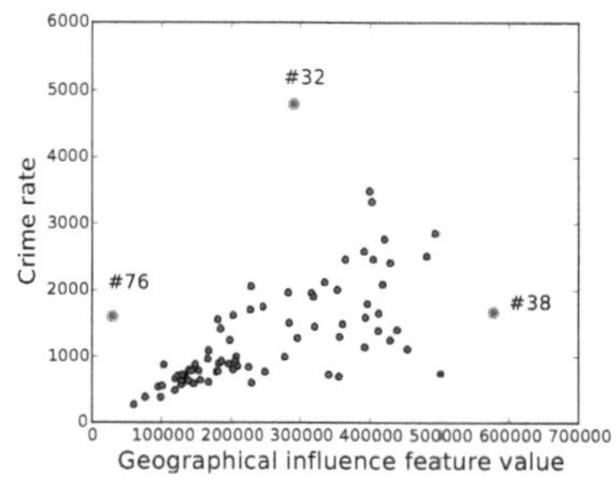

Figure 5: The correlation between geographical influence feature and crime rate. In the plot we marked out three outliers and their corresponding community area ID.

In Table 2 we show the Pearson correlation between POI category and crime rate. The category "professional" is most significantly correlated with the crime rate. Under the professional POI category, there are some venues with a large population concentration, such as transportation center, convention center, community center, and coworking space. In those venues, the population volume is high and residential stability is low, therefore the professional POI counts positively correlates with crime rate. One counter-intuitive observation is that "nightlife" category is not positively correlated with crime (-0.1553). This can be seen in Figure 4(a). The majority of nightlife venues in Chicago are located in the northern area, while most crime incidents occur in the downtown area.

5.3 Edge: Geographical Influence

Together with the US census demographics data, we also collected the boundary shape files of Chicago, which are used to calculate the geographical influence feature. Previous studies have also shown that the crime rate at one location is highly correlated with nearby locations [21, 11]. Such geographical influence is also frequently used in the literature [5, 29]. It is calculated as:

$$\vec{F^g} = W^g \cdot \vec{Y}, \tag{7}$$

where W^g is the spatial weight matrix. If region i and j are not geospatially adjacent, $w^g_{ij} = 0$; otherwise, $w^g_{ij} \propto distance(i, j)^{-1}$.

In Figure 5, we plot crime rate with respect to geographical influence calculated in Eq. 7. We observe an obvious positive correlation, which means if nearby neighborhoods have a high crime rate, the focal neighborhood is more likely to have a high crime rate. We also do observe a few outliers in Figure 5. These neighborhoods show different crime rate in their nearby neighborhoods compared to their own. For example, as we can also see in Figure 2, community area #38 locates in an area where the the neighbors have high crime rates but its crime rate is relatively low; in contrast, neighborhood #32 has a high crime rate even though its neighbors have relatively low crime. The community area #76 home of the O'Hare International Airport is far from most of other community areas, however its own crime rate is relative high.

5.4 Edge: Hyperlinks by Taxi Flow

In our Chicago taxi dataset, there are 1,048,576 taxi trips in total from October to December in 2013. For each trip, the following information are available: pickup/dropoff time, pickup/dropoff location, operation time, and total amount paid. We requested the taxi trip records from Chicago under the Illinois Freedom of Information Act. Figure 6 shows a visualization of the major flows at community level.

One of our hypotheses is that the social interaction among two community areas propagates crime from one region to another. The Chicago taxi data captures the social interactions among various community areas. To calculate this, we first map all taxi trips to community areas to get the taxi flow w_{ij} $\forall i, j \in \{1, 2, \cdots n\}$. Then the taxi flow lag is constructed by the product of social flow

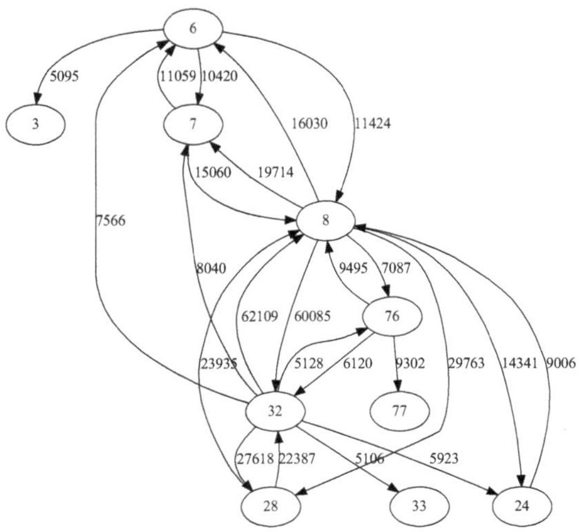

Figure 6: Major taxi flows between neighborhoods. The label on the edge shows the count of taxi trips commuting between two community areas from October to December months in 2013. We set a threshold (more than 5,000 trips) on the flow and only plot high volume flows. The label on a node is the ID of its corresponding community area. We can see that there are several hub community areas, such as #6, #8, #32, which are all in the downtown areas.

and the crime rate of neighboring regions as follows

$$\vec{F^t} = W^t \cdot \vec{Y}. \tag{8}$$

The taxi flow W^t is a matrix with entry w_{ij} denoting the taxi flow from i to j. Note that $\forall i$, $w^s_{ii} = 0$ in matrix W^t, because we have to exclude the crime in the focal area from its own predictor. The semantic of this taxi flow feature is how much crime in the focal area is contributed by its neighboring areas through social interaction.

The correlation between taxi flow and crime rate is shown in Figure 7. From the scatter plot, we can see that overall the crime rate is positively correlated with the taxi flow. There are two outliers clearly shown in Figure 7. The community area #32 is the downtown Loop, which has the highest crime rate and is hard to predict by taxi flow. Another anomalous community area (#47) has relatively low crime rate by itself. However, this area has a lot of in flows from high-crime communities.

6. EXPERIMENTS

6.1 Settings

We adopt leave-one-out evaluation to estimate the crime rate of one geographic region given all the information of all the other regions. When we construct the spatial/social lag variable for the training data, the effect of testing region is completely removed. For example, if region y_t is the testing region, the remaining $\{y_i\}\backslash y_t$ become the training set. For any y_j in the training set, its geographical influence feature and taxi flow feature are constructed from $\{y_i\}\backslash\{y_t, y_j\}$.

In the evaluation, we estimate the crime rate for testing community areas. The accuracy of estimation is evaluated by mean absolute error (MAE) and mean relative error (MRE).

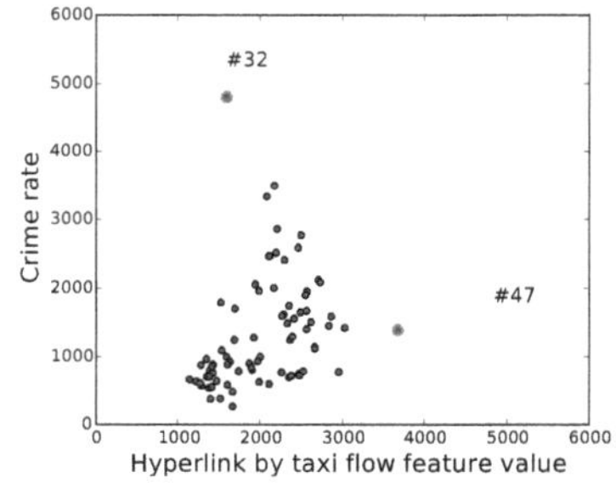

Figure 7: Correlation between taxi flow feature and crime rate. In the plot, we marked out two outliers and their corresponding community area ID.

$$MAE = \frac{\sum_i^n |y_i - \hat{y_i}|}{n} \tag{9}$$

$$MRE = \frac{\sum_i^n |y_i - \hat{y_i}|}{\sum_i^n y_i} \tag{10}$$

6.2 Performance Study

We evaluate the estimation accuracy under various feature combinations. The leave-one-out evaluation results are shown in Table 3. We run both the linear regression and the negative binomial regression on five consecutive years, 2010 – 2014. Both MAE and MRE are shown in the table. We have four types of features: demographics, POI, geographical influence and taxi flow. We test the various settings of feature combinations.

6.2.1 *Negative Binomial Regression vs. Linear Regression*

In Table 3, we can see that in different years and under most settings, the negative binomial regression significantly outperforms the linear regression (with only a few exceptions when using only demographic feature). When using all the features, NB is significantly better than LR with at least 6% improvement in relative error. One reason is that negative binomial regression is a count prediction model, which guarantees the prediction variable is non-negative . Another reason is that it is difficult to get very precise estimates of crime rate, and the negative binomial regression allows a large variance in the estimated crime rate. Therefore negative binomial is more appropriate for crime rate estimation than linear regression.

In the following discussions, we only refer to the performance of the negative binomial regression.

6.2.2 *POI Feature*

Adding POI features always improves the accuracy (see NB for column 2 vs. column1, column 6 vs. column 5, column 8 vs. column 7). The POI distribution reflects the functionality of a region. The most correlated POI major category is "professional", under which there are a lot of venues like transportation center and conventional center. These are locations with more dynamic movements of people. Such location information is not reflected in any of other features. POI thus provides unique information and it shows that using big data can benefit us in advancing the study of traditional crime inference problems.

Another issue that is worth discussing is whether POI is a surrogate of population features from demographics. That is, a region with POIs is a region with a higher population. However, as we

Table 3: Performance evaluation. Various feature combinations are shown in each column. The linear regression model and negative binomial results are compared by year group.

			Settings							
Column ID			1	2	3	4	5	6	7	8
Features[1]		Demo	✓	✓	✓	✓	✓	✓	✓	✓
		Geo					✓	✓	✓	✓
		POI		✓		✓		✓		✓
		Taxi			✓	✓			✓	✓
Year	Model[2]	Error								
2010	LR	MAE	394.41	416.98	408.09	406.93	394.78	432.45	402.25	416.41
		MRE	0.294	0.311	0.304	0.304	0.295	0.323	0.300	0.310
	NB	MAE	391.53	333.14	395.64	323.47	389.55	350.06	387.43	**320.75**
		MRE	0.292	0.249	0.295	0.241	0.290	0.261	0.289	**0.239**
2011	LR	MAE	380.22	409.30	396.97	401.11	379.61	422.94	389.39	408.91
		MRE	0.295	0.318	0.309	0.312	0.295	0.328	0.302	0.320
	NB	MAE	381.11	332.62	388.81	328.94	378.84	345.24	381.33	**335.97**
		MRE	0.296	0.259	0.302	0.256	0.294	0.268	0.296	**0.253**
2012	LR	MAE	378.91	412.95	401.54	412.20	376.53	423.88	399.25	419.93
		MRE	0.306	0.334	0.325	0.333	0.304	0.343	0.322	0.339
	NB	MAE	386.31	337.24	389.58	331.41	384.23	352.22	381.67	**345.49**
		MRE	0.312	0.273	0.315	0.268	0.310	0.284	0.308	**0.279**
2013	LR	MAE	367.89	420.81	390.75	402.75	369.24	433.48	388.92	412.31
		MRE	0.324	0.370	0.344	0.354	0.325	0.381	0.342	0.362
	NB	MAE	376.08	333.92	373.08	312.63	377.57	350.33	368.49	**319.86**
		MRE	0.331	0.294	0.328	0.275	0.332	0.308	0.324	**0.281**
2014	LR	MAE	331.28	375.53	349.00	350.31	329.93	386.90	345.79	361.28
		MRE	0.326	0.369	0.343	0.345	0.324	0.380	0.340	0.355
	NB	MAE	340.73	293.52	339.17	274.45	336.09	308.18	326.07	**273.27**
		MRE	0.335	0.289	0.334	0.270	0.331	0.303	0.321	**0.269**

[1] D – demographic features, G – geographical influence, P – POI features, T – taxi flow feature.
[2] LR – Linear Regression, NB – Negative Binomial Regression.

see from Table 3, adding POI in addition to demographics always outperforms the features without POI. This is because population from demographics reflects the number of residents in that region, but POI reflects dynamics of population (e.g., people go to venues for food, entertainment, or travel). Therefore, the dynamic population in POI further complements the residential population in demographics.

6.2.3 *Taxi Flow*

The taxi flow is shown to improve the inference accuracy (see NB for column 3 vs. column 1, column 7 vs. column 5, column 8 vs. column 6). This validates our hypothesis that crimes do not only correlate with nearby regions but also correlate through hyperlinks on the space (i.e., the taxi flow).

Comparing column 7 (D+G+T) with column 5 (D+G), we find that the improvement by taxi flow is not obvious. However, comparing column 8 (D+G+P+T) with column 6 (D+G+P), we observe a much significant accuracy boost. The reason could be that the taxi flow further complements the POI data. When POI information is missing from the predictor, the city dynamics captured by taxi flow are weakened as well.

6.3 Feature Construction

There are different ways to use the POI and taxi datasets. In this section, we share our insights into the more effective ways in constructing the features.

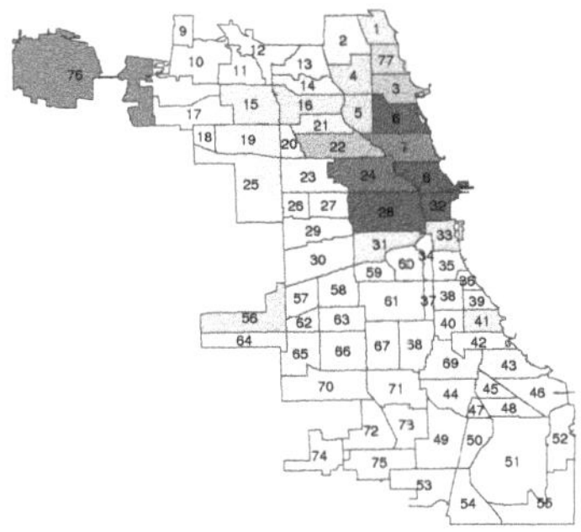

Figure 8: Absolute POI count distribution. In our crawled POI dataset, most community areas have less than 100 venues. Meanwhile, the downtown area there are over $10,000$ **venues for one community area, e.g. #8, #32.**

6.3.1 *POI Normalization*

The straightforward definition of POI distribution is calculated by normalizing the POI count in each category by the total POI counts. However, the POIs in Chicago are not evenly distributed. As shown in Figure 8, most POIs are in the downtown area and some areas only have a few POIs. If normalized by the total number of POIs in a neighborhood, two neighborhoods may show similar distributions but they are quite different. For example, a downtown neighborhood and a distant neighborhood may both have a high ratio of the food category but the downtown neighborhood has many more POIs in total and is more dynamic in population constitution. Therefore, using the raw count instead of normalized distribution is more effective. This is also demonstrated in estimation accuracy as shown in Table 4.

Table 4: Using POI count instead of POI percentage improve the estimation accuracy. Estimation for crime in 2014 with all other features.

Scheme	NB	
	MAE	MRE
POI count	273.27	0.269
POI percentage	283.16	0.278

6.3.2 *Taxi Flow Normalization*

The taxi flow represents the interactions among community areas. There are several different approaches to incorporate the taxi flow into the model. First, we can use the raw taxi count as a weight on crime from other neighborhoods. One issue with the raw count is the concentration of taxi trips distribution in the downtown area. Consider the following example. In the downtown area, the average taxi flow count is 1000 between any pair of community areas, while the average of suburbs is 100. When we propagate crime by raw taxi count, the same amount of crime in downtown is propagated with a 10 times higher coefficient than that of suburb.

To address this issue, we can normalize the taxi flow, and there are two different approaches to normalize. 1) We can normalize the taxi flow by the total incoming traffic of the destination community area, and the semantics of this normalization is splitting the crime in the destination to all its neighbors. 2) Alternatively, we can normalize the taxi flow by the outgoing total trips in the source community area. This normalization assumes the crime in each source community is spread out by the flow. The two normalization methods are shown in Figure 9.

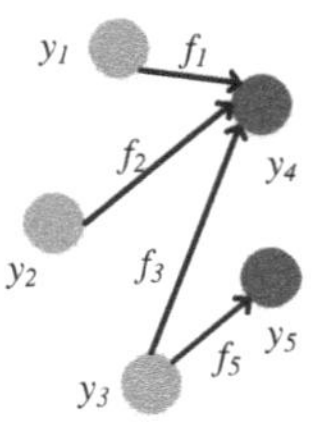

Normalization by source:

$$F_4^t = \frac{f_1}{f_1} y_1 + \frac{f_2}{f_2} y_2 + \frac{f_3}{f_3+f_5} y_3$$

Normalization by destination:

$$F_4^t = \frac{f_1}{f_1+f_2+f_3} y_1 + \frac{f_2}{f_1+f_2+f_3} y_2 + \frac{f_3}{f_1+f_2+f_3} y_3$$

Figure 9: Two different normalization schemes.

Table 5: Various approaches to construct taxi flow feature. Estimation for crime in 2013 with all other features.

Settings	NB	
	MAE	MRE
Taxi flow count	368.71	0.324
Taxi flow normalized by source	349.38	0.307
Taxi flow normalized by destination	319.86	0.281

In Table 5 we compare the different approaches to handle the taxi flow. Using raw taxi flow count is clearly not a good option, due to the unbalanced data distribution. We also observe that normalizing taxi flow by destination is better than normalization by source. The reason could be explained by the example given in Figure 9. Suppose the focal region is a transportation hub, which has a lot of isolated regions connected to it. If we normalize the crime by source region, then the taxi flow feature of focal region is overestimated, since the coefficients of its neighbors do not sum to one.

6.4 Feature Importance

In this subsection, we study the importance of features through significance tests and coefficient changes over the years.

6.4.1 *Significance Test*

From previous results, we see that combining POI features and taxi flow will help improve the estimation accuracy. Now we try to measure the significance of this accuracy boost by permutation tests. If a feature correlates with crime, when we randomly permute the values of this feature among neighborhoods, we will expect a higher error in crime estimation. So in each round of permutation, we can get an error in estimation. We compare the error with the original feature to the error distribution obtained from permutations. We conduct 1,000 rounds of permutations to approximately estimate the error distribution. The position of the original error in this distribution indicates the significance of this feature. For example, if the original error is smaller than 99% of the errors from the permutations, the p-value is 0.99.

Table 6: Estimated p-value for each feature. The p-value is defined as the possibility that a smaller error measure is observed under the null hypothesis.

Settings: D+S+P+T	LR		NB	
	MAE	MRE	MAE	MRE
	412.31	0.363	319.86	0.281
Feature	p-value			
D (demographics)	0.000	0.000	0.000	0.000
G (geographic inf.)	0.640	0.664	0.602	0.565
P (POI distribution)	0.025	0.025	0.001	0.001
T (taxi flow)	0.000	0.000	0.000	0.000

In Table 6, the p-values of different features are given. The demographics feature is the most significant with estimated p-value equals to 0.00. In all the $1,000$ random permutations of demographic feature, we never observe an error lower than the original error. The proposed POI distribution and taxi flow are significant as well, with a p-value of 0.5% and 1.3% for the negative binomial model. One interesting observation is that the geographical influence is not significant at all. One possible reason is that the demographics features capture the similarity of geographical neighbors, and therefore are surrogates of geographical influence.

6.4.2 *Coefficient Study*

In our regression model, the coefficient also indicates the importance of features. We normalize the values of all features to the range $[0, 1]$, so that coefficients are comparable. The top-6 features with the most significant coefficients are shown in Table 7. The top 3 rows in Table 7 are features with positive coefficients, which implies the positive correlation with Crime. The three features with negative coefficients are negatively correlated with crime.

By comparing the coefficients over different years, we observe that the coefficients are relatively stable with respect to time. The most important feature is always POI professional category, which represents many populated public areas. The other two important demographic features are disadvantage index and percentage black.

We also find three POI categories are among the top negatively correlated features. They are the residence, shop, and education categories. The reason is that at those places the population is relatively stable, which provides less opportunity for crime.

Table 7: The coefficients of the top-6 features over different years. There are 21 different features in total. Due to limited space, we only show the top 3 features with the highest positive/negative coefficients respectively.

Feature	Year				
	2010	2011	2012	2013	2014
POI professional	1.414	1.733	1.905	2.206	1.874
pct black	1.376	1.370	1.301	1.296	1.252
disadvantage index	1.237	1.055	1.270	1.700	1.462
POI education	-1.171	-1.265	-1.735	-2.041	-1.871
POI shops	-2.671	-2.747	-2.687	-2.549	-2.834
POI residence	-3.059	-2.719	-2.424	-2.151	-2.459

6.5 Improvements on Different Regions

The POI distributions are different from region to region. It is interesting to find out whether POI distribution is consistently positive in making the crime estimation better. We calculate the difference in estimation error (MAE) between two settings: 1) using demographics, geographical influence, taxi flow; and 2) using all these three features plus POI distribution. The similar measurement is calculated for the taxi flow feature. The results are shown in Figure 10. A positive difference (blue area) indicates that adding the new feature will help reduce the estimation error, while a negative difference (red area) indicates that the new feature adds more noise to the data.

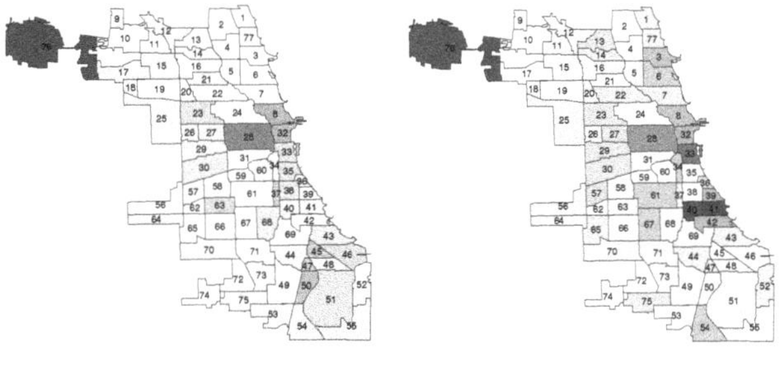

(a) POI (b) Taxi flow

Figure 10: Performance improvement per region by using POI or taxi flow features on 2014 crime. The difference of MAEs in estimating crime with/without POI feature is shown on the left, and the same measure of taxi flow is shown on the right. The color blue means the MAE is reduced by adding corresponding feature (i.e., better performance), while the red means the MAE is increased (i.e., worse performance). The color saturation indicates the value of difference.

It is interesting to find out that in the downtown area, i.e. community area #8, #32, #28, and #33, POI significantly improves the estimation accuracy. The reason is two fold. 1) The demographics information from census is mostly about the residing population in the focal area. However, in the downtown area there are a lot of floating population groups conducting various social activities, and this is not reflected by the census demographics. The POI information, on the other hand, reflects the functionality of a region, and plays a complementary role of demographic information. 2) In the downtown area, there are much more POIs than any other places, which provides more complete information about the community profile.

As for the taxi flow feature, it helps the most in those suburb area, because the taxi flow reflects the social interaction in those areas. In the downtown, the taxi flow feature incurs a relatively large estimation error. The reason is that the taxi flow distribution in Chicago is extremely skewed. Roughly 61% of the Chicago taxi trips have a destination in the downtown area, which may result in the model over-propagating crime estimates from all of Chicago into the downtown area.

7. CONCLUSION

In the social science literature, the demographics and geographical neighbors are known to exhibit strong correlations with crime. In this paper we solve the problem of crime rate inference with new features. More specifically, we propose to use POI features to assist the demographic features, and to use taxi flow as hyperlinks to supplement the geographical neighbors. The intuition behind the POI feature is that the POI distribution across community areas reflects profiles of the region functionality. The intuition behind the hyperlinks is that the taxi flow models the social interaction among nonadjacent regions, which potentially propagate crime or resources and information used in crime control. We adopt the negative binomial regression modal over the linear regression model, mainly because the count based regression models and guarantees positive prediction, while the linear regression may give negative crime rate as prediction. Both POI and taxi flow features from a publicly accessible dataset in Chicago are evaluated to be helpful. In the best scenario, the POI distribution and taxi flow reduces the prediction error by 17.6%.

8. ACKNOWLEDGEMENTS

The work was supported in part by NSF award #1544455, #1054389, and funding from NICHD R24-HD044943. The views and conclusions contained in this paper are those of the authors and should not be interpreted as reprinting any funding agencies.

9. REFERENCES

[1] Foursquare venues service. https://developer.foursquare.com/overview/venues.html.

[2] United states census bureau. http://www.census.gov.

[3] City of chicago data portal. https://data.cityofchicago.org/Public-Safety/Crimes-2001-to-present/ijzp-q8t2, 2015.

[4] ANSELIN, L. Under the hood: issues in the specification and interpretation of spatial regression models. *Agricultural economics 27*, 3 (2002), 247–267.

[5] ANSELIN, L., COHEN, J., COOK, D., GORR, W., AND TITA, G. Spatial analyses of crime. *Criminal justice 4*, 2 (2000), 213–262.

[6] BAUM, K. *Juvenile victimization and offending, 1993-2003.* US Department of Justice, Office of Justice Programs, Bureau of Justice Statistics, 2005.

[7] BOGOMOLOV, A., LEPRI, B., STAIANO, J., OLIVER, N., PIANESI, F., AND PENTLAND, A. Once upon a crime: towards crime prediction from demographics and mobile data. In *Proceedings of the 16th international conference on multimodal interaction* (2014), ACM, pp. 427–434.

[8] BRAITHWAITE, J. *Crime, shame and reintegration.* Cambridge University Press, 1989.

[9] BRANTINGHAM, P., AND BRANTINGHAM, P. Criminality of place. *European journal on criminal policy and research 3*, 3 (1995), 5–26.

[10] BUCZAK, A. L., AND GIFFORD, C. M. Fuzzy association rule mining for community crime pattern discovery. In *ACM SIGKDD Workshop on Intelligence and Security Informatics* (2010), ACM, p. 2.

[11] BURNELL, J. D. Crime and racial composition in contiguous communities as negative externalities: prejudiced household's evaluation of crime rate and segregation nearby reduces housing values and tax revenues. *American Journal of Economics and Sociology 47*, 2 (1988), 177–193.

[12] CHAINEY, S., TOMPSON, L., AND UHLIG, S. The utility of hotspot mapping for predicting spatial patterns of crime. *Security Journal 21*, 1 (2008), 4–28.

[13] COHEN, L. E., AND FELSON, M. Social change and crime rate trends: A routine activity approach. *American sociological review* (1979), 588–608.

[14] ECK, J., CHAINEY, S., CAMERON, J., AND WILSON, R. Mapping crime: Understanding hotspots.

[15] EHRLICH, I. On the relation between education and crime. In *Education, income, and human behavior*. NBER, 1975, pp. 313–338.

[16] FINKELHOR, D. *Childhood victimization: violence, crime, and abuse in the lives of young people: violence, crime, and abuse in the lives of young people*. Oxford University Press, USA, 2008.

[17] FOR DISEASE CONTROL, N. C., AND (CDC), P. Leading causes of nonfatal injury, united states 2001 - 2013. *Injury Prevention and Control: data and statistics* (2015).

[18] FREEMAN, R. B. The economics of crime. *Handbook of labor economics 3* (1999), 3529–3571.

[19] GARDNER, W., MULVEY, E. P., AND SHAW, E. C. Regression analyses of counts and rates: Poisson, overdispersed poisson, and negative binomial models. *Psychological bulletin 118*, 3 (1995), 392.

[20] GERBER, M. S. Predicting crime using twitter and kernel density estimation. *Decision Support Systems 61* (2014).

[21] GORMAN, D. M., SPEER, P. W., GRUENEWALD, P. J., AND LABOUVIE, E. W. Spatial dynamics of alcohol availability, neighborhood structure and violent crime. *Journal of studies on alcohol 62*, 5 (2001), 628–636.

[22] GRAIF, C. Toward a geographically extended perspective of neighborhood effects on children's victimization. *American Society of Criminology Annual Meeting* (2015).

[23] GRAIF, C., GLADFELTER, A. S., AND MATTHEWS, S. A. Urban poverty and neighborhood effects on crime: Incorporating spatial and network perspectives. *Sociology Compass 8*, 9 (2014), 1140–1155.

[24] GRAIF, C., AND SAMPSON, R. J. Spatial heterogeneity in the effects of immigration and diversity on neighborhood homicide rates. *Homicide Studies* (2009).

[25] HSIEH, C.-C., AND PUGH, M. D. Poverty, income inequality, and violent crime: a meta-analysis of recent aggregate data studies. *Criminal Justice Review 18*, 2 (1993), 182–202.

[26] JACOBS, J. *The death and life of great American cities*. Vintage, 1961.

[27] LAMBERT, D. Zero-inflated poisson regression, with an application to defects in manufacturing. *Technometrics 34*, 1 (1992), 1–14.

[28] MOHLER, G. O., SHORT, M. B., BRANTINGHAM, P. J., SCHOENBERG, F. P., AND TITA, G. E. Self-exciting point process modeling of crime. *Journal of the American Statistical Association* (2012).

[29] MORENOFF, J. D., AND SAMPSON, R. J. Violent crime and the spatial dynamics of neighborhood transition: Chicago, 1970–1990. *Social forces 76*, 1 (1997), 31–64.

[30] NAKAYA, T., AND YANO, K. Visualising crime clusters in a space-time cube: An exploratory data-analysis approach using space-time kernel density estimation and scan statistics. *Transactions in GIS 14*, 3 (2010), 223–239.

[31] OSGOOD, D. W. Poisson-based regression analysis of aggregate crime rates. *Journal of quantitative criminology 16*, 1 (2000), 21–43.

[32] PATTERSON, E. B. Poverty, income inequality, and community crime rates. *Criminology 29*, 4 (1991), 755–776.

[33] RATCLIFFE, J. H. A temporal constraint theory to explain opportunity-based spatial offending patterns. *Journal of Research in Crime and Delinquency 43*, 3 (2006), 261–291.

[34] SAHBAZ, O., AND HILLIER, B. The story of the crime: functional, temporal and spatial tendencies in street robbery. In *Proc of 6th International Space Syntax Symposium, Istanbul* (2007), pp. 4–14.

[35] SAMPSON, R. J., RAUDENBUSH, S. W., AND EARLS, F. Neighborhoods and violent crime: A multilevel study of collective efficacy. *Science 277*, 5328 (1997), 918–924.

[36] SHORT, M. B., D'ORSOGNA, M. R., PASOUR, V. B., TITA, G. E., BRANTINGHAM, P. J., BERTOZZI, A. L., AND CHAYES, L. B. A statistical model of criminal behavior. *Mathematical Models and Methods in Applied Sciences 18*, supp01 (2008), 1249–1267.

[37] TOOLE, J. L., EAGLE, N., AND PLOTKIN, J. B. Spatiotemporal correlations in criminal offense records. *ACM Transactions on Intelligent Systems and Technology (TIST) 2*, 4 (2011), 38.

[38] TRAUNMUELLER, M., QUATTRONE, G., AND CAPRA, L. Mining mobile phone data to investigate urban crime theories at scale. In *Social Informatics*. Springer, 2014, pp. 396–411.

[39] TRIBUNE, C. A tale of 3 cities: La and nyc outpace chicago in curbing violence, 2015.

[40] WANG, T., RUDIN, C., WAGNER, D., AND SEVIERI, R. Learning to detect patterns of crime. In *Machine Learning and Knowledge Discovery in Databases*. Springer, 2013.

[41] WANG, X., GERBER, M. S., AND BROWN, D. E. Automatic crime prediction using events extracted from twitter posts. In *Social Computing, Behavioral-Cultural Modeling and Prediction*. Springer, 2012, pp. 231–238.

[42] WIKIPEDIA. Community areas in chicago — wikipedia, the free encyclopedia, 2015.

[43] WOLFE, M. K., AND MENNIS, J. Does vegetation encourage or suppress urban crime? evidence from philadelphia, pa. *Landscape and Urban Planning 108*, 2 (2012), 112–122.

[44] YUAN, J., ZHENG, Y., AND XIE, X. Discovering regions of different functions in a city using human mobility and pois. In *ACM SIGKDD* (2012), ACM, pp. 186–194.

[45] ZHENG, Y., CAPRA, L., WOLFSON, O., AND YANG, H. Urban computing: concepts, methodologies, and applications. *ACM TIST 5*, 3 (2014), 38.

Improving the Sensitivity of Online Controlled Experiments: Case Studies at Netflix

Huizhi Xie
Netflix
100 Winchester Circle
Los Gatos, California, USA
kxie@netflix.com

Juliette Aurisset
Netflix
100 Winchester Circle
Los Gatos, California, USA
jaurisset@netflix.com

ABSTRACT

Controlled experiments are widely regarded as the most scientific way to establish a true causal relationship between product changes and their impact on business metrics. Many technology companies rely on such experiments as their main data-driven decision-making tool. The sensitivity of a controlled experiment refers to its ability to detect differences in business metrics due to product changes. At Netflix, with tens of millions of users, increasing the sensitivity of controlled experiments is critical as failure to detect a small effect, either positive or negative, can have a substantial revenue impact. This paper focuses on methods to increase sensitivity by reducing the sampling variance of business metrics. We define Netflix business metrics and share context around the critical need for improved sensitivity. We review popular variance reduction techniques that are broadly applicable to any type of controlled experiment and metric. We describe an innovative implementation of stratified sampling at Netflix where users are assigned to experiments in real time and discuss some surprising challenges with the implementation. We conduct case studies to compare these variance reduction techniques on a few Netflix datasets. Based on the empirical results, we recommend to use post-assignment variance reduction techniques such as post stratification [7] and CUPED [3] instead of at-assignment variance reduction techniques such as stratified sampling [2] in large-scale controlled experiments.

Keywords

Controlled experiment; Variance reduction; A/B testing; Randomized experiment; Sensitivity

1. BACKGROUND AND MOTIVATION

Controlled experiments are key for data-driven decisions in many technology companies. Running controlled experiments that are not sensitive enough to differences in business metrics caused by product changes can lead to suboptimal decisions with large revenue impact for companies like Netflix.

There are three ways to improve the sensitivity of controlled experiments: increasing sample sizes in the experiments, designing product changes that lead to large differences in business metrics, and reducing the sampling variance of business metrics.

The simplest way to increase sensitivity is to increase sample sizes. While the Netflix user base is very large, this option is not always practical. Many experimental product features affect only a small proportion of the user base, e.g., testing a new kids search experience on Android tablets has a relatively small audience, which limits the sample sizes. Moreover, while Netflix runs over a thousand experiments per year, there is always a desire to increase the pace of innovation by scaling up the number of experiments. With some experiments colliding with one another, available users for each experiment can become scarce. For these reasons, increasing the number of users assigned to experiments is often not feasible.

Two other avenues to improve the sensitivity of controlled experiments are explored in parallel at Netflix. Product managers lead cross-team efforts to focus on bold product changes that can lead to large positive differences in business metrics, while the experimentation team constantly seeks new experimentation methodologies to reduce the sampling variance of our business metrics.

This paper compares a few variance reduction techniques both theoretically and empirically based on a few Netflix datasets and provides guidance to experimenters on the choice of variance reduction techniques. Our primary contributions are threefold. First, we review the theory of three variance reduction techniques: stratified sampling [2], post stratification [7], and CUPED [3] and establish theoretical connections between them. Second, we describe an innovative implementation of stratified sampling at Netflix that addresses the challenges posed by assigning users to experiments in real time. Third, we conduct an empirical evaluation of these variance reduction techniques on a few Netflix datasets and compare their amount of variance reduction relative to simple random sampling.

2. CONTROLLED EXPERIMENTS AT NETFLIX

Netflix has a data-driven decision-making culture. We have learned through years of experimentation that using subjective intuition, even in a collective way, to make product decisions often yields the wrong answer. One way to

KDD '16 August 13-17, 2016, San Francisco, CA, USA

ACM ISBN 978-1-4503-4232-2/16/08.
DOI: http://dx.doi.org/10.1145/2939672.2939733

make product decisions is to hear what users have to say. But what users ask for and what actually works are very different. Running controlled experiments and making product decisions based on business metrics is the best way to bridge this gap. Business metrics should be chosen such that improving them is highly related to increasing the value users get from the Netflix service. See [6] for some examples where actual experiment results do not agree with subjective intuition in the movie/TV recommendation algorithm area and a more complete description of how controlled experiments are used to improve our movie/TV recommendation algorithms.

At Netflix, controlled experiments are leveraged in many different product areas such as movie/TV recommendation algorithms, user interface design, and messaging. Different product experiences in experiments are referred to as *cells*. In each experiment, we are typically interested in comparing various new experience(s), referred to as *test cell(s)*, with the current production experience, referred to as the *control cell*. For example, in a controlled experiment in the movie/TV recommendation algorithm area, the control cell maps to the current production algorithm and the test cell(s) map to new algorithm(s) we want to compare with the production one.

2.1 Test Audience

At Netflix, controlled experiments are run on both new and existing users [6]. New users are assigned to experimental conditions at the time of signup, while existing users can be assigned anytime after their free trial ends. While product decisions rely on results from both cohorts, they are more heavily based on results from new users since they have not been exposed to the Netflix experience before. For existing users, it is difficult to tease apart whether a movement in business metrics is simply due to a change in experience (change effect) [6] or whether it is caused by the new experience itself. One way to remove such change effect is to run experiments longer and observe if the difference in business metrics persists after a long time. But this slows down our pace of innovation. The other reason to favor results from new users is because they are more sensitive to product changes since they start with a free trial during which they are in an evaluation mode. Note that testing on new users is not a common practice in the industry but is very important for Netflix to make product decisions for the reasons just explained.

2.2 Business Metrics

Netflix's monthly subscription business model suggests a framework to define business metrics for controlled experiments. Our revenue comes solely from the monthly subscription fee that current users pay, and current users can cancel the subscription at anytime. Thus we believe maximizing revenue through product changes is closely related with maximizing the value we provide to our users. Revenue is proportional to the number of users that is affected by three processes: the acquisition rate of new users, current user cancellation rate, and the rate at which former users rejoin. The focus of this paper is on product changes that directly impact only current users. Hence the primary business metric of interest is current user cancellation rate or retention rate. However, there are some challenges with just looking at retention rate in product experiments.

First of all, as much as we hope that better product or user experience can increase user retention rate, it can be affected by many other factors that are not directly related to our product changes. Secondly, since our subscription is month by month, users typically choose to cancel their subscription by their next payment period. For new users, it typically takes a whole month to observe retention since they are assigned to the experiments at the beginning of their first payment period. For existing users, the wait time to observe retention varies depending on the number of days it takes from the start of the experiments to the users' next payment period.

Fortunately, we have observed that user engagement metrics are highly correlated with retention but are more sensitive. Moreover, we get to observe such engagement metrics from the start of an experiment. One good example of user engagement metrics is streaming hours. However, the relationship between streaming hours and retention is not linear. What we have learnt from historical data is that getting users that stream few hours per month to stream more has a much larger positive impact on retention than getting users that already stream a lot to stream a bit more. This is because those users with low streaming hours are more likely to be one of those on the fence of cancellation and are more sensitive to product changes.

So we summarize the distribution of streaming hours using I streaming thresholds T_i, $i = 1, ..., I$. For a given user, T_i is a binary metric indicating whether the user streamed more than H_i hours in a given time period. H_i's are chosen to minimize the loss of information from summarizing the distribution of streaming hours using these thresholds. Details are not covered in this paper. From a business perspective, these streaming thresholds allow decision makers to gain more insight on which part of the distribution of streaming hours is changed. While we have tried more sophisticated versions of streaming measurement in the past, these thresholds work well because they are easy to understand without much loss of information.

3. REVIEW ON VARIANCE REDUCTION TECHNIQUES

3.1 Terminology and Notation

We define all the users that can potentially be impacted by an experiment as the *population* for the experiment. Suppose there is one or more variable(s) that are correlated with the business metrics. These variables are measurable prior to an experiment and independent of the different experiences in the cells of the experiment. As an example, the signup country of a user is correlated with how likely the user is to retain but does not depend on the experiences tested in the experiment. We refer to these variables as *covariates* and denote them as X. The two sampling schemes considered in this paper are simple random sampling and stratified sampling. In stratified sampling, covariates are used to divide the population into K subpopulations called strata. For example, since Netflix is available in 190 countries, we can divide the population for an experiment in 190 strata based on the signup country covariate.

Now we introduce some terminology and notations used throughout the paper. Note that the following notations are used for both simple random sampling and stratified sampling.

- Random sample: a subset of users that are representative of the population
- Y: the business metric
- $T_i, i = 1..., I$: the binary streaming thresholds defined in Section 2.2
- $\mu = E(Y)$: the population mean of the business metric
- μ_k: the mean of the business metric for users in the kth stratum
- $\sigma^2 = var(Y)$: the population variance of the business metric
- σ_k^2: the variance of the business metric for users in the kth stratum
- p_k: proportion of the population in the kth stratum
- n_k: number of users from the kth stratum in a cell
- n: number of users in a cell from all the K strata, i.e., $n = \sum_{k=1}^{K} n_k$
- $Y_{11}, ...Y_{1n_1}, ...Y_{K1}, ..., Y_{Kn_K}$: business metrics of a random sample (either based on simple random sampling or stratified sampling) of users from the population where Y_{kj} is the business metric of the jth user from the kth stratum
- *Effect size*: difference between the population mean under the experience in the test cell and that in the control cell

Next we define two estimates of the population mean. The first is the standard simple sample average denoted as $\bar{Y}$. It is defined as

$$\bar{Y} = \frac{1}{n}\sum_{k=1}^{K}\sum_{j=1}^{n_k} Y_{kj}. \quad (1)$$

The second is a weighted average denoted as $\hat{Y}_{strat}$. It is defined as

$$\hat{Y}_{strat} = \sum_{k=1}^{K} p_k \bar{Y}_k, \quad (2)$$

where p_k is defined above and $\bar{Y}_k = \frac{1}{n_k}\sum_{j=1}^{n_k} Y_{kj}$ is the average of the business metric for users from the kth stratum. Note that, under stratified sampling, the two estimates in (1) and (2) are the same. More details around why this is true are in Section 3.3. However, these two estimates are not the same under simple random sampling. This is the reason why post stratification leads to variance reduction. See Section 3.4 for the details. The subscript *strat* is used in the weighted average estimate (2) because it comes from stratified sampling. Throughout the paper, we use E_{srs} and E_{strat} to denote the expectation of an estimate under simple random sampling and stratified sampling, respectively. Similarly, we use var_{srs} and var_{strat} to denote the variance of an estimate under simple random sampling and stratified sampling, respectively.

3.2 Overview

Variance reduction is a procedure to increase the precision of the sample estimate of some parameter such as the population mean. The sample estimate is typically based on a random sample of the population. While a well-known procedure in statistics, Monte Carlo simulation [8], and some other areas, its application in controlled experiments is relatively new. Next we review a few popular variance reduction techniques that can be easily applied to controlled experiments.

As a starting point, we briefly review the statistical inference in controlled experiments. Suppose we are interested in comparing a test cell and the control cell in an experiment. Denote the business metric in the test cell and the control cell as $Y^{(t)}$ and $Y^{(c)}$, respectively. We start with a pair of hypotheses. The null hypothesis is that $Y^{(t)}$ and $Y^{(c)}$ have the same mean and the alternative is that they do not. The sample size in the experiments at Netflix is at least in thousands. Regular two-sample t-test is thus applied to test the hypotheses. The t-test statistic is defined as follows.

$$\frac{\bar{Y}^{(t)} - \bar{Y}^{(c)}}{\sqrt{var(\bar{Y}^{(t)} - \bar{Y}^{(c)})}}, \quad (3)$$

where $\bar{Y}^{(t)}$ is an unbiased estimate for the population mean in the test cell and $\bar{Y}^{(c)}$ is an unbiased estimate for the population mean in the control cell. Thus $\bar{Y}^{(t)} - \bar{Y}^{(c)}$ is an unbiased estimate for the effect size. In controlled experiments, variance reduction is about reducing $var(\bar{Y}^{(t)} - \bar{Y}^{(c)})$. The sampling in our controlled experiments is without replacement because a user can not be assigned to two cells at the same time and the population is finite. Thus, strictly speaking, the samples in control and test are not independent from each other. But the users assigned to a single experiment are typically a small proportion of the Netflix user base. Hence the dependence is negligible and we have

$$var(\bar{Y}^{(t)} - \bar{Y}^{(c)}) = var(\bar{Y}^{(t)}) + var(\bar{Y}^{(c)}). \quad (4)$$

Equation (4) shows the equivalence between reducing the variance of the mean estimate in a single cell and reducing the variance of the effect size estimate. Therefore we focus the discussion that follows on variance reduction in a single cell. Fundamentally, variance reduction in a single cell of controlled experiments can be achieved by leveraging covariates that are measurable prior to the experiments and are correlated with the business metrics. Covariates can be used at different stages of an experiment. When used at-assignment, the covariates are leveraged during the process of assigning users to the cells, e.g., stratified sampling. When used post-assignment, the covariates are leveraged after the user assignment, e.g., post stratification and CUPED.

3.3 Stratified Sampling

Stratified sampling [2] is probably the most well-known at-assignment variance reduction technique. The basic idea of stratified sampling is to divide the population into strata, sample from each stratum independently, and then combine samples across each stratum to give an overall estimate. In stratified sampling, the sample size from the kth stratum n_k is fixed for given total sample size n and they have the following relationship

$$n_k = np_k, \quad (5)$$

where p_k is defined in 3.1 and $k = 1, ..., K$. In stratified sampling, the weighted average in (2) is typically used to estimate the population mean μ. As mentioned in Section 3.1, under stratified sampling, the two estimates in (1) and (2) are the same shown as follows.

$$\begin{aligned}\sum_{k=1}^{K} p_k \bar{Y}_k &= \sum_{k=1}^{K} p_k \frac{1}{n_k} \sum_{j=1}^{n_k} Y_{kj} \\ &= \sum_{k=1}^{K} \frac{n_k}{n} \frac{1}{n_k} \sum_{j=1}^{n_k} Y_{kj} \\ &= \frac{1}{n} \sum_{k=1}^{K} \sum_{j=1}^{n_k} Y_{kj}.\end{aligned} \tag{6}$$

The first equation in (6) follows from the definition of $\bar{Y}_k$. The second equation is true because of (5). Now we derive some statistical properties of the estimate in (2) under stratified sampling. We first show the estimate in (2) is unbiased under stratified sampling.

$$E_{strat}(\hat{Y}_{strat}) = \sum_{k=1}^{K} p_k E_{strat}(\bar{Y}_k) = \sum_{k=1}^{K} p_k \mu_k = \mu. \tag{7}$$

Secondly, the variance of the estimate in (2) under stratified sampling is

$$\begin{aligned}var_{strat}(\hat{Y}_{strat}) &= \sum_{k=1}^{K} p_k^2 var_{strat}(\bar{Y}_k) \\ &= \sum_{k=1}^{K} \frac{n_k^2}{n^2} \frac{1}{n_k} \sigma_k^2 \\ &= \frac{1}{n} \sum_{k=1}^{K} p_k \sigma_k^2.\end{aligned} \tag{8}$$

The first equation in (8) holds because sampling from the K strata is done independently from each other. σ_k^2 and n_k are defined in Section 3.1.

In simple random sampling, the standard simple sample average in (1) is used to estimate the population mean. Under simple random sampling, the estimate in (1) is unbiased shown as follows.

$$\begin{aligned}E_{srs}(\bar{Y}) &= E_{srs}(\frac{1}{n} \sum_{k=1}^{K} \sum_{j=1}^{n_k} Y_{kj}) \\ &= \frac{1}{n} \sum_{k=1}^{K} \sum_{j=1}^{n_k} E_{srs}(Y_{kj}) \\ &= \frac{1}{n} \sum_{k=1}^{K} \sum_{j=1}^{n_k} \mu \\ &= \frac{1}{n} n\mu \\ &= \mu.\end{aligned} \tag{9}$$

The variance of (1) under simple random sampling is derived as follows.

$$\begin{aligned}var_{srs}(\bar{Y}) &= var_{srs}(\frac{1}{n} \sum_{k=1}^{K} \sum_{j=1}^{n_k} Y_{kj}) \\ &= \frac{1}{n^2} \sum_{k=1}^{K} \sum_{j=1}^{n_k} var_{srs}(Y_{kj}) \\ &= \frac{1}{n^2} n\sigma^2 \\ &= \frac{1}{n} \sigma^2.\end{aligned} \tag{10}$$

Note that $var_{srs}(Y_{kj}) = \sigma^2$ because Y_{kj} are all random samples under simple random sampling from the distribution of Y. Next we make a connection between (8) and (10). First let Z denote the stratum number of a random observation from the distribution of Y under simple random sampling. Note that Z is a multinomial random variable that takes values $1, ..., K$ and $P(Z = k) = p_k$. Then we have

$$\begin{aligned}var_{srs}(Y) &= E_{srs}(var_{srs}(Y|Z)) + var_{srs}(E_{srs}(Y|Z)) \\ &= E_{srs}(\sum_{k=1}^{K} \sigma_k^2 I(Z = k)) + var_{srs}(\sum_{k=1}^{K} \mu_k I(Z = k)) \\ &= \sum_{k=1}^{K} \sigma_k^2 E_{srs}(I(Z = k)) + E_{srs}(\sum_{k=1}^{K} \mu_k I(Z = k))^2 \\ &\quad - (E_{srs}(\sum_{k=1}^{K} \mu_k I(Z = k)))^2 \\ &= \sum_{k=1}^{K} \sigma_k^2 p_k + \sum_{k=1}^{K} \mu_k^2 p_k - \mu^2 \\ &= \sum_{k=1}^{K} \sigma_k^2 p_k + \sum_{k=1}^{K} p_k (\mu_k - \mu)^2,\end{aligned} \tag{11}$$

where $I(Z = k)$ is an indicator variable with value 1 if $Z = k$ and 0 otherwise. Combing (10) and (11), we have

$$var_{srs}(\bar{Y}) = \frac{1}{n} \sum_{k=1}^{K} p_k \sigma_k^2 + \frac{1}{n} \sum_{k=1}^{K} p_k (\mu_k - \mu)^2. \tag{12}$$

To summarize the comparison between stratified sampling and simple random sampling, estimates in both sampling techniques are unbiased. But the variance of the estimate in stratified sampling is smaller than that in simple random sampling by $\frac{1}{n} \sum_{k=1}^{K} p_k (\mu_k - \mu)^2$. The intuition for variance reduction based on stratified sampling is that the variance of the estimate based on simple random sampling can be decomposed into within-strata variance and between-strata variance. Stratified sampling achieves variance reduction by removing the between-strata variance. Fundamentally, this is because the mean of the business metric is different across strata. From a sampling point of view, stratified sampling removes the variation of sample size from each stratum for a given total sample size n and thus reduces the variance of the estimate.

3.4 Post Stratification

Post stratification is a popular post-assignment variance reduction technique. It assumes simple random sampling but uses the estimate in (2) instead of (1). Note that, when simple random sampling is used, the estimates in (2) and (1) are different. This is because the sample size n_k from the kth stratum is not necessarily equal to np_k under simple random sampling. Here n_k, n, and p_k are defined in Section 3.1. In fact, $n_1, ..., n_K$ are all random under simple random sampling. The intuition behind post stratification is very simple. The weighted average (2) gives more weights to observations from the strata that are under-represented in the sample. Thus if a sample is badly balanced for some covariate such as signup country, the weighted average estimate automatically corrects for it. We now sketch the derivation of the variance of the estimate in (2) under simple random sampling.

$$\begin{aligned} var_{srs}(\hat{Y}_{strat}) &= E_{srs}(var_{srs}(\hat{Y}_{strat}|n_1, ..., n_K)) \\ &\quad + var_{srs}(E_{srs}(\hat{Y}_{strat}|n_1, ...n_K)) \\ &= E_{srs}(\sum_{k=1}^{K} p_k^2 var_{srs}(\bar{Y}_k|n_k)) + var_{srs}(\sum_{k=1}^{K} p_k\mu_k) \\ &= E_{srs}(\sum_{k=1}^{K} p_k^2 \frac{1}{n_k}\sigma_k^2) + var_{srs}(\mu) \\ &= \sum_{k=1}^{K} p_k^2\sigma_k^2 E_{srs}(\frac{1}{n_k}) \end{aligned} \tag{13}$$

What is remaining to calculate the variance of the estimate in (2) under simple random sampling is to calculate $E_{srs}(\frac{1}{n_k})$, where $k = 1, ..., K$. Note that, n_k is a Bernoullian random variable with expected value np_k for given sample size n. It can be shown that $E_{srs}(\frac{1}{n_k}) = \frac{1}{np_k} + \frac{1-p_k}{n^2p_k^2} + o(\frac{1}{n^2})$ [9], where $o(\frac{1}{n^2})$ is a residual term that converges to 0 faster than $\frac{1}{n^2}$ as $n \to \infty$. The proof in [9] is based on some complicated factorial expansions because it is for more general cases than the reciprocal of a Bernoullian random variable. In this paper, we provide a simpler proof based on Taylor expansion as follows.

$$\begin{aligned} E_{srs}(\frac{1}{n_k}) &= E_{srs}(\frac{1}{np_k} + (-\frac{1}{n^2p_k^2})(n_k - np_k) \\ &\quad + \frac{1}{n^3p_k^3}(n_k - np_k)^2) + o(\frac{1}{n^2}) \\ &= \frac{1}{np_k} + \frac{1}{n^3p_k^3}E_{srs}(n_k - np_k)^2 + o(\frac{1}{n^2}) \\ &= \frac{1}{np_k} + \frac{1}{n^3p_k^3}np_k(1-p_k) + o(\frac{1}{n^2}) \\ &= \frac{1}{np_k} + \frac{1}{n^2p_k^2}(1-p_k) + o(\frac{1}{n^2}), \end{aligned} \tag{14}$$

where the first equation is simply a Taylor expansion of $\frac{1}{n_k}$ at $\frac{1}{np_k}$ and the other equations follow from the fact that n_k is Bernoullian variable with mean np_k and variance $np_k(1 - p_k)$. Thus, we have

$$var_{srs}(\hat{Y}_{strat}) = \frac{1}{n}\sum_{k=1}^{K} p_k\sigma_k^2 + \frac{1}{n^2}\sum_{k=1}^{K}(1-p_k)\sigma_k^2 + o(\frac{1}{n^2}). \tag{15}$$

Since p_k's, μ_k's, K, and μ are finite values, we can always find a large enough n such that the following is true.

$$\frac{1}{n^2p_k^2}(1-p_k) + o(\frac{1}{n^2}) \le \frac{1}{n}\sum_{k=1}^{K} p_k(\mu_k - \mu)^2. \tag{16}$$

When equation (16) is true, we have $var_{srs}(\hat{Y}_{strat}) \le var_{srs}(\bar{Y})$. This shows that post stratification leads to variance reduction for large enough sample size. Hence for large enough n, the comparison of variance of the estimates based on simple random sampling, stratified sampling, and post stratification can be summarized as follows.

$$\begin{aligned} &var_{strat}(\hat{Y}_{strat}) = var_{srs}(\hat{Y}_{strat}) + O(\frac{1}{n^2}) = var_{srs}(\bar{Y}) + O(\frac{1}{n}), \\ &var_{strat}(\hat{Y}_{strat}) \le var_{srs}(\hat{Y}_{strat}) \le var_{srs}(\bar{Y}). \end{aligned} \tag{17}$$

Thus, although it is true that the variance of the estimate based on stratified sampling is the smallest, when n is large, the variance difference between post stratification and stratified sampling will be much smaller than that between simple random sampling and stratified sampling. This means that post stratification achieves similar variance reduction as stratified sampling when the sample size n is large. It is worth pointing out the derivation of the variance in post stratification requires a regularity condition that none of the n_k's is zero [7]. Although the derivation of variance is only of theoretical interest, in practice, we need a mechanism to estimate the mean for those strata that do not have any observation in a cell. One way is to pool or collapse similar strata [7]. This is potentially an issue for post stratification in practice.

3.5 CUPED

Another variance reduction technique is based on control variates. It has been used in Monte Carlo simulation [5]. One can think of the control variates here as covariates defined in Section 3.1. The control variates technique was applied to controlled experiments as a variance reduction technique in [3]. The authors name the technique CUPED (controlled experiments utilizing pre-experiment data) in their paper because the control variates in their paper are based on pre-experiment data. CUPED is also a post-assignment variance reduction technique because it is based on simple random sampling. Next we briefly review how CUPED works. Suppose the pre-experiment data X is a one-dimensional control variate. In CUPED, instead of looking at the business metric Y, we look at a new metric defined as

$$Y_{CUPED} = Y - \theta X, \tag{18}$$

where θ is some parameter that needs to be defined. Next we discuss how to choose θ to complete the definition of the new metric. For the variance of Y_{CUPED} under simple random sampling, we have

$$var_{srs}(Y_{CUPED}) = var_{srs}(Y) + \theta^2 var_{srs}(X) - 2\theta cov_{srs}(X, Y), \tag{19}$$

where $cov_{srs}(X, Y)$ is the covariance between X and Y under simple random sampling. Using simple calculus, we can show that $var_{srs}(Y_{CUPED})$ is minimized by choosing θ equal to $cov_{srs}(X, Y)/var_{srs}(X)$, where the minimal value is

$$var_{srs}(Y_{CUPED})_{min} = var_{srs}(Y)(1 - \rho^2), \tag{20}$$

where $\rho = corr_{srs}(X, Y)$ is the Pearson correlation between X and Y under simple random sampling. The intuition behind variance reduction using control variates is that the total variance of the business metric Y can be decomposed into two parts: the part that is caused by the variance of the control variate X, and the part that is explained by other unknown variables. By looking at the corrected metric Y_{CUPED}, we have removed the variance caused by X and thus the variance is reduced. So far, the discussion is all in the context of a single cell. It is clear that $E_{srs}(Y_{CUPED})$ is different from $E_{srs}(Y)$. In controlled experiments, we are typically interested in the difference between the means of the business metric in a test cell and the control cell. Hence the authors suggest using the same θ for different cells so that the difference between the means of the new metric Y_{CUPED} is the same as that of the original business metric Y. In practice, θ can be estimated based on pre-experiment data once we know X. Based on (20), X should be chosen to maximize the magnitude of $corr_{srs}(X, Y)$. In practice, the authors suggest using the same metric Y in the pre-experiment period because the same metric over different time periods typically correlate well. In our analysis, we take the authors' two suggestions: using the same θ across cells, and using the same business metric prior to experiment as the control variate.

There is also an interesting connection between CUPED and stratified sampling. When X is categorical, it can be mathematically shown that CUPED and stratified sampling (X is used to define strata in stratified sampling) is equivalent. For the detailed proof, please see [3].

4. NETFLIX'S IMPLEMENTATION OF STRATIFIED SAMPLING

We have learned through years of research that many factors not related to the product correlate with our business metrics. For example, the signup country of users correlates with retention. The most impactful factors are leveraged as covariates in stratified sampling to help reduce the sampling variance of business metrics. More covariates are leveraged for existing members since we know more about them. Results in Section 5 show that this extra information for existing users leads to significantly more variance reduction.

Prior to running an experiment, a target sample size is determined, and triggers for assigning users to the experiment are defined. For new users, the trigger is signing up for Netflix. For existing users, an example of trigger for a product change on the Netflix kids webpage could be a user visit to that page. The triggering rule and target sample size together decide the length of the recruitment period, which can last weeks. In this context, assigning users to cells happens in real-time when the trigger condition is satisfied.

Implementing stratified sampling in a real-time assignment scenario is rarely discussed and poses the challenge of having equal representation of the covariates in the test and control cells throughout the whole recruitment period. To address this issue, we rely on a queue system composed of one queue per experiment e and stratum s. Each queue consists of 100-slot segments. Prior to user assignment, the sampling rate for each cell in the experiment is specified. Sampling rate for a cell is defined as the share of users in the experiment that receive the experience in the cell. The cell sampling rate ranges between 0% and 100% in an increment of 1%. For each segment of 100 slots, the slots are mapped to cells such that the share of slots assigned to a cell exactly matches the sampling rate for that cell. Note that the increment cannot be more granular than 1% due to the 100-slot segment design.

Here is a simple example to illustrate the assignment in a single segment. Suppose we want to run an experiment with two cells and allocate 50% of the users to each of the two cells. We first get a sequence of integers between 1 and 100 as seen in Figure 1 (a) and then reshuffle this sequence as in Figure 1 (b). Finally we map integers 1-50 to Cell 1 and 51-100 to Cell 2 as in Figure 1 (c). As mentioned above, a queue consists of many 100-slot segments. The cell assignment in each 100-slot segment is done independently from each other within a single queue, and independently across queues. When a new user eligible for the experiment signs up, we first decide the strata that he falls into based on his covariate information and then assign him to the corresponding queue for his strata. He will then take the next available slot in the queue and gets assigned to the cell for the slot. A simple example of new user assignment with two strata and two cells is shown in Figure 2.

The implementation of stratified sampling based on our queue system does not always achieve perfect balance of strata across cells. This can diminish the amount of variance reduction based on stratified sampling. There are two factors that contribute to the imbalance.

Firstly, we only guarantee perfect balance within each segment of 100 slots. Thus the total sample size of a stratum across cells needs to be a multiple of 100 to achieve perfect balance. For example, if there are 100,090 users in a stratum prior to cell assignment, then the queue system guarantees balance for the first 100k users but not the last 90 users. For the last 90 users, the actual sampling rate in each cell may not exactly match the intended sampling rate. And thus, after cell assignment, the percent of users from each stratum may be different across cells. The rationale for having a segment size of 100 is mainly for the convenience of specifying sampling rate per cell (increment of 1%). Potentially we can decrease the segment size to achieve better balance but it also makes the sampling rate specification less granular, e.g., if we change the segment size to 50, then the sampling rate needs to be in increment of 2%. The impact of this imbalance depends on the sample size in each stratum.

The second factor preventing us from achieving perfect balance is that we usually have to use many machines to conduct the sampling because of both high volume of sampling requests and occasional failures of the machines. With M machines, there will be M queues for experiment e and stratum s. When a user eligible for an experiment signs up, he is first randomly assigned to a machine, and then assigned to a queue on the machine based on his covariate information, and finally he takes the next available slot in the queue and gets assigned to the cell for the slot. It is intuitive that with multiple machines, it is more difficult to achieve the strata balance across cells. For example, if the sample size of a stratum for the whole experiment is 100k, it would achieve perfect balance with a single machine but not necessarily with multiple machines because the number of users from the stratum on each single machine is not necessarily a multiple of 100. The likelihood to achieve perfect balance decreases as the number of machines increases. The impact of the number of machines on the variance reduction amount based on stratified sampling is quantified in the next section.

(a)	1	2	3	4	5	6	.	.	.	.	.	.	100
(b)	25	57	9	12	95	64	.	.	.	.	.	.	43
(c)	1	2	1	1	2	2	.	.	.	.	.	.	1

Figure 1: Illustration of Cell Assignment in One Segment: (a) generate a sequence of integers between 1 and 100, (b) random shuffling of the sequence of integers, (c) mapping of integers to cell

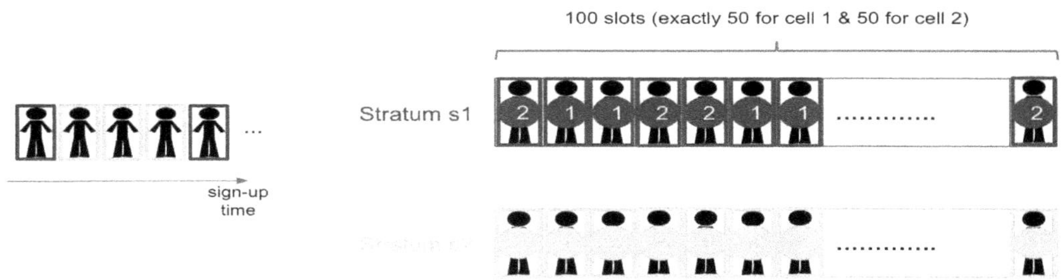

Figure 2: Illustration of stratified sampling with one machine for new users

5. EMPIRICAL EVALUATION

5.1 Evaluation Methodology

In this section, we compare the amount of variance reduction achieved by stratified sampling, post stratification and CUPED on a few datasets from Netflix. The business metrics considered are customer retention and seven out of the I streaming thresholds defined in Section 2.2. Simple random sampling is used as the baseline to estimate the amount of variance reduction achieved by each technique. The comparison is done on both new and existing users. For each user type, we collect covariates and business metrics for a cohort of users. We define these users as the population and repeatedly simulate A/A experiments, which are controlled experiments with two cells and zero effect size. In the case of stratified sampling, an A/A experiment is simulated by splitting users into two cells based on the implementation described in Section 4. For post stratification and CUPED, an A/A experiment is simulated by splitting users into two cells based on simple random sampling. After the user assignment to two cells in a single A/A experiment is determined, for each business metric, we compute an estimate of the effect size. For the simple random sampling baseline, this estimate is the difference of the simple sample averages in (1). For stratified sampling and post stratification, this estimate is the difference of the weighted averages in (2). For CUPED, this estimate is the difference of the averages for the corrected metric in (18). For each business metric and variance reduction technique, 100k A/A experiments are simulated independently from each other on the same cohort of users, yielding 100k estimates of the effect size. The sample variance of these estimates is then compared with the theoretical variance based on simple random sampling to quantify the amount of variance reduction for each metric and technique combination. For stratified sampling, we also estimated the variance reduction percentage pretending there is only one machine to get a sense of the additional variance introduced by the use of multiple machines. For new users, we do not have pre-experiment data for streaming and retention that can be used for CUPED. Thus, eight regression models (one per metric) were built on a different set of users from those used to simulate our A/A experiments. The predictors in the regression models are the same set of covariates used to define strata in stratified sampling. This ensures fair comparison between CUPED and stratified sampling. The predicted mean values of the metrics from the models are then used as pre-experiment data. For existing users, the same metric is used as the pre-experiment data for the streaming thresholds. We did not apply CUPED on retention for existing users since the amount of variance reduction for retention is very small based on the other techniques and we do not expect CUPED to make a significant difference. We report on the variance reduction point estimates along with error bars based on Bootstrap [4] as a measure of the uncertainty of the results based on a finite (although 100k is already pretty large) number of simulations.

5.2 Results

The resulting variance reduction estimates are presented in Figures 3 and 4, separately for new and existing users for each of the eight business metrics (retention and seven streaming thresholds). The results show that identifying covariates that are highly correlated with the business metrics is key for the success of any of these variance reduction techniques. The empirical results also align well with the theory in Section 3. Indeed, ignoring challenges posed by practical implementation, stratified sampling, post stratification and

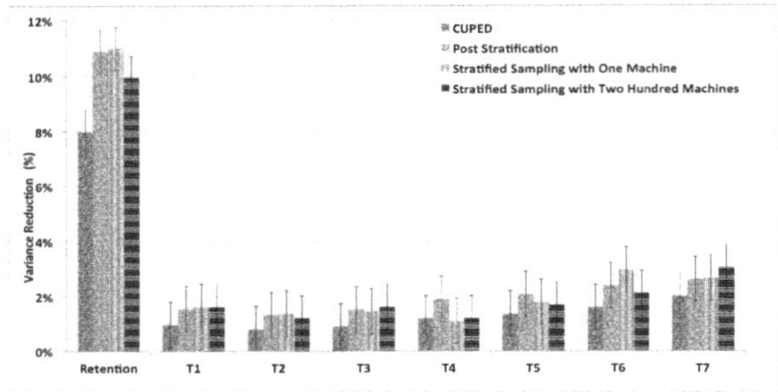

Figure 3: New users. Variance reduction results of stratified sampling, CUPED, and post stratification compared to simple random sampling

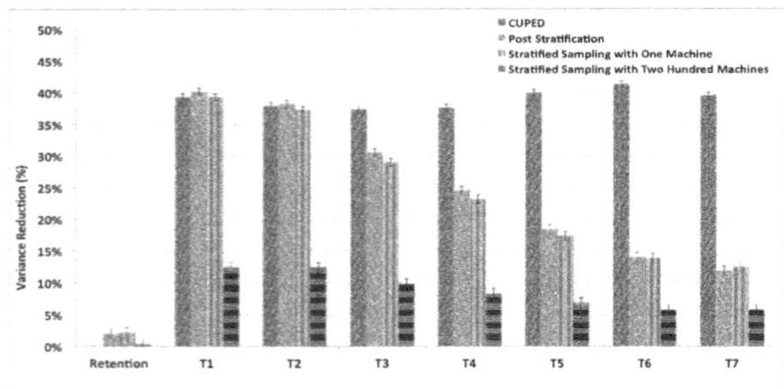

Figure 4: Existing users. Variance reduction results of stratified sampling, CUPED, and post stratification compared to simple random sampling

CUPED achieve similar variance reduction amount when leveraging the same covariates. However, in practice, the variance reduction achieved by stratified sampling can be severely impacted by the 100-slot design and the need to use multiple machines as described in Section 4. This is not the case for post stratification and CUPED which are post-assignment techniques. See the following subsections for more detailed findings.

5.2.1 Influence of Covariates

For new users, the amount of variance reduction achieved is very low regardless of the metric or the variance reduction technique used. This is due to the lack of covariates highly correlated with the business metrics for these users at the time of cell assignment. Indeed, the Pearson correlation between the covariates and business metrics ranges from 0.2 to 0.4 for new users.

For streaming thresholds, the variance reduction for existing users can be up to 40% because we included pre-experiment streaming activity as a stratification dimension or in the post-assignment correction. Note that for existing users, the lowest streaming threshold T_1 prior to the experiment is the only streaming threshold used as covariate in stratified sampling and post stratification. Thus it is expected that the amount of variance reduction becomes lesser as the streaming threshold moves further away from T_1 and the correlation between this covariate and these streaming thresholds becomes weaker.

For retention, while the amount of variance reduction is small for both new and existing users, it is higher for new users. The reason is because the covariates used to define strata for new users are more correlated with retention than for existing users. Also new users get a free trial in the first month and there is more user-level variation of retention than for existing users who have already passed the free trial period and whose retention metric becomes less sensitive.

5.2.2 Post Stratification Observations

For all the metrics and both user types, post stratification is comparable to stratified sampling with one machine. This is consistent with the theoretical understanding that post stratification achieves similar variance reduction as stratified sampling when the sample size is large. The sample size in the dataset used for evaluation is at the scale of hundreds of thousands.

5.2.3 Stratified Sampling Observations

As discussed in Section 3.3, from a sampling point of view, stratified sampling achieves variance reduction compared to simple random sampling because it removes the variation of the sample size from each stratum once the total sample size n is given. In Section 4, we described how the practical implementation of stratified sampling cannot completely remove this variation because of the use of a 100-slot queue system and the need to conduct sampling on multiple machines. The empirical evaluation shows that for existing users, variance reduction based on stratified sampling with multiple machines is less than half of that with one machine. This impact is not as clear for new users for whom the number of machines used for sampling is only one fifth of that for existing users. Also the increase in the number of machines tend to have a larger impact on existing users that have smaller strata sizes.

To provide some intuition around the impact of multiple machines, we run an evaluation procedure similar to the one described in Section 5.1 on a cohort of existing users. In this evaluation, we show the impact of number of machines on the sampling variance of the sample sizes of each stratum. Since there is more than one stratum, we define a weighted average of standard deviation metric as follows

$$\sum_{k=1}^{K} p_k \sigma_k, \tag{21}$$

where p_k is the proportion of users from stratum k in the population and σ_k is the standard deviation of the sample size from stratum k in a random sample for fixed total sample size n. The number of machines used for stratified sampling is varied from one to two hundred. For a given number of machines m, we simulate 100k A/A experiments to estimate σ_k. Each A/A experiment first randomly assigns users to machines and then for each machine splits users into two cells based on stratified sampling as described in Section 5.1. The estimates of σ_k are then plugged into (21) to get the estimate of the weighted average of standard deviation metric. The results are shown in Figure 5. Note that the variation of the weighted standard deviation metric monotonically increases as the number of machines increases. The error bars are calculated using the Bootstrap technique [4]. There is no error bar for simple random sampling because it is the theoretical value. So, as the number of machines increases, the variation of the sample size from each stratum increases, which translates to higher variance of the final es-

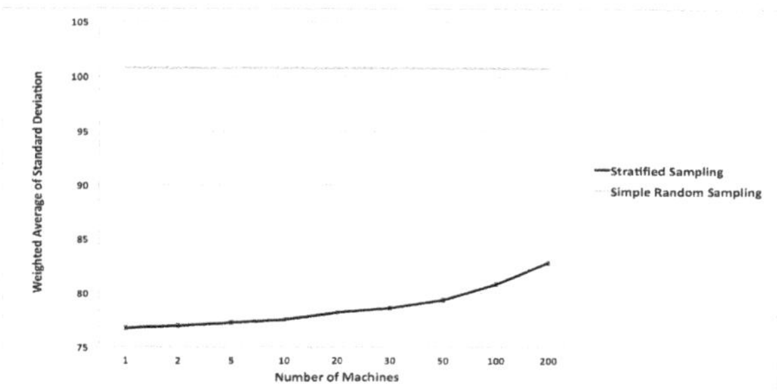

Figure 5: Impact of the number of machines used in stratified sampling on strata sample size variation

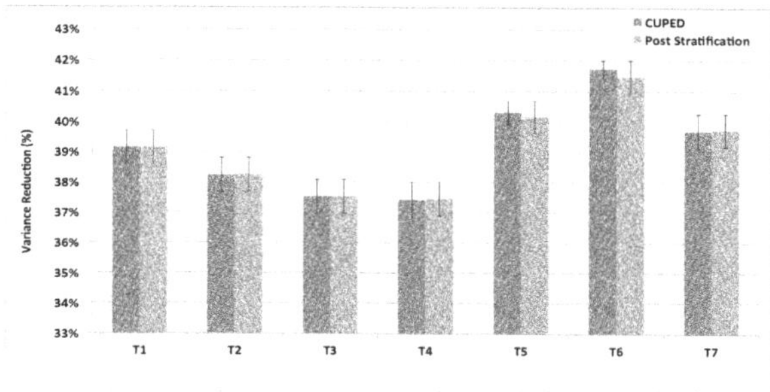

Figure 6: Existing users. Variance reduction of CUPED and post stratification using the same covariates compared to simple random sampling

timate based on stratified sampling and diminished variance reduction based on stratified sampling.

5.2.4 CUPED Observations

CUPED performs slightly worse than stratified sampling and post stratification for new users because the pre-experiment data in CUPED is essentially a one-dimensional summary of the covariates used to define strata and there is some loss of information in this summary.

For existing users, we have the flexibility of correcting streaming thresholds with the same metric prior to the experiment. Hence the amount of variance reduction is consistently around 40% for all the streaming thresholds. Finally, it is worth emphasizing that the difference in variance reduction between CUPED and the other techniques for high streaming thresholds on existing users in Figure 4 is due to the difference of covariates used in the techniques, not the techniques themselves. The comparison settings were set as such because the initial objective of this case study was to compare CUPED with what was used in production at Netflix. We also did a fair comparison between CUPED and post stratification by using exactly the same covariates for each of the streaming threshold metrics on existing users. The results in Figure 6 clearly show that these two techniques perform comparably when using the same covariates. This is expected due to the following two reasons.

- Post stratification achieves similar variance reduction as stratified sampling when the sample size is large, which is true here.
- Stratified sampling is equivalent to CUPED when the covariate is categorical, which is also true here since the covariates are binary streaming thresholds. For more on this point, please see the appendix of [3].

Comparisons with stratified sampling based on the same covariates are omitted since we expect stratified sampling to perform the same as post stratification given the large sample size in the data.

6. CONCLUSIONS

For companies that use controlled experiments to make product decisions, it is critical to run highly sensitive controlled experiments in order to not miss product changes that can have a substantial impact on user experience and revenue. In this paper, we focused on improving the sensitivity of controlled experiments by reducing sampling variance of the business metrics. We compared a few variance reduction techniques, both at-assignment (stratified sampling) and post-assignment (post stratification & CUPED). We showed that theoretically, these techniques achieve similar variance reduction when the sample size is large, which is typically the case in online controlled experiments. We applied them to a few Netflix datasets and our empirical results aligned with theory when the same set of covariates is used for all the techniques. However, in practice, stratified sampling performs worse than post-assignment techniques such as post stratification and CUPED because real-time experimental assignment requires a queue system and the use of multiple machines. Moreover, post-assignment techniques are cheaper to implement, and very flexible in choosing the covariates for post-assignment correction. It is thus recommended to apply post-assignment variance reduction techniques when running large-scale controlled experiments. Our results on new users emphasize that identifying covariates that are highly correlated with the business metrics is key for the success of variance reduction techniques. In cases where such covariates cannot be easily found, other methods to improve the sensitivity of controlled experiments should be explored. At Netflix we continuously research new user engagement metrics that are a better tradeoff between sensitivity and correlation with retention to help make better production decisions. In the context of TV/movie recommendation and search algorithms, we leverage offline experiments as a pre-selection mechanism to reduce the number of test cells in a single experiment run online. With fewer test cells , larger sample sizes can be used for each cell and sensitivity is thus improved. See [6] for a more complete description of the offline experiments method as well as its challenges. Another example is leveraging interleaving-based experiments [1] to remove the between-user variance associated with our traditional controlled experiment design. Finally, more sophisticated experimental designs such as fractional factorial designs [10] can be used to reduce the number of test cells when multiple changes are tested in one single experiment.

7. ACKNOWLEDGEMENTS

We are grateful to Bryan Gumm and Carlos Gomez-Uribe for designing the queue system for stratified sampling at Netflix. We would like to give many thanks to Carlos Gomez-Uribe and Harald Steck for their thoughtful comments on earlier drafts of this paper.

8. REFERENCES

[1] O. Chapelle, T. Joachims, F. Radlinski, and Y. Yue. Large-scale validation and analysis of interleaved search evaluation. *ACM Trans. on Information Systems*, 30(1), February 2012.

[2] W. G. Cochran. *Sampling Techniques*. Wiley, 1977.

[3] A. Deng, Y. Xu, R. Kohavi, and T. Walker. Improving the sensitivity of online controlled experiments by utilizing pre-experiment data. In *WSDM 13 Proceedings of the sixth ACM International Conference on Web Search and Data Mining*, pages 123–132, 2013.

[4] B. Efron and R. Tibshirani. *An Introduction to the Bootstrap*. Chapman & Hall, 1993.

[5] P. Glasserman. *Monte Carlo Methods in Financial Engineering*. Springer, 2003.

[6] C. A. Gomez-Uribe and N. Hunt. The Netflix recommender system: Algorithms, business value, and innovation. *ACM Trans. on Management Information Systems*, 6(4), December 2015.

[7] D. Holt and T. Smith. Post stratification. *J.R. Statist. Soc. A*, 142(1):33–46, 1979.

[8] C. P. Robert and G. Casella. *Monte Carlo Statistical Methods*. Springer, 2010.

[9] F. F. Stephan. The expected value and variance of the reciprocal and other negative powers of a positive bernoullian variate. *The Annals of Mathematical Statistics*, 16(1):50–61, March 1945.

[10] C. J. Wu and M. S. Hamada. *Experiments: Planning, Analysis, and Optimization*. Wiley, 2009.

Talent Circle Detection in Job Transition Networks

Huang Xu[†], Zhiwen Yu[†*], Jingyuan Yang[‡], Hui Xiong[‡*], Hengshu Zhu[♯]
[†]Northwestern Polytechnical University, Xi'an 710072, PR China
[‡]Rutgers University, [♯]Baidu Research-Big Data Lab
xuhuang@mail.nwpu.edu.cn, zhiwenyu@nwpu.edu.cn,
{jingyyan,hxiong}@rutgers.edu, zhuhengshu@baidu.com

ABSTRACT

With the high mobility of talent, it becomes critical for the recruitment team to find the right talent from the right source in an efficient manner. The prevalence of Online Professional Networks (OPNs), such as LinkedIn, enables the new paradigm for talent recruitment and job search. However, the dynamic and complex nature of such talent information imposes significant challenges to identify prospective talent sources from large-scale professional networks. Therefore, in this paper, we propose to create a job transition network where vertices stand for organizations and a directed edge represents the talent flow between two organizations for a time period. By analyzing this job transition network, it is able to extract talent circles in a way such that every circle includes the organizations with similar talent exchange patterns. Then, the characteristics of these talent circles can be used for talent recruitment and job search. To this end, we develop a talent circle detection model and design the corresponding learning method by maximizing the Normalized Discounted Cumulative Gain (NDCG) of inferred probability for the edge existence based on edge weights. Then, the identified circles will be labeled by the representative organizations as well as keywords in job descriptions. Moreover, based on these identified circles, we develop a talent exchange prediction method for talent recommendation. Finally, we have performed extensive experiments on real-world data. The results show that, our method can achieve much higher modularity when comparing to the benchmark approaches, as well as high precision and recall for talent exchange prediction.

CCS Concepts

•**Information systems → Clustering;**

Keywords

People Analytics; Talent Circle Detection.

*Corresponding authors.

KDD '16, August 13-17, 2016, San Francisco, CA, USA

DOI: http://dx.doi.org/10.1145/2939672.2939732

1. INTRODUCTION

When there is a scarcity of skilled talents, an emerging challenge for human resource management (HRM) is how to identify the right talent from the right source in an efficient manner. Professional recruiters usually invest a lot of resources in talent source acquisition, which is focused on identifying, assessing, and engaging the sources of skilled talent candidates through proactive recruiting techniques.

As a proactive recruiting strategy, the use of Online Professional Networks (OPNs), such as LinkedIn[1], for talent recruitment becomes popular in many firms. Indeed, there is rich information about talent career trajectories and the talent skills in OPNs data [17], which enables the new paradigm for talent recruitment and job search.

However, the dynamic and complex nature of this talent information imposes significant challenges to identify prospective talent sources from large-scale OPNs. More specifically, there are three unique challenges. First, there are too many people available in the network. For example, LinkedIn has reached over 400 million members around the world in October 2015. Thus, it is essential to provide a method for finding the candidate scope from many possible talent pools. Second, for different types of positions, hiring specialists usually need to consider different talent sources. Third, since people's job transition trajectories vary a lot [16] and lack of regularity, it is necessary to investigate people's job transition trajectories at the organizational level. Then, it is possible to capture the hidden recruitment patterns and identify the right talent sources.

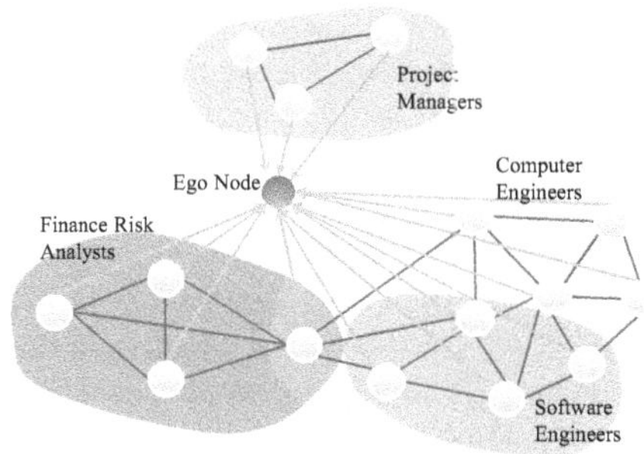

Figure 1: Circles in job transition network.

To address these challenges, in this paper, we propose to use an organization-level job transition network [3], which is generated from people's job transition trajectories. In the network, vertices stand for organizations and edges represent

[1]https://www.linkedin.com

the job transition amount among organizations for a time period. Also, the direction of edge indicates the job transition orientation and the weight of edge shows the quantity and the category of employees transferring between organizations. Moreover, if a given organization is used as a center node, an *ego network* can be formed by selecting all the neighbors and edges between them from job transition networks, as shown in Figure 1.

By analyzing this job transition network, we define a talent circle on the ego network to help identify prospective talent sources. A talent circle consists of organizations that have similar talent exchange patterns. With talent circles, the source of different types of talents are gathered together and can then be used for recruitment and job search. Specifically, recruiters can find candidates from organizations in most relevant circles. On the other hand, job seekers can locate the position targets in their related circles. For example, in Figure 1, the neighbor organizations of the ego have been separated into several circles with overlapping nodes or even in hierarchy. These different circles show different talent exchange patterns for talents on specific types of positions, such as financial risk analysts or software engineers.

Although the problem of ego network detection has been studied in social media [9] or co-authorship network fields [2], job transition network differs from the aforementioned scenarios in several aspects. First, the ego job transition network is much more densely connected and weighted. Since most of the organizations in an ego network have strong connections, the weight is important to distinguish the significance of edges. Second, the job transition network is direction sensitive, because the direction of edges has different meanings in different recruitment scenarios.

In light of the above, we propose a talent circle detection method for finding talent circles in the job transition networks. Specifically, we define node similarity based on talent exchange patterns and infer edge existence probability with hypothetical circles. Then, we compare the inferred probability with edge weight and refine the circle segmentation by maximizing Normalized Discounted Cumulative Gain (NDCG). Next, we label detected circles with representative words from job description to provide the semantic meaning for identified circles. Moreover, based on detected circles, we develop a talent exchange prediction method to show the effectiveness of the proposed model. Finally, we have performed extensive experiments on a large amount of real-world data. The results show that, our method can achieve much higher modularity when comparing to the benchmark approaches, as well as high precision and recall for talent exchange prediction.

2. FRAMEWORK OVERVIEW

To address the circle detection problem in job transition network, we design a framework that consists of data crawling, data transforming, modeling, learning and circle labeling. As shown in Figure 2, the framework consists of three main stages, namely network formation, feature extraction and circle detection.

Network Formation. In this stage, we obtain the raw data and transfer them into a formalized job transition network. The raw data are job experience records, in which each item contains a job title, a corresponding organization, a brief text description of work contents, and the beginning/end date of the job position. Specifically, we first crawl professional profiles from OPNs and transfer the inner resume into job transition trajectories by joining successive working experience items. Then, we aggregate all the trajectories into a weighted and directed network [21] at the organizational level. Finally, the ego network is defined as a subnetwork that consists of the neighbors of a specific node.

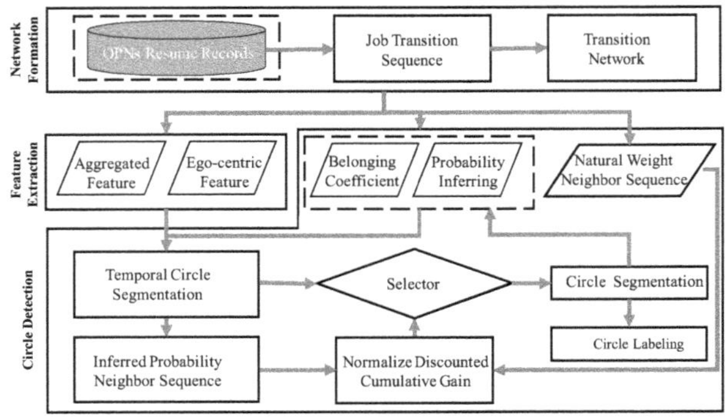

Figure 2: The framework of talent circle detection.

Feature Extraction. In this stage, we define similarity features according to the job transitions of nodes and the similarities between nodes. Specifically, we classify job titles into categories based on the job description posted by corresponding employees. Intuitively, organizations that exchange more employees and have more common preferences in job type distribution should be more similar to each other. Furthermore, organizations have homogeneous interactions with the ego node should be more similar than heterogeneous ones. Thus, the features used in similarity measurement can be derived from two aspects: aggregated and ego-centric personnel exchange. Specifically, aggregated personnel exchange features consist of job transition patterns centered by the node from all its neighbors; and ego-centric features consist of job transition patterns between nodes and the ego node. These features can capture the hiring characteristics of the organization. Here, the similarity is defined as the multiplicative inverse of Euclidean distance between nodes.

Circle Detection. In this stage, we conduct model learning process to determine node segmentation. In the model, we first put each node into one hypothetical circle and calculate the node-circle belonging coefficient based on the node similarity. Then, we remove a node from circles which it belongs to and then add it into other circles according to the level of *belongingness* and circle size. After that, we infer the possibility of edge existence based on the assumption that, if two nodes with high similarity and appear in tightly connected circles, an edge will be more possibly generated between them. Finally, we compare the inferred probability with edge weight by a customized version of NDCG and determine whether to accept the segmentation or not. The learning process is initiated as a single node circle sets and iterates until there is no update of objective function. After circle detection, we label the circles with top related organizations and keywords from job description. In particular, the learned circles can be further used for recruitment related applications, such as talent exchange prediction.

3. JOB TRANSITION NETWORK

In this section, we describe how to build the weighted job transition network, and how to extract features for measuring the similarity between nodes.

3.1 Preliminaries

We use a weighted and directed graph $\mathcal{G} =< V, E, W >$ to model job transitions between organizations for a time period (e.g., in 12 months). Specifically, each node $v_i \in V(i = 1, 2, ..., N)$ represents an organization, which could be a company, a university or a government department, etc. A directed edge $e_{i,j} \in E$ from v_i to v_j stands for the aggregated job transition from organization v_i to v_j. Moreover, the indegree (or outdegree) $deg^-(v_i)$ (or $deg^+(v_i)$) of node v_i is the number of edges ended at (or started from) v_i.

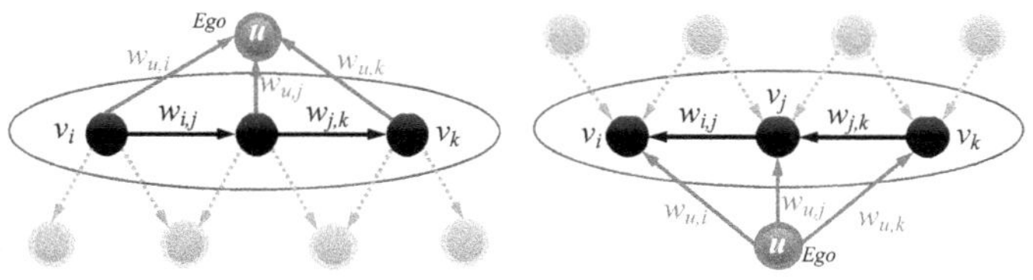

Figure 3: Directed and weighted ego network.

Application-Oriented Node Degree. In recruitment, different application scenarios concern different edge directions. For example, if the task is to discover where to find out candidates for a specific position in a company, the historical incoming transitions of that company are appropriate references. However, when job-seekers urge to know where to find the next job, they usually need to check the out-going transitions from the current company they are working for, and find out some companies which are ready for recruitment of qualified positions. Therefore, we use different degree definitions in these two scenarios. Specifically, we use $deg(v_i)$ to represent appropriate node degree while developing model. In the application of recruiting candidates, it is more meaningful to locate the source where employees come from, such that we set $deg(v_i) = deg^-(v_i)$, where the edge weight and transfer amount are calculated based on the selected direction of transitions. Accordingly, we set $deg(v_i) = deg^+(v_i)$ in the application of job position locating. As a result, the model is general for satisfying both application scenarios when using corresponding degree definition.

Edge Weight Definition. For a node v_i and its neighbors $\{v_j, j = 1, 2, ..., deg(v_i)\}$, weight $w_{i,j} \in W$ of edge $e_{i,j}$ is defined as the job transition percentage between v_i and v_j within a given time period. More precisely, we use n_i to denote the total number of transitions from (or to, depends on the application scenario) a node. The edge weight is then calculated as

$$w_{i,j} = \frac{\tau_{i,j}}{n_i}, \tag{1}$$

where $\tau_{i,j}$ is the amount of transitions between v_i and v_j. Note that, since we are only interested in one of the directions in our model for each scenario, edges will not be duplicated used in weight calculation. Furthermore, because the nodes in job transition network are densely connected, the weight is a critical indicator to distinguish the significance of edges. Thus we take the edge weight as an important determinant in both node similarity measurement and circle detection process.

Ego Network. The *ego network* in talent circle detection is a subset of the job transition network. Specifically, given a node u as the center node, the ego network is constituted of all the neighbors of u. For example, as shown in Figure 3, the neighbor node set (i.e., black nodes) in ellipses forms the ego network. In particular, different application scenarios require different edge sets. The left side of Figure 3 shows a network that is suitable for identifying talent source of the ego node, and the right side network is appropriate for job-seekers to reduce job search scope when chasing a new job. Note that, because the transition patterns should not be limited in the ego network, edge weights and transitions in the ego network are measured based on the whole network $\mathcal{G}$, but not measured by the traffic of subset nodes. Moreover, u is not included in its ego network. We use notation $G \subseteq \mathcal{G}$ to denote the ego network in our model.

3.2 Node Similarity

Intuitively, the similarity of two organizations could be derived from profile information, such as whether they are belonging to the same sector, located in the same city, or whether they have common business scope.

However, static profile based similarity is not suitable in talent circle detection from the perspective of recruitment. Ideally, the similarity should reflect employees' transition characteristics between organizations. In other words, organizations that share more job transitions and have more common preferences in job category distribution should be more similar to each other. Furthermore, since the primary goal is to find out the circles of the ego, organizations which have homogeneous interaction with ego should be more similar than heterogeneous ones. Thus, in this paper, the similarity is defined based on the historical job transitions. Specifically, the features used for similarity measurement can be derived from two aspects, namely aggregated and ego-centric personnel exchange.

Aggregated Personnel Exchange. This is defined as the categorical distribution of transitions to a node. In this paper, job positions in transitions are divided into 10 categories according to job title and the corresponding job description (the details are discussed in Section 6.1). The total amount of job transition n_i is separated into $\{n_{i,c}, c = 1, 2, .., 10\}$, where $n_{i,c}$ is the amount of transitions in job category c. Then, the transition proportion of each job title category with respect to the total transitions to organization v_i forms a categorical distribution vector

$$\alpha_i = [\alpha_i^1, \alpha_i^2, ..., \alpha_i^{10}], \alpha_i^c = \frac{n_{i,c}}{n_i}. \tag{2}$$

The vector captures the constitution of employees attracted (or offered in the application of recruitment) by the organization. In Figure 4, the solid lines illustrate the source of aggregated features of in-coming traffics. From the perspective of recruitment, two organizations with similar α may have analogous staffing strategies. Since the edge and the corresponding weight stand for the fraction of transitions between nodes, aggregated exchange could be treated as the extension of all the edges. Moreover, because the weight of edge is used as the objective in our model, it will be ignored in similarity measurement.

Ego-centric Personnel Exchange. This is the categorical distribution of transitions interfered by the ego node. From the viewpoint of the ego node, organizations may act as similar roles in talent exchange flows, even though they are different in staffing strategies. Specifically, two organizations are similar when they offering (or attracting) the same type of talents (e.g. hardware engineer) to (or from) the ego. Although the center node is excluded in its ego network, the

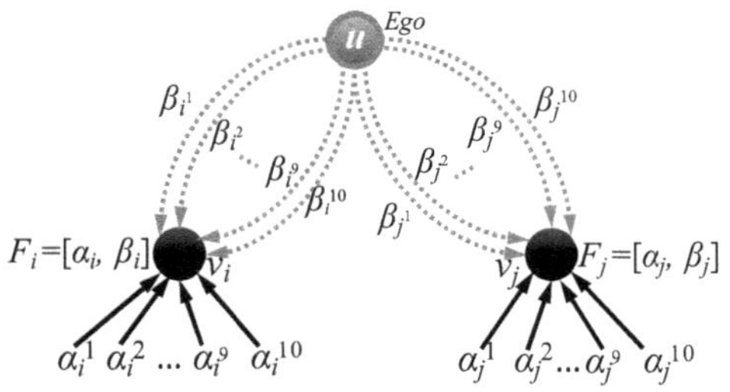

Figure 4: Similarity measurement illustration.

relationship between nodes and the ego is a determinative factor in circle detection. Particularly, two nodes are more likely to co-appear in a circle when they have common interaction patterns with the ego node. In fact, two organizations may be grouped into the same circle because they feed the ego with the same category of employees, even though they do not have the same organization scale or in the same sector. Ego-centric features are defined based on α_i, while the transitions between node u and v_i are considered. We use μ_i to denote the categorical distribution vector of transitions between u and v_i, and then define the feature vector as

$$\beta_i = [\beta_i^1, \beta_i^2, ..., \beta_i^{10}], \beta_i^c = \frac{\mu_i^c}{\alpha_u^c} \cdot w_{u,i}, \tag{3}$$

where α_u is the aggregated feature and $w_{u,i}$ is the weight of edge between u and v_i. Each dotted line in Figure 4 illustrates a dimension of ego-centric features of node v_i and v_j between the ego. β_i is the fine-grained transition categorical distribution normalized by aggregated transition categorical distribution. Indeed, two similar vectors indicate they interact with the ego in similar way, since the vector encodes the interaction pattern between the ego and organization. Based on the feature vectors α_i and β_i, similarity $Sim(v_i, v_j)$ is defined on the merged vector $F_i = [\alpha_i, \beta_i]$ and $F_j = [\alpha_j, \beta_j]$, as shown in Equation 4.

$$Sim(v_i, v_j) = \frac{1}{||F_i - F_j||_2}. \tag{4}$$

4. CIRCLE DETECTION MODEL

In this section, we introduce the details of our model for talent circle detection in the ego job transition network.

4.1 Basic Concepts

In this paper, we design a generative model to detect overlapping and hierarchical talent circles. As in the ego job transition network, two organizations should be assigned to a circle if they are closely connected and also similar to each other. The basic assumptions of our model have three aspects. First, two nodes have a possibility to form an edge when they are co-appearing in a circle. Second, circles that contain stronger connected nodes lead to a higher possibility to form edges among contained nodes. Third, two nodes in a circle with higher belongingness also have a higher edge existence possibility.

The probability of edges is generated based on the above assumptions. We then compare the inferred probability with the edge weight in an ordered manner. The objective of the model is to maximize the weighted similarity between the weight order of neighbors and the inferred probability of edges around an organization.

To build up the metrics of our model, we first define the concepts of *natural ordered neighbor sequence*, *circle* and *belonging coefficient* as follows.

Natural Ordered Neighbor Sequence. Given a node v_i, the *natural ordered neighbor sequence* A_i is the descending ordered list of neighbors according to the edge weight $\{w_{i,k}|e_{i,k} \in E\}$. Formally, we have

$$A_i = (..., v_j, v_{j+1}, ...),$$

where $w_{i,j} \geq w_{i,j+1}$. We use $A_{i,k}$ to refer to the k-th node in A_i. For example, if v_i connects to $\{v_1, v_2, v_3\}$ and weights among them satisfy $(w_{i,2} > w_{i,1}, w_{i,1} > w_{i,3})$, then $A_i = (v_2, v_1, v_3)$. The neighbors with the same edge weight are arranged by the indexing (e.g., alphabetic) order. When constructing the model for a specific organization, the ego node is excluded from the neighbor list.

Talent Circle. A *circle* is a subset of neighbors of an ego node, where nodes within a circle are closely connected and similar to each other. We use $\{C_m \in \mathbb{C}\}$ to denote circles, where $m = 1, 2, ..., M$ and $C_m \subseteq V$. Intuitively, on the one hand, if the circles are appropriately detected, nodes with strong connections should more likely be settled in the same circle than the nodes with weak connections. On the other hand, from the perspective of the node similarity, similar nodes are more likely to appear in the same circle. Meanwhile, circles could be hierarchical, which means circles with strongly connected nodes could be contained in circles with weakly connected nodes. Moreover, circles could also be overlapping. In other words, a node can belong to more than one circle.

Belonging Coefficient. Since circles may be overlapping, a node could more tightly belong to a circle than another circle. The *belonging coefficient* is defined as the tightness strength of a node to a circle. Specifically, we use a belonging matrix $U_{i,m} \in \mathbb{R}(0 \leq U_{i,m} \leq 1, i \in 1, 2, ..., N, m \in 1, 2, ..., M)$ to denote the belonging strength of node v_i to circle C_m, and a larger value of $U_{i,m}$ to indicate a tighter belongingness. In our model, $U_{i,m}$ is defined as the average mutual similarity between node v_i and the rest of the nodes in circle C_m, as shown in Equation 5. When there is only one node in a circle, the belonging coefficient is assigned to 1. In particular, the belonging coefficient affects the inferring of the edge existence probability in the model as well as the node-circle belonging dynamics in the learning process.

$$U_{i,m} = \frac{1}{|C_m| - 1} \sum_{v_j \in C_m, j \neq i} Sim(v_i, v_j). \tag{5}$$

4.2 Model Formalization

According to our assumptions, a pair of nodes within a circle has a possibility to generate an edge, and the generated edge weight is determined by two factors: the number of common circles they belong to, and the belonging coefficient of the node pair to the common circles. In reality, if two companies exchange employees more frequently, they should be more likely to be placed in the common circles. We use an iterative method to approximate the real segmentation and start from a simple temporary status where circles are hypothetically existing. Accordingly, the probability of two nodes forming an edge is defined based on node-circle belonging relation in the temporary status.

In a temporary status, all nodes are assigned into circles. We define an indicator $\rho(i, j)$ to capture the edge existence possibility (or weight strength) between node v_i and v_j. Specifically, the value of $\rho(i,j)$ is high if v_i and v_j are put into a common circle and have high belonging coefficients to the circle. For each node v_j which satisfies $|\{C_m|\{v_i,v_j\} \subseteq C_m\}| > 0$, $\rho(i,j)$ is defined as follows:

$$\rho(i,j) = \exp\{ \sum_{\{C_m|\{v_i,v_j\}\subseteq C_m\}} \frac{U_{i,m} \cdot U_{j,m}}{Sim(i,j)^{-1} - \mathcal{T}_m + \eta} \}, \quad (6)$$

where $\mathcal{T}_m$ is the minimal $U_{j,m}$ for all the $v_j \in C_m$, and η is the maximal $\mathcal{T}_m$ for all circles C_m. In other words, $\mathcal{T}_m$ is a similarity threshold of circle C_m, which indicates the tightness of nodes within a circle. η is used to guarantee that the value of $(-\mathcal{T}_m+\eta)$ is positive and has a higher value when $\mathcal{T}_m$ gets smaller. A smaller value of $\mathcal{T}_m$ reduces the value of $\rho(i,j)$, such that a pair of nodes in lower similarity threshold circles generates lower $\rho(i,j)$ value. On the contrary, $U_{i,m}$ and $U_{j,m}$ guarantee that $\rho(i,j)$ has a high value if both of the belonging coefficients are high.

Similar to the natural ordered neighbor sequence A_i, we arrange all the neighbors of node v_i according to $\rho(i,j)$ in descending order as $B_i = (..., v_j, v_{j+1}, ...)$, where $\rho_{i,j} \geq \rho_{i,j+1}$.

Let we use $B_{i,k}$ to refer to k-th node in B_i. Ideally, given a pair of nodes (v_j, v_l), if $w_{i,j} > w_{i,l}$ and the edge weight is well inferred, it should have $\rho_{i,j} > \rho_{i,l}$. The opposite relation indicates wrongly assigned circles. Thus we treat the *sequence difference* between A_i and B_i as the goodness of circle division. If $w_{i,j} > w_{i,l}$ and $\rho_{i,j} < \rho_{i,l}$, then the pair of nodes (v_j, v_l) is an *inversion* of A_i and B_i. The inversion number is the total inversions between two sequences as $inv(v_i) = |\{(v_j, v_l)|w_{i,j} > w_{i,l} \wedge \rho_{i,j} < \rho_{i,l}\}|$. According to the definition, there is no inversion when edge weights are perfectly inferred. In addition, the more error exists, the larger inversion number will be conducted.

However, the calculation of inversion number is computational complex, because the length and elements of A_i and B_i are not always match. Fortunately, since what we need is a metric that can measure the difference of two weighted sequences, we propose to use Normalized Discounted Cumulative Gain (NDCG)[7] for measuring the differences instead. Specifically, NDCG is a measure of ranking quality in information retrieval by calculating the weighted ranking results according to ideal ranking lists. When replacing *document* with *neighbors*, and *relevance* with *edge weight* in the definition, NDCG is suitable for measuring the difference between B_i and A_i. The basic assumptions of NDCG can be grafted on to measure sequence difference smoothly:

- Highly weighted neighbors are more meaningful when appearing earlier in B_i.
- Highly weighted neighbors are more meaningful than marginally weighted neighbors, which are in turn more meaningful than unconnected nodes.

By the migration of conceptions, Discounted Cumulative Gain (DCG) of node v_i is defined as follows.

$$DCG_i = \sum_{k=1}^{deg(v_i)} \frac{2^{w_{i,k}} - 1}{\log_2(k+1)}, \quad (7)$$

where k is the sequence order index in $B_{i,k}$. According to the definition, DCG_i increases when a node with higher weighted edge be moved before a lower one in B_i. In other words, DCG_i is high if B_i is close to A_i, especially when the prefix of B_i is close to the prefix of A_i. Ideal DCG_i ($IDCG_i$) is calculated based on the neighbor sequence of $A_{i,k}$, and it is the upper bound of DCG_i.

$NDCG_i$ is then defined as normalizing DCG_i by $IDCG_i$. Note that B_i is the list of neighbors that co-appear with v_i in circles, so the length of B_i is usually not equal to $|A_i|$ in reality. Typically, B_i may contain many elements as suffix that not belongs to A_i. For example, if nodes in A_i are (v_1, v_2), then $B_i' = (v_1, v_2, v_3, v_4)$ and $B_i'' = (v_1, v_2)$ will have the same $NDCG_i$. Thus we use set difference $A_i \triangle B_i$ to penalize it, and define objective function of our model in Equation 8:

$$\mathcal{F}_U = \sum_{i=1}^{N} (\frac{n_i}{\sum_i n_i} \cdot \frac{DCG_i}{IDCG_i} \cdot (1 - \frac{|A_i \triangle B_i|}{|A_i \cup B_i|})), \quad (8)$$

where U is the belonging coefficient matrix and acts as a dynamic parameter in the learning process. Meanwhile, $\mathcal{F}_U$ is related to the proportion of transitions such that a larger node has a higher priority.

5. MODEL LEARNING ALGORITHM

In this paper, we propose to use a bottom up learning algorithm starting from a simple node-circle belonging status to maximize objective Equation 8, as shown in Algorithm 1.

In the initial step, each node v_i is assigned to a corresponding circle C_i, such that $C_i = \{v_i\}, i = 1, 2, ..., N$. $U_{i,m}$ is assigned as an identity matrix, since the node-circle belonging coefficient is 1 if there is only one node in the circle. For each node, we first compute the natural ordered neighbor sequence $\{A_i\}$ according to $\{w_{i,k}|e_{i,k} \in E\}$. As illustrated in the left side of Figure 5, at step 0, U^0 is an identity matrix that encodes initial node-circle belonging relationships.

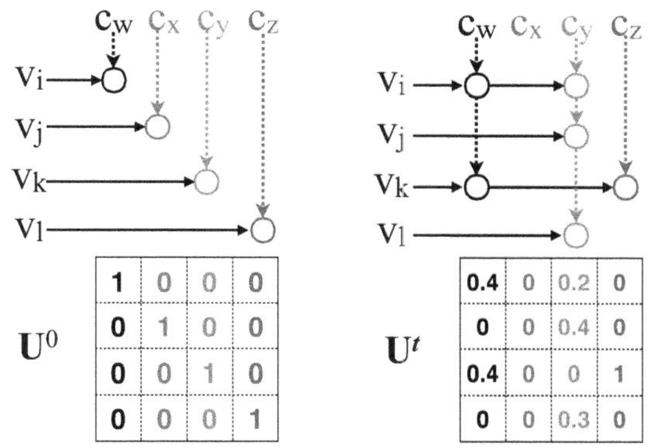

Figure 5: Learning process illustration.

In the learning process, the algorithm iteratively remove a node from circles it belongs to and add the node into other circles to maximize the objective function in Equation 8. In each step, the leaving and joining circles are determined by both the belonging coefficient and the circle size. Let we use notation $NC_i^t = \{C_m^t|v_i \in C_m^t\}$ to denote node-circle membership in iteration t, which is a binary version of non-zero elements in the corresponding row of $U_{i,m}$. The learning process then changes NC_i^t by adding and removing nodes in circles, and evaluates the value of $\mathcal{F}_U$ of the temporal status to decide whether accept or reject the change.

Specifically, in iteration t, for each node v_i, we first calculate the edge existence possibility according to Equation 6, and get ordered neighbor sequence B_i. Then, we adjust the node-circle membership as follows:

1. **Remove v_i from d_{rm} circles.** d_{rm} is determined by B_i, belongingness, and the number of circles which v_i belongs to. If B_i contains more nodes that not belong to A_i, then v_i should be removed from more circles. Meanwhile, the node should leave from lower $U_{i,m}$ circles in higher priority. Let $B_i \backslash A_i$ denote the set difference of B_i and A_i, then we define
$$d_{rm} = |NC_i^t| \cdot \frac{|B_i \backslash A_i|}{|B_i|}.$$
Next, we delete v_i from d_{rm} circles by randomly selecting circles in $\{m | m \in NC_i^t\}$ according to $P_r(i,m)$ which is the inverse order of $U_{i,m}$, as $P_r(i,m) = \frac{U_{i,m}}{\sum_m U_{i,m}}$.

2. **Add v_i to d_{add} circles.** To increase the value of $\mathcal{F}_U$, v_i should be added to more circles while A_i has many items not belonging to B_i. We define the number of circles to add as
$$d_{add} = \frac{1}{|NC_i|}(\sum_i |NC_i| - |NC_i|) \cdot \frac{|A_i \backslash B_i|}{|A_i|}.$$
Because A_i is much longer than B_i in the early stage of iteration, d_{add} is usually too large to converge. This may trigger the explosion of circles that v_i belongs to. Therefore, we set $\frac{1}{|NC_i|}$ to limit the scale of circle candidates. We first add nodes to circles with large size and high belongingness, and avoid adding nodes to empty circles. So v_i is added to d_{add} circles by randomly selecting circles in $\{m | m \notin NC_i^t\}$ according to probability distribution $P_a(i) = \frac{|C_j|}{\sum_{k \notin NC_i^t} |C_k|}$.

3. **Calculate temporary $\rho_{i,j}^t$.** We calculate $\rho_{i,j}^t$ (Equation 6) according to NC_i^t for all neighbors of v_i. Then, we form B_i^t by ordering $\rho_{i,j}^t$.

After the node-circle removing and adding step, we update $U_{i,m}$ for all the node-circle pairs and then calculate $\mathcal{F}_U^t$ based on $U_{i,m}$, A_i and B_i^t. If $\mathcal{F}_U^t > \mathcal{F}$, we accept the new circles, and set $NC_i = NC_i^t$ and $\mathcal{F} = \mathcal{F}_U^t$. The iteration repeats until $\mathcal{F}$ becoming stable after sufficient steps. When the iteration stops, $U_{i,m}$ contains the detected node-circle belonging relationship.

6. EXPERIMENTAL RESULTS

In this section, we evaluate our talent circle detection model with extensive experiments on real-world data.

6.1 Experimental Data

In this paper, we use a representative real-world data set from one of the largest commercial OPNs, to study the circle detection problem. Specifically, the data set contains 1.98 million professional profile pages from Sept. 2014 to Dec. 2015. Each page contains a job experience list in which each item shows the job title, the organization, the time period in a monthly granularity and a brief text about the job description [17]. According to the URL of organizations in resume records, there are 649,076 organizations in total. Since we are focusing on job-hopping behaviors among organizations, work experience records with keywords indicating freelancers like "freelance", "self employed" and "work at home" are neglected. Table 1 shows the detailed statistics of our data set.

Algorithm 1 Talent circle detection by maximizing NDCG

Require: Similarity matrix SIM, $IDCG$, A_i, Maximal iteration steps φ
Ensure: Node-circle belonging coefficient matrix U
  Initial: $U_{i,k} \leftarrow I$, $NC_i^0 \leftarrow \{v_i\}$, $\mathcal{F} \leftarrow 0$
  while $\mathcal{F}$ changed in last φ steps **do**
    Calculate $\rho_{i,j}^t$, then Arrange B_i
    for Node $v_i \in V$ **do**
      $d_{rm} \leftarrow |NC_i^t| \cdot \frac{|B_i \backslash A_i|}{|B_i|}$
      $rmc \leftarrow$ sample d_{rm} circles from NC_i by $P_r(i,m)$
      $NC_i^t \leftarrow setdiff(NC_i, rmc)$
      $d_{add} \leftarrow \frac{1}{|NC_i|}(\sum_i |NC_i| - |NC_i|) \cdot \frac{|A_i \backslash B_i|}{|A_i|}$
      $adc \leftarrow$ sample d_{add} circles by $P_a(i)$
      $NC_i^t \leftarrow setunion(NC_i^t, adc)$
    end for
    Calculare $U_{i,j}$
    $\mathcal{F}_U^t \leftarrow \mathcal{F}_U(NC^t, B_i, SIM, IDCG)$
    if $\mathcal{F}_U^t > \mathcal{F}$ **then**
      $\mathcal{F} \leftarrow \mathcal{F}_U^t$
      $NC_i \leftarrow NC_i^t$
    end if
  end while

There are three steps of data pre-processing, including *job transitions transformation*, *job title categorization* and *transition network initialization*.

Table 1: Job transition record statistics.

Data	Capacity	Data	Capacity
Resume	1,980,000	Job title	284,245
Transition	2,123,383	Category	10
Organization	649,076	Average flow	30

Job Transition Transformation. Items in job resume are transformed into job transitions by joining successive job record pairs. Specifically, we sort the resume items by starting time in ascending order, and then compare the end date to identify job-hooping activities, as shown in Figure 6. If the end date of record j satisfies $et_j < et_{j+1}$, then we treat

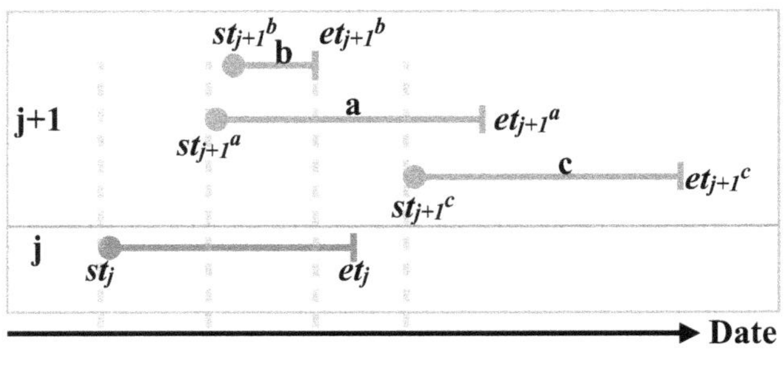

Figure 6: Transforming resume into job transition.

record pair j and $j+1$ as a transition, as case c of $j+1$ in the figure. If the end date of j is later than the start date of $j+1$, then we ignore the record pair j and $j+1$ because the $j+1$ time period is included by the period j (overlapping), as case b in Figure 6. Otherwise, as in case a in the figure, we check record $j+2$ (if it exists), and repeat the process until there is no more $j+1$ item. The job transition date is set as the start date of successor and the job title is determined by the title of predecessor when it changed during a transition.

Common transition date lasts from 1970s to the date when we collect data, and most of the transitions happening after 2000s. As shown in Figure 7, job transition frequency has a clear cycle of 12 months, so we use 12-month as a time window in our experiments.

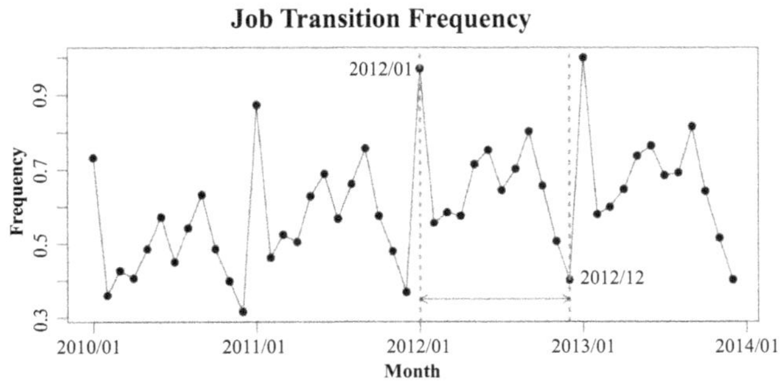

Figure 7: Aggregated job transition frequency.

Job Title Categorization. On professional profiles, users are free to specify their job titles, and usually write a short text description of their work [1]. In total, there are 284,245 different titles in our data set. In our experiments, we categorized the job titles into a few dozens of classes according to job functions by using online API from a third-party tool called Autocoder [2], which can classify job related content such as resumes and job description to a standardized hierarchy of occupation categories known as the Occupational Information Network. After that, we manually classified titles into 142 classes and further integrated into 10 major categories, as shown in Table 2.

Table 2: Job title category.

Category	#Subclass	#Title
High Tech	11	54,091
Finance	10	20,195
Professional and Business Services	21	75,565
Transportation	6	7,510
Consumer Goods	14	11,548
Goods-Producing Industries	6	7,850
Public Administration	22	27,994
Leisure and Hospitality	19	32,553
Education and Health Services	14	36,612
Manufacturing	19	10,327

Transition network initialization. We aggregated all the transitions at the organizational level and formed a job transition network. All the transitions from organization i to organization j form a direct edge starting from i and ending at j with the transition volume $n_{i,j}$. In average, there are 30 transitions between two organizations, and 84% of the flows happen among 20% of the nodes. Among all the transitions, approximately a quarter of the transitions took place within the same organization, and we ignored these loops because the ego is excluded in talent source identification.

6.2 Modularity based Evaluation

To evaluate the performance of our model in terms of circle detection, we compare our model with two state-of-the-art algorithms on modularity [10], which is a widely used metric in community detection [15]. Since the original definition of modularity is defined on non-overlapping communities, in our experiments we use an extension introduced in [12]. Specifically, we first choose two latest algorithms as baselines, namely Coordinate Ascent (**CA**) from social network analysis [9] and Simulated Annealing (**SA**) from co-authorship network analysis [2]. Meanwhile, we choose two classic algorithms as baselines, namely Random Walks (**RW**) based community detection [13] and Edge Betweenness (**EB**) based method [11]. Since there are some differences between network definitions, we follow the implication of **RW** and **EB** in [5], and from original websites[3,4] of four methods, respectively.

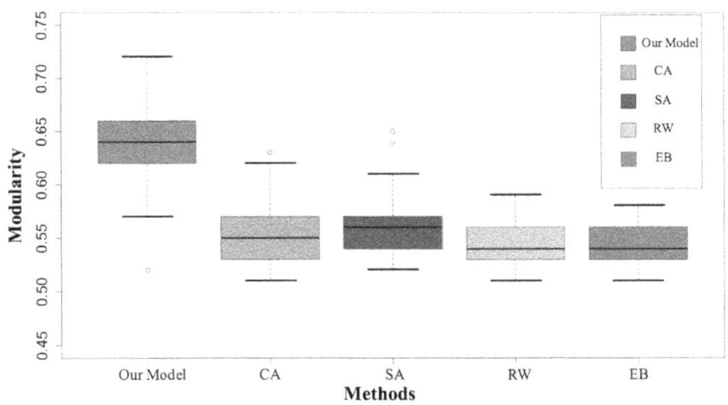

Figure 8: The comparison results of modularity.

Because the belongingness is usually normalized to have a summation of 1, we normalize the belonging coefficient $U_{i,m}$ by its row sum, i.e., $\overline{U}_{i,m} = \frac{U_{i,m}}{\sum_m U_{i,m}}$, and we set belonging coefficient of nodes as the multiplicative inverse of belonged circles in **CA** and **SA**. The coefficient is set to 1 in **RW** and **EB** since there is no corresponding definitions in these two methods. Since there is a modularity in each ego network, we pay more attention to the performance on majority egos and comparing the corresponding results of ego in other algorithms, as shown in Figure 8.

The result is based on the experiments on 7,000 egos which are the top 10 percent nodes in degree. There is an average of 5.6 circles and 3.1 organizations in each circle. As shown in Figure 8, the average modularity are 0.6376 (**Our Model**), 0.5536 (**CA**), 0.5652 (**SA**), 0.5464 (**RW**), and 0.5420 (**EB**), respectively. As a result, our method outperforms all other methods at least 7.2% in average. The majority of results of our method are also higher comparing to other methods in despite of few outliers with low modularity. The results clearly indicate that our method is more accurate for circle detection in terms of modularity in the weighted and densely connected job transition networks.

6.3 Circle Case Analysis

According to the model assumptions, organizations within a circle should have common interactions with the center organization and also exchange similar employees among each other. Thus different circles have different job transition characteristics. To this end, we select the results of several organizations for analysis.

To interpret the results, we rank the organizations in the circle according to the belonging coefficient and select top

[2]http://www.onetsocautocoder.com/plus/onetmatch

[3]http://cse.iitkgp.ac.in/resgrp/cnerg/circle/

[4]http://cseweb.ucsd.edu/ jmcauley/

ones as representative organizations. Besides, we extract related keywords from job description to facilitate the interpretation. We trace job transitions between ego and the set of companies in the circle, and extract job descriptions of these transitions. All the descriptions related to a circle are joined into a document, and thus a set of documents form as a corpus. After a removal of stop words, we arranged the words in a document according term frequency inverse document frequency (TF-IDF), and manually select several representative keywords in top 10% TF-IDF words.

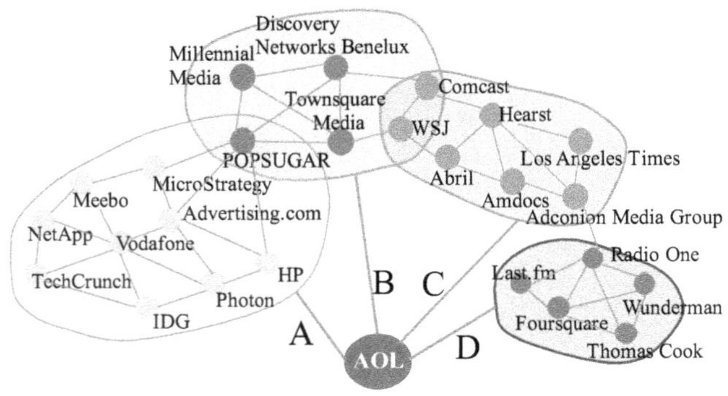

Figure 9: Circles of *AOL*. Organizations in circle (A) provide quantitative analysts. (B) provides digital marketing specialists. (C) provides customer operation support. (D) provides sales marketing analysts.

As shown in Table 3, we display the representative organizations and descriptive keywords for three ego examples, namely *Citi Bank*, *AOL*, and *Accenture* respectively. Four circles of each ego have been listed with corresponding keywords for job title description. For instance, since *Citi* is a corporate financial organization, most of the organizations in the *Citi* circles are focus on financial services. Although circle 1, 2, 3 of *Citi* are banking or related financial consulting services, the characteristics of talent sources from each circle are very different. For example, according the description of keywords, circle 1 mainly involves the talents for tasks such as corporate finance or project management, change management. While circle 2 focuses on job applicants specialized in corporate and financial risk management tasks, and circle 3 deals with talents for trading services, capital markets, or investment banking. The companies in circle 4 are mainly in IT services industry and the talent source from this circle are focusing on quantitative research, desk strategist, and quantitative analytics for *Citi* bank.

In summary, most of the companies in the circles for the ego are in the similar industry of the ego company, but different circle shows different needs of talent specialties. Similar observations can be found on the media and advertising company *AOL* (as illustrated in Figure 9) and the very successful consulting company *Accenture*. Keywords of job title summary based on the the top keywords of description is also listed in the last column of the result table.

6.4 Talent Exchange Prediction

One of the major application of talent circle detection in job transition network is to identify the source organization for selecting candidates in hiring. In fact, the detected circles are appropriate references for hiring different types of employees. For example, when the goal is to hire software engineer, recruiters can refer to the organizations appearing in circles which have labels in "computer software", "software engineer" or "programmer", etc. It is possible to precisely locate target organization by using the circles.

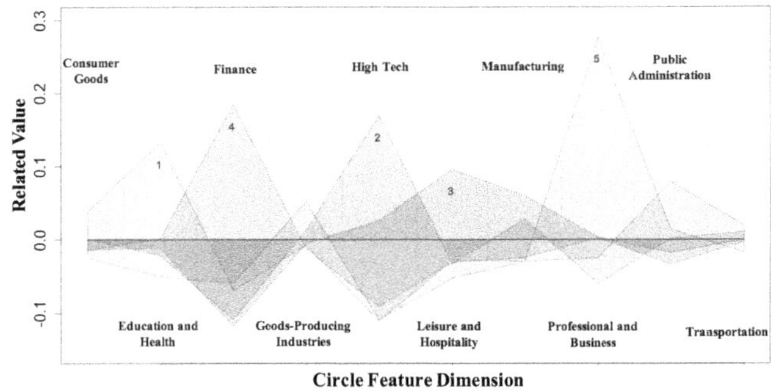

Figure 10: The feature distribution of typical circles of Citi bank.

However, enumerating related labels is inefficient when selecting circles for a job title category. As users are free to describe their works, there are too many alternative words for a title. There is a high possibility of mismatching by simply indexing keywords to solve the problem. Therefore, we design a quantitative method to identify related circles by ranking the average feature vectors. Specifically, the average feature of a circle C_m is defined as a vector FC_m where each dimension is defined as

$$FC_m^i = \frac{1}{|C_m|} \sum_{v_j \in C_m} \alpha_j^i.$$

For a given ego, FC_m can be normalized by subtracting the average circle feature $\frac{1}{M}\sum_m FC_m$, where M represents the number of circles. The normalized FC_m is treated as the "feature of a circle". Figure 10 shows the typical normalized circle feature distribution of ego "Citi", in which each area is the value of a circle feature in 10 dimensions. It indicates that different circles have different feature peak dimension combination [20]. This phenomenon also appears in circles of other egos. It suggests that average feature value is a reasonable way to identify different circle properties. We can then rank the circle features by different dimensions and select top ranked circles as related candidates.

Talent Exchange Prediction Problem. This problem refers to predict where employees will leave for from an ego, based on the detected circles. In real job market, majority of employees will go to the same set of companies where the forerunner in the same job type went, because the sector usually keeps stable and forms some specific job hooping trajectories. Although other employees may go to other companies, it is highly possible that they still stay in organizations which have similar labor demand. Therefore, we predict that the employees in a given category will go to the circles that labeled in the same category. By taking advantage of circle features, we design a simple talent exchange prediction mechanism.

For each given job title, we predict where employees with the title will leave for. Specifically, we first rank the circle feature [22, 19] according to the corresponding dimension in a descending order, and then select companies in top circles as the predicted destination. We use the job transition destination from the ego in the next year as ground truth. The prediction and evaluation procedures have three stages.

Table 3: Top circles: representative organization and keywords.

Ego	Circle	Top Organization	Top Keywords	Job Title Summary
Citi Bank	1	Capco, RBS Markets and International Banking, HSBC, PwC, Lehman Brothers, HSBC Global Banking and Markets, USAA	project, process, management, finance, back office, retail, firmwide, mssql, query, infrastructure	Corporate finance, Project management, Change management
	2	UBS, Credit Suisse, Barclays Investment Bank, Bank of Montreal, Newmark Grubb Knight Frank	stock, corporate, cash, compensation, extract, matlab, realtime, portfolio, oracle, model, data	Corporate/financial risk management
	3	YES Bank, John Hancock Financial Services, HSBC Private Bank, CHASE	finance, insurance, banker, private, systematic, equity, mortgage, rate, risk, business	Trading and Capital markets, Investment banking
	4	Sun Microsystems, Google, Palantir Technologies, D+H, Intel Corporation	visual, linear, predict, calculate, curve, java, system, algebra, compute, diagram, variable	Quantitative analytics, Desk strategist
AOL	1	Millennial Media, POPSUGAR, Discovery Networks Benelux, WSJ, Wunderman DC, Comcast, Townsquare Media	social, live, media, content, week, brand, advertise, broadband, freelance, independent, local, publish, editor	Digital marketing
	2	Thomas Cook, Foursquare, Last.fm, Radio One, Wunderman	accuracy, analyze, online, metric, sale, customer, website, trend, user response, webdata, revenue, adhoc, analyst, dashboard	Sales marketing, Digital sales
	3	Comcast, Adconion Media Group, Abril, Hearst, Los Angeles Times, Amdocs, WSJ	center, call, service, agent, maintain, quick, complaint, response, issue, communicate, customer, monitor	Customer operation, Sales operation and support
	4	IDG, Photon, TechCrunch, Vodafone, MicroStrategy, Advertising.com, Meebo, NetApp, Hewlett Packard Enterprise, POPSUGAR	data, report, media, web, strategy, advertise, market, analyze, feedback, hadoop, api, insight, module, benchmark, research, track, response, statistics, techniques	Web analytics, Quantitative research
Accenture	1	Cognizant, Logica, Deloitte Digital, Hewlett Packard Enterprise, Avanade, Gartner, Gtech	technology, enterprise, system, application, communication, defencework, enterprise, architecture	Business analyst, ERP, CRM, Enterprise Architecture
	2	Capgemini Consulting, Deloitte, EY, Alexander Mann Solutions, Towers Watson	agil, management waterfall, employee, execution, procurement, trainer	Technology project management
	3	Deloitte, Morgan Stanley, American Express, PwC, Standard Chartered Bank, Alexander Mann Solutions	e-source, spend, procurement, pension, finance, pay, pipeline, workforce, resource	Financial and Accounting services
	4	Microsoft, IBM, Google, Oracle, Amazon, Ebay, Cisco, Facebook, Tata Consultancy, CSC, Sopra Steria, EMC, Avanade, Altran	digit, advance, project, innovation, deploy, data, interface, module, architecture, technology, crm, methodology, network, database	System or Enterprise integration and implementation

First, for a given ego and title, we rank circle features by corresponding dimension in descending manner. Then we select organizations in top ranked circles as candidates. Finally, we compare predicted organization candidates with the companies which employees in the same title category leave for in the next 12 months.

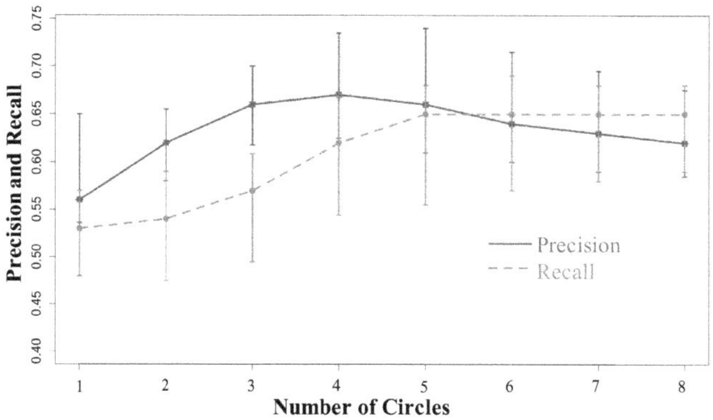

Figure 11: The precision and recall performance of talent exchange prediction.

We measure the precision and recall to evaluate the performance of talent exchange prediction. The circles are detected based on the data that have transitions during January 2013 and December 2013, and test data are the transitions during January 2014 and December 2014. Figure 11 shows the average, upper and lower bound of precision and recall for 10 job categories of *Citi*. As shown in the result, the precision and recall depend on the number of circles we used in prediction. We find that, the precision firstly increases with the increase of circles, and then reaches a peak of 73% in 4-5 circles, while it finally decreases when the number of circles larger than 6. The recall increases consistently with the number of circles, and stays stable after 6 circles in 65%. The results indicate that a majority of employees in a given job category will leave for companies that appears in the circles with corresponding characteristics. It suggests that the detected circles are appropriate node separation from the perspective of talent exchange flow.

7. RELATED WORK

In this section, we review two categories of literatures that are related to this paper, namely research on data mining for recruitment analysis, and research on circle detection in social networks.

Data mining for recruitment analysis. Recent years have witnessed the increasing popularity of using data mining techniques for addressing human resource management (HRM) problems [14]. The recruitment process is one of the important sub-domains of the HRM. Although many classic data mining tasks, such as classification, association rules and clustering [4, 6], have been performed to recruitment for personnel selection and talent prediction, only few existing work is focus on the analysis of job transition network for recruitment. For example, [3] proposed a real-time system for mining job-related patterns from social media by analyzing the job transition network. [17] showed a novel approach for modeling the professional similarity by mining professional career trajectories.

Circle detection in social networks. Social circle detection in ego networks is first proposed by McAuley and Leskovec [8, 9]. They proposed the node clustering problem and developed a model for identifying the circles including both network structure and user profile information from several popular social networks. Recently, [2] applied the techniques of automatic circle detection in an ego network on the field of co-authorship network by proposing an unsupervised method that combines both various node features and node similarity measures. Also, [18] used a multi-view clustering method for automatically detecting the social circles. Due to the different background in the job transition networks, although we have similar problem of discovering circles in the ego networks, the node features and node structures are very different. Therefore, different objective function and learning process have to be designed specifically for the job network scenario. To the best of our knowledge, this is the first attempt to detect circles for each company in a job transition network. We believe the findings from our model can further help to enhance the effectiveness of human resource tasks, such as staffing.

8. CONCLUSION

In this paper, we investigated how to identify the right talent sources for recruitment from Online Professional Networks (OPNs). Along this line, we first created a job transition network based on job transition trajectories at the organization level. Then, we proposed a talent circle detection model for extracting talent circles from the job transition network in a way that every circle includes the organizations with similar talent exchange patterns. With the help of these talent circles, the organizations can find the right talent for recruitment and the job seekers can locate suitable jobs for themselves. Moreover, based on these identified cycles, we developed a talent exchange prediction method to predict the possible destination companies for the job hopping employees. As shown in the experimental results on real-world OPNs data, our approach outperformed the benchmark methods in terms of modularity.

9. ACKNOWLEDGMENTS

This research was supported in part by the National Basic Research Program of China (No. 2015CB352400), the National Natural Science Foundation of China (No. 71329201, 61373119, 61332005, 61402369), Microsoft, and the Rutgers 2015 Chancellor's Seed Grant Program.

10. REFERENCES

[1] R. Bekkerman and M. Gavish. High-precision phrase-based document classification on a modern scale. In *SIGKDD*. ACM, 2011.

[2] T. Chakraborty, S. Patranabis, P. Goyal, and A. Mukherjee. On the formation of circles in co-authorship networks. In *SIGKDD*. ACM, 2015.

[3] Y. Cheng, Y. Xie, Z. Chen, A. Agrawal, A. Choudhary, and S. Guo. Jobminer: A real-time system for mining job-related patterns from social media. In *SIGKDD*. ACM, 2013.

[4] C.-F. Chien and L.-F. Chen. Data mining to improve personnel selection and enhance human capital: A case study in high-technology industry. *Expert Systems with applications*, 2008.

[5] G. Csardi and T. Nepusz. The igraph software package for complex network research. *InterJournal*, 2006.

[6] H. Jantan, A. R. Hamdan, and Z. A. Othman. Knowledge discovery techniques for talent forecasting in human resource application. *World Academy of Science, Engineering and Technology, Penang, Malaysia*, 2009.

[7] K. Järvelin and J. Kekäläinen. Cumulated gain-based evaluation of ir techniques. *TOIS*, 2002.

[8] J. Leskovec and J. J. Mcauley. Learning to discover social circles in ego networks. In *NIPS*, 2012.

[9] J. Mcauley and J. Leskovec. Discovering social circles in ego networks. *TKDD*, 2014.

[10] M. E. Newman. Modularity and community structure in networks. *PNAS*, 2006.

[11] M. E. Newman and M. Girvan. Finding and evaluating community structure in networks. *Physical review E*, 2004.

[12] V. Nicosia, G. Mangioni, V. Carchiolo, and M. Malgeri. Extending the definition of modularity to directed graphs with overlapping communities. *Journal of Statistical Mechanics: Theory and Experiment*, 2009.

[13] P. Pons and M. Latapy. Computing communities in large networks using random walks. In *Computer and Information Sciences-ISCIS 2005*. Springer, 2005.

[14] S. Strohmeier and F. Piazza. Domain driven data mining in human resource management: A review of current research. *Expert Systems with Applications*, 2013.

[15] Z. Wang, D. Zhang, X. Zhou, D. Yang, Z. Yu, and Z. Yu. Discovering and profiling overlapping communities in location-based social networks. *IEEE Transactions on Systems, Man, and Cybernetics: Systems*, 44(4):499–509, 2014.

[16] H. Xu, Z. Yu, H. Xiong, B. Guo, and H. Zhu. Learning career mobility and human activity patterns for job change analysis. In *ICDM*, pages 1057–1062. IEEE, 2015.

[17] Y. Xu, Z. Li, A. Gupta, A. Bugdayci, and A. Bhasin. Modeling professional similarity by mining professional career trajectories. In *SIGKDD*. ACM, 2014.

[18] Y. Yang, C. Lan, X. Li, B. Luo, and J. Huan. Automatic social circle detection using multi-view clustering. In *CIKM*. ACM, 2014.

[19] Z. Yu, Z. Wang, H. He, J. Tian, X. Lu, and B. Guo. Discovering information propagation patterns in microblogging services. *TKDD*, 10(1):7, 2015.

[20] Z. Yu, H. Xu, Z. Yang, and B. Guo. Personalized travel package with multi-point-of-interest recommendation based on crowdsourced user footprints. *IEEE Transactions on Human-Machine Systems*, 46(1):151–158, Feb 2016.

[21] J. Zhao, J. Wu, X. Feng, H. Xiong, and K. Xu. Information propagation in online social networks: a tie-strength perspective. *Knowledge and Information Systems*, 32(3):589–608, 2012.

[22] H. Zhu, E. Chen, H. Xiong, H. Cao, and J. Tian. Ranking user authority with relevant knowledge categories for expert finding. *World Wide Web*, 17(5):1081–1107, 2014.

Bid-aware Gradient Descent for Unbiased Learning with Censored Data in Display Advertising*

Weinan Zhang[1], Tianxiong Zhou[2,4], Jun Wang[2,3], Jian Xu[5]
[1]Shanghai Jiao Tong University, [2]University College London,
[3]MediaGamma Limited, [4]TukMob Inc., [5]TouchPal Inc.
{w.zhang, j.wang}@cs.ucl.ac.uk, tianxiong.zhou@tukmob.com, jian.xu@cootek.cn

ABSTRACT

In real-time display advertising, ad slots are sold per impression via an auction mechanism. For an advertiser, the campaign information is incomplete — the user responses (e.g, clicks or conversions) and the market price of each ad impression are observed only if the advertiser's bid had won the corresponding ad auction. The predictions, such as bid landscape forecasting, click-through rate (CTR) estimation, and bid optimisation, are all operated in the pre-bid stage with full-volume bid request data. However, the training data is gathered in the post-bid stage with a strong bias towards the winning impressions. A common solution for learning over such censored data is to reweight data instances to correct the discrepancy between training and prediction. However, little study has been done on how to obtain the weights independent of previous bidding strategies and consequently integrate them into the final CTR prediction and bid generation steps. In this paper, we formulate CTR estimation and bid optimisation under such censored auction data. Derived from a survival model, we show that historic bid information is naturally incorporated to produce Bid-aware Gradient Descents (BGD) which controls both the importance and the direction of the gradient to achieve unbiased learning. The empirical study based on two large-scale real-world datasets demonstrates remarkable performance gains from our solution. The learning framework has been deployed on Yahoo!'s real-time bidding platform and provided 2.97% AUC lift for CTR estimation and 9.30% eCPC drop for bid optimisation in an online A/B test.

Keywords

Unbiased Learning, Censored Data, Real-Time Bidding, Display Advertising

1. INTRODUCTION

The rise of real-time bidding (RTB) based display advertising and behavioural targeting provides one of the most significant cases for machine learning applied to big data. The major supervised learning tasks range from predicting the market price distribution and volume of a given ad impression type [4], estimating the click-through rate (CTR) [23] and conversion rate [17], to the optimisation of a bid [27, 38]. These data driven prediction and optimisation techniques enable ads to be more relevant and targeted to the underlying audience [38].

A challenging yet largely neglected problem in the aforementioned learning tasks is that common supervised learning requires the training and prediction data to follow the same distribution, but in the online display advertising case, the training data is heavily censored by the ad auction selection process [30]. For advertisers, specifically, the above prediction algorithms, e.g., CTR estimation and bid optimisation, are operated over the full volume bid request stream in order to evaluate each potential impression and automatically generate bid [39]. However, the auction selects the ad with the highest bid and displays it to the user. Only in this situation the corresponding user feedback, i.e., click and conversion, to this ad impression, along with the second price (or market price [1]) for this auction, are received by the advertisers as the labels of this data instance. Thus, as illustrated in Figure 1, the obtaining of a training instance is heavily influenced by its bid value; data instances with higher bid price (than the expected market price) would generate a higher probability of winning and thus higher chance to be in the training data. A consequence is that the learning will be overly focused on the instances with a high winning probability (high bid), while neglecting the cases where the probability is small. Such a bias is problematic as intuitively conversions or clicks from those low market-valued impressions are more crucial than those from high market-valued impressions in order to obtain a more economic solution. Ultimately advertisers not only need to identify the impressions that have high chance to be clicks/converted, but also (and equally importantly) require the cost of winning those impressions is relatively small. Thus, we need to have an unbiased learning framework that can take the final optimisation objective into account.

Typically, the bias problem is a missing data problem, which has been well-studied in the machine learning literature [8]. A direct solution would be to identify or assume the missing process and correct the discrepancy (e.g, [25, 22]) during the training. However, the data missing in RTB display advertising depends on both the advertiser's previous bidding strategy and the market competition, neither of them are known as a priori. There are some indirect solutions of alleviating the data bias such as by adding random ad selection probability in the bidding strategy [9], but a better solution would be to decouple the solution with the

*Work done while WZ, TZ were at UCL and JX was at Yahoo! US.

KDD '16, August 13-17, 2016, San Francisco, CA, USA

DOI: http://dx.doi.org/10.1145/2939672.2939713

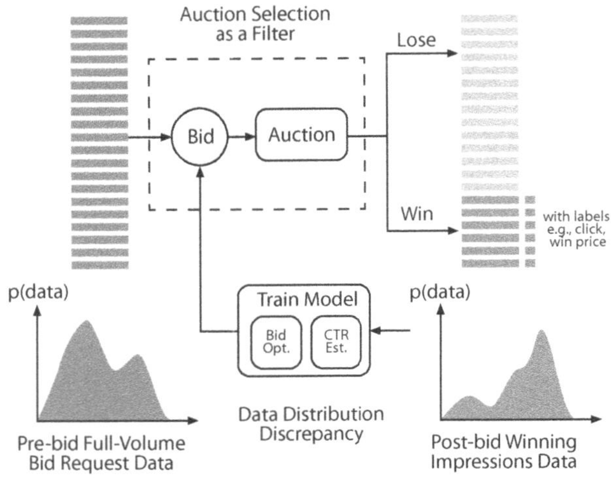

Figure 1: From an advertiser's perspective, the ad auction selection acts as a dynamic data filter based on bid value, which leads to distribution discrepancy between the post-bid training data (red) and the pre-bid prediction data (blue). The y-axis p(data) means the data p.d.f. while the x-axis is a 1-dimension abstraction of the data feature space.

previously employed bidding strategy (when acquiring the training data) and build a link to the final optimisation process.

In this paper, we consider both CTR estimation [23, 17] and bid optimisation [27, 38] together and propose a flexible learning framework that eliminates such auction-generated data bias towards a better learning and optimisation performance. According to the RTB auction mechanism, the labelled training data instance is observed only when the bid is higher than the market price. Inspired by the censored learning work in [1], we explicitly model the auction winning probability with a bid landscape based on a non-parametric survival model, i.e., [14], which is then estimated from the advertiser's historic bid. By importance sampling with the auction winning probability as propensity score [12], we naturally incorporate it into gradient derivation to produce a Bid-aware Gradient Descent (BGD) training scheme for both CTR prediction and bid optimisation tasks. Intuitively, our BGD shows that (i) the higher bid price the impression was won with, the lower valued gradient such data should generate; (ii) to generate a bid, historic bids will further adjust the gradient direction and provide a lower average budget for lower-bidden training instance when learning the bidding function. It is worth noticing that the proposed learning framework is generally applicable to various supervised learning and optimisation tasks mentioned above.

Besides the theoretical derivations, we also conduct empirical studies with the tasks of CTR estimation and bid optimisation on two large-scale real-world datasets. The results demonstrate large improvements brought from our solution over the start-of-the-art models. Moreover, the learning framework was also deployed on Yahoo! DSP in Sep. 2015 and brought 2.97% AUC lift for CTR estimation and 9.30% eCPC drop for bid optimisation over 9 campaigns in an online A/B test.

The rest of this paper is organised as follows. In Section 2 we discuss related work and compare it with ours. We then formulate the problem and propose our solutions for unbiased CTR estimation and bid optimisation under censored auction data in Section 3. Extensive offline empirical study based on two real-world datasets and online A/B test are provided in Section 4. Finally we conclude this paper and discuss future work in Section 5.

2. RELATED WORK

User Response Prediction. Click-through rate (CTR) estimation and conversion rate (CVR) estimation are critical in data driven targeted advertising as these techniques provide a quantification of the user's interest on a specific displayed ad, which in turn help advertisers better allocate budget across audiences [28, 33]. Essentially, CTR/CVR estimation is a probability regression problem where the positive instances are extremely sparse [11]. Various machine learning models with probability-related loss, such as cross entropy and log-likelihood, are used for user response estimation, including linear models such as logistic regression [17], Bayesian probit regression [9], FTRL regression [23], and non-linear ones such as factorisation machines [24] and gradient boosting tree models [11]. Nevertheless, to our best knowledge, none of the existing work considered the bias coming from the ad auction selection for the user response prediction purpose.

RTB Optimisation. Based on user response prediction, advertisers can estimate the value of a specific ad impression, which is the value of a response (click or conversion) multiplied by the predicted response rate (CTR or CVR) [17]. According to auction theory [7], the truth-telling bidding is the optimal strategy in second price auctions. However, when considering repeated auctions with volume and budget constraints, the optimal bidding strategy is not necessarily truth-telling [38, 37]. In RTB display advertising, with user response prediction and bid landscape forecasting [4], the bidding strategy determines how much to bid on a certain ad inventory. The authors in [27] proposed a linear bidding function w.r.t. the predicted CTR and the scaling parameter is tuned based on the market competition. In [3] the authors proposed to set the bid price as the truth-telling bid minus a value, which is dynamically tuned according to the current performance. In [38], the authors proposed a functional optimisation framework to induce the optimal bidding functions that maximises the target key performance indicator (KPI). Recently, a lift-based bidding strategy was proposed [32], where the bid price was set proportional to the user's CVR lift after seeing the ad impression. The authors claimed that such lift-based bidding strategy could substantially bring more customers to the advertisers. Again, none of the investigated work discussed the data bias problem which causes the data distribution discrepancy between the training and prediction stages.

Unbiased Offline Evaluation. As pointed out in [18], direct online evaluation and optimisation for a new solution are expensive and risky, which is also a dilemma in online advertising [2]. However, it is cheap and risk-free if the model can be optimised and evaluated using offline historic data that was previously collected using another (usually unknown) model. The authors in [19] proposed to use historic data for unbiased offline evaluation of news article recommendation models by replay and rejection sampling. Prerequisites of this approach are that the previous model generating the training data (called exploration model) is known, and that the evaluated policy has sufficiently explored all possible actions [15]. For cases where historic data is collected using a biased or non-stationary policy, the authors in [6] suggested an adaptive rejection sampling approach.

The authors in [36] further built a reinforcement learning framework which directly optimised the lower bound of inverse propensity score based policy value to reduce the training data bias from the historic policy. For cases where the exploration model is unknown, an evaluation scheme with estimated propensity scores and a lower bound of the data observation probability was proposed in [29]. In our case, the exploration model is known as we know the historic bid price for each bid request.

Learning with Missing Data. Handling missing data is a well-studied problem in machine learning [8]. A classic application is item recommendation with implicit feedback [25, 22]. The authors in [25] proposed uniform sampling of negative items for each user's positive-feedback item. The authors in [22] further proposed user response models to learn the missing data distribution instead of regarding it as completely random observations. With the idea that the popular but unrated items were more possible to be the true negative items for a user, the authors in [21, 26] proposed to sample the negative items more from the popular items and obtained significant recommendation improvement. More generally, the authors in [35] hypothesised that the unrated items with high predicted interest could actually be the negative samples to the user, and proposed dynamic negative item sampling which substantially improved the recommendation performance on implicit feedback data.

In online advertising, our work is closely related to [1, 31]. Similar to [1], we also employ a survival model [13] to estimate the market price. However, our purpose and setup are significantly different. The work in [31] specifically focused on forecasting and employing censored regression, while we aim at CTR estimation and bid optimisation. The authors in [1] considered bidding as a Markov decision process and formulated an online learning algorithm under the censored data. The underlying data bias was not considered in the bid optimisation and another potential drawback of this work is that a large amount of existing historic bidding data would not be utilised. Instead, we consider two distinctive training and prediction stages and develop models that can make use of any existing historic bidding data independent of previous bidding strategies. The main novelty of our work lies in deriving bid-aware gradient descent that directly incorporates the auction bias into the CTR prediction and bid generation processes to learn unbiased models.

3. METHODOLOGY

In online RTB display advertising, a bid request can be represented as a high dimensional feature vector [17]. Let us denote the vector as $\boldsymbol{x}$. Without loss of generality, we regard the bid requests as generated from an i.i.d. $\boldsymbol{x} \sim p_x(\boldsymbol{x})$ within a short period [38]. Based on the bid request $\boldsymbol{x}$, the ad agent (or demand-side platform, a.k.a. DSP) will then provide a bid $b_{\boldsymbol{x}}$ following a bidding strategy. If such bid wins the auction, the corresponding labels, i.e., user response y (either click or conversion) and market price z, are observed. Thus, the probability of a data instance $(\boldsymbol{x}, y, z)$ being observed relies on whether the bid b_x would win or not and we denote it as $P(\text{win}|\boldsymbol{x}, b_{\boldsymbol{x}})$. Formally, with the p.d.f. $q_x(\boldsymbol{x})$ denoting how the feature vector $\boldsymbol{x}$ is distributed within the observed training data $D = \{(\boldsymbol{x}, y, z)\}$, the generative process of creating the training data is summarised as:

$$\underbrace{q_x(\boldsymbol{x})}_{\text{impression}} = \underbrace{P(\text{win}|\boldsymbol{x}, b_{\boldsymbol{x}})}_{\text{auction selection}} \cdot \underbrace{p_x(\boldsymbol{x})}_{\text{bid request}}, \quad (1)$$

where the normaliser of $q_x(\boldsymbol{x})$ has been omitted for formula simplicity. Eq. (1) indicates the relationship (bias) between the p.d.f. of the pre-bid full-volume bid request data (prediction) and the post-bid winning impression data (training); in other words, the predictive models would be trained on D, where $\boldsymbol{x} \sim q_x(\boldsymbol{x})$, and be finally operated on prediction data $\boldsymbol{x} \sim p_x(\boldsymbol{x})$. In the following sections, we shall focus on the estimation of the winning probability $P(\text{win}|\boldsymbol{x}, b_{\boldsymbol{x}})$ and then introduce our solutions of using it for creating bid-aware gradients to solve CTR estimation and bid optimisation problems.

3.1 Auction Winning by Survival Models

The RTB display advertising uses the second price auction [34]. In the auction, the market price z is defined as the second highest bid from the competitors for an auction. In other words, it is the lowest bid value one should have in order to win the auction. Following [1], we take a stochastic approach rather than game theoretical, and assume the market price z is a random variable generated from a fixed yet unknown p.d.f. $p_z^{\boldsymbol{x}}(z)$; then the auction winning probability is the probability when the market price z is lower than the bid $b_{\boldsymbol{x}}$:

$$w(b_{\boldsymbol{x}}) \equiv P(\text{win}|\boldsymbol{x}, b_{\boldsymbol{x}}) = \int_0^{b_{\boldsymbol{x}}} p_z^{\boldsymbol{x}}(z)dz, \quad (2)$$

where to simplify the solution and reduce the sparsity of the estimation, the market price distribution is estimated on a campaign level rather than per impression $\boldsymbol{x}$ [4, 38]. Thus for each campaign, there is a $p_z(z)$ to estimate, resulting the simplified winning function $w(b_{\boldsymbol{x}})$, similar to [1, 38].

If we assume there is no data censorship, i.e., the ad agent wins all the bid requests and observes all the market prices, the winning probability $w_o(b_{\boldsymbol{x}})$ can directly come from the observation counting:

$$w_o(b_{\boldsymbol{x}}) = \frac{\sum_{(\boldsymbol{x}', y, z) \in D} \delta(z < b_{\boldsymbol{x}})}{|D|}, \quad (3)$$

where z is the historic market price of the bid request $\boldsymbol{x}'$, the indicator function $\delta(z < b_{\boldsymbol{x}}) = 1$ if $z < b_{\boldsymbol{x}}$ and 0 otherwise. We use it as a baseline of $w(b_{\boldsymbol{x}})$ modelling.

However, the above treatment is rather problematic as it does not take into account that in practice there are always a large portion of the auctions the advertiser loses ($z \geq b_{\boldsymbol{x}}$)[1], in which the market price is not observed in the training data. Thus, the observations of the market price are *right-censored*: when we lose, we only know that the market price is higher than our bid, but do not know its exact value. In fact, $w_o(b_{\boldsymbol{x}})$ is a biased model and over-estimates the winning probability. One way to look at this is that it ignores the counts for lost auctions where the historic bid price is higher than $b_{\boldsymbol{x}}$ in the denominator of Eq. (3). In this situation, the market price should have been higher than the historic bid price and thus higher than $b_{\boldsymbol{x}}$. As we will show in our experiment such estimator consistently over-estimate the actual winning probability.

In this paper, we use survival models [13] to handle the biased auction data. Survival models were originally proposed to predict patients' survival rate for a given time after certain treatment. As some patients might leave the investigation, researchers do not know their exact final survival

[1]In the iPinYou dataset [39] we tested, the overall auction winning rate of 9 campaigns is 23.8%, which is already a very high rate in practice.

period but only know the period is longer than the investigation period. Thus the data is right-censored. The auction scenario is quite similar: the integer market price[2] is regarded as the patient's underlying survival period from low to high and the bid price as the investigation period from low to high. If the bid b wins the auction, the market price z is observed, which is analogous to the observation of the patient's death on day z. If the bid b loses the auction, one only knows the market price z is higher than b, which is analogous to the patient's left from investigation on day b.

Specifically, we follow [1] by leveraging the non-parametric Kaplan-Meier Product-Limit method [14] to estimate the market price distribution $p_z(z)$ based on the observed impressions and the lost bid requests.

Suppose there is a campaign that has participated in N RTB display ad auctions. Its bidding log is a list of N tuples $\langle b_i, w_i, z_i \rangle_{i=1\ldots N}$, where b_i is the bid price of this campaign in the auction i, w_i is the boolean value of whether this campaign won the auction i, and z_i is the corresponding market price if $w_i = 1$. The problem is to model the probability of winning an ad auction $w(b_{\boldsymbol{x}})$ with bid price $b_{\boldsymbol{x}}$.

If we transform our data into the form of $\langle b_j, d_j, n_j \rangle_{j=1\ldots M}$, where the bid price $b_j < b_{j+1}$. d_j denotes the number of ad auction winning cases with the market price exactly valued $b_j - 1$ (in analogy to patients die on day b_j). n_j is the number of ad auction cases which cannot be won with bid price $b_j - 1$ (in analogy to patients survive to day b_j), i.e., the number of winning cases with the observed market price no lower than $b_j - 1$[3] plus the number of lost cases when the bid is no lower than $b_j - 1$. Then with bid price $b_{\boldsymbol{x}}$, the probability of losing an ad auction is

$$l(b_{\boldsymbol{x}}) = \prod_{b_j < b_{\boldsymbol{x}}} \frac{n_j - d_j}{n_j}, \tag{4}$$

which just corresponds to the probability a patient survives from day 1 to day $b_{\boldsymbol{x}}$. Thus the winning probability will be

$$w(b_{\boldsymbol{x}}) = 1 - \prod_{b_j < b_{\boldsymbol{x}}} \frac{n_j - d_j}{n_j}. \tag{5}$$

Note the calculation is Eq. (5) is highly efficient, i.e., $O(N)$. Table 1 gives an example of transforming the historic $\langle b_i, w_i, z_i \rangle$ data into the survival model data $\langle b_j, d_j, n_j \rangle$ and the corresponding winning probabilities calculated by Eqs. (5) and (3). We see that the Kaplan-Meier Product-Limit model, which is a non-parametric maximum likelihood estimator of the data [5], makes use of all winning and lost data to estimate the winning probability of each bid, whereas the observation-only counting model $w_o(b_{\boldsymbol{x}})$ does not. As we can see in the table $w_o(b_{\boldsymbol{x}})$ is consistently higher than $w(b_{\boldsymbol{x}})$. Later in experiment, we will further demonstrate such comparisons with real-world data in Figure 5.

3.2 Task 1: CTR Estimation

Generally, given a training dataset $D = \{(\boldsymbol{x}, y, z)\}$, where the data instance $\boldsymbol{x}$ follows the training data distribution $q_x(\boldsymbol{x})$, (the red data distribution in Figure 1), an *unbiased* supervised learning problem can be formalised into a loss-minimisation problem on prediction data distribution $p_x(\boldsymbol{x})$

Table 1: An example of data transformation of 8 instances with bid price between 1 and 4. Left: tuples of bid, win and cost $\langle b_i, w_i, z_i \rangle_{i=1\ldots 8}$. Right: transformed survival model tuples $\langle b_j, d_j, n_j \rangle_{j=1\ldots 4}$ and the calculated winning probabilities. Here we also provide a calculation example of $n_3 = 4$ shown as blue in the right table. The counted cases of n_3 in the left table are 2 winning cases with $z \geq 3 - 1$ and the 2 lost cases with $b \geq 3$, shown highlighted in blue color.

b_i	w_i	z_i
2	win	1
3	win	2
2	lose	×
3	win	1
3	lose	×
4	lose	×
4	win	3
1	lose	×

b_j	n_j	d_j	$\frac{n_j - d_j}{n_j}$	$w(b_j)$	$w_o(b_j)$
1	8	0	1	$1 - 1 = 0$	0
2	7	2	$\frac{5}{7}$	$1 - \frac{5}{7} = \frac{2}{7}$	$\frac{2}{4}$
3	4	1	$\frac{3}{4}$	$1 - \frac{5}{7}\frac{3}{4} = \frac{13}{28}$	$\frac{3}{4}$
4	2	1	$\frac{1}{2}$	$1 - \frac{5}{7}\frac{3}{4}\frac{1}{2} = \frac{41}{56}$	$\frac{4}{4}$

(the blue data distribution in Figure 1):

$$\min_{\boldsymbol{\theta}} \ \mathbb{E}_{\boldsymbol{x} \sim p_x(\boldsymbol{x})}[\mathcal{L}(y, f_{\boldsymbol{\theta}}(\boldsymbol{x}))] + \lambda \Phi(\boldsymbol{\theta}), \tag{6}$$

where $f_{\boldsymbol{\theta}}(\boldsymbol{x})$ is $\boldsymbol{\theta}$-parametrised prediction model to be learned; $\mathcal{L}(y, f_{\boldsymbol{\theta}}(\boldsymbol{x}))$ is the loss function based on the ground truth y and the prediction $f_{\boldsymbol{\theta}}(\boldsymbol{x})$; $\Phi(\boldsymbol{\theta})$ is the regularisation term that penalises the model complexity; λ is the regularisation weight. With Eqs. (1) and (2), one can use importance sampling to reduce the bias of the training data:

$$\mathbb{E}_{\boldsymbol{x} \sim p_x(\boldsymbol{x})}[\mathcal{L}(y, f_{\boldsymbol{\theta}}(\boldsymbol{x}))] = \int_{\boldsymbol{x}} p_x(\boldsymbol{x}) \mathcal{L}(y, f_{\boldsymbol{\theta}}(\boldsymbol{x})) d\boldsymbol{x}$$
$$= \int_{\boldsymbol{x}} q_x(\boldsymbol{x}) \frac{\mathcal{L}(y, f_{\boldsymbol{\theta}}(\boldsymbol{x}))}{w(b_{\boldsymbol{x}})} d\boldsymbol{x} = \mathbb{E}_{\boldsymbol{x} \sim q_x(\boldsymbol{x})} \Big[\frac{\mathcal{L}(y, f_{\boldsymbol{\theta}}(\boldsymbol{x}))}{w(b_{\boldsymbol{x}})} \Big] \tag{7}$$
$$= \frac{1}{|D|} \sum_{(\boldsymbol{x}, y, z) \in D} \frac{\mathcal{L}(y, f_{\boldsymbol{\theta}}(\boldsymbol{x}))}{w(b_{\boldsymbol{x}})} = \frac{1}{|D|} \sum_{(\boldsymbol{x}, y, z) \in D} \frac{\mathcal{L}(y, f_{\boldsymbol{\theta}}(\boldsymbol{x}))}{1 - \prod_{b_j < b_{\boldsymbol{x}}} \frac{n_j - d_j}{n_j}},$$

where the last equation is our empirical estimation. Based on this framework, if we obtain the auction winning probability $w(b_{\boldsymbol{x}})$, e.g., Eq. (5), we can eliminate the bias for each observed training data instance. Let us look at the case of CTR estimation with logistic regression [28]. With the logistic loss between the binary click label $\{-1, +1\}$ and the predicted probability and L2 regularisation, the framework of Eq. (7) is written as

$$\min_{\boldsymbol{\theta}} \frac{1}{|D|} \sum_{(\boldsymbol{x}, y, z) \in D} \frac{\log(1 + e^{-y \boldsymbol{\theta}^T \boldsymbol{x}})}{w(b_{\boldsymbol{x}})} + \frac{\lambda}{2} ||\boldsymbol{\theta}||_2^2, \tag{8}$$

where the winning probability $w(b_{\boldsymbol{x}})$ is estimated for each observation instance, which is independent from the CTR estimation parameter $\boldsymbol{\theta}$; the update rule of $\boldsymbol{\theta}$ is routine using stochastic gradient descent with the learning rate η. The derived *Bid-aware Gradient Descent* (BGD) of Eq. (8) is

$$\boldsymbol{\theta} \leftarrow (1 - \eta \cdot \lambda) \boldsymbol{\theta} + \frac{\eta \cdot y \cdot e^{-y \boldsymbol{\theta}^T \boldsymbol{x}} \cdot \boldsymbol{x}}{(1 + e^{-y \boldsymbol{\theta}^T \boldsymbol{x}})(1 - \prod_{b_j < b_{\boldsymbol{x}}} \frac{n_j - d_j}{n_j})}. \tag{9}$$

Discussion. From the equation above, we observe that with a lower winning bid $b_{\boldsymbol{x}}$, the probability $1 - \prod_{b_j < b_{\boldsymbol{x}}} \frac{n_j - d_j}{n_j}$ of seeing the instance in the training set is lower. However, the corresponding gradient from the data instance is higher and vice versa as it is in the denominator.

This is intuitively correct as when a data instance $\boldsymbol{x}$ is observed with low probability, e.g., 10%, we can infer there are 9 more such kind of data instances missed because of auction losing. Thus the training weight of $\boldsymbol{x}$ should be

[2]The mainstream ad exchange auctions require integer bid prices. Without a fractional component, it is reasonable to analogise bid price to survival days.

[3]We assume that if there is tie in the auction, the campaign will not get winning.

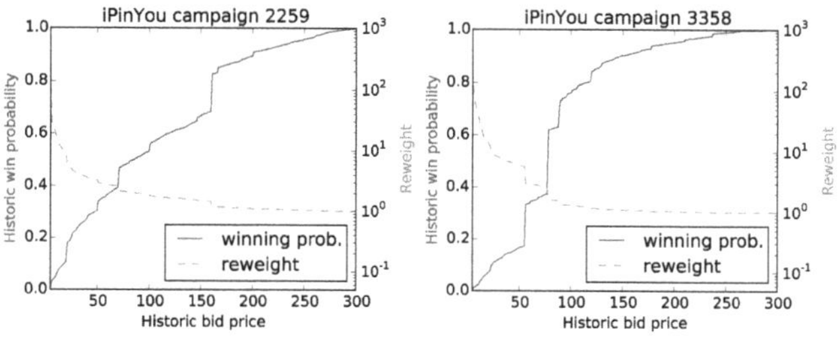

Figure 2: Winning probability and reweighting term in Eq. (9) against historic bid price.

multiplied by 10 in order to recover statistics from the full-volume data. By contrast, if the winning bid is extremely high, which leads 100% auction winning probability, then such data is observed from the true data distribution. Thus there will be no gradient reweighting on this data. Such nonlinear relationship has been well captured in our model in the gradient updates, as illustrated in Figure 2.

3.3 Task 2: Bid Optimisation

Another important problem in online advertising is bid optimisation, i.e. to find the optimal bidding strategy to maximise a campaign KPI, restricted by the campaign budget. Essentially, the bidding function is abstracted as a function mapping from the estimated CTR $f(\boldsymbol{x})$ to the bid price $b(f(\boldsymbol{x}))$.[4] According to [38], with the auction volume T and campaign budget B, it is a functional optimisation problem:

$$\arg\max_{b()} \; T\int_{\boldsymbol{x}} f(\boldsymbol{x})w(b(f(\boldsymbol{x})))p_x(\boldsymbol{x})d\boldsymbol{x} \tag{10}$$
$$\text{subject to } T\int_{\boldsymbol{x}} b(f(\boldsymbol{x}))w(b(f(\boldsymbol{x})))p_x(\boldsymbol{x})d\boldsymbol{x} = B.$$

With the auction selection, the observed data distribution is actually $q_x(\boldsymbol{x})$. By Eq. (1), Eq. (10) is written as

$$\arg\max_{b()} \; T\int_{\boldsymbol{x}} f(\boldsymbol{x})w(b(f(\boldsymbol{x})))\frac{q_x(\boldsymbol{x})}{w(b_{\boldsymbol{x}})}d\boldsymbol{x} \tag{11}$$
$$\text{subject to } T\int_{\boldsymbol{x}} b(f(\boldsymbol{x}))w(b(f(\boldsymbol{x})))\frac{q_x(\boldsymbol{x})}{w(b_{\boldsymbol{x}})}d\boldsymbol{x} = B.$$

Note that $w(b_{\boldsymbol{x}})$ is different from $w(b(f(\boldsymbol{x})))$, where $b_{\boldsymbol{x}}$ is the historic bid price for the bid request $\boldsymbol{x}$ while $b(f(\boldsymbol{x}))$ is the bid price we want to optimise.

The Lagrangian is

$$\mathcal{L}(b(f),\lambda) = \int_{\boldsymbol{x}} f(\boldsymbol{x})w(b(f(\boldsymbol{x})))\frac{q_x(\boldsymbol{x})}{w(b_{\boldsymbol{x}})}d\boldsymbol{x} - \lambda\int_{\boldsymbol{x}} b(f(\boldsymbol{x}))w(b(f(\boldsymbol{x})))\frac{q_x(\boldsymbol{x})}{w(b_{\boldsymbol{x}})}d\boldsymbol{x} + \frac{\lambda B}{T}, \tag{12}$$

According to the derivation of [38], the Euler-Lagrangian condition of Eq. (11) is

$$f(\boldsymbol{x})\frac{q_x(\boldsymbol{x})}{w(b_{\boldsymbol{x}})}\frac{\partial w(b(f(\boldsymbol{x})))}{\partial b(f(\boldsymbol{x}))} - \lambda\frac{q_x(\boldsymbol{x})}{w(b_{\boldsymbol{x}})}\Big[w(b(f(\boldsymbol{x}))) + b(f(\boldsymbol{x}))\frac{\partial w(b(f(\boldsymbol{x})))}{\partial b(f(\boldsymbol{x}))}\Big] = 0, \tag{13}$$

$$\Rightarrow \lambda w(b(f(\boldsymbol{x}))) = \Big[f(\boldsymbol{x}) - \lambda b(f(\boldsymbol{x}))\Big]\frac{\partial w(b(f(\boldsymbol{x})))}{\partial b(f(\boldsymbol{x}))}, \tag{14}$$

[4]We drop the CTR estimation parameter $\boldsymbol{\theta}$ here as it is not the parameter to optimise in this task.

where we see that the optimal bidding function $b(f(\boldsymbol{x}))$ depends on the winning function $w(b)$. For example, if

$$w(b(f(\boldsymbol{x}))) = \frac{b(f(\boldsymbol{x}))}{c + b(f(\boldsymbol{x}))}, \tag{15}$$

where c is a constant, then the corresponding optimal bidding function is

$$b_{\text{ORTB}}(f(\boldsymbol{x})) = \sqrt{\frac{c}{\lambda}f(\boldsymbol{x}) + c^2} - c. \tag{16}$$

For the solution of λ, the Euler-Lagrangian condition w.r.t. λ is

$$\partial\mathcal{L}(b(f(\boldsymbol{x})),\lambda)/\partial\lambda = 0 \tag{17}$$
$$\Rightarrow \int_{\boldsymbol{x}} b(f(\boldsymbol{x}),\lambda)w(b(f(\boldsymbol{x}),\lambda))\frac{q_x(\boldsymbol{x})}{w(b_{\boldsymbol{x}})}d\boldsymbol{x} = \frac{B}{T} \tag{18}$$
$$\Rightarrow \frac{1}{|D|}\sum_{(\boldsymbol{x},y,z)\in D} b(f(\boldsymbol{x}),\lambda)\frac{w(b(f(\boldsymbol{x}),\lambda))}{w(b_{\boldsymbol{x}})} = \frac{B}{|D|}. \tag{19}$$

The numeric solution of λ is highly efficient. A feasible solution of Eq. (19) is

$$\min_{\lambda}\sum_{(\boldsymbol{x},y,z)\in D}\frac{1}{2}\Big(\frac{b(f(\boldsymbol{x}),\lambda)w(b(f(\boldsymbol{x}),\lambda))}{1-\prod_{b_j<b_{\boldsymbol{x}}}\frac{n_j-d_j}{n_j}} - \frac{B}{|D|}\Big)^2. \tag{20}$$

As $b(f(\boldsymbol{x}),\lambda)$ always monotonically decreases w.r.t. λ and $w(b_{\boldsymbol{x}})$ monotonically increases w.r.t. $b(f(\boldsymbol{x}),\lambda)$, the objective of Eq. (20) is convex w.r.t. λ, which makes the solution of λ easy to obtain. The BGD to solve λ is via updating

$$\lambda \leftarrow \lambda - \eta\overbrace{\frac{1}{1-\prod_{b_j<b_{\boldsymbol{x}}}\frac{n_j-d_j}{n_j}}}^{\text{instance reweighting}}\overbrace{\Big(\frac{b(f(\boldsymbol{x}),\lambda)w(b(f(\boldsymbol{x}),\lambda))}{1-\prod_{b_j<b_{\boldsymbol{x}}}\frac{n_j-d_j}{n_j}} - \frac{B}{|D|}\Big)}^{\text{gradient direction}}\cdot \underbrace{\Big(\frac{\partial b(f(\boldsymbol{x}),\lambda)}{\partial\lambda}w(b(f(\boldsymbol{x}),\lambda)) + b(f(\boldsymbol{x}),\lambda)\frac{\partial w(b(f(\boldsymbol{x}),\lambda))}{\partial\lambda}\Big)}_{\text{bidding function gradient}}. \tag{21}$$

Discussion. Highlighted in Eq. (21), there are two factors related with the historic bid for updating λ: (i) the instance reweighting, similar with Eq. (9): a small historic bid $b_{\boldsymbol{x}}$ would generate a large weight, amplifying the importance of the training instance. (ii) The historic bid of the training instance also has an impact on the gradient direction, evidenced by the second factor of the update in Eq. (21).

The parameter λ converges when the second factor becomes zero. The ratio $B/|D|$ would ensure the budget to be allocated evenly across the new bids. The ratio between the winning rate of the new bid price $w(b(f(\boldsymbol{x}),\lambda))$ and that of the historic bid $1-\prod_{b_j<b_{\boldsymbol{x}}}(1-d_j/n_j)$ would adjust the discrepancy of the probability of seeing the impression in the training and that in the prediction.

To further understand this, Figure 3 illustrates the second factor (the gradient direction term) in Eq. (21) against historic bid price $b_{\boldsymbol{x}}$ on two sample campaigns with two new bids ($b(f(\boldsymbol{x}),\lambda) = 50$ and 100). We observe that when the historic bid is small, the gradient direction is more likely to stay positive and leads to higher λ value (as bidding function gradient term in Eq. (21) is always negative) in order to decrease the bid. For example, for a data instance that its historic bid $b_{\boldsymbol{x}}$ is low, the probability of observing the data instance is low, which means there are more similar or the same data instances that are missing in the training. If the

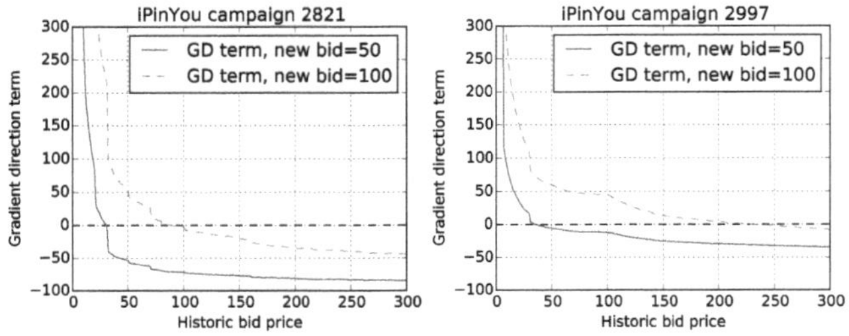

Figure 3: The gradient direction term in Eq. (21) against historic bid price $b_{\boldsymbol{x}}$ with two new bids $b(f(\boldsymbol{x}), \lambda)$.

new bid price $b(f(\boldsymbol{x}), \lambda)$ is high, then the optimal bid price $b(f(\boldsymbol{x}), \lambda)$ should be lower to avoid budget overspending in full-volume data, which is reflected on the positive value of the gradient direction factor to make λ higher and $b(f(\boldsymbol{x}), \lambda)$ lower.

Please note that with the pre-calculated reweighting factor $1/w(b_{\boldsymbol{x}}) = 1/(1 - \prod_{b_j < b_{\boldsymbol{x}}} \frac{n_j - d_j}{n_j})$, it is highly efficient to calculate the above BGD updating and solve λ.

4. EXPERIMENT

4.1 Datasets

Two real-world datasets are used in our repeatable offline empirical study[5]: iPinYou and TukMob.

iPinYou runs the largest DSP in China. The publicly available[6] iPinYou dataset consists of 64.75M bid records, 19.50M impressions, 14.79K clicks and 16K CNY expense on 9 conventional display ad campaigns from different advertisers during 10 days in 2013. According to iPinYou [20], the last 3-day data for each campaign is set as test data while the rest is training data.

TukMob is a major DSP focusing on mobile game and video display ads in China. TukMob dataset is our proprietary dataset which consists of 3.00M impressions, 96.45K clicks and 2.51K CNY expense on 63 campaigns in a video display ad market from Feb. to Aug. 2015. The first 5/6 data in the time sequence is set as training data while the rest is test data.

Each data instance of both datasets can be represented as a triple $(\boldsymbol{x}, y, z)$, where y is the user click binary feedback, z is the historic winning price of the auction, and $\boldsymbol{x}$ is the bid request and ad features of that auction. The auction features contain the information of the user (e.g. the user interest segments, IP address, browser, operation system, location), advertiser (e.g. the creative format and size), publisher (e.g. the auction reserve price, ad slot size, page domain and URL).

We mainly report the experimental results on iPinYou dataset for experiment reproducibility while the study on TukMob acts as an auxiliary part particularly for the high-CTR video ad marketplace to make our experiment more comprehensive.

The online A/B testing experiment is conducted based on Yahoo! DSP, a mainstream DSP in United States ad market. The training dataset comes from its ad log in Aug. and Sep. 2015 while the online A/B testing is performed on 9 campaigns during 7 days of Sep. 2015, which involves 117.1M impressions, 95.4K clicks and 68.6K USD expense.

[5]Experiment code link: https://github.com/wnzhang/rtb-unbiased-learning.

[6]Dataset link: http://data.computational-advertising.org

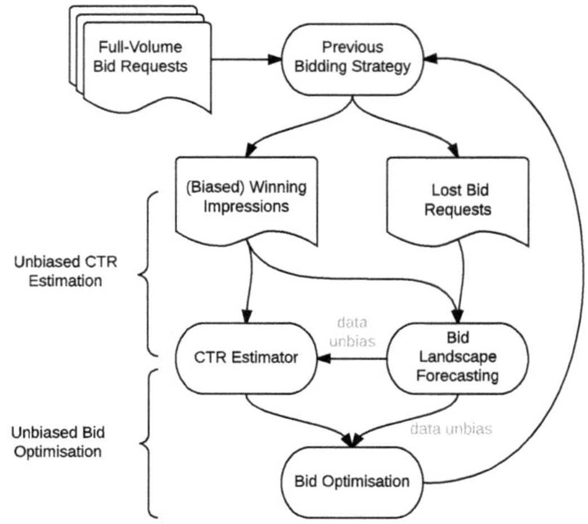

Figure 4: Experiment flow chart.

4.2 Experiment Flow

The experiment flow chart is shown in Figure 4. The original impression log data is reasonably assumed as full-volume bid request data in our experiment[7]. A truth-telling bidding strategy [17] is performed to simulate the historic bidding process and produce the winning (labelled but biased) impression data and lost (unlabelled) bid request data. Based on these two datasets, the bid landscape forecasting module as in Eq. (5) estimates the market price distribution which acts as the winning function in Eq. (1). Thus the observation bias of each data instance from the impression log is estimated. With Eq. (8), the unbiased CTR estimation is performed. Furthermore, with the unbiased CTR estimator and the winning function, the unbiased bid optimisation is performed via Eq. (11) to get the new bidding function, which is in turn operated in the next prediction stage.

4.3 Compared Settings

CTR estimation and bid optimisation are the two tasks we investigate in this work. For each of these tasks, we compare the following four training schemes:

- BIAS - The CTR estimation and bid optimisation are performed based on the impression data without considering any data bias, i.e., all $w(b_{\boldsymbol{x}})$ in Eqs. (8) and (11) are equal to 1. This is the routine training procedure used in most previous work [17, 27, 38].
- UOMP - The bias of each training data instance is estimated by the bid landscape forecastor purely based on the observed market prices from impression log, without using the lost bid request data, i.e., all $w(b_{\boldsymbol{x}})$ in Eqs. (8) and (11) are estimated by Eq. (3).
- KMMP - The bias of each training data instance is estimated by the bid landscape forecastor based on both observed market prices from impression log and the lost bid request data using Kaplan-Meier estimation, i.e., all $w(b_{\boldsymbol{x}})$ in Eqs. (8) and (11) are estimated by Eq. (5).

[7]This assumption is reasonable as this dataset is collected with fixed large bid to reduce the auction-selection bias [20].

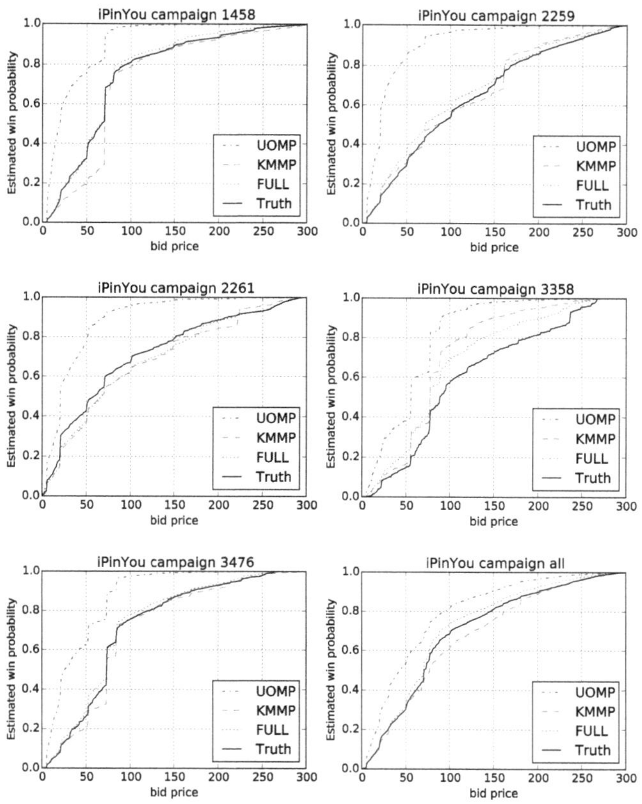

Figure 5: Winning probability against bid price (iPinYou).

- FULL - A progressive bidding strategy is performed to win all the bid requests via bidding extremely high. In such case the full-volume bid requests are collected with labels to train the CTR estimator and bid optimisation. In such setting, the data has no bias and is of full volume, and thus it is regarded as the (unrealistic) upper bound setting of the training.

4.4 Winning Probability Estimation

Before evaluating the practical CTR estimation and bid optimisation tasks, let us first take an analysis of the compared models' performance on winning probability estimation, i.e., $w(b_{\boldsymbol{x}})$ in Eq. (2).

First, Table 2 demonstrates the statistics of the full-volume data and the winning impression data by the 'historic' truth-telling bidding strategy as described in Section 4.2. As can be observed, for both datasets the winning impression data which is fed into BIAS, UOMP and KMMP training schemes is much smaller than the full-volume data which is fed into FULL training scheme.

Figure 5 shows the curves of winning probability w.r.t. the bid price with three compared settings, i.e., UOMP, K-MMP and FULL, on iPinYou dataset. As expected, all the curves start from 0 given the bid 0 and then increase as the bid price increases and finally converge to 1 when the bid price surpasses a threshold (300 for iPinYou dataset). The TRUTH curve is built from all the market price observations from the full-volume prediction data, regarded as the ground truth here. We observe that FULL curve is the closest one to TRUTH curve since FULL makes use of the full-volume training data and is naturally unbiased. The only reason of the slight difference between FULL and TRUTH is the data distribution shift between the training and prediction period. UOMP always over-estimates the winning probability, as pointed out in Section 3.1. Compared to UOMP, KMMP curve is much closer to TRUTH, which shows its advantage of making use of the lost bid request data to improve the winning probability estimation.

Table 3 presents the detailed Pearson correlation and KL-divergence between each of the three compared settings and TRUTH on iPinYou dataset. We observe that for all investigated campaigns, KMMP provides a much better estimation, i.e., higher Pearson correlation and lower KL-divergence, than UOMP, and it is even highly comparable with FULL on Pearson correlation. These results demonstrate the surprisingly large improvement that the lost and free bid request data brings to the estimation of winning probability (market price distribution).

Table 2: Winning data statistics: the full-volume data is used in FULL training scheme, while the winning data is used in BIAS, UOMP and KMMP training schemes (both datasets).

iPinYou Camp.	Full Vol.	Win Vol.	Win rate
1458	2,055,371	257,077	12.51%
2259	557,038	239,328	42.96%
2261	458,412	213,930	46.67%
2821	881,708	305,134	34.61%
2997	208,292	60,556	29.07%
3358	1,161,403	336,769	29.00%
3386	1,898,535	332,223	17.50%
3427	1,729,177	563,592	32.59%
3476	1,313,574	303,341	23.09%
all	10,263,506	3,973,989	38.72%
TukMob Camp.	Full Vol.	Win Vol.	Win rate
all	2,500,000	962,690	38.51%

Table 3: Winning probability estimation (iPinYou).

	Pearson Correlation			KL-Divergence		
Camp.	UOMP	KMMP	FULL	UOMP	KMMP	FULL
1458	0.9067	0.9903	0.9995	0.4053	0.1204	0.0407
2259	0.7811	0.9959	0.9980	0.7163	0.1870	0.0713
2261	0.9018	0.9947	0.9972	0.3483	0.1057	0.0346
2821	0.8234	0.9947	0.9931	0.5659	0.1421	0.0697
2997	0.8535	0.9285	0.9955	0.3862	0.1761	0.0210
3358	0.9269	0.9772	0.9926	0.5243	0.2652	0.1521
3386	0.9116	0.9821	0.9995	0.3232	0.1391	0.0444
3427	0.9743	0.9977	0.9996	0.1838	0.0762	0.0525
3476	0.9303	0.9979	0.9993	0.3807	0.1147	0.0451
all	0.9795	0.9958	0.9988	0.0893	0.0385	0.0237

4.5 CTR Estimation Results

With different biased or unbiased settings, we train the logistic regression model and evaluate its performance. Table 4 presents the detailed AUC and cross entropy performance of these 4 compared training schemes for each campaign in iPinYou dataset. Table 5 presents the AUC performance comparison on TukMob dataset. We can observe that (i) the proposed unbiased training schemes UOMP and KMMP always outperform the biased but widely adopted BIAS training scheme on all the test campaigns (except for 3476). Such consistent outperformance shows the effectiveness of our models in eliminating the training data instance bias which makes the prediction model generalise better on prediction data. (ii) Comparing the unbiased settings UOMP and KMMP and the upper bound oracle setting FULL, we can see KMMP outperforms UOMP for all the campaigns (except for 3476). For some campaigns, e.g., 1458 and 2997, KMMP

Table 4: CTR performance on iPinYou dataset.

Camp.	AUC (%)				Cross Entropy (‰)			
	BIAS	UOMP	KMMP	FULL	BIAS	UOMP	KMMP	FULL
1458	98.26	98.56	99.13	98.57	2.42	2.39	2.39	2.32
2259	60.27	60.94	62.00	67.37	4.04	4.03	4.02	4.00
2261	57.49	58.86	59.05	60.91	3.75	3.74	3.74	3.72
2821	59.25	59.69	60.28	62.36	7.07	7.06	7.04	6.92
2997	59.35	60.50	60.79	59.28	32.89	32.84	32.81	32.38
3358	96.59	96.78	97.01	97.32	4.48	4.47	4.38	4.36
3386	73.74	74.01	74.16	78.23	8.84	8.83	8.83	8.64
3427	96.04	96.42	96.78	97.02	3.37	3.37	3.33	3.31
3476	93.66	93.55	92.19	95.93	4.35	4.34	4.34	4.08
all	71.76	73.84	74.80	78.38	7.71	7.61	7.55	7.31

Table 5: CTR performance on TukMob dataset.

Camp.	AUC (%)			
	BIAS	UOMP	KMMP	FULL
all	60.49	60.51	60.67	60.96

even slightly outperforms FULL[8] which again shows the advantages of making use of the lost auction information for better estimating the instance bias.

Figure 6 shows the AUC and cross entropy on prediction data of all iPinYou campaigns for each training round. We can observe the unbiased UOMP and KMMP models learn stably and consistently outperform BIAS. FULL substantially outperforms other compared training schemes, which is not surprising as FULL obtains much more training data instances (as shown in Table 2) and the data distribution is unbiased.

Note that we do not compare calibration techniques [11] in our experiment because it is another dimension of reducing the model bias. If the training data is auction-biased, then the calibration based on that is still biased.

4.6 Bid Optimisation Results

For bid optimisation experiment, we mainly focus on the click performance improvement from bidding strategy parameter optimisation via Eqs. (16) and (19) instead of the difference of CTR estimation. Thus in our training/prediction environment, the logistic regression CTR estimator is trained based on a separate unbiased training data and is shared in all 4 compared training schemes of bid optimisation. For each training scheme, we train the optimal parameter λ in Eq. (19) via the biased or unbiased training data, then apply the corresponding bidding strategy Eq. (16) on prediction data to observe its performance.

We follow [38] to set the budget proportions to perform offline bid optimisation, where the train/test budget is set as 1/64, 1/32, 1/16, 1/8, 1/4 and 1/2 of the total expense of the train/test dataset. We cannot set the proportion as 1 because in such case one may simply bid infinity to win all the impressions and clicks in the data and just spend all the budget.

Table 6 shows the click performance of the 4 compared training schemes with 1/64 and 1/4 budget settings respectively for each iPinYou campaign. Table 7 shows the overall click and eCPC performance comparison against different budget settings on TukMob dataset. We can observe that the unbiased UOMP and KMMP consistently outperform the traditional BIAS which were used in the most of the previous bid optimisation work [16, 27, 38]. This shows the great potential of our proposed unbiased training schemes in bid optimisation. Furthermore, KMMP outperforms UOMP and it

[8]This is mainly caused by the local data distribution, which is not significant.

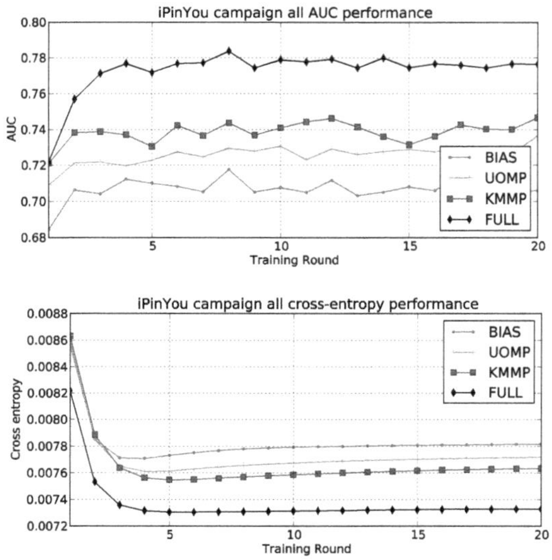

Figure 6: CTR performance training convergence (iPinYou).

Table 6: Bid optimisation click performance (iPinYou).

Camp.	1/64 budget setting				1/4 budget setting			
	BIAS	UOMP	KMMP	FULL	BIAS	UOMP	KMMP	FULL
1458	363	400	460	468	469	470	471	482
2259	5	5	5	7	49	51	51	50
2261	5	5	7	7	35	36	35	45
2821	18	18	23	27	65	91	106	134
2997	37	39	42	44	156	188	222	226
3358	86	117	137	140	183	198	220	221
3386	9	9	22	38	69	78	144	165
3427	103	119	154	169	242	262	286	314
3476	6	8	11	13	59	99	108	106
all	268	372	462	521	1,584	1,740	1,871	2,087

Table 7: Bid optimisation click performance (TukMob).

Budget Setting	Click Number				eCPC			
	BIAS	UOMP	KMMP	FULL	BIAS	UOMP	KMMP	FULL
1/32	846	848	866	871	9.25	9.23	9.04	8.99
1/16	1,829	1,831	1,863	1,838	8.56	8.55	8.40	8.52
1/8	3,721	3,721	3,774	3,775	8.42	8.42	8.30	8.29
1/4	7,181	7,178	7,226	7,257	8.72	8.72	8.67	8.63
1/2	13,127	13,132	13,163	13,019	9.54	9.54	9.52	9.62

is very close to the theoretic upper bound from FULL, in 17 out of 20 test cases, suggesting it is generally much better to leverage the winning probability obtained from the censored observations of both winning impressions and lost bid requests.

Figure 7 further provides the click, impression improvement percentages and eCPC drop percentage of the unbiased training schemes against BIAS with different budget settings. The improvements for clicks and impressions are positive for all budget settings and the eCPC drops are negative for all budget settings (except FULL on 1/2), which show the robustness of the unbiased training schemes. Also we can observe that KMMP dominates UOMP and heavily approach the upper bound FULL.

4.7 Online A/B Testing

We deployed the unbiased KMMP training scheme on Yahoo! DSP and performed online A/B testing for 9 campaigns during 7 days in Sep. 2015. For each campaign, we created two experiment buckets: control and treatment. Each was allocated 50% of the bid request traffic (based on user ID to avoid attribution conflicts), and 50% of the campaign's budget. The control bucket used gradient boosting decision tree

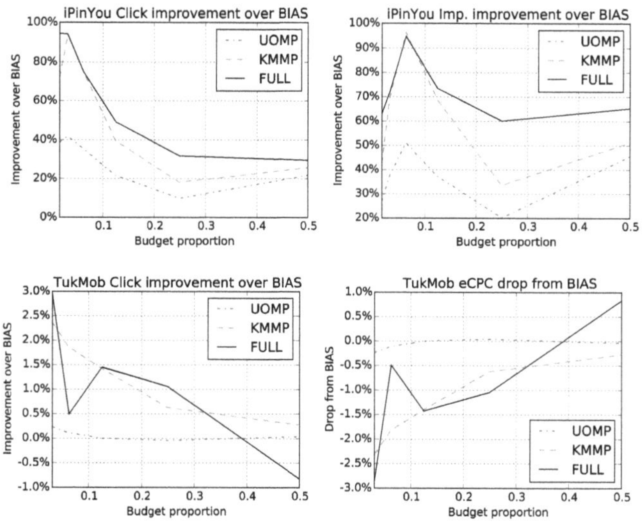

Figure 7: Improvement over BIAS w.r.t. budget proportions.

Table 8: Online A/B testing of CTR estimation (Yahoo!).

Camp.	BIAS AUC.	KMMP AUC	AUC Lift
C1	63.78%	64.12%	0.34%
C2	87.45%	88.58%	1.13%
C3	69.73%	75.52%	5.79%
C4	88.82%	89.55%	0.73%
C5	69.71%	72.29%	2.58%
C6	89.33%	90.70%	1.37%
C7	77.76%	78.92%	1.16%
C8	74.57%	76.98%	2.41%
C9	71.04%	73.12%	2.08%
all	73.48%	76.45%	2.97%

click predictor [11] trained with BIAS, while the click model used in the treatment bucket was trained with KMMP. The deployed bidding strategy is the conventional truth-telling bidding [17].

In order to perform an unbiased evaluation of the CTR estimation, we deployed a bidding agent performing very high constant bid in Sep. 2015 to collect an ad impressions dataset which can be regarded as full-volume unbiased test data. The training data was still the traditional biased ad impression dataset during Aug. and early Sep. 2015. Table 8 provides the detailed CTR estimation performance for each campaign and the overall performance. As can be observed, KMMP provided a consistent AUC improvement over BIAS across all investigated campaigns. The overall AUC was 73.48% for BIAS and 76.45% for KMMP, which was a very large improvement for CTR estimation task in practice.

Table 9 further presents the detailed performance of A/B testing of bid optimisation on the 9 campaigns. Figure 8 depicts the relative difference comparing the performance of KMMP againt BIAS. We found that with the same campaign budget the KMMP-trained model acquired more clicks (most of the time) but fewer impressions than the BIAS-trained one, which made its CTR much higher than BIAS. This is because there was less over-prediction on many cheap cases. In the biased training data, the over-predicted CTR on cheap cases were more likely to be sampled because the historic bidding strategy overbid on these cheap cases, vice versa on expensive cases. With the KMMP training scheme, the bidding strategy to-some-extent got rid of such bias to avoid over-prediction on cheap cases, which provided fewer impressions but more clicks.

Table 9: Online A/B testing of bid optimisation (Yahoo!).

Camp.	Impressions (M)		Clicks (K)		CTR (%)		eCPC ($/click)	
	BIAS	KMMP	BIAS	KMMP	BIAS	KMMP	BIAS	KMMP
C1	1.07	0.89	0.62	0.67	0.06	0.08	4.54	4.16
C2	7.73	6.02	0.94	1.19	0.01	0.02	7.49	5.89
C3	22.18	16.96	27.18	30.06	0.12	0.18	0.26	0.23
C4	0.37	0.12	0.61	0.61	0.16	0.49	2.46	2.48
C5	9.57	7.51	6.42	6.93	0.07	0.09	0.45	0.42
C6	0.32	0.22	0.46	0.46	0.14	0.21	2.17	2.18
C7	10.13	7.31	2.99	3.28	0.03	0.04	0.37	0.34
C8	1.04	0.52	1.04	1.13	0.10	0.22	1.92	1.78
C9	13.67	11.46	5.12	5.71	0.04	0.05	1.76	1.58
all	66.07	51.01	45.37	50.03	0.07	0.10	0.76	0.69

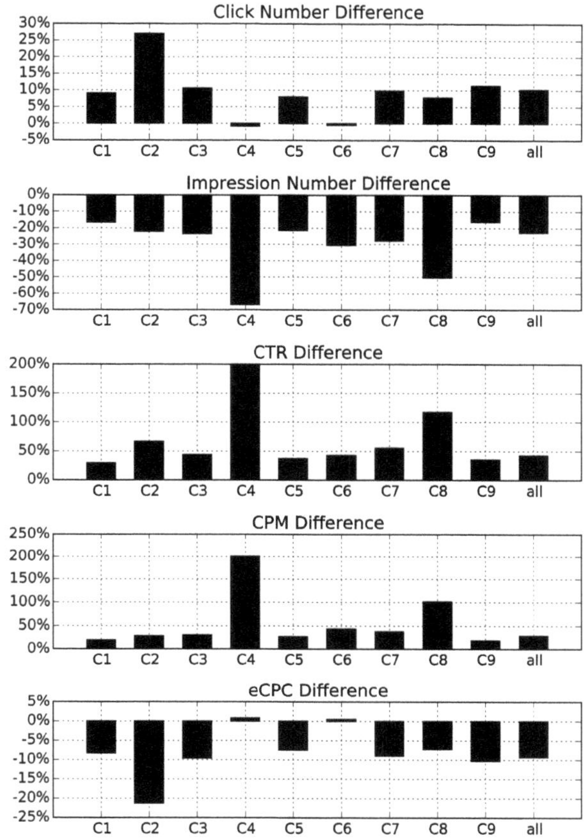

Figure 8: Relative performance difference between KMMP and BIAS in Yahoo! online A/B testing: (KMMP-BIAS)/BIAS.

Overall, with the same budget, the bidding strategy trained with KMMP achieved much better eCPC (9.30% drop) and CTR (42.8% rise) than the conventional one trained with BIAS. The KMMP-trained click model effectively alleviated over-prediction especially in the low-CTR region and thus became more efficient in acquiring clicks. Therefore, with the bidding strategy with unbiased KMMP-trained click model, campaigns could acquire clicks in a more cost-effective way.

5. CONCLUSIONS

In this paper, we studied the data observation bias problem in display advertising generated from the auction selection that would hurt the performance of various supervised learning models. To address this problem, we proposed a model-free learning framework that eliminates the model bias generated from censored auction data. The derived Bid-aware Gradient Descent (BGD) learning scheme naturally incorporates the historic auction and bid information, which is the main novelty of this paper. We found that the historic bid for each instance could influence both BGD learning weight and update direction. Comprehensive empirical study based on iPinYou and TukMob datasets demonstrated the large improvement of our learning framework over strong baselines in both CTR estimation and bid optimisation tasks. With light engineering work, the learning framework was deployed on Yahoo! DSP and brought 2.97% AUC lift in CTR estimation and 9.30% eCPC drop in bid optimisation over 9 campaigns.

It is important to point out that such learning framework is flexible with other supervised learning tasks than the investigated ones in this work, such as budget pacing and frequency capping in online advertising as well as other data science problems, such as interactive recommender systems [40], off-policy reinforcement learning [10], which are our planned future work.

Acknowledgement. We sincerely thank Quan Lu from Yahoo! US for his support of the online experiment. Weinan thanks the CSC funding for supporting the research.

6. REFERENCES

[1] K. Amin, M. Kearns, P. Key, and A. Schwaighofer. Budget optimization for sponsored search: Censored learning in MDPs. *UAI*, 2012.

[2] L. Bottou, J. Peters, J. Quinonero-Candela, D. X. Charles, D. M. Chickering, E. Portugaly, D. Ray, P. Simard, and E. Snelson. Counterfactual reasoning and learning systems: The example of computational advertising. *JMLR*, 14(1):3207–3260, 2013.

[3] Y. Chen, P. Berkhin, B. Anderson, and N. R. Devanur. Real-time bidding algorithms for performance-based display ad allocation. In *KDD*, pages 1307–1315. ACM, 2011.

[4] Y. Cui, R. Zhang, W. Li, and J. Mao. Bid landscape forecasting in online ad exchange marketplace. In *KDD*, pages 265–273. ACM, 2011.

[5] D. M. Dabrowska. Non-parametric regression with censored survival time data. *Scandinavian Journal of Statistics*, pages 181–197, 1987.

[6] M. Dudík, D. Erhan, J. Langford, and L. Li. Sample-efficient nonstationary policy evaluation for contextual bandits. In *Proceedings of the UAI*, 2012.

[7] B. Edelman, M. Ostrovsky, and M. Schwarz. Internet advertising and the generalized second price auction: Selling billions of dollars worth of keywords. *National Bureau of Economic Research*, 2005.

[8] P. J. García-Laencina, J.-L. Sancho-Gómez, and A. R. Figueiras-Vidal. Pattern classification with missing data: a review. *Neural Computing and Applications*, 19(2):263–282, 2010.

[9] T. Graepel, J. Q. Candela, T. Borchert, and R. Herbrich. Web-scale bayesian click-through rate prediction for sponsored search advertising in microsoft's bing search engine. In *ICML*, 2010.

[10] H. Hachiya, T. Akiyama, M. Sugiayma, and J. Peters. Adaptive importance sampling for value function approximation in off-policy reinforcement learning. *Neural Networks*, 22(10):1399–1410, 2009.

[11] X. He, J. Pan, O. Jin, T. Xu, B. Liu, T. Xu, Y. Shi, A. Atallah, R. Herbrich, S. Bowers, et al. Practical lessons from predicting clicks on ads at facebook. In *ADKDD*, pages 1–9. ACM, 2014.

[12] K. Hirano, G. Imbens, and G. Ridder. Efficient estimation of average treatment effects using the estimated propensity score, 2000.

[13] N. L. Johnson. *Survival models and data analysis*, volume 74. John Wiley & Sons, 1999.

[14] E. L. Kaplan and P. Meier. Nonparametric estimation from incomplete observations. *Journal of the American statistical association*, 53(282):457–481, 1958.

[15] J. Langford, A. Strehl, and J. Wortman. Exploration scavenging. In *ICML*, pages 528–535. ACM, 2008.

[16] K.-C. Lee, A. Jalali, and A. Dasdan. Real time bid optimization with smooth budget delivery in online advertising. In *ADKDD*, page 1. ACM, 2013.

[17] K.-C. Lee, B. Orten, A. Dasdan, and W. Li. Estimating conversion rate in display advertising from past erformance data. In *KDD*, pages 768–776. ACM, 2012.

[18] L. Li. Offline evaluation and optimization for interactive systems. In *WSDM*, pages 413–414. ACM, 2015.

[19] L. Li, W. Chu, J. Langford, and X. Wang. Unbiased offline evaluation of contextual-bandit-based news article recommendation algorithms. In *WSDM*, 2011.

[20] H. Liao, L. Peng, Z. Liu, and X. Shen. iPinYou global rtb bidding algorithm competition dataset. In *ADKDD*, 2014.

[21] Q. Lu, T. Chen, W. Zhang, D. Yang, and Y. Yu. Serendipitous personalized ranking for top-n recommendation. In *Web Intelligence*, 2012.

[22] B. M. Marlin and R. S. Zemel. Collaborative prediction and ranking with non-random missing data. In *RecSys*, 2009.

[23] H. B. McMahan, G. Holt, D. Sculley, M. Young, D. Ebner, J. Grady, L. Nie, T. Phillips, E. Davydov, D. Golovin, et al. Ad click prediction: a view from the trenches. In *KDD*, pages 1222–1230. ACM, 2013.

[24] R. J. Oentaryo, E.-P. Lim, J.-W. Low, D. Lo, and M. Finegold. Predicting response in mobile advertising with hierarchical importance-aware factorization machine. In *WSDM*, pages 123–132. ACM, 2014.

[25] R. Pan, Y. Zhou, B. Cao, N. N. Liu, R. Lukose, M. Scholz, and Q. Yang. One-class collaborative filtering. In *ICDM*, pages 502–511. IEEE, 2008.

[26] U. Paquet and N. Koenigstein. One-class collaborative filtering with random graphs. In *WWW*, 2013.

[27] C. Perlich, B. Dalessandro, R. Hook, O. Stitelman, T. Raeder, and F. Provost. Bid optimizing and inventory scoring in targeted online advertising. In *KDD*, 2012.

[28] M. Richardson, E. Dominowska, and R. Ragno. Predicting clicks: estimating the click-through rate for new ads. In *WWW*, pages 521–530. ACM, 2007.

[29] A. Strehl, J. Langford, L. Li, and S. M. Kakade. Learning from logged implicit exploration data. In *NIPS*, 2010.

[30] H. R. Varian. Online ad auctions. *The American Economic Review*, pages 430–434, 2009.

[31] W. C.-H. Wu, M.-Y. Yeh, and M.-S. Chen. Predicting winning price in real time bidding with censored data. In *KDD*, pages 1305–1314. ACM, 2015.

[32] J. Xu, X. Shao, J. Ma, K.-c. Lee, H. Qi, and Q. Lu. Lift-based bidding in ad selection. In *AAAI*, 2016.

[33] J. Yan, N. Liu, G. Wang, W. Zhang, Y. Jiang, and Z. Chen. How much can behavioral targeting help online advertising? In *WWW*, pages 261–270. ACM, 2009.

[34] S. Yuan, J. Wang, and X. Zhao. Real-time bidding for online advertising: measurement and analysis. In *ADKDD*, 2013.

[35] W. Zhang, T. Chen, J. Wang, and Y. Yu. Optimizing top-n collaborative filtering via dynamic negative item sampling. In *SIGIR*, pages 785–788. ACM, 2013.

[36] W. Zhang, U. Paquet, and K. Hofmann. Collective noise contrastive estimation for policy transfer learning. In *AAAI*, 2016.

[37] W. Zhang and J. Wang. Statistical arbitrage mining for display advertising. In *KDD*, pages 1465–1474. ACM, 2015.

[38] W. Zhang, S. Yuan, and J. Wang. Optimal real-time bidding for display advertising. In *KDD*, 2014.

[39] W. Zhang, S. Yuan, and J. Wang. Real-time bidding benchmarking with ipinyou dataset. *arXiv preprint arXiv:1407.7073*, 2014.

[40] X. Zhao, W. Zhang, and J. Wang. Interactive collaborative filtering. In *CIKM*, pages 1411–1420. ACM, 2013.

Author Index

www.ingramcontent.com/pod-product-compliance
Ingram Content Group UK Ltd.
Pitfield, Milton Keynes, MK11 3LW, UK
UKHW051419290926
15471UKWH00009B/1689

9 781450 346221